QUALITY OF LIFE
IN AMERICAN NEIGHBORHOODS

QUALITY OF LIFE IN AMERICAN NEIGHBORHOODS

Levels of Affluence, Toxic Waste, and Cancer Mortality in Residential Zip Code Areas

JAY M. GOULD

Edited by
Alice Tepper Marlin

PUBLISHED IN COOPERATION WITH
THE COUNCIL ON ECONOMIC PRIORITIES

Westview Press / Boulder and London

Copyright © 1986 by the Council on Economic Priorities

Published in 1986 in the United States of America by Westview Press, Inc.; Frederick A. Praeger, Publisher; 5500 Central Avenue, Boulder, Colorado 80301

Library of Congress Catalog Card Number: 85-31506
ISBN: 0-8133-7187-2

Composition for this book was provided by the Council on Economic Priorities.
This book was produced without formal editing by the publisher.

Printed and bound in the United States of America

 The paper used in this publication meets the minimum requirements of the American National Standard for Permanence of Paper for Printed Library Materials Z39.48–1984.

6   5   4   3   2   1

TABLE OF CONTENTS

PREFACE

Information, never before available, on levels of affluence and the quality of life in every Zip code area in which Americans reside is contained in this book. The Council On Economic Priorities (CEP), a non-profit research agency committed to the exploration of issues of corporate social responsibility, has been engaged in a study of the relationship between the generation and disposal of toxic waste and the regional variation in cancer mortality rates for some time. A CEP study, *Toxic Waste and Cancer: The Link Is Getting Stronger* (published in September, 1984), established a small but statistically significant association between cancer and toxic waste at the county level. For small counties with petrochemical concentrations, the association appeared to be particularly high. CEP chose therefore to continue its studies at the 5 digit Zip code level, because the average 5 digit Zip code area is one-tenth the size of the typical county.

Calculation of cancer mortality rates for any area requires data on the age composition of the area, since cancer mortality is in large part a function of age. When CEP requested 1980 Census data on the age breakdowns for Zip code areas from the Census Bureau, it was astonished to learn that the Census Bureau had no plans to publish any of the 1980 Zip code data. New Reagan Administration guidelines had decreed that complete publication of data for all Zip code areas would be too expensive, requiring the equivalent of 500 books of 500 pages each! Providing public access to such data required purchasing, editing, and processing the Census computer tapes, a task CEP has gladly assumed.

CEP decided that the new Census data, that had never before been available for analysis, should be compared with CEP measures of the "quality of life." Constructed for each Zip code area, these were measures of access to clean air and water or the degree to which the annual volume of toxic waste currently generated in an area exceeds the national average, and of toxic wastes deposited in the area from past industrial activities. These measures indicate a potential danger but do not take into account the quality of control in the management, recycling, or disposal of these wastes, which varies greatly from area to area.

Three striking findings resulted from this effort. First, an astonishingly wide variation among all Zip code areas in our measures of levels of affluence was uncovered. At one extreme are Zip code areas with average incomes per household well in excess of $100,000 (in 1984 $), with mean monthly rentals of more than $900 and average home values exceeding $400,000. At the other, are areas with incomes per household below $10,000, well below any reasonable definition of poverty. Second, these areas have disproportionately high levels of toxic waste concentrations. But, a perhaps unexpected finding, there are high income areas that lie in close proximity to areas with high toxic waste levels. This proximity poses a degree of danger of exposure to cancer risks. The pattern emerging is that very often both the rich and the poor live close enough to share some common environmental problems. Affluence no longer suffices in the evaluation of a safe place to live.

Figures published here may make grim reading for some. Others will find much information that will provide insights to a wide range of socio-economic and business problems associated with the geographic differences in the way Americans live. To find solutions to these problems, the information must be available for all to read and ponder.

Acknowledgments

This book has its roots in work Dr. Jay M. Gould began in 1976 when, as head of Economic Information Systems, Inc. and as a member of the Science Advisory Board of EPA, he developed a database methodology for estimating the industrial generation of toxic waste. The Council On Economic Priorities (CEP) is indebted to Dr. Charles Stryker, of the Trinet subsidiary of Control Data Corp., that now maintains the EIS databases, for permission to make use of these databases in this book. Valuable help and encouragement came from many of our advisors: Michael Podhorzer, of the Citizen Action Network, Dr. Henry Cole, of the National Campaign Against Hazardous Waste, Bridget Wieghart, who assisted in assembly of the tables, and Warren Barnett, who wrote the computer programs required by this book. We are deeply grateful to the Babcock Foundation of Winston-Salem, North Carolina, to the First Unitarian Society of Minneapolis and to the Arca Foundation of Washington, D.C. for grants to CEP to fund this ongoing research into the relation of toxic waste to cancer mortality.

QUALITY OF LIFE
IN AMERICAN NEIGHBORHOODS

1. INTRODUCTION

The Zip code area represents a geographic area whose boundaries have been established by the U.S. Post Office to facilitate the sorting and delivery of mail. Because it represents a way of breaking down our vast nation into some 36,000 small geographic units, which are additive to national totals, Zip code areas can be used for the social and economic demographic analysis of small areas. The U.S. can alternatively be broken down by states and the 3000 odd counties which compose the states. County lines, however, are frequently drawn quite arbitrarily, and since counties are on average about ten times larger than the typical Zip code area, many sharp divergences in the demographic characteristics of small communities and neighborhoods disappear in county aggregates and averages.

Ergo, the Zip code area has become, since its introduction some thirty years ago, the focus of laborious attempts on the part of direct mail marketing analysts to infer varying degrees of income levels and other demographic characteristics from published Census data on minor civil divisions or Census tracts.

Until 1980, the Census Bureau resisted all requests from business to permit analysis of Census data for 5 digit Zip code boundaries. Since the spring of 1983, however, computer tapes containing all 1980 Census data for all Zip code areas have been made available to the business community for the processing and analysis of marketing problems. Still no Zip code data has been, or will be, published by the Census Bureau for the general public.

2. POLITICAL SIGNIFICANCE OF THE ZIP CODE AREA

In this crucial time in the changing relationship of individuals in their role as taxpayers to traditional municipal, county, state, and federal political structures, availability of Census data on the human resources in each resident Zip code area greatly enhances the potential political significance of the Zip code area.

A common perception exists that as taxes become increasingly burdensome, these traditional political entities are providing fewer and fewer benefits to taxpayers in such important areas as better facilities for education, health care, clean water and air, and transportation—all bearing on the quality of life in America.

Neighborhoods and communities increasingly are perceived as political entities better suited to express those basic societal needs being neglected by the higher levels of political structures. Though not widely reported by the media, a spontaneous emergence of grass-roots organizations, including neighborhood health clinics, daycare centers, storefront schools, food co-ops, and environmental activist groups, has occurred in recent years. These are expressions of a community response to such local changes as withdrawal of a large supermarket chain from an inner city market, or a shut-down of a public hospital, the dissolution of a public education system, or the realization that the health of the community is at risk. CEP believes that sheer instinct for survival will spark the spread of community organizations in the coming decades, projected by most observers as an era of increasing public austerity.

The 5 digit Zip code area can be the fundamental building block in defining neighborhoods and communities. A neighborhood may consist of a single Zip code area, or as for example the Black community of Harlem in New York, could be defined to include several Zip code areas such as 10026, 10027, 10030, 10031, 10035, and 10037. Other New York neighborhoods never before defined statistically are Bedford-Stuyvesant, Canarsie, Greenwich Village, Williamsburg, Soho, etc. Every large city has such well-known neighborhoods: Watts in Los Angeles, San Francisco's Nob Hill, and Chicago's Loop.

One could conceive of a political breakdown of the national electorate into seven or eight thousand communities, defined along Zip code area lines, that could facilitate the expression of both local and national concerns about the quality of life. The definition of the boundaries of such communities can only be worked out locally, of course. In time, and possibly with the help of this book, local pressures may help develop such a community consciousness.

Data in this book can provide community organizers and activists with at least rough approximations of the size, degree of affluence, age composition, and toxic waste concentrations per capita for any combination of 5 digit Zip code areas. Sections 8 and 9 below, "How To Combine Zip Code Areas Into Neighborhoods," indicate how to calculate neighborhood cancer mortality rates. For those wanting more precise statistics, the entire Census database from which this book was taken will be available through an online database vendor or by way of special custom tailored computer print-outs ordered from CEP (See Section 9 and Appendix A).

3. DATA DEFINITIONS

Zip Codes

The five digit Zip code is a geographic code identifying all areas within the U.S. It does not necessarily adhere to the boundaries of cities, counties, states, or other political jurisdictions, however. The first digit of the Zip code divides the country into ten large groups of states numbered from zero in the Northeast to nine in the Far West. Within these areas, each state is divided into an average of 10 smaller geographic areas, identified by the second and third digits of the Zip code. The final two digits identify a local delivery area. Unfortunately, the sequence of the last two digits has little locational significance. While in large cities one could generally assume that successively numbered 5 digit Zip code areas lie in close proximity to each other, this is not true for areas lying outside of big cities. There the sequence of the last two digits is governed alphabetically by the place name assigned to each Post Office. Within large cities, Post Offices in each 5 digit Zip code area do not have place names assigned by the Postal Service.

Zip code data in this book has been listed by states, arranged in alphabetic sequence from Alabama to Wyoming. Within states, Zip code areas are listed in numeric sequence, but we provide the reader with some geographic orientation by printing the city names for each three digit sectional center.

Some 5,000 Zip code areas with less than 50 households are important to the Postal Service because of mail deliveries to business and industrial locations. These areas often have heavy concentrations of toxic waste, but receive little attention in this book since they are sparsely populated. The Zip directory making up the bulk of this book covers about 35,000 5 digit Zip code areas with more than 50 households, and is numbered from 2.1 to 2.352.

Population

All population figures in this book relate to April, 1980, when the total U.S. population was tabulated at 226.5 million persons. The typical residential 5 digit Zip code area has between 5,000 and 10,000 persons, or two to three thousand households. No attempt has been made to update the April, 1980 figures for population or households.

Households and Occupied Housing Units

In the calculation of percentages and means, both the number of private households and the number of occupied housing units are used. Both are generally interchangeable. A private household is defined by the Census to include all the persons occupying a housing unit. A housing unit is a house, an apartment, a group of rooms, or a single room that is occupied as separate living quarters. Separate living quarters are those in which occupants live and eat separately from other persons in the building and have direct access from outside the building or through a common hall.

The Census tabulated a total of 80.5 million households in April of 1980 as against 80.4 million occupied housing units. In the calculation of the monthly rental and value of owner occupied homes, the Census Bureau found it necessary to restrict the computation to specified groups of renters and owners. The Bureau, for example, excluded units on property of more than 10 acres. In such cases, value figures would be more a function of land value rather than of housing. Also co-ops, condominiums, mobile homes, trailers, boats, and vans are excluded from the definition of owner occupied units.

Group Quarters

All persons not living in households are classified as living in group quarters. This includes schools, hospitals, nursing homes, orphanages, correctional institutions, boarding houses, and military barracks. The presence of a significant number of such persons in any Zip code area listed here can be detected if the ratio of population to households is much higher than 2.8, the average size of a household.

Renter and Owner Occupied Units

A housing unit is "owner occupied" if the owner or co-owner lives in the unit, even if it is mortgaged or not fully paid for. All other occupied units are classified as "renter occupied," including units rented for cash rent and those occupied without payment of cash rent. The national share of owner occupied housing units was 64.4 percent. It has probably not changed much since that date because of the slow-down in new home construction since that year.

White Population

The percentage of population in each Zip code area classified as White, according to the self-identification of respondents, is shown. Non-White categories include Blacks, i.e., persons who indicated their race as Black or Negro, as well as persons who did not classify themselves in one of the specific race categories, but reported entries such as Jamaican, Black Puerto Rican, West Indian, Haitian or Nigerian. Also included as non-White are American Indians, Eskimos, Aleuts, Asians, and Pacific Islanders, accounting for 5.1 percent of total population. In 1980 the national White percentage was 83.2 and the Black percentage was 11.7.

Age Composition

Since the very young and older people are most vulnerable to exposure to toxic wastes, the percentage of the total population in each area under five years old and the percentage of those who are 65 and older are shown. The number of white males and the percentage that is 65 and older are also indicated since these figures enter into the calculation of white male cancer mortality rates. (White males account for the largest number of cancer deaths.) A significant age statistic is that in 1980, 10.0 percent of all white males were over 65 years of age—an important fact in the calculation of cancer mortality rates for white males.

Definition of Levels of Affluence

Three indicators of affluence levels, measured in terms of 1984 dollars, are the annual mean income per household, the mean monthly rental, and the mean value of owner occupied home. Several technical modifications of the Census data were performed to make these measures more meaningful.

Financial data collected by the Census Bureau from respondents relates to the year 1979, and, therefore, does not reflect the inflationary trend since that year. Based on Bureau of Labor Statistics data on cost of living changes for the period 1979 to 1984, the financial data were adjusted to reflect a 35 percent inflationary increase and for a 50 percent increase in the cost of housing. In addition, a perhaps arbitrary upward adjustment in the home value figures of 25 percent was made to compensate for understatement of home values by respondents wrongfully fearful their answers would be used for tax assessment purposes. (The Census Bureau would not offer an "official" estimate of the admitted degree of understatement. The 25 percent estimate was based on discussions with realtors in Los Angeles and New York where the understatement of home values appeared to be much greater.)

These adjustments produce the following national means for the year 1984: $27,413 for income per household; $315 for the mean monthly rent; and $97,650 for the mean value of all owner occupied homes. They preserve the relative financial levels of all areas, but probably underestimate them for high income neighborhoods in and around the metropolitan areas of New York, Chicago, Los Angeles, and San Francisco.

The figures yielded can be said to relate to the year 1984. A recent *Survey of Consumer Finances*, published in the September and December 1984 issues of the Federal Reserve Board Bulletin (FRB), offers support for the estimates for the year 1982. The FRB Survey estimated the mean income per family in 1982 (a recession year) at $26,259. Home ownership of non-farm families, according to the Survey, declined from 67 percent in 1977 to 60 percent in 1982, because of the increase in mortgage interest rates and the inflationary rise in housing prices. These, in turn, also boosted rents at a rate somewhat higher than the gain in inflation.

The Census Bureau does not calculate the mean value of rentals and homes. It prefers to calculate medians, which are based on a small number of class intervals and, therefore, do not show as much variation from area to area as would the mean value. In calculating the means in this book, CEP confined the calculations to specified groups of renters and owners as indicated above. Also the mean rental figure includes non-seasonal vacant rental units.

Finally, although the Census "suppresses" data on occupied units whenever fewer than 30 units are involved, it does not withhold the data for households. In all such cases, estimates of the missing figures were calculated on the basis of the national ratio between the mean rental or mean home value to income per household. All such estimates carry an asterisk (*).

4. Affluent Areas of the U.S.

The mean income per household in the U.S. in 1984 dollars was $27,400 as noted above. The range of variation in this mean turns out to be extraordinarily wide among all areas. Many areas have mean income levels below $10,000, and there is at least one area with an income level 20 times greater.

Also high and low income areas will frequently be found quite close geographically. The single most affluent area in the U.S. is Area 89413, in Reno, Nevada. It has only 200 persons, all white, with 80 percent owner occupancy, and a mean income per household of $201,000. Yet in the same city, not too far away is Area 89412, also with 200 persons, all white. In sharp contrast, it has a mean income only one tenth as large.

Another striking fact is that high income areas, defined as those with mean incomes about twice the national average, can be found in almost every state, even those generally regarded as low income states (see Table 1). One of the nation's most affluent areas is in Kentucky, Area 40027, a neighborhood of 200 persons. Known as Harrods Creek, east of Louisville, it has a mean household income of $156,000. The state of Kentucky, at the same time, has what may be the poorest single area in the nation: Area 40981, with a mean income of only $5,600.

Table 1 lists the single most affluent area in each state. In terms of size and relative importance, one could pick as the nation's leading area, 90210. This area, a section of Beverly Hills lying north of Wilshire Boulevard, has 22,000 persons, a mean income per household of $113,000, a mean monthly rental of $699, and a mean value of home of $425,000. Other noteworthy affluent neighborhoods include Area 60043, a section of Kenilworth, north of Chicago, Illinois. This area has a population of 2,700, a mean income of $117,000, a mean monthly rent of $846, and a mean home value of $350,000. The most affluent area in Michigan is Area 48025, in the Franklin section of Royal Oak, with a population of 3,000 and a mean income of $107,000. Of more importance is the larger Area 48013, Bloomfield Hills. It contains a population of 31,200 and a mean income of $88,000.

The most affluent area in New York is Area 10597 in Waccapuc Village in Westchester county. It has a small population of 500 persons and a mean income of $137,000.

. Table 1, most interestingly, suggests that even rural states have high income enclaves, and high income areas sometimes turn up in unexpected places. For example, here are some high income areas with few or no whites.

TABLE 1

The Richest Zip Code Area in Each State

State	Zip Code	Geographic Location	Pop. (Th.)	Mean Income Per H.H. Th. $	Mean Monthly Rent $	Mean Value Home Th. $
AL	35223	Mountainbrook Section, N. of Birmingham	10.4	68.0	382	233
AZ	85377	Carefree, North of Phoenix	1.1	67.1	298	317
AR	72212	Little Rock	8.2	55.3	401	165
CA	90210	Beverly Hills, No. of Wilshire Blvd.	21.6	113.2	699	425
CO	80111	Englewood Environs	15.7	66.7	616	246
CT	06840	New Canaan	17.9	77.6	669	333.7
DE	19807	Greenville Suburb of Wilmington	6.2	68.8	378	255
DC	20016	District of Columbia	25.5	51.0	521	282
FL	33158	Richmond Heights	5.7	78.6	676	235
GA	31411	Savannah	1.3	78.9	451	242
ID	83541	Lenore Suburb of Lewiston	.5	59.2	246	80
IL	60043	Kenilworth Suburb of Chicago	2.7	117.2	876	350
IN	46278	Indianapolis	2.4	58.8	536	157
IA	50324	Des Moines	.4	44.2	508	120
KS	66221	Shawnee Mission	.3	88.7	735	252
KY	40027	Harrod's Creek, East of Louisville	.2	156.4	320	161
LA	70773	Rougon Environs of Baton Rouge	.2	58.2	195	44
ME	04110	Brunswick Section of Portland	1.2	59.1	152	190
MD	21022	Brooklandville Section, Baltimore	.3	107.3	695	274
MA	02030	Dover	4.7	65.6	785	249
MI	48025	Franklin Section of Royal Oak	3.0	107.3	606	264
MN	55436	Southdale Section of Minneapolis	12.5	66.9	667	215
MS	39359	Sebastopol	.3	51.6	167	45
MO	63131	Des Moines Environs of St. Louis	17.9	73.7	578	229
MT	59403	Great Falls	.4	41.5	477	150
NB	68133	Omaha	.7	43.9	505	147
NV	89413	Reno	.2	201.3	1020	407
NH	03750	Etna, Environs of White River Junct.	.8	45.5	550	137
NJ	07620	Alpine Village Near Hackensack	1.5	106.6	876	333
NM	87122	Albuquerque	2.1	59.2	633	742
NY	10597	Waccapuc Village, Westchester	.5	139.2	534	350
NC	27706	Durham	2.2	59.2	1038	144
ND	58007	Ayr Po, Fargo	.2	40.6	221	44
OH	45243	Cincinnati	15.7	61.8	489	188
OK	73116	Oklahoma City	10.1	55.1	422	154
OR	97221	Portland	11.1	46.9	480	194
PA	19035	Philadelphia	3.8	90.1	678	283
RI	02806	Providence	16.2	42.8	461	137
SC	29503	Florence	.2	47.1	541	105
SD	57725	Rapid City, Caputa P.O.	.2	64.5	741	166
TN	37215	Nashville	18.2	49.8	445	185
TX	77069	Houston	6.3	74.0	341	241
UT	84060	Park City Section of Salt Lake City	4.5	42.8	340	229
VT	05445	Burlington (Charlotte)	2.0	37.3	410	118
VA	22101	McLean, North Virginia	28.7	65.7	810	264
WA	98040	Seattle	21.5	56.4	542	258
WV	26278	Buckhannon	.6	64.7	303	34
WI	53122	Elm Grove, South Milwaukee	6.8	77.4	518	222
WY	82727	New Castle (Rozef)	.5	40.7	443	149

State	Zip Code	Place Name	Pop. (th.)	% White	Mean Income Per Hhld ($th)
Ga.	31561	Sea Island	.3	.0	104.3
Fl.	33459	Lake Harbor	.6	21.0	86.6
Nb.	68133	Omaha	.7	.0	43.9
Oh.	44040	Cleveland	2.9	.0	74.3
Ok.	74009	Bowring	.2	.0	61.6
Pa.	19357	Mendenhall	.3	.0	87.2
Tx.	78851	Dryden	.2	.0	46.6
Va.	22940	Free Union	.9	.0	66.6

It is necessary to probe more deeply for a full explanation of these surprising figures. Sea Island, Georgia appears to be a resort area, with no resident white households. The Lake Harbor area is near Lake Okichobee, Florida but may include a few resident white households in Palm Beach, which could raise the mean household income. Area 74009, Bowring, Oklahoma, is located on an Indian reservation on which oil drilling rigs may be in operation. Probably only those familiar with each of these areas could provide a satisfactory explanation of the special circumstances involved in each case.

5. MEASURE OF THE QUALITY OF LIFE

A low income rural area, if it has not been exposed to the negative aspects of industrialization, should have access to clean air and clean water. Residents of high income urban areas, on the other hand, must often breathe polluted air and drink contaminated water. And if they suffer, as do apparently so many urban areas from excess cancer mortality rates, can hardly be said to enjoy a good life. It is in this sense that CEP has taken two environmental measures of exposure to toxic waste as measures of an area's "Quality of Life." (Many other measures can of course be chosen.) One is derived from an EPA database of 19,972 closed (i.e., inactive) hazardous waste sites from which EPA is to choose sites requiring Superfund clean-up expenditures. The other is a database carrying estimates for each area of the volume of toxic waste generated per capita in 1980.

Passage of the Resource Conservation and Recovery Act (RCRA) in 1976 has in large part increased understanding of the environmental dangers associated with industrial activity. Since 1970, under the authorization of the Solid Waste Disposal Act, the Environmental Protection Administration has funded considerable research in estimating the magnitude of industrial waste generation and disposal for specified locations in specified industries. Technical studies called *Effluent Limitation Guidelines* were authorized for organic chemicals, synthetic resins, pulp and paper, metal finishing, and many other industrial processes thought to be generating toxic wastes. These and other studies conducted by the National Institute of Occupational Safety led to a definition of hazardous or toxic wastes in terms of hundreds of specific chemical substances and industrial processes.

More recently, detailed studies were made by state environmental agencies of New York, Illinois, California, Missouri, and Massachusetts. These offered insights into the hazardous waste problem for a broad spectrum of industrial activity. For example, the New York State Department of Environmental Conservation released "An Inventory of Hazardous Waste Generation in New York State" in June of 1979. This study found significant waste generation and disposal problems in 1,170 out of 4,015 manufacturing locations, encompassing 205 different industries.

In 1980, in response to Section 3010 of RCRA, some 60,000 locations in the U.S. notified EPA they were engaged in the generation, transportation, and treatment of hazardous waste as defined by EPA.

In 1981, EPA made its first national survey of these locations and published the results in March of 1984. The results of these surveys suggest that toxic waste is generated in two different ways. First, there is the manufacture of petrochemical products. Here, a relatively small number of facilities generate as a by-product relatively high concentrations of toxic waste. Second, there is the industrial use of petrochemical products such as fuel, solvents, paints, greases, lubricants, etc. Here, a very large number of locations in as many as 300 different industries will generate relatively small amounts of toxic waste requiring safe disposal. Among the manufacturing industries generating significant amounts of toxic waste are the so-called process control industries like food, textiles, paper,and primary metals as well as wood and metal fabricating industries like machinery and automobiles. Even non-manufacturing industries like power utilities, hospitals, gasoline stations,and paint stores turn out to be small generators of toxic waste.

The relative importance of each industry is still a matter of some debate and controversy. Early surveys, such as the one conducted in New York State for the year 1979, indicated that 35 percent of all toxic waste generated came from the production of petrochemicals. This, however, is not as important in New York as it is in such states as New Jersey, Louisiana, or Texas. The *1981 National Survey of Hazardous Waste Generators*, conducted by EPA and released in 1984, attributes 71 percent of all toxic waste to the production of petrochemicals. CEP regards this as an overestimate, due to a failure on the part of EPA to define waste in dry-weight terms. (Thus a single chemical plant in this survey was credited with 27 percent of the total toxic waste generated in the U.S. because, in the words of its plant manager, "99 percent was water used in the advanced treatment process to make the waste safe.")

In constructing the CEP Toxic Waste Database used in this book, a somewhat arbitrary 50 percent weight was assigned to the petrochemical industries. The remainder was allocated to about 200 manufacturing and non-manufacturing industries in accordance with the results of all the various toxic waste surveys conducted to date. The choice of different sets of weights has little impact on the relative standing of counties or Zip code areas, because the petrochemical industries are still dominant in any set of weights.

Weights can be expressed as ratios of toxic waste per worker for each industry. When multiplied by the employment of a plant in a given industry, this yields an estimate of the potential toxic waste associated with that plant. (The basic assumption is that each plant in a given industry, by virtue of sharing a common technology of production, will generate toxic waste as a byproduct of production at the same rate per worker.) Thus, to produce such plant estimates that can then be summarized at the 5 digit Zip code area level, we need a database of establishments, with Standard Industrial Classification codes, employment estimates, and locational data.

Such a database is available commercially from the Trinet division of Control Data Corporation. It includes every establishment in the U.S. with 20 or more employees. This database accounts for about 90 percent of total U.S. private gross domestic output.

CEP, however, is responsible for developing ratios of toxic waste per worker in each of about 200 industries that are defined at the 4 digit level of detail in the U.S. Standard Industrial Classification system. These ratios have been used as "weights" in determining the relative importance of each establishment in the generation of toxic waste. This is assuming that each plant operates at a technological level equal to that of all other plants in a given industry. These weights can be changed in the future in accordance with new Toxic Waste Surveys to be conducted by EPA and other state environmental agencies.

Any significant change in these weights from future surveys may affect the relative standing of specific plants and companies as potential generators of toxic waste. The Trinet database carries ownership data on every establishment. So, if the toxic waste estimates for each plant are sorted by parent company, the major companies can be ranked. For the specific weights used here, the number one company is E.I. DuPont followed by General Motors and Union Carbide. Their respective shares of the national toxic waste total are 4, 3, and 2.5 percent. If the results of the latest EPA Toxic Waste study were taken literally, and 71 percent of the total toxic waste assigned to petrochemical production, the General Motors ranking would drop from number two to number five, and the top four companies would be DuPont, Union Carbide, Dow Chemical and Monsanto, in this order.

The procedure described above is a practical application of Input/Output analysis, an economic discipline for which Professor Wassily Leontief received the Nobel Prize in Economics in 1973.

In an Input/Output table, each industry in a national economy is arrayed both horizontally as a "selling" industry and vertically as a "buying" industry. A cell formed by the intersection of a row and column contains data on how much the selling industry sells to the buying industry in a given year. Therefore, all the items in a given column represent the costs of all materials, components, and services required by the buying industry. One can, therefore, conceive of a row representing the cost of the services of the waste disposal industry if it were to collect and treat the toxic waste of every industry that generates such waste. Thus every such industry would have a unit cost of waste disposal that could be expressed as the cost per worker in that industry.

Economists in the Department of Commerce are charged with the responsibility of estimating the unit costs of every buying industry, including the cost of waste disposal. Once these unit costs or ratios are established, they can be applied to a plant database, as was done above, to secure estimates (really inferences) about the volume of waste generated by each plant. All this is based on the assumption that each plant generates waste at the same rate as all other plants in that industry.

This assumption is, of course, an over-simplification. In actual practice there can be considerable divergence in the way each plant in a given industry will manage its waste. Yet since each plant in that industry does share a common technology, these estimates turn out in practice to be good first approximations. Ultimately, however, they should be verified by EPA.

These estimates of toxic waste are incomplete, however. Many industrial practices exposing people to dangers are not covered in the EPA definition of toxic waste. For example, no allowance is made for either dioxin released in the incineration of solid wastes at open waste sites or for polychlorinated biphenals (PCB) present in closed waste sites and deposited in unknown amounts all over the nation. Also omitted from the EPA toxic waste measures are radioactive wastes and toxic wastes generated and disposed of at military installations.

Indeed, radioactive and toxic wastes associated with military installations could represent the single most glaring deficiency in the monitor role of EPA. The Department of Energy has estimated that the cumulated volume of high-level radioactive waste through 1980 amounts to 347,000 tons at military installations as against only 4,000 tons at civilian reactors. (This estimate, however, ignores the large volume of used fuel assemblies that all nuclear reactors will someday have to dispose of.)

Most of the military radioactive wastes are now stored at four places: the Hanford reservation in Richland, Washington (Area 99352); Oak Ridge, Tennessee, (Area 37830); the Savannah River Plant, South Carolina (Area 29801); and the Idaho National Engineering Laboratory in Bonneville, Idaho (Area 83420).*

Toxic wastes at 400 to 800 military bases, according to Department of Defense Director of Environmental Policy Carl Schafer, would require clean-up expenditures of $5 to $10 billion. They consist of "toxic solvents and sludges from aircraft, tank and vehicle maintenance and weapons production, PCB's used as insulating material in electrical equipment and in military radar installations." (*New York Times*, March 3, 1985). These estimates do not include an estimated clean-up cost of $1 billion for wastes generated by the notorious Rocky Mountain Arsenal (Area 80640, just north of Denver, Colorado). The Arsenal has been described by one expert as "the most contaminated square mile on earth." Nor has any account been made for the nuclear bomb assembly Pantex plant in Amarillo, Texas, (Area 79069). With one further qualification one can now turn to the CEP estimates of per capita toxic waste for Zip code areas.

Toxic Emissions

The EPA definition of toxic waste is confined to liquid and solid wastes. It does not include toxic wastes emitted into the atmosphere. Spurred by the Union Carbide poison gas leak in Bhopal, India, responsible for 2000 deaths and 200,000 injuries, the House Subcommittee on Health and the Environment, headed by Henry A. Waxman, conducted the first major study of toxic emissions by plants owned by 86 leading petrochemical companies.

The survey indicated there is very little specific regulation of the tens of millions of pounds of toxic chemicals spewed into the air each year. Four major types of emissions were identified. The most important were the synthetic petroleum-based organic chemicals such as benzene, vinyl chloride, chloroform, carbon tetrachloride, acrylonitrile, and formaldehyde. Natural organic compounds such as chlorine and ammonia are considered of lesser importance. But carcinogenic emissions include fibers such as asbestos, and metals such as lead, bromine, mercury, cadmium, nickel, and arsenic.

The study confirmed, however, that the pattern of geographic distribution of toxic emissions duplicated roughly that of solid and liquid toxic waste generation. Heaviest concentrations of emissions are in Texas, Louisiana, West Virginia, Kentucky, Ohio, New Jersey, and New York. These same states have heavy concentrations of toxic waste

---

*According to *The Next Nuclear Gamble: Transportation and Storage of Nuclear Waste* by Marvin Resnikoff, published by the Council on Economic Priorities in 1983, the main danger to the public will come around the turn of the century, when all this high level waste from all reactors must be removed to a national burial ground. Resnikoff estimated that such a huge transport effort could result in 17 nuclear accidents per year, any one of which could be of the magnitude of Three Mile Island.

TABLE 2
Summary of CEP Toxic Waste Database, By 5 Digit Zip Code Areas

5 Digit Zip Code Areas	# of 5 Digit Areas	Toxic Waste Th. tons	Toxic Waste Bil lbs.	Toxic Waste % of Total	Population mil.	Population % of Total	Toxic Waste Lbs Per Cap.
Areas With No Resident Population	1,293	9,289	18.6	9.3	. . . .	. . .	. . .
Areas With Resident Population	36,000	90,711	181.4	90.7	226.5	100.0	800
Areas With Toxic Waste	14,893	90,711	181.4	90.7	190.3	84.0	953
Above Average Levels	3,443	73,851	147.7	73.8	38.9	17.2	3,797
Below Average Levels	11,450	16,660	33.3	16.7	151.4	66.8	219
Areas With No Toxic Waste	23,107	. . . .	. . . .	. . .	36.2	16.0	. . .
Totals, All Areas	40,000	100,000	200.0	100.0	226.5	100.0	883

generation. And, as in the case of toxic waste generation, the leading emitters of toxics were E.I. duPont, Dow Chemical, and Union Carbide. For this reason, the CEP database of toxic waste generation discussed below, while based on solids and liquids, can serve too as a relative indicator of toxic emissions.

The CEP Toxic Waste Database

Table 2 summarizes some of the characteristics of the CEP Toxic Waste Database arrayed by 5 digit Zip code areas. There are about 40,000 residential and business Zip code areas all told. Of these, some 4,000 have no residential population at all, and about 1,000 have fewer than 50 households. There are 1,293 industrial Zip code areas accounting for 9.6 percent of total toxic waste generation. This amount may present occupational exposure risks to its work force, although no people live there.

Of the 36,000 odd Zip code areas with resident population, 23,107 have no toxic waste generation at all within their boundaries. The remaining 14,893 areas can be divided into two groups: those with above average toxic waste levels and those with below average levels. For the nation as a whole, with a population of 226.5 million in 1980 and with 100 million tons of toxic waste generated in that year, there is a national average of 883 pounds per capita. (As noted above, this is conservative, since EPA in 1984 estimated toxic waste generation in 1981 as high as 264 million metric tons. This estimate does not allow for the dilution of some toxic wastes in the treatment stage.)

There are 11,450 areas with toxic waste levels below the national per capita average of 883 pounds. These areas, accounting for one-third of the national total waste and two-thirds of the total population, have an average per capita waste level of only 219 pounds. Thus the bulk of most 5 digit areas, 32,557 of the 36,000 in the Census Database, can for the moment be set aside as having little ascertainable exposure to toxic waste.

Attention should be centered on the 3,443 5 digit areas with above average toxic waste levels, since they account for three-quarters of all the toxic waste generated annually. With 39 million residents, these areas have toxic waste levels three times the national average.

Demographic characteristics of this high risk group shall be examined below. The number of people at risk is seen to be somewhat larger when this database is resummarized at the 4 digit Zip code level. On average, a 4 digit area is about three times larger than a 5 digit area. Thus many 5 digit areas with no toxic waste generated within their boundaries and no closed waste sites can still be subject to some degree of exposure if other nearby 5 digit areas within the same 4 digit area have heavy concentrations of toxic waste.

In fact, in the 4 digit areas with toxic waste presenting a public health problem to both workers and resident population, about 61 million persons are at risk. These areas deserve the most attention. They include those 5 digit areas having no waste generation within their own boundaries (and may have high levels of affluence and other indicators of material well-being), but are close to sources of waste generation in their 4 digit areas.

Table 3 lists in descending order of per capita waste the leading 400 4 digit Zip Code areas with respect to per capita toxic waste generation. Each has a toxic waste level more than twice the national average of 883 pounds. With a total resident populaiton of 19.7 million persons, these areas collectively account for nearly half of the nation's annual generation of toxic waste. The average toxic waste level for these areas is more than five times the national average.

The first dozen of these areas are sparsely populated sections of heavily industrialized cities or towns, so their extremely high per capita levels are perhaps not as alarming as on first view. Still, one wonders how the 25 residents of the first area in Table 3—Area 2619, Willow Island, West Virginia—would feel if they realized that plants in the area are generating toxic waste at a per capita rate 9,224 times the national average!

TABLE 3
Ranking of the Top 400 Four Digit Zip Codes
With Respect to Per Capita Toxic Waste Generation

ST	ZIP	POST OFFICE PLACE NAME	POPULATION	TOXIC WASTE (TONS)	LBS PER CAPITA	RATIO	SITES	RANK
WV	2619	WILLOW ISLAND	25	101,810	8,144,800	9,224.0	1	1
NY	1424	BUFFALO	52	158,760	6,106,154	6,915.2	9	2
MO	6316	ST. LOUIS	34	86,686	5,099,176	5,774.8	0	3
MO	6317	ST. LOUIS	62	65,720	2,120,000	2,400.9	1	4
FL	3368	TAMPA	24	20,757	1,729,750	1,959.0	2	5
NC	2823	CHARLOTTE	40	27,738	1,386,900	1,570.7	1	6
WV	2533	CHARLESTON	76	43,195	1,136,711	1,287.3	0	7
OK	7415	TULSA	16	6,043	755,375	855.5	1	8
CT	0672	WATERBURY	84	23,347	555,881	629.5	3	9
WV	2571	HUNTINGTON	36	7,139	396,611	449.2	1	10
AZ	8506	PHOENIX	26	2,943	226,385	256.4	0	11
NM	8718	ALBUQUERQUE	45	4,455	198,000	224.2	0	12
PA	1948	UWCHLAND	2,168	170,697	157,470	178.3	4	13
TX	7571	TYLER	171	13,252	154,994	175.5	4	14
TX	7828	SAN ANTONIO	237	17,162	144,827	164.0	0	15
NC	2828	CLINTON	12	789	131,500	148.9	0	16
VA	2400	ROANOKE	303	16,017	105,723	119.7	1	17
TN	3783	OAK RIDGE	28,162	1,268,844	90,110	102.1	8	18
FL	3373	ST. PETERSBURG	227	9,221	81,242	92.0	0	19
SC	2929	COLUMBIA	79	3,205	81,139	91.9	0	20
NC	2472	GREENSBORO	669	23,531	70,347	79.7	5	21
TX	7871	AUSTIN	5	170	68,000	77.0	0	22
CO	8093	COLORADO SPRINGS	60	1,826	60,867	68.9	2	23
WV	2501	CHARLESTON	8.698	243,422	55,972	63.4	4	24
IN	4628	INDIANAPOLIS	5,799	159,050	54,854	62.1	0	25
TX	7754	FREEPORT	49,341	1,150,881	46,650	52.8	18	26
VA	2321	RICHMOND	4,242	77,790	36,676	41.5	1	27
IN	4770	CANTON	996	17,394	34,928	39.6	21	28
AL	3655	MOBILE	12,423	213,727	34,408	39.0	0	29
SC	2980	AIKEN	42610	714,459	33,535	38.0	2	30
IN	3790	KNOXVILLE	1,833	30,180	32,930	37.3	5	31
NM	8719	ALBUQUERQUE	109	1,766	32,404	36.7	0	32
VA	2386	HOPEWELL	36,562	519,446	28,415	32.2	12	33
FL	3367	TAMPA	55	774	28,145	31.9	2	34
MI	4864	MIDLAND	61,891	857,6210	27,714	31.4	11	35
AL	3651	MOBILE	4,097	56,638	27,517	31.2	2	36
IA	5030	DES MOINES	4,059	55,371	27,283	30.9	5	37
NH	0174	BOLTON	11	144	26,182	29.7	0	38
NY	1464	ROCHESTER	198	2,504	25,293	28.6	0	39
TX	7876	AUSTIN	3,137	38,653	24,663	27.9	1	40
TX	7834	CORPUS CHRISTI	9,472	115,329	24,352	27.6	1	41
MI	4997	IRON MOUNTAIN	1,511	16,831	22,278	25.2	1	42
LA	7073	BATON ROUGE	34,652	348,016	20,086	22.8	16	43
KA	7076	BATON ROUGE	49,919	486,298	19,483	22.1	12	44
MA	0159	WILKONSVILLE	444	4,223	19,023	21.5	0	45
KY	4202	PADUCAH	30,998	250,868	16,186	18.3	9	46
TX	7759	TEXAS CITY	46,634	376,761	16,158	18.3	13	47
TX	7764	PORT ARTHUR	62,238	497,499	15,987	18.1	14	48
PA	1930	PAOLI	6,489	48,916	15,077	17.1	1	49
TX	7753	BAYTOWN	105,413	792,933	15,044	17.0	30	50
TOTAL — ABOVE AREAS			616,444	9,150,530	29,688	33.6	215	

TABLE 3
(CONTINUED)

ST	ZIP	POST OFFICE PLACE NAME	POPULATION	TOXIC WASTE (TONS)	LBS PER CAPITA	RATIO	SITES	RANK
CT	0634	GROTON	33,349	245,824	14,743	16.7	8	51
NY	1430	NIAGRA FALLS	85,967	618,479	14,389	16.3	78	52
MO	6414	KANSAS CITY	5,043	35,601	14,119	16.0	0	53
NJ	0802	DEEP WATER	80,148	559.735	13,968	15.8	11	54
CA	9067	SANTA FE SPRINGS	13,627	94,328	13,844	15.7	19	55
FL	3285	ORLANDO	138	935	13,551	15.4	1	56
MD	2155	CUMBERLAND	16,388	110,849	13,528	15.3	1	57
VA	2264	WINCHESTER	5,486	37,060	13,511	15.3	0	58
FL	3386	LAKELAND	17,485	116,796	13,360	15.1	9	59
KY	4010	LOUISVILLE	10,891	71,464	13,123	14.9	4	60
LA	7112	SHREVEPORT	6,709	43,097	12,848	14.6	0	61
TX	7757	HOUSTON	58,011	365,274	12,593	14,.3	14	62
TN	3766	KINGSPORT	82,427	509,111	12,353	14.0	9	63
TX	7763	BEAUMONT	47,796	277,554	11,614	13.2	12	64
OK	7460	PONCA CITY	33,401	193,473	11,585	13.1	5	65
MA	0178	WOODVILLE	13	75	11,538	13.1	0	66
LA	7077	BATON ROUGE	20,941	117,794	11,250	12.7	3	67
NJ	0880	NEW BRUNSWICK	49,041	273,345	11,148	12.6	8	68
TX	7765	BEAUMONT	46,648	259,807	11,139	12.6	14	69
WV	2514	CHARLESTON	15,772	84,414	10,704	12.1	14	70
SC	2923	COLUMBIA	31	165	10,645	12.1	0	71
IN	4762	MT. VERNON	14,079	69,650	9,894	11.2	9	72
WV	2530	CHARLESTON	66,321	317,976	9,589	10.9	14	73
KY	4112	ASHLAND	13,937	66,750	9,579	10.9	5	74
NY	1096	SUFFERN	43,648	207,021	9,486	10.7	5	75
MA	0115	SPINGFIELD	8,042	38,102	9,476	10.7	3	76
VA	2442	FREDERICKSBURG	29,588	136,693	9,240	10.5	7	77
IN	4631	GARY	81,218	373,475	9,197	10.4	21	78
TX	7797	VICTORIA	20,953	95,075	9,075	10.3	3	79
KS	6611	KANSAS CITY	21,912	99,389	9,072	10.3	14	80
MO	6337	ST. LOUIS	36,007	156,966	8,719	9.9	5	81
SC	2902	CAMDEN	21,652	93,907	8,674	9.8	0	82
AR	7201	LITTLE ROCK	50,679	211,953	8,365	9.5	8	83
PA	1616	NEW CASTLE	2,284	9,239	8,090	9.2	0	84
OH	4568	ATHENS	9,725	39,000	8,021	9.1	1	85
NC	2822	CHARLOTTE	2,534	9,921	7,830	8.9	0	86
TX	7525	DALLAS	7,177	27,999	7,802	8.8	2	87
LA	7060	LAKE CHARLES	105,742	411,952	7,792	8.8	9	88
OH	4526	CINCINNATI	55	212	7,709	8.7	0	89
AL	3560	FLORENCE	50,489	189,067	7,489	8.5	15	90
LA	7079	BATON ROUGE	14,060	51,906	7,383	8.4	3	91
AR	7265	HARRISON	25,927	95,601	7,375	8.4	3	92
FL	3383	LAKELAND	38,391	141,077	7,349	8.3	18	93
OH	4409	CLEVELAND	103,995	381,505	7,337	8.3	4	94
VA	2451	LYNCHBURG	6,172	22,290	7,223	8.2	0	95
TX	7752	BAYTOWN	69,821	252,105	7,221	8.2	12	96
LA	7005	LAKELAND	93,812	336,971	7,184	8.1	14	97
OH	4566	CHILLIUCOTHE	66,095	235,840	7,136	8.1	2	98
NJ	0890	NEW BRUNSWICK	77,505	272,691	7,037	8.0	8	99
WV	2614	PARKERSBURG	21,467	74,137	6,907	7.8	1	100
		TOTAL — ABOVE AREAS	2,349,043	17,584,180	14,971	17.0	611	

TABLE 3
(CONTINUED)

ST	ZIP	POST OFFICE PLACE NAME	POPULATION	TOXIC WASTE (TONS)	LBS PER CAPITA	RATIO	SITES	RANK
NY	1214	ALBANY	29,083	100,118	6,885	7.8	4	101
WY	8261	SHIRLEY BASIN	645	2,195	6,806	7.7	0	102
TX	7770	BEAUMONT	127,459	431,496	6,771	7.7	26	103
FL	3257	PENSACOLA	57,705	194,506	6,741	7.6	5	104
KY	4200	PADUCAH	56,026	187,576	6,696	7.6	7	105
MO	6412	KANSAS CITY	92,505	306,188	6,620	7.5	21	106
CA	9007	LOS ANGELES	338	1,085	6,420	7.3	0	107
NM	8822	CARLSBAD	31,132	97,190	6,224	7.1	8	108
VA	2298	CHARLOTTESVILLE	25,822	80,340	6,223	7.1	6	109
IA	5276	ROCK ISLAND	35,275	109,609	6,215	7.0	5	110
NJ	0790	SUMMIT	21,309	66,221	6,215	7.0	0	111
TX	7750	PASADENA	113,130	348,465	6,160	7.0	20	112
WV	2610	PARKERSBURG	68,880	212,107	6,159	7.0	10	113
WV	2553	HUNTINGTON	12,727	38,862	6,107	6.9	3	114
FL	3236	TALLAHASSEE	1,343	4,034	6,007	6.8	1	115
TX	7900	AMARILLO	22,513	67,196	5,790	6.8	15	116
CT	0638	NEW LONDON	31,533	93,935	5,958	6.8	2	117
WA	9842	TACOMA	11,415	33,786	5,920	6.7	34	118
CT	0677	WATERBURY	56,445	166,285	5,892	6.7	3	119
NJ	0703	NEWARK	189,072	547,790	5,795	6.6	57	120
WV	2606	WHEELING	27,914	80,766	5,787	6.6	5	121
WA	2411	ROANOKE	37,722	108,879	5,773	6.5	3	122
WI	5382	MADISON	13,454	38,591	5,737	6.5	1	123
SC	2941	CHARLESTON	28,074	80,165	5,711	6.5	1	124
ID	8327	POCATELLO	12,820	35,920	5,604	6.4	9	125
NY	1410	BUFFALO	26,379	73,154	5,546	6.3	8	126
WY	8293	ROCKY SPRINGS	26,976	74,262	5,506	6.2	3	127
AR	7250	BATESVILLE	20,693	56,647	5,475	6.2	6	128
KS	6746	SALINA	19,171	52,427	5,469	6.2	2	129
IN	3740	CHATTANOOGA	82,050	213,039	5,193	5.9	37	130
IL	6016	MELROSE PARK	60,119	155,875	5,186	5.9	4	131
AL	3650	MOBILE	36,573	94,482	5,167	5.9	12	132
NJ	0798	SUMMIT	10,537	26,818	5,090	5.8	5	133
ID	8323	POCATELLO	5,698	14,202	4,993	5.7	8	134
NJ	0885	NEW BRUNSWICK	110,327	275,100	4,987	5.7	28	135
NY	1297	PLATTSBURGH	12,222	30,179	4,938	5.6	0	136
PA	1934	SOUTH EASTERN	40,078	98,936	4,937	5.6	7	137
TX	7560	LONG VIEW	80,063	196,039	4,897	5.6	14	138
DE	1997	DOVER	36,931	90,428	4,897	5.6	4	139
NC	2846	HICKORY	31,409	76,249	4,855	5.5	3	140
AL	3658	MOBILE	27,791	66,790	4,807	5.4	3	141
LA	7089	BATON ROUGE	602	1,414	4,698	5.3	0	142
VA	2414	ROANOKE	29,986	70,313	4,690	5.3	2	143
KS	6704	WICHITA	20,653	48,287	4,676	5.3	5	144
DE	1970	WILMINGTON	53,995	125,522	4,649	5.3	18	145
NJ	0886	NEW BRUNSWICK	93,561	216,220	4,622	5.2	29	146
MA	0210	BOSTON	6,202	14,245	4,594	5.2	1	147
IL	6243	EFFINGHAM	13,676	30,914	4,521	5.1	11	148
CT	0649	NEW HAVEN	95,743	214,392	4,478	5.1	18	149
MI	4890	LANSING	29,803	66,615	4,470	5.1	8	150
TOTAL — ABOVE AREAS			4,424,613	23,400,034	10,577	12.0	1,093	

TABLE 3

(CONTINUED)

ST	ZIP	POST OFFICE PLACE NAME	POPULATION	TOXIC WASTE (TONS)	LBS PER CAPITA	RATIO	SITES	RANK
IL	6007	NORTH SUBURBAN	88,096	196,509	4,461	5.1	4	151
WV	2605	WHEELING	9,177	20,407	4,447	5.0	5	152
MI	4943	GRAND RAPIDS	26,475	58,785	4,441	5.0	8	153
NJ	0711	NEWARK	141,701	312,132	4,406	5.0	6	154
CT	0683	GREENWICH	38,173	83,744	4,388	5.0	0	155
NJ	0707	NEWARK	112,670	246,298	4,372	5.0	25	156
NJ	0887	NEW BRUNSWICK	89,293	195,138	4,371	5.0	28	157
TX	7741	HOUSTON	32,253	70,385	4,365	4.9	8	158
OH	4448	WARREN	94,879	206,494	4,353	4.9	8	159
IN	4662	SOUTH BEND	28,590	62,032	4,339	4.9	10	160
NY	1381	BINGHAMPTON	23,330	50,257	4,308	4.9	4	161
MA	0173	BEDFORD	15,699	33,637	4,285	4.9	7	162
DE	1972	NEW CASTLE	47,078	99,743	4,237	4.8	16	163
OH	4521	CINCINNATI	214,225	451,950	4,219	4.8	26	164
CO	8109	PUEBLO	2,896	6,057	4,183	4.7	0	165
TX	7566	LONGVIEW	28,218	58,757	4,165	4.7	8	166
IL	6132	LA SALLE	9,733	20,133	4,137	4.7	1	167
WV	2604	WHEELING	31,155	64,388	4,133	4.7	3	168
CA	9351	MOJAVE	21,942	45,121	4,113	4.7	1	169
MI	4805	ROYAL OAK	174,901	359,534	4,111	4.7	13	170
MI	4819	DETROIT	169,183	344,841	4,077	4.6	22	171
NV	8901	LAS VEGAS	27,445	55,392	4,037	4.6	14	172
IN	3847	COLUMBIA	29,545	59,161	4,005	4.5	11	173
PA	1837	WILKES-BARRE	1,559	3,121	4,004	4.5	0	174
IN	4720	COLUMBUS	53,507	106,806	3,992	4.5	18	175
NY	1246	KINGSTON	8,173	16,118	3,944	4.5	1	176
NY	1280	GLEN FALLS	43,468	85,370	3,928	4.5	17	177
IL	6052	SOUTH SUBURBAN	86,423	169,505	3,923	4.4	11	178
TX	7972	BIG SPRINGS	31,538	61,837	3,921	4.4	5	179
WV	2617	PARKERSBURG	12,681	24,829	3,916	4.4	2	180
OH	4311	COLUMBUS	42,567	83,271	3,912	4.4	9	181
MO	6310	SAINT LOUIS	150,561	293,828	3,903	4.4	35	182
OH	4304	COLUMBUS	25,006	48,659	3,982	4.4	2	183
AR	7161	PINE BLUFF	353	687	3,892	4.4	1	184
IL	6124	ROCK ISLAND	40,529	78,255	3,862	4.4	2	185
IL	6130	LA SALLE	11,374	21,707	3,817	4.3	0	186
NY	1215	ALBANY	19,882	37,930	3,816	4.3	3	187
TX	7700	HOUSTON	205,439	388,501	3,782	4.3	16	188
PA	1512	PITTSBURGH	65,422	122,929	3,758	4.3	7	189
TX	7840	CORPUS CHRISTI	70,184	130,883	3,730	4.2	14	190
NY	1476	JAMESTOWN	26,005	48,464	3,727	4.2	6	191
AR	7239		29,742	55,106	3,706	4.2	3	192
PA	1900	PHILADELPHIA	131,203	242,126	3,691	4.2	11	193
WV	2551	HUNTINGTON	15,338	28,063	3,659	4.1	1	194
MI	4815	DETROIT	114,334	207,312	3,626	4.1	5	195
MD	2154	CUMBERLAND	5,113	9,237	3,613	4.1	1	196
PA	1605	BUTLER	39,394	70,359	3,572	4.1	9	197
AK	9961	ANCHORAGE	19120	33,645	3,519	4.0	9	198
IL	6253	SPRING FIELD	10,233	18,003	3,519	4.0	3	199
MD	2103	BALTIMORE	44,386	77,413	3,488	4.0	2	200
TOTAL — ABOVE AREAS			7,184,804	28,964,893	8,063	9.1	1,514	

TABLE 3

(CONTINUED)

ST	ZIP	POST OFFICE PLACE NAME	POPULATION	TOXIC WASTE (TONS)	LBS PER CAPITA	RATIO	SITES	RANK
TN	3713	NASHVILLE	79,779	139,057	3,486	4.0	12	201
IN	4639	GARY	26,899	46,737	3,475	3.9	7	202
SC	2938	GREENVILLE	15,762	27,369	3,473	3.9	3	203
PA	1903	PHILADELPHIA	82,627	142,913	3,459	3.9	5	204
WY	8233	RAWLINS	4,477	7,682	3,432	3.9	2	205
MS	3956	GULFPORT	108,753	184,872	3,400	3.9	14	206
OH	4400	CLEVELAND	62,790	106,587	3,395	3.8	26	207
SC	2960	GREENVILLE	106,993	181,071	3,385	3.8	5	208
OH	4500	CINCINNATI	39,553	66,875	3,382	3.8	3	209
TN	3840	COLUMBIA	37,529	62,342	3,322	3.8	9	210
IL	3840	EAST ST. LOUIS	116,139	189,287	3,260	3.7	22	211
TX	7567	MARSHALL	32,708	52,981	3,240	3.7	6	212
IL	6100	ROCKFORD	25,346	41,025	3,237	3.7	5	213
SC	2911	COLUMBIA	52,225	84,420	3,233	3.7	9	214
NJ	0701	NEWARK	198,127	319,598	3,226	3.7	7	215
NY	1409	BUFFALO	60,580	97,730	3,226	3.7	23	216
OH	4575	MARIETTA	29,362	47,263	3,219	3.7	6	217
ID	8320	POCATELLO	61,317	98,444	3,211	3.6	7	218
CA	9074	LONG BEACH	139,156	220,594	3,170	3.6	27	219
MI	4928	JACKSON	27,022	42,788	3,167	3.6	3	220
LA	7056	LAFAYETTE	49,806	78,764	3,163	3.6	2	221
NJ	0881	NEW BRUNSWICK	119,239	188,174	3,156	3.6	20	222
OH	4401	CLEVELAND	41,424	65,246	3,150	3.6	8	223
MO	6480	JOPLIN	54,535	85,069	3,120	3.5	14	224
KS	6733	INDEPENDENCE	29,943	46,533	3,108	3.5	4	225
NJ	0795	MORRIS PLAINS	17,007	26,262	3,088	3.5	2	226
PA	1942	SOUTH EASTERN	42,525	65,553	3,083	3.5	12	227
NJ	0811	CAMDEN	14,700	22,635	3,080	3.5	4	228
IL	6245	EFFINGHAM	29,983	46,043	3,071	3.5	30	229
NJ	0741	PATERSON	52,056	79,666	3,061	3.5	13	230
WV	2540	MARTINSBURG	31,166	47,617	3,056	3.5	4	231
IL	6204	ST. LOUIS	67,012	102,049	3,046	3.5	16	232
IL	6108	ROCKFORD	44,032	66,978	3,042	3.5	4	233
PA	1774	WILLIAMSPORT	36,166	54,798	3,035	3.4	14	234
NV	8982	ELKO	6,819	10,312	3,024	3.4	17	235
NC	2780	ROCKY MOUNTAIN	76,207	115,189	3,023	3.4	11	236
KY	4020	LOUISVILLE	141,586	213,520	3,016	3.4	6	237
VA	2383	PETERSBURG	59,232	88,826	2,999	3.4	10	238
NC	2801	CHARLOTTE	35,640	53,280	2,990	3.4	3	239
AL	3566	SHEFFIELD	24,415	36,358	2,978	3.4	14	240
NJ	0851	TRENTON	20,033	29,827	2,978	3.4	3	241
IN	4790	LAFAYETTE	114,735	169,382	2,953	3.3	4	242
AR	7175	CAMDEN	21,983	32,390	2,947	3.3	6	243
PA	1634	OIL CITY	18,519	27,217	2,939	3.3	7	244
PA	1670	BRADFORD	20,768	30,508	2,938	3.3	4	245
IN	4657	SOUTHBEND	15,368	22,569	2,937	3.3	2	246
OH	4540	DAYTON	141,517	207,643	2,935	3.3	8	247
TX	7701	HOUSTON	210,988	309,221	2,931	3.3	31	248
KY	4110	ASHLAND	45,663	66,890	2,930	3.3	8	249
PA	1932	SOUTH EASTERN	34,326	50,206	2,925	3.3	8	250
TOTAL — ABOVE AREAS			4,424,613	23,400,034	10,577	12.0	1,093	

TABLE 3

(CONTINUED)

ST	ZIP	POST OFFICE PLACE NAME	POPULATION	TOXIC WASTE (TONS)	LBS PER CAPITA	RATIO	SITES	RANK
NC	2762	RALEIGH	93	136	2,925	3.3	0	251
VA	2263	WINCHESTER	19,493	28,465	2,921	3.3	2	252
TX	7908	AMARILLO	21,497	31,189	2,902	3.3	24	253
LA	7007	NEW ORLEANS	78,556	113,904	2,900	3.3	13	254
IL	6244	EFFINGHAM	27,732	40,160	2,896	3.3	5	255
TX	7906	AMARILLO	31,332	45,268	2,890	3.3	9	256
PA	1792	POTTSVILLE	14,639	21,083	2,880	3.3	3	257
IN	4620	INDIANAPOLIS	199,608	286,933	2,875	3.3	15	258
IA	5111	SIOUX CITY	32	46	2,875	3.3	0	259
PA	1632	OIL CITY	24,472	35,144	2,872	3.3	4	260
NC	2850	KINGSTON	48,064	69,007	2,871	3.3	4	261
VA	2282	HARRISONBURG	18,029	25,702	2,851	3.2	1	262
AR	7182	TEXARKANA	12,575	17,874	2,843	3.2	2	263
IL	6006	NORTH SUBURBAN	184,262	261,463	2,838	3.2	5	264
OH	4395	STEUBENVILLE	54,315	76,547	2,819	3.2	1	265
DC	2037	WASHINGTON D.C.	177	249	2,814	3.2	2	266
CT	0647	NEW HAVEN	74,274	104,448	2,813	3.2	8	267
PA	1906	PHILADELPHIA	119,505	167,877	2,810	3.2	16	268
IL	6209	SAINT LOUIS	21,984	30,872	2,809	3.2	10	269
TN	3762	BRISTOL	38,462	53,929	2,804	3.2	7	270
OH	4470	CANTON	123,865	173,065	2,794	3.2	21	271
OH	4523	CINCINNATI	277,203	386,166	2,786	3.2	10	272
LA	7034	THIBODAUX	42,916	59,742	2,784	3.2	3	273
NJ	0793	SUMMIT	29,944	41,550	2,775	3.1	11	274
OH	4462	CANTON	36,243	50,237	2,772	3.1	5	275
NJ	0782	ALLAMUCHY	37,152	51,429	2,769	3.1	12	276
NJ	0806	SOUTH JERSEY	75,160	103,990	2,767	3.1	30	277
IN	4784	TERRE HAUTE	18,568	25,593	2,757	3.1	5	278
PA	1935	SOUTH EASTERN	25,868	35,191	2,721	3.1	10	279
MI	4880	LANSING	29,332	39,802	2,715	3.1	6	280
SC	2906	COLUMBIA	31,347	42,526	2,713	3.1	1	281
IN	4651	SOUTH BEND	84,076	113,963	2,711	3.1	13	282
MA	0188	WOBURN	55,836	75,435	2,702	3.1	10	283
NC	2766	RALEIGH	43	58	2,698	3.1	2	284
NJ	0706	NEWARK	153,210	206,205	2,692	3.1	7	285
WV	2532	CHARLESTON	6,650	8,942	2,689	3.1	0	286
IL	6161	PEORIA	86,768	116,429	2,684	3.0	4	287
GA	3035	ATLANTA	21,598	28,981	2,684	3.0	5	288
VA	2450	LYNCHBURG	86,895	115,576	2,660	3.0	10	289
PA	1782	HARRISBURG	27,156	35,847	2,640	3.0	4	290
IL	6136	LA SALLE	40,268	52,965	2,631	3.0	9	291
SC	2981	AUGUSTA	23,144	30,442	2,631	3.0	4	292
WI	5340	RACINE	122,279	160,790	2,630	3.0	5	293
NC	2814	SALISBURY	52,798	69,433	2,630	3.0	15	294
OH	4430	AKRON	114,230	150,118	2,628	3.0	14	295
SC	2983	AUGUSTA	17,529	23,003	2,625	3.0	3	296
SC	2955	FLORENCE	55,776	72,680	2,606	3.0	4	297
NC	2820	CHARLOTTE	152,012	197,199	2,595	2.9	34	298
MO	6346	HANNIBAL	13,837	17,939	2,593	2.9	2	299
LA	7003	NEW ORLEANS	29,712	38,366	2,583	2.9	9	300
TOTAL — ABOVE AREAS			12,969,797	37,497,211	5,782	6.5	2,403	

TABLE 3

(CONTINUED)

ST	ZIP	POST OFFICE PLACE NAME	POPULATION	TOXIC WASTE (TONS)	LBS PER CAPITA	RATIO	SITES	RANK
MO	6410	KANSAS CITY	38,816	49,960	2,574	2.9	13	301
NC	2840	WILMINGTON	92,909	118,919	2,560	2.9	20	302
TN	3731	CHATTANOOGA	79,933	102,155	2,556	2.9	9	303
WA	9824	EVERETT	26,092	33,285	2,551	2.9	7	304
NJ	0875	TRENTON	109,302	138,997	2,543	2.9	11	305
TN	3770	KNOXVILLE	17,613	22,394	2,543	2.9	3	306
CA	9024	INGLEWOOD	167,292	212,382	2,539	2.9	10	307
FL	3245	PANAMA CITY	10,711	13,484	2,518	2.9	3	308
OH	4563	CHILLICOTHE	44,694	56,243	2,517	2.9	6	309
VA	2352	NORFOLK	15,496	19,494	2,516	2.9	3	310
CA	9150	BURBANK	86,993	109,211	2,511	2.8	5	311
NJ	0760	HACKENSACK	76,478	95,904	2,508	2.8	3	312
NJ	0700	NEWARK	203,510	254,488	2,501	2.8	41	313
IL	6000	NORTH SUBURBAN	133,072	165,891	2,493	2.8	8	314
MA	0211	BOSTON	113,647	141,497	2,490	2.8	3	315
CT	0610	HARTFORD	135,738	167,447	2,467	2.8	2	316
PA	1567	GREENSBURG	19,168	23,595	2,462	2.8	1	317
LA	7072	BATON ROUGE	41,598	51,188	2,461	2.8	7	318
KS	6720	WICHITA	108,248	132,958	2,457	2.8	9	319
IL	6060	CHICAGO	215,728	264,233	2,450	2.8	21	320
OH	4332	COLUMBUS	19,669	23,994	2,435	2.8	2	321
PA	1950	READING	24,746	32,468	2,428	2.8	6	322
MN	5674	THIEF RIVER FALLS	3,005	3,643	2,425	2.8	0	323
CA	9271	SANTA ANA	62,787	76,002	2,421	2.7	1	324
WA	9805	EVERETT	115,512	139,522	2,416	2.7	10	325
MA	0120	PITTSFIELD	53,423	64,470	2,414	2.7	2	326
TX	7751	HOUSTON	73,577	88,755	2,413	2.7	20	327
PA	1643	ERIE	18,494	22,294	2,411	2.7	2	328
NY	1090	SUFFERN	20,859	25,060	2,403	2.7	1	329
WY	8231	JEFFREY CITY	2,358	2,820	2,392	2.7	3	330
WV	2603	WHEELING	33,410	39,944	2,391	2.7	11	331
PA	1960	READING	151,204	180,620	2,389	2.7	12	332
NJ	0862	TRENTON	27,940	33,273	2,382	2.7	1	333
NY	1373	BINGHAMPTON	20,924	24,898	2,380	2.7	3	334
IN	4630	GARY	66,596	79,188	2,378	2.7	2	335
NM	8824	HOBBS	34,943	41,385	2,369	2.7	11	336
WY	8270	NEW CASTLE	5,103	6,024	2,361	2.7	3	337
NJ	0708	NEWARK	157,268	184,695	2,349	2.7	12	338
LA	7066	LAKE CHARLES	52,076	61,111	2,347	2.7	11	339
WI	5320	MILWAUKEE	263,150	308,372	2,344	2.7	17	340
NY	1346	UTICA	9,175	10,755	2,344	2.7	2	341
MO	6335	SAINT LOUIS	13,400	15,666	2,338	2.7	2	342
OH	4411	CLEVELAND	257,030	299,663	2,332	2.6	34	343
MO	6304	SAINT LOUIS	76,337	88,709	2,324	2.6	16	344
VT	0574	RUTLAND	5,556	6,456	2,324	2.6	0	345
OK	7410	TULSA	105,270	121,577	2,310	2.6	26	346
DC	2031	WASHINGTON D.C.	314	362	2,306	2.6	1	347
KY	4100	CINCINNATI	38,773	44,580	2,300	2.6	2	348
PA	1614	NEW CASTLE	49,879	56,770	2,276	2.6	4	349
OH	4580	LIMA	94,930	107,533	2,266	2.6	11	350
TOTAL — ABOVE AREAS			16,566,543	41,861,495	5,054	5.7	2,816	

TABLE 3

(CONTINUED)

ST	ZIP	POST OFFICE PLACE NAME	POPULATION	TOXIC WASTE (TONS)	LBS PER CAPITA	RATIO	SITES	RANK
SC	2930	SPARTANBURG	104,156	117,696	2,260	2.6	12	351
WY	8310	KEMMERER	3,584	4,037	2,253	2.6	2	352
PA	1501	PITTSBURGH	75,322	84,617	2,247	2.5	5	353
MI	4900	KALAMAZOO	176,599	197,080	2,232	2.5	29	354
NY	1278	MONTICELLO	9,605	10,653	2,218	2.5	0	355
IA	5105	SIOUX CITY	13,039	14,456	2,217	2.5	3	356
MI	4951	GRAND RAPIDS	102	113	2,216	2.5	0	357
OH	4571	ATHENS	20,891	23,141	2,215	2.5	5	358
TX	7790	VICTORIA	63,363	69,968	2,208	2.5	5	359
OK	7436	TULSA	27,433	30,130	2,197	2.5	22	360
CA	9050	TORRANCE	148,711	162,964	2,192	2.5	7	361
MN	5544	MINNEAPOLIS	45,580	49,720	2,182	2.5	4	362
NY	1415	TONAWANDA	59,387	64,672	2,178	2.5	39	363
OH	4403	CLEVELAND	110,074	119,747	2,176	2.5	15	364
SC	2965	GREENVILLE	61,039	66,256	2,171	2.5	7	365
RI	0290	PROVIDENCE	180,405	194,567	2,157	2.4	6	366
MD	2107	BALTIMORE	27,913	30,079	2,155	2.4	3	367
WA	9935	PASCO	49,983	53,152	2,127	2.4	5	368
OH	4504	CINCINNATI	78,082	82,814	2,121	2.4	9	369
NJ	0751	RIDGEWOOD	39,635	41,873	2,113	2.4	1	370
NC	2875	ASHEVILLE	45,470	47,998	2,111	2.4	4	371
AR	7173	EL DORADO	35,762	37,713	2,109	2.4	10	372
LA	7128	MONROE	18,742	19,625	2,094	2.4	2	373
NY	1230	SCHENECTADY	153,893	160,347	2,084	2.4	13	374
GA	3152	WAYCROSS	54,700	56,869	2,079	2.4	14	375
MS	3973	COLUMBUS	20,029	20,789	2,076	2.4	4	376
AZ	8563	TUCSON	40,881	42,410	2,075	2.4	5	377
NY	1402	BUFFALO	29,396	30,504	2,075	2.4	8	378
PA	1506	PITTSBURGH	123,175	127,479	2,070	2.3	12	379
TX	7762	BEAUMONT	35,213	36,334	2,064	2.3	3	380
PA	1893	SOUTH EASTERN	9,474	9,779	2,064	2.3	1	381
NJ	0750	PATERSON	114,288	117,784	2,061	2.3	11	382
MA	0145	WORCESTER	44,911	46,147	2,055	2.3	5	383
MA	0133	SPRINGFIELD	17,183	17,654	2,055	2.3	1	384
UT	8453	PROUD	16,062	16,500	2,055	2.3	7	385
ME	0469	BANGOR	4,438	4,558	2,054	2.3	3	386
IL	6090	KANAKEE	42,327	43,455	2,053	2.3	9	387
PA	1754	LANCASTER	48,936	50,097	2,047	2.3	7	388
TX	7610	FORT WORTH	173,033	176,926	2,045	2.3	26	389
MA	0270	PROVIDENCE	37,536	38,385	2,045	2.3	12	390
OH	4302	COLUMBUS	33,340	33,970	2,038	2.3	3	391
IN	4733	MUNCIE	46,311	46,937	2,027	2.3	3	392
MS	3957	GULFPORT	31,669	32,032	2,023	2.3	5	393
CA	9005	LOS ANGELES	74,145	74,950	2,022	2.3	7	394
OH	4414	CLEVELAND	163,957	165,711	2,021	2.3	19	395
MI	4944	GRAND RAPIDS	132,068	133,170	2,017	2.3	0	400
KS	6676	FORT SCOTT	27,235	27,358	2,009	2.3	3	397
NJ	0773	RED BANK	108,303	107,641	1,988	2.3	6	398
MI	4812	DETROIT	170,635	169,457	1,986	2.3	4	399
VT	0575	RUTLAND	13,610	13,486	1,982	2.2	0	400
TOTAL — ABOVE AREAS			19,408,239	44,961,422	4,581	5.2	3,256	

The top 50 areas include many which have been the subject of local environmental controversy for many years. Before commenting on these areas, it should be reemphasized again that these estimates of toxic waste generation do not take into account variations in the degree of care with which these wastes have been managed. So when specific plants and companies are referred to, no inferences can be drawn about the degree of environmental risk at various locations without a detailed examination of the actual local environmental problem and the steps taken to reduce adverse effects. It is the purpose of this book to stimulate such local examinations.

In the course of CEP studies there have been many indications that some plants do indeed manage their wastes quite well over a sufficiently long period of time. This demonstrates that the proper management of wastes is possible.

As indicated above, some of the most troublesome toxic waste problems are associated with military installations that are not subject to monitoring by EPA. Many of the top areas in Table 3 are the sites of large Federal facilities for the processing and enrichment of uranium and plutonium for nuclear weapons. Because these facilities are frequently operated by contractors, they are classified as chemical plants under the Standard Industrial Classification code 2819, Inorganic Industrial Chemicals. CEP estimated toxic waste for these plants by multiplying their large employment by the toxic waste per worker ratio derived from the experience of other plants classified as producers of inorganic industrial chemicals. This procedure makes no allowance for the radioactivity of plutonium, that makes the toxic waste problems at these sites far more dangerous.

As an example, the 18th ranking area in Table 3 is Area 3783, Oak Ridge, Tennessee. It has a toxic waste per capita level 102 times that of the nation, without any allowance for the radioactivity of the plutonium produced there. In confirmation of the danger to public health at this site, the Tennessee Department of Health and Environment disclosed in 1983 that 2.4 million pounds of mercury had been discharged into the East Fork Poplar Creek from the Oak Ridge Y-12 plant. The plant uses massive quantities of the highly toxic mercury in the production of lithium deuteride fuel for thermonuclear weapons.

Other nuclear installations can be found in Area 2980, Aiken, South Carolina; Area 4202 near Paducah, Kentucky; and in Area 9935 in Richland, Washington.

Table 3 also indicates high toxic waste rankings for many petrochemical installations in Texas and Louisiana, as in Area 7754, Freeport, Texas; Area 7834, Corpus Christi, Texas; Areas 7073 and 7076 in Baton Rouge, Louisiana; Area 7759, Texas City, Texas; Area 7764, Port Arthur, Texas; and Area 7753, Baytown, Texas.

Frequently petrochemical installations will be found fairly close to other process-control and metal working operations that also produce toxic waste. This is true for example of the 52nd ranking area, 1430, Niagra Falls, home of Love Canal and of such areas as the 33rd ranking Area, 2386, Hopewell, Virginia, with plants owned by Hercules, Allied Chemical, Firestone Rubber, ICI America, and Continental Can. All are within short distances from each other.

The 53rd ranking area, 0802, Deepwater, New Jersey, merits some comment. It is the home of a DuPont facility known as the Chambers Works. This plant was the subject of publicity in 1983 because it reported treating 40 million metric tons of toxic waste, or 27 percent of the national total in the EPA 1981 Survey of Hazardous Waste Generators. The report produced consternation since EPA had previously estimated annual generation of toxic waste at 60 million tons. The *New York Times* quoted the plant manager as explaining that "99 percent was water used in the advanced treatment process to make the water safe." Presumably only one percent, or 400,000 tons, represented the dry weight equivalent. (Incidentally this is close to CEP's own estimate of 463,000 tons for Area 08023.) Also, public health questions can be raised by the treatment process used by the Chamber Works. It requires the surface impoundment and evaporation of huge quantities of liquid toxic waste in ponds and lagoons covering many acres.

Closed Toxic Waste Sites

Love Canal dramatized the potential risks posed by the presence of thousands of abandoned, inactive toxic waste depositories all over the country; many covered over and forgotten. EPA is only in the early stages of assessing the environmental problems at each site. But it has already put close to 900 on a National Priority List for consideration of possible Superfund cleanup grants. A report released by the Congressional Office of Technology Assessment in March, 1985 estimated as many as 10,000 would require priority cleanup at an eventual cost of $100 billion.

As of this writing, about 20,000 closed sites have been assembled into an EPA database called ERRIS for Emergency and Remedial Response Information System. This file contains all locations that reportedly at some time accepted hazardous substances for transport, storage, treatment, or disposal, or where such substances have accidentally or illegally been spilled or dumped. This file has been used to indicate the number in each 5 digit Zip

Code area. These figures are shown in the tabular section of this book as a "Quality of Life" indicator to help trace the locational ties between the places where toxic waste is generated and treated and where it is or has been disposed of.

The Zip code locations of closed toxic waste sites give us another view of the geographic distribution of toxic waste, independent of the site of generation. In general, closed waste sites are located close to the places where toxic waste was being generated in 1980.

For example, the largest closed toxic waste site in Illinois is the U.S. Ecology Landfill in Zip code 61361 near Sheffield, Illinois. In operation from the late sixties to 1983, it accepted a wide variety of hazardous wastes, including acids, bases, organic solvents, pesticides, and sludges. Monitoring wells in the shallow aquifer at the site in 1983 indicated contamination with arenes, chlorinated hydrocarbons, ether, and PCBs. An estimated 450 persons within three miles of the site use this aquifer as a source of drinking water. Zip code 61361 itself contains no plant that was generating toxic waste in 1980. However, well within transport distance, several areas with high levels of toxic waste generation can be found. Such is the case of Areas 61322, 61327, 61354, 61360, and 61373.

Another example is a waste site near Darrow, Louisiana, in Area 70725. It does not appear in the statistical tabulation because it has less than 50 families. This site, called the Old Inger Oil Refinery, was started in 1976 to reclaim oil from nearby refinery wastes. A spill in 1978 contaminated a large surface area and the site was declared "abandoned" in 1981 when petrochoemicals were found to contaminate the drinking water for a few thousand persons within a three mile radius.

The list of ERRIS sites is expected to continue to grow as companies are encouraged by EPA to dig into their back waste management records. While not all sites are equally dangerous, the number deserving to be cleaned up is surely much greater than the 786 National Priority List sites carried at the end of 1984. At that time, EPA announced that a four year effort succeeded in "cleaning up" only six of the most dangerous sites. It should be noted that a Washington-based environmental network, the National Campaign Against Hazardous Waste, reported two of these six sites as posing only minor hazards. The number of ERRIS sites have been included in Table 3.

The top 400 toxic waste 4 digit areas, with 8.7 percent of the total population, includes 3,256 of the 19,972 ERRIS sites found to date (16 percent of the total). From the proximity of these sites to the major points of toxic waste generation accounting for nearly one half of the national total, CEP suggests that these 3,256 ERRIS sites may be the largest and probably the most deserving of investigation for a National Priority Listing.

6. RELATION OF INCOME LEVELS TO TOXIC WASTE

One would expect that income levels per household are systematically correlated, either directly or inversely, with other demographic characteristics. With some interesting exceptions in regard to toxic waste, this turns out to be quite true.

Table 4 summarizes key characteristics for all 5 digit Zip code areas arrayed in high to low sequence according to income per household. All 40,000 areas are covered here, including about 4,000 areas with no population at all and about 1,000 areas with fewer than 50 households. Summaries of characteristics are provided for each of five quintiles. Each quintile covers about one-fifth of the total population, or 45 million persons, representing successive income layers.

Thus for areas making up the most affluent 20 percent of the population, income per household averages out to $39,900, about 46 percent higher than the national average of $27,400. For each quintile, there is a steady

TABLE 4

Summary of Characteristics, Quintile Distribution,
5 Digit Areas in Order of Mean Household Income

Quintile	Pop. (mil.)	White %	His-panic % (mil.)	% of House holds Occup. (mil.)	% Owner Occup.	Mean H.H. Income (Th.)	Mean Monthly Rent $	Mean Value Home (Th.$)	Pop. % Under 5	Pop. % 65 & over	# Closed Toxic Sites	Tons Toxic Waste Gen. (Th.)	Lbs. Toxic Waste Per Cap.
First	45.3	91.7	3.7	15.8	71.7	39.9	429	164.2	6.3	8.8	2,462	17,887	789
Second	45.3	87.2	4.9	16.1	66.8	29.5	352	106.8	7.2	10.0	3,546	22,197	980
Third	45.3	84.4	5.3	16.3	65.5	25.5	301	82.4	7.3	11.9	4,131	20,755	916
Fourth	45.4	77.3	6.3	16.2	63.7	22.2	263	63.7	7.5	12.9	4,409	14,858	655
Fifth	45.2	75.2	11.9	16.1	54.4	20.2	271	54.4	7.8	12.9	5,434	24,303	1075
All Areas	226.5	83.2	6.4	80.5	64.4	27.4	315	97.6	7.2	11.3	19,972	100,000	883

downward progression in income levels to $20,200 per year for the poorest quintile. All other characteristics display the same steady progression. The White percentage declines from 91.7 in the richest quintile to 75.2 in the poorest quintile. The Hispanic percentage rises steadily from a low of 3.7 to a high of 11.9 for the poorest quintile. The owner occupancy percentage declines steadily from a high of 71.7 to a low of 54.4. Mean monthly rent declines fairly steadily from a high of $429 to a low of $263 in the fourth quintile. Residents of the poorest quintile have the highest ratio of renters, paying a mean monthly rental of $271. The mean value of owner occupied homes declines steadily from a high of $164,200 to a low of $54,400.

Even the percentages of the very young and old are systematically correlated to income levels. The richest quintile has only 6.3 percent of its population in the age group under five and only 8.8 percent in the 65 and over group. This is in contrast with the poorest quintile, with 12.9 percent and 11.9 percent in these two respective age groups.

With regard to the two measures of toxic waste, it is true that the richest quintile looks best. It has the smallest number of abandoned toxic waste sites discovered to date and the second lowest per capita level of toxic waste generation. (It should be noted, however, from the previous section that a "clean" 5 digit area can be close enough to a toxic waste area to share some environmental problems.) Thus, the richest quintile generated toxic waste at the level of 789 pounds per capita, 11 percent below the national average of 883 pounds. The poorest quintile had a level of 1,074 pounds per capita, 22 percent above the national average. It appears that for 5 digit areas, affluence can indeed purchase a degree of protection from direct exposure to toxic waste.

It is interesting to note, however, that the second highest level of toxic waste generation per capita is seen in the second quintile. This quintile has an income per household of $29,500, well above the national average. Equally interesting is the fact that for the third and fourth quintiles per capita levels of toxic waste generation declines as income levels decline.

Thus there is a paradox. The fourth quintile, with a mean household income level of only $22,000, 45 percent lower than that of the first quintile, has a toxic waste per capita level of only 655 lbs. Certainly, this is a far better showing than that of the richest quintile. This suggests that poor people living in non-industrial rural areas or those living in central city areas that had lost much of its industry by 1980, may be less exposed than residents of higher income areas. On the other hand, the poorest areas are all increasingly exposed to dangers emanating from abandoned waste sites containing toxic residues of past industrial activity.

The fact that many high income areas suffer from a close proximity to toxic waste concentrations is borne out by Table 5. It allows a closer look at the income levels of the 5 digit Zip code areas included in the top 400 four digit Zip areas.

Once again the 5 digit areas have been arrayed in high to low sequence according to income per household in Table 5. And again, all these areas have been divided into five quintiles. Each quintile has about 4 million residents. It is immediately apparent that income levels here have little direct relationship to toxic waste levels. The highest toxic waste levels (six times greater than the national average) can be found in the second quintile. Households in this quintile have a mean income of $31,100, well above the national average of $27,400.

On the other hand, the number of toxic waste sites does increase in each quintile—from 415 in the first to 707 in the fifth quintile—as the mean income level declines from $40,500 to $18,700. Table 6 yields a perhaps better perception of the ironies involved in location of high income areas in close proximity to toxic waste concentrations.

Table 6 lists the some of the most affluent 5 digit areas in the first quintile of Table 5, rearranged by state but

TABLE 5

**Summary of Characteristics of 5 Digit Areas Included in the Top 400
Digit Zip Code Areas With Respect to Toxic Waste**

(Quintile Distribution of All 5 Digit Zip Code Areas, in Order of Mean Household Income)

Quintile	Pop. (mil.) (mil.)	White %	His-panic %	% of House holds Occup. (mil.)	% Owner Occup.	Mean H.H. Income (Th.)	Mean Monthly Rent $	Mean Value Home (Th.$)	Pop. % Under 5	Pop. % 65 & over	# Closed Toxic Sites	Tons Toxic Waste Gen.(Th.)	Lbs. Toxic Waste Per Cap.
First	4.0	93.0	2.6	1.4	73.8	40.5	462	121.1	6.0	9.4	415	6,962	3510
Second	4.0	88.7	4.4	1.4	69.5	31.1	388	80.7	7.0	9.8	556	10,416	5234
Third	4.0	87.1	3.8	1.4	67.2	27.1	342	65.7	7.2	11.5	713	7,625	3823
Fourth	4.0	79.4	5.0	1.4	64.7	23.8	301	52.2	7.4	12.0	744	9,236	4637
Fifth	4.0	59.2	10.0	1.4	47.9	18.7	270	37.1	8.0	12.8	707	7,949	4087
All Areas	20.0	81.6	5.1	7.0	64.6	28.2	338	74.2	7.1	11.1	3135	42,189	4259

preserving the high to low income sequence. All areas have mean income levels higher than $50,000 per household. But some have population levels so small as to yield extremely high per capita toxic waste levels and, as such, of possibly misleading significance. (For this reason and because of space limitations, the tabulation of data for 5 digit areas in the Zip Directory omits areas with fewer than 50 households.)

Aside from areas with extremely small populations, Table 6 does include many large, high income areas, particularly in New Jersey and Pennsylvania where high toxic waste levels may come as a great surprise. Many of these have large waste generating facilities within the 5 digit Zip boundary. Others, like Area 19035, Gladwyne, Pennsylvania; Area 19357, Merion Station, Pennsylvania; and Area 19357, Mendenhall, Pennsylvania have no waste sites or generators within the 5 digit boundary. They do, however, fall into a 4 digit area with heavy toxic concentrations.

Most of these areas are predominantly white, have high monthly rentals, and high home values. Consider for example the case of Area 07417, Franklin Lakes, New Jersey. With a mean household income of $75,200 and a mean home value of $294,300, it has within its boundaries two toxic waste sites, and a per capita toxic waste level twice that of the nation, and lies in a four digit Zip area containing 13 toxic waste sites.

It is also interesting to note there are several high income areas in Table 6 with Black populations, such as Area 08858, Oldwhich, New Jersey; Area 19357, Mendenhall, Pennsylvania; Area 19421, Media, Pennsylvania; and Area 19421, Birchrunville, Pennsylvania.

On balance, the areas most exposed to the generation of toxic waste in 1980 are those with petrochemical and heavy industry. Often thought of as the heartland of middle America, industrial wage rates are higher than average in these areas. But when the ubiquitous spread of abandoned toxic waste sites are considered, both those in our study and the perhaps hundreds of thousands that some observers believe remain to be discovered, it is clear that few of us can be regarded as safe. One way to add precision to any accounting of who really has suffered from such exposures is to study the widespread geographic variation in cancer mortality rates. These are excessive in many areas that are both urban and rural, rich, poor, and middle class. One study under way at CEP will examine the differential impact on geographical variations in cancer mortality rates, by type of cancer, of several factors other than toxic waste. For example, the degree of urbanization of an area, measured in terms of population per square mile, appears to be a significant factor in explaining variations in cancer mortality. But urban areas also have more industrial activity than rural areas. So it does become important to find ways of isolating the differential impact of toxic waste and urbanization.

TABLE 6

High Income 5 Digit Areas Close to High Toxic Waste Concentrations, By State

Zip Code	Place Name	Pop.	% White	Mean Income Per H.H. Th. $	Mean Monthly Rent $	Mean Home Value Th. $	# Toxic Waste Sites 5 Digit	4 Digit	Tox. Waste Rel. to U.S. (883 lbs. per Capita) 5 Digit	4 Digit
California										
90743	Surfside	416	0	62.4	757	393.8	0	27	9	3.6
90056	Los Angeles	8,252	53	53.6	533	315.3	1	7	0	2.2
92715	Santa Ana	20,078	88	52.2	691	295.4	0	1	1.8	2.2
Connecticut										
06720	Waterbury	84	100	58.8	675	85.2	3	3	628.7	629.5
06490	Southport	2,364	99	51.4	657	240.3	0	18	5.5	5.1
District of Columbia										
20374	Washington	173	85	75.6	675	269.2	1	2	0	3.2
Illinois										
60521	Hinsdale	38,223	94	64.8	481	244.8	3	11	4.0	4.4
60062	North Brook	37,730	97	64.2	633	235.7	1	5	3.9	3.2
60077	Skokie	2,583	89	58.1	720	177.5	1	4	3.5	5.1
Kansas										
67206	Wichita	10,071	95	58.7	396	191.1	0	9	0	2.8
Louisiana										
70773	Rougon	185	30	58.2	195	43.8	0	3	0	12.7
Massachusetts										
01451	Harvard	3,729	99	51.9	471	189.0	0	5	0	2.3
Missouri										
63178	St. Louis	62	100	108.5	438	317.2	0	1	135.6	2400.9
63045	Hazelwood	68	100	53.9	619	124.8	0	16	97.9	2.6
64115	Kansas City	2,948	94	53.0	226	173.7	0	0	.2	16.0
New Jersey										
07078	Short Hills	12,838	97	91.0	648	297.9	0	25	.8	5.0
07931	Far Hills	2,132	98	84.3	547	224.3	0	11	4.1	3.1
07417	Franklin Lakes	8,788	99	75.2	901	294.3	2	13	2.0	3.5
07733	Holmdel	8,528	98	70.2	685	234.7	0	6	2.2	2.3
07079	South Orange	15,864	87	57.0	504	155.2	0	25	.2	5.0
07039	Livingston	28,040	96	55.8	740	181.2	1	57	.4	6.6
07901	Summit	21,309	93	55.4	583	226.1	0	0	7.0	7.0
08858	Oldwick	450	0	51.3	696	177.2	0	28	0	5.7
New York										
10964	Palisades	786	97	54.1	349	219.4	0	5	0	10.7
North Carolina										
28406	Wilmington	68	100	93.4	1073	320.3	1	20	0	2.9
28224	Charlotte	28	0	71.9	826	72.4	0	0	489.7	8.9
28234	Charlotte	34	100	59.1	255	210.6	0	1	11.0	1570.7
Pennsylvania										
19035	Gladwyne	3,755	98	90.1	678	283.3	0	5	0	3.9
19357	Menden Hall	287	0	87.2	1002	151.7	0	10	0	3.1
19066	Merion Station	5,686	98	67.2	547	176.9	0	16	0	3.2
19481	Valley Forge	1,296	0	62.5	409	230.0	2	4	92.2	178.3
19065	Media	663	0	56.9	420	185.1	0	16	0	3.2
15015	Bradford Woods	1,296	100	56.8	336	166.1	0	5	0	2.5
19421	Birchrunville	434	0	55.3	479	169.8	0	12	0	3.5
19034	Fort Washington	5,017	98	52.3	484	179.7	2	5	33.6	3.9
19004	Bala-Cynwyd	10,276	98	52.0	546	141.2	0	11	1.1	4.2
19425	Chester Springs	2,698	99	51.7	526	179.0	0	12	0	3.5
19006	Huntingdon Val.	19,993	99	50.9	515	162.8	2	11	.7	4.2
Texas										
75711	Tyler	77	100	136.0	502	484.3	1	4	0	175.5
75252	Dallas	13,737	99	54.8	175	232.7	0	2	0	8.8

7. RELATION OF TOXIC WASTE TO CANCER

Exposure to toxic waste poses many health hazards, among which cancer is the most ominous. The Council On Economic Priorities has for some time been conducting a study of the relationship between toxic waste concentrations and the variation in county cancer mortality rates. Initial findings, as published in the September, 1984 CEP Newsletter, *"Toxic Waste and Cancer: The Link Is Getting Stronger,"* are summarized below.

Of the 10 million American cancer deaths recorded since 1950, perhaps 16 percent, or more than one million, can be associated with occupational exposure to carcinogens and air and water pollution, according to a report of the Office of Technology Assessment of the U.S. Congress. A small but statistically significant association between higher cancer rates and above average toxic waste concentrations in 59 rural counties with petrochemical facilities was established in the Newsletter.

But in the Spring of 1984, an EPA survey of hazardous waste generators revealed that the bulk of all toxic wastes generated in the U.S. came as a result of operations conducted by petrochemical plants. CEP, at that point, decided to study cancer mortality in 59 rural counties that had at least one percent (or more) of its labor force engaged in petrochemical production and were therefore characterized by high levels of per capita toxic waste. It was found that in the 1950-59 decade these counties had below average cancer rates. Twenty years later (just about the time required for exposure to cancer risks to result in cancer deaths), these rural counties had cancer rates significantly above average.

It is worth examining in some detail how this fact can be demonstrated, for the technique involved is generally useful in our examination of cancer mortality rates for 5 digit Zip code areas, that are far smaller than counties in geographic size.

Table 7 contains a procedure developed to calculate the expected number of cancer deaths for any randomly selected group of white males. Statisticians have a simple but conclusive way to determine whether that section is really "random." If it is not, then it must be concluded that there is a forcce of mortality operating on that group significantly different from the force of mortality affecting other white males.

Since older persons are more likely to die of cancer than younger persons, in Table 7, for the year 1950 and then for 1970, the white male population has been divided into two groups: those over 65 years of age and those under 65.

The concept of the "expected" number of cancer deaths for any part of the U.S. therefore rests on the following proposition: Assume that for any given area the mortality rate for old people is the same as it is in the U.S. The only reason for that area to have a different "expected" mortality rate, therefore, would be if its proportion of old people differed from that of the nation as a whole.

Thus, an area with an older white male population than the U.S. would have an expected cancer mortality rate higher than the U.S. This is due to the higher "age-specific" mortality rate of older white males. The higher mortality rate will be weighted in the calculation procedure by the somewhat higher proportion of older white males (See Appendix B.).

All data in Table 7 came from either the Census Bureau or the National Cancer Institute (NCI). For the U.S. the "age-specific" cancer mortality rate for white males over 65 was .12350 for the period 1950-1959 (line 5). Thus, white males in the U.S. who were 65 years or older in 1950 died of cancer between 1950-59 at the rate of 12,350 per 100,000 white males. The age-specific rate for white males under 65 (line 6) is as expected, quite a bit lower; only .00813, or 813 deaths per 100,000 in this ten-year period. The combined mortality rate for both age groups (line 9) is .01687, or 1,687 deaths per 100,000. Multiplying this combined mortality rate by the 67,300,000 white males in 1950 yields an expected number of cancer deaths of 1,135,351 (line 10). This is aproximately equal to the recorded number 1,135,259 (line 11). Thus, the ratio of recorded to expected deaths for all white males in the U.S. is 1.00. Even greater agreement between the two numbers would be achieved if more decimal values were used in the calculations.

TABLE 7

Expected and Recorded White Male Cancer Deaths, 1950-59, 1970-79 in the U.S.A. and in 59 Rural Counties

Line No.	Source	U.S.		59 Rural Counties	
		1950-59	1970-79	1950-59	1970-79
1. # White Male (Th.)	Census	67,300	86,906	924.6	1215.2
2. # W.M. over 65 (Th.)	Census	5,101.3	7,615	62.1	92.8
3. Ratio of W.M. over 65	Line 2 ÷ Line 1	.0758	.0876	.0672	.0764
4. Ratio of W.M. under 65	1.00 – Line 1	.9242	.9124	.9328	.9236
5. Age Specific Mort. Rate for W.M. over 65	NCI	.12350	.14012	.12350	.14012
6. Age Spec. Mort. Rate for W.M. under 65	NCI	.00813	.00868	.00813	.00868
7. Weighted Age Spec. Rate W.M. over 65	Line 3 × Line 5	.00936	.01228	.00830	.01070
8. Weighted Age Spec. Rate W.M. under 65	Line 4 × Line 6	.00751	.00792	.00758	.00801
9. Expected W.M. Cancer Mortality Rate	Line 7 + Line 8	.01687	.02020	.01588	.01871
10. Expected Number of W.M. Cancer Deaths	Line 1 × Line 9	1,135,351	1,755,501	14,756	22,745
11. Recorded # Deaths	NCI	1,135,259	1,754,868	12,890	23,674
12. Crude W.M. Cancer Mortality Rate	Line 11 ÷ Line 1	.01687	.02019	.01371	.01948
13. Ratio, Rec. to Exp. W.M. Cancer Deaths	Line 11 ÷ Line 10	1.00	1.00	.88	1.04

Now consider the corresponding calculations for the 59 "rural petrochemical" counties.* Let us assume that in each decade each county has the same age-specific cancer mortality rates as the U.S. This is equivalent to assuming that white males in these counties were subject to the same exposure to carcinogens in the air, water, diet, tobacco, etc. as all other white males in the U.S. in those periods. But note that, on the whole, the 59 counties had a somewhat younger white male population than the U.S. in 1950-59—6.7 percent into the older age group as against 7.6 percent in the U.S. Thus, its expected cancer mortality rate in the earlier decade is .01588 (line 9)—6 percent lower than the corresponding national rate of .01687.

Allowing for a lowering of its expected mortality rate because of the relative youthfulness of these counties the recorded number deaths, (taken from the NCI files) 12,890, is 12 percent below the expected number of 14,576. It can be demonstreald that the divergence of the ratio of recorded to expected deaths (line 13) in this case is far too great to be due to chance. And, therefore, these counties appear not to have been subject to the same degree of exposure to carcinogens as all other counties in the U.S. in the period 1950-59.

But first consider the changes wrought over a twenty year period, by repeating this exercise for the years 1970-79 using the 1970 Census of Population for the demographic data in this decade.

Two significant changes raised the white male cancer mortality rate (line 9) for the ten-year period from 1,687 deaths per 100,000 to 2,020 per 100,000—a gain of twenty percent. This gain is due in part to the fact that the population has aged over the 20 years. Thus, the percentage of older persons increased from 7.58 to 8.76—a gain of 16 percent. The age specific rates for each age group also increased, however. Thus, for persons 65 and older, the cancer mortality rate went from 12,350 deaths per 100,000 in the early decade to 14,012 per 100,000 in the later decade—a gain of 13 percent. The rate for younger white males went up from 813 deaths per 100,000 to 868 per 100,000—a gain of seven percent.

It is evident from this table that an important change has also taken place in these rural petrochemical counties. In the earlier decade, they had below average cancer mortality rates. Twenty years later, however, they had above average cancer mortality rates. Table 7 shows that the number of recorded deaths for the 59 rural counties was four percent higher than the number of expected deaths for the 1970-79 decade. Is this change statistically significant or could it be dismissed as a "chance" result?

It is necessary to review the manner in which statisticians answer this question. Consider first the question of whether the four percent increase in the reported white male cancer deaths in rural petrochemical counties over the

*We define these as having less than 50,000 white males, and more than one percent of its total employment engaged in the production of petrochemicals in 1967-70. They include in order of size: Alabama: Morgan, Talledega, Washington; Arkansas: Saline, Baxter; Delaware: Sussex; Florida: Dixie; Georgia: Glynn; Idaho: Power; Indiana: Clark, Posey; Iowa: Clinton; Dansas: Butler, Cherokee; Kentucky: McCracken, Boyd, Marshall; Louisiana: Ascension, St. Charles, Plaquemines, Iberville, St. James; Michigan: Midland; Missouri: Bolivar, Yazoo, St. Charles, Jasper; New Jersey: Salem; New York: Chenango; North Carolinads: Rowan, New Hanover, Cleveland, Lenoir, Transylvania; Ohio: Pickaway, Union, Pike; Oklahoma: Kay; South Carolina: Aiken, York, Greenwood, Kershaw; Tennessee; Anderson, Carter, Roane, Hamblen; Texas: Orange, Gregg; Virginia: Montgomery, Augusta, Henry, Giles; Washington: Benton; West Virginia: Wood.

expected number in the 1970-79 period is statistically significant, since four percent may not appear to be a very large divergence.

The question of the statistical significance of an observed cancer mortality rate is quite important, literally a question of life or death to anyone living in an area exposed to an excessive risk of cancer. We would like to spend some time describing how statisticians answer this question.

(Readers familiar with statistical theory should forgive the author for perhaps excessive detail in this section. Others may welcome an opportunity to see how such theory accords with a common sense appreciation of the essential facts. CEP also firmly feels the need to demystify the technique of calculating cancer mortality rates that has too often been used in the past by government "experts" to conceal essential facts from the public. The statistical procedure depicted here is fairly standard except for one simplification. In the computerized calculation of expected cancer mortality rates, government epidemiologists divide the population into eighteen age groups to account for the influence of age on cancer mortality. CEP's use of only two age groups involves some loss of precision, but does not negate any of the conclusions.)

Let us engage in a hypothetical experiment. Imagine we had access to all records for all white males in the U.S. in the 1970-79 period. Now imagine that we drew a random sample of 1,215,000 white males from this "universe" and found that 23,674 had died of cancer in the decade. If the number of observed deaths is divided by the population, the result is what statisticians call the crude mortality rate. The rate in this case is .01948, or 1,948 deaths per 100,000. (Line 12 in Table 7). Although the corresponding crude mortality rate for the U.S. is 2,019 per 100,000, let us pretend this is unknown. The assumption for the moment is that the 1,215,200 white males were drawn at random from the universe of all white males in 1970, and that it is, therefore, an unbiased and representative sample of the universe.

Now let us continue with our imaginary experiment. Suppose we can continue to draw samples of 1,215,200 white males from the universe, record the crude mortality rate, and throw these records back into the "universe," take another sample of 1,215,200 records, calculate and record the mortality rate, etc., and continue this experiment hundreds of times.

We can perform this imaginary exercise because common sense tells us something about the results that can be expected. If the first sample was really representative of the universe of all white males, as each mortality rate is recorded, there will be about as many mortality rates above .01948 as below. And if after several dozen repetitions we record how many times the rate .01948 turned up, along with .01949, .01950, .01947, etc. and plotted these frequencies on a chart, we will find ourselves looking at the familiar bell shaped "normal curve," in which most of the rates would cluster about .01948.

The so-called normal curve occurs often as a natural phenomenon, and its properties have long been studied by statisticians. All symmetrical normal curves look alike except with respect to the degree of concentration or dispersion about the middle. This is measured by the "standard deviation," for which statisticians use the Greek letter sigma (σ). And, as in all normal curves, the area marked off by two standard deviations on either side of the mean contains 95 percent of all observations. The chance of a record falling outside this range is said to have a probability value of only five out of 100, and, as such, is usually regarded as "improbable" under the laws of chance. An area under the normal curve marked off by three standard deviations accounts for 99 percent of all observations. This leaves events outside the range with less than a one percent probability of occurring as a result of chance. The probabilities associated with events lying as far as four, five, or six standard deviations away from the mean are too small to have been precisely calculated, being of the order of one chance out of 10^4, 10^6, 10^7, etc., respectively.

Mathematicians are fond of noting that, given infinity, there is no event, no matter how small its probability, that can be mathematically ruled out. But statisticians, being for more practical, use two or three standard deviations as limiting the range for those events that can be attributed to chance.

It so happens that statisticians have a pretty good way of estimating the standard deviation of the imaginary normal distribution described above that is produced when the observed event is a percentage or proportion, or, as in this case, a mortality rate. The formula is:

$$\sigma_p = \sqrt{\frac{p(1-p)}{N}}$$

where σ_p is the standard deviation of the distribution of sample p's. In this case, p is the crude mortality rate of .01948. It is derived by dividing the recorded number of deaths in 1970-79 (23,674) by the total number of white males in 1970 (N = 1,215,200.), and $(1-p) = .98052$. By the phrase "distribution of sample p's" we are referring to our hypothetical experiment, in which for successive drawings of samples of 1,215,000 white males, we are calculating and recording the mortality rate, denoted by p.

And while we cannot really perform this experiment by continuing to draw these successive samples, yet this formula for the standard deviation tells us something about the shape and range of the normal curve describing the results of the hypothetical experiment. The calculated value of σ_p is .000125 and can be interpreted as follows: We can say that 95 percent of the crude mortality rates observed in the imaginary experiment will lie within the range of .01948 ± 2(.000125) or between .01923 and .01973, (i.e. mortality rates of 1,923 deaths per 100,000 and 1,973 deaths per 100,000).

Now let us introduce some of the information not used previously. First, the true mortality rate of all white males in the U.S. in this period was .02019. This is so far above the range of .01923 and .01973 that the assumption that the original 1,215,200 records were truly representative of all white males in the U.S. must be discarded.

And of course we know that the white males in the 59 counties were considerably younger than all white males in the U.S., and therefore it is really quite understandable that white males in these counties should have a lower crude cancer rate than that of all white males. What should be investigated is whether the recorded death rate for the white males in these counties is significantly higher than the expected rate for white males living in all other areas with the same age composition.

Let us use our knowledge of the imaginary distribution of sample mortality rates to change the original assumption. Could the original 1,215,200 records have been drawn from a universe of areas whose older white males made up 7.6 percent of all white males? The mean mortality rate for such a universe is given in line 9 of Table 7 as .01871 or 1,871 deaths per 100,000. How much higher than this rate is the recorded rate of .01948 for the 59 rural petrochemical counties?

The difference between an expected crude mortality rate of .01876 and the observed crude mortality rate of .01948 is .0072—a distance of about six standard deviations. This leaves the probability that the observed crude mortality rate for the 59 counties in 1970-79 could represent a random sample taken from the universe of all areas with a similar white male age mix at less than one out of several million.

The only distinctive characteristic of these particular 59 counties, aside from relative youthfulness, is that they have per capita petrochemical toxic waste levels nearly six times the national average. Heavy per capita toxic waste must, therefore, be regarded as a possible contributor to the demonstrated non-random excess in the recorded number of cancer deaths for these counties.

Turning now to a similar analysis of the data for 1950-59, a far different situation exists. In this decade, the recorded number of white male cancer deaths in the 59 counties was 12 percent below the expected number. Here again, however, the degree to which this level of cancer mortality falls below the expected level is far too great to be due to chance. The standard deviation of an imaginary distribution of mortality rates based on a continuous string of samples of 924,600 white males is .00012, according to the formula. (Applying the formula for the standard deviation of sample ps when p=.01371, and N=924,600 yields a value of .00012.)

The probability that the observed crude mortality rate of .01371 in a sample of 924,600 white males could be drawn from the same universe of white males of similar relative youthfulness with a corresponding mortality rate of .01588 (i.e. the "expected" mortality rate on line 9) can now be measured. But the difference between these two rates—.00217 represents a gap of more than seventeen standard deviations. This represents a result which can only happen by chance once in several trillion times!

It must be concluded that in the period 1950-59, these rural counties, with petrochemical facilities mainly of post World War II origin, had enjoyed enviably low cancer rates, of the kind associated with the pristine purity of rural life, untouched by the ills and stresses of industrialization.

The emergence of excessively high cancer rates in these rural counties over the twenty years under review corresponds with the 20 to 25 year latency period characteristic of exposure to carcinogens. The evidence points strongly to the high toxic waste levels that characterize the output of petrochemicals as playing an important role.

The significance of these findings is magnified by two additional considerations. First, the results are obtained in the face of the fact, as demonstrated below, that the number of cancer deaths reported in small rural counties is generally underestimated. This is due to the inability of the physician to correctly record the true county of residence of the deceased on a death certificate if the patient had moved to a large city in search of terminal care facilities.

In any case, death certificates do not record the county in which the victim worked.

Secondly, exposure to toxic wastes is a local phenomenon, associated with particular toxic waste sites or toxic waste generation, treatment, and disposal facilities. It would be unlikely for such facilities to affect the entire population of a county. Hence, these findings suggest the presence of extremely high cancer mortality rates in those 5 digit Zip code areas that are most heavily affected by toxic waste residues.

8. CANCER RATES IN SOUTHERN LOUISIANA

A series of three articles published in October 1984 in the *Wall Street Journal* have highlighted the association of high cancer rates with concentrations of petrochemical operations and toxic waste sites in southern Louisiana. An ABC television broadcast on Nov. 21, 1984 featured some preliminary CEP statistical findings on cancer rates in this area. The problem was visually dramatized by interviews with residents as they indicated the large number of households in the area hit by cancer. Information now available from government databases permits CEP to speculate about the number of possible cancer deaths in the 1970-79 period for every 5 digit zip code in the nation. The method of estimation has been applied to six parishes (the Louisiana term for county) in the New Orleans region, as illustrated in Tables 8 and 9. It suggests there may be a dozen Zip code areas with a total 1980 population of 213,400 that, in the aggregate, had cancer mortality rates as much as 68 percent higher than the rest of the nation. The smaller the area and the heavier its concentration of petrochemical toxic waste, the higher the cancer rate appears to be. In this demonstration, the worst area in the region would be the Hahnville Zip code area (70057) in St. Charles Parish with a possible cancer rate in the last decade about 18 times higher than normal. In Table 8, figures are assembled on the reported number of white male cancer deaths in each of six parishes in the greater New Orleans region for the years 1970-79. For all parishes, including Orleans, a total of 7,298 such deaths were reported (see column 8, Table 8).

Background information about the National Cancer Institute (NCI) county data on cancer deaths, published jointly by Environmental Protection Agency (EPA) and NCI in 1983 in a three volume report entitled *U.S. Cancer Rates and Trends, 1950-1979* is needed. In this database, cancer deaths are allocated to counties on the basis of the county of residence of the deceased as recorded on death certificates. A special NCI survey, "Accuracy of Cancer Death Certificates and Its Effect on Cancer Mortality Statistics" (published in the *American Journal of Health* in 1981) found the underlying cause of death as recorded on the death certificate was accurate for only about 65 percent of all cancer deaths. Misclassification and inaccuracies were found to affect the remaining 35 percent. The survey made no attempt to check on the accuracy of the indicated county of residence, even though NCI did find above average cancer rates in most large urban counties. This could reflect the fact that terminal patients seeking better hospital facilities tend to die in these urban counties rather than in the county where they lived and worked. Nevertheless, NCI data on cancer deaths are the only available information and can yield useful insights.

Data on age composition is essential in calculating the expected number of cancer deaths since cancer mortality is primarily a function of old age. Therefore, areas with an unusually young population would expect fewer cancer deaths.

Table 8 again makes use of our simplified method of estimating the expected "normal" number of deaths in each parish after due allowance for age composition differences. The one modification is the use of population data taken from the 1980 Census, rather than 1970. This permits the extension of the same method to 5 digit Zip code areas, for which only 1980 data are available. In 1980, 10.06 percent of all white males in the U.S. fell into the 65+ age group, whereas only 5.89 percent of the 250,000 white males in the five parishes excluding Orleans fell into this older category. In adjusting the number of expected deaths for age, CEP used the following method.

TABLE 8
Calculation of Expected and Excess White Male Cancer Deaths, 1970-79, Six Parishes in New Orleans Region

Column #	1	2	3	4	5	6	7	8	9	10	11
	White Males, 1980			col. 3	col. 2	Expected	Expected	Recorded	Ratio	Excess	Ratio
Parish Name	Th.	Ratio over 65	Ratio under 65	× .00834	× .11572	Mortality Rate, (4 + 5)	# Deaths (6 × 1)	# Deaths	(8/7)	Deaths (8-7)	of Chance Variation
Jefferson	186.5	.05965	.94035	.00784	.00690	.01474	2749	2418	.88	−331	.99
Plaquemines	10.2	.05768	.94232	.00786	.00667	.01453	148	139	.94	−9	.84
St. Bernard	29.6	.05863	.94137	.00785	.00679	.01464	433	463	1.07	30	1.10
St. Charles	13.9	.05202	.94798	.00791	.00602	.01393	194	156	.80	−38	85
St. John the Baptist	9.9	.05708	.94290	.00786	.00661	.01447	143	101	.71	−42	.81
TOTAL ABOVE	250.2	.05892	.94108	.00785	.00682	.01467	3667	3277	.89	−390	.99
Orleans	113.3	.12585	.87415	.00729	.01456	.02185	2476	4021	1.62	+1545	1.01
GRAND TOTAL	363.5	.07978	.92022	.00768	.00923	.01691	6143	7298	1.19	+1155	1.01
U.S. TOTAL	92,685.3	.10058	.89942	.00750	.01164	.01914	1,754,856	1,754,868	1.00	+ 12	1.00

TABLE 9
Calculation of Possible Number of Cancer Deaths in Twelve 5 Digit Zip Code Areas in New Orleans Region

	Total All 12 Areas	Gretna 70053	Harvey 70058	Westwego 70094	Belle Chasse 70037	Port Sulphur 70083	Chalmette 70043	Meraux 70075	Hahnville 70057	Lubing 70070	Norco 70079	Garyville 70051	La Place 70068
From Demographic Database:													
1. Total pop., 1980 (Th.)	213.4	55.7	27.6	38.7	9.9	4.5	33.6	5.4	3.2	9.5	4.4	2.7	18.2
2. # White Males, 1980 (Th.)	85.7	23.2	10.1	12.6	4.6	1.4	16.2	2.5	1.0	4.6	1.7	.4	7.4
3. # White Males 65 + (Th.)	4.10	1.04	.41	.64	.15	.15	.86	.09	.06	.19	.17	.06	.27
4. % W.M. over 65	4.8	4.5	4.1	5.1	3.3	10.7	5.3	3.6	6.0	4.1	10.0	15.3	3.7
5. Income per Household (Th.$)	28.5	29.8	28.4	23.0	29.5	23.2	28.7	24.8	29.0	36.9	29.0	19.9	33.8
From Environmental Database:													
6. # Closed Toxic Waste Sites	36	0	4	4	5	1	4	2	6	1	6	1	2
7. Tons Toxic Waste Generated (Th)	561.1	57.6	18.9	37.1	36.7	6.7	15.5	6.5	176.2	14.7	88.9	21.0	81.5
8. Lbs. Generated Per Capita	5259	2137	1367	1919	7406	3030	919	2417	111,693	3104	40,762	15,810	8,964
9. Ratio to Nat'l Av. (883 lbs.)	6.0	2.4	1.6	2.2	8.4	3.4	1.0	2.7	126.5	3.5	46.2	17.9	10.2
10. Toxic Waste % of Reg. Total (692 Th. Tons)	81.0	8.3	2.7	5.4	5.3	1.0	2.2	.9	25.5	2.1	12.9	3.0	11.8
From Public Health Database:													
11. % W.M. Over 65	4.80	4.50	4.10	5.11	3.30	10.7	5.3	3.6	6.0	4.1	10.0	15.3	3.7
12. Expected # Deaths	1,156	305	128	174	55	28	228	31	15	59	32	10	91
13. Allocation of 968 Excess	784	80	26	52	51	10	21	9	247	20	125	29	114
14. Total Deaths (12 + 13)	1,940	385	154	226	106	38	249	40	262	79	157	39	205
15. Ratio, Total to Expected (15/13)	1.68	1.26	1.20	1.30	1.93	1.36	1.09	1.29	17.47	1.34	4.91	3.90	2.25

The white male population in each parish was again divided into two groups—those under 65 years of age and those over. For the nation as a whole over the ten year period, white males who were under 65 in 1980 had a cancer mortality rate for the decade of 834 deaths per 100,000. Those in the 65 + group had a much higher rate—11,572 deaths per 100,000 persons. An "expected" number of cancer deaths for each parish can be calculated by simply weighting the national mortality rates (i.e. the "normal" death rates) for each age group by the actual age composition within the county. Thus, the "normal" national death rate for each age group, multiplied by the corresponding percentage of the population in each parish yields, after addition, the expected cancer mortality rate for the parish. Then, multiplying this rate by the white male population total for each parish yields the expected number of cancer deaths (Table 8, col. 7).

Column 8 shows the number of deaths per county as reported by NCI from death certificates. Columns 9 and 10 use these figures to calculate the ratio of the recorded to expected deaths and the differences between the two.

The significance of this table can best be illustrated by first drawing the reader's attention to the bottom line. Here it can be seen that the application of the indicated age-specific mortality rates for the younger and older groups to all white males in the U.S. in 1980 yields an "expected" number of deaths for the U.S. just about equal to the observed or recorded total.

Thus, if we assume that these parishes in Louisiana are random samples drawn from the universe of all white males, and are therefore subject to the same forces of mortality and exposure to the same degree to carcinogens in the air, water, diet, tobacco, etc., then column 7 yields estimates of the expected number of deaths in this 10-year period. Under this assumption, the ratio of observed to expected deaths will differ from 1.00 only because of chance variation. As is evident from a close examination of column 11, the ratio of chance variation diverges from 1.00 in accordance with sample size—the smaller the number of observed deaths, the greater the divergence from 1.00. For large samples of more than 1,000 observed deaths, the laws of chance offer the greatest opportunity for unusual events to balance out and the variation due to chance is therefore very limited.*

The figures in column 11 are taken from statistical tables that calculate the limits of variation due to chance based on the so-called five percent level of probability. The larger the divergence in the ratio of reported to expected deaths beyond the chance limits, the more unlikely the possibility that a given sample could be drawn from the same universe.

This background allows the reader to focus on the most important single fact revealed by this table. The 7,298 deaths recorded in all six parishes between 1970 to 1979 is 19 percent higher than the expected 6,143 deaths—with only a one percent divergence that could be attributed to chance. It therefore follows that a powerful force of mortality is lifting the cancer rate far above normal levels in this region. The power of that force can be measured by the fact that the probability of obtaining such a result by chance is only one out of several hundred million cases!

Several other surprises are contained in this table. The ratio of observed to expected deaths in Orleans is 1.62—an even more implausible result. The probability of securing such a result by chance is only one out of several hundred trillion! How can such a large divergence be explained, especially when New Orleans is a tourist city with little industry and only small amounts of petrochemicals either generated or deposited in the city?

Now let us examine the equally incredible but opposite scenario suggested for the five non-urban parishes that have some of the heaviest concentrations of toxic waste generation and disposal in the nation. Only 3,277 cancer deaths were recorded for these five parishes—11 percent fewer than the expected number of 3,667. Since only a two percent divergence can be attributed to chance for this number, the .89 ratio cannot be regarded as a chance result. But can it really be that toxic waste decreases the risk of cancer as these figures would suggest?

The solution to the puzzle is clear. Orleans' recorded total of 4,021 deaths must include many victims who actually lived and worked in the five adjoining parishes. How many can only be ascertained by examination of the hospital records of the deceased containing occupational and residential information necessary for proper allocation.

Urban bias in reported cancer rates is not, of course, unique to New Orleans. It affects all large cities in which better cancer care facilities are available. In the past, high urban cancer rates were attributed to heavy smoking and other associated "urban stress" factors. The Louisiana State Department of Health still attributes the state's high cancer mortality rate to a combination of "lifestyle and environmental factors." Yet there is no evidence that lifestyle differences, whatever we take that to mean, could explain the huge differences in cancer mortality under review here.

Additional evidence on the cause of the urban bias in the reporting of cancer deaths comes from an examination of the locational pattern of hospitals with facilities for the care of terminal cancer patients. The American Hospital Association maintains a database of all U.S. hospitals in which codes are carried to indicate the various types of services offered. This includes the availability of radioactive therapy, radioactive implants, catscan and nuclear resonance equipment, and other services useful in the care and treatment of cancer victims. The bulk of all such hospitals are to be found in a relatively small number of central counties of large metropolitan areas, all of whom report extremely high cancer mortality rates—rates far too high to be regarded as the result of chance variation.

Four such hospitals exist in New Orleans but none in the outlying parishes. They are the Touro Infirmary (351 beds), the Mercy Hospital of New Orleans (212 beds), the Ochsner Foundation Hospital (357 beds) and the Charity Hospital of Louisiana (617 beds).

Detailed statistics on all such hospitals in all counties will be presented in a companion CEP study. This study will attempt to adjust all reported county cancer mortality rates for this urban bias so as to evaluate the true relative importance of both an unbiased urbanization factor and the factor of toxic waste in the explanation of regional variations in cancer mortality.

Table 9 records some key demographic and environmental characteristics for 12 selected 5 digit Zip code areas taken from databases maintained by CEP. In particular, it includes data on the volume of toxic waste generated in 1980 developed by CEP from EPA information. Combined with EPA statistics on abandoned toxic waste sites, the data serves to measure both current and past toxic waste patterns.

---

*For very small areas with fewer than 100 observed deaths, the distribution of sample mortality rates is not quite symmetrical. For such small numbers, a special table is required to indicate the limits of chance variation. See Appendix B.

This information can be used to reallocate some of the excess cancer deaths attributed to New Orleans. It is reasonable to consider that in addition to transferring 377 (the deficit recorded for the five non-urban parishes), half the remainder, or 963 deaths in total, should be transferred. This conservative reallocation leaves New Orleans with 3,038 observed deaths—23 percent above the expected or normal number. For 3,038 observed deaths a two percent variation represents the limit attributable to chance. In other words, even 3,038 observed deaths in New Orleans for this period represents an excessively high number that is difficult to explain.

The 12 selected 5 digit Zip code areas shown in Table 9 are the ones most heavily saturated with refineries and abandoned toxic waste sites. They account for 81 percent of 692 thousand tons of toxic waste generated in the region in 1980. Allocation of the 963 excess deaths to these areas—on the basis of their share of toxic waste generation—may afford a more realistic idea of their possible cancer mortality rates.

These are not the "true" figures on the actual number of cancer deaths in each region; they are projections based on an hypothesis. But the calculations serve to dramatize the fact that in certain smaller areas heavily saturated by petrochemical waste, actual cancer mortality rates might be truly dismaying. Thus, the one dozen areas with a total population of 213,400 in 1980, show a possible white male annual cancer death rate 68 percent above normal. Hahnville, the worst single area in this scenario, with a per capita level of toxic waste generation of 111,693 pounds—127 times greater than the national average of 883 pounds per capita—also has a total of six abandoned toxic waste sites.

Table 9 suggests there are many questions that can only be resolved by further research. Concerned local officials, citizen groups, scholars, and university research teams could undertake it. Note for example that the combined mean income per household for the 12 Zip code areas is $28,500, a figure above the national average of $27,400. Does this mean it takes above average earnings to keep workers in these areas? Or does the fact that these areas have only 4.1 percent of the white males in the 65+ age group, as against 12.6 percent in Orleans parish, mean that few retired people elect to live in these areas? What is the significance of the presence in these areas of 36 closed toxic waste dumps, as taken from the EPA ERRIS file and listed in Table 10? The EPA file indicates dates of inspection by either state or EPA officials but contains no description of the findings. Four of these sites (those with asterisks) have been nominated for Superfund clean-up expenditures. These and many more questions remain. CEP has reason to believe that similar questions can be raised about other large metropolitan areas in Louisiana, New Jersey, Texas, West Virginia, and elsewhere.

The above findings were presented to staff members of the New York University Institute of Environmental Medicine and elicited the following observation. Although the calculations could be made more precise by the use of more detailed age-groupings, it was agreed that added precision would not alter the findings with respect to the non-random character of the ratios of observed to expected deaths.

Dr. Arthur C. Upton, head of the Institute and former head of the National Cancer Institute expressed willingness to offer the services of the Institute to local authorities to perform the special survey of death certificates that would test the degree of possible misallocation of deaths. The services of the Institute could also be made available to help perform the necessary epidemiological investigations of groundwater supplies to evaluate the possible linkages of toxic wastes to cancer in the area.

The 12 Zip code areas listed in Table 9 were those with the highest toxic waste levels. The 5 non-urban parishes, however, do include some small areas that do not have petrochemical waste sites or generating facilities. However, these areas too should have their true cancer mortality rates ascertained, for they may be close enough to suffer from contaminated water supplies. In Table 11, 15 Zip code areas along the Mississippi River are listed in geographic order following the Mississippi River, starting with Garyville, west of New Orleans, as it winds its way down through the Delta, past Venice into the Gulf of Mexico. Some additional key demographic and toxic waste data are included. Of the fifteen areas, only four have below average toxic waste levels. Heaviest concentrations are in the section around Hahnville.

The fifteen areas constitute a region with 104.3 thousand persons, largely white (84 percent), with somewhat better than average income per household levels ($29,900). They contain a combined average toxic waste level of 8700 pounds per person—about ten times the national average.

The truth about the annual number of white male cancer deaths in this and other regions of Louisiana is available in the files of the Louisiana State Department of Health. The Department has described the admittedly high cancer death rate in Louisiana as the combined result of "environmental and life style factors." The attitude of some state officials was indicated in the ABC television news program cited previously. Governor Edwin Edwards was quoted as saying "No one knows (the cause of cancer) . . . It is easy for a reporter to level an accusation or jump to a conclusion . . . but we must be more responsible."

TABLE 10
Closed Toxic Waste Sites In Selected
Zip Code Areas Near New Orleans

Zip Code	Place Name	Name of Site	Address	Last Date of Inspect.
70058	Harvey	Amsted Ind. Inc., Plexco Div.	4400 Peters Rd.	8/82
		Hydril Co.	200 Destrehan Ave.	3/80
		Metroplex Landfill	Peters Rd.	3/81
		National Environ. Controls	3317 Peters Rd.	11/79
70094	Westwego	Jefferson Disposal	US Hwy. 90, 6 mi. west of Westwego	6/79
		American Cyanamid	1800 River Rd.	12/80
		Paktank, La. Inc.	106 Bridge City Ave.	7/81
		Westwego Landfill	End of Lapaco Blvd.	3/83
70037	Belle Chasse	Chevron Chemical	Hwy. 23	1/81
		*Gulf Oil Alliance Refinery	Hwy. 23	7/84
		M & J Construction Co.	1202 Belle Chasse Hwy.	6/80
70083	Port Sulphur	Jefferson Lake Sulphur Co.	Lake Hermitage Hwy. 23	8/82
70043	Chalmette	Clean Co. Inc.	7007 St. Claude	1/82
		Koppers Co.	Unknown	12/84
		St. Bernard Parish Landfill	Paris Rd.	8/83
		Tenneco Oil Co.	Paris Rd.	6/81
70075	Meraux	ARCO Sinclair Gulf Refinery	St. Bernard Hwy. and Murphy Oil Co.	8/82
		Murphy Oil	2500 E. St. Bernard Hwy.	4/81
70057	Hahnville	Argus Chemicals	River Rd. Hwy. 3142	12/81
		Beker Industries	Hwy. 18, River Rd.	6/81
		Dolores Hanson Property	Hwy. 18	4/81
		Hooker Chemicals	Hwy. 18 and Hwy. 3142	10/79
		Shell Chemical, Taft Plant	Rt. 3142	9/80
		*Union Carbide	Hwy. 18 and Hwy. 3142	8/84
70070	Lubing	Monsanto Co.	River Rd.	8/81
70079	Norco	Good Hope Refinery	257 Prospect Ave.	6/81
		Browning Ferris	US Hwy. 61E	10/79
		Gatx Terminals Corp.	River Rd.	7/81
		RTL Corp.	573 Good Hope St.	3/81
		*Shell Chemical Co.	River Rd.	8/84
		*Shell Oil	Hwy. 61, River Rd.	7/84
70051	Garyville	Nalco Chemical	River Rd., Hwy. 44	2/80
70068	La Place	Cambridge Place East	1 block east of Cambridge Dr.	8/84
		E I Dupont	Hwy. 44	1/84

*Superfund notification

TABLE 11
Key Demographic and Environmental Indicators
In Selected 5 Digit Areas

Zip Code	PO Place Name	Pop. (Th.)	% White	Hhds Th.	Hh. Inc. (th.$)	Rent (Mo.) $	Home Value th.$	White Males Over 65 (th.)	White Males Over 65 (%)	Toxic Waste #of Sites	Toxic Waste Per Capita Relative
70051	Garyville	2.7	34	.8	19.9	136	66.2	.4	15	1	17.9
70068	La Place	18.2	80	5.4	33.8	320	106.1	7.4	4	2	10.2
70079	Norco	4.4	77	1.4	29.0	256	86.6	1.4	10	6	46.2
70057	Hahnville	3.0	60	1.0	29.0	314	94.3	1.0	6	6	126.5
70070	Luling	9.5	95	3.0	36.9	325	112.7	4.6	4	1	3.5
70037	Belle Chasse	9.9	91	2.8	29.5	360	118.0	4.6	3	5	8.4
70040	Braithwaite	1.2	72	.4	23.2	270	76.9	.4	12	1	8.0
70043	Chalmette	33.6	99	11.1	28.7	382	101.5	16.2	5	4	1.0
70047	Carlisle	7.1	83	2.1	32.9	313	106.6	3.0	4	1	.0
70046	Davant	1.4	0	.3	19.8	53	58.5	.0	.0	0	.0
70083	Port Sulphur	4.5	60	1.3	23.2	186	63.7	1.4	11	1	3.4
70050	Empire	1.3	69	.4	21.2	147	70.1	.4	7	0	.2
70041	Buras	5.2	84	1.6	26.7	302	72.3	2.3	5	0	.0
70038	Boothville	.6	70	.2	26.6	137	29.2	.2	11	0	.0
70091	Venice	1.7	93	.5	26.4	185	61.6	.8	3	1	7.6
Totals		104.3	84	32.3	29.9	343	97.8	44.4	5	29	9.8

The Governor (who has since been indicted for fraud) and the Department of Health could help the search for truth by releasing the data on cancer deaths in recent years by Zip code area. Failing that, it would still be possible for concerned citizens groups in Louisiana to assemble independent evidence of the number of cancer deaths in these areas. This can be accomplished either with help from local public agencies and hospitals or by dint of door-to-door canvasses. In some states, county records include death registries on file, complete with names and addresses, that would make possible a count by Zip code area.

A special door-to-door canvass of every household in a small neighborhood is not difficult when conducted under the auspices of local environmental "grass roots" agencies. The door-to-door survey can question each household about relatives dying of cancer over the past three-year or five-year period. The technique of estimating the expected number of white male cancer victims can be applied (exactly as indicated in Table 7 using data in this book) to establish ratios between the observed number of deaths and the expected number, as yielded by the survey. Appendix B contains a table indicating the lower and upper limits of chance variation applicable to any derived ratio for small numbers of observed deaths. For example, if in an area with 10 expected cancer deaths the canvass reveals as few as 20 observed deaths within any given period, the ratio of 2.0 could clearly be seen to fall outside the limits of chance variation. For twenty observed deaths, the chance limits of the ratio would range between .61 and 1.54. The larger the number of observed deaths, the smaller the range of chance variation. Thus, if in an area 100 deaths were observed over a five-year period, the limits of chance variation in the ratio of observed to expected deaths range between .82 and 1.22.

Generally speaking, an area with 1,000 white males should expect to have, over a five-year period, between 6 to 14 white male cancer deaths. If the number of observed deaths exceeds 20, the cancer rate in this area is alarmingly high.

9. How To Combine Zip Code Areas Into Neighborhoods

The 5 digit Zip code area has been referred to as a fundamental building block in defining neighborhoods and communities. The definition of such entities rests on decisions that must be made by local groups and depends on the nature of the community problem that must be addressed.

For example, as was demonstrated in the preceding section, a region covering 15 Zip code areas in Southern Louisiana delineates a fairly homogeneous population group that share very high toxic waste levels. To define such an area, it is necessary to reorder the 5 digit Zip code areas geographically. For this purpose, 5 digit local maps must be secured from local postmasters. It is a singular fact that the U.S. Postal Service does not carry a master set of such maps in Washington, D.C. (CEP is now engaged in developing a set of *proximal* maps for all 5 digit Zip code areas, in which the boundaries are approximated by computer.)

There are, of course, many issues other than environmental problems that merit analysis at the Zip code level. CEP databases, from which this publication was drawn, include hundreds of data elements for Zip code areas and counties taken from the Census Bureau, EPA, and the National Cancer Institute computer files. (See Appendix A for a description of the contents of these databases.)

Readers of this book will often be able to use the data here to obtain approximations of the key characteristics for combinations of areas. Thus, for the number of white persons, the reader should multiply the White percentage by population; for total household income one would multiply the number of households by the mean income per household, etc. To obtain estimates of the volume of toxic waste generated takes a bit more work. One must first multiply the area Toxic Waste Relative by 883 pounds to secure the per capita ratio for the combination of areas and then multiply by the corresponding population to obtain the total volume of toxic waste generated. When an area has a toxic waste relative greater than 100, it will generally be necessary to use Table 3 to establish the toxic waste tonnage for all the 5 digit areas in a leading toxic waste 4 digit area. (CEP will respond to requests for additional information on the toxic waste problem for any one area.)

For more accurate consolidations and the full range of data available, CEP will provide special computer printouts. The data is of such importance that CEP is certain the demand for it will be large enough to justify updating and maintaining the data for both offline and online use. This might include making the data available on personal computer diskettes. Interested readers can query CEP on this by writing to CEP Service Bureau, 30 Irving Place, New York, N.Y. 10003.

Table 12 illustrates some of the data elements omitted from this book for reasons of space but that are necessary to secure accurate totals for Table 11.

Another example of a public issue that can be illuminated with the help of Zip code data, is the use of figures on household income to calculate for each area an approximation of the amount of Federal personal income tax collections for any given year, to the extent that such tax collections are based on income levels.

Thus, in 1983, federal personal income taxes came to $285 bil. The total personal income of the nation's 80.5 million households, with a mean income of $27,400 per household came to about $2,205 billion. It can, therefore, be roughly estimated that about 13 percent of the income of each area will go to pay Federal personal income taxes.

Both the population and income data for each area can be used to make area allocations of such national budget items as federal expenditures for national defense, health, education, natural resources, and environmental controls. It will be found that for most areas (except for those relatively few in which defense contractor payrolls are concentrated), far more goes to the federal government than the value of federal benefits received.

CEP hopes this book will help evaluate geographic variations in cancer rates along the lines discussed in the previous section. Cancer now accounts for about 22 percent of all deaths in the U.S. There may, however, be areas of the nation where cancer may be accounting for as much as half. Those areas are not yet pinpointed, but CEP hopes to be able to do so in future reports.

Offered below are the latest (1982) age-adjusted cancer mortality rates per 10,000 persons in the U.S. by race and sex to illustrate that small area analyses of excess cancer can be carried out for males, females, white, and all other racial groups.

TABLE 12
Housing Units, Income and White Males
In Selected 5 Digit Areas

Zip Code	PO Place Name	Occupied Housing Units Renter	Occupied Housing Units Owner	Income of Households Th. $.	No. of White Males
70051	Garyville	214	548	15,463	67
70068	La Place	1106	4324	182,518	270
70079	Norco	368	1064	41,343	166
70057	Hahnville	352	661	28,254	61
70070	Lubing	709	2304	109,947	186
70037	Belle Chasse	1105	1766	83,662	153
70040	Braithwaite	59	349	9,750	49
70043	Chalmette	3139	7950	317,398	852
70047	Carlisle	376	1740	70,506	121
70046	Davant	40	282	6,586	0
70083	Port Sulphur	245	1080	31,267	148
70050	Empire	80	270	8,177	30
70041	Buras	399	1241	43,263	107
70038	Boothville	34	133	4,704	21
70091	Venice	65	429	12,702	27
Totals		8291	24,141	965,540	2258

Cancer Deaths per 10,000 persons (1982)

White Male	21.1
White Female	13.5
Other Male	27.9
Other Female	14.5

For any single year, it is obvious that a small area with only one thousand members of one of these four population groups would be reporting one or two cancer deaths if its cancer rate were normal. Although any reported number would reflect chance variation, the latter could be minimized by collecting data for a longer period, say five years. Thus, for an area with 1,000 white males and an average age composition, 20 such deaths over a five-year period would indicate a statistically significant doubling of the national rate.

Such a result would indicate the need for more intensive analysis by biometricians, epidemiologists, and environmental scientists. We do not deprecate these valuable expert services in evaluating the cause and magnitude of local environmental problems but we must find a way to direct attention to dangerous areas. EPA was created in response to public pressure but needs constant prodding to fulfill its mandate. If the risk to life can be dramatized at the local level, EPA can be forced to offer expert assistance.

Role of Litigation

As indicated in a report of the Congressional Office of Technology Assessment cited in CEP's September, 1984 Newsletter (Toxic Waste and Cancer), exposure to toxic wastes may account for 15 to 20 percent of all cancer deaths. If this is true, then the public has unknowingly been experiencing, slowly and over a period of decades, many environmental disasters that dwarf the recent Union Carbide accident in Bhopal, India. That incident, and the ensuing litigation, is likely to provide, after the fact, safeguards that should have been in place before.

It may very well be that only litigation can force negligent companies to upgrade the quality of waste management policies. There are large numbers of occupational cancer suits now being litigated all over the country.

Generally, they relate to single victims, for each of whom there could be a reasonable probability that factors other than exposure to toxic waste might be responsible.

However, for any single geographic area, in which a class action suit involves many victims sharing a common source of danger, the probability that other factors could be at fault sinks to near zero as the number of victims rises.

By focusing in this book on the environmental danger of industrial toxic waste, CEP believes it can make a contribution to the litigation of cases involving such exposures. Much evidence can be marshalled to upgrade the importance of industrial toxic waste in the explanation of high local cancer mortality rates, particularly in eliminating the spurious claim that cigarette smoking is the sole significant cause of cancer. The latter claim has been advanced in many such cases, despite the lack of evidence of significant regional differences in cigarette smoking.

In a forthcoming study, CEP will analyze the locational pattern of terminal cancer care facilities to correct for the urban bias in reported cancer mortality rates. The precise degree to which the factors of urbanization and toxic waste contribute to regional variations in cancer mortality will be established.

However, to forestall objections that the emphasis on the toxic waste factor represents an oversimplification of a very complex problem, CEP readily concedes that toxic substances can affect us in many other ways, some of which may have unusual regional concentrations that merit special study.

The presence of concentrations of radioactive waste in about 100 counties in which military and civilian nuclear facilities are located has been noted. Another example is the non-industrial contamination of groundwater supplies as a consequence of the use of pesticides and herbicides in farming. Since 83 percent of our water supply is consumed in agriculture as against only 8 percent in manufacturing, such contamination cannot be considered an example of industrial toxic waste but certainly merits a separate analysis. Then again, the use of chemical additives in processed foods and in other consumer goods exposes everyone to carcinogens. But we cannot give way to despair. Solutions will emerge as we bring a reasoned and systematic approach to the problem of environmental exposure to all toxic chemicals.

APPENDIX A

A Brief Description of the CEP Environmental and Public Health Database Service

CEP is acquiring, editing, and updating several government computer files bearing on environmental and public health issues. They are all geographically coded to the state, county, and 5 digit Zip code levels, and fall into three categories: Demographic, Public Health, and Environmental. It should be noted that the compilation of these databases by government agencies involved expenditures in the billions of dollars. Yet public access to this information has become increasingly difficult in recent years. The sheer volume of data in these databases is so great, and much of it is in such a state of constant change, that public access can best be provided by online networks; users can dial-up from personal computers equipped with telephone modems.

In the meantime, the databases will be available offline to interested parties at moderate fees. For example, CEP can generate standardized information packages for counties and 5 digit areas drawn from each of the three sets of databases, including digitized county and Zip code maps. University research teams can then perform in-depth public health analyses of local areas within any given distance from each of the 300 standard metropolitan areas. These analyses could be based on the techniques discussed here and the more detailed data available in these databases.

A. Demographic

CEP's 1980 Census files include nearly 1,000 separate items of information. These can be grouped into 31 categories of Population Characteristics, as indicated in Appendix Table 1.

B. Public Health

National Cancer Institute files are available, providing annual county data for the period 1950 to 1979 on the number of cancer deaths and age-adjusted cancer mortality rates, by race and sex, and for the following 35 different types of cancer:

All malignant neoplasms: lip; salivary gland; nasopharynx; other mouth and throat; esophagus; stomach; large intestine except rectum; rectum; bilinary passages of the liver; pancreas; nose, nasal cavaties and sinuses; larynx; trachea, bronchus, lung; male breast; female breast; cervix uteri; corpus uteri, etc.; ovary; prostate; testis; kidney; bladder; melanoma of skin; other skin; eye; brain and other parts of nervous system; thyroid gland; other endocrine glands; bone; connective tissue; Hodgkin's disease; lymphosarcoma and reticulosarcoma, etc.; multiple myeloma; leukemia; other, and unspecified sites.

Other public health databases available to CEP contain mortality and morbidity statistics from the National Center for Health Statistics and on hospital facilities from the American Health Association.

C. Environmental

Except for the volume estimates of the generation of toxic waste published here (available from the Trinet division of the Control Data Corporation for all states, counties, Zip code areas, and every business establishment in the U.S.) there are dozens of databases available from EPA and various state environmental agencies.

Some EPA databases contain detailed data on toxic waste generators, including detailed data on the composition of toxic waste discharged at the site and on open and closed waste sites, waste treatment facilities, etc. CEP has used one such database in this book (the ERRIS file) to indicate the number of closed toxic waste sites in each area.

The following is a brief commentary on some environmental databases that will be the subject of analysis in a forthcoming CEP study of the hazardous waste industry.

Various agencies of the United States federal government operate computerized data systems that maintain information on hazardous waste sites. Databases exist that identify locations contaminated by the mismanagement of hazardous wastes and facilities that currently generate, transport, treat, and dispose of hazardous wastes. The data range from the type and seriousness of damage caused by an uncontrolled dump to the technologies used to process every type and volume of hazardous waste handled by an operating facility. Certain data systems record the number of inspections, violations, and corrective actions occurring at a site. Others record the types and value of a site's insurance for sudden accidents or ground water contamination. Still others characterize the demographic and hydrogeological environment at a site or even the details of a transportation accident resulting in a spill of hazardous waste.

The U.S. Environmental Protection Agency (EPA) has assembled the following databases either at Research Triangle Park, in Durham, North Carolina, at its ten regional EPA offices, or by using contractors for programs authorized under the Resource Conservation and Recovery Act (RCRA) and the Comprehensive Environmental Response, Compensation, and Liability Act (CERCLA):

I. RCRA Databases

    A. "Hazardous Waste Data Management System" (HWDMS): HWDMS is EPA's most comprehensive hazardous waste data system. It contains a wide variety of information, some of which follows:

        1. Notification: Lists all generators, transporters, treatment, storage, and disposal facilities (TSDFs) that notified EPA of their activities (approximately 50,000 entries). Includes: names, addresses, facility type, waste types handled.

        2. Part A: Lists all TSDFs granted interim status for operating (approximately 5,000 to 10,000 entries). Includes: names, addresses, latitude, longitude, existence data, closure date, ownership, operator, processes, capacities, waste types, estimated quantities.

        3. Inspections: (Regional database) Lists all inspections taken at RCRA facilities. Includes: inspection date, type, status, responsible agencies, certain regions include regulation violated.

4. Enforcement: (Regional database) Lists all enforcement actions taken against RCRA facilities. Includes: enforcement type, status, violation type, penalties.

5. Financial Instruments: Lists financial instruments implemented at all RCRA facilities pursuant to Subpart G & H (sudden and non-sudden occurrences insurance, closure and post-closure assurance). Includes: instrument type, date, issuing institution, value, expiration date.

6. Major Facility Status Sheets: Outlines adequacy of all Major Handlers' (approximately 10,000 entries) ground water monitoring programs and financial instruments.

I. RCRA Databases (continued)

B. "Biennial Reports:" Many state governments are in the process of computerizing data reported through the manifest system that documents actual quantities of waste generated, transported, treated, stored, and disposed. States are required to send aggregate information to EPA regional offices. They in turn send aggregate data to EPA headquarters. The "Biennial Reports" system is based upon this aggregated data.

C. "RCRA Enforcement Management System:" This system is based upon two survey forms filled out by regional EPA offices concerning inspection and enforcement data. Although only in aggregate form, EPA claims the data is more accurate than that in HWDMS.

D. "National Survey:" EPA contracted Westat, Inc. to survey hazardous waste activities during 1981. The data results are computerized and more extensive than any other database on operating sites. The information includes: distance to nearest faults, and other geological data, along with information regarding quantities of waste actually handled, number of workers, pay scales for employees, detailed process data, and a wide variety of other information. It is, however, only a survey and does not include as large a universe as the other EPA systems.

E. "Surface Impoundment Assessment:" Contains extensive information on hazardous pits, ponds, and lagoons (approximately 200,000 entries).

F. "Open Dumps:" Contains information on all solid waste facilities not in compliance with RCRA including type of damage.

G. "Risk/Cost Assessment:" A complex computerized model that estimates risks and costs associated with any facility for which one can define certain parameters, including Zip code.

H. "Disposition of CERCLA Wastes Data Base:" Lists the RCRA sites that have received CERCLA wastes and the CERCLA sites that sent the waste (approximately 100 RCRA entries).

II. CERCLA Databases

A. "Emergency and Remedial Response Information System" (ERRIS): Includes: name, location, description of site, hazard, and status and type of inspection and corrective action (approximately 20,000 entries).

B. "Listing of Sites Scored with Hazard Ranking System:" Contains hazard scores for total migration, ground water, surface water, and air migration, fire and explosion, and direct contact (approximately 1,500 to 2,000 entries, including all "Superfund" sites).

C. "Listing of Potentially Responsible Parties:" Lists all identified parties suspected to have either owned, operated, shipped, carried, generated, or treated wastes disposed of at all Superfund sites.

D. "Remedial Investigations/Feasibility Studies:" Tracks status of clean-up measures taken at Superfund sites (database is reportedly under development).

Other federal agencies, including the Departments of Health and Human Services, Labor, and Transportation, also maintain information systems relating to hazardous wastes. These include:

III. Department of Health and Human Services

A. "Agency for Toxic Substances and Disease Control:" Lists all sites state governments have ordered closed or restricted to public use because of severe contamination by toxic substances (approximately 1,500 entries).

IV. Department of Labor

A. "OSHA Inspection History Listing:" Includes all inspections conducted by the federal Occupational Safety and Health Administration from 1972 to the present. It identifies type of inspection, regulation violated, hazardous substance involved, injuries, deaths, penalties, and abatement.

V. Department of Transportation

A. "Hazardous Materials Information System" (HMIS): Lists all transportation incidents involving hazardous materials from 1977 to the present. It identifies location, type of incident, material, shipper, carrier, amount spilled, injuries, deaths, and penalties.

B. "U.S. Coast Guard National Response Center Data System:" Lists all self-reported spills of hazardous materials. It identifies location, cause of spill, material, carrier, amount, injuries, deaths, remediation measures.

APPENDIX TABLE 1

Population and Housing Characteristics, 1980 Census

Population

Household relationship
Sex
Race
Age
Marital status
Spanish origin
School enrollment
Years of school completed
Nativity
Language spoken at home and ability to speak English
Ancestry
Residence in 1975
Labor force status in 1979
Veteran status and period of service
Work disability status
Transportation disability status
Children ever born
Labor force status
Place of work
Travel time to work
Means of transportation to work
Private vehicle occupancy (carpool arrangements)
Industry
Occupation
Class of worker
Number of weeks worked in 1979
Usual hours worked per week in 1979
Number of weeks unemployed in 1979
Income in 1979
Income type in 1979
Poverty status in 1979

Housing

Number of units at address
Complete plumbing facilities
Number of rooms
Tenure (whether owned or rented)
Vacancy status
Value (noncondominium)
Contract rent
Units in structure
Stories in structure and presence of passenger elevator
Year structure built
Year householder moved into unit
Source of water
Farm residence
Sewage disposal
Heating equipment
House heating fuel
Water heating fuel
Cooking fuel
Kitchen facilities
Number of bathrooms
Number of bedrooms
Telephone in housing unit
Air conditioning
Number of vehicles available
        (automobiles, vans, and light trucks)
Selected monthly homeowner costs
        (real estate taxes, property insurance, utilities,
        and regular mortgage payments

APPENDIX B

On the Calculation of the Expected Number of White Male Cancer Deaths in Small Areas

The calculation of cancer mortality rates has been the special province of epidemiologists and biometricians and as such, has been difficult for lay people to understand. We shall attempt to explain some of the basic concepts involved and suggest some short-cut methods of calculation that would be available to anyone living in an area troubled by the possibility of large scale exposures to toxic substances. CEP has used some, but not all, these concepts in Sections 7 and 8.

The national cancer mortality rate for white males is currently roughly of the order of .002. This means that each year American white males die of cancer at the rate of 200 deaths for every 100,000.

Mathematically, if D represents the national annual number of white male cancer deaths, and P represents the total number of white males, then M, the national cancer mortality rate can be expressed as:

$$M = \frac{D}{P}$$

The concept of an "age-specific" mortality rate for a specified age group:

$$M_s = \frac{D_s}{P_s}$$

where s stands for a specified age group, such as those in the 65+ age group.

It can be shown that:

$$M = \frac{D}{P} = \sum_{s=1}^{n} \left(\frac{D_s}{P_s} \right) \left(\frac{P_s}{P} \right)$$

Here n stands for the number of age groups into which the population has been divided. The expression on the right means that the national mortality rate can be derived by first calculating the mortality rate for each age group, weighting each rate by the percentage of the total population in that age group, and then adding the results for all age groups.

We will now apply all of these symbols to an area, using small letters to denote that we are now dealing with an area which in relation to the total universe of white males represents a small sample. We now obtain:

$$m = \frac{d}{p} = \sum_{s=1}^{n} \left(\frac{d_s}{p_s} \right) \left(\frac{p_s}{p} \right)$$

We shall call m the "crude" mortality rate for the area. The word crude denotes that this rate cannot be compared with the national rate, since the crude rate for the area is a function of the area's age composition. This may be quite different from that of the nation.

An "age-adjusted" mortality rate—m_a can be obtained by weighting the area's age-specific mortality rates by the relative importance that each age-group has in the nation:

$$m_a = \sum_{s=1}^{n} \left(\frac{d_s}{p_s} \right) \left(\frac{P_s}{P} \right)$$

The age-adjusted rate is difficult for lay people to calculate for a small area. It requires knowing the age at which each cancer victim died. It is easier to ascertain the total number of deaths in the area for comparison with the expected number of deaths. This can be calculated from the expected mortality rate for the area.

The area's expected mortality rate—m_e is based on the assumption that the population in each of the area's age groups (which we can now ascertain from the Census for each Zip code area) would be subject to the same force of mortality that is true for the nation as a whole. Since we can always secure the national age-specific mortality rates we have all the data we need to calculate

$$m_e = \sum_{s=1}^{n} \left(\frac{D_s}{P_s} \right) \left(\frac{P_s}{p} \right)$$

This, then, is the formula used in the text to illustrate how to ascertain if an area has an excessive cancer mortality rate. These formulas can be illustrated by dividing the 1980 population into two age groups—those over and under 65.

The current (1980) annual national age specific cancer rates for white males are roughly:

$$M_{65+} = .01240 \text{ (i.e. 1240 deaths per 100,000)}$$
$$\text{and } M_{65-} = .00084 \text{ (i.e. 84 deaths per 100,000)}$$

To show these are compatible with the national mortality rate of .002, we can calculate:

$$M = .90(.00084) + .10(.01240)$$
$$= .000756 + .001240 = .00200$$

Thus, the above calculations take into consideration the fact that in 1980, 90 percent of the national white male population was under 65. Accordingly, an area's expected mortality rate m_e is found in the same manner. Suppose an area had only five percent of its white male population in the 65 + age group. Then its expected cancer mortality rate in the absence of abnormal factors would be:

$$m_e = .95(.00084) + .05(.01240)$$
$$= .00080 + .00062 = .00142$$

Thus, a "normal" area with this age composition should expect only 142 deaths per 100,000 rather than 200. Correspondingly, an area that has 15 percent of its white male population in the 65 + group would have an expected mortality rate of:

$$m_e = .85(.00084) + .15(.01240)$$
$$= .00061 + .00186 = .00247$$

Thus, a "normal" area with so many older white males should expect to report 247 deaths per 100,000 instead of 200 per 100,000.

An area's expected mortality rate, when multiplied by the number of white males there, yields an estimated expected number of cancer deaths. This can then be compared with the actual reported number.

The Table below, reproduced from the Journal of the National Cancer Institute, vol. 28, No. 4, 1962, shows how to judge whether the ratio between expected and reported deaths is too large or too small to be attributed to chance. It includes estimates for observed deaths ranging from 1 to 1000. The table, prepared by Drs. W. Haenzel and D.B. Loveland, requires some explanation.

The usual tests of statistical significance of an observed statistic, such as the ratio of observed to expected deaths in an area, rest on the derivation of the standard deviation of that statistic and applying it to the familiar bell-shaped "normal curve." In this function, an area equivalent to two standard deviations on either side of the mean value will account for 95 percent of all cases. Hence an observed sample statistic that would fall in an area outside ±2 standard deviations can be said to fall outside the range of chance variation since the associated probability is less than five percent, or less than one chance out of twenty.

However, for small observed numbers of deaths such as one would expect (for example, areas with only 1000 white males), the assumption of "normality" breaks down because the probability of dying (i.e. the mortality rate) is so low (i.e. .002).

Visualizing the records of the number of reported white male deaths from successive randomly chosen areas with 1,000 white males helps explain this "small sampling" problem. We would obtain a series of discrete numbers something like: 2,1,2,3,0,2,1,4,0,2,3,1,2 etc. . . . After taking 100 or more records and summarizing the results, 2 would probably be the most frequently observed number but more discrete numbers will fall above rather than below 2. According to Table B-1 when the number of observed deaths is large (e.g. 1000), the normal curve does apply, and we would expect to find an equal number on either side of the mean and to find 95 percent of all recorded observations falling within ±6 percent of the expected number. For areas whose observed number of deaths is greater than 5,000, the variation in the observed number attributable to chance will be one percent or less.

Appendix Table B-1 records the lower and upper limit ratio of the observed number of deaths to the expected number that could be attributed to chance at the "95 percent confidence" level. This means that ratios falling outside these lower and upper limits would be regarded as having less than a one out of twenty probability value. The observed number of deaths, being based on a very small probability rate, is called a "Poisson-distributed" value.

TABLE B-1
Tabular values of 95 percent confidence limit factors
for estimates of a Poisson-distributed variable

Observed number on which estimate is based (n)	Lower limit factor (L)	Upper limit factor (U)	Observed number on which estimate is based (n)	Lower limit factor (L)	Upper limit factor (U)	Observed number on which estimate is based (n)	Lower limit factor (L)	Upper limit factor (U)
1	0.025	5.57	21	0.619	1.53	120	0.833	1.200
2	0.121	3.61	22	0.627	1.51	140	0.844	1.184
3	0.206	2.92	23	0.634	1.50	160	0.854	1.171
4	0.272	2.50	24	0.641	1.49	180	0.862	1.160
5	0.324	2.33	25	0.647	1.48	200	0.868	1.151
6	0.367	2.18	26	0.653	1.47	250	0.882	1.134
7	0.401	2.06	27	0.659	1.46	300	0.892	1.121
8	0.431	1.97	28	0.665	1.45	350	0.899	1.112
9	0.458	1.90	29	0.670	1.44	400	0.900	1.104
10	0.480	1.84	30	0.675	1.43	450	0.911	1.098
11	0.499	1.79	35	0.697	1.39	500	0.915	1.093
12	0.517	1.75	40	0.714	1.36	600	0.922	1.084
13	0.532	1.71	45	0.729	1.34	700	0.928	1.078
14	0.546	1.68	50	0.742	1.32	800	0.932	1.072
15	0.560	1.65	60	0.770	1.30	900	0.936	1.068
16	0.572	1.62	70	0.785	1.27	1000	0.939	1.064
17	0.583	1.60	80	0.798	1.25			
18	0.593	1.58	90	0.809	1.24			
19	0.602	1.56	100	0.818	1.22			
20	0.611	1.54						

ZIP DIRECTORY

INTRODUCTION TO ZIP DIRECTORY

Key statistics for each of 35,000 5 digit Zip code areas with 50 or more households, arranged in numeric sequence by state, have been tabulated in this directory. For reasons of space we have omitted about 5,000 areas with few or no residential mail deliveries. Many of these are, of course, important receivers of business mail.

The Postal Service does not assign geographic place names to 5 digit post offices falling within the boundaries of large cities. But for other 5 digit post offices, alphabetic place names have been assigned in the numeric sequence indicated by the last two digits of the Zip code. These place names can be found in both alphabetic and numeric sequence in the annual edition of the National Five Digit Zip Code & Post Office Directory, published by the National Information Data Center (a licensee of the U.S. Postal Service) as Section 10: "Numerical List of Post Offices By Zip Code and Sectional Center Facilities." In the tables to follow, we have provided the reader with some geographic orientation by printing the city name or area description for every three digit Zip code.

ZIP CODE MEASURES OF SIZE, LEVELS OF AFFLUENCE AND QUALITY OF LIFE

1=Population (th.); 2= % White; 3=Households (th.); 4=% Owner Occupied; 5=Mean Income Per Household (th.); 6=Mean Monthly Rent ($)*; 7=Mean Home Value (th.$)*; 8=% under 5; 9=% 65 and over; 10=White Males (th.); 11=% White Males, 65+; 12=# Toxic Waste Sites; 13=Toxic Waste Relative to US(883 lbs.per capita)**.

ALABAMA

ZIPCODE	1	2	3	4	5	6	7	8	9	10	11	12	13
ATLANTA													
30124	.8	100	.3	85	16.4	293	44.1	8	13	.4	10	0	.0
CHATTANOOGA													
30709	.2	100	.1	78	16.9	194*	60.1*	6	6	.1	7	0	.0
30731	.3	100	.1	83	16.4	188*	28.9	12	11	.2	11	0	.0
30738	.3	100	.1	92	14.9	171*	42.9	11	9	.1	9	0	.0
30752	.7	100	.2	87	19.8	83	54.7	12	9	.4	8	0	.0
COLUMBIS													
31833	1.1	80	.4	76	25.6	262	80.6	5	12	.5	13	0	.0
PANAMA CITY													
32440	.3	69	.1	91	16.6	261	64.6	6	7	.1	0	0	.0
PENSACOLA													
32533	.3	0	.1	76	17.8	240	79.1	10	11	.0	0	0	.0
32567	.2	0	.1	85	9.8	112*	27.8	9	22	.0	0	0	.0
BIRMINGHAM													
35005	10.4	85	3.4	87	25.5	325	63.1	8	9	4.4	7	2	.0
35006	2.4	85	.9	84	23.2	222	46.7	5	13	1.1	12	1	.0
35007	9.3	82	2.9	78	28.0	320	90.5	10	8	3.7	6	0	.1
35010	20.0	75	7.1	69	22.0	212	62.4	7	14	7.3	13	0	.4
35014	3.8	0	1.2	82	17.4	219	47.8	8	11	.0	9	0	.8
35016	12.3	100	4.4	78	21.8	234	61.8	6	11	6.0	10	0	.0
35019	1.4	100	.4	76	25.3	207	51.4	9	10	.6	9	0	.6
35020	87.0	57	29.4	72	22.5	248	61.5	8	13	23.7	10	0	.0
35031	6.4	99	2.3	81	17.8	211	48.1	7	13	3.1	11	0	.6
35033	2.7	100	.8	84	18.2	210*	26.6	6	7	.1	5	0	3.8
35034	3.8	0	1.2	66	22.2	199	47.7	8	11	.0	0	0	.0
35035	.8	74	.3	85	20.4	189	53.2	9	19	.3	19	0	.0
35036	.8	93	.3	67	16.7	319	37.1	6	16	.4	14	0	.0
35040	4.9	88	1.6	78	22.2	217	40.5	8	17	2.1	11	0	.4
35042	4.7	84	1.6	73	17.4	221	61.6	7	12	1.9	12	0	1.1
35043	1.7	0	.5	82	20.5	233	58.5	7	14	.7	28	0	.0
35044	6.6	72	2.2	72	23.9	317	90.9	9	10	2.3	8	0	7.8
35045	15.0	89	5.5	72	21.9	191	54.3	8	12	6.6	11	0	.0
35049	2.8	100	.9	76	18.8	205	60.3	7	15	1.4	9	0	.0
35051	5.3	88	1.8	83	20.9	258	55.0	9	9	2.3	9	0	.0
35053	1.5	100	.6	75	21.5	265	64.2	7	10	.7	15	0	.1
35054	5.2	94	.7	89	16.2	132	61.3	6	11	.8	11	0	.0
35055	33.3	100	12.1	88	24.0	201	82.0	8	12	15.9	11	0	.5
35061	2.1	0	.7	74	21.9	240	69.5	8	15	.0	0	0	3.7
35062	7.2	96	2.4	81	18.2	292	47.7	7	8	3.4	9	0	.0
35063	3.7	97	1.2	83	19.2	284	59.6	7	12	1.8	11	3	.4
35064	13.3	46	4.9	64	23.2	237	41.3	6	16	2.8	13	4	3.3
35068	5.5	99	1.9	84	26.3	267	67.4	6	16	2.5	7	2	.0
35070	.5	0	.1	78	17.4	321	72.3	7	9	.0	0	0	.0
35071	10.1	99	3.5	85	28.3	346	82.6	6	11	3.6	11	0	.0
35072	5.2	55	1.6	80	17.4	170	39.6	8	13	1.4	13	5	.2
35073	3.2	69	1.1	81	21.7	272	51.6	8	16	1.1	16	4	.0
35074	.5	0	.1	88	21.1	243*	43.9	9	11	.1	15	4	.0
35077	9.4	94	3.1	81	19.0	227	53.4	8	13	4.3	11	0	.0

ALABAMA

ZIPCODE	1	2	3	4	5	6	7	8	9	10	11	12	13
BIRMINGHAM													
35078	2.4	71	.8	77	19.8	184	60.4	8	10	.8	10	0	.0
35079	4.0	95	1.4	84	18.7	214	49.9	8	12	2.0	12	0	.0
35080	3.8	94	1.2	89	38.4	336	151.7	10	5	1.8	4	1	.6
35082	.2	0	.1	79	16.6	160	30.9	9	9	.0	0	0	.0
35083	2.3	100	.8	86	15.7	226	49.7	8	15	1.2	13	0	.0
35085	5.7	91	2.0	87	20.5	208	53.1	8	9	2.5	7	0	.0
35087	1.9	0	.7	80	17.9	207	46.4	4	13	.0	0	0	.0
35089	2.3	51	.7	79	16.9	262	41.8	7	11	.6	18	0	.7
35091	1.0	94	.3	85	22.5	182	51.8	7	9	.4	8	0	.0
35094	16.9	88	5.8	78	25.0	251	78.8	8	9	7.3	7	0	.7
35096	4.2	67	1.3	84	21.5	165	54.8	7	9	1.4	10	0	.0
35098	1.0	100	.3	79	19.7	244	43.8	10	10	.5	8	0	.0
BIRMINGHAM													
35111	3.8	97	1.3	86	28.0	276	82.7	7	9	1.9	8	0	.0
35112	.8	52	.2	89	17.5	209	26.7	11	7	.2	6	0	.0
35114	2.1	0	.7	81	26.1	258	81.2	10	6	.0	0	0	.6
35115	11.1	85	3.4	75	23.4	285	70.0	8	8	4.4	8	0	.1
35116	3.2	0	1.1	87	27.1	273	63.0	7	10	.0	0	0	.0
35117	4.3	100	1.5	90	27.2	355	74.5	8	7	2.1	7	0	.0
35118	4.4	80	1.5	87	26.9	328	55.8	8	11	1.7	10	0	.0
35119	.5	33	.2	80	16.1	223	35.5	5	13	.1	17	0	.0
35120	3.9	95	1.3	83	21.1	282	64.3	9	9	1.9	11	0	.0
35121	11.2	96	4.0	75	19.4	219	59.0	7	14	5.2	12	0	.0
35123	.1	100	.1	73	20.7	362	74.1	11	16	.1	16	0	.1
35124	7.0	96	2.4	87	33.1	403	112.7	8	4	3.3	3	0	.2
35125	12.5	87	4.1	81	24.4	243	70.6	7	10	5.3	9	0	.3
35126	12.6	94	4.2	89	27.6	305	83.6	9	7	5.8	6	1	.0
35127	7.1	100	2.3	93	33.5	335	87.6	7	10	3.4	7	0	.0
35129	.2	0	.1	0	14.5	237	51.6*	8	6	.0	0	0	.0
35130	3.7	87	1.2	77	22.5	237	50.6	7	10	1.6	10	0	.2
35131	3.1	85	1.1	82	18.4	177	40.1	7	13	1.3	11	0	.3
35133	2.7	100	.9	90	22.7	161	65.6	8	8	1.4	7	0	.0
35135	1.4	80	.6	82	17.9	227	85.8	12	9	.5	13	0	.0
35136	.4	62	.1	61	16.4	446	36.6	6	12	.1	6	0	.3
35137	.5	100	.2	34	20.0	148	42.3	8	13	.2	11	0	.0
35139	.3	100	.1	66	15.2	288	44.8	4	9	.1	7	0	.0
35142	1.5	94	.6	80	30.6	198	54.4	6	18	.8	14	0	.0
35143	.2	0	.2	79	21.2	182	47.8	6	8	.0	0	0	.1
35146	3.5	92	1.7	84	20.1	246	49.3	7	12	1.6	11	0	1.1
35147	1.8	99	.7	79	19.2	235	57.3	8	7	1.3	13	0	.4
35148	3.2	94	1.1	74	22.7	218	61.0	8	11	1.4	9	0	.0
35149	1.0	76	.3	86	17.3	161	22.4	7	16	.4	13	0	5.5
35150	25.9	78	9.1	71	21.3	227	56.1	8	13	9.6	11	0	.2
35160	27.9	64	8.7	67	19.7	225	56.6	8	10	8.6	10	0	.2
35171	2.5	92	.8	82	24.4	254	62.7	11	11	1.2	9	0	.0
35172	2.6	95	.9	82	22.4	217	58.1	6	12	1.1	11	0	.0
35173	10.5	95	3.5	83	27.2	340	84.4	8	9	4.9	7	0	.9
35175	3.7	100	1.3	76	21.6	215	55.0	7	10	1.9	9	0	.0

*=Estimated **1.0=883 lbs per person, 100++ indicates per capita toxic waste generation > than 100 times the U.S. average of 883 lbs per capita.

103001

ZIP CODE MEASURES OF SIZE, LEVELS OF AFFLUENCE AND QUALITY OF LIFE

1=Population (th.); 2= % White; 3=Households (th.); 4=% Owner Occupied; 5=Mean Income Per Household (th.$); 6=Mean Monthly Rent ($)*; 7=Mean Home Value (th.$)*;
8=% under 5; 9=% 65 and over; 10=White Males, 65+; 11=% White Males, 65+; 12=# Toxic Waste Sites; 13=Toxic Waste Relative to US(883 lbs.per capita)**.

ALABAMA

ZIP CODE	1	2	3	4	5	6	7	8	9	10	11	12	13
BIRMINGHAM													
35176	.7	100	.2	89	20.2	243	45.1	8	8	.4	8	0	.0
35178	2.5	71	.8	77	19.8	196	52.9	8	13	.9	11	1	1.0
35179	6.5	0	2.3	85	20.9	234	56.2	8	10	0	0	0	.
35180	9.0	93	3.1	80	24.0	247	71.1	7	10	4.1	8	0	.0
35182	.3	100	.1	97	19.6	225*	25.6	5	9	.2	9	0	.0
35183	.9	100	.3	83	23.5	244	47.5	6	10	.5	6	0	.0
35184	4.0	87	1.4	83	21.1	206	36.9	8	14	1.7	13	0	.0
35185	.3	100	.1	77	23.6	223	13.1	10	0	.2	0	0	.0
35186	2.3	91	.8	87	23.9	211	65.1	7	10	1.0	10	2	.0
35187	.5	66	.2	72	15.9	256	46.0	12	15	.2	13	0	.0
35188	1.1	93	.3	77	23.3	224	43.8	9	7	.5	2	0	.0
BIRMINGHAM													
35203	5.5	19	2.5	4	8.0	149	37.4	10	22	.3	32	0	2.8
35204	23.1	7	9.1	38	14.8	204	50.4	8	17	.6	22	2	.1
35206	21.6	64	11.8	22	18.2	282	69.9	4	18	6.4	9	0	1.4
35207	25.7	79	10.2	75	23.5	312	61.6	6	17	9.2	14	4	.1
35208	19.0	9	5.6	55	16.1	220	43.2	9	11	.9	14	0	1.1
35209	18.9	69	7.4	73	22.2	293	55.4	6	20	5.8	20	0	.0
35210	25.2	93	11.8	40	27.8	388	100.6	5	13	10.7	10	1	.1
35211	12.3	88	4.6	73	28.0	403	88.4	7	15	5.0	10	2	.5
35212	40.6	16	13.6	59	19.3	265	51.3	9	11	2.8	20	4	.0
35213	19.7	35	6.8	45	17.0	240	51.2	9	13	3.1	17	2	.2
35214	16.1	98	6.1	77	53.8	492	158.3	7	13	7.4	10	0	.2
35215	24.7	55	8.4	80	27.2	323	74.0	8	11	6.4	7	0	1.0
35216	44.0	98	15.5	70	28.2	369	85.6	8	6	20.9	8	1	.0
35217	26.3	97	10.8	52	37.8	440	151.0	5	9	12.0	8	2	.7
35218	19.5	73	6.7	75	22.8	283	57.7	7	15	6.6	12	6	.7
35221	14.6	35	5.4	47	16.4	239	44.9	8	15	2.3	16	0	.6
35222	6.5	65	2.1	79	19.4	222	44.8	7	15	.5	34	0	.0
35223	11.3	65	4.7	53	26.3	269	93.9	6	15	3.5	14	2	1.4
35224	10.4	100	3.9	81	68.0	382	232.6	6	14	4.8	11	0	.1
35226	8.9	58	3.2	79	20.8	261	42.0	7	18	2.4	16	3	.0
35228	23.0	98	7.8	80	43.9	441	145.2	7	6	11.0	6	0	.7
35233	1.8	8	.6	38	11.8	191	45.9	9	16	.6	14	0	6.9
35234	16.3	38	5.2	88	15.7	252	44.1	10	12	.6	29	4	.3
35235	13.0	98	4.3	77	35.7	385	100.6	8	7	6.4	5	0	.2
35243	15.4	98	5.5	77	42.8	452	159.8	8	6	7.4	5	0	.1
35244	3.4	98	1.0	98	51.5	262	158.2	12	2	1.7	0	0	.1
TUSCALOOSA													
35401	54.5	53	20.1	46	17.1	257	64.3	8	12	13.9	10	3	.5
35404	6.2	90	2.2	67	25.9	286	76.0	7	12	2.9	11	5	5.4
35405	19.9	83	7.4	60	27.0	332	88.2	7	6	8.3	5	0	.
35406	3.0	95	1.0	83	43.7	429	163.8	9	1	1.4	6	0	.0
35440	.2	0	.1	84	12.2	113	36.0	1	21	.0	0	0	.0
35441	1.4	40	.5	76	13.7	193	41.2	8	21	.3	17	0	.1
35442	5.9	37	1.8	68	16.3	189	54.2	9	14	1.1	13	0	.2
35443	2.7	12	.8	72	11.4	156	33.6	9	16	1.1	25	0	.0
35444	1.6	93	.5	83	20.2	280	50.4	9	14	.7	14	4	.0

ALABAMA

ZIP CODE	1	2	3	4	5	6	7	8	9	10	11	12	13
TUSCALOOSA													
35446	1.4	87	.5	84	20.5	105	41.3	5	8	.6	3	0	.0
35447	3.5	47	1.1	78	20.8	169	48.2	10	14	.8	11	0	.0
35449	.2	77	.1	66	28.6	177	24.8	6	9	.1	4	1	.0
35450	.9	19	.3	93	25.0	139	43.0	11	19	.1	16	0	.0
35452	2.3	100	.7	93	25.0	327	73.3	6	8	1.2	9	1	.0
35453	7.3	92	2.3	85	23.9	273	67.2	8	8	3.3	7	0	.0
35456	2.4	85	.8	88	28.8	282	60.5	8	8	1.1	9	0	.0
35458	.5	92	.2	90	23.8	159	37.0	3	12	.2	8	0	.0
35459	1.2	0	.3	67	15.9	131	40.9	13	13	.0	0	0	.0
35461	.7	55	.6	73	11.9	150	30.3	10	19	.5	17	0	.0
35462	6.2	27	2.0	63	17.5	206	58.8	10	17	.8	15	0	.0
35463	1.2	44	.3	77	18.8	455	47.2	5	12	.3	15	0	.0
35464	.6	13	.2	65	13.4	158	35.3	11	12	.0	17	0	.0
35466	5.3	80	1.8	78	18.4	171	48.5	6	16	2.2	15	0	.0
35469	.4	32	.4	80	13.9	160*	32.7	8	11	.1	11	0	.1
35470	4.5	64	1.4	66	20.7	227	73.4	10	9	1.1	6	0	.0
35474	3.6	84	1.1	76	20.0	170	52.4	8	14	1.1	11	0	.1
35476	24.4	84	8.0	74	24.6	272	79.9	7	11	10.0	8	0	6.2
35477	.9	12	.3	52	12.2	144	37.6	6	27	.1	16	0	.0
35478	.9	85	.3	84	25.2	234	60.0	8	7	.4	7	0	.1
35480	.8	68	.2	86	20.8	271	48.3	7	19	.2	21	0	.0
35481	4.3	83	1.4	74	18.9	172	44.7	9	13	1.4	12	1	.5
35486	4.3	83	1.0	0	6.2	242	22.1*	1	8	.7	1	0	.0
35490	2.1	97	.6	85	24.1	297	53.8	6	8	1.0	7	0	.0
BIRMINGHAM													
35501	29.8	93	10.4	77	23.4	246	69.6	8	12	13.4	10	0	1.5
35540	2.3	0	.8	86	17.9	184	44.2	6	12	.0	0	0	.0
35541	2.3	0	.8	87	19.7	270	53.1	5	10	.0	0	0	.0
35542	1.0	100	.4	80	27.5	135	32.2	7	17	.5	13	0	.4
35543	.9	96	.3	72	18.4	225	45.5	7	14	.5	13	0	.
35544	1.1	96	.4	77	15.9	149	49.8	7	19	.5	18	1	.5
35546	4.0	94	1.3	74	18.4	177	40.3	10	12	1.8	11	0	.1
35548	1.7	100	.5	71	17.9	143	37.7	8	18	.9	14	0	.2
35549	5.3	95	1.9	80	18.6	197	41.4	6	16	2.4	13	0	.1
35550	6.8	93	2.4	74	19.6	199	42.9	7	15	3.0	11	3	.1
35552	1.3	92	.4	75	17.6	183	38.3	9	11	.5	10	0	.0
35553	4.0	99	1.4	77	17.9	211	46.9	8	12	1.9	10	1	.1
35554	1.4	98	.5	88	21.1	103	34.1	7	15	.7	15	0	.0
35555	11.8	83	4.2	75	19.9	214	54.7	7	15	4.7	12	0	1.5
35559	.2	0	.1	85	14.5	155	47.9	3	8	.0	0	0	.
35560	.2	100	1.0	100	22.2	255*	43.1	6	11	.1	9	0	.
35563	4.4	94	1.6	72	18.9	173	57.8	7	15	2.0	14	1	2.7
35564	2.4	100	.8	77	16.7	176	48.7	8	11	1.1	8	0	.
35565	13.4	99	4.8	77	21.1	208	53.4	8	12	6.4	10	1	.4
35570	10.4	97	3.6	77	20.1	194	59.3	7	13	5.0	12	1	.9
35571	1.0	0	.3	84	16.0	255	42.8	6	23	.0	0	0	.0
35572	.3	99	.9	84	18.9	349	35.3	7	11	.5	11	0	.0
35574	1.6	86	.6	82	18.7	207	41.2	7	14	.7	14	1	.0

*=Estimated **1.0=883 lbs per person; 100++ indicates per capita toxic waste generation > than 100 times the U.S. average of 883 lbs per capita.

ZIP CODE MEASURES OF SIZE, LEVELS OF AFFLUENCE AND QUALITY OF LIFE

1=Population (th.); 2= % White; 3=Households (th.); 4=% Owner Occupied; 5=Mean Income Per Household (th.$); 6=Mean Monthly Rent ($)*; 7=Mean Home Value (th.$)*;
8=% under 5; 9=% 65 and over; 10=White Males (th.); 11=% White Males, 65+; 12=# Toxic Waste Sites; 13=Toxic Waste Relative to US(883 lbs.per capita)**;

ALABAMA

BIRMINGHAM

ZIP CODE	1	2	3	4	5	6	7	8	9	10	11	12	13
35575	1.0	0	.3	84	20.3	158	32.3	5	8		0	0	1.8
35576	3.1	86	1.1	80	19.9	200	46.7	.7	13	1.3	12	1	.0
35578	4.8	100	1.6	86	19.7	287	44.9	10	10	2.4	8	0	.0
35579	3.1	94	1.1	81	19.7	200	43.0	7	13	1.5	10	2	.0
35580	5.0	88	1.7	86	19.9	195	42.8	9	14	2.2	12	2	.2
35581	5.5	100	1.9	78	19.4	209	48.6	7	11	2.7	10	2	.0
35582	4.4	98	1.6	80	19.2	164	50.5	8	15	2.1	12	0	.0
35584	.8	66	.3	81	17.8	197	32.7	15	14	.2	11	0	.5
35585	1.2	100	.5	88	22.1	159	53.3	5	14	.6	15	0	.0
35586	4.9	83	1.7	72	20.2	189	53.9	8	13	2.0	13	0	.6
35587	1.5	99	.6	82	18.2	103	42.6	6	16		13	0	.0
35592	5.0	93	1.8	71	20.2	181	57.5	6	16	2.3	13	0	.2
35593	2.2	0	.8	85	20.2	181	44.5	8	11		0	0	.0
35594	7.3	96	2.8	71	20.6	231	51.8	6	16	3.3	15	1	.6

HUNTSVILLE

ZIP CODE	1	2	3	4	5	6	7	8	9	10	11	12	13
35601	38.6	82	14.2	64	24.6	262	75.7	7	11	15.1	8	10	11.0
35603	11.8	95	3.9	85	31.1	330	100.1	8	7	5.7	5	0	.0
35610	1.5	100	.6	79	19.2	248	48.3	10	14	.7	12	0	.0
35611	32.2	86	10.9	73	23.0	252	61.3	7	11	13.4	7	5	.8
35615	.4	24	.1	68	18.4	332	30.8	7	7		8	0	.0
35616	5.3	82	1.8	85	20.8	185	49.8	6	11	2.1	11	1	3.5
35618	2.8	53	.9	78	18.6	172	45.0	7	12	.8	7	0	.0
35619	4.0	90	1.3	79	19.6	269	51.2	8	11	1.9	8	1	3.7
35620	4.3	91	1.3	80	21.4	180	51.9	7	9	2.3	10	0	.0
35621	1.7	100	.6	85	21.5	242	55.6	8	12	.9	14	0	.0
35622	5.6	100	1.7	84	20.5	205	48.8	7	13	2.8	9	0	.0
35630	55.9	87	19.9	70	23.6	287	74.9	7	11	23.1	9	3	.2
35633	2.9	99	.9	94	39.7	380	110.5	7	4	1.4	3	0	.0
35640	18.3	95	6.4	78	23.1	272	68.1	8	10	8.6	7	2	.2
35643	3.6	65	1.1	79	18.7	222	50.5	8	11	1.9	11	2	3.3
35645	7.6	97	2.6	86	27.2	259	86.2	6	10	3.6	8	0	.0
35646	5.0	70	1.6	82	21.2	219	51.5	8	11	1.7	8	0	.0
35647	.9	97	.4	90	18.7	170	48.3	7	13	.5	6	1	.0
35648	3.4	100	1.1	83	21.3	209	59.1	8	12	1.7	11	0	.0
35650	10.2	93	3.4	77	20.4	221	60.2	8	12	4.6	9	0	.0
35651	1.2	97	.4	64	18.8	274	49.1	6	17	.9	14	1	.0
35652	6.5	94	2.3	85	22.0	252	63.9	6	12	3.1	10	0	.0
35653	17.0	93	6.1	75	21.5	223	59.6	7	13	7.7	11	0	.4
35660	24.4	83	9.0	74	25.5	286	70.6	7	11	9.8	10	14	3.3
35670	5.2	97	1.7	87	21.6	295	61.4	9	8	2.6	8	0	.0
35671	6.8	66	2.3	66	21.1	311	63.0	11	8	.6	6	1	.0
35672	1.1	82	.4	90	19.5	185	53.3	8	13	.5	9	4	.0
35673	4.9	98	1.6	82	21.7	217	66.4	9	7	2.3	5	0	.0
35674	18.0	85	6.3	77	23.2	263	62.9	7	11	7.5	9	4	1.8
35677	1.8	96	.6	86	15.9	165	46.3	5	11	.8	9	0	.0

HUNTSVILLE

ZIP CODE	1	2	3	4	5	6	7	8	9	10	11	12	13
35740	4.2	94	1.5	71	19.8	220	44.9	7	10	2.0	8	0	1.2
35741	1.9	91	.6	80	25.5	234	70.2	9	8	.8	0	0	.0
35742	.2	100	.1	62	33.8	224	54.9	6	13	.1	9	0	.0

ALABAMA

HUNTSVILLE

ZIP CODE	1	2	3	4	5	6	7	8	9	10	11	12	13
35744	2.2	98	.7	80	19.6	239	59.8	8	12	1.0	12	0	.0
35745	.2	100	.1	89	19.3	222*	68.9*	4	15	.1	16	0	.0
35746	.9	92	.3	81	19.5	114	50.6	12	8	.4	8	0	.0
35747	4.1	0	1.4	84	20.8	195	59.8	7	10	.0	0	0	.0
35748	3.6	84	1.2	75	21.7	195	47.7	6	11	1.4	8	0	.0
35749	4.0	74	1.2	86	24.5	258	63.6	8	8	1.5	7	4	.6
35750	3.4	98	1.1	90	21.7	218	58.0	7	8	1.7	9	0	.0
35751	.2	0	.1	70	8.8	126	39.4	11	18	.9	9	0	.0
35752	2.2	85	.7	83	21.9	150	60.4	8	11	.9	11	0	.0
35754	4.2	97	1.4	84	20.5	192	56.2	9	9	1.9	9	0	.0
35755	.3	0	.1	84	18.5	59	99.3	2	17	.0	0	0	.3
35758	10.9	73	3.5	78	25.7	302	82.9	8	8	3.9	6	0	.0
35759	.4	100	.1	87	31.2	209	89.3	8	13	.2	9	0	.3
35760	3.9	99	1.3	73	20.2	242	54.2	8	10	1.8	8	0	1.1
35761	4.5	89	1.4	77	19.1	279	54.5	8	12	1.9	10	0	.2
35763	3.0	97	1.0	75	20.0	260	60.2	10	9	1.4	9	0	.5
35764	.6	93	.2	82	13.8	151	35.7	6	14	.3	10	0	.0
35765	4.0	98	1.3	77	19.8	181	48.8	8	11	2.0	11	0	.8
35766	.1	100	.1	92	9.2	106*	40.7	5	28	.1	18	0	.0
35767	.1	100	.1	100	29.4	338*	21.9	12	18	.4	25	0	.0
35768	20.3	95	7.1	71	23.9	271	71.8	7	10	9.4	7	4	.6
35771	3.4	99	1.1	76	19.6	240	48.5	7	10	1.6	7	1	.0
35772	5.4	89	1.9	70	20.1	225	50.4	8	12	2.3	11	1	.7
35773	5.0	84	1.5	77	24.1	244	69.9	7	9	2.0	8	0	.0
35774	.1	100	.1	81	9.9	102	22.9	5	40	.0	30	0	.0
35775	.5	77	.1	90	19.8	209	47.8	8	7	.2	6	0	.1
35776	3.0	0	1.0	84	21.5	233	51.1	7	9		0	0	.0

HUNTSVILLE

ZIP CODE	1	2	3	4	5	6	7	8	9	10	11	12	13
35801	25.3	89	9.8	66	30.0	259	106.1	6	14	10.5	12	2	.2
35802	18.5	98	6.9	65	43.9	398	136.8	4	5	8.9	4	3	.5
35803	14.4	98	4.6	85	38.1	412	108.8	7	3	7.1	2	1	.0
35805	37.2	73	14.8	44	20.0	285	61.6	8	8	13.1	6	3	.8
35806	5.8	57	1.7	62	27.7	314	85.9	5	4	.6	4	1	1.9
35808	4.2	73	1.1	82	21.0	371	126.0	16	0	1.6	0	0	.0
35810	33.4	60	10.4	81	27.2	343	68.0	8	4	9.9	3	0	.1
35811	15.7	78	5.2	77	26.2	307	75.2	7	7	5.9	7	3	.0

GADSDEN

ZIP CODE	1	2	3	4	5	6	7	8	9	10	11	12	13
35901	40.1	80	14.5	70	25.0	243	69.5	7	13	15.1	11	1	1.9
35903	20.5	81	7.7	73	22.4	228	58.8	7	13	8.1	11	1	.4
35904	11.6	96	4.3	75	18.9	197	42.3	7	15	5.2	13	1	.2
35905	4.7	98	1.5	83	28.5	231	66.0	7	9	5.2	13	2	.0
35950	21.9	99	7.8	77	19.9	227	59.2	7	11	10.5	10	2	.2
35952	5.9	97	2.1	82	19.5	213	44.7	7	12	2.9	11	2	.2
35953	4.5	85	1.5	82	21.0	239	53.4	8	11	2.9	11	1	.1
35954	13.8	87	4.7	73	20.7	216	46.5	8	12	1.9	12	1	.0
35957	17.0	99	6.2	73	18.7	206	53.5	7	13	5.8	9	1	.3
35958	2.6	99	.9	84	21.3	170	50.5	8	8	1.4	8	1	.4
35959	4.0	90	1.3	77	19.2	223	59.9	8	10	1.8	10	0	.0
35960	6.9	90	2.5	76	19.6	161	63.4	6	15	3.0	12	0	.0

*=Estimated **1.0=883 lbs per person; 100++ indicates per capita toxic waste generation > than 100 times the U.S. average of 883 lbs per capita.

ZIP CODE MEASURES OF SIZE, LEVELS OF AFFLUENCE AND QUALITY OF LIFE

1=Population (th.); 2= % White; 3=Households (th.); 4=% Owner Occupied; 5=Mean Income Per Household (th.$); 6=Mean Monthly Rent ($); 7=Mean Home Value (th.$); 8=% under 5; 9=% 65 and over; 10=White Males (th.); 11=% White Males, 65+; 12=# Toxic Waste Sites; 13=Toxic Waste Relative to US(883 lbs.per capita)**.

ALABAMA

GADSDEN

ZIP CODE	1	2	3	4	5	6	7	8	9	10	11	12	13
35961	4.4	92	1.7	74	15.8	191	39.9	8	17	1.9	14	0	.0
35962	4.9	0	1.7	77	17.8	194	48.9	6	15	.0	0	0	.1
35963	1.4	100	.5	79	37.1	184	42.5	8	16	.7	15	0	.0
35966	3.4	99	1.1	85	18.6	259	43.3	9	7	1.7	6	0	.0
35967	17.4	96	6.5	75	20.4	243	59.5	7	14	8.0	12	0	.4
35971	4.5	0	1.6	81	18.9	204	48.2	8	12	.0	0	0	.0
35972	1.1	97	.4	79	22.0	216	58.0	5	12	.5	13	0	.0
35973	1.6	0	.6	73	15.9	225	41.5	6	14	.0	0	0	.0
35974	1.2	97	.5	77	19.0	174	46.8	4	17	.5	15	0	.0
35975	.7	100	.3	87	17.1	189	44.7	5	20	.3	17	0	.0
35976	13.1	93	4.8	72	21.6	222	70.7	8	13	5.8	11	1	.1
35978	4.2	100	1.5	79	19.3	228	50.3	8	12	2.0	11	0	.0
35979	.4	100	.1	94	17.8	205*	43.9	10	3	.2	6	0	.0
35980	3.2	0	1.1	84	19.1	192	47.2	6	12	.0	0	0	.0
35981	1.7	100	.6	88	26.4	165	39.5	6	13	.8	9	0	.0
35983	2.0	82	.6	85	22.2	194	51.5	8	10	.8	8	0	1.3
35984	1.4	0	.5	79	17.2	263	60.6	8	14	.0	0	0	.0
35986	5.7	0	2.1	81	20.1	213	55.3	7	10	.0	0	0	.0
35987	2.3	99	.8	85	20.3	185	45.7	7	12	1.1	9	0	.3
35988	1.1	0	.4	78	19.0	214	43.7	10	12	.0	0	0	.0
35989	2.2	98	.8	79	19.1	217	46.2	9	15	1.1	13	0	.7
35990	.3	100	.1	89	19.2	244	44.1	12	15	.1	11	0	.0

MONTGOMERY

ZIP CODE	1	2	3	4	5	6	7	8	9	10	11	12	13
36003	2.1	30	.6	73	18.6	151	40.5	10	14	.3	11	0	.0
36006	1.4	81	.5	77	15.1	179	42.0	8	18	.5	17	0	.1
36009	1.0	80	.3	83	15.1	159	38.0	8	13	.4	12	0	.0
36010	3.0	80	1.1	73	16.3	146	37.5	5	16	1.2	16	0	.0
36013	6.2	54	2.1	70	16.1	174	43.8	7	16	1.5	16	0	.1
36015	.1	0	.1	100	20.6	236*	86.3	0	35	.0	0	0	1.3
36016	3.9	50	1.4	71	15.2	142	38.4	8	15	1.0	14	0	.1
36017	2.0	63	.7	83	14.9	166	34.4	8	16	.6	15	0	.0
36020	.4	47	.1	86	22.5	182	64.8	9	7	.1	11	0	.0
36022	3.9	94	1.3	83	24.0	194	77.5	6	9	1.8	8	0	.0
36023	.9	87	.3	77	20.9	172	47.3	9	13	.4	7	0	.0
36024	4.4	81	1.6	80	21.9	173	61.9	6	14	1.7	14	0	.0
36025	4.5	68	1.0	81	26.5	220	69.0	7	9	1.7	7	0	.2
36026	.9	67	.3	92	21.0	104	60.5	8	13	.3	19	0	.2
36027	14.7	60	5.0	69	20.2	206	62.7	8	13	4.3	10	1	.2
36028	1.8	84	.7	66	14.0	138	38.0	5	21	.7	18	0	.0
36029	.8	35	.3	71	20.2	306	24.3	9	17	.1	17	0	.0
36030	1.0	0	.1	57	17.2	100	49.2	8	18	.0	0	0	.0
36031	.2	0	.1	51	6.0	303	28.4	4	40	.0	0	0	.0
36032	2.9	0	.9	77	19.0	152	46.9	10	13	.0	0	0	.8
36033	4.9	61	1.8	78	16.0	156	37.6	8	21	1.4	23	0	.0
36034	.9	71	.3	81	19.8	225	39.6	7	13	.4	11	0	.0
36035	2.3	69	.7	76	17.8	208	40.1	9	16	.8	14	0	.0
36036	1.9	0	.6	79	15.9	193	40.0	9	13	.0	0	0	.0
36037	13.5	61	4.6	69	19.0	185	51.7	9	14	3.8	11	1	.3

ALABAMA

MONTGOMERY

ZIP CODE	1	2	3	4	5	6	7	8	9	10	11	12	13
36038	.4	81	.1	67	15.0	211	35.1	6	13	.2	7	0	.0
36039	.5	13	.1	85	14.3	102	34.5	8	14	.0	0	0	.0
36040	4.8	8	1.2	76	11.9	133	38.1	12	9	.2	15	0	.0
36041	1.4	81	.5	79	14.1	248	34.9	6	13	.6	9	0	.0
36042	1.4	93	.4	84	17.4	51	41.5	6	13	.6	8	0	.0
36043	3.0	64	1.0	76	24.3	124	74.5	7	11	1.0	8	0	.0
36045	1.5	73	.4	89	20.5	140	51.2	12	15	.5	12	0	.0
36047	2.4	20	.6	70	14.4	179	48.9	9	9	.2	13	0	.0
36048	2.4	47	.8	79	16.1	91	37.2	8	15	.5	14	0	.0
36049	5.0	76	1.8	70	18.1	188	54.0	8	20	1.7	18	1	.7
36051	1.5	76	.5	87	23.8	178	43.9	5	12	.6	9	0	.0
36052	.4	28	.1	50	26.1	134	93.0*	9	7	.1	9	0	.0
36053	2.5	10	.7	78	12.6	137	26.9	8	13	.1	11	0	.1
36054	7.1	81	2.3	78	26.3	302	76.1	8	7	2.9	4	0	.0
36057	.6	40	.1	43	17.4	183	42.4	7	2	.2	0	0	6
36061	.5	59	.2	80	17.3	122	58.0	3	17	.2	10	0	.0
36064	2.2	58	.7	84	29.6	165	146.3	8	10	.6	6	3	.0
36067	26.2	81	8.3	80	26.0	311	74.7	8	13	10.5	6	3	.0
36069	2.3	48	.8	65	18.3	195	46.9	8	14	.3	13	0	.1
36071	1.0	59	.4	67	16.2	176	35.0	7	15	.3	14	0	.0
36075	2.2	18	.7	84	16.0	167	38.0	8	15	.2	15	0	.0
36076	.5	45	.1	58	27.2	213	39.0	12	15	.1	7	0	.7
36078	10.5	78	3.9	75	19.1	195	49.0	7	18	3.8	16	0	.7
36080	1.5	81	.5	84	22.2	180	58.8	6	16	.6	17	0	.0
36081	19.7	68	6.6	64	18.1	204	60.9	7	13	6.4	10	2	.3
36083	11.3	15	3.6	65	16.4	243	52.3	7	16	1.0	20	2	2.0
36088	7.4	1	2.1	52	19.6	245	75.1	7	9	.0	0	0	.0
36089	8.2	0	2.8	69	16.1	174	42.9	8	17	.0	0	0	.2
36091	2.3	79	.8	78	15.9	187	48.2	8	15	.8	17	0	.0
36092	15.1	74	4.9	81	24.0	205	76.6	8	11	5.5	10	0	.0

MONTGOMERY

ZIP CODE	1	2	3	4	5	6	7	8	9	10	11	12	13
36101	1.7	24	.2	81	22.2	297	57.2	3	0	.2	3	4	2.6
36104	19.5	16	7.3	28	12.6	185	47.2	10	15	1.5	13	2	.6
36105	16.7	27	5.6	68	21.1	283	56.5	9	11	2.0	22	0	.0
36106	12.6	84	5.0	67	31.7	329	112.8	6	15	4.8	11	0	.3
36107	10.7	86	4.5	59	19.9	253	56.3	7	20	4.1	16	0	1.0
36108	33.4	18	10.3	55	17.2	226	51.5	10	8	2.9	8	0	.9
36109	24.8	96	8.7	85	31.7	371	89.4	6	10	11.4	8	0	.9
36110	13.2	62	4.2	81	20.6	276	45.0	8	8	4.0	8	0	.5
36111	11.9	97	4.8	75	47.8	412	134.0	4	13	5.3	12	0	.1
36113	2.0	84	.5	3	30.1	436	107.4*10		0	.0	0	0	.0
36115	1.2	85	.4	4	23.3	383	100.6	13	0	.5	0	0	2.6
36116	26.0	87	9.7	62	27.9	361	89.3	9	5	10.7	3	0	.6
36117	11.8	76	4.3	61	30.7	365	111.1	7	3	4.5	1	0	.0

ANNISTON

ZIP CODE	1	2	3	4	5	6	7	8	9	10	11	12	13
36201	58.0	73	20.7	67	21.3	245	61.1	8	11	20.2	10	11	2.1
36203	13.4	93	4.8	76	23.1	289	64.2	8	9	6.2	8	1	.2
36205	7.6	69	.6	1	20.7	371	73.8*	5	0	3.6	0	0	.0
36250	2.6	96	.8	88	24.0	219	65.0	8	7	1.2	7	0	.0

*=Estimated **1.0=883 lbs per person; 100++ indicates per capita toxic waste generation > than 100 times the U.S. average of 883 lbs per capita.

ZIP CODE MEASURES OF SIZE, LEVELS OF AFFLUENCE AND QUALITY OF LIFE

1=Population (th.); 2= % White; 3=Households (th.); 4=% Owner Occupied; 5=Mean Income Per Household (th.$); 6=Mean Monthly Rent ($)*; 7=Mean Home Value (th.$)*;
8=% under 5; 9=% 65 and over; 10=White Males (th.); 11=% White Males, 65+; 12=# Toxic Waste Sites; 13=Toxic Waste Relative to US(883 lbs.per capita)**.

ALABAMA

ANNISTON

ZIPCODE	1	2	3	4	5	6	7	8	9	10	11	12	13
36251	5.2	86	1.8	71	17.8	177	44.5	8	16	2.2	15	0	.0
36253	.9	93	.3	88	24.1	315	59.6	4	4	.4	5	0	.0
36254	.1	79	.	76	14.2	178	45.9	10	24	.1	0	0	.0
36255	.9	100	.3	81	20.2	98	33.9	2	15	.5	17	0	.3
36256	1.2	80	.4	79	20.1	172	38.5	8	13	.5	6	0	.0
36257	.2	0	.	93	28.1	323*	90.3	0	18	.0	0	0	.0
36258	1.3	97	.4	88	23.9	286	58.0	9	9	.6	8	0	.0
36260	2.9	82	.9	85	21.5	265	62.1	7	8	1.1	8	2	.5
36261	.2	100	.1	87	15.2	174*	25.4	7	27	.1	21	0	.0
36262	1.1	100	.4	80	17.4	152	49.6	7	13	.5	11	1	.0
36263	.9	94	.	88	17.8	104	27.4	8	18	.4	18	0	.0
36264	8.3	90	2.7	77	20.9	199	52.7	7	12	3.8	11	0	.0
36265	15.8	89	5.2	63	21.2	258	69.1	6	9	6.8	7	1	.1
36266	4.8	79	1.7	75	19.6	178	51.9	7	18	1.8	17	0	.0
36267	.1	73	.1	61	10.1	135	37.2	0	35	.0	37	0	.0
36268	4.2	72	1.3	82	20.4	244	45.5	10	10	1.5	10	1	.1
36269	.7	0	.	86	20.8	176	41.2	5	11	.0	0	0	.0
36270	1.1	90	.3	80	19.6	302	26.0	8	8	.5	7	0	.0
36271	4.3	93	1.4	85	22.1	239	67.3	6	8	2.1	7	0	.0
36272	13.0	95	4.6	75	21.6	202	46.0	7	13	6.0	11	4	.2
36273	1.8	0	.7	80	17.8	317	57.3	9	12	.0	0	0	.0
36274	11.2	69	3.9	74	16.9	199	43.9	7	15	3.6	13	0	.3
36277	5.1	96	1.7	78	15.4	136	45.1	7	20	.8	23	0	.0
36278	3.2	72	1.2	83	24.7	334	64.9	6	5	2.4	4	0	.0
36279	2.2	90	.7	75	16.4	205	47.8	8	10	1.1	13	1	.0
36280	2.2	91	.8	85	21.4	218	55.3	10	10	1.0	12	0	.0
			.8	83	16.8	321	45.0	8	16	.9	17	0	.0

DOTHAN

ZIPCODE	1	2	3	4	5	6	7	8	9	10	11	12	13
36301	35.8	85	12.8	66	23.3	286	64.9	8	10	14.8	8	3	.9
36303	23.0	62	7.9	68	26.7	417	63.1	10	10	6.9	6	1	42.9
36310	6.1	60	2.1	78	20.3	251	82.1	9	9	1.8	13	2	.4
36311	2.5	80	.8	84	18.3	184	52.1	7	13	.9	10	0	.5
36312	5.8	81	1.9	74	19.2	149	45.7	7	12	.9	10	0	.5
36313	.3	50	.1	86	13.6	199	52.6	8	13	2.3	11	0	.0
36314	.3	100	.	72	13.7	237	25.8	2	22	.1	22	0	.0
36316	1.9	86	.7	91	28.3	185	54.0	3	27	.8	22	0	.0
36317	.8	0	.3	72	14.7	58	45.9	5	13	.0	14	0	.0
36318	1.1	92	.4	87	19.3	190	32.7	7	25	.0	0	0	.0
36319	2.4	77	.8	83	21.8	204	43.6	8	14	.5	10	0	.0
36320	2.4	80	.8	76	16.0	121	55.5	7	13	.9	11	0	.0
36321	.3	0	.	81	26.4	183	47.2	7	14	.9	14	0	.0
36322	7.0	81	2.5	54	21.1	164	71.5	8	8	1.8	13	0	.2
36323	8.7	79	3.0	77	20.1	283	67.7	10	5	2.9	4	0	.2
36330	23.5	82	8.1	68	23.9	195	52.8	7	14	3.4	12	0	.1
36340	6.3	86	2.2	77	19.7	285	78.0	8	9	9.6	7	0	.2
36343	1.7	56	.6	74	16.6	178	49.9	7	13	2.6	12	2	.2
36344	4.7	85	1.7	77	18.5	132	38.9	10	12	.5	15	0	.0
36345	5.5	73	2.0	77	20.0	191	47.9	8	17	2.0	15	0	.3
						181	53.8	8	15	1.8	15	0	.3

ALABAMA

DOTHAN (continued)

ZIPCODE	1	2	3	4	5	6	7	8	9	10	11	12	13
36346	1.3	98	.4	90	21.1	316	40.1	7	10	.6	11	0	.0
36349	.2	100	.1	94	17.5	201*	41.3	12	22	.4	21	0	.0
36350	4.1	88	1.5	63	18.1	217	52.5	5	10	1.8	9	0	.0
36351	3.3	85	1.2	79	18.9	167	45.2	6	13	1.3	11	0	.3
36352	3.5	90	1.2	84	18.2	204	50.4	7	10	1.5	9	0	.0
36353	2.1	59	.6	77	17.0	185	47.1	11	14	.6	13	0	.0
36360	19.2	80	6.7	68	20.9	227	65.3	8	11	7.5	9	2	.5
36362	8.9	76	1.5	3	21.3	384	75.8*11	8	14	4.3	0	1	.0
36370	.6	88	.2	76	16.7	88	48.5	3	14	.	0	0	.0
36371	.7	76	.3	83	20.2	182	49.3	7	13	.3	13	1	.0
36373	1.0	49	.3	81	16.8	202	47.3	12	12	.2	18	0	.0
36374	.3	73	.3	79	18.2	66	38.8	7	14	.3	13	0	.0
36375	4.7	86	1.6	83	18.0	195	40.6	7	13	2.0	12	0	.7
36376	2.0	82	.7	81	20.4	120	52.5	9	10	.8	10	0	.0

EVERGREEN

ZIPCODE	1	2	3	4	5	6	7	8	9	10	11	12	13
36401	9.2	55	3.2	75	17.8	195	41.9	9	16	2.5	14	3	.4
36420	18.2	86	6.9	77	19.7	188	51.5	6	16	7.4	14	0	2.2
36425	1.5	19	.5	80	13.4	182	37.3	9	21	.1	19	1	.0
36426	17.4	75	5.9	79	22.3	203	54.7	7	13	6.4	10	2	.8
36432	3.5	57	1.1	83	16.9	164	37.1	7	15	1.0	11	0	.0
36435	.9	0	.2	79	16.1	138	41.3	6	19	.1	2	0	.0
36436	.7	61	.2	90	15.3	184	41.7	15	9	.2	6	0	.4
36439	.4	0	.1	69	21.5	229	48.8	8	9	.0	0	0	.0
36441	3.5	79	1.3	73	17.7	206	47.8	9	12	1.3	12	0	.9
36442	3.3	84	1.3	71	15.8	192	38.8	5	19	1.3	17	2	.0
36444	1.1	52	.4	72	16.0	158	36.0	9	8	.2	7	0	.0
36445	3.5	76	1.3	80	19.3	203	44.2	8	16	1.2	17	0	.1
36446	.8	59	.7	79	18.3	204	35.6	11	11	.2	16	1	.0
36451	5.1	71	1.7	82	21.5	189	50.3	8	13	1.7	13	1	.0
36452	.3	0	.	33	11.3	141	13.1	9	20	.0	0	0	.0
36453	2.2	96	.8	77	26.7	165	42.5	6	18	1.0	18	0	.0
36454	.2	79	.1	92	21.8	251*	63.0	9	7	.1	0	0	.8
36455	.6	64	.2	81	14.2	167	23.0	9	19	.0	2	0	.0
36456	2.0	71	.8	84	14.7	155	29.0	7	15	.7	19	3	.4
36457	.2	71	.1	71	21.2	84	37.2	5	15	.1	20	0	.0
36458	.3	66	.1	83	19.3	211	64.8	15	10	.1	8	0	.0
36460	10.1	60	3.2	77	24.5	221	69.8	9	12	3.0	10	2	.0
36467	10.2	90	3.6	80	19.7	211	47.7	7	15	4.4	12	0	.4
36470	1.8	55	.4	54	15.4	191	30.3	8	4	.1	0	0	20.8
36471	.3	36	.5	78	22.9	136	44.1	11	15	.3	17	0	.4
36473	.3	100	.1	66	15.2	138	49.4	0	8	.1	5	0	.0
36474	2.8	83	1.0	80	16.2	230	41.5	9	7	1.2	17	0	.0
36475	1.6	61	.5	90	17.4	143	48.5	7	15	.5	18	0	.2
36476	.4	0	.	70	14.1	231	38.4	8	13	.0	0	0	.1
36477	4.5	88	1.6	66	23.9	174	40.4	9	15	2.0	12	0	.0
36480	1.8	72	.5	85	20.5	166	33.1	9	9	.6	9	0	.0
36481	1.5	16	.1	64	13.4	198	18.0	11	8	3.0	9	0	.0
36482	1.4	0	.5	80	16.1	140	34.3	10	9	.0	0	0	.0
36483	.5	98	.2	71	15.0	282	34.0	10	21	.3	23	0	.0

*=Estimated **1.0=883 lbs per person; 100++ indicates per capita toxic waste generation > than 100 times the U.S. average of 883 lbs.per capita.

103001

ZIP CODE MEASURES OF SIZE, LEVELS OF AFFLUENCE AND QUALITY OF LIFE

1=Population (th.); 2= % White; 3=Households (th.); 4=% Owner Occupied; 5=Mean Income Per Household (th.$); 6=Mean Monthly Rent ($)*; 7=Mean Home Value (th.$)*;
8=% under 5, 9=% 65 and over; 10=White Males (th.); 11=% White Males, 65+; 12=# Toxic Waste Sites; 13=Toxic Waste Relative to US(883 lbs.per capita)**.

ALABAMA — MOBILE

ZIPCODE	1	2	3	4	5	6	7	8	9	10	11	12	13
36502	17.2	57	5.3	73	19.4	225	50.6	8	12	4.9	10	0	.3
36505	.5	77	.4	85	25.5	234	61.2	8	9	.4	5	3	100++
36507	15.0	81	4.7	76	21.8	262	60.9	9	9	6.0	8	9	1.3
36509	3.1	94	1.0	72	21.3	261	57.4	12	12	1.4	10	0	1.0
36511	.5	90	.1	74	28.0	340	63.0	8	12	.2	16	0	.0
36512	.2	55	.1	71	17.7	186	64.8	3	30	.0	0	2	100++
36513	.3	83	.1	88	15.6	179*	24.5	15	5	.1	6	0	.0
36515	.6	0	.1	84	11.7	135*	33.0	12	8	.0	0	0	.0
36518	2.6	85	.9	80	22.3	180	55.6	9	11	1.1	10	0	.0
36521	2.7	93	.8	92	25.6	197	71.7	9	7	1.3	6	1	.0
36522	4.6	83	1.6	84	20.4	249	65.7	8	14	1.9	10	1	.1
36523	2.9	90	.9	84	20.5	327	59.6	9	10	1.3	7	0	.0
36524	1.5	64	.6	84	14.3	175	35.8	8	17	.4	18	0	.0
36525	2.5	85	.8	89	26.6	148	74.3	9	7	1.1	9	0	.0
36526	9.4	72	3.1	80	28.0	326	106.1	8	10	3.3	8	1	.0
36527	2.9	94	1.0	85	30.6	406	108.2	4	8	1.4	8	1	.0
36528	.4	100	.2	93	22.3	134	91.0	3	29	.2	26	0	.0
36529	.5	65	.1	81	18.6	265	35.7	10	8	.2	4	0	.0
36530	2.9	0	1.0	87	21.0	242	83.8	7	15	.0	0	0	.0
36532	13.0	87	4.9	75	25.0	310	90.8	6	18	5.4	17	0	.0
36535	10.0	82	3.4	78	25.5	275	75.4	8	15	3.9	14	0	.1
36538	.5	56	.2	89	10.5	158	45.7	3	20	.1	25	0	.0
36539	.5	87	.2	81	16.4	195	41.4	8	19	.2	15	0	.0
36540	.2	16	.1	83	11.0	126*	24.7	14	9	.0	42	0	.0
36541	9.0	83	2.7	82	25.3	311	69.5	11	6	3.7	5	0	.0
36542	1.8	0	.7	76	25.1	282	104.0	7	18	.0	0	0	.0
36543	.2	100	.1	88	11.1	147	35.3	15	12	.1	19	1	.0
36544	3.9	84	1.1	86	23.8	298	79.5	9	5	1.6	4	1	2.6
36545	8.8	59	2.8	76	25.1	213	57	8	12	2.6	11	0	.8
36548	1.2	60	.4	87	22.7	302	48.9	15	8	.4	6	0	.1
36549	1.1	83	.4	89	25.6	241	89.9	4	11	.4	14	0	.0
36550	.4	61	.3	94	16.8	193*	29.9	6	11	.1	8	0	.0
36551	3.3	82	1.1	80	21.6	271	63.2	8	9	1.4	9	0	.0
36552	.2	0	.1	100	28.0	322*	36.9	6	6	.0	0	0	.0
36553	3.7	36	1.0	88	20.1	187	43.4	10	7	.7	10	0	100++
36555	.7	98	.2	86	21.1	264	78.9	4	16	.3	15	0	.0
36558	3.2	66	1.0	84	18.0	227	39.1	8	11	1.0	13	0	.0
36559	.8	59	.3	96	37.1	357	162.1	9	13	.2	17	0	.0
36560	4.7	40	1.2	78	21.0	183	42.0	8	9	1.0	7	0	3.7
36561	1.1	0	.5	82	22.1	399	117.8	4	22	.0	0	0	.0
36562	1.4	86	.4	93	17.9	66	35.6	13	8	.6	6	0	.0
36564	.8	71	.3	88	31.7	350	169.4	5	15	.3	15	0	.0
36567	5.6	97	1.9	80	19.9	216	63.7	8	12	2.7	10	0	.0
36568	.7	84	.2	76	20.5	229	72.4	13	6	.2	7	0	.0
36569	.7	77	.2	72	18.9	145	46.3	8	16	.3	12	0	.0
36570	.5	54	.2	94	15.8	248	47.5	10	26	.1	22	0	.0
36571	12.0	95	4.0	76	27.5	332	73.9	8	6	5.7	5	2	.5
36572	3.4	92	1.1	87	28.4	335	79.6	8	7	1.6	6	0	.1
36575	7.3	99	2.3	89	27.1	274	83.7	10	5	3.6	4	0	.0

ALABAMA — MOBILE (continued)

ZIPCODE	1	2	3	4	5	6	7	8	9	10	11	12	13
36576	2.1	96	.7	86	21.2	220	70.1	6	7	1.0	7	0	.0
36578	.9	98	.3	87	18.1	295	49.3	10	8	.4	8	0	.0
36579	1.9	0	.6	81	20.3	197	50.0	9	17	.0	0	0	.0
36580	2.2	92	.7	85	21.5	312	63.6	6	10	1.0	10	0	.0
36581	.5	19	.1	78	21.5	247*	19.8	2	17	.0	0	0	.0
36582	15.8	85	5.2	78	24.4	314	77.7	9	9	6.7	6	3	9.5
36583	.6	100	.2	92	20.5	235*	38.4	11	12	.3	10	0	.0
36584	.7	88	.3	89	18.8	172	52.2	9	14	.3	3	0	.0
36585	1.1	80	.3	93	22.9	158	29.1	6	11	.5	9	0	.0
36586	.7	23	.2	72	16.3	555	39.5	11	4	.1	9	0	.0
36587	6.2	93	1.8	89	22.7	266	70.3	10	6	2.8	6	0	.0

MOBILE

ZIPCODE	1	2	3	4	5	6	7	8	9	10	11	12	13
36602	1.0	59	.5	9	11.3	167	71.5	2	29	.3	20	0	.6
36603	16.2	4	5.7	34	12.7	180	47.6	9	15	.3	30	5	.0
36604	12.6	60	5.3	53	20.6	264	73.5	7	20	3.4	19	0	.0
36605	35.6	63	12.0	65	21.4	254	62.2	9	10	10.9	9	1	.1
36606	20.7	82	8.8	64	22.4	323	67.1	9	18	7.8	8	1	.1
36607	9.5	64	3.9	55	21.4	247	71.4	7	24	2.4	22	2	.2
36608	44.3	90	15.1	66	32.6	350	115.8	7	7	19.6	6	2	.5
36609	49.1	93	17.4	67	32.1	384	103.9	8	6	22.5	6	1	.2
36610	33.0	14	10.1	46	12.9	201	39.0	12	10	2.1	13	2	.1
36611	7.9	95	3.1	70	21.7	240	59.2	6	15	3.5	12	4	10.3
36612	6.2	29	1.8	70	16.5	239	46.4	11	9	.9	14	2	.0
36613	10.2	87	3.1	86	24.6	309	68.9	8	8	4.4	7	0	.0
36617	22.8	1	6.6	66	17.4	226	54.9	8	9	.1	39	0	.0
36618	10.4	96	3.4	88	28.7	438	75.0	8	8	4.9	9	0	.0
36619	5.0	100	1.6	78	25.5	368	68.4	10	6	2.4	5	0	.0

SELMA

ZIPCODE	1	2	3	4	5	6	7	8	9	10	11	12	13
36701	44.9	50	15.0	60	19.9	230	63.5	9	12	10.5	9	10	.6
36720	.9	7	.2	64	12.6	191	37.5	14	8	.0	11	0	.0
36722	.4	40	.1	96	18.9	217*	25.6	6	16	.0	7	0	.0
36723	.6	0	.1	89	12.9	148*	84.6	11	8	.0	0	0	.0
36724	1.5	26	.4	46	15.3	232	47.7	8	11	.2	5	0	.0
36725	.9	46	.3	81	20.8	71	51.7	10	12	.2	4	0	.0
36726	5.3	0	1.7	72	18.6	180	52.0	10	14	.0	1	0	.1
36728	1.1	18	.3	76	19.0	166	28.2	10	16	.1	35	0	.0
36732	9.6	0	3.2	66	22.0	220	66.2	9	13	3.0	20	6	1.7
36736	1.4	32	.5	79	18.4	223	28.1	9	11	.5	15	0	.0
36738	1.2	17	.4	69	12.0	113	30.5	10	9	.2	11	0	.0
36740	1.5	18	.4	81	12.5	200	41.0	8	15	.2	7	0	.0
36742	2.1	53	.7	82	19.6	118	42.7	9	12	.6	6	1	.0
36744	7.6	6	2.4	73	16.9	160	47.6	10	16	.2	6	0	.0
36748	4.1	59	1.4	76	20.8	214	55.0	8	14	1.2	10	2	.0
36749	1.0	53	.3	82	16.8	86	66.1	12	12	.3	14	0	.0
36750	2.6	69	.9	82	20.7	199	44.2	10	12	.9	16	0	.0
36751	1.0	13	.3	71	8.9	168	21.7	16	18	.1	0	0	.0
36752	.4	45	.1	78	20.2	137	60.5	5	11	.1	10	0	.0
36753	.2	0	.1	89	12.5	274	83.7	10	5	.0	6	0	.0

*=Estimated **1.0=883 lbs per person; 100++ indicates per capita toxic waste generation > than 100 times the U.S. average of 883 lbs per capita.

ZIP CODE MEASURES OF SIZE, LEVELS OF AFFLUENCE AND QUALITY OF LIFE

1=Population (th.); 2= % White; 3=Households (th.); 4=% Owner Occupied; 5=Mean Income Per Household (th.$); 6=Mean Monthly Rent ($)*; 7=Mean Home Value (th.$)*; 8=% under 5; 9=% 65 and over; 10=White Males (th.); 11=% White Males, 65+; 12=# Toxic Waste Sites; 13=Toxic Waste Relative to US(883 lbs.per capita)**.

ALABAMA

ZIPCODE	1	2	3	4	5	6	7	8	9	10	11	12	13
SELMA													
36754	.5	29	.1	93	13.0	128	42.0	19	26	.1	53	0	.0
36756	7.7	53	2.4	69	16.9	210	53.7	9	17	1.9	13	0	.0
36758	1.4	66	.4	82	19.9	140	41.0	8	13	.4	7	0	.0
36759	1.1	26	.4	61	13.4	203	38.5	5	19	.2	26	0	.0
36761	1.5	22	.4	59	14.7	128	34.3	9	19	.2	17	0	.0
36762	.5	16	.1	85	18.2	38	60.8	13	10	.0	0	0	.0
36763	.4	0	.1	78	21.0	158	40.2	3	13	.0	0	0	.0
36765	1.4	19	.5	78	11.6	124	33.3	6	18	.1	7	0	.0
36766	.1	38	.1	67	12.5	139	38.2	8	41	.0	69	0	.0
36767	3.2	14	.9	56	12.9	140	43.3	11	15	.2	19	0	.0
36768	1.9	20	.5	57	15.2	137	26.6	9	16	.2	14	0	.0
36769	3.0	0	.9	83	16.2	140	41.1	11	18	.0	0	0	4.1
36772	.3	21	.1	61	18.4	83	47.9	18	18	.0	0	0	.0
36773	.4	18	.1	77	12.3	63	36.5	9	12	.0	19	0	.0
36775	1.8	13	.5	45	12.0	156	59.5	6	10	.1	6	0	.0
36776	1.9	0	.5	67	10.8	130	42.9	11	13	.0	0	0	.0
36778	.2	0	.1	39	8.6	93	28.1	9	10	.0	0	0	.0
36779	1.0	0	.3	70	17.5	201*	62.0	13	11	.1	0	0	.0
36780	.3	62	.2	73	14.0	175	48.0	9	14	.1	1	0	.0
36782	2.8	52	1.0	77	17.2	164	46.4	9	17	.7	15	0	.0
36783	1.3	50	.5	79	16.0	116	43.4	6	22	.3	16	0	.0
36784	7.1	64	2.2	78	22.8	191	53.4	8	12	.3	11	3	.0
36785	1.6	34	.5	67	21.3	172	33.7	9	13	2.3	17	0	.4
36786	4.7	0	1.4	64	12.1	163	36.3	10	14	.3	17	0	.0
36792	1.0	0	.3	89	19.5	95	35.8	7	9	.0	0	0	.0
36793	.6	94	.2	82	18.9	134	37.7	12	20	.3	17	0	.8
OPELIKA													
36801	29.9	68	10.2	66	23.0	231	70.9	8	10	9.8	7	5	.5
36830	34.0	79	12.6	45	18.7	287	95.4	5	5	14.3	3	3	.0
36850	3.7	41	1.1	67	16.9	170	39.0	7	13	.0	13	0	.0
36851	.3	30	.1	53	13.4	100	44.1	22	9	.0	61	0	.0
36852	1.9	88	.6	83	20.5	217	49.0	5	10	.8	9	0	.0
36853	5.5	71	1.9	79	22.0	198	61.1	6	15	1.9	14	0	.0
36854	5.9	69	2.0	80	20.3	207	49.5	7	13	1.9	13	3	.0
36855	1.5	54	.5	82	20.8	217	37.1	7	14	.4	17	0	.2
36856	.7	0	.2	82	19.4	99	36.5	8	6	.0	0	0	.0
36858	.7	16	.2	57	14.9	118	49.0	7	9	.1	33	1	1.5
36860	2.7	25	.9	69	14.7	168	37.2	9	16	.3	12	1	.8
36861	3.5	77	1.1	84	19.3	181	58.3	7	10	1.3	11	0	.0
36862	7.9	0	2.6	71	20.1	170	51.9	8	15	.0	1	0	.2
36863	12.1	64	4.3	69	19.0	207	46.9	8	15	3.5	14	1	1.6
36864	2.5	92	1.0	76	19.6	222	48.0	7	19	1.1	17	2	.8
36865	.4	59	.2	56	15.4	330	65.1	7	16	.1	10	0	.0
36866	3.6	59	1.2	81	17.6	172	44.5	8	12	1.0	13	0	.0
36867	40.1	70	13.9	63	19.6	215	52.7	8	10	13.4	8	1	.2
36871	1.3	0	.4	77	19.5	55	42.4	10	12	.0	0	0	.0
36872	3.0	68	1.0	85	21.4	218	40.4	7	13	1.0	12	0	.3
36874	3.2	0	1.1	82	21.8	125	46.1	7	9	.0	0	0	.0
36875	4.1	46	1.3	70	18.7	192	54.2	6	8	1.0	5	0	.0

ALABAMA

ZIPCODE	1	2	3	4	5	6	7	8	9	10	11	12	13
OPELIKA													
36876	2.4	93	1.0	82	22.4	277	51.6	4	15	1.1	14	0	.5
36877	5.1	79	1.7	83	23.1	216	57.7	6	8	2.0	7	0	.0
36879	1.1	42	.4	70	20.3	185	43.3	5	13	.2	10	0	.0
MERIDIAN													
36901	.9	24	.3	88	20.7	208	30.2	10	10	.1	12	0	.0
36902	.1	23	.1	77	9.7	111*	16.0	4	23	.0	0	0	.0
36904	4.8	62	1.6	79	22.6	213	65.4	8	11	1.5	9	1	1.3
36906	.3	17	.1	94	10.8	124*	44.5	7	6	.0	0	0	.0
36907	2.3	0	.7	73	14.9	124	39.1	6	15	.0	0	0	.0
36908	2.7	87	1.0	85	18.9	197	40.2	10	13	1.1	14	0	.0
36910	.2	48	.1	81	10.6	192	37.9*	13	24	.0	19	0	.0
36912	3.0	0	.9	81	15.3	140	38.6	9	12	.0	0	0	.0
36913	.2	0	.1	59	44.8	217	28.3	6	0	.0	1	0	.0
36915	.8	77	.2	81	17.5	161	32.8	6	7	.3	10	0	.0
36916	.7	60	.2	88	20.8	319	48.1	9	12	.2	6	1	5
36919	2.0	61	.7	84	14.8	182	38.8	9	17	.6	19	0	.0
36921	1.2	75	.4	93	19.7	167	53.6	7	12	.5	12	0	.0
36922	.8	28	.3	79	16.3	182	40.5	7	22	.1	8	0	.0
36925	4.5		1.4	67	23.6	155	46.2	10	16	.3		0	.0
CHATTANOOGA													
37328	.3	100	.1	51	13.6	90	49.7	9	17	.2	15	0	.0
37335	.3	100	.1	91	19.6	226*	54.4	2	9	.1	13	0	.0
COLUMBIA													
38449	3.3	96	1.1	77	21.2	253	53.7	7	9	1.6	8	0	.0
38481	1.0	100	.3	85	24.0	421	63.4	9	6	.5	5	0	.0
38488	.8	0	.3	90	20.8	181	60.6	7	15	.0	0	0	.0
MERIDIAN													
39322	.3	100	.1	92	22.6	260*	52.3	10	0	.2	0	0	.0
39362	.3	100	.1	92	21.9	252*	68.1	9	15	.1	12	0	.0
COLUMBUS													
39701	.6	68	.2	90	19.7	226*	53.9	9	14	.2	19	0	.0

*=Estimated **1.0=883 lbs per capita; 100++ indicates per capita toxic waste generation > than 100 times the U.S. average of 883 lbs per capita.

ZIP CODE MEASURES OF SIZE, LEVELS OF AFFLUENCE AND QUALITY OF LIFE

1=Population (th.); 2= % White; 3=Households (th.); 4=% Owner Occupied; 5=Mean Income Per Household (th.$); 6=Mean Monthly Rent ($)*; 7=Mean Home Value (th.$)*; 8=% under 5; 9=% 65 and over; 10=% White Males (th.); 11=% White Males, 65+; 12=# Toxic Waste Sites; 13=Toxic Waste Relative to US(883 lbs.per capita)**.

ALASKA

MILITARY (SEATTLE)

ZIPCODE	1	2	3	4	5	6	7	8	9	10	11	12	13
98733	2.1	81	.5	10	23.2	452	141.9	13	0	1.0	0	1	.0
98791	3.3	84	.7	1	28.8	437	102.5*	11	0	1.8	1	0	.0

ANCHORAGE

ZIPCODE	1	2	3	4	5	6	7	8	9	10	11	12	13
99501	16.8	74	7.0	30	36.6	382	164.3	8	6	6.7	6	5	.1
99502	27.6	90	9.2	72	50.2	542	169.4	9	1	12.9	1	5	.0
99503	24.1	86	9.9	45	38.6	439	161.1	7	3	10.6	3	2	.0
99504	53.3	84	18.9	62	43.9	495	159.1	9	2	23.0	1	1	.0
99505	8.3	75	1.8	3	23.5	489	141.3	16	0	3.7	0	1	.0
99506	7.0	84	1.5	2	26.1	578	178.4	12	0	3.5	0	1	.0
99507	17.7	94	5.7	79	50.9	523	188.1	9	1	8.6	1	0	.0
99508	.6	81	.2	63	46.5	583	138.4	12	0	.2	0	0	.0
99509	2.3	95	1.0	58	45.3	531	189.8	7	3	1.1	1	0	.0
99510	2.2	88	.9	55	44.2	481	171.0	9	3	1.0	0	2	.0
99511	2.5	91	.8	86	59.6	591	196.1	11	1	1.2	0	2	.0
99540	.2	88	.1	75	32.4	317	180.0	14	2	.1	0	3	.0
99550	.3	35	.1	64	26.6	634	61.2	12	4	.1	1	0	.0
99551	.4	10	.1	80	28.8	411	74.1	12	4	.0	0	0	.0
99554	.6	0	.1	90	17.1	314	25.8	11	4	.0	0	0	.0
99556	1.0	100	.3	84	29.0	186	77.5	8	8	.5	9	0	.0
99557	.5	31	.2	66	22.1	512	55.9	12	2	.1	0	2	.0
99559	4.4	25	1.3	47	33.3	449	65.1	12	2	.6	0	1	.0
99563	.5	0	.1	89	22.5	288	28.2	14	2	.2	0	0	.0
99567	3.5	92	1.1	75	43.0	398	142.7	11	2	1.7	2	0	.0
99568	2.0	100	.1	34	22.5	98	156.7	11	3	.1	0	4	.0
99571	.2	0	.2	0	32.2	654	114.8*	7	0	.0	0	0	.0
99572	.2	100	.1	65	43.9	624	118.8	11	16	.1	12	0	.0
99573	.9	75	.3	72	23.1	208	59.5	8	7	.4	7	0	.0
99574	2.2	82	.8	55	52.5	524	128.8	9	4	1.0	5	0	.0
99576	2.1	33	.6	57	42.7	598	86.9	10	4	.4	2	0	.0
99577	8.5	95	2.6	82	49.7	472	158.1	11	1	4.2	1	0	.0
99578	.2	0	.1	85	18.8	216*	16.4	16	7	.0	6	0	.0
99581	.5	8	.1	82	14.0	380	28.7	12	3	.0	3	0	.0
99585	.3	0	.1	95	20.0	230*	72.8	24	2	.0	2	0	.0
99587	.5	85	.1	87	39.7	234	54.7	8	7	.3	4	0	9.2
99588	.5	99	.3	60	39.7	323	123.9	7	2	.3	3	0	.0

ANCHORAGE

ZIPCODE	1	2	3	4	5	6	7	8	9	10	11	12	13
99602	.2	0	.1	63	10.3	360	46.3	15	8	.2	0	1	.0
99603	4.5	91	1.6	70	36.3	412	104.6	12	3	2.4	4	0	.0
99604	.6	0	.1	83	20.1	410	110.2	9	5	.1	0	0	.0
99606	.3	14	.1	70	17.4	735	143.5	15	2	.1	0	0	.0
99609	.4	0	.1	75	20.0	486	33.9	15	6	.0	0	0	.0
99610	.6	0	.2	88	35.3	666	100.4	8	3	.3	5	0	.0
99611	8.2	92	2.7	71	41.6	334	124.4	8	3	4.0	2	5	.0
99612	.4	0	.1	47	35.5	684	101.0	14	1	.0	0	2	9.2
99613	.4	74	.1	33	41.4	342	147.3	9	2	.2	3	1	.0
99614	.4	0	.1	92	29.7	342*	63.4	9	6	.3	2	1	.0
99615	9.0	77	2.7	52	44.8	623	145.8	10	2	3.9	2	1	.0
99620	.3	0	.1	93	22.4	258*	43.8	10	6	.0	0	0	.0

ALASKA

ANCHORAGE

ZIPCODE	1	2	3	4	5	6	7	8	9	10	11	12	13
99621	.5	0	.1	92	17.3	199*	20.9	10	7	.0	0	0	.0
99622	.3	0	.1	94	15.7	180*	46.6	13	2	.0	0	0	.0
99626	.3	0	.1	84	12.5	608	30.3	10	5	.0	0	0	.0
99627	.5	44	.2	50	28.4	496	86.2	10	4	.1	5	1	.0
99628	.3	0	.1	94	46.1	529*	47.9	8	3	.0	0	0	.0
99631	.2	0	.1	65	39.4	355	74.4	8	15	.0	0	0	.0
99632	.6	0	.1	76	33.8	111	41.7	12	2	.0	0	0	.0
99633	.4	0	.1	59	84.8	606	80.9	7	6	.0	0	0	.0
99634	.3	0	.1	77	18.7	198	29.2	9	3	.0	0	0	.0
99637	.3	0	.1	86	20.1	231*	91.5	9	3	.0	0	0	.0
99639	.3	82	.1	91	29.5	55	62.7	8	9	.2	8	0	.0
99641	.3	0	.1	96	12.5	144*	24.4	14	6	.0	0	0	.0
99643	.4	10	.1	87	18.2	383	91.9	12	0	.0	0	0	.0
99644	.2	0	.1	69	42.5	341	103.0	7	7	.0	0	0	.0
99645	8.3	95	2.6	75	37.9	401	125.8	10	5	4.1	5	2	.0
99649	.1	0	.1	66	34.9	448	64.4	4	3	.0	0	0	.0
99650	.3	0	.1	92	13.4	154*	18.0	14	5	.0	0	0	.0
99655	.4	0	.1	92	16.0	184*	116.2	15	6	.0	0	0	.0
99658	.4	15	.1	83	24.5	427	54.5	5	5	.0	0	0	.0
99659	.2	0	.2	80	17.7	239	52.1	13	5	.1	5	0	.0
99660	1.0	22	.2	82	34.2	395	93.1	8	4	.2	4	0	.0
99661	.6	44	.2	53	81.8	626	118.1	8	2	.2	2	0	.0
99662	.2	0	.1	28	19.6	225*	26.3	19	5	.2	2	0	.0
99663	.5	74	.2	49	24.9	320	82.9	6	3	.2	6	0	.0
99664	2.6	87	.9	58	33.8	393	98.4	8	6	1.2	6	0	.0
99669	5.7	96	1.9	78	37.9	369	130.3	11	3	2.9	2	1	.0
99671	.4	0	.1	16	18.9	238	59.1	18	1	.4	1	0	.0
99672	.8	95	.3	89	56.6	311	108.6	14	3	.4	3	0	.0
99674	.4	98	.1	93	26.7	258	86.9	11	14	.2	13	0	.0
99676	.5	91	.2	76	27.0	302	73.3	9	4	.2	2	0	.0
99678	.6	0	.1	67	20.6	391	106.1	13	3	.0	0	0	.0
99681	.3	0	.1	68	18.2	342	98.9	12	4	.0	0	18	.0
99682	.3	26	.1	53	23.7	233	78.9	13	4	.0	0	0	.0
99684	.8	0	.1	69	22.7	491	81.4	13	5	.1	5	1	.0
99685	1.3	66	.3	21	45.9	506	118.3	4	1	1.5	1	1	.0
99686	2.9	92	1.0	64	51.6	615	173.8	8	1	1.4	1	0	.0
99687	7.3	94	2.4	81	37.6	356	137.7	10	3	3.6	3	0	.0
99688	1.1	93	.3	78	27.3	293	121.7	9	3	3.5	2	0	.0
99689	.6	0	.2	65	39.5	506	84.1	6	3	.0	0	0	.0

FAIRBANKS

ZIPCODE	1	2	3	4	5	6	7	8	9	10	11	12	13
99701	35.5	86	12.9	58	39.2	393	117.9	9	3	16.3	3	9	.0
99702	5.5	85	1.3	10	24.9	641	112.8	13	9	2.6	1	0	.0
99703	5.9	79	1.4		21.6	383	65.6	17		2.7			.0
99704	.7	91	.2	69	51.7	457	79.1	8	0	.7	1	0	9.2
99705	1.4	89	.5	72	37.6	301	109.6	10	2	.7	3	1	8.9
99706	.6	90	.1	63	46.4	312	135.6	6	3	.3	1	0	.0
99707	3.1	93	1.2	61	43.3	442	131.6	7	3	1.6	4	0	.0
99708	1.6	90	.7	61	38.2	450	114.3	14	3	.8	0	0	.0
99712	.2	0	.1	95	22.0	252*	94.1	14	11	.0	0	0	.0

*=Estimated **1.0=883 lbs per person; 100++ indicates per capita toxic waste generation > than 100 times the U.S. average of 883 lbs per capita.

103001

ZIP CODE MEASURES OF SIZE, LEVELS OF AFFLUENCE AND QUALITY OF LIFE

1=Population (th.); 2= % White; 3=Households (th.); 4=% Owner Occupied; 5=Mean Income Per Household (th.$); 6=Mean Monthly Rent ($)*; 7=Mean Home Value (th.$)*; 8=% under 5; 9=% 65 and over; 10=White Males, 65+; 11=% White Males, 65+; 12=# Toxic Waste Sites; 13=Toxic Waste Relative to US(883 lbs.per capita)**.

ALASKA

ZIPCODE	1	2	3	4	5	6	7	8	9	10	11	12	13
FAIRBANKS													
99723	2.6	25	.7	38	52.8	526	97.2	9	4	.4	2	5	.0
99725	.3	0	.1	78	42.1	323	66.1	4	2	.0	0	0	.0
99729	.2	76	.1	48	19.8	252	54.3	8	3	.1	6	0	.0
99737	2.0	89	.6	72	33.7	329	75.8	8	5	1.0	1	0	.0
99738	.2	65	.1	61	19.9	162	34.6	8	4	.1	0	0	.0
99739	.2	0	.1	77	17.1	361	24.1	19	6	.0	0	0	.0
99740	.6	33	.2	64	22.8	297	55.0	14	5	.1	4	7	.0
99741	.4	29	.2	50	30.8	276	58.3	12	5	.1	0	0	.0
99742	.4	0	.1	91	18.8	216*	70.0	13	7	.0	0	3	.0
99743	.4	98	.1	57	46.6	258	88.6	8	2	.2	0	0	.0
99746	.2	0	.1	94	13.4	154*	56.8	15	3	.2	0	0	.0
99748	.3	0	.1	76	14.2	238	48.7	14	3	.0	0	0	.0
99749	.3	0	.1	76	29.4	766	91.6	16	5	.0	0	0	.0
99752	2.1	22	.6	50	36.3	636	84.3	11	5	.3	2	2	.0
99753	.2	0	.1	90	17.5	201*	39.4	12	8	.0	0	0	.0
99755	.1	0	.1	28	27.9	231	95.6	6	3	.0	0	0	.0
99760	.7	64	.3	73	31.0	328	61.9	10	5	.2	3	0	.0
99761	.3	0	.1	84	17.2	197*	61.3	9	8	.0	0	0	.0
99762	2.8	39	.8	44	35.4	584	62.6	9	5	.6	3	6	.0
99763	.5	0	.1	35	23.1	347	40.0	11	4	.0	0	0	.0
99764	.3	29	.1	85	28.8	331*	13.1	13	5	.1	0	0	.0
99765	.2	0	.1	78	19.9	201	14.4	11	4	.0	0	0	.0
99766	.5	8	.1	51	32.9	364	75.6	13	2	.0	0	2	.0
99768	.2	0	.1	77	13.6	232	55.3	10	2	.0	0	0	.0
99769	.5	0	.1	47	16.2	440	64.3	10	5	.0	0	0	.0
99770	.5	0	.1	77	17.0	524	60.5	14	5	.0	0	0	.0
99772	.4	12	.1	33	19.9	468	79.3	14	2	.0	0	0	.0
99777	.4	22	.1	51	21.6	352	40.4	9	4	.0	0	1	.0
99778	.2	0	.1	10	14.3	282	51.0*	15	8	.0	0	0	.1
99780	.9	77	.3	65	31.5	302	52.2	10	4	.4	6	0	.0
99782	.4	0	.1	77	47.6	387	61.5	15	5	.0	0	1	.0
99786	.2	20	.1	74	25.5	610	26.8	14	3	.0	0	0	.0
99787	.2	93	.1	55	50.5	366	47.7	7	0	.0	1	0	.0
99790	.4	53	.1	45	36.2	596	123.4	11	2	.2	1	3	.0
JUNEAU													
99801	14.3	83	5.2	65	44.6	551	154.3	9	5	6.1	4	2	.0
99802	.5	90	.2	59	58.1	739	140.3	4	2	.3	0	0	.0
99803	2.2	89	.8	58	48.4	699	164.0	11	2	1.0	3	0	.0
99820	.5	12	.1	57	22.9	297	88.6	14	9	.0	14	0	.0
99821	.9	0	.4	70	47.6	585	179.2	7	1	.0	0	0	.0
99824	1.4	94	.6	55	51.5	634	152.8	7	2	.7	0	0	.0
99826	.1	100	.1	39	27.5	354	56.9	10	0	.1	0	0	.0
99827	1.8	81	.6	67	31.9	377	93.8	8	4	.8	4	0	.0
99829	.8	32	.2	64	30.4	353	88.4	14	4	.0	0	0	.0
99830	.7	0	.2	66	35.5	353	66.8	11	3	.0	2	0	.0
99832	.2	80	.1	41	33.6	363	71.0	6	4	.1	0	0	.0
99833	2.9	85	1.0	67	42.3	484	124.8	10	6	1.3	6	1	.0
99835	7.9	75	2.5	52	44.0	564	156.4	10	4	3.2	6	1	.0
99840	.8	95	.3	54	44.2	501	123.9	12	5	.2	5	1	.0

ALASKA

ZIPCODE	1	2	3	4	5	6	7	8	9	10	11	12	13
JUNEAU													
99841	.2	96	.1	57	17.9	237	70.7	11	18	.1	16	0	.0
KETCHIKAN													
99901	11.3	85	4.0	53	40.3	512	134.1	9	5	5.1	5	1	.0
99921	.6	68	.2	60	31.7	495	68.9	8	4	.2	4	0	.0
99922	.3	0	.1	67	23.6	159	77.5	9	7	.0	0	0	.0
99925	.3	0	.1	69	33.8	411	97.5	12	2	.0	0	0	.0
99926	1.1	15	.3	71	34.0	472	72.8	11	6	.1	12	0	.0
99928	1.0	95	.3	91	41.5	407	121.5	13	7	.4	1	0	.0
99929	2.3	83	.8	60	37.2	408	107.6	8	7	1.1	6	0	.0
99950	.4	83	.1	28	41.8	199	28.1	10	1	.2	0	0	.0

*=Estimated **1.0=883 lbs per person; 100++ indicates per capita toxic waste generation > than 100 times the U.S. average of 883 lbs per capita.

ZIP CODE MEASURES OF SIZE, LEVELS OF AFFLUENCE AND QUALITY OF LIFE

1=Population (th.); 2= % White; 3=Households (th.); 4=% Owner Occupied; 5=Mean Income Per Household (th.$); 6=Mean Monthly Rent ($)*; 7=Mean Home Value (th.$)*;
8=% under 5; 9=% 65 and over; 10=White Males (th.); 11=% White Males, 65+; 12=# Toxic Waste Sites; 13=Toxic Waste Relative to US(883 lbs.per capita)**.

ARIZONA

PHOENIX

ZIPCODE	1	2	3	4	5	6	7	8	9	10	11	12	13
85003	9.2	61	3.8	33	18.4	235	97.5	8	13	3.0	12	1	.1
85004	6.3	68	2.7	24	20.1	303	87.9	8	18	2.4	20	2	6.5
85006	26.5	72	10.3	24	17.5	290	62.6	10	14	2.4	14	0	.0
85007	15.2	56	5.6	44	19.4	237	88.8	11	14	4.2	14	2	.0
85008	37.4	86	15.4	53	22.7	356	82.0	7	14	15.2	13	2	.9
85009	41.3	72	13.7	57	19.7	296	56.0	11	10	14.6	10	9	1.1
85012	6.9	87	3.0	49	31.9	362	167.5	5	21	2.8	19	0	.4
85013	18.6	93	8.6	52	29.3	399	118.4	5	21	7.9	17	0	.4
85014	24.5	91	12.1	39	23.9	396	106.0	6	15	7.0	12	0	.3
85015	30.3	91	13.4	46	24.5	406	88.3	6	13	10.7	13	0	.3
85016	31.2	94	14.7	49	28.4	423	123.0	4	15	13.9	13	0	.3
85017	24.7	92	9.8	64	23.6	373	76.7	7	10	10.8	9	0	.4
85018	37.3	97	16.2	58	36.5	407	162.8	4	14	17.2	12	1	.0
85019	21.1	91	7.1	70	28.8	438	88.9	6	6	9.3	9	0	.0
85020	27.8	96	11.8	64	29.8	377	131.9	7	15	12.7	12	0	.0
85021	64.4	96	23.6	66	32.1	405	118.0	6	9	29.8	8	0	.0
85022	15.3	97	5.8	88	31.2	509	138.0	7	12	7.2	12	0	.0
85023	38.7	96	12.4	84	35.7	487	127.4	8	14	18.8	5	2	.0
85024	8.5	96	2.8	89	28.2	556	102.5	11	6	4.1	4	1	.0
85027	5.9	98	2.2	92	28.0	377	123.6	9	2	2.9	12	0	1.0
85028	20.9	98	6.2	94	43.4	681	165.8	7	4	10.2	4	0	.0
85029	37.0	96	12.2	78	31.0	440	107.4	7	5	17.6	5	2	.5
85031	21.9	91	6.6	80	28.4	428	80.0	7	5	9.8	6	2	.0
85032	32.1	98	10.7	82	27.8	467	108.0	10	6	15.7	6	1	.0
85033	33.4	89	9.7	84	29.1	566	88.4	10	6	15.1	3	3	.0
85034	14.7	41	4.6	42	14.0	203	38.2	11	3	3.1	11	12	9.3
85035	27.6	79	7.8	78	28.6	551	82.2	12	4	11.1	3	0	.0
85037	8.5	86	2.5	84	30.0	501	93.1	9	5	3.7	2	0	.0
85039	1.3	96	.5	72	30.8	534	114.3	10	7	.5	5	1	.0
85040	41.8	46	12.7	71	22.5	317	68.4	10	7	9.8	7	0	.2
85041	27.1	55	7.2	82	23.1	313	58.3	11	5	7.5	7	1	.0
85043	3.7	92	1.4	78	24.1	395	95.3	11	9	1.6	8	3	.5
85044	5.7	96	2.2	95	38.4	579	130.8	7	8	2.7	8	0	.0

PHOENIX

ZIPCODE	1	2	3	4	5	6	7	8	9	10	11	12	13
85201	29.4	89	10.8	60	26.0	348	102.9	8	12	12.7	10	3	.5
85202	49.7	92	18.0	61	27.2	416	123.4	10	5	22.6	9	2	.0
85203	31.6	96	10.2	78	32.3	388	141.4	9	10	15.0	9	1	.0
85204	30.3	92	10.7	73	25.2	404	100.4	11	12	13.5	11	1	.0
85205	14.2	97	6.7	87	21.8	379	93.3	3	49	6.5	50	0	.1
85206	7.5	99	3.5	92	25.9	333	112.0	2	47	3.3	51	0	.3
85207	7.9	97	2.9	87	22.3	276	90.5	8	19	3.8	19	0	.0
85208	12.5	97	5.1	91	22.0	353	87.5	7	24	5.8	26	0	.0
85220	15.6	98	6.6	86	20.0	276	79.0	5	29	7.5	31	0	.0
85222	20.2	74	6.6	68	23.2	307	75.9	9	9	7.4	10	7	.0
85223	.9	0	.3	79	21.5	402	96.8	7	24	.0	0	0	.0
85224	40.6	84	12.9	67	25.0	345	110.6	11	7	17.1	7	11	.3
85227	.4	87	.1	84	25.0	287*	55.0	3	4	.2	0	0	.0
85228	9.2	70	2.9	67	21.2	236	53.7	8	10	3.2	12	0	.0
85230	.3	92	.1	58	24.8	327	114.8	15	4	.1	9	0	.0

ARIZONA

PHOENIX

ZIPCODE	1	2	3	4	5	6	7	8	9	10	11	12	13
85231	6.9	44	1.9	63	17.1	190	45.1	11	8	1.5	11	1	.1
85232	6.4	72	1.5	68	22.5	235	62.7	5	11	2.9	10	0	.0
85234	9.2	92	2.4	85	31.3	402	138.9	12	5	4.3	4	0	.0
85235	1.6	87	.5	87	26.3	182	30.8	7	9	.6	7	3	30.3
85236	1.7	82	.5	75	28.8	399	141.3	9	6	.8	9	0	.5
85237	3.8	89	1.2	82	29.2	325	66.9	9	5	1.8	5	0	.0
85238	4.8	88	1.5	80	23.3	225	76.6	10	8	2.2	8	1	.1
85239	2.9	56	.8	61	20.5	308	63.9	9	5	.9	8	0	.0
85241	.8	37	.2	60	19.2	199	72.1	5	4	.2	8	1	.0
85242	2.6	79	.7	76	22.8	240	82.4	8	6	1.1	7	0	.0
85243	.1	28	.1	92	10.9	125*	37.0	7	11	.0	41	0	.0
85247	7.3		1.7	62	15.2	205	26.3	13	17	.0	2	3	.0
85251	29.9	97	12.9	58	32.6	389	141.6	4	16	13.5	14	1	1.3
85253	29.2	98	10.3	87	58.7	598	252.2	3	10	13.9	10	0	.0
85254	19.7	99	5.8	95	45.8	796	191.0	7	4	9.8	8	0	.0
85255	.8	98	.3	85	54.7	81	381.8	8	7	.4	8	0	.1
85256	4.0	35	1.4	76	18.8	147	71.0	10	16	.6	44	1	.0
85257	27.6	97	10.4	76	30.4	467	111.6	5	12	13.5	14	4	.0
85258	7.9	97	3.1	78	52.5	510	239.2	4	9	3.8	10	0	.1
85259	.6	100	.2	100	47.2	542*	289.2	6	7	.3	8	0	.0
85260	6.1	97	1.7	93	54.1	474	248.9	6	2	3.0	2	0	1.1
85268	3.2	86	1.1	80	42.3	394	185.5	6	13	1.4	12	0	.0
85272	.7	91	.2	7	30.4	121	135.6	13	1	.3	1	0	1.8
85273	4.6	59	1.4	71	23.9	268	46.7	10	8	1.4	10	1	.9
85281	38.3	90	14.1	40	20.3	402	88.4	5	5	17.7	5	6	1.0
85282	45.3	94	15.8	70	34.1	512	129.7	6	5	21.2	5	3	.1
85283	26.7	81	8.0	80	36.4	572	143.5	10	3	10.8	3	3	.0
85284	1.9	92	.5	80	58.1	596	254.1	7	5	1.0	5	1	.0
85291	.4	92	.4	100	20.1	231*	56.7	10	9	.2	7	0	.0
85292	3.0	87	1.0	77	26.6	289	65.7	10	7	1.4	7	0	.0

PHOENIX

ZIPCODE	1	2	3	4	5	6	7	8	9	10	11	12	13
85301	43.8	85	16.3	58	23.0	363	92.2	8	10	17.8	9	1	.8
85302	23.3	94	7.8	81	34.1	453	129.3	8	10	10.8	8	0	.0
85303	9.7	88	3.2	63	25.1	426	109.8	11	4	4.3	3	0	.0
85304	12.0	96	3.5	90	34.6	623	124.4	10	5	5.6	4	0	.0
85306	18.3	96	5.3	90	34.7	633	124.5	9	3	8.8	2	0	.0
85307	4.4	76	1.1	17	20.7	349	85.7	15	1	1.7	0	0	.1
85308	9.8	98	3.3	91	33.4	565	128.7	9	4	4.8	4	0	.3
85310	.6	0	.6	96	34.5	397*	199.1	9	2	.0	4	1	.0
85320	.7	48	.3	56	24.8	388	55.0	7	22	.2	33	1	.0
85321	5.8	76	1.9	44	27.4	219	39.3	9	9	2.2	11	1	3.7
85322	.6	90	.2	65	16.2	177	135.6	4	6	.2	7	0	.0
85323	7.8	58	2.3	55	19.7	268	51.8	11	6	2.3	6	0	.0
85324	1.3	100	.6	82	19.8	293	59.0	7	31	.7	31	0	.8
85325	.5	100	.2	93	16.3	244	44.9	9	22	.2	32	0	.0
85326	11.4	84	3.6	71	25.5	319	82.0	9	7	4.8	7	1	3.7
85329	3.6	36	.8	78	17.7	252	40.5	12	6	.6	12	1	.0
85331	2.8	99	1.1	80	30.3	449	161.6	15	11	1.3	10	0	.0

*=Estimated **1.0=883 lbs per person; 100++ indicates per capita toxic waste generation > than 100 times the U.S. average of 883 lbs per capita.

ZIP CODE MEASURES OF SIZE, LEVELS OF AFFLUENCE AND QUALITY OF LIFE

1=Population (th.); 2= % White; 3=Households (th.); 4=% Owner Occupied; 5=Mean Income Per Household (th.$); 6=Mean Home Value (th.$); 7=Mean Monthly Rent ($); 8=% under 5; 9=% 65 and over; 10=White Males (th.); 11=% White Males, 65+; 12=# Toxic Waste Sites; 13=Toxic Waste Relative to US(883 lbs per capita)**

ARIZONA

PHOENIX

ZIPCODE	1	2	3	4	5	6	7	8	9	10	11	12	13
85332	.6	94	.2	75	11.8	209	51.4	5	22	.3	25	1	.0
85333	1.0	70	.3	30	16.4	239	41.3	10	4	.3	5	2	.0
85334	1.2	87	.4	61	22.3	230	73.5	9	6	.6	7	0	.0
85335	4.2	53	1.1	64	16.5	207	45.0	14	4	1.1	3	0	.0
85336	.5	31	.1	77	20.0	331	63.6	4	4	.1	6	0	.0
85337	3.1	65	.9	41	21.1	260	54.1	12	6	.1	6	2	.0
85338	3.3	87	1.1	58	28.1	422	94.9	9	6	1.1	6	6	.4
85339	2.8	79	.8	86	34.8	367	133.1	9	3	1.5	6	6	.0
85340	5.2	95	1.6	73	42.9	472	182.7	7	7	1.2	2	0	.0
85342	.6	90	.3	66	12.6	247	52.7	0	30	2.6	7	0	1.1
85343	.6	90	.3	65	24.8	360	66.7	18	6	.0	6	2	.0
85344	7.5	59	2.7	66	19.7	290	85.0	9	12	2.2	16	4	7.4
85345	24.8	83	7.7	81	26.4	347	112.8	9	11	2.2	11	1	.0
85346	1.3	0	.7	90	10.7	122	44.1	2	54	10.1	0	0	.0
85347	.6	76	.2	54	38.0	49	135.5*	12	2	.3	5	2	.0
85348	.7	87	.3	60	15.0	245	25.7	9	14	.3	18	0	.0
85350	3.0	37	.3	79	15.7	196	63.7	12	1	.5	6	2	.0
85351	6.9	38	1.8	78	20.0	233	60.4	9	5	1.4	8	0	.0
85352	35.0	100	19.9	96	25.4	386	111.7	0	76	14.8	79	0	.0
85353	.3	82	.1	56	15.5	164	77.2	14	13	.3	19	0	.0
85354	8.5	67	2.3	72	24.8	250	86.6	9	6	2.9	6	4	.6
85355	.8	85	.3	71	23.7	311	25.0	10	7	.4	7	0	.0
85356	.2	77	.1	86	19.8	227*	93.7	8	5	.1	12	0	.0
85357	2.2	69	.7	64	20.6	237	65.2	9	9	.8	10	0	.0
85358	.6	82	.3	52	21.8	156	68.5	17	6	.5	9	2	.0
85360	5.6	96	2.4	69	21.8	260	103.9	5	27	2.5	28	0	.0
85361	.3	0	.1	32	11.7	162	41.8*	19	5	1.4	8	0	.0
85362	.7	0	.3	86	18.0	240	57.3	6	15	.0	0	0	.0
85363	.7	0	.4	79	10.1	192	56.1	2	53	.0	0	0	.0
85364	2.3	99	1.3	79	14.1	329	60.0	68	.9	67	0	.1	
85371	63.4	82	21.8	69	23.6	334	81.3	9	11	26.7	13	6	.0
85372	.7	20	.2	43	23.1	225	43.6	16	4	1.4	13	0	.7
85373	.4	0	.3	95	16.0	150	121.5	10	9	1.0	10	0	.0
85375	6.1	69	3.2	96	31.2	344	132.1	0	62	.0	0	0	.0
85377	3.8	82	2.0	94	33.1	321	134.6	4	40	1.7	45	3	100++
	1.1	0	.5	90	67.1	298	316.9	1	29	.0	0	0	7.1

GLOBE

ZIPCODE	1	2	3	4	5	6	7	8	9	10	11	12	13
85501	12.3	94	4.4	76	23.7	283	73.0	9	13	5.6	12	3	.0
85530	1.4	4	.3	75	9.3	160	26.0	15	2	.0	0	0	.0
85531	.3	100	.1	79	17.2	57	46.7	14	4	.2	0	0	.0
85532	3.1	91	1.0	81	24.0	297	52.1	13	9	1.4	9	0	.7
85533	3.3	85	1.2	66	23.7	220	58.9	11	12	1.4	13	0	.0
85534	2.3	89	.7	79	23.4	152	52.5	10	9	1.0	10	0	.0
85536	.5	0	.3	92	18.8	232	74.8	5	10	.0	0	0	.0
85537	.2	100	.1	21	25.7	71	28.4	4	4	.1	3	0	.0
85539	5.0	90	1.7	76	23.5	232	47.2	9	12	.2	13	2	.0
85540	5.7	77	1.7	12	33.9	233	43.1	13	2	2.2	1	1	7.1
85541	7.2	97	3.0	81	18.3	342	98.9	5	21	3.3	22	1	.0
85542	.9	0	.2	72	22.7	221	41.3	8	6	.3			

ARIZONA

GLOBE

ZIPCODE	1	2	3	4	5	6	7	8	9	10	11	12	13
85543	2.0	96	.6	84	19.9	234	73.6	12	11	.9	12	1	.0
85544	1.2	100	.5	86	17.2	331	91.7	5	21	.6	23	0	.0
85545	.3	100	.2	75	23.1	140	120.9	7	24	.2	30	0	.0
85546	12.1	82	3.8	74	21.7	288	69.4	10	12	4.9	12	0	.0
85550	3.7	0	.8	68	16.1	238	34.2	12	4	.0	0	0	.0
85551	3.8	65	.9	84	20.8	188	48.6	9	9	.0	0	0	.6
85552	3.8	88	1.1	72	21.9	237	73.9	11	9	1.6	10	0	.4
85553	.3	100	.1	89	12.7	438	69.5	9	19	.0	26	0	.0
85554	.4	100	.2	81	21.1	282	64.3	13	10	.2	9	0	.0

TUCSON

ZIPCODE	1	2	3	4	5	6	7	8	9	10	11	12	13
85601	.6	89	.2	80	20.8	176	49.2	10	11	.3	14	0	.0
85602	6.0	95	2.2	76	21.1	233	69.8	6	17	2.7	17	4	2.3
85603	8.2	85	3.2	73	19.8	214	46.3	6	17	3.2	17	1	.1
85605	.7	62	.3	77	15.3	144	37.5	9	19	.2	26	0	.0
85606	.7	92	.3	85	25.2	278	87.7	4	19	.3	15	0	.6
85607	16.2	88	5.0	66	20.5	239	59.1	9	12	6.9	12	2	.4
85609	.2	100	.1	80	19.6	225*	83.1	0	42	.1	34	0	.0
85610	1.2	94	.4	63	21.4	177	56.0	10	11	.6	14	0	.0
85611	.4	100	.2	95	40.4	464*	65.6	0	12	.2	10	0	.0
85613	9.6	73	2.1	86	18.7	344	115.1	14	7	3.8	62	1	.0
85614	8.7	99	4.6	86	28.1	292	125.3	1	59	3.8	62	1	.2
85615	2.0	90	.7	80	26.8	221	95.2	8	10	.9	13	0	.0
85616	3.4	87	1.2	71	20.4	261	65.1	9	7	1.4	9	0	.0
85617	.9	97	.3	77	19.0	426	54.9	8	14	.4	14	0	.0
85618	2.3	67	.7	73	26.0	244	46.9	11	7	.8	6	0	.0
85619	.1	100	.1	64	16.5	174	26.5	0	0	.1	0	0	.0
85620	.6	75	.2	65	18.1	153	63.8	4	17	.2	7	0	.1
85621	17.7	78	5.0	62	23.7	299	86.6	11	8	6.5	7	1	.0
85623	3.0	82	.4	71	28.0	249	87.7	10	7	1.2	11	1	.0
85624	1.0	88	.4	73	18.3	204	63.4	7	25	.4	21	0	.1
85625	1.5	95	.6	84	19.4	205	80.1	7	33	.7	37	0	.0
85626	1.1	74	.3	92	37.4	87	37.4	11	8	.4	10	0	.7
85627	.2	83	.1	91	20.1	231*	49.8	11	23	.1	11	0	.0
85629	2.7	87	.8	75	26.8	362	120.4	7	5	1.2	6	4	.5
85630	1.6	97	.6	71	19.9	229	62.9	10	16	.8	16	0	8.8
85631	5.7	80	1.6	36	32.1	247	65.3	13	2	2.3	2	1	16.6
85632	.7	89	.2	68	18.7	160	53.4	6	12	.3	11	0	.0
85633	.3	0	.1	50	36.0	226	116.1	10	4	.1	0	0	.0
85634	7.2	8	1.7	72	14.3	206	24.3	11	6	.3	3	0	.3
85635	23.2	88	8.2	70	27.4	311	102.8	7	5	10.2	5	0	.0
85637	.4	100	.2	72	27.5	315	105.5	0	28	.2	33	0	.7
85638	1.9	91	.8	72	18.8	224	68.5	5	19	.8	22	3	.5
85640	2.4	88	.8	75	31.9	366	106.5	10	11	1.1	15	1	.0
85641	.3	0	.1	59	74.1	307	196.9	3	7	.0	0	0	.0
85643	7.3	87	2.4	71	20.1	265	59.6	7	12	3.3	12	3	.3

TUCSON

ZIPCODE	1	2	3	4	5	6	7	8	9	10	11	12	13
85701	5.6	59	2.6	19	11.2	184	64.0	8	19	1.6	23	0	.0
85704	42.9	95	14.9	83	34.8	446	143.8	8	10	20.2	10	4	.1
85705	65.1	82	26.8	60	19.5	285	86.2	7	15	26.1	15	3	.1

*=Estimated **1.0=883 lbs per person; 100++ indicates per capita toxic waste generation > than 100 times the U.S. average of 883 lbs per capita.

ZIP CODE MEASURES OF SIZE, LEVELS OF AFFLUENCE AND QUALITY OF LIFE

1=Population (th.); 2= % White; 3=Households (th.); 4=% Owner Occupied; 5=Mean Income Per Household (th.$); 6=Mean Monthly Rent ($)*; 7=Mean Home Value (th.$)*; 8=% under 5; 9=% 65 and over; 10=White Males (th.); 11=% White Males, 65+; 12=# Toxic Waste Sites; 13=Toxic Waste Relative to US(883 lbs.per capita)**.

ARIZONA

TUCSON

ZIPCODE	1	2	3	4	5	6	7	8	9	10	11	12	13
85706	62.6	71	18.7	79	23.3	323	75.6	11	6	22.0	7	10	.1
85707	6.1	80	1.3	1	19.2	340	68.3*	14	0	2.9	0	0	.0
85708	.4	80	.1	94	16.2	186*	109.4	12	0	.4	2	0	.0
85710	53.8	96	19.1	79	30.8	423	122.5	5	10	24.9	9	0	.0
85711	40.0	91	16.6	58	25.2	349	97.3	6	12	17.6	11	1	.0
85712	25.9	93	11.9	48	21.3	352	93.7	9	19	10.9	15	0	.0
85713	38.5	63	13.3	71	19.1	281	63.1	9	13	11.6	16	0	.0
85714	15.1	55	4.5	69	19.5	276	57.5	10	8	4.9	12	0	.1
85715	30.3	98	9.8	86	46.2	487	197.7	5	7	14.6	6	0	.2
85716	27.7	94	13.4	49	23.1	342	109.0	6	18	12.1	15	0	.4
85718	15.7	98	6.1	82	54.1	374	244.4	5	12	7.4	12	0	.0
85719	34.5	89	15.7	41	19.2	347	97.4	4	13	15.1	10	1	.2
85735	27.4	89	8.6	78	26.4	471	99.9	10	4	12.1	4	0	.0
85736	.6	88	.2	92	25.6	294*	102.0	7	8	.3	2	0	.0
85737	.6	84	.2	77	29.6	332	93.3	7	13	.3	15	0	.0
85738	.3	81	.1	94	23.7	272*	68.1	2	10	.2	10	0	.0
	1.0	98	.4	88	21.7	180	64.5	6	7	.5	5	0	.0

SHOW LOW

ZIPCODE	1	2	3	4	5	6	7	8	9	10	11	12	13
85901	6.0	92	1.9	80	25.0	343	99.1	12	7	2.7	0	0	.0
85911	1.1	0	.2	65	10.1	136	30.2	16	1	.0	0	0	.0
85912	.1	100	.1	100	14.3	165*	71.9	5	31	.1	14	0	.0
85920	.4	97	.2	75	22.9	189	93.4	11	6	.2	7	0	.0
85923	.3	87	.1	94	24.9	286*	47.4	17	6	.1	6	0	.0
85924	.6	0	.1	94	26.5	149	105.1	2	2	.2	0	0	.0
85925	2.2	97	.6	83	23.8	290	85.1	17	6	.6	11	0	.0
85926	.2	0	.0	61	17.2	328	40.8	4	10	.0	0	0	.0
85928	.9	0	.3	72	24.1	365	78.6	14	5	.4	5	0	.0
85929	3.7	98	1.3	83	26.4	332	92.5	9	10	1.8	12	0	1.0
85930	.6	13	.2	48	23.8	195	71.3	18	1	.1	0	0	.1
85933	.5	93	.2	82	26.2	306	77.1	6	8	.3	12	0	.0
85934	.1	100	.1	92	15.6	179*	58.3	15	13	.1	19	0	.0
85935	2.2	97	.8	79	26.6	318	134.0	7	8	1.1	9	0	.0
85937	4.0	87	1.2	80	28.4	291	85.9	13	5	1.8	6	1	.0
85938	4.3	88	1.1	81	28.7	298	95.0	14	4	2.0	4	1	1.0
85939	2.5	90	.8	82	25.5	367	85.5	10	8	1.1	7	0	.0
85941	2.0	99	.5	89	26.0	362	99.9	15	4	1.0	4	0	.0
85942	5.5	7	1.2	59	18.9	185	38.2	12	3	.3	2	0	.0
85943	.4	0	.1	79	10.3	147	66.5	8	5	.0	0	0	.0

FLAGSTAFF

ZIPCODE	1	2	3	4	5	6	7	8	9	10	11	12	13
86001	34.9	85	11.6	61	27.2	386	115.2	9	4	15.5	3	2	.0
86002	1.8	74	.7	45	22.2	336	86.9	9	5	.2	19	1	.0
86003	.4	72	.1	86	35.5	398	103.0	10	4	.7	27	0	.0
86011	5.2	84	.2	2	12.2	144	43.3*	4	0	.8	0	0	.0
86015	.4	68	.1	70	23.5	256	83.7*	5	2	.1	6	0	.0
86017	.4	100	.1	70	41.6	237	151.2	13	7	.2	0	0	.2
86020	2.0	4	.4	79	12.5	117	18.9	14	7	.0	0	0	.0
86021	1.5	100	.2	4	14.9	108	53.2*	24	5	.8	3	0	.1
86022	1.3	85	.4	78	20.5	264	71.9	9	7	.5	7	1	7.7

ARIZONA

FLAGSTAFF

ZIPCODE	1	2	3	4	5	6	7	8	9	10	11	12	13
86023	1.8	84	.5	29	26.3	223	56.9	6	1	.8	0	0	.0
86024	.2	100	.1	66	18.1	147	77.5	5	11	.1	10	0	.0
86025	6.7	65	2.1	66	22.3	315	85.1	10	6	2.2	6	0	.0
86029	.7	0	.1	47	9.6	233	41.6	4	19	.0	0	0	.0
86030	.7	0	.2	92	17.3	199*	50.1	10	19	.0	0	0	.0
86031	1.2	0	.3	42	11.9	136*	15.0	11	6	.9	4	0	.1
86032	1.6	98	.5	88	28.0	199	90.9	13	4	.9	2	1	.0
86033	6.6	8	1.5	62	22.9	167	26.4	15	4	.3	2	0	.0
86034	2.0	5	.5	62	21.8	304	37.3	15	8	.3	0	0	.0
86036	.2	30	.1	47	11.0	156	39.1*	10	0	.0	0	0	.0
86039	2.1	0	.5	72	11.7	243	31.4	15	7	.0	0	0	.0
86040	6.5	66	1.9	76	32.7	333	92.3	14	4	2.1	5	2	.0
86042	.9	4	.2	86	10.1	127	47.7	6	13	.0	0	0	.0
86043	1.2	0	.3	70	10.6	312	61.2	13	8	.0	0	0	.0
86044	2.8	0	.5	85	13.2	543	15.1	14	4	.4	2	0	.2
86045	7.9	9	1.8	52	20.2	192	40.1	14	3	.4	2	0	.0
86046	3.0	92	1.0	67	22.1	198	66.3	9	7	1.5	10	0	.1
86047	13.7	45	3.9	69	22.5	260	61.0	11	7	3.0	8	0	.0
86053	1.1	0	.2	66	15.4	253	39.3	18	5	.0	0	0	.0
86054	1.8	5	.4	58	17.5	239	18.7	18	3	.0	0	0	.0

PRESCOTT

ZIPCODE	1	2	3	4	5	6	7	8	9	10	11	12	13
86301	30.4	95	11.9	73	23.0	336	106.1	6	20	14.0	19	0	.0
86302	.3	100	.1	54	20.6	515	125.0	7	9	.1	5	0	1.9
86312	1.5	0	.6	78	20.3	288	91.6	6	15	.1	0	0	.0
86320	.6	93	.3	68	13.6	169	40.4	7	11	.3	11	0	.0
86321	2.7	94	1.7	17	23.7	82	73.2	12	4	1.3	3	1	.8
86322	4.4	99	1.7	84	22.3	293	92.7	6	18	2.2	18	0	.0
86323	3.1	98	1.1	83	20.4	314	81.6	9	9	1.5	9	0	.0
86324	1.3	79	.5	82	20.1	261	74.2	11	16	.5	16	0	.1
86325	1.4	0	.6	91	19.6	224	127.8	10	16	.6	15	0	.0
86326	8.0	95	3.0	74	20.3	314	88.8	8	20	3.6	18	0	.0
86327	1.0	0	.4	87	17.5	213	89.6	8	17	.2	33	0	.0
86329	.4	100	.2	87	16.6	118	44.4	3	31	.2	23	0	.2
86331	.5	97	.3	54	13.4	219	70.3	7	17	.2	23	0	.5
86332	.3	100	.1	85	17.4	158	45.0	10	38	.2	41	1	.0
86333	1.6	97	.7	75	17.2	247	54.9	5	28	.8	32	0	.0
86334	.2	0	.1	74	18.7	215*	50.9	9	21	.2	0	0	.0
86335	.6	84	.2	75	20.1	314	93.0	15	25	.3	30	0	.1
86336	6.1	99	3.0	76	24.4	458	171.2	3	31	2.9	31	0	.2
86337	.7	97	.3	65	24.6	187	38.9	9	5	.3	4	0	.0
86338	.4	100	.1	61	17.2	198*	127.6	6	15	.2	19	1	.0
86340	1.5	99	.7	84	31.0	509	154.8	4	27	.7	27	0	.0
86342	.4	100	.2	81	27.3	229	92.4	0	36	.2	37	0	.0

KINGMAN

ZIPCODE	1	2	3	4	5	6	7	8	9	10	11	12	13
86401	18.4	96	6.9	80	22.3	272	75.2	8	15	8.7	16	3	.2
86402	.4	100	.1	92	16.2	186*	77.5	0	45	.1	55	0	.0
86403	17.4	98	6.7	74	27.9	444	114.5	6	13	8.6	14	2	.1
86430	5.2	98	2.2	76	25.1	378	119.8	4	17	2.6	18	0	.1
86431	1.3	85	.4	78	16.7	157	27.2	6	19	.1	19	0	.0

*=Estimated **1.0=883 lbs per person; 100++ indicates per capita toxic waste generation > than 100 times the U.S. average of 883 lbs per capita.

ZIP CODE MEASURES OF SIZE, LEVELS OF AFFLUENCE AND QUALITY OF LIFE

1=Population (th.); 2=% White; 3=Households (th.); 4=% Owner Occupied; 5=Mean Income Per Household (th.$); 6=Mean Monthly Rent ($)*; 7=Mean Home Value (th.$)*;
8=% under 5; 9=% 65 and over; 10=% White Males (th.); 11=% White Males, 65+; 12=# Toxic Waste Sites; 13=Toxic Waste Relative to US(883 lbs.per capita)**.

ARIZONA

ZIPCODE	1	2	3	4	5	6	7	8	9	10	11	12	13
KINGMAN													
86433	.2	0	.1	91	19.1	219*	30.8	0	19	.0	0	0	.0
86434	1.0	0	.2	59	19.5	257	44.2	15	3	.0	0	0	.0
86435	.3	0	.1	86	10.9	56	15.5	4	6	.0	0	0	.0
86436	.5	0	.2	83	19.6	69	61.2	0	20	.0	0	0	.0
86438	.2	64	.1	91	24.0	276*	19.8	2	14	.1	18	1	.0
86440	2.7	92	1.1	80	21.4	308	87.5	6	19	1.2	23	0	.0
86441	.7	100	.3	94	14.1	220	47.7	5	32	.3	35	0	.0
86442	6.3	97	2.7	79	20.0	385	107.3	5	20	3.0	23	0	.0
86443	.1	100	.1	50	15.2	233	109.4	0	1	.1	0	0	.0
GALLUP													
86502	1.1	13	.2	58	15.1	106	24.0	11	7	.1	0	0	.0
86503	12.1	4	2.7	64	15.2	149	24.7	13	4	.2	5	0	.0
86504	4.0	8	.9	59	19.9	218	27.2	13	4	.2	27	0	.1
86505	7.4	5	1.7	63	12.7	152	17.7	13	6	.2	0	0	.0
86506	1.0	5	.2	77	17.1	207	17.3	8	8	.0	0	0	.0
86507	2.4	0	.5	76	11.7	160	19.3	17	6	.0	0	0	.0
86508	.7	0	.2	74	6.6	75*	13.1	18	2	.0	0	0	.0
86510	3.1	0	.5	78	11.8	115	68.6	10	4	.0	0	0	.0
86511	2.6	0	.5	66	16.0	211	24.2	13	5	.0	0	0	.0
86512	.9	36	.3	39	15.9	217	87.6	11	9	.1	17	0	.0
86514	2.5	9	.6	46	15.7	178	13.1	12	6	.2	5	0	.0
86515	3.8	11	.9	45	25.3	248	59.5	14	3	.0	5	0	.0
86535	.9	0	.2	60	12.5	124	13.1	14	3	.0	0	0	.0
86538	1.7	8	.4	45	17.5	222	21.8	13	3	.1	0	0	.0
86556	.6	0	.1	16	19.2	256	135.6	13	1	.0	0	0	.0
FARMINGTON													
87420	1.1	0	.3	94	10.1	43	19.8	11	10	.0	0	0	.0
LAS CRUCES													
88056	.1	59	.1	85	14.8	170*	52.6*	5	26	.0	33	0	.0
LAS VEGAS													
89046	.2	0	.1	76	35.0	913	66.5	0	0	.0	0	0	.0
SAN BERNARDINO													
92363	.3	93	.1	77	23.4	445	106.1	13	12	.2	11	0	.0

ARKANSAS

ZIPCODE	1	2	3	4	5	6	7	8	9	10	11	12	13
SPRINGFIELD													
65611	.1	100	.1	64	14.5	272	46.4	12	11	.1	4	0	.0
SPRINGFIELD													
65733	.2	100	.1	100	7.8	90*	41.3	0	50	.1	49	0	.0
65745	.2	100	.1	55	24.3	299	39.9	13	7	.1	0	0	.0
SHREVEPORT													
71075	.2	0	.1	85	19.6	225*	32.8	2	27	.0	0	0	.0
PINE BLUFF													
71601	29.4	36	9.8	57	17.1	224	49.6	8	15	5.2	15	12	2.0
71602	16.5	82	5.6	77	22.7	291	51.6	8	9	6.7	7	4	.4
71603	35.2	70	12.4	74	25.6	296	71.0	11	9	11.9	10	0	.0
71630	.8	64	.3	78	22.5	166	30.1	6	16	.2	14	0	2.1
71631	1.2	49	.4	74	14.3	153	27.7	9	16	.3	19	0	.0
71634	.3	100	.1	80	17.0	175	51.6	7	20	.2	27	0	.0
71635	14.7	78	5.2	77	23.0	257	56.3	8	11	5.4	9	5	3.7
71638	6.0	39	2.1	73	14.6	179	38.1	8	17	1.1	14	0	.0
71639	8.8	51	2.8	64	17.8	212	60.2	11	14	2.1	12	1	.2
71640	5.8	40	1.9	73	14.4	186	39.3	10	17	1.1	13	1	.0
71642	.8	66	.8	84	15.4	138	33.3	6	22	.3	24	0	.0
71643	2.6	42	.9	60	16.9	151	44.0	11	15	.9	4	0	.0
71644	3.2	77	1.1	65	18.0	150	36.5	5	9	1.1	4	0	.0
71646	6.5	88	2.1	84	17.0	191	48.5	8	14	2.6	12	1	1.2
71647	2.3	53	.8	91	14.0	193	43.6	8	16	1.0	14	0	.0
71648	.3	59	.1	82	25.3	248	30.5	6	11	.2	5	0	.0
71649	.3	59	.1	82	25.8	297*	45.6	6	12	.1	9	0	.0
71651	.2	76	.1	77	15.3	175*	26.6	7	22	.1	22	0	.0
71652	1.2	83	.5	81	18.5	158	34.5	7	18	.5	16	0	.0
71653	6.1	56	2.0	63	18.9	184	64.3	9	13	1.7	10	1	.0
71654	6.6	67	2.4	68	24.5	196	59.8	8	15	2.1	11	1	1.3
71655	14.0	76	4.8	71	20.8	223	60.2	8	12	5.2	10	0	.0
71658	1.2	50	.3	70	13.4	178	38.0	13	13	.3	10	0	.0
71659	.2	0	.1	79	10.4	119*	17.3	13	34	.4	18	0	.0
71660	1.1	73	.4	87	16.6	51	31.5	3	24	.4	18	0	.0
71661	.8	40	.3	67	15.5	174	60.2	9	24	.2	22	0	.0
71662	.5	35	.2	9	18.1	208*	62.0	6	15	.1	0	0	.0
71663	1.1	63	.4	64	19.5	159	67.5	8	13	.4	11	0	.1
71665	5.1	87	1.8	82	18.9	149	50.6	7	15	2.1	14	0	.0
71666	.4	51	.1	56	22.0	342	55.2	5	16	.6	9	0	.0
71667	6.6	83	2.2	80	18.9	217	51.2	7	14	2.7	11	1	1.0
71670	1.9	54	.6	67	17.6	199	41.9	8	15	.5	16	0	.0
71671	10.3	72	3.8	75	17.6	163	48.8	8	18	3.5	16	2	.0
71674	1.4	86	.5	69	15.3	146	43.6	10	15	.6	15	0	.0
71675	1.9	56	.7	85	17.2	163	40.5	10	16	.6	15	0	.0
71676	1.5	0	.5	70	15.0	156	46.3	10	22	.0	0	0	.0
71677	.4	49	.2	79	15.7	142	46.0	11	29	.5	21	0	.0
CAMDEN													
71701	23.3	66	8.5	74	20.5	194	54.5	8	15	7.4	13	7	.5
71720	3.3	71	1.2	77	18.7	188	36.0	7	17	1.2	15	0	.0
71722	.4	26	.1	92	18.0	207*	30.1	9	13	.1	40	0	.0
71724	.8	63	.3	63	18.8	220	40.9	9	10	.3	9	0	.0

*=Estimated **1.0=883 lbs per person; 100++ indicates per capita toxic waste generation > than 100 times the U.S. average of 883 lbs per capita.

ZIP CODE MEASURES OF SIZE, LEVELS OF AFFLUENCE AND QUALITY OF LIFE

1=Population (th.); 2= % White; 3=Households (th.); 4=% Owner Occupied; 5=Mean Income Per Household (th.$); 6=Mean Monthly Rent ($)*; 7=Mean Home Value (th.$)*; 8=% under 5; 9=% 65 and over; 10=% White Males (th.); 11=% White Males, 65+; 12=# Toxic Waste Sites; 13=Toxic Waste Relative to US(883 lbs.per capita)**.

ARKANSAS

CAMDEN

ZIP CODE	1	2	3	4	5	6	7	8	9	10	11	12	13
71725	1.0	30	.3	76	14.5	123	28.1	7	19	.2	22	0	.0
71726	1.7	42	.6	79	12.9	162	34.9	7	25	.3	24	0	.0
71730	35.8	73	13.6	70	22.3	232	61.5	8	15	12.2	13	10	2.3
71740	1.7	55	.7	70	22.3	136	31.9	8	25	.4	27	0	.0
71742	6.8	63	2.4	79	22.8	209	49.1	8	16	2.0	14	3	.5
71743	4.9	78	1.8	71	20.3	208	50.1	8	17	1.8	15	0	.0
71744	3.5	77	1.3	81	16.2	182	48.6	7	19	1.3	15	0	.0
71745	.4	37	.2	90	12.1	154	33.8	9	23	.1	19	0	.0
71749	1.7	54	.5	83	20.4	193	25.7	8	17	.4	18	0	.0
71751	2.2	63	.7	83	16.5	187	37.5	6	16	.7	15	0	.0
71752	.9	60	.4	83	15.9	167	36.7	6	22	.7	15	0	.0
71753	1.5	52	.5	77	15.0	168	29.2	9	19	.4	16	0	.0
71757	17.7	67	6.4	69	22.0	209	61.3	7	15	5.8	13	5	3.2
71758	.4	73	.1	86	26.3	303*	29.3	10	9	.1	11	0	.0
71762	.6	0	.1	76	16.2	131	36.3	5	31	.0	0	0	17.8
71763	3.4	95	.3	85	19.0	151	52.2	6	19	.4	18	1	2.4
71764	1.8	77	1.2	80	20.4	219	44.5	8	19	1.3	16	1	2.5
71765	2.8	74	.7	78	17.4	223	42.3	8	20	.7	24	0	.0
71766	2.7	50	1.0	84	17.2	167	32.8	7	18	.7	13	0	.0
71767	.1	100	.1	84	23.7	273*	34.2	6	26	.1	15	0	.0
71768	.3	68	.1	78	17.3	158	30.1	3	15	.1	18	0	.0
71770	3.9	56	1.3	81	17.3	165	39.7	9	14	1.0	14	0	.0
71772	.2	0	.1	63	19.5	191	31.4	6	13	.7	15	0	.1

TEXARKANA

ZIP CODE	1	2	3	4	5	6	7	8	9	10	11	12	13
71801	16.5	75	6.1	72	19.6	216	51.6	8	16	5.8	13	6	.1
71820	.1	100	.1	81	22.2	398	51.7	14	14	.1	8	0	.0
71823	8.4	76	2.8	80	26.0	217	59.6	9	13	3.1	10	2	4.7
71825	.8	82	.1	82	18.7	100	39.8	4	34	.0	0	0	.0
71826	1.9	0	.3	82	18.6	117	37.9	8	20	.3	20	0	.0
71827	1.1	67	.4	69	17.0	241	40.1	11	16	.4	16	0	.0
71832	8.4	96	3.0	89	18.3	212	24.6	9	17	3.8	15	0	.4
71833	2.4	99	.9	81	20.3	205	53.6	7	16	1.2	14	4	.0
71834	.6	70	.3	84	18.3	185	40.3	6	17	.2	15	0	.0
71835	1.4	88	.5	78	20.4	261	32.4	12	24	.6	16	2	.0
71836	3.1	77	1.1	80	18.3	157	41.4	8	13	1.3	13	1	.0
71837	3.8	99	1.2	81	20.9	180	42.0	11	10	1.9	10	0	.0
71838	1.5	33	.6	68	14.2	176	30.4	7	11	.3	27	0	.0
71839	.9	41	.3	64	14.1	146	32.1	11	15	.1	17	0	.0
71840	.2	100	1.0	100	15.9	183*	32.1	19	17	.1	18	0	.0
71841	.9	100	.3	82	22.5	231	36.0	9	11	.5	11	0	.0
71842	2.0	95	.7	85	17.4	180	38.1	9	16	1.0	15	0	.0
71845	2.9	50	1.0	74	17.4	170	42.8	8	17	.2	15	0	.0
71846	2.6	81	.9	80	17.8	163	38.1	9	16	.4	14	0	.0
71847	.7	78	.2	89	23.1	265*	33.4	8	17	.3	25	0	.0
71851	2.2	56	.7	80	18.2	214	44.6	7	14	.6	15	0	.0
71852	9.2	83	3.4	73	19.9	201	51.2	7	19	3.7	15	0	.1

ARKANSAS

TEXARKANA

ZIP CODE	1	2	3	4	5	6	7	8	9	10	11	12	13
71853	.9	0	.3	66	15.8	195	31.7	10	17	.0	0	0	.0
71855	1.0		.3	77	11.4	232	28.6	8	20	.0	0	0	.0
71857	7.1	74	2.7	76	19.2	166	43.3	7	21	2.5	19	2	.0
71858	2.1	59	.7	80	16.4	214	30.4	9	17	.6	19	0	.0
71859	.9	60	.3	90	22.2	141	44.3	16	12	.2	9	1	1.4
71860	3.9	59	1.4	73	14.8	177	34.4	8	20	1.0	21	0	.0
71861	2.3	91	.8	86	21.9	117	38.6	7	17	1.0	13	1	.0
71862	1.0	0	.4	87	15.8	136	27.8	6	25				.0
71865	.6	54	.2	81	20.0	176	31.6	11	11	.1	10	0	.0
71866	.9	0	.3	83	16.9	175	36.8	6	18	.0	0	0	.0

HOT SPRINGS NATIONAL PARK

ZIP CODE	1	2	3	4	5	6	7	8	9	10	11	12	13
71901	61.9	91	25.4	66	21.3	223	76.5	6	21	26.7	20	6	.2
71921	3.1	0	.1	83	18.3	169	41.0	7	16	.0	0	0	.5
71922	.3	0	.1	79	15.6	235	34.6	4	25	.0	0	0	.0
71923	15.4	77	5.1	67	22.1	238	67.4	6	13	5.6	10	2	.4
71929	2.4	0	.9	83	17.6	229	49.6	7	18	.0	0	0	.0
71930	.5	0	.2	83	21.2	202	35.5	6	16	.0	0	0	.0
71931	.8	100	.3	93	20.0	230*	20.1	19	9	.1	11	0	.0
71933	.8	98	.3	76	14.6	243	30.0	7	11	.4	11	0	.0
71934	.3	100	.1	91	16.0	285	32.3	0	10	.2	10	0	.0
71935	.6	0	.2	87	16.1	185*	34.6	7	25	.0	0	0	.0
71937	1.8	98	.6	71	17.4	183	38.8	8	15	.9	14	1	.0
71940	1.5	87	.6	86	19.0	175	45.9	5	17	.6	17	0	.1
71941	.5	96	.5	86	19.0	259	40.0	9	14	.8	11	0	.0
71942	.2	100	.1	89	19.3	221*	52.2	4	21	.1	16	0	.0
71943	3.3	99	1.2	77	17.4	235	50.9	7	17	1.6	14	0	.0
71944	1.1	96	.3	62	27.2	192	29.9	10	11	.5	10	0	.4
71945	1.1	100	.4	85	17.7	119	40.0	7	18	.5	13	0	.0
71946	1.0	100	.1	89	10.7	123*	17.6	0	37	.0	0	0	.0
71949	.5	100	.2	77	19.4	252	45.1	14	10	.2	11	0	.0
71950	.8	100	.3	73	15.1	223	38.0	7	12	.4	16	0	.0
71951	1.1	100	.6	94	26.2	301*	87.1	0	30	.1	23	0	.0
71952	.2	100	.1	25	10.8	134	13.1	11	18	.1	0	0	.0
71953	11.9	99	4.5	80	18.9	212	52.0	6	20	5.7	18	0	.1
71956	2.0	86	.7	82	19.7	223	28.0	6	14	.8	15	0	.0
71957	2.6	0	1.0	79	16.5	186	61.2	6	22				.0
71958	3.0	93	1.1	82	21.9	215	53.1	7	16	1.4	14	0	.0
71959	.2	0	.3	84	20.8	203	44.0	9	18				.0
71960	1.2	0	.4	75	17.3	181	30.9	5	15	.0	0	0	.0
71961	.6	0	.2	87	13.2	113	40.2	7	17	.0	0	0	.0
71962	1.1	52	.4	82	16.2	122	30.8	9	19	.3	20	0	.0
71964	2.7	0	.8	90	25.2	247	74.5	7	8				.0
71965	.2	100	.1	92	13.9	160*	71.8	6	25	.1	22	0	.0
71966	.2	100	.1	84	20.0	230*	91.9	13	17	.1	16	0	.0
71968	2.4	93	.8	88	18.4	234	66.2	5	18	1.1	19	1	.0
71969	.4	0	.2	82	14.6	126	36.3	8	14				.0
71970	.5	0	.2	92	13.0	153	42.2	6	23	.0	0	0	.0
71971	.6	0	.2	84	23.6	222	20.2	13	11	.0	0	0	.0
71972	.2	0	.1	69	12.8	428	22.3	9	17	.0	0	0	.1

*=Estimated **1.0=883 lbs per person; 100++ indicates per capita toxic waste generation > than 100 times the U.S. average of 883 lbs per capita.

ZIP CODE MEASURES OF SIZE, LEVELS OF AFFLUENCE AND QUALITY OF LIFE

1=Population (th.); 2= % White; 3=Households (th.); 4=% Owner Occupied; 5=Mean Income Per Household (th.$); 6=Mean Monthly Rent ($)*; 7=Mean Home Value (th.$)*;
8=% under 5; 9=% 65 and over; 10=White Males, 65+; 11=% White Males; 12=# Toxic Waste Sites; 13=Toxic Waste Relative to US(883 lbs.per capital)**.

ARKANSAS

HOT SPRINGS NATIONAL PARK

ZIPCODE	1	2	3	4	5	6	7	8	9	10	11	12	13
71973	.8	0	.3	74	17.3	229	46.3	11	15	.0	0	0	.0

LITTLE ROCK

ZIPCODE	1	2	3	4	5	6	7	8	9	10	11	12	13
72001	.6	0	.2	87	21.2	226	38.3	8	13	.0	0	0	.0
72002	7.4	96	2.4	82	25.2	261	76.4	7	7	3.5	6	0	.0
72003	1.2	92	.4	66	20.0	238	46.0	9	13	.6	15	0	.0
72004	3.2	32	.9	40	15.7	192	33.1	11	13	.5	7	2	.0
72005	.4	100	.2	64	12.4	139	29.0	3	21	.2	19	0	.2
72006	4.2	61	1.5	59	16.9	200	54.7	9	15	1.3	13	0	.2
72007	3.0	0	.9	84	21.1	334	72.8	7	9	.0	0	0	.1
72010	6.0	96	2.1	74	18.2	231	52.2	7	11	2.9	10	2	.1
72011	2.2	100	.8	84	21.7	268	54.8	7	10	1.1	10	2	100++
72012	6.0	96	2.2	77	18.2	255	58.9	7	15	2.8	13	.0	.0
72013	1.5	0	.5	81	19.5	193	34.8	9	16	.0	0	0	.0
72014	.2	100	.1	61	13.6	234	47.6	11	17	.1	11	0	.0
72015	31.9	96	10.6	79	25.6	270	69.9	7	11	15.1	9	4	.2
72016	1.7	93	.6	77	19.0	232	33.0	10	12	.8	11	0	.0
72017	1.0	69	.4	64	12.9	205	37.1	5	14	.4	11	0	.0
72020	4.2	100	1.5	83	15.7	170	39.7	7	15	2.1	13	2	.0
72021	7.0	61	2.5	59	16.3	206	54.5	10	15	2.0	11	1	.0
72022	2.9	100	1.0	84	29.0	333	83.8	6	6	1.4	5	1	.0
72023	8.9	99	2.8	79	24.8	254	77.3	8	8	4.3	8	0	.0
72024	4.2	88	1.5	70	22.4	228	58.5	5	16	1.8	15	1	.0
72025	.8	98	.3	98	14.8	170*	30.7	5	14	.4	14	0	.0
72026	.4	56	.1	56	18.2	278	39.9	5	11	.1	11	0	.0
72027	1.3	89	.4	91	19.7	226*	36.4	7	10	.6	12	0	.2
72029	3.0	71	1.1	65	15.7	189	47.0	7	18	1.0	15	1	.0
72030	.5	93	.2	92	14.8	353	28.6	6	18	.2	20	0	.0
72031	6.0	98	2.3	82	16.6	234	58.3	7	17	.9	15	2	.0
72032	31.4	90	10.4	68	23.2	281	78.8	7	10	13.6	8	7	.1
72036	2.0	37	.8	57	12.9	145	25.9	8	22	.4	20	0	.8
72038	.1	72	.1	45	14.7	217	65.2	9	17	.0	17	0	.0
72039	1.6	48	.1	74	29.7	341*	71.3	11	19	.0	16	1	.0
72040	3.3	83	.6	86	16.7	232	44.9	9	16	.7	16	0	.0
72041	1.5	93	.6	68	18.5	190	49.6	6	14	1.5	12	0	.0
72042	6.6	79	2.4	75	17.9	255	46.7	8	16	.6	13	1	.2
72044	.6	86	.2	64	19.3	220	50.4	8	16	2.7	12	1	.2
72045	.4	100	.2	93	18.5	581	95.2	10	16	.3	11	0	.0
72046	5.9	66	2.0	58	19.3	192	55.0	9	17	1.9	15	3	.0
72047	.6	100	.2	78	17.9	188	39.1	6	18	.3	26	0	.0
72048	.2	67	.1	60	11.5	132*	53.4	14	16	.0	24	0	.0
72051	.5	0	.2	86	15.3	206	32.6	6	15	.2	11	0	.0
72052	.2	100	.1	98	13.9	160*	41.4	5	18	.1	13	2	.0
72053	1.1	3	.3	67	13.5	195	36.8	8	19	.6	13	0	.0
72054	.3	100	.1	87	13.9	108	25.2	3	24	.0	26	0	.0
72055	1.3	85	.5	67	20.3	194	62.2	7	13	.6	14	0	.0
72057	.8	0	.3	81	15.9	203	58.1	4	17	.0	0	0	.0
72058	5.2	98	1.8	84	19.7	296	57.7	7	11	2.5	10	0	.0
72060	1.2	0	.4	82	15.7	148	44.8	8	19	.0	0	0	.0

ARKANSAS

LITTLE ROCK

ZIPCODE	1	2	3	4	5	6	7	8	9	10	11	12	13
72061	.4	98	.1	87	15.1	232	37.9	6	22	.2	18	0	.0
72063	1.2	84	.3	79	19.5	209	41.0	11	11	.5	8	0	.0
72064	2.7	84	1.0	78	18.9	194	64.6	8	14	1.1	14	0	.0
72065	2.3	86	.7	85	24.6	328	54.0	7	9	1.0	6	0	.0
72067	1.7	0	.7	86	17.4	202	79.9	6	17	.0	0	0	.0
72068	.4	0	.4	81	17.5	299	33.2	9	12	.0	0	0	.0
72069	3.0	35	1.0	62	15.1	167	41.2	8	20	.5	25	0	.0
72070	1.1	0	.4	78	16.7	177	50.7	2	16	.0	0	0	.2
72072	.8	68	.3	75	18.8	108	34.4	5	19	.3	17	0	.2
72073	1.6	78	.5	76	19.1	201	35.6	8	13	.6	14	1	.0
72074	.3	100	.1	54	12.6	213	25.6	14	15	.2	14	0	.0
72075	.3	100	.1	71	16.2	252	28.0	7	8	.1	9	0	.0
72076	33.7	86	10.7	57	22.3	302	74.4	11	8	15.1	3	5	.7
72079	.4	88	.1	80	25.3	367	51.3	10	4	.2	3	0	.0
72080	.3	100	.1	94	11.3	130*	29.5	11	13	.1	5	0	.0
72081	5.2	98	1.7	82	17.5	263	41.4	7	15	2.6	13	0	.0
72082	1.8	76	.7	68	15.2	202	41.2	7	15	.6	15	0	.0
72083	.3	54	.1	56	25.0	173	79.9	12	11	.1	10	0	.6
72084	1.2	77	.4	87	18.8	222	39.6	7	10	.5	13	0	.0
72085	.2	100	.1	81	13.7	212	35.4	7	16	.3	18	0	.0
72086	7.3	83	2.3	78	21.9	228	60.9	7	12	2.9	10	2	2.3
72087	.8	100	.3	84	19.5	256	51.3	6	9	.4	4	0	.0
72088	1.1	100	.5	93	21.2	130	92.7	2	24	.6	31	0	.0

LITTLE ROCK

ZIPCODE	1	2	3	4	5	6	7	8	9	10	11	12	13
72101	4.3	93	1.5	71	22.2	225	56.6	8	15	1.9	13	1	.1
72103	1.8	0	.6	74	16.8	227	40.3	6	13	.0	0	0	.0
72104	8.1	97	2.7	84	27.2	314	80.6	9	5	4.0	4	0	.0
72105	20.6	85	7.4	79	21.2	218	55.1	7	13	8.4	12	7	.6
72106	.5	100	.2	26	20.0	160	76.6	10	12	1.3	12	1	.8
72107	2.8	89	1.0	80	19.3	252	52.0	10	11	1.3	12	0	.0
72108	.4	0	.1	85	12.2	244	41.4	10	20	.0	0	0	.0
72110	.1	0	.1	65	40.0	248	43.8	10	10	.0	0	0	.0
72111	11.0	87	3.9	70	20.9	223	59.8	8	15	4.6	12	0	.5
72112	12.7	80	4.6	62	21.1	220	65.5	8	16	4.9	13	3	.4
72114	18.8	52	7.2	41	14.1	213	42.5	9	19	4.6	18	5	.3
72116	40.6	97	14.6	75	32.8	385	98.2	7	8	19.2	6	0	1.5
72117	14.8	63	4.9	71	20.3	277	49.2	9	11	4.5	9	1	.2
72118	25.5	93	9.5	73	24.5	313	68.4	8	8	11.5	7	2	.0
72121	1.8	0	.6	88	18.3	187	36.7	6	12	.3	26	0	.0
72122	.4	100	.1	95	19.6	225*	36.7	5	10	.2	11	0	.0
72123	.6	60	.2	72	11.2	204	29.6	9	20	.2	22	0	3.5
72125	1.1	100	.4	86	16.6	206	42.0	7	14	.5	16	0	.0
72126	2.7	0	1.0	82	19.6	217	51.4	8	16	.6	8	0	.0
72127	1.7	74	.6	78	17.9	203	43.8	8	13	.6	8	2	.0
72128	.8	90	.3	87	19.5	231	41.4	9	14	.4	12	0	.1
72130	1.2	83	.4	84	19.5	230	48.4	9	13	.5	12	0	.0
72131	3.2	99	1.2	84	14.8	232	50.2	6	21	1.5	21	0	.0

*=Estimated **1.0=883 lbs per person; 100++ indicates per capita toxic waste generation > than 100 times the U.S. average of 883 lbs per capita.

ZIP CODE MEASURES OF SIZE, LEVELS OF AFFLUENCE AND QUALITY OF LIFE

1=Population (th.); 2= % White; 3=Households (th.); 4=% Owner Occupied; 5=Mean Income Per Household (th.$); 6=Mean Monthly Rent ($)*; 7=Mean Home Value (th.$)*;
8=% under 5; 9=% 65 and over; 10=White Males (th.); 11=% White Males, 65+; 12=# Toxic Waste Sites; 13=Toxic Waste Relative to US(883 lbs.per capita)**.

ARKANSAS

LITTLE ROCK

ZIPCODE	1	2	3	4	5	6	7	8	9	10	11	12	13
72132	2.0	90	.7	85	25.2	387	53.9	7	8	.9	6	0	.1
72133	.3	100	.1	55	15.3	248	41.5	16	8	.1	4	0	.0
72134	.7	60	.2	71	18.4	243	50.9	10	11	.2	9	0	.0
72135	1.6	92	.6	87	24.5	234	63.9	8	13	.8	11	0	.0
72136	.6	0	.2	80	22.4	235	50.3	6	11	.0	0	0	.0
72137	1.5	100	.5	84	17.8	203	44.5	8	14	.8	15	0	.0
72139	.3	100	.2	81	10.2	216	33.0	7	34	.2	31	0	.2
72140	.4	84	.2	61	17.4	218	64.9	7	23	.1	19	0	.0
72141	.4	100	.1	90	17.2	161	22.7	2	15	.3	19	0	.2
72142	1.6	60	.5	68	22.3	214	64.4	12	12	.5	13	0	.0
72143	20.7	96	6.8	68	21.2	269	74.0	6	12	9.5	10	1	.4
72150	8.8	98	3.1	79	23.4	245	61.0	7	13	4.3	10	1	.1
72152	.8	30	.1	63	14.9	86	38.9	9	18	.0	9	0	.0
72153	2.7	0	1.0	82	17.1	145	74.2	6	21	.0	0	0	.0
72156	.4	0	.1	94	26.5	305*	45.7	11	11	.0	0	0	.0
72157	1.4	70	.5	87	18.8	215	41.2	8	13	.5	13	0	.0
72159	.4	100	.1	82	16.7	199	24.7	5	15	.2	14	0	.0
72160	13.0	76	4.9	65	24.5	253	81.5	8	13	4.8	11	0	.4
72164	1.2	23	.4	67	17.0	186	40.5	11	12	.1	14	0	.0
72165	.3	100	.1	100	13.9	160*	27.0	8	16	.1	9	0	.0
72166	.4	100	.1	76	23.2	267*	55.6	9	17	.3	15	0	.0
72167	1.3	0	.4	90	21.4	239	44.5	11	9	.0	0	0	.0
72168	1.2	0	.2	58	14.0	277	18.3	4	5	.0	0	0	.0
72169	.3	100	.1	68	15.2	154	43.3	12	13	.2	10	0	.0
72170	.4	100	.1	83	24.0	250	68.1	7	8	.1	6	0	.0
72173	3.5	98	1.1	81	21.5	261	63.2	7	8	1.7	7	0	.0
72176	.7	24	.2	49	13.9	226	37.1	9	18	.1	39	0	.0
72177	2.6	99	.9	79	17.9	190	49.4	9	13	1.3	14	0	2.0
72179	.3	84	.1	63	16.2	104	47.1	2	14	.1	6	0	
72180	.4	100		75	15.7	110	196.9	10	8	.2	6	0	.2
72183	.6	19	.2	83	14.8	203	30.7	2	20	.0	38	0	.8

LITTLE ROCK

ZIPCODE	1	2	3	4	5	6	7	8	9	10	11	12	13
72201	1.7	78	.6	9	12.7	247	39.4	2	15	.7	16	0	2.3
72202	17.3	31	7.1	34	18.2	275	54.4	9	16	2.3	17	0	.3
72203	2.3	91	.7	90	26.1	231	76.8	5	5	1.0	5	0	18.4
72204	38.0	52	13.3	65	21.9	306	59.9	9	10	9.3	11	3	.1
72205	24.5	92	11.2	56	28.1	372	90.0	5	18	9.7	14	0	.4
72206	35.1	44	12.0	61	19.7	252	56.2	10	10	7.8	8	3	.4
72207	23.4	97	9.8	71	45.1	454	144.5	6	12	10.5	10	0	.0
72208	.3	86	.1	80	16.1	357	45.4	4	10	.2	26	0	.0
72209	37.5	85	13.8	59	24.4	331	71.8	9	5	15.4	5	6	.2
72210	4.5	99	1.5	84	25.6	294	76.7	6	6	2.3	6	0	.0
72211	7.2	94	2.9	57	30.9	413	112.4	8	3	3.2	3	0	.0
72212	8.2	90	2.6	92	55.3	401	164.7	8	7	3.6	4	0	.0

MEMPHIS

ZIPCODE	1	2	3	4	5	6	7	8	9	10	11	12	13
72301	28.4	64	9.3	61	23.0	289	68.2	9	9	8.7	16	5	.3
72311	.3	41	.1	72	11.7	270	39.0	1	25	.2	7	0	.0
72313	.4	82	.1	67	22.0	213	27.9	2	15	.2	11	0	.0

ARKANSAS

MEMPHIS

ZIPCODE	1	2	3	4	5	6	7	8	9	10	11	12	13
72315	32.1	70	10.7	53	19.5	286	60.9	10	10	11.2	8	12	.9
72320	.6	27	.2	51	16.6	225	62.8	7	14	.1	19	0	.0
72321	.3	50	.1	44	18.1	306	59.8	7	11	.1	5	0	.0
72322	.4	81	.1	75	25.6	230	41.7	8	13	.1	23	0	.0
72324	2.2	93	.7	73	22.4	250	54.3	8	12	1.0	12	0	.0
72325	.4	21	.1	17	16.9	195*	29.5	19	4	.0	12	0	.0
72326	2.2	72	.7	78	16.0	174	51.6	9	12	.8	10	0	.2
72327	2.6	23	.7	48	15.1	173	39.1	10	11	.3	10	0	.0
72330	.5	26	.1	25	16.5	173	77.5	24	12	.1	21	0	.0
72331	.9	97	.3	79	19.7	290	30.8	8	10	.4	13	0	.0
72332	5.2	39	1.6	64	15.7	208	39.9	9	14	1.0	14	0	.0
72333	.5	0	.1	64	10.8	214	26.8	9	21	.0	8	0	.0
72335	2.5	40	.7	34	14.3	249	54.3	10	9	.5	8	0	2.3
72338	18.8	55	6.2	59	19.4	239	62.5	10	12	4.9	10	2	.7
72339	.2	28	.1	34	12.8	147*	13.1	5	11	.1	54	0	.0
72341	.7	32	.2	48	11.8	196	35.4	11	9	.1	2	0	.0
72342	.3	0	.1	78	12.1	195	31.4	10	11	.0	14	0	.0
72346	10.8	39	3.8	43	17.3	200	74.9	10	17	2.0	13	2	2.3
72347	1.3	48	.4	43	16.8	169	39.3	9	9	.3	8	0	.0
72348	1.4	97	.5	74	20.7	283	47.4	7	14	.7	14	0	.0
72350	4.4	41	1.5	42	14.8	212	65.7	9	13	.9	12	0	.0
72351	1.4	0	.4	58	21.2	212	44.0	10	14	.0	9	0	.0
72352	1.3	89	.2	57	19.2	243	42.1	11	8	.6	5	0	.0
72354	.2	30	.1	94	8.3	96*	25.7	8	17	.0	0	0	6.2
72355	2.7	90	1.0	59	18.8	196	45.8	9	15	1.1	13	0	.0
72358	2.7	38	.8	81	17.7	216	45.2	13	12	.5	8	0	.0
72359	2.3	57	.7	48	15.1	216	49.5	12	10	.7	8	0	.0
72360	1.0	19	.3	63	13.1	224	27.8	10	15	.1	14	0	6.2
72364	10.7	46	3.5	60	14.7	184	54.1	11	9	2.4	11	2	
72365	6.3	68	1.9	65	23.5	295	78.7	11	7	2.1	4	1	
72366	4.3	77	1.6	53	18.3	171	47.4	9	15	1.6	14	0	.8
72367	4.4	0	1.4	62	15.9	202	42.5	8	17	.0	0	0	.0
72368	.3	67	.1	19	9.0	192	37.2	5	15	.1	32	0	.0
72369	2.3	53	.7	68	12.5	247	48.6	9	12	.6	13	0	.0
72370	10.5	65	3.5	30	7.3	150	13.1	15	20	1.0	5	0	.4
72372	2.8	61	.8	49	19.4	230	54.0	10	11	.3	9	3	
72373	3.0	57	.9	82	18.5	133	54.0	10	11	.8	6	0	
72374	1.0	0	.3	57	17.2	186	48.0	8	13	.8	11	0	
72376	1.9	0	.5	75	13.2	203	28.3	7	16	.0	10	0	
72383	.2	42	.1	61	17.6	301	60.0	11	10	.1	4	1	
72384	2.0	0	.6	69	10.9	224	54.0	6	27	.0	0	0	
72385	.3	100		49	14.0	209	45.1	9	15	.0	26	0	
72386	2.3	78	.7	44	30.1	131	28.4	8	7	.3	0	0	
72387	.4	87	.3	58	20.8	224	51.9	9	13	.8	9	0	
72389	.2	40	.1	73	23.2	293	50.1	9	18	.2	16	0	
72390	12.5	55	4.1	28	19.1	280	29.5	7	4	3.4	0	0	9.5
72391	.3	100	.1	60	18.2	243	52.4	10	11	.2	9	3	
72392	.9	55	.3	74	15.8	204	51.9	9	13	.2	0	0	.3

*=Estimated **1.0=883 lbs per person; 100++ indicates per capita toxic waste generation > than 100 times the U.S. average of 883 lbs per capita.

ZIP CODE MEASURES OF SIZE, LEVELS OF AFFLUENCE AND QUALITY OF LIFE

1=Population (th.); 2= % White; 3=Households (th.); 4=% Owner Occupied; 5=Mean Income Per Household (th.$); 6=Mean Monthly Rent ($)*; 7=Mean Home Value (th.$)*; 8=% under 5; 9=% 65 and over; 10=% White Males (th.); 11=% White Males, 65+; 12=# Toxic Waste Sites; 13=Toxic Waste Relative to US(883 lbs.per capita)**.

ARKANSAS

MEMPHIS

ZIP CODE	1	2	3	4	5	6	7	8	9	10	11	12	13
72394	1.4	0	.4	48	15.5	215	33.5	11	12	.0	0	0	.0
72395	1.8	62	.5	46	22.8	228	57.3	11	10	.6	9	0	.0
72396	12.7	74	4.1	71	21.7	265	63.8	10	13	4.5	10	0	.4
72397	.3	100	.1	65	20.8	239*	36.4	7	2	.1	4	0	.0

JONESBORO

ZIP CODE	1	2	3	4	5	6	7	8	9	10	11	12	13
72401	43.7	94	16.1	66	23.9	286	76.0	8	11	20.0	9	4	1.1
72410	.9	0	.3	83	15.5	182	42.7	9	19	.0	0	0	.0
72411	2.3	98	.8	82	18.0	191	44.9	8	12	1.1	11	0	.0
72412	.9	100	.3	72	20.0	162	35.5	5	11	.5	10	0	.0
72413	.7	99	.3	79	19.0	223	38.1	6	21	.3	17	0	.0
72414	1.0	100	.4	65	16.7	185	34.0	5	16	.5	17	0	.0
72415	1.5	0	.6	83	16.0	171	36.4	7	16	.0	0	0	.4
72416	3.5	0	1.3	80	18.9	263	51.0	9	11	.0	0	0	.0
72417	2.2	98	.7	78	16.8	272	45.6	6	12	1.0	13	0	.2
72419	1.8	0	.6	68	15.4	202	38.7	6	13	.0	0	0	.2
72421	.9	100	.3	76	20.6	158	41.8	8	12	.4	10	0	.0
72422	6.7	0	2.4	74	16.3	232	49.7	8	16	.0	0	1	.3
72423	.1	100	.2	90	15.5	178*	48.4	12	14	.1	6	0	.0
72424	.1	100	.1	74	13.2	147	25.9	2	32	.1	31	0	.2
72425	1.0	100	.3	74	24.1	184	39.8	8	11	.5	10	0	.0
72426	.2	0	.1	37	11.1	207	29.1	4	17	.0	0	0	.0
72428	.7	100	.1	78	12.6	165	24.7	0	29	.1	22	0	.0
72429	.7	0	.2	77	26.8	168	40.9	6	16	.2	16	0	.0
72430	.7	100	.3	68	16.0	156	26.9	11	16	.3	12	0	.0
72431	.6	0	.2	62	14.8	224	44.1	9	13	.0	0	0	.3
72432	5.8	95	2.0	74	20.3	216	52.0	7	13	2.8	11	0	.0
72433	3.2	99	1.2	80	14.2	170	37.6	8	17	1.5	15	0	.0
72434	1.9	98	.7	79	15.9	140	41.5	9	18	.9	17	0	.0
72435	.9	100	.3	58	17.8	233	28.0	7	12	.5	9	0	.0
72436	.9	0	.3	83	15.9	219	35.3	11	15	.7	10	0	.0
72437	3.5	99	1.3	75	16.7	228	41.6	8	12	1.7	10	0	.0
72438	3.0	100	1.1	67	17.2	206	40.7	6	17	1.4	14	2	.0
72440	.4	100	.2	92	15.5	165	44.8	8	24	.2	21	0	.0
72441	.3	100	.1	95	21.2	243*	25.3	7	15	.1	10	0	.3
72442	4.1	99	1.5	69	17.7	196	44.6	8	14	1.9	12	1	.3
72443	2.8	100	1.1	76	17.0	200	42.4	7	14	1.4	12	0	.0
72444	1.7	100	.6	81	14.1	203	36.8	6	17	.8	16	0	.0
72445	2.0	100	.7	62	16.0	254	33.8	13	14	.1	11	0	.0
72447	1.8	100	.7	78	17.0	215	41.7	6	24	.9	19	1	.0
72448	.1	100	.1	93	12.7	145*	21.1	5	26	.1	25	0	.0
72449	.3	100	.1	84	14.2	280	29.3	6	11	.2	9	0	.0
72450	23.1	99	8.5	71	19.3	230	55.8	8	15	11.0	13	4	.9
72453	3.4	100	.2	72	12.8	145	30.6	9	19	.0	0	0	.0
72454	5.4	100	2.2	79	19.1	202	51.6	6	21	2.5	18	0	.0
72455	10.8	98	4.0	75	19.1	208	52.7	7	16	5.1	15	2	.5
72456	.8	100	.3	85	13.7	34	34.6	4	16	.4	16	0	.0
72457	.5	100	.2	88	14.8	261	40.2	8	23	.2	23	0	.0
72458	.5	0	.2	97	12.2	141*	46.9	9	12	.0	0	0	.0
72459	1.0	0	.4	84	11.6	188	40.4	9	22	.0	0	0	.0

ARKANSAS

JONESBORO

ZIP CODE	1	2	3	4	5	6	7	8	9	10	11	12	13
72460	.7	100	.2	82	15.1	142	23.0	10	7	.3	10	0	.0
72461	4.4	100	1.8	70	16.4	168	41.5	5	21	2.1	20	0	.0
72462	.6	100	.2	71	15.7	208	37.1	6	19	.3	16	0	.0
72464	.3	100	.2	71	18.3	172	26.2	4	24	.1	19	0	.0
72465	.2	100	.1	72	28.7	356	38.5	4	12	.1	10	0	.0
72466	1.2	100	.4	92	16.6	119	29.9	6	10	.6	13	0	.0
72467	2.9	79	.4	10	16.2	210	45.7	3	1	1.0	0	0	.0
72469	.9	100	.3	89	15.5	36	49.4	6	14	.5	12	0	.0
72470	.5	100	.2	79	14.9	98	28.5	6	19	.3	14	0	.0
72471	1.3	98	.5	78	15.3	151	40.2	8	15	.6	13	0	.0
72472	9.7	99	3.3	60	18.1	188	46.0	8	11	4.6	9	3	.2
72473	3.2	91	1.2	76	18.1	223	47.3	8	13	1.4	11	0	.0
72474	.9	0	.3	89	18.6	155	44.1	6	10	.0	0	0	.0
72475	2.2	100	.1	85	31.8	365*	61.4	11	21	.1	20	0	2.1
72476	7.7	98	2.8	69	19.7	225	51.2	6	16	3.6	14	0	2.8
72478	.5	100	.5	73	14.5	116	13.1	4	12	.3	9	0	.0
72479	2.0	99	.8	69	21.5	221	53.4	6	14	.9	16	0	.0
72482	1.4	0	.6	87	11.2	199	44.2	5	27	.7	0	0	.0

BATESVILLE

ZIP CODE	1	2	3	4	5	6	7	8	9	10	11	12	13
72501	20.7	96	7.4	72	19.9	279	62.9	8	14	9.7	11	6	6.2
72510	.3	0	.1	81	13.7	269	53.5	2	26	.0	0	0	.0
72512	1.9	100	1.8	86	18.3	233	86.4	2	47	.9	52	0	.0
72513	1.2	100	.6	84	17.7	308	60.8	8	15	.9	14	0	.0
72515	.2	100	.1	81	13.2	151*	28.4	3	34	.1	35	0	.0
72517	.3	100	.1	74	13.4	313	39.4	3	20	.1	18	0	.0
72519	2.2	99	.8	80	14.8	207	42.3	8	19	1.1	14	0	.2
72521	3.4	98	1.3	79	15.4	269	45.5	7	19	1.7	20	0	.0
72522	.8	100	.3	45	16.8	122	59.8	3	19	.1	16	0	.0
72523	.8	0	.3	87	15.1	194	41.0	8	16	.2	19	0	.0
72524	.4	92	.2	91	12.8	147*	43.8	5	23	.2	21	0	.0
72525	1.3	0	.6	70	24.4	160	88.7	6	33	.0	0	0	.0
72526	.4	0	.2	81	14.8	166	34.8	5	16	.0	0	0	.0
72527	.5	100	.2	88	17.1	286	56.0	7	18	.2	16	0	.0
72528	.2	100	.1	100	22.4	257*	19.0	2	10	.1	10	0	.0
72530	1.1	100	.4	90	13.8	212	22.4	7	9	.6	14	0	.0
72531	.5	100	.2	88	23.1	265*	53.8	10	20	.1	23	0	.1
72533	1.2	0	.4	86	14.9	186	40.0	10	13	.3	0	1	.0
72533	.4	100	.1	76	16.1	207	66.2	3	6	.2	7	0	.0
72534	1.1	0	.4	94	13.6	194	38.8	7	17	.1	0	0	.0
72536	.2	100	.2	87	15.0	201	43.3	6	22	.2	19	0	.0
72537	.6	0	.3	84	16.4	225	62.3	1	25	.0	0	0	.0
72538	.3	100	.3	84	20.1	231*	13.1	2	13	.1	20	0	.0
72539	.3	100	.1	89	20.3	248	47.5	2	14	.1	13	0	.0
72540	.2	0	.1	76	12.6	129	25.3	7	17	.2	7	0	.2
72541	.9	0	.4	86	20.6	194	75.3	4	47	.9	0	0	.0
72542	4.7	98	1.9	86	17.9	281	72.8	5	25	2.3	25	1	.0
72543	8.4	100	3.2	79	20.0	239	78.6	6	21	4.0	20	1	.4
72544	.5	100	.1	81	13.0	326	52.2	10	28	.2	27	0	.0
72546	.2	100	.1	83	25.1	289*	59.1	10	11	.1	10	0	.0

*=Estimated **1.0=883 lbs per person; 100++ indicates per capita toxic waste generation > than 100 times the U.S. average of 883 lbs per capita.

ZIP CODE MEASURES OF SIZE, LEVELS OF AFFLUENCE AND QUALITY OF LIFE

1=Population (th.); 2= % White; 3=Households (th.); 4=% Owner Occupied; 5=Mean Income Per Household (th.$); 6=Mean Monthly Rent ($); 7=Mean Home Value (th.$); 8=% under 5; 9=% 65 and over; 10=White Males (th.); 11=% White Males, 65+; 12=# Toxic Waste Sites; 13=Toxic Waste Relative to US(883 lbs.per capita)**.

ARKANSAS

BATESVILLE

ZIPCODE	1	2	3	4	5	6	7	8	9	10	11	12	13
72548	.1	0	.1	100	10.4	119*	55.6	0	27	.0	0	0	.0
72550	.6	0	.2	81	18.3	240	50.6	10	17	.0	17	0	.0
72553	.4	95	.2	72	20.5	300	61.7	10	18	.0	0	0	.0
72554	3.2	99	1.2	79	13.4	222	43.3	7	19	1.5	12	0	.0
72555	.2	100	.1	100	14.6	168*	31.8	8	15	.1	18	0	.0
72556	2.7	99	1.0	81	18.0	201	50.8	8	22	1.3	18	0	.1
72557	.2	0	.1	100	20.6	237*	30.6	5	5	.0	0	0	.0
72560	5.3	99	2.0	78	15.3	198	53.2	7	16	2.6	16	0	.0
72561	.8	0	.3	77	16.4	170	32.8	8	18	.0	0	0	.0
72562	1.8	96	.7	78	16.5	246	47.4	8	18	.8	16	0	.0
72564	.7	100	.2	80	18.5	267	42.2	4	7	.3	4	0	.0
72565	.7	100	.3	81	12.8	177	38.8	6	22	.3	22	0	.0
72566	.5	100	.2	84	11.1	250	53.3	11	24	.3	26	0	.0
72568	.3	89	.1	82	12.2	246	68.0	8	23	.1	28	0	.0
72569	1.3	100	.4	91	16.7	106	38.2	10	14	.6	13	0	.0
72571	.5	100	.2	86	14.1	270	35.1	4	8	.2	6	0	.0
72572	.2	0	.1	88	30.6	351*	82.3	4	17	.0	0	0	.0
72575	.3	100	.1	50	13.8	304	55.5	3	13	.1	12	0	.0
72576	2.6	0	1.0	83	15.3	205	52.4	7	25	.6	13	0	.0
72577	.8	0	.3	93	18.4	188	43.6	7	20	.1	21	0	.3
72579	.9	0	.3	74	18.4	232	49.2	12	12	.0	0	0	.0
72581	1.3	100	.1	77	17.0	192	69.8	3	15	.2	17	0	.0
72583	1.3	99	.5	89	15.2	236	38.4	6	16	.6	15	0	.0
72584	.3	100	.2	90	14.9	171*	38.6	0	7	.1	5	0	.0
72585	.2	100	.1	100	11.7	134*	41.6*	15	20	.1	28	0	.0
72587	.1	100	.1	84	8.0	92*	64.4	0	23	.1	27	0	.0
72588	.2	100	.1	61	10.9	125*	38.8*	7	16	.1	14	0	.0
72589	.1	100	.1	79	12.0	171	30.2	0	41	.0	23	0	.0

HARRISON

ZIPCODE	1	2	3	4	5	6	7	8	9	10	11	12	13
72601	20.6	100	7.8	76	20.4	255	70.7	7	16	9.7	13	2	.3
72610	.2	100	.1	86	16.4	188*	37.2	6	14	.1	21	0	.0
72611	1.5	100	.5	79	14.2	190	44.0	9	13	.0	0	0	.0
72615	.2	100	.1	90	14.2	163*	42.7	11	11	.1	8	0	.0
72616	6.1	100	2.3	81	18.2	223	55.8	8	18	2.9	18	0	.0
72617	.5	100	.2	76	14.8	132	34.2	8	19	.2	16	0	.0
72619	1.4	99	.7	87	16.7	246	73.0	4	36	.7	40	0	.0
72623	.4	0	.1	81	16.7	108	65.6	9	13	.2	0	0	.0
72624	.6	100	.2	76	12.9	171	37.5	15	9	.3	0	0	.0
72628	1.0	100	.4	74	15.9	231	66.6	6	24	.2	10	0	.0
72629	.4	0	.2	92	11.8	65	41.1	8	25	.1	23	0	.0
72632	4.0	100	1.9	77	19.0	139	27.4	5	26	1.9	22	0	.0
72633	1.8	0	.6	83	15.8	214	78.3	10	16	.0	0	0	.0
72634	2.7	100	.8	83	19.7	218	55.4	8	14	1.4	11	0	.0
72635	2.7	100	.9	87	20.1	220	54.5	7	20	.0	0	0	.0
72638	4.3	99	1.7	83	16.18	194	57.2	7	16	2.1	14	0	.0
72639	.3	100	.1	90	15.1	173*	33.3	6	7	.2	6	0	.0
72640	.3	100	.1	100	10.4	119*	39.7	7	0	.1	5	0	.0

ARKANSAS

HARRISON

ZIPCODE	1	2	3	4	5	6	7	8	9	10	11	12	13
72641	2.1	99	.7	77	15.0	273	50.1	9	15	1.1	14	0	.0
72642	1.3	0	.6	92	17.2	253	77.8	2	37	.0	0	0	.0
72644	2.1	99	.8	87	17.4	216	59.2	7	29	1.0	32	0	.0
72645	2.0	98	.8	89	15.2	287	36.7	8	18	.9	18	0	.0
72648	.6	100	.2	100	19.2	221*	68.4*	16	9	.1	18	0	.0
72650	4.6	100	1.7	79	15.0	150	47.7	7	17	2.2	16	0	.0
72651	.6	0	.3	91	14.2	172	48.3	7	17	.0	0	0	.0
72652	.2	100	.1	91	14.9	285	61.4	3	33	.0	0	0	.0
72653	18.4	99	7.6	84	8.8	101*	31.4*	6	17	.2	17	0	.0
72655	.6	100	.2	79	19.5	271	74.0	5	29	8.7	30	3	11.8
72656	.2	100	.1	90	11.3	132	23.9	1	17	.3	15	0	.0
72657	.4	100	.1	84	11.3	130*	51.8	0	44	.1	47	0	.0
72658	1.0	100	.3	89	14.2	203	39.5	5	7	.2	8	0	.0
72660	.2	100	.1	87	19.7	221	53.9	9	11	.5	10	0	.1
72661	.3	100	.1	86	14.2	205	38.2	3	30	.1	28	0	.0
72662	1.6	100	.6	86	16.6	288	55.7	0	28	.1	33	0	.0
72663	.4	0	.1	85	14.8	201	43.3	5	16	.9	15	0	.4
72666	.3	100	.1	86	15.2	65	43.8	15	16	.1	9	0	.0
72668	.4	100	.2	74	15.0	172*	13.1	7	9	.1	9	0	.0
72669	.3	0	.1	79	18.5	249	56.0	0	32	.2	30	0	.0
72670	.2	100	.1	60	9.8	131	30.8	6	15	.1	10	0	.1
72672	.3	91	.1	87	9.1	104*	32.3*	15	10	.1	16	0	.0
72675	1.6	99	.6	74	14.4	263	30.9	8	13	.1	16	0	.3
72677	.5	99	.2	82	16.0	190	30.3	8	17	.6	9	0	.0
72680	.3	100	.1	70	11.5	215	39.6	8	17	.2	18	0	.0
72682	.3	100	.1	79	9.4	189	36.9	4	15	.1	17	0	.0
72683	.4	100	.1	86	13.6	213	55.7	13	22	.1	22	0	.0
72684	.2	100	.1	80	15.3	175*	60.9	3	3	.2	2	0	.0
72685	.2	0	.2	95	8.8	101*	42.0	5	19	.0	0	0	.0
72686	.7	0	.2	86	19.3	222	55.8	12	10	.3	23	0	.0
72687	.5	100	.5	94	9.2	105*	13.1	7	21	.3	23	0	.0
	3.9	100	1.4	86	18.5	178	57.7	5	17	1.8	16	0	.0

FAYETTEVILLE

ZIPCODE	1	2	3	4	5	6	7	8	9	10	11	12	13
72701	47.1	95	17.1	55	21.7	308	84.5	6	9	22.6	8	2	.3
72711	.2	0		81	18.3	377	55.3	10	10	.8	0	0	.0
72712	16.6	98	6.5	77	23.0	275	84.5	7	21	7.9	20	1	.2
72717	.8	0	.3	85	20.9	468	83.5	3	15	.0	0	0	.0
72718	.5	97	.2	76	24.0	295	56.6	6	9	.3	7	0	.0
72719	.4	93	.2	75	18.6	173	49.3	5	16	.2	17	0	.9
72721	.4	100	.1	77	12.9	148*	63.6	10	13	.2	7	0	.0
72722	.7	92	.7	78	19.5	228	44.4	7	8	.9	8	0	.0
72727	2.0	99	.7	85	19.3	152	44.0	7	12	1.4	12	0	.0
72728	2.7	0		74	14.7	232	41.5	3	22	.0	0	0	.0
72729	.3	0	.1	65	12.0	311	18.0	4	8	.1	0	0	.0
72730	2.3	100	.7	81	22.6	314	64.4	8	18	.7	7	0	.0
72732	2.1	0	.8	88	20.0	271	75.7	8	14	.8	14	0	.0
72734	4.1	98	1.4	78	18.6	251	50.2	8	16	2.0	15	0	.0
72736	3.5	98	1.3	82	17.9	187	55.4	7	16	1.7	16	1	.6
72737	.3	100	.1	70	24.1	242	62.8	7		.1	5	0	.0

*=Estimated **1.0=883 lbs per person; 100++ indicates per capita toxic waste generation > than 100 times the U.S. average of 883 lbs per capita.

ZIP CODE MEASURES OF SIZE, LEVELS OF AFFLUENCE AND QUALITY OF LIFE

1=Population (th.); 2= % White; 3=Households (th.); 4=% Owner Occupied; 5=Mean Income Per Household (th.$); 6=Mean Monthly Rent ($)*; 7=Mean Home Value (th.$)*;
8=% under 5; 9=% 65 and over; 10=White Males (th.); 11=% White Males, 65+; 12=# Toxic Waste Sites; 13=Toxic Waste Relative to US(883 lbs.per capita)**.

ARKANSAS

ZIP CODE	1	2	3	4	5	6	7	8	9	10	11	12	13
FAYETTEVILLE													
72738	1.5	100	.5	87	17.5	101	51.5	6	13	.8	13	0	.0
72739	.5	100	.2	80	16.3	375	65.8	6	27	.3	23	0	.0
72740	6.4	98	2.3	81	16.7	206	51.1	8	18	3.1	17	0	.1
72741	.1	100	.1	66	15.0	261	44.3	4	21	.1	17	0	.4
72742	.6	0	.1	97	11.1	128*	41.5	15	8	.0	8	0	.0
72744	3.8	98	1.3	78	19.4	251	53.6	8	15	1.8	16	0	.0
72745	4.1	97	1.4	73	23.1	282	68.2	8	9	2.1	10	0	2.2
72747	.3	0	.1	64	15.7	239	44.0	9	14	.0	0	0	.0
72751	2.4	99	.9	85	20.1	273	58.0	7	15	1.2	13	0	.0
72752	.6	0	.2	86	11.6	170	38.7	5	11	.0	0	0	.0
72753	4.2	98	1.5	82	20.5	254	55.7	7	14	2.1	12	0	.0
72756	26.8	98	10.0	76	23.7	300	84.0	7	16	12.7	15	1	.3
72760	.6	0	.3	76	12.4	165	49.5	3	20	.0	0	0	.0
72761	11.5	96	4.0	69	22.7	241	68.4	8	15	5.4	13	1	.0
72764	34.0	98	12.0	72	23.2	288	71.9	8	11	16.3	9	1	.4
72768	1.0	0	.4	79	13.2	139	36.1	7	21	.0	0	0	.1
72769	.7	0	.1	65	17.0	243	50.2	10	16	.0	0	0	.0
72770	.3	0	.1	75	26.1	201	86.4	8	9	.0	0	0	.0
72773	.7	0	.3	88	19.2	203	32.3	10	8	.0	0	0	.0
72774	4.3	99	1.5	87	18.6	267	51.0	7	10	2.2	10	0	.0
72776	.3	100	.1	82	14.1	162*	65.6	6	28	.1	31	0	.0
RUSSELLVILLE													
72801	23.7	96	8.4	66	23.0	259	74.5	7	12	11.1	9	4	.5
72820	1.3	0	.5	80	15.7	281	34.2	4	13	.3			.5
72821	1.3	0	.5	83	16.7	186	40.1	6	14				.0
72823	5.9	95	2.1	80	18.3	244	46.0	7	14	2.8	12		.0
72824	1.4	96	.5	69	17.7	233	43.8	5	18	.7	18		.0
72826	.2	100	.1	75	11.5	80	47.7	13	13	.1	8		.0
72827	.2	100	.1	59	15.3	306	21.9	4	30	.1	31		.0
72828	.2	100	.1	72	9.8	98	39.5	5	27	.1	30		.0
72829	.2	100	.1	72	15.4	225	30.4	4	16	.1	19		.0
72830	9.6	96	3.6	71	20.4	217	55.1	8	19	4.4	16	2	.8
72832	.9	99	.4	67	14.1	193	33.3	7	20	.5	17		.0
72833	3.2	98	1.2	76	18.7	203	50.1	4	19	1.5	17		.0
72834	7.2	96	2.6	72	18.4	262	57.8	7	15	3.3	13	1	.1
72835	.6	100	.1	87	16.5	158	62.0	6	9	.3	11		.0
72837	4.7	98	1.6	86	18.8	212	49.9	6	13	2.4	13		.0
72838	.2	0	.1	83	11.5	110	37.9	9	28	.0	0		.0
72839	.2	100	.1	83	14.8	131	39.8	6	26	.1	29		.1
72840	1.8	99	.6	87	15.9	311	39.0	6	14	.8	14		.0
72841	.2	100	.1	88	27.4	315*	22.9	4	16	.1	18		.0
72842	2.1	100	.4	85	14.9	203	35.1	8	13	.6	13		.0
72843	2.1	98	.9	87	18.6	193	43.0	10	10	1.0	8		.0
72845	.5	100	.7	83	21.4	236	63.6	6	12	.3	13		.5
72846	2.7	99	.9	84	18.6	219	43.9	8	14	1.4	14		.1
72847	1.8	100	.6	80	16.2	214	53.8	7	14	.8	14		.0
72851	.4	100	.2	92	22.6	259*	45.6	4	13	.2	10		.0
72852	.2	100	.1	80	12.0	225	26.8	8	23	.1	33		.0
72853	1.9	100	.7	74	16.2	165	39.9	6	17	.9	15		.0

ARKANSAS

ZIP CODE	1	2	3	4	5	6	7	8	9	10	11	12	13
RUSSELLVILLE													
72854	.4	100	.2	75	13.5	101	84.2	5	15	.2	13	0	.0
72855	6.8	96	2.5	79	17.2	199	47.9	7	20	3.1	18	0	2.0
72856	.5	100		85	14.2	203	23.4	5	20	.3	20	0	.0
72857	1.7	99	.6	80	15.6	161	40.3	8	19	.9	17	0	.0
72858	1.2	0	.4	77	23.5	256	58.7	9	9	.0	9	1	.0
72860	.4	100	.1	90	16.3	165	23.5	11	14	.2	16	0	.0
72861	.3	100	.1	82	10.9	126*	22.3	6	11	.1	14	0	.0
72863	1.6	97	.5	84	20.3	170	47.0	5	9	.8	8	0	.0
72865	1.2	98	.3	89	17.5	217	46.9	5	14	.8	12	0	.0
FORT SMITH													
72901	25.1	89	10.3	55	20.2	245	56.3	7	17	10.2	13	4	2.9
72903	27.4	96	10.3	64	34.2	326	96.5	8	9	12.9	8	2	.0
72904	19.8	83	7.4	66	18.5	228	46.9	8	15	7.7	13	0	.0
72915	.5	100	.1	100	47.4	544*	132.8	9	1	.2	0	0	.0
72916	1.9	99	.6	89	23.7	239	62.0	9	10	1.0	9	0	.0
72921	7.5	97	2.6	77	20.6	253	59.1	9	12	3.6	10	0	.1
72922	.5	0		79	15.5	195	26.5	10	14	.0	14	0	.0
72923	3.8	94	1.3	76	21.6	315	59.6	10	6	1.7	6	0	.0
72926	.5	0	.2	97	17.1	197*	30.2	1	19	.0	0	0	.0
72927	7.4	99	2.5	76	17.2	198	49.6	8	18	3.5	15	1	.0
72928	.6	100	.2	70	18.5	199	36.5	10	15	.3	14	0	.0
72932	.5	0		72	19.9	198	33.0	6	7	.0	0	0	.0
72933	3.7	99	1.3	82	19.0	225	48.8	7	14	1.7	14	0	.1
72934	.7	86	.2	85	15.1	183	27.4	8	6	.3	5	0	.0
72935	.8	0	.3	84	21.4	166	61.0	5	13	.0	10	0	.0
72936	6.1	99	2.1	83	22.4	223	60.3	7	12	3.0	12	0	.0
72937	2.0	98	.7	80	23.3	259	49.1	8	13	.9	13	0	.0
72938	1.0	98	.3	85	16.6	199	31.2	4	23	.3	14	0	.0
72940	1.6	98	.6	86	16.7	168	42.2	6	15	.9	13	0	.0
72941	3.1	99	1.1	86	24.7	215	53.2	8	9	1.5	8	0	.1
72943	1.8	99	.7	82	15.9	167	33.3	7	18	.9	9	0	.0
72944	2.2	96	.8	79	18.1	207	37.1	5	16	1.1	16	0	.8
72945	.5	93	.2	79	17.1	188	34.4	14	15	.2	17	1	.0
72946	2.6	96	1.0	84	17.4	204	45.1	7	15	1.3	14	0	.0
72947	3.5	98	1.2	82	17.6	190	44.8	8	13	1.7	12	0	.1
72948	.6	88	.2	72	16.9	312	29.9	9	8	.2	3	0	.0
72949	8.5	95	3.1	75	17.3	215	53.2	6	17	4.0	15	0	.0
72950	.5	0	.2	90	11.7	129	39.7	9	26	.0	0	0	.0
72951	.8	0	.3	87	19.6	249	44.0	7	16	.0	0	0	.0
72952	2.0	97	.7	89	18.8	201	46.3	8	11	1.0	9	0	.0
72955	.4	0	.1	100	19.4	223*	50.4	6	14	.8	14	0	.0
72956	19.1	95	6.5	75	21.2	262	56.8	9	12	9.0	10	4	.6
72958	6.6	99	2.5	79	16.2	191	48.7	7	15	3.2	14	0	.6
72959	1.9	97	.6	84	15.9	191	41.8	11	11	.9	10	0	.0
POTEAU													
74937	.1	59		88	9.5	109*	17.5	0	36	.0	62	0	.0
TEXARKANA													
75501	2.0	94	.6	74	23.9	212	69.0	10	6	.9	6	3	.9
75502	29.4	74	10.7	69	20.4	240	54.9	8	14	10.3	12	2	.3

*=Estimated **1.0=883 lbs per person; 100++ indicates per capita toxic waste generation > than 100 times the U.S. average of 883 lbs per capita.

ZIP CODE MEASURES OF SIZE, LEVELS OF AFFLUENCE AND QUALITY OF LIFE

1=Population (th.); 2= % White; 3=Households (th.); 4=% Owner Occupied; 5=Mean Income Per Household ($); 6=Mean Monthly Rent ($); 7=Mean Home Value (th.$); 8=% under 5; 9=% 65 and over; 10=White Males (th.); 11=% White Males, 65+; 12=# Toxic Waste Sites; 13=Toxic Waste Relative to US(883 lbs.per capita)**.

ARKANSAS

ZIPCODE	1	2	3	4	5	6	7	8	9	10	11	12	13
TEXARKANA													
75556	.8	0	.3	91	16.5	257	32.6	3	12	.0	0	0	.0

CALIFORNIA

ZIPCODE	1	2	3	4	5	6	7	8	9	10	11	12	13
RENO													
89402	.1	100	.1	61	18.5	537	135.2	0	0	.1	0	0	.0
89439	.2	100	.1	88	35.2	405*	214.4	4	12	.1	17	0	.0
89448	.5	93	.2	29	24.5	509	168.5	9	1	.2	0	0	.0
89449	.8	96	.3	31	19.9	448	149.8	8	4	.4	4	0	.0
LOS ANGELES													
90001	44.2	32	12.2	37	16.2	283	66.7	13	7	6.9	4	4	1.3
90002	34.2	8	10.0	44	15.6	293	65.4	11	9	1.4	6	0	.0
90003	43.5	9	14.3	36	14.5	300	66.1	11	9	1.9	9	0	.3
90004	48.1	56	20.8	21	24.8	364	257.2	7	13	12.9	14	1	.0
90005	30.4	46	13.6	7	19.7	336	280.2	7	14	6.2	18	0	.0
90006	55.1	40	19.2	10	16.5	299	119.7	10	9	10.8	9	0	.0
90007	41.7	42	11.3	13	15.1	293	103.9	9	5	9.4	2	0	.1
90008	30.2	6	13.7	35	24.9	376	182.6	6	11	.7	40	0	.0
90010	.3	78	.2	0	16.8	329	59.7*	5	44	.1	38	0	1.0
90011	68.2	16	20.6	26	14.1	263	64.5	12	11	5.6	2	0	.2
90012	23.2	21	5.7	9	18.1	328	121.8	6	8	3.3	7	2	1.5
90013	6.1	47	2.2	0	8.9	174	31.5*	4	13	2.4	20	0	1.4
90014	2.7	49	1.8	1	6.9	175	24.4*	2	28	1.1	34	0	1.6
90015	18.0	35	5.8	3	13.5	243	103.5	12	6	3.3	9	1	.8
90016	39.6	10	16.1	38	20.6	344	108.7	7	11	1.9	17	0	.2
90017	20.1	55	8.6	1	13.0	221	107.5	9	12	6.4	17	0	2.0
90018	37.9	10	15.0	31	17.4	302	96.0	8	14	1.8	12	0	.0
90019	55.6	21	22.5	29	22.4	361	155.6	8	12	5.5	18	0	.1
90020	25.1	55	14.5	8	23.2	411	370.4	4	13	6.5	15	0	.0
90021	4.6	25	.8	3	10.3	183	51.1	5	4	.9	4	2	16.6
90022	59.3	52	16.6	40	19.5	315	103.0	11	9	14.7	11	2	1.0
90023	41.9	49	16.3	31	19.1	307	90.7	12	8	10.0	9	11	5.5
90024	38.8	90	16.3	43	60.7	618	405.0	5	10	15.4	11	0	.0
90025	33.6	80	18.3	19	28.5	531	288.6	3	14	12.1	12	2	.3
90026	65.9	44	23.3	24	20.8	326	136.7	9	10	14.3	11	0	.0
90027	43.1	78	20.9	23	28.4	390	287.9	4	18	16.1	16	0	.1
90028	25.9	75	14.2	5	16.0	343	163.0	5	14	10.5	12	0	.0
90029	34.0	60	12.9	12	17.7	338	148.0	8	11	9.8	10	0	.0
90031	34.9	49	9.9	33	19.5	312	109.0	10	9	8.4	8	1	1.0
90032	39.7	50	11.2	53	22.9	351	107.5	10	9	8.9	7	1	.1
90033	49.1	44	12.8	18	16.8	278	88.2	11	8	10.6	7	1	.4
90034	45.4	71	22.0	22	27.3	497	225.3	5	10	15.4	11	0	.4
90035	24.8	78	11.7	36	31.1	518	261.3	4	29	8.2	32	0	.4
90036	29.7	87	16.2	20	26.9	466	280.4	3	33	11.0	28	0	.4
90037	46.0	15	15.9	27	15.0	288	78.4	10	10	3.6	5	0	.3
90038	25.1	63	11.1	11	16.9	343	158.1	7	9	8.2	11	0	.1
90039	27.1	65	11.1	47	29.2	421	177.3	6	14	8.7	14	1	4.3
90040	8.2	74	2.3	50	23.2	338	106.2	11	7	3.0	8	8	22.5
90041	21.7	80	8.1	57	27.6	386	154.2	5	15	8.1	13	1	.0
90042	45.9	62	16.3	46	22.5	363	117.5	9	11	13.8	11	1	.0
90043	44.0	11	16.2	58	25.6	363	137.7	7	9	2.1	28	0	.1
90044	71.8	9	23.9	35	17.8	328	85.7	11	6	3.2	12	1	.0
90045	34.2	90	13.4	62	35.9	493	223.9	5	11	14.7	9	1	1.6
90046	44.6	92	24.8	22	29.4	472	310.8	2	22	20.2	18	0	.2

*=Estimated **1.0=883 lbs per person; 100++ indicates per capita toxic waste generation > than 100 times the U.S. average of 883 lbs per capita.

ZIP CODE MEASURES OF SIZE, LEVELS OF AFFLUENCE AND QUALITY OF LIFE

1=Population (th.); 2= % White; 3=Households (th.); 4=% Owner Occupied; 5=Mean Income Per Household (th.$); 6=Mean Monthly Rent ($)*; 7=Mean Home Value (th.$)*; 8=% under 5; 9=% 65 and over; 10=% White Males, 65+; 11=% White Males, 65+; 12=# Toxic Waste Sites; 13=Toxic Waste Relative to US(883 lbs.per capita)**.

CALIFORNIA

LOS ANGELES

ZIPCODE	1	2	3	4	5	6	7	8	9	10	11	12	13
90047	46.8	4	15.9	65	24.1	364	102.7	7	7	.9	32	1	.1
90048	22.6	93	11.8	30	29.2	535	270.2	2	32	9.2	28	0	.1
90049	35.3	94	15.9	49	65.3	646	415.4	3	13	15.2	13	1	.0
90056	8.3	53	3.4	68	53.7	533	315.3	4	14	2.1	22	1	.0
90057	30.7	52	13.7	4	15.8	309	118.2	8	13	8.1	17	0	.0
90058	3.6	22	1.0	13	11.7	221	65.3	14	6	.4	10	6	35.7
90059	31.6	5	8.9	45	15.9	274	70.6	12	8	.7	3	0	.2
90061	20.5	8	5.9	49	19.3	315	76.6	10	7	.8	10	0	.2
90062	25.1	5	9.2	46	18.1	322	83.7	11	8	.5	16	0	1.7
90063	51.5	45	12.4	41	20.0	310	88.3	11	8	11.1	8	2	.6
90064	24.0	82	10.2	58	38.6	509	295.9	5	16	9.1	16	0	.9
90065	39.7	59	11.1	54	27.3	358	142.4	9	11	9.1	9	0	.2
90066	51.9	79	21.7	44	30.2	469	240.8	6	10	19.8	9	0	.2
90067	1.1	96	.8	75	85.3	763	303.9*	1	38	.5	32	0	16.9
90068	22.9	87	12.4	42	41.0	472	316.1	3	12	11.0	10	3	.0
90069	20.6	91	13.2	25	41.1	532	366.6	1	17	10.1	14	0	.6

INGELWOOD

ZIPCODE	1	2	3	4	5	6	7	8	9	10	11	12	13
90201	77.9	74	23.4	27	19.1	366	112.6	13	7	28.0	7	0	.2
90210	21.6	93	8.7	72	113.2	699	424.8	3	18	9.4	19	0	.0
90211	6.8	95	3.3	33	35.7	635	389.9	2	21	2.7	18	0	.0
90212	11.2	96	5.4	26	46.6	641	411.4	2	22	4.4	19	0	.0
90220	42.4	9	11.4	60	23.4	343	79.4	10	4	2.0	8	1	1.0
90221	41.3	11	11.2	58	22.2	362	87.4	11	3	2.1	11	2	1.5
90222	25.6	9	6.6	59	20.0	325	73.8	10	6	1.1	5	1	.3
90230	45.9	71	18.0	54	33.1	519	211.4	6	9	15.8	9	2	1.1
90240	19.9	92	7.3	71	37.9	450	191.4	5	11	8.9	11	1	.7
90241	31.1	92	13.4	47	31.8	437	179.7	5	13	13.6	11	0	1.1
90242	31.6	88	12.0	49	27.9	439	143.4	7	10	13.7	7	0	.1
90245	13.7	95	6.0	41	34.2	506	231.1	5	8	6.4	7	2	21.4
90247	36.4	42	13.7	44	27.3	407	139.5	7	10	7.6	13	5	2.3
90248	9.6	49	4.9	74	31.5	428	140.6	4	9	2.3	11	2	3.8
90249	25.0	49	9.1	59	28.8	438	148.2	8	8	6.1	11	0	.0
90250	61.3	77	25.0	36	27.1	436	156.6	7	8	23.4	8	0	2.8
90254	18.2	94	9.2	35	35.5	588	280.1	3	6	9.2	4	0	.0
90255	58.5	74	18.8	32	19.4	319	110.0	12	9	21.0	9	1	.8
90260	25.5	79	8.7	41	27.5	483	148.7	9	6	10.0	6	0	.0
90262	49.3	39	14.2	51	21.7	369	102.0	12	7	9.2	12	0	1.0
90265	16.5	95	6.1	70	61.7	703	408.6	4	6	7.9	6	1	.0
90266	32.7	96	13.9	59	43.8	646	297.0	4	16	16.2	5	0	3.7
90270	22.0	65	6.6	33	20.0	326	103.2	13	7	7.1	7	0	.1
90272	21.8	95	8.4	80	69.4	696	399.9	4	11	10.0	11	0	.0
90274	62.9	90	20.7	85	72.3	744	391.2	4	5	27.7	5	1	.0
90277	33.0	92	15.7	40	34.9	596	263.8	4	10	15.2	8	1	.0
90278	33.8	90	13.1	44	33.2	593	189.9	6	5	15.3	4	0	1.1
90280	67.6	81	23.1	51	22.7	353	113.2	11	11	26.0	10	4	1.9
90290	4.1	95	1.7	76	48.2	625	296.1	6	8	2.1	8	0	.0
90291	55.1	82	28.2	27	35.9	572	253.3	4	8	23.5	7	3	.1

INGELWOOD

ZIPCODE	1	2	3	4	5	6	7	8	9	10	11	12	13
90301	29.3	44	12.1	24	22.0	419	128.9	9	11	6.2	16	1	.3

CALIFORNIA

INGELWOOD

ZIPCODE	1	2	3	4	5	6	7	8	9	10	11	12	13
90302	22.3	33	9.9	26	22.7	453	128.6	9	8	3.5	14	0	.1
90303	27.8	16	9.3	41	24.5	418	130.1	10	4	2.3	12	0	.0
90304	23.9	51	7.3	33	22.3	395	121.8	11	4	6.0	7	0	.0
90305	11.8	20	4.8	67	29.4	381	139.4	5	14	1.0	39	0	.0

SANTA MONICA

ZIPCODE	1	2	3	4	5	6	7	8	9	10	11	12	13
90401	5.6	90	3.6	5	19.5	413	324.9	2	23	2.4	16	0	1.1
90402	12.9	95	5.5	61	59.5	648	409.8	3	18	5.9	15	0	.0
90403	23.7	94	13.3	15	30.8	533	376.5	2	21	9.4	17	0	.0
90404	21.6	73	8.9	16	23.1	470	224.6	6	15	7.1	11	1	.8
90405	27.1	87	13.8	26	27.7	468	270.1	4	11	11.7	10	1	2.2

TORRANCE

ZIPCODE	1	2	3	4	5	6	7	8	9	10	11	12	13
90501	32.8	75	12.0	46	29.0	435	190.2	8	8	12.1	7	0	3.4
90502	13.9	66	4.4	66	31.3	447	154.9	7	10	4.4	9	1	1.0
90503	36.5	89	14.0	50	35.5	560	227.3	8	8	15.8	6	3	2.7
90504	30.9	76	11.2	63	35.9	516	185.4	5	7	11.5	6	1	.0
90505	34.6	89	13.2	57	38.7	566	255.6	9	9	14.9	7	0	.6

WHITTIER

ZIPCODE	1	2	3	4	5	6	7	8	9	10	11	12	13
90601	32.7	83	11.8	67	37.9	432	192.8	6	10	13.0	9	1	.5
90602	17.9	86	7.7	37	26.2	395	164.5	8	14	7.2	12	3	.6
90603	20.2	94	7.0	83	43.9	506	196.8	5	11	9.1	10	0	.0
90604	33.3	88	11.1	67	31.7	465	141.4	7	8	14.5	5	0	.0
90605	31.5	85	9.8	71	32.5	484	146.4	9	8	13.0	7	0	.0
90606	25.8	75	8.1	74	27.4	429	121.5	9	10	9.4	12	2	.3
90620	40.8	89	12.6	73	35.5	581	149.2	6	10	18.0	12	1	.0
90621	23.4	83	8.7	40	30.1	480	187.8	9	9	9.5	5	0	1.4
90623	15.5	82	4.7	76	43.8	575	216.5	7	6	6.3	2	0	.0
90630	44.1	89	13.8	72	39.1	566	195.3	6	4	19.1	3	0	.0
90631	49.7	89	17.9	61	34.5	465	184.7	7	8	21.6	5	1	.0
90638	40.2	91	17.2	84	37.6	544	157.3	6	8	18.0	5	2	.9
90640	52.9	61	17.8	51	28.5	415	168.5	9	11	14.8	12	2	.8
90660	85.2	79	25.2	68	28.2	469	120.0	9	6	32.8	5	2	.5
90670	53.5	71	15.4	71	27.4	407	118.0	9	7	18.5	7	1	15.6
90680	13.6	74	3.9	71	28.4	429	118.5	8	6	4.9	5	19	.3

LONG BEACH

ZIPCODE	1	2	3	4	5	6	7	8	9	10	11	12	13
90701	67.7	69	19.1	81	40.3	573	200.0	8	4	23.2	4	3	.1
90704	2.3	89	1.0	30	30.1	376	230.4	5	14	1.0	12	1	.9
90706	53.4	87	21.7	42	25.4	428	142.8	8	11	22.5	10	0	.2
90710	19.4	64	6.8	63	33.5	411	188.6	8	8	6.0	9	1	3.7
90712	28.9	91	10.6	75	33.9	522	153.1	6	10	12.7	9	0	.1
90713	28.2	94	9.6	82	34.1	611	144.8	6	8	12.9	7	0	.0
90715	17.4	77	5.5	59	30.2	522	138.6	9	9	6.7	3	0	.0
90716	10.5	60	3.1	47	22.3	400	102.7	12	5	3.1	7	0	.0
90717	20.2	86	8.4	45	27.9	459	196.9	7	10	8.2	9	0	.1
90720	22.0	94	7.6	68	41.3	569	226.2	5	8	10.1	7	0	.1
90723	35.6	72	11.0	45	22.9	395	110.4	12	8	12.5	8	2	.9
90731	51.9	75	20.2	37	24.9	396	169.9	8	11	19.6	11	2	.2
90732	25.1	87	8.4	74	40.9	510	236.8	6	11	10.5	9	1	.4
90740	23.6	65	12.5	74	27.8	560	237.4	2	38	9.8	28	2	.4

*=Estimated **1.0=883 lbs per person; 100++ indicates per capita toxic waste generation > than 100 times the U.S. average of 883 lbs per capita.

ZIP CODE MEASURES OF SIZE, LEVELS OF AFFLUENCE AND QUALITY OF LIFE

1=Population (th.); 2= % White; 3=Households (th.); 4=% Owner Occupied; 5=Mean Income Per Household (th.$); 6=Mean Monthly Rent ($); 7=Mean Home Value (th.$);
8=% under 5; 9=% 65 and over; 10=% White Males (th.); 11=% White Males, 65+; 12=# Toxic Waste Sites; 13=Toxic Waste Relative to US(883 lbs.per capital)**.

CALIFORNIA

ZIPCODE	1	2	3	4	5	6	7	8	9	10	11	12	13
LONG BEACH													
90742	1.4	92	.6	38	37.8	513	373.2	1	7	.8	9	0	.0
90743	.4	0	.2	50	62.4	757	393.8	5	2	.0	0	0	.0
90744	39.3	52	12.0	44	23.9	333	118.9	11	7	10.5	8	16	9.3
90745	46.8	54	13.1	74	32.7	479	143.0	7	6	12.6	7	6	1.2
90746	27.6	17	7.5	91	38.8	593	151.8	6	3	2.4	7	2	.0
LONG BEACH													
90802	28.5	84	17.1	20	16.0	316	140.5	4	30	11.6	24	0	2.6
90803	29.6	96	16.3	41	36.0	511	281.0	2	16	13.8	13	0	.0
90804	25.3	80	11.6	21	20.0	400	137.2	7	13	9.4	10	0	1.8
90805	62.7	73	24.8	46	23.9	403	117.9	9	12	22.1	12	2	.6
90806	33.5	55	13.7	35	21.1	358	124.0	9	14	8.7	17	0	.0
90807	26.5	91	12.0	58	33.7	466	187.5	5	23	11.0	19	1	2.6
90808	39.8	94	14.4	82	37.8	548	167.8	5	10	18.4	10	2	.0
90810	31.9	43	10.0	54	24.7	351	111.5	11	8	6.7	10	5	3.9
90813	40.4	47	15.0	14	14.5	313	98.5	13	10	9.6	12	1	1.2
90814	15.3	93	8.1	30	26.1	473	210.5	4	16	6.5	12	1	1.0
90815	37.3	92	13.9	73	38.1	580	177.2	5	11	16.5	11	0	.0
PASADENA													
91101	35.6	44	12.1	78	33.7	441	163.1	7	10	7.5	14	0	.2
91103	23.1	30	7.4	51	27.3	362	174.6	9	12	3.4	14	1	.1
91104	33.8	63	12.2	56	25.2	409	137.8	9	14	10.1	14	0	.0
91105	11.1	90	4.7	72	57.9	531	292.7	4	21	4.7	19	1	.8
91106	20.2	77	9.1	32	29.7	447	235.5	6	16	7.3	13	0	.0
91107	29.2	87	11.8	64	36.9	443	211.5	5	16	12.0	14	0	.4
91108	13.6	92	4.5	95	86.0	835	366.9	4	14	6.0	13	0	.0
GLENDALE													
91201	16.6	85	6.6	46	27.8	463	193.5	5	14	6.7	13	2	3.6
91202	16.5	95	7.5	53	34.3	495	251.2	4	21	6.9	18	0	.0
91203	8.1	89	3.8	22	21.8	450	147.5	6	15	3.2	12	0	2.9
91204	11.9	80	4.6	17	20.0	402	137.4	8	14	4.5	11	0	1.2
91205	26.9	82	12.1	21	21.0	416	159.7	6	16	10.1	13	0	.0
91206	21.7	89	10.3	42	32.4	459	270.8	4	19	8.5	15	0	.0
91207	8.5	93	3.5	65	42.8	500	306.0	3	19	3.6	17	0	.0
91208	12.7	95	5.2	71	42.1	560	261.5	5	17	5.7	15	0	.0
91214	27.7	95	9.9	76	38.4	559	192.0	6	8	13.1	7	0	.1
VAN NUYS													
91301	17.4	95	5.5	84	44.1	689	248.7	7	3	8.2	3	1	.0
91302	11.8	97	3.7	91	69.1	757	370.7	3	6	5.6	5	0	.1

CALIFORNIA

ZIPCODE	1	2	3	4	5	6	7	8	9	10	11	12	13
VAN NUYS													
91303	18.3	86	8.6	28	26.4	493	158.2	6	15	7.6	12	0	.6
91304	35.3	90	13.0	53	34.6	502	213.1	6	8	15.5	6	1	.7
91306	34.0	89	12.2	60	33.8	527	181.8	7	5	15.1	5	0	.0
91307	27.5	93	8.3	87	45.7	814	217.4	5	5	12.7	4	0	.0
91310	1.6	87	.5	73	31.7	487	146.9	4	11	.7	11	0	.0
91311	29.8	91	10.2	75	43.9	588	265.8	6	6	13.4	5	0	2.6
91316	23.9	95	10.6	49	45.3	578	296.5	4	15	10.8	14	0	.0
91320	24.9	94	.2	78	36.3	621	194.6	7	7	11.4	5	0	1.8
91321	16.5	92	6.2	70	32.5	447	195.2	6	13	7.4	12	2	.6
91322	.2	77	.1	73	37.8	414	257.3	7	13	.1	0	0	.0
91324	23.9	89	8.4	59	41.0	532	250.3	6	6	10.5	5	0	2.6
91325	24.3	89	8.7	61	42.5	529	269.5	5	6	10.7	5	0	.0
91326	22.6	89	7.1	84	54.5	584	306.6	6	3	10.1	3	0	.0
91331	67.8	53	17.5	70	28.1	450	127.8	10	3	18.1	5	0	.3
91335	52.3	90	20.4	54	29.6	504	127.4	8	6	22.8	8	0	.3
91340	25.0	60	7.2	59	25.0	421	120.7	11	7	8.4	9	0	.4
91342	50.1	75	14.9	76	32.7	484	153.6	8	7	18.5	6	0	.7
91343	38.0	86	13.3	59	35.3	502	194.5	7	6	16.5	6	0	.2
91344	45.6	90	14.8	80	42.3	609	214.9	5	6	20.2	5	0	.0
91345	14.2	84	4.6	78	34.0	576	156.2	7	8	5.9	7	0	.0
91351	19.8	87	5.3	86	36.8	582	178.6	8	3	9.5	3	2	1.6
91352	24.9	94	7.9	85	36.6	585	173.2	9	5	11.8	4	3	.8
91354	33.4	76	10.6	66	31.2	444	148.9	9	7	13.0	7	2	.8
91355	18.5	94	5.6	85	45.4	677	220.4	9	3	8.8	8	2	.5
91356	29.4	95	11.1	57	49.1	548	355.9	5	7	13.5	6	0	.1
91360	53.5	95	17.3	73	40.6	588	225.9	7	6	25.0	5	0	.2
91361	18.9	95	6.5	76	52.8	652	349.9	4	8	8.9	8	0	.1
91362	1.6	96	.4	81	43.0	871	204.1	9	1	2.0	2	0	.8
91364	20.2	96	7.1	81	52.8	632	283.2	4	9	9.6	7	0	.7
91367	22.0	94	7.7	79	49.6	708	270.2	4	9	10.4	5	0	.2
VAN NUYS													
91401	28.9	87	12.5	41	30.3	462	220.4	6	12	11.9	11	0	.1
91402	33.1	83	13.9	37	25.4	447	154.6	7	13	12.9	11	1	2.3
91403	19.3	93	9.9	50	41.7	527	306.9	4	16	8.4	14	0	.0
91405	30.2	84	13.8	31	26.2	445	181.0	6	10	12.6	9	0	.3
91406	35.7	88	14.7	51	29.6	497	169.9	6	8	15.7	8	1	.1
91411	16.8	82	7.3	34	25.5	439	178.2	6	13	6.7	11	1	1.1
91423	27.4	95	13.2	41	39.1	543	283.1	3	18	12.1	16	0	.0
91436	15.0	95	5.1	88	79.8	634	372.9	4	10	7.0	10	0	.0
BURBANK													
91501	13.1	92	5.9	42	29.9	481	212.2	5	11	5.5	15	0	.0
91502	7.9	84	3.4	12	20.0	406	143.9	9	13	3.2	10	1	5.00
91504	20.2	92	7.6	64	35.3	470	213.6	6	10	9.0	9	1	2.00
91505	28.5	92	12.7	56	28.1	469	161.2	5	16	12.5	15	1	.0
NORTH HOLLYWOOD													
91601	23.4	84	11.0	30	23.0	415	167.6	7	12	9.4	10	1	.1
91602	14.0	93	7.6	33	35.9	463	271.1	3	16	6.1	14	0	.0
91604	23.2	95	11.5	55	46.5	521	306.2	3	16	10.8	15	0	.0

*=Estimated **1.0=883 lbs per person; 100++ indicates per capita toxic waste generation > than 100 times the U.S. average of 883 lbs per capita.

ZIP CODE MEASURES OF SIZE, LEVELS OF AFFLUENCE AND QUALITY OF LIFE

1=Population (th.); 2= % White; 3=Households (th.); 4=% Owner Occupied; 5=Mean Income Per Household (th.$); 6=Mean Monthly Rent ($)*; 7=Mean Home Value (th.$)*; 8=% under 5; 9=% 65 and over; 10=White Males, 65 and over; 11=% White Males; 12=# Toxic Waste Sites; 13=Toxic Waste Relative to US(883 lbs.per capita)**

CALIFORNIA

ZIP CODE	1	2	3	4	5	6	7	8	9	10	11	12	13
NORTH HOLLYWOOD													
91605	37.9	75	13.2	50	27.5	441	155.9	9	8	14.3	8	3	2.0
91606	31.1	83	12.9	40	25.3	434	152.8	6	12	12.4	12	0	.0
91607	22.6	95	11.0	36	30.6	487	235.9	3	19	9.7	16	0	.0
ALHAMBRA													
91701	27.6	91	8.3	91	40.6	571	179.7	10	4	12.6	4	1	1.0
91702	42.9	78	13.8	57	25.9	420	113.2	10	7	16.3	6	8	1.2
91706	53.4	73	14.8	63	23.8	411	105.4	12	6	19.0	6	4	2.0
91710	59.0	87	17.0	78	33.5	475	146.4	10	4	26.4	4	2	.0
91711	32.1	88	10.0	71	41.7	471	185.8	5	10	13.8	8	0	.1
91720	52.3	81	15.9	69	30.7	412	140.7	9	7	20.8	6	1	.0
91722	26.6	88	8.8	77	31.3	525	126.4	8	7	11.6	6	0	.4
91723	14.9	93	6.0	45	27.3	429	150.1	7	12	6.3	6	1	1.2
91724	22.3	92	7.3	83	40.8	395	195.8	5	6	10.1	6	0	.1
91730	24.6	85	7.8	77	31.9	471	133.1	12	5	10.4	4	2	.3
91731	21.9	66	7.1	42	22.0	374	113.4	11	9	7.0	10	1	1.7
91732	41.6	72	12.9	45	22.3	386	119.8	11	9	14.5	9	1	1.1
91733	36.2	64	9.6	46	22.2	373	109.4	13	6	11.8	7	1	1.1
91739	2.9	85	.9	84	34.1	511	129.5	11	6	1.3	6	0	.3
91740	46.8	94	15.6	77	35.1	486	170.3	7	8	21.5	6	0	.2
91744	65.9	70	17.1	76	28.8	424	112.0	9	4	22.4	4	1	1.2
91745	43.8	78	12.4	87	44.5	599	201.4	7	3	17.2	3	2	.8
91746	25.4	67	6.3	82	30.6	474	118.2	9	4	8.3	4	3	.4
91750	29.8	79	9.3	68	33.3	465	158.8	9	6	11.5	4	0	.5
91752	27.0	88	9.3	75	33.1	486	171.6	7	11	11.3	10	0	.5
91754	12.2	91	4.3	62	25.3	333	134.0	8	16	5.4	14	1	.3
91759	53.6	49	18.5	57	31.5	452	184.7	7	3	12.3	12	1	.3
91760	19.9	91	5.2	88	30.0	180	111.6	6	10	.0	0	0	.0
91761	45.8	78	13.4	86	36.4	525	170.6	13	5	18.1	4	5	.5
91762	18.1	92	7.2	69	28.0	405	134.0	9	12	8.1	6	2	.2
91763	22.8	82	7.3	57	28.7	394	119.5	9	6	9.2	6	2	.3
91764	30.2	83	10.1	64	26.2	431	112.4	10	11	12.1	8	0	.3
91765	27.4	84	8.2	90	45.1	390	107.1	9	8	12.1	8	0	.0
91766	39.6	63	11.9	54	21.9	660	203.6	9	11	12.3	6	1	1.1
91767	34.0	66	12.3	60	25.0	362	100.2	8	11	10.6	11	0	.8
91768	21.9	63	7.0	56	24.1	401	109.5	9	10	7.0	7	0	.0
91770	49.9	63	15.2	56	25.1	375	110.5	9	10	15.0	11	1	.9
91773	22.7	87	7.4	78	37.0	403	126.9	7	8	7.8	7	1	.2
91775	19.7	89	7.7	68	35.5	500	175.3	6	15	14.6	8	0	.0
91776	28.4	73	10.5	47	25.0	424	137.6	8	14	9.5	14	1	.1
91780	28.6	91	10.6	66	30.6	465	155.3	6	15	12.1	12	0	.1
91786	50.8	91	18.7	63	35.8	437	174.6	6	8	22.1	7	2	1.2
91789	19.4	81	5.6	88	41.1	596	194.4	9	7	7.8	3	1	1.0
91790	35.3	84	11.3	75	33.0	488	135.3	9	7	14.6	7	0	.0
91791	23.5	87	8.1	73	40.8	499	187.8	6	6	10.2	5	2	.0
91792	23.5	59	7.7	65	35.7	576	167.2	11	2	6.8	2	1	.0
ALHAMBRA													
91801	39.5	76	16.9	37	25.0	420	163.0	7	16	13.0	15	0	.0
91803	25.2	67	9.1	55	27.4	419	152.4	7	15	7.7	15	1	.4

CALIFORNIA

ZIP CODE	1	2	3	4	5	6	7	8	9	10	11	12	13
SAN DIEGO													
92001	6.9	95	2.6	69	31.4	399	234.5	6	14	3.2	12	0	.0
92002	12.7	88	3.9	86	48.9	644	264.9	6	5	5.5	5	0	.0
92003	1.1	81	.4	90	46.2	150	287.4	4	14	.5	18	0	.0
92004	1.9	97	.9	73	30.4	273	173.8	4	23	1.0	24	0	.0
92005	.7	92	.3	67	17.5	160	66.2	7	15	.4	16	0	.0
92006	1.6	87	.5	63	23.2	254	115.7	7	10	.7	9	0	.0
92007	9.2	94	3.6	58	31.8	598	222.2	6	8	4.4	7	0	.0
92008	34.7	89	13.1	64	35.0	469	226.1	6	12	15.3	11	3	.1
92010	45.1	87	18.3	52	26.5	397	162.5	6	14	18.9	12	0	.0
92011	59.0	76	19.9	59	25.8	433	143.4	8	8	22.3	9	3	.0
92014	13.4	94	5.1	62	45.6	612	340.7	4	7	6.5	7	0	.0
92016	1.3	89	.4	72	28.5	400	173.8	9	4	.7	2	0	.1
92017	.0	0	.0	76	21.0	45	213.7	8	15	.0	0	0	.0
92020	50.7	95	18.9	48	30.5	417	213.1	7	10	23.1	8	1	.3
92021	60.6	95	22.4	62	25.9	400	178.2	7	11	27.6	9	0	.0
92024	27.9	92	10.5	63	33.0	520	238.8	6	10	12.9	9	0	.0
92025	38.6	90	14.3	54	28.5	407	206.2	8	13	16.6	12	3	.3
92026	19.0	93	7.3	69	29.4	470	189.2	7	15	8.6	16	0	.0
92027	29.0	92	10.5	67	28.3	463	161.9	7	15	12.9	13	0	.2
92028	23.2	86	8.0	69	32.6	404	219.1	7	15	9.8	17	1	1.2
92031	.5	0	.1	88	21.8	420	120.3	13	8	.1	3	2	.8
92032	22.6	80	7.7	33	21.1	417	129.4	12	9	9.5	4	3	.4
92034	.7	86	.3	66	19.0	284	62.4	6	17	.4	19	0	.5
92035	4.9	96	1.6	86	35.3	377	221.4	7	5	2.5	4	1	.5
92036	2.6	93	1.0	73	37.2	347	161.3	7	14	1.2	16	0	.3
92040	37.5	95	15.1	60	51.9	561	371.7	8	16	17.0	14	0	.8
92041	30.5	95	10.1	78	30.6	437	168.5	5	8	14.4	7	1	.0
92045	60.4	95	24.5	60	31.2	443	190.0	6	5	27.2	4	3	.9
92048	20.7	86	7.2	65	26.5	437	135.1	8	13	8.6	12	0	.0
92050	.3	81	.1	44	18.8	499	92.4	11	10	.1	11	5	.2
92054	44.6	54	14.9	37	19.1	337	110.3	11	9	11.6	4	2	.5
92055	79.0	76	29.3	51	24.3	394	143.8	10	6	29.8	11	0	.3
92059	17.3	65	.8	1	21.6	366	148.8	3	7	9.0	3	0	1.1
92060	1.0	40	.1	61	30.2	314	68.8	13	7	.2	13	0	.8
92061	.1	0	.1	53	33.2	122	129.7	7	6	.1	11	0	.1
92062	1.4	74	.5	70	35.2	159	251.7	7	18	.5	19	0	.0
92063	1.3	97	.5	81	33.9	446	193.5	9	6	.7	8	1	.9
92064	.5	92	.2	86	21.2	400	180.0	4	13	.2	15	0	.0
92065	31.7	93	9.9	77	36.0	520	199.7	7	4	14.9	4	0	.0
92066	14.9	96	4.9	76	30.7	439	183.1	8	8	7.1	8	0	.0
92067	4.7	2	1.7	92	99.9	847	419.8	4	18	2.2	18	0	.0
92068	1.5	41	.5	70	23.8	432	214.9	2	15	.3	30	0	.3
92069	25.9	92	9.8	78	31.1	454	186.8	7	20	11.5	21	0	1.3
92070	1.1	68	.4	60	22.8	385	174.5	6	10	.3	12	0	.0
92071	37.8	95	12.5	73	28.1	483	140.8	6	10	17.6	8	0	.2
92075	15.1	52	3.9	42	29.1	307	132.8	10	7	5.3	9	0	.0
92077	42.0	84	13.9	72	29.4	465	153.2	8	7	17.5	6	0	.2

*=Estimated **1.0=883 lbs per person; 100++ indicates per capita toxic waste generation > than 100 times the U.S. average of 883 lbs per capita.

ZIP CODE MEASURES OF SIZE, LEVELS OF AFFLUENCE AND QUALITY OF LIFE

1=Population (th.); 2=% White; 3=Households (th.); 4=% Owner Occupied; 5=Mean Income Per Household (th.$); 6=Mean Monthly Rent ($); 7=Mean Home Value (th.$); 8=% under 5; 9=% 65 and over; 10=White Males; 11=% White Males, 65+; 12=# Toxic Waste Sites; 13=Toxic Waste Relative to US(883 lbs.per capita)**.

CALIFORNIA

ZIPCODE	1	2	3	4	5	6	7	8	9	10	11	12	13
SAN DIEGO													
92078	3.7	89	1.2	76	36.5	519	179.8	9	4	1.6	2	0	.0
92082	7.4	83	2.5	79	33.9	486	232.5	7	11	3.2	12	0	.0
92083	53.1	86	19.9	65	27.0	422	168.7	7	16	22.0	16	1	.0
92086	.5	89	.2	78	45.2	386	136.7	4	24	.3	29	0	.0
SAN DIEGO													
92101	14.4	81	8.3	4	12.5	253	153.7	3	23	7.3	21	2	5.4
92102	32.0	40	11.6	33	16.3	310	102.6	9	9	6.2	10	0	.0
92103	27.8	92	15.4	30	24.6	369	232.5	3	24	11.9	18	0	.2
92104	34.0	85	17.1	29	19.1	374	133.3	6	19	13.2	16	0	.0
92105	42.4	69	17.5	39	19.4	364	113.7	10	11	14.1	11	0	.0
92106	17.1	96	6.8	68	47.0	495	280.1	4	15	8.0	14	0	.1
92107	25.4	96	12.5	37	25.2	424	216.8	4	11	12.7	9	0	.0
92108	5.9	94	3.8	37	27.0	475	212.7	1	7	2.7	6	0	.0
92109	43.8	95	22.6	28	26.3	461	257.0	3	13	20.4	11	1	.0
92110	21.3	87	9.5	42	25.2	412	184.6	6	13	9.1	11	1	.3
92111	40.3	75	13.3	55	28.2	439	150.6	7	6	14.7	5	4	.2
92113	32.2	27	9.9	37	16.4	300	82.8	11	8	4.7	6	0	.5
92114	46.4	33	13.3	73	25.2	409	119.1	10	4	7.6	6	0	.0
92115	43.7	88	18.8	46	23.4	409	149.7	4	16	18.1	15	0	.0
92116	29.0	88	15.1	32	21.3	373	164.8	6	18	11.9	15	0	.3
92117	50.9	91	19.3	61	30.1	479	165.7	5	8	22.5	7	0	.0
92118	15.3	95	6.4	44	34.7	484	306.1	4	15	7.0	13	0	.0
92119	23.8	94	8.2	76	36.8	511	190.2	5	6	11.0	8	0	.0
92120	27.6	95	10.0	77	39.8	527	212.9	4	9	12.7	8	1	.3
92121	1.5	93	.8	31	25.5	557	91.0*	1	7	.7	7	4	23.4
92122	18.8	92	7.0	64	38.5	568	257.7	7	5	8.5	6	0	.0
92123	23.9	83	7.9	54	30.3	488	153.7	6	9	9.8	5	2	8.4
92124	23.8	94	6.7	50	35.3	470	248.2	3	10	9.6	4	1	.0
92126	37.4	76	11.6	66	31.1	601	160.8	10	3	14.3	2	1	.0
92127	5.3	93	1.8	68	35.9	581	217.2	6	8	2.3	8	1	1.1
92128	12.6	98	5.6	87	41.9	578	250.4	3	37	5.8	37	0	.1
92129	18.8	79	6.0	64	33.6	440	217.4	12	3	7.3	3	0	.0
92131	6.9	93	2.1	83	44.9	720	251.8	8	2	3.3	2	1	1.4
92135	2.1	70	.1	0	31.0	501	110.4*	1	0	1.3	0	1	.7
92145	22.5	58	6.8	68	27.7	433	135.6	10	5	6.7	5	0	.0
92145	3.5	73	.8	48	22.6	448	258.4	3	0	2.1	0	0	.0
92154	43.0	62	11.9	69	25.5	442	134.8	10	4	13.7	4	0	.0
PALM SPRINGS													
92201	28.7	61	9.3	59	26.8	336	118.5	10	10	8.6	11	1	.0
92220	15.1	74	5.8	69	21.1	317	89.7	8	19	5.2	20	0	.0
92222	.8	100	.	70	18.1	58	75.5	5	32	.1	26	0	.0
92223	12.8	90	4.9	73	23.6	332	106.7	6	21	5.5	20	0	.1
92225	13.0	75	4.2	61	22.8	323	84.7	9	11	4.9	11	1	.0
92227	18.1	52	5.6	54	27.0	291	98.3	10	8	4.5	11	5	.0
92230	1.2	92	.5	74	14.3	191	60.7	7	25	.6	24	0	.0
92231	15.6	38	4.0	52	21.1	332	85.1	9	6	2.9	8	0	.0
92233	3.3	52	.9	63	22.1	282	71.5	11	8	1.0	12	1	.0
92235	4.5	83	1.8	70	24.8	358	127.9	7	19	1.7	23	0	.0
92236	10.0	44	2.4	61	21.2	293	73.0	13	5	2.2	6	0	.0

CALIFORNIA

ZIPCODE	1	2	3	4	5	6	7	8	9	10	11	12	13
PALM SPRINGS													
92239	.5	100	.2	72	24.1	271	93.7	11	5	.2	5	0	.0
92240	11.0	95	5.1	71	20.3	326	100.5	6	31	5.0	31	0	.0
92241	2.6	90	.7	33	31.3	135	79.2	9	3	1.3	4	0	.0
92243	29.8	64	9.4	59	27.9	340	103.1	10	8	9.6	9	0	.2
92249	2.4	16	.5	86	24.4	397	65.1	9	5	2.2	9	0	.0
92250	7.1	65	2.1	64	29.3	326	103.8	10	8	2.2	10	1	.0
92251	5.2	71	1.6	66	30.9	332	83.3	8	8	1.9	10	0	.0
92252	4.3	93	4.3	79	17.7	340	71.2	5	31	1.9	31	0	.0
92253	3.7	92	1.4	67	34.3	544	136.8	12	9	1.8	10	0	.0
92254	2.3	54	.5	48	24.2	315	80.2	11	10	.7	17	1	.0
92255	2.2	96	.9	77	21.6	311	90.2	8	23	1.1	24	0	.0
92257	2.3	82	1.1	75	16.2	234	43.9	2	33	.9	33	0	.0
92258	.4	0	.2	82	14.9	365	71.5	0	40	.2	18	0	.0
92259	.5	92	.5	92	21.4	155	45.3	5	18	.2	18	0	.0
92260	17.9	93	8.0	71	41.4	422	199.2	5	21	7.8	23	0	.0
92262	39.8	88	18.1	62	32.0	426	194.8	4	23	16.3	24	1	.0
92266	.5	77	.1	85	13.2	117	64.9	9	9	.1	11	0	.0
92268	.2	100	.1	82	17.0	233	87.8	4	31	.1	38	0	.0
92270	6.1	96	2.9	82	55.6	487	250.0	2	26	2.8	28	0	.0
92272	1.0	39	.4	46	17.7	217	30.5	6	13	.2	27	0	.0
92273	1.1	71	.3	71	21.0	281	59.5	9	9	.4	11	0	.0
92274	8.1	61	2.2	68	22.4	267	84.0	8	10	2.4	14	1	.0
92276	1.9	89	.9	86	23.9	396	75.9	5	23	.8	27	0	.0
92277	10.9	88	4.5	66	19.0	319	72.8	8	14	4.9	14	0	.0
92278	7.9	72	1.0	1	18.2	334	64.8*	9	0	.2	4	0	.0
92281	2.0	43	.6	53	21.7	266	66.6	11	7	.4	12	0	.0
92282	2.2	0	.1	91	22.6	245	66.7	8	8	.0	0	0	.0
92283	2.2	56	.8	65	16.3	170	44.0	8	17	.6	30	1	.0
92284	14.6	97	6.4	79	20.6	381	94.7	5	29	6.6	29	0	.3
SAN BERNARDINO													
92301	2.3	83	.9	55	16.9	288	80.4	10	9	1.0	8	0	.0
92302	2.5	85	.2	74	16.4	375	55.3	8	14	.2	12	0	.0
92305	.5	87	.2	69	31.1	371	121.3	7	10	.2	16	0	.0
92306	1.0	96	.5	83	21.1	298	114.8	7	25	.5	25	0	.0
92307	19.1	94	6.9	75	28.3	372	124.0	7	11	9.0	10	1	.0
92308	.1	0	.1	69	19.2	658	109.1	4	14	.9	10	0	.0
92309	.3	93	.1	27	13.0	168	59.1	9	5	.2	0	0	.3
92311	28.8	77	9.7	64	26.8	324	92.1	9	7	11.2	6	4	.0
92314	4.3	98	1.7	71	26.3	466	149.0	6	10	2.1	10	0	.0
92315	5.9	98	2.3	65	26.2	369	165.0	7	10	2.9	10	1	.0
92316	9.1	86	2.9	75	25.9	359	101.7	9	11	3.8	10	1	.0
92317	2.6	93	.9	77	36.4	487	233.4	6	7	1.2	7	0	.0
92318	.2	59	.	76	23.5	186	59.1	8	9	.9	0	0	.0
92320	5.6	96	2.3	84	23.8	386	124.1	6	28	2.6	27	0	.0
92321	1.3	97	.5	63	33.7	556	168.6	7	7	.6	5	0	.0
92322	.4	100	.2	85	22.1	408	106.1	9	17	.2	17	0	.3
92324	38.9	75	13.4	68	27.3	338	102.8	9	8	14.3	8	2	.3
92325	6.3	96	2.4	74	27.8	409	136.1	8	8	3.0	8	0	.0

*=Estimated **1.0=883 lbs per person; 100++ indicates per capita toxic waste generation > than 100 times the U.S. average of 883 lbs per capita.

ZIP CODE MEASURES OF SIZE, LEVELS OF AFFLUENCE AND QUALITY OF LIFE

1=Population (th.); 2= % White; 3=Households (th.); 4=% Owner Occupied; 5=Mean Income Per Household (th.$); 6=Mean Monthly Rent ($)*; 7=Mean Home Value (th.$)*; 8=% under 5; 9=% 65 and over; 10=White Males (th.); 11=% White Males, 65+; 12=# Toxic Waste Sites; 13=Toxic Waste Relative to US(883 lbs.per capita)**.

CALIFORNIA

SAN BERNARDINO

ZIPCODE	1	2	3	4	5	6	7	8	9	10	11	12	13
92326	.1	100	.1	74	35.3	421	175.6	0	8	.0	0	0	.0
92327	.3	81	.1	52	25.6	223	84.6	9	4	.1	4	0	.0
92328	.7	0	.4	39	20.9	125	28.4	7	7	.0	0	0	.0
92329	.3	62		71	22.9	154	135.2	1	19	.1	10	0	3.8
92330	16.1	89	6.5	69	20.1	309	110.5	7	17	6.9	17	0	.0
92335	59.8	84	19.8	72	25.9	345	96.7	9	3	24.5	8	4	1.2
92339	.5	0	.2	74	24.2	457	125.4	3	4	.0	0	0	.0
92341	.4	100	.1	88	21.2	217	133.9	9	9	.2	9	0	.0
92342	.8	86	.3	69	31.4	543	153.5	4	17	.4	17	0	.0
92345	54.4	95	24.4	75	21.6	346	112.9	5	36	23.6	36	0	.0
92346	21.0	94	7.6	82	24.1	387	100.4	8	14	9.8	14	0	.0
92347	24.0	87	8.3	77	29.9	379	120.9	8	8	10.0	8	0	.0
92348	1.8	87	.5	76	26.4	254	78.4	8	8	.8	10	0	.0
92349	3.4	96	1.7	90	19.0	305	96.4	2	41	1.6	45	0	.0
92352	2.9	97	1.2	67	25.4	403	163.7	7	11	1.4	12	0	.1
92354	2.9	99	1.0	77	48.4	468	249.2	6	6	1.4	6	0	.0
92356	11.2	78	4.3	45	24.7	401	117.3	7	5	.3	7	0	23.7
92358	3.4	94	1.3	75	17.4	385	147.0	6	13	3.9	12	0	.2
92359	.5	0	.2	87	23.2	238	78.6	6	16	1.7	16	2	.0
92360	.3	89	.1	77	26.6	136	105.0	9	13	.3	15	0	.0
92361	1.0	98	.3	95	33.8	253	157.0	5	23	.0	0	0	.6
92362	1.2	95	.3	75	20.6	538	135.9	8	3	.4	1	0	.3
92363	2.9	86	1.3	64	24.3	363	140.8	5	13	.9	17	0	.0
92364	5.8	86	2.3	80	24.3	353	129.6	4	27	1.3	28	0	.0
92365	.1	100	.1	51	18.0	263	71.4	7	16	2.6	17	0	.0
92366	1.5	86	.5	76	25.1	194	64.1*	0	17	.1	19	2	.0
92367	.3	100	.1	79	25.6	216	84.1	6	10	.7	7	0	.0
92368	2.1	97	.7	85	25.8	250	163.6	9	7	1.0	13	0	.0
92369	.9	80	.3	57	21.0	342	144.5	7	12	.4	11	1	.1
92370	1.3	69	.1	14	26.0	294	57.3	12	9	.3	7	1	.6
92371	20.9	68	7.1	79	22.1	207	92.7*	9	14	7.0	13	0	.0
92372	1.7	98	.6	82	22.1	346	114.3	8	16	.9	17	0	.3
92373	.4	89	.2	75	29.6	352	89.0	5	8	.2	11	0	.0
92378	50.6	87	18.4	67	31.4	387	143.9	7	12	20.8	11	1	.1
92380	44.2	78	14.3	79	29.4	374	107.3	9	7	16.8	7	0	.2
92381	.4	100	.1	75	27.6	295	124.7	9	9	.7	7	0	.2
92382	6.3	95	2.4	85	29.5	470	163.1	7	18	2.9	18	0	.0
92383	10.0	98	5.6	90	20.9	541	104.4	7	17	4.2	72	0	.0
92385	3.4	97	1.2	81	32.1	406	145.8	9	5	1.7	3	0	.0
92386	11.1	81	4.4	68	18.6	285	93.9	9	26	4.3	28	0	.7
92388	.2	100	.1	61	31.7	392	195.5	12	14	1.1	11	0	.0
92389	21.8	82	7.0	70	28.5	499	99.4	13	17	8.8	8	0	.0
92389	.5	94	.3	87	12.6	345	38.7	9	7	.3	56	0	.7
92390	5.4	92	1.8	72	34.2	503	212.0	8	9	2.6	9	0	.0
92391	1.1	0	.4	74	31.7	347	150.6	9	7	.0	0	0	.0
92392	25.7	77	8.7	54	31.7	348	101.3	10	8	10.4	9	0	2.0

CALIFORNIA

SAN BERNARDINO

ZIPCODE	1	2	3	4	5	6	7	8	9	10	11	12	13
92395	1.8	92	.7	83	25.7	463	179.2	8	9	.8	13	0	.0
92396	1.0	91	.1	76	26.3	422	90.0	7	7	.4	6	0	.0
92397	2.9	98	1.0	76	31.3	443	149.4	7	8	1.4	8	0	.0
92398	1.6	94	.6	72	23.3	208	61.9	9	12	.7	15	0	.0
92399	28.0	97	12.1	79	21.7	338	116.2	5	33	12.4	31	0	.0

SAN BERNARDINO

ZIPCODE	1	2	3	4	5	6	7	8	9	10	11	12	13
92401	1.4	72	.7	17	15.0	290	68.1	12	13	.5	12	0	.0
92403	.4	91	.1	58	25.2	365	110.7	4	7	.2	3	0	.8
92404	44.0	89	17.0	62	28.3	386	116.1	6	12	18.7	10	0	.0
92405	28.7	76	11.2	62	21.6	339	90.0	9	14	10.2	14	0	.0
92407	12.2	91	3.9	77	29.8	380	112.3	8	7	5.4	6	0	.1
92408	8.6	52	3.2	41	16.4	294	67.7	9	12	2.2	12	0	.0
92409	1.7	69	.1	11	34.8	470	124.1*	2	0	1.0	0	1	.0
92410	27.5	63	10.5	46	17.0	291	74.8	12	11	8.1	13	1	.0
92411	20.4	31	6.2	62	18.0	278	59.3	9	10	3.2	12	0	.0

RIVERSIDE

ZIPCODE	1	2	3	4	5	6	7	8	9	10	11	12	13
92501	15.1	81	6.5	43	20.2	328	112.4	8	14	5.8	11	1	.1
92503	43.0	84	13.6	68	28.0	457	121.5	11	7	17.8	6	1	.0
92504	40.5	84	13.9	68	29.5	433	129.9	7	8	16.3	7	2	.0
92505	24.9	83	8.2	66	27.8	452	127.0	9	8	10.1	7	0	.0
92506	30.7	92	11.6	76	38.5	432	155.4	6	11	13.5	10	0	.1
92507	30.5	65	11.5	43	25.1	389	155.2	8	9	9.9	9	2	.5
92508	5.6	73	1.9	42	24.2	338	107.1	5	8	3.2	5	2	.0
92509	36.1	81	11.7	74	26.4	400	119.3	9	8	14.4	8	1	.5
92518	3.6	69	.7	2	19.9	367	71.0*	11	1	1.5	0	0	.0

SANTA ANA

ZIPCODE	1	2	3	4	5	6	7	8	9	10	11	12	13
92621	28.3	92	10.1	68	37.8	446	199.3	6	13	13.0	5	3	.0
92624	6.0	90	2.3	66	35.7	575	237.0	6	12	2.6	11	0	.0
92625	12.9	97	5.5	61	61.4	669	404.4	3	11	5.9	11	0	.0
92626	40.4	91	14.3	54	37.7	597	215.0	5	5	18.3	4	2	.7
92627	43.4	90	18.8	33	24.9	508	176.6	6	10	19.4	8	1	.2
92629	12.0	94	4.8	48	35.4	565	239.2	6	6	5.7	5	0	.0
92630	34.4	93	11.5	76	39.2	670	248.1	7	6	15.7	6	0	.0
92631	29.0	90	12.3	40	32.2	483	211.7	4	8	12.7	6	3	.5
92632	18.5	79	6.8	43	27.5	456	154.2	9	10	7.1	8	0	.0
92633	34.4	87	12.0	64	36.4	494	188.2	7	7	14.5	7	1	.0
92635	20.3	93	6.9	78	53.2	569	257.8	4	8	9.3	6	0	.2
92640	38.4	89	13.9	61	31.0	497	154.0	7	9	16.7	6	0	.0
92641	24.7	89	8.9	61	31.4	493	167.6	6	11	10.6	9	1	.0
92643	31.8	84	10.0	56	29.7	486	143.1	10	7	13.1	6	2	.0
92644	15.4	84	5.7	49	30.2	527	156.0	7	7	6.4	6	0	.0
92645	18.3	92	5.5	86	40.6	678	174.6	6	4	8.3	3	0	.0
92646	58.5	92	19.4	76	39.2	656	223.7	6	6	26.5	5	1	.0
92647	55.8	89	19.0	50	34.2	574	196.8	7	5	24.4	4	1	.0
92648	25.2	93	10.8	33	28.2	553	236.2	6	8	11.9	6	0	.0
92649	31.1	93	11.9	62	45.0	606	281.9	6	7	14.4	6	3	.0
92651	20.4	97	9.7	56	43.0	560	356.0	4	14	10.0	11	0	.3
92653	34.7	96	18.0	87	31.4	648	246.7	3	52	13.8	46	0	.0
92655	5.4	85	2.1	56	25.5	424	137.1	8	11	2.2	8	0	.0

*=Estimated **1.0=883 lbs per person; 100++ indicates per capita toxic waste generation > than 100 times the U.S. average of 883 lbs per capita.

ZIP CODE MEASURES OF SIZE, LEVELS OF AFFLUENCE AND QUALITY OF LIFE

1=Population (th.); 2= % White; 3=Households (th.); 4=% Owner Occupied; 5=Mean Income Per Household (th.$); 6=Mean Monthly Rent ($)*; 7=Mean Home Value (th.$)*; 8=% under 5; 9=% 65 and over; 10=White Males (th.); 11=% White Males, 65+; 12=# Toxic Waste Sites; 13=Toxic Waste Relative to US(883 lbs.per capital)**.

CALIFORNIA

SANTA ANA

ZIP CODE	1	2	3	4	5	6	7	8	9	10	11	12	13
92660	22.9	98	9.6	63	62.9	713	379.3	3	13	10.7	11	1	.8
92661	4.6	98	2.1	42	46.5	567	396.2	2	12	2.2	10	0	.0
92662	3.7	97	1.8	35	44.6	638	424.0	2	12	1.6	10	0	.0
92663	20.2	97	9.6	45	44.6	579	346.4	2	11	10.3	8	1	.0
92665	16.1	93	5.5	69	35.8	571	187.4	6	7	7.2	5	1	.5
92666	12.4	90	5.2	41	26.1	477	162.2	9	12	5.2	9	0	.9
92667	37.7	91	12.2	70	41.9	524	247.0	6	6	16.9	5	3	.2
92668	16.4	86	6.2	41	27.2	516	147.9	7	12	6.7	9	0	.8
92669	23.9	87	6.9	75	45.1	571	201.7	4	4	10.6	3	0	.1
92670	36.0	86	11.2	74	39.3	542	201.4	5	5	15.3	4	0	.1
92672	30.3	91	12.6	50	32.2	501	263.9	7	14	13.6	13	0	.5
92675	74.1	94	23.8	84	43.7	703	241.1	8	6	34.5	6	0	.1
92676	.7	0	.3	73	30.8	484	173.9	9	3	.0	0	0	.0
92677	19.3	97	7.6	83	51.5	702	313.0	5	12	9.2	11	0	.3
92678	.9	98	.2	83	61.3	409	308.6	4	2	.5	0	0	.0
92680	43.0	90	17.6	44	31.8	529	207.2	6	8	18.7	6	1	.0
92683	68.6	85	23.2	65	33.4	529	180.7	7	7	28.8	6	0	.5
92686	31.9	93	9.8	85	45.6	647	243.0	8	4	14.8	3	1	.1

SANTA ANA

ZIP CODE	1	2	3	4	5	6	7	8	9	10	11	12	13
92701	39.0	75	14.0	34	25.6	428	161.2	9	9	14.7	7	0	.0
92703	40.7	51	15.4	58	25.4	471	122.9	11	6	10.3	7	0	.0
92704	58.4	65	17.4	59	29.2	553	153.5	10	5	18.7	5	2	.3
92705	29.3	93	9.7	73	60.2	526	311.1	4	6	13.6	5	2	2.5
92706	21.8	84	8.4	61	31.4	472	176.6	7	15	8.7	13	0	.
92707	42.6	67	12.9	54	29.2	480	143.7	9	6	14.6	6	0	.8
92708	58.2	89	17.5	78	42.1	624	226.2	6	6	25.4	4	1	3.2
92709	8.8	72	1.2	0	17.7	311	63.0*13	0	0	4.6	0	0	.
92710	.5	79	.1	0	25.9	368	92.1*11	8	3	.2	0	0	.1
92714	42.1	88	14.8	78	44.9	706	243.8	5	5	18.2	3	1	2.9
92715	20.1	88	6.6	62	52.2	691	295.4	5	5	8.7	4	0	1.7

ANAHEIM

ZIP CODE	1	2	3	4	5	6	7	8	9	10	11	12	13
92801	41.0	85	15.2	40	27.5	495	150.6	9	9	16.9	8	2	.
92803	29.4	88	11.5	46	28.4	483	171.7	7	10	12.1	9	1	1.2
92804	58.8	89	21.2	68	29.9	486	158.3	7	8	25.2	6	0	.0
92805	42.2	79	15.1	48	25.7	439	144.7	9	10	16.1	5	0	.8
92806	27.1	90	10.2	56	34.3	510	188.9	5	6	12.1	5	2	3.2
92807	34.1	88	10.6	81	49.2	678	263.2	8	2	15.1	2	3	.1

VENTURA

ZIP CODE	1	2	3	4	5	6	7	8	9	10	11	12	13
93001	16.7	84	6.9	37	21.2	352	148.2	9	12	6.9	11	0	.5
93003	68.6	91	26.1	63	31.3	493	185.1	6	12	30.0	11	1	.2
93010	50.0	90	16.5	75	37.6	475	209.1	7	11	22.6	11	0	.0
93013	14.2	82	5.4	59	32.5	487	240.2	6	13	5.7	13	1	.0
93015	11.9	71	3.7	61	26.2	333	129.4	10	12	4.2	14	2	.0
93017	38.8	88	13.6	38	26.9	519	236.3	5	5	17.0	4	0	.0
93021	9.0	82	2.7	71	33.3	560	159.9	11	4	3.8	4	1	.0
93022	5.2	95	1.8	75	31.3	469	163.3	8	10	2.4	9	0	.0
93023	18.6	96	7.0	71	30.2	456	186.7	6	19	8.5	17	0	.0
93030	123.4	62	38.3	54	27.9	431	140.4	10	7	37.9	7	11	.1
93040	1.5	68	.4	49	22.6	294	79.5	8	9	.5	13	1	.0

CALIFORNIA

VENTURA

ZIP CODE	1	2	3	4	5	6	7	8	9	10	11	12	13
93041	14.9	74	5.4	52	25.6	431	117.5	9	10	5.6	10	0	.0
93042	2.8	79	.6	0	20.8	355	74.0*12	0	0	1.3	0	1	.0
93043	2.9	77	.4	12	20.5	345	73.0*	9	0	1.6	0	1	.0
93060	24.4	69	8.0	57	26.2	335	138.3	9	13	8.1	15	1	.0
93063	37.0	93	11.1	82	35.5	640	178.1	8	4	16.9	3	1	.0
93065	43.4	93	11.7	84	39.1	710	178.3	8	3	20.3	3	2	.0
93066	.8	89	.3	60	42.7	375	192.7	15	8	.3	9	0	.0
93067	1.2	93	.6	29	23.4	503	187.7	4	9	.6	7	0	1.0

SANTA BARBARA

ZIP CODE	1	2	3	4	5	6	7	8	9	10	11	12	13
93101	24.9	81	11.8	22	20.0	433	198.4	6	17	9.1	13	0	.1
93103	16.6	79	6.8	46	27.0	498	246.2	6	14	6.4	13	1	.1
93105	22.8	95	9.4	60	34.1	550	269.8	8	23	4.9	19	0	.0
93108	10.7	98	4.1	70	56.2	551	368.5	4	20	4.9	18	0	.0
93109	10.7	89	4.4	58	32.8	568	239.6	4	13	4.7	11	0	.0
93110	12.7	94	5.1	67	37.2	532	293.9	3	20	5.7	18	0	.0
93111	16.5	91	5.3	78	43.3	631	269.3	5	7	7.2	6	0	.0

BAKERSFIELD

ZIP CODE	1	2	3	4	5	6	7	8	9	10	11	12	13
93201	.8	80	.3	72	19.5	296	31.3	13	19	.3	22	0	.0
93202	2.7	73	.8	68	21.6	317	72.5	10	8	.9	9	0	.0
93203	8.8	58	2.4	50	20.6	272	64.9	10	7	2.6	9	0	.0
93204	4.5	71	1.4	60	22.4	290	52.7	11	11	1.5	13	0	.0
93205	1.2	95	.6	84	19.9	357	79.2	3	30	.6	35	0	.0
93206	2.4	65	.8	40	25.4	302	93.3	9	12	.8	16	0	.0
93207	.2	100	.1	95	19.4	223*	112.2	7	16	.8	23	0	.0
93208	.2	79	.1	55	14.8	181	91.3	0	14	.1	16	0	.0
93210	7.9	80	2.7	59	26.0	327	83.8	9	11	3.1	11	4	.0
93212	9.9	59	2.9	59	23.8	238	60.9	11	7	2.9	8	1	.4
93215	19.1	44	5.6	55	21.8	303	83.7	10	11	4.1	11	1	.0
93218	.7	66	.2	73	35.1	320	76.4	9	6	.3	7	0	.0
93219	5.3	26	1.4	59	17.3	234	52.2	11	10	.7	12	0	.0
93220	.5	82	.2	37	31.4	234	121.4	16	1	.2	0	0	5.4
93221	8.7	88	3.1	66	24.3	305	94.1	8	16	3.7	15	0	.1
93223	5.6	65	1.6	66	17.6	262	65.2	12	8	1.7	11	1	.0
93224	1.0	95	.4	65	33.9	311	45.2	10	9	.5	8	2	.0
93225	3.2	97	1.2	77	28.7	347	114.5	7	12	1.5	13	0	.0
93226	.3	0	.1	63	21.8	158	156.1	10	15	.0	9	0	.0
93227	2.3	46	.6	66	18.1	335	57.9	12	6	.5	9	0	.0
93230	33.2	78	11.4	62	24.7	320	92.9	11	11	12.7	10	3	.9
93234	3.8	41	.8	30	19.4	263	69.1	14	3	.9	4	1	.0
93235	2.8	75	.9	74	21.1	312	68.6	11	11	1.1	13	0	.0
93238	1.9	0	.8	68	21.0	270	107.2	3	24	.0	0	0	.0
93239	1.4	61	.4	44	20.0	227	59.8	10	5	.5	8	2	.0
93240	6.1	98	2.8	84	20.4	343	94.3	4	30	2.9	33	0	.0
93241	11.3	59	3.2	56	18.3	274	66.3	12	9	3.4	10	0	.0
93242	2.6	82	.8	63	23.1	267	92.6	7	10	1.1	10	3	.9
93243	.5	92	.2	96	23.8	273*	102.4	8	10	.2	14	0	.9
93244	.4	0	.1	63	20.3	192	105.3	6	23	.0	0	2	.0
93245	20.4	79	6.0	50	23.7	344	110.3	11	5	8.6	4	1	.3
93247	11.3	70	3.8	65	23.2	278	82.5	9	13	3.9	14	0	.3

*=Estimated **1.0=883 lbs per person; 100++ indicates per capita toxic waste generation > than 100 times the U.S. average of 883 lbs per capita.

ZIP CODE MEASURES OF SIZE, LEVELS OF AFFLUENCE AND QUALITY OF LIFE

1=Population (th.); 2= % White; 3=Households (th.); 4=% Owner Occupied; 5=Mean Income Per Household (th.$); 6=Mean Monthly Rent ($)*; 7=Mean Home Value (th.$)*; 8=% under 5; 9=% 65 and over; 10=White Males (th.); 11=% White Males, 65+; 12=# Toxic Waste Sites; 13=Toxic Waste Relative to US(883 lbs.per capita)**

CALIFORNIA

BAKERSFIELD

ZIPCODE	1	2	3	4	5	6	7	8	9	10	11	12	13
93249	1.7	36	.4	17	19.9	296	80.9	11	1	.3	3	1	.0
93250	6.0	50	1.6	60	23.2	267	70.1	12	8	1.4	9	0	.0
93251	.7	77	.2	29	31.2	209	84.0	5	3	.3	3	1	.2
93252	1.4	87	.5	70	26.4	293	66.6	9	7	.6	8	2	4.2
93254	.8	98	.3	52	25.0	324	70.7	12	6	.4	2	0	.0
93255	.5	92	.3	78	17.6	286	70.5	8	30	.9	32	0	.0
93256	3.7	62	1.1	62	18.7	245	66.8	8	9	1.1	12	0	.0
93257	45.5	77	14.9	63	23.4	316	88.7	9	12	17.0	12	1	.0
93260	.1	0	.1	100	21.1	242*	131.0	0	30	.0	0	1	.0
93261	1.1	11	.3	48	17.0	246	39.8	16	12	.1	14	0	.0
93263	11.4	75	3.5	58	22.6	266	83.0	10	10	4	11	2	.6
93265	1.8	92	.7	63	20.8	207	105.4	6	19	.8	19	0	.0
93266	1.0	67	.4	50	21.7	264	67.1	10	7	.3	9	0	.0
93267	4.7	74	1.5	69	21.9	270	74.7	9	12	1.7	14	1	.0
93268	14.0	94	5.3	67	27.8	319	72.0	8	12	6.5	10	1	.0
93270	3.8	68	1.1	70	23.4	281	83.1	10	4	1.3	7	0	.0
93271	1.7	86	.6	64	30.6	384	142.7	4	18	.7	19	0	.0
93274	35.8	77	11.7	62	25.6	340	90.7	9	10	13.4	13	3	.0
93277	68.2	84	24.3	63	27.7	367	119.4	8	10	27.9	10	5	.1
93280	11.4	60	3.6	56	25.2	259	80.8	11	8	3.3	9	1	.0
93282	.2	100	.1	33	23.7	188	41.8	11	5	.1	0	0	.0
93285	3.8	92	.3	83	21.6	294	102.6	7	15	.4	15	0	.0
93286	2.0	58	1.0	82	16.2	332	107.6	5	35	1.0	42	0	.0
93286	6.4	58	2.0	64	20.7	266	83.1	11	9	1.8	11	0	.0

BAKERSFIELD

ZIPCODE	1	2	3	4	5	6	7	8	9	10	11	12	13
93301	10.3	85	4.8	42	28.4	317	120.5	7	18	4.1	16	1	1.7
93304	34.5	74	12.8	63	25.3	367	92.8	9	11	12.1	11	0	.0
93305	29.1	65	10.6	52	23.1	337	92.7	10	13	8.8	14	0	.0
93306	37.4	88	12.8	74	32.7	407	120.3	8	8	15.9	8	1	.0
93307	39.4	55	12.3	59	22.3	308	76.5	10	8	10.7	9	2	.1
93308	34.2	95	13.1	64	25.0	341	101.5	8	11	16.0	10	0	.6
93309	52.9	89	19.4	61	34.6	432	149.3	8	6	23.3	5	3	.0

SAN LUIS OBISPO

ZIPCODE	1	2	3	4	5	6	7	8	9	10	11	12	13
93401	39.7	90	14.7	48	24.8	433	167.8	3	11	18.7	8	3	.0
93402	11.2	93	4.4	66	24.1	490	156.7	7	16	5.2	15	0	.0
93406	3.2	88	.1	57	32.9	329	193.4	6	1	1.5	1	1	.0
93422	17.7	92	6.5	70	27.3	405	158.1	8	15	8.0	15	2	.9
93422	15.5	93	5.3	67	26.5	388	138.5	8	10	7.4	9	0	.9
93424	.5	96	.3	55	30.1	256	239.6	0	15	.3	13	0	.0
93426	.7	82	.3	68	23.1	325	138.6	3	15	.3	17	0	.0
93427	2.6	95	1.0	67	29.8	382	170.9	7	14	1.2	12	0	.0
93428	3.4	98	1.5	66	24.3	437	179.5	5	22	1.6	21	0	.0
93429	.2	67	1.3	30	30.3	385	48.8	8	6	.1	0	1	.0
93430	2.6	94	1.3	61	22.4	371	178.8	7	26	1.2	25	0	.0
93431	.1	100	.1	31	31.3	499	111.7*	0	12	.1	7	0	.0
93432	1.1	98	.4	79	24.4	241	152.7	3	6	.5	5	0	.0
93433	8.9	85	3.4	51	20.1	402	110.7	9	15	3.6	15	0	.0
93434	4.3	30	1.3	47	23.4	271	85.3	10	8	.6	13	0	.0

CALIFORNIA

SAN LUIS OBISPO

ZIPCODE	1	2	3	4	5	6	7	8	9	10	11	12	13
93436	36.4	83	12.7	57	27.8	382	128.3	7	7	15.3	6	1	.0
93437	8.2	79	2.1	8	20.8	351	78.0	15		3.6	0	0	.2
93438	.4	0	.1	73	42.5	549	151.4				0	0	.0
93440	1.1	90	.4	58	23.6	349	167.7	7	10	.4	12	0	.7
93441	1.0	95	.4	60	33.6	521	207.2	7	10	.4	11	0	.0
93442	10.3	95	4.6	57	22.3	385	146.6	5	23	4.6	21	2	.0
93444	6.6	86	2.1	77	28.7	355	156.4	8	10	2.7	12	0	.0
93445	4.4	77	1.6	63	19.2	387	109.9	9	12	1.7	13	0	.2
93446	15.3	88	5.6	62	25.7	357	127.7	8	12	6.5	13	3	.0
93449	5.3	95	2.7	53	22.8	401	175.6	3	23	2.4	24	0	.2
93450	.6	62	.2	31	30.7	275	84.8	6	8	.2	13	0	.0
93451	1.8	87	.6	55	29.2	273	93.6	8	9	.9	10	0	.0
93452	.3	100	.1	46	27.2	416	306.3	7	16	.2	21	0	.0
93453	2.8	96	1.0	73	26.4	359	132.2	6	11	1.3	11	0	.1
93454	63.6	79	21.5	62	28.6	393	131.7	8	9	24.3	9	2	.0
93456	.3	76	.1	84	21.6	227	123.6	7	15	.1	20	0	.0
93460	3.8	91	1.3	80	42.9	493	254.1	6	10	1.7	10	0	.0
93461	.7	0	.2	50	27.5	253	83.9	8	10	.0		0	.0
93463	4.8	96	1.9	64	38.8	473	251.2	5	21	2.2	18	0	.0
93465	3.8	97	1.4	86	31.5	463	183.6	8	11	1.9	10	0	.0

MOJAVE

ZIPCODE	1	2	3	4	5	6	7	8	9	10	11	12	13
93501	3.8	83	1.4	57	22.8	250	74.5	10	8	1.6	8	2	.0
93505	2.8	83	1.0	68	26.6	391	90.7	7	11	1.2	10	0	.0
93510	3.4	93	1.1	82	35.0	472	210.2	6	8	1.6	7	0	.0
93512	.2	0	.1	38	23.6	241	84.0*	9	10	.6	20	0	.0
93513	1.5	80	.6	75	24.2	352	121.6	9	17	.6	20	0	.0
93516	12.1	90	4.6	67	25.6	376	174.2	7	13	5.5	13	1	.0
93517	2.9	94	1.1	63	25.4	272	64.8	7	7	1.4	7	0	34.6
93518	.9	90	.3	60	24.7	361	134.3	4	5	.4	4	0	.0
93519	.6	96	.2	62	25.4	252	146.1	8	15	.3	12	0	.0
93523	.2	86	.1	41	18.7	138	66.5*12	9		.1	5	0	.0
93526	9.7	78	2.6	17	20.7	311	75.5	13	1	4.3	1	3	1.3
93527		94	.4	68	23.2	292	106.0	7	19	.4	14	0	.0
93528	1.6	95	.6	80	26.4	296	86.0	4	12	.8	11	0	.0
93529	.2	100	.1	72	15.7	89	72.8	16	20	.1	14	0	.0
93530	.7	0	.3	58	25.9	351	200.3	11	2	.0	0	0	.0
93531	.7	77	.1	66	10.8	135	39.1	5	18	.1	20	0	.0
93532	.4	81	.1	62	13.7	402	69.4	7	15	.2	20	0	.9
93534	1.2	80	.4	70	26.1	342	107.9	8	9	.5	13	0	.0
93541	62.4	91	22.5	69	29.7	398	125.1	7	10	27.8	8	1	.0
93543	.7	84	.2	52	25.2	265	126.3	10	5	.2	5	0	.0
93544	2.6	70	1.3	80	25.2	359	106.6	7	13	1.5	14	0	.0
93545	3.4	83	.6	88	30.3	355	163.4	2	16	.3	17	0	2.9
93546	2.0	89	.4	63	20.0	306	129.2	7	22	.9	23	2	.0
93549	4.6	98	2.0	42	31.1	431	297.2	7	1	2.5	1	0	.0
93550	.4	0	.1	47	16.7	176	41.5	5	13	.0	0	0	.0
93553	29.9	90	10.3	68	28.3	390	117.0	9	8	13.5	8	1	1.9
93554	.9	90	.3	94	28.9	309	121.8	9	19	.4	15	0	.0
	.2	100	.1		17.3	198*	43.0	3	22	.1	21		.0

*=Estimated **1.0=883 lbs per person; 100+ indicates per capita toxic waste generation > than 100 times the U.S. average of 883 lbs per capita.

ZIP CODE MEASURES OF SIZE, LEVELS OF AFFLUENCE AND QUALITY OF LIFE

1=Population (th.); 2= % White; 3=Households (th.); 4=% Owner Occupied; 5=Mean Income Per Household (th.$); 6=Mean Monthly Rent ($); 7=Mean Home Value (th.$); 8=% under 5; 9=% 65 and over; 10=White Males (th.); 11=% White Males, 65+; 12=# Toxic Waste Sites; 13=Toxic Waste Relative to US(883 lbs.per capita)**.

CALIFORNIA

MOJAVE

ZIP CODE	1	2	3	4	5	6	7	8	9	10	11	12	13
93555	24.6	91	8.6	65	32.8	376	108.8	8	5	11.6	5	1	.1
93558	.1	100	.1	53	21.5	83	13.1	0	20	.1	34	0	.0
93560	5.0	88	2.0	66	23.0	248	78.0	8	12	2.2	13	0	.0
93561	8.6	84	2.7	75	29.4	371	121.7	6	6	3.8	9	0	.0
93562	3.9	88	1.5	63	26.3	263	57.4	10	8	1.9	9	2	4.1

FRESNO

ZIP CODE	1	2	3	4	5	6	7	8	9	10	11	12	13
93601	1.3	90	.4	83	20.3	328	101.0	4	16	.6	12	0	.0
93602	2.1	97	.7	82	24.2	240	124.1	4	13	1.0	9	0	.0
93604	.6	96	.2	83	35.5	195	220.4	3	16	.3	12	0	.0
93605	.4	0	.3	21	27.8	242	128.6	14	0	.1	0	0	.0
93606	.9	30	.3	62	21.6	142	89.6	6	9	.1	11	0	.0
93607	1.7	64	.4	27	38.9	297	118.1	14	7	.1	11	0	.0
93608	1.7	49	.4	26	20.3	191	37.1	11	1	.5	2	0	.0
93609	4.7	83	1.4	57	24.0	291	90.9	8	10	2.0	11	0	.0
93610	9.2	91	3.1	61	21.6	320	80.2	9	14	4.2	12	0	.0
93612	43.1	90	15.5	57	28.2	390	146.1	8	7	18.7	6	0	.0
93614	2.5	98	.9	81	33.3	485	172.1	7	9	1.3	9	0	.0
93615	4.2	35	1.1	59	18.3	254	59.0	13	6	.7	8	0	.0
93616	2.4	66	.6	55	27.8	209	93.3	7	6	.9	5	1	.0
93618	15.9	67	5.1	64	23.2	291	93.2	9	12	5.2	13	2	.0
93620	6.8	76	2.2	57	25.6	271	83.0	10	12	2.5	12	3	.0
93621	6.7	83	.2	69	20.5	238	108.2	10	7	.3	6	1	.0
93622	6.8	58	2.0	35	22.0	249	107.1	12	6	2.0	7	0	.0
93623	.1	100	.1	64	31.5	362*	133.3	0	11	.1	12	0	.0
93624	1.6	68	.4	8	19.1	202	196.9	11	11	.6	2	1	.0
93625	4.4	67	1.4	65	31.6	286	105.0	9	14	1.4	13	1	.0
93626	.8	79	.2	83	24.8	386	136.3	2	13	.3	19	0	.0
93627	.2	38	.1		24.3	182	86.7*	13	11		.0	11	.1
93630	8.7	79	2.8	60	29.7	294	91.1	10	9	3.5	11	3	.0
93631	9.4	84	3.3	67	29.5	323	117.4	8	14	4.0	14	0	.0
93633	.3	94	.1	49	27.5	315*	126.9	13	0	.1	0	0	.0
93635	13.3	87	4.6	61	24.5	308	95.2	9	11	5.7	11	1	.0
93637	40.7	67	13.3	65	25.7	291	107.4	10	10	13.6	9	5	.0
93638	6.1	35	1.6	42	18.1	249	72.8	14	5	1.1	8	0	.0
93640	.5	100	.2	68	22.2	262	82.3	14	11	.2	13	0	.0
93641	2.2	82	.8	74	21.6	306	116.0	7	13	.9	14	1	.0
93643	4.8	98	1.9	79	27.6	363	140.3	6	19	2.3	21	1	.0
93644	.2	100	.1	92	18.6	214*	85.9	8	26	.1	26	0	.0
93645	6.1	65	1.9	68	23.1	294	83.9	10	9	2.1	10	2	.0
93646	6.1	52	1.8	69	19.8	253	76.6	10	13	1.6	13	0	.0
93647	7.2	55	1.8	50	19.3	214	65.3	11	6	2.0	6	0	.0
93648	.2	100	.1	67	18.6	208	173.4	9	35	.1	45	0	.0
93649	4.9	82	1.7	66	26.6	393	114.7	9	11	1.9	10	2	.0
93650	.6	0	.2	70	30.6	401	139.5	8	6	.7	0	0	.0
93651	.6	74	.2	61	22.4	220	67.5	4	8	.2	7	0	.0
93652	.7	85	.2	86	16.3	197	63.7	13	8	.3	8	0	.0
93653	.7	70	.2										
93654	17.1	70	5.3	65	25.3	319	106.2	8	13	5.8	14	0	.0
93656	3.9	78	1.7	57	24.7	284	81.8	9	11	1.6	11	0	.0
93657	21.4	77	6.6	66	28.4	316	118.6	9	10	8.3	10	0	.1

CALIFORNIA

FRESNO

ZIP CODE	1	2	3	4	5	6	7	8	9	10	11	12	13
93660	2.3	57	.7	45	23.4	234	75.1	12	6	.6	9	2	.0
93661	.4	39	.1	30	25.8	207	50.1	9	3	.1	0	0	.0
93662	18.2	64	5.6	64	26.2	298	95.5	9	11	5.8	13	0	.3
93664	.8	98	.3	52	37.4	375	208.3	8	1	.4	2	0	.0
93665	.8	32	.2	34	11.9	250	47.9	10	7	.2	7	0	.5
93666	.5	54	.1	33	17.0	217	24.5	17	6	.2	13	0	.0
93667	2.4	97	.4	87	31.2	329	192.1	4	9	1.6	8	0	.0
93668	1.1	82	.4	60	31.3	278	73.5	7	9	.5	9	0	.0
93670	.2	37	.1	24	14.7	216	37.2	27	0	.0	0	0	.1
93673	.7	68	.2	69	18.0	254	71.1	11	3	.3	5	0	.0

FRESNO

ZIP CODE	1	2	3	4	5	6	7	8	9	10	11	12	13
93701	10.0	53	3.7	24	13.8	271	65.0	13	9	2.6	11	0	.0
93702	33.5	63	11.9	52	17.3	298	74.5	11	14	9.8	17	1	.0
93703	23.1	84	9.6	56	22.1	335	93.3	7	14	9.1	13	0	.0
93704	25.2	89	10.5	63	33.7	389	142.0	6	14	10.4	13	0	.0
93705	28.9	84	11.2	61	26.2	396	105.2	8	11	11.5	11	0	.0
93706	32.0	33	9.8	54	19.0	281	73.2	9	11	5.4	11	0	.2
93710	32.4	86	11.1	62	32.8	378	155.2	7	11	13.5	5	0	.0
93711	34.8	86	11.5	81	44.2	419	193.7	8	7	14.7	7	0	.0
93721	3.7	65	2.0	10	13.3	232	98.2	13	9	1.2	33	0	3.5
93725	15.4	57	4.5	66	25.8	329	90.2	10	9	4.3	10	2	.0
93726	34.7	86	14.0	51	25.5	375	110.1	7	8	14.2	7	0	.0
93727	34.3	86	6.0	67	31.8	363	140.8	7	10	14.5	9	1	.0
93728	13.7	79		58	19.9	306	87.2	8	18	4.8	16	0	.1

SALINAS

ZIP CODE	1	2	3	4	5	6	7	8	9	10	11	12	13
93901	25.1	74	9.5	50	30.4	399	170.3	7	13	8.8	12	2	2.4
93905	29.9	50	8.9	43	22.4	386	108.0	13	7	7.2	10	0	.0
93906	29.1	72	9.7	62	28.4	441	128.8	8	7	10.2	7	0	.0
93907	13.2	80	4.1	78	31.9	471	170.3	9	7	5.3	6	1	.0
93908	9.2	75	2.7	78	49.3	417	263.5	7	6	3.4	6	0	.0
93920	.9	95	.4	44	20.6	314	437.5	10	11	.4	11	0	.0
93921	7.1	96	3.8	62	35.6	551	296.2	6	34	2.7	34	0	.0
93922	.2	100	.1	51	33.5	576	437.5	10	18	.1	19	0	.0
93923	8.1	97	3.3	78	47.5	640	330.6	3	17	3.7	16	0	.0
93924	5.1	96	2.1	69	39.0	537	283.9	6	13	2.4	13	1	.0
93925	2.2	23	.3	34	27.9	259	131.9	12	7	.1	15	0	.0
93926	4.0	50	1.1	45	23.1	336	107.6	11	9	1.0	10	0	.0
93927	5.8	54	1.5	52	23.9	319	102.5	13	6	1.5	6	1	.0
93928	1.0	57	.1	13	22.9	345	81.4*	6	0	.4	1	0	.0
93930	8.0	68	2.5	48	28.8	341	131.9	12	6	2.8	8	1	.0
93932	.6	98	.2	69	32.9	630	125.3	10	3	.3	9	0	.0
93933	13.9	62	4.6	52	25.9	479	149.3	9	4	4.4	4	0	.0
93940	30.5	89	12.3	41	28.5	490	207.8	6	11	13.6	9	0	.0
93941	22.1	54	3.5	13		328		13	17	7.7		0	.0
93950	16.3	91	1.9	50	25.6	504	189.9	5	19	6.7	14	0	.0
93953	4.9	96	4.9	86	61.2	711	358.8	3	22	2.3	23	0	.0
93954	.4	40	.1	31	24.2	249	59.1	11	9	.1	9	0	.0
93955	21.4	50	7.5	56	24.1	414	123.4	8	5	5.1	7	0	.0
93960	11.1	47		49	23.2	301	101.6	9	10	3.6	4	0	.1

*=Estimated **1.0=883 lbs per person; 100+ indicates per capita toxic waste generation > than 100 times the U.S. average of 883 lbs per capita.

ZIP CODE MEASURES OF SIZE, LEVELS OF AFFLUENCE AND QUALITY OF LIFE

1=Population (th.); 2= % White; 3=Households (th.); 4=% Owner Occupied; 5=Mean Income Per Household (th.$); 6=Mean Monthly Rent ($)*; 7=Mean Home Value (th.$)*; 8=% under 5; 9=% 65 and over; 10=White Males, 65+ and over; 11=% White Males (th.); 12=# Toxic Waste Sites; 13=Toxic Waste Relative to US(883 lbs.per capita)**.

CALIFORNIA

ZIP CODE	1	2	3	4	5	6	7	8	9	10	11	12	13
SALINAS													
93962	.5	74	.2	26	24.4	286	121.7	6	11	.2	10	1	.8
SAN FRANCISCO													
94002	24.7	91	9.8	59	39.7	552	281.7	4	8	10.9	7	2	.7
94005	2.9	94	1.4	55	30.3	461	181.6	4	9	1.3	8	0	2.0
94010	37.6	93	16.1	58	47.7	502	340.9	3	17	16.3	16	2	.7
94014	31.7	50	10.6	59	29.1	454	148.3	8	10	7.7	12	0	.0
94015	52.9	56	18.7	59	33.8	530	188.0	7	8	14.5	9	0	.0
94018	1.9	91	.8	66	33.2	509	214.8	7	6	1.0	7	0	.0
94019	9.5	91	3.3	74	36.6	535	232.6	7	8	4.3	6	0	.0
94020	1.4	94	.6	64	35.6	587	206.2	4	8	.8	3	0	.0
94021	.2	100	.1	53	30.9	575	136.7	6	4	.2	5	0	.0
94022	39.1	95	13.5	88	61.4	667	361.2	4	11	18.3	10	1	.0
94025	47.4	87	18.5	66	50.6	571	324.3	4	15	19.7	13	3	.6
94030	20.0	89	7.6	68	40.6	537	283.3	4	13	8.4	13	0	.6
94037	2.1	88	.7	78	39.9	577	225.0	9	6	1.3	7	0	.0
94038	2.6	98	.9	83	39.3	588	236.7	5	8	1.3	7	0	.0
94040	25.8	84	12.1	38	33.3	515	273.8	4	9	10.6	7	3	1.2
94041	10.3	83	5.3	30	25.1	458	199.8	5	14	4.2	12	1	.0
94043	24.5	73	10.7	32	30.1	507	183.7	6	7	9.1	5	1	1.5
94044	36.5	82	12.7	68	34.0	534	176.6	8	5	14.8	4	0	.0
94060	1.3	80	.4	63	32.4	327	222.4	8	5	.6	6	0	.0
94061	30.1	91	12.7	50	32.2	517	228.2	4	11	13.1	10	0	.0
94062	24.5	95	9.6	72	46.9	530	300.7	5	12	11.3	11	0	2.3
94063	23.7	77	9.2	41	25.6	430	163.6	5	14	9.3	8	2	1.3
94065	2.9	80	1.0	89	49.8	880	299.1	8	2	2.1	2	0	.0
94066	36.0	83	13.8	57	33.5	483	197.0	6	8	15.0	8	1	.0
94070	23.9	95	9.7	71	38.1	546	261.5	6	8	11.0	13	1	2.3
94074	.2	0	.1	49	38.0	146	325.2	0	12	.0	0	0	1.9
94080	49.7	74	17.5	62	32.3	480	183.0	7	8	17.3	9	8	2.2
94086	60.0	76	25.4	45	30.9	507	182.9	6	9	22.8	9	8	2.5
94087	46.2	88	17.0	63	40.8	558	245.1	5	7	20.1	5	0	.0
SAN FRANCISCO													
94102	22.2	53	12.9	4	13.6	272	192.6	4	17	8.0	20	0	.1
94103	18.5	48	8.5	4	15.0	271	182.9	6	14	6.0	14	1	1.2
94104	.1	40	.1	0	5.6	186	19.9*	0	21	.0	0	1	15.3
94105	.2	74	.2	4	12.8	251	45.5*	0	12	1.7	0	1	41.6
94107	10.5	61	4.7	31	22.9	365	174.7	6	13	3.5	12	1	5.9
94108	13.0	41	6.7	8	20.5	362	344.2	2	20	2.7	11	0	.4
94109	49.2	67	30.3	9	24.4	408	291.2	2	20	16.7	16	2	.0
94110	63.3	55	24.5	27	22.3	401	155.8	7	11	17.3	11	1	.6
94111	2.5	69	1.4	12	48.6	604	437.5	1	28	.9	23	0	3.3
94112	55.9	50	19.1	73	28.4	474	148.0	6	16	13.1	19	0	.0
94114	30.3	85	16.0	29	29.1	493	238.5	3	11	15.3	7	0	.0
94115	29.7	51	15.4	15	28.4	431	358.3	5	14	7.7	9	0	.0
94116	38.1	69	14.4	76	35.5	575	208.9	4	21	12.1	12	0	.0
94117	35.3	60	16.9	17	23.8	452	290.8	6	12	12.3	5	0	.0
94118	38.5	63	16.5	31	32.7	494	282.1	4	15	10.7	14	0	.0
94121	38.5	57	16.3	40	31.4	501	240.6	4	17	9.9	18	0	.0
94122	49.4	69	21.1	49	31.2	512	204.1	4	18	15.6	19	0	.0

CALIFORNIA

ZIP CODE	1	2	3	4	5	6	7	8	9	10	11	12	13
SAN FRANCISCO													
94123	23.3	92	14.3	21	34.4	523	355.6	2	20	8.9	17	0	.0
94124	21.6	18	6.8	57	22.4	345	121.7	6	12	2.2	17	5	2.2
94127	19.1	76	7.3	85	44.1	582	263.3	5	18	6.8	17	0	.0
94129	5.0	66	1.2	1	25.2	400	89.8*14	5	1	1.9	0	1	.3
94130	3.9	67	.8	0	21.6	352	77.1*14	4	0	1.6	0	0	.0
94131	27.9	75	12.7	48	33.6	523	222.6	5	10	10.7	10	0	.0
94132	23.0	64	9.8	44	32.3	541	215.4	4	22	6.3	26	0	.0
94133	28.0	37	12.0	16	29.0	414	239.2	3	18	5.6	14	0	.3
94134	31.5	37	9.9	66	28.2	369	145.7	8	11	5.6	18	0	.1
PALO ALTO													
94301	15.9	94	7.0	49	38.9	508	319.7	3	20	6.7	14	2	.0
94303	33.7	54	12.1	59	34.9	497	212.3	7	7	9.3	7	1	.0
94304	1.7	97	.9	9	45.9	739	426.9	0	29	.8	24	3	1.5
94305	11.1	82	1.9	35	37.5	385	378.3	5	2	.8	2	0	71.7
94306	22.0	89	9.6	52	36.1	538	256.9	4	11	9.5	9	0	1.2
SAN MATEO													
94401	24.1	75	10.7	39	28.1	505	180.1	6	15	8.7	12	1	.0
94402	24.0	90	9.6	68	46.1	574	301.4	4	15	10.1	14	0	.0
94403	32.7	88	13.3	55	34.3	558	232.1	5	13	13.7	12	0	.0
94404	24.7	82	9.6	61	47.8	643	327.6	4	6	10.2	4	0	.1
OAKLAND													
94501	63.9	79	26.6	41	29.0	427	194.6	6	12	24.9	10	3	.1
94507	8.2	97	2.6	91	72.9	661	350.8	4	6	4.0	6	0	.0
94508	4.2	90	1.0	53	29.9	388	177.7	4	8	1.8	7	0	.0
94509	43.9	90	15.4	67	29.9	402	131.1	9	7	19.2	7	5	.9
94511	1.8	87	.7	67	33.7	418	167.1	8	8	.6	7	0	.8
94512	.2	98	.1	75	25.9	348	178.1	2	22	.9	21	0	.8
94513	8.3	94	2.7	61	26.9	296	129.7	6	19	1.2	16	0	.0
94514	.2	96	.1	9	22.8	308	81.3*	8	11	.1	18	8	.0
94515	8.3	91	2.7	62	29.4	281	137.2	9	3	3.4	9	8	.0
94517	2.5	89	.8	86	36.0	380	213.9	5	7	1.2	9	1	.0
94518	5.4	93	2.4	61	30.3	340	157.5	4	28	2.2	30	0	.0
94519	7.6	91	2.3	90	47.6	597	256.4	6	3	3.6	3	1	1.3
94520	24.0	91	8.8	69	34.9	523	186.0	6	9	10.6	8	1	.2
94521	18.0	93	6.5	70	32.8	506	148.6	7	8	6.7	7	0	.0
94523	28.2	90	11.7	39	24.8	437	128.9	7	8	12.7	6	2	.0
94525	35.6	90	11.4	75	38.5	546	190.0	7	4	15.9	3	2	1.9
94526	26.7	94	10.3	62	34.4	512	180.1	6	8	12.4	7	1	.0
94530	2.7	95	1.2	61	26.9	296	129.7	6	5	1.2	16	2	.0
94533	26.4	96	8.3	89	57.6	310	187.4	6	12	12.7	4	1	.0
94535	22.5	73	9.5	66	34.1	465	145.7	4	16	7.8	17	0	.1
94536	47.4	76	16.3	63	28.9	391	121.1	8	5	18.0	5	3	.0
94538	11.2	71	2.2	3	19.1	312	127.8	6	13	.9	1	1	.0
94541	60.3	84	21.2	63	35.0	505	174.7	5	7	24.8	7	0	.1
94542	71.9	87	23.1	69	37.8	526	183.8	8	4	30.8	2	3	1.2
94544	44.5	80	17.6	47	27.9	415	145.7	7	12	17.3	1	1	.4
94545	6.2	78	2.2	56	37.8	225	225.9	7	13	2.5	3	0	.0
94546	40.9	93	16.1	69	35.3	461	184.6	5	12	18.2	10	0	.0

*=Estimated   **1.0-883 lbs per capita; 100++ indicates per capita toxic waste generation > than 100 times the U.S. average of 883 lbs per person.

ZIP CODE MEASURES OF SIZE, LEVELS OF AFFLUENCE AND QUALITY OF LIFE

1=Population (th.); 2= % White; 3=Households (th.); 4=% Owner Occupied; 5=Mean Income Per Household (th.$); 6=Mean Monthly Rent ($)*; 7=Mean Home Value (th.$)*;
8=% under 5; 9=% 65 and over; 10=White Males (th.); 11=% White Males, 65+; 12=# Toxic Waste Sites; 13=Toxic Waste Relative to US(883 lbs.per capita)**.

CALIFORNIA

OAKLAND

ZIPCODE	1	2	3	4	5	6	7	8	9	10	11	12	13
94547	6.0	48	1.8	92	44.1	776	208.9	12	3	1.5	2	3	2.1
94548	.4	0	.1	64	28.7	354	189.1	11	9	.8	0	0	.8
94549	25.3	96	9.1	75	53.0	525	297.4	5	9	11.8	9	0	.0
94550	51.9	93	17.6	71	35.1	492	163.4	8	6	24.1	5	5	.2
94553	34.8	92	13.0	70	33.4	417	165.8	7	9	15.9	8	14	3.7
94556	14.6	94	5.1	80	55.1	644	320.9	4	6	6.7	5	0	.0
94558	71.2	93	26.7	65	30.7	441	161.3	6	13	32.1	11	0	.3
94560	32.1	77	9.2	77	36.1	546	158.6	9	3	12.4	3	6	2.9
94561	7.7	87	2.8	76	28.1	313	146.9	8	10	3	4	11	.0
94562	.3	76	.1	36	55.2	506	191.1	3	10	.1	16	0	.0
94563	16.8	95	5.8	92	67.4	748	319.1	4	9	8.0	0	0	.1
94564	14.3	87	5.0	76	37.5	497	159.7	6	5	6.1	5	0	.0
94565	43.9	66	15.3	68	25.6	328	112.2	10	8	14.2	8	9	4.8
94566	52.2	92	16.0	76	40.1	545	199.6	6	4	24.0	3	1	.0
94567	.3	100	.3	67	23.6	791	106.4	17	22	.1	29	0	.0
94569	.2	0	.1	73	21.5	339	86.2	0	25	.0	0	0	.0
94571	3.7	93	1.5	64	28.1	317	113.8	6	16	1.7	15	0	.8
94572	8.3	75	2.8	70	31.9	363	152.7	10	7	3.0	8	1	.0
94573	.3	83	.1	56	32.7	309	147.3	6	9	.1	0	0	3.9
94574	8.4	92	3.4	62	29.8	419	194.4	5	25	3.5	23	0	.0
94576	.4	0	.1	52	27.3	432	162.7	6	24	.0	0	0	.9
94577	34.3	88	15.1	60	29.7	412	161.9	4	20	13.9	18	5	2.2
94578	29.0	84	12.6	49	27.2	425	142.2	5	11	11.5	12	6	.1
94579	16.4	88	6.1	78	33.0	482	142.2	5	11	6.9	12	1	.1
94580	20.3	89	7.3	78	33.1	516	135.4	5	9	8.7	9	2	.2
94583	24.1	92	7.7	85	46.0	722	231.7	8	3	11.1	3	2	7.3
94585	14.9	77	4.8	70	34.7	390	158.5	11	4	5.8	4	0	.4
94586	.8	93	.3	79	43.3	440	231.3	4	5	.4	5	0	.0
94587	38.9	60	11.8	70	33.6	513	157.8	10	5	11.5	5	6	.1
94590	86.1	65	31.8	65	26.4	353	110.9	8	11	27.7	12	1	.1
94592	2.9	84	.5	0	20.2	381	72.0*10	0	0	1.6	0	1	.0
94595	16.0	98	8.5	87	34.8	548	214.6	2	48	6.6	41	0	.0
94596	29.6	95	13.7	46	34.4	484	229.8	5	12	13.5	8	0	.1
94598	26.9	94	9.1	81	51.4	622	274.9	4	7	12.2	5	0	1.4
94599	2.8	95	.7	60	24.3	408	132.8	3	44	1.8	50	0	.0

OAKLAND

ZIPCODE	1	2	3	4	5	6	7	8	9	10	11	12	13
94601	37.7	31	13.5	38	19.8	317	83.5	9	11	5.4	19	6	1.9
94602	26.5	65	11.1	60	31.0	401	158.6	6	17	8.0	19	0	.0
94603	26.7	11	8.9	55	19.9	346	71.0	9	9	1.4	23	2	.2
94605	36.9	28	13.7	66	29.0	385	131.0	8	9	5.0	19	0	.0
94606	32.2	28	14.1	21	19.3	334	98.2	8	9	4.4	15	1	.0
94607	17.2	9	7.2	20	14.8	239	61.6	8	15	1.0	19	3	1.3
94608	19.6	18	8.9	19	19.0	315	75.8	5	15	2.8	13	7	5.1
94609	19.7	31	9.3	29	16.7	316	103.5	5	15	2.8	16	1	.1
94610	28.6	63	14.8	33	29.0	409	226.6	4	16	8.3	16	0	.0
94611	33.6	84	15.7	57	40.1	417	272.6	4	13	13.1	14	0	.0
94612	9.4	46	5.7	6	13.5	260	88.2	4	23	2.2	26	0	2.2
94618	15.5	86	6.3	59	34.7	452	222.4	4	18	6.2	16	0	.0
94619	22.0	54	8.6	67	32.1	402	151.7	6	14	5.5	20	0	.0

CALIFORNIA

OAKLAND

ZIPCODE	1	2	3	4	5	6	7	8	9	10	11	12	13
94621	23.8	8	8.3	48	17.5	299	67.6	10	10	.8	27	5	1.8
94626	.4	64	.1	0	26.0	384	92.7*15	0	0	.2	0	1	.0
94627	.9	68	.3	72	50.7	432	273.0	10	8	.3	10	1	1.4

BERKELEY

ZIPCODE	1	2	3	4	5	6	7	8	9	10	11	12	13
94702	15.2	34	7.1	45	19.6	337	107.5	4	15	2.4	13	0	.0
94703	18.0	49	8.4	33	21.0	362	131.0	5	11	4.4	4	0	.0
94704	17.9	78	8.0	8	15.4	391	220.0	2	6	7.6	3	2	.2
94705	13.6	88	6.0	44	34.5	450	273.6	4	11	5.6	8	0	.0
94706	14.4	77	6.7	54	26.8	448	152.6	4	18	5.1	16	2	.0
94707	12.9	90	5.1	81	45.4	544	240.9	4	16	5.4	14	0	.0
94708	11.9	90	4.8	80	48.2	584	265.2	4	14	5.3	13	0	.0
94709	10.3	84	5.4	16	23.0	413	222.8	3	9	4.3	6	0	.0
94710	7.8	36	3.2	30	18.4	287	84.6	11	7	1.4	6	4	12.5

RICHMOND

ZIPCODE	1	2	3	4	5	6	7	8	9	10	11	12	13
94801	20.3	32	7.9	43	19.1	301	95.3	9	12	3.1	16	3	7.2
94803	18.1	81	6.7	74	35.0	470	162.0	6	7	7.3	7	0	.0
94804	33.7	32	12.5	32	23.2	353	101.1	7	11	5.1	18	13	3.5
94805	12.3	73	5.1	68	28.0	429	128.2	8	13	4.3	13	1	.0
94806	39.6	65	14.6	60	25.7	393	107.8	8	8	4.3	8	1	4.6
94807	1.9	78	.9	10	23.5	483	83.7*11	9	8	.7	9	0	.0

SAN RAFAEL

ZIPCODE	1	2	3	4	5	6	7	8	9	10	11	12	13
94901	31.8	93	14.0	50	36.6	492	295.1	4	12	14.2	11	1	.0
94903	25.6	93	9.2	73	42.0	595	257.4	4	9	11.4	7	0	.1
94904	11.8	97	5.3	59	48.0	605	368.8	4	18	5.2	15	0	.0
94920	12.1	96	5.0	63	61.6	749	386.8	4	10	5.6	9	1	.2
94922	.2	0	.1	62	31.1	357*154.9		7	3	.0	0	0	7.3
94923	1.2	93	.5	58	26.1	356	203.7	7	16	.6	19	0	.4
94924	1.4	98	.6	59	26.5	575	181.7	6	8	.7	7	1	.0
94925	8.3	94	3.3	64	28.9	638	259.5	4	10	3.9	7	0	.0
94929	.3	92	.1	57	26.7	495	164.9	9	7	12.8	6	0	.0
94930	8.4	95	3.6	59	31.6	551	227.1	5	9	3.9	9	0	.1
94933	.8	97	.4	63	33.0	512	227.9	9	6	.4	3	0	.0
94934	2.6	89	.7	1	26.7	408	95.3*13	8	10	1.1	0	0	1.4
94937	1.1	96	.5	55	32.3	512	211.6	8	10	.5	10	0	.0
94938	.6	100		58	27.8	691	206.8	6	2	.3	2	0	.0
94939	5.9	97	2.7	47	41.3	598	318.9	4	10	2.7	7	0	1.9
94940	.7	88	.1	70	30.3	304	179.8	1	5	.7	10	0	.0
94941	26.8	94	11.5	60	44.1	602	310.7	5	10	12.2	8	0	.2
94946	.5	100	.1	75	43.2	745	387.0	2	3	.2	2	0	.0
94947	48.5	92	17.2	65	39.6	570	253.5	7	7	21.8	6	1	.0
94950	.2	100		7	29.7	489	105.8*15	0	.1	0	1	.0	
94951	3.1	92	1.1	70	33.5	402	225.9	4	10	1.4	10	0	.0
94952	45.7	94	16.3	67	30.6	452	172.1	7	10	21.0	9	1	.0
94956	1.4	98	.5	60	34.7	488	207.3	8	7	.3	8	0	.0
94957	2.6	97	.8	86	84.1	764	375.0	5	12	1.2	12	0	.0
94960	14.4	96	5.9	68	36.8	550	271.8	5	13	6.6	11	0	.0
94963	.5	100	.1	76	30.7	539	255.4	8	30	.2	9	0	.0
94964	3.2	45	.1		36.0	224	128.3*			1.3	1	0	.0

*=Estimated **1.0=883 lbs per person, 100++ indicates per capita toxic waste generation > than 100 times the U.S. average of 883 lbs per capita.

ZIP CODE MEASURES OF SIZE, LEVELS OF AFFLUENCE AND QUALITY OF LIFE

1=Population (th.); 2= % White; 3=Households (th.); 4=% Owner Occupied; 5=Mean Income Per Household (th.$); 6=Mean Monthly Rent ($); 7=Mean Home Value (th.$)*; 8=% under 5; 9=% 65 and over; 10=White Males (th.); 11=% White Males, 65+; 12=# Toxic Waste Sites; 13=Toxic Waste Relative to US(883 lbs.per capita)**.

CALIFORNIA

ZIPCODE	1	2	3	4	5	6	7	8	9	10	11	12	13
SAN RAFAEL													
94965	10.2	83	5.4	42	44.5	587	316.6	4	9	4.4	8	0	.1
94970	.8	88	.4	48	32.8	608	328.4	5	12	.4	12	0	.0
94971	.3	0	.2	38	16.9	301	167.3	14	9	.0	0	0	.0
94972	.2	100	.1	79	39.9	407	148.8	3	6	.0	11	0	.0
94973	1.3	0	.4	83	35.7	561	237.3	8	10	.0	0	0	.0
SAN JOSE													
95002	1.8	57	.5	54	26.2	329	85.4	10	5	.5	8	1	.0
95003	17.4	96	6.8	70	38.2	539	237.4	5	12	8.2	11	0	.0
95005	2.1	87	.7	72	29.0	396	168.0	11	10	.8	10	0	.0
95006	6.0	97	2.2	72	30.7	490	182.1	8	9	2.9	8	0	.0
95007	7.4	96	3.0	72	30.7	495	173.9	8	8	3.7	6	0	.0
95008	38.2	91	15.7	49	31.1	457	195.6	6	6	.3	6	0	.0
95010	8.8	96	4.2	42	21.5	512	185.3	6	5	17.0	7	0	.3
95012	6.6	52	2.0	57	24.4	491	166.1	11	7	1.6	11	2	.0
95017	43.3	90	15.7	63	41.9	612	251.6	5	6	19.6	5	3	1.4
95018	.5	87	.2	50	25.5	402	140.7	4	12	.2	7	1	.0
95019	6.6	96	2.6	68	26.9	466	152.1	8	8	3.2	7	0	.0
95020	4.1	75	1.3	60	24.0	390	120.8	10	10	1.5	11	0	.0
95023	27.9	70	8.6	60	31.8	396	175.9	10	8	9.5	9	1	1.1
95030	20.3	72	6.4	58	25.9	320	141.8	9	10	7.1	11	2	.0
95035	44.4	96	16.6	71	47.1	568	302.9	5	6	19.6	7	1	1.2
95037	37.8	72	11.4	72	35.1	575	168.6	9	4	14.1	7	3	.6
95039	24.0	81	7.3	73	39.8	472	246.8	9	6	9.7	6	2	.1
95041	.5	76	.7	73	25.4	243	96.7	2	14	.2	12	0	.0
95043	.7	0	.3	67	25.7	396	209.1	2	18	.0	0	0	.0
95045	.3	79	.1	46	27.9	321*	37.2	2	22	.1	22	0	.0
95046	2.9	72	.9	53	27.2	324	159.6	9	11	1.1	12	0	.0
95050	5.5	78	1.5	74	36.8	415	241.8	8	5	2.2	15	0	.0
95051	36.6	81	15.2	44	28.9	473	170.0	6	12	14.1	9	9	2.7
95054	48.9	85	18.8	51	34.9	554	184.0	6	6	20.7	5	0	2.1
95060	.7	84	.3	48	27.1	378	134.0	8	9	.3	7	0	7.6
95062	34.3	92	14.0	53	27.7	441	200.9	6	14	15.2	12	2	.2
95065	28.1	94	12.5	48	22.2	468	162.4	6	18	12.2	15	0	2.2
95066	5.3	94	1.8	75	31.9	387	215.4	6	8	2.6	6	1	.0
95073	9.9	97	3.6	76	36.1	507	233.5	6	13	4.7	12	1	.3
95075	30.9	95	9.9	89	62.3	592	356.7	4	8	14.4	6	0	.1
95076	7.8	94	3.2	71	27.7	477	215.5	7	17	3.5	15	0	.0
95075	.5	89	.1	62	25.0	192	162.3	19	5	.2	3	0	.0
95076	53.7	70	17.4	60	28.5	357	152.5	9	12	18.3	12	5	.0
SAN JOSE													
95110	14.6	59	4.8	35	21.2	382	120.7	9	11	4.3	11	3	2.5
95111	37.6	67	12.2	68	29.5	512	149.2	11	6	12.6	6	0	.0
95112	39.4	61	14.9	32	20.5	365	129.7	7	12	12.3	11	5	3.4
95113	.8	72	.6	62	11.5	165	121.9	3	9	.3	45	0	6.0
95114	.2	90	.1	67	44.5	511*	371.9	1	43	.3	45	0	.5
95116	31.3	45	9.9	38	21.6	395	117.3	11	9	6.7	12	1	.0
95117	22.8	85	9.8	36	29.2	497	191.3	6	7	9.3	7	0	.0
95118	30.5	90	10.3	64	35.4	567	176.8	7	5	13.7	7	0	.0

CALIFORNIA

ZIPCODE	1	2	3	4	5	6	7	8	9	10	11	12	13
SAN JOSE													
95119	9.6	84	2.7	76	37.4	605	183.6	9	3	4.0	1	0	.0
95120	31.2	92	8.9	92	54.3	742	287.6	6	3	14.3	2	1	.0
95121	25.3	63	7.5	81	38.0	624	173.3	11	3	8.0	3	0	.7
95122	54.5	50	14.5	68	32.3	509	152.0	11	3	13.7	3	0	.0
95123	50.7	85	15.6	71	36.6	610	181.6	9	4	21.2	3	0	.6
95124	45.8	92	15.6	72	37.9	587	191.5	6	6	20.8	5	0	.0
95125	40.7	89	16.6	70	34.9	483	202.0	6	17	16.9	15	0	.1
95126	20.2	80	9.5	36	25.5	439	176.8	6	13	7.8	11	0	.4
95127	44.7	66	13.7	76	33.6	506	164.1	8	7	14.5	7	0	.0
95128	26.7	84	11.8	44	28.2	459	171.5	6	14	10.5	12	0	.1
95129	35.1	90	12.9	57	37.9	554	213.5	5	5	15.8	4	0	.0
95130	10.6	91	4.6	57	33.7	560	179.2	5	5	5.8	4	0	.0
95131	10.6	65	3.3	81	33.8	686	180.7	11	3	3.4	3	1	.0
95132	35.5	72	10.3	81	41.3	638	193.3	9	2	13.0	1	0	2.6
95133	14.6	48	4.4	59	33.3	421	190.9	12	4	3.6	4	1	.9
95134	3.7	91	1.1	86	29.0	212	172.4	6	6	1.7	6	1	4.2
95135	5.2	87	2.1	91	45.2	563	203.9	6	24	2.2	26	0	.0
95136	24.8	86	7.5	82	39.5	635	200.9	9	4	10.4	4	0	.0
95138	2.2	72	.7	88	32.7	636	210.1	17	1	.8	1	0	.0
95139	6.5	86	1.9	81	40.7	754	190.1	11	1	2.8	2	0	.0
95148	2.9	60	.8	95	44.1	685	178.9	8	2	.9	2	0	.0
STOCKTON													
95202	6.2	67	3.4	6	11.6	208	118.3	6	20	2.1	19	0	.8
95203	13.8	64	5.9	52	19.0	240	82.7	7	19	4.1	17	2	.4
95204	26.5	86	11.1	70	26.6	329	101.4	6	18	10.4	17	0	.1
95205	45.3	68	15.5	64	20.6	276	66.9	9	12	15.1	13	1	.1
95206	25.4	31	7.8	53	18.3	238	55.7	10	11	3.8	13	0	.3
95207	39.8	79	15.5	50	28.2	350	129.6	7	9	15.0	8	0	.0
95208	.2	63	.1	85	29.8	342*126.9		0	11	.1	25	0	11.9
95209	25.2	86	8.8	67	36.0	382	154.5	9	4	10.7	4	0	.0
95210	16.2	75	5.5	59	26.2	341	103.5	12	6	6.0	6	0	.0
95212	5.9	91	2.1	89	37.4	294	174.4	5	12	2.7	12	0	.0
95220	5.1	88	1.7	78	31.5	257	144.4	5	23	2.3	11	1	.0
95221	1.4	98	.6	72	20.6	339	117.7	4	23	.6	22	0	.3
95222	1.9	98	.7	71	27.4	293	104.7	7	13	1.5	11	0	.0
95223	3.0	99	1.2	73	29.6	362	143.8	6	11	1.5	12	0	.0
95224	.5	96	.2	100	20.7	237*144.6		12	23	.2	22	0	.6
95225	.7	100	.2	72	33.9	392	145.2	3	8	.3	0	0	.0
95227	.4	79	.1	79	37.3	429*139.3		3	8	.2	23	0	.0
95228	.4	94	.2	80	28.8	303	151.5	4	16	.2	23	1	.4
95230	.7	100	.2	58	28.3	214	111.1	7	14	.3	15	0	.0
95231	3.6	50	.9	53	22.3	187	92.0	9	11	1.0	11	1	.0
95232	.3	94	.1	73	12.5	210	135.5	2	24	.1	21	0	.0
95233	.3	0	.1	84	26.2	393	134.1	4	18	.6	22	0	.0
95234	.3	44	.1	0	24.6	199	87.6*11	0	0	.1	0	2	.0
95236	3.5	90	1.2	72	33.3	281	142.4	6	12	1.6	13	1	.0
95237	2.3	88	.8	78	27.1	324	97.8	12	13	.9	13	0	.0
95240	44.1	90	17.0	62	27.1	326	119.7	7	15	19.1	14	1	.4
95245	1.3	0	.5	78	22.6	265	111.3	6	16	.0	0	0	.0

*=Estimated **1.0=883 lbs per person; 100++ indicates per capita toxic waste generation > than 100 times the U.S. average of 883 lbs per capita.

103031

ZIP CODE MEASURES OF SIZE, LEVELS OF AFFLUENCE AND QUALITY OF LIFE

1=Population (th.); 2= % White; 3=Households (th.); 4=% Owner Occupied; 5=Mean Income Per Household (th.$); 6=Mean Monthly Rent ($)*; 7=Mean Home Value (th.$)*;
8=% under 5; 9=% 65 and over; 10=White Males (th.); 11=% White Males, 65+; 12=# Toxic Waste Sites; 13=Toxic Waste Relative to US(883 lbs.per capita)**.

CALIFORNIA

STOCKTON

ZIPCODE	1	2	3	4	5	6	7	8	9	10	11	12	13
95246	.8	95	.3	79	27.8	204	114.5	6	11	.4	8	0	.0
95247	2.2	93	.8	80	21.3	333	133.8	6	21	1.0	21	0	.0
95248	.3	100	.1	61	12.5	395	82.4	6	10	.1	13	0	.0
95249	3.0	95	1.2	66	27.6	337	113.8	3	23	1.4	21	0	.1
95251	.3	100	.1	73	18.6	456	93.1	6	15	.1	12	0	.0
95252	1.7	0	.6	73	26.3	354	113.7	7	12	.0	0	0	.0
95253	.3	64	.1	75	19.1	337	79.1	7	19	.1	24	0	.0
95254	.2	100	.1	76	19.9	229*	148.4	10	12	.1	18	0	.0
95255	1.5	91	.6	80	20.8	357	92.3	8	16	.7	15	0	.3
95257	1.9	0	.6	72	15.5	231	98.9	3	25	.0	0	0	3
95258	.6	70	.6	61	22.2	287	113.4	8	9	.6	9	0	.0

STOCKTON

ZIPCODE	1	2	3	4	5	6	7	8	9	10	11	12	13
95301	20.7	80	6.8	53	25.9	353	101.7	11	6	8.2	5	0	.0
95303	.7	74	.2	60	29.4	283	82.9	7	6	.3	5	0	.0
95305	.2	100	.1	85	19.1	470	55.3	3	17	.1	11	0	.0
95306	.6	0	.1	68	19.7	344	86.6	6	16	.0	0	0	.0
95307	18.1	90	6.4	63	24.5	334	105.7	8	10	8.0	10	0	.0
95309	.1	100	.1	40	18.7	355	93.2	8	28	.1	22	0	.0
95310	1.5	98	.7	70	21.2	311	143.4	6	19	.7	19	0	.0
95311	1.2	0	.5	83	19.3	215	98.4	9	19	.0	0	0	.0
95312	.2	0	.1	73	23.9	267	78.4	8	9	.0	0	0	.0
95313	1.5	83	.5	50	33.0	231	76.2	10	10	.7	10	0	.2
95315	4.7	84	1.5	67	21.5	263	80.1	9	11	1.9	12	0	.0
95316	5.0	89	1.6	75	30.0	334	120.0	9	8	2.2	9	0	.0
95317	1.0	76	.3	43	21.9	226	117.0	12	4	.3	6	0	.0
95318	.5	97	.2	53	22.9	310	52.5	6	6	.2	13	0	.0
95319	2.6	90	.9	65	19.5	232	70.5	10	10	1.1	9	0	.0
95320	7.7	91	2.6	66	30.5	319	118.6	8	13	3.5	13	0	.1
95321	1.7	96	.7	63	23.2	327	137.3	9	11	.8	13	0	.0
95322	5.1	95	2.0	67	28.1	283	95.8	7	14	2.4	13	0	.2
95323	1.2	89	.4	61	25.1	348	86.3	7	9	.6	11	0	.0
95324	4.3	95	1.3	64	24.9	334	93.0	11	9	2.1	10	0	.0
95325	.2	0	.1	27	18.2	231	306.3	4	6	.0	0	0	.0
95326	5.7	87	1.8	63	27.7	281	124.0	8	9	2.5	9	0	.0
95327	4.9	85	1.5	71	21.2	340	115.2	5	13	2.2	13	0	.0
95328	1.8	90	.6	60	18.2	327	57.6	11	9	.8	10	0	.0
95329	1.0	100	.3	64	29.0	134	96.6	6	19	.3	17	0	.0
95330	4.6	59	1.4	74	23.6	311	84.0	9	7	1.4	14	2	22.5
95333	2.3	76	.6	56	25.6	218	69.1	7	7	.8	5	0	.0
95334	7.8	54	2.1	61	25.5	287	83.9	12	7	2.1	8	0	.0
95335	.2	87	.1	72	24.6	540	87.9	3	18	.1	17	0	.0
95336	32.9	89	11.1	63	27.5	369	109.5	9	8	14.3	8	3	.0
95337	5.9	94	2.3	77	22.2	376	122.8	6	19	2.7	18	0	.0
95340	53.0	76	18.9	56	25.4	329	107.6	9	9	19.8	8	0	.0
95342	1.2	66	.4	7	15.5	340	55.4*	1	2	.2	8	0	.1
95345	.5	85	.2	71	21.1	171	130.6	7	24	.2	28	0	.0
95346	1.0	97	.4	70	24.3	321	127.3	12	14	.4	15	0	.0
95347	.2	0	.1	22	27.5	83	97.9*	0	5	.0	0	0	.0
95350	57.9	93	21.6	66	31.0	371	125.4	7	11	25.6	0	0	.0

CALIFORNIA

STOCKTON

ZIPCODE	1	2	3	4	5	6	7	8	9	10	11	12	13
95351	58.4	83	20.2	62	23.1	317	89.7	10	11	23.8	12	2	.6
95354	6.6	90	3.3	41	18.5	267	102.9	6	22	2.9	20	0	.3
95355	29.9	91	10.5	65	31.2	408	143.0	8	7	13.3	7	0	.0
95360	4.2	89	1.5	60	23.7	290	87.1	8	16	1.8	15	0	.0
95361	16.7	93	6.1	68	27.1	328	124.5	7	13	7.6	12	0	.1
95363	6.7	68	2.1	59	25.9	269	88.1	9	10	2.2	12	0	.0
95364	.3	100	.1	60	24.8	288	120.7	3	11	.1	17	0	.0
95365	2.7	56	.7	59	19.5	233	59.1	13	8	.7	10	0	.3
95366	6.2	93	2.2	70	33.7	315	120.1	9	12	2.8	10	0	3.2
95367	6.7	76	2.0	70	23.8	286	104.7	9	9	.7	8	1	.8
95368	1.9	76	.6	58	22.5	250	67.1	9	10	.7	10	0	.3
95369	1.0	94	.4	33	17.3	253	58.0	9	11	.5	13	0	.0
95370	16.5	97	6.5	72	23.6	368	132.5	7	15	7.7	14	0	.1
95372	1.3	96	.5	77	23.9	482	124.6	10	15	.6	14	0	.0
95373	.2	0	.1	47	25.7	387	118.1	9	6	.0	0	0	.0
95374	1.4	84	.4	70	21.4	267	135.3	4	8	.6	6	0	.0
95375	.2	100	.1	100	47.1	541*	168.8	0	0	.1	0	0	.0
95376	26.7	81	8.9	63	26.9	315	114.9	8	10	10.8	10	2	.1
95379	2.8	94	.7	66	19.0	328	94.7	7	14	1.3	14	0	.1
95380	37.2	91	13.5	57	25.8	320	115.7	8	12	16.2	11	1	.0
95383	2.9	97	1.1	70	28.2	388	136.9	5	8	1.5	9	0	.0
95385	.4	26	.1	46	86.3	344	177.5	9	3	.0	0	0	.2
95386	4.2	94	1.5	73	25.2	314	99.6	8	14	1.9	14	0	.0
95387	.8	31	.2	40	25.1	246	44.4	13	7	.4	14	0	.0
95388	6.8	86	2.1	65	25.0	316	92.0	10	7	2.9	7	0	.0
95389	1.5	93	.4	20	25.8	157	69.3	3	1	.7	0	0	.0

SANTA ROSA

ZIPCODE	1	2	3	4	5	6	7	8	9	10	11	12	13
95401	58.2	90	22.5	58	25.1	437	153.0	8	13	25.1	12	3	.1
95404	28.3	94	11.9	59	31.9	399	194.0	6	16	12.5	13	0	.0
95405	37.1	97	14.6	71	31.9	505	183.8	5	18	16.7	16	0	.2
95410	.4	97	.4	62	16.7	231	127.1	8	4	.4	4	0	.0
95411	.8	79	.4	59	22.6	216	31.1	14	9	.2	4	0	.0
95412	.1	0	.1	86	24.4	281*	135.6	0	15	.0	0	0	.0
95415	1.1	95	.4	55	21.2	268	114.2	6	12	.6	13	0	.0
95416	1.2	99	.6	35	20.0	391	130.2	9	15	.6	10	0	.0
95417	.3	0	.1	79	27.6	348	118.1	11	20	.2	14	1	.0
95418	.2	94	.2	53	18.4	272	134.6	3	11	.2	14	0	.0
95419	.6	94	.2	76	37.5	378	105.6	7	12	.2	14	1	.0
95420	.4	100	.2	64	25.8	230	226.8	3	9	.3	9	0	.0
95421	1.0	96	.4	65	24.6	296	125.9	5	6	.5	6	0	.0
95422	8.8	95	3.8	78	16.5	307	83.5	5	25	4.0	28	0	.0
95423	2.5	94	.7	74	15.4	376	104.4	5	24	1.2	25	0	.4
95424	1.6	95	.7	72	18.9	262	125.5	8	23	.7	22	0	.0
95425	2.4	92	2.4	64	25.4	356	132.7	6	16	2.9	13	2	.3
95426	1.1	96	.4	77	26.3	494	121.9	4	21	.6	23	0	.0
95427	.3	100	.1	61	20.2	233*	149.7	7	4	.1	10	0	.4
95428	2.2	83	.7	74	24.5	255	134.0	6	9	1.0	10	0	.0
95431	1.8	87	.1	88	33.1	381*	180.0	2	3	.8	0	0	.8
95432	.2	82	.2	65	19.4	375	163.9	8	10	.2	11	0	.0

*=Estimated **1.0=883 lbs per person; 100++ indicates per capita toxic waste generation > than 100 times the U.S. average of 883 lbs per capita.

103001

ZIP CODE MEASURES OF SIZE, LEVELS OF AFFLUENCE AND QUALITY OF LIFE

1=Population (th.); 2= % White; 3=Households (th.); 4=% Owner Occupied; 5=Mean Income Per Household (th.); 6=Mean Monthly Rent ($); 7=Mean Home Value (th.$);
8=% under 5; 9=% 65 and over; 10=White Males (th.); 11=% White Males, 65+; 12=# Toxic Waste Sites; 13=Toxic Waste Relative to US(883 lbs.per capita)**

CALIFORNIA — SANTA ROSA

ZIP CODE	1	2	3	4	5	6	7	8	9	10	11	12	13
95433	.6	94	.2	44	19.5	439	136.4	8	7	.2	4	0	.0
95435	.3	48	.1	70	14.6	301	43.1	6	14	.1	30	0	.0
95436	4.4	95	1.7	67	24.4	418	142.5	8	12	2.1	12	0	.0
95437	12.3	96	4.9	67	23.8	387	139.8	6	14	5.8	12	2	.1
95439	.6	100	.2	56	30.0	366	186.8	12	14	.3	5	0	.0
95440	2.3	95	.9	66	21.5	327	130.3	7	8	1.1	5	0	.0
95441	1.9	73	.6	61	28.0	304	123.6	8	15	.7	18	0	.0
95442	2.6	96	1.1	54	26.1	392	172.0	6	11	1.2	8	0	.0
95444	.1	100	.1	83	15.5	256	56.9	3	44	.1	56	0	.0
95445	.5	91	.2	68	22.8	321	115.4	12	12	.2	13	0	.0
95446	1.2	98	.6	62	19.9	324	170.2	6	17	.6	18	0	.0
95448	4.0	94	1.8	56	20.5	358	133.9	9	15	1.9	16	1	.0
95449	13.3	91	5.0	62	29.0	405	163.9	7	15	6.0	14	0	.0
95450	.9	87	.3	52	23.3	206	103.4	6	12	.4	10	0	.0
95451	.4	92	.2	57	27.0	264	174.7	7	22	.2	22	0	.0
95452	5.1	92	2.0	79	23.1	287	151.6	6	20	2.3	20	0	.0
95453	1.7	97	.6	81	26.1	456	199.3	8	15	.6	18	0	.0
95454	7.8	95	3.3	72	24.5	342	132.2	7	20	3.5	16	0	.0
95455	2.1	86	.8	74	19.0	332	85.1	8	9	.9	12	0	.0
95456	.7	96	.3	47	17.7	278	90.9	6	8	.9	10	0	.0
95457	.7	0	.3	71	25.9	466	221.8	6	13	.7	12	0	.0
95458	.6	95	.3	81	25.2	564	135.6	6	15	.6	13	0	.0
95459	2.0	95	.9	75	15.5	211	84.6	4	34	.9	35	0	.0
95460	.4	0	.1	73	18.4	180	85.1	5	16	.8	12	0	.0
95461	1.6	98	.8	56	32.6	312	222.9	5	14	.7	13	3	.0
95462	2.4	96	.9	70	21.2	398	102.0	6	13	1.2	13	0	.0
95463	1.2	97	.6	54	16.5	346	123.2	6	18	.6	15	0	.0
95464	1.9	64	.8	76	18.6	118	66.4*	4	0	.8	0	0	.0
95465	1.2	94	.7	74	17.2	248	106.3	4	28	.8	35	0	.0
95466	.7	99	.3	43	22.6	416	186.6	6	13	.6	9	0	.0
95467	.2	92	.1	56	18.9	255	90.2	6	9	.6	11	0	.0
95468	1.1	87	.5	46	9.4	329	33.5*	3	15	.5	0	0	.0
95470	1.6	97	.5	45	21.3	294	101.3	6	9	.5	8	0	.0
95471	4.4	95	1.5	74	22.5	340	134.3	8	7	2.0	7	0	.0
95472	.5	0	.2	76	25.0	390	127.7	7	9	2.0	7	0	.0
95476	24.2	94	9.1	43	20.8	430	188.9	9	14	11.1	12	1	.0
95481	21.8	97	9.2	70	29.2	418	171.8	5	23	10.1	21	1	.0
95482	.3	82	.1	68	27.2	309	93.6	8	13	.1	7	0	.0
95485	23.2	92	8.6	62	25.8	388	135.6	8	13	10.3	11	0	.2
95486	2.1	87	.8	68	21.5	401	91.9	8	16	1.0	15	0	.0
95488	.2	100	.1	69	20.8	377	77.3	0	14	.0	13	0	.0
95489	.1	0	.2	77	14.6	203	130.0	13	24	.3	10	0	.0
95490	.6	92	.2	90	19.5	90	106.5	9	12	.3	10	1	.0
95492	9.0	94	3.3	65	23.9	363	113.0	9	12	4.2	12	1	.1
95494	6.8	84	2.4	73	26.8	389	145.5	7	14	2.8	14	1	.0
95495	.2	74	.1	61	20.6	112	126.9	17	4	.1	0	0	.0
95497	.3	100	.1	80	43.6	485	296.4	6	13	.2	13	0	.0

CALIFORNIA — EUREKA

ZIP CODE	1	2	3	4	5	6	7	8	9	10	11	12	13
95501	41.6	93	16.6	60	24.6	351	105.6	7	12	19.1	11	2	.0
95521	26.8	93	9.9	56	23.5	379	107.7	6	7	12.8	7	1	.0
95524	1.5	96	.5	76	33.6	362	147.3	8	6	.7	7	0	.0
95525	1.7	89	.7	65	24.8	372	94.8	6	8	.7	8	0	.0
95526	.9	94	.3	55	21.6	156	138.1	8	4	.5	6	0	.0
95527	.4	0	.1	54	22.8	209	75.8	10	9	.0	0	0	.0
95528	1.0	92	.3	73	22.6	421	117.7	6	10	.5	10	0	.0
95531	13.6	91	5.1	68	22.8	315	95.0	8	12	6.2	12	0	.0
95534	.4	100	.2	61	30.7	392	107.0	2	4	.2	2	0	.0
95536	3.0	96	1.1	64	27.3	301	112.3	6	13	1.5	12	1	.0
95537	.5	87	.2	47	22.5	303	79.6	3	7	.2	11	0	.0
95538	.9	92	.2	76	14.7	215	100.4	11	7	.2	13	1	.0
95540	9.2	95	3.6	67	23.7	352	97.5	7	15	4.2	13	2	.0
95543	.5	85	.2	52	21.4	270	105.7	12	12	.3	11	0	.0
95545	.2	0	.1	56	13.3	210	148.8	8	13	.3	11	0	.0
95546	2.4	22	.8	69	19.9	210	68.9	12	8	.3	17	15	1.2
95547	1.0	96	.4	76	28.1	329	104.7	6	8	.4	8	0	.0
95548	1.2	80	.5	65	23.2	284	82.5	7	11	.5	12	0	.0
95549	.5	95	.2	79	28.5	300	110.1	5	7	.2	6	0	.0
95550	.2	85	.1	44	29.8	210	30.6	8	7	.1	9	0	.0
95551	1.5	94	.5	59	26.6	345	105.1	9	11	.7	12	0	.0
95552	.2	100	.1	42	29.7	265	105.9*	11	5	.1	10	0	.0
95553	.8	100	.3	72	21.6	178	120.3	6	10	.4	11	0	.0
95554	.3	100	.1	87	13.5	182	98.0	8	29	.1	35	0	.0
95555	.7	94	.3	46	27.3	262	71.6	9	4	.3	5	0	.0
95556	.8	81	.3	48	19.3	230	79.4	9	8	.3	13	0	.0
95558	.3	100	.1	92	16.8	193*	65.6	6	18	.1	19	0	.0
95559	.1	0	.1	73	20.0	248	49.7	0	19	.0	0	0	.0
95560	1.6	94	.5	62	18.1	238	102.8	13	8	.9	18	0	.0
95562	2.5	90	.9	61	20.6	302	72.1	9	13	1.1	13	0	.0
95563	.7	90	.2	69	21.4	301	100.9	8	12	.3	9	0	.0
95564	.5	97	.1	19	29.1	308	54.5	12	1	.3	17	0	.1
95565	1.4	97	.4	27	26.6	211	93.3	7	8	.3	9	0	.0
95567	2.2	82	.8	64	21.0	314	106.9	5	17	.9	11	0	.0
95568	.3	93	.1	47	17.4	226	45.9	9	5	.1	6	0	.0
95569	.3	100	.1	60	21.9	260	123.3	8	13	.2	17	0	.0
95570	2.3	93	1.0	62	22.8	393	129.1	7	11	1.1	10	0	.0
95571	.4	79	.1	60	17.6	312	51.1	7	5	.2	6	1	.0
95573	1.5	90	.6	70	22.9	270	109.3	10	11	.8	12	0	.0

SACRAMENTO

ZIP CODE	1	2	3	4	5	6	7	8	9	10	11	12	13
95601	.2	0	.1	86	23.7	273	131.6	5	26	.0	0	0	.0
95603	29.4	96	11.1	70	28.8	399	152.9	6	15	13.6	14	0	.0
95605	10.4	68	4.1	47	19.0	245	70.1	9	11	3.7	16	1	.0
95607	.3	78	.2	90	24.7	284*	91.9	0	8	.1	12	0	.0
95608	52.2	95	20.0	61	32.9	374	162.1	5	9	23.8	7	0	.0
95610	65.0	94	23.5	69	29.5	429	124.6	7	9	29.9	6	0	.0
95612	1.5	74	.4	47	32.5	258	158.2	8	7	.1	0	0	1.7
95613	.4	81	.1	60	27.0	331	148.9	9	20	.1	0	0	.0
95614	1.1	97	.1	87	31.4	482	182.2	6	12	.6	9	0	.0

*=Estimated **1.0=883 lbs per person; 100++ indicates per capita toxic waste generation > than 100 times the U.S. average of 883 lbs per capita.

ZIP CODE MEASURES OF SIZE, LEVELS OF AFFLUENCE AND QUALITY OF LIFE

1=Population (th.); 2= % White; 3=Households (th.); 4=% Owner Occupied; 5=Mean Income Per Household (th.\$); 6=Mean Monthly Rent (\$); 7=Mean Home Value (th.\$); 8=% under 5; 9=% 65 and over; 10=White Males (th.); 11=% White Males, 65+; 12=# Toxic Waste Sites; 13=Toxic Waste Relative to US(883 lbs.per capita)**.

CALIFORNIA — SACRAMENTO

ZIP CODE	1	2	3	4	5	6	7	8	9	10	11	12	13
95615	.9	65	.3	41	29.9	266	105.8	9	8	.3	7	0	.1
95616	43.8	87	15.5	45	27.0	398	170.0	5	4	18.8	4	0	.1
95619	3.4	97	1.3	80	25.6	466	134.7	6	18	1.6	17	2	.1
95623	10.2	79	3.2	67	28.6	329	134.9	10	7	3.9	7	1	.0
95624	1.3	95	.4	80	25.7	383	148.7	8	9	.6	9	0	.0
95625	16.9	92	5.2	79	35.2	396	143.8	8	7	7.7	5	0	.4
95626	.3	73	.1	42	18.2	442	77.6	14	12	.1	20	1	.0
95627	4.1	92	1.2	87	28.9	370	98.5	12	5	1.8	5	0	.0
95628	1.9	85	.7	70	25.6	365	113.0	10	14	.8	15	0	.0
95629	34.1	95	12.0	72	38.2	420	181.9	6	5	16.3	5	0	.0
95630	.4	100	.2	72	16.9	342	77.5	6	11	.2	8	0	.0
95631	14.4	96	5.2	77	31.6	361	172.5	7	12	6.7	11	0	.8
95632	2.4	95	.8	87	26.4	412	129.0	9	11	1.3	12	0	.0
95633	9.8	91	3.2	72	27.8	309	112.5	8	12	4.4	12	0	.6
95634	1.4	95	.5	88	24.1	525	125.1	9	8	.7	11	0	.0
95635	1.4	94	.6	71	24.3	394	129.2	3	14	.7	12	0	.0
95636	.4	0	.1	60	26.3	263	115.7	5	15	.0	0	0	.0
95637	.3	100	.1	60	13.6	349	117.7	9	5	.1	0	0	.0
95638	.9	89	.2	80	23.2	213	85.5	8	28	.4	14	0	.0
95639	3.2	68	.2	72	34.7	539	151.6	5	4	.7	5	0	.0
95640	1.8	88	1.0	65	19.3	225	108.6	0	23	.1	24	0	.0
95641	4.4	74	1.0	62	26.5	300	106.4	7	9	1.5	8	1	.5
95642	.2	97	1.8	70	23.8	236	89.8	5	20	.6	21	0	.0
95643	.4	100	.1	89	25.9	359	122.6	4	21	.2	20	0	.0
95644	1.4	94	.4	77	23.5	270*	116.4	9	12	.1	12	0	.0
95645	1.4	77	.4	67	24.5	283	163.4	0	10	.2	13	0	.0
95646	1.4	100	.1	55	30.2	239	82.7	9	13	.5	17	0	.0
95648	8.1	87	2.7	75	41.6	400	233.9	0	0	.1	0	0	.0
95650	9.8	92	3.2	87	27.4	294	105.1	8	11	3.5	10	0	.1
95651	.2	100	.1	66	36.1	385	192.3	5	8	4.5	8	0	.0
95652	1.3	74	.1	0	25.0	253	120.6	5	9	.7	5	0	.0
95653	.4	42	.1	75	22.8	409	89.0*	5	1	.7	0	0	.2
95655	5.2	78	.1	2	19.5	225	65.4	8	7	.1	6	0	.0
95656	.3	96	.2	69	23.7	339	69.5*15	0	0	.2	4	0	.1
95658	4.7	94	1.6	85	30.3	60	126.6	8	25	.1	26	0	.0
95659	.4	0	1.2	84	25.8	355	174.8	5	11	2.1	9	1	.0
95660	20.7	81	10.2	66	22.4	450	126.0	5	17	1.7	18	0	.0
95662	31.2	95	8.0	64	25.3	295	107.8	6	15	9.8	14	0	.0
95663	24.3	92	.6	81	31.0	380	86.0	6	10	12.5	5	0	.0
95665	2.0	92	.6	89	32.7	449	132.9	8	6	11.6	6	0	.0
95666	2.0	94	.7	88	25.8	138	163.2	5	8	.9	6	0	.0
95667	3.4	99	1.4	84	22.4	355	134.6	7	15	1.0	17	0	.0
95668	1.7	97	.7	75	26.0	450	126.0	5	17	1.7	18	0	.0
95669	34.3	96	7.7	75	26.0	408	136.0	6	15	9.8	14	0	.0
95670	1.2	85	.2	74	33.0	244	151.7	8	5	1.6	4	0	.0
95672	20.7	0	12.4	56	26.2	309	152.0	6	14	.8	11	0	.0
95673	.8	90	1.4	82	26.4	355	134.6	5	8	1.0	17	0	.0
95674	10.3	90	3.4	77	30.8	513	141.2	6	12	.0	0	0	.0
	.7	81	.2	74	26.8	334	120.1	8	7	.2	8	0	.0

CALIFORNIA — SACRAMENTO

ZIP CODE	1	2	3	4	5	6	7	8	9	10	11	12	13
95675	.3	0	.1	81	16.2	286	55.2	15	11	.0	0	0	.0
95676	.4	80	.1	47	20.5	235*	112.3	11	10	.2	8	1	.0
95677	10.0	96	3.6	72	33.8	373	154.8	8	9	4.7	8	0	.0
95678	34.2	93	12.4	73	29.9	375	146.9	7	11	15.6	9	2	.0
95680	.2	0	.3	67	18.7	290	156.3	9	9	.0	0	0	.0
95681	.8	95	.3	83	19.5	300	85.3	12	6	.4	7	0	.4
95683	10.7	97	3.5	89	38.9	460	183.2	6	6	5.3	7	0	.0
95684	1.0	90	.4	80	44.8	440	282.2	6	16	.6	20	0	.0
95685	1.3	98	.5	86	21.6	270	96.5	9	11	.6	14	0	.0
95686	3.2	99	1.3	72	23.4	370	139.3	6	17	1.6	17	0	.3
95688	.9	74	.3	47	21.3	233	98.3	6	16	.3	13	0	.8
95689	48.0	85	.6	69	30.2	414	137.0	8	7	21.1	6	1	.0
95690	.6	94	.8	68	21.8	387	124.8	7	9	.3	7	0	.0
95691	14.7	63	2.5	49	30.7	245	124.8	6	14	.8	15	0	.6
95692	2.5	90	6.4	62	24.3	304	95.7	6	14	6.5	14	1	.3
95693	2.5	91	.8	62	25.1	291	89.1	9	13	1.0	14	0	.0
95694	5.0	97	.8	94	40.6	167	198.5	5	5	1.3	5	0	.0
95697	33.3	81	1.7	63	28.4	290	118.7	8	10	2.0	11	0	.4
95698	.6	71	.1	61	29.2	353	126.0	8	10	13.2	13	0	.0
95699	.2	86	.1	42	21.3	623	60.7	11	10	.3	10	0	.0
	.1	100	.1	100	14.9	171*	83.5	6	21	.1	14	0	.5

SACRAMENTO

ZIP CODE	1	2	3	4	5	6	7	8	9	10	11	12	13
95701	.4	100	.2	71	26.7	519	153.6	5	20	.2	17	0	.0
95702	2.6	92	.4	48	25.9	471	199.1	7	7	1.2	6	0	.0
95703	1.0	98	.4	86	25.0	167	136.8	3	18	.5	17	0	.0
95705	10.7	95	4.6	47	26.5	482	181.1	5	6	5.1	6	1	.0
95708	2.7	97	1.0	61	27.6	693	182.4	9	3	1.4	3	0	.0
95709	3.1	99	1.1	70	26.8	412	127.4	7	16	1.5	16	0	.1
95711	.9	0	.4	55	33.9	655	227.9	4	8	.0	0	0	.0
95712	.6	100	.6	78	26.4	506	207.7	7	13	.3	17	0	.0
95713	4.3	97	1.6	71	31.3	356	134.6	7	15	2.1	14	0	.2
95714	.2	100	.1	65	31.3	232	127.0	0	21	.1	25	0	.0
95717	.2	100	.1	74	21.3	285	102.2	8	23	.1	30	0	.1
95718	.5	0	.2	75	36.6	548	255.1	8	0	.1	26	0	.0
95719	2.6	95	1.2	39	22.1	424	167.7	8	5	1.2	5	0	.0
95720	1.0	100	.2	52	28.7	218	98.2	0	8	.0	17	0	.0
95722	3.0	98	1.0	88	30.3	545	158.0	6	10	1.5	10	0	.0
95726	4.5	98	1.8	78	23.3	435	133.9	7	14	2.1	14	1	.0
95727	.2	77	.1	79	26.1	53	96.7	3	10	.1	17	0	.0
95728	.2	0	.2	46	35.4	329	143.8	5	0	.0	0	0	.0
95729	3.8	81	1.7	21	21.9	450	188.7	7	5	1.6	4	0	.0
95730	5.0	97	1.9	54	31.8	560	276.8	6	3	1.5	2	0	.0
95731	5.4	98	2.2	50	27.5	488	191.4	8	6	2.6	6	0	.0
95732	.3	0	.1	79	19.4	242	373.3	3	0	.1	11	0	.0
95733	.9	98	.4	46	27.2	585	182.6	7	3	.4	4	0	.0
95734	5.1	97	1.9	65	32.6	476	182.5	8	4	2.6	4	1	.0
95736	.9	91	.4	59	30.9	383	109.2	7	17	.4	17	0	.0

*=Estimated **1.0=883 lbs per person; 100++ indicates per capita toxic waste generation > than 100 times the U.S. average of 883 lbs per capita.

ZIP CODE MEASURES OF SIZE, LEVELS OF AFFLUENCE AND QUALITY OF LIFE

1=Population (th.); 2= % White; 3=Households (th.); 4=% Owner Occupied; 5=Mean Income Per Household (th.$); 6=Mean Monthly Rent ($); 7=Mean Home Value (th.$); 8=% under 5; 9=% 65 and over; 10=White Males (th.); 11=% White Males, 65+; 12=# Toxic Waste Sites; 13=Toxic Waste Relative to US(883 lbs.per capita)**.

CALIFORNIA

SACRAMENTO

ZIPCODE	1	2	3	4	5	6	7	8	9	10	11	12	13
95814	13.9	64	7.9	7	13.7	213	104.1	4	22	5.2	22	2	.4
95815	19.7	81	8.7	46	18.8	280	75.6	8	14	7.5	14	0	.3
95816	16.2	83	9.3	27	18.0	285	117.1	4	23	6.0	18	1	.1
95817	12.5	56	5.5	49	16.9	264	70.2	8	17	3.3	17	0	.1
95818	21.3	66	9.7	55	25.2	280	127.7	6	22	6.3	22	1	.0
95819	17.1	95	7.6	77	29.1	390	128.5	4	24	7.2	22	1	.1
95820	30.2	68	11.9	67	21.3	305	74.2	8	14	9.7	15	1	.0
95821	30.7	92	14.0	50	26.6	334	131.2	6	12	13.3	11	0	.0
95822	40.8	54	14.0	70	28.7	341	107.9	6	12	10.2	14	0	.0
95823	33.7	73	12.5	65	27.0	340	110.6	8	7	11.7	8	1	.0
95824	19.8	62	7.1	56	19.6	300	75.1	10	10	5.8	12	1	.0
95825	48.6	93	21.9	49	34.1	399	173.2	4	10	21.5	9	0	.0
95826	39.8	82	15.1	62	29.3	387	127.1	8	5	16.1	4	3	.1
95827	13.6	81	4.9	70	29.2	454	122.8	4	9	5.6	4	0	.0
95828	19.2	73	6.7	77	27.7	371	104.4	8	9	7.0	9	1	.0
95829	.6	91	.2	90	86.8	125	122.9	7	5	.3	4	0	.0
95831	21.8	66	8.0	66	39.0	386	179.1	5	8	6.8	9	0	.0
95832	6.0	38	1.6	69	22.8	337	76.8	10	4	1.2	7	0	.0
95833	10.9	69	3.9	74	26.8	336	96.6	8	7	3.8	8	0	.0
95834	1.0	91	.4	82	38.2	193	131.7	7	10	.5	10	0	.3
95835	.5	85	.1	77	28.8	365	182.3	1	9	.1	9	0	.0
95837	.5	93	.1	79	27.6	455	105.7	4	7	.2	8	0	.0
95838	20.1	56	6.8	60	18.7	282	64.8	10	7	5.4	11	0	.0
95841	16.7	92	6.9	49	26.2	368	138.8	4	9	7.2	7	0	.0
95842	18.8	88	6.6	73	29.9	451	112.1	9	3	8.2	3	0	.0

MARYSVILLE

ZIPCODE	1	2	3	4	5	6	7	8	9	10	11	12	13
95901	30.9	85	11.6	56	21.7	277	89.5	8	10	12.8	10	2	.0
95903	7.2	78	1.9	7	18.2	335	117.3	15	1	3.1	1	1	.0
95910	.1	100		48	15.9	169	73.8	5	0	.1	0	1	.4
95912	2.1	81	.7	66	27.8	218	89.3	9	11	.9	12	0	.2
95913	.4	0	.1	69	32.7	293	86.8	7	12	.0	10	0	.0
95914	.9	92	.3	82	20.9	209	69.7	9	20	.4	23	0	.0
95916	.7	0	.2	85	19.1	177	104.6	6	15	.0	15	0	.0
95917	2.5	91	.9	74	30.7	285	82.9	7	15	1.1	15	0	.0
95918	.8	90	.3	89	30.7	343	147.2	5	10	.4	11	0	.0
95919	.9	91	.4	82	17.3	307	97.4	5	20	.4	19	0	.0
95920	.3	63	.1	55	27.5	158	42.1	10	23	.1	40	0	.0
95922	.8	0	.3	74	18.3	290	92.8	14	8	.0	8	0	.0
95923	.3	0	.1	75	39.0	398	173.2	4	10	.2	7	0	.0
95925	.4	100	.1	64	20.0	258	85.6	9	10	.2	12	0	.1
95926	60.9	94	24.3	51	23.3	356	125.9	6	10	27.9	9	3	.1
95931	.2	59	.1	45	23.4	260	56.0	12	6	.1	25	0	.0
95932	5.8	79	2.1	61	26.9	288	99.6	8	12	2.2	14	0	.0
95934	.6	85	.2	41	28.2	316	75.3	15	6	.3	7	0	.3
95935	.9	94	.3	67	16.3	288	84.7	6	19	.4	26	0	.0
95936	.5	99	.2	58	22.8	316	127.2	6	13	.3	11	1	.0
95937	.5	68	.2	71	23.2	235	78.4	6	11	.2	4	0	.0
95938	2.7	95	1.0	71	30.4	314	134.2	7	10	1.3	10	0	.0
95939	.5	82	.2	46	26.8	270	82.3	6	5	.2	6	0	.0

CALIFORNIA

MARYSVILLE

ZIPCODE	1	2	3	4	5	6	7	8	9	10	11	12	13
95941	.2	100	.1	73	19.3	185	71.1	5	6	.1	6	0	.0
95942	.7	0	.3	81	24.4	266	120.3	8	17	.0	0	0	.0
95943	1.0	99	.3	71	29.4	309	164.1	7	8	.5	7	0	.0
95945	23.4	97	9.5	72	23.4	370	136.8	6	20	10.7	19	3	.1
95946	3.3	97	1.2	86	31.2	579	180.9	7	13	1.6	14	0	.0
95947	1.8	93	.7	63	23.0	266	97.5	8	13	.8	11	0	.0
95948	9.0	83	3.1	65	22.2	252	93.1	8	15	3.6	16	0	.0
95950	.3	85	.1	61	18.8	234	65.3	9	20	.1	15	0	.0
95951	1.8	48	.5	63	21.0	337	71.7	10	11	.4	19	1	.3
95952	.1	100	.1	48	43.6	423	67.4	8	17	.1	22	0	.0
95953	5.7	81	2.0	63	23.2	246	87.9	8	11	2.3	11	2	.0
95954	5.8	99	2.4	90	21.6	364	118.9	9	25	2.8	27	0	.0
95955	1.0	87	.4	55	24.6	296	85.5	5	13	.4	14	0	.0
95956	.3	93	.1	62	25.8	244	137.9	16	8	.4	10	0	.0
95957	.9	87	.3	61	25.8	234	64.0	7	23	.3	24	0	.0
95958	.1	100	.1	58	20.4	115	63.8	13	12	.1	15	0	.0
95959	11.4	97	4.4	77	25.3	398	151.7	6	13	5.4	13	0	.0
95960	.7	94	.3	81	18.8	368	77.7	15	11	.4	11	0	.0
95961	5.8	86	2.0	68	18.1	266	62.8	9	12	2.5	13	0	.0
95962	.5	84	.5	69	21.0	235	53.1	6	10	.4	10	1	.3
95963	10.6	92	3.9	72	22.3	274	66.3	9	22	4.8	10	0	.0
95965	35.2	92	13.6	71	22.0	299	81.1	6	13	15.8	16	4	.3
95968	1.5	89	.5	81	18.4	322	56.4	5	19	.7	24	0	.1
95969	22.6	98	9.5	76	21.3	348	113.4	5	29	10.5	27	0	.0
95970	.7	75	.3	70	31.9	231	80.9	6	14	.3	17	0	.0
95971	5.5	94	2.4	63	24.0	336	118.8	7	10	2.7	9	3	.0
95972	.2	100	.1	90	23.3	267*	21.9	0	9	.1	8	0	.1
95974	.4	0	.2	89	36.3	231	107.7	14	16	.0	0	1	.0
95975	1.5	100	.6	81	28.5	453	159.4	5	12	.7	13	0	.4
95977	.4	100	.4	90	18.1	207*	103.7	0	18	.2	20	0	.2
95978	.3	0	.2	64	14.4	274	66.3	9	22	.0	1	0	.0
95979	.5	75	.1	74	23.5	299	81.1	6	13	.2	6	0	.0
95981	.1	100	.1	67	16.9	221	57.1	10	37	.1	41	0	.0
95982	2.4	95	.8	75	26.4	322	84.9	7	11	1.1	13	0	.0
95983	.4	0	.2	77	26.4	213	87.0	6	13	.0	0	0	.0
95984	.2	0	.1	39	14.5	238	69.4	16	27	.0	9	0	.0
95986	.2	100	.1	59	13.8	381	71.5	13	12	.1	9	0	.0
95987	2.3	84	.9	65	24.4	305	92.2	9	15	1.0	16	0	.0
95988	7.3	94	2.8	64	25.6	312	90.3	8	13	3.4	12	0	.0
95991	38.8	83	14.4	59	26.7	308	115.5	8	10	15.6	9	0	.1

REDDING

ZIPCODE	1	2	3	4	5	6	7	8	9	10	11	12	13
96001	43.7	96	17.3	61	25.3	330	120.2	7	12	20.3	11	0	.4
96002	17.4	96	6.2	65	26.8	414	114.5	8	9	8.1	8	0	.0
96003	2.1	96	.7	80	24.2	341	126.2	9	11	1.0	12	0	.0
96006	.5	0	.3	77	21.6	145	68.2	5	12	.0	0	0	.2
96007	19.2	96	7.0	69	21.5	336	100.6	8	11	8.9	11	2	.2
96008	1.1	99	.4	83	29.3	505	115.5	10	2	.6	3	1	.0
96009	.8	89	.3	83	27.9	234	100.8	7	14	.4	11	0	.0
96010	.3	82	.1	66	19.2	215	98.7	0	10	.0	0	0	.0

*=Estimated   **1.0=883 lbs per person, 100++ indicates per capita toxic waste generation > than 100 times the U.S. average of 883 lbs per capita.

ZIP CODE MEASURES OF SIZE, LEVELS OF AFFLUENCE AND QUALITY OF LIFE

1=Population (th.); 2= % White; 3=Households (th.); 4=% Owner Occupied; 5=Mean Income Per Household (th.$); 6=Mean Monthly Rent ($)*; 7=Mean Home Value (th.$)*;
8=% under 5; 9=% 65 and over; 10=White Males (th.); 11=% White Males, 65+; 12=# Toxic Waste Sites; 13=Toxic Waste Relative to US(883 lbs.per capita)**.

CALIFORNIA — REDDING

ZIPCODE	1	2	3	4	5	6	7	8	9	10	11	12	13
96011	.2	65	.1	61	10.4	219	13.1	10	7	.1	0	0	.1
96013	4.8	97	1.7	70	21.7	301	95.2	10	9	2.3	9	0	.0
96014	.2	100	.1	67	19.0	203	114.8	7	21	.2	22	0	.0
96015	.5	93	.1	82	12.8	288	44.3	10	13	.2	12	0	.0
96016	.3	100	.1	93	22.6	260*	96.9	4	16	.1	18	0	.0
96017	.3	100	.1	37	23.3	254	94.9	7	18	.1	24	0	.0
96019	4.2	94	1.6	76	21.5	328	81.1	7	13	2.0	13	1	.0
96020	2.3	94	.9	73	19.8	328	124.6	7	8	.5	9	1	.2
96021	8.6	95	3.2	75	19.8	304	80.6	7	14	4.0	15	0	.0
96022	7.0	97	2.2	77	25.0	422	106.8	9	8	3.4	8	0	.0
96023	1.2	95	.4	69	19.9	259	61.3	8	12	.6	12	0	.0
96024	.6	94	.3	90	22.4	178	124.9	5	19	.3	24	0	.0
96025	3.2	95	1.3	68	21.1	275	86.5	6	18	1.5	17	0	.0
96027	2.1	92	.8	72	20.0	278	94.5	8	12	.9	13	0	.0
96028	1.6	97	.6	70	25.2	290	124.1	6	11	.7	13	0	.0
96031	.2	0	.1	79	18.5	79	59.1	8	20	.2	13	0	.0
96032	2.0	94	.7	69	21.1	346	88.5	9	14	.9	17	1	.0
96033	.5	0	.2	57	21.9	349	150.0	13	5	.0	9	0	.0
96034	.3	0	.2	71	20.1	269	47.9	5	14	.0	0	0	.0
96035	2.3	94	.2	74	22.6	321	70.8	6	16	1.1	15	0	.1
96037	.4	0	.2	92	20.7	238*	68.3	11	16	.1	17	0	.0
96038	.8	91	.3	67	26.1	319	81.6	4	10	.4	11	0	.0
96039	1.9	72	.7	67	22.0	280	72.9	9	9	.7	9	0	.0
96040	.3	69	.2	59	23.1	173	194.7	16	7	.6	4	0	.0
96041	2.7	93	1.0	64	20.4	280	77.0	8	10	1.3	11	0	.0
96044	.8	86	.3	75	21.9	233	50.6	3	14	.4	13	0	.0
96045	.2	0	.1	75	19.8	118	86.5	10	5	.0	0	0	.0
96046	.4	0	.1	57	15.6	145	135.6	6	13	.0	9	0	.0
96047	.6	0	.2	84	15.8	283	63.6	13	14	.0	0	0	.0
96048	.5	89	.2	83	15.0	244	101.2	6	16	.2	23	0	.1
96050	.3	100	.1	56	11.8	267	69.1	5	20	.1	17	0	.0
96051	1.0	97	.4	84	21.3	354	136.9	2	15	.5	18	0	.0
96052	1.9	95	.4	65	21.2	320	88.0	7	13	.6	12	0	.0
96055	3.0	100	.2	74	17.6	173	55.7	11	10	.2	10	0	.0
96056	2.7	96	1.1	75	18.3	233	78.9	5	22	1.3	21	0	.0
96057	1.1	91	.4	84	19.0	390	85.5	7	18	.4	19	0	.0
96058	1.9	94	.7	69	23.4	297	87.8	7	16	.9	17	0	.0
96059	.7	97	.3	60	25.1	319	38.7	9	11	.3	9	0	.0
96062	.5	88	.2	76	22.0	77	93.8	3	16	.2	18	0	.0
96063	.5	100	.5	90	23.6	889	121.8	4	14	.2	8	0	.0
96064	.2	0	.1	65	23.1	183	161.2	4	8	.0	0	0	.0
96065	3.0	96	1.1	79	20.7	323	88.2	8	16	1.5	20	0	.0
96067	.7	81	.2	60	23.8	96	110.3	5	3	.6	12	0	.0
96068	5.9	95	2.1	70	26.4	329	130.2	9	10	2.8	9	0	.0
96069	.2	0		68	13.6	55	37.4	6	19	.0	0	0	.0
96071	.9	0	.3	87	26.5	128	99.2	6	8	.1	2	0	.0
96073	1.1	100	.1	69	17.0	215	142.2	5	5	.0	1	0	.0
96074	3.7	99	1.2	91	35.7	438	172.4	6	5	1.8	5	0	.0

CALIFORNIA — REDDING (continued)

ZIPCODE	1	2	3	4	5	6	7	8	9	10	11	12	13
96075	.3	93	.1	82	25.8	197	41.6	3	18	.1	19	0	.0
96076	.3	89	.1	66	18.5	278	91.9	0	5	.1	13	0	.0
96078	.2	0		78	22.5	282	68.0	3	17	.0	0	0	.0
96079	1.5	97	.6	51	17.1	330	78.4	7	18	.7	15	1	.0
96080	19.3	95	7.4	69	23.1	283	99.5	7	15	9.0	14	1	.0
96084	.7	100	.3	68	19.1	232	62.6	8	16	.4	9	0	.0
96086	.4	0	.1	59	22.5	323	73.6	13	3	.0	0	0	.0
96087	1.0	92	.4	78	25.0	338	100.3	7	14	.5	14	0	.0
96088	1.7	97	.7	80	21.9	354	125.0	9	17	.9	20	0	.1
96090	.4	98	.5	72	21.4	313	95.5	7	16	.6	18	0	.0
96091	.5	0	.2	59	20.5	389	121.6	11	10	.2	21	1	.0
96092	.5	100	.2	67	25.1	218	69.9	11	8	.3	10	0	.0
96093	3.6	96	1.3	74	25.9	343	111.0	7	12	1.7	11	1	.0
96094	4.5	83	1.7	69	22.3	277	87.0	9	12	1.8	12	0	.1
96096	.3	92	.1	62	23.9	387	122.1	3	19	.1	20	0	.0
96097	8.4	96	3.3	68	24.7	322	108.3	6	14	4.0	12	1	.0
96099	.2	100	.1	72	39.0	282	194.2	2	2	.1	5	0	.2

RENO

ZIPCODE	1	2	3	4	5	6	7	8	9	10	11	12	13
96101	4.7	96	1.7	72	24.6	267	80.6	7	13	2.2	12	0	.0
96103	1.1	100	.5	76	22.4	323	140.3	4	19	.6	19	1	.0
96104	.8	96	.1	68	32.4	236	85.7	10	14	.4	16	0	.0
96107	.7	76	.3	63	23.5	196	106.9	7	13	.3	18	0	.0
96109	.5		.2	77	21.2	363	81.3	8	8	.2	12	0	.0
96110	.2	100	.1	16	16.4	273	56.9	8	12	.1	6	0	.0
96112	.3	50	.3	65	15.6	212	85.7	17	16	.1	23	0	.1
96113	1.9	82	.6	56	23.3	290	63.8	8	7	.8	7	1	.0
96114	1.9	97	.6	80	31.0	324	106.1	7	10	.9	11	0	.0
96115	.2	100	.1	86	19.7	226*	182.1	0	19	.1	13	0	.0
96116	.2	100	.2	40	18.6	206	31.5	11	21	.1	23	0	.0
96117	.3	81	.1	69	21.7	323	59.7	12	13	.6	19	1	.0
96118	1.3	97	.5	64	24.4	264	89.4	6	15	.6	15	1	.0
96120	.5	74	.2	71	25.5	390	132.2	5	9	.2	12	1	.0
96121	.3	100	.1	75	16.4	430	77.2	16	10	.1	9	0	.0
96122	2.8	92	1	70	23.4	284	97.9	9	12	1.3	13	0	.1
96123	.1	100	.1	65	15.2	135	54.1*	0	40	.1	46	0	.0
96124	.2	96	.1	77	18.1	254	84.2	8	25	.1	28	0	.0
96125	.2		.1	76	20.4	313	134.1	8	21	.1	17	0	.0
96126	.3	100	.1	67	22.9	298	92.2	2	17	.1	13	0	.0
96128	.5		.2	79	28.7	260	114.6	5	5	.2	5	0	.0
96129	.2	100		59	20.6	300	95.4	4	13	.1	10	0	.0
96130	12.0	87	4.0	70	25.3	322	101.9	7	8	5.4	8	1	.0
96133	.1			77	26.4	303*	90.1	4	16	.1	0	0	.1
96134	2.1	93	.8	73	26.4	215	51.8	9	14	1.0	15	0	.0
96135	.3	100	.1	59	22.2	255*	148.8	14	8	.2	13	0	.0
96136	.1	83	.1	24	29.9	173	106.7*	11	5	.1	0	0	.0
96137	3.4	94	1.3	73	22.5	336	125.4	7	11	1.6	11	0	.2
96411	.1	87	.1	0	20.7	392	73.8*	6	6	.1	0	0	.0

*=Estimated **1.0=883 lbs per person; 100++ indicates per capita toxic waste generation > than 100 times the U.S. average of 883 lbs per capita.

ZIP CODE MEASURES OF SIZE, LEVELS OF AFFLUENCE AND QUALITY OF LIFE

1=Population (th.); 2= % White; 3=Households (th.); 4=% Owner Occupied; 5=Mean Income Per Household (th.$); 6=Mean Monthly Rent ($); 7=Mean Home Value (th.$); 8=% under 5; 9=% 65 and over; 10=White Males (th.); 11=% White Males, 65+; 12=# Toxic Waste Sites; 13=Toxic Waste Relative to US(883 lbs.per capita)**.

CALIFORNIA

ZIPCODE	1	2	3	4	5	6	7	8	9	10	11	12	13
KLAMATH FALLS													
97635	.2	100	.1	69	19.3	275	24.1	2	23	.1	20	0	.0

COLORADO

ZIPCODE	1	2	3	4	5	6	7	8	9	10	11	12	13
DENVER (NORTH)													
80002	14.4	97	6.0	58	26.1	391	115.0	7	9	6.9	8	8	.5
80003	32.1	94	10.5	73	33.9	455	127.0	8	4	15.0	3	0	.0
80004	31.0	97	10.5	72	36.3	437	137.0	6	6	14.7	4	0	.1
80005	18.0	96	5.3	93	44.0	652	165.9	9	2	8.7	2	0	.0
80010	31.3	82	13.0	45	23.6	364	98.7	9	7	12.4	7	0	.1
80011	36.3	89	13.3	68	28.6	406	113.1	8	5	15.8	5	0	.1
80012	40.9	90	15.1	69	34.0	466	134.7	9	3	18.0	5	0	.0
80013	24.4	91	7.7	89	37.3	669	130.1	13	1	11.3	1	0	.0
80014	22.1	96	9.9	71	38.6	437	158.2	6	7	10.2	6	1	.8
80015	8.0	92	2.6	90	42.9	685	161.7	11	1	3.8	0	0	.0
80016	1.5	97	.4	95	60.2	324	293.9	9	1	.7	1	0	.0
80020	36.7	95	11.8	81	36.0	508	133.2	11	6	17.8	2	1	1.4
80022	23.6	86	7.6	67	24.3	363	83.0	10	6	10.1	6	11	2.9
80024	.4	83	.2	61	25.8	376	102.6	3	7	.1	0	0	.0
80025	.2	100	.1	63	21.3	319	133.3	14	2	.1	0	0	.0
80026	10.9	91	4.0	77	29.2	462	126.2	10	6	5.0	6	1	.0
80027	6.3	94	2.5	73	28.8	445	116.9	9	8	3.0	7	0	1.3
80030	34.1	93	11.2	69	30.8	412	120.4	9	5	15.4	4	0	1.9
80033	25.0	97	10.1	56	29.7	416	132.5	6	14	11.2	12	2	.2
DENVER (SOUTH)													
80101	.2	100	.1	46	21.6	210	13.1	10	11	.1	13	0	.0
80102	1.9	99	.6	83	29.2	385	88.1	8	8	1.0	9	0	.0
80103	1.5	0	.5	75	33.7	280	76.8	7	6	.0	0	0	.0
80104	6.6	98	2.1	78	41.7	427	161.2	7	7	3.1	5	0	.0
80105	.7	100	.3	73	23.0	222	71.7	3	17	.3	17	0	.0
80106	1.0	100	.3	90	23.7	272*	92.3	11	6	.5	5	0	.0
80107	3.2	96	1.0	91	33.7	336	137.3	9	4	1.5	4	0	.0
80110	42.1	95	16.6	61	34.3	389	143.6	6	12	19.4	10	6	1.4
80111	15.7	97	4.7	88	66.7	616	245.5	7	1	7.7	1	0	.0
80112	14.0	97	4.1	92	52.4	676	183.8	9	1	6.8	1	0	.6
80116	2.0	98	.6	93	48.4	545	206.8	11	3	1.0	2	0	.0
80117	.6	0	.2	71	24.5	276	91.1	7	25	.0	0	0	.0
80118	1.1	98	.4	80	48.9	303	200.5	4	11	.5	14	0	.4
80120	22.4	97	8.6	59	32.1	373	142.2	5	10	10.3	8	1	.0
80121	17.6	97	5.6	86	46.4	539	181.2	6	3	8.4	3	0	.4
80122	24.3	97	7.5	89	44.9	584	165.4	8	3	11.6	2	0	.1
80123	52.6	96	16.0	92	45.1	662	167.4	10	2	25.5	2	0	.2
80124	3.4	99	1.0	92	39.6	696	134.7	13	2	1.7	1	0	.0
80125	.9	0	.3	66	42.9	324	221.1	8	5	.2	0	1	1.0
80131	.3	100	.1	91	33.0	308	94.7	0	7	.2	5	3	26.1
80132	3.1	100	1.0	89	41.8	521	194.0	5	5	1.6	5	0	.0
80133	1.2	97	.5	78	27.8	337	98.9	6	8	.6	7	0	.0
80134	8.8	98	2.6	91	53.9	596	219.1	7	3	4.4	3	0	.0
80135	2.4	98	.8	85	39.2	506	182.0	7	6	1.2	6	0	.0
80136	1.6	98	.5	77	29.2	325	104.2	10	8	.8	8	0	.0
80137	.2	89	.1	73	24.9	303	109.4	12	10	.1	20	0	1.0
DENVER													
80202	2.4	86	1.8	1	14.7	233	240.6	0	38	1.3	26	0	8.8
80203	17.2	83	11.9	9	17.2	279	112.3		16	7.4	12		.3

*=Estimated **1.0=883 lbs per person; 100++ indicates per capita toxic waste generation > than 100 times the U.S. average of 883 lbs per capita.

ZIP CODE MEASURES OF SIZE, LEVELS OF AFFLUENCE AND QUALITY OF LIFE

1=Population (th.); 2= % White; 3=Households (th.); 4=% Owner Occupied; 5=Mean Income Per Household (th.); 6=Mean Monthly Rent ($)*; 7=Mean Home Value (th.$)*; 8=% under 5; 9=% 65 and over; 10=White Males (th.); 11=% White Males, 65+; 12=# Toxic Waste Sites; 13=Toxic Waste Relative to US(883 lbs.per capita)**.

COLORADO

ZIP CODE	1	2	3	4	5	6	7	8	9	10	11	12	13
DENVER													
80204	29.0	61	10.7	34	18.9	263	85.1	11	11	8.6	13	3	.7
80205	30.2	21	11.2	42	15.9	256	83.9	9	11	3.2	11	4	.4
80206	21.2	89	11.3	33	25.8	355	161.8	4	16	8.5	11	0	.0
80207	24.3	25	8.0	75	27.9	449	111.3	8	7	2.9	12	0	.6
80209	20.6	96	10.8	51	30.8	368	142.1	4	19	9.3	16	2	.0
80210	33.7	96	15.4	60	29.1	404	124.8	4	16	15.4	14	0	.0
80211	36.1	73	13.7	52	20.8	323	90.7	8	15	12.2	15	0	.1
80212	18.2	90	8.0	61	23.5	351	98.2	6	20	7.8	18	1	.0
80214	13.0	95	5.5	44	24.0	375	101.5	7	14	5.9	11	0	.0
80215	27.4	97	11.1	55	35.0	423	157.1	5	12	12.8	10	0	.2
80216	9.5	60	3.3	58	18.1	295	69.9	10	12	2.8	15	15	8.8
80218	18.8	86	11.3	21	24.1	313	211.2	9	15	8.0	11	1	.2
80219	51.6	81	18.8	65	24.4	369	93.0	9	10	20.4	10	1	.0
80220	35.0	86	15.7	55	31.1	404	154.2	8	14	13.8	13	1	.0
80221	59.2	90	21.6	73	27.3	403	101.9	8	7	26.1	6	5	.1
80222	30.5	94	15.1	41	29.9	425	138.6	4	12	13.4	10	1	.3
80223	18.7	79	7.3	52	20.5	293	88.2	9	11	7.3	10	6	2.1
80224	18.1	91	8.3	58	34.7	466	148.1	4	10	7.6	10	0	.0
80226	48.5	96	17.3	72	34.7	466	127.9	5	7	22.7	6	0	.0
80227	21.9	95	7.6	73	41.0	483	158.8	6	4	10.1	3	0	.0
80228	19.1	96	6.4	73	39.4	488	144.5	6	3	9.2	3	0	.0
80229	28.8	87	9.2	70	29.0	416	100.2	10	4	12.5	3	0	.0
80230	3.8	76	.1	0	18.3	326	65.2*	2	0	2.3	1	1	.0
80231	23.6	90	12.3	49	30.5	415	170.4	5	16	10.0	13	0	.0
80233	29.5	92	9.2	75	32.6	469	113.1	7	4	13.4	3	0	.1
80234	10.3	92	3.8	70	41.6	427	149.1	7	4	4.7	4	0	1.4
80235	3.6	94	1.3	83	33.2	415	194.2	6	6	1.8	6	0	.0
80236	12.6	91	4.4	71	48.0	427	127.1	5	6	5.8	6	1	.0
80237	13.7	94	5.7	83	28.8	452	196.1	6	2	6.0	1	1	.0
80239	17.8	47	5.4	72	21.9	405	106.5	10	4	4.4	1	1	1.2
80240	1.5	76	.3	0	21.9	345	78.1*	11	0	.6	1	1	1.3
80241	2.7	94	.8	95	39.1	689	148.9	13	1	1.3	1	0	.1
BOULDER													
80301	12.9	94	5.0	71	35.3	417	196.3	7	4	6.3	3	4	7.5
80302	41.5	96	17.2	48	29.0	441	184.1	4	9	19.7	6	3	1.2
80303	38.9	95	14.4	56	33.5	504	174.7	5	5	19.3	4	2	.1
GOLDEN													
80401	42.6	97	15.4	73	37.6	432	165.6	6	6	21.4	5	5	.7
80420	.3	100	.1	65	27.6	346	72.6	7	5	.1	1	0	.0
80421	2.7	97	.9	81	28.5	438	141.6	8	5	1.3	5	0	.0
80422	.6	99	.2	75	26.0	402	117.9	10	4	.3	4	0	.0
80424	2.4	99	1.0	51	35.7	385	225.5	5	1	1.3	1	0	.0
80425	2.0	100	.5	53	16.9	485	95.3	7	14	.1	9	0	.0
80427	.3	96	.2	64	22.5	236	103.4	6	15	.2	17	1	1.2
80428	.2	100	.1	59	42.4	487*	166.3	11	0	.1	11	0	.0
80433	4.3	100	1.5	91	38.6	462	165.5	9	3	2.3	2	0	.0
80434	.2	100	.1	66	19.0	315	48.1	9	12	.1	10	0	1.1
80435	3.6	99	1.5	42	31.6	489	196.2	7	2	2.0	1	1	.0
80436	.5	0	.2	82	28.5	257	160.7	10	0	.0	0	0	.0
GOLDEN (cont.)													
80438	.8	0	.3	62	29.4	362	108.4	13	3	.4	0	2	.0
80439	14.6	99	4.9	81	47.7	564	212.1	6	4	7.4	3	2	.0
80440	.6	98	.2	66	26.5	331	91.3	6	14	.3	15	0	.0
80442	.7	99	.3	67	29.5	351	92.4	8	6	.3	3	0	.0
80443	2.0	98	.8	53	36.5	536	177.4	6	1	1.1	1	0	.0
80444	.9	98	.4	53	27.9	475	139.4	10	5	.4	4	0	.0
80446	2.1	99	.9	64	26.2	325	137.6	6	5	1.1	5	0	.1
80447	.9	100	.3	67	30.0	222	143.6	7	3	.4	4	0	.0
80448	.2	100	.1	64	23.9	165	56.9	12	0	.1	0	0	.0
80449	.1	100	.1	83	31.8	365*	54.6	0	19	.1	15	0	.2
80450	.6	99	.2	38	27.4	306	240.0	9	2	.3	1	0	.0
80451	.4	0	.2	67	26.7	387	94.3	10	4	.2	0	0	.0
80452	2.7	98	1.1	64	27.0	352	115.8	10	8	1.4	8	0	.0
80453	.3	100	.1	43	32.9	539	99.3	8	0	.1	7	0	.0
80454	1.2	98	.4	90	37.8	339	134.1	6	5	.7	5	0	.1
80455	1.1	98	.4	81	43.2	488	212.2	6	2	.6	2	0	.0
80457	.7	0	.3	63	30.2	550	121.0	14	7	.4	7	0	.0
80459	2.0	97	.7	69	26.3	336	102.3	14	8	1.0	8	2	.0
80465	8.6	85	2.9	68	30.7	357	78.4	10	4	3.9	4	2	.0
80466	11.4	95	3.6	87	42.0	577	161.1	11	2	5.4	2	2	.2
80467	1.9	97	.8	60	23.6	426	123.1	10	4	1.0	4	0	.0
80468	1.2	94	.5	59	25.0	366	75.9	5	16	.4	12	1	.1
80469	.3	100	.1	74	25.5	141	106.6	7	3	.6	3	0	.0
80470	1.5	0	.6	91	33.6	339	132.3	12	5	.1	3	0	.1
80471	.1	100	.1	79	31.8	389	99.6	8	5	.1	14	0	.0
80474	.2	0	.2	69	21.6	296	102.0	8	14	.1	4	0	.0
80475	.2	100	.2	57	16.0	431	106.4	9	12	.1	14	0	.0
80476	.2	100	.1	20	26.4	424	119.2	10	4	.1	4	1	.0
80477	7.6	99	2.8	64	34.7	416	199.2	7	3	4.0	4	2	1.2
80478	.2	0	.1	65	33.1	533	107.6	0	5	.1	7	1	1.3
80480	1.6	99	.6	63	27.2	270	85.2	8	7	.8	7	1	.1
80481	.4	99	.2	57	19.4	390	89.5	6	2	.2	2	0	.0
80483	.8	100	.3	71	24.3	358	109.6	10	8	.4	7	0	.1
80498	.9	97	.3	57	30.5	570	178.9	8	0	.4	0	0	.0
80499	.8	0	.4	47	32.9	323	234.0	3	0	.4	3	0	.0
LONGMONT													
80501	55.4	95	19.4	68	30.9	428	131.1	8	8	25.7	7	1	.2
80510	.3	0	.3	78	24.3	179	140.2	0	19	.0	5	0	.0
80512	1.5	97	.6	73	26.0	375	106.0	9	6	.7	7	0	.0
80513	5.7	96	1.8	80	30.4	374	129.9	7	9	2.7	9	0	.0
80514	2.3	94	.8	87	26.3	421	65.8	8	8	1.1	8	0	.0
80515	.2	100	.1	88	23.5	270*	108.8	7	7	.1	7	0	1.2
80516	2.9	94	.9	86	27.8	317	121.8	7	8	1.3	7	2	.0
80517	5.5	99	2.3	88	28.0	305	152.8	4	15	2.7	15	1	.0
80520	1.2	84	.3	88	25.4	385	96.9	12	4	1.5	4	0	.0
80521	25.2	93	9.4	51	22.6	399	105.2	5	8	11.6	6	6	.6
80524	21.9	93	8.6	63	26.1	346	137.1	7	11	10.0	10	1	.0

*=Estimated **1.0=883 lbs per person; 100++ indicates per capita toxic waste generation > than 100 times the U.S. average of 883 lbs per capita.

ZIP CODE MEASURES OF SIZE, LEVELS OF AFFLUENCE AND QUALITY OF LIFE

1=Population (th.); 2= % White; 3=Households (th.); 4=% Owner Occupied; 5=Mean Income Per Household (th.$)*; 6=Mean Monthly Rent ($)*; 7=Mean Home Value (th.$)*; 8=% under 5; 9=% 65 and over; 10=% White Males, 65+; 11=% White Males (th.); 12=# Toxic Waste Sites, 65+; 13=Toxic Waste Relative to US(883 lbs.per capita)**.

COLORADO

LONGMONT

ZIPCODE	1	2	3	4	5	6	7	8	9	10	11	12	13
80525	19.9	96	7.6	64	31.6	397	142.4	7	7	9.5	6	3	.5
80526	17.1	96	6.0	65	28.9	404	134.3	9	2	8.2	2	1	.0
80530	1.2	81	.3	68	25.7	427	85.6	11	8	.5	10	0	.1
80532	.2	100	.1	77	15.4	176*	85.6	15	22	.1	19	0	.0
80534	2.6	90	.9	70	25.3	343	91.2	10	11	1.2	8	0	23.6
80535	2.1	97	.8	70	23.8	466	111.2	10	6	.9	6	1	.0
80536	2.0	100	.5	70	20.5	506	136.5	11	17	.1	18	0	.1
80537	42.7	96	15.5	69	28.1	373	119.4	8	11	20.3	8	4	.3
80540	2.7	99	1.1	77	26.3	375	122.5	8	8	1.3	6	1	.1
80541	.1	100	.1	83	23.2	267*	99.9	0	0	.1	0	1	.0
80542	.4	93	.2	85	30.5	523	104.2	9	7	.2	6	1	.0
80543	1.9	75	.6	71	20.2	284	74.4	14	6	.7	7	0	.0
80544	.3	100	.1	82	29.2	444	127.6	10	15	.1	14	0	.2
80545	.3	100	.1	90	21.7	250*	77.7	8	15	.2	11	0	.0
80546	.2	70	.1	64	25.0	175	50.9	11	14	.1	11	0	.0
80547	.3	0	.1	61	24.9	312	96.0	3	16	.0	0	0	.0
80549	2.1	92	.7	75	24.3	304	93.4	8	6	1.0	5	0	.0
80550	5.2	95	1.8	65	25.7	317	105.0	9	11	2.4	10	0	1.5

BRIGHTON

ZIPCODE	1	2	3	4	5	6	7	8	9	10	11	12	13
80601	19.3	88	6.2	74	29.4	372	116.0	9	9	8.4	8	3	.0
80610	2.0	81	.7	59	22.6	245	83.6	8	14	.8	15	0	.0
80611	.3	0	.1	66	15.9	182*	17.5	4	16	.0	0	0	.0
80612	.2	0	.1	65	22.7	446	33.1	3	28	.0	0	0	.0
80614	.2	100	.1	59	21.3	342	123.5	13	10	.1	6	0	.1
80615	3.9	95	1.4	62	24.5	283	85.2	7	10	1.9	8	0	.8
80620	5.4	90	2.1	61	20.8	336	77.8	10	8	2.3	7	1	.2
80621	8.1	85	2.6	69	25.7	339	88.2	9	8	3.5	9	1	.1
80623	1.1	76	.3	87	25.6	274	72.7	13	5	.4	6	0	.0
80624	.6	81	.2	61	19.1	413	68.7	10	6	.2	5	0	.0
80631	62.0	90	22.5	57	24.9	310	110.4	8	9	26.6	8	5	.6
80640	2.8	95	1.0	75	28.1	369	120.6	8	6	1.2	6	3	6.2
80642	1.8	91	.5	78	24.0	342	88.6	8	8	.9	9	0	.0
80643	1.3	95	.4	60	21.4	209	78.3	8	9	.6	8	0	.0
80644	2.0	89	.6	71	23.8	269	84.3	8	7	.7	7	0	.0
80645	3.4	91	1.1	72	28.2	326	89.9	8	6	1.6	6	0	.0
80648	.4	94	.2	83	28.2	218	84.3	7	11	.2	12	0	.0
80649	.2	100	.1	74	13.4	331	28.7	10	21	.1	31	0	.0
80650	1.2	90	.4	79	21.7	250	69.7	10	5	.6	4	0	.3
80651	3.2	83	.9	68	25.1	341	93.1	10	7	1.3	8	0	4.1
80652	.6	0	.2	60	26.4	233	59.4	11	7	.0	0	0	.0
80653	.8	96	.2	43	18.0	309	39.1	9	10	.4	11	0	.0
80654	1.5	96	.5	69	27.8	246	72.2	10	9	.8	10	0	.0

FORT MORGAN

ZIPCODE	1	2	3	4	5	6	7	8	9	10	11	12	13
80701	13.7	97	4.9	68	25.2	297	87.2	9	12	6.4	10	0	.1
80720	2.5	100	1.0	73	21.3	207	67.3	6	18	1.2	15	0	.1
80721	.2	100	.1	63	26.7	206	42.5	11	23	.1	23	0	.0
80722	.5	100	.1	74	27.9	320*	77.0	10	6	.3	7	0	.0
80723	6.0	93	2.1	66	22.6	262	75.3	8	15	2.7	13	0	.2
80726	.6	92	.2	62	24.8	41	33.3	11	7	.3	6	0	.0

COLORADO

FORT MORGAN

ZIPCODE	1	2	3	4	5	6	7	8	9	10	11	12	13
80727	.5	93	.2	65	16.1	204	41.4	13	14	.2	16	3	.0
80728	.8	98	.3	73	21.8	170	43.3	9	22	.3	24	0	.0
80729	.6	0	.2	56	14.8	163	50.9	8	13	.0	0	0	.0
80731	1.7	99	.7	77	21.5	211	56.3	7	20	.8	17	0	.0
80733	.4	0	.2	52	20.3	155	40.2	8	8	.0	0	0	.2
80734	2.9	98	1.1	73	22.0	195	68.3	8	17	1.4	14	0	.2
80735	.4	100	.9	52	22.1	153	45.4	14	10	.2	13	0	.0
80736	.9	0	.3	73	27.1	216	39.3	11	8	.0	0	0	.3
80737	1.9	99	.8	71	20.0	182	59.2	7	21	.9	19	0	.0
80739	.2	100	.1	82	13.9	160*	49.5*11	11	21	.1	17	0	.0
80741	.8	0	.3	71	20.4	266	47.5	9	13	.0	0	0	.5
80742	.2	0	.1	65	18.5	212*	133.4	14	10	.0	0	0	.0
80743	1.2	100	.1	77	19.3	187	54.1	7	15	.6	17	0	.0
80744	.8	87	.3	72	23.0	208	31.2	8	12	.3	12	0	.7
80745	.2	100	.2	69	16.2	331	36.7	17	14	.0	11	0	.0
80747	.5	0	.2	80	19.4	266	28.3	7	15	.2	14	0	.0
80749	.5	91	.2	72	19.6	244	37.0	7	14	.2	14	0	.0
80750	.1	100	.1	74	12.1	139*	43.1*	6	32	.1	33	0	.0
80751	15.5	95	5.7	68	24.7	290	82.0	8	12	7.2	10	3	.3
80754	.2	100	.1	84	18.9	218*	34.6	3	14	.1	12	0	.0
80757	.3	100	.1	48	20.1	104	71.7*	0	7	.1	9	0	.0
80758	3.5	99	1.4	74	23.5	228	78.8	7	20	1.8	18	1	.0
80759	4.1	98	1.5	74	19.5	244	80.2	8	13	1.9	11	0	.0

COLORADO SPRINGS

ZIPCODE	1	2	3	4	5	6	7	8	9	10	11	12	13
80801	.4	0	.1	69	19.7	157	28.3	23	5	.0	0	0	.0
80802	.3	100	.1	70	19.4	221	74.6	10	10	.1	10	0	.0
80804	.4	0	.2	74	19.0	188	53.4	5	14	.0	0	0	.0
80805	.5	0	.2	70	21.6	285	57.8	10	6	.0	0	0	.0
80807	4.2	96	1.5	72	23.0	231	81.8	9	14	1.9	13	0	.0
80808	1.2	100	.7	71	23.0	174	76.5	9	10	.1	11	0	.0
80809	1.2	99	.5	84	32.1	448	139.2	6	13	.6	12	0	.0
80810	1.3	100	.5	75	21.9	207	56.5	10	15	.6	13	0	.0
80812	.3	100	.4	89	19.3	333	52.9	16	8	.3	8	0	.0
80813	.7	100	.3	69	19.7	264	64.9	7	14	.4	13	0	.1
80814	.7	0	.1	90	27.0	141	103.1	5	14	.6	6	0	.0
80815	1.1	0	.5	75	18.8	177	51.8	8	16	.2	12	0	.0
80816	.8	96	.3	79	21.5	434	104.8	8	7	.3	8	0	.0
80817	9.4	84	2.8	70	23.1	294	86.9	11	3	3.9	2	0	.3
80818	.2	0	.2	85	23.5	321	34.7	7	23	.0	0	0	.0
80819	1.0	97	.4	66	30.8	364	109.1	4	8	.5	6	0	.0
80820	1.2	100	.2	91	23.1	266*	82.4*	6	5	.6	5	0	.0
80821	1.1	99	.5	74	18.3	199	58.3	8	20	.5	18	0	.1
80822	.4	0	.1	96	32.6	375*	61.6	12	11	.4	0	0	.0
80823	.2	100	.1	71	22.3	235	32.9	9	14	.1	11	0	.1
80824	.3	90	.1	55	16.5	119	43.7	7	11	.2	10	0	.1
80825	.5	100	.1	82	15.7	169	40.8	8	19	.2	17	0	.0
80827	.4	100	.1	86	20.3	135	123.3	14	7	.2	6	0	2.1
80828	2.3	100	.9	73	22.7	204	71.2	6	18	1.1	15	0	.0
80829	4.5	98	2.1	53	23.3	268	100.6	5	11	2.2	11	0	.0

*=Estimated **1.0=883 lbs per person; 100++ indicates per capita toxic waste generation > than 100 times the U.S. average of 883 lbs per capita.

ZIP CODE MEASURES OF SIZE, LEVELS OF AFFLUENCE AND QUALITY OF LIFE

1=Population (th.); 2= % White; 3=Households (th.); 4=% Owner Occupied; 5=Mean Income Per Household (th.$); 6=Mean Monthly Rent ($)*; 7=Mean Home Value (th.$)*;
8=% under 5, 9=% 65 and over; 10=White Males (th.); 11=% White Males, 65+; 12=# Toxic Waste Sites, 65+; 13=Toxic Waste Relative to US(883 lbs.per capital)**.

COLORADO

ZIP CODE	1	2	3	4	5	6	7	8	9	10	11	12	13
COLORADO SPRINGS													
80830	.4	100	.1	81	18.3	210*	92.9	14	7	.2	13	0	.0
80831	2.2	99	.7	84	24.7	325	91.6	7	6	1.1	6	0	.0
80832	.5	100	.2	78	27.9	308	46.7	3	16	.3	8	0	.0
80833	.5	100	.2	71	26.5	181	80.2	7	18	.3	18	0	.0
80834	.4	100	.1	81	14.7	144	26.0	7	24	.2	22	1	.0
80835	.7	0	.3	82	19.2	195	54.2	6	21	.0	0	1	.0
80836	1.3	0	.5	77	21.5	194	59.4	8	12	.7	0	0	.0
80840	8.7	89	1.2	2	24.8	387	90.3	8	0	.7	0	0	.0
80860	.4	0	.2	80	16.0	162	42.5	4	14	5.4	0	0	.0
80861	.2	100	.1	89	23.4	269*	26.1	3	9	.1	10	0	.0
80863	5.5	99	1.8	77	28.9	395	123.6	7	5	2.8	5	0	.0
80864	.3	100	.1	80	32.8	335	116.8*	6	11	.1	8	0	.0
COLORADO SPRINGS													
80903	14.4	77	6.4	39	15.4	234	65.7	6	14	5.3	11	1	.6
80904	16.4	93	6.8	61	24.4	299	93.9	7	12	7.3	11	1	.0
80905	3.8	83	1.6	57	17.8	275	63.1	6	13	1.5	11	0	.0
80906	30.1	87	11.6	56	30.1	331	141.7	9	9	12.7	9	2	.3
80907	36.1	94	14.7	62	27.0	317	107.5	7	10	16.6	8	4	1.3
80908	6.7	99	2.0	88	36.4	454	152.9	6	4	3.3	4	0	.0
80909	37.3	92	14.8	59	25.0	309	99.7	6	11	16.1	9	0	.0
80910	24.8	75	8.8	50	21.3	327	82.1	10	7	8.9	6	0	.2
80911	20.4	86	6.2	80	20.4	412	85.9	7	3	8.8	3	0	.1
80913	13.2	66	1.8	0	15.7	336	55.8*10	8	0	8.0	0	1	.0
80915	14.4	90	4.9	72	29.4	378	112.8	8	3	6.5	3	0	.3
80916	14.4	81	4.8	54	21.8	350	91.1	13	4	5.8	2	0	.0
80917	18.7	93	6.2	68	31.3	381	124.1	8	2	8.6	2	0	.2
80918	18.2	93	5.7	78	33.4	422	127.3	9	4	8.5	2	1	.0
80919	5.7	95	1.7	92	50.8	716	198.6	6	4	2.7	2	0	.9
PUEBLO													
81001	29.6	84	10.5	67	23.2	279	74.2	8	10	12.0	9	1	.0
81003	14.0	82	5.4	56	18.7	222	61.3	7	15	5.6	14	0	.3
81004	27.8	82	11.0	66	22.2	253	61.7	7	19	10.7	18	2	2.1
81005	26.7	90	9.0	83	31.1	324	91.6	8	7	11.8	7	0	.0
81006	12.5	89	4.0	86	27.4	263	87.1	8	8	5.5	6	0	.0
81007	2.7	96	.9	77	29.0	344	116.3	6	4	1.3	5	1	.0
81008	6.3	94	2.3	82	30.4	349	98.6	7	8	2.8	8	1	.1
81019	1.2	96	.4	82	20.8	250	76.5	6	13	.5	12	0	.3
81020	1.0	93	.4	75	18.5	238	32.2	7	23	.4	25	0	.1
81022	1.3	78	.4	77	25.7	346	48.3	4	8	.6	8	0	.0
81023	1.0	97	.4	87	29.1	73	110.9	9	10	.5	11	0	.0
81024	.2	100	.1	100	23.3	268*	41.9	10	15	.1	13	0	.0
81025	1.3	83	.4	74	21.5	191	48.4	8	10	.6	11	0	.0
81027	.2	100	.1	76	25.7	160	17.9	9	10	.1	18	0	.1
81028	.3	79	.1	65	18.2	248	26.6	12	15	.1	11	0	.0
81029	.6	95	.2	79	17.3	161	34.9	8	11	.3	11	0	.0
81030	.2	90	.1	63	20.9	187	43.8	10	15	.1	13	0	.1
81033	.2	93	.1	79	13.2	58	27.4	6	13	.1	15	0	.0
81036	1.3	99	.5	75	22.7	155	54.3	7	15	.6	18	0	.1
81037	.1	0	.1	29	13.0	102	46.3*	9		.6	9	0	.0

COLORADO

ZIP CODE	1	2	3	4	5	6	7	8	9	10	11	12	13
PUEBLO													
81038	.6	92	.1	33	33.5	263	17.0	7	12	.4	13	0	.8
81039	2.1	96	.8	74	16.8	250	48.1	8	20	.9	17	0	.0
81040	.4	86	.1	49	9.8	208	16.3	8	23	.2	23	0	.0
81041	1.0	84	.3	64	19.8	174	38.9	10	10	.4	12	0	.0
81044	.2	100	.1	66	20.1	414	42.2	19	7	.1	12	0	.0
81045	.2	100	.1	84	14.5	166*	38.2	7	17	.1	18	0	.0
81047	1.7	92	.7	65	21.6	153	45.8	7	18	.1	17	0	.0
81049	.3	100	.1	81	22.3	322	19.7	3	14	.2	11	0	.0
81050	11.9	85	4.2	70	20.4	231	60.2	8	13	4.9	12	0	.0
81052	9.5	96	3.4	68	21.4	234	62.7	10	11	4.3	9	1	.0
81054	4.3	82	1.6	74	20.9	189	45.3	7	17	1.6	17	0	.5
81055	.9	0	.4	81	20.8	195	66.5	8	17	.0	0	0	.0
81057	.4	100	.4	58	28.8	288	35.2	4	13	.4	13	0	.0
81058	1.0	91	.3	74	16.1	234	38.4	7	14	.4	16	0	.0
81059	.1	78	.1	73	29.3	77	104.2*	0	7	.1	0	0	.0
81062	.6	93	.3	80	18.3	155	36.6	5	21	.3	22	0	.0
81063	1.8	92	.7	75	17.8	192	39.3	7	21	.7	20	0	.0
81064	.4	0	.2	83	16.4	218	24.3	2	21	.0	0	0	.0
81066	.1	100	.1	64	13.5	156*	48.2*21	0		.1	0	0	.0
81067	7.0	76	2.4	71	18.8	200	52.6	9	15	2.5	15	2	.1
81069	1.3	98	.4	84	27.3	292	86.3	9	12	.6	9	0	.0
81071	.2	100	.1	55	21.8	104	51.6	9	10	.1	11	0	.0
81073	2.3	97	.9	80	20.1	174	56.7	6	16	1.1	15	0	.0
81076	.5	0	.2	84	14.2	220	32.9	8	18	.1	0	0	.3
81077	.7	96	.3	78	18.9	230	64.8	7	15	.3	14	0	.0
81080	.1	0	.1	73	23.5	86	45.7	9	15	.6	0	0	.0
81082	11.9	89	4.3	67	18.9	235	67.3	7	18	5.2	17	1	.0
81084	.2	85	.2	80	23.4	35	58.7	7	6	.1	6	0	.0
81087	.2	0	.1	84	28.8	225	37.2	10	9	.0	0	0	.0
81089	4.9	85	1.8	72	18.6	213	45.0	7	19	2.1	17	0	.3
81090	1.6	96	.6	75	20.2	202	53.4	10	11	.8	11	0	8.3
81091	.5	0	.2	60	16.0	229	96.3	12	13	.0	0	0	.0
81092	.8	92	.3	76	23.6	208	53.9	8	13	.4	13	0	.0
ALAMOSA													
81101	11.1	80	3.7	67	22.9	271	75.0	9	9	4.4	9	0	.0
81120	2.4	39	.7	75	13.2	207	39.7	8	11	.5	7	0	.0
81122	2.7	96	1.0	77	26.4	268	110.3	8	11	1.3	11	0	.0
81123	.4	87	.1	77	25.7	188	56.7	6	9	.2	4	0	.0
81124	.4	68	.1	93	9.0	103*	21.5	14	6	.2	4	0	.0
81125	2.8	62	.9	63	18.0	224	53.0	9	9	.8	9	0	.0
81126	.2	0	.1	89	9.9	114*	31.3	11	17	.1	0	0	.0
81130	.8	100	.1	69	24.3	222	71.8	8	7	.4	6	0	1.7
81131	.2	0	.1	69	20.9	282	90.9	4	18	.0	0	0	.0
81132	2.9	83	.9	73	18.6	251	59.5	8	13	1.1	12	0	.0
81133	.5	77	.2	69	15.9	272	75.8	8	8	.2	8	0	.0
81136	.3	84	.1	57	19.6	273	29.9	8	17	.1	9	0	.0
81137	2.8	58	.9	71	20.4	179	73.9	9	11	.9	22	0	1.7
81140	1.8	84	.6	76	15.3	242	51.0	12	13	.7	13	0	.0
81141	1.3	72	.6	85	12.9	216	48.1	8	12	.5	10	0	.1

*=Estimated **1.0=883 lbs per person; 100++ indicates per capita toxic waste generation > than 100 times the U.S. average of 883 lbs per capita.

ZIP CODE MEASURES OF SIZE, LEVELS OF AFFLUENCE AND QUALITY OF LIFE

1=Population (th.); 2= % White; 3=Households (th.); 4=% Owner Occupied; 5=Mean Income Per Household (th.$); 6=Mean Monthly Rent ($)*; 7=Mean Home Value (th.$)*; 8=% under 5; 9=% 65 and over; 10=White Males (th.); 11=% White Males, 65+; 12=# Toxic Waste Sites; 13=Toxic Waste Relative to US(883 lbs.per capita)**.

COLORADO

ZIPCODE	1	2	3	4	5	6	7	8	9	10	11	12	13
ALAMOSA													
81143	.3	100		75	18.2	102	26.0	8	12	.2	15	0	.0
81144	6.7	77	2.3	73	21.4	262	62.1	9	12	2.5	12	2	1.9
81146	.4	87		56	17.8	223	118.1	7	2	.2	0	0	
81147	3.3	84	1.1	75	21.7	293	99.0	8	10	1.4	10	0	.0
81148	.4	57	.1	94	20.8	239*	41.3	13	7	.4	10	0	.3
81149	.9	96	.3	76	15.9	217	41.9	7	18	.4	16	1	.0
81150	.2	81	.1	74	11.4	236	43.9	7	12	.1	13	0	.0
81151	1.3	69	.4	81	16.7	217	41.8	11	8	.4	5	0	.0
81152	1.2	79	.4	72	12.1	147	41.5	8	15	.5	16	0	.0
81153	.4	87	.1	93	12.8	147*	43.7	3	19	.2	20	0	.0
81154	.5	100	.2	82	23.2	150	142.5	8	9	.3	12	0	.0
SALIDA													
81201	7.1	96	2.8	76	21.9	262	83.2	7	16	3.4	13	0	.1
81210	.2	100	.1	52	23.0	305	118.4	8	10	.1	14	0	.0
81211	5.3	98	1.6	72	24.7	341	100.2	9	6	2.8	6	0	.0
81212	20.8	95	7.4	73	20.7	265	89.2	6	19	9.9	16	2	.2
81221	.2	100	.1	86	16.4	188*	29.4	9	11	.1	8	0	.2
81223	.3	91	.1	58	18.2	382	82.1	7	10	.1	12	0	.0
81224	1.6	99	.7	50	26.4	410	191.5	5	3	.8	2	0	.0
81226	4.1	98	1.5	75	20.6	263	67.0	6	18	2.0	17	2	
81230	8.2	97	2.8	51	23.6	339	143.2	5	4	4.3	3	1	
81233	.6	0	.0	89	24.7	221	105.1	7	12	.0	4	0	.0
81235	.3	100	.1	62	28.4	262	107.9	4	8	.2	0	0	.0
81236	.3	100	.1	70	34.0	275	143.8	6	13	.2	10	0	.2
81237	.1	0	.0	60	33.3	427	95.4	13	7	.0	8	0	.0
81240	2.2	94	.6	87	24.3	277	94.3	10	8	1.0	8	0	.0
81242	.4	98	.2	75	21.5	305	104.5	11	15	.2	10	0	.0
81243	.1	100	.1	76	16.2	186*	91.9	12	21	.1	24	0	.0
81244	.2	100	.1	93	22.6	260*	40.3	2	19	.1	25	0	.0
81249	.2	95	.1	63	17.1	255	64.7	11	11	.0	0	0	.0
81250	.1	100	.1	79	13.4	154*	37.8	0	14	.1	25	0	.0
81252	1.0	98	.4	70	18.2	258	73.6	8	13	.5	12	0	.0
81253	.3	0	.1	82	22.8	383	88.6	7	19	.0	0	0	.0
DURANGO													
81301	21.0	92	7.6	65	25.6	381	117.8	7	8	9.8	7	1	.1
81320	.2	82	.1	82	17.3	199*	87.8	7	15	.6	11	0	.0
81321	10.5	93	3.7	76	24.6	340	83.8	10	9	4.8	8	1	.1
81323	2.7	95	.9	82	22.6	291	77.5	8	12	1.3	10	0	.0
81324	1.4	94	.5	81	21.6	266	53.8	10	10	.7	10	0	.0
81326	1.0	100	.3	80	18.7	497	95.4	11	7	.5	8	0	.0
81328	.9	89	.7	78	20.7	335	75.2	6	12	.8	11	0	.0
81331	.2	100	.1	89	18.5	213*	46.6	3	17	.8	14	0	.0
81334	1.0	0	.3	69	12.1	265	31.5	12	4	.0	0	0	.0
MONTROSE													
81401	16.8	96	6.0	77	25.2	321	95.9	8	12	7.9	11	4	.0
81410	1.1	100	.4	88	21.2	364	87.8	9	15	.6	13	0	.0
81413	2.8	99	1.2	83	16.3	258	88.3	5	22	1.4	22	0	.0
81415	1.0	100	.3	82	25.0	237	77.2	7	15	.5	13	0	.0
81416	9.3	96	3.4	74	18.9	264	78.1	8	17	4.4	16	4	.0

COLORADO

ZIPCODE	1	2	3	4	5	6	7	8	9	10	11	12	13
MONTROSE													
81418	1.0	0	.4	80	17.9	265	88.1	5	24	.0	0	1	.0
81419	2.8	93	1.1	77	21.1	247	84.3	8	18	1.3	21	1	.0
81422	1.1	97	.4	65	21.9	331	74.8	10	8	.5	9	3	.4
81423	1.2	99	.4	81	25.5	272	85.9	9	8	.7	7	0	.0
81424	1.7	98	.6	78	26.1	342	73.6	9	8	.9	6	0	.2
81425	3.3	94	1.1	78	20.3	280	76.8	8	13	1.5	13	1	.0
81427	.9	98	.3	73	23.8	269	118.5	7	16	.4	15	0	.2
81428	3.5	98	1.3	78	21.5	315	86.6	8	15	1.8	12	0	2.2
81429	.2	100	.1	76	16.3	347	21.9	17	18	.1	14	0	.0
81430	.2	100	.1	38	15.4	316	137.7	13	9	.2	8	1	.0
81431	.8	97	.1	78	24.6	260	44.8	12	6	.2	5	0	.0
81433	.8	95	.3	75	26.1	294	121.3	9	9	.4	8	0	.0
81434	.3	100	.1	61	21.1	306	73.4	11	4	.4	4	3	3.2
81435	1.6	98	.7	48	20.5	412	205.7	8	3	.8	1	2	.0
81436	.2	98	.2	20	28.2	166	100.6	8	1	.3	3	1	.9
GRAND JUNCTION													
81501	61.9	96	22.7	71	27.5	351	111.9	8	10	29.3	9	4	.3
81520	6.3	96	2.2	74	23.6	403	90.5	12	9	3.0	9	1	.2
81521	5.3	91	1.8	78	23.6	353	96.3	10	8	2.3	12	1	3.2
81522	.4	0	.1	86	34.1	392*	37.2	17	2	.3	1	0	.0
81524	.8	90	.3	81	24.4	267	79.5	7	13	.4	16	0	.0
81525	.8	82	.1	85	13.0	199	41.0	11	11	.1	20	1	.0
81526	3.8	98	1.4	73	23.8	318	116.7	8	16	1.9	14	1	.0
81527	.4	100	.2	61	22.9	351	45.9	2	6	2.6	3	0	.9
GLENWOOD SPRINGS													
81601	8.9	98	3.5	58	29.6	422	168.4	8	10	4.3	9	4	.0
81610	.4	96	.1	71	23.6	271	62.6	8	5	.2	5	1	.0
81611	7.5	99	3.4	49	37.3	503	382.0	4	2	4.0	2	0	.0
81615	.8	99	.4	44	47.1	452	423.2	2	0	.4	0	0	.0
81620	1.0	92	.4	25	33.3	701	407.1	5	0	.6	0	0	.0
81621	1.6	0	.4	58	27.3	489	226.1	2	7	.9	2	0	.0
81623	5.2	96	1.8	62	31.5	528	189.1	5	8	2.6	3	0	.0
81624	1.2	95	.4	75	18.2	275	78.7	7	15	.6	14	0	.0
81625	12.1	98	4.3	72	30.7	406	113.3	10	6	6.1	5	2	.0
81628	.7	100	.3	90	30.4	498	220.5	6	1	.4	0	0	.0
81630	.5	0	.1	78	21.5	353	105.6	8	11	.0	0	0	.0
81631	1.8	98	.6	71	29.5	466	179.4	8	3	.9	2	0	.0
81632	.4	98	.2	80	28.5	295	108.0	19	0	.2	0	0	.0
81635	.9	0	.3	77	26.0	295	108.0	7	10	.5	8	0	.0
81637	.8	96	.3	69	26.5	377	118.0	9	14	.4	11	0	.0
81638	.1	100	.1	48	37.2	428*	306.3	15	15	.1	16	0	.0
81639	2.3	97	.8	75	33.6	449	114.1	11	5	1.2	5	0	.1
81640	.4	0	.1	68	34.0	390*	156.2	7	6	.2	7	0	.0
81641	3.5	99	1.2	68	29.6	410	121.8	10	7	1.7	7	2	.0
81642	.2	100	.1	65	40.2	394	194.7	9	12	.1	20	0	.0
81643	.5	100	.2	83	19.8	257	82.1	9	16	.2	20	0	.0
81645	1.2	73	.4	61	28.6	502	158.7	9	5	.5	3	0	.0
81646	2.1	100	.9	86	36.0	413*	306.3	10	3	.1	0	4	.0

*=Estimated **1.0=883 lbs per person; 100++ indicates per capita toxic waste generation > than 100 times the U.S. average of 883 lbs per capita.

ICC6OI

I03OOI

ZIP CODE MEASURES OF SIZE, LEVELS OF AFFLUENCE AND QUALITY OF LIFE

1=Population (th.); 2= % White; 3=Households (th.); 4=% Owner Occupied; 5=Mean Income Per Household (th.$); 6=Mean Home Value (th.$)*; 7=Mean Monthly Rent ($)*; 8=% under 5; 9=% 65 and over; 10=White Males, 65+; 11=% White Males; 12=# Toxic Waste Sites; 13=Toxic Waste Relative to US(883 lbs.per capita)**.

COLORADO

ZIPCODE	1	2	3	4	5	6	7	8	9	10	11	12	13
GLENWOOD SPRINGS													
81647	2.2	96	.7	76	26.7	359	107.7	13	6	1.0	6	0	.0
81648	2.7	96	.9	69	31.7	314	88.5	9	4	1.4	4	0	.0
81649	.5	40	.1	72	25.4	309	78.3	9	1	.1	3	0	.0
81650	5.2	97	1.8	67	26.7	385	107.9	10	11	2.6	9	3	.0
81652	1.6	98	.6	85	25.3	340	97.5	7	11	.8	10	0	.0
81654	.4	100	.2	59	33.3	224	330.7	5	3	.2	0	0	.0
81656	.3	0	.1	68	23.6	404	369.4	12	7	.0	0	0	.0
81657	4.8	99	2.0	49	41.3	566	325.8	5	0	2.6	0	0	.0

CONNECTICUT

ZIPCODE	1	2	3	4	5	6	7	8	9	10	11	12	13
WORCESTER													
01570	.1	77	.1	87	28.8	331*	64.1	9	9	.1	11	0	.0
PROVIDENCE													
02804	.2	100	.1	86	24.7	284*	113.1	3	26	.1	29	0	.0
02891	.6	100	.2	92	48.3	498	113.0	12	4	.3	0	0	.0
HARTFORD													
06001	11.1	99	3.9	84	49.9	543	183.1	4	11	5.4	9	0	1.0
06002	18.6	71	6.4	74	35.9	471	120.4	5	15	6.2	16	1	1.2
06010	57.4	97	20.5	61	29.0	351	101.2	6	11	26.9	9	3	1.6
06013	5.5	100	1.7	93	36.8	512	129.7	7	5	2.7	5	0	.0
06016	4.3	96	1.5	56	30.2	432	117.4	8	7	2.1	7	1	1.3
06018	2.6	99	.9	67	22.4	340	90.6	6	22	1.2	18	1	1.4
06019	3.5	99	1.3	73	33.3	450	139.3	6	11	1.7	9	3	.0
06020	.6	100	.2	88	42.5	445	158.3	4	9	.3	10	0	.4
06021	.3	0	.1	80	34.9	422	107.3	8	8	.0	0	0	.0
06022	3.5	98	1.2	71	33.0	434	128.5	8	8	1.7	7	0	.2
06023	1.5	0	.5	90	32.9	428	115.9	5	8	.0	0	1	5.7
06024	.6	0	.2	78	22.0	459	90.9	7	9	.0	0	0	.0
06025	.4	100	.1	76	39.7	445	128.4	10	5	.2	6	0	8.3
06026	4.1	99	1.4	80	36.3	492	130.7	7	7	2.0	6	2	.6
06027	1.0	98	.3	88	33.7	430	124.4	9	7	.3	7	0	.2
06029	7.8	98	2.7	71	32.1	361	118.9	8	5	3.8	5	0	.0
06031	1.2	99	.5	75	34.4	421	104.2	4	21	.6	17	0	.0
06032	11.3	98	4.1	71	43.1	593	158.0	4	13	5.2	11	1	1.4
06033	21.5	99	7.4	76	43.7	446	159.3	6	13	10.4	7	1	.3
06035	6.3	99	2.1	88	39.6	466	133.3	7	7	3.1	6	0	.0
06037	13.6	99	4.7	85	33.9	340	123.3	5	13	6.6	11	2	3.0
06039	2.1	97	.8	73	34.7	447	148.9	3	26	1.0	23	0	7.9
06040	53.8	97	19.9	61	31.2	434	113.6	6	15	24.8	10	2	.9
06051	29.0	89	12.1	32	20.8	302	77.3	6	15	12.3	13	1	.5
06052	9.0	98	3.4	58	33.8	334	120.0	4	19	4.2	15	0	.1
06053	33.9	90	13.1	49	25.5	331	89.0	6	13	14.4	13	4	.4
06057	5.1	99	1.7	80	32.9	383	123.0	6	9	2.6	8	0	.0
06058	2.1	97	.6	70	34.6	369	123.4	7	14	1.0	12	0	.0
06059	1.1	100	.3	89	41.6	435	150.9	8	6	.5	4	0	.4
06060	1.1	0	.3	96	45.6	494	174.4	7	4	.1	0	0	.0
06061	.3	100	.1	72	20.6	505	91.2	10	7	.1	4	0	2.5
06062	17.0	97	6.2	71	28.8	359	97.7	6	11	8.0	9	5	2.2
06063	.5	96	.2	55	35.5	495	115.6	4	11	.2	13	1	.3
06065	.5	0	.2	89	31.0	405	108.1	3	13	.0	0	0	.7
06066	29.8	98	10.9	58	29.3	378	110.4	7	10	14.2	8	1	1.4
06067	14.5	97	5.4	49	32.0	491	124.9	5	13	7.1	14	4	.5
06068	1.5	99	.6	66	27.4	412	147.2	5	17	.0	0	0	.0
06069	2.3	99	.9	70	31.7	409	126.8	6	19	1.1	17	0	.0
06070	14.1	96	4.5	84	47.6	558	178.3	6	7	6.8	6	0	.4
06071	8.0	92	2.2	86	38.7	390	140.7	6	7	3.9	7	1	.0
06072	.6	100	.2	52	29.5	413	103.3	9	11	.3	8	0	2.7
06073	2.4	96	.8	82	47.4	467	152.4	5	10	1.2	8	0	1.1
06074	17.2	96	5.4	86	38.6	530	126.4	5	6	8.2	5	1	1.1
06075	.3	96	.1	83	24.2	333	74.9	5	0	.0	0	0	1.8

*=Estimated **1.0=883 lbs per person; 100++ indicates per capita toxic waste generation > than 100 times the U.S. average of 883 lbs per capita.

ZIP CODE MEASURES OF SIZE, LEVELS OF AFFLUENCE AND QUALITY OF LIFE

1=Population (th.); 2= % White; 3=Households (th.); 4=% Owner Occupied; 5=Mean Income Per Household (th.$); 6=Mean Monthly Rent ($)*; 7=Mean Home Value (th.$)*;
8=% under 5; 9=% 65 and over; 10=White Males (th.); 11=% White Males (th.); 12=# Toxic Waste Sites; 13=Toxic Waste Relative to US(883 lbs.per capita)**.

CONNECTICUT

HARTFORD

ZIPCODE	1	2	3	4	5	6	7	8	9	10	11	12	13
06076	12.9	99	4.5	70	27.0	334	95.4	7	11	6.2	9	0	.2
06077	.5	100	.2	76	25.6	338	73.4	7	19	.2	15	0	.1
06081	6.9	99	2.4	77	40.8	424	131.8	5	12	3.3	9	0	.0
06081	1.3	0	.5	53	27.8	381	110.6	9	9			0	.0
06082	42.6	97	13.2	78	31.7	396	94.4	6	8	20.3	6	1	.1
06084	9.7	99	2.9	91	36.3	386	119.0	7	5	4.8	4	2	.0
06085	6.0	99	2.1	73	34.9	455	116.5	6	10	2.8	8	0	.0
06088	4.3	97	1.6	67	27.4	407	91.1	4	12	2.0	11	0	.2
06089	1.7	100	.5	96	41.1	446	144.3	10	2			0	2.1
06090	.7	100		76	37.6	539	129.6	12	8	.3	4	0	.0
06091	.2	0	.1	87	26.7	307*	104.0	6	11			0	.0
06092	4.0	0	1.2	96	57.5	329	209.7	3	8			0	.0
06093	2.4	98	.8	87	32.2	455	119.3	7	7	1.2	6	0	.0
06094	.2	100	.1	78	29.6	330	112.2	0	9			1	.0
06095	25.3	88	8.6	75	34.4	455	111.0	6	12	10.8	10	2	1.9
06096	12.2	98	4.1	77	31.9	423	101.8	5	9	5.8	8	2	4.7
06097	.2	100	.1	69	33.5	372	106.5	8	11			0	.0
06098	13.1	99	4.7	66	26.4	317	96.9	6	13	6.3	10	0	.7

HARTFORD

ZIPCODE	1	2	3	4	5	6	7	8	9	10	11	12	13
06103	1.7	76	.9	1	23.6	362	83.9*	6	10	.7	10	0	.5
06105	18.9	64	10.3	12	20.2	322	147.1	6	15	5.6	17	2	.2
06106	46.4	68	17.1	22	18.3	294	78.8	8	12	14.8	13	1	.3
06107	19.1	99	7.3	85	47.8	545	159.8	4	20	8.7	18	1	.0
06108	23.5	95	9.3	44	26.3	389	97.5	6	12	10.8	11	1	13.8
06109	26.0	99	9.5	80	35.3	417	134.5	4	17	12.0	15	1	.0
06110	12.2	94	4.8	73	28.5	431	103.2	4	19	5.4	17	0	3.2
06111	28.8	98	10.3	79	33.8	455	116.7	5	12	13.6	10	2	1.9
06112	28.6	10	8.6	35	21.1	339	70.1	9	7	1.1	22	0	.0
06114	23.1	89	9.5	34	22.7	356	87.4	6	17	9.5	16	1	.2
06117	16.3	97	4.8	91	62.6	371	191.0	3	16	7.2	14	0	.0
06118	29.0	95	10.6	69	29.5	388	102.4	5	11	13.2	10	0	.0
06119	15.0	96	6.3	49	31.0	499	125.2	4	23	6.1	17	0	.0
06120	16.3	12	4.9	11	13.3	235	67.5	11	6	1.0	1	0	.1

WILLIMANTIC

ZIPCODE	1	2	3	4	5	6	7	8	9	10	11	12	13
06226	21.6	93	7.9	49	22.0	303	86.3	6	12	9.5	10	3	.4
06231	.5	97	.2	83	22.6	440	82.9	9	3	.2	3	1	.0
06232	2.5	99	.9	86	32.9	458	123.2	10	6	1.2	4	1	.0
06234	2.2	99	.7	86	34.6	392	108.0	9	7	1.1	7	2	.2
06235	4.0	99	1.3	82	31.6	373	98.7	6	8	2.0	10	0	.0
06237	.9	99	.3	72	24.5	375	86.9	5	12	.4	8	0	.0
06238	3.3	99	1.1	86	32.6	387	116.8	6	10	1.6	6	0	.0
06239	8.7	98	3.0	84	30.6	428	93.6	7	7	4.4	6	1	.0
06241	11.5	99	4.2	61	23.6	315	88.1	7	13	5.3	17	0	.0
06242	4.3	0	1.4	76	24.8	346	84.2	7	11	1.0	1	0	.8
06243	.8	97	.3	80	29.5	323	96.1	8	11	.4	11	0	.2
06244	.3	100	.1	66	22.2	310	57.3	7	9	.2	2	1	.2
06246	.3	0	.1	85	31.3	311	93.4	3	14	.0	0	0	.6
06247	1.5	98	.5	82	30.8	335	93.0	6	12	.8	11	0	.0

CONNECTICUT

WILLIMANTIC

ZIPCODE	1	2	3	4	5	6	7	8	9	10	11	12	13
06248	3.1	98	.9	87	35.5	437	116.2	8	5	1.6	6	0	.0
06249	4.1	0	1.3	86	29.0	344	96.5	7	6	.0	6	0	.0
06250	2.2	97	.7	72	31.3	413	102.8	5	11	1.1	10	0	.0
06251	1.3	95	.2	37	18.6	95	74.4	1	4	.7	3	0	.0
06253	.2	100	.1	45	19.6	336	69.9*	0	17	.1	14	0	.1
06254	1.6	0	.1	74	22.6	453	85.3	5	5			0	.0
06255	3.6	0	.5	86	32.6	291	109.9	5	7			0	.0
06256	1.5	100	.6	80	24.0	287	74.4	6	12	.7	10	1	.2
06258	.4	100	.2	68	26.0	287	76.5	7	10	.7	9	0	.0
06259	1.9	99	.6	64	41.1	401	87.1	8	20	.2	21	1	.6
06260	9.0	99		55	25.3	424	100.6	7	10	1.0	7	0	.7
06262	.9	100	.4	88	23.0	300	80.5	7	18	4.1	15	4	1.7
06263	.4	100	.2	60	22.0	314	75.9	6	20	.4	25	0	.0
06264	.4	100	.1	75	16.8	289	64.0	13	11	.2	13	0	.4
06266	.7	0	.2	86	27.6	355	95.0	2	11	.1	11	1	.0
06267	.6	100	.3	70	31.1	364	111.5	3	13			0	1.6
06268	15.4	94	2.7	50	26.7	323	90.5	3	13	.3	11	0	.0
06277	2.6	0	.9	79	29.5	359	126.7	2	3	7.1	3	0	.3
06278	1.1	98	.4	63	28.1	425	91.6	9	10	.5	7	0	.0
06279	2.7	99	1.0	60	26.9	424	101.6	6	7	1.2	7	0	.0
06280	1.2	99	.4	62	28.0	288	105.4	10	12	.6	11	0	.5
06281	3.3	100	1.1	81	33.9	397	107.8	6	10	1.5	9	1	.0
06282	1.1	100	.3	85	30.2	419	84.7	5	13	.5	10	0	.0

NEW LONDON

ZIPCODE	1	2	3	4	5	6	7	8	9	10	11	12	13
06320	28.0	81	10.5	38	22.1	330	88.7	7	13	11.1	11	0	.9
06330	3.0	99	1.1	62	26.3	292	81.2	9	12	1.5	11	0	.0
06331	3.5	98	1.2	83	27.7	341	94.2	8	8	1.7	7	0	.0
06332	1.1	100	.4	67	22.9	252	77.6	11	9	.5	6	0	.5
06333	5.2	99	1.6	83	35.2	450	129.5	7	6	2.5	5	0	.0
06334	1.8	99	.6	81	29.1	362	88.5	6	8	.9	7	0	.0
06335	6.8	97	2.2	77	34.9	499	119.3	4	4	3.3	4	1	3.8
06337	.2	100	.1	83	39.3	451*	111.8	4	3			0	.0
06339	7.6	95	2.3	81	33.3	433	105.1	8	3	3.6	0	0	.0
06340	33.3	91	10.1	40	25.0	378	99.4	10	5	17.0	5	1	16.7
06350	.3	100	.1	71	26.2	281	70.6	12	11	.1	4	0	1.0
06351	10.0	99	3.5	67	23.0	313	81.1	8	5	4.9	9	1	.6
06353	.5	100	.1	71	24.8	369	60.2	0	8	.3	9	0	.1
06354	4.7	99	1.6	63	23.9	312	77.8	8	11	2.3	8	0	.7
06355	10.4	98	3.7	76	32.8	458	117.3	5	11	5.0	9	1	.1
06357	8.7	98	3.2	74	31.7	467	112.1	5	10	4.2	7	0	.1
06359	3.6	0	1.1	86	31.7	438	102.0	7	5	.0	5	0	.2
06360	40.4	95	14.8	58	24.5	310	85.7	7	13	18.5	11	1	.4
06370	6.1	96	1.9	78	28.4	434	94.6	9	3	3.0	2	0	.0
06372	7.6	100	2.9	82	41.9	484	156.1	5	14	3.7	12	0	.6
06373	.4	0		74	24.5	397	105.0	5	16	.2	10	0	.0
06374	5.7	99	1.8	75	23.3	333	74.8	9	10	2.8	12	1	.6
06375	3.3	97	1.2	85	30.3	405	99.6	5	16	1.6	15	0	.0

*=Estimated **1.0=883 lbs per person; 100++ indicates per capita toxic waste generation > than 100 times the U.S. average of 883 lbs per capita.

ZIP CODE MEASURES OF SIZE, LEVELS OF AFFLUENCE AND QUALITY OF LIFE

1=Population (th.); 2= % White; 3=Households (th.); 4=% Owner Occupied; 5=Mean Income Per Household (th.$); 6=Mean Monthly Rent ($)*; 7=Mean Home Value (th.$)*; 8=% under 5; 9=% 65 and over; 10=White Males (th.); 11=% White Males, 65+; 12=# Toxic Waste Sites; 13=Toxic Waste Relative to US(883 lbs.per capita)**.

CONNECTICUT

NEW LONDON

ZIP CODE	1	2	3	4	5	6	7	8	9	10	11	12	13
06377	1.4	99	.4	79	22.7	306	78.9	8	10	.7	9	1	.0
06378	4.2	100	1.7	71	33.6	388	142.5	4	15	2.0	13	0	.6
06379	7.9	99	2.8	71	26.6	330	97.5	6	13	3.9	11	1	.1
06380	3.2	98	1.1	42	20.2	285	73.5	6	13	1.5	10	1	.1
06382	9.7	97	3.3	72	27.7	391	89.0	6	7	4.7	6	0	21.7
06383	.4	100	.1	79	27.1	256	90.0	7	10	.2	3	1	1.4
06384	2.5	99	.9	82	23.7	328	77.0	7	10	1.3	9	0	.0
06385	14.7	97	4.9	85	32.5	424	114.5	4	13	6.9	11	1	.0
06387	.9	100	.3	36	22.1	341	74.7	7	9	.	5	0	1.0
06388	.1	100	.1	67	31.5	512	137.7	0	44	.0	31	1	.0
06389	.2	100	.1	70	26.8	525	74.9	15	10	.1	0	0	2.2

NEW HAVEN

ZIP CODE	1	2	3	4	5	6	7	8	9	10	11	12	13
06401	19.0	92	7.0	57	25.4	347	101.7	7	14	8.2	11	1	1.2
06403	3.8	0	1.3	80	29.1	370	107.2	8	9	.0	6	5	.7
06404	.3	100	.1	74	24.7	431	97.1	7	11	.1	6	0	2.7
06405	23.4	98	9.1	66	31.7	472	136.2	5	12	11.0	10	2	.6
06409	.7	89	.2	65	26.9	471	113.4	4	9	.3	8	0	.6
06410	21.5	97	6.7	82	39.2	452	144.3	6	10	10.3	8	3	1.2
06412	3.1	98	1.1	78	31.5	395	111.6	5	15	1.4	12	2	.6
06413	11.3	97	3.9	76	30.2	445	116.9	7	10	5.3	9	0	2.1
06414	.3	100	.1	100	33.9	390*	118.9	12	5	.1	5	0	.0
06415	10.4	98	3.5	75	29.5	381	98.7	8	9	5.1	8	0	.5
06416	10.3	97	3.8	74	31.3	471	111.4	5	12	4.9	9	1	.1
06417	7.7	98	2.9	83	31.8	422	126.4	6	13	3.7	11	2	.1
06418	12.4	97	4.6	59	27.6	352	106.1	5	14	5.7	12	0	.3
06422	5.1	97	1.6	89	35.7	444	123.8	6	6	2.5	6	3	.4
06423	2.5	98	.9	82	30.8	395	104.2	6	11	1.2	11	0	.0
06424	8.2	100	2.7	79	30.3	393	101.9	7	12	4.1	7	1	2.2
06425	.4	100	.1	95	27.8	435	240.0	5	12	..	2	12	.4
06426	2.8	98	1.3	77	40.1	443	198.5	4	25	1.3	24	0	.6
06430	45.4	98	14.9	81	42.2	557	187.0	4	13	21.4	11	2	2.9
06432	7.6	99	2.6	92	46.7	525	184.3	5	14	3.7	13	2	1.1
06437	17.3	97	5.8	84	37.8	490	156.4	7	8	8.2	7	0	.0
06438	1.8	0	.6	83	38.4	366	142.4	5	11	..	0	2	.3
06439	.4	0	.	83	33.8	370	142.7	7	9	..	0	0	.5
06441	4.3	98	1.5	82	32.5	444	126.2	6	8	2.1	7	3	.0
06442	1.6	97	.6	73	30.8	395	104.2	6	11	.8	8	0	.0
06443	14.0	99	4.6	85	41.6	481	176.0	6	10	6.8	9	0	2.2
06444	.3	100	.1	95	27.8	319*	118.6	7	13	..	0	0	.4
06447	4.8	99	1.5	90	38.1	400	126.4	8	5	2.4	5	0	.0
06450	57.3	93	21.1	60	27.3	327	98.4	7	13	25.3	11	2	.5
06455	2.7	99	.9	82	32.6	374	105.6	6	8	1.3	8	1	.8
06456	.3	100	.6	85	45.0	638	149.6	2	14	..	2	15	.0
06457	39.1	89	14.2	49	26.2	358	107.8	6	12	16.8	11	1	.7
06460	50.9	97	17.5	76	32.2	492	121.5	6	10	24.2	8	1	1.8
06467	.8	0	.3	64	29.9	512	135.1	2	18	.0	0	0	3.2
06468	13.8	98	4.0	92	41.1	582	163.1	7	5	6.8	5	2	.0
06469	2.5	99	.9	76	27.2	422	103.7	7	15	1.2	14	1	.2
06470	12.3	98	3.7	88	44.1	527	177.3	6	9	5.9	7	4	.6

CONNECTICUT

NEW HAVEN

ZIP CODE	1	2	3	4	5	6	7	8	9	10	11	12	13
06471	6.4	0	2.1	88	33.5	445	116.7	6	9	.0	0	0	.2
06472	5.1	98	1.5	94	36.8	485	125.0	7	4	2.5	5	0	.2
06473	20.5	97	6.7	88	37.3	486	128.7	4	11	9.8	10	2	8.8
06475	9.3	97	3.3	82	32.7	508	134.3	5	16	4.3	13	2	.2
06477	13.2	98	4.2	94	46.5	592	182.5	5	11	6.5	10	0	2.7
06479	7.2	100	2.3	80	35.0	440	113.2	6	11	3.5	7	0	1.8
06480	8.3	96	2.8	74	32.6	353	114.9	5	11	3.9	9	1	1.2
06481	1.1	98	.4	66	29.1	350	98.4	2	9	.6	6	0	.8
06482	6.3	98	2.0	90	39.2	548	153.8	7	7	3.1	8	0	.1
06483	20.1	99	7.0	72	29.7	397	119.5	6	9	9.9	7	1	.2
06484	31.3	98	10.1	78	34.3	392	146.0	6	9	9.9	8	2	1.0
06487	.2	0	.1	43	35.4	342	151.0	4	21	.0	0	0	.1
06488	14.0	99	5.1	90	35.4	448	155.2	5	28	6.3	24	1	.1
06489	28.0	99	9.4	77	31.8	376	124.3	7	13	13.4	7	2	3.5
06490	2.4	99	.9	80	51.4	657	240.3	2	18	1.1	16	0	5.5
06491	.3	100	.9	74	24.5	356	113.1	4	16	.1	15	0	.0
06492	37.3	98	12.8	70	31.3	375	114.3	6	11	17.8	9	5	4.3
06497	50.5	93	18.4	81	32.0	439	125.3	5	15	22.3	13	13	6.1
06498	5.2	99	2.0	75	28.9	440	123.6	5	15	2.4	14	0	.5

NEW HAVEN

ZIP CODE	1	2	3	4	5	6	7	8	9	10	11	12	13
06511	54.2	51	22.6	24	20.1	362	103.2	6	13	13.1	15	0	.3
06512	27.5	100	9.9	72	26.5	421	88.8	5	14	13.2	12	2	.0
06513	31.2	85	12.0	40	19.3	327	82.2	5	12	12.0	13	0	.4
06514	24.2	93	9.0	62	28.2	492	103.8	4	17	10.4	14	2	.2
06515	17.5	75	6.4	44	27.6	391	107.6	5	15	10.4	16	1	1.0
06516	52.9	90	20.1	55	25.2	414	93.7	6	13	22.7	12	1	1.6
06517	14.8	87	5.6	73	33.4	436	118.5	5	20	5.8	17	0	.3
06518	12.6	97	4.2	83	36.3	465	128.8	5	14	5.6	13	1	.8
06519	16.5	37	5.5	23	15.0	341	43.9	10	15	2.9	9	0	.6
06525	12.1	97	3.9	90	53.6	479	201.2	5	10	5.9	15	3	1.4

BRIDGEPORT

ZIP CODE	1	2	3	4	5	6	7	8	9	10	11	12	13
06604	29.7	75	10.7	30	20.9	341	103.1	7	16	10.5	14	1	1.4
06605	23.2	69	8.7	32	20.2	354	101.1	9	12	7.4	13	0	2.1
06606	40.1	81	14.9	63	26.9	406	103.8	6	13	15.1	13	1	.4
06607	10.3	20	3.4	33	18.0	368	55.0	10	8	1.9	15	2	1.6
06608	9.9	55	6.4	19	15.2	297	76.6	12	8	4.8	10	1	.3
06610	19.9	88	8.2	53	22.4	374	94.1	6	19	8.0	17	0	.8
06611	33.2	98	10.1	94	44.4	499	181.5	4	10	15.8	9	0	.6
06612	4.3	100	1.3	94	59.4	752	257.1	5	10	2.1	9	1	.0

WATERBURY

ZIP CODE	1	2	3	4	5	6	7	8	9	10	11	12	13
06702	3.9	75	1.9	6	11.6	228	83.1	6	31	1.2	29	1	3.2
06704	24.4	63	8.6	47	20.9	256	62.3	7	13	7.4	14	0	.7
06705	23.2	94	8.7	47	24.0	351	71.4	6	16	10.0	14	1	.3
06706	15.3	82	5.2	51	24.5	310	70.2	7	12	6.1	12	2	.7
06708	26.3	97	9.7	59	26.1	327	84.2	5	16	11.9	14	1	.4
06710	9.8	82	3.8	38	24.0	323	78.8	7	17	3.7	15	1	1.0
06712	6.7	98	2.0	91	32.0	400	108.4	5	10	3.2	8	0	.2
06714	.2	0		32	14.5	317	91.0	5	8	.0	0	5	1.7
06716	12.9	98	3.9	90	31.5	439	93.0	5	8	6.3	7	8	.3

*=Estimated **1.0=883 lbs per person; 100++ indicates per capita toxic waste generation > than 100 times the U.S. average of 883 lbs per capita.

ZIP CODE MEASURES OF SIZE, LEVELS OF AFFLUENCE AND QUALITY OF LIFE

1=Population (th.); 2= % White; 3=Households (th.); 4=% Owner Occupied; 5=Mean Income Per Household (th.$); 6=Mean Monthly Rent ($); 7=Mean Home Value (th.$);
8=% under 5; 9=% 65 and over; 10=White Males (th.); 11=% White Males, 65+; 12=# Toxic Waste Sites; 13=Toxic Waste Relative to US($883 lbs.per capita)**.

CONNECTICUT

WATERBURY

ZIP CODE	1	2	3	4	5	6	7	8	9	10	11	12	13
06750	1.1	98	.4	73	31.0	373	100.5	6	13	.6	10	0	.8
06751	2.6	99	.9	82	32.3	374	136.1	6	11	1.3	9	0	.0
06752	1.6	98	.6	88	43.6	603	177.6	6	12	.8	10	0	.0
06753	.2	0	.0	81	29.7	740	143.2	4	14	.0	0	2	.0
06754	1.2	99	.4	84	35.7	412	126.4	5	19	.6	16	0	.2
06755	.5	100	.2	81	37.0	298	129.8	7	6	.3	5	0	.0
06756	1.7	98	.6	85	34.1	421	127.2	6	13	.8	13	0	.0
06757	1.6	0	.6	68	30.6	469	129.5	6	21	.0	0	1	1.5
06758	.3	0	.1	86	29.5	365	113.3	7	15	.0	0	0	.0
06759	5.7	99	1.9	75	36.2	429	132.3	5	15	2.7	12	0	.0
06762	6.2	98	2.1	89	39.9	467	149.0	5	13	3.0	12	1	1.0
06763	1.2	0	.4	78	29.7	448	115.0	5	10	.0	0	0	.0
06770	26.8	98	9.4	65	26.8	352	92.8	7	12	12.6	10	2	13.8
06776	18.4	98	6.2	71	32.9	445	136.0	8	10	8.7	8	1	.2
06777	1.7	100	.6	80	31.9	465	145.0	4	16	.8	13	0	.0
06778	.9	100	.3	88	32.6	346	109.4	5	5	.5	5	0	.0
06779	8.6	100	2.9	74	27.3	380	81.5	6	10	4.2	9	0	.2
06781	.3	0	.1	84	26.4	263	70.7	6	9	.0	0	0	.7
06782	2.2	99	.7	88	30.9	380	91.4	6	9	1.1	7	1	2.3
06783	1.4	0	.5	78	50.9	570	199.1	4	15	.0	0	0	.0
06784	2.4	100	.9	89	41.6	623	176.5	4	13	1.2	12	0	.0
06785	1.2	100	.3	82	39.7	440	171.1	5	9	.6	8	0	.0
06786	8.3	0	2.8	75	29.9	334	92.4	6	10	.0	0	0	1.0
06787	6.5	100	2.2	72	29.7	345	91.3	6	11	3.1	9	4	4.4
06790	34.0	98	13.0	66	25.6	304	90.9	5	16	15.9	14	1	1.1
06793	1.3	97	.4	83	45.0	576	179.8	7	16	.6	17	0	.0
06794	1.2	100	.5	70	38.0	443	154.3	7	13	.6	11	0	.0
06795	10.9	99	3.5	80	35.0	387	118.2	6	10	5.2	9	0	.8
06796	.9	0	.4	81	30.6	552	122.1	5	17	.0	0	1	.0
06798	7.0	99	2.6	67	38.7	511	167.0	5	13	3.4	11	2	.1

STAMFORD

ZIP CODE	1	2	3	4	5	6	7	8	9	10	11	12	13
06801	15.9	98	5.2	76	35.9	500	148.1	7	8	7.6	6	0	.5
06804	7.8	98	2.5	87	39.9	569	159.2	6	8	3.9	6	4	.2
06805	5.2	98	1.6	88	45.1	681	190.1	6	5	2.5	4	0	.0
06807	6.7	98	2.3	75	50.2	666	271.7	6	13	3.1	11	0	.0
06810	71.6	93	24.6	65	31.3	430	143.7	7	11	32.3	9	2	1.2
06820	19.7	99	6.5	87	74.6	750	288.9	5	11	9.4	9	0	1.7
06829	3.2	99	.7	70	40.7	578	169.3	5	12	.6	10	0	.9
06830	38.2	96	14.3	62	63.0	557	318.6	4	16	17.1	14	0	4.7
06840	17.9	98	6.1	80	77.6	669	333.7	4	10	8.5	8	0	.8
06850	15.9	89	5.8	64	35.4	479	175.0	6	11	6.8	10	0	.8
06851	24.4	92	8.9	72	36.3	487	168.9	5	11	10.8	9	1	1.9
06853	3.7	99	1.4	79	53.0	733	235.6	5	12	1.8	10	1	.1
06854	25.3	66	8.9	48	29.5	438	153.3	8	9	8.1	10	1	.8
06855	7.4	89	2.8	60	35.9	500	177.0	6	13	3.1	12	2	.5
06870	6.9	98	2.4	84	60.0	769	278.7	5	12	3.2	10	0	.8
06875	.8	95	.3	91	65.6	681	263.7	8	9	.4	9	1	.0
06876	.3	0	.1	100	60.5	695*	256.7	3	4	.0	0	0	.0
06877	19.9	99	6.4	82	50.9	619	231.0	5	7	9.7	5	1	.3

CONNECTICUT

STAMFORD

ZIP CODE	1	2	3	4	5	6	7	8	9	10	11	12	13
06878	8.0	97	2.6	87	67.0	672	295.3	5	10	3.8	9	0	.0
06880	25.6	98	8.8	82	65.8	701	276.4	4	10	12.2	8	0	1.2
06883	8.5	98	2.8	89	69.7	756	307.8	4	7	4.2	6	1	.0
06896	5.3	99	1.6	90	55.7	602	249.5	6	7	2.6	5	0	.1
06897	14.4	98	4.5	89	68.2	681	286.1	4	7	6.9	6	1	1.0

STAMFORD

ZIP CODE	1	2	3	4	5	6	7	8	9	10	11	12	13
06901	4.7	63	2.5	10	18.9	360	175.6	4	27	1.3	25	0	.7
06902	50.6	71	18.8	45	32.1	460	201.8	6	11	17.1	11	0	3.1
06903	13.9	96	4.3	93	74.8	885	304.5	5	7	6.5	7	0	.0
06905	17.7	95	6.9	66	41.0	575	188.6	5	14	7.9	13	0	.1
06906	7.3	95	2.9	65	36.8	622	164.8	5	12	3.3	10	0	1.9
06907	8.0	97	2.9	73	35.5	563	170.3	6	10	3.8	9	0	1.6

*=Estimated **1.0=883 lbs per person; 100++ indicates per capita toxic waste generation > than 100 times the U.S. average of 883 lbs per capita.

ZIP CODE MEASURES OF SIZE, LEVELS OF AFFLUENCE AND QUALITY OF LIFE

1=Population (th.); 2= % White; 3=Households (th.); 4=% Owner Occupied; 5=Mean Income Per Household (th.$); 6=Mean Monthly Rent ($)*; 7=Mean Home Value (th.$)*;
8=% under 5; 9=% 65 and over; 10=% White Males (th.); 11=% White Males, 65+; 12=# Toxic Waste Sites; 13=Toxic Waste Relative to US(883 lbs.per capita)**

DELAWARE

ZIP CODE	1	2	3	4	5	6	7	8	9	10	11	12	13
WILMINGTON													
19701	5.1	97	1.6	91	30.7	433	104.6	9	7	2.5	7	0	.0
19702	17.9	90	6.4	63	28.2	424	84.3	11	4	8.1	3	3	.5
19703	16.7	92	6.3	50	27.9	381	77.2	7	10	7.3	8	4	5.3
19706	2.0	85	.7	69	20.6	287	65.8	9	9	.8	7	5	
19707	6.2	95	2.0	85	47.8	671	157.2	9	13	2.9	10	1	91.4
19708	.3	86	.1	69	22.1	252	86.1	4	15	.1	11	1	.0
19709	5.8	84	1.9	73	27.6	317	88.7	7	9	2.4	4	4	.1
19710	.1	100	.1	58	59.4	590	317.7	5	20		9	5	.0
19711	42.8	94	13.1	60	32.3	394	109.4	5	5	19.3	4	6	
19713	29.2	92	10.0	63	29.6	347	78.4	9	3	13.4	3	1	2.9
19720	47.1	84	15.5	73	28.0	344	67.2	8	7	19.3	6	16	.3
19730	.6	86	.1	70	31.9	329	96.9	9	5	.3	3	0	4.8
19731	.3	85		83	19.3	95	56.9	6	12		10	0	.0
19733	.4	79	.1	79	23.7	242	76.4	3	10	.1	21	0	.0
19734	4.1	85	1.3	84	27.0	316	79.9	7	10	1.7	37	2	.1
19736	.3	100	.1	50	45.0	293	166.6	1	10	.2	9	0	1.0
WILMINGTON													
19801	13.4	13	5.2	34	14.8	225	38.8	9	14	.9	22	2	.4
19802	27.5	31	10.0	55	20.6	275	56.0	8	12	3.6	22	2	.1
19803	22.7	97	7.9	89	50.2	558	139.6	4	12	10.6	22	2	.4
19804	19.3	94	6.9	81	27.6	370	70.0	6	13	8.7	11	0	.1
19805	41.5	76	14.9	67	24.3	330	57.9	7	13	14.8	12	8	7.4
19806	9.6	89	4.9	42	29.6	371	112.8	3	28	3.4	20	0	.5
19807	6.2	93	2.3	64	68.8	378	255.2	4	16	2.7	14	0	.1
19808	33.2	97	11.5	81	35.8	410	97.9	5	7	15.6	7	1	.0
19809	16.0	88	6.2	65	29.4	380	90.4	7	13	6.6	12	0	3.8
19810	27.2	95	9.0	80	41.6	432	122.8	6	6	12.7	6	1	1.0
DOVER													
19901	49.2	75	15.9	59	25.7	331	90.2	8	6	18.5	6	5	.8
19930	.6	0	.3	78	24.3	52	149.1	3	23	.0	0	0	.0
19931	.3	0	.1	90	28.7	137	73.1	6	23		0	0	.0
19933	4.2	70	1.4	77	22.6	225	61.6	8	13	1.5	12	0	.6
19934	6.4	87	2.2	73	23.1	304	73.0	9	8	2.8	6	0	.4
19936	.5	65	.2	72	23.8	355	34.3	8	5	.2	4	0	.4
19937	.4	84	.1	68	22.7	311	95.6	9	8	.2	6	0	.0
19938	4.2	93	1.4	82	26.4	358	67.0	7	9	1.9	7	2	.0
19939	3.1	84	1.0	84	26.5	274	76.9	7	11	1.3	11	0	.0
19940	3.8	86	1.2	75	23.5	295	66.9	7	11	1.6	10	0	.0
19941	2.0	58	.6	69	17.4	233	55.3	11	6	.6	6	0	.6
19942	.2	0	.1	71	14.1	185	39.4	5	14	.6	3	0	.0
19943	6.7	83	2.2	82	22.6	310	76.7	8	8	2.7	7	0	.0
19944	.1	100	.1	81	35.0	267	109.4	3	22	.0	0	26	.0
19945	3.8	64	1.3	77	20.4	267	63.2	7	10	1.2	10	0	.6
19946	2.7	86	1.1	72	19.7	309	65.7	8	12	1.1	12	0	.6
19947	8.9	87	3.0	77	23.0	279	68.6	7	10	3.9	9	0	.0
19950	3.8	85	1.3	83	22.5	301	62.6	6	12	1.6	9	1	.1
19951	.4	72	.2	85	18.7	237	57.8	7	15	.1	8	0	.0
19952	5.7	85	2.0	76	22.2	279	63.7	9	12	2.4	12	0	.0
19953	3.0	94	.9	86	23.6	267	68.1	10	8	1.4	6	0	.0

DELAWARE

ZIP CODE	1	2	3	4	5	6	7	8	9	10	11	12	13
DOVER													
19954	1.0	78	.3	89	22.0	322	50.7	6	12	.4	10	2	.0
19955	.5	79	.2	77	23.0	252	59.5	10	10	.2	8	0	.1
19956	9.6	84	3.4	73	22.6	278	62.2	7	12	3.9	11	1	.2
19958	6.5	84	2.5	78	23.6	296	96.6	5	17	2.7	18	1	.9
19960	3.4	62	1.1	78	20.2	270	56.9	9	8	1.0	10	0	.0
19961	.2	100	.1	62	22.1	346	50.8	11	8	.1	4	0	.0
19962	3.3	84	1.2	70	17.8	343	69.9	9	5	1.4	4	1	.0
19963	11.2	88	4.2	73	23.5	295	80.3	7	15	4.8	13	0	1.1
19966	8.9	77	3.3	78	20.9	282	72.5	6	15	3.4	14	2	1.1
19967	.7	0	.3	92	21.2	221	82.5	5	21	.0	0	0	.0
19968	4.7	68	1.7	78	21.2	283	63.5	7	13	1.5	13	0	.2
19970	1.1	0	.5	83	27.5	294	96.4	7	20	.0	0	0	.0
19971	5.3	90	2.4	79	26.1	187	133.8	4	27	2.1	25	0	.0
19973	16.6	80	5.7	75	25.7	289	79.5	7	12	6.3	10	2	12.2
19975	4.0	68	1.3	73	22.7	272	85.8	8	11	1.3	13	0	.1
19977	9.5	81	2.8	73	25.7	305	79.6	6	15	3.9	11	2	.1
19979	.5	93	.2	85	25.5	383	70.5	5	5	.2	3	0	.0
19980	.3	85	.1	86	23.6	199	67.2	9	3	.1	2	0	.0
EASTON													
21636	.2	0	.1	90	21.4	245*	80.6	2	17	.0	0	0	.0
21649	.7	87	.2	81	18.5	329	68.5	6	14	.3	14	0	.0

*=Estimated **1.0=883 lbs per person; 100++ indicates per capita toxic waste generation > than 100 times the U.S. average of 883 lbs per person.

ZIP CODE MEASURES OF SIZE, LEVELS OF AFFLUENCE AND QUALITY OF LIFE

1=Population (th.); 2= % White; 3=Households (th.); 4=% Owner Occupied; 5=Mean Income Per Household (th.$); 6=Mean Monthly Rent ($)*; 7=Mean Home Value (th.$)*; 8=% under 5; 9=% 65 and over; 10=White Males (th.); 11=% White Males, 65+; 12=# Toxic Waste Sites; 13=Toxic Waste Relative to US(883 lbs.per capita)**.

DISTRICT OF COLUMBIA

WASHINGTON

ZIPCODE	1	2	3	4	5	6	7	8	9	10	11	12	13
20001	38.2	4	12.9	26	19.0	283	102.0	6	13	.9	12	0	.0
20002	62.6	12	23.0	38	24.3	336	114.4	6	12	4.0	6	0	.0
20003	27.4	34	10.8	38	31.4	404	181.7	4	10	5.0	5	1	.4
20005	7.4	37	4.8	6	17.7	296	166.3	3	17	5.0	14	0	.1
20006	1.2	87	1.0	1	24.4	349	87.0*	0	23	.5	12	0	18.5
20007	25.4	95	11.6	42	50.1	543	324.4	2	12	10.6	9	0	.0
20008	26.0	90	15.4	33	45.9	497	347.7	2	22	9.1	17	0	.0
20009	45.3	34	22.1	18	23.9	337	200.4	5	10	8.0	5	0	.0
20010	26.5	17	10.6	30	23.4	320	126.8	5	12	2.2	7	0	.1
20011	68.4	10	24.1	53	30.7	393	123.3	4	14	4.1	36	0	.0
20012	14.9	20	5.6	61	41.9	393	184.0	4	11	1.5	20	0	.0
20015	15.5	90	6.2	67	50.2	521	256.8	4	20	6.2	14	0	.0
20016	25.5	93	11.4	59	51.0	521	282.0	3	23	10.1	19	0	.0
20017	19.2	19	6.9	57	28.3	310	112.5	4	13	1.7	13	0	.0
20018	19.4	6	6.8	61	29.3	259	110.0	5	15	.5	37	0	.2
20019	72.2	1	25.9	32	21.7	284	85.7	7	8	.3	25	0	.0
20020	61.6	6	21.9	29	22.9	305	108.4	8	6	1.5	33	0	.0
20024	12.0	37	6.5	29	33.8	406	196.0	5	7	2.3	7	0	.0
20032	43.6	5	14.7	18	20.2	301	83.8	9	5	1.1	22	0	.1
20036	4.8	86	3.5	22	28.3	400	126.9	1	11	1.9	7	0	.1
20037	11.5	87	6.7	24	34.6	423	291.8	1	13	4.4	7	0	.4

GOVERNMENT

ZIPCODE	1	2	3	4	5	6	7	8	9	10	11	12	13
20319	.3	75	.1	0	39.1	491	139.4*	7	2	.2	0	0	.0
20332	6.3	71	1.4	0	27.7	397	98.8*	9	0	2.5	0	0	.0

FLORIDA

ZIPCODE	1	2	3	4	5	6	7	8	9	10	11	12	13
VALDOSTA													
31636	.3	11	.1	69	12.2	140*	27.7	6	21	.0	0	0	.0
ALBANY													
31792	.3	0	.1	81	10.1	85	26.3	10	3	.0	0	0	.0
JACKSONVILLE													
32002	1.5	0	.7	86	22.3	188	94.5	4	26	.0	0	0	.0
32007	.3	100	.3	88	18.2	111	39.2	0	16	.2	19	0	.0
32008	2.9	94	1.1	77	17.3	185	56.9	6	13	1.4	12	0	.0
32009	1.4	0	.5	92	29.9	251	54.3	7	6	.0	0	0	.0
32010	3.7	66	1.3	66	18.0	234	55.2	10	11	1.2	12	0	.0
32011	7.5	90	2.3	83	26.6	228	67.4	9	6	3.4	4	0	.0
32012	4.8	66	1.8	84	21.5	186	54.8	5	25	1.4	33	0	.0
32014	35.2	53	13.5	49	15.9	275	58.0	7	18	9.2	20	0	.4
32017	21.9	88	8.4	70	19.2	380	60.4	6	16	9.5	16	0	.0
32018	18.4	98	9.6	49	23.4	354	96.7	2	32	8.2	27	0	1.2
32019	37.4	98	15.5	79	21.7	396	88.4	5	20	17.9	19	0	.0
32028	2.3	85	.8	78	20.3	272	66.8	6	18	.8	22	0	1.1
32030	.9	100	.3	85	30.3	458	99.1	5	6	.4	4	0	.0
32031	3.8	65	1.4	82	20.8	221	60.7	7	11	1.2	11	0	.0
32032	8.2	100	3.4	86	19.3	327	69.9	5	24	4.0	23	0	.0
32033	2.0	58	.6	79	17.5	270	50.4	7	10	.6	10	0	.0
32034	12.6	80	4.4	73	27.8	250	73.1	7	10	5.0	8	0	.4
32036	2.2	100	1.1	72	21.8	292	88.1	4	26	1.1	27	0	.0
32037	3.0	97	1.3	83	27.6	419	111.0	3	24	1.4	26	0	.3
32038	2.3	76	.8	86	17.7	174	43.4	8	11	.8	10	0	.6
32039	.8	90	.3	92	18.8	112	76.8	1	32	.3	44	0	.0
32040	4.0	86	1.2	80	21.8	257	56.1	11	7	6.3	6	0	.4
32043	14.7	86	5.1	75	23.5	242	80.0	7	9	1.8	8	1	.3
32044	1.3	90	.5	76	17.5	258	58.2	9	12	6.3	13	0	.1
32045	2.8	0	.9	74	16.5	231	47.4	8	16	.6	0	0	.0
32046	5.7	91	1.8	76	23.2	254	58.5	7	7	2.6	7	0	.0
32047	1.1	96	.4	84	20.9	259	43.4	9	5	.5	5	0	.3
32048	4.5	96	1.7	90	17.7	235	57.1	5	21	2.2	22	0	.0
32052	5.4	61	1.8	75	17.4	171	50.6	8	14	1.6	13	0	.0
32053	1.5	95	.4	79	19.2	212	41.8	10	11	1.6	12	0	.1
32054	6.6	74	1.7	71	18.1	219	59.0	8	7	2.8	5	0	.0
32055	33.0	81	11.4	73	22.2	248	58.6	8	10	13.1	9	1	.3
32057	.6	100	.2	93	21.2	449	64.2	1	22	.3	22	0	.0
32058	1.3	89	.4	90	19.9	131	55.8	10	9	.5	7	0	.0
32059	8.7	86	2.4	76	22.2	228	60.9	8	10	3.7	22	0	.1
32060	3.0	90	.9	83	16.7	211	44.9	4	11	1.3	9	0	.1
32061	16.6	79	5.8	77	19.3	216	51.0	8	14	6.5	13	1	.0
32062	.3	0	.1	82	20.1	94	58.8	2	0	.5	5	0	.0
32063	1.3	89	.4	90	19.9	131	55.8	10	9	.3	7	0	.0
32066	8.7	86	2.4	76	22.2	228	60.9	8	10	3.7	9	0	.1
32068	8.2	97	2.5	86	24.8	282	87.6	8	6	4.0	5	0	.0
32069	21.1	90	8.9	76	21.8	182	78.6	4	26	8.8	25	0	.0
32071	1.3	88	.5	82	16.5	140	45.3	9	14	.6	10	0	.6
32072	.7	52	.2	79	14.5	199	31.4	2	13	.3	10	0	10.7
32073	37.5	95	11.6	74	31.5	471	105.5	8	5	17.5	4	0	.0

*=Estimated **1.0=883 lbs per person; 100++ indicates per capita toxic waste generation > than 100 times the U.S. average of 883 lbs per capita.

103001

ZIP CODE MEASURES OF SIZE, LEVELS OF AFFLUENCE AND QUALITY OF LIFE

1=Population (th.); 2= % White; 3=Households (th.); 4=% Owner Occupied; 5=Mean Income Per Household (th.$); 6=Mean Monthly Rent ($); 7=Mean Home Value (th.$); 8=% under 5; 9:% 65 and over; 10=% White Males (th.); 11=% White Males, 65+; 12=# Toxic Waste Sites; 13=Toxic Waste Relative to US(883 lbs.per capital)**.

FLORIDA

JACKSONVILLE

ZIP CODE	1	2	3	4	5	6	7	8	9	10	11	12	13
32074	38.9	97	15.6	80	28.6	419	106.5	4	21	17.8	20	0	.1
32077	23.5	78	8.2	71	21.1	218	53.3	9	11	8.8	10	0	.5
32079	.7	83		35	19.5	175	47.5	7	57	.2	57	0	.0
32080	2.9	77	1.0	76	16.9	249	68.1	9	10	1.1	12	0	.0
32081	1.0	91	.4	92	16.9	216	51.4	4	23	.5	24	0	.0
32082	5.8	98	2.2	80	38.1	341	158.4	5	12	2.7	13	0	.0
32083	3.5	60	.4	44	22.2	103	54.7	2	3	1.7	3	0	.0
32084	36.9	86	13.0	72	22.5	283	76.1	6	16	15.2	14	2	.3
32087	1.5	85	.5	84	19.9	250	41.6	9	7	.6	6	0	.1
32088	2.0	74	.7	81	16.2	268	59.0	9	18	.7	20	0	.0
32089	1.5	0	.7	88	17.7	262	56.5	3	26	.0	15	0	.0
32090	.5	62	.2	91	16.3	187*	25.0	4	17	.1	8	0	.0
32091	13.7	76	4.3	74	20.0	211	61.5	7	10	5.5	20	0	.0
32093	.8	66	.3	81	17.3	143	77.4	8	14	.3	20	0	.0
32094	1.0	87	.4	73	18.0	192	46.7	7	19	.5	18	0	.0
32096	1.9	68	.6	83	18.3	146	37.1	8	13	.7	6	0	.0
32097	5.8	85	1.8	84	23.7	264	59.6	9	6	2.5	5	0	3.3

JACKSONVILLE

ZIP CODE	1	2	3	4	5	6	7	8	9	10	11	12	13
32202	5.8	41	2.6	14	10.6	184	29.1	5	30	1.1	24	1	3.3
32204	11.6	48	4.7	31	16.9	263	40.3	7	23	2.4	19	0	.5
32205	57.3	90	22.5	69	22.7	312	52.5	7	13	24.5	10	11	1.1
32206	27.5	33	10.2	48	14.1	228	31.4	7	14	4.2	18	9	.6
32207	35.7	84	15.5	58	25.1	330	74.0	6	17	13.5	15	3	.3
32208	38.4	45	13.1	82	21.2	270	46.2	8	11	7.8	17	3	.3
32209	57.1	1	19.3	60	16.0	241	37.2	8	12	.3	11	0	.5
32210	78.4	90	28.4	65	28.0	376	75.2	7	8	34.8	6	0	.0
32211	61.7	92	23.3	56	28.6	376	80.7	7	6	27.9	5	1	.0
32212	3.9	80	.4		22.4	369	65.6	8	0	1.8	0	1	.3
32215	1.9	77	.2	27	14.0	372	41.8	7	7	1.2	0	0	.7
32216	50.7	91	19.1	59	29.1	372	76.5	7	7	22.5	6	1	.0
32217	29.5	96	11.0	66	36.7	410	115.8	7	7	13.7	7	0	.0
32218	27.3	92	9.0	75	25.5	350	56.1	8	7	12.5	6	1	.0
32219	8.6	65	2.8	78	20.9	313	46.8	8	7	2.7	7	1	.1
32220	4.7	0	1.5	79	23.4	297	62.4	9	5	.0	0	0	.5
32221	6.0	91	2.0	68	23.0	342	72.4	11	4	2.7	2	0	.0
32222	.2	0	.1	69	17.6	302	74.6	21	6	.0	0	0	.0
32223	10.5	94	3.4	93	37.0	386	121.8	9	9	4.8	7	0	.0
32224	2.0	94	.7	82	24.0	488	96.5	7	10	.9	9	0	.0
32225	4.9	95	1.6	88	40.4	333	124.9	6	5	2.3	3	0	.0
32226	4.4	96	1.4	90	29.9	290	80.5	9	6	2.2	4	1	.0
32227	2.7	82	.9	84	29.9	358	42.2*	8	7	1.0	1	0	4.7
32233	19.6	85	7.2	56	26.4	336	91.3	8	7	8.1	5	0	.3
32234	4.7	86	1.6	62	22.1	238	48.2	7	6	.4	7	0	.3
32250	18.7	92	7.5	82	25.7	336	77.5	5	11	8.2	9	0	.0
32265	.3	100	.1	82	18.0	223	32.7	10	3	.2	2	0	.0

TALLAHASSEE

ZIP CODE	1	2	3	4	5	6	7	8	9	10	11	12	13
32301	31.1	76	12.5	51	22.9	319	79.1	7	8	11.1	11	6	.1
32303	28.7	87	11.1	62	27.6	383	85.9	7	8	11.8	8	2	.0
32304	53.3	62	20.8	44	16.7	293	58.7	7	6	16.9	4	0	.0

FLORIDA

TALLAHASSEE

ZIP CODE	1	2	3	4	5	6	7	8	9	10	11	12	13
32308	19.9	83	6.6	80	37.3	401	117.0	7	7	7.9	5	0	.0
32312	12.1	86	4.0	86	44.7	405	138.7	6	7	5.1	6	0	.0
32320	3.8	73	1.3	77	16.3	218	45.5	7	15	1.4	11	0	.0
32321	2.7	83	.7	78	18.7	220	45.1	8	13	1.0	11	0	.0
32322	1.9	95	.7	84	19.7	153	45.6	8	15	.9	13	0	.0
32323	.2	100	.1	100	16.9	194*	66.0	0	68	.1	68	0	.2
32324	7.2	62	1.8	70	20.9	166	45.4	5	20	2.2	14	0	.2
32327	4.8	81	1.6	82	20.0	263	58.0	9	12	2.0	8	0	.2
32328	1.6	85	.6	70	14.9	180	57.9	10	10	.0	0	0	.0
32330	3.9	68	1.3	69	18.6	223	43.4	8	12	.3	13	0	.0
32331	1.5	54	.4	80	17.1	206	31.7	9	16	1.0	15	0	.2
32332	.5	15	.4	82	16.2	194	36.2	9	10	.1	19	0	.0
32333	8.0	0	2.4	73	18.7	195	53.7	10	9	.0	0	0	1.1
32334	1.1	100	.4	82	18.8	218	39.3	10	9	.6	9	0	.0
32336	.9	0	.3	66	16.1	125	29.4	7	22	.0	0	0	.0
32337	.3	60	.3	76	16.3	322	41.5	14	13	.1	0	0	.0
32340	9.3	53	3.0	70	16.5	184	54.3	8	13	2.3	14	0	.1
32343	.8	4	.?	81	13.6	212	26.3	17	9	.3	9	0	.2
32344	9.0	4	2.9	77	18.8	193	49.1	9	13	2.5	12	0	.2
32346	1.0	100	.5	84	17.8	202	56.4	6	18	.5	25	0	.0
32347	15.2	76	5.3	75	22.4	222	48.3	8	12	5.7	10	2	1.1
32350	.9	73	.3	86	19.2	171	50.7	5	17	.3	12	0	.1
32351	23.3	0	7.1	76	18.6	200	47.4	9	11	.0	0	2	48.1
32356	.4	0	.3	73	19.8	110	35	5	7	.0	0	2	.0
32358	.3	100	.3	77	15.1	68	44.6	7	31	.1	28	0	.0
32359	1.7	72	.6	76	18.5	178	55.6	8	14	.6	10	0	.0
32360	.9	100	.3	94	16.8	122	51.3	4	18	.5	16	1	40.6
32361	.9	100	.1	87	18.3	100	65.2*	6	10	.1	7	0	.0
32362	.3	100	.1	91	40.5	465*	15.5	0	9	.0	0	0	.7
32362	.8	91	.3	85	20.3	214	49.5	7	10	.4	7	0	.0

PANAMA CITY

ZIP CODE	1	2	3	4	5	6	7	8	9	10	11	12	13
32401	49.0	79	18.0	65	20.3	256	63.1	7	11	19.0	9	6	1.0
32403	4.6	78	.9	1	19.0	336	67.6*13	0	7	2.1	0	0	.0
32405	22.3	92	8.0	71	24.4	307	74.3	7	7	10.1	6	0	.3
32407	8.4	98	3.3	71	24.4	137	87.5	5	11	4.1	11	1	.1
32409	1.4	0	.5	84	19.5	263	49.2	7	8	.0	0	1	.1
32410	.5	100	.2	75	23.5	132	69.4	6	10	.2	9	0	.0
32420	.7	0	.3	84	12.4	206	26.3	7	17	.0	0	0	.0
32421	2.9	0	1.0	79	17.3	209	34.9	8	14	.2	0	0	.1
32422	.4	56	.1	87	18.3	144	37.4	16	16	.6	11	0	.0
32423	1.1	71	.4	82	14.5	235	30.9	6	22	.3	23	0	.3
32424	5.5	81	1.9	78	19.2	191	46.5	8	16	2.2	14	0	.3
32425	8.4	95	3.0	79	19.7	220	49.5	6	15	3.9	13	0	.2
32426	1.3	0	.4	79	12.3	145	40.6	7	17	.0	0	0	.1
32427	2.5	94	.9	82	14.0	171	32.2	8	12	1.2	9	0	.3
32428	8.8	85	3.2	82	17.6	176	49.2	7	16	3.5	16	0	.3
32430	.3	0	.1	84	20.7	179	42.5	0	25	.0	0	0	.1
32431	3.9	73	1.4	84	15.8	172	37.1	7	15	1.4	11	1	.0
32432	.4	82	.1	80	18.8	225	30.3	2	8	.2	8	0	.0

*=Estimated **1.0=883 lbs per person; 100++ indicates per capita toxic waste generation > than 100 times the U.S. average of 883 lbs per capita.

103001

ZIP CODE MEASURES OF SIZE, LEVELS OF AFFLUENCE AND QUALITY OF LIFE

1=Population (th.); 2= % White; 3=Households (th.); 4=% Owner Occupied; 5=Mean Income Per Household (th.$); 6=Mean Monthly Rent ($)*; 7=Mean Home Value (th.$)*;
8=% under 5; 9=% 65 and over; 10=White Males, 65+; 11=% White Males, 65+; 12=# Toxic Waste Sites; 13=Toxic Waste Relative to US(883 lbs.per capita)**.

FLORIDA

PANAMA CITY

ZIPCODE	1	2	3	4	5	6	7	8	9	10	11	12	13
32433	10.9	88	4.2	79	17.5	203	46.5	7	18	4.6	15	0	.0
32434	.2	100	.1	80	39.2	302	49.5	3	6	.1	9	0	.0
32437	.5	55	.2	84	13.5	117	21.2	4	18	.1	31	0	.0
32438	.9	0	.4	96	18.9	217*	45.0	5	26	.0	0	0	.0
32439	3.6	96	1.5	84	19.8	153	72.4	4	15	1.7	14	0	.0
32442	5.8	88	2.0	70	19.0	207	53.8	10	14	2.5	13	0	.3
32443	2.6	94	.9	85	20.3	210	38.1	7	12	1.2	12	0	.0
32444	1.9	59	.7	85	16.4	149	42.4	7	19	.6	16	0	.0
32445	9.0	88	2.9	86	26.9	320	75.9	7	7	3.9	7	1	.0
32446	1.7	79	.4	68	18.0	236	41.7	6	9	.7	8	0	.0
32448	16.2	71	5.8	73	20.3	213	55.3	8	14	5.6	11	1	.1
32449	.4	100	.1	88	34.7	399*	103.7	13	21	.1	26	0	.0
32455	.4	92	.	100	13.9	159*	16.7	13	19	.1	15	0	.0
32456	2.9	85	1.1	88	14.8	183	43.6	4	16	1.2	15	0	.0
32459	6.5	76	2.3	79	20.6	210	42.8	7	12	2.4	11	3	4.7
32460	1.0	0	.4	87	27.8	41	121.4	4	20	.0	0	0	.0
32461	4.6	71	1.2	78	18.3	138	39.7	6	8	1.9	6	0	.0
32462	2.3	94	.9	95	31.3	360*	75.1	7	22	.1	23	0	.0
32463	.5	72	.8	82	15.7	238	34.7	8	17	.8	18	0	.0
32464	3.0	99	.2	86	17.2	161	34.7	7	16	.6	14	0	.0
32465	4.3	98	1.1	87	14.6	223	31.2	7	14	1.4	13	0	.0
32466	1.3	86	1.5	79	16.6	194	40.2	9	11	1.9	11	0	.0
32466	1.3	100	.5	85	21.3	211	52.5	6	11	.7	11	0	.1

PENSACOLA

ZIPCODE	1	2	3	4	5	6	7	8	9	10	11	12	13
32501	20.3	35	7.6	53	17.8	224	45.6	7	19	3.2	22	1	.1
32503	34.5	68	13.0	70	24.7	315	74.8	6	13	11.0	11	0	.0
32504	47.1	87	16.4	69	26.4	347	82.6	7	9	11.9	5	0	.0
32505	32.9	69	11.5	66	18.7	280	45.6	9	8	10.9	8	2	.1
32506	42.3	94	14.6	75	25.3	340	73.5	8	6	19.4	6	0	.0
32507	22.8	86	8.7	63	22.5	299	70.3	9	11	9.6	10	0	.0
32508	4.8	83	.5	5	17.0	328	60.7*	6	0	3.0	0	1	.0
32530	1.0	73	.4	80	17.8	219	45.6	8	12	.4	10	0	.1
32531	2.4	93	.9	84	18.6	127	45.9	6	14	1.1	14	0	.7
32533	16.3	84	5.1	87	24.9	263	68.8	8	6	6.8	5	1	.0
32535	3.2	70	1.1	74	19.2	200	35.6	6	11	1.1	8	2	.5
32536	15.0	88	5.1	74	21.2	233	55.1	7	10	6.4	9	1	.3
32537	.5	94	.2	75	20.1	261	43.5	5	14	.2	7	0	.0
32541	3.9	99	1.5	74	28.5	122	113.3	5	8	1.9	7	0	.1
32542	10.3	77	2.3	11	17.8	326	81.9	13	0	4.6	0	0	.0
32544	2.2	77	.4	2	20.9	338	74.3*	0	7	1.0	1	12*	.1
32548	41.8	88	15.5	61	25.6	319	92.9	7	6	18.4	5	1	.1
32560	.7	83	.3	68	29.1	248	74.7	9	5	.3	5	1	.7
32564	14.1	98	5.0	78	34.7	365	120.5	6	6	6.9	6	1	.0
32565	1.4	98	.5	84	20.9	245	45.7	9	9	.7	8	0	.5
32567	5.0	98	1.7	82	17.3	218	52.9	7	13	2.4	11	0	.0
32568	2.1	84	.8	84	17.3	195	35.9	9	15	.0	15	0	.0
32569	7.9	89	2.8	62	23.0	324	88.3	8	5	3.7	5	0	.0
32570	35.6	91	11.7	74	21.6	282	64.4	8	11	16.3	6	3	3.4

FLORIDA

PENSACOLA

ZIPCODE	1	2	3	4	5	6	7	8	9	10	11	12	13
32577	.7	73	.2	76	17.2	261	33.0	8	11	.2	13	0	.0
32578	13.4	96	4.6	69	24.9	303	92.0	8	4	6.5	4	0	.0
32579	8.0	94	2.8	72	34.1	396	124.7	6	4	3.8	3	0	.0
32580	3.4	95	1.3	72	29.9	317	85.8	5	7	1.6	7	0	.0

GAINESVILLE

ZIPCODE	1	2	3	4	5	6	7	8	9	10	11	12	13
32601	65.6	71	24.9	51	21.3	341	80.7	7	7	23.1	6	2	.0
32602	1.8	67	.1	51	6.1	248	61.2	7	1	.7	2	0	15.8
32603	5.8	87	2.4	20	16.5	240	100.1	6	6	2.9	5	0	.0
32604	2.5	83	.	85	21.1	242*	83.1	0	6	1.1	1	0	.0
32605	21.8	95	7.5	76	35.7	480	101.1	7	6	10.2	5	1	.0
32607	6.3	97	2.5	46	27.5	487	101.1	4	7	3.1	5	1	.0
32608	15.0	91	7.1	29	14.5	390	79.0	5	4	7.2	3	0	.0
32615	7.6	71	2.5	77	23.0	257	80.2	9	9	2.7	8	0	.5
32616	.5	80	.2	74	15.1	236	36.4	4	16	.2	14	0	.0
32617	2.3	83	1.4	75	17.6	294	62.3	9	7	.9	8	1	.0
32618	4.0	69	1.2	81	21.3	232	57.7	9	10	1.4	10	0	.0
32619	1.8	98	.6	81	20.6	225	71.2	4	14	.8	15	0	.0
32620	6.1	95	2.4	77	16.6	288	67.8	6	20	2.7	20	3	.0
32621	2.0	81	.7	81	17.4	243	59.4	11	11	.7	13	0	.0
32622	1.2	87	.4	81	20.4	201	49.1	10	11	.5	8	0	.0
32624	.7	83	.2	75	34.0	327	75.3	10	3	.2	0	0	.0
32625	.9	0	.4	72	13.8	240	65.4	9	25	.0	0	0	.0
32626	4.8	83	1.7	80	22.3	170	54.6	6	12	2.0	12	0	.8
32627	2.8	80	.9	85	22.2	220	49.6	6	9	1.2	10	0	.0
32628	4.1	80	1.3	71	18.1	172	42.6	7	9	1.7	7	0	2.7
32629	9.5	92	3.7	81	24.9	340	96.7	5	21	4.2	23	0	1.0
32630	11.7	90	4.9	83	17.9	248	66.0	4	24	5.0	26	0	.3
32631	.1	100	.	56	27.3	151	96.4	9	0	.2	0	0	.0
32632	.3	54	.1	.	10.5	264	64.0	9	37	.1	0	0	.0
32634	1.0	100	.3	83	21.1	426	63.4	9	7	.1	1	0	.0
32635	1.0	96	.3	93	23.2	264	66.7	3	11	.5	11	0	.0
32636	4.2	98	1.7	95	19.1	165	71.5	4	27	2.0	29	0	.0
32637	3.9	96	1.6	88	18.2	289	51.1	4	23	1.9	26	0	.0
32639	.3	96	.1	84	12.8	264	78.1	6	22	.2	5	2	.5
32640	6.2	69	2.3	80	17.8	203	61.8	7	14	2.2	14	0	.3
32642	4.6	94	1.9	86	17.2	241	61.1	5	28	2.1	27	0	.0
32643	5.6	82	1.9	86	18.6	254	47.2	9	10	2.3	8	0	.1
32645	.2	84	.2	81	15.5	255	99.3	17	13	.1	19	0	.0
32646	6.5	98	2.7	84	17.7	277	83.3	5	25	3.2	27	0	.0
32647	1.0	100	.5	84	20.3	285	86.1	3	27	.5	34	0	.0
32648	.4	100	.3	85	19.1	115	42.6	9	17	.3	21	0	.1
32649	.7	98	.3	82	18.8	263	64.9	6	17	.9	19	0	.7
32650	1.9	97	.7	85	19.5	287	74.1	4	29	1.9	26	0	.0
32654	17.3	0	7.2	83	22.8	262*	36.3	5	34	8.0	29	0	.0
32656	.2	0	.1	86	23.4	302	89.1	5	17	.1	0	0	.0
32658	5.0	60	2.0	80	19.6	247	68.2	9	12	.2	12	0	.1
32659	.7	94	1.8	78	23.7	314	90.3	6	18	2.3	18	0	.0
32660	4.9	100	.3	78	21.9	365	102.6	6	19	.3	19	0	.0
32661	5.7	100	2.9	95	17.1	340	61.8	1	61	2.6	64	0	.0

*=Estimated   **1.0=883 lbs per person, 100++ indicates per capita toxic waste generation > than 100 times the U.S. average of 883 lbs per capita.

ZIP CODE MEASURES OF SIZE, LEVELS OF AFFLUENCE AND QUALITY OF LIFE

1=Population (th.); 2= % White; 3=Households (th.); 4=% Owner Occupied; 5=Mean Income Per Household (th.$); 6=Mean Monthly Rent ($)*; 7=Mean Home Value (th.$)*; 8=% under 5; 9=% 65 and over; 10=White Males (th.); 11=% White Males, 65+; 12=# Toxic Waste Sites; 13=Toxic Waste Relative to US(883 lbs.per capita)**.

FLORIDA

GAINESVILLE

ZIPCODE	1	2	3	4	5	6	7	8	9	10	11	12	13
32662	.2	100	.1	100	11.9	137*	33.0	11	9	.1	12	0	.0
32663	1.4	47	.1	86	14.0	161*	55.0	1	4	.4	2	0	9.2
32664	.7	77	.3	71	19.5	284	65.9	4	24	.3	28	0	.0
32666	2.9	92	1.2	86	23.2	237	94.0	5	19	1.3	17	0	.0
32667	2.7	69	1.0	78	23.0	237	61.8	6	13	1.0	13	0	.0
32668	1.5	80	.5	83	17.6	220	60.2	9	12	.6	13	0	.0
32669	4.5	77	1.5	82	21.3	240	64.3	7	8	1.7	6	0	.1
32670	49.5	77	18.1	69	22.3	281	75.1	7	15	18.2	15	3	.4
32671	20.8	88	7.7	80	22.6	329	81.4	5	16	8.9	16	0	.2
32672	4.0	90	1.6	73	22.6	395	87.3	4	25	1.8	28	0	.1
32673	1.4	97	.6	81	26.2	413	71.4	5	20	.6	23	0	.0
32679	3.8	96	1.5	85	17.2	219	72.3	4	24	1.7	21	0	.0
32680	2.3	95	.9	85	16.2	223	47.2	7	19	1.1	20	0	.0
32681	.7	80	.3	79	18.8	245	77.0	11	20	.3	20	0	.0
32682	.8	100	.3	86	17.2	566	50.2	6	18	.4	18	0	.0
32683	.2	0	.1	75	16.8	242	28.7	10	21	.0	17	0	.1
32684	1.4	87	.5	85	21.6	222	60.8	4	20	.6	13	0	.0
32685	.2	27	.1	51	14.8	185	26.6	11	17	.0	26	0	.0
32686	2.6	36	.8	80	18.3	102	37.3	7	14	.5	14	0	.0
32688	5.6	98	2.3	83	17.7	300	65.3	4	23	2.7	24	0	.0
32690	1.0	74	.4	83	20.6	306	68.7	7	15	.3	14	0	.0
32691	5.3	96	2.0	91	21.3	299	67.8	6	20	2.5	23	0	.0
32692	.4	100	.1	97	14.7	169*	60.8	7	11	.3	13	0	.0
32693	2.9	88	1.1	81	17.3	221	48.5	4	16	1.3	15	0	.0
32694	1.6	83	.6	78	18.3	245	52.2	7	14	.6	12	0	.0
32695	1.5	72	.6	75	18.9	235	49.7	6	13	.5	13	0	.1
32696	6.8	71	2.2	79	18.3	214	52.7	7	14	2.3	14	0	.1
32697	.2	0	.1	71	18.3	236	33.2	7	16	.0	0	0	.0
32698	.6	0	.3	93	17.4	218	72.9	4	39	.0	0	0	.0

ORLANDO

ZIPCODE	1	2	3	4	5	6	7	8	9	10	11	12	13
32701	31.7	90	11.8	59	29.4	438	112.2	6	8	13.9	8	0	.0
32702	1.8	0	.7	74	18.5	319	72.0	5	25	.0	0	0	.0
32703	29.5	78	9.7	75	23.7	267	75.2	8	9	11.5	9	0	.0
32705	1.5	97	.5	81	20.8	258	78.4	8	21	.7	21	0	.4
32706	.2	100	.1	86	15.4	70	50.2	0	57	.1	48	0	.0
32707	25.9	97	9.6	77	26.7	441	93.3	7	10	12.3	10	2	.1
32709	.7	0	.3	68	20.4	273	84.7	7	8	.0	0	0	.0
32710	.1	100	.1	100	20.9	240*	87.5	6	16	.1	13	0	.0
32711	9.0	82	3.3	73	23.7	261	87.1	5	19	3.6	18	0	.0
32713	5.6	99	2.6	88	21.4	311	63.7	4	40	2.5	38	0	.2
32720	36.5	86	13.9	73	21.9	289	74.0	5	21	14.9	19	1	.1
32722	.9	96	.4	95	24.9	53	82.9	7	14	.4	13	0	.0
32725	10.9	97	4.3	86	21.8	387	73.4	5	26	5.0	27	0	.0
32726	12.1	80	5.0	74	22.6	297	77.8	6	27	4.4	29	0	.0
32730	4.6	94	2.1	46	21.9	341	104.3	5	17	2.0	14	0	.2
32731	2.1	97	.8	81	21.1	306	65.6	8	13	1.0	12	0	.0
32732	1.4	94	.4	83	26.4	287	77.7	5	7	.7	8	0	.0
32733	.2	100	.1	94	37.1	426*	153.6	5	19	.1	25	0	.0
32734	.3	100	.1	80	25.8	384	152.5	4	16	.1	0	0	.0

FLORIDA

ORLANDO

ZIPCODE	1	2	3	4	5	6	7	8	9	10	11	12	13
32735	.1	100	.1	89	19.3	222*	162.7	6	32	.1	19	0	.8
32736	5.5	76	1.7	74	20.8	196	61.0	8	13	2.1	14	1	.0
32737	.7	0	.3	85	25.7	351	100.6	2	41	.0	0	0	.0
32739	.4	94	.2	49	13.0	221	46.3*	6	15	.2	20	0	.0
32740	.4	79	.1	57	19.5	457	124.5	12	23	.1	23	0	.0
32741	32.7	90	12.3	66	21.8	310	78.8	7	16	14.1	15	0	.1
32744	2.3	88	.8	86	18.9	276	57.0	9	15	.9	15	0	.0
32745	.2	79	.1	62	8.2	405	93.8	0	16	.1	10	0	.2
32746	2.9	99	1.1	87	29.6	201	95.0	6	13	1.4	12	0	8.2
32747	.6	38	.2	89	16.1	186*	39.4	0	15	.1	20	0	.0
32750	31.0	85	13.2	77	21.2	287	76.8	5	31	12.3	34	0	.2
32751	30.9	99	9.8	86	42.2	491	150.9	7	6	15.1	6	1	.1
32753	29.8	91	10.2	80	38.8	439	140.1	5	10	13.2	9	0	.0
32754	1.1	89	.3	66	15.8	279	42.4	11	11	.4	9	0	.0
32755	3.6	65	1.3	80	20.5	240	69.9	5	14	1.1	17	0	.7
32756	1.0	85	.4	63	17.2	295	72.8	4	19	.4	21	0	.0
32757	.8	83	.3	71	20.3	287	77.2	9	16	.4	18	0	.7
32759	11.3	85	4.9	76	23.3	336	43.6	5	31	4.3	31	0	.0
32760	1.0	48	.4	54	20.3	212	61.5	8	16	.4	9	0	.7
32761	8.7	97	2.8	81	23.1	359	65.3	9	15	4.1	7	0	.0
32762	1.1	80	.3	76	21.8	192	78.5	10	8	.4	9	0	.0
32763	11.9	97	5.4	87	18.7	326	64.0	5	8	5.3	34	0	.0
32764	1.5	80	.6	87	20.9	186	65.0	4	36	.6	14	0	.1
32765	7.5	78	2.7	80	26.8	258	85.8	6	11	2.9	11	0	.1
32766	.6	98	.2	92	22.6	212	87.9	6	14	.5	18	0	.1
32767	2.3	98	.8	90	21.4	199	63.0	7	19	1.1	16	0	.0
32768	1.9	55	.6	72	18.7	264	71.0	9	7	.6	5	0	.2
32769	14.8	96	5.7	79	21.2	281	71.0	6	22	6.8	20	0	.1
32771	38.2	67	13.6	69	20.8	275	63.4	7	13	12.2	12	5	.5
32775	3.2	85	1.0	90	24.4	209	65.1	6	10	1.4	10	0	.0
32776	.5	76	.2	80	20.5	180	82.4	3	26	.1	32	0	.1
32777	7.9	94	3.6	86	19.4	270	78.1	3	40	3.4	41	0	.1
32778	39.6	90	14.3	74	25.9	345	81.0	5	13	17.6	13	1	.1
32780	6.1	86	2.2	84	19.0	241	62.9	7	17	2.6	19	1	.1
32784	2.2	71	2.6	71	20.8	283	62.5	7	16	2.5	17	0	.1
32785	1.8	99	.6	86	45.7	438	204.7	5	8	.9	5	0	.1
32787	14.8	77	5.1	61	22.6	284	74.5	7	12	5.7	12	0	1.2
32789	25.2	87	10.5	66	30.1	359	128.9	4	22	10.1	20	0	.0
32792	23.3	97	9.2	51	28.2	436	100.7	4	12	10.3	10	1	.0
32797	.9	58	.4	70	18.5	137	86.8	7	28	.3	38	3	.4
32799	3.0	71	1.1	75	19.1	220	57.2	10	21	1.1	27	0	4.7

ORLANDO

ZIPCODE	1	2	3	4	5	6	7	8	9	10	11	12	13
32801	9.7	82	5.0	20	15.0	291	80.8	5	30	3.5	23	0	.1
32803	21.4	98	9.7	64	25.4	348	81.4	4	23	9.6	19	1	.6
32804	18.5	97	8.5	71	27.6	343	92.9	4	22	8.4	19	3	.4
32805	51.9	28	17.3	53	19.5	286	59.5	9	9	7.0	11	0	.5
32806	38.1	98	15.0	63	28.8	383	101.4	5	11	17.7	9	0	.1

*=Estimated **1.0=883 lbs per person; 100++ indicates per capita toxic waste generation > than 100 times the U.S. average of 883 lbs per capita.

ZIP CODE MEASURES OF SIZE, LEVELS OF AFFLUENCE AND QUALITY OF LIFE

1=Population (th.); 2= % White; 3=Households (th.); 4=% Owner Occupied; 5=Mean Income Per Household (th.$); 6=Mean Monthly Rent ($)*; 7=Mean Home Value (th.$); 8=% under 5; 9=% 65 and over; 10=White Males (th.); 11=% White Males, 65+; 12=# Toxic Waste Sites; 13=Toxic Waste Relative to US(883 lbs.per capita)**.

FLORIDA

ZIPCODE	1	2	3	4	5	6	7	8	9	10	11	12	13
ORLANDO													
32807	79.4	96	29.3	65	24.0	391	84.5	7	7	37.8	7	0	.2
32808	44.7	87	15.0	72	26.7	381	79.1	7	7	18.7	7	0	.1
32809	54.2	88	20.1	56	26.2	387	86.7	6	6	23.8	6	4	.3
32810	19.9	90	6.7	72	25.5	380	75.8	8	8	8.7	7	1	.0
32811	12.2	95	4.3	74	27.9	335	108.1	8	8	5.7	6	0	
32812	4.2	87	1.2	2	19.1	366	148.8	16	16	1.9	1	0	.0
ORLANDO													
32901	29.6	83	11.1	71	22.6	344	81.8	6	17	12.3	15	8	.7
32903	9.5	99	3.6	78	35.5	452	149.1	4	14	4.6	13	0	
32905	19.8	93	7.5	69	25.6	450	92.8	4	13	9.1	13	1	.0
32920	5.7	94	3.0	37	21.9	312	90.5	4	13	2.8	13	0	.1
32922	32.8	75	11.9	68	23.8	286	79.8	7	10	12.2	11	0	2.1
32925	1.7	78	.4	0	14.7	312	52.4*	8	0	.9	1	1	.3
32931	12.9	98	5.6	67	32.5	317	149.7	3	16	6.3	16	0	2.8
32935	33.6	97	12.4	77	25.9	387	84.0	5	12	15.8	11	1	.2
32937	26.9	94	9.5	66	30.8	390	129.8	6	9	12.5	9	1	
32948	2.0	66	.6	77	18.4	293	54.1	9	9	.6	11	0	.0
32949	.5	94	.2	67	20.9	184	79.0	4	9	.2	5	0	
32950	.7	94	.2	84	21.9	345	98.6	9	12	.3	11	0	1.2
32951	5.2	99	2.2	88	34.7	296	160.2	3	21	2.6	21	0	.1
32952	32.3	93	11.8	74	29.2	381	113.8	5	10	14.9	10	0	.0
32955	13.4	89	4.6	85	28.9	401	91.7	6	11	5.8	10	1	.8
32957	.8	100	.3	84	17.6	327	55.6	3	26	.4	23	0	.3
32958	8.4	99	3.7	87	21.4	362	83.1	3	32	4.1	34	0	.0
32959	1.3	65	.4	85	21.4	328	88.5	1	7	.7	5	0	.0
MIAMI													
32960	49.1	87	19.5	75	29.1	383	113.4	5	21	20.5	21	2	.5
32970	2.7	46	.8	64	16.9	219	65.3	5	13	.6	13	0	.3
32971	.3	100	.1	76	18.2	327	44.4	5	6	.1	5	0	.0
MIAMI													
33001	.5	89	.2	82	20.9	343	170.7	0	6	.2	8	0	.0
33004	12.9	68	5.4	57	20.5	351	98.5	5	20	4.4	22	1	.0
33009	39.9	89	21.2	72	25.0	444	118.1	2	49	16.0	54	0	.1
33010	38.4	87	13.6	40	20.2	354	80.1	5	15	15.8	14	6	.8
33012	58.5	88	19.0	56	25.2	435	98.4	6	10	24.0	9	0	.3
33013	28.6	94	9.1	71	25.5	399	83.8	5	12	12.9	11	3	.2
33014	32.2	94	11.5	54	33.9	499	145.5	6	14	14.3	15	1	1.3
33015	10.8	94	3.7	68	39.3	578	140.2	7	4	5.0	3	0	
33016	1.9	77	.8	82	25.5	524	251.5	5	9	.9	9	0	.8
33019	13.4	99	7.0	51	32.9	606	172.6	1	54	5.8	53	2	
33020	33.5	89	16.4	54	19.9	371	86.8	4	29	13.7	29	1	.1
33021	41.1	98	16.5	81	35.2	497	155.7	3	25	18.8	24	0	.0
33023	54.7	87	18.9	81	26.7	430	92.1	6	11	22.9	11	2	.0
33024	50.3	94	17.3	79	27.4	454	99.5	7	11	23.1	10	1	.1
33025	8.7	95	3.3	92	32.6	600	124.3	4	22	4.2	25	0	.6
33026	10.2	97	3.6	93	40.9	802	160.0	8	7	4.8	8	0	.0
33027	.5	100	.1	94	47.2	542*	213.6	6	6	.2	4	0	.0
33030	29.8	69	10.2	45	21.9	319	91.4	11	8	10.6	9	2	.2
33031	3.4	96	1.2	81	35.6	353	138.1	4	11	1.7	12	0	
33032	14.5	77	5.2	74	26.0	355		8	10	5.5	11	1	

FLORIDA

ZIPCODE	1	2	3	4	5	6	7	8	9	10	11	12	13
MIAMI													
33033	19.7	82	6.1	69	23.3	395	70.0	9	7	8.0	7	0	.0
33034	8.1	51	2.5	52	18.7	250	70.9	11	8	2.0	8	0	.0
33036	2.8	100	1.4	71	27.4	345	164.8	3	20	1.5	21	0	.0
33037	7.6	95	3.4	79	27.5	388	137.9	5	20	3.7	22	0	.1
33039	7.6	78	1.7	0	18.8	354	66.9*12	6	0	3.6	0	0	.0
33040	32.4	87	12.8	50	22.0	356	119.3	6	11	14.7	9	0	.0
33043	2.8	98	1.2	78	31.9	453	157.9	5	17	1.4	18	0	.0
33044	2.8	98	1.2	81	23.5	327	119.4	2	20	1.4	21	1	.0
33050	.2	100	.1	80	41.9	688	178.9	5	10	1	8	0	.3
33051	8.1	93	3.6	65	26.2	375	163.8	3	15	4.0	16	0	.0
33052	.9	99	.5	65	32.9	379	203.7	4	25	.5	25	0	.0
33054	.9	100	.4	66	21.6	519	137.9	6	16	.5	13	0	.1
33055	28.4	25	8.7	59	20.8	326	57.3	9	7	3.6	6	0	.0
33056	35.2	52	9.4	87	28.1	402	71.8	9	4	8.9	4	2	.3
33060	30.2	23	8.3	78	26.5	372	74.2	9	3	3.4	7	1	
33062	42.2	61	16.4	64	26.0	379	108.6	6	18	12.1	24	5	.3
33063	23.4	99	12.3	76	33.6	465	200.4	1	44	10.6	42	0	.0
33064	26.4	99	11.1	89	24.2	492	104.8	4	33	12.5	34	0	.0
33065	45.2	95	19.6	76	26.3	463	121.0	5	25	20.4	23	0	.1
33066	38.3	98	11.8	75	38.6	552	197.6	7	7	18.2	6	1	.0
33067	5.7	99	2.6	92	33.0	516	139.7	2	39	2.6	42	0	.0
33068	3.7	99	1.5	90	27.6	411	241.7	6	13	1.8	13	3	.0
33069	32.5	97	11.1	80	27.8	550	100.5	8	11	15.7	11	0	.0
33070	4.2	98	1.8	67	23.0	387	129.5	4	16	2.1	16	0	.0
MIAMI													
33125	41.6	78	15.2	36	19.4	355	85.6	4	20	14.8	18	0	.4
33126	24.1	93	9.1	42	23.4	450	88.8	8	14	10.4	13	0	.0
33127	31.3	20	9.8	37	16.1	302	58.7	9	7	3	13	1	.1
33128	6.2	53	2.7	8	11.0	281	73.2	5	28	1.6	32	0	.1
33129	9.4	96	4.4	47	35.6	489	139.4	3	23	4.1	19	0	
33130	18.6	79	8.4	10	13.6	314	80.7	4	26	6.6	24	0	.1
33131	2.9	92	1.2	28	27.8	351	99.0*	3	26	.8	28	0	
33132	2.9	64	1.7	13	13.3	226	37.2	5	19	1.2	24	0	1.8
33133	28.5	77	12.8	48	36.5	426	168.8	4	15	10.8	13	0	
33134	35.5	96	15.2	53	32.9	461	147.7	3	22	15.2	19	1	.0
33135	34.0	84	14.1	26	16.6	345	90.7	3	25	12.4	24	0	.0
33136	16.2	19	6.5	7	12.6	212	84.0	8	12	1.4	18	0	.5
33137	28.8	58	11.7	49	23.4	360	126.2	7	14	6.4	17	0	.0
33138	26.4	72	11.7	49	28.6	358	137.5	6	19	9.1	21	0	.1
33139	51.8	96	31.8	19	14.9	355	235.6	2	58	21.2	53	0	.0
33140	21.5	96	11.1	40	35.8	521	236.0	3	26	6.6	41	0	.1
33141	29.1	96	15.8	31	23.2	425	186.6	2	43	12.0	41	0	.0
33142	54.5	31	18.1	36	16.5	281	60.2	8	11	8.2	15	1	
33143	26.9	84	11.4	55	39.4	472	178.4	4	12	10.5	10	1	
33144	22.0	96	7.6	68	26.1	431	92.5	4	18	9.8	15	0	.0
33145	26.7	96	9.8	57	25.9	411	96.0	4	21	11.4	19	0	.0
33146	15.8	93	4.2	76	56.1	490	235.2	3	12	7.5	10	1	.5
33147	54.2	21	16.5	52	19.1	276	60.1	9	5	5.5	11	0	.4
33149	6.3	99	2.7	67	60.5	631	274.7	3	16	3.0	16	0	.0

*=Estimated **1.0=883 lbs per person; 100++ indicates per capita toxic waste generation > than 100 times the U.S. average of 883 lbs per capita.

103001

ZIP CODE MEASURES OF SIZE, LEVELS OF AFFLUENCE AND QUALITY OF LIFE

1=Population (th.); 2= % White; 3=Households (th.); 4=% Owner Occupied; 5=Mean Income Per Household (th.$); 6=Mean Monthly Rent ($); 7=Mean Home Value (th.$); 8=% under 5; 9=% 65 and over; 10=White Males (th.); 11=% White Males, 65+; 12=# Toxic Waste Sites, 65+; 13=Toxic Waste Relative to US(883 lbs.per capita)**.

FLORIDA

MIAMI

ZIPCODE	1	2	3	4	5	6	7	8	9	10	11	12	13
33150	27.3	33	10.0	42	18.1	281	71.1	9	12	4.2	23	0	.0
33154	11.7	98	6.4	51	42.6	595	203.9	1	57	4.9	56	0	.0
33155	42.1	96	14.4	77	32.7	483	106.3	4	13	19.3	12	0	.0
33156	28.6	97	10.3	69	54.9	554	259.5	4	8	13.6	7	0	.0
33157	57.3	77	18.7	72	34.3	434	135.9	8	7	21.7	5	1	.0
33158	5.7	98	1.7	97	78.6	676	234.5	4	8	2.8	4	0	1.0
33160	25.9	99	13.9	66	26.2	562	236.8	1	53	11.4	54	0	.0
33161	37.1	94	16.5	52	24.3	422	99.2	4	19	15.8	18	1	.0
33162	36.2	91	14.8	67	24.7	475	93.7	5	24	15.1	22	0	.0
33165	52.6	96	15.9	77	33.5	498	114.8	5	9	24.1	8	0	.1
33166	20.7	95	8.6	53	30.6	493	115.3	4	12	9.7	10	9	2.6
33168	16.8	54	5.5	68	24.2	364	73.6	8	8	4.4	10	0	.4
33169	20.2	82	7.4	83	25.7	410	78.0	6	15	8.0	15	0	.0
33170	27.7	78	10.0	69	28.8	507	90.7	5	9	10.6	9	0	2.8
33172	14.1	95	6.2	46	31.4	576	141.9	5	6	6.4	5	0	.0
33173	21.8	96	8.0	72	36.1	559	128.1	6	6	10.0	5	0	.0
33174	19.2	91	6.1	59	28.6	497	123.2	7	8	8.2	6	0	.0
33175	26.4	96	8.2	91	34.3	643	123.3	9	5	12.3	4	0	.3
33176	44.9	77	15.8	68	39.7	540	166.5	7	6	16.8	4	0	.0
33177	18.0	77	5.3	83	26.8	439	87.2	8	4	7.1	5	0	.0
33178	.4	100	.2	80	67.6	667	156.3	0	12	.2	11	0	.0
33179	26.9	98	11.7	84	29.7	477	158.7	4	36	12.0	34	0	15.3
33180	9.8	98	4.5	86	34.5	493	209.0	3	31	4.6	33	0	.0
33181	16.1	96	8.7	45	29.3	455	175.9	3	26	7.1	24	0	.0
33183	18.5	95	6.2	82	38.6	698	142.3	6	9	8.5	6	0	.0
33184	4.7	97	1.8	83	28.7	509	134.6	6	7	2.2	4	0	.0
33186	15.4	94	5.5	92	42.5	703	168.6	11	3	7.1	2	0	.0
33187	1.7	90	.6	80	26.9	337	146.5	4	4	.8	5	0	.0
33189	11.0	85	3.4	76	31.9	508	103.2	9	5	4.5	4	0	.0
33190	.4	85	.2	86	28.6	530	75.4	5	7	.2	13	0	.0
33193	2.7	97	1.0	90	35.1	590	133.5	8	12	1.3	12	0	.0
33196	.2	0	.1	7	29.6	450	105.5*	0	0	.0	0	0	.0

FORT LAUDERDALE

ZIPCODE	1	2	3	4	5	6	7	8	9	10	11	12	13
33301	11.8	97	6.1	49	34.2	379	219.4	2	24	5.8	19	2	.2
33304	17.0	96	9.2	45	25.5	381	136.8	3	26	7.6	21	2	.0
33305	12.3	99	5.7	61	30.9	453	166.8	3	22	5.6	18	2	.0
33306	3.9	100	1.9	67	32.5	477	201.2	2	26	1.8	21	0	.0
33308	28.3	99	14.0	76	39.9	507	236.5	1	37	12.4	34	0	.1
33309	23.7	98	9.6	81	26.9	484	102.2	5	17	10.9	15	1	1.7
33311	70.3	25	22.4	54	20.4	340	72.1	9	8	8.5	16	1	.0
33312	44.8	86	17.5	67	25.2	406	101.1	6	12	19.1	12	1	.0
33313	48.4	87	21.2	61	23.5	517	101.6	5	25	19.6	27	1	.0
33314	18.9	99	7.5	67	24.9	470	101.7	6	13	9.0	12	0	.0
33315	12.8	97	6.0	59	24.0	413	93.5	4	19	6.0	17	2	.7
33316	12.4	97	5.5	57	38.6	440	232.8	2	26	5.9	22	0	.5
33317	34.5	98	11.3	85	41.0	506	157.9	5	10	16.6	9	1	.0
33319	34.6	98	16.1	81	26.9	552	121.2	3	39	15.8	41	0	.0
33321	19.1	99	8.4	79	28.6	574	129.7	4	29	8.9	32	0	.1

FLORIDA

FORT LAUDERDALE

ZIPCODE	1	2	3	4	5	6	7	8	9	10	11	12	13
33322	23.8	99	10.3	93	25.0	521	126.6	3	37	11.0	39	0	.1
33323	5.3	96	1.6	98	36.4	807	132.8	10	3	2.6	3	0	.1
33324	13.0	97	5.4	79	34.6	629	234.4	4	13	5.9	17	0	.4
33325	12.0	99	4.1	93	29.0	494	181.0	7	8	5.9	8	1	.4
33326	1.1	0	.4	86	49.4	490	276.5	13	9	.0	0	0	.0
33328	13.8	99	4.5	90	38.9	563	156.8	7	8	6.7	8	0	.0
33330	3.6	95	1.1	93	57.1	277	230.8	5	3	1.6	2	0	.0
33331	2.3	0	.6	93	39.9	627	205.1	8	7	.5	3	0	.0
33332	1.1	100	.3	100	38.4	441*152.0	4	15	13.2	12	0	.1
33334	28.6	96	12.7	54	25.6	463	108.9	4	15	13.2	12	0	.1

WEST PALM BEACH

ZIPCODE	1	2	3	4	5	6	7	8	9	10	11	12	13
33401	23.3	52	9.9	34	21.2	353	81.6	7	19	5.8	20	0	.1
33403	11.1	93	4.7	58	28.2	479	94.7	5	17	5.1	18	1	.1
33404	28.9	37	10.7	69	26.0	344	87.6	7	17	4.9	33	1	.4
33405	18.8	98	8.1	69	27.3	376	89.4	4	22	8.5	19	0	.0
33406	46.5	98	17.7	77	26.8	439	98.0	6	16	21.7	14	1	.0
33407	23.7	69	9.4	60	24.0	350	76.9	6	17	7.7	16	3	.4
33408	16.8	99	7.0	82	37.9	508	173.8	3	22	8.1	21	0	.0
33409	29.6	98	13.7	82	20.9	404	85.3	4	40	13.1	38	0	.0
33410	22.3	99	8.0	78	36.4	583	144.6	5	9	10.7	8	1	.1
33411	11.1	97	4.5	89	33.6	565	147.8	7	21	5.6	22	0	.5
33430	20.6	39	6.4	38	22.7	277	77.7	10	7	4.1	7	0	.3
33431	18.4	98	7.9	78	39.1	566	189.6	6	25	8.5	25	0	.0
33432	34.2	96	13.8	77	43.2	514	185.2	3	24	15.5	24	0	.0
33433	11.8	99	4.7	92	40.8	614	203.5	5	21	5.6	22	0	.3
33434	6.0	98	2.4	87	28.6	384	142.8	7	21	2.8	22	0	.0
33435	39.7	83	17.0	85	24.9	409	107.7	5	36	15.0	41	0	.0
33436	35.9	99	2.8	92	29.2	261	146.6	2	36	2.8	37	0	1.1
33437	.1	95	.4	88	31.1	350	132.2	8	15	.5	15	0	.0
33438	1.2	83	.5	63	29.1	277	66.8	7	17	.5	23	0	.0
33439	.2	14	.1	0	18.0	150	64.1*	2	4	.0	0	0	2.5
33440	12.1	64	3.9	59	24.6	306	80.1	9	7	3.8	8	0	.1
33441	39.3	82	18.5	80	22.6	417	117.7	4	41	14.3	49	1	.4
33444	29.4	70	11.8	72	33.0	332	131.3	5	25	9.7	29	2	.2
33445	18.9	95	9.0	89	25.4	539	134.4	3	41	8.3	48	0	.0
33446	7.5	98	4.0	90	20.8	411	128.3	1	61	3.3	68	0	.0
33450	64.4	69	23.4	63	21.7	303	79.5	8	14	21.8	16	0	.0
33452	21.2	98	8.4	77	26.7	513	102.7	6	24	10.0	25	0	.3
33455	7.7	87	3.1	81	24.5	373	129.7	4	25	3.2	29	0	.0
33456	5.1	52	1.3	59	22.3	313	65.8	9	5	1.4	4	1	1.3
33457	12.2	98	5.3	83	26.7	296	113.8	3	29	5.9	29	0	.0
33458	24.2	95	9.3	83	36.1	439	146.1	6	18	11.2	17	0	.0
33459	.6	21	.2	44	86.6	180	79.2	13	10	.1	14	0	.0
33460	24.0	92	11.3	58	20.1	331	80.4	4	32	10.0	29	0	.0
33461	26.6	98	10.9	66	23.1	441	86.7	6	19	12.4	17	2	.3
33462	21.3	97	8.8	82	30.0	412	119.2	4	26	9.8	25	1	1.3
33463	24.5	98	9.5	86	28.4	408	106.6	6	20	11.7	21	2	.0
33470	4.3	95	1.2	93	35.4	306	130.0	9	3	2.1	3	0	.0
33471	4.0	81	1.5	72	17.5	279	58.2	7	13	1.6	14	0	.0

*=Estimated **=1.0=883 lbs per person; 100++ indicates per capita toxic waste generation > than 100 times the U.S. average of 883 lbs per capita.

ZIP CODE MEASURES OF SIZE, LEVELS OF AFFLUENCE AND QUALITY OF LIFE

1=Population (th.); 2= % White; 3=Households (th.); 4=% Owner Occupied; 5=Mean Income Per Household (th.$); 6=Mean Monthly Rent ($)*; 7=Mean Home Value (th.$)*; 8=% under 5; 9=% 65 and over; 10=% White Males (th.); 11=% White Males, 65+; 12=# Toxic Waste Sites; 13=Toxic Waste Relative to US(883 lbs.per capita)**.

FLORIDA

WEST PALM BEACH

ZIP CODE	1	2	3	4	5	6	7	8	9	10	11	12	13
33472	22.4	88	7.9	71	20.6	273	73.1	8	13	9.8	14	1	.1
33476	8.9	40	2.6	44	20.9	241	69.6	11	9	1.8	9	1	.1
33480	9.7	99	5.2	71	64.8	541	364.0	1	47	4.2	48	2	.0
33490	4.5	98	1.6	80	31.7	469	142.5	6	13	2.2	13	1	.0
33491	.2	0	.1	0	25.1	203	89.5*	8	0	.0	0	0	.0
33492	1.5	0	.6	76	18.3	385	87.1	6	22	.0	5	1	.3
33493	5.5	20	1.2	46	17.3	268	61.1	9	4	.5	5	0	.1
33494	31.9	94	13.5	77	27.0	387	126.4	5	28	14.3	28	0	.3

TAMPA

ZIP CODE	1	2	3	4	5	6	7	8	9	10	11	12	13
33501	1.5	99	.7	67	25.6	242	129.2	3	29	.7	27	0	.0
33502	.3	100	.1	71	22.8	173	63.6	3	16	.2	11	0	.0
33503	.6	97	.2	90	33.3	231	61.6	12	3	.3	3	0	.2
33505	42.4	96	17.2	76	26.0	357	98.4	5	24	18.9	21	0	.0
33507	41.2	99	19.3	71	20.1	374	80.9	4	37	18.3	35	0	.0
33508	19.7	73	6.7	70	20.2	281	71.2	8	15	6.9	15	1	.0
33510	5.6	100	2.7	67	26.7	239	140.4	2	34	2.6	33	0	.0
33511	32.0	97	10.1	82	32.6	452	97.8	6	6	15.4	5	0	.3
33512	50.0	94	19.1	84	19.9	293	69.4	5	22	22.8	23	1	.0
33513	6.6	82	2.1	80	18.6	257	52.6	5	17	2.8	18	0	.1
33514	1.3	87	.5	81	17.1	209	42.8	10	12	.5	13	0	.0
33515	60.3	91	27.6	70	24.5	362	95.7	4	31	25.1	32	0	.0
33516	53.8	97	23.3	73	26.4	367	104.2	3	30	24.0	26	0	.1
33519	22.3	97	9.1	76	27.1	340	128.1	5	22	9.8	22	0	.1
33520	10.4	97	4.5	70	24.9	405	105.1	6	19	4.9	19	1	1.2
33521	1.6	70	.6	75	19.4	199	62.0	7	16	.6	17	0	.2
33522	.7	0	.3	86	16.2	191	102.4	5	46	.0	0	0	.0
33523	.9	100	.3	83	23.4	343	95.6	4	29	.4	26	0	.0
33524	.2	100	.1	100	18.5	213*	29.2	2	15	.1	27	0	.0
33525	21.8	83	7.5	74	21.4	224	63.5	8	15	8.6	16	1	.1
33527	8.0	97	2.7	80	21.3	305	63.8	7	10	3.9	11	0	.0
33528	31.9	99	14.7	74	23.6	368	99.2	3	36	14.2	34	0	.0
33530	.7	100	.2	87	19.9	164	69.1	3	12	.3	4	0	.0
33531	.5	100	.2	80	17.2	240	73.4	6	25	.3	22	0	.0
33532	5.1	98	2.5	91	19.7	275	88.3	4	24	2.3	50	0	.0
33533	16.6	100	7.6	84	22.5	264	100.5	3	37	7.8	38	0	.0
33535	2.8	98	1.1	74	16.5	203	51.2	6	17	1.3	18	2	.0
33536	6.4	100	3.1	63	32.0	301	150.2	2	28	3.0	27	0	.0
33537	.2	100	.1	90	14.2	163*	39.7	8	19	.1	7	0	.0
33538	1.3	85	.4	65	15.3	181	25.6	5	11	.6	8	1	.2
33539	2.8	96	1.3	88	16.6	279	63.0	3	30	1.3	31	0	.0
33540	5.2	98	1.8	81	30.2	360	109.5	7	9	2.5	9	0	.0
33541	60.3	93	26.1	73	21.7	373	93.0	3	35	9.2	35	0	.3
33542	20.5	99	9.6	70	21.7	402	81.5	4	28	14.6	28	0	.0

TAMPA

ZIP CODE	1	2	3	4	5	6	7	8	9	10	11	12	13
33543	23.1	99	8.9	86	26.3	395	88.4	6	18	10.9	17	1	.2
33545	1.0	76	.4	77	21.9	226	102.3	5	16	.4	13	0	.1
33547	5.1	100	1.7	83	23.8	251	64.6	7	8	2.3	7	0	.0
33548	4.8	100	2.5	86	44.2	184	220.1	1	48	2.3	51	0	.0
33549	25.4	96	9.7	66	25.4	333	106.4	7	7	12.3	23	0	.0

FLORIDA

TAMPA

ZIP CODE	1	2	3	4	5	6	7	8	9	10	11	12	13
33550	.4	89	.1	65	18.4	296	62.8	9	13	.2	14	0	.0
33551	1.2	98	.4	81	26.7	128	107.1	4	10	.6	10	0	.0
33552	45.3	99	20.4	85	19.1	323	74.9	4	35	20.8	35	0	.8
33553	15.3	99	6.0	90	22.4	373	91.4	4	25	7.3	26	0	.0
33554	.4	100	.2	94	24.2	278*	42.0	5	16	.2	17	0	.0
33555	9.2	99	4.1	85	23.0	317	129.5	3	35	4.3	36	0	.0
33556	5.3	95	1.9	85	32.5	256	131.1	7	8	2.6	9	2	.1
33557	3.6	98	1.4	87	33.3	571	103.5	5	13	1.7	13	0	1.0
33558	.9	100	.3	85	19.2	231	73.5	11	13	.5	10	0	.3
33559	2.4	0	.1	84	27.8	302	162.8	3	27	.0	0	0	.1
33560	1.0	100	.4	76	28.7	249	108.4	6	28	.5	24	0	.0
33561	19.4	66	7.4	73	20.2	300	71.9	6	22	6.2	27	1	.8
33563	18.6	100	7.4	90	29.6	389	120.5	5	22	9.0	23	0	.0
33564	1.6	87	.5	75	19.8	262	68.0	3	10	.7	9	0	.2
33565	36.4	98	14.4	85	21.7	375	66.1	6	21	16.9	20	0	1.7
33566	41.0	84	14.2	75	21.8	279	61.8	8	12	16.5	11	6	1.7
33568	35.9	99	16.3	88	18.8	364	75.6	3	35	17.0	39	0	.2
33569	19.2	96	6.3	81	23.5	288	88.5	7	9	9.4	9	0	.0
33570	18.5	96	7.7	88	24.5	320	88.8	4	36	8.3	37	0	.3
33572	5.2	86	1.9	72	21.3	338	72.4	6	13	2.2	12	0	.0
33574	1.0	82	.5	50	21.2	311	64.9	0	5	.4	5	0	.0
33576	1.3	96	.5	74	20.6	300	73.1	6	17	.6	15	0	.0
33577	25.3	94	12.3	53	25.1	373	112.9	4	30	10.7	27	0	.1
33579	16.1	99	7.2	81	27.2	389	108.5	2	33	7.2	30	0	1.2
33580	30.4	71	11.9	75	23.9	332	95.9	6	21	10.3	24	0	.0
33581	36.3	99	16.7	75	29.4	476	134.5	3	31	16.5	30	0	.2
33582	23.7	98	8.9	85	28.1	476	104.2	6	17	11.0	17	0	.0
33583	11.9	99	4.8	86	27.2	467	123.0	5	20	5.7	20	1	.0
33584	14.5	91	4.8	79	24.7	333	77.1	8	7	6.5	7	1	.6
33585	.3	0	.1	76	14.4	293	64.8	7	22	.0	0	0	.0
33586	.2	100	.1	58	10.1	230	20.1	19	20	.1	9	0	3.1
33587	.5	100	.2	81	17.9	161	62.6	11	8	.3	9	0	.0
33588	.3	26	.1	79	38.7	284	66.0	7	6	.0	17	0	4.6
33589	16.4	91	6.4	74	24.6	296	95.5	5	21	7.2	21	1	3.3
33590	24.6	100	12.3	90	16.6	359	62.3	2	52	11.1	53	0	.0
33591	3.0	100	.1	91	20.4	444	58.6	4	24	.1	31	0	.0
33592	7.3	86	2.5	74	20.8	286	71.9	8	9	3.2	9	0	.0
33593	.6	55	.2	61	12.1	228	41.3	4	8	.2	13	0	.0
33594	11.6	97	3.9	90	30.8	349	102.9	7	9	5.6	9	0	.0
33595	32.7	99	15.2	88	23.7	350	98.7	3	41	14.8	41	1	.0
33596	7.9	98	3.6	85	20.5	298	73.8	3	43	3.6	45	0	3.1
33597	3.4	84	1.2	75	17.1	187	44.6	7	11	1.4	12	0	4.6
33598	1.7	60	.5	77	20.3	173	59.4	6	12	.5	15	0	3.3
33599	26.5	97	11.0	85	17.4	217	62.9	5	34	12.2	34	0	.0

TAMPA

ZIP CODE	1	2	3	4	5	6	7	8	9	10	11	12	13
33602	9.6	39	3.4	33	12.4	187	42.9	7	19	2.2	21	1	1.0
33603	20.5	84	8.4	65	20.7	300	51.7	6	17	7.8	17	1	.0
33604	31.9	91	13.5	66	18.0	269	50.4	7	18	13.6	16	0	.0
33605	23.0	34	8.2	51	14.0	204	34.3	8	17	3.5	23	3	.7

*=Estimated **1.0=883 lbs per person; 100++ indicates per capita toxic waste generation > than 100 times the U.S. average of 883 lbs per capita.

ZIP CODE MEASURES OF SIZE, LEVELS OF AFFLUENCE AND QUALITY OF LIFE

1=Population (th.); 2= % White; 3=Households (th.); 4=% Owner Occupied; 5=Mean Income Per Household (th.$); 6=Mean Monthly Rent ($); 7=Mean Home Value (th.$); 8=% under 5; 9=% 65 and over; 10=White Males (th.); 11=% White Males, 65+; 12=# Toxic Waste Sites; 13=Toxic Waste Relative to US(883 lbs.per capita)**.

FLORIDA

TAMPA

ZIPCODE	1	2	3	4	5	6	7	8	9	10	11	12	13
33606	15.9	81	7.2	44	23.3	270	107.5	5	16	6.4	13	0	.0
33607	22.9	50	8.4	62	17.9	231	51.3	6	16	5.3	17	0	.3
33608	5.4	77	1.0	9	18.8	309	59.9	12	0	2.6	0	1	.0
33609	38.6	96	16.7	69	33.0	355	103.0	5	18	17.2	15	0	.4
33610	36.1	45	12.1	70	19.7	263	48.1	8	11	8.0	12	2	.5
33611	26.2	95	10.8	65	24.5	367	65.9	6	14	11.8	11	0	.1
33612	51.8	94	20.2	52	20.8	350	70.4	5	10	23.5	9	1	.1
33614	47.9	94	17.5	61	25.6	395	74.6	6	8	21.8	6	0	.3
33615	30.7	97	10.8	73	28.1	368	87.1	6	8	14.1	7	0	.0
33616	9.9	81	3.2	76	23.4	360	55.4	8	5	3.9	4	1	.1
33617	34.0	94	12.9	54	27.8	425	97.3	6	6	15.5	5	1	1.0
33618	11.9	98	4.5	62	39.6	436	151.1	6	5	5.7	5	1	.0
33619	26.1	73	8.2	80	21.9	324	49.9	8	7	9.5	6	8	2.0
33624	16.0	96	5.3	89	43.2	412	128.9	8	5	7.7	4	2	.3

SAINT PETERSBURG

ZIPCODE	1	2	3	4	5	6	7	8	9	10	11	12	13
33701	17.1	85	9.9	26	14.3	228	56.0	4	45	6.3	44	2	.1
33702	32.1	98	14.3	66	22.0	377	82.9	4	26	14.4	23	0	.0
33703	23.3	99	10.2	86	25.3	375	89.7	4	26	10.6	23	0	.0
33704	16.4	99	7.8	69	24.9	309	94.2	3	33	7.3	28	0	.0
33705	31.2	61	12.7	55	18.9	274	69.2	6	22	8.7	26	0	.0
33706	15.7	100	7.9	64	28.3	345	135.8	4	34	7.2	32	0	.0
33707	23.9	99	12.0	69	21.3	354	80.2	3	40	10.1	36	1	.0
33708	16.2	99	8.4	73	23.9	362	104.2	2	38	7.3	35	0	.1
33709	22.3	99	10.1	80	20.1	340	66.4	5	32	9.9	28	0	.0
33710	34.5	99	14.9	82	24.4	379	76.5	4	26	15.6	23	0	.0
33711	18.8	55	7.3	73	20.2	335	59.9	7	15	4.9	23	0	.0
33712	27.5	35	10.3	53	20.2	304	66.7	7	13	4.5	15	0	.4
33713	28.0	97	13.6	73	17.1	318	55.8	5	34	12.1	30	0	.2
33714	16.5	98	7.9	69	15.7	264	48.0	6	34	7.3	28	0	.6
33715	2.0	99	1.0	81	49.9	565	222.7	1	38	.9	39	0	.0

LAKELAND

ZIPCODE	1	2	3	4	5	6	7	8	9	10	11	12	13
33801	72.6	82	27.3	64	21.5	296	62.9	7	17	28.2	16	4	.4
33802	1.0	100	1.6	85	24.5	281	77.0	6	11	.5	10	2	36.8
33803	48.8	96	17.1	76	32.1	405	103.0	6	11	22.8	10	1	.0
33820	.4	100	.2	76	39.9	217	68.8	9	12	.2	10	0	.0
33821	17.6	78	5.7	68	20.0	253	59.9	6	16	6.8	17	1	.1
33823	18.2	91	6.3	73	21.3	286	60.3	7	11	8.1	11	2	.7
33825	14.9	76	5.0	68	19.4	252	62.3	7	19	5.9	18	1	.0
33827	2.1	78	.7	75	24.6	286	62.9	5	18	.7	19	0	.0
33830	22.3	67	7.1	69	24.8	267	62.9	8	10	7.3	19	11	14.2
33834	5.2	80	1.6	78	21.2	192	47.0	11	10	2.0	11	0	.0
33835	1.0	0	.4	73	17.1	259	32.8	5	15	.0	7	0	.4
33837	4.5	85	1.4	73	20.3	255	54.0	5	13	1.9	13	0	.4
33838	2.4	78	.8	83	18.8	237	50.1	6	17	.9	22	0	.1
33839	2.9	98	.9	76	26.2	293	63.9	8	9	1.5	8	0	.0
33840	1.6	91	.6	72	19.5	270	48.6	12	10	.7	8	0	3.0
33841	8.2	72	2.5	75	22.6	272	53.2	11	10	3.0	11	5	4.9
33842	.5	0	.2	93	15.8	137	54.6	13	16	.0	0	0	.0
33843	6.0	82	2.1	74	19.4	211	51.9	6	21	2.4	24	0	.2

FLORIDA

LAKELAND

ZIPCODE	1	2	3	4	5	6	7	8	9	10	11	12	13
33844	17.3	66	5.4	71	21.2	257	59.9	7	14	5.7	17	0	.7
33846	1.4	97	.6	73	19.5	319	54.6	8	12	.7	12	0	.0
33847	.4	0	.2	73	19.1	244	30.9	11	17	.0	0	0	.0
33848	.6	97	.2	66	11.9	230	38.2	12	17	.3	13	0	.0
33849	3.7	99	1.2	83	22.4	323	75.4	10	7	1.8	7	0	1.5
33850	3.7	79	1.4	73	21.0	278	67.5	4	18	1.4	18	0	1.1
33851	1.4	66	.4	77	22.9	245	57.4	7	11	.5	14	0	.0
33852	10.2	83	4.0	81	18.7	244	77.4	5	25	4.1	30	0	.0
33853	21.2	76	8.0	76	21.3	216	68.3	6	19	7.8	21	0	.0
33854	.7	100	.5	0	14.7	257	52.4*	8	0	.3	85	0	.0
33855	.5	100	.3	93	25.7	418	91.9	2	48	.3	52	0	.0
33856	.8	100	.4	8	16.0	273	75.0	1	72	.4	74	0	.0
33857	1.2	100	.4	69	25.3	105	80.1	3	16	.6	17	0	.0
33858	.9	65	.3	70	18.4	185	39.1	4	12	.4	13	1	.0
33860	10.0	83	3.3	78	25.1	303	70.9	9	8	4.1	6	6	24.5
33863	.3	15	.3	75	19.0	356	33.1	12	6	.0	19	1	64.3
33864	1.0	85	.4	64	13.0	186	29.3	7	21	.4	25	1	.0
33865	.8	80	.3	85	29.7	168	32.8	8	11	.3	18	0	.0
33868	5.5	83	1.5	84	21.5	309	61.8	6	9	2.5	9	0	.0
33870	22.6	88	9.4	77	20.3	303	73.2	5	31	9.4	32	1	.0
33873	10.5	85	3.5	72	21.5	250	60.2	8	12	4.4	12	1	.1
33877	1.2	43	.3	65	14.0	176	33.4	7	12	.3	14	0	.5
33880	57.6	85	21.7	71	25.2	299	79.6	6	16	23.3	15	1	.4
33890	3.5	82	1.1	82	19.1	277	44.8	8	10	1.5	11	0	.0

FORT MEYERS

ZIPCODE	1	2	3	4	5	6	7	8	9	10	11	12	13
33901	38.5	62	15.0	51	21.7	295	80.1	8	16	11.4	19	1	.2
33902	1.0	93	.2	80	38.0	427	96.9	2	4	.6	4	2	4.0
33903	33.4	99	13.3	84	23.1	356	92.6	5	22	16.2	22	1	.0
33904	31.6	99	12.8	79	27.9	459	127.0	4	25	15.0	26	0	.0
33905	22.5	90	8.0	80	21.8	337	77.8	8	15	9.8	16	0	.0
33907	27.7	98	11.0	74	31.2	453	129.1	5	20	12.9	19	0	.0
33908	13.0	97	5.5	79	26.3	449	121.4	4	30	6.0	30	0	.0
33920	1.9	88	.7	80	19.6	233	69.3	5	18	.9	17	0	.0
33921	.7	90	.7	66	34.2	100	215.0	4	19	.3	18	0	.0
33922	1.0	100	.4	85	15.7	317	83.5	4	29	.5	27	0	.0
33923	9.1	97	4.0	80	21.2	222	95.2	6	27	4.3	27	0	.7
33924	.5	95	.3	44	31.9	68	202.8	3	19	.2	31	0	.1
33925	.3	100	.1	87	20.6	316	166.3	7	27	.2	31	0	.5
33926	.2	0	.1	21	9.8	161	34.9*	6	11	.0	0	0	.0
33927	.3	100	.8	100	14.2	163*	68.7	0	39	.1	42	0	.0
33928	1.8	92	.8	84	18.5	190	80.1	4	38	.8	39	0	.0
33929	1.0	95	.3	76	19.8	258	93.3	5	18	.5	17	0	.4
33930	.3	100	.1	77	16.7	480	74.7	2	16	.6	6	0	.0
33931	6.9	99	3.2	78	28.2	279	136.4	2	30	3.3	31	0	.1
33933	.3	0	.6	71	17.7	154	126.6	3	43	.3	0	0	.0
33934	14.9	48	4.8	42	16.5	210	85.8	11	4	3.8	6	1	3.0
33935	11.4	85	5.2	75	22.1	326	80.8	8	11	5.0	12	0	.0
33936	.5	97	.2	81	21.5	358	87.1	8	11	.2	40	1	.0
33937	4.7	100	2.1	79	40.6	339	231.6	2	23	2.3	25	0	.0

*=Estimated **1.0=883 lbs per person; 100++ indicates per capita toxic waste generation > than 100 times the U.S. average of 883 lbs per capita.

ZIP CODE MEASURES OF SIZE, LEVELS OF AFFLUENCE AND QUALITY OF LIFE

1=Population (th.); 2= % White; 3=Households (th.); 4=% Owner Occupied; 5=Mean Income Per Household (th.$); 6=Mean Home Value (th.$); 7=Mean Monthly Rent ($); 8=% under 5; 9=% 65 and over; 10=White Males (th.); 11=% White Males, 65+; 12=# Toxic Waste Sites; 13=Toxic Waste Relative to US(883 lbs.per capita)**.

FLORIDA

ZIPCODE	1	2	3	4	5	6	7	8	9	10	11	12	13
FORT MEYERS													
33939	.5	0	.2	76	30.6	441	118.7	11	14	.0	0	0	.0
33940	28.5	95	12.1	76	41.9	423	190.4	4	27	13.0	28	0	.0
33941	.3	100	.1	78	38.7	338	128.8	7	8	.1	9	0	.0
33942	28.6	97	11.8	75	28.4	376	130.6	5	20	13.4	20	0	.0
33943	.4	0	.2	61	34.1	415	83.9	0	14	.0	0	0	.0
33944	.1	100	.1	87	13.4	302	40.3	10	19	.1	19	0	.0
33945	.1	100	.1	100	37.0	425*	98.0	0	39	.1	37	0	.0
33946	.6	100	.3	87	32.0	168	201.6	0	39	.3	48	0	.0
33950	20.5	96	9.1	81	23.7	304	105.6	4	31	9.3	32	2	.0
33952	27.3	98	12.0	85	22.7	419	85.9	4	35	12.4	35	0	.0
33953	1.9	95	.8	91	23.9	338	81.5	5	17	.9	18	0	.0
33956	1.8	0	.9	92	20.4	331	104.7	1	38	.0	0	0	.0
33957	3.4	98	1.6	75	45.5	95	216.6	2	25	1.5	27	0	.0
33999	5.8	97	1.9	79	25.4	497	112.4	8	9	2.8	10	0	.0
DOTHAN													
36314	.6	94	.2	80	14.1	122	29.9	5	16	.3	12	0	.0
36340	.7	100	.2	77	15.7	65	14.9	7	17	.3	15	0	.0
EVERGREEN													
36426	.2	100	.1	84	15.7	180*	69.4	3	17	.1	9	0	.0
36441	.9	64	.3	80	17.5	191	36.8	8	19	.3	22	0	.0
36442	1.5	90	.5	82	18.1	237	40.8	8	14	.7	14	0	.0
36483	.3	82	.1	70	16.5	189*	43.1	9	5	.1	5	0	.0
MOBILE													
36502	2.6	85	.8	87	18.9	153	45.1	7	10	1.1	8	0	.0

GEORGIA

ZIPCODE	1	2	3	4	5	6	7	8	9	10	11	12	13
ASHEVILLE													
28909	.4	100	.2	91	13.4	255	32.5	3	19	.2	16	0	.0
ATLANTA													
30001	23.8	92	8.4	65	25.6	361	71.4	7	7	10.7	6	2	.3
30002	4.2	92	1.8	59	31.7	423	99.4	5	13	1.7	13	0	.0
30020	.3	100	.1	78	26.5	128	49.3	14	9	.1	11	1	3.5
30021	16.6	92	7.3	22	28.1	446	85.2	7	4	7.3	3	0	.0
30027	6.0	78	1.8	79	28.2	301	65.8	9	4	2.3	3	3	.6
30030	24.5	63	10.1	54	23.8	307	71.8	6	17	6.5	15	1	.1
30032	54.8	32	17.9	61	24.6	390	60.3	9	5	8.5	8	0	.0
30033	24.6	96	9.7	71	36.2	454	104.1	4	13	10.9	11	0	.0
30034	30.1	38	10.2	58	31.0	441	91.8	9	4	5.6	7	0	.0
30035	13.0	69	4.3	79	32.8	516	77.8	8	5	4.6	5	1	.0
30038	1.6	82	.7	42	38.0	462	135.5*	4	7	.7	7	0	.0
30049	11.0	73	3.4	84	33.1	355	79.2	8	5	4.1	5	1	.0
30050	29.7	94	10.4	62	26.0	345	59.2	8	6	13.4	5	6	.8
30057	10.8	97	3.5	84	28.9	350	73.1	8	8	5.2	7	1	.8
30058	24.2	83	8.0	79	31.7	369	93.7	7	7	10.0	6	3	.2
30059	19.2	99	6.7	80	28.6	360	76.1	6	8	9.2	6	4	.0
30060	47.3	90	17.5	53	24.3	315	73.6	8	7	20.8	5	6	2.6
30061	.2	100	.1	59	28.4	354	76.4	16	19	.1	19	0	4.6
30064	32.9	95	10.6	85	40.0	450	128.3	10	3	15.6	2	1	.9
30066	14.3	92	5.0	79	36.6	339	111.4	7	10	6.7	8	0	.9
30067	19.8	97	6.3	92	36.8	529	102.9	8	4	9.7	4	0	4.2
30070	46.6	97	17.2	62	42.1	459	150.7	6	3	22.4	2	1	.0
30071	.2	100	.1	100	41.8	481*	68.4	7	26	.1	26	0	.5
30073	13.9	95	5.3	61	31.4	436	102.9	7	4	6.6	3	4	2.0
30075	14.6	94	4.5	89	29.9	363	76.7	8	6	6.8	5	2	.5
30076	18.1	98	6.1	80	42.0	402	138.8	7	7	8.7	5	0	.0
30079	12.0	99	4.1	69	44.1	484	158.1	8	4	5.8	3	1	.6
30080	3.9	31	1.3	46	13.8	207	34.2	8	11	.6	13	6	.4
30083	42.5	94	16.8	52	28.0	382	80.8	6	7	19.2	6	2	.4
30084	36.0	95	12.5	62	34.4	417	103.0	7	5	16.7	4	2	.4
30087	25.8	98	8.6	76	36.8	466	108.3	6	7	12.3	5	9	4.2
30088	15.8	99	4.9	96	44.7	506	141.5	7	4	7.8	4	1	.0
30091	10.8	96	3.2	94	42.9	540	118.3	9	2	5.3	2	1	.0
30092	.3	0	.1	94	41.9	481*	123.9	0	0	.0	0	0	.0
30093	3.6	96	1.6	31	35.5	517	180.3	7	2	1.7	2	1	.3
ATLANTA													
30101	18.5	96	6.1	81	27.5	333	76.6	8	8	8.9	5	0	.0
30104	6.6	91	2.2	81	20.6	266	44.8	9	9	3.0	8	0	.0
30105	3.5	89	1.1	87	22.4	201	39.7	8	9	1.6	8	0	.5
30107	1.9	97	.7	76	23.1	161	59.4	6	10	1.0	9	0	.0
30108	6.3	86	2.3	82	21.1	237	51.8	6	13	2.6	11	2	.1
30110	7.8	90	2.7	76	21.5	250	59.9	7	13	3.5	10	1	.0
30113	3.5	93	1.2	80	19.6	223	49.0	5	12	1.5	8	0	.1
30114	20.6	96	6.8	78	22.4	274	64.4	7	11	9.6	9	0	.0
30117	34.3	80	11.5	64	22.4	252	71.5	7	10	13.2	9	4	1.8

*=Estimated **1.0=883 lbs per person; 100++ indicates per capita toxic waste generation > than 100 times the U.S. average of 883 lbs per capita.

ZIP CODE MEASURES OF SIZE, LEVELS OF AFFLUENCE AND QUALITY OF LIFE

1=Population (th.); 2= % White; 3=Households (th.); 4=% Owner Occupied; 5=Mean Income Per Household (th.$); 6=Mean Monthly Rent ($)*; 7=Mean Home Value (th.$)*;
8=% under 5; 9=% 65 and over; 10=White Males (th.); 11=% White Males, 65+; 12=# Toxic Waste Sites; 13=Toxic Waste Relative to US(883 lbs.per capita)**

GEORGIA — ATLANTA

ZIP CODE	1	2	3	4	5	6	7	8	9	10	11	12	13
30120	25.8	87	8.9	72	23.8	263	65.1	7	10	10.8	7	3	1.7
30123	.3	84		58	17.1	247	57.7	5	22	.1	19	0	.0
30124	2.3	87	.8	75	24.6	260	60.5	5	8	1.0	5	0	.0
30125	18.5	86	6.7	73	20.3	219	50.6	7	14	7.5	11	6	.0
30130	21.9	99	7.3	82	26.8	314	89.4	7	9	10.8	8	1	1.7
30132	15.5	97	5.3	80	22.4	249	62.9	8	9	7.5	7	0	.1
30133		100	.1	88	32.9	378*	69.5	9	11	.1	4	3	.0
30134	15.6	89	5.0	73	23.8	290	69.6	8	9	6.9	7	3	.0
30135	22.5	98	6.7	90	31.9	455	81.9	10	3	11.1	3	1	.1
30136	10.7	95	3.5	81	38.9	365	117.9	8	5	5.1	4	0	.0
30137	.7	64	.2	82	21.7	295	40.6	6	11	.2	11	0	.2
30138	.3	100	.1	77	16.0	386	33.1	4	21	.2	13	0	.0
30139	2.6	96	.9	84	18.7	252	39.7	7	12	1.3	10	0	.4
30140	.9	93	.4	78	16.1	327	40.4	5	12	.5	9	0	.0
30141	5.7	94	1.8	87	22.1	286	59.6	9	9	2.6	8	0	.2
30142	.3	0	.1	72	25.9	268	64.7	8	10	.1	8	0	.0
30143	7.4	98	2.7	77	21.8	274	60.1	6	13	3.6	10	1	.0
30144	18.2	97	5.7	87	32.2	409	94.7	8	4	8.8	3	0	.0
30145	2.7	88	.8	77	21.5	238	46.9	8	10	1.3	10	0	.4
30146	5.7	94	1.8	90	19.2	188	57.8	9	14	.1	7	1	.2
30147	4.6	98	1.6	78	22.4	283	49.3	6	11	2.2	10	1	.0
30148	.4	100		83	22.0	175	40.1	11	6		9	0	.0
30149	.8	0	.1	9	24.2	241	240.6	2	0	.0	0	0	.0
30151	.6	93	.2	83	17.1	300	32.8	7	13	.3	10	0	.0
30153	12.1	85	4.2	74	21.3	233	50.7	7	13	4.8	11	3	.2
30161	62.8	84	22.7	65	23.3	246	63.5	7	13	25.0	10	8	.5
30170	1.1	92	.4	83	20.3	160	44.9	7	13	.8	10	1	.0
30171	1.1	96	.4	75	22.2	213	56.4	8	8	.5	8	0	.0
30172	1.4	100	.5	80	21.5	255	42.7	5	14	.6	14	0	2.6
30173	4.0	96	1.3	78	24.9	312	61.2	7	11	1.9	8	0	.0
30174	2.8	97	.9	83	27.0	314	79.9	9	8	1.4	6	0	.0
30175	2.3	100	.8	86	16.7	184	37.1	7	13	1.1	12	0	.0
30176	5.1	95	1.9	76	20.2	151	47.2	6	14	2.3	11	0	.1
30177	.6	74	.2	64	23.0	249	41.4	10	17	.2	18	0	.0
30178	1.4	90	.4	78	21.6	253	52.7	7	11	.6	11	1	.6
30179	5.1	89	1.7	80	20.4	240	52.1	7	9	2.3	9	0	.0
30180	9.1	83	3.0	77	22.1	258	57.5	8	11	3.8	10	0	.2
30182	4.2	88	1.2	82	22.4	253	48.0	9	13	.7	8	0	.0
30183	1.5	98	.5	74	22.6	358	83.8	6	12	.8	12	1	.0
30184	1.8	100	.6	77	19.2	210	51.6	9	10	.9	11	1	.1
30185	2.2	88	.7	80	22.1	268	46.7	8	10	.7	9	0	.0
30186	.3	100	.1	82	14.9	186	31.2	12	5	1.4	9	0	.0
30187	4.2	88	1.2	87	26.9	331	73.7	8	7	1.8	6	0	.0

ATLANTA

ZIP CODE	1	2	3	4	5	6	7	8	9	10	11	12	13
30201	14.6	98	4.9	83	33.4	315	109.2	7	9	7.1	8	1	.0
30202	.3	72	.1	100	18.1	208*	58.0	9	25	.3	19	0	.0
30203	2.6	96	.9	80	22.3	294	58.2	9	11	1.2	9	0	.0
30204	9.5	63	3.1	69	20.7	226	50.7	8	12	2.8	10	3	.0

GEORGIA — ATLANTA

ZIP CODE	1	2	3	4	5	6	7	8	9	10	11	12	13
30205	1.3	97	.5	87	26.4	291	79.5	7	8	.7	7	0	.0
30206	1.8	52	.5	77	26.6	214	50.0	9	13	.4	18	0	.0
30207	21.2	86	7.0	76	26.4	329	77.6	8	8	8.9	7	6	.8
30208	13.3	95	3.9	94	37.1	473	106.7	8	4	6.3	4	0	.8
30209	26.4	72	8.5	73	24.1	238	63.9	8	11	9.1	9	6	1.8
30211	4.4	93	1.4	83	28.8	318	70.8	8	7	2.1	5	1	.0
30212	.1	100		48	10.1	181	38.0	0	49	.0	54	1	.0
30213	10.4	85	3.5	78	31.1	290	95.4	7	9	4.4	7	1	.1
30214	17.1	94	5.4	88	37.5	353	115.4	7	7	8.0	5	1	.0
30216	1.3	54	.4	70	19.2	274	38.6	9	16	.4	14	0	.2
30217	5.5	82	1.8	77	20.8	225	47.1	9	13	2.2	12	2	.1
30218	1.2	24	.3	51	19.7	127	38.3	7	8	.6	10	1	.0
30220	2.2	59	.8	79	18.2	189	45.0	7	16	.6	18	0	.2
30221	2.1	0	.7	79	33.2	387	102.8	9	6		0	0	5.3
30222	3.6	32	1.1	72	17.7	180	40.8	9	13	.0	0	0	.0
30223	46.4	71	15.6	64	23.5	249	63.5	8	11	15.9	9	3	.7
30228	6.1	87	2.0	77	30.7	303	75.9	9	9	2.7	8	1	.3
30229	.2	83		65	30.5	209	62.9	5	16		22	0	.2
30230	6.5	72	2.4	73	18.8	214	43.8	6	17	2.2	13	1	.2
30231	.3	32	.1	64	14.8	283	39.0	9	4	.0	0	0	.0
30233	11.2	66	3.4	72	22.8	241	60.2	7	10	3.9	9	0	.1
30234	1.4	44	.3	62	24.1	268	57.1	9	14	.3	18	0	.0
30235	.5		.3	72	20.1	184	53.8	8	10	.7	3	0	.7
30236	40.9	92	13.2	67	30.1	358	83.9	9	4	18.7	3	0	.7
30240	38.1	70	13.1	63	22.8	260	67.3	8	12	12.7	10	3	.3
30245	36.2	97	11.7	81	31.9	373	95.4	9	6	17.4	4	2	.7
30246	.2	0	.1	83	23.2	465	94.2	8	6		0	0	.0
30247	32.1	99	9.9	89	38.8	444	120.0	9	3	15.8	2	1	.0
30248	3.5	78	1.1	86	23.4	271	56.8	9	13	1.3	11	0	.7
30249	9.1	95	2.9	82	25.6	289	81.8	9	7	4.3	4	0	1.7
30250	.2	58	.1	59	21.2	314	30.9	8	10		8	0	.0
30251	1.5	58	.5	81	21.5	197	49.6	11	10	.4	13	0	.2
30252	.3	82	.1	84	27.0	178	54.4	9	3	1.0	8	0	.0
30253	11.7	64	3.6	73	26.4	247	74.2	7	12	3.6	11	1	.7
30255	1.6	79	.5	77	23.5	245	56.2	7	12	.6	10	1	.0
30256	1.6	88	.5	86	20.9	235	36.9	8	12	.7	11	0	.0
30257	2.5	77	.8	83	27.0	256	51.6	10	8	1.0	8	0	.2
30258	1.6	75	.5	77	18.5	218	45.3	8	15	.6	11	0	.0
30259	1.5	90	.5	81	27.9	201	63.9	7	10	.7	8	0	.3
30260	18.1	94	5.8	71	32.5	399	80.6	7	5	8.1	4	4	1.1
30261	.3	53	.1	84	23.4	80	36.6	15	46	.0	37	0	
30262	.8	76	.8	74	22.2	296	62.0	11	12	.3	12	0	.0
30263	27.1	71	9.3	70	25.4	289	68.7	8	11	1.0	10	3	.0
30265	1.4	59	.4	75	22.9	332	75.8	9	7	.4	7	0	.0
30266	.3	89	.1	81	22.0	220	57.3	9	20	.1	15	0	.3
30267	6.3	86	1.9	87	25.8	302	66.6	7	7	2.8	7	0	.0
30268	4.2	76	1.4	72	27.1	314	60.6	7	10	1.6	8	0	.0
30269	6.5	99	2.0	84	38.6	488	122.0	9	3	3.2	3	2	1.4
30270	1.6	95	.6	76	17.3	261	26.1	7	19	.7	16	0	.6

*=Estimated **1.0=883 lbs per person; 100++ indicates per capita toxic waste generation > than 100 times the U.S. average of 883 lbs per capita.

ZIP CODE MEASURES OF SIZE, LEVELS OF AFFLUENCE AND QUALITY OF LIFE

1=Population (th.); 2= % White; 3=Households (th.); 4=% Owner Occupied; 5=Mean Income Per Household (th.$); 6=Mean Monthly Rent ($)*; 7=Mean Home Value (th.$)*; 8=% under 5; 9=% 65 and over; 10=White Males (th.); 11=% White Males, 65+; 12=# Toxic Waste Sites; 13=Toxic Waste Relative to US(883 lbs.per capita)**.

GEORGIA — ATLANTA

ZIP CODE	1	2	3	4	5	6	7	8	9	10	11	12	13
30272	.2	100	.1	89	14.6	168*	52.3	12	23	.1	48	0	1.4
30273	5.3	98	1.7	92	32.7	461	78.8	11	5	2.6	4	0	.0
30274	22.9	97	7.7	63	30.5	370	75.6	8	5	11.1	4	3	.0
30275	.3	90	.1	69	11.9	305	30.9	2	35	.1	13	0	3.5
30276	3.6	63	1.2	77	21.9	240	52.2	7	11	1.2	12	1	.0
30277	2.7	91	.9	90	31.5	276	104.8	7	6	1.7	5	0	.0
30278	15.8	98	4.7	94	36.8	457	105.2	10	5	7.7	4	0	.0
30279	4.5	69	1.4	73	23.1	233		7	13	1.5	9	0	.1
30281	15.2	94	4.9	87	29.7	281	84.0	8	6	7.1	5	2	.0
30284	.5	88	.2	75	13.9	308	45.9	10	13	.5	9	0	.0
30285	.5	77	.1	66	27.7	167	49.5	12	9	.2	10	0	.0
30286	23.1	73	8.3	70	21.1	203	50.1	7	14	8.0	13	4	.3
30290	.2	71	.1	86	31.4	391	51.7	8	11	.1	8	0	.0
30291	5.0	100	1.9	65	26.6	115	82.2	6	9	2.0	6	0	.2
30292	1.8	82	.6	83	25.1	377	57.5	7	8	.7	10	0	.0
30293	3.6	85	1.1	75	20.4	361	63.3	8	10	.9	8	0	.1
30294	.2	55	.1	69	32.0	203	46.3	10	11	.1	8	0	.0
30295	2.5	100	.9	76	23.9	201	66.5	7	11	.9	8	0	.0
30296	12.8	73	3.8	94	36.5	494	97.7	8	3	5.9	3	0	.0

ATLANTA

ZIP CODE	1	2	3	4	5	6	7	8	9	10	11	12	13
30303	1.4	48	.3	3	10.6	169	37.9*	1	16	.5	16	3	10.0
30305	18.5	97	10.3	43	40.0	391	188.6	3	27	7.6	17	0	1.4
30306	18.5	94	9.5	49	27.6	341	111.9	4	17	8.4	12	0	1.2
30307	14.5	72	6.6	47	23.8	289	91.7	6	13	5.1	11	0	.1
30309	9.9	53	5.8	14	16.1	276	93.2	4	16	3.0	7	0	1.4
30310	15.1	90	9.3	27	28.6	349	166.8	8	14	6.8	9	0	.4
30311	38.8	16	13.2	50	16.1	252	42.2	8	11	3.0	21	5	.0
30312	40.0	5	14.4	44	22.5	338	71.0	8	5	.7	34	1	.0
30313	19.6	23	7.9	19	10.8	160	37.5	8	18	1.9	16	1	.5
30314	8.6	52	2.1	2	6.0	90	21.1	9	9	.9	3	0	.1
30315	34.3	1	12.2	36	13.7	204	40.2	5	16	3.2	0	5	.0
30316	43.5	23	14.0	37	14.7	220	39.7	10	10	4.7	13	5	.0
30317	35.7	24	11.6	59	20.9	321	47.2	7	10	4.1	14	0	.6
30318	20.8	4	6.2	51	16.2	246	40.3	8	9	.4	29	1	.1
30319	55.1	26	20.3	41	19.6	256	58.9	9	9	7.0	10	23	2.3
30324	28.2	91	11.6	52	33.3	389	114.1	5	11	11.9	9	2	.1
30326	13.3	93	7.0	36	28.6	412	106.6	3	16	5.7	13	0	.2
30327	.3	85	.1	11	37.6	510	30.4	2	1	.3	0	0	.3
30330	37.2	9	12.2	51	23.4	338	111.7	4	26	1.5	20	2	.0
30336	5.3	0	1.6	48	17.0	213	44.4	9	6	.0	0	9	.0
30337	24.2	51	10.1	29	22.3	342	67.1	8	8	6.0	0	0	10.5
30338	32.0	99	10.3	73	54.2	462	212.1	4	3	15.7	3	1	.4
30339	9.4	97	5.1	20	36.0	468	233.4	2	2	4.3	2	0	1.3
30340	17.4	97	6.2	62	33.4	435	97.9	6	4	8.2	3	8	6.7

GEORGIA — ATLANTA

ZIP CODE	1	2	3	4	5	6	7	8	9	10	11	12	13
30341	24.7	94	9.5	48	31.6	455	92.7	6	6	11.2	4	6	3.2
30342	17.8	97	8.4	57	41.2	463	165.0	4	13	7.8	11	0	.1
30344	37.0	58	14.4	50	24.7	329	66.7	7	11	9.8	13	9	.9
30345	19.0	96	7.5	58	40.3	478	132.6	4	5	8.7	6	2	.0
30349	35.2	59	12.8	57	29.5	354	82.5	8	5	10.1	6	2	.0
30354	21.6	41	7.4	47	20.5	301	54.0	10	6	4.2	9	5	3.00
30360	12.3	95	4.2	65	38.6	501	115.9	6	3	5.8	2	6	.0

SWAINSBORO

ZIP CODE	1	2	3	4	5	6	7	8	9	10	11	12	13
30401	12.6	69	4.3	65	20.4	192	52.9	9	11	4.2	9	2	.3
30410	.5	54	.5	67	22.7	146	45.5	10	10	.4	2	0	.0
30411	2.5	65	.9	78	14.6	174	38.4	7	15	.8	17	0	.0
30412	.1	0	.1	77	12.1	293	38.0	5	42	.0	0	0	.0
30413	2.0	41	.6	57	16.9	159	49.1	8	13	.4	15	0	.0
30414	.4	74	.1	80	22.7	104	67.7	5	15	.1	16	0	.8
30415	3.5	74	1.3	73	17.9	218	62.2	8	13	1.3	12	0	.0
30417	6.5	64	2.2	64	18.5	198	57.4	8	14	2.0	12	1	.0
30420	1.6	79	.6	65	18.8	186	46.1	8	17	.6	18	0	.0
30421	2.2	70	.8	74	15.5	153	43.8	7	15	.8	16	0	.0
30423	.2	70	.1	52	10.6	158	79.4	13	10	.1	8	0	.0
30425	1.4	61	.4	77	17.4	153	52.4	10	11	.1	9	0	.0
30426	1.2	42	.3	62	15.5	156	28.7	10	8	.3	6	0	.0
30427	7.9	74	2.8	67	16.0	230	50.6	9	13	2.8	11	0	.1
30428	2.3	74	.7	75	15.6	139	37.5	10	15	.8	12	0	.0
30429	.9	57	.3	67	16.0	204	42.8	12	8	.3	6	0	.0
30434	6.6	64	2.2	64	16.9	157	51.9	8	13	3.0	11	0	.8
30436	9.3	76	3.1	66	15.3	176	46.5	8	12	3.4	11	0	.0
30438	1.1	80	.4	74	16.3	190	43.7	4	14	.5	9	0	.0
30439	6.7	67	2.3	65	18.6	201	56.2	7	16	2.1	14	0	.2
30441	3.0	48	1.0	70	17.0	152	37.0	9	15	2.3	10	0	.0
30442	8.2	57	2.5	66	17.1	182	50.7	8	12	.9	14	0	.2
30445	2.5	67	.7	66	15.6	150	46.1	7	11	.9	6	0	.0
30446	1.2	60	.4	65	17.3	215	45.8	9	9	.4	8	0	.0
30449	.2	49	.1	71	17.4	143	39.0	10	11	.1	14	0	.1
30450	2.2	61	.6	68	15.8	185	52.1	9	10	.6	8	0	.0
30451	2.9	78	.1	60	16.9	288	45.9	9	36	.0	21	0	.0
30452	1.3	0	.4	65	20.7	158	27.0	9	14	.4	0	0	.2
30453	6.2	63	1.4	60	21.2	162	57.4	6	8	2.2	7	0	.0
30454	.5	100	.2	89	22.9	224	43.3	4	18	.2	23	0	.2
30455	.7	60	.2	74	13.6	203	37.6	7	14	.2	10	0	.0
30457	1.8	59	.6	70	15.2	188	44.1	11	14	.5	10	0	.2
30458	5.6	64	1.9	66	19.3	167	41.8	9	14	1.7	14	0	.0
30464	27.1	74	8.5	60	22.6	264	78.7	7	9	9.8	8	2	.0
30467	12.0	54	4.2	69	17.9	187	52.7	9	14	3.1	13	3	.8
30470	.8	91	.3	72	16.6	132	51.3	9	13	.4	8	0	.0
30471	3.5	61	1.1	80	16.8	153	39.7	10	16	1.0	18	0	.0
30473	2.6	78	.9	79	15.9	222	40.5	5	12	1.0	15	0	.5
30474	13.6	74	4.7	63	21.6	226	56.4	9	11	4.7	8	0	.0
30477	3.9	40	1.2	68	16.6	187	39.7	8	15	.7	16	1	.4

*=Estimated **1.0=883 lbs per person; 100++ indicates per capita toxic waste generation > than 100 times the U.S. average of 883 lbs per capita.

ZIP CODE MEASURES OF SIZE, LEVELS OF AFFLUENCE AND QUALITY OF LIFE

1=Population (th.); 2= % White; 3=Households (th.); 4=% Owner Occupied; 5=Mean Income Per Household (th.$); 6=Mean Monthly Rent ($); 7=Mean Home Value (th.$); 8=% under 5; 9=% 65 and over; 10=White Males (th.); 11=% White Males, 65+; 12=# Toxic Waste Sites; 13=Toxic Waste Relative to US(883 lbs.per capita)**.

GEORGIA

GAINESVILLE

ZIP CODE	1	2	3	4	5	6	7	8	9	10	11	12	13
30501	57.0	89	19.7	69	25.6	292	81.2	7	10	24.2	9	1	.5
30510	4.7	86	1.2	80	19.8	201	48.4	7	7	2.2	7	0	.4
30511	1.9	98	.7	84	17.5	321	51.3	6	16	1.0	13	1	.0
30512	8.4	99	3.1	83	16.5	223	52.1	6	15	4.1	14	1	.0
30513	6.1	100	2.3	80	17.1	199	46.7	7	17	2.9	14	1	.0
30516	1.2	86	.4	89	18.8	199	48.3	6	11	.4	10	0	.0
30517	1.9	99	.6	73	19.6	216	61.0	7	6	.9	6	0	.0
30518	17.0	92	5.7	77	24.2	288	73.8	8	10	7.7	8	1	.4
30520	2.9	97	1.1	82	16.9	177	54.6	5	16	1.4	13	0	.0
30521	3.3	90	1.2	81	20.8	159	54.1	5	16	1.5	16	1	.1
30522	.7	100	.2	81	16.3	167	60.4	2	15	.4	15	0	.0
30523	6.7	98	2.4	79	21.3	218	60.4	7	13	3.4	12	0	.1
30525	5.6	98	2.0	78	20.3	243	69.7	5	15	2.6	12	0	.6
30527	2.0	0	.7	84	21.2	293	57.5	6	13	.0	0	0	.0
30528	8.3	97	2.9	81	21.9	247	67.8	7	13	3.9	12	0	.0
30529	10.1	88	3.6	75	21.7	222	55.6	7	15	3.9	14	0	.4
30531	7.1	93	2.5	75	23.1	241	63.2	7	11	3.2	14	1	.6
30533	5.8	95	3.0	72	22.4	260	63.2	6	10	4.4	9	0	.5
30534	4.3	99	1.5	78	20.2	235	50.3	6	11	2.0	9	0	.0
30535	.5	0	.2	81	18.8	243	109.6	12	17	.0	0	0	.1
30537	1.9	97	.8	80	19.2	191	56.0	6	11	.9	10	0	.0
30538	.6	100	.2	59	14.8	258	39.0	6	12	.3	12	0	.0
30539	9.4	100	3.3	78	19.4	209	58.9	8	12	4.7	11	0	.3
30540	1.2	0	.4	85	17.2	234	49.8	4	14	.0	0	0	.0
30541	6.4	95	2.2	78	26.0	118	72.0	7	13	3.1	11	0	.1
30542	1.8	95	.6	80	23.8	283	57.9	6	12	.8	12	0	.1
30544	.3	100	.1	33	24.8	270	73.2	7	1	.1	11	0	.0
30545	3	0	.1	91	22.4	230	68.8	6	10	.8	4	0	2.8
30546	3.3	86	1.3	86	20.9	216	75.5	5	10	1.9	15	0	.0
30547	1.9	94	.7	72	24.0	175	46.4	9	13	.9	13	0	.0
30548	2.4	96	.8	76	23.5	170	60.6	7	9	1.2	11	0	.0
30549	7.1	83	2.4	73	19.8	234	55.8	6	10	2.9	8	0	.3
30552	.7	100	.7	78	18.0	236	52.3	3	23	.4	25	0	.0
30553	5.0	81	1.8	75	13.5	111	37.0	7	14	1.9	12	0	.0
30554	3.8	95	1.3	84	19.6	185	39.4	5	11	1.8	11	0	.0
30555	1.4	98	.6	75	17.9	231	81.9	5	17	.6	15	0	.0
30557	2.6	83	.9	81	18.3	199	73.5	9	11	1.0	8	0	.0
30558	2.1	97	.9	82	19.9	242	58.1	8	15	1.1	12	0	.2
30559	2.1	94	.7	87	13.5	237	66.1	6	14	.7	10	0	.0
30560	2.1	98	.7	86	22.1	103	59.8	7	13	1.0	10	0	.0
30562	.7	97	.8	78	29.4	331	81.9	9	3	2.1	1	0	.0
30563	2.5	0	.3	89	22.2	217	73.5	7	6	.8	8	0	.0
30564	2.0	0	.7	82	23.6	265	75.5	9	9	.6	13	0	.0
30565	2.1	94	.7	78	22.1	295	66.1	7	10	2.6	11	0	.0
30566	4.4	98	1.4	77	29.4	204	59.8	9	3	.5	15	0	.0
30567	1.5	97	.4	79	21.7	331	81.9	7	6	.6	10	0	.0
30568	1.3	100	.4	79	23.6	217	75.5	6	13	.6	13	0	.0
30571	1.6	91	.6	80	20.4	177	74.1	6	14	.7	14	0	.0

GEORGIA

GAINESVILLE

ZIP CODE	1	2	3	4	5	6	7	8	9	10	11	12	13
30572	.8	0	.3	87	15.7	289	71.4	6	11	.0	0	0	.0
30575	.9	100	.3	55	17.5	235	38.9	7	14	.5	13	0	.0
30576	1.0	0	.4	74	16.5	167	59.2	6	18	.0	0	0	.0
30577	19.6	87	6.9	73	21.0	216	56.7	7	13	8.2	11	10	.1
30580		100		93	33.5	385*	39.1	10	0	.1	0	0	.0
30581	.3	100	.1	74	14.4	494	62.0	9	6	.2	2	0	.0
30582	2.1	100	.6	84	14.9	216	54.4	5	14	1.0	10	0	.2

ATHENS

ZIP CODE	1	2	3	4	5	6	7	8	9	10	11	12	13
30601	18.6	44	7.0	42	16.0	225	47.4	8	10	4.0	6	2	1.0
30603	.3	84	.1	53	15.9	236	37.2	3	31	.1	8	0	.1
30604	.3	0	.2	73	23.5	281	57.5	8	6	.0	0	0	.0
30605	19.7	88	7.9	41	23.5	322	96.8	6	6	8.4	4	0	.0
30606	25.2	83	10.1	50	25.1	341	93.1	6	10	10.5	7	1	.0
30607	3.6	84	1.2	67	23.1	307	67.5	10	6	.0	4	0	.2
30619	.7	0	.3	88	24.4	210	75.4	9	12	.5	2	0	.1
30620	2.1	88	.7	76	21.8	272	51.4	6	10	.9	9	0	.0
30621	1.5	72	.5	75	23.1	237	60.0	7	10	.5	10	0	.0
30622	4.0	83	1.4	78	26.5	316	60.0	9	10	1.6	5	0	.0
30623	.4	63	.1	91	19.6	218	60.6	6	8	.1	7	0	.0
30624	2.1	72	.7	76	17.3	194	47.7	8	11	.8	8	0	.0
30625	.7	62	.3	80	23.2	163	52.5	9	17	.2	14	0	.0
30627	2.8	54	.7	81	18.9	200	38.0	5	16	.6	17	0	.0
30628	2.8	86	.9	82	23.3	180	62.8	7	9	1.2	8	1	.2
30629	2.9	78	.9	76	19.5	202	53.5	7	13	1.1	11	0	.0
30630	1.6	70	.5	74	22.4	159	57.7	9	12	.5	12	0	.1
30631	1.8	0	.7	72	16.0	167	35.3	7	19	.0	0	0	.0
30632	.6	53	.2	77	14.0	154	39.0	11	19	.2	9	0	.0
30633	5.2	97	1.7	86	21.0	199	51.9	9	9	2.5	8	0	2.8
30634	1.8	73	.6	77	17.3	287	40.5	7	14	.7	13	0	.0
30635	15.6	68	5.5	73	19.5	208	55.7	8	14	8.1	12	2	.4
30638	.1	100	.1	86	19.7	392	34.6	9	4	.1	0	0	.2
30639	.5	97	.1	58	21.1	230	64.4	6	5	.6	17	0	.0
30641	.7	91	.2	82	18.3	153	54.7	6	11	.2	8	0	.2
30642	6.0	50	2.0	76	17.6	204	46.4	9	13	1.4	9	0	.1
30643	12.6	77	4.3	78	20.8	199	58.6	9	13	4.8	12	0	1.2
30645	1.4	100	.5	85	19.7	259	42.3	7	13	.7	11	0	.0
30646	4.4	88	1.5	77	20.0	290	54.9	6	11	1.9	10	0	.0
30647	.4	100	.1	83	21.3	323	43.5	6	9	.2	9	0	.0
30648	2.3	58	.7	78	21.1	200	50.9	7	13	.7	14	0	.0
30650	8.4	56	2.7	73	22.0	205	64.9	8	12	2.3	10	1	1.3
30655	17.1	71	5.5	65	21.5	244	60.6	8	11	5.7	10	1	.1
30658	.1	34	.1	100	7.9	91*	35.0	20	28	.0	40	0	.0
30659		36	.1	89	13.2	152*	30.8	8	18	.2	27	0	.2
30660	.9	50	.3	65	13.1	184	36.0	6	23	.3	18	0	.0
30662	6.0	94	2.1	77	19.4	156	42.0	6	23	2.6	11	0	.1
30663	1.6	98	.5	69	21.7	235	54.2	9	15	.5	15	1	.0
30664	.1	36	.2	78	12.2	118	17.2	11	40	.0	65	0	.0
30665	.6	39	.2	66	13.5	196	30.6	10	8	.1	6	0	.0
30666	3.3	77	1.1	78	21.3	234	53.8	9	13	1.2	10	0	.0

*=Estimated **1.0=883 lbs per person; 100++ indicates per capita toxic waste generation > than 100 times the U.S. average of 883 lbs per capita.

ZIP CODE MEASURES OF SIZE, LEVELS OF AFFLUENCE AND QUALITY OF LIFE

1=Population (th.); 2= % White; 3=Households (th.); 4=% Owner Occupied; 5=Mean Income Per Household (th.$); 6=Mean Monthly Rent ($); 7=Mean Home Value (th.$); 8=% under 5; 9=% 65 and over; 10=White Males; 11=% White Males, 65+; 12=# Toxic Waste Sites; 13=Toxic Waste Relative to US(883 lbs.per capita)**.

GEORGIA

ATHENS

ZIPCODE	1	2	3	4	5	6	7	8	9	10	11	12	13
30667	.7	51	.2	73	18.3	199	53.1	11	11	.2	12	0	.0
30668	1.4	54	.5	81	17.1	179	37.8	5	17	.4	17	0	.0
30669	3.6	48	1.1	75	17.0	179	41.4	9	17	.8	18	0	.0
30671	.2	65	.1	73	19.1	220*	65.2	5	19	.1	20	0	.0
30673	8.2	55	3.0	75	20.8	222	55.0	8	13	2.2	12	0	.6
30677	7.0	90	2.2	78	28.9	297	88.4	7	7	3.1	7	1	.0
30678	.9	35	.3	82	17.3	111	36.6	11	14	.2	19	1	.0
30680	14.0	85	4.8	68	22.4	236	65.5	8	12	5.7	9	1	.2
30683	3.8	89	1.3	81	24.6	309	71.6	8	7	1.7	5	0	.3

CHATTANOOGA

ZIPCODE	1	2	3	4	5	6	7	8	9	10	11	12	13
30701	20.5	95	7.2	71	22.5	257	59.2	8	10	9.4	8	3	.6
30705	15.6	99	5.1	76	22.4	269	58.0	8	8	7.6	6	2	.3
30707	12.4	93	4.1	82	22.1	269	52.3	8	10	5.6	8	1	.1
30708	.3	100	.1	90	36.1	201	23.1	20	6	.2	8	0	.0
30709	.7	100	.2	78	18.7	267	27.9	11	11	.3	11	0	.0
30710	2.8	99	.9	87	26.0	218	80.3	9	7	1.4	6	0	.0
30711	2.0	100	.7	80	25.4	265	56.8	7	10	1.0	8	0	.0
30720	53.3	95	18.5	65	26.0	290	71.9	9	9	24.5	7	11	1.6
30724	.4	100	.1	82	25.4	226	51.5	7	9	.2	7	0	.3
30725	.3	100	.1	56	28.9	285	32.8	10	4	.2	4	0	1.5
30726	.2	100	.1	94	20.8	239*	86.2	9	6	.1	12	2	.2
30728	16.1	95	5.6	73	20.4	235	47.2	8	12	7.3	11	3	.2
30730	1.8	87	.6	73	17.9	201	40.2	8	8	.7	9	0	.2
30731	1.4	93	.3	66	16.0	149	35.6	5	15	.6	17	0	.0
30733	1.5	98	.5	81	20.3	219	40.0	9	12	.7	8	0	.0
30734	1.7	100	.5	71	19.2	212	36.1	9	14	.7	17	0	.1
30735	3.3	100	1.1	82	20.2	222	48.4	7	9	1.7	9	0	.2
30736	19.1	99	6.3	83	24.2	296	70.7	8	8	9.2	6	2	1.0
30738	2.7	0	.1	82	21.6	232	52.2	7	10	.8	6	0	.3
30739	2.5	0	.8	90	23.7	332	63.9	8	8	.2	4	0	.0
30740	4.9	98	1.6	81	25.9	276	68.9	11	10	2.4	8	0	.0
30741	27.7	98	9.9	79	21.3	300	52.5	7	11	13.1	9	2	.1
30742	5.2	98	1.8	66	24.0	256	64.9	6	10	2.4	6	0	.0
30746	.9	100	.3	79	23.8	312	73.3	10	8	.5	8	0	.4
30747	12.9	89	4.6	74	19.1	210	43.1	7	13	5.6	10	0	.1
30751	.4	100	.1	78	14.8	116	36.0	13	7	.2	7	0	.0
30752	7.2	99	2.4	80	18.8	268	49.5	8	9	3.5	8	0	.2
30753	5.3	97	1.9	84	21.0	221	36.4	8	12	2.5	11	0	1.0
30755	6.7	99	2.1	83	23.9	284	60.1	7	8	3.3	11	1	.0
30756	.4	100	.1	83	23.8	324	47.8	5	8	.8	5	0	.2
30757	1.7	92	.6	74	20.6	252	53.6	9	9	.8	6	0	.0

AUGUSTA

ZIPCODE	1	2	3	4	5	6	7	8	9	10	11	12	13
30801	.2	34	.1	49	20.6	131	62.7	8	10	.0	0	0	.0
30802	2.9	58	1.0	81	24.2	128	79.1	8	8	.9	0	1	.0
30803	.8	51	.8	74	14.2	176	38.9	7	24	.2	36	0	.0
30805	1.3	91	.4	85	23.3	216*	52.3	8	12	.6	13	0	.0
30806	.2	0	.1	94	18.8	216*	41.7	0	11	.1	0	0	.3
30807	.3	45	.1	76	17.1	140	32.4	4	10	.1	10	0	.2
30808	2.7	81	.9	78	19.6	200	54.8	9	10	1.1	9	0	.1

GEORGIA (continued)

AUGUSTA

ZIPCODE	1	2	3	4	5	6	7	8	9	10	11	12	13
30809	4.9	88	1.5	84	29.8	267	104.5	7	5	2.1	4	0	.0
30810	1.4	92	.5	70	19.9	164	41.8	6	18	.6	13	0	.0
30811	.3	45	.1	51	21.4	151	41.5	6	15	1.8	18	0	.0
30813	7.1	84	2.5	59	22.0	261	69.0	12	8	3.0	4	0	.6
30814	5.4	66	1.7	78	19.8	193	58.7	8	8	1.8	6	0	.0
30815	15.0	69	4.5	78	24.6	261	67.3	10	4	5.3	3	1	.0
30816	1.4	51	.4	74	16.3	178	47.3	11	8	.4	3	0	.0
30817	6.6	58	2.1	79	22.5	172	54.2	7	12	1.8	12	0	.2
30818	.2	92	.2	85	20.6	70	53.8	7	12	.1	6	0	.3
30819	.2	0	.2	68	11.7	87	30.8	12	8	.0	0	0	.0
30820	1.4	57	.5	81	21.6	175	31.8	8	14	.4	15	0	.1
30821	1.3	39	.4	80	14.5	224	32.1	10	10	.2	21	0	2.1
30822	.5	79	.2	72	15.8	106	45.7	7	13	.2	12	0	.1
30823	1.4	65	.4	76	18.4	99	35.4	8	14	.2	10	0	.2
30824	15.4	59	5.2	69	20.8	203	60.9	8	10	4.3	9	1	.0
30828	4.1	0	1.3	76	19.6	144	47.0	9	15	1.4	15	0	2.4
30830	11.2	46	3.7	63	19.5	198	57.1	9	12	2.5	9	4	.4
30833	4.3	47	1.4	62	17.4	175	48.4	9	12	1.0	12	0	.0

AUGUSTA

ZIPCODE	1	2	3	4	5	6	7	8	9	10	11	12	13
30901	29.6	8	10.2	37	12.9	195	34.9	8	13	1.1	18	3	1.5
30902	1.7	41	1.0	10	7.4	167	21.7	7	45	.9	51	0	.6
30904	32.8	73	13.5	56	20.7	279	57.7	7	15	11.1	14	0	.3
30905	14.1	52	.9	0	20.7	357	73.8*	4	5	5.3	0	1	.1
30906	54.1	68	17.4	72	24.8	325	57.2	9	2	17.8	5	5	.2
30907	26.6	91	8.4	86	32.7	420	85.0	9	4	12.0	3	0	2.4
30908	1.0	77	.3	93	41.3	184	137.3	5	6	.4	4	0	.0
30909	25.7	78	9.8	59	31.2	329	104.2	7	8	9.5	7	0	.0

MACON

ZIPCODE	1	2	3	4	5	6	7	8	9	10	11	12	13
31001	2.3	73	.8	81	16.9	183	36.5	7	14	.8	12	0	.0
31002	2.3	86	.8	82	18.3	147	35.4	7	16	.9	15	0	.0
31003	.2	62	.1	75	24.4	136	58.7	10	13	.1	17	0	.0
31004	.2	0	.1	69	46.3	138	82.1	0	19	.0	1	1	.0
31005	3.5	95	1.2	77	32.4	245	85.0	10	2	1.7	1	0	.0
31006	3.9	59	1.4	77	18.3	202	45.0	7	12	1.1	11	0	.0
31007	1.2	0	.3	62	16.0	170	51.1	9	18	1.0	11	0	.0
31008	6.0	84	2.0	79	24.8	257	71.6	9	6	2.5	4	0	.6
31009	1.1	71	.4	80	15.3	164	42.5	7	19	.4	14	0	.0
31011	.8	76	.3	81	17.9	129	38.7	8	11	.3	8	0	.0
31012	1.5	71	.5	72	14.5	187	39.9	10	13	.5	14	0	.1
31014	11.4	77	3.7	62	21.4	163	52.9	7	11	4.2	9	0	.5
31015	18.4	59	6.2	62	20.7	249	63.1	7	12	5.0	10	3	.0
31016	2.0	0	.5	66	20.4	225	37.7	10	10	.7	14	0	.0
31017	2.1	67	.8	73	16.8	128	46.9	7	17	.7	14	1	.0
31018	1.2	45	.4	72	18.9	138	39.1	7	13	.3	16	0	.0
31019	1.6	86	.5	81	22.4	153	52.7	9	14	.6	13	0	.3
31020	2.4	39	.7	77	18.3	210	41.0	12	9	.4	13	0	.2
31021	29.6	65	10.0	67	21.5	238	60.9	8	12	9.6	11	0	.0
31022	1.2	70	.4	77	21.0	244	60.3	9	10	.4	11	0	.1
31023	11.7	74	4.0	74	19.0	179	47.4	7	14	4.1	13	0	.1

*=Estimated **1.0=883 lbs per person; 100++ indicates per capita toxic waste generation > than 100 times the U.S. average of 883 lbs per capita.

ZIP CODE MEASURES OF SIZE, LEVELS OF AFFLUENCE AND QUALITY OF LIFE

1=Population (th.); 2= % White; 3=Households (th.); 4=% Owner Occupied; 5=Mean Income Per Household (th.$); 6=Mean Monthly Rent ($); 7=Mean Home Value (th.$); 8=% under 5; 9=% 65 and over; 10=% White Males, 65 and over; 11=% White Males (th.); 12=# Toxic Waste Sites; 13=Toxic Waste Relative to US(883 lbs.per capita)**.

GEORGIA — MACON

ZIPCODE	1	2	3	4	5	6	7	8	9	10	11	12	13
31024	10.2	58	3.4	74	21.8	198	61.7	7	12	2.9	11	0	.4
31025	.9	49	.3	67	19.2	130	49.9	3	16	.2	21	0	.0
31028	2.8	97	.9	83	29.5	359	71.6	9	3	1.4	2	0	.0
31029	10.8	60	3.5	71	21.7	240	56.9	6	12	3.0	11	0	.3
31030	15.9	41	5.1	65	21.5	232	59.7	8	10	3.2	9	2	2.1
31031	5.7	70	1.8	78	22.2	218	50.4	8	10	1.9	10	1	.2
31032	7.4	66	2.3	82	30.6	265	67.7	9	11	2.4	8	0	.2
31033	1.6	41	.5	84	19.8	205	44.6	7	10	.3	6	0	.1
31034	2.6	61	.8	66	20.2	229	51.0	7	6	1.2	6	0	.0
31035	1.4	57	.5	78	16.7	170	39.7	9	17	.4	18	0	.0
31036	9.5	62	3.2	72	20.2	225	59.4	8	12	2.8	10	0	.3
31037	1.9	76	.7	71	18.2	186	33.8	8	14	.7	11	0	.0
31038	.5	52	.3	75	16.2	206	33.5	5	12	.1	14	0	.0
31041	1.1	49	.3	78	15.2	226	33.5	8	19	.2	17	1	.0
31042	2.0	31	.6	78	22.7	186	42.4	11	9	.5	10	0	.0
31044	4.3	0	1.3	75	19.7	189	44.9	9	13	.0	9	0	1.0
31046	1.1	84	.4	67	23.3	180	87.6	8	11	.5	8	0	.0
31047	2.3	69	.7	84	26.6	217	74.4	10	5	.8	3	0	1.5
31049	1.7	92	.6	73	17.8	166	34.4	8	15	.7	14	0	.0
31051	5.3	62	.6	82	13.2	216	49.4	5	18	.0	37	0	.0
31052	5.3	81	1.6	88	28.8	267	78.7	8	6	2.2	6	0	.0
31054	1.6	61	.5	75	23.2	232	38.6	7	9	.2	11	0	.0
31055	5.2	66	1.8	76	19.8	189	49.7	8	16	.5	15	0	1.0
31057	2.2	0	.6	63	20.4	232	45.8	10	15	.0	8	0	.0
31058	1.0	84	.3	72	17.0	94	35.5	10	10	.5	10	0	.3
31059	1.0	5	.3	42	13.6	185	49.7	6	19	.0	81	0	.0
31060	2.4	81	.8	82	18.2	170	42.1	7	12	.1	11	0	.0
31061	31.1	62	9.6	66	24.8	213	68.2	8	11	9.2	10	4	2.2
31063	6.6	44	2.1	66	18.8	241	56.6	11	12	1.4	12	0	.1
31064	5.6	57	1.9	71	21.9	190	61.2	9	13	1.6	13	0	.0
31065	1.4	36	.4	62	18.3	263	50.1	8	12	.4	11	0	.0
31066	1.4	60	.4	79	34.0	353	46.4	10	9	.4	7	0	.0
31067	.4	53	.1	80	16.5	162	28.2	9	18	.1	14	0	.0
31068	3.1	50	1.1	78	17.5	194	45.1	7	12	.5	10	0	1.3
31069	11.6	65	3.8	72	26.2	273	72.2	10	13	3.8	8	5	.0
31070	1.3	0	.4	65	19.0	221	49.0	11	15	.0	0	0	.0
31071	1.0	0	.4	80	15.5	157	43.8	6	17	.0	0	0	.0
31072	1.2	87	.6	80	18.7	210	40.2	6	26	.5	24	0	.0
31075	.4	77	.1	76	17.9	154	48.8	7	14	.5	13	0	.0
31076	3.6	50	1.1	74	21.2	199	50.3	6	12	1.3	11	0	.0
31077	1.3	64	.5	69	13.6	115	40.0	8	16	.4	15	0	.0
31078	3.3	44	1.0	68	20.9	160	47.7	7	13	.7	12	0	.0
31079	3.2	60	1.0	67	18.9	205	37.6	9	13	.9	13	0	.0
31080	.4	71	.1	79	24.9	218	27.2	6	3	.1	7	0	.0
31081	.3	0	.1	64	14.0	99	60.7	7	19	.0	0	0	.0
31082	10.3	53	3.3	70	22.8	194	52.5	7	13	2.6	11	0	.3
31083	.2	82	.1	86	13.5	171	27.3	6	23	.1	21	0	.0
31084	.2	0	.1	85	13.9	104	32.0	11	11	.1	6	0	.0
31085	.7	0	.2	67	16.1	192	42.3	8	15	.0	0	0	.0

GEORGIA — MACON (cont.)

ZIPCODE	1	2	3	4	5	6	7	8	9	10	11	12	13
31086	.2	100	.1	100	37.0	425*	76.8	12	4	.1	5	0	.0
31087	8.3	24	2.4	75	17.5	166	34.2	8	13	1.0	13	0	.0
31089	3.9	97	1.3	66	18.4	189	47.8	9	14	.0	14	0	.1
31090	1.2	53	.4	80	20.3	219	33.6	7	12	.3	14	0	.0
31091	3.6	56	1.1	68	20.1	192	57.3	10	10	1.0	8	0	.0
31092	4.6	51	1.5	69	16.3	204	52.4	10	14	1.1	15	2	9.7
31093	50.5	81	17.2	67	27.7	301	70.6	8	5	20.3	4	0	9
31094	1.3	27	.3	52	18.8	161	33.1	13	6	.2	5	0	.0
31097	1.0	72	.4	71	18.5	147	40.6	8	13	.1	11	1	.0
31098	3.5	80	.7	9	22.3	372	26.7	11	0	1.7	0	0	.0

GEORGIA — MACON (31201 area)

ZIPCODE	1	2	3	4	5	6	7	8	9	10	11	12	13
31201	37.4	31	12.6	46	15.8	200	46.2	8	12	5.8	11	1	.3
31204	42.0	54	15.7	57	23.2	266	63.0	7	13	10.2	14	0	.2
31206	42.3	78	14.5	66	23.2	264	54.7	7	9	15.8	7	2	.2
31210	17.3	91	5.9	79	34.8	390	109.1	6	6	7.7	5	0	.8
31211	14.6	73	5.5	65	29.5	318	74.9	7	11	5.2	9	0	.0

GEORGIA — SAVANNAH

ZIPCODE	1	2	3	4	5	6	7	8	9	10	11	12	13
31301	.9	51	.3	55	14.5	313	49.2	13	4	.2	2	0	.0
31302	4.6	97	1.5	82	23.5	321	62.0	8	7	2.2	7	0	.0
31303	1.3	43	.4	77	16.8	151	51.7	10	13	.3	23	0	.3
31304	.7	34	.2	90	17.5	221	42.9	12	7	.1	12	0	.0
31305	3.0	66	1.0	79	18.4	214	53.4	7	10	1.0	8	0	.8
31307	.7	78	.2	76	17.0	358	51.0	6	8	.1	6	0	.1
31308	3.4	81	1.1	82	19.6	229	58.7	11	5	1.3	5	0	.0
31309	.2	58	.1	76	15.6	446	30.4	8	16	.1	21	0	.0
31312	4.5	78	1.4	83	22.3	289	56.7	10	10	1.7	9	0	.0
31313	29.5	65	7.2	40	19.7	331	79.4	11	2	11.3	2	0	2.2
31316	4.2	75	1.4	68	18.5	260	46.3	10	8	1.6	7	0	.1
31318	.4	76	.1	77	33.8	218	52.3	12	12	.1	0	0	.0
31319	.3	0	.1	100	13.4	154*	32.1	4	18	.0	0	0	.0
31320	4.4	79	1.5	79	17.6	225	54.3	8	12	1.8	5	0	.0
31321	4.4	72	1.4	75	20.1	202	51.9	10	10	1.2	9	0	.0
31322	3.5	98	1.1	80	26.6	330	69.7	8	6	1.7	4	0	.1
31323	1.8	14	.5	81	33.9	235	34.1	10	8	1.5	5	1	4.9
31324	4.4	80	1.4	79	22.3	338	77.6	9	6	1.8	5	1	.4
31326	4.4	90	1.4	84	24.5	292	71.3	8	7	1.2	14	0	.0
31328	2.6	97	1.0	64	26.6	308	82.4	5	18	1.1	7	0	.0
31329	4.2	79	1.3	80	22.8	253	58.4	8	10	1.7	7	0	.1
31331	3.6	55	1.3	87	16.5	257	37.1	8	12	1.1	11	0	.0
31332	.1	0	.1	89	17.8	204*	111.9	7	26	.0	0	0	.0
31333	.8	46	.3	57	13.3	291	45.1	13	5	.2	1	0	.0

GEORGIA — SAVANNAH (31401 area)

ZIPCODE	1	2	3	4	5	6	7	8	9	10	11	12	13
31401	51.5	19	18.4	38	15.6	233	51.2	8	9	4.6	11	4	.3
31404	35.8	63	13.2	57	20.5	279	53.5	8	12	10.4	13	1	1.8
31405	36.1	60	13.3	66	25.8	318	75.4	9	13	10.4	12	0	1.0
31406	45.3	89	15.7	69	31.1	410	86.4	8	7	19.7	6	0	.1
31407	3.5	91	1.2	69	24.9	252	54.8	7	11	1.5	8	5	1.1
31408	8.5	60	2.9	64	23.2	298	58.0	8	10	2.5	7		.1

*=Estimated **1.0=883 lbs per person; 100++ indicates per capita toxic waste generation > than 100 times the U.S. average of 883 lbs per capita.

103001

ZIP CODE MEASURES OF SIZE, LEVELS OF AFFLUENCE AND QUALITY OF LIFE

1=Population (th.); 2= % White; 3=Households (th.); 4=% Owner Occupied; 5=Mean Income Per Household (th.$); 6=Mean Monthly Rent ($)*; 7=Mean Home Value (th.$)*; 8=% under 5; 9=% 65 and over; 10=White Males (th.); 11=% White Males, 65+; 12=# Toxic Waste Sites; 13=Toxic Waste Relative to US(883 lbs.per capita)**

GEORGIA

SAVANNAH

ZIPCODE	1	2	3	4	5	6	7	8	9	10	11	12	13
31410	10.5	95	3.5	91	37.7	495	110.1	8	6	5.0	5	0	.0
31411	1.3	100	.5	89	78.9	451	242.3	5	13	.7	14	0	.0

WAYCROSS

ZIPCODE	1	2	3	4	5	6	7	8	9	10	11	12	13
31501	36.0	77	12.3	69	21.2	239	53.9	8	12	13.2	9	2	.2
31510	8.4	83	2.7	73	19.5	173	60.6	10	11	3.3	9	0	.1
31512	1.9	62	.6	67	17.0	177	59.3	10	10	.5	11	0	.0
31513	13.1	80	4.3	74	18.7	186	46.8	9	10	5.1	12	3	.1
31516	8.5	87	2.8	76	18.9	205	54.9	8	11	3.6	9	0	2.6
31518	.8	92	.3	75	14.5	152	84.6	9	13	.9	11	0	.0
31519	2.7	72	.9	70	15.9	186	43.9	9	13	.9	13	0	.0
31522	45.5	69	15.8	64	22.3	265	64.2	8	10	15.4	9	11	2.8
31532	9.2	91	3.8	65	35.7	403	137.8	5	15	9.3	13	0	.0
31533	.7	85	.3	82	16.1	242	34.9	12	9	.4	7	0	.0
31537	18.1	75	6.0	70	20.2	208	60.2	9	10	6.6	9	0	.1
31539	6.4	66	1.9	76	20.0	204	54.2	9	11	2.0	10	1	.0
31542	10.1	83	3.4	72	21.0	214	50.4	8	10	4.1	8	6	.1
31543	1.6	96	.5	79	19.6	250	41.2	10	8	.8	4	0	.0
31544	2.0	98	.6	87	19.0	176	36.7	9	12	.9	9	0	.0
31545	1.1	61	.4	86	16.1	209	47.2	11	12	.3	13	0	.0
31548	16.3	80	5.4	71	23.4	225	52.5	8	10	6.4	10	4	.9
31549	4.7	68	1.5	77	22.0	217	57.3	10	8	1.7	8	0	.0
31550	3.2	74	1.0	73	17.2	153	41.3	10	13	1.1	9	1	.0
31552	1.0	89	.3	66	17.2	176	23.6	5	7	.5	6	1	.0
31553	.8	89	.2	73	17.6	130	57.4	13	6	.3	5	0	.1
31554	1.0	89	.3	76	22.2	106	43.6	6	6	.5	8	0	.0
31555	2.9	92	1.0	85	17.8	192	40.6	7	10	1.3	10	0	.0
31557	3.5	84	1.3	74	15.8	179	38.0	6	13	1.5	10	0	.0
31558	2.0	83	.6	80	16.8	173	38.1	7	13	.8	14	0	.0
31560	2.5	80	.9	73	16.5	218	49.3	8	12	1.0	8	0	.0
31561	4.5	81	1.5	75	25.8	256	74.4	9	6	1.8	4	2	1.8
31563	2.3	77	.7	71	18.9	179	48.5	6	12	.7	10	0	.0
31564	.3	0	.1	83	104.3	1062	366.4	0	59	.0	0	0	.0
31565	1.6	72	.5	74	17.1	213	37.9	7	12	.6	13	0	.0
31566	.3	0	.1	82	20.2	323	37.5	5	5	.0	0	0	.0
31567	1.0	47	.3	85	18.1	161	46.2	3	6	.3	7	0	.0
31568	.8	78	.3	88	17.6	246	48.4	7	10	.4	4	0	.0
31569	1.0	90	.2	72	15.1	242	37.9	6	8	.3	7	0	.0

VALDOSTA

ZIPCODE	1	2	3	4	5	6	7	8	9	10	11	12	13
31601	59.8	67	19.8	59	22.5	268	71.3	8	9	19.7	7	11	.9
31605	.2	100	.1	82	27.7	318*	85.6	3	10	.1	14	0	.0
31620	8.6	67	2.8	71	20.1	227	50.1	9	12	2.8	11	3	.6
31623	1.8	73	.6	68	20.3	175	52.9	7	14	.7	15	0	.0
31624	.2	74	.1	81	16.3	105	27.5	2	11	.1	1	1	.0
31625	1.0	90	.4	78	17.4	109	33.1	6	8	.5	8	0	.0
31626	1.1	45	.3	70	17.0	173	29.8	6	12	.2	14	0	.0
31627	3.5	44	1.1	68	17.4	136	51.8	9	13	.8	15	0	.0
31628	.3	57	.9	60	16.2	169	37.1	8	21	.1	21	1	.0

GEORGIA

VALDOSTA

ZIPCODE	1	2	3	4	5	6	7	8	9	10	11	12	13
31629	1.0	48	.3	78	16.7	197	30.6	8	8	.2	17	1	.0
31630	.6	68	.2	80	17.6	117	38.0	7	12	.2	19	0	.0
31631	.8	77	.2	51	18.6	133	35.0	7	7	.3	4	0	.0
31632	5.1	80	1.7	74	19.9	232	58.6	8	11	2.0	10	0	.0
31634	5.1	69	1.6	64	19.4	168	45.0	9	10	1.7	9	3	.9
31635	4.0	78	1.3	69	18.1	222	50.9	9	12	1.5	12	0	.0
31636	4.4	88	1.5	75	22.2	263	79.4	8	8	1.9	7	0	.0
31637	2.8	83	.9	83	19.0	167	47.7	6	10	1.2	9	1	.0
31638	.6	59	.2	77	14.5	307	31.1	4	18	.2	16	0	.0
31639	8.3	89	3.0	69	20.1	211	52.0	8	12	3.5	9	2	.3
31641	1.1	64	.3	81	16.6	140	33.4	10	12	.3	10	0	.0
31642	3.6	72	1.2	65	16.0	189	43.1	9	12	1.3	12	1	.0
31643	9.7	52	3.1	64	18.0	191	48.3	8	15	2.4	14	0	.0
31645	2.0	86	.7	65	18.8	224	48.5	7	9	.5	8	0	.1
31646	1.1	97	.4	87	22.9	113	43.0	6	9	.5	10	0	.0
31647	2.1	76	.7	77	19.5	172	44.0	8	10	.8	10	0	.1
31648	.8	76	.3	78	17.4	159	37.2	9	12	.3	13	0	.0
31649	1.0	78	.3	74	17.4	115	37.0	8	16	.4	12	0	.0
31650	2.2	67	.7	80	17.7	133	41.0	9	9	.7	10	1	.6

ALBANY

ZIPCODE	1	2	3	4	5	6	7	8	9	10	11	12	13
31701	29.7	23	10.1	35	15.6	240	57.9	9	12	3.2	14	1	.0
31702	.1	59	.1	17	9.8	256	35.0*	0	27	.0	83	3	100++
31704	1.5	74	.3	6	19.7	365	118.1	10	0	.7	0	1	.0
31705	34.9	61	10.6	59	22.6	309	66.3	8	10	10.9	4	4	1.3
31707	36.0	80	12.3	67	33.8	371	103.0	8	6	13.9	5	3	.0
31709	23.4	59	7.5	62	21.1	237	69.0	8	13	6.4	10	4	1.0
31711	1.1	68	.3	80	21.9	145	45.0	7	10	.5	5	0	4.3
31712	1.1	86	.4	69	22.4	154	51.3	10	10	.5	9	0	.0
31713	2.6	42	.8	68	17.2	154	51.1	9	15	.6	11	0	.1
31714	7.0	58	2.3	62	19.7	234	57.0	10	11	2.0	12	2	.0
31715	1.8	34	.5	69	17.2	233	36.2	10	11	.3	16	0	.1
31716	2.2	51	.7	72	21.2	198	62.0	8	9	.5	5	0	19.
31717	17.5	63	5.9	70	21.6	235	55.1	8	13	5.5	10	5	.6
31720	.2	51	.2	72	18.8	189	38.3	10	21	.0	24	0	.0
31721	.2	39	.1	47	8.7	83	33.2	0	9	.0	0	0	.0
31722	.6	0	.2	66	15.0	209	34.8	8	21	.0	6	0	.0
31723	9.8	58	3.3	66	19.1	183	51.0	9	13	2.8	11	0	.0
31724	.6	44	.2	59	13.8	221	60.3	9	17	.1	8	0	.0
31725	1.4	84	.4	81	23.0	148	61.6	10	6	.6	5	0	.0
31726	.9	40	.3	70	17.1	160	40.7	6	16	.2	20	1	.0
31727	.5	92	.1	58	16.7	251	58.9	14	1	.2	2	0	.9
31728	15.5	66	5.2	74	17.7	216	51.8	8	13	4.9	13	0	.5
31729	.4	40	.1	56	20.5	108	93.3	8	8	.5	9	0	.6
31730	10.2	44	3.0	66	21.9	227	59.4	10	10	2.2	10	5	.0
31733	1.3	91	.5	77	25.3	195	88.9	6	11	.6	9	2	.1
31734	2.5	62	.8	64	16.2	161	41.0	8	15	.8	17	0	.0
31735	.6	59	.2	64	22.8	247	65.5	6	12	.8	6	0	1.0
31736	.7	43	.2	79	15.3	120	35.9	11	17	.2	2	0	.0
31737	7.1	67	2.4	71	18.6	171	57.0	8	14	2.3	14	0	.0

*=Estimated **1.0=883 lbs per person; 100++ indicates per capita toxic waste generation > than 100 times the U.S. average of 883 lbs per capita.

ZIP CODE MEASURES OF SIZE, LEVELS OF AFFLUENCE AND QUALITY OF LIFE

1=Population (th.); 2= % White; 3=Households (th.); 4=% Owner Occupied; 5=Mean Income Per Household (th.$); 6=Mean Monthly Rent ($)*; 7=Mean Home Value (th.$)*;
8=% under 5; 9=% 65 and over; 10=White Males (th.); 11=% White Males, 65+; 12=# Toxic Waste Sites; 13=Toxic Waste Relative to US(883 lbs.per capita)**.

GEORGIA — ALBANY

ZIP CODE	1	2	3	4	5	6	7	8	9	10	11	12	13
31738	2.2	72	.7	72	14.8	177	42.8	6	13	.8	16	0	.0
31740	6.6	46	2.2	70	18.7	162	46.9	9	17	1.5	14	0	.0
31741	1.4	28	.4	77	17.6	158	48.7	10	10	.1	12	0	.0
31742	10.3	38	3.2	58	18.5	206	54.4	9	12	1.9	12	2	.0
31743	1.1	23	.3	60	20.1	225	57.4	10	11	.1	5	0	.0
31744	3.8	66	1.2	71	19.3	170	45.0	8	12	1.2	16	0	.0
31745	8.2	68	2.7	78	19.3	197	55.8	9	13	2.7	12	0	.0
31746	2.3	45	.7	64	19.3	190	42.5	8	15	.5	11	0	.0
31747	.3	75	.1	81	14.2	225	19.8	8	13	.1	8	0	.0
31749	1.3	86	.4	87	19.0	218	53.8	9	9	.6	8	0	.0
31750	17.0	71	6.1	69	19.2	206	56.1	9	14	5.7	11	4	.4
31751	2.5	0	.9	69	17.2	179	37.9	6	16	.0	0	0	.0
31752	.5	15	.1	35	9.7	196	52.8	19	10	.0	26	0	.0
31753	.3	0	.1	76	16.4	234	50.2	8	16	.0		0	.0
31754	2.1	0	.7	69	15.2	160	43.4	8	15	.1	8	0	.0
31756	1.0	89	.3	76	22.9	162	48.3	4	8	.4	5	0	.0
31759	1.6	66	.5	77	19.4	188	57.1	8	11	.5	11	0	.0
31760	.9	100	.1	69	9.9	100	51.4	0	28	.1	13	0	.0
31761	1.9	73	.3	67	19.2	205	49.1	8	20	.3	13	0	.0
31763	1.9	46	.3	70	16.3	221	43.6	8	15	.4	12	0	.4
31764	9.2	84	3.0	73	28.0	288	78.5	9	6	3.9	3	1	.1
31765	1.4	38	.4	71	19.9	165	48.0	9	11	.3	17	0	.0
31766	2.3	69	.8	71	16.0	170	43.8	9	15	.7	12	0	.0
31767	.8	50	.3	62	16.5	148	45.2	7	17	.2	16	0	.0
31768	.6	19	.2	60	13.4	152	28.0	6	17	.4	10	0	.0
31769	26.4	74	9.1	64	20.3	235	58.5	8	12	9.3	11	10	.3
31770	2.4	46	.7	56	14.6	238	41.4	4	22	.0	10	0	.0
31771	3.2	84	1.1	68	19.4	170	48.6	9	13	.7	11	0	.0
31772	.5	0	.1	82	20.8	194	43.0	6	14	1.4	12	0	.0
31773	2.2	0	.8	84	20.6	277	51.8	10	5	.0	0	0	3.1
31774	5.8	82	1.9	70	18.9	203	40.5	9	13	.9	11	0	.0
31775	2.0	62	.7	68	18.4	188	52.3	8	15	1.6	13	1	.0
31776	2.0	86	.7	77	19.3	226	50.5	8	15	.8	14	0	.0
31777	.5	43	.2	75	28.9	109	38.2	7	15	.2	21	0	.0
31778	2.9	71	1.0	69	17.6	176	42.0	10	13	1.0	15	0	.0
31779	8.6	58	2.7	71	19.6	197	47.5	8	13	2.3	12	1	.6
31780	2.2	0	.7	70	17.3	182	49.2	7	15	.0	0	0	.0
31781	1.3	75	.4	79	19.7	196	44.7	7	11	.4	10	0	.0
31782	.4	92	.1	88	32.6	374*	78.8	5	8	.2	14	0	.0
31783	1.1	73	.3	69	20.1	170	36.5	6	15	.4	17	0	.0
31784	.6	77	.2	71	20.8	168	46.4	11	16	.3	19	0	.0
31785	.5	51	.2	77	22.6	120	50.6	8	11	.1	11	0	.0
31786	2.3	0	.7	61	25.4	167	62.7	8	14	.1	11	0	.0
31787	1.9	34	.6	73	17.9	168	52.1	11	12	.3	17	0	.0
31789	1.7	60	.5	69	24.1	222	55.3	5	7	.5	5	0	.0
31790	2.0	82	.7	78	18.5	246	54.9	9	17	.8	15	0	.0
31791	9.9	60	3.2	70	21.5	209	65.5	8	11	2.9	9	0	.0
31792	28.1	61	9.5	67	22.1	256	64.7	7	12	8.3	10	2	.4
31793	29.3	73	9.6	65	21.4	264	66.8	9	10	10.4	8	10	.4

GEORGIA — ALBANY (continued)

ZIP CODE	1	2	3	4	5	6	7	8	9	10	11	12	13
31795	1.7	69	.6	79	17.9	138	46.6	8	11	.6	10	0	.0
31796	1.4	68	.5	66	17.0	204	64.3	8	16	.4	15	0	.0
31797	2.1	70	.7	74	17.6	220	48.4	9	10	.8	8	0	.0
31798	1.4	72	.4	62	14.6	165	39.6	8	11	.5	10	0	.0

COLUMBIS

ZIP CODE	1	2	3	4	5	6	7	8	9	10	11	12	13
31801	1.1	58	.4	88	19.0	88	34.8	1	19	.3	6	0	.0
31803	4.3	0	1.3	70	17.2	191	48.8	8	13	.0	0	0	.0
31804	2.3	80	.8	81	25.6	231	74.1	7	10	.9	7	0	.0
31805	2.3	61	.7	64	16.7	199	43.2	9	9	.7	4	0	.0
31806	3.4	63	1.1	73	18.3	188	50.0	8	12	1.1	10	1	.2
31807	.8	77	.3	78	29.8	258	77.4	7	7	.3	3	1	.0
31808	1.9	88	.6	84	31.8	270	88.4	5	9	.8	10	0	.2
31810	.3	0	.1	76	17.2	284	30.9	8	6	.0	7	0	.0
31811	3.0	58	1.0	81	24.6	233	49.8	8	11	.9	9	0	.0
31812	.7	45	.2	64	17.8	134	29.0	7	15	.2	24	0	.0
31813	.3	22	.1	64	15.3	73	63.6	7	15	.0	12	0	.0
31814	.5	12	.1	55	11.7	168	13.1	7	3	.1	0	0	.0
31815	2.7	0	.8	65	14.9	180	41.1	7	15	.0	0	0	.0
31816	6.3	68	2.3	78	22.2	206	55.0	7	14	2.0	11	0	.4
31820	1.7	71	.5	67	26.1	240	103.7	8	11	.5	12	0	.1
31821	.4	56	.2	58	13.5	196	32.1	9	16	.1	12	0	.0
31822	4.1	61	1.5	72	20.6	274	59.2	9	12	1.3	10	0	.1
31823	.5	79	.2	89	22.7	90	52.0	6	20	.2	23	0	.0
31824	1.7	52	.5	71	17.6	137	46.3	8	11	.4	10	0	.0
31825	2.7	0	.9	72	15.8	137	38.3	8	15	.0	4	0	.0
31826	1.8	40	.6	73	20.3	173	38.6	6	10	.4	11	0	.0
31827	2.2	34	.7	71	20.5	140	50.8	7	14	.4	22	0	.0
31829	2.6	81	.7	89	29.5	80	111.2	10	9	.2	7	0	.3
31831	2.2	65	.8	74	20.3	226	38.5	7	11	.9	10	1	.0
31832	.2	55	.1	77	18.8	211	61.7	7	15	.6	11	0	.2
31833	6.8	54	2.5	68	28.3	101	28.8	8	19	.0	21	0	.2
31836	1.0	38	.3	84	21.5	186	44.0	9	13	.2	6	0	.0

COLUMBIS

ZIP CODE	1	2	3	4	5	6	7	8	9	10	11	12	13
31901	10.1	48	4.8	27	12.3	176	45.2	6	24	2.1	20	1	.2
31903	8.6	48	9.4	42	17.2	237	46.0	10	6	5.8	6	4	.6
31904	48.7	89	17.4	68	25.5	244	68.7	7	11	20.6	8	0	.0
31905	30.7	58	4.3	0	18.4	323	65.5*10	0	13.2	0	1		
31906	27.9	41	10.9	51	24.5	275	76.6	7	12	5.11		2	.2
31907	43.7	63	13.7	76	26.4	347	61.3	7	5	13.5	5		.0

TALLAHASSEE

ZIP CODE	1	2	3	4	5	6	7	8	9	10	11	12	13
32312	.2	70	.1	57	23.8	311	24.3	4	18	.1	9	0	.0
32324	.5	89	.2	91	18.1	308	85.8	7	13	.2	8	0	.5

CHATTANOOGA

ZIP CODE	1	2	3	4	5	6	7	8	9	10	11	12	13
37317	1.5	100	.6	87	18.1	162	47.2	6	14	.7	13	0	.0
37350	3.3	100	1.0	83	36.7	321	115.6	6	10	1.6	9	0	.0

CHATTANOOGA

ZIP CODE	1	2	3	4	5	6	7	8	9	10	11	12	13
37409	3.2	95	1.1	81	23.5	283	63.2	7	9	1.5	9	0	.4
37412	1.1	100	.4	75	20.9	314	38.5	10	12	.5	11	0	.4

*=Estimated   **1.0=883 lbs per person; 100++ indicates per capita toxic waste generation > than 100 times the U.S. average of 883 lbs per capita.

ZIP CODE MEASURES OF SIZE, LEVELS OF AFFLUENCE AND QUALITY OF LIFE

1=Population (th.); 2= % White; 3=Households (th.); 4=% Owner Occupied; 5=Mean Income Per Household (th.$); 6=Mean Monthly Rent ($); 7=Mean Home Value (th.$);
8=% under 5, 9=% 65 and over; 10=White Males (th.); 11=% White Males, 65+; 12=# Toxic Waste Sites; 13=Toxic Waste Relative to US(883 lbs.per capita)**.

HAWAII

HONOLULU

ZIPCODE	1	2	3	4	5	6	7	8	9	10	11	12	13
96701	35.5	27	10.7	64	39.4	580	262.6	7	5	5.3	3	2	.0
96703	.8	0	.2	61	28.2	538	147.4	8	4	.0	0	0	.0
96704	3.2	32	1.0	62	27.3	359	176.6	10	12	.6	6	13	.0
96705	1.2	13	.4	30	30.9	173	150.0	4	20	.1	14		1.6
96706	34.8	45	9.1	51	28.0	443	190.0	11	3	8.3	2	8	.5
96708	3.4	56	1.1	61	28.0	517	214.8	12	7	1.0	6	0	.0
96710	.4	0	.1	47	22.8	219	79.6	5	16	.0	0	0	.0
96712	6.8	45	2.1	39	31.2	483	235.3	8	7	1.6	4	0	.0
96713	1.3	32	.4	61	22.7	307	234.6	8	12	.2	18	1	.0
96714	1.6	68	.6	39	28.0	283	327.5	11	5	.6	0	0	.0
96715	.4	14	.2	75	28.4	251	126.3	7	11	.1	7	0	.0
96716	1.4	0	.5	37	26.3	294	166.0	11	18	.6	0	0	.0
96717	3.6	31	1.1	42	30.9	406	155.0	12	6	.6	4	0	.0
96718	.2	82	.1	40	33.1	417	95.8	17	3	.1	0	0	.0
96719	.8	33	.3	63	19.5	325	116.2	10	13	.1	7	0	.0
96720	38.5	33	12.2	60	28.9	390	138.5	9	10	5.4	8	2	.1
96725	1.8	28	.6	64	26.7	408	242.7	9	12	.4	4	0	.0
96727	3.6	39	1.1	62	25.5	280	116.0	9	15	.7	5	0	.0
96728	.6	31	.2	56	23.3	314	83.2	6	20	.1	22	0	.0
96729	.7	7	.2	100	24.2	278*	66.3	11	11	.0	0	0	.0
96730	1.2	43	.4	45	29.5	559	152.7	12	5	.3	8	0	.0
96731	1.2	29	.4	9	21.7	148	170.6	9	20	.2	12	0	.0
96732	13.7	20	4.1	69	33.0	444	201.3	7	12	1.4	0	1	.1
96734	47.7	62	14.0	63	39.0	560	260.3	9	5	15.1	5	1	.0
96740	10.5	62	3.5	55	31.9	315	232.4	9	6	3.3	8	0	.5
96741	3.0	49	1.0	62	31.1	461	196.9	8	10	.8	9	0	.0
96742	.1	0		0	12.7	145*	45.1*	0	26	.0	0	1	.0
96743	4.9	48	1.6	57	30.6	500	191.6	10	8	1.2	8	1	.3
96744	47.6	33	13.0	71	40.8	551	233.8	8	6	7.9	5	0	.0
96746	8.6	35	2.7	17	31.1	394	200.4	9	11	1.5	9	1	.0
96747	.9	17	.2	30	30.4	182	174.9	8	13	.0	1	0	1.0
96748	3.8	22	1.2	64	22.9	200	138.5	10	10	.5	11	0	.0
96749	3.4	36	1.0	79	25.5	306	89.2	10	10	.6	9	0	.3
96750	3.6	30	1.2	49	27.4	317	207.8	11	8	.5	4	0	.0
96751	.6	23		58	31.4	431	135.6	7	8	.1	13	0	.0
96752	3.1	25	.9	36	26.3	273	163.3	11	10	.4	6	1	.5
96753	6.8	60	2.4	53	32.2	215	296.0	8	7	2.0	8	0	.0
96754	1.1	0	.3	78	27.2	442	166.7	12	9		0	0	.0
96755	2.4	24	.7	72	22.2	314	127.8	8	13	.3	6	0	.0
96756	3.2	38	1.0	57	32.7	180	196.4	9	9	.6	5	0	.0
96757	.9	10	.2	12	27.5	196	136.5	12	4	.1	0	1	.0
96759	.7	35	.3	85	31.2	136	111.2*	9	6	.0	0	0	.0
96760	.7		.3	47	36.4	469	260.4	7	9	.2	4	0	.1
96761	10.4	44	3.5	34	24.0	461	188.2	15	3	2.4	9	2	.0
96762	4.7	30	.9	51	26.7	425	78.3	5	16		6	2	.0
96763	2.0	12	.6	68	22.9	201	97.5	8	10	.2	7	2	.0
96764	.6	28	.2	34	26.2	166	180.8	11		.1	13	0	3.2
96765	1.1	42	.3	79	34.9	481				.2	7	0	.0

HAWAII

HONOLULU

ZIPCODE	1	2	3	4	5	6	7	8	9	10	11	12	13
96766	8.8	23	2.7	62	31.3	406	177.9	8	12	1.0	7	4	.7
96768	3.8	61	1.3	59	36.8	520	224.0	11	5	1.2	5	0	.0
96769	1.3	0	.3	14	20.1	152	185.4	5	9	.0	0	0	.0
96770	.5		.2	0	17.9	210	63.8*	16	14	.0	0	1	.0
96771	1.4	37	.5	75	23.5	450	89.0	10	9	.3	4	0	.0
96772	1.5	24	.5	70	21.6	255	70.6	11	13	.2	13	2	.0
96774	.4	0	.1	37	18.9	139	93.2	8	13	.0	0	0	.0
96775	.5	23		8	23.1	149	82.4*	14	10	.0	25	0	.0
96776	.9	25	.3	17	24.2	154	77.1	10	10	.1	4	0	3.2
96777	1.8	23	.5	68	22.3	176	85.0	8	13	.2	4	0	.0
96778	4.6	45	1.5	71	21.9	439	91.1	11	8	1.0	6	0	1.0
96779	2.0	35	.6	53	30.4	439	210.2	10	11	.3	9	0	.1
96780	1.8	10	.4	24	20.7	205	117.0	10	12	.0	0	0	.0
96781	.8	30		30	23.6	440	86.2	7	17	.3	10	0	.2
96782	36.6	21	9.5	74	39.6	580	215.8	8	4	4.1	1	1	.0
96783	1.9	19	.5	66	23.5	262	102.6	12	13	.2	5	1	.0
96784	.8	0	.3	21	24.1	154	285.1	10	10	.0	0	0	5.8
96785	.7	62	.3	73	22.1	389	125.4	7	16	.3	27	0	.0
96786	39.3	43	11.6	30	24.4	430	185.0	13	5	8.9		0	.0
96787	.8	28	.2	72	24.8	539	123.2	6	11	1	8	1	.0
96788	3.8	38	1.1	73	34.9	654	224.2	9	6	.7	4	1	.0
96789	21.5	38	6.4	82	38.4	666	261.6	12	7	4.2	1	1	.0
96790	3.5	58	1.1	64	37.3	662	312.0	8	11	1.0	9	0	.0
96791	5.9	30	1.8	45	26.0	412	154.5	10	10	1.0	9	1	.3
96792	31.5	26	8.0	51	24.9	436	147.6	12	5	4.4	5	5	.0
96793	12.8	29	4.1	56	33.6	384	182.4	8	12	1.8	9	5	.0
96795	9.2	23	2.1	60	28.6	402	159.8	9	5	1.1	4	0	.0
96796	1.8	17	.6	46	30.0	296	149.0	8	15	.1	5	0	.0
96797	33.9	16	8.3	54	33.9	488	213.7	10	8	3.0	4	3	.1

HONOLULU

ZIPCODE	1	2	3	4	5	6	7	8	9	10	11	12	13
96813	17.6	27	6.9	40	30.0	433	202.9	5	12	2.6	11	2	1.4
96814	13.8	32	7.4	27	23.9	419	263.1	4	16	2.1	17	0	.2
96815	31.1	49	15.5	35	30.8	348	226.2	4	17	7.3	19	1	.0
96816	53.7	25	17.5	60	41.3	490	267.1	5	13	6.6	11	1	.5
96817	50.0	14	16.4	38	30.3	377	247.7	6	15	3.3	14	1	.5
96818	52.4	55	14.7	26	26.7	502	269.6	12	9	16.3	1	0	.0
96819	51.2	15	12.4	41	32.0	393	228.6	9	9	4.2	5	6	.1
96821	17.4	37	5.2	86	63.0	675	317.1	4	8	3.4	9	0	.0
96822	44.3	34	17.2	46	35.0	498	319.8	4	10	7.2	9	1	.0
96825	25.4	49	7.5	83	51.5	780	312.8	6	4	6.1	4	0	.0
96826	23.3	24	10.6	28	25.7	450	205.9	5	9	2.7	8	0	.0

*=Estimated **1.0=883 lbs per person; 100++ indicates per capita toxic waste generation > than 100 times the U.S. average of 883 lbs per capita.

ZIP CODE MEASURES OF SIZE, LEVELS OF AFFLUENCE AND QUALITY OF LIFE

1=Population (th.); 2= % White; 3=Households (th.); 4=% Owner Occupied; 5=Mean Income Per Household (th.$); 6=Mean Monthly Rent ($)*; 7=Mean Home Value (th.$)*; 8=% under 5; 9=% 65 and over; 10=White Males (th.); 11=% White Males, 65+; 12=# Toxic Waste Sites; 13=Toxic Waste Relative to US(883 lbs.per capita)**.

IDAHO

ZIPCODE	1	2	3	4	5	6	7	8	9	10	11	12	13
ROCK SPRINGS													
83120	.2	100	.1	78	32.9	378*	74.4	11	10	.1	9	0	.0
POCATELLO													
83201	59.8	95	20.7	69	26.2	275	85.7	11	8	28.2	7	7	3.7
83203	1.5	17	.5	73	19.8	279	54.9	12	6	.1	18	0	.2
83210	3.0	92	1.0	70	19.8	206	56.3	12	11	1.4	11	0	.0
83211	5.1	94	1.7	74	26.3	234	80.5	11	8	2.3	8	0	.4
83213	2.3	98	.8	77	23.7	206	66.5	11	12	1.2	11	0	.0
83214	.6	100	.2	82	24.0	245	74.2	21	14	.3	15	0	.0
83217	1.0	98	.3	88	23.1	237	63.1	12	12	.5	12	0	.0
83218	.4	93	.1	90	22.1	347	64.5	18	7	.2	9	0	.0
83221	20.5	90	6.2	78	24.4	249	79.7	13	8	9.2	9	1	.0
83223	1.5	100	.1	87	17.3	199*	73.7	8	12	.1	14	0	.0
83226	.2	0	.6	76	18.9	216	87.4	8	12	.0	0	0	.2
83227	.2	0	.1	58	23.1	198	90.3	8	9	.0	0	0	.0
83228	.5	100	.1	86	21.0	405	66.2	18	7	.1	7	0	1.2
83230	.2	100	.1	29	27.4	159	97.7*	4	8	.1	0	0	.0
83232	.3	0	.1	96	18.8	216*	71.5	15	12	.6	5	0	100++
83234	1.2	98	.4	91	21.5	193	57.9	11	13	.6	10	0	.0
83235	.1	100	.1	61	16.7	158	59.6*	4	9	.1	0	0	.0
83236	2.2	96	.6	89	20.3	164	75.4	11	10	1.1	9	2	.0
83237	.7	0	.2	79	18.3	200	78.4	17	17	.0	5	0	.1
83238	.2	100	.2	68	18.2	353	66.7	22	11	.1	10	0	.0
83239	.7	98	.2	88	23.0	285	68.6	12	10	.3	9	0	.0
83241	2.4	99	.7	75	20.6	289	71.6	12	10	1.2	9	0	.0
83244	.4	0	.1	60	18.2	420	83.6	15	8	.0	8	0	.0
83245	2.0	100	.6	88	29.5	207	79.7	12	5	1.0	5	0	.0
83246	.9	99	.3	75	19.9	186	62.4	6	15	.5	14	0	.0
83250	1.4	0	.4	92	23.3	306	73.6	10	9	.5	9	0	.0
83251	1.0	98	.4	76	17.9	154	56.5	9	14	.6	11	0	.0
83252	2.9	99	.9	83	17.2	208	58.2	11	18	1.4	15	0	.0
83253	.2	100	.1	64	29.3	337*	104.4*	10	12	.1	8	0	.0
83254	3.9	98	1.3	79	22.9	270	67.6	13	17	1.9	11	0	.0
83255	.8	0	.2	94	18.0	161	60.5	14	9	.0	0	0	.0
83256	1.0	96	.3	94	23.8	161	67.7	15	5	.5	4	0	.0
83260	.4	100	.1	96	26.8	308*	73.6	13	9	.2	8	0	.0
83261	.8	100	.3	81	23.5	212	67.7	15	15	.5	14	0	.0
83262	1.3	0	.4	90	17.3	169	83.0	13	11	.0	0	0	.0
83263	6.4	99	2.0	82	21.1	269	70.3	13	13	3.2	12	1	.0
83271	.7	93	.2	77	22.0	133	54.8	10	11	.3	10	0	.0
83272	.3	100	.1	91	20.4	235*	68.0	10	17	.1	18	0	.0
83274	6.6	97	1.9	84	23.8	303	77.3	14	8	3.1	8	1	.1
83276	4.9	98	1.6	75	26.7	332	86.0	15	6	2.4	5	4	16.5
83277	.2	100	.1	57	27.9	320*	46.9	12	19	.1	14	4	.0
83278	.2	100	.1	46	21.0	262	133.8	10	2	.0	4	0	.0
83286	.9	0	.2	83	23.9	221	85.4	14	10	.0	0	0	.0
TWIN FALLS													
83301	32.9	96	12.0	69	25.6	300	84.9	9	13	15.2	11	1	.1
83302	.3	0	.1	51	11.6	281	70.5	15	14	.0	0	0	.1
83311	.4	0	.2	73	18.6	172	68.8	10	8	.0	0	0	.0

IDAHO

ZIPCODE	1	2	3	4	5	6	7	8	9	10	11	12	13
TWIN FALLS													
83312	.2	100	.1	82	16.2	186*	196.9	6	26	.1	25	0	.0
83313	1.3	0	.5	82	20.8	338	95.5	9	10	.0	0	0	.0
83314	.7	96	.3	63	23.4	170	73.7	6	8	.4	8	1	.1
83316	8.5	96	2.9	71	21.2	247	65.5	9	15	4.0	15	1	.1
83318	14.8	91	4.8	73	23.2	256	77.6	12	10	6.7	10	2	.1
83320	.7	0	.2	79	17.7	268	62.9	19	8	.0	0	0	.0
83321	.7	75	.2	81	20.3	211	33.0	8	9	.2	7	0	.0
83323	1.2	78	.4	63	19.7	178	61.1	13	7	.5	6	0	.0
83324	.5	0	.1	76	20.9	221	41.2	14	9	.0	0	0	.0
83325	.9	96	.3	76	22.3	168	52.1	8	10	.4	13	0	.0
83327	.7	0	.3	74	21.3	206	57.7	8	12	.0	0	0	.0
83328	3.8	98	1.3	71	21.2	273	69.7	10	16	1.9	10	1	.2
83330	5.4	95	1.9	78	21.4	245	67.3	9	15	2.5	15	0	.0
83332	2.0	90	.7	74	18.9	224	83.1	9	18	.9	19	0	.0
83333	2.9	99	1.1	69	22.7	311	110.6	10	8	1.4	5	0	.0
83334	1.8	98	.6	72	22.3	248	55.4	12	10	.9	10	0	.0
83335	1.6	89	.5	61	21.7	198	59.2	12	10	.6	11	0	.1
83336	4.4	84	1.3	83	23.5	272	71.4	13	7	1.7	8	0	.1
83338	12.4	97	4.2	77	21.9	263	74	11	11	6.0	11	2	.2
83340	2.7	100	1.2	56	25.9	365	200.4	5	4	1.4	4	0	.0
83341	4.1	98	1.4	75	22.0	302	79.8	9	14	2.0	13	0	.0
83342	.9	100	.3	69	20.0	130	65.2	15	10	.5	10	0	.0
83343	.9	69	.1	56	20.3	59	57.4	6	5	.1	4	0	.0
83344	1.0	98	.4	63	23.2	188	54.1	12	5	.4	5	0	.0
83346	1.5	99	.4	77	17.6	219	83.0	16	11	.7	11	3	.0
83347	3.4	93	1.1	81	23.1	211	79.3	13	8	1.6	8	0	.3
83349	.8	0	.3	84	17.9	94	47.3	14	9	.0	0	0	.0
83350	12.2	86	4.0	77	21.9	218	67.2	12	9	5.2	9	3	.1
83352	1.9	97	.7	74	18.4	225	58.0	8	17	.9	16	0	.0
83353	2.1	99	.9	59	35.3	327	258.7	4	2	1.1	2	0	.0
83355	3.9	94	1.3	78	17.9	271	61.4	11	14	1.8	14	0	.0
POCATELLO													
83401	62.8	97	20.4	73	27.7	324	95.2	12	7	30.8	6	5	.5
83420	2.8	99	.9	81	21.6	267	67.1	9	10	1.4	9	0	.0
83421	.4	100	.1	83	16.6	190*	96.7	18	8	.2	10	0	.0
83422	1.7	99	.4	76	21.2	278	87.2	12	8	.6	8	0	.0
83423	.2	0	.2	72	18.0	174	51.1	11	9	.3	11	0	.0
83425	.6	95	.2	73	21.1	98	102.0	20	9	.3	9	1	.0
83427	1.2	100	.3	91	23.1	386	85.4	15	7	.6	7	0	.0
83428	.2	100	.1	100	27.0	310*	87.2	6	5	.2	5	0	.0
83431	.6	86	.2	89	21.0	246	84.1	15	9	.2	9	0	.5
83433	.2	100	.1	80	25.4	10	138.4	16	16	.1	26	0	.0
83434	1.2	94	.3	86	20.1	170	68.7	13	9	.6	7	1	.0
83435	.2	95	.2	54	17.7	458	56.9	18	5	.3	5	0	.0
83436	.5	95	.3	84	15.7	296	85.3	25	6	.2	5	0	.0
83437	.2	100	.1	61	19.0	253	67.7*13	6	.1	20	0	.0	
83438	.2	100	.1	64	17.9	324	59.1	7	20	.1	20	0	.0
83440	18.0	98	4.7	60	20.8	331	104.7	12	5	7.8	5	5	.0
83442	9.2	98	2.8	86	21.3	276	78.2	13	10	4.5	10	0	.0

*=Estimated **1.0=883 lbs per person; 100++ indicates per capita toxic waste generation > than 100 times the U.S. average of 883 lbs per capita.

ZIP CODE MEASURES OF SIZE, LEVELS OF AFFLUENCE AND QUALITY OF LIFE

1=Population (th.); 2= % White; 3=Households (th.); 4=% Owner Occupied; 5=Mean Income Per Household (th.$); 6=Mean Monthly Rent ($)*; 7=Mean Home Value (th.$)*; 8=% under 5; 9=% 65 and over; 10=White Males (th.); 11=% White Males, 65+; 12=# Toxic Waste Sites; 13=Toxic Waste Relative to US(883 lbs.per capita)**

IDAHO

ZIPCODE	1	2	3	4	5	6	7	8	9	10	11	12	13
POCATELLO													
83443	1.2	89	.4	72	21.8	263	70.7	10	5	.5	4	0	.0
83444	1.4	90	.4	71	17.9	235	69.5	16	9	.6	9	1	.0
83445	5.9	98	1.8	84	20.3	236	69.7	14	9	2.9	8	2	.0
83448	1.6	95	.4	95	22.5	321	106.7	20	6	.8	5	0	.0
83449	.2	100	.1	87	16.7	58	130.3	10	26	.8	26	0	.0
83450	1.0	97	.3	67	20.2	220	81.6	16	2	.5	2	0	.0
83451	.7	98	.2	95	19.3	243	75.0	11	15	.4	12	0	.0
83452	.8	100	.2	81	18.2	225	64.1	10	10	.4	9	0	.0
83454	1.0	100	.3	84	24.6	359	74.6	16	7	.5	8	0	.0
83455	.8	99	.3	77	15.0	182	62.1	13	12	.4	13	0	.5
83462	.3	100	.1	83	19.8	141	127.4	10	9	.1	12	0	.0
83464	.5	100	.2	64	16.3	207	55.1	7	3	.3	4	1	.0
83466	.3	100	.1	91	13.3	153*	126.4	14	10	.3	10	0	.0
83467	5.8	98	2.2	75	21.0	244	74.5	10	13	2.8	12	1	.0
LEWISTON													
83501	28.8	98	11.1	66	24.6	298	85.3	7	13	13.8	12	3	.3
83520	.3	100	.1	81	23.7	270	76.8	5	7	.2	9	1	1.1
83522	1.8	99	.6	74	19.7	192	74.2	11	12	.9	11	1	.0
83523	.9	99	.3	77	22.6	205	57.0	10	12	.5	11	0	.0
83524	.9	0	.3	73	22.6	382	56.2	12	9	.4	7	0	.0
83525	.5	0	.2	57	21.4	150	56.3	14	7	.2	7	1	.0
83526	.5	100	.1	91	15.1	173*	47.7	9	21	.1	19	0	.0
83530	5.1	99	1.9	74	24.9	224	71.9	8	13	2.6	12	3	.0
83531	.3	0	.1	72	33.5	385*	21.9	15	3	.1	3	0	.0
83533	.3	100	.1	80	44.0	194	82.6	12	0	.2	0	0	.3
83534	.2	0	.1	14	30.2	230	107.6*	15	0	.0	0	1	.0
83535	.9	0	.3	74	24.5	278	74.7	7	13	.9	13	0	.0
83536	3.6	99	1.2	79	21.5	190	74.8	9	12	1.8	11	0	.0
83537	1.1	99	.4	75	21.1	206	57.2	8	19	.6	17	0	.0
83539	2.3	99	.8	81	20.0	207	68.2	15	15	1.1	13	0	.0
83540	2.1	51	.7	64	19.4	182	73.2	10	14	.5	18	1	.0
83541	.5	100	.2	84	59.2	246	79.8	4	22	.3	23	0	.0
83543	.8	100	.3	75	20.9	159	51.8	9	14	.4	10	0	.0
83544	6.5	98	2.3	74	24.8	237	76.3	8	12	3.3	12	1	.0
83545	.4	100	.1	96	22.1	253*	53.8	6	15	.2	17	0	.3
83546	1.3	0	.4	74	32.1	253*	55.5	9	9	.2	9	0	.0
83547	.2	100	.1	93	25.0	288*	98.5	3	28	.1	36	0	.3
83549	1.0	100	.4	74	20.6	238	76.8	9	14	.5	15	0	.0
83552	.4	97	.1	77	20.2	246	49.9	9	13	.2	15	0	.0
83553	1.5	0	.5	80	23.5	244	48.8	13	6	.0	0	0	.0
83555	.5	0	.2	74	17.9	149	53.8	8	22	.0	0	0	.0
83555	.4	0	.1	74	19.3	198	61.9	8	14	.0	0	0	.0
BOISE													
83604	.9	88	.3	71	17.4	222	54.0	4	12	.4	13	1	.0
83605	31.7	92	10.9	70	22.9	289	83.5	11	11	14.3	13	3	.1
83610	1.0	100	.4	79	21.6	153	55.3	9	15	.6	14	0	.1
83611	1.4	98	.6	77	23.3	230	80.9	8	10	.7	11	0	.0
83612	1.9	98	.7	77	21.0	232	60.4	8	11	.9	11	0	.0
83615	.4	0	.1	78	27.3	252	91.8	10	9	.2	8	0	.0

IDAHO

ZIPCODE	1	2	3	4	5	6	7	8	9	10	11	12	13
BOISE													
83616	8.4	98	2.7	87	32.7	350	140.4	9	6	4.1	6	1	.0
83617	11.4	97	4.1	80	22.0	256	76.7	9	15	5.5	15	1	.0
83619	4.1	93	1.4	78	21.1	245	75.1	9	11	2.0	10	0	.0
83622	.6	0	.2	80	25.1	181	105.6	6	10	.0	0	0	.0
83623	1.6	94	.6	72	22.4	184	54.8	7	18	.7	20	1	.0
83624	1.1	95	.3	61	18.0	255	52.7	9	8	.5	7	1	.5
83626	.4	0	.1	65	25.6	263	72.8	12	10	.4	10	0	.0
83627	.5	92	.1	80	15.5	213	37.2	7	15	.2	11	0	.0
83628	3.4	89	1.1	76	17.9	220	58.0	9	15	1.5	16	1	.0
83629	1.1	0	.4	75	24.3	226	76.9	11	9	.4	13	0	.0
83631	.6	0	.2	74	22.0	142	78.6	7	10	.1	12	0	.0
83632	.2	0	.1	85	22.5	258*	62.7	11	16	.3	16	1	.0
83633	.7	58	.2	77	19.7	254	39.6	6	8	.1	0	0	.0
83634	7.4	99	2.2	83	24.7	342	91.5	13	4	3.8	3	1	.0
83635	.2	0	.1	81	21.3	418	96.6	7	4	.2	3	0	.0
83637	.1	100	.1	76	16.8	307	94.8	1	13	.1	19	0	.0
83638	3.6	99	1.3	66	24.5	272	117.5	8	7	1.9	7	0	.0
83639	2.1	83	.6	75	16.4	220	66.7	11	9	.9	10	3	.0
83641	1.8	97	.6	69	27.7	204	75.9	10	10	.9	10	0	.1
83642	16.0	98	5.4	77	28.7	330	119.6	10	10	7.7	8	1	.2
83644	1.7	97	.6	82	16.3	292	65.2	16	7	.8	6	0	.0
83645	.7	100	.3	74	12.8	210	52.6	9	26	.3	26	0	.1
83647	12.0	93	4.3	69	22.7	260	79.7	9	6	5.8	5	1	.3
83648	6.3	84	1.4	1	18.4	326	101.9	15	3	3.1	1	0	.0
83650	.2	0	.1	57	10.3	96	51.0	6	0	.0	0	0	.0
83651	40.6	93	13.9	72	22.5	297	84.1	12	18	18.0	12	4	.0
83654	1.0	0	.4	70	23.3	181	71.7	7	13	.2	1	0	.1
83655	3.2	98	1.1	78	17.7	205	60.9	10	16	1.6	17	0	.0
83656	.5	90	.2	71	17.3	274	60.1	7	15	.2	17	0	.0
83657	.2	100	.1	100	17.8	205*	74.9	8	20	.1	20	0	.0
83660	4.4	93	1.6	72	21.5	224	67.0	8	15	2.0	15	0	.0
83661	7.7	96	2.9	72	19.2	248	66.0	8	16	3.5	15	0	.0
83669	1.4	96	.5	75	22.4	286	74.3	12	15	.7	18	0	.1
83670	.3	100	.1	92	22.3	257*	82.4	5	4	.1	4	0	.3
83672	7.1	90	2.6	75	19.1	225	68.2	8	17	3.1	17	0	.0
83676	3.4	81	1.0	66	18.0	247	62.9	10	11	1.4	12	0	.0
BOISE													
83702	24.4	98	10.8	56	27.8	315	118.0	7	14	11.1	12	1	.0
83703	13.1	98	4.7	71	27.3	353	102.5	8	8	6.3	7	0	.2
83704	40.4	98	14.5	75	30.5	408	108.6	9	8	19.4	7	1	.0
83705	41.3	97	14.8	72	29.3	391	102.0	9	8	19.5	7	3	.1
83706	18.9	95	7.4	59	23.6	327	94.8	9	6	8.9	5	1	.1
83707	2.5	98	.5	94	31.9	402	120.4	4	2	1.6	2	3	2.7
SPOKANE													
83801	1.4	97	.4	89	23.7	200	91.9	9	7	.7	7	0	.0
83802	1.0	100	.1	9	22.7	152	80.7*21	4		.1	6	0	.0
83803	.5	0	.2	84	18.4	180	66.1	11	24	.0	0	1	.2
83804	.4	100	.2	86	14.9	209	44.6	2	17	.2	4	1	.0
83805	5.6	98	1.9	78	19.3	245	72.0	10	12	2.7	12	0	.0

*=Estimated **1.0=883 lbs per person; 100++ indicates per capita toxic waste generation > than 100 times the U.S. average of 883 lbs per capita.

PAGE 2.65

ZIP CODE MEASURES OF SIZE, LEVELS OF AFFLUENCE AND QUALITY OF LIFE

1=Population (th.); 2= % White; 3=Households (th.); 4=% Owner Occupied; 5=Mean Income Per Household (th.$); 6=Mean Monthly Rent ($)*; 7=Mean Home Value (th.$)*; 8=% under 5; 9=% 65 and over; 10=White Males (th.); 11=% White Males, 65+; 12=# Toxic Waste Sites; 13=Toxic Waste Relative to US(883 lbs.per capita)**.

IDAHO

SPOKANE

ZIP CODE	1	2	3	4	5	6	7	8	9	10	11	12	13
83806	.3	0	.1	73	24.1	152	36.2	2	13	.0	0	1	1.3
83808	.3	100	.1	51	20.6	109	25.8	5	11	.2	6	0	.0
83809	.3	100	.1	89	21.3	245*	196.9	11	10	.2	5	0	.0
83810	1.1	100	.4	87	27.7	80	78.2	8	11	.6	15	0	.0
83811	.8	0	.3	77	19.0	170	60.3	6	14	.0	0	0	.0
83813	.4	0	.1	85	19.4	407	115.0	10	5	.0	0	0	.0
83814	29.7	98	11.1	68	23.7	331	103.7	8	14	14.0	12	1	.0
83821	.2	100	.1	100	20.0	230*	106.2	6	25	.1	26	0	.0
83823	1.1	98	.4	79	23.4	242	68.9	10	9	.5	9	0	.0
83824	.3	56	.1	84	25.4	291*	76.1	0	16	.1	14	0	.0
83825	.1	100	.1	78	21.7	423	63.6	6	6	.1	10	0	.0
83827	.3	100	.1	68	18.9	167	30.8	6	10	.2	10	0	.0
83830	.8	0	.2	91	23.6	392	52.9	12	7	.0	0	0	.0
83832	1.4	99	.5	76	24.8	277	80.4	7	12	.7	12	0	.0
83833	.8	98	.3	89	22.9	151	81.0	4	23	.4	24	0	.4
83834	.3	100	.1	79	34.8	395	32.5	7	15	.1	9	0	.0
83835	7.5	99	2.6	83	24.6	328	120.3	8	8	3.7	9	1	.0
83836	.8	0	.3	83	18.8	194	112.3	5	20	.0	0	0	.0
83837	5.4	97	2.0	65	23.8	230	54.5	10	12	2.7	9	1	3.4
83839	1.2	100	.4	94	25.9	214	68.6	7	5	.6	6	1	.6
83840	.4	100	.1	78	22.9	262	58.8	11	13	.2	16	0	.0
83841	.4	100	.1	84	21.9	324	83.8	12	11	.2	12	0	.0
83843	19.8	98	7.0	51	22.5	299	102.2	6	8	10.1	5	2	.0
83845	.7	0	.3	86	17.6	232	58.3	11	9	.0	0	0	.0
83846	1.5	0	.5	81	20.7	231	38.5	8	12	.0	0	0	.4
83847	.8	0	.3	82	19.2	378	76.5	10	6	.0	0	0	.0
83848	2.4	100	.8	49	25.3	68	90.1*	6	4	.1	0	0	.0
83850	3.0	99	1.0	78	28.6	269	66.2	7	8	1.2	6	0	.0
83851	1.2	85	.4	72	25.8	258	62.7	10	9	.6	8	0	.6
83852	.2	100	.1	82	18.1	262	71.6	13	12	.1	14	0	.0
83854	12.3	98	4.1	83	23.9	303	64.3	8	6	5.9	6	1	.1
83855	.4	100	.1	78	29.1	311	98.1	11	13	.1	9	0	.0
83856	4.5	97	1.6	78	19.7	235	57.0	9	12	1.1	12	0	.0
83857	.4	100	.1	72	20.8	233	79.8	9	9	2.2	13	0	.3
83858	4.4	99	1.4	80	25.1	238	92.3	8	9	.7	12	0	.0
83860	2.2	98	.7	85	19.5	318	91.4	10	6	2.3	6	0	.0
83861	5.7	98	2.1	76	25.6	169	110.0	11	10	1.1	10	0	.0
83862	1.2	99	.4	87	19.1	237	72.6	8	11	2.8	10	0	.2
83864	9.9	99	3.6	74	20.6	312	68.7	10	5	4.7	7	1	.1
83865	.3	99	.1	86	9.2	105*	42.6	15	4	.0	0	0	.0
83866	.3	100	.1	84	24.0	307	101.4	9	12	.1	0	0	.0
83867	.6	0	.2	81	27.8	398	21.5	11	4	.0	0	0	.0
83868	1.2	0	.4	68	21.5	283	66.9	11	0	.1	0	0	.2
83869	1.4	99	.5	80	19.6	253	44.6	6	25	.7	12	0	.4
83870	.3	0	.1	93	15.9	228	73.6	9	12	.0	0	1	.0
83871	1.7	100	.6	74	22.3	183*	33.8	7	22	.9	11	0	.0
83872	.4	100	.1	79	22.1	316	85.5	3	10	.2	5	0	.2
83873	3.2	100	1.2	67	25.1	186	118.9	7	11	.0	0	0	1.1

IDAHO

ZIP CODE	1	2	3	4	5	6	7	8	9	10	11	12	13
SPOKANE													
83876	.6	88	.3	85	24.1	296	82.1	3	11	.3	15	0	.0
ELKO													
89832	.2	0	.1	77	24.5	282*	39.4	13	12	.0	0	0	.0
SPOKANE													
99156	1.3	97	.5	84	19.2	208	62.6	12	9	.7	9	0	.0

*=Estimated **1.0=883 lbs per person; 100++ indicates per capita toxic waste generation > than 100 times the U.S. average of 883 lbs per capita.

ZIP CODE MEASURES OF SIZE, LEVELS OF AFFLUENCE AND QUALITY OF LIFE

1=Population (th.); 2= % White; 3=Households (th.); 4=% Owner Occupied; 5=Mean Income Per Household (th.$); 6=Mean Monthly Rent ($)*; 7=Mean Home Value (th.$)*;
8=% under 5; 9=% 65 and over; 10=White Males, 65 and over; 11=% White Males, 65+; 12=# Toxic Waste Sites; 13=Toxic Waste Relative to US(883 lbs.per capita)**.

ILLINOIS

ZIPCODE	1	2	3	4	5	6	7	8	9	10	11	12	13
00648	.8	95	.3	66	36.0	404	135.6	6	13	.4	13	0	.0
WASHINGTON													
47591	.5	100	.2	76	24.3	266	53.1	7	9	.3	8	0	.0
BURLINGTON													
52601	.2	100	.1	64	26.5	215	72.9	2	9	.1	6	0	.0
ROCK ISLAND													
52761	.5	0	.2	79	25.6	260	92.7	10	13	.0	0	0	.0
MADISON													
53525	.2	100	.1	62	29.4	338*	95.1	11	11	.1	17	0	.0
NORTH SUBURBAN													
60002	13.4	99	4.5	78	33.6	413	117.1	7	10	6.6	9	1	.2
60004	42.7	97	13.5	81	45.5	546	167.2	6	7	20.0	6	0	.5
60005	24.0	97	8.3	79	45.7	504	176.4	5	10	11.2	7	1	1.3
60007	29.6	94	9.5	74	40.3	499	146.7	7	5	13.8	4	5	6.2
60008	22.8	94	8.4	57	37.0	457	142.8	7	5	10.7	4	1	5.7
60010	27.8	98	8.9	86	65.5	588	258.5	5	13	13.6	6	1	.5
60013	12.6	100	4.1	85	38.1	502	134.0	8	7	16.1	6	1	1.1
60014	30.8	99	9.8	80	38.9	492	146.7	7	7	15.1	6	3	1.0
60015	29.3	98	8.9	91	65.8	656	237.5	6	5	14.3	4	1	.4
60016	52.6	93	20.3	63	34.7	465	139.2	6	10	23.3	9	3	.5
60018	28.6	96	10.3	77	34.0	441	133.2	6	8	13.6	7	4	4.5
60020	5.6	99	2.4	63	26.0	349	92.0	6	18	2.7	15	0	.3
60021	3.3	99	1.3	79	32.3	436	116.2	8	12	1.6	9	1	.2
60022	8.7	94	2.9	89	94.7	606	301.4	4	11	4.0	11	0	.0
60025	45.2	96	15.3	79	51.4	540	202.2	6	9	21.3	7	1	.3
60030	13.3	98	4.4	80	36.8	455	122.3	7	6	6.6	6	4	.3
60031	10.8	95	3.9	75	37.7	486	130.6	7	6	5.1	6	1	3.1
60033	9.1	97	3.2	68	30.3	382	106.8	8	11	4.4	10	0	2.5
60034	1.5	98	.5	70	31.8	334	113.0	8	12	.7	10	0	3.4
60035	30.6	96	10.2	82	70.5	533	246.0	6	9	14.4	8	0	.3
60037	1.4	85	.2	0	35.3	503	125.7*	6	1	.7	0	1	.0
60040	4.1	90	1.7	34	26.3	462	129.1	5	16	1.7	13	0	.2
60041	7.0	98	2.4	79	31.2	432	106.9	8	10	3.4	8	0	2.6
60042	2.3	98	.8	86	31.8	522	98.9	9	8	1.1	7	0	.1
60043	2.7	99	1.1	93	117.2	846	349.7	5	9	1.3	9	0	.0
60044	7.0	99	2.4	82	54.3	498	204.7	6	10	3.4	7	2	2.3
60045	16.3	96	5.1	82	83.1	565	312.3	4	10	7.6	9	0	.0
60046	16.7	98	5.2	87	36.9	393	118.9	9	5	8.4	5	0	.0
60047	16.7	98	5.1	89	48.0	464	200.0	8	8	8.2	6	1	1.4
60048	21.9	97	6.9	79	47.3	461	194.0	6	8	10.3	6	1	1.3
60050	33.8	99	11.3	85	33.0	448	115.3	8	11	16.5	10	4	.0
60053	23.8	93	8.0	92	45.1	468	156.5	4	11	10.8	10	0	2.6
60056	54.2	95	19.5	66	40.0	485	160.1	6	7	25.3	6	1	.2
60060	22.5	96	7.2	71	37.1	472	135.7	8	5	10.9	4	0	.9
60061	9.7	93	3.6	71	37.5	525	157.9	11	4	4.4	1	0	.0
60062	37.7	97	12.2	87	64.2	633	235.8	6	8	18.1	7	1	3.9
60064	14.5	38	5.0	53	26.5	335	79.1	9	9	2.8	13	3	26.5
60067	57.7	96	20.1	67	43.0	469	184.7	7	5	27.0	4	0	.4
60068	39.7	99	13.5	86	47.7	520	177.6	4	14	18.6	11	1	.2

ILLINOIS

ZIPCODE	1	2	3	4	5	6	7	8	9	10	11	12	13
NORTH SUBURBAN													
60069	2.4	94	.8	78	33.7	443	140.4	9	6	1.1	4	0	1.3
60070	6.0	100	1.8	95	48.4	523	174.8	5	7	3.0	6	0	.3
60071	2.3	99	.8	73	34.0	425	145.6	7	9	1.2	8	0	1.7
60072	.8	0	.2	85	39.6	304	155.5	12	7	.0	1	0	21.3
60073	23.5	97	7.1	84	29.8	424	88.1	10	6	11.1	5	0	9.3
60075	.2	79	.1	24	12.8	376	179.0	15	4	.1	0	1	1.3
60076	52.8	92	19.9	73	41.7	512	151.8	4	15	22.8	15	1	3.6
60077	2.6	89	.9	96	58.1	720	177.5	12	5	1.1	13	1	3.5
60080	.2	100	.1	91	40.9	470*	107.0	8	5	.1	1	5	.5
60081	3.8	100	1.3	81	31.7	475	107.6	7	10	1.9	9	1	.5
60083	1.9	98	.6	82	42.4	369	177.1	6	5	1.0	5	0	.0
60084	8.9	99	3.0	76	33.1	453	130.0	7	8	4.3	6	1	.2
60085	78.1	76	27.9	59	29.2	358	97.1	9	8	28.7	9	9	1.5
60088	24.3	85	2.1	85	23.3	351	55.8	6	1	16.7	1	0	.0
60090	52.4	95	19.4	66	36.7	490	147.7	9	4	24.8	3	4	2.2
60091	28.2	97	9.8	85	64.2	638	228.4	5	13	13.0	10	4	.0
60093	19.8	98	6.9	85	83.7	662	301.9	5	12	9.4	10	0	.0
60096	5.6	98	1.8	77	35.7	435	105.5	9	4	2.8	3	0	.0
60097	7.1	98	2.4	87	28.2	514	104.8	9	11	3.5	10	1	.7
60098	18.6	99	6.5	66	33.3	381	136.1	7	12	9.0	6	1	.7
60099	24.8	84	8.0	69	30.5	390	100.7	10	7	10.1	6	0	.8
NORTH SUBURBAN													
60101	33.6	94	10.6	61	36.5	427	145.3	7	4	15.8	4	2	2.0
60102	13.9	99	4.3	88	37.6	503	134.9	9	5	6.9	4	1	.2
60103	66.7	94	19.7	86	36.9	475	125.6	11	2	31.3	2	2	.1
60104	19.8	60	6.4	79	32.3	417	94.4	8	9	5.8	12	1	4.3
60106	19.5	95	6.8	62	36.2	477	129.2	6	6	9.3	7	2	2.7
60108	12.6	95	3.9	83	42.0	405	161.5	9	6	5.9	4	1	.0
60109	.6	0	.2	71	32.3	353	120.9	9	12	.3	0	0	.1
60110	24.2	96	7.2	76	32.2	386	96.3	11	3	11.6	2	1	1.7
60111	.4	100	.1	65	31.2	410	127.3	12	12	.2	11	0	.0
60112	1.0	98	.4	79	29.1	467	88.8	10	8	.5	8	0	.2
60113	.6	98	.6	73	27.2	334	61.3	8	10	.3	10	0	.0
60115	36.3	93	10.9	44	26.2	370	109.8	4	7	16.3	5	2	.9
60118	10.3	98	3.5	73	40.2	447	157.3	6	8	4.9	7	0	.1
60119	4.4	99	1.3	79	41.2	462	170.7	8	7	2.2	6	0	.1
60120	71.1	89	25.9	61	30.6	378	118.0	9	11	30.4	9	7	.7
60126	47.8	97	16.1	84	42.8	499	141.4	6	12	22.5	10	0	.4
60129	.3	96	.2	57	30.1	263	85.2	7	13	.3	13	0	1.3
60130	15.2	89	7.7	38	26.6	394	88.5	5	17	6.3	13	0	2.7
60131	18.8	99	6.6	72	32.2	376	111.3	6	11	8.6	10	3	5.9
60134	10.3	99	3.7	77	41.4	489	156.1	6	11	4.9	8	3	2.4
60135	4.7	99	1.6	74	28.9	341	99.6	8	10	2.3	8	2	1.3
60136	.7	100	.2	76	40.0	465	135.6	11	6	.3	6	1	.5
60137	60.0	94	20.0	76	42.1	437	152.0	8	5	27.9	4	0	.0
60140	4.4	99	1.4	71	33.8	467	141.1	7	6	2.3	9	0	.5
60142	3.2	100	1.0	69	38.7	440	145.1	8	8	1.7	7	1	1.6
60143	10.7	97	3.4	74	46.2	493	161.6	7	7	5.3	6	0	.5
60144	.3	100	.1	68	32.0	351	132.6	7	7	.1	9	0	24.2

*=Estimated **1.0=883 lbs per person; 100++ indicates per capita toxic waste generation > than 100 times the U.S. average of 883 lbs per capita.

ZIP CODE MEASURES OF SIZE, LEVELS OF AFFLUENCE AND QUALITY OF LIFE

1=Population (th.); 2= % White; 3=Households (th.); 4=% Owner Occupied; 5=Mean Income Per Household (th.$); 6=Mean Monthly Rent ($)*; 7=Mean Home Value (th.$)*; 8=% under 5; 9=% 65 and over; 10=White Males (th.); 11=% White Males, 65+; 12=# Toxic Waste Sites; 13=Toxic Waste Relative to US(883 lbs.per capita)**.

ILLINOIS

NORTH SUBURBAN

ZIPCODE	1	2	3	4	5	6	7	8	9	10	11	12	13
60145	1.9	97	.6	72	31.4	327	98.2	9	8	1.0	8	0	.0
60146	2.2	0	.8	75	30.6	333	85.1	7	9	.0	0	0	.0
60148	47.6	96	16.5	74	38.2	522	129.6	7	7	22.5	6	0	.1
60150	1.7	0	.6	63	30.0	396	90.8	7	11	.0	6	0	.0
60151	2.7	99	.9	73	32.5	356	125.9	9	7	1.3	7	0	.9
60152	8.1	97	2.8	73	31.1	365	123.5	7	11	3.9	9	1	1.0
60153	54.3	54	17.9	74	30.1	404	106.4	7	11	14.0	14	4	2.0
60157	1.1	100	.3	95	46.8	628	170.6	7	3	.0	5	2	.0
60160	21.1	94	8.1	53	28.0	347	118.1	7	12	9.4	10	3	8.5
60162	8.4	98	3.1	68	34.7	452	116.0	5	11	4.0	8	1	2.0
60163	5.5	99	1.9	87	38.1	479	113.2	5	9	2.7	9	0	.2
60164	21.2	94	7.3	76	32.4	369	102.7	6	10	9.9	9	0	.4
60165	4.0	82	1.2	55	29.3	419	88.1	9	5	1.6	4	0	7.1
60170	.2	100	.1	84	38.0	310	132.9	8	14	.1	11	0	.3
60171	10.4	99	4.2	57	29.2	424	109.9	5	15	4.8	13	0	.4
60172	22.8	95	7.6	85	41.3	532	147.9	9	9	10.9	4	0	.9
60174	29.8	98	9.6	75	40.8	454	167.7	8	7	14.7	5	1	2.6
60176	11.5	96	4.3	51	31.7	393	121.4	7	6	5.6	4	3	3.2
60177	6.8	97	2.0	82	32.9	410	110.0	9	5	3.2	7	1	.3
60178	13.0	96	4.7	69	30.4	383	105.9	8	10	6.1	9	0	1.0
60180	1.4	99	.4	82	33.5	498	130.1	7	10	.7	9	0	3.8
60181	30.0	96	10.7	72	35.0	470	116.0	6	10	13.9	8	0	.3
60183	.2	100	.1	57	30.9	622	183.8	7	5	.1	7	0	2.1
60184	.8	0	.3	94	69.7	649	307.4	5	13	.4	0	0	.0
60185	22.4	92	7.0	72	37.2	408	140.4	9	7	10.4	6	4	2.0
60187	68.5	95	23.0	68	40.4	451	157.8	8	7	31.5	5	0	.4
60190	5.1	99	1.5	91	51.2	502	155.2	7	5	2.5	4	0	1.3
60191	13.4	85	4.3	86	43.7	485	134.4	7	6	6.2	7	2	.6
60193	32.4	96	10.7	80	39.2	537	156.0	8	4	15.4	3	0	.2
60194	29.5	94	10.6	68	35.5	515	138.1	9	6	13.6	3	1	.1
60195	28.0	94	10.3	57	39.1	528	150.2	8	2	13.5	1	1	3.7

EVANSTON

ZIPCODE	1	2	3	4	5	6	7	8	9	10	11	12	13
60201	41.4	75	14.5	52	39.8	510	192.8	4	16	14.3	11	0	.3
60202	32.3	75	13.5	45	36.2	503	158.2	5	11	11.3	10	0	.5
60203	4.8	88	1.6	92	61.3	649	197.7	6	11	2.1	10	0	.0

OAKPARK

ZIPCODE	1	2	3	4	5	6	7	8	9	10	11	12	13
60301	1.1	97	.7	18	28.5	440	101.4*	2	36	.4	24	0	.0
60302	34.3	86	14.9	46	33.7	417	150.0	6	16	13.5	12	0	.1
60304	19.4	85	6.8	64	32.7	399	102.1	7	10	7.9	9	0	.0
60305	12.4	98	4.0	78	57.2	466	213.8	4	16	5.4	13	0	.0

SOUTH SUBURBAN

ZIPCODE	1	2	3	4	5	6	7	8	9	10	11	12	13
60401	4.6	100	1.6	80	32.6	400	125.1	7	11	2.3	10	1	.3
60402	53.5	98	22.2	62	28.7	353	99.1	4	21	24.2	18	1	.1
60406	23.3	88	9.4	52	25.6	351	74.6	8	15	9.6	13	6	2.4
60407	1.6	100	.5	75	29.7	389	75.0	9	8	.8	7	0	
60408	3.2	98	1.0	82	30.2	363	75.5	11	6	1.5	5	0	1.0
60409	39.7	92	15.6	62	31.8	386	87.4	6	12	17.6	11	0	.8
60410	3.1	97	1.0	84	35.6	401	104.1	8	9	1.5	3	1	.0
60411	65.7	71	20.5	68	29.1	345	84.1	9	8	22.8	24	8	3.5

ILLINOIS

SOUTH SUBURBAN

ZIPCODE	1	2	3	4	5	6	7	8	9	10	11	12	13
60415	13.3	99	5.0	47	28.7	413	102.0	8	8	6.4	6	1	.4
60416	6.0	98	2.1	80	30.9	352	92.7	8	11	2.9	10	1	2.0
60417	12.3	98	3.8	80	41.3	435	143.8	8	7	6.1	6	0	.1
60418	.8	0	.2	80	31.0	400	98.6	6	7	.0	0	0	.0
60419	24.8	96	8.2	85	36.5	413	89.4	6	10	11.5	8	1	.0
60420	5.6	94	1.9	69	29.8	335	82.3	6	13	2.5	11	0	.1
60421	2.4	0	.8	77	36.9	392	116.2	8	6	.0	0	0	37.5
60422	8.4	93	2.7	96	75.6	622	211.7	5	9	3.8	8	0	.0
60423	12.3	98	3.6	88	41.5	471	160.1	10	5	6.0	4	1	2.0
60424	2.2	99	.8	71	29.8	383	78.2	8	9	1.0	8	1	.4
60425	10.6	88	3.4	87	40.9	439	119.0	7	9	4.5	8	0	.4
60426	57.3	29	16.9	70	27.3	360	62.6	9	7	8.0	11	2	.8
60429	15.4	87	4.9	84	37.7	458	97.0	8	7	6.5	6	0	.4
60430	20.5	97	7.4	85	40.0	501	121.7	5	14	9.5	11	1	.0
60431	.4	80	.1	0	8.4	148	30.1*	0	49	.1	38	0	100++
60432	22.6	55	6.6	59	25.0	323	63.8	10	8	6.3	11	3	.2
60433	19.0	62	6.0	66	28.9	332	67.7	9	9	5.6	12	2	.7
60435	58.0	94	21.2	67	33.3	338	102.5	8	11	8.0	9	1	.4
60436	22.1	80	7.8	70	30.7	323	86.6	8	11	8.7	10	6	2.3
60437	.3	100	.1	77	27.4	317	61.0	15	5	.1	13	0	.0
60438	29.7	98	10.6	71	35.5	429	101.5	6	10	14.2	10	3	.4
60439	47.0	91	14.2	81	36.0	383	117.4	11	4	21.3	9	9	1.7
60441	45.0	99	13.0	85	35.3	417	106.2	8	9	20.9	7	5	.4
60442	4.0	99	.9	76	33.3	403	119.9	10	8	2.0	7	0	.4
60443	12.1	86	3.9	80	37.3	466	116.8	10	8	5.1	5	1	1.2
60444	1.5	99	.5	65	31.3	388	86.0	8	7	.8	8	0	.1
60445	27.8	88	9.0	72	31.6	414	91.8	8	8	12.1	7	2	.0
60447	4.8	100	1.5	82	35.7	398	122.4	8	6	2.4	6	0	.0
60448	10.3	99	3.1	77	34.7	448	124.9	9	6	4.9	5	2	.0
60449	2.9	99	.9	73	35.8	424	130.0	8	12	1.5	8	0	.5
60450	15.0	99	5.4	64	31.1	374	102.9	8	7	7.4	10	3	.0
60451	13.5	99	4.1	83	37.0	454	122.6	9	5	6.7	5	1	.0
60452	25.9	97	7.6	79	37.9	417	116.0	8	7	12.5	5	1	.0
60453	60.7	99	20.8	78	37.1	446	118.5	8	5	28.3	11	0	.1
60455	14.1	98	4.6	76	30.9	413	104.4	8	10	6.7	8	0	3.2
60456	5.3	100	1.5	68	27.1	336	76.1	7	13	2.5	9	0	
60457	13.7	99	4.4	68	35.8	417	132.3	7	7	6.7	5	0	.1
60458	11.9	89	4.5	52	29.6	407	107.3	10	6	5.2	5	0	.0
60459	28.5	98	8.5	84	35.0	440	99.3	6	9	13.7	7	0	.1
60460	1.8	0	.6	68	30.9	346	71.5	8	11	.9	4	0	.5
60461	4.1	91	1.2	99	90.6	722	254.5	5	11	1.9	4	0	.0
60462	30.2	97	9.0	82	43.4	449	165.4	9	5	14.4	4	0	.0
60463	14.3	97	4.2	96	56.4	479	173.5	4	9	6.8	7	0	.0
60464	5.8	98	1.7	95	62.5	680	211.9	5	8	2.9	8	0	.0
60465	16.6	96	5.6	72	39.1	427	147.2	7	7	7.7	6	4	.0
60466	32.8	80	11.2	63	33.9	437	90.3	8	6	12.6	5	1	.2
60468	4.2	100	1.4	67	29.8	352	107.5	8	12	2.0	10	0	1.3
60469	4.8	95	1.3	74	29.1	364	70.4	8	8	2.2	5	0	.0
60470	.8	0	.3	71	29.9	348	56.0	8	11	.0			

*=Estimated **1.0=883 lbs per person; 100++ indicates per capita toxic waste generation > than 100 times the U.S. average of 883 lbs per capita.

ZIP CODE MEASURES OF SIZE, LEVELS OF AFFLUENCE AND QUALITY OF LIFE

1=Population (th.); 2= % White; 3=Households (th.); 4=% Owner Occupied; 5=Mean Income Per Household (th.$); 6=Mean Monthly Rent ($); 7=Mean Home Value (th.$); 8=% under 5; 9=% 65 and over; 10=White Males (th.); 11=% White Males, 65+; 12=# Toxic Waste Sites; 13=Toxic Waste Relative to US(883 lbs.per capita)**.

ILLINOIS

SOUTH SUBURBAN

ZIPCODE	1	2	3	4	5	6	7	8	9	10	11	12	13
60471	9.5	89	3.5	64	33.3	498	106.9	10	4	4.2	3	1	.0
60472	6.6	3	1.7	65	24.4	323	49.4	8	11	.1	19	0	.0
60473	24.9	98	7.5	95	44.7	416	125.7	5	10	11.9	8	2	.3
60474	.3	0	.3	90	28.1	315	62.4	8	17	.0	0	0	.0
60475	9.7	86	3.3	63	26.5	350	74.7	9	9	4.2	7	0	.0
60476	3.0	99	1.0	83	38.7	392	84.2	5	9	1.4	6	0	.4
60477	47.0	93	14.2	81	36.1	429	113.0	10	5	21.4	4	0	.0
60479	.6	0	.2	76	36.9	476	73.0	11	7	.1	0	0	.0
60480	4.0	95	1.4	78	37.9	417	145.6	7	6	1.9	7	0	.0
60481	9.5	96	3.2	74	30.3	359	84.7	8	10	4.6	9	2	.0
60482	13.1	99	4.8	66	32.0	400	106.3	7	10	6.3	8	0	7.4

SOUTH SUBURBAN

ZIPCODE	1	2	3	4	5	6	7	8	9	10	11	12	13
60501	11.1	77	3.9	53	28.2	349	87.6	8	11	4.1	9	3	.1
60504	3.4	99	1.1	79	51.5	485	142.8	8	8	1.7	7	1	1.7
60505	55.9	77	18.6	61	27.6	367	82.5	10	9	20.9	8	1	3.9
60506	36.0	88	12.7	67	35.5	390	108.5	9	10	15.1	9	1	.0
60510	15.4	94	5.2	69	35.3	413	140.6	8	10	7.1	8	0	.6
60511	1.8	100	.6	81	39.1	403	151.0	10	7	.9	6	0	1.2
60512	1.1	0	.6	92	45.6	375	142.0	7	9	.9	6	0	1.8
60513	19.5	99	7.4	75	32.2	429	109.1	6	14	9.2	12	0	2.3
60514	15.7	98	6.3	70	42.6	441	163.8	5	8	7.4	7	0	.0
60515	79.5	94	27.5	76	40.6	457	149.1	7	7	37.1	6	0	.0
60518	3.3	99	1.2	68	27.5	316	80.8	8	15	1.6	14	0	.0
60519	.4	100	.1	78	26.0	208	114.3	5	23	.9	19	0	2.3
60521	2.3	98	.8	64	30.8	389	108.1	8	12	1.1	10	0	.0
60522	38.2	94	12.5	79	64.8	481	244.8	6	9	17.5	8	3	4.0
60525	45.9	96	17.5	73	39.5	452	150.7	6	14	21.1	12	0	5.0
60530	.6	99	.2	63	25.2	449	80.6	9	9	.3	7	0	.0
60531	1.6	0	.6	64	31.2	383	87.8	6	13	.3	11	0	.1
60532	20.4	95	7.6	50	39.7	495	169.3	7	4	9.9	5	3	.4
60534	9.8	97	3.9	60	29.5	383	100.2	5	13	4.7	11	0	.7
60536	.4	0	.1	80	32.8	369	102.2	7	5	.0	0	0	.0
60537	.4	100	.1	77	32.3	290	77.0	13	9	.2	11	0	.0
60538	13.8	98	4.6	83	35.0	472	104.7	7	9	6.7	4	2	2.3
60540	55.6	96	17.0	61	48.7	485	181.1	5	5	26.4	4	1	.0
60541	2.3	94	.8	61	30.3	392	95.5	10	13	1.1	12	0	.0
60542	5.6	95	2.0	68	34.7	421	113.2	8	8	2.7	7	0	1.5
60543	8.0	98	3.7	70	36.3	381	143.6	7	6	3.9	5	0	.0
60544	11.9	99	3.7	78	37.6	437	129.1	8	5	5.8	5	0	.2
60545	7.1	94	2.3	72	30.4	359	103.6	9	8	3.3	7	0	.3
60546	16.2	100	6.5	74	37.1	430	146.5	4	19	7.6	16	0	.0
60548	7.3	98	2.6	72	29.2	402	101.4	9	11	3.5	10	0	.4
60549	.6	100	.2	71	32.6	389	94.1	8	9	.2	7	0	.0
60550	1.3	99	.5	66	25.6	282	86.4	6	16	.6	14	0	.2
60551	2.5	91	1.0	66	28.9	335	83.5	8	8	.8	7	0	.7
60552	3.0	100	1.0	74	30.2	409	108.3	9	10	1.3	7	0	.1
60553	.8	0	.3	68	30.6	403	71.7	6	11	1.5	9	0	.0
60554	2.4	99	.7	75	42.9	480	138.5	8	6	1.2	6	0	.4
60555	7.8	96	2.8	90	38.2	521	127.0	5	11	3.7	4	1	.1

ILLINOIS

SOUTH SUBURBAN

ZIPCODE	1	2	3	4	5	6	7	8	9	10	11	12	13
60556	1.6	99	.5	68	29.7	365	85.4	9	11	.8	10	0	.0
60557	.2	100	.1	66	24.4	255	84.7	5	11	.1	16	0	1.6
60558	12.9	100	4.3	95	54.8	641	184.2	5	11	6.3	10	0	.0
60559	34.7	93	12.2	64	37.9	467	151.6	8	8	15.8	6	0	.0
60560	7.1	99	2.4	69	36.1	373	138.1	8	10	3.5	8	1	.3

CHICAGO

ZIPCODE	1	2	3	4	5	6	7	8	9	10	11	12	13
60601	2.7	90	1.7	83	37.4	731	133.4*	1	17	1.3	12	0	8.4
60605	3.6	62	2.0	10	17.2	319	61.2*	1	24	1.2	25	1	1.6
60606	.7	70	.5	0	7.7	190	27.5*	3	21	.5	25	1	66.3
60607	10.6	51	4.3	16	20.1	283	140.5	6	12	3.2	16	2	7.2
60608	94.1	45	27.6	27	19.2	250	48.6	8	8	21.3	10	8	.9
60609	103.9	45	30.4	31	19.0	240	49.9	12	7	22.8	10	6	1.3
60610	47.8	53	23.7	24	35.0	388	386.8	7	10	12.1	12	1	.8
60611	19.9	92	13.0	33	56.4	552	437	5	20	8.7	18	2	3.8
60612	57.6	15	17.8	18	15.2	242	45.1	10	8	4.3	13	0	1.9
60613	53.6	70	26.2	24	25.3	349	114.0	6	14	18.0	13	0	1.2
60614	57.5	84	31.9	26	32.7	434	222.9	5	10	23.5	8	4	1.8
60615	54.8	26	25.3	19	22.0	341	168.3	6	14	7.5	9	4	1.0
60616	49.5	39	19.5	15	20.6	287	79.3	7	13	9.4	9	1	1.0
60617	107.6	39	33.5	60	29.4	312	68.7	8	8	20.0	12	6	2.9
60618	84.5	87	33.5	38	24.1	329	81.1	7	14	34.4	13	3	2.5
60619	85.5	2	32.0	45	25.0	352	68.8	6	12	.7	38	1	2.4
60620	100.6	5	30.1	54	28.9	361	76.7	8	9	2.4	20	4	.0
60621	68.1	1	20.8	28	16.7	316	47.1	8	12	.7	7	1	1.0
60622	85.4	55	28.8	21	18.9	270	56.2	10	9	23.6	12	1	1.8
60623	113.1	28	31.0	31	20.2	302	51.1	12	7	15.8	8	3	.6
60624	67.6	2	18.9	23	17.2	313	56.8	7	11	.4	13	0	.8
60625	78.7	80	29.6	30	25.7	353	107.1	6	14	30.1	13	3	.1
60626	51.7	78	24.3	14	22.0	361	120.8	6	15	19.1	12	3	.4
60627	26.8	50	9.0	44	24.6	299	71.6	10	5	6.0	6	5	.3
60628	107.6	5	29.3	67	28.1	371	66.9	8	11	2.8	22	8	4.2
60629	85.9	96	32.4	65	28.3	336	78.6	8	9	38.9	15	5	1.4
60630	49.3	97	19.7	64	30.1	386	109.9	4	19	22.0	15	0	.6
60631	27.3	99	10.3	75	27.3	353	132.4	6	15	13.2	27	0	3.1
60632	61.1	94	23.7	58	26.6	326	72.3	9	11	27.9	12	3	3.9
60633	15.6	97	5.5	76	31.2	304	77.1	8	17	7.6	10	5	5.9
60634	72.3	98	27.0	73	30.4	399	110.2	8	20	33.2	17	0	.0
60635	38.7	99	14.9	67	31.7	400	120.9	4	19	17.7	16	0	.4
60636	68.7	2	18.1	53	21.4	360	53.3	10	4	.8	18	2	3.1
60637	78.3	12	30.7	16	18.3	309	106.1	8	14	4.7	12	0	3.9
60638	58.4	90	20.0	77	31.8	379	89.7	5	11	25.5	14	9	5.5
60639	66.4	88	24.7	50	25.7	340	79.5	7	15	27.9	14	0	.0
60640	74.6	64	33.3	15	20.1	300	125.0	7	15	23.3	15	1	.4
60641	60.7	96	25.3	48	26.5	344	97.6	5	19	27.3	16	2	.7
60642	24.6	99	8.4	86	36.3	416	99.6	5	19	11.3	15	1	.1
60643	70.1	33	20.7	76	34.0	400	83.9	5	11	11.0	13	4	.3
60644	80.3	5	23.2	27	20.1	332	61.4	11	9	1.8	19	1	1.4
60645	42.9	91	17.8	52	34.6	432	146.7	5	23	17.7	22	1	1.0
60646	34.5	97	12.5	83	48.5	444	175.9	4	19	15.6	17	0	2.0

*=Estimated **+1.0=883 lbs per person; 100+ indicates per capita toxic waste generation > than 100 times the U.S. average of 883 lbs per capita.

ZIP CODE MEASURES OF SIZE, LEVELS OF AFFLUENCE AND QUALITY OF LIFE

1=Population (th.); 2= % White; 3=Households (th.); 4=% Owner Occupied; 5=Mean Income Per Household (th.$); 6=Mean Monthly Rent ($); 7=Mean Home Value (th.$)*; 8=% under 5; 9=% 65 and over; 10=White Males, 65+; 11=% White Males; 12=# Toxic Waste Sites; 13=Toxic Waste Relative to US(883 lbs.per capita)**.

ILLINOIS

CHICAGO

ZIP CODE	1	2	3	4	5	6	7	8	9	10	11	12	13
60647	101.1	68	34.4	28	20.8	296	53.4	10	9	33.4	10	2	.5
60648	33.1	97	11.0	79	37.9	461	145.6	4	15	15.3	12	1	2.4
60649	68.7	4	28.4	19	22.9	365	87.3	9	7	1.4	24	0	.0
60650	61.3	96	24.1	51	25.6	315	87.5	6	16	28.6	14	4	3.1
60651	80.1	36	24.1	43	23.3	337	59.8	10	16	14.3	11	0	.6
60652	39.8	99	12.9	91	37.1	464	92.4	5	12	19.1	10	0	.1
60653	62.6	1	22.3	8	11.7	222	55.6	9	13	.1	20	1	1.0
60655	31.9	99	11.2	83	32.7	421	89.2	9	17	15.1	14	0	.0
60656	46.4	98	18.3	66	34.3	490	139.9	4	15	21.8	12	1	.6
60657	68.1	82	37.0	23	27.9	408	112.5	5	15	26.2	12	1	.3
60658	15.7	98	5.6	55	33.3	424	108.9	8	6	7.6	5	0	3.3
60659	33.2	88	12.8	45	32.4	428	137.3	5	19	13.6	19	0	.0
60660	42.7	75	21.3	27	24.8	353	105.3	5	19	14.4	16	0	.0

KANKAKEE

ZIP CODE	1	2	3	4	5	6	7	8	9	10	11	12	13
60901	42.3	79	14.6	62	26.6	326	75.5	8	12	16.0	11	8	2.3
60910	1.4	98	.5	68	22.3	349	59.4	10	13	.3	11	0	.0
60911	1.4	100	.5	71	26.8	309	77.0	9	13	.7	12	0	1.1
60912	.7	81	.3	76	24.1	256	55.0	8	13	.3	13	0	.0
60913	1.5	0	.5	79	31.5	333	98.2	8	10	.0	0	0	.0
60914	15.9	96	5.3	68	31.3	392	99.3	9	6	7.4	5	0	.9
60915	11.6	99	4.1	72	25.4	358	69.8	8	10	5.6	8	0	6.1
60917	.7	0	.2	71	29.7	329	56.1	12	8	.0	0	0	.0
60918	1.0	0	.4	76	24.5	233	61.0	9	20	.0	0	0	.0
60919	.7	0	.2	69	22.4	233	44.3	10	16	.0	0	0	.0
60920	.2	0	.1	80	28.8	413	57.1	5	18	.0	0	0	.0
60921	1.7	99	.7	74	27.8	303	60.5	7	19	.8	17	0	.3
60922	2.8	93	.9	79	25.6	335	74.3	10	11	1.3	9	0	.0
60924	1.7	0	.6	78	26.8	277	82.2	7	17	.0	0	0	.0
60927	2.4	0	.8	71	28.6	320	78.6	9	14	.0	0	0	.0
60928	.8	100	.3	82	29.0	305	77.8	7	17	.4	14	0	.9
60929	.9	100	.3	82	27.4	228	57.8	6	22	.4	19	0	.0
60930	1.0	0	.4	67	24.7	304	64.1	7	23	.0	0	0	.0
60931	.7	0	.3	74	28.2	295	63.5	6	17	.0	0	0	.0
60932	.2	100	.1	85	24.3	233	35.4	14	18	.1	7	0	.0
60933	.4	0	.1	80	28.1	353	59.2	12	12	.0	0	0	1.3
60934	.4	100	.1	87	33.4	238	61.0	8	15	.2	14	0	.3
60935	.7	0	.3	71	27.5	321	77.2	10	11	.0	0	0	.1
60936	4.5	98	1.8	76	28.8	293	75.6	7	18	2.1	15	0	1.4
60938	2.3	99	.9	75	25.0	280	64.5	7	18	1.1	13	0	.0
60940	2.7	100	.9	72	29.5	362	100.6	7	12	1.3	12	0	.1
60941	1.9	0	.6	76	32.3	301	86.4	9	10	.0	0	0	.0
60942	7.5	97	2.7	71	24.2	245	59.8	8	14	3.5	11	0	.0
60944	1.2	0	.4	79	12.7	359	41.0	8	12	.0	0	0	1.4
60945	.2	100	.1	78	18.8	274	39.7	7	18	.1	15	0	.0
60946	.6	0	.2	69	29.4	271	51.3	9	13	.0	0	0	.1
60948	1.4	96	.5	80	28.5	400	93.1	6	11	.7	11	0	.0
60949	.6	100	.3	65	26.2	185	60.0	7	7	.3	5	0	.7
60950	5.8	93	1.8	65	26.9	300	85.7	7	12	2.7	11	0	.0
60951	1.0	100	.4	72	26.9	343	71.1	8	11	.5	10	0	.1

ILLINOIS

KANKAKEE

ZIP CODE	1	2	3	4	5	6	7	8	9	10	11	12	13
60952	.8	99	.3	73	25.5	256	52.2	7	18	.4	15	0	.0
60953	3.1	98	1.2	70	23.0	247	58.0	7	14	1.5	12	0	.6
60954	8.1	79	2.8	69	22.1	325	67.7	8	13	3.3	12	0	.0
60955	2.0	90	.7	76	24.1	307	56.1	7	17	.9	18	0	.0
60956	.2	100	.1	79	20.1	258	43.1	8	12	.1	15	0	.7
60957	5.7	100	2.1	73	26.7	279	73.8	7	14	2.7	11	0	.7
60959	1.3	0	.5	73	28.1	343	61.9	9	20	.0	0	0	.1
60960	1.4	0	.5	74	23.9	263	45.5	8	14	.0	0	0	.0
60961	.8	100	.3	73	27.8	346	76.0	6	13	.4	12	0	.0
60962	.7	100	.3	81	26.1	196	52.5	5	19	.3	18	0	.3
60963	2.0	99	.8	75	24.2	224	65.6	7	14	1.0	12	0	.0
60964	7.9	64	2.7	72	22.2	297	70.8	8	12	2.6	9	0	.0
60966	1.7	100	.7	75	23.7	318	55.1	6	18	.7	15	0	.0
60968	.6	100	.3	74	29.9	316	48.3	6	14	.3	15	0	.0
60970	7.7	99	2.9	72	25.7	287	72.7	7	17	3.6	13	0	.3
60973	.6	100	.2	72	27.1	354	57.1	7	7	.3	6	0	.0
60974	.3	100	.1	87	20.6	303	52.3	8	10	.2	7	0	.0

ROCKFORD

ZIP CODE	1	2	3	4	5	6	7	8	9	10	11	12	13
61001	1.0	0	.3	74	24.0	274	72.1	9	13	1.0	12	0	.0
61006	2.0	98	.7	62	27.6	295	69.9	9	14	.0	0	0	.0
61007	.6	0	.2	71	26.5	302	68.7	11	11	.0	0	0	.0
61008	21.7	96	7.6	68	29.4	345	92.5	8	11	10.2	9	5	4.2
61010	4.1	100	1.4	71	30.0	367	93.8	7	10	2.0	7	1	1.4
61011	1.7	99	.5	86	35.6	367	115.9	9	7	.8	8	0	.0
61012	1.7	99	.5	73	28.1	354	82.3	9	10	.9	10	0	.0
61013	.8	0	.3	92	27.1	454	73.4	10	14	.0	0	0	.0
61014	1.5	100	.5	74	25.1	331	59.9	7	14	.8	12	0	2.9
61015	1.0	0	.3	75	29.0	383	90.9	9	8	.0	0	0	.0
61016	2.4	100	.8	70	29.5	376	98.3	8	9	1.2	10	1	.4
61017	.2	97	.1	81	28.1	361	57.5	7	14	.1	19	0	.0
61018	1.2	0	.4	80	29.0	295	63.4	7	11	.0	0	0	.0
61019	2.0	100	.7	87	30.7	432	99.8	6	11	1.0	12	0	.0
61020	1.2	100	.4	79	28.8	328	92.9	6	7	.6	6	1	.0
61021	22.6	96	8.0	69	27.4	318	78.4	7	12	10.4	10	1	1.4
61024	2.1	98	.7	76	26.3	370	76.2	7	12	1.0	8	0	.0
61025	5.9	0	1.8	83	29.1	314	83.5	9	7	.9	10	1	2.9
61026	.7	100	.2	78	36.2	468	75.1	11	15	.8	12	0	.0
61028	2.3	100	.8	78	23.6	234	69.8	6	15	.3	11	0	.0
61030	2.3	100	.8	77	25.2	334	64.3	6	8	1.1	13	0	.0
61031	1.8	98	.6	70	29.6	381	68.4	7	18	.8	14	1	1.4
61032	33.6	92	13.0	68	26.5	300	76.7	7	14	14.4	12	3	.0
61036	5.7	100	2.1	73	28.0	258	82.2	7	15	2.7	12	1	1.8
61037	.2	97	.1	100	34.8	400*	79.5	7	11	.1	11	0	.1
61038	.8	99	.2	70	31.2	369	91.4	8	8	.4	9	0	.0
61039	.9	0	.3	75	29.1	286	78.4	9	10	.9	8	0	.7
61041	1.6	99	.6	62	24.8	258	59.7	7	13	.8	12	0	.0
61042	.7	0	.2	65	29.8	364	56.8	12	6	.8	12	0	.0
61043	.1	100	.1	88	23.9	275*	63.1	9	17	.1	14	0	.0
61044	.3	100	.1	84	28.3	315	64.6	8	6	.2	6	0	.1

*=Estimated **1.0=883 lbs per person; 100++ indicates per capita toxic waste generation > than 100 times the U.S. average of 883 lbs per capita.

ZIP CODE MEASURES OF SIZE, LEVELS OF AFFLUENCE AND QUALITY OF LIFE

1=Population (th.); 2= % White; 3=Households (th.); 4=% Owner Occupied; 5=Mean Income Per Household (th.$); 6=Mean Monthly Rent ($)*; 7=Mean Home Value (th.$)*; 8=% under 5; 9=% 65 and over; 10=White Males (th.); 11=% White Males, 65+; 12=# Toxic Waste Sites; 13=Toxic Waste Relative to US(883 lbs.per capita)**.

ILLINOIS

ROCKFORD

ZIPCODE	1	2	3	4	5	6	7	8	9	10	11	12	13
61045	.4	100	.2	72	28.4	325	72.3	9	15	.2	14	0	.0
61046	2.4	0	.9	75	25.1	305	62.9	7	16	.0	0	0	.6
61047	1.3	100	.4	75	27.3	394	58.1	8	9	.7	9	0	.0
61048	4.1	100	1.4	76	27.5	378	76.2	7	16	2.0	14	0	.1
61049	.5	100	.2	77	32.8	423	80.4	6	15	.2	13	0	19.9
61050	.5	100	.2	83	24.2	128	45.1	8	15	.2	14	0	.0
61051	1.9	100	.7	73	24.3	321	66.4	8	13	1.0	11	0	.0
61052	1.0	100	.3	77	30.2	460	90.7	7	8	.5	8	1	.0
61053	3.4	99	1.3	74	24.3	285	70.1	7	19	1.6	16	0	.9
61054	4.1	99	1.6	73	25.9	312	70.4	7	18	2.0	14	0	.0
61057	.2	100	.1	83	24.2	278*	57.6	12	12	.1	15	0	.0
61058	.2	100	.1	82	29.4	216	56.3	5	21	.1	16	0	.0
61059	.1	100	.1	87	21.1	243*	41.8	3	22	.1	22	0	.0
61060	1.6	99	.5	79	26.8	308	61.8	7	13	.8	11	0	.0
61061	6.8	100	2.5	71	28.1	347	84.7	6	13	3.3	11	0	1.8
61062	1.9	100	.7	75	27.0	312	69.8	7	10	1.0	9	0	.0
61063	3.5	100	1.2	80	31.7	337	83.4	7	11	1.7	9	1	.0
61064	4.5	0	1.6	68	25.8	327	71.3	5	15	.8	0	0	.4
61065	2.0	100	.6	85	31.1	341	91.9	8	8	1.0	8	0	.4
61067	1.1	0	.4	80	25.8	324	70.7	7	7	.5	11	0	.0
61068	13.0	95	4.7	62	27.8	328	83.8	8	11	6.0	10	3	.4
61070	1.0	100	.3	82	24.1	312	62.9	6	13	.5	12	0	.0
61071	16.3	95	5.6	74	29.1	313	70.9	9	10	7.5	9	0	1.3
61072	5.4	99	1.7	80	32.1	365	94.8	8	8	2.7	8	0	.0
61073	6.9	99	2.1	93	42.2	465	125.1	9	4	3.4	3	0	.5
61074	6.0	97	2.3	72	23.1	267	60.7	6	17	2.8	15	2	1.6
61075	1.0	100	.3	80	24.5	172	66.0	9	10	.5	10	0	.0
61077	.2	100	.1	67	23.3	341	69.8	9	14	.1	13	0	1.0
61078	1.8	100	.6	68	26.8	299	74.8	6	15	.8	12	0	.0
61079	.2	100	.1	69	23.5	377	57.9	12	11	.1	3	0	.1
61080	7.1	92	2.6	65	25.1	330	64.6	7	11	3.2	10	1	4.7
61081	24.0	94	8.5	69	32.0	364	82.2	7	11	11.0	10	1	4.4
61084	2.4	99	.8	80	32.9	422	104.8	6	5	1.2	5	0	.0
61085	3.7	100	1.3	75	24.1	292	70.1	8	15	1.8	13	1	2.7
61087	1.9	100	.8	80	22.4	281	56.4	7	17	.9	14	0	.7
61089	4.0	0	1.3	79	33.4	365	100.2	7	9	.0	0	2	.0

ROCKFORD

ZIPCODE	1	2	3	4	5	6	7	8	9	10	11	12	13
61101	.5	86	.3	6	9.1	176	21.9	0	43	.2	22	0	100++
61102	22.0	50	7.4	66	24.2	297	56.2	8	10	5.4	14	0	.7
61103	50.7	85	18.4	62	27.0	334	73.6	8	13	20.5	11	1	.7
61104	.2	92	.0	0	14.5	252	51.6*	4	27	.1	23	0	.6
61107	27.6	97	10.3	76	38.2	365	118.4	6	13	12.8	11	2	.0
61108	48.5	94	19.2	59	26.6	328	81.8	7	13	22.0	11	3	1.4
61109	26.0	94	14.2	82	33.9	446	89.6	8	12	6.12	4	5	.9
61111	43.4	98	17.7	63	28.0	307	86.7	8	14	18.7	13	6	1.6

ROCK ISLAND

ZIPCODE	1	2	3	4	5	6	7	8	9	10	11	12	13
61201	47.5	83	17.7	63	28.0	307	86.7	8	14	18.7	13	7	.0
61230	1.5	99	.5	75	29.7	352	77.2	10	10	7	7	0	.0

ILLINOIS

ROCK ISLAND

ZIPCODE	1	2	3	4	5	6	7	8	9	10	11	12	13
61231	6.1	99	2.2	72	27.2	330	77.8	7	16	2.9	13	0	.0
61232	1.3	98	.4	77	32.5	383	88.3	9	6	.6	6	0	.0
61233	.6	0	.2	85	28.3	350	85.6	16	8	.6	5	0	.0
61234	1.5	100	.6	64	26.1	342	76.9	9	14	.8	12	0	.0
61235	1.7	99	.6	77	29.2	305	80.2	8	13	.9	12	2	.0
61236	.5	96	.2	89	25.0	281	60.1	10	6	.2	5	0	.0
61238	3.9	99	1.4	75	28.7	316	80.2	7	15	2.0	13	0	.0
61239	.6	100	.2	86	27.2	335	66.9	8	11	.3	7	0	.0
61240	6.2	98	1.8	91	37.4	390	112.8	8	7	3.1	6	0	.9
61241	7.9	97	2.5	83	30.3	392	87.0	11	5	3.9	4	0	.0
61242	1.3	0	.5	72	33.2	404	95.4	7	8	.0	0	0	50.5
61243	.3	98	.1	54	26.6	277	57.5	7	6	.2	8	0	.0
61244	24.8	90	9.2	69	29.2	329	85.0	8	11	10.9	10	2	4.4
61250	.3	99	.1	73	30.0	348	85.1	9	10	1.6	9	0	.0
61251	.4	100	.1	67	27.0	204	71.1	10	8	.9	8	0	.6
61252	5.9	99	2.1	79	26.4	325	71.1	7	14	2.9	12	0	.0
61254	11.7	99	4.0	76	32.9	367	113.6	7	14	5.7	11	1	.3
61256	1.8	97	.5	85	33.9	401	89.0	8	4	.9	4	0	.0
61257	1.6	100	.5	73	29.9	367	82.0	8	9	.8	8	0	.6
61258	.2	100	.1	79	23.2	215	51.0	5	19	.1	17	0	.0
61259	1.0	0	.3	81	29.9	372	105.8	6	13	.6	13	0	.0
61260	1.1	100	.4	72	22.1	294	54.6	7	13	.6	14	0	.0
61261	1.2	0	.4	78	28.4	377	61.6	8	8	.9	8	0	.1
61262	1.0	100	.3	83	31.0	370	120.6	7	9	.5	8	0	.0
61263	.8	100	.3	84	25.4	155	64.0	8	13	.4	14	0	.6
61264	12.6	98	4.4	80	31.0	327	90.1	9	8	6.1	7	0	.9
61265	50.7	96	19.7	66	31.0	362	97.1	7	13	22.8	11	2	.9
61270	8.2	99	2.9	73	28.1	322	80.9	7	14	4.0	12	5	1.6
61272	1.5	99	.5	72	23.0	216	53.4	8	12	.8	12	0	1.6
61273	3.8	0	1.2	80	33.8	379	106.7	10	8	.7	7	0	.0
61274	.5	100	.2	60	31.3	299	55.9	9	7	.2	7	0	.0
61275	3.8	99	1.3	84	31.7	299	106.0	8	10	1.8	10	0	.0
61276	.4	100	.4	86	31.1	344	90.2	8	9	.9	9	0	.8
61277	4.0	100	1.5	67	25.8	323	71.6	7	15	2.1	13	0	.9
61278	.8	99	.3	86	31.5	394	89.3	8	9	.4	9	0	.0
61279	1.2	100	.4	73	28.0	414	88.2	8	13	.6	9	0	.0
61281	2.6	99	.8	88	32.0	375	113.9	9	8	1.3	7	0	.0
61282	8.6	91	2.9	74	28.6	379	79.7	8	10	3.9	8	0	.9
61283	2.1	99	.7	72	27.0	338	59.5	8	12	1.1	10	0	.9
61284	2.9	98	.9	86	35.9	355	115.7	7	7	1.4	7	0	.0
61285	2.2	99	.8	76	26.3	295	73.3	9	10	1.1	10	0	.0

LA SALLE

ZIPCODE	1	2	3	4	5	6	7	8	9	10	11	12	13
61301	11.4	98	4.5	69	23.1	269	70.5	6	19	5.3	16	0	4.3
61310	4.1	100	1.4	74	25.5	310	63.6	7	14	2.0	11	1	.0
61311	.4	100	.1	63	27.5	332	72.6	9	9	.2	11	0	.0
61313	.5	100	.2	63	28.4	384	64.7	9	11	.3	11	0	.0
61314	1.2	0	.4	75	24.8	279	47.7	5	8	.0	0	0	.1
61315	.5	100	.2	63	21.4	290	52.9	8	13	.2	11	0	.0

*=Estimated **1.0=883 lbs per person; 100++ indicates per capita toxic waste generation > than 100 times the U.S. average of 883 lbs per capita.

103001

ZIP CODE MEASURES OF SIZE, LEVELS OF AFFLUENCE AND QUALITY OF LIFE

1=Population (th.); 2= % White; 3=Households (th.); 4=% Owner Occupied; 5=Mean Income Per Household (th.$); 6=Mean Monthly Rent ($)*; 7=Mean Home Value (th.$)*; 8=% under 5; 9=% 65 and over; 10=White Males (th.); 11=% White Males, 65+; 12=# Toxic Waste Sites; 13=Toxic Waste Relative to US(883 lbs.per capita)**.

ILLINOIS — LA SALLE

ZIPCODE	1	2	3	4	5	6	7	8	9	10	11	12	13
61316	.3	0	.1	79	28.3	276	66.6	7	14	.0	0	0	.0
61317	.5	0	.2	90	29.6	263	67.1	7	18	.0	0	0	.0
61318	.7	99	.2	82	30.0	285	59.0	7	13	.3	14	0	2.0
61319	1.0	99	.4	78	26.7	303	64.2	6	13	.5	12	0	.0
61320	.7	0	.2	91	27.8	358	76.8	8	15	.0	0	0	.0
61321	.5	0	.2	74	42.5	419	58.1	6	15	.0	0	0	4.7
61322	2.0	91	.7	80	23.5	304	52.5	8	14	.9	14	1	.0
61323	.2	100	.1	88	19.6	225*	52.5*	6	17	.1	17	0	.0
61325	1.3	0	.4	79	32.3	413	82.1	7	12	.7	12	0	.0
61326	2.4	100	.9	77	30.8	266	86.2	8	12	1.2	10	0	.1
61327	1.1	99	.4	82	32.7	296	97.0	9	10	.5	10	0	32.5
61329	1.4	100	.5	74	27.3	319	71.9	6	18	.7	17	0	.0
61330	1.7	100	.6	68	27.1	308	76.5	6	12	.8	11	0	.0
61332	2.1	100	1	96	32.5	374*	46.2*	8	17	.1	14	0	.0
61333	.5	100	.2	74	26.4	342	57.4	8	13	.3	12	0	.0
61334	.9	100	.3	72	30.7	444	72.8	8	15	.4	16	0	.0
61335	.7	0	.2	64	29.3	247	85.6	6	11	.0	0	0	.0
61336	.7	100	.2	69	26.8	246	69.4	9	14	.4	13	0	.0
61337	.5	0	.2	82	29.2	327	65.0	5	12	.0	0	0	.0
61338	.5	0	.2	69	24.5	260	54.7	7	17	.0	0	0	.6
61339	.6	0	.2	74	26.4	266	80.4	9	9	.3	8	0	.0
61340	.4	100	.1	91	22.7	340	65.3	10	17	.2	16	0	.0
61341	7.3	100	2.6	77	28.2	269	87.2	8	14	3.6	11	0	2.4
61342	8.9	96	3.2	72	28.0	303	85.8	8	15	4.1	12	2	2.1
61344	.5	100	.2	78	27.3	207	51.4	9	11	.3	8	0	.0
61345	1.1	100	.4	75	27.4	245	69.9	10	13	.5	13	0	1.5
61346	.2	0	.1	78	27.8	287	31.4	9	13	.2	16	0	.0
61348	5.2	99	2.0	75	25.3	274	76.3	6	16	2.6	15	0	.0
61349	1.2	0	.4	70	25.7	300	61.8	7	17	.0	0	0	.1
61350	24.1	98	9.0	69	28.9	323	85.9	7	15	11.4	11	6	1.5
61353	1.2	100	.4	71	29.2	337	69.3	6	16	.6	14	0	.0
61354	11.7	99	4.4	77	28.8	325	83.8	6	14	5.6	11	1	3.8
61356	11.4	99	4.3	69	30.2	334	98.7	7	16	5.3	13	1	.8
61358	.8	100	3.2	84	28.0	250	72.2	6	13	.4	8	0	.0
61359	.4	100	.1	86	22.1	327	52.6	13	20	.1	22	0	.7
61360	3.1	99	1.0	79	28.9	328	86.7	9	9	1.5	9	2	31.5
61361	2.0	0	.7	71	26.3	279	56.2	7	17	.0	0	0	.0
61362	6.1	99	2.3	77	25.8	281	78.2	7	18	2.9	15	1	.5
61363	.3	100	.1	84	28.0	250	72.2	6	13	.1	10	0	.0
61364	24.1	98	8.7	74	27.5	304	71.5	7	14	11.5	11	3	.7
61367	.9	99	.3	79	30.0	338	72.2	7	6	.5	7	0	.0
61368	1.8	99	.6	74	27.2	339	69.8	6	13	1.0	11	1	.1
61369	1.9	0	.7	72	26.0	310	71.2	7	21	.0	0	0	.0
61370	1.5	0	.5	77	27.9	300	74.2	7	14	.1	10	0	.0
61371	.2	100	.1	76	28.0	387	76.2	7	6	.1	9	0	.2
61372	.3	0	.1	87	30.5	325	76.9	13	10	.0	0	0	.0
61373	2.1	99	.7	83	28.7	300	79.0	7	13	1.0	11	0	7.0
61375	1.1	99	.4	78	26.8	305	84.2	7	15	.6	13	0	.0
61376	2.6	0	.9	71	26.6	304	76.0	7	18	.0	0	0	.1

ILLINOIS — LA SALLE (continued) / GATESBURG

ZIPCODE	1	2	3	4	5	6	7	8	9	10	11	12	13
LA SALLE													
61377	1.6	99	.6	79	28.8	213	65.8	5	16	.8	14	0	.0
61378	.8	100	.3	55	35.5	390	64.6	8	8	.4	8	0	.0
61379	1.5	99	.6	76	25.1	297	65.6	8	14	.7	13	0	.0
GATESBURG													
61401	39.8	93	15.1	67	26.2	301	75.7	7	15	17.4	12	5	1.3
61410	5.0	98	1.8	77	23.4	285	64.3	9	13	2.4	11	1	.0
61411	.6	100	.2	67	27.7	325	55.8	10	16	.3	14	0	.0
61412	2.0	100	.7	77	25.4	316	75.3	7	14	1.0	13	0	.2
61413	1.4	100	.5	85	27.9	287	81.0	8	11	.7	11	0	.0
61414	1.2	100	.4	72	25.1	301	62.7	9	12	.6	10	0	.0
61415	2.5	100	.9	74	22.2	262	61.6	8	14	1.2	11	0	.0
61416	.3	100	.1	73	19.2	297	47.8	7	14	.2	12	0	.0
61417	.5	100	.1	78	22.1	266	59.7	15	10	.2	11	0	.2
61418	.8	99	.3	74	23.7	302	54.1	10	13	.4	12	0	.5
61419	.2	100	.1	73	21.6	298	55.8	4	15	.1	8	0	.0
61420	1.5	0	.6	79	25.7	207	53.0	7	17	.0	0	0	.0
61421	2.0	100	.7	74	27.2	305	67.2	8	14	1.0	12	0	.0
61422	4.3	0	1.6	80	23.9	239	54.1	9	14	.0	0	1	.2
61423	.8	100	.3	72	27.2	220	69.6	7	8	.4	7	0	.0
61425	.6	100	.2	84	25.6	123	52.6	5	20	.3	20	0	.6
61427	2.7	100	1.0	84	26.2	331	74.0	8	15	1.3	13	1	.0
61428	.8	100	.3	85	27.8	311	85.5	6	9	.4	8	0	.0
61430	.5	100	.2	89	25.4	354	52.6	8	5	.2	7	0	.0
61431	.6	0	.2	82	25.1	251	46.8	8	12	.0	0	0	.0
61432	.8	100	.3	78	25.2	306	58.3	10	16	.4	13	0	.0
61433	.2	100	.1	76	19.2	268	63.3	13	14	.1	12	0	.0
61434	4.1	0	1.6	74	26.5	255	64.8	8	18	.0	0	0	.0
61435	1.2	100	.4	71	32.9	100	67.2	4	19	.1	23	0	1.5
61436	.4	100	.2	78	25.0	318	61.1	10	10	.6	10	0	.0
61437	1.1	99	.4	77	25.0	274	73.8	9	10	.6	9	0	.0
61438	.9	0	.3	70	25.8	224	62.2	7	13	.0	0	0	.0
61439	.4	0	.1	85	31.0	301	71.6	7	8	.0	0	0	.0
61440	1.0	99	.4	79	23.1	259	51.9	8	17	.4	13	0	.0
61441	1.3	100	.5	79	24.3	280	46.0	7	14	.7	14	0	.0
61442	2.1	98	.8	74	22.7	296	46.0	7	14	.7	13	0	.1
61443	16.8	95	6.5	78	24.2	243	53.1	8	19	7.7	14	0	.4
61447	1.4	100	.5	75	24.2	388	58.5	7	18	.0	0	0	.0
61448	4.6	100	1.6	83	28.4	216	36.2	6	8	2.1	15	0	.1
61449	.6	0	.2	79	22.5	274	84.2	8	11	.0	0	0	.0
61450	2.1	0	.8	74	21.9	418	50.7	7	13	.0	0	0	.0
61451	.5	100	.4	75	23.1	243	53.1	8	12	.2	11	0	.0
61452	.4	0	1	72	19.6	388	52.2	8	14	.0	0	0	.2
61453	.9	0	.3	64	23.5	216	39.7	8	9	.0	0	0	.0
61454	1.0	0	.4	80	22.5	280	53.1	8	11	.0	0	0	.0
61455	24.1	94	7.5	56	23.6	292	77.8	9	11	11.2	7	3	.6
61458	1.1	0	.4	78	25.1	235	52.2	8	9	.0	0	0	.3
61459	.4	99	.1	86	23.5	182	39.7	8	11	.0	0	0	.0
61460	.4	100	.4	67	26.5	365	56.1	8	10	.2	9	0	.1
61462	13.3	0	4.8	70	25.3	277	68.2	8	15	6.0	12	1	.1

*=Estimated **1.0=883 lbs per person; 100++ indicates per capita toxic waste generation > than 100 times the U.S. average of 883 lbs per capita.

ZIP CODE MEASURES OF SIZE, LEVELS OF AFFLUENCE AND QUALITY OF LIFE

1=Population (th.); 2= % White; 3=Households (th.); 4=% Owner Occupied; 5=Mean Income Per Household (th.$); 6=Mean Monthly Rent ($)*; 7=Mean Home Value (th.$)*; 8=% under 5; 9=% 65 and over; 10=White Males (th.); 11=% White Males, 65+; 12=# Toxic Waste Sites; 13=Toxic Waste Relative to US(883 lbs.per capita)**.

ILLINOIS

GATESBURG

ZIPCODE	1	2	3	4	5	6	7	8	9	10	11	12	13
61465	1.4	99	.5	79	30.3	304	74.5	8	14	.7	12	0	.0
61466	.5	100	.5	83	26.1	330	57.0	9	11	.2	11	0	.0
61467	1.3	0	.5	72	30.3	292	69.7	8	12	.0	0	0	.0
61469	2.3	100	.9	80	21.7	260	61.1	8	13	1.1	12	0	.0
61470	.8	0	.3	79	23.5	270	43.7	7	22	.0	0	0	.0
61471	.2	0	.1	99	23.0	265*	41.0	7	20	.0	0	0	.0
61472	.8	99	.3	79	25.9	258	83.9	4	13	.4	13	0	.0
61473	2.4	0	.9	73	27.2	262	63.9	6	21	.0	0	0	.0
61474	.5	100	.2	78	22.9	261	70.4	5	16	.2	15	0	.0
61475	.3	100	.1	57	24.7	228	32.1	6	18	.1	13	0	.0
61476	.6	0	.2	69	26.7	140	53.0	7	13	.0	13	0	.0
61477	.9	0	.3	83	25.7	324	54.3	8	13	.0	0	0	.0
61478	.4	0	.2	67	25.9	228	37.6	5	11	.0	0	0	.0
61479	.2	100	.1	86	29.0	334*	76.6	13	7	.1	6	0	.2
61480	1.5	100	.6	73	26.5	288	63.6	7	17	.7	15	0	.0
61482	.9	100	.3	79	21.3	274	48.8	10	17	.4	15	0	.0
61483	2.4	99	.9	75	26.9	283	72.1	7	19	1.1	16	0	.0
61484	1.3	0	.5	80	20.4	267	45.3	7	19	.0	0	1	.3
61485	.7	100	.2	69	25.7	311	55.0	10	13	.4	14	0	.0
61486	1.9	100	.6	77	27.1	299	71.8	7	9	.9	9	1	.0
61488	1.1	99	.5	72	26.5	290	75.1	11	9	.7	8	1	.0
61489	1.1	99	.4	77	26.6	275	66.1	8	18	.6	14	0	.0
61490	1.3	100	.5	73	25.6	326	64.7	9	14	.7	12	0	.0
61491	2.6	0	1.0	74	27.0	277	73.5	7	15	.0	0	1	2.7

PEORIA

ZIPCODE	1	2	3	4	5	6	7	8	9	10	11	12	13
61501	2.5	100	1.0	79	21.6	246	50.7	7	20	1.2	16	1	.8
61516	.8	0	.3	81	29.1	209	75.9	9	15	.1	0	0	.8
61517	2.8	100	.9	83	33.4	352	103.5	9	11	1.4	10	0	.5
61519	.4	100	.1	86	25.3	249	45.7	6	11	.0	0	0	.0
61520	18.5	99	7.1	74	26.1	297	73.9	7	16	8.8	14	1	.0
61523	10.6	99	3.8	80	31.2	379	89.4	8	10	5.1	8	0	.1
61524	.3	100	.1	91	25.8	296*	50.9	12	13	.0	0	0	.0
61525	3.9	99	1.3	80	43.1	449	152.8	9	6	1.9	6	0	.0
61526	1.8	99	.5	88	35.7	585	125.3	9	7	.9	5	0	.0
61528	1.8	100	.5	92	38.8	342	107.5	7	7	.9	6	1	.0
61529	3.1	0	1.1	78	29.0	307	77.2	8	12	.9	9	0	.1
61530	5.9	98	1.9	71	29.7	306	100.7	9	14	2.8	11	0	.3
61531	4.2	0	1.5	76	25.3	356	71.7	8	15	.0	0	0	.1
61532	.8	100	.3	74	23.9	342	65.6	6	10	.5	8	0	.0
61533	1.1	100	.4	82	33.8	387	97.6	9	7	.6	7	3	.3
61534	1.9	0	.6	83	30.2	264	81.9	9	7	.7	6	0	.1
61535	.5	100	.2	84	44.9	455	123.2	9	12	.3	13	0	.4
61536	4.9	98	1.6	81	29.2	341	84.3	8	9	2.4	9	0	.0
61537	3.7	100	1.3	74	26.3	316	83.9	9	14	1.8	13	0	11.2
61539	.7	0	.2	85	28.0	416	69.9	7	15	.0	0	0	.0
61540	3.2	100	1.2	77	27.6	340	83.5	8	17	1.5	13	0	.1
61541	.2	0	.1	85	26.6	306*	58.5	5	26	.0	0	0	.7
61542	4.7	100	1.7	78	24.3	341	70.6	7	15	2.2	12	0	.0
61543	.3	100	.1	72	19.5	363	39.9	12	12	.0	0	1	.0

ILLINOIS

PEORIA

ZIPCODE	1	2	3	4	5	6	7	8	9	10	11	12	13
61544	1.2	0	.4	81	27.0	352	47.3	7	10	.7	0	0	.0
61545	.8	0	.2	75	27.7	457	73.9	10	9	.2	0	0	.0
61546	5.0	100	1.7	81	28.4	358	81.6	8	9	2.5	7	0	.0
61547	1.9	100	.6	92	38.5	446	122.7	9	6	1.0	5	1	23.2
61548	7.9	100	2.5	85	34.5	424	112.2	9	7	3.9	6	0	.1
61549	.2	100	.1	78	19.8	213	59.7	7	9	.1	9	0	.0
61550	16.1	100	5.6	76	40.4	427	142.2	8	9	7.7	8	0	.3
61552	.3	100	.1	76	26.5	402	62.0	15	7	.2	9	0	100++
61553	.3	0	.1	64	21.8	301	44.2	11	11	.0	0	0	.0
61554	45.4	99	16.6	72	28.9	335	84.5	9	10	21.7	8	2	.1
61559	2.9	0	1.0	77	29.5	359	86.1	7	12	.0	0	0	.4
61560	.6	0	.6	77	26.7	403	111.6	8	8	.0	0	0	.9
61561	2.7	100	.9	80	31.0	338	97.6	8	14	.0	0	0	.0
61562	.3	100	.1	93	32.1	369*	89.2	7	11	.2	6	0	.0
61563	.8	0	.3	86	21.8	334	55.3	7	11	.0	0	0	.0
61564	1.3	98	.4	80	23.8	335	59.6	13	5	.6	4	0	.0
61565	1.8	100	.6	78	31.8	312	96.0	6	7	1.0	7	0	.0
61567	.4	0	.4	84	22.1	213	47.8	8	10	.0	0	0	.0
61568	4.1	0	1.3	80	36.1	338	108.6	8	11	.4	4	0	.3
61569	1.2	0	.4	85	31.9	344	100.7	10	10	.9	9	2	.0
61570	2.0	99	.7	79	27.1	309	77.7	9	13	.7	8	0	.0
61571	19.9	99	6.7	77	33.1	422	94.5	8	7	9.7	6	2	.0
61572	1.3	100	.5	75	27.3	275	65.3	7	12	.7	10	0	.0

PEORIA

ZIPCODE	1	2	3	4	5	6	7	8	9	10	11	12	13
61603	.8	79	.5	16	15.4	186	26.4	3	20	.3	24	0	18.8
61604	23.9	85	9.3	57	22.6	299	63.9	9	14	9.3	13	1	1.3
61605	35.1	92	13.3	75	30.0	353	83.6	7	17	14.9	14	1	.0
61606	25.9	53	9.0	57	19.2	253	45.7	11	12	6.5	15	1	.0
61607	11.4	85	3.7	39	24.9	328	88.9	5	6	5.0	5	0	.6
61611	12.6	99	4.3	84	31.5	425	86.2	8	9	6.2	8	5	.2
61614	33.6	99	11.8	77	30.9	361	88.3	8	9	16.4	8	3	7.6
61615	41.1	94	16.2	66	39.1	424	122.1	6	12	18.5	10	0	.1
61616	12.1	93	4.3	77	39.0	403	131.4	8	7	5.6	7	0	.1

BLOOMINGTON

ZIPCODE	1	2	3	4	5	6	7	8	9	10	11	12	13
61701	52.5	94	21.1	61	27.7	310	100.2	8	12	23.1	9	3	.2
61720	.4	100	.1	64	39.0	382	64.0	9	14	.2	13	0	.0
61721	.7	100	.3	77	25.6	345	65.3	8	13	.4	12	0	.0
61722	.6	99	.2	68	30.3	221	63.3	8	11	.3	11	0	.6
61723	2.6	99	.9	77	26.0	310	70.2	8	15	1.3	12	1	.6
61724	.7	0	.3	75	27.1	234	54.2	10	15	.6	7	0	.0
61725	1.3	100	.4	77	32.4	364	100.1	10	7	.6	7	0	.6
61726	3.0	98	1.0	69	30.4	339	73.0	6	17	1.5	14	0	.6
61727	10.5	99	4.1	67	26.1	304	75.9	8	15	5.0	11	2	.6
61728	1.4	100	.5	71	28.0	283	66.5	9	19	.7	13	0	.5
61729	1.1	0	.3	82	32.4	343	122.5	11	6	.3	6	0	.0
61730	.5	100	.2	67	27.9	247	53.6	10	12	.3	12	0	.0
61731	.3	100	.1	70	25.2	341	57.8	5	12	.1	0	0	.7
61732	1.8	0	.6	80	29.1	299	76.5	8	12	.2	10	0	.0
61733	1.1	100	.4	72	31.5	393	92.6	8	7	.6	6	0	.0

*=Estimated **1.0=883 lbs per person; 100++ indicates per capita toxic waste generation > than 100 times the U.S. average of 883 lbs per capita.

ZIP CODE MEASURES OF SIZE, LEVELS OF AFFLUENCE AND QUALITY OF LIFE

1=Population (th.); 2= % White; 3=Households (th.); 4=% Owner Occupied; 5=Mean Income Per Household (th.); 6=Mean Monthly Rent ($)*; 7=Mean Home Value (th.$)*; 8=% under 5; 9=% 65 and over; 10=White Males (th.); 11=% White Males, 65+; 12=# Toxic Waste Sites; 13=Toxic Waste Relative to US(883 lbs.per capita)**.

ILLINOIS

BLOOMINGTON

ZIPCODE	1	2	3	4	5	6	7	8	9	10	11	12	13
61734	3.1	100	1.1	76	29.2	286	82.7	8	13	1.6	10	0	.0
61735	.4	100	.1	80	26.1	284	60.9	10	9	.2	10	0	.0
61736	1.1	0	.4	79	32.1	367	76.5	12	8	.0	0	0	.0
61737	.6	0	.2	78	28.3	408	76.9	6	14	.0	0	0	.0
61738	4.0	100	1.4	74	28.0	347	76.7	8	16	1.9	13	0	7.9
61739	4.7	99	1.7	72	30.3	367	80.9	8	18	2.2	14	0	.4
61740	1.6	99	.6	72	30.2	294	80.0	6	20	.8	17	0	.0
61741	2.1	0	.7	73	35.3	275	77.5	9	11	.0	0	0	.0
61742	.6	100	.2	79	33.3	392	100.5	12	11	.3	11	0	.0
61743	.3	95	.1	75	30.9	444	68.3	10	11	.2	8	0	.0
61744	2.0	100	.7	76	31.7	331	85.7	9	13	1.0	11	0	.2
61745	3.0	100	1.1	80	31.7	298	84.2	7	11	1.5	9	0	.0
61747	1.5	98	.5	77	28.1	322	82.0	9	19	.7	16	0	.0
61748	2.0	100	.7	80	35.4	439	104.3	6	8	1.0	8	0	.0
61749	.8	100	.3	74	25.5	304	59.9	9	13	.4	11	0	.9
61751	.1	100	.1	84	40.4	464*	42.8	9	27	.1	14	0	.0
61752	3.8	100	1.3	72	30.1	298	75.5	7	11	1.9	10	0	.0
61753	3.0	99	1.1	74	29.8	276	87.6	8	12	1.5	9	0	.0
61754	1.4	100	.5	72	26.8	399	68.9	8	13	.7	11	0	.0
61755	3.1	100	1.0	83	32.7	393	93.1	8	9	1.6	8	0	.2
61756	2.5	100	.9	75	28.2	328	71.8	8	11	1.2	9	0	.0
61759	1.6	100	.6	71	30.1	354	84.3	8	15	.8	12	0	.0
61760	2.6	100	1.0	82	27.4	292	68.7	7	19	1.2	17	1	.0
61761	36.2	92	9.9	61	29.5	413	110.2	5	5	15.7	4	0	.0
61764	14.5	87	4.7	68	29.5	317	83.6	6	14	6.2	11	1	.8
61769	.8	100	.3	78	28.3	334	60.5	10	15	.4	13	0	.0
61770	1.4	0	.5	69	25.3	283	55.9	9	13	.0	0	0	.0
61771	.8	0	.3	78	27.0	359	60.1	7	13	.0	0	0	.0
61772	.6	100	.2	76	37.4	432	96.0	5	8	.3	9	0	.1
61773	.6	0	.2	69	24.8	257	48.7	7	20	.0	0	0	.0
61774	1.1	0	.4	73	30.0	365	67.5	11	9	.0	0	0	.0
61775	.4	100	.1	58	30.0	340	73.3	11	7	.2	9	0	.2
61776	1.5	100	.5	78	37.8	316	104.6	8	8	.8	7	0	.0
61777	1.2	0	.4	73	30.4	314	66.8	10	9	.4	0	0	.0
61778	.9	99	.3	88	24.3	307	51.6	8	12	.4	11	0	.0

CHAMPAIGN (NORTH)

ZIPCODE	1	2	3	4	5	6	7	8	9	10	11	12	13
61801	45.8	87	15.9	49	25.7	374	96.9	6	7	19.6	6	1	.0
61810	.5	0	.2	68	31.6	283	63.3	5	15	.0	0	0	4.1
61811	.8	0	.3	75	28.3	231	68.5	9	10	.0	0	0	.0
61812	.5	0	.2	80	29.1	285	63.5	6	10	.0	0	0	.0
61813	2.2	99	.8	79	26.3	325	71.0	8	12	1.1	11	0	.0
61814	1.0	100	.3	85	26.1	406	82.5	12	11	.5	8	0	.0
61815	.4	100	.1	65	28.8	356	69.6	5	6	.2	5	0	.0
61816	.5	0	.2	77	27.8	413	64.3	7	16	.0	0	0	.0
61817	2.9	100	.9	83	31.3	395	85.8	7	13	.9	10	0	.0
61818	1.9	100	.6	78	27.1	329	72.4	10	13	.9	10	0	.0
61820	68.1	85	24.8	51	27.3	373	102.3	5	7	30.3	5	0	.1
61830	.6	100	.2	69	29.5	379	64.7	7	12	.3	10	0	.0
61831	.2	0	.1	74	24.5	287	51.9	8	12	.1	0	0	.0

ILLINOIS

CHAMPAIGN (NORTH)

ZIPCODE	1	2	3	4	5	6	7	8	9	10	11	12	13
61832	56.6	87	21.5	68	24.9	286	69.8	8	14	23.7	12	10	1.9
61839	.8	0	.3	62	32.5	306	66.7	9	8	.0	0	1	.0
61840	.7	0	.2	75	37.5	390	108.7	7	11	.0	0	0	.0
61841	1.6	0	.6	84	28.4	261	67.0	7	12	.0	0	2	.0
61842	3.4	100	1.3	69	28.5	350	76.0	8	16	1.7	14	0	1.0
61843	2.0	100	.7	73	28.6	281	77.7	8	11	1.0	9	0	.1
61844	1.1	99	.4	81	28.9	239	64.7	6	13	.5	9	0	.0
61845	.4	100	.1	65	28.9	353	48.9	6	8	.2	9	0	.0
61846	5.9	95	2.1	80	22.5	308	60.4	7	12	2.7	10	0	.5
61847	1.3	99	.4	75	28.4	294	80.2	8	15	.6	11	0	.0
61848	.3	100	.1	83	21.3	307	53.1	10	10	.1	9	0	.0
61849	1.9	0	.7	77	30.1	286	71.7	6	12	.0	0	0	.0
61850	.8	0	.3	78	24.0	301	45.9	11	8	.1	16	0	.0
61851	.6	100	.2	76	30.9	288	61.8	8	16	.3	12	0	.0
61852	.3	0	.1	77	33.2	213	53.8	6	20	.0	0	0	.0
61853	6.4	0	2.3	81	30.7	347	108.0	10	6	.0	0	0	.0
61854	1.4	0	.5	76	29.6	272	67.9	8	11	.0	0	0	.0
61855	.2	100	.1	85	27.7	188	59.9	5	15	.1	16	0	.0
61856	6.3	99	2.3	76	31.7	286	98.4	6	14	3.0	10	0	.3
61857	.2	0	.1	71	21.8	310	48.1	5	9	.0	0	2	.0
61858	2.9	0	1.0	80	27.0	348	77.1	9	7	.0	0	0	.1
61859	1.2	100	.4	81	28.7	326	72.6	9	10	.6	8	2	.0
61862	.6	0	.3	73	27.7	437	70.9	6	11	.0	0	0	.0
61863	1.0	100	.4	85	29.6	416	81.3	9	12	.5	11	0	.0
61864	1.2	99	.4	83	33.4	413	86.9	8	10	.6	9	0	.0
61865	1.5	0	.5	78	24.9	247	55.1	8	13	.3	14	0	.8
61866	21.5	86	6.1	42	24.6	273	85.9	9	14	10.4	3	0	.2
61870	1.7	100	.6	75	24.6	241	53.2	9	14	.8	11	0	.0
61871	.3	100	.1	89	26.0	385	82.7	10	20	.1	16	0	.0
61872	.8	0	.3	75	27.6	409	72.9	7	12	.0	0	0	.0
61873	3.9	100	1.4	79	30.3	297	93.8	8	7	1.9	6	0	.0
61874	2.1	93	.8	41	27.5	324	138.7	10	5	.9	5	0	.0
61875	.7	99	.3	66	32.0	299	105.7	6	11	.4	10	0	.0
61876	.9	0	.3	77	32.0	236	55.8	7	16	.0	0	0	.0
61877	1.3	0	.5	75	28.2	351	80.4	7	12	.8	10	0	.0
61878	1.5	98	.6	63	28.2	304	84.7	7	10	.8	9	0	.6
61880	3.2	0	1.1	75	29.3	296	80.5	9	8	.0	0	0	.0
61883	5.1	100	1.9	80	23.5	279	57.6	7	14	2.4	13	0	.1
61884	.9	0	.3	78	34.8	258	100.6	5	8	.0	0	0	.0

CHAMPAIGN (SOUTH)

ZIPCODE	1	2	3	4	5	6	7	8	9	10	11	12	13
61910	4.1	98	1.3	71	28.5	291	68.6	8	13	2.0	10	0	.0
61911	4.1	100	1.3	75	25.6	293	76.3	11	14	2.0	12	0	.2
61912	1.5	100	.5	81	26.9	341	58.3	10	10	.8	10	0	.0
61913	2.1	0	.8	75	25.8	318	63.3	8	14	.6	0	0	.0
61914	.6	100	.2	74	30.7	379	112.2	6	6	.3	7	0	.0
61917	.9	100	.3	70	23.2	235	41.8	11	14	.4	13	0	.0
61919	.7	100	.3	84	26.5	301	80.1	5	11	.4	10	0	.1
61920	22.8	96	7.2	59	23.3	343	80.3	5	10	10.2	7	1	.1

*=Estimated **1.0=883 lbs per person; 100++ indicates per capita toxic waste generation > than 100 times the U.S. average of 883 lbs per capita.

ZIP CODE MEASURES OF SIZE, LEVELS OF AFFLUENCE AND QUALITY OF LIFE

1=Population (th.); 2= % White; 3=Households (th.); 4=% Owner Occupied; 5=Mean Income Per Household (th.$); 6=Mean Monthly Rent ($); 7=Mean Home Value (th.$); 8=% under 5, 9=% 65 and over; 10=White Males (th.); 11=% White Males, 65+; 12=# Toxic Waste Sites; 13=Toxic Waste Relative to US(883 lbs.per capita)**.

ILLINOIS

CHAMPAIGN (SOUTH)

ZIPCODE	1	2	3	4	5	6	7	8	9	10	11	12	13
61924	2.9	100	1.1	73	24.4	242	62.2	7	19	1.4	16	0	.0
61925	.8	100	.3	82	34.0	349	86.2	9	12	.4	13	0	.0
61928	.8	100	.3	72	24.8	314	63.4	8	13	.4	10	0	.0
61929	.9	100	.3	80	26.2	328	59.0	6	18	.4	17	0	.0
61930	.7	100	.3	73	24.7	338	43.7	6	18	.3	14	0	.8
61931	1.3	0	.4	82	25.8	299	60.1	9	12	.0	14	0	.0
61932	.6	99	.2	79	26.2	319	48.2	7	16	.3	13	0	.0
61933	1.3	0	.5	78	21.4	220	57.6	9	19	.0	0	0	.2
61935	.6	94	.2	66	35.1	297	85.6	9	9	.3	0	0	.0
61936	.3	100	.1	79	28.9	327	52.9	3	4	.2	0	0	.0
61937	2.1	0	.7	76	27.2	258	63.7	7	15	.7	14	0	.0
61938	23.0	99	9.0	70	25.0	271	70.0	7	15	10.6	12	4	.0
61940	.4	100	.1	69	21.7	313	29.6	10	14	.2	13	0	.8
61941	.1	0	.1	91	19.6	225*	38.1	6	24	.0	0	0	.0
61942	1.5	100	.6	73	28.1	263	54.9	9	18	.9	14	0	.0
61943	1.9	99	.8	79	24.6	260	54.8	7	13	.9	11	0	.3
61944	14.6	100	5.7	75	22.8	263	61.4	7	16	6.9	13	1	.5
61949	.2	100	.1	66	17.1	296	37.6	9	14	.1	7	0	.0
61951	7.3	99	2.7	76	25.7	315	72.0	7	19	3.4	16	2	.6
61953	6.1	100	2.3	74	28.6	307	54.9	9	18	2.9	11	0	.3
61955	.3	100	.1	81	21.6	284	35.4	5	11	.1	6	2	.0
61956	3.1	99	1.1	77	27.4	289	65.6	7	11	1.5	9	1	.1
61957	2.1	99	.8	80	25.5	228	55.7	6	18	1.0	16	0	.0

SAINT LOUIS

ZIPCODE	1	2	3	4	5	6	7	8	9	10	11	12	13
62001	1.5	0	.5	84	27.7	313	72.4	5	20	.0	0	0	.0
62002	39.3	80	14.8	71	24.1	269	58.2	7	16	14.8	14	3	2.3
62006	.6	0	.2	97	21.4	245*	47.3	9	12	.0	0	0	.0
62009	1.9	0	.8	84	19.8	262	56.2	5	25	.0	0	0	.0
62010	8.9	99	3.0	84	26.9	330	69.3	8	8	4.3	8	0	.0
62011	.4	0	.1	79	18.5	285	31.4	13	13	.0	0	0	.0
62012	5.9	99	1.8	86	28.6	378	73.5	8	14	2.9	8	2	.0
62013	.6	100	.2	68	25.3	197	49.8	5	14	.3	14	0	.0
62014	3.7	99	1.2	84	25.8	223	62.6	8	12	1.9	11	0	.0
62015	.7	99	.2	73	24.2	242	71.1	5	13	.4	12	0	.0
62016	4.3	99	1.6	76	21.5	260	59.3	7	16	2.0	14	0	.0
62017	1.3	0	.5	82	23.8	290	57.1	7	16	.7	4	0	.0
62018	5.0	99	1.7	75	23.8	286	48.2	10	7	2.4	8	0	.0
62019	.5	100	.2	85	18.1	282	36.5	8	21	.1	21	0	.0
62021	.9	100	.3	90	28.7	365	91.8	6	11	.4	10	0	.0
62022	1.3	0	.4	86	29.3	392	77.1	8	8	.0	0	0	.0
62023	.1	100	.1	73	13.6	140	33.3	9	27	.0	21	0	.0
62024	14.1	100	5.2	75	27.3	297	70.5	6	12	6.7	10	1	2.8
62025	25.2	92	9.1	73	29.8	348	92.7	6	12	11.2	10	1	1.3
62027	.8	100	.3	60	19.9	267	35.7	5	15	.4	15	0	.0
62028	1.5	98	.3	66	29.3	303	76.9	5	4	.7	4	0	.0
62031	1.4	0	.5	76	22.9	182	46.0	7	11	.0	0	1	.0
62032	.9	99	.3	83	20.0	242	58.5	9	16	.5	14	0	.0
62033	5.1	100	2.0	83	22.5	229	57.1	8	17	2.4	14	0	.0
62034	3.2	99	1.1	86	31.1	353	96.2	7	12	1.6	6	0	.0

ILLINOIS

SAINT LOUIS

ZIPCODE	1	2	3	4	5	6	7	8	9	10	11	12	13
62035	14.4	96	4.7	89	33.1	354	85.6	6	9	6.7	8	1	.5
62036	.6	100	.2	85	22.0	312	56.6	4	18	.3	15	0	.0
62037	2.0	99	.7	81	23.8	218	56.3	9	11	1.0	10	0	1.0
62040	52.9	99	18.8	74	27.7	299	66.5	7	10	25.2	8	11	2.5
62044	2.2	100	.8	75	23.7	251	58.0	8	17	1.1	15	0	.0
62045	.6	0	.2	87	19.1	98	31.2	7	21	.0	0	0	.0
62046	.5	99	.2	75	37.0	399	81.4	9	8	.2	4	0	.7
62047	1.8	0	.6	73	21.6	245	61.3	6	19	.0	0	0	.0
62048	1.8	100	.7	77	26.2	273	46.2	7	14	.9	12	4	.0
62049	7.2	100	2.8	76	23.9	262	67.1	7	18	3.4	15	1	19.5
62050	.8	100	.3	64	17.8	160	24.6	7	13	.4	12	0	8.1
62051	1.1	0	.4	80	22.4	184	48.1	7	13	.1	0	0	.0
62052	11.0	99	4.0	76	25.2	284	63.1	7	15	5.2	12	1	.0
62053	.8	0	.3	78	17.4	172	42.2	6	27	.0	0	0	.0
62054	1.0	0	.3	77	21.0	280	44.9	8	12	.6	10	1	.0
62056	9.3	100	3.5	77	23.8	282	60.0	7	18	4.4	14	2	.3
62058	1.0	0	.4	85	21.5	280	45.1	6	19	.0	0	0	.0
62060	8.7	56	3.2	58	20.3	264	37.9	8	14	2.3	14	0	1.5
62061	1.2	99	.5	76	28.3	301	78.0	7	12	.7	10	0	.0
62062	1.2	97	.5	46	24.3	372	71.8	8	16	.6	13	0	.0
62063	1.3	100	.4	78	26.7	313	48.5	7	9	.7	8	0	.0
62064	.3	100	.1	81	21.2	244*	90.8	5	18	.2	16	0	.0
62065	.1	100	.1	88	22.4	258*	39.3	9	17	.1	14	0	.0
62067	1.6	0	.5	80	29.5	337	63.9	7	7	.0	0	0	.0
62069	3.4	0	1.3	83	21.2	276	57.9	7	24	.0	0	0	.0
62074	1.1	0	.4	85	24.2	271	52.0	7	16	.0	0	0	.0
62075	4.4	100	1.7	80	23.0	247	51.4	7	18	2.0	15	0	.0
62076	.2	0	.1	88	20.2	232*	47.1	9	19	.0	0	0	.0
62077	.5	100	.2	89	22.5	156	39.5	5	18	.1	16	0	.0
62078	.2	100	.1	88	16.4	188*	26.6	6	27	.1	20	0	.0
62079	.3	100	.1	84	28.7	297	58.9	3	18	.1	21	0	.0
62080	2.6	100	1.0	82	18.8	245	55.5	6	19	1.3	15	0	.0
62081	.4	100	.1	80	20.8	195	32.0	6	19	.2	18	0	.0
62082	3.6	100	1.4	77	19.4	240	44.0	8	16	1.7	15	0	.0
62083	.3	100	.1	85	19.4	273	45.8	8	15	.1	11	0	.0
62084	1.6	100	.6	71	25.4	321	53.2	5	14	.7	13	1	.0
62085	.3	100	.1	89	21.8	272	45.0	8	16	.1	11	0	.0
62086	1.6	100	.5	85	21.8	282	43.7	9	11	.8	10	0	.0
62087	2.3	99	.7	79	26.5	229	48.3	8	6	1.1	5	0	.0
62088	6.2	100	2.5	83	22.9	256	63.1	6	19	3.0	16	0	1.7
62089	.5	98	.2	80	22.0	231	47.4	7	18	.2	17	0	.0
62090	1.6	62	.6	66	17.5	249	35.0	6	12	.4	17	3	.0
62091	.4	100	.1	81	24.4	335	37.4	8	14	.2	14	0	.1
62092	3.5	100	1.3	71	19.9	239	44.6	7	21	.3	17	0	1.7
62093	.6	100	.3	87	19.6	324	38.6	6	20	.6	18	1	.0
62094	1.6	0	.6	78	20.4	250	47.8	6	18	.3	17	0	.0
62095	12.0	99	4.6	70	20.5	319	57.8	9	13	5.6	11	5	5.3
62097	2.2	0	.7	89	28.4	271	65.1	7	12	.0	5	0	.0

*=Estimated **=1.0-883 lbs per person; 100++ indicates per capita toxic waste generation > than 100 times the U.S. average of 883 lbs per capita.

ZIP CODE MEASURES OF SIZE, LEVELS OF AFFLUENCE AND QUALITY OF LIFE

1=Population (th.); 2= % White; 3=Households (th.); 4=% Owner Occupied; 5=Mean Income Per Household (th.$); 6=Mean Monthly Rent ($); 7=Mean Home Value (th.$)*; 8=% under 5; 9=% 65 and over; 10=% White Males (th.); 11=% White Males, 65+; 12=# Toxic Waste Sites; 13=Toxic Waste Relative to US(883 lbs.per capita)**

ILLINOIS — SAINT LOUIS

ZIPCODE	1	2	3	4	5	6	7	8	9	10	11	12	13
62201	13.1	25	4.5	43	15.1	229	37.3	9	12	1.6	11	10	28.6
62203	15.2	19	4.5	73	20.7	331	39.6	6	6	1.5	16	0	.0
62204	19.0	27	5.9	52	15.4	254	28.5	11	9	2.4	19	1	.0
62205	21.3	3	6.5	51	17.5	265	33.2	11	9	.2	23	1	1.8
62206	21.4	97	6.7	79	26.4	347	47.9	8	8	10.5	4	0	.0
62207	13.4	4	4.3	54	16.1	263	30.8	9	11	.3	11	2	.3
62208	12.6	98	4.3	84	31.7	386	84.9	6	12	5.9	10	0	.0
62214	.6	100	.2	77	26.7	189	71.0	8	13		13	0	.0
62215	1.2	100	.3	84	28.7	313	75.4	9	9	.6	7	0	.0
62216	1.0	100	.3	80	28.6	288	70.9	9	11	.5	11	1	.1
62217	1.1	100	.4	81	25.6	236	57.2	11	13	.6	13	1	.0
62218	1.3	0	.4	88	27.0	198	84.4	10	9	.6	0	0	.0
62219	1.1	0	.4	87	21.5	273	49.1	8	15	.0	0	0	.8
62220	.9	95	.4	29	17.3	243	67.4	5	31	.4	25	0	.4
62221	50.7	97	18.9	68	28.2	369	87.0	7	13	23.4	10	4	.0
62223	25.7	99	10.1	70	32.9	390	96.7	5	19	11.7	14	1	.1
62225	8.6	76	2.0	6	21.7	312	129.2	12	0	3.7	1	0	.0
62230	5.3	99	1.7	78	26.7	278	76.4	8	12	2.6	9	0	.0
62231	6.3	98	2.1	77	24.6	308	76.5	8	16	3.0	13	0	.4
62232	7.9	99	2.8	84	25.2	288	63.4	8	10	3.9	9	0	.0
62233	7.2	96	2.6	77	26.4	203	64.9	6	18	3.4	15	0	.1
62234	29.6	98	11.0	74	28.8	325	81.3	7	11	13.9	10	1	.0
62236	6.6	99	2.4	79	31.4	322	93.1	6	11	3.2	10	0	.0
62237	2.5	97	.9	84	26.2	285	58.2	8	12	1.2	10	0	.0
62238	.6	0	.3	82	22.6	216	42.3	9	11		10	1	.0
62239	3.9	99	1.5	71	24.1	267	58.6	7	13	1.9	10	1	.6
62240	2.7	95	1.0	76	25.2	332	57.6	9	10	1.3	9	1	.0
62241	1.1	100	.4	79	26.7	356	61.3	10	18	.5	18	0	.0
62242	1.8	0	.6	76	24.6	279	56.8	7	16	.0	0	0	.0
62243	5.0	98	1.7	80	28.0	296	86.2	9	11	2.4	10	1	.1
62244	.7	100	.3	83	22.7	261*	52.3	9	12	.4	12	0	.0
62245	2.0	100	.6	83	27.5	297	76.4	11	8	1.0	8	0	.0
62246	8.3	98	3.0	73	24.4	259	70.9	7	17	3.9	14	1	.2
62248	.6	0		76	29.0	347	83.2	11	15		0	0	.0
62249	10.8	99	3.7	77	28.9	344	86.3	8	13	5.1	11	1	.6
62250	.5	0	.2	81	26.1	305	70.1	9	13		10	1	.0
62252	.2	100	.1	90	26.6	306*	40.6	5	10	.1	10	0	.1
62253	.9	100	.3	83	21.3	254	59.4	8	14	.4	12	0	.0
62254	4.3	87	1.5	72	28.4	284	88.1	6	12	1.8	8	0	.0
62255	1.0	100	.4	77	24.3	337	47.0	7	11	.5	12	0	.0
62257	3.7	0	1.4	77	29.3	237	58.4	8	13		0	1	.0
62258	6.6	96	2.3	72	26.9	330	83.1	8	13	3.1	11	0	.3
62260	5.3	99	1.8	80	30.4	346	89.6	8	12	2.6	11	0	.1
62261	.3	0	.1	82	23.7	218	31.4	5	15		0	0	.0
62262	2.0	86	.8	83	17.1	231	44.2	5	20	.9	17	0	.0
62263	5.2	99	1.9	80	24.9	267	76.3	6	23	2.4	20	0	.3
62265	3.1	100	1.1	80	27.2	290	71.6	7	16	1.5	15	0	.1
62266	3.4	97	1.1	75	25.4	330	82.0	9	8	1.6	9	0	.0
62267	.2	100	.1	88	18.8	215*	74.9	4	20	.1	14	0	.0

ILLINOIS — SAINT LOUIS (continued)

ZIPCODE	1	2	3	4	5	6	7	8	9	10	11	12	13
62268	.8	0	.3	88	26.5	137	58.2	7	14	.0	0	0	.0
62269	15.3	96	5.3	77	32.6	420	100.5	7	9	7.2	7	0	.0
62271	2.1	100	.6	77	23.5	255	77.3	9	16	.0	0	0	.0
62272	1.6	100	.6	79	23.0	211	58.3	8	15	.8	13	0	.0
62273	.3	100	.1	74	27.9	362	65.8	10	14	.8	14	1	.0
62274	6.8	0	2.5	81	29.3	269	75.0	7	16	.0	0	1	.2
62275	2.8	100	1.0	81	24.3	241	63.1	7	12	1.4	11	0	.0
62277	1.8	0	.6	81	24.8	250	59.4	10	13	.0	0	0	.0
62278	5.6	99	1.9	83	30.8	256	82.5	8	17	2.7	14	0	.0
62280	.5	100	.5	78	26.3	250	44.9	4	13	.3	12	0	.0
62281	1.5	99	.5	81	27.2	390	77.8	8	12	.7	10	0	.0
62282	.5	100	.2	81	29.7	291	72.6	7	13	.7	13	0	.8
62283	.8	100	.3	83	29.6	267	70.4	6	17	.4	17	0	.0
62284	.8	99	.2	82	26.4	260	52.4	8	14	.4	14	0	.0
62285	1.4	99	.4	78	26.6	300	87.3	8	16	.7	13	0	.0
62286	7.2	90	2.6	77	27.1	289	71.3	9	14	3.1	12	2	.0
62288	3.1	100	1.1	83	28.1	288	80.0	8	14	1.5	13	0	.1
62289	.6	0	.2	74	24.3	334	59.3	9	14	.0	0	0	.0
62290	.4	0	.1	71	16.0	265	59.3	10	14	.0	0	0	.0
62292	1.0	99	.4	85	22.4	267	50.6	8	13	.5	11	0	.0
62293	4.2	100	1.4	80	27.9	338	89.1	7	11	2.0	9	0	.0
62294	1.7	100	2.1	82	31.7	327	95.7	8	7	3.1	5	0	.0
62295	.6	100	.6	73	27.3	277	64.8	10	11	.8	9	0	.0
62296	.6	100	.2	77	27.7	269	78.6	8	10	.3	6	0	.0
62297	.6	100	.2	84	25.5	274	66.8	11	18	.3	17	0	.0
62298	9.4	99	3.3	78	29.2	324	85.2	7	16	4.5	13	0	.0

QUINCY

ZIPCODE	1	2	3	4	5	6	7	8	9	10	11	12	13
62301	54.5	96	20.6	69	24.6	260	75.9	7	15	24.8	12	6	.8
62311	1.5	0	.9	83	20.8	223	35.9	6	28	.0	0	0	.0
62312	2.5	100	.4	77	19.0	186	41.5	6	20	1.2	17	0	.0
62313	.5	100	.2	80	25.8	120	35.3	11	13	.4	12	0	.0
62314	.8	99	.3	69	22.3	229	25.8	11	13	.4	14	0	.0
62316	.7	100	.3	78	19.7	160	39.7	8	24	.4	21	0	3.1
62318	.4	100	.2	78	26.6	135	38.1	8	19	.2	20	0	.0
62319	.4	99	.8	69	23.6	199	16.3	7	18	.0	0	0	.0
62320	2.4	99	.8	80	22.8	232	55.4	7	18	1.1	16	0	.0
62321	4.8	99	1.9	71	24.0	269	61.8	6	18	2.2	15	0	.0
62323	.4	100	.1	76	24.2	144	28.9	9	17	.2	13	0	.1
62324	1.6	0	.6	71	19.7	197	43.4	5	21	.0	0	0	.0
62325	.4	100	.1	79	20.4	276	44.7	10	16	.2	14	0	.0
62326	3.0	100	1.1	79	25.0	227	53.7	7	16	1.4	15	0	.6
62330	2.1	99	.8	77	24.1	234	53.8	8	15	1.0	14	0	.6
62334	.2	100	.1	77	22.1	353	41.4	8	16	.0	0	0	.0
62336	.2	100	.1	81	23.2	180	31.0	8	15	.1	10	0	.0
62338	1.4	0	.5	84	25.2	303	71.6	10	8	.5	8	0	.0
62339	.9	99	.3	87	22.7	213	50.6	8	24	.4	18	0	.0
62340	2.0	0	.7	76	22.0	208	49.5	9	15	.2	15	1	.0
62341	4.2	100	1.5	79	25.6	308	73.7	9	13	2.0	11	0	.1
62343	.2	100	.4	69	22.6	178	37.0	6	17	.5	16	0	.0

*=Estimated **1.0=883 lbs per person; 100++ indicates per capita toxic waste generation > than 100 times the U.S. average of 883 lbs per capita.

ZIP CODE MEASURES OF SIZE, LEVELS OF AFFLUENCE AND QUALITY OF LIFE

1=Population (th.); 2= % White; 3=Households (th.); 4=% Owner Occupied; 5=Mean Income Per Household (th.$); 6=Mean Monthly Rent ($); 7=Mean Home Value (th.$); 8=% under 5; 9=% 65 and over; 10=White Males, 65+; 11=% White Males; 12=# Toxic Waste Sites; 13=Toxic Waste Relative to US(883 lbs.per capita).

ILLINOIS

QUINCY

ZIP CODE	1	2	3	4	5	6	7	8	9	10	11	12	13
62344	.2	100	.1	81	19.9	366	15.8	6	17	.1	14	0	.0
62345	.4	100	.1	74	25.6	207	37.9	9	12	.2	11	0	.0
62346	.4	100	.1	69	23.2	174	39.6	4	15	.2	17	0	.0
62347	2.4	99	.7	83	22.5	317	57.3	10	9	1.2	9	0	.0
62348	.3	100	.1	75	22.9	237	68.7	10	9	.2	7	0	.0
62349	.8	100	.3	77	20.3	290	38.2	9	13	.5	12	0	.0
62351	2.0	100	.7	84	20.9	238	58.9	7	15	1.0	13	0	.0
62352	.3	100	.1	90	19.6	299	35.1	6	19	.1	18	0	.0
62353	3.9	100	1.6	75	19.3	221	53.7	7	22	1.9	18	0	.2
62354	1.9	0	.6	76	25.4	297	77.4	8	15	.0	0	0	.1
62355	1.2	100	.4	82	18.8	223	30.4	9	16	.6	15	0	.0
62356	.7	100	.3	79	21.2	272	35.7	6	19	.3	17	0	.0
62357	.3	100	.1	80	18.5	224	28.0	6	15	.2	16	0	.0
62358	1.0	100	.3	76	25.6	289	55.7	8	11	.5	10	0	.0
62359	.2	100	.1	88	21.7	231	46.4	4	16	.1	11	0	.0
62360	1.9	0	.6	83	25.3	239	67.3	11	10	.0	0	0	.0
62361	.8	0	.3	80	15.8	261	27.6	5	28	.6	15	0	.0
62362	.7	100	.1	79	20.4	221	42.9	3	20	.2	17	0	.0
62363	6.1	99	2.4	72	23.2	243	68.1	6	20	2.8	16	2	.0
62365	.7	100	.2	81	22.3	328	55.1	8	9	.4	8	0	.0
62366	1.7	0	.7	77	18.9	195	48.7	7	19	.0	0	0	.8
62367	1.6	0	.6	73	19.4	209	31.7	5	19	.0	0	0	.0
62370	.7	0	.3	78	18.4	257	33.0	6	17	.0	0	0	.0
62374	.7	100	.3	81	31.0	332	54.4	7	16	.2	12	1	.0
62375	.4	100	.2	83	19.7	171	46.5	4	9	.2	8	0	.1
62376	.4	100	.2	71	21.0	162	33.0	6	13	.2	15	0	.0
62378	.4	100	.4	82	23.8	241	69.9	8	15	.6	14	0	.0
62379	1.0	0	.4	80	19.0	185	45.9	9	16	.2	16	0	8.8
62380	2.5	98	.9	81	22.3	249	55.3	8	14	1.2	12	0	.0

EFFINGHAM

ZIP CODE	1	2	3	4	5	6	7	8	9	10	11	12	13
62401	16.5	100	5.9	74	28.6	287	87.1	8	13	7.9	11	0	.0
62410	1.6	99	.6	82	23.3	313	58.9	7	11	.8	10	1	.7
62411	4.2	100	1.5	74	24.0	284	69.1	10	16	2.0	13	0	.0
62413	.5	0	.2	87	22.3	307	43.2	9	19	.0	0	0	.0
62414	1.8	100	.6	83	22.3	202	50.2	9	14	1.0	13	1	.0
62415	1.6	0	.6	84	16.0	209	29.9	8	24	.0	0	0	.0
62417	3.3	99	1.3	79	20.6	266	49.8	7	17	1.6	14	5	8.8
62418	2.2	0	.8	78	20.7	229	56.8	7	15	.0	0	0	.0
62419	.6	0	.2	81	21.5	211	41.0	6	11	.0	0	0	.0
62420	5.1	100	2.0	80	24.7	264	55.0	7	20	2.3	16	1	.3
62421	1.0	100	.4	84	22.9	243	56.9	6	12	.8	15	0	.0
62422	1.3	100	.4	81	20.3	215	52.7	8	15	.6	13	0	.0
62423	.7	0	.2	83	24.9	190	60.4	9	10	.0	0	0	.0
62424	1.9	100	.6	79	25.8	237	58.4	11	11	1.0	14	0	.0
62425	.6	100	.2	89	24.0	176	51.9	7	14	.3	15	0	.0
62426	1.2	0	.4	78	19.9	186	40.2	8	15	.0	0	0	.0
62427	1.7	0	.6	84	20.7	170	47.7	6	13	.0	0	0	.0
62428	3.1	100	1.3	79	19.8	222	56.4	7	20	1.5	18	0	.0

ILLINOIS

EFFINGHAM

ZIP CODE	1	2	3	4	5	6	7	8	9	10	11	12	13
62431	1.2	100	.4	85	19.8	249	32.2	6	16	.7	15	0	.0
62432	.7	100	.2	92	23.3	117	46.5	6	18	.3	20	0	.0
62433	1.1	99	.4	79	23.6	246	47.5	5	18	.6	17	0	.9
62434	.5	0	.2	83	24.4	131	40.5	7	17	.0	0	0	.0
62436	.6	100	.2	90	20.2	212	40.8	7	11	.3	9	0	.0
62438	.5	100	.2	81	22.9	336	34.3	5	19	.2	17	0	.0
62439	8.8	99	3.4	73	24.4	233	59.1	6	20	4.0	14	11	7.8
62440	1.3	99	.4	83	25.2	325	56.0	13	10	.6	10	0	.0
62441	6.9	100	2.6	77	22.5	229	64.1	8	17	3.3	14	3	12.0
62442	2.9	0	1.1	82	24.6	200	45.1	6	17	.0	0	0	.0
62443	1.5	0	.5	85	23.5	277	54.4	7	13	.0	0	4	.0
62444	.5	100	.1	79	24.3	261	46.6	4	9	.3	9	0	.0
62445	.9	100	.3	81	21.5	220	46.0	8	14	.4	15	0	.1
62446	.5	100	.3	89	24.0	164	50.0	6	18	.3	15	0	.0
62447	3.1	100	1.1	79	23.6	206	66.9	8	11	3.1	15	2	.0
62448	6.5	100	2.4	80	25.0	254	65.0	8	17	3.1	15	2	1.0
62449	3.7	99	1.4	80	22.0	236	52.5	6	19	1.8	16	0	.0
62450	12.7	100	5.0	75	24.5	250	64.5	7	16	6.0	13	17	2.3
62451	2.7	0	1.1	77	24.0	214	52.5	8	16	.0	0	0	.0
62452	.6	0	.3	91	24.3	206	30.0	8	10	.0	0	0	.0
62454	11.0	100	4.3	78	26.0	284	63.5	7	17	5.3	14	9	6.8
62458	2.6	100	1.0	81	23.3	144	50.0	7	17	1.0	4	0	.0
62459	.3	100	.1	94	20.2	232*	54.9	6	21	.1	20	0	.0
62460	1.7	0	.6	85	24.5	216	42.6	10	13	.5	13	1	.0
62461	.9	100	.3	89	26.7	307	74.5	9	12	.5	13	0	.4
62462	1.1	0	.3	86	27.6	198	55.0	8	11	.0	0	0	.0
62463	1.3	0	.5	77	24.0	226	53.1	9	15	.0	0	0	.0
62464	.1	100	.1	82	20.0	230*	45.3	13	13	.1	16	0	.0
62465	.9	99	.4	84	23.6	184	45.3	6	22	.4	20	0	.0
62466	3.1	99	1.1	82	20.5	241	43.0	8	19	1.5	17	2	.0
62467	3.4	100	1.0	86	31.3	233	88.0	11	8	1.7	8	1	.0
62468	2.6	100	1.0	81	23.8	215	61.0	8	14	1.3	12	0	.0
62469	9.3	96	3.3	86	27.8	215	58.2	7	12	1.2	12	0	.0
62471	1.0	100	.3	73	23.1	250	67.2	7	18	4.5	14	1	.2
62473	1.0	100	.3	86	23.3	342	61.6	12	8	.5	8	0	.0
62474	.5	100	.4	80	24.6	204	45.2	7	13	.0	0	0	.0
62475	.2	100	.2	85	24.2	149	42.9	8	11	.3	13	0	.0
62476	2.2	0	.8	86	23.6	224	51.0	9	19	.0	0	0	.0
62477	1.1	95	.4	81	19.9	190	37.5	7	18	.5	15	0	11.1
62479	1.0	100	.3	92	28.1	140	58.3	9	15	.3	12	0	.0
62480	1.1	100	.4	82	20.7	273	42.5	5	13	.1	11	0	.7
62481	.5	100	.2	89	24.5	78	37.4	6	18	.2	15	0	.0

SPRINGFIELD (EAST)

ZIP CODE	1	2	3	4	5	6	7	8	9	10	11	12	13
62501	1.6	0	.5	80	29.6	364	74.0	8	8	.0	8	0	.0
62510	2.0	99	.8	74	24.7	294	60.0	6	18	1.0	14	0	.7
62511	.3	100	.1	74	18.5	158	43.6	5	9	.1	11	0	.0
62512	.6	0	.2	62	32.1	379	57.4	7	12	.0	0	0	.0
62513	2.5	99	.9	75	28.7	267	66.4	8	11	1.3	10	1	.0

*=Estimated   **1.0=883 lbs per person; 100++ indicates per capita toxic waste generation > than 100 times the U.S. average of 883 lbs per capita.

ZIP CODE MEASURES OF SIZE, LEVELS OF AFFLUENCE AND QUALITY OF LIFE

1=Population (th.); 2= % White; 3=Households (th.); 4=% Owner Occupied; 5=Mean Income Per Household (th.$); 6=Mean Monthly Rent ($)*; 7=Mean Home Value (th.$)*; 8=% under 5; 9=% 65 and over; 10=White Males (th.); 11=% White Males, 65+; 12=# Toxic Waste Sites; 13=Toxic Waste Relative to US(883 lbs.per capita)**.

ILLINOIS

SPRINGFIELD (EAST)

ZIP CODE	1	2	3	4	5	6	7	8	9	10	11	12	13
62514	1.6	0	.6	82	25.7	295	67.0	10	12	.0	0	0	.0
62515	1.0	0	.4	69	31.0	351	89.3	9	10	.0	0	0	.0
62517	.4	100	.1	78	23.0	287	46.2	9	15	.2	15	1	.0
62518	.5	100	.2	74	25.6	358	70.1	6	14	.3	10	0	.0
62520	2.0	99	.7	85	28.7	309	86.5	9	9	1.0	8	0	.0
62521	45.9	85	16.5	77	30.2	342	82.3	8	11	19.1	10	1	.1
62522	21.6	81	8.4	61	26.9	299	77.0	8	15	8.1	13	6	.0
62523	.6	55	.3	0	10.3	216	36.7*14	15	0	.2	14	0	5.9
62526	42.4	92	16.1	74	27.7	333	77.3	8	12	18.7	10	1	2.5
62530	1.3	99	.5	82	26.5	381	65.7	8	15	.6	13	0	.0
62531	2.1	0	.8	74	25.9	284	70.0	8	13	.0	0	1	.0
62532	.2	100	.1	83	28.9	329	79.3	7	0	.0	0	0	.0
62533	1.1	100	.4	77	31.4	216	75.1	9	13	.5	12	0	.0
62534	1.4	100	.5	76	24.6	202	70.6	8	13	.7	9	0	.0
62535	.8	0	.3	85	32.6	426	83.5	7	9	.0	0	0	.0
62536	.7	100	.2	97	30.5	350*117.1	7	8	.4	8	0	.4
62537	.2	100	.1	84	31.2	347	66.0	13	4	.1	0	0	.0
62538	.6	100	.2	74	27.8	310	71.0	7	16	.5	13	0	.0
62539	1.8	0	.6	74	32.1	342	72.8	7	9	.0	0	2	23.1
62540	1.6	100	.6	82	24.7	257	50.1	8	13	.8	11	0	.4
62543	.8	97	.2	72	25.9	291	74.8	6	14	.4	14	1	.0
62544	2.0	0	.7	76	29.8	328	82.9	7	17	.0	0	0	.0
62545	.7	100	.2	71	28.2	401	83.5	9	11	.4	12	0	.0
62546	2.0	0	.7	71	25.8	324	61.6	7	14	.0	0	0	.0
62547	.9	0	.4	74	26.4	298	62.2	9	18	.0	0	0	.0
62548	2.6	100	1.0	70	27.9	317	78.2	6	18	1.2	14	0	1.5
62549	5.4	99	1.7	80	33.0	344	97.8	10	5	2.7	4	0	1.6
62550	3.1	99	1.1	79	30.2	279	74.6	8	13	1.5	10	0	.0
62551	1.0	0	.3	76	25.0	243	57.3	7	11	.0	0	0	.0
62552	1.1	99	.4	78	31.7	333	88.1	7	9	.6	9	0	.0
62553	.7	100	.3	80	24.1	280	54.5	12	13	.4	14	0	.5
62554	1.6	100	.5	87	34.0	392	86.9	7	4	.8	3	0	.0
62555	.7	0	.2	81	30.3	377	69.0	8	10	.0	0	0	.0
62556	.5	100	.2	77	25.9	324	49.8	5	12	.0	0	0	.1
62557	8.1	99	3.1	75	21.9	248	48.9	7	17	3.8	14	1	.5
62558	3.7	100	1.3	79	30.9	389	88.1	7	10	1.8	9	0	.0
62560	1.6	0	.6	77	28.7	270	70.9	9	7	.0	0	0	.0
62561	4.1	98	1.4	86	28.6	387	88.9	10	7	2.0	8	0	.0
62563	4.6	99	1.5	85	36.0	426	114.1	7	7	2.3	6	0	.0
62565	7.7	100	2.9	77	25.3	251	65.4	7	18	3.7	15	0	.1
62568	15.2	99	5.8	74	25.5	314	93.4	7	16	7.1	12	2	.7
62570	.6	100	.2	94	25.8	293	44.4	6	15	.3	13	0	.0
62571	1.6	0	.5	81	22.4	285	42.5	10	12	.0	0	0	.0
62572	.6	0	.2	77	28.8	217	66.2	6	12	.0	0	0	.0
62573	1.7	98	.6	72	32.5	253	78.1	9	8	.9	7	0	.0

SPRINGFIELD (WEST)

ZIP CODE	1	2	3	4	5	6	7	8	9	10	11	12	13
62601	.5	100	.2	68	22.3	86	55.7	9	16	.3	11	0	.0
62610	.3	100	.1	90	18.6	341	38.0	12	14	.2	11	0	.0

ILLINOIS

SPRINGFIELD (WEST)

ZIP CODE	1	2	3	4	5	6	7	8	9	10	11	12	13
62611	1.3	100	.5	78	27.5	351	83.4	7	16	.6	13	0	.0
62612	2.1	0	.8	70	27.5	328	66.4	6	14	.0	0	0	.0
62613	2.7	0	1.0	73	26.0	334	81.4	9	12	.0	0	1	.2
62615	4.5	99	1.5	76	26.4	334	78.0	9	15	2.2	13	0	.4
62617	1.1	0	.4	80	24.7	243	45.4	9	14	.0	0	0	.0
62618	8.0	100	2.9	78	24.2	255	57.9	7	16	3.9	12	1	.3
62621	1.5	0	.6	76	23.8	210	52.3	7	15	.0	0	0	.0
62623	.2	100	.1	80	26.8	204	57.1	7	7	.1	9	0	.0
62624	.9	100	.3	82	21.9	215	35.7	8	13	.5	13	0	.0
62625	.7	0	.2	91	34.8	442	104.9	9	6	.0	0	0	.0
62626	8.3	98	3.0	74	25.8	274	75.0	7	17	3.8	14	2	.3
62627	1.5	100	.5	72	24.5	232	48.7	8	15	.7	14	1	.0
62628	1.0	100	.3	83	29.1	346	57.8	6	14	.5	13	0	.0
62629	6.6	99	2.1	83	33.0	394	101.1	9	5	3.2	4	0	.0
62630	.7	100	.3	71	23.6	208	45.6	7	18	.4	17	0	.0
62631	.3	100	.1	91	39.8	457*	54.4	6	12	.2	10	0	.0
62633	.9	0	.4	70	26.6	308	57.9	8	16	.0	0	0	.0
62634	.8	0	.3	59	31.6	354	84.5	6	15	.0	0	0	.0
62635	.9	100	.3	75	23.0	343	71.0	8	19	.4	17	0	.0
62638	1.5	100	.5	74	28.8	310	62.4	9	11	.8	10	0	.6
62639	.6	100	.2	74	23.7	307	55.6	8	9	.3	8	0	.0
62640	3.7	0	1.4	74	23.7	329	68.1	7	16	.0	0	0	.0
62642	1.8	0	.6	72	27.4	240	75.5	7	15	.0	0	0	.0
62643	.7	100	.3	72	24.4	334	60.0	8	15	.4	13	0	.0
62644	7.2	0	2.7	73	24.5	279	69.8	8	15	.0	0	1	.5
62649	.8	0	.3	73	21.3	283	44.2	12	11	.0	0	0	.0
62650	27.7	95	10.1	65	26.5	276	78.6	7	15	12.3	12	1	.1
62655	.9	0	.3	72	25.0	334	53.1	9	10	.0	0	0	.0
62656	19.8	95	6.9	67	26.0	308	82.9	9	15	9.1	11	2	.6
62661	1.2	0	.4	73	22.7	324	72.3	7	9	.0	0	0	.0
62663	.4	100	.3	79	23.1	274	43.0	7	14	.2	15	0	.0
62664	3.6	100	1.4	75	28.7	232	75.0	7	17	1.7	16	0	.0
62665	1.8	100	.7	77	23.0	205	47.6	8	12	.9	12	0	.1
62666	.8	0	.3	75	22.8	329	51.9	9	12	.0	0	0	.0
62667	.7	100	.3	76	21.7	217	49.5	5	13	.3	14	0	.0
62668	1.6	0	.6	78	22.1	280	58.3	9	15	.0	0	0	.0
62670	2.5	0	.3	75	28.8	316	86.8	6	12	.0	0	0	.0
62671	.7	100	.3	64	28.3	363	56.5	7	16	.3	15	0	.0
62672	.3	0	.1	89	23.1	201	53.1	8	16	.0	0	0	.1
62673	.6	100	.2	81	29.0	262	70.0	12	12	.3	13	0	.0
62674	1.6	0	.6	75	21.2	267	43.2	8	17	.0	0	0	.0
62675	5.6	100	2.0	76	28.8	294	91.0	6	17	2.7	13	0	.0
62676	.7	100	.3	83	29.4	392	73.8	13	9	.3	8	0	.0
62677	.3	100	.1	78	31.7	354	93.2	7	11	.0	0	0	.1
62681	5.5	100	2.2	74	22.7	253	69.5	7	19	2.6	15	0	.0
62682	1.3	99	.5	78	25.8	292	65.3	6	14	.6	13	0	.0
62684	2.3	99	.8	86	33.4	445	111.3	8	6	1.1	6	0	.0
62685	1.5	84	.5	82	22.8	271	54.7	9	13	.6	11	0	.0
62686	1.1	100	.8	82	18.3	205	37.2	10	14	.1	9	0	.0

*=Estimated **1.0=883 lbs per person; 100++ indicates per capita toxic waste generation > than 100 times the U.S. average of 883 lbs per capita.

ILLINOIS

ZIP CODE MEASURES OF SIZE, LEVELS OF AFFLUENCE AND QUALITY OF LIFE

1=Population (th.); 2= % White; 3=Households (th.); 4=% Owner Occupied; 5=Mean Income Per Household (th.$); 6=Mean Monthly Rent ($); 7=Mean Home Value (th.$); 8=% under 5; 9=% 65 and over; 10=White Males (th.); 11=% White Males, 65+; 12=# Toxic Waste Sites; 13=Toxic Waste Relative to US(883 lbs.per capita)**

ILLINOIS

ZIPCODE	1	2	3	4	5	6	7	8	9	10	11	12	13
SPRINGFIELD (WEST)													
62688	1.1	72	.4	72	25.5	267	63.9	8	14	.0	0	0	.0
62689	.7	0	.3	88	23.0	307	46.0	8	12	.0	0	0	.0
62690	4.6	98	1.7	75	24.5	301	68.5	8	16	2.1	13	0	.0
62691	2.8	99	1.1	73	24.5	299	64.5	7	16	1.3	13	0	.0
62692	2.3	0	.9	77	26.3	265	57.1	7	18	.0	0	0	.0
62693	1.4	100	.5	68	29.3	402	80.5	8	11	.7	10	0	.0
62694	3.4	100	1.3	72	22.7	209	57.8	5	20	1.7	16	0	.0
62695	.5	100	.2	79	26.1	322	67.7	12	5	.2	5	0	.0
SPRINGFIELD													
62701	1.1	90	.8	4	14.5	227	101.2	2	27	.5	19	2	5.5
62702	45.3	92	17.8	65	23.6	284	70.8	8	13	19.3	10	1	.2
62703	33.7	78	13.2	67	23.8	316	67.8	8	14	12.3	13	4	.1
62704	40.8	97	17.6	60	33.4	364	110.1	6	15	17.7	12	0	.0
62707	13.4	98	4.5	86	37.5	393	135.5	7	8	6.5	6	1	.0
CENTRALIA													
62801	24.7	93	9.5	74	23.9	264	57.9	7	16	10.7	13	7	.7
62803	1.1	0	.4	80	26.2	291	70.4	7	17	.0	0	0	.1
62805	.6	100	.2	71	19.4	264	30.9	9	23	.0	20	0	.0
62806	3.7	0	1.5	81	20.8	245	57.3	7	20	.0	0	3	3.1
62807	.9	100	.3	86	21.9	173	45.3	10	15	.5	13	0	.0
62808	1.6	99	.6	88	19.6	249	44.5	6	20	.8	18	1	.0
62809	.2	100	.1	90	20.4	235*	44.0	3	13	.1	12	0	2.7
62810	1.0	99	.3	77	21.2	242	49.8	8	12	.5	13	1	.0
62811	3.3	100	1.1	85	21.9	187	59.6	7	13	.5	16	0	.0
62812	11.8	0	4.7	74	23.2	272	58.7	6	19	.0	0	1	.0
62814	1.9	0	.7	86	24.1	275	60.2	9	12	.0	0	0	.0
62815	.6	100	.2	73	24.6	203	35.9	9	9	.2	9	0	.0
62816	1.6	99	.5	87	24.5	209	55.1	10	12	.8	12	0	.0
62817	.7	100	.3	89	19.5	144	38.4	8	17	.3	19	0	.0
62818	.7	100	.2	82	20.5	159	52.2	9	17	.3	20	2	.0
62819	.6	99	.2	89	20.1	273	30.9	9	12	.3	19	0	.0
62820	.3	100	.1	81	22.2	245	33.0	7	16	.2	13	0	.0
62821	9.0	99	3.6	72	24.4	281	64.0	6	20	4.2	18	6	.3
62822	3.5	0	1.5	77	19.8	223	46.6	6	23	.0	0	2	.1
62823	1.8	99	.7	86	20.4	203	50.2	8	20	.9	16	0	.0
62824	2.0	100	.8	83	20.6	221	45.2	6	20	.9	18	5	.0
62825	.3	100	.1	94	19.6	226*	36.9	7	18	.1	15	0	.0
62827	1.6	0	.6	72	25.7	203	51.7	6	19	.0	0	4	.0
62828	1.4	100	.5	86	21.8	191	51.8	5	20	.7	17	1	.0
62829	.1	100	.1	86	18.1	208*	46.5	5	13	.1	8	0	.0
62830	1.1	99	.4	82	23.6	237	62.7	7	13	.5	13	0	.0
62831	.7	100	.3	83	18.9	93	40.4	5	18	.3	15	0	.0
62832	9.9	96	3.8	78	23.8	265	59.6	7	18	4.5	13	2	.0
62833	.5	100	.2	92	25.6	294*	41.0	8	10	.2	12	0	.0
62835	1.6	100	.6	80	21.3	159	46.5	6	16	.8	14	0	.5
62836	.7	100	.2	83	27.1	194	71.1	7	14	.8	14	0	.0
62837	9.3	100	3.7	78	22.5	204	61.8	6	18	4.3	15	12	2.2
62838	1.6	100	.6	82	22.6	102	44.7	7	17	.8	14	0	.0
62839	7.2	0	2.8	77	19.8	233	53.3	7	20	.0	0	1	1.2

ILLINOIS

ZIPCODE	1	2	3	4	5	6	7	8	9	10	11	12	13
CENTRALIA													
62841	.2	0	.1	91	22.1	253*	34.1	6	15	.0	0	0	.0
62842	.9	100	.3	88	20.7	207	45.4	8	15	.4	16	0	.0
62843	.1	100	.1	87	18.4	212*	34.5	8	14	.1	14	0	.0
62844	2.7	0	1.1	75	22.8	213	51.0	7	18	.0	0	2	1.0
62846	.5	0	.2	89	21.3	165	45.4	5	19	.0	0	0	.0
62848	.8	98	.3	73	24.7	343	69.6	8	11	.4	12	0	.4
62849	1.9	99	.7	87	20.7	202	45.3	7	16	.4	15	0	.0
62850	.4	100	.1	88	21.4	246*	42.8	5	15	.2	15	0	.0
62851	.4	100	.2	82	22.9	78	41.5	7	18	.2	17	0	.0
62853	.6	100	.2	86	25.0	279	42.6	7	11	.3	10	0	.0
62854	2.0	99	.7	82	20.0	270	46.0	9	14	1.0	14	0	.0
62856	.3	0	.1	94	19.0	219*	42.7	3	9	.0	0	0	.0
62857	.2	100	.1	95	20.7	261*	41.0	4	20	.1	15	0	.0
62858	3.4	100	1.2	82	20.6	211	51.8	7	17	1.6	15	1	.0
62859	6.1	99	2.5	77	18.7	219	53.5	6	21	2.8	18	2	.2
62860	.5	100	.2	87	17.6	423	45.3	5	20	.3	23	0	.0
62861	.2	0	.1	80	13.1	165	20.3	4	23	.0	0	0	.0
62862	.5	0	.2	85	21.7	201	41.5	10	15	.0	0	0	.0
62863	11.2	99	4.3	73	26.3	247	66.3	8	15	5.3	13	24	.8
62864	25.4	94	10.1	72	24.3	281	66.1	7	16	11.1	14	10	.9
62865	1.8	0	.6	90	26.2	121	53.3	6	10	.4	15	0	.0
62867	.7	100	.3	87	16.8	95	38.6	7	15	.0	0	0	.0
62868	2.3	0	.8	84	20.7	206	44.3	9	15	.0	0	0	.4
62869	3.0	99	.8	79	22.2	196	51.8	7	17	1.4	16	1	.0
62870	2.2	97	.8	84	23.0	275	48.0	7	18	1.1	16	0	.0
62871	.8	100	.3	78	24.7	274	53.1	7	17	.4	15	0	.0
62872	.9	98	.3	90	23.4	337	60.1	9	11	.4	12	1	.3
62874	.4	100	.2	93	17.5	167	28.1	6	24	.2	22	0	.0
62875	1.3	99	.5	84	22.6	217	49.0	7	18	.6	17	0	.1
62876	.2	100	.2	88	15.8	135	38.9	2	40	.1	41	0	.0
62877	.7	97	.2	83	26.5	268	51.4	11	15	.4	15	0	.0
62878	.4	100	.1	87	25.7	152	34.1	4	18	.2	17	0	.0
62879	.2	100	.1	74	12.4	237	19.0	7	15	.0	15	0	.0
62880	.7	0	.3	84	24.8	237	61.2	7	17	.0	0	1	.0
62881	12.0	99	4.3	78	24.7	275	66.4	7	15	5.7	12	8	.4
62882	2.9	99	1.1	68	20.4	262	42.9	6	15	1.4	12	1	.3
62883	.7	100	.2	90	24.1	197	55.9	9	16	.3	17	0	.0
62884	3.3	100	1.2	80	24.7	218	50.5	7	17	1.6	13	2	.0
62885	.9	97	.3	80	21.1	145	49.8	6	17	.5	16	0	.0
62886	.6	100	.2	86	22.4	212	36.4	6	16	.3	15	0	.5
62887	.4	100	.2	87	19.4	353	36.4	3	18	.2	11	0	.0
62888	2.3	99	.7	84	28.9	232	62.0	9	12	1.2	12	0	.0
62889	.7	100	.2	87	23.2	332	68.4	8	15	.4	16	0	.0
62890	2.4	97	.9	85	18.6	231	47.5	7	15	.0	0	1	.0
62891	.7	100	.3	88	24.6	217	42.6	7	17	.4	14	0	.5
62892	.4	0	.1	84	24.1	206	52.4	8	15	.8	15	0	.0
62893	.8	98	.3	85	23.6	293	62.1	9	14	.4	15	0	.0
62894	1.0	0	.3	90	26.9	185	53.7	8	12	.0	0	0	.0
62895	2.2	99	.8	79	20.9	194	59.5	8	18	1.1	16	0	.2

*=Estimated **1.0=883 lbs per person; 100++ indicates per capita toxic waste generation > than 100 times the U.S. average of 883 lbs per capita.

ZIP CODE MEASURES OF SIZE, LEVELS OF AFFLUENCE AND QUALITY OF LIFE

1=Population (th.); 2= % White; 3=Households (th.); 4=% Owner Occupied; 5=Mean Income Per Household (th.$); 6=Mean Monthly Rent ($)*; 7=Mean Home Value (th.$)*; 8=% under 5; 9=% 65 and over; 10=% White Males (th.); 11=% White Males, 65+; 12=# Toxic Waste Sites; 13=Toxic Waste Relative to US(883 lbs.per capita)**.

ILLINOIS

ZIP CODE	1	2	3	4	5	6	7	8	9	10	11	12	13
CENTRALIA													
62896	13.6	100	5.3	77	21.3	252	53.4	7	19	6.4	15	6	.1
62897	.5	100	.2	79	22.3	352	47.1	8	20	.2	18	0	.0
62898	1.4	0	.5	81	25.2	374	67.6	8	9	.9	0	0	.0
62899	1.7	100	.6	83	20.7	141	45.1	6	19	.9	18	0	.0
CARBONDALE													
62901	35.1	84	12.7	39	19.8	323	89.5	4	6	15.9	5	2	.0
62905	.6	100	.2	73	17.6	204	45.9	8	13	.3	12	0	.0
62906	8.0	99	3.2	81	24.5	252	73.3	8	26	3.9	24	1	.1
62907	1.9	100	.7	77	22.2	243	50.0	8	15	1.0	15	0	.0
62908	.5	94	.2	82	24.8	54	35.3	9	5	.3	0	0	.0
62910	2.5	92	1.0	82	17.5	193	42.7	7	15	1.1	12	0	.0
62911	.3	83	.1	85	21.2	243*	24.2	4	11	.2	10	0	.0
62912	.3	0	.2	87	20.2	101	50.8	9	9	.0	0	0	.0
62914	6.5	52	2.6	55	15.8	336*	58.7	23	20	1.5	21	1	.7
62915	1.1	0	.4	71	19.1	156	43.0	7	12	.0	0	0	.7
62916	.8	0	.3	88	24.2	270	57.1	9	14	.6	11	0	.0
62917	3.1	88	1.2	82	20.8	240	51.4	6	19	1.3	16	1	.0
62918	6.7	99	2.6	70	24.1	293	70.3	8	11	3.3	9	3	3.4
62919	1.5	100	.5	78	19.6	178	42.0	6	12	.7	8	0	.2
62920	2.6	97	.9	76	22.9	231	54.4	5	15	1.3	14	0	.0
62921	.5	0	.2	63	16.7	279	42.2	6	20	.0	0	0	.0
62922	2.7	100	1.0	87	22.9	122	62.1	6	14	1.4	13	0	.1
62923	.7	100	.3	87	19.7	201	30.2	4	18	.3	18	2	.0
62924	2.5	99	.9	76	23.0	312	59.2	9	9	1.2	7	1	.0
62926	2.1	96	.8	81	20.5	153	47.1	9	15	1.0	13	0	.0
62927	.5	0	.2	85	19.3	278	31.2	4	17	.0	0	0	.0
62928	.2	100	.1	69	20.0	316	27.7	9	11	.1	11	0	.2
62930	7.5	100	3.0	77	21.2	202	54.2	6	23	3.4	18	0	.0
62931	1.7	100	.7	79	16.3	133	49.5	6	15	.9	16	0	.0
62932	1.6	96	.6	81	23.4	256	52.5	8	15	.7	12	0	.0
62933	.9	97	.3	77	22.3	333	67.0	5	19	.4	13	0	.1
62934	1.2	0	.4	80	20.1	179	49.9	7	15	.0	0	0	.0
62935	2.1	100	.8	80	19.9	203	51.3	7	21	1.0	19	2	.0
62938	2.7	96	1.0	74	18.3	163	49.0	4	17	1.4	18	0	.0
62939	2.1	0	.8	86	23.4	277	67.9	6	16	.0	0	1	.0
62940	.7	0	.2	85	20.5	220	37.4	5	18	.3	0	0	.0
62941	.7	90	.3	87	19.6	169	48.4	10	12	.3	12	0	.0
62942	.5	0	.4	76	20.2	226	40.5	7	17	.0	0	0	.1
62943	.2	0	.2	81	17.2	71	28.0	9	22	.0	0	1	.0
62946	14.7	97	5.8	75	22.5	259	59.3	6	18	6.7	15	8	.0
62947	.5	100	.2	71	18.1	147	48.7	13	14	.2	12	0	.0
62948	12.0	100	4.8	75	22.4	263	54.3	6	19	5.5	15	4	.7
62949	1.1	0	.4	79	19.6	175	42.4	8	17	.0	0	0	.0
62950	.4	100	.2	73	25.9	287	57.4	9	21	.2	22	0	.0
62951	5.4	100	2.0	84	21.6	209	49.6	6	17	2.5	15	0	.0
62952	3.2	100	1.2	72	19.7	216	48.1	5	15	1.5	11	0	.1
62953	.6	85	.2	75	21.7	190	31.6	5	12	.3	12	2	.1
62954	.6	100	.2	83	19.8	278	62.5	7	15	.3	12	0	3.7

ILLINOIS

ZIP CODE	1	2	3	4	5	6	7	8	9	10	11	12	13
CARBONDALE													
62956	1.1	99	.5	82	20.8	176	38.7	5	23	.5	25	0	.0
62957	1.3	100	.5	79	21.2	280	55.1	8	12	.6	13	0	.0
62958	1.8	98	.7	74	25.6	304	72.6	5	8	.9	8	0	.0
62959	21.7	98	8.4	77	23.6	278	66.7	7	15	10.2	12	17	.1
62960	11.3	94	4.3	79	22.3	239	54.8	7	18	5.1	15	1	6.1
62961	.2	100	.1	99	21.7	249*	37.2	2	13	.1	15	0	.0
62963	1.1	51	.4	61	12.1	181	25.8	11	16	.3	12	0	.2
62964	2.6	55	.9	69	16.2	194	37.6	11	18	.7	19	0	.0
62965	.9	100	.3	77	16.2	169	71.7	5	12	.1	12	0	.0
62966	16.5	92	6.3	68	22.5	275	67.0	7	14	7.4	11	0	.0
62967	.3	100	.1	79	16.3	296	46.1	5	17	.2	14	0	.0
62969	.6	0	.3	96	16.2	186*	44.6	5	19	.0	19	0	.0
62970	.9	82	.3	80	17.3	250	39.7	5	20	.4	15	0	.1
62972	.4	100	.1	100	17.2	198*	29.4	8	22	.2	20	0	.0
62973	.2	80	.1	92	14.2	164*	27.0	0	31	.1	29	0	.0
62974	1.2	100	.4	88	20.7	183	50.7	10	10	.6	11	0	.0
62975	.3	0	.1	75	18.5	165	49.2	7	11	.0	0	0	.0
62976	.9	0	.3	78	15.3	150	36.5	7	16	.4	16	0	.0
62977	1.7	100	.7	83	23.3	296	68.0	6	18	.8	15	2	.2
62979	1.6	99	.6	78	22.4	222	58.9	5	19	.8	18	0	.0
62982	1.3	100	.5	77	16.4	220	40.2	7	22	.8	18	1	.0
62983	2.7	99	1.0	83	17.9	239	39.5	6	19	1.3	19	1	.0
62984	.9	99	.3	75	18.5	201	49.7	7	16	.4	14	0	.4
62985	1.0	100	.3	78	21.9	396	40.8	8	17	.5	17	0	.0
62987	2.0	0	.7	81	21.7	200	39.2	10	17	.8	11	0	.0
62988	1.1	80	.4	84	19.4	217	39.6	8	16	.8	16	0	.0
62990	.4	100	.1	83	18.6	138	32.9	3	18	.6	16	0	.0
62991	1.0	100	.4	100	22.8	262*	60.7	4	16	.2	16	2	.0
62992	.3	78	.1	82	16.6	159	29.2	11	21	.4	15	0	.0
62993	.7	16	.3	66	14.4	113	40.1	5	17	.4	0	0	.0
62994	.9	0	.2	83	24.9	288	49.0	7	18	.8	13	1	.0
62995	3.8	90	1.2	76	19.3	230	62.5	5	16	1.8	13	1	.0
62996	.7	75	.2	78	23.4	251	53.3	7	19	.3	13	0	.0
62997	.9	100	.3	78	22.7	243	50.0	12	17	.4	15	0	.0
62998	.6	0	.2	79	29.3	250	42.5	11	13	.4	13	1	20.4
62999	2.3	100	.9	82	20.4	212	39.0	7	20	1.1	16	0	.0
FLAT RIVER													
63673	.1	0	.1	64	19.2	169	62.7	0	25	.0	0	0	.0

*=Estimated **1.0=883 lbs per person; 100++ indicates per capita toxic waste generation > than 100 times the U.S. average of 883 lbs per capita.

ZIP CODE MEASURES OF SIZE, LEVELS OF AFFLUENCE AND QUALITY OF LIFE

1=Population (th.); 2= % White; 3=Households (th.); 4=% Owner Occupied; 5=Mean Income Per Household (th.$); 6=Mean Home Value (th.$)*; 7=Mean Monthly Rent ($)*; 8=% under 5; 9=% 65 and over; 10=White Males (th.); 11=% White Males, 65+; 12=# Toxic Waste Sites; 13=Toxic Waste Relative to US(883 lbs.per capita)**.

INDIANA

ZIPCODE	1	2	3	4	5	6	7	8	9	10	11	12	13
TOLEDO (WEST)													
43526	.3	0	.1	88	27.6	289	99.3	13	8	.0	0	0	.0
CINCINNATI (WEST)													
45003	.9	0	.3	70	21.0	240	57.2	10	13	.0	0	0	.0
45030	4.4	100	1.3	83	27.2	291	87.7	9	8	2.2	7	0	.0
45056	.4	0	.1	58	25.0	260	58.9	12	7	.0	0	0	.0
DAYTON													
45347	.2	100	.1	89	31.3	360*	74.4	0	7	.1	4	0	.0
LIMA													
45813	.2	100	.1	76	28.6	352	84.6	13	9	.1	7	0	.0
45846	.2	100	.1	82	21.3	244*	71.5	4	13	.1	11	0	.0
INDIANAPOLIS (NORTH)													
46001	13.9	99	4.8	77	25.8	290	61.1	9	10	6.8	8	0	.0
46011	39.1	81	13.5	80	30.6	303	76.5	8	10	15.5	10	1	1.0
46012	19.7	97	7.0	74	26.7	296	65.0	6	9	9.1	9	0	.1
46013	10.2	96	3.8	77	29.3	309	68.3	7	8	4.6	8	0	.1
46014	14.6	95	6.2	64	21.2	280	46.1	8	15	6.4	13	1	1.1
46016	4.6	90	2.1	45	17.7	227	39.8	8	16	1.9	10	1	.1
46017	2.7	0	1.0	81	27.4	323	58.1	7	11	1.0	9	0	.1
46030	3.2	99	1.0	77	26.1	357	71.8	8	11	1.6	8	0	.0
46031	1.9	0	.7	81	27.1	231	68.3	7	9	1.0	8	0	.0
46032	26.9	99	8.6	76	50.7	471	175.9	6	5	13.1	4	0	.3
46034	4.1	100	1.5	78	31.2	352	106.1	8	8	2.1	7	0	.0
46035	1.2	0	.4	80	25.2	245	50.8	8	12	1.0	7	0	.0
46036	13.2	100	4.8	75	24.3	258	49.4	8	14	6.3	11	3	1.3
46038	.3	100	.3	61	22.5	296	58.3	9	10	.2	5	0	.0
46039	.9	100	.3	83	29.4	270	54.6	8	11	.4	9	0	.0
46040	6.1	99	2.1	80	28.3	320	74.0	7	12	3.0	11	1	.5
46041	23.0	99	8.3	70	25.8	261	60.8	8	14	10.9	11	2	.3
46044	3.3	100	1.1	82	27.0	304	64.4	7	9	1.7	8	0	.1
46048	.9	0	.3	81	21.3	278	43.1	8	11	.3	9	0	.0
46050	1.6	0	.6	84	28.7	317	58.6	6	11	.9	5	1	.2
46051	2.8	100	1.0	80	26.1	287	47.1	8	14	1.1	12	0	.0
46052	18.0	99	6.6	75	28.1	278	65.5	9	12	8.6	10	1	.1
46055	1.5	98	.5	71	26.2	305	78.3	7	12	.7	7	0	.7
46056	2.4	0	.8	80	32.5	320	94.3	8	7	.6	8	2	2.3
46057	1.2	0	.4	83	28.7	267	74.4	10	9	1.2	9	0	.0
46058	1.9	0	.6	71	26.8	278	61.1	7	12	.9	8	0	.0
46060	27.9	99	9.3	80	27.3	369	64.4	9	15	13.4	11	2	.3
46063	.5	100	.2	78	34.4	346	117.5	8	13	.3	6	1	1.2
46064	9.5	94	2.8	82	29.0	295	81.5	6	6	4.9	5	1	.0
46065	2.4	100	.6	82	25.3	279	74.5	7	16	1.1	12	0	.0
46067	.1	100	.1	93	21.8	251*	38.5	14	7	1.3	8	0	.1
46069	3.0	0	1.0	83	32.1	288	86.0	8	8	.8	7	0	.0
46070	5.8	100	2.0	81	26.9	290	70.3	9	14	1.2	13	1	.1
46071	2.6	100	.9	80	25.5	288	67.0	8	11	1.0	10	0	.7
46072	9.6	99	3.5	75	27.0	275	72.7	7	14	4.6	11	2	.7
46074	5.8	100	1.9	78	32.6	270	103.9	9	8	2.9	6	0	3.2

ZIPCODE	1	2	3	4	5	6	7	8	9	10	11	12	13
INDIANAPOLIS (NORTH)													
46075	1.8	100	.6	78	31.4	407	77.9	7	8	.9	7	0	.2
46076	1.8	98	.6	80	28.1	317	62.5	7	10	.0	0	0	.0
46077	9.6	98	3.2	81	44.6	398	162.4	7	8	4.5	5	1	.0
INDIANAPOLIS (SOUTH)													
46102	.4	100	.1	82	25.6	340	49.1	7	9	.2	8	0	.0
46103	.5	100	.1	85	30.0	251	56.0	10	8	.3	7	0	.0
46104	1.1	0	.4	82	26.3	280	60.7	8	10	.0	0	0	.9
46105	1.6	99	.6	83	26.8	335	59.4	9	13	.8	13	0	.0
46106	3.6	100	1.2	85	31.5	368	90.5	9	9	1.8	7	0	.8
46107	11.1	99	4.2	70	27.1	306	62.5	6	15	5.0	11	1	.0
46110	.5	0	.2	83	33.4	242	79.5	9	9	.0	0	0	.0
46111	.6	100	.2	77	23.6	309	48.5	10	10	.3	8	0	.0
46112	16.4	99	5.2	87	35.9	335	99.6	8	6	8.0	4	0	.0
46113	4.7	0	1.5	89	35.0	190	85.0	7	5	.0	0	1	.0
46114	.2	100	.2	90	26.6	305*	61.4	3	18	.0	20	0	.0
46115	2.0	100	.6	80	27.1	228	57.6	8	11	1.0	11	0	.0
46116	.2	100	.1	60	15.8	349	67.1	12	9	.1	0	0	.3
46117	.7	100	.2	84	24.7	326	68.8	9	8	.4	6	0	.0
46118	4.4	100	1.4	84	28.8	298	76.6	8	8	.0	0	0	.0
46120	4.2	100	1.5	81	24.3	282	64.9	7	15	2.1	13	0	.0
46121	2.8	99	.7	86	29.8	314	87.4	7	10	1.4	8	0	.0
46122	12.5	100	4.1	81	33.1	358	96.8	8	8	6.1	7	0	.1
46124	8.7	93	2.7	69	22.9	275	61.9	8	7	4.0	7	0	.1
46126	4.9	99	1.6	88	30.1	287	79.5	8	7	2.4	6	0	.1
46127	.4	100	.2	82	22.2	447	45.5	7	16	.2	16	0	.0
46128	1.6	100	.5	84	25.6	309	65.3	8	10	.8	7	0	.0
46130	2.2	100	.7	80	24.6	198	55.0	6	17	.1	13	0	.0
46131	18.8	98	6.2	81	31.9	284	94.2	8	9	10.4	9	2	.0
46133	1.1	99	.3	71	27.8	297	78.1	7	14	8.5	10	1	1.4
46135	16.6	97	5.1	78	20.8	240	48.8	8	10	.5	9	0	.2
46140	26.3	99	8.7	75	26.2	272	77.7	5	12	8.0	9	1	.0
46142	33.7	100	11.1	77	31.5	329	91.6	7	9	12.8	7	2	2.2
46144	.2	93	.1	77	34.4	281	105.4	7	8	16.4	4	0	.2
46146	.2	0	.2	93	23.1	266*	68.5	7	18	.2	7	0	.0
46147	2.5	100	.8	78	20.3	273	51.0	12	16	.1	8	0	.0
46148	5.0	99	1.6	81	29.9	273	70.1	11	11	1.2	9	0	.0
46149	1.7	0	1.7	73	24.9	266	61.6	7	12	2.4	11	0	.2
46150	.9	100	.3	81	30.0	358	85.5	8	9	.0	0	0	.0
46155	26.1	100	8.8	77	27.2	260*	50.8	8	21	12.7	8	1	1.2
46156	1.7	100	.5	87	22.6	224	52.4	9	11	.9	9	0	.1
46157	2.9	100	.5	86	29.7	287	76.4	7	8	1.4	8	0	.0
46158	16.1	100	5.2	80	31.3	319	81.5	8	8	8.1	7	0	.5
46160	4.9	0	1.7	82	25.2	294	69.7	8	12	.0	0	0	.0
46161	2.2	0	.7	80	26.4	296	72.6	8	13	.0	0	2	.2
46162	.5	0	.2	62	23.7	344	86.8	7	14	.0	0	2	.2
46163	6.0	100	1.8	88	36.8	331	110.0	7	5	3.0	4	2	.7
46164	2.6	100	1.0	88	28.9	359	85.4	6	10	1.3	9	0	.0

*=Estimated **1.0=883 lbs per person; 100++ indicates per capita toxic waste generation > than 100 times the U.S. average of 883 lbs per capita.

ZIP CODE MEASURES OF SIZE, LEVELS OF AFFLUENCE AND QUALITY OF LIFE

1=Population (th.); 2= % White; 3=Households (th.); 4=% Owner Occupied; 5=Mean Income Per Household (th.$); 6=Mean Monthly Rent ($)*; 7=Mean Home Value (th.$)*;
8=% under 5; 9=% 65 and over; 10=White Males (th.); 11=% White Males, 65+; 12=# Toxic Waste Sites; 13=Toxic Waste Relative to US(883 lbs.per capita)**.

INDIANA

ZIPCODE	1	2	3	4	5	6	7	8	9	10	11	12	13
INDIANAPOLIS (SOUTH)													
46165	1.5	99	.5	85	26.9	294	66.9	8	10	.7	8	0	.0
46166	1.8	100	.6	78	22.6	281	61.2	5	9	.9	8	0	.0
46167	3.1	100	1.0	87	32.3	329	91.4	8	10	1.5	9	0	.0
46168	18.4	98	6.0	80	33.4	335	96.3	7	8	9.3	6	3	.5
46171	1.5	0	.5	86	24.7	235	53.4	6	11	.0	0	0	.5
46172	2.4	100	.8	83	24.8	283	52.7	7	12	1.2	10	0	.0
46173	12.1	99	4.3	69	22.6	266	59.8	7	14	5.7	12	0	.0
46175	.7	99	.3	83	21.6	153	42.9	7	18	.3	13	0	.1
46176	23.9	98	8.7	72	25.9	245	67.9	8	12	11.3	8	3	.6
46180	1.2	0	.4	83	27.0	245	70.2	8	12	.0	0	0	.0
46181	3.4	99	1.1	85	28.9	320	88.8	7	8	1.7	7	0	.0
46182	1.8	100	.6	82	27.0	289	66.3	7	13	.9	12	1	.1
46183	.2	100	.2	83	35.9	337	72.5	7	3	.1	0	0	.0
46184	7.5	99	2.3	89	29.0	393	69.3	9	4	3.7	4	0	.0
46186	1.5	100	.5	84	25.8	359	67.3	7	11	.7	10	0	.0
INDIANAPOLIS													
46201	45.0	96	17.4	54	19.4	262	36.6	9	14	20.2	10	1	.2
46202	19.1	32	8.0	29	13.9	177	34.5	7	16	2.9	16	1	2.1
46203	46.5	87	16.0	66	21.0	246	40.7	9	11	19.7	10	5	.5
46204	4.5	60	2.8	0	10.7	177	38.2*	1	32	1.5	20	3	14.8
46205	40.0	30	14.4	43	22.4	290	54.9	9	11	5.4	14	0	.3
46208	44.4	34	16.6	62	27.4	265	76.1	9	16	7.1	12	2	.3
46216	3.1	65	.4	9	22.5	293	80.2*	7	0	.7	7	0	.0
46217	15.0	98	4.9	92	37.5	407	97.4	7	7	7.3	6	0	.0
46218	46.5	30	14.7	70	22.6	274	40.6	9	8	6.6	13	1	.4
46219	40.1	96	15.5	70	28.1	322	68.6	8	15	17.6	12	0	.9
46220	35.8	97	15.5	67	35.7	411	103.5	6	16	15.9	12	0	.2
46221	8.7	95	3.0	61	19.1	251	31.4	9	11	3.9	10	2	2.7
46222	41.3	74	15.1	60	22.3	295	42.0	9	11	15.0	10	5	.6
46224	45.5	95	19.6	45	28.2	357	79.9	9	9	20.2	7	1	.1
46225	10.5	94	3.9	54	18.6	240	32.9	9	14	4.6	11	2	6.3
46226	50.6	72	18.4	64	31.5	366	74.0	7	6	17.9	6	1	.3
46227	66.6	98	24.8	61	30.1	343	84.7	7	10	31.1	8	1	.0
46229	9.1	97	2.9	87	34.5	309	91.8	6	10	4.3	8	2	.2
46231	7.0	94	2.3	55	30.6	392	85.1	8	8	3.3	6	1	.0
46234	13.3	98	4.5	86	34.7	395	105.4	8	5	6.5	4	2	2.9
46236	24.6	84	9.1	48	25.1	296	81.5	10	3	9.8	4	0	.6
46239	9.1	97	2.9	87	34.5	309	91.8	6	10	4.3	8	2	.2
46240	13.6	98	5.9	59	38.1	418	121.5	5	14	6.3	12	0	.2
46241	43.5	99	15.0	73	26.0	311	59.5	8	8	21.2	7	4	1.4
46250	11.0	98	3.9	61	47.9	452	153.9	6	6	4.9	5	0	.6
46254	13.2	76	5.4	34	25.7	291	82.5	10	3	4.9	4	0	.6
46256	9.1	96	3.4	66	42.9	274	154.2	7	3	4.2	3	0	.3
46259	4.3	0	1.4	93	35.1	408	97.8	8	7	.0	0	0	.0
46260	28.6	78	11.0	47	39.5	413	145.7	7	10	10.5	9	3	10.0
46268	6.4	90	2.4	65	30.8	312	103.8	7	13	2.7	8	0	.0
46278	2.4	88	.8	89	58.8	536	157.3	6	8	1.0	6	0	.0
46280	5.8	99	2.0	84	34.3	393	97.4	8	7	2.8	7	0	.0

INDIANA

ZIPCODE	1	2	3	4	5	6	7	8	9	10	11	12	13
GARY													
46301	1.0	0	.4	64	31.9	359	132.7	4	12	.0	0	0	.0
46302	.6	0	.2	87	36.4	314	91.2	4	9	.0	0	0	.6
46303	11.5	100	3.7	76	29.5	386	80.2	10	8	5.8	8	1	.0
46304	17.3	99	5.9	73	34.2	414	101.7	8	8	8.6	7	1	.0
46307	36.2	99	11.3	77	37.9	441	118.4	8	9	17.5	7	0	10.1
46310	9.4	100	2.9	85	30.9	384	95.3	11	7	4.7	7	0	.1
46311	12.1	97	3.6	87	40.8	406	116.3	9	4	4.7	4	0	.0
46312	39.8	48	13.6	43	25.5	241	66.4	9	10	9.5	12	18	.0
46319	19.9	98	6.9	66	34.7	447	90.0	8	6	9.9	9	3	21.1
46320	19.6	67	7.1	44	21.9	256	50.6	9	9	6.6	10	17	.2
46321	20.7	97	6.8	88	50.1	560	144.8	6	10	9.8	9	4	6.1
46322	26.1	97	8.5	81	38.9	462	100.6	7	8	12.7	6	0	.0
46323	26.3	96	9.5	68	32.6	369	74.8	8	8	12.5	7	1	.0
46324	25.7	96	9.5	75	30.1	350	73.0	8	12	11.9	10	0	.0
46327	13.3	94	4.9	68	25.9	304	59.7	8	12	6.1	10	2	.1
46340	1.0	100	.3	76	29.9	361	74.3	8	9	.5	7	0	.0
46341	7.7	99	2.4	85	34.2	384	104.5	9	8	3.8	7	0	.0
46342	30.0	99	10.2	80	33.4	389	81.1	8	9	14.5	8	0	9.6
46345	.3	0	.1	64	21.4	269	60.6	13	9	.7	0	0	.0
46346	1.6	88	.5	77	23.0	302	52.2	13	4	.7	4	0	.0
46347	3.3	100	1.0	81	31.5	357	94.5	8	8	1.6	6	0	.0
46348	1.3	100	.5	79	26.7	338	69.7	11	12	.6	12	0	.0
46349	2.9	99	.9	79	27.6	364	86.2	9	7	1.5	6	0	.0
46350	38.5	99	13.9	75	28.7	305	81.6	7	12	18.1	10	6	1.3
46351	.2	100	.1	94	26.0	299*	77.8	8	11	.1	13	0	.0
46355	.3	100	.1	80	28.6	508	79.9	11	7	.1	5	0	.0
46356	11.3	100	3.5	80	32.9	422	97.2	9	9	5.6	6	2	.0
46360	51.5	84	17.5	71	28.5	304	74.9	8	11	21.2	9	8	1.3
46365	.9	100	.3	77	27.4	356	73.2	11	7	.5	7	0	.6
46366	5.9	100	1.9	81	23.7	303	63.7	9	11	2.9	9	0	.0
46368	28.8	98	9.7	77	34.5	420	96.1	9	6	14.0	5	3	.9
46371	2.8	0	.9	83	28.7	347	82.8	7	9	.0	0	0	.4
46372	.2	0	.1	89	24.2	278*	72.0	8	7	.0	0	0	.0
46373	3.9	100	1.1	92	43.8	525	160.6	8	4	2.0	5	0	.0
46374	1.2	99	.4	81	24.0	368	66.1	7	22	.6	15	0	.6
46375	9.5	98	3.5	60	35.7	478	132.2	9	5	4.7	5	3	.5
46376	.5	94	.1	87	28.3	290	63.1	11	14	.2	10	0	.1
46377	.6	100	.2	71	24.0	363	48.0	7	13	.3	10	0	.0
46379	.4	99	.1	73	20.1	361	35.3	12	10	.1	9	0	.0
46380	.2	100	.1	81	27.4	216	56.1	6	7	.1	5	0	1.9
46381	.3	100	.1	88	27.2	350	65.2	11	5	.1	4	0	.0
46382	1.6	98	.6	84	30.4	339	72.2	8	11	.8	11	0	.0
46383	56.4	98	18.1	75	34.8	387	107.6	8	7	27.0	6	6	.5
46390	2.4	99	.8	81	30.0	407	85.2	7	9	1.2	8	0	1.1
46391	4.7	92	1.4	82	30.0	361	89.0	7	9	2.4	5	2	.6
46392	4.9	99	1.4	81	28.9	379	81.9	10	7	2.5	5	0	.0
46393	.4	0	.1	88	26.9	456	76.9	5	13	.3	0	1	.0
46394	14.6	97	5.7	62	29.6	266	71.9	6	16	6.8	14	4	6.8

*=Estimated **1.0=883 lbs per person; 100++ indicates per capita toxic waste generation > than 100 times the U.S. average of 883 lbs per capita.

ZIP CODE MEASURES OF SIZE, LEVELS OF AFFLUENCE AND QUALITY OF LIFE

1=Population (th.); 2= % White; 3=Households (th.); 4=% Owner Occupied; 5=Mean Income Per Household (th.$); 6=Mean Monthly Rent ($); 7=Mean Home Value (th.$); 8=% under 5; 9=% 65 and over; 10=White Males (th.); 11=% White Males, 65+; 12=# Toxic Waste Sites; 13=Toxic Waste Relative to US(883 lbs.per capita)**.

INDIANA

ZIPCODE	1	2	3	4	5	6	7	8	9	10	11	12	13
GARY													
46402	18.1	14	5.8	43	20.6	229	39.0	11	8	1.3	24	3	11.0
46403	19.7	49	6.8	63	30.1	314	62.3	11	6	4.6	10	2	.1
46404	29.6	3	9.0	66	28.4	282	52.6	9	6	.4	28	3	1.0
46405	14.4	93	4.6	82	28.9	385	54.5	9	7	6.7	7	2	.1
46406	20.5	37	5.9	66	26.1	316	42.2	10	7	3.8	12	12	.3
46407	29.3	1	10.1	46	19.6	251	42.8	8	13	.2	26	0	.0
46408	23.3	66	8.3	78	29.2	321	57.3	9	10	7.3	12	0	.0
46409	16.8	46	5.3	74	27.0	350	44.7	9	8	3.9	14	0	.0
46410	31.5	97	10.5	78	36.8	437	96.1	11	10	14.8	8	1	.0
SOUTH BEND													
46501	3.5	99	1.2	82	23.8	305	64.8	8	13	1.7	10	0	.0
46502	3.0	0	.1	86	24.2	281	77.3	9	15	.0	0	0	.7
46504	3.0	99	1.1	77	26.7	300	64.3	7	14	1.5	13	0	.9
46506	8.2	99	2.8	83	27.4	261	76.3	8	10	4.0	9	9	1.3
46507	5.7	99	2.0	80	29.3	308	88.5	9	8	2.8	7	0	2.2
46508	.3	0	.1	85	24.5	319	52.9	10	11	.0	0	0	6.1
46511	3.0	99	1.0	83	24.2	292	61.5	9	12	1.7	10	1	.0
46514	4.4	98	1.6	78	27.3	266	87.5	9	14	2.2	12	0	.0
46524	76.5	92	27.8	72	28.2	288	74.4	8	10	33.6	8	10	3.1
46526	1.7	0	.6	82	22.7	245	65.6	9	11	.0	0	1	.0
46530	33.6	98	11.4	73	26.7	302	75.6	9	10	15.9	8	5	1.1
46531	9.7	98	2.9	97	41.8	439	124.9	8	4	4.9	4	2	.2
46532	1.1	0	.4	85	23.8	287	48.5	8	12	.0	0	0	.0
46534	2.1	99	.7	81	25.9	322	56.9	5	11	1.0	1	0	.5
46536	10.4	99	3.6	79	21.0	277	65.6	8	13	5.0	12	0	.4
46537	3.0	99	1.0	87	35.7	298	67.8	8	11	1.5	10	0	1.2
46538	.7	0	.3	81	20.0	264	48.6	9	12	.0	0	0	.1
46539	3.3	100	1.1	85	28.5	302	93.1	9	9	1.7	9	0	.1
46540	2.2	99	.8	79	25.2	247	64.8	9	12	1.7	11	1	.4
46542	6.5	99	1.9	81	26.2	337	81.2	10	7	3.2	6	1	3.1
46543	3.1	97	1.0	79	27.4	261	68.7	10	10	1.5	10	4	1.4
46544	1.9	100	.6	84	23.2	295	65.1	13	11	.9	11	0	2.8
46550	50.2	98	19.5	67	25.2	298	65.3	7	12	23.3	10	4	.6
46552	9.2	100	3.0	77	26.0	268	74.0	10	9	4.5	7	1	3.1
46553	4.7	100	1.6	82	27.2	325	66.4	7	13	2.3	8	0	.4
46555	2.6	98	.8	83	28.6	312	76.2	9	9	1.2	8	0	1.2
46561	3.8	99	1.4	82	27.5	299	71.0	7	11	1.9	10	0	.1
46562	2.4	0	.9	78	20.7	351	80.6	6	17	.0	0	0	.1
46563	.2	0	.1	90	29.8	355	72.1	7	6	3.7	5	0	.1
46565	7.3	99	2.3	90	29.8	329	97.6	8	11	3.6	3	5	.0
46566	.2	0	.1	91	22.9	263*	35.2	9	13	.0	0	4	1.4
46567	7.5	99	2.8	77	28.8	329	97.6	8	11	3.6	10	0	1.4
46570	1.1	99	.4	86	23.1	254	63.8	8	11	.2	8	0	.2
46571	3.7	99	.9	83	22.9	248	71.3	13	8	1.8	6	1	10.1
46573	2.9	100	1.0	82	27.2	316	74.7	8	13	1.5	11	0	4.2
46574	7.5	100	2.7	80	24.6	295	65.8	7	15	3.7	13	0	.1
46580	24.3	98	8.6	78	28.0	314	83.4	7	7	11.6	0	1	1.9

INDIANA

ZIPCODE	1	2	3	4	5	6	7	8	9	10	11	12	13
SOUTH BEND													
46590	3.7	94	1.2	59	21.8	249	77.3	9	9	1.6	8	0	.0
46595	.2	100	.1	83	29.0	383	62.9	10	15	.1	17	0	.0
SOUTH BEND													
46601	2.8	82	1.3	18	15.4	213	47.6	4	31	1.0	25	0	.4
46613	13.2	81	5.0	75	20.6	306	34.5	9	15	5.2	15	3	.6
46614	26.0	98	9.3	83	33.5	320	84.1	7	11	12.3	10	6	1.4
46615	16.2	94	6.9	69	25.7	367	57.3	7	17	7.0	15	0	.0
46616	8.1	86	3.2	64	22.5	286	49.6	9	12	3.3	10	0	.0
46617	12.0	74	4.4	72	31.9	357	73.2	6	16	4.4	15	2	.1
46618	2.3	50	1.1	36	13.9	213	34.2	9	16	7.6	16	0	1.7
46619	21.3	75	7.6	84	23.9	275	48.4	7	13	7.6	13	8	.2
46625	2.6	38	.9	27	12.1	170	24.1	7	28	.4	36	0	.0
46628	26.0	77	9.4	79	25.2	323	50.9	9	13	9.7	12	9	2.5
46635	7.4	98	2.3	96	40.9	519	100.5	5	7	3.5	7	0	.0
46637	14.9	95	5.3	69	32.3	413	81.8	6	9	7.1	8	0	.0
FORT WAYNE													
46701	5.5	100	2.0	84	23.8	261	64.3	8	12	2.7	10	0	.9
46702	2.4	0	.8	82	23.5	253	50.0	8	12	.0	0	0	.5
46703	12.4	98	4.4	75	25.4	257	80.6	7	13	6.2	10	0	1.1
46704	.6	100	.1	85	24.8	456	49.3	7	10	.7	11	0	.0
46705	1.8	100	.6	80	24.8	266	54.8	9	13	.7	12	0	.2
46706	12.8	100	4.6	81	28.0	281	78.8	8	12	6.2	9	2	1.8
46710	3.3	99	1.0	84	25.2	258	68.4	8	11	1.6	9	0	.0
46711	5.7	100	1.9	81	26.3	277	82.5	10	15	2.7	12	0	1.3
46714	13.6	99	4.9	76	27.7	260	77.3	8	13	6.4	10	1	.5
46723	4.7	99	1.5	84	26.2	302	60.9	8	11	2.3	9	0	1.3
46725	6.6	99	2.1	89	29.0	308	77.8	9	12	3.3	7	0	.5
46730	17.3	99	6.0	83	26.2	273	72.7	7	12	8.3	10	3	.2
46731	1.2	99	.4	87	23.6	381	55.2	9	9	.6	9	0	.4
46732	.6	100	1.9	73	31.5	340	61.9	9	14	.3	16	0	3.1
46733	1.8	99	.6	85	23.3	248	59.5	12	11	.9	10	0	1.4
46737	17.4	97	5.9	82	27.4	255	74.3	8	10	8.5	9	0	2.8
46738	4.3	100	1.6	88	27.2	298	88.8	8	7	2.1	13	4	.6
46740	6.7	98	2.3	82	25.7	272	60.6	9	10	3.2	8	2	3.1
46741	3.5	100	1.1	78	22.1	247	61.1	13	10	1.7	9	0	.4
46742	5.3	99	1.6	91	35.1	389	97.8	9	7	2.7	6	0	1.2
46743	3.0	99	1.1	87	27.0	280	80.1	7	12	1.5	11	0	.1
46746	.9	100	.3	87	24.4	301	69.0	11	11	.4	12	0	.1
46747	1.5	0	.5	82	36.0	276	89.3	7	7	.0	0	0	1.5
46748	3.1	99	1.0	82	28.3	293	67.2	9	9	1.7	9	0	.8
46750	2.0	0	.7	88	24.2	225	61.2	7	6	2.7	6	0	.7
46755	2.6	99	.8	87	30.0	372	95.9	11	6	1.5	11	0	.1
46759	25.9	99	9.1	77	26.2	299	65.0	8	13	12.3	10	1	1.6
46760	11.3	0	4.0	74	24.5	268	68.4	9	11	5.4	8	0	2.3
46761	1.1	100	.8	85	25.8	194	53.4	9	11	.0	0	0	.0
46763	8.2	99	.4	81	24.2	225	58.3	6	17	.6	15	0	.9
46764	1.3	99	2.7	79	25.1	267	70.6	8	13	.7	8	0	.9

*=Estimated **1.0=883 lbs per person; 100++ indicates per capita toxic waste generation > than 100 times the U.S. average of 883 lbs per capita.

ZIP CODE MEASURES OF SIZE, LEVELS OF AFFLUENCE AND QUALITY OF LIFE

1=Population (th.); 2= % White; 3=Households (th.); 4=% Owner Occupied; 5=Mean Income Per Household (th.); 6=Mean Monthly Rent ($)*; 7=Mean Home Value (th.$)*;
8=% under 5; 9=% 65 and over; 10=White Males (th.); 11=% White Males, 65+; 12=# Toxic Waste Sites; 13=Toxic Waste Relative to US(883 lbs.per capita)**.

INDIANA

FORT WAYNE

ZIPCODE	1	2	3	4	5	6	7	8	9	10	11	12	13
46765	.6	100	.2	81	29.7	378	72.1	5	6	.3	5	0	.0
46766	.7	100	.2	76	29.6	354	59.8	11	8	.3	6	0	.0
46767	5.5	99	1.9	77	25.0	233	64.5	10	10	2.7	8	1	.5
46770	1.9	0	.6	82	28.1	277	68.5	8	11	.0	6	0	.6
46771	.2	100	.1	79	27.0	117	37.2	9	6	.1	6	0	1.4
46772	2.5	100	.7	86	26.0	367	71.6	13	9	1.3	8	0	.1
46773	4.0	0	1.3	85	28.1	273	71.1	9	11	.0	8	0	.1
46774	14.5	99	4.4	85	31.5	363	77.5	8	6	7.2	5	0	.0
46776	1.3	100	.4	85	22.0	272	55.0	8	13	.7	11	0	.1
46777	5.1	100	1.7	87	28.6	347	86.0	9	9	2.5	8	1	1.1
46778	.1	100	.1	89	19.4	223*	41.4	5	16	.1	3	0	.0
46779	1.8	0	.6	83	25.7	261	61.7	8	12	.0	7	0	.0
46781	.9	100	.3	88	26.9	276	62.8	10	12	.5	12	0	.0
46783	4.5	98	1.5	83	29.7	285	92.2	9	10	2.2	8	0	.1
46784	2.7	99	.8	82	25.4	277	63.1	9	9	1.4	7	0	.0
46785	1.4	98	.4	93	27.5	267	63.4	9	11	.7	10	0	1.1
46786	.3	100	.1	78	23.9	316	41.9	8	7	.3	7	0	1.0
46787	3.6	100	1.3	82	23.8	269	65.2	9	13	1.8	10	0	.3
46788	2.2	100	.6	94	23.7	227	90.3	8	5	1.1	10	0	.2
46789	.5	0	.2	88	23.7	285	47.5	13	13	.0	7	0	.0
46791	.9	0	.3	84	27.0	324	67.0	8	13	.0	0	0	.0
46792	4.1	99	1.3	81	26.5	273	54.8	7	21	1.8	14	0	.0
46793	3.9	0	1.3	83	26.5	259	63.0	9	10	.0	0	0	.0
46794	1.2	99	.6	90	26.2	239	53.6	7	11	.6	10	0	.2
46795	4.5	0	1.6	86	25.0	317	70.7	9	10	.0	0	0	.0
46796	.1	90	.0	90	19.9	229*	30.6	8	17	.1	19	0	.5
46797	3.3	0	1.1	87	32.0	308	91.6	9	7	.0	0	0	.0
46798	1.5	0	.5	85	31.1	348	90.2	7	9	.0	0	0	.0
46799	.5	100	.2	93	28.2	377	70.0	11	7	.3	4	0	.0

FORT WAYNE

ZIPCODE	1	2	3	4	5	6	7	8	9	10	11	12	13
46802	3.1	68	1.4	22	12.8	199	25.5	7	17	1.1	13	0	12.3
46804	17.7	35	5.8	54	18.2	240	29.9	11	8	3.1	10	1	2.2
46805	26.5	94	9.8	67	34.9	293	102.1	8	9	12.2	9	0	.9
46806	24.7	97	10.6	59	25.5	315	67.3	6	17	10.9	13	1	.2
46807	29.9	67	10.5	78	24.5	325	48.1	10	10	9.5	12	1	.0
46808	19.5	96	7.4	68	29.0	327	70.8	8	14	8.8	11	0	.1
46809	26.3	98	10.0	74	24.1	283	56.1	8	12	12.5	10	4	1.8
46815	10.5	98	4.0	73	26.4	282	67.6	8	13	4.9	10	0	.8
46816	49.1	96	16.2	76	37.1	413	104.2	8	10	23.5	4	0	.0
46818	15.9	91	5.9	65	27.8	323	79.8	8	10	6.9	7	0	.0
46819	4.0	98	1.4	79	28.5	345	87.1	9	9	2.0	8	1	2.0
46825	8.6	98	3.0	78	33.8	368	93.0	7	6	4.2	6	0	.0
	19.0	98	6.4	73	35.4	289	107.8	11	8	8.9	6	2	.0

KOKOMO

ZIPCODE	1	2	3	4	5	6	7	8	9	10	11	12	13
46901	78.0	93	28.2	73	28.5	311	73.6	8	8	35.0	7	4	1.6
46910	2.9	99	1.1	81	24.5	279	58.0	8	14	1.4	12	0	.0
46911	1.5	98	.5	87	28.2	316	61.1	9	12	.7	10	0	.0
46913	1.2	0	.4	81	30.3	289	86.1	10	6	.0	0	0	.0
46914	2.2	96	.8	75	26.3	251	70.5	8	8	1.1	7	0	.0

INDIANA

KOKOMO

ZIPCODE	1	2	3	4	5	6	7	8	9	10	11	12	13
46915	.7	100	.2	77	29.9	360	70.9	8	17	.3	14	0	.0
46916	.7	100	.2	81	22.7	250	34.4	9	12	.1	11	0	.0
46917	1.9	100	.7	77	27.4	317	58.5	7	14	.9	12	0	.6
46919	2.5	99	.9	77	27.1	284	65.8	7	11	1.2	9	0	.1
46920	1.2	99	.4	83	28.2	348	74.3	8	12	.6	11	0	.3
46923	7.2	100	2.6	75	25.3	266	65.8	7	12	3.5	11	0	.4
46926	1.7	99	.6	82	23.3	301	56.5	6	11	.9	8	1	.0
46928	5.6	99	2.0	77	25.2	265	60.8	7	11	2.6	10	0	.5
46929	3.6	99	1.3	77	26.2	265	66.6	7	16	1.7	12	0	.2
46930	.4	100	.1	91	23.0	159	53.6	9	7	.2	3	0	.0
46931	.3	100	.1	83	22.6	315	51.5	9	11	.1	7	0	.0
46932	3.9	100	1.3	84	31.5	268	78.5	8	7	1.9	7	3	.0
46933	6.7	99	2.3	79	24.3	270	60.0	8	9	3.1	7	0	.0
46936	5.6	99	1.9	81	30.2	314	86.6	7	9	2.7	7	0	.1
46937	.1	100	.1	81	23.4	315	45.7	11	22	.1	22	0	.3
46938	4.5	100	1.6	87	26.4	286	49.5	8	8	2.2	8	0	.2
46939	2.5	100	.9	80	20.8	263	49.7	8	14	1.2	12	0	.1
46940	2.5	100	.8	83	26.3	286	71.8	7	13	1.2	12	0	.1
46941	1.2	100	.4	83	26.7	325	50.2	8	7	.6	10	1	.2
46943	.3	100	.3	91	21.3	175	43.0	6	18	.2	19	1	.9
46945	.2	100	.2	83	24.2	418	51.4	3	15	.1	15	0	.1
46946	.2	100	.1	74	21.4	308	31.4	6	4	.2	4	0	.6
46947	29.6	98	10.8	75	25.6	264	62.4	7	13	13.9	10	2	7.9
46950	.8	100	.3	82	27.7	419	58.6	11	14	.8	13	0	.3
46951	2.3	99	.8	85	24.3	115	49.7	7	13	1.1	12	0	.5
46952	52.7	88	18.7	69	25.9	260	65.4	7	12	22.6	10	3	1.5
46957	.7	0	.2	87	25.5	177	50.9	6	9	.0	0	0	.2
46958	.6	95	.2	88	20.9	249	68.9	6	17	.2	19	0	.8
46959	.4	99	.1	95	22.6	288	45.3	5	11	.3	4	0	.0
46960	1.0	96	.3	85	21.9	260	50.1	8	14	.5	12	0	.0
46961	.2	100	.1	82	25.8	297*	39.7	5	5	.1	5	0	.6
46962	10.0	99	3.3	73	25.5	281	71.3	8	14	4.6	10	1	.1
46965	.2	0	.1	100	22.5	259*	47.7	0	23	.0	0	0	7.9
46968	.2	0	.1	89	15.9	183*	26.0	11	4	.2	13	0	.0
46970	24.1	97	8.8	75	23.9	257	61.1	8	12	11.4	10	2	.5
46971	4.7	82	1.1	82	18.0	334	62.4	15	1	1.2	1	1	.1
46974	1.2	98	.4	87	25.7	162	68.4	8	9	.6	9	3	.5
46975	12.7	98	4.7	79	25.1	280	72.1	8	14	6.1	11	3	.5
46977	.2	100	.1	93	24.0	275*	46.4	8	16	.0	15	0	.0
46978	2.2	100	.8	79	25.6	305	64.3	8	12	.3	10	0	.5
46979	4.2	100	1.3	89	33.9	334	92.2	7	7	2.1	6	1	.1
46982	1.9	99	.9	85	22.7	313	56.5	9	12	.9	11	2	.5
46983	.3	0	.1	87	23.1	279	44.9	12	10	.0	0	0	.8
46984	.2	100	.1	96	40.7	468*	105.2	6	7	.2	10	0	1.0
46985	1.4	0	.5	81	24.7	298	50.7	8	14	.0	14	0	.0
46986	1.9	100	.6	83	28.4	337	70.7	7	10	.9	9	0	.0
46987	.9	98	.3	84	28.9	310	70.9	6	8	.5	7	0	.8
46988	.9	100	.3	81	26.6	235	62.7	8	14	.5	11	0	.8
46989	4.7	99	1.2	73	23.6	299	72.0	5	6	2.3	6	0	1.0

*=Estimated **1.0=883 lbs per person; 100++ indicates per capita toxic waste generation > than 100 times the U.S. average of 883 lbs per capita.

ZIP CODE MEASURES OF SIZE, LEVELS OF AFFLUENCE AND QUALITY OF LIFE

1=Population (th.); 2= % White; 3=Households (th.); 4=% Owner Occupied; 5=Mean Income Per Household (th.$); 6=Mean Monthly Rent ($)*; 7=Mean Home Value (th.$)*;
8=% under 5; 9=% 65 and over; 10=White Males (th.); 11=% White Males, 65+; 12=# Toxic Waste Sites; 13=Toxic Waste Relative to US(883 lbs.per capita)**.

INDIANA

KOKOMO

ZIPCODE	1	2	3	4	5	6	7	8	9	10	11	12	13
46990	1.1	0	.4	88	29.5	296	63.6	7	10	.0	0	0	1.0
46991	1.9	100	.6	84	25.0	272	56.0	8	11	.9	9	0	.2
46992	21.0	99	7.4	73	25.6	275	64.8	8	11	10.1	10	5	.6
46994	2.8	0	1.0	80	27.5	323	63.6	8	11	.0	0	0	.1
46995	.2	100	.1	100	28.6	329*	47.4	8	14	.1	25	0	5.6
46996	6.7	99	2.5	79	23.7	271	69.1	8	15	3.2	13	0	.5
46998	.2	100	.1	87	25.8	350	43.3	11	10	.1	6	0	.0

CINCINNATI

ZIPCODE	1	2	3	4	5	6	7	8	9	10	11	12	13
47001	9.7	100	3.4	77	25.0	294	72.9	7	12	4.8	10	0	.2
47006	8.5	100	2.7	80	27.3	291	87.6	8	13	4.2	11	0	.1
47011	.6	100	.2	89	22.2	162	58.5	8	11	.3	11	0	.0
47012	8.5	99	2.8	76	25.2	275	73.3	8	12	4.2	10	1	.0
47016	.9	100	.3	75	25.9	273	77.6	11	9	.5	8	0	.0
47017	.5	0	.2	83	19.8	179	49.4	7	13	.0	0	0	.6
47018	3.1	100	1.0	77	25.2	295	71.7	7	13	1.5	10	0	.0
47020	.7	100	.2	82	18.8	203	39.8	7	14	.3	16	0	.0
47022	1.8	100	.6	88	28.0	253	82.4	8	10	.9	10	0	.0
47023	1.7	100	.5	83	20.2	181	49.5	9	12	.9	11	0	.0
47024	3.6	0	1.1	85	19.4	222	46.4	8	11	6.3	9	0	.0
47025	13.2	97	4.5	78	27.7	261	87.4	8	11	.6	9	1	.6
47030	1.3	100	.4	83	21.4	248	58.8	9	8	.6	9	0	.0
47031	4.6	100	1.4	83	23.9	289	63.6	9	10	.2	9	0	.1
47032	2.7	0	.8	86	23.4	316	65.3	9	9	2.2	9	0	.0
47033	.1	100	.1	66	21.7	335	48.6	6	0	.0	60	56	.0
47034	.2	100	.1	78	19.0	292	62.1	5	13	.1	7	0	.0
47035	.3	100	.1	80	20.7	316	52.9	12	6	.1	7	0	.0
47036	1.2	0	.3	76	25.0	272	77.8	5	23	.0	0	0	.0
47037	4.1	100	1.4	82	21.0	208	62.9	7	15	2.0	14	0	.1
47038	.9	98	.3	79	22.2	274	48.2	8	10	.1	10	0	.4
47040	4.3	98	1.5	76	23.1	210	68.8	8	14	2.1	12	0	.0
47041	4.6	99	1.4	82	25.2	275	77.3	11	8	2.3	7	0	.6
47042	3.5	100	1.2	77	20.4	225	72.5	9	15	1.7	12	0	.1
47043	4.2	99	1.6	80	19.1	223	56.7	7	17	2.1	14	0	.0

LOUISVILLE

ZIPCODE	1	2	3	4	5	6	7	8	9	10	11	12	13
47102	7.6	100	2.3	80	20.2	265	44.0	10	8	3.9	7	0	.1
47106	3.5	100	1.1	86	26.1	256	73.2	9	8	1.8	8	0	.3
47108	2.4	100	.8	85	18.6	203	41.2	10	12	1.2	10	0	.4
47110	.6	0	.2	86	24.3	300	54.9	8	8	.0	0	0	.0
47111	9.6	98	3.1	72	23.9	262	65.0	9	8	4.6	8	1	.5
47112	10.4	98	3.6	83	24.7	264	76.5	9	12	5.0	10	0	.3
47114	.3	100	.1	99	28.3	326*	50.8	6	8	.1	4	0	.0
47115	1.7	100	.5	89	23.2	332	58.9	9	9	.8	10	0	.0
47116	.6	0	.2	93	20.4	69	57.1	7	12	.0	0	0	.1
47117	3.5	99	1.1	89	24.1	242	66.6	8	10	1.7	9	0	.0
47118	3.2	99	1.1	84	18.3	200	45.0	9	14	1.6	13	0	.0
47119	7.6	100	2.2	90	33.7	384	100.4	8	6	3.8	5	0	.0
47120	2.4	100	.2	90	20.7	219	54.5	8	8	.4	8	0	.0
47122	7.0	99	2.1	91	27.9	344	76.8	8	6	3.4	6	0	.0
47124	.5	100	.2	89	28.4	396	62.9	4	11	.3	10	0	.0

INDIANA

LOUISVILLE

ZIPCODE	1	2	3	4	5	6	7	8	9	10	11	12	13
47125	1.3	99	.4	84	20.3	197	56.0	7	10	.6	8	0	.0
47126	3.0	100	.9	84	26.2	419	68.4	8	8	1.4	7	0	.0
47130	58.0	92	20.9	64	25.2	311	70.3	8	9	25.5	7	5	1.0
47135	.9	99	.3	87	20.7	122	56.1	6	16	.4	13	0	.0
47136	2.9	99	.5	89	28.3	334	86.0	9	7	1.4	5	0	.0
47137	1.3	0	.5	84	19.2	196	51.9	8	17	.0	0	0	.0
47138	3.8	100	1.2	86	22.7	268	61.9	8	11	1.9	11	0	.0
47140	2.6	100	.4	86	19.6	233	50.5	8	12	1.3	10	0	.0
47141	1.0	0	.3	88	23.0	199	58.3	7	14	.0	0	0	.3
47142	.7	99	.3	86	21.6	248*	53.5	8	14	.3	13	0	.1
47143	1.9	0	.3	86	26.8	282	77.0	9	8	.0	0	0	.0
47145	2.2	100	.8	87	20.1	260	52.4	7	12	1.1	10	0	.0
47147	1.2	99	.4	87	25.0	241	56.8	9	13	.6	11	0	.0
47150	44.9	95	16.5	68	24.7	278	69.4	7	13	20.2	10	2	.3
47160	.2	100	.1	90	20.2	232*	51.1	7	14	.1	11	0	.0
47161	2.3	0	.7	82	24.3	246	70.7	8	6	.0	0	0	.1
47162	.6	0	.6	67	20.0	315	62.3	16	0	.0	0	0	.0
47163	1.3	0	.4	96	22.9	202	61.3	6	10	.0	0	0	.0
47165	2.7	100	.9	87	24.7	349	67.3	8	9	1.3	9	0	.0
47166	4.2	100	1.3	81	22.4	245	62.1	9	7	2.1	6	0	.3
47167	1.2	0	.4	88	30.8	304	74.4	11	7	.0	0	0	.0
47170	12.3	100	4.4	82	21.8	245	61.2	8	14	6.0	12	0	.0
47172	10.9	99	3.8	81	23.1	273	61.1	7	13	5.3	11	0	.1
47175	9.2	100	.0	86	28.1	339	75.5	8	8	4.5	7	1	.0
47177	.8	0	.3	89	21.2	126	37.5	8	12	.0	0	0	.0
	1.3	0	.4	92	21.5	221	52.9	7	3	.0	0	1	.0

COLUMBUS

ZIPCODE	1	2	3	4	5	6	7	8	9	10	11	12	13
47201	53.5	97	19.0	73	31.3	335	90.4	7	9	25.1	7	18	4.5
47220	4.8	100	1.7	84	24.3	258	65.7	9	15	2.3	13	1	.3
47222	2.5	98	.5	77	21.0	243	43.2	11	6	.1	8	0	.3
47223	.4	100	.5	78	20.9	257	47.9	6	8	1.3	7	0	.3
47224	.2	100	.4	86	20.9	341	61.7	8	13	.2	13	0	.3
47225	.3	100	.2	70	17.3	306	33.9	10	15	.1	12	0	.1
47226		0	.1	83	23.7	249	47.3	11	8	.1	8	0	.0
47227	1.1	100	.4	92	24.3	207	55.5	7	11	.6	9	0	.1
47229	3.9	100	1.4	80	23.0	304	53.8	7	10	1.9	9	1	.0
47230	1.9	0	.7	88	22.5	259	55.5	8	11	.0	0	0	.0
47231	1.1	0	.4	87	21.9	176	51.8	7	13	.0	0	0	.0
47232	2.5	98	.8	87	27.3	277	78.2	7	9	.0	0	1	.3
47234	1.6	99	.6	79	25.0	292	61.9	6	14	.8	13	0	.0
47235	1.6	0	.5	86	23.6	223	51.9	8	10	.1	4	0	.1
47236	.1	95	.1	91	22.1	254*	47.1	10	12	.1	13	0	.0
47240	18.8	100	6.4	75	24.2	272	72.2	9	13	9.1	11	4	.6
47243	5.7	97	1.6	78	22.9	315	68.5	8	9	2.6	8	0	.0
47244	.7	0	.3	83	27.4	338	57.9	9	9	.0	0	0	.0
47246	4.8	98	1.5	84	25.9	275	68.7	10	10	2.3	8	1	.0
47247	.2	100	.1	82	19.1	231	42.8	11	13	.1	9	0	.0
47250	20.3	98	7.2	72	23.9	291	71.4	8	7	9.7	11	2	.7
47260	.7	100	.7	86	20.8	201	43.8	8	13	1.0	12	1	.2

*=Estimated **1.0=883 lbs per person; 100++ indicates per capita toxic waste generation > than 100 times the U.S. average of 883 lbs per capita.

ZIP CODE MEASURES OF SIZE, LEVELS OF AFFLUENCE AND QUALITY OF LIFE

1=Population (th.); 2= % White; 3=Households (th.); 4=% Owner Occupied; 5=Mean Income Per Household (th.$); 6=Mean Monthly Rent ($)*; 7=Mean Home Value (th.$)*; 8=% under 5; 9=% 65 and over; 10=% White Males (th.); 11=% White Males, 65 and over; 12=# Toxic Waste Sites; 13=Toxic Waste Relative to US(883 lbs.per capita)**.

INDIANA

COLUMBUS

ZIP CODE	1	2	3	4	5	6	7	8	9	10	11	12	13
47263	.2	100	.1	96	19.8	227*	39.8	6	13	.1	14	0	.0
47264	1.3	100	.4	88	20.8	177	46.1	8	13	.6	12	0	.0
47265	14.6	99	4.9	81	24.7	298	64.1	8	10	7.1	7	0	1.2
47270	.9	100	.3	87	23.0	273	51.7	10	9	.5	7	0	.0
47272	1.8	100	.6	84	23.3	240	56.2	10	9	.9	8	0	.0
47273	1.7	0	.5	86	27.2	176	70.6	7	6	.0	8	1	.0
47274	23.0	99	8.3	79	24.1	291	70.8	8	12	11.0	10	2	.6
47280	1.5	0	.5	92	28.9	358	66.2	8	3	.0	0	0	.0
47281	1.5	0	.5	88	21.2	201	47.0	8	13	.0	0	0	.0
47282	.4	100	.2	81	16.1	358	44.3	7	18	.2	15	0	.1
47283	3.6	100	1.2	81	23.0	275	56.0	8	10	1.8	9	0	.0

MUNCIE

ZIP CODE	1	2	3	4	5	6	7	8	9	10	11	12	13
47302	51.4	93	18.2	75	25.0	281	60.9	7	10	23.0	8	7	.9
47303	25.8	87	8.1	58	20.6	326	50.1	5	11	9.8	8	0	.1
47304	19.2	96	7.3	73	33.5	344	88.6	6	10	8.8	9	0	1.9
47305	6.4	90	2.8	31	15.1	220	31.3	7	12	2.8	9	0	4.5
47320	4.7	100	1.6	81	25.6	293	60.9	8	11	2.3	9	0	.0
47324	.2	0	.1	79	23.7	241	49.2	7	13	.0	0	0	.0
47325	.9	0	.3	81	25.0	301	49.0	7	12	.0	0	0	.0
47326	2.0	100	.6	86	25.4	304	46.2	8	11	1.0	10	0	.0
47327	5.0	99	1.8	73	25.4	282	62.7	7	12	2.4	10	0	.4
47330	5.6	100	1.9	80	23.5	309	65.5	8	10	2.8	9	0	.3
47331	27.2	98	9.6	72	23.1	278	65.0	8	11	12.9	9	2	3.8
47334	3.4	100	.1	82	29.7	337	72.8	6	9	1.6	8	0	.0
47335	.9	100	.3	84	20.0	222	46.6	6	15	.4	13	0	.0
47336	5.0	100	1.8	79	23.5	245	49.0	7	11	2.4	11	0	.1
47337	.2	98	.1	89	24.1	200	54.1	11	11	.0	6	0	.0
47338	3.3	0	1.2	83	22.9	291	55.4	7	11	.0	0	0	.0
47339	.7	100	.3	83	23.8	253	54.8	6	13	.3	11	0	.0
47340	3.4	99	1.2	82	22.9	246	60.1	7	12	1.6	9	0	.1
47341	3.2	99	1.2	82	25.4	285	61.5	9	9	1.1	10	0	.0
47342	3.3	99	1.1	78	27.1	287	61.6	8	11	1.6	9	0	.0
47344	.2	100	.1	89	20.6	237*	49.0	8	15	.1	11	0	.0
47345	1.3	0	.4	76	26.7	315	58.8	5	8	.0	0	0	.0
47346	4.2	0	1.5	77	28.0	283	72.0	7	13	.0	0	1	1.6
47348	12.1	100	4.3	81	23.1	259	54.0	7	13	5.8	10	0	.3
47351	.4	100	.1	79	24.1	244	52.2	8	13	.2	13	0	.0
47352	1.2	100	.4	66	22.4	267	64.5	8	14	.6	12	0	.0
47353	5.2	100	1.8	73	22.5	274	66.5	8	13	2.5	11	0	.3
47354	1.5	100	.5	81	22.4	266	55.1	6	12	.8	11	0	.0
47355	3.4	100	1.2	78	23.8	256	50.6	7	11	1.7	10	0	.1
47356	5.8	99	2.0	85	26.8	300	71.0	7	10	2.8	8	0	.0
47357	1.5	100	.5	73	23.5	306	56.0	7	11	.6	11	0	.6
47358	1.2	0	.4	80	21.2	155	46.5	8	15	.0	0	0	.0
47359	3.5	0	1.2	80	23.3	275	52.0	7	11	.0	0	2	.0
47360	1.6	100	.5	81	24.3	282	59.2	9	10	.8	9	0	.1
47361	.3	100	.1	82	22.5	229	58.9	6	22	.2	17	0	.6
47362	32.8	98	11.7	75	23.9	256	59.3	7	13	15.4	10	3	.7
47366	.2	100	.1	91	20.3	234*	33.8	15	11	.1	1	0	.0

INDIANA

MUNCIE

ZIP CODE	1	2	3	4	5	6	7	8	9	10	11	12	13
47367	.2	100	.1	88	25.1	288*	48.0	3	13	.1	9	0	.0
47368	3.0	100	1.0	80	25.1	266	60.5	7	14	1.5	11	0	.0
47369	1.5	99	.6	82	20.4	245	44.4	9	15	.0	0	0	.0
47370	.4	0	.2	78	22.7	247	49.2	8	11	.0	0	0	.4
47371	13.0	100	4.7	78	22.0	231	55.1	8	14	6.2	12	0	.0
47373	2.6	99	.9	85	23.2	173	48.7	7	11	1.3	10	0	.0
47374	52.6	92	19.4	66	23.9	258	64.6	7	13	22.6	11	3	1.1
47380	2.6	100	.9	81	22.0	256	44.8	9	10	1.3	10	0	.0
47382	.3	0	.1	81	21.9	198	40.4	8	13	.0	0	0	1.7
47383	2.8	99	.9	77	28.1	313	68.7	8	8	1.3	6	0	.0
47384	2.0	100	.7	87	25.2	259	54.2	6	11	1.0	10	0	.0
47385	1.8	0	.6	83	26.0	265	58.8	6	13	.0	0	0	.0
47386	1.4	100	.4	85	24.3	296	73.5	8	6	.7	4	0	.0
47387	.8	0	.3	80	26.3	345	58.4	6	12	.0	0	0	.0
47388	.4	0	.2	93	23.0	339	51.0	8	12	.0	0	0	1.8
47390	5.9	99	2.2	78	23.1	241	59.8	8	11	2.9	8	1	.0
47392	.3	100	.1	94	24.7	284*	60.0	4	11	.1	9	0	.0
47393	1.5	100	.5	79	24.5	309	63.2	6	8	.4	9	0	.0
47394	9.6	0	3.6	72	23.0	250	59.7	8	14	.7	0	0	.5
47396	5.3	100	1.9	80	29.4	327	72.0	7	11	2.6	8	0	.0

BLOOMINGTON

ZIP CODE	1	2	3	4	5	6	7	8	9	10	11	12	13
47401	90.8	95	31.1	54	23.3	320	82.4	5	7	42.3	6	12	.2
47420	.2	100	.1	85	28.1	212	39.6	8	11	.1	12	0	2.8
47421	26.7	99	10.1	80	23.5	244	59.8	7	14	12.6	11	6	.1
47424	8.2	100	3.1	82	22.1	213	61.1	7	16	4.0	14	0	.1
47427	1.0	97	.6	89	18.4	281	34.2	6	21	.5	21	0	.0
47429	4.9	99	1.6	82	24.8	258	70.7	11	7	2.4	6	0	.0
47431	.6	0	.2	82	22.0	211	46.3	5	13	.0	0	0	.0
47432	4.6	96	1.7	81	19.3	222	45.1	7	15	2.1	12	0	.5
47433	3.2	100	1.0	82	23.2	251	50.7	6	14	1.5	12	0	.0
47434	.3	100	.1	90	17.4	200*	42.1	6	10	.1	10	0	.0
47435	1.3	100	.1	92	17.7	204*	40.8	6	9	.1	11	0	.0
47436	1.3	100	.5	88	22.4	156	47.6	6	12	.7	12	0	.0
47437	.2	100	.2	79	19.8	183	30.8	16	13	.1	12	0	.0
47438	4.8	100	1.8	84	22.0	201	43.0	8	16	2.3	12	0	1.6
47441	9.5	100	3.8	82	21.4	238	54.6	7	18	4.4	14	0	.2
47443	1.6	99	.6	77	20.2	219	44.9	10	14	.8	12	0	.2
47446	9.6	100	3.4	81	22.6	252	51.3	7	12	4.7	11	0	.7
47448	6.3	100	.4	78	25.1	340	85.8	6	11	3.1	10	0	.0
47449	.5	0	.2	83	18.8	302	42.2	5	11	.0	0	0	.0
47451	1.1	0	.4	89	21.6	234	45.2	6	11	.1	0	0	.0
47452	4.5	99	1.7	83	19.9	240	53.5	8	15	2.2	13	0	1.6
47453	.4	0	.2	94	25.4	137	49.4	4	15	.0	0	0	.0
47454	7.1	0	2.6	81	20.1	210	54.9	9	14	.0	0	0	.0
47455	.2	100	.1	87	20.7	446	25.2	9	18	.0	0	0	.0
47456	.8	100	.5	83	21.3	317	45.2	9	10	.4	9	0	.0
47458	.2	100	.1	92	27.9	321*	34.8	5	5	.1	0	0	.0
47459	2.0	99	.7	86	22.5	210	59.5	8	5	1.0	8	0	.0
47460	8.5	100	3.1	81	22.5	269	60.2	7	13	4.2	10	1	.0

*=Estimated **1.0=883 lbs per person; 100+ indicates per capita toxic waste generation > than 100 times the U.S. average of 883 lbs per capita.

ZIP CODE MEASURES OF SIZE, LEVELS OF AFFLUENCE AND QUALITY OF LIFE

1=Population (th.); 2= % White; 3=Households (th.); 4=% Owner Occupied; 5=Mean Income Per Household (th.$); 6=Mean Monthly Rent ($); 7=Mean Home Value (th.$);
8=% under 5; 9=% 65 and over; 10=White Males (th.); 11=% White Males, 65+; 12=# Toxic Waste Sites; 13=Toxic Waste Relative to US(883 lbs.per capita)**.

INDIANA

ZIPCODE	1	2	3	4	5	6	7	8	9	10	11	12	13
BLOOMINGTON													
47462	3.1	99	1.0	91	22.2	290	53.2	9	8	1.5	7	1	.3
47464	.3	0	.1	93	17.4	200*	34.7	6	11	.0	0	0	.0
47465	.8	100	.3	82	20.8	275	56.1	4	15	.4	14	2	.0
47468	1.2	98	.5	84	27.3	262	91.7	7	13	.6	13	0	.0
47469	1.8	98	.6	79	18.3	169	51.4	7	12	.9	11	0	.0
47470	1.2	0	.4	91	21.3	340	46.3	10	9	.7	9	0	.0
47471	2.6	0	1.1	83	18.8	192	49.1	6	20	1.1	20	0	.0
WASHINGTON													
47501	16.5	99	6.3	75	20.9	229	61.0	7	16	7.8	13	4	.6
47512	4.7	0	1.9	80	19.5	250	39.0	7	19	.0	0	0	.3
47513	1.6	0	.6	82	21.1	183	61.6	9	13	.0	0	0	.0
47514	.2	100	.1	96	28.2	324*	80.2	4	14	.1	15	2	.0
47515	.7	0	.3	87	16.6	206	50.0	8	13	.0	0	0	.0
47516	1.2	100	.4	84	21.9	256	52.1	8	13	.6	11	0	.0
47519	.6	100	.2	86	23.0	331	49.2	11	7	.3	7	0	.0
47520	3.4	100	1.1	78	19.4	195	51.3	8	16	1.6	14	0	.0
47521	.5	100	.2	86	31.0	226	92.9	9	9	.0	0	0	.0
47522	.7	94	.2	40	23.1	146	35.9	10	2	.3	2	2	.0
47523	3.3	0	1.1	76	24.7	241	70.6	10	14	1.3	10	0	.3
47524	.6	0	.2	69	17.1	195	38.4	5	18	.0	0	0	.0
47525	.4	100	.1	87	22.3	276	59.7	9	12	.0	0	0	.0
47527	1.7	100	.5	86	24.0	225	68.7	9	10	.9	10	0	.0
47529	1.4	99	.6	80	20.4	284	44.8	6	20	.7	15	0	.0
47531	.8	99	.3	91	25.7	216	70.8	7	13	.4	13	2	.1
47532	4.4	99	1.2	88	29.0	164	84.1	8	9	2.2	7	2	.0
47535	.6	100	.2	90	20.3	262	42.5	6	29	.3	21	0	.0
47537	.9	0	.3	88	22.5	377	64.3	10	12	.0	0	0	.0
47541	1.1	100	.3	84	24.5	276	70.1	8	16	.0	0	1	.1
47542	8.3	100	2.8	77	25.5	266	68.8	8	12	4.0	10	2	.0
47546	15.7	100	5.3	88	23.6	247	57.8	7	5	7.8	5	4	.6
47550	.8	0	.3	79	23.8	157	61.4	8	11	.0	0	0	.0
47551	.5	100	.1	82	23.6	303	91.1	9	14	.0	0	1	.0
47553	7.4	100	2.4	91	21.8	280	70.1	8	10	3.6	9	1	.0
47555	.3	100	.1	78	23.8	197	48.9	5	9	.0	0	0	.0
47556	.3	100	.1	79	20.1	274*	75.6	6	16	.1	22	0	.0
47557	1.4	0	.5	82	22.3	231*	61.5	8	17	.0	0	1	.0
47558	2.8	100	.8	84	21.4	258	56.1	9	10	1.4	9	0	.9
47561	1.7	100	.6	83	22.9	331	51.4	7	15	.8	12	0	.9
47562	4.1	0	.5	86	20.6	261	52.1	9	12	.4	0	3	.0
47564	1.3	100	1.3	86	21.4	188	58.3	6	15	.6	14	0	.0
47567	6.9	99	2.6	85	23.0	277	57.4	7	17	3.2	15	5	.2
47568	.8	100	.3	80	22.2	244	50.0	7	16	.4	13	0	.1
47574	.3	100	.1	82	25.7	228	47.5	10	11	.1	13	0	.0
47575	1.0	100	.3	86	26.0	447	75.8	9	8	.5	7	0	.0
47576	.3	97	.1	92	19.2	305	71.1	9	12	.2	11	1	.0
47577	1.4	97	.5	79	27.8	221*	63.4	6	9	.9	7	2	.0
47578	.9	100	.3	82	21.9	251	50.3	8	17	.5	15	0	.0

ZIPCODE	1	2	3	4	5	6	7	8	9	10	11	12	13
WASHINGTON													
47579	.6	0	.2	86	36.3	307	143.7	5	18	.0	0	1	.3
47580	.2	100	.1	84	25.3	303	73.0	13	10	.1	8	0	.0
47581	4.1	100	1.5	83	19.5	206	45.7	7	13	2.0	16	1	.1
47584	.2	100	.2	94	24.4	280*	49.5	6	16	.1	16	0	.0
47585	.5	100	.2	88	24.3	276	53.5	8	19	.2	17	2	.0
47586	11.7	99	4.3	83	24.7	239	73.1	8	13	5.7	11	4	.4
47587	.3	100	.1	90	20.9	500	41.0	5	15	.2	13	0	.0
47588	.8	100	.3	81	22.7	221	61.3	7	15	.4	13	1	.0
47590	.9	100	.3	88	24.9	231	50.2	6	14	.4	11	0	.0
47591	28.2	98	10.9	69	22.5	284	69.8	6	14	13.4	11	11	.7
47596	.3	100	.1	85	28.5	321	36.0	4	20	.2	20	1	.0
47597	1.2	100	.5	80	20.6	267	50.9	6	15	.6	13	1	.0
47598	3.3	98	1.3	85	22.9	224	52.7	7	14	1.6	12	2	.0
EVANSVILLE													
47601	12.3	99	4.3	81	27.7	247	73.4	7	12	5.9	10	4	.0
47610	5.5	100	1.8	81	26.2	320	72.1	9	8	2.8	7	2	.0
47611	1.3	100	.5	76	23.1	266	59.9	8	16	.7	15	0	.0
47612	1.2	0	.4	81	24.2	304	54.5	7	13	.0	0	0	.2
47613	2.7	100	.9	85	27.5	306	73.9	7	10	1.3	10	2	.0
47615	1.6	99	.5	84	24.2	232	55.4	9	9	.8	8	2	.0
47616	.5	100	.2	78	21.6	274	48.1	7	17	.2	18	0	.0
47617	.5	100	.2	92	25.8	158	57.0	6	19	.3	15	0	.3
47619	1.4	99	.5	84	27.4	330	73.3	8	11	.7	10	1	.2
47620	14.1	98	4.9	75	27.7	279	82.5	7	11	6.8	9	9	11.2
47630	17.8	98	5.7	83	35.9	369	118.9	9	6	8.6	5	2	.7
47631	2.1	100	.8	70	24.0	274	68.9	7	16	1.0	13	5	.0
47633	2.7	0	.9	83	26.9	316	70.0	8	12	.0	0	0	.0
47634	5.3	0	1.8	83	24.4	239	67.1	9	11	.0	0	2	.0
47635	5.3	98	1.8	77	24.6	251	66.8	7	15	2.5	13	2	.7
47636	.1	100	.1	84	18.5	161	36.1	8	16	.1	14	0	.0
47637	1.5	0	.5	86	22.9	308	54.2	7	10	2.1	10	0	.0
47638	3.3	99	1.1	85	29.5	332	93.3	9	9	2.8	13	3	.0
47639	3.2	0	1.1	83	30.5	257	88.3	8	10	1.7	7	1	.0
47640	1.2	100	.4	88	25.5	208	41.8	7	13	1.4	13	1	.2
47648	4.3	99	1.5	83	28.7	349	71.6	8	11	2.1	10	0	.4
47649	1.0	0	.3	79	25.7	293	69.5	5	10	.1	2	0	.0
47660	5.9	100	2.2	80	24.6	306	61.2	6	16	2.8	13	1	.3
47665	2.9	100	1.0	82	23.4	181	59.4	7	14	1.4	12	0	.2
47666	2.1	100	.8	84	21.9	271	51.7	9	16	1.0	13	1	.9
47670	12.4	95	4.8	75	25.1	272	64.4	7	16	5.7	12	12	.1
47683	.4	100	.1	88	23.5	235	43.5	10	9	.2	9	0	.0
EVANSVILLE													
47708	1.0	92	.5	3	16.2	266	13.1	2	23	.5	18	13	4.9
47710	25.0	96	9.3	61	22.7	274	66.4	7	14	11.1	11	3	.6
47711	33.8	99	13.0	75	27.0	298	77.9	7	12	15.9	11	4	.5
47712	35.6	99	13.0	78	28.0	314	79.7	9	15	17.1	10	7	.4
47713	18.6	54	7.5	45	17.1	229	44.6	9	12	4.6	14	1	.0
47714	31.0	95	11.8	72	26.4	339	67.2	6	14	13.6	12	3	.0
47715	24.5	96	9.7	56	33.1	387	105.7	6	13	11.0	10	1	.0

*=Estimated **1.0=883 lbs per person; 100++ indicates per capita toxic waste generation > than 100 times the U.S. average of 883 lbs per capita.

ZIP CODE MEASURES OF SIZE, LEVELS OF AFFLUENCE AND QUALITY OF LIFE

1=Population (th.); 2= % White; 3=Households (th.); 4=% Owner Occupied; 5=Mean Income Per Household (th.$); 6=Mean Monthly Rent ($); 7=Mean Home Value (th.$); 8=% under 5; 9=% 65 and over; 10=White Males (th.); 11=% White Males, 65+; 12=# Toxic Waste Sites; 13=Toxic Waste Relative to US(883 lbs.per capita)**.

INDIANA

TERRE HAUTE

ZIPCODE	1	2	3	4	5	6	7	8	9	10	11	12	13
47802	28.3	95	10.6	70	26.6	299	72.0	7	12	12.9	10	9	.1
47803	18.2	97	6.9	82	28.8	333	74.7	6	17	8.8	13	1	.0
47804	13.2	95	5.2	71	20.5	272	40.3	7	20	5.7	14	1	.5
47805	12.6	97	4.4	82	28.3	318	72.3	7	8	6.0	7	3	.5
47807	17.8	84	7.5	47	16.8	249	30.7	8	14	6.9	11	2	2.5
47831	.4	100	.1	95	28.2	325*	41.2	5	12	.2	14	0	.0
47832	1.1	0	.4	83	23.6	268	40.3	7	15	.0	0	1	.0
47833	.9	100	.3	90	22.6	174	37.3	8	21	.5	18	0	.1
47834	17.3	99	6.4	79	22.6	270	57.7	8	15	8.2	12	0	.0
47836	.2	100	.1	90	18.9	217*	30.1	6	19	.1	19	4	.5
47837	1.0	100	.4	88	20.1	193	42.3	7	14	.0	0	0	.0
47838	2.3	0	.9	83	21.6	195	47.2	7	16	1.0	0	0	.0
47840	1.4	100	.5	89	23.5	301	59.7	8	13	.7	11	1	.7
47841	2.2	100	.8	84	21.2	216	50.3	7	20	1.1	18	2	.0
47842	10.1	100	4.0	79	21.2	271	52.8	7	18	4.7	15	0	.0
47845	.3	100	.1	89	18.7	182	29.7	7	21	.1	16	0	5.7
47846	.8	100	.3	78	23.7	232	50.4	8	18	.4	16	1	.0
47847	1.5	0	.5	81	20.4	257	50.7	8	15	.0	0	0	.0
47848	1.9	100	.7	87	23.1	225	44.7	7	17	.9	14	2	.2
47849	.5	0	.2	77	22.3	358	39.9	3	14	.0	0	0	.0
47850	3.1	100	1.1	84	22.3	325	54.0	7	13	1.5	10	1	.6
47851	.2	100	.1	86	14.1	196	36.8	8	19	.1	15	0	.0
47853	.3	100	.1	93	26.4	303*	50.6	8	15	.1	7	0	.0
47854	.8	0	.4	88	22.2	222	40.7	5	15	.0	0	0	2.7
47855	1.1	97	.4	85	19.9	209	32.7	8	14	.3	8	0	.0
47857	.4	100	.1	87	23.2	222	45.1	7	13	.2	10	0	.0
47858	.8	0	.3	88	23.3	122	55.5	10	13	.0	0	0	.0
47859	1.0	100	.4	78	22.9	139	46.3	9	16	.5	16	0	.1
47860	.4	100	.1	93	18.7	169	25.2	9	12	.2	8	0	.0
47861	.7	0	.2	82	25.5	321	48.2	8	13	.0	0	1	.0
47862	1.8	0	.7	83	20.9	202	44.7	7	14	.0	0	0	.0
47863	.3	100	.1	87	21.6	462	41.5	8	5	.1	15	1	.0
47865	.6	100	.2	80	14.7	368	29.5	4	15	.1	0	0	.0
47866	.6	0	.2	76	21.9	203	57.0	5	17	.0	0	1	.0
47868	1.6	97	.6	90	22.0	189	54.2	6	17	.9	18	0	.0
47869	.2	100	.1	84	20.3	175	41.9	6	23	.2	10	0	.0
47870	.1	100	.1	78	20.0	325	52.0	8	18	.1	15	0	.0
47871	.3	100	.1	80	22.2	292	55.2	7	16	.2	11	0	.0
47872	6.8	99	2.6	78	22.6	223	69.6	6	17	3.3	14	1	.1
47874	4.0	0	1.4	87	26.1	266	56.6	5	12	.0	0	0	.0
47875	.4	100	.2	80	16.4	257	32.5	8	28	.2	26	0	.0
47876	1.0	91	.1	100	40.6	466*	58.6	0	27	.0	8	0	.0
47877	.1	100	.1	57	22.3	300	65.4	6	0	.1	15	1	.0
47878	.5	0	.2	80	27.2	252	47.5	6	13	.0	0	0	.0
47879	2.9	0	1.1	83	20.4	272	47.3	8	17	.0	0	0	.3
47880	.2	100	.1	82	17.2	305	43.9	16	17	.1	22	0	.0
47881	.5	100	.1	91	21.9	228	51.5	8	13	.2	10	0	.0
47882	8.3	100	3.2	79	23.5	262	59.9	7	19	3.8	14	2	.4
47884	.4	0	.2	91	20.3	221	32.0	7	16	.0	0	0	.0

INDIANA

ZIPCODE	1	2	3	4	5	6	7	8	9	10	11	12	13
TERRE HAUTE													
47885	10.9	99	3.7	84	25.2	261	57.4	8	11	5.3	10	3	.0
LAFAYETTE													
47901	4.9	97	2.2	21	16.1	256	67.2	7	18	2.3	15	1	1.5
47904	15.6	97	6.4	64	21.8	301	59.6	8	11	7.2	7	1	1.1
47905	46.0	98	16.6	73	29.2	321	90.9	8	8	22.0	7	1	1.7
47906	48.2	94	13.1	45	26.6	349	124.1	5	5	24.2	3	0	.0
47917	.6	95	.2	70	28.8	260	34.3	6	15	.3	18	0	.7
47918	6.9	100	2.5	70	24.8	236	54.7	7	14	3.3	11	2	.0
47920	2.1	99	.7	82	28.8	352	82.0	9	7	1.0	6	0	.8
47921	1.2	100	.5	80	24.1	300	51.8	8	18	.6	18	0	.0
47922	1.7	100	.6	74	23.7	227	66.4	8	18	.8	18	0	.0
47923	2.9	100	1.0	82	27.4	288	72.3	9	10	.1	0	1	.7
47924	.2	100	.1	84	20.2	341	46.6	5	23	.1	20	0	.2
47925	.3	100	.1	88	25.9	487	67.0	12	13	.1	14	0	.0
47926	.4	99	.1	83	25.7	348	50.5	11	9	.0	0	0	.0
47928	2.4	99	.9	85	22.0	259	50.4	8	11	1.2	10	0	.0
47929	.9	0	.3	65	26.4	299	63.4	6	14	.0	0	0	.0
47930	1.1	100	.4	81	26.4	338	61.0	9	11	.5	10	0	.0
47931	.3	100	.1	80	25.7	221	44.8	10	7	.1	7	0	.0
47932	6.0	0	2.1	78	26.4	297	77.0	7	12	.0	0	1	.6
47933	24.8	99	9.1	72	26.0	277	73.4	7	13	12.2	10	1	1.0
47940	1.5	100	.5	83	24.1	204	52.2	7	14	.7	12	0	.0
47941	.8	100	.8	70	29.1	377	73.1	8	9	.4	9	0	.0
47942	.8	100	.3	69	23.9	338	53.5	6	16	.4	10	0	.0
47943	.7	100	.2	64	27.5	357	62.2	8	9	.3	8	0	.0
47944	4.2	100	1.5	73	26.8	317	72.4	8	14	2.1	13	1	.2
47946	2.0	99	.7	73	27.5	287	71.5	9	14	1.0	12	0	.0
47948	1.5	0	.5	74	25.9	251	68.5	8	15	.0	0	0	.4
47949	1.3	100	.5	78	21.8	257	53.9	8	15	.6	13	0	.0
47950	1.1	0	.4	84	26.0	250	50.0	8	15	.0	0	0	.0
47951	2.6	0	1.0	71	27.8	304	79.9	7	16	.0	0	0	2.2
47952	2.4	100	.9	81	22.2	251	46.7	7	14	1.2	12	0	.0
47954	2.5	100	.8	78	25.1	294	53.1	7	15	1.2	12	0	.0
47955	1.0	0	.4	80	27.1	178	60.0	7	11	.0	0	0	.1
47957	1.9	100	.7	83	24.1	293	52.9	9	12	.9	10	0	.0
47958	.2	100	.1	79	19.6	247	32.9	6	10	.1	13	1	.0
47959	3.0	0	1.1	76	22.9	311	61.2	8	12	.0	0	0	.0
47960	13.8	99	5.2	79	24.0	304	81.1	7	14	6.6	12	2	.3
47963	2.4	99	.9	69	24.0	274	62.0	8	14	1.2	11	0	.2
47964	.2	100	.1	64	26.1	303	39.4	10	5	.0	0	0	.0
47965	.7	100	.2	85	24.3	280	54.8	10	16	.3	12	0	.0
47966	.7	100	.3	79	23.6	278	39.5	8	12	.4	10	2	.0
47967	.8	100	.3	74	28.4	310	55.0	8	13	.4	11	0	.0
47968	.9	0	.3	79	21.9	223	60.0	6	11	.0	0	0	.3
47969	.3	100	.1	86	24.1	267	44.9	6	20	.2	12	0	.0
47970	1.8	99	.7	78	21.5	291	59.8	8	13	.9	11	0	.0
47971	2.0	0	.7	75	24.4	296	60.6	8	15	.0	0	0	.3
47974	1.3	99	.5	82	26.5	309	55.5	8	12	.6	11	0	5.5
47975	.7	0	.3	70	25.9	306	53.0	6	14	.0	0	0	.0

*=Estimated **1.0=883 lbs per person; 100++ indicates per capita toxic waste generation > than 100 times the U.S. average of 883 lbs per capita.

ZIP CODE MEASURES OF SIZE, LEVELS OF AFFLUENCE AND QUALITY OF LIFE

1=Population (th.); 2= % White; 3=Households (th.); 4=% Owner Occupied; 5=Mean Income Per Household (th.$); 6=Mean Monthly Rent ($)*; 7=Mean Home Value (th.$)*;
8=% under 5; 9=% 65 and over; 10=White Males (th.); 11=% White Males, 65+; 12=# Toxic Waste Sites; 13=Toxic Waste Relative to US(883 lbs.per capita)**.

INDIANA

ZIPCODE	1	2	3	4	5	6	7	8	9	10	11	12	13
LAFAYETTE													
47977	2.4	100	.8	72	29.5	261	72.4	7	13	1.1	12	0	1.5
47978	11.2	99	3.6	72	27.0	343	76.9	8	12	5.4	10	0	.5
47980	1.3	0	.4	73	26.5	325	58.7	10	12	.0	0	0	.0
47981	.7	99	.2	74	33.5	375	78.9	8	9	.4	6	0	.0
47982	.2	100	.1	85	29.6	427	54.5	12	10	.1	8	0	.0
47983	.4	100	.2	87	23.3	311	48.7	4	22	.2	20	0	.0
47985	.5	0	.2	90	21.3	245*	36.5	10	10	.0	0	0	.0
47987	4.2	100	1.5	82	23.0	263	51.2	8	13	2.0	10	0	.0
47989	1.3	0	.5	81	22.7	326	50.4	6	15	.0	0	0	.0
47990	1.7	0	.6	78	24.2	274	54.1	6	14	.0	0	0	.0
47991	1.4	99	.4	75	24.3	289	54.2	10	8	.7	7	0	.1
47992	1.3	100	.4	77	26.6	349	86.6	6	13	.7	8	1	.0
47993	3.8	100	1.3	77	26.9	271	63.8	7	13	1.9	11	0	.0
47994	.7	0	.3	81	25.9	279	46.2	7	11	.0	0	0	1.5
47995	1.7	100	.6	75	23.7	278	65.8	10	16	.8	15	0	.3
47997	.2	100	.1	90	21.8	250*	41.6	9	15	.1	19	0	.0
KALAMAZOO													
49099	.6	0	.2	86	21.0	233	63.6	10	6	.0	0	0	.0

IOWA

ZIPCODE	1	2	3	4	5	6	7	8	9	10	11	12	13
DES MOINES													
50001	.4	100	.2	83	20.9	274	57.0	6	10	.2	12	0	.0
50002	1.8	0	.6	82	20.3	258	49.1	7	19	.0	0	0	.0
50003	4.7	100	1.7	79	29.6	263	92.5	7	13	2.3	10	0	.0
50005	1.1	100	.3	79	24.1	354	56.8	7	9	.5	7	0	.0
50006	2.2	100	.8	70	23.4	307	62.1	8	17	1.1	14	0	.1
50007	.3	100	.1	75	31.4	399	81.1	9	7	.1	8	0	.1
50008	.5	100	.1	80	18.1	197	32.1	9	24	.0	0	0	.3
50009	7.4	99	2.4	77	30.2	385	100.3	9	6	3.5	4	3	.4
50010	49.3	95	15.4	50	27.1	363	117	5	24	24.5	4	3	.4
50020	1.8	0	.7	73	19.3	255	48.0	7	21	.0	0	0	.1
50021	18.3	99	6.2	67	32.8	405	111.2	8	4	8.7	3	2	.0
50022	9.6	99	3.8	72	23.9	251	70.2	8	18	4.6	15	1	.0
50025	4.4	0	1.6	77	24.2	262	68.4	7	19	.0	0	1	.0
50026	.9	0	.3	56	22.7	290	39.7	10	20	.0	0	0	.0
50027	.4	0	.2	70	14.2	245	19.7	5	24	.0	0	0	1.5
50028	1.4	0	.5	82	20.3	347	61.9	7	18	.0	0	0	.3
50029	1.0	100	.4	68	22.4	221	41.2	6	21	.5	17	0	.0
50032	.4	96	.2	100	28.6	329*	57.0	12	17	.2	12	0	.0
50034	.6	100	.2	64	23.7	379	70.4	4	4	.3	4	0	.0
50035	2.2	100	.7	86	29.5	338	95.5	9	8	1.1	6	0	.1
50036	16.2	99	6.2	73	25.3	284	73.9	7	17	7.5	13	0	.1
50038	.5	0	.2	79	26.1	315	148.4	11	18	.2	20	0	.0
50039	.4	100	.2	69	27.4	82	46.5	7	18	.2	0	0	.0
50040	.3	100	.1	85	21.8	204	43.4	4	22	.2	0	0	.0
50042	.4	100	.2	75	19.4	356	31.9	6	9	.2	8	0	.0
50043	.2	100	.1	81	19.5	289	27.0	7	25	.1	17	0	.0
50044	1.3	100	.4	81	23.0	277	46.9	9	11	.7	12	0	.1
50045	.2	100	.2	100	20.9	240*	18.7	13	6	.1	0	0	.0
50046	1.3	99	.5	79	28.4	340	83.8	9	11	.6	13	0	.0
50047	4.9	100	1.7	79	28.8	330	89.1	9	11	2.4	13	0	.1
50048	1.0	0	.4	79	20.5	122	32.0	8	20	.0	0	0	.0
50049	7.3	99	3.0	75	20.6	196	60.6	7	20	3.4	16	0	.1
50050	1.1	0	.4	68	22.0	293	38.2	8	14	.0	0	0	.0
50051	.5	100	.2	88	22.0	376	40.3	8	13	.3	11	0	.0
50052	.2	100	.1	85	20.9	240*	19.8	9	9	.1	4	0	.0
50054	3.4	99	1.2	79	22.8	274	65.6	8	12	1.7	10	1	.1
50055	.8	100	.3	78	22.6	336	59.2	6	18	.4	16	0	.0
50056	1.3	99	.5	74	42.0	311	68.8	12	10	.6	8	0	.1
50057	.3	100	.1	85	18.1	188	26.1	0	0	.1	0	0	.0
50058	2.7	0	.9	71	23.0	266	66.8	9	15	.1	4	0	.0
50060	.6	100	.2	78	20.6	222	56.5	6	23	.3	17	0	.4
50061	.9	0	.3	83	40.0	467	142.1	7	8	.0	0	0	.0
50062	.8	0	.2	86	20.7	185	50.6	6	14	.0	0	0	.0
50063	2.1	99	.8	74	30.6	256	87.4	8	14	1.1	11	1	.0
50064	.2	100	.1	89	21.2	244*	18.1	9	8	.1	4	0	.1
50065	.6	100	.2	81	14.4	221	25.1	4	15	.3	17	0	.0
50066	.4	100	.2	53	21.8	289	40.0	8	8	.2	6	0	.4
50067	.4	100	.1	87	19.1	311	35.9	10	13	.2	15	0	.0
50068	.6	100	.2	65	17.5	290	22.4	7	18	.3	14	0	.0

*=Estimated **1.0=883 lbs per person; 100++ indicates per capita toxic waste generation > than 100 times the U.S. average of 883 lbs per capita.

ZIP CODE MEASURES OF SIZE, LEVELS OF AFFLUENCE AND QUALITY OF LIFE

1=Population (th.); 2= % White; 3=Households (th.); 4=% Owner Occupied; 5=Mean Income Per Household (th.$); 6=Mean Monthly Rent ($)*; 7=Mean Home Value (th.$); 8=% under 5; 9=% 65 and over; 10=White Males (th.); 11=% White Males, 65+; 12=# Toxic Waste Sites; 13=Toxic Waste Relative to US(883 lbs.per capita)**.

IOWA

ZIP CODE	1	2	3	4	5	6	7	8	9	10	11	12	13
DES MOINES													
50069	1.0	99	.3	78	27.9	309	84.4	12	5	.5	6	0	.0
50070	1.4	0	.5	85	24.4	342	61.9	5	17	.0	0	0	.0
50071	1.6	99	.6	74	22.8	282	40.3	5	19	.7	18	0	.0
50072	2.2	0	.7	77	25.4	293	73.6	9	13			0	.0
50073	.7	100	.2	80	28.2	267	78.6	3	9	.4	8	0	.0
50074	.2	100	.1	91	16.5	190*	66.3	7	10	.1	5	0	.0
50075	.9	100	.3	82	29.9	271	63.6	8	14	.4	14	0	.0
50078	2.0	0	.8	78	20.5	222	50.2	7	22	.0	0	0	.2
DES MOINES													
50101	.2	100	.1	59	23.9	344	54.8	9	5	.1	4	0	.0
50102	.1	100	.1	100	14.1	162*	52.4	0	26	.1	23	0	.0
50103	.6	100	.3	81	16.1	236	32.7	5	25	.3	27	0	.4
50104	.2	100	.1	83	23.6	285	59.7	3	28	.1	33	0	.0
50105	.8	99	.3	73	29.6	377	89.0	9	5	.4	6	0	.0
50106	1.5	100	.5	68	28.6	289	69.9	8	12	.7	12	0	.0
50107	1.5	100	.6	71	20.1	234	45.5	9	21	.7	18	0	.0
50108	.5	100	.2	80	15.0	210	21.4	7	17	.3	16	1	.0
50109	1.6	100	.5	74	30.8	302	98.5	10	9	.8	7	0	.0
50110	.4	100	.1	80	23.7	248	30.2	12	16	.2	13	0	.3
50111	3.1	99	1.1	76	31.7	374	111.6	9	7	1.5	6	0	.0
50112	11.3	99	3.9	67	26.2	283	82.2	7	13	5.3	10	0	.8
50115	3.1	100	1.3	77	20.6	215	54.6	7	23	1.4	20	0	.4
50116	.3	100	.1	96	20.5	235*	39.2	1	17	.1	21	1	.1
50117	.4	100	.1	70	21.6	203	83.4	5	8	.2	0	0	.3
50118	.8	98	.3	92	25.8	272	72.7	7	10	.4	6	0	.0
50119	.4	0	.1	74	27.1	311	71.1	7	17	.2	14	0	.2
50120	.3	100	.1	75	21.1	338	36.3	11	15	.2	13	0	.0
50122	1.6	100	.6	74	24.7	193	63.0	8	19	.8	16	0	.3
50123	1.0	100	.5	69	17.5	249	43.1	6	25	.5	24	0	.0
50124	2.3	100	.8	75	26.7	333	102.3	10	10	1.1	9	2	.8
50125	14.3	99	5.0	71	27.0	294	96.0	7	12	6.8	9	0	.0
50126	8.4	99	3.0	73	26.7	305	77.8	7	15	4.1	13	1	.1
50128	.6	0	.2	83	21.8	191	45.5	5	18	.0	0	0	.0
50129	6.2	100	2.5	74	25.2	272	70.4	7	21	3.0	16	0	.3
50130	1.7	0	.6	74	25.8	268	71.1	7	17	.0	0	0	.0
50131	.4	0	.2	53	35.1	166	160.1	14	2	.0	0	0	.2
50132	.5	0	.2	72	23.0	329	47.0	6	15	.0	0	0	.0
50133	.7	0	.3	79	12.5	159	30.4	9	17	.3	9	0	.0
50134	.6	100	.2	68	30.1	303	98.3	5	10	.3	9	0	.3
50135	.7	100	.6	82	27.8	304	70.8	7	13	.9	12	2	.8
50136	2.3	100	.3	80	19.9	239	38.8	9	17	.4	14	0	.0
50137	.1	100	.1	73	41.5	135	48.9	14	0	.0	0	0	.0
50138	11.5	99	4.0	75	25.0	285	72.4	8	16	5.8	14	0	.1
50139	1.4	100	.5	78	21.6	155	49.1	9	16	.7	15	0	.0
50140	3.3	98	1.0	69	19.5	216	60.4	5	13	1.5	10	0	.1
50141	.9	100	.2	71	26.2	306	56.1	8	9	.3	7	0	.1
50142	.9	98	.3	82	28.4	290	73.7	10	9	.4	9	0	.0
50143	.7	100	.2	71	24.1	296	45.1	9	12	.4	12	0	.0

IOWA

ZIP CODE	1	2	3	4	5	6	7	8	9	10	11	12	13
DES MOINES													
50144	3.2	100	1.3	74	18.2	187	46.0	6	26	1.4	22	0	.0
50146	.6	0	.2	83	17.6	235	43.9	6	18	.0	0	0	.0
50147	.7	100	.3	73	13.5	193	30.5	7	20	.4	18	0	.0
50148	.5	100	.3	74	17.9	457	42.9	10	20	.2	18	0	.0
50149	.7	100	.4	83	18.5	169	29.8	10	18	.5	19	0	.0
50150	.2	100	.4	85	20.1	264	44.1	5	19	.6	19	0	.0
50151	.9	0	.3	94	18.1	336	40.0	9	15	.0	5	0	.2
50153	.9	100	.3	69	23.6	282	52.7	10	6	.5	5	0	.0
50154	.5	99	.3	66	23.9	379	55.8	9	16	.3	19	0	.0
50155	.3	100	.3	70	18.7	399	22.9	8	24	.2	25	0	.0
50156	3.7	99	1.4	76	26.9	313	70.5	7	15	1.8	12	0	.8
50157	1.2	0	.4	69	25.0	260	48.3	6	0	.0	0	0	.7
50158	31.9	98	11.9	70	27.7	331	78.8	7	14	15.0	12	0	.7
50160	.4	100	.2	78	24.0	274	70.2	9	10	.2	8	0	.0
50161	1.8	100	.7	77	25.9	298	69.3	8	15	.9	12	0	.0
50162	1.2	100	.5	77	25.2	314	61.6	10	14	.6	14	0	.0
50163	1.0	0	.4	85	18.3	289	43.1	10	15	.0	0	0	.0
50164	.5	99	.3	84	21.5	293	50.7	7	18	.5	16	0	.0
50166	1.5	0	.5	80	27.1	263	57.6	10	10	.4	19	0	.0
50167	.8	100	.3	79	24.3	273	71.9	7	20	.4	17	0	.0
50168	.8	100	.3	78	25.1	259	55.0	6	16	1.1	13	0	.1
50169	2.2	99	.8	77	25.5	305	78.6	8	17	1.4	9	0	.0
50170	2.9	100	1.0	78	25.5	286	65.5	9	10	1.3	16	1	.0
50171	2.7	100	1.0	78	22.7	279	67.6	8	15			0	2.4
50172	.3	0	.1	87	23.7	272*	40.0	6	17	.4	9	0	.0
50173	.8	97	.2	78	28.6	383	43.4	6	10	.4	9	0	.5
50174	1.4	0	.5	80	18.4	234	31.7	8	15	.0	0	0	.0
DES MOINES													
50201	7.3	99	2.6	73	26.1	322	84.4	7	14	3.5	11	0	.0
50206	2.7	100	1.0	61	26.2	308	63.0	7	8	.4	6	0	.1
50207	1.0	100	.7	72	21.8	269	58.1	10	18	.9	12	0	.0
50208	19.5	99	7.6	72	25.7	261	54.8	9	14	9.4	12	2	1.0
50210	1.6	0	.6	86	22.5	266	54.4	8	13	2.8	5	0	.0
50211	5.9	99	1.7	87	32.4	432	103.1	10	5	2.8	4	1	.0
50212	3.1	99	1.2	78	25.3	318	72.7	8	19	1.5	15	0	.0
50213	6.1	100	2.4	75	20.0	251	62.5	6	18	3.0	16	0	.5
50214	.6	0	.2	68	30.1	512	85.6	6	8	.0	0	0	.0
50216	2.0	100	.7	80	22.3	237	74.7	8	22	.5	5	1	.0
50217	.6	100	.3	80	23.2	254	46.9	4	14	.3	16	0	.3
50218	.1	100	.1	86	25.6	294*	36.0	8	3	.1	0	0	.0
50219	10.4	99	3.5	72	27.1	315	90.9	7	14	4.9	12	1	1.2
50220	8.3	100	3.2	71	25.6	259	70.9	8	17	3.9	14	2	.3
50222	.5	100	.2	79	16.9	330	42.7	8	14	.2	13	0	.1
50223	4.0	100	1.0	71	20.3	217	55.8	9	20	.3	16	0	.0
50225	2.7	100	1.0	75	22.6	282	70.8	9	13	1.3	7	0	.0
50226	2.3	98	.7	78	33.5	411	99.6	9	18	1.1	7	1	.1
50228	2.2	0	.8	73	24.4	317	74.5	8	18	1.1	11	0	.0
50229	.9	98	.3	88	30.7	589	96.7	11	8	.5	10	0	.0
50230	.7	100	.5	68	23.0	159	61.4	11	16	.7	16	0	.0

*=Estimated **1.0=883 lbs per person; 100++ indicates per capita toxic waste generation > than 100 times the U.S. average of 883 lbs per capita.

ZIP CODE MEASURES OF SIZE, LEVELS OF AFFLUENCE AND QUALITY OF LIFE

1=Population (th.); 2= % White; 3=Households (th.); 4=% Owner Occupied; 5=Mean Income Per Household (th.$); 6=Mean Monthly Rent ($)*; 7=Mean Home Value (th.$)*; 8=% under 5; 9=% 65 and over; 10=White Males (th.); 11=% White Males, 65+; 12=# Toxic Waste Sites; 13=Toxic Waste Relative to US(883 lbs.per capita)**.

IOWA

DES MOINES

ZIPCODE	1	2	3	4	5	6	7	8	9	10	11	12	13
50231	.2	100	.1	81	28.5	363	42.7	2	13	.1	10	0	.0
50232	.7	100	.1	77	33.1	359	54.7	6	8	.4	7	0	.0
50233	1.5	0	.6	79	23.0	282	54.4	8	14	.0	0	0	.0
50234	.6	100	.2	78	19.2	269	48.8	10	11	.3	5	0	.0
50235	.6		.3	69	24.7	177	40.1	5	20	.0			.0
50236	1.3	100	.5	85	24.0	255	81.1	13	13	.6	10	0	.0
50237	2.0	100	.6	84	30.0	437	93.6	8	8	1.0	8	0	.0
50238	1.3	100	.5	75	19.1	273	48.1	7	16	.6	13	0	.0
50239	.3	0	.1	75	16.4	431	36.5	15	11	.0	0	0	.0
50240	1.7	100	.6	86	27.8	316	69.1	9	9	.8	9	0	.0
50242	.6	100	.2	80	18.8	58	39.2	7	16	.3	15	0	.0
50243	.3	100	.1	90	27.6	443	59.2	7	10	.2	10	0	.0
50244	1.8	0	.6	68	26.6	342	89.9	9	12	.0	0	0	.0
50246	.9	100	.3	70	27.7	228	59.5	8	15	.5	12	0	.2
50247	2.2	0	.8	75	25.0	242	64.2	7	18	.0	0	0	.0
50248	3.8	0	1.4	72	26.8	283	91.5	7	20	.0	0	0	.0
50249	1.5	0	.6	71	22.4	233	57.4	7	19	.0	0	0	.0
50250	2.5	0	.9	76	22.4	254	60.8	7	17	.0	0	0	.0
50251	1.4	100	.5	79	27.1	232	73.0	7	15	.7	14	0	.1
50252	.4	0	.1	86	23.6	265	44.6	2	12	.0	0	0	.2
50254	.5	100	.2	93	11.9	213	21.0	2	20	.3	23	0	.0
50256	.6	100	.2	86	21.7	240	42.6	10	7	.3	5	0	.0
50257	.6	0	.2	87	21.0	213	52.1	6	19	.1	11	0	.0
50258	.9	0	.4	80	21.0	242	54.9	7	17	3.2	16	0	.0
50261	1.4	100	.5	81	28.2	326	93.5	12	12	.3	19	0	.0
50262	.5	0	.2	70	16.2	250	26.0	14	11	.0	0	0	.0
50263	3.7	100	1.3	79	33.6	330	117.4	7	7	.0	0	0	.1
50264	.7	100	.2	79	20.7	318	32.2	5	19	.3	19	0	.0
50265	22.5	98	8.5	66	37.9	441	124.9	6	9	10.5	7	0	.2
50269	1.3	0	.5	81	16.9	264	29.9	12	16	.0	0	0	.0
50271	.2	100	.1	89	22.3	256*	39.1	6	16	.1	10	0	.0
50272	.9	0	.4	75	22.5	269	50.3	6	20	.0	0	0	.0
50273	6.7	100	2.4	86	19.9	266	27.2	8	13	3.2	11	0	1.1
50274	.6	100	.2	75	23.8	245	70.7	7	21	.3	16	0	.0
50275	.5	0	.2	78	21.2	311	43.6	5	14	.3	19	0	.0
50276	3.0	0	.9	83	19.8	233	43.1	6	14	.0	0	0	.0
50277	.6	99	.2	69	27.0	313	69.6	7	9	1.5	8	0	.2
50278	1.0	0	.4	63	30.1	225	49.6	5	18	.3	19	0	.0

DES MOINES

ZIPCODE	1	2	3	4	5	6	7	8	9	10	11	12	13
50309	3.8	68	2.1	10	12.3	220	35.7	4	22	1.3	17	3	4.3
50310	29.3	95	12.0	73	30.7	426	90.4	7	13	12.9	10	1	.0
50311	21.1	93	8.4	52	26.1	338	88.0	6	11	9.3	9	0	.1
50312	17.0	93	7.6	57	35.6	411	123.0	6	18	7.1	12	0	.0
50313	16.9	96	6.9	77	24.6	344	65.4	7	14	7.7	12	3	1.1
50314	13.4	53	5.2	35	17.3	278	45.0	9	13	5.3	12	0	.0
50315	38.8	97	14.1	73	27.3	393	74.8	8	8	17.8	7	1	.2
50316	16.8	82	6.7	62	20.5	330	57.5	8	18	6.1	15	4	.2
50317	41.6	97	14.7	80	27.0	363	69.4	8	10	19.3	8	6	.6

IOWA

DES MOINES

ZIPCODE	1	2	3	4	5	6	7	8	9	10	11	12	13
50320	6.3	98	2.5	75	25.2	369	88.7	11	6	3.2	6	0	2.4
50321	6.7	97	2.4	64	43.1	394	157.0	7	5	3.0	5	2	1.8
50322	27.8	98	10.2	70	37.9	434	127.7	7	6	13.2	5	1	.6
50323	2.3	98	.7	77	35.7	498	102.6	6	4	1.1	4	0	.0
50324	.4	100	.1	94	44.2	508*	119.5	4	18	.2	16	0	.0

MASON CITY

ZIPCODE	1	2	3	4	5	6	7	8	9	10	11	12	13
50401	32.3	99	12.6	70	25.2	282	77.1	7	15	14.7	12	1	.2
50420	.4	100	.2	57	21.6	296	44.8	9	25	.3	25	1	.0
50421	3.4	100	1.3	76	27.1	252	77.8	6	20	1.6	19	1	.6
50423	3.6	100	1.3	74	27.1	272	65.8	9	18	1.8	14	0	.4
50424	2.1	0	.8	80	22.0	254	58.4	6	21	.0	0	0	.0
50426	.1	100		96	13.6	156*	26.9	6	45	.1	40	0	.0
50428	9.6	99	3.7	74	26.8	302	96.0	6	14	4.6	13	2	.0
50430	.9	100	.3	70	23.4	185	53.4	6	14	.5	11	0	.0
50431	.3	100	.1	80	19.0	297	51.2	10	28	.1	24	0	.0
50432	.3	100	.1	79	19.0	252	49.7	12	21	.2	15	0	.0
50433	.4	100	.1	70	24.3	65	35.4	4	8	.2	4	0	.7
50434	.6	99	.2	84	24.1	271	56.7	6	20	.3	22	0	.0
50435	.9	100	.3	82	25.9	260	69.5	7	12	.5	11	0	.0
50436	6.4	99	2.3	74	24.5	259	76.1	9	13	3.1	11	1	1.8
50438	4.4	100	1.5	81	26.2	313	75.8	9	12	2.1	10	1	.5
50439	.5	100	.2	80	28.5	243	49.3	4	23	.2	20	0	.0
50440	.5	100	.2	76	26.4	229	56.3	10	26	.2	19	0	.0
50441	6.3	99	2.5	72	24.0	271	74.2	7	19	3.0	15	1	.8
50444	.5	100	.2	83	25.6	127	59.7	9	17	.2	17	0	.0
50446	.7	100	.3	75	29.1	259	61.9	9	16	.3	13	0	.0
50447	1.5	0	.6	70	25.0	261	64.8	6	21	.0	0	0	.7
50448	1.0	100	.4	78	24.5	220	70.0	9	10	.5	8	0	.0
50449	1.0	100	.4	75	21.0	248	58.9	9	19	.5	17	0	.2
50450	3.1	100	1.2	76	23.2	240	73.4	8	21	1.5	17	1	3.2
50451	.8	100	.3	73	19.8	246	46.6	11	17	.4	15	0	.0
50452	1.0	0	.4	74	25.9	268	58.2	10	26	.0	0	0	.0
50453	.7	0	.3	77	20.3	272	64.2	9	10	.1	11	0	.0
50454	.2	100	.1	85	20.2	221	43.8	3	3	.1	0	0	.0
50455	.6	100	.2	77	18.6	172	31.7	9	13	.3	11	0	.0
50456	2.1	98	.8	78	27.5	235	59.6	7	20	1.0	18	0	.0
50457	.6	0	.2	79	23.4	374	41.4	10	19	.0	0	2	.0
50458	2.3	0	.8	85	25.9	262	70.9	8	14	.0	0	0	.0
50459	3.3	99	1.3	77	23.1	205	69.8	6	22	1.6	12	0	.0
50460	.5	100	.2	92	29.2	248	47.0	10	6	.3	5	0	.0
50461	6.3	0	2.4	79	29.6	275	69.8	6	19	.3	5	0	.0
50464	.9	100	.3	80	25.7	309	64.9	10	12	.4	10	0	.0
50465	.4	100	.2	77	22.6	173	41.6	4	31	.2	32	0	.0
50466	2.2	0	.8	81	22.7	235	50.1	9	20	.0	0	0	.0
50467	.3	100	.1	85	34.9	387	62.1	10	8	.1	5	0	3.2
50469	2.0	99	.7	75	25.9	268	58.7	10	12	.9	10	0	.0
50468	1.8	100	.6	77	23.3	294	66.0	9	16	.9	13	2	.0
50470	.4	100	.2	77	19.1	247	37.9	6	20	.9	15	2	.0
50471	.9	100	.3	78	23.3	230	54.2	5	12	.5	12	0	.0

*=Estimated **1.0=883 lbs per person; 100++ indicates per capita toxic waste generation > than 100 times the U.S. average of 883 lbs per capita.

ZIP CODE MEASURES OF SIZE, LEVELS OF AFFLUENCE AND QUALITY OF LIFE

1=Population (th.); 2= % White; 3=Households (th.); 4=% Owner Occupied; 5=Mean Income Per Household (th.$); 6=Mean Monthly Rent ($); 7=Mean Home Value (th.$); 8=% under 5; 9=% 65 and over; 10=% White Males (th.); 11=% White Males, 65+; 12=# Toxic Waste Sites; 13=Toxic Waste Relative to US(883 lbs.per capital)**.

IOWA

MASON CITY

ZIPCODE	1	2	3	4	5	6	7	8	9	10	11	12	13
50472	2.2	100	.8	79	26.3	283	63.2	8	20	1.1	16	0	.0
50473	.4	100	.1	71	24.1	304	43.9	6	23	.2	17	0	.0
50475	2.1	97	.8	73	21.4	321	64.7	8	16	1.0	15	0	.6
50476	1.0	100	.3	83	26.7	232	51.5	11	15	.5	12	0	.0
50477	.4	0	.2	74	28.0	317	57.0	8	10	.5	16	0	.0
50478	1.1	97	.4	72	22.5	284	51.0	9	17	.5	16	0	.0
50479	.9	100	.4	72	23.3	268	59.8	9	15	.5	14	0	.0
50480	1.4	0	.5	84	24.8	306	60.9	5	25	.0	0	0	.0
50482	.9	99	.4	72	26.7	246	87.3	8	12	.5	9	0	.0
50483	1.3	100	.4	65	25.7	285	68.5	10	10	.7	10	0	.0
50484	.6	100	.2	60	20.7	218	44.7	7	16	.3	12	1	.0

FORT DODGE

ZIPCODE	1	2	3	4	5	6	7	8	9	10	11	12	13
50501	34.0	96	12.6	69	25.9	299	78.4	7	15	15.2	12	10	.6
50510	1.5	0	.6	73	25.2	284	75.1	10	23	.0	0	0	.0
50511	8.5	100	3.0	71	26.3	292	88.2	9	14	4.1	11	1	1.3
50514	2.1	99	.7	73	25.5	274	69.8	8	14	1.0	12	0	1.7
50515	.5	100	.2	66	23.0	227	36.1	10	15	.4	12	0	.0
50516	.9	100	.3	80	26.0	262	73.5	12	10	.4	10	0	.3
50517	1.8	0	.6	66	25.4	240	57	9	18	.2	0	0	.0
50518	.4	100	.1	75	28.6	315	65.1	7	12	.2	12	1	.0
50519	1.0	99	.4	72	24.0	193	44.9	10	13	.6	11	0	.0
50520	.3	100	.1	65	15.2	278	40.4	4	13	.2	8	0	.3
50522	1.3	100	.4	76	22.6	265	54.7	7	13	.7	12	0	.0
50523	.9	100	.3	64	29.2	316	61.9	7	10	.4	7	0	.0
50524	.8	100	.3	79	28.8	200	58.0	9	13	.5	12	0	.3
50525	4.1	98	1.6	71	26.0	233	69.8	8	19	2.0	16	1	.0
50527	.6	100	.2	51	23.9	209	20.7	14	11	.3	9	0	.0
50528	.6	100	.2	66	26.8	215	54.8	6	15	.7	12	0	.0
50529	1.1	98	.4	84	22.3	340	62	13	10	.4	11	0	.0
50530	1.4	100	.5	74	24.2	252	52.4	7	20	.7	17	0	.3
50531	.4	100	.2	76	27.5	233	51.3	11	14	.2	13	0	.0
50532	1.2	100	.5	70	23.1	330	61.5	10	15	.7	12	0	.0
50533	5.1	99	1.8	71	24.3	283	64.0	7	16	2.4	12	0	1.1
50536	1.0	100	.6	76	21.7	246	56.6	8	17	.5	16	0	.0
50538	5.6	99	1.9	72	24.9	289	69.5	7	16	2.8	13	3	.5
50539	.7	0	.3	76	25.4	224	50.3	5	24	.0	0	0	.0
50540	.8	0	.3	79	19.2	235	56.6	7	23	.2	16	1	.0
50541	1.7	100	.6	69	22.7	229	44.5	6	17	.9	15	0	.0
50542	1.4	99	.5	66	22.7	213	43.7	7	15	.7	13	0	.0
50543	1.4	0	.5	72	27.3	296	59.7	8	14	.7	0	0	.0
50544	1.8	100	.6	68	26.1	248	61.9	6	21	.9	18	0	.1
50545	.7	0	.3	78	29.8	240	62.0	6	17	.5	0	0	.0
50546	.4	100	.1	64	24.4	280*	40.5	6	22	.5	7	0	1.1
50548	6.2	0	2.4	74	26.9	230	35.8	6	18	2.8	13	3	.5
50550	.3	100	.1	53	20.2	173	72.6	6	2	.1	0	0	.8
50551	.4	0	.1	64	23.7	169	39.7	6	7	.2	6	0	.0
50554	2.3	0	.9	75	27.6	234	65.8	6	20	.3	0	0	.7
50556	.5	0	.2	69	23.7	260	36.3	3	15	.0	0	0	.0

FORT DODGE (continued)

ZIPCODE	1	2	3	4	5	6	7	8	9	10	11	12	13
50557	1.2	0	.5	84	20.8	248	59.0	4	19	.6	8	0	.0
50558	.8	0	.3	85	23.2	242	53.8	7	17	.2	16	0	.0
50559	.5	0	.2	81	31.3	227	56.8	11	18	.1	10	0	.0
50560	.9	0	.4	68	21.0	218	37.3	3	20	.0	27	0	.0
50561	.8	0	.3	66	24.9	267	48.0	9	15	.0	0	0	.0
50562	.9	100	.3	76	21.5	257	58.4	5	18	.4	14	0	.0
50563	3.1	100	1.1	75	29.3	256	76.9	8	16	1.5	14	0	.9
50565	.9	0	.4	65	23.6	213	32.3	5	15	.0	0	0	.9
50566	.6	0	.2	83	36.2	336	52.4	6	15	.0	0	2	.0
50567	.4	0	.1	69	22.7	234	36.7	9	18	.0	0	0	.0
50568	1.7	0	.7	70	24.0	276	60.5	7	17	.6	8	0	.0
50569	1.2	100	.4	81	24.7	298	51.7	10	9	.6	8	0	.3
50570	.4	100	.1	80	23.5	206	40.8	4	16	.2	16	0	.0
50571	.9	100	.3	64	22.7	265	38.1	13	13	.5	10	0	.3
50573	3.1	100	1.2	85	19.3	222*	26.3	8	22	.1	27	0	.0
50574	1.5	0	.5	76	24.5	258	75.9	7	20	.0	0	0	.4
50575	.6	100	.3	74	18.9	282	43.3	6	23	.7	21	0	.0
50576	.7	100	.3	76	23.1	217	32.8	13	12	.3	12	0	.0
50577	.3	0	.1	76	22.2	287	34.6	9	23	.3	0	0	.0
50578	1.1	0	.4	72	25.5	200	46.0	7	18	.2	15	0	.0
50579	3.3	100	1.3	75	24.7	228	59.6	5	23	1.5	21	1	.3
50580	.3	100	.1	71	29.3	336*	44.8	5	8	.2	11	0	.0
50581	1.5	0	.5	72	24.7	288	46.7	9	19	.0	0	0	.0
50583	4.1	100	1.6	68	25.0	257	45.3	6	12	2.0	9	0	.0
50585	1.6	0	.7	78	24.4	223	53.4	7	19	.0	15	1	.6
50586	.6	100	.2	65	26.4	309	62.4	11	12	.3	9	0	.6
50588	11.5	99	4.1	69	28.8	288	85.8	7	16	5.4	13	2	.0
50590	1.3	100	.6	70	21.6	276	62.1	6	18	.7	14	0	.0
50591	.5	100	.2	74	26.1	178	56.7	8	17	.2	17	0	.6
50594	.4	100	.2	72	22.9	254	58.5	5	14	.2	13	0	.0
50595	10.1	100	3.8	73	26.6	308	76.0	7	16	4.8	13	3	.5
50597	1.7	100	.6	76	22.4	251	61.0	10	16	.8	19	0	.1
50598	1.3	0	.4	77	24.4	286	59.4	8	13	.3	0	0	.0
50599	.5	100	.2	59	28.9	231	50.9	13	10	.3	8	0	.0

WATERLOO

ZIPCODE	1	2	3	4	5	6	7	8	9	10	11	12	13
50601	3.9	100	1.2	78	24.9	308	63.3	5	19	1.6	14	0	.2
50602	1.9	99	.7	79	23.1	204	61.9	6	19	.9	17	0	.2
50603	.8	100	.3	82	22.8	211	49.2	6	13	.4	9	0	.0
50604	2.0	100	.7	78	23.5	252	77.4	9	18	1.0	15	0	.0
50605	.3	100	.1	81	19.4	133	48.8	11	15	.1	10	0	.1
50606	1.1	98	.4	80	22.9	303	43.2	5	20	.6	16	0	.0
50607	.7	100	.2	80	26.1	283	40.1	8	15	.3	15	0	.0
50609	.5	0	.2	60	28.0	380	40.7	7	16	.3	19	0	.1
50611	.6	0	.2	83	22.6	179	44.9	8	17	.3	8	0	.0
50612	.4	100	.1	81	30.4	405	71.1	8	17	.2	6	0	.0
50613	38.5	98	12.3	68	31.3	380	102.8	7	8	18.3	13	4	.3
50616	12.2	99	4.5	77	24.9	258	73.7	7	17	5.7	13	3	3.9
50619	2.7		.2	75	21.2	260	61.0	9	16	.0	0	0	.0

*=Estimated **1.0=883 lbs per person; 100++ indicates per capita toxic waste generation > than 100 times the U.S. average of 883 lbs per capita.

ZIP CODE MEASURES OF SIZE, LEVELS OF AFFLUENCE AND QUALITY OF LIFE

1=Population (th.); 2= % White; 3=Households (th.); 4=% Owner Occupied; 5=Mean Income Per Household (th.$); 6=Mean Home Value (th.$)*; 7=Mean Monthly Rent ($)*;
8=% under 5; 9=% 65 and over; 10=White Males (th.); 11=% White Males, 65+; 12=# Toxic Waste Sites; 13=Toxic Waste Relative to US(883 lbs.per capita)**.

IOWA

WATERLOO

ZIPCODE	1	2	3	4	5	6	7	8	9	10	11	12	13
50621	1.6	0	.6	75	28.6	287	86.6	7	19	.0	0	0	.5
50622	3.0	100	1.0	84	30.3	317	106.0	8	9	1.5	9	0	.1
50624	1.5	0	.5	77	26.1	338	87.5	7	12	.0	0	0	.0
50625	1.3	100	.5	75	21.4	195	53.2	8	20	.7	17	0	.3
50626	1.8	100	.6	71	28.0	338	81.9	10	8	.9	6	0	.0
50627	4.3	99	1.6	74	23.9	293	65.3	9	17	2.1	12	1	.9
50628	1.8	100	.6	78	19.9	158	40.5	7	17	1.0	16	0	.0
50629	2.4	100	.7	83	33.3	327	75.4	10	10	1.2	8	0	.0
50630	2.1	0	.7	80	25.0	238	72.9	9	16	.0	0	0	.1
50631	.2	100	.1	86	22.2	271	57.6	5	23	.1	22	0	.0
50632	1.2	100	.4	76	28.2	271	59.1	6	16	.5	15	0	.0
50633	.6	100	.2	65	22.6	297	57.9	9	7	.3	6	0	.0
50634	.8	0	.2	82	30.7	323	86.9	10	10	.0	0	0	.0
50635	1.8	100	.7	73	25.7	242	64.9	6	21	.9	18	0	.0
50636	2.8	100	1.0	76	23.1	243	58.5	9	16	1.3	14	0	.0
50638	3.8	100	1.4	76	27.1	264	77.4	7	19	1.8	15	1	.1
50641	1.7	99	.6	82	22.5	384	62.6	13	13	.9	11	0	.0
50642	.7	100	.2	74	22.5	394	63.7	7	12	.4	10	0	.3
50643	3.0	99	.9	83	36.5	413	102.1	9	8	1.5	7	1	.0
50644	9.7	99	3.3	75	25.0	281	75.0	8	12	4.7	10	0	.1
50645	1.7	100	.6	79	21.4	213	62.5	9	11	.9	10	0	.0
50647	1.6	0	.6	79	27.4	328	94.6	10	8	.0	0	0	.2
50648	4.1	99	1.3	79	28.7	336	77.4	10	10	2.1	9	0	.0
50650	1.1	99	.4	75	24.2	276	41.9	6	15	.5	13	0	.0
50651	4.2	100	1.4	77	28.5	241	82.5	8	14	2.1	11	0	.0
50652	.2	100	.1	82	20.3	141	52.4	8	19	.1	12	0	.0
50653	.9	100	.3	70	22.9	255	44.7	6	17	.4	13	0	.0
50654	.7	100	.2	83	31.0	121	44.1	3	14	.4	18	0	.0
50655	.9	100	.3	68	24.2	236	59.5	7	14	.5	12	0	.0
50658	3.0	100	1.1	80	22.2	283	64.6	6	13	1.6	13	0	.3
50659	6.8	100	2.3	79	23.4	285	82.0	9	16	3.3	13	0	.2
50660	1.4	0	.5	85	26.1	333	71.1	9	12	.0	0	0	.0
50662	8.9	99	3.3	80	24.3	382	66.4	8	17	4.2	14	0	.4
50664	.1	100	.1	90	19.7	226*	68.9	0	0	.1	0	0	1.3
50665	3.4	99	1.2	82	27.4	246	76.4	7	15	1.6	13	0	.3
50666	1.1	100	.4	86	23.4	238	64.9	9	15	.6	13	0	.2
50667	.6	100	.2	85	30.1	462	85.0	16	6	.3	6	0	.0
50668	1.5	100	.5	81	31.6	354	80.8	11	14	.7	13	0	.0
50669	2.7	0	1.0	72	30.0	276	77.4	6	20	.0	0	0	.0
50670	2.3	0	.8	80	25.6	277	73.5	9	13	.0	0	0	.0
50671	.5	91	.3	91	30.0	332	45.5	8	15	.2	16	0	.0
50672	.3	0	.3	74	22.0	277	61.3	7	17	.0	0	0	.2
50673	.3	100	.1	80	24.3	382	65.8	7	9	.1	8	0	.0
50674	4.4	0	1.5	80	23.2	276	66.7	6	18	.0	0	0	.4
50675	2.8	99	1.0	77	26.4	314	77.4	6	18	1.3	15	0	.0
50676	2.2	0	.8	86	27.7	291	68.7	6	15	.0	0	1	.0
50677	11.7	99	3.9	72	27.0	321	95.8	7	13	5.6	10	2	.6
50680	1.5	0	.2	82	31.6	314	61.4	7	18	.0	0	0	.0
50681	.6	100	.2	76	24.2	315	54.0	9	13	.3	13	0	.0

IOWA

WATERLOO

ZIPCODE	1	2	3	4	5	6	7	8	9	10	11	12	13
50682	1.9	0	.6	74	24.8	256	73.1	11	10	.0	0	0	.0

WATERLOO

ZIPCODE	1	2	3	4	5	6	7	8	9	10	11	12	13
50701	34.7	98	12.8	73	33.3	383	103.8	8	10	16.7	8	2	.3
50702	20.8	97	8.1	69	27.8	371	83.7	7	13	9.6	11	0	.0
50703	22.9	69	8.1	69	22.3	292	57.6	10	13	7.5	13	2	.2
50706	1.3	0	.4	96	34.2	395	69.1	10	4	.0	0	1	.0
50707	8.6	91	3.0	83	24.7	336	66.7	10	7	3.9	8	0	.0

CRESTON

ZIPCODE	1	2	3	4	5	6	7	8	9	10	11	12	13
50801	10.4	99	4.1	73	22.6	246	61.2	8	17	4.9	13	2	.6
50830	1.8	0	.6	73	18.0	225	45.0	9	19	.0	0	0	.0
50833	3.0	0	1.2	71	19.0	201	42.5	5	22	.0	0	0	.0
50836	.6	100	.2	83	16.4	209	18.9	8	30	.3	24	0	.0
50837	.6	100	.2	82	16.8	257	35.0	10	19	.3	18	0	.0
50840	.7	0	.3	77	17.9	213	35.1	13	23	.0	0	0	.0
50841	3.9	100	1.5	77	20.5	201	56.4	7	21	1.9	18	2	.0
50843	.8	0	.3	73	24.2	213	33.7	9	17	.3	17	0	.1
50845	.9	0	.3	78	21.5	192	26.9	6	15	.0	0	0	.0
50846	1.5	0	.6	78	20.6	230	42.6	8	21	.0	0	0	.3
50847	.1	100	.1	86	18.0	207*	27.9	3	27	.1	19	0	.0
50848	.6	0	.2	84	16.6	308	24.0	9	9	.0	0	0	.0
50849	3.4	99	1.4	75	21.8	220	62.2	6	23	1.7	19	1	.0
50850	.4	0	.1	88	22.6	282	107.2	9	10	.0	0	0	.0
50851	2.0	0	.8	75	21.8	205	58.9	7	26	.0	0	0	.5
50853	1.1	0	.4	77	21.6	212	40.8	6	20	.0	0	0	.0
50854	2.9	99	1.1	77	19.9	234	55.3	6	25	1.3	22	0	.0
50857	.4	100	.2	87	16.2	114	25.0	7	13	.2	15	0	.0
50858	1.0	100	.4	66	16.3	216	43.0	12	17	.5	15	0	.0
50859	.8	100	.3	73	21.6	158	34.6	10	17	.4	19	0	.0
50860	.3	100	.1	79	16.7	83	18.5	7	26	.2	23	0	.0
50861	.4	100	.2	80	20.8	195	15.8	5	17	.2	16	0	.0
50862	.2	100	.1	89	12.7	146*	20.3	7	24	.1	17	0	.0
50863	.4	100	.1	79	19.3	225	26.2	5	28	.1	18	0	.0
50864	2.5	100	1.0	75	18.2	169	40.9	8	26	1.2	23	0	.0

SIOUX CITY

ZIPCODE	1	2	3	4	5	6	7	8	9	10	11	12	13
51001	2.4	99	.9	75	20.3	200	61.2	9	23	1.1	19	0	.1
51002	2.9	0	1.0	77	24.5	293	64.1	7	12	.0	0	0	.0
51003	1.7	100	.5	75	27.0	256	67.7	9	11	.8	10	1	1.7
51004	1.4	100	.5	77	20.4	268	55.1	11	16	.6	15	0	.0
51005	1.9	0	.7	77	24.2	289	67.9	7	20	.0	0	0	.0
51006	1.6	100	.6	72	26.1	234	50.1	9	18	.8	16	0	.0
51007	.8	100	.3	75	23.1	333	70.0	7	11	.4	10	0	.3
51008	.1	100	.1	86	25.6	295*	57.8	4	16	.1	13	0	.7
51009	.2	100	.1	100	18.5	212*	43.8	5	20	.1	18	0	.0
51010	.7	100	.3	69	26.3	289	19.5	10	16	.4	16	0	.0
51012	8.9	99	3.3	69	26.9	245	68.8	8	16	.0	0	1	.3
51014	.7	0	.3	59	22.3	161	56.4	12	11	.0	0	0	.7
51016	1.6	100	.6	80	20.6	230	45.7	8	18	.8	17	0	.0
51018	.6	100	.2	69	14.3	310	48.5	9	13	.3	11	0	.0
51019	1.2	100	.5	74	22.5	259	45.6	9	16	.6	13	0	.0

*=Estimated **1.0=883 lbs per person; 100++ indicates per capita toxic waste generation > than 100 times the U.S. average of 883 lbs per capita.

ZIP CODE MEASURES OF SIZE, LEVELS OF AFFLUENCE AND QUALITY OF LIFE

1=Population (th.); 2= % White; 3=Households (th.); 4=% Owner Occupied; 5=Mean Monthly Rent ($)*; 6=Mean Income Per Household (th.$); 7=Mean Home Value (th.$);
8=% under 5; 9=% 65 and over; 10=White Males (th.); 11=% White Males, 65+; 12=# Toxic Waste Sites; 13=Toxic Waste Relative to US(883 lbs.per capita)**.

IOWA

ZIPCODE	1	2	3	4	5	6	7	8	9	10	11	12	13
SIOUX CITY													
51020	.9	100	.4	69	25.2	224	40.3	7	17	.5	14	0	.0
51022	1.1	100	.4	80	27.0	270	54.2	9	13	.6	9	0	.0
51023	3.6	98	1.3	76	22.3	193	58.8	8	14	1.7	11	2	.2
51024	1.7	0	.5	74	29.8	289	84.5	9	8	.0	0	1	.0
51025	2.3	0	.9	72	21.5	217	59.6	6	21	.0	0	0	.0
51026	1.1	100	.4	71	23.1	357	51.0	7	18	.5	17	0	.0
51027	1.4	100	.5	79	25.1	261	61.0	8	10	.7	8	0	.0
51028	2.3	99	.8	69	23.6	227	63.4	7	19	1.2	16	0	.0
51029	.4	100	.2	64	20.7	324	44.5	11	7	.2	5	0	.0
51030	1.4	100	.5	75	25.0	327	81.5	10	12	.7	11	0	.0
51031	11.2	99	3.8	70	27.6	291	83.6	8	14	5.3	11	1	.1
51033	.8	100	.3	63	24.7	123	41.2	9	13	.4	15	0	.0
51034	2.3	100	.9	77	20.9	245	54.9	7	24	1.1	22	0	.0
51035	2.1	100	.8	76	25.4	232	59.6	8	16	1.0	14	0	.0
51036	1.0	100	.1	70	20.0	347	76.8	15	6	.4	7	0	.0
51037	.5	100	.1	74	23.7	293	57.6	10	13	.2	16	0	.0
51038	1.8	98	.6	79	27.1	305	70.9	10	10	.9	12	0	.0
51039	2.2	0	.8	79	24.2	231	61.0	10	13	.0	0	0	.0
51040	3.9	99	1.5	73	20.8	203	57.2	7	22	1.8	18	0	.1
51041	5.8	99	1.8	80	25.9	257	88.7	8	14	2.8	11	0	.7
51044	.3	100	.1	84	17.1	86	37.2	9	10	.2	8	0	.0
51045	.8	100	.3	80	21.4	279	52.9	15	6	.1	4	0	.0
51046	2.1	100	.8	79	22.2	221	68.4	8	20	1.0	18	0	.0
51047	1.0	0	.4	69	21.8	273	40.1	6	18	.0	0	0	.1
51048	.6	100	.2	85	21.1	245	36.4	5	27	.3	22	0	.0
51049	.9	100	.3	79	27.3	242	47.6	6	20	.5	17	0	.6
51050	3.1	0	1.0	76	23.9	262	67.5	9	15	.0	0	0	.0
51052	1.3	0	.4	82	26.1	284	64.6	8	8	.2	0	0	.3
51053	1.4	0	.5	79	26.9	233	55.2	9	18	.6	15	0	.1
51054	3.3	99	1.1	59	26.3	396	86.0	10	7	1.6	7	0	.3
51055	1.3	99	.5	70	27.7	245	68.7	8	12	.6	12	1	9.8
51056	.6	100	.2	75	18.0	235	40.3	4	17	.3	17	0	.0
51058	1.6	100	.6	72	24.8	236	49.4	7	16	.8	14	0	.0
51059	1.0	0	.4	87	22.2	255*	31.5	8	14	.2	18	0	.0
51060	1.0	100	.4	75	19.6	353	50.9	7	20	.5	20	0	.0
51061	.8	100	.3	69	25.8	249	39.0	9	11	.3	10	0	.0
51062	.8	0	.3	84	27.7	311	65.5	10	14	.0	0	0	.0
51063	1.2	99	.4	68	22.4	343	55.6	6	20	.6	15	1	.0
SIOUX CITY													
51101	.6	90	.4	2	9.9	153	35.4*	0	47	.3	35	0	4.0
51103	18.2	93	6.3	69	20.6	285	53.9	9	12	7.9	10	0	.1
51104	19.3	99	7.1	75	35.1	380	92.3	7	15	8.9	12	0	.0
51105	10.7	93	4.5	50	17.3	252	45.8	9	14	4.7	12	0	.5
51106	26.1	99	9.1	78	27.3	343	73.7	8	12	12.2	9	0	.0
51107	.1	100	.1	55	23.3	232	44.7	5	16	.0	0	1	5.0
51108	6.6	99	2.3	79	27.2	362	74.3	9	10	3.1	9	1	.3
51109	3.2	98	1.2	79	23.5	325	50.2	7	17	1.5	14	1	.1
SHELDON													
51201	6.4	0	2.2	72	24.5	259	73.9	9	14	.0	0	1	.0

IOWA

ZIPCODE	1	2	3	4	5	6	7	8	9	10	11	12	13
SHELDON													
51230	.5	100	.1	85	21.8	89	40.0	11	16	.2	17	0	.0
51231	.4	0	.1	75	40.9	221	45.6	6	9	.0	0	0	.0
51232	1.1	100	.4	82	25.6	250	52.3	5	15	.6	14	0	.0
51234	1.5	100	.5	79	26.9	308	64.4	12	10	.7	9	0	.3
51235	1.2	100	.5	75	26.6	254	53.1	10	7	.6	7	0	.0
51237	2.1	0	.8	70	21.3	290	56.8	8	20	.0	0	1	.2
51238	1.4	100	.5	83	29.7	272	68.8	11	13	.7	11	1	.2
51239	2.8	99	.9	87	23.3	269	70.2	13	13	.0	1	0	.0
51240	1.8	0	.6	73	20.5	272	67.7	10	14	.0	0	0	.0
51241	1.5	100	.5	87	26.4	250	69.7	13	11	.2	14	0	.0
51242	.9	100	.3	91	34.1	377	70.0	8	20	.2	14	0	.0
51243	.9	100	.3	77	19.8	183	47.8	9	16	.4	15	0	.0
51245	1.7	0	.6	79	24.3	208	56.5	10	23	.0	0	0	.1
51246	3.9	0	1.5	70	25.6	212	71.6	8	17	.0	0	1	.2
51247	4.4	99	1.4	78	23.5	245	73.6	8	16	2.2	14	1	.3
51248	2.2	100	.8	79	25.2	234	71.1	8	16	1.1	14	1	.1
51249	4.4	100	1.6	78	24.7	243	66.1	8	20	2.1	16	0	.0
51250	5.7	99	1.7	78	26.1	274	90.4	9	12	2.7	10	0	.1
SPENCER													
51301	13.4	99	5.1	68	27.0	322	89.0	8	14	6.3	11	3	.2
51331	1.1	99	.5	78	21.7	290	85.2	6	17	.5	16	0	.0
51333	.7	0	.3	81	26.3	223	41.9	7	17	.0	0	0	.0
51334	9.4	99	3.4	73	25.1	280	68.8	8	15	4.5	12	0	.1
51338	1.3	100	.5	76	23.4	267	70.4	9	9	.6	6	0	.0
51340	.2	0	.1	93	22.5	259*	52.5	6	22	.6	6	0	.0
51341	.9	100	.3	63	11.8	222	42.3	11	8	.1	4	0	.0
51342	1.6	0	.6	72	21.6	302	53.6	8	17	.0	0	0	.3
51343	.3	100	.1	79	22.8	243	47.8	4	25	.2	25	0	.0
51345	.7	100	.3	53	21.3	250	30.0	8	19	.4	18	0	.0
51346	2.9	99	1.1	79	24.3	210	62.9	7	20	1.4	18	0	.2
51347	1.7	0	.6	79	23.8	248	61.9	7	20	.5	16	0	.0
51350	.7	100	.2	71	25.5	257	39.9	7	15	.3	12	0	.0
51351	4.0	100	1.6	74	25.1	254	93.9	8	16	1.9	14	2	.0
51352	.2	100	.1	50	16.4	188*	26.3	2	13	.1	10	0	.0
51354	1.2	0	.4	83	25.5	215	57.5	6	13	.1	4	0	.0
51355	.5	0	.2	81	30.3	282	151.7	4	28	.2	25	0	.0
51357	.9	100	.3	69	31.9	340	68.9	9	9	.4	8	0	.3
51358	1.6	0	.6	74	24.3	202	58.2	10	17	.0	0	0	.0
51360	7.2	0	2.7	75	27.1	295	112.4	8	15	.0	0	0	.2
51363	.2	100	.1	92	22.5	258*	48.7	2	26	.1	28	0	.0
51364	.7	0	.3	79	26.0	240	49.0	10	15	.0	0	0	.0
51365	.5	0	.2	81	25.0	309	53.3	9	15	.0	0	0	.0
51366	.5	0	.2	73	24.7	236	41.6	8	15	.0	0	2	.1
CARROLL													
51401	12.4	100	4.2	72	28.6	310	85.5	9	13	5.9	10	1	.5
51430	.9	0	.3	75	25.6	353	52.6	10	12	.0	0	0	.0
51431	.6	100	.2	91	22.1	188	52.5	5	20	.3	24	0	.0
51433	1.0	100	.4	66	22.3	232	36.4	6	22	.5	20	0	.0
51436	1.0	100	.4	83	20.8	267	54.0	6	16	.5	15	0	.1

*=Estimated **1.0-883 lbs per person; 100++ indicates per capita toxic waste generation > than 100 times the U.S. average of 883 lbs per capita.

ZIP CODE MEASURES OF SIZE, LEVELS OF AFFLUENCE AND QUALITY OF LIFE

1=Population (th.); 2= % White; 3=Households (th.); 4=% Owner Occupied; 5=Mean Income Per Household (th.$); 6=Mean Monthly Rent ($)*; 7=Mean Home Value (th.$)*;
8=% under 5; 9=% 65 and over; 10=White Males (th.); 11=% White Males, 65+; 12=# Toxic Waste Sites; 13=Toxic Waste Relative to US(883 lbs.per capita)**.

IOWA

CARROLL

ZIPCODE	1	2	3	4	5	6	7	8	9	10	11	12	13
51439	1.4	100	.5	73	23.0	277	53.4	7	17	.7	15	0	.0
51440	.5	100	.2	77	21.8	178	46.5	11	16	.3	14	0	.0
51441	.6	99	.2	85	21.3	251	58.8	15	11	.3	11	0	.0
51442	8.6	98	3.1	72	26.1	303	82.1	8	14	4.1	11	1	.2
51443	2.0	100	.7	76	25.9	283	68.8	10	15	1.0	14	0	.0
51444	.4	100		86	26.3	259	46.3	11	15		15	0	.0
51445	3.3	0	1.3	71	24.2	246	68.0	7	17		0	0	.3
51446	.7	0	.3	75	24.3	183	45.4	4	16	.0	0	0	.0
51447	.4	100	.1	80	19.9	245	37.6	9	7	.2	5	0	.0
51448	.8	100	.3	89	28.2	184	55.9	8	19	.4	17	0	.2
51449	2.7	99	1.1	73	23.7	253	58.0	7	23	1.2	18	0	.0
51450	1.9	0	.8	74	23.2	279	63.5	9	18	.0	0	0	.0
51451	.2	0	.1	81	21.2	293	28.7	11	19	.0	0	0	.0
51452	.2	100	.1	81	21.0	230	49.0	10	17	.1	17	0	.0
51453	1.2	0	.4	71	19.8	164	37.0	10	14	.0	0	0	.0
51454	2.3	0	.9	72	20.0	219	56.5	10	20	.0	0	0	.0
51455	2.5	0	.8	75	21.7	190	52.3	6	19	.0	0	0	.2
51458	2.0	0	.7	79	24.1	252	56.7	6	20	.0	0	0	.0
51460	.1	100	.1	94	16.0	184*	34.0	3	19	.1	18	0	.0
51461	1.4	0	.5	80	27.7	317	62.7	7	20	.0	0	0	.7
51462	1.5	97	.6	71	20.3	259	44.7	9	17	.1	15	0	.0
51463	.7	100	.2	70	21.5	212	50.8	9	14	.4	10	0	.0
51465	1.0	0	.3	78	22.5	272	43.3	14	10	.3	13	1	.1
51466	1.4	0	.5	76	22.6	260	59.2	9	21	.3	17	0	.0
51467	.9	100	.3	73	26.1	337	53.9	6	10	.5	9	0	.0

OMAHA

ZIPCODE	1	2	3	4	5	6	7	8	9	10	11	12	13
51501	65.6	98	23.5	71	26.0	311	63.6	8	11	30.6	9	6	.5
51520	.3	100	.1	78	18.6	353	23.5	18	13	.2	9	0	.0
51521	2.3	100	.9	76	24.2	264	58.5	7	17	1.1	13	0	.0
51523	.5	100	.2	77	22.8	293	45.9	4	17	.2	16	0	.0
51525	1.4	100	.5	71	28.7	304	57.9	8	13	.7	10	0	.0
51526	1.6	0	.5	82	27.4	358	80.8	8	8	.5	0	0	.0
51527	.9	100	.3	74	23.4	227	51.7	14	9	.0	5	0	.0
51528	1.4	0	.5	76	21.1	290	56.8	10	11	.0	0	0	.0
51529	2.4	100	.8	70	23.0	258	50.4	6	18	1.2	17	0	.0
51530	1.1	100	.3	76	22.5	235	54.4	8	15	.6	13	0	.0
51531	1.1	0	.4	75	23.0	238	62.4	4	31	.0	0	0	.0
51532	1.0	100	.5	75	23.8	281	42.2	6	15	.5	14	0	.0
51533	1.1	99	.5	69	26.0	229	51.5	6	18	.6	17	0	.0
51534	7.1	100	2.3	72	25.7	288	75.7	8	12	3.5	9	2	.1
51535	2.5	0	1.0	73	22.2	252	58.9	5	22	.0	0	0	.2
51536	.6	100	.2	72	20.1	217	39.0	10	6	.3	5	0	.0
51537	7.3	100	2.6	72	25.7	257	71.5	7	15	3.6	13	1	.1
51540	.6	100	.2	84	24.3	289	41.4	5	14	.3	17	0	.0
51541	.6	0	.2	77	31.2	323	59.9	7	20	.0	0	0	.0
51542	.8	0	.3	91	22.3	327	87.9	7	13	.0	0	0	.0
51543	.7	100	.3	74	19.1	226	40.1	7	18	.3	13	0	.0
51544	.9	0	.4	65	20.8	188	38.6	7	16	.0	0	0	.0
51545	.6	100	.3	79	17.5	258	28.5	3	22	.3	17	0	.0

IOWA

OMAHA

ZIPCODE	1	2	3	4	5	6	7	8	9	10	11	12	13
51546	3.0	99	1.1	73	21.8	262	55.8	8	17	1.4	13	0	.0
51548	.7		.2	71	29.1	327	67.8	8	10	.3	12	0	.0
51549	.5	100	.2	71	24.8	242	33.5	4	14	.2	12	0	.0
51550	.2	0	.1	82	15.3	192	41.4	9	12	.0		0	.2
51551	1.9	0	.7	77	22.2	239	55.1	11	16	.0	1	0	.0
51552	.4	100	.1	76	21.4	321	42.2	15	17	.2	20	0	.0
51553	.9	100	.3	72	24.6	266	61.4	10	16	.5	14	0	.0
51554	.2	100	.1	89	28.8	330*	70.6	16	5	.1	0	0	.0
51555	5.2		1.9	73	23.8	247	59.3	8	16	.0	0	0	.0
51556	.6	100	.2	68	21.4	292	45.5	9	14	.3	12	0	.0
51557	.9	100	.3	75	27.9	223	59.7	4	13	.4	13	0	.0
51558	.7	0	.3	81	20.7	232	33.9	8	11	.0	0	0	.0
51559	1.8	99	.6	74	24.9	259	59.7	7	11	.9	12	0	.0
51560	2.4	100	.9	72	22.7	268	64.2	7	19	1.2	17	0	.1
51561	1.2	100	.4	86	25.3	315	53.7	10	10	.6	10	0	.0
51562	.7	100	.2	89	22.5	317	42.5	8	18	.3	19	0	.0
51563	1.0	100	.3	84	23.0	99	51.2	9	16	.4	16	0	.2
51564	.7	100	.3	76	22.5	266	43.2	7	17	.4	15	0	.0
51565	.7	100	.2	75	24.6	309	40.6	5	11	.3	10	0	.0
51566	8.5	99	3.4	70	24.3	250	64.3	8	19	3.9	16	2	.7
51570	1.2	0	.4	74	24.3	270	59.9	8	16	.4	10	0	.0
51571	.8	100	.2	78	26.3	397	42.8	9	12	.3	13	0	.0
51572	.6	100	.2	81	16.8	237	39.4	7	15	.7	16	0	.0
51573	1.4	99	.5	84	23.0	215	62.3	7	19	.7	19	0	.0
51575	1.0	0	.3	83	29.1	220	83.6	9	11	.5	12	0	.5
51576	1.2	100	.4	75	25.4	464	89.9	8	11	.6	11	0	.0
51577	1.5	0	.6	66	20.8	252	47.5	12	21	.1	26	0	.0
51578	.1	100	.1	89	16.8	193*	49.4	12	24	.1		0	.0
51579	2.5	100	.9	72	19.8	218	54.7	7	19	1.2	15	0	.0

OMAHA

ZIPCODE	1	2	3	4	5	6	7	8	9	10	11	12	13
51601	7.9	100	3.2	64	22.3	237	59.6	7	20	3.7	16	0	.0
51630	.3	100	.1	89	24.8	285*	21.5	2	17	.1	19	0	.0
51631	.4	100	.1	79	17.2	200	42.3	12	25	.2	17	0	.0
51632	7.5	99	2.8	78	19.3	286	64.3	7	19	3.6	15	0	.0
51636	.8	100	.3	78	19.3	286	22.7	9	20	.4	17	0	.0
51637	.3	0	.1	89	23.4	221	40.7	9	14	.9	14	0	.0
51638	1.7	100	.6	69	23.6	254	50.8	7	14	.6	13	0	.0
51639	1.2	100	.5	70	23.5	202	56.3	9	17	1.0	18	0	.0
51640	2.2	99	.9	72	20.8	234	49.7	6	20	.3	4	0	.1
51645	1.5	100	.5	64	19.7	293	29.4	14	6	.7	18	0	.2
51646	1.1	0	.4	83	18.2	277	40.7	8	18	.3	17	0	.0
51647	.2	0	.1	84	20.2	232*	38.8	8	17	.2		0	.0
51648	.4	100	.1	64	22.1	254*	83.0	10	19	.2	22	1	.1
51649	.5	100	.2	74	26.4	229	36.5	10	13	.3	10	0	.0
51650	.2	100		89	18.0	207*	28.4	7	27	.1	25	0	.0
51651	.2	0	.1	83	19.7	296	39.2	10	21	.0		0	.0
51652	2.0	0	.8	72	20.1	290	56.2	8	21	.7	16	0	.0
51653	1.4	99	.5	69	23.3	271	64.2	7	18	.7	16	0	.0
51654	.7		.2	77	21.2	370	38.5	8	16	.0		0	.0

*=Estimated **1.0=883 lbs per person; 100++ indicates per capita toxic waste generation > than 100 times the U.S. average of 883 lbs per capita.

ZIP CODE MEASURES OF SIZE, LEVELS OF AFFLUENCE AND QUALITY OF LIFE

1=Population (th.); 2= % White; 3=Households (th.); 4=% Owner Occupied; 5=Mean Income Per Household (th.$); 6=Mean Monthly Rent ($); 7=Mean Home Value (th.$);
8=% under 5, 9=% 65 and over; 10=% White Males (th.); 11=% White Males, 65+; 12=# Toxic Waste Sites; 13=Toxic Waste Relative to US(883 lbs.per capita)**.

IOWA

ZIPCODE	1	2	3	4	5	6	7	8	9	10	11	12	13
DECORAH													
52134	.5	100	.2	78	23.7	276	41.6	6	17	.3	15	0	.0
52135	.9	100	.4	79	20.2	286	50.9	7	21	.4	16	0	.0
52136	6.4	100	2.3	78	25.2	246	63.1	7	20	3.2	16	0	.3
52140	.7	100	.6	68	16.6	280	36.2	5	13	.4	10	0	.0
52141	1.6	100	.6	80	24.1	269	59.0	8	19	.8	16	0	.0
52142	2.2	97	.7	70	21.9	239	55.4	7	16	1.1	13	0	.0
52144	1.5	100	.5	89	26.8	267	63.0	7	11	.8	8	1	.0
52146	.8	100	.4	81	16.9	287	54.0	7	17	.4	14	0	.0
52147	1.3	100	.5	82	25.0	249	49.1	9	18	.7	17	0	.0
52151	2.3	0	.8	80	20.3	241	57.2	6	18	.8	0	0	1.7
52155	1.5	100	.5	79	23.6	307	71.7	10	11	.8	12	0	.0
52156	1.5	100	.5	77	23.4	168	46.7	8	14	.5	0	0	.6
52157	1.7	96	.7	66	20.6	222	60.9	9	10	.8	10	0	.1
52158	.5	0	.2	76	18.6	255	48.4	5	23	.2	20	1	.2
52159	2.4	98	.9	77	18.6	226	44.6	6	12	1.1	16	0	.0
52160	.9	99	.3	80	22.5	242	57.8	6	18	.5	14	0	.0
52161	1.7	100	.5	78	21.5	290	48.5	9	17	.8	10	0	.1
52162	3.3	0	1.2	79	21.4	277	66.4	9	13	.2	0	0	.0
52163	.4	100	.2	77	21.8	235	63.8	5	16	.2	26	0	.0
52164	.4	100	.1	71	19.1	191	50.5	12	2	.6	1	0	.0
52165	1.1	100	.4	75	29.2	288	38.7	8	15	.6	15	0	.0
52166	.2	100	.1	94	19.8	245	54.8	1	17	.1	10	0	.0
52168	.4	100	.2	84	26.5	305*	67.8	9	22	.2	18	1	.0
52169	.5	0	.2	77	20.2	292	52.7	5	16	.4	9	0	.0
52170	.7	100	.2	89	26.2	101	46.1	11	6	.7	6	0	.0
52171	1.4	100	.5	81	22.7	264	38.6	8	12	.8	12	0	.0
52172	6.8	0	2.3	76	17.2	225	37.7	8	18	.0	0	2	.6
52175	4.2	0	1.5	77	21.6	257	63.4	7	18	.0	0	0	.3
CEDAR RAPIDS													
52201	1.4	0	.4	86	24.1	293	65.2	9	8	.0	0	0	.0
52202	1.0	100	.3	78	28.6	342	78.7	10	10	.5	12	0	.0
52203	1.3	100	.4	73	29.8	341	99.4	4	13	.6	8	0	4.2
52205	7.4	98	2.3	75	25.8	266	74.1	6	9	3.9	7	0	.1
52206	1.2	0	.4	80	28.3	411	79.4	10	12	.0	0	0	.0
52207	.6	99	.2	66	26.8	210	33.5	13	8	.4	20	0	.0
52208	3.7	99	1.4	77	21.1	295	50.7	7	23	1.7	20	0	.0
52209	1.2	100	.4	81	25.1	216	65.7	7	16	.4	9	0	.0
52210	.8	100	.3	72	19.8	259	48.7	11	10	.4	9	0	.0
52211	2.4	100	.9	75	23.6	280	55.2	8	22	1.2	18	0	.0
52212	.5	100	.2	67	18.4	260	46.3	8	10	.3	10	0	.1
52213	3.1	0	1.0	82	25.8	248	74.4	8	10	.0	0	1	.0
52214	3.2	0	1.1	79	25.5	321	69.7	7	13	.1	0	0	.0
52215	1.1	98	.4	83	18.6	225	41.4	10	13	.5	14	0	.0
52216	1.7	99	.6	65	23.4	311	62.8	6	18	.8	14	0	.0
52217	.8	100	.3	82	18.6	270	46.8	6	15	.4	12	1	.0
52218	1.8	100	.6	79	23.7	283	59.9	6	13	.9	12	0	.0
52219	.2	100	.1	71	24.4	280*	50.7	10	10	.1	8	0	.0
52220	.2	100	.1	81	29.3	336*	62.0	7	11	.0	0	0	.0

IOWA

ZIPCODE	1	2	3	4	5	6	7	8	9	10	11	12	13
OMAHA													
51656	.1	100	.1	93	21.4	246*	49.8	4	19	.1	18	0	.6
DUBUQUE													
52001	72.6	99	24.1	70	29.2	314	91.5	7	12	34.2	9	5	1.9
52030	.3	100	.1	77	21.3	224	49.8	8	18	.2	16	1	.0
52031	5.3	99	1.7	81	26.9	260	77.1	7	12	.8	4	0	.0
52032	1.6	99	.4	84	22.9	303	72.6	9	4	.8	3	0	.0
52033	3.2	99	.9	82	25.1	253	72.2	10	12	1.6	10	1	.0
52035	1.1	100	.4	87	22.5	261	61.8	7	10	.5	9	0	.0
52036	.1	0	.1	91	23.6	272*	64.0	7	11	.7	17	0	.0
52037	1.7	0	.6	82	26.4	365	71.0	9	9	.0	0	0	.0
52038	.5	100	.2	93	25.1	220	53.7	16	10	.3	11	0	.0
52039	1.2	0	.3	90	32.9	27	86.2	8	9	.0	0	0	.0
52040	5.6	0	1.7	83	29.6	336	86.0	9	11	.0	0	1	.1
52041	1.9	100	.6	77	26.4	246	64.8	10	9	.9	8	0	.0
52042	1.6	100	.6	81	22.0	276	59.7	8	16	.8	10	0	.1
52043	2.9	100	1.1	70	21.7	209	69.7	7	17	1.5	14	1	.2
52044	.3	100	.5	68	18.2	175	33.0	8	9	.3	11	0	.0
52045	2.4	99	.6	79	26.3	328	74.5	11	7	1.3	7	0	.0
52046	2.0	100	.6	79	26.9	370	75.2	13	9	1.0	7	0	.1
52047	.8	100	.3	75	28.1	260	49.2	9	8	.4	6	0	.0
52048	.6	100	.2	78	24.1	283	58.3	13	14	.3	16	0	.0
52049	1.5	0	.5	79	24.2	318	65.5	7	16	.0	9	0	.3
52050	.7	100	.2	77	23.2	251	40.5	5	8	.4	9	0	.0
52051	.3	0	.1	73	25.1	418	27.0	10	10	.0	7	1	.0
52052	.8	100	.3	78	23.2	229	68.4	9	18	1.9	16	0	.0
52053	1.4	100	.3	89	30.9	437	68.4	6	6	.7	6	0	.0
52054	1.2	100	.4	82	28.1	264	79.3	8	8	.7	5	0	.0
52055	.1	100	.1	89	13.1	150*	25.3	9	35	.0	33	2	.6
52056	.3	100	.1	88	30.3	352	67.3	11	10	.3	9	0	.3
52057	7.9	99	2.8	75	23.8	288	78.1	9	14	3.7	11	1	.3
52060	9.5	100	3.5	72	24.1	276	76.4	8	16	4.5	15	0	.6
52064	.6	99	.1	68	26.5	362	58.1	7	14	.3	12	0	.0
52065	1.2	100	.3	82	34.0	360	63.4	11	10	.6	10	0	.0
52068	1.8	100	.5	83	37.5	154	137.8	12	4	1.0	4	0	.0
52069	2.1	100	.7	80	25.7	283	72.5	10	15	1.1	14	0	.0
52070	1.5	0	.6	77	23.4	259	57.1	9	11	.0	0	0	.0
52071	.2	100	.6	80	41.2	268	69.4	11	9	.1	9	0	.0
52072	.5	100	.2	76	27.9	128	38.8	8	10	.3	10	0	.0
52073	1.5	100	.4	86	29.6	237	93.1	8	8	.8	8	0	.0
52074	.4	100	.1	79	39.2	300	44.5	10	7	.2	5	0	.0
52075	.2	100	.1	87	19.5	224*	61.9	6	16	.1	13	0	.0
52076	2.7	99	1.0	77	22.0	269	61.5	8	20	1.3	18	0	.1
52077	.5	100	.2	85	22.1	264	35.2	7	29	.0	25	0	.0
52078	1.1	100	.3	75	25.5	243	68.6	10	10	.6	12	0	.0
52079	1.0	0	.2	79	27.3	542	98.2	15	7	.0	0	0	.0
DECORAH													
52101	12.7	99	4.0	69	23.8	282	80.8	6	14	5.9	12	1	.0
52132	1.9	0	.7	74	22.8	246	58.8	8	18	.0	0	0	.0
52133	.6	100	.2	81	22.5	168	41.5	12	14	.3	12	0	.0

*=Estimated **1.0=883 lbs per person; 100++ indicates per capita toxic waste generation > than 100 times the U.S. average of 883 lbs per capita.

ZIP CODE MEASURES OF SIZE, LEVELS OF AFFLUENCE AND QUALITY OF LIFE

1=Population (th.); 2= % White; 3=Households (th.); 4=% Owner Occupied; 5=Mean Income Per Household (th.$); 6=Mean Monthly Rent ($)*; 7=Mean Home Value (th.$)*; 8=% under 5; 9=% 65 and over; 10=White Males (th.); 11=% White Males, 65+; 12=# Toxic Waste Sites; 13=Toxic Waste Relative to US(883 lbs.per capita)**.

IOWA

CEDAR RAPIDS

ZIP CODE	1	2	3	4	5	6	7	8	9	10	11	12	13
52222	1.0	0	.3	81	19.9	243	25.5	10	17	.0	0	0	.0
52223	1.3	0	.4	77	24.6	235	87.6	9	14	.0	0	0	1.2
52224	2.3	0	.8	72	26.4	281	74.7	8	18	.0	0	0	.0
52225	.6	0	.2	87	21.3	308	32.9	8	16	.0	0	0	.0
52227	1.0	0	.4	75	27.9	437	90.4	6	11	.0	0	0	.0
52228	2.0	0	.6	83	39.5	337	100.5	7	14	.0	0	0	.0
52229	.8	0	.3	79	23.9	281	40.3	7	14	.0	0	0	.1
52231	.5	100	.2	80	22.6	225	38.9	6	18	.3	15	0	.0
52232	.2	100	.1	84	23.3	235	33.4	0	15	.1	12	0	.0
52233	4.7	100	1.8	65	26.8	371	87.8	10	5	2.3	4	0	.0
52235	.6	100	.2	73	26.5	402	81.5	11	12	.3	13	0	.0
52236	.5	100	.2	63	30.5	361	89.0	13	10	.3	9	1	.0
52237	1.8	0	.6	77	22.4	250	52.6	10	12	.0	0	0	.0
52240	58.1	95	21.4	51	26.6	362	114.2	6	7	26.7	5	3	.3
52241	6.8	96	3.0	31	25.4	403	105.2	7	5	3.1	3	2	.0
52247	4.5	99	1.4	75	25.0	299	86.9	9	16	2.1	14	0	.0
52248	2.0	99	.7	73	23.2	224	54.0	9	21	1.0	17	0	.2
52249	.9	0	.3	84	25.4	290	64.4	6	21	.0	0	0	.0
52251	.6	100	.2	64	26.4	257	37.3	9	10	.3	10	0	.2
52253	2.1	0	.7	82	26.7	271	77.7	8	11	.0	0	0	.0
52254	1.1	0	.4	71	23.8	268	54.6	7	14	.0	0	0	.0
52255	1.2	100	.5	83	24.9	377	62.3	6	20	.6	18	0	.0
52257	.3	100	.1	91	24.8	236	50.3	8	13	.2	11	0	.2

CEDAR RAPIDS

ZIP CODE	1	2	3	4	5	6	7	8	9	10	11	12	13
52301	4.1	100	1.6	76	24.3	319	60.5	7	16	2.0	12	0	.0
52302	22.1	99	7.6	77	31.9	342	90.1	7	9	10.8	7	2	.3
52305	.7	0	.2	78	27.6	406	68.5	16	13	.0	0	1	.0
52306	2.0	99	.7	68	22.5	268	62.1	10	16	.9	12	1	.0
52307	.3	100	.1	57	23.5	301	96.8	2	13	.1	13	1	.0
52308	.2	100	.1	90	20.8	239*	34.3	6	19	.1	11	0	.0
52309	.5	100	.1	92	25.5	176	39.4	3	8	.2	8	0	.4
52312	6.0	100	2.2	75	25.5	289	74.6	7	17	2.9	15	0	.0
52313	.4	100	.1	84	15.9	183*	42.0	2	23	.0	0	0	.0
52314	4.8	98	1.4	72	26.1	300*	62.6	5	7	.2	4	0	.0
52315	1.2	100	.4	70	31.5	321	91.6	7	9	.2	7	1	.0
52316	1.8	100	.7	82	26.5	302	79.9	7	14	1.3	11	0	.1
52317	2.9	99	.7	77	22.9	277	52.2	6	22	.8	17	0	.0
52318	1.0	0	.3	73	30.1	363	118.6	11	5	.6	0	0	.0
52319	.1	100	.1	0	13.4	148	47.9*	0	21	2.0	24	0	.0
52320	1.4	99	.5	72	20.3	245	55.7	6	18	.7	18	0	.0
52321	.5	100	.2	79	19.5	214	41.2	8	11	1.3	14	0	.0
52322	2.5	99	.8	70	26.3	433	68.0	7	9	1.5	7	1	.0
52323	1.1	100	.4	80	21.9	174	38.4	8	21	.6	11	0	.0
52324	1.1	99	.4	80	30.5	416	87.7	9	8	.6	17	0	6.5
52325	.7	0	.2	76	26.4	246	59.4	7	8	.0	5	0	.0
52326	.6	0	.2	86	22.5	268	52.8	9	13	.2	9	0	.0
52327	2.3	99	.8	72	27.7	276	79.9	7	7	1.2	9	0	.0
52328	.6	100	.2	96	33.7	388*	104.3	7	21	4.0	18	1	.2

IOWA

CEDAR RAPIDS

ZIP CODE	1	2	3	4	5	6	7	8	9	10	11	12	13
52329	.9	100	.3	87	23.6	325	57.5	9	13	.4	12	0	.0
52330	1.0	0	.3	86	25.3	249	62.4	8	12	.0	0	0	.0
52331	.4	100	.1	78	19.1	435	80.0	11	12	.2	5	0	.0
52332	1.7	99	.6	83	24.5	322	68.7	10	8	.8	7	0	.0
52333	3.9	0	1.3	84	34.4	377	108.4	7	11	.4	0	0	.0
52334	.1	100	.1	70	24.8	177	43.8	8	15	.2	11	0	.2
52335	.4	100	.2	71	20.3	74	40.1	6	21	.2	21	0	.0
52336	2.4	100	.8	82	29.6	294	76.3	8	9	1.1	8	2	.0
52337	.9	100	.4	75	28.6	327	69.7	8	16	.4	16	0	.3
52338	1.8	100	.6	89	30.8	438	105.1	7	7	.9	7	0	.0
52339	4.3	84	1.5	76	19.8	262	59.0	8	16	1.7	15	0	.2
52340	.4	0	.2	63	20.8	350	71.6	6	8	.0	0	0	.0
52341	1.1	0	.3	96	30.6	351*	103.7	12	5	.0	0	0	.0
52342	3.6	98	1.3	75	24.6	271	63.5	8	17	1.7	15	0	.3
52343	.2	100	.1	93	20.3	233*	41.2	7	13	.1	13	0	.0
52345	.6	100	.2	84	22.1	268	56.5	8	14	.3	14	0	.0
52346	1.1	100	.4	80	28.9	278	74.9	8	12	.6	11	0	.0
52347	1.6	0	.6	78	23.9	299	61.3	8	18	.6	0	0	.3
52349	7.3	100	2.7	74	26.4	240	72.0	8	16	3.5	13	1	.0
52351	.3	100	.1	71	27.5	283	91.9	9	7	.2	7	0	4.6
52352	1.9	100	.6	83	26.6	282	70.4	8	10	1.0	8	0	.0
52353	8.9	100	3.3	73	25.8	302	70.2	7	18	4.2	14	1	.2
52354	.6	0	.2	67	26.0	408	36.7	9	8	.0	0	0	.0
52355	.5	100	.2	81	28.3	47	41.7	4	19	.2	20	0	.2
52356	2.5	100	.9	77	23.1	278	66.1	7	17	1.2	14	0	.0
52357	.2	100	.1	51	21.0	207	72.9	7	19	.1	8	0	.0
52358	3.3	98	1.2	72	29.6	352	93.1	8	13	1.6	12	0	.0
52359	.2	99	.1	93	29.5	339*	31.2	3	20	.1	20	0	.0
52361	3.6	99	1.2	79	28.5	306	76.5	8	11	1.8	15	0	.4
52362	1.3	100	.5	77	21.8	306	49.4	9	16	.7	11	0	.0

CEDAR RAPIDS

ZIP CODE	1	2	3	4	5	6	7	8	9	10	11	12	13
52401	8.4	93	3.2	62	26.9	275	96.8	7	14	3.9	11	0	3.2
52402	35.7	98	13.3	66	29.6	373	91.7	7	10	16.6	8	2	.5
52403	23.2	94	9.0	70	35.3	333	108.1	7	13	10.4	10	2	.0
52404	26.5	97	10.3	67	25.6	355	70.2	8	11	12.3	9	3	.7
52405	24.3	99	8.5	77	30.0	405	80.5	8	9	11.5	7	0	.4

OTTUMWA

ZIP CODE	1	2	3	4	5	6	7	8	9	10	11	12	13
52501	33.6	99	13.1	77	24.3	276	56.8	7	18	15.8	14	0	.9
52530	.7	100	.4	91	21.8	263	49.8	6	18	.5	19	0	.0
52531	6.5	99	2.6	75	21.1	248	55.6	7	21	3.1	17	1	.2
52533	1.3	100	.4	80	24.6	179	42.7	8	14	.7	13	0	.0
52534	.4	0	.1	93	21.4	246*	45.4	8	7	.0	0	0	.0
52535	1.0	100	.4	84	24.2	259	47.7	10	20	.5	20	0	.0
52537	1.5	100	.5	86	23.0	326	36.3	7	12	.7	12	1	.0
52540	1.9	100	.7	77	22.1	242	62.3	8	17	1.0	13	0	.1
52542	.5	0	.2	91	23.8	245	42.1	7	13	.0	0	0	.0
52543	.4	100	.1	69	18.8	221	41.3	8	15	.2	8	0	.0
52544	8.7	98	3.5	96	29.5	339*	66.9	7	10	4.0	18	1	.2

*=Estimated **1.0=883 lbs per person; 100++ indicates per capita toxic waste generation > than 100 times the U.S. average of 883 lbs per capita.

103001

ZIP CODE MEASURES OF SIZE, LEVELS OF AFFLUENCE AND QUALITY OF LIFE

1=Population (th.); 2= % White; 3=Households (th.); 4=% Owner Occupied; 5=Mean Income Per Household (th.$); 6=Mean Monthly Rent ($)*; 7=Mean Home Value (th.$); 8=% under 5; 9=% 65 and over; 10=White Males (th.); 11=% White Males, 65+; 12=# Toxic Waste Sites; 13=Toxic Waste Relative to US(883 lbs.per capita)**.

IOWA

OTTUMWA

ZIPCODE	1	2	3	4	5	6	7	8	9	10	11	12	13
52549	.9	100	.3	83	18.7	310	25.8	10	16	.4	17	1	.0
52550	.9	100	.3	88	15.2	213	22.7	8	23	.4	23	0	.0
52551	.7	100	.3	87	14.7	148	46.4	4	26	.3	29	0	.0
52552	.9	100	.3	86	19.0	219	47.2	5	15	.4	14	0	.0
52553	1.9	0	.7	81	21.5	280	54.1	8	11	.0	.0	0	.0
52554	1.8	0	.7	82	20.5	207	32.1	6	17	.0	0	0	.0
52555	.4	100	.2	89	19.4	153	35.2	12	13	.2	10	0	.0
52556	12.6	98	4.4	73	23.0	271	66.6	7	16	6.1	12	1	.7
52560	.6	100	.2	81	20.3	417	25.7	4	12	.3	13	0	.0
52561	1.0	97	.4	84	23.0	313	60.4	8	20	.5	19	0	.1
52563	1.8	99	.7	73	25.6	230	43.6	6	18	.9	16	0	.0
52565	2.3	0	.8	73	18.1	237	54.9	9	20	.0	0	1	.7
52566	.2	100	.1	86	21.9	456	36.5	9	11	.1	11	0	.0
52567	.4	100	.1	91	22.4	116	41.4	4	14	.2	15	0	.2
52568	.2	100	.1	86	20.4	234*	37.7	5	10	.2	15	0	13.9
52569	.9	100	.3	84	19.2	66	42.0	7	9	.5	7	0	.0
52570	1.2	0	.4	81	21.0	273	32.8	6	18	.0	0	0	.1
52571	1.5	100	.6	81	19.6	180	52.9	6	16	.8	16	1	.0
52572	1.5	100	.6	80	19.5	223	38.5	9	19	.7	15	0	.0
52573	.2	100	.1	97	9.9	114*	30.4	9	12	.1	10	0	.0
52574	1.1	100	.4	92	16.5	302	34.7	9	16	.5	15	0	.2
52575	.5	98	.2	79	20.5	260	27.8	5	11	.3	9	0	.0
52576	.7	100	.2	74	22.6	166	39.2	5	14	.3	13	0	.0
52577	14.6	98	5.7	71	22.3	282	63.8	7	17	6.8	14	2	.1
52580	.6	98	.5	79	21.3	378	52.3	8	12	.3	13	0	.0
52581	.5	100	.2	83	17.7	356	69.3	6	16	.3	17	0	.0
52583	.4	0	.2	96	14.3	165*	34.8	3	38	.0	0	0	.0
52584	.4	100	.2	80	15.8	223	31.3	6	20	.2	20	1	.0
52585	1.1	98	.4	83	22.3	298	35.2	11	18	.5	10	0	.0
52586	.6	100	.2	67	19.8	249	30.0	6	16	.3	13	0	.0
52588	.3	100	.1	100	15.8	181*	19.6	3	16	.1	21	0	.0
52589	.2	100	.1	69	17.2	198*	61.4*	8	15	.1	18	0	.0
52590	1.5	100	.6	77	15.9	205	35.9	7	23	.7	18	1	.0
52591	3.6	100	1.3	78	22.8	266	58.2	6	23	1.7	19	0	.0
52593	.2	100	.1	80	20.1	644	40.7	4	13	.1	10	0	.0
52594	.5	100	.2	86	15.3	233	17.2	14	12	.2	7	0	.0
52595	.6	96	.2	54	23.0	304	65.8	10	7	.3	0	0	.0

BURLINGTON

ZIPCODE	1	2	3	4	5	6	7	8	9	10	11	12	13
52601	34.2	96	12.9	73	26.5	289	73.1	7	15	15.5	12	2	1.8
52619	1.0	97	.4	76	26.0	315	53.9	11	13	.5	14	0	.4
52620	.7	0	.3	80	19.7	190	28.0	7	21	.0	0	0	.0
52621	.8	100	.3	71	20.1	281	46.6	12	18	.4	17	1	.0
52623	1.9	100	.6	78	31.2	284	80.2	11	11	1.0	10	1	.0
52624	.3	100	.1	89	24.4	474	61.5	11	18	.2	8	0	.0
52625	2.6	0	.9	79	26.7	238	74.8	8	14	.0	0	0	.0
52626	1.5	94	.6	81	25.3	336	44.4	8	13	.7	13	0	.0
52627	16.1	94	5.8	73	26.7	296	70.5	6	13	7.6	10	6	2.0
52630	.7	0	.3	86	32.0	374	39.0	11	7	.0	0	0	.0
52632	16.1	96	6.0	73	24.7	271	60.1	8	15	7.3	12	12	2.4

IOWA

BURLINGTON

ZIPCODE	1	2	3	4	5	6	7	8	9	10	11	12	13
52635	.7	100	.3	68	16.5	321	44.4	7	16	.4	14	0	.0
52637	2.6	100	.9	81	28.9	269	73.1	10	17	1.2	13	0	.4
52638	.6	97	.7	62	25.6	374	71.9	9	4	.3	4	1	3.0
52639	2.1	98	.7	86	23.4	318	64.8	8	12	1.1	11	0	.0
52640	1.5	0	.6	80	23.3	236	59.7	7	17	.0	.0	0	.0
52641	10.7	98	3.9	74	24.7	266	78.0	7	15	5.1	12	1	.4
52642	.1	100	.1	84	14.7	169*	30.0	10	29	.1	31	0	.0
52644	.6	100	.2	61	29.9	357	42.2	4	13	.3	13	0	.0
52645	3.3	100	1.2	83	24.0	288	67.2	8	13	1.6	13	0	.8
52646	.9	0	.3	66	23.9	301	43.6	11	12	.0	0	0	.0
52647	.2	100	.2	86	19.9	292	59.9	8	20	.1	19	0	.0
52649	1.1	99	.4	83	26.2	278	43.1	6	14	.5	11	0	.0
52650	.8	100	.2	75	24.8	314	85.0	6	12	.4	12	0	.2
52651	.8	100	.3	79	20.6	152	31.3	3	23	.4	22	0	.0
52653	3.4	99	1.3	79	26.3	295	72.1	7	16	1.6	15	1	.0
52654	1.5	0	.6	82	24.5	306	62.4	7	16	.0	0	0	.0
52655	5.0	99	2.0	75	26.5	325	76.9	6	11	2.4	9	2	.2
52656	2.7	98	.8	78	26.4	307	82.7	6	12	1.4	10	3	.1
52658	1.2	97	.4	82	34.6	274	89.5	7	8	.7	7	0	.0
52659	1.7	99	.6	73	25.3	234	58.9	9	20	.8	17	0	.2
52660	.3	100	.1	70	30.8	104	89.3	9	8	.2	4	0	.0

ROCK ISLAND

ZIPCODE	1	2	3	4	5	6	7	8	9	10	11	12	13
52701	.2	0	.1	97	32.8	376*	48.8	15	2	.0	0	0	.0
52720	.4	99	.1	71	27.1	395	59.4	6	11	.6	13	0	.1
52721	1.0	100	.4	75	29.5	367	78.9	7	10	.5	8	0	.0
52722	28.9	98	9.9	75	39.0	445	121.4	8	6	13.9	5	2	1.4
52726	3.9	98	1.1	89	38.7	408	121.2	8	5	2.0	4	0	.0
52727	.6	100	.2	75	35.6	296	105.8	7	7	.3	8	0	.0
52728	1.3	97	.4	84	28.7	359	64.0	9	7	.6	7	0	14.7
52729	1.0	100	.2	73	24.7	344	64.7	7	15	.5	13	0	.0
52730	5.5	0	1.8	81	30.3	322	82.5	9	6	.0	0	0	2.0
52731	1.2	0	.3	83	27.8	341	59.0	6	13	.0	0	0	.0
52732	34.3	98	12.7	72	26.4	324	71.1	7	14	15.9	12	5	2.4
52737	.3	0	.1	94	23.0	264*	47.1	10	11	.0	0	0	.0
52738	3.3	98	1.2	75	27.4	279	66.7	7	15	1.6	13	0	.0
52739	.6	87	.2	77	23.4	269*	39.0	5	21	.3	19	0	.0
52742	6.5	100	2.3	73	28.0	313	91.3	7	13	3.3	11	0	.0
52745	.8	100	.3	66	31.8	414	82.1	10	9	.4	7	0	.0
52746	.9	100	.3	89	34.0	524	101.3	7	3	.5	3	0	.0
52747	2.0	100	.7	74	30.4	350	89.7	8	13	.9	11	1	.0
52748	5.6	98	1.7	67	33.9	435	113.1	11	3	2.7	2	0	.1
52750	.7	0	.2	84	27.3	385	72.3	10	10	.0	0	0	.0
52751	1.3	0	.5	80	29.4	302	79.4	9	16	.0	0	0	.1
52753	4.1	99	1.3	82	31.9	310	66.7	11	13	.2	8	0	.0
52754	1.4	0	.5	76	26.5	243	65.3	6	7	.0	0	0	.0
52755	1.9	100	.7	74	25.7	310	76.5	8	15	.9	12	0	.0
52756	2.2	0	.7	88	38.0	304	120.6	8	6	.0	0	1	.0
52757	.4	0	.2	78	30.2	370	66.3	6	13	.0	0	0	.0

*=Estimated **1.0=883 lbs per person; 100++ indicates per capita toxic waste generation > than 100 times the U.S. average of 883 lbs per capita.

ZIP CODE MEASURES OF SIZE, LEVELS OF AFFLUENCE AND QUALITY OF LIFE

1=Population (th.); 2= % White; 3=Households (th.); 4=% Owner Occupied; 5=Mean Income Per Household (th.$); 6=Mean Monthly Rent ($)*; 7=Mean Home Value (th.$)*; 8=% under 5; 9=% 65 and over; 10=White Males, 65+; 11=% White Males; 12=# Toxic Waste Sites; 13=Toxic Waste Relative to US(883 lbs.per capital)**.

IOWA

ZIP CODE	1	2	3	4	5	6	7	8	9	10	11	12	13
ROCK ISLAND													
52758	.3	100	.1	84	27.5	453	77.9	7	10	.1	8	0	.0
52759	.3	0	.1	72	31.0	359	66.8	4	3	.0	0	0	.0
52760	.7	100	.1	78	29.4	396	56.2	7	7	.3	5	0	.3
52761	30.2	96	10.6	74	27.5	307	83.6	9	12	13.9	10	5	7.9
52765	.5	100	.2	59	31.1	397	72.0	7	4	.3	0	0	.0
52766	.8	0	.3	90	22.2	429	59.1	9	19	.4	0	0	.0
52767	.6	100	.2	83	42.0	596	102.8	4	24	.3	19	0	1.9
52768	1.6	0	.5	74	29.4	365	93.1	10	8	.3	0	0	3.7
52769	.9	100	.8	67	29.6	480	91.3	9	8	.5	6	0	.0
52772	4.9	99	1.8	73	24.1	272	75.6	8	16	2.4	14	1	.0
52773	2.6	0	.9	76	31.7	326	102.1	8	7	.0	0	1	.4
52774	.1	100	.1	62	18.8	328	72.3	8	15	.1	9	1	1.0
52776	4.0	94	1.5	72	28.1	279	78.4	9	15	1.8	14	0	.1
52777	1.5	100	.5	79	26.6	361	63.5	7	16	.7	13	0	.3
52778	3.8	100	1.3	70	29.0	385	87.5	9	10	1.8	10	1	2.8
DAVENPORT													
52801	1.3	83	.8	0	10.6	219	37.7*	6	29	.5	21	0	5.5
52802	13.9	92	5.2	61	23.2	317	58.8	9	12	6.2	10	2	.4
52803	30.0	87	11.4	59	27.3	322	88.9	8	13	12.8	11	0	.2
52804	29.2	95	10.5	76	29.6	397	87.6	8	12	13.3	10	0	.2
52806	24.8	95	8.3	70	31.8	446	97.7	10	5	11.7	4	2	.0
52807	7.8	92	3.2	39	35.4	405	153.0	8	5	3.6	4	0	.0
ROCHESTER													
55953	.3	100	.1	74	20.1	248	23.0	7	28	.1	22	0	.0
55954	.3	100	.1	72	21.4	245*	42.3	6	13	.2	10	0	.0
55974	.3	100	.1	81	19.6	158	69.9*	7	10	.2	15	0	.0
MANKATO													
56027	.3	0	.1	67	25.7	295*	91.4*	6	16	.0	0	0	.0
56029	.3	100	.1	92	23.4	269*	62.3	14	11	.1	1	0	.0
SAINT JOSEPH													
64461	.2	100	.1	68	25.4	291*	90.4*	0	22	.1	29	0	.0
OMAHA													
68110	3.4	99	1.1	88	27.4	420	49.9	10	5	1.7	4	0	.0

KANSAS

ZIP CODE	1	2	3	4	5	6	7	8	9	10	11	12	13
HARRISONVILLE													
64742	.3	100	.1	84	21.4	150	89.3	15	15	.1	18	0	.0
KANSAS CITY													
66002	14.7	91	4.9	71	23.0	231	58.5	7	16	6.3	12	2	.7
66006	4.9	97	1.6	73	24.5	270	73.8	7	12	2.3	11	0	.0
66007	2.3	98	.7	84	33.6	403	88.9	8	8	1.1	7	0	.0
66008	.3	0	.1	71	22.6	351	54.2	10	13	.0	0	0	.0
66010	.8	97	.3	82	18.7	180	30.1	3	25	.3	22	0	1.9
66012	8.1	91	2.6	75	29.2	265	78.4	9	11	3.6	8	2	2.2
66013	1.2	0	.4	80	32.8	427	122.4	9	9	.0	0	0	.0
66014	.4	0	.2	89	21.2	131	24.2	6	19	.0	0	0	.0
66015	1.0	0	.4	79	19.7	213	38.7	9	19	.0	0	0	.0
66016	.4	100	.1	86	23.7	37	65.3	7	12	.0	0	0	.2
66017	.4	0	.1	87	24.2	197	47.0	6	24	.0	14	0	.0
66018	4.1	98	1.3	74	29.8	271	89.2	9	8	2.0	8	1	1.5
66019	.4	97	.2	21	10.9	211	29.5	0	83	.8	85	0	.0
66020	1.7	99	.5	89	25.5	240	67.2	7	12	.8	11	0	.0
66021	2.1	100	.6	83	26.2	301	69.8	12	5	1.0	5	0	1.3
66023	1.1	99	.5	79	23.2	193	43.1	8	11	.6	11	0	.0
66024	1.1	83	.4	76	16.0	248	29.0	8	14	.4	11	0	.2
66025	4.0	99	1.4	73	27.8	294	71.9	9	11	1.9	9	1	21.5
66026	.5	0	.2	79	24.0	139	36.8	4	11	.1	1	0	.0
66027	8.0	75	1.6	1	30.4	444	111.8	10	0	3.5	0	0	.0
66030	4.9	98	1.7	73	27.6	300	89.6	10	10	2.4	8	0	1.3
66032	5.1	100	2.0	78	20.5	220	56.8	7	23	2.5	20	0	.0
66035	1.4	97	.3	92	24.4	131	36.3	8	14	.4	14	0	.0
66038	.3	100	.1	72	21.1	178	50.9	6	21	.7	20	0	.0
66039	.9	98	.3	89	16.6	267	18.6	8	17	.1	19	0	.0
66040	2.1	98	.8	87	20.1	141	26.8	8	21	.4	22	0	.0
66041	.5	100	.2	80	21.9	181	50.8	8	20	1.0	19	0	.9
66042	.6	99	.2	85	22.5	332	41.5	7	17	.3	13	0	.0
66044	4.7	86	1.2	85	21.7	133	32.9	4	21	.3	19	0	.0
66048	57.6	86	20.5	67	25.4	287	73.9	7	13	12.8	11	5	1.0
66050	1.4	99	.5	84	24.7	319	71.3	6	10	.7	7	0	.1
66052	1.4	99	.5	83	26.4	368	69.6	6	13	.7	11	0	.0
66053	3.2	99	1.1	79	27.0	314	77.4	9	12	1.6	9	0	.0
66054	2.1	97	.7	85	22.6	211	64.0	8	10	1.1	10	0	.0
66056	1.4	100	.5	81	20.4	190	50.8	6	18	1.1	10	0	.1
66058	.5	100	.2	88	18.2	234	28.0	5	20	.3	15	0	.1
66060	1.2	99	.4	85	22.2	268	45.5	6	17	.3	17	0	.0
66061	41.7	96	13.4	71	33.5	408	111.4	10	5	19.7	4	4	.4
66064	6.0	94	2.2	76	22.9	204	48.4	7	18	2.7	16	5	.5
66066	2.1	98	.7	85	23.2	207	60.2	6	18	1.0	15	0	.1
66067	13.8	95	5.2	72	24.1	261	62.9	7	18	6.3	15	0	.4
66070	1.3	99	.5	89	31.4	410	100.0	5	13	.6	12	0	.0
66071	9.2	96	3.3	76	28.5	250	73.9	7	15	4.3	12	1	.3
66072	.9	0	.3	86	20.7	209	37.8	7	18	1.0	10	1	.0
66073	2.1	99	.8	82	25.0	251	66.7	7	12	1.0	10	1	1.0

*=Estimated **1.0=883 lbs per person; 100++ indicates per capita toxic waste generation > than 100 times the U.S. average of 883 lbs per capita.

ZIP CODE MEASURES OF SIZE, LEVELS OF AFFLUENCE AND QUALITY OF LIFE

1=Population (th.); 2=% White; 3=Households (th.); 4=% Owner Occupied; 5=Mean Income Per Household (th.$); 6=Mean Monthly Rent ($)*; 7=Mean Home Value (th.$)*;
8=% under 5; 9=% 65 and over; 10=White Males (th.); 11=% White Males, 65+; 12=# Toxic Waste Sites; 13=Toxic Waste Relative to US(883 lbs.per capita)**.

KANSAS

ZIPCODE	1	2	3	4	5	6	7	8	9	10	11	12	13
KANSAS CITY													
66075	2.3	99	.9	76	19.8	215	44.6	8	23	1.1	20	1	.0
66076	1.9	99	.7	83	23.0	259	55.6	7	16	1.0	14	0	.0
66078	.8	100	.3	89	22.0	180	48.8	10	12	.3	13	0	.0
66079	.7	100	.2	84	36.1	138	39.5	9	11	.3	11	0	.0
66080	1.0	99	.2	88	21.7	179	48.3	5	19	.5	14	0	.0
66081	.2	98	.1	81	19.2	160	38.6	4	21	.1	18	0	.0
66083	4.3	98	1.3	86	31.6	382	95.6	9	7	2.1	6	1	.0
66085	3.4	99	1.0	91	45.7	303	177.2	8	3	1.7	2	0	.0
66086	4.6	97	1.5	84	28.2	304	73.7	8	10	2.2	9	0	.0
66087	2.2	99	.8	73	21.7	230	46.2	8	17	1.1	15	0	.0
66088	2.5	99	.9	80	24.5	191	58.3	7	18	1.2	17	0	.0
66090	2.8	99	1.0	79	21.2	222	53.9	8	16	1.4	14	2	.0
66091	.4	0	.2	84	17.4	141	40.6	10	16	1.0	0	2	.2
66092	3.0	100	1.0	85	26.0	272	64.5	7	14	1.4	12	0	.0
66093	.8	100	.3	82	22.1	280	27.2	6	18	.4	17	0	.0
66094	.4	84	.1	77	19.5	62	40.0	8	11	.2	12	0	.0
66095	.9	99	.3	83	21.4	298	40.5	7	13	.5	13	0	.0
66097	1.0	96	.3	85	22.7	264	44.6	5	23	.5	19	0	.0
KANSAS CITY													
66101	18.3	43	7.6	50	15.2	186	27.5	8	20	3.7	17	2	.2
66102	30.9	77	12.6	61	22.0	267	50.6	8	15	11.0	13	7	.0
66103	14.6	86	6.4	44	19.4	338	46.4	8	11	6.0	9	1	1.8
66104	37.6	46	12.5	74	23.4	278	49.6	8	11	8.2	14	4	.0
66105	3.4	92	1.2	58	17.8	252	26.0	10	12	1.5	10	7	33.1
66106	26.3	90	9.1	74	27.0	280	71.8	8	9	11.5	7	8	.9
66109	14.0	93	4.5	87	34.3	407	90.9	7	6	6.5	5	0	.0
66111	7.8	91	2.7	78	28.0	338	62.5	8	6	3.6	6	1	4.3
66112	11.2	81	4.0	61	30.6	382	81.7	7	7	4.4	5	0	.0
66113	2.8	91	1.0	87	26.4	300	73.8	9	13	1.2	9	0	.1
SHAWNEE MISSION													
66202	17.1	98	7.5	60	31.5	442	97.4	5	11	8.0	10	0	.0
66203	20.5	95	7.5	67	32.7	399	99.8	5	8	9.4	6	3	.2
66204	19.0	98	7.3	60	31.1	522	89.9	8	7	8.9	7	0	.0
66205	15.2	97	6.1	84	37.1	440	107.6	6	15	7.0	13	0	.1
66206	11.3	98	4.0	97	61.4	609	182.1	5	13	5.5	12	1	.0
66207	15.4	98	5.3	86	59.9	656	180.8	5	13	5.9	7	0	6.3
66208	24.5	99	9.3	88	52.0	561	146.5	6	12	11.6	10	0	.1
66209	3.0	98	1.0	97	67.6	776*	237.7	7	5	1.5	5	0	3.5
66210	2.9	0	1.2	79	42.3	466	208.0	9	2	1.2	0	1	7.8
66211	3.7	97	.9	90	57.7	825	286.5	8	7	.2	6	0	.0
66212	33.7	97	12.3	67	39.4	500	135.0	6	9	15.6	5	1	.0
66213	.3	100	.1	61	39.4	594	204.4	7	4	.1	4	2	.2
66214	9.4	96	3.4	54	37.4	459	134.0	7	4	4.4	2	0	.0
66215	16.8	96	5.7	74	41.5	457	143.7	9	5	8.0	3	0	1.6
66216	14.6	97	4.7	80	39.3	447	136.6	9	2	7.1	2	0	.0
66217	.9	95	.3	82	37.5	589	152.6	9	9	.5	6	1	.0
66218	1.5	95	.5	94	44.1	632	131.7	8	4	.7	2	1	.0
66219	.2	0	.1	82	48.4	350	173.2	6	12	.0	0	0	19.3
66220	.7	0	.2	95	57.9	441	208.0	7	3	.0	0	0	.0

KANSAS

ZIPCODE	1	2	3	4	5	6	7	8	9	10	11	12	13
SHAWNEE MISSION													
66221	.3	0	.1	85	88.7	735	251.7	4	0	.0	0	0	.0
66223	.5	100	.2	75	26.0	428	114.4	11	13	.3	10	1	1.3
66224	.6	94	.2	93	57.1	543	295.7	2	3	.3	1	0	.0
TOPEKA													
66402	1.9	97	.7	81	22.8	165	58.8	6	21	.9	18	0	.0
66403	.8	97	.2	90	23.4	247	74.5	15	5	.4	3	0	.0
66404	.9	0	.3	87	16.9	213	43.6	9	18	.0	0	0	.0
66406	.7	100	.2	79	23.3	142	46.4	7	13	.4	11	0	.0
66407	.7	100	.2	76	22.5	156	38.6	8	16	.3	15	0	.0
66408	.5	100	.2	66	23.7	302	52.5	9	20	.3	18	0	.0
66409	.6	100	.2	84	19.5	181	63.7	9	17	.3	17	0	.0
66410	1.5	99	.5	92	32.1	253	108.9	7	7	.8	8	0	.0
66411	.3	100	.1	87	22.2	255*	46.1	10	14	.8	15	0	.0
66412	1.7	100	.7	79	19.1	181	36.6	6	25	.8	21	0	.1
66413	.4	100	.1	85	20.9	240*	69.6	7	16	.2	17	0	.0
66414	2.2	99	.8	80	22.9	195	53.3	7	17	1.1	15	0	.0
66415	2.6	98	.8	86	24.5	224	61.9	10	7	1.3	6	0	.0
66416	1.0	100	.4	81	20.8	225	39.2	9	23	.5	21	0	.0
66417	.5	0	.5	85	16.5	177	18.8	10	15	.5	20	0	.0
66418	.5	0	.5	83	23.9	328	41.0	8	12	.5	12	0	.0
66419	.2	100	.2	95	22.1	254*	39.7	9	19	.2	18	0	.0
66422	.5	100	.5	68	22.0	150	50.0	7	11	.2	8	0	.1
66423	.5	99	.4	90	21.4	275	38.9	5	22	.5	21	0	.2
66424	1.1	98	.3	80	19.6	159	39.1	8	17	.3	17	0	.0
66425	.7	98	.2	75	20.9	263	49.7	5	23	.6	23	1	.0
66427	.6	99	.8	84	21.3	189	43.2	6	17	.8	17	0	.0
66428	1.8	99	.6	87	19.9	226	24.6	9	18	.6	18	0	.3
66429	.6	97	.4	88	26.5	297	76.6	10	7	.3	7	0	.0
66431	.4	98	.3	81	22.4	209	42.4	12	16	.4	15	0	.0
66433	.7	99	.3	88	24.7	241	33.5	13	15	.0	17	0	.0
66434	.6	100	.1	81	19.7	95	32.3	7	23	.2	19	0	.1
66436	.2	97	.2	72	22.8	219	61.8	7	19	2.5	17	0	.2
66438	5.6	98	2.0	77	23.7	237	56.6	7	21	2.4	25	0	.0
66439	5.0	100	.3	78	14.9	156	31.9	7	26	.2	22	1	.2
66440	.3	84	3.1	77	17.1	165	40.2	7	23	1.2	7	1	.1
66441	1.5	96	1.5	86	27.5	423	68.4	8	7	.7	0	0	.3
66442	22.2	74	8.3	53	22.4	277	47.0	11	0	8.5	5	3	.0
66448	21.1	60	3.2	1	17.2	348	47.0	8	23	.1	19	0	.0
66449	.2	100	.1	66	21.5	246	31.9	4	15	.4	15	0	.0
66450	.9	0	.3	77	20.5	270	45.4	5	18	.0	17	0	.0
66451	.3	100	.1	82	19.0	162	27.1	5	18	.1	18	0	.0
TOPEKA													
66501	.2	0	.1	94	20.0	230*	35.0	7	19	.2	19	0	.0
66502	40.0	93	15.4	53	23.4	318	93.2	7	7	19.2	6	3	.0
66506	5.3	85	.6	7	8.4	155	78.3	3	0	2.2	0	0	.0
66507	.2	0	.3	82	34.3	327	74.0	6	13	.1	18	0	.0
66508	4.9	100	1.9	74	25.5	327	59.7	8	21	2.3	16	1	.4

*=Estimated **1.0=883 lbs per person; 100++ indicates per capita toxic waste generation > than 100 times the U.S. average of 883 lbs per capita.

ZIP CODE MEASURES OF SIZE, LEVELS OF AFFLUENCE AND QUALITY OF LIFE

1=Population (th.); 2= % White; 3=Households (th.); 4=% Owner Occupied; 5=Mean Income Per Household (th.$); 6=Mean Monthly Rent ($); 7=Mean Home Value (th.$); 8=% under 5; 9=% 65 and over; 10=%White Males (th.); 11=% White Males, 65+; 12=# Toxic Waste Sites; 13=Toxic Waste Relative to US(883 lbs.per capita)**

KANSAS

TOPEKA

ZIP CODE	1	2	3	4	5	6	7	8	9	10	11	12	13
66509	1.9	82	.6	86	23.0	271	58.1	10	8	.8	7	0	.0
66510	.9	99	.3	82	21.6	305	41.7	8	13	.4	13	0	.0
66512	2.5	100	.8	87	27.4	324	79.2	7	8	1.3	7	0	.0
66514	1.3	97	.4	66	28.6	342	101.7	11	5	.6	4	0	.0
66515	.6	0	.0	78	24.0	155	35.1	7	17	.0	0	0	.0
66516	.5	93	.2	85	20.4	133	40.4	8	17	.2	17	0	.0
66517	1.8	84	.7	34	16.1	202	47.2	16	4	.8	3	0	.0
66518	.3	0	.1	80	18.9	124	17.2	3	21	.0	0	0	.0
66520	.5	100	.2	74	19.0	190	44.0	7	16	.2	16	0	.0
66521	1.2	99	.5	81	18.2	243	42.6	6	25	.6	21	0	.0
66522	.3	0	.1	77	16.0	197	19.8	10	10	.0	0	0	.0
66523	3.8	99	1.4	78	23.0	222	59.8	6	24	1.8	19	0	.0
66524	2.1	99	.8	83	24.8	285	71.5	7	16	1.1	14	0	.0
66526	.7	97	.2	82	23.9	149	49.2	7	11	.3	13	0	.0
66527	.3	0	.1	71	18.8	136	26.9	12	15	.0	0	0	.0
66528	.2	99	.3	87	20.8	231	33.1	9	14	.4	12	0	.0
66529	.2	0	.1	59	17.0	212	32.8	19	21	.0	0	0	.0
66531	1.2	98	.5	77	19.4	247	52.5	7	19	.6	17	0	.0
66532	.7	0	.3	71	18.7	225	35.3	8	17	.0	0	0	.0
66533	1.6	97	.5	83	27.1	291	70.4	6	16	.8	13	0	.0
66534	3.2	99	1.2	79	22.6	208	58.7	7	23	1.5	19	0	1.0
66535	1.6	96	.6	78	19.6	250	68.2	10	8	.8	8	0	.0
66536	2.1	99	.9	76	26.0	264	70.3	8	16	1.1	12	0	.9
66537	1.3	0	.4	87	23.3	263	47.9	8	14	.0	0	0	.0
66538	3.6	100	1.2	79	21.1	198	61.9	7	18	1.1	16	1	.1
66539	2.2	99	.7	77	29.2	325	93.2	8	8	1.1	7	0	.0
66540	.7	97	.2	90	20.2	308	23.3	11	14	.3	13	0	.0
66541	.4	100	.2	81	17.2	320	22.8	5	16	.3	22	0	.0
66542	1.9	94	.7	87	32.6	396	115.4	5	7	.9	8	0	.0
66543	.4	98	.2	91	20.8	169	76.6	4	18	.2	16	0	.0
66544	.4	100	.2	84	18.8	194	23.3	5	22	.2	15	0	.0
66546	1.0	0	.3	74	27.9	219	78.6	11	8	.4	0	1	.0
66547	4.9	98	1.8	79	23.1	245	69.5	9	15	2.4	12	0	.5
66548	1.0	100	.4	79	21.7	159	49.3	4	20	.5	22	0	.3
66549	1.1	0	.4	78	21.8	225	43.4	6	20	.0	0	0	.0
66550	.3	98	.1	85	20.9	253	38.2	7	20	.3	18	0	.0
66551	.7	100	.3	85	21.1	230	23.3	11	14	.2	19	0	.0
66552	.5	0	.2	82	22.0	232	27.1	10	16	.0	0	0	.0
66554	.5	100	.2	84	21.1	225	61.1	8	17	.3	17	0	.0

TOPEKA

ZIP CODE	1	2	3	4	5	6	7	8	9	10	11	12	13
66603	2.5	84	1.4	19	15.0	231	47.5	7	15	.9	13	1	.2
66604	28.5	91	11.6	70	28.8	312	89.2	6	15	12.3	11	0	.0
66605	19.2	86	6.6	79	28.4	303	82.9	8	8	8.0	8	0	.0
66606	13.1	92	5.3	63	26.0	330	83.2	6	19	5.4	15	0	.0
66607	12.2	61	4.4	63	18.0	240	44.0	11	13	3.5	14	0	.1
66608	7.9	89	3.0	67	19.8	235	48.7	9	13	3.5	12	2	1.3
66609	5.6	93	2.3	66	26.1	311	95.7	8	5	2.6	3	0	.0
66610	1.0	93	.3	95	47.5	548	152.8	6	3	.5	2	0	.0
66611	11.8	93	5.1	59	32.0	400	101.9	7	13	5.1	10	0	.0

KANSAS

TOPEKA

ZIP CODE	1	2	3	4	5	6	7	8	9	10	11	12	13
66612	4.1	73	2.3	17	15.3	235	44.3	5	24	1.3	17	0	3.2
66614	17.8	96	6.7	72	34.9	346	105.4	7	7	8.2	6	0	.0
66615	.4	100	.2	73	27.4	197	92.7	6	9	.2	9	1	.0
66616	7.3	87	2.7	81	23.3	292	52.4	7	15	3.1	14	1	.0
66617	7.3	97	2.3	87	33.7	290	93.9	8	8	3.6	7	1	.0
66618	5.4	98	1.7	90	35.6	357	104.5	8	5	2.7	5	1	.1
66619	.9	77	.2	29	28.7	175	87.1	8	2	.3	0	0	1.4

FORT SCOTT

ZIP CODE	1	2	3	4	5	6	7	8	9	10	11	12	13
66701	12.5	95	5.1	71	21.1	219	56.4	7	20	5.5	16	3	.6
66710	1.0	0	.4	88	16.8	235	31.8	9	20	.0	0	0	.0
66711	.8	0	.3	84	19.3	170	23.5	7	23	.0	0	0	.0
66712	1.6	97	.7	80	17.3	202	47.0	7	28	.7	25	0	.5
66713	6.1	95	2.4	74	20.0	205	48.0	7	17	2.7	12	0	.0
66714	.2	100	.1	95	16.4	188*	21.0	5	16	.1	13	0	.0
66716	.7	0	.3	82	20.8	125	35.2	6	20	.0	0	0	.0
66717	1.0	0	.4	84	19.0	227	33.4	8	17	.0	0	0	.0
66720	13.0	96	5.1	74	23.6	259	58.4	8	18	5.9	13	3	.8
66724	.4	99	.4	90	19.3	203	35.9	7	19	.5	15	0	.5
66725	5.7	98	.3	80	21.1	173	44.3	6	21	2.6	17	1	.5
66730	.1	0	.1	70	22.5	287	42.1	7	19	.2	20	0	.0
66732	.4	100	.1	94	21.6	248*	29.0	8	19	.2	18	0	.0
66733	2.5	99	1.0	78	20.9	182	50.3	6	19	1.2	18	0	.0
66734	.3	100	.1	77	21.1	256	46.7	8	20	.2	17	0	.9
66735	.3	0	.1	100	25.0	288*	47.8	12	12	.0	0	0	.0
66736	4.8	98	1.9	77	19.8	201	48.5	7	22	2.2	20	0	.4
66738	.4	0	.7	86	18.0	131	29.1	8	22	.0	0	0	.0
66739	6.0	97	2.2	79	18.9	197	40.3	8	14	2.8	11	0	5.0
66740	.5	100	.2	87	21.3	162	38.7	10	18	.3	15	0	4.8
66741	.3	0	.1	85	19.7	450	26.8	7	15	.0	0	0	.0
66742	.3	0	.1	84	19.4	234	47.6	10	10	.0	0	0	.0
66743	.6	99	.2	83	19.1	181	51.0	6	22	2.3	18	0	.0
66744	.4	88	.2	88	20.1	159	25.8	5	17	.0	1	0	.0
66746	.3	100	.1	85	18.2	71	28.8	6	19	.0	21	0	.2
66748	3.1	97	1.2	80	22.3	253	52.6	7	20	1.4	16	1	1.2
66749	9.0	97	3.5	76	22.2	228	53.6	9	18	4.0	15	1	1.4
66751	.9	99	.3	79	17.6	207	30.7	11	15	.5	14	1	.0
66753	1.3	99	.5	81	19.9	167	38.8	8	18	.6	18	0	.2
66754	.4	99	.2	83	16.6	237	31.2	7	22	.2	18	0	.0
66755	1.2	99	.5	78	20.3	185	40.6	6	20	.2	21	0	.1
66756	1.2	99	.5	84	16.9	167	27.9	4	27	.6	23	0	.0
66757	4.5	99	1.8	75	19.5	199	48.8	8	20	2.1	16	2	1.9
66758	.3	0	.1	86	16.8	183	24.8	6	18	.0	0	0	.0
66761	.3	100	.1	84	20.7	47	33.2	4	22	.0	0	0	.0
66762	25.6	97	10.4	65	20.0	239	57.7	6	18	11.7	14	3	2.4
66767	.6	100	.2	79	22.0	239	32.3	6	28	.3	25	0	.0
66769	.6	100	.2	77	23.4	204	34.2	7	10	.3	9	0	.0
66770	.4	0	.1	77	24.6	295	54.7	9	11	.0	0	0	.4
66771	1.1	99	.4	85	20.3	173	43.7	9	18	.6	16	0	.2
66772	.4	100	.2	82	20.8	131	34.3	10	21	.2	21	0	.0

*=Estimated **1.0=883 lbs per person; 100++ indicates per capita toxic waste generation > than 100 times the U.S. average of 883 lbs per capita.

ZIP CODE MEASURES OF SIZE, LEVELS OF AFFLUENCE AND QUALITY OF LIFE

1=Population (th.); 2= % White; 3=Households (th.); 4=% Owner Occupied; 5=Mean Income Per Household (th.$); 6=Mean Monthly Rent ($)*; 7=Mean Home Value (th.$)*; 8=% under 5; 9=% 65 and over; 10=White Males (th.); 11=% White Males, 65+; 12=# Toxic Waste Sites; 13=Toxic Waste Relative to US(883 lbs.per capita)**.

KANSAS

ZIPCODE	1	2	3	4	5	6	7	8	9	10	11	12	13
FORT SCOTT													
66773	.9	98	.4	86	18.2	204	31.6	5	22	.4	18	1	.0
66775	.3	100	.1	88	17.8	234	25.9	11	18	.2	11	0	.0
66776	1.3	99	.5	84	19.3	236	44.5	8	16	.6	16	0	.0
66777	.8	95	.4	83	16.8	190	34.2	6	26	.4	26	0	.1
66778	.2	0	.1	77	13.6	132	18.7	5	15	.0	0	0	.0
66779	.8	0	.3	75	20.9	151	49.6	9	26	.0	0	0	.0
66780	1.1	0	.4	83	17.5	186	18.7	8	16	.0	0	0	.0
66781	1.3	98	.5	82	18.5	246	34.2	7	18	.6	16	0	.0
66782	.2	100	.1	91	17.3	199*	20.7	6	20	.6	14	0	.0
66783	3.1	98	1.2	77	18.8	243	50.1	7	24	1.5	21	0	.0
TOPEKA													
66801	29.6	94	11.0	61	25.3	292	77.7	8	11	13.4	9	1	.6
66830	.4	0	.2	76	17.7	181	35.5	3	27	.0	0	0	.0
66833	.4	100	.2	80	23.4	251	39.7	3	17	.2	14	0	.0
66834	1.0	100	.4	83	20.3	191	44.4	7	21	.5	19	0	.0
66835	1.3	98	.5	77	23.0	261	62.2	11	12	.7	11	0	.0
66838	.2	100	.1	91	17.9	206*	36.1	5	26	.1	26	0	.0
66839	4.3	99	1.7	91	24.7	308	55.4	7	20	2.1	18	0	.0
66840	.8	0	.3	75	16.8	215	26.7	5	18	.0	0	0	.0
66842	.3	0	.1	80	21.8	33	47.4	6	15	.0	0	0	.0
66843	.4	0	.1	83	28.8	331*	28.6	5	14	.0	0	1	1.1
66845	1.2	99	.5	80	18.9	204	47.8	6	29	.6	20	0	.0
66846	3.3	99	1.4	71	22.0	219	58.5	7	25	1.5	23	0	.4
66847	.2	100	.1	86	17.6	202*	38.2	8	11	.1	6	0	.0
66848	.4	96	.2	78	16.9	206	39.1	9	19	.2	15	0	.0
66849	.6	98	.2	80	22.1	201	40.4	5	15	.3	14	0	.0
66850	.3	0	.1	72	21.1	234	30.1	11	16	.0	0	0	.0
66851	1.0	98	.4	76	17.6	234	35.7	5	23	.4	21	0	.0
66852	.9	0	.3	80	21.4	225	46.2	7	17	.0	0	0	.0
66853	.6	100	.2	76	19.2	238	27.6	4	18	.3	17	0	.0
66854	1.0	0	.3	81	21.2	300	48.9	10	16	.9	20	0	.0
66856	1.6	99	.6	84	24.7	306	59.5	9	15	.8	13	0	.0
66857	1.1	99	.4	81	19.5	224	36.5	8	21	.6	20	0	.0
66858	.6	0		87	21.8	231	29.3	6	17	.0	0	0	.0
66859	.3	91	.1	89	23.2	138	21.3	4	18	.1	15	0	.0
66860	1.8	98	.7	78	22.3	221	45.1	6	21	.9	20	0	.0
66861	3.3	100	1.3	72	24.3	279*	28.6	2	31	1.5	22	0	.0
66862	.2	0	.1	72	24.3	209	40.6	8	12	.0	0	0	.0
66864	.5	0	.2	86	24.3	280	58.1	9	16	.0	0	0	.0
66865	1.1	0	.4	81	22.6	231	45.2	6	22	1.0	17	0	.0
66866	2.1	98	.8	73	20.8	289	45.2	6	16	.4	16	0	.2
66868	.8	99	.3	78	21.0	226	46.5	8	18	.4	16	0	.0
66869	.8	99	.3	66	20.2	259*	24.1	7	22	.1	17	0	.0
66870	.2	100	.1	87	20.2	269	36.1	9	21	.7	19	0	.0
66871	1.3	99	.5	78	20.2	209	42.1	6	22	.6	20	0	2.1
66872	1.1	100	.4	79	19.1	167	31.6	7	26	.2	28	0	.0
66873	.4	100	.2	76	18.8								
SALINA													
66901	8.1	100	3.1	70	21.0	195	55.7	7	21	3.7	16	0	.0

KANSAS

ZIPCODE	1	2	3	4	5	6	7	8	9	10	11	12	13
SALINA													
66930	.3	100	.1	96	17.4	200*	19.0	4	24	.1	20	0	.0
66931	.2	100	.1	77	18.3	202	27.1	6	17	.1	16	0	.0
66932	.3	100	.1	82	21.0	506	24.4	7	15	.2	12	0	.0
66933	.6	100	.2	78	17.6	183	23.8	9	17	.3	17	0	.1
66935	3.6		1.5	76	20.6	189	50.1	6	26	.0	0	0	.1
66936	.7	0	.3	75	18.6	115	25.9	9	19	.0	0	0	.0
66937	1.1	0	.5	76	20.5	145	38.4	7	22	.0	0	0	.0
66938	1.3	99	.6	78	17.8	171	34.7	7	24	.7	20	0	.0
66939	.3	99	.3	79	16.2	123	34.2	7	22	.4	19	0	.7
66940	.6	100	.2	84	14.8	120	23.4	8	21	.0	0	0	.0
66941	.6	0	.2	82	22.3	201	37.0	8	20	.0	0	0	.0
66942	.4	100	.3	81	12.3	142*	13.4	3	27	.2	30	0	.8
66943	.8	100	.8	78	16.9	158	40.8	8	30	.4	25	0	.8
66944	.5	97	.2	83	16.7	84	23.5	7	25	.2	23	0	.0
66945	1.4	100	.5	78	23.1	182	38.5	6	23	.7	20	0	.0
66946	.2	100	.1	74	16.3	188*	20.0	5	18	.1	17	0	.0
66948	.8	0	.3	81	17.7	167	26.6	4	30	.0	0	0	.0
66949	.9	99	.4	79	17.5	258	30.9	9	27	.4	22	0	.0
66951	1.0	0	.4	85	19.7	134	42.9	8	22	.0	0	0	.0
66952	.9	0	.4	85	12.7	116	20.2	7	31	.2	17	0	.0
66953	1.0	100	.3	84	19.0	132	47.9	7	24	.2	27	0	.0
66955	.2	0	.1	81	17.5	335	29.9	4	38	.2	18	0	.0
66956	1.7	100	.7	76	20.0	145	42.7	6	24	.2	18	0	.1
66958	.5		.2	82	18.4	141	33.3	9	22	.8	20	0	.0
66959	.3	100	.1	89	15.6	87	27.7	8	17	.2	17	0	.0
66960	.3	100	.2	85	14.6	111	17.0	4	31	.2	27	0	.0
66962	.4	100	.2	84	18.9	121	36.2	7	18	.2	18	0	.0
66963	.4	100	.1	86	19.4	121	25.2	9	20	.2	21	0	.0
66964	.4	100	.2	81	16.1	108	22.9	8	24	.2	27	0	.0
66966	.8	100	.3	84	15.0	116	29.5	4	31	.4	19	0	.0
66967	2.8	99	1.2	81	19.2	159	49.9	6	25	1.3	20	1	.9
66968	2.2	0	.9	77	20.7	152	49.4	7	26	.0	0	0	.2
66970	.2	100	.1	85	17.4	199*	34.4	4	20	.1	14	0	.0
WICHITA													
67001	.8	100	.2	80	30.0	343	80.3	7	11	.4	10	0	.0
67002	2.6	99	.9	76	29.5	318	92.4	9	5	1.3	5	0	4.5
67003	3.3	0	1.4	72	19.9	197	56.0	6	24	.0	0	0	.0
67004	1.0	0	.4	82	26.4	256	49.8	6	18	.0	0	0	.0
67005	17.6	94	6.9	71	24.4	259	59.2	8	16	7.9	13	5	1.8
67008	.6	100	.2	82	30.0	345*	39.9	6	17	.3	15	0	.0
67009	1.1	99	.4	81	24.0	262	43.4	7	21	.5	17	0	.3
67010	11.0	99	4.0	78	29.3	278	78.3	8	13	5.3	11	2	.0
67013	3.0	99	1.1	82	28.4	301	71.9	8	13	1.5	11	0	.0
67016	.3	100	.1	93	24.0	276*	53.9	7	17	.2	14	0	.0
67017	1.4	98	.4	78	31.4	390	74.9	10	7	.7	6	0	.0
67018	.2	0	.1	79	22.0	165	23.3	5	27	.0	0	0	.0
67019	1.0	99	.4	78	23.9	194	45.0	6	20	.5	17	0	.0
67020	2.0	99	.7	76	22.1	263	54.5	9	16	.9	15	0	6.1
67022	2.1	98	.9	75	20.9	211	44.5	6	29	1.0	25	1	.1

*=Estimated **1.0=883 lbs per person; 100++ indicates per capita toxic waste generation > than 100 times the U.S. average of 883 lbs.per capita.

ZIP CODE MEASURES OF SIZE, LEVELS OF AFFLUENCE AND QUALITY OF LIFE

1=Population (th.); 2= % White; 3=Households (th.); 4=% Owner Occupied; 5=Mean Income Per Household (th.$); 6=Mean Monthly Rent ($)*; 7=Mean Home Value (th.$)*; 8=% under 5; 9=% 65 and over; 10=White Males, 65+; 11=% White Males, 65+; 12=# Toxic Waste Sites; 13=Toxic Waste Relative to US(883 lbs.per capita)**.

KANSAS

WICHITA

ZIPCODE	1	2	3	4	5	6	7	8	9	10	11	12	13
67023	.3	0	.1	76	25.2	266	34.2	5	25	.0	0	1	.0
67024	1.3	97	.5	76	18.8	185	29.2	7	26	.6	27	0	.1
67025	2.6	99	.9	80	28.8	323	71.0	9	13	1.3	10	0	.2
67026	3.7	98	1.2	83	31.9	333	89.0	8	8	1.8	7	0	.0
67028	.3	100	.1	71	19.1	107	21.7	7	27	.1	21	0	.0
67029	1.3	0	.5	78	23.3	154	47.8	5	25	.0	0	0	.0
67030	2.0	0	.5	89	31.4	298	88.7	9	9	.0	0	0	.0
67031	2.0	99	.6	81	28.1	287	64.2	11	15	.9	13	0	.0
67035	.9	98	.3	71	22.9	209	44.3	7	20	.5	17	0	.3
67037	12.9	98	4.1	80	35.7	470	105.0	7	4	6.3	3	0	.0
67038	.7	95	.3	69	21.0	239	41.3	6	22	.4	18	0	.0
67039	2.5	97	.9	78	25.7	267	45.8	7	15	1.2	12	0	.0
67041	.2	100	.1	89	27.8	319*	68.2	7	3	.1	4	0	.0
67042	15.1	97	5.9	70	24.8	267	65.5	7	16	6.9	13	5	7.2
67045	4.5	99	1.9	73	20.5	225	46.7	6	26	2.1	23	0	.0
67047	.8	99	.4	84	18.7	137	34.0	6	23	.4	23	0	.0
67050	1.4	100	.4	84	28.7	389	82.4	9	10	.7	9	0	.0
67051	.6	99	.2	75	21.4	273	36.6	11	19	.3	18	0	.0
67052	4.2	97	1.2	82	33.2	359	121.7	10	4	2.1	3	0	.0
67053	.4	100	.1	83	20.4	209	57.3	5	45	2.3	39	0	.0
67054	2.3	100	1.0	74	24.0	211	58.7	8	20	1.1	16	0	.0
67056	2.9	99	1.1	71	26.2	265	72.7	8	18	1.4	14	0	.0
67057	.2	0	.1	71	21.5	161	36.0	5	18	.1	14	0	.0
67058	2.7	99	.9	75	23.1	234	52.2	6	23	.9	19	0	1.0
67059	1.2	99	.4	76	22.4	204	48.6	9	19	.6	18	0	.0
67060	7.0	97	2.1	79	30.7	377	72.2	9	5	3.3	4	0	.0
67061	.3	100	.1	87	21.4	40	27.7	6	26	.1	25	0	.0
67062	3.4	97	1.0	72	27.8	283	89.4	6	11	1.7	8	1	.0
67063	3.7	99	1.3	80	23.7	259	61.9	6	21	1.7	16	0	.0
67065	.4	0	.2	71	21.4	283	31.5	8	17	.0	0	0	.0
67066	.4	100	.2	70	30.5	215	53.8	10	6	.2	4	1	.0
67067	.2	0	.1	83	23.4	391	56.1	19	7	.0	0	0	.6
67068	4.9	98	1.9	75	23.6	220	61.1	7	19	2.3	15	1	.0
67070	1.6	97	.7	78	23.0	197	54.5	7	23	.7	18	0	.7
67071	.2	100	.1	58	24.7	98	30.1	13	12	.1	8	0	.0
67072	.3	0	.1	80	19.5	66	29.3	4	20	.0	0	0	.0
67073	.3	100	.1	93	20.7	238*	38.6	7	12	.2	13	0	.0
67074	1.4	98	.5	73	25.7	189	62.4	7	16	.7	14	0	.0

WICHITA

ZIPCODE	1	2	3	4	5	6	7	8	9	10	11	12	13
67101	1.8	98	.6	87	28.6	305	86.4	9	5	.9	5	1	1.5
67103	.4	0	.1	73	25.4	235	40.2	11	13	.0	0	0	.0
67104	3.0	99	1.2	73	29.3	210	61.8	8	19	1.5	17	1	.1
67105	.3	100	.1	65	22.3	179	37.1	8	9	.1	9	0	.0
67106	.4	0	.1	74	38.8	302	79.0	5	10	.0	0	0	.0
67107	2.7	99	1.0	75	24.6	212	74.7	8	19	1.3	15	0	1.4
67108	1.6	100	.5	80	28.4	311	68.3	7	16	.8	12	0	.0
67109	.6	0	.2	78	24.1	193	40.5	8	12	.0	0	0	.0
67110	6.3	98	2.1	84	30.0	328	85.3	9	7	3.0	5	1	.0
67111	.4	98	.1	67	24.5	308	63.6	6	16	.2	17	0	.0

KANSAS

WICHITA

ZIPCODE	1	2	3	4	5	6	7	8	9	10	11	12	13
67112	.4	100	.1	80	20.5	202	28.0	6	26	.2	25	1	.0
67114	1.3	94	7.2	71	25.1	297	71.8	8	16	8.5	13	1	.3
67117	1.2	95	.3	59	22.9	204	87.5	4	15	.5	11	0	.0
67118	.8	0	.3	77	24.0	253	55.2	9	15	.0	0	0	.2
67119	1.5	99	.6	78	26.9	192	55.7	6	19	.7	17	1	.0
67120	.8	99	.1	94	31.7	108	88.5	5	10	.4	8	0	.0
67121	.3	0	.3	76	15.0	223	56.3	6	17	.0	0	0	.0
67122	.3	0	.1	77	19.7	215	24.8	9	21	.0	0	0	.0
67123	.8	0	.3	80	24.2	276	44.6	6	17	.0	0	3	.3
67124	8.3	97	3.3	73	24.5	274	62.2	7	18	3.8	15	2	.2
67127	1.0	0	.4	74	24.3	255	39.6	7	21	.0	0	0	.5
67128	.3	0	.1	83	21.8	250*	36.6	15	15	.0	0	0	.0
67131	.3	0	.1	69	23.6	162	28.9	4	15	.0	0	0	.0
67132	.3	100	.1	82	24.1	209	57.0	12	8	.2	3	0	7.2
67133	3.0	98	.9	89	35.0	369	112.3	9	15	1.5	4	0	.1
67134	.4	99	.2	78	19.4	224	31.2	9	12	.2	15	0	.0
67135	2.3	98	.8	81	28.5	282	70.1	9	21	1.1	8	0	.0
67137	.3	0	.3	82	21.7	247	29.8	7	16	.0	0	0	.0
67138	.6	0	.2	76	20.7	175	41.0	7	16	.2	3	0	.0
67140	.9	98	.4	83	23.3	226	37.5	5	24	.5	23	0	.0
67142	.3	100	.1	74	24.0	156	34.3	5	20	.2	18	0	.0
67143	.2	100	.1	85	16.4	122	22.4	11	18	.1	11	0	.0
67144	2.2	99	.7	86	31.1	311	83.4	11	6	.1	5	0	.7
67146	1.7	99	.6	81	25.7	280	66.8	9	12	.8	11	0	.0
67147	5.9	99	2.0	81	33.1	320	86.7	7	9	2.9	8	0	.7
67149	.3	99	.1	86	28.6	340	82.6	10	10	.4	9	0	.0
67150	.2	100	.1	60	15.0	191	19.3	16	11	.1	10	0	.0
67151	.5	100	.2	64	25.1	284	43.2	8	17	.2	16	0	.0
67152	9.8	95	3.9	73	25.0	250	61.7	8	18	4.4	15	0	5.8
67154	1.4	99	.4	82	29.4	289	68.6	7	16	.7	12	0	.6
67155	.3	100	.1	78	24.0	276*	32.0	8	14	.2	14	0	.0
67156	14.5	94	5.3	71	25.3	262	61.8	7	16	6.4	13	4	.0
67159	.4	100	.2	65	19.2	270	35.6	7	16	.2	13	0	.7

WICHITA

ZIPCODE	1	2	3	4	5	6	7	8	9	10	11	12	13
67202	1.4	87	.9	2	12.2	226	21.9	8	23	.7	18	2	.0
67203	30.6	93	13.6	56	25.3	371	76.4	7	16	13.4	13	2	39.6
67204	19.3	92	7.2	75	29.5	347	82.9	11	11	8.6	9	3	.1
67205	1.4	0	.5	79	24.1	344	75.8	11	6	.0	0	0	.1
67206	10.1	95	3.9	68	58.7	396	191.1	5	10	4.7	9	0	.0
67207	18.1	91	7.6	44	33.4	464	113.8	7	4	8.1	4	0	.1
67208	20.2	88	8.2	64	32.4	354	100.7	6	13	8.6	11	1	.0
67209	7.3	98	2.5	70	39.1	412	117.6	7	7	3.5	6	1	3.0
67210	6.1	78	2.2	29	19.6	321	54.3	13	5	2.4	5	2	22.4
67211	22.4	94	10.3	55	21.6	299	60.0	8	17	10.0	14	1	.3
67212	25.7	96	8.4	79	36.7	438	99.0	9	5	12.2	5	0	.0
67213	24.6	94	9.9	59	21.6	316	55.4	8	14	11.1	11	0	.9
67214	24.0	31	8.9	43	16.9	274	47.1	9	11	3.8	11	2	.0
67215	1.2	97	.4	88	34.5	149	118.9	6	5	.6	5	0	2.2
67216	21.2	89	7.5	70	26.3	373	64.1	11	5	9.4	5	2	.0

*=Estimated **1.0=883 lbs per person; 100++ indicates per capita toxic waste generation > than 100 times the U.S. average of 883 lbs per capita.

ZIP CODE MEASURES OF SIZE, LEVELS OF AFFLUENCE AND QUALITY OF LIFE

1=Population (th.); 2= % White; 3=Households (th.); 4=% Owner Occupied; 5=Mean Income Per Household (th.$); 6=Mean Monthly Rent ($); 7=Mean Home Value (th.$); 8=% under 5; 9=% 65 and over; 10=% White Males, 65+; 11=% White Males (th.); 12=# Toxic Waste Sites; 13=Toxic Waste Relative to US(883 lbs.per capita)**.

KANSAS

WICHITA

ZIP CODE	1	2	3	4	5	6	7	8	9	10	11	12	13
67217	29.0	95	10.3	76	29.3	405	69.7	9	5	13.8	5	0	.2
67218	24.5	93	10.8	58	28.8	345	86.3	7	16	10.4	12	2	1.1
67219	11.1	45	3.3	67	24.1	337	57.2	11	4	2.5	6	7	.6
67220	7.7	72	2.7	67	36.7	440	107.6	6	6	2.8	4	0	.0
67221	3.3	74	.6	0	24.2	354	86.2*	10	6	1.5	0	1	.0
67222	2.0	89	.6	87	44.4	623	133.1	10	3	.9	3	0	3.6
67228	.3	100	.6	78	45.4	675	146.5	6	7	.2	8	0	.0
67230	3.5	96	1.2	91	60.7	407	177.4	7	6	1.7	6	0	.0
67232	.2	0	.1	100	40.6	467*	110.2	5	1	.1	0	0	.0
67233	2.8	96	.9	88	28.6	267	75.1	10	5	1.4	4	0	.0
67235	1.0	100	.3	96	48.8	308	149.4	5	2	.5	3	0	.0
67236	.4	94	.1	100	43.0	495*	107.0	4	2	.2	3	0	13.5

INDEPENDENCE

ZIP CODE	1	2	3	4	5	6	7	8	9	10	11	12	13
67301	14.7	92	5.8	74	24.0	241	62.0	8	18	6.4	15	1	.4
67330	1.6	99	.6	80	23.8	203	62.2	7	18	.8	15	0	.1
67332	.3	0	.1	74	21.0	133	27.8	6	17	.0	0	0	.0
67333	3.1	96	1.2	79	20.7	218	44.2	7	21	1.4	19	0	.3
67334	.1	94	.1	80	12.0	105	27.4	5	39	.1	34	0	.0
67335	4.0	99	1.5	83	19.1	210	37.9	8	18	1.9	16	0	.4
67336	2.4	93	.9	72	16.9	170	36.6	6	22	1.1	20	0	.5
67337	18.5	87	7.1	73	23.5	241	50.3	8	17	7.6	14	3	5.4
67340	.5	0	.2	84	18.5	318	40.3	9	14	.0	5	0	.0
67341	.3	100	.1	91	21.9	251*	29.0	8	10	.1	5	0	.0
67342	1.1	98	.4	81	20.9	155	45.1	8	17	.5	15	0	.0
67344	1.0	100	.4	85	17.9	210	34.4	7	19	.5	16	0	.0
67345	.2	0	.1	81	14.7	57	24.5	7	14	.0	0	0	.0
67346	.5	100	.2	84	17.3	152	20.6	7	20	.3	19	0	.0
67347	.5	100	.2	80	22.4	264	31.8	8	19	.2	17	0	.0
67349	1.4	98	.6	79	16.9	144	38.1	6	31	.9	27	0	.0
67351	.5	96	.2	86	23.0	274	31.7	8	20	1.5	17	0	1.2
67352	.8	98	.3	81	19.3	128	32.6	7	21	6.8	13	1	.3
67353	.8	0	.3	82	18.8	140	31.5	7	31	.0	0	0	.0
67354	.8	0	.3	81	19.3	150	26.7	8	14	.0	0	0	.0
67355	.2	86	.1	86	15.5	178*	33.3	9	20	.5	24	0	.0
67356	3.2	96	1.3	76	19.9	213	47.5	8	16	1.1	14	0	2.4
67357	15.7	91	5.9	76	22.3	239	54.5	8	16	6.8	25	1	.0
67360	.5	0	.2	87	17.5	182	26.6	5	20	.2	21	0	.0
67361	2.4	96	1.0	80	22.4	188	47.8	5	27	1.1	24	0	.6
67363	.4	98	.1	79	18.3	156	55.0	7	19	.0	0	0	.0
67364	.3	0	.1	87	18.6	233	33.4	7	26	.0	0	0	.0

SALINA

ZIP CODE	1	2	3	4	5	6	7	8	9	10	11	12	13
67401	44.7	95	17.1	69	25.9	290	73.5	8	12	20.3	10	5	.9
67410	9.7	98	3.7	74	22.5	211	61.1	7	19	4.6	15	1	.5
67414	.2	0	.1	83	15.5	250	21.4	7	15	.0	0	0	.0
67416	1.1	99	.4	89	29.2	359	68.5	6	13	.5	9	0	2.4
67417	.4	100	.2	86	18.5	87	22.2	9	16	.1	14	0	.0
67418	.4	100	.2	75	22.4	147	20.1	8	25	.2	21	0	.0
67420	5.8	99	2.2	72	21.7	212	62.6	7	21	2.7	16	0	.6
67422	.8	99	.3	84	23.2	190	52.2	8	16	.4	11	0	.0

KANSAS

SALINA (continued)

ZIP CODE	1	2	3	4	5	6	7	8	9	10	11	12	13
67423	.3	0	.1	79	20.1	126	22.3	6	26	.0	0	0	.0
67425	.6	95	.2	85	24.2	322	44.5	5	20	.3	21	0	.0
67427	.6	0	.2	87	24.5	190	39.2	4	20	.0	0	0	.0
67428	1.8	100	.6	77	23.9	260	52.5	8	16	.9	14	0	.0
67429	.2	0	.1	97	22.9	264*	34.7	8	21	.0	0	0	.8
67430	.9	100	.4	76	19.5	180	44.4	8	17	.5	15	0	.0
67431	2.2	98	.8	73	22.1	254	60.4	8	15	1.1	12	0	.8
67432	6.5	0	2.6	75	21.1	210	58.8	7	23	.0	0	0	1.7
67434	.3	0	.1	82	27.6	349	73.7	11	12	.0	0	0	.0
67435	.4	0	.1	90	23.5	84	44.1	5	17	.0	0	0	.0
67436	1.0	100	.4	79	19.4	217	33.5	7	25	.5	23	0	.2
67437	1.7	99	.7	80	18.5	179	45.3	7	26	.8	21	0	.0
67438	.4	100	.1	82	21.5	170	46.3	10	18	.2	15	0	.2
67439	3.2	99	1.3	75	20.1	214	55.9	7	24	1.5	20	1	3.0
67441	1.2	97	.4	76	20.6	208	45.7	8	19	.6	18	0	.0
67442	.2	100	.2	86	21.4	140	47.1	7	13	.1	11	0	.2
67443	1.5	100	.5	78	26.2	243	65.0	10	9	.7	10	0	.4
67444	.8	98	.3	83	22.7	114	34.3	9	21	.4	21	0	.2
67445	1.0	100	.4	83	17.4	178	37.2	5	24	.5	21	0	.0
67446	.8	100	.3	84	18.3	153	43.3	9	27	.4	27	0	.1
67447	.4	0	.2	75	19.6	158	28.1	8	13	.0	0	0	.2
67448	1.2	99	.4	78	25.1	271	44.9	8	18	.6	18	0	.0
67449	3.7	99	1.5	75	21.0	199	44.7	6	24	1.7	19	0	1.6
67450	.7	0	.2	83	20.4	202	35.5	5	26	.2	15	0	.0
67451	1.2	0	.5	80	23.9	156	44.8	8	21	.6	18	0	.0
67452	.4	100	.2	87	19.9	263	17.8	9	27	.2	23	0	.0
67453	.9	97	.3	73	21.2	243*	21.8	7	15	.1	16	0	.0
67454	.3	97	.1	82	17.7	153	36.9	11	14	.4	11	0	.0
67455	2.4	99	1.0	79	18.5	164	45.0	7	28	1.2	22	0	.1
67456	3.8	98	1.3	74	22.1	252	67.3	5	21	1.8	17	0	.2
67457	.9	99	.3	83	21.0	190	41.1	7	25	.4	17	0	.0
67458	.3	100	.1	74	19.7	188	28.9	6	18	.2	17	0	.0
67459	.9	0	.3	80	19.9	207	35.1	3	20	.0	0	0	.0
67460	13.5	97	5.1	74	26.2	301	81.0	7	14	6.3	11	1	8.5
67463	.3	100	.3	81	22.4	258*	49.8	4	23	.1	19	0	.0
67464	1.1	0	.4	78	21.3	212	39.9	6	25	.4	17	0	.0
67466	1.0	100	.4	83	16.8	145	28.5	5	27	.5	23	0	.0
67467	2.7	99	1.0	77	20.8	193	52.2	7	22	1.3	19	0	1.2
67468	.4	0	.2	87	20.4	198	34.7	9	13	.3	9	0	.0
67470	.6	99	.2	86	28.5	283	58.9	6	11	.3	9	0	.0
67472	.6	100	.2	92	15.9	182*	25.2	4	33	.1	36	0	.0
67473	2.6	100	1.0	79	20.1	213	47.9	7	23	1.2	18	0	.2
67474	.4	0	.2	82	16.2	166	18.8	8	31	.0	0	0	.0
67475	.3	98	.1	89	16.8	108	36.8	8	31	.0	0	0	.2
67478	.1	100	.1	77	15.5	210	25.3	7	29	.1	26	0	.0
67479	.5	0	.2	79	36.2	174	50.3	7	14	.0	0	0	.0
67480	1.7	0	.6	84	23.9	216	50.7	7	15	.0	0	0	.2
67481	.8	0	.3	82	17.3	177	33.7	7	21	.0	0	0	.2
67483	.4	0	.2	84	21.2	180	52.2	4	22	.0	0	0	.3

*=Estimated **1.0=883 lbs per person; 100++ indicates per capita toxic waste generation > than 100 times the U.S. average of 883 lbs per capita.

ZIP CODE MEASURES OF SIZE, LEVELS OF AFFLUENCE AND QUALITY OF LIFE

1=Population (th.); 2= % White; 3=Households (th.); 4=% Owner Occupied; 5=Mean Income Per Household (th.$); 6=Mean Monthly Rent ($)*; 7=Mean Home Value (th.$)*;
8=% under 5; 9=% 65 and over; 10=White Males, 65+; 11=% White Males, (th.); 12=# Toxic Waste Sites; 13=Toxic Waste Relative to US(883 lbs.per capita)**;

KANSAS

SALINA

ZIPCODE	1	2	3	4	5	6	7	8	9	10	11	12	13
67484	.5	99	.2	88	16.6	196	42.8	8	23	.2	16	0	.1
67485	.6	0	.2	76	21.4	239	52.5	6	11	.0	0	0	1.2
67487	1.3	98	.5	75	20.0	257	66.5	10	17	.6	14	0	.0
67490	1.3	0	.5	85	19.3	196	37.1	6	28	.0	0	0	.0
67491	.4	0	.1	81	23.9	178	39.8	8	13	.0	0	0	.0
67492	.3	100	.1	90	21.1	97	41.5	7	20	.2	17	0	.0

HUTCHINSON

ZIPCODE	1	2	3	4	5	6	7	8	9	10	11	12	13
67501	50.2	94	19.1	72	25.7	288	73.4	8	13	22.7	11	8	1.4
67505	2.4	96	.9	63	23.4	213	67.8	7	16	1.1	11	0	.0
67510	.4	0	.1	81	23.8	260	48.5	4	18	.0	0	0	.0
67511	.5	97	.2	80	25.1	270	58.5	12	13	.2	13	0	.0
67512	.3	97	.1	90	23.9	220	36.2	6	21	.2	19	0	7.5
67513	.2	100	.1	86	16.0	184*	31.2	1	29	.2	17	0	.0
67514	1.0	99	.4	76	22.9	231	45.5	9	24	.5	22	0	.0
67515	.2	100	.1	81	27.2	90	37.1	9	19	.1	18	0	.0
67516	.6	0	.3	82	19.3	155	41.4	5	27	.0	0	0	.0
67519	.3	100	.1	73	20.3	211	39.6	4	25	.1	25	0	.0
67520	.5	100	.2	80	18.7	245	32.6	11	23	.2	17	0	.0
67521	.4	100	.1	86	19.4	223*	23.6	8	17	.2	15	0	.0
67522	2.0	99	.7	87	27.3	276	72.6	7	17	1.0	15	0	.0
67523	.5	100	.2	84	26.2	187	48.2	5	19	.3	17	0	.0
67524	1.0	94	.4	72	25.0	197	42.4	10	13	.5	11	0	.7
67525	1.4	0	.5	84	23.9	186	47.5	6	15	.0	0	0	.2
67526	3.3	99	.7	77	22.5	230	62.3	7	17	1.5	14	0	.0
67529	.5	99	.2	81	21.2	248	45.4	9	19	.2	16	0	.0
67530	20.8	97	7.7	71	27.6	293	82.0	9	12	9.8	10	2	.6
67543	1.9	99	1.1	78	25.3	270	50.5	7	22	1.0	10	0	.0
67544	4.4	97	1.7	77	23.0	252	60.6	8	18	2.1	16	0	.7
67545	.4	100	.1	82	26.4	303*	40.0	5	19	.2	20	0	.2
67546	2.3	100	.8	86	26.4	229	72.4	6	18	1.1	16	0	.6
67547	2.6	98	1.1	76	20.4	179	50.5	7	22	1.3	19	1	.1
67548	1.8	100	.7	79	21.3	204	54.4	6	25	.9	19	0	1.2
67549	.3	0	.1	71	21.7	192	45.9	8	16	.0	0	0	.0
67550	6.5	93	2.5	73	23.3	232	64.1	6	17	2.9	15	0	.2
67552	.9	93	.4	76	22.3	231	44.3	9	17	.4	16	0	4.4
67553	.2	100	.1	92	16.3	188*	25.2	6	33	.1	30	0	.0
67554	5.0	97	2.0	76	24.2	213	57.7	7	19	2.3	16	0	2.8
67556	.5	0	.2	87	20.2	140	34.9	5	17	.0	0	0	.0
67557	.9	0	.3	81	19.0	202	37.1	9	23	.0	0	0	.3
67560	2.2	100	.9	79	23.5	197	65.4	8	19	1.1	16	1	.0
67561	1.8	99	.7	80	22.2	280	52.4	9	14	.9	12	0	.0
67563	.5	0	.8	80	22.5	146	45.9	8	16	.0	0	0	.0
67564	.5	100	.2	82	18.5	235	36.3	7	19	.3	18	0	.0
67565	6	0	.2	91	21.1	174	46.5	11	21	.0	0	0	.0
67566	.7	99	.3	74	24.9	263	58.8	8	12	.3	11	0	.0
67567	.7	0	.3	76	21.7	256	43.4	7	13	.0	0	0	.0
67568	.4	98	.2	83	20.6	194	43.6	7	23	.2	22	0	.0
67569	.5	0	.2	81	21.7	281	32.6	8	16	.0	0	0	.6
67570	1.4	98	.5	82	22.8	243	57.5	6	18	.7	15	0	.0

KANSAS

HUTCHINSON

ZIPCODE	1	2	3	4	5	6	7	8	9	10	11	12	13
67572	.7	0	.3	85	24.8	217	52.5	6	24	.0	0	0	.6
67573	.3	0	.1	83	26.8	239	35.9	7	22	.0	0	0	.0
67574	.4	91	.1	77	21.9	194	47.4	7	12	.2	12	0	.0
67575	.4	100	.2	71	21.5	212	50.8	4	17	.2	16	0	.0
67576	2.1	98	.8	80	22.0	213	54.1	6	23	1.0	20	0	.3
67577	.3	100	.1	77	31.2	468	56.6	9	16	.2	15	0	.0
67578	1.9	98	.8	81	19.6	208	47.0	6	27	.9	24	0	.1
67579	3.3	97	1.2	76	25.3	218	55.6	6	18	1.5	15	0	.0
67581	.7	100	.3	87	19.2	194	39.0	6	23	.3	23	0	.0
67582	.3	100	.1	95	22.0	253*	34.5	1	17	.2	17	0	.0
67583	.7	98	.3	77	18.8	259	39.0	8	22	.3	18	0	.0
67584	.5	0	.2	67	22.2	193	44.7	7	14	.0	0	0	.0

HAYS

ZIPCODE	1	2	3	4	5	6	7	8	9	10	11	12	13
67601	20.8	99	7.4	66	25.0	262	88.1	8	8	9.9	7	3	.3
67621	.6	100	.2	80	18.2	129	36.5	9	27	.3	23	0	.0
67622	.9	100	.4	88	19.9	101	29.6	6	23	.4	20	0	.0
67623	.5	100	.2	80	18.2	202	19.2	3	26	.2	23	0	.0
67625	.3	75	.1	85	17.1	149	39.6	5	24	.1	27	0	.0
67626	.2	100	.1	80	16.2	88	32.5	9	23	.1	16	0	.0
67627	.1	100	.1	78	19.5	224	40.7	10	19	.1	12	0	.0
67628	.1	100	.1	94	21.3	245*	16.7	7	11	.1	16	0	.0
67629	.3	0	.1	84	21.1	29	29.8	4	21	.0	0	0	.0
67631	.5	100	.2	85	22.7	240	35.8	11	16	.2	13	0	.0
67632	.4	100	.1	97	21.7	250*	45.6	10	12	.2	12	0	.0
67633	.1	100	.1	86	12.3	141*	21.9	9	29	.1	27	0	.0
67634	.5	100	.2	88	14.2	191	30.6	6	24	.2	19	0	.0
67635	.3	100	.1	83	19.3	159	29.2	7	10	.1	11	0	.0
67636	.2	100	.1	92	21.7	249*	18.1	1	31	.2	33	0	.0
67637	2.8	98	1.0	78	21.8	202	54.0	8	19	1.3	16	1	.7
67638	.4	0	.1	79	16.5	113	34.1	8	22	.1	21	0	.0
67639	.3	100	.1	80	25.5	251	51.5	7	14	.1	21	0	.0
67640	.3	100	.1	81	22.9	221	42.5	8	16	.3	15	0	.0
67642	2.5	97	1.0	73	24.3	213	56.5	8	18	1.2	14	0	.0
67643	.4	100	.2	77	20.0	102	18.6	7	17	.2	14	0	.2
67644	.4	100	.2	80	14.0	65	23.5	5	28	.2	25	0	.0
67645	.6	100	.2	85	20.5	232	29.0	7	21	.3	19	0	.0
67646	1.0	100	.4	88	20.7	158	41.3	5	22	.4	20	0	.0
67647	.4	0	.2	80	18.0	169	32.1	11	10	.0	0	0	.0
67648	.8	100	.3	85	20.2	160	32.1	9	30	.4	29	0	.0
67649	.4	0	.3	75	16.9	195	34.6	7	25	.0	0	0	.7
67650	.5	100	.1	81	20.3	182	37.0	6	18	.3	20	0	.0
67651	.8	98	.3	81	18.9	83	28.5	8	21	.4	20	0	.0
67653	.2	100	.1	82	18.7	213	25.9	7	18	.2	15	0	.0
67654	4.5	99	1.8	74	21.8	170	55.7	6	21	2.2	16	0	.5
67656	.3	0	.1	77	20.8	188	40.9	11	5	.0	0	0	.0
67657	.5	0	.2	77	25.0	210	36.0	12	19	.0	0	0	.0
67658	.2	0	.1	66	16.5	91	21.9	17	24	.0	0	0	.0
67659	.2	100	.1	84	23.1	266*	49.4	3	18	.1	18	0	.6
67661	4.3	99	1.6	74	22.7	188	62.5	6	21	2.1	17	0	1.5

*=Estimated **1.0=883 lbs per person; 100++ indicates per capita toxic waste generation > than 100 times the U.S. average of 883 lbs per capita.

ZIP CODE MEASURES OF SIZE, LEVELS OF AFFLUENCE AND QUALITY OF LIFE

1=Population (th.); 2= % White; 3=Households (th.); 4=% Owner Occupied; 5=Mean Income Per Household (th.$); 6=Mean Monthly Rent ($)*; 7=Mean Home Value (th.$)*;
8=% under 5; 9=% 65 and over; 10=White Males (th.); 11=% White Males, 65+; 12=# Toxic Waste Sites; 13=Toxic Waste Relative to US(883 lbs.per capita)**.

KANSAS

HAYS

ZIPCODE	1	2	3	4	5	6	7	8	9	10	11	12	13
67663	3.0	100	1.1	77	23.4	191	59.7	8	17	1.4	14	0	.0
67664	.4	100	.2	84	18.5	241	30.2	7	26	.2	21	0	.0
67665	6.3	98	2.5	77	26.9	215	66.9	7	18	3.0	16	1	.2
67667	2.3	100	.1	92	19.1	219*	55.4	10	10	.1	11	0	.0
67669	2.3	98	1.0	77	20.7	171	47.4	7	24	1.1	21	1	.0
67671	2.0	100	.6	87	23.5	217	66.0	10	15	1.0	13	0	.0
67672	3.0	100	1.2	78	23.0	185	64.0	8	22	1.4	19	1	.2
67673	.2	100	.1	85	17.0	196*	17.1	1	18	.1	12	0	.0
67675	.2	100	.2	82	17.9	206*	16.9	5	28	.2	28	0	.0
67676	.4	100	.1	86	25.3	204	26.4	6	14	.2	12	0	.0

COLBY

ZIPCODE	1	2	3	4	5	6	7	8	9	10	11	12	13
67701	6.7	100	2.4	70	25.9	223	83.2	8	12	3.2	10	2	.3
67730	2.3	99	.9	75	21.0	167	65.7	8	21	1.1	18	0	.0
67731	.8	0	.4	74	23.6	142	42.9	5	22	.0	0	0	.0
67732	.7	97	.3	79	24.1	196	52.8	10	13	.3	12	0	.0
67733	.2	0	.1	81	27.1	311*	41.6	1	11	.0	0	0	.0
67734	.3	100	.1	79	23.6	163	62.8	13	13	.2	8	0	.0
67735	7.0	95	2.6	75	23.6	240	67.7	8	13	3.3	11	1	.1
67736	.3	0	.1	62	24.6	138	20.8	12	12	.0	0	0	.0
67737	.7	0	.2	92	19.3	270	64.6	10	11	.7	0	0	.0
67738	.9	0	.3	86	21.6	234	50.3	5	12	.0	0	0	.0
67739	.5	0	.2	76	24.5	194	26.0	8	18	.0	0	1	.0
67740	2.1	100	.8	83	22.3	186	68.8	9	19	1.0	16	0	.1
67741	.5	95	.2	79	21.0	314	33.9	4	14	.3	14	0	.0
67743	.3	100	.1	81	19.8	128	48.9	10	15	.9	23	0	.0
67744	.4	100	.1	82	25.7	373	31.8	6	15	.2	13	0	.0
67745	.5	0	.2	71	18.5	209	30.9	9	15	.0	0	0	.0
67746	.3	100	.1	71	18.1	83	32.8	11	2	.2	11	0	.0
67747	.2	100	.1	68	24.2	186	36.9	5	10	.1	7	0	.0
67748	3.1	100	1.2	78	22.2	199	66.7	7	16	1.5	13	0	.1
67749	3.2	100	1.3	75	22.9	217	59.7	7	23	1.6	19	0	.3
67751	.5	0	.1	88	17.9	160	45.4	3	14	.0	0	0	.0
67752	1.6	100	.6	78	21.1	202	67.2	9	20	.8	18	0	1.5
67753	.4	100	.2	80	18.6	185	30.2	7	24	.2	19	0	.0
67755	.2	100	.1	72	20.8	239*	32.1	12	10	.1	11	0	.0
67756	2.6	99	1.0	79	21.1	182	56.7	8	19	1.2	16	0	.0
67757	.7	100	.7	78	21.0	190	37.2	9	17	.4	15	0	.1
67758	1.5	99	.5	77	19.6	186	61.7	7	15	.8	14	0	.0
67759	.2	100	.2	86	20.2	232*	35.5	10	16	.1	13	0	.0

DODGE CITY

ZIPCODE	1	2	3	4	5	6	7	8	9	10	11	12	13
67761	.3	100	.1	91	21.7	250*	40.7	11	9	.1	11	0	.0
67762	.3	0	.1	75	20.9	262	59.6	10	13	.0	0	0	.0
67764	.4	100	.2	84	18.6	151	40.6	9	17	.2	16	0	.0
67830	20.5	92	7.5	69	26.0	268	78.6	9	11	9.1	9	2	.8
67831	1.4	0	.6	75	31.5	362*	112.2*	5	7	.1	9	0	.0
67833	.1	100	.4	77	24.1	180	45.2	6	24	.0	0	0	.1
67834	1.0	98	.4	85	21.3	245*	21.5	6	25	.1	21	0	.0
67835	2.2	100	.8	77	25.8	240	70.3	9	13	.5	22	1	.0

KANSAS

DODGE CITY

ZIPCODE	1	2	3	4	5	6	7	8	9	10	11	12	13
67836	.1	0	.1	68	22.1	294	24.9	9	15	.0	0	0	.0
67837	1.0	96	.3	75	25.7	222	67.7	10	10	.5	10	0	.0
67838	.9	88	.3	69	24.3	240	58.4	11	8	.4	6	0	.0
67839	1.7	0	.7	76	22.5	161	60.2	9	18	.0	0	0	.2
67840	.2	0	.1	69	24.0	18	23.0	5	26	.0	0	0	.0
67841	.4	0	.1	82	19.1	197	59.1	8	14	.0	0	0	.0
67842	.4	100	.2	70	22.0	248	37.3	9	18	.2	19	0	.0
67843	.4	0	.1	10	14.7	45	52.5*	0	65	.2	19	0	.0
67844	.9	100	.4	80	20.9	260	44.2	4	27	.5	21	0	.0
67846	21.9	89	7.6	70	27.8	306	82.0	10	8	9.6	8	2	.2
67849	.5	0	.2	79	22.5	138	39.5	5	14	.0	0	0	.0
67850	.6	94	.2	81	23.4	89	54.9	12	11	.3	10	0	.0
67851	1.5	96	.4	70	25.3	267	76.8	11	4	.7	4	0	.7
67853	.8	0	.3	72	24.6	205	64.9	14	6	.7	0	0	.0
67854	1.4	98	.6	79	24.2	168	49.7	6	22	.7	19	0	.0
67855	1.9	91	.1	69	25.4	213	78.9	10	8	.9	8	0	.0
67856	.1	100	.1	85	21.0	242*	21.9	3	12	.1	11	0	.0
67857	.2	100	.2	91	19.8	227*	20.8	6	10	.1	10	0	.0
67859	.7	100	.2	68	24.3	271	62.7	10	10	.3	6	0	.0
67860	2.4	94	.9	76	26.9	221	68.1	10	10	1.1	9	1	.0
67861	2.5	87	.9	71	22.9	202	73.4	10	11	1.1	11	0	.0
67862	.4	93	.2	81	27.2	146	57.7	8	13	.2	13	0	.7
67863	.5	0	.2	67	23.8	233	45.2	7	13	.1	0	0	.0
67864	2.5	100	.9	77	21.4	214	57.7	8	18	1.2	15	0	.2
67865	1.0	0	.4	74	23.6	193	50.6	6	18	.6	0	0	.1
67867	1.3	98	.4	72	28.4	197	64.2	9	16	.6	15	0	.0
67868	.2	100	.1	80	23.4	284	42.7	11	7	.1	5	0	.0
67869	1.5	96	.5	70	23.5	268	71.7	10	11	.7	9	0	.0
67870	1.9	89	.7	61	26.0	197	57.5	13	8	.8	7	1	1.9
67871	5.5	97	2.0	77	25.8	216	79.3	9	13	2.7	12	3	.9
67874	.2	100	.1	62	19.9	110	29.5	7	20	.1	17	0	1.4
67877	1.9	95	.6	72	24.5	257	79.2	9	8	.9	7	0	.1
67878	2.2	98	.9	78	21.4	196	59.8	7	19	1.1	16	1	.0
67879	1.8	97	.7	78	25.3	165	60.5	8	14	.9	14	1	.0
67880	6.8	92	2.3	71	28.8	261	80.8	9	8	3.1	7	3	.9
67882	.5	0	.1	78	26.7	397	84.3	10	7	.0	0	0	.0

LIBERAL

ZIPCODE	1	2	3	4	5	6	7	8	9	10	11	12	13
67901	16.1	84	5.9	69	29.4	307	72.6	10	9	6.8	8	8	.6
67950	2.5	95	.9	77	25.0	207	61.6	9	9	1.2	9	1	.0
67951	4.1	95	1.5	78	26.8	267	68.7	10	13	1.9	12	2	.0
67952	.6	95	.2	70	28.5	106	81.7	9	7	.3	0	0	.0
67953	.2	0	.1	77	32.2	370*	50.8	8	10	.0	0	1	.3
67954	.6	92	.2	65	21.9	259	55.1	11	10	.3	10	0	.0

HASTINGS

ZIPCODE	1	2	3	4	5	6	7	8	9	10	11	12	13
68943	.1	100		76	14.7	169*	32.1	5	19	.1	15	0	.0

MCCOOK

ZIPCODE	1	2	3	4	5	6	7	8	9	10	11	12	13
69021	.1	100	.1	89	21.2	244*	75.6*	0	34	.0	29	0	.0

*=Estimated **1.0=883 lbs per person; 100++ indicates per capita toxic waste generation > than 100 times the U.S. average of 883 lbs per capita.

ZIP CODE MEASURES OF SIZE, LEVELS OF AFFLUENCE AND QUALITY OF LIFE

1=Population (th.); 2= % White; 3=Households (th.); 4=% Owner Occupied; 5=Mean Income Per Household (th.$); 6=Mean Monthly Rent ($)*; 7=Mean Home Value (th.$)*; 8=% under 5, 9=% 65 and over; 10=White Males (th.); 11=% White Males, 65+; 12=# Toxic Waste Sites; 13=Toxic Waste Relative to US(883 lbs.per capital)**.

KENTUCKY

ZIP CODE	1	2	3	4	5	6	7	8	9	10	11	12	13
HUNTINGTON													
25661	1.2	0	.4	66	28.5	292	95.0	5	10	.0	0	0	.2
25678	.3	100	.1	68	18.4	248	52.7	11	5	.1	4	0	.0
KNOXVILLE													
37762	2.5	100	.7	76	14.0	198	26.6	10	8	1.3	7	0	.0
MCKENZIE													
38226	.2	100	.1	90	22.3	257*	30.9	13	6	.1	6	0	.0
COOKEVILLE													
38551	.2	100	.1	100	9.9	114*	58.3	14	11	.1	14	0	.0
LOUISVILLE (EAST)													
40003	1.3	0	.5	71	19.8	228	62.2	8	17	.0	0	0	.0
40004	15.6	91	4.9	78	24.7	250	69.5	9	9	6.9	8	0	.1
40006	3.3	100	1.1	78	20.3	235	63.8	7	12	1.6	10	1	.0
40007	.3	100	.1	60	15.8	221	61.7	6	15	.1	19	0	.0
40009	2.8	92	1.0	78	19.7	243	62.5	7	12	1.2	9	0	.0
40011	1.3	100	.4	81	16.1	123	41.1	9	12	1.0	8	0	.0
40012	2.2	98	.7	78	24.8	196	64.4	10	8	1.1	9	0	.0
40013	.6	100	.2	77	17.8	235	43.7	7	12	.3	9	0	.0
40014	3.2	98	.9	83	22.2	259	65.4	9	7	1.6	5	0	.0
40017	10.0	99	3.1	86	29.7	356	98.3	9	5	4.9	4	3	.4
40018	.3	100	.1	73	24.5	293	81.0	7	9	.1	8	0	.0
40019	3.3	88	1.2	73	20.4	176	57.6	7	14	1.4	11	0	.1
40020	.4	51	.1	74	19.2	256	59.1	10	14	.3	13	0	.0
40022	1.1	87	.4	70	29.8	430	113.8	6	11	.6	8	0	.0
40023	1.2	94	.4	76	33.9	312	95.6	6	9	.6	9	0	.0
40026	.5	100	.1	81	51.1	588*	258.1	8	3	.2	6	0	.0
40027	.5	100	.1	58	156.4	320	160.6	3	6	.1	6	0	.0
40031	.2	100	2.8	80	28.5	337	97.2	6	6	5.7	5	0	.1
40033	10.9	90	3.6	72	20.6	201	62.6	9	13	4.8	11	0	.3
40036	11.4	89	.1	49	10.4	97	38.0	27	8	.1	12	0	.0
40037	2.8	0	.7	89	22.0	210	54.1	9	11	.6	10	0	.0
40040	.9	100	.3	75	20.4	192	48.3	9	18	.4	22	0	.0
40045	2.7	100	.9	79	21.2	225	61.1	7	13	1.3	11	0	.0
40046	1.1	0	.4	77	20.4	192	58.6	7	10	.0	0	0	.0
40047	7.2	99	2.3	86	27.2	331	75.7	10	6	3.6	4	0	.3
40048	.4	100	.1	0	11.7	176	41.6*	5	72	.1	64	0	.1
40050	1.2	89	.5	74	20.6	237	61.5	7	23	.5	19	2	.0
40051	3.6	100	1.0	86	21.1	224	48.4	11	9	1.9	9	0	8.2
40052	.5	100	.2	81	12.5	75	34.4	3	12	.2	10	0	.0
40055	.8	0	.3	82	23.2	308	68.7	6	8	.0	0	0	.0
40056	1.6	89	.5	83	36.5	290	128.5	7	13	.7	10	0	.0
40057	2.9	98	1.1	78	18.6	195	56.3	7	14	1.4	13	0	.0
40058	.1	100	.1	73	11.4	342	33.7	11	26	.0	11	0	.0
40059	7.6	92	2.4	86	54.9	498	173.6	6	7	3.5	6	0	.0
40060	1.0	100	.3	79	13.7	308	45.3	12	5	.5	5	1	.0
40062	.3	100	.1	92	18.1	208*	38.7	16	9	.5	7	0	.2
40065	16.1	87	5.6	69	24.9	258	75.0	13	7	6.7	12	0	.7
40067	1.0	65	.3	83	27.4	372	75.5	3	7	.3	5	0	.0
40068	.9	0	.3	77	24.3	328	62.0	5	11	.0	0	0	.0

KENTUCKY

ZIP CODE	1	2	3	4	5	6	7	8	9	10	11	12	13
LOUISVILLE (EAST)													
40069	7.6	86	2.5	75	22.0	184	61.7	7	13	3.3	12	0	.0
40070	1.0	0	.3	69	22.0	203	61.1	6	10	.0	0	0	.0
40071	5.3	97	1.8	72	22.2	236	70.8	7	11	2.7	10	0	.0
40075	1.0	0	.3	83	18.7	215*	36.5	4	15	.0	0	0	.0
40076	1.8	97	.6	87	25.2	284	74.3	8	10	.9	12	0	.0
40077	.6	100	.6	87	21.9	178	58.1	9	10	.3	8	0	.0
40078	1.7	97	.6	84	15.4	268	42.6	8	10	.8	9	0	.0
LOUISVILLE (WEST)													
40104	1.2	100	.4	76	16.7	180	33.7	9	8	.6	4	0	.0
40106	.3	100	.1	77	20.9	180	34.4	10	2	.2	0	0	.0
40107	1.6	100	.5	83	21.9	222	42.0	6	10	.8	8	0	.0
40108	5.5	97	1.8	75	23.4	252	73.7	7	7	2.6	8	3	29.2
40109	2.3	100	.7	88	27.1	279	65.7	7	4	1.2	4	1	.0
40110	.3	0	.1	91	18.1	208*	22.5	11	7	.0	0	0	2.8
40111	2.0	99	.7	72	17.1	194	42.4	9	13	.9	12	0	.0
40114	.3	100	.1	88	18.5	108	34.8	6	18	.1	17	0	.0
40115	.7	100	.2	84	18.3	210*	75.2	10	14	.3	17	0	.0
40117	.6	93	.2	82	23.5	267	53.1	8	9	.9	6	0	.0
40118	8.7	99	2.8	83	23.2	304	47.3	9	7	4.3	6	0	.0
40119	1.1	71	.4	82	18.1	128	46.5	8	17	.0	0	0	.4
40121	31.2	71	4.4	1	18.7	354	126.9	9	0	16.3	0	0	.0
40140	.3	100	.1	84	14.8	64	47.3	1	21	.3	22	0	.1
40141	.3	100	.1	91	13.8	158*	27.7	13	2	.1	0	0	.0
40142	1.7	93	.5	82	22.9	205	53.0	9	8	.3	1	0	.0
40143	4.9	95	1.7	79	21.2	231	66.7	8	15	2.3	13	0	.3
40144	1.5	95	.5	84	22.9	265	51.6	6	9	.7	8	0	.0
40145	.7	100	.3	90	17.6	219	34.6	7	11	.4	8	0	.0
40146	2.9	91	1.0	83	19.4	186	53.1	8	12	1.2	12	0	.0
40150	4.3	99	1.4	84	22.5	255	48.7	6	9	2.1	8	0	.0
40152	.5	100	.2	81	16.9	206	56.6	6	7	.3	10	0	.3
40155	1.8	83	.7	24	15.9	246	50.4	15	4	.8	4	0	.0
40157	1.0	0	.3	92	18.7	368	38.8	14	14	.0	0	0	.0
40160	15.7	81	5.5	58	22.5	296	84.8	11	3	6.4	3	1	.0
40161	.3	100	.1	91	11.1	127*	38.6	4	17	.1	12	0	.0
40162	2.8	100	.8	82	24.2	325	86.3	11	5	1.4	3	0	.0
40165	16.5	99	5.0	85	26.4	266	77.2	7	7	8.1	6	1	.0
40170	.2	100	.1	79	10.0	149	24.3	3	34	.2	37	0	.0
40171	.3	100	.1	71	12.8	148*	48.0	10	13	.2	17	0	.0
40174	.3	100	.1	94	14.1	162*	38.5	6	21	.1	18	0	.0
40175	7.4	96	2.4	78	22.1	258	64.9	8	7	3.5	6	0	.0
40176	1.0	100	.3	95	18.1	329	37.4	10	11	.5	9	0	.0
40177	2.1	98	.7	61	21.1	163	41.1	12	7	1.0	5	1	.0
40178	.3	100	.1	89	14.6	269	33.2	9	39	.1	46	0	.0
LOUISVILLE													
40202	5.8	43	2.6	3	8.2	151	22.5	10	25	1.2	19	1	7.1
40203	23.4	47	10.4	22	11.5	181	24.4	8	22	5.0	16	1	2.0
40204	17.4	95	7.9	46	20.2	286	57.7	6	17	7.5	11	0	.1
40205	25.8	99	10.4	73	33.8	328	102.3	5	22	11.2	16	0	.1
40206	21.3	95	9.2	50	25.6	312	81.7	5	17	9.3	13	0	.4

*=Estimated **1.0=883 lbs per person; 100++ indicates per capita toxic waste generation > than 100 times the U.S. average of 883 lbs per capita.

ZIP CODE MEASURES OF SIZE, LEVELS OF AFFLUENCE AND QUALITY OF LIFE

1=Population (th.); 2= % White; 3=Households (th.); 4=% Owner Occupied; 5=Mean Income Per Household (th.$); 6=Mean Monthly Rent ($)*; 7=Mean Home Value (th.$)*;
8=% under 5; 9=% 65 and over; 10=White Males (th.); 11=% White Males, 65+; 12=# Toxic Waste Sites; 13=Toxic Waste Relative to US(883 lbs.per capita)**.

KENTUCKY

LOUISVILLE

ZIPCODE	1	2	3	4	5	6	7	8	9	10	11	12	13
40207	29.5	98	12.1	77	43.5	384	124.8	5	19	12.9	15	0	.1
40208	14.1	85	6.0	43	17.0	239	37.5	6	14	5.8	12	1	.6
40209	4.2	93	1.6	62	17.2	252	34.4	8	16	2.0	12	2	.1
40210	21.7	15	7.3	59	17.0	202	33.7	9	12	1.5	17	4	.9
40211	32.6	5	10.9	59	17.4	229	35.8	9	12	.8	24	8	6.0
40212	24.9	52	7.9	68	18.4	246	30.5	9	10	6.2	11	3	1.0
40213	24.6	90	8.9	74	25.3	306	56.1	7	11	10.7	9	3	6.6
40214	43.8	96	17.2	60	24.3	306	66.8	7	11	19.8	9	1	.1
40215	26.0	93	10.3	60	17.9	229	41.7	8	15	11.1	12	0	.0
40216	47.2	92	17.2	75	25.8	302	61.5	7	9	21.3	8	20	1.3
40217	14.4	95	6.1	72	20.4	274	47.4	5	25	6.2	19	1	.6
40218	31.6	71	12.0	52	24.5	317	69.8	7	9	10.4	8	1	.6
40219	42.7	94	14.5	69	26.4	301	66.0	8	6	19.6	5	5	1.3
40220	27.4	96	10.1	71	31.9	389	90.7	6	12	12.3	9	0	.0
40222	40.0	94	13.9	75	43.1	398	133.1	7	9	18.4	6	2	.0
40223	15.5	92	5.5	73	44.2	422	135.0	6	7	7.2	6	0	.0
40228	8.3	95	2.5	87	34.2	421	87.6	4	8	3.8	4	0	.0
40229	28.4	98	8.2	83	25.5	326	60.6	10	3	13.8	2	0	.0
40243	9.7	97	3.3	79	38.0	370	117.1	9	7	4.6	6	0	.0
40258	24.7	98	7.9	86	27.4	329	61.4	8	6	11.8	5	0	.0
40272	35.6	97	11.2	84	27.7	342	62.6	8	5	17.2	4	1	.0
40291	23.3	95	7.5	82	32.3	365	87.7	9	4	11.3	4	0	.0
40299	20.1	95	6.8	78	31.0	364	88.4	8	6	9.5	5	1	.6

LEXINGTON (NORTH)

ZIPCODE	1	2	3	4	5	6	7	8	9	10	11	12	13
40308	.7	0	.2	75	22.8	236	55.2	11	8	.0	0	0	.2
40310	1.1	95	.4	85	20.9	235	52.5	6	15	.5	11	1	.0
40311	7.1	98	2.5	69	19.2	219	48.5	7	14	3.4	12	0	.0
40312	4.7	0	1.4	80	17.5	267	49.0	10	9	.0	0	0	.0
40313	1.6	100	.6	69	18.0	222	56.8	7	13	.8	8	0	.1
40316	.3	100	.1	80	12.0	251	31.9	8	10	.2	4	0	.0
40317	.2	100	.1	64	16.7	95	33.1	10	7	.1	14	0	.0
40319	.4	100	.1	58	22.7	328	75.3	12	11	.2	13	0	.0
40322	1.9	97	.7	82	14.8	186	42.0	9	13	.9	12	0	.0
40324	18.2	93	6.0	66	24.2	264	83.7	9	10	8.2	8	0	.9
40329	1.3	0	.5	70	15.3	148	38.5	9	13	.0	0	0	.2
40330	.1	100	.1	54	11.7	203	17.5	5	25	.1	12	0	.0
40333	16.2	95	5.9	74	21.3	232	64.4	7	14	7.4	12	0	.0
40336	.2	100	.1	84	18.5	213*	39.1	8	12	.1	16	0	.0
40337	12.2	100	4.0	74	18.0	238	46.4	8	13	.4	13	0	.1
40339	3.5	0	1.1	79	16.9	219	45.0	8	7	.0	0	0	.0
40342	12.2	96	4.2	80	23.8	338	68.9	8	12	4.7	12	0	.0
40345	.7	93	.2	87	13.8	270	59.0	5	15	.3	10	0	.1
40346	.7	100	.1	89	13.8	245	43.3	10	5	.3	10	0	.0
40347	2.9	88	1.0	55	25.9	283	84.4	8	11	1.2	11	0	.0
40348	1.0	96	.3	60	18.3	244	45.2	6	15	.5	13	0	1.2
40350	.2	100	.1	74	17.4	200*	70.3	13	15	.1	19	0	.0
40351	17.1	98	5.1	66	18.9	225	64.7	9	9	8.0	8	4	.0
40353	16.6	94	5.8	68	22.0	242	67.2	9	11	7.5	9	4	.2
40355	.4	84	.1	75	12.5	143*	31.7	15	23	.1	20	0	.0
40356	20.0	95	6.6	70	24.5	290	87.6	9	8	9.3	7	1	.1
40357	.3	95	.1	75	19.4	335	52.7	7	16	.1	15	0	.0
40358	.7	100	.2	78	13.4	103	38.1	9	11	.4	13	0	.0
40359	6.0	99	2.2	76	18.1	187	53.8	8	17	2.9	15	0	.2
40360	5.2	97	1.9	73	18.2	173	55.9	7	17	2.4	16	0	.0
40365	.2	100	.1	66	10.8	257	71.6	14	13	.1	10	0	.2
40370	1.3	0	.4	72	20.0	185	48.8	8	7	.0	0	0	.0
40371	2.1	100	.7	70	15.3	210	33.7	8	12	1.0	9	0	.0
40372	1.3	100	.4	67	22.8	313	69.4	7	5	.7	5	0	.0
40374	1.9	93	.6	69	16.8	188	43.9	9	10	.9	7	0	.0
40376	.2	100	.1	69	19.7	53	30.3	9	12	.1	15	0	.0
40379	2.5	99	.8	78	22.0	282	62.3	6	14	1.2	13	0	.1
40380	5.9	100	1.8	74	18.4	214	55.8	9	11	2.9	9	1	.0
40381	.2	100	.2	100	17.0	196*	63.2	3	9	.1	15	0	.0
40383	14.6	92	4.8	71	28.2	307	95.6	7	9	6.6	8	4	.6
40385	1.4	0	.5	84	20.9	314	58.3	4	15	.0	0	0	.0
40388	.2	59	.1	80	16.3	125	39.9	6	13	.5	13	0	.0
40390	5.1	98	1.4	80	16.7	179	47.1	7	15	2.0	15	0	.0
40391	27.5	93	9.6	56	20.2	272	84.4	8	10	12.5	8	1	.9

LEXINGTON (SOUTH)

ZIPCODE	1	2	3	4	5	6	7	8	9	10	11	12	13
40402	2.1	100	.8	79	13.2	155	45.1	9	17	1.0	20	0	.2
40403	14.0	97	4.8	66	19.5	261	64.6	9	10	6.6	9	0	.7
40404	1.2	94	.2	70	14.3	297	73.0	5	14	.5	3	0	.0
40407	.2	100	.1	73	15.6	230	23.0	5	14	.1	18	0	.0
40409	2.8	100	1.0	79	22.8	235	43.0	6	15	1.4	12	0	.1
40412	.3	100	.1	85	11.3	262*	55.0	7	6	.2	6	0	.0
40417	.1	100	.1	80	16.1	185	31.2	7	6	.1	14	0	.0
40419	4.0	97	1.3	77	16.1	180	42.5	7	14	2.0	14	0	.1
40422	19.8	89	6.9	68	25.1	252	76.7	6	12	8.4	9	0	.0
40426	.2	100	.2	64	10.9	163	19.3	6	13	.2	12	0	.2
40434	.4	100	.1	85	16.7	138	45.0	11	4	.2	3	0	.9
40437	3.4	0	.1	74	15.0	188	39.6	9	13	.1	12	0	.0
40440	2.9	0	1.0	76	17.3	247	39.3	7	10	.1	14	0	.0
40442	1.2	100	.4	82	14.0	120	29.0	8	12	.6	16	0	.2
40445	8.9	93	3.3	73	18.6	188	64.3	8	15	4.0	13	0	.0
40447	6.1	100	1.9	77	10.4	193	38.1	9	13	.1	3	0	.0
40452	.2	100	.1	90	18.3	129	35.1	8	9	.1	11	0	.0
40455	.2	100	.1	80	16.5	289	16.5	3	14	.1	16	0	.0
40456	7.6	100	2.6	75	15.0	117	45.7	10	8	3.7	12	0	.1
40460	1.0	97	.3	87	9.6	191	32.9	8	13	.5	13	0	.0
40461	2.4	99	.8	68	15.4	155	56.0	8	18	1.2	17	0	.0
40464	.2	100	.1	84	17.4	224	35.3	10	9	.1	9	0	1.2
40468	1.9	89	.7	75	18.3	46	61.0	7	15	.8	15	0	.0
40472	1.8	100	.6	73	20.1	224	37.6	5	17	.9	14	0	.0
40475	36.0	91	11.1	57	21.0	271	80.0	6	15	15.5	7	3	.6

*=Estimated **1.0=883 lbs per person; 100+ indicates per capita toxic waste generation > than 100 times the U.S. average of 883 lbs per capita.

103001

ZIP CODE MEASURES OF SIZE, LEVELS OF AFFLUENCE AND QUALITY OF LIFE

1=Population (th.); 2= % White; 3=Households (th.); 4=% Owner Occupied; 5=Mean Income Per Household (th.$); 6=Mean Monthly Rent ($)*; 7=Mean Home Value (th.$)*; 8=% under 5; 9=% 65 and over; 10=White Males (th.); 11=% White Males, 65+; 12=# White Males; 13=Toxic Waste Sites; 13=Toxic Waste Relative to US(883 lbs.per capita)**.

KENTUCKY

ZIPCODE	1	2	3	4	5	6	7	8	9	10	11	12	13
LEXINGTON (SOUTH)													
40481	.7	100	.2	71	14.3	129	33.8	9	14	.3	16	1	.0
40484	8.8	93	3.1	76	18.6	203	57.8	7	14	4.0	13	0	.0
40486	2.1	100	.7	77	14.0	202	43.5	8	14	1.1	14	0	.0
40488	.2	100	.1	63	6.8	124	16.8	3	17	.1	32	0	.0
40489	3.7	100	1.2	79	16.4	182	48.6	8	11	1.9	9	0	.0
40495	.1	100	.1	100	24.5	281*	52.3	0	5	.1	0	0	.0
LEXINGTON													
40502	51.2	95	20.5	54	32.2	381	136.0	7	9	22.9	7	0	.1
40503	37.1	98	13.1	69	31.1	370	105.2	7	8	17.4	6	2	.0
40504	24.4	94	10.0	46	24.9	332	95.6	9	9	10.8	7	0	.2
40505	36.2	89	13.3	64	24.7	316	78.1	7	9	15.4	7	0	2.8
40507	1.9	74	.9	27	16.1	226	57.2*	0	21	.9	21	1	3.7
40508	31.1	57	10.9	27	13.1	247	46.5	6	11	9.2	7	0	.2
40509	3.2	87	1.2	36	23.1	394	73.1	7	7	1.4	3	0	.3
40511	18.9	68	6.1	54	28.8	342	102.7	9	6	6.7	6	4	.0
FRANKFORT													
40601	42.5	91	15.9	64	26.1	290	80.9	7	10	18.6	9	1	.4
CORBIN (WEST)													
40701	21.2	100	7.7	72	21.5	238	63.6	8	14	10.1	11	0	.1
40729	5.1	96	1.6	84	18.1	275	55.1	7	10	2.5	9	0	.0
40730	.2	100	.1	68	11.3	166	36.3	3	16	.1	25	0	.0
40734	3.2	100	1.1	78	16.3	226	46.5	11	13	1.5	13	0	.0
40737	.8	100	.2	79	21.2	321	55.1	9	11	.4	9	0	.0
40741	26.4	99	8.8	83	18.8	247	46.9	10	6	12.9	7	0	.2
40754	.2	100	.1	78	19.9	247	68.8	8	11	.1	10	2	.2
40755	.3	100	.1	73	8.4	97*	22.4	8	8	.1	0	0	.0
40759	2.1	100	.7	77	16.9	296	53.9	14	3	.1	4	0	.0
40763	.6	100	.1	78	15.0	190	30.5	11	12	1.0	11	0	.0
40769	14.7	99	4.9	65	12.2	199	22.6	8	11	.3	11	1	.2
40771	1.8	99	.6	69	14.8	232	32.8	7	18	.9	17	1	.0
CORBIN (EAST)													
40801	.8	99	.3	81	21.3	214	35.4	6	17	.4	18	1	.0
40803	.4	100	.1	76	14.2	163*	30.7	9	6	.2	4	0	.0
40806	2.5	97	.8	73	22.0	247	64.1	12	7	1.2	5	0	.1
40807	1.1	89	.4	90	23.1	305	45.9	16	16	.5	14	0	.0
40808	.3	100	.1	76	14.3	158	33.2	11	14	.2	12	0	.0
40810	1.5	100	.4	69	17.2	205	36.5	8	8	.8	6	0	.0
40812	.4	100	.1	81	15.8	210	47.8	9	11	.2	13	0	.0
40813	.7	100	.2	80	15.9	245	36.1	10	8	.3	5	0	.0
40815	1.7	100	.5	63	17.6	217	32.7	10	8	.8	8	0	.0
40817	.4	100	.1	44	18.3	195	59.1	13	10	.2	17	0	.0
40819	1.0	100	.3	57	30.5	243	29.9	13	0	.4	9	0	.0
40820	.6	100	.2	82	13.7	218	34.4	7	13	.3	2	0	.0
40822	.4	100	.1	74	19.6	116	26.6	12	12	.3	9	0	.0
40823	6.0	95	2.1	65	19.7	218	47.0	9	12	2.7	9	0	.0
40824	.6	100	.2	80	30.5	274	34.8	8	9	.3	8	0	.0
40825	.3	100	.1	75	19.9	156	39.9	10	10	.1	13	0	.0
CORBIN (EAST) *(continued)*													
40826	.6	0	.2	64	21.6	204	46.7	9	10	.0	0	0	.0
40827	1.0	100	.2	69	23.9	140	37.4	13	10	.5	0	0	.0
40828	3.9	95	1.2	69	18.7	202	30.8	9	10	1.8	8	0	.0
40829	.6	100	.2	62	23.4	195	35.1	6	4	.3	4	1	.0
40830	.7	0	.2	69	22.4	204	29.1	5	8	.0	0	0	.0
40831	7.2	92	2.7	53	21.9	219	63.0	8	15	3.1	11	1	.1
40840	1.2	100	.4	62	17.6	185	33.8	11	5	.6	6	1	.0
40843	.4	100	.2	65	13.2	194	18.7	8	7	.2	11	1	.0
40844	.5	100	.2	83	13.3	141	34.2	11	8	.3	2	0	.0
40845	.8	100	.3	77	12.6	130	32.2	8	12	.4	13	0	.0
40846	.3	100	.1	83	20.5	349	41.8	12	4	.1	3	0	.0
40847	1.3	92	.4	80	16.3	224	32.2	10	10	.5	5	0	.0
40849	.5	100	.1	69	12.6	271	18.7	10	5	.3	5	0	.0
40853	.1	100		79	15.6	179*	35.4	10	18	.1	13	0	.0
40854	1.9	0	.7	76	23.0	301	51.0	8	11	.0	0	0	.0
40855	1.6	66	.6	80	25.9	277	40.8	8	13	.5	9	1	.0
40856	.3	100	.1	90	30.1	210	27.0	9	18	.2	20	0	.0
40858	.3	100		100	11.7	135*	24.0	9	25	.2	21	0	.0
40863	.8	100	.3	89	22.5	259	44.3	7	7	.4	13	0	.0
40865	.5	100	.2	84	17.5	256	35.3	11	13	.4	13	0	.0
40867	.3	100	.1	77	24.9	132	41.4	4	10	.3	8	0	.0
40868	.8	100	.2	84	23.1	152	53.6	2	8	.1	0	0	.0
40870	.7	0	.2	78	28.4	215	32.4	8	4	.4	2	0	.2
40873	2.6	100	.9	67	24.1	202	49.0	13	4	1.3	14	0	.2
40874	.2	100	.1	63	18.4	165	13.1	13	9	.1	7	0	.0
CORBIN (CENTRAL)													
40902	1.5	100	.5	62	12.1	194	28.1	6	10	.8	10	0	.0
40903	1.1	100	.4	69	15.4	155	43.4	11	11	.5	8	0	.0
40905	.5	100		77	19.7	340	43.2	5	6	.3	6	0	.2
40906	9.1	95	3.1	66	17.3	227	55.1	7	15	4.1	12	1	.0
40913	.6	100	.2	45	18.0	171	34.7	15	6	.3	6	0	.0
40914	.8	100	.3	70	18.0	204	44.9	7	5	.4	4	0	.0
40915	1.1	100	.3	59	13.6	220	56.0	12	5	.5	2	0	.0
40921	.3	100	.1	78	13.3	153*	34.1	9	20	.2	17	0	.1
40923	.5	100	.2	90	13.9	159*	63.5	14	17	.3	14	0	.0
40925	.9	0	.2	78	16.8	108	34.7	9	8	.0	8	0	.0
40927	.9	94	.3	73	14.5	154	33.7	10	11	.4	12	0	.0
40928	.2	94	.1	59	14.6	318	51.9*	9	11	.2	13	0	.0
40930	.4	100	.2	53	9.6	236	34.7	9	5	.1	5	0	.0
40935	2.5	100	.7	62	14.1	203	46.6	7	9	1.2	9	0	.0
40939	.6	100	.2	77	20.7	115	33.4	4	4	.3	4	0	.0
40940	.6	100	.2	90	14.7	144	22.0	7	18	.3	15	0	.0
40941	.8	100	.3	74	10.8	164	25.7	17	5	.4	4	0	.0
40943	1.0	96	.3	79	14.9	125	48.8	10	8	.5	8	0	.0
40944	.7	0	.1	46	9.3	116	20.0	7	3	.0	0	0	.0
40949	.9	100	.3	67	13.1	257	40.4	6	10	.5	10	0	.0
40951	.2	100	.1	75	22.9	341	21.9	7	10	.1	11	0	.0
40953	.7	100	.2	70	15.6	257	44.8	8	1	.4	0	0	.0

*=Estimated **1.0=883 lbs per person; 100++ indicates per capita toxic waste generation > than 100 times the U.S. average of 883 lbs per capita.

ZIP CODE MEASURES OF SIZE, LEVELS OF AFFLUENCE AND QUALITY OF LIFE

1=Population (th.); 2= % White; 3=Households (th.); 4=% Owner Occupied; 5=Mean Income Per Household; 6=Mean Monthly Rent ($)*; 7=Mean Home Value (th.$)*; 8=% under 5; 9=% 65 and over; 10=White Males; 11=% White Males, 65+; 12=# Toxic Waste Sites; 13=Toxic Waste Relative to US(883 lbs.per capita)**.

KENTUCKY

CORBIN (CENTRAL)

ZIP CODE	1	2	3	4	5	6	7	8	9	10	11	12	13
40955	.3	100	.1	71	14.6	219	30.1	10	6	.2	7	0	.0
40958	.8	100	.3	78	16.6	264	49.0	10	9	.4	5	0	.0
40962	17.0	98	5.1	70	16.7	195	46.3	9	9	8.3	9	3	.0
40963	.5	0	.2	86	16.3	187*	43.7	6	13	.0	0	0	.0
40964	.2	0	.1	54	24.9	294	49.3	17	10	.0	10	0	.0
40965	15.6	95	5.6	63	19.2	254	54.3	13	8	7.1	10	0	.2
40970	.4	100	.1	71	8.7	79	26.1	8	17	.3	11	0	.0
40972	1.7	100	.5	70	10.9	207	32.2	11	13	.9	13	0	.0
40977	9.3	99	3.0	64	18.2	227	55.5	8	12	4.3	10	0	.1
40978	.2	100	.1	86	10.0	115*	20.2	14	12	.1	10	0	.0
40979	.4	100	.1	61	15.5	133	37.7	17	6	.2	11	0	.0
40980	.3	100	.1	80	7.9	91*	13.1	10	2	.2	11	0	.0
40981	.2	100	.1	46	5.6	179	25.0	9	0	.2	0	0	.0
40982	.5	100	.1	83	11.1	174	17.7	5	0	.0	0	0	.0
40983	.4	0	.1	58	10.6	242	44.2	13	10	.2	0	0	.0
40988	.7	100	.2	69	11.1	231	29.0	8	9	.3	10	0	.0
40989	.4	100	.1	77	16.6	44	33.2	9	7	.3	3	0	.0
40993	.4	100	.1	68	17.9	229	33.3	11	8	.3	3	0	.0
40995	.3	100	.1	65	8.4	81	18.6	4	17	.2	0	0	.0
40997	.5	100	.2	66	8.7	227	19.3	8	18	.2	2	0	.0
40999	.6	100	.2	69	11.0	124	33.3	12	1	.3	20	0	.0

CINCINNATI

ZIP CODE	1	2	3	4	5	6	7	8	9	10	11	12	13
41001	10.5	100	3.2	85	29.9	315	88.4	8	6	5.2	5	0	.0
41002	2.5	99	.9	69	20.5	245	53.7	8	14	1.3	12	0	.4
41003	2.0	99	.6	80	21.6	224	45.4	8	11	1.0	11	0	.0
41004	3.4	100	1.2	75	17.9	242	53.3	7	15	1.6	14	0	.0
41005	7.5	99	2.3	82	30.2	361	95.7	10	6	3.7	6	0	.5
41006	3.4	99	1.1	76	24.3	277	62.7	9	8	1.7	7	0	.0
41007	3.0	100	.9	83	25.2	267	75.7	7	10	1.5	11	0	.1
41008	6.3	96	2.4	61	21.3	239	66.2	8	13	2.9	12	2	15.7
41010	2.5	99	.9	79	19.0	170	37.7	8	11	1.3	12	0	.0
41011	33.8	91	13.1	47	22.3	250	80.0	8	15	14.4	11	1	.1
41014	10.7	97	3.9	59	21.7	291	44.5	8	16	4.9	11	0	.5
41015	19.6	99	6.9	71	23.2	271	57.8	8	14	9.0	10	2	.0
41016	9.7	99	3.6	71	24.8	330	57.2	8	12	4.5	9	1	.5
41017	24.1	99	8.0	73	35.3	392	112.2	8	10	11.6	8	1	.5
41018	23.9	97	7.9	75	27.9	343	73.2	9	9	11.4	6	0	.5
41030	2.4	0	.8	79	23.2	275	73.2	9	9	.0	0	3	.0
41031	13.6	97	4.9	64	20.4	226	74.6	7	16	6.4	13	3	1.0
41033	1.8	100	.6	87	21.4	170	59.6	10	11	.9	11	0	.0
41034	.8	0	.3	64	17.3	151	53.3	11	10	.0	0	0	.0
41035	5.5	99	1.8	81	22.7	300	64.9	8	10	2.7	10	2	.0
41039	2.6	98	.9	70	18.3	237	47.7	8	15	1.3	15	0	.1
41040	5.7	97	2.1	71	18.5	242	52.5	9	7	2.9	13	0	.3
41041	6.2	97	2.3	74	19.0	212	60.5	6	16	2.9	13	1	.1
41042	23.4	99	7.8	67	29.4	326	90.9	9	6	11.2	5	1	.0
41043	1.5	100	.6	81	20.0	166	41.5	4	19	.7	16	0	2.6
41044	1.1	0	.4	73	16.0	129	40.5	4	16	.0	0	0	.0
41045	1.3	92	.3	63	19.9	199	58.8	9	10	.6	10	0	.0
41046	1.3	100	.4	81	20.0	344	35.3	8	11	.6	11	1	.0
41048	3.3	100	1.1	81	29.6	288	86.8	6	9	1.6	8	0	.1
41049	1.7	100	.6	79	14.4	228	42.5	6	13	.9	14	0	.0
41051	11.0	100	3.3	84	30.7	382	85.3	9	6	5.5	5	0	.0
41055	1.6	94	.5	64	17.8	191	53.0	7	13	.8	11	0	.0
41056	14.6	91	5.3	62	21.0	244	64.5	8	14	6.4	11	1	.8
41059	2.3	100	.8	84	28.9	190	70.2	9	10	1.1	8	0	.0
41063	2.5	0	.8	90	25.2	332	74.6	7	8	.9	7	0	.0
41064	2.0	100	.7	70	17.3	228	45.7	7	17	1.0	16	0	.1
41065	.2	100	.1	89	15.9	182*	21.9	8	11	.6	6	0	.0
41071	25.6	96	9.2	51	19.9	251	46.3	9	13	11.4	10	0	.2
41073	7.6	0	2.8	70	22.4	295	51.3	8	15	.0	8	0	.1
41075	16.1	100	5.9	73	32.4	369	93.9	9	10	3.3	8	0	.2
41076	9.8	99	3.2	81	30.2	317	84.4	7	9	4.8	8	0	.1
41080	1.4	0	.4	80	25.5	423	85.8	9	10	.0	0	0	.0
41083	1.0	100	.4	75	18.8	298	39.4	6	14	.5	14	0	.0
41085	1.2	0	.4	81	25.9	346	54.2	9	9	.0	5	0	.0
41086	1.0	97	.4	81	25.9	105	48.2	9	12	.5	8	1	.0
41091	3.3	100	1.0	86	32.1	393	98.6	10	7	1.6	7	0	.0
41092	1.7	0	.5	80	25.8	232	73.4	8	5	.0	0	2	.0
41093	2.0	0	.7	78	15.1	149	40.3	11	10	.0	0	0	.0
41094	6.4	99	2.1	80	30.3	339	94.7	9	8	3.2	7	2	.0
41095	2.6	97	.9	69	22.4	255	65.6	8	14	1.2	11	0	.4
41096	.1	0	.1	55	24.2	350	85.1	7	12	.0	0	0	.0
41097	4.6	100	1.6	75	22.8	222	56.1	7	16	2.3	14	1	.0
41098	1.3	100	.5	75	17.4	301	39.1	6	12	.6	11	0	.1

ASHLAND (NORTH)

ZIP CODE	1	2	3	4	5	6	7	8	9	10	11	12	13
41101	45.7	98	16.6	73	27.4	268	69.3	7	12	21.4	10	8	3.3
41121	1.9	100	.5	79	22.7	196	62.8	8	4	1.0	4	0	.0
41124	1.1	100	.4	67	14.1	90	31.0	5	19	.6	17	0	.0
41127	.3	100	.1	86	24.1	277*	63.1	8	9	.2	14	0	.0
41128	.3	100	.1	60	17.4	300	47.2	5	9	.1	8	0	.0
41129	10.3	99	3.4	79	24.8	250	69.6	8	11	5.1	9	5	14.6
41132	.3	100	.1	89	18.7	186	23.4	4	13	.2	11	0	.0
41135	.1	100	.1	76	10.6	197	13.1	0	20	.1	11	0	.0
41137	.3	100	.1	72	16.5	171	33.5	12	7	.2	10	0	.0
41139	9.1	0	3.0	85	26.7	346	60.8	8	7	.0	0	0	.0
41141	2.5	99	.7	82	16.5	200	42.0	10	6	1.3	7	1	.0
41142	.5	100	.2	81	17.8	166	35.3	10	6	.2	7	0	.0
41143	11.3	100	3.6	80	20.6	233	63.4	9	11	5.6	10	0	.0
41144	8.6	99	2.8	79	22.2	264	56.9	9	11	4.1	9	3	3.1
41145	.2	100	.1	82	10.7	149	17.5	8	21	.1	16	0	.0
41146	.8	100	.2	98	20.5	236*	28.6	7	9	.4	9	0	.3
41149	.3	100	.2	75	18.8	210	34.2	7	9	.2	7	0	.0
41153	.7	100	.1	70	14.6	162	35.2	13	5	.1	4	0	.0
41156	.4	100	.1	91	27.3	365	61.1	16	2	.2	4	0	.0
41158	.6	0	.2	80	23.0	315	58.0	4	19	.2	2	0	.0
41159	.5	100	.2	65	12.2	57	14.7	11	18	.2	12	0	.0

*=Estimated **1.0=883 lbs per person; 100++ indicates per capita toxic waste generation > than 100 times the U.S. average of 883 lbs per capita.

ZIP CODE MEASURES OF SIZE, LEVELS OF AFFLUENCE AND QUALITY OF LIFE

1=Population (th.); 2= % White; 3=Households (th.); 4=% Owner Occupied; 5=Mean Income Per Household (th.$); 6=Mean Monthly Rent ($)*; 7=Mean Home Value (th.$)*;
8=% under 5; 9=% 65 and over; 10=White Males (th.); 11=% White Males, 65+; 12=# Toxic Waste Sites; 13=Toxic Waste Relative to US(883 lbs.per capita)**.

KENTUCKY

ASHLAND (NORTH)

ZIPCODE	1	2	3	4	5	6	7	8	9	10	11	12	13
41163	.4	100	.1	83	21.6	249*	59.5	10	9	.2	12	0	.0
41164	11.4	100	3.7	80	15.5	197	44.1	8	12	5.6	10	0	.0
41166	.8	0	.2	66	17.5	281	48.3	12	6	.0	0	0	.0
41168	2.8	100	.9	83	21.6	286	43.8	9	7	1.3	6	0	.0
41169	6.7	99	2.3	79	33.4	268	87.0	6	10	3.3	7	2	.7
41170	.3	100	.1	47	19.3	203	48.1	14	2	.1	4	0	.0
41171	3.5	100	1.2	77	16.3	198	62.4	10	14	1.7	15	0	.0
41173	.7	100	.2	86	13.9	56	36.2	12	10	.4	9	0	.0
41174	1.1	100	.4	84	20.8	225	56.1	4	7	.4	6	0	.0
41175	5.2	0	1.8	83	19.0	197	51.7	7	12	.0	0	4	.5
41180	8.0	99	2.6	71	16.5	186	48.2	9	11	3.9	11	0	.0
41183	2.0	0	.7	71	13.6	157	27.5	11	17	.5	17	0	.0
41184	.2	100	.1	89	27.0	327	62.0	8	8	.0	0	0	.0
41189	.2	100	.1	100	23.2	266*	13.1	9	1	.1	0	0	.0

ASHLAND (SOUTH)

ZIPCODE	1	2	3	4	5	6	7	8	9	10	11	12	13
41201	.2	100	.1	78	12.0	138*	65.6	4	14	.1	13	0	.0
41203	.8	100	.2	81	26.7	260	46.1	9	9	.4	10	0	.0
41204	.8	100	.3	76	14.5	332	22.5	13	7	.5	6	0	.0
41208	.2	100	.1	43	17.1	103	65.6	14	7	.1	15	0	.0
41214	.7	100	.2	80	24.4	264	61.3	11	12	.4	9	0	.0
41215	.3	100	.1	83	16.7	192*	16.7	7	4	.2	3	0	.0
41216	1.2	100	.4	76	22.0	354	91.6	11	11	.6	8	0	.0
41219	1.2	100	.4	79	16.0	220	63.8	9	14	.6	12	0	.0
41220	.3	100	.1	94	17.4	200*	50.3	15	10	.1	10	0	.0
41222	1.9	100	.6	84	22.5	218	77.9	10	10	.9	10	0	.0
41223	.7	100	.2	90	21.5	359	58.0	10	12	.4	12	0	.0
41224	5.3	100	1.7	79	24.4	255	59.0	10	8	2.6	7	1	.0
41225	.3	100	.1	81	25.9	257*	38.4	11	7	.2	6	0	.0
41226	.2	100	.1	91	22.3	297*	41.6	11	28	.1	26	0	.0
41228	.5	100	.2	91	15.7	236	36.7	7	4	.2	8	0	.0
41229	.4	100	.1	88	20.6	237*	45.4	11	4	.2	3	0	.0
41230	10.0	100	3.4	75	19.6	238	59.2	8	13	4.9	12	1	.0
41231	1.4	100	.4	78	22.7	216	60.9	11	7	.6	8	2	.0
41232	.9	100	.3	51	17.8	362	91.4	11	12	.4	14	0	.4
41235	.8	100	.3	85	19.7	289	61.5	7	5	.4	6	0	.0
41236	.3	100	.1	92	16.7	251*	30.8	8	4	.2	3	0	.0
41238	1.1	100	.4	81	21.4	323	66.1	4	10	.6	11	0	.0
41240	1.4	0	.5	80	17.1	277	32.0	6	12	.0	0	0	.0
41250	4.8	0	1.8	62	27.8	277	98.4	5	13	.0	14	0	.0
41251	1.3	0	.4	82	25.6	175	61.8	12	5	.4	6	0	.0
41254	.3	100	.4	92	16.7	305	57.4	8	13	.2	3	0	.0
41255	.6	100	.2	67	16.7	97	58.8	11	11	.3	10	0	.0
41256	1.2	0	.4	87	20.6	224	52.7	9	6	.0	0	0	.0
41257	1.4	0	.5	72	19.4	215	72.6	9	10	.3	21	0	.0
41259	.8	100	.2	72	16.0	193	60.1	8	20	.4	11	0	.0
41260	.5	100	.3	84	18.6	193	47.0	4	9	.3	2	0	.0
41262	1.1	100	.4	76	16.3	223	48.0	18	8	.6	7	0	.0

KENTUCKY

ASHLAND (SOUTH)

ZIPCODE	1	2	3	4	5	6	7	8	9	10	11	12	13
41263	.6	100	.2	76	23.3	263	61.2	13	13	.3	12	0	.0
41264	.4	100	.1	68	20.9	348	62.9	10	6	.2	6	0	.0
41265	2.2	0	.7	84	22.9	284	60.5	12	11	.0	0	0	.0
41266	.2	100	.1	100	17.7	203*	56.9	11	21	.1	14	0	.0
41267	.6	100	.2	87	31.5	315	51.1	12	7	.3	6	0	.7
41268	.6	100	.2	80	18.4	222	53.2	9	10	.2	12	0	.0
41269	.2	100	.1	86	14.2	163*	32.8	8	17	.1	15	0	.0
41271	.4	0	.2	78	13.4	276	31.5	3	11	.0	9	0	.0
41274	.5	100	.2	75	20.0	251	66.7	13	7	.2	7	0	.0

CAMPTON (SOUTH)

ZIPCODE	1	2	3	4	5	6	7	8	9	10	11	12	13
41301	4.8	0	1.7	69	14.6	146	50.7	10	12	.0	0	0	.0
41306	.7	100	.3	61	12.9	150	24.0	14	5	.4	7	0	.0
41307	.3	100	.1	65	13.8	260	49.3*	7	18	.1	16	0	.0
41311	6.0	100	2.0	76	16.4	225	47.5	8	16	2.9	14	0	.0
41314	5.1	100	1.6	72	12.5	147	42.4	6	14	.4	12	0	.0
41317	.7	100	.2	80	19.9	105	25.9	6	13	.2	4	0	.0
41329	.3	100	.1	68	16.4	267	17.1	14	9	.2	4	0	.0
41332	1.6	0	.6	71	12.3	131	44.9	9	7	.2	25	0	.0
41333	.1	100	.1	65	14.2	153	13.1	5	28	.1	27	0	.0
41339	8.2	99	2.7	68	19.4	218	55.5	10	11	4.0	10	1	.0
41340	.2	100	.1	64	17.7	165	19.5	10	6	.1	10	0	.0
41342	.2	100	.1	54	11.9	122	28.4	3	13	.1	13	0	.0
41344	.3	100	.1	73	8.0	173	39.7	6	13	.1	15	0	.0
41348	1.5	100	.4	76	20.0	64	42.0	10	9	.8	9	0	.0
41355	.2	100	.1	89	23.8	273*	57.3	6	14	.4	17	0	.0
41357	.5	0	.2	72	35.2	278	54.2	7	10	.0	0	0	.0
41360	.5	0	.3	73	22.1	188	32.9	13	11	.1	6	1	.0
41363	.3	100	.1	90	15.4	177*	85.6	18	3	.1	0	0	.0
41364	.5	100	.2	96	14.1	163*	16.6	7	18	.2	22	0	.0
41365	.5	100	.1	96	16.5	189*	30.3	9	9	.3	8	0	.0
41366	.3	100	.1	61	13.7	107	56.9	9	2	.2	6	0	.0
41367	.4	100	.1	80	24.3	280*	52.5	11	8	.2	5	0	.0
41368	.3	100	.1	71	13.2	218	32.6	8	5	.1	5	0	.0
41369	.3	0	.3	68	19.4	138	26.5	11	3	.0	0	0	.0
41377	.3	100	.3	84	15.0	172*	41.6	7	9	.1	10	0	.0
41384	.3	100	.1	65	11.2	129*	65.6	14	7	.1	6	0	.0
41385	1.0	100	.2	51	14.3	215	34.9	9	5	.5	6	0	.0
41386	.1	100	.1	71	5.7	66*	91.5	9	20	.1	12	0	.0
41390	.3	100	.1	70	32.4	232	51.6	9	17	.2	18	0	.0
41396	.3	100	.1	85	20.8	239*	42.0	9	19	.2	22	0	.0
41397	.2	100	.1	80	13.1	151*	17.0	9	8	.1	5	0	.0

CAMPTON (NORTH)

ZIPCODE	1	2	3	4	5	6	7	8	9	10	11	12	13
41407	.3	100	.1	73	10.7	100	45.0	9	15	.2	14	0	.0
41408	.4	100	.1	85	12.5	200	30.3	5	8	.2	6	0	.0
41409	.3	100	.2	58	15.1	203	13.1	5	7	.1	10	0	.0
41412	.1	100	.3	79	16.4	188*	42.1	0	12	.1	14	0	.0
41421	.3	100	.1	88	10.9	156	20.7	15	4	.2	8	0	.0
41422	.2	100	.1	81	11.8	255	13.1	0	21	.1	21	0	.0

*=Estimated **1.0=883 lbs per person; 100++ indicates per capita toxic waste generation > than 100 times the U.S. average of 883 lbs per capita.

ZIP CODE MEASURES OF SIZE, LEVELS OF AFFLUENCE AND QUALITY OF LIFE

1=Population (th.); 2= % White; 3=Households (th.); 4=% Owner Occupied; 5=Mean Income Per Household (th.$); 6=Mean Monthly Rent ($)*; 7=Mean Home Value (th.$)*;
8=% under 5; 9=% 65 and over; 10=White Males (th.); 11=% White Males, 65+; 12=# Toxic Waste Sites; 13=Toxic Waste Relative to US(883 lbs.per capita)**.

KENTUCKY

CAMPTON (NORTH)

ZIP CODE	1	2	3	4	5	6	7	8	9	10	11	12	13
41425	.8	99	.3	73	11.2	172	37.1	5	13	.4	10	0	.0
41426	.6	100	.2	72	22.6	180	75.3	13	11	.3	10	0	.0
41427	.2	100	.1	74	16.4	188*	13.1	11	6	.1	6	0	.0
41429	.3	100	.1	84	18.7	214*	51.0	11	6	.2	8	0	.0
41431	.2	100	.1	77	15.8	165	56.9	5	2	.1	5	0	.0
41435	.2	100	.1	59	12.8	147*	37.2	10	11	.1	13	0	.0
41441	.3	100	.1	76	10.8	242	74.1	2	19	.1	14	0	.0
41457	.1	100	.1	63	18.0	177	35.2	16	4	.2	3	0	.0
41464	.1	100	.1	77	12.8	143	60.8	6	17	.1	13	0	.0
41465	.8	100	.2	71	12.8	253	43.1	11	10	.5	8	0	.2
41467	7.6	0	2.4	76	19.0	205	62.5	10	9	.0	0	0	.0
41469	.2	100	.1	100	7.0	81*	13.1	11	4	.1	0	0	.0
41472	.2	100	.1	100	9.1	105*	13.1	5	16	.1	30	0	.0
41474	7.0	0	2.4	73	17.5	217	67.9	8	12	.0	0	0	.0
41477	.3	100	.1	82	19.0	218*	82.2	7	0	.1	10	0	.0
41477	.2	100	.1	79	23.0	218	59.2	17	13	.1	18	0	.0

PIKEVILLE (EAST)

ZIP CODE	1	2	3	4	5	6	7	8	9	10	11	12	13
41501	21.0	99	7.2	69	23.5	296	87.2	9	9	10.1	8	3	.0
41510	.3	100	.1	91	12.6	145*	31.1	0	19	.2	18	0	.0
41511	.6	100	.1	71	18.2	204	16.0	18	0	.3	0	0	.0
41512	1.3	100	.4	90	25.4	314	77.4	5	7	.6	5	0	.0
41513	.9	100	.3	85	23.9	217	51.9	9	9	.5	7	0	.0
41514	1.6	100	.5	76	19.8	288	63.9	6	8	.7	9	0	.0
41515	.1	0	.1	88	14.9	172*	31.8	0	0	.0	0	0	.0
41517	.7	100	.2	75	25.1	228	38.0	11	8	.3	13	0	.0
41518	.3	100	.1	86	19.6	225*	35.7	3	14	.1	7	0	.0
41519	1.2	100	.4	82	18.2	287	54.9	7	11	.6	11	0	.0
41520	.4	100	.1	82	17.2	137	33.1	17	2	.2	8	0	.0
41521	.2	100	.1	93	20.4	234*	59.3	11	15	.1	12	0	.0
41522	5.7	0	1.8	78	23.7	248	61.4	10	7	.0	0	4	.0
41523	.3	100	.1	65	13.5	285	35.9	8	10	.1	17	0	.0
41524	.8	100	.2	75	23.9	189	77.0	3	6	.4	8	1	.0
41525	.2	100	.1	86	11.2	207	30.0	11	13	.2	13	0	.0
41526	.2	100	.1	81	17.8	221	111.7	6	9	.1	12	0	.0
41527	.6	100	.2	77	29.6	332	81.8	7	15	.3	13	0	.0
41528	2.0	0	.6	83	22.3	317	35.5	11	7	.3	13	0	.0
41529	.1	100	.1	89	15.8	182*	39.6	0	34	.1	29	0	.0
41530	.4	100	.1	62	17.3	172	39.8	6	17	.2	20	0	.0
41531	1.4	96	.5	89	19.6	305	45.0	8	15	.7	12	0	.0
41534	.7	0	.3	79	17.5	127	32.0	9	13	.0	0	0	.0
41535	.6	88	.2	72	20.9	178	51.4	7	12	.3	9	0	.0
41536	.5	100	.1	86	25.4	419	42.7	7	7	.3	3	0	.0
41537	3.5	0	1.2	86	22.0	193*	47.6	7	15	.2	2	0	.0
41538	.5	100	.2	69	15.3	413	26.7	9	11	.2	16	0	.0
41539	1.8	0	.5	76	24.2	303	57.7	14	3	.0	0	0	.0
41540	.5	0	.2	93	19.9	200	62.8	12	5	.0	0	0	.0
41542	.8	100	.2	70	15.2	235	48.6	8	6	.5	5	0	.0
41543	.7	0	.3	89	19.7	134	24.5	10	7	.5	7	0	.0
41544	1.0	100	.3	78	29.2	254	57.8	9	7	.5	7	0	.0

PIKEVILLE (EAST) (continued)

ZIP CODE	1	2	3	4	5	6	7	8	9	10	11	12	13
41545	.3	100	.1	86	20.6	237*	91.9	9	16	.1	18	0	.0
41546	.4	100	.1	64	16.9	257	28.0	8	3	.2	3	0	.0
41547	.6	100	.2	80	19.0	379	39.5	14	7	.3	5	0	.0
41548	1.4	100	.4	78	20.7	212	59.4	7	4	.6	3	1	.0
41549	1.2	100	.4	76	28.7	290	67.0	12	9	.6	7	0	.0
41551	.3	100	.1	71	16.4	210	26.1	17	8	.1	5	0	.0
41552	.2	100	.1	85	17.6	369	47.9	5	9	.1	6	0	.0
41553	1.0	100	.8	86	27.3	258	64.0	6	5	.1	5	0	.0
41554	2.4	0	.8	75	20.6	246	54.0	12	7	1.5	5	0	.0
41555	.8	100	.3	89	21.4	139	33.2	9	15	.0	15	0	.0
41557	2.0	100	.6	82	25.1	275	74.0	11	6	.4	6	0	.1
41558	1.0	0	.3	82	21.9	204	47.1	12	6	1.0	6	0	.0
41559	1.3	100	.4	76	21.8	235	52.4	9	7	.6	5	0	.0
41560	1.1	100	.4	78	19.9	263	88.3	8	7	.5	6	0	.0
41561	.5	100	.1	71	27.0	249	47.7	5	2	.2	2	0	.0
41563	3.2	0	1.0	80	20.9	215	48.4	12	6	.0	5	0	.0
41564	.5	100	.1	73	25.1	200	37.3	4	7	.8	5	0	.0
41565	1.6	100	.5	82	23.0	253	75.1	11	13	.1	14	0	.0
41566	.3	100	.1	83	15.0	195	34.4	7	4	.2	0	0	.0
41567	.6	0	.2	93	26.5	263	44.2	4	5	.4	0	0	.0
41568	.8	100	.3	44	21.6	255	37.2	12	10	.5	8	0	.0
41569	.9	100	.1	64	16.2	196	45.6	10	3	.2	3	0	.0
41570	.3	100	.1	74	26.0	299*	52.6	2	15	.8	13	0	.0
41571	1.5	100	.5	79	27.7	219	59.6	11	8	.4	7	0	.0
41572	.8	100	.2	86	20.0	105	75.3	7	7	.0	4	0	.0
41572	4.9	0	1.7	83	20.1	237	58.5	8	11	1.7	0	0	.0

PIKEVILLE (WEST)

ZIP CODE	1	2	3	4	5	6	7	8	9	10	11	12	13
41601	1.7	100	.6	75	24.5	298	77.1	10	7	.0	0	0	1.1
41602	.9	100	.3	80	22.9	258	65.4	13	10	.4	9	0	.0
41603	1.1	100	.3	90	19.9	393	58.3	10	6	.5	8	0	.0
41604	.5	100	.1	93	13.6	156*	29.1	10	0	.2	0	0	.0
41605	1.9	0	.7	78	23.3	310	71.1	10	17	.0	0	0	.0
41606	.3	100	.1	85	20.4	323	30.8	8	5	.1	5	0	.0
41607	.3	100	.1	80	21.0	241*	16.0	14	7	.1	10	0	.1
41612	.2	100	.2	82	16.8	163	40.7	10	12	.4	12	0	.0
41614	.4	100	.1	82	18.4	284	20.8	4	8	.2	5	0	.0
41615	.8	100	.2	79	20.6	174	52.5	12	3	.4	2	0	.0
41616	.7	100	.2	90	24.0	276*	41.7	6	8	.3	9	0	.0
41619	.8	0	.2	70	23.2	183	47.8	10	14	.3	9	0	.0
41621	.5	100	.1	87	22.3	314	42.1	7	7	.3	9	0	.1
41622	.4	100	.2	77	18.0	161	70.9	3	14	.2	16	0	.0
41623	1.3	0	.4	71	16.1	218	41.9	9	7	.0	0	0	.0
41625	.4	100	.1	78	12.4	153	86.0	4	14	.2	15	0	.0
41626	.6	100	.2	65	17.4	119	53.0	8	10	.3	5	0	.0
41627	.4	100	.1	85	17.7	309	49.7	7	12	.3	9	0	.0
41629	.6	100	.2	80	15.0	114	29.7	11	5	.2	8	0	.0
41630	1.7	100	.6	74	18.9	144	48.2	10	10	.8	6	0	.0
41631	.9	100	.3	82	15.7	99	49.6	9	6	.5	6	0	.0
41632	1.0	100	.3	81	18.7	215*	45.0	11	3	.2	3	0	.0

*=Estimated **1.0=883 lbs per person; 100++ indicates per capita toxic waste generation > than 100 times the U.S. average of 883 lbs per capita.

ZIP CODE MEASURES OF SIZE, LEVELS OF AFFLUENCE AND QUALITY OF LIFE

1=Population (th.); 2= % White; 3=Households (th.); 4=% Owner Occupied; 5=Mean Income Per Household (th.$); 6=Mean Monthly Rent ($)*; 7=Mean Home Value (th.$)*;
8=% under 5; 9=% 65 and over; 10=White Males (th.); 11=% White Males, 65+; 12=# Toxic Waste Sites; 13=Toxic Waste Relative to US(883 lbs.per capita)**.

KENTUCKY

PIKEVILLE (WEST)

ZIPCODE	1	2	3	4	5	6	7	8	9	10	11	12	13
41633	.5	100	.2	76	13.4	184	22.1	5	11	.2	11	0	.0
41635	2.4	100	.8	73	18.9	303	40.1	12	8	1.2	9	1	.8
41636	.3	100	.1	100	14.2	163*	35.6	0	17	.2	16	0	.0
41637	.4	100	.1	56	21.3	152	56.8	6	0	.2	0	0	.0
41639	.7	100	.2	72	10.5	176	26.9	13	8	.4	8	0	.0
41640	1.4	100	.4	78	20.2	207	40.7	11	10	.7	10	0	.0
41641	.2	100	.1	58	20.7	120	41.6	3	7	.1	0	0	.3
41642	.5	100	.2	76	17.2	299	60.2	12	14	.3	14	0	.0
41643	.3	100	.1	52	17.7	162	47.7	5	9	.3	2	0	.0
41645	1.4	0	.4	78	22.7	212	54.2	11	10	.1	0	0	.0
41647	.9	100	.3	81	20.8	109	59.5	10	8	.5	6	1	.1
41648	.1	100	.1	73	23.7	177	47.7	0	18	.1	12	0	.0
41649	2.9	0	1.0	69	20.8	229	55.0	9	10	.6	10	0	.0
41650	1.2	100	.4	79	16.6	180	35.8	8	10	.6	10	0	.0
41651	.3	100	.1	84	16.2	187*	108.1	11	4	.1	0	0	.0
41653	10.8	100	3.7	69	24.7	255	87.5	8	13	5.3	11	0	.0
41654	1.0	100	.1	88	17.6	129	46.6	15	10	.2	12	1	.1
41655	1.0	100	.3	81	17.7	197	52.4	18	7	.5	7	1	.0
41659	.6	100	.2	62	20.4	408	144.6	7	8	.3	13	0	.6
41660	1.1	100	.4	82	14.8	121	33.7	8	12	.6	7	0	.0
41663	.3	74	.1	66	16.3	113	72.1	9	13	.1	8	0	.0
41664	.2	100	.1	88	22.7	261*	56.9	14	0	.2	0	0	.0
41666	1.2	100	.4	82	21.2	197	44.0	8	10	.1	0	0	.0
41667	1.2	0	.4	89	16.6	171	33.8	11	4	.4	10	1	.0
41668	.5	100	.2	78	17.5	282	61.8	7	17	.2	9	0	.0
41669	.8	82	.3	68	17.2	230	37.7	7	9	.3	6	0	.0

HAZARD (WEST)

ZIPCODE	1	2	3	4	5	6	7	8	9	10	11	12	13
41701	14.1	96	4.8	70	23.1	243	61.7	9	12	6.4	10	0	.0
41711	.3	100	.1	91	20.1	230*	15.2	16	6	1.2	4	0	.0
41712	.7	100	.1	74	19.8	113	35.6	7	6	.6	5	0	.0
41713	.4	100	.1	81	19.9	333	39.6	11	8	.2	6	0	.0
41714	.8	0	.2	52	13.8	225	24.7	13	7	.0	0	0	.0
41715	.2	0	.1	71	11.8	236	16.8	20	9	.0	0	0	.0
41719	1.3	100	.4	74	22.4	158	50.3	10	9	.6	10	0	.0
41720	.3	100	.1	66	16.1	308	18.6	8	6	.1	6	0	.0
41721	.6	100	.2	59	14.6	209	31.9	8	8	.3	6	0	.0
41722	1.1	100	.4	87	18.2	256	38.6	10	12	.6	8	0	.0
41723	1.5	100	.4	74	14.0	160	25.2	14	10	.8	10	0	.0
41725	.7	100	.2	74	9.2	274	28.6	8	10	.3	11	0	.0
41727	.8	100	.3	74	21.0	193	63.2	14	5	.4	2	0	.0
41728	.3	100	.1	67	13.1	150	27.2	9	13	.2	15	0	.0
41729	1.2	0	.4	72	23.6	78	44.5	13	9	.0	0	0	.0
41730	.4	100	.1	75	17.5	99	19.1	14	7	.1	4	0	.0
41731	.7	0	.2	74	9.2	153	26.3	8	9	.2	9	0	.0
41732	.2	100	.1	80	15.0	134	48.2	3	5	.1	3	0	.0
41733	.2	100	.1	47	19.3	192	37.9	4	0	.1	0	0	.0
41735	.4	100	.1	41	19.1	209	24.4	13	3	.2	6	0	.0
41736	.4	100	.1	64	14.0	123	47.1	10	7	.2	7	0	.0
41739	1.1	100	.3	87	19.8	227*	39.6	10	11	.5	8	0	.0

KENTUCKY

HAZARD (WEST)

ZIPCODE	1	2	3	4	5	6	7	8	9	10	11	12	13
41742	.5	100	.2	77	18.1	297	30.6	12	13	.2	16	0	.0
41743	.4	100	.1	82	19.6	142	33.1	3	10	.2	7	0	.0
41745	.4	100	.1	81	17.6	138	29.7	10	7	.2	0	0	.0
41746	.7	100	.2	66	20.3	254	46.1	8	7	.4	7	0	.0
41747	.5	0	.1	87	17.5	377	19.3	9	12	.0	0	0	.0
41749	3.7	100	1.3	75	17.8	193	39.2	9	12	1.8	11	0	.0
41751	.6	100	.2	84	19.0	220	64.5	6	10	.3	10	1	1.2
41754	.7	100	.2	84	18.3	135	24.9	7	9	.4	8	0	.0
41756	.3	100	.1	32	34.5	166	47.6	3	2	.1	0	0	.0
41757	.3	100	.1	78	17.4	255	28.4	15	7	.1	10	0	.0
41759	.4	92	.2	84	16.7	304	40.7	3	19	.2	11	0	.0
41762	.9	100	.2	54	10.6	233	24.9	11	4	.5	0	0	.0
41763	.9	100	.2	59	20.2	220	57.1	9	4	.5	3	0	.0
41764	.8	100	.3	81	21.7	218	31.8	10	12	.4	10	0	.0
41765	.3	100	.1	65	14.8	230	38.0	6	6	.2	6	0	.0
41766	.2	100	.1	80	25.5	293*	25.4	7	7	.1	1	0	.0
41770	.2	0	.1	69	10.9	135	42.7	3	7	.0	0	0	.0
41772	.2	0	.1	80	11.5	312	19.0	8	13	.0	0	0	.0
41773	1.8	0	.5	78	16.4	256	27.6	11	5	.1	6	0	.6
41774	2.4	100	.7	81	21.6	254	40.4	8	6	1.2	6	0	.0
41775	.3	100	.1	78	15.7	97	57.8	3	7	.2	9	0	.0
41776	1.6	0	.5	64	15.8	219	30.1	12	6	.2	0	0	.0
41777	.8	100	.2	45	16.0	192	35.1	10	2	.4	0	0	.0
41778	.8	100	.2	94	24.7	283*	56.7	5	7	.2	7	0	.0

HAZARD (EAST)

ZIPCODE	1	2	3	4	5	6	7	8	9	10	11	12	13
41801	.4	100	.2	90	31.3	428	32.9	3	18	.2	11	0	.0
41804	.8	100	.3	64	16.4	138	51.4	11	12	.4	11	0	.0
41805	.4	100	.1	90	20.6	172	60.5	13	10	.2	13	0	.0
41806	.1	100	.1	75	20.0	194	25.4	13	0	.1	0	0	.0
41810	.6	100	.2	82	14.4	185	27.9	8	12	.3	7	0	.0
41811	.3	100	.1	49	12.8	257	45.7*14	3	.1	0	0	.0	
41812	.1	100	.1	76	16.6	105	21.4	12	9	.2	7	0	.0
41814	.3	100	.1	82	22.5	200	27.8	7	8	.1	11	0	.0
41815	1.3	100	.4	60	16.0	235	48.5	10	9	.7	9	0	.0
41816	.3	89	.1	83	17.8	285	31.2	9	16	.1	16	0	.0
41817	.6	0	.2	69	13.0	178	28.8	1	6	.2	9	0	.0
41818	.1	100	.1	77	10.7	123*	32.1	16	19	.1	13	0	.0
41819	.4	100	.2	75	16.0	193	18.4	15	9	.1	12	0	.0
41821	.5	100	.2	86	20.7	159	26.0	9	9	.3	7	0	.0
41822	2.2	100	.7	66	22.7	206	63.1	9	13	1.0	13	0	.0
41823	.2	100	.1	88	11.5	132*	19.7	3	4	.1	0	0	.0
41824	1.2	100	.4	78	17.6	203	45.7	8	10	.6	9	0	.0
41825	1.1	100	.4	67	15.2	220	23.9	10	9	.6	10	0	.0
41826	1.5	100	.5	82	16.3	170	37.4	8	11	.8	12	0	.0
41827	1.0	100	.2	79	12.9	253	45.7	9	11	1.0	13	0	.0
41828	1.0	100	.3	67	22.8	156	48.7	9	9	.6	9	0	.0
41829	.4	100	.1	51	17.3	293	59.2	7	2	.2	3	0	.0
41830	.5	100	.1	79	13.1	86	43.4	2	16	.2	15	0	.0
41831	.8	100	.2	83	28.8	244	63.0	7	6	.4	5	0	.0

*=Estimated **1.0=883 lbs per person; 100++ indicates per capita toxic waste generation > than 100 times the U.S. average of 883 lbs per capita.

ZIP CODE MEASURES OF SIZE, LEVELS OF AFFLUENCE AND QUALITY OF LIFE

1=Population (th.); 2= % White; 3=Households (th.); 4=% Owner Occupied; 5=Mean Income Per Household (th.$); 6=Mean Monthly Rent ($)*; 7=Mean Home Value (th.$); 8=% under 5; 9=% 65 and over; 10=White Males (th.); 11=% White Males, 65+; 12=# Toxic Waste Sites; 13=Toxic Waste Relative to US(883 lbs.per capita)**.

KENTUCKY

HAZARD (EAST)

ZIPCODE	.1	2	3	4	5	6	7	8	9	10	11	12	13
41832	.6	100	.2	60	16.0	255	52.3	12	5	.3	6	0	.0
41833	.3	100	.4	74	14.1	131	25.3	9	10	.1	13	0	.0
41834	.6	100	.2	67	15.8	122	32.8	9	4	.3	6	0	.0
41835	.9	87	.3	89	20.1	143	35.8	12	13	.4	9	0	.0
41836	.6	100	.2	86	20.8	191	65.4	14	6	.5	5	0	.0
41837	.9	100	.3	83	19.3	228	43.1	8	8	.5	11	0	.0
41838	1.0	100	.3	73	17.3	198	26.7	9	11	.5	9	0	.0
41839	1.2	0	.3	71	20.7	170	69.9	11	11	.5	11	0	.0
41840	1.8	0	.6	69	17.5	169	37.1	11	8	.0	8	0	.1
41843	.8	100	.3	89	17.3	60	49.2	13	9	.4	8	0	.0
41844	1.1	100	.3	59	17.5	190	62.8	11	4	.5	4	0	.0
41845	.4	100	.1	69	17.1	120	82.8	5	3	.5	3	0	.0
41847	.6	87	.2	75	18.8	209	36.5	5	13	.3	15	0	.0
41848	.3	100	.1	83	15.8	114	47.9	6	11	.1	4	0	.0
41849	.3	100	.1	69	17.2	199	25.8	9	18	.1	15	0	.0
41850	.2	100	.1	83	20.9	344	35.2	8	3	.1	0	0	.0
41855	.9	100	.3	73	16.1	196	39.2	12	9	.5	7	0	.0
41856	.3	100	.1	75	16.1	132	43.9	15	9	.2	12	0	.0
41857	.3	100	.1	92	18.1	208*	65.0	17	8	.2	7	0	.1
41858	6.0	99	2.0	72	20.5	216	62.1	9	11	2.8	10	0	.0
41859	.4	100	.1	78	27.6	220	48.8	8	11	.2	10	0	.0
41860	.2	100	.1	81	25.3	291*	30.2	18	2	.2	3	0	.0
41861	.2	100	.1	62	18.4	220	56.0	5	13	.1	8	0	.0
41862	.9	100	.3	69	14.5	267	25.1	12	7	.4	7	0	.2

PADUCAH

ZIPCODE	.1	2	3	4	5	6	7	8	9	10	11	12	13
42001	56.0	89	21.5	70	24.3	267	67.7	7	14	23.4	11	7	7.5
42020	1.1	97	.4	91	22.0	223	52.8	5	15	.5	15	0	.0
42021	1.5	0	.6	90	18.6	277	40.0	4	20	.0	0	0	.5
42022	2.8	100	1.0	100	11.6	133*	31.1	4	25	.1	15	0	.0
42023	2.8	100	1.1	83	19.3	197	42.5	6	20	.0	0	0	.0
42024	1.6	95	.6	85	18.9	291	45.1	5	17	.7	14	0	.0
42025	15.4	100	5.6	86	22.0	258	62.3	7	15	7.5	14	0	.0
42026	.2	100	.1	89	10.6	122*	40.8	12	21	.1	24	0	.0
42027	1.8	96	.7	90	22.2	87	53.5	7	10	.8	9	0	.0
42028	.9	100	.3	90	18.5	172	37.0	4	22	.3	24	0	.1
42029	5.9	100	2.0	87	27.9	326	67.9	7	13	2.9	11	9	96.1
42030	.2	100	.1	97	14.3	164*	25.9	7	22	.1	30	0	.1
42031	4.2	89	1.5	77	22.0	203	48.7	7	17	1.8	15	0	.0
42032	.3	69	.1	82	16.9	116	30.1	6	21	.1	17	0	.0
42034	.3	100	.1	77	16.8	192*	39.6	14	11	.2	7	0	.0
42035	1.1	100	.3	79	24.5	293	58.8	6	19	.4	15	0	.0
42036	1.1	100	.4	87	16.1	186	33.8	8	10	.1	8	0	.0
42038	4.3	93	1.4	78	22.3	227	69.7	4	13	2.3	10	0	.0
42039	1.7	100	.5	90	25.2	180	47.3	8	9	.3	13	0	.0
42040	.8	100	.3	79	22.7	247	56.9	6	20	.4	16	0	.0
42041	4.7	89	1.9	66	19.2	208	51.6	8	24	1.9	21	0	.5
42044	2.6	100	1.0	87	27.5	206	93.5	8	14	1.3	16	0	.1
42045	1.9	0	.7	76	23.6	286	67.2	7	14	.1	0	0	.2
42046	.2	100	.1	69	18.5	212*	79.9	9	26	.1	36	0	.0

KENTUCKY

PADUCAH

ZIPCODE	1	2	3	4	5	6	7	8	9	10	11	12	13
42047	.2	100	.1	73	24.8	194	56.9	8	7	.1	7	0	.0
42048	1.6	0	.7	86	16.7	219	55.7	5	22	.0	0	0	.0
42049	1.5	98	.6	84	18.0	300	52.7	7	23	.7	22	0	.0
42050	4.9	80	1.7	72	20.1	218	45.6	7	16	1.8	13	0	.1
42051	2.7	0	.9	86	22.6	332	50.8	8	12	.0	0	0	.0
42053	3.7	99	1.4	85	22.0	285	54.4	8	17	1.8	15	0	.0
42054	.7	100	.3	81	17.1	53	66.6	11	25	.3	23	0	.0
42055	2.1	97	.8	85	21.5	231	66.5	6	23	1.0	18	0	.1
42056	2.2	96	.8	87	21.8	175	55.2	7	22	1.0	18	0	.0
42058	2.0	0	.7	93	24.8	164	62.7	11	6	.0	0	0	.0
42059	.2	100	.1	83	13.8	159*	25.3	5	13	.1	9	0	.0
42060	.2	0	.1	85	18.5	347	27.0	7	23	.0	0	0	.0
42064	8.2	99	3.1	81	19.7	200	48.0	7	18	3.9	15	1	.2
42066	21.3	94	8.2	75	21.1	232	59.4	6	19	9.5	16	1	.4
42069	.6	100	.2	88	18.2	206	47.8	4	16	.3	15	0	.0
42070	.5	100	.1	83	26.6	272	41.7	14	7	.2	6	0	.0
42071	24.5	96	8.7	70	22.1	243	72.2	5	14	11.2	12	3	.1
42076	.7	0	.2	91	14.8	171*	55.8	6	16	.2	12	0	.0
42078	2.0	0	.7	84	19.2	265	48.2	6	15	.1	0	0	.0
42079	1.1	100	.4	84	20.5	236	52.7	9	18	.6	14	0	.0
42081	1.9	0	.8	85	18.2	224	54.1	4	20	.2	0	0	.0
42082	1.5	100	.5	90	25.3	277	53.8	7	11	.8	9	0	.0
42083	.7	100	.2	84	18.6	144	38.6	9	7	.2	8	0	.0
42084	.9	100	.3	91	12.6	145*	14.5	5	14	.1	9	0	.1
42085	1.2	96	.5	87	24.4	106	44.9	6	21	.5	17	0	.0
42086	2.6	96	1.0	88	30.2	288	62.3	7	9	1.2	9	0	.0
42087	2.6	97	1.0	85	22.9	193	57.4	7	14	1.2	13	0	1.9
42088	2.6	95	1.0	84	20.5	164	48.8	6	17	1.2	17	0	.0

BOWLING GREEN (EAST)

ZIPCODE	1	2	3	4	5	6	7	8	9	10	11	12	13
42101	65.0	91	22.5	62	22.9	284	81.8	7	10	28.7	8	4	.8
42120	2.1	100	.7	80	17.1	230	34.3	6	11	1.0	11	0	.0
42122	2.2	96	.7	82	24.0	261	80.2	11	7	1.0	4	0	.0
42123	.6	100	.2	77	17.7	224	63.8	4	20	.3	15	0	.0
42127	5.1	94	1.8	69	19.0	190	54.3	7	13	2.3	12	0	.1
42129	6.1	99	2.2	78	16.4	196	45.8	7	16	3.0	15	0	.0
42133	1.6	94	.6	75	16.1	145	51.4	5	17	.7	17	0	.0
42134	14.1	87	5.0	70	21.6	241	65.9	8	14	5.9	12	1	2.1
42140	.4	100	.4	79	16.4	91	41.6	7	16	.6	18	0	1.0
42141	24.0	95	8.7	70	21.4	228	63.8	7	14	10.8	12	0	1.0
42151	.4	100	.2	76	27.2	148	73.7	4	8	.2	7	0	.0
42153	.3	100	.1	70	16.6	190*	29.5	6	19	.1	18	0	.0
42154	.8	86	.2	74	42.9	207	34.6	7	7	.3	5	0	.0
42155	.2	100	.1	87	21.2	244*	75.6*	7	16	.1	17	0	.0
42156	.1	100	.1	79	20.0	105	66.7	0	9	.1	5	0	.0
42157	.9	100	.3	82	16.0	383	48.4	10	11	.5	11	0	.1
42159	1.0	85	.3	90	21.5	262	64.4	6	15	.4	14	0	.0
42160	1.7	94	.6	73	18.2	222	51.5	8	12	.8	10	0	.0
42163	.2	100	.1	77	14.6	168*	44.8	12	18	.1	22	0	.0
42164	11.5	98	4.3	74	19.1	177	50.1	8	16	5.5	13	0	.1

*=Estimated **1.0=883 lbs per person; 100++ indicates per capita toxic waste generation > than 100 times the U.S. average of 883 lbs per capita.

ZIP CODE MEASURES OF SIZE, LEVELS OF AFFLUENCE AND QUALITY OF LIFE

1=Population (th.); 2= % White; 3=Households (th.); 4=% Owner Occupied; 5=Mean Income Per Household (th. $); 6=Mean Monthly Rent ($); 7=Mean Home Value (th.$); 8=% under 5; 9=% 65 and over; 10=%White Males (th.); 11=% White Males, 65+; 12=# Toxic Waste Sites; 13=Toxic Waste Relative to US(883 lbs.per capita)**.

KENTUCKY

ZIPCODE	1	2	3	4	5	6	7	8	9	10	11	12	13
BOWLING GREEN (EAST)													
42166	2.2	98	.8	86	15.7	175	38.7	8	15	1.1	13	0	.0
42167	9.1	96	3.2	72	16.1	167	45.0	7	15	4.3	13	0	.1
42170	1.2	87	.4	79	31.2	271	58.9	5	14	.5	13	0	.0
42171	3.8	94	1.4	83	19.5	233	51.4	8	16	1.8	14	0	.0
BOWLING GREEN (WEST)													
42201	.1	100	.1	91	25.8	296*	38.3	0	10	.1	10	0	.0
42202	2.6	87	1.0	65	19.8	207	51.1	7	15	1.1	12	0	.0
42203	.3	100	.1	85	12.4	142*	28.2	16	17	.1	17	0	.0
42204	.8	84	.3	85	20.0	125	38.9	5	21	.4	20	0	.0
42206	3.8	93	1.3	78	19.5	209	56.9	8	16	1.7	15	1	.0
42207	1.3	100	.4	86	16.4	164	43.7	5	12	.7	13	0	.0
42210	2.9	0	1.1	82	17.3	207	48.5	7	15	.0	15	0	.0
42211	8.3	91	3.0	78	21.3	218	63.6	7	16	3.7	14	0	.2
42214	.6	100	.2	87	18.1	208*	39.2	4	22	.3	16	0	.0
42215	1.3	64	.4	87	19.2	211	41.9	6	13	.4	14	0	.0
42216	.6	100	.2	90	16.5	120	54.5	3	16	.3	13	0	.0
42217	3.3	91	1.1	84	24.0	229	44.5	7	13	1.5	11	0	.0
42220	6.3	91	2.2	77	17.3	207	47.8	7	16	2.8	14	1	.0
42223	17.8	59	2.6	0	14.8	332	52.6*	12	0	7.1	0	0	.0
42232	.6	77	.2	74	26.2	117	53.3	11	17	.2	22	1	.4
42234	2.5	78	.8	73	22.7	192	51.2	11	14	.9	13	0	.0
42236	.9	85	.3	81	23.0	261	51.1	7	12	.4	11	0	.0
42240	37.6	75	13.2	66	22.4	219	65.1	8	13	13.5	11	3	.2
42250	.6	91	.2	92	18.3	304	67.2	8	8	.3	7	0	.0
42251	.2	100	.1	90	15.3	176*	37.1	6	21	.1	18	0	.0
42254	.4	61	.1	67	15.9	179	45.5	6	17	.1	10	0	.0
42256	3.0	0	1.0	82	18.7	236	45.0	8	13	.9	9	0	.0
42257	.4	100	.1	100	19.5	224*	52.6	5	5	.2	7	0	.0
42258	.2	100	.1	86	23.7	273*	47.9	21	4	.1	0	0	.0
42259	1.0	90	.3	79	13.9	216	35.2	8	9	.4	10	0	.0
42261	7.7	99	2.6	75	18.0	173	47.4	9	14	3.8	13	0	.0
42262	2.7	75	1.0	21	14.3	324	70.1	17	5	2.0	16	0	.0
42265	1.3	78	.5	72	20.6	219	54.8	4	16	.5	13	0	.0
42266	2.3	70	.7	72	22.2	271	58.9	8	11	.8	10	0	.0
42268	1.0	100	.3	87	19.0	102	31.9	6	7	.5	8	0	.0
42273	.4	0	.1	93	21.2	101	42.2	6	17	.0	9	0	.0
42274	2.0	93	.6	88	22.4	445	63.3	9	8	.9	9	0	.0
42275	.5	100	.2	80	12.7	164	26.3	10	19	.3	11	0	.0
42276	13.1	90	4.7	69	20.6	215	61.9	8	14	5.7	13	6	.4
42280	.2	100	.1	83	18.3	210*	23.5	6	16	.1	25	0	.0
42284	.2	100	.1	62	13.4	233	47.7*	6	13	.1	10	0	.0
42285	.5	100	.2	98	19.3	222*	34.6	8	13	.3	15	0	.0
42286	1.5	83	.5	72	25.4	225	71.9	8	13	.6	8	0	.0
42287	.4	0	.2	72	14.4	198	32.8	8	13	.1	0	0	.0
OWENSBORO													
42301	72.3	95	25.9	68	25.1	279	76.1	8	11	32.6	9	8	1.0
42320	7.1	97	2.6	77	22.3	262	62.2	9	14	3.4	13	1	.1
42321	.8	0	.2	74	15.7	270	40.8	6	13	.0	0	0	.0
42322	.2	100	.1	100	25.7	295*	47.4	10	7	.1	0	0	.0

KENTUCKY

ZIPCODE	1	2	3	4	5	6	7	8	9	10	11	12	13
OWENSBORO													
42323	.8	100	.3	90	26.1	406	62.9	8	11	.4	7	0	.0
42324	1.3	95	.4	73	20.8	275	52.3	8	11	.6	14	0	.0
42325	2.1	100	.7	87	22.9	307	54.2	8	11	1.0	11	0	.0
42326	.6	100	.2	85	17.8	273	38.5	12	13	.3	11	0	.0
42327	3.9	100	1.4	77	20.5	208	67.8	7	14	1.9	13	0	.0
42328	1.4	87	.5	87	21.9	276	54.2	9	11	.4	0	2	.0
42330	9.4	96	3.4	80	23.4	255	58.5	9	14	4.4	12	2	.0
42332	.5	92	.2	78	12.2	190	24.0	10	14	.2	11	1	.0
42333	1.0	0	.3	77	15.6	46	38.3	8	14	.2	0	0	.0
42337	2.2	91	.7	86	22.5	314	42.6	8	15	1.0	13	0	2.4
42338	.2	100	.1	89	20.8	239*	68.9	4	19	.1	0	0	.0
42339	.8	0	.3	89	18.8	126	39.1	6	12	.0	0	0	.0
42340	.4	100	.1	87	21.0	248	45.8	6	14	.2	5	0	.0
42343	1.7	0	.6	83	18.6	234	39.9	9	17	.6	0	0	.0
42344	1.2	100	.4	80	18.2	318	41.0	10	15	.6	10	1	1.5
42345	11.2	91	3.7	82	26.1	274	70.3	8	14	4.9	11	0	.0
42347	5.0	98	1.8	81	24.2	289	66.9	6	17	2.4	15	0	.1
42348	4.3	99	1.4	86	20.5	229	64.6	10	10	2.2	10	4	3.4
42349	1.4	100	.5	80	17.5	139	36.9	8	12	.7	13	0	.0
42350	1.6	0	.5	84	23.4	152	44.1	7	13	.6	0	0	.0
42351	3.7	98	1.2	78	25.1	223	66.1	9	10	1.9	9	1	.0
42352	2.3	100	.8	78	21.5	184	51.5	8	13	1.1	12	0	.0
42354	.3	100	.1	94	21.4	246*	56.9	15	4	.2	4	0	.2
42355	1.7	100	.7	85	25.5	188	64.9	7	10	.8	0	2	.0
42357	.1	0	.1	92	19.5	224*	24.3	0	8	.0	8	0	.0
42361	.8	100	.3	90	19.7	168	33.8	6	12	.4	12	1	.0
42365	.1	100	.1	100	16.6	191*	27.7	0	32	.1	35	0	.0
42366	4.9	100	1.5	86	26.4	348	80.3	9	8	2.5	8	0	.0
42367	.4	0	.3	79	20.3	301	41.2	13	17	.3	8	0	.0
42368	.9	0	.2	88	21.6	248*	55.2	9	13	.1	13	0	.0
42369	.5	98	.2	81	19.3	261	37.9	8	12	.3	12	0	.0
42370	.2	100	.1	79	11.0	149	30.2	3	17	.1	6	0	.0
42371	.7	100	.3	90	22.0	230*	33.2	6	18	.4	17	0	.0
42372	2.0	96	.7	82	22.0	260	55.3	6	15	1.0	15	0	.0
42374	.3	100	.1	80	20.4	202	38.4	4	17	.2	16	0	.0
42375	.2	100	.1	88	24.0	276*	46.6	6	3	.1	6	0	.2
42376	4.6	99	1.6	84	23.3	301	67.3	9	9	2.4	8	2	.2
42378	2.8	0	.8	91	24.4	207	60.4	9	9	.8	0	0	.0
EVANSVILLE													
42402	.5	100	.2	75	21.8	494	64.5	10	17	.2	14	0	.0
42403	.1	100	.1	85	21.1	243*	52.0	0	15	.1	13	0	.0
42404	2.8	100	1.1	81	23.7	295	51.4	8	16	1.4	14	2	.0
42406	2.9	91	.8	77	22.9	302	58.0	9	10	1.3	9	0	.0
42408	7.4	100	2.6	76	21.9	211	40.9	5	15	3.4	12	0	.1
42409	2.2	98	.9	80	21.4	193	54.4	8	14	1.0	13	0	.0
42410	2.3	70	.9	83	21.4	224	37.5	7	20	.8	16	0	.0
42411	1.7	98	.6	87	24.0	200	55.8	8	11	.8	8	0	.0
42413	1.5	100	.5	81	24.9	340	61.9	8	6	.7	6	0	.0

*=Estimated **1.0=883 lbs per person; 100++ indicates per capita toxic waste generation > than 100 times the U.S. average of 883 lbs per capita.

ZIP CODE MEASURES OF SIZE, LEVELS OF AFFLUENCE AND QUALITY OF LIFE

1=Population (th.); 2= % White; 3=Households (th.); 4=% Owner Occupied; 5=Mean Income Per Household (th.$); 6=Mean Monthly Rent ($); 7=Mean Home Value (th.$);
8=% under 5; 9=% 65 and over; 10=% White Males; 11=% White Males, 65+; 12=# Toxic Waste Sites; 13=Toxic Waste Relative to US(883 lbs.per capita)**.

KENTUCKY

EVANSVILLE

ZIPCODE	1	2	3	4	5	6	7	8	9	10	11	12	13
42420	32.8	92	12.3	66	26.0	304	72.2	8	12	14.5	9	4	1.6
42431	26.3	91	9.6	71	26.6	285	71.6	8	13	11.5	10	7	.8
42436	.7	100	.2	90	24.7	413	45.5	8	18	.4	20	0	.0
42437	9.5	70	2.5	73	26.0	264	66.4	6	9	3.3	9	3	.0
42440	1.2	96	.4	83	20.5	208	38.5	7	15	.6	13	0	1.5
42441	1.7	0	.5	77	21.7	249	52.4	5	14	.0	0	0	.0
42442	3.4	97	1.1	87	22.8	212	40.0	10	10	1.7	10	0	.0
42444	.3	100	.1	70	29.6	263	47.6	7	16	.2	18	0	.0
42445	11.4	93	4.3	74	20.5	216	53.6	6	19	5.0	16	0	.2
42450	5.3	85	2.1	75	20.6	214	40.1	8	18	2.2	15	0	.2
42451	1.0	100	.3	81	24.4	326	55.2	5	7	.5	9	0	.0
42452	2.2	100	.6	75	29.9	355	69.4	9	8	1.1	9	0	.0
42453	.7	0	.3	91	16.5	228	24.1	7	13	.0	0	0	.0
42455	2.9	99	1.0	76	22.6	232	47.8	7	17	1.4	13	0	.0
42456	1.6	100	.6	88	21.0	197	48.2	10	14	.8	12	0	.0
42457	.3	0	.1	59	22.9	423	54.0	7	6	.0	0	0	.2
42458	.8	100	.3	88	26.8	340	69.2	6	13	.4	12	0	.0
42459	5.2	94	2.0	78	25.2	231	53.9	8	16	2.4	12	1	.0
42460	.2	100	.1	100	21.0	241*	53.8	8	11	.1	5	0	.0
42461	1.9	95	.6	86	24.9	240	46.0	10	9	.9	8	1	.0
42462	1.5	94	.4	69	25.7	351	65.8	11	8	.7	8	0	.0
42463	.3	82	.1	91	21.5	83	31.4	8	10	.1	10	0	.0
42464	2.1	98	.7	79	22.6	267	53.9	8	12	1.1	12	0	.0

SOMERSET (NORTH)

ZIPCODE	1	2	3	4	5	6	7	8	9	10	11	12	13
42501	27.6	98	9.8	74	20.6	229	66.6	7	14	13.0	12	0	.4
42516	1.0	100	.3	84	12.1	239	31.2	7	9	.5	7	0	.0
42518	1.7	98	.6	82	17.1	173	54.6	6	9	.8	9	0	.0
42519	1.7	99	.6	79	16.8	188	56.9	8	11	.9	10	0	.0
42528	1.5	100	.5	84	14.8	97	40.2	8	11	.7	7	0	3.4
42532	.7	100	.2	89	16.2	186*	56.2	9	4	.4	6	0	.0
42533	1.0	0	.4	73	18.5	252	48.4	9	12	.3	4	1	1.0
42536	.2	100	.1	80	15.6	179*	62.9	5	21	.1	17	0	.0
42539	9.0	100	3.1	77	15.4	187	41.9	8	14	4.4	13	0	.2
42541	.6	0	.2	82	16.8	187	41.9	13	13	.0	0	0	.1
42544	3.2	0	1.1	84	24.0	141	67.5	6	12	.3	18	0	.0
42550	.2	100	.1	75	13.6	212	46.8	8	12	.1	0	0	.0
42553	3.2	100	1.2	76	14.8	205	52.0	8	14	.4	4	0	.0
42558	.9	100	.3	91	14.4	121	29.2	6	10	.9	4	0	.0
42564	.5	100	.1	68	18.1	276	68.3	9	9	.3	8	0	.0
42565	.5	0	.2	78	11.2	110	37.4	3	18	.0	0	0	.0
42566	.8	100	.3	70	12.3	191	25.0	11	13	.4	14	0	.0
42567	4.3	100	1.4	81	16.7	182	45.5	7	11	2.1	9	0	.0

SOMERSET (SOUTH)

ZIPCODE	1	2	3	4	5	6	7	8	9	10	11	12	13
42602	8.7	100	3.0	80	10.4	240	26.9	7	7	4.1	6	0	.0
42603	.6	100	.2	79	13.0	137	42.2	7	14	.4	13	0	.0
42606	.2	100	.1	64	11.3	172	32.0	11	5	.2	13	0	.0
42611	.5	100	.2	66	11.4	131*	84.7	14	12	.1	18	0	.0
42613	.6	100	.2	90	10.5	55	22.5	10	16	.3	20	0	.0

KENTUCKY

SOMERSET (SOUTH)

ZIPCODE	1	2	3	4	5	6	7	8	9	10	11	12	13
42628	.4	100	.1	67	14.5	167*	66.9	3	15	.2	11	0	.0
42629	4.3	98	1.5	83	17.2	179	45.7	6	17	2.1	14	0	.2
42631	.2	100	.2	90	11.9	137*	29.8	9	13	.1	14	0	.0
42633	14.0	98	4.8	75	14.8	171	46.8	8	13	6.7	12	2	.0
42634	.4	100	.1	79	9.3	251	23.9	16	8	.2	6	0	.0
42635	3.8	95	1.1	72	14.1	223	44.5	8	10	1.8	10	0	.0
42638	.5	100	.2	73	12.4	250	34.9	8	13	.2	5	0	.2
42640	9.2	0	3.3	71	11.6	131	25.5	8	12	.1	13	0	.0
42643	1.4	100	.4	72	11.0	192	20.5	9	14	.7	9	0	.0
42647	4.1	100	1.2	78	15.3	218	43.4	9	10	2.1	10	0	.0
42649	1.2	95	.4	86	12.7	215	28.4	9	12	.6	14	0	.0
42653	3.4	100	1.2	69	15.5	217	46.3	9	11	1.6	9	0	.0
42655	.4	100	.1	78	19.8	218	32.1	12	11	.2	5	0	.0

ELIZABETHTOWN

ZIPCODE	1	2	3	4	5	6	7	8	9	10	11	12	13
42701	28.4	94	10.0	75	24.5	254	75.4	8	10	12.9	9	6	.6
42711	.3	0	.1	94	13.4	154*	26.4	2	17	.0	0	0	.0
42712	1.7	0	.5	86	16.7	126	36.7	11	13	.0	0	0	.0
42713	1.8	95	.6	79	15.4	176	34.6	6	10	.9	10	0	.0
42714	.7	100	.3	81	11.8	202	26.9	11	23	.3	25	0	.0
42715	.4	100	.4	85	15.3	176*	17.8	3	24	.2	25	0	.0
42716	1.3	100	.5	80	18.4	248	45.5	6	16	.7	14	0	.0
42717	4.7	93	1.7	70	16.4	152	47.2	7	15	2.1	14	1	.1
42718	19.3	94	6.9	75	20.9	230	64.3	9	12	8.7	11	0	.2
42721	3.4	0	1.2	82	15.5	205	36.2	7	16	.0	0	0	.0
42722	.7	0	.3	80	15.1	138	39.9	6	14	.0	0	0	.0
42723	.7	100	.3	78	16.8	132	29.1	3	6	.4	7	0	.0
42724	4.0	97	1.3	80	20.2	257	49.2	8	8	1.9	6	0	.0
42726	3.5	0	1.2	84	17.0	170	42.8	9	13	.0	0	0	.0
42728	11.1	95	4.1	81	17.5	191	50.2	6	16	5.1	15	0	.2
42729	1.0	100	.3	85	17.1	140	44.6	10	13	.5	15	0	.0
42730	.3	100	.1	64	19.4	223*	13.1	7	7	.1	6	0	.0
42731	.3	100	.5	69	15.0	101	135.6	4	12	.2	13	0	.1
42732	1.6	0	.5	94	21.8	211*	44.4	9	11	.0	0	0	.0
42733	1.2	0	.4	83	16.6	69	50.4	6	9	.0	0	0	.0
42735	.3	100	.1	95	16.4	188*	67.1	11	15	.1	7	0	.0
42736	1.6	97	.5	88	16.8	193*	50.3	8	11	.8	8	0	.0
42740	1.4	93	.5	79	26.2	245	63.5	9	12	.8	11	0	.0
42741	.6	93	.2	88	18.4	211*	38.9	7	14	.3	14	0	.0
42743	9.2	96	3.4	80	17.5	173	50.1	7	16	4.3	14	1	.5
42746	1.6	95	.6	75	34.4	90	46.0	6	12	.8	8	0	.0
42748	7.2	93	2.7	80	20.0	217	59.7	6	15	3.3	13	1	.0
42749	4.5	85	1.7	73	16.3	189	45.2	8	13	1.8	12	0	.1
42752	1.0	100	.3	91	15.5	179*	37.4	3	16	.5	16	0	.0
42753	.7	100	.2	85	16.2	80	32.5	10	6	.3	6	0	.0
42754	11.6	100	4.1	82	19.1	227	55.2	7	13	5.6	12	0	.3
42757	2.4	98	.9	81	15.3	94	43.8	7	19	1.1	19	0	.3
42758	.2	100	.1	100	27.4	315*	44.8	8	18	.1	32	0	.0

*=Estimated **1.0=883 lbs per person; 100++ indicates per capita toxic waste generation > than 100 times the U.S. average of 883 lbs per capita.

ZIP CODE MEASURES OF SIZE, LEVELS OF AFFLUENCE AND QUALITY OF LIFE

1=Population (th.); 2= % White; 3=Households (th.); 4=% Owner Occupied; 5=Mean Income Per Household (th.$); 6=Mean Monthly Rent ($); 7=Mean Home Value (th.$); 8=% under 5; 9=% 65 and over; 10=White Males (th.); 11=% White Males, 65+; 12=# Toxic Waste Sites; 13=Toxic Waste Relative to US(883 lbs.per capita)**.

KENTUCKY

ELIZABETHTOWN

ZIPCODE	1	2	3	4	5	6	7	8	9	10	11	12	13
42759	.2	0	.1	78	13.5	155*	41.9	6	20	.0	0	0	.0
42761	.6	100	.2	73	13.0	197	36.8	9	8	.3	6	0	.0
42762	.2	100	.1	89	18.9	217*	24.2	0	19	.1	25	1	2.2
42764	.5	92	.2	88	12.4	140	38.8	5	12	.2	11	0	.0
42765	4.2	92	1.5	73	18.5	154	50.5	7	14	1.9	12	0	.0
42768	.2	100	.1	59	13.2	152*	17.0	11	17	.1	17	0	.0
42772	.3	63	.1	77	14.0	171	29.3	9	10	.1	0	0	.0
42776	2.3		.8	79	16.4	194	52.1	7	14	.0	0	0	.4
42782	.9	0	.3	82	15.4	197	56.2	9	14	.1	18	0	.0
42783	.2	100	.8	48	13.8	159*	47.0	14	15	.1	18	0	.0
42784	2.2	98	.8	88	17.2	236	44.6	10	18	1.1	0	0	.0
42788	.5	100	.2	74	17.7	157	50.3	8	10	.3	12	0	.0

LOUISIANA

NEW ORLEANS

ZIPCODE	1	2	3	4	5	6	7	8	9	10	11	12	13
70001	43.9	95	17.7	53	28.2	421	107.4	7	10	19.9	8	2	.0
70002	39.3	96	15.3	51	35.4	442	163.4	5	7	18.1	6	1	.0
70003	50.7	89	16.4	77	34.5	412	111.8	8	6	22.2	5	0	.0
70005	28.8	98	12.0	61	33.0	430	137.4	5	15	13.3	13	0	.0
70030	3.8	94	1.2	87	25.8	189	73.0	10	6	1.8	6	0	.0
70031	1.2	73	.3	86	29.6	422	81.1	7	7	.4	6	0	.2
70032	10.3	99	3.6	80	29.4	336	88.0	4	14	4.8	11	0	.0
70036	1.1	79	.3	81	22.4	229	54.5	7	8	.4	11	0	8.3
70037	9.9	91	2.8	62	29.5	367	118.0	9	4	4.6	3	5	.0
70038	.6	70	.2	80	26.6	137	29.2	11	8	.2	11	3	.0
70039	2.8	40	.8	70	25.1	199	78.7	14	6	.6	12	1	7.9
70040	1.2	72	.4	86	23.2	270	76.9	10	6	.4	5	0	.0
70041	5.2	84	1.6	76	26.7	302	72.3	10	6	2.3	5	0	.0
70042	.4	0	.1	60	11.7	167	25.1	9	5	.0	0	0	.4
70043	33.6	99	11.1	72	28.7	382	101.5	8	6	16.2	5	0	1.0
70046	1.4	0	.3	88	19.8	53	58.5	9	5	.6	4	1	.0
70047	7.1	83	2.1	82	32.9	343	106.6	9	7	3.0	7	0	.9
70049	3.1	0	.7	76	21.6	219	61.3	7	9	.0	9	0	.2
70050	1.2	69	.4	77	21.2	147	70.1	10	8	.4	4	1	.0
70051	2.7	34	.8	72	19.9	133	66.2	8	8	.4	15	3	17.9
70052	3.4	79	1.0	83	34.1	223	89.6	8	6	1.3	6	3	41.1
70053	55.7	84	19.1	58	29.8	363	104.5	8	5	23.2	5	6	2.4
70057	3.2	60	1.0	65	29.0	314	94.3	12	5	1.0	4	6	100++
70058	27.6	72	9.2	57	28.4	370	95.7	10	4	10.1	4	4	1.5
70062	68.1	83	21.4	65	31.0	411	114.4	8	10	28.0	3	3	.1
70066	2.0	10	.6	72	13.3	328	43.4	10	10	.1	0	0	.8
70067	18.2	98	5.4	77	20.2	222	68.1	11	5	7.4	4	6	.0
70068	9.5	80	3.0	80	33.8	320	106.1	11	5	4.6	4	4	10.1
70070	4.7	95	1.4	77	36.9	375	112.7	9	6	1.2	2	1	3.5
70071	52.9	51	15.6	76	26.1	187	83.8	11	5	17.7	7	2	.0
70072	5.4	68	1.6	76	27.2	290	89.6	11	5	2.5	4	4	2.1
70075	5.4	93	1.6	79	24.8	294	88.1	16	5	2.5	4	2	2.7
70076	.5	9	.2	70	18.8	102	86.9	14	6	.2	36	0	.0
70078	1.1	36	.3	74	22.8	213	68.7	7	9	.4	13	6	.0
70079	4.4	77	1.4	76	29.0	256	86.6	12	9	1.7	10	6	46.1
70080	1.3	89	.5	82	22.8	256	64.5	9	9	.6	9	1	.0
70083	4.5	60	1.3	80	23.2	186	63.7	10	9	1.4	11	9	3.4
70084	2.1	54	.7	87	25.9	222	76.4	9	6	.6	9	0	.2
70085	6.7	92	2.0	70	22.2	218	71.1	14	8	3.0	6	13	.6
70086	2.7	27	1.0	74	23.0	214	74.8	9	9	.4	9	0	9.0
70087	1.7	9	.6	85	20.8	232	67.1	9	9	.1	9	2	2.7
70090	7.2	0	2.0	87	29.1	154	76.7	5	5	.8	5	0	.0
70091	1.7	93	.5	83	26.4	185	61.6	12	5	.8	5	3	7.5
70092	8.2	80	2.3	83	24.1	280	64.8	5	5	3.3	4	4	.0
70094	38.7	66	11.5	69	23.0	280	64.8	10	5	12.6	5	0	2.1

NEW ORLEANS

ZIPCODE	1	2	3	4	5	6	7	8	9	10	11	12	13
70112	8.5	29	3.7	5	11.0	196	77.9	8	16	1.2	22	0	1.8
70113	18.0	3	7.1	11	11.4	223	54.6	9	15	.3	6	2	.0
70114	58.5	54	20.0	49	27.7	307	112.7	9	5	15.7	6	2	.2

*=Estimated **1.0=883 lbs per person; 100++ indicates per capita toxic waste generation > than 100 times the U.S. average of 883 lbs per capita.

ZIP CODE MEASURES OF SIZE, LEVELS OF AFFLUENCE AND QUALITY OF LIFE

1=Population (th.); 2= % White; 3=Households (th.); 4=% Owner Occupied; 5=Mean Income Per Household (th.$); 6=Mean Monthly Rent ($)*; 7=Mean Home Value (th.$)*;
8=% under 5; 9=% 65 and over; 10=White Males (th.); 11=% White Males, 65+; 12=# Toxic Waste Sites; 13=Toxic Waste Relative to US(883 lbs.per capita)**.

LOUISIANA

NEW ORLEANS

ZIP CODE	1	2	3	4	5	6	7	8	9	10	11	12	13
70115	51.7	45	21.6	30	23.7	325	156.2	7	15	10.7	13	0	.0
70116	22.6	29	10.5	19	17.2	303	82.9	7	13	3.9	7	0	.0
70117	70.0	20	23.4	40	16.1	277	59.1	10	10	6.6	18	2	.1
70118	47.2	49	17.1	41	26.5	356	142.4	6	12	11.1	11	0	.0
70119	54.0	41	21.8	30	18.2	297	76.2	6	16	10.4	18	0	.8
70121	15.1	84	6.4	59	23.0	319	81.0	6	19	6.2	16	1	.2
70122	51.7	50	19.0	58	26.4	300	102.5	6	14	11.6	19	1	.1
70123	28.7	93	9.9	75	34.8	378	126.4	7	8	13.2	7	0	.1
70124	24.7	99	10.5	67	37.6	477	149.3	4	22	11.0	17	0	.1
70125	30.6	28	11.7	30	20.2	277	129.5	9	14	3.9	17	0	.0
70126	50.8	34	15.7	50	24.9	302	94.9	9	7	8.5	9	2	.0
70127	26.2	68	9.4	55	29.8	422	104.7	8	5	8.9	6	0	.0
70128	10.2	62	3.1	85	34.9	421	123.7	10	5	3.2	4	0	.0
70129	11.9	39	3.4	44	24.0	348	101.5	13	5	2.3	7	0	.0
70130	20.6	46	9.1	15	21.7	282	170.8	9	12	4.6	16	1	2.7
70131	.3	84	.1	46	13.5	205	41.6	5	7	.1	9	0	.4

THIBODAUX

ZIP CODE	1	2	3	4	5	6	7	8	9	10	11	12	13
70301	35.8	81	11.0	66	29.0	291	93.3	8	8	14.3	7	1	1.8
70339	4.8	0	1.4	89	23.2	158	60.8	12	6	.0	0	0	.6
70340	2.5	78	.7	71	32.6	404	87.0	13	3	1.1	0	0	.2
70341	3.7	41	1.0	79	22.9	149	73.5	8	10	.8	14	0	2.6
70342	4.4	88	1.5	63	22.8	352	99.9	9	3	1.9	6	0	.1
70343	3.6	98	1.0	88	30.1	266	91.7	9	9	1.7	4	0	.5
70344	6.6	91	1.8	89	24.1	290	62.5	12	4	1.4	1	1	.5
70345	10.6	95	3.4	84	29.4	290	85.2	10	5	3.1	6	0	.0
70346	11.5	48	3.5	63	23.3	196	71.9	10	6	5.1	10	0	.0
70352	.2	2	.1	66	30.2	184	62.8	8	10	.0	2	0	.0
70353	.2	39	.1	59	35.6	120	56.9	14	7	.0	10	0	10.7
70354	5.1	100	1.5	87	26.8	285	74.0	8	6	2.5	5	0	.0
70355	.3	100	.1	61	16.0	183*	72.1	8	10	.3	11	0	.0
70356	3.0	43	.9	76	21.9	253	60.5	9	7	.6	6	0	.2
70357	3.4	90	1.1	75	23.3	236	59.1	8	8	1.5	10	0	.0
70358	2.1	97	.7	62	23.2	301	66.9	9	9	1.1	6	0	5.8
70359	4.9	72	1.4	74	26.6	352	95.7	12	9	1.8	3	0	.1
70360	68.9	82	22.1	68	30.4	340	97.7	10	7	28.3	5	5	.3
70371	.4	100	.1	90	21.4	200	51.0	12	10	.9	7	0	.0
70372	2.3	76	.7	82	26.4	221	85.0	10	11	.9	5	0	.3
70373	2.8	94	.9	74	27.8	235	82.6	8	7	1.3	6	2	1.7
70374	8.1	94	2.6	78	27.5	240	79.6	8	8	3.7	7	1	1.5
70375	.7	100	.1	73	24.9	238	61.1	9	8	.4	5	0	.0
70377	4.3	80	1.2	85	26.1	271	69.5	9	9	1.8	5	0	1.5
70380	27.2	85	8.8	64	32.1	332	100.3	9	11	11.6	5	1	.0
70390	7.2	64	2.2	72	22.0	269	64.7	11	9	2.4	9	0	1.4
70391	1.4	0	.3	79	23.3	210	66.3	12	10	.0	0	0	.0
70392	5.9	64	1.9	64	30.4	297	105.2	10	10	2.0	8	0	.4
70393	1.3	59	.4	81	29.0	167	73.8	6	8	.4	5	0	.0
70394	13.2	80	4.0	75	27.5	242	79.0	10	8	5.2	7	1	.0
70395	3.5	82	1.1	79	31.1	303	94.7	12	6	1.6	9	0	.0
70397	1.8	87	.5	92	21.8	185	62.6	13	6	.5	5	0	.0

LOUISIANA

HAMMOND

ZIP CODE	1	2	3	4	5	6	7	8	9	10	11	12	13
70401	33.2	70	10.3	64	22.2	255	85.2	9	8	11.4	7	1	.0
70420	2.0	88	.8	79	22.3	249	79.1	9	11	1.0	11	0	.0
70422	11.5	57	3.7	76	19.0	187	62.2	9	12	3.1	11	0	.1
70426	2.1	0	.6	75	17.8	214	48.8	10	14	.0	0	0	.0
70427	23.1	73	8.6	72	20.1	202	52.2	8	14	8.0	11	0	.5
70431	2.1	100	.8	88	25.7	353	95.1	8	12	1.1	10	0	.4
70433	21.9	85	7.1	72	31.4	303	133.9	8	10	9.1	8	2	2.4
70436	.4	28	.4	72	30.6	198	61.3	11	11	.1	0	0	.2
70437	4.1	81	1.3	83	32.7	226	89.5	9	11	1.7	7	0	.0
70438	13.8	69	4.6	78	18.9	207	56.1	9	11	4.7	10	2	.0
70441	4.8	0	1.5	79	17.8	245	57.5	10	12	.2	9	0	.1
70442	.3	100	.1	71	18.9	212	65.9	14	14	.2	8	0	.1
70443	7.5	76	2.1	81	21.8	205	63.6	10	11	2.8	14	0	.0
70444	9.0	62	2.9	80	19.5	187	49.5	9	14	2.8	8	0	.3
70445	6.3	73	2.1	87	26.3	224	94.9	10	10	2.4	11	1	.0
70446	2.0	90	.8	85	23.1	280	76.1	11	11	.9	9	0	.0
70447	2.2	78	.8	78	20.1	261	78.8	11	13	.9	9	0	.0
70448	10.9	90	3.5	77	33.7	389	139.1	8	9	4.9	7	1	1.4
70449	2.1	92	.7	90	21.5	227	51.6	9	11	1.0	10	1	.0
70450	2.4	66	.8	81	20.5	261	52.1	8	11	.8	8	0	.0
70451	.9	51	.3	62	24.0	196	96.5	12	15	.2	8	0	.3
70452	8.1	94	2.5	85	27.0	251	96.5	9	6	3.7	6	1	.3
70453	.3	72	.1	75	13.2	281	50.7	12	10	.1	19	0	.0
70454	13.7	78	4.4	77	21.6	216	69.8	10	11	5.2	10	2	.0
70455	.7	0	.3	87	17.4	151	64.0	5	20	.0	2	0	.0
70456	3.4	51	1.1	76	18.5	220	53.6	8	9	.9	8	0	.0
70458	51.7	88	16.3	81	32.4	407	109.5	9	5	22.8	4	3	.1
70459	1.0	89	.4	76	20.3	280	66.5	11	14	.4	10	0	.0
70462	3.9	76	1.3	84	20.0	227	66.5	9	7	1.0	8	0	.0
70463	.4	82	.2	75	20.4	246	51.2	10	13	.8	8	0	.0
70464	.3	100	.1	74	33.4	384*	48.0	3	4	.2	4	0	.0
70465	.9	39	.3	67	15.6	148	44.1	9	5	.2	4	0	3.9
70466	3.3	86	1.1	80	20.4	225	73.9	10	5	1.4	8	0	.0
70467	2.7	74	.9	89	18.0	178	56.1	11	12	1.0	13	0	.0

LAFAYETTE

ZIP CODE	1	2	3	4	5	6	7	8	9	10	11	12	13
70501	41.1	48	13.1	57	21.5	299	74.6	8	10	9.6	9	0	.4
70502	.3	83	.1	76	25.5	243	42.1	15	6	.2	8	0	8.6
70503	21.4	97	7.3	70	45.9	477	163.4	6	5	10.4	4	4	.0
70504	.4	88	.4	80	15.8	102	56.3*	2	4	.2	5	0	.2
70505	5.5	88	1.7	80	30.8	318	116.4	9	5	2.4	5	1	1.5
70506	28.8	91	11.2	56	32.6	445	117.8	9	6	13.0	5	1	.0
70507	7.5	89	2.3	77	35.3	438	125.0	10	2	3.4	4	0	.0
70508	11.3	95	3.6	78	42.4	480	162.8	11	2	5.4	2	0	.0
70510	23.4	81	7.9	70	24.9	250	69.8	10	10	9.4	8	5	.0
70512	8.8	77	2.7	79	20.4	188	66.5	9	10	3.4	9	0	.4
70513	.6	93	.2	24	29.0	157	86.0	8	9	.3	10	0	.0
70514	2.8	0	.8	71	26.3	246	75.0	10	8	1.4	7	1	6.1
70515	3.3	84	1.1	78	20.2	224	39.0	12	6	1.4	13	1	.3
70516	1.3	82	.4	66	19.3	177	71.1	9	6	.5	5	0	.0

*=Estimated **1.0=883 lbs per person; 100++ indicates per capita toxic waste generation > than 100 times the U.S. average of 883 lbs per capita.

ZIP CODE MEASURES OF SIZE, LEVELS OF AFFLUENCE AND QUALITY OF LIFE

1=Population (th.); 2= % White; 3=Households (th.); 4=% Owner Occupied; 5=Mean Income Per Household ($); 6=Mean Monthly Rent ($); 7=Mean Home Value (th.$); 8=% under 5; 9=% 65 and over; 10=% White Males, 11=% White Males; 12=# Toxic Waste Sites; 13=Toxic Waste Relative to US(883 lbs.per capita)**.

LOUISIANA

LAFAYETTE

ZIPCODE	1	2	3	4	5	6	7	8	9	10	11	12	13
70517	16.2	70	5.0	78	22.8	219	71.1	10	8	5.7	8	0	.3
70518	7.5	83	2.4	84	29.0	317	110.9	9	6	3.1	6	0	.3
70519	.5	55	.2	72	26.8	213	77.6	7	14	.2	23	1	.0
70520	9.0	78	2.8	81	24.9	264	103.4	10	6	3.5	5	0	.0
70521	.8	94	.3	87	22.7	346	81.2	8	12	.4	10	0	.0
70522	1.0	87	.3	71	32.1	221	97.6	12	10	.7	7	0	.0
70523	1.8	36	.5	71	18.0	203	39.7	13	7	.3	14	0	.0
70524	.6	55	.2	65	16.3	310	46.8	13	7	.2	11	0	.0
70525	11.0	78	3.4	73	20.9	197	59.0	10	11	4.0	10	1	.3
70526	20.6	78	6.8	65	23.4	230	72.1	10	10	7.7	10	3	.2
70528	3.2	89	1.0	77	23.7	274	64.4	8	9	1.4	8	0	.0
70529	5.9	85	1.9	75	26.8	322	94.3	9	6	2.6	6	0	.0
70531	1.0	0	.3	85	24.9	201	52.9	9	5	.9	0	1	3.5
70532	2.8	68	1.0	77	21.4	223	40.2	8	12	.9	12	0	.0
70533	5.9	93	1.8	79	26.3	205	71.2	9	12	2.6	10	2	.0
70534	.7	0	.2	73	26.9	181	56.1	11	7	.0	0	0	.0
70535	19.6	78	6.5	71	22.8	252	60.3	11	10	7.5	9	0	.1
70537	.8	0	.3	87	22.0	252*	31.3	11	7	.0	0	0	.0
70538	16.9	57	5.2	64	25.3	268	73.6	9	10	4.7	11	1	.2
70540	.4	29	.1	32	31.7	178	120.9	4	2	.1	11	0	6.2
70541	1.3	42	.4	80	15.9	199	52.3	6	15	.2	20	0	.0
70542	3.7	94	1.3	83	25.5	263	60.6	10	11	1.7	10	0	.0
70543	3.1	93	1.0	82	27.8	211	57.3	9	9	1.4	11	1	.0
70544	12.1	48	3.5	75	25.2	229	66.7	9	8	2.9	7	0	.3
70546	16.5	80	5.3	71	24.7	252	70.2	11	9	6.5	10	3	1.6
70548	9.3	92	3.3	76	20.7	233	61.7	7	15	4.2	13	4	.0
70549	4.7	91	1.6	68	21.5	221	53.1	10	11	2.1	10	0	.0
70550	.9	44	.3	77	20.3	168	54.1	13	4	.2	5	0	.0
70551	.9	76	.3	74	19.6	201	58.9	8	10	.3	10	0	.3
70552	2.3	78	.6	76	27.1	188	78.7	9	12	1.0	9	0	.3
70554	5.0	77	1.8	64	18.1	203	51.4	7	11	1.9	11	0	.0
70555	3.7	84	1.3	85	27.6	288	105.8	7	12	1.5	11	1	.4
70556	.5	83	.3	69	20.5	168	50.4	9	12	.3	10	0	.0
70557	.5	0	.1	88	22.0	225	39.5	9	9	.0	3	0	.0
70558	.7	0	.3	67	33.2	381	94.2	16	9	.1	8	0	.0
70559	2.0	99	.6	85	19.8	170	45.4	10	11	1.0	9	0	.0
70560	49.3	75	15.6	70	28.8	295	85.6	9	8	18.3	7	2	3.6
70569	.5	87	.1	87	28.3	209	65.4	9	5	.2	10	0	.0
70570	37.2	51	12.0	69	20.5	225	67.4	9	11	9.2	10	3	1.3
70575	1.0	100	.1	79	26.6	344	87.0	9	9	.1	8	0	.0
70576	1.0	100	.4	83	20.7	166	48.9	9	11	.5	11	0	.0
70577	4.6	80	1.4	73	21.5	210	53.9	10	8	1.8	9	0	.0
70578	13.9	79	4.3	68	25.1	239	71.1	10	11	5.3	10	1	.4
70580	.2	100	.1	83	17.4	159	44.6	7	16	.1	24	0	.0
70581	.9	70	.3	81	25.5	267	60.5	10	9	5.3	7	0	.0
70582	17.6	61	5.1	77	23.8	204	72.5	10	8	.6	7	0	.0
70583	6.3	90	2.1	79	25.9	326	89.8	9	9	2.8	6	0	.0
70584	5.4	69	1.6	78	24.0	243	82.9	8	9	1.8	8	0	.0
70585	.6	100	.2	83	19.9	198	43.0	7	11	1.3	11	0	.0

LOUISIANA

LAFAYETTE

ZIPCODE	1	2	3	4	5	6	7	8	9	10	11	12	13
70586	20.7	72	6.9	68	18.4	198	51.2	10	12	7.3	11	1	.1
70589	3.5	60	1.1	73	17.5	142	50.8	9	15	1.1	12	0	.0
70591	5.1	78	1.6	73	25.5	206	64.5	10	11	1.9	9	0	.0
70592	4.4	86	1.4	77	29.2	285	106.5	9	8	1.9	7	0	.0

LAKE CHARLES

ZIPCODE	1	2	3	4	5	6	7	8	9	10	11	12	13
70601	66.5	58	23.1	64	25.4	302	76.2	9	10	18.7	10	4	13.3
70602	.2	71	.1	85	34.2	593	140.5	8	17	.1	7	5	100++
70605	38.3	91	12.9	74	34.1	406	109.8	8	6	17.3	5	0	.0
70606	.3	0	.1	89	26.9	542	96.1	11	4	.0	8	0	.0
70630	1.1	95	.3	69	29.1	181	81.1	7	13	.5	8	0	13.1
70631	3.9	89	1.2	80	28.2	307	58.2	11	7	1.8	6	0	.0
70632	.9	93	.3	85	31.3	258	119.5	9	11	.4	5	0	.0
70633	8.9	79	2.7	79	25.8	227	55.1	8	11	3.7	9	2	1.0
70634	21.9	82	7.3	76	24.8	254	68.3	9	10	8.8	9	2	2.6
70637	.4	100	.2	85	13.6	156*	58.1*	13	16	.4	15	0	2.8
70638	.9	94	.3	86	24.6	262	54.3	7	14	.4	10	0	.0
70639	.7	0	.2	89	26.9	309*	29.4	11	13	.0	7	0	.1
70640	.8	63	.3	77	24.3	172	32.6	12	7	.3	7	0	.3
70641	.2	100	.1	100	34.0	391*	121.2*	4	25	.1	23	1	.2
70643	1.0	96	.3	85	38.9	222	71.8	8	9	.4	11	1	.1
70644	.3	100	.1	66	24.0	135	88.4	10	8	.1	3	0	.0
70645	1.7	99	.6	81	24.2	243	77.5	12	11	.9	9	0	.0
70646	.6	100	.6	91	19.8	139	49.2	9	7	.3	7	0	.0
70647	5.6	85	1.7	79	25.9	289	67.1	9	8	2.5	8	0	.3
70648	5.3	83	1.9	81	22.6	170	55.4	9	11	2.1	10	0	1.6
70650	.3	100	.1	87	25.8	143	54.7	4	15	.1	17	0	.0
70652	1.1	87	.1	83	27.9	318	47.5	10	9	.5	9	0	.0
70653	3.0	87	1.1	83	21.7	128	36.3	12	12	1.2	10	0	.0
70654	.3	100	.1	84	15.1	144	34.1	5	17	.2	21	0	.0
70655	2.8	67	1.4	79	20.3	139	46.2	7	12	.9	16	0	.0
70656	4.4	97	.6	83	19.0	278	33.5	10	10	2.1	9	0	.0
70657	2.2	0	.6	85	26.5	267	68.6	10	5	.0	6	0	.0
70658	.8	100	.3	87	28.2	299	47.2	9	14	.4	12	0	.0
70659	1.5	97	.5	68	21.6	259	55.3	10	5	.9	9	0	.0
70660	1.1	100	.3	88	20.0	127	41.1	11	11	.6	10	0	.0
70661	2.6	93	.9	82	20.5	148	37.6	8	10	1.1	9	1	.0
70662	.3	0	.1	94	20.0	230*	28.3	11	7	.0	9	0	.0
70663	30.9	95	10.2	78	30.7	329	86.9	9	8	14.5	7	6	.9
70669	6.5	85	3.4	82	28.8	303	76.3	9	7	2.9	9	4	10.4

BATON ROUGE

ZIPCODE	1	2	3	4	5	6	7	8	9	10	11	12	13
70710	1.9	84	.5	79	29.5	251	91.3	10	4	.8	3	1	.0
70711	2.9	82	1.0	72	19.1	200	65.9	8	8	1.1	9	0	17.3
70712	5.1	0	.1	21	16.4	61	56.9	1	0	.0	0	0	.0
70714	18.5	85	5.4	84	31.9	374	92.4	9	5	7.9	5	0	.0
70715	1.8	38	.6	59	17.2	178	46.2	9	15	.3	16	1	.0
70716	1.3	15	.4	76	14.6	181	83.1	10	9	.1	9	1	.0
70717	.2	76	.1	61	14.6	279	87.3	10	14	.1	9	0	.0
70718	.2	0	.1	88	25.2	290*	86.3	8	23	.0	23	0	.0

*=Estimated **1.0=883 lbs per person; 100 indicates per capita toxic waste generation > than 100 times the U.S. average of 883 lbs per capita.

103001

ZIP CODE MEASURES OF SIZE, LEVELS OF AFFLUENCE AND QUALITY OF LIFE

1=Population (th.); 2= % White; 3=Households (th.); 4=% Owner Occupied; 5=Mean Income Per Household (th.$); 6=Mean Monthly Rent ($)*; 7=Mean Home Value (th.$)*;
8=% under 5; 9=% 65 and over; 10=White Males (th.); 11=% White Males, 65+; 12=# Toxic Waste Sites; 13=Toxic Waste Relative to US(883 lbs.per capital**.

LOUISIANA

BATON ROUGE

ZIPCODE	1	2	3	4	5	6	7	8	9	10	11	12	13
70719	3.4	58	1.0	84	29.9	219	79.2	9	7	1.0	6	0	.1
70720	.5	81	.1	60	28.1	281	78.2	15	5	.2	7	0	.0
70721	.8	26	.2	71	28.0	241	47.7	6	20	.1	21	0	51.9
70722	5.3	0	1.5		21.6	207	68.8	9	11	.0	0	0	.0
70723	2.4	33	.7	69	21.6	136	57.1	11	11	.4	15	1	30.1
70725	1.1	29	.3	76	21.8	254	60.5	7	7	.2	10	2	.0
70726	30.2	93	9.4	86	27.4	319	98.3	10	7	13.8	5	3	.0
70728	.5	0	.2	88	40.7	304	88.1	9	21	.0	5	0	.0
70729	.8	67	.2	76	20.8	219	90.8	10	12	.3	4	1	.0
70730	2.7	53	.7	80	24.8	259	73.0	10	9	.8	8	0	.0
70733	1.1	86	.3	79	24.5	335	78.9	12	6	.4	7	0	.0
70734	.8	57	.3	91	27.8	56	67.6	10	9	.2	0	0	.0
70736	1.3	57	.4	76	23.8	313	82.5	11	8	.3	3	10	100++
70737	.5	54	.2	73	20.2	244	57.4	8	8	.1	17	0	.0
70739	20.7	87	6.4	81	29.6	316	86.5	9	6	9.1	5	3	.0
70740	7.5	95	2.1	92	37.2	307	142.3	8	4	3.6	3	0	.0
70742	1.1	70	.3	82	26.9	142	63.3	10	7	.4	5	0	.0
70743	.5	25	.1	65	17.4	223	88.8	14	8	.0	0	0	.0
70744	.2	100	.1	100	33.6	386*	106.5	11	8	.1	8	0	.1
70746	2.9	97	.9	87	21.1	279	66.0	9	8	1.5	6	0	.0
70747	.1	0	.1	46	12.7	31	45.1*27	24	.0	0	0	.0	
70748	7.4	55	1.7	73	21.9	214	59.5	6	13	2.1	11	0	.4
70749	1.4	95	.5	80	22.4	368	82.3	9	11	.7	7	0	.0
70750	.5	84	.2	75	17.6	127	63.6	9	6	.4	16	0	.0
70751	.7	35	.2	77	13.9	180	46.8	7	13	.1	18	0	.0
70752	.6	65	.2	71	21.7	114	90.7	7	10	.2	9	0	1.0
70753	1.5	53	.5	65	17.2	183	60.7	8	8	.4	7	0	.0
70754	5.2	98	1.6	84	25.0	257	70.3	10	6	2.7	8	0	.0
70755	1.8	93	.6	84	27.5	205	82.1	7	10	.8	7	0	.0
70756	.5	53	.2	78	31.7	148	68.7	9	12	.1	13	1	.0
70757	2.4	40	.8	76	20.3	204	56.9	13	11	.5	13	3	.0
70759	1.7	71	.6	79	21.1	123	55.4	6	15	.6	12	0	.0
70760	7.9	0	2.4	69	20.0	219	68.9	8	11	.0	0	1	.0
70761	.9	43	.3	62	18.3	210	55.7	8	14	.2	12	0	.0
70762	.9	78	.3	55	28.8	357	81.9	13	15	.4	14	0	.0
70763	1.7	85	.5	87	27.4	111	90.1	10	6	.7	4	0	.0
70764	17.9	59	5.6	71	25.2	241	73.0	8	10	5.2	8	4	60.5
70767	12.7	55	3.9	72	25.6	240	74.0	8	9	3.6	7	7	1.1
70769	7.8	87	2.4	86	28.7	312	94.8	11	8	3.3	6	6	.4
70770	3.4	90	.9	94	33.7	454	105.5	12	5	1.6	19	0	.0
70772	.9	43	.3	82	20.1	142	63.2	9	13	.2	11	0	.0
70773	.9	30	.3	45	58.2	195	43.8	6	13	.0	16	3	.0
70774	4.2	100	1.2	88	27.8	427	86.9	11	5	2.1	4	0	.0
70775	4.7	50	1.4	66	28.8	252	87.3	9	12	.8	8	0	.4
70776	2.1	0	.4	80	35.8	193	66.7	8	7	.0	0	3	100++
70777	3.5	70	1.1	89	26.3	214	81.1	10	6	1.2	6	0	.2
70778	2.0	78	.6	87	27.2	217	69.0	8	10	.7	9	0	.0
70780	1.1	51	.4	71	24.3	146	73.7	8	9	.3	6	0	.0

LOUISIANA

BATON ROUGE

ZIPCODE	1	2	3	4	5	6	7	8	9	10	11	12	13
70781	.4	75	.1	87	26.0	206	57.9	8	5	.1	4	1	.0
70782	.5	70	.1	38	10.5	200	152.7	10	6	.2	9	0	.0
70783	2.4	67	.2	81	25.0	146	92.6	14		.8	10	0	.0
70784	.2	55	.1	71	17.9	206*	21.9	7	23	.1	38	0	.0
70785	7.9	93	2.5	82	26.0	262	86.8	10	8	3.6	5	1	.0
70786	.7	92	.2	94	36.2	324	101.6	7	8	.4	8	0	.0
70787	.5	8	.1	58	14.2	242	86.4	4	15	.0	0	0	.0
70788	4.6	49	1.4	52	19.3	210	72.1	9	13	1.0	18	1	.0
70789	.9	29	.3	76	17.4	138	50.4	11	17	.1	9	0	.0
70791	14.1	63	4.2	81	28.9	282	87.6	10	8	4.5	7	2	.8

BATON ROUGE

ZIPCODE	1	2	3	4	5	6	7	8	9	10	11	12	13
70802	46.0	17	16.9	39	15.3	246	51.1	9	10	4.6	6	1	.1
70805	39.1	64	14.0	58	23.3	313	63.3	10	8	12.3	10	4	1.8
70806	27.4	76	12.3	43	28.1	355	123.1	6	15	9.6	12	1	.0
70807	26.5	5	7.7	62	20.2	247	64.4	10	6	.8	7	6	2.4
70808	32.7	86	13.3	54	33.2	380	145.0	6	9	14.0	8	6	.0
70809	13.9	95	5.4	56	39.7	435	154.8	6	6	.6	6	1	.0
70810	12.5	72	3.8	87	38.2	462	125.3	11	6	2.4	6	2	.0
70811	18.1	67	5.6	85	30.1	347	92.6	10	5	5.9	5	2	.0
70812	11.8	47	3.6	77	26.7	345	72.4	12	4	2.7	4	0	.0
70814	14.3	97	4.8	80	34.5	420	111.2	9	5	6.9	4	0	.1
70815	37.4	97	12.6	71	38.2	441	129.3	6	6	17.6	5	1	.0
70816	34.2	97	11.6	69	38.4	429	149.3	10	3	16.5	2	3	.4

SHREVEPORT

ZIPCODE	1	2	3	4	5	6	7	8	9	10	11	12	13
71001	5.0	56	1.8	74	21.1	157	53.2	8	17	1.3	16	0	13.1
71002	.0	0	.1	63	19.7	123	34.7	3	30	.0	0	0	.0
71003	1.1	65	.4	79	24.0	128	39.5	7	16	.4	11	0	1.0
71004	1.0	0	.3	54	27.6	160	64.2	5	19	.0	0	0	.0
71006	5.5	65	1.8	86	25.9	266	79.0	8	10	1.9	6	1	.1
71007	.3	69	.1	100	16.5	189*	49.6	6	15	.8	17	0	.0
71008	.9	52	.4	79	13.7	178	34.7	7	26	.2	35	1	.0
71009	1.2	100	.4	83	26.7	202	71.5	6	8	.6	7	3	.0
71016	2.0	77	.6	81	19.7	204	42.9	7	13	.8	12	0	.0
71017	1.1	80	.4	80	19.3	114	56.0	8	17	.6	17	1	.0
71018	2.4	70	1.0	78	18.6	136	39.7	9	20	.8	17	2	.0
71019	9.0	65	3.0	73	18.2	196	55.8	9	14	2.8	13	0	.1
71021	1.7	74	.6	64	14.5	148	40.2	10	6	.4	14	0	.0
71023	2.6	74	.9	82	21.5	154	51.7	8	9	1.0	13	0	.0
71024	1.1	69	.4	85	25.2	96	47.0	6	16	.4	9	0	60.5
71027	1.2	26	.4	85	17.6	202*	40.8	6	14	.2	13	0	1.1
71028	2.2	36	.8	73	15.1	141	35.9	9	19	.4	19	0	.0
71029	.6	0	.2	61	22.2	122	65.6	9	9	.2	5	0	.0
71030	1.1	37	.3	73	25.5	183	68.8	8	13	.0	16	0	.0
71031	1.7	75	.4	91	18.1	56	30.8	6	16	.4	9	0	.4
71032	.6	60	.6	77	23.8	144	74.4	9	14	.5	13	0	.0
71033	2.0	62	.7	78	22.7	184	73.6	10	12	.6	5	0	100++
71034	.3	83	.1	81	13.0	159	23.0	9	23	.1	30	0	.2
71037	11.3	83	3.6	86	30.5	296	99.6	9	5	4.7	3	0	.0
71038	5.8	64	2.1	71	19.9	167	53.2	9	18	1.7	14	2	.1

*=Estimated **1.0=883 lbs per person; 100++ indicates per capita toxic waste generation > than 100 times the U.S. average of 883 lbs per capita.

ZIP CODE MEASURES OF SIZE, LEVELS OF AFFLUENCE AND QUALITY OF LIFE

1=Population (th.); 2= % White; 3=Households (th.); 4=% Owner Occupied; 5=Mean Income Per Household (th.$); 6=Mean Monthly Rent ($); 7=Mean Home Value (th.$);
8=% under 5; 9=% 65 and over; 10=White Males (th.); 11=% White Males, 65+; 12=# Toxic Waste Sites; 13=Toxic Waste Relative to US(883 lbs.per capita)**.

LOUISIANA — SHREVEPORT

ZIP CODE	1	2	3	4	5	6	7	8	9	10	11	12	13
71039	1.8	67	.7	82	20.7	211	59.2	11	15	.6	14	1	.0
71040	8.2	0	2.8	72	19.6	179	58.5	7	19	.0	0	0	.1
71043	.7	64	.2	72	20.3	184	40.1	9	9	.2	10	0	.0
71044	.6	64	.2	82	16.8	113	51.8	8	23	.2	20	1	.0
71045	.6	92	.2	86	16.8	118	30.7	8	25	.2	14	0	.0
71046	1.1	55	.4	79	24.2	121	33.7	4	13	.3	8	0	.0
71047	7.3	76	2.2	85	26.6	250	88.5	8	6	2.9	5	0	.0
71048	.3	36	.1	70	14.8	213	52.6	2	19	.1	22	0	9.3
71049	3.6	76	1.4	76	20.1	212	53.2	7	18	1.3	16	0	.0
71050	.3	83	.1	81	27.5	316*	62.8	5	13	.1	4	0	.0
71051	1.9	60	.6	73	21.8	116	72.4	7	10	.6	7	1	.0
71052	13.5	48	4.8	71	21.0	223	51.1	9	16	3.2	15	0	.2
71055	21.8	61	7.7	72	21.4	233	64.8	8	14	6.4	11	0	.3
71059	.4	46	.1	79	19.0	218*	52.3	16	7	.1	24	0	.0
71060	2.2	75	.7	74	27.0	188	52.2	8	15	.8	13	1	.0
71063	2.1	79	.8	69	20.5	168	37.4	10	14	.8	13	0	.9
71064	1.1	57	.3	76	19.7	176	30.0	12	18	.3	14	0	.0
71065	5.1	0	1.7	80	18.0	147	44.7	8	17	.0	0	0	.2
71066	1.4	69	.5	78	18.7	206	39.3	11	15	.5	16	0	.3
71067	.5	34	.1	64	14.6	273	34.7	8	14	.1	4	1	.0
71068	1.9	70	.6	81	19.6	281	59.2	12	11	.7	12	1	.1
71069	4.0	64	1.5	79	18.4	149	44.8	6	18	1.3	17	0	.0
71070	1.2	66	.4	76	13.2	182	23.4	6	21	.4	18	0	.0
71071	1.4	56	.5	85	18.0	223	38.1	9	18	.5	19	0	.0
71072	2.5	93	.9	79	27.0	141	53.5	8	15	1.2	12	1	.0
71073	1.4	85	.5	78	22.1	159	64.1	5	16	.6	13	1	.0
71075	7.5	71	2.8	79	20.6	206	59.2	10	13	2.9	13	0	5.2
71078	1.5	82	.5	74	22.5	195	56.5	8	14	.6	13	4	1.2
71079	.3	79	.1	82	26.4	235	92.1	7	10	.6	6	0	.0
71080	.4	36	.1	57	10.9	67	44.2	6	26	.0	49	0	.0
71081	.1	31	.1	84	16.1	180	45.5	21	19	.1	16	0	5.2
71082	5.5	100	2.1	100	24.5	185*	47.5	7	17	2.2	15	0	1.2

SHREVEPORT

ZIP CODE	1	2	3	4	5	6	7	8	9	10	11	12	13
71101	15.1	28	6.3	30	14.5	180	47.9	8	19	2.0	22	3	.3
71103	17.6	20	6.2	46	15.1	211	43.6	9	16	1.5	17	1	1.8
71104	16.4	80	7.4	56	25.0	291	77.5	7	20	5.6	16	0	.0
71105	19.8	97	8.4	68	37.2	405	108.3	6	14	8.9	12	0	.4
71106	34.1	58	11.5	75	36.8	290	107.1	8	11	9.3	10	3	.5
71107	27.7	46	9.0	72	25.1	280	73.0	10	8	6.3	8	1	.5
71108	27.6	82	9.7	78	26.3	326	67.7	8	10	10.9	8	0	.0
71109	34.2	30	11.4	68	21.4	273	57.1	10	10	4.7	17	3	.2
71111	5.5	72	1.1	68	21.6	345	77.0*	12	0	2.3	0	1	1.0
71112	23.4	82	8.1	56	24.4	265	83.2	9	8	9.3	6	2	.2
71115	25.0	90	8.6	72	27.3	356	76.8	8	6	11.1	4	2	.0
71118	6.3	87	2.5	61	34.7	407	119.7	7	5	2.7	7	0	.2
71119	15.9	97	5.3	74	32.6	390	98.0	9	4	7.6	8	1	.0
71129	6.7	82	2.4	73	33.3	347	102.9	8	7	2.9	7	0	1.1

*=Estimated **1.0-883 lbs per person; 100++ indicates per capita toxic waste generation > than 100 times the U.S. average of 883 lbs per capita.

LOUISIANA — MONROE

ZIP CODE	1	2	3	4	5	6	7	8	9	10	11	12	13
71201	25.4	67	9.7	54	28.5	291	106.9	7	13	7.5	10	1	1.0
71202	33.4	39	10.3	67	16.4	218	47.8	12	11	6.2	12	0	.0
71203	32.0	74	10.3	67	26.0	308	80.2	9	6	12.0	5	2	.9
71216	.3	61	.1	51	17.4	154	60.2	2	19	.1	6	0	.0
71218	.2	0	.1	91	13.5	155*	46.2	0	21	.0	0	0	.0
71219	1.2	95	.4	89	23.7	151	43.0	8	13	.5	13	0	.0
71220	27.5	63	9.4	76	19.5	199	53.0	9	13	8.4	11	4	.6
71222	3.4	65	1.3	80	15.8	153	50.9	7	26	1.0	27	0	.0
71223	1.1	0	.3	69	12.2	174	46.9	17	20	.0	0	0	.0
71225	2.7	81	.9	86	26.4	211	64.2	7	10	1.1	8	1	.0
71226	1.7	56	.6	82	16.4	153	36.3	8	15	.4	16	0	.0
71227	2.4	79	.9	81	19.1	109	66.5	8	12	.9	12	1	.0
71229	1.5	47	.4	80	16.2	105	39.7	10	12	.3	10	0	.2
71230	.5	90	.2	66	23.6	135	60.9	9	11	.2	6	0	.0
71232	7.8	58	2.5	74	21.0	153	55.1	9	15	2.0	15	2	.3
71233	.3	89	.1	90	16.4	151	50.9	6	6	.1	5	0	.9
71234	3.0	89	1.0	84	25.6	210	66.7	9	12	1.3	8	0	.0
71235	4.0	73	1.5	80	23.1	160	51.7	7	15	1.5	13	1	.0
71237	1.4	61	.5	75	14.6	140	47.1	7	15	.4	15	0	.0
71238	1.5	87	.3	87	20.3	195	53.4	9	15	.6	10	0	.0
71239	.3	45	.1	58	20.3	234*	38.8	17	8	.1	12	0	.1
71240	.2	0	.1	60	14.0	149	52.0	7	30	.0	0	0	.0
71241	8.2	72	2.7	85	21.4	200	60.3	8	13	2.9	12	0	.0
71242	.8	100	.3	89	23.9	214	73.5	7	13	.3	13	0	2.3
71244	.2	69	.1	79	24.5	135	59.2	0	6	.1	8	0	.0
71245	5.2	94	1.0	64	21.2	229	71.3	4	5	2.0	5	0	.0
71247	2.1	69	.8	83	19.9	162	46.9	7	16	.7	15	0	.0
71249	1.1	100	.1	86	10.4	119*	47.1	15	15	.6	30	0	.0
71250	.8	73	.2	33	17.6	119	53.6	12	6	.3	3	0	.0
71251	9.5	66	3.5	72	18.7	186	52.8	9	17	3.1	14	0	.0
71253	.8	94	.2	83	29.2	208	67.8	7	10	.3	6	0	.0
71254	9.9	32	3.0	64	17.0	163	62.3	11	13	1.6	12	0	.0
71256	.5	44	.2	85	13.2	136	33.8	10	25	.3	25	0	.1
71259	2.1	56	.7	72	14.2	123	47.1	8	16	.6	17	0	.0
71260	3.7	74	1.3	86	17.0	168	43.3	8	16	1.3	17	0	.0
71261	2.7	0	.8	77	16.4	151	46.4	8	18	.0	0	0	.0
71263	8.0	87	2.7	84	16.4	144	55.8	7	16	3.4	15	0	.0
71264	1.3	52	.4	66	24.3	238	97.7	7	10	.3	3	0	.4
71266	2.3	79	.8	79	16.5	140	41.7	11	13	.9	10	0	.0
71268	2.5	76	.9	93	19.6	148	56.7	9	21	.9	21	0	.0
71269	12.4	66	4.1	75	20.7	186	54.5	10	16	3.9	14	0	.0
71270	27.1	71	8.7	62	22.2	296	80.8	6	11	9.7	8	4	.2
71275	1.9	54	.6	86	20.5	169	45.4	6	14	.5	9	0	.2
71276	1.5	60	.5	65	20.0	145	43.9	12	13	.4	12	0	.0
71277	2.0	65	.7	89	20.4	174	37.8	6	19	.6	20	1	.0
71279	.7	82	.2	91	18.9	192	79.0	12	4	.6	20	0	.0
71280	2.4	85	.8	87	27.8	212	67.9	8	11	.3	7	1	.0
71281	1.0	0	.3	82	28.8	338	98.5	11	5	1.0	0	0	18.5
71282	14.1	36	4.6	67	17.0	149	53.1	11	15	2.4	11	0	.0

*=Estimated **1.0-883 lbs per person; 100++ indicates per capita toxic waste generation > than 100 times the U.S. average of 883 lbs per capita.

ZIP CODE MEASURES OF SIZE, LEVELS OF AFFLUENCE AND QUALITY OF LIFE

1=Population (th.); 2= % White; 3=Households (th.); 4=% Owner Occupied; 5=Mean Income Per Household (th.$); 6=Mean Monthly Rent ($)*; 7=Mean Home Value (th.$)*; 8=% under 5; 9=% 65 and over; 10=White Males (th.); 11=% White Males, 65+; 12=# Toxic Waste Sites; 13=Toxic Waste Relative to US(883 lbs.per capita)**.

LOUISIANA

MONROE

ZIPCODE	1	2	3	4	5	6	7	8	9	10	11	12	13
71286	.7	0	.2	75	29.7	341*	44.6	6	7	.0	0	1	.0
71289	.5	48	.1	61	25.1	190	19.7	7	14	.1	0	0	.0
71291	41.7	92	14.8	74	25.4	269	71.6	8	10	18.6	8	2	.2
71295	15.1	69	5.2	75	17.6	191	54.7	9	16	5.0	15	0	.4

ALEXANDRIA (EAST)

ZIPCODE	1	2	3	4	5	6	7	8	9	10	11	12	13
71301	69.1	59	23.8	59	23.0	290	72.7	9	11	19.6	9	3	.2
71316	.3	100	.1	90	21.9	193	44.8	2	0	.1	0	0	.0
71318	.2	71	.1	82	11.9	137*	13.1	0	27	.0	27	0	.0
71320	.2	67	.1	100	15.5	178*	32.3	5	17	.1	28	0	.0
71322	8.3	65	2.7	67	20.2	181	53.5	8	15	2.5	13	1	.0
71323	.9	100	.3	79	16.3	172	55.8	8	17	.5	9	0	.0
71325	1.9	51	.6	71	16.6	137	36.2	10	19	.4	20	0	.0
71326	2.0	57	.6	79	15.7	124	39.0	9	13	.6	12	0	.0
71327	3.4	76	1.4	78	17.3	176	53.5	9	12	1.6	11	0	.0
71328	4.0	100	1.3	88	20.6	227	55.7	8	11	2.1	9	0	.0
71330	.3	0	.1	59	21.0	241*	46.9	11	17	.9	0	0	.0
71331	1.2	100	.4	87	26.2	270	68.2	6	13	.6	15	0	.0
71333	.7	58	.3	78	17.6	123	45.7	8	17	.2	13	0	.0
71334	10.7	56	3.5	71	19.5	158	56.3	9	12	2.9	8	0	.1
71336	2.2	79	.7	82	22.3	124	42.1	8	12	.9	11	0	.0
71339	2.6	87	.8	80	17.3	177	54.5	10	11	.2	10	0	.0
71340	1.4	87	.5	87	21.6	160	47.8	6	14	.6	18	0	.0
71341	2.8	97	.9	90	17.1	187	49.0	9	14	1.3	12	0	.1
71342	9.3	85	3.4	80	21.7	212	52.4	7	15	3.7	13	0	.0
71343	8.4	77	2.8	82	20.7	241	60.2	11	10	.9	9	0	.0
71346	3.6	53	1.2	70	23.2	172	53.7	10	13	.9	10	0	.0
71347	.2	0	.1	75	15.3	178	34.2	2	17	.0	0	0	.1
71348	.3	100	.1	100	24.0	276*	98.9	13	2	.1	16	0	.1
71350	4.6	63	1.4	76	15.3	157	57.3	9	10	1.4	16	0	.1
71351	11.1	73	3.7	77	17.9	185	57.3	9	10	3.9	10	0	.0
71353	2.6	66	.8	72	17.3	171	41.4	8	12	.9	9	0	.0
71354	1.8	96	.6	89	27.5	294	59.1	6	14	.9	12	0	.1
71355	2.3	82	.8	87	19.0	168	47.1	7	15	.9	14	0	.0
71356	.3	30	.1	56	15.9	124	32.1	8	17	.3	18	0	.0
71357	3.2	54	1.1	64	20.0	208	56.1	10	15	.2	22	0	.2
71358	1.6	34	.5	85	13.0	134	37.8	13	16	.3	13	0	.0
71360	37.6	90	11.6	73	25.8	280	73.2	8	9	16.3	17	2	.0
71362	1.6	92	.5	83	17.4	167	47.0	6	20	.7	16	0	.1
71363	.3	100	.1	93	9.9	114*	24.4	3	18	.2	23	0	.0
71365	.3	100	.1	100	26.5	305*	40.3	2	26	.2	18	0	.2
71366	2.8	0	1.0	72	19.0	124	55.9	8	16	.6	16	0	.0
71367	1.3	87	.4	87	19.2	150	32.6	6	16	.6	6	0	.1
71368	2.2	52	.7	69	15.5	168	40.6	9	16	.5	14	0	.0
71369	3.0	64	1.0	78	18.9	156	44.4	9	15	1.0	15	0	.2
71371	1.9	89	.7	88	22.4	240	41.4	10	15	.9	13	0	.0
71372	.3	78	.1	61	27.3	173	28.4	3	20	.1	13	0	.0
71373	7.8	71	2.5	80	25.3	244	59.9	8	9	2.7	6	0	.0
71375	2.1	32	.7	71	14.0	116	38.8	9	17	.4	11	0	.0
71377	.4	46	.1	72	23.7	215	45.3	10	11	.1	6	0	.9

LOUISIANA

ALEXANDRIA (EAST)

ZIPCODE	1	2	3	4	5	6	7	8	9	10	11	12	13
71378	3.4	54	1.1	73	14.9	143	52.6	7	15	.8	14	0	.0

ALEXANDRIA (WEST)

ZIPCODE	1	2	3	4	5	6	7	8	9	10	11	12	13
71403	3.2	100	1.1	89	25.6	254	59.8	9	9	1.6	8	0	.0
71404	.8	84	.3	97	19.5	205	42.1	7	11	.3	11	0	.0
71405	.2	100	.1	72	31.7	201	94.7	10	7	.3	4	0	.0
71406	.4	100	.1	80	26.6	305*	78.5	11	13	.2	10	0	.0
71407	.7	100	.2	79	18.2	190	50.2	9	16	.3	12	0	.0
71409	5.1	70	1.7	80	21.8	173	60.3	9	8	1.7	6	0	.0
71410	.2	100	.1	62	19.5	134	32.4	0	16	.1	9	0	.9
71411	.3	73	1.3	83	17.9	159	39.8	9	15	1.1	10	0	.0
71412	.4	100		88	23.3	368	24.0	12	12	.2	10	0	.0
71414	.8	45	.2	73	14.5	218	62.3	12	10	.2	15	0	.0
71415	1.0	80	.4	87	14.9	154	37.8	9	14	.4	15	0	.0
71416	.7	49	.2	66	16.8	135	30.3	8	14	.2	14	0	.0
71417	5.4	56	1.8	77	19.2	186	48.6	7	15	1.5	14	0	.0
71418	5.6	76	2.0	74	20.8	192	58.6	7	16	2.1	14	0	.0
71419	2.1	84	.7	79	19.2	82	47.7	5	14	.9	13	0	.0
71421	.4	53	.3	71	37.1	426*	125.7	0	14	.7	17	0	.1
71422	1.9	77	.7	82	18.2	218	35.5	13	13	.7	10	0	.0
71423	3.2	97	1.2	93	20.4	217	52.1	9	16	1.4	14	0	.0
71424	1.0	93	.3	92	28.2	324*	56.8	4	13	.5	11	0	.0
71425	.3	100	.1	100	16.8	193*	41.2	25	12	.2	17	0	.0
71427	.4	100	.1	79	13.7	171	35.0	4	14	.2	16	0	.1
71429	3.6	81	1.4	89	18.7	165	53.6	8	20	1.5	22	0	.0
71430	2.2	93	.8	84	22.0	212	40.9	7	9	1.0	10	0	.1
71432	.9	0	.4	80	16.6	166	29.2	5	23	.0	0	0	.0
71433	4.1	84	1.4	80	16.8	241	39.1	9	13	1.7	10	0	.1
71435	2.6	95	1.0	86	20.9	214	46.6	10	16	1.2	13	0	.1
71436	1.2	0	.5	98	22.2	255*	34.4	5	18	.0	0	0	.0
71438	.9	89	.3	89	22.5	287	54.0	9	24	.9	9	0	.0
71439	1.9	99	.7	87	22.3	135	48.5	7	11	.9	6	0	.1
71440	.4	85	.1	61	15.8	187	49.2	2	8	.2	4	0	.0
71441	.5	85	.1	82	18.8	146	44.1	10	9	.2	4	0	.0
71444	.3	100	.1	100	21.8	250*	25.3	14	9	.1	5	0	.0
71445	.3	100	.1	65	15.5	143	51.4	8	22	.1	28	0	.0
71446	23.4	79	8.3	59	18.4	258	66.3	11	8	9.4	8	0	.1
71447	1.1	80	.4	91	17.8	116	42.7	7	13	.4	15	0	.0
71449	9.8	76	3.5	75	20.2	182	57.7	9	16	3.6	14	0	.0
71450	1.6	82	.5	86	17.7	77	74.8	6	19	.6	18	0	.0
71452	.2	0	.1	19	11.1	110	39.6*	8	25	.0	0	0	.0
71454	3.0	85	1.1	79	18.7	175	43.9	5	15	1.3	13	0	.1
71455	.7	67	.2	94	17.1	121	31.5	6	7	.2	5	0	.0
71456	1.1	23	.3	66	14.0	128	40.4	8	6	.1	9	0	.2
71457	24.3	59	8.2	63	21.2	250	75.4	9	12	6.9	10	0	.0
71459	14.4	54	2.1	12	17.0	335	63.8	10	0	5.3	0	0	.0
71461	2.3	81	.8	34	22.5	319	79.1	17	3	1.0	3	0	.1
71462	1.5	68	.5	83	20.3	171	47.6	9	9	.5	12	0	.1
71463	10.0	73	3.5	71	18.4	181	47.6	9	13	3.6	11	0	.9

*=Estimated **1.0=883 lbs per person; 100++ indicates per capita toxic waste generation > than 100 times the U.S. average of 883 lbs per capita.

ZIP CODE MEASURES OF SIZE, LEVELS OF AFFLUENCE AND QUALITY OF LIFE

1=Population (th.); 2= % White; 3=Households (th.); 4=% Owner Occupied; 5=Mean Income Per Household (th.$); 6=Mean Monthly Rent ($); 7=Mean Home Value (th.$);
8=% under 5; 9=% 65 and over; 10=White Males (th.); 11=% White Males, 65+; 12=# Toxic Waste Sites; 13=Toxic Waste Relative to US(883 lbs.per capita)**.

LOUISIANA

ZIPCODE	1	2	3	4	5	6	7	8	9	10	11	12	13
ALEXANDRIA (WEST)													
71465	3.6	96	1.3	83	20.4	196	54.7	8	13	1.7	12	1	.0
71466	.2	100	.1	77	28.5	255	56.9	9	4	.1	0	0	.0
71467	3.4	99	1.2	81	22.9	222	53.6	10	12	1.7	12	1	1.5
71468	.8	100	.3	76	17.3	207	58.3	9	15	.4	16	0	.0
71469	3.5	83	1.2	77	17.2	182	53.1	8	12	1.4	9	0	.0
71471	.3	22	.1	95	13.1	151*	28.2	7	12	.0	0	0	.0
71472	.2	100	.1	84	20.2	61	19.4	9	35	.1	24	0	.0
71473	.9	0	.3	87	18.9	262	25.5	10	21	.0	0	0	.0
71474	.6	100	.2	82	22.1	175	56.5	8	10	.3	8	0	.0
71475	.2	100	.1	73	18.8	200	56.9	5	29	.1	28	0	.0
71477	1.1	100	.4	80	23.8	263	66.5	5	11	.6	10	0	1.9
71479	1.1	98	.4	88	19.3	218	36.1	8	17	.5	15	0	.0
71480	.8	0	.3	90	19.9	212	28.4	6	17	.0	0	0	.0
71483	11.5	67	4.1	72	17.5	188	54.6	9	15	3.8	14	0	2.3
71485	.5	69	.2	75	18.4	174	44.8	5	9	.2	9	0	.8
71486	4.9	75	1.7	78	16.3	169	46.2	8	14	1.7	15	0	.1
CAMDEN													
71749	1.0	52	.4	82	18.0	128	45.9	8	13	.2	14	0	.0
71765	.2	0	.1	85	11.5	132*	22.4	8	27	.0	0	0	.0

MAINE

ZIPCODE	1	2	3	4	5	6	7	8	9	10	11	12	13
PORTSMOUTH													
03830	.2	100	.1	92	20.5	236*	47.6	4	14	.1	12	0	.0
03852	.2	100	.1	96	22.0	253*	72.7	5	10	.1	8	0	.0
PORTSMOUTH													
03901	4.2	0	1.4	77	24.3	301	67.7	6	10	.0	0	0	.2
03902	2.3	100	.9	86	25.8	401	124.6	9	11	1.1	11	0	.0
03903	5.0	99	1.7	82	27.5	409	96.4	8	9	2.5	7	0	.0
03904	6.8	98	2.6	66	24.6	352	80.8	7	14	3.1	12	1	.1
03905	1.7	96	.6	83	30.7	492	99.0	7	13	.8	10	0	.1
03906	4.1	99	1.3	85	23.1	302	80.5	9	10	2.0	7	0	.0
03907	1.7	99	.8	67	22.2	349	137.7	3	23	.8	20	0	4.8
03908	4.1	99	1.4	70	23.3	367	76.6	8	13	2.0	11	0	.0
03909	3.8	100	1.3	78	31.8	432	105.5	6	15	1.9	10	0	.0
03910	1.6	0	.6	73	20.8	399	99.7	4	13	.0	0	0	.0
03911	.6	0	.2	65	39.0	348	204.8	5	14	.0	0	0	.0
PORTLAND													
04001	.5	0	.2	83	27.1	322	66.7	6	14	.0	0	0	.0
04002	2.6	100	.8	89	22.8	261	75.6	9	10	1.3	8	0	.0
04003	1.0	0	.4	78	23.8	422	114.8	5	25	.0	0	0	.0
04004	.7	0	.2	85	27.1	409	76.4	10	9	.0	0	0	.0
04005	21.9	99	7.7	56	21.3	275	77.9	7	13	10.4	10	2	.3
04006	2.7	100	.9	50	24.9	391	129.3	6	19	.2	16	0	.0
04008	3.6	100	1.3	84	22.3	381	69.8	8	7	1.3	6	0	.1
04009	.9	100	.3	76	20.1	282	65.3	5	16	1.7	13	0	.1
04010	18.5	97	6.3	81	18.5	268	67.9	6	12	8.9	6	1	.5
04011	.5	100	.2	60	23.6	353	87.8	6	12	.2	9	0	.2
04014	1.9	100	.6	68	21.3	410	113.8	7	14	.2	9	0	.0
04015	.3	100	.1	87	21.0	320	69.5	9	11	.9	9	0	.0
04017	1.5	99	.5	100	11.9	137*	61.8	8	27	.1	23	0	.1
04020	1.5	100	.5	84	19.6	319	64.0	8	12	.7	9	0	.0
04021	5.3	100	1.6	87	31.2	423	99.2	6	7	2.6	6	1	.0
04022	.4	100	.2	87	22.8	286	78.7	6	23	.2	22	0	.1
04024	.8	100	.3	93	19.7	167	65.6	5	14	.4	13	0	.0
04027	3.5	100	1.1	90	21.4	303	65.2	8	11	1.7	10	0	.4
04029	.6	0	.2	73	22.5	374	72.2	7	11	.5	11	0	.0
04030	1.2	0	.4	87	23.5	327	73.8	10	8	.4	8	0	.0
04031	.2	100	.1	92	24.7	284*	67.0	2	14	.1	7	0	1.6
04032	6.3	99	2.2	77	24.3	367	79.6	7	9	3.0	10	0	.0
04037	2.4	99	.9	73	20.9	263	71.8	7	18	1.1	14	0	.3
04038	11.3	99	3.4	80	25.9	345	83.2	6	9	5.5	7	1	.1
04039	4.3	99	1.5	82	22.7	356	74.6	8	10	2.1	9	1	.4
04040	2.1	99	.8	86	18.6	328	68.8	9	14	1.1	12	0	.0
04041	.6	99	.2	86	17.4	307	52.4	6	14	.3	13	0	.0
04042	2.4	100	.8	88	24.3	306	70.7	11	9	1.2	7	0	.0
04043	6.6	99	2.4	77	27.5	362	97.5	6	17	3.1	15	2	.4
04046	3.8	99	1.5	82	29.3	376	112.7	5	16	1.8	12	0	.3
04047	1.8	99	.6	85	20.3	313	58.4	7	14	.8	11	1	.3
04048	2.2	100	.8	85	21.4	323	65.7	9	11	1.1	10	1	.1
04049	.2	100	.1	78	19.6	367	81.2	19	9	.1	12	0	.0
04051	.7	0	.2	88	20.6	357	69.2	7	13	.0	0	0	.0

*=Estimated **1.0=883 lbs per person; 100++ indicates per capita toxic waste generation > than 100 times the U.S. average of 883 lbs per capita.

103001

ZIP CODE MEASURES OF SIZE, LEVELS OF AFFLUENCE AND QUALITY OF LIFE

1=Population (th.); 2= % White; 3=Households (th.); 4=% Owner Occupied; 5=Mean Income Per Household (th.$); 6=Mean Monthly Rent ($)*; 7=Mean Home Value (th.$)*; 8=% under 5; 9=% 65 and over; 10=% White Males (th.); 11=% White Males, 65+; 12=# Toxic Waste Sites; 13=Toxic Waste Relative to US(883 lbs.per capital)**.

MAINE

PORTLAND

ZIPCODE	1	2	3	4	5	6	7	8	9	10	11	12	13
04054	.4	100	.2	80	22.1	241	106.3	6	27	.2	11	0	.0
04055	1.8	100	.7	85	18.9	307	75.1	6	13	.9	12	0	.0
04056	.1	100	.1	79	18.2	210*	74.9	6	23	.1	24	0	.0
04058	.2	100	.1	95	18.4	212*	43.3	9	7	.1	9	0	.0
04060	.2	100	.1	88	20.6	237*	65.1	7	11	.1	9	0	.0
04061	.6	0	.1	85	23.2	443	75.6	12	5	.0	7	0	.0
04062	3.5	100	1.1	82	27.5	381	86.8	6	9	1.7	7	0	.1
04063	.3	0	.2	62	14.8	222	72.0	0	49	.0	0	0	.0
04064	6.0	100	2.3	63	19.4	316	62.8	7	12	2.9	9	2	.0
04066	1.0	100	.4	69	24.9	350	102.1	9	12	.5	11	0	.0
04068	.2	0	.1	78	25.9	244	58.5	5	21	.0	0	0	.0
04069	1.6	100	.8	89	24.0	304	75.0	5	6	.9	5	0	.1
04071	2.3	0	.8	88	26.0	435	90.5	7	11	.9	10	0	.1
04072	13.6	100	4.8	71	23.2	308	76.3	7	12	6.5	10	3	.4
04073	14.0	100	5.1	64	20.3	258	66.0	8	15	6.6	11	2	4.7
04074	11.7	98	4.2	79	27.9	460	96.9	7	8	5.6	8	0	.9
04075	2.9	100	1.0	84	23.9	269	75.0	9	8	1.5	7	0	.0
04076	.3	100	.2	79	25.0	302	98.1	9	12	.1	12	0	.1
04077	.6	98	.2	87	30.1	500	103.8	9	10	.6	14	0	.9
04078	.4	100	.2	78	35.6	334	143.2	7	9	.2	7	0	.0
04079	.6	100	.2	80	31.4	420	131.7	5	8	.3	8	1	.0
04080	.3	100	.1	88	21.0	209	58.3	10	18	.1	18	0	.0
04082	7.6	100	2.4	83	24.3	326	79.9	8	8	3.8	7	0	.0
04083	4.8	99	1.5	74	21.2	238	73.5	6	14	2.3	13	0	3.4
04084	.6	0	.2	80	22.5	338	81.7	6	16	.2	12	0	.0
04085	2.2	99	.7	88	22.6	372	69.3	11	6	1.1	6	0	.0
04086	6.3	98	2.1	72	23.8	429	84.4	9	8	3.0	7	0	.0
04087	1.2	98	.4	88	20.8	273	65.8	7	10	.6	8	3	.7
04088	.2	100	.1	95	25.3	291*	89.1	3	22	.1	20	0	.0
04090	4.7	99	1.9	77	21.5	338	82.7	7	14	2.3	13	1	.4
04091	.7	0	.3	94	20.3	183	55.0	8	12	.1	6	0	.3
04092	16.2	100	5.8	64	24.1	322	74.3	8	11	7.6	10	1	1.4
04093	3.4	99	1.1	87	24.7	359	72.3	10	7	1.6	7	0	.0
04094	.5	100	.2	85	18.1	263	53.7	10	15	.3	10	0	.0
04095	.3	0	.1	91	20.5	306	70.2	10	17	.1	6	0	.0
04096	6.8	0	2.5	66	29.0	429	109.5	7	11	2.3	13	0	.1

PORTLAND

ZIPCODE	1	2	3	4	5	6	7	8	9	10	11	12	13
04101	17.0	98	8.2	15	15.6	306	59.0	6	18	7.7	12	3	.4
04102	17.7	98	7.2	46	22.2	322	82.6	6	15	8.0	12	0	.3
04103	26.0	99	9.7	61	23.8	353	76.4	6	17	11.4	13	0	.1
04104	.3	100	.1	100	30.3	349*	72.0	1	8	.2	11	1	8.7
04105	6.6	100	2.4	88	33.7	392	115.6	5	16	3.1	13	0	.1
04106	22.5	99	8.1	68	23.4	374	72.3	6	14	10.6	11	1	.5
04107	8.3	0	2.9	88	40.1	468	121.8	6	12	.4	23	0	.0
04108	.8	100	.4	71	15.1	362	53.9	6	23	.4	23	0	.0
04110	1.2	0	.4	97	59.1	152	189.9	5	11	.0	0	0	.1

AUBURN

ZIPCODE	1	2	3	4	5	6	7	8	9	10	11	12	13
04210	24.2	99	8.8	61	22.0	273	71.4	7	14	11.4	11	3	.1
04216	.7	100	.2	87	22.2	176	55.6	8	13	.3	11	0	.0

MAINE

AUBURN

ZIPCODE	1	2	3	4	5	6	7	8	9	10	11	12	13
04217	2.8	100	1.0	76	19.8	297	58.2	8	12	1.4	10	0	.0
04219	1.3	98	.4	82	17.1	282	47.8	7	12	.7	9	0	.1
04220	2.0	99	.6	89	20.7	262	54.2	9	10	1.0	10	1	.0
04221	1.2	0	.4	87	20.6	245	60.5	7	11	.7	10	0	.0
04223	.2	100	.2	64	15.3	374	51.0	4	16	.1	24	0	.0
04224	2.9	0	1.0	84	21.9	269	51.4	6	14	.1	0	0	.1
04225	1.2	100	.4	82	20.3	283	54.0	5	12	.5	10	0	.0
04226	.1	100	.1	94	18.0	207*	60.0	4	11	.1	12	0	.0
04227	.2	100	.1	85	24.8	285*	42.2	3	6	.1	6	0	.0
04228	.4	100	.1	83	27.9	380	65.8	6	1	.2	2	0	.0
04230	.4	100	.2	80	22.4	292	59.6	12	10	.2	10	0	.0
04231	1.6	100	.2	94	19.9	166	54.2	5	6	.9	5	0	.1
04233	2.3	100	.8	79	22.9	263*	82.4	7	5	.1	3	0	.0
04234	13.6	100	4.8	71	16.9	306	45.5	7	12	6.5	19	2	.4
04236	3.0	98	.9	88	22.5	358	75.3	8	8	1.5	8	2	.0
04237	.3	0	.1	89	25.0	231	62.3	2	11	.0	7	0	.0
04238	.7	100	.2	78	21.1	275	67.0	9	7	.4	7	0	3.2
04239	4.6	100	1.5	79	26.8	219	71.0	9	8	2.3	7	2	.0
04240	40.8	99	15.0	48	20.0	262	71.0	6	15	18.6	12	0	.2
04250	3.0	99	1.0	80	19.1	360	67.9	9	9	1.5	8	0	.2
04251	.7	0	.2	78	21.6	399	64.8	8	2	.3	9	0	.0
04252	6.5	99	2.2	77	21.7	334	70.1	10	9	3.2	7	0	.0
04253	.4	100	.1	91	23.2	312	61.9	8	12	.2	13	0	.0
04254	4.6	100	1.7	73	22.5	238	58.7	6	11	2.2	11	0	2.9
04255	.3	100	.1	92	18.4	212*	54.3	9	18	.1	12	0	.0
04256	4.4	99	1.4	84	21.8	276	56.2	8	10	.0	10	0	.0
04257	3.6	100	1.3	70	22.1	280	46.8	6	13	1.7	10	2	.0
04258	.2	100	.1	80	37.0	305	67.7	8	4	.1	3	0	.0
04259	2.0	0	.6	87	21.9	284	67.0	8	11	.6	8	0	.0
04260	2.2	100	.7	87	21.4	349	72.4	8	8	1.0	8	0	.4
04261	.2	95	.1	97	18.6	214*	54.7	4	5	.8	8	0	.0
04263	1.8	99	.6	85	21.4	221	55.9	9	12	.8	7	0	.0
04265	.8	100	.3	88	21.4	247	66.3	9	10	.4	10	0	.9
04266	.2	100	.1	75	21.6	181	67.5	8	19	.1	30	0	.0
04267	.4	99	.1	91	21.7	213	62.1	8	13	.2	15	0	.0
04268	4.6	0	1.8	73	18.8	247	63.8	6	18	.3	9	0	.0
04270	2.5	100	.9	86	18.9	242	61.9	7	11	1.3	7	0	.0
04271	.2	91	.1	91	41.2	474*	118.5	13	12	.6	6	0	.2
04273	.5	100	.2	100	28.0	322*	75.6	6	7	.2	11	0	.0
04274	1.8	97	.5	80	24.9	308	78.4	6	6	.9	5	0	.1
04275	.3	100	.1	100	23.5	270*	41.0	3	18	.1	13	0	8.7
04276	7.7	99	2.9	59	23.3	258	60.0	6	14	3.7	12	1	2.7
04278	.4	100	.1	92	23.4	269*	58.5	5	11	.2	15	0	.1
04279	.2	96	.1	96	25.4	292*	53.7	7	16	.1	12	0	.0
04280	3.8	99	1.2	85	20.7	322	64.9	4	10	1.9	7	0	.1
04281	4.8	100	1.7	73	18.9	262	59.7	7	14	2.2	13	0	.0
04282	2.9	100	1.0	80	23.1	326	69.1	9	8	1.4	7	0	.0
04284	.7	0	.3	88	26.4	308	80.7	9	11	.0	0	0	.0
04285	.4	100	.4	83	21.4	271	55.6	6	11	.2	10	0	.0

*=Estimated **1.0=883 lbs per person; 100++ indicates per capita toxic waste generation > than 100 times the U.S. average of 883 lbs per capita.

ZIP CODE MEASURES OF SIZE, LEVELS OF AFFLUENCE AND QUALITY OF LIFE

1=Population (th.); 2= % White; 3=Households (th.); 4=% Owner Occupied; 5=Mean Income Per Household (th.$); 6=Mean Monthly Rent ($); 7=Mean Home Value (th.$);
8=% under 5; 9=% 65 and over; 10=White Males (th.); 11=% White Males, 65+; 12=# Toxic Waste Sites; 13=Toxic Waste Relative to US(883 lbs.per capita)**.

MAINE

ZIPCODE	1	2	3	4	5	6	7	8	9	10	11	12	13
AUBURN													
04289	1.8	100	.6	81	19.5	251	51.2	7	21	.9	17	0	.0
04290	1.4	0	.5	89	22.5	286	53.4	8	12	.0	0	0	.0
04291	.3	100	.1	74	25.2	437	55.0	15	5	.2	4	0	.0
04292	.4	100	.1	93	19.0	218*	47.1	11	13	.2	11	0	.0
04294	2.9	0	1.0	83	24.5	285	65.7	9	12	.0	0	0	.1
AUGUSTA													
04330	26.6	99	9.9	59	22.4	296	72.7	7	14	12.6	11	0	.4
04341	1.3	100	.4	84	18.8	324	57.5	7	10	.6	8	0	.0
04342	.8	100	.3	90	21.1	343	65.1	9	11	.4	9	0	.0
04343	.5	100	.2	85	23.2	245	76.7	3	15	.2	8	0	.0
04345	15.5	99	5.4	75	21.4	299	62.7	7	13	7.3	11	0	.1
04347	3.7	100	1.4	70	24.7	269	77.7	6	13	1.8	10	0	.0
04348	.7	0	.3	91	21.4	338	72.4	10	12	.0	0	0	.0
04349	.5	0	.2	85	24.2	86	66.4	7	10	.0	0	0	.0
04350	1.7	100	.6	89	22.4	230	70.5	9	8	.9	7	0	.0
04351	.6	100	.2	85	33.6	361	108.5	5	11	.3	10	0	.0
04352	1.2	0	.5	80	19.6	235	60.1	8	13	.0	7	0	.0
04353	1.4	100	.3	86	20.4	301	58.0	10	7	.7	7	0	.0
04354	.9	0	.3	90	20.9	321	62.4	8	7	.7	7	0	.0
04355	1.6	99	.6	89	24.6	338	73.7	7	10	.8	9	0	.1
04357	2.8	100	1.0	81	19.7	284	54.8	7	16	1.4	14	0	.0
04358	.6	0	.2	91	22.0	713	68.1	6	13	.0	0	0	.0
04359	.5	100	.3	81	26.9	250	48.3	8	10	.3	13	0	.0
04361	.9	0	.3	84	21.5	181	65.1	10	10	.0	0	0	.0
04363	1.3	100	.4	88	22.7	320	64.9	9	8	.7	9	0	.0
04364	6.1	0	2.1	77	25.3	319	78.8	7	13	.0	0	0	.2
BANGOR													
04401	40.4	99	14.6	57	22.1	304	73.7	6	12	18.8	9	0	.2
04406	.5	100	.1	92	17.9	187	47.7	8	11	.2	11	0	.0
04408	.2	100	.1	75	17.6	431	42.8	4	19	.1	12	0	.0
04410	.8	0	.3	81	16.8	127	53.5	9	10	.0	0	0	.0
04411	.9	100	.3	83	23.1	292	59.4	9	11	.4	11	0	.0
04412	11.7	100	4.1	73	23.9	305	76.0	6	12	5.5	9	0	.4
04413	.2	100	.1	100	15.7	181*	29.3	6	17	.0	13	0	.0
04414	.9	0	.3	85	19.6	191	38.9	7	17	.0	0	0	.0
04415	.7	0	.3	82	20.8	247	43.6	6	12	.0	0	0	.0
04416	5.1	100	1.8	78	20.7	232	65.0	7	11	2.5	10	0	1.6
04417	.3	100	.1	98	17.3	199*	33.4	7	10	.1	12	0	.0
04418	.3	0	.1	92	21.6	249*	67.7	8	2	.0	0	0	.0
04419	3.0	100	.9	89	21.2	296	67.9	8	7	1.5	7	0	.0
04421	1.2	99	.3	77	26.7	323	125.2	2	12	.8	6	0	.0
04422	1.0	97	.3	75	19.6	319	53.0	8	6	.5	7	0	.0
04423	.8	0	.3	85	16.9	255	45.5	8	8	.0	0	0	.0
04424	1.1	0	.4	86	17.0	242	33.2	5	15	.0	0	0	.0
04426	5.3	98	1.9	77	17.8	269	49.7	7	13	2.4	11	0	.0
04427	2.3	99	.8	80	19.1	260	57.1	9	10	1.2	9	0	.0
04428	.8	0	.3	81	20.3	346	59.5	7	7	.0	0	0	.0
04429	3.1	99	1.0	88	22.7	298	75.6	8	7	1.5	7	0	.0
04430	2.4	0	.8	82	27.2	250	67.7	7	7	.0	0	0	2.4

MAINE

ZIPCODE	1	2	3	4	5	6	7	8	9	10	11	12	13
BANGOR													
04431	.4	100	.1	79	22.4	318	62.7	7	8	.2	4	0	.0
04433	.5	100	.2	93	24.4	175	55.6	11	11	.2	8	0	.0
04434	.7	0	.2	84	18.3	305	46.6	9	11	.2	0	0	.0
04438	.8	98	.3	92	18.7	382	47.8	10	10	.4	9	0	.0
04441	1.4	0	.6	72	17.8	239	53.6	7	17	.0	0	0	.0
04442	.6	0	.9	78	24.8	254	45.5	6	15	.0	0	0	.0
04443	2.4	99	.9	74	17.8	247	45.8	7	18	1.2	15	0	.4
04444	.7	100	.2	82	27.2	363	78.2	4	13	.3	16	1	.9
04445	3.1	100	1.0	83	25.2	406	82.5	8	7	1.5	5	0	.0
04446	.2	100	.1	91	15.8	182*	47.9	14	7	.1	5	0	.1
04448	1.8	0	.6	80	20.7	217	56.7	9	11	.9	7	0	.0
04449	.7	98	.2	83	21.2	333	55.8	10	7	.4	11	0	.1
04450	.9	0	.3	87	19.3	298	56.6	9	8	.4	5	0	.0
04451	.4	100	.2	85	18.3	124	39.7	8	12	.2	7	0	.0
04453	.7	0	.2	90	17.7	255	43.0	10	12	.4	0	0	.0
04454	.1	100	.1	78	8.9	102*	13.1	6	31	.0	42	0	.0
04455	.8	0	.3	86	20.2	253	53.8	9	8	.4	8	0	.0
04456	1.3	100	.4	90	20.6	279	71.8	9	7	.7	5	0	.0
04457	4.7	100	1.6	79	20.5	236	60.5	8	13	2.2	11	0	3.1
04458				91	19.7	271	63.1	13	5				
04459	1.6	100	.6	79	21.9	242	45.8	11	5	.9	3	0	.1
04460	2.0	0	.6	86	25.0	274	54.9	10	10	1.1	6	0	.0
04461	1.8	100	.7	83	22.4	310	62.0	6	8	.9	6	0	.1
04462	7.7	100	2.7	84	26.6	323	68.7	9	9	3.8	7	0	.5
04463	3.1	99	1.1	84	19.8	237	42.0	8	9	.2	0	0	.0
04464	.8	0	.3	91	17.3	235	41.1	6	13	.4	0	0	.4
04465	.3	100	.1	91	15.3	175*	46.4	5	18	.2	18	0	1.1
04468	8.7	100	3.2	66	20.6	279	63.3	8	14	4.0	12	0	.0
04472	1.2	94	.4	50	18.1	288	55.2	7	11	.6	9	0	.0
04473	10.6	98	4.0	87	22.6	344	83.3	3	6	5.5	6	0	1.4
04474	3.2	100	1.1	88	25.1	363	75.6	3	6	1.6	9	0	.0
04475	.5	100	.2	90	19.4	188	42.5	6	14	.2	16	0	.0
04476	.9	0	.3	86	22.2	274	60.9	6	20	.4	20	0	.1
04478	.2	100	.1	74	13.3	153*	50.7	3	28	.1	30	0	.0
04479	.9	0	.3	81	17.8	181	53.7	7	14	.4	14	0	.0
04485	.2	100	.1	87	18.0	207*	37.3	12	18	.1	18	0	.0
04487	1.0	0	.3	88	17.3	241	34.2	7	7	.3	7	0	.0
04488	.6	99	.2	91	18.5	347	48.3	8	7	.3	7	0	.0
04489	.6	0	.2	70	20.7	380	62.2	8	12	.1	12	0	.1
04490	.3	100	.1	87	17.7	272	62.2	6	8	.1	8	0	.0
04491	.3	100	.1	74	19.0	240	30.6	6	15	.1	15	0	.0
04492	.2	100	.1	92	18.4	211*	44.5	11	18	.1	19	0	.0
04493	.6	100	.2	89	23.0	260	53.6	6	9	.3	5	0	.0
04495	.3	100	.1	85	20.7	324	44.1	8	10	.1	6	0	.0
04496	2.7	98	.9	82	20.2	305	71.3	6	12	1.3	12	0	.0
04497	.4	100	.1	85	14.4	211	22.9	6	13	.2	13	0	.1
PORTLAND													
04530	12.4	98	4.4	63	22.3	339	71.0	7	13	5.9	10	1	1.3
04537	1.4	100	.5	83	20.8	331	83.1	7	13	.7	13	0	.1

*=Estimated **1.0=883 lbs per person; 100++ indicates per capita toxic waste generation > than 100 times the U.S. average of 883 lbs per capita.

ZIP CODE MEASURES OF SIZE, LEVELS OF AFFLUENCE AND QUALITY OF LIFE

1=Population (th.); 2= % White; 3=Households (th.); 4=% Owner Occupied; 5=Mean Income Per Household (th.$); 6=Mean Monthly Rent ($); 7=Mean Home Value (th.$); 8=% under 5; 9=% 65 and over; 10=% White Males (th.); 11=% White Males, 65+; 12=# Toxic Waste Sites; 13=Toxic Waste Relative to US(883 lbs.per capita)**.

MAINE

PORTLAND

ZIP CODE	1	2	3	4	5	6	7	8	9	10	11	12	13
04538	2.0	100	.8	71	19.9	321	85.8	5	21	.9	15	0	.3
04539	.4	100	.2	89	19.6	369	75.4	8	20	.2	16	0	.0
04543	1.8	0	.8	77	19.6	305	98.0	6	23	.0	0	0	.0
04544	.6	100	.3	89	23.1	257	99.2	7	19	.3	16	0	1.5
04546	.2	100	.1	87	16.8	220	68.2	6	17	.1	15	0	.0
04547	1.0	0	.4	83	20.4	335	67.8	7	14	.0	0	0	.0
04548	.5	0	.2	85	22.7	393	98.9	5	22	.0	0	0	.0
04551	.4	100	.1	85	21.3	399	92.3	9	14	.0	12	0	.0
04553	1.3	99	.5	82	21.2	341	77.1	7	19	.6	15	0	.0
04554	.6	100	.3	91	19.3	331	87.7	4	27	.3	25	0	.0
04555	.7	100	.2	88	22.4	277	67.3	10	11	.3	10	0	.0
04556	1.0	0	.4	90	17.6	341	73.7	7	19	.0	0	0	.0
04558	.3	100	.1	89	16.1	278	91.9	9	23	.2	17	0	.0
04562	.4	100	.1	87	20.3	410	78.1	5	14	.2	9	0	.0
04563	.4	100	.1	89	22.8	393	110.2	7	20	.2	21	0	.5
04564	.4	100	.2	90	18.2	209*	79.8	7	22	.1	22	0	.4
04565	.4	100	.1	87	21.0	252	48.9	4	10	.0	11	0	.0
04567	.2	100	.1	81	26.3	327	71.7	9	18	.1	13	0	.0
04568	.5	0	.2	80	18.6	349	87.7	4	20	.0	0	0	.5
04571	.3	100	.1	87	22.3	378	77.8	5	16	.2	19	0	.0
04573	4.6	0	1.6	85	19.2	296	68.0	7	16	.0	0	0	.4
04574	.1	100	.1	81	29.7	271	101.7	4	22	.1	25	0	.0
04575	.9	0	.3	86	16.8	232	56.5	8	12	.0	0	0	.0
04576	.2	100	.1	71	20.2	178	99.5	1	23	.1	15	0	.0
04578	.5	100	.2	91	22.3	262	117.0	5	18	.2	15	0	2.0
04579	4.3	0	1.5	82	22.3	392	84.6	8	10	.0	0	0	.1
04580	1.6	0	.5	85	26.3	325	73.8	7	9	.0	0	0	.1

BANGOR

ZIP CODE	1	2	3	4	5	6	7	8	9	10	11	12	13
04605	8.8	100	3.3	77	20.0	298	71.6	6	16	4.1	13	0	.1
04606	1.1	99	.3	91	15.4	260	55.0	7	13	.5	14	0	.0
04607	1.2	0	.4	82	17.4	276	55.6	6	13	.0	0	0	.1
04609	3.8	100	1.5	67	20.8	328	69.0	5	20	1.7	16	0	.0
04611	.7	0	.3	87	11.7	302	42.3	7	17	.0	0	0	.0
04612	2.0	100	.1	94	19.8	228*	69.5	3	12	.1	10	0	.0
04613	.3	100	.1	80	16.0	270	65.9	11	13	.6	18	0	.5
04614	1.3	100	.5	80	20.6	319	74.5	7	18	.6	18	0	.0
04615	.2	100	.1	86	18.2	209*	53.6	6	16	.1	15	0	.0
04616	.4	100	.2	78	17.4	362	61.7	5	23	.2	20	0	.0
04617	.6	99	.2	91	16.4	241	71.6	8	17	.3	15	1	.0
04618	.4	100	.2	86	15.0	170	59.8	8	17	.2	14	0	.0
04619	4.4	100	1.6	85	15.6	271	69.5	7	14	.1	6	0	.0
04622	1.1	0	.5	81	13.9	198	52.4	7	20	.5	13	0	.0
04623	.7	0	.3	81	14.9	177	53.6	9	18	.8	6	0	.1
04624	.2	100	.2	84	19.3	544	82.2	5	16	.1	21	1	.0
04626	.4	100	.1	88	15.6	235	63.3	11	9	.2	8	0	.0
04627	1.0	100	.4	72	16.1	197	69.5	7	19	.5	15	0	.0
04628	.6	0	.5	81	15.8	181*	40.0	12	16	.0	0	0	.0
04630	1.6	98	.6	84	18.9	274	54.0	8	9	.8	6	0	.0
04631	2.0	98	.8	77	15.1	264	39.0	7	21	.9	17	0	.1

MAINE

BANGOR

ZIP CODE	1	2	3	4	5	6	7	8	9	10	11	12	13
04634	1.2	99	.4	88	15.2	280	59.2	8	14	.6	12	0	.2
04637	.2	100	.1	92	17.0	195*	50.4	3	16	.1	19	0	.0
04638	.2	100	.1	88	17.6	203*	54.8	8	14	.1	12	0	.0
04640	.7	0	.3	83	22.7	275	56.5	9	13	.0	0	0	.0
04642	.1	100	.1	78	16.5	420	50.8	9	12	.1	13	0	.0
04643	1.0	100	.4	87	16.5	238	53.0	7	15	.5	15	0	.0
04644	.2	100	.1	69	22.0	495	71.4	2	36	.1	17	0	.0
04648	.6	100	.2	95	17.6	202*	46.0	11	11	.3	9	0	.0
04649	1.5	99	.5	82	13.1	211	49.6	9	17	.7	14	0	.0
04650	.2	100	.2	90	16.7	192*	40.3	4	19	.1	17	0	.0
04652	2.4	0	.9	78	15.5	222	41.2	6	21	.0	0	0	.0
04653	.5	100	.2	80	16.7	352	59.2	8	16	.3	11	0	.0
04654	3.5	100	1.2	78	19.3	281	63.7	7	15	1.8	13	0	.0
04655	.5	98	.2	84	15.6	366	55.6	10	13	.2	11	0	.0
04656	.4	0	.2	87	21.1	334	82.8	4	19	.0	0	0	.0
04657	.2	100	.1	84	22.1	254*	74.5	2	11	.1	6	0	.0
04658	1.5	100	.5	85	16.4	256	55.4	7	17	.7	16	0	.0
04659	.1	0	.1	93	12.7	146*	57.9	3	14	.0	0	0	.0
04660	.9	100	.3	86	21.4	311	86.9	8	16	.4	16	0	.0
04661	.7	0	.3	91	20.7	238*	75.1	2	22	.0	0	0	.1
04662	.3	0	.1	71	26.4	301	90.6	3	18	.0	0	0	.0
04664	.3	98	.1	81	13.9	325	41.4	6	5	.1	7	0	.0
04665	.2	100	.2	96	17.7	204*	41.8	8	5	.1	16	0	1.2
04666	1.2	100	.4	89	16.1	308	41.8	11	13	.6	13	0	.0
04667	1.3	59	.4	85	12.8	128	64.2	10	10	.4	16	0	1.7
04668	1.5	77	.5	84	19.7	232	62.9	9	11	.6	13	0	.0
04669	.2	96	.1	80	19.2	299	73.2	3	23	.1	25	0	.0
04671	.3	100	.1	92	14.8	287	55.3	7	17	.2	16	0	.0
04675	.3	100	.1	74	24.3	320	81.2	8	14	.2	13	0	.0
04676	.7	0	.1	87	14.0	284	60.3	9	12	.5	14	0	.0
04677	.3	0	.1	87	20.4	316	101.2	4	14	.0	0	0	.1
04679	1.6	100	.6	67	21.9	304	85.8	7	16	.8	13	0	1.2
04680	.7	99	.2	85	15.5	235	54.6	6	13	.3	10	0	.0
04681	1.5	0	.6	81	15.1	257	57.0	6	16	.0	0	0	1.7
04684	.9	100	.3	79	19.3	292	69.0	5	18	.6	16	0	.0
04685	1.0	100	.1	68	13.6	245	62.0	6	9	.1	4	0	.0
04686	.2	100	.1	79	15.6	147	42.2	11	13	.1	10	0	.0
04689	.3	95	.1	91	19.4	223*	55.3	3	23	.1	17	0	.0
04690	.3	100	.1	86	18.1	347	61.3	3	21	.1	28	0	.0
04691	.2	100	.1	90	17.9	206*	75.0	7	12	.1	6	0	.0
04692	.1	100	.3	85	16.3	290	46.8	6	9	.1	13	0	.0
04693	1.1	97	.1	55	15.9	301	64.7	11	9	.6	7	1	.0
04694	2.7	0	.9	87	24.6	299	67.5	8	9	.0	0	1	3.8

HOULTON

ZIP CODE	1	2	3	4	5	6	7	8	9	10	11	12	13
04730	10.2	98	3.5	74	18.5	277	51.4	8	14	4.8	13	5	.4
04732	2.1	99	.7	80	20.5	267	52.3	7	10	1.1	9	0	.0
04733	1.1	100	.1	95	18.7	215*	46.0	9	7	.0	6	0	.0
04734	.5	0	.3	89	17.3	253	44.0	12	8	.0	0	0	.0
04735	.8	100	.3	87	14.9	327	38.5	6	14	.4	15	0	.0

*=Estimated **1.0=883 lbs per person; 100++ indicates per capita toxic waste generation > than 100 times the U.S. average of 883 lbs per capita.

ZIP CODE MEASURES OF SIZE, LEVELS OF AFFLUENCE AND QUALITY OF LIFE

1=Population (th.); 2= % White; 3=Households (th.); 4=% Owner Occupied; 5=Mean Income Per Household (th.$); 6=Mean Monthly Rent ($); 7=Mean Home Value (th.$); 8=% under 5, 9=% 65 and over; 10=White Males (th.); 11=% White Males; 12=# Toxic Waste Sites, 65++; 13=Toxic Waste Relative to US(883 lbs.per capita)**;

MAINE

HOULTON / ROCKLAND

ZIPCODE	1	2	3	4	5	6	7	8	9	10	11	12	13
HOULTON													
04736	12.2	98	4.1	74	18.9	295	57.4	7	10	5.8	9	0	.0
04738	.2	100	.1	83	15.5	301	51.5	8	10	.1	12	0	.1
04739	.9	100	.3	70	19.4	191	57.4	7	25	.5	25	0	.0
04740	1.6	0	.5	83	17.8	236	48.6	8	12	.0	0	0	.4
04742	4.2	0	1.4	74	18.1	250	51.8	8	11	.0	0	0	.0
04743	5.4	98	1.6	73	20.2	235	62.6	8	10	2.6	9	0	.0
04744	.3	100	.1	100	29.8	343*	58.0	4	7	.0	7	0	.0
04745	.5	100	.2	83	23.2	211	55.8	7	10	.2	8	0	.0
04746	.4	100	.1	71	21.9	163	52.6	2	18	.2	20	0	.0
04747	1.5	0	.5	82	19.3	219	49.8	9	10	.0	0	0	.0
04749	.3	100	.1	92	19.5	224*	36.6	7	8	.2	11	0	.3
04750	2.9	96	.9	70	19.5	273	47.6	8	8	1.4	8	0	.0
04751	6.7	85	1.6	70	19.6	296	65.6	6	14	3.4	0	1	.0
04756	5.1	0	1.7	70	24.5	252	68.5	7	9	.0	0	0	2.0
04757	1.7	98	.5	81	19.1	234	55.2	7	10	.9	11	0	.0
04758	2.2	99	.7	75	16.7	233	44.4	8	16	1.0	14	0	.0
04759	.2	100	.1	80	17.6	359	27.8	13	13	.1	11	0	.0
04760	1.4	97	.4	85	15.3	192	44.8	8	10	.7	9	0	.0
04761	.1	100	.1	93	13.7	157*	49.9	9	17	.1	14	0	.0
04762	.8	0	.2	90	19.2	254	49.2	6	14	.5	10	0	.0
04763	1.0	0	.3	83	19.2	198	44.5	6	15	.4	7	0	.0
04765	1.8	0	.6	74	17.2	244	48.2	8	14	.0	0	0	.0
04768	.6	100	.2	90	27.6	97	48.3	9	7	.3	6	0	.1
04769	11.5	99	3.8	66	22.2	296	62.1	7	10	5.5	8	0	.2
04772	1.0	100	.3	80	21.6	242	60.2	7	11	.5	10	0	.0
04773	.7	100	.3	93	26.3	345	50.2	8	9	.4	7	0	.0
04774	1.3	0	.4	81	18.5	204	50.2	8	12	.0	0	0	.0
04776	.8	0	.2	92	19.2	84	54.2	9	9	.0	0	0	.0
04777	.7	0	.2	94	18.3	146	43.4	8	14	2.0	0	0	.0
04779	.3	0	.1	75	13.2	238	37.5	8	14	.0	0	0	.0
04780	.7	0	.2	89	19.1	289	44.6	8	7	.0	0	0	.0
04781	.7	0	.2	91	22.1	239	56.8	7	9	.0	0	0	.0
04782	.2	100	.1	79	13.1	220	27.0	7	14	1.0	18	0	.0
04783	.7	98	.2	83	17.6	189	46.0	5	14	.3	14	0	.0
04784	.4	100	.1	72	21.3	216	55.7	7	22	.2	19	0	.0
04785	4.0	99	1.3	68	16.5	200	48.0	6	13	1.9	11	0	.0
04786	2.2	0	.7	84	18.5	281	52.1	9	10	.0	0	0	.0
04787	.6	0	.2	90	20.1	432	43.7	9	13	.0	0	0	.1
ROCKLAND													
04841	9.5	100	3.6	65	19.1	313	59.9	7	16	4.4	13	2	3.4
04843	4.8	0	2.0	70	22.8	355	88.1	5	22	.0	0	0	.3
04846	.2	100	.1	82	24.2	223	102.8	3	22	.1	24	0	.0
04847	.3	0	.1	83	16.9	216	52.5	9	8	.0	0	0	.0
04848	.5	100	.2	78	15.9	265	71.4	4	17	.3	14	0	.0
04849	1.9	99	.7	82	18.8	342	68.2	6	13	.9	11	0	.1
04852	.1	99	.1	60	13.1	292	64.5	6	13	.1	18	0	.0
04853	.4	97	.2	78	17.3	292	89.7	5	15	.1	13	0	.0
04854	1.1	0	.4	85	24.5	386	80.4	7	22	.0	0	0	.0
04855	.2	100	.1	68	19.5	280		7	22	.1	24	0	.0

MAINE

ROCKLAND / WATERVILLE

ZIPCODE	1	2	3	4	5	6	7	8	9	10	11	12	13
ROCKLAND													
04856	1.2	100	.5	76	22.9	416	97.2	5	20	.5	17	0	.1
04857	.4	100	.2	89	20.0	227	66.9	5	24	.2	19	1	.0
04858	.5	100	.2	83	21.7	425	73.4	6	16	.3	16	0	.0
04859	.7	100	.3	87	20.6	362	71.5	7	12	.3	13	0	.0
04860	1.0	0	.4	88	21.3	323	86.7	5	20	.0	0	0	.2
04861	3.6	99	1.2	78	20.6	302	68.1	5	14	1.9	11	0	.1
04862	2.7	100	.9	85	20.1	249	65.9	7	13	1.3	11	1	.2
04863	.5	0	.5	80	17.4	268	49.6	6	18	.0	0	0	.0
04864	2.1	100	.7	83	18.8	333	63.6	6	11	1.2	9	0	.0
04865	.4	100	.1	88	22.6	311	69.2	9	8	.2	4	0	.0
WATERVILLE													
04901	27.2	99	9.4	60	22.1	278	74.7	6	13	12.5	10	0	.4
04910	1.8	0	.6	86	20.4	298	63.0	12	11	.0	0	0	.0
04911	1.6	99	.5	82	15.9	256	42.7	7	11	.8	11	0	.0
04912	.8	100	.2	86	15.9	250	36.9	5	9	.0	0	0	.0
04915	8.7	100	3.1	74	18.0	260	60.3	8	13	4.1	11	0	.0
04917	1.1	99	.4	81	25.7	283	66.7	10	9	.5	9	0	.0
04918	.6	0	.2	87	25.4	360	71.8	4	15	.0	0	0	.0
04920	1.8	0	.6	80	17.4	237	47.7	7	16	.0	0	0	.0
04921	1.5	0	.5	86	17.5	209	49.0	8	12	.0	0	0	.0
04922	1.2	0	.4	88	16.9	225	48.2	9	10	.0	0	0	.2
04923	.6	0	.2	77	14.8	356	45.9	11	13	.0	0	0	.0
04924	1.0	0	.3	86	16.5	312	56.9	9	10	.0	0	0	.1
04926	.7	0	.3	84	26.3	412	76.3	8	5	.0	0	0	.2
04927	3.1	99	1.0	88	21.5	229	59.8	7	8	1.5	7	0	.5
04928	2.0	100	.7	77	19.0	225	49.2	7	13	1.0	11	1	.0
04929	.6	0	.2	90	17.0	217	41.4	7	9	.0	0	1	.6
04930	5.8	0	2.0	76	19.5	303	54.1	7	13	.0	0	0	1.1
04932	1.0	100	.3	89	20.5	222	52.0	5	8	.5	8	0	.0
04936	.1	100	.1	78	8.6	195	43.2	4	26	.1	20	0	.0
04937	5.8	100	2.0	71	20.2	269	65.8	7	13	2.8	11	0	.0
04938	7.8	99	2.5	71	21.1	286	62.0	6	11	3.5	10	1	.6
04939	.2	100	.1	94	14.3	164*	40.2	8	18	.1	15	0	.0
04940	.2	100	.1	100	24.2	278*	47.4	0	26	.1	37	0	.1
04941	.7	0	.2	88	15.6	379	43.1	9	11	.0	0	0	.0
04942	.9	0	.3	90	15.8	178	44.8	6	9	.0	0	0	.0
04943	2.0	100	.6	82	17.7	255	50.1	8	12	1.0	9	0	.2
04945	1.4	99	.5	71	20.6	236	52.0	7	14	.7	11	0	.0
04947	1.3	0	.5	77	18.7	224	64.4	7	14	.0	0	0	.1
04949	1.1	100	.4	82	16.7	188	53.7	10	13	.5	8	0	.0
04950	3.8	100	1.3	72	19.1	249	56.6	6	17	1.8	15	0	.6
04951	.5	100	.2	90	20.1	284	52.3	11	13	.2	11	0	.6
04952	.9	100	.3	89	17.0	260	58.5	9	10	.5	9	0	.0
04953	3.4	100	1.2	76	17.5	259	61.8	9	12	1.6	9	0	.1
04954	.2	0	.1	95	18.3	210*	44.1	9	12	.0	0	0	.0
04955	1.1	100	.4	88	18.4	300	52.0	7	13	.5	10	0	.0
04956	.7	100	.6	87	17.4	206	45.4	10	10	.3	9	0	.4
04957	.7	0	.1	81	19.4	291	53.2	7	9	.0	0	0	.3
04958	1.6	100	.6	86	17.2	236	49.0	7	15	.8	14	0	.3

*=Estimated **1.0=883 lbs per person; 100++ indicates per capita toxic waste generation > than 100 times the U.S. average of 883 lbs per capita.

ZIP CODE MEASURES OF SIZE, LEVELS OF AFFLUENCE AND QUALITY OF LIFE

1=Population (th.); 2= % White; 3=Households (th.); 4=% Owner Occupied; 5=Mean Income Per Household (th.$); 6=Mean Monthly Rent ($)*; 7=Mean Home Value (th.$)*;
8=% under 5; 9=% 65 and over; 10=White Males, 65+; 11=% White Males, 65+; 12=# Toxic Waste Sites; 13=Toxic Waste Relative to US(883 lbs.per capita)**.

MAINE

WATERVILLE

ZIPCODE	1	2	3	4	5	6	7	8	9	10	11	12	13
04961	.4	100	.2	89	17.8	230	42.0	7	14	.2	15	0	.0
04962	1.8	100	.6	91	22.0	208	60.8	8	12	.9	11	0	.0
04963	6.4	0	2.1	80	22.2	274	67.6	9	9	.0	0	0	.0
04964	.2	100	.1	80	26.6	74	71.3	1	20	.1	17	0	.2
04966	1.8	100	.6	80	18.9	237	49.4	7	14	.9	13	0	.0
04967	5.0	100	1.6	77	19.9	316	58.5	8	13	2.4	11	1	.3
04969	.4	100		83	18.7	148	63.3	10	7	.2	9	0	.0
04970	1.2	0	.5	77	19.7	203	58.4	5	17	.0	0	0	.0
04971	1.0	0	.3	85	16.8	203	51.1	9	10	.0	0	0	.0
04973	.4	0	.1	75	19.7	198	58.5	11	5	.0	0	0	.0
04974	2.0	100	.7	80	18.0	261	63.2	8	13	1.0	9	1	4.7
04975	.4	100	.1	90	18.7	206	62.9	11	9	.2	9	0	3.6
04976	10.1	100	3.5	72	20.1	254	64.5	8	13	4.7	11	2	.0
04979	1.0	0	.4	81	14.9	286	47.3	10	13	.0	0	0	.1
04981	1.6	0	.2	85	19.4	271	56.2	7	14	.3	11	0	.0
04982	.6	100	.2	72	20.2	190	54.9	6	11	.3	11	0	.0
04983	1.3	0	.5	85	18.6	232	46.1	7	13	.0	0	0	.1
04984	.5	100	.2	88	17.7	294	56.9	8	11	.2	8	0	.0
04985	.2	100	.1	81	18.6	64	33.3	6	19	.1	24	0	.0
04986	1.3	99	.4	84	15.2	149	53.2	7	9	.6	9	0	.0
04987	.5	98	.4	83	14.8	331	51.1	9	11	.3	11	0	.0
04988	1.5	100	.5	74	17.8	249	57.1	6	9	.8	9	0	.0
04989	1.5	100	.5	75	24.7	284	64.1	8	12	.8	7	0	.0
04990	.3	98	.1	84	11.8	261	29.4	8	7	.1	8	0	.0
04992	.4	100	.1	63	16.6	299	56.0	18	13	.2	8	0	.0

MARYLAND

ZIPCODE	1	2	3	4	5	6	7	8	9	10	11	12	13
JOHNSTOWN													
15545	.2	100	.1	89	28.9	331*	58.8	0	11	.1	6	0	.0
15558	.1	100	.1	100	11.2	129*	33.1	0	19	.1	18	0	.0
YORK													
17321	7	100	.2	87	28.9	526	116.5	1	6	.3	5	0	.0
SOUTHEASTERN													
19362	.5	0	.1	92	28.6	431	139.3	3	10	.0	0	0	.0
WILMINGTON													
19709	.2	100	.1	26	25.5	129	72.5	4	20	.1	27	0	.0
19711	2.0	0	.6	98	46.0	495	136.6	10	2	.0	0	0	.0
DOVER													
19940	3.6	89	1.3	80	23.3	297	70.2	6	11	1.5	8	0	4.7
19973	.5	89	.2	83	20.0	239	49.0	10	15	.2	22	0	3.6
19975	.3	27	.1	72	21.4	264	56.7	7	4	.0	0	0	.0
WASHINGTON													
20011	.3	10	.1	18	20.8	454	110.4	5	6	.0	37	0	.0
20014	23.3	59	9.5	37	27.3	395	121.3	6	10	6.6	11	0	.0
20015	22.6	93	10.2	44	44.6	538	222.2	4	15	9.9	12	1	.2
20015	25.5	95	10.9	59	60.5	586	279.3	3	18	11.0	16	0	.0
20016	15.0	95	5.6	81	72.6	701	277.3	5	14	6.7	13	0	.7
20018	.8	44	.3	92	33.8	241	106.0	7	16	.1	35	0	.0
20019	.2	0	.1	35	24.9	429	80.2	4	4	.0	0	0	.0
20021	28.3	34	10.0	45	30.5	377	103.0	8	4	4.6	7	0	.0
20022	38.6	57	11.9	80	45.7	525	138.7	7	5	11.0	3	1	.0
20023	29.4	45	11.7	30	27.5	422	103.8	8	5	6.4	3	0	.0
20027	41.0	11	11.9	66	30.5	391	85.4	7	5	2.1	12	0	.7
20028	35.3	45	13.0	39	30.0	421	104.0	8	6	7.7	9	0	.0
20031	41.8	53	15.3	56	35.9	433	119.5	6	7	10.6	9	0	.0
20034	34.0	92	11.7	84	67.1	691	258.5	4	9	15.1	9	0	.0
GOVERNMENT													
20331	.4	92	.2	94	23.3	268*	166.3	13	0	.2	0	1	5.0
20335	9.6	73	2.1	1	24.7	376	100.6	12	0	4.1	0	0	.0
PRINCE GEORGES													
20601	28.2	86	8.3	80	36.0	450	118.3	9	3	12.2	2	0	.0
20606	.5	76	.2	71	20.2	357	104.5	9	18	.2	16	0	.5
20607	3.7	88	1.2	84	36.7	485	127.8	6	8	1.5	8	1	.0
20608	.3	34	.1	60	27.7	341	76.5	9	21	.1	18	0	.0
20609	1.1	81	.4	77	21.5	232	78.7	4	13	.5	15	0	.5
20610	.3	60	.1	77	32.4	239	110.5	5	2	.1	0	0	.0
20611	.9	75	.3	52	25.9	370	106.4	8	9	.4	10	0	.0
20612	.4	81	.2	57	20.3	305	77.4	9	6	.2	0	0	.0
20613	8.6	65	2.5	85	32.3	393	110.6	7	7	2.8	7	0	.0
20615	.3	100	.1	83	20.8	543	81.7	12	18	.2	17	0	.0
20616	4.1	77	1.2	86	33.7	371	99.0	7	5	1.6	4	0	.5
20617	1.0	70	.3	79	34.9	392	137.5	6	3	.3	5	0	.0
20618	.6	89	.2	71	27.4	586	96.0	3	9	.3	9	0	.0
20619	3.4	92	1.2	80	30.6	358	119.0	8	8	1.6	6	1	.0
20620	.6	73	.2	67	27.0	283	92.4	5	5	.2	3	0	.0
20621	1.6	52	.4	84	25.7	239	102.3	11	8	.1	10	0	.0
20622	3.4	77	.9	78	31.9	443	130.4	9	5	1.4	6	0	.0

*=Estimated **1.0=883 lbs per person; 100++ indicates per capita toxic waste generation > than 100 times the U.S. average of 883 lbs per capita.

ZIP CODE MEASURES OF SIZE, LEVELS OF AFFLUENCE AND QUALITY OF LIFE

1=Population (th.); 2= % White; 3=Households (th.); 4=% Owner Occupied; 5=Mean Income Per Household (th.$); 6=Mean Monthly Rent ($); 7=Mean Home Value (th.$); 8=% under 5; 9=% 65 and over; 10=White Males (th.); 11=% White Males, 65+; 12=# Toxic Waste Sites; 13=Toxic Waste Relative to US(883 lbs.per capita)**.

MARYLAND

PRINCE GEORGES

ZIPCODE	1	2	3	4	5	6	7	8	9	10	11	12	13
20623	1.1	68	.3	87	35.3	465	107.0	7	5	.4	3	0	.0
20624	.7	73	.2	74	27.9	229	105.1	8	3	.3	2	0	.0
20625	.8	100	.3	90	21.2	495	81.1	6	28	.4	24	0	.0
20626	.5	91	.	88	19.8	346	105.5	3	13	.2	10	0	.0
20627	.2	76	.1	79	11.5	362	54.4	4	11	.1	11	0	.0
20628	.4	0	.2	71	27.1	162	111.8	4	15	.0	11	0	.0
20629	.3	39	.1	86	23.8	461	95.3	11	17	.1	11	0	.0
20630	.4	72	.1	66	20.4	341	103.7	8	23	.1	23	0	.0
20632	.3	83	.1	64	41.6	615	117.4	6	2	.1	0	0	.0
20634	2.1	82	.6	64	32.0	435	110.9	8	6	.9	5	0	.0
20635	.2	85	.2	64	19.2	401	57.7	15	6	.1	5	0	.0
20636	5.8	90	1.9	77	31.2	418	120.1	7	8	2.5	6	0	.0
20637	2.4	62	.7	74	31.6	330	108.8	5	7	.8	6	0	.0
20639	6.2	74	1.8	87	34.9	353	143.0	6	7	2.3	5	0	.0
20640	7.9	72	2.4	73	31.1	329	86.2	8	8	2.9	6	1	.0
20650	10.1	82	2.9	78	37.2	445	131.2	7	7	4.1	4	1	.0
20653	7.0	89	2.3	65	27.6	356	128.5	8	11	3.1	8	0	.0
20656	12.5	78	4.5	52	26.2	363	110.7	10	7	4.9	3	0	.0
20657	.5	77	.2	70	25.6	294	74.0	15	12	.2	10	0	.0
20658	4.0	78	1.4	83	29.5	518	105.6	8	12	1.6	13	0	.0
20659	1.2	61	.4	82	27.6	285	99.5	7	9	.4	10	0	.0
20660	10.2	86	2.8	80	29.5	373	104.6	10	6	4.3	6	1	.0
20662	2.3	67	.1	62	36.3	316	93.4	8	9	.9	9	0	.0
20664	2.5	43	.7	80	24.5	262	78.9	9	10	.5	12	0	.0
20667	.4	58	.7	73	27.5	374	92.9	11	5	.3	8	0	.0
20670	3.5	39	.1	78	26.3	225	84.4	5	5	.1	7	0	.0
20674	.8	85	.6	1	22.2	365	79.2*	11	0	1.8	0	1	.0
20675	1.6	83	.3	79	24.1	412	92.2	6	14	.4	15	0	.0
20676	1.6	61	.4	89	36.8	730	132.0	8	6	.5	7	0	.0
20677	1.6	58	.4	88	29.8	469	114.3	6	11	.6	16	0	.0
20678	5.8	81	1.4	77	37.9	469	149.1	8	8	.6	6	0	.0
20680	1.2	73	1.8	83	31.1	247	106.8	9	10	2.0	9	0	.0
20684	1.1	88	.5	71	26.8	440	127.7	2	11	.5	12	0	.0
20685	2.3	54	.3	64	26.4	466	101.6	6	5	.3	0	0	.0
20686	1.1	81	.7	80	29.0	383	108.6	8	9	.1	7	0	.0
20687	3.5	93	.2	56	40.5	306	143.9	1	2	.5	3	0	.0
20688	.8	85	.6	83	22.1	288	105.0	4	13	.4	9	1	.0
20689	1.3	47	.3	61	26.7	398	160.2	9	6	.3	6	0	.3
20690	.3	0	.1	86	28.3	284	136.8	8	2	.0	0	0	.0
20692	1.1	81	.4	78	30.1	454	93.8	8	7	.4	12	0	.0
20693	.6	74	.3	73	31.2	415	104.3	7	9	.2	7	0	.0
20695	3.7	95	1.1	92	41.7	441	142.7	6	5	1.7	3	0	1.1
PRINCE GEORGES													
20702	.8	92	.3	92	57.2	482	254.2	7	10	.4	9	0	.0
20703	.4	100	.1	83	61.7	987	160.2	2	9	.2	8	0	.0
20704	.3	51	.1	72	28.5	741	155.7	8	13	.1	8	0	.0
20705	17.8	84	6.4	62	37.0	474	133.8	6	5	7.6	5	4	.1
20710	7.8	56	3.5	22	33.8	398	89.6	8	8	2.0	3	9	.9

MARYLAND

PRINCE GEORGES

ZIPCODE	1	2	3	4	5	6	7	8	9	10	11	12	13
20715	29.6	92	8.2	88	45.8	713	126.7	5	4	13.6	3	1	.0
20716	11.9	82	3.4	90	47.2	644	145.4	9	4	4.9	3	0	.0
20720	1.8	87	.5	83	40.6	580	158.1	5	7	.7	0	0	.0
20722	5.4	68	1.9	70	24.6	339	79.1	8	13	1.7	12	0	.0
20727	.5	83	.1	78	55.3	636*	295.8	5	4	.2	2	0	.0
20729	4.1	92	1.2	89	51.8	595	190.7	8	4	1.8	4	0	.0
20730	1.5	95	.9	56	44.5	547	178.8	8	10	.7	10	1	.0
20732	2.7	80	.9	76	29.7	416	94.3	8	8	1.1	6	1	.0
20733	1.9	75	.6	91	32.0	488	101.0	8	7	.7	4	0	.0
20734	2.9	98	.9	81	41.4	464	165.3	9	6	1.5	5	0	.2
20735	21.2	73	6.2	91	42.9	655	119.6	6	5	7.7	5	0	.0
20740	30.2	91	8.0	61	36.1	487	118.6	6	3	13.8	4	0	.0
20751	6.1	96	1.9	86	42.5	486	155.3	7	7	2.9	6	0	.0
20753	1.7	89	1.9	83	29.4	408	118.3	5	15	.7	11	0	.0
20754	1.9	76	.6	66	33.2	446	150.9	7	8	.8	6	0	.0
20755	4.2	96	1.3	92	40.0	445	160.8	7	5	2.1	5	0	.0
20758	14.1	73	3.1	0	20.7	333	73.7*	13	0	5.9	10	1	.0
20759	.5	74	.2	64	31.4	245	122.6	3	11	.2	10	1	.0
20760	1.1	77	.4	96	46.6	308	202.7	7	8	.0	0	0	.0
20765	68.9	87	25.0	55	38.4	495	173.8	9	4	29.4	3	2	.1
20767	12.0	57	.3	84	27.7	308	120.8	6	16	.8	28	0	.6
20768	.2	90	4.2	83	40.5	530	150.5	10	3	5.4	3	0	.3
20769	2.9	0	.1	45	30.2	667	178.8	10	16	.0	0	0	.3
20770	20.3	82	.7	86	44.0	615	142.1	4	8	1.2	5	0	.3
20777	2.4	86	9.1	35	30.8	478	84.6	6	6	8.4	5	0	.0
20780	1.9	78	.7	79	38.7	389	179.5	5	5	.9	5	0	.0
20781	.3	95	.5	95	51.9	523	219.4	5	7	.1	9	0	.0
20782	10.8	90	.1	100	58.7	675*	163.5	3	7	.1	19	0	.4
20783	26.8	83	4.0	51	27.2	391	92.6	7	12	4.3	2	0	.2
20784	34.2	58	10.4	43	30.0	414	120.2	7	12	7.1	14	1	.1
20785	28.3	59	13.2	43	30.3	434	120.8	7	7	9.9	9	1	.6
20786	33.0	66	9.7	56	34.4	435	104.9	7	5	9.2	5	0	.0
20794	5.9	20	10.0	51	31.8	374	95.7	9	4	3.3	9	0	.0
20795	8.1	61	1.9	78	33.5	346	120.6	11	8	1.2	5	0	.0
20796	20.6	93	7.3	81	45.8	572	175.1	5	11	9.3	10	0	.0
PRINCE GEORGES													
20801	31.2	61	9.9	64	38.6	422	119.2	7	3	9.5	3	0	.0
20811	37.5	85	13.3	55	33.4	448	126.5	7	5	16.1	4	1	.0
20820	19.3	85	7.6	27	32.3	448	150.5	8	2	8.1	2	0	.0
20822	5.1	77	1.8	88	31.5	283	129.2	7	9	2.1	7	0	.0
20831	8.1	63	3.6	26	21.3	346	81.8	7	13	2.3	14	0	.0
20832	2.8	95	1.0	78	24.2	413	86.2	11	10	1.3	8	0	.1
20836	9.2	92	2.5	93	47.6	678	185.9	6	4	4.2	3	0	.0
20837	3.5	75	1.0	86	36.5	290	143.2	7	6	1.3	4	0	.1
20840	4.3	91	1.3	87	39.5	534	133.6	11	3	2.0	2	0	.0
20850	16.1	76	5.8	48	27.8	407	92.0	6	6	6.1	5	0	.0
20851	22.7	85	7.4	72	44.6	508	182.8	6	7	6.5	5	1	.0
20852	14.4	91	4.9	64	38.7	547	117.8	7	3	6.6	3	0	.1

*=Estimated **1.0=883 lbs per person; 100++ indicates per capita toxic waste generation > than 100 times the U.S. average of 883 lbs per capita.

103001

ZIP CODE MEASURES OF SIZE, LEVELS OF AFFLUENCE AND QUALITY OF LIFE

1=Population (th.); 2= % White; 3=Households (th.); 4=% Owner Occupied; 5=Mean Income Per Household (th.$); 6=Mean Monthly Rent ($)*; 7=Mean Home Value (th.$)*;
8=% under 5; 9-% 65 and over; 10=White Males (th.); 11=% White Males, 65+; 12=# Toxic Waste Sites; 13=Toxic Waste Relative to US(883 lbs.per capita)**.

MARYLAND

PRINCE GEORGES

ZIP CODE	1	2	3	4	5	6	7	8	9	10	11	12	13
20852	24.5	88	9.7	51	43.9	523	221.1	4	11	10.0	8	0	.1
20853	30.4	88	8.9	83	51.5	512	179.6	5	4	13.4	3	0	.0
20854	37.3	90	10.0	94	82.1	783	300.0	5	3	16.6	2	0	.0
20855	8.7	91	2.3	90	50.8	600	182.8	7	3	3.9	2	0	.0
20860	1.0	71	.4	50	45.5	365	146.3	3	36	.3	22	0	.5
20863	1.7	100	.7	34	27.6	399	108.2	7	6	.8	9	0	1.5
20867	2.1	83	.9	80	27.4	457	114.5	5	7	.9	16	0	.0
20868	.4	68	.1	52	33.9	605	157.1	11	8	.1	9	0	.0
20869	.7	75	.2	76	38.5	443*	151.2	5	7	.3	14	0	.0
20870	34.3	60	10.4	84	42.7	575	130.8	7	4	10.4	3	0	.0
20880	.6	0	.2	88	45.1	580	145.9	4	14	.0	0	0	.0
20881	.8	92	.3	73	35.0	564	161.8	3	12	.4	10	0	.0

SILVER SPRINGS

ZIP CODE	1	2	3	4	5	6	7	8	9	10	11	12	13
20901	30.3	82	11.5	67	40.0	457	148.8	6	12	12.1	12	0	.0
20902	39.7	83	14.3	64	38.9	533	142.5	6	10	15.8	10	0	.0
20903	16.5	64	6.1	43	36.4	450	151.1	6	8	4.9	10	0	.0
20904	36.8	82	11.7	73	49.7	518	197.8	5	6	14.9	5	1	.1
20906	40.5	83	15.3	66	38.4	546	153.1	5	11	15.7	10	0	.0
20910	30.6	70	14.3	35	32.3	453	160.1	5	17	9.6	17	1	.6

BALTIMORE

ZIP CODE	1	2	3	4	5	6	7	8	9	10	11	12	13
21001	16.5	80	5.9	57	26.9	307	92.8	7	7	6.5	7	1	.1
21005	6.3	65	.8	3	20.6	361	73.4*	8	0	2.8	0	1	.0
21009	4.3	95	1.7	64	31.2	376	105.0	7	6	2.1	5	1	.0
21010	.5	85	.2	0	24.3	247	86.6*	6	1	.1	3	0	.0
21012	14.0	95	4.4	85	43.6	575	158.0	7	5	6.7	4	1	.0
21013	3.5	0	1.0	94	46.9	379	167.8	6	5	.0	6	0	.0
21014	27.4	96	9.2	70	34.7	392	125.0	7	6	12.7	7	0	.0
21017	.3	76	.1	19	23.5	236	144.8	6	5	.3	7	0	.0
21021	.6	94	.2	95	34.3	614	101.4	4	16	.3	12	0	.0
21022	.3	100	.1	37	107.3	695	273.8	5	12	.1	13	0	4.5
21023	.4	0	.1	77	33.5	413	102.7	7	19	.0	0	0	.0
21024	.4	0	.1	61	22.5	381	72.8	5	13	.0	0	0	.0
21027	.4	86	.1	70	17.3	263	82.4	3	23	.1	25	0	.0
21028	2.5	94	.8	86	40.7	356	137.7	7	4	1.2	3	1	.0
21029	2.7	96	.8	78	51.5	389	206.6	5	7	1.3	5	1	.0
21030	18.2	95	7.8	33	34.1	462	150.8	5	9	8.4	7	1	7.5
21032	6.1	88	1.8	78	38.7	337	89.7	10	4	2.6	6	0	.1
21034	28.5	95	9.7	77	42.0	404	167.4	4	7	13.5	6	0	.0
21035	21.4	78	7.3	65	43.3	511	170.6	7	3	8.1	1	1	.0
21036	1.0	95	.3	68	39.6	479	145.6	6	10	.5	5	0	.0
21037	12.4	95	4.3	85	34.6	610	160.1	9	3	5.9	3	0	.0
21040	18.2	85	5.6	64	27.2	337	154.7	5	5	7.7	3	0	.0
21043	28.5	95	9.7	68	42.0	486	140.1	7	11	13.5	6	1	.0
21044	21.4	92	7.3	65	43.3	511	170.6	8	5	8.1	2	1	.0
21045	27.7	76	9.6	68	39.6	479	145.6	10	3	10.2	3	0	.0
21046	3.5	85	1.5	94	48.1	610	160.1	9	3	1.5	5	1	1.4
21048	10.2	98	2.9	91	45.4	385	154.7	5	5	5.1	4	0	.0
21050	8.0	96	2.4	82	34.7	441	126.5	8	5	3.9	6	0	.1

MARYLAND

BALTIMORE

ZIP CODE	1	2	3	4	5	6	7	8	9	10	11	12	13
21051	.4	100	.1	74	35.3	460	120.0	3	8	.2	9	0	.0
21052	1.0	94	.2	67	28.1	395	59.2	4	13	.6	13	0	.4
21053	2.1	100	.7	85	33.1	358	121.7	7	9	1.1	8	0	.0
21054	8.3	87	2.4	86	38.1	341	138.4	8	3	3.6	2	0	.6
21056	.4	100	.2	76	92.0	495	280.6	8	25	.2	23	0	.6
21057	3.7	96	1.1	90	63.7	352	211.6	4	10	1.7	7	0	2.8
21061	73.0	91	26.5	58	29.4	393	96.1	7	6	32.7	7	3	.4
21071	1.5	96	.5	71	50.9	333	153.7	3	17	.7	11	0	.0
21074	8.2	0	2.7	77	33.3	372	110.2	6	9	.0	0	0	3.1
21076	4.0	84	1.3	88	30.0	376	110.3	5	8	1.7	8	0	.0
21077	.4	92	.2	82	34.9	335	101.3	10	1	.2	0	0	8.2
21078	13.7	84	4.8	59	27.4	278	95.2	6	12	5.6	9	3	2.8
21082	.6	0	.3	79	47.3	497	147.1	7	4	.0	0	0	.0
21084	5.5	98	1.7	89	36.4	451	130.1	8	6	2.7	6	0	.0
21085	15.5	93	4.9	81	34.1	420	110.2	6	4	7.2	3	0	.0
21087	4.1	99	1.4	88	38.8	303	142.9	5	10	2.1	9	0	.0
21088	.6	100	.2	93	32.8	272	115.0	5	15	.3	10	0	.0
21090	10.1	98	3.4	81	37.1	406	109.9	4	8	4.8	8	1	.0
21092	1.0	100	1.0	100	24.1	277*	140.1	0	23	.0	20	0	.5
21093	26.9	95	9.1	82	48.0	461	156.9	4	11	12.2	9	1	.2

BALTIMORE

ZIP CODE	1	2	3	4	5	6	7	8	9	10	11	12	13
21102	4.5	99	1.5	73	30.5	345	104.3	8	9	2.1	8	0	.0
21104	2.1	95	.6	86	37.3	449	145.2	6	6	1.0	5	0	.0
21105	.3	100	.1	69	29.5	284	145.5	3	2	.4	4	0	1.6
21106	.9	88	.3	84	27.2	319	105.2	7	10	.3	8	0	.0
21107	1.7	95	.5	93	29.9	289	110.7	7	4	.8	3	0	.0
21108	9.9	94	3.0	77	37.6	476	140.1	7	4	4.5	3	0	.0
21111	3.5	96	1.2	84	43.5	554	149.4	7	5	1.6	12	0	.0
21113	7.8	88	2.5	69	32.7	452	110.2	7	5	3.4	4	0	3.4
21114	12.8	96	4.5	77	42.1	576	165.2	8	4	6.1	3	0	.0
21117	18.8	85	6.8	41	33.4	381	151.9	7	7	7.7	6	0	.0
21120	4.0	100	.4	82	38.1	419	138.6	6	6	2.0	6	1	1.6
21122	39.1	96	12.3	86	33.2	414	111.2	6	7	18.8	6	0	.0
21128	2.6	99	.9	95	40.4	336	129.0	2	11	1.3	11	0	.0
21130	.5	89	.2	56	17.7	335	55.6	9	10	.2	9	0	.0
21131	4.9	96	1.4	93	50.7	616	201.6	5	6	2.4	6	0	.0
21144	20.1	74	6.2	67	30.0	383	116.4	11	3	7.6	6	0	.0
21146	20.4	93	6.4	90	47.7	534	169.1	5	11	9.5	5	0	.0
21152	2.2	96	.8	78	44.4	518	150.5	7	7	1.0	10	1	1.6
21153	.8	90	7.8	65	32.4	376	326.2	6	7	.4	15	0	.0
21154	5.8	92	1.8	81	27.1	348	118.2	6	7	2.7	6	0	.1
21155	1.5	100	.5	80	35.2	509	120.1	8	6	.8	3	2	.0
21156	.3	100	.3	73	32.2	323	135.3	6	13	.2	12	0	.1
21157	33.3	97	11.1	72	29.6	327	110.4	6	10	15.6	9	2	.0
21160	1.6	100	.5	79	25.3	373	126.5	6	6	.7	6	2	.0

*=Estimated **1.0=883 lbs per person; 100++ indicates per capita toxic waste generation > than 100 times the U.S. average of 883 lbs per capita.

ZIP CODE MEASURES OF SIZE, LEVELS OF AFFLUENCE AND QUALITY OF LIFE

1=Population (th.); 2=% White; 3=Households (th.); 4=% Owner Occupied; 5=Mean Income Per Household (th.$); 6=Mean Monthly Rent ($); 7=Mean Home Value (th.$);
8=% under 5, 9=% 65 and over; 10=% White Males (th.); 11=% White Males, 65+; 12=# Toxic Waste Sites; 13=Toxic Waste Relative to US(883 lbs.per capita)**.

MARYLAND

ZIPCODE	1	2	3	4	5	6	7	8	9	10	11	12	13
BALTIMORE													
21161	3.2	97	1.1	78	32.5	418	110.6	8	10	1.6	8	0	.1
21162	2.8	95	.9	86	33.1	473	99.7	4	10	1.3	9	0	.6
21163	1.6	83	.4	80	32.8	499	113.3	6	7	.7	3	0	.0
BALTIMORE													
21201	17.0	29	7.5	7	14.5	228	68.1	7	16	2.5	20	6	2.5
21202	25.7	21	8.4	9	13.9	240	44.8	8	7	3.4	8	3	.3
21204	38.8	96	14.8	59	42.9	479	153.2	3	18	16.2	15	0	.3
21205	24.9	46	8.9	47	17.7	298	28.0	8	12	5.5	13	2	1.0
21206	55.4	76	20.9	61	25.6	348	70.3	6	12	20.2	12	0	.0
21207	73.1	49	27.0	55	29.7	401	86.7	6	9	17.2	12	2	.2
21208	26.4	94	10.0	70	48.6	488	143.3	4	14	12.0	13	0	.2
21209	19.6	90	8.2	46	37.1	471	134.0	5	14	8.3	14	0	.7
21210	12.2	96	5.7	41	43.7	496	177.9	3	23	5.1	20	0	.0
21211	20.9	93	8.2	56	21.3	324	47.0	6	17	9.0	13	0	.3
21212	37.6	65	13.9	65	33.4	379	108.4	6	15	10.8	16	0	.0
21213	51.8	32	16.7	53	20.0	310	44.0	7	12	7.5	17	1	.8
21214	22.7	87	8.9	72	26.1	319	72.1	6	17	9.2	15	1	.0
21215	82.4	21	27.2	46	23.3	353	59.0	6	13	7.5	34	0	.0
21216	47.6	1	15.3	52	21.5	324	43.7	6	12	.3	34	0	.0
21217	59.2	7	22.3	21	15.6	260	42.8	7	14	2.3	14	1	.0
21218	61.9	36	22.9	42	23.6	316	66.0	6	12	10.6	15	1	.0
21219	8.1	95	2.8	77	29.7	371	83.4	6	11	3.7	10	0	43.1
21220	36.2	90	12.8	56	25.6	361	82.2	8	6	16.2	6	0	.6
21221	42.8	95	16.2	51	25.7	328	79.6	7	8	19.8	8	0	.1
21222	64.8	93	22.5	71	28.4	352	69.1	5	9	30.0	8	6	.7
21223	42.4	39	13.4	39	16.1	289	26.9	8	11	8.0	12	1	.3
21224	56.5	95	21.5	70	21.8	279	45.4	6	15	25.5	13	5	3.3
21225	37.8	63	13.2	52	21.5	253	64.7	6	10	11.4	10	5	.2
21226	6.8	80	2.5	53	19.9	258	56.5	7	11	2.7	11	16	.9
21227	40.6	95	14.3	68	27.8	347	86.1	6	10	18.6	9	2	2.6
21228	40.4	89	13.7	76	34.2	390	111.8	4	17	16.7	14	0	.1
21229	56.7	44	19.8	58	25.4	330	59.9	6	16	12.1	15	0	.0
21230	37.6	81	13.2	62	20.2	301	45.7	7	14	14.5	11	3	3.9
21231	18.0	58	6.9	36	15.4	215	34.6	8	13	5.2	14	3	5.0
21234	65.7	91	24.8	65	29.0	398	90.9	6	11	28.6	10	0	.0
21237	23.3	95	8.4	68	33.9	440	108.0	7	6	10.7	6	0	.0
21239	24.6	86	9.2	58	29.2	342	98.0	6	9	10.3	8	5	.5
21239	29.6	56	11.4	59	27.6	367	68.5	5	14	7.2	16	0	.0
ANNAPOLIS													
21401	36.4	74	12.8	68	37.8	390	164.6	6	9	13.5	8	1	.0
21402	6.3	90	.4	9	29.9	425	258.1	4	0	4.7	0	2	.0
21403	21.9	76	8.6	53	32.4	420	149.7	6	11	8.0	11	0	.0
21405	.5	100	.2	97	39.9	458*	178.6	3	20	.2	19	0	.0
CUMBERLAND													
21502	47.2	97	18.2	68	22.6	243	65.1	6	16	21.3	13	2	.1
21520	1.4	0	.4	82	24.8	237	64.4	7	13	.0	0	0	.0
21521	1.8	99	.6	81	22.9	223	45.3	6	13	.9	11	0	.0
21523	.2	100	.1	78	27.9	257	67.3	4	18	.1	21	0	.0
21524	.8	100	.3	90	19.5	233	52.5	2	17	.4	13	0	.0

MARYLAND

ZIPCODE	1	2	3	4	5	6	7	8	9	10	11	12	13
CUMBERLAND													
21525	.3	100	.1	91	17.8	205*	34.1	16	4	.2	4	0	.0
21528	.4	100	.2	76	16.9	306	39.6	6	21	.2	13	0	.0
21529	.7	100	.3	98	21.0	241*	46.4	3	17	.3	18	0	.0
21530	1.4	99	.5	82	19.9	268	54.8	6	10	.8	11	0	.0
21531	2.5	100	.9	82	17.4	170	64.4	7	13	1.2	13	0	.0
21532	14.5	97	4.6	72	21.4	251	64.7	5	13	6.6	10	3	.0
21536	3.0	100	1.0	78	19.5	266	69.9	8	16	1.5	16	0	.0
21538	.8	100	.3	80	16.8	175	29.6	8	18	.4	14	0	.0
21539	3.2	100	1.3	70	17.5	190	42.6	7	21	1.5	17	0	.0
21540	.4	100	.1	74	21.7	189	33.6	3	24	.2	21	0	58.9
21541	.9	100	.3	77	23.5	212	88.3	8	4	.4	3	0	.0
21542	1.1	0	.4	75	23.2	208	56.6	8	13	.0	0	1	.0
21543	1.4	100	.4	69	26.2	202	57.2	7	12	.2	12	0	.0
21545	2.2	100	.8	77	19.0	217	50.3	8	15	1.0	13	0	.0
21546	.2	100	.1	100	11.3	130*	24.6	11	8	6.2	1	0	.0
21550	12.9	100	4.3	77	22.1	279	73.5	8	12	.1	8	1	.0
21555	1.5	0	.5	80	18.4	210	57.6	8	14	.0	0	1	.0
21557	2.0	100	.6	89	21.9	246	62.3	7	11	.1	11	0	.0
21561	2.1	0	.7	76	21.4	257	60.5	8	9	.0	0	0	.0
21562	3.8	100	1.5	75	21.3	215	53.2	6	15	1.8	12	0	.0
EASTON													
21601	13.5	77	5.4	60	27.3	345	127.2	5	18	4.8	17	1	.7
21607	.4	59	.1	81	22.5	163	77.1	12	7	.1	16	0	.2
21610	.4	100	.2	75	22.1	244	74.8	11	15	.2	14	0	.0
21611	.2	100	.1	93	18.6	214*	46.1	3	21	.1	7	0	.0
21613	.4	100	.4	87	31.2	550	140.2	4	24	.2	21	0	.3
21617	17.0	68	6.5	60	22.8	275	76.1	6	18	5.5	16	3	.3
21619	4.7	79	1.6	65	27.4	332	99.0	5	18	1.7	14	0	.3
21620	2.8	81	1.0	87	29.9	242	107.8	7	10	1.1	10	0	.0
21622	9.9	76	3.7	69	25.3	294	92.6	5	14	3.6	12	0	1.5
21623	.7	76	.2	76	30.3	202	94.6	7	8	.3	10	0	.0
21624	.7	77	.3	72	20.6	321	83.6	8	11	.4	9	0	.0
21625	1.2	84	.4	84	49.0	392	80.8	3	16	.7	27	0	.0
21626	1.9	71	.6	77	25.5	318	74.4	7	5	.7	5	0	.0
21628	.5	100	.1	84	14.4	165*	46.0	8	13	.3	14	0	1
21629	6.0	82	2.2	72	20.0	272	94.1	7	10	.5	6	0	.0
21631	1.8	81	.7	84	24.2	279	79.3	6	15	1.2	13	0	.1
21632	5.8	81	2.2	76	23.8	229	67.3	7	15	2.4	13	0	.0
21634	.5	100	.5	71	22.0	248	60.5	7	13	2.2	11	0	.0
21635	.8	82	.3	89	18.3	219	70.9	7	19	.5	22	0	.0
21636	1.0	91	.4	82	20.5	374	78.0	7	19	.3	22	0	.0
21637	.4	84	.1	84	21.9	283	55.5	7	12	.2	10	0	.0
21638	2.3	70	.8	65	24.4	288	137.3	7	11	.8	15	0	.0
21639	2.6	93	.9	81	22.1	256	73.7	7	15	1.2	14	0	.0
21640	1.0	96	.4	79	22.7	302	70.1	7	15	.5	18	0	.0
21641	.2	100	.6	87	19.2	236	62.8	4	19	.9	15	0	.2
21643	4.2	53	1.4	75	20.1	289	60.6	6	13	1.0	19	0	.0
21644	.2	100	.1	62	23.4	164	66.5	16	4	.1	0	0	.0

*=Estimated **1.0=883 lbs per person; 100++ indicates per capita toxic waste generation > than 100 times the U.S. average of 883 lbs per capita.

ZIP CODE MEASURES OF SIZE, LEVELS OF AFFLUENCE AND QUALITY OF LIFE

1=Population (th.); 2= % White; 3=Households (th.); 4=% Owner Occupied; 5=Mean Income Per Household (th.$); 6=Mean Monthly Rent ($)*; 7=Mean Home Value (th.$)*; 8=% under 5; 9=% 65 and over; 10=White Males (th.); 11=% White Males, 65+; 12=# Toxic Waste Sites; 13=Toxic Waste Relative to US(883 lbs.per capita)**.

MARYLAND

EASTON

ZIPCODE	1	2	3	4	5	6	7	8	9	10	11	12	13
21645	.9	84	.3	77	28.6	281	102.2	6	16	.4	8	0	.0
21647	.3	75	.1	72	28.8	246	117.4	5	6	.1	0	0	.1
21648	.2	85	.1	79	18.4	345	78.8	0	8	.1	6	0	.5
21649	1.1	87	.4	78	19.8	332	50.3	11	16	.5	13	0	.0
21650	.2	100	.1	77	20.8	239*	59.5	11	26	.5	16	0	.0
21651	2.3	75	.7	76	22.5	248	72.5	8	11	.8	9	0	.0
21652	.3	100	.1	95	18.4	212*	91.6	12	25	.1	27	0	.0
21653	.2	100	.1	90	24.5	282*	70.6	0	16	.1	14	0	.0
21654	1.2	80	.5	74	32.2	435	180.6	3	28	.5	29	0	.2
21655	3.6	71	1.2	77	24.6	302	75.8	9	12	1.3	12	0	3.4
21657	1.0	80	.3	82	28.2	394	74.7	4	11	.4	14	0	.2
21658	2.2	84	.8	78	32.4	258	150.3	4	11	.8	14	0	.2
21659	1.1	68	.3	92	26.8	76	53.6	5	15	.4	12	0	.3
21660	2.5	81	.8	79	22.0	315	65.5	5	13	1.0	11	0	.0
21661	2.9	83	1.1	78	19.4	325	57.6	6	19	1.1	17	0	.0
21663	2.8	73	.8	65	30.3	288	137.8	7	20	.3	13	0	.0
21664	2.7	77	1.2	70	28.2	352	145.8	5	22	.9	22	0	.0
21666	.6	100	.2	90	22.0	227	55.7	7	14	.2	13	0	.0
21667	5.5	95	1.9	88	32.1	459	115.4	7	10	2.6	9	0	.0
21668	.4	72	.2	57	19.9	421	57.0	10	9	.1	0	0	.0
21669	1.4	93	.5	72	23.2	289	73.1	8	11	.7	9	0	.0
21670	1.6	62	.1	79	17.0	195*	46.4	4	32	.1	30	0	11.8
21671	.9	100	.1	93	25.5	116*	36.0	5	38	.0	39	0	.8
21673	.9	100	.1	85	25.5	339	90.7	7	17	.5	16	0	.0
21675	2.2	78	.8	70	32.8	367	110.7	8	13	.9	8	0	.3
21676	.3	100	.1	82	20.0	288	43.4	3	22	.1	23	0	.0
21677	.4	84	.1	94	27.5	316*	61.4	3	23	.2	29	0	.2
21678	.4	81	.1	76	21.8	383	71.2	7	13	.1	15	0	.0
21679	1.5	62	.6	79	22.1	226	59.9	5	13	.5	17	0	.0
	.3	78	.1	85	30.5	614	86.6	8	4	.1	0	0	.0

FREDERICK

ZIPCODE	1	2	3	4	5	6	7	8	9	10	11	12	13
21701	48.2	90	16.9	63	29.6	386	110.8	7	11	20.6	9	2	.5
21710	1.6	85	.5	74	27.5	310	98.5	13	9	.7	9	0	11.8
21711	.9	100	.1	80	23.7	371	76.6	5	13	.4	15	0	.0
21712	.4	100	.1	79	18.9	115	63.2	7	7	.2	7	0	.0
21713	6.5	100	2.2	79	28.3	334	85.4	6	14	3.1	10	0	.0
21714	.5	96	.2	58	39.2	263	142.8	9	3	.1	0	0	.2
21715	.2	100	.1	91	32.4	372*	106.9	12	3	.1	0	0	.0
21716	4.5	94	1.5	76	26.1	305	77.3	9	10	2.1	8	0	.0
21717	.4	86	.1	72	41.0	433	147.3	11	6	.2	6	0	.0
21718	2.8	83	.7	77	28.6	271	74.7	4	13	.2	10	0	.0
21719	1.6	80	.7	34	22.8	358	70.3	9	4	1.2	4	0	.0
21720	.2	100	.1	67	22.3	337	66.0	0	25	.1	26	0	.0
21721	.3	100	.1	64	30.5	229	78.5	4	6	.2	5	0	.0
21722	3.7	0	1.2	79	26.3	302	77.1	6	9	.0	0	0	.0
21723	.6	67	.2	87	38.8	322	125.6	7	9	.2	9	0	.0
21725	.3	100	.1	65	22.0	338	120.2	2	15	.1	17	0	.0
21727	5.1	99	1.1	60	27.4	336	76.3	5	10	2.6	8	0	.0
21733	1.0	100	.3	90	29.3	393	79.2	5	10	.5	8	0	.0

MARYLAND

FREDERICK

ZIPCODE	1	2	3	4	5	6	7	8	9	10	11	12	13
21734	1.1	99	.5	55	24.2	323	66.4	5	12	.5	11	0	.0
21736	.3	100	.1	90	36.8	423*	113.4	4	3	.1	0	0	.0
21737	.6	0	.2	84	45.0	356	179.6	7	7	.1	0	0	.0
21738	1.1	94	.3	89	48.8	321	194.4	6	5	.6	5	0	.0
21740	69.6	93	25.2	59	25.1	285	85.8	6	13	31.2	10	4	1.2
21750	4.0	100	1.5	76	20.0	264	76.9	5	12	2.0	10	0	2.3
21753	.3	0	.1	70	39.8	466	69.7	0	3	.1	0	0	.0
21754	3.4	94	1.0	91	42.2	395	142.9	10	3	1.6	2	0	.0
21755	2.7	0	.9	78	31.6	435	110.0	8	6	.0	0	0	.0
21756	1.9	100	.7	75	29.3	333	81.3	5	8	1.0	8	0	.0
21757	1.9	100	.6	74	26.7	385	90.7	8	9	1.0	7	0	.1
21758	3.0	93	1.0	79	25.9	335	98.9	7	10	1.3	9	0	.3
21760	.9	100	.3	81	25.2	335	78.2	10	5	.5	5	0	.0
21762	.5	89	.1	77	31.2	363	74.7	7	10	.2	7	0	.0
21764	.3	0	.1	76	26.1	319	109.5	0	12	.0	2	0	.0
21766	.5	100	.2	74	16.9	229	66.0	8	12	.3	10	0	.3
21767	1.3	0	.5	72	25.9	349	78.9	10	12	.9	12	0	.0
21769	7.0	99	2.2	81	33.8	296	76.6	9	14	3.4	6	0	.0
21770	3.2	97	.9	92	41.9	450	143.4	6	3	1.6	3	0	.1
21771	14.8	95	4.4	83	35.1	444	131.2	9	6	7.0	5	0	.3
21773	3.0	100	1.0	81	28.8	325	98.8	5	8	1.5	7	0	.0
21774	.3	77	.1	64	35.9	385	111.2	8	18	.1	16	0	.0
21776	4.1	94	1.3	74	29.9	332	104.5	8	6	1.9	6	0	3.5
21777	.6	0	.2	76	27.0	315	87.5	4	5	.0	0	0	.3
21778	.3	100	1.1	80	25.1	377	87.3	6	9	.3	7	0	.0
21779	.4	0	.5	82	28.3	333	95.5	8	11	.2	12	0	.3
21780	.5	99	.8	66	21.5	310	86.7	4	9	.2	12	0	.0
21782	.8	99	.2	78	25.6	333	73.3	6	10	.4	7	0	.0
21783	6.3	99	2.1	75	28.0	284	87.6	9	8	3.2	8	0	.2
21784	20.5	94	5.9	84	36.3	388	126.3	6	8	9.6	7	0	.1
21787	6.1	99	2.9	73	26.8	313	89.2	6	9	2.9	9	0	.3
21788	8.4	99	2.9	73	26.8	344	90.4	6	10	4.0	9	1	.0
21791	3.8	94	1.3	72	28.6	339	88.5	6	12	1.8	10	1	.0
21793	6.3	96	1.9	84	35.2	486	108.9	10	5	3.0	3	0	3
21794	.9	88	.3	84	44.1	327	186.7	4	6	.4	3	0	.0
21795	7.8	98	2.7	70	28.4	339	82.0	4	15	3.7	13	2	.5
21797	5.3	97	1.6	87	36.7	381	159.9	7	8	2.6	6	0	.0
21798	1.5	99	.5	72	28.2	360	96.1	6	10	.7	11	0	.0

SALISBURY

ZIPCODE	1	2	3	4	5	6	7	8	9	10	11	12	13
21801	43.6	77	15.4	66	26.5	332	84.0	6	12	15.8	10	3	.2
21810	.2	82	.1	75	23.4	362	78.4	4	10	.1	10	0	.1
21811	8.7	69	3.1	72	24.1	315	78.7	8	13	2.9	12	1	.4
21813	1.3	85	.5	71	19.2	201	89.8	6	12	.5	9	0	.0
21814	.4	82	.2	86	22.9	332	43.6	4	10	.2	6	0	.0
21816	.5	52	.2	84	21.9	197	51.2	5	20	.1	7	0	.0
21817	5.7	79	2.2	70	18.9	234	54.9	6	19	2.1	18	1	1.8
21820	.2	59	.1	86	18.4	201	44.9	5	35	.1	42	0	.0
21821	.5	86	.2	79	19.4	296	70.1	8	13	.2	12	0	.0

*=Estimated **1.0=883 lbs per person; 100++ indicates per capita toxic waste generation > than 100 times the U.S. average of 883 lbs per capita.

ZIP CODE MEASURES OF SIZE, LEVELS OF AFFLUENCE AND QUALITY OF LIFE

1=Population (th.); 2= % White; 3=Households (th.); 4=% Owner Occupied; 5=Mean Income Per Household; 6=Mean Monthly Rent ($)*; 7=Mean Home Value (th.$)*; 8=% under 5; 9=% 65 and over; 10=White Males (th.); 11=% White Males, 65+; 12=# Toxic Waste Sites; 13=Toxic Waste Relative to US(883 lbs.per capita)**.

MARYLAND

SALISBURY

ZIPCODE	1	2	3	4	5	6	7	8	9	10	11	12	13
21822	1.9	51	.6	79	20.6	268	60.6	10	6	.5	4	0	.0
21823	.1	100	.1	100	15.3	176*	25.1	0	27	.0	13	0	.0
21824	.3	100	.1	88	15.4	177*	45.1	10	29	.1	26	0	.0
21826	2.9	66	1.1	64	18.5	325	54.8	8	11	.9	8	0	.2
21829	.7	80	.3	68	17.5	205	46.0	5	14	.3	19	0	.0
21830	2.2	87	.8	81	24.5	274	79.6	8	14	1.0	12	0	.0
21834	.2	63	.1	74	23.2	248	83.6	14	3	.1	8	0	.0
21835	.4	62	.1	75	27.6	269	52.3	9	2	.1	0	0	.0
21837	1.9	70	.7	84	21.9	320	54.3	6	12	.6	11	0	.0
21838	1.3	54	.5	91	19.7	198	46.8	5	19	.3	20	1	.0
21840	.4	42	.2	79	17.1	258	55.9	5	26	.1	49	0	.1
21841	.7	56	.2	83	18.5	217	72.9	8	12	.2	5	0	.0
21842	6.5	97	2.9	64	26.8	230	131.3	4	13	3.0	12	0	.0
21849	2.4	93	.8	82	23.9	313	70.2	8	8	1.1	8	0	.0
21850	1.7	92	.6	72	21.9	255	67.9	6	13	.7	11	0	.0
21851	7.0	63	2.5	70	22.3	234	62.4	6	14	2.1	14	0	.0
21853	5.8	55	1.9	70	21.3	260	58.6	7	15	1.6	15	0	.0
21856	1.2	0	.4	73	22.7	214	51.7	6	14	.0	0	0	.0
21857	.4	55	.1	71	15.4	209	50.7	13	12	.1	0	0	.0
21858	.1	100	.1	100	7.6	87*	37.1	24	13	.1	7	0	.0
21861	.8	91	.3	90	23.2	291	53.4	4	17	.4	15	1	.0
21863	4.6	66	1.7	68	22.5	268	68.0	6	16	1.5	14	0	.0
21865	.5	49	.3	68	20.3	220	55.2	8	9	.2	10	0	.0
21866	.5	66	.2	87	22.2	383	47.2	3	31	.2	22	0	.0
21867	.2	100	.1	93	9.0	104*	23.6	9	28	.1	19	0	.0
21869	1.1	59	.4	73	25.1	236	54.2	5	14	.3	16	0	.4
21870	.1	100	.1	100	20.8	239*	47.9	4	21	.1	25	0	.0
21871	1.9	56	.6	89	20.5	208	55.1	7	9	.6	11	0	.1
21874	1.5	63	.2	76	22.0	337	67.5	8	9	.2	16	0	.0

BALTIMORE

ZIPCODE	1	2	3	4	5	6	7	8	9	10	11	12	13
21901	8.2	97	2.6	76	28.2	342	92.0	6	11	3.9	8	1	.5
21902	1.2	79	.1	8	34.7	251	123.7*	4	23	.7	25	0	.8
21903	3.4	96	1.2	69	29.5	275	85.2	6	12	1.6	9	0	.0
21904	5.2	81	1.4	74	24.6	280	79.0	6	6	2.2	7	0	.1
21911	5.5	98	1.8	77	27.8	329	86.0	8	8	2.8	7	0	.0
21913	1.3	75	.5	61	23.1	278	58.7	5	11	.5	9	0	.0
21914	.8	97	.3	72	22.0	317	70.5	7	13	.4	10	0	.0
21915	2.5	94	.8	79	23.9	325	80.3	6	10	1.2	8	1	.0
21917	1.4	100	.4	80	28.2	270	83.1	6	8	.7	7	0	.0
21918	2.5	98	.8	78	28.5	291	71.1	7	10	1.3	12	0	.0
21919	1.5	98	.6	80	24.2	350	82.5	3	22	.7	19	0	.0
21920	1.5	100	.1	72	27.5	356	94.7	10	0	.2	0	0	.0
21921	23.7	95	7.7	73	26.7	302	83.5	8	8	11.0	7	6	1.4
21930	.1	74	.1	65	60.6	696*	73.4	8	24	.0	32	0	1.3

MARTINSBURG

ZIPCODE	1	2	3	4	5	6	7	8	9	10	11	12	13
25425	.7	100	.2	85	25.9	581	71.7	9	11	.4	10	0	.0
25434	.2	100	.1	61	24.2	139	49.7	2	20	.2	18	0	.0

MARYLAND

CUMBERLAND

ZIPCODE	1	2	3	4	5	6	7	8	9	10	11	12	13
26726	.3	100	.1	82	21.4	205	49.9	4	11	.1	4	0	.0

*=Estimated **1.0=883 lbs per person; 100++ indicates per capita toxic waste generation > than 100 times the U.S. average of 883 lbs per capita.

ZIP CODE MEASURES OF SIZE, LEVELS OF AFFLUENCE AND QUALITY OF LIFE

1=Population (th.); 2= % White; 3=Households (th.); 4=% Owner Occupied; 5=Mean Income Per Household (th.$); 6=Mean Monthly Rent ($)*; 7=Mean Home Value (th.$)*; 8=% under 5; 9=% 65 and over; 10=White Males (th.); 11=% White Males, 65+; 12=# Toxic Waste Sites; 13=Toxic Waste Relative to US/883 lbs.per capita)**.

MASSACHUSETTS

SPRINGFIELD

ZIP CODE	1	2	3	4	5	6	7	8	9	10	11	12	13
01001	18.6	99	6.8	67	27.3	397	73.2	5	14	8.7	11	1	.6
01002	23.6	92	7.8	44	26.0	439	99.1	4	6	10.9	5	0	.0
01003	10.7	94	.1	0	20.1	53	71.6*	0	0	5.2	0	1	.0
01007	3.4	0	1.2	79	27.4	271	68.1	7	14	.0	0	1	.5
01008	8.0	98	2.7	71	25.5	334	77.4	7	9	3.9	9	1	.0
01009	1.0	99	.3	89	29.2	333	81.9	7	11	.5	10	0	.0
01010	1.4	100	.5	68	26.0	311	66.9	4	11	.7	11	0	.0
01011	2.1	98	.7	76	25.5	300	73.7	7	15	1.0	13	0	.0
01012	1.7	99	.6	85	22.8	326	66.8	6	12	.9	10	0	.1
01013	.5	100	.2	73	21.8	317	60.7	7	9	.3	9	0	.0
01020	23.3	99	8.7	52	21.6	278	61.2	6	15	10.6	11	3	.6
01022	30.7	99	11.3	64	24.3	331	64.7	6	13	14.5	11	1	.2
01026	1.4	81	.3	75	18.6	314	66.2*	0	16	.6	0	0	.2
01027	16.4	99	6.0	63	25.4	340	69.5	7	9	7.9	9	2	1.0
01028	12.9	100	4.3	87	32.2	288	84.2	5	13	6.2	10	1	2.3
01029	.5	100	.2	88	23.6	360	77.0	7	10	.2	16	0	.0
01030	7.7	99	2.5	81	28.3	330	80.6	10	6	3.7	5	0	.0
01031	1.2	0	.4	51	19.9	279	53.7	7	14	.0	0	0	.3
01032	.3	100	.1	89	26.1	226	79.0	5	13	.2	13	1	.0
01033	5.4	99	1.7	82	29.0	356	72.9	6	7	2.7	6	1	.0
01034	1.4	100	.5	84	26.0	367	90.8	8	9	.7	9	0	.0
01035	4.2	99	1.5	78	29.1	435	90.3	5	14	2.1	11	0	.0
01036	4.8	99	1.5	88	29.1	334	86.4	6	9	2.3	8	0	.0
01037	.5	100	.1	73	29.2	380	82.3	8	12	.3	11	0	.0
01038	2.0	100	.8	71	25.9	319	86.8	6	13	1.0	11	1	.2
01039	1.1	99	.4	79	23.9	361	65.8	6	11	.5	10	0	.0
01040	44.7	86	16.6	38	22.0	258	67.1	7	18	17.6	15	5	.9
01050	2.0	99	.4	78	24.1	330	67.2	7	9	1.0	7	0	.0
01053	1.3	0	.4	73	30.6	370	81.5	5	15	.0	0	0	.6
01054	1.3	99	.5	79	30.6	535	93.9	7	7	.5	5	0	.0
01056	17.8	99	6.0	76	28.1	371	71.5	5	10	8.7	9	0	.1
01057	5.9	99	2.1	82	27.9	299	71.3	8	11	2.9	9	0	.5
01059	.4	82	.2	34	24.0	421	116.9	2	23	.2	25	0	.4
01060	26.2	98	9.9	52	23.7	348	72.8	5	15	12.1	12	1	.0
01066	.6	0	.2	81	25.5	258	75.3	5	2	.0	0	0	.0
01068	1.0	98	.4	85	25.4	308	73.2	8	11	.5	10	0	.0
01069	8.1	99	2.8	70	24.1	308	65.6	6	14	3.8	11	1	.8
01070	.4	100	.1	80	22.0	324	79.7	10	12	.4	9	1	2.3
01071	.8	98	.3	74	25.3	355	66.8	7	10	.4	9	1	.2
01072	.7	98	.3	79	28.3	518	79.3	7	6	.4	5	0	.0
01073	4.1	0	1.4	86	28.1	426	78.5	5	7	.0	0	1	.0
01074	.8	0	.3	51	21.8	262	70.5	8	13	.0	0	0	.0
01075	16.6	98	5.3	71	27.1	363	74.9	4	12	6.9	11	0	.2
01077	7.4	99	2.5	76	27.1	394	72.0	7	6	3.7	6	1	.1
01079	.9	0	.3	66	26.1	350	63.1	3	14	.0	0	0	.2
01080	2.6	100	1.0	58	23.0	319	58.7	8	13	1.2	10	0	.9
01081	1.1	0	.3	86	25.4	370	62.3	6	6	.0	0	0	.2
01082	9.1	99	3.4	65	23.3	294	71.4	6	14	4.3	12	1	.2

MASSACHUSETTS

SPRINGFIELD

ZIP CODE	1	2	3	4	5	6	7	8	9	10	11	12	13
01083	2.2	97	.8	68	23.6	251	56.5	8	13	.0	0	3	2.9
01085	37.0	97	12.6	66	26.8	339	76.9	6	12	16.9	10	3	.9
01088	.4	100	.2	82	24.4	303	83.1	4	11	.2	16	0	.0
01089	27.0	99	10.5	57	25.6	334	73.8	5	13	12.7	10	0	1.3
01092	1.0	0	.4	72	24.9	278	55.6	4	17	.0	0	0	.3
01093	.4	100	.2	76	28.1	388	98.2	4	15	.2	14	0	.0
01094	.3	98	.1	84	27.1	321	63.9	5	8	.2	8	0	.0
01095	12.5	98	4.0	91	40.1	376	104.1	5	8	6.1	7	1	.0
01096	1.9	98	.7	78	24.2	361	76.1	7	11	.9	10	0	.0
01097	.7	99	.2	71	25.9	376	82.1	8	8	.4	5	0	.0
01098	1.1	100	.4	90	27.9	415	81.9	7	10	.5	10	0	.2

SPRINGFIELD

ZIP CODE	1	2	3	4	5	6	7	8	9	10	11	12	13
01103	1.2	92	.8	0	14.2	310	50.6*	0	38	.6	28	1	3.5
01104	22.3	92	8.5	58	21.0	295	48.6	6	20	9.4	16	1	1.0
01105	13.1	66	5.9	12	14.9	276	40.6	8	16	3.9	15	1	.0
01106	16.7	98	5.2	95	52.9	582	134.8	5	11	7.7	10	0	1.3
01107	12.2	51	3.9	28	14.1	290	57.5	10	9	2.8	13	0	2.3
01108	26.2	97	10.4	45	22.4	356	57.4	7	16	11.6	13	0	.0
01109	32.1	41	9.7	53	20.3	320	41.9	7	10	6.3	12	0	.3
01118	14.6	97	5.2	81	27.9	367	61.4	6	15	6.7	14	0	.0
01119	12.1	89	4.2	75	24.8	375	53.5	6	11	5.3	11	0	.0
01128	2.8	95	.9	93	31.2	539	65.7	8	10	1.3	8	0	.0
01129	7.3	86	2.4	82	28.8	447	58.8	6	8	3.0	7	0	.0
01151	8.0	92	3.1	51	21.4	286	51.8	7	13	3.5	12	3	10.7

PITTSFIELD

ZIP CODE	1	2	3	4	5	6	7	8	9	10	11	12	13
01201	53.4	97	20.0	61	25.6	313	69.6	6	14	24.2	11	2	2.7
01222	.7	100	.2	79	20.8	490	73.4	9	12	.3	12	4	1.8
01223	1.2	99	.4	79	26.5	428	68.7	5	15	.6	15	0	.0
01224	.3	100	.1	86	26.4	323	67.8	8	14	.1	12	0	.0
01225	2.9	100	1.0	83	24.2	311	69.7	7	9	1.5	8	0	2.1
01226	6.7	0	2.3	76	28.8	358	70.8	6	13	.0	0	1	.0
01229	.2	100	.1	85	22.3	426	82.3	8	20	.0	18	0	.5
01230	7.4	97	2.8	64	24.9	347	88.0	6	20	3.3	17	0	.1
01235	2.5	100	.8	76	23.1	311	63.7	9	12	1.2	12	0	.0
01236	2.1	97	.7	77	24.1	388	69.6	5	14	1.0	11	0	.8
01237	2.6	99	.9	80	25.3	358	66.1	5	11	1.3	10	2	.1
01238	6.1	100	2.0	71	28.0	334	69.3	5	12	3.0	10	4	.4
01240	5.8	99	1.8	69	29.5	386	97.3	5	16	2.7	11	1	.2
01242	.7	100	.2	77	27.6	458	61.3	8	13	.4	6	1	2.3
01243	.4	98	.1	92	21.4	353	64.3	8	13	.2	10	0	.0
01244	.3	0	.1	88	18.8	350	64.8	7	22	.0	0	1	.0
01245	.6	99	.3	74	30.3	422	105.0	4	15	.3	11	0	.0
01247	20.5	99	7.6	54	20.3	264	56.9	5	15	9.5	13	3	.0
01252	.2	100	.1	76	36.1	349	84.9	7	19	.1	19	0	.0
01253	.6	0	.2	85	25.0	278	72.3	7	12	.6	0	0	.0
01254	1.2	99	.4	92	34.2	492	103.0	6	10	.6	9	0	.0
01255	.7	0	.2	80	21.5	373	71.4	3	24	.3	11	0	.0
01256	.6	0	.2	89	24.7	329	69.4	6	7	.0	0	0	.0

*=Estimated **1.0=883 lbs per person; 100++ indicates per capita toxic waste generation > than 100 times the U.S. average of 883 lbs per capita.

ZIP CODE MEASURES OF SIZE, LEVELS OF AFFLUENCE AND QUALITY OF LIFE

1=Population (th.); 2= % White; 3=Households (th.); 4=% Owner Occupied; 5=Mean Income Per Household (th.$); 6=Mean Monthly Rent ($)*; 7=Mean Home Value (th.$)*;
8=% under 5; 9=% 65 and over; 10=White Males (th.); 11=% White Males, 65+; 12=# Toxic Waste Sites; 13=Toxic Waste Relative to US(883 lbs.per capita)**.

MASSACHUSETTS

PITTSFIELD

ZIPCODE	1	2	3	4	5	6	7	8	9	10	11	12	13
01257	1.8	98	.8	68	25.7	378	96.9	5	14	.9	10	0	.1
01258	.4	0	.2	75	25.2	388	86.5	4	17	.0	0	0	.0
01259	.2	100	.1	64	37.8	477	86.5	5	10	.1	8	0	.0
01260	.2	100	.1	86	28.2	487	50.3	8	19	.1	8	0	18.0
01262	2.4	99	1.0	61	31.5	357	100.1	5	15	1.1	11	0	.0
01264	.3	0	.1	86	30.8	273	94.2	7	11	.0	0	0	.0
01266	.8	0	.3	81	32.1	434	95.9	5	14	.0	0	0	.0
01267	9.1	97	2.8	72	30.8	365	94.1	4	14	4.3	11	0	.1
01270	.5	0	.2	86	27.8	137	77.1	10	10	4.3	11	0	.3

SPRINGFIELD

ZIPCODE	1	2	3	4	5	6	7	8	9	10	11	12	13
01301	18.7	99	7.3	57	22.9	308	65.7	6	16	8.7	12	1	1.1
01330	1.2	99	.5	74	24.5	341	84.1	7	11	.6	10	1	.0
01331	12.5	99	4.4	73	23.2	271	56.6	7	16	5.9	14	1	3.2
01337	2.0	100	.7	84	25.9	298	72.4	7	12	1.0	11	0	.0
01338	.2	100	.1	86	22.5	259*	75.9	3	17	1.0	11	0	.0
01339	1.4	99	.5	75	21.9	307	63.1	7	12	.7	21	0	.0
01340	1.4	100	.5	82	24.6	323	63.4	7	13	.7	11	0	1.1
01341	1.1	100	.4	77	28.5	337	84.6	8	10	.7	11	0	1.2
01342	.3	100	.1	20	41.5	686	137.8	6	15	.2	11	0	.0
01345	.6	100	.2	84	26.2	238	63.1	6	11	.3	11	0	.9
01346	.2	0	.1	87	26.6	305*	51.0	10	18	.0	0	0	5.9
01347	.2	100	.1	91	22.6	260*	56.3	8	8	.1	12	0	16.1
01349	1.5	0	.7	78	15.3	483	35.7	0	20	.0	11	0	.0
01351	1.7	0	.6	76	21.5	265	59.3	6	15	.7	21	0	1.1
01355	.5	0	.2	81	26.9	362	68.8	8	10	.7	11	0	.0
01360	2.5	99	.9	90	24.3	433	69.0	8	14	.6	9	0	.0
01364	7.5	99	2.7	69	25.3	317	71.5	6	14	1.2	13	1	.0
01366	.9	100	.3	75	20.7	235	54.0	7	14	3.6	11	1	.3
01367	.5	0	.2	82	31.0	355	88.4	5	15	.4	7	0	6.5
01368	.3	100	.2	96	24.1	292	74.6	6	13	.0	13	0	.0
01370	4.0	99	1.5	69	20.3	234*	62.3	12	15	1.9	14	1	.1
01373	4.9	99	1.8	74	27.4	339	65.6	6	11	2.4	10	1	1.4
01375	2.9	97	1.3	33	19.8	394	92.6	4	7	1.5	6	0	.0
01376	6.6	99	2.6	60	22.3	271	63.6	6	15	3.1	13	1	.5
01379	.5	0	.2	72	21.2	356	64.0	9	7	.6	9	0	.4
01380	.2	100	.1	79	17.8	244	58.9	6	5	.1	0	0	.0

WORCESTER

ZIPCODE	1	2	3	4	5	6	7	8	9	10	11	12	13
01420	42.1	97	15.2	53	22.8	302	65.4	6	14	18.7	11	6	.9
01431	3.0	0	1.0	83	28.4	399	71.1	6	11	.0	0	0	2.4
01432	2.2	100	.7	89	27.8	350	73.5	9	9	1.1	8	0	.1
01433	7.0	87	2.6	43	23.0	367	79.1	9	3	4.0	7	2	2.2
01436	9.0	80	1.5	2	22.0	369	45.9	11	0	4.4	0	0	.1
01437	4.6	99	.8	85	26.4	208	60.1	5	13	1.5	12	1	.5
01438	1.2	100	.4	86	24.7	265	59.1	4	17	.6	15	0	.0
01440	18.1	99	7.0	53	22.8	279	63.6	6	17	8.4	14	2	.5
01450	5.7	99	1.8	74	34.4	478	117.5	7	8	1.8	6	1	.1
01451	3.7	99	1.2	85	51.9	471	189.0	6	5	1.8	4	0	.0

MASSACHUSETTS

WORCESTER

ZIPCODE	1	2	3	4	5	6	7	8	9	10	11	12	13
01452	1.8	99	.6	88	27.3	382	71.4	8	8	.9	8	0	.4
01453	33.7	97	12.4	54	24.7	325	77.2	7	12	15.5	9	4	3.0
01460	8.3	98	2.9	65	32.7	437	110.7	7	9	4.1	7	0	.5
01462	7.3	99	2.5	85	32.3	386	83.0	6	9	3.6	7	0	.1
01463	3.4	0	1.1	89	32.5	365	108.0	9	9	.0	0	0	.0
01464	4.4	93	1.5	65	25.9	362	83.4	7	8	2.1	7	0	.0
01465	.1	0	.1	78	35.7	522	95.5	6	0	.0	0	0	.0
01466	1.0	100	.3	81	25.9	303	62.6	9	9	.5	10	0	.2
01467	.3	100	.1	83	43.9	324	110.4	3	9	.1	11	0	.0
01468	1.9	100	.6	82	25.1	289	68.5	9	9	1.0	7	1	.8
01469	5.9	100	1.9	80	29.1	380	84.1	11	6	.9	9	1	.1
01472	.4	100	.1	95	35.6	409*	95.0	9	10	.2	12	1	3.9
01473	5.1	99	1.7	87	30.2	326	82.9	7	9	2.5	8	1	1.4
01474	1.3	100	.4	95	31.3	299	82.9	6	8	.6	7	0	.0
01475	6.7	0	2.2	66	22.7	267	58.0	7	13	.0	0	1	.3
01477	.3	100	.1	46	18.8	383	48.2	18	12	.2	7	0	.3

WORCESTER

ZIPCODE	1	2	3	4	5	6	7	8	9	10	11	12	13
01501	14.9	100	5.1	83	29.2	355	73.9	5	12	7.2	11	2	.6
01503	1.9	98	.6	85	33.8	445	100.3	6	9	.9	9	0	.0
01504	6.9	100	2.3	65	24.0	293	68.8	7	10	3.3	7	0	.1
01505	2.6	98	1.0	78	34.1	358	100.4	5	9	1.3	7	0	.3
01506	2.8	100	1.0	77	23.0	334	65.6	6	13	1.4	12	0	.1
01507	2.5	100	.8	82	27.0	351	71.1	9	8	1.2	8	0	.2
01508	1.5	0	.5	65	23.2	355	76.5	9	7	.0	0	0	.1
01509	.3	100	.3	75	26.9	321	83.6	8	7	.2	10	0	.0
01510	12.7	96	4.7	52	23.1	303	71.7	7	14	5.7	11	3	.1
01515	1.9	99	.7	81	24.1	345	67.4	7	12	1.0	11	1	.1
01516	3.9	0	1.3	76	25.3	345	74.8	8	10	.0	0	0	.3
01517	.4	0	.1	82	28.9	444	88.7	8	8	.0	0	0	.2
01519	1.8	98	.7	65	24.1	350	74.7	8	12	.9	13	0	.0
01520	3.9	99	3.8	79	33.4	377	101.8	8	12	1.9	7	1	.0
01522	11.2	100	2.1	88	36.6	396	95.3	6	14	5.4	11	2	.2
01523	2.1	98	.7	77	32.1	419	98.0	6	10	2.1	6	1	.0
01524	4.2	98	1.2	84	32.0	319	88.7	7	9	2.1	9	2	.3
01525	6.3	98	1.9	77	27.4	317	69.8	7	10	2.9	12	2	.6
01526	1.2	100	.4	49	23.4	365	71.7	7	14	.5	9	0	.1
01527	15.8	100	5.2	82	23.1	256	62.9	6	16	7.8	13	1	.1
01529	1.3	100	.4	75	27.9	342	78.8	6	12	.9	9	0	.3
01530	.9	0	.2	92	33.0	419	68.8	8	13	.0	0	0	.6
01531	.7	98	.2	74	26.8	370	61.5	5	17	.3	0	0	.0
01532	10.7	97	3.3	79	37.8	426	105.3	8	6	5.1	4	0	.2
01534	3.6	97	1.2	64	25.3	259	81.9	7	15	1.7	12	0	.8
01535	4.8	99	1.4	75	31.8	267	65.5	6	12	2.1	11	0	.1
01536	1.4	99	1.7	75	31.8	321	86.3	9	11	2.3	9	1	.5
01537	1.1	99	.4	69	25.7	403	62.4	8	9	.7	9	0	.1
01538	.4	100	.4	58	21.6	333	68.2	8	12	.5	8	0	.1
01539	.4	100	.1	69	25.6	354	71.4	2	35	.2	26	0	2.7
01540	10.0	100	3.3	85	25.8	350	68.4	8	9	4.7	6	0	.4

*=Estimated **1.0=883 lbs per person; 100++ indicates per capita toxic waste generation > than 100 times the U.S. average of 883 lbs per capita.

ZIP CODE MEASURES OF SIZE, LEVELS OF AFFLUENCE AND QUALITY OF LIFE

1=Population (th.); 2= % White; 3=Households (th.); 4=% Owner Occupied; 5=Mean Income Per Household (th.$); 6=Mean Monthly Rent ($)*; 7=Mean Home Value (th.$)*;
8=% under 5; 9=% 65 and over; 10=White Males, 65+; 11=% White Males, 65+; 12=# Toxic Waste Sites; 13=Toxic Waste Relative to US(883 lbs.per capita)**.

MASSACHUSETTS

WORCESTER

ZIP CODE	1	2	3	4	5	6	7	8	9	10	11	12	13
01541	2.0	99	.7	90	37.4	424	111.1	8	6	1.0	5	0	.0
01542	1.7	100	.5	79	27.7	258	69.6	8	8	.8	7	1	.4
01543	4.3	99	1.4	71	27.3	372	75.7	7	9	2.2	7	0	.9
01545	22.7	97	8.2	69	31.9	416	95.9	6	12	10.8	10	3	.3
01549	.2	0	.1	85	46.9	453	113.2	4	8	.0	0	0	.0
01550	20.2	97	7.3	51	22.4	281	71.3	7	15	9.2	13	2	.3
01560	2.6	100	.9	48	25.6	324	74.9	8	12	1.2	11	0	.3
01561	1.9	79	.5	53	23.9	309	86.9	5	7	.7	8	0	.3
01562	10.7	99	3.7	63	25.2	322	69.8	9	11	5.2	8	2	.0
01564	1.4	100	.5	69	31.6	294	86.3	5	10	.6	6	0	.1
01565	3.6	99	1.1	87	32.1	469	97.1	6	6	1.8	6	0	.0
01566	4.1	0	1.3	81	36.3	354	92.2	6	8	.0	0	0	.8
01568	3.0	99	1.0	81	28.5	261	98.1	7	10	1.5	8	0	.0
01569	6.9	99	2.3	70	27.0	290	81.0	7	13	3.4	10	1	.2
01570	23.2	99	8.5	57	23.3	278	76.0	6	14	11.1	12	3	.5
01581	13.7	98	4.9	55	34.4	486	120.6	5	11	6.6	8	5	2.5
01583	5.5	98	1.8	81	34.1	375	92.7	5	10	2.8	9	0	1.2
01585	3.2	0	1.1	75	27.3	364	74.1	7	7	.0	0	1	.1
01586	.4	100	.1	93	27.4	315*	83.4	5	9	.2	6	0	.1
01587	.9	100	.3	59	26.2	324	80.3	10	9	.4	7	0	.4
01588	7.9	99	2.7	55	25.9	318	83.0	8	14	3.7	12	1	.0
01590	.4	100	.2	29	19.3	243	71.1	7	19	.2	16	0	21.5

WORCESTER

ZIP CODE	1	2	3	4	5	6	7	8	9	10	11	12	13
01603	21.3	98	7.9	66	29.3	391	73.9	5	19	9.6	15	0	.1
01604	17.4	98	6.3	45	21.4	298	53.7	5	18	7.9	14	2	.1
01605	30.1	98	11.1	45	22.8	326	60.8	6	15	13.6	12	0	.4
01606	24.5	88	8.8	35	20.2	291	62.9	8	16	9.5	14	1	1.3
01607	17.9	99	6.7	66	26.6	367	64.9	6	16	8.4	14	3	5.0
01608	6.3	98	2.6	43	19.4	283	53.8	8	15	2.7	16	1	.7
01609	3.5	72	1.4	5	12.7	269	45.4*	6	21	1.2	19	0	1.9
01610	18.2	93	6.4	33	29.6	324	117.7	4	16	8.3	12	3	.0
01611	22.8	91	7.6	24	17.6	283	49.0	6	14	10.0	12	1	.7
01612	1.8	0	.6	68	27.2	389	60.1	6	9	.0	0	0	.0
01612	3.7	98	1.2	94	39.1	445	112.9	4	9	1.7	7	0	.0

FRAMINGHAM

ZIP CODE	1	2	3	4	5	6	7	8	9	10	11	12	13
01701	65.2	95	24.0	53	33.1	470	117.5	5	11	28.8	9	4	1.3
01718	.8	96	.3	52	52.0	824	185.3*	5	9	.3	1	0	.0
01720	18.5	98	6.2	66	41.5	498	154.0	7	6	9.0	4	3	.3
01721	9.2	98	3.1	73	35.2	467	100.7	7	7	4.5	5	4	4.0
01730	15.7	93	4.4	65	38.9	463	139.4	7	7	7.8	7	0	4.8
01740	2.5	99	.8	87	40.7	420	139.7	6	8	1.3	5	1	.5
01741	3.3	99	1.0	93	55.5	422	187.6	6	6	1.6	6	0	.0
01742	16.4	98	5.2	75	50.8	636	179.5	5	10	7.8	7	1	.3
01745	.4	100	.2	80	31.9	516	89.7	2	17	.2	20	0	6.4
01746	12.7	98	3.9	83	37.0	438	112.2	5	11	6.2	4	2	.4
01747	3.9	100	1.3	69	29.4	342	88.5	4	17	1.8	14	1	.1
01748	6.9	99	2.3	83	34.9	392	110.3	8	8	3.4	6	1	.1
01749	16.5	99	5.4	70	31.1	381	89.8	7	11	8.0	6	1	1.5
01752	30.6	97	10.9	55	28.9	424	94.9	7	11	14.3	8	3	.4

MASSACHUSETTS

FRAMINGHAM

ZIP CODE	1	2	3	4	5	6	7	8	9	10	11	12	13
01754	9.6	98	3.5	66	28.0	434	87.4	6	12	4.6	10	2	.5
01756	3.2	98	1.0	83	30.0	332	102.6	7	11	1.5	9	0	.0
01757	23.4	99	8.2	59	27.6	365	93.2	7	11	11.0	9	2	.2
01760	29.5	97	10.1	73	34.8	470	107.2	5	11	13.8	8	3	.3
01770	4.0	100	1.2	91	62.5	623	214.2	6	6	2.0	5	0	.0
01773	5.7	99	1.8	81	40.6	400	132.5	6	7	2.8	5	0	1.8
01773	4.7	98	1.7	82	64.4	638	233.1	5	11	2.2	10	0	.1
01775	5.1	97	1.6	90	43.2	580	139.6	7	7	2.5	6	0	.3
01776	14.1	98	4.1	93	55.6	486	173.8	5	8	6.8	4	3	.3
01778	12.0	99	3.9	90	54.2	439	166.4	5	8	5.9	7	1	.3

WOBURN

ZIP CODE	1	2	3	4	5	6	7	8	9	10	11	12	13
01801	36.6	99	12.3	61	30.2	462	92.0	6	10	17.5	8	15	1.5
01803	23.4	97	6.9	83	38.4	580	107.5	6	5	11.3	4	7	1.3
01810	26.4	99	8.8	75	41.7	428	152.9	6	10	12.6	7	5	1.8
01821	27.7	99	8.1	85	32.6	462	89.5	8	5	13.6	4	2	.1
01824	25.7	99	7.7	89	39.4	453	113.4	6	11	12.4	5	2	1.1
01826	21.2	99	6.8	76	29.6	409	82.4	7	8	10.3	7	5	.0
01827	1.7	100	.5	90	36.0	448	115.4	8	6	.8	6	0	.2
01830	46.8	98	17.2	51	23.4	324	75.0	7	16	21.3	12	3	.4
01833	5.8	0	1.9	82	31.9	311	100.2	7	8	.0	0	0	.0
01834	5.0	100	1.5	86	33.9	430	87.6	6	7	2.5	5	1	.0
01840	3.6	70	1.6	6	13.5	239	42.0	9	26	1.3	27	1	1.6
01841	37.7	85	14.0	31	18.3	305	68.5	9	15	14.8	13	2	.3
01843	21.9	96	6.8	41	22.6	327	77.5	7	14	9.8	11	7	.8
01844	36.7	99	12.7	68	27.2	367	89.4	7	13	17.2	11	4	4.9
01845	20.1	98	6.8	60	33.8	486	141.3	5	13	9.4	10	3	.2
01850	14.4	98	5.2	47	22.6	363	66.1	8	11	6.7	6	2	.2
01851	25.8	98	9.1	44	24.5	374	77.1	8	11	11.8	9	0	.3
01852	29.3	94	10.5	45	22.9	304	80.5	7	13	13.1	11	5	.3
01854	22.9	97	7.9	33	19.7	312	69.8	6	15	10.4	10	3	.2
01860	4.5	99	1.6	76	26.5	362	77.6	8	7	2.1	9	1	.4
01862	9.2	98	2.6	78	32.4	472	89.8	7	7	4.6	6	8	6.3
01863	5.5	99	1.9	68	30.3	425	91.6	7	10	2.6	8	0	.1
01864	11.3	99	3.5	81	34.8	476	107.1	6	5	5.5	6	1	.3
01867	22.9	99	7.3	80	36.9	506	116.1	6	10	11.1	8	2	.3
01876	24.4	99	6.4	91	35.0	376	95.5	7	8	12.1	7	7	.1
01879	5.7	99	1.8	77	29.4	436	82.5	8	7	2.8	6	0	.2
01880	24.3	99	8.5	71	31.9	426	106.9	8	13	11.5	10	1	.7
01885	.7	0	.3	97	46.2	531*	178.5	8	9	.0	0	0	.0
01886	13.5	99	4.0	86	38.3	416	115.3	7	6	6.7	5	1	.2
01887	17.3	100	5.0	92	33.0	421	94.2	7	7	8.6	8	0	8.6
01890	20.7	98	6.7	78	46.4	543	164.4	5	13	9.6	10	0	.2

LYNN

ZIP CODE	1	2	3	4	5	6	7	8	9	10	11	12	13
01901	.2	99	.1	0	12.3	258	43.7*	4	20	.0	0	5	61.7
01902	38.8	93	16.0	35	20.4	329	60.3	7	17	16.7	13	1	.0
01904	17.4	99	6.2	69	29.4	389	78.2	5	17	9.7	12	0	2.9
01905	22.0	94	8.2	46	22.0	328	66.6	7	14	9.7	12	2	.7
01906	24.8	99	8.2	79	30.0	414	89.5	5	12	11.8	10	2	.7
01907	13.8	99	5.0	73	38.3	535	131.2	4	17	6.5	14	0	.0

*=Estimated **1.0=883 lbs per person; 100++ indicates per capita toxic waste generation > than 100 times the U.S. average of 883 lbs.

ZIP CODE MEASURES OF SIZE, LEVELS OF AFFLUENCE AND QUALITY OF LIFE

1=Population (th.); 2= % White; 3=Households (th.); 4=% Owner Occupied; 5=Mean Income Per Household (th.); 6=Mean Monthly Rent ($); 7=Mean Home Value (th.$);
8=% under 5; 9=% 65 and over; 10=White Males (th.); 11=% White Males, 65+; 12=# Toxic Waste Sites; 13=Toxic Waste Relative to US(883 lbs.per capital)**.

MASSACHUSETTS

ZIPCODE	1	2	3	4	5	6	7	8	9	10	11	12	13
LYNN													
01908	3.9	0	1.4	67	36.9	497	130.2	5	14	.0	0	0	.0
01913	13.9	99	5.1	53	24.4	350	76.3	8	13	6.5	10	4	.9
01915	37.4	99	13.7	59	29.5	396	104.4	5	13	17.2	10	3	.6
01921	4.3	99	1.2	93	53.5	825	199.4	6	5	2.1	4	0	.0
01922	1.8	0	.6	78	34.8	424	106.5	8	6	.0	0	0	.0
01923	23.4	99	7.9	72	33.0	431	105.4	5	12	11.0	9	3	1.1
01929	3.2	0	1.2	72	27.0	407	96.1	6	14	.0	0	0	.7
01930	27.7	100	10.5	56	26.8	367	98.2	6	14	13.1	11	1	.4
01936	1.1	0	.4	74	55.1	774	182.9	5	9	.0	0	0	
01937	1.0	99	.1	74	34.1	424	103.4	0	14	.0	0	0	.7
01938	11.1	99	4.1	69	30.3	360	106.7	6	12	5.4	8	1	.3
01940	11.2	98	3.5	93	50.3	396	158.3	4	12	5.5	8	0	
01944	5.4	99	1.9	65	45.8	503	175.5	5	12	2.6	9	0	.0
01945	20.1	99	7.9	71	39.6	514	159.5	4	14	9.3	11	0	.0
01949	3.9	100	1.3	82	29.5	391	90.9	7	10	1.9	9	3	6.1
01950	24.7	99	8.9	65	25.9	389	87.2	6	13	11.6	10	0	
01960	46.0	98	15.7	70	30.3	375	96.8	5	11	21.6	9	8	.8
01966	6.3	99	2.8	66	50.1	780	212.5	0	10	.1	0	0	1.4
01969	3.9	99	1.3	69	29.9	417	94.1	7	9	1.9	9	1	
01970	38.2	97	15.0	42	24.0	376	88.4	5	16	16.9	13	7	.8
01982	5.8	99	1.9	83	36.1	363	120.6	6	8	2.9	6	0	
01983	5.9	100	1.8	85	47.6	435	162.0	5	10	2.9	6	0	
01984	2.9	99	.9	80	51.1	299	155.8	3	10	1.8	9	1	1.9
01985	2.9	99	1.1	92	36.8	577	123.6	7	8	.0	0	0	3.6
SOUTH POSTAL ANNEX													
02019	14.3	99	4.3	83	30.2	350	79.9	8	6	7.1	5	1	.5
02020	.6	100	.2	65	26.0	504	77.1	4	10	.3	8	1	.0
02021	17.7	99	5.4	77	38.4	451	118.0	6	10	8.6	8	6	3.1
02025	7.2	99	2.4	76	51.2	510	169.9	5	12	3.4	9	1	.1
02026	25.3	99	8.3	79	34.6	423	103.2	5	13	12.0	10	1	1.2
02030	4.7	99	1.5	91	65.6	785	248.5	5	10	2.3	9	1	.0
02032	2.5	0	.8	80	34.7	462	100.9	4	10	1.2	0	1	
02035	14.1	99	4.6	65	32.8	431	98.2	6	10	6.9	7	1	1.9
02038	18.3	99	5.5	72	30.7	371	92.0	6	14	8.7	6	1	3.6
02041	1.2	0	.4	83	27.2	535	76.2	6	14	.0	0	1	.2
02043	20.0	99	6.2	84	43.3	513	136.1	6	10	9.5	8	3	.5
02045	9.7	100	3.2	72	25.4	400	70.8	6	10	4.6	6	1	.1
02047	.8	100	.3	90	43.1	451	103.7	6	11	4.1	8	0	.2
02048	13.4	99	4.5	63	29.0	415	89.7	7	7	6.5	6	5	.6
02050	17.4	99	5.7	76	32.8	460	97.5	8	7	8.4	6	1	.1
02051	1.0	100	.3	86	44.6	580	126.4	6	5	.5	6	1	
02052	10.3	99	3.1	79	43.5	446	140.5	6	7	5.1	5	1	1.5
02054	8.5	99	2.5	80	33.0	360	105.6	8	8	4.1	6	1	.2
02055	6.9	99	2.3	72	37.4	433	124.9	7	12	3.3	11	1	
02056	6.2	93	1.6	86	36.2	336	119.8	6	6	3.2	5	3	3.0
02059	.3	87	.1	100	36.6	420*	106.8	13	6	.1	8	0	.0
02060	7.1	99	2.2	82	38.9	356	115.7	5	10	3.5	0	0	.3
SOUTH POSTAL ANNEX													
02061	9.2	99	2.8	90	42.5	400	125.2	6	8	4.4	6	0	.0
02062	29.9	99	10.5	58	31.8	470	101.4	5	13	13.9	10	1	1.5
02065	.5	100	.2	63	18.8	569	69.9	7	23	.2	25	0	.0
02066	9.0	99	2.9	82	37.6	595	107.2	5	11	4.3	9	0	.0
02067	13.6	95	4.3	89	43.6	457	123.2	7	8	6.4	6	0	.1
02071	.7	100	.6	63	33.3	531	102.9	6	11	.3	0	0	1.1
02072	26.4	97	8.5	73	30.9	425	85.5	6	11	12.4	9	0	.6
02081	15.7	98	4.7	84	37.4	438	107.4	6	9	7.8	6	1	.5
02090	13.2	99	4.2	91	46.5	455	138.0	5	11	6.4	9	1	.3
02093	7.6	99	2.2	81	30.7	383	94.7	7	10	3.7	7	2	.2
BOSTON													
02108	3.7	95	2.1	27	43.2	526	404.3	2	12	1.6	10	0	1.4
02109	2.5	95	1.0	24	36.3	400	91.9	1	10	1.4	7	0	10.4
02110	1.7	96	1.1	13	41.8	613	148.9*	2	17	.8	19	0	11.5
02111	4.0	33	1.5	4	22.3	405	79.5*	4	12	.9	10	0	2.0
02113	6.8	0	3.5	14	19.0	332	112.0	2	15	.0	0	0	.0
02114	11.7	95	6.5	9	28.3	529	239.6	2	11	5.8	9	0	.8
02115	25.1	80	10.0	5	18.2	388	125.3	3	9	10.0	5	0	.3
02116	19.9	79	10.4	20	33.6	461	169.6	2	11	7.7	8	0	.1
02118	19.9	36	8.8	11	18.1	282	156.3	5	10	4.2	9	1	12.8
02119	24.5	12	8.6	19	16.3	249	34.8	8	10	1.3	13	2	.6
02120	11.4	36	4.2	12	17.6	267	57.5	7	7	2.1	6	0	.2
02121	24.4	5	8.8	17	16.3	285	51.9	9	8	.5	6	0	.2
02124	49.3	43	16.3	36	21.3	370	48.7	7	14	8.8	9	1	.3
02125	29.2	60	10.0	28	20.8	330	58.3	7	10	9.9	13	1	.3
02126	26.8	25	8.8	44	19.6	281	43.0	8	10	8.3	11	2	.3
02127	30.7	99	12.7	26	23.7	401	58.6	8	17	14.2	20	3	.9
02129	13.4	97	5.3	32	21.8	280	70.4	5	12	5.7	10	2	.8
02130	36.1	71	13.0	32	23.5	359	80.6	5	15	11.5	15	3	.1
02131	32.2	94	11.4	49	25.0	367	66.4	6	18	13.0	14	0	.0
02132	26.7	98	9.8	69	30.4	439	84.9	4	20	12.0	15	0	.5
02134	19.0	84	8.9	11	17.4	426	70.3	3	9	7.7	7	0	.7
02135	37.1	90	15.3	22	21.8	426	86.9	3	16	14.2	13	1	.4
02136	25.4	95	9.6	51	24.5	360	62.2	6	16	11.2	13	1	.7
02138	35.4	88	13.8	28	31.0	456	200.2	3	11	15.0	7	10	1.0
02139	32.7	77	13.5	17	20.1	360	76.2	4	14	11.7	11	2	2.2
02140	16.3	79	7.0	25	25.0	376	117.9	5	14	5.7	11	2	20.5
02141	10.4	94	4.2	22	19.1	280	57.4	6	14	4.6	12	0	.3
02142	.8	82	.4	0	28.2	512	100.6*	1	5	.3	8	0	
02143	25.6	95	10.4	28	25.6	384	72.2	5	14	11.5	11	1	.0
02144	26.7	97	10.0	36	26.7	422	76.2	4	18	13.0	11	0	.0
02145	24.6	98	9.3	35	21.5	378	67.2	6	11	11.4	10	1	.2
02148	53.6	92	20.7	25	30.4	525	189.0	3	18	20.9	14	0	42.4
02149	37.2	97	14.1	41	23.0	372	85.0	6	16	16.9	11	6	3.0
02150	25.5	92	9.7	27	18.8	333	66.5	7	17	11.1	16	2	1.5
02151	42.4	99	16.4	49	23.1	387	85.2	5	15	19.9	12	0	.3

*=Estimated **1.0=883 lbs per person; 100++ indicates per capita toxic waste generation > than 100 times the U.S. average of 883 lbs per capita.

ZIP CODE MEASURES OF SIZE, LEVELS OF AFFLUENCE AND QUALITY OF LIFE

1=Population (th.); 2= % White; 3=Households (th.); 4=% Owner Occupied; 5=Mean Income Per Household (th.$); 6=Mean Monthly Rent ($); 7=Mean Home Value (th.$); 8=% under 5; 9=% 65 and over; 10=White Males (th.); 11=% White Males, 65+; 12=# Toxic Waste Sites; 13=Toxic Waste Relative to US(883 lbs.per capita)**.

MASSACHUSETTS

BOSTON

ZIP CODE	1	2	3	4	5	6	7	8	9	10	11	12	13
02152	19.5	99	7.4	48	27.8	449	93.2	4	16	8.9	12	0	.0
02154	58.2	97	20.6	45	28.4	454	104.2	5	12	26.8	9	5	1.8
02155	58.5	96	20.3	58	27.4	423	93.2	5	15	26.1	12	6	.1
02158	14.0	96	4.8	53	39.9	533	147.8	4	14	6.3	11	1	.6
02159	17.7	95	6.0	81	54.3	598	137.9	5	14	7.8	13	0	1.7
02160	9.5	97	3.6	56	37.0	569	137.9	5	14	4.2	10	1	.1
02161	6.7	94	2.3	85	44.0	586	142.1	6	14	2.9	13	0	.1
02162	1.4	90	.5	81	37.4	472	135.4	5	22	.5	16	0	3.0
02163	1.3	85	.4	0	28.4	539	101.2*	3	1	.7	0	0	.0
02164	2.6	93	.9	48	29.9	520	105.5	5	15	1.1	11	1	1.1
02166	11.9	96	3.9	77	42.9	573	146.8	5	15	5.4	13	0	.0
02167	6.7	98	2.4	55	37.0	569	135.6	4	14	2.9	11	0	.0
02168	16.6	96	5.6	59	52.6	639	204.7	3	20	6.8	18	1	1.0
02169	5.9	97	1.9	93	65	678	194.5	6	13	2.7	10	0	.0
02170	54.0	99	21.8	47	25.2	410	80.4	5	18	24.2	14	2	1.0
02171	13.3	99	5.0	52	26.0	401	78.5	4	19	5.9	14	0	.1
02172	17.5	99	6.8	54	28.3	495	80.1	5	14	8.2	11	0	1.0
02173	34.4	98	13.2	47	28.5	515	108.5	5	16	15.2	12	3	.7
02174	29.4	96	9.7	86	49.3	602	161.5	4	12	13.6	9	3	3.5
02176	48.2	98	18.6	56	31.0	517	113.4	4	17	21.6	13	0	.0
02178	33.8	99	11.9	66	32.1	433	103.1	4	15	15.6	11	0	.1
02180	26.2	98	9.7	60	40.2	559	165.4	4	15	11.5	15	0	.3
02181	18.3	99	6.5	63	30.4	459	104.4	5	14	8.4	11	0	.1
02184	26.3	97	8.4	81	53.5	542	196.4	5	13	11.1	11	1	.1
02186	36.2	99	11.5	78	33.7	434	92.9	4	17	17.0	10	2	.5
02187	17.4	97	5.3	89	42.3	452	121.8	4	16	7.8	14	0	.1
02188	8.7	98	3.1	73	35.3	482	111.1	5	19	3.9	16	0	.0
02189	15.3	98	5.6	58	27.6	430	79.7	5	14	6.9	10	2	.1
02190	14.2	99	5.0	60	28.3	433	77.4	5	10	6.6	9	0	.5
02191	16.1	99	5.4	63	30.0	475	87.0	5	10	7.7	7	0	.0
02192	10.0	0	3.3	82	30.8	417	74.0	5	10	.0	0	0	.0
02193	19.5	98	6.4	86	48.8	500	155.8	6	13	9.2	10	1	.0
02194	11.2	96	3.3	88	81.8	717	270.3	4	11	5.0	10	0	.3
02195	8.4	98	2.9	75	42.6	633	130.5	4	14	3.9	12	0	2.4

BOSTON

ZIP CODE	1	2	3	4	5	6	7	8	9	10	11	12	13
02215	16.5	88	6.2	2	14.2	390	306.3	1	4	7.4	2	0	.3

BROCKTON

ZIP CODE	1	2	3	4	5	6	7	8	9	10	11	12	13
02322	5.0	0	1.6	76	29.4	381	75.7	6	10	.0	0	0	1.5
02324	17.2	96	5.1	65	27.4	424	82.5	6	8	8.2	8	2	.1
02327	.8	100	.3	77	22.4	407	63.3	9	11	.4	8	0	.0
02330	4.5	96	1.4	90	26.2	455	74.3	12	7	2.1	8	0	.0
02333	11.7	98	3.7	89	43.6	490	142.6	7	9	5.7	7	0	.0
02334	9.7	98	3.0	81	27.5	362	76.6	9	7	4.7	7	2	.4
02337	1.0	100	.3	77	37.1	550	95.5	6	8	.5	11	0	.7
02338	.2	100	.1	75	28.7	401	81.8	0	7	.1	7	0	.0
02339	5.4	99	1.8	92	26.3	450	77.5	8	13	2.6	12	1	.0
02341	11.4	99	3.1	92	36.9	529	108.0	7	6	5.6	5	3	.2
02343	8.2	96	2.9	87	30.1	383	81.2	8	7	3.9	5	0	.0
02343	11.2	96	3.4	83	30.1	388	73.1	8	5	5.3	7	0	2.2

MASSACHUSETTS

BROCKTON

ZIP CODE	1	2	3	4	5	6	7	8	9	10	11	12	13
02345	2.9	0	1.0	85	24.9	447	79.7	7	12	.0	0	0	.0
02346	22.3	98	7.3	74	24.3	343	75.5	8	12	10.5	10	3	.1
02350	.6	94	.2	94	20.3	279	50.7	10	12	.3	11	0	.0
02351	13.5	100	4.3	71	28.9	401	80.4	7	10	6.5	7	0	.1
02355	1.7	94	.5	98	27.7	318*	74.4	12	5	.8	6	0	.0
02356	8.4	99	2.4	79	34.4	338	106.4	6	6	4.0	6	0	.0
02359	12.6	99	3.7	90	30.0	387	81.7	8	6	6.1	5	1	.0
02360	34.2	97	11.5	71	26.7	375	89.6	9	12	15.9	10	3	.7
02364	5.2	99	1.9	76	27.1	384	79.2	7	14	2.5	11	1	.1
02366	.7	92	.3	88	22.0	491	79.7	6	12	.3	11	0	.0
02367	2.0	98	.6	94	29.9	443	93.4	8	6	1.0	5	0	.0
02368	28.2	96	9.3	73	31.1	475	83.6	5	12	13.0	10	2	.7
02370	15.7	99	4.8	69	25.3	399	68.6	7	7	7.5	7	2	.6
02375	7.2	97	2.3	77	33.8	509	94.4	7	7	3.6	6	0	.2
02379	6.4	0	2.1	86	29.3	357	81.4	6	11	.0	0	0	.7
02381	.9	100	.4	61	26.6	433	84.2	6	10	.5	8	0	.0
02382	13.5	99	4.2	75	27.3	366	72.6	8	8	6.4	8	0	.3

BROCKTON

ZIP CODE	1	2	3	4	5	6	7	8	9	10	11	12	13
02401	60.6	94	22.5	44	22.4	341	74.8	7	14	27.0	11	3	.3
02402	34.6	91	10.5	72	25.5	320	64.5	8	9	15.2	7	1	27.3
02403	.4	0	.1	92	46.9	539*	128.5	8	8	.0	0	0	.1

BUZZARDS BAY

ZIP CODE	1	2	3	4	5	6	7	8	9	10	11	12	13
02532	7.7	98	2.6	71	24.2	372	77.0	6	16	4.0	12	0	.0
02534	.7	92	.1	84	31.5	370	117.8	4	11	.3	12	0	.0
02535	.6	87	.6	69	19.9	343	168.5	5	21	.3	20	0	.0
02536	13.0	92	4.7	76	24.7	467	88.9	7	11	5.8	11	0	.0
02537	2.8	0	.9	87	31.8	456	117.3	8	16	.0	0	0	.0
02538	3.2	87	.7	82	21.9	422	69.9	9	14	1.4	14	1	.0
02539	2.3	0	1.0	73	23.6	428	138.6	6	17	.0	0	2	.0
02540	6.4	97	2.7	66	27.7	361	118.5	4	23	2.8	17	1	.1
02541	.4	0	.4	58	23.4	533	114.1	3	35	.0	0	0	.0
02542	2.1	95	.6		18.1	340	64.5*	16	1		1		1.1
02543	1.6	98	.6	65	32.8	439	148.6	4	15	.8	12	0	.3
02553	1.5	0	.5	85	27.4	391	83.1	5	13	.0	0	0	2.4
02554	4.8	98	2.0	68	31.4	475	172.1	5	17	2.2	14	2	.3
02556	2.0	98	.7	82	26.9	446	119.7	6	18	1.0	15	0	.3
02557	2.0	90	.8	79	19.3	327	87.2	6	22	.9	14	1	.0
02558	1.8	84	.7	64	18.2	271	54.6	5	19	.7	18	0	.0
02559	2.1	96	.8	84	29.3	436	95.2	7	20	1.0	17	1	.1
02561	.8	100	.3	63	22.5	427	72.0	11	15	.4	20	0	.0
02562	.7	100	.2	81	29.8	396	97.5	2	10	.3	10	0	.0
02563	4.5	98	1.7	88	30.7	428	106.4	5	15	2.1	13	1	.0
02564	.6	90	.3	66	26.6	606	191.9	11	15	.2	11	0	.0
02568	3.3	97	1.5	65	23.5	394	81.0	6	18	1.4	13	1	.7
02571	9.5	88	3.4	70	22.7	320	65.0	6	15	4.0	14	1	.1
02574	.9	94	.4	81	35.3	408	154.8	5	21	.4	24	0	.3
02575	.5	99	.2	65	24.1	403	127.1	8	13	.3	11	0	.2
02576	2.9	90	1.1	81	19.2	369	66.4	10	18	1.2	17	0	.0

*=Estimated **1.0=883 lbs per person; 100++ indicates per capita toxic waste generation > than 100 times the U.S. average of 883 lbs per capita.

ICCE01

ZIP CODE MEASURES OF SIZE, LEVELS OF AFFLUENCE AND QUALITY OF LIFE

1=Population (th.); 2= % White; 3=Households (th.); 4=% Owner Occupied; 5=Mean Income Per Household (th.$); 6=Mean Monthly Rent ($); 7=Mean Home Value (th.$);
8=% under 5; 9=% 65 and over; 10=% White Males; 11=% White Males, 65+; 12=# Toxic Waste Sites; 13=Toxic Waste Relative to US($883 lbs.per capita)**.

MASSACHUSETTS

ZIPCODE	1	2	3	4	5	6	7	8	9	10	11	12	13
BUZZARDS BAY													
02601	11.7	93	4.8	58	20.5	426	84.3	5	20	4.9	16	0	.3
02630	1.6	99	.5	82	33.6	494	157.0	5	19	.8	15	0	.0
02631	5.0	99	1.9	80	23.7	400	108.0	7	22	2.3	20	1	.0
02632	7.3	99	2.7	86	28.9	504	111.3	5	18	3.4	17	0	.0
02633	3.7	99	1.7	77	26.6	396	137.2	3	31	1.8	30	2	.0
02635	1.8	98	.8	83	28.3	429	120.8	5	18	.9	13	0	.0
02637	.5	100	.2	75	31.3	579	157.7	6	11	.2	13	0	.0
02638	2.4	97	.9	85	26.5	531	114.1	6	24	1.1	21	1	.0
02639	2.6	99	1.3	59	17.8	383	86.2	3	34	1.1	31	0	.0
02641	1.9	98	.8	85	29.6	442	124.5	4	25	.9	26	0	.0
02642	1.7	100	.7	88	27.6	444	112.1	4	25	.8	23	1	.0
02643	1.1	100	.5	83	33.4	384	178.3	4	25	.6	20	0	.0
02644	1.4	96	.5	81	23.0	472	87.8	10	6	.7	7	0	.0
02645	5.4	95	2.1	82	22.1	394	93.9	6	24	2.5	22	2	.0
02646	1.8	0	.8	84	25.4	333	125.1	2	37	.0	0	0	.0
02647	.3	87	.1	66	36.6	411	195.6	7	22	.2	26	0	.0
02648	2.7	96	1.0	86	26.7	467	102.7	7	11	1.2	11	1	.0
02649	3.0	81	1.1	68	27.7	391	105.9	7	18	1.1	18	0	.0
02650	.8	0	.4	81	25.5	444	147.4	3	25	.0	0	0	.1
02651	1.6	100	.6	77	21.4	455	97.0	7	16	.8	16	0	.0
02652	.9	98	.3	71	22.0	372	120.2	7	13	.5	14	0	.0
02653	3.8	0	1.7	61	23.4	371	125.1	4	31	1.0	0	0	.0
02655	2.9	94	1.3	83	30.5	517	144.2	4	29	1.2	29	1	.0
02657	3.6	100	1.8	49	18.4	320	97.9	4	17	1.8	13	0	.0
02659	.7	100	.3	78	21.6	285	100.6	11	32	.3	23	0	.0
02660	4.0	98	1.6	79	22.5	430	92.1	6	21	1.7	21	0	.0
02661	.7	100	.3	77	24.3	522	97.2	6	21	.3	26	0	.0
02662	.8	100	.3	93	28.9	271	157.8	7	25	.4	25	1	.0
02663	.6	99	.2	79	19.4	413	117.5	3	28	.3	25	0	.0
02664	8.2	99	3.5	80	23.6	359	97.8	3	33	3.5	29	3	.0
02666	.5	100	.2	84	25.2	420	149.8	1	27	.3	23	3	.0
02667	1.6	99	.6	64	21.9	359	119.1	8	20	.8	17	1	.0
02668	1.8	100	.6	87	28.4	468	107.9	13	12	.9	10	0	.0
02669	.8	0	.3	77	24.9	424	129.7	4	26	.0	0	0	.0
02670	1.5	98	.7	79	22.0	389	105.2	4	31	.7	29	0	.0
02671	1.0	100	.5	80	20.4	466	97.9	2	44	.4	38	0	.0
02672	.5	92	.2	88	30.3	662	128.1	4	25	.2	23	0	.0
02673	6.2	99	2.5	80	22.0	439	85.8	6	22	2.9	20	1	.0
02675	3.7	99	1.6	87	24.8	522	117	4	30	1.7	29	2	.0
PROVIDENCE													
02702	3.4	99	1.1	85	26.8	374	84.6	7	8	1.7	9	0	.4
02703	34.2	98	11.8	62	27.2	331	76.8	7	11	16.2	9	12	2.5
02712	.3	100	.1	76	28.0	345	70.7	3	11	.2	8	0	1.4
02714	.4	100	.2	92	21.2	217	65.4	5	18	.2	3	1	.0
02715	2.1	0	.7	81	28.3	366	72.3	6	11	.0	0	1	8.8
02717	4.1	97	1.2	91	29.4	327	87.2	9	6	2.0	4	2	.2
02718	4.2	98	1.3	82	26.5	403	66.9	8	7	2.0	7	0	.4
02719	16.4	97	5.8	72	23.6	322	64.0	6	15	7.9	12	4	.2
02720	29.9	99	10.9	37	20.9	273	70.4	7	18	13.4	14	4	.1

MASSACHUSETTS

ZIPCODE	1	2	3	4	5	6	7	8	9	10	11	12	13
PROVIDENCE													
02721	26.7	99	10.1	29	17.0	234	58.0	7	15	12.1	12	1	.3
02723	17.7	99	6.6	29	17.6	231	61.0	7	16	8.1	12	0	.0
02724	17.8	99	7.0	32	17.6	248	55.9	7	17	8.1	14	0	.3
02725	2.7	0	.9	86	28.9	336	75.8	4	14	.0	0	0	.1
02726	16.4	99	5.5	80	28.1	317	83.5	5	12	7.8	10	2	.1
02738	3.9	89	1.5	78	33.7	499	127.5	6	14	1.7	10	0	.3
02739	5.7	98	2.0	79	30.9	410	101.5	6	12	2.7	10	0	1.2
02740	45.3	84	17.6	43	18.5	263	56.1	7	18	17.1	15	4	.4
02743	8.7	99	3.0	83	24.9	315	69.5	5	11	4.2	10	2	.0
02744	13.7	94	5.2	36	18.5	261	58.8	8	15	6.0	13	0	.6
02745	22.6	97	8.4	61	22.6	298	62.3	6	15	10.3	13	1	.6
02746	17.0	96	6.4	24	16.9	252	66.7	8	15	7.5	12	0	.7
02747	12.4	97	3.8	87	28.7	396	83.0	5	10	6.0	9	0	.0
02748	10.4	98	3.7	78	27.4	312	86.5	5	16	4.8	13	0	.0
02760	19.3	99	6.8	65	28.2	355	88.0	7	10	9.3	7	1	1.2
02762	5.9	0	2.1	71	29.5	411	89.6	6	11	.0	0	0	3.3
02763	1.7	0	.5	69	31.2	358	92.4	8	7	.0	0	0	1.3
02764	3.1	99	1.0	84	28.5	225	85.2	6	11	1.6	9	0	.3
02767	12.3	98	3.6	76	28.0	397	76.5	8	8	5.4	7	0	.1
02768	9.1	98	2.8	87	31.8	355	82.0	8	7	4.3	6	1	.0
02769	7.6	99	2.4	86	32.7	390	99.2	6	8	3.7	6	0	.0
02770	2.6	97	.8	91	29.7	401	93.6	8	7	1.3	6	0	.1
02771	12.3	99	4.0	85	32.0	330	94.1	6	10	5.9	9	3	.0
02777	15.4	99	4.9	87	27.9	331	79.0	6	10	7.5	9	0	.0
02780	43.4	97	15.2	56	23.5	317	66.9	7	13	20.0	11	6	1.2
02790	13.1	99	4.3	82	27.0	380	85.6	6	9	6.5	8	0	.1
02791	.4	0	.2	63	23.0	547	129.2	7	16	.0	0	0	.6
PROVIDENCE													
02801	.3	0	.1	73	26.4	464	115.3	6	32	.0	0	0	.0
02861	.1	100	.1	100	19.5	224*	65.6	0	44	.1	44	0	.0
HARTFORD													
06018	.2	100	.1	77	28.4	379	64.6	2	14	.1	12	0	.0
06076	.1	100	.1	73	18.4	469	58.4	14	11	.1	13	0	.0

*=Estimated **1.0=883 lbs per person; 100++ indicates per capita toxic waste generation > than 100 times the U.S. average of 883 lbs per capita.

103001

ZIP CODE MEASURES OF SIZE, LEVELS OF AFFLUENCE AND QUALITY OF LIFE

1=Population (th.); 2= % White; 3=Households (th.); 4=% Owner Occupied; 5=Mean Income Per Household (th.$); 6=Mean Monthly Rent ($)*; 7=Mean Home Value (th.$)*;
8=% under 5; 9=% 65 and over; 10=White Males (th.); 11=% White Males, 65+; 12=# Toxic Waste Sites; 13=Toxic Waste Relative to US(883 lbs.per capita)**.

MICHIGAN

ZIPCODE	1	2	3	4	5	6	7	8	9	10	11	12	13
TOLEDO (WEST)													
43540	.2	100	.1	71	27.8	417	76.4	3	18	.1	14	0	.0
43560	.2	63	.1	73	30.0	149	81.2	4	6	.1	0	0	.0
TOLEDO													
43611	.2	100	.1	100	47.7	548*	101.9	0	13	.1	16	0	.0
43612	2.2	97	.8	90	29.1	318	96.9	7	11	1.0	7	0	.0
43613	3.2	98	.9	85	34.4	376	97.4	7	5	1.6	5	0	.0
SOUTH BEND													
46507	.2	100	.1	90	22.8	262*	109.1	9	14	.1	12	0	.0
FORT WAYNE													
46737	.3	0	.1	78	23.5	284	41.3	9	6	.0	0	0	.0
ROYAL OAK													
48001	10.5	99	3.7	82	29.0	323	87.5	8	12	5.3	10	0	.0
48002	1.9	0	.6	89	30.6	497	92.2	10	6	.0	0	0	.0
48003	4.1	99	1.2	81	33.4	384	92.7	8	8	2.0	7	0	.2
48004	2.9	99	1.1	86	25.5	384	93.2	7	14	1.4	14	0	.1
48005	3.8	0	1.1	85	34.4	399	64.9	7	9	.0	0	0	.1
48006	1.5	0	.4	87	27.9	424	131.7	6	7	.0	0	0	.0
48008	8.5	98	3.5	71	41.1	567	176.2	6	12	3.9	9	0	1.6
48009	21.0	99	8.2	80	55.3	653	240.1	5	14	9.9	10	0	.6
48010	19.7	98	6.4	91	82.2	630	251.7*	3	9	9.5	8	1	1.2
48011	31.2	94	10.1	88	70.7	738	258.4	3	9	14.2	8	0	8.0
48013	3.9	97	1.2	82	26.3	566	70.5	4	10	1.4	8	0	.4
48014	9.3	97	3.5	63	27.8	356	72.4	5	20	4.1	15	0	.1
48015	23.0	100	7.0	87	42.5	449	127.1	5	12	11.2	7	0	.8
48016	15.1	99	5.4	75	32.9	417	79.6	6	9	7.2	7	1	.6
48017	37.8	97	13.1	73	54.8	550	184.9	5	13	18.3	6	0	1.7
48018	6.5	98	2.1	90	34.4	461	100.0	8	8	3.3	6	0	.3
48020	16.0	99	5.2	88	39.6	503	96.2	6	5	8.0	5	0	.4
48021	38.3	99	13.4	90	32.2	428	70.1	6	13	18.2	12	0	.1
48022	2.5	100	.7	89	29.8	355	73.4	8	6	1.3	9	1	.1
48023	3.1	100	1.1	82	28.3	368	80.7	6	9	1.6	9	0	.1
48024	30.3	98	11.6	68	35.8	489	109.1	5	12	14.3	9	4	.0
48025	17.9	99	5.8	97	107.3	606	263.8	4	10	1.4	10	0	.6
48026	21.2	99	6.7	74	36.5	386	105.8	6	8	10.0	6	0	1.7
48027	4.1	98	1.2	87	26.0	337	65.0	8	10	2.0	6	0	.0
48028	1.2	100	.4	95	27.7	458	83.2	4	22	.6	25	0	.0
48029	2.9	0	.9	88	36.5	490	115.9	8	3	.0	0	1	.0
48030	20.9	99	7.4	78	26.0	372	47.8	8	9	10.0	8	1	.5
48031	14.8	98	4.6	91	33.5	453	106.4	9	7	7.3	5	4	.1
48033	44.0	96	13.7	83	25.6	349	87.0	6	5	21.2	5	1	.0
48034	27.3	92	12.2	42	40.7	573	199.6	4	15	11.8	14	0	.5
48035	17.9	99	5.8	81	39.9	535	127.6	7	5	8.9	5	1	1.9
48036	.6	100	.2	73	29.4	435	120.4	6	7	.4	5	1	.2
48038	2.6	100	.8	83	40.2	364	87.3	8	10	1.4	6	0	.0
48039	10.1	100	3.5	84	26.8	369	112.0	8	13	4.9	11	0	.2
48040	7.1	99	2.6	90	31.7	355	80.9	6	11	3.4	10	2	.2
48041	2.9	97	.8	84	31.7	417	86.5	8	8	1.4	8	0	.6

MICHIGAN

ZIPCODE	1	2	3	4	5	6	7	8	9	10	11	12	13
ROYAL OAK													
48042	24.1	99	7.5	87	40.1	414	138.9	7	5	12.0	4	2	.2
48043	70.0	90	24.6	64	31.4	385	91.3	8	8	30.6	7	3	.9
48044	23.2	99	7.9	86	37.5	427	128.7	10	4	11.4	4	0	.1
48045	31.3	97	10.6	71	34.3	389	105.6	8	6	15.4	5	1	.4
48047	16.4	99	5.4	75	33.7	378	106.9	9	6	8.2	5	1	.0
48048	6.1	86	1.9	86	27.4	377	72.7	12	7	2.6	7	1	.5
48049	2.5	99	.7	92	34.2	385	80.3	8	6	1.2	7	0	.5
48050	12.8	97	4.5	92	40.8	599	140.9	8	6	6.0	5	3	2.3
48051	14.5	100	4.8	84	36.8	379	110.1	9	5	7.1	4	1	.3
48052	.5	100	.2	78	21.0	491	76.3	4	17	.2	19	0	.0
48053	29.0	52	9.4	61	26.6	354	60.7	8	11	7.3	12	2	23.1
48054	38.2	98	14.1	70	33.4	413	94.4	7	8	18.3	6	1	.0
48055	31.2	92	11.1	67	29.4	339	72.1	9	8	13.9	6	4	2.8
48057	19.3	82	7.2	66	30.5	377	75.7	8	9	7.6	9	1	.1
48058	29.3	53	9.7	54	23.5	312	41.5	11	8	7.5	10	0	.2
48060	58.2	94	20.8	69	26.2	347	65.3	8	11	26.2	9	5	.7
48062	11.4	100	3.5	83	32.8	380	92.8	7	9	5.7	7	0	.0
48063	55.2	98	18.1	75	44.0	464	153.3	9	8	26.4	7	8	.8
48065	14.0	97	4.2	83	39.3	353	122.1	6	8	8.8	6	2	.8
48066	54.3	98	18.2	79	30.3	407	67.4	8	8	25.7	6	6	.6
48067	29.7	99	11.6	72	30.6	397	70.7	7	13	14.1	10	0	.4
48069	3.3	99	1.2	86	38.2	425	107.5	6	14	1.6	11	0	1.8
48070	7.2	99	2.5	97	59.2	686	130.3	7	13	3.5	13	0	.1
48071	35.4	97	12.8	72	31.1	393	70.3	7	7	16.7	6	2	2.6
48072	24.4	98	9.2	80	32.5	417	76.5	6	13	11.4	10	0	.1
48073	35.2	99	14.0	73	34.8	457	89.6	6	11	16.4	9	0	.2
48074	3.2	95	.9	90	29.3	335	71.8	5	7	1.6	5	0	.0
48075	22.8	76	8.8	62	46.5	613	112.8	5	18	8.2	19	0	1.0
48076	30.0	96	10.2	82	46.4	576	126.3	6	12	13.9	11	0	.3
48077	63.9	97	19.5	81	40.7	465	121.4	7	5	30.6	4	2	3.6
48078	45.1	99	14.8	83	36.7	435	111.1	8	6	21.9	3	1	1.2
48079	11.3	99	3.8	80	33.3	334	91.6	6	9	5.4	10	0	2.8
48080	28.4	99	11.0	79	33.3	492	82.9	5	15	13.1	12	0	.1
48081	26.4	99	9.0	91	37.1	470	91.3	7	10	12.8	8	0	.2
48082	21.8	99	6.9	88	36.2	437	81.2	6	8	10.5	6	1	.2
48084	35.8	96	13.9	58	40.3	516	134.0	7	8	16.6	6	2	4.5
48085	24.3	98	9.0	87	38.1	463	108.7	7	8	12.0	5	0	.1
48087	41.3	99	12.5	78	40.8	377	126.0	8	4	20.3	3	5	1.8
48088	18.3	99	6.5	68	33.4	424	97.7	8	5	9.4	4	0	1.0
48089	38.6	98	12.7	81	28.8	442	59.1	8	8	18.8	6	2	3.6
48091	35.9	98	12.7	80	31.2	385	68.7	9	9	17.4	8	1	4.5
48092	29.1	99	9.5	81	39.6	454	95.2	6	9	14.2	6	0	2.3
48093	57.5	99	18.8	84	39.7	447	100.5	7	8	27.5	7	0	.1
48094	.9	100	2.6	84	40.2	401	131.8	6	5	4.5	5	1	.2
48095	8.1	99	2.6	88	36.3	437	100.3	7	7	3.9	7	0	.1
48096	7.8	99	3.6	46	29.9	351	113.5	7	6	4.0	5	1	7.1
48097	5.3	99	1.7	84	25.3	335	61.4	8	13	2.6	12	1	.1
48098	31.7	95	9.4	94	53.3	588	165.6	8	3	15.1	3	1	.1

*=Estimated **=1.0=883 lbs per person; 100+ indicates per capita toxic waste generation > than 100 times the U.S. average of 883 lbs per capita.

ZIP CODE MEASURES OF SIZE, LEVELS OF AFFLUENCE AND QUALITY OF LIFE

1=Population (th.); 2= % White; 3=Households (th.); 4=% Owner Occupied; 5=Mean Income Per Household (th.$); 6=Mean Monthly Rent ($)*; 7=Mean Home Value (th.$)*; 8=% under 5; 9=% 65 and over; 10=% White Males, 65+; 11=% White Males (th.); 12=# Toxic Waste Sites; 13=Toxic Waste Relative to US(883 lbs.per capita)**;

MICHIGAN

DETROIT

ZIP CODE	1	2	3	4	5	6	7	8	9	10	11	12	13
48101	34.2	98	12.1	88	38.7	453	88.3	5	11	16.4	10	2	.0
48103	37.0	90	14.4	67	36.7	474	129.8	6	9	16.1	7	2	.2
48104	54.9	88	21.8	34	30.2	484	144.6	5	5	24.5	4	1	.1
48105	25.7	80	9.9	38	33.7	444	159.2	7	5	10.2	4	0	.1
48111	32.9	92	11.5	73	33.0	471	94.6	8	6	15.4	5	3	.5
48116	28.7	99	9.3	82	39.1	422	130.0	8	7	14.2	6	5	.4
48117	9.7	95	3.0	88	32.9	321	95.3	9	6	4.8	5	1	.0
48118	9.0	98	2.9	78	33.2	418	95.9	9	6	4.8	8	0	.7
48120	6.2	98	2.2	41	34.1	437	96.1	8	11	3.2	9	0	.6
48122	12.3	96	4.7	70	29.2	375	54.3	6	9	5.8	8	0	.9
48124	37.0	99	14.0	86	39.3	364	104.0	4	14	17.7	12	0	.8
48125	27.7	98	9.1	91	33.4	464	67.3	7	11	13.3	7	0	.2
48126	36.2	98	14.5	68	27.6	370	72.1	6	18	16.9	15	2	1.3
48127	40.0	98	14.1	85	39.9	458	103.9	4	11	18.9	9	0	.0
48128	11.3	100	4.4	94	41.5	577	112.7	4	15	15.4	13	1	.5
48130	7.2	99	2.4	78	37.6	429	125.6	8	8	3.6	7	1	.6
48131	5.3	100	1.8	72	29.1	400	81.2	8	9	2.6	3	0	.6
48133	4.8	96	1.6	84	30.0	377	78.7	8	7	2.3	6	1	.2
48134	11.1	99	3.9	91	31.7	348	90.5	8	6	5.5	5	2	.0
48135	35.6	99	11.1	88	35.7	449	74.4	7	6	17.5	5	0	.1
48137	9.3	98	3.0	92	39.3	502	89.3	6	8	4.5	6	0	.0
48138	9.3	98	3.0	92	58.4	526	174.5	5	7	4.5	6	0	.5
48139	1.2	100	.4	90	29.1	404	89.4	7	6	.6	7	0	.5
48140	3.3	99	1.0	87	32.2	397	93.1	8	8	1.7	4	0	.9
48141	35.2	42	11.8	65	26.9	337	54.0	8	14	17.1	7	1	.6
48143	.7	100	.2	88	38.2	361	105.4	8	11	.4	9	1	.6
48144	6.6	99	1.9	91	35.6	444	101.0	8	9	3.3	5	1	.2
48145	3.5	99	1.1	86	31.4	422	90.8	8	9	1.7	7	1	.3
48146	45.1	98	16.5	79	30.6	377	62.7	7	10	21.4	8	0	.2
48150	31.0	99	10.0	93	39.3	552	94.3	6	8	15.0	8	2	5.7
48152	27.8	98	9.2	85	39.9	427	117.7	6	9	13.4	7	0	.0
48154	46.1	99	13.5	95	48.1	458	124.6	5	5	22.4	9	0	.0
48157	1.4	98	.5	74	24.6	216	55.2	11	9	.7	7	0	.4
48159	5.6	93	1.8	83	35.0	446	100.6	8	8	2.8	6	1	.1
48160	10.8	91	3.4	84	30.0	390	71.3	7	9	5.0	6	0	.0
48161	53.8	97	18.2	76	33.0	428	96.5	8	7	25.2	8	1	.5
48164	6.1	96	1.8	70	28.9	349	81.3	8	11	2.9	8	0	.6
48165	3.3	99	1.2	88	35.2	409	98.2	7	7	1.6	6	0	.6
48166	7.8	100	2.5	81	32.0	334	141.8	6	6	4.0	9	1	.0
48167	25.0	96	7.8	83	30.4	406	76.8	9	6	11.7	5	0	.4
48169	11.5	96	3.6	80	40.8	448	168.0	5	5	5.6	6	0	.2
48170	37.0	98	3.6	85	33.8	455	108.0	6	7	17.7	6	1	.6
48173	10.3	99	12.8	73	41.4	414	141.4	8	8	8.1	6	1	1.5
48174	31.1	85	10.2	72	36.5	392	88.3	9	13	13.2	5	2	.6
48175	.2	0	.1	77	29.9	367	73.0	3	5	.2	0	0	1.9
48176	11.4	99	3.7	79	28.6	278	101.2	11	9	5.5	6	3	.2
48177	.4	100	.1	79	26.4	314	76.0	7	7	.2	7	0	2.4
48178	13.0	99	4.3	78	34.0	398	121.2	7	7	6.4	7	0	.4

MICHIGAN

DETROIT

ZIP CODE	1	2	3	4	5	6	7	8	9	10	11	12	13
48179	2.7	100	.8	88	34.9	379	84.3	8	6	1.4	5	5	.0
48180	77.6	90	24.5	71	31.5	386	69.8	9	5	36.8	4	3	.2
48182	12.5	99	3.8	87	36.9	380	96.8	8	6	6.3	6	0	.0
48183	41.4	98	13.6	74	37.5	366	106.0	8	6	19.9	4	8	5.2
48184	21.3	94	7.1	68	31.3	355	72.3	7	7	9.6	7	5	6.5
48185	84.3	96	29.0	82	32.6	412	79.1	7	9	39.4	5	0	.1
48187	35.1	95	11.1	76	40.0	486	135.7	7	3	16.6	3	0	.0
48188	12.5	97	4.3	76	33.4	347	122.1	10	4	6.0	6	0	.2
48189	7.0	96	2.2	72	31.9	459	93.1	8	7	3.5	6	1	.6
48190	.3	73	.1	95	30.6	352*	62.4	0	15	.1	8	0	.0
48191	2.3	92	.7	90	36.6	368	92.2	7	5	1.1	6	0	.0
48192	51.4	98	18.4	68	31.1	357	78.2	7	11	24.2	8	15	7.0
48195	32.1	98	11.0	77	35.0	430	77.4	8	5	15.5	5	7	.4
48197	83.1	78	29.7	52	29.4	388	88.9	8	8	31.8	4	7	4.8

DETROIT

ZIP CODE	1	2	3	4	5	6	7	8	9	10	11	12	13
48201	24.5	35	14.7	2	9.8	172	57.8	5	25	5.1	25	1	.3
48202	32.7	15	13.6	24	16.9	248	39.6	6	17	2.5	20	4	.6
48203	69.1	34	25.1	46	21.5	307	38.3	8	11	11.5	15	1	.5
48204	59.8	3	20.6	53	21.5	316	34.6	8	9	1.0	34	0	.4
48205	61.1	86	23.6	76	25.6	343	41.0	7	17	25.0	16	0	.1
48206	51.8	3	19.3	36	18.7	286	40.2	8	12	.6	24	0	.9
48207	34.3	15	13.9	28	19.9	304	32.3	7	18	2.4	29	0	.9
48208	24.6	10	9.9	30	14.9	259	25.2	8	15	1.3	23	0	.5
48209	46.1	81	16.5	48	21.3	277	26.1	9	12	18.1	11	4	4.7
48210	48.2	54	17.6	56	20.4	283	24.4	8	15	12.6	14	1	.6
48211	26.1	33	9.1	43	20.5	276	21.1	9	14	14.7	17	5	2.7
48212	49.1	63	18.2	63	20.4	268	27.2	7	17	14.7	17	3	3.4
48213	61.8	22	19.8	59	20.0	313	32.4	9	9	6.4	19	1	.7
48214	53.2	14	20.1	56	20.0	303	35.1	7	14	3.3	23	4	.9
48215	39.5	18	12.8	41	17.3	304	29.8	8	11	3.3	16	2	4.2
48216	11.6	49	4.1	32	15.6	251	22.8	10	13	2.9	15	0	1.5
48217	13.7	13	4.2	80	13.7	273	39.6	8	9	4.1	8	2	4.0
48218	12.9	66	4.7	66	23.6	268	39.6	7	9	14.9	9	2	2.2
48219	62.9	52	22.2	77	29.4	398	51.2	8	11	12.4	15	2	3.8
48220	29.7	87	11.1	71	25.9	388	50.6	6	8	2.5	16	0	.1
48221	54.1	10	17.2	79	33.7	407	60.0	6	10	15.0	10	0	1.2
48223	42.0	73	15.5	71	28.3	397	47.7	9	9	20.7	10	0	.0
48224	51.5	84	20.3	79	27.5	374	50.3	9	9	7.7	17	2	.0
48225	17.1	99	6.8	83	52.0	483	78.0	7	14	.7	17	2	.6
48226	3.0	39	1.4	3	17.9	246	20.5	3	10	.7	15	2	21.8
48227	74.8	13	23.4	70	25.7	377	41.5	9	6	4.5	24	1	1.3
48228	70.9	61	26.0	73	25.7	304	38.6	8	8	20.7	14	2	.6
48229	14.5	58	5.1	62	26.1	301	42.5	8	10	4.1	12	2	10.3
48230	19.7	99	7.3	75	52.0	483	176.8	5	14	9.1	21	2	.0
48234	52.2	40	18.2	78	25.2	351	37.7	8	13	3.3	32	0	1.8
48235	61.8	12	20.2	82	30.4	387	48.4	8	8	8.3	13	0	.0
48236	34.4	99	12.1	94	65.8	562	176.2	4	15	16.4	15	0	.0
48237	33.9	87	12.8	70	31.1	464	72.5	7	16	13.9	15	0	.8
48238	63.1	99	21.5	54	21.9	328	35.4	8	37	6.4	37	0	.7

*=Estimated **1.0=883 lbs per person; 100++ indicates per capita toxic waste generation > than 100 times the U.S. average of 883 lbs per capita.

ZIP CODE MEASURES OF SIZE, LEVELS OF AFFLUENCE AND QUALITY OF LIFE

1=Population (th.); 2= % White; 3=Households (th.); 4=% Owner Occupied; 5=Mean Income Per Household (th.$); 6=Mean Monthly Rent ($)*; 7=Mean Home Value (th.$)*;
8=% under 5; 9=% 65 and over; 10=White Males (th.); 11=% White Males, 65+; 12=# Toxic Waste Sites; 13=Toxic Waste Relative to US(883 lbs.per capita)**.

MICHIGAN

ZIPCODE	1	2	3	4	5	6	7	8	9	10	11	12	13
DETROIT													
48239	42.7	99	15.0	93	35.9	428	78.3	6	11	20.7	10	1	.5
48240	22.2	99	7.3	93	34.0	458	70.4	7	10	10.7	8	0	.0
FLINT													
48401	1.3	99	.5	86	22.7	302	59.0	8	15	.6	15	0	.0
48410	.1	100	.1	88	14.4	165*	26.3	8	20	.1	14	0	.0
48412	3.5	98	1.0	88	33.0	361	76.5	8	7	1.7	6	0	.0
48413	7.7	99	2.6	80	23.6	282	66.2	9	14	3.7	11	1	.2
48414	2.5	99	.7	88	29.0	461	60.4	9	8	1.3	5	1	.0
48415	9.2	98	2.8	89	30.7	367	72.4	8	6	4.5	5	0	.0
48416	4.6	99	1.4	82	25.2	359	64.8	9	9	2.3	8	0	1.0
48417	3.6	94	1.0	86	28.2	303	63.7	10	5	1.7	6	0	.0
48418	3.2	99	.9	90	35.4	375	76.7	10	5	1.6	5	0	.0
48419	2.6	99	.9	85	22.4	283	55.4	8	14	1.2	13	0	.0
48420	22.9	99	7.2	81	31.7	337	78.3	9	6	11.3	5	2	.1
48421	6.2	98	1.8	87	30.7	359	77.1	10	5	3.0	5	0	.1
48422	5.0	96	1.6	85	22.4	312	56.4	8	12	2.3	11	0	.3
48423	26.4	99	9.1	74	33.3	359	83.2	8	6	12.8	5	1	.0
48426	1.1	99	.3	84	24.7	309	49.9	8	10	.6	10	0	.0
48427	3.1	99	1.1	83	23.1	305	58.9	7	16	1.5	16	0	.2
48428	3.2	99	.9	88	34.6	300	83.3	6	5	1.6	5	0	.6
48429	9.7	98	3.2	82	28.9	342	66.1	10	8	4.7	7	0	.0
48430	23.3	99	7.5	84	36.0	368	104.5	7	8	11.4	6	1	1.1
48432	3.8	0	.8	88	23.5	283	60.1	7	11	1.0	11	0	.7
48433	23.6	99	7.7	88	37.9	405	96.1	7	7	11.3	6	0	.3
SAGINAW (WEST)													
48434	.2	0	.2	87	16.1	185*	64.5	4	36	.6	6	0	.0
48435	1.9	99	.6	87	29.2	452	63.4	7	7	.9	6	0	.1
48436	3.0	99	.8	84	45.3	397	84.3	9	3	1.6	2	0	.0
48437	.8	93	.3	84	35.0	351	69.8	8	7	.4	7	0	.0
48438	3.8	99	1.1	92	40.7	367	105.7	8	6	1.9	6	0	.0
48439	25.9	98	8.5	77	44.8	422	115.1	6	6	12.5	4	3	3.5
48440	.3	100	.1	88	29.8	232	72.3	9	18	.1	8	0	.0
48441	4.7	99	1.6	83	20.9	302	54.3	8	15	2.3	14	1	12.3
48442	15.5	97	4.9	84	33.9	355	94.1	8	8	7.4	6	0	.3
48444	6.9	95	2.1	79	30.1	346	76.3	9	10	3.2	8	0	.3
48445	1.8	99	.6	82	21.2	332	48.0	8	13	1.0	11	0	.0
48446	25.6	98	8.0	77	30.3	336	79.4	9	9	12.3	7	1	.2
48449	4.4	99	1.4	88	32.1	246	75.9	9	5	2.2	4	0	1.1
48450	3.8	99	1.5	84	22.3	302	63.8	6	21	1.9	20	0	.0
48451	9.0	100	2.9	85	35.3	382	99.7	7	7	4.5	5	0	.5
48452	1.1	100	.3	93	27.9	415	68.1	10	6	.6	6	0	.0
48453	5.3	100	1.7	78	27.4	326	68.2	9	12	2.6	10	0	1.1
48454	2.5	0	.4	84	22.4	427	52.8	6	10	.8	9	0	.0
48455	5.7	99	1.7	86	40.3	463	103.8	7	5	2.8	5	0	.0
48456	1.1	0	.4	86	21.2	322	42.0	9	15	.2	10	0	.0
48457	8.3	96	2.5	89	32.1	352	70.2	8	7	4.0	6	0	.0
48458	25.4	76	8.7	81	28.4	338	58.1	7	8	9.4	6	0	.0
48460	2.5	98	.7	84	31.5	367	79.5	9	10	1.2	9	0	.0
48461	6.0	99	1.8	87	29.9	333	67.3	7	7	3.0	7	0	.3
48462	9.0	100	2.6	89	38.8	451	115.8	6	5	4.6	5	0	.0

MICHIGAN

ZIPCODE	1	2	3	4	5	6	7	8	9	10	11	12	13
FLINT													
48463	4.5	98	1.4	91	32.1	356	74.9	9	6	2.3	5	1	.0
48464	2.3	99	.7	88	28.2	296	61.5	10	6	1.2	5	0	.0
48465	.8	100	.2	87	22.1	344	65.8	8	10	.4	9	0	.0
48466	1.6	99	.5	81	24.0	330	53.7	9	10	.8	9	0	.1
48467	2.5	99	.9	83	19.3	151	63.3	6	19	1.2	18	0	.1
48468	1.6	100	.6	84	19.5	284	48.4	7	18	.8	17	0	.0
48469	1.2	98	.5	83	19.8	321	73.7	7	31	.5	29	0	.0
48470	1.0	100	.3	85	23.2	210	50.9	8	15	.5	13	0	.0
48471	5.5	98	1.9	83	24.4	298	62.9	8	12	2.6	11	0	.4
48472	2.1	100	.7	82	22.1	355	55.4	9	12	1.0	11	0	.0
48473	16.9	98	5.2	89	37.8	392	88.0	8	5	8.2	5	0	.4
48475	3.0	100	1.0	83	21.7	292	58.7	7	13	1.6	12	0	.7
48476	1.0	0	.3	89	27.2	424	60.0	8	7	.0	7	0	.0
FLINT													
48502	1.7	75	.5	4	15.6	275	73.0	3	19	.7	11	0	12.0
48503	37.6	60	14.7	58	26.0	307	62.3	8	13	10.5	13	3	.0
48504	63.4	76	23.1	75	30.6	374	65.2	8	10	22.8	10	2	.0
48505	53.6	21	16.8	64	24.3	362	39.8	9	6	5.4	11	1	.0
48506	37.3	97	12.3	77	27.5	325	54.7	9	9	17.4	7	0	1.1
48507	42.1	91	16.0	71	31.5	359	75.6	7	9	18.5	8	0	.8
48509	9.8	100	3.2	93	37.1	419	77.3	6	8	4.8	7	0	.0
48519	7.5	99	2.5	84	30.2	266	67.4	7	8	3.6	6	0	.0
48529	11.5	96	4.3	70	24.3	342	47.5	8	7	5.4	7	0	.3
SAGINAW (WEST)													
48601	62.9	44	20.1	69	23.5	340	44.5	10	11	13.3	11	4	.5
48602	36.2	96	11.3	73	26.8	323	63.0	7	14	16.3	12	5	.7
48603	49.5	96	17.1	71	35.8	399	101.1	9	9	22.9	7	2	.0
48604	12.8	93	4.2	83	31.1	412	64.3	8	9	5.8	8	1	.0
48607	4.9	19	1.9	28	12.3	283	31.0	9	13	4.1	21	0	3.4
48610	2.0	99	.8	89	17.2	299	50.5	8	20	1.0	22	0	.0
48611	5.9	99	1.8	87	31.6	350	78.9	7	7	3.0	6	1	.0
48612	7.6	100	2.7	86	21.6	302	56.8	7	12	3.8	12	5	1.4
48613	1.1	98	.3	92	23.0	504	50.9	9	8	.6	9	0	.0
48614	1.4	0	.4	89	25.0	378	59.1	8	8	.6	8	0	.0
48615	3.3	98	1.1	84	24.1	299	51.2	8	12	1.6	11	1	.0
48616	8.5	98	2.6	86	29.7	356	69.9	8	8	4.2	7	0	.3
48617	8.9	99	3.1	77	22.8	264	59.7	8	12	4.2	11	0	.3
48618	4.3	99	1.4	87	25.0	294	59.1	9	8	2.1	7	0	.0
48619	.5	0	2.9	91	17.0	207	40.3	6	20	.0	0	0	.0
48621	1.2	0	.4	83	22.1	238	58.1	7	16	.2	11	0	.2
48622	5.0	100	1.7	87	21.7	316	56.1	7	14	2.5	13	2	.5
48623	9.0	99	2.8	86	35.3	368	89.1	8	6	4.4	6	2	.2
48624	11.8	99	4.2	84	20.2	266	59.6	7	15	5.8	15	1	.6
48625	9.6	99	3.6	85	17.3	279	45.5	7	17	4.6	17	1	.8
48626	6.3	100	1.9	89	32.6	377	83.3	7	7	3.1	6	2	.8
48627	.4	99	.6	88	16.5	198	55.9	8	14	.0	2	1	.0
48628	1.9	99	.6	91	27.0	364	68.0	8	6	1.0	6	1	.5
48629	5.1	99	2.0	85	18.0	240	59.8	6	19	2.5	20	1	.1
48630	.5	100	.2	72	17.4	150	45.8	6	20	.2	16	0	.0

*=Estimated **1.0=883 lbs per person; 100++ indicates per capita toxic waste generation > than 100 times the U.S. average of 883 lbs per capita.

ZIP CODE MEASURES OF SIZE, LEVELS OF AFFLUENCE AND QUALITY OF LIFE

1=Population (th.); 2= % White; 3=Households (th.); 4=% Owner Occupied; 5=Mean Income Per Household (th.$); 6=Mean Monthly Rent ($)*; 7=Mean Home Value (th.$)*;
8=% under 5; 9=% 65 and over; 10=White Males (th.); 11=% White Males, 65+; 12=# Toxic Waste Sites; 13=Toxic Waste Relative to US(883 lbs.per capita)**.

MICHIGAN

SAGINAW (WEST)

ZIP CODE	1	2	3	4	5	6	7	8	9	10	11	12	13
48631	4.8	99	1.5	87	29.7	376	69.3	8	8	2.4	8	2	.1
48632	3.2	99	1.2	89	18.9	317	47.6	6	17	1.6	18	0	.0
48633	.6	100	.2	88	15.5	349	46.3	6	20	.3	22	0	.0
48634	5.0	99	1.5	89	31.1	321	77.0	9	6	2.6	5	0	.1
48635	1.6	0	.6	88	15.4	200	55.8	7	18	.0	9	2	.0
48636	.7	100	.3	91	16.2	248	42.2	6	21	.4	19	2	1.3
48637	3.7	98	1.2	89	27.7	347	65.3	8	10	1.8	10	0	.0
48640	56.5	97	19.0	77	34.5	364	96.6	8	7	27.2	6	11	34.4
48647	3.5	0	1.3	86	18.8	287	50.8	7	15	.0	7	0	.0
48649	1.9	98	.6	84	26.5	314	62.5	9	7	1.0	7	0	.4
48650	8.2	98	2.6	86	26.9	295	64.1	9	9	4.0	8	0	.8
48651	1.5	0	1.1	89	17.9	287	56.5	5	21	.7	10	0	.0
48652	1.5	98	.5	92	23.1	311	56.2	9	10	.7	10	1	1.0
48653	5.8	100	2.2	85	20.6	292	63.5	7	15	2.9	15	3	.4
48654	2.0	99	.7	77	15.8	273	50.8	6	15	.9	15	0	.2
48655	6.5	99	2.1	85	27.9	322	65.4	8	8	3.1	8	0	.0
48656	3.1	0	1.3	87	16.7	303	46.5	9	22	.0	6	0	.8
48657	7.0	99	2.3	85	26.3	383	73.5	8	5	3.5	6	2	.0
48658	5.1	98	1.7	84	22.7	279	56.9	7	13	2.5	11	0	.1
48659	2.6	100	.8	88	21.5	350	57.3	9	11	1.3	11	1	.0
48661	7.8	100	2.8	83	21.9	305	62.0	7	13	3.8	13	1	1.2
48662	1.8	98	.6	83	24.3	323	53.2	9	9	1.8	7	2	.0

SAGINAW (EAST)

ZIP CODE	1	2	3	4	5	6	7	8	9	10	11	12	13
48701	1.7	98	.6	88	24.9	342	57.4	7	11	.9	10	0	.0
48703	2.6	100	1.0	86	21.5	210	70.9	6	18	1.3	19	1	1.8
48705	.5	0	27.5	90	14.9	261	49.4	7	20	.0	0	0	.0
48706	77.4	97	27.5	79	27.8	308	66.7	8	11	36.3	9	6	1.8
48720	1.3	0	.4	77	22.0	278	53.0	8	14	.0	0	0	.6
48721	1.2	100	.1	82	16.3	364	60.6	6	19	.0	1	18	.2
48722	4.3	97	1.3	89	37.2	367	80.1	7	5	2.0	5	1	1.2
48723	12.8	98	4.2	78	25.7	303	71.5	7	11	6.0	11	2	.8
48725	2.4	98	1.0	89	17.9	244	55.6	8	6	1.1	23	0	.3
48726	5.6	99	1.9	81	26.2	315	69.5	8	14	2.8	12	2	1.4
48727	1.3	100	.4	81	23.1	377	50.0	6	7	.0	7	0	.0
48728	.3	0		89	18.6	52	46.8	8	16	.0	0	0	.2
48729	1.7	99	.5	87	23.0	346	59.5	8	8	.9	8	0	.0
48730	4.2	99	1.7	83	20.8	262	62.7	6	21	2.0	20	0	.6
48731	2.0	99	.7	88	22.1	301	60.3	10	11	.0	9	0	.9
48732	12.6	97	4.5	67	27.4	361	63.1	8	9	5.8	9	0	.2
48733	2.3	98	.8	85	27.6	325	61.3	8	10	1.1	9	0	.0
48734	6.4	99	2.0	77	38.8	390	112.5	7	14	3.0	10	1	1.2
48735	1.3	0	.4	85	23.3	329	55.6	7	13	.0	0	0	.0
48737	1.1	100	.5	89	17.0	281	47.5	5	23	.5	25	0	.0
48738	1.3	99	.5	83	18.3	164	68.9	6	21	.6	20	0	.0
48739	3.4	0	1.4	88	15.8	185	50.1	5	24	.0	0	0	.1
48740	1.7	99	.6	83	16.8	188	50.0	6	23	1.0	22	1	.1
48741	1.8	99	.6	89	25.4	374	59.0	8	11	.9	10	0	.0
48742	1.7	100	.6	86	19.7	266	69.6	5	20	.8	19	1	.0
48743	.2	100	.1	72	17.9	332	50.4	10	15	.1	15	0	.0

MICHIGAN

SAGINAW (EAST)

ZIP CODE	1	2	3	4	5	6	7	8	9	10	11	12	13
48744	4.1	98	1.3	85	26.1	340	62.5	8	10	2.1	10	0	.2
48745	1.2	96	.4	93	18.3	220	50.1	6	16	.6	16	0	.0
48746	8.4	99	2.5	89	30.0	330	68.1	8	6	4.1	6	0	.1
48747	1.8	98		89	29.2	338	75.0	8	9	.9	9	0	.0
48748	1.2	0	.5	87	17.2	281	54.1	5	22	.0	9	2	1.0
48749	1.0	100	.4	91	19.3	306	52.9	7	11	.5	13	1	
48750	8.0	97	3.0	73	20.7	231	67.0	8	11	3.7	10	3	.3
48753	5.2	85	1.3	0	16.6	331	59.2*16	0		2.5	0	1	1.0
48754	1.1	0	.4	85	23.6	397	47.0	7	9	.0	9	0	.0
48755	3.0	98	1.1	83	24.3	311	74.5	7	19	1.5	17	0	.4
48756	3.2	99	1.4	85	16.3	314	43.0	9	14	1.6	15	0	.0
48757	4.2	99	1.4	87	30.6	325	80.4	9	12	2.0	18	0	.0
48758	.4	100	.1	96	37.4	430*	68.0	7	12	2.2	12	0	1.8
48759	4.0	98	1.5	81	22.5	328	61.3	7	15	1.9	14	0	.0
48760	1.1	97	.3	87	26.6	304	58.4	8	9	.5	8	0	.6
48761	.8	98	.3	95	16.0	264	46.7	4	24	.4	22	0	.0
48762	1.0	100	.3	90	19.7	343	68.4	6	18	.5	17	0	.0
48763	4.8	99	1.7	82	21.5	278	65.1	6	18	2.3	16	1	1.8
48765	1.1	0	.3	87	19.6	226	50.1	8	12	.0	10	0	.0
48766	1.3	99	.4	88	18.3	295	51.3	6	14	.7	14	0	.0
48767	2.4	99	.8	87	25.8	316	54.0	7	13	1.2	11	0	.6
48768	9.6	97	3.1	84	28.0	315	67.8	8	8	4.6	7	0	.3
48769	.1	100		75	22.1	331	59.6	9	7	.1		0	.0
48770	1.7	99	.6	79	17.6	223	43.0	8	13	.9	13	1	.0

LANSING

ZIP CODE	1	2	3	4	5	6	7	8	9	10	11	12	13
48801	12.9	97	4.1	71	25.1	304	60.5	8	12	5.9	9	3	4.3
48806	1.9	99	.6	86	24.3	326	49.8	9	14	.9	13	0	.0
48807	1.3	0	.4	87	24.2	315	54.1	11	9	.0	0	0	.0
48808	3.7	99	1.1	84	30.1	406	72.1	7	5	1.9	5	1	3.6
48809	9.5	99	3.2	78	23.7	276	54.5	9	12	4.6	10	2	2.2
48811	3.2	98	1.1	79	23.6	301	52.4	8	11	1.6	10	1	
48812	.3	0	.1	58	20.5	380	45.9	12	5	.0	0	2	.2
48813	18.7	98	6.1	78	28.9	314	71.3	8	9	8.9	7	2	.4
48815	1.6	100	.5	88	27.2	273	62.9	9	9	.9	8	0	.0
48816	.3	100	.1	85	30.2	347	73.9	10	13	.1	14	0	.6
48817	6.4	99	2.1	76	28.9	329	68.9	8	7	3.1	7	0	.6
48818	2.3	99	.7	83	21.7	355	54.0	8	15	.9	16	1	.0
48819	2.3	99	.7	88	30.8	397	54.0	8	7	1.1	6	0	.9
48820	10.0	98	3.0	86	36.0	415	96.2	7	6	4.9	5	0	.2
48821	4.6	98	1.6	91	36.9	323	99.1	6	12	2.2	11	0	.0
48822	2.3	98	.7	95	34.0	450	99.7	7	5	1.2	6	0	.6
48823	43.8	92	16.2	39	29.7	416	119.5	6	6	19.7	5	3	.1
48824	17.0	91	.0	0	14.1	347	50.1*	0	0	7.7	0	2	.0
48827	12.2	99	3.9	82	30.7	341	76.1	8	9	5.9	8	2	.0
48829	3.2	98	1.0	78	22.6	304	52.0	7	12	1.4	11	0	.6
48831	3.4	99	1.1	83	26.1	343	60.5	7	11	1.7	10	1	.1
48832	1.3	99	.4	86	24.4	288	59.3	8	8	.6	8	0	.0
48834	1.9	98	.6	89	22.4	223	59.1	10	11	1.0	11	0	.1
48835	3.2	100	.9	83	29.8	339	72.4	10	15	1.6	6	0	.0

*=Estimated **1.0=883 lbs per person; 100++ indicates per capita toxic waste generation > than 100 times the U.S. average of 883 lbs per capita.

ZIP CODE MEASURES OF SIZE, LEVELS OF AFFLUENCE AND QUALITY OF LIFE

1=Population (th.); 2= % White; 3=Households (th.); 4=% Owner Occupied; 5=Mean Income Per Household (th.$); 6=Mean Monthly Rent ($)*; 7=Mean Home Value (th.$); 8=% under 5, 9=% 65 and over; 10=White Males (th.); 11=% White Males, 65+; 12=# Toxic Waste Sites; 13=Toxic Waste Relative to US(883 lbs.per capita)**.

MICHIGAN

LANSING

ZIP CODE	1	2	3	4	5	6	7	8	9	10	11	12	13
48836	7.7	98	2.5	82	29.5	376	84.5	8	8	3.7	7	2	.1
48837	15.3	98	5.3	77	32.6	361	89.9	7	8	7.3	7	3	.0
48838	14.2	98	5.1	76	24.3	296	62.0	7	13	6.6	10	4	1.3
48840	9.0	97	3.7	55	30.4	389	86.8	6	6	4.2	9	1	.0
48841	.9	100	.3	86	28.5	507	57.7	9	10	.5	9	1	.0
48842	14.3	98	5.1	71	29.7	373	82.5	8	6	6.8	4	2	.0
48843	26.9	99	8.3	80	34.0	374	108.0	7	9	13.3	7	8	1.8
48845	1.0	0	.3	87	25.4	278	41.0	9	12	.0	0	0	.0
48846	16.0	87	4.6	75	26.6	305	56.6	6	11	7.4	7	3	.8
48847	6.3	99	2.2	78	23.4	308	55.9	6	9	3.1	9	1	.0
48848	6.4	99	1.9	87	31.5	340	75.9	9	5	3.2	5	0	.0
48849	5.3	98	1.8	77	25.8	308	63.2	9	11	2.6	10	1	.3
48850	3.5	98	1.3	80	20.6	290	53.2	7	14	1.7	13	1	.2
48851	2.0	0	.7	87	26.1	344	58.4	10	8	.0	0	1	.0
48852	.2	100	.1	89	24.2	278*	34.0	12	12	.1	14	0	.0
48853	.7	100	.2	88	23.8	318	51.9	9	11	.3	6	1	.0
48854	14.9	97	4.9	79	31.1	373	72.4	9	7	7.2	9	1	1.7
48856	1.0	100	.4	84	24.9	300	46.5	8	14	.5	9	0	.0
48857	2.0	98	.6	87	27.5	342	63.5	7	6	1.0	5	0	.0
48858	37.8	96	10.7	58	24.4	351	77.0	6	6	17.1	5	6	.2
48860	1.4	0	.4	83	26.6	284	52.7	9	7	.0	5	0	.0
48861	1.6	97	.5	87	30.0	394	65.5	9	9	.8	8	0	.0
48862	.2	100	.1	91	24.1	277*	38.9	6	14	.1	12	0	.0
48864	13.4	95	4.7	61	42.9	453	142.0	5	6	6.3	7	6	.0
48865	1.4	99	.4	85	22.9	327	53.9	9	9	.4	9	0	.2
48866	4.3	98	1.4	86	28.0	332	62.5	9	11	2.1	9	1	.1
48867	29.6	99	10.3	76	26.9	333	64.9	8	11	14.2	9	5	1.2
48870	2.0	100	.1	93	19.4	222*	41.2	10	12	.1	9	0	.0
48871	1.6	98	.5	84	30.1	341	76.5	7	11	.8	10	0	.0
48872	5.9	99	1.9	87	28.9	423	74.0	8	9	2.9	6	1	.0
48873	1.7	100	.4	90	30.6	339	66.9	8	7	.9	6	0	.0
48874	.2	0	.1	93	21.0	241*	37.1	8	14	.0	0	0	.0
48875	8.9	100	2.7	80	29.6	360	72.8	10	4	4.4	7	1	.0
48876	2.5	97	.8	80	31.4	401	70.3	10	4	1.2	4	0	.0
48877	.7	99	.7	86	20.5	289	46.9	8	5	.4	7	0	.0
48878	2.1	99	.5	87	23.3	252	52.9	9	10	1.1	7	0	.0
48879	15.6	98	5.0	82	29.9	369	77.2	9	9	7.4	7	1	.6
48880	7.5	98	2.5	78	23.3	298	50.6	8	13	3.6	10	3	.0
48881	3.8	99	1.3	78	25.1	246	65.9	8	10	1.8	8	4	.4
48882	.4	100	.1	86	28.6	367	66.1	7	3	.2	5	0	.0
48883	6.3	99	2.0	84	24.9	323	61.5	9	7	3.2	7	1	.0
48884	3.0	99	1.0	85	22.8	310	55.7	8	10	1.5	10	0	.0
48885	.7	97	.8	86	23.8	378	46.9	8	11	.4	10	0	.0
48886	1.9	99	.7	86	20.5	289	48.8	5	14	1.0	16	0	.0
48888	5.6	98	1.9	83	22.7	283	52.9	9	12	2.1	11	1	.0
48889	1.5	99	.5	88	22.1	269	44.4	8	10	.7	11	0	.0
48890	2.0	99	.6	89	28.3	345	65.6	6	7	1.0	6	0	1.8
48891	2.5	99	.8	84	20.9	334	49.4	9	11	1.2	10	1	.0
48892	4.2	98	1.3	83	27.9	408	78.6	10	7	2.1	7	0	.3

MICHIGAN

LANSING

ZIP CODE	1	2	3	4	5	6	7	8	9	10	11	12	13
48893	2.9	99	1.0	89	22.4	343	69.0	9	10	1.4	11	2	.0
48894	.9	0	.3	79	27.1	306	72.5	7	13	.0	0	0	.0
48895	9.2	99	3.1	79	35.6	334	95.2	7	7	4.7	5	0	.5
48896	.9	100	.3	82	20.1	276	40.0	7	14	.1	11	0	20.9
48897	1.5	0	.5	88	26.7	335	57.8	8	9	.0	0	1	.0

LANSING

ZIP CODE	1	2	3	4	5	6	7	8	9	10	11	12	13
48906	29.7	85	10.8	67	25.6	329	62.5	9	8	12.4	8	4	.4
48910	77.9	85	29.3	60	27.6	373	66.8	9	8	31.4	7	4	.6
48912	21.1	85	8.5	52	24.7	360	67.3	7	10	8.6	8	2	.1
48915	12.3	53	4.3	64	25.4	386	57.2	9	6	3.1	9	3	.1
48948	26.8	95	10.0	63	34.5	401	99.5	6	7	12.3	6	2	.1
48933	3.3	77	1.9	8	17.1	275	63.9	6	18	1.2	11	2	.0

KALAMAZOO

ZIP CODE	1	2	3	4	5	6	7	8	9	10	11	12	13
49001	43.9	89	16.4	65	24.4	351	56.7	8	12	18.5	10	5	7.0
49002	37.2	97	12.9	74	33.5	380	91.1	7	5	17.7	4	1	.4
49004	14.2	96	4.9	86	30.2	383	72.4	7	8	6.8	7	4	.0
49007	38.6	76	14.6	47	23.5	341	72.4	7	11	14.1	8	8	1.1
49008	25.5	92	7.9	60	35.1	356	103.7	6	8	11.2	7	0	.0
49009	17.1	95	6.6	58	28.8	342	103.3	8	8	7.9	6	1	.0
49010	13.6	96	4.7	82	25.7	315	62.5	8	12	6.4	11	4	.2
49011	2.1	99	.7	85	27.3	289	54.0	6	12	1.0	11	0	.0
49012	3.1	99	1.1	79	31.0	363	82.0	5	11	1.5	10	0	.1
49013	5.0	86	1.7	75	19.6	294	52.2	9	14	2.1	12	3	.4
49014	.4	0			13.0	178	47.4*	0		.0			70.0
49015	31.4	93	11.9	71	28.8	349	67.0	8	11	13.8	4	4	.2
49017	63.6	86	23.8	73	26.2	304	57.6	7	12	26.1	10	2	.1
49021	5.4	99	1.7	87	27.9	304	59.5	8	8	2.7	6	0	.9
49022	41.3	51	14.4	61	20.1	300	46.0	10	11	10.2	14	5	.3
49026	1.5	98	.5	81	22.4	265	53.9	9	11	.7	9	0	.0
49027	5.9	79	2.1	72	17.6	285	51.5	5	18	1.1	17	3	.1
49028	1.7	100	.7	80	23.5	285	54.1	8	13	1.5	11	3	2.0
49029	.2	99	.1	91	24.1	368	48.7	8	13	.1	8	0	.0
49030	1.5	0	.6	85	21.5	350	49.2	8	15	.7	7	0	.0
49031	2.6	78	.9	79	23.8	298	65.6	8	13	3.1	12	2	.5
49032	7.8	99	2.7	73	23.7	320	60.7	11	9	3.1	7	2	1.7
49033	2.7	73	.9	88	30.0	421	72.9	10	7	1.3	7	0	.0
49034	2.0	88	.6	85	30.6	345	73.5	11	15	1.0	8	0	.6
49035	.2	85	.1	81	22.9	424	61.9	11	12	.1	15	3	.0
49036	20.9	0	7.5	75	25.8	322	63.8	8	10	10.1	10	4	.4
49038	11.2	99	3.9	74	26.4	341	66.3	8	8	5.3	7	7	.0
49040	2.9	98	1.1	82	22.3	338	56.4	9	15	1.4	15	0	.0
49042	4.7	99	1.5	79	23.1	324	62.1	7	10	2.3	8	1	1.4
49043	5.1	98	.8	76	15.8	312	42.2	8	19	.1	12	2	.0
49045	5.5	0	1.9	77	23.7	313	57.5	5	10	3.1	7	0	.5
49046	6.5	92	2.2	75	26.5	351	63.5	7	13	3.2	10	2	.1
49047	15.4	98	5.4	89	22.5	297	57.5	8	12	6.6	10	0	.5
49050	1.4	89	.5	75	28.2	352	62.2	10	8	.1	6	4	.0
49051	2.0	99	.7	93	31.8	375	67.0	8	8	1.0	6	0	.0
49052	4.2	98	1.3	89	28.6	261	54.4	10	9	.5	9	0	.3

*=Estimated **1.0-883 lbs per capita toxic waste generation per person; 100++ indicates per capita toxic waste generation > than 100 times the U.S. average of 883 lbs per capita.

ZIP CODE MEASURES OF SIZE, LEVELS OF AFFLUENCE AND QUALITY OF LIFE

1=Population (th.); 2= % White; 3=Households (th.); 4=% Owner Occupied; 5=Mean Income Per Household (th.$); 6=Mean Monthly Rent ($)*; 7=Mean Home Value (th.$)*;
8=% under 5; 9=% 65 and over; 10=White Males (th.); 11=% White Males, 65+; 12=# Toxic Waste Sites; 13=Toxic Waste Relative to US(883 lbs.per capita)**.

MICHIGAN

KALAMAZOO

ZIP CODE	1	2	3	4	5	6	7	8	9	10	11	12	13
49053	5.2	99	1.8	73	30.6	323	78.4	8	8	2.6	6	0	.0
49055	4.8	97	1.6	83	24.7	363	66.2	8	10	2.3	9	1	.0
49056	2.9	88	1.0	87	19.2	315	50.8	7	13	1.3	12	0	.5
49057	6.2	95	2.1	76	21.7	316	52.4	9	10	2.9	8	1	.5
49058	15.5	98	5.4	81	27.0	310	59.1	8	12	7.5	10	8	.5
49060	1.6	0	.6	77	45.8	417	110.0	6	10	.0	0	0	.0
49061	1.6	94	.5	80	25.3	340	61.5	6	10	.0	9	0	.0
49064	3.7	89	1.3	73	22.8	316	75.1	8	13	1.7	12	0	.0
49065	5.0	97	1.6	79	26.4	288	65.5	8	13	2.3	11	0	.1
49066	.9	0	.3	87	22.9	360	46.3	9	9	.0	0	0	.2
49067	4.2	99	1.4	83	24.6	322	58.6	8	11	2.1	11	0	.0
49068	14.2	98	5.0	77	28.0	322	74.9	7	12	6.7	9	4	2.2
49070	2.0	99	.7	82	25.3	301	66.2	8	8	1.0	7	0	.0
49071	5.4	98	1.8	85	27.2	304	78.1	9	7	2.7	7	2	.3
49072	3.4	98	1.1	83	23.8	308	56.2	9	10	1.7	9	1	.1
49073	4.4	99	1.5	80	24.4	312	50.1	10	11	2.2	10	0	.0
49074	.5	0	.1	0	5.3	107	18.7*	0	49	.0	0	0	.0
49075	.4	100	.1	69	19.1	282	46.8	12	3	.2	0	0	.0
49076	3.8	98	1.2	75	24.4	309	46.3	7	9	1.9	9	1	.2
49077	.9	100	.3	83	22.0	419	61.8	9	19	.1	24	0	.6
49078	9.2	99	3.2	80	26.7	327	64.9	8	9	4.4	8	1	.7
49079	10.8	96	3.9	76	25.7	299	76.9	7	13	5.1	11	0	.3
49080	11.8	98	3.9	80	29.1	347	78.7	7	10	5.7	8	6	.5
49081	.7	100	.3	83	34.8	555	76.1	12	7	.3	3	3	4.1
49082	5.7	100	2.0	79	22.9	321	62.3	8	10	2.8	9	2	1.1
49083	5.8	100	2.0	84	41.0	341	123.0	7	7	2.9	5	1	.1
49084	.3	100	.1	59	15.0	331	52.4	2	13	.1	7	0	.1
49085	22.4	98	8.5	72	31.7	333	89.1	6	13	10.3	10	3	1.7
49087	4.3	100	1.4	81	29.2	318	82.1	7	7	2.1	6	1	.1
49088	2.8	0	.9	92	30.3	430	81.5	7	9	1.0	11	0	.0
49089	1.9	99	.6	84	23.2	294	47.9	9	11	1.0	11	1	2.2
49090	15.3	84	5.5	73	24.1	288	67.0	8	13	6.3	8	1	1.1
49091	17.0	99	6.3	74	26.2	293	66.7	8	13	8.1	10	3	.1
49092	2.4	100	.8	83	24.9	350	53.5	7	11	1.2	10	1	1.2
49093	16.6	92	6.0	78	24.7	330	65.2	8	13	7.4	10	1	1.1
49094	4.1	99	1.4	83	25.1	317	50.4	7	12	2.0	11	4	.3
49095	1.8	69	.6	81	22.2	318	56.2	8	17	.6	14	0	.7
49096	3.1	99	.9	89	26.0	384	56.9	9	10	1.6	9	2	.0
49097	8.4	100	2.8	82	31.1	351	80.8	9	7	4.1	7	0	.4
49098	5.9	97	2.1	76	24.9	322	63.4	7	10	2.8	10	0	.6
49099	5.2	0	1.8	81	25.5	345	68.0	8	10	.0	0	1	.7

KALAMAZOO

ZIP CODE	1	2	3	4	5	6	7	8	9	10	11	12	13
49101	2.8	98	1.0	82	26.8	405	77.3	9	8	1.3	7	0	7.3
49102	1.4	89	.3	86	30.5	90	66.4	3	23	.6	19	1	.0
49103	11.7	86	3.9	57	25.9	324	83.5	8	9	4.9	8	1	.0
49106	3.9	99	1.3	74	26.9	283	77.5	8	14	2.0	10	1	2.0
49107	10.9	94	3.8	75	27.6	305	61.9	8	11	5.0	10	0	.7
49111	3.6	93	1.2	81	25.0	331	61.1	6	10	1.7	9	1	1.7
49112	8.6	99	3.0	81	28.3	344	77.4	8	9	4.2	7	0	.0

MICHIGAN

KALAMAZOO

ZIP CODE	1	2	3	4	5	6	7	8	9	10	11	12	13
49113	2.4	99	.8	81	25.0	345	57.6	9	9	1.2	8	1	.3
49115	.3	0	.1	84	26.0	299*	93.3	13	10	.0	0	0	.0
49116	.6	97	.2	84	19.4	362	79.3	3	24	.3	19	0	.0
49117	5.1	100	1.8	77	27.5	337	83.2	7	12	2.5	11	1	.1
49119	.4	100	.1	76	23.7	378	54.1	5	9	.2	6	0	5.8
49120	36.1	93	13.1	77	26.0	317	61.1	7	11	16.2	9	9	.6
49125	2.2	97	.8	88	24.5	318	82.9	6	22	1.1	21	0	1.4
49126	1.7	91	.6	77	24.2	285	55.8	7	10	.8	9	1	.2
49127	10.3	98	3.7	71	30.4	395	95.1	8	7	5.1	6	0	.4
49128	4.4	99	1.5	83	25.3	282	64.6	8	13	2.1	10	0	.0
49129	1.4	88	.6	71	22.0	279	62.8	10	18	.6	11	1	.0
49130	1.8	0	.7	84	30.9	314	81.0	8	8	.0	0	1	.5

JACKSON

ZIP CODE	1	2	3	4	5	6	7	8	9	10	11	12	13
49201	40.6	88	12.1	73	29.1	307	78.0	6	7	18.5	6	3	.9
49202	21.5	95	8.4	67	23.6	357	46.4	7	17	9.5	13	0	1.0
49203	41.3	84	14.7	73	28.3	342	64.9	8	11	16.6	9	2	1.0
49220	2.0	98	.6	82	27.9	283	61.4	8	10	1.0	8	0	.0
49221	35.6	93	11.9	73	27.0	348	68.8	8	11	15.7	8	1	2.9
49224	17.2	79	5.6	68	23.0	284	52.6	8	11	6.7	9	3	.8
49227	1.2	100	.4	80	23.0	286	48.0	9	9	.6	10	0	.0
49228	5.5	98	1.9	80	28.3	381	73.4	8	12	2.6	10	1	.7
49229	2.6	99	.8	81	28.9	378	76.2	7	10	1.3	9	0	.0
49230	8.2	100	2.9	86	29.4	378	86.0	8	10	4.0	8	1	.1
49232	2.2	99	.7	86	22.4	375	48.2	8	13	1.1	12	0	.2
49233	2.0	0	.9	85	27.3	371	65.7	7	10	.6	10	0	.0
49234	2.7	98	.9	85	35.4	389	85.2	8	10	1.4	10	0	.7
49235	2.3	98	.7	85	29.0	438	54.2	8	7	1.1	8	0	.0
49236	4.4	99	1.5	82	30.8	350	81.5	8	9	2.1	7	1	2.3
49237	2.8	99	.9	79	25.2	350	63.1	7	7	1.4	8	0	.0
49238	1.9	99	.6	79	28.3	366	66.0	9	9	.6	10	0	.6
49240	5.9	98	1.8	86	30.6	370	74.5	7	10	2.9	10	0	.0
49241	2.5	99	.8	85	25.4	338	59.4	9	8	1.3	8	0	.6
49242	13.7	99	4.8	73	23.4	297	64.4	7	14	6.5	12	5	1.3
49245	5.0	100	1.7	80	23.2	290	50.0	8	10	2.5	8	0	.1
49246	2.8	99	.9	91	33.3	348	84.5	9	6	1.4	6	1	.0
49247	5.6	100	1.9	82	24.7	332	52.8	8	13	2.7	11	0	.6
49248	1.1	99	.7	81	25.6	325	51.3	9	9	.5	10	0	.0
49249	2.3	0	.7	90	27.3	388	79.0	9	10	1.6	9	0	.0
49250	4.8	98	1.7	81	26.8	307	57.5	7	11	2.4	11	3	1.8
49251	6.0	98	1.9	82	27.5	344	65.4	8	7	2.9	6	1	.0
49252	2.5	100	.8	77	27.0	298	62.2	8	12	1.2	10	0	2.0
49253	3.2	99	1.1	81	24.9	286	73.7	8	9	1.6	9	0	.0
49254	3.9	100	1.4	84	25.9	362	54.9	6	11	1.9	10	1	1.3
49255	1.3	100	.4	86	22.7	219	45.7	9	11	.6	10	0	.0
49256	4.1	99	1.4	79	23.8	304	55.3	8	13	2.0	11	1	1.3
49257	.2	0	.1	82	23.3	419	43.4	10	6	.0	0	0	.0
49259	2.3	0	.7	86	27.7	387	59.1	11	7	.0	0	0	.7
49261	.8	100	.3	75	23.7	316	55.0	8	11	.4	6	0	.2
49262	1.3	99	.4	84	23.7	320	45.9	10	7	.7	7	0	.1

*=Estimated **1.0=883 lbs per person; 100++ indicates per capita toxic waste generation > than 100 times the U.S. average of 883 lbs per capita.

ZIP CODE MEASURES OF SIZE, LEVELS OF AFFLUENCE AND QUALITY OF LIFE

1=Population (th.); 2= % White; 3=Households (th.); 4=% Owner Occupied; 5=Mean Income Per Household (th.$); 6=Mean Monthly Rent ($); 7=Mean Home Value (th.$); 8=% under 5; 9=% 65 and over; 10=% White Males (th.); 11=% White Males, 65+; 12=# Toxic Waste Sites; 13=# per capita toxic waste**

MICHIGAN

JACKSON

ZIP CODE	1	2	3	4	5	6	7	8	9	10	11	12	13
49263	.3	100	.1	77	27.9	396	51.7	3	8	.1	5	0	.0
49264	1.6	99	.5	89	28.3	375	62.5	8	6	.8	6	0	.0
49265	2.8	99	.9	84	27.3	368	69.5	5	8	1.4	7	0	.0
49266	2.8	100	1.0	82	27.1	274	56.5	5	12	1.3	12	0	.1
49267	3.4	98	1.0	87	32.3	370	91.1	7	8	1.7	7	0	.1
49268	1.3	98	.5	75	27.9	356	56.6	6	12	.7	12	0	.1
49269	5.0	99	1.6	82	29.4	365	72.4	9	7	2.5	7	0	.1
49270	5.6	0	1.7	87	30.8	408	86.7	7	8	.0	8	0	.0
49271	5.6	99	.7	83	21.9	296	42.5	9	11	.1	9	0	.0
49272	2.0	100	.7	89	29.1	398	68.6	7	7	1.0	6	0	.5
49274	3.8	100	1.2	82	22.3	305	53.2	9	12	1.9	12	1	.0
49275	.2	93	.1	84	24.4	281*	66.6	11	5	.1	5	0	.3
49276	1.0	96	.4	82	26.1	323	78.1	5	16	.5	16	1	.0
49277	2.8	100	.8	91	28.3	344	71.9	8	7	1.4	7	0	.0
49279	.8	100	.3	87	29.1	252	56.4	8	10	.4	6	2	.8
49282	.4	100	.1	95	25.1	288*	62.4	6	14	.2	6	0	.0
49283	3.3	99	.9	65	29.7	303	84.3	6	11	1.5	8	0	.6
49284	2.8	99	1.0	82	24.5	352	57.1	8	11	1.4	9	0	.4
49285	4.3	99	1.3	81	30.6	427	80.6	8	11	2.1	10	0	.1
49286	12.2	98	4.2	81	31.0	376	80.9	8	8	5.9	7	1	3.0
49287	2.0	0	.6	81	32.0	345	79.2	8	9	.0	0	0	.0
49288	1.6	100	.5	83	25.3	367	47.3	6	13	.8	12	0	.0
49289	2.8	100	1.0	80	21.0	398	34.1	9	15	.1	7	1	100++

GRAND RAPIDS (EAST)

ZIP CODE	1	2	3	4	5	6	7	8	9	10	11	12	13
49301	6.6	99	2.1	93	42.2	436	127.0	8	7	3.4	7	0	10.6
49302	3.9	99	1.3	87	32.5	343	88.4	8	9	1.9	8	0	.0
49303	.9	95	.3	83	23.5	280	52.4	9	12	.4	12	0	.5
49304	2.8	73	.6	80	15.6	231	38.4	7	26	1.0	24	1	.0
49305	1.8	100	.7	88	17.6	301	42.1	7	19	.9	19	0	.0
49306	4.2	98	1.3	94	35.7	451	87.7	6	7	2.1	8	1	.3
49307	21.7	96	5.8	58	22.8	316	71.5	6	7	10.8	5	1	1.1
49309	1.3	81	.5	87	16.4	268	35.8	7	21	.5	20	0	.0
49310	2.1	95	.7	86	20.7	352	47.1	9	11	1.0	10	1	.0
49312	2.2	93	.1	78	17.5	274	38.9	8	15	.1	12	0	.0
49315	7.5	99	3.4	91	34.3	367	87.5	8	7	3.7	7	0	.3
49316	6.2	99	1.9	87	32.9	378	94.9	10	7	3.1	7	1	.2
49318	1.3	0	.4	86	26.5	328	59.9	9	8	.0	0	0	.0
49319	8.7	99	2.7	86	26.4	268	62.8	10	8	4.3	8	0	.1
49320	.3	0	.1	85	18.6	327	48.3	7	19	.0	0	0	.0
49321	9.7	99	3.2	83	30.6	315	76.2	8	6	4.9	5	0	.0
49322	2.2	0	.9	88	20.7	258	48.5	8	15	.3	5	0	.0
49323	5.4	98	1.5	90	29.1	363	69.2	11	5	2.7	5	0	.0
49325	1.5	0	.5	86	26.4	352	47.7	8	7	.1	0	1	.0
49326	2.2	98	.8	89	22.5	274	56.9	7	10	.2	9	0	.3
49327	6.0	96	2.0	84	22.4	302	54.9	10	10	2.8	9	0	.0
49328	2.7	97	.9	87	27.0	310	57.3	10	10	1.3	9	0	.0
49329	3.7	99	1.2	85	21.6	278	51.4	9	11	1.8	10	1	.3
49330	3.6	98	1.0	90	27.4	317	58.4	10	6	1.7	5	1	.6
49331	10.9	99	3.5	85	29.8	340	72.4	9	10	5.2	8	2	.6

GRAND RAPIDS (EAST) (continued)

ZIP CODE	1	2	3	4	5	6	7	8	9	10	11	12	13
49332	2.1	93	.8	89	19.5	269	56.8	6	15	1.0	15	0	.0
49333	5.8	99	1.9	89	30.4	314	75.7	9	8	2.9	8	2	.0
49335	.5	96	.2	79	27.3	336	64.7	11	4	.3	4	0	.7
49336	2.7	98	.9	84	20.5	292	41.1	9	11	1.3	11	1	.2
49337	7.5	99	2.7	89	21.8	289	59.4	7	15	3.6	15	0	.2
49338	1.6	98	.5	79	19.9	330	50.5	8	10	.8	10	1	.0
49339	1.3	100	.4	89	24.3	332	56.1	8	7	.7	7	1	.0
49340	2.8	95	.9	81	19.6	248	49.7	9	10	1.3	10	0	.0
49341	15.0	99	4.9	86	33.2	302	86.6	8	7	7.3	6	1	.5
49342	1.2	0	.4	85	22.3	288	57.6	7	6	.0	6	1	.0
49343	3.5	100	1.1	89	24.7	370	54.5	9	9	1.7	9	0	.0
49344	2.7	95	.7	84	25.9	341	67.7	8	10	1.3	11	0	.5
49345	8.8	99	3.0	83	28.1	307	64.7	9	9	4.3	9	0	.3
49346	2.3	100	.8	87	23.6	326	75.6	7	14	1.2	15	0	.8
49347	.8	100	.4	85	24.9	284	56.2	7	11	.7	9	0	.0
49348	6.3	99	2.1	85	27.9	309	71.7	7	11	3.1	9	1	.0
49349	5.6	94	.9	81	18.5	283	40.2	7	15	2.6	14	1	.1

GRAND RAPIDS (WEST)

ZIP CODE	1	2	3	4	5	6	7	8	9	10	11	12	13
49401	6.2	95	.4	64	24.7	372	82.9	8	5	2.9	4	0	.0
49402	1.0	92	.4	88	16.8	195	44.1	7	15	.4	19	0	.0
49403	2.5	92	.7	87	27.5	318	63.0	8	7	1.2	7	0	.5
49404	6.3	99	2.0	84	27.7	331	68.5	9	8	3.1	7	0	.3
49405	1.6	98	.5	87	20.7	275	47.0	7	13	.8	14	0	.0
49406	1.0	96	.5	72	23.1	347	87.3	5	14	.5	12	2	.2
49408	6.5	92	2.1	81	23.0	294	64.0	9	11	3.0	10	4	.0
49409	.6	100	.2	74	23.0	348	57.4	8	10	.3	9	1	4.1
49410	1.2	100	.5	87	17.6	296	42.1	7	17	.6	17	0	.0
49411	1.5	91	.5	90	21.2	333	45.7	7	13	.7	14	0	.1
49412	10.1	99	3.3	81	25.1	297	69.3	8	13	4.9	11	0	.2
49415	4.9	98	1.5	88	29.7	290	62.1	8	8	2.4	8	2	.2
49417	20.9	99	7.3	76	28.1	332	76.6	8	11	10.0	8	6	1.6
49418	15.8	99	5.2	83	34.1	384	87.0	8	11	7.7	6	1	.7
49419	4.9	98	1.6	86	26.5	372	73.1	10	9	2.4	8	0	.0
49420	5.7	94	1.9	79	23.1	277	53.2	7	14	2.6	12	1	.3
49421	4.3	98	1.5	88	19.6	273	48.4	9	12	2.1	11	0	.2
49423	57.2	94	19.1	79	30.1	349	86.4	8	11	26.3	9	10	3.0
49425	2.6	98	.8	86	26.8	312	48.4	8	7	1.3	6	2	.0
49426	13.2	99	3.9	91	30.4	363	88.1	10	7	6.5	6	1	.1
49427	3.2	100	.1	87	22.7	261*	78.5	3	20	.1	30	0	.0
49428	20.6	99	5.8	93	34.1	376	92.3	9	6	10.1	5	0	.0
49431	16.0	98	6.2	74	23.6	276	64.3	7	16	7.5	14	5	5.1
49434	.2	100	.1	63	35.4	372	115.6	7	0	.1	0	0	.0
49435	3.2	0	.9	91	30.9	410	75.1	8	15	.0	1	0	.0
49436	1.2	97	.4	84	21.5	308	57.1	7	13	.6	11	0	.0
49437	5.9	98	1.9	85	27.1	322	64.3	8	9	2.8	9	2	8.7
49440	.9	74	.5	11	9.8	207	71.0	9	12	.3	20	3	2.3
49441	38.4	94	14.1	75	27.6	316	67.3	7	12	17.3	13	13	.5
49442	40.2	81	13.9	68	20.5	274	39.7	9	12	15.4	10	8	1.7
49444	26.8	61	9.3	73	21.1	297	41.1	11	10	7.9	11	10	.4

*=Estimated **1.0=883 lbs per person; 100++ indicates per capita toxic waste generation > than 100 times the U.S. average of 883 lbs per capita.

ZIP CODE MEASURES OF SIZE, LEVELS OF AFFLUENCE AND QUALITY OF LIFE

1=Population (th.); 2= % White; 3=Households (th.); 4=% Owner Occupied; 5=Mean Income Per Household (th.$); 6=Mean Monthly Rent ($)*; 7=Mean Home Value (th.$)*; 8=% under 5; 9=% 65 and over; 10=% White Males; 11=% White Males, 65+; 12=# Toxic Waste Sites; 13=Toxic Waste Relative to US(883 lbs.per capita)**.

MICHIGAN

GRAND RAPIDS (WEST)

ZIPCODE	1	2	3	4	5	6	7	8	9	10	11	12	13
49445	18.3	96	6.1	87	30.7	368	78.7	7	9	8.7	7	10	1.0
49446	1.9	96	.6	89	25.1	294	59.8	7	9	.9	8	0	.0
49448	3.1	0	1.0	88	25.4	267	61.6	7	9	.0	0	1	.3
49449	2.5	98	.9	82	23.3	303	69.3	8	17	1.2	16	0	.3
49450	2.0	78	.5	79	17.3	298	41.7	9	15	.8	11	0	.9
49451	5.0	98	1.5	88	25.6	349	55.9	8	6	2.4	5	0	.1
49452	1.9	96	.6	86	19.7	297	52.9	11	9	.9	9	1	.3
49453	1.5	99	.7	68	26.3	309	91.3	4	19	.7	16	1	.6
49454	3.9	98	1.4	81	21.0	295	54.7	8	14	1.9	13	1	.0
49455	4.2	96	1.4	83	23.5	320	52.8	9	13	2.0	12	1	.0
49456	12.7	99	4.5	82	31.3	355	93.7	7	8	6.3	8	3	.6
49457	6.0	93	2.0	82	23.3	310	53.3	10	6	2.9	7	1	.0
49458	.5	0	.2	90	19.4	217	41.7	11	0	.0	0	0	.0
49459	1.3	97	.4	82	17.8	330	41.7	11	9	.7	10	1	.0
49460	3.5	99	1.1	90	32.6	369	97.8	9	6	1.7	6	1	.0
49461	7.0	99	2.4	81	27.0	336	66.6	7	12	3.4	9	8	2.3
49464	12.8	98	4.2	86	29.2	367	79.5	9	11	6.2	10	1	1.4

GRAND RAPIDS

ZIPCODE	1	2	3	4	5	6	7	8	9	10	11	12	13
49503	34.0	76	13.9	43	19.2	266	53.5	8	14	11.9	12	2	1.7
49504	58.6	97	21.7	71	25.9	291	70.0	8	12	27.2	10	14	.8
49505	48.2	96	16.5	77	28.5	319	74.0	7	12	22.4	11	1	.8
49506	56.6	87	18.6	73	39.4	395	111.7	7	12	23.0	10	0	.1
49507	37.2	60	12.6	70	22.8	299	50.5	11	10	10.5	11	3	.6
49508	60.7	95	22.3	69	28.4	369	81.6	8	8	27.7	7	6	1.1
49509	50.8	96	18.5	70	27.6	342	65.2	8	8	23.6	7	5	.5

TRAVERSE CITY

ZIPCODE	1	2	3	4	5	6	7	8	9	10	11	12	13
49601	17.6	99	6.4	78	23.0	288	61.3	8	13	8.3	11	4	1.2
49610	.3	100	.1	70	34.7	404	117.9	3	6	.9	2	1	.0
49611	.4	0	.3	90	21.0	309	39.5	6	11	.2	4	0	.0
49612	.8	0	.3	87	19.7	351	65.2	7	16	.0	0	0	.0
49613	.7	0	.9	86	19.3	256	55.5	6	22	.9	19	0	.0
49614	2.5	98	.9	87	23.4	271	66.3	7	15	.6	14	0	.0
49615	2.8	99	1.0	82	22.8	301	77.0	7	18	1.4	11	1	.2
49616	1.6	97	.6	87	18.5	314	52.6	7	15	.7	14	1	.0
49617	2.2	98	.8	81	21.8	266	74.8	7	14	1.1	15	0	2.5
49618	.5	100	.2	89	23.5	256	45.1	8	7	.2	5	0	.0
49619	.9	95	.3	87	18.8	230	37.6	6	15	.4	14	0	.0
49620	1.3	0	.3	86	22.5	322	84.4	7	10	.2	4	0	.0
49621	1.9	99	.6	86	26.5	257	82.4	7	12	1.0	13	1	.0
49622	2.0	99	.7	89	19.7	259	61.3	5	20	.9	19	0	.1
49623	.8	0	.3	86	15.6	292	38.5	8	14	.2	0	0	.0
49625	1.0	99	.4	87	17.5	285	43.6	7	15	.5	16	0	.0
49626	.5	0	.2	90	25.3	264	51.7	5	12	.0	0	1	.0
49627	.2	0	.1	82	30.0	416	114.3	6	13	.0	0	0	.0
49628	.6	0	.1	79	18.4	273	39.6	8	15	.9	15	0	.1
49630	2.0	99	.7	75	24.1	329	77.7	9	16	.9	14	0	1.9
49631	1.1	0	.4	78	23.9	225	104.4	6	14	.4	0	0	.0
49632	5.3	99	1.8	81	20.0	234	47.8	9	14	2.6	12	2	.3

MICHIGAN

TRAVERSE CITY

ZIPCODE	1	2	3	4	5	6	7	8	9	10	11	12	13
49633	2.1	0	.7	88	16.1	293	54.8	9	15	.0	0	0	.0
49634	.2	100	.2	84	21.7	300	39.6	3	16	.1	16	0	18.4
49635	3.0	98	1.1	81	23.5	268	66.9	5	17	1.4	14	1	.3
49636	.3	100	.1	63	26.8	313	154.3	2	15	.2	9	0	.0
49637	1.8	97	.6	84	23.6	372	74.2	10	11	.8	12	0	.3
49638	.2	0	.5	89	20.5	275	44.0	6	15	.8	13	1	.0
49639	1.6	100	.5	90	21.8	339	54.1	7	13	.8	13	0	.0
49640	1.3	96	.5	79	18.8	321	69.3	5	16	.6	16	0	.0
49642	.6	17	.3	79	12.8	383	30.6	6	10	.0	10	0	.0
49643	2.8	98	.9	83	21.9	316	73.1	11	7	1.4	8	1	.0
49644	1.3	99	.4	94	15.5	29	57.8	3	24	.5	26	2	.6
49645	5.9	98	2.1	85	23.7	263	51.3	8	19	.6	19	0	.0
49646	1.2	96	.4	82	26.4	346	60.5	9	11	2.9	11	7	.5
49648	3.1	96	1.2	84	26.4	365	102.3	7	15	.6	15	0	.5
49649	.7	96	.3	85	21.8	371	63.5	9	15	1.5	8	0	.0
49650	5.0	0	.2	88	26.5	222	74.5	11	9	.7	0	1	.1
49651	1.3	99	1.8	85	20.9	284	56.4	7	14	2.4	14	1	.0
49653	.5	99	.4	84	24.9	359	91.6	8	13	.7	13	0	.0
49654	2.1	0	.7	80	24.5	370	125.4	6	22	.0	0	0	.0
49655	1.3	0	.7	92	21.4	174	53.5	7	12	.0	0	1	.1
49656	2.5	99	.4	88	16.7	267	38.4	7	14	.6	14	0	.0
49657	2.5	99	.8	89	20.5	294	52.4	10	11	1.2	10	3	.5
49659	4.1	99	1.4	85	19.8	247	51.9	9	11	2.0	11	3	.1
49660	13.9	99	5.2	75	22.7	282	62.7	6	15	6.6	13	3	2.8
49663	3.9	100	1.4	83	18.7	291	48.2	8	15	1.9	13	2	.1
49664	1.4	98	.5	78	21.6	389	74.5	8	13	.7	15	2	.0
49665	3.7	0	1.3	84	19.1	297	49.8	7	13	.0	0	0	1.3
49667	.5	0	.2	84	17.6	334	41.3	3	11	.0	0	0	.0
49668	2.4	99	.9	84	19.5	333	48.8	6	14	1.1	14	3	.1
49670	1.4	96	.5	77	23.5	293	96.5	7	16	.6	17	2	.6
49674	1.1	0	.4	74	22.9	246	124.3	6	22	.0	0	0	.0
49675	2.1	98	.4	85	26.3	304	76.8	7	15	1.0	16	0	.2
49676	2.1	99	.8	86	21.3	269	54.5	6	17	1.0	13	1	.0
49677	5.8	99	2.1	80	21.1	259	47.4	7	15	2.8	11	5	1.8
49679	.9	0	.3	83	19.3	263	47.4	8	17	.0	0	0	.0
49680	1.2	0	.4	85	21.4	312	52.4	6	7	.0	0	1	.0
49681	.5	95	.1	80	23.9	293	45.8	6	15	.4	14	0	.0
49682	2.5	97	.3	79	25.7	356	97.2	9	6	1.2	11	3	.2
49683	1.1	97	.4	85	16.8	381	45.5	6	7	.5	14	0	.0
49684	46.4	99	16.5	74	27.0	289	93.3	5	20	22.0	9	11	.3
49688	2.2	99	.7	87	21.3	289	49.5	7	12	1.1	13	0	.0
49689	1.0	99	.4	85	18.3	284	38.1	6	16	.5	16	0	.0
49690	3.4	99	1.2	80	27.0	382	100.0	10	9	1.7	9	1	.0

GAYLORD

ZIPCODE	1	2	3	4	5	6	7	8	9	10	11	12	13
49701	1.0	96	.4	79	19.1	257	61.9	5	17	.4	14	1	.0
49705	.7	0	.2	94	21.2	291	49.3	9	8	.0	0	0	.0
49706	2.3	100	.8	84	19.9	290	64.0	9	13	1.1	14	0	.0
49707	26.2	100	9.2	80	23.6	265	62.6	7	12	12.6	10	6	.5
49709	3.0	99	1.2	87	16.7	242	55.3	7	20	1.5	20	3	.0

*=Estimated **=1.0=883 lbs per person; 100++ indicates per capita toxic waste generation > than 100 times the U.S. average of 883 lbs per capita.

ZIP CODE MEASURES OF SIZE, LEVELS OF AFFLUENCE AND QUALITY OF LIFE

1=Population (th.); 2= % White; 3=Households (th.); 4=% Owner Occupied; 5=Mean Income Per Household (th.$); 6=Mean Monthly Rent ($); 7=Mean Home Value (th.$); 8=% under 5; 9=% 65 and over; 10=White Males, 65+; 11=% White Males (th.); 12=# Toxic Waste Sites; 13=Toxic Waste Relative to US(883 lbs.per capita)**.

MICHIGAN — GAYLORD

ZIPCODE	1	2	3	4	5	6	7	8	9	10	11	12	13
49710	.4	91	.1	84	16.5	265	69.5	3	14	.2	18	0	.0
49712	6.2	98	2.2	81	21.4	311	61.9	9	12	2.9	11	3	1.5
49713	1.2	98	.4	78	19.6	331	60.1	7	12	.6	10	0	.0
49715	1.8	76	.6	86	20.3	223	42.0	11	12	.7	17	0	.0
49716	.5	94	.2	84	22.6	329	100.4	4	15	.3	17	0	.0
49718	.6	99	.2	88	16.6	84	53.3	6	17	.3	16	0	.0
49719	1.4	96	.5	84	23.2	266	74.4	7	16	.7	16	1	.0
49720	7.6	98	2.8	76	24.9	315	80.2	8	11	3.7	10	4	1.0
49721	12.3	98	4.3	81	21.8	269	63.3	8	13	5.9	12	2	.2
49722	.4	0	.1	70	27.5	357	84.8	6	11	.1	11	0	.0
49723	.3	95	.1	89	15.2	116	61.4	12	21	.2	16	0	.0
49724	.9	96	.3	87	20.4	204	41.4	9	9	.4	9	0	.2
49725	.7	86	.3	92	17.7	255	51.4	5	18	.3	20	1	.0
49726	.8	95	.3	91	18.2	491	61.2	5	15	.4	13	2	.0
49727	5.2	98	1.8	85	20.4	308	57.7	8	15	2.5	13	4	.4
49728	.4	95	.1	77	14.4	140	51.7	11	12	.2	11	0	.0
49729	1.4	0	.5	86	21.2	304	57.9	9	14	.5	16	0	.8
49730	1.0	0	.3	83	21.5	308	47.8	10	13	.2	20	0	.0
49733	.3	0	1.0	98	17.0	195*	30.5	6	17	.0	0	0	.0
49735	1.0	0	.3	88	19.0	311	52.6	6	11	.3	0	0	.0
49736	12.0	99	3.9	82	25.0	381	77.5	9	10	5.8	9	2	.2
49738	.4	0	.2	90	16.5	229	45.5	7	19	.0	0	1	.0
49740	7.3	99	2.6	83	21.9	281	62.1	8	13	3.5	12	1	.0
49743	4.5	97	1.7	80	25.1	294	98.9	7	14	2.1	12	1	.0
49744	1.0	98	.4	91	18.3	302	54.8	8	15	.7	9	0	.0
49745	.9	0	.2	85	20.0	326	54.3	7	10	.5	16	0	.0
49746	.4	94	.2	87	17.3	275	49.3	9	18	.2	20	0	.0
49747	3.0	100	1.0	84	17.0	225	54.1	8	14	1.5	14	1	.1
49748	1.7	0	.6	93	18.3	195	72.6	6	18	.3	10	1	.1
49749	.3	0	.3	82	14.4	243	26.9	7	17	.0	0	0	.0
49751	2.6	100	1.1	84	20.6	249	70.2	6	18	1.3	18	1	.0
49752	1.1	99	.4	89	19.3	292	55.6	5	16	.6	17	0	.0
49753	.3	100	.1	81	22.3	152	41.7	7	4	.2	3	0	.0
49755	1.9	0	.6	67	18.4	248	52.4	9	12	.4	12	0	.0
49756	1.4	97	.5	93	17.7	229	48.5	9	10	.3	15	1	.0
49757	2.5	99	1.0	83	18.4	287	64.0	9	20	1.2	20	1	.9
49759	.5	76	.2	91	19.2	255	89.4	7	13	.2	13	0	.0
49760	1.0	0	.3	45	17.2	252	48.7	7	13	.0	0	0	.0
49762	.6	0	1.0	90	17.6	155	50.3	9	15	1.5	14	0	.0
49763	.7	81	.2	88	17.6	243	49.8	7	15	.3	11	0	.0
49764	.5	100	.2	85	16.9	387	63.5	4	22	.2	23	0	.0
49765	.3	0	.1	93	21.5	191	58.9	4	11	.2	20	0	.9
49766	3.7	99	1.3	85	17.6	269	53.5	7	16	1.8	15	0	.0
49768	.3	90	.1	82	23.3	281	71.0	9	12	1.3	12	1	.3
49769	1.1	90	.4	82	18.0	218	44.5	7	15	.1	11	1	.0
49770	12.0	98	4.2	81	18.1	251	50.9	7	11	.5	11	0	.2
49774	1.4	97	.5	69	26.2	331	86.9	7	12	5.5	13	0	.0
49776	2.3	0	.7	87	20.4	217	47.7	7	15	.7	14	0	.0

MICHIGAN — GAYLORD

ZIPCODE	1	2	3	4	5	6	7	8	9	10	11	12	13
49777	.3	100	.1	91	18.4	376	85.5	6	17	.1	16	0	.0
49779	5.6	98	2.0	84	23.8	261	62.1	8	16	2.7	13	2	.0
49780	1.3	97	.4	83	19.3	233	46.2	8	12	.6	11	0	.0
49781	4.1	88	1.5	76	20.7	254	52.8	8	13	1.8	13	1	.0
49782	.3	0	.1	91	17.7	309	70.7	6	12	.0	0	0	.0
49783	18.2	91	6.4	73	20.8	237	51.8	7	13	8.1	11	6	.3
49788	1.2	68	.2	0	18.6	86	66.2*	9	0	.6	0	0	.0
49789	.2	0	.1	97	19.3	221*	44.4	8	9	.0	0	0	.3
49791	.3	0	.1	88	18.1	316	60.9	8	25	.0	0	0	.0
49792	.3	100	.1	79	15.9	232	29.9	9	12	.2	12	0	.0
49793	.3	0	.1	90	17.7	324	51.6	3	19	.2	16	0	.1
49795	1.5	100	.5	77	18.7	324	49.5	8	13	.8	13	0	.0
49796	.4	98	.1	67	22.6	334	65.2	5	7	.2	6	0	.6
49797	.2	100	.1	87	26.4	549	89.7	6	8	.1	10	0	.0
49799	1.4		5	81	18.1	238	47.3	8	13	.0	0	0	.1

IRON MOUNTAIN (EAST)

ZIPCODE	1	2	3	4	5	6	7	8	9	10	11	12	13
49801	17.7	100	6.8	79	22.6	297	63.9	7	17	8.6	15	5	.6
49805	.1	100	.1	93	11.0	126*	24.1	5	47	.1	48	0	.6
49806	.4	0	.2	82	23.0	320	69.2	8	13	.0	0	0	.0
49807	3.0	0	.9	87	23.1	279	60.2	8	9	.0	0	1	.0
49808	.3	0		70	15.6	181	42.6	5	12	.0	0	0	.0
49810	.4	100	.1	88	19.9	261	56.5	12	8	.2	6	0	.0
49812	1.0	100	.3	86	16.3	258	55.8	9	13	.5	12	1	.0
49813	.3	96			21.2	244*	46.1	3	28	.1	1	0	.1
49814	1.7		.5	91	24.9	216	49.2	10	10	.0	0	0	.0
49815	.5			89	21.6	288	46.8	8	15	.0	0	0	.0
49816	.7			83	19.1	214	44.6	8	12	.0	0	0	.0
49817	.6	91			19.1	310	47.8	5	8	.3	10	0	.0
49818	1.0	99	.3	94	20.8	406	70.5	11	8	.5	10	0	.0
49820	.5		.3	94	16.0	249	70.2	7	16	.7	0	0	.0
49821	1.4	100	.5	88	18.0	220	59.3	10	15	.7	13	2	.0
49822	.2	0		81	20.5	291	66.4	3	25	.2	6	0	.0
49825	.5	100		81	19.6	171	45.0	9	12	.3	11	0	.0
49827	.3			79	17.9	259	47.1	8	16	.3	0	0	.0
49829	19.0	99	7.0	70	22.9	262	65.7	9	14	8.9	12	5	1.0
49833	.5	100		78	23.4	200	68.8	12	9	.4	9	0	.0
49834	.2	100		91	17.3	199*	39.4	8	23	.1	19	0	.0
49835	1.0	87		85	19.9	301	47.4	8	15	.4	17	1	.0
49836	.8		.3	86	17.7	249	47.2	12	15	.3	11	0	.0
49837	8.9	99	2.9	84	24.8	267	68.6	9	11	4.4	10	2	1.3
49838	.3			76	15.5	219	40.3	4	18	.2	6	0	.0
49839	.5	100		77	14.9	190	53.3	4	17	.3	20	0	.0
49840	.8	93		90	21.3	249	49.8	6	14	.4	16	1	.4
49841	4.3	97	1.5	78	25.0	265	68.4	9	6	2.2	15	2	.0
49843	7.6	88	2.0	10	18.0	341	48.5	17	0	3.9	0	1	.0
49844	.2	100		93	16.7	192*	45.5	8	13	.1	13	0	.0
49847	1.0			86	18.9	258	42.6	6	13	.0	0	1	.3
49848	.2	100		74	15.0	274	43.0	8	17	.1	18	0	.0
49849	13.2	99	4.8	75	25.7	260	59.9	9	13	6.4	11	5	.1

*=Estimated **1.0=883 lbs per person; 100++ indicates per capita toxic waste generation > than 100 times the U.S. average of 883 lbs per capita.

PAGE 2.148

ZIP CODE MEASURES OF SIZE, LEVELS OF AFFLUENCE AND QUALITY OF LIFE

1=Population (th.); 2= % White; 3=Households (th.); 4=% Owner Occupied; 5=Mean Income Per Household (th.$); 6=Mean Monthly Rent ($)*; 7=Mean Home Value (th.$)*;
8=% under 5; 9=% 65 and over; 10=White Males (th.); 11=% White Males, 65+; 12=# Toxic Waste Sites; 13=Toxic Waste Relative to US($883 lbs.per capita)**

MICHIGAN

IRON MOUNTAIN (EAST)

ZIPCODE	1	2	3	4	5	6	7	8	9	10	11	12	13
49851	.2	100	.1	86	13.2	151*	43.1	12	8	.1	9	0	.0
49852	.2	100	.1	91	18.3	210*	49.4	5	15	.1	17	1	.0
49853	1.0	0	.4	86	18.0	154	50.1	7	15	.0	0	1	.0
49854	6.4	93	2.3	79	20.1	250	48.4	7	17	2.8	16	0	.3
49855	33.1	96	10.7	60	24.8	328	81.3	7	8	15.9	7	4	.1
49858	14.3	100	5.4	77	22.7	262	62.0	8	14	6.9	12	1	1.1
49861	.7	0	.2	94	22.0	303	40.6	9	12	.0	0	1	.9
49862	4.5	97	1.7	75	22.6	251	56.7	8	14	2.2	13	1	.9
49863	.2	100	.1	88	15.1	173*	32.8	8	18	.1	19	0	.0
49865	.3	0	.1	90	24.6	266	30.4	9	18	.0	0	0	.0
49866	8.1	100	2.9	73	25.4	271	63.1	8	12	4.0	12	0	.0
49868	5.6	96	1.9	83	21.8	268	48.2	8	14	2.7	13	1	.0
49870	3.3	0	1.3	83	21.0	297	56.1	6	20	.0	0	0	.0
49871	.7	100	.2	82	24.3	298	53.9	5	19	.4	17	0	.0
49872	.2	100	.1	89	17.8	200	49.1	7	13	.2	12	0	.0
49873	.2	100	.1	91	17.6	202*	61.9	7	10	.1	14	0	.0
49874	1.3	98	.3	79	21.1	309	63.3	8	18	.6	16	0	.0
49876	1.4	100	.4	88	22.6	378	69.0	16	10	.7	11	1	.0
49878	3.7	96	1.3	88	20.5	268	63.8	8	14	1.8	16	0	.0
49879	1.4	100	.6	83	24.6	230	44.5	5	15	.7	14	0	.0
49880	1.4	98	.5	86	18.0	293	38.8	6	13	.7	15	0	.4
49881	.3	100	.1	91	18.1	265	43.6	9	19	.2	18	0	.0
49883	.2	100	.1	90	11.5	133*	31.6	5	13	.1	15	0	.0
49884	.7	90	.2	90	21.1	226	36.3	6	6	.3	4	0	.0
49885	1.7	0	.5	81	22.2	320	67.6	10	7	.0	0	1	.5
49886	.4	0	.1	92	17.7	230	44.2	10	15	.0	0	0	.0
49887	2.4	100	.9	83	18.1	204	58.5	6	19	1.2	18	1	.0
49890	.2	96	.1	95	16.2	186*	36.3	3	19	.0	21	0	.0
49891	.6	0	.2	87	17.9	232	45.4	9	13	.0	0	0	.0
49892	1.5	100	.5	91	24.2	336	54.4	8	11	.8	11	0	.2
49893	1.7	100	.5	89	22.5	228	59.1	10	9	.8	9	0	.0
49894	1.0	100	.3	88	22.7	288	61.7	8	7	.5	6	0	.0
49895	.5	0	.2	96	16.3	187*	57.6	4	9	.5	9	0	.0
49896	1.2	84	.4	78	20.4	311	45.4	13	9	.5	12	0	.1

IRON MOUNTAIN (WEST)

ZIPCODE	1	2	3	4	5	6	7	8	9	10	11	12	13
49901	.5	0	.2	88	14.7	335	27.2	7	23	.0	0	0	.2
49902	.2	0	.1	85	17.1	167	35.1	3	19	.0	0	0	.0
49903	.4	100	.1	80	16.2	141	31.1	5	20	.2	17	0	.0
49905	1.5	0	.5	84	18.5	258	29.7	8	14	.0	0	0	.0
49906	.2	0	.1	83	13.4	360	53.6	10	31	.0	0	0	.0
49908	2.0	82	.7	75	20.3	180	56.9	10	12	.9	14	1	1.3
49910	.6	0	.2	88	17.9	217	37.1	5	16	.0	0	0	.0
49911	3.6	98	1.5	83	17.8	190	34.7	6	22	1.7	20	1	.0
49912	1.1	99	.4	88	16.0	220	37.5	6	19	.6	18	0	.0
49913	8.6	100	3.3	76	17.0	236	37.2	7	22	4.3	20	0	.0
49915	1.0	0	.4	88	16.8	254	40.8	5	20	.0	0	0	.0
49916	2.7	0	.9	79	20.8	355	55.2	9	13	.2	17	0	.0
49917	.3	100	.1	88	13.2	244	28.3	6	26	.1	21	0	.0
49919	.4	100	.1	91	18.3	276	39.0	3	27	.2	29	0	.0

MICHIGAN

IRON MOUNTAIN (WEST)

ZIPCODE	1	2	3	4	5	6	7	8	9	10	11	12	13
49920	4.3	100	1.7	85	18.7	225	50.3	6	25	2.1	22	0	.0
49921	.4	100	.4	80	26.5	322	50.4	11	21	.2	23	0	.0
49922	1.2	0	.4	84	20.2	246	53.0	7	15	.0	0	0	.0
49925	.9	0	.3	89	19.5	220	38.8	8	15	.0	0	0	.0
49927	.5	0	.2	86	17.0	284	36.2	4	19	.1	12	0	.0
49929	.3	100	.3	90	19.7	272	35.4	6	11	.1	0	0	.1
49930	7.0	98	2.5	62	19.1	300	50.7	5	19	3.5	16	1	.1
49931	9.4	97	2.3	49	20.9	385	66.3	4	6	5.7	14	1	.1
49934	1.2	99	.4	81	17.6	274	34.6	7	17	.5	14	0	.0
49935	5.8	99	2.3	80	19.8	230	50.8	7	20	2.8	20	2	.0
49938	10.6	99	4.3	80	17.8	246	36.3	5	22	5.0	19	1	.0
49942	.2	100	.1	85	15.7	347	31.6	5	20	.1	18	0	.0
49943	.1	0	.1	79	12.6	159	32.3	6	33	.0	0	0	.0
49945	2.4	0	.9	81	17.0	235	40.5	8	20	.0	0	0	.2
49946	4.3	89	1.5	75	19.9	208	59.0	8	16	1.9	15	2	.0
49947	.8	82	.2	82	18.7	294	35.6	4	13	.4	14	0	.0
49948	.9	0	.3	90	16.6	247	32.6	8	22	.6	0	0	.0
49950	.9	0	.4	90	14.7	145	29.1	5	32	.7	0	0	.0
49952	.9	100	.2	94	16.1	185*	42.4	5	21	.1	20	1	.0
49953	3.9	99	1.4	80	23.4	236	47.7	6	17	1.9	16	1	1.1
49955	.5	100	.2	98	17.8	205*	31.7	5	25	.2	20	0	3.8
49958	1.4	0	.5	84	17.6	229	40.7	4	17	.1	0	0	.0
49959	.5	0	.2	86	21.2	283	29.8	5	22	.2	17	0	.0
49960	.2	100	.1	81	19.8	239	34.4	8	19	.2	1	0	.0
49961	.1	0	.1	85	17.8	204*	23.3	4	22	.0	0	0	.0
49962	.3	0	.1	94	17.1	196*	78.0	8	25	.0	0	0	.0
49963	1.0	0	.4	73	16.6	279	41.7	8	16	.0	0	0	.0
49964	1.3	0	.6	76	18.3	190	43.3	7	23	.0	0	0	.0
49965	.5	100	.2	82	17.2	129	32.6	8	24	.3	26	0	.0
49967	.6	0	.2	85	17.9	186	23.7	5	15	.1	0	0	.0
49968	3.1	98	1.1	83	17.6	215	33.2	6	19	1.5	17	1	.0
49969	.9	89	.4	85	19.1	211	48.8	9	17	.4	16	0	.0
49970	.4	0	.1	91	20.7	149	49.7	9	11	.0	0	0	.0
49971	1.2	98	.4	73	26.5	282	41.8	7	5	.6	5	1	33.0

RHINELANDER

ZIPCODE	1	2	3	4	5	6	7	8	9	10	11	12	13
54540	.2	100	.1	78	19.6	307	71.3	5	27	.1	24	0	.0

*=Estimated **1.0=883 lbs per person; 100++ indicates per capita toxic waste generation > than 100 times the U.S. average of 883 lbs per capita.

ZIP CODE MEASURES OF SIZE, LEVELS OF AFFLUENCE AND QUALITY OF LIFE

1=Population (th.); 2= % White; 3=Households (th.); 4=% Owner Occupied; 5=Mean Income Per Household (th.$); 6=Mean Monthly Rent ($); 7=Mean Home Value (th.$);
8=% under 5; 9=% 65 and over; 10=% White Males, 65+; 11=% White Males (th.); 12=# Toxic Waste Sites; 13=Toxic Waste Relative to US(883 lbs.per capita)**.

MINNESOTA

ZIPCODE	1	2	3	4	5	6	7	8	9	10	11	12	13
MASON CITY													
50459	.2	100	.1	69	20.7	372	56.9	4	20	.1	20	0	.0
SPENCER													
51347	.3	0		57	16.3	113	52.5	9	6	.0	0	0	.0
51360	.2	100	.1	80	22.6	346	80.4	11	5	.1	5	0	.0
DECORAH													
52134	.1	100	.1	74	14.3	165*	70.0	6	21	.1	27	0	.0
52155	.2	100	.1	80	21.4	231	70.0	12	16	.1	18	0	.0
SAINT PAUL													
55001	2.6	0	.8	92	44.6	471	156.8	7	6	.0	0	0	.0
55002	1.8	100	.1	82	17.2	288	61.7	10	16	.1	16	0	.0
55003	3.4	99	.7	79	34.9	338	103.4	6	17	.9	13	1	.1
55005	2.9	0	1.0	93	30.5	398	96.0	10	4	.0	0	0	.0
55007	1.5	99	.5	79	20.4	226	70.4	8	14	1.5	11	0	.0
55008	8.9	99	2.9	76	25.7	254	50.3	8	10	4.3	12	1	.3
55009	6.6	99	2.2	80	27.7	312	88.3	8	14	3.3	11	1	.1
55011	5.3	99	1.5	96	32.9	271	95.3	9	12	2.7	2	0	.0
55012	1.4	100	.4	92	29.6	620	112.5	11	2	.7	7	0	.0
55013	3.4	100	1.0	86	28.8	306	97.5	9	9	1.7	10	1	.1
55014	8.4	97	2.4	92	36.5	332	106.0	8	14	4.2	2	1	.1
55016	18.7	97	5.0	94	37.7	374	105.4	11	2	9.3	1	3	.1
55017	.7	99	.2	87	23.9	598	114.8	10	2	.3	17	0	.0
55018	.8	99	.2	76	27.5	464	66.1	7	17	.4	10	0	.0
55019	.9	100	.3	88	28.6	327	71.0	8	10	.4	14	0	.0
55020	1.2	0	.3	94	34.6	233	82.3	9	13	.0	0	0	.0
55021	22.7	99	7.8	75	34.6	212	106.1	8	5	10.9	11	1	.4
55024	8.8	99	2.8	77	24.5	265	84.5	14	10	4.3	7	0	.0
55025	13.3	99	4.2	78	29.5	343	106.1	8	8	6.5	7	0	.0
55026	.2	100	.1	96	32.0	354	121.8	8	6	.1	11	0	.0
55027	2.7	100	.8	81	21.8	250*	57.2	11	10	1.4	10	0	.0
55029	.1	100	.8	72	26.6	358	75.5	7	12	.1	12	0	.0
55030	1.8	99	.5	91	19.0	185	77.6	11	6	.9	5	0	.6
55031	1.4	100	.4	88	30.3	319	106.0	10	6	.7	6	0	.6
55032	1.9	0	.6	89	32.6	446	103.4	8	9	.0	0	0	.0
55033	19.3	99	6.0	75	24.9	353	80.5	8	9	9.6	6	1	.6
55037	3.3	95	1.2	81	31.0	346	111.1	9	8	1.6	14	0	.0
55038	4.8	99	1.4	91	19.0	265	61.1	9	15	2.5	5	0	.5
55040	6.2	99	1.8	88	32.9	360	115.2	9	5	3.1	6	0	.5
55041	6.9	99	2.6	79	28.1	305	85.6	10	6	3.3	15	1	1.3
55042	6.4	99	2.0	90	23.5	275	83.0	8	18	1.1	9	0	.0
55043	3.5	99	1.1	88	36.7	329	147.8	8	5	.2	13	0	.0
55044	10.4	99	3.1	86	33.5	477	147.8	8	8	.9	11	0	.0
55045	3.5	100	1.4	81	36.3	489	118.3	10	5	1.8	5	0	.6
55046	2.4	100	.7	92	24.3	475	139.1	6	20	.9	12	0	.6
55047	2.1	99	.7	91	25.3	375	99.6	8	11	1.8	18	0	.0
55048	.3	86	.7	74	35.4	273	81.4	7	9	1.2	10	0	.0
55051	1.8	100	.6	91	25.9	241	70.0	8	16	3.5	15	0	.0
55052	7.3	100	2.7	79	21.8	276	67.5	8	14	.8	13	0	.1

MINNESOTA

ZIPCODE	1	2	3	4	5	6	7	8	9	10	11	12	13
SAINT PAUL													
55053	.9		.3	86	26.9	438	71.4	6	12	.0	0	0	.0
55054	.3	100		85	26.1	371	80.8	12	13	.1	10	0	.0
55055	4.5	99	1.5	74	30.3	387	117.2	9	7	2.2	6	0	.6
55056	5.8	99	1.8	85	25.2	287	85.4	9	12	2.2	11	0	.1
55057	15.9	98	4.2	72	29.3	323	107.5	6	9	7.7	7	2	.6
55060	22.8	99	8.0	74	25.8	306	92.0	8	12	11.1	10	1	1.0
55063	5.9	99	2.1	80	20.8	245	74.6	8	17	2.9	16	1	.2
55065	1.3	100	.4	84	30.5	356	93.5	9	10	.7	10	0	.0
55066	15.7	99	5.8	74	25.6	263	82.8	7	14	7.5	14	3	.6
55067	.2	100	.1	89	21.5	247*	52.8	11	13	1.1	16	0	.0
55068	9.9	98	2.8	84	34.2	475	111.9	11	3	5.0	3	4	.1
55069	3.1	99	.1	82	25.9	297	77.1	8	14	1.5	13	0	.1
55070	.3	100	.1	68	25.2	420	93.7	8	4	.2	6	0	.0
55071	5.2	98	1.6	84	29.7	322	93.9	8	6	2.5	6	0	3.3
55072	2.8	99	.6	75	20.2	220	56.4	7	15	1.4	14	0	.0
55073	2.3	99	.6	96	33.2	282	121.3	8	15	1.1	5	0	.0
55074	1.0	0	.3	89	27.5	245	82.2	10	10	.1	5	0	.2
55075	38.5	99	13.3	74	30.3	369	105.4	8	8	18.5	7	2	.2
55079	4.7	99	1.4	96	29.1	343	95	8	5	2.4	4	0	.1
55080	2.0	100	.7	88	22.7	245	78.9	8	14	1.1	14	0	.0
55081	.7	100	.1	60	17.7	221	63.3	7	14	.1	14	0	.0
55082	23.3	97	7.1	80	34.7	335	124.6	8	8	11.5	14	0	.0
55084	1.1	99	.4	79	24.6	268	82.2	8	14	.5	14	0	.0
55085	.9	100	.1	80	31.1	418	92.7	14	8	.2	6	0	.0
55087	.4	100	.1	95	23.3	268*	72.5	15	3	2.4	4	0	.0
55088	1.4	0	.4	91	31.1	488	106.1	10	6	.0	0	0	.0
55089	1.5	93	.3	82	32.1	268	93.3	12	8	.3	7	0	.0
55090	.8	100	.1	81	26.1	376	81.0	9	8	.7	10	0	1.5
55092	6.2	99	2.0	90	30.3	306	102.3	11	6	3.2	5	0	.0
SAINT PAUL													
55101	15.8	88	6.5	37	21.4	327	82.9	8	17	6.5	15	3	2.7
55102	16.5	91	7.1	42	21.6	264	79.2	6	20	7.1	16	1	.4
55103	13.4	78	5.1	42	18.4	270	74.8	9	17	4.4	14	1	.7
55104	46.3	81	17.8	55	25.6	329	89.1	7	13	17.9	11	4	.5
55105	30.0	98	11.3	63	30.0	379	118.0	5	13	13.1	11	2	.0
55106	49.2	96	18.7	63	25.1	330	88.6	8	14	22.2	11	4	.3
55107	15.2	87	5.4	60	23.1	318	80.2	9	15	6.2	12	4	3.9
55108	15.3	94	5.6	51	26.7	342	109.5	7	16	6.8	12	0	.1
55109	31.5	98	10.4	74	31.7	376	112.3	8	8	15.1	6	2	.1
55110	39.5	98	12.4	84	41.3	414	140.7	8	5	19.3	4	1	.4
55112	59.5	97	19.9	73	37.2	422	135.7	8	5	28.4	4	4	.4
55113	40.6	97	15.0	68	37.0	427	130.2	5	10	19.2	8	3	1.2
55114	1.3	98	.7	22	19.1	278	76.9	3	16	.6	10	0	19.9
55115	.4	99	1.3	87	40.9	521	133.2	6	7	2.1	7	0	.0
55116	22.0	97	9.7	58	33.9	376	126.1	5	21	9.4	16	1	2.7
55117	36.6	91	14.0	60	26.9	371	95.3	8	12	15.8	11	1	.1
55118	24.4	98	9.4	65	36.8	422	134.5	5	14	11.2	12	1	5.9
55119	47.8	97	16.9	69	31.7	414	110.5	8	12	22.6	6	1	.1
55120	1.9	0	.6	96	46.1	707	128.1	5	9	.0	0	0	.1

*=Estimated   **1.0=883 lbs per person; 100++ indicates per capita toxic waste generation > than 100 times the U.S. average of 883 lbs per capita.

1=Population (th.); 2= % White; 3=Households (th.); 4=% Owner Occupied; 5=Mean Income Per Household (th.$); 6=Mean Monthly Rent ($)*; 7=Mean Home Value (th.$)*;
8=% under 5; 9=% 65 and over; 10=White Males (th.); 11=% White Males, 65+; 12=# Toxic Waste Sites; 13=Toxic Waste Relative to US(883 lbs.per capita)**.

MINNESOTA

ZIPCODE	1	2	3	4	5	6	7	8	9	10	11	12	13
SAINT PAUL													
55121	5.8	95	1.9	55	35.7	485	139.4	10	3	2.8	3	0	2.1
55122	10.8	95	3.7	61	31.4	428	123.1	10	1	5.1	1	0	.3
55123	4.0	99	1.2	90	42.3	641	159.9	11	3	2.0	3	1	1.0
55124	21.8	97	6.4	87	40.0	501	143.0	11	1	10.6	1	0	.0
55150	.2	0	.1	69	23.7	286	89.3	5	14	.0	0	0	.0
MINNEAPOLIS													
55301	.9	100	.2	87	32.8	371	97.2	12	5	.5	5	0	.0
55302	4.8	99	1.7	87	25.4	239	104.6	8	15	2.4	16	1	.1
55303	45.6	98	13.4	80	33.6	377	116.3	10	5	22.5	4	1	.3
55307	3.1	0	.1	78	22.6	213	77.5	9	18	.0	0	0	.1
55308	1.7	0	.5	80	25.0	353	86.1	10	7	.0	0	0	.0
55309	4.3	99	1.4	84	25.6	330	89.6	10	8	2.2	9	0	.4
55310	2.1	0	.7	80	22.8	220	62.2	8	15	.0	0	0	.0
55312	1.7	99	.7	84	24.4	216	66.6	7	14	.8	13	0	.0
55313	11.9	99	3.7	82	28.4	304	107.3	10	10	5.8	10	0	.0
55314	1.5	0	.5	85	21.6	278	57.4	6	19	.0	0	0	.0
55315	1.5	0	.5	83	28.8	330	101.8	9	11	.0	0	0	.0
55316	9.1	100	2.8	80	35.1	429	112.1	12	3	4.6	3	0	.0
55317	3.8	99	1.2	78	42.6	429	156.8	9	3	2.0	2	0	.0
55318	10.8	99	3.8	73	31.0	370	123.3	9	7	5.4	6	1	1.8
55319	2.7	100	.8	87	25.1	391	99.7	10	11	1.4	10	0	.0
55320	2.7	99	.8	85	26.7	339	86.2	10	8	.2	8	0	1.3
55321	4.0	100	1.3	81	25.8	262	81.3	8	16	2.0	14	0	.0
55322	2.3	100	.7	85	29.1	316	96.1	7	8	1.2	7	1	.0
55323	.1	100	.1	100	43.4	499*	98.8	13	8	.1	7	0	.0
55324	1.0	0	.4	86	25.4	306	85.6	6	16	.6	16	0	.0
55325	3.2	100	1.1	83	24.7	264	82.4	8	17	1.6	15	0	.1
55327	3.2	0	.8	93	38.1	402	124.3	11	3	.0	0	0	.0
55328	5.4	100	1.7	80	29.7	298	95.3	10	10	2.7	8	0	1.3
55329	1.8	99	.6	82	17.5	243	61.1	10	15	.9	14	0	.0
55330	13.3	99	4.0	86	31.4	372	107.7	10	8	6.6	6	0	.1
55331	13.6	99	4.8	75	46.9	452	191.7	6	8	6.7	7	0	.0
55332	2.4	0	.9	78	19.8	226	58.8	7	21	.0	0	0	.0
55333	1.0	98	.7	77	20.7	202	52.9	7	23	.5	23	0	1.2
55334	2.1	98	1.1	81	25.3	240	76.4	8	16	1.5	14	0	.0
55335	2.1	99	.7	82	23.7	262	63.6	8	16	.0	0	0	6.7
55336	6.5	100	2.4	79	24.3	310	83.4	8	15	3.2	14	0	.1
55337	35.9	97	12.1	73	39.5	458	149.4	8	2	17.3	2	1	.7
55338	1.1	100	.3	82	23.5	350	70.2	8	14	.5	14	0	.0
55339	1.0	100	.3	86	25.3	209	87.9	9	15	.5	15	0	.0
55340	5.4	99	1.6	91	41.6	410	148.7	10	3	2.8	3	1	.3
55341	2.7	100	1.0	67	26.5	317	98.7	9	10	1.4	17	0	.4
55343	63.6	98	22.7	71	40.3	455	152.7	7	7	30.6	6	1	6.7
55344	4.8	98	1.7	83	46.1	580	164.4	9	3	2.4	3	1	.3
55349	3.2	99	1.1	82	23.7	287	80.2	9	14	1.6	12	0	.1
55350	13.1	99	4.7	74	26.0	286	91.2	8	13	6.3	11	1	.7
55352	5.2	99	1.6	85	30.2	381	100.3	10	10	2.6	8	0	.1
55353	2.8	0	.9	82	22.9	313	71.3	9	13	.2	6	0	.0

MINNESOTA

ZIPCODE	1	2	3	4	5	6	7	8	9	10	11	12	13
MINNEAPOLIS													
55354	2.6	100	.9	80	24.2	299	90.0	8	13	1.4	12	3	1.0
55355	8.8	98	3.2	76	22.8	273	77.1	8	17	4.1	15	0	1.2
55356	4.2	99	1.3	86	51.7	410	174.4	8	8	2.0	7	0	.7
55357	2.0	98	.6	85	31.6	369	120.9	11	6	1.0	6	1	.0
55358	3.7	100	1.1	87	29.3	302	87.0	10	10	1.9	9	0	.1
55359	4.4	99	1.4	84	37.6	386	123.3	8	8	2.2	6	1	.0
55360	1.4	0	.4	87	26.8	345	90.7	10	7	.0	6	0	.0
55361	.2	98	.1	89	57.8	664*	211.3	3	4	.1	4	0	1.1
55362	7.6	99	2.4	83	28.9	310	104.0	11	8	3.7	7	1	.0
55363	2.2	99	.6	86	26.1	272	78.4	11	7	1.1	6	0	.0
55364	13.0	99	4.6	78	35.4	464	147.9	8	7	6.6	6	4	.0
55366	.4	0	.2	86	15.5	216	45.3	11	21	.6	6	0	.0
55367	.9	100	.3	77	22.3	316	85.2	9	15	.4	14	0	.0
55368	2.0	0	.7	78	26.4	276	81.8	9	13	.0	0	0	.1
55369	24.7	98	7.8	90	38.6	469	128.6	11	4	12.3	3	0	1.6
55370	.8	100	.2	90	29.5	281	90.2	7	15	.4	14	0	.0
55371	9.8	99	3.2	82	23.9	275	78.4	10	12	4.9	10	0	.0
55372	12.3	99	3.6	86	42.2	460	146.0	9	5	6.3	5	0	4.2
55373	3.3	100	1.1	89	28.6	285	106.8	11	5	1.6	5	0	.0
55374	4.0	100	1.1	88	35.2	357	119.7	10	4	2.0	4	0	2.1
55375	1.4	100	.3	84	29.8	380	101.3	6	6	.7	6	0	.0
55376	3.2	99	.9	87	31.1	309	110.7	9	6	1.6	6	0	1.6
55378	3.0	99	1.0	75	35.2	395	121.0	10	4	1.6	3	1	3.2
55379	12.9	99	4.1	75	31.3	367	114.0	7	7	6.3	6	4	1.0
55381	2.0	0	.7	84	24.1	238	65.7	9	15	.0	0	0	.0
55382	3.0	99	1.0	89	22.9	311	87.5	8	16	1.5	15	0	.0
55384	1.5	99	.7	28	26.6	451	144.0	5	20	.7	13	0	4.2
55385	1.7	0	.6	79	20.7	236	61.1	9	16	.0	0	0	.0
55386	.6	100	.6	74	31.7	359	100.1	8	11	.3	11	0	2.1
55387	4.5	100	1.5	73	31.5	305	119.1	8	14	2.2	12	0	.2
55388	3.4	100	1.1	83	27.1	347	101.3	10	10	1.7	8	0	.1
55389	2.7	0	.8	86	21.9	285	68.3	11	11	.0	9	0	.0
55390	1.8	99	.6	81	25.7	271	86.0	10	9	.9	8	1	.0
55391	24.5	99	8.1	82	56.0	481	200.0	6	7	11.8	6	0	.6
55395	2.3	100	.7	81	28.3	330	85.0	9	14	1.2	12	0	.6
55396	2.7	99	1.0	80	20.9	196	63.0	8	20	1.3	18	0	.4
55397	2.1	100	.7	85	25.7	315	89.3	12	10	1.1	9	0	.2
55398	4.6	98	1.4	92	27.0	412	85.0	11	6	2.3	6	0	.0
MINNEAPOLIS													
55401	1.8	93	1.3	29	16.7	240	59.4*	0	45	.7	24	0	3.6
55402	.8		.3	81	10.7	222	38.0*	0	15	.2	11	0	34.2
55403	12.6	91	8.3	11	19.2	302	278.0	2	17	5.7	11	1	.2
55404	24.6	75	12.3	8	13.4	268	72.5	6	21	8.5	16	2	1.5
55405	16.0	82	7.5	35	27.2	346	139.1	6	12	6.2	11	2	1.4
55406	33.2	95	14.7	68	24.7	363	87.9	6	19	14.5	15	3	1.8
55407	36.0	82	15.3	54	23.0	365	84.9	9	12	13.4	14	0	.3
55408	28.7	84	15.1	21	19.5	353	99.9	5	12	10.9	8	0	.7
55409	22.2	83	8.7	68	31.4	425	112.0	6	14	8.2	10	0	.0
55410	21.0	98	8.6	77	35.9	488	123.1	6	16	9.5	12	0	.0

*=Estimated **1.0=883 lbs per person; 100++ indicates per capita toxic waste generation > than 100 times the U.S. average of 883 lbs per capita.

ZIP CODE MEASURES OF SIZE, LEVELS OF AFFLUENCE AND QUALITY OF LIFE

1=Population (th.); 2= % White; 3=Households (th.); 4=% Owner Occupied; 5=Mean Income Per Household (th.$); 6=Mean Monthly Rent ($); 7=Mean Home Value (th.$); 8=% under 5; 9=% 65 and over; 10=% White Males (th.); 11=% White Males, 65+; 12=# Toxic Waste Sites; 13=Toxic Waste Relative to US(883 lbs.per capita)**.

MINNESOTA

MINNEAPOLIS

ZIPCODE	1	2	3	4	5	6	7	8	9	10	11	12	13
55411	30.0	62	11.3	49	19.2	288	73.1	10	12	8.8	13	0	.9
55412	22.2	96	9.1	78	24.6	355	81.6	7	18	10.0	15	1	.1
55413	10.8	96	5.1	38	20.5	315	82.7	7	17	4.8	11	1	.1
55414	21.6	90	8.3	25	20.3	373	99.5	3	7	9.7	11	1	6.2
55415	.9	81	.2	2	11.2	278	39.9*	2	7	.3	7	3	2.8
55416	25.5	98	11.3	62	38.6	469	134.6	5	17	11.4	14	0	21.0
55417	26.7	96	10.6	83	30.5	436	103.2	6	17	12.3	15	0	2.0
55418	32.1	99	13.2	70	27.2	345	96.9	6	16	15.0	13	0	.1
55419	19.0	97	7.4	77	35.8	462	124.7	5	16	8.4	13	0	1.2
55420	32.8	96	12.5	63	33.0	490	111.9	6	15	15.4	13	1	1.8
55421	27.8	98	10.5	65	29.7	387	104.3	6	10	13.0	8	2	1.9
55422	31.0	98	11.5	77	35.8	429	118.5	5	14	14.2	12	1	1.2
55423	38.3	98	15.4	66	30.7	409	109.3	5	11	17.5	9	0	.0
55424	10.0	99	3.6	90	53.6	621	190.2	5	14	4.7	11	0	.4
55426	24.9	98	9.9	68	33.4	430	114.9	5	12	11.4	9	0	.5
55427	27.3	97	9.3	73	38.3	447	131.5	6	13	12.8	9	0	.7
55428	32.1	98	10.9	64	31.6	423	110.1	8	7	15.1	5	1	.5
55429	26.2	97	9.6	62	31.7	385	105.2	7	5	12.4	5	0	.1
55430	22.4	95	8.1	71	28.6	419	94.1	8	9	10.2	8	0	.3
55431	20.8	98	6.7	82	40.8	454	132.1	5	6	9.9	4	2	2.1
55432	37.9	98	12.7	71	33.8	413	116.3	7	4	18.5	4	1	.6
55433	33.9	99	9.4	85	34.8	407	105.5	9	3	16.8	2	0	.0
55434	26.4	98	7.9	93	33.0	451	104.1	10	1	13.0	2	0	.0
55435	18.5	98	7.8	63	50.8	547	229.0	3	16	8.3	11	1	3.3
55436	12.5	99	4.6	82	66.9	667	215.4	3	12	6.1	11	0	.0
55437	18.1	97	5.9	77	46.0	518	156.0	5	5	8.7	4	0	.0
55438	10.1	97	3.5	85	48.4	553	184.7	8	5	4.9	4	0	.0
55441	16.9	97	6.0	66	37.7	483	147.0	7	4	8.4	5	0	3.0
55443	14.5	94	5.2	86	31.1	443	210.1	10	3	7.1	3	0	.0
55444	7.7	98	2.4	86	35.2	434	119.1	10	3	3.6	2	0	.0
55445	4.3	98	1.3	93	37.8	568	135.5	13	1	2.1	2	0	.0
55454	6.6	86	2.7	9	14.7	271	50.4	3	11	2.8	9	0	.4

DULUTH (EAST)

ZIPCODE	1	2	3	4	5	6	7	8	9	10	11	12	13
55601	.4	100	.1	68	32.5	287	66.3	8	7	.2	8	0	.0
55602	.3	0	.1	80	21.9	283	40.3	4	20	.1	6	0	.0
55603	.8	97	.3	70	26.9	243	52.1	10	5	.4	6	0	.0
55604	2.6	97	1.0	74	22.8	250	77.8	6	16	1.3	14	0	.0
55605	.3	0	.1	55	25.1	313	36.0	10	8	.0	0	0	.0
55606	.1	0	.1	68	16.3	186	34.8	6	19	.0	0	0	.0
55607	.1	0	.1	72	21.2	168	57.2	4	5	.0	0	0	.0
55609	.4	100	.1	85	24.9	488	78.6	9	9	.0	0	2	.0
55611	.2	100	.1	100	27.0	310*	73.4	9	17	.1	24	0	.0
55612	.4	95	.1	75	28.8	226	103.5	6	16	.1	12	1	.0
55613	.3	97	.1	53	28.7	242	72.9	7	10	.1	11	0	.0
55614	3.8	0	1.1	91	40.2	348	63.2	8	3	.0	0	0	.0
55615	.3	0	.1	71	20.2	139	71.9	6	19	.0	0	0	.0
55616	7.2	100	2.7	81	26.2	260	64.1	8	16	3.6	14	1	.3

MINNESOTA

DULUTH (WEST)

ZIPCODE	1	2	3	4	5	6	7	8	9	10	11	12	13
55702	.4	94	.1	95	24.9	286*	83.7	10	10	.2	12	0	.0
55703	.9	0	.3	90	21.3	137	53.6	10	14	.0	0	0	.0
55704	1.0	99	.4	84	20.8	327	56.5	8	15	.5	16	0	.0
55705	5.0	100	1.7	82	26.8	284	68.7	7	11	2.5	10	0	.0
55706	2.9	98	.9	94	30.0	361	60.2	8	4	.1	4	0	.0
55707	2.0	100	.7	91	22.2	255	63.2	9	11	1.1	12	1	.0
55708	1.5	99	.6	81	26.4	289	56.5	7	14	.8	12	1	3.1
55709	3.7	100	1.3	87	22.8	257	57.0	8	12	1.9	11	0	.0
55710	1.6	98	.5	93	35.2	453	104.3	7	5	.8	3	0	.0
55711	.6	89	.2	77	25.4	244	47.1	10	9	.3	8	0	.0
55712	.5	98	.1	91	15.8	275	39.7	8	14	.2	14	0	.0
55713	1.3	99	.5	85	24.1	203	53.0	6	15	.7	15	2	1.2
55716	.5	100	.2	85	19.8	255	37.8	9	16	.3	13	0	.0
55717	.3	100	.1	87	19.8	69	79.5	18	19	.1	25	0	.0
55718	2.6	99	.8	84	24.8	276	68.2	9	13	1.3	11	0	.4
55719	7.0	99	2.7	81	25.7	278	60.4	7	16	3.4	14	0	.2
55720	14.9	95	5.3	80	24.4	275	66.6	7	13	6.9	11	2	1.2
55721	2.4	97	.5	89	23.8	298	74.3	10	10	1.2	10	0	.0
55722	1.1	0	.1	87	25.6	228	58.9	5	15	.1	25	0	.0
55723	2.4	98	.4	80	21.2	256	64.6	10	17	1.2	17	0	.1
55724	.3	100	.1	93	19.8	227*	69.1	5	19	.2	16	0	.0
55726	1.5	100	.3	86	18.6	349	50.0	10	20	.5	17	0	.0
55727	.2	98	.1	98	29.2	336*	62.6	7	9	.2	9	0	.0
55731	6.9	99	2.8	76	22.3	223	64.6	6	20	3.4	17	0	.4
55732	2.4	98	.7	92	27.3	342	62.6	12	6	1.3	6	0	.0
55733	3.8	99	1.1	91	30.5	416	85.1	8	5	1.9	5	0	.0
55734	8.1	99	3.2	74	24.8	302	68.2	8	15	4.0	13	0	.0
55735	1.3	100	.5	86	16.7	169	66.5	7	18	.7	18	0	.0
55736	1.9	100	.6	85	19.1	208	41.9	7	17	1.0	18	0	.0
55738	.2	100	.6	97	29.0	333*	60.0	17	4	.1	2	0	.0
55740	.5	93	.2	80	19.0	278	41.6	4	9	.3	12	0	.0
55741	4.2	98	1.5	85	27.3	267	75.0	9	9	2.1	8	1	.0
55742	.4	0	.1	88	28.2	168	79.5	12	4	.0	0	0	.0
55744	18.3	99	6.4	78	25.4	314	79.7	8	11	9.0	10	1	.4
55746	22.2	99	8.1	76	26.5	278	69.1	8	14	10.7	12	1	.4
55748	1.2	0	.4	76	18.0	227	58.0	9	12	.0	0	0	.0
55750	3.2	0	1.0	92	34.3	243	63.1	7	3	.0	0	0	.0
55751	1.9	100	.6	93	30.5	246	76.4	12	6	1.0	7	0	.0
55752	.5	97	.2	86	14.7	363	38.1	10	19	.3	24	0	.0
55753	1.4	0	.6	88	23.8	161	49.1	8	15	.0	0	0	.2
55754	.7	100	.2	96	27.1	312*	45.3	9	8	.4	6	0	.0
55755	.3	0	.1	95	22.6	259*	41.6	10	12	.0	0	0	.0
55756	.2	100	.1	96	14.5	166*	51.6	13	11	.1	12	1	.0
55757	.9	0	.3	85	18.6	239	34.5	8	14	.0	0	0	.2
55758	.4	0	.1	97	30.4	350*	40.1	12	5	.0	0	0	.0
55760	2.5	95	.9	80	17.2	225	76.1	8	18	1.2	18	0	.2
55761	.3	100	.1	85	21.2	318	44.8	11	10	.1	10	0	.0
55762	.4	100	.1	89	19.3	398	64.9	5	9	.2	9	0	.0

*=Estimated **1.0=883 lbs per person; 100++ indicates per capita toxic waste generation > than 100 times the U.S. average of 883 lbs per capita.

ZIP CODE MEASURES OF SIZE, LEVELS OF AFFLUENCE AND QUALITY OF LIFE

1=Population (th.); 2= % White; 3=Households (th.); 4=% Owner Occupied; 5=Mean Income Per Household (th.$); 6=Mean Monthly Rent ($)*; 7=Mean Home Value (th.$)*;
8=% under 5; 9=% 65 and over; 10=% White Males, 65+; 11=% White Males; 12=# Toxic Waste Sites; 13=Toxic Waste Relative to US(883 lbs.per capita)**.

MINNESOTA

DULUTH (WEST)

ZIPCODE	1	2	3	4	5	6	7	8	9	10	11	12	13
55763	.6	100	.2	90	28.4	166	73.3	7	8	.4	8	8	.0
55764	.7	96	.2	90	22.5	225	41.0	6	16	.3	15	2	.0
55765	1.1	98	.4	89	24.2	204	38.6	11	12	.6	14	0	.0
55767	3.3	99	1.1	75	20.5	240	71.4	6	19	1.7	17	0	.1
55768	3.1	98	1.1	75	29.7	366	78.0	8	7	1.5	7	2	.4
55769	2.4	99	.9	80	24.4	229	52.3	10	13	1.1	13	1	.0
55771	1.1	97	.4	84	20.5	131	56.2	7	17	.6	18	0	.0
55772	.4	0	.1	48	15.5	194	24.6	15	7	.0	0	0	.0
55773	.8	100	.3	81	26.1	403	62.2	7	10	.0	0	0	.0
55775	1.8	0	.6	91	29.1	201	73.6	10	10	.0	18	0	.0
55778	.1	100	.1	91	15.3	176*	40.5	6	18	.1	18	0	.0
55779	2.4	99	.7	92	27.8	313	88.9	8	6	1.2	7	0	.0
55780	.3	60	.1	83	21.1	256	58.9	14	5	.1	0	0	.0
55781	.3	100	.1	82	27.6	524	103.3	9	12	.1	12	2	.0
55782	1.7	100	.3	98	23.7	272*	49.2	11	15	.4	18	0	.6
55783	1.5	98	.5	89	19.5	352	72.2	11	11	.8	16	0	.0
55785	.4	100	.1	95	18.9	217*	41.4	8	11	.2	12	0	.0
55786	.3	100	.1	91	23.7	272*	34.9	5	15	.2	11	0	.0
55787	.5	0	.2	88	15.8	265	50.0	6	17	.0	0	0	.6
55788	.3	93	.1	79	24.5	282*	40.5	9	4	.0	18	0	.0
55790	1.9	93	.7	84	23.3	180	76.2	7	18	.9	18	0	.0
55792	13.1	98	5.5	63	23.9	255	72.4	7	18	6.1	14	3	.0
55793	.6	99	.2	91	22.3	167	50.4	6	13	.0	0	0	.0
55795	1.1	99	.4	85	17.4	265	58.1	8	14	.6	11	0	.0
55796	.3	0	.1	85	20.3	258	55.0	9	14	.8	16	0	.0
55797	1.5	96	.4	92	24.5	358	67.9	11	6	.8	7	1	.0
55798	.6	0	.2	87	16.6	297	43.7	11	20	.0	0	0	.0
55799	.8	97	.3	95	25.5	248	58.7	11	9	.4	8	0	.0

DULUTH

ZIPCODE	1	2	3	4	5	6	7	8	9	10	11	12	13
55802	2.6	96	1.3	67	15.7	224	66.5	3	37	1.2	31	7	2.3
55803	15.7	99	5.2	90	33.0	425	84.4	7	9	7.7	8	0	.1
55804	14.4	99	4.9	89	33.1	439	89.1	7	14	6.9	11	0	.0
55805	12.8	91	5.8	38	16.1	270	55.8	7	19	5.1	15	0	.1
55806	11.0	95	4.9	50	18.0	282	51.3	8	16	5.4	15	0	.0
55807	11.6	99	4.5	76	21.5	293	54.9	6	19	5.4	15	0	.4
55808	6.5	98	2.4	77	22.4	267	61.9	8	13	3.1	11	0	.0
55810	8.0	99	2.8	84	26.1	283	66.2	8	11	3.9	9	2	.0
55811	23.6	98	7.7	76	28.7	399	85.1	6	11	11.3	9	0	.0
55812	10.3	99	3.7	54	32.5	387	94.9	5	11	4.7	8	0	.0

ROCHESTER

ZIPCODE	1	2	3	4	5	6	7	8	9	10	11	12	13
55901	72.6	98	26.5	67	31.0	350	112.3	8	10	33.1	7	3	.5
55909	1.5	99	.5	86	24.4	216	61.4	7	19	.0	11	0	.0
55910	1.0	97	.3	89	23.3	321	63.6	10	9	.5	9	0	.0
55912	29.2	99	11.1	78	26.5	257	69.2	7	16	14.0	13	0	.0
55917	4.0	100	1.4	84	23.5	233	74.4	9	16	2.0	14	0	.0
55918	1.1	100	.4	80	20.9	288	58.8	9	15	.6	13	0	.0
55919	.9	0	.3	90	21.5	489	63.0	8	14	2.0	7	0	.0
55920	4.0	99	1.2	87	29.3	285	106.5	9	7	2.0	7	2	.0
55921	4.9	100	1.7	79	23.1	219	69.4	7	16	2.4	14	0	.0

MINNESOTA

ROCHESTER

ZIPCODE	1	2	3	4	5	6	7	8	9	10	11	12	13
55922	.9	0	.4	82	16.7	179	51.1	7	17	.0	0	1	.0
55923	3.8	100	1.3	81	25.2	290	78.0	9	16	1.9	13	0	.1
55924	1.5	0	.5	81	25.5	312	68.6	9	11	.5	0	0	.0
55925	1.1	100	.3	85	22.3	243	69.0	9	13	1.1	13	0	.0
55926	.9	0	.3	84	24.3	247	51.6	7	10	1.5	13	0	.4
55927	3.2	100	1.1	84	25.2	260	79.1	9	16	1.5	13	0	.0
55929	.8	100	.3	79	22.4	310	64.3	6	12	.4	10	0	.0
55931	.3	100	.1	89	18.3	359	68.0	6	30	.1	28	0	.0
55932	1.8	100	.6	82	24.9	284	82.9	11	13	.9	11	0	.0
55933	.2	100	.1	87	18.5	90	74.6	12	17	.1	15	0	.2
55934	2.6	98	.8	80	25.6	307	91.9	9	8	1.3	8	1	.0
55935	.9	100	.9	88	18.6	250	59.8	10	13	.5	13	0	.0
55936	1.8	99	.6	81	21.0	221	63.7	8	17	.9	15	0	.0
55938	.2	100	.1	68	22.2	181	51.3	13	18	.1	18	0	.0
55939	1.9	100	.7	79	20.0	187	62.0	6	20	.9	16	0	.0
55940	2.5	99	.8	81	23.1	264	74.9	8	19	1.2	17	0	.2
55941	1.2	100	.4	79	21.5	281	70.6	9	13	.6	12	0	.0
55943	3.1	100	1.1	80	21.5	215	66.1	8	17	1.6	14	0	.1
55944	4.7	100	1.6	84	27.1	253	90.4	11	9	2.4	8	0	.0
55945	1.2	0	.4	86	24.1	276	61.4	8	12	1.6	17	0	.0
55946	3.2	99	1.2	80	24.2	239	70.0	7	20	1.6	17	0	.1
55947	6.2	100	2.1	79	26.6	357	93.2	8	9	3.2	9	0	.0
55949	1.8	99	.7	76	19.4	193	54.9	9	19	.9	17	0	.0
55950	2.3	100	.9	94	28.8	331*	55.1	3	19	.1	21	0	.0
55951	1.5	0	.6	78	20.6	176	58.0	7	20	.2	20	0	.0
55952	2.4	99	.8	76	24.0	269	75.8	9	14	1.2	12	0	.0
55953	1.1	100	.4	81	18.4	220	60.0	9	15	.6	15	0	.0
55955	.7	0	.7	93	24.9	232	87.3	11	10	.9	10	0	.0
55956	1.4	0	.2	84	23.3	275	70.8	9	12	.1	12	0	.0
55957	.8	0	.2	79	24.7	269	61.0	6	8	.5	8	0	.0
55958	.6	0	.2	80	24.7	276	85.1	6	15	.5	15	0	.0
55959	1.7	0	.5	89	28.5	255	59.0	8	5	1.3	5	0	.0
55960	2.3	99	.8	88	28.3	319	104.6	9	7	1.2	6	0	.5
55961	.5	99	.2	88	25.7	427	60.3	8	20	.3	17	0	.0
55962	.8	99	.3	87	18.1	182	51.5	9	15	.4	14	0	.0
55963	3.9	99	1.3	81	27.5	282	95.5	8	12	1.9	9	1	1.5
55964	3.7	100	1.2	83	24.7	302	78.5	9	15	1.9	12	0	.0
55965	2.6	99	.9	77	27.1	238	60.6	7	17	1.3	15	0	.0
55967	.8	0	.1	89	27.1	231	90.4	9	10	.0	10	0	.0
55968	.2	100	.3	87	18.0	207*	62.4	0	27	.1	27	0	.0
55969	.9	100	.3	87	24.3	361	77.2	11	10	.5	8	0	.0
55970	1.0	100	.4	84	24.5	174	59.0	8	16	.5	16	0	.0
55971	2.8	100	1.0	79	20.8	256	64.6	8	18	1.3	17	0	.3
55972	3.4	99	1.1	76	23.7	241	76.3	9	15	1.7	13	0	.9
55973	.3	0	.9	68	19.6	66	60.8	8	21	.3	20	0	.0
55974	2.5	99	.9	78	19.7	230	60.8	8	22	1.2	20	0	.4
55975	4.6	100	1.6	79	23.4	204	69.7	7	17	2.2	14	2	.0
55976	6.2	99	2.0	83	27.7	315	89.2	9	10	3.1	9	0	.0

*=Estimated **1.0=883 lbs per person; 100++ indicates per capita toxic waste generation > than 100 times the U.S. average of 883 lbs per capita.

ZIP CODE MEASURES OF SIZE, LEVELS OF AFFLUENCE AND QUALITY OF LIFE

1=Population (th.); 2= % White; 3=Households (th.); 4=% Owner Occupied; 5=Mean Income Per Household (th.$); 6=Mean Monthly Rent ($)*; 7=Mean Home Value (th.$)*; 8=% under 5; 9=% 65 and over; 10=% White Males; 11=% White Males, 65+; 12=# Toxic Waste Sites; 13=Toxic Waste Relative to US(883 lbs.per capital)**.

MINNESOTA

ROCHESTER

ZIPCODE	1	2	3	4	5	6	7	8	9	10	11	12	13
55977	.3	100	.1	91	28.3	325*	52.6	14	7	.2	7	0	.0
55978	.3	100	.1	90	26.3	368	67.7	14	14	.2	14	0	.0
55979	.8	0	.3	79	21.1	235	69.3	10	11	0	0	0	.0
55981	3.3	99	1.2	78	22.3	230	81.8	7	21	1.6	18	0	.0
55982	.5	0	.2	87	22.1	251	44.6	7	15	.0	0	0	.0
55983	1.3	0	.5	82	25.7	226	74.9	7	20	.0	0	0	.1
55985	2.0	0	.7	81	23.3	201	71.1	8	15	.0	0	0	.0
55986	.5	0	.2	81	19.7	242	48.1	8	15	.0	0	0	.0
55987	32.9	99	11.3	70	23.6	285	74.2	6	14	15.2	12	4	1.1
55988	.4	100	.1	87	23.6	227	60.5	9	4	.2	3	0	.0
55990	1.1	0	.4	87	20.8	237	45.1	8	16	.0	0	0	.0
55991	1.2	0	.4	82	26.1	365	103.1	10	8	.0	0	0	.0
55992	3.8	99	1.3	84	25.6	295	88.9	8	16	1.9	15	0	.2

MANKATO

ZIPCODE	1	2	3	4	5	6	7	8	9	10	11	12	13
56001	46.0	98	15.9	63	25.8	306	97.3	7	10	21.6	8	8	.4
56007	23.6	98	8.8	73	24.8	295	75.8	7	16	11.1	13	3	.9
56009	2.0	100	.7	81	26.1	233	68.8	8	14	1.0	12	0	.0
56010	1.4	100	.5	79	21.5	272	56.4	6	20	.7	18	0	.0
56011	4.4	99	1.4	79	25.6	289	83.0	8	14	2.2	12	0	.0
56013	5.8	99	2.1	75	25.6	234	69.1	7	19	2.7	15	0	.2
56014	1.1	97	.4	77	21.7	276	50.5	8	16	.5	15	0	.0
56016	1.1	99	.4	86	25.5	310	77.2	8	11	.7	12	0	.0
56017	1.4	99	.4	86	24.2	269	87.2	13	12	.7	12	0	.0
56019	1.5	0	.5	80	18.5	243	45.4	9	18	.0	0	0	.0
56020	.2	100	.3	88	20.2	232*	56.5	4	22	.1	23	0	.0
56021	.9	0	.3	88	25.8	217	86.5	8	12	.0	0	0	.3
56022	.2	100	.1	81	25.8	235	40.3	5	24	.0	27	0	.0
56023	.7	98	.3	82	23.2	249	40.2	8	20	.4	21	0	.0
56024	2.0	0	.6	81	25.1	274	85.3	13	5	.0	0	0	.0
56025	1.0	100	.3	84	21.7	462	60.6	7	14	.5	12	0	.3
56026	2.0	99	.7	86	25.0	281	69.9	7	13	1.1	13	0	.0
56027	1.3	97	.5	79	19.0	225	42.0	8	19	.6	17	0	.0
56028	1.0	0	.4	89	23.4	262	69.0	7	15	.0	0	0	.0
56029	.9	100	.3	79	22.7	239	64.4	9	15	.5	13	0	.0
56031	13.7	99	5.3	71	25.1	268	81.3	8	16	6.5	14	1	.8
56032	.4	100	.1	91	26.3	284	67.6	8	15	.2	19	0	.0
56033	.5	0	.2	73	21.8	273	51.7	10	18	.0	0	0	.0
56034	.7	0	.2	82	25.6	288	69.1	11	11	.0	0	0	.0
56035	.5	100	.2	92	21.5	375	69.1	7	18	.3	14	0	.0
56036	2.3	99	.8	83	23.6	279	62.2	7	14	1.2	14	0	.0
56037	1.7	100	.6	79	25.7	265	72.1	9	15	.9	13	0	.0
56039	1.4	0	.5	74	22.0	333	49.3	9	14	.0	0	0	.0
56041	1.4	0	.5	81	21.8	289	60.4	7	15	.0	0	0	.0
56042	.9	0	.3	80	25.5	263	56.2	5	15	.0	0	0	.0
56043	.6	99	.2	82	23.8	306	61.6	8	15	.3	14	0	.1
56044	2.0	0	.6	80	23.3	207	60.2	8	14	.0	0	0	.0
56045	.9	0	.3	85	24.9	277	69.1	10	12	.0	0	0	.0
56047	.1	100	.1	96	27.0	310*	50.3	11	16	.1	17	0	.0
56048	3.9	100	1.3	83	23.2	256	69.6	10	14	2.0	12	0	.2

MINNESOTA

MANKATO

ZIPCODE	1	2	3	4	5	6	7	8	9	10	11	12	13
56050	1.4	99	.5	80	28.4	256	85.9	11	6	.7	4	0	.0
56051	1.0	100	.4	83	23.2	268	56.1	6	17	.5	14	0	.0
56052	.9	98	.3	86	21.1	320	66.4	8	12	.4	12	0	.0
56054	.9	0	.3	81	22.6	169	59.8	9	18	.0	0	0	.3
56055	3.6	100	1.3	78	25.3	267	76.8	8	17	1.8	14	0	.1
56057	3.6	99	1.2	81	22.5	222	76.0	8	18	1.8	16	0	.0
56058	6.0	100	2.0	77	27.4	272	89.8	7	14	3.0	13	0	.9
56060	.6	0	.2	79	20.6	300	35.5	5	21	.0	0	0	.0
56062	3.4	98	1.2	76	22.3	241	65.0	9	18	1.6	15	0	.0
56063	1.9	100	.6	84	29.5	371	109.5	8	12	1.0	10	0	.0
56065	2.8	0	1.0	78	23.5	275	70.5	8	17	.0	0	0	.0
56068	1.3	0	.5	80	25.4	272	64.8	8	17	.0	0	0	.1
56069	3.7	100	1.3	83	22.4	252	70.5	8	17	1.8	15	0	.0
56071	6.3	100	2.0	82	27.8	332	95.8	8	14	3.1	12	0	.3
56072	2.8	0	1.0	82	25.3	250	64.0	8	17	.0	0	0	.0
56073	17.1	99	5.7	78	25.4	263	84.2	8	13	8.2	11	0	.5
56074	2.2	100	.7	82	26.2	257	82.0	8	12	1.1	11	0	.0
56075	.2	0	.1	94	21.2	244*	63.9	7	19	.0	0	0	.0
56076	.4	0	.1	86	24.2	258	55.9	6	12	.0	0	0	.0
56078	.6	0	.2	80	22.9	248	65.1	13	8	.0	0	0	.1
56080	.5	0	.2	86	27.4	323	81.8	12	9	.0	0	0	.0
56081	6.4	98	2.4	75	23.4	219	68.2	7	18	3.1	16	0	.0
56082	11.3	99	3.2	73	24.6	268	95.0	6	13	5.5	11	1	.0
56083	1.4	100	.9	77	23.5	215	51.6	9	10	.7	11	0	.2
56084	.1	0	.1	86	16.4	189*	55.3	12	23	.0	0	0	.2
56085	6.3	99	2.2	77	24.2	223	67.6	9	17	3.1	15	0	.0
56087	3.9	100	1.4	84	22.2	244	62.3	6	21	1.9	18	0	.0
56088	2.5	100	.9	77	25.2	273	66.8	8	18	1.2	15	0	.1
56089	.8	100	.3	83	18.0	270	49.0	13	16	.0	0	0	.1
56090	.8	100	.3	82	23.6	360	59.1	11	18	.4	17	0	.0
56091	.5	100	.2	75	22.5	319	55.9	9	15	.2	10	0	.0
56092	.4	97	.2	77	23.5	154	44.4	8	16	.2	14	0	.0
56093	11.6	98	4.1	76	25.6	287	81.8	9	13	5.7	10	1	.1
56096	2.7	99	1.0	82	22.2	265	71.1	8	17	1.3	15	0	.0
56097	4.5	99	1.6	75	22.7	227	64.3	9	17	.9	13	0	.3
56098	2.9	97	1.1	72	22.0	253	59.0	8	20	1.4	16	0	.0

WINDOM

ZIPCODE	1	2	3	4	5	6	7	8	9	10	11	12	13
56101	6.6	100	2.5	75	26.3	276	78.1	8	16	3.1	14	0	.6
56110	2.3	100	.8	84	22.0	297	56.4	8	15	1.2	12	0	.0
56111	.6	0	.2	80	28.7	255	41.2	8	12	.0	0	0	.0
56112	.3	100	.1	86	19.5	416	56.1	9	8	.2	6	0	.0
56113	.4	100	.1	84	17.8	392	30.6	10	11	.2	11	0	.0
56114	.6	0	.2	83	19.3	250	34.1	8	17	.0	0	0	.0
56115	1.8	99	.6	82	18.4	239	51.6	10	17	.9	15	0	.0
56116	.6	100	.2	80	20.7	174	49.7	9	13	.3	13	0	.0
56117	.5	0	.2	82	22.2	338	42.0	7	13	.0	0	0	.0
56118	.8	0	.2	75	20.5	366	52.1	9	13	.0	0	0	.0
56119	.8	100	.4	78	20.2	284	59.7	9	13	.6	11	0	.0
56120	1.5	99	.5	78	20.7	257	50.7	9	14	.8	14	0	.0

*=Estimated **1.0=883 lbs per person; 100++ indicates per capita toxic waste generation > than 100 times the U.S. average of 883 lbs per capita.

ZIP CODE MEASURES OF SIZE, LEVELS OF AFFLUENCE AND QUALITY OF LIFE

1=Population (th.); 2= % White; 3=Households (th.); 4=% Owner Occupied; 5=Mean Income Per Household (th.$); 6=Mean Monthly Rent ($)*; 7=Mean Home Value (th.$)*;
8=% under 5; 9=% 65 and over; 10=% White Males, 65+; 11=% White Males (th.); 12=# Toxic Waste Sites; 13=Toxic Waste Relative to US(883 lbs.per capita)**.

MINNESOTA

WINDOM

ZIP CODE	1	2	3	4	5	6	7	8	9	10	11	12	13
56121	1.0	100	.4	83	23.8	262	47.9	10	17	.5	14	0	.0
56122	.8	0	.3	81	19.3	147	50.1	10	12	.0	0	0	.0
56123	.9	0	.3	79	20.3	167	41.6	9	16	.0	0	0	.0
56126	.5	0	.2	74	20.7	243	22.0	8	14	.0	0	0	.0
56127	.7	0	.2	74	25.1	269	50.7	10	12	.0	0	0	5.1
56128	2.5	0	.8	83	20.9	256	62.3	9	15	.0	0	0	.0
56129	1.0	100	.3	82	21.1	320	42.2	7	22	.5	19	0	.0
56131	2.4	99	.8	84	22.6	321	68.1	7	18	1.2	14	0	.0
56132	.8	99	.3	74	21.7	225	47.6	8	10	.4	10	0	.0
56133	.4	100	.1	78	23.4	263	43.2	9	17	.2	15	0	.0
56134	.7	0	.2	83	22.3	192	42.0	10	11	.0	0	0	.0
56136	1.5	100	.5	80	16.9	181	45.1	5	25	.7	21	0	.0
56137	1.8	0	.6	76	22.2	275	54.5	8	18	.0	0	0	.0
56138	.9	100	.3	89	23.2	279	54.2	8	20	.4	17	0	.0
56139	.6	100	.2	84	17.2	251	37.0	6	16	.3	14	0	.0
56141	.6	100	.2	91	20.4	314	44.4	8	14	.3	15	0	.0
56142	1.5	0	.5	76	18.0	160	49.9	8	21	.0	0	0	.0
56143	5.5	100	2.1	73	22.1	260	71.6	8	17	2.7	15	0	1.1
56144	1.3	100	.5	79	18.5	284	46.3	7	17	.6	14	0	.0
56145	.9	100	.3	80	19.2	394	43.5	10	17	.5	15	0	.0
56147	1.8	100	.7	66	28.7	186	33.9	12	3	.9	16	0	.0
56150	3.2	0	1.2	81	22.1	275	54.7	8	18	.9	16	0	.0
56151	.9	100	.3	79	18.8	168	43.0	9	10	.5	10	0	.0
56152	2.2	100	.8	78	21.0	187	50.8	7	20	.2	12	0	.0
56153	.2	100	.1	94	17.6	202*	49.0	6	27	.1	31	0	1.4
56155	6.4	98	2.5	88	21.0	350	36.1	7	14	.2	12	0	.0
56157	.7	99	.2	71	23.4	221	73.6	8	17	3.0	15	1	.1
56158	.5	100	.2	76	22.2	241	60.2	11	10	.4	12	0	.0
56159	3.3	100	1.3	80	24.3	459	43.3	9	12	1.6	21	0	.4
56160	.3	100	.1	86	21.8	222	65.6	7	24	.2	13	0	.0
56161	.4	100	.1	82	24.0	312	57.0	10	15	.2	22	0	.0
56164	6.6	99	2.6	72	20.4	214	59.7	7	19	3.1	16	0	1.4
56165	.5	100	.2	75	23.9	339	44.8	7	13	.2	12	0	.0
56166	.4	0	.1	75	16.8	148	38.8	7	20	.0	0	0	.0
56167	.9	0	.3	76	23.6	315	50.3	6	16	.0	0	0	.4
56168	1.3	100	.5	77	19.0	237	43.9	11	14	.7	14	0	.0
56169	.8	100	.3	81	18.6	196	52.9	10	17	.5	17	0	.0
56170	.3	0	.1	84	18.1	230	33.4	9	20	.0	0	0	.0
56171	2.2	99	.8	74	24.3	220	63.4	6	18	1.1	15	0	.0
56172	3.5	99	1.4	76	22.1	241	68.1	7	18	1.7	16	0	.0
56173	.4	0	.2	85	19.3	134	32.7	9	19	.0	0	0	.0
56174	.7	100	.3	83	22.6	232	53.3	9	16	.4	16	0	.0
56175	3.3	100	1.3	76	20.5	206	56.7	7	22	1.6	18	0	.0
56176	1.3	0	.5	79	23.2	200	60.2	7	25	.0	0	0	.4
56178	2.2	99	.8	80	18.3	243	56.8	8	19	1.1	18	0	.1
56179	.4	100	.1	81	13.3	221	33.0	11	12	.2	12	0	.0

WINDOM (continued)

ZIP CODE	1	2	3	4	5	6	7	8	9	10	11	12	13
56180	1.6	100	.6	73	19.6	185	44.6	7	20	.8	20	0	.0
56181	1.5	97	.5	79	23.2	268	61.6	5	15	.7	13	1	.5
56183	1.9	100	.7	81	20.2	241	49.4	6	23	.9	19	0	.0
56185	.9	100	.3	83	20.1	273	36.1	10	12	.5	12	0	.0
56186	.6	100	.2	78	17.7	375	37.9	8	15	.3	14	0	.0
56187	12.1	99	4.5	72	25.2	295	77.8	7	16	5.8	14	0	.0

WILLMAR

ZIP CODE	1	2	3	4	5	6	7	8	9	10	11	12	13
56201	19.4	99	6.9	66	25.3	304	92.0	7	14	9.2	12	0	.2
56207	.4	100	.1	72	18.6	274	49.1	11	10	.2	9	0	.0
56208	3.1	100	1.2	78	18.7	200	50.5	7	23	1.5	22	0	.1
56209	2.5	99	.9	83	20.8	269	74.7	9	15	1.2	14	0	.2
56211	.8	0	.3	83	18.9	261	28.2	7	15	.0	0	0	.0
56212	1.0	100	.4	84	17.0	195	29.2	7	13	.5	13	0	.0
56214	.9	100	.3	77	21.9	266	46.1	6	22	.5	21	0	.1
56215	5.7	99	2.1	75	20.8	193	62.7	8	17	2.7	15	0	1.2
56216	.7	0	.2	86	24.8	315	55.0	7	12	.0	0	0	.0
56218	1.0	99	.4	81	20.0	195	34.3	8	18	.5	17	0	.0
56219	1.1	94	.4	83	17.8	293	33.4	6	27	.5	23	0	.0
56220	4.1	100	1.5	76	17.7	238	54.8	7	20	2.1	18	0	.0
56221	1.3	100	.5	77	19.6	216	51.5	9	16	.2	13	0	.0
56222	2.4	100	.9	79	21.9	249	61.4	7	20	1.2	18	0	.0
56223	2.0	99	.7	81	20.1	176	53.8	8	21	1.0	18	0	.1
56224	.5	0	.2	87	20.4	128	43.5	7	22	.0	0	0	.1
56225	1.3	0	.5	77	17.8	208	41.1	6	25	.0	0	0	.0
56226	.3	100	.1	88	18.8	165	46.0	9	13	.2	12	0	.0
56227	.4	100	.2	89	20.5	483	58.9	9	10	.2	10	0	.0
56228	1.1	0	.4	79	21.0	211	54.2	10	19	.0	0	0	.0
56229	1.7	98	.6	73	22.0	178	67.4	11	13	.8	12	0	.0
56230	1.1	100	.4	78	25.0	247	63.7	10	14	.0	0	0	.0
56231	.2	0	.2	83	18.0	332	57.8	8	14	.2	13	0	.0
56232	3.1	99	1.2	78	22.5	228	61.8	8	21	1.5	20	0	1.2
56233	.7	100	.3	86	18.6	329	44.5	9	10	.4	11	0	.0
56235	.9	0	.3	86	18.3	292	41.6	9	15	.0	0	0	.0
56236	.6	0	.2	70	23.8	217	38.6	7	9	.0	0	0	.0
56237	.9	100	.3	76	21.2	247	45.3	8	19	.5	18	0	.0
56239	.6	99	.2	70	23.8	180	57.1	15	13	.0	0	0	.0
56240	1.5	0	.5	76	21.0	228	43.5	7	20	.0	0	0	.0
56241	4.8	97	1.8	72	22.8	199	73.0	7	17	2.3	15	0	.6
56243	1.1	100	.6	80	21.7	243	58.3	8	13	.9	13	0	.0
56244	1.8	100	.6	80	21.4	241	56.0	11	13	.4	11	0	.0
56245	.6	0	.2	81	20.8	171	41.1	8	19	.0	0	0	.0
56246	.5	100	.2	88	22.4	377	77.5	9	16	.3	21	0	.0
56247	1.1	100	.4	87	17.5	201*	35.1	5	12	.1	10	0	.0
56248	1.2	0	.4	82	19.8	203	43.2	7	15	.0	0	0	.0
56249	.6	100	.3	78	20.1	237	40.8	9	5	.3	4	0	.0
56251	.9	99	.3	76	25.3	282	79.2	9	12	.5	11	0	.0
56252	1.4	99	.5	76	20.0	246	58.3	8	15	.7	14	0	.0
56253	1.3	0	.5	70	20.0	237	57.9	6	15	.0	0	0	.0
56254	.2	100	.1	73	18.7	215*	22.3	4	18	.1	19	0	.0

*=Estimated **1.0=883 lbs per person; 100+ indicates per capita toxic waste generation > than 100 times the U.S. average of 883 lbs per capita.

103001

ZIP CODE MEASURES OF SIZE, LEVELS OF AFFLUENCE AND QUALITY OF LIFE

1=Population (th.); 2= % White; 3=Households (th.); 4=% Owner Occupied; 5=Mean Income Per Household (th.$); 6=Mean Monthly Rent ($)*; 7=Mean Home Value (th.$)*;
8=% under 5; 9=% 65 and over; 10=White Males, 65+; 11=% White Males (th.); 12=# Toxic Waste Sites; 13=Toxic Waste Relative to US(883 lbs.per capital)**.

MINNESOTA

WILLMAR

ZIPCODE	1	2	3	4	5	6	7	8	9	10	11	12	13
56255	.6	100	.2	72	18.8	218	45.6	7	19	.3	18	0	.0
56256	3.6	99	1.4	75	21.4	174	63.1	7	22	1.7	20	0	.1
56257	.7	100	.2	85	16.5	208	27.2	9	18	.3	18	0	.0
56258	13.4	98	4.4	66	26.1	291	89.0	8	10	6.6	18	2	.1
56260	1.2	100	.4	75	20.9	252	45.0	8	12	.6	11	0	.0
56262	1.0	100	.4	82	19.1	158	44.2	7	20	.5	20	0	.0
56263	.7	100	.3	76	23.8	105	51.6	10	12	.4	10	0	.0
56264	2.4	0	.8	79	21.0	251	59.5	8	18	.3	16	0	.5
56265	9.0	100	3.4	74	22.7	251	65.6	8	18	4.3	16	1	.1
56266	1.9	100	.7	85	21.4	239	55.1	9	20	.9	17	0	.0
56267	7.2	97	2.5	65	22.0	266	72.5	7	14	3.4	12	0	.0
56270	1.6	92	.6	76	22.7	189	55.2	10	12	.8	10	0	.0
56271	1.1	99	.4	82	16.6	320	47.8	7	15	.6	17	0	.0
56273	2.1	100	1	91	19.9	229*	17.4	5	23	.1	19	0	.0
56274	.3	100	.1	87	19.0	197	31.2	3	26	1.6	14	0	.0
56275	.7	100	.2	85	25.2	315	60.1	10	12	.4	12	0	.0
56276	.5	100	.2	88	19.0	320	27.9	7	12	.2	13	0	.0
56277	3.9	100	1.4	74	22.7	231	73.0	8	15	1.9	12	0	.2
56278	3.7	0	.4	75	20.6	225	63.5	7	22	.0	0	0	.1
56279	1.2	0	.4	88	23.1	311	72.6	10	12	.4	14	0	.0
56280	.7	100	.2	79	17.0	176	38.8	9	15	.4	14	0	.0
56281	.3	100	.1	90	31.2	359*	91.4	9	9	.1	10	0	.9
56282	2.3	100	.3	80	21.8	268	66.6	11	13	1.1	13	0	.0
56283	6.3	100	2.4	74	24.2	269	80.5	8	17	3.0	14	0	.1
56284	2.7	100	.9	78	23.9	230	57.5	8	18	1.3	16	0	.0
56285	1.5	100	.5	79	22.6	201	43.0	7	19	.0	0	0	.2
56288	3.4	99	1.2	81	25.4	356	105.6	9	13	1.7	13	0	.0
56289	.8	100	.3	81	16.7	286	50.0	10	17	.4	17	0	.0
56291	.7	0	.2	85	19.7	159	38.6	6	11	.0	0	0	.0
56292	.9	0	.3	78	18.8	226	40.2	8	18	.0	0	0	.0
56293	1.5	100	.5	73	20.8	177	54.5	7	16	.8	12	0	.0
56294	1.0	100	.2	85	17.4	200*	63.1	3	34	.1	36	0	.0
56295	.4	0	.2	86	15.9	174	33.1	11	19	.0	0	0	.0
56296	2.9	99	1.1	77	22.0	231	55.0	7	24	1.4	22	0	.0
56297	1.0	98	.4	77	20.3	207	41.5	8	17	.5	17	0	.0

SAINT CLOUD

ZIPCODE	1	2	3	4	5	6	7	8	9	10	11	12	13
56301	56.6	98	18.0	65	26.0	338	90.4	7	9	27.0	8	3	.3
56307	4.1	100	1.2	84	21.5	240	67.9	11	13	2.1	12	0	.2
56308	17.4	98	6.4	70	22.1	271	86.7	8	15	8.2	14	1	.2
56309	.9	98	.4	87	19.1	232	61.5	7	22	.6	21	0	.0
56310	3.6	100	1.0	91	25.4	282	86.5	11	7	1.9	7	0	.2
56311	.9	0	.3	79	18.2	281	43.1	8	22	.0	0	0	.0
56312	2.8	100	.8	79	20.3	206	60.6	9	15	1.4	14	0	.0
56313	1.1	100	.1	93	17.2	198*	49.9	10	20	.1	15	0	.0
56314	1.1	100	.1	84	18.5	329	48.8	9	14	.6	15	0	.0
56315	1.5	100	.5	85	19.6	231	63.7	10	15	.8	15	0	.0
56316	1.7	0	.6	81	17.3	208	46.9	10	19	.0	0	0	.0
56318	1.1	0	.4	87	18.4	143	51.4	11	12	.0	0	0	.0

MINNESOTA

SAINT CLOUD

ZIPCODE	1	2	3	4	5	6	7	8	9	10	11	12	13
56319	1.2	0	.4	92	21.4	233	80.2	7	15	.0	0	0	.0
56320	5.4	100	1.5	86	27.4	322	89.7	10	9	2.7	9	0	.0
56323	.7	100	.2	81	21.0	304	41.3	5	15	.4	12	0	.0
56324	1.0	99	.3	85	21.3	303	69.4	6	17	.5	17	0	.0
56325	.3	100	.1	90	25.1	289*	64.4	10	14	.2	13	0	.0
56326	1.6	0	.5	87	16.2	174	47.8	10	18	.3	14	0	.0
56327	.6	100	.2	85	22.9	264	62.8	8	15	.3	14	0	.0
56328	.2	100	.1	88	17.6	202*	46.8	4	20	.1	23	0	.0
56329	5.4	100	1.6	87	21.0	268	63.8	10	12	2.7	11	1	.1
56330	1.0	100	.3	93	20.3	302	51.5	9	10	.0	0	0	.0
56331	1.9	100	.5	91	26.0	217	59.3	8	11	1.0	10	0	.0
56332	.9	100	.3	91	20.1	348	65.9	9	11	.0	0	0	.0
56333	.1	100	.1	86	18.3	210*	53.8	20	15	.1	13	0	.0
56334	4.8	100	1.8	74	20.4	221	71.8	8	20	2.3	17	1	.1
56335	.3	100	.3	86	24.5	290	70.7	12	15	.2	14	0	.0
56336	1.4	99	.5	85	16.9	171	70.0	7	16	.7	15	0	.0
56338	1.1	0	.4	86	16.5	128	64.2	7	12	.0	0	0	.0
56339	1.1	100	.4	86	20.0	256	52.0	9	23	.0	0	0	.0
56340	2.0	0	.7	85	19.9	252	59.5	9	11	.0	0	0	.2
56342	2.3	96	.9	83	18.1	207	68.3	6	22	1.1	24	0	.2
56343	1.2	100	.4	86	17.7	245	61.0	7	16	.6	15	0	.0
56345	13.8	99	4.6	77	21.3	236	65.9	9	15	6.5	13	2	.3
56347	6.2	99	2.1	81	19.4	218	64.1	8	16	3.1	15	0	.3
56349	.7	100	.3	88	21.6	234	53.9	8	21	.4	19	0	.0
56350	.6	0	.3	81	16.1	182	45.3	8	16	.0	0	0	.0
56352	4.9	100	1.5	82	22.7	233	67.2	9	12	2.5	11	0	.0
56353	6.4	99	2.2	80	21.8	250	62.9	8	16	3.2	14	0	.1
56354	1.0	0	.4	86	23.6	286	71.0	8	17	.0	0	0	.6
56355	.5	0	.2	78	15.6	153	48.1	5	14	.0	0	0	.0
56356	.3	100	.2	84	25.7	308	61.1	11	21	.0	16	0	.0
56357	.9	99	.3	89	22.9	326	59.4	8	10	.4	11	0	.0
56358	2.3	98	.8	88	19.5	302	57.9	10	11	1.2	13	0	.0
56359	3.0	85	1.0	81	18.9	188	60.7	8	15	1.3	15	0	.0
56360	3.7	100	1.3	83	17.9	216	64.1	7	18	1.8	17	0	.1
56361	2.5	99	1.8	86	17.5	235	50.3	7	20	1.3	18	0	.0
56362	5.5	100	1.8	82	24.1	239	83.5	9	14	2.8	13	0	.0
56363	.2	100	.1	91	26.5	304*	54.4	7	19	.1	16	0	.0
56364	4.9	100	1.4	88	19.0	202	62.2	11	12	2.5	11	0	.0
56367	4.3	100	1.3	88	26.1	307	89.2	12	5	2.2	6	0	.2
56368	3.3	100	.9	86	22.8	260	73.2	10	9	1.7	9	0	.0
56369	.6	100	.2	53	24.2	312	70.5	7	10	.3	5	0	.0
56371	1.0	100	.3	90	17.7	203*	35.6	13	16	.1	13	0	.0
56373	2.3	100	.7	84	20.0	255	67.5	12	10	1.2	9	0	.0
56374	6.8	99	1.5	84	27.8	283	92.1	9	17	2.7	7	0	.0
56376	.2	100	.1	86	14.6	168*	56.6	13	27	.1	27	0	.0
56377	3.1	99	1.1	73	29.0	332	100.4	13	4	1.6	3	1	.0
56378	1.5	99	.5	81	22.0	242	69.8	8	14	3.6	13	0	1.7
56379	1.7	0	.6	79	25.4	318	83.6	9	12	4.6	10	0	.0
56380	1.1	0	.4	87	15.6	206	46.6	10	17	.3	18	0	.0

*=Estimated **1.0=883 lbs per person; 100++ indicates per capita toxic waste generation > than 100 times the U.S. average of 883 lbs per capita.

ZIP CODE MEASURES OF SIZE, LEVELS OF AFFLUENCE AND QUALITY OF LIFE

1=Population (th.); 2= % White; 3=Households (th.); 4=% Owner Occupied; 5=Mean Income Per Household (th.$); 6=Mean Monthly Rent ($)*; 7=Mean Home Value (th.$)*; 8=% under 5; 9=% 65 and over; 10=White Males (th.); 11=% White Males, 65+; 12=# Toxic Waste Sites; 13=Toxic Waste Relative to US(883 lbs.per capita)**.

MINNESOTA

SAINT CLOUD

ZIP CODE	1	2	3	4	5	6	7	8	9	10	11	12	13
56381	2.6	100	1.0	82	18.5	199	65.8	7	23	1.3	22	2	.0
56382	1.5	0	.5	92	19.2	132	51.0	6	13	.0	0	0	.0
56384	.3	0	.1	77	13.1	205	50.3	6	32	.5	0	0	.0
56385	1.0	100	.3	90	18.6	207	58.1	9	15	.5	14	0	.0
56386	.5	100	.2	89	18.6	199	54.2	8	21	.2	23	0	.0
56387	3.5	99	1.2	58	22.9	373	71.9	8	11	1.6	9	0	.0

BRAINERD

ZIP CODE	1	2	3	4	5	6	7	8	9	10	11	12	13
56401	26.3	99	9.3	76	22.2	268	74.7	8	13	12.5	12	1	.3
56431	6.9	99	2.7	83	17.9	217	73.1	6	22	3.4	21	0	.1
56433	1.3	0	.5	88	17.8	234	46.2	7	21	.0	0	0	.0
56434	.2	100	.1	75	17.2	213	33.0	11	26	.1	31	0	.0
56435	1.9	98	.7	88	14.9	208	55.3	9	17	.9	18	0	.0
56437	1.4	100	.5	83	16.1	163	37.1	9	15	.7	15	0	.0
56438	2.7	0	.9	82	17.9	205	58.3	10	14	.3	0	0	.0
56440	1.6	99	.6	90	16.9	288	48.8	9	21	.8	19	0	.3
56441	3.0	98	1.2	73	17.9	179	54.5	8	22	1.3	20	2	.4
56442	1.1	0	.5	91	21.9	187	114.2	5	26	.0	0	0	.0
56443	1.1	0	.4	89	17.3	252	78.7	5	16	.0	0	0	.0
56444	3.0	99	1.1	86	20.7	242	77.4	7	19	1.5	19	0	.0
56446	2.0	100	.7	86	15.1	212	51.5	10	17	1.0	15	0	.0
56447	.5	98	.1	89	15.6	129	72.4	8	21	.0	20	0	.0
56448	1.1	0	.1	95	14.2	164*	66.6	8	17	.0	0	0	.0
56449	1.1	100	.3	89	19.1	239	50.9	10	9	.6	9	0	.0
56450	.7	0	.1	90	17.3	301	67.3	7	18	.0	0	0	.0
56451	.8	99	.2	88	16.3	188*	55.5	9	11	.4	11	0	.0
56452	1.3	0	.5	87	18.8	197	75.3	5	25	.0	20	0	.0
56453	1.0	100	.1	88	15.8	199	34.0	10	19	.0	5	0	.0
56455	.8	98	.3	81	19.9	241	44.7	7	20	.3	21	0	.0
56456	.2	0	.1	90	16.0	184*	54.8	8	15	.0	0	0	.0
56458	.3	0	.1	90	20.1	263	46.1	4	19	.0	0	0	.0
56459	.2	100	.2	84	22.5	411	80.3	6	20	.1	20	0	.0
56460	.2	100	.2	72	18.0	161	55.4	8	3	.1	5	0	.0
56461	1.1	99	.4	83	21.5	243	62.6	10	11	.6	11	0	.0
56464	3.7	99	1.2	86	16.0	172	51.3	10	17	1.9	16	0	.0
56465	1.3	0	.5	94	20.2	320	82.6	7	16	.0	0	0	.0
56466	2.1	0	.7	86	17.1	219	55.9	7	15	.0	0	0	.0
56467	1.6	0	.6	87	18.0	221	65.2	5	16	.0	0	0	.0
56468	.7	0	.3	88	23.5	293	90.2	7	13	.3	21	0	.0
56469	1.0	100	.4	89	17.1	174	43.0	7	18	.5	16	0	.0
56470	7.9	98	2.9	77	18.9	203	63.6	7	19	3.6	18	0	.0
56472	3.6	100	1.4	85	19.3	223	83.9	7	18	1.8	18	0	.0
56473	1.7	0	.6	88	17.7	258	59.4	9	14	.0	0	0	.0
56474	3.6	99	1.3	82	16.8	203	68.2	7	21	1.7	21	0	.0
56475	1.4	99	.4	91	18.6	158	52.6	10	13	.7	11	0	.0
56477	2.9	99	1.0	85	16.6	209	42.9	9	14	1.4	15	1	.0
56479	5.9	100	2.0	76	20.5	273	52.6	8	15	2.9	14	0	.0
56481	2.2	100	.7	89	16.3	252	46.0	8	14	.1	13	0	.0
56482	7.7	99	2.7	74	20.3	223	61.6	8	15	3.7	13	1	.1
56484	2.6	92	1.0	79	21.1	220	75.9	5	21	1.2	19	0	.0

MINNESOTA

DETROIT LAKES

ZIP CODE	1	2	3	4	5	6	7	8	9	10	11	12	13
56501	14.1	97	5.3	73	22.2	240	82.2	7	16	6.7	14	0	.1
56510	1.5	99	.5	77	20.9	222	57.1	6	22	1.5	20	0	.0
56511	1.5	100	.5	89	21.5	303	77.9	7	14	.8	15	0	.0
56513	.2	100	.1	84	27.9	290	98.2	3	5	.1	4	0	.0
56514	3.5	0	1.2	83	22.5	216	69.2	9	16	.0	0	1	.1
56515	2.5	100	1.0	83	19.9	273	76.0	5	25	1.2	25	0	.0
56516	.4	0	.2	85	14.9	155	23.5	8	14	.0	0	0	.0
56517	.4	0	.1	82	21.2	213	34.9	8	14	.0	0	0	.0
56518	.4	0	.1	88	21.6	333	52.7	7	10	.0	0	0	.0
56519	.6	97	.2	85	27.0	269	61.4	8	11	.3	13	0	.0
56520	4.6	98	1.6	72	23.8	247	62.6	7	17	2.2	14	0	.0
56521	.8	84	.2	85	21.2	333	59.2	9	9	.3	8	0	.0
56522	.6	98	.2	87	22.9	231	41.3	9	9	.0	0	0	.0
56523	.7	98	.3	79	22.9	270	58.4	10	18	.3	15	0	.0
56524	.6	100	.2	90	16.0	158	57.0	7	18	.3	20	0	.0
56527	1.1	0	.4	85	16.0	210	46.0	8	19	.0	0	0	.0
56528	1.2	100	.4	88	15.9	258	62.8	7	20	.6	17	0	.0
56529	2.6	99	.9	74	25.7	305	74.6	10	7	1.3	6	0	.3
56530	.4	100	.1	90	18.6	79	39.3	10	13	.2	9	0	.1
56531	2.4	100	.9	79	22.1	266	61.8	7	22	1.2	20	0	.0
56533	.3	0	.1	90	18.3	228	39.2	6	19	.0	0	0	.0
56534	1.1	0	.4	92	17.2	241	62.8	9	15	.0	0	0	.0
56535	1.4	0	.5	79	16.9	188	51.0	5	25	.0	0	0	.0
56536	.8	98	.3	85	26.2	243	61.7	10	13	.4	12	0	.0
56537	17.8	100	6.5	72	24.0	294	78.5	7	16	8.5	14	1	.1
56540	2.3	99	.8	83	19.2	175	54.8	7	24	1.2	22	0	.0
56542	3.1	98	1.1	81	16.9	210	52.7	5	21	1.5	19	0	.0
56543	.4	98	.1	89	31.8	317	38.7	9	11	.2	10	0	.3
56544	4.5	98	1.4	84	21.5	225	71.2	9	13	2.3	14	0	.1
56545	1.1	100	.4	86	19.3	313	49.2	9	16	.2	14	0	.0
56546	.4	100	.1	88	23.4	333	75.0	9	9	.2	14	0	.0
56547	2.4	97	.8	82	26.6	297	92.4	9	9	1.2	7	0	.0
56548	1.1	0	.4	77	24.8	207	53.9	7	22	.0	0	0	.0
56549	3.9	99	1.3	82	22.2	218	73.6	9	13	1.9	13	0	.0
56550	.5	0	.2	82	23.2	267	59.1	9	23	.0	0	0	.0
56551	2.3	100	.9	82	15.6	183	55.5	6	24	1.1	23	0	.0
56552	.6	100	.2	86	15.6	86	48.0	10	17	.3	18	0	.0
56553	.4	0	.1	94	23.9	275*	42.7	8	14	.0	0	0	.0
56554	2.2	98	.7	87	23.8	225	80.4	8	17	1.1	16	0	.0
56556	1.3	99	.5	79	17.2	220	47.0	6	27	.7	25	0	.0
56557	2.8	91	1.0	78	17.4	228	54.5	8	21	1.3	20	0	.0
56560	33.2	98	10.8	63	26.8	313	97.1	6	9	15.5	7	2	.0
56566	.6	20	.1	68	17.2	209	62.4	10	7	.0	12	0	.0
56567	3.1	100	1.1	82	18.1	165	48.7	8	19	1.6	17	0	.4
56568	.2	98	.2	91	19.2	220*	29.3	3	27	.0	0	0	.0
56569	1.0	73	.3	88	16.3	186	43.9	10	11	.4	15	0	.0
56570	.8	94	.3	84	17.5	113	39.8	7	16	.4	18	0	.1
56571	.9	99	.4	89	18.1	188	70.7	7	20	.5	20	0	.1
56572	4.2	99	1.6	79	21.4	191	77.0	5	21	2.1	20	0	.1

*=Estimated **1.0=883 lbs per person; 100++ indicates per capita toxic waste generation > than 100 times the U.S. average of 883 lbs per capita.

ZIP CODE MEASURES OF SIZE, LEVELS OF AFFLUENCE AND QUALITY OF LIFE

1=Population (th.); 2= % White; 3=Households (th.); 4=% Owner Occupied; 5=Mean Income Per Household (th.$); 6=Mean Monthly Rent ($); 7=Mean Home Value (th.$); 8=% under 5; 9=% 65 and over; 10=White Males; 11=% White Males, 65+; 12=# Toxic Waste Sites; 13=Toxic Waste Relative to US(883 lbs.per capita)**.

MINNESOTA

DETROIT LAKES

ZIP CODE	1	2	3	4	5	6	7	8	9	10	11	12	13
56573	4.4	100	1.6	80	20.7	249	70.2	8	18	2.2	15	2	.1
56574	.4	0	.1	95	29.2	336*	60.3	11	12	.0	0	0	.0
56575	.8	55	.2	69	14.7	178	36.1	6	11	.2	20	0	.0
56576	.8		.3	90	18.1	300	83.1	6	17	.2	17	0	.0
56578	1.2	96	.4	89	21.1	343	78.4	9	11	.6	11	0	.0
56579	1.4	100	.5	80	19.6	258	43.2	8	17	.7	16	0	.0
56580	1.0	0	.3	89	31.0	438	97.5	9	8	.0	0	0	.2
56581	.4	0	.2	88	20.5	260	36.3	7	26	.0	0	0	.0
56583	.2	100	.1	86	25.0	105	30.3	9	15	.1	15	0	.0
56584	2.0	99	.7	82	17.4	197	45.3	9	22	1.0	20	0	.0
56585	1.1	0	.4	82	18.5	158	48.9	8	22	.0	0	0	.0
56586	1.7	100	.6	85	20.8	221	62.1	7	20	.9	22	0	.0
56587	1.3	99	.5	91	18.0	285	63.8	10	19	.7	19	0	.0
56588	.7	100	.2	91	16.5	243	62.4	6	17	.4	16	0	.0
56589	1.8	80	.6	86	17.9	225	54.5	8	12	.7	14	0	.0
56590	.6	0	.2	84	19.8	239	48.0	6	18	.0	0	0	.0
56591	.4	11	.2	63	12.3	191	33.2	11	10	.0	11	0	.0
56592	.6	0	.2	93	15.7	243	36.9	6	22	.0	0	0	.0
56593	.6	100	.2	80	27.1	228	49.3	7	18	.3	16	0	.0

BEMIDJI

ZIP CODE	1	2	3	4	5	6	7	8	9	10	11	12	13
56601	21.7	95	7.2	73	21.9	311	72.5	7	10	10.2	9	2	.1
56621	4.6	89	1.6	80	17.8	206	50.9	7	16	2.1	16	0	.0
56622	.4	0	.1	93	19.2	221*	43.6	13	10	.0	0	0	.0
56623	2.6	0	1.0	80	18.6	168	60.2	5	17	.0	0	0	2.7
56625	.2	0	.1	86	18.2	209*	45.1	1	6	.1	15	0	.0
56626	.4	50	.1	78	15.2	302	43.1	9	15	.1	15	0	.0
56627	.7	0	.2	72	17.0	187	47.1	9	7	.0	0	1	.0
56628	1.7	99	.6	87	18.3	171	66.7	19	17	.9	17	0	.0
56629	.3	100	.1	87	13.5	221	21.4	6	31	.1	32	0	.0
56630	2.2	99	.7	83	17.0	252	58.1	5	19	1.1	20	0	.0
56632	.3	89	.1	83	12.6	197	67.5	5	20	.1	21	0	.0
56633	3.5	58	1.2	74	17.6	214	49.0	9	14	.1	19	0	.2
56634	1.6	98	.6	83	17.1	171	46.2	6	23	.8	21	0	.0
56636	4.1	84	1.4	85	20.0	231	64.9	11	13	1.7	13	0	.0
56637	.2	100	.1	98	22.1	254*	63.4	7	17	.1	16	0	.0
56639	.3	100	.1	87	23.2	350	118.1	12	22	.1	22	0	.6
56641	.4	62	.1	83	13.7	151	35.1	9	12	.2	13	0	.0
56644	1.0	0	.4	91	16.6	241	36.6	6	24	.8	13	0	.0
56646	.5	0	.2	87	15.5	289	23.9	7	21	1.7	0	0	.0
56647	.5	98	.1	86	20.6	233	61.9	9	11	.2	9	0	.6
56649	10.4	97	3.7	77	25.2	237	71.6	6	11	4.9	9	0	.6
56650	.8	97	.3	82	16.5	156	39.7	9	21	.4	21	0	.0
56651	.6	87	.2	93	16.9	277	48.8	8	16	.3	19	0	.0
56652	.5	0	.2	87	16.0	184*	40.3	8	15	.2	0	0	.0
56653	1.9	99	.6	86	22.4	216	52.5	10	14	.9	14	0	.0
56654	.2	100	.1	91	21.8	250*	79.9	0	16	.1	30	0	.0
56655	1.0	97	.4	84	15.1	285	82.6	6	19	.5	21	0	.0
56657	.3	0	.1	89	17.3	195	65.0	4	31	.0	0	0	.0
56660	.5	0	.1	92	15.5	179*	42.6	12	14	.0	0	0	.0

MINNESOTA

BEMIDJI

ZIP CODE	1	2	3	4	5	6	7	8	9	10	11	12	13
56661	1.1	0	.4	74	12.0	183	40.6	6	24	.0	0	0	.0
56662	.4	100	.2	92	14.0	73	76.0	1	33	.2	35	0	.0
56664	.4	97	.1	81	14.8	162	39.4	8	15	.2	17	0	.0
56666	.6	12	.1	51	16.7	216	38.7	16	4	.0	0	0	.0
56667	.7	95	.2	91	16.7	95	40.3	8	11	.3	12	0	.1
56668	.5	0	.2	88	29.2	409	72.0	6	8	.0	0	1	.0
56669	.5	100	.2	96	15.5	178*	54.0	13	12	.3	12	0	.0
56670	.9	0	.2	66	18.2	150	23.7	12	7	.0	0	0	.0
56671	.4	3	.4	78	25.5	156	39.3	12	5	.0	0	0	.0
56672	1.4	99	.6	86	17.5	187	60.7	8	17	.7	17	0	.0
56673	.4	0	.2	85	26.2	98	57.3	9	14	.2	18	0	.0
56676	1.0	98	.3	86	15.9	334	33.2	13	10	.5	11	0	.0
56678	.6	100	.2	85	17.2	278	61.4	14	11	.3	10	0	.0
56679	1.9	98	.6	81	23.7	208	63.1	13	6	.9	4	0	.0
56680	.1	0	.1	87	19.0	218*	74.2	11	21	.0	0	0	.0
56681	.4	88	.2	80	18.0	198	41.1	7	21	.2	20	0	.0
56683	.5	100	.2	88	16.0	166	67.2	7	14	.3	15	0	.0
56684	.5	0	.2	85	12.3	240	27.6	8	22	.0	0	0	.0
56685	.1	100	.1	100	13.3	153*	35.8	6	19	.1	15	0	.0
56686	.9	100	.3	87	17.3	246	38.4	13	19	.5	19	0	.0
56687	.5	0	.1	85	20.2	263	66.1	11	7	.0	0	0	.0
56688	.6	0	.1	93	13.6	157*	51.0	3	19	.0	0	0	.0

THIEF RIVER FALLS

ZIP CODE	1	2	3	4	5	6	7	8	9	10	11	12	13
56701	13.4	99	4.8	74	23.9	237	74.7	8	15	6.4	12	0	2.7
56710	.6	97	.6	81	19.6	211	58.4	5	17	.3	16	0	.0
56712	.4	100	.4	79	32.6	375*	53.0	10	12	.2	13	0	.0
56713	1.5	100	.5	83	21.8	195	61.8	10	11	.8	11	0	.0
56714	1.3	100	.5	89	20.2	141	41.5	10	15	.7	16	0	.0
56715	.6	100	.2	79	20.2	111	37.7	12	10	.3	12	0	.0
56716	10.6	97	3.6	69	24.3	249	72.0	8	14	4.9	11	2	.2
56721	10.3	97	3.5	68	25.7	246	84.7	8	11	4.8	9	1	.1
56722	.6	0	.2	86	25.9	107	58.0	12	10	.3	9	0	.0
56723	1.1	100	.3	83	31.8	292	78.0	9	8	.6	8	0	.0
56724	.3	100	.1	91	15.8	182*	24.5	13	9	.2	10	0	.0
56725	1.4	99	.5	85	17.6	232	45.5	10	11	.8	13	0	.0
56726	.6	0	.6	86	19.9	237	52.9	7	18	.4	9	0	.0
56727	1.0	0	.3	83	16.9	152	58.0	12	10	.6	8	0	.0
56728	2.0	100	.3	79	22.9	214	78.0	11	15	.6	8	0	.0
56729	.2	100	.1	82	19.0	317	25.8	7	21	.2	10	0	.0
56731	.1	100	.1	86	22.8	262*	31.2	8	23	.1	27	0	.0
56732	1.5	0	.5	80	19.0	197	53.4	10	18	.8	9	0	.6
56733	.4	100	.4	80	27.6	159	57.8	10	13	.5	12	0	.0
56734	.6	100	.6	86	17.4	127	42.8	4	18	.3	20	0	.0
56735	1.0	100	.4	84	17.2	172	31.1	8	21	.1	19	0	.0
56736	.9	0	.3	82	18.1	221	70.6	9	13	.5	13	0	.0
56737	1.3	100	.4	89	16.1	221	41.2	8	15	.7	17	0	.0
56738	1.7	100	.6	86	18.9	219	45.4	9	16	.9	15	0	.0
56742	.4	0	.4	81	16.2	172	47.7	9	22	.4	22	0	.0
56744	.8	100	.3	87	22.2	241	59.7	8	16	.4	13	0	10.0

*=Estimated **1.0=883 lbs per person; 100++ indicates per capita toxic waste generation > than 100 times the U.S. average of 883 lbs per capita.

ZIP CODE MEASURES OF SIZE, LEVELS OF AFFLUENCE AND QUALITY OF LIFE

1=Population (th.); 2= % White; 3=Households (th.); 4=% Owner Occupied; 5=Mean Income Per Household (th.$); 6=Mean Monthly Rent ($)*; 7=Mean Home Value (th.$)*;
8=% under 5; 9=% 65 and over; 10=White Males, 65+; 11=% White Males; 12=# Toxic Waste Sites, 13=Toxic Waste Relative to US($883 lbs.per capita)**.

MINNESOTA

ZIPCODE	1	2	3	4	5	6	7	8	9	10	11	12	13
THIEF RIVER FALLS													
56746	.3	100	.1	87	15.1	139	21.9	9	14	.2	17	0	.0
56748	.9	100	.3	81	18.0	109	39.1	9	10	.5	10	0	.0
56750	3.1	100	1.0	79	19.9	209	52.2	8	16	1.6	15	0	.1
56751	4.7	99	1.7	81	21.8	254	70.4	8	16	2.4	16	0	2.9
56754	.8	96	.2	87	21.8	204	49.0	10	9	.4	10	0	.0
56755	.2	100	.2	88	24.1	395	26.4	4	22	.1	25	0	.0
56756	.4	100	.1	93	19.5	225*	67.7	7	15	.2	16	0	.0
56757	1.6	0	.5	85	22.8	172	65.9	7	14	.0	0	0	.0
56758	.7	0	.2	83	15.4	77	36.8	11	19	.0	0	0	.0
56759	.4	100	.1	97	13.0	149*	49.0	8	16	.2	19	0	.0
56760	.5	100	.2	93	27.1	95	42.2	7	10	.3	8	0	.0
56761	.5	100	.2	96	16.1	185*	36.0	8	12	.3	13	0	.0
56762	3.2	0	1.2	78	21.9	178	65.2	8	19	.0	0	0	.0
56763	2.8	97	1.0	75	21.2	297	67.6	10	12	1.4	11	1	.0
SIOUX FALLS													
57060	.2	100	.1	82	30.3	348*	107.8*	5	9	.1	11	0	.0

MISSISSIPPI

ZIPCODE	1	2	3	4	5	6	7	8	9	10	11	12	13
BIRMINGHAM													
35582	1.0	100	.3	89	15.7	168	40.4	7	16	.5	13	0	.0
MOBILE													
36587	.5	100	.2	100	20.1	231*	50.3	4	19	.3	17	0	.0
MERIDIAN													
36907	.2	16	.1	76	12.7	146*	56.9	4	9	.0	0	0	.0
MEMPHIS													
38017	3.0	64	.8	74	22.7	239	68.4	10	6	.9	5	1	.0
38039	.6	7	.1	100	17.3	199*	40.7	12	8	.0	30	0	.0
38057	.5	60	.1	82	17.1	197*	65.5	6	10	.2	12	0	.0
38067	.3	100	.1	87	14.6	320	32.8	4	29	.2	26	0	.0
MEMPHIS													
38601	1.9	0	.6	84	20.2	167	42.2	7	11	.0	0	0	.0
38602	.2	59	.1	57	24.5	245	35.6	12	26	.1	19	0	.0
38603	3.0	77	1.0	85	18.7	194	49.9	9	14	1.2	12	0	.3
38606	12.3	60	3.9	79	19.3	236	59.3	9	13	3.7	14	0	.2
38609	.3	23	.1	26	16.6	137	13.1	5	6	.0	0	0	.0
38610	3.3	76	1.0	76	16.3	187	42.9	7	14	1.2	13	0	.4
38611	8.4	51	2.4	82	18.9	193	48.6	9	10	2.2	7	0	.9
38614	26.8	39	8.9	54	18.3	225	62.8	10	13	5.0	9	3	.9
38617	1.1	16	.3	49	11.9	135	28.6	8	15	.1	24	0	.0
38618	9.2	56	2.8	79	21.0	221	55.6	10	12	2.5	12	0	.0
38619	4.5	0	1.4	62	16.7	182	52.3	9	16	.0	0	0	.0
38620	2.3	49	.7	76	15.9	249	47.8	10	12	.5	14	0	.0
38621	2.0	0	.7	68	15.4	121	34.0	10	15	.0	0	0	.1
38622	.9	62	.3	78	15.4	155	39.5	7	13	.3	12	0	.0
38623	.5	24	.1	70	12.1	181	27.5	8	18	.1	15	0	.0
38625	.8	100	.3	90	15.5	129	45.8	4	12	.4	9	0	.3
38626	1.9	0	.5	46	16.1	149	53.0	12	13	.0	0	0	1.6
38627	1.2	80	.4	81	16.1	119	53.3	9	18	.4	17	0	.0
38628	.3	0	.1	68	10.4	215	35.3	20	13	.3	12	0	.0
38629	1.0	93	.4	86	16.8	225	49.7	4	18	.5	20	0	.0
38630	.4	0	.1	26	8.2	298	28.4	20	4	.0	0	0	.3
38631	1.6	15	.5	61	11.0	131	36.1	14	14	.1	13	0	1.6
38632	9.5	71	3.2	76	23.8	224	75.4	7	12	3.3	9	0	.0
38633	2.2	93	.7	84	19.1	215	48.9	6	14	.9	15	0	.6
38635	13.1	33	3.7	71	17.8	188	61.1	9	12	2.1	10	3	.3
38637	5.9	98	1.7	86	26.9	442	59.4	10	8	2.9	3	0	1.6
38638	.6	82	.1	61	21.2	234	44.2	4	18	.1	17	0	.0
38639	1.6	0	.4	56	13.5	141	48.7	11	15	.0	0	0	.0
38641	1.4	64	.4	57	22.8	249	81.2	7	14	.4	10	0	.6
38642	1.9	28	.5	68	18.4	183	54.6	13	10	.3	15	0	.0
38643	3.4	57	1.2	63	18.2	194	41.7	8	16	1.0	15	0	.0
38644	.6	0	.2	57	15.4	172	40.3	14	13	.0	0	0	.0
38645	2.3	40	.7	63	19.0	299	57.7	9	16	.4	16	0	.0
38646	4.8	43	1.5	70	17.2	191	54.7	11	15	.9	14	1	.0
38647	.8	32	.2	66	19.1	151	43.6	9	12	.1	12	0	.0
38649	.4	74	.2	77	16.5	288	47.0	8	8	.1	0	0	.0
38650	2.9	93	1.0	80	18.5	175	48.7	6	13	1.4	12	0	.0
38651	3.9	57	1.1	79	27.6	218	83.9	8	8	1.0	3	0	.0

*=Estimated **1.0=883 lbs per person; 100++ indicates per capita toxic waste generation > than 100 times the U.S. average of 883 lbs per capita.

ZIP CODE MEASURES OF SIZE, LEVELS OF AFFLUENCE AND QUALITY OF LIFE

1=Population (th.); 2= % White; 3=Households (th.); 4=% Owner Occupied; 5=Mean Income Per Household (th.$); 6=Mean Monthly Rent ($); 7=Mean Home Value (th.$); 8=% under 5; 9=% 65 and over; 10=% White Males (th.); 11=% White Males, 65+; 12=# Toxic Waste Sites; 13=Toxic Waste Relative to US(883 lbs.per capita)**.

MISSISSIPPI

MEMPHIS

ZIPCODE	1	2	3	4	5	6	7	8	9	10	11	12	13
38652	13.6	82	4.8	72	19.2	219	60.5	8	15	5.2	13	4	.7
38654	7.7	74	2.3	80	24.1	267	91.4	7	9	2.8	8	3	1.9
38655	21.2	73	7.9	63	20.7	298	79.3	7	11	7.8	8	1	.2
38658	1.5	77	.5	84	17.7	191	51.9	10	15	.5	12	0	.7
38659	2.6	75	.9	77	17.3	234	56.7	8	12	1.0	12	0	.0
38661	1.3	0	.4	85	17.4	106	58.4	11	9	.0	0	0	.0
38663	9.7	83	3.4	77	17.6	220	47.4	8	16	3.9	14	1	.9
38664	.9	22	.3	25	12.0	166	53.6	9	14	.1	7	0	.9
38665	1.5	77	.6	69	19.9	197	45.1	5	10	.6	10	0	.0
38666	5.9	48	2.0	74	16.9	230	51.9	8	17	1.4	14	0	.9
38668	9.3	64	2.7	63	21.7	262	75.0	7	11	2.9	10	1	.2
38670	2.1	0	.6	66	12.1	217	42.2	10	14	.0	14	0	.0
38671	17.8	95	5.3	84	29.9	377	71.8	7	4	8.3	3	1	.0
38673	.6	37	.1	84	18.6	215	32.7	6	11	.1	5	0	1.8
38674	.9	61	.9	93	17.3	80	47.0	11	17	.3	16	0	.0
38676	6.7	0	2.0	49	15.7	197	59.3	11	12	.0	0	2	.0
38677	4.5	80	.6	16	16.2	201	97.4	8	1	1.9	0	0	.0
38679	.6	45	.2	83	19.8	116	44.1	9	7	.1	2	0	.0
38680	5.5	86	1.7	81	23.7	245	71.1	12	6	2.5	6	0	.0
38683	4.6	97	1.6	79	15.3	173	37.8	9	12	2.2	10	0	.0
38685	1.2	58	.4	78	17.7	200	52.3	9	14	.4	11	0	.0

GREENVILLE

ZIPCODE	1	2	3	4	5	6	7	8	9	10	11	12	13
38701	51.6	47	16.6	62	20.9	267	59.4	10	11	11.7	8	7	.7
38720	2.0	38	.3	42	13.2	159	50.0	9	11	.3	11	0	.0
38721	1.2	33	.6	65	17.2	169	50.4	10	15	.3	18	0	1.9
38722	.3	0	.3	47	10.6	207	26.0	10	11	.5	0	0	.0
38723	.2	67	.1	69	12.9	284	40.8	4	12	.0	15	0	.0
38724	1.7	0	.5	44	20.5	178	31.5	14	11	.3	16	0	.0
38725	.8	33	.3	41	17.7	257	43.4	10	12	.3	16	0	.0
38726	2.0	52	.6	39	12.4	207	33.3	12	8	.5	11	0	.0
38730	.2	0	.1	64	9.2	106*	32.8	16	7	.0	0	0	.0
38732	19.6	53	5.9	63	21.8	250	68.8	9	10	4.9	9	4	2.9
38736	.8	32	.3	38	15.4	141	41.3	4	13	.1	22	1	.0
38737	4.2	0	1.4	66	16.8	203	53.0	9	15	2.4	2	2	.6
38738	2.6	44	.6	39	26.2	79	93.5*	1	1	.4	2	0	.0
38739	.2	40	.1	35	23.8	248	79.5	4	21	.0	0	0	.0
38740	1.5	0	.4	47	14.4	178	59.0	9	17	.0	13	0	.0
38742	.4	0	.1	83	14.4	258	18.6	10	9	.0	0	0	.0
38744	1.8	37	.6	58	15.9	201	40.5	9	11	.3	7	0	.0
38745	.4	42	.4	45	16.5	206	88.9	12	7	.1	0	0	.0
38746	1.5	24	.4	55	16.0	212	36.1	10	10	.0	14	0	.0
38748	6.2	32	1.7	59	16.9	163	43.9	11	12	.9	10	1	.0
38749	.2	43	.1	26	13.2	216	145.2	12	15	.1	22	0	.0
38751	12.9	39	3.9	63	20.4	236	60.4	11	12	2.4	12	0	.6
38753	2.1	45	.6	54	23.3	242	60.9	8	14	.4	14	0	.1
38754	2.3	44	.7	64	19.8	163	51.4	8	11	.5	10	0	.0
38755	.3	21	.1	43	21.4	179	46.6	8	16	.0	0	0	.0
38756	9.1	44	3.0	58	17.0	227	44.5	11	12	2.0	9	1	.8

MISSISSIPPI

GREENVILLE

ZIPCODE	1	2	3	4	5	6	7	8	9	10	11	12	13
38758	.5	14	.1	17	12.6	284	13.1	7	14	.0	11	0	.0
38759	1.7	54	.5	62	17.8	234	48.0	10	12	.5	13	0	.0
38760	1.0	7	.3	69	12.3	227	30.1	14	11	.0	0	0	.0
38761	3.6	24	.9	55	13.5	194	34.9	11	12	.4	10	0	.0
38762	3.8	0	1.0	64	12.7	228	42.8	12	11	.0	0	0	.0
38764	1.0	20	.3	54	14.8	225	36.8	8	16	.1	19	0	.0
38765	.5	0	.1	33	19.7	227*	39.9	13	8	.0	0	0	.0
38767	.4	75	.1	61	19.7	372	90.1	10	3	.1	0	0	.0
38768	.3	0	.1	42	16.1	190	51.4	21	14	.0	0	0	.2
38769	3.5	27	1.0	59	15.3	191	44.5	11	14	.5	15	1	.5
38771	4.6	0	1.4	64	18.3	186	51.3	11	16	.0	0	0	.0
38772	.4	30	.0	0	19.7	148	70.1*	9	5	.1	18	0	.0
38773	4.7	0	1.5	63	14.9	186	41.7	9	14	.0	0	0	.0
38774	3.4	26	1.1	63	14.9	174	38.7	10	19	.4	15	0	.0
38775	.2	57	.1	64	14.3	98	70.8	11	3	.1	0	0	.0
38776	.2	57	.6	32	31.1	357*	109.4	8	10	.0	10	1	.0
38778	2.0	20	.6	49	14.1	176	36.3	13	15	.2	12	0	.0
38781	.3	73	.2	63	31.8	194	57.7	11	11	.1	5	0	.0
38782	.5	0	.2	76	7.4	185	24.5	8	20	.0	0	0	.0
38783	.4	0	.1	40	14.1	214	22.8	2	13	.0	13	0	.2

TUPELO

ZIPCODE	1	2	3	4	5	6	7	8	9	10	11	12	13
38801	33.7	80	12.0	66	23.7	262	80.5	8	11	12.8	8	8	1.2
38821	11.6	83	4.2	77	18.9	206	58.3	7	15	4.5	12	1	.2
38824	3.2	71	3.2	75	17.4	211	49.5	7	15	3.1	13	0	.0
38826	2.4	59	.8	85	22.9	246	82.7	9	12	.7	9	0	.0
38827	2.6	0	.9	81	20.3	209	53.4	7	15	.0	0	0	2.8
38828	3.2	93	1.2	86	17.3	166	38.4	6	15	1.5	12	0	.0
38829	16.6	90	5.8	78	18.7	202	51.3	7	14	7.1	12	0	.0
38833	2.4	100	.9	82	18.6	265	47.2	8	13	1.2	11	0	.2
38834	24.7	91	9.1	72	23.0	251	63.0	7	13	10.9	10	7	1.0
38838	1.5	100	.2	84	17.6	243	44.7	5	14	.7	7	0	.0
38839	.5	79	.5	85	15.7	235	46.1	7	15	.2	16	0	.1
38841	1.5	89	.6	80	16.6	181	48.5	7	19	.7	17	0	.0
38843	10.4	89	3.5	80	19.7	188	57.9	6	13	4.5	12	0	.2
38844	.3	100	.1	79	15.6	169	29.4	6	10	.9	11	0	.0
38846	1.3	100	.6	87	20.2	155	45.3	8	14	.7	11	0	.0
38847	1.8	100	.6	86	17.0	151	41.7	7	15	1.0	8	0	1.6
38848	.9	0	.3	85	17.8	145	40.1	6	21	.0	0	0	.0
38849	2.9	87	1.1	80	17.8	205	45.9	6	15	1.3	11	0	.0
38850	3.4	73	1.2	80	15.9	189	44.1	9	14	1.2	12	0	.1
38851	7.7	70	2.6	74	19.4	206	50.2	8	13	2.5	11	0	.1
38852	9.1	95	3.4	77	20.8	203	55.3	7	13	4.2	12	0	1.1
38855	3.4	98	1.2	88	18.4	242	49.0	6	12	1.7	9	0	.0
38856	1.6	99	.5	86	21.5	131	52.8	6	14	.8	12	0	.0
38857	1.7	100	.5	83	23.4	363	56.3	7	5	.8	8	0	.6
38858	6.5	79	2.1	81	18.3	231	48.9	9	12	2.5	11	0	.1
38859	1.0	100	.3	79	16.9	221	34.1	15	9	.5	11	0	.0
38860	6.6	51	2.1	77	18.3	203	49.5	9	12	1.6	11	0	.1
38862	2.4	65	.7	76	19.2	284	56.3	9	10	.8	10	0	.0

*=Estimated **1.0=883 lbs per person; 100++ indicates per capita toxic waste generation > than 100 times the U.S. average of 883 lbs per capita.

ZIP CODE MEASURES OF SIZE, LEVELS OF AFFLUENCE AND QUALITY OF LIFE

1=Population (th.); 2= % White; 3=Households (th.); 4=% Owner Occupied; 5=Mean Income Per Household (th.$); 6=Mean Monthly Rent ($)*; 7=Mean Home Value (th.$)*;
8=% under 5; 9=% 65 and over; 10=% White Males, 65+; 11=% White Males; 12=# Toxic Waste Sites; 13=Toxic Waste Relative to US(883 lbs.per capita)**.

MISSISSIPPI

TUPELO

ZIPCODE	1	2	3	4	5	6	7	8	9	10	11	12	13
38863	13.8	86	5.0	80	19.8	197	57.2	7	14	5.7	13	0	.3
38864	1.2	0	.4	86	17.9	274	34.7	7	14	.0	0	0	.0
38865	4.7	87	1.5	85	17.4	105	46.4	8	11	2.0	11	0	.0
38866	5.5	93	1.9	75	19.1	228	60.7	8	11	2.6	10	0	.0
38868	5.1	56	1.6	78	18.7	230	57.9	10	11	1.4	10	0	.4
38869	.5	94	.2	64	20.5	272	52.3	11	13	.3	13	0	.0
38870	2.3	92	.8	82	19.4	167	51.0	8	12	.1	12	0	.0
38871	1.3	89	.4	85	17.1	137	39.1	7	13	.6	10	0	.0
38873	2.7	89	1.0	81	18.2	188	43.5	7	16	1.2	17	0	.2
38874	.2	0	.1	86	13.1	294	41.1	8	17	.0	0	0	.0
38876	1.2	97	.4	83	21.3	180	47.3	6	15	.6	15	0	.3
38877	.7	74	.4	84	38.7	164	57.3	18	13	.1	10	0	.0
38878	2.7	77	.9	79	16.8	208	41.8	8	13	1.0	13	0	.0
38879	1.8	69	.6	68	19.6	280	56.1	8	9	.6	7	3	.9
38880	.3	100	.1	85	23.0	218	39.1	2	8	.1	10	0	.0

GRENADA

ZIPCODE	1	2	3	4	5	6	7	8	9	10	11	12	13
38901	18.4	58	6.2	68	20.6	219	60.3	8	12	5.0	10	5	.9
38913	.4	100	.2	76	18.1	198	41.3	8	12	.2	17	0	.0
38914	.7	75	.3	77	13.7	280	41.1	7	22	.3	27	0	.0
38915	4.4	75	1.5	76	16.9	191	50.6	7	13	1.6	13	0	.0
38916	4.7	73	1.6	77	17.8	194	55.1	9	16	1.6	17	0	.0
38917	2.1	76	.7	83	18.2	168	57.0	10	16	.8	17	0	.0
38920	.9	72	.3	67	14.0	99	46.0	7	13	.3	14	0	.0
38921	6.0	46	2.0	72	17.1	208	47.4	8	17	1.3	17	0	.0
38922	3.8	56	1.3	75	16.9	161	52.3	7	14	1.0	13	0	.0
38923	1.5	33	.2	76	13.5	269	38.0	8	11	.3	18	0	.0
38924	1.6	13	.4	47	10.1	164	27.9	13	11	.1	20	0	.0
38925	2.4	57	.9	77	17.6	170	43.2	8	18	.7	23	0	.0
38926	.2	100	.4	81	13.8	159*	69.3	8	8	.1	4	0	2.3
38927	1.1	64	.4	78	12.6	290	32.7	7	17	.3	14	0	.0
38928	.9	21	.3	25	23.0	240	31.3	9	6	.1	2	0	.0
38929	.9	41	.3	71	19.9	95	53.6	8	14	.4	18	0	.2
38930	29.3	49	9.8	51	19.1	236	72.1	10	14	6.7	12	1	.2
38940	2.0	58	.6	72	16.2	150	31.9	8	14	.5	15	0	.0
38941	6.7	16	1.6	53	19.1	210	49.1	8	9	.5	7	0	.0
38943	.4	55	.2	84	18.4	211*	48.3	3	21	.1	12	0	.0
38944	1.6	23	.4	29	15.2	182	70.1	14	10	.2	11	0	.0
38946	.5	49	.1	62	20.6	238	62.1	5	22	.1	19	0	.0
38947	1.1	56	.4	75	17.9	195	48.9	9	18	.3	21	0	.0
38948	1.9	0	.6	80	14.5	158	27.1	9	19	.0	0	0	.0
38949	.3	100	.1	89	18.3	211*	20.4	0	17	.2	14	0	.0
38950	.8	30	.2	59	14.3	106	39.2	10	9	.1	4	0	.0
38951	1.2	61	.4	80	16.7	198	38.4	6	21	.7	28	0	.0
38952	1.3	29	.4	34	12.5	207	36.7	8	11	.2	9	0	.0
38953	.6	78	.2	67	14.3	194	49.2	12	12	.3	19	0	.0
38957	1.7	54	.6	64	18.9	234	43.8	10	13	.5	19	0	.0
38958	.8	49	.3	59	17.8	214	56.5	11	14	.2	12	0	.0
38961	.3	0	.1	14	10.9	193	38.9*	19	8	.0	0	0	.0
38961	.6	57	.2	74	18.3	180	43.4	7	16	.2	8	0	.0

MISSISSIPPI

GRENADA

ZIPCODE	1	2	3	4	5	6	7	8	9	10	11	12	13
38962	.4	32	.1	57	17.4	212	24.9	13	6	.1	0	0	.0
38963	3.2	26	.8	50	11.9	182	38.3	13	11	.4	10	0	.0
38964	.8	15	.2	23	15.0	292	60.9	13	10	.0	28	0	.0
38965	8.6	71	3.1	78	17.3	202	46.9	9	17	2.9	15	0	2.0
38966	1.5	0	.5	59	20.0	175	44.4	9	17	.0	0	0	.0
38967	8.6	62	2.9	72	16.7	207	50.3	8	16	2.5	13	0	.4

JACKSON

ZIPCODE	1	2	3	4	5	6	7	8	9	10	11	12	13
39038	9.2	33	2.9	56	17.2	189	52.7	11	13	1.5	11	2	.0
39039	2.6	53	.8	67	19.2	304	57.5	13	13	.7	11	1	.0
39040	3.0	53	1.0	79	18.2	159	44.4	7	14	.8	13	0	.0
39041	3.7	0	1.1	75	17.4	147	41.3	11	11	.0	5	0	.0
39042	22.9	81	7.1	88	32.3	397	115.5	9	7	9.3	12	0	.4
39044	2.7	68	.8	81	19.9	286	55.3	8	10	.9	12	0	.0
39045	1.4	12	.4	87	11.4	158	34.6	6	16	.1	16	0	.9
39046	21.8	27	6.4	68	18.0	221	54.8	10	13	2.8	13	3	.1
39049	.3	35	.1	87	11.2	204	31.3	11	15	.1	10	0	.0
39050	.7	28	.7	78	28.9	110	47.1	11	12	.1	15	0	.0
39051	13.6	65	4.6	84	16.1	227	50.5	8	15	4.3	15	0	.0
39054	.8	28	.1	44	19.2	185	59.5	11	12	.1	15	0	.0
39055	.4	40	.1	71	13.8	159*	28.8	10	11	.1	11	0	.0
39056	16.6	84	5.2	73	31.7	378	103.0	7	6	6.9	5	3	2.1
39057	1.7	61	.5	87	20.5	183	35.5	9	9	.5	12	0	.0
39059	10.2	52	3.4	79	18.1	161	49.8	9	14	2.6	13	0	.2
39061	.9	2	.3	68	18.7	215*	91.9	10	13	.1	16	0	.6
39062	.6	69	.6	73	16.2	182	43.3	14	12	.2	16	0	.6
39063	3.9	0	1.4	78	14.7	191	43.1	7	17	.1	15	0	1.4
39064	.3	25	.1	67	14.6	117	61.9	12	15	.0	0	0	.0
39066	4.4	0	1.3	76	22.9	181	40.2	8	14	.7	0	0	.0
39067	1.6	74	.5	83	14.6	177	32.4	8	11	.6	18	0	.7
39069	5.1	15	1.5	72	13.9	182	43.2	11	12	.4	21	0	1.6
39071	4.2	21	1.2	75	18.9	204	57.1	11	11	.2	11	0	.0
39073	13.2	84	4.5	85	25.2	276	81.9	8	9	5.4	6	2	.1
39074	12.3	56	4.1	77	17.6	215	49.6	9	13	3.3	13	0	.0
39077	.2	48	.2	79	13.2	126	71.6	8	10	.1	10	1	.8
39078	1.0	51	.3	74	16.4	253	37.7	11	13	.2	6	0	.0
39079	2.2	37	.5	68	13.7	160	36.4	6	13	.4	16	0	.2
39080	.2	47	.1	42	20.5	218	13.1	16	19	.2	16	0	.0
39081	.4	8	.1	77	13.8	196	47.2	11	16	.0	39	0	.0
39082	1.0	62	.4	89	16.2	100	42.9	8	18	.3	14	0	.0
39083	10.0	43	3.3	76	18.9	198	49.4	9	16	2.1	12	1	.8
39086	1.3	27	.5	78	16.1	236	40.7	10	17	.2	11	0	.0
39087	.2	76	.2	94	16.9	194*	34.8	0	19	.1	0	0	1.6
39088	.7	46	.2	45	19.3	212	54.6	20	16	.1	23	0	.1
39090	12.8	63	4.6	74	17.5	172	38.5	8	17	3.8	15	2	.3
39092	2.6	63	.8	90	15.1	172	38.8	9	13	.1	11	0	.8
39093	.2	100	.1	97	29.5	339*	55.1	15	17	.1	13	0	.0
39094	2.9	60	1.0	86	17.5	199	35.3	9	17	.9	18	0	.4
39095	7.8	0	2.6	73	16.3	183	41.9	9	17	.0	0	0	.0
39096	4.0	57	.2	72	15.8	231	46.7	7	11	.0	0	0	.0

*=Estimated **1.0=883 lbs per person; 100++ indicates per capita toxic waste generation > than 100 times the U.S. average of 883 lbs per capita.

ZIP CODE MEASURES OF SIZE, LEVELS OF AFFLUENCE AND QUALITY OF LIFE

1=Population (th.); 2= % White; 3=Households (th.); 4=% Owner Occupied; 5=Mean Income Per Household (th.$); 6=Mean Monthly Rent ($)*; 7=Mean Home Value (th.$)*; 8=% under 5; 9=% 65 and over; 10=White Males (th.); 11=% White Males, 65+; 12=# Toxic Waste Sites; 13=Toxic Waste Relative to US(883 lbs.per capita)**.

MISSISSIPPI

JACKSON

ZIP CODE	1	2	3	4	5	6	7	8	9	10	11	12	13
39097	1.7	0	.5	61	14.9	180	37.1	8	14	.0	0	0	.0
39098	.2	33	.1	76	16.8	454	58.2	14	11	.0	21	0	.0

JACKSON

ZIP CODE	1	2	3	4	5	6	7	8	9	10	11	12	13
39107	.3	51	.1	82	16.4	393	34.6	10	6	.1	14	0	.0
39108	2.6	62	.9	84	14.3	164	35.2	9	18	.8	18	0	.0
39110	5.3	78	1.7	85	36.3	446	117.1	9	9	2.1	6	0	.2
39111	8.4	76	2.7	81	20.2	237	53.4	7	15	3.1	14	0	.0
39113	.5	19	.2	70	18.6	164	39.5	9	14	.1	8	0	.0
39114	9.1	66	2.9	82	18.6	199	50.7	10	11	2.9	10	0	1.4
39115	.5	18	.1	27	14.4	168	17.3	12	8	.1	0	0	.0
39116	2.7	84	.9	80	16.5	198	48.7	9	13	1.1	14	0	.0
39117	8.9	79	3.0	78	19.6	194	46.0	8	12	1.1	10	0	.0
39119	5.2	57	1.7	85	18.1	188	42.0	9	15	3.4	13	1	.0
39120	37.7	50	12.6	71	20.9	236	63.5	11	11	1.4	9	8	.7
39140	2.4	59	.8	77	19.2	193	53.4	10	15	.7	13	1	.0
39144	1.2	20	.3	73	13.7	125	29.3	10	15	.7	13	1	.0
39145	4.6	74	1.4	79	21.2	148	50.8	8	11	1.7	23	0	.2
39146	3.9	20	1.1	72	14.3	167	42.7	11	13	.4	9	0	.0
39149	1.8	47	.5	84	17.0	192	36.3	10	13	.3	10	0	.0
39150	7.0	31	2.3	72	20.3	158	56.7	9	14	1.2	11	1	.5
39151	.1	0	.	84	24.8	285*	67.8	11	12	.0	11	1	.0
39152	1.1	83	.3	79	13.2	202	38.4	11	14	.5	12	0	.7
39153	3.5	81	1.1	87	21.5	197	51.4	7	14	1.4	13	0	.0
39154	5.5	65	1.6	72	21.7	193	72.0	7	11	1.7	6	1	.7
39156	.9	69	.3	71	24.4	254	54.5	8	10	.3	6	1	.7
39157	.8	86	.3	75	25.1	225	77.8	6	9	.3	6	0	.0
39160	4.8	42	1.4	55	17.9	216	62.6	9	11	1.0	14	0	2.1
39161	3.0	34	.9	74	12.3	154	41.9	8	15	.5	18	0	.0
39162	.6	52	.2	46	18.6	211	64.5	6	12	.2	0	0	.0
39163	.4	0	.1	92	14.7	169*	37.9	22	0	.0	0	0	.0
39165	.3	33	.1	81	17.1	137	43.8	9	12	.0	0	0	.2
39166	1.1	17	.3	55	12.8	183	42.9	9	17	.1	16	0	.0
39167	.5	79	.2	90	23.0	208	67.5	5	11	.2	8	0	.0
39168	6.6	52	2.0	82	16.7	188	53.2	8	11	1.7	12	7	.7
39169	3.5	0	1.1	59	13.2	194	42.6	13	13	.0	9	0	.0
39170	5.3	58	1.7	84	22.5	245	71.1	9	11	1.4	10	0	.0
39172	2.0	0	.4	66	24.7	283*	45.0	5	12	.0	0	0	.0
39174	5.1	0	1.5	65	13.6	257	36.5	8	8	.0	0	0	.0
39176	2.2	53	.7	76	18.0	160	42.6	7	15	.9	19	1	.0
39177	.5	0	.2	50	16.6	208	44.5	9	13	.6	14	0	.0
39179	1.5	28	.4	62	21.3	217	68.8	14	9	.0	0	0	.1
39180	50.7	62	17.0	66	25.1	174	48.0	10	13	.2	17	15	.3
39189	3.0	61	1.0	85	15.5	281	71.7	9	11	.3	8	0	.0
39190	.6	75	.2	62	15.5	159	36.4	9	18	.9	19	0	.1
39191	5.9	72	1.8	84	28.3	226	77.8	9	13	.6	13	0	.0
39192	2.4	54	.8	78	20.6	195	32.7	7	14	.2	12	0	.0
39193	2.4	0	.1	26	61.4	705*	56.9	1	24	.0	0	15	.5

MISSISSIPPI

JACKSON

ZIP CODE	1	2	3	4	5	6	7	8	9	10	11	12	13
39194	19.1	49	6.4	62	18.7	210	55.5	9	14	4.5	11	3	3.1

JACKSON

ZIP CODE	1	2	3	4	5	6	7	8	9	10	11	12	13
39201	.9	60	.6	3	15.6	276	223.1	4	25	.2	12	0	34.2
39202	12.4	48	5.4	28	19.9	295	97.3	8	17	2.7	16	1	.0
39203	16.8	8	5.7	29	12.4	265	43.3	11	11	.6	22	1	.0
39204	21.0	68	7.9	57	21.9	297	69.7	8	11	6.7	10	3	.1
39206	24.7	57	9.5	63	29.2	454	86.4	8	9	6.2	11	1	.7
39208	23.4	88	7.8	78	26.2	337	77.6	9	6	9.9	4	6	.7
39209	36.2	48	12.7	63	21.1	325	58.0	10	10	8.0	12	2	.1
39211	24.2	98	9.3	72	48.2	472	152.8	7	7	11.4	7	0	.0
39212	31.7	97	11.0	83	30.5	378	85.5	8	6	15.0	5	0	.1
39213	39.9	12	12.0	63	19.7	270	60.8	10	8	2.3	5	3	.0
39216	4.3	95	2.0	54	42.3	311	139.5	10	28	1.8	22	0	1.4
39218	.2	0	.1	81	14.7	223	48.1	22	6	.0	0	1	4.3

MERIDIAN

ZIP CODE	1	2	3	4	5	6	7	8	9	10	11	12	13
39301	68.9	69	24.1	64	21.6	246	65.7	8	13	22.8	10	11	.2
39320	1.3	78	.5	87	22.6	102	71.8	8	14	.5	13	0	.0
39322	1.6	60	.5	80	20.5	187	39.8	14	10	.6	9	0	.0
39323	1.2	95	.4	83	16.6	223	41.5	8	15	.6	14	0	.0
39324	.3	100	.1	85	15.2	145	48.6	4	4	.1	7	0	.5
39325	3.9	86	1.3	91	22.1	274	53.9	7	12	1.6	9	0	.7
39326	.7	48	.2	75	14.2	235	42.0	8	18	.2	23	0	.7
39327	3.2	75	1.1	82	18.8	205	55.4	6	13	1.3	11	0	.2
39328	4.8	47	1.6	82	16.0	170	48.0	8	16	1.1	18	0	.0
39330	1.9	75	.6	82	19.2	254	48.1	9	18	.7	10	0	.0
39332	1.5	65	.6	83	16.0	158	39.2	6	20	.5	16	0	.0
39335	2.7	45	.8	71	28.9	222	68.5	11	12	.6	14	0	.1
39336	1.4	76	.5	83	20.1	248	42.9	10	9	.5	6	0	.0
39337	1.4	93	.5	85	18.0	315	44.3	8	15	.6	15	0	.0
39338	.6	56	.2	86	15.7	230	39.8	10	16	.6	17	0	.0
39339	15.6	60	5.4	79	18.9	202	56.2	9	15	4.5	14	7	1.4
39341	6.6	41	2.1	74	17.6	185	52.0	10	13	1.3	13	0	.0
39342	.3	0	.1	52	21.2	333	76.8	8	12	.0	0	1	.0
39343	.5	38	.1	89	14.3	148	34.9	5	10	.1	16	0	.0
39345	6.4	54	2.2	81	17.9	164	53.3	8	18	1.6	16	0	.2
39346	2.3	62	.7	85	18.9	143	44.3	6	14	.7	13	0	.0
39347	1.3	0	.4	82	15.6	182	57.6	8	18	.3	16	0	.0
39348	1.1	49	.4	96	14.1	192	31.5	8	17	.3	16	0	.0
39350	19.2	66	6.4	79	19.0	198	54.1	9	13	6.1	13	1	.3
39352	.9	0	.3	85	12.6	115	28.2	7	14	.1	0	0	.0
39353	.3	12	.1	68	15.2	146	32.0	15	9	.1	23	0	.0
39354	1.7	50	.6	79	14.1	161	46.6	8	21	.4	18	0	.0
39355	7.2	75	2.5	84	20.7	224	53.9	9	14	2.6	13	0	.0
39356	.8	55	.3	78	13.2	182	30.4	7	8	.3	20	0	.0
39358	1.7	43	.5	72	18.0	176	37.9	11	10	.3	9	0	.1
39359	.3	86	.1	82	51.6	167	45.2	7	17	.1	12	0	2.3
39360	4.4	0	1.4	83	16.3	157	40.7	9	14	.0	0	0	.2
39361	2.4	40	.8	76	14.3	136	40.7	6	14	.4	13	1	.0
39362	2.8	53	.9	92	17.4	93	50.8	10	14	.7	13	0	.0

*=Estimated **1.0=883 lbs per person; 100++ indicates per capita toxic waste generation > than 100 times the U.S. average of 883 lbs per capita.

ZIP CODE MEASURES OF SIZE, LEVELS OF AFFLUENCE AND QUALITY OF LIFE

1=Population (th.); 2= % White; 3=Households (th.); 4=% Owner Occupied; 5=Mean Income Per Household (th.$); 6=Mean Monthly Rent ($)*; 7=Mean Home Value (th.$)*;
8=% under 5; 9=% 65 and over; 10=% White Males (th.); 11=% White Males, 65+; 12=# Toxic Waste Sites; 13=Toxic Waste Relative to US(883 lbs.per capita)**.

MISSISSIPPI

MERIDIAN

ZIP CODE	1	2	3	4	5	6	7	8	9	10	11	12	13
39363	2.2	78	.7	88	18.5	201	45.0	9	13	.8	10	0	.8
39364	2.1	49	.7	80	18.9	195	68.0	11	9	.5	7	0	.0
39365	7.3	86	2.8	84	15.9	150	49.8	7	20	3.0	17	0	.0
39366	1.7	25	.5	89	14.8	189	32.0	14	14	.2	11	0	.0
39367	13.5	65	4.4	81	18.2	186	52.8	10	11	4.2	9	0	.1

LAUREL

ZIP CODE	1	2	3	4	5	6	7	8	9	10	11	12	13
39401	65.5	72	22.8	65	21.3	272	72.7	8	10	22.5	8	6	2.0
39421	5.7	0	.9	89	17.2	161	44.3	10	12	.0	0	0	.0
39422	5.7	63	1.9	83	19.4	198	60.9	9	13	1.7	11	1	.3
39423	2.4	62	.7	87	17.1	184	35.0	10	8	.8	6	0	.0
39425	1.6	85	.5	84	19.3	218	45.8	4	11	.7	9	0	.2
39426	5.7	95	1.8	87	21.9	317	74.7	7	10	2.7	8	0	.0
39427	1.3	71	.4	86	20.0	212	52.2	9	12	.5	12	0	.0
39428	8.5	67	2.9	84	19.3	183	52.8	9	14	2.8	6	4	.0
39429	17.5	68	5.8	78	20.2	198	60.5	9	13	5.7	10	3	.2
39437	11.0	84	3.5	81	19.3	172	53.8	7	12	4.5	10	1	.0
39439	4.9	0	1.6	81	18.4	192	46.4	8	12	.0	0	0	.3
39440	40.9	74	14.8	73	21.9	221	66.4	8	13	14.5	11	7	.3
39450	1.5	67	.4	95	16.3	125	33.5	11	5	.5	11	0	.0
39451	3.4	85	1.0	86	17.4	152	48.2	9	12	1.4	12	0	.0
39452	15.9	91	5.1	87	20.9	202	56.7	9	11	7.2	9	5	.0
39455	7.0	82	2.3	84	17.7	202	48.3	8	10	2.9	8	1	.6
39456	.9	54	.3	87	13.0	163	39.0	11	16	.2	14	0	.0
39457	1.0	96	.7	98	20.0	230*	62.4	6	12	.5	4	0	.0
39459	2.1	89	.7	85	19.2	240	54.5	6	12	.9	10	0	.0
39460	1.4	74	.4	92	16.0	36	51.4	9	12	.5	5	0	.0
39461	1.4	100	.4	86	16.0	184*	41.1	13	5	.5	2	0	2.0
39462	1.1	88	.4	85	16.6	234	50.4	10	13	.5	11	0	.0
39463	.5	0	.2	82	27.5	248	61.2	6	1	1.0	0	1	.1
39464	2.0	98	.7	86	16.7	193	56.1	8	13	1.0	13	0	2.4
39465	8.2	98	2.9	70	20.3	279	56.4	8	9	3.8	8	0	.7
39466	18.9	81	6.4	77	21.3	244	68.0	9	11	7.6	9	0	2.0
39470	8.6	85	2.8	83	20.9	198	58.7	8	10	3.6	6	4	.0
39474	6.9	0	2.2	87	19.5	209	52.8	8	14	.0	0	1	.1
39475	6.4	91	2.0	89	20.3	226	59.0	8	13	2.8	8	1	2.4
39476	6.4	88	2.0	85	17.8	178	46.6	10	10	2.8	8	0	.0
39477	.9	92	.3	90	22.7	265	45.5	6	10	.4	10	1	6.7
39478	2.3	60	.7	87	19.1	197	37.9	13	11	.7	7	0	.0
39479	3.0	96	1.0	86	17.4	285	62.5	7	8	1.4	7	0	.0
39480	2.6	83	.8	89	24.2	141	59.4	9	13	1.0	12	0	.1
39481	1.3	92	.4	92	19.0	413	55.2	6	10	.6	10	0	.0
39482	5.9	85	2.0	87	17.5	221	46.0	8	12	2.6	11	0	.0
39483	5.1	79	1.7	85	18.3	219	46.7	9	12	2.0	11	0	.0
39484	.2	100	.1	100	17.9	206*	56.0	16	12	.1	20	0	.0

GULFPORT

ZIP CODE	1	2	3	4	5	6	7	8	9	10	11	12	13
39501	51.2	66	17.9	60	22.0	265	69.4	8	11	16.8	10	9	.8
39503	19.0	92	5.7	82	25.6	363	76.6	10	5	8.8	4	3	.6
39520	12.7	87	4.2	76	23.1	283	75.2	8	12	5.6	10	0	.0
39530	18.6	68	7.3	49	17.7	218	55.2	8	15	5.9	14	3	.1

MISSISSIPPI

GULFPORT

ZIP CODE	1	2	3	4	5	6	7	8	9	10	11	12	13
39531	19.8	86	6.9	34	22.2	315	80.4	11	6	8.6	6	0	.0
39532	22.1	94	7.1	80	24.6	327	74.3	9	5	10.2	5	0	.0
39533	.3	76	.1	79	24.3	412	92.3	10	4	.1	3	2	1.6
39550	.4	48	.1	79	14.4	335	29.0	7	8	.1	14	0	.0
39551	.3	100		84	14.5	256	67.9	3	25	.2	27	0	.0
39552	2.0	84	.6	85	22.8	305	53.9	8	8	.8	7	1	1.5
39553	13.4	88	4.2	73	26.7	284	78.5	12	4	5.9	3	1	.0
39555	.3	100	.1	83	18.1	327	34.2	10	14	.1	22	0	.0
39556	.5	90	.2	78	18.7	225	50.0	13	9	.2	6	1	.0
39558	.5	0	.1	89	23.3	339	42.5	9	14	.0	0	0	.0
39560	14.5	96	4.8	74	26.8	350	83.4	8	7	6.8	5	0	.2
39561	.7	83	.5	95	20.7	238*	59.8	11	8	.1	9	0	.0
39563	19.3	36	5.7	77	24.1	252	57.5	10	7	3.5	10	4	3.9
39564	30.9	93	10.0	77	26.9	344	83.6	7	7	14.2	6	3	.0
39567	43.5	86	14.3	68	25.4	261	66.1	9	7	19.1	6	7	7.8
39571	12.0	76	3.9	78	23.1	285	75.5	8	12	4.4	12	0	4.0
39572	1.6	75	.6	90	22.2	161	68.5	8	10	.6	9	0	6.6
39573	3.2	89	.8	86	21.1	197	53.0	9	8	1.5	5	0	.0
39576	3.8	97	1.1	91	22.3	328	65.7	8	6	1.1	9	1	2.7
39577	4.3	90	1.5	78	22.6	273	72.4	7	15	1.8	15	1	.2

MCCOMB

ZIP CODE	1	2	3	4	5	6	7	8	9	10	11	12	13
39601	21.8	68	7.4	74	20.3	241	62.6	9	14	7.2	12	4	.7
39629	4.9	77	1.6	87	19.7	218	47.0	8	11	1.9	11	0	.0
39630	1.0	41	.4	76	13.8	162	31.4	8	19	.2	19	1	1.3
39631	3.3	0	1.1	81	16.6	183	48.7	7	18	.2	2	0	.0
39633	1.4	0	.4	75	16.1	196	40.4	11	10	.0	0	1	.2
39635	.7	59	.2	75	16.9	312	46.5	9	6	.2	4	1	2.3
39638	.5	39	.2	79	15.4	188	42.9	9	15	.8	18	3	.0
39641	3.6	76	2.4	86	21.1	205	48.7	9	11	1.3	10	0	1.0
39643	1.0	83	1.2	81	18.2	188	53.1	9	17	.5	15	0	.0
39645	5.8	57	1.7	83	19.2	168	46.7	9	15	1.5	14	0	.1
39647	.8	93	.3	86	17.2	140	60.6	12	11	.4	11	0	.0
39648	19.6	60	7.0	68	19.2	208	57.7	9	15	5.4	13	2	.0
39652	7.8	45	2.4	79	16.6	187	55.2	10	12	1.7	12	1	1.0
39653	3.1	79	1.2	82	18.0	145	49.7	7	18	1.2	15	0	.0
39654	5.8	73	3.0	84	22.3	239	56.7	8	13	2.1	10	0	1.3
39656	1.1	39	.8	92	17.5	201*	55.0	8	11	.4	12	0	.0
39657	2.8	57	.8	81	16.6	186	60.8	10	13	.7	6	0	.0
39661	2.8	38	.9	82	15.3	136	41.4	7	14	.5	19	1	.0
39662	.9	73	.3	75	17.2	356	56.5	9	11	.3	6	0	.0
39663	3.1	49	1.0	90	21.0	216	48.1	9	14	.8	11	0	.0
39664	1.9	78	.7	85	15.8	114	50.9	7	12	.7	11	0	.0
39665	.9	64	.3	91	19.3	222*	48.3	8	8	.3	8	0	.0
39666	6.6	63	2.2	81	20.4	219	72.8	7	13	2.1	14	0	.1
39667	11.3	55	3.6	81	18.9	211	54.2	9	15	3.0	16	0	.0
39668	1.0	34	.3	89	15.5	137	32.8	7	18	.2	27	0	.0
39669	6.0	26	1.9	69	15.0	198	53.4	7	15	.8	16	1	.0

*=Estimated **1.0=883 lbs per person; 100++ indicates per capita toxic waste generation > than 100 times the U.S. average of 883 lbs per capita.

ZIP CODE MEASURES OF SIZE, LEVELS OF AFFLUENCE AND QUALITY OF LIFE

1=Population (th.); 2= % White; 3=Households (th.); 4=% Owner Occupied; 5=Mean Income Per Household (th.$); 6=Mean Monthly Rent ($)*; 7=Mean Home Value (th.$)*; 8=% under 5; 9=% 65 and over; 10=White Males (th.); 11=% White Males, 65+; 12=# Toxic Waste Sites; 13=Toxic Waste Relative to US(883 lbs.per capita)**.

MISSISSIPPI

COLUMBUS

ZIPCODE	1	2	3	4	5	6	7	8	9	10	11	12	13
39701	50.7	65	16.6	61	21.7	274	75.2	9	9	15.9	6	10	.7
39730	12.1	60	3.9	72	19.2	218	59.1	8	13	3.5	9	2	3.8
39735	4.0	72	1.4	79	17.7	253	47.0	10	17	1.4	17	2	.1
39736	.5	41	.2	71	15.7	179	44.4	11	11	.1	15	0	.0
39737	.5	65	.2	90	21.7	249*	79.5	9	18	.1	23	0	.0
39739	2.8	23	.9	69	13.2	153	37.4	9	16	.3	17	0	.0
39740	3.2	80	1.1	83	19.9	210	59.7	5	12	1.2	12	0	.0
39741	1.7	60	.5	88	21.4	118	48.3	10	12	.5	13	0	.0
39743	2.6	19	.7	79	15.4	135	43.6	11	13	.2	17	0	.0
39744	6.0	77	2.0	76	18.4	197	51.9	7	18	2.2	17	4	1.3
39745	.8	82	.2	78	12.7	252	45.2	9	12	.3	13	0	.7
39746	2.6	79	.9	83	23.3	156	59.9	9	9	1.0	10	1	.0
39747	2.7	0	.9	82	13.5	197	35.6	9	17	.0	0	0	11.3
39750	2.9	73	.9	81	17.1	228	41.6	9	13	1.1	9	0	.3
39751	1.6	69	.5	83	18.6	163	48.7	7	12	.6	19	0	.4
39752	2.3	91	.8	84	15.9	123	45.9	7	15	1.0	12	0	.0
39754	.1	57	.1	92	16.0	184*	57.6	0	20	.0	0	0	.0
39755	1.1	45	.4	72	14.4	111	41.9	10	17	.2	24	0	.0
39756	2.4	25	.7	74	16.3	150	40.4	12	9	.3	6	2	.1
39759	26.8	62	9.3	59	20.1	275	78.9	8	9	8.6	6	0	.1
39766	5.2	82	2.4	51	28.7	260	124.5	1	11	2.4	1	1	.0
39767	1.9	81	.6	88	19.2	248	59.6	8	13	.8	13	0	.0
39769	1.2	93	.4	82	17.7	117	38.0	6	16	.6	15	0	.0
39771	1.8	70	.6	76	14.6	246	45.2	8	17	.6	17	0	.0
39772	2.1	100	.1	96	15.2	175*	55.3	5	17	.1	8	0	.0
39773	16.6	49	.7	79	15.1	182	33.2	10	15	.5	18	0	.0
39776	16.6	51	5.4	71	21.0	230	54.1	9	12	4.0	10	0	.3
	1.8	66	.6	87	18.5	144	48.2	9	14	.6	13	0	.0

MISSOURI

ZIPCODE	1	2	3	4	5	6	7	8	9	10	11	12	13
OMAHA													
51640	.2	100	.1	49	15.4	177*	74.4	7	16	.1	18	0	.0
BURLINGTON													
52626	.2	100	.1	84	26.8	308*	56.9	6	11	.1	13	0	.0
SAINT LOUIS													
63001	.2	100	.1	65	24.8	356	37.0	14	9	.1	15	0	.0
63010	27.0	100	8.5	82	29.6	366	79.6	9	5	13.2	9	0	.0
63011	66.6	97	21.1	81	40.9	511	130.8	8	5	31.9	4	23	.1
63012	6.3	100	2.0	89	29.9	331	86.5	11	5	3.2	3	2	.1
63013	1.4	0	.4	87	26.7	257	72.4	14	7	.0	0	1	.0
63014	.8	96	.3	76	23.8	213	42.7	10	17	.4	18	0	.7
63015	1.3	0	.4	84	25.6	273	73.7	8	8	.3	0	0	.0
63016	4.7	99	1.5	91	26.6	273	77.4	9	8	2.4	8	0	.0
63017	32.7	97	10.1	83	55.1	543	204.7	7	9	15.3	6	9	.1
63018	.1	100	.1	87	21.0	242*	63.9	12	18	.1	25	2	.3
63019	4.0	91	1.5	76	25.2	311	69.7	15	7	1.7	12	1	1.6
63020	15.4	98	5.1	80	24.1	272	61.2	8	12	7.5	10	0	.2
63023	3.4	0	1.1	87	25.8	285	69.8	6	9	3.4	8	6	.0
63025	8.2	99	2.6	83	28.7	300	81.2	10	8	4.1	8	6	.0
63026	27.5	99	9.1	85	29.4	379	88.8	11	5	13.6	15	15	2.5
63028	18.2	98	6.0	80	25.6	332	71.3	9	11	8.6	10	4	.0
63030	.2	100	.1	86	27.5	316*	43.8	21	0	.1	0	0	.0
63031	50.0	96	15.5	85	32.7	426	74.6	8	7	23.7	5	0	.0
63033	47.4	91	15.8	77	36.3	398	97.4	9	7	20.9	6	0	.0
63034	7.2	94	2.1	95	40.6	569	126.4	8	6	3.5	5	2	.0
63036	.3	100	.1	90	22.5	259*	82.3	9	4	.2	4	1	.0
63037	2.5	99	.9	84	22.1	223	60.2	7	15	1.3	15	1	.7
63038	2.6	99	.9	88	40.6	470	179.4	5	11	1.3	10	6	.0
63039	1.2	96	.4	73	28.8	272	68.5	8	8	.6	8	7	.0
63040	.1	100	.1	85	17.0	350	106.4	0	30	.1	23	0	.0
63041	.4	100	.2	92	22.8	262*	86.0	11	18	.2	14	0	.7
63042	21.3	94	7.7	67	30.7	401	77.7	6	5	9.6	5	4	3.7
63043	23.0	96	8.0	71	34.2	482	91.1	6	5	11.0	3	5	3.3
63044	18.1	97	6.2	74	33.3	454	98.7	6	9	8.4	7	4	1.0
63047	.2	100	.7	68	16.8	322	41.2	21	33	.1	19	0	29.1
63048	1.9	97	.7	81	26.1	297	60.2	4	9	.9	7	1	7.7
63049	11.2	99	3.6	84	29.1	342	77.4	10	5	5.7	5	2	.0
63050	9.6	99	3.0	85	26.2	318	77.9	9	8	4.8	4	3	.0
63051	9.4	99	2.9	86	29.4	392	78.9	9	5	4.8	4	5	.0
63052	12.5	100	3.9	85	30.6	377	82.5	10	5	6.2	4	7	.0
63053	.3	100	.1	66	27.6	366	59.5	7	10	.2	10	0	.0
63055	1.4	0	.4	78	35.7	287	90.4	8	4	.2	4	0	.0
63056	1.5	0	.5	84	21.6	180	64.4	4	15	.0	0	2	.0
63060	1.6	100	.5	73	25.5	261	55.7	9	11	.8	10	1	.0
63061	.1	100	.1	66	30.9	356*	109.4	13	0	.1	20	0	.0
63066	.2	100	.2	81	22.9	240	103.7	15	12	.1	20	0	.0
63068	3.6	99	1.3	82	23.9	238	68.3	7	16	1.8	14	0	.0
63069	10.6	99	3.5	73	28.4	292	87.7	9	8	5.2	7	2	.0
63070	5.3	100	1.6	85	27.4	341	68.3	10	4	2.6	4	2	.2
63071	.6	100	.3	78	13.2	153	68.1	7	19	.3	17	3	.1

*=Estimated **1.0=883 lbs per person; 100++ indicates per capita toxic waste generation > than 100 times the U.S. average of 883 lbs per capita.

ZIP CODE MEASURES OF SIZE, LEVELS OF AFFLUENCE AND QUALITY OF LIFE

1=Population (th.); 2= % White; 3=Households (th.); 4=% Owner Occupied; 5=Mean Income Per Household (th.$); 6=Mean Monthly Rent ($)*; 7=Mean Home Value (th.$)*; 8=% under 5; 9=% 65 and over; 10=% White Males (th.); 11=% White Males, 65+; 12=# Toxic Waste Sites; 13=Toxic Waste Relative to US(883 lbs.per capita)**.

MISSOURI

SAINT LOUIS

ZIP CODE	1	2	3	4	5	6	7	8	9	10	11	12	13
63072	2.2	90	.7	87	23.1	315	52.4	6	9	1.0	7	0	.0
63074	18.3	98	7.5	56	25.6	363	59.1	6	9	8.5	8	0	.0
63077	8.1	99	2.9	77	21.4	234	60.0	9	12	3.9	12	2	.2
63079	.2	100	.1	90	17.9	206*	45.3	5	14	.1	13	0	33.1
63080	10.4	100	3.7	77	21.5	258	56.4	8	13	5.0	11	3	.4
63084	10.6	98	3.5	81	26.0	270	69.2	8	12	5.2	9	3	.5
63087	.4	100	.1	86	24.4	375	42.0	7	11	2.0	7	0	.0
63088	4.2	97	1.5	56	23.0	359	56.5	8	13	2.0	10	5	3.9
63089	3.7	98	1.2	86	27.1	255	99.4	10	8	1.7	9	3	.0
63090	14.7	99	5.0	78	28.7	285	83.5	8	13	6.9	11	1	.9
63091	1.0	0	.4	86	23.4	212	45.6	7	16	.0	0	0	.1

SAINT LOUIS

ZIP CODE	1	2	3	4	5	6	7	8	9	10	11	12	13
63101	.8	86	.7	0	12.8	314	45.4*	6	65	.3	61	4	7.4
63102	1.0	84	.8	2	25.1	386	13.1	6	18	.4	19	9	100++
63103	8.4	42	4.1	2	16.2	319	124.1	9	23	1.5	30	6	11.8
63104	23.5	58	8.9	31	17.1	199	63.1	9	13	6.4	12	5	12.3
63105	14.4	96	6.4	44	47.1	487	200.2	4	20	6.1	18	0	.4
63106	18.3	10	6.8	17	11.2	167	23.9	9	16	.9	17	6	2.7
63107	28.8	20	8.8	43	16.4	247	26.9	10	11	2.5	20	4	.0
63108	24.6	46	11.3	21	22.7	287	110.9	7	24	5.0	19	1	2.0
63109	30.9	100	14.4	62	25.6	322	83.7	5	30	13.0	23	0	.0
63110	24.7	67	10.0	38	18.8	263	52.6	8	13	8.0	13	8	5.2
63111	24.7	97	10.7	48	19.5	259	44.8	6	23	10.7	15	9	4.4
63112	35.9	9	12.0	35	18.0	261	61.5	8	12	1.5	14	1	.0
63113	30.2	1	10.9	41	15.5	247	30.3	7	19	1.2	29	0	.0
63114	43.3	92	16.4	72	25.8	379	56.0	7	12	19.2	11	4	.0
63115	36.9	2	12.8	52	19.4	281	38.4	8	12	.3	32	1	1.8
63116	50.2	98	22.0	59	22.4	283	57.4	6	21	22.2	17	3	.5
63117	11.9	84	5.0	62	33.2	350	103.0	5	19	4.4	15	0	.2
63118	36.5	98	15.5	38	18.0	236	39.0	7	18	16.2	13	5	2.6
63119	33.4	88	12.7	79	33.2	419	96.0	6	16	13.8	14	0	.8
63120	20.5	6	6.0	62	26.5	285	31.5	10	6	.5	31	3	6.8
63121	35.7	44	12.7	69	26.5	347	57.3	7	12	7.1	17	2	.0
63122	40.0	93	14.8	81	37.8	451	115.8	6	16	17.4	13	2	.3
63123	54.5	99	20.9	76	31.1	386	84.9	5	14	25.8	12	1	.1
63124	10.5	98	4.0	80	91.2	453	281.4	3	21	4.8	19	2	3.2
63125	37.2	99	13.6	74	27.6	353	74.3	6	13	17.7	10	2	.3
63126	18.0	99	6.4	86	38.3	437	105.8	5	10	8.5	9	1	.7
63127	4.2	97	1.6	83	41.7	467	144.2	5	22	1.9	16	0	.6
63128	26.5	99	8.6	83	41.8	436	131.7	6	18	12.8	13	5	5.3
63129	34.9	98	11.2	77	34.8	391	113.3	7	16	16.9	15	1	.0
63130	38.0	55	13.6	64	29.7	365	91.1	6	12	10.0	14	0	.1
63131	17.9	97	5.6	95	73.7	578	229.3	5	10	8.2	9	5	.1
63132	15.4	66	6.1	67	34.9	413	103.0	6	16	4.6	20	0	9.8
63133	11.7	29	3.8	74	21.1	281	37.4	9	11	1.6	17	3	5.3
63134	23.4	62	7.6	74	26.7	389	52.7	9	7	7.0	8	3	.1
63135	25.0	93	8.8	82	30.8	383	65.0	7	13	11.2	11	0	.1
63136	59.0	60	20.9	74	26.8	375	56.8	7	12	16.6	15	3	.2
63137	22.9	95	8.5	85	29.0	355	64.8	6	15	10.3	14	7	.0

MISSOURI

SAINT LOUIS

ZIP CODE	1	2	3	4	5	6	7	8	9	10	11	12	13
63138	21.7	93	7.9	59	31.6	377	88.3	6	10	9.6	8	1	.0
63139	28.7	98	12.1	63	23.6	290	58.7	5	23	12.4	18	6	.9
63140	4.5	1	1.4	54	14.9	245	35.6	10	14	.0	0	0	.5
63141	47.7	95	17.6	64	48.0	516	168.7	5	9	21.8	8	4	.3
63143	13.1	92	6.1	47	20.2	295	49.5	6	15	5.7	12	3	1.3
63144	9.7	87	4.3	62	28.3	300	85.9	6	17	3.9	15	9	3.9
63147	14.2	50	5.2	69	21.8	258	46.4	7	19	3.2	27	37	6.3

SAINT LOUIS

ZIP CODE	1	2	3	4	5	6	7	8	9	10	11	12	13
63301	80.2	98	26.8	77	31.4	367	89.3	9	6	38.8	5	13	.1
63330	.2	100	.1	97	17.5	201*	31.3	8	18	.1	22	0	.0
63332	1.1	0	.4	81	25.9	253	79.6	7	13	.1	8	0	.0
63333	.9	100	.3	87	17.7	195	26.5	5	16	.4	13	0	.0
63334	5.9	94	2.2	78	22.1	209	57.0	8	17	2.7	14	1	.1
63336	1.4	88	.5	62	31.8	201	47.1	5	14	.6	10	0	.0
63339	1.2	96	.4	84	17.6	307	26.5	12	8	.6	8	2	.0
63341	1.2	97	.1	90	34.0	434	96.4	10	12	.6	12	2	.0
63342	.2	100	.1	79	27.5	338	75.0	25	16	.1	18	0	.0
63343	3.4	97	1.1	79	24.4	227	53.5	5	17	1.6	13	0	.0
63344	1.1	95	.4	79	20.3	179	51.2	10	19	1.5	17	0	.0
63345	.6	0	.2	80	20.2	274	36.9	10	12	.0	1	0	.0
63347	1.4	0	.4	86	19.9	270	53.9	9	12	.0	11	0	.0
63348	2.2	98	.7	83	35.5	218	87.1	7	9	1.1	8	0	.0
63349	1.1	98	.4	79	22.7	267	45.6	11	15	.6	11	0	.0
63350	.4	100	.4	67	22.2	269	39.7	4	24	.6	28	0	.2
63351	1.4	98	.5	83	23.7	289	55.8	8	17	.7	15	0	.0
63352	1.6	0	.6	78	23.6	197	39.9	8	12	.0	15	0	.0
63353	5.7	95	2.1	71	23.2	231	53.2	7	19	2.5	15	2	6.0
63357	2.9	0	.9	79	29.8	231	90.2	8	12	.0	7	0	.0
63359	1.3	97	.5	87	18.6	224	31.2	8	23	.7	25	0	.0
63361	3.6	96	1.4	82	21.8	218	56.1	7	18	1.6	17	1	.0
63362	1.8	97	.6	81	20.3	267	51.9	8	13	.8	11	1	.0
63363	1.7	98	.6	74	21.2	233	44.4	8	16	.8	12	0	.0
63364	.1	98	.1	87	26.0	298*	63.9	17	14	.0	0	0	.0
63366	18.8	99	5.8	84	29.9	374	77.7	8	6	9.1	4	5	.2
63367	4.1	97	1.3	78	45.4	399	167.3	6	4	2.0	3	0	.1
63369	1.6	0	.5	85	27.2	395	71.3	10	16	.0	7	0	.0
63373	1.2	100	.4	80	41.0	219	68.6	10	8	.4	6	0	.2
63376	25.5	98	7.4	89	34.3	430	93.7	12	3	12.6	3	3	13.8
63377	1.8	98	.6	83	21.2	271	48.0	8	15	.9	15	0	.0
63379	7.2	95	2.5	84	25.8	269	68.6	8	15	3.3	13	2	.1
63381	.4	0	.1	96	19.2	220*	30.5	14	15	.0	1	0	.0
63382	4.6	93	1.8	77	22.8	220	47.3	7	18	2.0	15	1	.0
63383	7.1	99	2.6	80	24.7	289	76.6	7	17	3.4	14	0	2.4
63384	2.3	94	.9	77	19.0	206	37.2	7	20	3.8	9	16	.1
63385	8.3	94	2.6	81	26.2	297	77.4	8	15	3.3	13	2	.0
63386	1.3	0	.5	92	26.2	297	56.4	6	15	.0	0	1	.0
63387	.2	0	.1	72	15.4	206	19.4	2	26	.0	0	0	.0
63388	.6	0	.2	80	20.8	206*	76.1	13	14	.0	0	0	.0
63389	2.9	95	1.0	81	24.1	261	55.6	7	12	1.5	9	0	.0

*=Estimated **1.0=883 lbs per person; 100++ indicates per capita toxic waste generation > than 100 times the U.S. average of 883 lbs per capita.

ZIP CODE MEASURES OF SIZE, LEVELS OF AFFLUENCE AND QUALITY OF LIFE

1=Population (th.); 2= % White; 3=Households (th.); 4=% Owner Occupied; 5=Mean Income Per Household (th.$); 6=Mean Monthly Rent ($); 7=Mean Home Value (th.$); 8=% under 5; 9=% 65 and over; 10=White Males, 65+; 11=% White Males; 12=# Toxic Waste Sites; 13=Toxic Waste Relative to US(883 lbs.per capita)**.

MISSOURI

ZIPCODE	1	2	3	4	5	6	7	8	9	10	11	12	13
SAINT LOUIS													
63390	3.8	88	1.3	83	23.6	232	65.1	7	14	1.6	16	3	1.1
HANNIBAL													
63401	21.9	94	8.3	70	22.2	240	52.6	8	17	9.7	14	1	.1
63430	.9	0	.3	81	23.3	191	43.2	6	13	.0	.0	0	.0
63431	.3	100	.1	58	26.9	203	95.7*	17	14	.2	19	0	.0
63432	.8	100	.2	79	20.2	155	45.5	11	12	.4	13	0	.0
63433	.2	100	.1	60	11.2	129*	19.1	0	18	.1	12	0	.0
63434	.4	0	.2	77	20.8	98	25.2	4	12	.0	0	0	.0
63435	3.8	97	1.4	68	20.9	232	57.6	6	16	1.8	14	0	.0
63436	1.3	100	.5	78	22.5	218	48.0	7	18	.7	17	0	.0
63437	2.1	98	.8	79	16.1	175	35.2	7	24	.9	23	0	.2
63438	.5	100	.2	94	20.8	302	39.0	8	15	.3	10	0	.0
63439	.2	100	.2	75	15.5	113	31.6	6	27	.1	30	0	.0
63440	1.3	0	.5	83	18.4	214	37.7	9	13	.0	.0	0	.2
63441	1.3	95	.4	84	21.3	138	31.6	9	11	.4	10	0	.0
63443	.6	99	.2	74	15.8	182	24.3	8	17	.3	22	0	.0
63445	4.2	100	1.6	76	20.6	244	50.8	9	19	.2	16	0	.0
63446	.8	100	.3	87	18.1	155	24.0	5	18	.3	16	0	.0
63447	1.3	93	.5	77	17.9	190	31.9	6	23	.6	18	0	.0
63448	1.8	92	.7	83	21.5	183	49.6	7	15	.8	15	1	.2
63450	.4	100	.1	48	30.4	96	63.8	7	20	.2	18	0	.0
63451	.4	100	.1	69	22.0	239	41.6	6	24	.2	24	0	.0
63452	1.4	99	.5	73	19.5	195	50.2	8	17	.7	16	0	.0
63453	.4	100	.1	83	19.5	248	45.5	6	9	.2	7	0	.0
63454	.9	0	.3	88	22.2	263	62.2	13	8	.8	15	0	.2
63456	3.9	94	1.4	78	22.1	229	58.0	9	16	1.8	15	0	.0
63457	.2	100	.1	89	28.3	266	30.8	3	14	.9	16	0	.0
63458	.2	100	.1	89	20.6	236*	27.3	3	30	.1	32	0	.2
63459	3.3	95	1.2	83	23.9	285	58.6	9	14	1.5	13	0	.0
63460	.5	100	.2	91	18.8	212	33.2	7	23	.3	21	0	.0
63461	5.4	96	2.0	71	23.3	242	62.2	7	19	2.6	16	1	7.4
63462	1.6	0	.6	77	20.2	196	49.2	5	25	.0	0	0	.0
63463	.6	100	.2	86	16.5	497	47.1	8	11	.3	11	0	.0
63465	.6	0	.2	85	19.2	246	40.8	4	20	.0	0	0	.0
63468	3.3	99	1.3	78	19.6	185	34.2	10	16	1.6	19	1	.0
63469	1.5	100	.6	77	19.6	250	66.7	11	7	.7	12	0	.0
63471	.8	0	.3	84	21.5	174	43.8	7	21	.0	0	1	.0
63472	.6	0	.3	79	20.2	124	32.3	9	13	.2	10	0	.1
63473	.4	100	.2	77	18.0	200	22.4	7	18	.4	15	0	.0
63474	.7	100	.3	73						.3		0	.0
KIRKSVILLE													
63501	20.7	97	7.6	61	21.2	271	68.5	6	13	9.3	10	2	.4
63530	1.2	100	.4	86	21.1	146	31.3	5	18	.6	14	0	.0
63531	.8	100	.2	74	16.6	188	27.4	7	16	.4	13	0	.0
63532	1.5	0	.6	92	18.4	212	33.7	8	17	.3	21	0	.0
63533	.8	98	.3	83	22.7	159	33.6	5	18	.3	20	0	.0
63534	.9	99	.4	82	18.7	178	35.7	4	22	.4	18	0	.0
63536	.9	0	.4	84	15.1	189	32.2	6	24	.2	10	0	.0
63537	2.5	99	.9	80	21.0	187	57.6	7	24	1.1	18	0	.0

MISSOURI

ZIPCODE	1	2	3	4	5	6	7	8	9	10	11	12	13
KIRKSVILLE													
63538	.5	100	.2	89	23.5	288	18.9	6	20	.3	23	0	.0
63539	.3	100	.1	81	18.3	185	18.9	2	21	.2	13	0	.0
63540	.5	100	.1	91	36.4	419*	16.1	4	23	.1	24	0	.0
63541	.2	100	.2	86	18.4	127	32.4	5	22	.0	25	0	.0
63543	.5	0	.2	77	17.6	167	18.7	12	20	.0	.0	0	.0
63544	1.0	100	.4	84	16.2	85	22.1	7	22	.5	18	0	.0
63545	1.3	100	.5	82	17.3	206	34.9	6	23	.6	19	0	.0
63546	1.4	100	.5	73	18.2	220	52.6	7	14	.7	14	0	.0
63547	.6	100	.2	81	17.2	96	24.0	8	18	.3	14	0	.0
63548	1.5	100	.6	73	20.3	217	53.4	6	21	.7	16	0	.1
63549	2.5	0	1.0	76	19.0	197	50.1	5	25	.0	0	0	.3
63551	.5	0	.2	89	15.3	162	25.1	7	22	.0	0	1	.0
63552	7.8	96	3.1	78	21.7	222	56.7	7	20	3.5	17	0	.2
63555	3.4	0	1.4	76	20.2	211	47.1	5	24	.0	.0	0	.0
63556	3.7	99	1.4	78	17.7	220	43.1	7	22	1.8	20	0	.1
63557	.4	100	.1	91	15.5	122	18.0	3	5	.2	5	0	.3
63558	1.1	100	.4	83	21.6	215	38.8	10	18	.6	16	0	.0
63559	1.6	0	.5	81	19.5	176	39.4	8	12	.0	0	0	.0
63560	.3	0	.1	89	14.4	165*	27.3	6	27	.0	0	0	.0
63561	1.5	100	.6	86	18.2	108	31.1	7	20	.7	15	0	.0
63563	.6	0	.2	70	16.4	252	14.0	7	20	.0	0	0	.0
63565	4.4	100	1.7	79	18.4	208	49.5	6	23	2.0	19	0	.0
63567	.2	100	.1	78	19.2	236	26.8	1	23	.1	23	0	.0
FLAT RIVER													
63601	12.3	100	4.6	75	19.5	260	40.6	8	15	5.9	12	1	.0
63620	1.5	100	.5	79	17.5	181	34.7	7	17	.7	16	3	.0
63621	1.4	99	.5	72	17.1	177	55.1	6	19	.7	18	0	.2
63622	.9	100	.3	77	17.2	196	40.7	6	11	.4	10	0	.0
63623	1.0	98	.3	85	17.9	95	42.9	5	21	.5	18	0	.0
63624	3.1	100	1.1	80	18.3	214	36.9	7	15	1.5	12	1	.0
63625	.6	100	.3	86	18.6	153	47.9	8	12	.3	16	0	.0
63626	.3	100	.1	78	17.1	269	69.4	9	11	.1	13	0	.0
63627	2.0	98	.7	88	23.5	219	73.3	8	14	1.0	13	0	.0
63628	9.2	100	3.2	82	23.0	231	59.9	7	14	4.5	13	1	.3
63629	1.9	0	.6	79	19.0	224	40.5	8	11	.5	9	0	.2
63630	2.9	98	.8	86	20.4	216	40.9	8	12	1.5	13	1	.0
63631	.8	100	.2	86	20.5	216	44.9	12	11	.4	10	0	.1
63633	.7	0	.3	87	15.0	140	37.5	5	15	.0	0	0	.0
63636	.6	0	.3	80	15.4	256	29.6	4	24	.0	0	0	.0
63637	1.0	100	.3	75	19.4	247	32.0	10	15	.5	9	0	.0
63638	3.0	100	1.1	76	16.4	215	46.3	9	15	1.4	13	0	.0
63640	15.7	98	5.5	81	21.4	251	60.7	7	18	7.3	16	1	.1
63644	.4	100	.4	77	23.8	213	28.5	17	4	.4	2	5	.0
63645	9.3	99	3.5	80	17.5	217	45.2	7	18	4.4	16	2	.0
63648	1.4	0	.5	80	18.6	223	33.9	9	13	.0	.0	0	.0
63650	4.2	99	1.4	79	20.0	239	56.0	8	19	1.9	14	1	.0
63653	1.4	100	.5	84	20.0	269	29.6	8	15	.7	11	0	.0
63654	.8	100	.3	79	17.5	232	46.7	5	13	.4	13	0	.0

*=Estimated **1.0=883 lbs per person; 100++ indicates per capita toxic waste generation > than 100 times the U.S. average of 883 lbs per capita.

ZIP CODE MEASURES OF SIZE, LEVELS OF AFFLUENCE AND QUALITY OF LIFE

1=Population (th.); 2= % White; 3=Households (th.); 4=% Owner Occupied; 5=Mean Income Per Household (th.$); 6=Mean Monthly Rent ($)*; 7=Mean Home Value (th.$)*; 8=% under 5; 9=% 65 and over; 10=White Males, 65+; 11=% White Males; 12=# Toxic Waste Sites; 13=Toxic Waste Relative to US(883 lbs.per capita)**.

MISSOURI

FLAT RIVER

ZIPCODE	1	2	3	4	5	6	7	8	9	10	11	12	13
63655	1.5	100	.6	75	15.7	186	29.8	5	23	.7	20	0	.0
63656	.5	100	.2	77	14.4	215	36.4	9	17	.2	16	0	.0
63660	3.0	99	.4	86	16.8	152	37.3	10	11	1.4	11	0	.1
63662	.9	100	.4	92	14.3	165*	45.7	5	25	.5	23	0	.1
63663	.8	97	.3	71	18.0	277	37.3	9	13	.4	11	1	.1
63664	6.8	99	2.4	74	18.6	225	51.9	9	12	3.3	10	2	.6
63665	.4	100	.1	78	17.8	207	83.1	8	10	.2	11	0	.0
63670	9.7	100	3.2	83	25.1	292	74.1	8	13	4.7	11	0	.0
63673	2.1	99	.7	87	23.9	223	48.0	8	11	1.1	10	0	.0
63675	.2	100	.1	86	16.1	185*	41.6	13	8	.1	0	0	.0
63676	.4	100	.1	78	21.2	155	47.8	11	4	.2	3	0	.0

CAPE GIRARDEAU

ZIPCODE	1	2	3	4	5	6	7	8	9	10	11	12	13
63701	38.8	94	14.0	65	24.7	300	81.4	6	12	17.2	10	3	.6
63730	3.0	100	1.1	84	20.8	199	52.1	7	13	1.5	13	0	.1
63732	.7	100	.3	86	20.8	174	43.4	4	22	.4	22	0	.1
63735	1.1	87	.4	70	15.0	115	28.2	3	20	.4	23	0	.0
63736	2.7	78	.9	73	18.7	218	55.2	9	10	1.1	9	0	.0
63738	.3	100	.1	81	12.1	139*	21.7	6	22	.1	32	0	.0
63739	.3	100	.1	78	20.6	289	35.5	11	10	.2	7	0	.0
63740	5.1	0	2.0	76	19.0	203	46.5	8	15	.0	0	0	.0
63742	.2	0	.1	86	20.3	275	38.4	10	12	.0	0	0	.0
63743	.1	100	.1	87	12.7	145*	32.2	0	32	.0	35	0	.0
63744	.6	100	.2	81	18.6	217	36.6	9	12	.3	11	0	.0
63747	.4	100	.1	94	17.4	199*	39.4	10	21	.2	21	0	.1
63748	.9	100	.1	93	24.0	113	59.8	9	12	.4	12	0	.0
63750	.1	100	.1	74	9.7	293	13.1	3	13	.1	9	0	.0
63751	.8	0	.3	83	17.9	199	48.2	4	15	.4	14	0	.0
63752	.9	0	.3	88	17.0	260*	56.0	4	15	.4	14	0	.0
63753	.2	100	.1	94	25.4	96	51.2	7	14	.0	0	0	.0
63754	2.6	100	.9	83	22.9	210	52.7	7	12	1.3	9	0	.0
63755	13.2	99	4.7	81	24.4	257	76.4	7	14	6.4	12	0	.3
63758	.2	100	.1	91	23.4	367	60.7	6	13	.2	11	0	.1
63762	2.9	100	1.1	92	18.1	216	61.9	10	12	1.5	15	1	.1
63763	.2	100	.1	83	14.9	167	40.6	8	16	.0	15	0	.0
63764	1.6	0	.6	79	11.9	98	91.9	13	17	.0	15	0	.0
63766	.9	100	.3	94	17.6	199	48.2	4	15	.4	14	0	.0
63767	1.0	0	.3	88	17.0	200	41.9	8	19	.4	14	0	.0
63769	1.0	0	.3	94	19.1	219*	37.8	8	16	.4	22	0	.1
63770	.2	100	.1	100	21.1	243*	64.1	13	12	.0	16	0	.0
63771	2.5	93	.9	76	19.4	168	43.4	8	12	1.2	12	0	.0
63772	.2	100	.1	73	20.6	237*	44.4	12	13	.1	5	0	.0
63775	14.1	100	4.9	81	20.0	253	62.9	9	17	6.9	15	1	.1
63780	3.3	100	1.1	81	23.4	272	56.9	7	10	1.6	9	0	.0
63781	1.0	0	.1	81	19.2	243	49.8	11	16	.0	0	0	.0
63782	.3	100	.3	72	16.4	152	26.8	12	25	.2	32	0	.0
63784	.4	95	.2	76	18.8	141	36.2	9	12	.2	9	0	.0
63785	.8	100	.3	87	29.2	106	62.2	9	8	.5	7	0	.0
63787	.9	100	.3	78	13.6	117	30.3	6	16	.5	14	0	.0

MISSOURI

SIKESTON

ZIPCODE	1	2	3	4	5	6	7	8	9	10	11	12	13
63801	23.4	90	8.2	66	22.5	253	68.0	9	12	9.8	10	2	.1
63820	.3	100	.1	80	15.8	183	24.0	9	16	.2	13	0	.0
63821	.3	98	.5	62	14.8	176	26.5	7	17	.6	15	0	.0
63822	3.3	98	1.2	75	16.7	188	44.1	7	15	1.6	11	0	.0
63823	1.1	100	.4	78	18.5	205	51.0	6	20	.5	16	0	.0
63824	.1	100	.1	83	16.1	185*	38.9	9	26	.0	20	0	.0
63825	4.0	100	1.5	79	16.8	170	42.3	6	18	1.9	15	0	.0
63826	.2	100	.1	78	15.0	173*	31.8	6	16	.1	10	0	.0
63827	1.3	72	.7	53	17.7	146	36.6	6	13	.5	18	0	.0
63828	.2	100	.2	78	13.3	122	26.2	6	19	.1	19	0	.0
63829	1.5	99	.6	69	15.5	191	31.4	6	21	.7	18	0	.0
63830	9.3	75	3.4	57	18.1	214	45.1	9	15	3.3	12	1	.5
63833	.4	55	.1	48	13.0	91	35.0	8	14	.1	27	0	.0
63834	7.6	69	2.6	62	19.9	190	54.3	9	16	2.5	14	0	.0
63837	1.7	97	.6	72	15.7	189	36.0	8	14	.8	12	0	.0
63839	.5	0	.2	62	18.0	227	36.9	7	17	.0	0	0	.1
63841	11.4	99	4.4	75	19.9	229	59.1	7	16	5.2	14	0	1.3
63845	6.4	95	2.2	68	18.3	186	41.7	9	13	2.9	12	0	.0
63846	2.0	91	.7	74	19.1	209	39.8	7	12	.9	11	0	.1
63847	.1	100	.1	78	14.4	176	30.6	6	41	.1	38	0	.0
63848	2.0	100	.8	55	16.1	189	37.1	7	14	.9	16	0	.0
63849	.3	80	.1	65	16.8	215	34.4	16	10	.1	4	0	.0
63850	.1	100	.1	61	17.8	123	38.1	9	22	.1	16	0	.0
63851	6.0	59	2.1	57	14.4	195	34.9	10	17	1.7	14	1	.1
63852	1.6	100	.6	66	20.7	194	43.5	8	12	.8	10	0	.0
63853	.4	0	.1	63	16.5	223	34.5	7	16	.0	0	0	.0
63855	1.4	96	.5	69	15.7	142	39.1	8	18	.7	18	0	.0
63857	13.3	93	5.1	63	19.1	221	53.4	8	14	5.8	12	0	.0
63860	.3	0	.1	87	26.7	307*	35.3	7	8	.0	0	0	.0
63862	2.6	73	.9	71	17.0	186	39.5	10	13	.9	13	0	.0
63863	8.1	86	2.9	70	16.9	210	50.4	8	14	3.3	14	0	.3
63866	.9	86	.3	70	17.5	154	32.4	11	12	.4	9	0	.1
63867	1.3	93	.5	68	20.3	217	52.4	6	13	.6	13	0	.0
63868	1.2	100	.5	79	15.9	206	30.1	7	18	.6	18	0	.0
63869	4.1	68	1.5	62	19.5	190	57.4	10	12	1.3	9	0	.0
63870	1.9	81	.6	62	17.1	184	35.0	7	15	.7	16	0	.0
63871	.3	78	.3	50	14.0	245	22.2	7	9	.1	6	0	.0
63873	6.1	83	2.2	61	18.2	218	51.0	9	13	2.4	14	0	.0
63874	.5	100	.2	75	19.0	271	32.8	11	14	.3	10	0	.0
63876	2.6	0	1.0	68	17.0	186	42.3	5	23	.0	0	0	.0
63877	4.9	79	1.7	59	17.4	205	44.5	9	16	1.9	14	0	.0
63878	.2	100	.1	57	8.7	153	20.9	11	20	.1	18	0	.0
63879	1.3	71	.5	59	12.9	167	28.9	10	16	.4	12	0	.0
63882	.7	58	.3	75	15.3	209	33.1	6	20	.3	15	0	.0

POPLAR BLUFF

ZIPCODE	1	2	3	4	5	6	7	8	9	10	11	12	13
63901	28.9	95	10.9	69	19.2	227	56.6	7	15	12.7	13	0	.0
63931	.2	100	.1	87	14.1	162*	50.2*	7	12	.1	11	0	.0
63932	1.5	82	.5	88	17.1	286	30.0	6	14	.6	15	0	.0
63933	4.4	100	1.6	74	15.0	195	41.1	7	18	2.1	15	1	.0

*=Estimated **1.0=883 lbs per person; 100++ indicates per capita toxic waste generation > than 100 times the U.S. average of 883 lbs per capita.

ZIP CODE MEASURES OF SIZE, LEVELS OF AFFLUENCE AND QUALITY OF LIFE

1=Population (th.); 2= % White; 3=Households (th.); 4=% Owner Occupied; 5=Mean Income Per Household (th.$); 6=Mean Monthly Rent ($); 7=Mean Home Value (th.$); 8=% under 5; 9=% 65 and over; 10=White Males (th.); 11=% White Males, 65+; 12=# Toxic Waste Sites; 13=Toxic Waste Relative to US(883 lbs.per capita)**.

MISSOURI

POPLAR BLUFF

ZIP CODE	1	2	3	4	5	6	7	8	9	10	11	12	13
63934	.6	0	.2	74	11.3	178	28.3	7	24	.0	0	0	.0
63935	8.4	99	3.1	81	14.1	210	46.6	8	20	4.0	19	0	.1
63936	.8	100	.3	88	22.0	126	39.2	1	13	.4	13	0	.0
63937	2.2	0	.7	81	14.6	139	35.4	8	12	.0	0	0	.0
63939	1.0	100	.3	86	15.7	154	36.7	3	11	.5	13	0	.0
63940	1.7	100	.6	75	15.9	224	39.4	7	17	.9	18	0	.0
63941	.5	100	.2	76	12.9	198	30.1	7	16	.3	20	0	.0
63942	.5	100	.2	76	13.8	71	16.5	11	24	.3	28	0	.0
63943	.9	95	.3	84	16.1	204	25.1	8	16	.4	15	0	.0
63944	.9	99	.4	80	13.7	183	38.7	1	25	.5	21	0	.3
63947	1.0	92	.4	82	12.5	235	38.3	7	13	.5	10	0	.0
63951	.2	100	.1	83	20.2	150	22.6	9	18	.1	12	0	1.5
63952	.3	100	.1	70	14.9	308	57.1	2	6	.2	4	0	.0
63953	.5	100	.2	61	13.3	214	23.8	9	25	.2	26	0	.1
63954	1.6	99	.6	80	14.1	174	34.3	6	22	.7	21	0	.4
63955	1.7	84	.6	66	11.5	149	34.0	10	15	.7	9	0	.0
63956	.4	100	.1	83	10.7	143	28.0	15	8	.2	4	0	.0
63957	1.0	100	.4	81	17.1	205	37.8	5	21	.5	23	0	.0
63959	.2	100	.1	76	26.6	306*	26.4	10	8	.1	6	0	.0
63960	2.9	95	.9	80	16.1	182	38.7	6	18	1.4	16	0	.0
63961	1.8	100	.7	79	12.4	140	31.6	4	18	.9	18	0	.0
63963	2.0	100	.7	100	7.9	91*	23.0	3	4	.9	10	0	.0
63964	.5	90	.2	59	16.1	224	20.3	2	11	.2	7	0	.0
63965	2.4	0	.9	72	18.1	202	47.0	7	15	.0	0	0	.0
63966	1.0	100	.4	83	16.5	190	53.6	11	15	.5	16	0	.2
63967	.8	100	.6	80	15.1	178	35.5	5	21	.0	0	0	.0

KANSAS CITY

ZIP CODE	1	2	3	4	5	6	7	8	9	10	11	12	13
64001	.7	100	.3	77	26.4	274	54.4	8	17	.4	14	0	.0
64011	2.4	97	.8	82	24.7	264	69.0	8	17	.0	0	0	.1
64015	15.2	97	5.2	73	28.8	323	81.1	9	6	7.3	5	0	.0
64016	29.5	97	9.5	79	34.6	424	101.0	10	4	14.3	4	0	.0
64017	3.9	99	1.3	79	26.3	233	64.6	9	8	1.9	8	0	.7
64018	.5	100	.2	87	24.0	226	44.4	8	12	.3	13	0	.6
64019	1.5	100	.5	89	26.1	215	60.6	6	17	.3	17	0	.0
64020	3.4	99	1.3	79	22.8	334	48.6	8	8	.2	14	0	1.0
64021	.8	100	.3	73	22.7	230	59.8	7	25	.4	16	0	.2
64022	.2	100	.1	79	21.5	362	34.7	6	14	.1	9	0	.0
64024	14.8	97	5.2	80	22.8	396	34.2	7	12	1.1	15	0	.1
64028	2.4	100	.8	73	25.2	226	70.5	9	11	6.9	8	0	.0
64029	3.2	99	1.1	88	30.1	328	78.9	2	16	1.6	6	0	.0
64030	25.3	90	8.9	85	30.6	373	82.9	10	7	11.2	6	4	.0
64034	2.6	100	.9	87	30.0	335	67.0	9	4	5.1	13	2	.0
64035	1.1	97	.4	80	36.8	365	45.0	6	7	.6	5	0	.0
64036	.5	93	.2	74	21.3	296	29.6	7	22	.3	19	0	1.0
64037	6.1	94	2.4	72	18.4	285	63.4	9	18	.2	14	0	.0
64040	4.7	99	1.7	82	22.9	267	59.8	6	20	2.7	16	0	.2
64048	3.2	99	.9	90	22.3	235	50.3	9	17	2.3	13	0	.0

MISSOURI

KANSAS CITY

ZIP CODE	1	2	3	4	5	6	7	8	9	10	11	12	13
64050	25.3	97	10.2	57	22.7	262	55.8	7	15	11.5	11	1	3.0
64052	24.2	98	10.2	73	26.9	339	65.2	7	16	11.1	14	1	1.0
64053	7.1	99	2.8	65	20.9	316	38.3	9	14	3.4	10	1	.0
64054	4.6	99	4.6	62	24.2	271	55.0	8	12	2.3	11	3	.0
64055	32.1	98	11.6	80	33.1	391	84.3	6	11	15.3	7	0	.0
64056	15.1	97	4.8	70	30.3	350	73.5	7	11	4.7	3	1	.0
64057	7.4	98	2.4	78	31.5	335	94.0	10	6	3.6	5	0	.0
64058	5.2	97	1.6	85	32.8	482	73.0	9	7	2.6	4	0	.0
64060	3.9	99	1.3	81	40.1	348	116.8	8	7	2.0	5	0	.0
64061	1.9	100	.6	91	26.2	235	47.4	7	10	.9	8	0	.3
64062	4.6	100	1.4	90	29.4	241	68.1	9	14	2.3	7	1	.0
64063	32.1	98	12.4	64	31.4	373	108.6	7	14	14.7	10	1	1.5
64067	6.4	94	2.4	71	22.9	239	60.4	7	17	2.9	13	0	.1
64068	20.9	97	7.0	72	32.2	338	95.6	7	8	9.9	6	2	.4
64070	1.7	100	.5	85	33.9	268	78.9	9	5	.9	6	0	.0
64071	.8	95	.2	85	20.9	209	40.7	6	16	.3	14	0	.0
64072	.3	0	.1	77	22.4	300	36.5	9	8	.0	7	1	.0
64073	.3	100	.1	77	17.3	297	30.7	5	10	.0	7	0	.0
64074	.6	97	.2	82	26.3	348	30.9	7	13	.3	14	0	.0
64075	6.4	99	2.1	80	26.9	277	69.7	9	10	3.0	7	1	.0
64076	5.9	98	2.1	85	26.7	245	66.8	7	13	2.9	11	0	.2
64077	2.0	0	.7	83	23.8	265	49.5	9	13	.0	0	0	.0
64078	.3	99	.1	81	29.9	340	95.3	8	8	.1	7	0	.0
64079	4.3	99	1.5	70	30.5	339	78.4	5	9	2.1	8	1	.1
64080	6.3	99	2.3	77	26.3	250	60.3	8	13	2.2	8	1	.1
64083	4.4	99	1.4	91	34.2	386	113.9	8	10	2.2	12	0	.1
64084	1.6	99	.5	89	25.7	384	67.7	5	4	.8	4	0	.0
64085	8.1	95	3.1	76	23.5	244	57.8	7	18	3.7	14	0	.0
64088	1.1	100	.4	86	30.1	311	62.8	6	7	.5	7	0	.0
64089	3.5	99	1.3	73	28.6	248	80.7	6	16	1.7	13	0	.1
64090	.2	0	.1	90	22.2	255*	25.1	7	11	.0	0	0	.7
64091	.3	0	.1	92	29.5	339*	65.6	8	6	.0	0	0	.6
64092	.2	100	.1	100	47.7	548*	72.9	3	19	.1	17	0	.0
64093	19.2	93	5.9	59	22.3	264	78.4	5	9	8.7	7	1	.1
64096	1.3	100	.5	74	21.9	203	53.7	7	21	.6	18	0	.0
64097	.5	98	.5	77	25.6	343	54.9	6	12	.7	10	0	.0
64098	2.6	98	.9	71	25.9	276	79.0	8	14	1.2	12	0	.1

KANSAS CITY

ZIP CODE	1	2	3	4	5	6	7	8	9	10	11	12	13
64105	1.9	89	1.5	1	12.9	198	46.1*	0	36	.9	33	2	7.1
64106	9.0	45	3.9	9	14.1	210	29.2	8	19	2.0	19	3	4.0
64108	8.9	43	3.2	32	18.0	207	27.6	10	13	2.0	9	6	6.4
64109	19.0	28	8.0	32	16.2	183	42.0	8	15	2.6	17	0	.1
64110	22.5	47	8.6	49	22.3	295	51.6	8	10	5.1	13	0	.2
64111	22.2	86	8.6	67	18.4	271	67.4	4	18	8.9	13	1	.2
64112	10.4	96	6.8	22	26.5	385	135.5	5	31	3.9	18	0	.0
64113	12.9	99	4.9	90	51.3	569	149.9	9	16	6.0	13	0	.0
64114	25.3	98	10.9	75	31.9	468	93.1	5	22	11.5	18	0	.1
64116	14.0	97	6.3	50	28.5	356	87.4	5	13	6.2	11	4	.2
64117	13.9	98	5.0	66	27.5	354	69.0	8	7	6.5	6	0	.0

*=Estimated **1.0=883 lbs per person; 100++ indicates per capita toxic waste generation > than 100 times the U.S. average of 883 lbs per capita.

ZIP CODE MEASURES OF SIZE, LEVELS OF AFFLUENCE AND QUALITY OF LIFE

• 1=Population (th.); 2= % White; 3=Households (th.); 4=% Owner Occupied; 5=Mean Income Per Household (th.$); 6=Mean Monthly Rent ($)*; 7=Mean Home Value (th.$)*;
8=% under 5; 9=% 65 and over; 10=White Males (th.); 11=% White Males, 65+; 12=# Toxic Waste Sites; 13=Toxic Waste Relative to US(883 lbs.per capita)**.

MISSOURI — KANSAS CITY

ZIPCODE	1	2	3	4	5	6	7	8	9	10	11	12	13
64118	33.6	97	12.7	68	32.1	406	92.6	7	6	16.0	6	1	.0
64119	23.6	98	8.1	76	33.5	443	86.9	7	6	11.5	5	2	3.1
64120	.8	95	.4	64	20.2	244	19.3	6	23	.4	14	7	100++
64123	10.4	97	4.3	65	20.8	275	42.6	8	17	4.6	13	0	.0
64124	14.3	90	5.9	49	18.3	215	34.3	8	18	5.8	15	0	.0
64125	2.6	93	1.0	65	19.6	265	28.1	8	16	2.7	12	1	35.9*
64126	7.2	80	2.8	64	20.6	297	29.7	9	13	2.7	14	4	6.7
64127	25.2	47	9.8	53	16.0	210	25.7	9	16	5.5	13	3	.4
64128	20.2	12	6.9	63	19.6	258	30.2	8	13	1.2	16	0	.0
64129	11.7	79	4.6	65	24.8	347	58.8	8	9	4.5	8	6	6.3
64130	35.5	8	11.3	72	21.6	316	34.7	8	9	1.2	33	1	.2
64131	23.6	80	9.7	60	28.4	394	82.4	7	17	8.5	16	1	.5
64132	18.9	37	7.6	66	23.0	363	40.1	9	8	3.2	14	2	.6
64133	33.5	95	12.9	77	31.7	394	85.6	6	11	15.2	10	5	.0
64134	24.4	89	8.1	82	31.2	478	71.7	8	5	10.8	5	0	.0
64136	.9	100	.3	70	26.2	349	64.3	9	7	.5	7	0	.0
64137	10.9	93	3.7	69	34.1	447	86.0	7	5	5.0	4	0	5.2
64138	26.3	94	9.4	76	33.3	416	84.1	6	8	12.1	7	0	.0
64139	3.6	96	1.4	64	35.5	294	132.0	5	8	1.9	7	1	.1
64146	2.9	94	.8	92	53.0	226	173.7	5	11	1.2	8	0	.2
64147	1.2	100	.5	86	33.9	230	96.5	5	10	.7	10	0	.0
64149	.5	78	.2	7	11.4	212	40.7*	8	18	.1	18	0	.0
64150	.4	0	.1	66	41.5	638	109.9	8	6	.0	0	0	.2
64151	1.5	96	.6	33	26.5	329	106.9	8	13	.7	9	0	.0
64152	14.0	96	5.1	66	34.6	339	111.0	8	5	6.7	5	1	.4
64153	16.8	96	5.7	73	36.3	405	115.1	8	4	8.1	3	2	.4
64154	1.0	99	.2	61	32.7	500	93.8	11	8	.3	9	0	1.2
64155	6.8	98	2.3	82	36.7	584	98.2	7	3	3.3	5	0	.0
64156	.8	0	.3	79	35.5	416	99.2	9	3	.3	3	0	.0
64157	.5	100	.3	89	27.3	398	101.9	6	9	.6	7	0	.0
64161	.5	0	.2	84	32.3	383	62.9	9	5	.3	7	3	.0
64163	.6	95	.3	40	24.6	350	57.7	8	14	.3	6	0	.4
64164	.2	100	.1	73	23.6	231	54.3	6	5	.3	6	0	.0
64165	1.5	96	.6	57	35.4	641	111.8	6	4	.1	0	0	.0
64...	.2	100	.1	57	20.0	207	54.6	12	0	.1	0	0	.0

SAINT JOSEPH

ZIPCODE	1	2	3	4	5	6	7	8	9	10	11	12	13
64401	1.4	99	.4	85	32.5	344	82.2	11	8	.7	7	0	.0
64402	2.9	100	1.2	76	18.5	199	50.2	7	23	1.3	17	0	.3
64421	.7	100	.2	83	24.7	336	58.7	8	11	.4	9	1	.0
64422	.4	0	.2	76	17.2	184	33.3	7	12	.0	0	0	.0
64423	1.0	100	.4	75	20.8	183	36.6	8	17	.5	17	0	.0
64424	4.3	99	1.9	70	19.8	207	45.3	6	24	2.0	19	0	.2
64425	.3	0	.1	70	19.4	75	38.7	16	6	.3	6	0	.0
64426	.5	95	.2	78	16.7	287	24.9	8	18	.0	0	0	.0
64427	.8	0	.3	82	18.9	185	22.3	6	19	.6	18	0	.0
64428	1.2	100	.5	79	19.7	176	34.3	7	21	.6	18	0	.0
64429	6.7	99	2.6	75	22.3	235	60.9	8	18	3.2	16	0	.0
64430	.7	100	.3	84	20.7	223	38.6	7	18	.4	20	0	.0
64431	.6	100	.2	70	17.3	147	33.9	11	18	.1	16	0	.0

MISSOURI — SAINT JOSEPH

ZIPCODE	1	2	3	4	5	6	7	8	9	10	11	12	13
64434	.6	100	.2	77	21.0	174	37.6	9	10	.3	13	0	.0
64436	.7	100	.2	83	26.0	351	49.4	8	15	.4	15	0	.0
64437	.7	0	.3	78	14.4	141	28.7	6	31	.0	0	0	.0
64438	.4	0	.1	85	14.4	251	20.1	10	17	.0	0	0	.0
64439	1.7	98	.6	81	25.2	172	59.5	9	15	.8	12	0	.0
64440	.6	99	.6	82	23.9	386	40.4	8	15	.3	23	0	.0
64441	.3	100	.1	80	14.4	164	44.4	5	28	.1	31	0	.0
64442	.8	0	.3	80	20.0	208	42.0	8	15	.0	0	0	.0
64443	1.2	100	.4	78	32.4	269	53.8	7	12	.6	12	0	.0
64444	1.2	0	.4	76	22.3	227	69.7	11	9	.0	0	0	.0
64445	.4	0	.1	76	17.9	180	26.8	5	23	.0	0	0	.0
64446	1.6	0	.7	70	20.4	223	45.4	6	18	.0	0	0	.0
64448	1.1	100	.3	81	28.1	277	61.6	9	16	.6	6	0	.0
64449	.6	100	.2	80	18.5	248	27.9	15	18	.3	13	0	.0
64451	.6	0	.3	85	24.1	204	43.8	3	21	.0	0	0	3.1
64452	.2	100	.1	100	19.9	229*	41.9	10	15	.1	8	0	.0
64453	.3	0	.1	84	15.7	131	18.9	4	22	.0	0	0	.0
64454	2.3	100	.8	79	25.7	265	75.6	7	14	1.2	11	0	.0
64455	.6	100	.2	77	16.5	146	23.6	6	25	.3	26	0	.1
64456	1.9	0	.8	76	17.9	195	36.6	6	26	.2	13	0	.0
64457	.4	100	.1	83	16.5	184	18.4	7	13	.2	13	0	.0
64458	.3	100	.1	83	20.6	186	41.7	6	12	.1	12	0	.0
64459	.7	95	.2	83	22.8	294	54.3	11	20	.3	18	0	.0
64461	.7	100	.5	81	16.3	196	44.6	9	21	.3	26	0	.2
64463	.8	100	.1	78	19.2	228	48.4	6	24	.9	21	0	.0
64464	.1	100	.1	100	13.5	155*	48.0*	0	14	.1	11	0	.0
64465	2.9	98	1.0	83	25.9	284	66.3	7	12	1.4	11	0	.0
64466	.8	0	.3	69	19.0	139	29.3	8	21	.0	0	0	.1
64467	.8	100	.3	90	16.7	163	17.1	5	23	.1	25	0	.0
64468	12.3	98	4.1	60	23.6	268	78.2	7	13	5.9	10	1	.2
64469	2.2	0	.8	76	20.0	223	48.7	7	21	.2	13	0	.1
64470	2.1	99	.8	74	18.9	199	49.0	6	24	1.0	19	0	.0
64471	.7	100	.3	82	15.3	236	27.1	7	27	.3	26	0	.2
64473	1.8	99	.7	80	18.5	220	46.0	8	24	.8	22	0	.0
64474	.8	100	.8	79	23.7	247	41.5	7	15	.4	13	0	.0
64475	.6	99	.7	77	17.2	93	19.2	9	15	.3	14	0	.0
64476	.5	0	.6	80	18.5	214	34.2	8	13	.0	0	0	.0
64477	2.9	91	1.0	77	23.6	231	70.0	7	17	1.2	13	0	.1
64478	.3	98	.1	67	21.3	204	24.7	6	10	.2	10	0	.0
64479	.9	99	.3	80	19.5	203	42.0	7	18	.5	17	0	.0
64480	.4	100	.1	79	18.9	158	20.1	7	17	.2	19	0	.0
64481	1.2	100	.5	81	15.5	239	35.3	6	22	.6	20	0	.0
64482	2.8	99	1.1	65	21.6	245	58.2	5	23	1.3	19	0	.2
64484	1.7	100	.6	82	22.9	357	53.8	10	10	.9	8	0	.0
64485	6.2	100	2.2	79	23.0	244	63.1	8	17	2.9	14	0	.0
64486	.6	100	.2	80	14.4	168	21.3	7	21	.3	17	0	.1
64487	1.0	100	.4	74	18.0	148	27.6	9	23	.5	20	0	.0
64489	2.4	100	.9	82	18.6	204	43.7	11	18	1.2	19	0	.0

*=Estimated **1.0=883 lbs per person, 100++ indicates per capita toxic waste generation > than 100 times the U.S. average of 883 lbs per capita.

ZIP CODE MEASURES OF SIZE, LEVELS OF AFFLUENCE AND QUALITY OF LIFE

1=Population (th.); 2= % White; 3=Households (th.); 4=% Owner Occupied; 5=Mean Income Per Household (th.$); 6=Mean Monthly Rent ($)*; 7=Mean Home Value (th.$); 8=% under 5; 9=% 65 and over; 10=White Males (th.); 11=% White Males, 65+; 12=# Toxic Waste Sites; 13=Toxic Waste Relative to US(883 lbs.per capita)**.

MISSOURI

SAINT JOSEPH

ZIPCODE	1	2	3	4	5	6	7	8	9	10	11	12	13
64490	2.1	99	.7	79	19.8	252	49.7	7	14	1.1	13	0	.0
64491	3.0	98	1.1	66	21.7	249	58.1	6	18	1.4	15	0	.0
64492	.7	0	.3	78	21.7	248	67.7	3	17	.0	0	0	.0
64493	.5	100	.2	70	22.8	368	50.3	5	16	.3	14	0	.0
64494	.9	0	.4	84	20.6	176	40.8	5	16	.1	0	0	.0
64496	.3	100	.1	66	18.9	314	48.7	19	12	.1	7	0	.0
64497	.5	0	.2	87	18.4	176	32.1	7	20	.0	0	0	.0
64498	.5	0	.2	70	25.9	280	33.9	11	17	.0	0	0	.0
64499	.3	100	.1	98	15.8	182*	14.9	8	20	.1	24	0	.0

SAINT JOSEPH

ZIPCODE	1	2	3	4	5	6	7	8	9	10	11	12	13
64501	15.6	89	6.5	46	17.0	199	42.8	7	19	6.2	15	4	2.9
64503	14.7	98	5.1	77	23.2	254	54.4	9	10	7.0	8	0	.6
64504	12.3	97	4.5	79	20.8	260	42.2	7	14	5.9	12	4	5.6
64505	12.5	99	4.6	75	23.3	271	57.9	7	15	5.9	13	3	.0
64506	15.8	96	5.9	67	31.9	324	105.2	7	16	7.1	12	1	.0
64507	13.2	97	5.1	73	22.1	278	53.5	6	18	5.8	15	2	.0

CHILLICOTHE

ZIPCODE	1	2	3	4	5	6	7	8	9	10	11	12	13
64601	12.3	98	4.8	72	23.6	245	65.7	7	18	5.6	15	0	.7
64620	.4	0	.2	90	16.4	99	37.9	9	17	.0	0	0	.0
64622	.7	100	.3	78	19.4	160	33.2	8	15	.3	12	0	.0
64623	.8	100	.3	84	18.4	187	24.8	8	22	.4	21	0	.0
64625	1.9	0	.8	82	19.5	199	41.6	7	23	.0	0	1	.0
64626	.9	0	.4	80	16.0	195	27.5	7	23	.0	0	0	.0
64628	6.6	99	2.8	84	14.4	232	22.9	7	18	.3	16	0	.0
64630	1.0	99	.4	78	20.9	231	46.7	7	23	3.0	19	0	.2
64631	1.3	99	.4	83	18.1	205	26.8	6	20	.0	0	0	.0
64632	1.0	99	.5	87	19.2	180	41.8	7	19	.7	17	0	.0
64633	6.5	96	2.6	70	21.4	196	61.5	7	20	2.9	16	0	.1
64635	.7	100	.3	83	22.9	134	30.8	6	16	.4	17	0	.0
64636	.3	100	.1	78	14.2	204	19.2	4	18	.2	13	0	.0
64637	.8	0	.3	88	19.5	140	32.6	7	18	.0	0	0	.0
64638	.7	100	.3	75	22.7	125	27.5	8	17	.3	16	0	.0
64639	.3	0	.1	86	28.7	282	32.0	13	22	.3	16	0	.0
64640	3.2	100	1.3	75	21.1	222	55.2	6	24	1.5	19	0	.0
64641	.8	100	.4	80	16.1	114	26.1	5	20	.4	16	0	.0
64642	.9	0	.4	76	32.4	260	28.6	9	23	.0	0	0	.0
64643	1.3	0	.5	78	17.9	192	35.8	9	20	.0	0	0	.0
64644	2.6	96	1.0	78	19.6	216	44.3	7	23	2.9	16	0	.1
64645	.4	100	.2	85	20.1	90	17.1	4	19	.2	20	0	.0
64646	.4	0	.1	80	15.9	35	31.8	9	16	.0	0	0	.0
64647	.5	0	.2	81	18.1	157	32.6	9	18	.0	0	0	.0
64648	2.2	0	.7	79	18.0	228	36.0	11	14	.0	0	0	.0
64649	.7	100	.2	91	22.3	235	38.1	6	16	.4	14	1	.0
64650	.6	100	.2	77	20.1	184	34.2	10	16	.3	16	0	.0
64651	.7	0	.3	84	16.7	141	31.0	6	24	.0	0	0	.0
64652	.7	100	.2	76	18.7	195	24.9	8	15	.3	14	0	.0
64653	.9	0	.3	80	18.5	179	31.7	6	18	.0	0	0	.0
64655	.4	100	.1	80	17.4	200*	31.2	9	17	.2	19	0	.0

MISSOURI

CHILLICOTHE

ZIPCODE	1	2	3	4	5	6	7	8	9	10	11	12	13
64656	.4	100	.2	75	18.3	177	23.0	4	30	.2	23	0	.0
64657	.5	0	.2	83	15.7	233	18.8	4	25	.0	0	0	.0
64658	4.1	99	1.6	79	21.3	201	51.6	8	23	1.8	19	0	.1
64659	.9	99	.4	79	20.6	201	53.3	5	25	.4	24	0	.0
64660	.6	100	.2	81	24.4	225	35.2	5	23	.3	20	0	.0
64661	1.2	0	.5	76	16.2	193	37.5	6	19	.1	7	0	.0
64664	.4	100	.1	88	22.4	244	35.4	10	12	.2	16	0	.0
64665	.2	0	.1	90	12.5	144*	21.3	3	29	.0	0	0	.0
64667	.5	100	.2	75	21.7	76	30.0	6	18	.3	17	0	.0
64668	2.1	96	.8	72	21.7	194	47.0	8	20	1.0	18	1	.0
64670	1.3	0	.5	81	17.5	135	26.4	6	25	.0	0	0	.0
64671	1.5	0	.5	87	20.4	202	45.6	6	17	.0	0	0	.0
64672	.4	0	.1	75	14.6	167*	25.8	6	16	.2	18	0	.0
64673	2.8	100	1.2	79	17.3	184	42.0	6	27	1.3	23	0	.0
64674	.6	0	.3	85	17.9	128	22.0	8	20	.1	12	0	.0
64676	.3	100	.1	81	22.5	258*	32.2	11	14	.1	12	0	.0
64677	.4	0	.4	93	20.7	75	71.5	6	16	.0	0	0	.0
64679	1.0	0	.4	78	19.2	148	26.3	9	18	.0	0	0	.0
64681	.4	100	.2	70	19.2	238	25.3	7	20	.2	18	0	.0
64682	.4	100	.2	89	18.5	272	33.4	7	18	.2	17	0	.0
64683	9.3	99	3.8	74	19.1	226	55.4	6	21	4.3	16	1	.9
64686	.4	0	.1	77	20.9	197	43.3	10	18	.0	0	1	.0
64688	.7	0	.2	69	22.3	195	31.0	9	13	.0	0	0	.0
64689	.6	0	.2	77	21.6	250	41.8	6	10	.2	13	0	.1

HARRISONVILLE

ZIPCODE	1	2	3	4	5	6	7	8	9	10	11	12	13
64701	9.8	99	3.5	71	26.9	288	74.6	7	12	4.8	9	1	.1
64720	2.9	100	1.1	79	21.4	240	47.2	8	16	1.4	13	0	.0
64722	.6	98	.3	79	18.9	166	30.8	7	17	.3	17	0	.0
64723	.7	100	.3	79	22.5	191	49.0	10	17	.4	19	1	.0
64724	2.1	99	.8	76	20.2	214	47.8	6	26	1.0	22	0	.0
64725	1.8	98	.6	78	25.6	192	55.6	11	11	.9	10	0	.0
64726	.4	98	.1	85	22.7	150	29.5	5	18	.2	15	0	.0
64728	.5	100	.2	79	23.4	156	43.6	10	13	.2	13	0	.0
64730	6.8	98	2.7	72	21.5	247	57.3	7	22	3.2	19	1	.1
64733	1.2	0	.5	89	21.4	184	42.5	7	20	.0	0	0	.0
64734	1.4	99	.4	94	33.2	240	47.2	8	16	.7	9	1	.0
64735	11.2	98	4.4	71	21.9	271	91.6	7	10	5.3	13	1	1.6
64738	.8	96	.3	83	14.8	260	64.7	7	21	.3	17	0	.0
64739	.9	98	.4	84	23.3	211	30.7	2	19	.5	20	0	.0
64740	.4	100	.5	78	17.2	144	42.6	3	19	.0	0	0	.0
64741	.4	0	.1	76	23.5	154	29.6	8	15	.0	0	0	.0
64742	1.8	100	.7	74	25.3	189	42.3	7	14	.9	14	0	.0
64743	2.2	0	.3	75	22.3	240	55.6	6	16	.9	14	0	.0
64744	.7	100	.3	78	18.0	222	39.9	12	7	.3	7	0	.0
64745	.6	0	.2	87	14.9	187	48.0	7	23	3.7	20	0	.1
64746	.7	100	.4	89	25.0	171*	21.0	4	25	.0	0	0	.0
64747	.7	100	.8	76	22.6	354	51.0	8	9	.5	11	0	.0
64748	.9	99	.3	78	18.4	268	51.7	7	11	1.1	10	0	.0
64750	.4	100	.1	90	17.2	198	37.4	9	15	1.0	18	0	.0

*=Estimated **1.0=883 lbs per person; 100++ indicates per capita toxic waste generation > than 100 times the U.S. average of 883 lbs per capita.

ZIP CODE MEASURES OF SIZE, LEVELS OF AFFLUENCE AND QUALITY OF LIFE

1=Population (th.); 2= % White; 3=Households (th.); 4=% Owner Occupied; 5=Mean Income Per Household (th.$); 6=Mean Monthly Rent ($)*; 7=Mean Home Value (th.$)*; 8=% under 5; 9=% 65 and over; 10=% White Males (th.); 11=% White Males, 65+; 12=# Toxic Waste Sites; 13=Toxic Waste Relative to US(883 lbs.per capita)**.

MISSOURI

HARRISONVILLE

ZIP CODE	1	2	3	4	5	6	7	8	9	10	11	12	13
64751	.3	100	.1	77	17.2	151	58.2	6	26	.2	39	0	.0
64752	.7	100	.3	78	16.8	204	25.9	6	23	.4	25	0	.0
64753	.4	100	.2	87	20.8	249	32.1	6	14	.2	15	0	.0
64754	.3	100	.1	82	17.8	244	45.6	10	14	.2	15	0	.3
64755	2.3	99	.9	73	20.6	168	47.5	5	19	1.1	18	1	.0
64756	.6	0	.3	88	18.2	147	33.5	6	22	.0	0	0	.0
64759	6.3	99	2.4	74	18.5	245	52.9	7	21	2.9	18	2	.0
64760	.3	82	.1	83	16.1	283	16.6	13	8	.1	10	0	.1
64761	1.3	100	.5	86	20.6	194	45.0	6	17	.6	17	0	.4
64762	1.6	99	.6	82	18.4	159	35.0	7	22	.7	20	0	.0
64763	1.3	0	.5	75	15.3	218	44.4	6	27	.0	0	0	.0
64767	.4	91	.2	84	22.6	258	32.5	8	14	.0	0	0	.0
64770	1.3	0	.5	80	14.1	213	18.2	8	24	.2	23	0	.0
64771	.5	0	.2	77	22.2	209	44.9	7	17	.0	0	0	.0
64772	12.6	99	4.8	83	20.2	299	32.5	10	15	5.6	14	1	.2
64776	3.1	100	1.2	70	21.2	231	55.5	7	18	1.6	21	0	.0
64778	.4	0	.2	76	16.4	171	51.4	5	22	.0	0	0	.0
64779	2.6	100	1.1	79	21.1	242*	35.2	10	12	1.3	20	0	.0
64780	.8	99	.3	77	16.0	218	24.0	10	16	.4	14	0	.0
64781	.1	100	.1	76	31.3	158	41.1	3	62	.0	74	0	.0
64783	.8	0	.3	72	15.9	180	29.4	7	19	.0	0	0	.0
64784	1.4	0	.6	75	19.2	168	40.9	7	19	.0	0	1	.0
64788	1.3	99	.5	81	20.5	251	37.5	5	25	.6	15	0	.0
64790	1.0	0	.4	79	20.1	203	36.8	10	14	.0	0	0	.0

JOPLIN

ZIP CODE	1	2	3	4	5	6	7	8	9	10	11	12	13
64801	54.5	97	21.5	69	21.3	250	59.6	7	14	24.8	11	14	3.5
64830	.5	98	.2	86	18.2	225	33.2	12	14	.3	12	0	.0
64831	4.1	99	1.5	77	18.0	152	48.8	7	17	2.0	16	0	4.9
64832	.5	0	.2	83	19.1	185	33.6	6	16	.0	1	0	.0
64833	.5	100	.2	83	15.4	186	28.6	10	9	.1	12	0	.3
64834	5.0	99	1.6	87	21.4	273	54.0	8	8	2.5	7	0	.5
64835	1.9	99	.7	80	16.5	232	31.8	10	13	.9	10	0	.1
64836	17.8	97	6.7	75	22.2	224	58.0	8	17	8.2	14	5	.7
64840	1.9	99	.7	85	21.0	226	56.1	5	13	.9	12	0	.1
64841	.6	100	.2	80	19.4	215	34.5	7	16	.3	12	0	.0
64842	.7	100	.3	86	16.0	119	38.8	5	25	.4	23	0	.0
64843	2.6	98	1.0	82	17.5	179	41.9	8	14	.7	14	0	.0
64844	3.6	99	1.3	79	16.6	253	38.3	7	14	1.8	12	1	.0
64846	.7	0	.2	90	18.2	158	58.8	5	11	.0	0	0	.0
64847	.4	0	.2	66	9.9	235	29.5	8	22	.2	17	0	.0
64848	.7	100	.2	78	17.6	203*	31.4	11	7	.4	7	0	.0
64849	.2	0	.1	76	18.1	145	26.1	9	14	.0	0	0	.0
64850	16.9	97	6.3	74	20.3	210	61.6	7	15	7.8	13	3	.4
64853	.5	100	.2	84	15.9	203	40.8	8	18	.0	17	0	.0
64854	2.4	98	.9	66	16.7	174	52.2	8	13	1.2	11	0	.1
64855	1.5	100	.5	87	16.8	306	33.5	7	13	.7	12	0	.0
64856	1.3	98	.4	78	18.4	165	43.4	9	16	.6	13	0	.0
64857	.3	100	.1	84	19.1	212	26.0	5	11	.1	8	0	.0

MISSOURI

JOPLIN

ZIP CODE	1	2	3	4	5	6	7	8	9	10	11	12	13
64859	1.0	100	.3	87	21.3	266	41.9	6	9	.6	7	0	.0
64861	1.0	100	.4	96	16.1	59	37.5	4	23	.5	21	0	.0
64862	2.8	100	1.1	80	19.5	198	44.0	7	18	1.4	15	0	.0
64863	1.2	95	.4	72	16.1	209	33.0	8	16	.5	16	0	.3
64864	.2	100	.2	64	18.5	206	47.1	6	13	.1	13	0	.0
64865	4.0	96	1.5	86	19.5	214	48.3	6	14	1.9	12	0	.0
64866	.7	0	.2	82	14.6	308	45.3	7	17	.0	0	0	.0
64867	1.1	100	.4	80	16.4	197	25.9	5	14	.6	10	0	.1
64870	8.0	99	3.2	72	20.2	199	46.7	7	17	3.7	12	2	.4
64873	.9	0	.3	87	19.0	238	33.6	2	15	.0	0	0	.0
64874	.7	99	.3	80	14.2	195	47.7	7	23	.3	18	0	.0

JEFFERSON CITY

ZIP CODE	1	2	3	4	5	6	7	8	9	10	11	12	13
65001	.4	100	.1	91	21.1	173	44.3	15	13	.2	15	0	.0
65010	1.2	0	.5	70	21.3	251	67	8	15	.0	1	0	.0
65011	1.5	100	.5	86	15.7	148	45.3	11	14	.8	13	0	.0
65013	2.8	100	1.1	79	19.1	184	44.6	7	18	1.4	14	1	1.2
65014	1.9	100	.8	84	19.0	179	35.6	6	20	.9	17	0	.0
65016	1.3	99	.4	84	21.6	240	68.0	12	15	.6	12	0	.0
65017	1.3	100	.4	83	16.3	144	37.8	12	9	.7	11	0	.0
65018	5.8	99	2.2	81	20.2	226	56.2	6	20	2.8	18	0	.5
65020	6.9	99	2.7	78	20.4	246	82.9	6	16	3.3	15	0	.5
65022	.6	77	.1	73	17.1	198	34.0	5	10	.2	11	0	.0
65023	1.4	100	.5	88	23.4	222	64.3	9	14	.7	14	0	.0
65024	1.4	100	.5	79	19.1	153	37.5	5	25	.7	21	0	.0
65025	.8	100	.3	84	16.9	195	24.7	9	12	.7	18	0	.0
65026	9.3	99	3.7	79	19.6	215	61.2	7	18	4.3	15	1	.4
65032	1.2	100	.4	87	18.9	176	60.6	11	15	.6	12	0	.0
65034	.4	100	.2	75	12.8	263	24.4	9	27	.2	22	0	.0
65035	1.5	100	.5	89	22.1	78	54.3	10	11	.8	9	0	.0
65036	.3	0	.1	80	13.5	174	31.4	8	30	.0	0	0	.3
65037	2.4	0	1.1	83	18.5	293	87.0	3	26	.0	0	0	.0
65038	.2	100	.1	66	56.9	284	116.7	3	17	.1	20	0	.5
65039	1.3	100	.5	95	31.0	245	74.1	4	10	.7	9	0	.1
65040	.2	100	.1	100	21.6	248*	53.5	3	0	.1	0	0	.7
65041	5.3	100	1.9	79	21.7	211	60.4	8	21	2.6	18	1	.1
65043	5.5	96	1.9	82	26.9	305	82.2	9	5	2.7	5	0	.0
65046	1.1	100	.4	89	20.1	209	44.8	11	18	.6	18	0	.0
65047	.4	100	.2	74	17.2	210	80.9	7	12	.2	14	0	.0
65049	2.1	99	.9	75	24.6	294	134.1	4	11	1.0	10	0	.0
65050	.5	100	.1	96	19.3	222*	24.7	16	6	.3	5	0	.3
65051	3.8	100	1.3	77	21.6	196	61.1	7	17	2.0	17	0	.0
65052	.7	0	.3	85	17.0	231	47.8	5	22	.0	0	0	.0
65053	.9	100	.3	86	23.9	227	65.5	7	11	.5	10	0	.0
65054	.2	100	.3	89	25.6	253	54.8	12	9	.5	8	0	.0
65058	1.3	98	.5	89	21.0	179	46.2	7	18	.3	18	0	1.5
65059	.8	0	.3	88	24.3	325	40.1	7	20	.0	0	0	.0
65061	.6	100	.3	92	19.5	114	39.6	5	28	.3	27	0	.0
65063	2.1	97	.7	81	30.2	309	64.4	8	9	1.0	7	1	.0
65064	.5	94	.2	90	15.6	73	32.4	4	17	.2	18	0	.0

*=Estimated **1.0=883 lbs per person; 100++ indicates per capita toxic waste generation > than 100 times the U.S. average of 883 lbs per capita.

ZIP CODE MEASURES OF SIZE, LEVELS OF AFFLUENCE AND QUALITY OF LIFE

1=Population (th.); 2= % White; 3=Households (th.); 4=% Owner Occupied; 5=Mean Income Per Household (th.$); 6=Mean Monthly Rent ($); 7=Mean Home Value (th.$); 8=% under 5; 9=% 65 and over; 10=White Males (th.); 11=% White Males, 65+ and over; 12=# Toxic Waste Sites; 13=Toxic Waste Relative to US(883 lbs.per capita)**.

MISSOURI

ZIP CODE	1	2	3	4	5	6	7	8	9	10	11	12	13
JEFFERSON CITY													
65065	2.6	99	1.1	76	24.1	286	112.5	6	15	1.3	14	0	.0
65066	5.2		2.0	82	19.7	247	52.7	6	19	.0	2	0	.0
65067	.3	100	.1	93	21.4	246*	36.6	14	7	.2	0	0	.0
65068	.6	100	.2	81	18.7	195	40.8	10	18	.3	16	0	.0
65069	.6	100	.3	84	18.7	78	35.8	5	28	.3	25	0	.0
65072	.8	100	.3	87	20.4	250	79.6	6	17	.4	21	0	.3
65074	2.3	0	.8	86	21.1	204	63.1	6	15	.0	7	0	.0
65075	.7	100	.2	79	22.4	176	53.0	10	9	.4	7	0	.0
65076	.7	100	.2	92	24.2	269	60.1	15	8	.4	7	0	.0
65077	.6	0	.2	76	28.1	185	34.8	3	7	.0	7	1	.0
65078	2.2	98	.9	86	15.3	203	51.4	5	26	1.1	24	0	.0
65079	2.1	100	.9	91	18.1	183	87.2	5	24	1.1	27	0	.0
65080	.7	0	.2	89	31.1	248	71.7	4	9	.0	0	0	.2
65081	3.1	96	1.1	76	21.6	218	51.6	7	13	1.5	11	0	.5
65082	1.3	100	.4	75	21.6	251	62.1	9	14	.7	14	0	.0
65083	.2	100	.1	71	16.2	187*	42.4	11	20	.1	16	0	.0
65084	5.5	98	2.0	79	18.1	194	52.0	8	20	2.5	17	0	.2
65085	1.0	100	.3	89	27.5	197	62.2	7	14	.5	10	1	.5
JEFFERSON CITY													
65101	51.8	91	18.0	67	28.0	300	84.7	7	11	23.4	8	5	.7
COLUMBIA													
65201	86.9	90	30.3	52	25.6	346	94.1	6	7	38.0	5	3	.1
65230	.8	96	.3	83	16.7	89	29.6	8	20	.4	19	0	.0
65231	2.5	95	.9	76	23.2	175	58.6	11	14	1.2	15	0	.0
65232	.3	0	.1	84	22.6	259*	36.3	5	13	.3	0	0	.0
65233	9.0	92	3.3	73	22.6	250	60.4	7	18	4.0	14	0	.3
65236	2.0	93	.8	74	18.6	188	49.5	7	25	.9	21	0	.0
65237	1.1	89	.4	74	20.4	229	39.1	5	13	.5	14	0	.0
65239	1.1	100	.4	79	25.4	174	60.3	10	9	.6	10	0	.0
65240	5.8	99	2.2	80	24.8	248	59.7	7	16	2.8	13	0	.4
65243	1.9	100	.6	83	19.6	278	54.1	13	11	1.0	12	0	.0
65244	.7	100	.1	80	22.3	175	41.6	6	24	.4	20	0	.0
65246	2.2	66	.6	81	16.8	180	23.7	3	30	.1	31	0	.0
65247	2.5	100	.9	84	25.5	234	67.6	9	11	1.2	10	0	.0
65248	4.5	87	1.7	71	22.2	293*	44.5	4	14	.3	13	0	.0
65250	.7	0	.2	86	21.0	231	54.2	5	19	.6	15	0	.0
65251	17.1	92	5.5	71	24.4	330	29.4	10	11	.0	0	0	.0
65254	2.2	91	.8	79	21.9	281	65.0	6	14	7.6	12	0	.1
65255	2.5	100	.9	85	21.3	189	54.6	8	21	.9	17	0	.0
65256	1.6	100	.6	80	24.6	239	73.4	12	4	.6	4	0	.4
65257	.5	96	.2	80	18.0	248	31.3	9	16	.8	17	0	.0
65258	2.2	100	.5	80	15.8	312	28.1	9	16	.2	12	0	.1
65259	2.7	93	.9	85	21.3	216	50.6	9	15	1.3	11	1	.8
65260	.5	100	.2	82	18.3	129	33.5	7	8	.3	7	1	.8
65261	1.4	95	.6	79	20.3	192	43.6	6	23	.7	21	0	.0
65262	.7	0	.2	89	27.3	229	86.3	10	7	.0	7	0	.0
65263	2.1	98	.8	84	17.8	227	40.5	7	21	.6	20	0	.0
65264	1.1	99	.3	83	24.0	211	63.0	8	16	.6	12	0	.0
65265	16.5	93	6.2	75	24.0	246	63.0	8	12	7.4	17	3	.8

MISSOURI

ZIP CODE	1	2	3	4	5	6	7	8	9	10	11	12	13
COLUMBIA													
65270	18.1	92	6.6	70	22.3	248	61.0	8	18	7.9	14	1	1.4
65274	1.6	99	.6	77	21.0	209	44.8	9	19	.8	13	0	.0
65275	3.2	98	1.3	80	20.4	195	52.0	6	22	1.5	16	0	.0
65276	1.6	99	.6	81	20.4	196	43.4	9	19	.8	16	0	.0
65278	.2	100	.1	97	18.3	211*	44.2	9	22	.8	18	0	.0
65279	1.1	100	.4	74	28.0	274	66.8	7	17	.6	14	0	.0
65280	.3	100	.1	75	21.3	203	29.5	7	7	.2	7	0	.0
65281	3.8	95	1.4	79	24.3	197	54.1	6	21	1.7	19	0	.0
65283	.3	100	.1	66	15.9	183*	50.3	12	14	.1	8	0	.0
65284	1.8	97	.7	86	21.5	226	53.1	7	17	.9	16	0	.0
65285	.6	100	.2	84	30.9	449	60.5	7	6	.3	5	0	.0
65286	.3	82	.1	80	16.4	272	19.9	8	16	.1	17	0	.0
65287	.3	100	.1	77	22.8	140	26.9	2	24	.1	26	0	.0
SEDALIA													
65301	28.9	94	11.3	75	22.2	262	57.2	7	17	12.8	14	5	.9
65305	4.3	82	1.0	87	19.5	337	69.5*	15	0	2.1	0	1	.0
65320	.7	0	.2	87	19.8	228*	52.2	19	18	.0	0	0	.1
65321	.7	94	.2	77	21.6	218	47.9	10	19	.3	18	0	.0
65322	.7	94	.2	88	21.8	132	44.4	5	17	.3	17	0	.3
65323	.8	99	.2	81	16.9	301	32.9	6	19	.4	17	0	.0
65324	.9	100	.4	91	14.5	166*	47.1	1	28	.0	0	0	.0
65325	2.6	100	1.0	84	17.8	253	52.1	6	21	1.2	18	0	.0
65326	1.5	0	.6	93	15.1	164	50.2	4	23	.0	0	1	.0
65327	.3	0	.1	84	23.4	267	50.9	6	22	.0	0	0	.6
65329	.5	0	.2	77	20.9	139	28.4	3	16	.0	0	0	.0
65330	.6	92	.5	86	19.7	111	44.7	16	19	.0	0	0	.0
65332	1.3	0	.3	86	21.0	222	39.5	7	17	.0	0	0	.0
65333	.9	99	.3	86	21.9	141	29.5	9	14	.4	17	0	.0
65334	.7	100	.3	66	22.0	228	50.9	12	8	.4	7	0	.0
65335	.5	99	.2	89	27.2	317	37.6	7	7	.4	7	0	.4
65336	4.3	90	1.7	54	20.2	236	64.3	12	6	2.1	7	0	.0
65337	2.0	99	.7	70	22.3	205	48.8	9	12	1.0	10	1	.0
65338	2.3	99	.9	86	17.7	149	46.4	4	26	1.1	24	0	.8
65339	.9	94	.3	60	20.5	338	39.4	9	15	.4	16	0	.0
65340	14.9	94	5.5	68	21.8	270	69.8	7	16	6.7	13	0	.1
65344	.6	0	.2	73	22.7	112	45.7	5	26	.0	0	0	.0
65345	.4	100	.1	93	23.5	270*	45.2	5	12	.2	10	0	.0
65346	.4	0	.2	71	24.8	285*	51.8	3	10	.2	0	0	.2
65347	.9	97	.3	82	19.2	222	31.1	8	19	.4	17	0	.1
65348	1.0	99	.4	90	18.9	154	44.5	9	17	.4	15	0	.1
65349	3.1	90	1.3	75	19.5	182	42.6	7	24	1.3	21	0	.2
65350	1.7	98	.6	90	26.5	229	62.1	7	13	.8	12	0	.1
65351	2.9	99	.9	78	20.7	238	44.8	8	18	1.4	18	1	.1
65354	.6	100	.2	83	17.6	126	40.4	8	14	.3	13	0	.0
65355	5.2	99	2.2	81	18.4	230	53.2	6	22	2.5	22	0	.0
65360	4.5	99	1.8	83	23.0	188	45.3	7	23	2.1	20	0	.0
ROLLA													
65401	23.0	96	7.9	65	22.7	263	70.7	6	10	11.9	8	2	.2
65438	2.4		.8	79	14.4	154	40.2	7	17	.0	0	0	.2

*=Estimated **1.0=883 lbs per person; 100+ indicates per capita toxic waste generation > than 100 times the U.S. average of 883 lbs per capita.

ZIP CODE MEASURES OF SIZE, LEVELS OF AFFLUENCE AND QUALITY OF LIFE

1=Population (th.); 2= % White; 3=Households (th.); 4=% Owner Occupied; 5=Mean Income Per Household (th.$); 6=Mean Monthly Rent ($)*; 7=Mean Home Value (th.$)*; 8=% under 5; 9=% 65 and over; 10=White Males, 65+; 11=% White Males (th.); 12=# Toxic Waste Sites; 13=Toxic Waste Relative to US(883 lbs.per capita)**.

MISSOURI

ROLLA

ZIP CODE	1	2	3	4	5	6	7	8	9	10	11	12	13
65439	.4	90	.2	65	16.6	206	38.3	13	15	.2	16	0	2.5
65440	.4	100	.2	74	13.5	189	31.4	6	29	.2	39	2	5.8
65441	3.3	99	1.1	76	21.3	169	55.5	10	13	1.6	12	0	.0
65444	.7	99	.2	91	17.5	137	33.8	5	17	.3	17	0	.0
65446	.5	100	.2	83	13.2	309	28.5	8	7	.3	6	0	.0
65449	.4	100	.2	85	22.5	258*	26.4	4	30	.2	37	0	.0
65452	2.9	98	1.1	84	17.4	211	42.2	5	15	1.4	17	0	.0
65453	6.2	99	2.3	81	18.6	247	50.8	7	19	3.0	19	0	.3
65456	6.5	100	.2	88	20.7	238*	21.0	7	12	.3	9	0	.0
65459	5.8	99	2.2	82	19.5	185	44.2	7	13	2.8	11	0	.0
65461	.3	100	.1	91	19.2	293	34.6	8	14	.2	16	0	.0
65462	1.3	0	.4	85	16.9	125	36.8	10	10	.0	16	0	.0
65463	1.3	100	.5	82	16.0	146	44.6	3	16	.2	15	0	.0
65464	.5	0	.2	92	19.0	218*	32.2	10	7	.0	7	0	.0
65466	1.5	100	.6	79	15.7	185	45.3	5	18	.7	16	0	.0
65470	.6	0	.3	79	15.5	129	40.5	8	20	.1	0	0	.0
65471	.1	100	.1	65	18.0	53	39.6	0	4	.1	0	0	.0
65473	21.1	74	2.8	1	18.6	358	66.4*	8	0	11.3	0	1	.0
65479	.5	100	.1	90	12.6	129	20.4	10	9	.3	8	0	.0
65483	4.5	99	1.7	73	18.4	207	57.5	8	18	2.1	15	1	.3
65484	.2	100	.1	94	14.2	163*	27.6	0	22	.1	15	0	.0
65486	2.8	100	1.0	83	18.3	246	47.8	7	17	1.4	14	0	.0

ROLLA

ZIP CODE	1	2	3	4	5	6	7	8	9	10	11	12	13
65501	.2	100	.1	57	18.2	167	23.0	7	2	.1	4	0	.0
65529	.3	100	.1	83	16.7	181	25.7	3	10	.1	0	0	.0
65534	.3	100	.1	50	13.1	316	42.9	14	16	.1	25	0	.0
65535	1.3	0	.5	78	18.3	238	41.5	7	15	.0	0	1	.0
65536	19.8	98	7.3	76	19.9	243	59.3	7	13	9.5	13	1	.3
65540	.6	100	.2	81	16.5	62	41.6	4	13	.3	11	0	.0
65541	.2	100	.1	100	14.8	171*	36.5	9	23	.1	27	0	.0
65542	4.1	100	1.6	79	14.9	220	46.3	8	19	2.0	16	0	.5
65543	.4	100	.1	93	17.5	201*	31.9	6	14	.1	9	0	.0
65548	4.5	100	1.7	74	14.2	164	44.6	7	16	2.2	15	0	.1
65552	1.1	0	.4	76	20.3	202	51.3	6	11	.0	0	0	.0
65555	1.0	100	.4	86	18.3	215	41.1	5	12	.5	10	0	1.1
65556	4.8	98	1.8	79	18.2	152	48.0	9	18	2.3	15	1	.1
65557	.3	0	.1	91	15.0	172*	53.1	6	14	.0	0	1	1.0
65559	6.9	99	2.5	75	19.4	227	57.1	6	19	3.4	19	3	.0
65560	13.0	99	4.8	76	18.5	198	55.6	7	17	6.2	15	0	.7
65564	.1	100	.1	90	8.2	95*	29.4*	0	48	.1	56	0	.0
65565	4.1	100	1.6	77	18.3	174	42.4	8	23	2.0	20	2	.0
65566	1.2	99	.4	90	29.2	215	65.1	9	7	.6	7	1	2.7
65567	1.1	0	.4	82	18.9	212	41.0	11	9	.3	0	0	1.0
65570	.5	100	.2	70	18.1	150	34.8	7	9	.3	7	0	.0
65571	2.1	100	.8	82	14.6	173	42.2	6	14	1.0	13	0	.0
65572	2.1	100	.1	100	22.6	259*	28.3	8	17	.1	10	0	.0
65578	.2	100	.1	84	19.2	220*	40.6	7	27	.1	29	1	.0
65580	.7	100	.2	73	20.3	233*	58.9	5	14	.4	17	0	.0

MISSOURI

ROLLA

ZIP CODE	1	2	3	4	5	6	7	8	9	10	11	12	13
65582	1.9	100	.7	83	21.6	171	42.7	6	16	1.0	14	0	.0
65583	9.8	88	3.7	67	21.0	227	64.0	7	7	4.2	6	0	.0
65588	2.3	100	.8	79	15.1	189	35.8	8	14	1.1	16	0	.3
65589	.2	100	.1	81	19.0	195	37.9	12	13	.1	8	0	.0
65590	1.0	100	.3	75	13.5	323	25.1	9	17	.5	19	0	.0
65591	.7	100	.2	88	19.8	428	29.2	9	9	.3	8	0	.0

SPRINGFIELD

ZIP CODE	1	2	3	4	5	6	7	8	9	10	11	12	13
65601	.8	100	.3	88	17.9	130	37.2	3	17	.4	15	0	.0
65603	.2	97	.1	78	15.9	204	39.6	6	18	.1	19	0	.0
65604	2.7	99	1.0	81	21.4	220	48.7	6	19	1.3	16	0	.0
65605	8.7	99	3.4	76	17.8	200	57.6	7	20	4.0	17	1	.1
65606	3.1	99	1.2	81	13.6	219	34.3	6	16	1.5	16	1	.0
65608	3.0	99	.3	81	15.5	207	48.7	8	18	3.7	16	1	.2
65609	.7	100	.2	77	17.4	198	42.3	9	19	.4	15	0	.0
65610	2.6	99	1.0	84	20.1	226	56.1	6	16	1.3	17	0	.0
65611	1.0	0	.4	83	17.5	237	87.6	5	21	.0	0	0	.0
65612	1.0	0	.3	87	21.7	312	52.9	5	11	.0	0	0	.0
65613	.9	99	.3	71	19.3	217	60.1	7	18	1.3	16	0	.1
65614	.5	100	3.2	91	15.0	192	24.5	8	29	.3	29	0	.0
65616	8.0	99	3.3	76	22.4	250	87.5	5	21	3.8	20	2	.0
65617	1.0	100	.3	87	22.9	263*	53.9	9	8	.5	8	0	.0
65618	.2	100	.1	100	28.0	322*	99.9*	11	20	.1	24	0	.0
65619	2.4	99	.8	87	28.5	326	75.9	10	5	1.2	4	1	.0
65620	.4	100	.1	83	21.6	142	76.3	11	8	.2	7	0	.0
65622	6.3	99	2.3	83	17.2	199	44.8	6	21	.1	17	0	.0
65623	.2	100	.1	83	15.8	232	38.6	4	10	.1	8	0	.0
65625	5.4	100	2.1	78	19.5	211	65.5	6	22	2.5	20	1	.4
65626	.9	0	.3	93	14.9	171*	38.7	8	14	.0	0	0	.0
65627	.4	0	.2	88	11.3	329	50.2	5	30	.0	0	0	.0
65629	.7	100	.3	86	16.8	233	28.6	6	10	.3	8	0	.0
65630	1.8	99	.6	89	16.9	194*	37.2	10	16	.1	19	0	.0
65631	1.8	99	.6	81	19.7	198	44.8	8	10	.9	5	0	.0
65633	2.5	99	.8	80	19.4	229	40.4	7	13	1.1	13	0	.0
65634	3.0	99	1.1	84	18.7	166	45.3	8	17	1.2	7	0	.0
65635	.7	99	.2	87	22.7	108	46.5	7	18	.2	17	0	.0
65637	.5	0	.3	88	16.6	190*	41.9	10	7	.9	5	0	.0
65638	.9	0	.3	93	12.8	147*	118.1*	6	17	.1	8	0	.0
65640	.5	0	.3	96	15.5	51	28.8	5	15	.0	0	0	.0
65641	.7	100	.2	77	16.9	209	86.0	2	31	.0	0	0	.0
65644	1.9	97	.7	89	21.2	126	41.3	5	13	.9	14	1	.3
65646	1.8	99	.7	91	18.4	151	33.2	7	16	.9	15	1	.0
65647	.6	98	.6	88	18.5	224	45.4	7	14	.8	15	0	.0
65648	3.4	99	1.1	88	23.1	182	68.2	6	9	1.6	9	0	.0
65649	1.1	99	.5	80	14.0	175	31.2	8	17	.6	16	0	.0
65650	.9	100	.8	93	13.0	156	47.1	3	30	.9	14	0	.0
65652	2.2	95	.7	79	20.4	205	46.6	4	14	1.1	11	0	.0
65653	3.1	0	1.4	83	17.8	188	70.2	4	32	.0	0	1	.0
65654	.1	100	.1	82	16.0	184*	40.8	10	41	.0	0	0	.0

*=Estimated **1.0=883 lbs per person; 100++ indicates per capita toxic waste generation > than 100 times the U.S. average of 883 lbs per capita.

ZIP CODE MEASURES OF SIZE, LEVELS OF AFFLUENCE AND QUALITY OF LIFE

1=Population (th.); 2= % White; 3=Households (th.); 4=% Owner Occupied; 5=Mean Income Per Household (th.$); 6=Mean Monthly Rent ($); 7=Mean Home Value (th.$); 8=% under 5; 9=% 65 and over; 10=White Males (th.); 11=% White Males, 65+; 12=# Toxic Waste Sites; 13=Toxic Waste Relative to US(883 lbs.per capita)**.

MISSOURI — SPRINGFIELD

ZIP CODE	1	2	3	4	5	6	7	8	9	10	11	12	13
65655	2.6	98	1.0	77	18.1	180	55.9	4	21	1.2	21	0	.0
65656	3.5	99	1.2	85	17.2	160	60.0	7	16	1.7	15	0	.0
65657	.2	100	.1	100	12.9	148*	28.4	19	17	.1	17	0	.0
65658	.4	100	.1	100	20.5	235*	83.5	0	26	.2	42	0	.0
65659	.3	0	.1	94	23.3	268*	34.5	4	17	.0	0	0	.0
65660	.2	100	.1	91	18.0	206*	13.1	5	17	.1	20	0	.0
65661	2.4	99	1.0	80	17.4	171	49.6	6	28	1.1	24	0	.0
65662	1.0	0	.4	90	17.9	186	46.1	7	14	.0	0	0	.0
65663	1.4	100	.5	84	20.7	275	43.1	10	10	.8	8	0	.0
65667	3.0	98	1.1	80	15.3	172	39.1	9	16	1.5	14	0	.0
65668	1.0	100	.3	86	14.9	244	63.2	7	21	.5	18	0	.0
65669	1.0	100	.3	83	20.5	236	57.9	7	11	.5	9	0	.0
65672	2.9	0	1.1	82	20.3	193	74.9	7	20	.0	0	0	.0
65674	2.1	98	.9	80	14.8	152	38.6	4	26	1.0	25	0	.0
65675	.1	100	.1	88	13.6	156*	31.9	9	27	.1	28	0	.0
65676	.3	0	.1	68	13.0	111	63.5	4	10	.5	0	0	.0
65677	1.0	98	.3	89	17.1	293	29.1	13	13	.5	14	0	.0
65679	.7	0	.3	83	15.1	220	54.5	4	17	.5	0	0	.0
65680	.6	100	.3	95	15.5	267	38.1	7	24	1.0	20	0	.0
65681	.9	100	.4	84	15.1	294	71.0	8	24	.4	29	0	.0
65682	2.1	99	.8	77	20.0	182	40.4	7	23	1.0	0	0	.0
65685	.7	0	.3	74	18.8	152	30.8	8	20	.0	0	0	.0
65686	1.8	0	.8	86	25.1	372	101.7	3	37	.0	0	0	.0
65689	4.6	99	1.6	75	18.5	195	51.9	7	17	2.2	16	0	.0
65690	1.1	0	.4	84	15.7	104	49.0	8	17	.2	19	0	.0
65692	1.1	100	.4	79	13.6	170	28.0	8	17	.0	0	0	.0

SPRINGFIELD

ZIP CODE	1	2	3	4	5	6	7	8	9	10	11	12	13
65702	.3	99	.1	87	19.5	216	37.5	4	15	.2	14	0	.0
65704	3.4	99	1.2	77	17.4	181	46.2	8	14	1.6	13	0	1.9
65705	3.1	100	1.0	82	17.8	226	48.3	7	18	1.4	15	1	.3
65706	8.5	100	3.0	80	20.1	230	63.4	8	15	4.1	13	1	.3
65707	9.0	0	3.4	80	17.6	160	40.4	7	18	4.1	0	1	.3
65708	9.0	100	3.4	75	20.8	222	60.1	7	18	4.2	14	0	.4
65710	.7	0	.2	78	19.5	199	51.0	5	14	.0	0	0	.0
65711	8.6	100	3.3	78	19.0	210	45.2	6	18	4.1	16	0	.0
65712	5.7	100	2.1	79	20.2	215	55.4	8	19	2.7	16	0	.0
65713	5.7	99	.7	81	17.6	185	40.4	10	13	1.1	13	0	.0
65714	5.7	99	2.1	83	24.7	282	75.2	9	10	2.8	9	2	.2
65717	1.8	99	.6	85	17.2	181	34.1	7	14	.9	12	0	.0
65719	.2	100	.1	72	14.0	161*	74.4	12	21	.2	27	0	.0
65720	.5	100	.2	98	17.4	200*	26.9	3	8	.3	8	0	.0
65721	7.1	99	2.5	79	23.5	251	75.0	7	12	3.4	10	0	.0
65722	.9	100	.3	86	15.6	166	42.8	10	14	.5	12	0	.2
65723	3.1	0	1.1	79	19.4	181	45.1	9	15	.2	0	0	.0
65724	.6	100	.3	95	14.1	162*	59.4	7	27	.4	28	0	.0
65725	1.7	99	.6	82	20.2	282	49.0	7	8	.9	7	0	.0
65726	1.1	97	.1	27	21.8	219	71.5	1	5	.5	4	0	.0
65727	.4	100	.1	69	13.8	265	91.9	7	14	.2	23	0	.0
65729	.2	100	.1	85	12.1	139*	42.1	7	37	.1	36	0	.0

MISSOURI — SPRINGFIELD

ZIP CODE	1	2	3	4	5	6	7	8	9	10	11	12	13
65730	.1	0	.1	83	15.6	180*	91.9	3	14	.0	0	0	.0
65731	.3	100	.1	77	16.9	242	79.7	9	11	.1	17	0	.0
65732	.7	100	.2	87	14.5	201	32.2	10	17	.3	17	0	.0
65733	.4	100	.1	80	14.5	232	51.4	8	17	.2	15	0	.0
65734	2.7	99	1.0	80	18.4	156	49.3	10	15	1.3	12	0	.0
65735	.2	100	.2	89	16.7	192*	83.1	8	30	.1	21	0	.0
65737	3.7	99	1.4	85	19.6	247	82.8	4	17	1.9	17	0	.0
65738	6.4	99	2.3	80	25.4	291	66.0	8	11	3.1	10	0	.0
65739	.3	100	.1	84	15.2	168	68.6	6	10	.1	2	0	.0
65740	.7	100	.3	91	18.7	245	53.0	5	24	.4	27	0	.0
65742	5.9	0	2.0	86	26.1	198	88.1	7	10	.0	0	0	.1
65745	1.3	98	.5	80	16.1	161	35.2	6	16	.6	14	0	.0
65746	4.7	99	1.6	84	21.2	176	40.1	10	11	2.3	9	0	.9
65747	1.9	97	.9	92	18.8	267	79.1	4	29	.2	33	0	.0
65752	.4	100	.2	92	18.4	132	29.6	4	26	.2	26	0	.0
65753	1.9	100	.7	80	19.3	250	53.9	9	14	.9	13	0	.0
65754	.3	100	.1	84	20.5	304	35.3	8	21	.2	15	0	.0
65755	.4	100	.1	84	13.1	158	17.0	7	16	.2	12	0	.0
65756	.6	0	.6	84	12.3	130	25.6	10	22	.2	0	0	.0
65757	3.8	99	1.3	82	23.7	282	68.9	8	11	1.9	10	0	.0
65759	.9	0	.3	90	17.1	194	50.8	4	19	.9	13	0	.0
65760	.2	100	.1	81	11.7	205	41.8	14	8	.1	6	0	.0
65761	.8	100	.3	91	16.6	128	60.6	2	23	.4	26	0	.4
65762	.1	0	.1	78	17.6	202*	16.8	3	22	.2	0	0	.0
65764	.8	96	.3	96	27.1	311*	54.2	11	17	.4	22	0	.0
65766	.2	96	.1	100	12.8	147*	43.8	12	34	.5	28	0	.0
65767	1.5	99	.6	82	19.5	241	50.9	7	23	.7	21	0	.0
65768	.3	100	.1	82	13.2	152*	56.9	10	10	.2	16	0	.0
65769	2.2	99	.8	86	18.0	208	46.6	8	14	1.0	14	7	3.4
65770	2.3	100	.8	86	18.6	168	47.0	9	12	1.2	10	1	.0
65771	.6	0	.2	90	21.0	204	42.2	11	8	.0	0	0	.0
65772	1.5	0	.5	88	18.2	255	43.2	8	9	.5	0	0	.0
65773	.6	100	.4	81	13.5	164	26.3	6	7	.2	12	0	.0
65774	1.0	100	.4	76	16.6	216	34.3	2	25	.5	28	0	.0
65775	16.8	100	6.3	77	17.6	228	59.5	7	16	8.0	14	1	.5
65777	.3	96	.1	81	18.1	114	25.4	4	21	.1	22	0	.0
65778	.5	100	.2	84	11.4	131*	27.6	12	6	.3	3	0	.0
65779	1.5	0	.6	84	16.1	176	55.7	4	19	.0	0	0	.0
65781	4.2	99	1.4	80	23.7	269	74.9	8	9	2.1	9	0	.0
65785	3.8	99	1.5	82	17.8	170	59.0	5	24	1.8	23	0	4.6
65786	1.2	100	.5	89	13.6	187	44.6	7	16	.6	18	0	.0
65787	1.0	100	.4	80	17.9	213	90.8	3	19	.5	22	0	.0
65788	.3	100	.1	83	18.7	123	49.6	9	9	.2	12	0	.0
65789	1.4	98	.4	91	15.1	90	39.0	9	13	.7	13	0	.0

SPRINGFIELD

ZIP CODE	1	2	3	4	5	6	7	8	9	10	11	12	13
65790	.8	97	.3	80	13.5	263	33.4	8	15	.3	13	0	.0
65791	4.4	100	1.8	79	15.5	174	46.9	6	23	2.1	20	0	.0
65793	5.2	98	1.9	76	16.1	180	45.1	7	16	2.5	13	0	.0

SPRINGFIELD

ZIP CODE	1	2	3	4	5	6	7	8	9	10	11	12	13
65802	34.5	95	13.1	62	19.2	267	50.7	8	13	15.5	11	1	.8

*=Estimated **1.0-883 lbs per person; 100++ indicates per capita toxic waste generation > than 100 times the U.S. average of 883 lbs per capita.

ZIP CODE MEASURES OF SIZE, LEVELS OF AFFLUENCE AND QUALITY OF LIFE

1=Population (th.); 2= % White; 3=Households (th.); 4=% Owner Occupied; 5=Mean Income Per Household (th.$); 6=Mean Monthly Rent ($)*; 7=Mean Home Value (th.$)*;
8=% under 5; 9=% 65 and over; 10=White Males, 65+; 11=% White Males; 12=# Toxic Waste Sites; 13=Toxic Waste Relative to US(883 lbs.per capita)**.

MISSOURI

ZIPCODE	1	2	3	4	5	6	7	8	9	10	11	12	13
SPRINGFIELD													
65803	36.1	96	13.2	66	19.7	246	53.6	8	12	16.2	10	4	.2
65804	34.0	99	13.6	71	32.8	334	101.0	5	12	16.1	10	3	.6
65806	10.2	96	5.5	25	12.6	230	40.0	5	4	4.3	13	1	.0
65807	41.2	98	14.2	73	26.7	328	79.0	7	9	19.1	8	0	.0
FORT SCOTT													
66739	.5	0	.2	77	22.1	269	80.7	3	11	.0	.0	0	.0
66756	.1	100	.1	86	14.6	168*	23.4	5	29	.0	23	0	.0
66762	.2	100	.1	84	27.9	320*	48.1	9	9	.1	8	0	.0
HARRISON													
72616	.2	100	.1	87	11.6	133*	47.0	5	18	.1	22	0	.0
FAYETTEVILLE													
72732	.3	100	.1	67	13.9	236	45.9	11	13	.1	15	0	.0
72751	.3	100	.1	91	17.7	204*	55.5	10	2	.1	0	0	.0

MONTANA

ZIPCODE	1	2	3	4	5	6	7	8	9	10	11	12	13
BILLINGS													
59001	1.1	100	.4	70	16.0	176	84.5	4	21	.5	19	0	.0
59003	1.4	0	.4	65	20.5	250	65.2	11	5	.0	0	0	.0
59006	.7	88	.2	84	28.2	253	81.9	8	9	.3	8	0	.0
59007	.1	100	.1	85	14.2	163*	38.8	4	23	.1	30	0	.0
59008	.1	0	.1	78	20.0	129	42.3	12	23	1.4	19	0	.0
59011	2.8	99	1.1	72	19.3	199	68.8	7	19	.1	20	0	.0
59012	.3	65	.1	39	17.9	103	63.6*	16	12	.1	14	0	.0
59014	1.6	97	.6	74	19.3	176	64.7	5	16	.7	14	0	.0
59015	.5	100	.2	62	18.4	279	77.7	10	7	.2	10	0	.0
59016	.6	0	.2	40	18.4	226	43.2	9	4	.0	0	0	.0
59018	.6	0	.2	84	18.0	279	56.4	7	10	.0	0	0	.1
59019	2.2	0	.8	75	20.5	243	78.4	8	19	.0	23	1	.0
59022	1.7	11	.4	54	23.4	189	43.0	17	3	.2	9	0	.0
59024	.5	100	.2	68	17.5	334	50.8	13	8	.3	9	0	.0
59025	.2	100	.1	44	32.6	375*	91.9	15	0	.1	14	0	.0
59026	.2	100	.1	77	18.3	143	71.6	11	11	.1	14	0	.0
59027	.3	100	.1	62	40.5	321	120.5	8	3	.1	7	0	.0
59028	.3	100	.1	81	20.0	230*	74.9	8	10	2.0	9	0	.0
59029	.5	100	.2	81	17.7	228	55.7	10	20	.2	19	0	.1
59030	.7	0	.3	55	19.6	191	71.1	7	10	.1	10	0	.0
59031	.3	0	.1	61	24.0	267	47.2	17	0	.0	0	0	.0
59032	.5	100	.2	64	24.8	189	38.4	8	9	.3	7	0	.0
59034	5.0	83	1.7	66	22.9	267	80.8	8	11	2.0	11	2	.0
59036	1.6	99	.7	76	19.8	173	40.2	9	18	2.0	18	0	.0
59037	1.0	100	.4	84	29.4	356	108.1	8	6	.5	8	0	.1
59038	.9	99	.3	68	20.7	245	55.2	7	12	.4	11	0	.1
59041	1.3	0	.5	81	23.8	231	87.1	10	14	.6	13	0	.0
59043	2.1	0	.6	55	15.4	240	56.4	13	5	.0	0	0	.0
59044	7.9	98	2.8	76	25.6	249	87.3	9	11	3.8	3	0	1.8
59046	.5	0	.2	83	16.6	202	37.2	6	15	.0	0	0	.0
59047	10.2	100	4.0	72	23.3	250	78.0	16	7	.5	14	1	.0
59050	1.6	28	.4	69	21.7	242	45.4	11	7	.2	8	0	.0
59052	.2	100	.1	79	20.6	95	61.8	16	5	.1	8	0	.0
59053	.2	0	.1	71	21.3	60	35.5	8	27	.0	0	0	.1
59054	.4	0	.1	69	19.2	263	27.2	12	9	.1	15	0	.0
59055	.1	100	.1	58	23.8	113	21.9	16	12	.1	15	0	.0
59057	.2	0	.1	85	20.9	238	91.9	14	26	.2	9	0	.0
59059	.2	100	.1	90	14.8	170*	23.3	9	12	.1	9	0	.0
59061	.2	100	.1	45	18.1	208*	25.5	0	27	.0	52	0	.0
59063	1.1	0	.4	83	28.2	373	93.2	13	8	.1	13	0	.0
59064	.2	100	.1	87	17.3	199*	35.9	9	11	.1	8	0	.0
59065	.2	100	.1	58	14.7	172	52.4*	0	7	.2	8	0	.0
59066	.5	34	.1	72	20.5	102	53.3	9	6	.1	20	0	.1
59068	2.5	0	1.1	69	18.1	253	72.7	7	25	.2	16	0	.0
59069	.4	86	.3	70	18.7	330	49.9	11	20	.5	14	0	.0
59070	.8	100	.3	79	21.7	262	83.6	9	12	.9	15	0	.0
59072	3.7	100	1.5	76	19.3	207	47.2	8	17	1.9	15	0	.0
59074	.6	98	.2	79	18.5	209	46.2	5	11	.3	10	0	.0
59075	.3	42	.1	100	16.4	188*	17.5	11	12	.1	0	0	.0

*=Estimated **1.0=883 lbs per person; 100++ indicates per capita toxic waste generation > than 100 times the U.S. average of 883 lbs per capita.

ZIP CODE MEASURES OF SIZE, LEVELS OF AFFLUENCE AND QUALITY OF LIFE

1=Population (th.); 2= % White; 3=Households (th.); 4=% Owner Occupied; 5=Mean Income Per Household (th.$); 6=Mean Monthly Rent ($)*; 7=Mean Home Value (th.$); 8=% under 5; 9=% 65 and over; 10=White Males (th.); 11=% White Males, 65+; 12=# Toxic Waste Sites; 13=Toxic Waste Relative to US(883 lbs.per capita)**.

MONTANA

ZIPCODE	1	2	3	4	5	6	7	8	9	10	11	12	13
BILLINGS													
59078	.2	100	.1	84	22.8	203	37.5	14	8	.1	10	0	.0
59079	1.3	100	.4	86	30.5	352	121.4	7	2	.7	3	0	.0
59080	.3	0	.1	77	22.7	165	123.2	5	14	.1	8	0	.0
59085	.2	100	.1	71	24.8	285*	26.3	0	12	.1	7	0	.0
59086	.6	100	.2	70	19.2	237	49.5	11	16	.3	16	0	.0
59087	.5	100	.2	75	16.4	73	30.1	7	13	.2	12	0	.0
59088	1.0	96	.4	74	20.8	215	71.6	9	16	.5	17	0	.0
59089	.4	18	.1	86	11.6	134*	27.9	19	13	.0	65	0	.0
BILLINGS													
59101	54.0	94	20.5	60	23.6	296	93.7	9	9	24.9	7	6	.0
59102	40.9	98	14.7	75	34.0	400	117.9	7	10	19.5	8	1	.4
59103	.2	100	.1	76	37.9	393	159.1	17	4	.1	8	5	100++
WOLF POINT													
59201	5.3	69	1.9	63	23.3	221	67.8	10	10	1.8	11	1	.0
59211	.5	100	.1	87	23.5	434	33.6	7	12	.3	18	0	.0
59212	.5	95	.2	94	25.4	292*	35.1	9	20	.1	23	1	.0
59213	.8	31	.2	71	23.0	193	50.8	11	14	.1	36	0	.0
59214	.3	100	.1	83	11.8	51	29.2	7	16	.1	20	0	.0
59215	1.6	100	.5	80	21.0	179	66.5	9	10	.2	20	0	.0
59218	1.4	94	.5	79	23.5	281	52.5	6	17	.7	13	0	.0
59219	.3	97	.1	92	26.5	304*	20.8	10	10	.7	10	0	.0
59221	1.7	97	.6	77	22.5	377	63.1	10	10	.8	9	1	.0
59222	.5	100	.1	81	23.4	346	29.9	10	12	.3	12	0	.0
59223	.5	96	.1	48	33.2	273	88.4	5	2	.3	1	0	.0
59225	.7	42	.2	65	15.9	206	29.2	20	4	.1	4	0	.0
59226	.6	100	.2	80	22.3	229	43.7	5	10	.3	6	0	.0
59230	6.0	97	2.3	64	24.2	229	77.3	8	13	2.8	12	0	.0
59231	.6	87	.2	0	20.6	48	73.3*	16	1	.2	3	0	.0
59241	.5	0	.2	83	16.7	122	32.3	5	25	.2	20	0	.0
59242	.2	68	.1	92	29.4	338*	33.1	6	14	.1	10	0	.0
59243	.5	100	.1	50	22.6	299	46.7	10	4	.3	3	0	.0
59247	.6	0	.2	71	25.7	232	58.3	5	10	.3	3	0	.0
59248	.9	0	.3	78	22.0	156	54.2	5	10	.0	0	0	.0
59250	.4	0	.2	73	18.3	160	30.6	6	12	.3	3	0	.0
59252	.2	100	.1	76	24.1	170	57.0	8	12	.1	12	0	.0
59253	.3	100	.1	84	19.8	215	31.4	11	13	.1	16	0	.0
59254	2.9	99	1.1	73	23.0	332	78.6	8	18	.1	15	0	.0
59255	2.8	37	.8	62	24.4	233	47.0	13	4	.5	4	0	.0
59257	.2	100	.1	90	32.0	367*	30.1	12	7	.1	4	0	.0
59258	.2	100	.1	82	26.9	290	32.4	12	14	.2	13	0	.0
59259	.7	100	.3	79	23.3	250	30.9	5	16	.1	15	0	.0
59260	.3	100	.1	100	22.8	262*	81.1*	14	11	.4	7	0	.0
59261	.6	0	.2	79	18.4	140	35.0	5	19	.0	0	0	.0
59262	.9	0	.3	76	27.5	416	64.5	9	6	.3	14	0	.0
59263	.2	99	.7	80	22.2	214	57.0	8	19	.9	17	0	.0
59270	8.7	97	3.1	68	27.7	329	93.7	10	11	4.3	9	0	.0
59274	3.1	100	.1	74	17.1	128	58.0	11	11	.2	14	0	.0
59275	6.1	100	.2	83	27.1	196	46.9	10	15	.3	14	0	.0
59276	.1	100	.1	72	23.1	295	20.2	6	17	.1	18	0	.0

MONTANA

ZIPCODE	1	2	3	4	5	6	7	8	9	10	11	12	13
MILES CITY													
59301	12.6	97	4.8	68	23.5	257	72.4	8	13	6.0	12	2	.1
59311	.2	100	.1	72	18.1	462	48.1	5	20	.1	15	0	.0
59313	3.2	99	1.2	76	25.3	209	69.2	9	12	1.6	10	0	.0
59315	.2			69	21.2	243*	75.4*	13	4		7	0	.0
59317	1.7	98	.6	73	24.3	245	72.5	9	9	.8	8	0	.0
59318	.2	100	.1	77	15.2	174*	54.1*	12	6	.1	3	0	.0
59322	.2	100	.1	81	27.7	318*	56.1	9	8	.1	9	0	.0
59323	2.3	99	.7	73	34.5	256	93.7	14	1	1.2	1	0	.1
59324	1.2	0	.4	82	17.3	213	38.7	6	18	.0	0	0	.0
59326	.4	96	.1	79	14.8	230	27.3	5	17	.2	16	0	.0
59327	3.6	100	1.3	73	26.8	242	76.5	10	10	1.8	8	0	.0
59330	10.5	98	3.8	73	25.3	303	82.5	9	10	5.3	8	0	.1
59336	.2	100	.1	71	22.6	260*	34.0	8	28	.1	22	0	.0
59337	1.0	0	.4	79	19.7	261	42.2	9	13	.0	0	0	.0
59338	.2	100	.1	88	9.2	105*	83.1	13	0	.1	18	0	.0
59339	.3	100	.1	97	17.5	201*	56.9	11	9	.1	21	0	.0
59343	.1	100	.1	62	25.2	289*	89.6*	3	21	.1	21	0	.0
59344	.5		.2	83	18.5	269		13	6	.2	4	0	.0
59347	.5	100	.2	76	29.8	342*	42.2	13	6	.2	4	0	.0
59349	1.4	98	.5	77	16.9	175	44.3	8	17	.7	18	0	.0
59351	.3	0	.1	85	25.3	291*	32.8	6	11	.3	6	0	.0
59353	1.4		.5	76	18.7	200	53.8	7	15	.5	9	0	.0
GREAT FALLS													
59401	17.8	95	7.3	58	23.5	228	80.9	8	14	8.3	11	0	.1
59403	.4	100	.1	94	41.5	477*	150.1	9	9	.4	2	3	.0
59404	19.8	96	6.8	80	30.3	319	96.0	7	7	9.4	6	2	3.00
59405	32.1	93	11.9	54	23.9	285	89.0	9	10	14.4	9	2	.0
59410	.8	92	.3	64	20.8	223	49.7	10	7	.4	7	0	.0
59411	.2		.1	86	31.2	359*	30.3	0	4	.8	8	0	.0
59412	1.5	99	.6	80	21.8	209	72.0	8	18	.8	17	0	.0
59414	1.1	96	.4	60	23.2	282	60.6	8	9	.6	9	2	.0
59416	.6	100	.3	69	30.4	105	51.8	9	7	.3	6	0	5.00
59417	4.5	0	1.2	53	18.8	257	63.8	13	6	.0	0	0	.0
59419	.3	100	.1	92	36.8	423*	24.1	6	3	.2	6	0	.0
59420	1.5	100	.5	63	21.9	323	32.6	7	7	.7	7	0	.0
59421	2.8	99	1.1	75	23.0	269	66.2	6	14	.7	14	0	.0
59422	.2	97	.1	73	20.9	211	66.1	6	18	1.3	17	0	.0
59424	4.0	100	1.5	69	16.2	186*	18.6	8	21	.3	9	0	.0
59425	5.3	99	1.9	68	27.2	211	66.2	8	14	2.4	10	2	.0
59427	.6	90	.2	75	25.4	243	74.7	9	11	.8	17	0	1.0
59430	.4	0	.1	73	23.1	198	58.5	8	11	.3	14	0	.0
59432	.7	0	.2	81	24.3	279*	42.3	5	9	.1	7	0	.0
59433	.2	0	.1	80	23.0	241	62.9	4	19	.1	17	0	.0
59434	1.8	99	.6	63	16.7	389	48.4	9	16	.2	6	0	.0
59436	.3	0	.1	80	24.1	260	65.9	9	13	1.0	14	0	.0
59440	2.3	99	.8	78	29.2	318	74.5	8	16	1.0	9	0	.0
59442	.8	95	.3	73	23.6	239	67.2	8	15	1.2	13	0	.9
59443	.4	100	.1	80	20.1	199	76.0	5	4	.4	11	0	.9
59444	.1	100		72	16.3	333	58.2*	5	7	.2	7	0	.0

*=Estimated   ***1.0=883 lbs per person; 100++ indicates per capita toxic waste generation > than 100 times the U.S. average of 883 lbs per capita.

ZIP CODE MEASURES OF SIZE, LEVELS OF AFFLUENCE AND QUALITY OF LIFE

1=Population (th.); 2= % White; 3=Households (th.); 4=% Owner Occupied; 5=Mean Income Per Household (th.$); 6=Mean Monthly Rent ($)*; 7=Mean Home Value (th.$)*;
8=% under 5; 9=% 65 and over; 10=% White Males, 65 and over; 11=% White Males, 65+; 12=# Toxic Waste Sites; 13=Toxic Waste Relative to US(883 lbs.per capita)**.

MONTANA

GREAT FALLS

ZIPCODE	1	2	3	4	5	6	7	8	9	10	11	12	13
59446	.6	100	.3	74	22.0	254	37.8	9	13	.3	14	0	.0
59447	.3	0	.1	73	24.8	367	47.7	14	14	.0	0	0	.0
59448	.9	0	.2	84	16.1	89	65.4	17	14	.0	0	0	.0
59450	.5	100	.2	69	26.1	242	42.8	8	14	.3	14	0	.0
59451	.4	100	.1	94	18.9	217*	13.1	11	8	.2	6	0	.0
59452	.6	0	.2	73	19.4	247	60.3	5	10	.0	0	0	.0
59453	.3	100	.1	77	17.9	255	31.9	11	9	.2	8	0	.0
59454	.3	100	.1	73	24.1	174	19.1	14	13	.1	10	1	.0
59456	.3	100	.1	69	26.6	306*	94.8*	7	5	.2	9	0	.0
59457	10.0	98	3.7	73	20.7	231	72.0	17	17	4.8	15	2	.0
59460	.2	100	.1	86	27.9	203	46.3	9	7	.1	5	0	.0
59462	.3	0	.1	89	23.4	191	36.2	1	15	.0	0	0	.0
59463	.3	71	.1	76	14.0	127	62.5	0	7	.1	7	0	.0
59464	.5	100	.2	58	19.7	273	41.9	10	14	.2	19	0	.0
59465	.2	100	.1	61	20.4	290	45.9	10	5	.1	8	0	.0
59467	.2	100	.1	12	16.3	228	58.0*	16	6	.1	8	0	.0
59468	.7	100	.2	88	26.9	279	83.6	13	6	.4	5	0	.0
59469	.3	100	.1	83	30.9	135	95.1	14	11	.1	14	0	.0
59471	.4	0	.2	83	31.3	324	30.7	6	25	.0	0	0	.0
59472	.8	0	.3	92	25.3	168	57.2	11	9	.0	0	0	.0
59474	3.6	95	1.4	67	23.1	243	63.8	10	13	1.6	11	0	.4
59477	.4	0	.1	64	18.3	177	67.3	5	8	.0	0	0	.0
59479	1.1	0	.4	70	19.7	203	50.3	9	18	.0	0	0	.0
59480	.3	100	.1	86	15.9	300	42.1	5	18	.2	15	0	.0
59482	.7	99	.3	85	22.8	179	40.1	11	14	.4	13	1	.0
59483	.6	0	.2	85	19.0	275	77.6	13	12	.2	4	0	.0
59484	.6	100	.2	46	32.6	284	49.3	7	7	.2	4	0	.0
59485	.6	0	.2	87	24.2	278*	74.8	13	7	.0	0	0	.0
59486	1.2	93	.5	71	21.7	257	48.3	11	18	.6	20	0	.0
59487	1.2	97	.4	75	27.5	427	80.6	7	5	.6	5	0	.0
59489	.4	97	.2	75	9.6	218	37.9	7	19	.2	22	0	.0

HARVE

ZIPCODE	1	2	3	4	5	6	7	8	9	10	11	12	13
59501	14.6	94	5.3	65	27.0	288	90.8	9	9	6.8	8	2	.1
59520	1.6	99	.6	81	24.8	222	59.7	9	13	.1	11	0	.0
59521	1.8	10	.4	59	18.5	202	44.0	12	6	.1	17	0	.0
59522	1.7	99	.6	69	25.4	244	60.2	9	12	.9	12	0	.4
59523	2.9	92	1.1	68	23.1	205	67.6	9	17	1.3	16	1	.0
59524	.6	42	.2	70	26.6	344	44.3	12	5	.1	8	0	.0
59525	.4	100	.1	80	25.8	296*	47.7	7	19	.2	20	0	.0
59526	2.4	49	.7	58	17.3	215	54.2	11	11	.5	15	0	.0
59527	.6	11	.2	61	12.4	233	49.8	7	6	.0	0	0	.0
59528	.3	0	.1	61	22.4	244	43.4	5	10	.0	0	0	.0
59529	.2	100	.1	91	25.9	298*	17.5	3	13	.1	17	0	.0
59530	.2	100	.1	76	19.6	197	19.4	5	29	.1	32	0	.0
59531	.5	0	.2	88	26.5	180	61.9	10	9	.0	0	0	.0
59532	.3	100	.1	72	30.8	226	49.0	9	9	.2	5	0	.0
59533	.2	100	.1	100	31.6	168*	52.2*	0	0	.1	17	0	.0
59535	.1	100	.1	54	31.6	363*	112.7*	11	23	.1	22	0	.0
59538	3.5	95	1.2	69	19.0	231	67.9	11	14	1.6	16	0	.0

MONTANA

HARVE

ZIPCODE	1	2	3	4	5	6	7	8	9	10	11	12	13
59540	.7	0	.2	72	24.8	225	58.7	11	9	.5	8	2	.0
59542	.5	0	.1	66	24.5	321	59.6	9	1	.1	25	0	.0
59543	.2	0	.1	100	11.5	132*	40.9*	12	27	.9	6	0	.0
59544	.2	0	.1	55	17.4	242	21.3	3	9	.0	5	0	.0

HELENA

ZIPCODE	1	2	3	4	5	6	7	8	9	10	11	12	13
59601	36.8	98	13.8	67	26.4	291	94.0	8	10	17.5	8	2	.1
59631	.2	100	.1	77	11.2	163	25.5	6	20	.1	25	0	.0
59632	1.8	97	.6	70	20.4	229	59.7	9	6	.9	6	0	.0
59635	2.0	98	.6	91	33.0	375	119.8	8	5	1.0	5	0	.0
59638	4.3	98	1.4	86	24.8	337	75.1	12	6	2.1	6	0	2.3
59639	.3	0	.1	53	20.8	240*	60.5	15	12	.0	0	0	.0
59643	.7	100	.3	68	17.6	202	80.9	2	19	.4	18	0	.0
59644	.3	71	.1	70	20.3	181	46.3	7	12	.2	9	0	.0
59645	2.6	99	.9	81	21.6	240	70.2	8	12	1.3	11	0	.0
59647	1.8	100	.6	73	21.6	261	61.2	7	11	.9	12	0	.0
59648	.4	100	.2	71	26.6	306*	70.0	6	25	.3	21	0	.0

BUTTE

ZIPCODE	1	2	3	4	5	6	7	8	9	10	11	12	13
59701	37.5	97	14.5	70	22.9	205	63.3	7	15	17.7	13	2	1.3
59710	.3	100	.1	66	20.4	101	91.0	11	3	.2	6	0	.0
59711	11.8	97	4.3	75	23.0	175	54.0	11	14	5.7	13	1	.0
59713	.3	100	.1	76	20.3	581	47.8	10	11	.1	10	0	.0
59714	4.2	99	1.4	74	23.8	296	90.3	12	7	2.0	8	0	.1
59715	31.7	98	10.9	55	24.2	330	113.7	6	7	16.1	5	4	.0
59716	.3	100	.1	49	22.6	327	193.8	3	0	.1	0	0	.0
59721	.3	100	.1	87	15.1	174*	28.4	9	18	.2	17	0	.1
59722	5.9	95	1.9	71	22.3	194	62.1	6	12	3.1	10	0	.0
59725	6.7	98	2.4	64	21.3	221	81.4	10	12	3.3	10	1	.0
59727	.2	0	.1	70	19.8	53	86.0	12	8	.0	0	0	.0
59728	.3	0	.1	76	23.4	260	61.2	12	7	.0	0	0	.0
59729	1.3	98	.5	62	18.9	318	112.8	11	14	.2	17	0	.0
59730	.9	98	.4	65	23.2	337	75.2	5	13	.4	12	0	.1
59731	.2	100	.1	56	24.2	173	86.2*	10	14	.1	25	2	.4
59732	.2	100	.1	26	17.1	196*	60.8*	6	9	.1	7	0	.0
59735	.2	100	.1	58	20.4	235*	46.0	9	35	.1	23	0	.0
59736	.1	100	.1	58	23.9	263	80.7	4	25	.1	37	1	.0
59739	.5	0	.2	82	26.3	153	34.7	6	12	.4	9	0	.0
59741	2.8	99	.9	83	22.9	204	87.4	9	9	1.4	9	0	.0
59743	.2	100	.1	84	19.5	98	68.7	7	9	.1	9	0	.0
59747	.2	100	.1	100	17.6	202*	68.1	0	14	.1	14	0	.0
59748	.1	100	.1	100	17.6	202*	68.1	14	19	.1	20	1	.0
59752	1.2	49	.7	58	18.6	207	66.4	9	20	.1	6	0	.0
59754	1.9	99	.7	73	23.3	221	63.6	6	14	1.0	13	1	.0
59755	.9	0	.4	71	17.8	185	67.7	8	18	.0	0	0	.0
59756	.3	0	.1	71	18.2	169	44.0	9	15	.0	0	0	.0
59758	.5	93	.2	88	27.2	160	96.8*	1	8	.3	6	0	.0
59760	1.0	100	.4	61	24.8	287	67.3	6	7	.7	13	0	4.1
59761	2.6	97	.9	81	23.4	170	67.4	7	12	1.3	13	1	.0
59761	.4	95	.1	69	17.0	165	21.9	1	19	.0	0	0	.0

*=Estimated **1.0=883 lbs per person, 100++ indicates per capita toxic waste generation > than 100 times the U.S. average of 883 lbs per capita.

ZIP CODE MEASURES OF SIZE, LEVELS OF AFFLUENCE AND QUALITY OF LIFE

1=Population (th.); 2= % White; 3=Households (th.); 4=% Owner Occupied; 5=Mean Income Per Household (th.$); 6=Mean Monthly Rent ($)*; 7=Mean Home Value (th.$)*; 8=% under 5; 9=% 65 and over; 10=White Males (th.); 11=% White Males, 65+; 12=# Toxic Waste Sites; 13=Toxic Waste Relative to US(883 lbs.per capita)**.

MONTANA

ZIPCODE	1	2	3	4	5	6	7	8	9	10	11	12	13
BUTTE													
59762	.2	100	.1	80	13.7	157	74.4	3	32	.1	24	0	.0
MISSOULA													
59801	64.7	97	24.5	58	25.8	326	110.8	7	9	31.1	7	3	.3
59806	.1	0		24	13.6	431	54.4	0	6		7	0	.0
59807	.2	100	.1	37	22.5	350	94.3	7	11	.1	6	0	.0
59820	.8	93	.3	70	23.2	191	61.4	13	7	.4	8	0	.0
59821	1.8	54	.6	78	21.8	239	69.4	12	6	.5	6	0	.0
59823	1.1	100	.4	77	30.2	275	106.0	12	4	.6	2	0	.0
59824	1.2	0		83	18.5	246	74.2	9	16	.6	0	0	.0
59825	1.4	98	.5	85	26.7	250	110.3	8	4	.7	3	0	.0
59826	.2	100	.1	53	18.0	363	127.4	0	25	.1	24	0	.0
59827	.2	100	.1	85	25.9	179	83.1	9	11	.1	12	0	.0
59828	2.0	95	.8	82	19.8	212	88.8	5	13	1.0	14	0	.0
59829	2.1	96	.7	72	22.6	218	71.8	7	9	1.0	10	0	.0
59831	.4		.1	70	16.0	270	60.1	13	10	1.0	10	0	.0
59832	.7	97	.3	66	25.0	204	64.7	9	13	.4	11	0	.0
59833	2.5	96	.8	85	26.6	339	97.9	10	6	1.2	7	0	.0
59834	1.3	0	.4	90	36.1	441	112.2	12	3	.6	2	0	.0
59836	.2	100	.1	75	24.0	276*	85.4*	5	3	.1	5	0	.0
59837	.3	100		81	24.9	115	60.5	7	11	.1	9	0	3.6
59840	8.7	98	3.5	75	20.3	247	87.5	6	19	4.2	17	0	.0
59841	.4	100	.1	65	19.2	249	57.2	23	0	.2	0	0	.0
59843	.1	100	.1	66	21.7	249*	77.2*	9	13	.1	0	0	.0
59844	.3	100	.1	73	12.4	132	74.4	4	14	.1	12	0	.0
59845	1.1	94	.5	69	13.8	167	43.0	8	29	.5	31	0	.0
59846	.7	100	.2	82	27.0	455	113.2	8	6	.3	7	0	.0
59847	3.0	99	1.0	84	29.5	261	102.4	10	4	1.5	5	0	.1
59848	.2	100	.1	87	28.3	326	100.9*	9	21	.1	19	0	.0
59851	.6	100	.2	70	21.6	316	104.5	9	18	.2	26	1	.2
59853	.8	100	.3	90	19.3	150	51.0	12	11	.4	10	0	.0
59854	.3	100	.1	82	25.2	289*	53.5	8	8	.1	9	0	.0
59855	.6	83	.2	81	20.7	133	72.6	11	6	.3	5	0	.0
59856	.3	100	.1	97	18.3	210*	46.2	4	17	.1	25	1	.0
59858	1.6	98	.6	78	19.4	149	42.2	7	16	.8	16	1	.2
59859	2.4	98	.8	73	23.6	240	68.5	9	12	1.2	12	0	.1
59860	6.2	95	2.5	71	19.8	240	96.4	7	19	2.8	17	0	.0
59864	4.8	73	1.5	71	22.2	231	71.9	10	12	1.7	13	0	.0
59865	2.2	70	.7	72	19.9	229	64.2	10	11	.7	14	0	.0
59866	.7	100	.3	72	21.6	172	74.9	9	8	.0	0	0	.2
59868	1.3	0	.4	79	22.1	208	74.9	10	6	.0	0	0	.1
59870	5.1	99	1.7	81	22.1	316	93.0	10	11	2.4	9	0	.0
59872	2.2	99	.8	75	23.0	225	75.8	10	9	1.1	9	0	.0
59873	2.6	99	.9	76	22.4	183	69.7	9	9	1.4	8	1	.0
59874	.7	100	.3	85	20.0	125	103.5	6	12	.4	13	0	.0
59875	2.0	95	.7	81	21.5	339	87.7	6	11	1.0	11	0	.0
KALISPELL													
59901	27.9	98	10.1	74	25.0	288	91.7	8	11	13.4	10	2	.2
59910	.1	100	.1	89	12.5	144*	178.0	0	39	.1	33	0	.0
59911	4.4	99	1.5	82	23.7	248	120.3	10	13	2.2	13	0	.0

MONTANA

ZIPCODE	1	2	3	4	5	6	7	8	9	10	11	12	13
KALISPELL													
59912	8.4	99	2.9	76	25.3	293	84.8	8	8	4.3	7	1	.9
59913	.3	0	.1	71	22.1	173	67.1	6	11	.0	0	0	.0
59914	.3	100	.1	76	21.3	158	70.6	18	12	.1	7	0	.0
59915	.2	23	.1	100	12.2	141*	100.9	5	21	.0	62	0	.0
59917	2.8	97	.9	72	20.0	224	65.5	8	8	1.3	7	0	.0
59918	.4	0	.1	73	20.9	182	57.4	11	14	.0	0	0	.0
59919	.6	100	.2	65	17.6	211	78.6	12	12	.3	17	0	.0
59920	.6	0	.2	91	27.4	308	62.3	10	3	.0	0	0	.0
59922	1.0	0	.3	81	23.9	203	136.1	4	13	.0	0	0	.4
59923	10.9	98	3.8	77	24.1	243	82.0	8	8	5.4	7	1	.0
59925	.5	93	.1	80	22.0	284	115.2	8	17	.3	19	0	.0
59926	.7	95	.2	77	26.3	312	56.1	11	7	.4	9	0	.0
59927	.3	100	.1	74	22.8	176	36.8	7	2	.1	4	0	.0
59930	.4	0	.1	85	22.1	123	46.8	12	7	.0	7	0	.0
59931	.1	100	.3	100	30.7	353*	163.2	0	38	.1	42	0	.0
59932	.8	100	.3	79	26.5	315	111.9	5	15	.4	21	0	.0
59934	.2	100	.2	59	16.2	402	57.7*	14	4	.1	7	0	.0
59935	3.0	99	1.1	70	20.1	260	66.5	13	8	1.5	7	1	.0
59936	.3	100	.1	44	25.5	224	148.8	12	0	.1	0	0	.0
59937	7.8	99	3.1	68	24.5	311	91.0	8	10	3.8	8	0	.0

*=Estimated **1.0=883 lbs per person; 100++ indicates per capita toxic waste generation > than 100 times the U.S. average of 883 lbs per capita.

ZIP CODE MEASURES OF SIZE, LEVELS OF AFFLUENCE AND QUALITY OF LIFE

1=Population (th.); 2= % White; 3=Households (th.); 4=% Owner Occupied; 5=Mean Income Per Household (th.$); 6=Mean Monthly Rent ($)*; 7=Mean Home Value (th.$)*;
8=% under 5; 9=% 65 and over; 10=White Males (th.); 11=% White Males, 65+; 12=# Toxic Waste Sites; 13=Toxic Waste Relative to US(883 lbs.per capita)**.

NEBRASKA — OMAHA

ZIPCODE	1	2	3	4	5	6	7	8	9	10	11	12	13
68001	.2	100	.1	89	12.8	147*	20.1	19	26	.1	30	0	.0
68002	1.9	100	.7	77	25.7	286	74.0	7	12	1.0	11	0	.0
68003	3.6	99	1.3	78	24.4	244	61.5	8	16	1.8	14	0	.0
68004	1.3	99	.5	74	21.0	225	51.4	7	16	.6	13	0	.0
68005	24.2	93	8.5	63	31.0	408	94.4	7	4	11.5	4	1	.2
68007	1.5	0	.6	78	28.1	324	77.3	10	7	.0	0	0	.0
68008	8.8	100	3.0	72	26.6	250	79.6	7	14	4.0	11	0	.3
68014	.5	0	.2	71	19.4	286	25.5	10	17	.0	0	0	.0
68015	1.1	100	.4	84	26.5	265	58.1	7	14	.6	11	0	.0
68016	.3	100	.1	93	34.1	392*	76.2	7	7	.2	10	0	.0
68017	1.7	0	.5	83	25.9	297	67.3	9	13	.0	0	0	.0
68018	.5	0	.3	81	24.6	179	53.4	7	8	.0	0	0	.0
68019	.7	0	.3	74	22.9	170	29.3	4	18	.0	0	0	.0
68020	1.1	95	.4	73	18.5	227	42.5	8	17	.6	16	0	.0
68022	6.5	99	1.8	90	36.1	350	118.8	9	6	3.1	5	0	.4
68023	1.6	99	.5	84	29.8	232	84.0	7	8	.8	9	2	3.4
68025	27.5	100	10.4	69	26.2	295	69.4	7	14	13.1	7	1	.9
68028	3.3	99	1.0	85	29.5	350	83.0	8	7	1.7	6	0	.0
68029	1.0	100	.3	73	22.2	280	54.2	8	15	.5	15	0	.0
68030	.6	0	.2	83	24.1	291	65.2	7	15	.0	0	0	.6
68031	2.2	0	.8	71	25.3	215	54.1	9	18	.0	0	0	.0
68033	.4	100	.1	78	22.0	218	57.0	7	15	.2	14	0	.0
68034	.8	100	.3	84	24.9	282	62.6	8	11	.4	10	0	.0
68035	.2	0	.1	88	23.8	273*	66.9	6	9	.0	0	0	.0
68036	.4	0	.1	67	18.9	270	25.5	15	16	.8	15	0	.1
68037	1.7	0	.6	82	26.4	273	56.3	7	17	.8	15	0	.1
68038	2.0	100	.8	74	22.8	196	54.4	7	25	1.0	21	0	.0
68039	1.2	6	.3	30	15.0	192	20.5	13	8	.2	29	0	.0
68040	.4	100	.1	86	24.2	380	41.2	6	10	.2	10	0	.0
68041	.9	99	.4	74	28.7	246	72.2	8	11	.3	16	0	.3
68044	.6	99	.2	81	26.7	184	70.6	5	13	.3	15	0	.0
68045	2.2	0	.8	68	21.3	206	48.3	6	23	.0	0	0	.0
68046	8.3	98	2.5	75	33.6	404	97.8	7	5	4.0	4	1	.0
68047	2.3	100	.8	73	23.0	195	69.3	7	17	1.1	15	5	1.5
68048	9.1	98	3.1	74	25.6	283	74.0	9	11	4.4	9	1	.0

LINCOLN

ZIPCODE	1	2	3	4	5	6	7	8	9	10	11	12	13
68050	.8	100	.3	85	16.8	239	37.5	8	17	.4	16	0	.0
68055	.5	0	.2	67	21.5	227	31.7	6	17	.0	0	0	.1
68057	2.1	100	.8	74	22.8	188	53.7	7	20	1.0	18	0	.0
68059	2.3	99	.7	85	32.5	374	82.0	10	7	1.2	7	0	.0
68061	2.8	100	1.1	72	20.8	249	60.0	8	19	1.3	16	0	.0
68062	.4	0	.1	83	24.9	209	56.2	9	14	.0	0	0	.0
68063	.3	100	.1	81	21.4	269	45.4	8	27	.1	28	0	.0
68064	3.1	100	.8	71	27.8	277	75.1	9	10	1.5	8	1	5.5
68065	1.2	0	.4	89	24.6	298	58.4	9	15	.0	0	0	.0
68066	4.5	100	1.8	74	23.8	247	61.0	7	23	2.1	19	2	.0
68067	1.3	87	.7	76	21.3	192	47.7	9	16	.3	16	0	1.5
68069	2.0	100	.7	80	33.0	311	94.7	8	11	1.0	10	1	.0
68070	.8	100	.3	82	16.5	217	37.0	6	15	.4	14	0	.0
68071	1.5	24	.4	44	18.7	189	62.4	12	8	.2	15	0	.0

NEBRASKA — OMAHA (continued)

ZIPCODE	1	2	3	4	5	6	7	8	9	10	11	12	13
68073	1.6	99	.5	85	27.9	304	68.1	11	10	.8	8	0	.0
68102	4.2	76	2.4	2	16.9	181	21.8	3	27	1.9	24	4	8.5
68104	36.7	83	13.8	73	24.9	326	55.9	8	13	14.4	12	1	.0
68105	23.0	97	10.2	44	20.8	254	55.5	6	18	10.3	14	5	.2
68106	21.7	97	8.8	72	27.1	379	55.3	6	16	9.9	13	1	.0
68107	24.8	88	9.4	70	21.4	235	44.3	7	15	10.4	14	4	4.5
68108	14.0	94	5.6	54	18.4	254	35.9	8	17	6.2	15	3	3.7
68110	10.1	40	3.8	56	15.5	201	24.8	9	15	1.9	18	6	4.2
68111	30.2	35	10.3	62	17.8	256	29.2	10	10	4.9	13	1	.0
68112	13.2	91	4.5	84	26.5	335	55.0	7	14	5.7	13	2	.2
68113	3.4	76	1.4	60	18.2	328	64.8*	11	0	1.8	0	1	.0
68114	17.0	97	6.8	60	41.8	458	123.0	8	14	7.7	12	0	1.4
68117	8.6	98	2.8	79	25.7	364	57.9	8	8	4.1	6	0	.6
68118	.8	100	.3	97	33.4	150	132.1	7	6	.5	5	0	.4
68122	1.9	94	.6	87	32.8	530	93.2	8	15	.8	9	0	.0
68123	15.0	87	4.0	35	27.9	381	120.7	12	1	6.7	1	4	.0
68124	17.6	98	5.9	76	44.9	405	122.5	6	9	8.3	7	0	.0
68127	18.7	98	7.4	48	29.1	339	89.5	7	3	9.2	2	4	.4
68128	9.7	95	3.0	67	28.2	366	80.1	11	2	4.5	2	0	.0
68130	4.5	99	1.3	96	41.3	388	121.4	12	1	2.2	1	0	.0
68131	13.4	82	6.2	28	17.5	270	46.1	6	15	4.9	10	1	.1
68132	15.1	97	6.5	49	32.2	311	109.7	6	13	6.7	10	0	.0
68133	.7	0	.2	97	43.9	505*	146.6	5	6	.6	10	0	.0
68134	28.8	96	10.6	96	31.0	380	115.0	13	6	13.1	6	1	.0
68135	.6	100	.2	96	36.2	416*	118.2	11	5	.8	4	0	.1
68137	20.8	98	6.3	79	36.6	408	98.2	12	3	10.0	3	0	.4
68138	2.7	98	.9	86	31.3	550	102.6	14	1	1.4	2	0	.0
68142	1.0	100	.4	91	25.5	350	92.2	13	0	.5	0	0	.0
68144	25.0	99	7.9	76	39.9	354	110.4	8	4	12.0	3	1	.0
68147	11.1	91	3.5	75	27.7	353	71.2	10	4	5.1	4	3	.0
68152	5.9	81	1.8	80	38.2	236	110.2	8	6	2.4	7	2	6.1
68154	14.2	97	5.0	68	42.3	441	136.9	8	5	6.8	5	0	.0
68157	5.7	98	1.6	86	33.9	452	84.0	9	2	2.8	2	0	.0
68164	10.3	96	3.6	73	32.1	400	99.4	14	2	4.9	1	0	.0

LINCOLN

ZIPCODE	1	2	3	4	5	6	7	8	9	10	11	12	13
68301	1.3	100	.4	81	22.4	265	59.4	8	14	.7	13	0	.0
68303	.6	99	.2	79	15.5	145	31.7	6	29	.3	27	0	.0
68304	.4	100	.1	91	24.5	150	50.8	5	15	.2	17	0	.0
68305	4.7	100	1.9	71	23.1	225	57.8	7	21	2.2	17	1	.4
68307	.5	0	.2	79	20.1	279	47.4	8	24	.0	0	0	.0
68309	.2	100	.1	92	17.4	200*	26.1	5	13	.1	9	0	.0
68310	15.6	100	5.9	70	22.7	247	65.5	7	18	7.3	15	8	1.1
68313	1.0	0	.4	70	22.5	244	47.9	9	16	.2	9	0	.0
68314	.3	100	.1	75	16.1	292	35.3	7	12	.2	9	0	.0
68315	.3	100	.1	87	21.3	134	16.6	8	18	.2	19	1	.0
68316	.5	100	.2	83	24.0	244	41.9	7	11	.3	10	0	.0
68317	1.1	100	.4	88	26.8	182	67.3	10	14	.6	12	0	.0
68318	.7	99	.3	75	19.9	278	30.8	8	16	.4	16	0	.0

*=Estimated **1.0=883 lbs per person; 100++ indicates per capita toxic waste generation > than 100 times the U.S. average of 883 lbs per capita.

ZIP CODE MEASURES OF SIZE, LEVELS OF AFFLUENCE AND QUALITY OF LIFE

1=Population (th.); 2= % White; 3=Households (th.); 4=% Owner Occupied; 5=Mean Income Per Household (th.$); 6=Mean Monthly Rent ($); 7=Mean Home Value (th.$); 8=% under 5; 9=% 65 and over; 10=White Males (th.); 11=% White Males, 65+; 12=# Toxic Waste Sites; 13=Toxic Waste Relative to US(883 lbs.per capita)**.

NEBRASKA

LINCOLN

ZIP CODE	1	2	3	4	5	6	7	8	9	10	11	12	13
68319	.8	96	.3	80	28.2	273	52.4	9	15	.4	14	0	.0
68320	.5	100	.2	75	21.8	274	34.5	7	14	.2	14	0	.0
68321	.4	97	.2	82	16.5	196	42.0	10	17	.2	22	0	24.9
68322	.6	100	.2	75	21.7	166*	51.3	9	19	.3	15	0	.0
68324	.5	0	.1	76	15.3	176*	32.6	9	12	.0	0	0	.0
68325	.3	100	.1	73	18.6	258	38.0	5	14	.2	15	0	.0
68326	.4	100	.2	84	22.3	269	38.2	8	23	.2	24	0	.0
68327	.4	0	.1	79	24.6	183	46.6	12	14	.0	0	0	.0
68328	.5	0	.2	82	20.1	187	30.2	5	20	.0	0	0	.2
68329	.8	100	.3	88	19.6	140	50.8	8	18	.2	15	0	.0
68331	.9	99	.3	83	17.4	286	41.9	5	22	.0	0	0	.0
68332	.2	100	.1	93	17.1	197*	75.4	8	13	.4	12	0	.0
68333	6.4	99	2.2	72	25.7	289	21.1	7	16	3.0	15	0	.0
68335	.8	100	.4	83	24.6	275	53.2	4	21	.4	20	0	.0
68336	.5	0	.2	90	25.7	332	77.7	11	8	.0	0	0	.0
68337	.7	0	.2	66	14.0	372	20.6	4	16	.0	0	0	.0
68338	.4	100	.2	86	26.4	368	41.7	9	19	.2	19	0	.0
68339	.7	100	.2	83	29.9	436	88.7	6	19	.4	8	0	.2
68340	1.5	98	.6	74	19.4	202	45.7	6	23	.7	21	1	2.9
68341	1.3	0	.5	77	29.8	256	57.2	6	17	.7	17	0	.8
68342	.7	100	.3	81	25.9	239	41.4	9	19	.4	19	0	.6
68343	.4	0	.5	76	22.6	248	52.3	4	20	.0	0	0	.6
68344	1.1	100	.2	94	25.7	295*	50.9	6	19	.6	14	0	.3
68345	.4	100	.2	87	15.1	157	23.7	4	30	.2	31	0	.0
68346	.6	100	.2	63	25.4	261	40.3	6	15	.3	16	0	.0
68347	1.3	99	.5	87	27.4	373	76.3	10	9	.7	8	0	.0
68348	.4	100	.1	78	19.3	215	34.1	8	25	.2	21	0	.0
68349	1.0	99	.4	76	26.7	273	63.0	6	17	.5	12	0	.0
68350	.3	0	.1	73	19.2	164	31.8	4	19	.7	21	1	.0
68351	1.2	0	.4	80	21.7	292	45.6	4	23	.0	0	0	.0
68352	6.4	99	2.6	74	20.6	215	49.6	6	22	3.0	19	0	.0
68354	1.3	100	.5	72	22.9	188	48.3	7	18	.6	14	1	.6
68355	6.5	99	2.6	70	19.9	209	53.5	5	23	3.0	18	0	.3
68357	.6	0	.2	74	19.0	376	53.0	5	12	.2	13	0	.0
68358	.9	97	.3	77	24.3	308	55.6	10	21	.4	17	0	.0
68359	1.7	0	.7	72	22.7	198	58.2	5	23	.3	16	0	.0
68360	.7	100	.7	93	28.6	360	53.3	13	10	.7	10	1	.2
68361	3.1	99	1.2	73	22.3	243	67.7	8	20	1.5	15	0	.1
68365	.3	100	.1	77	21.7	248	41.1	8	16	.2	13	0	.0
68366	1.0	0	.4	74	24.9	332	59.2	6	10	.4	17	0	.0
68367	.7	100	.3	80	20.8	160	34.8	7	18	.3	16	0	.0
68368	.6	0	.2	77	22.3	302	51.0	4	9	.1	0	0	.0
68370	2.6	0	1.0	80	22.6	235	56.0	7	21	1.5	15	0	.0
68371	1.7	0	1.2	81	24.8	221	84.1	9	20	1.0	9	0	.2
68372	1.5	100	.5	87	25.4	255	76.2	9	13	.7	12	0	.0
68374	.2	100	.1	72	26.3	391	40.2	8	9	.1	17	0	.0
68375	.2	100	.1	96	21.1	242*	20.6	1	18	.1	17	0	.1
68376	1.9	99	.8	77	20.3	187	43.3	6	28	.9	25	0	.1

NEBRASKA

LINCOLN

ZIP CODE	1	2	3	4	5	6	7	8	9	10	11	12	13
68377	.5	100	.2	64	18.1	108	54.4	6	12	.3	9	1	.0
68378	.9	100	.3	72	23.5	249	47.5	10	18	.4	16	0	.0
68381	.3	100	.1	90	24.2	243	16.4	7	9	.2	8	0	.0

LINCOLN

ZIP CODE	1	2	3	4	5	6	7	8	9	10	11	12	13
68401	.7	100	.2	67	20.6	287	47.4	9	10	.4	8	2	.0
68402	.9	100	.3	92	30.6	445	90.4	8	7	.5	7	0	.0
68404	.7	100	.2	79	24.4	412	101.5	10	8	.4	11	0	.0
68405	3.3	99	1.0	69	23.9	241	74.1	7	13	1.8	10	0	.0
68406	.7	100	.3	75	17.1	241	45.6	4	28	.3	25	0	.0
68407	.8	100	.3	80	25.6	199	57.5	4	16	.3	14	0	.0
68409	.8	100	.3	72	29.4	402	75.5	10	10	.4	10	0	.0
68410	8.6	100	3.4	71	22.3	248	59.1	7	20	4.0	17	2	.2
68413	.6	0	.2	70	18.5	344	44.4	7	12	.0	0	0	.7
68414	.8	100	.2	74	22.7	302	30.7	5	26	.2	27	0	.0
68415	.8	99	.3	81	22.3	253	38.4	6	18	.4	16	0	.0
68416	.4	100	.2	70	15.6	266	22.3	6	23	.2	21	0	.0
68417	.4	100	.1	70	16.2	373	33.9	11	12	.2	8	0	.0
68418	.9	100	.3	77	25.7	340	55.1	7	14	.5	11	0	.0
68419	.1	100	.1	69	23.4	310	60.9	3	22	.1	15	0	2.9
68420	1.8	100	.6	78	16.9	158	34.5	5	32	.8	27	0	.8
68421	1.3	94	.4	64	20.2	230	48.2	8	8	.6	7	0	.0
68422	.6	0	.2	79	25.9	272	59.2	8	14	.0	0	0	.0
68423	.8	0	.3	88	25.0	291	90.9	8	17	.0	0	0	.0
68424	1.0	100	.3	84	25.8	257	52.7	10	15	.5	12	0	.0
68428	.2	0	.3	79	30.6	281	83.7	8	11	.2	17	0	.0
68429	.4	100	.1	74	10.5	308	21.6	3	14	.2	19	0	.0
68430	.5	100	.2	85	36.1	172	98.0	8	10	.2	13	0	.1
68431	1.2	100	.6	76	17.6	128	32.1	9	11	.6	17	0	.0
68433	.2	87	.1	78	13.7	220	20.1	11	11	.3	0	0	.0
68434	7.5	97	2.4	68	26.1	273	81.8	8	14	3.5	11	1	.0
68436	.8	100	.3	81	28.9	277	49.9	8	13	.4	13	0	.0
68437	.4	98	.2	77	19.0	145	24.2	7	25	.2	23	0	.0
68438	.6	0	.1	93	39.5	453*	70.9	8	13	.0	0	0	.0
68439	.6	100	.2	77	26.7	285	38.9	9	9	.4	8	0	.0
68440	.2	100	.1	90	18.2	209*	20.2	3	24	.2	17	0	.0
68441	.4	100	.2	86	18.9	73	28.6	7	20	.2	19	0	.0
68442	.5	100	.2	74	27.5	263	35.5	4	13	.2	13	0	.0
68443	1.2	100	.4	88	18.3	272	44.3	11	21	.6	17	0	.0
68444	.2	100	.1	73	23.3	167	41.3	14	7	.1	6	0	.0
68445	.2	100	.1	78	18.5	203	22.9	11	10	.2	17	0	.0
68446	2.3	100	.7	80	24.7	274	72.6	7	24	1.2	18	0	.0
68447	.7	100	.3	80	16.2	223	30.4	4	20	.3	19	0	.0
68448	.6	100	.2	77	18.7	223	44.3	5	26	.3	24	0	.0
68450	2.7	0	1.1	76	20.3	165	52.2	6	23	.0	0	0	.0
68452	.2	0	.1	82	17.0	71	25.7	8	21	.0	0	0	.0
68453	.5	100	.2	72	19.2	250	29.7	12	21	.2	20	0	.0
68454	.7	100	.3	78	26.7	228	61.5	11	15	.4	15	0	.2
68455	1.0	100	.2	77	26.5	163	58.9	7	14	.5	14	0	.0
68456	1.1	0	.4	73	25.5	264	50.0	6	23	.9	25	0	.1

*=Estimated **1.0=883 lbs per person; 100++ indicates per capita toxic waste generation > than 100 times the U.S. average of 883 lbs per capita.

ZIP CODE MEASURES OF SIZE, LEVELS OF AFFLUENCE AND QUALITY OF LIFE

1=Population (th.); 2= % White; 3=Households (th.); 4=% Owner Occupied; 5=Mean Income Per Household (th.$); 6=Mean Monthly Rent ($)*; 7=Mean Home Value (th.$)*; 8=% under 5; 9=% 65 and over; 10=% White Males, 65+; 11=% White Males; 12=# Toxic Waste Sites; 13=Toxic Waste Relative to US(883 lbs.per capita)**.

NEBRASKA

LINCOLN

ZIP CODE	1	2	3	4	5	6	7	8	9	10	11	12	13
68457	.5	0	.2	79	13.7	274	27.6	4	27	.0	0	0	.0
68458	.3	0	.1	78	19.4	300	48.9	10	13	.0	0	0	.0
68460	1.0	100	.4	67	21.6	319	41.5	8	11	.5	11	0	.1
68461	.4	100	.1	94	37.8	434*	90.1	0	2	.2	0	0	.0
68462	2.3	99	.7	79	30.8	343	89.0	8	7	1.1	7	3	2.0
68463	1.6	0	.6	74	22.7	239	54.0	7	21	.0	0	2	11.8
68464	.7	100	.3	89	19.2	90	24.4	8	20	.3	18	0	.0
68465	2.2	100	.9	80	21.2	218	54.1	7	28	1.1	24	0	.0
68466	2.5	99	1.0	79	19.5	204	45.6	5	27	1.2	23	0	.0
68467	9.4	99	3.5	69	25.9	270	74.9	7	16	4.3	12	1	.3

LINCOLN

ZIP CODE	1	2	3	4	5	6	7	8	9	10	11	12	13
68502	28.7	96	12.4	53	26.2	329	91.6	6	14	12.9	11	0	.1
68503	12.8	85	5.2	41	18.3	298	56.3	8	11	5.6	9	0	.0
68504	12.7	97	5.1	53	22.0	333	69.3	7	9	5.9	7	0	.5
68505	14.5	99	4.8	77	33.2	398	87.5	6	6	7.0	6	0	.0
68506	24.6	98	9.1	76	34.8	385	109.3	7	11	11.3	10	0	.0
68507	12.0	99	4.5	74	27.3	334	75.9	8	10	5.9	9	0	.6
68508	13.9	92	4.6	14	14.4	250	52.7	5	22	6.4	6	1	1.6
68510	20.4	98	8.5	60	26.7	339	92.6	5	17	9.0	12	0	.0
68512	4.8	97	1.7	67	36.4	423	118.2	11	2	2.3	1	1	.5
68516	12.4	99	4.2	75	35.0	439	118.6	9	5	6.0	3	0	.0
68520	.7	100	.2	88	55.2	807	151.4	9	3	.3	5	0	.0
68521	12.1	96	4.4	75	25.1	316	80.1	12	6	5.7	5	1	.2
68522	3.7	92	1.4	86	27.5	332	82.8	11	5	1.9	4	1	.1
68524	3.4	97	1.0	25	22.3	328	68.1	14	1	1.6	1	1	2.9
68528	2.1	95	.8	66	30.0	321	102.7	9	8	1.0	1	0	.9

COLUMBUS

ZIP CODE	1	2	3	4	5	6	7	8	9	10	11	12	13
68601	22.6	99	8.2	74	26.9	281	83.5	9	12	10.8	10	0	1.5
68620	3.7	0	1.4	67	22.7	186	56.3	9	18	.0	0	0	.0
68621	.6	98	.2	77	28.0	496	86.1	8	8	.3	8	0	.2
68622	.4	100	.1	65	22.2	224	39.1	13	9	.2	7	1	.8
68623	.5	100	.2	65	16.3	130	18.8	8	15	.2	12	0	.0
68624	1.2	100	.4	76	24.1	291	65.8	9	12	.6	10	0	.0
68626	.7	100	.3	77	20.1	335	50.4	7	17	.4	16	1	.0
68627	1.0	100	.4	79	17.1	187	32.7	5	18	.5	18	0	.0
68628	1.1	100	.4	72	20.4	269	40.6	8	16	.6	16	0	.0
68629	1.9	100	.7	80	21.8	175	46.2	4	25	1.0	20	0	.0
68631	.6	100	.2	73	18.8	234	45.8	12	12	.3	11	0	.0
68632	3.8	100	1.4	73	21.7	233	56.3	9	24	1.8	21	1	.1
68633	1.7	99	.6	79	19.4	213	53.6	9	17	.8	15	0	.0
68634	.5	100	.2	90	21.8	282	64.0	13	11	.3	12	0	.2
68635	.6	99	.2	83	24.5	338	31.7	7	15	.3	14	0	.0
68636	1.8	100	.7	80	15.0	177	50.2	7	20	.9	17	0	.0
68637	.4	100	.2	72	16.6	375	31.2	5	22	.1	23	0	.0
68638	2.2	0	.8	80	18.4	166	46.1	7	22	.5	18	0	.0
68640	1.9	0	.6	78	19.0	215	44.8	9	18	.6	16	0	.2
68641	1.6	99	.6	75	20.1	288	40.8	7	19	.8	17	0	.0
68642	2.2	0	.6	81	25.5	283	52.5	8	12	.0	0	0	.0
68643	1.3	99	.5	80	19.8	240	47.0	7	16	.6	16	0	.0

NEBRASKA

COLUMBUS

ZIP CODE	1	2	3	4	5	6	7	8	9	10	11	12	13
68644	1.2	100	.4	80	24.0	254	55.2	10	10	.6	8	0	4.1
68647	.7	100	.3	82	22.3	284	50.6	10	17	.4	15	0	.0
68648	.5	100	.2	76	22.1	253	48.0	6	21	.2	21	0	.0
68649	2.1	99	.7	78	25.8	275	59.1	9	16	1.0	13	0	.0
68650	.1	100	.1	83	19.9	229*	40.6	8	7	.0	6	0	.0
68651	1.7	99	.6	81	24.0	199	51.1	8	19	.8	15	1	.0
68652	1.1	100	.4	81	15.4	213	28.8	10	14	.5	15	0	.0
68653	.9	100	.3	81	23.4	252	50.0	11	14	.5	16	0	.0
68654	.3	100	.1	76	15.3	176	34.1	6	24	.5	22	0	.0
68655	.3	100	.1	86	17.8	225	38.2	10	15	.1	12	0	.0
68657	.5	100	.5	74	23.0	410	36.9	13	14	.2	17	0	.0
68658	.8	100	.3	83	23.4	234	52.6	9	22	.4	20	0	.0
68659	.3	100	.1	79	30.0	289	38.2	9	9	.2	10	0	.0
68660	1.6	0	.6	78	22.4	146	47.5	9	22	.2	10	0	.0
68661	5.4	99	2.0	76	22.7	255	61.9	8	20	2.6	18	0	.0
68662	1.2	100	.5	72	20.2	191	56.1	8	15	.6	14	0	.0
68663	1.2	100	.4	81	20.9	199	45.8	10	13	.6	11	0	.0
68664	.4	100	.1	76	20.3	211	43.4	9	17	.2	12	0	3.2
68665	1.3	0	.4	80	19.0	181	37.5	9	16	.2	12	0	.0
68666	1.8	97	.7	76	21.4	159	54.0	5	27	.0	0	1	.1
68669	.7	100	.2	83	24.7	67	28.6	6	15	.4	13	0	.0

NORFOLK

ZIP CODE	1	2	3	4	5	6	7	8	9	10	11	12	13
68701	25.9	99	9.4	68	26.2	300	80.4	9	12	12.3	10	2	.7
68710	1.1	100	.4	81	22.0	221	50.0	8	12	.6	12	1	.0
68711	.2	100	.1	71	23.7	77	15.3	4	5	.1	3	0	.7
68713	3.2	100	1.1	73	19.6	233	54.1	9	18	1.6	17	0	.1
68714	1.9	99	.7	73	22.4	211	61.7	8	17	.9	15	0	.0
68715	1.5	0	.5	80	26.8	301	69.2	9	15	.0	0	0	.0
68716	1.4	100	.5	76	22.9	188	55.4	7	20	.7	16	0	.1
68717	.3	100	.1	78	17.3	254	37.6	15	20	.2	18	0	.0
68718	2.6	98	1.0	75	17.9	188	47.7	8	20	1.3	17	0	.0
68719	.2	100	.2	89	14.7	58	22.8	12	19	.1	19	0	.0
68720	.5	100	.2	77	22.1	250	46.0	7	14	.3	11	0	.0
68722	.9	100	.3	78	17.9	229	34.4	10	27	.5	26	0	.0
68723	.7	0	.3	74	19.4	184	45.0	5	19	.0	0	0	.0
68724	.3	100	.1	87	21.3	173	32.4	10	18	.1	18	0	.0
68725	.6	100	.2	77	18.2	253	42.6	9	17	.3	13	0	.0
68726	1.1	99	.4	79	15.2	168	45.4	10	13	.5	11	0	.0
68727	.6	100	.2	74	16.9	190	41.4	6	25	.5	22	0	.0
68728	.3	100	.1	78	14.2	163*	35.4	7	28	.1	21	1	.0
68729	2.2	0	.9	76	19.3	182	49.5	5	21	.0	0	0	.0
68730	2.2	0	.7	77	20.4	208	63.4	11	12	.0	0	0	.0
68731	2.6	93	.8	78	28.9	365	77.7	11	6	1.2	5	0	1.8
68732	.4	100	.1	80	18.5	186	27.8	5	10	.2	8	0	.0
68733	1.6	99	.6	70	23.6	222	44.7	9	20	.8	19	0	.0
68734	.1	100	.1	81	21.0	140	42.5	12	15	.1	5	0	.0
68735	1.4	100	.5	83	19.6	203	47.4	8	14	.7	12	1	.0
68736	.9	100	.3	75	21.5	353	49.2	10	12	.5	10	1	.0
68737	.1	100	.1	60	33.1	124	36.0	12	11	.1	10	0	.0

*=Estimated **1.0=883 lbs per person; 100++ indicates per capita toxic waste generation > than 100 times the U.S. average of 883 lbs per capita.

ZIP CODE MEASURES OF SIZE, LEVELS OF AFFLUENCE AND QUALITY OF LIFE

1=Population (th.); 2= % White; 3=Households (th.); 4=% Owner Occupied; 5=Mean Income Per Household (th.$); 6=Mean Monthly Rent ($); 7=Mean Home Value (th.$); 8=% under 5; 9=% 65 and over; 10=White Males; 11=% White Males, 65+; 12=# Toxic Waste Sites; 13=Toxic Waste Relative to US(883 lbs.per capita)**.

NEBRASKA — NORFOLK

ZIPCODE	1	2	3	4	5	6	7	8	9	10	11	12	13
68738	.2	100	.1	65	18.0	288	70.9	13	8	.1	7	0	.0
68739	3.8	0	1.1	80	24.8	225	61.0	11	13	.0	11	0	.3
68740	.8	100	.3	83	21.6	371	61.5	16	13	.4	11	0	.0
68741	.5	100	.2	65	18.7	384	58.5	6	4	.3	6	0	.0
68742	.4	0	.2	73	15.7	252	44.8	7	15	.0	0	0	.0
68743	1.0	100	.3	77	20.9	323	59.2	8	10	.5	12	1	.0
68744	1.9	0	.8	72	18.7	184	49.5	7	19	.0	0	0	.0
68745	.8	100	.3	73	13.6	208	33.4	7	17	.4	16	0	.0
68746	.3	100	.1	74	25.5	293*	36.1	6	11	.1	8	0	.0
68747	3.2	100	1.1	74	21.9	257	55.5	10	17	1.6	13	0	.1
68748	1.0	0	.4	76	21.9	242	43.2	5	14	.0	0	0	.0
68752	.1	100	.1	70	18.4	330	13.1	7	13	.1	10	0	.0
68753	.4	100	.2	93	15.1	173*	21.7	9	27	.2	24	0	.0
68755	2.6	100	1.0	75	20.6	186	60.9	9	21	1.2	17	0	.2
68756	1.0	100	.3	79	16.6	300	39.9	9	20	.5	19	0	.0
68757	1.5	0	.6	74	18.7	239	44.3	8	22	.0	0	0	.0
68758	.4	100	.2	72	18.1	161	23.8	9	18	.2	20	0	.0
68759	1.2	67	.4	58	17.3	156	70.6	10	16	.4	19	0	.0
68760	.7	0	.2	84	12.9	214	38.6	10	13	.7	0	0	.0
68761	1.0	100	.1	62	23.1	275	33.5	11	11	1.4	15	0	.0
68762	5.7	100	2.1	73	20.5	250	68.0	9	14	2.8	12	0	.0
68763	1.0	100	.4	77	18.6	147	41.9	8	22	.5	20	0	.0
68764	1.6	100	.6	80	22.2	213	54.1	7	17	.8	16	0	.2
68765	.5	100	.6	83	18.9	215	25.8	12	20	.0	0	0	.0
68766	3.1	100	1.1	76	21.6	249	67.8	9	17	1.6	14	0	.1
68767	.9	100	.3	75	18.7	252	39.8	8	17	.4	15	0	.0
68768	2.5	100	1.0	78	19.5	208	54.4	6	24	.8	22	0	.0
68769	1.8	0	.6	74	20.3	225	54.9	8	20	.0	0	0	.0
68770	2.2	100	.7	76	20.9	157	53.8	8	17	1.0	15	0	.0
68771	.3	100	.1	80	16.3	120	19.8	10	23	.2	0	0	.0
68773	.4	100	.1	80	18.7	233	71.2	7	25	.2	19	0	.0
68774	11.3	100	4.0	70	25.8	318	69.1	9	11	5.2	9	0	.0
68776	1.2	96	.4	82	16.8	217	45.9	5	19	.7	18	0	.2
68777	1.0	100	.4	72	22.1	270	53.7	9	15	.5	14	0	.0
68778	2.7	100	1.0	72	23.6	248	62.1	7	18	1.4	16	0	.1
68779	1.2	100	.4	73	13.7	188	40.2	13	16	.6	12	0	.0
68780	1.7	99	.6	71	17.2	208	54.5	9	25	.8	22	0	.0
68781	.2	100	.1	89	17.9	206*	26.0	10	17	.1	20	0	.0
68782	1.4	100	.5	79	15.2	237	43.6	7	23	3.1	11	0	.2
68783	2.0	100	1.0	72	23.6	248	57.2	8	22	2.9	14	0	.1
68784	.4	100	.1	73	20.3	188	37.5	8	10	.2	25	0	.0
68785	1.4	100	.5	82	21.4	166	43.3	6	23	.4	15	0	.0
68786	6.5	99	2.2	66	23.5	248	84.0	6	14	.7	17	0	.0
68787	5.8	100	2.0	73	25.5	216	75.7	8	17	3.1	11	0	.0
68788	.3	100	.7	82	15.2	279	20.6	10	21	2.9	14	0	.1
68789	.9	100	.4	77	19.2	260	49.9	6	15	.2	25	0	.0
68790	2.3	100	.9	74	21.8	238	62.6	6	19	.4	15	0	.0
68791	.5	100	.2	83	15.8	241	38.9	3	17	1.1	17	0	.0
68792													

NEBRASKA — GRAND ISLAND

ZIPCODE	1	2	3	4	5	6	7	8	9	10	11	12	13
68801	41.4	98	15.2	67	26.4	309	83.9	8	13	19.5	11	5	.9
68810	1.6	0	.6	73	23.1	270	59.3	12	7	.0	0	0	.5
68812	.8	0	.3	79	24.2	346	55.8	8	13	.0	0	0	.0
68813	.7	100	.2	77	23.5	254	33.3	7	13	.3	10	0	.0
68814	1.0	0	.4	76	18.0	164	36.3	9	23	.0	0	0	.0
68815	.9	0	.3	74	18.9	153	38.8	8	18	.0	0	0	.0
68816	.2	100	.1	90	20.1	231*	36.9	3	25	.1	21	0	.0
68817	.7	100	.2	88	13.1	261	27.8	7	17	.3	16	0	.0
68818	5.3	100	1.9	88	26.4	276	75.4	7	17	2.5	13	2	.1
68819	.3	100	.1	88	17.0	195*	27.1	12	22	1.6	16	2	.0
68820	.5	100	.2	84	21.7	249*	41.1	12	10	.2	8	0	.0
68821	.3	0	.1	76	10.9	125*	17.2	11	17	.0	0	0	.0
68822	5.3	99	2.0	71	22.9	209	67.9	8	19	2.5	16	0	.4
68823	2.8	100	1.1	71	17.7	158	48.6	7	21	1.3	19	0	.2
68824	1.4	99	.5	79	23.8	188	59.0	10	12	.7	10	0	.0
68825	1.1	100	.4	79	19.7	258	36.9	9	26	.5	22	0	.0
68826	4.1	99	1.5	72	23.0	230	56.8	8	18	2.0	15	0	.3
68827	.8	100	.3	72	22.5	218	66.7	10	10	.4	10	0	.0
68828	.4	100	.1	77	23.4	74	33.5	4	19	.2	20	0	.3
68829	.2	100	.1	68	14.8	320	20.5	14	11	.1	15	0	.0
68831	.9	0	.3	74	24.4	181	47.4	7	12	.0	0	0	.0
68832	1.5	98	.5	71	27.0	329	87.4	8	9	.7	9	1	.2
68833	.5	100	.2	61	17.8	249	25.3	8	16	.8	18	0	.2
68834	.4	0	.1	88	19.9	63	41.1	13	13	.3	0	0	.0
68835	.5	100	.1	78	17.9	251	32.9	10	13	.3	14	0	.3
68836	1.5	99	.6	76	24.0	200	56.8	9	13	.7	11	0	.0
68837	.2	100	.1	79	17.8	205*	32.4	1	16	.1	12	0	.0
68838	.5	100	.1	82	25.4	186	25.4	5	14	.2	13	0	.0
68840	2.5	98	.9	74	24.6	232	66.4	8	17	1.2	15	0	.3
68841	.8	100	.3	79	24.6	231	41.7	8	7	.5	5	0	.0
68842	1.0	100	.3	74	16.7	183	35.6	11	21	.5	17	0	.0
68843	1.1	99	.4	66	24.9	287	61.7	8	13	.5	11	0	.0
68844	.3	100	.1	74	20.2	242	32.1	10	10	.2	8	0	.2
68846	.3	100	.1	69	24.9	156	44.4	5	22	.2	21	0	.0
68847	25.5	98	8.8	61	25.0	312	90.8	8	10	11.9	8	4	.7
68850	9.4	98	3.4	70	26.9	282	72.2	9	12	4.6	9	2	1.4
68852	.6	100	.3	87	14.8	86	35.3	7	22	.1	21	0	.0
68853	2.1	100	.8	72	16.6	172	50.3	7	25	1.0	24	0	.0
68854	.7	0	.2	88	20.8	244	51.8	10	12	.2	13	0	.0
68855	.6	100	.2	85	17.1	197	29.9	8	16	.3	18	0	.0
68856	.7	100	.1	80	26.2	198	43.7	8	18	.4	13	0	.0
68859	.8	100	.3	79	18.4	150	31.6	7	23	.4	19	0	.0
68860	.5	100	.2	77	14.1	106	37.1	11	19	.2	21	0	.1
68861	.2	100	.2	76	21.7	306	66.5	12	10	.1	13	0	.0
68862	3.7	100	1.4	73	20.1	191	59.0	8	20	1.8	16	0	.0
68863	1.3	0	.5	77	23.2	242	59.7	9	13	.0	0	0	.1
68864	1.3	0	.4	80	23.7	240	44.0	7	19	.0	0	0	.0
68865	1.0	0	.3	84	25.6	268	81.3	11	4	.0	0	1	.0

*=Estimated **1.0=883 lbs per person; 100++ indicates per capita toxic waste generation > than 100 times the U.S. average of 883 lbs per capita.

ZIP CODE MEASURES OF SIZE, LEVELS OF AFFLUENCE AND QUALITY OF LIFE

1=Population (th.); 2=% White; 3=Households (th.); 4=% Owner Occupied; 5=Mean Income Per Household (th.$); 6=Mean Monthly Rent ($)*; 7=Mean Home Value (th.$); 8=% under 5; 9=% 65 and over; 10=White Males (th.); 11=% White Males, 65+; 12=# Toxic Waste Sites; 13=Toxic Waste Relative to US(883 lbs.per capita)**.

NEBRASKA

GRAND ISLAND

ZIPCODE	1	2	3	4	5	6	7	8	9	10	11	12	13
68866	.9	100	.3	78	21.8	234	62.5	9	13	.4	11	0	.0
68868	.2	100	.1	92	16.2	186*	44.4	9	20	.1	14	0	.0
68869	2.4	99	.9	77	20.1	204	49.3	6	22	1.2	18	0	.0
68870	.4	100	.1	75	21.5	177	61.1	13	8	.2	9	0	.0
68871	.3	100	.3	74	16.8	165	27.4	7	19	.2	16	1	.0
68872	1.0	100	.3	80	28.4	241	65.5	14	9	.5	7	0	.0
68873	3.0	100	1.1	76	19.1	196	62.2	8	22	1.4	19	0	.0
68875	.7	100	.3	81	18.1	147	40.4	5	17	.4	15	0	.0
68876	1.8	95	.6	71	22.9	242	57.3	8	17	.8	16	0	.0
68878	.4	100	.2	79	19.9	255	35.5	9	23	.2	22	0	.0
68879	.5	100	.3	78	19.3	294	36.6	7	18	.2	16	0	.0
68882	.7	100	.3	83	15.3	194	30.2	10	21	.4	21	0	.0
68883	2.5	98	.8	70	24.6	269	63.8	8	13	1.3	12	0	.0

HASTINGS

ZIPCODE	1	2	3	4	5	6	7	8	9	10	11	12	13
68901	25.8	99	10.1	63	24.0	279	83.4	7	16	12.0	12	14	.7
68920	1.7	100	.7	79	21.2	166	56.8	6	26	.8	22	0	.0
68922	1.6	100	.7	76	18.0	186	57.1	6	26	.8	25	0	.0
68924	1.4	0	.4	66	24.2	257	65.7	6	13	.0	0	0	.0
68925	.5	100	.2	78	24.8	332	49.6	8	14	.2	15	0	.1
68926	1.0	0	.4	77	17.1	143	29.8	6	32	.2	0	0	.0
68927	1.3	100	.5	73	22.4	189	57.1	9	18	.6	18	0	.0
68928	.6	100	.2	79	20.8	238	30.4	9	16	.3	15	0	.0
68929	.8	100	.3	78	17.4	109	26.8	5	29	.2	25	0	.0
68930	1.5	100	.6	78	17.5	150	52.0	7	18	.7	18	0	.0
68932	.8	100	.3	82	19.6	179	39.1	7	23	.4	18	0	.0
68933	1.2	0	.5	72	21.8	211	56.2	7	14	.2	0	1	.1
68934	.3	100	.1	88	16.9	390	25.0	7	13	.2	14	0	.0
68935	1.0	100	.4	73	18.3	178	40.3	9	26	.5	19	0	.0
68936	.4	0	.1	83	16.6	181	23.3	8	20	.0	0	0	.0
68937	1.4	99	.5	86	23.5	283	69.9	6	22	.7	19	0	.0
68938	.8	0	.3	72	21.4	196	52.6	11	15	.0	0	0	.0
68939	1.6	99	.7	80	20.1	173	48.3	6	29	.7	26	0	.0
68940	.5	0	.2	76	20.2	297	55.2	5	12	.0	0	0	.0
68941	1.0	99	.3	81	23.8	224	59.4	10	11	.5	12	1	.2
68942	.7	100	.3	80	18.4	202	23.9	7	17	.4	17	0	.0
68943	.5	0	.2	93	23.2	248	25.1	4	19	.0	0	0	.0
68944	1.7	99	.6	72	21.7	193	56.0	8	18	.8	18	1	.7
68945	.3	100	.1	68	33.0	171	55.9	12	19	.2	15	0	.0
68946	.1	100	.1	84	23.1	266*	24.4	6	12	.1	11	0	.0
68947	.7	100	.3	83	21.5	161	48.7	9	24	.3	24	0	.0
68948	.5	0	.2	75	12.5	161	33.7	9	16	.0	0	0	.0
68949	6.8	99	2.6	72	25.9	212	71.5	8	19	3.1	15	0	.7
68950	.4	100	.2	84	16.8	189	39.8	5	23	.2	22	0	.0
68952	.2	100	.1	84	21.2	182	23.8	2	25	.1	29	0	.0
68954	.1	100	.1	88	25.2	290*	54.4	8	10	.1	15	0	.0
68955	1.5	0	.5	77	26.3	353	90.5	9	7	.0	0	0	.0
68956	1.2	0	.4	81	23.3	308	58.5	4	18	.0	0	0	.0
68957	.8	100	.3	86	17.5	226	37.1	10	18	.4	17	0	.0
68958	.8	99	.3	71	21.7	220	63.2	8	12	.4	12	0	.0
68959	4.0	99	1.5	74	24.5	249	73.0	7	21	1.9	17	1	.0
68960	.3	100	.1	79	20.9	61	21.1	8	22	.1	18	0	.0
68961	1.0	0	.4	82	19.0	121	41.6	7	23	.0	0	0	.0
68962	.2	100	.1	75	21.9	252*	20.8	13	22	.1	26	0	.0
68964	.2	100	.1	89	13.3	168	22.2	3	41	.1	46	0	.0
68966	.9	100	.4	79	18.3	190	36.7	7	21	.4	20	0	.0
68967	1.6	100	.6	75	20.3	184	46.3	8	20	.8	23	0	.0
68970	1.8	99	.8	75	19.5	153	48.8	6	27	.2	20	0	.0
68971	.5	100	.5	77	21.3	212	62.4	6	20	.2	20	0	.0
68972	.4	0	.1	77	18.3	218	15.2	8	13	.0	0	0	.3
68973	.6	100	.2	82	25.8	207	60.6	11	11	.3	12	0	.0
68974	.4	100	.2	73	24.8	232	31.7	10	12	.2	13	0	.0
68975	.2	100	.1	74	27.2	324	27.2	9	8	.1	9	0	.0
68976	.4	100	.2	66	27.2	207	34.9	8	8	.2	8	0	.0
68977	.5	0	.2	77	20.2	151	26.5	6	20	.0	0	0	.0
68978	3.2	100	1.3	73	20.6	180	51.6	7	21	1.0	18	2	.3
68979	2.1	100	.8	78	22.2	228	52.7	6	20	1.0	18	0	.0
68980	.4	98	.1	73	25.0	333	69.5	4	7	.2	6	0	.0
68981	.5	100	.3	71	23.2	218	36.2	9	10	.3	9	0	.0
68982	.8	0	.3	78	22.1	306	56.9	9	13	.0	0	0	.0

MCCOOK

ZIPCODE	1	2	3	4	5	6	7	8	9	10	11	12	13
69001	10.3	99	3.9	72	26.5	258	72.3	8	15	4.8	12	2	1.0
69020	.3	0	.2	70	23.7	198	38.4	4	18	.0	0	0	.0
69021	1.8	99	.8	74	18.6	160	49.0	6	24	.9	21	1	.0
69022	1.9	100	.7	75	17.0	184	47.8	8	25	.9	23	0	.0
69023	.4	100	.2	71	15.9	227	34.8	10	23	.2	13	1	.1
69024	1.5	100	.6	81	19.7	223	54.9	10	14	.7	16	1	.0
69025	1.5	99	.6	68	20.4	192	59.1	6	18	.7	16	1	.0
69026	.4	100	.1	91	19.2	27	17.5	6	21	.2	20	2	.0
69027	.2	100	.5	67	18.7	214*	63.4	9	9	.1	10	0	.0
69028	.9	0	.3	86	24.4	266	56.9	5	19	.0	0	0	.0
69029	.5	100	.2	92	18.1	124	27.0	5	17	.3	17	0	.0
69030	.5	100	.2	71	23.2	106	33.6	10	13	.3	13	0	.0
69032	.5	99	.3	76	19.0	117	44.2	9	15	.2	12	0	.0
69033	2.7	98	1.0	78	20.8	216	70.8	9	15	1.3	12	0	.0
69034	1.3	100	.5	77	19.4	183	54.4	10	18	.7	15	0	.0
69035	.3	0	.1	80	26.9	309*	80.4	14	4	.0	4	0	.0
69036	.3	100	.1	74	12.4	181	22.0	11	22	.8	13	0	.0
69037	.2	100	.2	68	24.2	356	32.6	8	21	.1	21	0	.0
69038	.6	100	.3	73	21.5	159	38.8	10	19	.3	19	0	.0
69039	.2	100	.1	78	22.4	146	19.4	9	16	.1	6	0	.0
69040	.7	99	.3	78	16.9	196	32.6	8	19	.4	17	0	.0
69041	.2	100	.1	67	20.0	100	18.7	10	11	.1	10	0	.0
69043	.9	100	.3	78	21.1	326	48.9	6	20	.3	12	0	.0
69044	1.2	100	.4	74	21.5	239	38.8	10	20	.6	18	0	.0
69045	1.4	100	.5	83	20.6	97	45.3	6	17	.6	17	0	.0
69046	.4	0	.1	86	18.6	221	21.1	6	15	.0	0	0	.0

*=Estimated **1.0=883 lbs per person; 100++ indicates per capita toxic waste generation > than 100 times the U.S. average of 883 lbs per capita.

ZIP CODE MEASURES OF SIZE, LEVELS OF AFFLUENCE AND QUALITY OF LIFE

1=Population (th.); 2= % White; 3=Households (th.); 4=% Owner Occupied; 5=Mean Income Per Household (th.$); 6=Mean Monthly Rent ($)*; 7=Mean Home Value (th.$)*; 8=% under 5; 9=% 65 and over; 10=% White Males (th.); 11=% White Males, 65+; 12=# Toxic Waste Sites; 13=Toxic Waste Relative to US(883 lbs.per capita)**.

NEBRASKA

NORTH PLATTE

ZIP CODE	1	2	3	4	5	6	7	8	9	10	11	12	13
69101	29.3	97	10.8	70	29.1	320	83.7	9	12	13.9	10	3	.0
69120	1.3	100	.5	74	22.3	181	44.9	8	21	.7	17	1	.0
69121	.3	100	.1	72	18.5	180	32.9	5	21	.2	21	0	.0
69122	.9	0	.4	76	23.2	254	55.4	6	22	.0	0	0	.0
69123	1.0	100	.4	76	30.1	270	67.6	8	17	.5	13	0	.0
69125	.5	0	.2	76	17.5	107	36.1	9	21	.0	0	0	.0
69127	.9	97	.3	71	19.9	315	63.8	8	9	.4	9	0	.0
69128	.4	100	.2	85	19.1	117	27.8	11	16	.2	14	0	.0
69129	1.6	97	.6	77	21.3	142	55.4	7	21	.8	18	0	.0
69130	6.1	95	2.3	71	23.5	257	66.1	9	13	2.8	12	1	2.7
69131	.7	100	.3	76	20.1	184	40.9	5	12	.4	11	0	.0
69133	.5	99	.2	73	25.8	215	43.1	7	14	.2	15	0	.0
69134	.6	0	.2	75	19.8	286	44.1	4	13	.0	0	0	.0
69138	4.6	100	1.7	76	21.0	257	64.3	8	17	2.3	15	1	.0
69140	1.9	0	.7	78	22.0	227	68.7	8	20	.0	0	0	.0
69141	.5	100	.2	76	18.3	269	31.5	11	19	.2	15	1	3.4
69142	.2	100	.1	76	16.8	273	42.4	9	9	.1	8	1	.0
69143	1.8	95	.6	87	24.6	182	67.0	7	10	.9	9	0	.0
69144	.3	100	.1	76	42.1	263	78.8	11	19	.2	13	0	.0
69145	4.1	100	1.5	72	23.1	235	63.3	8	14	2.0	12	1	.1
69146	.2	0	.1	91	16.4	188*	47.6	6	11	.0	0	0	.0
69147	.8	100	.3	78	18.0	160	46.2	3	24	.4	22	0	.6
69148	.3	100	.1	66	27.1	172	68.7	3	18	.2	16	2	.0
69149	.9	100	.4	71	25.0	204	37.2	6	16	.5	15	0	.0
69150	.5	93	.2	80	17.2	216	48.7	12	19	.3	18	1	.0
69151	.8	100	.3	74	21.4	366	50.4	10	11	.4	11	0	.0
69152	1.1	98	.3	78	22.6	254	54.1	8	19	.5	16	0	.0
69153	6.8	99	2.6	73	25.2	243	75.0	8	14	3.2	12	2	.2
69154	1.6	99	.7	73	21.9	171	57.0	7	21	.8	18	0	.7
69155	1.1	100	.4	72	22.8	267	54.6	9	15	.5	13	0	.0
69156	.7	0	.3	83	26.7	150	44.5	6	17	.0	0	0	.0
69161	.2	0	.1	63	13.3	35	19.1	10	15	.0	0	2	.6
69162	7.7	98	3.0	71	23.2	219	59.2	8	15	3.6	13	2	.0
69165	2.1	98	.7	69	26.2	326	68.0	9	15	1.0	14	1	.0
69166	.7	0	.2	69	28.3	235	53.4	8	12	.2	9	0	.0
69167	.5	100	.2	74	21.6	209	35.2	7	16	.2	16	0	.0
69168	.4	0	.2	65	24.7	289	58.0	5	16	.0	0	0	.2
69169	.7	98	.3	67	25.0	281	39.2	10	13	.3	14	0	.7
69170	.3	100	.1	78	19.4	35	34.4	8	18	.2	19	0	.0

VALENTINE

ZIP CODE	1	2	3	4	5	6	7	8	9	10	11	12	13
69201	4.1	99	1.6	74	23.8	276	65.8	8	16	2.0	14	0	.0
69210	3.4	0	1.3	75	18.5	208	58.7	8	19	.0	0	0	.0
69211	.4	100	.1	59	20.2	366	26.0	6	10	.2	12	0	.0
69212	.2	100	.1	52	25.7	296*	33.5	18	10	.1	13	0	.0
69214	.4	100	.1	68	31.9	317	21.0	12	8	.2	9	0	.0
69216	.2	0	.1	59	20.4	222	32.2	9	19	.0	0	0	.0
69217	.8	100	.3	79	15.8	122	41.9	8	19	.4	17	0	.0
69218	.3	94	.1	80	19.6	225	21.3	6	18	.2	14	0	.0
69219	.1	100	.1	70	19.8	398	41.6	8	42	.1	29	0	.0
69221	.3	100	.1	65	23.6	261	18.0	14	14	.1	9	0	.0

ALLIANCE

ZIP CODE	1	2	3	4	5	6	7	8	9	10	11	12	13
69301	12.2	95	4.6	70	28.3	325	79.8	10	12	5.8	10	0	.1
69333	.3	100	.1	66	27.4	260	34.6	3	7	.2	8	0	.0
69334	2.9	94	1.0	67	16.8	167	52.8	9	15	1.3	15	0	.4
69335	.1	100	.1	43	30.3	348*	21.9	0	23	.1	30	0	.0
69336	2.7	99	1.1	70	19.2	227	56.7	7	20	1.4	18	0	.0
69337	7.2	97	2.5	64	22.0	261	68.6	7	13	3.4	10	0	.0
69339	1.9	99	.8	78	20.4	177	40.8	7	22	.9	18	0	.0
69340	.2	100	.1	77	16.0	313	57.1*	9	9	.1	3	0	.0
69341	11.2	93	3.8	73	25.1	269	73.7	9	11	5.1	10	0	1.1
69343	3.6	92	1.3	68	25.8	220	60.5	9	15	1.6	13	0	.0
69345	.5	100	.2	71	25.2	143	30.9	6	12	.2	11	0	.0
69346	.7	0	.3	73	25.6	281	38.4	8	20	.0	0	0	.0
69347	1.8	99	.7	79	23.9	173	45.2	7	21	.9	17	0	.0
69348	1.9	98	.7	68	23.3	226	49.6	11	12	.9	11	0	.0
69349	.2	89	.1	78	21.5	263	49.6	8	9	.1	8	0	.0
69350	.6	100	.2	64	19.4	216	33.6	6	15	.3	14	0	.0
69351	.3	90	.1	42	16.0	113	21.9	15	15	.2	12	0	.1
69352	1.0	85	.3	68	19.7	220	44.7	11	11	.5	10	0	1.3
69354	.2	100	.1	75	20.7	368	25.2	18	19	.1	24	0	.0
69355	.2	100	.1	82	25.7	278	48.5	6	18	.1	10	0	2.1
69356	2.0	93	.7	65	23.0	271	59.6	8	9	.9	9	0	.0
69357	4.5	90	1.6	71	21.7	239	65.1	8	14	2.0	13	0	.1
69358	2.3	96	.8	68	21.5	207	54.6	7	13	1.1	12	1	.0
69360	1.8	93	.7	71	18.7	213	53.8	9	18	.8	16	0	.0
69361	17.3	93	6.6	66	23.0	273	75.5	8	14	7.6	13	3	.0
69366	.4	0	.1	42	16.6	266	19.3	17	4	.0	0	0	.0
69367	.3	100	.1	83	24.9	287*	23.6	10	18	.1	19	0	.0

*=Estimated **1.0=883 lbs per person; 100++ indicates per capita toxic waste generation > than 100 times the U.S. average of 883 lbs per capita.

ZIP CODE MEASURES OF SIZE, LEVELS OF AFFLUENCE AND QUALITY OF LIFE

1=Population (th.); 2= % White; 3=Households (th.); 4=% Owner Occupied; 5=Mean Income Per Household (th.$); 6=Mean Monthly Rent ($)*; 7=Mean Home Value (th.$);
8=% under 5; 9=% 65 and over; 10=% White Males; 11=% White Males, 65+; 12=# Toxic Waste Sites; 13=Toxic Waste Relative to US(883 lbs.per capita)**.

NEVADA

ZIPCODE	1	2	3	4	5	6	7	8	9	10	11	12	13
SALT LAKE CITY													
84083	.4	97	.2	44	17.6	396	196.9	2	3	.2	6	0	.0
LAS VEGAS													
89001	.9	98	.3	71	29.6	283	73.2	12	4	.5	3	1	.0
89003	.8	95	.4	61	19.4	244	54.1	10	15	.4	15	3	.0
89004	.2	0	.1	79	22.9	815	84.8	3	9	.0	0	0	.0
89005	10.0	98	3.8	78	30.7	388	132.9	5	17	4.8	17	2	.0
89007	.4	76	.1	69	17.5	265	97.7	16	10	.2	9	0	.0
89008	1.1	88	.4	66	17.7	180	51.0	7	19	.4	19	0	.0
89013	.4	98	.2	78	21.4	236	34.5	3	19	.2	25	3	.0
89015	24.3	93	8.0	76	29.6	390	114.0	10	7	11.3	6	8	5.1
89017	.2	100	.1	80	26.1	175	70.5	11	7	.1	7	0	.0
89018	1.5	90	.5	47	22.0	351	390.6	8	5	.7	4	0	.0
89019	.9	80	.3	66	24.1	201	39.4	8	8	.5	6	0	.0
89020	.7	95	.3	88	23.6	304	34.8	9	10	.4	10	1	.0
89021	1.0	0	.3	88	34.4	285	116.3	4	4	.4	4	0	.0
89024	1.0	100	.3	83	22.0	284	77.7	15	9	.5	10	0	.0
89025	.6	64	.2	58	20.2	191	59.3	12	3	.3	2	0	.0
89030	46.0	60	14.3	61	24.1	367	85.1	11	5	13.9	6	0	.0
89040	1.8	98	.6	91	25.0	144	84.7	7	21	.9	22	1	.0
89041	3.3	92	1.1	82	25.8	293	130.5	6	10	1.5	11	0	.0
89042	.7	94	.3	79	19.4	310	68.8	9	18	.4	18	0	.0
89043	.8	94	.3	68	21.4	225	74.1	16	12	.4	12	2	.0
89045	.5	100	.2	51	24.8	97	88.2*	9	0	.3	0	2	.4
89046	.7	0	.4	70	21.4	270	82.6	0	28	.0	0	2	2.1
89047	.2	100	.1	71	30.4	194	13.1	14	3	.1	4	0	28.6
89049	2.5	96	1.1	54	27.6	333	70.1	9	9	1.3	4	2	.8
LAS VEGAS													
89101	32.3	84	14.4	31	20.5	330	97.1	7	12	14.5	12	0	.1
89102	34.6	90	13.8	50	34.3	392	173.6	6	8	15.8	7	1	.0
89103	16.1	93	6.0	79	32.8	500	144.4	7	6	7.4	4	1	.0
89104	25.8	91	11.0	67	29.6	425	121.7	5	15	11.6	15	1	.0
89106	25.6	35	8.2	45	22.8	319	110.1	10	7	4.4	9	0	.0
89107	28.5	95	9.8	78	35.8	533	126.5	6	13	13.4	5	0	.0
89108	23.2	93	8.2	77	34.1	508	135.7	7	5	10.9	8	0	.2
89109	44.0	91	24.0	19	26.0	459	187.9	3	11	20.9	11	0	.0
89110	42.1	86	14.0	69	26.2	380	111.7	10	5	18.6	5	0	.0
89117	6.5	92	2.2	88	36.3	713	148.7	10	2	3.0	2	0	.0
89118	3.4	95	1.0	88	43.8	602	195.5	10	3	1.6	4	0	.0
89119	15.3	92	6.3	51	29.8	445	154.3	5	7	7.1	7	0	.0
89120	13.3	93	4.3	85	42.4	676	178.3	7	4	6.2	3	0	.0
89121	41.7	94	15.5	83	36.4	565	148.1	7	5	19.3	8	0	.0
89122	11.4	92	3.9	72	27.8	470	110.2	8	5	5.1	5	0	.0
89128	8.8	91	2.6	88	37.4	834	130.8	9	3	4.1	2	0	.0
ELY													
89301	4.4	92	1.7	71	27.4	309	64.2	7	10	2.0	9	3	.0
89310	.5	94	.2	71	18.3	388	39.2	5	9	.2	9	3	.0
89311	.2	100	.1	47	11.4	249	71.1	13	4	.1	0	0	.0
89314	.1	0	.1	100	16.8	193*	21.9*	15	16	.0	0	0	.0
89315	1.3	99	.5	78	25.4	178	58.9	6	17	.6	13	2	.1

NEVADA

ZIPCODE	1	2	3	4	5	6	7	8	9	10	11	12	13
ELY													
89316	.8	96	.3	68	20.2	373	71.6	6	9	.4	9	3	.0
89317	.3	100	.1	79	14.8	78	75.3	21	11	.1	9	0	.0
89318	1.5	93	.6	83	23.1	236	40.9	8	15	.7	14	1	.0
89319	.4	100	.1	92	25.9	125	37.7	8	3	.3	2	0	8.1
RENO													
89402	.7	100	.3	63	46.4	696	342.2	4	6	.4	9	0	.0
89403	2.4	92	.8	73	29.1	420	138.1	9	6	1.1	5	2	.0
89404	.1	0	.1	18	10.0	255	35.7*	6	13	.0	0	0	.0
89405	.4	89	.1	24	26.6	212	94.6*	15	8	.4	2	2	.1
89406	13.9	92	5.0	66	23.5	329	107.0	8	12	6.4	12	1	.0
89408	3.3	96	1.1	81	30.2	385	113.4	13	5	1.5	5	0	.0
89409	.8	87	.3	60	25.0	225	31.6	8	5	.4	5	2	.0
89410	6.7	95	2.3	77	31.6	507	151.9	8	9	3.1	10	2	.1
89411	.3	100	.1	61	52.4	576	397.4	8	8	.1	12	0	.0
89413	.2	100	.1	51	37.2	233	37.2	8	5	.1	4	0	.0
89414	.2	100	.1	81	201.3	1020	407.2	2	11	.1	9	0	.0
89415	.3	100	.1	68	18.5	593	30.6	5	7	.1	6	0	.0
89416	4.0	88	1.5	72	21.5	301	69.1	8	13	1.7	12	1	.0
89418	1.2	73	.4	30	23.5	224	53.3	7	2	.5	0	2	.0
89420	2.8	88	1.0	61	24.3	296	75.6	9	12	1.3	12	7	.0
89421	.2	100	.2	87	18.6	213*	28.7*	6	17	.1	16	0	1.4
89422	.7	0	.2	63	19.2	168	32.8	9	6	.0	0	1	.0
89423	.3	100	.2	85	20.4	157	35.8	0	24	.0	0	5	.0
89424	3.4	97	1.2	77	42.7	517	163.2	8	10	1.8	9	1	.0
89425	.3	0	.1	45	25.8	246	52.5	8	13	.1	4	0	.0
89426	.5	93	.2	45	25.8	296*	91.9*	10	4	.3	10	0	.0
89427	.2	79	.1	47	21.8	219	13.1	12	7	.1	10	1	.0
89429	.6	97	.2	71	21.8	378	46.5	6	8	.3	8	0	.0
89430	1.8	97	.7	87	23.5	582	87.9	7	12	.9	13	0	.0
89431	.4	100	.1	58	25.8	309	130.2	13	6	.2	6	0	.1
89437	52.0	93	19.2	63	30.6	521	128.7	7	7	23.8	6	0	.4
89440	.5	23	.2	45	30.3	540	107.8*	4	2	.5	8	1	.4
89442	1.0	99	.4	78	34.4	482	211.6	3	12	.5	8	1	.4
89444	.9	96	.4	66	26.0	300	135.9	7	11	.4	10	0	.3
89445	.7	61	.2	85	22.6	293	94.5	7	11	.2	16	0	.0
89447	1.3	99	.5	78	21.6	315	101.9	4	15	.6	13	0	.0
89448	7.4	89	2.7	65	25.3	315	102.4	8	8	3.3	8	3	.0
89449	5.0	92	2.1	73	23.1	338	87.8	5	18	2.4	19	2	.0
89450	2.9	99	1.2	63	46.2	603	326.7	4	10	1.5	9	0	.3
89450	3.0	96	1.4	54	34.6	471	242.3	4	5	1.5	5	0	.0
89450	5.9	98	2.3	59	44.1	640	341.9	6	5	2.9	5	0	.0
RENO													
89501	3.4	83	2.0	10	25.2	405	155.8	3	15	1.6	15	0	.2
89502	28.6	91	13.0	37	26.2	465	137.2	5	10	13.1	9	0	.5
89503	22.0	94	9.2	54	29.6	488	135.6	5	10	10.7	9	0	.5
89505	2.5	94	.8	81	43.2	724	142.1	9	2	2.0	2	0	1.9
89506	18.2	94	5.9	75	31.3	587	125.8	9	3	8.8	3	0	.0
89509	30.3	97	13.2	56	39.6	535	220.3	4	12	14.2	11	1	.0

*=Estimated **1.0=883 lbs per person; 100++ indicates per capita toxic waste generation > than 100 times the U.S. average of 883 lbs per capita.

ZIP CODE MEASURES OF SIZE, LEVELS OF AFFLUENCE AND QUALITY OF LIFE

1=Population (th.); 2= % White; 3=Households (th.); 4=% Owner Occupied; 5=Mean Income Per Household (th.$); 6=Mean Monthly Rent ($); 7=Mean Home Value (th.$);
8=% under 5; 9=% 65 and over; 10=White Males, 65+; 11=% White Males, 65+ and over; 12=# Toxic Waste Sites; 13=Toxic Waste Relative to US(883 lbs.per capita)**.

NEVADA

ZIP CODE	1	2	3	4	5	6	7	8	9	10	11	12	13
RENO													
89510	.6	72	.2	89	31.8	516	119.7	16	3	.2	5	0	2.3
89511	9.7	97	3.5	88	43.0	461	204.5	7	7	4.8	7	0	.0
89512	13.4	80	5.8	40	21.7	372	115.2	7	13	5.2	11	0	.0
89523	.2	100	.1	100	45.1	518*	166.4	0	6	.1	6	0	.0
CARSON CITY													
89701	37.2	94	13.9	66	30.3	433	155.2	6	9	17.7	8	2	.2
ELKO													
89801	10.9	90	4.1	67	27.9	289	104.9	7	10	5.1	8	4	.0
89820	3.7	91	1.3	64	27.7	356	98.5	11	5	1.8	3	10	6.1
89821	.2	90	.1	77	22.2	615	47.6	7	0	.1	0	3	.0
89822	1.3	90	.5	65	24.2	229	51.6	9	11	.6	10	4	.4
89823	.7	100	.3	62	37.6	431*	133.8*	9	9	.1	14	0	.0
89825	.3	100	.1	31	20.0	213	70.3	13	2	.4	2	0	.0
89828	.3	100	.1	89	28.1	175	116.0	13	3	.2	14	0	.0
89830	.2	0	.1	63	19.5	98	32.8	13	8	.0	0	1	.0
89832	.8	8	.2	58	13.6	178	31.6	9	7	.0	0	0	.0
89834	.2	73	.1	27	36.1	135	28.4	0	8	.1	10	0	.0
89835	1.7	91	.6	58	23.1	271	58.1	11	8	.8	7	0	.1

NEW HAMPSHIRE

ZIP CODE	1	2	3	4	5	6	7	8	9	10	11	12	13
LYNN													
01913	.6	100	.2	90	35.6	502	118.2	4	11	.3	10	0	.0
MANCHESTER													
03031	8.1	99	2.4	91	45.6	497	155.5	7	5	4.0	5	0	.5
03032	2.3	99	.7	91	32.5	425	95.2	9	5	1.2	6	0	.0
03033	2.2	99	.7	85	31.3	464	103.4	8	7	1.1	6	0	.0
03034	.7	98	.2	90	30.0	384	88.7	9	9	.4	6	0	.0
03036	3.1	99	1.0	92	29.0	437	97.7	7	8	1.5	8	0	.4
03037	2.0	99	.7	88	27.1	376	91.6	8	10	1.0	9	1	.2
03038	18.6	99	6.5	63	28.0	398	92.7	9	8	9.1	6	0	.0
03040	.2	100	.1	85	29.3	336*	85.8	6	3	.1	1	0	.0
03041	.4	100	.2	84	36.6	400	121.2	4	3	.2	3	0	.0
03042	4.0	99	1.2	82	27.5	343	79.1	7	15	1.9	12	0	.0
03043	.8	100	.3	87	29.2	586	102.5	5	12	.4	13	0	.0
03044	1.9	100	.6	87	27.7	376	79.8	7	10	.9	10	0	.1
03045	7.9	99	2.3	80	29.0	365	87.2	6	12	3.7	9	0	.0
03047	1.0	100	.3	80	24.1	371	86.1	6	11	.5	10	0	.2
03048	2.8	99	.9	76	25.4	404	82.0	9	9	1.4	8	0	.1
03049	3.1	99	1.0	90	39.1	517	140.8	8	10	1.6	10	2	.0
03051	17.1	99	5.1	80	32.5	465	102.7	9	4	8.4	4	3	1.3
03053	12.9	99	4.1	83	32.3	506	113.3	9	4	6.4	4	1	.7
03054	15.4	98	4.7	92	35.6	553	101.8	9	3	7.7	3	2	1.7
03055	9.7	99	3.4	64	27.6	422	105.0	7	11	4.6	9	3	1.3
03057	1.3	0	.4	86	34.6	526	118.3	7	7	.0	0	0	.4
03060	68.4	98	24.7	56	29.2	427	97.5	7	10	32.3	7	7	1.0
03070	1.7	0	.5	79	27.9	457	99.3	7	7	.5	7	1	.0
03071	2.4	100	.8	83	26.5	326	85.0	11	9	1.2	8	0	.2
03073	.4	100	.2	81	24.2	563	75.3	4	20	.2	22	0	.0
03076	8.1	99	2.4	84	33.1	518	104.2	7	11	4.1	9	1	.2
03077	6.3	98	2.2	82	22.0	383	79.2	9	11	3.1	10	2	.0
03079	23.7	98	7.9	74	30.5	444	95.3	6	7	11.5	7	1	1.0
03082	1.0	98	.3	86	30.6	398	77.3	8	7	.5	8	0	.0
03084	.6	0	.2	79	36.2	464	100.6	5	11	.0	0	0	.2
03086	2.9	0	1.0	72	25.7	376	90.1	8	12	.0	1	0	.6
03087	5.6	99	1.7	91	42.4	536	127.6	9	6	2.8	4	0	.0
MANCHESTER													
03101	2.6	97	1.5	80	12.5	206	68.2	5	28	1.2	17	1	5.3
03102	37.3	99	13.0	66	27.7	352	105.4	7	11	17.8	11	1	.0
03103	40.8	99	14.6	56	24.1	341	79.0	7	11	19.4	9	0	.4
03104	31.6	99	11.7	53	27.6	372	97.8	6	15	14.5	11	0	.0
03106	3.5	99	1.2	77	27.6	328	88.3	7	8	1.7	6	1	2.7
CONCORD													
03216	1.0	100	.4	80	22.1	316	68.9	7	14	.5	14	0	.0
03217	2.4	99	.9	66	21.6	286	63.8	9	12	1.2	11	0	.2
03218	1.3	0	.5	93	24.2	399	71.0	7	11	.0	0	0	.0
03220	1.8	0	.6	84	23.6	395	67.0	8	13	.0	0	0	.0
03221	1.7	99	.6	78	22.2	356	83.2	7	17	1.7	12	0	.0
03222	3.4	100	1.3	79	22.3	279	69.2	7	14	1.7	14	1	.4
03223	1.9	100	.9	72	25.3	228	83.0	8	9	.9	7	0	.0
03224	1.4	97	.5	87	28.3	282	93.1	8	9	.7	8	0	.0

*=Estimated **1.0=883 lbs per person; 100++ indicates per capita toxic waste generation > than 100 times the U.S. average of 883 lbs per capita.

ZIP CODE MEASURES OF SIZE, LEVELS OF AFFLUENCE AND QUALITY OF LIFE

1=Population (th.); 2= % White; 3=Households (th.); 4=% Owner Occupied; 5=Mean Income Per Household (th.$); 6=Mean Monthly Rent ($)*; 7=Mean Home Value (th.$)*; 8=% under 5; 9=% 65 and over; 10=White Males (th.); 11=% White Males, 65+; 12=# Toxic Waste Sites; 13=Toxic Waste Relative to US(883 lbs.per capita)**.

NEW HAMPSHIRE

CONCORD

ZIPCODE	1	2	3	4	5	6	7	8	9	10	11	12	13
03225	1.2	100	.4	81	25.7	433	70.1	8	8	.6	7	0	.0
03226	1.9	100	.7	84	25.2	366	120.0	6	15	1.0	16	0	.0
03227	.5	100	.2	90	25.2	308	93.0	3	21	.2	18	0	.0
03229	2.8	100	1.0	86	31.5	357	96.2	6	10	1.4	8	0	.7
03230	.9		.3	81	22.9	340	57.6	5	14	.0	0	0	.0
03231	.4	100	.1	80	21.7	233	70.1	8	14	.2	14	0	.0
03232	.2	100	.1	74	30.1	495	127.3	8	10	.1	15	0	.0
03233	.2	100	.1	63	27.3	390	68.6	7	17	.1	22	0	.0
03234	2.6	99	.9	80	24.1	378	82.5	8	18	1.2	14	0	.0
03235	8.8	99	3.1	64	22.3	304	66.9	8	14	4.1	11	1	1.4
03237	.9	98	.3	89	24.7	426	81.0	10	10	.5	9	0	.0
03240	.7	99	.2	88	22.4	335	56.6	7	13	.4	15	0	.0
03241	.3	100	.1	81	19.9	323	64.1	12	15	.1	19	0	.0
03242	3.3	0	1.0	69	23.8	309	81.1	6	8	.0	0	0	.0
03243	.7	0	.3	85	23.5	347	66.1	9	11	.3	0	0	.0
03244	4.5	100	1.7	76	23.6	259	72.4	6	13	2.2	12	1	.3
03245	.4	100	.2	74	19.7	340	113.2	8	16	.0	12	0	.0
03246	23.7	99	8.6	66	24.4	330	89.3	7	13	11.4	11	1	.4
03251	1.3	100	.5	74	22.4	296	72.3	5	15	.7	13	0	.4
03252	.2	100	.1	78	19.5	380	74.1	5	0	.1	0	0	.3
03253	5.2	100	1.9	77	22.5	318	90.3	7	14	2.6	12	0	.0
03254	.6	0	.3	75	23.8	309	101.6	4	22	.0	0	0	.0
03255	.5	100	.2	77	36.1	367	96.6	8	13	.3	15	0	.0
03256	.6	100	.2	67	22.7	290	80.1	9	10	.3	11	0	.0
03257	2.9	98	1.0	78	36.0	384	153.6	4	20	1.1	19	0	.0
03258	.6	0	.2	81	23.4	333	75.1	9	11	.0	0	0	.0
03259	.2	100	.1	85	23.2	266*	74.9	4	21	.1	23	0	.0
03260	.4	0	.1	69	24.7	320	88.0	7	11	.0	0	0	.0
03261	1.9	0	.7	81	23.4	319	80.0	7	12	.0	1	0	.0
03262	.8	100	.3	64	20.7	272	66.8	6	13	.4	11	0	.0
03263	3.7	99	1.4	73	22.6	314	67.3	7	13	1.8	11	0	.1
03264	7.2	99	2.2	63	20.4	365	76.0	4	9	3.4	8	0	.1
03265	.2	0	.1	67	19.8	363	70.3	6	14	.0	0	0	.0
03266	1.5	0	.5	84	20.3	293	66.9	7	12	.2	12	1	.0
03268	.6	0	.2	92	24.0	266	72.1	8	8	.0	0	0	.0
03269	.4	0	.1	90	27.0	425	85.5	10	9	.0	0	0	.0
03272	.1	100	.1	100	22.6	260*	90.4	9	7	.1	0	0	.0
03273	.2	100	.1	73	27.4	385	97.1	10	8	.1	9	0	.0
03275	7.8	99	2.8	71	24.7	337	77.9	7	10	3.8	8	0	.0
03276	5.8	99	2.0	70	22.3	287	69.1	7	13	2.8	12	0	.2
03278	2.0	99	.7	80	25.0	352	76.2	8	12	1.0	10	0	.4
03279	.7	99	.3	87	21.8	285	49.7	7	14	.3	11	0	.0
03280	.3	100	.1	94	19.3	222*	68.6	7	15	.1	22	0	.0
03281	3.0	99	1.0	83	24.8	355	87.3	9	9	1.5	9	0	.0
03282	.4	0	.1	87	21.9	329	61.3	6	7	.0	0	0	.0
03284	.4	100	.1	86	24.4	350	76.2	8	13	.2	12	0	.0
03287	.7	99	.2	88	23.1	300	79.3	9	17	.3	17	0	.0
03289	.3	0	.1	69	25.3	351	92.1	5	12	.0	0	0	1.6
03290	.4	100	.1	93	28.4	326*	93.2	5	9	.2	0	0	.0

NEW HAMPSHIRE

CONCORD

ZIPCODE	1	2	3	4	5	6	7	8	9	10	11	12	13
03291	.4	0	.1	82	27.1	384	81.7	7	6	.0	0	0	.9
03293	.2	100	.1	81	18.6	377	79.9	5	13	.1	10	0	.0

CONCORD

ZIPCODE	1	2	3	4	5	6	7	8	9	10	11	12	13
03301	45.0	99	16.2	65	26.5	363	86.9	6	14	21.2	10	5	.4

KEENE

ZIPCODE	1	2	3	4	5	6	7	8	9	10	11	12	13
03431	25.5	100	9.1	64	25.2	355	80.7	6	13	11.7	10	0	1.2
03440	2.5	99	.8	71	22.5	349	68.2	8	10	1.3	8	0	.1
03441	.6	0	.2	71	21.1	303	57.9	3	5	.0	0	0	.0
03442	.8	100	.3	76	21.9	391	75.1	10	14	.4	12	0	1.7
03443	1.4	100	.5	81	25.1	406	85.2	6	12	.7	11	0	.0
03444	.4	100	.3	64	33.4	416	111.3	8	10	.5	8	0	.0
03445	.4	100	.4	86	29.9	482	64.9	9	6	.2	5	0	.0
03447	1.9	100	.7	85	25.2	348	70.3	7	14	.9	14	0	.4
03448	.6	100	.2	89	24.7	396	56.1	8	12	.3	7	0	.0
03449	1.2	99	.5	81	35.6	383	114.3	5	19	.6	18	0	.5
03450	.6	0	.6	79	24.5	371	90.5	8	12	.0	0	0	.4
03451	3.6	100	1.3	75	22.1	287	68.6	7	13	1.7	12	0	.5
03452	3.9		.5	62	23.1	319	64.2	7	16	.9	14	0	.5
03454	.6	100	.2	81	50.5	406	132.0	8	16	.3	12	0	1.5
03455	2.2	0	.8	72	23.7	352	68.2	6	15	.0	0	0	.0
03456	.5		.2	85	22.8	350	51.3	8	8	.1	8	0	.2
03457	.4	100	.1	85	21.1	376	81.2	4	11	.2	9	0	.0
03458	3.2	99	1.9	68	30.4	404	115.5	6	19	2.4	16	1	2.2
03461	.9		.9	77	26.3	439	87.5	8	8	.9	0	0	.0
03462	.6	100	.2	85	26.8	381	101.6	6	9	.3	8	0	.0
03464	.4		.2	69	21.8	367	60.4	7	15	.1	10	0	.0
03465	2.1	99	.7	69	21.2	361	65.8	8	10	1.0	10	1	.2
03467	1.8	99	.6	86	28.4	360	87.0	6	15	.9	12	0	.0
03468	.3	0	.1	64	19.6	578	83.6	8	9	.0	0	0	.3
03469	1.8	99	.6	78	24.8	426	69.1	7	10	.9	8	0	.2
03470	3.8	99	1.3	77	19.8	321	61.6	9	11	1.8	10	0	.1

LITTLETON

ZIPCODE	1	2	3	4	5	6	7	8	9	10	11	12	13
03561	14.4	100	6.4	67	19.9	253	67.4	7	15	3.0	12	0	2.0
03570	14.4	100	5.5	62	20.8	231	58.2	6	16	6.9	13	1	2.1
03574	1.0	0	.4	72	21.0	191	65.3	8	10	.3	8	0	.0
03576	3.4	99	1.2	66	20.7	247	57.7	8	13	1.7	12	1	.2
03579	.9	100	.4	87	22.7	172	44.0	6	16	.2	14	0	.0
03580	.9	96	.4	67	22.4	252	87.9	4	21	.4	19	0	.8
03581	3.1	69	1.3	69	20.7	275	62.9	6	16	.0	0	0	.6
03582	2.6	100	1.0	73	21.7	244	51.6	6	12	.0	2	0	.6
03583	.8	0	.3	90	23.0	227	76.5	7	16	.0	10	0	.0
03584	3.7	100	1.2	72	22.3	269	56.4	9	11	1.7	7	0	.4
03585	2.3	100	.8	76	22.3	255	67.5	6	14	1.1	11	0	.5
03588	.9	100	.3	79	20.6	298	56.5	11	9	.5	7	0	.0
03590	1.3	100	.4	78	21.6	239	48.3	10	8	.6	8	0	1.4
03592	1.0	100	.1	85	21.2	287	56.1	7	10	.5	11	0	.1
03595	.5	99	.2	67	18.6	279	71.8	7	9	.2	8	0	.0
03597	.4	100	.1	66	22.1	240	51.9	6	12	.2	9	0	.0
03598	2.7		1.0	78	18.9	272	56.7	7	15	.0	0	0	.0

*=Estimated **1.0=883 lbs per person; 100++ indicates per capita toxic waste generation > than 100 times the U.S. average of 883 lbs per capita.

ZIP CODE MEASURES OF SIZE, LEVELS OF AFFLUENCE AND QUALITY OF LIFE

1=Population (th.); 2= % White; 3=Households (th.); 4=% Owner Occupied; 5=Mean Income Per Household (th.$); 6=Mean Monthly Rent ($)*; 7=Mean Home Value (th.$)*; 8=% under 5; 9=% 65 and over; 10=White Males (th.); 11=% White Males, 65+; 12=# Toxic Waste Sites; 13=Toxic Waste Relative to US(883 lbs.per capita)**.

NEW HAMPSHIRE

BELLOWS FALLS

ZIPCODE	1	2	3	4	5	6	7	8	9	10	11	12	13
03601	.3	100	.1	88	20.8	265	76.1	6	23	.2	19	0	.0
03602	1.8	99	.6	84	24.8	297	72.8	7	11	.9	10	0	.0
03603	4.2	100	1.5	78	23.3	308	67.6	7	13	2.0	12	1	.4
03604	.1	100	.1	76	26.6	347	57.7	2	7	.0	0	0	.0
03605	.3	0	.1	85	19.8	446	66.3	5	8	.0	0	0	.0
03606	.2	100	.1	93	18.2	209*	64.9	8	9	.1	12	0	.0
03607	.3	100	.1	94	20.8	238*	56.3	9	11	.2	9	0	.0
03608	2.2	100	.8	72	27.4	322	96.3	7	13	1.1	10	0	.0

WHITE RIVER JUNCTION

ZIPCODE	1	2	3	4	5	6	7	8	9	10	11	12	13
03741	2.9	99	1.0	80	20.7	311	60.0	7	11	1.4	10	1	.0
03743	15.7	100	5.9	59	22.6	304	69.2	7	15	7.5	12	2	.2
03746	.3	100	.1	83	22.8	412	74.2	10	7	.1	10	0	.0
03748	3.8	99	1.4	79	23.4	290	76.3	7	11	1.9	9	0	.0
03749	.5	0	.1	88	23.1	475	60.2	6	13	.0	0	0	.0
03750	.8	97	.3	73	45.5	550	137.3	9	9	.4	10	0	.0
03751	.3	100	.1	73	22.5	433	75.5	4	17	.1	12	0	.0
03752	.5	100	.2	91	26.1	260	74.2	7	12	.3	13	0	.0
03753	.6	99	.3	84	32.9	490	129.0	6	14	.3	12	0	.0
03754	.2	100	.1	76	23.2	265	58.9	3	16	.1	0	0	3.0
03755	7.8	94	1.7	54	38.0	498	168.9	2	8	4.2	6	1	.1
03766	.6	100	3.0	89	24.5	176	68.8	6	16	.3	15	0	.0
03768	7.4	99	3.0	58	23.9	324	81.0	7	13	3.4	11	0	1.4
03769	1.1	98	.4	78	29.3	404	94.7	6	9	.5	9	0	.0
03770	.5	0	.2	83	24.6	456	75.6	3	17	.4	0	0	.0
03771	.5	0	.2	75	24.0	489	93.4	7	12	.8	0	0	.2
03772	.6	0	.2	85	23.9	248	77.5	7	12	.1	0	0	.0
03773	.2	100	.2	87	31.9	367*	100.0	9	16	.1	13	0	.0
03774	.2	100	2.6	70	23.8	322	63.8	8	13	3.5	11	0	.6
03777	7.2	100	.4	73	22.5	261	75.3	10	11	.1	0	0	.6
03779	1.2	0	.3	77	23.9	332	78.9	5	18	.4	15	0	.0
03780	.9	100	.1	84	18.8	290	58.8	5	20	.0	0	0	.0
03781	.3	100	.1	76	14.9	139	49.8	8	15	.1	5	0	.0
03782	.3	100	.3	78	27.9	430	89.6	6	9	.4	7	0	.0
03784	3.5	99	1.4	76	27.7	371	106.2	5	15	1.5	8	0	.0
03785	2.5	100	.9	69	19.1	268	57.7	6	24	1.2	23	0	.0

PORTSMOUTH

ZIPCODE	1	2	3	4	5	6	7	8	9	10	11	12	13
03801	27.7	94	9.9	43	23.0	351	92.2	8	10	12.9	7	3	.9
03809	1.7	99	.6	77	21.9	328	76.8	6	17	.8	14	0	.0
03810	.6	0	.2	86	26.4	205	117.5	3	18	.0	0	0	.0
03811	4.4	99	1.4	87	35.9	302	118.6	7	6	2.2	5	0	.0
03812	.5	100	.2	82	20.9	261	79.0	6	14	.3	13	0	.0
03813	1.1	0	.4	81	21.1	280	77.5	6	10	.1	0	0	.0
03814	1.9	0	.7	82	19.8	256	73.5	5	17	.0	0	0	.2
03815	3.5	99	1.4	49	26.6	381	95.5	9	11	1.5	8	0	.0
03816	.3	100	.9	90	20.7	197	86.7	9	21	.2	18	0	.0
03817	.5	100	.2	89	21.4	350	74.8	6	15	.2	12	0	.0
03818	3.2	0	1.2	72	19.9	263	76.7	8	13	.0	0	0	.2
03819	.7	0	.2	86	28.0	406	91.3	6	10	.5	0	0	.5

NEW HAMPSHIRE

PORTSMOUTH

ZIPCODE	1	2	3	4	5	6	7	8	9	10	11	12	13
03820	26.7	99	10.0	55	24.3	346	86.6	6	11	12.7	8	3	.5
03824	12.1	98	2.6	56	29.6	402	129.2	3	4	5.7	4	0	.0
03825	3.9	99	1.3	84	25.8	360	84.4	9	7	2.0	6	2	.0
03826	.8	100	.7	69	29.1	345	99.7	8	5	.5	7	0	.4
03827	2.0	100	.7	93	29.8	464	101.1	7	11	1.0	9	0	.0
03830	.4	99	.1	92	20.1	185	68.9	4	18	.1	18	0	.0
03832	.2	0	.1	72	17.7	278	71.7	7	15	.2	0	0	.0
03833	12.8	99	4.7	72	27.0	364	106.1	6	15	6.2	11	2	.7
03835	4.5	0	1.6	71	20.9	290	59.0	9	11	.3	1	0	.1
03836	.7	99	.3	87	21.2	194	89.4	5	17	.3	17	0	.5
03837	.7	0	.3	86	23.3	304	73.0	9	17	.0	0	0	.1
03838	.4	0	.1	72	16.2	402	68.5	5	11	.0	0	0	.2
03840	1.8	99	.6	80	31.3	448	113.1	7	8	.9	6	0	.0
03841	3.0	0	1.0	91	34.0	365	106.3	6	11	.0	0	0	.1
03842	10.6	100	4.1	64	28.6	376	113.4	5	12	5.1	10	0	.0
03844	1.4	99	.5	91	37.1	373	148.4	5	11	.7	10	0	.0
03845	.6	100	.6	70	21.1	330	87.6	4	14	.3	9	0	.0
03846	.7	0	.3	73	31.2	256	110.4	3	12	.0	0	0	.0
03848	4.0	0	1.4	85	29.0	417	90.5	5	10	.0	0	0	.5
03849	.5	0	.2	76	23.4	319	81.5	9	15	.2	6	0	.1
03850	.4	100	.2	93	30.7	392	130.1	3	27	.2	27	0	.2
03851	1.0	97	.4	86	22.6	262	61.7	6	11	.5	9	0	.0
03852	.4	100	.2	91	21.3	151	58.1	4	9	.1	0	0	.0
03853	.4	100	.2	83	28.6	263	149.0	5	27	.2	26	0	.2
03854	1.0	100	.3	77	36.5	483	183.1	2	19	.0	0	0	.0
03855	1.1	0	.4	89	24.5	413	76.6	7	12	.1	0	0	.0
03856	.6	100	.2	74	27.6	386	85.6	10	10	.3	9	0	6.3
03857	5.1	99	2.0	55	24.0	355	88.2	5	11	2.5	9	0	.0
03858	.4	100	.1	86	25.4	226	87.9	7	7	.1	0	0	.0
03859	.4	100	.1	94	32.0	367*	76.5	12	6	.2	7	0	.0
03860	3.4	0	1.5	60	20.9	324	90.3	5	14	.0	0	0	.1
03862	3.4	99	1.2	84	35.5	470	131.5	6	8	1.6	8	0	.0
03864	1.4	0	.5	87	23.9	334	84.3	7	22	.0	0	0	.0
03865	7.9	100	2.5	79	30.5	445	93.5	7	8	4.0	7	0	.1
03867	22.6	100	8.1	70	23.8	334	74.2	7	13	10.9	11	1	.0
03869	3.7	100	1.3	55	22.8	340	68.8	5	14	.5	10	0	.0
03871	.5	100	.2	76	31.7	468	143.8	5	9	1.8	13	0	.0
03872	1.9	100	.7	78	36.5	489	187.7	4	22	.3	19	0	.0
03873	.9	100	.3	86	20.5	307	78.6	7	19	.9	17	0	.0
03874	5.9	0	.3	90	28.8	550	90.8	12	6	.1	0	1	1.6
03875	.4	100	2.4	60	24.7	409	94.3	6	11	.0	0	0	.0
03878	9.6	99	.1	81	24.8	412	91.9	6	13	.2	11	0	1.6
03881	1.4	0	3.5	62	23.9	311	77.8	7	11	.2	8	0	1.5
03883	.3	100	7.9	95	29.5	338*	75.0	5	17	4.5	8	2	.0
03884	.8	100	.3	85	20.8	276	74.2	7	15	.2	10	0	.0
03885	2.5	99	.8	82	30.1	439	94.1	7	8	1.7	8	0	.0
03886	.7	0	.3	86	34.9	428	120.5	7	8	1.2	7	0	.0
03887	1.6	98	.5	92	21.5	317	69.2	9	11	.8	11	0	.0

*=Estimated **1.0=883 lbs. per person; 100++ indicates per capita toxic waste generation > than 100 times the U.S. average of 883 lbs per capita.

103001

ZIP CODE MEASURES OF SIZE, LEVELS OF AFFLUENCE AND QUALITY OF LIFE

1=Population (th.); 2= % White; 3=Households (th.); 4=% Owner Occupied; 5=Mean Income Per Household (th.$); 6=Mean Monthly Rent ($)*; 7=Mean Home Value (th.$)*; 8=% under 5; 9=% 65 and over; 10=% White Males (th.); 11=% White Males, 65+; 12=# Toxic Waste Sites; 13=Toxic Waste Relative to US(883 lbs.per capita)**.

NEW HAMPSHIRE

PORTSMOUTH

ZIPCODE	1	2	3	4	5	6	7	8	9	10	11	12	13
03890	.4	100	.2	83	19.5	162	75.6	8	18	.2	13	0	.6
03894	4.0	100	1.6	79	25.2	264	100.3	6	19	1.8	16	0	.0
03896	.2	100	.1	59	27.6	290	55.9	8	8	.1	5	0	.0

PORTLAND

ZIPCODE	1	2	3	4	5	6	7	8	9	10	11	12	13
04037	.3	100	.1	84	19.1	234	77.8	15	13	.1	10	0	.0

WHITE RIVER JUNCTION

ZIPCODE	1	2	3	4	5	6	7	8	9	10	11	12	13
05089	1.0	100	.4	89	22.4	277	81.5	4	11	.5	10	0	.0

BELLOWS FALLS

ZIPCODE	1	2	3	4	5	6	7	8	9	10	11	12	13
05101	.8	0	.3	69	19.7	310	54.6	9	19	.0	0	0	.4

NEW JERSEY

NEWARK

ZIPCODE	1	2	3	4	5	6	7	8	9	10	11	12	13
07001	10.7	94	4.0	64	31.2	484	91.1	5	9	5.0	9	0	6.1
07002	65.2	94	25.5	39	26.3	343	100.3	5	15	29.0	13	16	2.6
07003	47.8	95	18.6	53	29.0	436	103.9	5	16	20.9	13	1	.9
07005	13.7	96	4.7	71	37.0	472	152.5	5	14	6.4	12	9	3.9
07006	32.9	96	10.4	78	44.7	533	167.8	6	10	15.2	16	6	3.5
07008	20.6	91	6.9	69	30.7	372	92.3	6	10	9.0	10	9	5.2
07009	12.7	95	3.8	78	40.6	564	145.3	4	15	5.7	11	0	.7
07010	21.5	97	9.0	48	33.0	439	121.6	5	16	9.9	13	1	.1
07011	32.2	97	12.9	51	25.4	411	102.8	6	19	14.4	16	4	2.8
07012	11.9	98	5.0	57	32.6	418	125.2	4	18	5.5	16	0	8.6
07013	26.5	99	9.6	76	35.7	468	136.2	4	18	12.5	13	0	.2
07014	3.8	97	1.4	73	32.4	441	112.2	4	16	1.8	16	1	73.0
07016	24.6	96	8.3	81	40.4	518	132.0	5	12	11.4	9	0	3.3
07017	44.6	15	16.1	26	22.5	387	66.7	8	9	3.0	22	0	.3
07018	33.1	14	12.8	23	21.9	378	64.5	7	12	2.2	33	0	.0
07020	4.6	95	2.1	28	31.8	530	97.3	5	11	2.2	10	5	4.5
07021	2.4	99	.7	93	71.3	498	277.3	4	12	1.1	11	0	.0
07022	10.5	98	4.2	40	24.9	403	106.0	5	16	4.9	13	0	.1
07023	7.8	93	2.5	93	41.6	601	132.6	7	7	3.5	6	0	.1
07024	32.4	89	14.8	27	39.1	593	161.1	4	17	13.5	17	0	.1
07026	26.9	98	10.8	44	23.6	397	96.7	6	16	12.5	13	1	.3
07027	4.8	0	1.7	64	31.1	459	107.0	5	12	.0	0	1	2.0
07028	7.9	97	2.4	89	52.6	555	146.2	5	16	3.6	10	0	.2
07029	14.3	80	5.2	35	25.3	369	80.9	7	11	6.4	10	0	5.8
07030	42.3	80	15.5	13	19.6	296	82.8	8	10	17.0	10	2	.5
07032	52.2	99	19.4	51	28.2	404	105.2	5	14	24.1	12	33	4.8
07033	8.2	97	2.7	82	32.4	531	111.3	5	11	3.9	11	3	16.7
07034	10.0	96	3.6	58	33.0	505	108.1	7	6	4.8	5	0	.0
07035	8.8	98	2.6	74	34.9	515	115.1	6	14	4.0	9	0	.2
07036	39.6	83	14.8	59	29.5	395	99.3	5	14	15.8	14	18	20.5
07039	28.0	96	8.5	97	55.8	740	181.3	5	8	13.2	8	1	.4
07040	22.9	95	8.0	80	41.2	470	124.7	5	16	10.3	14	0	.2
07041	6.7	98	2.7	65	41.7	589	152.1	4	20	3.1	18	0	.3
07042	26.4	58	10.3	43	35.0	458	149.9	5	17	6.9	13	1	.1
07043	12.1	95	4.2	79	56.2	580	171.1	5	14	5.4	12	0	.5
07044	14.0	96	5.1	69	43.5	581	137.5	5	16	6.2	14	0	.0
07045	5.9	98	1.7	93	52.9	489	185.8	5	7	2.9	9	3	.2
07046	4.4	99	1.2	96	68.9	791	239.2	5	5	2.2	4	0	.1
07047	47.7	94	19.2	36	25.6	383	83.5	5	16	21.1	13	4	2.1
07050	31.1	40	12.2	25	23.2	370	72.5	7	12	5.7	17	1	.1
07052	39.5	95	14.0	68	40.9	487	135.3	5	16	17.6	14	1	1.3
07054	27.8	94	10.0	51	35.6	470	153.5	6	16	10.3	14	6	1.9
07055	52.5	63	19.2	26	21.1	351	97.8	8	12	15.8	14	2	2.4
07057	10.6	97	4.5	43	25.8	402	119.2	5	12	4.9	11	1	.4
07058	4.1	92	1.1	92	50.2	556	195.8	6	11	2.0	15	0	.3
07060	52.6	72	18.9	54	35.8	421	157.8	6	11	17.9	10	2	.1
07062	14.0	43	4.7	68	31.2	424	91.9	7	9	3.0	11	0	.1
07063	13.2	42	3.9	70	30.4	431	85.0	8	8	2.8	12	0	.9
07064	4.4	97	1.3	86	35.2	403	103.9	5	7	2.1	6	2	14.6

*=Estimated **1.0=883 lbs per person; 100++ indicates per capita toxic waste generation > than 100 times the U.S. average of 883 lbs per capita.

ZIP CODE MEASURES OF SIZE, LEVELS OF AFFLUENCE AND QUALITY OF LIFE

1=Population (th.); 2= % White; 3=Households (th.); 4=% Owner Occupied; 5=Mean Income Per Household (th.$); 6=Mean Monthly Rent ($); 7=Mean Home Value (th.$); 8=% under 5; 9=% 65 and over; 10=White Males (th.); 11=% White Males, 65+; 12=# Toxic Waste Sites; 13=Toxic Waste Relative to US(883 lbs.per capita)**.

NEW JERSEY

ZIP CODE	1	2	3	4	5	6	7	8	9	10	11	12	13
NEWARK													
07065	26.7	80	9.8	65	30.5	403	94.0	6	12	10.3	11	2	12.4
07066	16.7	99	5.6	80	39.0	496	140.4	4	10	8.0	9	1	1.5
07067	20.2	94	6.1	80	41.3	515	124.4	5	7	9.3	6	0	.0
07068	5.3	96	1.8	76	46.9	746	175.4	5	10	9.3	9	0	1.7
07070	19.1	95	6.9	61	34.0	448	124.4	5	15	8.6	12	2	.8
07071	20.3	99	7.3	61	29.3	432	111.6	5	14	9.5	12	5	6.5
07072	6.2	98	2.3	57	28.3	435	109.6	5	13	2.9	11	6	31.3
07073	7.8	96	3.1	42	24.8	410	109.4	5	15	3.6	12	7	7.8
07074	3.0	98	1.2	73	27.8	453	102.8	5	12	1.4	12	1	18.7
07075	7.9	98	2.8	76	34.9	510	124.9	5	13	3.7	11	1	3.4
07076	17.1	85	5.5	86	46.7	549	158.2	5	9	5.9	9	1	2.2
07077	2.5	98	.8	81	34.1	393	97.3	5	9	1.3	8	3	6.7
07078	12.8	97	4.3	91	91.0	648	297.9	5	14	6.0	14	3	.8
07079	15.9	87	5.2	73	57.0	504	155.2	4	14	6.6	12	0	.2
07080	20.5	94	6.3	92	36.4	471	106.4	7	9	9.6	6	8	5.5
07081	14.0	96	5.5	67	39.5	482	155.7	5	21	6.2	19	0	2.6
07082	3.8	95	1.1	93	46.7	614	175.3	8	5	5.0	5	0	.0
07083	47.1	96	17.2	79	32.8	459	118.9	4	19	21.0	17	4	5.5
07087	68.8	86	25.7	21	21.6	351	82.3	7	12	27.9	11	0	.0
07088	3.1	7	1.0	59	23.4	435	69.7	5	14	.1	15	0	.0
07090	33.6	94	11.3	81	49.7	532	173.1	5	11	15.2	9	0	.0
07092	7.5	97	2.4	96	57.9	685	207.6	4	12	3.5	12	2	1.2
07093	45.8	86	18.3	20	22.3	342	70.8	6	14	18.3	10	0	.1
07094	13.7	98	4.9	63	35.5	457	118.8	5	12	6.4	10	3	3.3
07095	16.7	91	5.3	66	30.1	388	99.3	5	11	7.5	10	7	.9
NEWARK													
07102	11.9	17	4.7	5	13.0	237	57.0	7	11	1.2	10	3	2.0
07103	54.7	5	17.1	11	13.2	246	31.1	10	9	1.2	20	4	.1
07104	54.8	57	18.8	20	18.3	308	63.5	10	9	14.8	11	1	1.5
07105	42.1	87	14.1	27	22.8	299	55.1	7	9	18.2	11	34	10.6
07106	35.5	42	12.3	37	22.2	361	62.8	7	12	7.2	20	0	.0
07107	41.4	39	14.5	23	16.2	308	48.1	8	12	7.2	18	0	.2
07108	37.6	2	12.1	17	15.9	279	49.8	9	7	.3	24	0	.1
07109	35.4	94	13.1	50	27.9	441	95.4	5	13	15.5	12	1	1.2
07110	29.0	96	10.6	66	32.9	463	113.8	5	14	13.1	12	1	15.0
07111	61.6	57	24.8	31	22.1	387	64.7	7	14	16.0	11	1	.4
07112	37.6	1	12.5	25	20.7	370	64.9	9	5	.2	21	0	.0
07114	13.5	22	5.2	12	11.2	186	37.3	9	13	1.3	15	4	18.1
ELIZABETH													
07201	24.8	56	8.2	33	23.0	376	66.3	7	9	6.8	10	15	3.4
07202	31.4	91	12.6	31	23.9	383	73.7	6	17	13.2	15	2	.7
07203	20.6	70	7.6	60	28.2	373	87.1	6	13	6.9	13	1	.4
07204	13.4	98	5.0	58	30.5	459	101.1	5	12	6.3	10	1	.3
07205	21.5	67	7.2	73	31.3	428	86.3	6	11	7.0	14	1	5.1
07206	23.6	60	7.3	32	20.2	309	58.0	9	8	6.9	9	2	1.1
07208	26.4	88	10.9	33	27.8	405	96.3	6	16	10.9	14	0	.0
JERSEY CITY													
07302	30.3	48	11.0	16	17.3	261	46.4	9	10	6.9	14	12	3.4
07304	41.7	42	14.9	27	21.3	304	55.1	8	12	8.3	15	11	1.0

NEW JERSEY

ZIP CODE	1	2	3	4	5	6	7	8	9	10	11	12	13
JERSEY CITY													
07305	59.7	43	19.8	38	23.6	319	58.7	8	10	12.0	15	9	.6
07306	51.5	71	20.1	21	21.0	312	55.6	7	14	17.3	15	0	4.3
07307	40.3	90	15.1	34	22.1	327	60.2	7	12	17.0	10	2	.1
PATERSON													
07401	5.9	99	1.7	90	64.2	764	216.6	5	9	2.8	7	0	4.3
07403	7.8	99	2.6	73	30.5	547	111.1	7	7	3.9	6	1	.1
07405	15.4	99	4.9	82	43.5	508	165.2	6	7	7.5	6	1	.2
07407	18.4	97	6.7	63	29.0	450	110.8	5	15	8.5	13	4	2.8
07410	32.2	98	11.6	81	37.4	493	133.6	4	14	15.3	13	4	4.9
07416	5.3	99	1.8	75	27.3	462	86.5	7	12	2.5	10	5	.2
07417	8.8	99	2.5	94	75.2	901	294.3	5	7	4.4	6	2	1.9
07418	1.6	98	.4	98	32.5	373*	113.5	10	4	.8	7	0	.0
07419	4.2	99	1.5	69	30.4	515	99.9	8	9	2.0	8	0	.6
07420	5.1	97	1.5	78	28.7	497	92.7	7	10	2.3	8	2	.0
07421	5.6	97	1.8	86	28.9	535	94.4	11	7	2.7	6	0	.0
07422	4.8	100	1.5	91	30.7	607	96.1	11	6	2.4	6	0	.0
07423	9.6	98	3.0	92	52.0	706	178.9	6	8	4.6	4	1	.0
07424	22.7	99	8.2	76	33.6	523	128.0	5	11	10.8	9	1	2.2
07428	1.3	100	.4	76	33.7	601	101.7	8	4	.6	4	0	.0
07430	12.1	93	3.7	79	45.9	607	193.2	5	8	5.6	7	4	1.0
07432	7.4	0	2.6	74	35.1	586	136.9	6	13	.0	0	0	.8
07435	2.6	100	.8	82	40.5	557	153.1	6	8	1.3	6	0	.9
07436	13.5	99	3.8	91	44.8	666	150.4	6	6	6.6	4	7	.3
07438	8.8	99	2.7	89	35.4	479	117.0	8	7	4.3	4	0	.0
07439	2.7	96	.8	88	29.6	487	94.2	9	6	1.3	6	0	.3
07440	5.4	100	1.6	87	36.1	418	129.9	6	7	2.6	4	1	.3
07442	10.6	99	3.5	79	36.2	470	118.3	5	10	5.0	8	1	2.9
07444	8.4	0	2.6	91	44.4	540	146.0	4	9	.0	0	2	.4
07446	12.9	97	4.2	79	44.4	639	182.4	6	8	6.1	7	1	.8
07450	25.2	95	8.3	80	57.4	680	202.5	5	12	11.3	10	1	.8
07452	12.6	95	4.8	94	49.5	725	160.1	6	12	5.3	11	0	.4
07456	12.6	96	3.6	93	39.0	664	138.5	7	9	6.2	7	0	.2
07457	2.5	100	.8	80	34.9	496	110.7	6	9	1.3	7	1	2.4
07458	10.7	98	3.2	94	77.9	625	313.3	4	9	5.2	7	0	2.1
07460	3.2	0	1.0	96	31.0	612	103.3	9	5	.0	0	0	.1
07461	13.7	99	4.2	75	29.1	453	107.6	9	6	6.8	7	2	.0
07462	2.9	99	.9	89	32.1	438	115.5	6	10	1.4	6	1	.0
07463	5.3	97	1.7	87	43.4	590	139.8	6	8	2.5	7	2	.3
07465	5.0	98	1.5	78	35.4	543	132.8	9	7	2.5	7	2	.0
07470	47.0	97	14.3	81	43.8	498	160.1	5	10	22.3	8	1	1.0
07480	14.2	98	4.1	90	34.9	550	122.4	8	6	6.9	5	0	.0
07481	15.5	98	4.8	93	54.8	673	214.6	5	10	7.4	9	1	.1
PATERSON													
07501	32.7	39	10.9	18	15.1	328	56.1	10	9	6.1	14	6	1.5
07502	12.7	91	4.4	56	25.0	386	89.6	5	16	5.3	15	0	.0
07503	16.5	79	5.8	36	20.5	362	76.5	8	13	6.1	13	0	.7
07504	12.9	37	3.8	45	31.3	416	90.7	8	7	2.3	15	0	2.7
07505	1.9	59	1.0	2	11.8	233	41.9*	6	16	.5	18	0	4.2
07506	18.2	100	6.8	66	30.5	500	125.6	5	17	8.5	14	3	2.7

*=Estimated **1.0=883 lbs per person; 100++ indicates per capita toxic waste generation > than 100 times the U.S. average of 883 lbs per capita.

ZIP CODE MEASURES OF SIZE, LEVELS OF AFFLUENCE AND QUALITY OF LIFE

1=Population (th.); 2= % White; 3=Households (th.); 4=% Owner Occupied; 5=Mean Income Per Household (th.$); 6=Mean Monthly Rent ($); 7=Mean Home Value (th.$); 8=% under 5; 9=% 65 and over; 10=% White Males, 65+; 11=% White Males; 12=# Toxic Waste Sites; 13=Toxic Waste Relative to US(883 lbs.per capita).

NEW JERSEY

ZIPCODE	1	2	3	4	5	6	7	8	9	10	11	12	13
PATERSON													
07508	19.4	99	6.9	63	29.2	449	130.5	5	17	9.0	14	2	1.0
07512	11.2	98	3.4	82	34.1	486	130.4	4	12	5.0	11	0	3.1
07513	11.1	57	3.4	36	22.6	351	75.9	9	9	3.0	13	0	1.2
07514	17.4	44	6.1	33	21.9	371	78.7	8	12	3.3	19	0	1.5
07522	21.7	39	7.1	24	17.9	355	58.7	7	8	4.1	12	1	.0
07524	11.4	55	3.8	30	19.2	377	69.6	9	9	3.0	12	0	3.4
HACKENSACK													
07601	36.0	74	15.7	28	28.9	499	113.6	5	14	12.8	12	0	.6
07603	8.3	96	2.9	66	32.6	522	106.3	6	12	3.8	9	0	.0
07604	11.9	99	4.3	72	36.0	490	129.4	4	15	5.6	13	0	.5
07605	8.0	94	3.1	60	39.7	444	146.8	5	15	3.5	13	0	.6
07606	2.2	98	.7	60	30.1	494	118.8	6	12	1.1	11	1	11.3
07607	9.9	97	3.6	71	32.7	495	121.8	5	15	4.5	13	2	4.9
07620	1.5	97	.5	80	106.6	876	333.1	5	8	2.3	10	0	.0
07621	25.6	94	8.7	72	34.1	496	118.0	5	12	11.6	11	0	.0
07624	8.2	94	2.6	89	45.7	631	171.8	5	10	3.8	9	1	.0
07626	7.6	95	2.3	91	44.0	721	151.8	5	13	3.5	11	1	.4
07627	5.0	94	1.5	94	60.8	786	202.8	5	10	2.3	8	0	.0
07628	18.3	96	6.1	76	35.4	501	118.5	5	13	8.4	11	0	.0
07630	7.7	96	2.2	94	45.7	587	149.5	5	11	3.5	8	0	.0
07631	23.7	54	8.6	52	37.9	453	150.8	5	14	5.9	14	1	1.5
07632	5.7	89	1.7	93	64.6	672	273.1	4	11	2.5	10	0	4.2
07640	4.5	95	1.3	94	55.0	650	188.3	6	8	2.1	7	0	.0
07641	3.5	94	1.1	97	54.9	1041	212.1	5	11	1.6	11	0	.0
07642	10.2	98	3.1	91	46.2	542	167.8	6	8	4.9	8	0	.0
07643	9.4	96	3.7	45	31.0	500	119.0	5	10	4.4	8	0	2.0
07644	24.0	96	9.3	43	26.5	446	108.5	6	12	10.9	10	3	1.9
07645	7.3	98	2.3	78	46.3	652	204.5	6	11	3.5	9	0	1.2
07646	16.9	96	6.2	62	32.7	382	131.7	5	14	7.6	12	0	.0
07647	5.2	95	1.5	83	39.2	590	150.1	5	8	2.4	8	1	23.8
07648	4.4	96	1.3	91	48.1	602	181.8	5	8	2.1	8	0	.2
07649	8.7	97	2.8	90	53.2	639	200.9	4	12	4.1	10	0	.0
07650	13.7	93	5.5	40	29.3	472	118.8	5	11	6.0	13	1	.9
07652	26.5	96	7.6	92	44.2	665	160.7	4	11	12.2	12	1	1.2
07656	8.5	97	2.8	78	42.5	584	165.5	5	9	4.1	11	1	.1
07657	10.3	99	3.9	56	32.1	481	144.6	4	16	4.8	14	2	5.5
07660	12.7	98	4.9	52	31.3	475	104.4	5	13	5.8	10	0	.1
07661	11.1	98	4.1	73	39.4	521	139.4	5	16	5.1	13	0	.0
07662	19.7	99	6.9	76	33.3	504	118.1	5	12	9.3	10	0	1.4
07666	39.0	72	12.9	79	42.0	471	127.1	5	13	13.6	13	0	.1
07670	13.6	95	4.6	82	59.3	647	215.9	5	15	6.0	13	1	1.1
07675	40.1	96	12.3	87	48.2	585	183.6	5	14	18.6	7	0	.1
REDBANK													
07701	31.9	87	11.7	71	37.4	457	133.3	5	16	12.9	13	0	.1
07703	5.0	71	1.2	2	22.8	390	81.3*	11	0	23	.0	2.0	.0
07710	.1	0	.1	87	25.0	288*	105.4	0	23	.0	0	0	.0
07711	2.1	99	.8	81	40.4	340	159.8	6	16	1.1	14	0	.1
07712	34.5	70	13.6	38	25.6	358	127.7	6	14	11.4	14	1	1.0
07716	7.5	93	2.5	73	33.1	492	113.7	6	14	3.3	10	1	.0

NEW JERSEY

ZIPCODE	1	2	3	4	5	6	7	8	9	10	11	12	13
REDBANK													
07717	2.3	100	1.0	53	27.7	437	130.3	4	27	1.0	22	0	.0
07718	6.2	100	1.8	92	33.0	511	99.0	7	6	3.0	5	1	.0
07719	18.7	95	7.2	63	26.6	386	96.5	6	16	8.6	13	6	.2
07720	4.8	94	2.0	42	20.9	383	74.6	7	18	2.1	15	0	.1
07721	1.9	60	.6	50	24.7	475	76.9	7	8	.5	8	2	.1
07722	7.5	97	2.1	91	59.3	627	234.3	4	7	3.6	6	1	.0
07723	2.6	98	.9	85	69.3	435	267.4	5	13	1.3	13	0	.2
07724	16.7	82	6.4	56	30.6	436	117.2	6	9	6.7	8	5	.8
07726	22.0	94	6.6	91	38.7	489	144.7	6	11	10.1	10	0	.1
07727	5.7	93	1.8	71	30.0	425	105.1	7	9	2.7	8	6	1.3
07728	34.1	90	10.8	76	33.8	421	129.6	6	12	15.1	10	4	.8
07730	17.9	97	5.0	89	37.5	485	115.5	7	7	8.4	5	0	.0
07731	18.0	96	5.4	87	31.1	374	102.9	7	7	8.4	7	1	.0
07732	5.6	99	2.3	55	27.8	452	93.6	5	12	2.8	10	1	.0
07733	8.5	98	2.2	95	70.2	685	234.7	5	5	4.2	4	0	2.1
07734	20.5	99	6.5	70	24.1	402	72.5	8	11	9.7	9	0	.0
07735	22.3	93	7.5	71	25.7	384	75.6	7	11	10.0	9	3	10.0
07737	4.4	99	1.4	87	32.1	434	102.3	7	9	2.2	8	0	.0
07738	5.5	95	1.7	85	46.6	283	174.2	6	9	2.6	6	0	.0
07739	5.5	100	1.9	96	49.5	649	159.2	6	11	2.6	11	0	.0
07740	30.2	76	11.8	41	24.0	382	94.5	7	14	10.6	14	1	.1
07746	8.1	91	2.0	92	48.9	371	174.5	8	7	3.8	5	2	.0
07747	24.1	94	8.1	74	37.0	448	129.3	6	10	11.0	8	4	.1
07748	20.6	98	5.9	93	47.9	355	167.1	6	7	3.4	5	0	.3
07750	3.3	97	1.4	71	44.6	469	151.3	4	12	.0	12	0	.0
07751	8.4	94	2.3	95	49.5	496	174.7	6	9	3.9	4	1	.2
07753	30.5	67	10.5	70	27.8	395	85.3	6	12	9.8	12	0	.1
07755	5.7	100	1.8	88	38.0	462	124.9	6	12	2.7	9	0	.0
07756	4.4	99	2.2	47	18.0	310	66.5	3	45	1.6	33	0	.2
07757	5.0	99	1.7	85	35.3	316	134.4	6	11	2.3	9	0	.5
07758	4.7	98	1.5	81	27.5	392	83.4	7	11	2.2	8	0	.2
07760	10.4	97	3.7	75	54.8	521	206.1	5	11	4.9	8	0	.0
07762	10.1	99	4.1	64	33.6	530	150.6	4	22	4.6	18	0	.3
07764	7.4	99	2.2	83	38.2	363	145.1	4	12	3.4	10	0	.3
07765	.3	100	.1	76	32.0	675	121.4	3	2	.2	2	0	.0
DOVER													
07801	33.1	92	11.5	60	33.2	496	119.3	6	9	15.0	8	5	.9
07820	.4	100	.1	43	25.6	419	116.4	6	15	.2	10	0	.0
07821	8.0	98	2.3	86	36.0	454	126.0	7	13	.8	10	3	.0
07822	1.1	100	.4	77	31.7	428	146.1	7	6	.5	10	0	.2
07825	5.3	100	1.9	70	28.7	333	94.8	6	12	2.6	10	3	21.7
07826	6.0	99	1.9	82	35.2	404	144.5	6	11	2.9	9	0	.0
07828	5.2	100	1.8	80	30.2	441	106.6	7	13	2.6	12	0	.0
07829	10.8	97	3.9	49	30.6	470	118.6	9	5	5.1	5	3	.0
07830	.3	100	.3	80	32.6	285	110.2	8	10	.1	12	1	.0
07832	5.1	98	1.6	87	43.0	490	172.2	6	7	2.4	6	1	.1
07833	2.6	100	.8	79	29.2	396	115.0	7	13	1.3	12	0	.0
07834	.3	100	.3	79	28.2	455	91.2	9	10	.8	10	0	.0
07834	15.4	98	4.9	88	39.1	540	138.8	6	9	7.3	7	0	.2

*=Estimated **1.0=883 lbs per person; 100++ indicates per capita toxic waste generation > than 100 times the U.S. average of 883 lbs per capita.

ZIP CODE MEASURES OF SIZE, LEVELS OF AFFLUENCE AND QUALITY OF LIFE

1=Population (th.); 2= % White; 3=Households (th.); 4=% Owner Occupied; 5=Mean Income Per Household (th.$); 6=Mean Monthly Rent ($)*; 7=Mean Home Value (th.$)*; 8=% under 5, 9=% 65 and over; 10=White Males (th.); 11=% White Males, 65+; 12=# Toxic Waste Sites; 13=Toxic Waste Relative to US(883 lbs.per capita)**.

NEW JERSEY

DOVER

ZIPCODE	1	2	3	4	5	6	7	8	9	10	11	12	13
07836	8.1	97	2.5	74	40.4	549	155.9	8	4	4.0	3	0	.1
07837	.2	100	.1	60	22.3	441	99.5	10	11	.1	16	0	.0
07838	1.7	96	.5	80	30.3	475	119.9	8	10	.8	8	3	13.0
07840	18.3	98	6.4	60	32.3	452	125.3	7	11	8.4	8	3	2.6
07843	12.3	97	3.8	89	28.2	427	101.4	6	6	6.1	5	0	.7
07844	.7	0	.3	73	32.8	552	104.7	11	5	.0	0	0	.0
07845	3.1	98	1.0	79	33.5	449	119.5	5	13	1.5	3	0	.0
07846	.3	0	.1	60	42.5	478	148.5	7	5	.0	0	0	.0
07847	2.0	95	.7	74	27.6	618	106.3	6	8	.9	11	1	.0
07848	2.0	99	.7	78	31.4	415	102.6	6	11	.5	7	1	6.2
07849	6.6	99	2.3	82	32.5	474	125.2	7	10	.9	7	1	.2
07850	6.8	98	2.1	86	34.8	483	109.3	8	8	3.3	8	0	.0
07851	.4	98	.2	73	24.6	558	112.7	9	4	3.4	3	0	.0
07852	.8	100	.3	86	34.3	301	106.2	5	21	.0	12	4	.4
07853	9.1	98	2.6	88	43.3	308	121.5	7	11	4.5	4	3	1.9
07856	2.6	99	.9	64	33.7	591	180.3	9	9	1.3	6	3	2.2
07857	3.6	99	1.3	48	27.7	510	126.2	6	10	1.7	9	1	.0
07860	21.0	98	6.9	72	30.4	503	102.4	7	12	9.9	9	1	.4
07863	3.2	98	1.0	87	27.1	431	113.0	7	15	.0	8	0	.0
07865	1.6	94	.5	76	29.0	443	95.0	9	11	.8	8	8	.4
07866	19.0	97	6.0	84	38.7	568	127.4	7	7	9.2	5	5	.5
07871	14.4	99	4.5	87	43.9	526	130.6	7	7	7.1	6	6	.1
07874	8.8	98	2.8	89	33.6	461	150.9	6	4	4.3	7	0	.0
07875	.6	100	.3	74	30.2	539	107.1	10	6	.8	4	0	.0
07876	9.3	98	2.6	94	43.7	549	91.3	11	11	4.5	5	1	1.9
07877	.3	98	.1	70	20.3	616	153.5	7	6	.0	6	0	.0
07878	1.2	0	.4	95	39.1	290	114.2	14	11	.1	0	0	.0
07880	.2	87	.1	91	35.1	590	109.1	7	5	.0	5	1	.2
07881	11.6	100	4.1	38	30.5	403*	98.2	3	1	5.4	4	0	.2
07882	9.7	98	3.4	68	28.4	406	107.2	6	10	4.6	11	7	.1
07885		98		70	30.3	420	97.6	6	9		6	2	

SUMMIT

ZIPCODE	1	2	3	4	5	6	7	8	9	10	11	12	13
07901	21.3	93	7.8	66	55.4	583	226.1	4	15	9.1	12	0	7.0
07920	11.0	99	3.4	86	55.7	478	224.7	4	8	5.3	6	1	.0
07921	1.5	100	.5	82	56.0	745	235.0	4	10	.8	9	0	.0
07922	12.2	99	3.5	92	54.9	702	189.2	5	8	5.8	9	1	2.7
07924	6.7	99	2.3	78	55.1	582	232.8	4	12	3.0	9	0	.0
07926	1.4	100	.4	91	53.5	502	246.3	5	9	.7	9	0	.0
07927	2.1	94	.7	88	38.2	614	152.8	6	6	1.0	6	1	13.2
07928	17.0	98	6.0	79	54.5	648	208.5	5	13	8.0	11	2	.0
07930	5.9	99	1.7	84	45.7	632	203.3	5	7	2.8	6	2	.2
07932	2.1	98	.7	65	84.3	547	224.3	5	13	1.0	11	0	4.1
07933	7.7	99	2.7	90	49.7	947	190.5	5	7	3.8	7	0	.9
07934	2.7	96	.9	89	43.6	715	161.4	6	7	1.3	5	0	1.9
07935	1.1	99	.4	73	43.7	517	194.8	4	17	.5	16	0	.3
07936	.8	100	.2	82	44.5	576	191.0	1	25	.3	16	0	1.0
07938	9.3	96	2.6	93	42.5	564	176.0	6	7	4.4	6	7	7.6

NEW JERSEY

SUMMIT (continued)

ZIPCODE	1	2	3	4	5	6	7	8	9	10	11	12	13
07940	16.4	93	4.8	69	44.3	560	183.3	4	11	7.4	9	2	.0
07945	7.4	99	2.2	86	58.9	711	250.3	4	9	3.5	7	0	.0
07946	5.0	95	1.2	91	46.5	553	187.6	4	13	2.9	15	0	.2
07950	17.0	93	5.3	73	43.7	553	176.1	6	11	7.7	9	2	3.5
07960	34.9	83	12.4	57	45.9	498	196.2	5	13	13.6	11	0	.7
07961	.9	93		100	62.3	715*	281.4	3	23	.1	3	2	.0
07970	5.8	96	1.5	90	53.8	410	213.8	3	9	2.8	3	0	.0
07974	12.6	97	4.2	77	48.7	533	183.1	4	9	5.9	7	1	1.4
07976	.3	100	.4	88	83.4	456	308.3	4	16	.6	16	0	.0
07977	2.0	97	.3	53	39.0	496	204.0	6	10	.5	7	1	1.6
07978	.3	100	.1	73	51.6	554	186.2	3	14	.2	13	0	.0
07979	.7	100		77	92.9	465	264.2	5	7	.3	4	0	.2
07980	1.9	0	.6	77	41.6	534	156.6	6	11	.0	7	1	6.0
07981	8.6	97	2.6	92	44.6	545	162.3	5	8	4.2	7	4	5.7

SOUTH JERSEY

ZIPCODE	1	2	3	4	5	6	7	8	9	10	11	12	13
08001	1.6	86	.5	81	29.5	335	65.8	5	11	.7	9	1	.0
08002	21.4	94	7.6	70	34.2	417	98.1	5	13	9.5	11	4	.9
08003	27.0	93	7.4	97	55.1	664	153.5	6	9	12.5	13	0	.2
08004	9.9	89	3.0	90	28.6	400	95.5	4	7	4.3	6	1	.1
08005	8.9	96	2.9	89	23.6	515	77.8	11	11	4.2	11	1	.4
08006	.9	0	.4	88	31.7	390	156.6	4	22	.0	7	1	.0
08007	6.1	96	2.2	67	26.9	330	71.8	7	8	2.9	7	2	.3
08008	8.4	99	3.8	80	27.0	343	144.0	3	28	4.0	26	0	.0
08009	12.3	89	3.8	83	32.0	397	92.5	7	8	5.2	8	3	1.6
08010	12.7	84	4.6	60	29.3	393	81.7	7	7	5.2	8	0	.0
08011	2.1	100	1.1	100	22.8	262*	89.2	8	12	.9	9	1	100++
08012	34.6	95	11.1	70	31.0	367	92.2	8	16	16.1	15	1	.0
08014	.6	100	.2	80	23.7	404	55.7	8	13	.3	13	5	57.5
08015	20.3	79	6.3	83	25.3	384	68.6	10	4	8.0	5	1	.0
08016	22.3	78	7.8	64	26.1	340	75.6	7	11	8.2	10	10	2.8
08018	.7	100		100	23.4	269*	83.5	3	22	.1	12	0	.1
08019	.7	93	.2	75	25.2	419	68.6	7	14	.3	3	1	.1
08020	2.0	97	.6	79	30.8	344	99.2	7	16	.9	11	1	.0
08021	45.2	91	17.6	51	25.7	381	75.7	8	7	19.7	6	1	1.9
08022	2.5	100	.8	76	32.3	406	109.4	7	9	.0	0	0	.2
08023	.5	100	.2	91	21.5	246	36.9	7	17	.3	17	1	100++
08025	.5	97	.1	95	33.8	389*	98.2	8	7	.3	6	0	.0
08027	2.5	97	.8	88	30.8	416	79.9	8	7	1.2	6	2	2.7
08028	15.7	79	5.0	55	23.5	319	73.0	6	8	6.0	7	3	39.1
08029	5.8	0	2.0	79	27.2	220	73.2	6	13	.0	0	0	.3
08030	15.3	99	5.5	73	21.9	334	49.7	6	14	7.4	11	1	.3
08031	13.7	98	4.5	72	27.0	301	69.8	6	8	6.6	7	0	3.9
08032	.3	93	.3	89	34.1	392*	81.7	8	8	.4	6	0	.0
08033	18.6	98	7.2	71	40.0	426	126.0	5	16	8.4	13	0	1.9
08034	20.3	96	6.8	83	43.4	465	112.2	5	13	9.4	8	0	.8
08035	8.4	100	3.1	77	31.5	348	87.7	5	17	3.9	13	0	.0
08036	.6	0	.2	83	26.0	442	73.3	6	8	.0	0	0	.8
08037	21.3	90	6.8	74	28.4	316	87.1	6	12	9.2	11	1	2.0

*=Estimated **1.0=883 lbs per person; 100++ indicates per capita toxic waste generation > than 100 times the U.S. average of 883 lbs per capita.

ZIP CODE MEASURES OF SIZE, LEVELS OF AFFLUENCE AND QUALITY OF LIFE

1=Population (th.); 2= % White; 3=Households (th.); 4=% Owner Occupied; 5=Mean Income Per Household (th.$); 6=Mean Monthly Rent ($)*; 7=Mean Home Value (th.$)*; 8=% under 5; 9=% 65 and over; 10=White Males (th.); 11=% White Males, 65+; 12=# Toxic Waste Sites; 13=Toxic Waste Relative to US(883 lbs.per capita)**.

NEW JERSEY

SOUTH JERSEY

ZIP CODE	1	2	3	4	5	6	7	8	9	10	11	12	13
08093	8.6	93	3.2	63	24.3	380	63.8	7	11	3.8	9	0	8.6
08094	25.2	87	8.1	84	25.9	352	77.5	9	8	10.8	8	0	.7
08095	.5	85	.2	89	26.7	292	70.3	10	2	.2	0	6	1.1
08096	31.5	91	10.6	75	30.1	382	78.5	7	10	13.8	8	10	1.4
08097	3.8	96	1.1	90	34.1	410	94.5	5	8	1.8	8	1	.0
08098	7.0	81	2.4	73	29.8	357	86.2	6	14	2.6	11	2	.0

CAMDEN

ZIP CODE	1	2	3	4	5	6	7	8	9	10	11	12	13
08102	9.0	17	2.6	38	13.4	282	19.6	11	7	.8	16	2	.8
08103	18.4	10	5.9	54	15.5	293	24.3	9	10	.9	16	1	.6
08104	26.4	39	9.4	60	17.2	275	29.6	9	11	4.6	19	0	.4
08105	32.0	41	10.8	54	16.1	261	32.7	11	10	6.1	16	1	.1
08106	10.8	100	4.1	71	25.8	319	69.1	6	17	5.1	14	0	.0
08107	14.8	97	6.2	60	23.9	354	66.0	5	19	6.1	15	0	.0
08108	19.4	100	7.3	74	27.8	341	75.5	5	16	9.1	13	0	.2
08109	21.9	95	7.6	79	31.2	343	80.3	6	14	9.7	11	0	3.4
08110	14.7	91	5.2	84	26.1	351	62.7	6	14	6.4	13	4	3.4

ATLANTIC CITY

ZIP CODE	1	2	3	4	5	6	7	8	9	10	11	12	13
08201	12.8	96	4.3	88	30.8	436	109.2	8	9	6.1	9	0	.0
08202	2.3	100	1.0	81	30.0	186	206.7	4	21	4.0	20	0	.0
08203	8.3	98	3.4	61	27.3	452	153.1	4	16	4.0	14	0	.0
08204	16.8	94	6.4	74	22.3	340	79.9	9	20	7.7	17	3	.0
08210	7.2	84	2.6	82	25.6	427	86.1	7	19	2.8	17	2	.0
08212	.3	98	.1	77	19.6	423	98.0	4	35	.1	29	0	.0
08213	.7	100	.2	89	38.3	386	92.7	1	7	.3	9	3	1.6
08214	.5	0	.1	95	34.3	394*	77.3	2	8	.7	14	0	15.4
08215	8.9	84	3.2	74	25.5	317	78.0	7	14	3.7	13	0	30.1
08217	.8	64	.2	84	22.7	331	79.5	8	17	.3	18	1	9.1
08218	.4	0	.1	85	30.0	456	84.9	9	8	.0	7	0	1.0
08219	.6	100	.2	90	21.0	238	72.0	7	9	.3	7	0	.0
08220	.2	0	2.7	100	27.2	313*	144.8	14	15	4.7	10	1	.3
08221	8.5	99	.2	92	37.9	472	145.3	6	10	4.1	8	1	.0
08223	2.5	0	1.0	87	29.0	446	137.2	7	17	.0	7	0	.0
08224	.7	100	.3	78	24.1	345	88.3	6	19	.4	15	0	.0
08225	7.8	99	2.5	92	35.1	510	115.4	4	14	3.7	12	0	.1
08226	14.0	94	6.3	59	27.4	446	153.1	4	26	6.0	23	0	.7
08230	3.0	98	1.0	84	26.7	338	124.3	10	15	1.4	14	0	.1
08231	.4	100	.1	84	34.8	399*	85.2	5	20	.2	16	0	.6
08232	25.4	65	9.2	73	22.9	328	77.1	8	14	7.7	14	1	.0
08240	2.4	89	.7	56	22.9	552	98.0	5	6	1.2	5	0	.0
08241	1.0	0	.3	93	31.8	415	117.9	8	11	.4	8	0	.0
08242	2.6	98	.9	80	22.9	383	86.7	6	15	1.2	16	0	.0
08243	2.6	98	1.1	75	28.7	438	143.0	5	22	1.2	20	0	.0
08244	10.4	97	4.3	56	24.2	409	101.6	6	18	4.7	16	0	1.8
08245	.2	100	.1	68	24.3	361	79.8	10	3	.1		0	.0
08246	.5	100	.2	79	22.7	400	77.2	9	12		12	3	.0
08247	1.3	98	.6	75	27.5	300	206.4	3	30	.6	25	0	.0
08248	.1	100	.1	100	24.4	280*	170.5	0	35	.1	30	0	.0
08250	.5	92	.2	92	23.8	497	98.7	11	12	.3	9	0	.5
08251	6.9	100	3.0	86	17.6	408	57.0	6	26	.0	26	0	.0

NEW JERSEY

SOUTH JERSEY

ZIP CODE	1	2	3	4	5	6	7	8	9	10	11	12	13
08038	.3	0	.1	84	20.8	350	57.1	3	15	.0	0	0	.0
08039	.4	0	.1	70	27.5	312	73.0	2	8	.0	0	0	.0
08041	.7	99	.2	72	37.1	372	83.5	8	9	.3	11	1	.2
08042	.4	100	.1	81	31.2	391	95.7	4	6	.3	8	0	.0
08043	9.4	91	3.6	49	35.2	478	114.2	6	6	4.2	5	2	.0
08045	3.0	1	1.1	75	26.8	255	70.3	5	12	.0	0	1	.4
08046	40.2	59	11.0	96	36.9	686	74.7	7	3	11.5	3	0	
08048	.6	0	.2	73	22.6	445	66.8	7	16	.0	0	2	.8
08049	6.0	87	2.0	79	27.9	325	67.7	7	8	2.6	6	0	
08050	9.5	99	3.5	89	24.7	476	84.8	9	14	4.6	13	2	
08051	6.0	97	2.0	73	27.3	424	73.8	7	10	2.8	10	3	
08052	20.5	94	8.5	51	25.6	419	72.0	5	11	9.3	10	1	.6
08053	22.8	97	7.1	80	38.4	468	118.2	7	6	10.8	4	2	.1
08054	17.1	94	5.3	82	40.9	551	122.7	7	4	7.7	7	4	
08055	20.6	99	6.5	81	39.8	483	139.7	7	9	9.9	5	0	
08056	1.5	91	.5	80	36.6	259	115.1	8	8	.7	7	0	
08057	16.2	93	5.4	87	44.8	452	145.0	5	16	7.0	12	1	2.1
08059	4.9	0	1.9	81	24.7	345	65.2	5	16	.0	0	1	.0
08060	24.7	84	8.8	67	28.3	384	79.3	7	9	10.1	9	3	.5
08061	.6	83	.2	86	28.5	432	60.0	4	12	.0	3	16	.0
08062	4.2	92	1.4	72	26.1	361	108.0	9	9	1.8	9	2	.0
08063	3.6	99	1.1	85	23.7	419	59.9	9	9	1.8	8	1	.0
08064	1.8	84	.5	57	24.7	148	76.3	1	15	1.3	12	0	.0
08065	7.0	87	2.2	73	28.5	403	71.2	6	12	2.9	7	0	1.6
08066	9.2	77	3.4	58	24.6	360	63.1	8	10	3.5	10	13	15.4
08067	1.8	81	.5	76	24.9	363	70.0	7	10	.7	10	6	30.1
08068	8.3	68	2.7	71	25.1	350	75.6	8	17	2.6	7	0	
08069	14.0	77	5.1	62	23.4	297	55.5	8	12	5.2	11	3	1.0
08070	12.9	99	4.5	79	28.9	298	72.0	6	10	6.3	8	3	.0
08071	10.3	99	3.6	73	28.6	371	80.9	7	14	4.7	10	1	.3
08072	.7	72	.2	76	24.7	432	55.3	8	10	.3	7	0	.0
08073	.3	100	.1	72	26.7	419	125.8	8	15	.2	6	0	28.2
08074	.4	0	.1	72	41.6	373	102.6	4	7	.0	0	0	.0
08075	26.1	95	8.8	72	29.8	364	85.4	7	9	12.1	4	1	.1
08077	19.4	93	5.8	92	41.9	425	108.0	4	9	8.9	7	0	.7
08078	8.7	99	3.0	75	26.0	369	69.3	6	10	4.2	9	1	.1
08079	13.0	71	4.6	61	24.2	287	58.5	8	13	4.5	13	0	.6
08080	13.6	94	4.1	89	33.2	457	102.4	10	7	6.4	5	1	.0
08081	16.1	81	4.9	91	29.4	377	89.8	4	13	6.5	4	0	.0
08083	12.5	88	3.9	77	30.9	377	89.8	6	8	5.4	6	0	.0
08084	8.0	95	2.6	76	29.6	311	82.2	6	9	3.7	7	0	.0
08085	5.7	82	2.0	74	28.7	346	84.1	9	11	2.3	10	1	.0
08086	5.0	96	1.9	66	25.7	429	72.3	8	8	2.5	7	2	1.8
08087	11.4	99	4.3	85	22.4	402	75.7	7	17	5.5	17		.0
08088	18.2	97	6.1	92	29.5	419	107.1	8	15	8.7	14	3	.0
08089	4.1	73	1.2	90	27.3	381	88.5	12	6	1.5	4	0	.0
08090	9.2	90	2.7	91	34.6	380	80.1	6	6	4.2	5	0	.0
08091	5.6	92	1.7	86	35.9	344	124.3	8	7	2.5	5	0	.5
08092	1.7	100	.6	86	22.7	333	71.2	6	8	.8	12	0	.0

*=Estimated **1.0=883 lbs per person; 100++ indicates per capita toxic waste generation > than 100 times the U.S. average of 883 lbs per capita.

ZIP CODE MEASURES OF SIZE, LEVELS OF AFFLUENCE AND QUALITY OF LIFE

1=Population (th.); 2= % White; 3=Households (th.); 4=% Owner Occupied; 5=Mean Income Per Household (th.$); 6=Mean Monthly Rent ($); 7=Mean Home Value (th.$);
8=% under 5; 9=% 65 and over; 10=White Males (th.); 11=% White Males, 65+; 12=# Toxic Waste Sites; 13=Toxic Waste Relative to US(883 lbs.per capita)**.

NEW JERSEY

ZIPCODE	1	2	3	4	5	6	7	8	9	10	11	12	13
ATLANTIC CITY													
08252	.8	32	.3	79	18.0	272	55.4	3	22	.1	45	0	.0
08260	13.9	92	5.8	64	21.3	320	99.8	5	20	6.1	18	0	.0
08270	5.5	80	1.5	81	22.5	275	69.2	7	10	2.6	10	1	2.2
SOUTH JERSEY													
08302	39.5	68	13.4	66	22.8	334	59.2	8	12	12.7	13	3	.1
08310	.5	82	.2	91	29.6	285	78.1	3	15	.2	18	1	4.9
08311	1.7	72	.5	82	21.9	304	39.9	5	12	.6	13	0	.0
08312	5.8	82	1.8	76	24.6	395	62.9	11	7	2.3	7	3	.2
08313	.2	0		87	25.2	290	67.4	11	14	.0	0	0	.0
08314	.4	100	.1	85	25.1	150	39.4	3	9	.2	4	0	.0
08315	.4	0	.1	86	22.6	289	33.7	9	10	.0	0	0	.0
08316	.5	0	.2	82	23.4	326	54.6	2	10	.0	0	0	.2
08317	.9	93	.3	88	25.7	424	83.2	9	11	.4	9	0	.0
08318	6.5	96	2.2	84	28.2	325	75.8	7	11	3.1	10	1	.0
08319	.6	91	.2	90	26.6	373	72.1	11	9	.3	11	0	.0
08321	.3	100	.1	82	14.8	371	45.7	4	28	.1	27	0	.0
08322	7.7	91	2.4	87	24.9	393	73.9	10	9	3.4	7	0	.5
08323	.3	91	.1	79	34.6	462	73.4	3	13	.2	20	0	.0
08324	.4	100	.2	89	17.2	608	31.2	10	19	.2	23	0	.0
08326	1.6	91	.5	74	26.0	426	75.6	7	11	.7	11	1	.0
08327	1.8	63	.7	77	24.6	387	37.6	3	5	.7	5	0	.0
08328	1.1	91	.4	78	36.6	327	68.2	8	6	.5	5	0	.0
08329	.2	100	.1	93	25.7	296*	58.3	3	17	.5	7	0	1.1
08330	14.2	90	4.7	79	27.1	426	91.3	8	9	6.2	8	1	.4
08332	30.7	89	11.0	66	23.7	330	59.7	8	11	13.1	11	3	.5
08340	.6	0	.2	97	25.4	292*	90.0	6	12	.0	0	0	.1
08341	2.0	91	.7	71	24.4	473	72.5	6	14	.8	13	1	.0
08342	.4	0	.1	72	16.2	401	34.7	1	3	.0	0	0	.0
08343	3.1	96	1.0	88	27.0	355	78.5	9	10	1.6	8	0	.5
ATLANTIC CITY													
08344	6.6	88	2.2	87	25.1	379	70.2	6	12	2.8	10	2	.1
08345	.8	89	.3	83	20.7	286	39.5	5	13	.4	11	0	.3
08346	1.0	10	.3	87	20.8	296	48.6	6	12	.1	33	0	.0
08347	.3	58	.6	71	19.7	523	55.8	13	8	.1	5	0	.1
08348	.4	0	.2	91	26.1	410	50.3	7	8	.0	0	0	.1
08349	2.7	51	.8	76	22.8	281	38.3	8	12	.4	7	1	.2
08350	1.0	78	.3	83	30.1	526	76.8	11	10	.7	12	1	.0
08352	1.0	64	.2	88	25.4	166	70.3	10	9	.3	7	0	.0
08353	.6	94	.2	73	25.7	389	55.9	8	9	.3	7	0	.0
08360	54.0	80	17.4	67	25.5	364	77.4	7	12	20.0	12	5	.5
ATLANTIC CITY													
08401	40.2	46	16.7	31	18.2	281	86.7	5	24	8.1	28	0	.0
08402	9.1	99	3.8	76	39.0	410	196.4	3	22	4.2	19	0	.0
08403	1.3	100	.6	84	32.5	561	201.0	3	37	.6	30	0	.2
08406	11.8	98	5.1	53	29.6	499	154.1	4	22	5.2	20	0	.0
TRENTON													
08501	3.7	92	1.2	76	33.6	454	110.0	7	11	1.7	10	0	.0
08502	7.8	97	2.1	93	47.8	624	184.8	8	4	3.8	3	2	3.6
08505	14.7	84	4.6	68	30.1	419	85.3	5	9	6.3	8	6	.2
08510	1.4	94	.4	87	36.9	429	164.1	10	7	.7	7	1	.0

NEW JERSEY

ZIPCODE	1	2	3	4	5	6	7	8	9	10	11	12	13
TRENTON													
08511	.9	88	.3	67	24.4	370	77.2	8	10	.4	11	0	.0
08512	10.5	91	4.2	57	35.6	445	150.9	6	13	4.5	13	1	5.1
08514	2.2	92	.7	78	31.8	390	107.4	5	9	1.0	7	1	.0
08515	.6	0	.2	75	37.8	427	117.7	9	12	.0	0	0	.0
08518	4.5	88	1.7	72	27.6	345	76.8	6	11	1.8	8	0	2.9
08520	22.8	92	7.8	64	35.2	486	120.4	8	8	9.9	6	4	.2
08525	4.7	97	1.7	76	36.2	480	137.3	5	12	2.1	11	1	.4
08526	.3	0	.1	87	30.9	355*	63.4	3	6	.0	0	0	.0
08527	25.2	96	7.6	83	29.6	431	95.5	7	10	11.8	9	10	.0
08528	.9	98	.3	68	27.5	372	135.3	4	15	.5	10	1	.0
08530	6.8	96	2.5	68	27.9	437	104.4	6	13	3.2	10	2	.1
08533	4.0	97	1.3	69	24.2	397	82.6	9	6	1.9	9	0	.1
08534	5.9	97	2.0	88	50.0	540	176.5	5	9	2.9	9	0	.1
08535	.2	0	.1	62	24.2	263	132.0	5	13	.0	8	0	.0
08536	4.7	92	2.7	15	32.5	510	168.3	5	3	2.3	2	1	1.1
08540	33.7	88	10.8	57	50.2	483	228.7	3	11	15.0	8	4	1.1
08550	3.9	93	1.1	92	51.3	903	185.2	6	6	1.8	5	4	.9
08551	3.3	100	1.2	79	36.4	369	151.6	6	7	1.6	6	0	.1
08553	.8	94	.3	72	41.4	516	181.0	5	13	.6	3	2	.0
08554	3.6	96	1.3	85	27.3	362	65.4	6	13	1.6	12	0	.4
08555	.8	95	.3	89	35.4	716	95.0	8	10	.4	12	0	.1
08556	.1	0	.1	87	38.7	444*	132.3	0	0	.0	0	0	.0
08557	.5	100	.1	75	34.6	393	133.1	6	4	.2	4	0	.4
08558	2.8	91	.8	87	52.5	512	195.5	4	7	1.3	6	1	.0
08559	3.7	98	1.2	78	36.5	499	145.8	8	9	1.8	8	0	3.7
08560	2.9	0	1.0	88	41.0	382	150.6	6	13	.0	0	1	.0
08561	.3	0	.1	85	28.5	273	94.4	6	17	.0	0	1	18.0
08562	4.3	91	1.5	70	24.9	334	105.3	9	11	1.9	6	2	.0
TRENTON													
08608	1.3	46	.8	2	10.7	210	38.3*	9	15	.3	21	0	.2
08609	16.4	40	5.6	38	17.7	314	35.2	8	13	3.0	16	0	.3
08610	37.2	94	13.7	75	28.4	403	75.6	5	13	16.7	11	1	.0
08611	24.1	80	8.8	62	20.4	321	36.8	7	15	9.3	14	0	.6
08618	41.9	38	14.9	50	23.9	320	61.8	8	12	7.2	18	1	.6
08619	21.4	97	7.9	71	31.1	423	96.2	5	13	9.9	10	7	.8
08620	5.2	94	1.8	71	28.7	381	94.3	6	9	2.4	8	0	5.4
08628	9.7	92	3.2	65	40.1	480	132.1	4	15	4.2	12	1	4.7
08629	10.9	92	4.0	77	24.6	367	53.4	6	11	4.7	14	0	.0
08638	34.3	67	11.6	73	29.1	366	85.8	6	11	11.0	11	5	1.4
TRENTON													
08640	16.3	61	.8	2	18.1	348	80.1	8	7	.0	0	0	.2
08641	8.2	74	1.9	8	21.0	348	74.8	14	0	3.6	0	0	.3
08648	11.0	94	3.1	69	38.4	521	132.3	3	12	5.0	9	0	.0
08690	15.5	98	4.8	86	36.9	481	111.0	6	7	7.3	6	0	.2
08691	11.8	96	1.4	80	37.8	438	142.3	5	8	1.9	6	0	1.2
TRENTON													
08701	39.9	83	15.0	69	24.5	399	92.0	9	24	15.3	22	7	.3
08720	.9	93	.3	84	35.8	240	149.3	0	16	.4	11	0	1.8
08721	11.3	100	3.5	84	25.0	467	81.1	8	13	5.4	11	3	.0
08722	7.7	99	.4	89	37.8	502	79.5	9	10	3.7	9	0	.0

*=Estimated **1.0=883 lbs per person; 100++ indicates per capita toxic waste generation > than 100 times the U.S. average of 883 lbs per capita.

ZIP CODE MEASURES OF SIZE, LEVELS OF AFFLUENCE AND QUALITY OF LIFE

1=Population (th.); 2= % White; 3=Households (th.); 4=% Owner Occupied; 5=Mean Income Per Household (th.$); 6=Mean Monthly Rent ($)*; 7=Mean Home Value (th.$)*; 8=% under 5; 9=% 65 and over; 10=White Males (th.); 11=% White Males, 65+; 12=# Toxic Waste Sites; 13=Toxic Waste Relative to US(883 lbs.per capita)**.

NEW JERSEY

TRENTON

ZIPCODE	1	2	3	4	5	6	7	8	9	10	11	12	13
08723	50.9	99	17.9	82	27.0	452	90.9	7	15	24.2	13	1	.0
08730	4.1	92	1.5	80	40.1	589	155.7	5	17	1.8	15	0	.0
08731	10.6	99	4.0	91	23.9	501	86.1	6	21	5.0	20	0	.0
08732	1.6	100	.6	84	26.1	390	97.9	6	15	.8	16	0	.0
08733	11.6	88	4.7	87	22.7	354	79.3	6	34	4.8	34	1	.0
08734	3.7	100	1.2	89	27.7	433	92.9	9	9	1.9	9	0	.0
08735	3.1	100	1.4	78	26.2	330	123.3	5	30	1.4	30	0	.0
08736	9.8	99	3.7	77	29.8	440	115.3	6	17	4.6	14	0	.6
08738	1.1	0	.5	96	57.1	372	259.7	1	22	.0	0	0	.1
08739	.9	100	.4	84	27.8	433	142.2	5	20	.4	20	0	.0
08740	1.4	100	.6	72	19.5	407	68.8	6	22	.7	20	0	.0
08741	2.3	0	.3	87	27.9	503	98.1	5	19	.9	19	0	.0
08742	24.6	99	9.3	74	27.6	483	106.1	5	18	11.4	15	0	.0
08750	4.3	100	1.5	84	40.9	593	177.9	3	20	2.0	18	0	.0
08751	3.3	99	1.6	54	18.6	345	92.4	6	21	1.6	19	0	.0
08752	2.1	99	1.0	68	25.9	248	120.1	5	26	1.0	23	0	.0
08753	81.4	97	29.6	87	26.1	448	92.2	6	21	37.3	20	4	3.8
08758	3.6	0	1.5	92	23.5	535	82.0	5	27	.0	0	1	.0
08759	14.6	99	8.2	98	17.8	288	74.4	1	70	5.9	73	6	.0

NEW BRUNSWICK

ZIPCODE	1	2	3	4	5	6	7	8	9	10	11	12	13
08801	3.8	90	1.1	83	43.0	535	186.1	5	8	1.7	6	0	.0
08802	3.0	99	.9	87	34.4	464	142.7	7	10	1.5	10	0	.1
08803	.2	100	.7	40	22.9	350	91.5	9	5	.1	6	0	.0
08804	2.3	100	.7	85	33.3	452	115.7	7	10	1.2	9	0	.2
08805	11.4	96	4.1	60	32.9	459	124.1	6	12	5.5	11	2	51.9
08807	23.2	97	7.0	88	46.3	600	170.7	5	7	11.1	5	5	1.0
08808	.4	0	.1	86	26.6	359	71.4	7	10	.0	0	1	.6
08809	4.6	92	1.3	72	35.9	544	145.4	4	7	2.2	5	0	.0
08810	1.8	89	.6	88	37.7	609	126.9	7	8	.7	8	4	36.7
08812	11.2	98	3.8	77	33.7	440	118.2	6	11	5.4	8	1	.2
08816	36.4	95	10.8	85	44.7	540	145.6	6	8	17.1	4	1	.0
08817	69.9	93	23.3	67	38.0	478	128.1	6	8	31.9	7	14	5.0
08821	.5	100	.2	90	32.3	388	118.9	5	13	.9	9	3	.6
08822	16.6	99	5.5	69	37.3	503	160.3	5	11	7.9	8	3	3.0
08823	1.1	91	.3	84	35.0	626	136.7	11	15	.4	5	0	.0
08824	8.8	88	2.5	88	41.4	557	125.7	8	3	3.8	2	0	.0
08825	3.4	0	1.2	71	30.0	487	115.9	8	11	.0	0	1	.1
08826	3.8	99	1.2	77	36.5	423	138.1	7	14	1.9	11	0	.9
08827	3.9	99	1.2	76	36.4	426	148.6	9	8	1.9	7	0	.0
08828	1.0	99	.3	82	30.7	335	83.3	8	11	.5	10	0	.2
08830	3.3	100	1.1	80	35.8	421	115.1	5	7	1.6	6	0	.0
08831	15.4	97	4.9	84	31.5	473	101.3	6	25	7.4	23	2	1.5
08832	10.8	90	4.1	83	31.7	523	70.1	8	9	4.6	9	4	.5
08833	1.7	94	.8	36	55.3	500	194.8	9	7	.9	5	5	.3
08835	6.3	98	1.9	87	30.6	441	98.3	5	9	3.2	5	0	2.4
08836	3.2	0	1.0	93	58.3	800	199.5	5	5	.0	0	0	1.2
08840	17.0	92	5.9	79	39.3	468	120.5	5	11	7.4	9	4	1.2
08846	13.5	98	4.5	76	33.0	476	108.9	6	9	6.4	7	11	2.2

NEW JERSEY

NEW BRUNSWICK

ZIPCODE	1	2	3	4	5	6	7	8	9	10	11	12	13
08848	6.7	99	2.2	84	33.0	530	130.7	6	10	3.3	9	1	.7
08850	8.6	99	2.9	86	37.1	450	126.0	6	11	4.2	9	0	.2
08852	3.5	93	1.3	83	32.4	468	125.3	6	12	1.7	9	8	5.2
08853	5.3	98	1.5	84	40.0	599	162.5	6	10	2.5	7	2	3.4
08854	42.2	79	12.3	66	35.5	455	115.5	6	4	17.3	4	8	5.3
08857	30.1	96	9.4	62	34.8	458	113.1	6	6	14.2	4	4	1.9
08858	.5	100	.2	76	51.3	696	177.2	4	15	.0	0	0	.0
08859	20.2	95	6.5	57	33.9	463	113.3	7	6	9.7	5	6	14.9
08861	41.2	78	14.2	46	23.4	369	79.2	7	13	15.2	13	11	.1
08863	13.1	96	4.7	72	33.4	420	98.3	5	10	6.2	9	6	10.7
08865	29.9	98	10.9	68	25.7	330	77.2	6	13	14.0	11	8	8.5
08867	3.1	100	.9	84	48.8	412	165.2	6	8	1.6	6	0	.0
08869	6.1	99	2.2	63	48.8	422	110.7	5	14	2.9	11	2	10.7
08870	.5	100	.2	80	38.1	385	192.4	14	4	.3	6	0	.0
08872	10.8	99	3.5	85	34.6	399	106.1	5	9	5.1	8	15	2.2
08873	28.2	72	9.0	71	37.6	482	120.6	7	8	10.0	4	4	2.2
08876	29.3	93	10.8	64	35.9	494	136.9	6	8	13.1	7	8	12.0
08879	20.5	98	6.8	74	29.9	431	90.1	6	11	9.8	9	1	.1
08882	14.4	94	5.1	70	30.1	401	92.6	6	13	6.5	11	0	.1
08884	13.9	98	4.2	88	35.3	440	109.6	9	5	6.9	3	0	.3
08885	.2	100	.1	77	34.9	594	194.2	9	27	.1	30	0	.0
08886	2.4	99	.8	77	30.8	426	99.3	7	14	1.2	12	0	.4
08887	.4	100	.7	73	27.9	466	111.8	4	6	.2	4	0	.1
08888	.4	93	.2	67	35.1	481	124.6	6	5	.2	5	0	.2
08889	5.5	99	1.7	90	42.6	478	174.6	7	6	2.8	5	5	.0
08890	.1	100	.1	0	8.2	323	29.1*	7	41	.0	0	0	.0

NEW BRUNSWICK

ZIPCODE	1	2	3	4	5	6	7	8	9	10	11	12	13
08901	35.7	60	13.3	32	22.9	389	80.5	7	10	10.7	11	4	1.1
08902	21.4	93	7.7	58	36.8	513	138.8	6	9	9.6	8	2	16.0
08904	13.4	91	5.6	42	31.3	465	118.1	5	13	5.7	11	0	.0

MONTICELLO

ZIPCODE	1	2	3	4	5	6	7	8	9	10	11	12	13
12771	2.2	98	.8	67	28.6	391	98.6	7	11	1.1	10	0	.0

*=Estimated **1.0=883 lbs per person; 100++ indicates per capita toxic waste generation > than 100 times the U.S. average of 883 lbs per capita.

ZIP CODE MEASURES OF SIZE, LEVELS OF AFFLUENCE AND QUALITY OF LIFE

1=Population (th.); 2= % White; 3=Households (th.); 4=% Owner Occupied; 5=Mean Income Per Household (th.); 6=Mean Home Value (th.$)*; 7=Mean Monthly Rent ($)*; 8=% under 5; 9=% 65 and over; 10=White Males (th.); 11=% White Males, 65+; 12=# Toxic Waste Sites; 13=Toxic Waste Relative to US(883 lbs.per capita)**.

NEW MEXICO

ZIPCODE	1	2	3	4	5	6	7	8	9	10	11	12	13
EL PASO													
79835	.2	60	.1	71	19.2	302	74.2	3	8	.0	0	0	.0
GLOBE													
85534	.3	100	.1	74	18.2	203	41.0	8	19	.2	16	0	.0
GALLUP													
86504	.4	0	.1	51	17.2	169	23.7	10	6	.0	0	0	.0
86508	.4	0	.1	84	5.1	59*	29.2	12	2	.0	0	0	.0
86515	.9	0	.2	59	25.9	256	27.6	19	3	.0	0	0	.0
ALBUQUERQUE													
87001	2.2	8	.4	88	16.7	94	63.2	12	4	.1	11	0	.6
87002	12.6	84	4.6	82	21.5	264	82.4	8	15	5.0	15	3	.0
87004	5.3	55	1.6	79	21.3	252	81.3	8	8	1.4	10	1	.0
87005	1.0	0	.2	84	33.1	398	61.5	18	4	.0	2	0	.4
87006	.5	76	.2	94	16.0	183*	46.4	13		.2	7	1	.0
87007	.3	20	.1	63	18.3	211*	71.8	6	13	.2	0	0	.0
87008	1.1	96	.4	87	32.8	553	121.3	7	6	.5	2	0	.6
87010	.5	95	.2	68	13.4	94	46.6	20	4	.2	0	1	.0
87012	.4	25	.1	78	14.6	78	40.7	4	14	.1	1	0	.0
87013	4.4	29	1.2	78	14.8	128	34.8	11	8	.6	16	0	.0
87015	1.2	39	.3	76	20.8	139	45.6	12	5	.2	11	0	.4
87016	1.6	92	.5	92	25.2	93	122.1	6	7	.8	5	0	.2
87017	1.9	75	.6	79	17.9	198	54.0	8	12	.7	12	0	.3
87018	.4	19	.1	73	14.8	206	31.7	6	10	.0	0	0	.1
87020	.3	0	.1	25	22.7	53	81.0*	17	0	.1	0		.2
87021	14.3	81	4.4	72	32.0	298	82.6	11	3	6.0	3	0	.1
87022	4.8	90	1.6	76	27.6	294	70.5	15	3	2.3	1		.0
87023	2.2	3	.6	92	24.0	253	63.9	10	7	.0	2	0	.0
87024	.5	84	.1	92	17.5	201*	75.7	8	14	.4	12	0	.1
87025	1.7	7	.4	86	15.1	233	78.8	12	6	.1	0	0	.1
87026	.8	82	.3	76	23.6	238	97.7	10	13	.4	14	0	.0
87027	2.5	4	.6	81	18.5	219	87.7	9	5	.1	20	0	.0
87028	.4	30	.1	64	19.7	262	16.5	13	7	.1	30	0	.0
87031	.2	66	.2	100	12.5	144*	43.2	23	27	.1	48	1	.0
87032	.3	100	.1	73	26.9	40	13.1	9	20	.2	20	0	.0
87034	13.1	77	4.0	89	22.8	270	96.8	9	7	5.2	3	0	.0
87035	2.3	81	.8	85	19.5	205	75.1	11	6	.9	5	1	.0
87036	1.9	66	.8	79	15.2	171	42.7	7	16	.6	16	0	.1
87037	1.2	19	.2	82	15.6	204	20.8	8	4	.1	0	0	.0
87038	.9	0	.2	83	25.9	111	81.0	16	6	.0	0	0	.0
87040	.6	9	.2	89	16.3	64	45.3	12	18	.0	43	0	.0
87041	1.6	28	.4	80	20.0	260	64.4	11	11	.2	27	0	.0
87042	.6	68	.2	95	25.7	296*	159.0	14	7	.1	10	0	.0
87043	2.2	82	.8	84	21.6	257	110.9	10	6	.9	5	0	.0
87044	1.8	64	.4	100	24.3	279*	48.5	8	8	.1	8	0	.0
87045	.9	6	.1	95	11.5	248	40.7	18	2	.1	15	1	.0
87046	.2	50	.1	90	21.9	251*	39.2	14	5	.4	21	0	.0
87047	2.8	95	.8	91	28.5	293	143.3	7	6	.8	6	0	.0
87048	4.3	87	1.4	79	33.7	379	170.0	7	7	1.9	8	0	.1

NEW MEXICO

ZIPCODE	1	2	3	4	5	6	7	8	9	10	11	12	13
ALBUQUERQUE													
87049	1.2	10	.2	90	23.6	212	70.8	13	10	.1	39	0	.0
87050	.9	73	.1	72	25.9	223	107.8	12	5	.1	14	1	.0
87051	.9	20	.3	74	21.5	232	58.3	14	3	.1	0	0	.0
87052	2.3	3	.4	86	14.9	93	44.4	11	5	.0	0	0	.0
87053	.8	15	.2	87	16.8	102	52.0	13	9	.1	38	0	.0
87055	.5	84	.2	95	23.4	268*	51.2	12	10	.2	7	0	.0
87056	.3	100	.1	87	21.0	134	135.6	6	11	.2	12	0	.0
87059	2.7	87	.9	88	27.9	151	87.4	10	5	1.2	5	1	.0
87060	.2	62	.1	100	13.9	160*	43.4	15	5	.1	4	0	.0
87061	.2	29	.1	93	12.7	146*	14.7	7	49	.0	0	0	.9
87062	.4	84	.1	89	18.7	56	76.9	9	7	.0	0	0	61.5
87063	.2	74	.1	73	24.0	276*	17.2	12	4	.1	4	0	.2
87068	3.4	95	1.2	91	28.8	332	123.0	8	7	1.6	7	0	.1
ALBUQUERQUE													
87102	24.5	63	8.9	44	14.8	255	60.0	9	14	7.4	13	7	.3
87103	.1	87	.1	72	19.1	431	148.8	11	11	.1	0	5	.1
87104	12.5	74	4.5	60	23.4	267	96.7	8	11	4.5	11	4	.2
87105	65.9	72	19.3	76	21.9	289	76.4	10	6	23.3	7	4	.1
87106	25.9	77	11.6	44	21.0	303	98.5	6	11	9.7	10	1	.1
87107	29.3	77	10.6	66	26.3	323	99.1	7	9	11.0	9	4	.3
87108	35.5	79	16.4	38	20.0	309	88.1	8	12	13.5	11	0	.1
87109	31.6	89	12.7	61	30.6	372	131.4	8	6	14.3	6	3	.2
87110	42.4	91	16.7	71	30.6	356	105.3	4	12	18.7	10	0	.1
87111	33.2	94	10.8	81	39.9	390	139.2	6	4	15.4	4	0	.0
87112	44.6	91	15.9	67	30.0	417	104.3	7	7	19.6	6	5	.1
87113	2.9	86	1.1	86	22.8	340	90.1	8	10	1.2	11	5	.0
87114	12.9	85	4.0	83	32.0	324	118.5	9	6	5.4	7	0	.1
87116	5.4	79	1.6	0	16.8	287	59.7*	19	0	2.1	0	3	.0
87118	1.4	84	.4	0	24.4	417	86.9*	13	0	.6	0	0	.0
87120	6.7	86	2.4	92	33.7	551	113.6	11	3	2.9	3	5	.0
87122	2.1	98	.7	92	59.2	633	241.8	7	11	1.1	1	3	.0
87123	28.4	85	10.5	69	28.1	337	118.7	9	7	11.7	7	1	.0
87124	10.1	95	3.7	87	25.5	368	99.5	7	16	4.7	16	0	.1
GALLUP													
87301	25.5	46	8.0	62	24.5	303	91.9	11	6	5.8	5	3	1.3
87310	.7	0	.1	79	18.1	208*	69.7	12	3	.0	0	0	.0
87311	1.9	0	.4	39	14.5	284	14.5	14	3	.0	0	0	.0
87312	.6	20	.2	55	16.7	308	68.4	5	4	.1	0	0	.1
87313	3.3	0	.8	64	19.3	189	20.9	13	4	.0	1	0	.3
87315	.2	49	.1	61	9.1	105*	13.1	14	5	.1	16	0	.0
87316	.9	0	.3	62	19.5	263	36.6	10	2	.0	0	0	.0
87317	1.4	12	.3	85	23.8	209	30.5	11	4	.1	4	0	.0
87319	1.1	14	.3	90	13.6	274	95.6	13	7	.1	3	0	.0
87320	.8	0	.2	96	15.1	173*	21.6	13	7	.2	0	0	.0
87321	1.9	32	.5	64	16.5	153	40.0	16	9	.3	11	0	.0
87322	.4	10	.1	79	9.8	192	196.9	16	8	.1	0	0	.0
87323	3.4	25	.8	68	16.8	251	48.1	12	4	.4	2	0	.0
87324	.4	0	.1	87	11.9	137*	23.2	14	5	.0	0	0	.0
87325	5.2	0	1.4	79	16.6	198	24.8	13	5	1.2	0	0	.0

*=Estimated **1.0=883 lbs per person; 100++ indicates per capita toxic waste generation > than 100 times the U.S. average of 883 lbs per capita.

ZIP CODE MEASURES OF SIZE, LEVELS OF AFFLUENCE AND QUALITY OF LIFE

1=Population (th.); 2= % White; 3=Households (th.); 4=% Owner Occupied; 5=Mean Income Per Household (th.$); 6=Mean Monthly Rent ($)*; 7=Mean Home Value (th.$)*; 8=% under 5; 9=% 65 and over; 10=White Males (th.); 11=% White Males, 65+; 12=# Toxic Waste Sites; 13=Toxic Waste Relative to US(883 lbs.per capita)**.

NEW MEXICO

ZIPCODE	1	2	3	4	5	6	7	8	9	10	11	12	13
GALLUP													
87326	.8	0	.2	68	12.0	166	19.5	15	6	.0	0	0	.0
87327	6.2	4	1.2	61	16.2	227	49.9	12	5	.1	0	0	.1
87328	2.5	0	.5	26	16.9	169	16.6	19	3	.0	0	0	.0
FARMINGTON													
87401	37.8	80	13.0	73	28.6	348	101.5	11	6	15.3	5	6	.4
87410	9.5	88	3.2	78	25.9	315	88.8	10	8	4.1	7	2	.0
87412	.4	74	.2	60	19.8	146	67.4	10	16	.2	14	0	.0
87413	8.2	72	2.6	79	22.4	286	92.0	12	6	2.9	5	2	.0
87415	1.0	95	.4	80	31.6	211	119.4	8	5	.5	4	0	1.1
87416	3.0	18	.8	90	21.9	128	41.0	11	3	.3	0	1	.0
87417	3.5	71	1.1	83	25.9	266	101.6	14	5	1.3	4	1	.0
87418	.2	68	.1	48	20.3	237	77.7	21	5	.2	8	1	.0
87420	9.9	4	2.2	59	17.9	229	33.8	14	4	.2	0	0	.0
87421	1.3	23	.4	81	16.7	171	39.2	11	4	.1	5	1	.0
87461	1.7	5	.4	47	17.0	194	13.1	11	7	.0	0	0	.0
SANTA FE													
87501	66.8	82	23.5	65	26.6	379	131.7	8	9	26.9	8	1	.0
87510	.4	69	.1	78	9.0	232	45.9	11	16	.1	20	0	.0
87511	.8	41	.3	82	14.2	159	77.3	10	5	.1	2	0	.0
87513	.4	0	.1	87	13.1	144	54.0	10	10	.0	0	0	.0
87515	.7	47	.2	73	17.5	385	58.4	10	4	.2	9	0	.0
87519	.4	17	.1	60	15.7	273	58.6	10	12	.0	2	0	.0
87520	.3	0	.1	100	26.3	302*	47.9	5	11	.0	0	0	.0
87521	1.4	67	.5	71	19.9	199	69.4	8	8	.4	10	0	.0
87522	.4	40	.1	75	6.6	81	27.8	6	18	.1	21	0	.0
87523	2.3	37	.7	84	16.5	259	65.7	14	8	.4	7	0	.0
87524	3.4	43	.1	73	12.4	224	28.0	2	15	.1	13	0	.0
87527	.4	63	.1	80	22.9	390	53.3	3	6	.1	8	0	.0
87528	1.1	52	.3	82	15.4	179	37.2	7	11	.3	12	0	.0
87529	1.7	0	.5	55	17.9	191	41.6	13	3	.0	0	0	.0
87530	1.3	36	.4	75	15.7	214	87.8	8	15	.2	18	0	.0
87531	.9	52	.2	83	17.4	224	48.1	9	10	.1	13	0	.0
87532	.9	25	.3	94	16.5	102	75.0	8	9	.3	8	0	.0
87533	.2	0	.1	91	13.6	157*	67.0	13	12	.1	20	0	.0
87535	11.1	54	3.6	78	17.8	216	86.8	9	8	2.8	7	0	.0
87537	2.8	45	.9	87	19.9	279	90.5	9	8	.6	9	0	.0
87540	.5	0	.2	63	21.4	328	81.3	10	9	.0	0	0	.0
87543	.9	36	.3	94	16.5	210*	75.0	8	9	.1	20	0	.0
87544	17.7	95	6.3	73	39.3	366	149.0	6	4	8.6	4	1	1.2
87547	.2	2	.1	50	9.0	345	37.8	4	5	.0	0	0	.0
87548	.2	29	.1	100	20.3	233*	37.2	8	9	.0	33	0	.0
87549	.2	30	.1	72	15.3	55	28.4	9	32	.1	21	0	.0
87551	.4	42	.1	95	10.9	125*	42.8	7	21	.1	16	0	.0
87552	1.8	94	.5	78	17.8	223	57.3	7	6	.3	5	0	.0
87553	1.0	62	.3	85	14.5	173	47.9	10	12	.3	7	0	.0
87556	1.7	66	.6	75	19.3	241	80.9	11	7	.6	7	1	.0
87557	2.6	36	.8	85	17.0	220	87.3	11	7	.5	8	0	.1
87558	.6	0	.2	51	23.6	287	181.2	12	0	.0	0	0	.0

NEW MEXICO

ZIPCODE	1	2	3	4	5	6	7	8	9	10	11	12	13
SANTA FE													
87560	.7	68	.2	89	13.8	159*	24.9	14	7	.2	4	0	.0
87561	.2	14	.1	78	9.9	245	40.8	11	13	.0	0	0	.0
87562	.2	60	.1	84	7.1	398	13.1	19	0	.1	0	0	.0
87564	.3	63	.1	46	12.3	141*	166.3	4	0	.1	0	0	.0
87565	.3	82	.1	90	11.3	129*	33.4	19	6	.2	8	0	.0
87566	2.4	25	.7	79	12.4	208	69.9	9	8	.3	2	0	.0
87567	1.2	47	.3	66	18.0	188	84.4	13	5	.2	14	0	.0
87571	8.0	48	2.9	71	20.4	269	97.0	8	11	1.8	9	1	.0
87574	.6	91	.2	60	29.9	486	100.0	8	10	.3	6	0	.1
87575	.6	62	.2	83	13.3	47	47.6	9	15	.2	7	0	.0
87577	.2	0	.1	51	21.1	104	75.1*	1*	3	.0	0	0	.0
87578	.6	29	.2	87	13.7	100	39.2	18	10	.1	0	0	.0
87579	.5	30	.2	84	15.4	109	46.7	8	8	.1	6	0	.0
87581	.3	58	.1	59	8.6	71	42.8	18	11	.1	0	0	.0
87582	1.1	39	.4	89	17.2	147	55.3	14	9	.3	6	0	.0
87583	.3	100	.1	56	16.1	166	43.1	5	10	.2	7	0	.0
LAS VEGAS													
87701	17.1	70	5.5	67	16.4	194	57.5	9	12	5.9	11	0	.0
87711	.6	71	.2	94	10.5	56	24.9	13	12	.1	2	13	.0
87712	.1	0	.1	70	11.1	73	18.0	14	4	.0	0	0	.0
87713	.2	76	.1	68	5.5	95	15.8	7	16	.1	13	0	.0
87714	1.1	98	.4	56	15.3	200	43.5	8	15	.5	13	0	.0
87715	.5	38	.2	76	12.1	188	27.1	13	17	.1	30	0	.0
87718	.8	93	.3	61	21.3	255	158.7	10	8	.4	12	0	.1
87722	.3	84	.1	74	14.7	152	23.7	6	12	.1	10	0	.0
87723	.4	59	.1	80	11.8	118	23.0	7	14	.1	12	0	.0
87725	.2	40	.2	53	9.2	48	35.5	3	9	.0	35	0	.0
87728	.5	89	.2	62	19.8	140	42.5	11	11	.2	9	1	.0
87731	.5	75	.2	62	14.7	202	47.6	3	14	.2	20	0	.0
87732	1.0	48	.4	75	12.3	227	36.5	8	13	.3	7	0	.0
87733	.3	79	.1	66	14.4	213	19.0	10	14	.1	13	1	.0
87734	.3	40	.1	78	12.9	148*	13.1	10	24	.1	54	0	.0
87735	.2	42	.1	100	10.7	123*	15.2	5	14	.0	0	0	.0
87740	8.8	84	3.1	72	22.6	210	69.5	9	13	3.6	13	3	.0
87742	.3	45	.1	67	16.0	184*	62.5	4	9	.0	0	0	.0
87743	.5	0	.2	74	17.9	249	33.3	5	22	.0	0	0	.0
87745	.5	72	.2	81	16.3	143	17.7	6	13	.1	25	0	.0
87747	2.3	72	.8	71	16.3	178	47.1	4	14	.9	12	0	.0
87752	.6	75	.2	73	15.1	125	26.7	10	15	.2	20	0	.0
87753	.2	100	.1	82	34.9	401*	66.2	4	13	.1	14	0	1.2
SOCORRO													
87801	8.5	90	2.8	69	19.9	240	73.2	8	8	3.9	8	3	.1
87821	.4	95	.1	73	18.2	197	29.4	7	9	.2	7	0	.0
87824	.2	0	.1	77	14.2	343	51.8	13	7	.1	16	0	.0
87825	2.2	46	.6	76	13.4	205	31.7	14	8	.5	11	0	.0
87827	.1	69	.1	69	12.9	110	35.3	9	18	.3	7	0	.0
87829	.5	82	.2	66	15.2	216	53.3	9	13	.2	14	0	.0
87830	1.1	96	.4	77	21.0	180	57.5	10	12	.6	13	0	.1
87831	.2	100	.1	77	13.5	155*	47.7	13	20	.1	24	0	.0

*=Estimated **1.0=883 lbs per person; 100++ indicates per capita toxic waste generation > than 100 times the U.S. average of 883 lbs per capita.

ZIP CODE MEASURES OF SIZE, LEVELS OF AFFLUENCE AND QUALITY OF LIFE

1=Population (th.); 2= % White; 3=Households (th.); 4=% Owner Occupied; 5=Mean Income Per Household (th.$); 6=Mean Monthly Rent ($)*; 7=Mean Home Value (th.$)*;
8=% under 5; 9=% 65 and over; 10=% White Males (th.); 11=% White Males, 65+; 12=# Toxic Waste Sites; 13=Toxic Waste Relative to US(883 lbs.per capita)**.

NEW MEXICO

ZIPCODE	1	2	3	4	5	6	7	8	9	10	11	12	13
SOCORRO													
87832	.4	0	.2	87	23.6	230	40.1	7	15	.0	0	0	.0
TRUTH OR CONSEQUENCES													
87901	5.5	96	2.6	68	13.8	132	49.2	5	33	2.5	33	0	.5
87930	.7	0	.2	74	13.6	156*	41.5	5	11	.0	0	0	.0
87931	.3	100	.1	74	11.4	131*	43.9	7	17	.1	28	0	.0
87933	.2	0	.1	82	16.0	184*	38.4	6	7	.0	0	0	.0
87935	.5	100	.2	85	15.0	229	80.1	10	35	.2	31	0	.0
87936	.4	92	.2	71	16.0	155	20.1	10	16	.2	6	0	.0
87937	2.2	93	.8	73	15.0	148	38.9	9	14	1.0	13	2	.1
87940	.5	68	.1	71	13.2	152*	34.8	14	10	.1	10	0	.0
87941	.4	84	.1	71	13.4	53	24.8	2	10	.1	10	0	.0
87942	.7	0	.3	77	15.2	117	50.5	5	31	.0	0	0	.0
LAS CRUCES													
88001	58.7	82	20.2	63	23.6	279	88.7	8	8	23.2	8	2	.0
88002	3.1	77	.8	2	19.1	272	53.3	15	0	1.3	0	1	.0
88003	2.6	71	.3	53	19.8	239	99.3	4	2	1.1	2	0	.4
88009	1.0	98	.3	4	34.0	217	121.1*	17	0	.5	0	2	9.4
88021	.8	0	.2	77	20.3	32	58.1	13	6	.1	0	0	.0
88023	8.9	77	2.5	73	18.1	219	55.7	11	6	3.4	6	3	.3
88024	3.5	65	1.1	75	20.7	231	50.3	10	8	1.0	9	6	.0
88026	.4	81	.7	78	21.5	247*	75.6	3	2	.2	1	7	.0
88027	2.1	81	.7	72	17.8	201	42.6	11	10	.8	10	0	.1
88028	.7	88	.2	78	16.4	143	64.2	10	4	.3	5	0	.0
88029	.5	100	.2	75	18.1	323	43.9	10	16	.1	14	0	.1
88030	.7	92	.7	79	14.3	174	57.6	9	15	.7	16	3	.0
88032	14.8	85	5.3	73	18.1	215	60.9	8	17	6.1	19	3	.1
88033	1.0	56	.3	88	17.0	269	53.9	11	8	.3	7	0	.0
88036	.7	73	.3	83	20.5	221	133.1	7	4	.3	7	0	.0
88038	.4	52	.1	24	32.5	219	43.9	3	39	.1	39	0	.5
88039	.3	100	.1	63	17.3	190	71.2	6	6	.1	0	0	.0
88040	.2	97	.1	75	18.0	119	51.6	5	31	.1	26	0	.0
88041	.7	0	.3	43	50.9	591	181.5*	17	14	.8	0	0	2.1
88042	.2	100	.3	88	19.7	71	33.0	8	16	.0	0	1	.0
88043	2.0	87	.7	95	14.2	164*	59.3	3	28	.1	20	0	1.5
88044	2.8	52	.7	84	24.9	249	44.3	9	12	.9	12	2	.0
88045	3.7	95	1.3	61	19.2	206	58.2	11	9	.7	13	0	.1
88046	2.3	79	.7	66	19.1	175	46.7	10	12	1.7	9	0	.1
88047	4.2	78	1.3	67	19.1	220	85.5	8	9	1.6	8	0	.1
88048	1.6	92	.4	79	22.3	236	81.9	11	7	.8	10	0	.1
88049	.6	100	.6	78	19.9	132	52.3	13	2	.3	7	0	.1
88052	.3	96	.2	71	29.1	110	85.2	5	11	.4	6	0	.0
88053	.2	100	.1	75	28.0	281	44.3	12	4	.4	15	0	.0
88056	2.0	87	.3	85	23.0	189	76.8	4	17	.1	17	0	1.5
88058	.3	64	.1	69	17.5	93	48.1	9	7	.1	9	0	.0
88061	14.1	86	4.7	73	23.6	254	78.4	9	10	6.0	10	1	.1
88063	4.7	82	1.2	64	18.3	248	64.3	9	3	2.0	5	1	.0
88065	1.1	85	.3	21	34.0	297	83.1	11	3	.5	2	0	2.0
88072	.3	66	.1	74	12.8	159	22.4	15	12	1.1	11	1	.0

NEW MEXICO

ZIPCODE	1	2	3	4	5	6	7	8	9	10	11	12	13
CLOVIS													
88101	39.5	80	13.5	64	22.7	254	68.2	10	9	15.9	8	3	.0
88115	.2	0	.1	78	23.8	250	43.2	3	14	.0	0	0	.0
88116	.6	0	.2	78	17.5	106	35.5	6	17	.0	0	0	.0
88118	.3	100	.1	83	31.9	195	25.3	12	11	.1	10	0	.0
88119	2.3	90	.9	79	17.3	161	43.2	6	21	1.0	20	0	.0
88120	.3	100	.1	90	28.1	346*	35.4	6	16	.2	21	0	.0
88121	.2	0	.1	93	30.1		27.4	2	20	.0	0	0	.0
88122	.2	0	.1	16	34.7	399*	123.6*	1	14	.0	0	0	.0
88124	1.0	98	.4	84	17.9	140	36.7	5	30	.4	25	1	.1
88130	.5	80	.1	68	18.5	205	55.2	7	12	5.4	13	2	.0
88132	.4	0	.1	67	19.0	218*	67.6*	0	40	.0	0	0	.0
88135	.7	69	.3	79	22.4	254	50.6	7	12	.5	17	0	.0
ROSWELL													
88201	45.9	86	16.8	71	22.2	258	64.6	8	15	19.0	14	2	.2
88210	13.9	76	4.9	73	23.4	235	58.4	9	12	5.1	11	4	1.1
88220	31.1	87	10.9	72	23.6	279	69.1	9	13	13.1	12	8	7.0
88230	2.9	91	.8	72	15.3	191	43.1	11	9	1.3	9	0	.0
88231	3.4	91	1.2	76	26.0	226	44.6	12	9	1.5	8	1	.0
88232	1.5	97	.5	68	18.5	169	48.9	11	9	.7	7	1	.0
88240	34.9	85	12.0	72	28.5	316	73.5	10	8	14.8	11	7	2.6
88250	.3	88	.1	67	22.6	65	45.1	10	4	1.1	5	0	.0
88252	3.2	81	1.1	60	27.9	137	47.6	11	7	1.3	7	1	.0
88253	.6	75	.2	57	23.4	204	40.3	5	6	.2	3	0	.0
88254	.3	50	.1	25	14.1	162*	50.1*	4	9	.1	1	6	.0
88255	.2	100	.1	80	17.9	206*	13.1	4	4	.1	7	0	.0
88256	1.8	99	.5	80	20.8	213	38.0	10	9	.9	9	1	.0
88260	12.2	74	4.0	75	25.0	285	62.4	11	9	4.6	9	3	.0
88263	.2	100	.1	84	23.0	264*	42.7	2	13	.2	11	0	.4
88265	.4	100	.1	57	35.2	91	55.8	8	4	.2	7	0	29.3
88267	1.4	88	.5	72	20.4	231	39.3	8	9	.6	9	2	.1
CARRIZOZO													
88301	1.5	80	.6	75	15.9	169	43.5	7	13	.6	13	2	.1
88310	27.1	86	9.7	66	22.3	264	68.1	8	7	11.6	7	1	.0
88312	1.0	100	.1	91	33.9	390*	139.0	4	18	.5	21	0	.0
88316	1.0	94	.4	86	17.1	238	64.8	6	18	.5	17	0	.0
88317	1.1	91	.4	77	23.9	292	74.6	13	6	.5	6	1	.0
88318	.6	88	.1	56	24.8	75	19.3	2	11	.3	11	0	.0
88321	.3	38	.1	75	12.0	64	31.4	10	26	.1	58	0	.0
88323	.3	87	.1	29	17.7	129	41.6	6	5	.2	2	0	.0
88325	.6	0	.2	83	24.8	150	96.5	2	10	.8	10	1	.0
88330	7.3	78	1.6	6	17.8	336	70.6	14	3	3.4	0	0	.0
88336	.2	0	.1	58	29.2	341	126.9	9	8	.0	1	0	.0
88337	1.5	94	.5	85	22.0	304	70.4	9	8	.7	6	0	.0
88338	.1	0	.1	86	23.9	274*	130.5	9	12	.0	0	0	.0
88339	.4	100	.1	69	17.0	317	74.8	9	9	.2	10	0	.0
88340	1.9	0	.5	37	17.3	205	44.3	14	3	.0	3	0	.1
88341	.2	64	.1	93	15.3	176*	64.2	13	24	.1	35	0	.0
88344	.2	100	.1	71	32.2	396	51.0	19	13	.1	5	0	.0
88345	5.4	94	2.1	71	26.5	300	111.3	7	12	2.5	11	1	.0

*=Estimated   **1.0=883 lbs per person; 100++ indicates per capita toxic waste generation > than 100 times the U.S. average of 883 lbs per capita.

ZIP CODE MEASURES OF SIZE, LEVELS OF AFFLUENCE AND QUALITY OF LIFE

1=Population (th.); 2= % White; 3=Households (th.); 4=% Owner Occupied; 5=Mean Income Per Household (th.$); 6=Mean Monthly Rent ($)*; 7=Mean Home Value (th.$)*; 8=% under 5; 9=% 65 and over; 10=White Males (th.); 11=% White Males (th.); 12=# Toxic Waste Sites; 13=Toxic Waste Relative to US(883 lbs.per capita)**.

NEW MEXICO

CARRIZOZO

ZIPCODE	1	2	3	4	5	6	7	8	9	10	11	12	13
88346	.9	87	.3	81	19.7	122	73.4	8	12	.4	12	0	.0
88348	.3	85	.1	76	22.5	259*	40.6	21	14	.1	17	0	.0
88352	3.5	90	1.2	76	19.6	245	49.0	7	13	1.6	13	0	.0
88353	.8	92	.3	76	14.0	118	23.6	7	12	.3	13	0	.0
88354	.1	0	.1	62	16.7	192*	166.3	0	53	.0	0	0	.0

TUCUMCARI

ZIPCODE	1	2	3	4	5	6	7	8	9	10	11	12	13
88401	8.1	81	3.0	71	19.1	199	46.3	8	16	3.1	16	2	1.3
88410	.2	100	.1	100	50.2	577*	13.1	0	19	.1	10	0	.0
88414	.1	100	.1	79	7.6	87*	42.8	5	23	.0	16	0	.0
88415	3.2	98	1.1	75	21.3	188	56.6	8	19	1.5	16	2	.0
88416	.2	100	.2	77	14.4	158	41.6	8	23	.1	21	0	.0
88418	.3	100	.2	72	20.9	364	23.1	7	21	.1	22	0	.0
88419	.3	0	.1	73	23.1	265*	39.1	7	5	.0	0	0	.0
88421	.1	0	.1	62	8.7	165	13.1	0	33	.0	0	0	.0
88426	1.0	99	.3	84	21.7	231	63.7	7	18	.5	19	0	.0
88427	.3	100	.1	45	24.3	279*	86.6*	4	19	.1	15	0	.0
88430	.3	100	.2	72	21.9	168	26.6	7	13	.1	11	0	.0
88434	.6	94	.2	82	20.8	130	33.9	10	10	.3	13	0	.0
88435	2.9	82	1.0	68	16.5	189	52.1	9	12	1.2	14	0	.0
88436	.2	100	.1	47	16.2	53	57.7*	13	11	.1	19	0	.0
88439	.1	100	.1	100	9.5	109*	33.7*	0	47	.1	46	0	.0

NEW YORK

PITTSFIELD

ZIPCODE	1	2	3	4	5	6	7	8	9	10	11	12	13
01266	.1	100	.1	80	23.7	242	102.9	2	17	.1	17	0	.0

RUTLAND

ZIPCODE	1	2	3	4	5	6	7	8	9	10	11	12	13
05764	.3	0	.1	92	23.4	268*	49.0	6	6	.0	0	0	.0
05775	.2	100	.1	94	23.3	267*	48.0	6	4	.1	5	0	.0

STAMFORD

ZIPCODE	1	2	3	4	5	6	7	8	9	10	11	12	13
06840	1.5	99	.5	92	40.5	558	195.8	7	5	.8	4	0	.0

NEW YORK

ZIPCODE	1	2	3	4	5	6	7	8	9	10	11	12	13
10001	17.1	77	9.0	10	21.2	389	75.4*	3	18	6.2	17	0	3.2
10002	78.1	38	28.7	6	15.5	248	126.9	7	13	13.8	19	0	.0
10003	48.2	85	28.0	8	30.4	500	379.4	3	12	19.9	11	0	1.6
10004	3.6	83	.7	0	25.4	393	90.5*	14	1	2.0	0	0	1.9
10005	.4	90	.3	3	37.9	733	134.4*	2	0	.2	0	0	2.0
10006	.1	100	.1	4	36.6	417	130.4*	0	40	.1	45	0	13.5
10007	1.9	75	.6	12	21.4	511	76.2*	1	2	.9	4	0	3.4
10009	57.0	62	26.5	3	19.6	346	83.1	6	15	15.8	16	0	.0
10010	25.5	85	14.4	5	34.4	553	306.3	3	14	10.3	13	0	1.2
10011	47.0	87	28.1	7	28.7	484	186.2	2	15	20.6	11	0	1.1
10012	22.5	81	11.7	8	25.0	412	437.5	4	11	9.4	9	0	.5
10013	22.3	47	8.9	7	20.8	382	74.2*	3	14	6.1	11	0	2.9
10014	30.1	93	19.4	5	28.5	473	338.6	2	11	14.5	8	0	.6
10016	40.0	91	26.6	4	34.5	570	189.3	2	14	15.9	12	0	1.1
10017	13.6	89	10.0	5	37.7	566	315.6	2	15	5.1	13	0	4.8
10018	3.1	64	2.1	5	12.8	321	45.5*	3	10	1.2	8	0	9.7
10019	34.0	82	21.5	5	29.0	491	103.5*	3	16	13.5	16	0	.2
10021	103.8	95	62.5	16	53.7	623	428.5	3	18	42.6	15	0	1.1
10022	32.9	95	22.1	22	54.2	639	270.3	2	19	14.4	18	0	.0
10023	58.8	87	36.7	8	36.7	555	339.1	2	19	23.7	16	0	1.1
10024	62.9	84	35.3	10	35.6	511	437.5	3	14	25.0	12	0	.0
10025	98.6	60	46.7	3	24.0	427	179.4	4	12	28.3	11	0	.0
10026	25.7	2	10.2	1	11.3	240	40.4*	7	14	2.2	12	0	.0
10027	56.4	23	23.4	4	16.1	281	47.7	6	13	6.3	8	0	.0
10028	93.6	92	52.4	16	45.9	546	367.9	4	14	38.5	12	0	.0
10029	75.1	26	27.9	6	15.3	255	91.9	7	10	8.8	11	0	.0
10030	25.0	1	11.2	3	12.1	237	108.5	5	18	.1	18	0	.0
10031	52.1	17	20.6	3	15.1	308	97.6	8	13	4.5	10	0	.0
10032	57.1	33	21.4	2	16.7	336	52.5	8	12	8.8	12	0	.0
10033	50.0	56	19.1	2	19.3	371	100.6	8	15	12.5	19	0	.0
10034	36.1	57	15.1	3	18.7	332	131.3	8	15	9.2	17	0	.0
10035	29.4	19	10.1	3	11.6	219	122.3	8	9	2.7	12	0	.1
10036	17.5	73	10.0	2	16.0	332	57.0*	4	11	7.3	11	0	10.4
10037	19.1	3	8.9	4	17.1	313	74.4	4	19	.2	5	0	.1
10038	13.4	47	5.1	19	22.7	334	80.9*	5	14	3.2	16	1	.1
10039	24.1	4	10.0	6	14.2	252	50.4*	7	10	.4	2	0	.0
10040	39.0	59	16.0	2	18.5	353	13.1	8	19	10.2	22	0	.0
10044	7.2	72	2.1	16	44.1	603	157.1*	5	20	2.3	16	0	.1

STATEN ISLAND

ZIPCODE	1	2	3	4	5	6	7	8	9	10	11	12	13
10301	35.3	75	13.3	36	28.2	384	126.2	6	14	12.7	14	2	.0
10302	14.3	88	5.0	56	26.5	385	82.5	6	13	6.0	12	0	.4
10303	15.0	76	4.9	50	24.3	331	78.4	8	9	5.4	9	2	3.2

*=Estimated **1.0=883 lbs per person; 100++ indicates per capita toxic waste generation > than 100 times the U.S. average of 883 lbs per capita.

ZIP CODE MEASURES OF SIZE, LEVELS OF AFFLUENCE AND QUALITY OF LIFE

1=Population (th.); 2= % White; 3=Households (th.); 4=% Owner Occupied; 5=Mean Income Per Household (th.$); 6=Mean Home Value (th.$)*; 7=Mean Monthly Rent ($)*;
8=% under 5, 9=% 65 and over, 10=White Males (th.); 11=% White Males, 65+; 12=# Toxic Waste Sites, 13=Toxic Waste Relative to US(883 lbs.per capita)**.

NEW YORK

STATEN ISLAND

ZIPCODE	1	2	3	4	5	6	7	8	9	10	11	12	13
10304	32.4	69	10.7	45	29.4	331	131.5	7	11	10.6	11	0	.0
10305	30.0	96	10.4	54	28.0	412	102.3	5	11	13.9	10	2	1.6
10306	49.4	98	16.1	64	31.5	432	106.6	6	11	23.2	9	0	.0
10307	6.0	99	2.0	75	28.5	446	95.4	7	11	2.9	9	2	1.6
10308	24.5	99	7.4	78	34.9	480	109.9	7	7	11.9	5	0	.0
10309	10.6	89	2.8	82	34.2	451	115.1	6	8	4.9	7	1	.0
10310	21.6	79	7.2	55	28.4	351	99.8	7	12	8.0	11	0	.0
10312	43.5	97	12.7	84	37.1	483	118.5	9	5	20.6	4	1	.0
10314	69.4	94	22.0	67	34.3	458	114.5	7	9	31.9	8	2	.0

BRONX

ZIPCODE	1	2	3	4	5	6	7	8	9	10	11	12	13
10451	36.7	23	13.4	9	16.0	323	64.5	8	9	3.7	14	0	.3
10452	55.3	20	19.8	3	12.6	331	43.6	12	5	5.0	8	0	.0
10453	64.5	18	23.0	4	13.0	340	66.1	12	5	5.4	9	0	.0
10454	35.4	25	11.3	3	11.4	216	42.4	9	6	4.0	6	0	.8
10455	30.6	29	10.2	3	12.6	266	56.6	9	7	4.1	7	0	.0
10456	69.8	13	23.4	5	12.8	277	54.9	8	8	3.9	12	0	.0
10457	58.9	22	21.1	5	13.2	331	51.0	11	7	6.0	11	1	.0
10458	65.1	60	24.8	5	16.3	341	59.2	9	14	18.0	16	1	.1
10459	25.7	26	8.9	6	11.7	276	48.7	9	9	3.0	4	0	.3
10460	41.8	32	15.0	7	14.1	287	56.6	9	9	6.1	14	0	.1
10461	48.2	94	19.1	32	24.1	387	89.5	5	19	21.3	17	0	.4
10462	64.2	77	29.1	14	21.1	356	84.8	5	25	22.0	26	0	.0
10463	65.2	78	27.4	10	27.6	440	111.9	5	22	22.7	22	0	.0
10464	4.2	98	1.6	58	30.5	470	97.1	7	15	2.4	13	0	.3
10465	41.4	90	13.6	55	27.5	359	83.8	6	13	18.0	11	0	.0
10466	56.3	40	19.8	37	23.0	343	82.1	6	13	10.3	19	0	.0
10467	79.6	65	34.0	10	20.2	354	84.3	6	21	23.3	24	1	.0
10468	64.6	49	25.2	3	16.8	367	69.1	9	14	14.1	20	0	.0
10469	57.3	50	19.3	49	26.4	364	89.5	5	17	13.2	21	0	.0
10470	15.0	87	5.8	31	26.0	390	89.4	7	20	6.0	18	0	.1
10471	23.7	87	9.1	26	39.1	511	206.2	4	20	9.6	17	0	.0
10472	61.4	39	21.2	16	17.8	333	77.8	9	9	11.0	12	0	.0
10473	55.1	29	17.7	20	21.1	330	74.4	7	7	7.5	8	0	.0
10474	9.5	25	3.1	10	13.7	296	74.4	10	5	1.2	3	1	.0
10475	40.2	64	16.2	13	25.2	396	86.0	3	23	11.6	27	0	2.5

WESTCHESTER

ZIPCODE	1	2	3	4	5	6	7	8	9	10	11	12	13
10501	.9	98	.3	96	41.4	404	140.8	6	9	.4	8	0	.0
10502	4.8	95	1.5	89	57.6	560	163.3	5	9	2.2	7	1	2.9
10504	5.9	99	1.8	87	71.5	679	254.9	5	8	2.9	8	1	.1
10505	.2	100	.1	76	26.2	464	119.9	2	44	.1	41	0	.0
10506	4.7	98	1.4	91	66.5	587	248.9	5	7	2.2	7	1	.0
10507	5.1	83	1.5	57	44.8	547	164.1	5	11	2.0	10	0	.0
10509	12.9	98	4.3	76	34.7	471	118.9	6	11	6.2	10	5	.1
10510	9.0	95	2.7	77	30.7	453	101.5	4	16	.0	0	0	.0
10511	2.1	0	.7	72	30.7	296	74.4	4	16	.0	0	0	9.7
10512	19.9	99	6.4	79	33.9	516	107.3	7	9	9.7	8	4	.0
10514	10.0	96	3.1	93	81.2	749	244.1	6	14	4.6	12	5	.0
10516	5.0	99	1.8	67	31.6	461	112.7	6	6	2.5	12	1	.0
10517	.7	94	.3	65	40.3	528	105.0	8	4	.3	4	0	.0

NEW YORK

WESTCHESTER

ZIPCODE	1	2	3	4	5	6	7	8	9	10	11	12	13
10518	.3	100	.1	84	41.9	634	157.3	2	33	.2	24	0	.0
10519	.7	100	.2	77	38.6	475	120.4	4	14	.4	11	0	1.0
10520	10.9	98	4.2	57	39.5	502	145.8	5	15	4.9	11	3	.0
10521	.5	92	.2	97	45.2	519*	147.4	4	6	.2	6	0	.4
10522	10.2	91	3.6	56	42.1	476	166.7	4	13	4.5	10	1	.4
10523	6.5	75	2.3	70	37.5	470	127.0	4	11	2.4	10	0	.5
10524	2.7	99	.8	81	45.0	619	158.6	4	14	1.3	13	0	.0
10526	.9	100	.3	81	45.4	609	161.1	9	6	.5	5	0	.0
10527	1.0	0	.3	92	56.3	641	192.0	7	2	.0	0	0	.0
10528	12.0	97	4.2	58	53.7	557	249.5	5	12	5.4	12	0	.0
10530	14.1	88	5.6	52	47.2	614	169.6	6	10	5.8	10	0	.0
10532	5.6	94	1.6	85	35.7	426	131.6	5	9	2.7	9	0	1.6
10533	7.2	94	2.5	69	57.6	545	202.4	5	10	3.3	10	0	.8
10535	.6	0	.2	50	33.2	530	93.0	0	17	.0	0	0	.8
10536	9.4	97	2.8	85	57.6	584	198.1	5	7	4.4	7	0	.0
10537	1.7	0	.6	75	28.5	545	83.3	9	9	.0	0	0	.0
10538	17.5	97	6.2	66	58.7	523	231.2	5	14	7.9	12	0	.0
10541	1.2	87	.3	85	34.5	424	110.6	5	11	.6	9	0	1.1
10542	.3	99	.1	75	29.3	493	118.8	7	8	.1	6	1	.9
10543	19.0	100	6.9	55	44.1	694	110.7	2	6	10.5	12	0	1.7
10546	1.2	96	.3	86	57.0	471	198.7	7	7	.5	7	0	.5
10547	5.0	95	1.5	63	36.7	501	108.9	9	9	2.4	7	0	.2
10548	4.5	90	1.1	80	36.5	381	109.3	5	13	2.4	15	0	.3
10549	14.7	94	5.0	57	42.7	523	176.7	6	11	6.7	8	0	.2
10550	36.3	37	13.4	24	21.9	390	83.9	7	13	6.1	18	0	1.1
10552	20.3	84	8.4	38	33.1	420	143.3	5	19	7.7	18	0	.0
10553	10.1	21	3.5	46	28.7	439	99.2	7	12	1.0	22	1	1.3
10560	2.3	99	.8	90	52.4	575	169.4	8	9	.0	0	0	.2
10562	25.4	80	8.4	56	35.7	447	129.3	5	12	9.8	10	1	.6
10566	34.4	86	11.6	62	31.4	426	107.1	7	11	14.1	9	1	.3
10570	11.5	96	3.8	75	45.5	564	168.4	4	10	5.4	8	1	1.3
10573	31.4	85	11.5	50	31.8	447	169.9	6	15	12.4	13	0	.2
10576	4.2	98	1.3	90	68.8	602	271.0	5	9	2.0	8	0	.0
10577	3.9	90	.6	75	57.5	674	304.6	4	5	1.6	4	0	.6
10578	2.2	99	.8	86	48.8	606	137.0	6	16	1.0	7	0	1.6
10579	7.0	99	2.1	85	38.1	560	125.1	6	10	3.4	9	1	.9
10580	16.5	94	5.5	69	63.3	657	255.9	5	13	7.2	11	0	1.3
10583	39.0	93	13.1	76	75.3	624	255.6	4	12	17.3	12	0	.2
10587	1.3	0	.4	92	33.5	332	95.8	9	11	.0	0	0	.0
10588	2.2	0	.6	85	36.3	450	102.7	6	7	.0	0	0	.0
10589	3.6	98	1.3	93	51.6	775	182.4	5	17	1.6	13	0	1.1
10590	3.9	98	1.2	87	51.3	560	184.0	5	8	2.0	8	0	.0
10591	19.4	88	7.2	42	38.5	437	163.5	5	14	7.8	13	0	5.2
10594	2.7	98	.8	94	44.7	582	158.9	3	12	1.3	11	0	.0
10595	7.3	88	2.0	79	40.7	498	157.4	5	12	3.2	10	0	.2
10596	1.7	98	.6	67	26.4	433	85.4	7	12	.8	12	0	.2
10597	.5	100	.2	68	139.2	534	350.0	6	2	.2	4	0	.0
10598	25.4	94	7.5	92	44.4	535	126.0	6	8	12.2	6	0	.0

*=Estimated **1.0=883 lbs per person; 100++ indicates per capita toxic waste generation > than 100 times the U.S. average of 883 lbs per capita.

ZIP CODE MEASURES OF SIZE, LEVELS OF AFFLUENCE AND QUALITY OF LIFE

1=Population (th.); 2= % White; 3=Households (th.); 4=% Owner Occupied; 5=Mean Income Per Household (th.$); 6=Mean Monthly Rent ($)*; 7=Mean Home Value (th.$)*;
8=% under 5; 9=% 65 and over; 10=White Males (th.); 11=% White Males, 65+; 12=# Toxic Waste Sites; 13=Toxic Waste Relative to US(883 lbs.per capita)**.

NEW YORK

ZIP CODE	1	2	3	4	5	6	7	8	9	10	11	12	13
WHITE PLAINS													
10601	7.2	62	3.7	5	22.9	416	122.0	5	24	1.8	22	1	.5
10603	16.0	70	6.3	50	33.8	504	129.0	5	12	5.1	12	1	.0
10604	9.4	87	3.4	48	32.6	521	152.2	4	12	3.8	11	0	.3
10605	16.3	89	6.1	56	48.9	511	196.5	5	15	6.6	13	0	.1
10606	13.2	70	4.7	44	32.7	449	152.0	5	16	4.3	15	0	1.1
10607	6.1	63	2.0	82	42.7	452	141.7	6	10	1.9	7	0	.0
YONKERS													
10701	58.6	68	21.9	25	24.4	382	116.2	7	13	18.7	14	1	.5
10703	21.4	92	7.9	41	28.8	401	101.8	6	14	9.2	12	0	.1
10704	32.5	98	12.4	43	30.0	459	113.0	6	15	15.0	17	0	.3
10705	33.6	83	13.2	26	25.9	373	123.6	6	15	13.1	14	0	.1
10706	8.9	93	3.2	60	43.8	504	156.1	4	15	3.9	12	0	1.3
10707	16.0	92	5.7	58	37.9	487	158.8	5	15	6.9	13	0	4.0
10708	24.0	96	9.8	43	48.2	545	244.9	4	18	10.2	15	0	.0
10709	3.4	97	1.3	81	43.2	482	185.3	5	15	1.5	13	0	.0
10710	27.6	93	9.8	53	36.6	503	133.6	4	13	12.3	11	0	.0
NEW ROCHELLE													
10801	33.2	66	11.9	38	26.4	397	122.6	5	16	10.0	15	0	.4
10803	13.0	95	4.2	70	53.0	538	182.2	5	14	5.9	12	0	.2
10804	14.6	94	4.7	88	71.9	605	200.1	5	13	6.6	13	0	.0
10805	19.3	90	7.9	20	29.9	480	139.8	5	17	7.9	13	0	.1
SUFFERN													
10901	20.9	96	6.9	68	38.8	512	139.1	6	10	9.7	8	1	2.7
10912	.7	0	.2	86	32.6	806	97.7	12	7			1	
10913	4.9	97	1.4	94	46.0	538	137.9	5	6	2	4	2	.1
10914	.9	97	.3	95	44.4	893	119.7	6	7	.5	5	0	.0
10915	.3	100	.2	61	24.7	340	71.1	4	9	.2	11	0	.0
10916	2.4	91	.7	81	31.4	370	103.8	4	14	2	8	0	.0
10917	1.9	0	.6	62	30.6	451	108.2	8	7	1.1	0	0	15.5
10918	7.3	91	1.9	74	30.6	433	92.9	6	10	3.6	12	0	.3
10919	.9	100	.3	88	28.1	254	82.5	5	11	.4	12	0	.0
10920	8.0	98	2.3	80	39.6	535	123.5	7	7	3.9	5	0	.1
10921	3.0	99	1.0	84	29.2	412	83.7	6	13	1.4	11	0	.1
10922	1.1	99	.4	63	26.0	391	77.4	9	10	.5	8	0	.0
10923	6.9	96	2.0	69	31.5	483	105.1	6	8	4.7	5	0	.0
10924	10.3	94	3.2	69	31.5	380	92.1	6	13	4.7	11	3	.0
10925	4.3	99	1.6	74	29.8	296	80.3	6	13	2.1	12	0	.0
10926	1.4	97	.5	73	27.6	394	87.1	5	16	.6	16	0	.0
10927	8.8	75	2.6	48	26.7	437	77.8	9	10	3.2	9	1	.3
10928	4.8	85	1.8	55	24.5	355	70.2	5	13	1.8	12	0	.0
10930	4.6	97	1.4	86	34.4	353	108.6	8	8	2.2	7	0	.0
10931	.9	51	.3	69	27.7	510	66.6	8	11	.4	14	0	.0
10932	.3	84	.1	84	28.5	419	79.3	4	20	.1	19	0	.0
10933	.4	0	.1	60	23.3	417	65.4	12	10	.0	0	0	.0
10940	43.9	91	14.8	61	25.2	380	73.1	8	13	19.1	11	2	1.9
10950	20.2	98	5.6	76	32.9	497	100.9	10	7	9.9	9	2	.0
10952	24.1	97	6.4	69	40.2	542	141.1	10	6	11.7	5	0	.1
10953	.7	84	.3	65	28.3	450	82.6	4	19	.3	16	1	2.3
10954	15.0	92	4.6	80	40.6	522	126.3	6	10	6.7	20	0	.0

NEW YORK

ZIP CODE	1	2	3	4	5	6	7	8	9	10	11	12	13
SUFFERN													
10956	30.1	97	8.2	90	49.6	555	156.7	6	6	14.4	4	0	.0
10958	2.8	93	.7	77	30.0	495	78.8	6	6	1.3	5	0	.0
10960	14.1	68	5.2	46	31.5	480	117.2	6	12	4.5	13	3	.0
10962	7.1	83	1.5	84	49.4	543	146.6	6	15	2.9	13	0	3.8
10963	2.6	78	.7	71	25.7	370	70.9	7	7	1.1	8	0	.4
10964	.8	97	.3	85	54.1	349	219.4	3	34	.3	23	0	.0
10965	15.6	98	5.0	76	39.1	521	120.1	5	10	7.4	7	1	28.1
10968	2.3	88	.9	44	33.6	509	127.4	6	11	1.0	9	1	.0
10969	1.1	91	.4	66	18.8	313	62.7	6	16	.5	18	0	.0
10970	4.7	97	1.5	80	39.9	538	172.6	7	13	2.1	7	1	.0
10973	1.4	100	.4	81	26.5	416	82.7	10	12	.0	8	0	1.5
10974	3.3	97	1.1	71	34.0	499	95.3	6	10	1.6	8	0	.0
10975	.4	0	.2	22	21.8	494	78.4	8	0	.0	0	0	.0
10976	.8	95	.1	94	46.5	534*	149.0	3	23	.2	0	0	.0
10977	46.4	79	14.7	58	34.7	453	121.9	8	7	17.6	7	1	.1
10979	.2	100	.1	89	27.2	312*	88.8	6	6	.1	6	0	.0
10980	11.4	99	3.5	84	33.3	479	109.4	7	9	5.5	6	2	2.7
10981	.4	99	.1	80	34.4	385	109.2	3	5	3.3	7	0	.1
10983	7.0	95	2.0	89	46.5	510	137.8	4	9	3.3	7	0	.0
10984	4.8	92	.7	88	39.8	307	125.0	5	7	2.3	6	0	.4
10985	.3	100	.1	73	20.3	240	73.8	7	30	.2	37	0	.0
10986	1.0	96	.4	66	29.3	430	114.7	7	10	.4	10	0	.0
10987	2.7	98	.9	69	53.1	524	171.1	4	9	1.4	4	0	1.8
10988	.8	0	.2	73	21.5	330	66.9	4	17	.0	0	1	.0
10989	7.4	93	2.5	84	38.1	560	121.8	8	10	3.3	7	0	.0
10990	11.1	93	3.5	74	31.3	393	97.8	8	10	5.0	8	5	.0
10992	4.2	94	1.4	79	32.3	414	97.7	9	9	1.9	8	1	.0
10993	5.7	83	1.9	51	24.0	379	77.0	6	12	2.1	9	2	.0
10994	7.5	96	2.1	88	46.8	570	147.4	6	6	3.5	5	2	1.8
10996	8.1	91	1.0	1	32.2	483	114.7*	6	0	.4	0	0	.0
10998	1.4	97	.4	80	32.6	430	85.5	7	7	.7	6	0	.0
QUEENS													
11001	19.6	96	6.8	74	33.3	480	106.5	5	15	8.8	12	0	.1
11003	34.9	93	11.4	79	32.4	460	88.1	5	12	15.5	12	0	.0
11004	18.1	93	6.8	52	31.6	422	103.6	5	14	8.0	13	0	.1
11005	3.0	94	1.6	0	59.9	817	213.3*	3	17	.3	21	3	.0
11010	24.6	99	8.1	85	33.5	449	96.1	4	15	11.6	13	1	.0
11020	7.4	82	2.6	71	58.7	506	230.2	4	12	3.0	13	0	.7
11021	16.9	93	7.0	49	53.4	599	242.5	4	17	7.1	15	0	1.3
11023	7.5	98	2.6	89	63.3	692	219.8	5	14	3.6	14	0	.0
11024	7.8	94	2.3	90	92.6	647	294.4	4	9	3.9	8	0	.0
11030	16.5	96	5.4	84	70.8	544	256.1	5	14	7.6	12	0	.0
11040	40.3	97	12.9	91	40.4	480	123.7	4	15	18.3	14	2	1.4
11050	28.6	95	10.0	68	50.6	615	199.7	5	11	13.0	10	0	.5
LONG ISLAND CITY													
11101	24.0	54	9.3	10	17.0	265	65.4	7	12	6.3	13	3	8.5
11102	32.8	73	12.7	16	19.9	339	80.0	7	13	11.4	14	2	.3
11103	36.3	90	14.8	21	21.1	342	92.4	6	16	15.3	14	0	.4
11104	24.8	83	11.9	10	22.0	349	88.8	5	10	9.2	20	0	.5

*=Estimated   **1.0=883 lbs per person; 100++ indicates per capita toxic waste generation > than 100 times the U.S. average of 883 lbs per capita.

ZIP CODE MEASURES OF SIZE, LEVELS OF AFFLUENCE AND QUALITY OF LIFE

1=Population (th.); 2= % White; 3=Households (th.); 4=% Owner Occupied; 5=Mean Income Per Household (th.$)*; 6=Mean Monthly Rent ($)*; 7=Mean Home Value (th.$)*; 8=% under 5; 9=% 65 and over; 10=White Males, 65+; 11=% White Males (th.); 12=# Toxic Waste Sites; 13=Toxic Waste Relative to US(883 lbs.per capita)**.

NEW YORK

ZIPCODE	1	2	3	4	5	6	7	8	9	10	11	12	13
LONG ISLAND CITY													
11105	38.5	91	14.8	31	22.8	354	93.5	6	15	16.3	13	0	.2
11106	39.2	83	17.3	14	20.5	316	86.1	6	18	14.7	17	0	.2
BROOKLYN													
11201	45.2	66	20.7	15	29.4	406	276.4	5	13	15.3	12	8	.7
11203	79.8	15	25.3	35	23.4	380	80.4	8	7	5.5	20	0	.
11204	69.4	96	26.0	33	22.2	353	103.1	7	17	31.1	15	0	.
11205	33.5	22	12.5	14	15.9	293	76.9	9	7	3.5	9	1	.7
11206	63.8	28	21.1	8	13.0	250	46.2	8	7	8.1	8	0	.7
11207	96.9	24	20.8	16	17.3	342	61.6	10	7	10.9	13	0	5.9
11208	73.6	38	22.7	27	16.8	329	56.8	10	8	13.0	12	2	.2
11209	68.6	95	31.3	22	26.2	380	135.1	5	23	29.6	18	0	.2
11210	53.6	68	19.7	38	28.2	396	102.9	7	15	16.7	17	1	.0
11211	73.0	70	24.3	12	14.6	267	50.7	13	9	24.7	10	3	.0
11212	76.5	5	25.2	11	14.9	296	76.9	10	5	1.6	16	0	1.1
11213	57.3	9	19.9	15	16.6	335	104.8	10	8	2.6	15	0	.0
11214	76.3	96	30.3	26	22.6	374	97.5	7	18	33.6	16	0	.0
11215	67.0	75	26.8	23	22.3	350	104.0	7	12	23.8	12	3	.0
11216	50.1	2	20.6	14	14.3	296	66.7	8	9	.4	15	0	.1
11217	33.1	40	13.7	14	20.4	323	167.3	7	8	6.6	9	0	.1
11218	62.6	81	24.9	22	22.1	374	80.8	7	17	23.4	17	1	.1
11219	70.9	92	25.8	24	20.5	357	111.2	9	18	30.9	17	0	.1
11220	66.8	13	22.2	18	13.9	328	87.9	9	12	23.4	13	3	.0
11221	37.6	87	15.2	20	18.8	273	52.1	11	7	4.0	7	0	.
11222	37.6	87	15.2	20	18.8	273	59.8	7	13	15.6	12	10	1.6
11223	72.3	92	27.8	32	22.3	359	102.2	6	17	31.3	15	0	.1
11224	46.7	59	17.8	14	17.7	289	105.4	7	20	12.5	28	2	.0
11225	59.1	10	21.7	12	19.4	365	87.3	9	6	2.9	20	1	.0
11226	95.0	19	34.7	9	18.7	389	93.1	10	7	7.9	21	0	.0
11227	79.8	87	31.7	32	26.1	329	89.4	7	17	31.7	16	0	.0
11228	39.9	99	14.9	51	26.2	380	114.1	5	17	18.5	15	1	.0
11229	73.1	94	30.0	35	25.7	379	93.5	4	20	31.8	18	1	.0
11230	74.1	89	30.7	22	24.5	387	108.8	7	20	30.4	19	0	.0
11231	36.9	68	13.9	18	19.7	299	99.7	8	11	12.2	11	0	1.2
11232	20.3	68	7.6	24	16.9	307	59.2	9	9	6.4	15	3	1.4
11233	56.0	4	20.2	16	14.6	300	52.6	10	8	1.0	10	0	.1
11234	80.6	95	28.5	61	30.4	423	98.8	5	13	36.4	12	0	.0
11235	74.4	94	33.8	23	22.8	386	102.2	4	26	32.2	24	0	.0
11236	80.4	81	28.4	45	26.8	400	87.0	6	13	31.4	14	1	.0
11237	47.2	73	17.6	16	15.0	303	65.6	10	12	15.8	13	2	.0
11238	49.4	11	19.2	12	16.9	329	79.1	8	9	2.7	17	0	2.0
FLUSHING													
11354	43.1	80	17.4	29	26.8	424	121.3	5	19	15.7	18	0	.
11355	62.7	67	24.9	25	25.9	444	101.7	6	14	19.2	16	0	.
11356	16.7	97	5.9	54	27.3	413	99.8	6	13	18.3	11	2	.7
11357	40.3	96	14.2	65	35.5	503	132.5	4	14	18.3	14	0	.
11358	34.8	96	12.8	59	31.5	431	118.7	5	16	15.6	13	0	.
11359	.6	67	.2	0	24.8	403	88.3*	17	1	.2	0	0	.
11360	18.7	94	7.1	45	41.8	682	154.0	4	10	8.5	10	0	.
11361	27.3	89	10.1	52	31.4	467	113.5	5	14	11.4	12	1	.0

NEW YORK

ZIPCODE	1	2	3	4	5	6	7	8	9	10	11	12	13
FLUSHING													
11362	16.8	96	6.4	75	38.5	529	145.3	4	14	7.8	13	0	.0
11363	7.8	94	2.9	63	40.2	547	161.4	5	13	3.5	10	0	.0
11364	32.6	94	12.5	48	35.2	457	124.5	5	14	14.7	13	0	.0
11365	34.9	91	14.0	45	33.3	427	113.9	5	18	14.9	18	0	.0
11366	12.7	78	4.8	72	35.1	492	117.5	5	17	4.7	19	0	.0
11367	35.5	86	14.2	33	29.8	411	108.1	6	14	14.7	14	0	.1
11368	67.5	47	22.6	24	20.8	412	73.4	8	10	15.2	11	0	.0
11369	24.3	37	9.1	52	24.9	388	81.3	6	15	4.2	17	0	.1
11370	28.7	72	8.5	43	28.2	442	100.8	4	10	10.1	10	1	.0
11372	55.4	80	24.7	17	23.9	399	105.5	6	19	19.4	18	0	.0
11373	78.4	65	29.6	24	24.9	431	93.0	6	12	23.9	13	0	.0
11374	40.1	90	19.2	15	24.0	468	117.3	6	23	15.8	22	0	.4
11375	71.3	91	33.3	18	32.4	510	157.2	4	23	29.0	22	0	.0
11377	72.1	78	29.1	23	24.2	375	92.1	6	15	25.5	15	0	.1
11378	31.2	99	12.1	52	25.7	368	91.1	5	18	14.3	15	1	.0
11379	29.3	98	11.2	58	27.8	395	103.2	5	19	13.4	16	0	1.2
JAMAICA													
11411	21.1	11	5.8	89	33.4	472	84.0	6	8	.9	36	1	.0
11412	33.7	2	9.8	73	27.6	440	73.5	6	9	.3	43	0	.0
11413	36.9	11	10.5	79	31.7	470	82.8	6	6	2.0	21	1	.4
11414	29.1	98	10.1	63	33.7	481	117.3	4	11	13.7	10	0	.1
11415	17.5	89	8.0	12	26.9	437	140.2	5	19	7.3	15	0	.1
11416	17.4	96	6.2	47	24.5	380	68.0	6	14	7.8	12	0	.1
11417	25.0	97	9.0	56	25.5	401	74.3	6	15	11.4	13	0	1.6
11418	28.3	86	10.7	39	26.0	372	79.0	7	15	11.5	13	0	.3
11419	32.8	76	10.3	60	25.1	372	67.4	7	12	11.1	12	0	.0
11420	36.2	55	11.5	67	26.0	398	69.7	7	11	9.5	13	1	.0
11421	28.3	96	10.9	53	27.1	366	71.6	6	18	12.6	16	1	.0
11422	25.7	79	8.2	72	32.4	485	82.8	6	10	9.9	9	0	.0
11423	27.3	50	9.2	52	29.0	400	101.9	7	13	6.3	18	1	.0
11426	18.9	96	6.7	75	32.3	409	93.0	5	15	8.6	14	1	.0
11427	21.1	79	7.1	57	32.1	390	93.0	5	15	7.9	14	0	.0
11428	16.1	81	5.3	69	29.5	397	76.2	5	12	6.9	12	0	1.2
11429	23.3	18	6.2	76	30.7	447	77.7	6	7	1.8	19	0	1.4
11432	42.9	63	16.9	31	28.7	423	129.8	6	16	12.4	17	0	.1
11433	24.1	4	7.6	48	20.3	301	61.9	7	12	.5	25	0	.0
11434	50.1	7	16.9	52	25.0	359	67.4	7	11	1.8	38	0	.5
11435	44.0	51	16.0	25	24.9	429	69.4	6	11	10.5	13	1	.0
11436	15.5	2	4.6	72	15.0	453	60.0	7	9	2.7	41	0	.0
HICKSVILLE													
11501	21.1	96	7.7	58	32.5	524	102.0	5	13	9.6	11	0	1.2
11507	7.1	97	2.2	94	47.2	549	137.3	4	10	3.4	9	0	.1
11509	2.5	100	.9	83	53.0	729	160.2	4	11	1.2	10	0	.0
11510	32.5	94	10.4	86	39.2	537	97.6	6	10	14.7	9	0	.0
11514	5.0	97	1.7	73	33.7	542	94.8	5	11	2.3	12	0	2.5
11516	8.1	98	2.9	66	44.2	570	148.2	5	14	3.8	12	0	.
11518	12.1	99	4.3	66	35.3	505	104.0	6	12	5.7	10	0	.1
11520	38.6	64	12.8	59	30.3	497	78.5	6	10	11.8	11	1	.8
11530	28.7	89	8.9	72	54.9	620	178.1	4	14	13.1	11	2	1.4

*=Estimated **1.0=883 lbs per capita. **1.0=883 lbs per person; 100++ indicates per capita toxic waste generation > than 100 times the U.S. average of 883 lbs per capita.

ZIP CODE MEASURES OF SIZE, LEVELS OF AFFLUENCE AND QUALITY OF LIFE

1=Population (th.); 2= % White; 3=Households (th.); 4=% Owner Occupied; 5=Mean Income Per Household (th.$); 6=Mean Monthly Rent ($)*; 7=Mean Home Value (th.$)*; 8=% under 5; 9=% 65 and over; 10=White Males (th.); 11=% White Males, 65+; 12=# Toxic Waste Sites; 13=% Toxic Waste Relative to US(883 lbs.per capita)**.

NEW YORK

HICKSVILLE

ZIPCODE	1	2	3	4	5	6	7	8	9	10	11	12	13
11542	25.7	90	8.5	63	38.3	519	133.0	5	13	11.2	10	1	.6
11545	11.1	98	3.7	87	65.3	609	232.1	4	11	5.3	11	0	.4
11547	.9	100	.3	81	39.7	622	108.0	2	12	.5	10	1	.6
11548	2.6	87	.4	76	42.2	560	151.1	3	7	1.0	7	0	.3
11550	44.6	45	14.9	47	28.4	451	80.6	7	10	9.3	12	1	.1
11552	22.4	85	7.0	87	37.9	556	97.4	5	11	9.0	11	1	.1
11553	20.6	69	5.9	83	31.1	458	75.3	6	13	6.5	12	0	.0
11554	36.3	96	10.9	88	38.9	405	95.6	6	7	17.3	7	1	.1
11557	7.6	98	2.6	77	68.2	598	190.2	4	12	3.6	11	0	.1
11558	8.9	99	2.9	66	28.9	500	95.2	5	12	4.2	10	0	1.4
11559	6.5	96	2.3	63	56.4	614	208.2	5	14	3.0	13	0	.0
11560	6.8	97	2.3	77	54.5	589	196.5	5	11	3.0	10	0	.0
11561	38.2	89	14.8	44	30.8	483	92.6	5	20	16.1	18	0	.0
11563	23.1	99	8.2	67	34.6	521	96.4	5	15	10.7	12	0	.6
11565	9.9	99	3.2	94	41.9	508	103.8	5	15	4.7	14	0	.0
11566	38.2	99	11.5	94	45.3	588	108.6	6	9	18.3	8	0	.0
11568	3.3	77	.8	85	113.8	769	368.5	3	7	1.2	8	0	.0
11569	1.6	0	.6	72	38.2	625	121.0	6	18	1.0	8	0	.0
11570	28.1	90	9.9	65	43.2	502	136.1	6	16	11.8	13	0	.6
11572	32.2	99	10.1	88	41.0	531	108.0	5	9	15.6	7	0	.1
11575	14.2	10	3.7	77	31.7	614	71.9	8	5	.6	19	0	.0
11576	12.2	94	4.1	91	86.3	593	266.2	6	7	5.6	7	0	.2
11577	12.0	92	4.1	80	55.5	553	180.8	5	11	5.4	10	0	.1
11579	5.5	97	2.1	70	36.9	519	140.0	5	14	2.5	10	0	.0
11580	36.2	98	12.3	80	44.7	493	95.9	5	14	17.0	12	0	.4
11581	21.3	98	7.0	83	44.7	531	122.2	4	10	10.1	9	0	.0
11590	39.3	75	12.2	81	39.6	558	97.0	6	9	14.4	9	1	1.1
11596	11.5	98	3.8	84	42.0	560	126.9	5	13	5.3	11	0	.0
11598	13.8	99	4.4	83	61.6	583	174.1	5	11	6.6	10	0	.0

FAR ROCKAWAY

ZIPCODE	1	2	3	4	5	6	7	8	9	10	11	12	13
11691	49.7	56	17.4	23	18.9	308	83.6	8	19	12.3	21	0	.0
11692	15.7	21	5.1	22	17.7	288	62.0	10	10	1.5	24	0	.0
11693	11.9	73	4.4	37	20.1	298	54.6	6	19	4.0	22	0	.4
11694	19.8	94	7.6	41	31.0	392	141.5	5	26	8.5	22	1	.0
11696	7.0	68	2.4	50	22.9	344	75.5	5	14	2.4	12	0	2.3
11697	3.6	99	1.3	98	30.6	233	79.3	6	20	1.7	18	0	.0

HICKSVILLE

ZIPCODE	1	2	3	4	5	6	7	8	9	10	11	12	13
11701	24.4	55	7.8	72	29.8	540	80.4	7	12	6.3	12	0	.2
11703	17.6	99	5.2	81	34.8	583	77.8	6	7	8.5	6	0	.0
11704	37.8	87	11.3	76	30.7	567	74.6	6	7	15.9	6	3	.2
11705	8.3	98	2.6	74	36.0	510	89.4	7	8	4.0	6	1	.1
11706	54.1	87	16.2	74	30.9	508	72.2	7	8	23.1	7	2	.2
11709	7.0	99	2.3	72	35.7	584	133.5	5	10	3.5	8	0	.1
11710	37.1	98	11.3	89	39.8	514	98.8	5	8	17.7	7	0	.1
11713	8.2	66	2.4	77	31.2	539	78.4	8	8	2.9	10	0	.1
11714	26.3	99	7.8	89	36.2	530	90.2	5	8	13.0	7	1	4.6
11715	4.1	98	1.3	84	32.6	512	77.7	6	12	2.0	10	0	1.5
11716	9.7	99	3.0	75	28.9	507	77.7	7	11	4.6	9	0	3.9

NEW YORK

HICKSVILLE

ZIPCODE	1	2	3	4	5	6	7	8	9	10	11	12	13
11717	46.5	85	10.7	86	31.9	507	64.4	6	9	19.4	7	0	.3
11718	3.2	0	1.1	88	47.9	563	101.1	6	12	.0	0	0	.0
11719	3.1	96	1.0	87	34.4	431	89.0	9	7	1.5	6	1	.0
11720	27.7	97	7.4	88	32.2	594	68.9	8	5	13.2	4	0	.0
11721	6.6	99	2.2	87	43.1	650	134.1	5	10	3.2	9	0	.0
11722	29.8	74	7.8	75	28.1	533	61.5	8	9	10.8	9	2	.8
11724	2.1	0	.6	88	61.9	612	216.0	4	8	.0	0	0	.0
11725	23.7	99	6.4	91	41.8	659	96.2	5	8	11.5	3	2	.6
11726	15.3	86	4.8	76	31.6	554	72.4	7	8	6.3	7	0	.8
11727	19.0	87	6.2	67	31.2	489	70.4	10	6	8.0	5	0	.2
11729	30.6	92	8.7	84	33.7	537	79.8	5	6	13.7	5	1	1.4
11730	13.9	99	4.1	84	34.2	559	79.2	7	8	6.7	6	1	.0
11731	40.7	98	11.4	91	39.5	606	101.9	6	7	19.9	5	1	.0
11732	4.0	98	1.2	94	61.3	834	161.9	5	7	1.9	7	0	.0
11733	14.6	95	4.3	80	45.3	608	122.8	6	6	6.7	6	0	.0
11735	25.1	95	7.6	73	34.1	541	87.8	6	9	11.4	7	4	6.8
11738	13.6	97	3.7	90	31.2	519	72.9	10	7	6.3	6	0	.0
11739	1.5	100	.5	92	57.1	333	136.9	4	7	.4	6	0	5.8
11740	9.3	97	2.9	85	42.6	427	115.9	6	10	4.4	7	0	.9
11741	25.2	96	6.9	84	31.8	571	76.5	10	4	12.0	4	0	.0
11742	9.0	98	2.6	69	30.9	536	72.9	10	5	4.3	5	0	.0
11743	44.8	93	14.4	83	49.4	552	151.3	5	10	20.3	8	1	.0
11746	79.3	94	22.7	85	43.5	529	129.7	6	7	36.5	5	0	.8
11751	12.6	97	2.4	73	31.9	489	81.5	7	10	6.0	8	0	.2
11752	9.6	98	2.6	88	31.9	567	71.0	6	6	4.6	4	0	.0
11753	10.3	97	3.3	90	57.3	567	168.9	5	5	5.0	5	0	.0
11754	20.7	96	5.1	84	36.2	525	92.8	6	13	9.5	10	2	.3
11755	7.9	99	2.3	75	32.7	533	87.5	5	7	3.7	5	0	.0
11756	47.3	99	13.6	90	35.7	624	74.4	7	7	22.8	7	0	.3
11757	45.7	98	14.1	78	30.0	500	73.4	7	8	22.1	7	0	.3
11758	63.7	97	18.8	91	41.3	541	98.8	5	8	30.3	6	0	.0
11762	26.5	99	7.4	97	43.5	613	96.5	5	6	12.9	5	0	.0
11763	22.0	89	6.1	86	30.0	611	68.4	6	7	9.7	4	1	.0
11764	8.1	99	2.4	87	37.3	586	92.5	8	8	4.0	6	0	.0
11765	.6	98	.6	81	137.8	908	311.5	2	15	.3	16	0	2.3
11766	6.9	98	2.0	91	34.3	632	86.7	11	5	3.4	4	0	.0
11767	9.5	99	2.6	84	35.0	546	96.4	7	6	4.6	5	0	.0
11768	22.5	99	7.0	83	45.3	570	142.0	5	9	11.2	8	0	.2
11769	9.5	99	2.9	76	35.1	478	86.1	6	7	4.6	5	0	.0
11770	.2	100	.1	77	28.2	341	204.6	9	10	.1	6	0	.0
11771	8.1	94	2.9	60	47.4	532	187.2	5	13	3.7	10	0	.2
11772	37.4	94	12.9	59	26.4	481	70.9	8	12	16.7	10	2	.3
11776	20.0	96	5.5	81	30.9	493	72.4	7	8	9.4	6	1	.3
11777	7.8	97	2.5	71	41.1	493	133.9	6	13	3.5	9	1	.3
11778	9.0	99	3.2	74	26.3	512	71.4	8	15	4.3	13	0	.3
11779	42.8	99	12.9	77	29.0	501	71.1	8	8	20.9	6	1	.1
11780	12.7	99	3.9	86	40.1	547	121.2	5	14	5.9	10	0	.0
11782	15.6	99	4.7	79	32.6	494	83.6	8	7	7.4	7	0	.1
11783	23.4	99	6.8	93	40.7	553	91.3	6	7	11.5	6	0	.0

*=Estimated **1.0=883 lbs per person; 100++ indicates per capita toxic waste generation > than 100 times the U.S. average of 883 lbs per capita.

ZIP CODE MEASURES OF SIZE, LEVELS OF AFFLUENCE AND QUALITY OF LIFE

1=Population (th.); 2= % White; 3=Households (th.); 4=% Owner Occupied; 5=Mean Income Per Household (th.$); 6=Mean Monthly Rent ($)*; 7=Mean Home Value (th.$)*; 8=% under 5; 9=% 65 and over; 10=% White Males (th.); 11=% White Males, 65+; 12=# Toxic Waste Sites; 13=Toxic Waste Relative to US(883 lbs.per capita)**.

NEW YORK

ZIPCODE	1	2	3	4	5	6	7	8	9	10	11	12	13
HICKSVILLE													
11784	22.8	97	6.4	78	28.4	528	64.6	9	6	10.9	5	5	.0
11786	4.5	99	1.3	89	40.8	671	110.0	9	5	2.3	4	1	.3
11787	53.2	99	15.1	83	38.6	527	100.3	5	7	25.7	5	1	1.5
11789	5.6	99	1.9	73	24.6	524	67.1	9	13	2.7	12	1	.0
11790	20.1	90	4.4	90	43.3	733	100.5	4	6	9.2	5	0	.0
11791	23.9	98	7.3	94	52.0	487	156.6	5	7	11.4	6	2	1.0
11792	4.9	97	1.6	82	32.4	528	102.6	5	11	2.4	9	0	.0
11793	33.5	99	10.7	94	37.4	506	91.3	7	8	16.4	7	0	.0
11795	28.0	99	7.7	92	37.4	577	88.2	6	8	13.5	6	1	.0
11796	4.0	99	1.3	82	30.8	532	67.2	6	11	2.0	8	0	.0
11797	7.0	97	2.1	74	60.1	770	233.4	4	17	3.0	8	1	.6
11798	12.5	30	3.1	72	31.0	594	71.6	9	4	1.9	5	1	.4
HICKSVILLE													
11801	42.5	98	13.2	88	36.8	542	89.4	5	9	20.3	8	3	.7
11803	30.4	98	8.9	97	46.6	625	116.9	5	6	14.7	5	2	1.9
11804	5.8	100	1.6	98	49.0	700	118.9	5	4	2.9	4	0	1.3
RIVERHEAD													
11901	15.9	75	5.9	72	22.0	420	73.1	7	19	5.7	21	1	.0
11930	1.3	96	.6	77	33.9	420	155.8	3	15	.6	16	0	.0
11931	1.2	92	.5	80	24.5	423	91.7	9	23	.5	20	1	2.2
11932	.6	76	.3	80	38.4	541	169.4	7	17	.3	17	0	.0
11933	3.7	91	1.4	85	27.3	485	75.0	8	16	1.6	15	1	7.0
11934	5.4	91	1.8	78	27.3	438	77.1	8	12	2.4	10	0	.0
11935	2.9	99	1.1	88	28.4	407	125.4	5	22	1.3	19	1	.6
11937	8.7	94	3.6	81	31.0	440	143.7	5	19	3.9	17	0	.0
11939	.7	93	.3	80	27.6	447	115.3	3	34	.3	31	0	.0
11940	3.5	97	1.1	85	29.1	470	85.2	8	13	1.6	10	0	.0
11941	1.6	0	.6	71	23.5	415	95.7	6	15	1.0	14	1	.0
11942	3.1	99	1.2	85	25.2	384	105.1	7	20	1.4	20	0	.0
11944	3.8	85	1.4	67	25.9	369	86.4	5	25	1.4	23	1	.0
11946	9.0	99	3.6	75	26.1	405	100.1	5	22	4.3	21	1	.0
11947	.9	100	.3	78	26.0	529	97.7	4	16	.4	12	0	.0
11948	.8	0	.1	83	31.4	404	102.3	11	14	.0	12	0	.0
11949	3.6	98	1.5	48	24.3	477	77.5	9	10	1.8	9	0	.0
11950	11.3	93	3.1	73	23.7	512	57.3	12	4	5.2	4	1	.0
11951	9.3	99	3.0	77	26.4	534	52.9	6	21	1.9	20	0	.0
11952	4.2	97	1.5	72	24.7	516	113.2	7	15	1.9	18	1	.0
11953	6.5	90	2.1	70	32.0	367	110.1	6	19	1.4	15	0	.0
11954	2.8	96	1.1	74	26.1	458	69.6	6	11	1.3	8	0	1.2
11955	.7	88	.2	73	26.7	485	92.1	5	15	.3	18	0	.0
11956	.4	90	.2	77	27.2	451	124.0	3	21	.2	20	0	.0
11957	.9	100	.4	72	24.0	516	116.9	3	29	.4	32	1	.0
11958	.7	89	.3	86	28.6	546	113.2	7	16	.0	15	0	.0
11959	1.0	81	.4	73	39.1	472	216.0	4	19	.4	15	0	.1
11960	1.0	100	.4	93	42.1	451	197.9	6	14	.5	16	0	.0
11961	7.8	98	3.3	91	23.9	551	73.6	10	32	3.4	28	0	.0
11962	.3	88	.1	89	32.4	217	175.6	7	15	.2	14	0	.0
11963	5.3	94	2.3	79	27.4	458	136.5	5	23	2.4	21	1	1.1
11964	1.4	100	.6	81	31.7	383	136.3	4	27	.6	26	1	.0

NEW YORK

ZIPCODE	1	2	3	4	5	6	7	8	9	10	11	12	13
RIVERHEAD													
11965	.7	99	.3	87	36.3	309	170.7	3	36	.3	30	0	.0
11967	18.1	97	5.1	84	24.7	555	61.0	12	6	8.7	6	2	.0
11968	10.7	86	4.0	76	36.3	381	140.9	4	18	4.4	16	0	.0
11970	.5	100	.2	85	28.1	404	88.8	5	24	2.2	16	0	.0
11971	4.6	99	1.9	84	27.8	470	119.5	5	27	.4	12	0	.0
11972	.9	86	.3	56	21.9	397	77.4	6	12	.4	12	0	.0
11973	.2	69	.1	0	23.3	429	82.9*	15	0	.1	0	0	5.8
11975	.3	0	.2	62	26.2	367	205.6	9	37	.6	15	2	.0
11976	1.3	95	.5	85	41.0	286	196.0	6	15	.0	0	0	.0
11977	1.1	0	.4	71	32.1	379	153.9	6	12	1.5	17	2	.9
11978	3.9	82	1.5	69	33.2	437	156.0	6	17	1.1	12	1	.0
11980	2.2	95	.7	81	26.0	479	74.2	8	16	1.1	12	1	.9
ALBANY													
12007	.2	100	.1	59	26.3	302*	73.9	20	8	.1	9	0	.0
12008	.5	100	.2	78	33.1	358	67.2	7	8	.3	7	0	.0
12009	5.5	99	1.9	78	28.6	381	77.6	7	10	2.7	9	0	.3
12010	31.1	97	12.1	62	22.0	239	61.1	5	19	14.2	17	6	.3
12015	2.4	99	.8	71	23.4	323	54.6	7	17	1.1	15	0	.0
12017	.2	100	.1	71	23.8	416	66.9	3	16	.1	11	0	.0
12018	6.4	100	2.0	80	26.8	347	69.6	7	9	3.2	8	2	.0
12019	12.5	98	3.8	81	37.7	482	105.0	7	6	6.2	5	0	.0
12020	18.5	99	6.2	76	26.3	317	72.2	8	10	9.0	8	4	.0
12022	1.0	99	.4	76	26.3	287	56.8	8	16	.5	13	1	.6
12023	1.5	99	.5	73	27.5	394	53.4	8	11	.8	9	0	.2
12024	.3	93	.3	82	25.4	505	49.7	4	19	.1	17	0	.0
12025	4.5	93	1.6	88	22.2	256	60.1	6	13	2.2	12	1	.0
12027	3.4	99	1.1	86	36.6	401	89.8	6	5	1.7	4	0	1.1
12028	1.0	93	.3	89	22.7	377	59.4	9	17	.6	9	0	.0
12029	1.1	93	.3	72	29.5	343	71.9	4	12	.6	11	0	.0
12031	.9	99	.3	86	22.4	326	53.7	9	5	.4	9	1	.0
12032	7.1	100	2.5	77	27.2	257	60.7	6	11	3.4	9	1	.0
12033	1.1	98	.4	67	19.5	325	73.8	6	12	3.4	9	1	.0
12035	.3	0	.4	91	18.2	325	54.2	6	13	.3	12	0	.0
12036	.3	100	2.3	62	22.1	209*	44.1	7	16	.2	16	1	.2
12037	4.0	96	1.4	70	24.5	323	67.2	6	14	1.9	11	0	.0
12040	.3	100	.2	71	23.0	403	61.3	12	4	.0	5	0	.0
12041	.7	100	.2	73	30.9	395	55.1	4	6	.4	4	5	.0
12042	.5	100	.2	78	29.4	321	80.0	8	11	.3	12	0	.0
12043	8.0	98	2.3	62	22.1	298	69.8	4	12	3.6	10	1	.0
12045	.8	78	.4	39	17.7	222	84.1	8	10	.4	7	1	.0
12046	.8	100	.2	88	33.0	245	82.6	9	11	.4	9	0	.0
12047	20.7	99	8.1	52	23.3	272	69.1	7	15	9.6	13	2	.0
12050	3.0	100	.95	95	22.4	258*	59.2	0	16	.1	16	1	.0
12051	3.0	98	1.1	73	25.9	318	60.8	7	16	1.4	13	1	.2
12052	1.0	98	.3	88	25.9	410	53.6	8	11	1.6	7	0	.0
12053	3.3	100	1.0	86	26.2	309	67.7	10	8	1.6	7	0	.0
12054	14.6	99	5.4	79	39.0	441	98.8	6	15	6.8	13	1	.0
12056	1.8	100	1.8	82	26.2	284	79.3	6	10	.9	8	0	.0
12057	1.4	100	.6	81	24.5	217	58.5	6	26	.0	0	1	.1

*=Estimated **1.0=883 lbs per person; 100++ indicates per capita toxic waste generation > than 100 times the U.S. average of 883 lbs per capita.

ZIP CODE MEASURES OF SIZE, LEVELS OF AFFLUENCE AND QUALITY OF LIFE

1=Population (th.); 2= % White; 3=Households (th.); 4=% Owner Occupied; 5=Mean Income Per Household (th.$); 6=Mean Monthly Rent ($)*; 7=Mean Home Value (th.$)*; 8=% under 5; 9=% 65 and over; 10=White Males (th.); 11=% White Males, 65+; 12=# Toxic Waste Sites; 13=Toxic Waste Relative to US(883 lbs.per capita)**.

NEW YORK — ALBANY

ZIPCODE	1	2	3	4	5	6	7	8	9	10	11	12	13
12058	1.3	100	.4	79	23.2	336	58.1	8	12	.7	10	0	.0
12059	1.4	100	.5	85	26.4	328	81.1	10	7	.7	6	0	.0
12060	1.2	100	.5	88	26.5	267	73.1	5	22	.6	19	0	.0
12061	6.4	97	2.2	72	32.0	425	81.9	6	8	3.0	7	2	.2
12062	1.3	100	.4	83	23.9	225	58.4	9	8	.7	7	0	.0
12063	.4	100	.1	84	26.0	431	67.3	7	7	.2	9	0	.0
12064	.5	97	.2	79	17.1	284	38.1	8	20	.2	18	0	.0
12065	25.5	98	8.5	72	33.9	435	105.0	7	5	12.4	5	2	.0
12066	1.7	100	.6	83	25.1	351	61.6	8	11	.8	10	0	.0
12067	1.3	100	.4	82	28.8	449	66.7	8	13	.6	10	0	.0
12068	2.6	100	.9	75	20.3	253	47.2	4	12	1.2	11	1	.2
12069	.3	0	.2	72	21.6	348	31.2	5	17	.0	0	0	.0
12070	1.4	0	.5	82	22.0	251	53.2	8	11	.0	0	0	.0
12071	.3	100	.1	87	21.9	224	46.4	11	13	.1	11	0	.0
12072	2.2	100	.7	81	22.9	287	45.1	8	11	1.1	10	1	1
12074	2.5	100	.8	89	23.9	267	65.4	8	7	1.3	5	0	.0
12075	2.4	0	.8	79	25.7	346	81.5	7	12	.0	0	0	.0
12076	1.2	0	.4	89	22.8	256	53.2	6	14	.0	14	0	.0
12077	3.2	91	1.0	76	35.6	391	93.9	5	8	1.5	8	1	.0
12078	25.0	98	9.4	65	21.8	246	57.7	7	17	11.5	14	4	.2
12082	.5	0	.2	85	24.2	303	49.7	13	7	.0	0	0	.0
12083	2.3	100	.9	82	23.5	365	71.2	7	16	.9	14	1	.0
12084	2.8	96	1.2	30	31.9	452	97.5	4	14	1.2	12	2	.0
12085	.8	91	.3	30	21.1	403	65.0	7	22	.2	19	0	4.8
12086	1.9	100	.6	84	24.4	225	62.7	5	11	.9	11	0	.0
12087	.9	100	.3	82	23.9	267	64.1	7	12	.5	11	0	.0
12089	.2	0	.1	68	20.3	234*	52.0	5	22	.0	0	1	.0
12090	5.5	99	1.9	71	22.0	302	52.0	7	15	2.6	13	3	.4
12092	1.0	98	.3	84	27.9	384	66.0	6	9	.5	9	0	.2
12093	1.2	99	.4	81	17.9	196	55.0	5	17	.6	14	0	.0
12094	1.9	100	.6	83	21.6	357	58.2	8	12	.9	13	0	.6
12095	13.2	98	4.8	69	22.8	274	51.0	8	11	6.2	13	6	.6
12099	.2	96	.1	82	21.4	280	40.8	9	7	.1	9	0	.0

ALBANY

ZIPCODE	1	2	3	4	5	6	7	8	9	10	11	12	13
12106	2.4	99	.8	79	29.8	399	86.6	7	13	1.2	10	0	.0
12107	.2	0	.1	93	26.8	308*	77.6	23	2	.0	0	0	.0
12108	.5	100	.2	89	19.4	53	67.4	4	11	.2	7	0	.0
12110	17.2	97	5.8	71	33.8	463	83.7	6	9	8.1	7	0	.2
12114	.4	99	.2	75	26.9	366	67.3	5	12	.1	12	0	.0
12115	.2	0	.1	85	23.8	488	55.4	0	17	.0	0	0	.0
12116	1.6	100	.6	83	21.6	296	50.1	7	12	.8	10	0	.0
12117	3.2	99	1.1	86	22.8	274	51.0	8	11	1.6	11	0	.0
12118	9.5	100	3.4	60	25.2	291	68.1	8	13	4.5	11	3	.1
12120	.5	99	.2	84	23.5	284	73.0	7	14	.3	14	0	.0
12121	1.5	0	.4	91	26.8	312	81.5	7	6	.7	6	0	.0
12122	3.9	99	1.4	79	21.7	274	59.4	6	16	1.9	14	0	.0
12123	4.9	99	1.6	74	26.1	319	59.7	7	10	2.5	9	1	.0
12124	.6	97	.2	88	30.8	389	64.2	8	8	.3	7	0	.0
12125	.7	0	.2	63	25.5	300	71.2	8	9	.0	0	0	.0

NEW YORK — ALBANY

ZIPCODE	1	2	3	4	5	6	7	8	9	10	11	12	13
12126	.2	97	.1	65	21.3	337	56.4	3	15	.1	10	0	1.4
12130	1.5	0	.5	73	24.5	352	60.9	10	7	.0	0	0	.0
12131	.2	100	.1	80	19.9	371	51.8	4	15	.1	16	0	.0
12132	.4	100	.2	83	22.5	312	62.0	8	18	.2	16	0	.2
12133	.5	100	.1	87	23.2	497	47.4	6	4	.3	3	0	.0
12134	3.5	100	1.3	78	20.9	237	59.2	8	13	1.7	11	0	.0
12136	.8	100	.3	57	14.9	287	57.1	5	29	.4	27	0	.0
12137	1.5	0	.8	90	27.9	349	66.0	8	12	.4	12	0	.0
12138	2.4	99	.8	83	22.7	322	53.0	7	11	1.2	11	1	.0
12139	.2	100	.2	87	23.3	267*	98.2	1	16	.1	14	0	12.3
12140	.4	0	.2	66	24.5	238	51.7	9	9	.0	0	0	.0
12141	.3	100	.1	90	34.0	391*	76.8	8	0	.1	0	0	.0
12142	.3	0	.1	85	18.0	309	48.1	11	4	.0	0	0	.0
12143	5.0	100	1.7	66	27.7	359	75.1	6	10	2.4	10	4	.0
12144	18.4	98	6.6	66	24.9	324	60.5	6	12	8.6	10	4	12.3
12147	.5	94	.2	84	24.2	359	82.2	5	14	.3	14	0	.0
12148	2.3	96	.8	88	36.6	293	97.5	8	9	1.1	9	0	.0
12149	1.8	100	.6	82	20.3	246	56.4	7	12	.9	9	0	.0
12150	1.0	100	.3	76	31.6	232	74.9	10	5	.4	9	1	.1
12151	.9	98	.3	80	24.5	289	56.0	6	10	.4	11	0	.0
12153	.9	0	.3	84	28.2	371	65.1	12	8	.0	0	0	.0
12154	2.4	99	.7	79	27.6	240	58.6	9	9	1.2	10	0	.0
12155	1.5	99	.3	79	18.1	218	49.1	7	18	.7	18	0	.0
12156	.9	0	.3	87	27.8	336	56.9	6	12	.0	0	0	.0
12157	3.6	0	1.1	81	22.2	276	61.9	6	13	.0	0	0	.0
12158	5.0	98	1.7	79	28.3	381	74.7	7	9	2.4	9	1	17.0
12159	3.7	98	1.6	54	37.5	448	113.5	5	13	1.8	11	0	.0
12160	.8	99	.3	81	24.0	335	62.9	9	12	.4	12	0	.0
12161	.3	0	.1	63	34.5	418	63.0	9	13	.0	0	0	.0
12163	.2	100	.1	77	22.7	370	70.0	6	6	.1	0	0	.0
12164	.5	0	.2	78	21.7	236	72.1	9	20	.0	0	0	.5
12165	.4	0	.2	79	30.4	447	96.1	4	13	.0	0	0	.0
12166	1.2	99	.4	86	21.6	201	45.2	7	12	.6	11	0	.2
12167	2.4	98	.9	70	22.1	282	66.0	7	18	1.2	15	4	1.3
12168	1.3	99	.4	80	22.2	289	68.4	8	12	.7	11	0	.3
12169	.3	100	.1	86	20.5	62	52.8	5	18	.2	18	0	.0
12170	5.7	99	1.9	77	24.5	196	63.2	9	10	2.8	9	3	.4
12172	1.6	100	.6	66	19.1	329	49.9	8	14	.7	12	0	.4
12173	1.6	96	.5	75	24.8	344	71.0	10	7	.7	7	1	.1
12174	.6	100	.2	87	22.7	313	65.5	6	15	.3	8	0	.0
12175	.6	79	.2	80	18.2	289	51.7	5	13	.3	14	0	.5
12176	.3	100	.1	91	22.6	260*	67.9	15	7	.1	8	0	.7
12177	1.0	100	.4	87	27.9	296	61.4	10	14	.6	11	0	.2
12180	66.1	94	23.1	52	22.9	270	65.3*	6	14	30.1	11	4	.2
12181	.2	0		0	11.1	736	39.6*	7	14	.0		3	100++
12182	15.3	98	5.6	59	22.2	271	53.6	7	14	7.0	11	0	.7
12183	2.7	0	1.1	47	22.5	278	47.4	6	16	.0		2	7.6
12184	5.3	98	1.8	79	27.4	335	88.0	7	13	2.5	10	0	.0

*=Estimated **1.0=883 lbs per person; 100++ indicates per capita toxic waste generation > than 100 times the U.S. average of 883 lbs per capita.

ZIP CODE MEASURES OF SIZE, LEVELS OF AFFLUENCE AND QUALITY OF LIFE

1=Population (th.); 2= % White; 3=Households (th.); 4=% Owner Occupied; 5=Mean Income Per Household (th.$); 6=Mean Monthly Rent ($)*; 7=Mean Home Value (th.$)*; 8=% under 5; 9=% 65 and over; 10=% White Males (th.); 11=% White Males, 65+; 12=# Toxic Waste Sites; 13=Toxic Waste Relative to US(883 lbs.per capita)**.

NEW YORK

ALBANY

ZIPCODE	1	2	3	4	5	6	7	8	9	10	11	12	13
12185	1.8	0	.6	78	26.6	307	54.6	8	7	.0	0	0	.0
12186	5.7	0	1.8	80	33.5	392	92.0	7	7	.0	0	0	.3
12187	.7	0	.2	72	22.9	314	58.4	5	13	.0	0	0	.0
12188	8.7	99	3.1	66	26.4	282	68.7	6	11	4.2	9	6	11.2
12189	16.4	99	6.9	43	22.5	300	54.4	5	16	7.5	12	4	2.3
12190	.6	99	.2	84	17.9	224	56.6	6	18	.3	18	0	.0
12191	.5	0	.2	87	22.2	382	62.9	8	8	.0	0	0	.0
12192	2.7	77	.8	62	20.6	270	59.0	4	12	1.1	12	0	.0
12193	1.8	0	.6	85	23.4	415	65.9	7	11	.0	0	0	.0
12194	.2	100	.1	69	18.8	209	48.2	2	9	.1	6	0	.0
12195	.3	0	.1	74	21.4	281	59.5	6	21	.0	0	0	.0
12196	2.1	98	.7	82	28.1	322	77.9	6	13	.9	9	0	.0
12197	1.9	0	.7	79	18.8	236	54.7	6	17	.0	0	0	.0

ALBANY

ZIPCODE	1	2	3	4	5	6	7	8	9	10	11	12	13
12202	11.6	58	4.7	33	17.5	257	40.3	7	13	3.0	14	0	.1
12203	30.6	96	12.1	51	29.6	393	83.1	4	15	13.3	12	0	.0
12204	7.5	86	3.2	32	27.5	356	104.0	6	17	2.9	16	0	1.6
12205	27.9	96	10.1	74	28.0	421	70.0	6	12	13.1	10	6	.1
12206	17.4	78	7.4	36	18.0	293	52.1	7	19	6.0	17	0	.0
12207	2.3	54	1.4	2	9.0	162	13.1	3	33	.6	35	0	.1
12208	22.9	95	9.2	47	26.4	365	83.8	4	18	9.8	14	0	.0
12209	9.6	96	3.6	65	25.7	370	63.5	6	20	4.1	16	0	.0
12210	10.2	53	5.1	18	16.3	266	56.1	7	11	2.7	12	0	.0
12211	13.1	96	3.4	93	47.2	496	110.8	4	13	6.0	10	0	.0
12250	.3	100	.3	66	19.8	351	75.1	8	25	.1	22	0	.0

SCHENECTADY

ZIPCODE	1	2	3	4	5	6	7	8	9	10	11	12	13
12302	26.7	98	9.3	84	31.9	372	75.6	6	14	12.6	11	2	.0
12303	27.6	99	10.0	75	25.8	326	66.4	6	14	12.8	12	3	.1
12304	21.5	94	8.0	62	22.8	318	56.4	6	14	9.4	11	0	.0
12305	4.4	96	2.6	16	16.2	239	81.8	4	29	1.9	21	0	74.5
12306	25.0	98	9.1	77	25.8	348	65.9	6	14	12.0	12	1	.3
12307	8.7	73	3.7	29	15.5	252	30.1	8	13	3.0	13	0	.0
12308	15.9	96	6.0	49	23.7	317	67.0	6	16	7.0	11	0	.0
12309	24.1	96	8.8	80	37.9	408	96.2	6	13	11.0	11	4	.0

KINGSTON

ZIPCODE	1	2	3	4	5	6	7	8	9	10	11	12	13
12401	39.5	93	15.1	61	24.0	342	68.3	6	16	16.9	13	2	.4
12404	2.5	96	.9	78	20.2	304	61.8	7	13	1.3	12	0	.0
12405	.5	100	.2	73	17.5	291	60.3	8	20	.2	28	0	.0
12406	.5	97	.2	67	12.9	272	42.8	9	23	.2	25	0	.0
12407	.3	100	.1	90	20.0	229*	57.1	7	11	.1	1	0	.0
12409	.7	100	.3	77	36.7	432	98.6	4	18	.3	17	0	.0
12410	1.1	100	.4	88	21.8	250*	44.5	0	13	.1	14	0	.0
12411	.6	100	.2	94	22.5	307	61.6	10	10	.3	14	0	.0
12412	.5	0	.2	90	30.3	294	74.7	4	14	.0	0	0	.0
12413	2.2	0	.9	70	17.3	285	63.3	5	20	.0	0	0	.0
12414	10.4	94	3.8	66	23.4	300	66.9	6	18	4.5	14	2	.4
12415	.3	100	.1	85	18.2	758	38.6	8	20	.1	29	0	.1
12417	.3	0	.1	86	20.4	330	35.3	9	14	.0	0	0	.0
12418	.4	98	.1	81	22.6	315	80.7	5	14	.2	11	0	.0

*=Estimated **1.0=883 lbs per person; 100++ indicates per capita toxic waste generation > than 100 times the U.S. average of 883 lbs per capita.

NEW YORK

KINGSTON

ZIPCODE	1	2	3	4	5	6	7	8	9	10	11	12	13
12419	.5	100	.2	80	26.3	466	74.3	11	11	.3	17	0	.0
12420	.3	0	.1	83	20.6	825	77.4	3	25	.0	0	0	.0
12421	.3	100	.1	77	31.4	508	98.2	5	16	.1	15	0	.0
12422	.3	0	.1	85	21.7	398	61.0	5	14	.0	0	1	.0
12423	1.0	98	.3	81	19.5	296	70.2	6	19	.5	18	0	.2
12424	.2	0	.1	78	19.5	208	61.1	9	13	.0	0	0	.0
12427	.2	0	.1	71	21.6	17	72.3	1	23	.0	0	0	.0
12428	7.2	85	2.5	57	21.9	344	65.3	6	14	3.1	13	1	.5
12429	.5	100	.1	77	23.7	165	70.1	10	13	.3	12	0	.0
12430	.8	96	.3	80	17.5	265	56.3	4	20	.4	17	0	.0
12431	1.1	0	.4	74	20.6	275	72.3	7	17	.0	0	0	.0
12432	.7	100	.1	68	21.1	315	54.1	10	19	.3	16	0	.0
12433	.3	100	.1	72	21.0	471	78.0	4	23	.2	23	0	.0
12434	.7	100	.3	82	17.1	191	44.5	4	12	.4	9	0	.0
12435	.4	93	.1	69	20.0	329	67.7	4	9	.3	10	0	.0
12436	.3	0	.1	72	21.5	518	67.3	6	18	.0	0	0	.0
12437	.1	100	.1	79	15.3	471	50.7	4	30	.1	27	0	.0
12439	.5	0	.2	77	20.6	327	74.8	6	20	.0	0	0	.0
12440	1.8	0	.7	64	20.7	348	58.2	6	13	.4	9	0	.3
12442	.9	99	.4	64	17.9	270	86.9	5	21	.4	19	0	.0
12443	1.2	0	.4	84	36.9	395	73.0	5	13	.1	25	0	.0
12444	.2	98	.1	79	17.9	331	53.6	4	27	.1	25	0	.0
12445	.3	100	.1	84	18.1	275	66.7	3	17	.1	19	0	.0
12446	3.7	98	1.4	71	21.7	301	63.0	7	17	1.8	18	0	.0
12447	.2	100	.2	87	18.5	212*	71.2	4	60	.1	63	0	.0
12448	.3	100	.1	46	31.8	399	79.0	5	10	.2	8	0	.0
12449	2.4	97	.8	68	30.1	379	77.6	8	4	1.1	4	0	.0
12450	.2	100	.1	74	19.6	97	74.5	4	16	.1	13	0	.0
12451	1.2	100	.4	82	22.6	322	70.3	5	18	.6	16	0	.0
12452	.2	100	.2	77	19.6	285	49.7	4	26	.1	24	0	.0
12453	.5	100	.2	83	27.3	196	59.6	8	27	.2	29	0	.0
12454	.2	100	.1	76	25.9	224	68.4	4	18	.1	24	0	.0
12455	1.9	99	.8	72	23.4	302	64.5	5	19	.9	16	0	.0
12456	1.4	98	.4	87	24.8	307	53.7	9	8	.7	9	3	.3
12457	.7	0	.3	82	24.8	255	80.4	10	11	.6	14	0	.0
12458	2.9	74	.7	71	23.3	294	64.5	6	8	1.1	9	0	.0
12459	.2	100	.1	84	23.1	265*	68.0	3	9	.1	17	0	.0
12460	.4	100	.1	77	21.4	359	67.0	9	24	.2	21	0	.0
12461	.8	0	.3	82	25.3	301	65.9	5	14	.6	16	0	.0
12462	.3	100	.1	74	27.3	314*	66.2	7	18	.1	24	0	.0
12463	.9	100	.3	72	22.6	227	76.0	6	16	.5	16	0	.0
12464	1.1	0	.4	73	18.5	231	66.4	5	22	.0	0	0	.0
12465	.3	99	.1	72	15.4	140	52.0	2	23	.2	22	0	.0
12466	2.4	0	.9	69	26.6	376	69.9	7	11	.0	0	0	.0
12468	1.1	100	.3	80	20.1	293	65.0	7	17	.6	14	0	.0
12469	.7	98	.3	87	18.5	265	55.8	8	20	.4	21	0	.0
12470	.5	100	.2	76	15.9	366	70.7	6	10	.3	10	0	.0
12471	.8	0	.2	77	27.9	425	61.8	10	7	.0	0	0	.0
12472	1.5	98	.6	64	22.2	347	55.7	6	13	.7	11	0	.0

ZIP CODE MEASURES OF SIZE, LEVELS OF AFFLUENCE AND QUALITY OF LIFE

1=Population (th.); 2= % White; 3=Households (th.); 4=% Owner Occupied; 5=Mean Income Per Household (th.$); 6=Mean Monthly Rent ($)*; 7=Mean Home Value (th.$)*; 8=% under 5; 9=% 65 and over; 10=White Males (th.); 11=% White Males, 65+; 12=# Toxic Waste Sites; 13=Toxic Waste Relative to US(883 lbs.per capita)**.

NEW YORK

KINGSTON

ZIP CODE	1	2	3	4	5	6	7	8	9	10	11	12	13
12473	.4	100	.1	93	15.3	281	96.0	6	14	.2	14	0	.0
12474	1.1	99	.4	74	19.8	267	54.5	7	19	.6	18	0	.0
12475	.4	100	.1	84	25.8	497	68.9	14	1	.2	0	0	.0
12476	.1	100	.1	88	25.2	290*	86.1	12	24	.0	13	3	.1
12477	15.8	99	5.6	74	25.6	307	68.1	6	13	7.6	11	3	.0
12479	.3	93	.1	89	26.7	307*	63.5	3	18	.1	18	0	.0
12480	.6	0	.2	72	18.3	209	59.4	14	11	.7	12	1	.0
12481	1.5	97	.5	83	27.1	401	85.8	6	14	.7	0	1	.0
12482	.7	0	.3	71	19.4	323	63.1	9	17	0	15	0	2.4
12483	.4	82	.1	78	21.3	246	83.8	9	12	.2	8	0	.0
12484	2.6	98	.9	83	31.1	422	74.4	4	11	1	2	0	.1
12485	.8	100	.4	67	17.2	202	75.3	5	18	.4	15	0	.0
12486	1.5	97	.5	86	26.9	326	65.1	5	14	.8	13	0	.1
12487	1.9	0	.7	86	27.1	368	66.4	5	15	.0	0	0	.0
12489	.6	97	.2	74	24.7	300	61.5	2	11	.3	12	0	.0
12490	.3	100	.1	87	21.5	219	61.6	6	20	.2	16	0	.0
12491	2.7	97	.9	87	32.6	502	88.4	4	8	1.3	6	0	.3
12492	.3	0	.1	77	23.0	251	58.5	6	25	.0	0	0	.0
12493	.5	84	.1	57	22.8	411	77.1	0	6	.0	2	5	.0
12494	.7	0	.3	82	22.3	312	68.3	3	8	.0	0	0	.0
12495	.4	100	.1	80	30.8	238	93.3	8	29	.0	28	0	.0
12496	1.4	100	.5	74	23.0	296	82.3	5	19	.7	17	0	.0
12498	5.0	96	2.0	70	33.0	437	98.1	6	10	2.3	10	0	2.7

POUGHKEEPSIE

ZIP CODE	1	2	3	4	5	6	7	8	9	10	11	12	13
12501	2.9	98	1.0	59	31.9	388	80.6	7	9	1.4	8	1	.0
12502	.9	0	.3	81	20.6	382	72.1	5	21	.0	0	0	1.0
12503	.4	96	.2	75	22.4	417	81.1	8	14	.0	0	0	.0
12504	.6	84	.1	14	21.4	414	76.4*	0	3	.2	3	0	.0
12507	.4	91	.1	47	24.4	245	107.6	4	6	.2	6	0	.0
12508	18.4	81	6.3	54	25.7	369	68.8	7	13	7.3	12	6	.4
12510	.2	0	.1	89	23.8	273*	88.8	4	17	.0	1	0	.0
12511	.4	88	.1	41	19.0	226	46.1	0	40	.3	46	0	1.1
12512	.4	92	.1	96	32.6	375*	84.1	2	5	.2	2	0	.0
12513	1.4	95	.5	79	29.0	330	82.4	4	16	.7	15	0	.1
12514	2.2	99	.7	87	36.9	438	96.6	8	11	1.1	9	2	.6
12515	1.3	96	.5	67	25.3	404	65.2	6	12	.6	11	0	.0
12516	1.4	0	.4	75	23.2	472	87.7	3	15	.0	0	0	.0
12517	.4	100	.1	66	17.6	365	66.5	5	12	.2	11	0	.0
12518	4.6	98	1.6	64	28.4	414	86.9	7	12	2.1	11	1	.2
12520	3.4	99	1.3	65	30.4	406	91.8	6	10	1.6	10	0	.6
12521	1.5	98	.6	77	20.8	355	74.4	6	18	.7	19	0	.0
12522	4.8	96	1.7	74	25.9	372	80.9	8	16	2.2	15	5	.0
12523	1.6	98	.6	76	22.6	329	76.5	6	17	.8	16	0	.1
12524	9.6	94	3.3	71	33.1	454	96.2	6	10	4.3	8	2	1.6
12525	2.7	99	.9	72	25.5	390	74.5	7	13	1.3	11	0	.3
12526	3.2	98	1.2	74	22.2	272	75.0	4	19	1.4	19	0	.0
12527	.2	85	.1	86	28.5	434	70.2	13	4	.7	5	1	.0
12528	9.6	97	3.3	66	25.9	394	76.6	6	12	4.5	10	0	.0
12529	2.3	99	.8	77	24.0	294	78.1	6	18	1.1	18	0	.0

NEW YORK

POUGHKEEPSIE

ZIP CODE	1	2	3	4	5	6	7	8	9	10	11	12	13
12531	2.3	99	.7	79	28.7	449	98.0	8	16	1.1	10	0	.0
12533	14.5	97	4.4	87	34.6	509	109.3	7	7	7.0	6	3	.0
12534	16.2	90	6.3	56	21.0	253	65.2	6	18	7.0	17	1	.9
12537	.4	0	.1	51	33.7	498	92.0	8	10	.0	0	0	.0
12538	14.3	96	4.5	72	31.6	404	88.9	6	7	7.1	6	3	.0
12540	3.9	98	1.2	85	32.0	434	116.6	7	8	1.9	8	1	.0
12541	.8	95	2	68	23.8	294	70.2	5	30	.3	15	0	.0
12542	4.7	96	1.6	66	25.7	338	85.0	6	11	2.2	11	0	.0
12543	2.0	98	.7	62	24.8	340	59.6	10	9	1.0	8	0	.0
12544	.4	100	.1	96	25.9	298*	60.2	4	15	.2	17	0	.0
12545	4.4	89	1.4	64	34.4	416	100.9	5	14	1.9	11	0	.3
12546	3.0	96	1.0	70	24.7	393	73.1	8	16	1.4	14	3	.3
12547	2.0	98	.7	75	24.8	409	78.3	6	11	1.0	10	0	.0
12548	.9	79	.3	62	18.5	387	72.5	11	10	.4	8	0	.0
12549	5.7	99	1.8	78	28.8	413	74.2	8	11	2.9	9	0	.0
12550	63.3	82	21.7	59	25.1	338	70.9	8	11	24.8	11	11	.2
12560	.3	100	.1	96	25.2	289*	76.9	0	25	.2	23	0	1.8
12561	12.2	91	3.9	61	24.5	407	84.2	5	8	5.4	8	0	.0
12563	4.6	99	1.5	82	30.5	391	95.2	7	11	2.3	10	3	.0
12564	4.8	97	1.7	68	34.7	380	113.3	8	15	2.3	12	3	.0
12565	1.8	99	.6	65	21.2	251	58.3	5	19	.9	16	0	.0
12566	5.8	100	2.0	78	24.9	400	70.5	6	12	2.9	11	0	.0
12567	2.6	97	.9	75	24.2	320	77.0	6	17	1.2	14	0	.2
12568	1.0	91	.3	72	20.8	340	69.8	6	10	.4	12	1	.0
12569	7.2	99	2.6	77	31.2	415	93.9	6	10	3.5	10	3	.0
12570	2.9	99	.9	81	31.9	340	117.5	7	15	1.5	10	2	.0
12571	6.6	99	2.2	78	26.9	400	82.5	6	14	3.1	12	5	.0
12572	8.5	99	2.8	73	29.3	411	91.5	4	19	3.9	14	0	.1
12574	.5	88	.2	69	23.9	322	72.8	6	16	.2	14	0	.0
12575	1.2	96	.4	75	27.0	454	80.1	8	13	.5	11	0	.0
12577	1.3	98	.4	86	33.8	348	98.8	7	9	.7	8	0	.0
12578	1.8	0	.4	78	32.4	421	103.2	7	10	.3	7	1	.1
12580	3.7	98	1.1	81	31.4	464	86.2	6	16	1.7	13	0	.2
12581	2.4	99	.8	73	29.2	397	93.2	5	14	1.3	15	0	.0
12582	4.6	66	.8	86	34.1	570	110.6	6	5	1.7	7	0	.0
12583	1.6	99	.5	67	21.2	335	68.0	10	14	.8	15	0	.0
12584	.5	86	.2	78	26.5	353	73.9	6	12	.2	13	100++	.0
12585	.6	0	.2	69	29.7	517	84.8	3	11	.0	0	0	.0
12586	9.7	100	3.4	71	24.2	335	65.6	8	11	4.6	10	0	.2
12588	.2	100	.2	83	27.2	253	65.6	8	5	.3	4	0	.0
12589	8.6	93	2.4	79	27.3	363	75.5	7	10	4.1	9	2	.0
12590	31.2	93	10.2	66	34.0	440	95.7	7	13	14.4	5	2	.1
12592	2.5	83	.2	54	25.5	310	80.9	2	14	1.1	12	0	.0
12594	3.6	86	1.0	68	25.0	314	93.3	6	12	1.5	10	1	.3

POUGHKEEPSIE

ZIP CODE	1	2	3	4	5	6	7	8	9	10	11	12	13
12601	42.3	78	15.1	42	24.2	347	78.5	6	14	15.5	13	4	.3
12603	36.5	95	12.6	76	35.7	431	96.2	6	10	17.0	9	5	.2

MONTICELLO

ZIP CODE	1	2	3	4	5	6	7	8	9	10	11	12	13
12701	11.4	80	4.4	52	21.3	294	75.1	7	14	4.4	15	1	.1

*=Estimated **1.0=883 lbs per person; 100++ indicates per capita.toxic waste generation > than 100 times the U.S. average of 883 lbs per capita.

ZIP CODE MEASURES OF SIZE, LEVELS OF AFFLUENCE AND QUALITY OF LIFE

1=Population (th.); 2= % White; 3=Households (th.); 4=% Owner Occupied; 5=Mean Income Per Household (th.$); 6=Mean Monthly Rent ($)*; 7=Mean Home Value (th.$)*; 8=% under 5; 9=% 65 and over; 10=White Males, 65+; 11=% White Males; 12=# Toxic Waste Sites; 13=Toxic Waste Relative to US(883 lbs.per capita)**.

NEW YORK

MONTICELLO

ZIPCODE	1	2	3	4	5	6	7	8	9	10	11	12	13
12719	.7	0	.3	88	17.8	240	69.1	2	35	.0	0	0	.0
12720	.4	0	.3	69	19.3	310	64.9	5	15	.8	15	0	.0
12721	3.7	96	1.3	77	22.6	313	70.7	5	13	1.7	14	1	.0
12722	.2	0	.1	73	22.2	444	75.9	22	6			0	.0
12723	2.0	82	.6	75	20.5	302	63.9	6	14	.8	15	0	.0
12724	.3	100	.1	80	19.3	177	59.4	3	28	.2	26	0	.0
12725	.2	100	.1	64	17.6	334	60.6	14	14	.1	7	0	.0
12726	.9	98	.3	88	21.7	291	57.4	7	14	.4	13	0	.0
12727	.1	100	.1	90	16.0	184*	60.7	8	33	.1	31	0	.0
12729	1.1	96	.4	80	20.5	322	65.3	8	10	.5	10	0	.0
12732	.7	0	.3	73	21.4	325	81.4	6	16	.3	5	0	.0
12733	.6	92	.1	36	17.9	345	54.5	12	2	.3	2	0	.0
12734	1.3	88	.4	70	23.4	388	60.4	6	11	.5	11	0	.0
12737	.7	98	.1	84	19.7	332	78.6	4	27	.4	27	0	.0
12738	.2	100	.1	40	25.5	458	70.6	4	14	.1	14	0	.0
12739	.3	90	.1	79	23.4	291	46.9	7	19	.1	16	0	.0
12740	1.7	95	.6	82	22.3	371	85.6	7	12	.7	13	0	.0
12741	.3	0	.1	64	19.7	301	67.3	10	12	.0	0	0	.0
12742	.3	100	.1	71	23.4	291	79.8	4	0	.1	0	0	1.5
12743	.2	100	.1	68	22.2	352	127.1	4	19	.1	16	0	.0
12745	.2	100	.1	69	24.5	298	54.8	3	25	.1	20	0	.0
12746	.7	0	.3	75	16.9	386	78.3	3	21	.0	0	1	10.7
12747	1.2	0	.5	79	16.1	235	62.5	6	13	.0	0	0	.0
12748	1.7	99	.7	74	21.8	286	73.1	4	19	.4	14	0	.0
12749	.3	100	.1	96	20.6	237*	67.4	0	15	.1	9	0	.0
12750	1.5	100	.6	77	21.1	273	67.6	4	25	.5	26	0	.0
12751	1.1	80	.3	43	28.3	338	71.6	2	9	.2	5	0	.0
12752	.3	100	.1	87	23.7	345	71.0	5	29	.5	9	0	.0
12753	.2	100	.1	78	15.4	180	59.1	1	24	.1	28	0	.0
12754	6.5	91	2.5	57	20.0	308	68.5	6	20	2.9	18	0	.0
12758	3.9	99	1.3	68	18.7	322	57.8	7	14	2.0	13	0	.0
12759	.9	95	.2	65	16.2	105	75.7	9	6	.4	7	0	.0
12760	.9	99	.2	77	15.2	271	43.7	2	26	.3	22	0	.0
12762	.5	100	.2	78	24.8	374	72.4	9	9	.3	10	0	.0
12763	1.0	88	.3	70	21.8	283	60.5	6	13	.5	17	0	.0
12764	1.5	95	.6	81	21.7	299	71.9	5	27	.7	24	0	.0
12765	.6	100	.2	88	22.6	274	91.0	7	8	.3	0	0	.0
12766	.5	100	.3	74	20.3	230	49.2	5	18	.2	13	0	.0
12768	1.0	88	.3	83	19.3	361	64.2	2	9	.5	9	0	.0
12769	.2	84	.1	60	16.2	151	52.4	0	23	.1	31	0	.0
12770	.3	0	.1	79	19.7	309	61.1	9	16	.0	0	0	.0
12771	11.6	96	4.5	62	21.3	315	61.4	7	14	5.2	11	3	1.6
12775	1.0	97	.4	85	29.2	266	90.0	7	20	.5	19	0	.0
12776	2.0	0	.7	80	23.3	262	69.1	7	23	.3	0	0	.0
12778	.4	100	.2	86	14.6	318	56.7	4	41	.2	45	0	.0
12779	2.6	80	.8	43	21.6	289	82.0	6	9	.1	10	0	.0
12780	1.8	99	.7	84	22.9	354	72.1	7	14	.9	15	0	.0
12781	.3	88	.1	93	16.2	186*	55.5	0	16	.7	16	0	.0
12782	.3	0	.1	82	18.7	293	40.8	6	17	.0	0	0	.0

NEW YORK

MONTICELLO

ZIPCODE	1	2	3	4	5	6	7	8	9	10	11	12	13
12783	1.4	91	.5	65	19.3	237	80.6	6	11	.7	10	0	.0
12785	.7	100	.2	90	20.6	304	65.9	9	6	.4	4	0	.0
12786	.5	100	.2	92	19.2	175	60.1	5	25	.2	21	0	47.4
12787	.9	100	.3	79	24.0	249	60.4	6	8	.5	6	0	.0
12788	2.4	72	.6	84	23.8	294	66.9	5	11	.9	13	0	.0
12789	1.3	83	.5	59	27.4	245	78.7	7	17	.5	20	1	.0
12790	3.0	96	1.1	80	22.2	401	67.1	7	14	1.5	12	1	.0
12791	.7	100	.2	83	23.4	316	60.2	4	13	.3	9	0	.0
12792	.4	100	.1	92	22.3	621	73.2	2	15	.1	18	0	.0

GLENS FALLS

ZIPCODE	1	2	3	4	5	6	7	8	9	10	11	12	13
12801	40.9	99	14.6	65	24.6	319	71.5	7	13	18.9	10	15	4.6
12808	.7	100	.1	89	16.2	186*	75.3	7	24	.1	30	0	.0
12809	2.4	0	.8	82	22.3	262	56.8	6	15	.0	0	2	1.9
12810	.4	0	.1	76	18.6	310	42.5	7	11	.1	0	0	.0
12811	.3	100	.1	90	19.7	226*	50.1	8	12	.1	10	0	.0
12812	.4	100	.1	73	22.6	283	65.4	3	15	.1	14	0	.0
12814	1.4	0	.5	74	21.9	282	78.3	6	13	.0	0	0	.0
12815	.3	0	.1	82	17.8	246	58.2	9	13	.0	0	0	.0
12816	3.8	99	1.4	76	20.5	311	56.1	7	18	1.8	15	0	.0
12817	1.7	98	.6	74	17.1	280	73.4	8	16	.8	12	0	.0
12819	.2	100	.1	74	21.2	389	50.4	7	14	.1	16	0	.0
12820	.4	0	.1	60	44.1	393	227.0	3	14	.1	17	0	.0
12821	1.7	34	.1	81	25.0	124	61.3	1	0	.5	0	0	.0
12822	5.3	100	1.9	75	23.2	274	54.1	7	12	2.6	10	1	1.1
12823	.1	100	.1	80	16.4	110	45.4	3	14	.1	8	0	.0
12824	.6	100	.2	90	29.6	185	104.7	7	10	.3	7	0	.0
12826	.2	100	.1	91	21.5	248*	32.1	0	27	.1	30	0	.0
12827	3.2	99	1.0	78	23.0	321	61.1	6	9	1.5	8	0	.0
12828	8.2	99	2.6	79	23.1	308	57.1	7	12	3.8	9	0	.5
12831	6.4	98	2.1	82	25.2	368	72.6	9	14	3.2	9	8	.0
12832	5.3	99	1.7	74	21.8	294	55.5	7	15	2.5	13	2	.0
12833	3.1	97	.9	84	22.9	328	80.9	8	8	1.6	8	0	2.0
12834	5.5	0	1.9	75	22.0	293	61.0	7	14	.0	0	1	.0
12835	1.9	99	.7	86	19.4	270	56.1	8	13	.9	13	0	.5
12836	.7	0	.2	77	18.7	246	65.5	6	14	.1	8	0	.0
12837	.4	100	.1	78	22.9	233	61.9	8	9	.3	7	0	.0
12838	.5	0	.2	86	22.4	306	56.4	8	8	.2	8	0	.0
12839	12.5	100	4.3	70	22.4	288	55.2	8	11	6.0	9	3	.9
12842	1.1	100	.4	80	17.3	232	59.4	7	18	1.5	17	0	.0
12843	.5	98	.1	89	19.6	150	56.1	8	8	.8	10	0	.5
12844	.1	100	.1	93	55.1	633*	136.7	0	21	.1	21	0	.0
12845	4.4	97	1.6	69	25.2	327	101.2	6	12	2.2	11	0	2.0
12846	2.6	100	.9	79	20.1	314	62.2	6	12	1.3	11	0	.0
12847	.7	0	.3	79	21.0	285	73.3	6	16	.0	0	0	.0
12848	.2	100	.1	81	21.4	347	55.6	4	17	.1	13	0	.0
12849	.3	100	.1	70	25.1	376	56.0	6	7	.2	4	0	.0
12850	1.5	0	.5	87	20.4	283	67.0	7	9	.3	0	0	.0
12851	.5	100	.2	81	20.9	303	65.8	5	19	.3	13	0	.0
12852	.7	0	.2	86	25.5	290	51.1	6	11	.0	0	0	.0

*=Estimated **1.0=883 lbs per person; 100++ indicates per capita toxic waste generation > than 100 times the U.S. average of 883 lbs per capita.

103001

ZIP CODE MEASURES OF SIZE, LEVELS OF AFFLUENCE AND QUALITY OF LIFE

1=Population (th.); 2= % White; 3=Households (th.); 4=% Owner Occupied; 5=Mean Income Per Household (th.$); 6=Mean Monthly Rent ($)*; 7=Mean Home Value (th.$)*; 8=% under 5; 9=% 65 and over; 10=White Males, 65+; 11=% White Males; 12=# Toxic Waste Sites, 13=Toxic Waste Relative to US(883 lbs.per capita)**

NEW YORK

GLENS FALLS

ZIP CODE	1	2	3	4	5	6	7	8	9	10	11	12	13
12853	1.4	100	.5	75	20.5	243	53.6	5	18	.6	15		.1
12854	.5	100	.2	84	27.7	510	72.5	6	9	.2	4		.0
12855	.1	100	.1	88	14.2	163*	56.8	6	20	.1	13		.0
12857	.4	100	.2	80	15.6	251	43.2	12	11	.2	9		.0
12859	.9	100	.3	90	23.9	283	54.4	12	11	.5	7		.0
12860	.9	0	.2	73	19.2	266	50.6	2	8	.0	0		.0
12861	.5	100	.2	81	19.1	322	46.3	6	16	.3	13		.0
12863	.5	0	.2	64	25.5	356	52.5	9	6	.0	0		.0
12865	2.6	0	.9	82	21.5	293	51.6	7	14	.0	0		.2
12866	30.3	96	10.6	61	23.7	314	78.0	7	11	13.5	9	3	.1
12870	1.4	0	.5	77	19.6	252	65.4	5	16	.0	0		.0
12871	3.3	100	1.1	77	22.0	252	55.0	7	13	1.6	10		.0
12873	.6	0	.2	87	23.3	216	61.5	7	19	.0	0		.0
12878	.6	100	.2	89	19.2	215	47.2	6	17	.3	16		.0
12883	5.4	0	1.9	74	22.8	288	57.7	7	14	.0	3		1.4
12884	.6	100	.2	65	18.7	315	44.6	7	10	.3	7		.0
12885	4.3	100	1.5	77	20.1	297	60.0	8	13	2.0	11		.0
12886	.2	0	.1	83	22.0	273	63.2	11	20	.0	0		1.9
12887	5.0		1.8	71	21.0	292	47.1	7	14	.0	0		.0

PLATTSBURGH

ZIP CODE	1	2	3	4	5	6	7	8	9	10	11	12	13
12901	31.5	98	10.4	56	22.7	310	80.6	6	11	14.3	8		.1
12903	7.6	85	1.7	3	18.8	334	54.9	13	9	3.9	0		.0
12910	1.5	99	.5	83	19.7	297	44.0	8	9	.7	5		.0
12912	2.3	0	.8	72	19.5	271	53.0	6	15	.0	0		.0
12913	.8	99	.3	76	19.0	321	61.6	10	11	.4	9		.0
12914	1.4	72	.4	89	22.3	338	43.2	11	11	.5	8		.0
12915	1.4	100	.1	80	18.5	127	34.7	4	12	.0	11		.0
12916	1.8	0	.6	78	19.7	273	48.8	8	13	.9	12		.0
12917	1.3	0	.4	78	21.4	258	48.0	7	9	.0	0		.0
12918	2.1	0	.7	76	22.5	363	63.2	8	8	.0	11		.0
12919	2.8	100	1.0	73	23.3	284	58.9	7	10	1.5	8		1.3
12920	2.3	100	.8	78	19.0	269	42.4	6	14	1.1	13		.0
12921	2.2	100	.7	77	22.5	319	77.3	8	6	1.1	5		1.9
12923	.6	0	.2	84	19.5	203	47.3	5	12	.0	0		.0
12926	1.9	98	.6	87	21.5	265	51.1	7	9	.9	8		.0
12927	.2	0	.1	86	23.3	154	60.3	5	13	.0	0		.0
12928	1.8	100	.6	76	21.0	267	56.8	8	13	.9	12		.0
12929	4.0	62	.5	69	25.1	327	46.4	4	5	1.6	4		.0
12930	.6	100	.2	76	32.7	204	40.5	8	12	.3	11		.0
12932	2.1	0	.4	70	21.2	275	58.5	7	24	.0	0		.0
12934	.9	0	.3	85	19.1	234	39.5	9	11	.3	0		.0
12935	1.5	99	.5	82	19.0	203	41.0	9	10	.8	8		.0
12936	.5	0	.2	77	24.4	251	67.6	7	13	.0	0		.0
12937	1.7	93	.5	82	22.5	273	48.8	8	7	.8	7		.0
12938	.2	100	.1	83	22.4	408	36.0	10	9	.1	9		.0
12939	.3	100	.1	63	19.1	355	46.3	6	12	.1	10		.0
12940	.2	100	.1	74	16.3	261	35.4	7	10	.1	13		.0
12941	.9	0	.3	81	22.9	298	77.1	7	14	.0	0		.0
12942	.5	99	.2	80	24.6	226	78.8	6	20	.3	21		.0

NEW YORK

PLATTSBURGH (continued)

ZIP CODE	1	2	3	4	5	6	7	8	9	10	11	12	13
12943	.4	100	.2	83	23.4	291	71.9	5	24	.2	19	0	.0
12944	3.9	100	1.3	76	22.4	262	61.5	7	11	1.9	10	0	.0
12945	.4	0	.1	74	23.6	215	77.9	9	16	.7	14	0	.0
12946	4.7	99	1.8	61	23.8	243	85.2	5	15	2.2	12	0	.0
12949	.3	0	.1	78	32.1	321	45.4	9	8	.3	0	0	.0
12950	.7	100	.2	88	19.7	303	59.3	7	9	.3	9	0	.0
12952	.8	100	.2	93	19.3	437	28.4	4	8	.4	7	0	.0
12953	12.2	99	4.3	64	20.9	260	58.5	7	15	5.7	12	0	.0
12955	.4	0	.1	94	18.4	211*	38.8	3	13	.0	0	0	.0
12956	1.2	0	.4	80	21.3	267	37.7	7	8	.8	11	0	.0
12957	1.6	100	.5	82	18.9	273	47.5	8	9	.8	11	0	.0
12958	1.5	100	.5	82	25.5	239	53.9	5	13	.7	14	0	.0
12959	1.2	100	.3	72	17.5	245	84.4	12	9	.6	10	0	.0
12960	1.0	100	.3	78	19.1	343	41.8	4	14	.6	8	0	.0
12961	.3	100	.1	84	19.2	319	44.7	11	11	.1	10	0	.0
12962	4.6	0	1.4	84	25.8	388	68.0	9	5	.0	0	0	.0
12964	.2	100	.1	84	23.8	274*	57.0	4	20	.1	21	0	.0
12965	.3	100	.1	78	20.4	241	48.9	6	13	.1	9	0	.0
12966	2.4	98	.7	82	20.8	262	48.9	10	8	1.2	8	0	.0
12967	.9	99	.3	79	23.2	243	40.0	6	10	.5	9	0	.0
12968	.1	86	.1	70	15.9	260	50.8	3	9	.1	6	0	.0
12969	.3	0	.1	87	13.3	178	52.3	12	17	.0	0	0	.0
12970	1.2	99	.2	57	38.9	215	67.2	2	4	.8	2	0	.0
12972	5.0	99	1.6	81	24.3	365	77.6	8	8	2.4	7	0	.0
12973	.2	0	.1	82	20.5	355	32.2	2	12	.0	0	0	.0
12974	1.9	100	.7	78	21.1	253	48.0	6	15	.9	14	0	.0
12975	.1	100	.1	67	28.5	351	55.8	5	10	.3	0	0	.0
12976	.1	100	.1	71	27.4	318	89.3	7	11	.1	11	0	.0
12977	.5	76	.1	62	21.7	145	64.2	0	6	.1	0	0	.1
12978	1.0	100	.4	84	14.9	224	43.3	17	8	.3	4	0	.0
12979	2.8	99	1.0	68	24.8	292	71.5	7	13	1.3	10	0	24.6
12980	1.4	99	.5	85	18.9	204	34.1	8	13	.7	11	0	.0
12981	1.9	100	.6	87	21.9	335	51.1	5	9	1.0	6	0	.0
12983	7.7	99	3.1	57	20.5	255	63.8	6	16	3.5	13	0	.0
12985	.9	100	.3	75	17.2	321	43.5	7	13	.4	11	0	.1
12986	6.4	99	2.2	71	21.0	222	54.8	6	13	3	11	0	.0
12987	.3	100	.1	83	18.3	343	62.8	7	18	.1	17	0	.0
12990	.1	100	.1	71	18.5	308	44.5	8	22	.1	25	0	.0
12992	3.6	100	1.1	77	20.6	296	56.1	8	8	.3	0	0	.0
12993	1.6	77	.6	77	21.7	343	58.5	6	16	1.3	10	0	.0
12994	.3	0	.1	85	17.9	289	42.2	6	20	.7	11	0	.0
12996	1.8	0	.6	81	22.7	303	61.4	6	15	1.0	6	0	.0
12997	1.0	0	.4	78	21.5	281	74.0	7	13	.3	0	0	.0
12998	1.7	100	.2	70	17.9	259	35.8	13	15	.3	0	0	.2

SYRACUSE

ZIP CODE	1	2	3	4	5	6	7	8	9	10	11	12	13
13020	.2	100	.1	77	23.6	418	75.6	6	17	.1	13	0	.0
13021	44.0	95	15.6	63	23.5	297	62.0	6	15	19.9	13	3	.8
13026	.5	96	.5	71	23.8	300	65.8	5	9	.6	12	0	.0
13027	20.9	98	7.0	74	29.2	350	75.4	8	9	8.9	7	2	.2

*=Estimated **1.0=883 lbs per person; 100++ indicates per capita toxic waste generation > than 100 times the U.S. average of 883 lbs per capita.

ZIP CODE MEASURES OF SIZE, LEVELS OF AFFLUENCE AND QUALITY OF LIFE

1=Population (th.); 2= % White; 3=Households (th.); 4=% Owner Occupied; 5=Mean Income Per Household (th.$); 6=Mean Monthly Rent ($); 7=Mean Home Value (th.$);
8=% under 5; 9=% 65 and over; 10=% White Males (th.); 11=% White Males, 65+; 12=# Toxic Waste Sites, 13=Toxic Waste Relative to US(883 lbs.per capita)**.

NEW YORK
SYRACUSE

ZIP CODE	1	2	3	4	5	6	7	8	9	10	11	12	13
13028	1.0	0	.4	81	21.5	286	67.1	6	12	.0	0	0	.0
13029	4.6	98	1.5	83	28.4	340	69.7	9	9	2.2	8	0	.0
13030	4.4	0	1.4	90	26.6	320	59.3	8	6	.9	6	0	.0
13031	15.2	99	5.0	78	34.9	443	85.4	5	7	7.3	6	0	.1
13032	11.5	98	3.8	75	24.4	307	55.4	8	10	5.6	8	2	.0
13033	3.0	98	.9	82	24.9	293	57.9	9	9	1.5	9	0	.0
13034	7.2	99	.6	86	36.1	316	59.3	7	11	1.0	11	1	.0
13035	7.2	99	2.2	77	36.1	323	109.6	6	9	3.3	8	0	.0
13036	6.7	100	2.2	78	25.1	343	68.7	6	10	3.3	10	0	.0
13037	7.8	99	2.6	81	25.4	327	62.9	9	8	3.8	9	0	.1
13039	.4	0	.1	66	22.8	355	55.7	3	4	.0	0	0	.0
13040	1.8	100	.6	76	18.9	292	48.3	8	15	.9	12	0	.0
13041	16.5	98	5.1	84	31.8	426	76.2	10	4	8.2	4	0	.0
13042	2.0	0	6	81	22.4	365	46.9	8	10	.0	0	0	.0
13044	2.2	0	.7	84	26.1	336	70.3	8	7	1.8	8	1	.0
13045	29.6	99	10.0	57	21.9	301	71.3	6	12	13.5	10	3	1.8
13050	.6	0	.2	81	23.8	202	47.9	10	11	.0	0	0	.0
13051	1.9	100	.6	89	21.0	213	45.1	5	6	.2	3	0	.0
13052	1.9	100	.6	79	21.2	268	52.1	9	8	.9	7	0	.0
13053	3.6	99	1.3	71	24.0	322	80.0	9	10	1.7	8	0	.0
13054	1.9	100	.5	82	22.5	335	56.9	11	6	.0	0	0	.0
13055	.7	100	.2	85	18.0	335	45.5	10	7	.4	8	1	.0
13056	.2	100	.1	84	27.1	357	47.2	3	10	.1	9	0	.0
13057	15.7	99	5.4	76	28.3	353	65.8	6	10	7.6	8	0	3.4
13060	2.8	100	1.0	78	26.7	398	78.4	6	8	1.4	7	0	.2
13061	.8	98	.3	79	22.9	289	54.8	8	11	.4	9	0	.0
13062	.3	100	.1	88	25.7	245	75.5	3	21	.2	10	0	.0
13063	1.3	0	.4	75	27.5	375	70.1	7	7	.2	10	1	.4
13064	.8	100	.3	82	23.4	304	65.6	4	15	.4	15	0	.0
13065	6.0	99	2.3	78	24.1	362	68.5	7	9	3.0	9	0	.4
13066	12.1	99	4.4	79	47.5	476	121.2	5	11	5.7	9	0	.1
13068	4.3	99	1.4	72	23.0	333	74.7	8	6	2.1	6	0	.0
13069	24.9	99	8.8	88	23.3	308	63.5	8	11	11.8	10	0	.0
13071	1.1	99	.4	79	19.1	228	49.5	8	10	.5	8	0	.0
13072	.8	89	.2	90	21.0	225	36.7	6	10	.4	9	0	.0
13073	5.8	100	2.0	75	23.2	280	58.3	8	13	2.8	10	2	.0
13074	4.0	100	1.3	83	21.6	307	56.8	8	9	2.0	8	0	.0
13076	1.7	0	.5	87	25.3	419	55.9	9	10	.0	0	0	.0
13077	6.8	99	2.3	78	24.1	291	68.5	6	9	3.3	10	0	.0
13078	6.0	99	1.8	86	27.4	362	92.3	4	8	3.0	7	12	.0
13080	3.5	100	1.1	83	36.1	294	60.6	7	10	1.9	8	0	.0
13081	1.2	100	.4	85	26.1	290	64.6	7	15	.6	15	0	.1
13082	4.4	99	1.5	83	23.4	247	64.6	8	6	2.1	6	0	.0
13083	1.5	0	.5	78	27.1	360	67.8	7	9	2.1	9	0	.4
13084	3.8	98	1.2	79	22.3	291	76.6	7	10	3.9	10	0	.0
13087	.4	100	.1	57	20.1	294	62.9	9	15	.3	18	0	.0
13088	49.0	97	16.7	64	30.6	407	78.7	8	6	23.1	5	2	.4
13092	2.2	100	1.5	85	23.1	322	62.4	7	9	1.1	9	0	.0
13093	.3	100	.1	74	25.9	589	62.1	0	5	1.5	5	0	.1

NEW YORK
SYRACUSE

ZIP CODE	1	2	3	4	5	6	7	8	9	10	11	12	13
13094	.2	100	.1	93	30.9	355*	74.8	3	21	.1	14	1	.0

SYRACUSE

ZIP CODE	1	2	3	4	5	6	7	8	9	10	11	12	13
13101	2.5	99	.8	72	23.2	322	59.2	7	7	1.2	6	0	.0
13102	.4	100	.1	90	20.9	240*	60.2	3	8	.1	13	0	.0
13103	.4	100	.1	91	20.8	239*	65.1	12	8	.4	4	0	.0
13104	10.2	98	3.5	74	40.5	375	119.6	6	8	4.9	7	0	.1
13108	6.1	99	2.0	77	29.5	343	85.7	7	10	3.0	9	0	.0
13110	2.4	99	.8	85	25.6	353	78.0	11	10	1.2	10	0	.0
13111	1.4	99	.4	87	18.5	392	47.8	10	11	.7	9	0	.1
13112	1.7	0	.5	90	29.4	361	63.9	8	11	.0	0	0	.0
13113	.4	100	.1	82	24.0	315	49.3	11	11	.2	10	0	.0
13114	5.6	98	1.7	78	25.1	338	62.1	9	8	2.7	7	1	.0
13115	.5	0	.2	77	26.8	296	74.0	8	16	.0	7	0	.0
13116	3.7	98	1.1	79	29.0	309	68.3	9	10	1.8	8	0	.0
13117	.3	100	1.6	74	20.6	360	53.1	9	10	.2	11	0	.0
13118	5.0	99	1.6	82	23.4	288	53.2	9	11	2.5	9	0	.0
13119	.3	100	.3	71	27.6	249	51.0	11	6	.2	7	0	.0
13120	2.8	70	1.0	85	24.6	326	55.0	8	11	.9	12	0	.0
13121	.2	0	.1	95	26.0	298*	55.5	5	11	.0	0	0	.0
13122	.7	100	.2	63	23.9	379	56.7	10	11	.3	6	0	.0
13123	.5	0	.1	90	21.6	268	50.3	13	4	.0	0	0	.0
13124	.4	100	.1	84	17.3	148	36.9	11	6	.1	11	0	.0
13126	36.7	99	11.6	67	24.6	330	65.0	7	10	17.9	8	6	1.0
13129	.2	100	.1	83	16.3	187*	26.0	4	11	.1	5	0	.0
13130	.3	100	.1	92	23.9	274*	39.5	6	16	.1	11	0	.0
13131	3.2	99	1.0	85	25.2	281	57.8	8	8	1.6	7	0	.0
13132	4.0	97	1.2	89	26.2	373	65.2	11	5	2.0	4	0	.0
13133	.2	0	.1	59	20.5	271	49.1	10	2	.0	0	0	.0
13134	.8	90	.1	86	23.8	235	40.9	7	13	.1	8	0	.0
13135	.3	99	2.0	76	25.9	354	67.1	7	8	2.9	8	0	.0
13136	.5	0	.1	86	20.7	288	33.6	10	7	.0	8	0	.0
13138	.4	100	.1	71	47.4	498	99.9	8	8	.2	4	0	.0
13140	4.3	99	1.4	82	22.5	334	50.2	8	10	2.1	9	0	.0
13141	.9	0	.3	76	26.2	253	56.9	10	8	.0	0	0	.0
13142	5.8	100	2.1	69	23.4	291	58.7	8	13	2.9	10	1	.3
13143	2.6	99	1.3	81	20.6	306	50.2	9	10	1.3	10	0	.2
13144	1.5	99	.4	79	18.9	276	40.0	11	9	.7	9	0	.0
13145	1.5	0	.5	82	25.7	326	59.6	8	13	.0	0	0	.0
13146	2.5	98	.8	80	23.4	326	47.4	12	12	1.2	11	0	.1
13147	.7	0	.3	82	22.7	323	56.1	9	10	.0	8	0	.0
13148	11.3	99	4.0	70	25.9	321	65.9	6	11	5.4	9	0	1.9
13150	.2	0	.1	100	32.7	375*	66.3	3	8	.0	0	0	.0
13151	.2	100	.1	82	25.1	150	38.2	7	11	.1	9	0	.0
13152	8.1	100	2.8	81	34.6	377	109.7	6	12	3.9	10	0	.0
13153	.6	100	.2	90	24.7	346	50.8	11	12	.3	8	0	.1
13154	.2	0	.1	69	18.3	329	36.2	14	13	.0	0	0	.0
13155	.6	0	.2	74	20.4	264	40.0	7	14	.0	0	0	.0
13156	1.5	100	.5	86	25.3	182	58.2	7	10	.7	7	0	.0
13157	1.4	0	.5	71	18.0	345	44.5	9	10	.7	0	0	.0

*=Estimated **1.0=883 lbs per person; 100++ indicates per capita toxic waste generation > than 100 times the U.S. average of 883 lbs per capita.

ZIP CODE MEASURES OF SIZE, LEVELS OF AFFLUENCE AND QUALITY OF LIFE

1=Population (th.); 2= % White; 3=Households (th.); 4=% Owner Occupied; 5=Mean Income Per Household (th.$); 6=Mean Monthly Rent ($)*; 7=Mean Home Value (th.$)*;
8=% under 5; 9=% 65 and over; 10=White Males (th.); 11=% White Males, 65+; 12=# Toxic Waste Sites; 13=Toxic Waste Relative to US(883 lbs.per capita)**.

NEW YORK

ZIPCODE	1	2	3	4	5	6	7	8	9	10	11	12	13
SYRACUSE													
13158	.7	0	.2	78	21.0	293	50.3	8	14	.0	0	0	.0
13159	4.3	99	1.4	73	27.7	332	72.6	7	8	2.1	7	1	.7
13160	1.9	98	.6	82	25.0	333	65.8	8	14	1.0	12	0	.8
13161	.4	100	.1	84	24.3	269	47.6	12	9	.2	9	0	.0
13162	.6	100	.2	83	17.1	338	28.6	15	12	.2	9	0	.0
13163	.4	97	.1	90	27.7	431	63.5	7	15	.2	15	1	4.3
13164	1.9	98	.6	81	27.8	352	71.5	6	14	1.0	12	0	.0
13165	10.6	99	3.7	80	24.0	306	58.6	7	13	5.1	10	3	.4
13166	4.6	99	1.5	84	25.2	313	63.6	8	10	2.2	8	0	.0
13167	2.5	100	.8	84	22.9	248	71.5	9	6	1.3	4	0	.0
SYRACUSE													
13202	7.2	39	3.6	3	11.9	222	33.4	8	14	1.5	22	2	2.5
13203	17.8	95	8.1	33	21.1	310	69.3	6	19	7.3	15	0	.1
13204	26.8	84	10.6	35	18.7	266	41.8	8	13	10.5	12	2	.2
13205	24.5	63	9.2	45	19.3	306	47.2	8	19	6.7	20	0	.0
13206	19.3	98	8.1	58	23.7	328	58.4	6	16	8.7	13	1	.5
13207	17.6	85	6.5	65	25.4	346	56.1	7	18	6.9	13	0	.0
13208	24.0	98	10.2	51	20.5	317	52.6	7	18	10.8	11	1	1.2
13209	14.0	99	5.0	74	27.3	300	70.2	6	12	6.7	10	0	.0
13210	30.0	79	10.0	29	18.7	333	66.8	4	8	11.9	6	1	.1
13211	7.5	99	2.8	74	24.9	391	52.3	5	12	3.5	11	0	3.0
13212	26.1	97	8.6	73	30.0	387	68.3	6	7	12.2	6	1	.0
13214	10.4	92	3.3	75	34.9	333	92.0	5	13	4.6	10	4	.2
13215	11.2	98	3.5	73	36.0	467	96.9	5	13	5.4	12	1	.1
13219	17.8	99	6.1	86	32.2	385	75.1	7	13	8.4	11	0	.0
13224	9.4	72	3.6	68	35.9	366	89.7	7	12	3.2	15	0	.5
UTICA													
13302	1.3	99	.4	88	21.6	245	46.5	11	9	.7	8	0	.0
13303	1.1	0	.4	82	26.0	349	73.8	8	6	.0	0	0	.0
13304	1.7	97	.6	86	28.1	320	78.1	7	12	.9	11	0	.3
13305	.6	0	.6	77	24.8	358	60.8	12	11	.4	7	0	3.7
13308	2.8	98	.8	85	22.2	303	56.6	6	10	1.4	7	0	.0
13309	5.2	100	1.7	76	21.6	248	52.0	5	8	2.5	12	0	.9
13310	.6	100	.3	77	18.0	236	42.4	5	13	.3	14	0	.2
13312	.2	100	.1	90	20.0	230*	67.0	4	20	.1	23	0	.0
13313	.7	0	.2	86	23.2	310	37.7	12	9	.0	0	0	.0
13314	.5	99	.1	86	19.3	213	36.9	5	13	.3	12	0	.0
13315	1.0	100	.3	89	23.5	366	48.2	8	13	.5	13	0	.6
13316	6.3	0	2.0	75	23.5	323	53.9	8	12	.3	0	0	.6
13317	4.2	99	1.5	68	22.8	265	48.0	7	17	2.0	14	1	.2
13318	1.1	96	.3	89	20.5	384	44.8	7	7	.5	8	0	.1
13319	1.2	100	.5	62	22.6	336	45.5	5	17	.5	14	0	.5
13320	2.0	99	.7	79	18.4	228	47.4	7	16	1.0	15	0	.0
13321	1.3	0	.5	69	24.6	324	64.3	6	11	.0	0	0	.0
13322	1.3	0	.4	78	24.3	307	56.1	8	10	.0	0	2	.1
13323	10.1	99	2.9	76	31.5	350	75.4	5	11	5.0	8	0	.0
13324	2.0	100	.6	82	20.4	303	44.9	9	11	1.0	10	0	.0
13325	1.0	100	.3	83	23.7	240	42.1	8	11	.5	8	0	.0
13326	5.2	99	2.0	65	24.3	333	81.2	6	22	2.4	19	0	.1

NEW YORK

ZIPCODE	1	2	3	4	5	6	7	8	9	10	11	12	13
UTICA													
13327	2.0	0	.6	83	22.0	251	51.8	7	12	.0	0	8	.0
13328	1.2	99	.4	73	24.2	316	57.6	7	12	.5	8	0	.0
13329	3.9	99	1.5	70	18.0	231	44.2	8	16	1.8	13	1	.1
13331	.3	100	.1	80	19.7	257	73.3	4	19	.1	11	0	.0
13332	2.3	99	.7	81	22.4	245	43.1	7	11	1.1	11	0	.0
13333	.3	100	.1	88	19.1	412	64.6	4	13	.1	8	0	.0
13334	1.1	100	.4	74	19.3	334	40.9	9	18	.5	12	0	.0
13335	1.4	99	.4	77	21.0	249	52.7	7	12	.7	8	0	.0
13336	.2	100	.1	100	27.8	319*	40.5	8	9	.1	8	0	.0
13337	1.0	100	.4	84	22.5	221	72.5	2	16	.4	17	0	.0
13338	1.0	98	.4	84	18.6	135	42.0	6	14	.5	14	0	.0
13339	6.6	100	2.3	77	21.0	254	41.8	7	12	3.3	10	0	.0
13340	7.4	100	2.6	76	21.9	251	63.6	8	11	3.6	10	4	.1
13342	.3	0	.1	86	20.5	434	44.0	6	17	.0	0	0	.0
13343	1.7	99	.5	83	20.3	290	48.3	11	12	.8	11	0	.0
13345	.3	100	.1	90	19.0	218*	50.5	10	11	.1	10	0	.0
13346	5.4	96	1.0	66	25.0	316	76.9	3	10	2.7	9	0	.4
13348	1.0	100	.4	77	19.6	325	49.3	6	16	.1	14	0	.0
13350	10.9	99	4.1	62	21.0	270	54.7	5	16	5.0	13	1	.6
13352	.1	0	.1	75	17.0	240	37.1	2	24	.0	0	0	.0
13354	3.1	99	1.0	82	25.2	283	71.2	7	8	1.5	8	0	.0
13355	.7	100	.2	91	22.9	168	41.9	8	12	.4	11	0	.0
13357	12.7	98	4.5	69	21.9	242	48.3	8	14	6.0	11	4	.6
13360	.3	100	.3	86	19.5	211	65.6	5	10	.2	8	0	.0
13361	.7	0	.2	87	23.3	243	43.8	8	18	.1	8	0	.0
13362	.3	100	.1	82	23.7	181	40.3	10	10	.1	8	0	.0
13363	2.5	100	.8	84	25.8	368	58.5	9	6	1.3	6	0	.0
13364	.3	0	.1	71	18.1	283	34.6	10	10	.0	0	0	.0
13365	9.9	100	3.7	64	19.8	222	44.8	6	19	4.6	16	3	.3
13367	7.4	99	2.5	75	24.4	255	58.3	7	14	3.6	10	3	.1
13368	1.3	99	.4	84	21.7	243	51.2	8	10	.6	10	2	2.3
UTICA													
13401	.3	100	.1	82	36.9	306	54.3	5	3	.1	0	0	.9
13402	1.2	100	.4	76	21.3	326	47.9	9	10	.6	10	0	.0
13403	5.0	95	1.2	84	27.3	290	73.5	5	18	2.3	15	0	.0
13404	.2	100	.1	89	22.9	263*	35.8	3	8	.1	8	0	.3
13406	.9	99	.3	75	21.9	296	45.4	9	13	.4	13	0	.3
13407	5.7	100	2.0	78	21.9	238	52.1	7	13	2.8	11	1	.0
13408	3.9	96	.7	75	22.9	275	64.2	3	4	2.0	11	0	.0
13409	2.0	0	.6	74	22.6	276	47.1	8	10	.0	0	0	.0
13410	.6	0	.2	73	19.8	262	38.4	7	20	.5	14	0	.0
13411	3.3	100	1.1	74	18.4	271	42.9	8	17	1.5	14	0	.3
13413	14.4	99	5.0	78	31.9	428	82.6	5	15	6.8	12	2	.4
13415	.2	0	.1	86	17.8	204*	46.3	6	18	.0	0	0	.0
13416	2.0	99	.6	74	21.1	297	52.4	10	10	.4	17	0	.2
13417	3.6	100	1.6	52	20.7	307	60.1	5	19	1.6	16	0	.0
13418	.3	100	.1	89	20.5	319	31.1	12	6	.2	7	0	.0
13419	.2	96	.1	75	19.9	331	42.1	7	12	.1	8	0	.0
13420	1.3	99	.5	77	22.5	311	72.4	5	18	.6	16	0	.0

*=Estimated **1.0=883 lbs per person; 100++ indicates per capita toxic waste generation > than 100 times the U.S. average of 883 lbs per capita.

ZIP CODE MEASURES OF SIZE, LEVELS OF AFFLUENCE AND QUALITY OF LIFE

1=Population (th.); 2= % White; 3=Households (th.); 4=% Owner Occupied; 5=Mean Income Per Household (th.$); 6=Mean Monthly Rent ($); 7=Mean Home Value (th.$); 8=% under 5; 9=% 65 and over; 10=White Males, 65+; 11=% White Males; 12=# Toxic Waste Sites; 13=Toxic Waste Relative to US(883 lbs.per capita)**.

NEW YORK

UTICA

ZIPCODE	1	2	3	4	5	6	7	8	9	10	11	12	13
13421	13.4	99	4.9	64	22.7	293	54.2	7	14	6.1	11	2	.0
13424	2.8	100	.8	80	25.9	329	64.8	6	11	1.4	8	1	.3
13425	1.9	0	.6	74	20.3	267	48.9	8	10	.0	0	0	.6
13426	.3	94	.1	91	20.2	232*	37.5	1	23	.2	20	1	.0
13428	1.4	99	.5	79	24.9	297	60.2	7	20	.8	19	1	.0
13431	1.6	0	.5	82	23.7	313	60.5	6	12	.0	0	0	.0
13432	1.7	100	.6	89	20.8	239*	51.2	13	0	.0	0	0	.0
13433	.4	0	.1	77	19.6	284	42.3	8	11	.0	0	0	.0
13435	.2	100	.1	81	22.5	286	51.1	6	8	.2	8	0	.0
13436	.5	100	.2	65	22.4	261	64.5	3	15	.1	12	0	.0
13437	3.1	100	.2	85	17.3	199*	50.1	6	17	.2	18	0	.0
13438	3.9	100	1.0	81	24.1	260	52.5	7	8	.0	0	0	.0
13439		100	1.4	78	20.3	262	53.6	7	15	2.0	15	0	.4
13440	52.4	95	17.9	60	23.7	316	65.2	11	24	5.2	24	5	.4
13452	4.8	100	1.6	77	19.5	249	42.7	9	13	2.3	11	2	.0
13454	1.0	0	.3	77	19.2	219	38.8	9	8	.0	0	0	.0
13456	3.9	0	1.2	84	26.3	331	69.2	8	10	.0	0	0	.0
13457	.4	0	.1	75	17.2	327	43.0	11	11	.0	0	0	.0
13459	2.2	99	.7	81	20.5	318	48.1	7	14	1.1	12	0	.2
13460	3.8	100	1.3	75	21.8	269	55.1	7	12	1.8	9	0	.0
13461	2.9	100	1.0	81	26.7	243	62.2	6	13	1.4	10	0	.1
13464	1.0	0	.3	78	17.5	200	41.1	7	10	.0	0	2	8.0
13466	.1	100	.1	83	15.0	219	39.6	7	22	.1	22	0	.0
13468	.5	100	.1	84	18.4	408	52.0	8	19	1.6	18	0	.0
13469	.8	100	.3	90	24.4	339	74.8	4	11	.4	8	0	.0
13470	2.8	100	.8	92	18.5	158	32.4	7	13	.4	15	0	.0
13471	.1	98	.1	84	22.3	297	48.5	8	7	1.4	7	0	.0
13472	.8	0	.1	57	20.1	266	35.6	8	18	.0	0	0	.0
13473	.2	100	.3	75	27.4	288	52.5	10	10	.4	10	0	.5
13475	2.9	0	.3	75	24.1	188	56.9	3	12	.0	0	0	.0
13476	1.2	100	1.0	72	25.1	315	64.1	8	10	1.4	7	0	.1
13477	3.5	100	.4	88	23.8	227	66.9	6	7	.6	6	0	.0
13479	1.7	99	1.1	88	27.8	325	54.7	4	10	1.8	9	0	.0
13480	3.3	99	1.0	85	28.0	322*	52.7	5	22	1.6	4	0	.0
13484	.3	93	.1	70	22.5	318	56.5	7	13	1.1	10	0	.0
13485	.9	99	.3	91	24.7	284*	43.6	3	17	.1	4	0	.0
13486	.8	0	.3	74	16.8	293	40.7	10	11	.5	13	0	.0
13488	.6	100	.2	85	24.1	312	63.8	5	12	.1	7	0	.5
13489	1.6	99	.2	79	18.3	136	37.3	4	17	.0	0	0	.6
13490	3.4	99	1.1	84	24.1	270	48.1	8	9	.3	6	0	.0
13491	13.0	0	4.4	80	25.5	337	75.8	9	9	1.4	7	0	.0
13492	1.7	100	.5	80	21.3	260	53.9	9	9	.6	8	0	.0
13493	.3	100	.1	79	18.3	299	70.4	6	11	.0	0	0	.8
13494	2.3	100	1.0	71	20.9	267	42.3	12	6	.8	5	0	.6
13495		99	.3	81	20.9	108	47.9	9	15	.1	18	0	.0

UTICA

ZIPCODE	1	2	3	4	5	6	7	8	9	10	11	12	13
13501	45.2	90	17.5	49	20.0	246	63.0	7	18	18.6	16	4	.1
13502	40.2	95	14.7	60	21.0	258	53.5	6	16	17.9	13	4	.1

NEW YORK

WATERTOWN

ZIPCODE	1	2	3	4	5	6	7	8	9	10	11	12	13
13601	36.4	98	13.4	58	21.7	279	58.4	7	15	16.4	11	8	.8
13605	3.9	99	1.3	76	20.8	283	53.7	8	13	1.8	11	8	.0
13606	2.1	0	.6	82	23.3	281	53.7	8	9	.0	0	0	.0
13607	2.2	0	.8	76	21.2	313	62.4	5	19	.0	0	0	2.1
13608	1.5	0	.5	78	21.2	254	42.8	10	6	.0	0	0	.0
13611	.2	100	.1	71	14.4	215	32.1	8	29	.1	30	0	.0
13612	3.0	95	.9	67	25.0	309	61.7	11	6	1.5	5	0	.0
13613	2.3	99	.7	81	21.2	271	53.8	7	8	1.2	7	0	.0
13614	.3	100	.3	75	17.0	374	37.9	9	6	.2	5	0	.0
13615	1.2	0	.4	67	23.9	261	63.6	6	11	.3	8	0	.5
13616	.7	100	.2	84	19.8	372	54.3	9	11	.3	6	0	.0
13617	11.5	99	3.0	64	22.4	311	69.6	6	9	5.6	7	1	.0
13618	1.6	0	.6	81	20.8	276	50.2	5	20	.0	0	0	.5
13619	9.3	0	3.2	69	20.7	252	52.2	8	13	.0	0	0	.0
13620	1.5	0	.4	87	21.8	222	51.7	10	7	.0	0	0	.0
13621	.7	95	.3	80	26.7	228	48.9	11	5	.3	6	0	.0
13622	1.5	100	.5	82	21.1	305	51.2	10	10	.7	13	0	.0
13624	3.7	99	1.3	78	19.4	276	57.7	7	16	1.7	13	0	.8
13625	1.4	100	.5	85	22.3	287	56.3	8	11	.7	9	0	.0
13626	1.6	0	.5	81	21.4	298	41.3	8	10	.0	0	0	.0
13628	.3	0	.1	93	23.0	265*	42.8	4	17	.0	0	1	19.3
13630	1.2	0	.4	78	18.2	306	37.6	7	10	.0	0	0	.0
13632	.4	100	.1	81	21.3	272	30.3	5	6	.2	7	0	.0
13633	.5	100	.1	88	22.3	184	36.2	10	6	.2	5	0	.0
13634	3.2	100	1.1	80	22.3	336	49.9	8	12	.5	11	0	.0
13635	1.1	100	.3	79	16.4	282	37.3	9	9	.4	8	0	.7
13636	.3	100	.2	80	21.1	339	38.5	10	13	.6	9	0	.7
13637	2.5	0	.6	82	24.1	313	56.4	7	9	.2	2	0	.0
13638	2.0	0	.5	73	22.6	300	70.1	5	6	.0	0	0	.5
13639	.5	100	.3	92	20.9	240*	37.0	6	10	.0	0	0	.0
13642	8.8	100	3.0	68	19.3	277	46.3	9	11	4.2	10	1	.0
13643	.4	100	.1	68	25.4	380	48.7	11	4	.3	6	0	.2
13645	.3	0	.1	90	19.8	197	46.9	5	8	.1	9	0	.0
13646	2.0	99	.7	81	17.7	238	43.4	8	16	1.0	15	0	.4
13647	.4	100	.2	71	26.2	321	89.7	6	12	.2	11	0	.0
13648	.8	84	.2	84	18.5	220	39.0	10	11	.7	0	0	.7
13649	.2	100	.1	84	27.4	273	50.1	18	10	.1	8	0	.0
13650	.6	0	.2	85	22.6	189	47.3	4	8	.0	0	0	.5
13651	.3	0	.1	87	22.2	313	56.5	8	9	.0	0	0	.0
13652	1.8	100	.6	83	17.8	259	36.6	6	11	1.0	15	1	.0
13653	.2	0	.1	76	18.6	381	30.4	6	2	.0	0	0	.0
13654	2.0	100	.4	70	20.1	281	47.1	10	11	.1	8	0	.0
13655	1.4	7	.4	90	20.0	223	41.8	6	11	.0	0	0	.9
13656	1.8	99	.5	79	21.2	310	45.7	8	8	.9	9	0	.7
13658	2.1	0	.6	83	20.7	386	58.4	6	9	.1	7	0	.0
13659	.5	0	.2	82	18.6	234	29.9	6	14	.0	0	0	.0
13660	1.9	0	.6	78	20.5	340	47.1	6	11	.0	0	0	.0
13661	1.3	100	.4	83	19.7	216	52.0	9	8	.7	8	0	.9
13662	18.3	99	6.5	72	25.6	293	65.5	7	12	8.6	10	5	1.9

*=Estimated **1.0=883 lbs per person; 100++ indicates per capita toxic waste generation > than 100 times the U.S. average of 883 lbs per capita.

ZIP CODE MEASURES OF SIZE, LEVELS OF AFFLUENCE AND QUALITY OF LIFE

1=Population (th.); 2= % White; 3=Households (th.); 4=% Owner Occupied; 5=Mean Income Per Household (th.$); 6=Mean Monthly Rent ($)*; 7=Mean Home Value (th.$)*;
8=% under 5; 9=% 65 and over; 10=White Males (th.); 11=% White Males, 65+; 12=# Toxic Waste Sites; 13=Toxic Waste Relative to US(883 lbs.per capita)**.

NEW YORK

WATERTOWN

ZIPCODE	1	2	3	4	5	6	7	8	9	10	11	12	13
13664	.6	0	.2	78	19.3	269	61.6	7	13	.0	0	0	.0
13665	1.0	0	.3	75	16.8	259	35.8	7	14	.0	0	0	1.3
13666	.5	0	.2	82	24.1	276	36.8	5	11	.0	0	1	8.9
13667	3.5	100	1.1	76	21.8	297	53.7	8	8	1.7	7		.0
13668	3.4	100	1.2	76	22.3	332	54.9	10	9	1.7	8		.0
13669	16.9	99	5.5	68	22.0	286	50.9	6	15	7.8	12		.0
13670	.6	0	.2	82	17.7	318	35.6	6	10	.0	0		.1
13672	.9	0	.3	75	18.7	315	46.7	9	9	.0	0		.0
13673	1.7	0	.5	76	21.3	304	44.5	10	10	.0	0		.0
13674	.3	100	.1	73	28.1	420	51.4	5	15	.2	12		.0
13675	.2	100	.1	92	22.6	260*	38.8	3	11	.1	15		.0
13676	16.8	98	4.3	59	21.7	323	65.6	5	7	8.9	5		.0
13678	1.4	100	.4	94	30.9	355*	72.0	13	6	.7	2		.0
13679	1.4	100	.4	84	17.6	292	49.1	10	11	.1	7		.0
13680	1.1	100	.3	79	19.0	245	41.9	11	11	.6	12		.0
13681	.9	97	.3	80	23.6	356	40.8	11	8	.4	8		.0
13682	.7	99	.2	84	23.6	372	46.8	8	9	.3	8		.0
13683	.2	33	.1	88	15.4	177*	42.2	3	19	.0	0		.0
13684	1.0	0	.3	89	17.0	291	36.5	9	12	.0	0		.0
13685	1.5	0	.5	77	23.1	259	53.2	8	12	.2	13		.0
13687	.5	100	.2	86	20.5	194	48.7	7	15	.2	13		.0
13690	1.3	100	.5	78	21.0	253	52.5	8	13	.6	12		.0
13691	2.1	0	.7	82	20.3	261	38.6	7	12	.0	0		.0
13693	.5	100	.2	93	19.2	202	44.2	6	17	.2	15		.0
13694	1.5	100	.5	81	24.3	326	55.7	8	11	.7	10		.0
13695	.2	98	.1	81	20.6	233	44.2	3	9	.1	5		.2
13696	.3	100	.1	92	21.0	241*	46.1	13	7	.2	3		.0
13697	2.1	0	.6	81	25.7	291	50.2	7	8	.0	0		.0
13698	.1	100	.1	84	15.2	218	39.6	14	17	.2	17		.0

BINGHAMTON

ZIPCODE	1	2	3	4	5	6	7	8	9	10	11	12	13
13730	2.5	99	.9	77	21.6	290	55.9	7	12	1.2	12	0	.0
13731	1.1	99	.4	78	18.6	324	51.4	5	15	.6	14	0	.0
13732	8.2	98	2.4	88	34.8	345	91.8	8	5	4.0	4	0	.2
13733	4.8	99	1.7	76	22.8	303	56.6	8	13	2.3	13	3	11.3
13734	1.2	99	.4	83	23.2	243	53.5	6	10	.6	11	0	.0
13736	2.1	99	.7	85	22.3	317	56.3	9	7	1.0	6	0	.0
13739	.9	0	.3	80	18.7	269	47.7	6	13	.0	0	0	.0
13740	.5	100	.2	79	19.3	288	57.7	4	13	.2	14	0	.0
13742	.3	100	.1	96	20.9	240*	33.9	6	16	.7	19	0	.0
13743	3.2	99	.4	82	22.8	299	58.5	9	8	1.5	8	0	.0
13744	1.2	0	.4	85	24.2	338	71.0	6	8	.0	0	0	.0
13745	.3	0	.1	94	25.2	289*	76.6	6	6	.0	0	0	.0
13746	2.6	100	.9	89	23.0	281	62.9	6	10	1.3	9	0	.0
13747	.1	100	.1	53	14.8	460	65.6	0	31	.0	0	0	.0
13748	4.0	98	1.3	86	26.3	413	76.0	7	9	2.0	9	0	.1
13749	.2	0	.1	88	26.7	353	50.7	7	2	.0	0	0	.0
13750	.8	0	.3	78	18.0	327	53.0	6	15	.0	0	0	.0
13751	.3	0	.1	85	23.9	446	40.5	9	7	.0	0	0	.0
13752	.7	0	.2	84	19.2	316	50.4	11	16	.0	0	0	.0

NEW YORK

BINGHAMTON

ZIPCODE	1	2	3	4	5	6	7	8	9	10	11	12	13
13753	5.9	98	1.6	67	22.0	328	66.7	4	14	2.8	11	0	.0
13754	3.7	100	1.3	77	21.9	257	58.1	7	13	1.8	12	1	.2
13755	1.2	100	.5	84	19.4	230	56.8	5	19	.6	19	0	.0
13756	.6	92	.2	79	20.0	229	66.9	7	5	.3	0	1	.0
13757	.6	100	.2	82	23.7	353	62.6	7	13	.3	15	0	.8
13760	47.7	98	17.4	68	28.9	328	85.1	6	11	22.6	9	5	.8
13774	.3	100	.1	81	18.6	213*	65.4	8	8	.0	0	0	.0
13775	1.6	0	.6	79	22.2	297	57.1	9	15	.0	0	0	.0
13776	.9	0	.2	81	22.0	279	57.9	5	15	.0	0	0	.0
13777	.3	0	.3	87	26.3	365	79.1	7	8	.1	12	0	.0
13778	2.0	100	1.0	78	24.4	310	65.8	8	9	3.0	8	1	2.2
13780	.9	0	.3	89	21.6	331	48.1	8	8	.0	0	0	.0
13782	.9	0	.3	76	19.6	310	56.1	9	13	.0	0	0	.0
13783	2.5	98	.9	71	21.4	223	53.3	9	17	1.2	14	1	1.2
13784	.3	100	.1	77	25.4	421	53.6	9	5	.2	5	0	.0
13785	.2	100	.1	78	19.7	314	41.3	11	16	.1	12	0	.0
13786	.3	0	.1	88	20.9	240	47.3	10	11	.0	9	0	.0
13787	2.8	100	1.0	81	24.0	278	63.1	7	10	1.4	9	0	.0
13788	1.0	0	.3	65	20.4	245	54.8	5	16	.2	14	0	5.1
13790	19.9	99	8.0	60	22.0	294	65.4	5	18	9.1	14	1	.3
13794	.2	100	.1	68	17.6	303	56.6	12	7	.1	8	0	.0
13795	4.1	99	1.4	74	25.1	358	69.1	8	7	2.0	6	0	.1
13796	.4	0	.4	79	23.0	242	52.9	5	13	.0	0	0	.0
13797	1.4	99	.5	83	20.4	287	57.0	9	8	.7	8	0	.0

BINGHAMTON

ZIPCODE	1	2	3	4	5	6	7	8	9	10	11	12	13
13801	1.0	99	.3	93	20.3	323	39.0	9	10	.6	9	1	.0
13802	1.0	100	.3	86	26.0	137	59.1	6	12	.5	8	0	.0
13803	3.5	100	1.1	76	21.3	263	50.7	8	10	1.7	8	0	.5
13804	.5	94	.5	81	22.6	176	41.5	6	10	.2	0	0	.0
13806	.3	0	.3	69	18.8	313	38.2	9	15	.0	0	0	.0
13807	1.0	100	.6	74	19.4	254	57.1	9	14	.6	9	0	.0
13808	1.8	100	.5	78	22.2	240	55.1	7	14	.9	12	0	1.6
13809	1.5	0	.5	81	22.4	263	48.9	8	13	.0	0	0	.0
13810	.9	97	.3	79	19.8	235	61.4	7	12	.5	11	0	.0
13811	4.2	100	1.4	82	26.7	290	73.5	9	9	2.0	8	0	.0
13812	2.5	99	.7	84	25.1	292	56.2	8	9	1.3	7	0	.1
13813	1.3	88	.5	91	24.9	320	66.1	9	6	.6	6	0	.0
13814	1.5	98	.5	81	22.7	348	58.6	8	14	.6	8	0	.1
13815	13.9	98	5.1	66	24.4	288	65.8	8	11	6.5	11	4	8.1
13820	21.6	97	7.0	59	21.5	330	64.4	4	13	9.6	11	2	.1
13825	2.7	99	.9	78	23.9	314	67.1	7	10	1.3	9	0	.0
13826	.1	100	.1	95	16.0	183*	58.2	0	24	.1	33	0	.0
13827	12.0	98	4.2	74	27.3	287	75.0	7	10	5.7	8	5	2.0
13830	4.9	99	1.6	77	21.1	281	54.0	7	16	2.4	14	0	.0
13832	.6	0	.3	83	17.9	203	42.1	10	8	.0	0	0	.1
13833	4.0	100	1.3	88	22.0	254	66.2	9	8	2.0	8	1	.0
13834	.2	100	.1	80	12.7	202	36.7	13	21	.1	10	0	.0
13835	1.0	100	.3	79	20.5	217	45.7	9	7	.5	6	2	.0
13836	.2	100	.1	55	18.1	293	69.0	7	13	.1	12	0	.0

*=Estimated **1.0=883 lbs per person; 100++ indicates per capita toxic waste generation > than 100 times the U.S. average of 883 lbs per capita.

103001

ZIP CODE MEASURES OF SIZE, LEVELS OF AFFLUENCE AND QUALITY OF LIFE

1=Population (th.); 2= % White; 3=Households (th.); 4=% Owner Occupied; 5=Mean Income Per Household (th.$); 6=Mean Monthly Rent ($); 7=Mean Home Value (th.$); 8=% under 5; 9=% 65 and over; 10=White Males (th.); 11=% White Males, 65+; 12=# Toxic Waste Sites; 13=Toxic Waste Relative to US(883 lbs.per capita)**.

NEW YORK

BINGHAMTON

ZIP CODE	1	2	3	4	5	6	7	8	9	10	11	12	13
13838	5.8	99	2.2	63	23.3	307	57.4	7	14	2.8	11	3	2.0
13839	1.3	0	.4	84	21.8	299	47.7	10	13	.0	0	0	.0
13840	.3	100	.1	61	20.0	342	57.8	18	6	1.1	6	0	.0
13841	.5	100	.2	79	19.6	258	46.5	8	11	.3	7	0	.0
13842	.3	93	.1	81	29.4	247	81.8	4	18	.1	16	0	.0
13843	1.5	100	.5	81	21.0	292	54.9	3	12	.7	11	0	.0
13844	.8	98	.2	83	18.2	315	47.4	7	8	.4	8	0	.0
13845	.5	100	.1	67	18.3	285	57.2	14	27	.2	28	0	.0
13846	.5	100	.1	78	23.1	325	58.4	14	10	.3	8	0	.0
13847	.2	100	.1	80	28.2	292	48.8	4	7	.1	8	0	.2
13849	3.5	100	1.4	79	22.6	287	67.3	8	14	1.7	10	1	.0
13850	18.6	98	6.2	80	33.9	383	92.4	6	8	9.1	8	2	.1
13856	6.4	98	2.3	75	23.4	269	52.3	7	15	3.0	12	1	.4
13859	.2	100	.1	87	21.1	348	39.9	3	12	.1	19	0	.0
13860	.1		.1	60	19.7	240	59.4	5	10	.0	9	0	.0
13861	.9	98	.3	84	22.3	353	63.0	8	10	.1	9	0	.0
13862	3.5	100	1.2	76	23.9	270	67.8	9	11	1.8	9	0	.0
13863	.4	100	.1	78	23.3	305	44.1	9	7	.2	9	0	.0
13864	1.2	0	.4	81	22.4	356	52.3	8	7	.0	0	0	.0
13865	5.6	99	1.8	80	22.8	329	71.4	8	8	2.8	7	0	.6

BINGHAMTON

ZIP CODE	1	2	3	4	5	6	7	8	9	10	11	12	13
13901	26.6	95	8.7	56	21.6	251	74.9	5	14	12.0	11	2	.3
13903	26.0	96	9.3	68	28.9	312	88.1	6	11	12.0	10	0	.0
13904	10.1	96	3.7	69	22.9	299	61.9	7	16	4.6	13	1	.0
13905	31.5	97	12.9	49	22.8	305	77.6	5	18	14.2	15	0	.0

BUFFALO

ZIP CODE	1	2	3	4	5	6	7	8	9	10	11	12	13
14001	8.1	99	2.7	75	25.6	301	72.8	7	12	4.0	10	8	1.0
14003	1.3	89	.7	82	25.1	289	49.9	8	5	.6	6	2	.0
14004	11.2	97	3.2	85	29.0	309	84.7	6	11	5.6	9	0	.3
14005	1.8	100	.5	83	25.4	245	68.7	8	7	.9	6	0	.0
14006	11.5	99	3.8	81	25.4	338	58.1	7	10	5.6	9	4	.1
14008	1.5	0	.4	77	26.3	388	62.3	8	8	.0	0	0	.1
14009	4.7	100	1.6	73	25.2	280	64.2	9	9	2.3	9	2	.9
14011	7.5	85	1.9	86	22.8	262*	70.0	10	12	.1	8	3	.0
14012	2.3	97	.7	81	24.2	296	63.5	6	9	3.4	9	0	.3
14013	1.5	74	.5	80	26.0	288	65.9	9	9	1.1	9	1	.0
14020	23.3	96	8.5	67	23.6	312	51.2	9	11	.5	9	0	.0
14024	1.6	99	.5	83	25.1	312	67.8	7	15	10.5	13	3	.9
14025	2.6	0	.1	84	22.9	286	44.6	9	10	.8	9	0	.0
14027	.3	0	.1	80	32.9	383	89.7	6	7	.0	0	1	.0
14028	1.3	98	.4	83	20.7	282	70.6	5	15	.0	0	9	.0
14030	1.4	0	.1	81	30.2	265	75.8	5	12	.7	9	2	37.1
14031	7.2	99	2.5	77	28.8	246	69.2	6	12	3.4	14	0	.4
14032	3.4	0	1.0	87	33.7	320	117.5	4	18	.0	1	0	.2
14033	2.3	99	.7	81	32.2	290	91.1	9	7	.0	0	0	.0
14034	1.8	98	.6	82	30.1	290	86.7	5	9	1.2	7	0	.0
14035	.4	98	.1	78	26.0	304	42.3	6	15	.8	14	1	.0
14036	3.8	99	1.2	80	24.3	290	64.0	7	10	1.9	8	0	.9

NEW YORK

BUFFALO

ZIP CODE	1	2	3	4	5	6	7	8	9	10	11	12	13
14037	1.1	0	.3	82	26.5	305	73.7	7	8	.0	0	0	.0
14040	2.1	100	.6	86	33.2	288	73.4	6	6	1.1	7	0	.0
14041	.4	0	.1	71	20.3	346	42.0	11	13	.0	0	0	.0
14042	3.1	99	1.1	75	23.1	287	61.3	8	11	1.5	9	0	.0
14043	27.3	93	9.0	81	27.9	347	76.5	8	11	13.1	7	6	.4
14047	6.4	99	2.0	84	29.1	405	69.9	10	7	3.1	6	0	.0
14048	18.5	93	6.8	83	23.5	289	62.0	7	16	8.1	14	2	.0
14051	7.7	96	2.4	88	44.9	441	132.7	6	6	3.6	5	0	1.9
14052	16.3	100	5.4	78	32.6	360	100.5	6	12	7.8	9	0	.1
14054	1.4	100	.4	82	29.5	336	63.3	9	6	.7	5	0	.0
14055	1.2	0	.2	72	20.9	229	63.2	10	6	.0	0	0	.0
14056	1.0	0	.3	84	30.6	330	65.4	8	14	.0	0	0	.0
14057	7.8	99	2.4	84	31.5	294	83.8	6	8	3.9	7	1	.1
14058	2.5	95	.8	82	27.6	302	64.8	6	8	1.2	7	0	.0
14059	9.1	100	2.9	88	34.8	334	103.5	5	9	4.6	8	1	.5
14060	.5	100	.1	95	17.6	202*	45.0	7	11	.3	10	0	.0
14061	.5	88	.2	75	20.4	225	55.7	6	8	.2	6	0	.0
14062	3.5	99	1.2	82	24.8	300	62.4	6	11	1.7	10	0	.0
14063	14.6	97	4.5	67	24.6	349	82.2	5	10	6.8	10	0	.0
14065	1.0	99	.3	83	22.9	309	60.4	10	8	.5	8	0	.1
14066	1.0	99	.3	84	22.5	251	51.6	8	8	.5	8	0	.0
14067	5.0	97	1.6	88	28.6	370	67.0	6	12	2.4	9	2	.0
14068	2.8	93	.8	59	28.3	325	100.4	10	16	1.1	7	0	.0
14069	.8	100	.3	74	34.2	366	107.8	6	16	.5	4	0	.1
14070	5.6	88	2.1	71	22.0	284	57.5	7	14	2.3	12	4	3.5
14072	16.8	97	5.4	79	35.1	398	97.4	7	7	8.1	5	0	.6
14075	41.4	100	13.9	76	30.9	370	85.6	7	10	19.7	8	2	.0
14080	4.1	99	1.3	76	24.9	333	83.7	8	8	2.1	7	0	.0
14081	2.4	72	.8	79	22.0	318	50.0	6	13	.9	14	0	.0
14083	.4	100	.1	75	27.8	263	64.4	9	9	.2	10	1	.0
14085	.2	100	.1	88	26.8	308*	67.6	5	13	.1	11	0	.0
14086	4.1	0	1.3	92	33.3	383	81.6	5	9	.4	0	0	.4
14091	21.4	99	7.2	77	28.4	331	78.4	6	12	10.2	10	2	.5
14092	1.2	65	.3	71	22.2	296	57.6	7	7	.4	6	0	.0
14094	10.3	96	3.5	81	38.6	451	107.0	5	12	4.7	10	7	.0
14098	3.0	97	1.0	81	25.2	341	56.4	8	11	1.4	11	1	.1

BUFFALO

ZIP CODE	1	2	3	4	5	6	7	8	9	10	11	12	13
14101	1.9	100	.6	81	22.9	291	52.5	7	15	1.0	13	1	.0
14102	1.4	100	.4	87	31.1	385	91.6	9	9	.7	8	1	.0
14103	11.4	93	4.0	71	24.7	329	57.8	8	13	5.0	11	1	.6
14105	4.6	99	1.5	84	28.6	313	55.6	7	11	2.3	10	2	33.3
14107	1.4	100	.1	82	29.9	255	68.1	6	12	.3	10	3	15.8
14108	5.3	97	1.6	86	29.1	318	70.2	7	12	2.5	11	0	.0
14111	3.7	97	1.2	73	25.5	311	63.8	9	9	1.7	8	2	.0
14112	.3	100	.1	87	27.2	423	59.6	5	12	.1	9	0	.0
14113	1.0	100	.3	82	29.0	319	75.7	10	9	.5	8	0	.0
14120	51.9	98	17.9	69	27.5	349	74.6	7	9	25.0	8	15	3.1
14125	3.7	99	1.3	80	26.2	311	60.0	7	10	1.8	9	0	.3

*=Estimated **1.0=883 lbs per person; 100++ indicates per capita toxic waste generation > than 100 times the U.S. average of 883 lbs per capita.

ZIP CODE MEASURES OF SIZE, LEVELS OF AFFLUENCE AND QUALITY OF LIFE

1=Population (th.); 2= % White; 3=Households (th.); 4=% Owner Occupied; 5=Mean Income Per Household (th.); 6=Mean Monthly Rent ($)*; 7=Mean Home Value (th.$)*;
8=% under 5, 9=% 65 and over; 10=% White Males, 65+; 11=% White Males (th.); 12=# Toxic Waste Sites; 13=Toxic Waste Relative to US(883 lbs.per capita)**

NEW YORK

BUFFALO

ZIPCODE	1	2	3	4	5	6	7	8	9	10	11	12	13
14126	1.1	0	.4	62	23.3	335	56.9	8	14	.0	0	0	.0
14127	22.7	99	7.4	72	37.0	432	107.6	6	10	11.1	8	2	.3
14129	1.6	97	.5	76	23.8	272	60.8	6	9	.8	8	0	.0
14130	.4	100		77	19.4	285	43.8	10	9	.2	6	0	.0
14131	5.0	100	1.5	85	26.3	373	76.7	7	11	2.5	9	7	.0
14132	5.4	90	1.7	83	29.9	358	82.7	7	9	2.5	7	0	.0
14133	.3	100	.1	94	25.2	289*	55.9	6	6	.2	7	0	.0
14134	.7	100	.2	85	28.5	346	66.1	5	6	.3	8	0	.0
14135	.3	100		64	28.7	281	90.4	5	15	.1	13	0	.0
14136	5.4	98	1.9	76	23.1	297	65.7	6	14	2.4	11	0	.5
14138	1.9	0	.6	86	22.4	332	50.4	7	12	.0	0	0	.0
14139	2.3	100	.8	87	30.1	307	80.4	6	11	1.2	11	0	.1
14141	7.4	99	2.4	73	25.0	310	67.0	8	13	3.6	11	3	.6
14143	1.4	0	.5	78	28.4	284	69.4	8	9	.1	9	1	.5
14145	1.7	100	.5	81	27.2	383	74.6	9	9	.8	9	0	.0
14150	59.4	98	21.2	71	29.3	356	72.4	6	9	28.3	8	39	2.4
14167	1.6	0	.5	88	24.0	244	63.5	10	9	.0	0	0	.0
14168	.4	29	.1	84	20.6	158	51.5	9	15	.1	14	0	.0
14169	.3	100	.1	75	26.3	303	86.6	2	6	.2	2	3	.0
14170	2.2	100	.7	87	31.2	341	85.2	8	11	1.1	10	1	3.6
14171	1.8	97	.6	83	22.5	306	55.6	8	11	.9	10	0	.0
14172	3.3	98	1.2	85	26.9	339	73.4	7	9	1.6	12	1	1.6
14173	.3	100	.1	74	22.0	330	72.4	9	10	.4	11	0	.3
14174	5.7	98	1.9	80	35.0	416	102.1	7	8	2.8	7	0	.4

BUFFALO

ZIPCODE	1	2	3	4	5	6	7	8	9	10	11	12	13
14201	17.1	64	7.6	17	15.5	245	52.4	7	17	4.9	18	4	.0
14202	2.9	70	1.9	4	14.2	229	101.4	1	30	1.0	30	3	3.0
14203	1.7	46	.6	5	9.7	265	37.2	5	17	.4	30	4	20.5
14204	14.6	17	6.0	20	12.0	210	19.2	8	14	1.2	11	4	1.6
14206	28.3	91	11.1	63	21.2	252	45.6	6	16	12.2	14	2	1.2
14207	25.6	96	10.5	49	19.8	261	36.6	7	15	11.7	13	8	1.4
14208	17.4	7	6.0	44	17.6	300	31.2	6	13	.6	27	0	.0
14209	10.2	48	4.5	28	23.8	313	77.8	4	24	1.9	28	0	.2
14210	21.0	97	7.3	51	21.7	272	38.2	8	11	9.6	9	7	11.0
14211	42.7	51	16.2	48	18.2	278	32.3	8	13	9.9	18	1	.5
14212	21.8	80	9.3	45	17.6	235	40.3	6	18	8.1	16	1	.0
14213	31.7	91	12.4	38	17.6	283	33.0	7	15	13.3	13	1	2.3
14214	25.4	69	9.0	46	23.9	329	61.5	6	13	8.2	11	1	.4
14215	49.4	61	19.2	58	21.0	289	44.8	7	17	13.7	20	2	2.0
14216	26.8	95	11.1	52	26.0	324	71.4	6	18	11.4	15	0	.1
14217	27.3	99	10.5	69	26.4	338	66.0	6	17	12.6	13	1	.0
14218	24.2	89	8.9	57	24.5	259	62.0	7	12	10.4	12	4	4.9
14219	14.1	99	4.9	68	27.6	335	65.7	7	15	6.4	13	6	2.7
14220	31.0	98	10.8	67	24.9	303	51.6	7	13	14.1	11	7	2.8
14221	52.8	96	17.9	77	40.9	450	115.6	5	11	24.3	8	1	.0
14222	15.9	92	7.2	29	24.1	290	98.4	3	16	6.5	12	0	.0
14223	27.8	99	10.2	82	30.3	367	74.2	5	15	12.9	13	0	.0
14224	45.1	99	14.3	78	30.3	367	82.3	6	10	21.7	8	3	.1
14225	42.2	100	15.2	75	27.3	342	67.4	5	14	20.0	11	10	.9

NEW YORK

BUFFALO

ZIPCODE	1	2	3	4	5	6	7	8	9	10	11	12	13
14226	33.3	96	12.7	73	34.3	391	92.0	5	16	14.8	14	2	.0
14227	28.7	97	9.7	64	27.6	380	76.9	7	16	13.7	6	0	.3
14228	1.2	86	.6	37	22.9	262	111.3	8	15	.5	13	0	.0

NIAGRA FALLS

ZIPCODE	1	2	3	4	5	6	7	8	9	10	11	12	13
14301	17.9	91	7.4	46	19.2	259	51.0	7	20	7.4	19	18	.0
14303	9.9	82	4.3	45	20.9	285	47.1	6	18	3.7	16	16	10.6
14304	34.4	95	12.1	74	26.6	323	67.7	6	10	15.9	9	35	.5
14305	23.8	76	8.4	61	23.3	255	57.6	7	13	8.4	13	4	.9

ROCHESTER

ZIPCODE	1	2	3	4	5	6	7	8	9	10	11	12	13
14411	11.7	92	3.9	75	26.1	320	58.0	6	13	5.3	12	1	.0
14413	.4	86	.1	58	17.8	335	39.1	12	13	.2	14	0	.9
14414	6.1	99	2.1	72	27.2	350	80.9	8	10	3.0	8	0	.1
14415	.2	100	.1	84	21.8	367	55.1	5	13	.1	13	0	.0
14416	3.1	99	1.0	82	28.8	308	70.6	8	9	1.5	9	1	.0
14417	.4	0		73	16.1	374	69.5	4	18	.0	0	0	.0
14418	1.2	100	.5	85	18.6	172	50.4	9	15	.6	17	0	.5
14420	18.5	93	5.4	54	27.7	422	82.1	5	6	8.4	5	4	.0
14422	2.0	100	.6	81	32.5	334	69.9	9	7	1.0	6	0	.0
14423	4.7	92	1.5	81	28.3	311	78.7	8	10	2.1	7	1	2.3
14424	24.1	98	8.0	69	27.6	374	79.4	7	12	12.0	12	1	.0
14427	2.2	98	.7	72	23.1	287	52.9	8	12	1.1	9	0	.0
14428	5.5	98	1.8	86	32.8	394	86.5	8	8	2.6	6	1	1.6
14432	5.0	99	1.7	76	25.6	298	64.1	6	13	2.5	11	0	.3
14433	4.6	96	1.5	80	23.2	315	50.8	7	13	2.1	11	0	.4
14435	2.4	0	.8	82	26.4	356	76.5	8	8	.0	0	0	.6
14437	9.6	98	3.5	70	24.1	299	58.5	7	12	4.6	10	0	.6
14441	.5	0	.2	86	22.8	343	59.8	8	15	.3	14	0	.0
14443	.2	98		84	31.5	409	83.8	5	11	.2	10	0	.6
14445	9.3	99	3.6	61	28.7	396	74.9	7	12	4.5	11	3	.3
14449	.2	62	.1	40	20.2	227	57.5	2	7	.1	9	0	1.2
14450	33.4	97	11.3	72	38.2	423	110.7	7	7	15.6	5	4	.3
14453	.3	100	.1	90	50.0	574*	106.4	9	8	.2	4	0	.8
14454	9.2	98	2.1	58	27.0	402	88.8	8	7	3.8	7	4	4.4
14456	21.4	93	7.4	64	24.1	303	64.5	5	13	9.5	11	2	.6
14461	.2	100		87	26.6	356	61.1	8	12	.2	11	0	.3
14462	.5	99	.2	79	27.0	358	58.2	5	8	.3	10	0	.6
14463	.2	100	.1	88	33.7	387*	49.5	7	11	.1	7	0	.6
14464	5.8	98	1.8	81	30.9	360	80.9	11	4	2.8	3	1	.3
14466	1.3	98	.4	85	23.5	163	72.1	9	10	.6	8	0	.3
14467	8.9	92	2.8	67	34.3	406	81.9	7	7	4.1	7	1	1.2
14468	13.7	92	4.2	82	35.0	400	86.2	8	7	6.8	6	2	.3
14469	4.9	99	1.6	79	28.7	325	80.7	8	8	2.4	7	0	.8
14470	6.2	98	2.1	75	28.2	318	64.7	8	11	3.0	9	0	1.0
14471	2.5	99	1.0	80	27.8	367	77.4	7	14	1.3	14	1	1.2
14472	5.6	100	1.9	76	35.5	419	108.9	6	9	2.7	8	1	.3
14475	.2	100	.1	88	29.9	279	85.9	8	10	.1	7	0	.0
14476	.2	95		85	31.2	362	66.5	8	7	.1	6	0	.0
14477	1.6	84	.5	76	25.2	313	57.8	9	8	.7	10	0	.0
14478	.8	95	.1	56	28.2	327	75.3	2	4	.2	14	0	.0

*=Estimated **1.0=883 lbs per person; 100++ indicates per capita toxic waste generation > than 100 times the U.S. average of 883 lbs per capita.

ZIP CODE MEASURES OF SIZE, LEVELS OF AFFLUENCE AND QUALITY OF LIFE

1=Population (th.); 2= % White; 3=Households (th.); 4=% Owner Occupied; 5=Mean Income Per Household (th.$); 6=Mean Monthly Rent ($); 7=Mean Home Value (th.$); 8=% under 5; 9=% 65 and over; 10=% White Males (th.); 11=% White Males, 65+; 12=# Toxic Waste Sites; 13=Toxic Waste Relative to US(883 lbs.per capita)**.

NEW YORK

ROCHESTER

ZIPCODE	1	2	3	4	5	6	7	8	9	10	11	12	13
14479	.3	100	.1	73	24.7	321	48.1	5	16	.2	16	0	.0
14480	.8	98	.3	56	20.1	387	81.6	6	14	.4	12	1	.1
14481	1.5	100	.5	80	25.5	344	68.5	6	12	.8	11	3	.8
14482	8.7	97	2.9	69	27.1	326	76.2	7	13	4.1	10	1	.0
14485	3.7	98	1.2	72	26.8	323	85.2	8	9	1.7	8	0	.0
14486	.3	100	.1	75	32.6	322	83.1	6	16	.1	19	0	.0
14487	3.9	99	1.3	81	28.0	379	78.5	7	11	2.0	10	2	.0
14488	.3	100	.1	89	23.7	273*	62.1	5	23	.1	26	0	.0
14489	7.8	93	2.8	72	23.0	281	51.8	7	6	3.5	13	0	.4

ROCHESTER

ZIPCODE	1	2	3	4	5	6	7	8	9	10	11	12	13
14502	8.2	99	2.5	87	32.6	388	79.5	8	6	4.1	6	2	.4
14504	1.8	100	.7	83	24.6	306	55.5	5	19	.8	17	0	.2
14505	5.0	97	1.5	89	28.4	295	74.1	9	8	2.4	8	0	.2
14507	1.1	100	.4	86	52.2	539	142.3	13	8	.2	9	0	.1
14508	1.1	98	.4	81	20.6	297	62.5	7	16	.5	15	0	.0
14510	.2	100	.1	70	20.6	298	65.7	14	17	.1	12	0	.0
14511	5.0	99	1.8	68	22.8	317	62.0	8	14	2.4	12	0	.0
14512	.8	94	.3	86	26.6	304	66.7	6	10	.4	7	0	.0
14513	4.1	99	1.5	82	24.5	316	68.3	7	14	2.0	13	2	.1
14514	14.4	97	5.1	66	24.7	333	67.5	8	13	6.7	11	1	.2
14516	2.4	0	.8	57	32.6	427	83.5	7	8	1.6	7	1	.0
14517	2.3	99	.8	79	24.9	321	63.6	6	13	1.1	10	0	.3
14518	.2	100	.1	100	28.0	321*	42.8	0	12	.1	12	0	.0
14519	8.2	97	2.7	84	31.8	331	82.7	8	7	4.0	6	0	.6
14520	2.3	100	.9	64	25.0	386	71.9	7	17	.8	20	0	.1
14522	8.8	99	3.2	78	23.2	311	59.0	5	14	4.4	13	1	.2
14525	2.7	99	.8	70	26.5	306	66.9	7	11	1.4	9	2	.2
14526	14.8	98	4.9	81	41.3	407	111.4	6	7	7.0	5	0	.0
14527	11.6	99	4.4	75	22.9	283	65.8	6	17	5.5	12	3	.2
14529	.3	0	.1	85	22.4	382	56.0	5	15	.0	0	0	.0
14530	5.9	99	2.1	69	22.3	304	55.9	8	11	2.9	10	1	.0
14532	4.0	100	1.4	76	25.3	312	61.9	6	11	1.9	10	0	.0
14533	.9	100	.3	78	23.9	278	65.6	13	11	1.1	12	0	.1
14534	23.5	97	7.2	91	55.3	526	148.9	5	11	11.3	6	3	.0
14536	.8	100	.3	73	18.2	270	48.3	10	15	.4	17	0	.0
14537	.5	100	.2	90	25.2	254	55.0	5	9	.2	8	0	.0
14538	.1	100	.1	81	28.1	277	86.9	0	34	.4	24	0	.0
14539	.6	0	.2	90	26.5	338	63.0	6	11	.0	0	1	.0
14541	2.4	93	.7	64	24.5	357	71.4	11	9	1.2	9	0	.0
14542	.3	0	.1	81	19.9	372	38.0	4	20	.0	0	0	.0
14543	2.6	0	.9	89	37.9	333	93.7	5	8	.0	0	0	.0
14544	1.7	100	.6	87	24.3	498	74.8	8	13	.1	12	0	.1
14545	.2	0	.1	80	24.0	358	43.6	5	12	.0	0	0	.0
14546	4.5	95	1.5	69	32.9	492	80.7	7	8	2.1	7	1	.0
14547	.8	100	.3	88	36.0	378	76.8	12	9	.2	8	0	.0
14548	3.9	100	1.3	81	25.5	329	67.4	10	10	1.9	8	0	.3
14549	.4	100	.1	84	22.7	259	55.9	5	12	.2	8	0	.0

NEW YORK

ROCHESTER

ZIPCODE	1	2	3	4	5	6	7	8	9	10	11	12	13
14550	1.5	0	.5	81	22.7	247	55.9	6	17	.0	0	1	8.9
14551	5.4	90	1.8	74	26.1	333	59.6	9	12	2.3	9	0	.1
14555	1.6	95	.6	77	23.0	243	57.9	6	9	.8	10	0	.0
14557	.3	100	.1	88	31.0	443	67.5	4	11	2.1	10	0	.8
14558	.3	100	.1	100	31.5	362*	56.0	5	20				.0
14559	14.2	98	4.6	80	35.7	415	89.7	7	6	7.0	6	4	.0
14560	1.8	0	.6	88	25.5	370	63.6	8	10	.0	0	1	.0
14561	2.2	99	.7	79	22.8	426	56.4	7	14	1.1	10	0	.0
14564	9.9	99	3.2	76	30.9	384	100.8	7	6	4.8	5	0	.4
14565	.3	100	.3	87	24.8	402	59.3	8	6	1.6	4	0	.0
14568	3.4	99	1.1	84	31.4	395	84.4	8	6	1.6	4	0	.2
14569	6.1	100	2.1	71	24.4	319	62.0	7	16	2.8	11	0	.2
14571	1.1	97	.4	73	23.3	245	58.9	7	13	.6	11	0	.0
14572	4.5	98	1.5	85	22.9	328	58.1	7	11	2.2	9	0	.1
14580	32.3	97	10.9	75	37.6	378	101.0	6	9	15.2	7	2	2.7
14584	.2	0	.1	69	24.3	345	46.3	9	7	.0	0	2	.0
14585	.2	100	.1	83	27.6	283	69.3	9	14	.1	7	1	.0
14586	3.2	93	1.1	67	31.1	482	78.7	9	6	1.6	6	0	.0
14588	1.1	93	.4	72	26.9	271	40.5	1	52	.5	46	0	.4
14589	6.8	92	2.3	84	29.4	301	68.0	7	10	3.1	9	0	.1
14590	4.8	96	1.7	81	22.3	316	49.5	7	14	2.3	14	0	.0
14591	1.6	0	.5	84	24.9	335	59.1	7	13	.0	0	1	.0
14592	.4	99	.2	77	29.9	350	59.7	6	13	.0	0	0	.3

ROCHESTER

ZIPCODE	1	2	3	4	5	6	7	8	9	10	11	12	13
14604	1.6	82	1.0	0	10.1	197	35.8*	1*	29	.6	22	0	1.3
14605	16.2	22	5.6	28	15.1	286	24.7	7	10	1.7	15	1	2.3
14606	29.0	94	10.2	67	27.2	354	65.1	7	10	13.1	9	3	2.1
14607	16.6	90	9.9	16	20.7	326	81.3	4	14	7.3	11	1	2.7
14608	15.1	33	5.7	29	17.3	287	32.7	7	10	2.3	10	1	.2
14609	48.5	84	18.4	67	25.8	357	60.1	7	14	19.1	14	1	.1
14610	16.3	95	7.2	57	40.4	451	106.8	5	20	7.0	16	1	1.1
14611	22.0	46	7.9	47	19.5	313	34.6	9	12	4.8	9	5	.3
14612	26.8	99	10.1	64	31.9	392	82.8	7	11	12.8	9	1	.5
14613	15.7	95	6.1	50	24.4	318	51.5	8	12	7.0	9	1	.5
14614	1.8	80	.7	22	5.6	126	20.1*	0	43	.4	45	1	5.5
14615	17.8	95	7.1	58	29.5	375	71.6	7	8	8.1	8	1	.0
14616	30.3	97	11.3	75	31.8	383	75.4	5	12	12.1	11	1	.0
14617	25.4	99	9.1	86	38.2	437	90.4	5	15	12.0	13	2	.0
14618	21.6	98	7.8	77	47.4	458	130.4	4	14	9.6	12	0	.0
14619	16.8	50	5.9	71	27.2	372	45.3	9	10	3.9	16	0	.1
14620	27.2	85	11.5	37	22.0	338	61.1	6	22	10.4	17	1	.0
14621	38.4	67	14.8	48	20.0	327	40.4	8	18	11.5	20	1	.0
14622	13.8	98	5.3	84	31.8	397	77.6	6	15	6.5	14	0	.0
14623	28.1	92	8.9	51	28.0	429	71.1	6	9	13.6	8	1	1.9
14624	34.7	97	11.2	81	35.4	422	87.1	6	9	16.2	8	6	.6
14625	11.7	98	4.4	84	39.7	495	117.5	5	11	5.6	11	0	.8
14626	23.3	97	7.8	76	36.1	394	90.1	5	8	11.0	6	1	1.0

JAMESTOWN

ZIPCODE	1	2	3	4	5	6	7	8	9	10	11	12	13
14701	46.1	97	17.8	62	21.5	254	60.8	7	17	20.7	14	1	1.8

*=Estimated **1.0=883 lbs per person; 100++ indicates per capita toxic waste generation > than 100 times the U.S. average of 883 lbs per capita.

ZIP CODE MEASURES OF SIZE, LEVELS OF AFFLUENCE AND QUALITY OF LIFE

1=Population (th.); 2= % White; 3=Households (th.); 4=% Owner Occupied; 5=Mean Income Per Household (th.$); 6=Mean Monthly Rent ($)*; 7=Mean Home Value (th.$)*;
8=% under 5; 9=% 65 and over; 10=% White Males, 65+; 11=% White Males (th.); 12=# Toxic Waste Sites; 13=Toxic Waste Relative to US(883 lbs.per capita)**.

NEW YORK

JAMESTOWN

ZIPCODE	1	2	3	4	5	6	7	8	9	10	11	12	13
14706	6.3	99	2.0	81	26.1	333	73.8	8	10	2.9	8	1	.4
14707	.3	100	.1	80	20.0	311	41.4	4	19	.1	17	0	.0
14708	.2	100	.1	82	18.7	164	37.9	10	15	.1	14	0	.0
14709	1.7	99	.6	79	17.5	207	42.6	9	10	.8	10	0	.0
14710	3.4	100	1.1	85	25.7	325	67.4	6	12	1.7	11	0	.0
14711	1.5	100	.5	76	17.3	267	44.8	7	16	.7	12	0	.0
14712	3.2	0	1.1	86	26.4	300	77.5	6	13	.0	0	0	.0
14714	.4	0	.1	85	23.7	401	42.2	6	8	.0	0	0	.0
14715	3.2	99	1.1	78	20.4	298	41.8	9	12	1.6	10	1	.0
14716	2.4	99	.8	76	22.6	265	54.8	9	12	1.2	10	0	.8
14717	.7	100	.2	85	18.0	286	46.3	12	11	.4	13	0	.0
14718	2.0	91	.6	81	23.2	331	55.5	7	11	.9	10	0	.0
14719	3.0	100	1.0	81	21.0	264	48.6	8	12	1.5	11	0	.1
14720	1.0	99	.4	65	19.7	311	34.3	6	20	.5	19	0	.0
14721	.3	100	.1	76	20.1	269	45.2	9	7	.1	4	0	.0
14722	.3	100	.2	60	18.0	355	122.4	0	44	.1	32	1	2.1
14723	1.5	100	.5	80	22.4	291	41.8	8	11	.7	10	1	.0
14724	2.1	0	.7	76	21.5	284	58.7	9	13	.0	8	0	.0
14726	1.8	100	.7	81	17.3	292	37.1	15	7	.9	5	0	.0
14727	4.9	100	1.7	77	23.8	270	61.5	9	12	2.4	11	1	1.0
14728	1.0	100	.3	82	25.7	236	86.8	8	10	.0	8	0	.0
14729	.9	0	.3	80	20.7	311	51.9	9	10	.0	0	0	.0
14730	.3	0	.1	72	21.9	274	53.6	3	14	.0	0	0	.0
14731	1.6	99	.6	68	22.4	299	60.7	6	11	.8	10	1	3.0
14732	.5	99	.2	90	22.7	291	37.8	11	11	.3	11	0	.4
14733	4.6	100	1.7	68	21.4	259	51.8	6	15	2.2	13	1	.4
14735	2.1	100	.7	77	18.9	247	48.2	7	9	1.0	8	0	.0
14736	.6	100	.2	80	25.0	223	73.7	6	11	.3	10	0	.0
14737	4.3	99	1.5	80	19.5	258	48.5	7	14	2.1	12	1	.1
14738	3.8	100	1.3	84	25.9	303	58.8	9	13	.3	11	0	.2
14739	2.8	97	1.0	80	19.1	274	36.3	9	13	1.3	12	2	.1
14740	1.4	0	.6	87	24.0	265	60.4	7	22	.0	0	0	.0
14741	1.9	96	.6	86	22.9	276	55.9	7	9	.0	9	0	.0
14742	.4	100	.2	76	25.5	335	82.0	7	21	.2	19	0	.0
14743	1.5	100	.5	85	23.7	296	52.1	9	8	.8	7	0	.1
14744	1.9	96	.4	66	23.8	229	71.5	3	6	.8	7	0	.0
14745	.2	0	.1	73	17.0	266	50.2	8	21	.0	0	0	.0
14746	.4	0	.2	92	19.3	335	44.1	6	8	.0	0	1	.0
14747	2.4	94	.8	84	24.3	381	47.1	10	8	.3	10	0	.2
14748	.7	94	.3	86	19.6	277	54.4	5	13	.3	6	0	.0
14749	.2	100	.1	89	19.6	225*	26.0	5	13	.1	16	0	.0
14750	4.9	98	1.9	78	28.9	349	83.5	6	13	2.3	11	0	1.9
14752	.2	0	.1	85	20.1	243	31.2	4	19	.7	8	0	.0
14753	1.4	99	.5	85	20.8	281	39.0	11	10	.7	8	0	.0
14754	2.6	100	.8	88	21.7	292	42.4	8	11	.3	11	0	.2
14755	2.8	100	1.0	78	21.6	247	47.6	6	14	1.4	11	0	.0
14756	.3	100	.1	66	27.6	322	66.2	2	5	.1	2	0	.0
14757	3.5	99	1.3	78	21.8	236	66.4	7	14	1.7	12	0	.1
14759	.2	100	.1	91	21.0	241*	67.4	10	13	.1	8	0	.0

NEW YORK

JAMESTOWN

ZIPCODE	1	2	3	4	5	6	7	8	9	10	11	12	13
14760	23.1	97	8.8	64	21.9	263	57.6	7	15	10.5	12	6	4.7
14766	.3	100	.1	79	20.3	319	45.5	8	8	.1	6	6	.0
14767	1.5	0	.1	83	22.0	287	50.0	9	9	.5	0	0	.0
14769	1.1	100	.4	78	23.8	409	57.6	7	13	.5	9	0	.0
14770	2.8	99	.9	78	23.7	306	61.1	8	7	1.4	6	1	.0
14772	3.7	99	1.2	79	21.9	310	55.4	8	12	1.9	11	0	.7
14774	.4	100	.1	78	20.5	304	35.6	6	19	.2	15	0	.0
14775	3.0	98	1.0	74	20.5	276	46.4	8	12	1.5	12	0	.0
14777	.7	100	.2	81	20.0	319	46.4	8	15	.3	12	0	.0
14779	8.5	92	3.1	69	19.0	195	40.0	7	17	3.7	15	0	.1
14781	2.1	100	.7	82	22.4	277	51.6	10	10	1.1	11	1	.0
14782	2.3	99	.7	84	22.8	285	49.6	9	7	1.2	6	0	.0
14783	.4	0	.1	76	15.1	288	59.2	9	20	.0	0	0	.1
14784	1.0	99	.3	85	22.0	289	44.3	8	14	.0	0	1	.0
14785	.2	100	.1	82	22.6	242	68.6	4	16	.2	14	0	.0
14786	.3	100	.1	77	19.2	303	32.7	4	16	.2	17	0	.0
14787	5.5	98	2.1	74	23.4	255	67.6	7	15	2.6	13	0	.7
14788	.5	100	.2	69	19.0	260	54.1	6	14	.2	19	0	.1

ELMIRA

ZIPCODE	1	2	3	4	5	6	7	8	9	10	11	12	13
14801	4.9	99	1.6	80	21.5	280	49.4	9	9	2.4	9	0	.0
14802	5.0	97	.5	43	23.0	321	67.7	11	2	2.5	1	0	.1
14803	1.2	98	.4	68	24.4	329	61.0	9	4	.6	4	0	.0
14804	1.3	99	.5	76	22.3	292	57.2	8	13	.7	12	0	.0
14805	1.1	99	.4	83	21.2	329	51.4	9	8	.6	8	0	3.0
14806	2.4	100	.8	78	19.2	215	48.0	8	11	1.2	10	0	.0
14807	2.8	100	1.0	81	22.7	231	58.2	7	12	1.4	11	2	.4
14808	2.1	100	.7	77	18.9	247	48.2	8	9	2.2	13	1	.4
14809	2.3	98	.8	80	22.5	319	48.1	7	14	1.1	11	0	.4
14810	12.2	98	4.2	73	21.5	270	55.6	7	15	6.1	16	1	.1
14812	3.7	98	1.1	88	22.2	337	46.9	11	7	1.8	7	0	.2
14813	3.0	97	1.0	72	20.6	272	47.3	9	14	1.4	13	0	.1
14814	2.2	97	.7	80	37.4	378	104.8	8	7	1.0	8	4	.0
14815	.6	0	.2	94	22.4	253	45.4	8	8	.4	4	0	.0
14816	.7	100	.2	90	22.0	409	56.4	12	9	.4	4	0	.0
14817	1.8	98	.7	77	20.6	425	64.3	6	9	.9	8	0	.2
14818	1.4	96	.5	85	24.1	356	51.9	6	15	.7	15	0	.0
14819	.7	0	.2	82	20.9	332	38.6	8	10	.7	5	0	.0
14820	.8	100	.2	85	20.2	387	37.1	9	8	.4	5	0	.0
14821	3.4	99	1.2	84	25.9	339	60.0	9	8	1.6	4	0	.0
14823	4.3	100	1.5	78	19.1	242	43.5	7	13	2.1	11	0	.2
14824	.7	99	.3	78	17.9	285	47.6	9	14	.3	7	0	1.9
14825	.9	98	.3	78	19.1	267	57.8	8	10	.5	10	0	.0
14826	1.9	99	.6	89	21.3	252	45.6	7	14	.9	13	0	.0
14827	.3	100	.1	78	27.2	401	58.7	10	4	.2	3	0	.0
14830	21.8	97	8.4	68	26.7	298	65.8	6	13	10.1	11	3	.2
14836	1.1	100	.4	78	23.4	323	47.1	6	13	.5	11	0	.1
14837	3.5	99	1.3	78	20.1	245	56.4	6	14	2.0	13	1	.1
14838	.2	100	.1	90	20.7	347	57.9	11	7	.1	6	0	.0

*=Estimated **1.0=883 lbs per person; 100++ indicates per capita toxic waste generation > than 100 times the U.S. average of 883 lbs per capita.

ZIP CODE MEASURES OF SIZE, LEVELS OF AFFLUENCE AND QUALITY OF LIFE

1=Population (th.); 2= % White; 3=Households (th.); 4=% Owner Occupied; 5=Mean Income Per Household (th.$); 6=Mean Monthly Rent ($)*; 7=Mean Home Value (th.$)*; 8=% under 5; 9=% 65 and over; 10=% White Males (th.); 11=% White Males, 65+; 12=# Toxic Waste Sites; 13=Toxic Waste Relative to US(883 lbs.per capita)**.

NEW YORK

ELMIRA

ZIPCODE	1	2	3	4	5	6	7	8	9	10	11	12	13
14839	.8	100	.3	82	19.3	254	39.0	8	12	.4	11	0	.0
14840	3.3	100	1.2	77	24.8	281	69.2	8	12	1.7	10	1	.2
14841	.2	0	.1	90	19.2	220*	79.6	13	10	.3	12	0	.0
14842	.5	100	.2	82	23.5	300	58.4	14	11	.3	12	0	.0
14843	14.4	98	5.4	68	21.1	238	46.1	8	16	6.6	13	1	.2
14845	20.6	98	7.0	81	28.1	348	73.0	7	11	9.7	9	2	.1
14846	.6	100	.6	87	21.8	336	45.7	8	9	.3	8	0	.0
14847	2.2	99	.8	82	22.3	329	56.9	7	12	1.1	9	0	.0
14850	52.4	92	19.2	43	23.9	382	93.1	5	9	23.8	7	3	.7
14854	.3	100	.1	85	23.4	271	67.0	5	13	.8	8	0	.0
14855	.9	100	.3	85	18.8	330	44.6	10	11	.5	11	0	.4
14856	.4	0	.1	80	22.1	329	47.9	4	15	.0	0	0	.0
14858	1.4	100	.1	89	23.0	333	55.3	9	8	.7	8	0	.0
14859	1.0	99	.3	90	23.6	314	56.5	6	11	.5	11	0	.0
14860	.9	0	.3	81	22.6	316	43.2	7	15	.8	6	0	2.5
14861	1.6	100	.5	86	22.5	308	55.8	9	7	.8	6	1	.0
14863	.2	100	.1	79	21.6	205	59.4	9	11	.1	6	0	.0
14864	.6	100	.6	82	22.1	345	61.1	7	12	.8	13	0	.0
14865	2.7	99	1.0	74	20.2	313	56.7	6	18	1.3	13	0	2.5
14867	4.6	98	1.7	84	24.6	400	66.0	8	9	2.2	8	0	.0
14868	.3	100	.1	94	26.2	301*	47.2	4	18	.2	11	0	.0
14869	1.3	0	.4	83	23.2	267	55.2	8	9	.2	11	0	.0
14870	8.5	98	3.2	77	29.7	335	79.0	6	11	4.0	10	0	2.7
14871	5.1	98	1.6	88	31.3	329	72.5	6	7	2.4	7	0	.0
14872	.6	0	.2	88	22.7	321	60.2	6	11	.2	0	0	.0
14873	2.0	95	.7	87	19.4	233	43.3	7	13	1.0	12	0	.0
14874	.3	100	.1	89	21.7	503	48.7	11	10	.2	13	0	.0
14876	.1	0	.1	91	25.3	291*	39.2	10	18	.0	0	0	.0
14877	.5	100	.2	78	18.5	299	32.7	10	12	.3	10	0	.0
14878	.6	0	.2	96	20.2	232*	47.8	5	18	.0	0	0	.0
14879	1.9	0	.6	82	22.8	272	54.5	8	10	.0	0	0	.0
14880	1.8	0	.6	81	20.7	275	50.9	8	11	.1	13	0	.0
14881	.2	100	.1	74	26.4	392	76.1	3	11	.2	8	0	.0
14882	3.2	97	1.1	77	27.9	387	77.6	7	6	1.7	5	3	.0
14883	3.3	97	1.1	82	22.0	324	58.3	8	9	1.5	7	0	.0
14884	.4	0	.1	77	19.1	244	58.1	9	15	.0	0	0	.0
14885	.8	99	.2	76	19.2	321	37.1	8	10	.4	9	0	.0
14886	5.6	99	1.9	81	23.4	316	70.1	7	10	2.7	9	0	.0
14887	.2	100	.1	78	15.8	173	38.4	6	15	.1	22	0	.0
14888	.6	0	.2	81	20.3	374	51.7	11	18	.0	0	0	.0
14889	1.5	98	.5	85	19.8	286	51.3	7	13	.8	12	0	.0
14890	.2	100	.1	73	21.6	300	48.6	7	14	.1	13	0	.0
14891	4.5	99	1.6	72	23.2	266	60.9	6	15	2.1	14	0	6.6
14892	8.0	99	2.8	72	21.6	297	57.9	7	14	3.8	11	0	.4
14893	.4	99	.1	79	16.1	222	37.9	5	16	.2	15	0	.0
14894	1.6	99	.6	86	20.5	328	55.8	7	13	.8	12	0	.0
14895	10.7	99	4.0	70	22.2	266	59.6	8	16	5.2	12	2	1.5
14896	.2	0	.1	84	23.3	347	45.7	5	0	.2	2	0	.0
14897	.8	100	.3	71	18.1	264	38.0	6	15	.4	13	0	.0

NEW YORK

ZIPCODE	1	2	3	4	5	6	7	8	9	10	11	12	13
ELMIRA													
14898	1.1	100	.4	81	17.1	251	39.6	10	11	.5	12	0	.0
ELMIRA													
14901	18.7	88	6.9	50	18.3	251	54.1	7	15	7.5	12	2	.8
14903	9.0	87	2.9	69	22.8	264	63.2	4	12	4.0	11	2	2.0
14904	19.4	96	7.3	63	20.2	288	49.4	8	15	8.6	13	3	.0
14905	10.4	98	3.9	69	30.2	338	84.5	7	16	4.6	15	1	.0
ERIE													
16428	.3	100	.1	90	23.2	267*	42.2	3	0	.1	0	0	.0
WELLSBORO													
16923	.3	100	.1	86	18.9	163	44.8	9	11	.2	13	0	.0
16942	.2	0	.1	88	16.1	185*	29.9	2	17	.0	0	0	.0
MONTROSE													
18847	.4	100	.1	81	19.4	152	56.8	6	14	.2	13	0	.0

*=Estimated **1.0=883 lbs per person; 100++ indicates per capita toxic waste generation > than 100 times the U.S. average of 883 lbs per capita.

ZIP CODE MEASURES OF SIZE, LEVELS OF AFFLUENCE AND QUALITY OF LIFE

1=Population (th.); 2= % White; 3=Households (th.); 4=% Owner Occupied; 5=Mean Income Per Household (th.$); 6=Mean Monthly Rent ($)*; 7=Mean Home Value (th.$)*; 8=% under 5; 9=% 65 and over; 10=White Males (th.); 11=% White Males, 65+; 12=# Toxic Waste Sites; 13=Toxic Waste Relative to US(883 lbs.per capita)**.

NORTH CAROLINA

ZIPCODE	1	2	3	4	5	6	7	8	9	10	11	12	13
NORFOLK													
23457	.7	0	.2	84	19.2	277	64.7	13	5	.0	0	0	.0
FARMVILLE													
23927	.3	54	.1	71	17.5	71	52.1	11	8	.1	4	0	.0
ROANOKE													
24171	.3	0	.1	96	30.0	344*	82.6	4	12	.0	0	0	.0
LYNCHBURG													
24580	.3	75	.1	73	19.7	64	56.9	7	15	.1	8	0	.0
24598	1.6	44	.5	64	16.3	177	51.9	8	14	.3	16	0	.0
GREENSBORO (WEST)													
27006	6.8	95	2.4	87	29.5	266	105.6	6	8	3.2	7	0	.0
27007	1.2	100	.5	81	19.1	262	85.9	7	15	.6	15	0	.0
27009	1.8	71	.6	80	19.9	205	59.6	5	11	.6	11	0	.0
27010	.2	100	.1	84	27.5	241	91.3	1	15	.1	6	0	.0
27011	4.2	95	1.6	85	20.3	176	62.9	6	11	1.9	8	0	.3
27012	11.8	97	4.0	84	34.2	296	115.3	7	8	5.5	5	0	1.0
27013	3.4	71	1.1	82	23.7	178	60.9	7	12	1.2	11	0	.5
27014	1.7	85	.6	79	20.8	254	46.4	8	13	.7	11	0	.0
27016	1.6	98	.6	91	23.1	205	58.7	7	10	.8	9	0	.0
27017	6.1	97	2.1	79	22.0	236	66.7	7	11	2.9	9	0	.0
27018	5.1	94	1.8	84	22.1	274	63.2	6	12	2.4	12	0	.0
27019	3.3	98	1.1	78	26.9	218	73.3	7	9	1.6	9	0	.5
27020	4.6	99	1.7	83	19.9	189	62.4	6	14	2.2	13	0	.0
27021	10.7	100	3.7	85	23.9	292	71.1	7	8	5.1	16	0	.3
27022	1.2	96	.4	78	21.4	148	57.7	4	18	.5	18	0	.0
27023	5.2	97	1.9	83	29.8	297	90.0	7	8	2.6	7	0	.3
27024	1.8	0	.6	84	19.8	155	41.0	7	15	.0	0	0	.0
27025	10.0	78	3.4	73	22.6	237	65.5	8	11	3.8	9	0	.5
27027	4.2	94	1.7	72	20.0	212	50.1	5	14	1.8	12	0	.0
27028	16.4	88	5.6	82	22.7	224	68.3	7	11	7.1	9	0	.7
27030	33.2	94	11.9	76	20.7	229	58.5	7	12	15.1	9	0	.2
27031	.2	100	.1	86	22.2	154	64.2	0	22	.1	18	0	.0
27040	6.9	96	2.3	90	38.6	302	97.2	7	8	3.3	8	0	.5
27041	5.7	95	2.0	74	22.6	205	63.8	7	11	2.7	8	0	.4
27042	.7	92	.3	81	20.3	233*	54.9	6	16	.3	19	0	1.1
27043	3.7	95	1.3	79	21.5	245	63.3	7	10	1.8	8	0	.0
27045	6.0	92	2.3	82	26.1	260	76.1	5	10	2.7	10	0	.0
27046	1.6	94	.5	83	20.2	315	56.6	8	11	.7	9	0	.0
27047	.9	0	.3	81	20.2	175	49.5	6	14	.0	8	0	.0
27048	6.9	87	2.3	82	24.7	253	69.1	7	10	3.0	8	0	.2
27049	.2	100	.1	78	16.4	172	42.3	2	35	.1	31	0	.0
27050	2.8	90	.9	85	23.4	259	77.1	5	9	1.3	7	0	.0
27051	5.1	90	1.9	83	26.6	247	67.2	6	11	2.3	8	0	.4
27052	7.8	82	2.6	80	21.0	226	60.5	6	11	3.2	9	1	.0
27053	2.5	87	.9	79	19.7	136	59.1	8	14	1.1	11	0	.0
27054	1.9	70	.7	82	22.6	233	56.5	7	13	.7	13	0	.0
27055	9.8	95	3.4	82	22.7	225	65.2	5	12	4.6	10	1	.1
WINSTON SALEM													
27101	18.6	45	7.8	39	17.4	253	57.9	6	15	3.8	11	1	.3
27103	22.9	93	9.6	65	26.4	320	77.8	6	11	9.8	9	0	.3

NORTH CAROLINA

ZIPCODE	1	2	3	4	5	6	7	8	9	10	11	12	13
WINSTON SALEM													
27104	20.5	95	8.5	66	41.1	347	139.6	5	11	9.2	9	0	.0
27105	45.2	34	15.8	51	19.2	277	57.8	7	11	7.1	10	6	.5
27106	26.7	88	10.6	67	36.3	351	112.6	5	9	11.2	8	0	.0
27107	51.6	78	18.6	71	23.7	304	63.4	6	10	19.2	9	3	.0
GREENSBORO (EAST)													
27201	.3	0	.1	80	23.3	225	46.7	6	13	.0	0	0	.0
27202	.3	51	.1	74	22.3	185	47.1	0	1	.1	0	0	.3
27203	34.5	93	12.7	75	24.5	263	69.2	6	11	15.6	9	0	.4
27207	2.7	80	.9	90	20.9	240*	44.9	6	12	.0	12	0	.0
27208	1.6	97	.5	81	21.5	250	48.5	9	10	.8	8	0	.0
27209	3.2	83	1.1	78	19.9	260	47.9	6	11	1.3	9	0	.4
27212	1.3	57	.4	76	31.4	244	43.0	6	7	.4	7	0	.0
27213	.1	79	.1	86	21.7	250*	67.0	0	14	.0	0	0	.0
27214	5.4	66	1.7	76	26.7	246	72.4	7	7	1.9	8	0	.0
27215	58.8	78	21.7	71	24.8	283	69.3	6	11	21.7	10	1	.6
27228	.2	100	.1	75	16.3	245	40.0	8	20	.1	19	0	3.5
27229	3.6	62	1.2	79	18.4	197	53.6	7	10	1.1	9	0	.0
27230	2.0	100	.1	73	16.8	327	32.7	9	28	.1	24	0	2.0
27231	2.0	59	.6	82	23.1	299	60.8	6	7	.6	7	0	.0
27232	.3	100	.1	90	17.7	210	34.7	4	16	.1	23	0	.0
27233	2.3	97	.8	88	26.5	247	71.3	5	8	1.2	7	0	.0
27235	1.1	100	.4	90	30.8	269	77.4	4	10	.5	8	0	.1
27239	5.6	100	2.0	82	19.9	198	56.4	7	12	2.7	12	0	.0
27242	2.4	64	.7	80	18.3	189	41.5	7	8	.7	6	0	.0
27243	2.4	72	.9	83	21.0	210	49.3	7	12	.9	11	0	.3
27244	8.2	84	2.4	77	23.2	255	62.9	6	9	3.4	9	0	.7
27248	2.9	96	1.1	86	19.9	174	44.9	6	13	1.3	13	0	.7
27249	6.7	82	2.4	72	23.9	252	62.2	7	11	2.7	9	0	.7
27252	.7	63	.3	79	23.2	186	54.9	4	14	.6	12	0	1.2
27253	16.9	88	6.2	74	23.7	273	64.4	5	12	7.0	8	1	.3
27258	3.8	80	1.3	83	23.7	299	44.9	6	11	1.5	11	1	.7
27260	56.5	69	20.5	56	24.8	282	76.2	7	12	18.7	11	5	.7
27262	12.1	90	4.7	69	28.6	317	76.7	5	17	4.8	14	1	.2
27263	17.0	96	6.1	74	23.9	266	64.5	8	9	8.0	9	1	.3
27278	13.5	77	4.7	75	25.7	340	70.4	8	9	5.0	8	0	.5
27281	1.7	62	.5	78	20.1	187	61.4	6	11	.5	10	0	.7
27282	6.7	97	2.3	79	33.8	337	112.7	6	8	3.2	10	5	.7
27283	2.2	99	.8	82	26.0	290	96.9	6	12	1.1	10	0	1.2
27284	27.3	97	9.5	78	27.7	301	83.6	7	13	13.1	6	4	.3
27288	24.8	84	9.3	77	22.1	231	52.9	6	13	9.7	11	3	.5
27291	1.4	49	.5	76	16.9	114	61.8	6	12	.3	12	0	.0
27292	55.0	89	19.6	75	22.9	261	62.9	6	10	23.8	8	7	.4
27298	2.7	87	2.7	83	21.8	241	61.9	6	13	3.0	11	1	.3
27299	3.0	97	1.0	81	20.7	283	50.5	5	11	1.5	8	0	.1
GREENSBORO (EAST)													
27301	4.8	94	1.6	82	27.3	296	81.3	6	7	2.2	6	1	.0
27302	12.4	70	4.3	82	22.6	227	60.9	7	11	4.2	9	2	.4
27305	1.4	35	.5	79	20.2	162	41.0	6	12	.2	12	0	.0

*=Estimated **1.0-883 lbs per person; 100++ indicates per capita toxic waste generation > than 100 times the U.S. average of 883 lbs per capita.

ZIP CODE MEASURES OF SIZE, LEVELS OF AFFLUENCE AND QUALITY OF LIFE

1=Population (th.); 2= % White; 3=Households (th.); 4=% Owner Occupied; 5=Mean Income Per Household (th.$); 6=Mean Monthly Rent ($); 7=Mean Home Value (th.$); 8=% under 5; 9=% 65 and over; 10=% White Males; 11=% White Males, 65+; 12=# Toxic Waste Sites; 13=Toxic Waste Relative to US(883 lbs.per capita)**.

NORTH CAROLINA

GREENSBORO (EAST)

ZIPCODE	1	2	3	4	5	6	7	8	9	10	11	12	13
27306	5.6	58	1.9	78	19.1	233	49.1	8	16	1.6	14	0	.0
27310	1.2	94	.4	81	29.5	337	115.1	7	8	.6	9	0	.0
27311	3.5	62	1.1	73	19.6	183	47.5	8	10	1.1	10	0	.0
27312	7.4	71	2.8	76	23.5	316	71.7	5	12	2.6	10	0	.2
27313	3.8	92	1.3	83	29.8	284	96.3	5	8	1.7	9	0	.1
27314	.9	72	.3	73	17.4	236	57.2	2	9	.3	11	0	.0
27315	1.6	92	.6	77	21.9	275	58.6	4	10	.7	8	0	.0
27316	1.8	89	.8	83	23.2	214	56.4	6	13	2.2	10	0	.0
27317	9.6	94	3.4	79	23.0	251	61.6	7	12	4.3	8	1	1.0
27320	33.6	71	11.7	71	23.4	242	62.5	7	12	11.5	10	4	.3
27325	6.0	87	2.2	82	20.5	216	46.9	7	10	2.5	9	0	.0
27326	3.7	73	1.2	71	21.6	231	60.6	8	9	1.4	9	0	.0
27330	37.9	77	13.1	73	24.2	265	69.5	8	10	14.1	8	7	1.5
27340	.2	85	.1	46	21.6	227	45.6	3	12	.1	15	0	5.4
27341	4.2	91	1.4	89	20.2	161	50.8	7	13	1.9	12	0	.0
27342	.4	0	..	86	38.1	83	78.6	7	2	.0	0	0	.0
27343	1.7	0	.5	71	18.7	155	53.4	7	13	.0	0	0	.0
27344	11.4	75	4.1	80	24.0	231	62.8	6	12	4.1	11	2	.3
27349	2.7	83	1.0	82	20.6	158	66.3	6	13	1.0	14	0	.0
27350	3.7	99	1.3	89	21.0	320	69.7	9	8	1.8	7	0	.0
27351	2.0	75	.2	91	15.1	194	42.3	5	18	.1	12	0	1.0
27355	2.0	75	.9	80	21.2	201	60.3	7	11	.8	11	0	.0
27356	2.8	96	1.0	82	19.6	192	42.4	8	12	1.4	11	0	.0
27357	3.7	93	1.2	78	21.7	238	63.2	6	11	1.7	10	1	.2
27358	5.0	93	1.7	76	25.8	263	87.7	6	9	2.2	7	0	1.6
27359	.5	100	.2	85	19.6	208	44.9	7	17	.3	16	0	5.3
27360	34.2	86	12.2	69	22.3	261	61.9	7	11	14.4	9	4	.2
27370	8.9	93	3.0	82	25.1	248	74.2	6	7	4.2	6	0	
27371	7.2	84	2.5	72	21.1	212	59.4	7	11	2.9	10	7	.5
27373	.1	100	.1	64	24.8	188	64.1	5	20	.1	11	0	.1
27374	1.1	97	.4	63	22.6	241	76.0	7	10	.6	10	0	1.0
27376	2.8	75	.9	84	26.3	296	84.2	8	10	1.1	11	0	.2
27377	2.1	86	.7	92	25.9	252	75.1	5	8	1.0	6	1	.2
27379	4.9	49	1.5	73	19.7	227	53.8	6	11	1.3	10	0	

GREENSBORO

ZIPCODE	1	2	3	4	5	6	7	8	9	10	11	12	13
27401	19.0	28	7.5	33	18.0	273	58.6	6	14	2.2	13	2	.2
27403	17.5	94	7.7	59	24.9	323	81.4	5	17	7.4	13	2	2.4
27405	41.2	68	15.3	58	23.6	332	69.4	7	8	13.3	8	7	.5
27406	44.8	55	15.4	64	24.8	308	79.3	7	8	12.2	7	1	.1
27407	25.7	88	9.8	58	28.0	338	86.6	7	7	10.9	6	4	.3
27408	20.4	96	8.3	75	41.2	393	124.3	5	11	9.1	9	0	
27409	5.9	87	2.5	51	26.8	400	91.3	7	4	2.5	3	11	3.5
27410	23.7	95	8.1	79	44.0	418	144.7	5	8	11.0	7	2	.2

RALEIGH

ZIPCODE	1	2	3	4	5	6	7	8	9	10	11	12	13
27501	5.8	84	2.0	68	21.2	232	64.8	9	9	2.4	5	0	.2
27502	10.8	68	3.6	78	26.4	287	84.0	7	10	3.6	8	5	1.8
27503	2.6	83	.9	72	30.9	352	88.9	6	10	1.1	7	0	.0
27504	8.3	82	2.9	61	18.4	212	62.1	7	12	3.3	12	0	.0
27505	3.0	79	1.0	80	22.2	325	63.1	7	12	1.1	9	0	.0

NORTH CAROLINA

RALEIGH

ZIPCODE	1	2	3	4	5	6	7	8	9	10	11	12	13
27506	2.6	94	.6	63	18.5	246	73.9	7	7	1.2	2	0	.0
27507	.3	57	.1	66	28.3	116	43.6	7	5	.1	9	0	2.6
27508	.7	59	..	80	16.9	252	46.8	6	14	.2	16	0	.7
27509	5.1	67	.9	77	27.2	240	70.9	4	8	1.8	7	3	.4
27510	7.8	81	3.8	22	16.8	386	81.5	4	4	2.9	2	1	.0
27511	.9	96	8.5	76	36.0	421	120.3	7	3	11.8	3	0	.0
27514	1.6	84	15.7	52	29.0	373	134.7	5	7	19.0	5	5	.1
27520	10.6	75	3.6	70	22.3	281	65.0	7	8	4.0	6	2	2.1
27521	3.2	90	1.2	74	17.4	229	56.1	8	15	1.4	11	0	.0
27522	5.2	63	2.7	69	22.5	256	64.6	7	10	1.6	8	0	2.8
27524	7.5	89	2.7	72	18.4	233	62.1	6	12	2.3	10	1	.0
27525	6.6	52	2.3	67	18.7	248	46.0	5	13	1.7	11	0	6.4
27526	9.0	78	3.2	68	21.9	249	71.0	6	13	3.3	10	0	.5
27529	15.7	91	5.3	75	28.6	366	78.4	8	5	6.9	3	0	.0
27530	64.5	66	21.5	54	21.6	264	75.8	8	8	21.3	6	5	.3
27536	33.2	58	11.1	63	20.3	244	63.6	7	12	9.2	10	1	.9
27541	2.8	35	.8	69	19.0	244	58.7	7	7	.5	9	0	.0
27542	6.5	78	2.3	70	19.5	193	57.5	7	12	2.4	10	1	2.0
27544	3.2	43	1.0	72	17.7	175	59.4	6	12	.7	14	0	.0
27545	6.6	86	2.2	75	27.7	321	85.7	8	5	2.8	4	1	.0
27546	9.2	69	3.0	73	20.8	225	58.8	6	11	3.1	10	0	.0
27549	14.5	58	4.7	71	19.4	240	61.6	7	13	4.0	11	0	.1
27551	1.5	40	.6	77	14.2	119	57	6	11	1.7	10	1	.4
27552	.3	0	.1	94	25.4	292*	45.6	5	2	.0	0	0	.0
27553	2.0	0	.6	69	16.0	125	58.6	8	13	.6	16	0	.0
27555	.5	85	.2	69	17.6	207	37.9	4	16	.2	16	0	.0
27556	.2	39	.2	77	17.4	132	32.9	5	11	.1	15	0	.0
27557	4.2	70	.4	70	18.1	207	50.2	6	10	1.4	8	1	.0
27559	1.8	64	1.0	73	20.7	270	52.3	7	12	.6	7	4	11.8
27560	2.9	78	1.0	73	28.7	282	57.4	5	9	7.3	11	1	14.6
27562	1.4	53	.4	77	20.1	216	59.0	9	13	3.8	9	1	.0
27563	3.6	0	1.2	73	17.6	195	49.0	8	14	3.3	14	0	.1
27565	18.7	50	6.2	67	20.6	217	63.9	6	12	4.4	11	0	.3
27568	.9	90	.3	66	21.5	283	58.7	5	13	.4	8	0	.0
27569	4.6	87	1.6	68	21.5	226	55.4	6	9	2.0	9	0	.0
27570	.2	0	.2	72	15.7	180*	32.9	7	7	.1	8	0	.0
27571	.4	100	.1	85	28.6	235	75.2	5	14	.1	8	0	.0
27572	3.5	74	1.2	78	21.8	216	62.0	7	10	1.3	9	0	.0
27573	22.4	69	7.7	69	21.6	240	58.5	7	12	7.3	11	4	.5
27576	10.3	78	3.7	64	19.1	250	57.4	8	11	3.8	9	2	.1
27577	15.1	76	5.4	66	21.2	259	71.8	7	12	5.4	9	4	.2
27581	1.5	65	.4	75	25.4	205	63.8	6	10	.5	11	0	.0
27582	.8	60	.2	78	17.0	154	53.1	8	14	.4	14	0	.3
27583	2.3	75	.8	77	21.6	242	58.4	7	7	.9	8	0	.0
27584	.9	27	.2	74	17.9	169	45.0	10	8	.1	11	0	.0
27587	11.9	76	4.1	68	26.0	250	70.6	7	10	4.6	8	0	.3
27589	7.0	33	2.2	63	16.8	194	50.8	8	14	1.1	16	0	.0
27591	8.7	73	3.0	74	23.7	263	73.4	9	9	3.2	6	2	.0

*=Estimated **1.0=883 lbs per person; 100++ indicates per capita toxic waste generation > than 100 times the U.S. average of 883 lbs per capita.

ZIP CODE MEASURES OF SIZE, LEVELS OF AFFLUENCE AND QUALITY OF LIFE

1=Population (th.); 2= % White; 3=Households (th.); 4=% Owner Occupied; 5=Mean Income Per Household (th.); 6=Mean Monthly Rent ($)*; 7=Mean Home Value (th.$)*; 8=% under 5; 9=% 65 and over; 10=White Males (th.); 11=% White Males, 65+; 12=# Toxic Waste Sites; 13=Toxic Waste Relative to US(883 lbs.per capita)**.

NORTH CAROLINA

ZIPCODE	1	2	3	4	5	6	7	8	9	10	11	12	13
RALEIGH													
27592	2.8	86	1.0	65	19.5	304	85.5	4	11	1.2	9	0	.0
27593	.3	76	.1	89	21.5	246	43.9	0	15	.1	12	0	.0
27594	.2	60	.1	86	16.3	214	33.8	8	17	.0	20	0	.0
27596	2.8	81	1.0	74	23.9	216	66.4	7	10	1.2	10	0	.0
27597	12.3	69	4.2	69	21.2	257	67.3	7	11	4.0	9	0	.1
RALEIGH													
27601	9.6	12	3.7	21	13.7	238	53.6	6	16	.5	10	1	.1
27603	17.5	81	7.0	56	21.7	273	72.3	7	10	7.1	6	4	.6
27604	25.3	88	9.6	62	28.7	346	91.1	7	6	10.6	4	3	.8
27605	4.0	92	2.2	28	20.4	334	92.6	2	22	1.5	14	0	.0
27606	19.5	87	7.9	38	25.5	397	99.3	5	4	9.2	3	1	.2
27607	17.8	82	6.1	51	31.0	353	108.7	4	7	7.5	7	2	1.7
27608	9.8	96	4.6	59	31.1	348	107.0	4	22	4.2	17	0	.1
27609	36.7	92	13.6	63	38.3	409	135.0	6	5	16.3	3	3	.2
27610	31.1	30	10.6	57	22.1	343	65.0	7	7	4.5	8	1	.0
27612	20.4	93	7.1	77	42.2	435	142.2	7	5	9.4	4	0	.0
27614	3.1	87	1.0	86	39.4	297	168.1	5	6	1.3	3	0	.0
DURHAM													
27701	21.8	36	9.3	28	16.4	272	59.6	7	16	3.6	14	3	.6
27703	21.0	67	7.4	57	23.0	293	59.9	7	10	6.7	11	4	.0
27704	23.1	66	8.1	63	24.6	366	64.0	7	10	7.1	10	0	.3
27705	29.3	84	12.0	47	23.8	331	91.3	6	12	11.6	8	0	.4
27706	2.2	97	.1	78	59.2	1038	144.4	0	2	1.3	2	1	.0
27707	32.4	42	12.0	52	27.9	360	95.4	6	10	6.6	9	0	.0
27712	11.0	94	3.6	93	37.0	455	107.6	7	4	5.1	3	2	.0
27713	9.7	61	3.2	82	30.5	422	82.8	6	6	2.9	3	0	.0
ROCKY MOUNT													
27801	59.2	63	21.3	60	23.0	281	73.5	7	11	17.8	8	9	3.4
27805	3.9	0	1.3	70	17.0	207	45.5	10	12	.8	0	0	.0
27806	3.1	52	1.1	82	17.3	208	45.1	7	15	.8	17	0	17.9
27807	3.7	67	1.4	63	19.7	182	55.5	9	10	1.2	8	0	.0
27808	1.8	85	.7	79	18.0	216	65.3	9	22	.7	17	0	.0
27809	4.5	31	1.3	71	19.0	183	60.1	7	9	.7	8	0	.0
27810	4.5	59	1.6	77	18.0	193	48.5	8	16	1.3	14	0	.0
27811	.6	55	.2	68	23.5	377	70.0	14	2	.1	0	0	.0
27812	3.6	0	1.1	60	20.2	219	61.8	7	11	.3	0	1	.0
27813	.6	89	.2	73	20.9	219	60.2	7	11	.3	5	0	.0
27814	.8	58	.3	83	15.8	215	60.9	11	17	.3	0	0	.0
27816	2.3	51	.7	63	15.7	200	57.8	6	14	.5	17	0	.0
27817	5.4	67	1.8	80	18.9	245	50.1	9	9	1.8	9	1	.0
27818	1.5	29	.4	78	19.3	148	43.3	8	13	.2	12	0	.0
27819	.5	30	.2	69	15.4	266	48.4	15	11	.1	13	0	.0
27820	2.7	68	.9	81	21.4	177	48.1	6	13	.9	11	2	12.7
27821	.4	27	.2	95	12.3	141*	34.6	7	17	.0	16	0	.0
27822	5.9	69	1.9	72	23.4	222	68.3	8	8	2.0	0	0	.3
27823	10.1	21	3.0	59	15.7	224	49.7	8	14	.9	15	3	.0
27824	1.9	60	.6	75	14.7	236	41.9	8	17	.5	19	1	.0
27825	.4	52	.1	73	19.2	214	66.4	13	16	.1	18	0	.0
27826	.8	58	.3	90	15.9	261	56.9	6	24	.2	19	0	.0

NORTH CAROLINA

ZIPCODE	1	2	3	4	5	6	7	8	9	10	11	12	13
ROCKY MOUNT													
27827	.3	84	.1	63	18.8	272	55.4	5	15	.1	11	0	.0
27828	7.9	55	2.8	56	19.4	224	68.2	7	12	2.1	9	4	.3
27829	2.3	62	.7	58	18.7	150	53.0	6	12	.7	13	0	.0
27830	4.5	58	1.5	62	20.3	227	55.4	7	13	1.2	10	1	.2
27831	3.7	0	1.1	78	15.9	206	41.3	11	10	.5	13	0	.0
27832	2.2	50	.8	73	17.6	207	32.6	8	14	.5	13	0	.0
27833	.3	20	.3	75	20.7	164	50.1	9	23	.0	0	0	.0
27834	56.8	69	18.9	55	23.4	307	91.5	7	7	18.9	5	10	1.4
27837	2.5	61	.9	67	22.5	259	55.9	7	10	.8	9	0	.0
27839	3.4	0	.8	71	18.6	160	45.6	3	11	.0	0	1	.0
27840	.9	55	.3	60	19.6	257	46.1	8	10	.2	7	0	.0
27842	1.3	38	.9	88	30.1	260	90.5	5	6	.1	6	0	.0
27843	1.3	47	.5	71	15.2	177	38.5	8	7	.3	10	0	.0
27844	2.4	0	.7	61	15.3	130	33.8	8	9	.0	0	0	.0
27845	2.9	0	.7	70	18.0	240	48.8	3	9	.0	0	0	.0
27846	2.7	67	.9	76	18.6	197	51.2	8	12	.9	10	0	.0
27847	1.0	16	.3	70	14.3	145	35.4	13	17	.1	29	0	.0
27848	1.0	0	.0	69	16.6	147	36.8	0	24	.0	0	0	.0
27849	2.5	19	.7	66	17.3	192	46.8	9	11	.2	13	1	1.4
27850	5.7	37	1.9	67	17.2	184	55.9	7	16	1.0	22	0	.0
27851	4.6	77	1.5	65	21.0	233	65.9	8	7	1.8	7	0	.0
27852	2.6	62	.9	56	17.6	199	55.8	7	13	.7	14	0	.5
27853	.6	19	.2	69	12.2	154	33.6	9	7	.0	0	0	.0
27854	1.1	68	.6	79	14.7	368	23.4	2	29	.1	35	0	.3
27855	6.3	46	1.8	71	21.7	267	57.8	6	15	1.5	2	0	.2
27856	11.3	56	3.8	64	24.9	225	67.8	8	11	3.1	11	0	.0
27857	2.2	35	.7	63	15.5	225	47.4	7	8	.4	12	0	.0
27859	.2	44	.1	55	26.6	106	46.7	0	27	.1	33	0	.0
27860	2.4	61	.8	71	22.7	263	47.2	8	11	.7	7	0	.0
27861	.3	17	.1	59	12.6	219	34.6	3	19	.0	13	0	.5
27862	4.5	29	1.6	67	35.5	118	51.5	8	7	.8	7	0	.0
27863	4.5	83	1.9	73	21.2	211	63.3	6	11	1.9	7	0	.5
27864	4.0	52	1.2	63	19.6	243	54.9	9	8	1.0	6	1	.3
27865	1.6	91	.5	76	19.4	273	53.1	8	8	.7	9	0	.0
27866	1.0	40	.3	65	18.3	197	32.4	8	15	.2	18	0	.2
27867	.2	47	.1	58	29.0	89	63.8	5	39	.1	29	0	.0
27868	.2	81	.1	72	29.4	259	64.6	5	6	.4	9	0	.0
27869	2.8	28	.8	74	19.0	198	40.8	4	18	.4	22	0	.0
27870	23.4	77	8.2	70	20.6	263	53.9	7	11	8.6	10	1	.8
27871	5.4	0	1.8	61	18.3	253	56.0	8	13	.0	0	0	.0
27872	.4	70	.2	74	17.9	101	49.5	7	15	.1	15	0	.0
27873	.5	80	.5	57	22.8	238	47.1	8	10	.9	6	0	.0
27874	6.2	41	2.2	60	16.6	200	57.3	9	13	1.2	10	1	.3
27875	.8	47	.3	86	16.8	33	51.5	5	16	.7	11	0	.0
27876	1.8	42	.3	75	15.3	234	43.1	6	17	.4	22	0	.0
27877	.6	34	.2	80	22.3	189	46.0	6	12	.1	15	0	8.3
27878	1.4	62	.5	72	21.3	237	55.0	7	8	.4	10	0	.2
27879	.5	28	.2	71	13.7	182	42.8	8	14	.1	31	0	.0
27880	1.9	66	.6	62	19.5	204	58.0	7	9	.7	6	0	.0

*=Estimated **1.0=883 lbs per person; 100++ indicates per capita toxic waste generation > than 100 times the U.S. average of 883 lbs per capita.

ZIP CODE MEASURES OF SIZE, LEVELS OF AFFLUENCE AND QUALITY OF LIFE

1=Population (th.); 2=% White; 3=Households (th.); 4=% Owner Occupied; 5=Mean Income Per Household (th.); 6=Mean Monthly Rent ($)*; 7=Mean Home Value (th.$)*;
8=% under 5; 9=% 65 and over; 10=% White Males; 11=% White Males, 65+; 12=# Toxic Waste Sites; 13=Toxic Waste Relative to US(883 lbs.per capita)**

NORTH CAROLINA

ROCKY MOUNT

ZIPCODE	1	2	3	4	5	6	7	8	9	10	11	12	13
27960	.7	100	.3	81	20.6	167	85.5	4	10	.3	13	0	.0
27962	8.5	61	2.9	72	23.1	216	62.4	8	10	2.6	9	4	1.5
27964	.2	100	.1	100	29.6	340*	99.8	0	21	.1	26	0	.0
27965	.4	84	.1	93	22.8	262*	33.8	3	10	.2	8	0	.0
27966	.6	70	.2	77	22.9	511	59.6	13	13	.1	17	0	.0
27967	.6	32	.2	72	40.4	233	46.1	15	16	.1	14	0	.9
27969	.2	0	.1	50	10.9	177	14.5	16	22	.0	0	0	.0
27970	4.3	0	1.2	77	20.8	227	51.4	9	10	.0	0	0	.0
27973	.8	80	.2	88	26.8	308*	58.8	4	17	.3	21	0	.0
27974	1.0	79	.4	77	15.7	214	42.1	6	17	.4	14	0	.0
27976	1.7	67	.6	77	22.1	240	56.1	7	11	.4	8	0	.0
27978	.1	100	.1	95	30.7	353*	74.1	3	24	.1	20	0	.9
27979	1.3	51	.5	81	21.6	197	54.5	5	12	.3	15	0	.9
27980	1.7	61	.6	76	18.5	233	42.2	9	12	.5	11	0	.0
27981	1.0	100	.4	91	18.7	290	66.0	8	6	.5	5	0	.7
27982	.1	100	.1	38	22.0	224	91.9	13	6	.1	9	0	.0
27983	8.0	43	2.8	76	17.6	206	50.3	7	14	1.6	14	0	.0
27985	.5	48	.1	70	10.7	187	49.3	5	16	.1	11	0	.0
27986	1.1	49	.4	73	17.9	249	39.2	7	16	.2	13	2	.0

CHARLOTTE

ZIPCODE	1	2	3	4	5	6	7	8	9	10	11	12	13
28001	22.6	89	8.4	74	21.7	255	61.8	6	14	9.6	12	0	.3
28006	1.0	0	.4	75	25.0	255	73.9	2	11	.0	0	0	.0
28007	.7	0	.3	75	18.8	253	47.5	8	13	.0	0	0	11.4
28009	1.8	47	.7	78	20.1	270	47.8	6	19	.4	26	1	5.1
28012	16.0	93	5.6	61	23.1	243	64.8	6	11	7.3	9	0	.8
28016	11.6	92	3.9	74	23.7	253	58.6	7	9	5.2	7	0	9.1
28017	2.4	91	.6	61	24.7	249	75.1	7	6	1.1	5	0	.0
28018	4.3	96	1.5	78	20.2	232	56.1	8	15	2.0	12	0	.0
28019	1.2	93	.5	83	18.2	235	37.5	5	17	.5	16	0	1.2
28020	2.2	0	.9	84	18.1	159	40.8	8	11	.4	0	0	.0
28021	9.4	92	3.3	76	23.9	257	63.1	7	13	4.2	11	0	3.8
28023	9.5	94	3.6	80	22.1	239	59.6	6	14	4.3	12	0	.3
28024	1.0	94	.4	85	24.5	223	54.3	5	11	.5	5	0	3.5
28025	43.8	86	15.8	74	24.7	253	70.0	6	12	18.3	10	8	.1
28031	2.2	72	.8	71	24.0	252	52.2	8	14	.7	10	0	.4
28032	2.2	95	.8	72	18.3	219	37.6	5	18	.9	15	1	2.5
28033	1.5	92	.5	80	24.4	194	64.0	7	8	.7	7	0	.0
28034	12.8	90	4.3	71	22.9	268	62.1	6	8	5.6	6	0	.5
28036	6.1	83	1.7	78	31.2	259	115.6	5	8	2.8	6	0	1.1
28037	5.5	94	1.9	86	30.4	319	116.0	9	6	2.6	5	0	.0
28038	.7	77	.2	56	24.0	295	57.2	6	4	.3	4	0	.0
28039	1.4	28	.5	59	17.7	257	39.0	7	11	.7	13	0	.0
28040	4.6	95	1.6	77	19.8	233	52.2	6	13	2.1	9	0	.0
28041	.8	0	.2	78	20.9	313	62.7	8	16	.0	0	0	.1
28042	.5	91	.2	68	20.3	234	64.2	4	22	.7	23	0	.3
28043	19.2	87	6.7	68	21.6	245	57.3	8	12	7.9	10	0	.6
28052	83.0	84	29.0	67	25.3	291	66.7	7	10	33.3	8	1	1.1
28071	1.8	98	.7	85	18.8	172	66.8	6	13	.9	11	0	.0
28072	1.5	73	.5	77	24.6	299	69.0	7	12	.5	11	0	.6

NORTH CAROLINA

ROCKY MOUNT

ZIPCODE	1	2	3	4	5	6	7	8	9	10	11	12	13
27881	.1	52	.1	61	12.2	76	36.1	1	30	.0	61	0	.0
27882	5.6	54	1.8	65	20.1	220	57.7	7	12	1.5	10	4	.1
27883	3.6	56	1.2	61	19.3	193	61.8	7	12	1.0	14	0	.0
27884	1.3	65	.4	68	19.1	282	58.9	7	9	.4	7	0	.0
27885	1.4	57	.5	69	15.5	183	45.0	11	12	.4	6	0	.0
27886	20.5	58	6.7	66	22.1	259	63.0	8	10	5.7	8	2	.9
27887	.3	0	.1	69	22.8	148	22.8	8	9	.0	0	0	.0
27888	2.3	55	.7	55	23.6	196	71.6	5	10	.6	10	0	.0
27889	21.2	72	7.6	69	20.8	253	74.0	8	12	7.3	10	3	.6
27890	4.2	38	1.5	49	15.6	216	56.6	8	15	.8	15	0	.1
27891	5.2	29	1.5	59	16.9	180	47.3	11	10	.7	10	0	.0
27892	13.9	63	4.7	66	20.8	255	65.2	7	10	4.1	10	1	.9
27893	45.3	62	15.9	54	22.9	280	78.3	7	10	13.2	8	2	.9
27897	2.1	46	.7	74	20.3	210	40.8	8	13	.5	13	0	.0

ROCKY MOUNT

ZIPCODE	1	2	3	4	5	6	7	8	9	10	11	12	13
27909	28.6	63	9.8	65	20.0	277	66.0	7	12	8.7	9	1	.0
27910	11.5	48	4.0	64	20.0	253	57.5	7	13	2.6	12	2	.0
27915	.9	0	.3	86	22.6	30	73.9	4	8	.0	0	0	.0
27916	.2	0	.1	93	17.8	205*	104.6	9	16	.0	0	0	.1
27917	.3	86	.1	89	15.6	193	55.5	2	20	.1	10	0	.0
27919	1.3	75	.4	84	16.5	199	50.5	5	18	.5	14	0	.0
27921	2.8	65	.9	79	25.1	301	67.9	8	10	.9	12	0	.0
27923	.6	86	.3	64	15.4	243	41.5	10	9	.2	19	0	6.7
27924	3.8	43	1.2	67	16.4	225	47.5	7	12	.8	12	0	.0
27925	3.6	60	1.3	78	16.0	238	45.9	8	16	1.1	17	0	.0
27926	1.0	44	.3	65	18.1	177	63.2	3	16	.2	16	0	.0
27928	2.4	63	.8	75	17.8	165	52.0	9	11	.7	12	0	.0
27929	.5	100	.2	70	21.7	315	87.3	6	11	.5	11	0	6.7
27932	10.6	57	3.7	68	20.3	260	68.5	7	14	2.9	13	1	.1
27935	1.1	85	.4	79	19.6	299	55.8	8	13	.5	11	0	.0
27937	2.7	31	.9	80	17.3	160	46.8	6	14	.4	18	0	.0
27938	1.5	0	.5	80	25.1	262	50.1	9	14	.0	0	0	.0
27939	.9	82	.3	79	19.5	222	49.3	2	13	.3	12	0	.0
27941	1.0	0	.1	100	15.3	176*	69.2	8	39	.5	1	0	.0
27942	1.0	38	.3	71	15.7	182	53.1	8	14	.2	6	0	.0
27943	2.6	99	1.0	69	21.5	248	79.7	5	12	1.4	12	0	.0
27944	7.8	60	2.6	75	18.4	224	56.2	8	16	2.3	16	0	.0
27946	1.1	70	.4	89	26.5	95	55.4	4	16	.4	20	0	.0
27947	.4	62	.1	79	16.7	192*	64.5	1	19	.1	13	0	.0
27948	2.2	99	1.0	62	21.7	460	98.9	6	9	1.1	9	0	.0
27949	1.5	100	.7	92	26.4	227	126.1	7	14	.7	14	0	.0
27950	.5	100	.2	78	19.1	365	56.2	9	9	.3	6	0	.0
27953	.4	100	.2	91	26.8	323	48.9	1	13	.2	9	0	.0
27954	3.0	75	1.1	80	23.3	301	81.8	7	18	1.0	16	0	.0
27956	.5	75	.1	62	19.2	279	69.0	6	6	.2	9	0	.0
27957	1.7	48	.5	71	16.2	164	57.3	5	12	.4	16	1	.0
27958	4.5	79	1.5	81	20.4	278	64.1	4	9	1.9	6	0	.0
27959	1.2	99	.5	61	30.7	400	126.3	3	14	.5	13	0	.0

*=Estimated **1.0=883 lbs per person; 100++ indicates per capita toxic waste generation > than 100 times the U.S. average of 883 lbs per capita.

103001

ZIP CODE MEASURES OF SIZE, LEVELS OF AFFLUENCE AND QUALITY OF LIFE

1=Population (th.); 2= % White; 3=Households (th.); 4=% Owner Occupied; 5=Mean Income Per Household (th.$); 6=Mean Monthly Rent ($)*; 7=Mean Home Value (th.$)*; 8=% under 5; 9=% 65 and over; 10=% White Males, 65+; 11=% White Males (th.); 12=# Toxic Waste Sites; 13=Toxic Waste Relative to US(883 lbs.per capita)**

NORTH CAROLINA

CHARLOTTE

ZIP CODE	1	2	3	4	5	6	7	8	9	10	11	12	13
28073	3.0	82	1.0	77	21.5	248	53.5	9	8	1.2	8	1	.9
28075	5.2	92	1.7	89	30.0	294	93.8	7	3	2.3	3	1	.3
28076	1.6	78	.6	76	19.0	238	37.4	6	13	.6	10	0	1.1
28077	.8	92	.3	75	24.4	242	38.1	4	11	.4	10	0	.0
28078	8.9	83	3.0	83	26.5	253	93.4	6	13	3.6	11	0	.0
28079	6.1	94	2.0	88	26.5	308	75.4	9	6	2.9	6	0	.4
28080	2.9	84	1.0	80	23.1	232	62.5	9	9	1.2	7	0	.0
28081	39.2	85	14.4	66	23.3	239	57.7	9	14	15.8	12	2	.6
28086	19.4	81	6.7	63	23.3	244	60.8	7	10	7.7	10	0	4.5
28088	3.2	91	1.2	79	22.8	259	57.0	5	16	1.3	15	0	.6
28089	.4	85	.1	86	22.8	109	60.8	8	17	.1	12	0	.0
28090	6.6	78	2.3	80	20.6	176	48.4	6	16	2.6	15	0	.0
28091	2.4	54	.8	79	20.8	214	45.9	7	13	.6	7	0	.0
28092	26.0	92	9.2	75	23.0	265	64.3	6	10	11.5	9	1	.6
28097	2.1	100	.7	81	22.8	327	61.0	9	7	.1	5	0	.0
28098	3.3	93	1.2	65	21.1	243	48.1	8	13	1.4	9	2	11.3

CHARLOTTE

ZIP CODE	1	2	3	4	5	6	7	8	9	10	11	12	13
28101	1.1	97	.4	41	25.0	222	57.8	7	7	.6	4	0	.6
28102	.2	38	.1	48	18.1	162	37.7	10	8	.0	8	0	.0
28103	7.8	74	2.7	80	24.3	251	58.9	8	11	2.8	12	0	.5
28105	27.7	95	8.8	87	38.3	398	125.9	8	5	1.6	4	1	.4
28107	3.7	91	1.3	86	25.3	181	78.4	7	6	.6	8	0	.0
28108	.7	76	.2	83	26.1	350	62.8	2	6	.3	3	0	2.5
28109	1.0	91	.3	40	24.9	254	73.5	7	11	.4	4	0	.0
28110	35.4	83	11.9	70	24.9	286	76.1	7	10	14.2	7	5	1.0
28114	3.1	94	1.1	80	20.9	214	52.6	6	12	1.4	10	0	.0
28115	21.6	87	7.9	77	24.5	258	75.1	6	11	9.2	10	0	.3
28119	2.4	28	.7	69	17.0	187	50.4	6	16	.1	13	0	.0
28120	13.1	89	4.6	78	24.0	274	61.6	7	10	5.6	8	2	3.4
28123	.5	0	.2	87	18.4	248	60.5	2	14	.0	5	0	.0
28124	3.9	92	1.3	80	25.3	218	65.7	7	11	1.7	9	0	.2
28125	1.3	94	.5	87	23.8	226	63.1	7	12	.6	10	0	.0
28126	.6	82	.2	84	25.1	141	93.7	1	16	.2	11	0	.0
28127	5.0	86	1.6	85	26.4	231	73.6	7	11	2.0	11	0	.4
28128	6.7	84	2.3	80	20.1	194	54.9	8	11	2.8	11	2	.1
28129	4.6	92	1.6	84	20.0	346	56.5	0	13	2.0	10	0	.0
28130	.3	100	.1	73	29.4	177	60.2	8	16	.1	14	1	.0
28133	2.3	77	.7	83	21.0	280	41.8	9	12	.9	10	0	.0
28134	8.1	90	2.9	80	33.0	368	103.2	9	5	3.6	5	2	.9
28135	2.8	66	.9	79	20.7	134	48.0	7	12	.8	10	0	.0
28136	.5	87	.2	77	25.3	123	62.0	7	10	.9	12	2	.2
28137	1.9	96	.7	78	25.0	218	63.1	7	8	.9	8	0	.1
28138	5.7	99	2.0	84	24.0	260	58.9	7	14	2.8	7	0	.6
28139	12.6	88	4.7	78	20.9	240	63.7	6	13	5.4	12	1	.3
28144	52.8	79	19.1	71	24.2	264	70.5	6	13	20.4	11	15	2.9
28150	46.1	76	15.9	70	24.2	269	68.7	7	11	16.7	9	3	1.1
28159	3.0	88	1.2	69	24.2	280	48.1	5	20	1.6	17	2	1.0
28160	4.5	77	1.7	73	18.3	224	41.9	5	18	1.6	17	2	1.8
28163	3.8	99	1.3	88	25.3	172	58.5	4	10	1.9	8	0	.3

NORTH CAROLINA

CHARLOTTE

ZIP CODE	1	2	3	4	5	6	7	8	9	10	11	12	13
28164	9.3	88	3.0	77	25.3	283	64.6	8	8	4.0	6	1	.6
28166	5.0	76	1.7	83	23.2	284	67.7	6	10	1.9	9	2	.5
28167	1.9	81	.6	79	20.2	140	44.3	10	12	.8	12	0	.0
28168	6.5	91	2.2	84	20.9	139	57.6	7	10	2.9	11	1	.0
28169	.2	66	.1	68	15.6	200	50.3	5	19	.1	14	0	.0
28170	14.4	52	4.7	72	19.9	241	54.4	8	14	3.6	13	0	.2
28173	7.2	78	2.3	79	31.3	276	78.3	6	11	2.8	11	0	.0
28174	5.1	76	1.3	75	25.1	296	72.6	6	6	2.0	5	0	.0

CHARLOTTE

ZIP CODE	1	2	3	4	5	6	7	8	9	10	11	12	13
28201	.2	100	.1	0	23.3	184	83.2*	10	0	.1	0	2	100++
28202	4.5	0	1.9	6	12.3	186	70.9	5	17	.0	17	4	7.2
28203	11.6	50	5.0	41	18.2	243	72.5	6	17	2.5	17	6	1.2
28204	5.5	59	2.6	24	15.4	236	79.2	6	19	1.4	14	5	.5
28205	43.4	77	18.3	48	15.1	355	60.7	6	15	15.7	11	6	.1
28206	13.3	16	4.9	28	15.1	273	39.1	9	10	1.1	10	0	2.0
28207	8.4	98	3.5	68	49.3	295	192.6	4	23	3.4	16	11	.1
28208	47.7	53	16.9	52	21.6	385	57.5	8	8	12.2	8	0	1.8
28209	17.4	96	8.0	58	27.5	385	89.4	5	16	7.7	13	6	.9
28210	44.8	73	15.3	65	32.1	404	97.1	7	5	15.9	4	2	1.9
28211	40.3	94	14.8	72	46.6	482	168.0	5	4	18.3	3	4	.0
28212	36.4	94	13.0	71	32.3	421	101.3	7	5	16.9	4	1	.6
28213	27.7	61	9.9	58	24.9	362	72.0	7	5	8.4	5	2	.1
28214	9.2	94	3.1	87	33.1	415	84.5	6	6	4.2	6	5	.0
28215	24.3	79	8.3	67	28.1	381	81.7	7	9	9.4	3	2	.0

FAYETTEVILLE

ZIP CODE	1	2	3	4	5	6	7	8	9	10	11	12	13
28301	23.0	48	7.6	61	23.9	297	59.9	9	9	2.3	7	7	.4
28303	56.8	69	19.1	58	19.7	266	62.3	9	7	13.5	5	1	.0
28304	36.6	75	16.6	70	25.4	334	86.6	9	4	12.6	4	0	.0
28305	50.7	66	3.0	60	24.2	364	69.0	5	14	19.1	2	12	1.1
28306	7.1	76	7.3	65	25.0	302	86.0	8	7	2.2	6	1	1.1
28307	21.3	56	4.8	0	19.2	266	53.4	10	0	8.0	0	2	.0
28308	37.9	72	.5	75	17.6	337	62.6*	8	0	15.8	0	0	.8
28315	2.9	62	2.2	0	20.1	356	71.7*	8	7	1.3	7	5	.0
28318	6.1	81	1.1	75	19.3	207	58.5	9	9	2.3	9	2	.0
28320	3.3	81	2.8	82	18.5	229	51.3	9	10	1.5	5	0	.0
28322	8.1	15	.1	72	22.6	165	40.3	7	14	3.3	4	1	.0
28323	.3	54	.7	62	22.6	218	51.4	6	7	.5	1	0	1.0
28325	2.1	67	.2	73	17.0	165	36.8	7	12	.2	5	2	.0
28326	.6	76	1.4	79	19.6	226	49.6	9	7	1.7	7	0	.0
28327	4.4	82	2.7	80	20.3	241	57.9	11	11	3.1	9	0	.2
28328	7.9	62	7.3	66	19.7	232	63.0	7	12	6.4	10	1	.0
28330	21.5	93	.2	66	22.2	232	28.7	13	12	.3	12	2	3.7
28331	.6	100	.3	68	20.2	234	42.3	7	10	.1	4	1	2.4
28332	.3	78	.9	81	18.5	242	55.8	10	10	.4	3	3	.1
28333	.9	63	2.8	73	20.7	231	63.2	10	11	2.9	2	2	.3
28334	8.8	76	7.4	66	20.5	165	57.8	7	12	2.5	17	2	.4
28337	20.5	59	2.9	79	20.8	230	63.3	7	9	2.6	10	2	.0
28338	3.8	65	1.3	76	19.4	227	51.7	5	11	1.2	10	0	.3

*=Estimated **1.0=883 lbs per person, 100++ indicates per capita toxic waste generation > than 100 times the U.S. average of 883 lbs per capita.

ZIP CODE MEASURES OF SIZE, LEVELS OF AFFLUENCE AND QUALITY OF LIFE

1=Population (th.); 2= % White; 3=Households (th.); 4=% Owner Occupied; 5=Mean Income Per Household (th.$); 6=Mean Monthly Rent ($)*; 7=Mean Home Value (th.$)*; 8=% under 5; 9=% 65 and over; 10=White Males (th.); 11=% White Males, 65+; 12=# Toxic Waste Sites; 13=Toxic Waste Relative to US(883 lbs.per capita)**

NORTH CAROLINA — FAYETTEVILLE

ZIPCODE	1	2	3	4	5	6	7	8	9	10	11	12	13
28339	5.8	76	2.1	79	19.1	233	44.6	6	14	2.1	13	0	.4
28340	11.6	39	3.5	62	20.1	246	53.1	8	9	2.2	8	0	.0
28341	3.8	55	1.3	70	16.6	219	48.9	8	14	1.0	13	0	.0
28342	.4	94	.1	58	20.9	308	66.0	7	22	.0	17	0	.0
28343	.9	0	.3	60	16.0	199	46.8	7	11	.0	10	0	.0
28344	1.8	67	.6	77	18.9	202	50.6	8	12	.6	10	0	.0
28345	12.6	68	4.4	73	21.0	218	50.6	7	12	4.0	9	1	.1
28347	1.0	0	.3	76	16.8	156	30.1	7	13	.0	9	0	.0
28348	11.8	81	3.9	81	21.7	253	60.9	9	6	4.6	5	0	.0
28349	3.2	59	1.0	81	19.3	269	49.7	6	14	.9	13	0	.0
28350	.4	87	.2	78	18.3	215	55.5	8	21	.2	20	0	.0
28351	3.9	71	1.3	70	20.7	216	42.5	8	10	1.3	11	1	.2
28352	23.9	60	7.6	67	23.7	249	64.8	8	9	6.9	6	4	.7
28355	.1	0	.1	80	23.7	197	77.9	9	20	.0	6	0	.1
28356	2.8	74	.9	76	22.2	203	56.4	9	6	1.1	6	0	.0
28357	1.7	40	.5	77	15.9	151	50.0	7	8	.6	7	1	.3
28358	39.1	56	12.9	66	21.8	239	60.9	8	9	10.4	9	3	.2
28362	.3	0	.1	44	24.0	89	196.9	14	5	.0	0	0	.0
28363	.9	0	.3	84	17.2	264	43.4	7	10	.0	8	0	.0
28364	11.3	17	2.9	74	17.7	197	41.2	11	8	.9	8	0	.9
28365	13.0	66	4.4	69	18.7	231	53.7	7	13	4.1	10	0	.4
28366	3.5	67	1.2	73	17.6	206	64.0	7	12	1.2	11	0	.0
28367	.4	63	.1	74	13.8	165	47.3	11	11	.0	9	0	.0
28368	.8	70	.1	74	23.1	188	50.2	6	9	.2	9	0	.0
28369	2.2	64	.6	69	15.7	200	46.6	10	7	.7	5	0	.1
28371	2.6	58	.8	75	21.1	206	60.5	8	11	.7	14	0	.0
28372	9.8	10	2.1	70	18.3	211	51.3	8	7	.5	8	0	.7
28373	1.5	83	.5	77	17.6	232	43.5	11	10	2.0	9	0	.3
28374	4.2	74	1.7	79	33.7	213	63.1	6	27	1.5	29	0	.1
28375	.3	0	.1	84	17.4	246	37.7	3	9	.9	8	0	.0
28376	15.0	48	4.4	66	20.7	268	58.2	10	9	3.5	7	1	.3
28377	9.1	33	2.8	71	17.6	206	45.4	10	10	1.4	14	0	.2
28378	.3	24	.1	44	15.2	256	13.1	11	23	.0	17	0	.0
28379	26.3	77	9.3	74	21.8	237	50.4	8	11	9.7	9	4	.9
28382	6.1	72	2.1	74	18.3	233	47.9	7	13	2.1	11	0	.1
28383	7.0	17	2.1	70	16.5	180	45.3	10	11	.5	28	0	.0
28384	8.0	52	2.4	68	17.6	232	43.5	11	10	2.0	8	1	.3
28385	2.6	68	.8	80	20.4	213	67.0	6	11	.9	9	0	.0
28386	3.5	18	1.0	82	16.6	247	40.3	9	6	.3	8	0	.0
28387	11.5	67	4.4	66	26.3	283	97.3	7	18	3.6	18	1	.3
28390	16.9	61	5.9	38	16.2	275	58.1	10	9	5.4	7	0	.0
28391	3.3	81	1.1	79	21.6	242	53.0	6	10	1.3	8	0	.0
28392	1.4	65	.4	84	16.6	206	49.1	9	9	.4	7	0	.0
28393	2.0	54	.7	77	16.7	222	47.7	7	13	.5	19	0	.0
28394	3.7	87	1.5	83	28.4	311	121.6	4	22	1.6	25	0	.1
28395	2.3	63	.8	76	17.0	210	46.0	6	11	.7	7	0	.0
28396	2.5	34	.8	74	21.8	202	52.1	9	11	.5	13	0	.3
28398	6.0	53	2.0	69	19.5	258	54.2	10	10	1.5	7	0	.1
28399	1.4	40	.4	91	13.9	217	39.8	7	16	.3	24	0	.0

NORTH CAROLINA — FAYETTEVILLE

ZIPCODE	1	2	3	4	5	6	7	8	9	10	11	12	13
28401	24.5	48	9.3	46	15.6	221	42.2	7	15	5.4	10	7	10.9
28403	45.1	91	16.9	68	28.3	329	87.7	6	10	19.6	8	3	.0
28404	.3	12	.1	81	13.7	307	32.8	9	14	.0	17	2	3.1
28405	22.7	79	7.4	81	27.1	316	78.2	7	7	8.7	6	2	.0
28420	2.6	80	.9	76	16.9	234	50.3	7	10	1.0	10	0	.0
28421	1.2	41	.4	83	17.6	199	42.7	9	11	.2	13	0	.0
28422	3.1	71	1.0	83	20.1	229	53.0	10	10	1.1	10	0	.0
28423	2.2	24	.7	78	18.6	189	44.3	8	9	.3	7	0	.0
28424	.8	0	.2	52	16.6	256	34.6	5	9	.0	0	0	1.8
28425	5.9	58	2.0	79	20.6	271	53.6	7	12	1.7	10	2	.4
28428	2.6	97	.2	63	19.9	265	67.4	6	14	1.2	12	2	.0
28429	5.2	75	1.8	83	25.9	323	63.0	8	6	2.0	6	3	5.7
28430	1.9	84	.6	70	20.3	127	51.9	8	11	.8	7	0	.0
28431	7.1	71	2.5	72	16.1	197	52.8	8	10	2.5	9	1	.8
28432	1.6	81	.6	77	17.1	170	36.3	6	10	.6	12	0	.0
28433	4.9	51	.6	81	18.0	240	45.2	8	13	1.2	11	0	.1
28434	1.4	20	.5	83	16.8	196	44.8	8	13	.5	21	0	.0
28435	1.8	51	.6	78	19.2	199	57.2	11	12	.5	7	0	.0
28436	1.6	78	.5	90	21.9	192	48.1	8	8	.6	8	0	.0
28437	.2	100	.1	85	21.4	188	19.1	12	8	.1	8	0	.9
28438	1.8	60	.6	79	15.8	154	41.8	9	8	.5	6	0	.4
28439	1.7	58	.6	72	16.7	211	50.5	8	11	.4	7	0	.0
28441	3.0	65	1.0	77	17.7	227	41.6	8	14	1.0	12	0	.3
28442	2.6	55	.9	85	17.9	215	51.1	7	11	.1	10	0	.0
28443	3.1	72	.6	88	23.1	184	84.0	7	10	1.1	12	0	.0
28444	2.0	46	.6	76	13.0	206	46.4	10	13	.5	16	0	.0
28445	2.6	96	1.0	72	19.9	172	72.3	6	13	1.3	12	0	.0
28446	.2	71	.1	90	20.6	237*	50.6	10	7	.1	18	1	1.2
28447	1.1	0	.1	76	16.7	145	48.0	9	14	.0	0	0	.0
28448	1.0	42	.4	74	15.9	144	33.4	5	12	.2	19	0	.0
28449	.7	90	.2	66	15.9	216	70.7	9	11	.3	11	0	.0
28450	1.3	75	.4	75	27.1	248	86.4	5	18	.5	12	0	.0
28451	8.5	73	2.8	79	21.5	274	59.1	9	7	3.1	6	6	.3
28452	.4	40	.1	84	10.9	125*	39.8	4	7	.1	0	6	.0
28453	1.9	50	.7	84	15.8	181	37.6	8	10	.5	13	0	.0
28454	2.2	0	.7	88	15.9	175	44.3	8	8	.6	10	0	.0
28455	1.4	82	.5	81	16.6	191*	52.5	8	12	.7	10	5	6.6
28456	3.5	39	1.1	87	20.2	152	52.5	5	11	.8	9	0	.0
28457	3.1	54	1.1	82	17.3	179	52.1	7	14	.9	9	0	.0
28458	5.3	0	1.9	75	17.1	197	42.8	7	13	.2	10	0	.3
28459	6.5	79	2.3	86	19.6	219	69.7	7	12	2.5	12	0	.0
28460	2.9	88	1.0	74	17.5	170	60.1	9	7	1.3	6	0	.0
28461	7.7	85	2.9	76	22.2	257	68.7	6	14	3.2	13	2	21.8
28462	4.6	78	1.6	87	19.0	72	58.8	7	11	.1	0	0	.3
28463	6.8	74	2.3	73	18.6	160	48.6	8	10	2.4	10	0	.0
28464	1.6	42	.5	77	15.7	177	47.6	8	10	.3	10	0	.0
28466	7.9	69	2.7	81	19.3	208	53.4	8	12	2.7	10	1	.6
28471	1.4	68	.5	85	20.6	232	42.6	8	8	.5	9	1	.0
28472	16.2	40	5.8	72	19.5	246	61.1	8	12	5.5	10	6	.2

*=Estimated **1.0=883 lbs per person; 100++ indicates per capita toxic waste generation > than 100 times the U.S. average of 883 lbs per capita.

ZIP CODE MEASURES OF SIZE, LEVELS OF AFFLUENCE AND QUALITY OF LIFE

1=Population (th.); 2= % White; 3=Households (th.); 4=% Owner Occupied; 5=Mean Income Per Household (th.$); 6=Mean Monthly Rent ($)*; 7=Mean Home Value (th.$)*;
8=% under 5; 9=% 65 and over; 10=White Males, 65+; 11=% White Males (th.); 12=# Toxic Waste Sites; 13=Toxic Waste Relative to US(883 lbs.per capita)**

NORTH CAROLINA

ZIPCODE	1	2	3	4	5	6	7	8	9	10	11	12	13
FAYETTEVILLE													
28478	2.5	54	.9	87	17.7	194	41.3	10	13	.6	9	0	.0
28479	1.4	65	.5	84	19.2	197	58.2	7	8	.5	10	0	.0
28480	2.9	99	1.4	43	32.7	403	152.9	2	10	1.5	8	0	.0
KINSTON													
28501	46.5	62	16.2	60	21.4	245	73.2	7	11	13.9	8	4	3.3
28508	1.2	84	.4	66	16.2	144	47.7	9	8	.5	8	0	.0
28509	.4	77	.1	85	21.7	198	54.2	7	22	.1	14	0	.0
28510	1.3	73	.5	87	22.5	201	64.7	11	11	.5	9	0	.0
28511	.8	100	.3	92	16.6	202	53.8	3	29	.3	21	0	.0
28512	1.1	97	.5	58	23.4	242	107.7	5	6	.6	7	1	.0
28513	8.6	61	2.9	63	18.5	249	61.4	8	12	2.5	10	1	.0
28515	2.3	47	.8	79	17.3	243	44.9	5	14	.1	13	0	.0
28516	8.7	78	3.1	76	21.7	219	63.9	6	11	3.3	11	0	.9
28518	5.0	86	1.8	78	18.2	177	49.1	6	11	2.1	11	0	.1
28519	1.0	97	.1	67	20.7	217	63.2	6	14	.5	12	1	2.1
28520	.3	100	.7	86	18.1	213	63.9	7	18	.2	13	0	.0
28521	2.0	75	.7	85	17.4	116	51.7	5	13	.8	11	0	.0
28522	2.2	72	.7	57	9.3	241	13.1	5	28	.1	7	0	.0
28523	2.2	54	.7	74	22.7	183	53.4	6	11	.5	11	1	.0
28524	.5	100	.2	91	23.4	408	69.6	9	6	.2	8	0	.0
28525	2.0	80	.7	66	24.4	235	50.5	7	9	.8	8	0	.0
28526	3.0	60	1.0	72	17.3	193	45.8	7	9	.9	9	0	.0
28527	.6	73	.1	85	19.4	225	58.0	6	6	.9	3	0	.0
28528	.3	100	.1	100	27.7	319*	95.5	10	27	.1	19	0	.0
28529	1.0	81	.3	86	18.1	213	45.5	7	13	.4	11	0	.8
28530	5.7	57	1.9	71	21.3	228	62.7	8	9	1.6	7	0	.0
28531	1.9	0	.7	88	16.1	210	57.8	7	10	.0	6	2	.0
28532	19.2	76	6.1	42	20.3	337	73.0	15	3	7.6	2	0	.0
28537	.3	0	.2	89	14.4	203	31.2	4	34	.0	1	1	.0
28538	2.0	47	.6	66	20.6	220	57.8	10	6	.5	4	0	.0
28539	5.5	90	2.0	59	19.3	221	73.7	10	5	2.5	3	1	.0
28540	51.8	78	17.5	59	21.5	300	69.3	10	4	21.2	3	2	.2
28542	26.9	67	1.5	0	23.9	393	85.1*	3	0	15.1	0	0	.0
28543	5.9	61	1.8	4	12.0	280	42.8*	29	0	1.8	0	0	.0
28544	5.1	64	1.8	30	13.8	249	59.1	15	3	1.7	2	0	4.2
28550	.1	43	.1	83	13.7	157*	33.4	6	24	.0	0	0	.1
28551	9.7	53	3.2	66	18.3	224	56.7	8	9	2.5	5	0	.0
28552	.5	0	.2	83	18.7	269	35.6	4	19	.0	0	0	.0
28553	.6	0	.2	88	22.6	230	56.3	3	14	.0	0	0	.1
28554	.5	68	.2	70	21.3	203	37.0	2	16	.2	6	0	.0
28555	4.0	68	1.3	75	19.4	247	52.7	8	7	1.5	8	0	.0
28556	.9	66	.3	79	19.8	159	41.5	8	9	.3	13	0	.0
28557	11.5	90	4.4	73	24.7	274	92.8	6	14	4.9	12	2	.0
28560	38.2	71	14.2	68	23.0	266	78.1	8	10	13.1	8	6	.4
28570	10.7	91	3.9	71	20.5	247	68.3	9	8	5.2	11	0	.0
28571	1.6	58	.6	80	21.3	230	68.3	5	16	.4	13	0	.0
28572	4.5	84	1.6	77	19.6	178	52.5	8	12	1.9	10	0	.0
28573	2.2	50	.7	79	20.8	260	65.2	6	12	.5	13	0	.0
28574	7.1	86	2.4	75	24.0	204	52.6	8	9	3.0	12	0	.0

NORTH CAROLINA

ZIPCODE	1	2	3	4	5	6	7	8	9	10	11	12	13
KINSTON													
28575	.6	0	.2	80	17.8	342	88.6	7	4	.0	0	0	.0
28577	.5	100	.1	87	26.1	227	47.2	8	29	.3	35	0	.2
28578	2.2	87	.8	72	18.9	286	52.9	11	11	.9	6	0	.0
28579	.3	0	.1	84	17.0	250	68.1	7	21	.0	0	0	.0
28580	8.2	56	2.7	69	20.7	227	63.1	8	11	2.3	9	0	.0
28581	.3	0	.1	84	17.8	372	38.3	9	21	.0	0	0	.0
28582	.5	76	.2	77	17.4	298	40.0	6	14	.2	3	0	.0
28583	.3	77	.1	85	18.8	283	53.4	7	14	.1	13	0	.0
28584	4.7	95	1.8	77	22.6	283	73.6	7	12	2.3	12	0	.3
28585	4.0	55	1.2	78	19.4	171	53.0	9	11	1.0	13	0	.0
28586	5.1	77	1.8	82	17.2	182	43.8	8	11	1.9	9	0	.6
28589	.4	28	.1	76	14.9	232	46.0	6	13	.0	24	0	.0
28590	.3	100	.1	100	24.0	276*	51.8	7	15	.1	11	0	.0
	3.9	58	1.3	71	19.5	303	66.2	8	10	1.1	8	0	.3
HICKORY													
28601	58.3	91	21.1	69	25.9	291	80.6	7	9	25.5	7	12	.5
28604	4.1	99	1.2	76	18.1	74	80.9	6	9	2.1	6	0	.0
28605	2.4	99	1.0	69	26.9	290	112.6	4	14	1.2	13	0	.0
28606	1.7	85	.6	86	17.9	207	47.9	6	11	.7	8	0	.1
28607	19.6	98	6.2	60	19.8	301	90.0	9	7	9.2	6	0	.1
28609	3.8	83	1.2	86	24.5	266	62.6	8	10	1.6	9	0	4.2
28610	5.8	89	1.9	80	23.7	273	67.9	7	7	2.6	6	0	.0
28611	.3	83	.1	76	19.9	203	25.9	10	5	.1	6	0	.0
28613	7.4	98	2.5	84	22.4	203	56.2	7	8	3.7	6	0	.6
28614	13.8	96	4.8	81	25.7	282	74.4	8	6	6.4	7	2	.6
28615	.3	100	.1	95	15.6	179*	37.9	2	5	.0	4	0	.8
28616	2.2	0	.8	85	14.6	206	40.7	5	14	.0	0	0	.0
28617	.6	98	.2	84	17.4	212	56.2	3	8	.7	16	0	.6
28618	1.5	98	.5	73	17.0	191	62.1	8	15	.7	16	0	.6
28619	1.4	98	.5	81	16.7	262	70.1	10	12	1.1	11	0	.6
28621	2.4	95	.9	74	21.6	213	62.2	5	13	1.1	11	0	.0
28622	9.1	99	3.4	81	21.6	213	62.0	5	15	4.1	13	1	.6
28623	2.5	99	.9	78	15.2	246	46.2	8	11	1.2	11	0	.0
28624	1.4	0	.5	88	14.3	133	49.2	6	16	.8	12	0	.0
28626	1.8	96	.6	79	18.8	222	62.2	5	12	.8	12	0	.0
28627	1.2	0	.4	85	15.9	209	59.8	5	15	.0	0	0	.0
28628	1.1	100	.4	73	12.3	211	53.6	7	16	.5	15	0	.0
28629	2.3	93	.8	80	21.1	238	55.8	6	9	1.0	8	0	.0
28630	.3	98	.1	62	18.8	224	88.2	12	13	.2	0	0	.1
28631	12.8	98	4.4	77	21.9	252	59.8	7	9	6.1	7	0	.2
28634	.7	100	.3	87	11.2	139	40.7	6	23	.3	22	0	.0
28635	3.7	80	1.1	82	20.5	181	57.8	6	10	1.4	9	0	.0
28636	3.0	0	.9	87	21.0	164	67.3	8	6	.0	0	0	.0
28637	3.7	95	1.3	85	21.7	228	56.7	9	12	1.8	11	0	.6
28638	2.0	91	.7	69	22.7	282	56.3	6	8	.8	6	0	.6
28640	9.4	99	3.1	77	23.4	259	65.2	8	5	4.7	4	1	.1
28641	3.4	99	1.2	79	19.5	204	78.6	5	16	1.6	11	0	.1
28642	.2	100	.2	93	15.9	183*	54.8	4	30	.1	25	0	.0
	5.3	86	1.9	79	18.9	204	53.4	6	13	2.3	12	0	.3

*=Estimated **1.0-883 lbs per person; 100++ indicates per capita toxic waste generation > than 100 times the U.S. average of 883 lbs per capita.

ZIP CODE MEASURES OF SIZE, LEVELS OF AFFLUENCE AND QUALITY OF LIFE

1=Population (th.); 2= % White; 3=Households (th.); 4=% Owner Occupied; 5=Mean Income Per Household (th.$); 6=Mean Monthly Rent ($)*; 7=Mean Home Value (th.$)*;
8=% under 5; 9=% 65 and over; 10=White Males (th.); 11=% White Males, 65+; 12=# Toxic Waste Sites; 13=Toxic Waste Relative to US(883 lbs.per capital)**.

NORTH CAROLINA

HICKORY

ZIP CODE	1	2	3	4	5	6	7	8	9	10	11	12	13
28643	3.5	0	1.3	87	14.7	211	48.2	5	16	.0	0	1	.4
28644	1.7	97	.6	84	20.0	194	57.4	6	10	.8	10	0	.0
28645	43.3	92	15.0	76	21.5	232	59.9	6	11	19.5	9	14	.7
28646	1.2	0	.5	84	23.1	84	91.7	5	16	.0	0	0	.0
28647	.2	100	.1	92	22.6	260*	78.8	7	19	.1	16	0	.0
28649	1.1	100	.4	90	18.2	150	40.0	5	10	.5	10	0	.0
28650	8.3	92	2.9	83	21.7	250	57.1	7	9	3.7	8	1	.2
28651	5.1	0	1.8	82	23.0	239	67.2	7	11	.0	0	0	.0
28652	.2	100	.1	100	16.9	194*	63.6	0	25	.1	24	0	.0
28653	.2	100	.1	81	26.0	135	80.9	9	4	.1	0	0	.0
28654	2.8	93	1.0	81	22.8	217	62.0	8	13	1.3	10	0	.0
28655	40.9	88	13.9	74	22.5	254	66.0	6	11	17.7	9	5	.6
28657	6.1	100	2.1	83	17.0	163	58.8	7	11	2.9	9	0	.0
28658	18.3	91	6.5	78	25.9	278	70.5	7	11	8.2	9	3	.2
28659	19.9	94	7.1	77	22.7	261	68.4	6	10	9.1	9	1	.1
28660	1.0	95	.4	76	22.3	221	53.8	7	16	.5	16	0	.0
28661	1.5	100	.2	74	23.6	157	69.0	5	5	.3	5	0	.0
28662	.1	100	.1	53	19.1	304	37.2	7	30	.1	25	0	12.0
28663	.7	100	.3	90	23.7	68	57.4	10	15	.3	13	0	.2
28664	.2	0	.1	86	17.8	80	36.6	3	21	.0	0	0	.9
28665	1.5	100	.6	88	22.9	87	48.4	8	13	.8	14	1	.0
28666	1.2	100	.4	78	19.9	208	43.5	7	9	.6	10	0	.0
28667	1.0	0	.3	84	20.0	287	35.5	5	8	.0	0	0	.0
28668	.2	100	.1	88	14.2	163*	50.8	23	14	.1	17	0	.1
28669	2.5	85	.9	88	18.2	89	50.4	8	9	1.1	11	0	.0
28670	2.6	95	.8	89	18.7	267	69.9	7	12	1.1	11	2	.7
28671	1.0	0	.4	80	25.5	259	54.8	5	14	.8	12	0	.2
28673	2.4	85	.8	86	27.7	227	65.7	5	16	.9	13	0	.0
28675	5.5	97	2.1	79	18.7	225	98.8	6	9	2.6	14	0	.1
28676	2.8	100	1.0	90	19.8	219	63.7	6	16	1.3	11	0	.0
28677	49.0	81	17.2	74	23.2	267	69.9	7	12	19.0	10	6	.7
28678	2.8	90	1.0	84	22.5	259	54.8	5	14	1.2	12	0	.2
28679	1.4	100	.5	81	14.0	140	59.5	7	16	.7	13	0	.2
28681	16.9	92	5.7	82	22.3	239	69.5	7	9	7.6	10	0	.1
28682	.2	100	1.0	84	25.0	288*	80.3	0	24	.0	0	0	.0
28683	1.5	0	.5	95	18.8	178	58.0	7	12	.0	0	0	.0
28684	1.6	100	.6	89	13.7	90	51.0	8	14	.8	13	0	.2
28685	1.9	95	.7	75	14.8	149	43.6	9	15	.9	12	0	.1
28686	.2	100	.1	71	18.3	889	119.4	16	8	.2	9	0	.0
28689	1.4	95	.5	85	17.7	216	65.2	5	16	.7	14	0	.0
28690	8.5	98	3.3	75	21.5	227	67.4	6	11	3.9	9	1	.4
28692	3.1	0	1.1	79	18.4	220	64.6	8	15	.0	0	0	.0
28693	1.5	100	.5	86	16.0	170	46.9	9	12	.8	13	0	.2
28694	5.5	98	2.0	81	20.3	220	68.9	7	13	2.6	12	0	.1
28697	10.1	92	3.6	76	27.2	281	88.9	7	9	4.5	6	0	.1
28698	1.5	100	.5	78	16.8	156	60.0	8	12	.8	9	0	.0

ASHEVILLE

ZIP CODE	1	2	3	4	5	6	7	8	9	10	11	12	13
28701	2.0	100	.7	85	23.2	107	58.5	7	9	1.0	8	0	1.8
28704	7.9	99	2.8	80	28.1	346	89.4	6	13	3.8	5	1	1.8

NORTH CAROLINA

ASHEVILLE

ZIP CODE	1	2	3	4	5	6	7	8	9	10	11	12	13
28705	6.5	100	2.4	82	16.9	203	51.5	6	15	3.2	13	0	.0
28706	.2	0	.1	70	26.8	349	72.3	13	0	.0	0	2	5.3
28707	.2	100	.1	71	17.4	395	70.4	3	6	.1	6	0	.0
28708	.4	100	.1	93	17.6	202*	17.0	0	16	.2	21	0	.0
28709	1.7	100	.6	79	16.1	192	51.0	5	12	.8	11	0	.0
28710	.3	100	.1	74	20.4	251	59.8	8	24	.8	18	0	.0
28711	8.4	94	3.1	74	21.2	325	67.7	5	17	3.7	15	2	.4
28712	13.8	93	4.8	77	24.3	265	77.6	7	14	6.3	12	5	.4
28713	7.4	94	2.7	75	16.0	199	57.1	6	17	3.4	14	2	.1
28714	12.4	98	4.4	79	17.5	200	58.7	6	14	5.9	12	0	.1
28715	13.6	100	4.7	83	22.7	255	72.4	6	13	6.6	11	0	.0
28716	16.1	98	5.9	77	21.8	214	58.7	6	14	7.6	13	0	2.8
28717	1.1	100	.4	79	24.7	283	126.6	6	15	.2	16	0	.0
28718	.5	100	.2	73	25.0	335	102.1	6	19	.2	17	1	.0
28719	4.9	16	1.5	76	15.0	219	61.9	11	6	.3	9	0	.5
28721	6.5	99	2.4	76	20.2	235	68.8	6	12	3.2	11	0	.1
28722	2.1	97	.6	86	24.8	276	94.7	4	20	1.0	20	1	.0
28723	7.0	96	1.6	55	18.8	228	84.5	5	8	3.4	4	0	.3
28724	.4	100	.1	65	19.7	252	94.9	9	8	.2	7	0	.1
28725	.6	0	.9	64	18.5	175	74.4	8	7	.8	10	0	.5
28726	2.5	97	.9	77	18.7	293	62.2	6	10	1.2	8	1	.0
28727	.2	0	.1	40	17.6	331	70.0	11	12	.0	0	0	.6
28728	.8	0	.3	88	24.6	220	57.0	6	15	.0	0	2	.0
28729	1.7	98	.8	86	26.2	291	93.3	6	11	.8	10	0	.0
28730	4.1	100	1.4	78	22.7	309	73.8	7	11	2.0	10	0	.5
28731	3.1	99	1.2	83	23.9	273	56.0	5	13	.0	9	0	.1
28732	7.5	95	2.6	78	22.6	282	83.3	9	12	3.5	8	5	.0
28734	15.7	97	6.0	78	20.0	288	76.0	7	10	3.5	17	1	1.7
28735	2.1	100	1.0	83	16.5	224	72.1	5	17	7.3	17	1	.1
28736	.7	100	1.0	70	19.9	91	22.2	0	29	.0	16	0	.0
28738	3.6	100	1.3	83	21.5	332	126.7	3	30	.3	27	0	.0
28739	2.1	99	.7	67	18.7	273	56.0	5	13	1.0	10	0	.3
28740	36.7	95	14.7	77	23.9	289	87.9	5	22	16.4	19	2	.1
28741	2.8	100	1.0	80	14.9	174	44.8	9	14	.4	18	3	.0
28742	2.1	100	1.0	91	22.3	183	104.3	6	24	1.0	20	0	.0
28743	3.6	100	1.3	83	23.1	332	86.1	7	12	.3	16	1	.1
28745	2.2	99	.8	64	19.1	190	33.7	8	16	.0	13	0	.0
28746	1.2	100	.4	83	24.6	355	71.4	3	20	.4	18	0	.3
28747	1.2	100	.4	95	20.9	217	91.9	5	14	.6	20	2	.1
28748	5.5	0	.7	83	20.9	206	91.9	6	13	.0	13	0	.0
28750	.2	100	1.9	83	20.9	304	69.5	5	13	.3	27	2	.0
28751	1.5	100	.1	70	13.8	159*	39.5	15	11	.1	0	0	.3
28752	24.6	95	.8	78	24.2	194	93.7	2	18	.8	15	0	.1
28753	6.3	98	8.7	77	20.3	232	58.0	7	12	11.4	10	3	4.0
28754	2.0		3.0	78	16.5	172	49.9	6	15	4.1	14	0	.0
28755	.3	0	.1	80	18.9	220	73.7	6	13	3.0	11	1	.2
28756	2.4	95	.8	77	16.3	185	54.5	7	33	.0	0	0	1.4
28757	.8	98	.4	42	17.2	196	47.0	7	12	1.1	11	0	.3
28758	1.0		.4	83	20.6	270	73.8	7	9	.0	0	0	4.9

*=Estimated **1.0=883 lbs per person; 100++ indicates per capita toxic waste generation > than 100 times the U.S. average of 883 lbs per capita.

ZIP CODE MEASURES OF SIZE, LEVELS OF AFFLUENCE AND QUALITY OF LIFE

1=Population (th.); 2= % White; 3=Households (th.); 4=% Owner Occupied; 5=Mean Income Per Household (th.$); 6=Mean Monthly Rent ($)*; 7=Mean Home Value (th.$)*; 8=% under 5; 9=% 65 and over; 10=White Males (th.); 11=% White Males, 65+; 12=# Toxic Waste Sites; 13=Toxic Waste Relative to US(883`lbs.per capital)**.

NORTH CAROLINA

ZIPCODE	1	2	3	4	5	6	7	8	9	10	11	12	13
ASHEVILLE													
28761	4.8	96	1.5	88	22.1	195	54.3	6	9	2.2	8	0	.0
28762	6.0	93	2.1	79	19.8	235	57.1	7	12	2.8	11	1	.1
28763	.9	100	.4	80	20.5	160	74.5	6	18	.4	15	0	.0
28766	.7	97	.3	87	20.8	239*	74.7	8	13	.3	5	0	.0
28768	4.6	92	1.6	88	25.6	254	79.6	6	10	2.2	8	2	2.7
28770	.3	100	.1	49	20.9	324	60.6	14	15	.3	10	2	.0
28771	6.6	94	2.3	81	18.1	198	57.4	8	13	3.1	13	2	.0
28772	1.8	0	.6	79	27.2	205	57.3	8	9	.0	0	0	.8
28773	2.0	0	.7	78	19.1	280	62.1	7	20	.0	0	0	.0
28774	.3	100	.1	87	13.2	201	41.8	6	23	.2	23	0	.0
28775	.3	0	.1	88	15.7	64	77.6	7	10	.0	0	0	.0
28776	1.0	0	.4	69	24.6	367	78.3	5	6	.0	0	3	4.9
28777	8.0	98	2.8	84	20.5	219	62.8	7	14	3.8	12	1	.4
28778	7.6	96	2.6	79	21.1	263	60.3	6	11	3.5	9	2	.8
28779	10.0	97	3.7	77	20.6	240	63.0	6	15	4.6	13	0	.0
28780	.2	100	.1	75	21.7	72	62.1	8	20	.1	19	0	.0
28781	.8	100	.3	90	11.0	257	37.4	1	22	.4	22	0	.0
28782	4.9	86	2.1	78	26.5	308	98.1	9	29	1.9	27	0	.0
28783	1.2	0	.4	66	16.0	120	60.4	9	8	.1	9	0	.0
28784	.6	100	.2	88	26.3	347	40.0	5	12	.3	12	0	2.4
28786	19.5	97	7.0	75	20.7	233	73.5	5	13	9.1	11	3	.4
28787	10.6	100	3.8	80	21.1	286	67.9	7	11	5.1	10	0	.2
28788	.4	100	.1	78	23.8	231	94.2	8	12	.2	14	0	.0
28789	2.9	85	1.0	85	17.8	183	63.2	6	12	1.2	15	0	.2
28790	1.4	0	.5	82	21.5	242	67.4	12	11	.0	0	0	.0
ASHEVILLE													
28801	14.7	46	6.3	38	15.0	204	48.9	5	21	2.8	18	0	.5
28802	.4	71	.1	84	29.0	333*	91.9	0	6	.2	4	0	11.0
28803	19.1	85	7.4	69	25.4	332	85.3	6	15	7.5	12	0	.5
28804	16.5	99	6.5	74	29.4	338	95.9	6	15	7.8	13	2	.0
28805	13.2	96	5.1	70	25.3	330	80.8	5	13	6.0	12	2	.0
28806	31.2	94	11.9	70	20.7	277	57.7	7	13	13.8	11	4	.2
ASHEVILLE													
28901	4.9	98	1.9	78	16.3	199	59.4	5	17	2.3	16	0	.3
28902	1.0	0	.4	90	15.4	177*	44.9	5	9	.0	0	0	.0
28904	5.4	99	2.0	85	17.4	186	61.3	6	18	2.7	18	0	.1
28905	1.7	0	.6	86	17.5	191	54.4	10	10	.0	0	0	.4
28906	11.4	95	4.0	80	16.7	199	53.5	7	15	5.2	13	1	.5
28909	.3	100	.1	89	16.3	187*	58.6	9	14	.2	8	0	.0
GREENVILLE													
29322	.7	87	.2	77	20.6	265	72.8	6	8	.3	7	0	.0
29323	.7	0	.2	91	23.2	266*	45.1	6	7	.0	0	0	.0
29340	.8	72	.3	79	24.4	158	58.0	8	20	.3	20	0	.0
29356	.8	85	.3	78	17.6	164	51.3	9	18	.4	20	0	.0
FLORENCE													
29582	.6	86	.2	85	39.2	446	88.2	7	10	.2	16	0	.0
CHARLOTTE													
29709	.4	57	.1	86	14.9	249	30.7	7	11	.1	20	0	.0
29728	.4	89	.1	90	15.4	270	59.9	9	12	.2	7	0	.0

NORTH CAROLINA

ZIPCODE	1	2	3	4	5	6	7	8	9	10	11	12	13
GAINESVILLE													
30537	.3	100	.1	85	19.4	222*	56.1	4	27	.1	32	0	.0
CHATTANOOGA													
37317	.3	100	.1	93	19.1	219*	34.2	7	10	.1	14	0	.0
37333	.1	100	.1	91	10.5	121*	38.0	6	12	.1	16	0	.0
37391	.2	100	.1	100	15.0	172*	30.2	16	22	.1	18	0	.0
JOHNSON CITY													
37691	.3	100	.1	100	14.7	169*	50.3	5	17	.1	9	0	.0

*=Estimated **1.0=883 lbs per person; 100++ indicates per capita toxic waste generation > than 100 times the U.S. average of 883 lbs per capita.

103001

ZIP CODE MEASURES OF SIZE, LEVELS OF AFFLUENCE AND QUALITY OF LIFE

1=Population (th.); 2= % White; 3=Households (th.); 4=% Owner Occupied; 5=Mean Income Per Household (th.$); 6=Mean Monthly Rent ($); 7=Mean Home Value (th.$)*; 8=% under 5; 9=% 65 and over; 10=White Males (th.); 11=% White Males, 65+; 12=# Toxic Waste Sites; 13=Toxic Waste Relative to US(883 lbs.per capita)**.

NORTH DAKOTA

ZIPCODE	1	2	3	4	5	6	7	8	9	10	11	12	13
THIEF RIVER FALLS													
56744	.3	100	.1	80	19.3	404	99.5	10	11	.1	13		.0
MOBRIDGE													
57638	.4	100	.1	80	14.4	319	31.2	12	11	.2	13	0	.0
57648	.3	100	.1	100	16.7	191*	59.3*	5	5	.2	4	0	.0
FARGO													
58001	.4	0	.1	79	21.9	371	60.3	8	15	.0	0	0	.0
58003	.2	100	.1	81	17.0	191	26.7	9	18	.1	13	0	.0
58004	.3	0	.1	67	27.5	139	73.4	7	12	.0	0	0	.0
58005	.5	0	.1	89	32.0	299	94.6	8	12	.0	0	0	.0
58006	.6	0	.2	64	29.4	229	64.6	7	23	.0	0	0	.0
58007	.2	100	.1	77	40.6	221	43.8	13	12	.1	8	0	.0
58008	.3	100	.1	85	31.4	236	40.5	6	17	.2	15	0	.0
58009	.2	100	.1	69	29.4	338*	37.2	8	21	.2	19	0	.0
58011	.5	98	.2	77	27.3	279	45.6	6	16	.2	15	0	.0
58012	1.9	99	.7	64	25.5	260	77.4	8	14	.9	11	0	.8
58013	.3	100	.1	90	20.3	234*	20.5	8	14	.2	12	0	.2
58014	.1	100	.1	73	17.2	342	22.0	3	22	.1	19	0	.0
58015	.3	0	.1	92	27.6	317*	62.1	8	15	.0	0	0	.0
58016	.2	100	.1	86	20.9	225	28.7	5	13	.1	14	0	.0
58017	.6	100	.1	84	23.1	215	24.5	8	17	.3	14	0	.0
58018	.4	100	.1	85	23.4	155	53.6	10	16	.2	16	0	.0
58021	.6	0	.2	87	25.6	234	72.5	8	14	.0	0	0	.0
58022	.3	100	.1	84	25.7	251	20.2	5	22	.1	18	0	.0
58023	.3	100	.1	74	20.7	126	56.4	6	10	.1	13	0	.1
58027	1.8	0	.7	75	21.5	228	43.7	8	22	.0	0	0	.0
58028	.3	100	.1	75	15.6	258	19.8	10	17	.1	18	0	.0
58029	.2	100	.1	88	30.6	354*	52.7	7	13	.1	10	0	.0
58030	1.0	100	.3	83	25.6	197	41.1	6	17	.5	16	0	.0
58031	.4	100	.2	85	21.0	221	32.5	8	22	.2	22	0	.0
58032	.9	100	.3	77	19.6	215	44.6	8	20	.4	18	0	.0
58033	.3	100	.1	79	14.4	224	24.2	7	28	.1	24	0	.0
58035	.5	100	.1	77	27.8	201	51.9	10	21	.2	18	0	.0
58036	.4	0	.1	80	25.9	207	53.1	8	18	.0	0	0	.0
58037	.2	100	.1	89	18.4	211*	19.5	10	12	.1	9	0	.0
58038	.5	100	.2	88	32.7	281	61.6	12	9	.3	8	0	.3
58040	1.0	0	.4	71	24.1	286	67.3	9	9	.0	0	0	2.0
58041	2.0	0	.7	80	19.1	171	48.1	7	22	.0	0	0	.0
58042	1.2	100	.4	94	34.0	381	110.1	12	5	.6	5	0	.0
58043	.3	100	.1	83	23.5	246	20.7	7	14	.2	13	0	.0
58045	2.4	99	.9	73	26.1	243	67.8	8	18	1.2	17	0	.2
58046	.9	0	.4	71	21.5	231	44.2	7	19	.0	0	0	.0
58047	1.4	0	.7	87	30.2	276	116.7	11	9	.0	0	0	.0
58048	.6	99	.2	76	26.3	170	44.6	5	18	.3	16	0	.0
58049	.5	0	.2	84	19.5	166	30.7	4	17	.0	0	0	.0
58051	1.2	99	.5	80	29.7	236	82.9	8	17	.6	18	0	.1
58052	.8	0	.3	77	20.3	294	42.6	5	20	.2	16	0	.0
58053	1.7	100	.6	84	20.3	144	42.7	7	24	.8	23	0	.0
58054	3.6	100	1.3	73	22.1	222	69.1	8	18	1.8	17	0	.2
58056	.2	100	.1	76	27.1	311*	20.5	6	10	.1	11	0	.0

NORTH DAKOTA

ZIPCODE	1	2	3	4	5	6	7	8	9	10	11	12	13
FARGO													
58057	.2	100	.1	87	16.1	206	14.0	7	20	.1	18	0	.0
58058	.2	0	.1	87	22.5	195	26.5	13	10	.0	0	0	.0
58059	.5	98	.2	77	28.5	436	88.4	8	7	.3	6	0	.0
58060	1.2	0	.5	78	22.0	193	38.0	6	16	.0	0	0	.0
58061	.5	100	.2	77	25.2	228	55.8	10	13	.3	13	0	.0
58062	.3	0	.1	83	21.2	83	18.1	4	21	.0	0	0	.0
58063	.5	0	.2	79	24.5	170	42.4	10	11	.0	0	0	.0
58064	.6	100	.2	69	26.1	187	30.4	8	13	.3	12	0	.0
58067	.4	0	.2	75	21.2	250	35.2	11	14	.2	15	0	.0
58068	.5	0	.2	84	19.2	151	25.9	11	17	.1	0	0	.0
58069	.3	100	.1	93	18.9	217*	22.6	12	12	.1	15	0	.0
58071	.5	0	.2	72	21.3	253	50.9	8	21	.0	0	1	.0
58072	9.3	99	3.5	63	23.1	230	83.3	7	18	4.4	15	0	.0
58075	10.3	97	3.2	57	25.9	296	82.7	8	11	5.3	8	1	.8
58077	.7	0	.2	86	23.2	169	60.3	7	20	.0	0	0	.0
58078	10.4	99	3.5	65	27.4	294	96.0	11	4	5.2	4	1	.2
58079	.5	100	.2	84	33.9	238	55.0	7	14	.3	14	0	.0
58081	1.0	100	.4	79	24.9	238	42.8	7	16	.5	15	0	.0
FARGO													
58102	39.5	98	14.7	52	26.2	304	103.4	7	9	19.0	8	1	.5
58103	25.0	98	9.9	59	29.7	339	110.8	8	11	12.2	7	0	.0
GRAND FORKS													
58201	54.7	95	18.3	48	25.2	302	98.5	9	7	26.4	5	4	.1
58205	.6	100	.1	74	18.6	352	66.2*	10	22	.3	0	1	.0
58210	.8	100	.3	83	20.7	195	54.6	7	22	.4	23	0	.3
58212	.8	100	.3	78	19.3	259	40.7	9	25	.4	22	0	.4
58213	.4	100	.2	89	21.4	194	42.4	7	13	.2	14	0	.2
58214	.5	0	.1	90	21.6	197	62.8	6	17	.0	0	0	.0
58215	.2	0	.1	87	19.1	219*	31.4	15	15	.2	16	0	.3
58216	.3	100	.1	97	19.0	218*	20.1	5	27	.1	22	0	.2
58217	.2	100	.1	89	25.2	289*	26.3	5	14	.1	17	0	.0
58218	.9	98	.3	78	22.4	253	70.7	9	15	.4	14	0	.2
58220	.4	99	.2	76	24.6	267	74.8	8	16	1.2	13	0	.0
58222	.4	100	.2	87	20.6	331	39.5	9	26	.2	25	0	.0
58223	.5	100	.4	84	23.5	272	75.5	7	12	.7	12	0	.0
58225	1.0	0	.4	76	23.5	192	55.6	8	18	.7	16	0	2.0
58227	.8	98	.3	81	18.1	251	37.7	4	18	.1	17	0	.0
58228	1.1	95	.4	63	21.0	230	41.6	7	17	.4	14	0	.0
58229	.4	100	.1	93	23.4	187	85.8	9	6	.6	6	0	.6
58230	1.1	100	.4	84	19.2	221*	36.9	10	11	.6	13	0	.2
58231	.6	100	.6	76	27.0	183	58.8	7	12	.3	18	0	.0
58235	1.4	0	.8	86	18.1	251	37.7	7	16	.7	16	0	.0
58237	7.0	97	2.3	71	21.6	274	71.8	8	14	3.3	13	0	.0
58238	.3	100	.1	96	18.0	207*	35.2	6	18	.2	16	0	.1
58239	.3	100	.1	88	21.2	264	13.1	7	18	.1	19	0	.0
58240	1.4	100	.5	80	21.9	237	57.2	7	25	.0	0	0	.0
58241	.3	100	.1	80	25.9	107	30.4	9	15	.2	12	0	.2
58243	.8	0	.3	82	18.1	302	60.7	9	16	.0	0	0	.0

*=Estimated **1.0=883 lbs per person; 100++ indicates per capita toxic waste generation > than 100 times the U.S. average of 883 lbs per capita.

103001

ZIP CODE MEASURES OF SIZE, LEVELS OF AFFLUENCE AND QUALITY OF LIFE

1=Population (th.); 2= % White; 3=Households (th.); 4=% Owner Occupied; 5=Mean Income Per Household (th.$); 6=Mean Monthly Rent ($)*; 7=Mean Home Value (th.$)*;
8=% under 5; 9=% 65 and over; 10=% White Males ●5+; 11=% White Males (th.); 12=# White Males; 13=Toxic Waste Sites; Toxic Waste Relative to US(883 lbs.per capita)**

NORTH DAKOTA

GRAND FORKS

ZIPCODE	1	2	3	4	5	6	7	8	9	10	11	12	13
58244	.3	0	.1	78	19.7	344	31.9	7	18	.0	0	0	.0
58248	.1	100	.1	71	14.3	268	16.5	4	15	.1	12	0	.0
58249	3.7	100	1.3	75	24.0	218	81.4	8	17	1.8	14	0	.0
58250	.5	100	.2	91	18.1	109	27.9	7	22	.2	24	0	.0
58251	2.1	98	.8	71	23.5	176	69.7	7	16	1.1	13	0	.0
58253	.2	100	.1	88	20.2	232*	74.4	8	8	.4	12	0	.0
58254	.8	100	.3	76	16.1	183	47.6	5	29	.4	26	0	.0
58256	.8	98	.3	86	22.8	309	82.3	14	10	.4	10	0	.0
58257	2.7	99	.9	61	24.0	263	74.6	5	21	1.3	18	0	.0
58258	.3	100	.1	86	19.8	219	58.6	6	16	.2	13	0	.0
58259	.9	0	.3	81	21.4	296	58.0	5	18	.0	0	0	.0
58260	.5	0	.2	88	19.5	225	26.4	5	18	.0	0	0	.0
58261	.9	0	.4	79	19.1	187	50.5	7	20	.0	0	0	.0
58262	.3	100	.1	71	17.9	338	26.2	8	32	.2	34	0	.0
58265	.7	0	.2	83	19.7	229	45.3	11	17	.0	0	0	.0
58266	.4	98	.1	81	19.5	211	31.4	5	14	.2	15	0	.0
58267	2.0	100	.7	72	22.9	271	66.2	8	21	1.0	20	0	.0
58269	.4	0	.1	89	21.1	251	40.6	6	26	.0	0	0	.0
58270	2.5	99	.9	78	19.8	215	62.9	7	19	1.3	18	0	.0
58271	.8	100	.3	83	23.2	272	60.8	7	12	.4	11	0	.1
58273	.5	0	.2	89	15.8	277	44.6	8	26	.0	0	0	.0
58274	.5	0	.2	82	17.6	128	42.5	8	17	.0	0	0	.0
58275	1.1	0	.4	74	22.5	222	61.1	9	19	.0	0	0	.0
58276	.9	0	.3	80	23.6	330	77.1	10	13	.0	0	0	.0
58277	.8	0	.3	87	26.8	282	56.0	8	12	.0	0	0	.0
58278	.4	100	.1	76	22.9	173	30.2	11	20	.2	17	0	.0
58281	1.4	99	.4	90	30.9	245	96.3	11	8	.7	7	0	.0
58282	2.1	0	.7	71	20.2	232*	23.0	7	13	.2	16	0	.0

DEVILS LAKE

ZIPCODE	1	2	3	4	5	6	7	8	9	10	11	12	13
58301	9.9	96	3.5	64	24.2	257	76.5	8	15	4.6	13	0	.0
58311	.3	100	.1	86	22.7	105	24.2	5	20	.2	25	0	.0
58313	.3	100	.1	88	17.9	228	24.2	11	15	.2	16	0	.0
58315	.3	100	.1	78	16.0	183*	19.1	5	11	.2	13	0	.0
58316	4.4	0	1.2	57	18.7	173	49.3	13	6	.0	0	0	.0
58317	.5	100	.2	77	23.9	243	27.4	4	29	.3	30	0	.0
58318	4.4	98	1.5	77	22.8	275	72.0	6	17	2.2	16	0	.0
58320	.2	100	.1	92	26.8	277*	21.2	14	7	.1	6	0	.0
58321	.3	100	.1	90	24.1	158	26.4	4	22	.2	19	0	.0
58322	.1	100	.1	76	21.9	251*	19.0	3	9	.1	8	0	.0
58323	.3	100	.1	91	20.8	239*	24.2	5	11	.1	14	0	.0
58324	2.0	99	.8	72	22.6	251	74.2	6	22	1.0	19	0	.0
58325	.3	100	.1	79	23.5	256	50.7	7	14	.2	15	0	.0
58327	.4	100	.1	85	34.0	323	43.1	8	6	.2	6	0	.0
58329	2.8	34	.7	69	15.8	185	38.9	13	9	.5	14	0	.0
58330	.7	0	.3	87	17.8	131	41.5	5	27	.2	16	0	.0
58331	.3	100	.1	72	25.1	201	29.4	9	12	.2	11	0	.0
58332	.9	100	.3	88	21.7	189	33.0	5	18	.4	21	0	.0
58335	1.2	0	.3	19	16.2	121	80.2	18	4	.0	0	0	.0

NORTH DAKOTA

DEVILS LAKE

ZIPCODE	1	2	3	4	5	6	7	8	9	10	11	12	13
58336	.3	0	.1	95	20.8	239*	13.1	4	19	.0	0	0	.0
58338	.3	100	.1	79	21.5	182	25.5	13	18	.1	20	0	.0
58341	3.4	100	1.2	71	20.6	248	62.6	7	21	1.6	19	0	.0
58342	.2	100	.1	86	13.7	157*	16.8	7	29	.1	28	0	.0
58343	.2	0	.1	83	18.4	212*	22.3	6	17	.0	0	0	.0
58344	1.4	0	.5	72	22.5	223	58.3	6	23	.0	0	0	.0
58345	.3	100	.3	93	15.1	174*	25.5	7	23	.2	21	0	.0
58346	1.1	0	.4	73	24.1	195	49.7	7	19	.0	0	0	.0
58348	1.2	99	.5	76	21.0	204	46.4	7	24	.6	22	0	.3
58351	.7	100	.3	69	22.4	198	44.3	6	24	.3	21	0	.0
58352	.8	100	.3	84	24.3	290	62.1	10	17	.4	19	0	.0
58353	.2	100	.1	84	16.3	188*	43.9	2	8	.1	6	0	.0
58355	.3	95	.3	50	22.0	316	22.9	10	7	.2	6	0	.0
58357	.4	88	.1	75	20.2	230	50.6	8	16	.2	21	0	.0
58359	.4	100	.1	91	13.7	157*	19.7	9	10	.2	11	0	.0
58361	.4	100	.1	89	17.0	39	21.3	10	19	.2	22	0	.0
58362	.2	100	.1	89	15.3	175*	31.0	6	11	.1	13	0	.0
58364	.2	0	.1	92	19.9	228*	70.8*	6	14	.0	0	0	.0
58365	.7	0	.3	78	20.4	200	39.3	10	17	.6	14	0	.1
58366	1.3	94	.5	73	21.5	194	68.0	8	13	.8	16	0	.0
58367	2.3	70	.8	66	22.4	254	68.0	9	14	.8	18	0	.0
58368	4.2	99	1.5	72	21.7	266	67.6	7	21	2.0	18	0	.1
58369	.8	60	.3	86	23.3	235	43.3	9	12	.3	21	0	.0
58370	.9	25	.3	80	17.5	181	59.4	15	5	.1	7	0	.0
58372	.3	0	.1	82	17.1	242	21.5	8	18	.2	17	0	.0
58373	.3	100	.1	94	29.5	339*	32.3	6	8	.1	10	0	.0
58374	.8	0	.4	81	18.0	177	36.4	8	22	.2	16	0	.0
58377	.6	100	.2	69	21.8	172	35.8	9	17	.3	18	0	.0
58379	.3	0	.1	55	14.2	134	37.3	16	7	.0	0	0	.0
58380	.5	0	.2	80	20.7	230	50.3	4	16	.0	0	0	.0
58381	.4	0	.1	76	20.7	202	28.3	7	18	.2	11	0	.0
58382	.9	0	.3	70	31.9	404	58.9	10	11	.2	11	0	.0
58384	.3	100	.1	84	18.2	192	37.6	7	22	.4	23	0	.0
58385	.3	100	.1	69	24.3	220	37.2	12	8	.2	8	0	.0
58386	.3	100	.1	90	25.2	227	21.1	4	18	.1	16	0	.0

JAMESTOWN

ZIPCODE	1	2	3	4	5	6	7	8	9	10	11	12	13
58401	18.5	98	6.8	65	24.7	276	86.9	8	13	8.7	11	0	.3
58410	.2	0	.1	85	23.8	135	52.2	7	7	.0	0	0	.0
58411	.1	100	.1	95	19.3	221*	16.7	4	9	.1	7	0	.0
58413	1.7	99	.7	83	18.0	175	54.6	5	27	.8	26	0	.6
58416	.7	100	.3	84	19.5	142	37.6	6	22	.4	22	0	.6
58417	.2	100	.1	75	26.0	230	30.6	11	11	.1	10	0	.0
58418	.5	100	.2	85	19.0	357	28.7	7	22	.3	21	0	.0
58420	.4	100	.1	86	28.7	123	67.3	11	15	.2	18	0	.0
58421	3.5	0	1.2	72	25.0	262	64.2	8	17	.0	0	0	.1
58422	.3	100	.1	83	20.5	303	18.2	6	20	.2	16	0	.0
58423	.3	100	.1	85	22.3	329	28.4	7	12	.1	15	0	.0
58424	.5	100	.2	84	25.0	251	61.4	5	15	.3	16	0	.0

*=Estimated **1.0=883 lbs per person; 100++ indicates per capita toxic waste generation > than 100 times the U.S. average of 883 lbs per capita.

ZIP CODE MEASURES OF SIZE, LEVELS OF AFFLUENCE AND QUALITY OF LIFE

1=Population (th.); 2= % White; 3=Households (th.); 4=% Owner Occupied; 5=Mean Income Per Household (th.$); 6=Mean Monthly Rent ($); 7=Mean Home Value (th.$);
8=% under 5; 9=% 65 and over; 10=White Males (th.); 11=% White Males, 65+; 12=# Toxic Waste Sites; 13=Toxic Waste Relative to US(883 lbs.per capita)**.

NORTH DAKOTA — JAMESTOWN

ZIP CODE	1	2	3	4	5	6	7	8	9	10	11	12	13
58425	1.8	100	.7	75	21.4	187	59.6	7	21	.9	18	0	1.5
58426	.4	100	.2	67	16.7	171	37.9	9	13	.2	14	0	.0
58428	.3	100	.1	96	15.3	176*	32.9	6	15	.2	12	0	.0
58429	.5	0	.2	78	16.9	269	17.8	9	15	.0	0	0	.0
58430	.2	100	.1	78	16.9	170	15.8	4	18	.1	18	0	.0
58431	.3	100	.1	91	15.3	175*	23.1	8	12	.1	9	0	.0
58432	.2	100	.1	79	29.1	334*	53.2	4	13	.1	15	0	.0
58433	1.6	100	.6	83	22.8	178	55.2	7	18	.8	16	0	.0
58435	.3	100	.1	91	26.7	307*	92.4	7	13	.1	15	0	.5
58436	2.5	99	.9	69	19.6	206	56.7	6	20	1.2	17	0	.0
58438	1.1	99	.4	79	22.2	199	48.8	5	21	.6	20	0	.0
58439	.4	0	.1	82	12.7	141	28.6	8	17	.0	0	0	.0
58440	.4	100	.1	87	19.7	393	14.3	6	8	.2	8	0	.0
58441	.5	100	.1	78	21.3	189	17.0	10	9	.2	8	0	.0
58442	.9	100	.3	88	21.3	213	40.2	6	19	.5	19	0	.0
58443	.3	100	.1	70	18.7	217	39.8	6	13	.2	14	0	.0
58444	.6	100	.1	77	17.0	189	31.7	10	18	.3	17	0	.0
58445	.2	100	.1	56	18.5	243	44.0	7	14	.0	0	0	.0
58447	.2	100	.1	74	20.0	305	71.4*	11	11	.1	7	0	.0
58448	.6	0	.2	82	21.3	232	40.4	6	17	.0	0	0	.0
58450	.1	100	.1	93	21.9	252*	29.8	5	17	.0	15	0	.4
58451	.5	100	.1	75	20.3	246	23.1	4	16	.2	20	0	.0
58455	.5	100	.2	83	15.9	183	34.5	7	18	.3	17	0	.0
58456	.9	0	.4	84	17.7	300	35.2	10	15	.2	11	0	.0
58458	2.0	99	.7	75	18.2	146	38.8	6	28	1.0	15	0	.0
58460	.6	100	.2	87	19.3	225	56.1	8	18	.3	14	0	.2
58461	.8	0	.3	90	17.8	198	31.8	8	15	.0	0	0	.0
58464	1.2	100	.4	80	21.7	112	36.5	6	20	.1	4	0	.0
58465	.5	100	.2	90	17.9	249	34.5	6	17	.2	16	0	.0
58466	.2	100	.1	100	18.5	175	31.3	5	16	.1	17	0	.0
58467	.9	100	.5	85	15.7	180*	17.5	2	19	.2	21	0	.0
58471	.3	100	.1	84	18.9	224	39.6	8	19	.5	15	0	.2
58472	3.0	99	1.0	81	16.0	195	38.5	7	15	.2	7	0	.0
58474	.6	100	.1	84	16.6	197	18.2	10	8	.2	12	0	.0
58475	.3	100	.1	74	19.5	259	28.4	7	12	.3	16	0	.0
58476	.5	100	.2	82	21.8	239	76.7	9	18	.2	14	0	.0
58477	.3	100	.1	83	16.3	210	34.9	8	21	1.5	17	0	.0
58478	.4	100	.1	84	25.5	210	28.2	11	14	.1	8	0	.0
58479	.2	100	.1	85	15.1	230	42.0	9	14	.3	0	0	.0
58480	.5	0	.2	74	17.9	230*	40.5	1	17	.3	12	0	.0
58481	.2	100	.1	99	22.8	262*	40.5	1	17	.1	22	0	.0
58482	1.1	0	.4	76	18.3	197	55.6	9	17	.1	17	0	.0
58483	.6	100	.2	89	15.1	164	20.7	5	20	.2	3	0	.0
58486	.4	100	.2	79	17.1	213	33.8	11	15	.3	16	0	.2
58487	.6	0	.2	89	14.8	191	32.5	8	9	.2	14	0	.0
58488	.6	100	.2	86	21.2	210	31.3	11	14	.1	0	0	.0
58489	.2	100	.1	82	15.6	240	41.0	6	13	.3	15	0	.0

NORTH DAKOTA — JAMESTOWN / BISMARCK

ZIP CODE	1	2	3	4	5	6	7	8	9	10	11	12	13
JAMESTOWN													
58490	.4	100	.1	73	20.7	178	28.9	12	11	.2	9	.0	.0
58492	.7	0	.2	81	21.4	202	38.5	10	14	.0	0	0	.0
58494	.5	0	.2	88	19.4	146	27.7	8	16	.0	0	0	.0
58495	2.0	0	.8	80	18.4	188	55.1	6	22	.3	13	0	.3
58496	.5	100	.2	82	18.5	201	21.3	10	15	.3	13	0	.0
58497	.5	0	.2	88	24.3	300	55.4	5	10	.0	0	0	.0
BISMARCK													
58501	51.3	97	18.4	65	29.7	335	109.8	9	8	24.2	7	1	.2
58520	.4	0	.1	78	19.8	237	36.7	5	19	.0	0	0	.0
58521	.4	0	.1	82	19.9	308	91.4	12	13	.0	1	0	.0
58523	3.6	97	1.2	75	29.9	299	91.8	9	11	1.8	9	1	.0
58524	.4	100	.1	85	22.7	275	17.1	9	6	.2	5	0	.0
58528	.6	7	.1	41	12.8	123	16.8	16	4	.0	0	0	.0
58529	.9	0	.3	80	15.4	236	54.3	8	17	.0	0	0	.0
58530	1.4	95	.5	76	26.5	198	74.0	12	8	.7	8	0	.5
58531	.4	100	.2	88	24.0	402	35.9	8	11	.2	12	0	.0
58532	.5	100	.2	81	17.8	213	40.6	9	9	.3	10	0	.0
58533	.9	99	.5	79	17.6	220	60.0	7	22	.1	19	0	.0
58534	.6	48	.1	80	25.6	204	91.3*	8	13	.1	22	0	.1
58535	.9	100	.3	75	14.7	236	48.8	5	16	.5	14	0	.1
58538	1.7	12	.4	30	23.0	176	47.1	14	4	.1	10	0	.0
58540	2.4	96	.9	81	22.5	215	64.6	7	19	1.1	16	0	.0
58541	.6	0	.2	77	17.6	241	42.9	9	11	.0	0	0	.0
58542	.9	0	.2	92	11.6	133*	16.7	11	5	.0	0	0	.0
58543	.3	100	.1	100	20.6	237*	64.3	14	13	.1	17	0	.0
58544	.7	100	.3	89	17.4	99	34.6	7	15	.3	14	0	.2
58545	3.4	99	1.2	80	26.1	352	87.2	8	10	1.7	10	0	.0
58547	.2	100	.1	79	23.2	266*	84.5	4	8	.1	4	0	.0
58549	.4	100	.1	89	28.2	249	15.6	8	12	.2	14	0	.0
58552	2.6	100	.9	81	19.9	158	63.8	8	16	1.3	15	0	.1
58553	.3	100	.1	84	23.6	195	53.7	8	5	.1	5	0	.0
58554	18.4	99	6.2	76	27.1	279	89.6	11	8	9.2	6	2	1.1
58558	.7	0	.2	93	25.6	294*	85.3	11	4	.0	0	0	.0
58559	.4	100	.1	93	21.1	87	41.4	17	12	.2	12	0	.0
58560	.3	100	.1	90	23.0	264*	34.2	11	17	.1	15	0	.0
58561	1.7	100	.6	87	16.7	187	63.5	6	19	.9	17	0	.7
58563	.8	99	.3	79	18.5	221	52.9	13	7	.4	12	0	.1
58564	.3	0	.1	88	14.3	164*	24.2	5	2	.2	2	0	.0
58565	.4	0	.1	6	34.4	263	45.8	7	3	.0	0	0	.7
58566	.2	100	.1	83	15.7	181*	61.7	4	18	.1	24	0	.0
58568	.6	88	.3	71	16.4	286	37.6	10	8	.3	6	0	.1
58569	2.3	72	.8	83	12.4	243	15.3	13	6	.1	11	0	.0
58571	.3	86	.1	86	15.2	298	23.9	9	4	.2	3	0	.0
58572	1.1	0	.3	88	27.9	186	65.9	14	8	.9	14	0	.0
58573	.3	0	.1	79	21.1	279	32.6	8	15	.1	8	0	.7
58575	1.0	100	.3	89	17.1	221	40.1	5	26	.5	26	0	.0
58576	1.5	0	.5	84	18.6	213	62.6	10	17	.0	0	0	.1
58576	1.6	99	.5	82	23.2	156	72.0	11	14	.8	13	0	.0

*=Estimated **1.0=883 lbs per person; 100++ indicates per capita toxic waste generation > than 100 times the U.S. average of 883 lbs per capita.

ZIP CODE MEASURES OF SIZE, LEVELS OF AFFLUENCE AND QUALITY OF LIFE

1=Population (th.); 2= % White; 3=Households (th.); 4=% Owner Occupied; 5=Mean Income Per Household (th.$)*; 6=Mean Monthly Rent ($)*; 7=Mean Home Value (th.$)*; 8=% under 5; 9=% 65 and over; 10=White Males (th.); 11=% White Males, 65+; 12=# Toxic Waste Sites; 13=Toxic Waste Relative to US(883 lbs.per capita)**.

NORTH DAKOTA

ZIP CODE	1	2	3	4	5	6	7	8	9	10	11	12	13
BISMARCK													
58577	2.2	99	.8	75	30.3	284	79.1	11	8	1.1	8	0	.0
58579	1.5	99	.5	77	19.2	238	64.1	10	17	.8	17	0	.0
58580	.8	0	.3	80	25.6	334	51.2	10	9	.0	0	0	.0
58581	.5	100	.2	95	14.8	250	26.5	7	19	.3	16	0	.0
DICKINSON													
58601	19.3	99	6.4	70	26.8	332	99.2	9	10	9.7	8	2	.1
58620	.3	100	.1	89	14.5	167*	16.5	12	14	.2	12	0	.0
58621	1.6	99	.6	78	23.1	223	65.2	7	19	.8	15	0	.0
58622	2.2	100	.7	78	25.3	308	62.3	9	10	1.1	9	2	.0
58623	3.0	99	1.1	76	22.8	222	84.9	9	14	1.4	11	1	.0
58625	.5	100	.1	82	21.6	246	39.5	10	8	.2	10	0	.0
58626	.4	92	.1	84	23.4	165	55.3	6	16	.2	21	0	.0
58627	.3	0	.1	84	30.4	488	108.4*	16	3	.0	0	0	.0
58630	.7	0	.2	79	22.4	262	62.1	12	5	.0	0	0	.0
58631	1.7	100	.6	82	18.3	194	52.3	6	19	.9	17	0	.0
58632	.3	0	.1	69	21.8	226	55.1	8	7	.0	0	0	.0
58634	.3	100	.1	85	23.7	230	57.8	9	9	.0	8	0	.0
58636	1.0	73	.4	78	19.5	168	46.8	6	12	.3	15	0	.0
58637	.2	100	.1	77	18.0	345	22.7	8	7	.1	6	0	.0
58638	1.6	0	.6	79	16.5	173	42.5	7	19	.0	0	0	.0
58639	2.3	0	.9	73	23.3	224	76.0	8	19	.0	0	0	.0
58640	1.3	0	.5	66	23.9	293	69.2	10	17	.0	1	0	.0
58641	.4	100	.1	81	21.2	244*	19.3	18	9	.1	14	0	.0
58642	.4	100	.1	87	15.1	285	68.1*	12	2	.2	2	0	.0
58643	.3	100	.1	82	15.1	140	28.6	10	19	.1	22	0	.0
58645	.3	0	.1	66	37.1	233	56.7	5	10	.0	0	0	.0
58646	2.1	0	.8	79	18.6	215	54.8	7	17	.0	0	0	.0
58647	1.7	0	.6	82	21.9	220	59.5	6	14	.0	1	0	.0
58649	.6	0	.2	76	18.6	209	50.1	6	15	.0	0	0	.2
58650	.7	100	.2	85	19.5	180	46.5	7	11	.4	10	0	.0
58651	.6	100	.2	80	24.3	197	29.3	7	12	.3	13	0	.0
58652	1.4	0	.5	81	18.6	182	53.6	5	13	.0	0	3	.3
58653	.7	0	.3	86	26.5	257	72.6	10	10	.0	0	0	.0
58654	.4	0	.1	88	24.7	174	27.2	10	13	.0	0	0	.0
58655	.5	97	.1	82	19.4	218	73.9	12	5	.2	6	0	.0
58656	.5	100	.2	88	22.9	292	51.5	6	17	.3	13	0	.0
MINOT													
58701	39.3	98	14.3	68	26.2	273	91.3	8	10	18.7	9	2	.1
58704	9.8	86	2.5	6	18.4	330	13.1	15	0	4.7	0	0	.0
58710	.8	100	.3	90	15.2	102	34.4	5	21	.4	21	0	.0
58711	.3	0	.1	87	18.0	280	21.6	8	21	.0	0	0	.0
58712	.2	100	.1	94	18.3	211*	17.2	6	16	.1	19	0	.0
58713	.1	100	.1	92	18.3	211*	16.9	4	38	.1	41	0	.0
58714	.2	100	.1	88	22.6	271*	35.4	13	11	.1	12	0	.0
58716	.2	100	.1	93	22.6	260*	37.1	13	17	.1	15	0	.0
58718	1.0	100	.3	90	23.8	168	50.1	12	10	.5	10	0	.0
58721	.9	100	.3	83	18.7	181	44.7	5	19	.4	18	0	.0
58722	1.2	0	.4	80	24.9	306	77.9	11	7	.0	0	0	.0
58723	.3	100	.2	86	11.7	256	29.0	7	37	.2	32	0	.0

NORTH DAKOTA

ZIP CODE	1	2	3	4	5	6	7	8	9	10	11	12	13
MINOT													
58725	.6	100	.2	78	20.0	280	43.1	5	12	.3	11	0	.0
58727	.5	99	.2	82	18.1	244	26.9	4	25	.3	28	0	.3
58730	1.8	100	.7	78	22.3	194	54.9	7	22	.9	21	0	.0
58731	.3	0	.1	83	17.9	256	45.3	7	12	.0	0	0	.0
58732	.2	100	.1	92	21.1	243*	13.1	7	14	.1	13	0	.0
58733	.4	100	.1	87	26.8	291	68.8	6	7	.2	6	0	.0
58734	.6	0	.2	84	18.9	143	31.9	5	17	.0	0	0	.0
58735	.5	100	.2	89	17.9	75	31.1	7	18	.2	21	0	.0
58736	.8	100	.2	76	15.8	211	32.6	7	20	.4	18	0	.0
58737	.3	100	.2	75	18.1	205	17.4	3	32	.2	28	0	.0
58738	.2	100	.1	96	16.6	190*	54.2	3	14	.1	13	0	.0
58740	.8	0	.3	81	23.8	292	65.2	7	12	.0	0	0	.0
58741	.7	0	.2	81	19.2	191	32.8	7	22	.0	0	0	.7
58744	.4	0	.1	93	17.8	205*	37.1	8	10	.0	0	0	.0
58746	2.2	100	.9	76	21.2	253	53.5	7	22	1.1	20	0	.0
58747	.2	100	.1	87	17.7	53	13.1	4	19	.1	16	0	.0
58748	.3	100	.1	84	14.0	232	29.7	17	23	.1	26	0	.0
58750	.7	0	.2	80	25.3	168	56.7	8	6	.0	0	0	.0
58752	.5	97	.2	84	18.2	238	43.4	8	18	.2	19	0	.9
58755	.2	100	.1	89	25.9	297*	27.8	7	13	.1	13	0	.0
58756	.4	100	.2	88	20.2	133	33.6	5	19	.2	19	0	.0
58757	.6	6	.1	58	15.8	190	78.6	9	4	.0	15	0	.0
58758	.4	0	.2	93	18.3	210*	46.5	4	19	.0	0	0	.7
58759	.9	100	.3	78	19.3	306	43.7	8	14	.5	14	0	.0
58760	.5	100	.2	84	17.3	260	31.0	9	19	.2	15	0	.0
58761	1.5	0	.6	80	21.7	254	60.7	8	21	.0	0	0	.0
58762	.4	100	.1	69	20.2	279	42.1	15	8	.2	8	0	1.2
58763	2.6	58	.8	67	21.9	240	58.6	10	10	.8	15	1	.0
58765	.5	100	.2	86	18.8	150	21.5	6	25	.2	27	0	.0
58768	.4	0	.1	95	28.5	327*	60.3	8	5	.0	0	0	.0
58769	.3	99	.1	89	19.9	242	26.1	6	15	.2	15	0	.0
58770	1.4	79	.5	69	19.8	191	43.4	10	18	.6	20	0	.0
58771	.7	0	.2	88	18.4	164	16.2	5	14	.0	0	0	.0
58772	.3	100	.1	85	20.6	232	21.2	7	9	.2	6	0	.0
58773	.9	98	.3	79	18.5	160	47.6	10	16	.4	14	0	.0
58775	.3	54	.1	73	25.3	323	42.3	9	11	.1	19	0	.0
58776	.4	99	.1	80	23.7	114	35.3	12	8	.2	6	0	.0
58779	.2	100	.1	91	19.6	225*	13.1	7	9	.1	13	0	.0
58781	.6	100	.3	85	20.4	126	29.7	4	16	.3	15	0	.0
58782	.7	100	.3	88	23.7	270	51.5	8	9	.4	20	0	.0
58783	.6	0	.1	79	22.6	235	35.5	8	19	.0	0	0	.0
58784	2.1	100	.8	82	19.7	281	28.7	7	19	1.0	18	0	.0
58785	1.2	97	.3	78	21.7	216	57.5	8	19	.6	2	0	.0
58788	1.0	100	.3	90	18.8	192	49.0	9	16	.7	13	0	.0
58789	.5	100	.3	83	14.7	171	25.5	8	22	.3	17	0	.0
58790	1.6	99	.6	73	20.8	191	62.9	8	21	.8	18	1	.0
58792	.4	0	.1	86	19.4	223*	40.7	8	19	.0	0	0	.0

*=Estimated **1.0=883 lbs per person; 100++ indicates per capita toxic waste generation > than 100 times the U.S. average of 883 lbs per capita.

ZIP CODE MEASURES OF SIZE, LEVELS OF AFFLUENCE AND QUALITY OF LIFE

1=Population (th.); 2= % White; 3=Households (th.); 4=% Owner Occupied; 5=Mean Income Per Household (th.$); 6=Mean Monthly Rent ($)*; 7=Mean Home Value (th.$)*;
8=% under 5; 9=% 65 and over; 10=White Males (th.); 11=% White Males, 65+; 12=# Toxic Waste Sites; 13=Toxic Waste Relative to US(883 lbs.per capita)**.

NORTH DAKOTA

MINOT

ZIPCODE	1	2	3	4	5	6	7	8	9	10	11	12	13
58793	1.1	0	.4	86	23.5	205	59.7	9	19	.0	0	0	.2
58794	.2	100	.1	84	15.8	216	29.3	12	15	.1	16	0	.0
58795	.4	100	.2	83	21.1	247	30.4	8	22	.2	21	0	.0

WILLISTON

ZIPCODE	1	2	3	4	5	6	7	8	9	10	11	12	13
58801	16.7	97	6.0	70	29.2	341	98.1	9	10	8.2	9	1	.8
58830	.4	100	.2	83	22.2	241	31.1	7	19	.3	19	0	.0
58831	.7	98	.2	76	22.3	402	48.9	9	9	.4	9	0	.0
58833	.2	100	.1	86	17.5	177	13.1	6	25	.1	25	0	.0
58835	.5	0	.2	86	24.2	316	47.6	9	14	.0	0	0	.0
58838	.3	0	.1	83	14.9	346	36.5	13	9	.0	0	0	.0
58843	.3	0	.1	83	21.2	222	62.8	5	12	.0	0	0	.0
58844	.3	0	.1	77	21.6	176	36.3	7	11	.0	0	0	.0
58845	.6	0	.2	70	21.4	276	30.6	7	18	.0	0	0	.0
58847	.3	0	.1	91	23.6	128	59.1	12	16	.0	0	0	.0
58849	1.0	0	.4	83	23.1	244	44.3	10	13	.0	0	0	.1
58852	2.3	99	.8	78	29.6	207	67.2	10	11	1.2	10	0	.0
58853	.4	29	.1	74	26.1	192	78.6	14	4	.0	0	0	.0
58854	3.1	98	1.1	76	26.5	319	75.9	9	12	1.6	11	0	.1
58856	.3	100	.1	87	25.4	247	27.7	6	14	.1	17	0	.0

WOLF POINT

ZIPCODE	1	2	3	4	5	6	7	8	9	10	11	12	13
59221	.7	95	.2	70	25.8	436	36.5	8	9	.3	11	0	.0
59270	.2	100	.1	88	34.5	397*	74.4	6	16	.1	15	0	.0

OHIO

NEW CASTLE

ZIPCODE	1	2	3	4	5	6	7	8	9	10	11	12	13
16146	.7	90	.3	81	27.3	317	54.1	10	13	.4	14	0	.0

COLUMBUS (NORTH)

ZIPCODE	1	2	3	4	5	6	7	8	9	10	11	12	13
43001	1.9	0	.6	88	30.0	291	84.0	6	10	.9	0	0	.0
43002	1.7	100	.6	79	28.9	237	127.5	6	6	.9	5	0	1.0
43003	2.4	0	.8	79	24.2	282	63.8	7	11	1.0	6	0	.5
43004	2.1	98	.7	82	46.9	383	132.8	6	8	.1	6	0	.0
43005	.2	100	.1	72	24.3	156	44.3	8	12	.1	11	0	.5
43006	.5	0	.2	81	19.9	212	45.6	10	12	.0	10	0	.0
43007	.4		.1	88	25.6	322	68.1	9	9	.0	0	0	.0
43009	2.3	0	1.0	67	17.9	243	40.2	8	15	.0	0	0	.0
43010	1.3	0	.4	85	26.0	274	67.9	7	9	.0	0	0	.0
43011	.3	100	.1	81	27.0	470	52.4	8	6	.2	5	0	.0
43013	1.0	100	.3	83	24.8	307	81.0	7	12	2.1	11	0	.0
43014	2.8	0	.9	71	24.0	273	66.6	11	12	.5	11	0	.5
43015	27.4	96	9.2	75	23.0	257	63.4	9	13	12.9	7	4	1.9
43017	8.7	98	2.9	79	47.0	440	181.5	9	4	4.2	3	0	6.7
43018	.3	100	.1	95	23.0	264*	61.9	0	33	.1	26	0	.0
43019	7.3	100	2.4	81	23.9	296	72.3	8	10	3.7	8	0	.1
43021	4.0	99	1.3	87	35.0	373	126.9	6	8	2.0	8	0	.0
43022	3.2	99	.7	72	26.8	330	94.3	5	6	1.6	6	0	.0
43023	8.9	98	2.5	82	35.5	358	124.5	5	7	4.4	7	2	3.7
43026	4.4	0	1.5	76	27.2	290	84.0	6	9	4.9	4	1	5.5
43027	9.9	100	3.1	84	29.6	399	82.7	9	5	4.1	4	1	31.9
43028	.2	0	.2	90	17.1	197*	40.7	9	16	.3	10	0	.0
43029	2.2	99	.7	81	23.8	317	81.2	9	10	1.1	10	0	.0
43031	.5	100	.2	67	28.9	355	60.7	7	7	.3	4	0	.0
43033	8.0	100	2.6	81	28.0	292	85.3	7	8	3.9	6	0	7.0
43036	.5	100	.1	65	22.7	296	64.1	7	15	.3	11	0	.2
43037	.3	0	.1	80	19.2	230	41.1	6	14	.0	0	0	.4
43040	.4	0	.2	80	19.8	233	47.4	5	12	1.5	12	0	.0
43044	15.5	96	5.2	73	26.6	319	87.5	8	10	1.1	10	0	7.0
43045	4.7	98	1.6	75	25.7	277	69.3	8	7	.3	4	0	.0
43046	1.6	0	.5	74	26.1	328	64.1	10	12	3.9	6	0	.2
43048	3.0	99	1.1	76	26.4	294	72.1	6	14	1.5	12	0	.4
43050	2.0	100	.7	69	20.0	232	66.3	8	13	1.1	11	0	.0
43054	9.4	72	1.2	88	22.3	274	70.2	7	14	11.9	6	1	1.4
43055	3.7	99	1.2	88	34.3	441	113.7	7	7	1.9	6	0	.9
43060	66.7	97	24.5	69	25.4	298	75.6	7	12	31.1	10	11	.9
43061	1.6	98	.5	73	23.0	396	54.3	10	11	.8	10	0	.0
43062	2.1	98	.7	85	28.5	345	83.6	8	11	1.1	9	0	.0
43065	13.1	98	4.2	84	29.9	324	97.1	7	6	6.4	5	0	.6
43066	8.2	98	2.7	77	29.2	487	101.6	8	7	4.0	6	0	.0
43067	5.1	95	1.6	86	36.9	359	143.8	8	7	2.5	5	0	.0
43068	1.1	100	.3	79	29.5	303	81.6	6	8	.5	8	0	.0
43070	27.1	97	9.4	70	32.5	401	60.2	8	5	13.0	4	0	.0
43071	2.3	100	.7	89	22.0	253*	58.5	5	27	.1	27	0	.0

*=Estimated **1.0=883 lbs per person; 100++ indicates per capita toxic waste generation > than 100 times the U.S. average of 883 lbs per capita.

ZIP CODE MEASURES OF SIZE, LEVELS OF AFFLUENCE AND QUALITY OF LIFE

1=Population (th.); 2= % White; 3=Households (th.); 4=% Owner Occupied; 5=Mean Income Per Household (th.$); 6=Mean Monthly Rent ($)*; 7=Mean Home Value (th.$)*; 8=% under 5; 9=% 65 and over; 10=White Males (th.); 11=% White Males, 65+; 12=# Toxic Waste Sites; 13=Toxic Waste Relative to US(883 lbs.per capital)**.

OHIO

ZIPCODE	1	2	3	4	5	6	7	8	9	10	11	12	13
COLUMBUS (NORTH)													
43072	4.6	99	1.6	79	25.4	301	73.2	8	10	2.3	9	1	.0
43073	.2	100	.1	84	19.6	356	64.1	3	32	.1	27	0	.0
43074	6.5	99	2.1	86	30.1	367	93.4	8	9	3.2	7	0	.3
43076	6.2	100	2.1	85	25.4	326	70.5	6	11	3.1	10	0	.0
43077	.3	100	.1	68	23.9	317	50.2	7	11	.9	9	0	.0
43078	18.4	95	6.6	71	24.8	294	76.4	7	13	8.4	11	1	2.4
43080	4.2	99	1.5	75	23.8	274	63.5	8	10	2.1	6	0	.0
43081	38.8	98	12.0	81	35.7	408	121.2	8	6	18.6	4	0	.2
43083	.2	100	.1	94	23.7*	273*	55.8	5	12	.1	9	0	.0
43084	.8	0	.3	76	27.5	324	55.3	9	9	.2	9	0	.0
43085	28.4	96	9.2	87	48.3	393	155.6	6	7	13.4	5	1	.3
COLUMBUS (SOUTH)													
43101	.5	0	.2	78	21.4	245	50.4	7	10	.0	0	0	.0
43102	3.4	0	1.1	78	24.5	278	72.1	8	9	.0	0	0	.7
43103	6.7	100	2.2	72	26.7	320	83.0	9	7	3.3	7	1	.1
43105	6.5	100	2.1	80	28.8	334	95.3	8	9	3.3	6	0	.6
43106	1.6	96	.5	62	22.5	355	53.6	8	9	.3	9	0	.6
43107	2.9	99	1.0	85	26.8	290	67.4	9	12	1.4	11	0	.8
43110	7.1	98	2.3	81	36.7	350	118.0	6	10	3.3	9	0	.2
43111	.3	0	.1	71	19.3	327	36.4	10	18	.0	0	0	.0
43112	4.1	99	1.3	85	29.6	301	96.2	8	7	2.1	7	0	.0
43113	21.3	98	7.4	68	25.5	304	83.2	8	10	1.9	8	0	.0
43115	1.3	99	.4	70	26.1	274	55.0	7	7	.7	9	8	8.7
43116	.3	100	.1	72	23.1	289	45.0	7	8	.0	8	1	.0
43117	.3	100	.1	84	21.6	286	43.8	5	11	.3	5	0	.0
43119	7.8	98	2.5	86	34.4	370	103.7	10	4	3.9	4	0	.0
43121	.1	100	.1	71	16.8	223	47.5	8	10	.1	9	0	.0
43123	29.9	97	9.8	77	31.1	346	93.0	7	7	1.2	10	2	.7
43125	7.9	97	2.7	76	28.9	374	95.2	9	6	4.6	9	4	.0
43126	.5	0	.2	76	21.6	346	73.0	7	18	.0	0	0	.0
43127	.4	0	.1	93	18.4	211*	29.4	9	7	.0	0	0	.0
43128	2.4	94	.8	68	21.5	296	50.2	7	10	1.2	10	0	.0
43130	51.5	99	18.5	71	26.7	300	81.3	7	12	24.6	9	4	.7
43135	3.5	100	1.1	81	21.5	257	59.7	8	9	1.8	9	0	.0
43136	.6	100	.2	68	29.3	416	82.5	4	7	.3	5	0	.0
43137	3.3	99	1.1	71	25.6	284	79.4	10	8	1.7	6	0	.0
43140	16.9	99	5.5	71	26.2	238	62.7	7	13	7.3	11	4	.0
43143	5.3	91	5.2	67	26.2	307	85.0	7	9	7.9	8	0	.4
43144	.7	100	1.8	61	22.6	288	71.1	8	11	.4	12	0	.4
43145	1.8	0	.6	70	17.4	193	27.7	6	14	.0	0	0	.0
43146	7.9	97	1.9	74	24.9	291	68.8	8	10	4.0	7	0	.0
43147	11.6	99	3.4	84	31.8	342	113.4	6	7	5.7	2	0	.0
43148	1.7	99	.6	94	39.1	460	129.9	6	9	.0	0	0	.0
43149	2.2	100	.7	75	19.9	334	58.2	10	11	.8	0	0	.0
43150	1.7	100	.5	78	22.8	322	63.8	6	16	.8	13	0	.0
43151	.4	0	.1	84	25.1	270	67.1	11	12	.0	0	0	.0
43152	.9	100	.3	79	19.9	271	51.4	9	10	.4	12	0	.0
43153	1.2	99	.4	63	18.9	125	42.1	6	14	.0	0	0	.0

OHIO

ZIPCODE	1	2	3	4	5	6	7	8	9	10	11	12	13
COLUMBUS (SOUTH)													
43154	1.9	0	.6	85	23.3	313	75.2	10	8	.0	0	0	.0
43155	1.8	100	.6	87	26.1	302	73.8	8	9	.9	10	0	.0
43156	.3	100	.1	80	17.9	290	50.1	3	12	.2	10	0	.0
43157	.5	100	.2	82	19.9	310	46.0	6	11	.2	6	0	.0
43158	.3	0	.1	80	21.1	189	42.0	8	8	.0	0	0	.0
43160	20.4	97	7.4	65	21.8	289	65.1	8	14	9.4	12	3	.3
43162	6.4	100	2.1	77	29.8	302	80.4	7	7	3.2	6	0	.3
43163	.1	100	.1	76	17.7	173	52.6	8	15	.1	20	0	.0
43164	2.4	99	.8	68	23.6	276	61.2	8	8	1.2	8	0	.0
COLUMBUS													
43201	37.9	80	15.8	14	13.2	300	55.1	5	5	16.6	3	0	.7
43202	21.2	94	10.0	33	13.9	325	69.5	6	11	9.6	7	0	.0
43203	11.8	6	5.2	27	13.9	193	46.3	3	23	.2	23	0	.0
43204	39.1	93	14.9	66	24.1	323	66.3	8	12	17.0	10	2	.1
43205	20.1	17	7.2	31	15.4	244	48.6	9	11	1.7	12	1	.2
43206	29.4	68	11.5	53	21.1	319	59.9	8	11	9.4	11	0	.9
43207	46.0	75	15.1	70	23.0	261	59.7	8	8	16.7	8	7	.3
43209	30.0	84	12.1	59	34.9	321	134.6*	7	14	11.7	13	0	.5
43210	11.8	87	.5		9.8	249	34.9*	1	0	5.4	0	0	.0
43211	30.7	42	10.1	65	19.2	304	45.5	9	7	5.4	10	1	.5
43212	19.2	98	9.7	37	24.4	352	104.7	5	14	8.4	9	1	.8
43213	29.2	94	12.2	48	27.1	367	89.6	7	8	12.8	7	0	.5
43214	27.8	98	12.1	67	30.4	363	100.5	5	19	12.1	15	0	.2
43215	12.4	79	5.9	7	12.3	273	60.4	4	17	5.3	10	4	4.5
43217	.3	77	.4	79	19.2	214	68.3*	8	10	3.6	12	0	.7
43219	27.5	29	9.0	65	22.7	255	66.6	6	9	3.6	12	0	.5
43220	33.0	98	13.0	62	46.1	408	174.1	5	7	15.4	6	0	.3
43221	22.4	98	9.2	79	42.6	458	139.9	5	16	10.3	10	0	.4
43222	6.3	90	2.9	35	14.3	246	33.8	10	13	2.7	10	3	.7
43223	30.8	83	10.4	59	19.7	252	57.0	9	10	12.5	8	0	.0
43224	41.9	86	16.9	58	23.6	297	69.2	8	11	17.2	8	1	.0
43227	62.8	87	23.4	60	26.8	346	77.7	8	6	26.3	5	3	1.2
43228	32.5	94	12.9	47	24.6	302	81.8	9	6	14.7	4	3	.0
43229	56.7	94	22.3	49	29.5	383	100.5	8	5	25.8	4	3	.0
43230	22.0	95	7.3	74	33.9	373	107.5	7	5	10.3	4	2	.0
COLUMBUS													
43302	56.1	96	19.7	71	25.1	315	77.2	8	10	26.1	8	5	1.6
43311	16.8	96	6.1	70	24.1	296	69.3	8	12	7.8	9	0	.5
43314	3.2	99	1.1	84	26.0	292	81.4	7	9	1.6	9	0	.0
43315	5.3	100	1.8	83	23.7	272	63.8	7	10	2.6	8	0	.1
43316	6.2	99	2.0	75	22.9	280	67.8	9	11	3.0	10	0	.0
43317	.2	100	.1	65	24.9	212	44.8	8	29	.1	23	0	.0
43318	3.2	100	1.1	83	22.4	274	63.9	9	11	1.5	11	0	.0
43319	.6	100	.2	82	22.8	279	75.7	9	13	.3	13	0	.0
43320	1.6	0	.5	83	24.5	293	63.6	6	16	.2	10	0	.0
43321	.4	100	.1	80	23.0	202	38.5	6	9	.0	13	0	.0
43322	.5	0	.2	85	24.8	253	61.0	4	12	.0	0	0	.0
43323	.6	100	.2	88	25.4	386	74.6	9	13	.3	12	0	.0

*=Estimated **1.0=883 lbs per person; 100++ indicates per capita toxic waste generation > than 100 times the U.S. average of 883 lbs per capita.

ZIP CODE MEASURES OF SIZE, LEVELS OF AFFLUENCE AND QUALITY OF LIFE

1=Population (th.); 2= % White; 3=Households (th.); 4=% Owner Occupied; 5=Mean Income Per Household (th.$); 6=Mean Monthly Rent ($)*; 7=Mean Home Value (th.$)*;
8=% under 5; 9=% 65 and over; 10=White Males (th.); 11=% White Males, 65+; 12=# Toxic Waste Sites; 13=Toxic Waste Relative to US(883 lbs.per capital)**.

OHIO

COLUMBUS

ZIPCODE	1	2	3	4	5	6	7	8	9	10	11	12	13
43324	2.3	99	.8	84	24.6	285	90.5	8	14	1.1	12	0	.0
43325	.2	100	.1	82	24.4	302	53.3	5	10	.1	11	0	11.1
43326	14.1	99	5.1	73	24.0	268	64.6	8	15	6.6	12	2	3.6
43330	.2	100	.1	73	19.9	288	38.4	12	16	.1	13	0	.0
43331	3.7	0	1.5	84	19.7	240	53.5	7	20	.0	9	0	.0
43332	2.5	99	.8	78	24.7	259	67.8	8	11	1.2	9	0	.0
43333	.6	100	.2	78	23.0	389	47.8	10	6	.3	4	0	.1
43334	4.2	0	..	87	25.2	342	72.1	9	7	.0	9	0	.0
43335	.2	0	.1	80	22.7	368	39.5	8	12	.0	12	0	.1
43337	1.1	98	.4	82	29.7	344	80.5	8	9	.1	9	0	.0
43338	7.5	99	2.7	80	24.1	280	74.0	8	13	3.7	12	0	1.2
43340	1.4	0	.5	81	21.8	234	58.2	8	12	.0	6	0	.0
43341	.8	100	.3	93	25.3	266	64.3	7	6	.4	6	0	.0
43342	3.2	99	1.1	84	29.1	283	84.2	7	10	1.6	7	0	.0
43343	1.4	100	.5	82	22.7	314	54.2	8	11	.6	10	0	.0
43344	4.9	99	1.8	76	24.2	287	70.0	8	13	2.4	11	0	.0
43345	1.0	96	.3	76	23.6	259	58.0	12	8	.0	8	0	.0
43347	1.6	0	.5	85	21.3	308	55.1	10	9	.0	9	0	.0
43348	1.9	0	.8	75	17.9	230	60.0	7	19	.0	7	0	.0
43349	.2	100	.1	75	22.0	263	40.0	4	11	.1	11	0	.0
43350	.2	100	.1	74	18.5	281	43.3	7	6	.1	9	0	.0
43351	9.8	99	3.5	73	25.7	315	78.8	8	16	4.6	12	0	.4
43356	1.1	100	.4	84	26.1	282	106.1	5	10	.5	11	0	.0
43357	3.9	100	1.3	75	25.9	273	82.4	9	11	1.9	9	1	.2
43358	2.2	0	.8	85	25.9	273	56.2	8	12	.0	9	1	.7
43359	.9	100	.3	80	22.1	197	53.6	10	15	.4	15	0	.0
43360	1.0	0	.3	86	23.5	174	67.2	7	11	.0	0	0	.8

TOLEDO (EAST)

ZIPCODE	1	2	3	4	5	6	7	8	9	10	11	12	13
43402	32.1	95	9.3	51	25.1	380	111.2	5	14	14.1	5	0	.2
43406	1.9	99	.6	78	23.9	358	67.1	8	9	.9	8	0	.0
43407	.7	96	.2	86	27.8	228	72.1	4	9	.3	9	0	.0
43408	.4	0	.1	87	25.5	345	61.8	7	22	.0	9	0	.0
43410	10.0	98	3.3	79	27.3	323	75.5	9	9	4.9	7	1	2.6
43412	4.0	0	1.3	81	28.3	358	86.8	8	8	.0	9	0	.7
43413	1.3	98	.4	82	23.8	327	66.1	8	9	.6	9	0	.0
43414	.9	0	.3	56	25.6	303	75.4	8	8	.0	7	0	.1
43416	2.6	98	1.0	81	29.7	353	89.2	6	14	1.3	12	1	.6
43420	33.4	94	11.6	73	26.9	326	80.9	8	11	15.2	9	2	.7
43430	5.1	99	1.6	84	32.4	362	88.0	8	8	2.4	7	0	.0
43431	4.7	97	1.5	82	28.8	316	77.9	7	10	2.3	9	0	.2
43432	1.2	100	.4	89	29.9	304	96.8	10	7	.6	6	0	.0
43433	1.2	100	.1	78	33.4	413	58.0	18	14	.9	14	1	2.6
43434	.7	89	.1	84	12.0	149*	31.7	3	11	.5	12	0	.0
43435	1.6	99	.5	83	26.5	394	70.8	8	10	.8	7	0	.0
43437	.6	0	.2	88	26.1	287	58.2	10	8	.0	8	0	.0
43438	.1	100	.1	88	15.0	172*	83.2	5	47	.1	56	0	.0
43439	.1	0	.1	71	23.8	289	85.2	1	16	.0	0	0	.0
43440	4.2	99	1.6	85	24.4	281	79.4	9	17	2.0	16	0	.1
43442	1.2	96	.4	80	28.5	320	75.1	9	13	.6	11	0	.0

OHIO

TOLEDO (EAST)

ZIPCODE	1	2	3	4	5	6	7	8	9	10	11	12	13
43443	1.4	100	.5	84	27.5	359	85.8	6	13	.7	11	1	.1
43445	1.1	96	.4	80	27.9	424	81.5	8	9	.6	10	0	.0
43447	3.1	0	1.0	87	33.9	352	99.6	7	7	.0	0	1	3.7
43449	7.5	100	2.6	77	27.3	319	88.1	7	13	3.7	11	0	1.4
43450	3.2	98	1.1	76	28.8	354	95.4	8	12	1.6	10	1	.5
43451	1.3	97	.4	81	25.7	396	87.3	8	10	.6	9	1	.0
43452	14.6	98	5.4	76	27.1	300	91.0	7	12	6.9	11	4	.1
43456	.5	0	.2	91	25.7	428	96.0	5	24	.0	0	0	.0
43457	1.9	99	.6	81	28.3	318	69.0	9	6	.9	7	1	.0
43458	.4	89	.1	86	24.6	387	56.1	10	6	.2	5	0	.0
43460	6.7	96	2.5	72	35.6	366	112.0	7	11	3.1	10	1	.2
43462	1.2	0	.4	84	25.6	282	72.9	7	8	.0	0	0	.0
43463	.2	0	.1	87	28.2	438	74.3	8	11	.0	0	0	.0
43464	1.6	0	.5	78	24.7	356	65.5	7	8	.0	0	0	.0
43465	5.9	98	2.1	79	29.6	337	87.8	8	8	3.0	7	2	.8
43466	2.2	0	.7	80	25.1	347	65.5	10	10	.0	0	1	.0
43467	.2	100	.1	88	25.2	290*	47.6	6	10	.1	6	1	.0
43468	.5	0	.2	69	30.8	495	93.2	8	5	.0	0	0	.0
43469	3.0	95	1.1	78	33.2	329	91.3	7	12	1.4	10	0	.6

TOLEDO (WEST)

ZIPCODE	1	2	3	4	5	6	7	8	9	10	11	12	13
43501	1.1	99	.3	80	21.1	276	48.2	10	11	.5	10	0	.0
43502	5.8	97	2.0	77	31.4	329	95.6	8	13	2.7	11	0	1.4
43504	1.0	100	.3	82	32.5	391	92.2	6	9	.5	7	0	.0
43506	14.3	98	5.4	74	27.2	312	81.0	9	12	6.9	10	2	1.3
43511	.9	0	.3	80	26.8	293	65.2	9	14	.0	0	0	.0
43512	29.3	95	9.8	77	29.6	321	81.8	9	11	13.8	7	0	.7
43515	7.1	98	2.4	82	26.5	342	87.1	10	9	3.4	8	1	.2
43516	3.2	97	1.2	81	25.2	281	71.0	8	15	1.5	11	0	3.9
43517	3.5	99	.5	81	25.4	297	67.3	9	12	1.7	11	0	.7
43518	2.7	99	.1	85	27.1	331	60.0	8	10	1.3	7	0	1.1
43521	2.7	99	.9	78	21.8	285	58.6	6	12	1.3	10	0	1.8
43522	2.9	99	1.0	79	28.5	348	91.2	9	8	1.4	7	0	.0
43523	.2	100	.1	83	28.1	386	55.8	11	11	.1	11	0	.0
43524	1.5	96	.5	79	26.1	335	70.0	8	14	.7	14	0	.0
43525	.5	0	.2	84	25.1	287	73.1	7	16	.0	0	0	.0
43526	6.2	99	2.1	79	25.3	284	64.8	9	12	2.9	10	0	.4
43527	2.8	94	.9	78	26.7	327	65.8	8	13	1.3	10	0	.0
43528	8.1	90	2.6	80	28.5	343	82.3	8	8	3.7	7	0	.0
43529	.3	85	.1	89	22.3	230	29.9	9	14	.1	21	0	.0
43531	.2	100	.1	88	18.1	426	32.1	10	19	.1	18	0	.0
43532	3.9	98	1.3	82	26.8	325	75.6	7	9	1.9	8	0	.0
43533	1.4	0	.9	77	27.2	344	68.6	10	7	.0	0	0	.1
43534	1.5	98	.5	79	23.5	351	66.0	9	16	.1	14	0	.0
43535	.9	95	.3	84	27.8	276	66.8	10	13	.4	12	0	1.0
43536	.6	100	.2	89	29.1	289	64.8	8	8	.3	6	0	.0
43537	20.3	97	7.1	76	35.6	376	117.2	8	7	9.6	6	4	.4
43540	1.3	99	.4	82	28.3	333	81.1	9	11	.7	8	0	.5
43541	.3	81	.1	80	24.7	185	46.3	9	11	.1	18	0	.0

*=Estimated **1.0=883 lbs per person; 100++ indicates per capita toxic waste generation > than 100 times the U.S. average of 883 lbs per capita.

ZIP CODE MEASURES OF SIZE, LEVELS OF AFFLUENCE AND QUALITY OF LIFE

1=Population (th.); 2= % White; 3=Households (th.); 4=% Owner Occupied; 5=Mean Income Per Household (th.$); 6=Mean Monthly Rent ($)*; 7=Mean Home Value (th.$)*; 8=% under 5; 9=% 65 and over; 10=White Males (th.); 11=% White Males, 65+; 12=# Toxic Waste Sites; 13=Toxic Waste Relative to US(883 lbs.per capita)**.

OHIO

TOLEDO (WEST)

ZIPCODE	1	2	3	4	5	6	7	8	9	10	11	12	13
43542	2.6	0	.7	88	34.7	293	103.7	5	14	.0	0	0	.0
43543	7.7	100	2.8	78	24.1	258	62.5	8	13	3.8	11	0	2.0
43545	13.2	98	4.7	73	28.0	326	87.1	8	12	6.3	9	0	.8
43548	.3	100	.1	76	26.6	468	88.2	7	9	.2	9	0	.0
43549	.8	0	.3	88	28.6	401	74.6	9	12	.7	7	0	.0
43551	1.4	99	.4	90	29.9	353	73.5	8	9	.7	7	0	.0
43552	21.9	98	7.7	76	34.5	374	127.3	9	9	10.5	7	2	3.6
43553	.4	91	.1	69	30.1	353	88.3	14	4	.2	0	0	.0
43554	2.1	0	.7	83	25.2	287	63.2	8	10	.0	0	0	2.7
43555	.3	100	.1	79	27.2	338	70.0	9	15	.9	10	0	.0
43556	1.8	98	.6	85	27.1	295	67.3	9	9	.9	7	0	.0
43557	2.7	97	.9	83	26.9	325	69.1	9	10	1.3	9	0	.9
43558	13.7	97	4.3	82	29.3	379	92.2	8	9	6.5	7	1	.1
43560	21.3	98	7.0	76	40.3	418	126.8	7	9	9.9	9	1	.5
43565	.4	0	.2	86	25.5	365	76.4	10	15	.0	0	0	.0
43566	5.2	0	1.7	84	33.7	384	120.6	8	8	.7	8	0	.5
43567	11.0	96	3.8	75	26.1	365	87.3	8	11	5.1	10	0	2.5
43569	2.9	97	.9	76	25.2	321	65.7	10	9	1.4	7	0	.0
43570	3.1	100	1.0	83	26.4	298	72.5	8	11	1.5	10	0	2.3
43571	4.3	98	1.3	81	33.8	416	122.0	8	9	2.1	7	1	.6

TOLEDO

ZIPCODE	1	2	3	4	5	6	7	8	9	10	11	12	13
43602	5.6	8	2.3	28	10.1	169	34.0	9	19	.3	10	0	.8
43604	6.2	86	2.7	23	12.4	214	34.1	9	19	2.5	14	0	.4
43605	35.6	91	12.9	63	21.5	270	48.7	10	12	15.4	10	3	.4
43606	30.6	76	12.0	60	31.4	357	107.6	9	16	10.5	15	1	.3
43607	35.9	35	13.1	65	22.2	322	55.5	8	12	5.9	15	1	.6
43608	23.3	78	8.6	69	21.1	295	44.4	8	14	8.5	13	2	.5
43609	31.3	90	11.8	60	21.0	303	49.9	9	11	13.5	10	2	.3
43610	10.7	29	3.5	50	19.9	303	46.2	10	6	1.6	12	1	1.5
43611	25.4	93	8.3	75	27.0	275	74.9	8	10	11.5	8	4	.1
43612	34.9	98	13.3	72	27.0	348	69.9	8	13	16.5	10	7	5.8
43613	36.9	98	14.1	77	29.1	368	81.0	6	13	17.5	11	0	.4
43614	32.9	96	12.9	64	34.0	379	117.0	6	13	14.9	10	2	.1
43615	30.9	92	11.3	74	33.8	355	103.3	7	9	14.2	8	1	.1
43616	17.0	96	5.8	72	31.9	362	98.2	6	11	7.9	9	5	.0
43617	4.0	97	1.4	79	29.2	480	99.3	8	8	1.9	6	1	.2
43618	2.0	99	.6	86	30.5	309	79.1	8	7	1.0	8	0	.0
43619	7.8	96	2.6	78	28.5	358	90.1	10	7	1.5	6	1	.0
43620	9.7	35	3.5	27	16.4	222	59.5	9	15	1.5	18	1	.0
43623	22.7	98	8.5	70	37.8	382	122.7	5	11	10.6	23	1	.0
43624	2.9	48	1.5	4	10.3	193	26.3	5	22	.7	23	1	2.9

ZANESVILLE (SOUTH)

ZIPCODE	1	2	3	4	5	6	7	8	9	10	11	12	13
43701	57.7	94	20.9	72	23.0	255	65.3	8	13	25.5	10	6	.6
43711	7.4	99	2.8	89	17.8	205*	37.1	8	21	3.5	17	0	.2
43713	.1	100	.1	75	17.3	248	57.6	7	16	3.5	13	0	.2
43715	.1	100	.1	87	23.5	199*	34.8	4	26	.1	24	0	.0
43716	2.5	0	.8	84	23.5	276	64.4	8	10	.0	0	0	.0
43717	.3	100	.1	77	21.5	278	37.8	4	10	.1	6	0	.0
43718	3.5	100	1.1	83	25.6	340	63.9	8	13	1.7	11	0	.0

OHIO

ZANESVILLE (SOUTH)

ZIPCODE	1	2	3	4	5	6	7	8	9	10	11	12	13
43719	2.4	99	.8	86	25.5	291	57.4	6	11	1.1	8	0	.0
43720	1.2	0	.4	86	24.4	221	63.3	9	8	.0	9	0	.0
43722	.7	100	.2	86	20.2	224	32.1	7	13	.3	15	0	.0
43723	5.0	100	1.8	76	28.6	258	49.6	9	11	2.4	9	0	.5
43724	6.2	100	2.2	75	22.4	266	61.1	8	15	3.0	13	0	.9
43725	23.5	97	8.7	70	23.3	266	62.2	8	15	10.7	12	2	2.5
43727	1.2	99	.4	84	26.2	237	61.4	6	10	.6	10	0	.0
43728	1.4	73	.5	84	20.5	223	45.1	7	15	.5	15	0	.0
43730	2.3	98	.8	83	18.7	193	32.4	7	17	1.1	14	0	.0
43731	5.6	0	2.0	79	19.9	213	42.1	8	13	.0	0	0	.0
43732	1.5	0	.5	85	24.3	303	43.5	9	12	.5	9	0	.0
43733	.1	100	.1	85	14.3	165*	24.2	23	9	.1	1	0	.0
43734	1.1	100	.5	82	22.1	255	64.3	6	20	.1	0	1	.5
43735	.5	100	.2	74	23.1	313	52.1	7	14	.2	12	0	.0
43738	.2	100	.1	77	22.0	310	43.3	7	5	.1	6	0	.0
43739	1.4	100	.5	83	25.1	268	63.3	7	10	.7	8	1	.0
43740	.3	0	.2	86	21.4	223	64.3	7	18	.7	11	0	.0
43741	.7	99	.2	76	21.2	301	56.8	11	11	.4	13	0	.0
43743	.2	0	.1	99	18.0	206*	25.1	7	20	.0	0	0	.0
43746	1.1	0	.3	87	24.7	213	64.5	8	9	.5	9	0	.0
43747	1.0	100	.6	89	26.2	162	59.6	8	10	.0	0	0	.0
43748	1.9	0	.6	83	22.9	283	45.7	9	10	.8	13	0	.0
43749	1.6	100	.5	83	22.2	305	55.6	10	14	.8	13	0	.0
43754	1.5	0	.5	81	21.0	270	53.3	10	15	.8	0	0	.5
43755	1.6	100	.6	86	23.2	263	48.3	7	14	.8	13	0	.0
43756	5.3	99	1.9	74	22.5	266	66.1	7	16	2.5	15	1	1.2
43757	.2	100	.1	75	30.2	462	59.6	9	11	.1	7	0	.0
43758	3.3	96	1.1	79	20.6	248	54.6	9	12	1.5	10	0	.0
43759	.4	100	.4	65	24.8	245	56.6	8	24	.2	22	0	.0
43760	1.2	99	.5	90	24.5	259	72.2	5	8	.6	8	0	.0
43762	4.7	99	1.4	71	26.0	277	79.9	6	11	2.3	9	2	.0
43764	7.8	100	2.7	73	20.9	257	53.7	9	11	.0	0	1	.5
43766	1.7	100	.6	85	19.7	150	29.8	8	11	.9	11	0	.0
43767	1.2	100	.4	84	28.1	341	86.7	12	7	.6	8	0	.0
43768	.4	100	.1	78	17.5	194	50.1	5	21	.2	16	0	.0
43770	.1	0	.1	72	14.9	235	49.7	6	32	.0	0	0	.0
43771	1.7	100	.6	87	21.8	226	52.7	7	11	.9	8	1	1.0
43772	1.8	100	.6	89	22.1	286	50.3	8	12	.9	12	0	.0
43773	2.7	0	.9	80	20.3	252	45.5	8	16	.9	10	0	.0
43777	4.2	100	1.4	81	20.2	245	44.4	9	10	2.1	10	0	.0
43778	.8	100	.3	90	19.8	384	45.7	9	14	.4	13	0	.0
43779	.9	100	.3	82	26.7	315	57.0	9	10	.4	10	0	.0
43780	1.7	0	.6	86	22.9	264	54.1	9	13	.0	0	0	.2
43782	1.2	0	.4	83	18.3	259	27.5	7	15	.2	0	0	.0
43783	3.5	100	1.2	82	23.0	255	60.1	7	10	.1	22	0	.8
43784	.2	100	.1	83	19.5	203	45.3	7	24	.1	9	0	.0
43785	.2	100	.1	96	23.6	272*	29.2	9	8	.5	8	0	.0
43787	2.6	98	.9	84	19.2	211	48.3	10	12	1.3	11	0	.0
43788	.9	0	.3	77	20.2	200	36.2	8	14	.0	0	0	.0

*=Estimated   **1.0=883 lbs per person; 100++ indicates per capita toxic waste generation > than 100 times the U.S. average of 883 lbs per capita.

ZIP CODE MEASURES OF SIZE, LEVELS OF AFFLUENCE AND QUALITY OF LIFE

1=Population (th.); 2= % White; 3=Households (th.); 4=% Owner Occupied; 5=Mean Income Per Household (th.$); 6=Mean Monthly Rent ($)*; 7=Mean Home Value (th.$)*;
8=% under 5; 9=% 65 and over; 10=%White Males (th.); 11=% White Males, 65+; 12=# Toxic Waste Sites; 13=Toxic Waste Relative to US(883 lbs.per capita)**

OHIO

ZANESVILLE (SOUTH)

ZIPCODE	1	2	3	4	5	6	7	8	9	10	11	12	13
43791	.3	0	.1	72	19.4	321	43.2	6	14	.0	0	0	.0
43793	5.8	100	2.1	78	22.7	246	61.9	7	15	2.8	12	0	.0

ZANESVILLE (NORTH)

ZIPCODE	1	2	3	4	5	6	7	8	9	10	11	12	13
43802	1.0	100	.3	81	21.0	249	43.1	6	6	.5	7	0	.0
43804	2.3	100	.6	83	21.3	241	67.6	8	8	1.2	8	0	.0
43810	.2	100	.1	85	31.6	363*	24.4	10	12	.1	9	0	.0
43811	1.0	0	.3	85	25.2	266	54.5	7	8	.0	8	0	.0
43812	21.0	97	8.1	72	24.7	254	66.6	7	14	9.7	11	0	1.0
43821	3.3	100	1.2	80	22.3	257	55.2	8	12	1.6	10	3	.2
43822	3.5	0	1.2	81	24.9	255	61.8	8	11	.0	0	0	.0
43824	2.6	0	.8	87	24.5	291	59.4	9	8	.0	0	0	.0
43830	3.9	98	1.3	85	27.2	256	87.4	9	6	1.9	6	0	.0
43832	7.0	98	2.5	80	21.2	250	52.0	7	15	3.3	14	0	.0
43836	.2	100	.1	66	29.3	382	57.3	8	12	.1	13	0	.4
43837	1.8	99	.6	83	20.8	242	48.4	10	12	.9	11	0	.0
43840	1.2	0	.4	86	23.3	276	64.6	9	11	.0	0	0	.0
43842	.4	0	.1	81	24.2	307	45.5	9	11	.0	0	0	.0
43843	.7	100	.2	86	21.3	372	45.5	5	11	.4	9	0	.0
43844	3.2	100	1.1	84	21.4	218	58.6	8	12	1.6	11	0	.0
43845	4.9	99	1.7	82	25.3	307	65.8	7	14	2.3	12	1	.4

STEUBENVILLE

ZIPCODE	1	2	3	4	5	6	7	8	9	10	11	12	13
43901	2.7	99	1.3	81	24.3	279	61.9	7	15	1.3	13	0	.0
43902	2.4	100	.1	80	20.2	249	46.1	12	12	1.2	12	0	.0
43903	2.4	100	.8	82	21.9	228	55.5	8	11	1.2	10	0	.0
43905	.4	0	.1	79	19.3	196	42.6	7	18	.0	0	0	.4
43906	13.8	96	5.1	65	21.4	256	60.7	7	14	6.3	13	0	.0
43907	6.8	93	2.4	74	23.1	246	65.3	8	15	3.1	14	3	.0
43908	1.5	0	.6	83	26.8	300	34.9	9	8	.0	0	0	.0
43909	.3	100	.1	64	25.3	366	50.9	7	12	.0	0	0	.0
43910	4.2	98	1.3	92	24.9	286*	43.6	3	8	2.1	7	0	.0
43912	7.7	95	2.9	72	23.6	312	57.3	8	15	3.5	12	1	1.0
43913	2.2	0	.8	75	25.3	245	62.6	7	13	.0	6	0	.4
43915	1.8	100	.6	82	25.1	234	61.8	6	13	.9	12	0	.0
43916	.4	100	.1	100	33.7	388*	78.3	0	4	.2	5	0	56.8
43917	3.3	96	.7	87	27.9	353	61.0	7	15	1.6	14	0	.4
43920	29.7	97	10.8	72	24.9	251	60.3	8	13	13.8	11	3	.1
43925	.2	100	.1	89	22.2	255*	39.2	4	6	.0	0	0	.0
43926	.5	99	.2	73	26.8	300	34.9	9	8	.3	11	0	.0
43927	.4	0	.1	72	25.3	366	50.9	7	12	.0	0	0	.0
43928	1.2	100	.1	92	24.9	286*	43.6	3	7	.1	6	0	.0
43930	1.2	100	.1	84	27.0	312	57.3	8	8	.6	6	0	1.2
43931	.5	100	.2	92	29.1	269	80.2	9	6	.6	6	0	.0
43932	1.4	98	.4	85	24.6	325	50.3	8	12	.3	4	0	.0
43933	2.1	99	.7	85	24.6	232	65.6	10	10	.7	10	0	.0
43934	1.0	97	.4	81	24.7	245	55.2	3	20	1.1	10	0	.0
43935	11.8	96	4.6	67	23.9	268	63.2	6	17	5.2	18	0	1.2
43937	.5	100	.2	73	23.9	372	43.3	7	20	.3	14	0	.0
43938	7.9	97	2.7	81	27.7	241	60.1	6	11	3.8	10	0	.2
43939	.8	97	.3	90	25.9	359	64.5	7	13	.4	11	0	.0

OHIO

STEUBENVILLE

ZIPCODE	1	2	3	4	5	6	7	8	9	10	11	12	13
43940	1.0	100	.4	88	21.2	245	42.6	4	14	.5	11	0	.0
43941	.3	100	.1	84	22.9	290	27.9	3	20	.2	25	0	.0
43942	3.3	99	1.2	79	26.2	276	65.1	7	12	1.6	10	0	.0
43943	4.5	98	1.6	85	26.1	284	56.6	6	11	2.2	10	1	.0
43944	2.7	0	.9	85	29.7	193	73.7	7	10	.0	0	0	.0
43945	3.4	99	1.1	87	22.4	249	46.5	7	12	1.7	11	0	.0
43946	2.4	0	.8	82	24.7	288	63.5	7	12	.0	0	0	.0
43947	6.3	100	2.4	79	25.0	288	69.9	6	14	3.0	12	0	.3
43948	1.4	87	.5	80	23.4	203	56.8	8	13	.6	14	0	.0
43950	13.1	97	4.6	76	28.9	374	96.5	7	11	6.2	10	0	.0
43951	.4	100	.2	79	24.4	228	45.7	5	10	.2	9	0	.0
43952	40.8	89	15.0	67	27.0	270	45.2	6	14	16.9	12	1	4.2
43960	.2	0	.1	100	19.2	220*	30.8	4	28	.0	0	0	.0
43961	.4	0	.1	74	27.0	320	55.5	6	7	.0	0	0	.0
43962	.2	100	.1	87	24.5	282*	71.4	2	23	.1	19	0	.0
43963	1.8	0	.7	65	24.6	283	67.1	7	21	.0	0	0	.0
43964	12.1	99	4.3	79	28.4	270	66.5	7	11	5.8	10	3	.4
43967	.2	100	.1	62	17.5	233	40.0	4	11	.1	14	0	.0
43968	9.2	96	3.3	79	23.8	228	55.5	7	12	4.2	11	0	.0
43971	1.6	99	.6	63	26.5	280	64.4	6	16	.7	13	1	1.6
43972	.3	92	.7	98	30.4	350*	51.2	3	12	.1	12	0	.0
43973	2.0	100	.7	87	20.9	289	44.0	8	16	1.0	16	0	.6
43974	.3	100	.3	85	21.0	397	53.7	10	14	.2	13	0	.0
43976	1.5	0	.5	82	28.2	293	64.5	5	10	.0	0	0	.0
43977	2.4	99	.8	78	28.2	247	58.1	8	13	1.2	11	0	.6
43981	.5	100	.2	87	23.9	308	51.0	5	13	.2	12	0	.4
43983	.6	100	.2	84	24.8	193	41.0	6	15	.3	14	0	2.5
43985	.4	100	.2	88	20.7	211	29.8	4	19	.3	14	0	8.5
43986	.6	0	.2	84	23.2	268	51.2	9	12	.2	19	0	1.5
43988	2.9	100	1.0	81	21.3	239	60.2	7	14	1.4	11	0	.0

CLEVELAND

ZIPCODE	1	2	3	4	5	6	7	8	9	10	11	12	13
44001	19.2	99	6.4	84	31.6	357	108.8	6	9	9.4	8	1	.6
44003	3.9	98	1.3	80	23.3	325	70.5	8	15	1.9	13	0	.4
44004	39.7	94	14.4	72	25.2	301	73.3	7	13	17.8	11	25	5.7
44010	1.3	99	.4	85	28.2	344	89.2	8	9	.6	8	2	.4
44011	7.2	99	2.1	84	34.1	422	112.7	7	10	3.6	7	2	.5
44012	13.2	99	4.3	85	36.3	419	120.5	7	7	6.4	5	4	8.5
44017	19.7	94	6.8	72	32.2	384	104.8	8	10	8.8	7	1	1.5
44021	6.0	100	1.9	79	30.6	376	111.3	9	12	3.0	8	0	.6
44022	24.7	96	8.2	88	53.7	515	194.0	5	11	11.7	7	4	.6
44024	18.7	99	6.0	81	32.6	412	131.5	8	11	9.1	7	1	.4
44026	13.1	99	3.9	94	44.6	492	161.1	6	6	6.5	5	1	.0
44028	8.0	100	2.3	88	34.4	454	115.4	7	5	4.0	5	0	.1
44030	17.1	98	8.1	78	28.2	312	71.1	7	13	8.1	11	1	1.2
44032	1.4	97	.4	84	24.3	310	59.5	9	7	.6	6	0	.0
44034	1.2	99	.4	74	23.8	264	76.7	8	11	.6	11	0	.0
44035	68.9	88	24.4	68	27.7	316	87.7	8	9	29.2	8	12	3.5
44039	21.5	99	6.4	87	35.3	398	110.0	9	4	10.7	3	1	.0
44040	.8	97	.3	88	74.6	386	274.6	3	15	.0	0	0	.0

*=Estimated **1.0=883 lbs per person; 100++ indicates per capita toxic waste generation > than 100 times the U.S. average of 883 lbs per capita.

ZIP CODE MEASURES OF SIZE, LEVELS OF AFFLUENCE AND QUALITY OF LIFE

1=Population (th.); 2= % White; 3=Households (th.); 4=% Owner Occupied; 5=Mean Income Per Household (th.$); 6=Mean Monthly Rent ($)*; 7=Mean Home Value (th.$)*; 8=% under 5; 9=% 65 and over; 10=White Males; 11=% White Males, 65+; 12=# Toxic Waste Sites; 13=Toxic Waste Relative to US(883 lbs.per capita)**.

OHIO

ZIPCODE	1	2	3	4	5	6	7	8	9	10	11	12	13
CLEVELAND													
44041	13.9	98	4.7	74	25.8	332	81.5	7	11	6.5	9	3	.0
44043	1.5	100	.6	57	22.6	261	68.3	10	6	.8	5	0	.0
44044	11.4	99	3.3	89	33.8	358	103.1	8	6	5.7	6	1	.0
44045	.4	100	.1	75	29.8	338	87.9	7	8	.2	4	1	2.7
44046	2.4	94	.7	89	31.1	315	107.2	9	7	1.1	7	0	.0
44047	8.8	97	2.9	78	26.7	341	83.4	8	7	4.2	8	0	.2
44048	2.7	100	.7	86	29.0	364	79.0	7	18	1.3	15	0	.0
44049	.3	100	.1	79	31.6	362	81.8	7	8	.2	8	0	.0
44050	4.1	0	1.2	83	31.0	361	99.5	10	5	.0	0	0	.3
44052	37.9	81	13.4	66	24.7	276	77.4	9	12	14.5	11	0	.1
44053	16.5	93	5.9	62	31.8	337	112.4	6	7	7.5	7	0	.1
44054	12.4	99	3.8	83	30.5	364	90.7	9	6	6.1	5	1	.0
44055	25.3	70	8.1	68	24.6	286	64.7	9	9	8.6	10	1	4.8
44056	6.7	98	1.9	94	37.6	429	119.2	9	2	3.3	5	2	2.9
44057	18.4	99	5.6	81	30.7	418	100.6	9	7	9.1	6	1	.2
44060	53.5	99	17.0	84	37.9	493	121.6	8	6	26.3	5	4	1.0
44062	9.6	100	2.5	68	24.9	380	100.4	13	7	4.7	6	1	.1
44065	3.7	0	1.1	84	34.8	418	121.5	7	7	.0	0	2	.0
44067	15.4	97	4.8	84	28.3	454	129.3	5	8	7.5	7	0	2.2
44068	1.0	100	.8	78	28.9	236	89.2	4	4	.5	3	0	.7
44070	36.5	98	12.3	78	35.9	440	122.5	6	9	17.4	7	0	.0
44072	4.0	0	1.3	90	44.7	450	181.8	6	8	.0	0	1	.0
44074	12.1	78	3.6	64	28.4	321	99.4	6	10	4.5	8	1	.4
44076	2.5	96	.9	76	26.0	299	83.3	9	10	1.2	6	0	3.6
44077	42.4	94	14.8	71	29.2	366	103.4	8	10	19.4	7	8	2.3
44080	.3	98	.3	65	27.6	379	95.5	7	11	.2	9	0	.9
44081	5.4	99	1.6	85	30.5	406	106.3	7	5	2.7	7	1	5.8
44082	1.4	96	.4	81	22.6	306	69.7	8	9	.7	9	0	.0
44084	2.7	96	.8	86	27.8	364	89.4	7	14	1.3	13	0	2.2
44085	2.4	98	.7	86	27.7	346	87.8	10	7	1.2	8	0	.0
44086	2.2	98	.7	85	29.5	378	103.9	8	8	1.1	9	0	.2
44087	8.4	92	2.7	79	33.4	312	108.8	8	6	3.8	4	1	5.2
44088	.2	90	.1	78	28.4	726	79.0	6	8	.1	3	0	.0
44089	15.4	96	5.1	78	31.1	371	102.6	8	7	7.5	6	0	.0
44090	9.6	99	3.1	78	28.2	311	94.7	8	10	4.7	8	0	.9
44092	21.3	97	7.5	72	31.8	429	105.8	5	9	10.1	8	2	37.5
44093	1.4	98	.5	81	23.2	284	60.2	8	12	.7	12	0	.0
44094	70.1	99	24.7	75	32.8	425	104.3	6	9	33.7	8	2	.7
44099	1.6	89	.5	77	26.0	338	82.4	9	13	.7	11	0	7.0
CLEVELAND													
44102	57.4	94	21.8	42	20.4	282	49.7	9	11	26.1	9	8	1.8
44103	36.3	32	14.3	31	14.7	214	25.9	8	15	5.6	17	2	3.2
44104	42.2	5	15.2	26	13.2	194	33.8	11	10	.1	30	8	2.0
44105	63.2	45	22.0	60	22.0	293	44.9	9	10	13.6	13	3	2.1
44106	42.0	37	16.5	26	19.6	269	73.9	9	16	7.6	10	0	2.9
44107	62.2	99	27.1	44	27.8	365	100.6	6	15	28.0	11	0	.5
44108	48.8	4	16.4	47	21.2	307	39.5	8	10	.9	17	0	.7
44109	50.7	95	19.3	57	22.4	296	61.7	8	14	23.0	11	7	.8
44110	30.5	65	12.6	44	20.3	286	49.5	8	13	9.1	15	5	7.0

OHIO

ZIPCODE	1	2	3	4	5	6	7	8	9	10	11	12	13
CLEVELAND													
44111	47.2	96	18.7	69	25.2	339	73.2	8	16	21.1	13	7	1.2
44112	45.0	17	17.5	39	21.5	312	59.9	8	10	3.3	25	1	1.1
44113	23.5	73	8.6	27	14.0	197	31.2	9	12	8.4	12	13	4.2
44114	5.4	71	3.3	10	20.5	330	31.6	3	22	2.1	17	1	14.7
44115	7.9	20	3.8	4	9.3	159	18.5	8	14	1.0	24	3	10.3
44116	21.1	99	8.9	67	40.9	437	149.1	4	19	9.6	15	0	.5
44117	12.3	87	5.6	49	26.2	323	100.5	4	20	4.9	17	2	6.5
44118	48.3	76	17.0	73	36.3	448	107.9	7	12	17.6	13	0	.2
44119	15.9	99	6.5	67	25.8	336	80.1	5	22	7.3	18	0	.2
44120	51.5	31	21.7	46	26.9	360	94.2	6	14	7.2	18	0	.4
44121	39.9	89	15.1	78	32.2	407	97.2	5	17	16.3	16	0	.0
44122	35.9	74	13.2	71	52.6	571	167.6	5	17	11.9	17	1	1.1
44123	20.2	96	8.7	65	27.4	394	88.5	5	18	11.5	15	0	.0
44124	45.9	98	18.0	67	39.0	470	145.3	4	18	20.7	16	1	.0
44125	33.5	96	12.4	81	28.2	366	83.5	6	14	15.1	13	10	1.1
44126	19.3	99	7.6	74	35.2	400	123.5	5	17	8.8	14	0	.0
44127	9.8	94	3.8	55	18.9	236	28.8	8	14	4.5	12	2	13.5
44128	38.8	14	14.0	67	27.9	425	66.7	6	9	2.5	22	1	3.3
44129	32.1	99	12.3	76	30.1	381	97.3	5	15	14.9	13	1	.0
44130	56.1	99	21.1	68	33.6	412	117.1	5	12	26.5	10	2	2.4
44131	21.8	99	6.9	95	40.5	486	138.1	4	12	10.5	11	2	2.2
44132	17.9	86	7.3	58	29.0	413	91.7	6	12	7.5	12	1	.3
44133	17.7	98	6.1	83	36.2	452	133.7	6	8	8.6	7	1	.0
44134	44.1	98	15.6	84	31.2	404	99.7	5	13	20.9	11	0	.0
44135	35.4	91	12.4	80	27.0	280	70.6	8	12	15.4	10	1	.9
44136	28.6	97	9.2	78	41.3	381	150.4	5	13	13.8	4	1	.6
44137	29.6	96	10.7	85	28.6	385	80.5	6	14	13.7	12	0	.4
44138	12.8	99	4.5	84	32.6	431	116.0	7	9	6.2	9	0	.1
44139	14.8	97	4.8	86	42.5	501	163.4	6	8	7.1	7	3	4.7
44140	17.8	99	6.4	93	45.9	366	144.4	7	9	8.7	8	0	.0
44141	19.0	97	6.4	80	41.3	447	159.3	5	9	9.3	9	2	.3
44142	26.2	98	7.7	89	34.4	399	95.7	5	4	12.7	3	4	4.1
44143	21.4	96	8.2	66	35.8	424	146.7	4	13	9.6	11	0	.6
44144	23.5	99	9.8	70	26.8	333	87.6	5	18	10.9	15	0	1.4
44145	19.5	99	6.8	80	42.1	455	147.9	5	13	9.3	11	1	.5
44146	34.3	84	13.3	64	29.7	383	96.5	5	11	13.8	10	11	5.6
44147	2.4	95	.7	76	44.2	433	139.8	3	10	1.2	8	1	2.2
AKRON													
44201	5.9	99	1.8	89	27.5	405	85.1	6	7	2.9	7	0	.0
44202	11.1	98	3.6	91	44.4	534	145.3	6	5	5.4	5	0	1.1
44203	45.1	97	16.3	73	25.3	302	77.8	7	13	20.9	11	12	2.4
44210	.4	100	.1	69	43.8	458	203.1	10	5	.2	4	0	.1
44212	31.0	99	8.9	84	35.5	442	115.0	9	3	15.3	2	0	.4
44214	1.6	99	.5	81	32.7	359	81.5	7	7	.8	6	0	.0
44215	1.7	100	.6	79	25.3	426	77.8	7	6	.8	5	0	.0
44216	9.4	99	2.8	88	32.1	448	105.4	7	6	4.7	5	1	.0
44217	3.8	0	1.2	81	24.5	226	81.0	10	10	.0	0	0	.0
44221	33.3	99	12.6	67	27.2	369	76.8	7	10	15.7	8	1	1.3
44223	14.6	99	5.4	79	32.2	325	101.8	5	12	6.9	12	2	.1

*=Estimated **1.0=883 lbs per person; 100++ indicates per capita toxic waste generation > than 100 times the U.S. average of 883 lbs per capita.

ZIP CODE MEASURES OF SIZE, LEVELS OF AFFLUENCE AND QUALITY OF LIFE

1=Population (th.); 2= % White; 3=Households (th.); 4=% Owner Occupied; 5=Mean Income Per Household (th.$); 6=Mean Monthly Rent ($)*; 7=Mean Home Value (th.$)*; 8=% under 5; 9=% 65 and over; 10=% White Males (th.); 11=% White Males, 65+; 12=# Toxic Waste Sites; 13=Toxic Waste Relative to US(883 lbs.per capita)**.

OHIO

AKRON

ZIP CODE	1	2	3	4	5	6	7	8	9	10	11	12	13
44224	29.3	98	10.1	72	35.7	458	123.1	7	7	14.2	5	1	.3
44230	7.5	99	2.4	85	29.1	373	101.2	8	7	3.7	6	0	.0
44231	6.6	99	2.2	83	29.6	373	93.0	8	8	3.3	7	0	.0
44232	.1	100	.1	57	21.4	401	71.0	0	25	.1	20	0	.5
44233	5.2	100	1.5	92	39.0	497	152.6	6	6	2.6	6	0	.0
44234	3.1	97	.8	76	28.7	373	109.9	5	7	1.5	6	0	.0
44235	1.3	0	.4	86	26.3	473	95.8	12	7		0	0	.0
44236	13.5	98	4.2	85	50.2	533	193.4	6	6	6.7	4	0	.0
44240	43.7	96	15.9	57	26.0	363	97.3	7	6	20.7	5	2	1.2
44251	.8	0	.3	90	48.6	350	155.4	6	7	.0	0	0	.3
44253	2.5	99	.7	92	32.2	402	113.9	6	4	1.2	4	0	.0
44254	4.7	99	1.6	92	32.8	280	99.0	8	10	3.9	8	0	.2
44255	7.8	99	2.5	83	29.7	373	100.8	9	8	3.9	7	0	.1
44256	32.3	97	10.7	76	34.4	366	132.2	8	8	15.6	7	2	.9
44260	13.4	99	4.2	84	31.4	417	97.5	8	6	6.5	6	1	1.3
44262	4.8	98	1.5	81	36.0	409	117.1	7	4	2.4	3	1	.3
44264	2.9	98	1.1	76	32.2	405	132.2	8	9	1.4	9	0	.0
44265	.5	0	.2	68	26.3	394	85.6	9	7	.0	0	0	.8
44266	31.3	96	10.9	73	25.4	347	83.0	8	10	14.6	8	3	.4
44270	8.0	100	2.7	72	26.2	326	82.3	8	9	3.9	7	3	3.1
44272	4.1	99	1.3	82	31.9	497	97.8	8	8	2.0	6	1	.0
44273	4.8	99	1.5	84	31.5	380	113.4	8	7	2.4	7	0	.0
44274	4.2	100	1	49	30.0	518	117.2	8	6	.1	0	0	.5
44275	2.4	100	.7	86	29.4	332	94.5	8	10	.0	1	0	.0
44276	1.8	0	.6	84	27.3	391	95.8	6	9	1.2	6	0	1.2
44278	15.6	99	5.2	79	33.5	400	112.7	7	5	7.6	7	1	2.9
44280	3.8	0	1.0	87	39.8	469	138.1	6	9	.0	0	0	.1
44281	21.3	99	7.5	77	30.3	347	108.0	7	10	10.3	9	3	.3
44285	.2	100	.1	64	32.7	289	69.8	8	10	.1	5	0	.6
44286	4.7	100	1.4	86	37.4	443	141.7	5	11	2.3	8	1	.0
44287	5.0	100	1.5	86	26.5	292	75.3	8	8	2.6	6	0	.0
44288	5.4	96	1.6	59	24.3	168	78.7	11	5	2.5	4	0	.0

AKRON

ZIP CODE	1	2	3	4	5	6	7	8	9	10	11	12	13
44301	19.8	89	7.6	70	22.1	294	60.0	8	15	8.2	14	0	2.8
44302	7.3	77	3.2	41	19.3	268	51.1	8	12	2.7	9	0	.0
44303	9.6	88	2.9	51	33.7	327	125.6	6	19	3.9	14	0	.1
44304	8.0	70	2.9	21	15.1	261	31.9	8	11	2.7	6	0	.5
44305	27.8	91	10.3	70	23.6	302	58.2	8	14	12.1	11	6	1.2
44306	27.8	74	10.6	60	19.4	273	49.4	8	12	9.6	12	1	2.9
44307	12.9	15	4.7	46	16.4	239	37.8	9	13	.8	10	1	.1
44308	.9	78	.4	2	7.2	87	25.8*	0	37	.4	30	0	18.3
44310	27.6	85	10.9	58	21.9	307	54.8	8	14	11.0	12	2	.7
44311	10.4	72	3.9	41	15.6	245	32.5	8	14	3.5	11	0	1.5
44312	34.1	99	12.9	78	25.2	352	73.0	6	12	16.4	10	2	.0
44313	37.1	97	14.2	72	44.8	461	155.9	5	15	16.7	12	2	.2
44314	22.8	99	8.9	71	22.6	324	56.8	7	13	10.7	10	1	.7
44319	23.8	99	8.5	82	30.6	400	101.2	6	10	11.7	9	1	.0
44320	27.3	33	9.4	71	23.9	308	58.7	8	10	4.2	15	0	.0
44321	7.5	93	2.4	90	37.7	495	126.2	6	8	3.5	8	0	2.5

OHIO

YOUNGSTOWN

ZIP CODE	1	2	3	4	5	6	7	8	9	10	11	12	13
44401	2.7	100	.8	91	31.4	320	96.2	7	6	1.4	6	0	.0
44402	3.3	99	1.1	85	31.9	327	93.6	8	7	1.6	6	0	.0
44403	4.6	99	1.6	88	32.4	431	101.5	6	10	2.2	9	0	.1
44404	1.6	100	.5	80	29.2	343	78.3	6	10	.8	11	0	.0
44405	11.6	88	4.1	79	23.6	226	60.8	6	13	5.0	12	1	.3
44406	15.6	99	.8	79	37.0	358	121.8	8	8	7.5	8	0	.2
44408	8.8	100	3.2	72	26.8	312	84.1	6	12	4.3	10	1	.8
44410	14.5	99	4.8	80	33.1	360	104.3	8	7	7.0	7	0	.0
44411	2.5	0	.8	88	22.7	327	80.9	8	10	.0	0	1	.0
44412	2.5	98	.8	89	30.3	463	87.3	8	6	1.2	6	0	.0
44413	7.8	100	2.8	78	24.6	308	68.0	7	13	3.8	12	1	.7
44415	.2	100	.2	80	25.0	518	43.6	10	3	.1	7	0	.0
44417	1.9	0	.6	87	33.2	390	91.5	9	6	.0	5	0	.0
44418	1.3	100	.4	83	32.9	339	91.5	10	8	.7	5	2	.9
44420	18.9	98	7.0	74	28.7	334	76.6	7	11	8.9	10	1	.2
44423	2.1	100	.7	78	24.5	349	64.7	8	10	1.0	9	0	.3
44425	18.2	97	6.1	80	30.5	325	82.2	7	10	8.6	8	0	.2
44427	1.5	0	.5	78	24.8	329	60.6	8	8	.0	0	0	.2
44428	3.9	0	1.2	81	27.5	338	76.8	8	10	.7	5	0	.4
44429	3.3	100	1.0	77	25.4	339	65.3	9	9	1.6	7	0	.0
44430	4.8	99	1.5	85	25.1	292	58.6	7	9	2.3	8	1	.0
44431	4.7	100	1.6	83	26.5	294	65.3	8	10	2.3	8	0	.0
44432	11.1	99	3.7	80	24.2	287	64.8	8	12	5.4	10	0	.1
44436	4.8	97	1.7	86	26.2	263	71.9	6	8	2.2	11	0	.6
44437	4.9	96	1.9	91	30.6	375	70.9	8	7	2.4	10	1	.0
44438	5.3	93	1.9	76	26.3	308	57.4	7	11	2.4	10	0	6.00
44439	.3	0	.1	84	21.4	341	72.9	15	13	1.8	9	0	.3
44440	3.8	99	1.2	71	28.3	323	84.4	9	12	1.8	9	0	.6
44441	1.8	0	.6	88	25.8	368	72.7	8	9	.0	0	0	.6
44442	4.0	0	1.3	83	26.6	382	85.3	7	8	.0	0	0	.9
44443	2.3	0	.7	84	26.0	317	83.7	10	7	.0	0	0	.6
44444	11.3	98	4.0	74	25.3	305	73.1	7	9	5.5	8	2	.6
44445	2.9	0	1.0	82	23.2	227	72.8	10	8	.0	0	0	.9
44446	25.8	98	9.5	69	26.6	299	71.1	6	12	12.2	10	11	.5
44449	.7	100	.2	90	26.9	333	69.1	8	9	.4	4	0	.0
44450	2.1	93	.7	82	26.2	346	76.8	9	10	1.0	9	0	.1
44451	3.1	100	1.0	83	29.8	308	91.4	8	8	1.5	9	0	.3
44452	2.7	99	.8	83	29.4	348	82.5	8	18	1.3	15	0	.3
44453	.2	100	.1	64	25.3	369	72.3	6	7	1.3	6	0	.0
44454	1.0	100	.3	86	25.6	396	63.1	6	10	.5	6	0	.0
44455	1.7	0	.5	89	23.7	301	59.2	7	8	.0	0	0	.0
44460	26.6	100	9.6	76	25.0	313	75.4	7	12	12.6	10	0	1.00
44470	3.8	0	1.2	91	31.5	401	90.8	8	7	.0	0	0	.0
44471	13.7	97	4.9	79	24.5	290	59.8	6	13	6.4	10	1	.0
44473	4.4		1.5	85	32.6	348	89.7	5	7	5.0	7	4	14.7
44481	10.6	95	3.4	84	31.5	228	91.5	7	10	5.0	6	0	.0
44483	33.1	91	12.3	67	29.0	303	78.6	6	13	14.2	11	3	1.9
44484	26.0	87	8.8	79	32.2	317	94.6	7	10	11.1	9	0	.0
44485	25.2	77	9.0	65	25.2	283	62.2	8	10	9.1	9	1	.5

*=Estimated **1.0=883 lbs per person; 100++ indicates per capita toxic waste generation > than 100 times the U.S. average of 883 lbs per capita.

ZIP CODE MEASURES OF SIZE, LEVELS OF AFFLUENCE AND QUALITY OF LIFE

1=Population (th.); 2= % White; 3=Households (th.); 4=% Owner Occupied; 5=Mean Income Per Household (th.$); 6=Mean Monthly Rent ($)*; 7=Mean Home Value (th.$)*;
8=% under 5; 9=% 65 and over; 10=White Males (th.); 11=% White Males, 65+; 12=# Toxic Waste Sites; 13=Toxic Waste Relative to US(883 lbs.per capita)**.

OHIO

ZIPCODE	1	2	3	4	5	6	7	8	9	10	11	12	13
YOUNGSTOWN													
44490	.9	100	.3	86	24.0	324	53.9	7	11	.4	7	0	.8
44491	2.5	97	.7	87	29.4	382	91.7	8	7	1.3	7	0	.0
44493	.3	100	.1	88	38.5	442*	58.4	11	15	.1	20	0	.0
YOUNGSTOWN													
44502	18.4	70	6.7	73	20.3	280	43.4	7	14	6.0	14	2	.2
44503	.7	81	.5	59	7.7	118	50.3	8	39	.3	26	0	16.1
44504	6.9	74	2.5	56	27.4	333	68.0	6	18	2.4	16	0	.0
44505	29.2	58	10.7	62	25.0	284	67.5	7	12	8.2	13	1	.5
44506	8.1	43	2.7	65	17.9	314	28.3	9	13	1.7	16	2	.1
44507	13.6	63	5.0	80	19.3	283	42.6	9	15	3.9	16	1	.0
44509	15.5	98	5.8	80	24.3	295	55.3	6	16	7.2	14	4	.8
44510	6.3	24	2.3	48	15.6	178	31.2	10	13	.7	20	0	.0
44511	30.6	78	10.7	80	29.1	325	74.4	7	12	11.3	11	0	.0
44512	34.6	99	13.2	70	30.3	372	99.7	6	15	16.1	12	1	.4
44514	22.1	100	7.3	88	32.8	368	92.7	7	10	10.8	9	0	.0
44515	28.4	98	10.3	67	28.1	345	77.7	7	7	13.7	7	0	.7
CANTON													
44601	39.0	91	13.9	71	24.6	284	69.1	7	12	17.1	10	6	1.4
44606	6.1	99	1.6	81	23.9	246	91.2	11	16	3.1	7	0	.1
44607	.2	100	.1	84	23.4	304	43.5	6	22	.2	27	0	.0
44608	2.5	0	.9	87	26.2	291	72.2	9	12	1.0	11	0	.4
44609	3.7	99	1.2	82	26.2	276	73.1	8	11	1.8	11	0	.0
44610	.7	100	.2	66	24.2	305	115.1	17	8	.4	7	0	.3
44611	1.5	100	.5	84	25.4	259	72.2	8	8	.7	4	0	.5
44612	3.8	0	1.3	71	30.0	344	105.8	9	7	1.0	9	0	.0
44613	2.2	100	.1	80	25.7	302	68.7	8	13	1.0	9	0	.3
44614	10.0	99	3.0	82	29.6	339	97.2	9	6	4.8	5	0	.3
44615	9.5	100	3.2	79	22.4	255	70.0	7	13	4.6	12	0	.9
44618	5.7	100	1.7	83	27.7	326	96.0	9	10	2.9	9	0	.0
44619	.4	100	.4	59	30.9	266	79.8	6	10	.2	14	0	.0
44620	1.2	0	.4	83	25.5	374	77.9	6	12	.2	11	0	.3
44621	4.7	96	1.6	76	19.9	281	51.0	7	12	2.1	11	1	.1
44622	16.0	98	5.9	77	25.1	302	80.1	7	14	7.5	12	4	6.9
44624	2.9	100	.7	81	23.6	246	76.4	13	6	1.4	6	1	1.0
44625	1.5	0	.4	86	28.3	355	71.3	7	7	.7	0	0	.0
44626	3.3	100	1.1	86	29.1	336	76.4	8	10	1.7	11	0	.0
44627	3.5	100	.8	80	22.0	222	76.7	15	6	1.8	6	0	.0
44628	1.0	0	.3	82	23.4	283	54.3	8	11	1.0	0	0	.0
44629	2.2	100	.8	85	23.4	295	68.8	8	14	.0	13	0	.5
44630	.5	0	.2	75	22.7	335	61.8	5	14	.0	6	0	.0
44632	8.5	99	2.7	75	32.4	374	109.6	8	7	4.3	6	1	3.9
44633	1.7	100	.5	80	23.8	307	74.9	12	8	.8	7	0	.0
44634	2.0	100	.6	86	34.9	458	86.1	7	11	1.0	10	1	.1
44636	.3	100	.1	92	41.7	480*	127.6	5	9	.2	11	0	7.6
44637	2.2	0	.9	78	23.8	282	62.4	8	10	.0	0	0	.0
44638	1.1	0	.4	76	26.0	299	65.2	8	11	.0	0	0	.0
44639	.2	100	.1	85	23.5	261	43.4	8	11	.1	0	0	.0
44640	.2	0	.1	96	23.3	268*	40.6	5	14	.0	0	0	.0
44641	19.7	100	6.2	77	29.6	367	94.0	8	14	9.5	9	2	.4

OHIO

ZIPCODE	1	2	3	4	5	6	7	8	9	10	11	12	13
CANTON													
44643	3.4	0	1.2	87	27.1	269	82.8	7	9	.0	0	0	.0
44644	4.5	98	1.5	83	27.7	308	89.3	8	9	2.2	8	2	.1
44645	2.2	100	.7	76	26.7	297	93.3	11	5	1.1	4	0	.0
44646	63.8	94	22.3	75	27.6	319	82.4	7	11	28.8	9	4	1.7
44650	.2	100	.1	86	21.9	174	69.4	5	33	.1	21	0	.0
44651	.7	100	.2	83	22.1	255	60.6	9	8	.4	9	0	.0
44653	.7	0	.2	74	21.7	302	46.2	9	12	.0	0	0	1.4
44654	13.8	100	3.8	72	24.0	267	91.1	11	11	6.6	9	0	.0
44656	2.3	0	.8	86	24.7	321	58.9	7	9	.0	0	0	.0
44657	11.0	99	3.7	80	26.9	281	75.7	8	9	5.4	7	3	.6
44659	.4	0	.1	75	25.0	268	77.7	14	7	.0	0	0	.0
44661	.4	100	.1	86	25.5	151	51.7	11	11	.1	8	0	.0
44662	9.4	100	3.1	83	27.5	317	78.8	7	10	4.6	9	0	.6
44663	24.6	99	9.4	74	24.3	304	76.7	7	14	11.5	11	7	.6
44666	2.5	100	.8	84	27.8	364	85.2	6	10	1.3	8	0	.0
44667	12.1	96	4.1	69	27.2	335	85.6	9	10	5.5	9	1	2.6
44669	1.2	0	.8	83	26.2	149	79.4	8	16	.0	0	0	.0
44670	.4	100	.1	89	24.6	377	66.4	4	14	.2	13	0	.0
44671	.4	100	.1	77	30.8	263	66.0	2	16	.2	14	0	.1
44672	5.9	99	2.2	63	21.8	399	55.2	7	18	2.6	13	0	.2
44675	1.4	0	.5	85	24.2	244	64.8	9	10	.0	0	0	.4
44676	3.8	0	1.3	78	24.6	321	81.2	8	9	.0	0	0	.1
44677	2.9	98	.9	74	29.8	347	97.9	10	6	1.4	8	0	.6
44678	.4	100	.1	87	23.7	374	48.0	7	9	.2	5	0	.3
44680	3.2	0	1.6	74	25.8	275	78.3	8	11	.0	0	0	.5
44681	5.5	0	1.1	78	24.4	301	84.6	11	11	.0	0	0	.3
44682	1.0	100	.4	84	24.2	306	61.1	6	10	.4	9	0	.3
44683	8.9	98	3.2	73	21.2	276	53.9	8	14	4.2	11	1	.9
44685	16.9	99	5.5	87	35.9	432	119.8	7	5	8.3	4	0	.0
44687	.5	100	.1	83	27.5	396	87.6	7	38	.2	19	0	.2
44688	3.2	95	1.1	78	28.9	266	65.2	8	11	1.5	10	1	.0
44689	.6	100	.2	80	23.0	361	57.1	9	13	.3	14	0	.0
44690	.3	100	.1	82	23.5	263	82.6	13	16	.1	15	0	5.2
44691	36.4	97	12.9	67	28.1	311	104.1	7	11	17.2	9	2	1.0
44695	1.5	0	.5	84	22.4	261	55.0	8	15	.0	0	0	.2
44697	.3	0	.1	93	42.4	487*	108.0	5	5	.0	0	0	1.4
44699	.9	100	.3	82	21.9	136	35.5	6	12	.5	10	0	.0
CANTON													
44702	1.0	87	.8	8	8.5	154	34.5	1	40	4	29	2	31.6
44703	12.5	97	5.3	43	20.2	252	58.1	8	14	5.5	11	0	1.6
44704	7.3	41	2.6	61	20.4	270	39.8	7	11	1.6	13	0	.4
44705	23.6	81	7.9	72	22.8	280	55.8	8	9	9.3	9	5	.4
44706	20.8	96	7.3	77	25.4	303	65.8	7	8	9.6	8	7	8.6
44707	14.1	64	5.2	56	18.3	209	52.3	8	13	4.4	13	6	1.6
44708	25.1	99	9.8	73	29.5	346	91.5	6	14	11.6	12	0	.0
44709	19.5	98	7.9	63	28.7	314	92.6	5	16	8.7	13	0	1.4
44710	11.3	97	4.2	76	24.2	308	60.7	7	15	5.1	13	0	.0
44714	9.8	93	3.7	73	29.9	348	85.1	7	17	4.2	15	0	.1
44718	8.7	98	3.3	64	37.6	338	142.9	5	11	4.1	9	0	.0

*=Estimated **1.0=883 lbs per person; 100++ indicates per capita toxic waste generation > than 100 times the U.S. average of 883 lbs per capita.

ZIP CODE MEASURES OF SIZE, LEVELS OF AFFLUENCE AND QUALITY OF LIFE

1=Population (th.); 2= % White; 3=Households (th.); 4=% Owner Occupied; 5=Mean Income Per Household (th.$); 6=Mean Monthly Rent ($); 7=Mean Home Value (th.$); 8=% under 5; 9=% 65 and over; 10=White Males (th.); 11=% White Males, 65+; 12=# Toxic Waste Sites; 13=Toxic Waste Relative to US(883 lbs.per capita)**.

OHIO

CANTON

ZIP CODE	1	2	3	4	5	6	7	8	9	10	11	12	13
44720	30.8	99	10.5	77	35.8	377	115.7	6	9	14.9	8	2	.3
44721	10.4	99	3.4	85	35.4	384	109.9	7	6	5.2	5	0	.0
44730	6.3	92	2.2	84	26.9	307	75.6	7	11	2.9	10	1	.2

MANSFIELD

ZIP CODE	1	2	3	4	5	6	7	8	9	10	11	12	13
44802	1.1	0	.3	84	25.7	355	83.8	9	10	.0	.0	0	.0
44804	1.2	0	.4	90	28.9	375	76.4	8	11	.0	.0	0	.0
44805	29.8	98	10.4	72	24.9	305	80.8	8	12	14.0	10	2	1.0
44807	2.5	100	.9	78	26.1	260	72.3	7	11	1.2	11	0	.0
44809	.5	100	.2	86	29.4	331	68.0	8	11	.3	14	0	.0
44811	12.7	99	4.5	77	27.9	329	81.6	9	11	6.2	9	0	.7
44813	6.4	99	2.2	81	25.4	291	76.1	8	10	.8	7	0	.3
44814	2.8	99	.8	79	31.0	318	87.9	7	7	1.4	7	1	.0
44815	.9	97	.3	84	27.3	299	63.9	10	10	.5	8	0	.7
44816	.3	100	.1	78	24.2	264	84.4	8	13	.1	10	0	9.2
44817	1.4	0	.5	84	23.7	294	71.5	7	11	.0	.0	0	8.3
44820	2.9	100	.9	79	24.3	272	66.7	10	11	1.5	9	0	.7
44822	2.6	99	.8	85	23.8	254	65.0	9	8	1.3	7	0	.0
44824	4.3	100	1.3	88	33.9	385	97.7	7	5	2.1	3	0	1.8
44825	.2	100	.1	75	16.7	247	43.8	6	17	.0	.1	0	.0
44826	1.5	0	.5	90	26.2	244	77.5	9	7	.0	.0	0	.0
44827	5.6	98	1.9	82	25.2	277	64.4	8	8	2.9	9	0	.3
44828	.3	97	.1	85	27.9	323	54.7	6	7	.1	5	0	.0
44829	.1	100	.1	75	26.6	241	62.4	3	21	.1	16	0	3.4
44830	22.1	93	7.8	75	26.2	306	74.8	9	11	9.1	8	0	2.2
44833	22.2	99	8.2	72	24.2	261	70.2	7	13	10.4	10	1	1.1
44836	2.9	98	.9	76	25.5	348	68.9	10	14	1.4	10	0	.0
44837	3.6	0	1.2	85	23.7	247	64.2	10	9	.0	.1	0	.0
44839	10.8	100	3.9	75	31.8	354	65.1	7	11	5.3	9	0	.4
44840	2.3	100	.8	79	26.3	274	78.7	7	10	1.1	10	0	.8
44841	.9	100	.3	82	25.4	333	59.5	9	14	.4	14	0	.0
44842	5.4	98	1.9	72	26.3	242	74.6	6	15	2.7	11	0	.0
44843	2.7	0	.9	79	28.7	326	79.2	6	7	.0	.1	0	3.4
44844	.6	100	.2	88	22.6	246	64.8	10	8	.3	9	1	.0
44846	3.1	100	1.0	78	30.7	325	99.3	6	11	1.6	10	0	1.8
44847	3.9	99	1.3	73	27.8	289	81.6	9	11	1.9	9	0	.0
44848	.3	100	.1	82	21.6	307	62.2	10	10	.1	7	0	.0
44849	2.4	100	.8	84	23.5	318	62.4	8	13	1.2	10	0	1.3
44850	.4	100	.1	72	23.4	307	61.5	5	15	.2	9	0	.0
44851	1.5	97	.6	78	24.0	257	74.7	10	10	.2	9	0	.0
44853	1.5	0	.7	81	25.1	316	83.0	12	7	.0	0	0	.0
44854	2.2	0	.7	80	28.3	267	72.1	7	9	.0	0	0	.0
44855	1.2	0	.4	79	23.0	251	64.9	8	11	.0	1	0	.0
44856	.3	100	.1	95	25.4	292*	56.3	6	10	.2	13	0	.0
44857	20.6	98	7.3	70	27.0	300	84.5	8	11	9.6	9	0	1.8
44859	1.2	0	.4	83	24.1	343	72.1	7	9	.0	0	0	.0
44860	.2	100	.1	80	19.8	311	44.2	10	7	.1	8	0	.0
44861	.3	0	.1	90	30.4	349*	74.7	4	11	.0	0	0	11.0

OHIO

MANSFIELD

ZIP CODE	1	2	3	4	5	6	7	8	9	10	11	12	13
44863	.5	99	.2	52	22.4	279	63.9	11	15	.2	15	0	.0
44864	2.5	0	.8	81	25.5	281	59.4	7	10	.0	0	0	.0
44865	2.9	99	.9	78	26.1	269	67.9	8	7	1.4	6	0	2.7
44866	1.6	0	.5	84	24.7	301	69.5	8	9	.0	0	0	.0
44867	2.2	100	.7	83	26.5	288	74.2	9	10	1.1	8	2	.0
44870	45.8	86	16.5	68	27.0	297	81.7	8	11	19.1	12	4	1.4
44874	.4	100	.1	71	22.5	237	52.0	9	10	.2	10	0	.0
44875	14.8	99	5.3	76	26.6	268	77.8	7	13	7.1	10	0	.6
44878	3.3	99	.9	86	25.8	319	60.3	11	7	1.6	7	0	.6
44880	1.5	99	.5	84	27.2	315	84.3	10	7	.8	7	0	.0
44881	6.4	99	2.2	89	24.5	341	59.4	9	12	.2	11	0	.0
44883	30.2	98	10.3	73	25.2	295	78.9	8	12	14.3	9	1	9.2
44887	1.2	100	.4	82	26.8	305	62.0	8	8	.6	8	0	.0
44889	5.3	99	1.7	85	28.8	361	94.1	8	9	2.6	7	0	.7
44890	10.3	98	3.5	76	27.0	274	72.0	9	11	4.9	8	0	.5

MANSFIELD

ZIP CODE	1	2	3	4	5	6	7	8	9	10	11	12	13
44902	4.6	70	2.0	38	14.7	205	34.7	9	15	1.5	14	3	5.9
44903	31.2	82	10.9	70	23.6	269	66.8	8	10	12.4	8	0	
44904	11.3	99	3.8	78	30.3	332	97.2	8	6	5.4	5	0	2.4
44905	16.8	95	5.8	80	25.2	315	60.9	7	8	8.0	7	0	.5
44906	17.9	96	6.6	72	27.6	301	77.5	7	10	8.3	9	0	3.5
44907	16.4	98	6.6	68	27.7	325	87.7	6	17	7.5	14	0	.5

CINCINNATI (WEST)

ZIP CODE	1	2	3	4	5	6	7	8	9	10	11	12	13
45001	1.2	87	.4	58	23.1	253	44.6	8	8	.5	7	1	100++
45002	8.0	99	2.6	79	28.1	333	81.6	8	7	4.0	7	0	2.7
45003	.9	0	.3	74	25.2	314	59.2	5	14	.0	0	0	3.3
45004	.2	100	.1	65	19.9	321	58.4	8	11	.1	3	0	.0
45005	29.2	99	9.4	76	28.3	294	86.7	8	6	14.4	5	2	.1
45011	39.0	87	13.5	63	22.4	264	75.2	9	10	16.6	8	3	.7
45013	44.5	99	15.8	76	29.7	334	94.4	7	11	21.1	9	4	.3
45014	33.2	97	11.6	70	34.4	426	115.9	8	5	16.0	4	0	.2
45015	13.6	100	5.1	75	23.8	328	66.4	8	14	6.3	10	0	.2
45030	12.2	100	4.0	80	28.5	310	90.1	10	8	6.0	7	3	2.3
45032	.4	0	.1	64	20.9	341	66.0	11	10	.0	0	0	.0
45033	.2	100	.2	92	20.8	203	52.4	6	23	.3	18	1	.0
45034	.5	100	.1	53	27.8	462	59.5	14	10	.2	7	0	.0
45036	19.0	93	5.8	64	28.1	357	105.6	6	11	9.2	8	0	.1
45039	4.8	99	1.5	91	39.2	419	122.9	8	9	2.4	5	0	.2
45040	12.4	99	4.1	83	34.7	383	108.2	9	5	6.1	4	2	.2
45041	.4	100	.1	67	19.6	335	88.4	15	14	.2	16	0	56.6
45042	65.3	91	23.7	67	27.5	318	88.6	7	11	28.6	9	0	2.4
45050	4.2	97	1.4	71	35.5	336	112.1	6	11	1.9	8	0	.2
45052	2.7	0	.9	78	29.3	275	96.2	8	9	.2	4	0	.0
45053	2.0	100	.6	90	32.7	300	134.3	9	6	1.0	6	0	10.1
45054	1.0	100	.4	78	25.5	284	90.1	7	8	.5	6	0	.0
45055	.2	100	.1	84	27.9	316	84.8	5	5	.1	5	0	1.1
45056	24.3	95	6.0	48	24.0	353	106.8	4	5	11.2	4	1	.0
45061	.2	100	.1	85	24.3	312	78.0	4	13	.1	11	1	7.8

*=Estimated **1.0=883 lbs per person; 100++ indicates per capita toxic waste generation > than 100 times the U.S. average of 883 lbs per capita.

ZIP CODE MEASURES OF SIZE, LEVELS OF AFFLUENCE AND QUALITY OF LIFE

1=Population (th.); 2= % White; 3=Households (th.); 4=% Owner Occupied; 5=Mean Income Per Household (th.$); 6=Mean Monthly Rent ($); 7=Mean Home Value (th.$);
8=% under 5; 9=% 65 and over; 10=White Males (th.); 11=% White Males, 65+; 12=# Toxic Waste Sites; 13=Toxic Waste Relative to US(883 lbs.per capita)**.

OHIO

ZIP CODE	1	2	3	4	5	6	7	8	9	10	11	12	13
CINCINNATI (WEST)													
45062	.9	100	.3	74	29.5	315	83.7	7	11	.4	8	0	.0
45063	.3	100	.1	100	35.0	403*	80.2	3	10	.1	7	1	.0
45064	2.7	99	.9	85	27.9	330	87.9	7	9	1.4	8	0	.0
45065	3.4	100	1.1	73	23.3	333	60.6	10	5	1.7	4	0	.0
45066	5.6	99	1.8	83	34.0	422	106.9	8	5	2.8	4	0	.0
45067	8.0	0	2.6	79	30.7	338	87.6	8	6	.0	0	0	.0
45068	6.9	99	2.2	79	28.8	318	103.8	7	10	3.4	8	1	.0
45069	18.7	98	5.8	83	39.9	401	136.5	8	4	9.3	3	1	.0
45070	.3	100	.1	84	23.0	291	54.0	11	6	.1	10	0	.0
CINCINNATI (EAST)													
45101	2.4	99	.9	68	23.5	306	71.9	9	9	1.2	9	0	.0
45102	12.5	99	4.1	68	26.3	329	89.0	10	7	6.1	6	2	.0
45103	16.2	99	5.2	75	28.0	239	92.8	10	8	7.7	7	0	1.0
45106	10.6	99	3.5	78	27.4	342	76.0	9	9	5.2	7	0	.0
45107	7.6	99	2.5	76	25.3	305	71.3	10	10	3.6	8	0	.3
45108	.2	100	.1	78	18.5	277	45.5	6	26	.1	39	0	.1
45111	.5	66	.2	77	21.3	377	61.8	9	8	.2	6	0	.0
45113	2.3	100	.7	83	23.5	353	73.5	8	8	1.2	8	0	.0
45115	.2	0	.1	72	18.2	219	41.2	4	27	.0	0	0	.0
45118	2.5	99	.8	85	26.3	342	76.0	7	13	1.3	12	0	.0
45120	2.6	98	.8	73	23.3	339	64.1	9	10	1.3	8	1	.0
45121	6.8	99	2.3	73	22.5	268	73.6	9	14	3.3	12	2	.1
45122	9.5	100	2.9	88	28.0	354	80.4	9	5	4.7	5	1	.1
45123	8.6	98	3.1	67	20.0	260	54.4	8	13	4.0	11	0	.1
45130	2.7	100	.9	82	25.1	314	78.3	10	10	1.3	9	0	.0
45131	.3	98	.1	59	18.5	244	50.7	8	15	.1	15	0	.0
45132	.3	0	.1	85	15.6	169	43.8	12	15	.0	0	0	.0
45133	17.3	97	6.1	74	21.2	244	64.8	8	15	8.1	13	1	.5
45135	3.0	99	1.1	74	20.6	258	60.3	7	14	1.4	13	0	.0
45140	26.3	98	8.2	82	33.3	357	106.9	9	5	12.9	4	0	.2
45144	4.3	100	1.5	73	17.5	257	47.5	7	13	2.1	13	0	.1
45146	1.3	0	.4	76	22.7	275	60.0	9	9	.0	0	0	.1
45147	.4	100	.1	82	35	383	109.7	10	7	.2	6	0	.1
45148	1.5	100	.4	77	25.5	329	60.1	10	8	.8	7	0	.0
45150	23.3	99	7.8	73	29.7	367	101.8	8	7	11.1	7	0	.0
45152	6.3	100	2.0	77	28.5	368	89.8	8	6	3.1	7	0	.0
45153	1.5	0	.5	74	25.4	288	66.8	9	6	.0	0	0	.1
45154	5.2	99	1.6	81	23.3	320	70.7	9	11	2.5	9	0	.0
45155	.4	100	.1	85	13.6	218	37.7	5	20	.2	15	0	.2
45157	8.2	98	2.5	76	27.8	310	94.8	10	7	3.9	6	0	.0
45158	.4	100	.1	78	25.9	304	65.5	13	6	.2	7	0	.0
45159	2.4	99	.8	73	25.9	282	66.6	9	12	1.1	11	0	.1
45160	.9	99	.4	58	27.0	336	69.7	5	6	.5	5	0	.0
45162	2.7	98	.7	83	30.9	369	89.5	7	6	1.5	6	0	.0
45164	.3	100	.1	69	17.6	298	49.5	5	25	.1	26	0	.0
45166	.2	100	.1	63	23.4	292	67.9	12	0	.1	0	0	.0
45167	3.9	94	1.4	68	20.6	256	58.4	8	15	1.8	13	0	.1
45168	1.3	100	.5	77	18.5	275	60.3	7	16	.7	16	0	.0

OHIO

ZIP CODE	1	2	3	4	5	6	7	8	9	10	11	12	13
CINCINNATI (EAST)													
45169	4.8	99	1.7	68	21.8	287	56.5	8	13	2.3	11	1	.2
45171	4.1	99	1.3	84	21.4	278	62.3	9	13	2.0	11	0	.0
45172	.2	0	.1	66	17.8	337	42.0	13	5	.0	0	0	.0
45174	2.0	100	.7	95	48.9	583	162.9	4	12	1.0	10	0	.0
45176	5.8	100	2.0	78	25.8	267	80.4	7	10	2.9	8	1	.0
45177	17.0	96	6.2	66	24.8	297	80.4	7	12	7.8	10	0	.6
CINCINNATI													
45202	6.8	78	3.9	13	18.6	252	103.3	3	21	2.9	17	4	6.9
45203	3.4	0	1.2	2	9.7	132	100.6	15	6	.0	0	3	1.6
45204	10.8	98	3.9	40	19.3	259	47.1	9	11	5.2	9	3	1.1
45205	25.8	96	9.8	48	21.3	274	60.1	9	13	11.5	10	0	.0
45206	15.6	26	3.0	20	17.8	243	90.3	7	17	2.0	13	0	.0
45207	9.9	13	3.0	53	18.2	276	51.8	7	14	.7	8	0	1.6
45208	18.7	91	8.4	52	40.0	444	151.1	5	20	7.5	14	0	.4
45209	12.6	97	5.7	49	22.5	285	69.0	7	17	5.4	13	0	4.2
45210	14.0	38	6.3	9	8.8	160	67.2	10	13	2.5	13	1	.0
45211	59.2	98	23.0	63	28.2	306	93.0	6	16	27.0	13	1	.3
45212	29.3	97	11.8	50	23.3	276	68.0	7	14	13.1	11	4	7.7
45213	15.1	53	5.8	64	29.4	312	86.9	7	15	3.6	17	0	.6
45214	15.7	40	6.2	22	12.8	171	37.5	10	13	3.1	11	1	2.8
45215	35.9	73	13.3	58	31.3	334	105.1	6	13	12.5	10	10	8.6
45216	12.6	90	4.6	54	23.7	271	62.8	7	19	5.2	15	4	1.6
45217	8.2	69	3.2	51	23.3	278	74.2	8	15	2.6	14	5	47.3
45218	5.2	99	1.8	71	34.0	382	96.7	6	8	2.5	7	0	.3
45219	19.0	55	8.6	23	16.0	276	58.4	10	10	5.5	8	0	.1
45220	15.5	77	7.3	29	24.1	320	123.3	4	13	5.7	9	2	1.4
45223	17.7	75	7.0	41	20.7	313	55.2	9	11	6.2	10	2	1.4
45224	24.5	73	9.0	67	30.5	339	92.5	6	18	7.9	16	0	.6
45225	16.5	34	6.2	17	13.7	210	39.9	12	12	2.6	12	1	1.4
45226	8.7	93	3.6	56	32.7	289	114.8	8	12	3.9	10	0	.8
45227	22.2	63	8.5	62	26.9	331	75.9	7	15	6.4	15	1	.5
45229	20.8	14	8.3	27	20.5	249	101.7	7	16	1.5	18	0	2.4
45230	40.7	99	14.3	73	35.3	234	114.1	7	10	19.4	8	0	.0
45231	48.2	86	15.6	79	32.5	360	90.6	8	7	20.0	7	1	40.5
45232	10.3	31	3.3	20	16.8	375	59.0	9	11	1.5	7	3	1.5
45233	4.3	98	1.5	67	25.5	191	82.3	9	12	2.1	8	2	.4
45236	26.8	90	10.5	72	32.3	321	98.8	5	17	11.7	14	1	3.8
45237	26.1	58	11.3	46	25.9	412	93.7	9	11	6.7	22	1	14.6
45238	57.1	98	19.6	73	32.5	322	107.2	7	11	26.9	9	1	.8
45239	63.6	96	21.1	78	31.3	307	93.4	8	9	29.7	8	1	.1
45240	29.7	73	8.7	84	37.2	345	98.8	9	6	10.8	2	0	.1
45241	16.4	98	5.8	75	36.1	485	117.3	5	17	8.1	5	4	3.8
45242	27.2	97	8.9	81	45.9	415	152.1	6	17	12.8	7	1	1.7
45243	19.8	99	6.1	91	61.8	440	188.4	4	14	7.5	12	1	1.0
45244	19.8	99	6.1	81	38.8	489	124.4	8	5	9.6	4	1	1.0
45245	11.7	99	4.0	74	32.0	338	100.6	8	5	5.8	4	0	.2
45246	12.0	91	4.4	60	33.7	366	103.2	7	10	5.2	8	0	4.4
45247	7.0	98	2.0	93	36.1	447	108.6	6	17	3.5	6	4	.0

*=Estimated **1.0=883 lbs per person; 100++ indicates per capita toxic waste generation > than 100 times the U.S. average of 883 lbs per capita.

ZIP CODE MEASURES OF SIZE, LEVELS OF AFFLUENCE AND QUALITY OF LIFE

1=Population (th.); 2= % White; 3=Households (th.); 4=% Owner Occupied; 5=Mean Income Per Household (th.$); 6=Mean Monthly Rent ($); 7=Mean Home Value (th.$); 8=% under 5; 9=% 65 and over; 10=White Males (th.); 11=% White Males, 65+; 12=# Toxic Waste Sites; 13=Toxic Waste Relative to US(883 lbs.per capita)**.

OHIO

DAYTON

ZIP CODE	1	2	3	4	5	6	7	8	9	10	11	12	13
45301	.2	100	.1	96	33.3	382*	75.1	9	3	.1	0	1	1.4
45302	3.0	0	.9	83	27.6	343	80.0	10	9	.0	0	0	.0
45303	2.4	0	.8	74	27.0	271	62.0	9	9	.0	0	0	1.0
45304	7.1	100	2.4	78	25.6	329	83.6	8	10	3.4	9	0	.0
45305	6.1	100	2.0	92	36.9	396	109.6	6	6	3.1	6	0	.0
45306	2.3	99	.7	81	27.6	360	83.9	9	8	1.2	6	0	.0
45307	.3	100	.1	78	18.2	340	44.8	8	19	.1	16	0	.1
45308	4.9	99	1.5	78	22.8	297	58.5	9	9	2.4	8	1	.0
45309	10.7	100	3.8	78	28.3	297	91.9	7	10	5.3	9	0	.2
45310	.3	100	.1	89	24.0	296	65.1	7	7	.6	8	0	.0
45311	5.9	98	1.9	81	25.6	304	72.6	9	8	2.8	8	0	.0
45312	1.3	0	.4	83	28.0	294	88.9	7	9	.0	0	0	.0
45314	4.0	95	1.0	61	21.9	292	81.7	6	7	1.8	7	0	.0
45315	2.0	99	.7	82	33.1	332	116.6	4	9	1.0	8	0	.2
45316	.2	0		48	18.0	267	74.2	4	15	.0	0	0	.0
45317	1.1	0	.4	75	20.5	304	59.7	7	11	.0	0	0	.0
45318	5.6	99	1.9	79	25.4	282	79.9	7	12	2.7	9	0	.0
45319	.3	100	.1	66	23.2	233	55.5	1	15	.1	6	0	.2
45320	11.6	99	4.3	72	25.2	273	75.0	7	14	5.6	11	2	10.5
45321	1.2	100	.2	75	24.6	292	66.9	10	12	.6	12	0	.2
45322	20.1	99	6.7	83	31.8	395	96.0	8	9	9.6	5	0	.1
45323	2.1	99	1.8	78	31.5	336	93.9	7	4	2.6	5	0	.0
45324	35.0	95	12.7	63	27.1	334	84.2	7	6	16.5	5	4	3.6
45325	2.6	99	.8	82	29.8	329	84.9	8	8	1.3	7	0	
45326	1.1	0	.4	78	26.5	376	72.3	8	11	.0	0	0	.0
45327	8.4	98	2.9	78	29.4	327	83.9	7	9	4.1	8	0	.2
45328	.6	100	.2	80	21.5	262	55.0	10	13	.3	12	0	.1
45329	2.2	100	.7	97	22.7	260*	61.7	6	12	.1	10	0	1.3
45330	.7	0	.2	85	23.7	313	57.1	7	11	.0	0	0	.0
45331	23.2	99	8.2	75	24.7	290	74.0	8	15	10.9	8	4	1.9
45332	.7	98	.2	83	21.2	231	51.0	8	12	.3	12	0	.0
45333	1.3	100	.4	82	27.0	253	70.5	8	8	.7	7	0	.0
45334	2.0	0	.7	79	25.2	323	66.5	9	11	.0	0	0	3.6
45335	6.1	97	2.0	77	25.8	314	81.2	8	8	2.9	7	0	
45336	.2	100		88	25.5	293*	54.0	6	14	.1	12	0	.0
45337	1.9	100	.7	85	26.5	303	83.6	8	10	1.0	9	0	.0
45338	4.6	0	1.6	79	26.2	265	79.5	7	9	.0	0	0	.1
45339	1.9	0	.6	85	27.3	270	102.6	7	9	.0	0	0	.0
45340	.7	0	.2	85	26.7	289	63.1	8	11	.0	0	0	.0
45341	4.0	100	1.5	82	25.9	350	75.3	7	9	2.0	8	0	.0
45342	22.0	98	8.2	69	27.0	327	86.7	7	10	10.7	8	1	.1
45344	17.9	99	5.8	81	28.2	349	77.5	8	7	8.8	6	1	1.6
45345	6.9	99	2.3	79	27.5	318	74.0	7	9	3.4	8	0	.0
45346	2.6	100	.9	81	25.7	286	67.6	8	10	1.3	9	0	.0
45347	4.2	100	1.5	78	24.2	282	63.8	7	12	2.1	10	0	.0
45348	1.3	96	.3	85	26.0	279	61.6	10	9	.6	8	0	.1
45349	.4	100	.1	83	21.9	302	56.7	7	13	.2	10	0	1.6
45350	2.0	100		90	28.2	324*	66.1	7	11	.1	13	0	.0
45351	.3	0	.1	92	31.9	367*	74.8	5	13	.0	0	0	.0

OHIO

DAYTON

ZIP CODE	1	2	3	4	5	6	7	8	9	10	11	12	13
45352	.2	100	.1	87	21.6	340	36.0	10	21	.1	20	2	.0
45353	.2	100	.1	86	27.3	314*	43.2	7	6	.1	6	0	.0
45354	.8	0	.3	84	24.6	286	62.4	6	15	.0	0	0	.0
45356	25.0	96	9.1	73	24.6	298	70.7	8	12	11.4	10	2	.1
45358	.5	100	.2	83	26.7	302	73.4	6	6	.2	5	0	.0
45359	1.2	98	.5	77	22.5	348	66.9	11	17	.6	16	0	.0
45360	.4	100	.1	80	21.1	335	43.3	8	10	.2	10	0	.0
45361	.2	100	.1	70	20.1	336	49.9	10	16	.1	17	0	.0
45362	1.4	99	.4	83	26.6	224	69.7	10	10	.7	8	0	.0
45363	1.1	100	.3	85	31.4	285	93.3	9	8	.6	8	0	.1
45365	26.9	98	9.3	72	25.7	321	80.9	9	10	12.7	9	2	2.2
45368	4.3	99	1.5	68	25.4	267	74.7	7	12	2.0	10	0	.0
45369	3.1	99	1.0	85	26.3	357	88.9	7	9	1.5	9	0	.0
45370	2.5	98	.8	86	32.4	320	128.2	7	6	1.2	5	0	.0
45371	14.0	100	4.8	79	31.2	335	104.9	6	9	6.9	7	0	.8
45372	.4	0	.1	83	23.6	200	60.2	6	18	.0	0	0	.0
45373	28.1	96	10.1	71	27.8	322	93.6	8	11	13.0	9	2	1.6
45377	14.4	99	5.4	64	31.3	358	94.8	8	7	6.9	6	0	.5
45378	.6	0	.2	65	29.3	289	64.5	13	8	.0	0	0	.0
45380	4.9	0	1.7	75	25.6	240	72.2	9	12	.0	0	0	1.4
45381	5.6	99	1.9	77	25.5	269	71.9	7	9	2.8	9	0	.9
45382	1.3	100	.4	82	24.7	275	60.5	8	10	.7	9	0	.0
45383	6.8	99	2.4	76	27.0	329	88.3	7	11	3.3	10	0	.0
45384	2.4	99	2.4	53	28.4	299	114.0	9	8	.3	0	1	.5
45385	42.2	91	14.2	77	29.4	325	92.3	8	18	18.8	6	4	.6
45387	5.3	80	2.0	63	30.1	327	99.3	5	8	2.0	7	0	.4
45388	.9	0	.3	81	28.2	309	81.7	10	10	.0	0	0	.1
45389	.7	100	.2	76	24.0	253	50.1	8	13	.3	11	0	.0

DAYTON

ZIP CODE	1	2	3	4	5	6	7	8	9	10	11	12	13
45402	2.5	82	1.6	10	17.3	157	101.0	3	32	1.0	22	2	6.1
45403	20.9	96	8.0	53	18.8	269	46.1	9	12	9.6	10	2	1.8
45404	15.9	88	6.0	52	18.0	228	47.3	10	11	6.6	10	2	2.6
45405	25.5	90	12.0	43	22.0	276	63.9	7	16	10.5	13	0	.0
45406	33.1	40	12.8	56	22.3	261	59.7	9	13	6.3	13	0	8.4
45407	17.4	0	6.1	43	14.8	235	35.8	9	12	.0	0	0	.1
45408	14.3	2	5.1	50	17.1	233	42.8	9	10	.1	16	0	.5
45409	12.0	96	4.0	51	30.8	350	111.5	4	13	6.3	9	0	2.1
45410	19.8	98	8.0	55	19.7	268	49.1	8	14	9.3	11	2	1.2
45414	22.6	97	8.4	68	27.4	321	87.3	6	9	10.6	8	2	3.3
45415	13.2	97	4.7	80	39.4	420	118.9	5	12	6.2	10	0	.0
45416	8.1	79	2.7	83	26.6	358	55.9	8	13	2.9	10	1	.0
45417	15.2	2	5.6	59	17.9	276	38.2	8	10	.1	16	0	8.4
45418	6.6	0	2.1	78	27.8	296	69.8	7	5	.0	0	2	.0
45419	16.5	99	6.6	71	35.6	337	123.5	4	19	7.3	15	0	.1
45420	27.9	99	11.8	68	23.9	302	64.1	6	16	12.7	12	0	.0
45424	44.6	94	14.3	77	32.0	414	91.1	9	11	21.0	3	1	.0
45426	17.5	76	6.8	60	28.7	382	84.8	6	10	6.2	12	0	.1
45427	13.4	45	4.4	67	20.8	255	45.7	5	14	3.0	10	2	.2
	27.9	99	10.9	73	38.0	375	119.8	5	14	13.1	12	1	.1

*=Estimated **1.0=883 lbs per person; 100++ indicates per capita toxic waste generation > than 100 times the U.S. average of 883 lbs per capita.

ZIP CODE MEASURES OF SIZE, LEVELS OF AFFLUENCE AND QUALITY OF LIFE

1=Population (th.); 2= % White; 3=Households (th.); 4=% Owner Occupied; 5=Mean Income Per Household (th.$); 6=Mean Monthly Rent ($)*; 7=Mean Home Value (th.$)*; 8=% under 5; 9=% 65 and over; 10=White Males (th.); 11=% White Males, 65+; 12=# Toxic Waste Sites; 13=Toxic Waste Relative to US(883 lbs.per capita)**.

OHIO

ZIPCODE	1	2	3	4	5	6	7	8	9	10	11	12	13
DAYTON													
45430	6.1	98	1.9	91	38.8	440	112.4	7	5	3.0	4	0	.0
45431	25.0	93	8.5	57	28.2	314	90.9	9	5	11.6	4	0	.1
45432	16.1	97	5.6	82	30.8	359	83.4	7	6	7.7	6	2	.0
45433	4.1	86	1.0	3	27.7	439	98.7*	11				0	.2
45439	9.5	100	3.9	73	22.9	386	65.4	7	12	4.5	10	6	4.5
45440	17.9	98	6.4	69	35.7	398	121.7	5	6	8.4	5	0	.2
45449	18.9	98	7.2	70	31.0	366	92.8	7	6	9.0	5	2	.5
45459	37.4	97	12.8	77	44.0	427	159.1	6	8	17.7	6	0	.0
SPRINGFIELD													
45501	3.1	96	.3	87	37.8	504	91.7	1	21	1.3	16	0	27.9
45502	13.3	98	4.4	83	29.6	309	101.1	6	8	6.6	7	2	.0
45503	31.0	95	11.3	71	26.0	297	76.4	7	12	14.2	9	1	.0
45504	19.4	98	7.5	67	29.9	310	90.6	6	15	9.0	12	1	.3
45505	26.2	86	10.1	58	20.5	261	55.5	8	14	10.5	11	0	.3
45506	19.5	60	7.2	61	20.5	257	57.7	8	13	5.6	12	2	.0
CHILLICOTHE													
45601	49.5	93	16.8	69	25.3	284	75.2	7	11	23.1	10	4	.6
45610	.3	100	.3	74	28.5	431	82.9	6	6	.6	6	0	.0
45612	4.2	99	1.5	74	19.9	231	54.0	8	14	2.1	13	0	.0
45613	2.8	93	.9	81	18.8	229	52.7	8	9	1.3	8	0	.0
45614	3.5	89	1.2	81	23.5	288	63.6	10	10	1.6	9	0	.0
45616	1.2	100	.4	69	16.2	214	46.6	10	8	.6	9	0	.0
45617	.1	100	.1	66	27.8	201*	66.1	8	8	.1	5	0	.0
45618	.1	100	.1	80	14.9	171*	44.3	5	28	.1	24	0	.0
45619	8.8	100	3.0	72	22.4	289	70.9	9	9	4.2	9	0	.0
45620	1.3	0	.5	81	22.9	231	55.4	7	13	.0	0	0	.0
45621	.6	98	.2	70	15.8	309	36.1	8	13	.3	11	0	.0
45622	.4	0	.1	83	19.3	339	62.8	11	10	.0	0	0	.0
45623	3.0	100	1.0	80	19.1	286	57.0	10	12	1.5	12	0	.0
45624	.2	100	.1	85	21.8	251*	29.5	5	17	.1	19	0	.0
45627	.2	0	.1	82	17.3	137	48.0	8	6	.0	0	0	.0
45628	1.0	0	.3	76	18.2	273	42.5	8	11	.0	0	0	.7
45629	3.7	92	1.3	73	22.4	244	67.2	7	12	1.7	10	0	.0
45630	3.0	0	1.0	81	22.1	281	64.2	8	8	.0	0	0	.0
45631	.8	0	.3	79	21.1	359	55.1	9	18	.0	0	0	.4
45633	16.0	96	5.6	72	25.1	302	78.6	7	13	7.4	11	0	3.8
45634	1.2	0	.2	67	24.7	248	51.6	8	7	.0	0	0	.0
45635	1.8	0	.6	77	17.5	260	41.8	8	17	.0	0	0	.0
45638	.2	100	.1	71	17.8	243	42.3	9	6	.1	7	0	.0
45640	25.5	97	9.1	70	21.8	253	62.7	8	13	11.6	10	5	3.9
45643	13.8	99	4.9	74	21.1	287	63.3	7	13	6.6	11	1	.0
45644	2.8	0	.1	76	15.5	247	64.2	16	10	.0	0	0	.0
45645	2.3	100	1.0	77	24.0	277	73.6	6	12	1.4	9	0	.9
45646	.4	100	.7	84	23.4	301	62.5	9	13	.0	0	0	.0
45647	2.0	0	.7	76	16.8	174	40.7	8	13	.0	0	0	.0
45648	12.0	91	3.4	82	22.4	262	59.0	8	10	5.8	9	0	.0
45649	.8	0	.2	73	20.3	267	62.1	7	9	.0	0	0	.0
45650	.4	100	.1	76	15.0	119	34.9	11	16	.2	13	0	.0
CHILLICOTHE (cont.)													
45651	4.7	100	1.6	77	19.3	253	55.3	8	12	2.3	11	0	4.9
45652	3.2	100	1.0	82	19.6	213	50.4	8	12	1.6	10	0	.0
45653	3.4	0	1.1	88	23.9	336	66.5	9	11	.0	0	0	.0
45654	.7	0		79	20.7	226	36.9	4	11	.0	0	0	.0
45655	.6	0	.2	80	17.9	245	62.0	7	11	.0	0	0	.7
45656	6.1	98	2.0	76	18.6	285	48.1	8	12	2.9	11	0	.1
45657	2.3	0	.7	77	16.8	239	42.4	10	10	.0	0	0	.0
45658	1.5	98	.5	80	18.4	202	44.5	7	14	.8	14	0	.0
45659	3.0	99	.9	78	20.2	220	43.5	9	9	1.5	10	0	.0
45660	6.5	0	2.2	73	17.0	256	48.1	8	12	.0	0	0	.0
45661	5.3	99	1.7	73	19.1	247	52.8	8	13	2.6	10	1	99.9
45662	45.3	96	17.4	67	20.0	243	54.8	8	16	20.2	13	1	.0
45669	9.0	100	3.1	81	23.1	312	77.6	8	9	4.4	8	0	.0
45670	.4	100	.1	74	17.7	225	45.3	7	12	.2	12	0	.0
45671	.3	0	.1	76	17.7	226	37.5	7	15	.0	0	0	.0
45672	1.5	0	.5	87	20.1	252	47.0	10	10	.3	11	0	.0
45673	.6	100	.2	77	20.1	275	56.9	10	12	.3	11	0	.0
45674	.9	95	.2	55	24.0	258	57.9	4	7	.4	7	0	.0
45675	.2	100	.1	84	26.4	304*	118.1	9	4	.0	4	0	.0
45676	.3	0	.1	100	23.9	275*	84.5	17	3	.0	0	0	.0
45678	1.1	0	.4	76	15.2	220	45.3	7	15	.0	0	0	.1
45679	2.4	100	.8	77	17.2	290	54.1	10	12	1.2	12	0	.6
45680	11.7	94	4.0	76	26.1	336	78.2	8	8	5.5	8	0	.3
45681	.2	100	.1	69	18.2	259	39.0	7	8	.1	8	0	.0
45684	2.6	100	.8	73	19.4	245	47.0	8	9	1.0	11	0	.0
45685	.6	0	.2	82	19.1	219	54.7	7	10	.0	0	0	.0
45686	2.0	100	.6	82	20.3	195	64.8	7	11	1.0	11	0	.0
45688	.6	98	.2	85	17.8	195	67.0	9	13	.0	10	0	.0
45690	11.4	99	4.1	71	19.3	179	34.7	10	10	5.5	10	0	.1
45692	9.1	99	3.3	70	21.6	274	67.1	7	14	4.3	12	1	.0
45693	7.1	99	2.4	76	20.8	248	54.7	8	14	3.5	12	0	.6
45694	10.8	99	3.7	78	20.1	289	72.9	8	13	5.3	12	0	.3
45695	.2	100	.1	78	23.9	324	72.0	9	10	.1	9	0	.0
45696	1.6	0	.9	78	18.4	220	44.8	8	11	.3	12	3	.0
45697	3.6	0	1.2	78	20.7	303	56.5	7	12	.0	0	0	.0
45698	.4	100	.4	79	18.2	203	38.2	9	13	.2	11	0	.0
ATHENS													
45701	28.9	93	8.7	53	20.8	337	87.0	5	7	13.7	6	2	.0
45710	4.1	100	1.4	78	20.4	260	62.1	9	11	2.0	11	1	.0
45711	1.1	83	.4	83	17.1	254	45.3	8	14	.4	13	1	.0
45712	.2	100	.1	93	26.0	298*	76.0	7	12	.1	13	0	.9
45713	.2	100	.1	92	19.7	227*	51.0	8	21	.1	20	0	.0
45714	10.7	97	3.9	73	25.8	339	82.7	7	10	5.0	9	0	4.8
45715	2.6	100	.9	78	25.7	251	68.2	9	14	1.3	12	0	.3
45716	.6	100	.2	86	20.1	311	47.8	7	9	.3	9	0	.0
45719	1.2	99	.5	82	19.3	256	40.4	7	14	.6	12	0	.0
45723	2.9	0	1.0	82	21.1	242	56.2	9	12	.0	0	2	.0
45724	1.2	82	.4	89	21.3	229	55.1	9	10	.5	10	0	.0

*=Estimated **1.0=883 lbs per person, 100++ indicates per capita toxic waste generation > than 100 times the U.S. average of 883 lbs per capita.

ZIP CODE MEASURES OF SIZE, LEVELS OF AFFLUENCE AND QUALITY OF LIFE

1=Population (th.); 2= % White; 3=Households (th.); 4=% Owner Occupied; 5=Mean Income Per Household (th.$); 6=Mean Monthly Rent ($); 7=Mean Home Value (th.$);
8=% under 5; 9=% 65 and over; 10=% White Males (th.); 11=% White Males, 65+; 12=# Toxic Waste Sites; 13=Toxic Waste Relative to US(883 lbs.per capita)**.

OHIO — LIMA

ZIPCODE	1	2	3	4	5	6	7	8	9	10	11	12	13
45809	.3	100	.1	90	24.0	279	75.1	6	17	.1	13	0	.0
45810	7.7	99	2.5	62	23.5	279	75.3	6	8	3.9	6	0	.0
45812	2.1	97	.7	75	24.6	265	56.3	8	9	1.0	8	0	.0
45813	3.7	99	1.2	88	27.8	259	66.2	9	9	1.8	8	1	.8
45814	2.4	0	.8	84	25.1	317	74.5	7	16	.0	0	0	.0
45815	.3	94	.1	87	18.5	212*	46.5	16	9	.1	9	0	.0
45816	.3	100	.1	88	21.9	301	43.8	6	13	.1	10	0	.0
45817	5.5	99	1.8	78	27.3	283	85.2	6	17	2.6	13	0	1.0
45819	.3	100	.2	98	21.5	247*	51.3	9	20	.1	17	0	.0
45820	.6	100	.2	88	24.7	261	61.9	9	13	.3	11	0	.0
45821	1.5	97	.5	86	25.9	261	66.2	8	7	.7	6	0	.0
45822	17.2	99	6.1	77	26.7	293	81.6	8	12	8.3	10	3	1.3
45826	.4	100	.1	81	34.6	286	90.6	11	11	.2	9	0	.4
45827	2.1	99	.6	87	29.0	292	77.0	10	11	1.1	10	0	.3
45828	6.0	99	1.9	83	32.1	289	83.3	11	9	2.9	7	0	4.4
45830	5.9	99	1.6	83	26.4	262	75.8	9	10	2.8	9	0	.0
45831	3.1	99	1.0	86	27.8	281	62.1	9	8	1.5	8	0	.2
45832	2.9	99	1.0	86	27.3	277	81.6	9	13	1.4	9	0	.0
45833	11.2	100	3.6	83	26.6	291	73.5	8	12	5.4	10	0	1.0
45835	.7	0	.2	78	23.2	335	51.8	7	14	.0	0	0	.0
45836	1.6	99	.5	84	24.6	257	52.9	7	10	.8	9	0	.0
45837	.3	100	.1	75	20.0	285	49.4	9	10	.1	7	0	.0
45840	45.4	97	16.7	71	28.1	311	90.4	11	11	21.1	9	6	.5
45841	.9	100	.3	77	27.0	367	69.1	11	11	.5	10	0	.0
45843	4.1	100	1.4	81	24.9	271	65.2	9	9	2.1	9	0	.6
45844	3.0	100	.9	91	30.4	283	85.2	11	8	1.5	8	0	.0
45845	2.6	100	.8	87	30.1	266	84.8	9	14	1.4	8	0	.0
45846	2.4	100	.7	85	26.0	278	74.4	10	10	2.1	9	0	.1
45848	.3	100	.1	92	29.3	337*	85.4	10	14	.2	12	0	2.1
45849	1.4	100	.5	85	24.5	242	55.2	8	11	.7	12	0	.0
45850	1.7	0	.6	86	27.5	317	62.7	9	10	.3	0	0	.0
45851	.6	98	.2	88	27.4	231	59.8	11	14	.3	11	0	.0
45853	1.1	0	.3	92	34.1	279	77.5	11	9	.1	0	0	.0
45854	1.6	0	.5	84	26.7	337	76.5	7	12	.0	0	0	2.1
45855	.3	0	.1	83	22.8	303	40.5	12	6	.1	0	0	.0
45856	5.4	93	1.6	82	26.2	258	67.9	9	10	2.5	10	0	.0
45858	3.1	98	1.0	80	26.4	290	73.1	9	11	1.5	9	0	.0
45859	.7	100	.2	78	24.8	226	49.0	6	9	.3	8	0	.0
45860	1.9	100	.4	87	33.2	382	85.7	7	12	1.0	13	0	.0
45861	.3	0	.1	82	19.1	351	38.2	15	10	.7	0	0	.0
45862	1.8	100	.6	86	23.8	285	58.9	8	12	.9	10	0	.0
45863	1.3	100	.1	86	27.0	340	55.7	11	10	.6	8	0	.0
45864	.2	100	.1	82	27.8	212	68.2	9	13	.2	11	0	.0
45865	4.3	100	1.3	85	29.2	290	89.1	9	13	2.2	15	0	.8
45866	.2	100	.1	83	20.1	211	42.0	8	14	.1	9	0	.0
45867	1.0	100	.3	83	27.0	298	73.4	9	13	.5	11	0	.1
45868	.7	98	.2	86	27.4	378	69.3	9	11	.4	8	0	.0
45869	3.9	100	1.3	82	28.8	281	86.8	11	13	1.9	11	0	2.2
45870	.5	0	.2	73	24.4	208	45.4	9	6	.1	22	0	.0

OHIO — ATHENS

ZIPCODE	1	2	3	4	5	6	7	8	9	10	11	12	13
45726	.4	100	.1	78	17.2	271	45.9	9	8	.2	8	0	.0
45727	.6	100	.2	82	20.1	266	32.5	10	12	.3	11	0	.0
45728	.1	100	.1	76	19.8	213	24.0	3	17	.1	10	0	.0
45729	1.1	98	.4	90	26.2	255	77.5	10	6	.6	5	0	.8
45732	4.7	99	1.7	75	16.9	221	37.2	9	14	2.3	13	0	.0
45734	.4	0	.1	77	18.6	144	38.2	6	18	.0	0	0	.0
45735	1.5	96	.5	76	18.7	273	50.2	8	9	.7	8	0	.0
45739	.2	0	.1	93	17.5	202*	50.4	3	11	.7	0	0	.0
45740	.7	0	.2	82	20.1	292	36.3	7	13	.0	0	0	1.0
45741	.6	0	.2	85	19.6	256	44.2	8	14	.0	0	0	.0
45742	2.8	99	.9	93	26.1	311	72.8	9	9	1.4	8	0	.0
45743	1.0	100	.9	83	20.3	232	53.9	8	11	.5	10	0	.0
45744	3.0	98	1.0	79	22.8	282	61.6	9	14	1.5	13	1	1.3
45745	1.1	0	.4	75	15.3	193	28.2	10	18	.0	7	0	.4
45746	.4	100	.1	78	16.4	235	28.1	10	12	.1	10	0	.0
45750	29.4	99	10.4	70	25.1	288	77.6	7	12	14.0	12	1	3.6
45760	4.1	98	1.6	72	20.0	237	47.3	6	16	1.9	13	0	.1
45761	1.5	100	.4	73	17.1	211	35.9	10	7	.6	7	0	.0
45763	1.5	100	.5	83	23.2	294	56.8	6	18	.2	16	0	.1
45764	7.7	98	2.8	70	18.6	259	46.2	7	14	3.7	11	0	.0
45766	1.4	100	.5	82	19.2	271	40.3	9	9	.7	9	0	.0
45767	3.2	0	1.1	77	21.6	215	56.5	8	13	.0	0	0	.0
45768	1.8	0	.6	82	24.5	288	66.2	7	11	.0	0	0	.0
45769	6.7	98	2.3	79	21.6	259	55.7	8	13	3.2	12	0	.0
45770	.6	100	.2	79	14.4	195	28.7	7	19	.3	15	0	.0
45771	2.8	100	1.0	77	18.8	256	54.6	9	14	1.4	12	0	.0
45772	1.6	0	.6	84	18.5	268	44.6	8	13	.0	0	0	.0
45773	.5	0	.2	79	19.8	291	70.7	6	13	.0	0	0	.1
45774	2.1	99	.9	73	20.4	313	64.7	5	12	.9	10	0	.0
45775	1.7	99	.5	69	16.8	282	31.8	9	11	.9	0	0	.0
45776	.6	100	.2	85	22.0	272	53.5	8	9	.8	9	0	.0
45778	1.0	100	.2	85	20.3	310	46.5	8	13	.3	11	0	.0
45779	1.1	99	.4	82	17.1	205	38.1	10	10	.4	8	0	.0
45780	2.1	99	.9	73	19.8	291	55.8	6	11	.5	9	0	2.1
45782	.5	0	.2	83	20.1	196	48.1	10	10	.9	0	0	.0
45783	.3	100	.1	92	19.7	351	59.5	5	18	.2	16	0	.0
45784	2.3	98	.7	88	27.1	302	79.3	9	8	1.1	7	0	.0
45785	.4	100	.1	92	20.4	234*	44.6	9	14	1.0	13	0	.0
45786	2.8	99	.9	84	23.9	278	70.2	8	8	.2	8	0	.0
45787	.2	0	.1	96	25.0	288*	39.9	6	11	.0	0	0	31.1
45788	.9	100	.3	81	25.5	257	62.4	8	7	.5	10	0	.0
45789	.3	100	.1	72	17.4	265	55.6	6	7	.1	8	0	.0

OHIO — LIMA

ZIPCODE	1	2	3	4	5	6	7	8	9	10	11	12	13
45801	27.7	89	9.7	64	22.8	269	62.7	9	10	12.0	9	2	1.4
45804	22.7	73	8.1	66	20.9	266	49.0	10	12	7.7	11	6	4.2
45805	23.7	91	8.7	74	31.9	354	94.0	8	12	10.3	10	2	1.6
45806	10.4	99	3.5	84	32.1	344	93.7	8	8	5.1	7	0	.0
45807	9.6	99	3.2	81	30.5	385	93.3	8	7	4.7	7	0	.0
45808	.5	0	.2	84	26.1	296	45.1	9	6	.0	0	0	.0

*=Estimated   **=1.0-883 lbs per person; 100+ indicates per capita toxic waste generation > than 100 times the U.S. average of 883 lbs per capita.

ZIP CODE MEASURES OF SIZE, LEVELS OF AFFLUENCE AND QUALITY OF LIFE

1=Population (th.); 2= % White; 3=Households (th.); 4=% Owner Occupied; 5=Mean Income Per Household (th.$); 6=Mean Monthly Rent ($)*; 7=Mean Home Value (th.$)*; 8=% under 5; 9=% 65 and over; 10=% White Males; 11=% White Males, 65+; 12=# Toxic Waste Sites; 13=Toxic Waste Relative to US(883 lbs.per capita)**.

OHIO

ZIPCODE	1	2	3	4	5	6	7	8	9	10	11	12	13
LIMA													
45871	1.8	100	.6	84	28.3	314	76.3	6	15	.9	13	0	.0
45872	3.9	97	1.3	80	24.4	270	62.7	9	11	1.9	9	0	2.5
45873	3.0	99	.9	87	26.7	295	62.8	10	8	1.5	7	0	.1
45874	2.3	0	.8	87	25.2	243	61.2	9	10	.0	0	0	.6
45875	9.4	99	2.9	84	28.9	262	89.2	10	11	4.6	9	1	.7
45876	.8	100	.3	89	28.1	300	71.6	8	11	.4	8	0	.0
45877	2.0	0	.7	85	28.1	305	77.4	8	16	.0	0	2	4.1
45879	6.5	95	2.2	80	26.2	285	63.0	9	10	3.0	8	0	.0
45880	2.8	100	.9	83	28.5	271	63.0	8	12	1.4	10	1	.0
45881	1.2	99	.4	84	29.4	303	68.1	7	10	.6	8	0	.0
45882	3.2	100	1.1	85	27.7	265	65.3	8	15	1.5	12	0	.0
45883	3.4	100	.8	89	31.9	286	87.9	10	8	1.7	6	0	.0
45885	12.3	100	4.3	77	24.6	287	70.6	11	11	5.9	9	0	.4
45886	.5	100	.2	83	25.6	257	41.1	10	13	.3	9	0	1.0
45887	4.7	100	1.6	81	26.3	272	65.6	7	12	2.3	9	1	2.8
45888	.3	100	.1	89	24.0	216	55.9	5	11	.2	8	0	.0
45889	.9	100	.3	87	26.4	271	84.9	7	10	.4	10	0	.0
45890	.6	0	.2	85	27.2	365	58.6	8	12	.0	0	1	.0
45891	15.7	98	6.0	77	25.7	296	73.6	8	15	7.4	12	1	1.0
45893	.3	100	.1	85	22.7	229	57.6	6	10	.1	7	0	.0
45894	.8	100	.3	87	28.9	186	51.6	9	16	.4	16	0	.0
45895	16.0	99	5.5	79	26.0	280	79.6	8	12	7.8	10	0	1.6
45896	2.1	100	.7	80	23.9	303	67.6	8	10	1.0	9	0	.0
45897	.2	100	.2	79	29.2	165	54.7	6	5	.1	5	0	.0
45898	1.2	0	.4	86	23.6	310	54.3	7	17	.0	0	0	.0
45899	.3	95	.1	94	25.6	294*	55.4	8	9	.1	8	1	1.0
MUNCIE													
47374	.5	100	.1	86	24.4	289	72.5	8	8	.3	8	0	.0
47390	4.2	98	1.4	74	21.0	245	59.9	9	13	2.0	11	0	.0
JACKSON													
49256	.3	97	.1	76	25.1	356	81.8	15	15	.1	18	0	.0

OKLAHOMA

ZIPCODE	1	2	3	4	5	6	7	8	9	10	11	12	13
JOPLIN													
64831	.1	0	.1	55	15.3	240	78.8	0	17	.0	0	0	.0
64863	.9	76	.3	84	13.9	63	36.6	8	17	.3	21	0	.0
64865	.9	95	.3	84	23.5	359	62.3	10	12	.4	12	0	.0
INDEPENDENCE													
67336	.5	94	.2	77	21.7	155	45.2	17	12	.3	12	0	.0
67337	.2	86	.1	72	28.3	257	91.4	16	7	.1	9	0	.0
67361	.2	100	.1	84	19.3	222*	31.0	5	15	.1	21	0	.0
LIBERAL													
67901	.5	100	.2	100	32.2	370*	105.9	9	15	.3	19	0	.0
67950	.4	0	.1	76	20.5	236*	28.4	17	15	.0	0	0	.0
TEXARKANA													
71836	.2	0	.1	85	12.0	138*	18.6	12	22	.0	0	0	.0
HOT SPRINGS NATIONAL PARK													
71945	.2	100	.1	100	15.3	176*	13.1	0	17	.1	26	0	.0
FAYETTEVILLE													
72734	.3	74	.1	93	19.0	219*	19.0	5	7	.1	7	0	.0
72747	.5	83	.2	70	18.6	283	68.2	8	19	.2	26	0	.0
72761	2.3	91	.8	81	18.3	229	42.2	8	13	1.1	10	0	.1
FORT SMITH													
72901	3.8	92	1.3	83	20.4	243	52.6	8	10	1.8	10	0	.0
72955	.2	0	.1	78	20.7	164	34.9	12	12	.0	0	0	1.6
OKLAHOMA CITY													
73002	1.3	93	.5	80	20.4	182	43.5	8	13	.6	10	0	.0
73004	.8	100	.2	72	22.0	230	55.5	9	7	.4	15	0	.0
73005	10.1	67	3.5	70	19.9	225	55.4	8	16	3.2	17	1	.1
73006	3.4	72	1.2	74	18.6	205	47.9	8	14	1.2	15	2	.0
73007	1.0	53	.3	75	28.3	174	62.8	9	9	.3	16	0	.4
73008	23.1	96	8.4	68	28.9	333	84.4	7	9	10.3	7	2	.4
73009	1.6	86	.6	78	21.0	175	46.2	7	16	.7	17	0	.0
73010	6.9	96	2.3	84	26.7	257	72.3	8	8	3.4	21	1	1.6
73011	.5	93	.2	77	16.6	114	35.0	7	16	.2	16	0	.0
73014	1.4	90	.5	83	24.9	323	57.6	8	16	.7	20	0	.0
73015	3.8	71	1.3	73	20.4	181	51.3	9	7	1.2	22	4	.0
73016	.8	0	.3	82	24.4	289	55.9	7	13	.7	13	0	.0
73017	1.9	95	.6	81	22.2	175	32.0	7	15	.9	12	0	.0
73018	19.2	88	7.5	71	22.6	273	63.1	8	16	7.8	13	2	.9
73020	13.5	95	4.3	90	29.7	325	91.3	8	6	6.4	5	0	.9
73021	.4	0	.2	74	25.2	200	65.8	16	10	.0	0	0	.0
73024	.7	97	.2	79	28.4	232	74.4	6	21	.3	17	0	.4
73025	.3	0	.1	78	25.1	137	19.9	12	6	.2	16	0	.0
73026	2.8	82	.1	82	5.6	139	20.1*	0	0	1.3	0	0	.0
73027	1.6	90	.6	81	23.4	249	73.0	7	12	.7	11	0	.0
73028	3.1	91	1.2	76	23.5	250	59.8	9	17	1.3	14	0	13.2
73029	1.8	90	.7	78	20.6	208	42.3	9	18	.8	16	1	1.0
73030	4.0	94	1.5	75	20.8	212	54.9	8	16	1.9	13	2	1.2
73031	.3	0	.1	64	20.8	236	48.5	11	4	.0	0	1	.0
73032	.2	0	.1	66	16.4	114	22.9	10	18	.0	0	0	.0
73033	.7	88	.2	74	27.3	196	56.5	9	18	.3	20	0	.0
73034	39.0	94	12.8	72	36.9	365	134.4	8	15	18.0	5	3	.0

*=Estimated **1.0=883 lbs per person; 100++ indicates per capita toxic waste generation > than 100 times the U.S. average of 883 lbs per capita.

ZIP CODE MEASURES OF SIZE, LEVELS OF AFFLUENCE AND QUALITY OF LIFE

1=Population (th.); 2= % White; 3=Households (th.); 4=% Owner Occupied; 5=Mean Income Per Household (th.$); 6=Mean Monthly Rent ($)*; 7=Mean Home Value (th.$); 8=% under 5; 9=% 65 and over; 10=White Males (th.); 11=% White Males, 65+; 12=# Toxic Waste Sites; 13=Toxic Waste Relative to US(883 lbs.per capita)**.

OKLAHOMA

OKLAHOMA CITY

ZIPCODE	1	2	3	4	5	6	7	8	9	10	11	12	13
73035	2.5	89	1.0	83	19.0	229	38.3	8	20	1.1	18	0	.0
73036	15.8	86	5.6	72	24.2	258	63.0	8	15	6.7	12	1	.4
73037	2.3	83	.8	80	20.3	209	53.1	9	15	.9	17	3	.0
73038	.6	100	.2	89	24.0	233	64.3	6	21	.9	3	0	.0
73039	.6	100	.2	89	24.0	233	64.3	6	21	.9	3	0	.0
73040	2.6	81	1.0	73	21.6	248	44.6	9	20	1.0	20	0	.5
73041	.7	85	.3	78	23.7	176	26.7	11	17	.3	24	0	.0
73042	1.2	74	.4	66	18.7	210	52.3	10	15	.4	18	0	.0
73043	.3	100	.1	68	20.4	202	44.5	8	12	.2	12	0	.0
73044	16.6	84	5.9	71	22.7	218	65.0	8	16	6.7	13	1	.1
73045	6.0	95	2.1	92	24.4	276	78.1	8	9	2.8	8	0	.0
73046	.3	77	.1	75	17.3	92	20.4	5	11	.1	0	0	.0
73047	2.4	97	1.0	75	25.8	226	60.6	6	21	1.1	18	0	.0
73048	1.6	100	.6	77	24.8	182	58.8	10	21	.8	16	0	.0
73049	3.7	81	1.2	84	25.7	264	64.4	10	13	1.5	10	2	.0
73050	1.0	0	.2	48	14.5	236	33.3	7	6	.0	0	0	.0
73051	5.3	92	1.5	77	20.5	238	56.9	6	12	2.6	10	0	.0
73052	6.6	96	2.4	79	25.4	257	55.4	7	15	3.2	12	6	.0
73053	1.1	92	.4	71	32.8	150	90.9	6	16	.5	12	0	.0
73054	1.7	85	.6	81	24.2	214	58.9	8	10	.7	7	0	.0
73055	8.7	96	3.3	78	19.7	237	57.9	7	18	4.1	15	1	.1
73056	.6	0	.6	89	22.7	255	30.6	5	16	.0	0	0	.0
73057	2.6	94	.9	82	22.1	252	44.7	9	17	1.2	17	1	.1
73058	.2	57	.1	85	18.7	99	27.3	7	25	.1	14	0	.0
73059	2.3	97	.9	84	26.4	195	56.3	8	17	1.1	15	0	.0
73061	1.1	99	.4	80	23.8	252	57.4	9	9	.5	8	0	.5
73062	2.2	88	.9	81	18.2	171	44.7	5	26	.9	24	0	.6
73063	.7	0	.3	84	24.5	286	32.7	6	12	.0	0	0	.0
73065	8.4	97	2.5	92	33.2	448	86.0	9	3	4.1	3	0	.0
73066	2.4	99	.8	89	28.8	454	86.8	7	4	1.2	4	1	1.6
73067	1.4	95	.5	75	22.7	291	67.6	8	12	.6	10	0	.0
73068	1.8	97	.6	93	24.3	68	65.9	6	9	1.0	10	0	1.6
73069	5.5	97	1.9	80	23.2	288	77.2	9	9	2.7	7	0	.0
73071	41.5	93	16.1	53	27.1	345	107.9	6	19	19.5	6	1	23.8
73073	7.4	87	.2	61	45.5	477	83.1	2	15	.7	19	0	.1
73074	23.8	91	8.9	62	26.2	366	94.8	9	4	10.9	5	2	1.5
73075	.4	0	.1	88	19.4	175	37.5	5	19	.5	0	0	.0
73077	.8	93	.3	74	19.0	244	42.0	9	20	.4	15	0	.0
73078	6.5	91	2.4	74	21.0	245	55.0	7	18	2.8	16	1	.0
73079	1.2	89	.4	78	21.8	194	32.5	9	11	.5	8	2	.1
73080	3.1	97	1.2	79	19.4	183	48.4	6	20	1.4	19	0	.0
73081	7.7	35	2.6	82	21.9	235	54.9	9	11	1.3	9	0	1.5
73082	7.5	90	2.8	72	19.6	177	50.3	8	20	3.3	19	1	.0
73084	.4	0	.1	70	12.6	117	25.7	7	14	.0	0	0	.0
73086	6.4	97	2.0	87	28.0	290	92.5	8	7	3.1	6	1	.0
73087	.9	98	.3	87	27.8	226	65.1	9	10	.5	8	0	.0

OKLAHOMA

OKLAHOMA CITY

ZIPCODE	1	2	3	4	5	6	7	8	9	10	11	12	13
73091	1.1	96	.4	80	25.4	228	60.7	12	6	.5	4	1	.0
73092	1.2	98	.5	75	20.7	246	48.8	9	19	.6	20	0	.0
73093	1.8	98	.6	81	28.5	315	94.4	7	7	.8	5	1	.0
73095	1.5	89	.5	80	20.7	317	51.9	4	17	.6	18	0	.0
73096	11.0	93	3.9	55	25.8	279	87.8	7	9	5.1	7	2	.1
73097	.4	0	.1	90	26.9	668	47.3	1	6	.0	0	2	.1
73098	4.4	90	1.6	76	19.8	216	50.9	6	18	1.9	17	2	5.5
73099	24.2	97	7.9	80	35.1	419	101.1	10	5	11.6	4	0	.0

OKLAHOMA CITY

ZIPCODE	1	2	3	4	5	6	7	8	9	10	11	12	13
73102	2.1	63	1.3	3	11.8	197	79.5	3	20	.8	23	1	1.3
73103	6.4	72	3.3	26	19.7	251	113.0	8	15	2.2	11	0	.3
73104	4.3	17	1.7	25	13.4	179	49.1	8	14	.4	11	0	2.0
73105	7.1	13	2.7	60	23.0	261	73.0	8	8	.4	19	2	.2
73106	13.9	79	6.2	40	17.0	240	56.3	9	16	5.1	13	2	1.4
73107	24.7	92	11.7	68	22.7	304	61.6	7	22	10.2	18	1	.2
73108	15.2	78	8.6	55	16.5	210	39.6	11	12	5.6	12	1	2.0
73109	19.1	90	8.0	60	18.1	247	50.6	8	22	7.8	18	3	.9
73110	42.7	89	16.0	66	27.6	360	77.3	8	7	18.1	6	2	.9
73111	19.8	9	6.5	69	23.5	250	62.8	9	10	.9	25	1	.1
73112	30.9	95	15.0	62	29.2	400	88.0	5	20	13.4	16	0	.6
73114	15.1	63	5.7	66	24.9	382	71.0	9	7	4.7	8	2	.0
73115	28.9	88	10.4	73	26.3	335	67.8	8	8	12.5	6	0	.1
73116	10.0	81	4.5	78	55.1	422	153.8	4	18	4.5	16	1	.0
73117	7.6	10	3.1	56	16.3	198	46.9	7	18	.7	7	3	.5
73118	14.8	86	7.2	64	25.0	324	84.1	7	22	5.8	18	2	.9
73119	29.9	94	11.8	70	21.2	300	49.4	9	11	13.5	9	3	.9
73120	25.9	94	10.2	82	46.8	464	141.5	7	10	11.7	8	0	.0
73121	3.2	23	1.1	85	33.7	325	97.5	6	10	.4	14	3	.0
73122	13.7	96	5.6	65	32.2	387	97.0	9	6	6.3	9	0	.6
73127	22.9	88	9.1	47	26.8	330	101.6	8	6	9.9	8	2	.6
73128	2.0	97	.8	80	24.5	361	68.3	12	6	.9	5	4	1.0
73129	21.1	81	7.8	66	18.3	265	40.1	11	12	8.3	12	10	.1
73130	12.2	86	4.1	83	26.2	306	71.4	9	6	5.3	6	2	.0
73131	.2	100	.1	100	48.1	553*	140.3	3	6	.1	0	1	23.8
73132	29.5	95	10.6	66	39.5	386	142.3	8	5	13.5	3	1	.0
73135	11.9	82	6.0	66	26.8	414	77.5	11	5	4.3	4	0	.0
73139	14.5	94	6.0	51	32.2	452	105.3	7	5	6.9	4	0	.0
73141	2.6	94	1.0	76	21.9	249	56.0	11	3	1.2	11	0	.1
73145	3.1	76	.1	1	24.8	328	88.4*10	3	6	.1	0	2	1.5
73149	5.4	90	2.0	70	23.6	335	57.9	10	6	2.5	5	3	.0
73150	1.5	97	.5	72	24.8	388	77.5	10	3	.7	2	1	.1
73153	.5	0	0	94	27.7	452	143.5	7	6	.0	1	4	.0
73159	24.6	94	8.8	78	31.0	401	82.9	8	5	11.4	4	0	.0
73160	34.3	95	10.8	78	29.7	400	81.7	10	3	16.1	3	5	.1
73165	1.2	98	.4	81	31.9	230	122.8	4	7	.6	5	1	.0
73170	3.9	97	1.2	87	41.1	562	131.0	9	4	1.8	4	0	.0

ARDMORE

ZIPCODE	1	2	3	4	5	6	7	8	9	10	11	12	13
73401	30.3	83	11.4	71	24.2	260	66.0	8	16	12.0	14	8	1.4
73430	.5	0	.2	86	29.3	84	87.3	3	19	.0	0	0	.0

*=Estimated **1.0=883 lbs per person, 100++ indicates per capita toxic waste generation > than 100 times the U.S. average of 883 lbs per capita.

PAGE 2.246

ZIP CODE MEASURES OF SIZE, LEVELS OF AFFLUENCE AND QUALITY OF LIFE

1=Population (th.); 2= % White; 3=Households (th.); 4=% Owner Occupied; 5=Mean Income Per Household (th.$); 6=Mean Home Value (th.$)*; 7=Mean Monthly Rent ($)*; 8=% under 5; 9=% 65 and over; 10=% White Males (th.); 11=% White Males, 65+; 12=# Toxic Waste Sites; 13=Toxic Waste Relative to US(883 lbs.per capita)**.

OKLAHOMA

ARDMORE

ZIP CODE	1	2	3	4	5	6	7	8	9	10	11	12	13
73432	.8	95	.3	88	13.6	368	48.4	7	17	.4	14	0	.1
73435	.3	0	.3	92	18.3	211*	23.3	13	11	.0	11	0	.0
73436	.3	80	.1	82	16.8	149	32.5	7	9	.1	11	0	.0
73437	.3	92	.1	75	19.9	229*	14.6	4	9	.1	6	0	.0
73438	4.5	93	1.7	75	21.8	219	40.6	8	17	2.0	15	2	.0
73439	3.9	91	1.6	82	17.7	194	54.6	5	23	1.8	22	1	.0
73440	.3	91	.2	95	13.3	153*	37.1	5	22	.1	28	0	.0
73441	.3	79	.1	89	13.6	228	22.8	0	18	.1	18	0	.0
73442	.6	0	.2	89	24.0	216	24.0	8	10	.0	0	1	.0
73443	2.0	93	.7	77	22.3	274	56.6	9	11	.9	11	0	.0
73446	5.9	91	2.3	76	20.4	183	50.6	5	21	2.5	19	0	.4
73447	1.0	95	.4	65	19.7	204	42.7	7	12	.5	11	1	.0
73448	5.0	90	1.9	78	21.2	207	51.6	7	19	2.1	17	1	.0
73449	1.2	95	.5	79	18.7	179	57.8	5	13	.6	13	0	.0
73450	1.2	85	.5	71	15.5	171	33.9	6	11	.5	10	0	.0
73451	1.2	33	.1	100	14.7	169*	38.6	3	23	.0	36	1	.0
73452	.2	86	.1	73	17.8	212	43.6	6	17	.1	20	0	.0
73453	.3	100	.1	89	30.9	355*	40.7	8	7	.2	8	0	.0
73455	.7	89	.3	82	16.1	173	35.1	5	23	.3	21	0	.0
73456	2.7	93	1.0	73	16.3	163	35.1	8	19	1.2	17	0	.0
73458	.6	78	.2	84	19.1	252	48.5	8	18	.2	20	0	.0
73459	.9	96	.3	67	20.1	200	38.0	10	11	.4	10	0	.0
73460	4.5	83	1.6	69	15.3	188	51.1	7	17	1.8	17	1	.0
73461	.7	88	.3	82	10.2	151	27.8	7	23	.3	25	1	.0
73463	3.6	95	1.4	79	19.3	212	39.7	7	16	1.7	15	2	.0

LAWTON

ZIP CODE	1	2	3	4	5	6	7	8	9	10	11	12	13
73501	40.6	71	15.0	57	20.3	238	60.5	10	10	14.3	9	3	.1
73503	15.9	62	1.4	0	22.8	349	81.2*	6	0	7.5	0	1	.0
73505	43.6	80	14.3	67	25.6	332	74.5	10	5	17.1	5	0	.0
73520	.2	96	.1	67	19.9	126	19.6	14	18	.1	18	0	.0
73521	24.6	83	8.5	60	20.9	255	59.8	10	10	10.3	8	4	.0
73526	2.1	96	.7	71	19.8	209	50.6	9	13	.9	12	0	.0
73527	2.4	79	.8	78	19.3	207	59.4	8	11	1.0	12	0	.0
73528	.8	0	.3	89	26.2	210	53.3	6	15	.4	15	0	.0
73529	5.5	96	2.0	77	21.1	225	49.5	9	15	2.6	14	0	.0
73530	.8	88	.3	68	22.6	171	48.3	4	14	.4	16	0	.0
73531	.5	97	.2	85	18.7	318	52.7	6	16	.2	11	0	.0
73532	.8	92	.3	83	22.2	210	57.7	8	22	.4	24	0	.2
73533	27.3	93	10.6	78	26.0	291	68.7	8	15	12.3	12	6	1.6
73537	1.0	97	.4	83	18.4	204	39.3	5	33	.4	28	0	.0
73538	2.2	86	.8	82	20.9	248	52.6	5	11	.9	12	0	.0
73539	.4	92	.1	74	16.3	188*	24.0	1	14	.2	12	0	.0
73540	.4	87	.1	58	14.2	255	42.9	8	15	.2	11	0	.0
73541	2.2	92	.8	82	21.3	131	50.0	7	13	1.0	12	0	.0
73542	7.0	74	2.7	72	18.6	228	52.1	9	18	2.4	18	0	.0
73543	1.2	93	.4	85	22.5	301	62.8	10	6	.6	6	0	.0
73544	1.2	91	.5	74	15.7	137	36.7	8	33	.5	35	0	.0
73546	1.6	83	.6	76	18.1	163	48.1	7	21	.6	19	0	.0
73547	2.0	92	.7	75	18.4	146	41.4	5	18	1.0	15	0	.0

OKLAHOMA

LAWTON

ZIP CODE	1	2	3	4	5	6	7	8	9	10	11	12	13
73548	.4	0	.2	82	18.3	225	45.9	6	18	.0	0	0	.0
73549	.5	86	.2	81	17.9	318	24.1	9	15	.2	17	0	.0
73550	3.6	83	1.5	77	18.2	132	50.5	7	25	1.4	25	2	.0
73552	1.5	64	.4	79	20.3	172	57.6	7	10	.5	11	0	.0
73554	3.8	91	1.6	79	19.2	173	44.3	5	28	1.6	23	0	.0
73555	.4	92	.1	76	14.4	205	25.7	10	19	.2	15	0	.0
73556	.3	75	.1	68	16.8	201	39.0	6	14	.1	18	0	.0
73557	.4	87	.2	55	15.9	122	24.4	8	12	.2	10	0	.0
73559	.7	95	.3	67	12.0	207	28.7	8	15	.3	17	0	.0
73560	.9	77	.3	68	14.3	166	34.3	8	12	.3	14	0	.0
73562	.8	0	.3	86	18.2	164	47.1	8	19	.3	0	0	.4
73564	.8	94	.4	78	21.0	216	42.6	10	20	.4	17	0	.0
73565	1.4	94	.6	70	16.3	164	37.8	6	27	.6	22	0	.0
73566	2.2	89	.9	74	18.2	156	46.3	8	22	1.0	18	0	.0
73567	.8	92	.3	76	18.3	197	43.7	9	11	.4	8	0	.0
73568	1.8	86	.7	72	16.6	168	41.9	6	23	.7	20	0	.0
73569	.8	89	.3	73	18.6	136	35.7	8	19	.4	20	0	.0
73570	2.0	77	.7	79	25.0	138	37.2	6	20	.7	21	0	.0
73571	.3	80	.1	80	18.8	135	66.8*	2	23	.0	0	0	.0
73572	4.0	88	1.5	78	18.7	176	52.1	8	17	1.7	16	3	.5
73573	2.9	94	1.1	74	21.8	169	49.6	8	20	1.3	18	0	.0

CLINTON

ZIP CODE	1	2	3	4	5	6	7	8	9	10	11	12	13
73601	9.9	83	3.7	69	24.6	268	68.7	8	17	4.0	18	3	.0
73620	1.3	98	.4	86	25.8	266	62.5	12	14	.6	13	1	.0
73622	.4	0	.2	77	24.3	158	50.5	6	16	.2	4	2	.0
73624	2.5	94	.7	71	27.1	319	51.6	14	14	1.2	4	2	.0
73625	.6	94	.2	71	21.7	149	34.5	6	11	.3	10	0	.0
73626	1.2	96	.5	85	24.7	299	54.8	11	11	.6	8	0	.0
73627	.7	0	.3	89	21.7	209	34.6	7	25	.8	19	0	.0
73628	1.8	99	.7	76	28.8	195	57.5	8	22	.8	19	1	.0
73632	4.1	98	1.6	80	24.7	251	60.2	7	22	1.9	18	1	.0
73638	.9	100	.4	62	18.1	208*	90.1	0	23	.1	25	0	.0
73639	.9	98	.4	84	21.7	182	42.7	6	16	.4	16	0	.0
73641	1.1	99	.4	80	21.3	176	44.0	6	21	.5	19	0	.0
73642	.2	100	.1	100	21.3	245*	45.9	9	21	.2	20	0	.0
73644	11.7	95	4.4	77	25.0	295	62.6	9	16	5.4	13	1	.0
73645	1.8	95	.7	80	19.0	190	41.1	7	29	.8	26	6	.0
73646	.2	100	.1	84	22.2	255*	52.3	10	16	.1	13	0	.0
73647	.8	88	.3	65	21.0	120	42.3	7	7	.3	6	0	1.6
73650	1.3	74	.4	81	18.4	226	43.2	9	11	.5	16	0	.0
73651	5.4	86	2.2	73	18.2	157	49.6	8	23	2.2	20	1	1.9
73654	1.1	0	.4	86	26.3	128	50.4	7	24	.0	0	1	.0
73655	.9	96	.5	86	18.2	139	32.0	2	28	.5	24	0	.0
73658	.4	97	.1	82	29.8	130	37.2	10	18	.2	19	0	.0
73659	.2	100	.2	84	17.1	123	41.9	6	37	.3	35	0	.0
73660	.5	100	.2	68	28.7	185	46.1	12	13	.0	0	3	.0
73661	.5	100	.2	95	27.6	124	35.5	5	23	.3	26	0	.0
73662	5.0	97	1.9	71	19.9	230	50.8	8	20	2.3	16	2	.0
73663	1.6	87	.6	84	22.0	149	55.1	8	19	.7	18	0	.0

*=Estimated **1.0=883 lbs per person; 100++ indicates per capita toxic waste generation > than 100 times the U.S. average of 883 lbs per capita.

ZIP CODE MEASURES OF SIZE, LEVELS OF AFFLUENCE AND QUALITY OF LIFE

1=Population (th.); 2= % White; 3=Households (th.); 4=% Owner Occupied; 5=Mean Income Per Household (th.$); 6=Mean Monthly Rent ($)*; 7=Mean Home Value (th.$)*;
8=% under 5; 9-% 65 and over; 10=White Males (th.); 11=% White Males, 65+; 12=# Toxic Waste Sites; 13=Toxic Waste Relative to US(883 lbs.per capita)**.

OKLAHOMA

ZIPCODE	1	2	3	4	5	6	7	8	9	10	11	12	13
CLINTON													
73664	1.2	0	.5	82	17.2	163	41.4	5	27	.0	0	0	.0
73665	.3	100	.1	88	25.3	291*	56.6	11	15	.2	18	0	.0
73666	.5	100	.2	82	17.8	205*	50.1	10	16	.2	19	0	.0
73667	.9	97	.4	81	26.0	299	50.2	9	17	.4	15	0	.0
73669	2.0	92	.8	79	26.0	232	53.8	5	21	.8	17	1	.0
73673	.4	99	.2	83	17.9	31	23.5	2	34	.2	29	0	.0
ENID													
73701	53.4	94	20.4	72	27.6	338	81.8	8	13	24.2	10	12	.9
73716	.8	0	.3	86	22.2	208	45.4	5	22	.0	0	0	.0
73717	7.6	97	3.1	69	25.7	223	64.2	6	19	3.6	16	0	.0
73718	.3	0	.3	92	26.3	158	44.8	8	16	.0	0	0	.0
73719	.2	100	.1	82	14.9	135	43.6	6	20	.1	12	0	.0
73720	.4	100	.1	91	28.8	331*	74.1	7	22	.2	21	0	.0
73721	.3	100	1	100	29.9	343*	78.8	8	4	.2	2	0	.0
73722	.4	100	.1	77	26.8	167	65.7	8	13	.2	12	0	.0
73723	.2	100	.1	85	25.2	233	18.8	2	15	.1	10	0	.0
73724	2.2	86	.8	79	28.4	222	44.0	7	15	.5	14	0	.0
73725	.2	100	.1	81	25.8	297*	37.2	8	15	.2	20	0	.0
73726	.9	98	.3	74	25.1	184	45.8	5	25	.4	24	0	.0
73727	.3	0	.1	78	31.7	222	60.6	7	23	.0	0	0	.1
73728	2.7	99	1.2	82	23.5	191	49.5	6	26	1.3	21	0	.0
73729	.7	0	.3	77	25.7	267	53.5	11	17	.0	0	1	.0
73730	1.0	98	.4	83	20.7	188	38.9	6	17	.5	16	0	.0
73731	.3	0	.1	77	22.8	243	52.6	5	21	.3	12	0	.0
73733	.3	100	.1	81	25.9	299	49.8	4	9	.1	5	0	.0
73734	1.4	91	.5	80	27.6	303	63.3	9	11	.6	11	1	.0
73735	.6	97	.2	79	24.9	263	74.8	10	12	.3	12	1	.0
73736	.5	0	.2	82	30.9	316	76.7	5	19	.0	0	0	.0
73737	4.1	97	1.6	79	26.7	244	74.8	7	19	1.9	15	0	.8
73738	1.7	98	.6	81	21.9	226	51.8	7	22	.8	20	0	.8
73739	.5	0	.2	89	22.5	256	45.0	9	20	.6	13	0	.0
73741	1.1	94	.3	77	25.2	276	53.7	8	17	.6	13	0	.0
73742	3.8	95	1.4	79	27.2	256	77.0	9	17	1.8	15	1	.0
73743	.2	100	.1	74	30.6	337	50.5	10	12	.1	10	0	.0
73744	.3	0	.1	76	26.2	197	49.3	4	25	.0	0	0	.0
73747	.5	100	.2	84	20.6	236*	50.4	10	14	.2	9	0	.0
73749	.6	0	.3	82	23.4	201	38.2	7	32	.3	11	0	.0
73750	6.2	93	2.3	78	25.7	290	81.0	8	16	2.8	13	0	.0
73753	.5	100	.2	75	23.7	368	65.4	12	8	.3	8	0	.0
73754	1.1	99	.3	82	27.4	368	83.0	12	6	.5	6	0	.0
73755	.5	92	1.4	85	19.1	296	82.2	10	9	.2	11	0	.0
73756	.5	0	.2	64	22.4	258*	66.8	5	14	.0	0	0	.0
73757	.5	100	.1	85	16.1	186*	21.8	0	17	.1	11	0	.0
73758	.4	100	0	79	20.7	324	32.6	6	27	.0	0	0	.0
73759	2.3	98	.9	75	23.3	262	59.5	7	20	1.1	18	1	.0
73760	.5	0	.2	88	25.5	65	72.8	7	23	.0	0	0	.0
73761	.7	100	.3	81	20.9	295	42.1	7	28	.4	22	1	.0
73762	2.0	100	.8	81	27.0	287	84.9	10	10	1.0	7	1	.1
73763	2.2	98	.9	81	26.0	251	63.5	7	22	1.1	18	0	.1

OKLAHOMA

ZIPCODE	1	2	3	4	5	6	7	8	9	10	11	12	13
ENID													
73764	.2	100	.1	49	29.3	183	98.0	9	3	.0	5	0	.0
73766	1.4	99	.5	81	22.4	271	48.7	6	20	.6	17	0	.3
73768	1.3	98	.4	79	26.5	325	59.3	12	9	.6	9	0	.0
73771	.9	100	.1	73	18.7	120	24.4	12	9	.3	20	1	1.8
73772	5.7	85	2.2	72	23.4	199	45.2	6	30	2.3	13	1	.2
73773	1.9	99	.7	83	27.2	250	64.4	8	17	.9	7	0	.0
WOODWARD													
73801	16.4	97	5.9	71	29.4	359	75.9	10	9	7.8	7	14	1.0
73832	1.2	98	.5	79	22.5	181	47.3	7	21	.6	19	0	2.5
73834	1.7	97	.7	83	23.5	212	50.9	6	22	.8	18	0	.0
73835	.4	100	.1	82	23.1	200	41.6	9	31	.2	28	0	.0
73838	.6	100	.3	84	20.1	269	50.8	5	28	.3	30	0	.0
73840	.8	0	.3	84	22.7	298	50.5	8	17	.5	0	0	.3
73841	1.0	94	.3	77	21.3	188	50.9	5	14	.5	11	0	.0
73842	.8	95	.3	85	30.1	163	54.7	8	13	.6	15	0	.0
73843	1.2	100	.5	81	23.1	288	43.9	8	18	.6	14	0	.0
73844	.4	100	.2	76	33.2	125	46.1	9	19	.2	20	0	.1
73847	.1	100	.1	77	29.7	354	38.1	3	23	.1	25	0	2.8
73848	2.4	99	1.0	81	26.8	243	52.6	8	18	1.2	15	0	.0
73849	.2	100	.1	67	27.0	311*	96.3*	7	27	1	20	0	.0
73851	.2	100	.1	85	21.8	188	40.7	8	22	1	25	0	.0
73852	2.2	99	.8	84	23.9	240	62.5	8	18	1.1	15	1	.0
73853	.6	100	.1	85	31.8	177	73.5	11	12	.3	12	0	.0
73855	.3	100	.1	82	31.0	309	52.2	13	11	1	10	0	.0
73856	.3	0	.1	82	33.8	388*	28.3	6	9	.0	0	0	.0
73857	.7	0	.2	83	31.3	261	68.1	8	17	.0	0	0	.0
73858	2.2	0	.9	75	23.7	239	62.0	9	20	.7	21	0	.1
73859	1.5	99	.6	76	20.6	209	48.8	13	23	.9	24	1	.0
73860	1.9	97	.8	81	18.7	184	35.1	6	27	.9	24	1	.0
LIBERAL													
73901	.1	100	.1	57	19.8	159	40.3	10	26	.1	27	0	.0
73931	.8	100	.3	82	23.2	205	46.3	12	9	.4	9	0	.0
73932	2.5	97	1.0	80	25.4	261	65.8	9	16	1.1	14	1	.0
73933	2.3	95	.9	79	20.7	187	48.8	7	16	1.1	14	1	.0
73937	.9	100	.1	69	21.8	155	48.1	8	10	.4	18	0	.0
73938	.3	100	.3	81	23.0	231	47.0	6	14	.4	13	0	.0
73939	1.4	93	.4	53	23.4	162	55.6	9	5	.7	4	0	.0
73942	10.0	94	3.6	74	27.8	276	76.3	10	10	4.7	8	4	1.3
73944	.5	95	.2	72	22.8	181	43.4	5	21	1.2	15	0	.0
73945	2.6	97	1.0	84	26.6	237	63.0	9	12	1.2	13	0	.0
73947	.7	96	.3	71	26.8	202	38.1	7	18	.6	17	0	.1
73948	.3	0	.1	58	20.6	156	27.5	8	7	.0	0	0	.0
73950	1.1	98	.5	79	21.9	235	58.6	8	16	.6	14	0	.0
73951	1.1	98	.4	83	26.0	279	65.2	9	8	.6	7	0	1.0
TULSA													
74001	.5	88	.2	79	17.8	157	27.0	9	12	.2	12	0	.0
74002	2.1	86	.8	81	19.8	169	34.2	7	23	.9	20	3	11.7

*=Estimated **1.0=883 lbs per person; 100++ indicates per capita toxic waste generation > than 100 times the U.S. average of 883 lbs per capita.

ZIP CODE MEASURES OF SIZE, LEVELS OF AFFLUENCE AND QUALITY OF LIFE

1=Population (th.); 2= % White; 3=Households (th.); 4=% Owner Occupied; 5=Mean Income Per Household (th.$); 6=Mean Monthly Rent ($)*; 7=Mean Home Value (th.$)*; 8=% under 5; 9=% 65 and over; 10=White Males (th.); 11=% White Males, 65+; 12=# Toxic Waste Sites; 13=Toxic Waste Relative to US(883 lbs.per capita)**.

OKLAHOMA

TULSA

ZIP CODE	1	2	3	4	5	6	7	8	9	10	11	12	13
74003	38.6	92	15.3	75	32.4	312	86.8	7	13	16.9	11	4	.6
74008	10.4	95	3.5	83	28.8	311	94.6	8	8	4.9	7	0	.0
74009	.2	0	.1	75	61.6	210	57.0	8	10	.0	0	0	.0
74010	8.9	86	3.2	75	20.6	215	48.0	8	16	3.7	12	2	.2
74012	49.7	95	15.7	82	33.4	417	108.4	10	4	23.7	4	4	.2
74015	4.0	92	1.5	83	30.2	236	92.6	8	6	1.8	7	2	12.9
74016	4.1	84	1.4	80	21.6	244	49.2	8	14	1.8	12	0	.0
74017	25.5	88	8.7	77	27.4	308	84.5	8	10	11.2	8	1	.3
74020	6.1	95	2.3	81	25.4	256	74.7	7	15	2.9	12	2	.0
74021	9.5	94	3.2	84	27.8	312	79.6	7	8	4.4	7	0	.0
74022	1.7	91	.6	87	23.5	262	56.3	8	11	.8	9	0	.0
74023	11.4	91	4.6	77	23.5	236	53.5	8	18	5.0	15	7	1.4
74026	1.1	94	.4	76	19.3	211	39.0	8	15	.5	12	0	.0
74027	1.3	90	.4	73	20.2	291	29.0	7	11	.6	13	1	.0
74028	2.1	91	.8	70	19.8	173	41.0	10	13	.9	12	0	.0
74029	5.1	85	2.0	78	23.6	258	55.9	7	14	2.1	11	0	.5
74030	4.3	95	1.7	77	21.6	170	38.7	8	22	2.0	18	3	.0
74031	.2	89	.1	86	25.0	228	52.3	10	13	.6	17	0	.0
74032	1.3	98	.5	86	25.0	219	48.1	10	13	.6	13	0	.2
74033	1.6	82	.5	91	23.5	285	65.2	12	3	.6	2	0	.0
74034	.2	100	.1	84	14.5	233	39.5	14	12	.1	15	0	.0
74035	4.2	78	1.5	72	20.8	228	47.0	7	14	1.7	13	0	.0
74036	4.2	92	1.3	83	27.1	285	79.9	8	7	1.9	6	0	.0
74037	6.9	94	2.3	84	31.1	386	101.0	8	8	3.2	6	1	.1
74038	2.1	98	.7	82	24.2	223	41.5	8	8	1.1	8	0	.0
74039	2.4	91	.8	85	21.9	235	50.4	9	8	1.1	8	1	.0
74040	.1	100	.1	77	13.7	131	22.3	4	25	.1	21	0	.0
74041	1.5	87	.5	78	22.1	380	66.5	9	6	.6	5	0	.0
74042	.4	78	.1	86	16.9	166	29.9	8	15	.2	14	0	.0
74043	.2	100	.1	69	20.1	152	67.7	10	5	.1	6	0	.0
74044	5.2	96	1.8	87	27.6	322	84.0	7	7	2.5	7	2	.2
74045	.3	0	.1	87	20.2	113	34.6	6	31	.0	0	0	.0
74046	.1	100		41	12.8	101	13.1	6	37	.1	35	0	.0
74047	3.5	91	1.1	80	25.6	269	62.1	6	10	1.6	12	1	.1
74048	6.8	85	2.7	79	22.9	195	48.8	8	19	2.8	16	3	.0
74050	1.2	87	.4	78	18.3	187	34.6	8	11	.6	11	0	.0
74051	1.4	83	.5	83	20.2	297	60.2	10	6	.6	6	0	.0
74053	1.4	78	.5	78	17.5	113	33.1	6	18	.6	18	0	.0
74053	2.4	95	.8	86	30.1	337	82.9	7	7	1.2	5	1	.0
74054	.6	93		78	20.8	87	56.0	7	10	.3	9	1	.0
74055	11.9	94	3.8	81	31.4	312	96.6	9	4	5.6	3	0	.0
74056	6.5	74	2.6	71	23.5	204	49.8	8	18	2.3	16	0	.0
74058	4.3	86	1.7	74	21.8	211	48.9	8	19	1.8	19	1	.0
74059	3.2	96	1.3	83	21.6	232	57.6	7	15	1.5	13	3	.2
74060	.7	95		87	21.5	269	52.1	7	12	.3	12	0	.0
74061	1.7	91	.6	79	23.2	176	42.4	9	13	.7	13	0	.0
74062	.8	95	.3	81	19.2	184	47.5	7	14	.4	16	0	.0
74063	22.4	93	7.5	78	28.1	289	80.1	8	8	10.4	6	7	1.6
74066	25.2	87	9.0	76	24.2	296	69.4	8	12	10.6	10	6	.2

OKLAHOMA

TULSA

ZIP CODE	1	2	3	4	5	6	7	8	9	10	11	12	13
74068	.2	0		89	16.2	75	17.1	11	12	.0	0	0	.0
74070	7.2	87	2.5	83	25.0	287	62.4	8	10	3.1	9	0	.0
74071	.2	75	.1	87	15.5	141	19.2	10	18	.1	3	1	.0
74072	1.8	92	.7	85	20.0	227	43.2	6	13	.8	14	0	.2
74073	3.5	89	1.2	80	28.9	246	56.5	7	11	1.6	10	0	.0
74074	43.0	91	14.6	49	20.7	310	91.2	6	7	20.2	6	4	.2
74079	4.7	90	1.7	78	21.4	203	48.1	6	15	2.1	14	2	.6
74080	1.5	97	.5	84	23.6	347	57.9	6	9	.7	9	0	.0
74081	1.8	97	.6	94	25.3	179	80.9	7	9	.9	8	0	.0
74082	.2	0	.1	94	20.2	232*	35.2	6	12	.1	7	1	100++
74083	1.0	91	.3	90	24.0	182	46.4	10	11	.5	13	2	8.4
74084	1.0	87	.3	80	22.4	138	30.1	9	11	.4	15	1	.3
74085	2.7	96	1.0	76	21.5	179	39.0	8	16	1.3	12	2	.2

TULSA

ZIP CODE	1	2	3	4	5	6	7	8	9	10	11	12	13
74102	.4	100	.1	86	35.4	406*	103.1	2	28	.1	7	1	100++
74103	.9	68	.2	19	13.4	140	19.5	1	12	.5	13	2	8.4
74104	15.5	88	7.4	51	19.4	310	71.4	6	19	6.4	15	1	.3
74105	32.2	95	13.8	56	36.0	389	135.0	5	13	14.3	11	2	.2
74106	26.6	20	9.3	63	17.4	215	40.8	9	14	2.4	17	0	.1
74107	22.0	86	8.0	70	22.2	246	62.2	9	11	3.3	9	1	1.5
74108	7.7	89	2.4	69	27.3	376	77.3	12	3	3.3	3	0	.0
74110	16.2	72	6.6	65	17.3	276	41.2	10	15	5.5	12	2	.0
74112	23.2	93	10.3	69	25.5	365	73.8	6	16	10.1	14	2	.3
74114	18.2	96	7.6	83	43.3	387	127.3	6	20	7.9	16	0	.4
74115	28.0	88	10.7	74	21.9	310	52.4	10	9	12.1	8	9	2.0
74116	2.8	89	1.2	52	24.4	349	82.9	8	6	1.8	7	3	2.3
74119	4.7	87	3.2	33	21.1	306	121.1	3	24	1.8	13	2	2.3
74120	6.9	85	3.7	33	20.2	241	91.3	5	17	2.7	13	2	1.1
74126	16.5	30	4.6	76	20.0	353	40.5	11	5	2.4	10	0	.4
74127	19.9	80	7.6	69	22.1	237	59.8	9	13	7.6	13	1	.4
74128	13.8	93	5.0	70	29.3	386	83.4	8	5	6.4	4	1	.0
74129	19.1	93	4.3	62	30.7	386	97.3	7	8	8.8	4	2	.0
74130	2.5	67	1.0	79	23.1	293	48.7	9	7	.9	7	0	.0
74131	1.0	96	.3	90	28.6	321	106.8	4	4	.5	4	0	1.4
74132	4.8	94	1.5	89	37.8	392	109.2	8	4	2.2	5	2	.0
74133	12.7	97	4.3	78	47.3	424	158.7	8	3	6.1	3	0	.0
74134	4.7	90	1.6	67	31.8	395	95.8	11	2	2.1	1	0	.0
74135	24.1	94	10.6	57	37.6	397	97.3	8	6	10.5	11	1	.1
74136	28.2	94	11.9	44	23.1	402	230.9	6	5	12.9	4	0	.6
74138	.6	83	.4	88	29.9	407	95.2	11	11	.4	10	1	.0
74145	34.2	94	13.5	62	33.0	404	108.1	7	5	15.8	4	1	1.2

TULSA

ZIP CODE	1	2	3	4	5	6	7	8	9	10	11	12	13
74301	11.3	82	4.2	76	20.1	209	54.4	6	20	4.5	18	1	.2
74330	1.9	94	.7	87	22.7	221	62.7	8	12	.8	12	0	.0
74331	3.8	91	1.6	79	18.8	207	64.5	5	20	1.7	21	0	.0
74332	1.4	90	.5	88	20.4	292	43.6	9	16	.6	16	0	.2
74333	.8	95	.3	89	20.7	215	32.1	7	9	.5	9	0	.0
74335	.4	0	.1	89	11.7	121	19.3	7	11	.0	0	3	13.3
74336	.7	92	.3	83	18.9	304	47.5	7	21	.3	19	0	.0

*=Estimated **1.0=883 lbs per person; 100++ indicates per capita toxic waste generation > than 100 times the U.S. average of 883 lbs per capita.

ZIP CODE MEASURES OF SIZE, LEVELS OF AFFLUENCE AND QUALITY OF LIFE

1=Population (th.); 2= % White; 3=Households (th.); 4=% Owner Occupied; 5=Mean Income Per Household (th.$); 6=Mean Monthly Rent ($); 7=Mean Home Value (th.$);
8=% under 5; 9=% 65 and over; 10=White Males (th.); 11=% White Males, 65+; 12=# Toxic Waste Sites; 13=Toxic Waste Relative to US(883 lbs.per capita)**.

OKLAHOMA

TULSA

ZIP CODE	1	2	3	4	5	6	7	8	9	10	11	12	13
74337	2.4	89	.7	81	21.4	294	68.7	9	11	1.0	10	1	.0
74338	2.1	74	.7	78	16.0	238	41.6	7	9	.8	11	0	.0
74339	2.8	82	1.1	74	17.0	217	37.9	6	15	1.0	14	0	.0
74340	.8	89	.4	88	16.8	215	70.7	5	26	.3	28	0	.0
74342	1.4	71	.5	88	16.7	97	57.6	8	14	.5	11	0	.0
74343	2.4	88	.9	79	17.0	184	50.8	5	19	1.0	17	0	.0
74344	6.9	88	2.8	84	18.2	215	78.1	4	26	2.9	28	1	.0
74346	4.3	74	1.5	76	15.6	192	44.7	8	18	1.5	19	0	.0
74347	1.1	52	.3	80	15.3	275	48.5	9	10	.2	13	0	.0
74349	.5	87	.2	68	14.6	243	61.7	8	21	.2	24	0	.0
74350	.7	93	.3	79	14.7	214	51.7	5	23	.3	24	0	.0
74351	.4	53	.1	62	9.9	149	37.2	12	10	.1	0	0	.0
74352	5.1	80	1.8	85	18.5	204	49.3	7	14	2.0	15	0	.0
74354	17.9	88	6.8	74	21.8	212	60.8	7	14	7.4	12	1	.2
74358	.5	83	.2	68	21.5	198	37.8	13	7	.2	7	0	.0
74359	.5	30	.1	85	14.1	215	46.1	9	9	.1	16	0	.0
74360	2.3	88	.8	69	13.6	148	22.1	8	13	.9	10	0	.1
74361	13.7	91	5.0	74	23.4	268	66.7	8	14	6.0	12	17	4.9
74363	2.7	78	.8	82	19.7	212	37.1	8	10	1.1	9	0	.0
74364	1.0	82	.4	87	19.5	166	32.5	7	14	.4	16	0	.0
74365	4.4	69	1.4	78	17.5	240	51.8	10	12	1.5	13	1	.0
74366	1.4	76	.6	77	15.8	140	53.8	7	15	.5	20	0	.0
74367	.5	87	.2	79	11.5	173	28.5	6	18	.4	16	0	.0
74368	.2	49	.1	75	12.5	225	50.4	5	29	.3	35	0	.0
74369	1.3	88	.5	84	21.6	206	40.3	6	18	.6	15	1	.1
74370	1.5	79	.5	81	20.8	160	45.8	7	14	.6	16	0	.0

MUSKOGEE

ZIP CODE	1	2	3	4	5	6	7	8	9	10	11	12	13
74401	49.7	75	19.0	70	21.9	247	60.6	8	15	17.8	13	12	.2
74421	3.1	75	.4	81	20.8	194	55.1	9	13	1.1	15	0	.0
74422	1.2	63	.3	69	15.5	235	23.7	7	13	.4	15	0	.0
74423	.9	91	.3	83	19.0	181	37.3	9	10	.4	9	0	.0
74425	.6	89	.3	81	15.2	257	39.4	4	17	.3	17	0	.0
74426	7.6	83	2.9	76	17.2	195	50.1	6	18	3.0	17	0	.2
74427	.7	95	.3	90	19.1	280	70.9	5	17	.3	22	0	.0
74428	.7	92	.3	86	18.2	243	68.8	6	17	.3	20	0	.0
74429	8.2	88	2.6	76	25.7	250	74.7	7	10	3.6	7	0	.0
74430	.5	0	.2	78	17.2	206	40.4	10	14	.0	0	0	.0
74431	.9	84	.3	86	19.1	246	31.1	6	15	.3	17	0	.0
74432	6.7	83	2.6	79	17.8	196	58.0	6	24	2.7	24	0	.0
74434	5.4	88	1.8	81	23.0	260	60.9	8	10	2.4	9	1	.2
74435	1.8	87	.6	85	18.0	257	55.2	9	12	.8	12	0	8.6
74436	3.9	81	1.4	83	18.5	205	44.8	6	17	1.5	15	0	.0
74437	10.2	87	3.8	80	17.8	212	45.9	6	19	4.2	17	1	.0
74438	.3	79	.1	76	11.2	221	17.9	7	23	.7	18	0	.0
74439	.4	71	.1	87	17.5	162	32.0	7	19	.3	17	0	.0
74441	4.0	71	1.4	80	18.5	217	54.5	8	11	1.4	14	0	.0
74442	.7	89	.4	85	21.1	162	36.6	3	20	.4	25	0	.0
74445	2.5	87	.9	77	19.2	198	42.4	9	13	1.1	12	0	.0
74446	.9	86	.3	78	20.8	233	48.4	7	11	.4	9	0	.0

OKLAHOMA

MUSKOGEE

ZIP CODE	1	2	3	4	5	6	7	8	9	10	11	12	13
74447	20.0	71	7.3	69	18.9	207	48.5	7	17	7.2	13	6	.5
74450	1.4	81	.5	86	20.3	280	72.0	7	7	.6	8	0	.0
74451	2.2	84	.8	82	22.4	313	60.7	8	19	.9	21	0	.0
74452	.3	76	.8	69	18.0	317	46.6	8	6	1	5	0	.0
74454	2.1	80	.8	79	19.6	205	47.0	6	17	.8	13	0	.0
74455	2.5	88	1.0	77	15.8	149	31.4	6	15	1	14	1	.0
74456	.4	60	.1	65	22.3	193	59.1	6	7	1	6	0	.0
74457	.5	64	.2	92	18.4	320	46.9	8	8	.2	5	0	.0
74458	.2	0	.1	82	9.7	188	29.7	9	22	.0	0	0	.0
74460	.5	93	.2	89	21.5	292	24.0	6	13	.2	13	0	.0
74461	.2	81	.1	90	13.9	190	29.0	8	16	.1	6	0	.0
74462	5.9	89	2.4	76	16.6	186	47.9	7	20	2.6	18	0	.0
74463	.5	15	.2	69	13.8	190	39.0	7	14	.1	0	0	.1
74464	19.8	71	6.8	67	17.8	216	65.8	8	12	6.7	11	0	.2
74466	.3	0	.1	67	10.5	206	24.6	2	14	.2	0	0	.0
74467	11.5	87	4.3	79	21.2	245	63.1	8	17	4.8	16	0	.3
74468	.4	100	.1	85	18.4	253	23.7	7	13	.1	11	0	.0
74469	2.0	87	.6	78	20.0	170	57.5	9	9	.8	9	0	.0
74470	1.5	82	.5	74	14.9	211	42.9	9	14	.6	13	0	.0
74471	1.2	66	.4	93	18.6	197	44.9	5	10	.4	9	0	.0
74472	.2	0	.1	72	16.3	203	54.3	4	10	.0	0	0	.0

MCALESTER

ZIP CODE	1	2	3	4	5	6	7	8	9	10	11	12	13
74501	24.1	87	8.9	74	20.6	222	54.1	7	16	10.1	12	2	.2
74521	.3	72	.1	72	16.7	91	29.6	6	13	.1	14	0	.0
74522	.4	79	.1	80	14.9	189	33.0	6	20	.0	21	0	.1
74523	5.9	89	2.3	74	16.3	175	41.1	6	21	2.5	20	0	.1
74525	7.6	87	2.7	69	17.2	175	45.2	8	18	3.1	18	4	.0
74528	.3	66	.1	61	15.3	143	38.8	7	23	.1	30	0	.0
74530	.9	95	.3	83	14.1	116	23.7	7	24	.0	0	0	.0
74531	.9	95	.3	80	13.8	122	31.9	6	14	.4	11	0	.0
74533	.9	90	.3	80	17.8	141	40.0	5	11	.5	11	0	.0
74534	.4	82	.1	81	18.7	151	25.0	7	6	.2	5	0	.0
74535	.1	0	.1	77	20.1	57	27.4	6	15	.0	0	0	.0
74536	1.8	86	.7	72	15.9	169	39.8	9	17	.8	17	0	.0
74538	4.0	88	1.5	75	16.4	165	36.7	6	23	1.6	21	0	.0
74540	.7	0	.1	79	16.5	189*	50.3	6	21	.0	0	0	.0
74542	.8	83	.2	72	15.1	174*	53.5	5	12	.4	9	0	.0
74543	.4	86	.1	95	15.3	176*	35.6	5	22	.2	15	0	.1
74546	.8	87	.3	78	16.1	138	32.5	6	18	.2	17	0	.0
74547	4.0	81	1.4	76	18.1	163	37.6	7	18	1.5	15	0	.1
74548	1.0	95	.3	86	20.0	200	32.6	10	13	.5	7	0	.0
74552	.4	86	.4	79	18.2	168	36.4	7	22	.4	20	0	.0
74553	1.6	93	.5	73	17.7	156	27.0	7	17	.7	18	0	.1
74554	1.7	88	.1	76	16.1	196	42.0	6	14	.7	14	1	.0
74555	.7	86	.2	86	19.0	74	32.7	4	9	.3	6	0	.0
74556	.3	86	.1	81	14.6	128	22.1	9	24	.1	22	0	.0
74557	.5	100	.2	85	18.8	99	41.3	8	8	.3	10	0	.0
74558	.4	100	.1	63	17.3	293	30.6	10	11	.2	7	0	.0
74560	.7	87	.3	78	18.9	122	30.8	9	12	.3	14	0	.0

*=Estimated **1.0=883 lbs per person; 100++ indicates per capita toxic waste generation > than 100 times the U.S. average of 883 lbs per capita.

1=Population (th.); 2=% White; 3=Households (th.); 4=% Owner Occupied; 5=Mean Income Per Household (th.); 6=Mean Monthly Rent ($)*; 7=Mean Home Value (th.$)*; 8=% under 5, 9=% 65 and over; 10=% White Males (th.); 11=% White Males, 65+; 12=# Toxic Waste Sites; 13=Toxic Waste Relative to US(883 lbs.per capita)**.

OKLAHOMA

MCALESTER

ZIPCODE	1	2	3	4	5	6	7	8	9	10	11	12	13
74561	2.3	90	.8	75	17.5	173	31.9	8	17	1.1	13	0	.0
74562	.9	86	.3	84	16.3	207	42.4	7	10	.4	17	1	.0
74563	1.8	83	.6	82	14.9	176	32.7	6	16	.8	17	0	.0
74565	.8	93	.8	76	16.5	173	33.4	8	12	.4	7	1	.0
74567	.8	0	.1	76	18.9	62	30.4	8	14	.9	0	0	.0
74569	1.4	66	.3	80	13.1	169	28.7	6	9	.6	8	2	.2
74570	1.2	95	.5	85	18.9	127	32.5	9	19	.6	21	0	.0
74571	3.6	70	1.3	63	16.3	179	40.9	7	21	1.2	22	0	.0
74572	1.0	79	.3	59	13.9	179	31.6	11	11	.4	10	0	.0
74574	1.0	74	.4	86	12.1	115	53.9	6	18	.4	19	0	.0
74576	.2	100	.1	92	11.3	130*	28.0	0	27	.1	28	0	.0
74577	.4	83	.1	66	18.2	152	25.3	6	9	.2	9	0	.0
74578	5.9	85	2.0	70	18.1	188	44.5	6	15	2.4	14	0	.0

PONCA CITY

ZIPCODE	1	2	3	4	5	6	7	8	9	10	11	12	13
74601	33.4	91	13.0	75	27.0	302	79.6	8	14	14.7	12	5	13.1
74630	1.0	0	.3	81	20.3	259	35.6	7	17	.0	0	0	.1
74631	9.3	96	3.7	76	23.0	241	51.6	8	19	4.2	15	4	.2
74632	.3	0	.3	79	20.4	229	33.0	6	18	.2	14	0	.0
74633	.5	93	.2	74	18.9	127	19.0	6	18	.2	14	0	.0
74636	.4	100	.2	88	25.4	214	36.6	4	20	.2	20	0	.0
74637	2.4	80	1.0	72	17.9	191	38.0	6	20	.9	19	0	.0
74640	.5	99	.2	64	28.9	491	42.6	7	16	.2	16	0	.0
74641	.2	89	.2	75	20.2	435	83.1	5	20	.2	22	0	.0
74642	.5	97	.2	67	22.7	250	38.5	8	20	.2	26	0	.0
74643	.8	0	.3	83	24.3	212	42.5	11	25	.0	0	0	.0
74644	.6	74	.2	58	22.1	309	34.2	10	8	.0	7	0	.0
74646	.3	0	.1	96	28.0	322*	45.0	4	19	.0	0	1	.0
74647	3.9	90	1.4	76	23.6	213	55.1	6	18	1.6	17	0	.0
74650	.9	85	.4	69	15.9	210	23.7	6	22	.4	26	1	.0
74651	.8	62	.3	75	21.7	223	31.1	8	16	.3	18	0	.0
74652	1.2	93	.5	75	20.6	150	23.6	7	19	.6	13	1	.0
74653	4.3	92	1.5	74	22.0	213	57.7	6	17	1.9	15	0	.4
74654	.2	100	.1	94	19.6	226*	14.5	14	25	.1	27	0	.0

DURANT

ZIPCODE	1	2	3	4	5	6	7	8	9	10	11	12	13
74701	17.0	90	6.6	62	18.3	230	57.0	7	16	7.2	14	3	.4
74720	.6	86	.2	79	18.1	180	34.5	8	16	.3	10	0	.0
74721	.1	100	.1	89	14.7	169*	29.0	6	37	.1	59	0	.0
74722	.3	57	.1	67	12.4	233	31.6	4	7	.1	14	0	.0
74723	1.5	85	.5	84	18.0	198	29.7	7	14	.6	16	0	.0
74724	.4	66	.1	51	14.8	131	49.3	14	7	.1	10	0	.0
74726	2.0	93	.8	82	13.8	176	31.3	7	24	.9	21	0	.0
74727	2.1	80	.8	77	13.9	153	34.0	7	19	.8	18	0	.0
74728	11.0	84	3.7	74	18.3	208	49.1	8	12	4.6	12	3	.0
74729	2.0	91	.7	80	14.6	154	33.7	6	21	.9	19	1	.0
74730	2.2	95	.8	82	19.2	196	45.8	7	15	1.0	14	0	.0
74731	1.2	87	.5	88	16.7	159	43.8	4	16	.5	20	0	.0
74733	1.9	84	.7	77	17.2	187	40.4	9	16	.8	11	0	.0
74734	1.2	88	.4	84	15.8	83	36.1	6	12	.6	11	0	.0
74735	1.6	87	.6	78	16.9	242	38.3	6	16	.7	12	1	.0

OKLAHOMA

DURANT

ZIPCODE	1	2	3	4	5	6	7	8	9	10	11	12	13
74736	1.0	97	.3	83	24.1	239	23.6	8	8	.5	9	0	.0
74737	.2	100	.1	66	14.4	191	33.5	12	11	.1	7	0	.0
74738	.7	52	.3	77	13.1	192	22.4	8	18	.2	17	0	.0
74740	3.4	75	1.1	80	16.6	199	33.4	8	16	1.3	14	0	.0
74741	.9	87	.4	78	19.9	152	34.1	6	10	.4	9	0	.0
74743	10.2	74	3.8	80	18.0	180	46.5	8	17	3.6	15	3	.1
74745	10.9	71	4.0	85	17.1	198	48.9	9	16	3.6	13	2	.0
74747	.2	0	.1	63	14.9	176	28.4	7	28	.0	0	0	.0
74748	.3	100	.3	59	14.2	178	40.4	4	14	.2	10	0	.0
74750	.3	86	.1	86	23.9	96	36.8	10	9	.1	5	0	.0
74751	.5	0	.2	70	16.4	167	19.1	6	9	.0	0	0	.0
74754	.3	71	.1	61	18.1	181	40.8	11	15	.1	18	0	.0
74755	.2	100	.1	78	15.2	175*	24.1	4	9	.1	9	0	.0
74756	.6	90	.2	88	16.1	111	22.5	10	20	.2	14	0	.0
74759	1.4	79	.5	74	14.5	161	31.1	7	17	.6	16	0	.0
74760	.2	78	.1	60	16.7	184	59.5*	3	19	.1	31	0	.0
74761	.2	100	.1	91	27.4	315*	20.2	0	19	.1	19	0	.0
74764	3.3	86	1.1	75	20.2	224	41.5	11	14	1.4	11	1	.9
74766	2.1	77	.6	84	20.5	171	31.7	10	5	.8	5	1	.6

SHAWNEE

ZIPCODE	1	2	3	4	5	6	7	8	9	10	11	12	13
74801	35.2	89	13.2	72	22.4	258	65.0	7	16	14.7	13	2	.2
74820	25.8	88	9.7	68	21.5	242	65.8	7	16	10.7	14	2	.1
74824	1.1	0	.4	78	22.0	240	35.2	9	8	.0	0	0	.0
74825	2.3	86	.8	77	17.4	157	39.6	8	16	1.0	14	1	.6
74826	1.2	94	.4	79	16.9	262	27.7	4	18	.5	18	0	.0
74827	.4	100	.2	89	12.7	192	24.6	5	27	.3	22	0	.0
74829	.9	13	.3	68	15.5	212	29.6	10	16	.1	4	0	.0
74830	.5	83	.2	57	20.7	210	30.5	9	10	.1	9	0	.0
74831	.9	95	.3	87	16.7	104	26.0	5	18	.4	15	0	.0
74832	.9	0	.3	81	23.5	204	43.4	10	10	.3	10	0	.0
74833	.7	40	.2	85	16.3	79	23.2	7	15	.1	19	0	.0
74834	5.7	92	2.1	80	21.0	228	61.0	8	18	2.4	14	2	.1
74836	.3	49	.1	58	14.5	256	19.5	7	17	.1	40	0	.4
74837	.5	79	.2	72	17.0	211	29.5	6	10	.2	11	0	.0
74838	.3	0	.1	55	19.1	322	45.9	11	18	.0	0	0	.0
74839	.9	74	.3	79	16.2	141	31.1	6	18	.4	21	3	.0
74840	1.3	78	.5	87	25.9	204	43.8	9	13	.5	14	0	.0
74842	.2	100	.1	71	18.6	241	36.5	3	15	.2	16	0	.0
74843	.2	0	.1	76	22.1	254*	47.6	7	36	.5	18	0	.0
74844	.3	0	.1	73	19.5	271	39.2	9	18	.3	22	0	.0
74845	.5	82	.2	70	12.5	181	24.4	8	26	.2	24	0	.0
74848	8.2	84	3.3	74	16.7	200	40.8	6	23	3.2	22	2	.0
74849	3.6	85	1.2	74	17.4	197	41.8	5	17	1.5	15	2	.1
74850	.3	89	.1	83	14.8	183	35.5	3	9	.2	3	0	.0
74851	5.2	93	1.6	87	25.1	243	64.8	8	8	2.4	7	1	.0
74852	1.2	94	.4	83	17.8	186	43.5	8	18	.5	9	0	.0
74854	2.4	84	.8	80	19.8	186	32.4	7	17	.9	17	0	.0
74855	3.2	89	1.1	84	23.4	256	57.2	8	12	1.4	13	0	.0
74856	.9	85	.3	81	17.2	197	29.0	8	20	.4	21	1	.0

*=Estimated **1.0=883 lbs per person; 100++ indicates per capita toxic waste generation > than 100 times the U.S. average of 883 lbs per capita.

ZIP CODE MEASURES OF SIZE, LEVELS OF AFFLUENCE AND QUALITY OF LIFE

1=Population (th.); 2= % White; 3=Households (th.); 4=% Owner Occupied; 5=Mean Income Per Household (th.$); 6=Mean Monthly Rent ($); 7=Mean Home Value (th.$)*;
8=% under 5; 9=% 65 and over; 10=% White Males, 65+; 11=% White Males; 12=# Toxic Waste Sites; 13=Toxic Waste Relative to US(883 lbs.per capita)**.

OKLAHOMA

SHAWNEE

ZIP CODE	1	2	3	4	5	6	7	8	9	10	11	12	13
74857	3.2	93	1.0	89	27.1	223	75.2	9	5	1.6	5	0	.0
74859	6.0	83	2.4	72	15.6	141	40.4	6	22	2.3	24	0	.1
74860	1.3	91	.4	93	20.8	152	38.1	7	14	.6	11	0	.0
74863	.7	96	.2	90	22.7	116	67.7	8	21	.3	11	0	.0
74864	4.0	97	1.5	82	18.3	245	52.5	6	18	1.9	15	0	.0
74865	1.6	95	.6	79	17.6	229	39.6	6	18	.7	14	0	.0
74866	.4	0	.1	75	20.0	158	37.8	7	6	.0	0	2	.0
74867	1.3	55	.4	84	15.6	284	31.7	10	13	.4	17	0	.0
74868	12.3	85	4.8	73	21.6	220	56.9	8	17	5.0	14	3	.3
74869	.6	93	.2	89	17.2	182	38.9	5	11	.3	14	0	.0
74871	2.3	89	.8	79	19.0	157	37.9	9	15	.9	14	0	.0
74872	2.8	92	1.1	82	16.5	201	44.9	8	24	1.2	22	0	.0
74873	7.4	93	2.6	84	21.9	250	56.9	8	14	3.3	12	2	.0
74875	1.2	95	.4	82	18.5	204	39.0	7	20	.5	18	0	.9
74878	1.4	94	.5	78	22.2	200	35.7	5	10	.7	9	0	.0
74880	2.1	72	.8	77	16.9	146	35.1	6	19	.8	18	0	.0
74881	2.6	90	1.0	81	19.6	159	52.0	8	14	1.2	14	0	.0
74882	.2	100	.1	88	15.6	179*	46.0	10	3	.1	0	0	.0
74883	2.8	73	1.1	78	14.8	144	35.5	6	23	.9	22	0	.0
74884	7.8	68	2.9	71	18.1	174	43.7	7	20	2.5	20	1	.0

POTEAU

ZIP CODE	1	2	3	4	5	6	7	8	9	10	11	12	13
74901	1.5	97	.6	68	17.2	195	36.9	6	17	.7	11	0	.0
74930	1.6	95	.6	80	17.6	159	38.1	5	17	.7	17	0	.0
74931	1.2	0	.3	70	14.6	170	41.3	11	10	.8	0	0	.0
74932	1.7	96	.5	71	19.4	207	41.3	7	5	.8	5	0	.0
74934	.3	0	.1	71	15.6	220	44.8	13	25	.0	0	0	.0
74935	.2	76	.1	74	12.2	101	30.4	5	13	.1	9	0	.0
74936	.4	88	.1	71	14.8	228	36.2	12	11	.2	9	0	.0
74937	4.5	94	1.7	78	18.1	185	40.1	7	21	2.0	17	1	.0
74939	.7	85	.2	77	15.6	153	26.4	1	12	.4	9	0	.0
74940	1.4	91	.5	79	16.8	201	40.0	10	9	.7	11	0	.0
74941	2.1	94	.7	75	15.9	125	31.4	7	16	.9	15	0	.0
74942	.3	0	.1	73	15.8	189	30.6	11	10	.0	0	0	.0
74943	.1	0	.1	100	23.2	266*	30.1	3	11	.0	0	0	.0
74944	1.3	97	.4	78	19.9	93	23.7	8	15	.7	13	1	.0
74945	.7	62	.3	79	13.3	150	30.8	9	20	.2	20	0	.0
74946	.4	60	.1	35	13.9	142	27.5	9	10	.1	6	0	.0
74947	.3	0	.1	75	14.8	227	27.3	4	15	.0	0	0	.0
74948	8.4	85	2.7	82	18.7	207	45.7	7	10	3.6	10	0	.0
74949	.3	0	.1	59	15.4	229	48.4	16	14	.1	11	0	.0
74951	1.7	92	.6	76	16.8	179	38.8	9	14	.8	11	0	.0
74953	8.2	92	3.1	71	21.2	216	54.6	8	18	3.6	16	0	.0
74954	2.3	91	.8	90	22.3	168	59.8	9	11	1.0	10	0	.0
74955	11.7	85	4.1	74	18.4	196	53.8	7	14	4.7	12	3	.9
74956	1.2	91	.4	88	16.0	231	34.3	13	16	.6	18	0	.0
74957	.9	71	.3	78	11.7	146	31.4	7	17	.3	17	0	.0
74959	5.8	83	2.0	76	17.4	198	42.9	7	13	2.3	13	1	.0
74960	10.7	57	3.5	73	15.9	185	46.9	7	13	3.0	14	0	.1
74962	5.4	74	1.8	77	19.1	208	51.7	8	15	2.0	14	0	.0

OKLAHOMA

POTEAU

ZIP CODE	1	2	3	4	5	6	7	8	9	10	11	12	13
74963	.6	94	.2	95	14.2	163*	38.6	11	7	.2	6	0	.0
74964	2.0	85	.6	83	15.9	242	42.2	7	9	.8	8	0	.0
74965	4.5	84	1.5	74	16.0	186	37.8	9	16	1.8	17	1	.0
74966	3.3	93	1.2	80	16.7	183	46.9	8	16	1.5	15	0	.0

AMARILLO

ZIP CODE	1	2	3	4	5	6	7	8	9	10	11	12	13
79005	.1	100	.1	92	18.4	211*	65.4*	0	19	.1	23	0	.0

*=Estimated **1.0=883 lbs per person; 100++ indicates per capita toxic waste generation > than 100 times the U.S. average of 883 lbs per capita.

ZIP CODE MEASURES OF SIZE, LEVELS OF AFFLUENCE AND QUALITY OF LIFE

1=Population (th.); 2= % White; 3=Households (th.); 4=% Owner Occupied; 5=Mean Income Per Household (th.$); 6=Mean Monthly Rent ($); 7=Mean Home Value (th.$); 8=% under 5; 9=% 65 and over; 10=% White Males; 11=% White Males, 65+; 12=# Toxic Waste Sites; 13=Toxic Waste Relative to US(883 lbs.per capita)**

OREGON

BOISE

ZIP CODE	1	2	3	4	5	6	7	8	9	10	11	12	13
83610	.1	100	.1	45	27.1	176	96.7*	15	11	.1	7	0	.0
83628	.3	100	.1	60	17.9	205*	63.6*	18	4	.2	4	0	.0
83660	.3	0	.1	75	13.2	101	41.1	6	11	.0	0	0	.0
83672	.5	84	.2	67	15.2	271	35.7	8	9	.2	6	0	.0

PORTLAND

ZIP CODE	1	2	3	4	5	6	7	8	9	10	11	12	13
97001	.2	100	.1	82	24.4	195	39.6	13	13	.1	8	0	.0
97002	4.8	98	1.6	83	33.0	425	157.0	8	9	2.3	8	0	.0
97004	4.0	99	1.2	91	38.4	580	139.5	8	5	2.0	5	0	.0
97005	85.3	94	31.4	62	33.2	453	133.6	9	6	39.2	5	1	1.7
97008	.4	0	.1	60	30.4	179	128.4	10	8	.2	0	0	.0
97009	12.0	98	3.8	88	34.0	448	146.5	7	7	6.0	7	0	.0
97011	.7	97	.3	76	26.4	326	94.1	10	5	.3	3	0	.0
97013	14.2	98	4.9	73	29.1	391	124.1	8	11	6.8	10	1	.0
97014	1.0	96	.4	63	32.2	287	80.2	8	10	.5	8	0	.0
97015	8.3	99	3.0	80	31.4	357	141.9	8	8	4.1	8	1	1.1
97016	6.2	98	2.1	78	26.8	271	87.6	8	11	3.1	11	1	1.1
97017	2.2	98	.7	86	27.4	307	107.8	8	9	1.1	8	0	.0
97018	.6	0	.2	87	27.1	251	105.9	7	19	.0	0	0	.0
97019	2.6	96	.9	82	29.5	408	133.0	8	8	1.2	7	0	.0
97020	.3	95	.1	76	24.2	469	73.5	10	12	.1	16	0	.5
97021	1.1	100	.4	75	29.2	242	68.3	9	13	.6	12	1	.0
97022	3.0	100	.9	82	28.9	354	124.0	7	6	1.3	6	0	.0
97023	8.1	96	2.7	79	27.9	359	116.5	8	8	4.0	8	0	.0
97024	.2	100	.1	85	24.1	277*	105.0*	11	11	.1	8	0	.0
97026	2.4	85	.7	72	24.3	329	83.8	9	8	1.0	8	0	.0
97027	9.8	98	3.5	73	29.9	411	120.9	7	13	4.6	10	0	.0
97028	9.8	98	3.5	37	24.3	285	92.8	6	8	4.6	8	0	.0
97029	.4	100	.1	66	24.3	489	118.4	8	12	.1	12	0	.0
97030	41.1	96	14.3	82	30.9	477	128.9	9	8	19.4	6	0	.0
97031	12.1	90	4.7	76	26.7	309	105.1	8	13	5.4	7	3	1.1
97032	3.5	91	1.2	78	26.1	448	96.2	8	14	1.5	14	0	.0
97034	29.5	98	10.8	74	46.3	540	193.5	5	14	14.1	7	0	.0
97037	1.1	99	.4	56	21.4	269	125.0	6	11	.6	11	0	.0
97038	9.3	97	3.0	76	25.0	258	49.4	8	11	4.5	10	2	3.6
97039	.5	96	.2	67	33.7	349	93.3	9	13	.3	13	0	.0
97040	.9	0	.3	84	26.7	267	119.8	8	12	.0	13	0	.0
97041	2.3	98	.8	72	27.1	271	103.2	9	10	1.1	9	0	.0
97042	2.8	99	.9	86	29.7	298	92.8	6	7	1.5	6	0	.0
97044	34.2	90	11.4	65	29.9	248	68.7	9	10	16.5	12	0	.0
97045	6.3	98	2.3	73	29.8	412	127.6	9	9	3.2	7	1	1.1
97049	.7	95	.3	81	29.8	339	95.7	7	10	.3	10	0	.0
97050	.4	0	.2	68	28.7	269	125.0	11	4	.0	0	0	.0
97051	10.0	98	3.7	66	23.1	234	102.7	8	10	4.8	11	2	.0
97053	2.4	99	.8	86	25.0	326	48.7	11	12	1.2	8	0	.0
97054	1.2	97	.4	81	26.7	307	72.3	8	6	.6	5	0	.0
97055	10.1	98	3.4	79	27.7	415	92.8	9	9	4.9	8	0	.0
97056	7.1	97	2.5	77	28.3	328	111.6	8	11	3.4	11	1	1.2
97058	17.0	97	6.6	68	25.8	296	92.7	7	15	8.0	13	2	.6

OREGON

PORTLAND

ZIP CODE	1	2	3	4	5	6	7	8	9	10	11	12	13
97060	12.0	98	4.0	76	33.5	482	129.2	9	6	6.0	6	1	.8
97062	8.6	97	3.2	52	31.6	476	147.1	10	2	4.2	2	0	1.2
97063	1.0	97	.3	71	32.1	148	48.5	11	8	.5	9	0	.0
97064	2.9	98	1.0	77	23.2	299	78.3	11	14	1.4	14	0	.0
97065	.7	98	.3	65	24.4	268	58.4	9	14	.4	13	0	.0
97067	.9	99	.4	73	26.3	428	136.2	6	6	.5	5	0	.0
97068	14.1	98	5.0	78	37.2	474	154.9	7	7	6.9	6	0	.4
97070	4.6	97	1.8	76	38.4	460	183.2	6	12	2.2	11	0	.6
97071	16.5	90	5.8	76	24.6	368	89.5	8	23	7.3	22	0	.2

PORTLAND

ZIP CODE	1	2	3	4	5	6	7	8	9	10	11	12	13
97101	2.8	96	1.0	78	23.3	370	96.5	8	11	1.4	11	0	.0
97102	.1	100	.1	66	21.0	175	139.6	0	34	.1	46	0	.0
97103	17.1	95	6.4	63	27.5	270	90.3	8	12	8.1	10	2	.0
97106	2.9	97	.9	79	29.8	314	140.0	10	8	1.4	8	0	.0
97107	1.2	80	.5	80	22.8	295	84.1	6	17	.4	17	0	.0
97108	.8	97	.3	64	20.3	325	110.3	12	12	.4	13	0	.0
97109	.5	95	.2	75	20.4	464	81.2	11	4	.2	2	0	.0
97110	1.0	100	.5	54	19.6	307	121.2	4	15	.5	12	0	.0
97111	2.4	98	.8	82	24.4	354	78.6	8	14	1.1	13	0	.0
97112	1.5	96	.5	70	26.1	257	96.2	12	13	.7	12	0	.0
97113	8.5	94	2.9	71	27.8	424	116.1	9	9	4.1	8	1	.1
97114	3.7	91	1.3	77	25.5	348	95.5	9	12	1.7	13	0	.0
97115	2.0	97	.7	90	31.2	446	125.9	11	9	.9	10	0	.0
97116	15.6	95	5.5	62	24.6	331	113.4	8	13	7.3	11	1	.7
97117	.4	100	.2	91	29.0	333*	138.1	3	13	.2	14	0	.0
97118	1.0	97	.4	72	17.5	266	77.4	5	21	.5	24	0	.0
97119	3.9	96	1.2	74	31.7	331	127.1	9	6	1.8	5	0	.0
97120	.3	0	.1	94	23.0	265*	110.4	8	8	.0	0	0	.0
97121	.5	95	.2	75	20.5	297	75.1	8	13	.3	16	0	.0
97122	.6	98	.2	60	18.7	305	84.7	10	5	.3	6	0	.0
97123	37.6	96	12.9	67	30.5	452	129.8	9	9	17.6	8	1	.1
97125	.3	100	.1	92	30.7	353*	144.7	7	0	.2	0	0	.0
97127	1.2	89	.4	80	21.8	377	74.2	8	16	.5	18	0	.0
97128	17.3	96	6.4	64	25.7	342	108.7	7	13	8.1	13	1	.7
97130	.5	99	.2	72	21.2	297	106.5	4	27	.2	24	0	.0
97131	1.5	99	.6	85	24.4	244	100.2	6	15	.7	15	0	.5
97132	15.9	97	5.4	70	27.7	384	110.9	9	12	7.5	10	1	.4
97133	.6	88	.2	76	22.6	338	81.5	9	12	.3	11	2	.0
97134	.2	100	.1	62	30.3	141	129.7	7	36	.1	34	0	.0
97135	.7	89	.3	66	22.7	348	100.6	4	18	.3	18	0	.1
97136	1.6	98	.7	81	19.0	224	91.9	6	24	.7	24	0	.0
97137	1.3	90	.4	62	30.3	322	93.4	7	8	.7	8	0	.0
97138	8.5	98	3.6	63	23.2	302	105.4	7	19	4.0	18	2	.0
97140	8.0	98	2.8	77	33.6	396	158.2	6	9	4.0	8	0	.2
97141	10.8	99	4.2	69	25.4	291	97.8	8	14	5.2	13	1	.7
97143	.2	100	.1	50	23.2	335	71.0	0	14	.1	12	0	.0
97145	.2	93	.1	71	22.6	327	126.8	5	44	.1	44	0	.0
97146	4.1	97	1.6	72	26.6	311	96.9	8	14	2.0	13	1	.0
97147	.4	97	.2	54	19.6	238	77.5	6	25	.2	23	0	.1

*=Estimated **1.0=883 lbs per person; 100++ indicates per capita toxic waste generation > than 100 times the U.S. average of 883 lbs. per capita.

ZIP CODE MEASURES OF SIZE, LEVELS OF AFFLUENCE AND QUALITY OF LIFE

1=Population (th.); 2= % White; 3=Households (th.); 4=% Owner Occupied; 5=Mean Income Per Household (th.$); 6=Mean Monthly Rent ($); 7=Mean Home Value (th.$); 8=% under 5; 9=% 65 and over; 10=White Males, 65+; 11=% White Males, 65+; 12=# Toxic Waste Sites; 13=Toxic Waste Relative to US(883 lbs.per capita)**.

OREGON

ZIPCODE	1	2	3	4	5	6	7	8	9	10	11	12	13
PORTLAND													
97148	2.7	95	.8	84	29.0	359	85.3	9	9	1.3	9	0	.0
97149	.3	100	.1	71	24.6	346	162.1	0	28	.2	26	0	.0
PORTLAND													
97201	20.7	94	11.1	42	32.4	369	203.2	3	17	9.2	12	4	.5
97202	37.8	93	16.6	51	25.3	387	106.3	6	15	16.6	12	1	.6
97203	25.1	89	9.5	56	22.0	343	77.7	9	13	10.8	12	10	.9
97204	1.5	95	.8	26	15.1	270	93.3	7	16	.8	16	0	.3
97205	5.6	93	4.3	5	17.7	282	269.3	1	30	2.7	24	0	.2
97206	43.7	94	17.9	63	17.7	415	82.8	8	14	19.6	12	2	.2
97209	5.9	90	4.2	3	11.5	203	168.1	2	25	3.4	18	2	1.8
97210	9.5	96	5.1	30	25.9	301	205.3	3	18	4.4	14	16	8.6
97211	29.4	58	10.9	68	22.7	394	80.6	9	13	7.9	15	5	.6
97212	24.7	74	9.6	67	28.2	374	114.8	7	15	8.6	12	0	.0
97213	23.6	93	12.9	61	23.7	392	94.6	6	19	12.2	15	0	.0
97214	23.2	90	11.4	35	19.8	324	93.1	6	17	9.8	12	3	1.5
97215	16.3	95	6.8	64	26.2	411	104.7	6	18	7.1	15	0	.0
97216	11.4	94	4.5	68	26.6	436	96.0	7	12	5.0	11	0	.0
97217	30.2	80	12.5	66	23.3	358	79.0	8	16	11.7	16	8	2.3
97218	12.1	89	5.2	63	22.3	362	89.8	8	15	5.2	15	6	.6
97219	31.9	95	12.5	66	35.3	474	141.7	6	14	14.9	9	0	.4
97220	25.5	95	10.1	62	26.4	405	96.3	6	13	11.4	11	3	.2
97221	11.1	97	4.2	74	46.9	480	194.3	5	10	25.9	9	4	.4
97222	55.6	97	20.8	67	29.8	422	118.9	7	11	17.4	12	2	.7
97223	37.2	97	15.3	63	31.7	441	141.4	7	14	17.4	12	2	.7
97225	20.4	98	8.4	65	45.3	468	180.6	4	11	9.6	11	0	1.8
97227	3.9	43	1.4	42	16.1	300	80.5	12	11	.8	9	3	
97229	19.9	96	7.2	65	40.8	482	170.0	7	4	9.7	4	1	.2
97230	28.1	94	10.5	65	32.8	432	118.5	6	8	12.8	8	2	.8
97231	3.2	98	1.2	77	34.4	386	134.7	5	10	1.7	8	0	.0
97232	10.3	92	5.3	36	21.5	339	116.6	4	22	4.0	15	0	1.8
97233	26.1	96	10.1	55	26.0	411	99.3	8	8	12.0	7	0	.0
97236	23.2	96	8.6	61	27.0	401	111.2	8	10	10.6	8	1	.0
97266	27.5	95	10.4	65	27.6	414	103.5	9	11	12.8	10	1	.1
SALEM													
97301	39.1	94	15.1	55	22.9	352	93.8	8	14	17.5	11	2	.1
97302	42.1	97	16.3	65	30.3	351	118.3	7	11	19.6	10	0	.1
97303	54.4	94	20.8	61	24.8	364	94.2	9	12	24.5	10	3	.0
97304	14.5	97	5.6	68	29.6	304	121.4	7	16	6.7	13	0	.1
97305	1.8	96	.6	85	22.1	274	99.0	7	12	.8	14	0	.1
97321	41.1	98	15.3	63	26.5	343	102.3	8	9	19.6	8	2	1.6
97324	1.0	99	.4	71	21.1	264	83.1	9	11	.5	12	0	.0
97325	4.9	99	1.4	82	28.3	377	105.4	8	5	2.4	4	0	.0
97326	.9	100	.3	70	18.6	327	95.1	10	9	.4	10	0	.0
97327	2.5	99	.9	84	24.0	329	86.0	8	11	1.3	12	0	.0
97329	.2	0	.1	55	18.5	168	59.7	21	11	.0	0	0	.0
97330	52.7	94	18.8	51	25.4	361	122.0	6	8	25.2	6	4	.2
97336	.5	100	.2	83	23.9	285	68.0	6	10	.2	10	0	.0
97338	13.1	98	4.6	73	24.8	323	94.1	8	13	6.2	11	0	.2
97341	.9	100	.5	60	19.8	304	125.0	8	19	.5	19	0	.0

OREGON

ZIPCODE	1	2	3	4	5	6	7	8	9	10	11	12	13
SALEM													
97342	.4	98	.2	62	22.1	246	73.4	10	8	.2	6	0	.0
97343	.6	100	.2	72	23.3	350	73.5	14	2	.4	2	0	.0
97344	.9	98	.3	81	20.6	330	59.8	7	11	.4	10	0	.0
97345	.7	96	.3	80	20.0	278	116.4	7	11	.3	14	0	.6
97346	.6	97	.2	76	23.0	242	85.3	9	14	.6	22	0	.0
97347	1.3	88	.4	70	23.1	320	75.1	9	14	.6	14	0	.0
97348	1.3	98	.5	66	27.6	337	97.9	10	12	.6	11	0	5.1
97350	.3	95	.1	65	25.8	197	44.1	10	8	.2	10	0	.4
97351	5.4	88	1.9	73	22.1	295	77.2	11	11	2.3	11	0	.8
97352	3.9	94	1.3	76	26.0	318	102.9	11	10	1.8	11	0	.0
97355	23.0	97	8.2	74	23.8	333	89.0	7	13	10.9	12	1	.1
97357	.3	99	.8	71	22.1	293	91.5	9	8	.9	0	0	.0
97358	2.1	99	.8	79	26.1	289	89.6	7	14	1.1	14	0	.0
97359	.2	100	.2	76	21.7	323	59.7	5	4	.1	6	0	.0
97360	1.7	97	.7	72	24.3	313	76.1	10	16	.8	16	0	.0
97361	7.6	95	2.7	55	21.5	300	97.1	7	6	3.4	6	1	.0
97362	4.1	92	1.3	62	20.4	347	84.5	17	13	1.7	13	0	.0
97364	.4	100	.2	90	37.7	433*	110.8	9	20	.2	19	0	.0
97365	9.0	98	3.8	58	26.8	339	109.6	7	14	4.2	13	0	.0
97366	1.0	97	.4	75	24.9	338	122.0	2	14	.5	16	0	.0
97367	6.5	98	3.0	63	21.3	265	100.0	6	22	3.0	21	0	.0
97368	2.0	97	.8	79	21.2	377	110.7	6	24	.0	24	0	.0
97369	1.0	100	.4	44	16.8	229	143.4	0	22	.1	24	0	.0
97370	6.5	98	2.3	71	26.9	348	104.4	9	11	3.2	8	0	.0
97371	.5	98	.2	71	29.0	434	61.8	12	14	.0	0	0	.6
97372	.3	0	.1	58	13.7	297	52.2	4	4	.0	0	0	.0
97374	4.9	99	1.6	86	26.8	311	105.3	7	10	2.5	9	0	.0
97375	1.6	89	.4	78	18.7	339	92.9	6	16	.7	12	0	.2
97376	.7	94	.3	69	26.8	378	116.9	7	11	.4	13	0	.1
97377	1.0	97	.4	75	24.5	298	110.1	7	12	.5	9	0	.2
97378	4.8	99	1.7	74	25.3	328	82.3	7	15	2.3	14	0	.0
97380	1.6	89	.6	80	24.7	351	108.3	11	11	.7	12	0	.2
97381	10.5	98	3.7	75	26.1	338	105.6	8	15	5.0	13	0	.0
97383	6.0	97	2.1	72	27.4	345	98.7	9	12	2.9	9	0	.2
97384	.3	0	.4	77	20.0	431	62.3	9	17	.0	0	0	.0
97385	1.7	0	.6	84	28.7	331	108.6	12	17	.0	0	0	.0
97386	10.8	98	3.9	74	22.4	291	81.1	7	14	5.3	13	0	.0
97388	1.0	97	.5	84	34.2	242	163.0	2	23	.5	25	0	.0
97389	1.1	0	.4	55	26.9	306	106.6	5	11	.0	0	0	.1
97390	.5	84	.2	84	21.4	201	108.9	9	26	.1	8	0	.1
97391	5.1	97	1.9	73	27.6	298	83.2	8	9	2.5	9	2	.1
97392	3.8	97	1.3	81	26.3	338	102.1	7	11	1.8	8	0	1.3
97393	.4	87	.3	0	30.6	206	109.1*	7		.2			.5
97394	3.5	98	1.5	75	23.3	278	98.5	7	25	1.7	25	0	.0
97396	2.7	95	.9	76	21.7	315	69.2	13	13	1.3	12	0	.0
EUGENE													
97401	39.7	96	16.7	48	25.2	344	129.7	5	10	18.7	8	4	.1
97402	35.2	95	14.1	48	21.7	350	100.1	8	9	16.6	8	0	.8
97403	11.6	94	3.8	56	26.7	360	155.5	4	7	5.6	6	0	.0

*=Estimated **1.0=883 lbs per person; 100++ indicates per capita toxic waste generation > than 100 times the U.S. average of 883 lbs per capita.

ZIP CODE MEASURES OF SIZE, LEVELS OF AFFLUENCE AND QUALITY OF LIFE

1=Population (th.); 2= % White; 3=Households (th.); 4=% Owner Occupied; 5=Mean Income Per Household (th.$); 6=Mean Monthly Rent ($)*; 7=Mean Home Value (th.$)*;
8=% under 5; 9=% 65 and over; 10=White Males (th.); 11=% White Males, 65+; 12=# Toxic Waste Sites; 13=Toxic Waste Relative to US(883 lbs.per capita)**.

OREGON
EUGENE

ZIPCODE	1	2	3	4	5	6	7	8	9	10	11	12	13
97404	25.1	97	8.7	74	28.0	427	108.1	8	7	12.0	7	0	.0
97405	39.7	96	14.9	67	32.2	425	136.6	6	10	18.5	8	3	.0
97409	.2	77	.1	91	24.7	284*	128.3	6	20	.1	24	0	.0
97410	.7	95	.3	84	23.8	181	113.9	8	15	.3	12	0	.0
97411	5.7	97	2.2	74	20.8	270	89.8	6	16	2.7	14	0	.0
97412	.5	0	.3	69	27.0	203	83.4	11	6	.0	0	0	.0
97413	.8	0	.3	81	23.9	276	133.3	6	13	.0	0	0	.0
97414	.3	0	.1	75	29.4	282	48.1	11	14	.0	0	0	.0
97415	9.2	98	3.6	76	24.7	357	114.9	7	18	4.4	19	0	.0
97416	1.1	0	.4	76	25.1	197	93.6	12	12	.0	13	0	.0
97417	2.3	96	.8	67	24.0	306	91.6	8	14	1.0	13	0	.0
97419	1.2	98	.4	84	25.1	224	130.1	9	9	.6	9	0	.0
97420	27.1	96	10.2	68	25.4	339	85.8	8	11	13.0	10	2	.2
97423	7.7	96	2.9	73	23.8	287	83.0	7	15	3.6	15	0	.1
97424	14.9	98	5.2	73	26.4	349	108.4	8	11	7.2	7	0	.0
97425	.2	100	.1	55	23.0	294	116.3	6	6	.1	7	0	.0
97426	6.3	97	2.2	79	27.0	348	104.5	8	9	3.1	9	0	.1
97427	.5	100	.1	79	25.6	228	78.6	9	8	.2	8	0	.0
97428	.2	100	.1	54	32.5	291	112.3	9	26	.0	16	0	.2
97429	.8	0	.3	72	16.2	264	95.6	14	17	.1	4	0	.0
97430	.2	93	.1	59	15.6	221	56.5	8	7	.1	5	0	.0
97431	2.1	0	.7	82	25.3	309	116.4	10	8	.0	0	0	.0
97432	.5	0	.3	78	26.4	392	84.7	11	11	.0	0	0	3.0
97434	.5	100	.3	60	21.5	206	85.5	18	9	.2	7	0	.0
97435	2.5	99	.9	71	20.9	279	80.0	11	12	1.2	12	0	.3
97436	.9		.4	77	21.4	286	76.9	11	18	.5	11	0	.0
97437	2.7	93	.8	90	27.1	340	141.2	5	6	1.3	7	0	.0
97438	1.2	95	.4	77	28.1	355	116.6	6	7	.6	9	0	.2
97439	8.8	96	3.5	73	21.5	310	97.6	8	19	4.2	20	0	.0
97441	.4	100	.1	71	15.9	276	50.3	11	10	.1	12	1	19.6
97442	1.9	95	.7	73	24.4	287	68.6	9	14	.9	15	0	.0
97443	2.0	91	.6	70	25.3	308	110.5	6	9	1.0	9	0	.2
97444	4.5	97	1.7	72	26.4	290	110.5	9	14	2.2	13	0	.1
97446	3.2	97	1.1	72	26.1	330	99.3	9	8	1.6	13	0	.0
97447	.9	98	.4	45	21.7	278	81.0	10	9	.5	11	0	.0
97448	10.0	98	3.6	72	25.4	324	116.2	8	13	4.8	12	0	.2
97449	1.6	95	.7	80	22.9	235	79.1	5	17	.8	19	1	.0
97450	.7	0	.2	73	24.1	245	96.4	8	38	.3	37	0	.0
97451	.4	100	.1	85	24.1	230	99.3	9	8	.2	11	0	.2
97453	1.3	96	.4	76	23.6	312	79.8	10	8	.6	10	0	.0
97454	1.6	95	.6	76	26.5	309	85.1	8	11	.8	11	0	.2
97456	1.3	0	.5	81	23.2	276	97.2	6	9	.0	9	0	.0
97457	2.5	98	.8	76	22.9	297	88.3	9	8	1.2	8	0	.2
97458	9.1	97	3.0	77	24.9	313	85.2	10	8	4.4	7	0	.0
97459	15.3	98	5.4	71	22.7	280	72.2	9	13	2.6	12	0	.2
97461	.7	0	.2	73	28.0	339	100.1	8	11	7.4	10	1	.2
97462	3.7	98	1.3	83	23.1	262	107.2	12	11	1.8	13	0	.0
97463	4.7	95	1.7	75	23.6	248	78.1	7	12	2.2	12	0	.0

OREGON
EUGENE

ZIPCODE	1	2	3	4	5	6	7	8	9	10	11	12	13
97465	2.0	99	.8	72	19.2	239	85.7	8	15	1.0	16	0	.0
97466	1.0	92	.4	66	18.4	292	56.5	10	13	.5	15	0	.0
97467	6.6	98	2.5	70	24.5	263	94.9	8	14	3.2	14	0	.0
97469	3.0	98	1.0	73	25.2	303	74.2	11	7	1.5	8	0	.1
97470	40.0	98	14.6	70	26.7	357	104.5	8	11	19.4	10	0	.0
97473	.2	0	.1	88	15.5	150	111.8	3	30	.0	0	0	.0
97476	.8	100	.1	64	25.9	324	91.9	9	6	.2	6	0	.0
97477	55.1	97	20.7	59	24.5	358	103.9	9	8	26.2	8	4	.5
97479	6.4	97	2.2	76	21.3	328	84.0	10	10	3.1	8	0	.0
97480	.5	86	.2	58	28.4	301	59.5	6	7	.3	6	0	.0
97481	.9	100	.3	84	27.9	182	103.7	8	8	.4	8	0	.0
97484	.3	0	.3	74	22.2	33	109.6	0	3	.0	3	0	.2
97486	.7	100	.3	94	21.3	401	145.9	6	10	.3	6	0	.2
97487	6.2	98	2.1	75	25.7	321	109.2	9	9	3.0	8	0	.0
97488	.9	99	.4	63	26.1	319	129.4	6	18	.4	18	0	.0
97490	.2	100	.1	72	17.9	455	69.1	9	21	.0	21	0	.0
97491	.4	0	.2	76	25.8	343	86.1	2	14	.0	14	0	.0
97492	.6	0	.2	75	25.7	285	78.4	11	15	.0	15	0	.2
97493	.4	88	.1	77	26.2	260	84.0	9	23	.3	26	0	.0
97494	.2	100	.1	58	28.6	238	65.6	3	3	.1	4	0	.0
97495	1.0	95	.4	68	40.8	370	146.3	6	8	.4	11	0	.0
97496	5.0	99	1.7	68	23.6	326	86.7	9	8	2.5	8	0	.0
97497	1.3	0	.5	74	19.0	238	82.9	7	9	.0	9	0	.0
97498	1.3	98	.5	74	19.8	247	122.6	4	21	.6	20	0	.0
97499	1.8	98	.6	76	25.9	308	89.1	9	13	1.0	13	0	.0

MEDFORD

ZIPCODE	1	2	3	4	5	6	7	8	9	10	11	12	13
97501	60.4	97	22.8	66	25.8	368	109.7	8	14	28.6	12	4	.3
97502	17.5	97	5.8	78	26.5	370	101.8	7	10	8.4	9	0	.0
97520	18.3	95	7.2	58	23.4	334	121.1	6	11	8.4	11	0	.0
97522	.7	0	.2	78	24.3	214	52.5	7	11	.2	5	0	.0
97523	5.2	97	1.9	77	17.8	311	86.1	9	17	2.5	17	0	.0
97524	7.7	97	2.5	81	24.6	396	100.1	9	9	3.7	9	0	.0
97525	4.4	99	1.6	81	23.8	382	110.6	7	12	2.3	11	0	.0
97526	47.3	98	17.8	73	21.8	364	110.9	7	16	22.5	15	3	.1
97530	5.8	98	2.2	78	25.5	347	120.2	6	16	2.9	16	0	.0
97531	.5	95	.2	63	14.9	256	70.5	8	19	.3	14	0	.0
97532	1.5	98	.5	78	22.3	294	100.0	7	11	.7	12	1	.1
97533	.2	0	.3	70	15.4	330	87.5	13	10	.0	0	0	.0
97534	.6	0	.3	81	17.0	165	75.5	5	13	.0	0	0	.0
97535	2.5	90	1.0	66	22.6	345	98.4	7	15	1.1	16	0	.0
97536	.9	95	.3	69	23.3	246	88.0	7	8	.4	7	0	.0
97537	5.5	97	2.0	81	22.0	344	114.6	7	16	2.6	16	0	.0
97538	1.7	100	.5	84	20.0	303	79.4	10	10	.9	10	0	.0
97539	1.4	97	.6	72	20.0	294	104.9	6	20	.7	22	0	.0
97540	4.6	97	1.7	74	23.1	304	108.6	7	15	2.2	15	0	.0
97541	1.2	97	.4	79	22.8	261	105.7	6	8	.7	8	0	.0
97543	.5	100	.5	83	24.8	286	74.4	3	7	.2	8	0	.0
97544	1.5		.5	83	19.4	279	100.4	7	12	.0	0	0	.0

*=Estimated **1.0=883 lbs per person; 100++ indicates per capita toxic waste generation > than 100 times the U.S. average of 883 lbs per capita.

103001

ZIP CODE MEASURES OF SIZE, LEVELS OF AFFLUENCE AND QUALITY OF LIFE

1=Population (th.); 2= % White; 3=Households (th.); 4=% Owner Occupied; 5=Mean Income Per Household (th.$); 6=Mean Monthly Rent ($); 7=Mean Home Value (th.$); 8=% under 5; 9=% 65 and over; 10=White Males (th.); 11=% White Males, 65+; 12=# Toxic Waste Sites; 13=Toxic Waste Relative to US(883 lbs.per capita)**.

OREGON

ZIP CODE	1	2	3	4	5	6	7	8	9	10	11	12	13
KLAMATH FALLS													
97601	46.7	95	17.4	67	24.0	290	84.1	8	11	22.3	10	0	.1
97620	.2	100	.1	58	22.0	253*	78.4*	0	16	.1	24	0	.0
97621	.4	81	.1	95	17.9	206*	38.2	3	3	.2	14	0	.0
97622	.9	97	.3	74	22.1	180	38.8	11	2	.5	3	0	.0
97623	1.7	99	.6	75	21.3	163	70.4	10	8	.9	7	0	.0
97624	2.6	78	.9	82	19.4	262	65.2	9	11	1.0	11	0	.0
97625	.3	100	.1	100	23.2	266*	81.1	0	11	.2	12	0	.0
97627	1.0	95	.4	85	25.4	272	120.8	12	5	.2	5	0	.0
97630	5.3	95	2.0	75	25.4	273	68.7	8	12	2.6	12	0	.0
97632	1.1	98	.4	79	24.4	287	69.9	7	16	.6	15	0	.0
97633	1.5	95	.6	72	24.2	219	65.8	9	13	.8	12	0	.0
97634	.3	0	.1	89	32.9	208	108.5	9	10	.0	0	0	.0
97635	.2	100	.1	33	21.2	270	115.2	13	16	.0	15	0	.0
97636	.5	0	.2	55	20.2	194	51.7	7	8	.0	0	0	.0
97638	1.0	93	.4	68	15.3	224	39.7	11	7	.5	10	0	.0
97639	.5	80	.2	96	16.3	187*	54.3	5	25	.2	23	0	.0
BEND													
97701	42.0	98	15.7	71	28.0	380	114.6	8	9	20.7	9	1	.1
97720	5.3	94	2.0	73	26.3	255	60.6	7	11	2.6	10	0	.0
97721	.2	100	.1	48	23.5	185	83.6*	11	10	.1	11	0	.0
97730	.2	100	.1	37	16.5	312	120.1	10	15	.1	17	0	.0
97731	.5	94	.2	56	26.4	219	104.0	11	2	.3	0	0	.0
97732	.2	0	.1	50	21.4	231	39.7	4	15	.0	0	0	.0
97733	.5	88	.2	68	20.5	266	57.8	1	2	.2	3	0	.0
97734	1.3	96	.5	66	23.8	365	76.8	8	10	1.1	7	0	.0
97735	.7	100	.3	88	12.8	147*	45.6*	12	6	.1	0	0	.0
97737	.7	96	.3	39	34.6	189	70.8	7	9	.4	8	0	.0
97738	2.0	99	.6	86	28.1	265	69.7	12	8	1.0	7	0	.0
97739	4.2	98	1.5	88	20.2	301	81.8	7	14	2.1	15	0	.0
97741	7.7	91	2.7	70	24.2	259	88.4	9	10	3.5	10	0	.1
97750	.4	0	.2	66	19.1	211	38.2	6	19	.0	0	0	.0
97753	.9	0	.3	81	26.4	416	103.4	8	10	.0	0	0	.0
97754	11.8	96	4.4	73	24.4	304	83.3	8	13	5.6	13	0	.0
97756	12.1	99	4.2	72	23.9	344	100.5	9	11	5.8	10	0	.2
97759	2.1	98	.9	69	27.1	385	155.5	8	11	1.1	19	0	.2
97760	2.5	98	1.0	84	20.7	362	85.2	8	19	1.1	13	1	.0
97761	2.3	8	.6	56	26.4	262	97.1	11	2	.2	8	0	.0
PENDLETON													
97801	19.5	93	7.1	61	26.5	300	89.7	8	12	8.9	10	0	.2
97810	.8	72	.3	79	28.4	250	57.5	7	16	.3	23	0	.0
97812	.8	95	.3	64	25.8	274	57.9	5	9	.4	11	1	.0
97813	1.2	99	.4	70	20.9	287	77.0	9	10	.5	10	0	.1
97814	11.6	98	4.5	73	22.9	291	71.8	8	16	5.6	14	0	.3
97818	2.1	94	.7	65	29.7	292	105.3	9	5	1.0	5	0	.1
97820	1.1	98	.4	76	24.1	281	84.5	9	9	.5	8	0	.1
97823	1.1	0	.5	69	22.6	187	52.4	7	18	.0	0	0	.0
97824	1.1	0	.4	79	23.7	334	76.7	10	15	.0	0	0	.0
97825	.3	98	.1	84	19.1	230	43.1	8	12	.2	12	0	.1
97826	1.2	92	.4	69	22.2	323	57.9	9	10	.6	10	0	.0

OREGON

ZIP CODE	1	2	3	4	5	6	7	8	9	10	11	12	13
PENDLETON													
97827	2.7	98	.9	81	21.4	274	65.2	9	10	1.3	12	1	.1
97828	3.2	99	1.2	70	22.1	250	93.1	9	17	1.5	16	0	.0
97830	.8	0	.8	70	19.2	206	47.3	9	17	.0	0	0	.0
97833	.8	0	.3	75	19.0	213	67.5	6	20	.0	0	0	.0
97834	1.2	99	.4	75	16.8	215	65.2	4	17	.6	15	0	.0
97835	.4	100	.1	53	30.5	258	73.4	6	18	.2	12	0	.0
97836	2.3	99	.9	67	27.2	264	65.4	8	15	1.1	13	0	.0
97837	.2	100	.1	52	27.7	338	65.6	3	7	.1	6	0	.0
97838	16.1	94	5.8	65	25.2	326	89.9	10	10	7.5	9	2	.1
97839	.6	96	.2	75	25.6	333	67.2	12	4	.3	5	0	.0
97840	.2	100	.1	18	16.7	194	13.1	14	5	.1	0	0	.0
97841	.6	100	.2	67	23.7	255	76.6	11	13	.3	12	0	.0
97842	.2	100	.1	73	20.1	53	91.9	3	23	.1	16	0	.0
97843	.7	0	.2	64	28.2	324	82.1	9	9	.0	0	0	.0
97844	1.8	95	.6	82	25.2	216	80.1	10	9	.9	10	0	.3
97845	2.8	98	.7	70	26.0	311	85.3	7	11	1.3	10	0	.5
97846	2.0	98	.7	80	21.9	301	86.7	8	10	1.0	10	0	.0
97848	.2	100	.1	63	16.6	175	61.3	11	13	.1	13	0	.0
97850	15.4	98	5.8	66	24.2	303	84.2	8	12	7.5	11	1	.3
97856	.4	0	.2	72	20.9	165	41.2	6	11	.0	0	0	.0
97857	.4	100	.1	73	23.5	191	61.6	7	16	.2	19	0	.0
97859	.1	100	.1	74	17.3	199*	20.8	5	7	.1	12	0	.0
97862	9.5	95	3.5	70	21.4	265	76.0	8	18	4.4	17	0	.3
97864	.3	97	.1	68	15.1	231	42.5	6	17	.1	20	0	.5
97865	1.1	98	.4	85	23.6	216	76.0	10	14	.5	14	0	.0
97867	.7	99	.3	70	21.2	321	44.5	9	17	.4	16	0	.4
97868	2.4	95	.9	76	24.0	245	69.0	9	9	1.2	10	0	.0
97869	1.4	99	.5	73	23.1	263	67.9	9	15	.7	14	0	.0
97870	.6	0	.3	85	16.6	112	59.2	6	21	.0	0	0	.0
97873	.3	100	.1	77	22.5	160	27.8	10	13	.2	11	0	.0
97874	.3	100	.1	78	19.9	201	42.9	9	17	.2	18	0	.0
97875	2.2	94	.7	71	23.4	363	72.4	11	6	1.0	6	0	.0
97876	.9	97	.3	78	23.8	335	119.2	12	6	.5	8	0	.0
97877	.2	100	.1	81	17.0	227	44.5	6	19	.1	17	0	.0
97880	.9	84	.4	56	23.5	207	56.2	14	6	.1	9	0	.0
97882	4.3	89	1.4	66	24.6	348	56.4	13	5	1.9	6	0	.1
97883	2.6	99	.9	77	20.6	317	74.3	8	14	1.3	12	0	.0
97884	.3	0	.1	47	19.7	248	35.2	11	5	.0	0	0	.0
97885	1.5	100	.6	73	22.3	252	64.3	5	16	.8	12	0	.0
97886	1.0	98	.4	74	20.8	331	55.5	7	11	.5	10	0	.1
BOISE													
97901	2.0	100	.1	97	22.7	261*	53.8	1	18	.1	26	0	.0
97903	.1	100	.1	59	18.2	101	64.8*	0	5	.1	27	0	.3
97904	.2	100	.1	70	17.2	40	26.4	19	18	.1	21	0	.1
97905	.2	100	.1	83	22.0	237	30.8	4	16	.1	18	0	.0
97906	.3	100	.1	81	16.7	192*	27.8	0	28	.1	27	0	.0
97907	.7	0	.3	75	17.2	185	38.2	7	15	.0	0	0	.1
97910	.8	94	.3	72	23.4	284	45.9	13	5	.4	7	0	.0
97911	1.0	100	.1	60	14.4	161	48.9	8	23	.1	28	0	.0

*=Estimated **1.0=883 lbs per person; 100++ indicates per capita toxic waste generation > than 100 times the U.S. average of 883 lbs per capita.

ZIP CODE MEASURES OF SIZE, LEVELS OF AFFLUENCE AND QUALITY OF LIFE

1=Population (th.); 2= % White; 3=Households (th.); 4=% Owner Occupied; 5=Mean Income Per Household (th.$); 6=Mean Monthly Rent ($)*; 7=Mean Home Value (th.$)*;
8=% under 5; 9=% 65 and over; 10=White Males (th.); 11=% White Males, 65+; 12=# Toxic Waste Sites; 13=Toxic Waste Relative to US(883 lbs.per capita)**.

OREGON

BOISE

ZIPCODE	1	2	3	4	5	6	7	8	9	10	11	12	13
97913	5.3	71	1.7	70	20.0	227	59.2	10	13	1.9	16	0	.1
97914	14.0	87	4.9	67	22.3	270	83.6	9	12	6.0	11	1	.1
97918	4.2	94	1.5	76	20.3	214	62.1	8	16	1.9	18	0	.0

PENNSYLVANIA

ZIPCODE	1	2	3	4	5	6	7	8	9	10	11	12	13
MONTICELLO													
12723	.4	100	.1	84	20.3	316	63.4	6	12	.2	9	0	.0
12764	1.0	100	.4	88	17.8	299	79.7	5	21	.5	22	0	.0
BINGHAMTON													
13754	.3	0	.1	81	16.9	314	59.6	7	12	.0	0	0	.0
13783	.3	0	.1	84	20.8	318	54.8	11	14	.0	0	0	.0
BINGHAMTON													
13812	.8	0	.3	86	22.0	308	48.9	7	8	.0	0	0	.0
JAMESTOWN													
14721	.7	100	.2	84	23.9	179	52.1	8	8	.3	9	0	.0
14754	.3	96	.1	90	18.7	214*	47.0	7	9	.1	9	1	.0
ELMIRA													
14892	1.5	99	.5	75	22.9	342	56.3	7	12	.7	11	0	.0
14894	1.5	0	.5	78	21.5	285	53.2	10	9	.0	0	1	.0
PITTSBURGH													
15001	38.3	86	13.5	77	29.3	302	77.8	6	12	15.9	11	2	3.2
15003	16.1	96	6.3	66	25.2	273	67.5	5	18	7.3	17	2	1.1
15004	.4	100	.1	84	18.7	320	48.4	2	13	.2	14	1	.0
15005	9.6	99	3.2	79	30.7	328	92.9	7	10	4.6	9	2	.0
15006	.6	99	.2	92	26.1	497	55.1	5	11	.3	15	0	.0
15007	.4	0	.2	89	27.2	144	80.4	4	29	.0	0	2	2.7
15009	16.5	98	5.9	73	32.3	333	94.5	6	17	7.7	13	0	.7
15010	34.9	93	12.3	71	27.9	318	78.5	6	12	15.6	11	1	2.2
15012	17.2	98	6.4	77	25.7	288	76.6	6	13	8.2	12	0	.0
15014	4.5	98	1.7	65	22.6	254	54.5	5	19	2.0	16	0	5.9
15015	1.3	100	.4	94	56.8	336	166.1	5	6	.7	5	0	.0
15017	14.2	95	5.0	74	29.7	390	89.6	5	16	6.5	13	3	6.1
15018	1.6	96	.5	81	32.4	315	72.8	4	15	.8	16	0	.0
15019	1.7	100	.6	85	26.5	305	66.3	6	9	.9	8	0	.0
15020	.2	100	.1	89	24.0	170	44.3	3	27	.1	29	0	.0
15021	8.5	98	2.8	78	29.4	288	75.9	6	11	4.0	10	0	.1
15022	13.6	98	5.5	73	24.9	255	62.0	6	18	6.2	15	1	.2
15024	9.1	100	3.1	84	30.7	347	79.0	6	10	4.4	9	0	1.7
15025	18.7	81	7.0	68	25.8	272	64.8	6	16	7.2	14	3	2.3
15026	3.4	99	1.2	89	30.7	385	89.0	8	10	1.7	9	1	.0
15027	2.7	0	.9	85	32.3	345	77.0	5	8	.0	0	0	.0
15028	.3	100	.1	83	18.5	416	39.7	2	19	.1	18	0	.1
15030	1.4	96	.6	71	21.8	280	46.1	5	21	.7	22	0	.6
15031	.5	0	.2	71	29.6	325	76.1	7	3	1.2	3	0	.0
15032	.7	100	.2	87	19.8	203	48.3	4	22	.3	17	0	.0
15033	7.6	86	2.9	63	21.0	226	40.1	5	19	3.1	17	0	1.1
15034	2.5	0	1.0	71	23.2	253	54.6	6	18	.0	0	0	1.2
15035	3.0	99	3.1	66	23.6	335	58.9	5	17	1.4	15	0	.3
15036	.2	100	.1	80	20.7	418	51.6	3	18	.1	17	0	.0
15037	13.8	97	4.6	85	29.4	300	75.8	6	10	6.6	9	0	.1
15038	.7	0	.2	75	29.5	280	58.7	12	11	.0	0	1	.0
15042	8.5	96	2.9	86	28.4	309	78.1	2	10	4.1	8	1	1.7
15043	2.4	98	.7	87	29.6	325	76.1	7	3	1.2	3	0	.0
15044	14.9	99	4.8	87	34.8	294	109.0	7	7	7.5	6	0	.0
15045	6.3	100	2.3	68	24.0	297	52.9	5	15	3.0	14	0	.0

*=Estimated **1.0=883 lbs per person; 100++ indicates per capita toxic waste generation > than 100 times the U.S. average of 883 lbs per capita.

ZIP CODE MEASURES OF SIZE, LEVELS OF AFFLUENCE AND QUALITY OF LIFE

1=Population (th.); 2=% White; 3=Households (th.); 4=% Owner Occupied; 5=Mean Income Per Household (th.$); 6=Mean Monthly Rent ($)*; 7=Mean Home Value (th.$)*;
8=% under 5; 9=% 65 and over; 10=White Males (th.); 11=% White Males, 65+; 12=# Toxic Waste Sites; 13=Toxic Waste Relative to US(883 lbs.per capita)**

PENNSYLVANIA — PITTSBURGH

ZIPCODE	1	2	3	4	5	6	7	8	9	10	11	12	13
15046	.7	90	.3	74	27.1	347	61.9	10	9	.3	9	0	.5
15047	.5	100	.2	94	25.7	296*	60.6	4	16	.2	13	0	.0
15049	1.1	100	.4	82	26.0	313	54.3	4	11	.5	8	0	.0
15050	2.8	99	.8	87	30.3	331	87.9	8	7	1.5	8	0	.0
15051	.7	0	.2	85	20.0	270	58.0	3	19	.0	0	3	3.2
15052	4.6	97	1.5	90	33.2	371	79.7	7	9	2.3	9	0	.0
15053	.3	100	.1	85	22.6	321	79.0	8	14	.1	6	0	.0
15054	.9	0	.3	78	22.0	299	38.4	9	12	.0	0	0	38.0
15055	.8	91	.3	73	25.0	269	56.6	4	16	.4	13	0	.1
15056	1.6	95	.6	69	26.1	359	61.9	5	16	.7	14	1	1.7
15057	10.6	97	3.6	81	27.4	311	79.7	7	12	4.9	10	1	.0
15059	6.2	83	2.3	59	26.0	219	52.9	7	12	2.4	11	1	.3
15060	1.2	99	.4	79	27.7	307	68.5	7	13	.6	11	0	.0
15061	17.6	97	6.0	77	31.4	372	89.7	6	9	8.4	8	4	10.2
15062	12.1	90	4.8	75	24.8	196	58.9	4	19	5.2	18	1	5.4
15063	14.7	97	5.4	77	25.9	267	68.1	5	16	6.9	14	1	1.0
15064	.9	79	.3	34	15.9	206	52.9	11	8	.1	3	0	.0
15065	14.4	98	5.4	73	27.2	280	68.7	5	15	6.7	13	0	.1
15066	15.2	95	5.5	71	26.0	309	68.5	7	12	7.0	10	4	.4
15067	2.7	99	1.0	85	23.6	274	57.9	6	12	1.3	12	0	.0
15068	44.4	95	16.7	71	25.3	282	75.0	6	15	20.1	13	2	1.4
15071	7.2	97	2.4	84	29.7	343	78.2	6	10	3.6	8	1	.3
15072	.4	68	.2	88	21.0	135	34.5	5	27	.1	10	0	.1
15074	11.4	94	4.1	72	26.5	306	69.4	7	11	5.2	10	3	.8
15075	.3	100	.1	53	22.4	318	49.1	4	10	.1	10	1	.0
15076	1.3	100	.5	69	23.3	332	56.4	5	15	.6	10	0	.0
15077	.2	0	.1	66	32.5	373	70.4	7	9	.0	0	0	30.2
15078	.9	88	.3	78	18.9	242	49.1	8	12	.4	13	0	.0
15081	.7	0	.2	78	28.0	395	63.0	9	15	.0	0	2	.2
15082	.6	100	.2	88	29.4	289	55.2	4	11	.3	8	0	.0
15083	1.2	97	.4	81	30.4	247	74.3	7	14	.6	12	0	.0
15084	11.8	99	4.5	65	23.1	254	58.3	7	14	5.7	12	1	.0
15085	8.9	99	3.1	84	30.7	292	84.5	6	11	4.3	10	1	.4
15086	.5	100	.2	82	30.5	337	103.6	6	5	.3	8	0	2.6
15087	.5	100	.2	59	19.4	264	38.0	5	15	.2	15	0	.0
15088	1.2	96	.4	65	26.1	284	50.2	4	18	.6	13	0	4.3
15089	7.4	98	2.7	80	27.1	212	68.2	7	13	3.5	11	1	.2
15090	7.9	99	2.5	84	39.9	435	133.3	6	9	3.9	7	0	.0
15091	.3	100	.1	81	22.4	392	72.5	8	14	.1	12	0	.2
15092	.4	0	.1	83	28.3	401	49.6	6	14	.0	0	0	.0

PENNSYLVANIA — PITTSBURGH

ZIPCODE	1	2	3	4	5	6	7	8	9	10	11	12	13
15101	22.8	98	7.2	82	40.5	454	122.9	6	7	11.0	5	1	.0
15102	31.5	98	10.3	82	37.7	454	111.7	6	8	15.5	15	0	.4
15104	17.2	69	6.8	54	18.4	217	36.4	6	17	8.5	17	0	2.3
15106	22.1	99	8.5	64	27.1	348	76.2	5	14	10.2	14	1	1.1
15108	37.0	95	13.0	70	32.0	384	97.9	9	12	16.9	7	4	.3
15110	10.1	77	4.1	58	20.8	247	46.1	7	18	3.6	18	10	100++
15112	4.3	97	1.8	60	23.2	260	54.5	6	18	2.0	16	0	2.8
15116	16.5	98	5.3	89	28.1	460	103.4	6	10	7.9	8	1	4.9

PENNSYLVANIA — PITTSBURGH

ZIPCODE	1	2	3	4	5	6	7	8	9	10	11	12	13
15120	24.7	91	10.0	67	24.4	250	63.2	5	18	10.5	15	0	7.9
15122	25.4	93	9.3	81	28.6	310	72.1	5	12	11.5	11	4	3.2
15126	4.3	99	1.5	82	27.7	306	76.7	6	10	2.1	9	3	.0
15127	.7	100	.2	74	48.3	580	127.5	4	16	.3	14	0	.0
15131	10.2	95	3.4	74	31.2	439	96.3	10	5	4.8	4	0	.0
15132	10.3	99	3.8	79	21.9	394	84.4	5	15	5.0	12	1	.0
15133	33.4	87	13.2	60	21.9	262	47.6	6	18	13.5	16	1	.4
15135	8.7	99	3.1	86	27.0	306	61.3	5	13	4.2	12	0	.1
15136	5.2	99	1.9	80	32.4	451	88.1	6	12	2.5	10	0	.1
15137	26.8	96	10.1	66	25.1	264	69.0	6	15	12.3	14	2	1.3
15139	13.1	91	4.9	75	27.9	359	66.9	5	11	5.8	10	0	.0
15140	7.0	99	2.7	55	33.3	420	101.8	4	20	3.1	15	1	1.3
15142	4.2	99	1.7	54	22.0	276	50.0	4	15	1.9	13	0	.0
15143	.2	0	.1	87	23.1	425	48.7	5	11	.3	14	0	.3
15144	16.7	94	6.0	74	46.1	412	131.2	5	14	7.5	12	1	3.6
15145	5.2	100	2.0	71	25.5	310	63.9	5	14	2.5	12	1	.1
15146	9.4	99	3.9	58	23.8	311	58.1	6	16	4.2	14	0	.2
15147	31.1	92	11.0	72	34.1	467	98.9	6	7	13.9	7	1	1.0
15148	21.3	87	7.3	81	29.2	359	75.5	6	10	9.0	9	1	1.0

PENNSYLVANIA — PITTSBURGH

ZIPCODE	1	2	3	4	5	6	7	8	9	10	11	12	13
15201	3.5	98	1.5	57	20.5	251	46.7	6	20	1.5	16	0	11.8
15202	18.3	92	7.2	65	22.6	263	51.2	5	18	7.7	15	8	3.2
15203	24.2	98	10.4	49	25.9	368	79.0	5	18	10.5	14	0	.4
15204	12.1	98	5.3	57	18.0	231	32.3	4	20	5.6	17	2	.0
15205	12.0	91	4.3	73	26.1	325	62.7	5	16	5.1	14	0	4.7
15206	25.9	88	10.1	59	26.1	329	77.2	6	12	10.7	10	0	.5
15207	43.2	61	18.3	40	22.9	339	71.4	5	17	12.1	16	3	.3
15208	17.9	88	6.6	73	23.3	266	51.8	5	15	7.4	14	1	.1
15209	19.6	24	7.3	48	22.8	304	80.8	6	16	2.0	17	0	.3
15210	14.7	100	5.4	76	25.5	313	76.9	5	15	6.9	13	0	.2
15211	22.7	78	8.6	64	21.5	240	48.6	8	14	9.5	13	1	.3
15212	15.4	98	6.2	60	24.4	345	52.9	5	15	7.1	11	1	.1
15213	42.6	87	17.4	54	20.2	259	51.6	6	19	17.3	17	3	.2
15214	29.5	69	12.7	24	22.1	332	80.3	3	16	9.8	12	1	.3
15215	23.2	73	7.9	62	22.5	257	62.6	6	13	7.9	13	1	.3
15216	15.3	98	5.6	67	37.0	364	122.8	4	16	7.1	15	1	1.3
15217	30.6	98	11.8	64	29.0	369	80.7	4	19	13.8	11	0	.0
15218	29.4	96	12.2	54	37.2	422	126.4	4	17	12.8	16	1	.2
15219	17.9	96	7.1	65	26.1	349	76.4	5	17	7.8	15	0	1.2
15220	23.6	29	9.0	27	16.1	266	40.1	5	14	2.9	14	0	2.6
15221	21.4	95	8.4	64	31.0	443	90.1	5	13	9.6	10	0	.4
15222	45.3	65	18.6	52	25.0	351	73.5	6	16	13.3	16	1	.0
15223	1.9	85	.7	14	20.9	246	28.4	0	29	.8	21	0	17.7
15224	9.2		3.7	65	22.7	329	66.0	5	18	5.3	18	1	.4
15225	16.1	76	6.6	44	19.4	275	44.5	4	20	5.3	18	0	.2
15226	1.4	99	.7	53	24.3	301	66.7	4	18	.7	16	10	100++
15227	17.8	99	6.4	80	25.9	367	70.5	6	16	8.4	13	0	1.7
15228	35.2	100	13.4	72	28.4	371	83.4	5	14	16.5	12	0	.0
15228	18.0		5.3	68	41.4	447	128.0	5	17	8.3	12	0	.0

*=Estimated **1.0=883 lbs per person; 100++ indicates per capita toxic waste generation > than 100 times the U.S. average of 883 lbs per capita.

ZIP CODE MEASURES OF SIZE, LEVELS OF AFFLUENCE AND QUALITY OF LIFE

1=Population (th.); 2= % White; 3=Households (th.); 4=% Owner Occupied; 5=Mean Income Per Household (th.$); 6=Mean Monthly Rent ($)*; 7=Mean Home Value (th.$)*; 8=% under 5; 9=% 65 and over; 10=White Males (th.); 11=% White Males, 65+; 12=# Toxic Waste Sites; 13=Toxic Waste Relative to US(883 lbs.per capita)**.

PENNSYLVANIA

ZIP CODE	1	2	3	4	5	6	7	8	9	10	11	12	13
PITTSBURGH													
15229	16.0	100	6.0	75	28.7	404	84.0	5	16	7.3	13	0	.0
15232	12.7	89	6.8	21	26.6	386	164.5	3	17	4.8	13	0	.1
15233	4.9	31	1.6	33	16.5	205	49.4	4	13	1.0	12	0	6.2
15234	17.0	99	6.1	72	29.0	405	82.3	5	12	7.9	10	0	.0
15235	48.4	90	16.8	82	33.0	416	89.4	6	11	21.2	10	3	.0
15236	34.9	99	12.2	78	35.2	389	100.0	6	11	16.9	9	2	.1
15237	40.1	98	14.1	80	39.0	422	124.1	6	10	18.9	8	0	.0
15238	11.4	97	4.0	82	60.7	376	174.5	5	10	5.5	8	3	3.9
15239	21.4	97	6.5	79	33.0	409	89.8	7	5	10.5	4	1	.0
15240	.5	100	.2	74	32.5	322	83.7	4	12	.3	13	0	2.4
15241	20.4	99	6.2	91	61.0	519	172.8	5	7	9.9	6	2	.0
15243	16.4	98	5.0	96	52.4	642	133.2	5	18	7.3	13	0	.1
WASHINGTON													
15301	52.9	94	19.0	68	26.1	308	81.5	7	14	23.5	11	7	1.3
15311	1.5	0	.5	88	26.4	165	63.4	7	11	.0	0	0	.0
15312	4.0	99	1.3	78	26.2	289	63.3	8	11	2.0	10	1	.0
15313	.6	100	.2	86	24.0	199	61.5	7	18	.3	16	0	.0
15314	3.9	99	1.5	81	24.9	260	63.7	6	14	1.9	13	0	.0
15316	1.0	0	.4	88	23.1	248	33.1	7	15	.0	0	0	.0
15317	29.0	97	9.7	76	33.4	326	114.9	6	10	13.8	9	1	1.1
15320	5.4	100	2.0	77	24.3	245	69.7	7	13	2.5	12	0	.0
15321	1.0	96	.6	77	25.4	351	76.4	7	11	.5	6	0	.9
15322	2.8	92	.8	84	24.1	212	47.0	6	14	1.3	12	0	.7
15323	4.9	99	1.6	75	23.3	268	72.2	8	13	2.4	12	0	.0
15324	.8	0	.3	83	26.4	301	47.7	5	15	.0	0	0	.0
15325	.7	100	.2	87	19.5	329	36.2	7	20	.3	15	0	.0
15326	.2	100	.1	69	19.2	270	64.6	8	11	.1	6	0	.0
15327	1.6	98	.5	80	21.9	270	49.2	9	12	.8	11	0	.0
15329	2.0	100	.6	82	24.3	207	69.2	7	15	.1	12	0	.0
15330	5.1	97	1.6	86	28.7	369	101.3	8	7	2.5	6	1	1.0
15331	1.3	97	.5	86	24.7	319	47.6	6	16	.6	16	0	.0
15332	8.7	99	3.1	87	27.6	312	84.0	5	12	4.2	10	0	.0
15333	2.6	99	1.0	81	21.9	290	42.0	9	9	1.2	20	2	.0
15334	.2	100	.1	86	23.4	400	99.6	4	12	.1	12	0	.0
15336	.2	100	.1	97	22.8	262*	69.2	7	15	.1	11	0	.0
15337	.8	0	.3	72	19.0	257	66.9	9	13	.0	0	0	.0
15338	2.0	99	.7	82	23.7	244	52.7	7	14	.0	15	0	.7
15339	.4	92	.1	90	24.9	290	42.0	9	9	.2	4	0	.0
15340	1.6	100	.5	73	33.0	400	99.6	4	12	.8	13	0	.5
15341	.8	99	.3	73	19.1	168	52.0	9	14	.4	12	0	.0
15342	5.2	94	1.9	73	27.9	327	85.7	5	13	2.3	11	1	1.1
15344	1.8	98	.6	85	23.6	191	61.2	6	11	.9	11	0	.0
15345	2.2	93	.8	79	23.4	272	46.5	8	14	1.0	12	0	.0
15346	.9	92	.3	88	21.6	132	48.7	7	14	.4	12	0	.5
15347	1.0	97	.4	78	27.1	283	71.4	4	12	.5	12	0	1.1
15348	.4	100	.1	82	19.9	341	44.8	8	9	.2	12	0	.0
15349	1.7	100	.6	81	26.0	312	71.5	8	13	.8	12	0	.0
15350	.9	95	.4	73	19.4	283	33.5	7	20	.4	20	1	4.8

PENNSYLVANIA

ZIP CODE	1	2	3	4	5	6	7	8	9	10	11	12	13
WASHINGTON													
15351	1.2	100	.5	84	22.2	316	24.3	9	19	.6	15	0	.0
15352	1.0	0	.3	65	17.5	219	49.7	9	14	.0	0	0	.0
15354	.5	0	.2	78	20.9	169	42.7	6	14	.0	0	1	.0
15357	1.8	0	.6	80	25.2	257	64.8	7	15	.0	0	0	.0
15358	.9	100	.3	94	24.6	300	49.6	7	13	.5	13	0	.0
15359	.2	100	.1	76	22.2	258	57.0	7	18	.1	17	1	.0
15360	1.8	99	.6	87	26.8	331	74.5	7	12	.9	12	1	.1
15361	.2	100	.1	84	26.8	228	41.2	12	24	.1	22	0	.0
15362	.9	100	.3	73	19.7	294	88.0	8	11	.4	11	0	2.7
15363	.8	0	.4	72	22.5	310	59.9	2	22	.0	0	1	.0
15364	.8	0	.3	74	22.2	203	61.3	9	9	.0	0	0	.0
15365	.2	98	.1	69	20.8	248	53.1	5	10	.1	8	0	.0
15366	.3	100	.1	89	33.9	316	55.6	4	12	.2	11	0	.0
15367	2.5	100	.8	88	37.3	425	130.5	8	7	1.2	5	0	.4
15368	.7	100	.3	86	20.3	360	26.4	3	26	.3	21	0	.0
15370	12.7	99	4.4	63	23.5	275	76.2	7	15	6.0	12	0	.0
15376	1.6	100	.6	86	23.7	205	69.2	8	15	.8	12	0	41.8
15377	1.0	0	.3	79	18.4	183	52.0	9	12	.0	0	0	.0
15378	.2	67	.1	66	21.9	260	39.8	3	20	.1	33	0	.0
15379	.2	83	.1	80	29.4	221	45.3	2	19	.1	21	0	.6
15380	.7	100	.2	71	19.4	182	53.6	7	12	.3	9	0	.0
UNIONTOWN													
15401	37.3	94	13.9	65	23.1	258	66.9	6	16	16.0	14	3	.0
15410	1.1	92	1.1	89	22.9	144	40.1	7	13	.5	17	0	.0
15411	.6	100	.2	81	21.7	308	58.4	7	15	.3	15	0	.0
15413	.4	98	.1	92	26.7	308	40.7	5	22	.2	19	0	.0
15416	.9	87	.3	81	20.9	273	27.1	6	17	.3	18	0	.0
15417	.5	100	.1	66	14.7	275	40.7	2	8	.2	6	0	.0
15419	10.3	94	4.0	70	22.1	205	51.7	7	17	4.5	15	2	.6
15420	4.7	94	1.3	56	22.8	280	70.7	4	12	2.1	11	0	.0
15421	.4	72	.1	91	24.3	356	31.0	5	10	.2	10	0	.0
15422	.7	100	.3	83	28.1	241	96.2	11	8	.3	6	0	.0
15423	.3	0	.1	67	23.6	258	34.2	4	11	.3	12	0	.0
15424	2.1	0	.7	85	27.2	282	61.7	5	11	.2	12	0	.0
15425	22.4	97	8.1	76	17.6	246	49.2	8	19	10.4	11	3	1.3
15427	1.5	88	.5	68	21.4	259	57.6	6	13	.6	13	0	.0
15428	2.0	100	.7	86	21.5	274	46.1	7	14	1.0	12	0	.0
15430	.5	100	.2	77	21.1	238	47.6	8	13	.2	12	0	.0
15431	5.5	99	1.9	82	23.1	315	34.2	5	15	2.7	11	0	.0
15432	.5	99	.2	82	19.4	249	48.0	7	13	.6	12	0	.0
15433	.9	100	.3	77	24.7	303	63.3	8	10	1.0	12	0	.0
15434	.4	100	.2	84	24.0	224	43.8	5	12	.2	12	0	.0
15435	1.0	93	.4	82	20.2	271	42.0	6	18	.4	17	0	.0
15436	3.4	98	1.1	74	20.2	268	30.0	6	14	1.6	12	0	.1
15437	2.1	100	.6	73	21.1	243	48.6	7	14	1.1	15	0	.0
15438	2.6	99	1.0	84	26.4	262	69.1	8	13	1.3	12	0	.0
15439	.3	100	.1	91	15.4	273	36.2	4	14	.1	12	0	.0

*=Estimated **1.0=883 lbs per person; 100++ indicates per capita toxic waste generation > than 100 times the U.S. average of 883 lbs per capita.

ZIP CODE MEASURES OF SIZE, LEVELS OF AFFLUENCE AND QUALITY OF LIFE

1=Population (th.); 2= % White; 3=Households (th.); 4=% Owner Occupied; 5=Mean Income Per Household (th.$); 6=Mean Monthly Rent ($); 7=Mean Home Value (th.$); 8=% under 5; 9=% 65 and over; 10=White Males (th.); 11=% White Males, 65+; 12=# Toxic Waste Sites; 13=Toxic Waste Relative to US(883 lbs.per capita)**.

PENNSYLVANIA

UNIONTOWN

ZIP CODE	1	2	3	4	5	6	7	8	9	10	11	12	13
15440	.3	100	.1	75	17.0	195*	49.8	6	14	.2	9	0	.0
15442	3.0	97	1.1	78	21.7	225	41.0	6	15	1.4	16	1	.0
15443	.5	85	.2	89	20.3	356	32.4	8	17	.3	12	0	.0
15444	.7	76	.3	72	23.6	207	45.4	4	25	.3	21	0	.0
15445	3.5	99	1.3	80	26.1	296	79.7	6	13	1.7	12	0	.0
15446	.8	100	.2	67	22.4	289	69.4	7	9	.4	8	0	.0
15447	.3	0	.1	86	19.0	159	26.1	6	19	.0	26	0	.0
15448	.2	100	.1	92	17.1	196*	30.3	0	26	.1	32	0	.0
15449	.4	100	.1	73	14.1	368	25.8	12	15	.1	12	0	.0
15450	.8	92	.3	85	23.0	303	30.5	10	12	.4	9	0	.0
15451	.7	0	.3	76	19.8	235	47.4	2	10	.0	0	0	.0
15452	.3	70	.1	85	26.4	303*	28.4	0	10	.1	10	0	.0
15454	.4	83	.2	74	19.3	224	33.4	7	19	.2	15	0	.0
15455	.5	100	.1	92	20.5	300	31.8	3	14	.3	8	0	.0
15456	3.2	99	1.1	84	19.7	255	47.2	8	12	1.5	11	0	.0
15457	.1	100	.1	73	14.6	192	43.8	10	15	.1	16	0	.0
15458	1.4	86	.5	83	22.1	236	48.9	4	25	.6	22	0	.0
15459	1.6	0	.5	73	18.0	279	56.2	7	16	.0	0	0	.0
15460	.3	0	.1	78	22.0	233	28.2	8	13	.1	0	0	.0
15461	5.7	95	2.1	67	22.5	244	58.9	7	15	2.6	15	1	.0
15462	.5	100	.2	73	21.0	256	42.7	7	13	.2	14	0	.0
15463	.5	100	.2	78	18.1	176	48.6	7	13	.1	12	0	.0
15464	1.3	100	.4	81	21.8	174	50.4	7	8	.6	7	0	.0
15465	.5	100	.2	85	25.5	273	41.5	7	11	.2	12	0	.0
15466	.6	99	.2	81	23.9	182	39.2	5	15	.0	0	2	.0
15467	.4	0	.1	64	19.8	148	40.4	16	7	.0	0	0	39.8
15468	3.2	97	1.1	80	22.4	260	42.9	6	16	1.5	14	0	.0
15469	2.3	100	.7	83	19.1	318	45.6	10	10	1.2	10	1	.0
15470	.9	100	.3	75	17.2	237	56.3	5	11	.4	0	0	.0
15472	.3	100	.1	56	18.9	279	36.0	8	17	.1	17	0	.0
15473	4.1	0	1.5	83	26.5	270	73.8	7	13	.0	0	0	.0
15474	2.6	98	.9	73	22.1	260	51.2	10	13	1.3	10	0	.0
15475	2.5	89	.9	58	20.8	226	49.1	6	12	1.0	10	0	.0
15476	.5	87	.2	78	19.7	186	30.7	5	11	.2	13	0	.0
15477	1.4	100	.6	76	24.8	234	53.1	5	18	.7	16	0	.0
15478	6.1	100	2.0	75	20.8	254	52.6	7	13	3.0	12	1	.0
15479	2.4	96	.9	75	24.1	219	57.0	6	15	1.1	13	0	.0
15480	2.2	0	.7	73	24.3	297	48.8	9	7	.0	0	0	.0
15482	.9	100	.3	76	21.1	314	38.9	4	15	.4	14	0	.1
15483	.4	100	.1	77	24.3	259	60.0	6	15	.0	0	0	.0
15484	.4	100	.1	88	25.3	174	47.3	12	8	.2	11	0	.0
15485	.2	100	.1	82	17.0	262	47.7	10	15	.1	12	0	.0
15486	2.4	96	.8	81	27.1	244	54.2	8	11	1.2	9	0	.0
15487	.2	100	.1	60	17.8	377	20.1	11	18	.1	13	0	.0
15488	.2	100	.1	59	18.3	404	52.4	3	22	.1	31	0	.0
15489	.6	100	.2	90	19.5	230	29.6	7	13	.3	11	0	.0
15490	2.4	96	.9	87	22.0	204	37.7	8	8	.2	13	0	.0
15491	.2	71	.1	57	20.7	272	22.2	2	12	.1	12	0	.3
15492	.2	0	.1	83	20.7	190	39.5	3	11	.0	0	0	.0

PENNSYLVANIA

JOHNSTOWN

ZIP CODE	1	2	3	4	5	6	7	8	9	10	11	12	13
15501	15.7	99	5.8	68	24.7	307	80.7	7	13	7.4	11	3	.6
15520	.4	100	.1	79	19.3	273	40.8	6	24	.2	28	0	.0
15521	1.6	0	.5	84	21.0	254	57.2	9	9	.0	0	0	.0
15522	11.3	99	4.2	74	21.8	251	75.8	6	15	5.4	12	1	.6
15530	4.8	100	1.6	77	23.9	262	66.0	8	15	2.3	12	0	.0
15531	4.1	0	1.4	75	24.8	272	62.2	7	10	.0	0	0	.0
15532	.3	100	.1	78	17.3	134	36.1	4	13	.2	9	0	.7
15533	1.2	100	.3	86	19.2	295	65.7	9	8	.6	6	0	.0
15534	.9	100	.3	86	21.7	243	59.3	6	11	.4	10	0	.0
15535	1.2	100	.4	82	20.0	188	61.0	10	12	.6	10	0	.0
15536	.4	0	.1	86	17.2	182	71.7	6	12	.0	0	0	.0
15537	7.7	100	2.7	75	20.7	257	66.2	6	13	3.7	11	0	.0
15538	.4	100	.2	90	20.1	195	56.2	10	10	.2	8	0	.0
15539	.2	100	.1	86	19.6	266	49.6	5	14	.1	9	0	.0
15540	.3	100	.1	82	18.0	338	50.1	4	21	.1	22	0	.0
15541	3.3	0	1.1	79	23.4	335	68.8	8	10	.0	0	0	.0
15542	1.5	100	.5	82	22.0	193	46.7	6	12	.8	9	0	.0
15543	.4	0	.1	82	23.6	271*	71.2	9	11	.0	0	0	.0
15544	.2	100	.1	87	19.8	297	44.7	13	27	.1	31	0	.0
15545	3.1	100	1.1	83	20.1	224	50.9	7	13	1.5	12	0	.0
15546	.5	100	.2	79	23.5	318	34.9	12	12	.2	10	0	.5
15547	.6	0	.3	83	25.4	245	77.8	7	22	.0	0	0	.0
15549	.2	100	.1	75	23.5	320	48.8	9	6	.1	5	0	.0
15550	1.7	99	.6	85	18.8	225	57.8	8	15	.8	14	0	.0
15551	.9	0	.3	86	19.3	263	50.5	10	10	.0	0	0	.0
15552	6.5	100	2.2	78	19.8	220	54.4	9	14	3.1	12	1	.0
15553	.2	100	.1	85	21.1	242*	40.2	6	18	.1	13	0	.0
15554	2.2	0	.7	84	20.5	249	62.8	8	11	.0	0	0	.0
15555	.1	100	.1	90	17.7	203*	38.5	7	17	.1	18	0	.0
15557	3.9	100	1.3	80	23.2	287	59.6	8	12	1.5	12	0	.0
15558	1.6	100	.6	80	20.0	208	56.0	7	14	.8	12	0	.5
15559	1.7	100	.6	82	20.5	170	58.8	9	10	.9	10	0	.0
15560	.3	100	.1	75	26.5	248	64.1	5	8	.2	6	0	.0
15561	.3	100	.1	88	24.8	444	68.8	4	12	.1	10	0	.0
15562	.4	100	.1	78	20.6	227	82.7	7	17	.2	16	0	1.1
15563	3.5	100	1.2	84	23.2	256	62.1	6	12	1.8	10	0	.0
15564	.2	100	.1	88	19.2	264	54.9	10	21	.1	25	0	.0

GREENSBURG

ZIP CODE	1	2	3	4	5	6	7	8	9	10	11	12	13
15601	59.3	98	21.1	69	28.4	307	95.5	6	12	27.5	10	1	1
15610	2.9	0	1.0	87	25.5	316	79.6	10	6	.0	0	0	.0
15611	.9	0	.4	78	20.4	280	60.5	12	14	.0	0	0	.0
15612	.6	100	.2	80	21.4	201	65.4	4	13	.3	11	0	.0
15613	14.9	99	5.2	81	25.9	283	76.5	7	12	7.2	11	5	1.2
15615	.3	100	.1	70	22.1	305	56.8	16	9	.1	3	0	.0
15616	.3	100	.1	70	22.0	233	61.2	9	6	.1	4	0	.0
15617	.5	100	.2	85	20.7	370	56.5	8	14	.2	13	0	.0
15618	2.5	97	.9	84	24.8	251	58.8	7	12	1.2	10	0	.3
15619	.5	93	.2	75	28.8	347	61.5	8	8	.3	5	0	.0
15620	1.4	100	.5	79	23.8	335	53.2	5	11	.7	7	0	.0

*=Estimated **1.0=883 lbs per person; 100++ indicates per capita toxic waste generation > than 100 times the U.S. average of 883 lbs per capita.

ZIP CODE MEASURES OF SIZE, LEVELS OF AFFLUENCE AND QUALITY OF LIFE

1=Population (th.); 2= % White; 3=Households (th.); 4=% Owner Occupied; 5=Mean Income Per Household (th.$); 6=Mean Monthly Rent ($); 7=Mean Home Value (th.$); 8=% under 5; 9=% 65 and over; 10=White Males (th.); 11=% White Males, 65+; 12=# Toxic Waste Sites; 13=Toxic Waste Relative to US(883 lbs.per capita)**.

PENNSYLVANIA

GREENSBURG

ZIPCODE	1	2	3	4	5	6	7	8	9	10	11	12	13
15621	.2	0	.1	67	18.9	273	42.5	0	32	.0	0	0	.0
15622	1.0	100	.4	69	21.4	178	72.2	6	11	.5	8	0	.0
15623	.8	0	.3	79	24.5	350	49.1	5	15	.0	0	0	.0
15624	.8	0	.3	72	22.7	340	64.9	2	6	.1	13	0	.0
15625	.2	100	.1	88	25.5	221	78.5	10	18	.2	13	0	.3
15626	5.0	99	1.9	77	26.7	300	93.4	7	16	2.4	13	2	.0
15627	7.0	99	2.5	82	23.3	299	65.4	7	12	3.4	10	0	.0
15628	.6	100	.2	75	24.9	265	83.8	7	10	.3	8	0	.0
15629	1.0	100	.4	80	20.3	275	41.4	7	20	.5	19	0	.2
15630	.3	82	.1	94	17.9	206*	41.9	7	10	.1	15	0	.0
15631	1.3	98	.5	71	19.5	284	43.4	7	15	.6	14	0	.0
15632	7.3	98	2.5	84	31.4	348	100.5	7	9	3.6	9	3	.0
15633	.5	100	.2	84	21.4	214	37.6	4	8	.2	5	0	.0
15634	.8	100	.3	82	24.3	261	41.9	4	8	.4	9	0	.0
15635	.4	100	.1	75	22.0	245	37.8	3	27	.2	21	0	.0
15636	.8	100	.3	79	27.3	223	77.5	10	17	.4	14	1	.0
15637	2.3	98	.8	80	25.2	303	69.4	9	17	1.1	16	0	.0
15639	1.5	0	.5	74	22.2	309	67.0	9	13	.2	11	0	.1
15640	.5	0	.1	85	24.9	239	70.8	6	11	.0	0	0	.0
15642	45.1	99	15.0	80	29.7	266*	45.4	8	6	21.9	7	1	.5
15644	20.9	97	7.8	75	24.1	345	89.7	7	8	9.6	13	0	2.2
15646	.3	100	.1	78	19.7	287	69.0	6	15	.3	14	0	.0
15650	29.1	99	10.2	75	26.6	137	50.4	5	13	14.0	11	2	2.2
15656	11.8	98	4.1	81	30.9	304	78.7	7	12	.4	12	0	.3
15658	9.1	99	3.3	77	30.2	308	104.8	6	15	4.4	13	0	1.1
15660	.5	100	.1	78	24.9	332	92.5	5	15	.2	7	0	.0
15661	.7	100	.3	87	23.1	299	48.1	6	5	.4	13	0	.1
15662	.4	100	.2	78	18.3	240	63.7	7	22	.2	7	0	.0
15664	.4	90	.1	76	35.2	359	46.5	13	8	.2	18	0	.0
15665	1.7	97	.5	84	24.8	405*	81.3	9	11	.8	2	0	2.3
15666	16.6	99	5.8	90	24.9	251	66.8	6	12	.0	4	0	.1
15668	11.0	98	3.4	82	41.2	281	67.8	6	13	5.3	11	0	.4
15670	4.4	0	1.5	85	25.9	396	140.4	6	6	.3	5	0	.0
15671	.8	100	.3	86	23.1	337	80.5	9	9	.2	0	0	.0
15672	4.0	97	1.5	62	26.7	252	79.4	8	8	.4	7	0	13.1
15673	1.4	97	.5	80	25.2	357	94.5	5	17	1.9	3	0	.1
15674	.7	100	.2	94	27.5	269	64.8	6	12	.6	13	0	.0
15675	2.1	99	.7	85	26.3	402	76.5	11	9	.3	15	0	.2
15676	.8	100	.3	71	24.6	213	69.0	10	8	1.0	13	0	.0
15677	.5	100	.2	83	34.5	296	59.6	9	9	.4	7	0	.0
15678	.9	100	.3	63	26.4	298	100.3	6	19	.3	3	0	.3
15679	3.6	100	1.1	86	26.7	347	64.7	8	12	.0	9	0	.0
15680	.3	100	.1	82	23.5	297	75.4	6	20	.2	15	0	.1
15681	5.0	100	1.7	80	23.7	249	47.1	7	10	2.5	10	1	.1
15683	9.8	99	3.5	76	23.8	253	64.7	7	13	4.6	11	1	.2
15684	1.0	92	.3	84	22.6	253	50.2	7	13	.5	11	4	.0

PENNSYLVANIA

GREENSBURG

ZIPCODE	1	2	3	4	5	6	7	8	9	10	11	12	13
15685	.5	100	.2	76	21.3	404	43.1	4	19	.3	16	0	.0
15686	1.2	98	.4	80	29.1	352	96.5	8	9	.6	7	0	.6
15687	1.5	100	.5	85	26.5	284	72.9	7	14	.7	13	0	.0
15688	.9	100	.3	78	22.7	242	55.9	8	11	.4	10	0	.0
15689	.4	100	.2	71	24.6	282	51.9	6	10	.2	13	0	.0
15690	11.2	96	4.4	86	23.1	259	57.7	6	18	5.2	15	1	.0
15691	1.0	100	.4	86	22.5	261	39.5	9	9	.2	7	0	.0
15692	.4	100	.1	85	23.9	408	56.8	7	18	.4	16	0	.0
15693	.4	100	.1	68	20.9	202	51.0	4	24	.2	11	0	.2
15694	.2	100	.1	63	16.8	263	61.0	9	20	.1	19	0	.0
15695	.4	0	.1	72	22.2	253	58.2	11	4	.0	0	0	.1
15696	1.0	100	.4	76	25.6	246	61.8	5	10	.5	11	0	.0
15697	3.7	100	1.6	70	23.1	309	66.2	8	15	1.8	12	1	2.5
15698	1.0	100	.4	75	19.4	254	52.2	8	15	.5	12	1	.0

INDIANA

ZIPCODE	1	2	3	4	5	6	7	8	9	10	11	12	13
15701	33.8	97	10.5	61	27.0	368	98.0	5	10	15.1	8	1	.1
15710	.4	0	.2	87	26.4	241	51.7	5	11	.0	0	0	.0
15711	.5	0	.2	81	19.0	250	51.5	7	14	.0	0	1	.0
15712	.5	0	.1	88	21.3	119	38.0	5	15	.0	1	0	.0
15713	.3	100	.1	91	21.3	245*	41.6	8	20	.1	0	0	.0
15714	5.9	100	2.1	77	22.0	270	52.1	8	14	2.9	13	0	.0
15715	.9	0	.3	81	23.0	313	53.2	5	15	.0	0	0	.0
15716	1.2	0	.4	78	21.9	334	57.9	6	13	.0	2	2	.2
15717	10.6	98	3.7	76	24.7	270	74.5	6	13	5.1	13	0	.3
15721	.4	0	.1	69	21.7	330	50.5	9	9	.0	0	0	.0
15722	2.8	0	.9	86	24.4	280	61.2	9	11	.0	0	0	.0
15724	3.0	0	.9	85	21.8	294	63.5	8	16	.0	0	0	.0
15725	1.4	100	.5	91	25.3	329	68.7	6	11	.7	10	0	.0
15727	.3	100	.1	76	24.1	360	33.2	4	15	.1	18	0	.1
15728	4.2	0	1.4	81	22.8	304	53.6	8	12	.0	4	0	.0
15729	1.6	0	.5	85	20.5	298	51.4	9	10	.0	5	0	.0
15730	.6	100	.1	86	26.8	170	57.9	9	9	.1	3	0	.0
15731	.6	0	.2	78	26.8	329	56.2	7	12	.3	8	0	.0
15732	1.6	0	.5	83	23.9	292	59.3	8	13	.0	11	2	.1
15733	.2	100	.1	93	14.5	166*	23.3	4	16	.1	13	0	.4
15734	.5	100	.2	78	26.7	228	37.9	3	15	.3	5	0	.0
15736	.7	0	.3	66	23.5	245	82.8	8	18	.0	0	0	.0
15737	.9	0	.3	84	23.4	355	33.5	7	10	.2	13	0	.1
15738	.6	100	.2	84	22.0	344	42.5	7	14	.0	9	0	.0
15739	.7	0	.2	84	21.3	316	46.0	7	17	.0	13	0	.0
15742	1.0	0	.7	79	18.3	151	57.1	9	19	.0	8	0	.2
15743	.2	100	.1	66	16.6	288	41.0	7	18	.1	12	0	.0
15745	.4	100	.1	90	21.1	311	60.2	8	17	.2	13	0	.0
15746	.9	100	.3	88	21.0	196	80.1	8	12	.1	13	0	.0
15747	2.0	0	.6	84	25.7	177	67.2	7	8	.0	8	0	.0
15748	7.6	100	2.6	78	25.1	306	71.7	8	8	3.8	8	0	1.2
15750	.3	84	.1	85	21.5	330	71.0	7	0	.1	0	0	.0
15752	.2	100	.1	70	25.4	329	71.0	6	13	.1	12	0	.1
15753	.6	100	.2	85	26.0	310	42.9	10	13	.3	9	0	.0

*=Estimated **1.0=883 lbs per person; 100++ indicates per capita toxic waste generation > than 100 times the U.S. average of 883 lbs per capita.

ZIP CODE MEASURES OF SIZE, LEVELS OF AFFLUENCE AND QUALITY OF LIFE

1=Population (th.); 2= % White; 3=Households (th.); 4=% Owner Occupied; 5=Mean Income Per Household (th.$); 6=Mean Monthly Rent ($)*; 7=Mean Home Value (th.$)*; 8=% under 5; 9=% 65 and over; 10=White Males (th.); 11=% White Males, 65+; 12=# Toxic Waste Sites; 13=Toxic Waste Relative to US(883 lbs.per capita)**.

PENNSYLVANIA

ZIPCODE	1	2	3	4	5	6	7	8	9	10	11	12	13
INDIANA													
15754	.7	0	.2	96	26.6	306*	50.1	5	11	.0	0	0	.0
15756	.2	0	.1	90	20.4	311	36.7	5	17	.0	0	0	.0
15757	2.0	0	.7	83	23.7	268	51.2	10	12	.0	0	0	.0
15759	2.6	100	.8	80	26.0	299	68.7	10	10	1.3	9	0	.0
15760	2.6	100	.1	90	18.6	213*	30.1	3	26	.1	27	0	.0
15762	.9	100	.3	90	32.4	338	66.9	11	8	.5	4	0	.0
15764	.2	100	.1	86	24.6	283*	86.0	15	12	.1	14	0	.0
15765	1.6	100	.5	86	24.4	254	75.6	9	10	.8	12	0	.0
15767	14.8	99	5.4	73	23.2	234	66.7	8	15	7.0	12	1	.6
15770	.3	100	.1	83	32.3	237	74.9	8	13	.2	12	0	.0
15771	1.0	0	.3	86	23.6	202	54.0	7	15	.0	0	0	.0
15772	2.0	0	.6	85	19.2	231	47.1	7	15	.0	0	0	.0
15773	.5	0	.2	90	28.5	516	43.8	7	10	.0	0	0	.0
15774	3.1	100	1.0	84	25.2	292	71.5	8	10	1.6	10	0	.0
15775	2.5	100	.8	81	24.2	284	52.1	10	15	1.2	15	0	.0
15777	.2	100	.1	76	11.8	271	35.2	9	27	.1	26	0	.0
15778	.2	100	.1	79	19.7	226	40.3	9	17	.1	12	0	.0
15779	1.0	96	.1	74	31.0	338	56.6	2	38	.4	31	0	.7
15780	.3	100	.1	83	19.7	229	50.3	7	10	.1	7	0	.0
15781	.2	100	.1	91	18.3	210*	39.6	2	25	.1	21	0	.0
15783	.2	98	.1	81	20.7	191	46.6	8	13	.1	11	0	.0
DU BOIS													
15801	17.8	100	6.5	73	25.9	287	70.1	7	15	8.4	12	2	.7
15821	.2	100	.1	77	24.9	225	50.4	3	6	.1	14	0	.7
15822	.2	100	.1	85	22.7	261*	33.6	4	14	.1	14	0	.0
15823	1.5	0	.5	80	25.4	343	67.1	9	9	.0	0	0	.0
15824	5.6	100	2.0	78	27.5	284	73.2	7	12	2.8	11	3	.4
15825	9.9	100	3.5	78	23.4	295	67.9	7	18	4.7	15	0	.8
15827	.4	100	.1	88	18.5	258	49.6	5	11	.2	11	0	.0
15828	.2	100	.1	93	19.4	223*	69.1	6	15	.1	17	0	.0
15829	1.3	0	.4	82	26.4	311	66.9	6	11	.0	1	0	.0
15831	.4	100	.1	76	19.7	212	52.7	18	5	.2	4	0	.0
15832	.4	100	.2	85	20.4	185	50.2	5	14	.2	15	0	.0
15834	5.9	100	2.3	70	21.1	233	61.1	7	14	2.9	11	0	.2
15840	2.1	100	.7	85	24.1	335	62.4	7	12	1.0	9	0	.0
15841	4.9	99	1.7	77	23.1	436	43.3	4	11	.2	10	0	.0
15845	3.1	100	1.0	84	24.1	332	56.2	8	14	1.6	9	2	.0
15846	1.3	0	.4	83	21.9	281	58.4	8	11	.0	0	0	.0
15847	.4	100	.1	84	24.1	332	58.0	8	13	.2	5	0	.0
15848	1.0	0	.3	83	24.1	281	58.4	8	11	.0	0	0	.0
15849	1.3	0	.5	84	21.9	332	58.0	8	13	.3	6	0	.0
15850	.3	100	.1	89	16.7	284	44.8	12	11	.0	0	0	.0
15851	7.0	100	2.4	80	22.3	219	57.9	8	13	3.4	12	0	.0
15853	8.1	100	2.9	74	23.5	256	70.9	7	14	.3	9	0	6.0
15856	.7	100	.2	85	20.6	325	74.4	9	7	.3	9	0	.0
15857	15.3	100	4.8	79	29.7	308	80.3	6	12	7.4	10	5	1.3
15860	1.1	0	.4	85	21.0	227	52.4	7	15	.0	0	0	.0
15861	.2	0	.1	92	19.0	219*	46.5	4	21	.1	10	1	.0
15863	.2	100	.1	85	20.6	187	43.9	9	13	.1	10	0	.0

PENNSYLVANIA

ZIPCODE	1	2	3	4	5	6	7	8	9	10	11	12	13
DU BOIS													
15864	2.1	100	.7	82	23.9	232	51.1	9	13	1.1	11	0	.0
15865	1.8	100	.7	71	22.9	192	55.5	7	16	.9	14	0	.1
15866	.3	100	.1	84	25.1	372	50.6	7	13	.1	12	0	.0
15868	1.6	0	.5	90	25.7	272	67.7	8	13	.0	0	0	.0
15870	1.5	0	.5	85	22.5	248	56.2	9	12	.0	0	0	.0
JOHNSTOWN													
15901	9.2	82	4.1	32	15.6	227	32.3	5	25	3.2	22	1	7.2
15902	20.4	96	7.2	58	21.1	274	52.9	7	14	9.4	11	0	.2
15904	17.1	99	6.2	73	28.9	344	83.9	6	12	8.2	10	1	.2
15905	25.7	99	9.3	77	31.9	339	83.4	6	15	12.1	13	0	.2
15906	17.0	96	6.3	68	21.0	246	48.4	6	11	7.9	13	0	.0
15909	7.6	98	2.6	77	23.6	252	56.2	7	12	3.6	11	0	.0
15920	.5	100	.4	89	25.9	257	66.5	11	11	.5	11	2	.0
15921	1.1	100	.4	74	20.1	251	34.6	6	20	.5	18	1	.0
15922	.3	100	.1	89	23.3	267*	57.1	12	8	.1	6	0	.0
15923	2.3	99	.8	87	23.2	275	55.7	7	10	1.2	9	0	.0
15924	1.3	100	.5	91	20.2	282	40.0	6	10	.6	12	0	.0
15925	.4	100	.1	60	20.1	154	46.2	8	10	.2	10	0	.0
15926	1.2	0	.3	83	23.5	229	58.1	8	13	.4	9	0	.0
15927	1.4	100	.5	80	19.6	312	45.1	6	18	.7	15	0	.0
15928	1.1	100	.4	83	31.9	296	85.1	7	12	.5	11	0	.0
15929	.2	100	.1	67	20.3	201	78.5	16	14	.1	13	0	.0
15930	.6	100	.2	83	20.0	227	39.0	5	15	.3	13	0	.0
15931	10.4	98	3.1	74	28.3	344	81.1	7	14	5.0	13	0	.0
15934	.2	100	.2	84	18.6	277	78.3	8	15	.2	14	0	.0
15935	4.2	0	1.5	85	23.4	259	61.7	8	12	.0	0	0	.4
15936	2.0	100	.7	82	20.9	267	51.9	8	14	1.0	12	0	.0
15937	1.0	100	.4	80	20.8	300	42.6	7	12	.5	11	0	.1
15938	2.9	0	.9	84	25.8	265	48.1	7	13	.2	11	0	.0
15940	2.6	99	.5	74	22.5	310	64.6	6	6	1.3	6	0	.0
15942	2.3	100	.7	92	22.3	359	59.6	6	6	1.2	5	0	.0
15943	5.4	100	1.8	81	23.4	297	51.3	7	13	2.6	11	0	.0
15944	3.7	100	1.2	85	24.5	258	73.9	8	10	1.8	9	0	.2
15945	.3	100	.1	100	28.6	329*	49.5	0	9	.1	9	0	.1
15946	8.4	0	2.9	79	24.1	250	58.6	8	13	.0	0	2	.1
15948	.8	0	.3	91	26.4	373	45.7	4	12	.0	0	0	.0
15949	.8	100	.3	92	23.8	96	48.7	9	11	.4	10	0	.0
15951	1.1	100	.3	86	23.1	233	41.1	6	12	.5	11	1	.0
15952	1.4	0	.5	72	24.8	369	71.3	11	5	.2	9	0	.2
15953	.2	100	.1	85	18.5	158	36.0	8	7	.1	6	0	.1
15954	2.9	100	1.0	84	23.6	293	62.4	9	8	1.4	7	0	.0
15955	2.0	100	.8	79	22.3	309	55.3	9	10	1.0	9	0	.6
15956	4.1	100	1.4	83	23.8	227	45.9	7	13	2.0	12	0	.0
15957	.6	0	.3	86	19.5	287	52.6	6	13	.0	0	0	.0
15958	2.5	0	.7	87	27.6	277	68.0	9	7	.3	9	0	.0
15959	.4	100	.1	89	28.7	242	56.3	10	6	.2	8	0	.0
15960	.8	100	.2	84	24.1	325	46.9	7	10	.4	11	0	.0
15961	1.3	100	.5	88	22.3	280	47.6	8	15	.6	12	0	.0
15962	.4	100	.1	86	25.7	335	53.7	6	15	.2	14	0	.0

*=Estimated **1.0=883 lbs per person; 100++ indicates per capita toxic waste generation > than 100 times the U.S. average of 883 lbs per capita.

ZIP CODE MEASURES OF SIZE, LEVELS OF AFFLUENCE AND QUALITY OF LIFE

1=Population (th.); 2= % White; 3=Households (th.); 4=% Owner Occupied; 5=Mean Income Per Household (th.$); 6=Mean Monthly Rent ($)*; 7=Mean Home Value (th.$)*;
8=% under 5; 9=% 65 and over; 10=White Males (th.); 11=% White Males (th.); 12=# Toxic Waste Sites; 13=Toxic Waste Relative to US(883 lbs.per capital)**.

PENNSYLVANIA

ZIPCODE	1	2	3	4	5	6	7	8	9	10	11	12	13
JOHNSTOWN													
15963	13.3	100	4.7	74	23.5	248	61.6	6	14	6.3	12	1	.2
BITLER													
16001	56.9	99	20.1	72	27.9	301	83.8	7	12	27.3	10	2	1.6
16020	1.0	99	.4	79	22.5	315	49.5	6	18	.5	17	0	.0
16022	.7	0	.3	81	26.4	186	56.9	8	10	.0	0	1	.0
16023	3.5	0	1.1	86	24.6	264	78.1	8	12	6.8	0	0	.0
16024	.4	100	.1	72	22.8	318	56.0	6	6	.2	7	0	4.8
16025	5.7	100	1.8	85	25.5	262	65.0	8	11	2.9	9	0	.0
16027	.5	100	.2	87	29.6	279	72.1	8	13	.1	11	0	.0
16028	2.5	0	.8	74	22.5	250	58.2	7	18	.0	0	0	.8
16029	.9	100	.3	84	26.7	226	60.2	6	6	.4	6	0	.2
16030	.5	100	.2	80	26.4	294	57.7	6	13	.1	14	0	.0
16033	6.8	99	2.2	80	26.9	283	89.0	8	11	3.2	10	1	4.3
16034	1.5	100	.5	89	24.9	220	64.9	8	9	.7	8	0	.0
16035	.3	0	.1	91	21.0	242*	46.9	10	17	.0	0	0	.0
16036	.5	100	.2	77	27.2	337	52.0	7	18	.2	16	0	.0
16037	3.7	100	1.2	82	28.2	325	97.8	8	8	1.9	7	1	.2
16038	3.1	0	1.0	84	26.4	267	58.4	8	13	.0	0	0	.0
16039	.2	100	.1	100	40.3	463*	75.4	2	15	.1	10	0	.0
16040	1.0	0	.3	86	25.8	233	48.4	7	12	.0	0	1	.2
16041	2.0	0	.7	80	23.4	184	55.0	7	11	.0	0	0	.9
16045	1.4	100	.6	67	23.4	385	49.1	5	21	.7	19	0	.0
16046	11.9	99	3.7	81	30.6	385	105.0	10	8	5.8	6	2	2.9
16047	.2	100	.1	87	29.3	337*	87.1	7	15	.1	20	0	.0
16048	.2	100	.1	83	24.4	272	49.9	8	14	.1	11	0	.0
16049	3.5	0	1.2	80	22.4	250	50.5	6	13	.1	0	0	.0
16050	1.6	0	.5	81	24.9	235	52.0	7	12	.0	0	2	.0
16051	2.7	100	.9	85	24.7	325	80.0	9	8	1.4	6	0	89.7
16052	2.0	100	.9	88	26.2	256	79.9	9	8	1.0	8	0	.0
16053	3.1	100	.3	88	29.9	298	84.3	7	9	1.6	8	0	.0
16054	.6	100	.2	84	19.8	315	54.5	5	14	.3	11	0	.0
16055	7.7	100	2.5	86	28.3	329	93.2	8	9	3.8	8	1	.0
16056	3.9	0	1.3	80	28.1	336	91.5	6	11	.0	0	0	3.0
16057	10.8	97	2.7	71	25.4	330	73.9	5	7	5.0	7	1	.0
16059	7.0	100	2.2	88	30.1	326	104.8	7	9	3.5	7	0	.0
16061	2.2	98	.7	87	26.9	330	71.7	7	11	1.1	10	1	.0
16063	8.9	99	3.1	78	27.6	315	86.5	7	13	4.2	9	0	1.4
NEW CASTLE													
16101	44.8	94	16.0	72	22.7	248	54.7	7	14	19.7	12	3	.2
16102	6.2	100	2.2	81	24.5	301	59.2	6	12	3.0	12	0	.4
16105	16.0	99	5.8	86	32.6	317	86.4	6	14	7.6	12	0	.0
16110	.3	100	.1	84	28.1	296	63.5	5	12	.2	11	0	.4
16111	1.2	99	.3	83	23.3	280	59.8	9	8	.6	8	0	.0
16112	1.4	100	.5	84	25.0	333	58.7	6	15	.7	14	1	.3
16113	.5	100	.1	95	31.1	358*	84.4	7	4	.2	3	0	.0
16114	.6	100	.2	85	26.9	257	53.0	8	5	.3	4	0	.0
16115	3.9	100	1.3	85	27.2	329	73.0	8	11	2.0	10	0	.0
16116	2.3	100	.8	87	21.8	278	67.7	8	11	1.1	10	0	.1
16117	19.6	99	7.1	76	24.4	284	64.9	7	14	9.3	12	5	1.1

PENNSYLVANIA

ZIPCODE	1	2	3	4	5	6	7	8	9	10	11	12	13
NEW CASTLE													
16120	2.2	100	.7	89	25.7	325	66.2	9	9	1.1	7	0	.0
16121	8.9	64	3.3	72	22.7	276	40.8	6	16	2.7	17	1	.0
16123	2.0	99	.7	84	31.8	364	92.0	7	10	1.0	9	0	.0
16124	2.1	99	.7	84	24.2	245	56.4	7	8	1.0	8	0	.0
16125	21.0	99	7.3	78	26.0	300	67.0	6	14	10.0	11	2	.7
16127	14.3	98	4.5	75	25.5	304	71.3	5	14	6.8	12	1	.5
16130	2.2	0	.7	90	22.7	317	60.9	8	10	.0	0	0	.5
16131	.8	0	.3	87	24.0	198	61.2	8	9	.0	0	0	.0
16132	.8	100	.2	98	25.2	290*	43.2	1	11	.3	13	0	.0
16133	1.7	0	.5	81	24.5	299	61.3	9	11	.0	0	0	.0
16134	3.7	99	1.3	84	22.4	257	62.4	7	14	1.8	13	0	.5
16136	1.3	99	.5	72	24.0	313	54.8	6	14	.6	14	0	.2
16137	11.8	99	3.9	82	26.1	303	71.7	8	11	5.9	9	0	.2
16140	1.5	0	.2	95	30.1	346*	71.6	4	13	.0	0	0	.0
16141	.3	0	.8	88	25.9	340	66.7	8	8	3.6	8	0	.0
16142	7.6	97	2.0	73	25.9	328	79.2	6	10	3.6	8	0	.4
16143	3.5	0	1.1	81	29.4	330	81.9	7	8	.0	0	0	.4
16145	2.5	99	.9	82	21.7	274	58.7	7	12	1.2	13	1	.2
16146	33.6	95	12.6	70	26.0	303	62.6	6	15	15.1	13	2	3.7
16150	10.0	99	3.6	80	28.6	289	70.8	5	13	4.8	11	0	2.0
16151	.2	100	.1	78	21.1	294	55.3	7	21	.0	9	0	.0
16153	2.8	0	1.0	85	24.3	314	57.8	8	14	.0	0	0	.0
16154	3.1	99	1.0	80	25.5	308	75.4	9	6	1.6	5	0	.0
16156	3.1	100	1.0	80	24.9	319	67.3	9	10	1.6	10	0	.1
16157	4.0	98	1.4	83	26.0	304	60.7	8	12	2.0	12	1	.0
16159	6.0	96	2.0	88	30.1	352	70.9	7	10	2.9	9	0	.0
16160	1.2	0	.4	89	26.7	311	58.4	8	8	.6	8	0	13.6
16161	1.1	84	.4	84	24.4	262	35.8	6	12	.5	10	0	4.5
BUTLER													
16201	19.3	100	7.0	71	23.6	264	70.9	6	15	9.2	13	2	.0
16210	1.0	100	.3	78	21.4	222	50.5	6	12	.5	11	1	.0
16212	.5	100	.2	83	25.9	325	74.6	7	13	.2	15	0	.0
16214	.3	100	.1	68	18.4	244	45.5	10	14	.2	9	0	.0
16218	9.9	97	2.7	61	24.7	324	82.6	9	9	4.6	8	2	.1
16222	1.1	0	.4	79	27.5	226	62.0	9	9	.0	0	1	.0
16223	2.4	98	.8	80	21.4	273	54.8	7	13	.0	0	0	.4
16224	.4	100	.2	77	27.3	201	58.9	8	17	.2	16	0	.0
16226	1.2	100	.4	80	21.9	231	57.3	7	13	.6	12	0	.0
16228	10.2	98	3.9	76	23.4	269	62.4	6	14	4.9	12	1	.1
16229	4.9	99	1.8	72	25.9	259	48.3	8	13	2.4	12	0	.4
16230	.6	100	.1	84	21.7	274	49.5	8	13	.3	12	0	.3
16232	4.6	100	1.6	86	24.7	279	72.8	8	12	2.2	10	1	.1
16233	.9	0	.3	81	21.8	249	54.2	7	18	.0	0	0	.0
16235	1.3	100	.4	90	28.1	191	75.0	9	10	.6	9	0	.4
16236	.4	100	.1	66	19.6	353	39.3	10	12	.2	12	0	.0
16238	.4	100	.2	80	25.5	199	57.5	7	19	.2	13	1	.0
16239	1.7	0	.6	85	21.0	235	57.8	5	16	.0	0	0	.0
16240	1.9	99	.6	80	22.6	294	54.6	8	11	.0	0	0	.0

*=Estimated **1.0=883 lbs per capita.   **1.0=883 lbs per person; 100++ indicates per capita toxic waste generation > than 100 times the U.S. average of 883 lbs per capita.

ZIP CODE MEASURES OF SIZE, LEVELS OF AFFLUENCE AND QUALITY OF LIFE

1=Population (th.); 2= % White; 3=Households (th.); 4=% Owner Occupied; 5=Mean Income Per Household (th.$); 6=Mean Monthly Rent ($); 7=Mean Home Value (th.$); 8=% under 5; 9=% 65 and over; 10=White Males (th.); 11=% White Males, 65+; 12=# Toxic Waste Sites; 13=Toxic Waste Relative to US(883 lbs.per capita)**.

PENNSYLVANIA

BUTLER

ZIPCODE	1	2	3	4	5	6	7	8	9	10	11	12	13
16242	5.3	100	2.0	73	23.3	225	62.8	7	16	2.6	14	0	.0
16244	.3	100	.1	73	21.0	169	52.9	9	10	.1	11	0	.0
16246	.5	100	.2	65	21.2	244	56.0	17	7	.2	5	0	.0
16248	3.9	0	1.3	78	23.1	198	53.4	8	14	.0	10	0	.0
16249	2.1	100	.7	78	23.2	274	67.6	9	12	1.0	10	0	.0
16250	.6	0	.2	27	16.2	201	37.6	10	15	.0	0	0	.0
16253	.2	100	.1	81	22.6	171	34.4	3	14	.0	11	0	.0
16254	3.6	98	1.2	83	27.9	262	87.4	9	9	1.7	8	0	.0
16255	2.1	100	.7	77	27.5	263	58.9	8	17	1.0	13	0	.0
16256	1.3	100	.4	85	21.7	204	54.5	15	10	.7	9	0	.0
16258	1.7	100	.6	77	21.7	294	62.1	7	10	.8	7	4	.0
16259	2.3	100	.8	83	21.5	192	47.3	7	15	1.1	13	1	.1
16262	2.8	0	1.0	88	24.3	204	69.0	10	10	.2	10	0	.0
16263	.4	100	.2	73	18.4	224	44.5	3	29	.2	25	0	.5

OIL CITY

ZIPCODE	1	2	3	4	5	6	7	8	9	10	11	12	13
16301	20.3	99	7.4	71	26.5	290	58.3	7	14	9.5	11	2	1.9
16311	.5	100	.2	92	22.4	126	55.4	7	22	.2	16	0	.0
16313	2.3	0	.8	85	21.6	242	50.5	9	13	1.1	0	1	.5
16314	5.5	100	1.8	85	23.3	272	62.0	8	11	2.7	10	0	.2
16316	5.3	100	1.9	77	26.6	314	75.5	6	12	2.6	10	0	.0
16317	1.4	0	.4	89	28.0	316	67.4	11	6	.6	6	0	.0
16319	1.3	100	.5	82	22.8	266	63.1	8	14	.6	12	1	.8
16321	.2	100	.1	77	17.4	274	52.0	3	26	.1	25	1	.0
16322	.2	100	.1	74	23.0	285	49.2	6	11	.1	11	1	3.8
16326	20.1	100	7.3	74	25.4	269	64.3	7	13	9.5	11	3	.0
16327	2.7	99	.9	79	23.4	312	73.6	9	11	1.3	9	0	.0
16328	.3	0	.1	89	21.0	277	57.9	8	10	.1	11	0	.0
16329	.5	100	.2	83	30.0	257	42.4	10	19	.3	8	1	6.4
16333	.5	100	.2	86	20.7	321	52.8	8	8	.3	25	1	.0
16334	.5	100	.5	84	27.3	190	43.4	7	26	.2	7	0	.0
16335	31.8	96	11.6	65	25.0	215	76.1	6	15	14.4	12	1	.8
16340	2.1	100	.7	91	23.6	274	72.1	6	11	.7	11	1	.1
16341	2.0	100	.7	82	22.7	239	52.3	7	11	1.0	11	1	.3
16342	3.4	98	.8	76	22.9	260	62.7	8	12	1.7	9	0	.0
16343	.6	100	.2	88	22.6	228	54.5	6	11	.3	10	0	42.8
16344	.7	0	.3	81	23.7	391	50.7	6	12	.3	10	1	45.7
16345	3.4	99	1.2	90	24.6	270	43.2	8	12	1.7	11	1	.0
16346	3.4	99	1.2	75	27.1	233	68.0	10	11	1.4	9	2	.0
16347	2.8	99	1.0	79	27.1	306	74.4	10	9	1.7	14	2	.3
16350	2.4	99	.8	84	23.8	285	50.5	6	15	1.4	14	0	.0
16351	1.8	100	.6	81	23.0	308	60.2	9	8	.9	14	0	.0
16352	.3	100	.1	91	28.4	234	47.9	8	15	.2	9	0	.0
16353	3.1	100	1.1	81	20.4	326*	50.0*	7	13	1.5	14	2	2.3
16354	13.4	99	4.7	73	23.9	265	57.7	7	12	6.4	10	0	.0
16360	1.2	0	.4	81	21.7	278	59.0	7	10	.0	0	1	.0
16361	.3	100	.1	94	31.0	272	61.7	7	4	.2	5	0	.0
16362	1.1	0	.4	83	23.8	356*	47.7	6	11	.0	0	0	.0

PENNSYLVANIA

OIL CITY

ZIPCODE	1	2	3	4	5	6	7	8	9	10	11	12	13
16364	1.3	0	.4	80	23.3	242	61.6	8	10	.0	0	0	.0
16365	23.0	100	8.5	69	25.6	287	69.1	7	16	10.8	13	5	2.4
16370	.3	0	.1	85	18.0	146	46.8	3	24	.0	0	0	.0
16371	3.6	0	1.2	77	25.7	277	62.5	7	15	.3	0	1	.0
16372	.6	100	.2	78	20.3	278	54.7	9	19	1.0	18	0	.0
16373	3.7	100	1.3	83	24.2	221	59.6	7	15	1.8	14	1	.0
16374	1.7	100	.6	92	22.9	112	52.6	8	13	.8	15	0	.0

ERIE

ZIPCODE	1	2	3	4	5	6	7	8	9	10	11	12	13
16401	4.4	99	1.5	76	22.9	258	62.8	8	12	2.1	10	0	.1
16402	1.0	100	.3	87	23.4	341	49.0	8	7	.0	0	0	.0
16403	5.5	99	1.8	78	22.4	271	61.0	7	13	2.7	12	0	.1
16404	3.0	99	1.0	85	21.7	245	49.7	8	10	1.5	10	0	.0
16405	.9	100	.3	91	27.6	345	61.0	7	13	.4	11	0	.0
16406	3.5	0	1.1	83	23.1	275	55.7	8	12	.5	12	0	.0
16407	11.9	100	4.2	74	23.1	271	63.3	9	11	5.7	10	0	1.2
16410	2.1	100	.6	82	22.6	349	63.3	9	8	.0	0	0	.0
16411	1.4	0	.4	88	26.0	469	71.1	7	7	.0	0	1	.0
16412	10.7	98	3.1	58	23.9	359	91.2	6	4	5.0	4	0	.1
16414	.9	100	.3	84	17.7	347	65.1	5	20	.4	20	1	.0
16415	6.6	100	2.1	89	36.0	289	108.7	7	8	3.3	8	1	.7
16416	.3	100	.1	83	23.0	314	42.6	11	10	.1	8	0	.0
16417	7.3	99	2.3	82	25.4	283	78.6	7	11	3.4	11	0	.2
16420	.7	100	.2	94	23.3	242	38.4	8	10	.4	12	0	.0
16421	2.5	99	.7	82	26.4	247	73.1	8	7	1.3	7	2	.0
16422	.3	100	.1	89	19.0	240	45.1	4	21	.2	17	0	.0
16423	4.0	99	1.3	83	26.4	326	76.2	8	7	2.0	6	2	1.3
16424	3.5	100	1.3	79	21.3	254	62.6	7	14	1.7	13	1	1.1
16426	3.7	99	1.1	88	27.9	261	86.4	10	6	1.8	6	0	.0
16427	.3	99	.1	85	24.1	225	61.1	9	8	.7	8	0	.0
16428	12.2	100	4.1	75	27.4	295	80.9	9	10	6.0	9	1	.3
16433	5.3	100	1.7	85	25.4	275	65.0	8	11	2.6	10	2	8.9
16434	2.3	100	.7	88	21.1	311	48.9	12	8	1.1	7	0	.0
16435	1.9	99	.6	83	20.8	249	49.4	7	12	.9	12	0	.0
16436	.6	100	.2	88	22.4	299	51.9	6	13	.3	14	0	.0
16438	8.3	99	2.8	78	22.3	302	56.9	9	10	4.1	10	0	.3
16440	.7	100	.2	81	22.1	260	54.0	8	11	.4	9	0	.0
16441	7.8	100	2.4	85	25.5	295	74.1	9	7	3.9	7	1	1.3
16442	2.7	99	.8	84	26.3	308	68.2	10	10	1.4	6	0	.0
16443	1.5	100	.5	80	25.1	219	59.6	8	12	.7	11	0	.0

ERIE

ZIPCODE	1	2	3	4	5	6	7	8	9	10	11	12	13
16501	2.4	91	1.4	1	7.6	180	27.0*	10	15	1.0	26	2	43.7
16502	19.4	94	7.5	45	21.4	305	53.4	9	14	8.3	10	1	1.2
16503	20.1	76	7.3	49	18.5	266	40.5	9	12	9.1	12	1	.9
16504	20.6	95	7.1	73	25.8	322	67.7	6	14	9.1	12	0	.4
16505	18.8	99	7.2	77	30.9	330	93.8	6	13	8.7	11	3	.1
16506	17.6	98	5.9	83	32.4	411	97.8	6	8	8.6	7	2	.7
16507	12.8	83	5.0	40	17.9	269	43.0	9	12	5.0	12	2	1.3
16508	19.4	99	8.1	75	26.8	337	70.5	9	15	9.0	12	2	.0
16509	24.9	98	8.7	81	32.3	393	94.7	6	12	12.0	8	2	.2

*=Estimated **1.0=883 lbs per person, 100++ indicates per capita toxic waste generation > than 100 times the U.S. average of 883 lbs per capita.

ZIP CODE MEASURES OF SIZE, LEVELS OF AFFLUENCE AND QUALITY OF LIFE

1=Population (th.); 2= % White; 3=Households (th.); 4=% Owner Occupied; 5=Mean Income Per Household (th.$); 6=Mean Monthly Rent ($)*; 7=Mean Home Value (th.$)*;
8=% under 5; 9=% 65 and over; 10=White Males (th.); 11=% White Males, 65+; 12=# Toxic Waste Sites; 13=Toxic Waste Relative to US(883 lbs.per capita)**.

PENNSYLVANIA

ERIE

ZIPCODE	1	2	3	4	5	6	7	8	9	10	11	12	13
16510	26.7	92	8.3	80	26.2	283	72.9	8	7	12.2	6	1	.4
16511	12.8	94	4.5	73	26.0	260	77.4	7	12	5.5	10	2	.3

ALTOONA

ZIPCODE	1	2	3	4	5	6	7	8	9	10	11	12	13
16601	35.4	98	13.0	72	21.8	256	51.2	7	16	16.1	13	3	.1
16602	37.7	99	14.0	70	22.0	292	54.4	7	16	17.1	13	3	.1
16611	2.1	100	.7	79	20.2	326	66.1	8	11	1.1	10	0	.0
16613	1.6	0	.5	84	22.0	282	51.0	8	8	.0	0	0	.0
16616	.2	0	.1	90	20.3	233*	49.2	8	13	.0	0	0	.0
16617	3.2	0	1.1	82	23.4	279	54.7	6	16	.2	0	0	.0
16619	.7	100	.2	83	22.4	258	34.6	7	10	.3	9	0	.0
16620	.4	0	.2	87	18.6	275	46.9	8	16	.0	0	0	.0
16621	.6	0	.2	85	18.9	332	54.5	6	16	.1	0	0	.0
16622	.2	100	.1	97	18.4	212*	44.3	8	12	.1	16	0	.0
16623	.4	96	.1	84	20.6	242	61.5	10	12	.2	13	0	.0
16624	.3	100	.1	88	18.9	220	64.7	9	11	.2	7	0	.0
16625	3.2	100	1.1	81	20.2	252	52.8	8	9	1.5	6	2	.8
16627	2.4	100	.9	77	20.7	216	45.7	7	15	.6	0	0	.0
16629	.2	100	.1	88	19.5	225*	41.4	5	16	.1	15	0	.0
16630	5.6	100	1.7	73	23.9	281	59.6	8	12	2.5	9	0	.1
16631	.2	100	.1	79	19.5	369	49.2	14	14	.1	15	0	1.0
16633	.2	100	.1	79	15.6	230	45.0	8	25	.1	24	0	.0
16634	.5	100	.2	90	15.9	437	39.1	5	17	.2	16	0	.0
16635	10.1	100	3.5	79	24.0	371	72.5	9	9	4.9	8	2	.5
16636	.3	0	.1	80	22.5	298	57.1	9	12	.0	0	0	.0
16637	2.8	0	.9	80	22.1	361	53.9	11	17	.4	18	0	.0
16639	.9	100	.3	83	20.8	170	45.7	7	12	.3	11	0	.0
16640	.6	100	.2	68	24.9	242	55.3	7	14	.1	12	0	.0
16641	3.4	100	1.1	82	22.4	261	45.7	8	14	1.7	12	0	.0
16644	.4	0	.1	79	26.8	312	55.1	10	7	.0	0	0	.0
16645	.2	100	.1	80	25.0	256	52.1	9	14	.1	10	0	.0
16646	2.9	99	1.0	85	23.8	260	55.0	7	12	1.4	11	0	.0
16647	.9	0	.3	83	22.0	241	76.1	9	12	.2	0	0	.0
16648	15.1	100	5.2	73	26.7	340	78.6	6	15	7.2	12	0	.8
16650	2.0	0	.7	79	19.0	204	48.6	6	12	.2	0	0	.0
16651	3.6	0	1.3	83	21.7	234	52.5	6	15	.2	6	0	.0
16652	15.1	96	5.1	69	21.8	258	67.6	5	13	7.2	10	3	.0
16655	1.5	100	.5	80	20.8	205	51.7	5	11	.7	8	0	.0
16656	1.5	100	.4	85	23.1	287	42.7	9	11	.7	11	0	.0
16657	1.0	100	.3	82	20.0	212	60.6	8	12	.5	11	0	.0
16659	.3	100	.1	88	20.1	293	52.3	8	18	.1	14	0	.1
16660	.1	0	.1	75	19.9	272	49.3	9	15	.0	0	0	.0
16661	1.3	99	.5	83	19.7	274	45.4	6	18	.6	18	0	.0
16662	4.8	100	1.6	77	23.2	298	70.6	8	15	2.3	11	0	.0
16663	.8	100	.3	81	19.9	340	46.0	8	11	.1	14	0	.0
16664	1.7	0	.5	79	25.0	242	62.1	9	9	.0	0	0	.1
16665	.7	100	.2	70	26.0	348	67.7	11	13	.3	16	0	.0
16666	3.7	100	1.3	82	20.8	267	47.3	9	13	1.8	13	0	.0
16667	1.2	100	.4	87	19.8	219	62.5	9	11	.6	11	0	.0
16668	4.6	0	1.4	77	21.6	251	51.7	9	14	.1	0	0	.0

PENNSYLVANIA

ALTOONA

ZIPCODE	1	2	3	4	5	6	7	8	9	10	11	12	13
16669	2.0	100	.7	82	20.7	232	54.7	9	10	1.0	9	1	.4
16670	.3	100	.1	91	21.0	320	52.7	7	8	.2	11	0	.0
16671	.7	100	.3	86	23.1	304	55.6	6	17	.4	14	0	.0
16672	.2	100	.1	77	11.9	220	29.0	8	22	.1	20	0	.0
16673	5.5	100	1.9	77	23.5	253	59.5	8	12	2.7	10	0	.8
16674	1.0	100	.1	73	16.1	268	31.9	7	13	.5	11	0	.0
16677	.5	100	.2	88	21.6	423	39.6	0	13	.2	11	0	.0
16678	3.0	0	1.1	73	18.4	243	47.6	6	15	.0	0	0	.0
16679	1.0	100	.4	75	18.9	197	35.3	6	12	.5	10	0	.0
16680	.6	100	.2	90	20.9	182	51.7	4	15	.3	14	0	.0
16681	.2	100	.1	89	14.5	166*	34.3	6	27	.1	23	0	.0
16682	.6	100	.2	96	18.2	210*	38.0	3	7	.1	0	0	.0
16683	.6	100	.2	72	22.7	337	73.0	10	10	.3	9	0	.0
16684	.5	100	.2	51	20.7	353	57.8	14	6	.3	8	0	.7
16685	.3	0	.1	84	17.8	268	53.8	10	9	.1	8	0	.0
16686	14.3	100	5.1	74	22.3	258	56.3	7	14	6.8	11	4	1.4
16689	.4	100	.1	85	18.8	155	51.0	4	14	.2	16	0	.0
16691	.2	100	.2	92	19.4	222*	56.0	6	22	.2	23	1	.0
16692	.9	100	.3	86	21.8	276	46.0	9	11	.4	11	1	.1
16693	4.3	100	1.5	73	21.5	253	48.0	7	13	2.1	11	0	.0
16694	.3	100	.1	91	17.8	204*	29.2	6	8	.1	4	0	.0
16695	.8	100	.3	82	23.9	262	60.1	8	14	.4	11	0	.0

BRADFORD

ZIPCODE	1	2	3	4	5	6	7	8	9	10	11	12	13
16701	20.8	99	7.8	71	23.7	273	58.4	6	16	9.7	13	4	3.3
16720	1.7	0	.6	84	20.3	264	52.0	8	11	.0	0	2	.2
16724	.2	100	.1	83	24.4	184	47.0	5	15	.1	16	0	.2
16725	.3	100	.1	77	24.1	242	53.8	17	9	.2	7	1	.0
16726	.3	100	.1	91	20.7	498	45.3	4	21	.2	19	0	.0
16727	.5	100	.1	97	31.0	357*	57.7	10	17	.2	17	0	.0
16729	1.1	100	.4	87	21.8	253	50.7	6	16	.5	15	0	.1
16730	.3	100	.1	64	12.3	251	52.2	18	21	.3	15	0	.1
16731	3.6	100	1.2	79	21.6	226	50.7	7	13	1.8	26	1	.0
16732	.5	100	.2	90	19.8	342	43.8	6	12	1.1	8	0	.0
16733	.3	100	.1	83	20.7	111	30.3	13	9	.2	6	0	.0
16734	.4	0	.1	86	19.0	244	33.4	5	14	.2	0	0	.0
16735	7.7	99	2.9	73	22.3	204	51.0	7	17	3.7	15	0	.1
16738	1.4	0	.5	86	24.7	276	51.8	9	11	.1	0	0	.1
16739	.1	100	.1	77	16.5	252	47.5	5	15	.1	0	0	.0
16740	1.3	0	.5	81	19.9	241	45.4	6	17	.2	6	1	.0
16743	4.8	100	1.7	75	21.5	280	57.7	7	13	2.3	12	0	.0
16744	.5	0	.2	94	28.9	323	54.7	4	13	.0	0	0	.0
16745	.7	100	.2	91	23.5	232	44.6	8	9	.3	7	0	.0
16746	1.3	100	.4	78	19.5	281	47.7	8	12	.7	10	0	.0
16748	2.3	99	.8	75	20.9	272	49.3	7	13	1.2	12	1	.0
16749	4.8	99	1.6	78	22.8	253	53.0	8	17	2.3	15	1	1.9
16750	.6	0	.2	78	19.8	234	47.8	9	9	.0	0	0	.0

STATE COLLEGE

ZIPCODE	1	2	3	4	5	6	7	8	9	10	11	12	13
16801	41.3	95	16.0	38	23.2	406	121.0	4	6	21.0	4	2	.4
16802	12.5	95	.18	18	17.0	227	102.0	0	6.2	6.2	0	0	.0

*=Estimated **1.0=883 lbs per person; 100++ indicates per capita toxic waste generation > than 100 times the U.S. average of 883 lbs per capita.

ZIP CODE MEASURES OF SIZE, LEVELS OF AFFLUENCE AND QUALITY OF LIFE

1=Population (th.); 2= % White; 3=Households (th.); 4=% Owner Occupied; 5=Mean Income Per Household (th.$); 6=Mean Monthly Rent ($)*; 7=Mean Home Value (th.$)*; 8=% under 5; 9=% 65 and over; 10=White Males, 65+; 11=% White Males; 12=# Toxic Waste Sites; 13=Toxic Waste Relative to US(883 lbs.per capita)**.

PENNSYLVANIA

STATE COLLEGE

ZIPCODE	1	2	3	4	5	6	7	8	9	10	11	12	13
16820	.9	99	.3	86	22.0	187	63.2	7	13	.4	13	0	.0
16821	.3	100	.1	78	18.3	309	41.6	10	16	.1	18	0	.0
16822	2.1	100	.7	85	23.4	317	57.6	7	9	1.1	9	1	1.0
16825	18.1	97	6.0	73	24.9	288	75.0	6	11	8.9	8	2	2.4
16826	.3	0	.1	70	24.6	339	48.4	7	10	.4	0	0	.4
16827	.8	100	.3	85	21.3	281	49.3	8	9	.4	9	1	.0
16828	2.9	0	1.0	79	34.1	382	100.6	4	7	.0	9	1	.9
16829	3.7	100	1.3	81	23.7	336	81.6	8	9	1.8	9	1	.0
16830	16.1	98	5.9	89	21.5	269	57.4	8	11	7.6	11	0	.3
16832	.4	0	.1	71	23.2	267	64.4	8	14	.1	12	0	.0
16833	5.4	100	1.9	79	21.1	312	47.9	6	13	2.7	11	2	.2
16834	.3	100	.1	87	22.7	259	59.6	7	12	.1	11	0	.2
16835	.4	99	.1	91	26.0	299*	56.6*	3	13	.1	13	1	.0
16836	1.2	100	.4	87	19.1	418	55.3	4	12	.7	12	0	4.1
16838	2.1	100	.7	84	23.1	287	54.0	7	11	.6	11	1	.0
16839	.7	100	.2	95	26.3	304	54.7	7	13	.3	10	0	.0
16840	.6	100	.2	78	21.4	233	39.8	5	16	.3	20	1	.0
16841	4.3	100	1.4	82	15.4	335	47.7	8	17	.3	18	0	.0
16843	1.0	0	.4	83	22.9	298	63.0	9	9	.0	0	0	.0
16844	2.2	100	.7	80	19.8	266	62.0	9	11	1.0	6	0	.0
16845	1.0	0	.3	91	21.8	282	63.4	10	6	.0	9	0	.0
16847	.4	100	.2	92	22.3	234	52.5	8	9	.0	9	1	.0
16848	.6	100	.2	90	24.0	396	58.8	5	12	.3	7	0	.0
16849	.5	100	.2	81	22.2	298	61.3	8	11	.3	7	0	.3
16851	.9	0	.3	82	18.4	268	48.1	4	12	.0	2	0	.0
16852	.3	0	.1	66	36.7	399	102.2	7	10	.1	12	0	.0
16853	1.8	0	.6	88	21.2	345	64.2	10	11	1.6	11	0	.0
16854	.5	100	.2	76	21.5	283	64.3	5	10	.3	10	2	.3
16855	.3	100	.1	81	20.6	251	63.4	6	17	.9	9	0	.0
16856	.2	100	.1	84	21.9	252*	39.7	4	5	.1	8	0	.0
16858	3.1	100	1.0	84	30.4	360	52.2	8	11	1.6	11	0	.0
16859	.6	100	.2	88	31.8	448	103.9	6	6	.3	11	0	.0
16860	.5	100	.2	80	23.4	239	60.7	6	14	.3	11	0	.3
16861	.4	100	.1	83	22.4	242	48.4	7	8	.3	7	0	.0
16863	.9	100	.3	79	22.3	190	42.8	10	10	.2	8	0	.0
16865	1.7	97	.5	86	22.6	317	48.9	8	6	.7	8	0	.0
16866	9.2	100	3.4	88	22.6	231	65.5	8	11	4.2	11	1	.4
16868	.9	100	.3	73	26.3	239	49.5	6	8	.5	7	0	.0
16870	2.9	98	1.0	78	21.0	326	84.5	7	10	1.4	5	1	.0
16871	.1	100	.1	90	19.9	265	73.9	8	21	.1	18	1	.0
16872	1.0	100	.3	82	22.6	229*	29.8*	6	11	.5	11	0	.0
16874	1.3	0	.4	83	24.9	277	52.7	8	7	.5	9	0	.0
16875	2.6	100	.9	80	22.1	300	62.8	7	10	1.3	10	3	.0
16876	.5	100	.1	92	21.0	273	63.1	8	6	.3	8	0	.3
16877	1.2	0	.4	80	22.7	234	42.8	7	11	.8	6	0	.7
16878	1.9	0	.6	87	20.9	257	65.5	7	8	.8	6	0	.2
16879	.6	100	.2	87	20.8	248	49.5	7	5	.4	5	2	.6
16881	2.3	0	.7	88	22.3	201	56.4	11	9	.8	13	0	.5

PENNSYLVANIA

STATE COLLEGE

ZIPCODE	1	2	3	4	5	6	7	8	9	10	11	12	13
16882	.3	100	.1	81	19.3	298	45.3	8	8	.2	7	0	.0

WELLSBORO

ZIPCODE	1	2	3	4	5	6	7	8	9	10	11	12	13
16901	10.1	100	3.6	76	23.3	254	67.7	7	15	4.8	12	3	.3
16910	.2	100	.1	76	18.2	320	44.8	6	13	.1	11	0	.0
16911	2.0	100	.7	83	22.4	253	55.9	8	9	.2	11	1	.0
16912	2.2	99	.7	74	23.2	207	58.8	6	13	.9	11	2	.9
16914	2.2	100	.7	82	20.2	315	61.2	9	9	.9	11	1	.9
16915	5.2	99	1.8	76	21.1	266	66.7	7	15	2.5	13	3	.7
16917	1.4	100	.5	80	22.1	249	61.6	7	11	.7	10	0	.2
16920	2.2	99	.8	70	19.3	221	47.7	7	15	1.0	15	1	.0
16921	.6	0	.2	79	18.6	257	61.6	8	19	.0	1	1	.0
16922	2.3	99	.8	75	19.8	222	49.7	7	14	1.1	10	1	.4
16923	1.5	100	.5	80	18.2	252	46.1	7	14	.7	13	1	.1
16925	2.1	100	.7	84	19.0	312	56.7	7	11	1.1	13	1	.0
16926	.8	0	.3	85	19.1	229	54.3	7	9	.2	5	0	.0
16927	.6	0	.2	81	20.0	162	42.9	10	8	.3	5	0	.0
16928	1.3	100	.5	78	20.8	190	47.0	7	13	.7	12	0	.0
16929	.6	100	.2	86	21.7	244	65.4	8	8	.9	8	0	.0
16930	1.2	0	.4	85	20.1	231	62.6	8	10	.2	5	0	.3
16931	.4	100	.1	82	17.8	177	43.8	10	6	.2	5	1	.0
16932	.6	100	.2	78	20.5	193	53.7	9	7	.3	5	0	.0
16933	6.6	98	1.9	70	22.2	243	78.0	5	9	3.1	8	0	.0
16935	1.3	99	.4	83	19.9	279	69.5	11	8	.6	8	1	.0
16936	.7	100	.7	84	20.6	242	57.1	8	9	.7	7	1	.0
16937	2.0	100	.2	89	13.6	156*	39.0	4	12	.2	14	0	.0
16938	.8	0	.3	84	21.0	264	57.5	4	18	.0	0	0	.0
16939	.3	100	.1	82	19.1	270	31.8	8	8	.1	3	0	.0
16940	.2	100	.1	80	20.6	255	61.7	7	10	.0	8	0	.3
16942	.9	0	.3	79	19.9	268	46.4	11	11	.0	8	0	.3
16943	.6	0	.2	72	18.5	237	39.8	9	12	.0	0	0	.0
16947	4.7	100	1.6	76	23.0	278	62.5	7	16	2.1	13	0	.0
16948	1.6	99	.5	76	20.9	240	52.6	8	11	.8	11	0	.0
16950	3.3	99	1.1	68	18.4	210	48.4	7	14	1.6	12	0	.2

HARRISBURG

ZIPCODE	1	2	3	4	5	6	7	8	9	10	11	12	13
17002	.6	100	.2	80	18.8	316	62.8	10	12	.3	11	0	.0
17003	10.7	99	3.3	75	27.2	315	79.4	7	9	5.2	8	1	3.3
17004	4.4	100	1.3	82	23.8	231	65.6	9	11	2.1	9	0	.0
17005	.4	100	.1	77	22.6	173	39.4	7	10	.2	7	0	.0
17006	.9	98	.3	77	18.8	229	55.0	7	16	2.0	5	0	.0
17007	4.2	99	1.4	79	30.6	430	101.4	8	6	2.0	5	0	.0
17008	.2	100	.1	79	27.4	275	104.1	3	10	.1	9	0	.0
17009	2.4	100	.9	72	21.7	271	47.7	5	15	.0	0	1	10.9
17010	.9	0	.3	70	22.1	273	73.3	7	10	1.3	9	0	.2
17011	.5	97	12.3	75	35.0	395	102.5	5	13	15.5	11	2	.7
17013	1.2	96	15.5	68	27.2	359	87.2	6	11	20.6	9	6	.2
17014	1.9	100	.2	82	20.5	218	53.0	10	5	.2	9	1	.6
17016	.6	98	.3	83	29.0	326	73.8	2	37	.4	24	1	.1
17017	2.3	100	.7	88	24.1	236	55.5	6	14	.8	13	0	.0

*=Estimated **1.0=883 lbs per person; 100++ indicates per capita toxic waste generation > than 100 times the U.S. average of 883 lbs per capita.

103001

ZIP CODE MEASURES OF SIZE, LEVELS OF AFFLUENCE AND QUALITY OF LIFE

1=Population (th.); 2= % White; 3=Households (th.); 4=% Owner Occupied; 5=Mean Income Per Household (th.$); 6=Mean Monthly Rent ($)*; 7=Mean Home Value (th.$)*;
8=% under 5; 9=% 65 and over; 10=White Males (th.); 11=% White Males, 65+; 12=# Toxic Waste Sites; 13=Toxic Waste Relative to US(883 lbs.per capital)**.

PENNSYLVANIA

HARRISBURG

ZIP CODE	1	2	3	4	5	6	7	8	9	10	11	12	13
17018	4.4	0	1.5	82	30.3	346	84.5	7	8	.0	9	0	.0
17019	10.4	100	3.5	81	28.1	340	90.1	7	8	5.1	11	8	.0
17020	7.5	100	2.6	77	25.0	282	70.0	7	9	3.7	8	0	.0
17021	.9	0	.3	82	19.0	202	37.6	8	11	.0	10	0	.1
17022	19.3	99	6.2	70	27.9	337	89.3	7	13	9.2	11	4	.1
17023	3.1	100	1.1	78	25.0	275	62.8	7	13	1.5	10	0	.3
17024	1.3	100	.4	89	22.4	313	65.3	7	10	.7	10	0	.0
17025	10.9	99	4.1	72	26.7	398	70.8	6	9	5.2	9	0	.0
17026	2.4	0	.8	74	26.1	285	75.5	10	8	.0	8	0	.0
17027	1.5	96	.5	63	33.4	404	89.1	2	2	.6	7	0	.0
17028	3.0	0	1.0	79	27.2	330	83.4	7	6	.0	6	0	.0
17029	.5	100	.2	85	26.1	389	54.6	8	4	.0	3	0	.0
17030	.8	100	.3	81	21.2	249	50.0	7	15	.4	13	0	.0
17032	6.6	99	2.2	83	24.9	313	72.5	7	9	3.2	10	0	.0
17033	16.4	97	6.0	54	30.5	402	114.7	5	14	7.8	11	0	.1
17034	3.0	99	1.2	60	24.7	352	61.5	6	11	1.4	10	0	.0
17035	.6	100	.2	83	18.3	230	47.5	6	11	.3	11	0	.0
17036	12.4	99	4.4	72	28.8	367	96.0	7	9	6.1	8	1	.0
17037	.7	99	.3	81	19.7	324	62.7	5	11	.4	10	0	.0
17038	5.4	99	1.8	76	25.2	289	74.2	8	8	2.7	7	0	.0
17040	2.0	100	.7	83	23.9	282	65.0	9	9	1.0	8	0	.0'
17041	.2	100	.1	70	27.9	324	71.6	15	30	.1	27	0	.0
17042	55.9	98	20.1	68	25.7	287	69.5	6	13	26.7	12	11	.9
17043	5.8	100	2.6	55	27.3	366	86.8	6	19	2.6	15	0	.2
17044	23.3	99	9.0	67	20.7	262	55.0	6	16	10.7	13	6	.3
17045	2.4	0	.8	80	22.9	278	61.7	8	12	.9	9	0	.0
17047	1.8	99	.6	84	24.1	281	67.4	7	9	.9	9	0	.0
17048	3.7	99	1.4	78	22.1	240	47.8	6	15	1.8	12	0	.0
17049	2.5	100	.9	78	22.0	226	63.4	9	13	1.2	11	0	1
17051	4.0	100	1.3	85	22.8	270	51.9	8	10	2.0	8	0	.0
17052	1.7	0	.7	83	20.3	242	43.7	9	11	.0	9	0	.0
17053	4.3	100	1.5	85	24.9	325	70.5	8	10	2.1	9	0	1.2
17054	.2	0	.1	75	20.3	250	52.8	8	14	.0	7	0	.0
17055	39.3	98	13.6	75	32.0	393	101.8	6	9	18.7	7	1	.6
17056	.2	100	.1	59	16.9	228	45.6	12	18	.1	12	0	.0
17057	21.0	96	7.7	66	26.3	350	73.4	7	11	9.8	9	4	.4
17058	1.2	99	.4	73	19.2	260	39.9	7	15	.6	13	0	.0
17059	5.9	100	2.1	80	24.3	250	61.2	7	14	2.8	11	0	.0
17060	3.7	100	1.4	81	19.7	265	45.3	7	10	.7	8	0	1.1
17061	6.6	99	2.4	73	22.5	260	62.9	7	16	3.1	12	0	1.2
17062	3.3	100	1.2	81	23.5	250	65.2	8	12	.0	9	0	.0
17063	3.5	100	1.2	75	21.6	268	55.3	8	9	.0	7	1	.1
17064	1.0	100	.4	84	32.4	442	111.0	7	12	.5	11	1	.0
17065	3.2	98	1.1	78	25.8	347	74.1	7	10	1.6	8	1	1.1
17066	6.0	92	2.2	66	18.3	215	45.7	6	14	2.6	11	2	.0
17067	10.6	100	3.4	78	26.7	297	78.0	8	13	5.2	10	0	5.4
17068	3.3	100	1.2	76	24.7	299	76.8	8	13	1.6	9	0	.0
17069	.2	100	.1	72	27.2	390	63.8	9	10	.1	9	0	.0
17070	16.6	98	6.1	79	31.1	369	90.8	6	10	8.0	8	1	.2

PENNSYLVANIA

HARRISBURG

ZIP CODE	1	2	3	4	5	6	7	8	9	10	11	12	13
17071	.1	100	.1	93	17.8	204*	39.0	10	13	.1	9	0	.0
17073	3.6	100	1.2	80	26.8	283	68.1	6	13	1.8	11	0	.0
17074	6.1	100	2.1	78	22.7	279	60.5	7	11	3.0	10	0	.0
17075	.5	0	.2	75	19.4	229	40.1	11	15	.0	10	0	.1
17078	13.1	99	4.8	71	27.6	332	85.4	6	13	6.2	10	0	.1
17080	.4	100	.1	89	21.7	255	47.7	11	7	.2	5	0	.0
17081	.4	100	.1	77	27.6	162	67.7	7	4	.2	4	0	.0
17082	3.0	100	1.0	80	20.8	257	56.4	6	13	.0	0	0	.0
17083	.5	100	.2	67	25.7	301	60.1	6	12	.2	12	0	.0
17084	3.1	100	1.0	83	27.6	252	66.2	7	12	1.5	10	0	.1
17085	.5	0	.2	70	25.0	377	62.5	9	8	.0	9	0	.0
17086	1.9	100	.7	78	22.5	223	57.8	9	13	.9	10	0	.0
17087	2.5	100	.8	84	28.2	297	75.0	7	10	1.2	10	0	.0
17088	1.0	0	.4	76	31.4	311	72.5	11	10	.0	5	0	.1
17090	3.1	99	1.0	85	24.9	275	74.3	5	5	1.6	5	0	.0
17093	1.0	100	.4	94	29.6	403	66.4	6	7	.5	7	0	.0
17094	2.0	100	.7	77	22.4	276	59.5	7	11	1.0	9	0	.0
17097	1.3	100	.5	84	21.7	245	41.8	8	11	.6	8	0	.0
17098	2.7	100	1.0	82	21.4	228	47.8	6	14	1.3	11	0	.3
17099	1.4	100	.5	77	23.4	332	44.0	9	13	.0	11	1	.0

HARRISBURG

ZIP CODE	1	2	3	4	5	6	7	8	9	10	11	12	13
17101	.2	83	1.6	4	16.4	254	71.1	2	42	.7	27	3	1.9
17102	8.5	54	4.3	29	17.5	245	31.0	5	19	2.2	16	0	.0
17103	13.1	38	5.0	53	19.9	268	40.3	7	14	2.2	17	0	.0
17104	21.1	67	8.0	55	20.7	282	41.9	9	12	6.4	14	1	.0
17109	25.0	90	10.5	57	28.8	391	81.5	5	15	10.4	14	1	.0
17110	18.7	65	7.1	66	29.4	333	74.6	7	13	5.7	14	0	.0
17111	20.1	93	7.4	67	32.0	375	87.6	6	12	8.9	10	1	.1
17112	23.4	97	8.1	79	33.3	408	96.6	7	7	11.2	6	1	.7
17113	11.5	77	4.4	74	25.5	257	54.9	5	15	4.1	13	1	8.4

CHAMBERSBURG

ZIP CODE	1	2	3	4	5	6	7	8	9	10	11	12	13
17201	40.4	96	14.7	69	25.5	304	79.9	7	12	18.4	10	2	.3
17211	.4	0	.1	86	19.4	171	54.4	8	18	.0	0	0	.0
17212	.8	99	.3	80	22.8	219	66.8	6	8	.4	7	1	.6
17213	.6	100	.2	88	18.8	276	40.4	10	11	.3	10	0	.0
17214	1.3	97	.5	69	25.6	404	85.2	8	11	.6	7	0	.0
17215	.3	100	.1	78	18.0	158	46.8	10	16	.1	14	0	.0
17217	.2	100	.1	83	24.9	182	45.7	6	9	.1	11	0	.0
17219	.4	100	.1	78	15.2	216	29.3	7	13	.2	15	0	.0
17220	.6	0	.2	73	23.0	286	63.9	12	13	3.1	12	0	1.2
17221	.6	100	.2	81	23.4	254	56.6	8	15	.3	15	0	.0
17222	7.5	98	2.7	82	26.8	349	74.1	6	11	3.7	10	1	.1
17223	.3	0	.1	77	17.8	293	48.4	6	7	.0	0	0	.4
17224	1.4	0	.5	80	21.5	181	56.3	4	14	.0	0	0	.0
17225	12.2	99	4.1	73	27.8	306	81.5	6	9	6.1	7	0	.1
17228	1.1	0	.4	79	19.2	224	58.6	7	10	.0	0	0	.0
17229	1.0	0	.3	88	20.6	200	53.0	9	11	.0	0	0	.0
17231	.2	100	.1	80	15.9	267	52.9	8	19	.1	17	0	.0
17232	.2	100	.1	87	27.9	320*	53.0	6	10	.1	10	0	.0

*=Estimated **1.0=883 lbs per person; 100++ indicates per capita toxic waste generation > than 100 times the U.S. average of 883 lbs per capita.

ZIP CODE MEASURES OF SIZE, LEVELS OF AFFLUENCE AND QUALITY OF LIFE

1=Population (th.); 2= % White; 3=Households (th.); 4=% Owner Occupied; 5=Mean Income Per Household (th.$); 6=Mean Monthly Rent ($)*; 7=Mean Home Value (th.$)*; 8=% under 5; 9=% 65 and over; 10=White Males (th.); 11=% White Males (th.); 12=# Toxic Waste Sites; 13=Toxic Waste Relative to US(883 lbs.per capita)**.

PENNSYLVANIA

CHAMBERSBURG

ZIPCODE	1	2	3	4	5	6	7	8	9	10	11	12	13
17233	4.6	98	1.7	74	22.6	236	62.6	8	12	2.1	11	0	1.3
17235	.7	100	.3	80	24.9	330	70.1	4	16	.3	14	0	.0
17236	6.9	97	2.3	73	24.8	264	69.4	9	10	3.3	10	0	.4
17238	1.3	0	.4	80	20.3	230	54.3	7	10	.0	0	0	.0
17239	.2	100	.8	78	19.5	236	40.1	10	18	.1	17	0	.0
17240	2.4	100	.8	86	23.0	275	66.2	10	9	1.2	9	0	.0
17241	8.6	99	2.8	81	22.9	286	70.5	9	10	4.3	8	0	.0
17243	1.3	100	.5	80	20.7	224	45.8	8	15	.6	14	3	.0
17244	1.6	0	.5	83	23.6	280	62.5	8	9	.0	0	0	.0
17246	.3	0	.1	79	30.1	304	66.8	9	9	.0	0	0	.0
17247	.5	100	.1	65	22.2	533	54.9	1	52	.0	36	0	.2
17249	.5	100	.2	90	16.3	256	37.6	4	17	.2	12	0	.0
17250	.7	100	.2	71	23.1	335	61.1	7	6	.4	6	0	.0
17251	.3	100	.1	89	24.3	318	54.7	5	12	.1	11	0	.0
17252	3.2	99	1.2	81	25.0	266	71.5	8	10	1.6	9	0	.0
17253	.3	0	.1	85	20.7	292	39.2	8	13	.0	0	0	.0
17254	.5	0	.2	88	21.5	432	76.4	11	13	.0	0	0	.0
17255	.9	100	.3	84	20.5	273	52.4	8	7	.4	5	0	.0
17256	.4	100	.1	69	30.2	266	73.5	12	7	.2	7	0	100++
17257	19.1	99	6.0	71	23.8	303	72.6	6	9	9.2	7	0	.4
17260	1.1	0	.4	81	19.0	310	40.3	8	10	.0	0	0	.0
17261	1.1	97	.1	65	24.8	144	66.7	2	56	.5	48	0	.5
17262	.8	100	.3	79	19.3	265	58.7	8	9	.4	9	0	.0
17263	.9	100	.2	80	32.9	400	86.3	6	6	.4	3	0	.0
17264	2.1	0	.7	87	19.7	243	53.5	9	7	.2	5	0	.0
17265	.5	100	.2	84	21.8	223	60.3	9	10	.2	10	0	.0
17266	.3	0	.1	93	27.3	314*	67.1	5	14	.0	24	0	.0
17267	2.0	100	.6	80	18.8	254	62.6	9	10	1.0	11	2	.0
17268	22.4	99	8.4	70	25.4	292*	74.6	6	13	10.7	12	2	1.0
17270	.2	100	.1	100	25.1	285	51.4	10	11	.0	15	0	.0
17271	.5	100	.1	88	24.5	307	44.3	9	8	.2	8	0	.0
17272	.3	100	.1	90	22.8	332	77.2	15	2	.1	0	1	.0

YORK

ZIPCODE	1	2	3	4	5	6	7	8	9	10	11	12	13
17301	2.6	99	.8	83	26.8	301	80.9	7	7	1.3	6	0	.0
17302	2.3	98	.8	75	24.4	360	73.3	8	10	1.1	8	0	.0
17303	.7	98	.3	73	24.7	338	74.8	8	11	.3	8	0	.0
17304	1.9	0	.6	78	24.6	324	71.6	9	9	.2	6	0	.1
17306	.5	96	.2	82	23.5	289	71.3	8	17	.2	16	0	.0
17307	3.8	99	1.4	70	24.7	312	77.5	5	12	1.9	12	0	1.4
17308	2.0	100	.6	87	28.2	424	90.4	9	7	1.0	7	0	.2
17309	2.0	99	.6	86	22.1	361	85.4	7	10	1.0	11	0	.0
17310	.2	100	.1	72	30.5	332	82.0	7	24	.1	24	0	.0
17311	.6	99	.2	77	27.3	376	77.9	5	11	.3	8	0	.0
17312	.5	100	.2	88	22.7	375	82.7	6	12	4.2	23	1	.0
17313	8.8	99	3.2	69	26.3	352	81.7	6	10	1.8	8	0	.2
17314	3.6	98	1.2	75	24.5	297	79.2	8	10	8.1	9	0	.0
17315	16.5	98	5.6	84	27.9	338	86.1	7	7	.0	6	0	4.5
17316	4.4	0	1.5	79	24.7	289	85.5	7	10	.0	0	0	.0
17317	.5	0	.2	85	26.9	271	63.5	3	21	.0	1	0	.0

PENNSYLVANIA

YORK

ZIPCODE	1	2	3	4	5	6	7	8	9	10	11	12	13
17318	.5	100	.2	87	31.2	199	74.5	8	7	.2	3	0	4.9
17319	5.9	99	2.0	85	31.0	355	92.7	9	5	2.9	4	1	.0
17320	3.6	98	1.2	80	25.5	365	82.2	6	12	1.8	11	0	.0
17321	1.1	97	.4	81	24.6	301	84.8	6	17	.5	13	0	.0
17322	3.8	100	1.2	84	26.5	376	84.4	9	6	1.9	5	0	.1
17323	.2	0	.1	69	19.9	341	47.8	7	15	.0	0	0	.0
17324	3.6	99	1.2	83	23.9	310	67.0	6	10	1.8	10	0	.2
17325	21.5	97	7.3	67	24.9	316	90.2	6	13	10.0	11	1	.3
17327	6.3	100	2.2	78	27.8	306	85.4	6	10	3.1	9	0	.4
17331	34.6	99	12.9	68	25.1	304	81.8	6	14	16.6	11	3	.0
17339	3.5	100	1.2	87	29.9	343	91.5	10	6	1.8	6	1	.0
17340	7.1	99	2.4	72	24.6	298	76.4	7	12	3.5	10	0	.1
17342	.7	100	.2	67	28.0	350	66.9	4	9	.2	8	2	.0
17343	.2	0	.1	94	26.8	308*	69.0	5	8	.1	8	0	.0
17344	2.9	100	1.0	61	25.2	324	65.0	8	9	1.3	8	0	.0
17345	4.8	99	1.8	73	24.8	368	73.3	6	9	2.4	9	0	.0
17347	3.6	0	1.3	83	27.2	300	79.0	6	11	.0	8	2	.0
17349	4.7	100	1.6	84	30.2	315	66.0	4	9	2.4	7	0	.4
17350	8.4	100	2.6	79	25.1	320	99.5	5	8	2.4	7	0	.1
17352	.2	0	.3	78	23.5	378	75.2	8	9	4.0	5	1	.0
17353	2.4	97	.8	76	22.9	287	86.5	8	9	1.1	8	0	.0
17355	.3	100	.1	58	22.3	277	76.8	10	14	.1	11	0	.0
17356	13.9	99	5.0	78	25.4	315	78.7	10	10	.1	12	0	.4
17361	3.6	99	1.4	80	30.6	338	97.1	6	12	1.7	8	0	.2
17362	9.6	99	3.1	86	29.0	371	94.9	7	5	4.7	8	3	.0
17363	4.8	99	1.6	83	28.2	314	84.6	8	11	2.4	10	1	.0
17364	2.5	100	.8	85	27.5	320	92.7	8	9	1.3	7	0	.0
17365	2.2	100	.2	88	28.6	303	81.4	7	12	1.1	5	1	.0
17366	3.8	100	1.3	79	27.0	356	87.6	9	8	1.8	8	4	.0
17368	5.4	99	1.9	78	24.1	288	67.5	9	7	2.7	9	0	.0
17370	4.2	100	1.4	83	30.1	232	65.7	8	8	2.1	7	4	1.0
17371	.4	0	.1	85	26.2	369	72.7	8	10	1.3	9	0	.0
17372	2.6	99	.9	78	25.2	302	71.8	8	10	1.3	9	0	.1

YORK

ZIPCODE	1	2	3	4	5	6	7	8	9	10	11	12	13
17401	1.1	89	.7	6	11.8	190	38.8	3	33	.4	21	0	.0
17402	34.0	99	12.1	78	32.8	421	100.2	5	12	16.0	10	5	2.1
17403	42.8	85	16.2	65	27.7	294	81.2	6	15	17.0	14	6	1.1
17404	48.6	93	18.7	69	24.6	301	72.8	6	13	21.7	12	4	.2
17406	5.6	100	2.0	80	27.7	315	84.1	7	11	2.7	10	2	.0
17407	1.9	100	.6	88	33.3	358	100.8	7	9	.9	7	0	.0

LANCASTER

ZIPCODE	1	2	3	4	5	6	7	8	9	10	11	12	13
17501	4.0	96	1.5	76	30.1	371	90.9	7	11	1.9	10	0	.0
17502	2.0	0	.7	78	25.5	320	74.8	8	8	.0	9	0	.0
17503	.3	0	.1	88	24.0	275*	83.1	6	10	.0	0	0	.0
17505	1.6	0	.4	70	25.3	292	109.8	12	12	.0	0	0	.1
17506	.6	100	.2	75	30.0	313	82.4	5	12	.3	11	0	.0
17507	.5	100	.2	87	27.0	347	82.6	3	23	.2	20	0	.1
17508	.7	100	.3	80	26.3	304	84.1	5	19	.3	12	0	.1

*=Estimated **1.0=883 lbs per person; 100++ indicates per capita toxic waste generation > than 100 times the U.S. average of 883 lbs per capita.

ZIP CODE MEASURES OF SIZE, LEVELS OF AFFLUENCE AND QUALITY OF LIFE

1=Population (th.); 2= % White; 3=Households (th.); 4=% Owner Occupied; 5=Mean Income Per Household (th.$); 6=Mean Home Value (th.$)*; 7=Mean Monthly Rent ($)*; 8=% under 5; 9=% 65 and over; 10=White Males (th.); 11=% White Males; 12=# Toxic Waste Sites; 13=Toxic Waste Relative to US(883 lbs.per capita)**.

PENNSYLVANIA

LANCASTER

ZIPCODE	1	2	3	4	5	6	7	8	9	10	11	12	13
17509	3.6	98	1.0	74	26.8	335	87.1	11	12	1.7	9	0	.6
17512	15.5	97	5.5	70	24.1	272	65.9	7	14	7.1	10	2	.7
17516	3.5	99	1.1	81	27.6	293	86.2	7	9	1.7	9	0	.0
17517	8.3	0	2.7	81	27.9	346	81.2	8	11	.0	9	2	.4
17518	.7	100	.2	77	25.8	291	93.4	10	10	.4	10	0	.0
17519	3.6	0	1.1	81	29.0	320	80.9	7	9	.1	8	0	.0
17520	3.7	98	1.3	85	32.6	309	92.7	6	8	1.8	7	1	.4
17522	21.1	99	7.2	69	26.5	323	83.4	8	12	10.1	10	0	.5
17527	4.3	100	1.4	74	25.7	349	80.7	9	10	2.1	8	0	.2
17528	.3	100	.1	72	27.8	347	71.3	4	13	.2	9	0	.0
17529	2.4	100	.7	68	28.8	316	89.1	15	9	1.1	8	0	.0
17532	2.0	0	.6	79	24.6	329	90.1	10	7	.0	7	0	.0
17533	.2	100	.1	67	22.4	323	43.2	3	2	.1	5	0	.0
17534	.6	100	.2	66	28.3	234	92.2	4	9	.3	9	0	.1
17535	1.8	100	.5	72	28.2	356	85.7	12	6	.9	5	0	.0
17536	1.2	0	.4	73	22.2	315	83.9	11	9	.0	7	0	.1
17537	.3	100	.1	87	27.3	255	119.8	5	20	.2	18	0	.5
17538	3.6	98	1.3	86	32.0	341	105.1	6	10	1.7	10	0	.3
17540	7.5	99	2.5	70	32.0	385	102.2	8	8	3.6	7	0	1.0
17543	20.4	99	6.8	77	32.5	350	92.8	8	13	9.8	10	2	2.1
17545	16.8	99	5.7	75	28.0	328	87.3	8	10	8.1	9	5	1.4
17547	4.0	97	1.5	64	25.2	325	70.7	8	9	2.0	9	0	9.3
17550	1.1	0	.3	87	30.5	346	82.2	9	10	.0	8	0	.0
17551	7.9	96	2.0	64	25.6	318	92.4	4	9	3.4	7	2	.0
17552	10.6	99	3.8	69	29.4	325	85.7	9	9	5.1	7	2	.3
17554	2.4	98	.9	67	27.8	306	81.4	7	12	.1	9	0	.0
17555	4.4	98	1.2	81	25.3	389	85.7	12	8	2.0	8	1	.0
17557	10.2	97	3.2	72	29.6	363	94.4	4	9	4.9	9	0	5.3
17560	3.5	99	1.2	82	24.6	331	81.6	8	7	1.7	7	0	.0
17562	3.5	99	1.1	69	25.3	316	81.8	8	10	1.7	9	0	.0
17563	2.8	99	.9	78	29.0	313	77.7	9	8	1.4	7	1	.0
17565	1.9	100	.6	87	29.2	451	80.0	8	6	1.0	6	0	.0
17566	7.6	100	2.5	72	27.2	329	90.3	9	13	3.6	10	0	.5
17567	.7	100	.3	66	23.5	304	70.9	4	20	.1	9	0	1.4
17569	2.6	0	.9	80	28.3	353	70.6	6	9	.0	7	2	.3
17570	.2	100	.1	69	22.2	248	89.8	10	27	.1	10	0	1.3
17572	3.0	0	.9	70	27.2	329	92.2	11	10	.0	9	0	.0
17573	1.3	0	.5	64	25.6	345	83.1	6	10	.0	8	0	.0
17575	.2	100	.1	16	18.6	314	66.1*	10	10	.1*10	0	.0
17576	.3	100	.1	78	28.2	340	108.4	2	9	.1	10	0	.0
17577	.2	0	.1	78	23.1	338	67.6	0	38	.0	6	0	.0
17578	4.6	100	1.4	82	29.5	298	81.5	10	6	2.2	6	0	.0
17579	4.4	100	1.5	77	28.7	325	93.3	10	11	2.1	10	0	.0
17580	.3	100	.1	45	21.6	261	52.7	8	2	.1	6	0	.1
17581	1.3	98	.4	71	24.8	370	78.6	8	15	.6	12	0	.0
17582	2.1	98	.7	75	27.2	309	86.0	10	9	1.0	9	0	.0
17583	.1	100	.1	65	19.6	315	71.8	5	10	.1	11	0	.0
17584	5.0	98	1.8	81	29.1	360	97.5	5	11	2.4	9	0	.0

PENNSYLVANIA

LANCASTER

ZIPCODE	1	2	3	4	5	6	7	8	9	10	11	12	13
17601	35.6	98	12.4	71	36.4	403	118.9	6	12	16.8	9	2	1.3
17602	36.9	78	13.7	51	22.0	310	68.3	8	13	13.7	13	1	.1
17603	50.6	95	19.7	60	24.8	326	83.2	6	15	22.7	13	4	.3

WILLIAMSPORT

ZIPCODE	1	2	3	4	5	6	7	8	9	10	11	12	13
17701	60.1	97	22.0	61	22.7	283	70.8	7	14	27.4	12	7	1.6
17720	.4	100	.1	87	20.4	202	52.5	12	10	.2	8	0	.0
17721	2.0	0	.7	86	23.1	282	60.4	7	9	.0	0	0	.0
17724	4.8	100	1.7	71	19.9	240	55.6	7	14	2.3	13	0	.1
17726	.2	100	.2	81	23.5	263	67.7	6	14	.1	17	0	.3
17728	4.9	100	1.7	85	24.2	273	77.5	8	8	2.4	7	0	.0
17729	.2	100	.2	78	16.2	162	52.4	5	17	.1	17	1	.0
17730	.3	100	.1	63	14.9	176	48.6	7	20	.1	12	0	.0
17731	.3	100	.1	88	23.6	240	69.1	4	21	.1	20	1	.0
17734	.2	100	.1	81	17.1	237	31.6	16	12	.1	15	0	.0
17737	5.3	100	1.9	80	23.7	289	69.9	7	12	2.6	10	0	.0
17738	.2	100	.1	83	19.2	179	54.7	1	15	.1	11	0	.7
17740	12.3	99	4.2	75	22.8	292	64.9	8	12	6.0	10	1	.0
17742	.2	0	.1	98	20.8	240*	56.0	8	7	.0	0	0	.0
17744	3.1	100	1.1	87	22.3	314	68.8	7	9	1.6	8	0	6.4
17745	17.8	99	6.2	64	22.3	267	68.9	6	13	8.3	11	11	.0
17747	2.0	100	.7	88	21.9	273	55.7	8	11	1.0	10	1	.0
17748	.2	100	.1	80	21.5	169	57.0	11	14	.1	15	0	.0
17749	.4	100	.1	83	23.8	267	59.6	7	12	.2	12	0	.0
17750	.2	100	.2	92	29.9	343*	66.6	5	17	.1	15	0	.4
17751	6.6	100	2.2	81	23.4	304	65.8	8	9	3.3	8	8	.4
17752	5.0	97	1.6	79	23.4	256	64.0	7	10	2.5	8	0	.0
17754	11.8	100	4.1	84	27.2	344	88.1	6	13	5.8	11	3	.6
17756	10.3	98	3.5	82	24.3	281	73.9	8	11	4.8	10	0	1.5
17758	.8	0	.3	84	18.9	175	56.8	6	16	.0	8	0	.0
17760	.6	100	.1	84	19.6	152	44.8	9	10	.3	10	0	.0
17762	.6	100	.2	91	23.8	235	61.6	4	15	.3	12	0	.0
17763	.6	100	.2	78	18.0	234	51.3	6	8	.3	8	0	.0
17764	3.5	100	1.4	73	19.3	214	40.8	7	18	1.7	17	0	.4
17765	1.1	0	.4	84	19.3	228	40.7	7	12	.0	8	0	.0
17767	.2	100	.1	83	22.8	286	55.7	9	13	.1	14	0	.0
17768	.2	100	.2	91	21.9	251*	53.5	6	9	.1	8	0	.0
17770	.2	100	.1	82	22.7	261*	43.0	5	3	.1	2	0	.0
17771	2.8	100	.9	82	20.2	255	64.4	8	8	1.4	8	0	.0
17772	2.2	100	.8	84	23.3	272	65.3	7	9	1.1	8	0	1.5
17774	1.0	0	.3	86	18.5	200	58.5	8	13	.0	6	0	.0
17776	.3	100	.1	77	24.4	218	63.5	6	9	.1	8	0	.0
17777	6.2	0	2.1	75	22.2	291	68.3	7	12	.0	1	0	.1
17778	.3	100	.1	76	19.4	283	39.2	8	16	.1	16	0	.0
17779	.6	100	.2	61	28.0	214	102.3	5	16	.3	14	1	2.0

HARRISBURG

ZIPCODE	1	2	3	4	5	6	7	8	9	10	11	12	13
17801	18.5	100	7.1	59	19.8	241	55.6	7	15	8.6	12	3	.1
17810	1.8	99	.6	83	23.4	254	63.0	9	11	.9	10	1	.0
17812	1.4	100	.5	80	26.1	283	54.8	7	10	.7	10	1	.0
17813	1.7	100	.6	83	22.8	202	55.1	8	12	.8	11	0	.3

*=Estimated **1.0=883 lbs per person; 100++ indicates per capita toxic waste generation > than 100 times the U.S. average of 883 lbs per capita.

ZIP CODE MEASURES OF SIZE, LEVELS OF AFFLUENCE AND QUALITY OF LIFE

1=Population (th.); 2= % White; 3=Households (th.); 4= % Owner Occupied; 5=Mean Income Per Household (th.$); 6=Mean Monthly Rent ($); 7=Mean Home Value (th.$); 8=% under 5; 9=% 65 and over; 10=White Males; 11=% White Males, 65+; 12=# Toxic Waste Sites; 13=Toxic Waste Relative to US(883 lbs.per capita)**.

PENNSYLVANIA — HARRISBURG

ZIPCODE	1	2	3	4	5	6	7	8	9	10	11	12	13
17814	4.2	98	1.4	77	20.6	269	63.8	7	13	2.1	12	1	.0
17815	25.1	99	8.3	69	23.1	330	70.3	5	12	11.7	11	3	.1
17820	4.9	100	1.8	82	20.8	288	61.1	6	14	2.4	13	1	.0
17821	17.1	99	5.6	75	25.6	286	68.4	6	16	7.9	13	3	4.7
17823	1.2	100	.4	82	24.2	234	52.6	7	14	.6	13	0	.0
17824	2.9	100	1.0	87	24.0	313	71.5	6	14	1.4	13	0	.0
17825	.1	100	.1	88	13.2	152*	17.5	0	28	.0	22	0	.0
17827	.7	100	.3	80	24.4	258	56.5	6	10	.4	10	0	.0
17828	.2	100	.1	83	19.7	227*	39.2	7	14	.1	10	0	.0
17829	.2	100	.1	81	20.5	229	49.0	5	23	.1	15	0	.0
17830	2.1	100	.7	83	21.8	223	51.1	6	10	1.0	8	0	.0
17831	.5	0	.2	64	21.6	293	65.4	5	19	.0	0	0	.2
17832	.9	100	.4	81	19.1	255	38.7	5	19	.4	17	0	.1
17833	.5	0	.2	88	27.2	386	63.4	7	10	.7	10	0	.0
17834	3.8	100	1.4	87	18.9	270	40.7	6	17	1.8	14	0	.0
17835	.6	0	.1	80	21.0	320	52.2	3	19	.0	0	0	.6
17836	.3	100	.1	94	26.1	300*	57.8	3	2	.1	3	0	.0
17837	15.8	93	4.3	69	27.6	332	88.1	4	11	7.4	8	0	.1
17838	.4	100	.1	81	27.6	336	58.0	6	4	.2	5	0	.1
17840	.5	100	.2	64	16.8	218	27.6	5	18	.2	14	0	.0
17841	3.7	100	1.2	84	22.4	248	51.9	8	10	1.8	9	0	.1
17842	6.4	99	2.1	82	22.0	277	59.2	8	9	3.2	8	2	.0
17844	7.4	100	2.6	77	21.6	289	66.5	9	11	3.7	9	0	.1
17845	1.7	100	.6	84	21.1	286	51.8	8	9	.8	9	0	.0
17846	3.3	0	1.1	77	21.3	275	67.8	8	14	.0	0	1	.6
17847	12.0	99	4.4	70	22.8	272	64.2	6	12	5.8	10	3	2.7
17850	.4	97	.1	71	22.7	277	40.3	13	8	.2	12	0	.0
17851	10.2	100	4.2	77	17.7	226	34.0	5	22	4.7	19	2	.4
17853	2.7	0	.8	86	21.3	264	58.2	9	7	.0	0	0	.0
17855	.9	100	.3	75	23.6	293	61.2	5	10	.4	9	0	.0
17856	2.7	100	.7	89	25.0	326	64.5	8	9	1.4	7	1	.2
17857	6.9	100	2.6	79	22.5	271	63.6	6	15	3.3	13	1	.2
17859	2.4	100	.8	83	20.3	282	60.5	7	18	1.1	15	1	.1
17860	1.6	0	.6	84	21.1	286	51.8	8	13	.0	0	0	.0
17861	.2	100	.1	78	22.2	285	46.7	4	16	.1	9	0	.1
17862	.5	0	.2	69	19.4	278	45.9	6	12	.0	12	0	.0
17864	2.1	100	.7	82	19.8	218	51.0	7	18	1.1	9	1	.6
17866	.3	100	.1	76	17.7	285	57.2	7	18	.1	14	0	.0
17867	.8	100	.3	80	18.5	184	30.7	8	18	.4	16	0	.0
17868	.2	100	.1	76	24.6	304	54.2	9	16	.1	10	1	.7
17870	1.3	100	.4	86	30.5	323	73.4	6	12	.6	10	1	.2
17872	12.5	99	3.7	75	26.4	289	72.1	5	11	6.2	8	2	.1
17876	22.8	100	8.9	73	17.4	207	35.1	5	21	10.4	17	3	.1
17877	3.3	100	.4	78	22.2	255	72.0	5	18	2.1	14	1	.1
17878	1.5	100	.5	85	22.0	314	48.5	9	10	.8	8	1	.0
17881	1.7	100	.7	79	22.8	235	37.8	7	16	.8	15	2	.0
17882	.2	0	.1	78	28.5	438	40.4	6	11	.0	0	0	.0
17884	.3	100	.1	54	20.7	279	53.9	8	18	.1	18	0	.0

PENNSYLVANIA — HARRISBURG (cont.) / POTTSVILLE

ZIPCODE	1	2	3	4	5	6	7	8	9	10	11	12	13
HARRISBURG													
17886	.6	0	.2	53	23.4	304	66.5	7	12	.0	0	0	.0
17887	.6	100	.2	95	23.3	270	56.2	6	11	.3	10	1	.0
17888	.4	100	.1	91	15.6	267	32.3	8	18	.2	23	0	.0
17889	2.2	0	.7	87	25.8	240	76.7	7	7	.0	0	1	.0
POTTSVILLE													
17901	27.3	98	10.1	72	21.4	236	50.3	6	16	12.5	13	1	.0
17920	.3	100	.1	88	18.6	253	37.7	7	20	.2	16	0	1.1
17921	7.3	100	2.7	77	21.6	220	45.9	7	17	.0	0	0	.0
17922	2.7	0	.9	88	25.7	283	66.5	7	8	.0	0	0	.5
17923	.7	100	.2	85	19.3	199	33.6	6	22	.3	19	2	.0
17925	.5	100	.2	89	20.6	246	48.7	6	15	.2	10	0	.0
17927	1.3	100	.5	84	18.2	226	32.3	6	16	.6	13	0	.0
17929	1.9	100	.7	78	23.8	335	52.6	6	11	.9	10	1	1.0
17930	.7	100	.2	66	22.9	254	43.5	7	16	.3	12	0	.0
17931	6.7	100	2.5	80	20.9	243	50.7	5	17	3.2	14	0	.0
17933	.3	100	.1	86	21.4	269	68.5	5	11	.1	14	0	.6
17934	.6	100	.3	86	15.9	248	21.9	5	29	.3	22	0	.0
17935	2.3	0	.9	79	17.4	234	31.1	6	17	.0	0	0	.1
17936	1.2	100	.8	81	23.7	286	51.7	7	12	.6	9	0	.1
17938	2.4	100	.8	82	23.2	270	56.3	7	12	1.2	12	0	.0
17940	.3	100	.1	91	23.1	266*	27.5	5	13	.1	8	0	.1
17941	.8	100	.3	75	20.8	271	46.3	7	13	.4	16	0	.2
17942	.2	100	.1	91	20.6	237*	59.4	7	23	.1	28	0	.1
17943	.7	100	.2	87	19.2	225	49.1	6	10	.3	8	0	.0
17944	.4	100	.1	83	19.3	224	47.4	3	14	.2	11	0	.6
17945	.2	100	.1	39	15.9	189	23.7	4	13	.1	6	0	2.7
17946	.5	100	.2	90	18.5	143	21.4	4	24	.3	22	0	.0
17948	7.3	99	3.0	75	18.5	176	30.5	5	25	3	20	2	.4
17949	.5	100	.2	84	20.1	317	23.3	4	19	.2	16	0	.0
17951	.4	100	.5	95	20.3	233*	52.8	6	17	.2	11	0	.1
17952	.4	100	.4	92	19.3	201	29.7	9	18	.2	12	0	.2
17953	.6	100	.2	75	19.9	230	34.6	4	19	.3	19	0	.1
17954	6.3	0	2.4	72	19.8	211	39.7	5	18	.3	8	0	.1
17955	.3	100	.1	93	18.6	214*	29.4	6	21	.1	19	1	.0
17957	.4	100	.2	89	18.4	221	39.2	5	16	.2	8	0	.0
17959	1.6	0	.6	77	19.7	216	41.2	5	19	.0	0	0	.0
17960	3.1	100	1.0	85	25.2	242	67.3	7	13	.0	0	0	.0
17961	5.3	0	1.9	81	28.2	280	76.3	6	11	.1	9	1	.6
17963	8.0	100	2.8	82	26.5	236	76.6	8	11	.0	0	1	.0
17964	.8	100	.2	76	24.2	184	52.4	8	12	.4	8	0	.0
17965	2.7	100	1.0	79	22.1	268	44.9	6	15	1.3	13	1	.0
17967	2.5	0	.9	82	21.8	234	57.6	7	16	.3	19	0	.2
17968	.4	100	.2	86	19.3	219	49.3	6	12	.2	9	0	.2
17970	4.4	100	1.7	74	18.7	219	39.0	4	18	2.1	14	1	.1
17972	10.7	100	3.8	78	22.6	236	58.5	6	17	5.1	15	0	.0
17974	.4	100	.1	86	23.9	247	55.4	4	15	.2	11	0	.0
17975	.4	100	.2	81	12.7	249	34.8	4	22	.2	19	2	.0
17976	9.6	0	4.1	72	17.1	213	34.8	10	25	4.4	21	2	.0
17978	.4	100	.1	54	23.2	374	51.9	8	12	.0	0	0	.0

*=Estimated **1.0=883 lbs per person; 100++ indicates per capita toxic waste generation > than 100 times the U.S. average of 883 lbs per capita.

ZIP CODE MEASURES OF SIZE, LEVELS OF AFFLUENCE AND QUALITY OF LIFE

1=Population (th.); 2= % White; 3=Households (th.); 4=% Owner Occupied; 5=Mean Income Per Household (th.); 6=Mean Monthly Rent .($); 7=Mean Home Value (th.$)*; 8=% under 5; 9=% 65 and over; 10=White Males (th.); 11=% White Males, 65+; 12=# Toxic Waste Sites; 13=Toxic Waste Relative to US(883 lbs.per capita)**.

PENNSYLVANIA

POTTSVILLE

ZIPCODE	1	2	3	4	5	6	7	8	9	10	11	12	13
17979	.4	100	.1	82	21.9	317	55.2	3	11	.2	14	0	1.1
17980	3.7	100	1.4	78	21.7	242	49.8	6	13	1.7	9	0	.4
17981	3.2	100	1.1	85	20.5	266	36.1	7	15	1.5	12	1	.0
17982	.5	100	.2	91	20.3	234	41.5	3	18	.2	19	0	.2
17983	1.7	0	.6	91	22.9	155	62.1	8	18	.2	19	0	.4
17985	.9	100	.3	78	17.8	264	58.7	9	13	.4	12	0	.0

LEHIGH VALLEY

ZIPCODE	1	2	3	4	5	6	7	8	9	10	11	12	13
18011	3.1	100	1.1	85	26.7	304	79.3	8	10	1.5	9	0	.1
18012	.2	100	.1	82	24.3	345	49.3	0	36	.1	30	0	.0
18013	13.5	100	5.0	75	25.0	320	72.7	6	15	6.5	12	1	.3
18014	8.8	100	3.0	85	30.2	336	91.9	6	14	4.4	9	0	.2
18015	28.5	93	9.4	65	25.8	294	71.1	5	13	13.7	10	3	.0
18017	39.2	95	13.6	75	34.2	351	105.8	6	10	18.0	9	2	.4
18018	33.3	97	13.4	63	26.4	323	74.6	5	16	15.2	13	1	.3
18030	.9	100	.3	73	23.6	270	60.1	6	16	.4	15	0	.0
18031	3.4	99	1.1	84	29.1	346	100.8	8	9	1.7	7	0	.0
18032	9.3	99	3.4	77	26.0	297	70.9	7	10	4.4	8	1	1.0
18034	4.7	100	1.4	84	35.4	370	119.6	6	7	2.3	7	0	.2
18035	.1	100	.1	90	28.6	329*	121.1	4	4	.1	4	1	.5
18036	10.5	99	3.3	88	34.1	337	106.1	6	11	5.1	9	0	.1
18037	5.5	0	1.9	82	29.7	306	77.9	6	10	.0	0	0	.2
18038	2.4	100	.8	84	27.4	309	91.2	10	5	1.2	6	1	1.2
18041	4.2	100	1.5	74	26.6	341	86.4	8	11	2.0	8	0	1.0
18042	61.2	95	22.0	70	25.2	315	78.6	6	14	27.9	11	5	1.2
18046	.4	99	.2	51	25.2	460	75.8	7	14	.2	11	0	.0
18049	15.1	99	5.6	79	32.2	349	98.6	5	12	7.4	10	1	.3
18051	1.0	99	.4	82	37.8	362	102.3	11	12	.5	14	1	12.8
18052	21.5	98	8.2	62	29.2	420	83.3	5	11	10.3	10	1	.0
18053	1.9	100	.6	90	27.5	321	85.9	10	6	1.0	6	0	.0
18054	3.4	99	1.1	84	29.2	395	100.5	8	11	1.6	10	0	3.1
18055	8.8	100	3.3	80	28.7	304	82.1	6	13	4.2	12	2	.0
18056	1.1	98	.4	92	24.7	372	121.1	10	14	.5	14	2	.0
18058	4.2	100	1.5	88	24.0	328	81.7	7	12	2.1	11	0	.0
18059	.7	100	.3	85	27.4	362	90.5	7	13	.4	13	0	.0
18060	.2	100	.1	72	29.8	325	105.1	10	7	.1	9	0	.0
18061	.1	100	.1	93	25.9	298*	79.8	2	10	.1	6	0	.0
18062	8.7	98	2.9	85	33.9	384	103.6	7	8	4.4	7	2	.4
18063	.8	100	.3	77	28.9	336	86.4	8	12	.1	4	0	.2
18064	16.4	100	5.7	78	28.0	343	87.2	6	15	7.7	12	5	1.1
18065	.5	100	.1	80	38.1	261	88.0	9	6	.2	9	0	.0
18066	3.5	100	1.2	81	28.0	332	61.8	7	11	1.7	9	1	.0
18067	14.3	100	4.9	82	28.1	287	78.2	7	11	6.9	10	2	.1
18068	.3	100	.1	79	22.7	336	84.2	8	23	.1	22	0	.4
18069	3.9	99	1.4	88	30.1	343	111.2	7	10	1.9	7	1	.0
18070	.8	0	.3	93	27.5	286	88.0	9	10	.2	0	0	.1
18071	8.9	100	3.3	79	25.7	286	61.8	7	15	4.3	13	0	1.0
18072	5.9	0	2.1	78	24.8	321	73.2	7	14	.0	8	1	.0
18073	5.5	100	1.9	80	29.5	306	95.7	7	9	2.8	8	0	.2
18074	2.8	0	.9	91	30.7	315	105.8	6	11	.0	0	0	.0

PENNSYLVANIA

LEHIGH VALLEY

ZIPCODE	1	2	3	4	5	6	7	8	9	10	11	12	13
18076	1.9	100	.6	85	30.2	342	85.3	9	10	1.0	8	0	.2
18077	2.1	100	.8	76	34.6	418	105.8	8	11	1.1	9	0	.0
18078	3.2	99	1.1	75	32.7	391	112.1	6	8	1.5	8	0	.0
18079	.9	100	.3	93	26.6	713	75.0	10	9	.5	10	0	.0
18080	9.1	100	3.2	77	26.6	284	75.1	11	9	4.5	9	0	.4
18081	.6	0	.2	85	29.1	320	105.1	3	12	.0	0	0	.0
18083	.6	0	.2	70	25.0	384	81.3	5	13	.0	0	0	24.5
18084	.5	100	.2	79	30.7	288	88.3	6	8	.2	5	0	.0
18085	.9	0	.2	83	26.1	361	84.9	6	13	.0	5	0	.2
18086	.5	100	.2	86	30.6	435	85.0	10	13	.3	11	0	.0
18087	.8	0	.4	45	23.0	378	79.9	4	12	.0	0	0	3.4
18088	6.2	100	2.1	90	27.5	298	86.2	6	9	3.1	8	2	.6
18091	4.6	99	1.6	72	25.7	337	75.6	7	10	2.2	9	0	1.1
18092	2.0	98	.6	84	35.9	379	115.4	6	7	1.0	6	0	1.0

ALLENTOWN

ZIPCODE	1	2	3	4	5	6	7	8	9	10	11	12	13
18101	4.0	82	1.6	21	13.5	197	37.1	5	32	1.3	30	0	7.0
18102	40.2	93	17.0	53	19.9	277	47.4	6	18	17.4	15	2	.3
18103	57.8	95	21.4	67	29.1	340	87.0	5	10	26.5	10	3	.5
18104	34.0	99	12.3	76	33.8	375	107.5	5	17	15.7	14	2	.3
18106	5.0	98	1.7	84	33.5	459	115.6	8	8	2.4	7	0	.3

WILKES-BARRE

ZIPCODE	1	2	3	4	5	6	7	8	9	10	11	12	13
18201	38.8	99	15.1	63	21.3	247	54.7	5	19	17.8	16	12	.7
18210	.8	0	.3	85	25.1	306	78.0	5	18	.0	0	0	.0
18211	1.0	100	.3	82	24.9	197	69.3	9	12	.5	7	0	.0
18212	.3	0	.1	71	22.8	302	60.8	6	12	.0	0	0	.0
18214	2.1	0	.8	84	21.4	258	61.7	6	13	.1	22	0	.0
18215	.2	100	.1	58	18.8	197	26.1	0	30	.7	15	0	.0
18216	1.5	100	.6	78	21.1	206	52.9	4	19	.7	15	0	.0
18218	2.8	0	1.2	80	18.1	215	33.3	4	24	.0	6	0	.0
18219	2.4	99	.9	78	32.8	370	98.8	7	12	1.1	9	0	7.3
18220	.5	100	.3	91	21.3	280	32.7	6	15	.3	11	0	.0
18221	.7	100	.3	95	19.4	290	47.9	3	18	.3	19	0	.0
18222	5.4	89	1.6	86	25.0	310	72.7	7	10	2.4	16	0	.0
18223	.3	100	.1	100	17.0	195*	33.9	10	26	.1	16	12	.0
18224	7.6	100	2.8	75	21.4	242	46.5	6	18	3.6	14	2	.1
18225	.4	100	.1	87	25.6	607	60.9	1	12	.2	4	0	.0
18229	6.1	100	2.0	79	22.2	242	51.5	6	15	2.9	13	2	.0
18230	.5	0	.2	60	17.9	209	43.0	6	15	.3	21	0	.0
18231	.7	100	.3	81	19.5	212	49.3	5	22	.3	24	0	.0
18232	4.5	0	1.9	78	19.8	213	32.9	4	22	.0	27	0	.8
18234	.5	100	.5	80	22.4	208	53.6	3	22	.2	27	0	.2
18235	15.8	99	5.7	75	24.1	271	67.1	7	13	7.6	11	1	.0
18237	3.7	100	1.4	70	18.7	204	47.5	4	20	1.7	17	0	.0
18239	.3	100	.3	81	21.0	353	37.7	3	22	.3	21	0	.0
18240	3.8	100	1.4	82	23.1	283	50.9	4	16	1.8	12	0	.1
18241	1.0	99	.4	71	20.9	259	48.7	7	16	.5	13	0	.0
18242	.4	100	.2	86	16.0	339	25.9	4	16	.2	14	0	1.0
18243	.6	100	.2	73	22.7	337	59.5	9	8	.3	9	0	.0
18244	.4	100	.2	82	23.8	284	44.7	5	13	.2	11	0	.0

*=Estimated **1.0=883 lbs per person; 100++ indicates per capita toxic waste generation > than 100 times the U.S. average of 883 lbs per capita.

ZIP CODE MEASURES OF SIZE, LEVELS OF AFFLUENCE AND QUALITY OF LIFE

1=Population (th.); 2= % White; 3=Households (th.); 4=% Owner Occupied; 5=Mean Income Per Household (th.$); 6=Mean Monthly Rent ($); 7=Mean Home Value (th.$); 8=% under 5; 9=% 65 and over; 10=White Males (th.); 11=% White Males, 65+; 12=# Toxic Waste Sites; 13=Toxic Waste Relative to US(883 lbs.per capita)**.

PENNSYLVANIA

WILKES-BARRE

ZIPCODE	1	2	3	4	5	6	7	8	9	10	11	12	13
18245	.3	100	.1	88	21.0	280	41.8	3	16	.2	11	0	.0
18246	.2	100	.1	81	20.0	271	39.5	4	14	.1	13	0	.0
18247	.2	100	.1	100	28.7	330*	90.8	3	7	.1	9	0	.0
18248	.5	0	.2	84	19.5	259	36.4	8	23	.0	0	0	.0
18249	2.2	0	.7	87	24.9	348	88.3	9	9				.0
18250	3.2	100	1.2	84	22.6	234	38.6	6	18	1.5	14	0	.0
18251	.2	100	.1	73	28.0	314	70.5	0	15	.1	8	0	.0
18252	13.3	99	5.0	76	21.7	225	49.8	6	17	6.3	15	3	.5
18254	1.1	100	.4	84	22.5	250	52.6	6	16	.5	12	1	.0
18255	4.5	99	1.6	83	22.2	216	59.1	5	18	2.1	15	0	.2
18256	.5	100	.2	86	22.5	207	45.6	7	13	.2	10	0	.0

LEHIGH VALLEY

ZIPCODE	1	2	3	4	5	6	7	8	9	10	11	12	13
18301	16.5	98	5.4	71	24.3	343	84.8	6	13	7.6	11	3	.5
18321	.6	100	.1	75	25.5	437	101.8	8	10	.3	9	0	.0
18323	1.3	100	.4	72	29.4	313	97.0	5	11	.6	10	0	.0
18324	1.5	98	.1	52	30.4	103	129.5	12	23	.1	21	0	.0
18325	1.5	100	.6	71	24.7	456	89.7	6	12	.8	15	0	.0
18326	2.8	99	1.2	74	23.8	293	84.8	8	18	.7	13	0	.0
18327	.7	97	.2	42	23.8	344	94.3	5	17	1.3	14	0	.0
18328	1.6	100	.6	85	24.4	379	81.2	4	9	.3	10	1	22.2
18330	1.4	99	.5	87	26.0	169	77.1	6	17	.8	18	0	.0
18331	.7	0	.2	84	23.3	241	85.7	11	11	.7	12	0	.4
18332	1.6	100	.6	83	25.1	395	80.9	6	11	.0	8	0	.0
18333	.6	0	.2	84	23.6	361	87.9	8	14	.9	0	0	.0
18334	.7	0	.2	91	22.8	307	85.1	4	8	.0	0	0	.0
18335	.8	100	.2	81	23.2	147	82.2	10	9	.9	8	0	.0
18336	3.3	100	1.2	79	24.7	409	85.6	5	17	1.6	16	1	.0
18337	4.2	99	1.6	75	24.7	324	69.1	6	16	1.9	17	1	.1
18340	.2	100	.1	70	18.6	363	95.8	7	11	.3	19	1	.0
18341	.4	96	.2	76	27.9	207	65.0	8	23	.2	3	0	.0
18342	.4	0	.1	66	26.3	440	100.1	6	8	.0	0	0	.7
18343	2.2	99	.8	81	23.9	301	86.5	0	13	.0	0	0	.0
18344	1.8	99	.7	69	27.5	381	90.5	6	13	.9	13	0	.1
18346	1.6	100	.6	92	22.5	519	92.7	6	12	.3	9	0	.0
18347	1.6	100	.5	75	23.7	436	84.1	3	20	.8	11	1	.1
18350	1.1	0	.4	81	26.6	257	88.3	6	10	.0	0	0	.0
18351	.7	100	.3	64	22.4	336	98.0	7	12	.3	14	0	.0
18352	.3	0	.1	78	26.1	352	69.7	5	12	.3	11	0	.4
18353	3.8	99	1.3	82	25.3	301	102.5	3	8	1.9	11	1	.0
18354	.8	0	.2	90	24.9	313	87.0	8	12	.4	0	0	.0
18355	.5	100	.2	80	23.9	432	103.9	5	9	.2	13	0	.0
18356	.6	100	.2	73	26.7	450	99.1	8	12	.2	14	0	.0
18360	18.5	98	7.1	68	24.7	320	91.1	6	15	8.7	12	2	15.0
18370	.5	100	.2	63	22.5	434	96.8	3	17	.2	19	0	.0
18372	1.1	100	.4	69	25.4	272	104.7	8	6	.6	4	0	.0

SCRANTON

ZIPCODE	1	2	3	4	5	6	7	8	9	10	11	12	13
18403	6.0	0	2.0	79	22.6	287	56.7	6	15	0	0	0	1.4
18405	.4	100	.4	70	20.6	323	82.0	7	19	.2	12	0	.0

PENNSYLVANIA

SCRANTON

ZIPCODE	1	2	3	4	5	6	7	8	9	10	11	12	13
18407	16.2	100	5.9	67	21.7	212	51.2	6	17	7.4	14	2	.3
18410	.5	100	.2	86	24.2	234	66.3	4	17	.2	14	0	.0
18411	18.3	99	5.8	82	34.1	352	94.4	6	11	8.8	9	1	.2
18413	.5	100	.2	81	22.6	408	93.5	11	7	.1	4	3	.0
18414	5.0	100	1.7	82	28.6	312	90.6	7	10	2.5	8	0	.0
18415	.2	100	.1	77	19.1	299	74.4	11	24	.1	19	0	.0
18416	.2	100	.1	92	33.6	386*	86.2	11	9	.1	3	0	.1
18417	.8	0	.3	82	17.3	275	62.5	8	18	.0	0	0	.0
18419	3.6	100	1.3	79	23.0	264	72.1	8	10	1.8	9	0	.0
18420	.1	100	.1	71	20.4	238	73.8	6	18	.1	10	0	.0
18421	3.9	0	1.5	78	21.3	213	52.5	6	21	.0	0	0	3.2
18423	.2	100	.1	71	18.2	386	71.4	7	15	.1	15	0	.0
18424	2.8	100	1.0	84	24.5	277	76.2	6	11	1.4	10	0	.0
18425	.8	100	.3	79	18.9	343	86.3	5	18	.4	17	0	.0
18426	1.5	100	.6	89	21.0	256	82.0	4	19	.7	19	0	.0
18427	.3	100	.1	80	20.3	395	66.6	6	21	.1	17	0	.0
18428	5.1	100	2.1	82	22.7	305	86.9	6	20	2.5	19	0	.0
18431	11.8	100	4.3	74	22.3	293	74.7	7	17	5.5	13	1	.0
18433	6.3	99	2.2	78	20.8	228	58.0	6	16	3.1	13	0	.1
18434	5.0	99	1.8	71	21.7	270	54.0	5	18	2.3	15	0	.0
18435	.2	100	.1	84	20.5	161	78.5	9	28	.1	20	0	.0
18436	7.4	0	2.4	86	22.8	326	80.1	8	10	.0	0	0	.4
18437	.7	0	.3	74	19.0	300	57.1	6	12	.0	0	0	.0
18438	.7	0	.3	86	30.0	392	99.4	4	16	.0	0	0	.0
18439	.5	100	.2	83	18.4	244	61.7	9	10	.2	10	0	.0
18440	.6	97	.1	81	29.6	264	67.7	4	9	.2	5	1	.0
18441	.2	100	.1	80	17.1	232	75.3	7	16	.1	19	0	.0
18443	.5	100	.2	82	22.4	237	67.1	7	15	.2	10	0	.0
18444	10.8	100	3.6	83	25.4	341	80.0	8	11	5.3	10	0	.1
18445	.2	100	.4	75	22.7	287	75.2	6	20	.0	0	0	.0
18446	.4	96	.1	76	22.1	317	64.4	6	17	.2	11	0	.0
18447	10.7	99	3.8	71	24.1	268	60.9	8	13	4.8	13	0	.1
18451	.2	100	.1	88	24.5	277*	131.6	4	9	.1	9	0	.0
18452	5.3	99	1.9	79	24.5	277	69.7	6	13	2.5	11	1	.1
18453	.9	100	.3	84	23.6	301	67.9	9	11	.4	12	0	.1
18455	.4	100	.1	75	20.4	234*	61.3	8	15	.1	18	0	.1
18456	.4	100	.4	72	23.0	350	77.3	5	12	.2	14	0	.0
18457	.2	0	.1	64	20.7	237*	68.3	7	27	.0	0	1	.0
18458	.9	100	.4	88	26.6	276	91.7	8	11	.5	16	0	.1
18459	.9	100	.4	65	20.6	297	81.7	5	12	1.9	11	0	.0
18462	.4	100	.1	87	19.8	242	62.5	7	14	.2	13	0	.0
18463	.4	100	.1	90	19.4	223*	43.7	5	9	.0	0	0	.0
18464	.6	0	.1	85	25.0	155	81.3	6	15	.3	17	0	.0
18465	1.1	100	.4	81	21.1	266	111.3	6	19	.3	17	1	.1
18466	3.2	90	1.2	61	22.0	319	59.3	7	19	1.4	9	0	.0
18470	1.7	100	.6	83	20.4	253	62.0	6	16	.9	18	0	.0
18471	1.1	0	.4	86	44.9	348	131.8	8	12	.2	0	0	.1
18472	3.7	98	1.2	83	22.2	267	65.6	6	15	1.9	12	0	.1
18473	.4	100	.1	80	17.0	274	58.0	6	14	.2	14	0	.0

*=Estimated **1.0=883 lbs per person; 100++ indicates per capita toxic waste generation > than 100 times the U.S. average of 883 lbs per person.

ZIP CODE MEASURES OF SIZE, LEVELS OF AFFLUENCE AND QUALITY OF LIFE

1=Population (th.); 2= % White; 3=Households (th.); 4=% Owner Occupied; 5=Mean Income Per Household (th.$); 6=Mean Monthly Rent ($)*; 7=Mean Home Value (th.$)*;
8=% under 5; 9=% 65 and over; 10=White Males (th.); 11=% White Males, 65+; 12=# Toxic Waste Sites, 13=Toxic Waste Relative to US(883 lbs.per capita)**.

PENNSYLVANIA

SCRANTON

ZIPCODE	1	2	3	4	5	6	7	8	9	10	11	12	13
18503	2.0	96	.9	9	11.3	224	38.4	3	29	1.0	20	0	3.7
18504	24.4	100	9.4	58	20.0	257	49.9	6	18	11.3	14	0	.0
18505	23.3	100	9.0	59	20.9	239	59.5	6	18	10.7	15	3	.3
18507	5.8	100	2.0	81	24.6	298	64.7	6	11	2.8	10	1	1.0
18508	14.8	97	5.4	56	19.5	274	47.0	7	16	6.5	12	1	.0
18509	16.2	99	5.5	55	23.5	275	64.4	5	18	6.5	15	1	.3
18510	14.7	97	5.6	43	20.5	260	57.5	5	23	6.3	18	0	.2
18512	14.6	100	5.4	69	21.6	251	58.0	6	18	6.8	14	3	.4
18517	6.5	100	2.3	76	20.9	265	60.1	6	14	3.0	13	3	.2
18518	8.9	100	3.4	71	21.6	270	63.8	5	18	4.1	15	0	.1
18519	6.1	0	2.4	67	18.8	246	54.8	6	20	.0	0	0	.0

WILKES BARRE

ZIPCODE	1	2	3	4	5	6	7	8	9	10	11	12	13
18601	.3	100	.1	86	20.3	366	41.3	9	10	.2	7	0	.0
18603	20.2	100	7.5	74	22.1	291	64.2	6	15	9.6	12	3	1.4
18610	1.0	100	.4	83	21.2	380	73.5	7	15	.5	15	0	.0
18612	14.3	96	4.4	84	29.3	401	85.7	6	11	6.6	10	0	.0
18614	2.2	0	.6	78	20.4	264	61.3	7	16	.0	0	1	.2
18615	1.7	99	.6	84	21.4	284	71.8	5	13	.0	9	0	.0
18616	.8	100	.3	83	17.2	255	60.8	6	25	.4	19	0	.0
18617	2.2	100	.9	61	17.4	233	35.7	6	28	1.0	25	0	.0
18618	3.1	100	1.1	77	24.0	353	74.1	8	12	1.5	11	0	.0
18619	.2	100	.1	87	18.4	211*	73.3	5	13	.1	11	0	.0
18621	5.2	100	1.8	84	20.9	287	63.0	7	14	2.6	12	1	.0
18622	.2	100	.2	76	21.6	241	64.8	6	10	.1	15	0	.0
18623	2.4	0	.8	76	23.9	281	56.4	9	12	.2	18	0	.3
18624	.3	100	.1	79	23.9	316	92.2	5	15	.2	18	0	.0
18626	.3	100	.1	83	24.6	252	76.9	9	13	.1	9	0	.0
18627	.2	100	.1	88	23.9	274*	67.3	11	12	.2	14	0	.0
18628	.3	0	.1	77	15.7	303	47.7	5	27	.0	15	0	10.1
18629	1.6	100	.5	75	22.6	324	58.7	10	10	.8	9	0	.0
18630	2.7	99	.7	80	23.1	362	63.6	6	11	1.4	10	0	.1
18631	1.3	100	.4	89	23.8	264	65.1	6	10	.3	6	1	.0
18632	.5	100	.2	87	21.8	251	45.8	7	19	.2	16	0	.0
18634	16.7	100	6.6	64	19.2	239	52.7	4	20	7.6	15	1	.4
18635	3.5	99	1.3	74	21.9	275	61.6	7	13	1.7	10	0	.0
18636	1.6	100	.5	77	19.4	273	45.5	8	15	.8	16	1	.0
18637	.5	0	.2	86	25.2	292	69.0	6	10	.0	0	0	.0
18640	18.7	0	6.5	72	21.4	283	59.1	5	16	.0	0	0	.0
18641	9.4	0	3.2	79	22.1	258	60.3	5	14	.0	0	0	.3
18642	4.7	0	1.7	77	21.0	288	52.2	5	18	.0	0	0	.7
18643	13.3	100	4.7	73	22.1	281	62.1	6	15	6.2	13	1	.3
18644	8.9	100	3.2	76	22.4	305	67.1	5	16	4.1	14	2	.2
18651	11.3	0	4.3	66	19.0	244	46.6	5	19	.0	0	0	.0
18653	.4	0	.1	87	24.9	286*	62.3	8	31	.0	0	0	.7
18655	6.6	100	2.3	77	20.7	271	58.6	7	14	3.2	12	0	.0
18656	1.8	99	.6	84	21.4	255	64.5	7	10	.9	7	1	.0
18657	11.4	99	3.8	78	25.1	298	74.1	8	11	5.6	8	0	.0
18660	3.4	100	1.1	88	22.8	311	63.5	7	10	1.7	10	0	.0
18661	5.0	100	1.6	83	22.6	306	63.0	6	13	2.6	12	0	.1

PENNSYLVANIA

WILKES BARRE

ZIPCODE	1	2	3	4	5	6	7	8	9	10	11	12	13
18701	2.3	98	1.5	8	15.7	309	40.0	1	50	1.0	33	0	.7
18702	58.2	98	22.2	61	20.4	263	57.5	6	17	26.3	13	4	.2
18704	36.5	100	14.3	63	23.2	308	66.5	5	19	16.6	15	3	.1
18705	19.7	99	7.3	71	21.3	269	54.2	5	16	9.0	13	2	.1
18706	9.0	99	3.2	71	21.0	270	48.2	6	14	4.2	12	1	.1
18707	11.1	100	3.4	86	30.0	313	85.4	8	8	5.3	7	1	.5
18708	7.9	100	2.6	87	29.4	341	79.9	6	10	3.8	10	0	.1
18709	3.8	0	1.5	62	18.3	271	48.8	5	20	.0	0	0	.0

MONTROSE

ZIPCODE	1	2	3	4	5	6	7	8	9	10	11	12	13
18801	7.7	100	2.6	77	22.2	261	70.8	7	13	3.8	11	0	.0
18810	6.4	99	2.3	70	20.5	235	58.9	8	15	3.0	11	0	1.1
18812	1.1	100	.3	89	28.1	210	87.7	11	6	.6	6	0	.0
18814	.2	95	.1	88	23.2	267*	50.5	9	22	.1	17	0	.1
18816	.2	100	.1	74	21.1	183	67.2	9	14	.1	9	0	.0
18817	.4	100	.1	87	25.0	385	57.7	5	17	.2	9	0	.0
18818	1.0	0	.5	85	25.0	311	72.9	8	9	.0	0	0	.0
18821	.2	0	.1	73	21.6	293	53.7	8	11	.0	0	0	.1
18822	3.4	99	1.1	81	22.8	308	57.9	8	11	1.7	10	0	.5
18823	.3	100	.1	80	20.6	238	63.1	7	16	.2	13	0	.0
18824	1.4	0	.5	79	20.3	250	50.8	9	9	.1	9	0	.0
18826	1.3	100	.5	84	21.0	239	58.4	7	13	.3	7	0	.0
18827	.1	100	.1	79	18.9	240	41.6	8	17	.1	14	0	.0
18829	.8	0	.3	77	19.5	332	45.4	10	12	.1	5	0	.0
18830	.9	99	.3	80	26.0	259	69.6	6	10	.1	7	0	.0
18831	1.1	99	.5	83	21.7	247	69.5	6	11	.6	11	0	.0
18832	1.7	99	.5	82	23.5	311	60.7	9	9	.9	8	1	.0
18833	1.9	0	.6	84	21.7	274	56.6	9	10	.9	10	0	.0
18834	3.2	99	1.1	76	22.8	286	65.7	8	12	1.6	12	2	.0
18837	1.7	100	.5	77	20.2	266	56.5	9	10	.8	9	0	.0
18839	.2	0	.1	76	18.7	290	49.0	11	16	.6	11	0	.0
18840	10.3	99	3.7	69	23.1	317	60.0	6	13	4.8	12	0	.1
18842	.3	0	.1	79	19.6	114	59.2	9	5	.2	3	0	.0
18843	.3	100	.1	75	23.0	255	66.7	9	13	.2	12	1	.0
18844	1.4	0	.5	85	21.1	306	61.0	6	12	.2	12	0	7.4
18845	.4	100	.2	69	17.5	308	67.3	11	10	.4	12	0	.0
18846	.7	100	.2	83	21.5	305	57.5	9	14	.4	14	1	.0
18847	5.3	100	1.8	79	21.1	275	45.7	7	14	2.6	10	2	.0
18848	9.5	100	3.4	70	23.1	266	68.3	7	12	4.7	10	8	1.1
18850	2.3	0	.7	80	21.8	328	56.7	9	8	.8	9	0	.0
18851	.7	0	.2	82	22.3	223	56.4	9	12	.0	0	0	.0
18853	3.6	100	1.2	77	22.0	277	61.6	8	11	1.8	9	1	.0
18854	1.7	0	.6	78	24.0	310	62.1	9	11	.0	0	1	.0

SOUTHEASTERN

ZIPCODE	1	2	3	4	5	6	7	8	9	10	11	12	13
18901	28.2	99	9.3	70	35.5	421	141.6	6	14	13.5	9	1	.6
18911	.4	94	.1	77	27.8	513	107.9	7	12	.2	11	0	.0
18912	.1	100	.1	82	32.2	536	100.0	7	10	.2	7	0	.0
18913	.4	93	.1	81	35.5	517	136.6	4	7	.5	3	0	.0
18914	.3	100	.1	65	29.9	505	197.0	5	10	.1	6	1	.5

*=Estimated **1.0=883 lbs per person; 100++ indicates per capita toxic waste generation > than 100 times the U.S. average of 883 lbs per capita.

ZIP CODE MEASURES OF SIZE, LEVELS OF AFFLUENCE AND QUALITY OF LIFE

1=Population (th.); 2= % White; 3=Households (th.); 4=% Owner Occupied; 5=Mean Income Per Household (th.$); 6=Mean Monthly Rent ($); 7=Mean Home Value (th.$); 8=% under 5; 9=% 65 and over; 10=White Males (th.); 11=% White Males, 65+; 12=# Toxic Waste Sites; 13=Toxic Waste Relative to US(883 lbs.per capita)**.

PENNSYLVANIA — SOUTHEASTERN

ZIPCODE	1	2	3	4	5	6	7	8	9	10	11	12	13
18915	.2	0	.1	68	32.5	594	92.2	10	8	.0	0	3	35.8
18916	.8	0	.3	77	21.7	365	109.4	9	6	.0	0	0	1.3
18917	1.7	99	.7	31	24.4	455	89.0	12	10	.9	9	0	.1
18920	.4	100	.2	88	33.9	497	116.3	3	21	.9	19	0	.0
18921	.5	100	.1	85	30.2	530	94.9	6	5	.3	3	0	.0
18922	.2	100	.1	90	30.9	355*	128.4	0	8	.1	5	0	.0
18923	.4	100	.2	65	30.7	342	122.9	7	10	.2	10	0	.0
18924	.2	100	.1	74	26.3	408	105.0	6	8	.1	0	0	1.0
18925	2.7	99	.7	91	48.5	580	174.7	5	5	1.4	5	0	.0
18926	.4	0	.1	89	33.3	453	142.7	5	4	.0	0	0	.2
18927	.4	0	.1	88	33.9	383	135.0	2	8	.0	0	1	.0
18928	.5	100	.2	71	41.3	603	201.4	3	21	.0	14	0	.0
18929	.9	0	.3	79	42.2	423	129.9	7	7	.3	0	0	.2
18930	1.7	100	.6	83	28.6	458	113.1	8	8	.9	9	0	.5
18931	.2	100	.1	39	26.1	411	158.1	3	26	.1	13	0	.0
18932	.6	94	.2	84	32.1	456	95.6	3	10	.3	11	0	.0
18933	.3	100	.2	65	41.1	386	157.1	1	13	.3	9	0	1.1
18934	.6	100	.2	94	42.8	492*	173.9	5	8	.3	0	0	.0
18935	.3	0	.1	67	28.6	452	81.9	5	4	.3	0	0	.0
18938	5.6	99	2.1	68	41.9	516	169.8	4	11	2.8	8	0	.7
18940	9.8	98	3.3	81	42.4	478	141.4	6	9	4.7	7	0	.7
18942	2.4	99	.7	79	32.8	395	116.9	7	7	1.2	7	0	.0
18943	.4	93	.1	89	29.2	500	113.3	5	8	.2	6	0	.3
18944	12.1	99	4.1	79	31.6	362	104.4	6	11	6.0	9	0	.0
18946	.5	0	.2	81	33.0	246	136.1	8	24	.0	0	0	.0
18947	2.6	0	.9	81	36.5	421	125.7	4	9	.0	0	0	.4
18949	.6	100	.2	68	25.7	441	106.3	10	9	.3	6	0	.3
18950	.7	94	.2	73	30.9	584	111.4	4	9	.4	0	3	2.3
18951	22.8	99	8.2	77	26.8	320	91.7	8	13	10.9	11	1	.2
18953	.4	100	.1	76	28.8	551	103.7	4	11	.2	11	0	10.3
18954	6.8	100	1.8	96	42.5	591	147.7	10	4	3.4	3	0	.3
18955	1.5	99	.5	70	27.0	305	84.1	8	17	.7	16	0	1.0
18956	.3	100	.1	58	31.8	537	158.6	8	13	.1	15	0	.0
18957	.3	100	.1	88	27.7	318*	90.6	8	5	.2	4	0	.0
18960	8.0	99	2.6	82	29.7	373	96.9	7	11	3.9	9	1	2.5
18962	.6	0	.2	70	33.9	390	100.5	11	8	.0	0	1	.0
18963	.5	100	.2	83	46.1	417	183.9	10	12	.3	14	0	.1
18964	9.8	98	3.5	68	31.0	349	96.9	7	14	4.6	11	0	.2
18966	33.5	99	9.5	91	41.2	504	132.4	6	7	16.2	5	1	.3
18968	.3	100	.1	79	29.4	439	94.8	8	9	.0	0	0	.0
18969	9.7	99	3.3	75	30.6	382	100.8	9	7	4.7	8	0	.4
18970	.8	99	.3	66	27.8	405	80.8	9	7	.0	0	0	.1
18971	.4	0	.1	78	27.5	373	92.8	3	16	.0	0	0	.0
18972	2.3	0	.9	78	26.2	390	105.8	8	11	.0	0	2	.0
18974	38.8	97	11.1	74	34.6	418	106.9	7	6	18.5	4	6	2.3
18976	10.4	99	3.2	72	35.6	482	123.9	7	5	5.2	5	0	.4
18977	2.9	100	.9	92	52.1	573	192.6	5	5	1.5	5	0	2.1
18979	.3	100	.1	77	30.5	373	98.6	7	5	.3	10	0	.0
18980	.5	100	.2	75	29.5	366	132.3	7	11	.3	10	0	.3
18981	.2	100	.1	68	25.6	326	129.9	13	14	.1	10	0	.0

PHILADELPHIA

ZIPCODE	1	2	3	4	5	6	7	8	9	10	11	12	13
19001	18.6	96	6.4	84	34.8	421	92.4	6	12	8.5	11	0	.0
19002	23.8	92	8.0	73	40.5	495	130.8	5	10	10.6	8	3	12.4
19003	14.3	86	5.6	60	32.8	465	108.0	5	18	5.8	14	0	.0
19004	10.3	98	3.8	76	52.0	546	108.2	4	12	4.8	14	0	1.1
19006	20.0	99	6.4	80	50.9	515	162.8	4	12	9.5	10	2	.6
19007	22.5	88	7.9	62	24.8	306	65.8	7	11	9.5	10	6	8.9
19008	21.8	98	7.1	85	38.1	474	123.4	4	14	10.2	11	0	1.1
19010	19.7	91	6.8	59	47.2	499	187.1	4	16	7.4	13	0	1.5
19012	6.3	97	2.2	88	42.7	347	108.5	6	15	2.9	14	0	.1
19013	52.9	46	18.3	56	19.6	261	41.9	8	13	11.5	15	5	1.5
19014	18.4	94	5.7	84	33.0	371	93.3	7	8	8.4	11	1	.2
19015	16.9	95	5.9	77	29.4	421	76.1	8	8	7.9	7	3	.0
19017	1.2	93	.1	79	39.0	503	137.4	2	63	.4	43	0	.0
19018	25.7	98	9.8	65	27.5	395	74.9	7	12	11.9	10	0	.2
19020	58.0	94	20.7	58	27.8	394	87.9	9	6	27.0	6	5	.5
19022	1.5	92	.5	44	22.0	230	58.7	10	8	.7	7	1	7.4
19023	23.9	92	7.9	73	22.8	295	48.6	8	14	10.3	10	4	.2
19025	4.3	96	1.2	99	56.7	675	155.5	5	5	2.1	5	0	1.0
19026	33.8	98	12.2	71	31.7	371	89.5	6	15	15.4	12	1	.0
19029	2.3	0	.9	76	24.5	331	63.2	5	14	.0	0	0	16.0
19030	12.5	97	4.1	78	32.7	408	85.1	8	6	5.9	6	1	11.2
19031	4.5	99	1.4	90	43.6	522	123.2	4	21	2.1	14	0	.3
19032	8.2	99	2.4	85	29.1	394	78.9	8	11	4.0	10	1	.3
19033	8.4	95	2.8	81	30.4	405	80.7	5	12	3.9	10	0	.3
19034	5.0	98	1.6	76	52.3	484	179.7	5	12	2.5	10	2	33.6
19035	3.8	98	1.2	90	90.1	678	283.3	3	13	1.7	11	0	.0
19036	15.6	97	5.3	76	27.3	366	63.0	7	8	7.4	7	0	.1
19037	1.6	90	.6	46	29.4	493	107.4	4	11	2.5	13	0	1.3
19038	22.7	94	8.1	78	32.2	434	91.8	6	15	10.2	13	1	.0
19039	.3	0	.1	74	43.8	433	225.9	3	12	.0	0	0	.0
19040	20.1	99	7.1	70	32.0	414	96.6	6	11	9.6	9	3	1.6
19041	5.5	93	1.8	60	65.7	506	244.0	1	17	2.5	13	0	.3
19043	3.1	96	1.0	78	30.1	366	78.9	5	11	1.4	10	1	.3
19044	11.4	95	4.0	64	31.5	403	102.7	6	8	5.3	7	1	1.2
19046	15.6	98	6.0	62	53.3	543	171.1	4	25	6.5	19	1	1.0
19047	45.6	96	15.4	74	31.2	404	97.7	7	7	21.6	1	5	1.5
19050	30.0	85	11.6	66	27.7	371	71.4	6	18	11.6	15	1	.4
19052	.3	100	.1	90	35.5	453	91.2	0	7	.1	21	0	.4
19054	20.4	97	6.4	78	33.5	441	76.2	8	5	10.0	4	0	.1
19055	16.0	99	4.6	94	31.9	527	70.4	8	5	7.8	4	1	.0
19056	16.6	98	.1	98	35.7	380	88.8	6	6	7.8	5	0	.0
19057	19.1	93	5.7	82	31.6	442	71.4	7	5	8.9	4	1	1.6
19061	20.1	98	6.8	71	27.9	385	80.0	7	9	9.5	8	1	.3
19063	29.0	92	10.5	69	36.9	406	131.9	5	14	12.9	10	4	1.3
19064	25.9	98	8.4	90	39.0	543	112.1	5	13	12.2	11	2	.4
19065	.7	0	.2	90	56.9	420	185.1	4	8	.0	0	2	.0
19066	5.7	98	1.9	82	67.2	547	176.9	5	16	2.6	14	0	.0

*=Estimated **1.0=883 lbs per person, 100++ indicates per capita toxic waste generation > than 100 times the U.S. average of 883 lbs per capita.

ZIP CODE MEASURES OF SIZE, LEVELS OF AFFLUENCE AND QUALITY OF LIFE

1=Population (th.); 2= % White; 3=Households (th.); 4=% Owner Occupied; 5=Mean Income Per Household (th.); 6=Mean Monthly Rent ($)*; 7=Mean Home Value (th.$)*; 8=% under 5; 9=% 65 and over; 10=White Males (th.); 11=% White Males, 65+; 12=# Toxic Waste Sites; 13=Toxic Waste Relative to US(883 lbs.per capita)**.

PENNSYLVANIA

PHILADELPHIA

ZIP CODE	1	2	3	4	5	6	7	8	9	10	11	12	13
19067	38.2	94	13.1	74	38.0	395	128.1	6	8	17.5	7	3	1.0
19070	7.0	91	2.4	74	29.1	380	85.3	6	11	3.0	9	1	.1
19072	10.5	99	4.1	62	49.5	536	177.5	5	14	4.8	11	0	.0
19073	13.9	100	4.5	80	45.3	508	168.8	4	13	6.6	11	0	.0
19074	6.6	100	2.2	74	26.9	363	67.7	7	9	3.3	8	0	.0
19075	7.9	98	2.7	88	37.2	449	107.8	5	12	3.7	11	0	.2
19076	6.6	98	2.5	63	25.4	370	69.2	7	12	3.1	11	0	.4
19078	12.9	99	4.6	70	30.3	367	78.0	6	11	6.0	8	0	.0
19079	10.5	57	3.4	72	25.4	311	54.7	6	10	2.9	9	0	4.8
19081	10.7	97	3.5	74	40.1	486	114.1	4	13	5.0	10	0	.1
19082	38.5	96	15.8	66	22.8	338	57.9	9	16	16.9	15	1	.0
19083	38.3	99	12.7	87	34.7	429	104.4	6	14	18.2	12	2	.0
19085	8.0	97	1.7	89	83.7	678	264.3	3	8	4.2	7	0	.0
19086	10.9	99	3.6	90	47.0	516	128.9	5	13	5.1	11	0	.0
19087	25.6	95	9.3	65	49.6	532	183.2	4	11	11.4	9	2	3.4
19090	21.5	87	7.5	70	31.8	457	92.0	6	12	9.0	10	1	.3
19094	4.9	96	1.7	68	27.1	270	75.4	6	12	2.3	10	0	.0
19095	6.0	93	2.2	61	51.0	477	138.3	3	26	2.6	26	0	.0
19096	6.9	99	2.8	69	56.8	492	183.8	5	26	3.0	20	0	.2

PHILADELPHIA

ZIP CODE	1	2	3	4	5	6	7	8	9	10	11	12	13
19102	4.4	86	3.1	15	29.8	465	117.9	1	12	1.8	12	0	1.2
19103	19.6	93	13.4	20	30.7	461	192.5	1	28	7.6	22	0	.9
19104	54.1	40	18.5	26	14.6	287	34.2	5	11	12.5	4	5	.5
19106	5.5	95	3.2	37	45.2	567	287.9	2	11	2.6	10	2	2.1
19107	9.2	84	5.7	9	20.4	366	162.0	2	14	1.2	12	0	3.8
19111	63.2	99	25.3	67	25.6	361	72.5	5	21	28.5	17	0	.1
19112	2.9	99	.5	2	25.1	370	89.3*	9	0	1.6	0	1	19.7
19113	2.0	81	.7	67	25.5	366	70.0	6	11	.0	8	2	15.9
19114	33.1	95	11.1	64	28.8	408	75.1	6	10	15.1	8	1	.0
19115	31.2	98	11.8	62	30.2	416	100.2	4	17	14.4	15	1	.5
19116	29.8	98	10.4	64	28.9	379	95.7	6	10	14.0	8	1	.1
19117	14.3	88	5.5	58	44.6	399	130.5	4	20	8.3	17	1	.0
19118	20.6	95	7.7	64	45.8	516	141.3	4	23	8.3	19	1	.1
19119	31.7	35	12.2	64	29.2	335	73.6	5	15	4.9	14	0	.0
19120	63.4	90	24.1	76	22.1	302	40.9	7	17	26.5	15	1	.4
19121	56.8	2	19.5	35	12.3	199	22.2	8	13	.5	5	1	.0
19122	23.8	24	6.6	39	13.6	215	30.5	9	7	2.8	11	0	.6
19123	14.3	21	5.1	23	12.6	155	37.8	10	12	1.5	23	1	1.2
19124	63.0	93	24.0	74	21.9	266	44.8	7	14	4.9	11	0	.0
19125	26.4	99	9.3	73	18.8	232	24.8	7	14	12.5	11	0	4.3
19126	23.8	46	8.1	67	30.5	339	67.0	5	14	5.0	18	0	.0
19127	6.5	96	2.2	72	21.3	311	36.0	6	14	3.0	12	1	1.4
19128	39.3	96	15.2	66	26.9	413	70.1	6	16	17.4	13	0	.0
19129	13.1	52	4.7	57	22.2	220	55.8	7	11	3.1	14	0	.4
19130	23.1	60	10.2	34	24.8	372	75.3	5	16	6.6	15	0	12.5
19131	50.0	27	19.6	54	21.9	381	39.6	5	19	5.6	34	1	.9
19132	56.6	2	19.0	60	15.7	264	20.8	7	11	.6	28	1	.9
19133	36.8	19	10.2	45	13.0	244	16.8	10	7	3.5	11	0	.6
19134	60.4	98	22.3	78	19.1	264	26.9	7	16	27.8	13	5	1.1

PENNSYLVANIA

PHILADELPHIA

ZIP CODE	1	2	3	4	5	6	7	8	9	10	11	12	13
19135	33.9	99	12.7	77	24.0	299	50.3	7	16	16.0	13	1	1.3
19136	40.5	93	13.6	74	25.7	305	58.9	6	14	17.9	12	2	.8
19137	8.8	100	3.2	87	21.1	296	38.9	5	15	4.2	13	5	11.1
19138	41.3	8	12.9	79	23.0	335	37.2	8	7	1.4	34	0	.0
19139	51.4	7	19.6	54	17.0	264	26.1	6	15	1.7	25	0	.0
19140	68.5	30	22.7	63	16.4	270	22.5	9	11	9.7	16	1	.4
19141	40.3	24	13.9	57	20.3	318	36.3	7	12	4.5	26	0	.1
19142	30.9	87	11.0	78	21.0	277	33.0	6	15	12.5	13	2	.8
19143	86.3	12	29.0	63	19.7	291	31.3	7	8	4.7	17	1	.0
19144	51.2	32	20.6	42	20.5	296	37.5	6	15	7.2	20	0	.2
19145	57.3	72	20.5	69	20.4	243	48.9	6	14	19.2	15	1	2.1
19146	41.1	26	16.4	51	16.7	280	35.1	6	18	4.9	11	0	1.0
19147	36.3	73	15.2	51	21.1	301	61.6	6	15	12.4	15	1	.5
19148	56.6	92	20.5	77	19.8	308	41.5	6	15	24.2	14	1	.3
19149	50.2	99	19.5	85	24.8	343	56.2	5	20	23.0	17	1	.0
19150	29.1	12	10.1	80	27.1	394	54.9	8	7	1.5	37	0	.0
19151	40.9	66	15.3	72	27.8	388	62.7	5	18	12.4	19	1	.0
19152	32.8	98	13.1	68	25.8	370	78.5	4	26	14.4	22	0	.0
19153	13.0	65	4.9	66	25.6	393	57.7	7	8	4.1	11	2	.5
19154	42.1	97	12.1	82	31.9	358	69.4	8	5	20.0	4	0	.9

SOUTHEASTERN

ZIP CODE	1	2	3	4	5	6	7	8	9	10	11	12	13
19301	6.5	90	2.2	77	44.7	535	143.5	6	9	2.9	8	1	17.0
19310	2.0	94	.7	79	28.2	330	85.4	9	10	1.0	10	0	1.5
19311	3.3	83	1.1	62	30.6	387	100.5	7	9	1.3	7	0	2.3
19312	10.3	97	3.2	85	52.9	541	181.6	4	8	4.8	7	0	.0
19317	.4	0	.1	83	30.0	345	148.3	6	4	.0	4	1	.0
19318	5.3	99	1.8	86	51.7	598	190.0	5	7	2.7	6	0	.0
19319	.5	94	.2	60	28.8	365	110.0	3	31	.3	27	0	.0
19320	1.3	16	.1	91	35.0	165	133.7	1	17	1.1	17	0	3.3
19330	34.3	78	11.3	72	27.9	330	83.4	8	11	13.5	11	8	.3
19331	3.8	97	1.2	79	29.7	370	100.3	6	7	1.8	7	0	10.8
19333	.5	94	.2	74	45.5	451	147.4	4	22	.7	14	0	.0
19335	23.0	93	7.7	69	46.0	395	192.1	4	12	2.7	11	0	1.8
19341	8.9	98	2.9	69	34.3	413	114.2	8	7	10.5	6	1	.0
19342	6.6	93	1.9	84	38.2	483	132.3	6	5	4.3	4	2	24.6
19343	3.8	98	1.1	81	43.4	511	165.1	4	8	3.2	7	1	.0
19344	6.9	99	2.1	82	36.1	418	129.0	7	7	1.9	6	0	.0
19347	.4	100	.1	87	28.0	336	98.3	10	10	3.3	8	3	.0
19348	12.7	88	4.4	60	34.2	548	142.8	5	5	5.3	4	0	3.0
19350	3.6	97	1.1	85	38.5	463	135.2	6	15	12	12	0	.0
19351	.2	96	.1	67	37.2	361	131.6	7	7	1.8	7	0	.0
19352	2.5	94	.5	79	27.2	326	90.2	8	9	.0	6	3	.0
19354	.3	52	.1	83	33.5	359	91.7	6	22	.6	14	0	.0
19355	18.0	100	6.1	73	40.1	280	114.9	5	14	.2	11	1	4.0
19357	.3	95	.1	92	42.6	506	149.2	5	8	8.4	8	9	.0
19358	.9	0	.2	87.2	1002*	151.7		6	11	.3	6	1	.0
19360	.5	72	.2	61	27.1	409	48.0	7	7	.3	6	0	.3
19362	3.5	95	.1	77	34.0	373	101.0	6	7	.0	7	0	.0
19362			1.1		23.9	378	84.0	10	7	1.7	7		

*=Estimated **1.0=883 lbs per person; 100++ indicates per capita toxic waste generation > than 100 times the U.S. average of 883 lbs per capita.

ZIP CODE MEASURES OF SIZE, LEVELS OF AFFLUENCE AND QUALITY OF LIFE

1=Population (th.); 2= % White; 3=Households (th.); 4=% Owner Occupied; 5=Mean Income Per Household (th.$); 6=Mean Monthly Rent ($); 7=Mean Home Value (th.$); 8=% under 5; 9=% 65 and over; 10=White Males (th.); 11=% White Males, 65+; 12=# Toxic Waste Sites; 13=Toxic Waste Relative to US(883 lbs.per capita)**.

PENNSYLVANIA

SOUTHEASTERN

ZIP CODE	1	2	3	4	5	6	7	8	9	10	11	12	13
19363	9.2	93	3.1	67	24.7	279	83.5	8	12	4.2	10	1	1.0
19365	5.0	91	1.7	77	27.3	326	79.2	8	10	2.2	8	0	.1
19367	.5	0	.2	74	27.7	421	67.8	6	13	.0	7	0	.9
19369	.7	99	.3	79	23.6	280	81.0	9	9	.4	7	0	.0
19372	2.4	87	.9	50	28.8	497	96.0	9	7	1.0	6	0	2.2
19373	1.2	79	.2	87	44.6	590	173.6	9	2	1.0	5	0	.0
19374	1.5	73	.4	56	27.2	320	105.4	9	4	.5	4	0	.2
19375	.8	96	.3	65	36.8	433	135.6	4	10	.4	7	0	.0
19376	.4	0	.1	87	46.6	116	112.7	4	10	.0	0	1	.0
19380	67.4	90	22.1	66	35.5	417	135.0	6	8	29.3	6	4	1.2
19390	6.0	87	2.0	78	29.5	341	91.7	8	8	2.6	8	0	.0

SOUTHEASTERN

ZIP CODE	1	2	3	4	5	6	7	8	9	10	11	12	13
19401	71.5	87	24.3	66	28.6	379	88.1	6	13	30.3	10	1	.6
19403	19.8	94	6.8	65	35.9	497	112.6	6	6	9.1	6	0	.0
19405	5.8	98	2.3	59	24.0	347	64.5	6	14	2.7	12	2	.4
19406	22.1	95	8.0	68	39.5	493	114.7	5	7	10.2	6	15	2.0
19409	.6	100	.1	44	36.4	444	118.0	5	7	.3	14	1	.0
19420	.2	100	.1	74	40.5	238	124.5	5	5	.1	0	0	.0
19421	.4	0	.1	82	55.3	479	169.8	5	8	.0	0	0	.0
19422	5.8	96	1.9	77	49.9	611	167.7	5	7	2.7	6	1	1.0
19423	.3	100	.1	75	33.4	261	133.3	6	6	.1	0	0	.0
19425	2.7	99	.9	78	51.7	526	179.0	7	7	1.3	6	0	.0
19426	16.1	90	4.5	75	32.6	526	110.1	6	6	7.4	6	2	.9
19428	16.9	94	6.2	65	27.1	403	76.9	5	5	7.6	10	9	7.5
19430	.3	100	.1	100	32.3	371*	93.5	7	23	.2	16	0	.7
19435	.5	100	.1	79	34.1	369	84.9	7	7	.2	20	0	.0
19436	.8	93	.2	93	78.1	393	210.7	4	46	.3	33	0	2.4
19437	1.0	98	.3	94	88.8	1020*	263.6	3	10	.4	12	0	.0
19438	8.4	99	2.7	76	36.1	438	126.5	7	9	4.2	7	1	.9
19440	14.2	95	5.1	58	29.7	382	106.8	8	8	6.7	7	2	1.2
19442	1.0	100	.3	83	33.8	531	107.7	4	11	.5	12	1	1.6
19443	.3	100	.1	60	27.6	425	119.0	3	15	.2	17	5	34.8
19444	8.1	99	2.5	88	48.3	437	136.1	6	10	3.8	8	0	.7
19446	37.6	96	13.4	66	32.3	429	109.6	7	11	17.3	8	8	.3
19450	.5	100	.2	93	37.1	356	154.0	5	7	.3	11	0	.7
19451	1.1	100	.4	48	29.6	480	175.7	4	12	.1	18	0	2.4
19453	1.9	93	.7	46	27.8	456	76.1	7	11	.1	9	0	.0
19454	11.5	93	4.3	60	34.0	462	114.6	6	8	5.2	4	2	2.0
19456	.7	91	.2	90	30.1	506	108.1	6	8	.4	6	2	5.2
19457	.6	100	.2	80	23.6	397	81.0	8	3	.3	22	2	4.5
19460	26.7	95	9.2	71	29.3	371	95.9	6	10	12.4	8	1	.5
19462	5.7	94	2.1	67	39.3	555	119.8	4	12	2.6	12	5	.9
19468	51.4	93	18.4	69	27.7	334	82.4	7	12	23.0	10	4	2.0
19470	.3	0		65	31.1	342	86.1	7	14	5.8	10	2	.3
19472	.4	100	.1	83	33.5	480	75.3	5	11	.2	8	0	.0
19473	5.5	100	1.8	75	30.3	397	103.1	8	6	2.7	8	0	.0
19474	1.2	100	.4	79	35.1	453	108.0	9	6	.6	4	0	5.9
19475	8.5	96	2.8	66	25.7	309	87.2	7	11	4.1	9	0	2.3

PENNSYLVANIA

SOUTHEASTERN

ZIP CODE	1	2	3	4	5	6	7	8	9	10	11	12	13
19477	1.2	0	.1	86	68.4	393	241.0	1	62	.0	0	0	5.8
19478	.8	0	.3	79	27.4	430	81.3	7	9	.0	0	0	.0
19480	.4	98	.1	66	27.4	437	119.3	8	8	.2	7	0	.0
19481	1.3	0	.4	82	62.5	409	230.0	5	10	.0	0	2	92.2
19486	.5	100	.9	79	35.1	410	110.5	4	9	.3	6	2	100++
19490	.8	97	.3	70	41.8	422	160.1	7	11	.4	9	1	.8
19492	.8	0	.3	82	30.0	286	93.5	6	13	.0	0	0	.0

READING

ZIP CODE	1	2	3	4	5	6	7	8	9	10	11	12	13
19501	1.1	99	.4	68	27.9	305	76.6	6	16	.5	14	0	.0
19503	1.3	99	.4	73	30.0	371	77.6	7	11	.6	11	1	3.2
19504	3.0	100	.9	79	29.0	365	91.4	7	6	.0	0	0	.0
19505	2.9	100	1.0	81	28.8	359	82.4	9	8	1.5	7	0	.1
19506	4.5	100	1.5	78	28.8	369	91.5	9	7	2.3	3	0	.0
19507	2.7	97	.8	83	25.6	296	81.9	7	10	1.3	8	0	.0
19508	11.2	99	3.9	80	27.7	332	75.0	7	11	5.5	10	5	6.1
19510	1.2	97	.4	81	26.8	308	64.7	5	15	.6	13	0	.2
19511	.5	100	.1	85	28.8	243	71.2	6	12	.3	11	0	.0
19512	14.8	99		77	26.6	328	82.2	7	12	7.2	10	5	1.0
19516	.2	98	.1	76	22.1	214	61.2	6	19	.1	14	0	.0
19517	.3		.1	83	19.4	267	50.6	4	12	.1	0	0	.0
19518	7.4	98	2.4	76	31.0	383	90.8	7	7	3.6	7	0	3.0
19519	.3	100	.3	83	32.0	333	65.9	0	23	.1	30	0	.0
19520	4.7	98	.7	80	30.9	397	101.9	8	8	2.3	8	0	.0
19522	10.4	100	3.6	83	28.4	323	78.5	7	11	5.1	5	0	.7
19523	.3	100	.1	88	17.7	198	64.2	15	12	.1	0	0	.0
19525	.5	100	1.5	83	32.4	335	96.2	6	9	4.0	4	0	.0
19526	.8	99	3.2	72	25.7	279	68.4	6	14	4.3	12	1	.1
19529	2.0	99	.7	79	28.7	303	77.6	7	11	1.0	0	0	.0
19530	11.2	98	3.3	69	27.0	360	85.0	5	9	5.2	10	0	2.8
19533	3.4	99	.6	83	30.4	330	88.5	6	11	1.7	10	0	.7
19534	1.5	100	.6	76	26.2	300	75.4	6	11	.7	11	0	.7
19536	.6	100	.2	70	24.0	329	50.8	5	17	.1	11	0	.0
19538	.2	100	.1	60	21.6	303	71.7	3	12	.1	14	0	.0
19539	3.4	0	.1	82	29.1	353	72.5	6	9	2.0	14	0	2.3
19540	8.1	99	2.8	84	30.5	324	83.7	6	10	4.0	1	0	.1
19541	1.9	0	.6	83	25.6	312	77.0	6	12	.0	0	0	.0
19542	1.1	100		83	40.1	300	82.6	7	9	.0	0	0	.0
19543	1.9	0	.7	73	31.0	460*	60.7	9	11	.0	0	0	2.8
19544	.3	100	.1	78	20.6	341	100.7	7	18	.1	17	0	.0
19545	.8	100	.1	81	31.5	327	45.2	6	7	.3	7	0	.3
19547	3.4	100	1.2	76	30.1	377	72.6	6	12	.0	0	0	.0
19548	.2	45	.1	62	22.1	400	87.8	6	19	.1	11	0	.6
19549	.6	100	.1	82	24.7	552	91.9	9	12	.2	9	0	.0
19550	.6	97	.2	68	22.6	316	46.4	9	11	.3	11	0	.0
19551	4.0	99	1.3	81	29.6	277	63.3	7	10	2.0	10	1	.3
19553	.5	0	.2	91	31.7	312	77.0	6	12	.0	0	0	.0
19554	.5	100	.2	70	24.6	266	67.5	6	11	.3	10	0	.0
19555	3.5	100	1.3	82	28.1	337	73.3	7	11	1.7	10	3	.1
19557		98		78	24.3	344	75.0	9	18	.1	20	0	.0

*=Estimated **1.0=883 lbs per person; 100++ indicates per capita toxic waste generation > than 100 times the U.S. average of 883 lbs per capita.

ZIP CODE MEASURES OF SIZE, LEVELS OF AFFLUENCE AND QUALITY OF LIFE

1=Population (th.); 2= % White; 3=Households (th.); 4=% Owner Occupied; 5=Mean Income Per Household (th.$); 6=Mean Monthly Rent ($); 7=Mean Home Value (th.$); 8=% under 5; 9=% 65 and over; 10=White Males (th.); 11=% White Males, 65+; 12=# Toxic Waste Sites; 13=Toxic Waste Relative to US(883 lbs.per capita)**.

PENNSYLVANIA

ZIPCODE	1	2	3	4	5	6	7	8	9	10	11	12	13
READING													
19559	.5	100	.2	78	25.3	319	53.4	7	13	.3	13	0	.1
19560	6.9	100	2.6	82	28.7	337	70.3	4	14	3.4	12	2	1.7
19562	2.3	100	.8	73	26.3	323	70.5	5	25	1.1	15	1	1.9
19564	.3	100	.1	76	28.3	358	63.7	9	13	.1	9	0	.0
19565	5.2	99	1.7	80	29.7	334	85.9	5	16	2.6	13	0	.1
19567	3.9	98	1.3	72	26.5	312	69.8	8	10	1.9	9	0	.4
READING													
19601	29.7	77	12.5	50	19.8	261	43.3	7	17	10.5	17	1	2.5
19602	17.0	83	7.4	48	17.0	233	32.9	6	20	6.3	18	2	4.0
19604	23.3	96	9.1	72	23.1	299	47.1	6	17	10.5	14	1	4.3
19605	14.6	99	5.4	88	28.8	331	79.5	4	15	7.1	13	2	1.7
19606	24.6	99	9.1	82	29.8	367	80.4	5	13	11.8	12	0	.0
19607	19.5	98	7.7	72	28.9	370	83.0	6	14	9.0	15	1	.0
19608	10.4	99	3.7	71	30.3	351	90.6	7	11	5.0	10	3	.6
19609	10.9	98	4.0	87	32.1	406	85.8	4	13	5.2	11	0	.0
19610	10.7	98	3.9	71	42.3	446	137.3	6	15	4.9	13	1	.5
19611	10.6	85	4.0	61	21.9	269	63.4	7	21	4.0	20	0	.0
WILMINGTON													
19711	.4	0	.1	91	47.4	425	181.5	6	9	.0	0	0	.0
BALTIMORE													
21088	.2	100	.1	93	30.2	347*	97.1	8	6	.1	6	0	.0
CUMBERLAND													
21502	.3	100	.1	85	23.3	216	72.3	5	14	.2	14	0	.0
21530	.7	97	.2	88	20.3	131	53.5	7	10	.3	11	0	.0
21536	.3	100	.1	79	15.9	245	52.0	16	12	.1	12	0	.0
FREDERICK													
21750	.5	0	.2	85	19.7	128	68.1	9	9	.0	0	0	.0
WHEELING													
26033	.7	0	.2	72	15.8	178	34.2	5	12	.0	0	0	.0
YOUNGSTOWN													
44436	1.3	0	.4	82	26.1	270	71.1	11	7	.0	0	0	.0
44442	.2	100	.1	100	22.8	262*	61.4	12	34	.1	37	0	.0

RHODE ISLAND

ZIPCODE	1	2	3	4	5	6	7	8	9	10	11	12	13
WORCESTER													
01504	.2	100	.1	81	23.7	314	103.3	5	12	.1	8	0	.0
PROVIDENCE													
02801	.4	100	.1	84	30.5	419	122.5	5	19	.2	21	0	.0
02802	.4	100	.2	30	20.8	267	76.6	4	21	.2	19	0	.0
02804	2.6	98	.9	85	26.0	406	91.1	7	10	1.3	9	0	.4
02806	16.2	99	5.2	89	42.8	461	136.8	5	10	7.9	8	0	.0
02807	.6	0	.3	66	23.5	372	172.4	4	18	.0	0	0	.1
02808	3.3	98	1.2	71	22.9	341	97.2	7	12	1.6	11	0	.5
02809	20.1	99	6.4	64	25.2	312	106.2	6	14	9.9	12	1	.3
02812	.9	93	.9	80	28.0	334	89.7	6	7	.4	10	0	.0
02813	1.6	0	.6	70	25.1	400	102.6	7	18	.0	0	2	.0
02814	5.0	0	1.6	86	26.5	329	89.8	7	10	.0	0	0	.0
02815	.2	100	.1	83	22.8	348	61.6	3	15	.1	16	0	.0
02816	28.9	99	9.5	80	27.7	326	87.8	7	8	14.2	7	3	2.7
02817	.2	100	.1	76	32.9	523	258.5	5	3	.1	7	0	.0
02818	15.1	99	5.3	74	38.8	363	141.0	5	10	7.2	8	2	1.0
02822	2.7	97	.9	79	25.2	354	93.5	8	7	1.3	7	0	.2
02823	.1	100	.1	89	17.3	199*	79.8	4	4	.1	8	0	96.0
02824	.5	100	.5	65	32.4	410	97.7	5	13	.1	13	0	.1
02825	3.8	99	1.2	84	30.7	368	98.8	7	9	1.9	8	1	.0
02826	.9	99	.3	79	28.4	331	86.7	6	7	.5	4	0	.0
02827	.8	100	.3	95	27.9	320*	97.6	10	6	.4	4	0	.6
02828	6.9	99	2.1	85	36.2	342	108.0	5	9	3.4	7	1	.6
02829	.8	100	.2	79	28.8	313	90.2	5	5	.3	1	0	.0
02830	2.7	98	.8	65	25.1	285	85.6	8	17	1.2	13	0	.1
02831	2.3	99	.8	83	33.5	421	122.6	6	8	1.1	7	0	.6
02832	2.8	99	.8	79	23.4	357	86.6	6	8	1.4	7	0	4.5
02833	.5	100	.5	95	30.5	351*	96.0	16	0	.0	2	0	.0
02835	4.1	99	1.5	82	27.2	425	127.3	6	13	1.9	10	0	.1
02836	1.2	100	.4	74	26.6	315	104.8	8	10	.5	8	1	1.4
02837	2.6	99	.9	80	30.4	377	130.8	6	16	1.3	12	0	.0
02838	3.4	100	1.3	39	23.2	287	77.7	5	19	1.5	14	0	.4
02839	1.4	100	.5	78	24.7	389	85.4	7	8	.7	8	0	11.4
02840	46.1	91	16.7	45	24.7	369	108.8	7	12	20.2	10	4	.1
02852	21.2	99	7.0	70	30.5	381	107.1	7	10	10.1	7	4	3.1
02857	7.5	99	2.3	89	29.3	361	105.3	5	10	3.7	8	0	.0
02858	.4	100	.1	60	23.7	290	70.7	5	12	.2	11	0	.0
02859	5.3	100	1.8	71	23.1	306	79.2	8	13	2.5	10	2	1.2
02860	45.0	95	18.3	36	19.6	268	76.3	7	16	20.0	13	2	1.7
02861	27.5	99	10.3	66	24.9	320	75.3	5	16	12.6	13	1	.7
02863	17.0	94	6.6	25	17.9	243	59.9	7	17	7.4	14	1	1.5
02864	26.9	99	8.8	75	31.3	273	102.4	5	11	13.0	9	3	1.5
02865	13.2	99	4.7	72	31.9	360	108.3	5	13	6.3	11	5	4.5
02871	13.5	98	4.6	75	30.3	408	121.0	6	9	6.6	8	2	.3
02873	.2	100	.1	100	28.0	322*	69.6	10	4	.1	5	0	.0
02874	2.3	98	.8	79	31.2	474	122.1	6	8	1.1	7	0	.0
02875	.7	100	.2	53	27.9	208	103.9	6	6	.4	5	0	1.6
02876	4.1	99	1.5	71	27.7	309	95.6	6	14	2.0	12	3	1.6
02877	.7	100	.2	80	29.8	391	118.4	10	12	.3	11	0	.5

*=Estimated **1.0=883 lbs per person; 100++ indicates per capita toxic waste generation > than 100 times the U.S. average of 883 lbs per capita.

ZIP CODE MEASURES OF SIZE, LEVELS OF AFFLUENCE AND QUALITY OF LIFE

1=Population (th.); 2= % White; 3=Households (th.); 4=% Owner Occupied; 5=Mean Income Per Household (th.$); 6=Mean Monthly Rent ($); 7=Mean Home Value (th.$); 8=% under 5; 9=% 65 and over; 10=White Males (th.); 11=% White Males (th.); 12=# Toxic Waste Sites; 13=Toxic Waste Relative to US(883 lbs.per capita)**.

RHODE ISLAND

PROVIDENCE

ZIPCODE	1	2	3	4	5	6	7	8	9	10	11	12	13
02878	13.5	99	4.6	82	26.9	338	92.1	5	11	6.5	10	2	.0
02879	8.9	95	3.2	74	29.1	365	108.6	6	11	4.2	10	1	.0
02880	.2	0	.1	62	32.7	551	133.9	10	21	.0	3	0	1.5
02881	6.5	97	.9	55	30.6	337	127.6	2	3	3.0	3	0	.0
02882	11.3	98	4.3	54	26.5	443	110.7	6	10	5.6	9	0	.0
02883	2.9	92	1.1	67	25.0	261	85.6	8	15	1.2	10	0	3.7
02885	10.6	99	3.8	57	23.7	314	92.2	6	15	5.0	12	0	.8
02886	37.5	99	13.1	71	28.5	383	78.9	6	12	17.8	10	0	.5
02888	21.7	99	8.0	81	27.9	383	73.7	5	16	17.2	14	3	.9
02889	21.4	99	7.2	78	27.4	361	75.8	6	12	10.1	9	0	.0
02891	17.4	99	6.3	65	27.7	362	113.8	7	14	8.3	11	0	1.1
02892	2.3	99	.7	87	29.7	405	103.8	6	13	1.1	11	0	.5
02893	28.8	99	10.6	55	23.9	314	83.0	7	11	13.6	9	1	2.0
02894	.6	0	.2	80	24.0	294	86.2	8	7	.0	0	2	18.2
02895	53.4	98	19.4	42	21.3	267	82.8	7	15	24.4	12	1	.7
02898	1.5	100	.5	79	28.4	345	100.0	10	7	.8	5	0	.2

PROVIDENCE

ZIPCODE	1	2	3	4	5	6	7	8	9	10	11	12	13
02903	8.2	90	4.3	12	17.0	260	89.3	3	25	3.4	20	2	6.0
02904	24.8	98	9.8	50	20.8	287	86.4	5	18	11.2	14	1	1.8
02905	25.5	74	8.9	51	22.9	282	62.5	8	12	8.9	11	2	7.0
02906	29.1	85	11.6	41	33.7	393	137.9	4	14	11.5	11	0	.0
02907	23.9	51	8.6	29	16.0	271	47.7	10	12	5.7	14	0	2.6
02908	34.7	95	12.7	49	21.7	296	70.7	5	16	15.0	14	1	.4
02909	34.2	93	13.9	33	17.0	256	60.4	7	17	14.7	14	0	2.0
02910	25.9	98	9.0	70	25.2	365	74.1	4	18	12.1	15	4	1.4
02911	14.4	99	5.2	68	27.8	322	85.3	5	14	6.6	11	0	1.7
02914	23.7	89	8.6	55	27.2	305	75.0	6	17	9.7	14	3	3.9
02915	18.7	97	6.7	67	26.7	374	76.5	6	14	8.6	12	1	.4
02916	7.3	97	2.8	74	29.1	310	95.5	6	17	3.3	14	1	6.5
02917	10.3	100	2.9	74	27.5	302	94.3	5	11	5.1	9	3	2.2
02919	24.3	100	8.0	75	27.8	323	90.0	5	13	11.7	10	2	1.1
02920	34.9	99	12.9	69	29.3	359	99.7	4	15	16.2	13	2	1.0

WILLIMANTIC

ZIPCODE	1	2	3	4	5	6	7	8	9	10	11	12	13
06260	.2	100	.1	61	26.1	339	87.9	6	10	.1	6	0	.0

SOUTH CAROLINA

CHARLOTTE

ZIPCODE	1	2	3	4	5	6	7	8	9	10	11	12	13
28073	1.0	94	.3	84	25.1	402	72.5	9	8	.4	6	0	.0

CHARLOTTE

ZIPCODE	1	2	3	4	5	6	7	8	9	10	11	12	13
28173	.3	0	.1	100	21.2	243*	91.0	7	7	.0	0	0	.0

FAYETTEVILLE

ZIPCODE	1	2	3	4	5	6	7	8	9	10	11	12	13
28343	.9	39	.2	69	16.5	173	40.6	11	6	.2	9	0	.0
28345	.9	68	.3	75	20.4	170	35.3	9	12	.3	6	0	.0

FAYETTEVILLE

ZIPCODE	1	2	3	4	5	6	7	8	9	10	11	12	13
28439	.8	86	.3	71	17.7	296	74.1	9	12	.4	14	0	.0
28463	1.3	59	.4	69	13.6	54	44.5	8	11	.3	19	0	.0

COLUMBIA

ZIPCODE	1	2	3	4	5	6	7	8	9	10	11	12	13
29001	2.2	35	.6	71	18.3	132	53.0	9	9	.4	7	0	.0
29002	.3	0	.1	93	30.9	355*	122.7	3	14	.0	0	0	.0
29003	7.1	47	2.3	72	18.8	199	56.9	8	12	1.6	12	1	.5
29006	8.5	75	2.9	78	19.2	191	54.5	8	12	3.1	10	0	.1
29009	2.5	64	.8	83	20.5	227	51.9	8	13	.8	15	0	1.3
29010	11.4	48	3.6	74	20.0	217	53.0	10	11	2.6	12	0	.2
29014	1.7	56	.5	81	20.6	148	54.7	9	11	.5	13	0	.0
29015	1.4	17	.4	70	19.5	129	38.3	6	18	.1	35	0	.0
29016	4.7	69	1.5	86	25.2	247	79.0	8	7	1.6	5	0	.0
29018	4.3	25	1.2	73	17.5	203	47.7	8	11	.5	10	0	.6
29020	21.7	63	7.6	76	24.3	248	73.9	8	11	6.6	8	0	9.8
29030	2.2	0	.6	69	22.5	252	51.0	5	11	.5	10	0	.0
29031	1.8	0	.6	83	18.4	226	37.4	12	12	.0	1	0	8.9
29032	.7	71	.7	83	20.3	245	48.4	8	7	.8	4	0	.0
29033	13.4	86	4.8	73	26.3	368	66.1	6	8	5.5	6	0	.7
29036	5.9	92	2.0	91	32.5	363	105.2	6	11	2.7	10	4	.0
29037	.9	52	.7	63	20.0	166	50.7	7	10	.2	8	0	.0
29038	2.2	52	.7	73	18.8	184	52.3	6	10	.5	10	0	.0
29039	2.7	66	.9	74	19.5	207	54.7	8	9	.9	6	0	.0
29040	4.3	48	1.3	75	20.1	292	57.4	10	5	1.1	4	0	.0
29041	.2	33	.1	50	22.6	192	58.1	10	5	.2	6	0	.0
29042	7.3	0	2.2	66	16.7	207	75.6	9	8	.2	8	0	.6
29044	5.6	77	1.7	81	22.9	238	52.9	9	8	1.8	10	0	.0
29045	5.6	77	1.7	85	26.4	294	50.6	8	4	2.1	5	1	6.3
29046	.6	24	.2	60	17.8	205	79.6	6	10	.1	5	0	.0
29047	3.3	60	1.1	80	17.7	198	33.5	6	10	.1	10	0	.0
29048	3.6	0	1.1	82	19.0	196	60.3	5	9	.1	12	0	.0
29050	.6	28	.2	60	14.5	220	53.5	8	16	.1	10	0	.0
29051	.6	38	.2	69	15.0	174	29.4	1	15	.1	12	0	.0
29052	1.9	0	.6	91	18.1	139	46.5	9	3	.7	3	0	.0
29053	5.9	90	1.8	88	23.2	345	41.7	10	5	2.7	6	0	3.6
29054	3.6	92	1.2	92	23.4	221	58.1	8	9	1.7	9	0	.0
29055	5.1	74	1.7	74	21.7	229	69.1	7	12	1.8	10	0	.0
29056	3.4	33	1.0	76	19.1	231	40.0	10	10	.6	12	0	.0
29058	4.5	59	1.4	83	22.0	126	44.7	7	13	1.3	11	0	.0
29059	6.7	33	2.0	75	17.4	229	49.4	8	10	1.1	12	0	3.6
29061	7.6	48	2.3	84	25.3	296	76.9	10	7	1.9	9	0	.0
29062	2.4	75	.7	75	13.0	268	29.4	3	10	.0	17	0	.0
29063	8.9	86	2.9	92	32.6	511	99.4	10	5	3.9	10	0	10.5

*=Estimated **1.0=883 lbs per person; 100++ indicates per capita toxic waste generation > than 100 times the U.S. average of 883 lbs per capita.

ZIP CODE MEASURES OF SIZE, LEVELS OF AFFLUENCE AND QUALITY OF LIFE

1=Population (th.); 2= % White; 3=Households (th.); 4=% Owner Occupied; 5=Mean Income Per Household (th.$); 6=Mean Monthly Rent ($)*; 7=Mean Home Value (th.$)*; 8=% under 5; 9=% 65 and over; 10=White Males (th.); 11=% White Males, 65+; 12=# Toxic Waste Sites; 13=Toxic Waste Relative to US(883 lbs.per capita)**.

SOUTH CAROLINA

COLUMBIA

ZIP CODE	1	2	3	4	5	6	7	8	9	10	11	12	13
29065	.9	27	.3	82	23.7	155	78.4	5	9	.2	5	1	.0
29067	8.8	80	2.9	79	21.4	169	47.0	7	12	3.5	10	0	.2
29069	4.9	52	1.5	78	18.1	184	56.4	8	12	1.3	13	0	.0
29070	8.7	84	3.0	82	20.9	213	63.4	7	12	3.6	11	1	.1
29072	24.1	92	7.8	84	27.9	331	88.5	8	8	10.9	6	1	.3
29074	.1	47	.1	86	17.1	196*	73.2	0	34	.4	47	0	.0
29075	1.7	74	.6	85	24.7	200	67.2	4	13	.6	14	0	.0
29076	.2	66	.1	85	18.1	140	55.1	13	17	.1	19	0	.0
29078	6.9	78	2.2	85	25.8	243	73.9	8	6	2.7	5	2	.0
29079	.5	25	.2	73	19.3	215	33.6	2	14	.1	27	0	.0
29080	4.4	0	1.2	72	16.0	188	50.2	9	10	.4	0	0	.0
29081	1.8	52	.6	78	17.5	206	41.3	6	14	.4	10	0	.0
29082	.7	53	.2	82	17.3	229	39.0	9	9	.1	6	0	.0

COLUMBIA

ZIP CODE	1	2	3	4	5	6	7	8	9	10	11	12	13
29101	3.3	73	1.1	81	21.2	157	57.4	10	9	1.2	10	0	.0
29102	12.9	44	4.1	74	19.7	216	61.5	8	11	2.7	12	1	.3
29104	2.2	0	.6	70	19.2	224	44.5	8	9	.0	0	1	.2
29105	1.0	64	.3	73	18.5	175	44.3	5	11	.3	7	0	.0
29107	2.3	79	.7	86	18.3	160	48.2	7	8	.9	8	0	.0
29108	17.8	65	6.4	72	21.6	206	58.7	6	15	5.6	14	0	.7
29111	1.5	52	.4	70	19.3	163	59.7	9	7	.4	5	0	.0
29112	3.8	52	1.2	78	18.2	177	42.9	10	11	1.0	13	0	.0
29113	2.0	44	.6	80	18.1	114	47.8	7	8	.4	9	0	.0
29114	2.5	54	.7	74	17.0	200	58.6	7	10	.7	10	0	.1
29115	42.4	45	13.6	66	21.4	245	66.2	7	10	9.1	10	9	4.5
29121	1.4	41	.4	66	16.1	144	69.4	7	10	.3	10	0	.0
29123	2.4	87	.8	85	22.9	251	58.5	5	7	1.1	5	0	.0
29124	.4	73	.1	71	20.3	243	32.3	5	8	.1	7	0	.0
29125	3.0	28	.8	68	15.1	170	44.0	8	12	.4	3	1	.6
29126	2.4	72	.7	86	26.5	237	63.1	7	10	.8	8	0	.0
29127	4.4	68	1.4	85	23.7	147	68.3	8	12	1.5	13	0	.0
29128	4.3	21	1.1	77	18.4	158	46.6	8	7	.0	0	0	.0
29130	4.2	41	1.2	79	20.4	186	52.5	7	13	.8	13	0	.1
29131	.8	16	.2	62	17.0	167	45.6	5	11	.1	20	0	.6
29132	.2	37	.1	54	13.7	203	62.5	3	0	.0	0	0	.0
29133	1.0	33	.3	71	15.6	217	36.1	12	12	.2	12	0	.0
29134	.3	14	.1	79	13.2	141	41.8	4	5	.0	1	0	.0
29135	7.0	43	2.3	75	19.7	195	55.9	8	12	.8	5	2	.1
29137	2.8	0	.1	69	18.1	155	48.7	5	11	.0	0	0	.0
29138	8.6	65	2.9	81	20.0	212	55.8	8	14	2.7	13	0	.1
29142	3.0	0	.9	78	24.9	193	86.9	13	11	.0	0	0	.0
29143	.2	70	.1	83	27.7	318*	54.6	4	21	.1	25	1	.0
29145	.9	70	.3	80	18.3	123	58.7	8	15	.3	11	0	.5
29146	1.7	52	.6	78	18.6	135	48.7	11	12	.4	12	0	.0
29147	.1	0	.1	69	13.8	178	32.9	8	24	.0	0	0	.0
29148	5.1	0	1.6	72	16.5	195	48.5	6	14	.0	0	1	2.1
29150	64.9	58	21.2	66	21.1	259	65.4	9	8	18.4	6	3	.5
29152	7.0	75	1.5	1	18.5	330	74.4	13	0	3.1	0	0	.0

SOUTH CAROLINA

COLUMBIA

ZIP CODE	1	2	3	4	5	6	7	8	9	10	11	12	13
29160	5.0	69	1.6	82	20.9	219	56.5	9	10	1.7	9	1	.0
29161	9.8	48	3.0	70	18.4	223	57.7	9	11	2.3	9	0	.0
29162	2.5	69	.7	76	19.0	222	49.6	11	9	.9	8	0	.0
29163	1.8	0	.5	71	15.8	146	49.2	11	9	.0	0	0	.0
29164	3.1	61	1.0	72	17.7	187	48.6	7	14	.9	13	0	.0
29166	.1	62	.4	69	15.5	123	49.3	8	8	.1	8	0	.0
29168	1.7	0	.5	69	18.5	258	67.2	7	5	.0	0	1	.0
29169	.2	92	15.5	71	25.5	343	76.2	8	6	19.9	5	3	.8
29175	.3	54	.1	92	18.9	217*	40.5	9	6	.1	7	0	.0
29178	4.7	79	1.7	82	21.9	208	42.4	6	15	1.8	12	1	.5
29180	13.1	44	4.2	75	19.0	210	52.4	8	12	2.7	12	1	.0

COLUMBIA

ZIP CODE	1	2	3	4	5	6	7	8	9	10	11	12	13
29201	16.9	61	5.8	33	17.5	256	56.2	4	14	4.9	12	4	1.7
29203	51.0	25	14.9	63	20.1	293	58.0	8	9	6.0	13	1	.0
29204	40.2	55	13.7	61	25.7	298	90.7	7	9	10.6	8	1	.0
29205	27.0	78	12.1	48	23.8	309	90.9	6	14	9.7	12	2	5.7
29206	36.9	84	13.0	63	35.1	398	118.1	8	6	14.9	6	0	.1
29209	25.1	71	8.4	70	28.7	377	85.5	5	4	8.7	4	1	1.0
29210	45.7	87	15.7	60	32.0	412	105.1	7	3	19.8	3	1	.0

GREENVILLE

ZIP CODE	1	2	3	4	5	6	7	8	9	10	11	12	13
29301	45.0	59	15.1	59	21.6	279	63.8	7	10	12.8	8	2	5.0
29302	32.3	87	11.8	71	31.6	318	100.3	6	10	13.5	8	4	.3
29303	26.7	86	9.7	66	23.9	270	56.1	7	13	10.9	10	2	.2
29304	.2	73	.1	92	22.6	260*	61.7	4	0	.1	0	4	100++
29320	1.1	97	.4	72	18.0	244	30.2	3	13	.5	11	0	1.7
29321	2.6	87	.9	90	18.8	155	40.7	6	14	1.1	10	0	1.2
29322	4.9	91	1.6	84	23.8	185	60.3	7	12	2.3	10	0	.0
29323	9.4	85	3.1	79	21.3	225	52.7	7	10	3.8	8	0	.2
29324	.4	71	.1	76	16.3	374	19.2	9	18	.2	17	0	.0
29325	16.4	74	4.8	71	22.5	220	60.0	6	11	5.9	8	1	1.5
29329	.5	100	.2	80	20.2	284	33.3	8	16	.3	15	0	.0
29330	5.3	88	1.9	78	20.2	215	51.4	6	11	2.1	9	0	1.6
29331	1.2	79	1.1	76	18.1	286	58.5	3	16	.1	14	0	.0
29332	.7	41	.2	59	19.7	77	39.8	9	16	.2	22	0	.0
29333	.4	100	.3	69	21.1	303	38.1	6	5	.1	0	0	.1
29334	4.7	86	1.6	79	24.2	260	61.3	7	9	2.0	8	0	.6
29335	3.5	71	1.1	83	22.0	175	43.8	6	10	1.2	8	0	.0
29336	.7	87	.2	59	21.5	329	52.4	10	8	.3	5	1	.0
29338	.4	0	.4	69	19.7	239	38.1	11	5	.8	0	2	.1
29346	31.1	77	10.2	73	22.9	230	62.6	7	10	11.6	8	5	.6
29349	18.2	100	6.1	78	17.4	194	21.1	6	18	7.5	17	0	.1
29351	1.9	87	.8	78	25.6	278	69.9	7	11	.9	8	3	1.9
29353	4.3	93	1.3	76	22.5	219	42.1	5	14	1.1	11	1	1.7
29355	.6	78	.2	94	20.6	200	46.5	6	11	1.1	12	0	.2
29356	5.9	95	2.2	83	20.8	36	59.4	6	12	2.8	13	0	.0
29360	18.6	70	6.6	72	22.9	200	64.5	7	12	6.2	10	1	.3
29364	1.0	0	.4	87	19.5	248	56.0	6	10	.0	0	0	1.6
29365	4.7	90	1.7	81	23.7	240	57.0	9	13	2.1	11	2	3.0

*=Estimated **1.0=883 lbs per person; 100++ indicates per capita toxic waste generation > than 100 times the U.S. average of 883 lbs per capita.

ZIP CODE MEASURES OF SIZE, LEVELS OF AFFLUENCE AND QUALITY OF LIFE

1=Population (th.); 2= % White; 3=Households (th.); 4=% Owner Occupied; 5=Mean Income Per Household (th.$); 6=Mean Monthly Rent ($); 7=Mean Home Value (th.$); 8=% under 5; 9=% 65 and over; 10=% White Males, 11=% White Males, 65+ and over; 12=# Toxic Waste Sites; 13=Toxic Waste Relative to US(883 lbs.per capita)**.

SOUTH CAROLINA

GREENVILLE

ZIPCODE	1	2	3	4	5	6	7	8	9	10	11	12	13
29368	.8	98	.2	81	28.2	207	52.4	6	5	.4	3	0	.0
29369	4.2	82	1.3	88	31.6	251	77.7	6	7	1.7	4	0	.3
29370	.9	53	.3	86	23.2	267*	58.4	11	6	.3	7	0	.0
29372	3.1	82	1.1	80	18.6	214	42.6	6	11	1.2	12	1	.5
29373	1.3	82	.5	80	18.2	178	34.6	7	17	.5	15	0	.5
29374	2.5	97	.9	84	23.2	279	57.6	9	10	1.2	10	0	.0
29375	.3	100	.1	67	26.3	278	40.7	2	7	.1	9	0	.0
29376	4.1	81	1.3	87	26.4	289	67.9	7	8	1.5	6	2	1.0
29377	1.0	91	.4	81	20.3	208	33.0	5	18	.3	16	1	.3
29378	.9	82	.3	62	14.0	192	27.7	7	11	.3	18	1	.0
29379	20.4	74	7.1	76	21.5	203	50.9	7	12	7.1	9	9	.9
29384	1.9	67	.6	89	20.5	155	47.2	9	9	.6	12	0	.0
29385	4.1	70	1.3	81	24.1	229	49.4	8	9	1.4	7	2	.0
29388	9.7	82	3.5	74	21.9	216	49.1	7	13	3.9	11	1	.5

CHARLESTON

ZIPCODE	1	2	3	4	5	6	7	8	9	10	11	12	13
29401	10.2	84	5.0	38	31.1	352	211.7	4	21	3.8	14	0	.4
29402	.1	0	.1	89	30.5	350*	67.5	4	8	.0	16	1	100++
29403	29.0	15	9.4	36	16.1	262	59.0	7	13	1.8	16	1	.0
29404	7.5	81	1.6	10	20.3	346	58.3	14	0	3.5	0	1	.0
29405	53.6	68	18.7	57	21.7	313	65.0	9	5	18.6	4	8	.8
29406	33.6	74	12.4	49	22.9	284	78.7	9	7	12.4	6	4	3.8
29407	51.6	79	19.1	62	28.6	383	91.9	8	8	19.4	7	0	.0
29408	21.1	83	2.3	5	18.5	348	42.6	8	11	13.6	0	1	.1
29409	2.1	95	1.0	0	38.5	207	137.2*	1	1	.0	0	0	.1
29410	1.8	79	.4	40	21.2	294	52.4	6	4	.4	7	0	.0
29412	26.2	76	8.5	78	29.6	369	90.5	7	7	9.8	7	0	.0
29426	.9	18	.3	76	11.3	176	42.1	6	14	.1	33	0	.0
29427	1.5	16	.1	90	20.8	240*	60.1	8	6	.1	12	0	.0
29429	1.5	19	.4	81	18.6	376	62.4	6	14	.2	8	0	.0
29430	.1	100	.1	100	10.2	117*	25.2	9	18	.1	32	0	.0
29431	3.4	82	1.0	88	23.8	222	57.0	7	8	1.3	8	0	.0
29432	2.8	56	.9	76	20.4	181	42.5	7	15	.8	17	0	.0
29433	.2	71	.1	89	21.7	249*	66.0	4	21	.1	31	0	.9
29435	1.9	57	.6	93	20.3	264	49.0	3	11	.5	11	0	.1
29436	3.1	25	.8	85	20.3	216	52.7	8	8	.4	5	0	.0
29437	1.6	0	.5	85	21.1	216	52.4	7	10	.8	10	2	.0
29438	1.5	28	.5	71	20.1	105	68.2	7	11	.1	21	0	.0
29439	1.5	100	.7	54	24.0	283	80.8	5	11	.8	9	0	.0
29440	25.4	54	7.9	76	23.4	270	73.5	10	9	6.7	8	3	1.2
29441	.8	23	.2	78	23.1	216	24.4	12	6	.1	7	0	.0
29445	19.4	84	5.9	74	26.0	377	74.6	10	2	8.4	1	0	2.6
29446	1.4	26	.4	77	13.1	193	55.3	6	11	.2	10	0	.0
29447	.8	44	.3	81	18.3	263	59.2	5	7	.1	4	0	.0
29448	2.4	51	.8	84	20.6	244	49.2	9	9	.6	9	0	.0
29449	.2	42	.1	82	17.7	143	47.7	6	14	.7	26	0	2.6
29450	2.3	15	.6	88	16.8	374	42.8	13	7	.1	0	0	.0
29451	3.9	96	1.5	70	31.9	399	126.5	5	7	1.9	7	0	.0
29452	.4	37	.2	72	13.6	230	37.0	11	17	.1	24	0	.0
29453	.8	31	.2	89	21.5	195	38.2	10	10	.1	14	0	.7

SOUTH CAROLINA

CHARLESTON (continued)

ZIPCODE	1	2	3	4	5	6	7	8	9	10	11	12	13
29455	10.3	51	3.1	83	23.1	342	69.9	8	8	2.6	8	1	.2
29456	16.7	88	5.1	80	26.4	389	81.3	11	2	7.6	1	0	.0
29458	2.9	29	.9	85	21.0	254	53.5	8	10	.4	11	0	.0
29460	2.3	29	.6	81	21.8	201	50.3	9	8	.3	6	0	.0
29461	18.3	69	5.9	80	24.1	298	77.1	8	7	6.4	5	0	.1
29464	22.9	75	7.7	74	31.8	408	106.9	8	6	8.4	4	0	3.6
29468	1.7	0	.5	92	12.1	236	32.6	8	12	.0	8	0	.0
29470	3.0	48	.9	85	19.3	249	48.0	7	8	.7	8	0	.0
29471	1.6	49	.5	85	17.7	218	58.0	6	8	.4	11	0	.0
29472	6.4	43	1.8	84	21.2	290	50.7	7	8	1.4	8	0	.2
29473	.5	11	.5	94	12.4	142*	44.5	9	7	.0	0	0	.0
29474	1.4	39	.4	85	20.0	189	48.0	5	15	.3	14	0	.0
29475	2.3	50	.7	78	17.8	242	40.2	12	12	.6	8	0	.0
29477	5.5	46	.5	79	18.5	218	47.3	8	13	1.2	12	0	.1
29479	5.2	32	1.5	80	17.5	248	60.2	9	8	.8	7	0	.2
29480	.5	39	.5	70	20.0	230*	48.5	10	4	.1	7	0	.0
29481	2.1	40	.6	83	22.9	166	37.8	6	12	.4	17	0	.2
29482	1.9	97	.7	68	34.6	433	142.2	5	11	.3	8	0	.2
29483	42.2	82	13.2	76	28.0	329	95.5	9	5	17.3	4	3	.4
29487	2.4	19	.7	84	18.6	226	56.8	8	12	.2	22	0	.3
29488	17.4	65	5.9	73	20.0	265	65.2	8	11	5.5	9	0	.2
29492	.7	33	.2	73	24.9	129	64.0	9	13	.1	22	0	.0
29494	4.7	0	1.3	82	17.7	196	57.5	9	9	.0	0	1	.1

FLORENCE

ZIPCODE	1	2	3	4	5	6	7	8	9	10	11	12	13
29501	65.9	67	21.9	69	25.2	283	78.5	8	8	21.1	6	3	2.2
29503	.2	80	.1	100	47.1	541*	105.1	10	6		5	0	
29510	10.7	52	3.2	80	21.4	209	50.9	8	7	2.8	7	0	.2
29511	3.4	86	1.1	75	18.4	224	53.8	9	11	1.4	8	0	.2
29512	20.4	48	6.3	70	20.4	224	52.3	9	10	4.7	8	0	.4
29516	1.2	65	.4	77	18.0	200	43.1	8	11	.4	9	2	.0
29518	2.0	57	.6	83	20.1	212	62.5	10	7	.5	7	0	.0
29519	.4	8	.1	62	17.6	241	37.5	8	7	.0	8	0	.0
29520	12.3	60	4.4	65	20.8	274	62.4	8	12	3.6	10	1	.9
29525	2.6	45	.8	68	16.9	198	54.7	7	11	.6	10	0	.9
29526	27.9	77	9.3	73	22.1	252	71.8	9	7	10.7	7	3	.4
29527	1.2	21	.3	83	16.7	128	48.7	10	9	.1	16	0	.0
29530	2.2	76	.2	79	18.9	269	59.0	8	8	.8	8	2	.9
29532	24.7	54	7.9	71	21.1	223	70.0	8	11	6.3	7	0	.9
29536	16.4	59	5.1	61	19.7	228	54.4	10	10	4.7	10	0	.3
29540	.4	66	.1	73	19.2	155	42.8	15	11	.1	4	0	.0
29541	6.1	56	1.8	82	20.3	193	53.4	9	6	1.6	5	0	1.0
29543	.8	56	.2	72	17.4	213	51.8	9	5	.2	14	0	.0
29544	3.6	92	1.2	76	17.6	220	70.0	8	7	1.6	7	0	.0
29547	2.4	59	.7	80	16.9	220	50.1	13	8	.5	3	0	1.2
29550	26.4	68	8.6	73	23.3	240	70.3	9	9	8.8	6	0	.0
29554	10.6	0	3.1	74	19.0	190	55.4	9	8	.0	0	1	1.1
29555	5.4	69	1.7	76	19.1	192	54.3	9	9	1.8	7	1	12.1
	13.5	38	4.1	76	19.6	190	60.4	9	10	2.5	8	2	5.1

*=Estimated **1.0=883 lbs per person; 100++ indicates per capita toxic waste generation > than 100 times the U.S. average of 883 lbs per capita.

ZIP CODE MEASURES OF SIZE, LEVELS OF AFFLUENCE AND QUALITY OF LIFE

1=Population (th.); 2= % White; 3=Households (th.); 4=% Owner Occupied; 5=Mean Income Per Household (th.$); 6=Mean Monthly Rent ($)*; 7=Mean Home Value (th.$)*; 8=% under 5; 9=% 65 and over; 10=White Males; 11=% White Males, 65+; 12=# Toxic Waste Sites; 13=Toxic Waste Relative to US(883 lbs.per capita)**

SOUTH CAROLINA

FLORENCE

ZIPCODE	1	2	3	4	5	6	7	8	9	10	11	12	13
29560	14.1	45	4.4	65	18.6	188	59.4	10	10	3.0	9	1	.3
29563	2.9	58	.9	63	18.3	223	54.6	10	7	.8	6	0	.0
29564	1.4	17	.4	71	16.7	202	37.1	7	17	.1	23	0	.0
29565	6.2	55	2.0	67	16.7	215	50.3	10	10	1.5	9	0	.0
29566	1.0	62	.3	77	18.5	344	73.8	7	9	.3	7	0	.0
29567	1.1	28	.3	60	15.6	141	50.2	8	10	.2	12	0	.0
29568	3.2	28	.9	86	18.0	259	43.0	8	6	.5	4	0	.0
29569	10.7	64	3.5	72	17.9	193	61.6	10	10	3.4	10	0	.2
29570	4.9	68	1.5	67	17.7	170	35.5	8	12	1.5	10	0	.0
29571	14.9	52	4.7	70	19.9	226	62.7	9	10	3.7	8	1	.3
29574	13.1	50	4.3	68	19.1	217	57.2	9	11	3.1	10	0	.1
29576	4.9	84	1.9	82	23.7	227	120.5	6	16	2.1	18	0	.0
29577	36.0	86	12.8	61	26.5	338	119.3	8	15	15.2	8	3	.1
29580	2.1	0	.6	79	15.3	166	43.8	11	11	.2	0	0	.0
29581	5.1	57	1.7	68	15.5	242	52.0	8	11	1.3	9	1	.1
29582	7.2	75	2.8	72	23.1	289	98.1	6	13	2.6	15	0	.0
29583	5.4	58	1.7	76	18.2	199	57.8	9	11	1.5	10	0	.2
29584	2.6	86	.9	86	20.6	170	46.7	6	5	1.1	6	0	.0
29585	3.4	60	1.3	69	25.4	388	129.3	7	11	1.0	13	0	.1
29586	.3	56	.1	64	21.5	245	63.4	14	4	.0	0	0	.0
29589	.8	11	.2	75	18.0	249	42.6	13	14	.0	23	0	.0
29590	2.7	0	.8	81	16.5	139	41.0	6	10	.0	0	0	.0
29591	4.6	79	1.4	77	18.2	239	48.8	8	10	1.7	8	0	.0
29592	1.1	0	.3	70	15.7	132	22.9	11	10	.0	0	0	.1
29593	3.6	37	1.0	71	17.5	191	52.5	11	8	.7	2	1	1.5
29594	.4	40	.1	65	14.9	399	49.4	6	27	.0	25	0	.0
29595	.3	11	.1	70	14.9	278	34.2	7	11	.0	0	0	.0
29596	.4	77	.1	81	21.8	250	41.8	12	5	.2	5	0	13.7

GREENVILLE

ZIPCODE	1	2	3	4	5	6	7	8	9	10	11	12	13
29601	13.7	39	5.7	25	17.3	273	79.6	6	18	2.4	16	1	1.2
29604	.2	49	.1	23	17.5	202	147.9	0	0	.0	0	0	46.5
29605	31.8	63	11.5	69	25.5	275	71.3	7	11	9.2	12	0	.0
29607	26.7	65	9.4	61	27.8	279	92.2	7	8	8.7	10	0	.1
29609	34.5	90	13.2	64	23.8	294	71.8	7	7	14.7	10	0	.2
29611	44.2	85	15.9	65	20.1	294	52.8	7	11	18.0	9	0	.4
29615	23.4	97	9.0	63	35.7	399	113.8	6	6	11.0	5	0	.5
29620	11.4	66	4.0	79	22.2	227	58.2	8	12	3.6	11	0	.4
29621	52.7	80	18.8	70	24.3	266	70.3	7	11	20.1	9	2	1.8
29622	.2	67	.1	78	22.5	231	68.1	7	8	.3	13	0	.3
29624	17.6	79	6.3	72	20.9	261	56.5	7	10	6.8	8	0	.2
29627	13.7	83	4.8	79	24.1	228	56.4	8	11	5.5	10	0	.4
29628	3.6	60	1.2	79	18.3	196	36.7	8	13	1.0	12	0	1.1
29629	.4	100	.1	77	18.4	225	25.8	8	11	.1	14	0	
29630	7.4	91	2.8	64	21.8	233	65.6	9	9	3.5	8	0	.8
29631	9.1	85	3.5	53	27.6	273	104.2	5	9	4.2	7	1	1.3
29635	.8	100	.2	74	18.1	179	41.8	11	11	.4	7	0	.0
29636	.5	0	.2	69	19.2	287	19.4	3	13	.8	0	0	6.7
29638	2.5	64	.9	85	20.4	205	45.2	6	15	.8	15	0	.0
29639	1.9	73	.6	70	19.9	212	58.2	5	13	.7	10	0	.0

SOUTH CAROLINA

GREENVILLE

ZIPCODE	1	2	3	4	5	6	7	8	9	10	11	12	13
29640	34.8	92	11.9	79	24.7	264	69.3	7	9	15.7	7	2	.5
29643	1.3	97	.5	77	23.2	288	56.9	6	10	.6	9	0	.0
29644	8.2	73	2.7	78	22.8	235	60.3	7	11	2.8	7	3	.0
29645	5.1	65	1.6	81	26.4	187	60.0	7	8	1.7	8	0	.7
29646	43.7	71	15.1	68	23.9	241	70.9	7	11	14.6	9	2	3.3
29651	33.0	88	11.5	77	24.8	270	73.5	7	10	14.0	8	5	4.1
29653	5.0	67	1.8	88	23.7	214	55.4	5	13	1.7	9	0	.0
29654	8.3	86	3.5	72	22.0	204	55.4	6	12	3.5	10	0	.3
29655	5.9	77	2.1	81	19.2	175	43.3	6	14	1.3	13	0	.1
29656	.5	92	.2	77	18.6	305	31.8	6	14	.3	10	1	3.4
29657	7.9	94	2.7	82	22.7	221	58.4	8	10	3.6	8	1	.7
29658	.1	100	.1	69	10.7	161	83.1	0	45	.0	41	0	.0
29659	.4	84	.1	69	12.4	97	40.9	9	17	.2	16	0	.1
29661	4.6	94	1.6	74	21.0	240	47.2	7	3	2.2	8	0	.1
29662	7.2	90	2.3	82	32.2	420	90.4	7	3	3.3	2	0	1.2
29664	1.0	0	.4	76	15.9	234	34.3	5	22	.1	0	0	.0
29665	.3	100	.1	86	17.6	311	23.1	13	21	.1	15	0	.2
29666	5.9	72	2.1	80	22.0	221	53.8	7	13	2.1	12	0	.6
29667	.7	76	.7	78	20.2	267	47.0	9	7	.3	6	0	.1
29669	9.2	88	3.2	83	23.3	250	49.2	7	11	3.9	6	0	.2
29670	6.3	72	2.3	71	22.6	242	60.3	8	10	4.4	10	0	.3
29671	13.7	94	4.7	79	25.0	212	56.0	8	9	6.4	7	2	1.2
29673	14.5	90	4.9	88	25.4	294	68.0	7	9	6.6	7	0	.6
29676	2.5	0	.3	78	18.6	259	59.4	7	10	.0	0	0	1.1
29677	.7	95	.3	78	26.9	189	62.7	8	9	.3	9	0	.8
29678	22.1	84	8.0	75	22.8	240	68.4	8	11	9.1	9	1	1.0
29681	18.6	88	6.1	83	28.6	329	85.1	9	6	8.1	4	4	1.2
29682	3.1	100	1.1	79	21.0	201	66.3	9	11	1.5	8	0	.4
29683	.3	100	.3	88	17.0	307	31.1	9	26	.3	27	1	4.9
29684	3.4	83	1.1	80	20.7	163	58.0	9	8	1.4	8	1	.0
29685	.7	100	.2	86	23.3	212	50.5	7	9	.4	10	0	.0
29686	.2	100	.2	78	20.6	240	80.1	6	7	.1	0	0	.1
29687	21.3	87	7.3	75	28.3	347	78.7	8	7	9.2	6	1	1.2
29688	.5	84	.5	53	27.9	178	114.2	7	12	.8	3	0	.4
29689	2.0	84	.6	83	22.5	273	67.3	9	12	.8	13	0	.0
29690	13.0	92	4.3	82	25.3	274	58.8	8	9	6.0	8	3	.4
29691	8.1	94	3.0	71	21.7	206	56.7	8	12	3.6	9	0	.4
29692	4.1	87	1.6	83	20.3	170	40.4	5	17	1.7	17	1	1.0
29693	10.4	92	3.6	76	20.0	178	51.4	7	11	4.8	9	0	1.0
29696	2.9	96	1.0	84	23.3	160	60.0	8	8	1.4	5	0	2.5
29697	8.0	88	2.8	83	24.0	227	54.5	7	10	3.4	8	0	.4

CHARLOTTE

ZIPCODE	1	2	3	4	5	6	7	8	9	10	11	12	13
29702	5.8	86	2.0	82	20.9	179	47.6	7	12	2.4	9	1	2.0
29703	.5	82	.1	64	42.6	284	56.1	7	4	2.3	3	0	2.8
29704	1.9	65	.6	83	21.6	264	76.5	8	8	.6	6	1	.8
29705	.2	100	.1	84	14.0	335	17.2	0	8	.1	8	0	.0
29706	19.5	59	6.4	77	21.8	198	52.1	8	12	5.4	11	0	1.7
29710	12.1	84	4.1	83	31.9	289	104.9	7	10	5.1	8	0	.3

*=Estimated **1.0=883 lbs per person; 100++ indicates per capita toxic waste generation > than 100 times the U.S. average of 883 lbs per capita.

ZIP CODE MEASURES OF SIZE, LEVELS OF AFFLUENCE AND QUALITY OF LIFE

1=Population (th.); 2= % White; 3=Households (th.); 4=% Owner Occupied; 5=Mean Income Per Household (th.$); 6=Mean Monthly Rent ($)*; 7=Mean Home Value (th.$)*; 8=% under 5; 9=% 65 and over; 10=White Males, 65+; 11=% White Males; 12=# Toxic Waste Sites; 13=Toxic Waste Relative to US(883 lbs.per capita)**.

SOUTH CAROLINA

CHARLOTTE

ZIPCODE	1	2	3	4	5	6	7	8	9	10	11	12	13
29712	1.5	69	.4	95	27.1	328	68.5	6	12	.5	6	0	.0
29714	1.7	59	.5	85	20.6	248	51.5	11	6	.5	5	0	1.8
29715	15.1	91	5.2	81	27.9	279	82.6	6	8	6.7	5	2	.2
29717	1.1	74	.4	88	21.3	211	53.5	8	14	.4	11	0	.2
29718	3.1	64	1.0	83	19.0	155	49.0	6	14	.9	11	0	.0
29720	38.9	76	13.0	72	23.7	254	58.2	8	9	14.4	8	2	.6
29724	.3	100	.1	14	19.6	211	35.0	2	14	.2	12	0	.0
29726	.9	59	.3	79	22.3	224	50.6	4	10	.2	11	0	.0
29727	.8	70	.3	75	14.0	127	33.8	9	13	.3	9	0	.0
29728	7.5	64	2.3	75	20.5	231	51.6	10	6	2.3	9	2	.3
29729	1.3	57	.5	78	22.7	170	51.1	7	14	.3	12	0	.0
29730	62.7	73	20.3	70	25.5	308	73.7	7	9	21.6	8	7	1.2
29741	1.9	88	.7	77	19.2	165	36.4	5	11	.9	10	0	.1
29742	1.9	59	.5	85	21.4	221	42.3	9	9	.6	7	0	.0
29743	.8	94	.3	79	23.4	116	37.9	6	10	.4	8	0	.3
29744	.4	26	.1	76	25.5	175	68.5	13	7	.1	0	0	.0
29745	12.4	73	3.9	74	22.4	248	62.2	8	10	4.4	8	0	.6

AUGUSTA

ZIPCODE	1	2	3	4	5	6	7	8	9	10	11	12	13
29801	39.7	69	14.1	76	26.1	287	78.1	7	10	13.3	9	2	40.7
29809	2.9	70	.9	83	26.7	182	52.7	9	7	1.0	5	0	.0
29810	5.6	0	1.8	70	17.9	210	48.4	9	12	2.0	0	0	.1
29812	8.8	67	3.0	71	21.4	259	62.9	9	10	2.8	7	4	7.0
29813	.4	76	.1	90	18.4	165	40.3	7	16	.6	2	0	.0
29814	.4	38	.1	51	15.2	170	31.5	12	11	.1	19	0	.0
29816	2.0	86	.7	82	17.8	201	37.1	7	11	.8	23	0	.8
29817	5.3	0	1.6	73	19.5	173	45.6	9	11	.8	6	0	.8
29819	.7	59	.2	84	24.0	164	56.5	7	12	.1	0	0	.0
29821	.6	37	.2	68	16.6	122	36.2	8	14	.1	14	0	.0
29822	1.2	90	.4	75	21.5	256	45.1	9	9	.5	9	0	5.1
29824	6.4	49	2.1	75	19.6	201	52.1	8	13	1.5	11	3	2.2
29826	.4	31	.1	93	21.5	247*	48.0	8	7	.7	7	0	.0
29827	3.6	43	1.1	68	18.8	178	54.6	9	12	.7	11	0	.2
29828	1.5	92	.5	59	20.7	198	38.0	6	6	.6	2	0	.0
29829	5.1	82	1.8	76	23.1	237	56.0	5	11	2.1	9	2	2.1
29831	3.1	78	1.0	78	27.9	241	57.3	9	10	1.3	6	0	.0
29832	5.4	43	1.7	65	20.3	220	61.2	9	11	1.1	10	0	.0
29834	2.3	96	.8	71	20.4	239	34.4	5	10	1.1	12	2	3.2
29835	5.3	0	1.6	76	19.4	181	47.9	8	10	.1	0	0	.2
29836	1.0	14	.3	67	16.5	169	23.3	7	16	.5	23	1	43.9
29838	.2	100	.1	87	24.5	282*	104.9	11	7	.1	4	0	.0
29839	.2	80	.1	50	30.4	128	49.8	15	2	.1	0	0	.0
29840	.4	0	.1	46	15.7	125	52.7	2	10	.7	11	0	.0
29841	34.1	80	11.6	77	26.0	311	72.2	8	8	13.3	7	2	.2
29842	1.5	52	.5	84	22.2	233	52.2	12	8	.4	6	0	.2
29843	1.6	66	.5	72	19.1	220	43.5	6	12	.5	10	0	.0
29844	.2	66	.1	82	15.7	117	51.8	5	16	.1	16	0	.0
29845	1.0	26	.3	86	18.8	97	46.8	9	10	.1	16	0	.0
29846	.3	54	.1	92	24.6	283*	53.6	14	12	.1	9	0	.0
29847	2.5	41	.7	69	21.9	216	52.6	8	9	.5	9	0	.1

SOUTH CAROLINA

AUGUSTA

ZIPCODE	1	2	3	4	5	6	7	8	9	10	11	12	13
29848	.7	0	.2	68	20.7	171	44.9	7	11	.0	0	5	.0
29849	.4	53	.1	60	19.9	161	51.8	4	9	.1	3	0	.0
29850	.4	100	.1	89	19.9	285	35.3	10	10	.2	10	1	.4
29851	3.9	90	1.4	80	19.4	213	39.9	10	11	1.7	7	0	2.4
29852	.9	15	.1	58	15.6	100	35.4	16	12	.0	0	0	.0
29853	5.0	57	1.7	71	24.3	213	53.2	9	10	1.4	8	0	.2
29856	.9	87	.3	87	18.0	233	38.8	8	10	.4	12	0	.0

SAVANNAH

ZIPCODE	1	2	3	4	5	6	7	8	9	10	11	12	13
29902	30.8	68	10.0	58	23.5	345	91.8	11	6	11.1	5	5	.2
29905	7.8	70	.4	20	21.4	334	76.1*	4	0	4.4	0	1	.0
29910	2.4	62	.9	76	21.5	243	87.8	6	11	.7	14	0	.0
29911	1.5	51	.5	72	16.1	166	42.0	10	11	.4	22	0	.0
29912	.3	30	.1	62	19.4	183	34.0	1	14	.0	26	0	.0
29914	.4	34	.1	100	20.5	235*	51.2	4	5	.1	28	0	.0
29915	.2	56	.1	63	16.5	189*	43.0	7	17	.4	16	0	.3
29916	1.3	56	.5	92	13.6	135	41.2	10	15	.4	16	0	.0
29918	4.1	37	1.3	71	19.0	176	51.2	10	11	.7	9	0	.0
29920	5.0	41	1.6	86	21.6	277	83.5	7	12	.7	9	0	2.5
29921	.3	41	.1	87	19.6	128	36.1	7	14	.1	16	5	.5
29922	1.2	0	.4	61	18.7	176	29.8	10	17	.7	0	1	.0
29923	.4	0	.1	85	13.0	160	38.8	7	5	.1	0	0	.0
29924	4.3	73	1.5	73	23.3	207	64.5	8	9	1.5	8	2	1.9
29927	4.9	45	1.3	79	20.0	277	55.3	11	7	1.0	6	0	.0
29928	11.9	85	4.9	71	42.5	230	232.9	6	15	4.8	18	0	.2
29929	1.2	59	.4	84	18.4	284	52.0	8	11	.4	11	1	100++
29931	.2	54	.1	66	10.8	344	105.2	15	22	.1	12	1	.0
29932	.3	0	.1	33	17.4	150	56.8	11	11	.1	13	0	.0
29934	1.0	16	.3	59	11.1	137	69.1	5	12	.1	13	0	.0
29935	3.0	69	1.1	39	19.8	366	61.9	9	6	.4	4	0	.0
29936	8.1	45	2.5	79	19.0	238	63.5	11	12	1.8	11	0	.0
29939	.3	12	.1	61	11.6	144	34.1	17	17	.2	22	0	.0
29940	1.5	16	.4	82	14.6	283	65.7	8	13	.2	17	0	.0
29941	.7	0	.2	100	14.6	168*	51.1	13	7	.0	18	0	.0
29943	.3	68	.1	82	15.5	173	37.8	8	23	.1	7	0	.0
29944	3.2	58	1.1	80	21.6	223	53.0	8	11	.9	7	0	.0
29945	4.8	18	1.3	77	15.9	167	40.6	7	10	.4	10	0	.3

*=Estimated **1.0=883 lbs per person; 100++ indicates per capita toxic waste generation > than 100 times the U.S. average of 883 lbs per capita.

103001

ZIP CODE MEASURES OF SIZE, LEVELS OF AFFLUENCE AND QUALITY OF LIFE

1=Population (th.); 2= % White; 3=Households (th.); 4=% Owner Occupied; 5=Mean Income Per Household (th.$); 6=Mean Monthly Rent ($)*; 7=Mean Home Value (th.$)*;
8=% under 5; 9=% 65 and over; 10=White Males (th.); 11=% White Males, 65+; 12=# Toxic Waste Sites; 13=Toxic Waste Relative to US(883 lbs.per capita)**.

SOUTH DAKOTA

ZIPCODE	1	2	3	4	5	6	7	8	9	10	11	12	13
SIOUX CITY													
51001	.3	0	.1	62	23.6	271*	57.8	8	10	.0	0	0	.0
51023	.2	100	.1	74	22.0	253*	65.6	6	16	.1	20	0	.0
WINDOM													
56144	.2	100		73	27.8	367	69.6	14	15	.1	11	0	.0
WILLMAR													
56219	.4	90	.1	74	18.3	183	52.9	8	9	.2	11	0	.0
SIOUX FALLS													
57001	1.9	99	.7	72	16.9	225	51.6	8	21	.9	19	0	.5
57002	.9	0	.3	69	19.1	273	65.7	10	10	.0	0	0	.0
57003	1.4	99	.5	85	23.2	271	72.8	10	10	.7	10	0	.5
57004	3.5	0	1.3	73	18.5	179	61.4	8	21	1.0	4	0	.2
57005	3.4	99	1.0	89	30.4	348	96.9	11	4	1.7	4	0	.0
57006	17.2	99	5.6	58	22.1	273	83.9	6	9	8.5	7	3	.3
57010	.5	99	.2	73	25.0	297	57.8	11	8	.5	5	0	.0
57012	1.1	0	.4	82	18.3	160	42.1	6	22	.9	15	0	.0
57013	4.1	0	1.5	76	22.2	216	63.4	9	17	.0	0	1	1.2
57014	1.7	0	.7	76	15.6	186	40.0	7	27	.0	0	0	.0
57015	.7	0	.3	89	22.2	138	52.1	10	15	.7	10	0	.0
57016	.5	98	.2	74	22.1	194	47.4	5	15	.3	14	0	.0
57017	1.2	100	.4	72	18.5	193	55.6	9	13	.6	12	1	.4
57018	1.5	0	.5	76	20.4	253	60.9	9	14	.0	4	0	.0
57020	.8	98	.3	86	25.5	322	71.9	16	5	.4	4	0	.0
57021	.3	100	.1	78	15.1	143	25.9	7	15	.2	11	0	.0
57022	3.9	99	1.3	75	23.7	226	69.0	9	17	1.9	15	0	.0
57023	.3	100	.1	95	21.1	243*	18.0	8	8	.1	8	0	.0
57024	.5	0	.2	75	20.1	253	36.1	5	13	.0	0	0	.0
57025	2.7	99	1.0	72	22.0	210	62.6	10	16	1.3	13	0	.2
57026	1.3	0	.4	79	18.1	200	43.3	8	18	.0	0	0	.0
57027	.2	100	.1	91	24.1	277*	32.5	9	10	.1	8	0	.0
57028	3.3	90	1.0	70	20.7	215	56.5	8	20	1.4	20	0	.5
57029	2.7	99	1.0	83	19.0	247	52.4	11	25	1.3	22	1	3.4
57030	1.8	100	.6	77	22.7	275	68.5	10	16	.9	13	0	.8
57031	.6	98	.3	72	19.5	172	50.9	8	21	.3	19	0	.0
57032	1.4	99	.5	86	27.1	321	84.9	12	6	.7	6	0	.0
57033	2.8	99	.9	78	24.2	271	78.8	10	9	1.4	9	0	.2
57034	.9	100	.3	76	19.6	199	36.5	9	21	.4	21	0	.1
57035	1.1	99	.4	76	23.7	215	54.6	9	13	.6	12	0	2.0
57036	.9	100	.4	79	19.4	215	34.7	8	20	.4	19	0	.3
57037	1.1	100	.4	78	16.9	199	39.3	8	22	.6	18	0	.1
57038	2.9	99	1.0	79	24.5	282	71.2	11	8	1.4	8	0	.1
57039	3.2	99	1.1	82	22.3	200	64.0	9	18	1.6	16	0	.2
57040	.6	100	.2	86	16.8	97	32.7	6	19	.3	21	0	.0
57042	7.9	99	3.0	66	19.0	216	59.4	8	19	3.7	15	2	1.1
57043	1.7	99	.6	87	19.6	170	41.8	7	21	.8	20	0	.2
57044	.3	100	.1	84	18.1	215	42.3	9	15	.1	14	0	.0
57045	1.4	99	.5	80	18.0	197	39.6	6	25	.7	22	0	.2
57046	.7	92	.2	75	20.7	310	49.9	11	10	.4	10	0	.0
57047	.3	100	.1	73	19.0	224	20.4	8	14	.2	15	0	.0
57048	1.1	100	.3	73	19.2	193	40.3	9	12	.6	13	0	.0

SOUTH DAKOTA

ZIPCODE	1	2	3	4	5	6	7	8	9	10	11	12	13
SIOUX FALLS													
57049	.8	99	.3	72	19.2	271	43.4	9	6	.4	6	0	.0
57050	.2	100	.1	92	17.0	195*	29.8	2	11	.1	14	0	.0
57051	.6	100	.2	71	12.5	212	19.9	6	19	.3	16	0	.0
57052	.6	100	.2	85	13.9	160*	24.8	11	16	.3	15	0	.0
57053	2.0	0	.7	81	21.4	144	53.8	7	20	.0	0	0	.0
57054	.7	100	.3	79	21.2	194	38.2	8	15	.4	15	0	.0
57055	.6	0	.2	74	24.7	342	85.8	9	10	.0	0	0	.0
57057	.2	100	.1	85	18.0	230	62.1	7	17	.1	21	0	.0
57058	2.3	0	.8	73	18.7	191	53.3	9	17	.0	0	0	.4
57059	2.1	99	.8	83	16.4	195	43.0	8	23	1.0	20	0	.0
57060	.4	0	.1	74	22.0	162	47.0	8	10	.0	0	0	.0
57061	.1	100	.1	89	16.0	184*	35.5	10	35	.1	29	0	.0
57062	2.1	90	.6	62	18.7	237	54.1	7	7	.1	5	0	.0
57063	.4	97	.2	76	18.1	219	54.8	9	16	.5	19	0	.0
57064	1.1	100	.3	81	27.2	293	84.8	11	5	.4	4	0	.0
57065	.4	100	.1	81	16.5	183	45.6	11	12	.2	10	0	.0
57066	2.0	0	.8	78	14.3	187	44.7	8	26	.0	0	0	.0
57067	.6	100	.3	87	19.1	450	43.7	11	13	.3	11	0	.0
57068	1.4	99	.5	85	24.1	262	72.4	9	8	.7	7	0	.0
57069	11.1	96	3.5	54	21.1	262	85.7	6	7	5.3	6	0	.2
57070	1.6	0	.6	71	18.0	210	35.9	9	21	.0	0	0	.0
57071	2.2	99	.8	81	21.7	194	66.8	8	15	1.1	14	0	3.4
57072	.7	100	.3	82	21.2	309	37.6	9	16	.4	16	0	.1
57073	.2	100	.1	72	17.8	203	37.7	9	17	.1	17	0	.0
57074	.2	100	.1	83	23.4	268*	19.9	9	7	.1	5	0	.0
57075	.7	100	.3	81	23.5	255	59.6	9	17	.4	16	0	.0
57076	.6	97	.2	80	15.0	377	23.6	10	13	.3	15	0	.0
57077	.8	100	.3	84	21.6	218	60.3	8	14	.4	14	0	.0
57078	14.9	97	5.3	64	23.7	276	79.2	7	13	6.8	10	1	.5
SIOUX FALLS													
57101	6.7	99	2.0	87	31.7	312	122.4	9	7	3.3	5	3	3.5
57102	2.2	97	.7	6	9.8	148	125.0	0	15	.7	12	1	1.6
57103	23.9	98	8.4	66	29.0	312	91.9	9	6	11.4	5	1	.0
57104	21.1	96	9.1	48	20.0	268	63.9	6	15	5.6	11	1	1.1
57105	25.6	99	9.7	71	30.8	354	102.5	5	13	11.5	11	0	.0
57106	11.7	98	4.2	69	27.1	345	100.2	12	6	5.6	5	0	.0
57107	.5	100	.2	63	29.5	328	109.0	7	13	.3	13	1	2.6
WATERTOWN													
57201	18.5	99	6.9	67	22.4	247	72.4	9	14	8.8	11	3	.2
57211	.3	0	.1	91	16.7	191*	23.8	10	17	.1	5	1	.0
57212	2.1	100	.7	80	17.1	217	49.6	8	21	1.0	19	0	1.6
57213	.4	100	.2	83	14.7	167	31.9	8	13	.2	10	0	.0
57214	.1	100	.1	89	20.4	235*	24.3	0	25	.1	22	0	1.1
57215	.2	100	.2	84	19.7	227*	23.7	7	11	.1	16	0	.0
57216	1.1	100	.4	83	15.4	201	57.4	9	15	.6	14	1	.1
57217	.3	100	.3	86	16.3	384	17.3	13	22	.2	23	0	.0
57218	.5	100	.5	89	16.3	187*	21.9	5	14	.2	11	0	.0
57219	.7	100	.7	80	16.2	234	29.6	4	29	.4	27	0	.0
57220	.9	100	.3	85	22.0	199	44.1	8	10	.5	9	0	.0

*=Estimated **1.0=883 lbs per person; 100++ indicates per capita toxic waste generation > than 100 times the U.S. average of 883 lbs. per capita.

ZIP CODE MEASURES OF SIZE, LEVELS OF AFFLUENCE AND QUALITY OF LIFE

1=Population (th.); 2= % White; 3=Households (th.); 4=% Owner Occupied; 5=Mean Income Per Household (th.$); 6=Mean Monthly Rent ($)*; 7=Mean Home Value (th.$)*; 8=% under 5; 9=% 65 and over; 10=% White Males, 65+; 11=% White Males, 65 and over; 12=# Toxic Waste Sites; 13=Toxic Waste Relative to US(883 lbs.per capital)**.

SOUTH DAKOTA

WATERTOWN

ZIPCODE	1	2	3	4	5	6	7	8	9	10	11	12	13
57221	.8	0	.3	78	13.9	157	23.4	5	27	.0	0	0	.0
57222	.2	100	.1	92	17.2	197*	18.1	8	22	.1	24	0	.0
57223	1.2	0	.4	85	18.8	222	30.4	8	18	.0	0	0	.0
57224	.2	0	.1	87	15.3	191	30.4	7	17	.0	0	0	.0
57225	2.1	100	.8	75	18.4	192	42.9	7	22	1.0	18	0	.1
57226	2.1	100	.8	81	18.2	215	44.5	7	20	1.1	17	0	.0
57227	.5	99	.2	84	19.4	113	46.1	5	15	.2	14	0	.0
57231	2.1	100	.8	76	17.0	171	43.8	8	21	1.0	17	0	.0
57232	.4	0	.2	81	19.0	198	33.8	5	31	.0	0	0	.1
57233	.2	0	.1	86	20.7	125	13.6	10	15	.0	0	0	.4
57234	1.3	100	.5	77	16.5	268	40.8	8	23	.6	21	0	.0
57235	.7	99	.2	85	20.1	242	40.3	11	10	.4	12	0	.5
57236	.4	100	.1	87	16.3	188*	17.4	15	14	.0	14	0	.0
57237	.7	100	.3	84	12.2	206	27.4	7	22	.2	22	0	.0
57238	.3	100	.1	88	21.0	206	36.3	13	12	.3	11	0	.0
57239	.4	98	.1	89	14.1	80	33.3	9	15	.2	19	0	.0
57241	.9	0	.3	85	15.4	207	43.0	9	15	.0	0	0	.0
57242	.5	100	.1	81	17.2	223	27.7	10	9	.0	8	0	.0
57243	.6	0	.2	86	18.7	203	23.6	7	9	.3	22	0	.0
57244	.1	100	.1	92	14.1	162*	14.7	12	24	.1	23	0	.0
57245	.1	100	.1	85	19.8	228*	46.3	9	13	.1	17	0	.0
57246	.3	100	.1	80	16.6	191*	31.9	10	22	.1	26	0	.0
57247	.3	100	.1	81	17.4	199*	36.5	12	10	.1	13	0	.0
57248	.9	100	.3	85	18.3	125	39.2	6	26	.4	23	0	.0
57249	1.3	0	.5	76	17.4	177	32.0	7	23	.3	16	0	.0
57250	.2	97	.1	85	19.5	172	19.1	10	17	.1	19	0	.0
57251	.2	0	.1	90	15.6	180*	17.4	4	19	.0	0	0	.0
57252	5.5	100	1.9	73	21.7	243	67.9	8	16	2.6	13	0	.1
57255	.6	100	.2	78	16.6	147	22.2	6	22	.3	21	0	.0
57256	.2	0	.1	88	12.8	147*	18.6	9	19	.1	23	0	.0
57257	.8	40	.2	60	13.1	185	24.8	10	11	.2	21	0	.0
57258	.6	100	.2	85	13.9	212	23.7	7	13	.3	13	0	.0
57259	.7	0	.2	80	14.1	152	21.7	9	17	.1	13	0	.0
57260	1.4	96	.5	79	20.4	194	50.8	9	20	.7	16	0	.0
57261	.5	100	.2	79	16.7	134	29.9	6	30	.3	30	0	.0
57262	4.9	70	1.6	59	18.9	194	48.6	10	16	1.7	18	0	.0
57263	.6	100	.2	76	17.4	233	31.9	12	16	.3	14	0	.0
57264	.3	100	.1	83	15.7	117	25.7	7	18	.2	17	0	.0
57265	.3	100	.1	85	15.5	205	26.2	9	21	.2	22	0	.0
57266	.7	94	.3	74	15.8	166	23.4	6	18	.4	21	0	.0
57268	.6	100	.2	77	17.7	218	27.5	5	17	.3	16	0	.0
57269	.5	0	.2	83	20.9	257	38.2	8	15	.0	0	0	.0
57270	.9	81	.4	76	14.8	143	29.7	7	18	.7	24	0	.0
57271	.4	100	.1	89	12.3	60	15.9	9	22	.2	19	0	.0
57272	.3	100	.1	73	12.1	211	19.2	9	24	.1	26	0	.0
57273	1.6	75	.6	70	14.9	174	31.8	9	16	.6	17	0	.0
57274	3.7	0	1.4	72	18.6	235	54.5	8	20	.0	0	0	.0
57276	1.3	99	.4	80	16.6	220	45.2	10	17	.7	15	0	.1
57278	.9	0	.3	75	13.2	179	28.8	8	16	.0	0	0	.0

SOUTH DAKOTA

WATERTOWN

ZIPCODE	1	2	3	4	5	6	7	8	9	10	11	12	13
57279	1.2	98	.4	79	16.1	175	36.7	6	24	.6	22	0	.0

MITCHEL

ZIPCODE	1	2	3	4	5	6	7	8	9	10	11	12	13
57301	16.3	97	6.1	64	20.3	240	61.5	9	16	7.5	13	2	.3
57310	1.4	0		63	15.0	162	53.3*	11	7	.0	0	0	.0
57311	1.5	100	.5	79	16.9	157	38.4	10	13	.7	11	0	.0
57312	.7	100	.2	84	17.8	214	25.9	8	19	.3	19	0	.0
57313	1.6	0	.6	82	15.7	184	41.7	7	20	.0	0	0	.0
57314	.6	100	.2	79	13.7	194	21.1	7	19	.3	19	0	.1
57315	1.3	100	.5	86	18.4	212	33.5	5	20	.6	18	0	.0
57316	.7	0	.1	83	25.9	77	16.6	7	17	.0	0	0	.4
57317	.7	0	.2	78	14.9	204	28.7	7	16	.0	0	0	.0
57319	1.2	0	.4	76	16.5	187	38.7	6	25	.0	0	0	.5
57321	.7	0	.3	89	13.3	104	20.0	8	18	1.2	13	0	.0
57322	.5	100	.2	83	17.6	233	13.1	12	10	.2	8	0	.0
57323	.5	100	.2	78	13.2	108	22.0	10	24	.3	20	0	.0
57324	.6	0	.3	82	16.9	239	46.5	5	25	.2	24	0	.0
57325	2.9	88	1.1	71	18.9	222	69.8	9	14	1.2	13	0	.2
57328	1.5	100	.5	79	15.3	221	39.4	9	17	.7	16	0	.0
57329	.3	0	.1	83	18.2	165	35.5	9	9	.2	8	0	.0
57330	.8	100	.3	75	14.0	231	27.8	8	13	.4	13	0	.0
57331	.6	0	.2	82	18.7	236	46.5	7	7	.1	0	0	.0
57332	.9	100	.4	84	13.4	219	35.1	11	21	.5	17	0	.0
57334	1.0	0	.3	65	18.6	256	37.8	9	13	.0	0	0	.0
57335	.5	100	.2	73	16.0	166	18.0	7	18	.3	18	0	.0
57337	.3	100	.1	81	14.3	159	21.2	11	16	.4	14	0	.0
57338	.3	0	.1	94	9.8	113*	22.4	8	24	.0	0	0	.0
57339	1.1	8	.3	26	14.0	167	25.9	9	5	.0	0	0	.0
57340	.4	0	.1	83	21.9	138	33.8	6	9	.0	0	0	.1
57341	.1	0	.1	75	16.6	197	15.9	11	9	.0	0	0	.0
57342	.8	0	.3	77	11.4	151	26.0	9	21	.0	0	0	.0
57344	.3	100	.1	90	12.8	330	27.0	11	12	.1	7	0	.0
57345	1.8	0	.6	81	18.3	196	45.1	6	21	.0	0	0	.0
57348	.9	100	.3	75	17.8	134	26.9	11	12	.0	0	0	.0
57349	2.1	0	.8	77	16.4	161	39.3	7	25	.4	10	0	.0
57350	15.4	99	6.0	68	22.7	239	59.5	8	15	7.3	12	0	.2
57353	1.4	0	.5	81	16.3	267	29.9	10	13	.0	0	0	.0
57355	1.4	0	.5	76	14.1	197	34.8	9	18	.0	0	0	.0
57356	1.9	75	.6	72	16.0	165	41.9	9	16	.7	18	0	.0
57359	1.0	0	.3	84	17.1	257	35.6	8	17	.4	10	0	.0
57361	.4	0	.1	26	12.9	147	38.3	18	3	.0	0	0	.0
57362	2.8	100	1.1	71	19.2	165	56.4	7	20	1.1	18	0	.0
57363	1.1	99	.4	80	19.0	223	29.0	8	13	.6	13	0	.1
57365	.3	90	.1	74	18.1	240	36.0	11	10	.2	13	0	.0
57366	2.6	0	1.0	81	17.1	201	44.1	7	18	.4	10	0	.0
57368	1.3	98	.5	79	17.9	176	39.2	8	14	.7	12	0	.0
57369	2.5	100	.9	78	17.9	258	46.9	9	16	1.2	13	0	.0
57370	.9	81	.3	80	15.9	143	41.8	8	10	.4	11	0	.0
57371	.4	100	.1	59	14.7	108	17.3	6	11	.2	14	0	.0
57373	.9	0	.3	75	16.7	75	45.7	9	12	.3	10	0	.0

*=Estimated **1.0-883 lbs per person; 100++ indicates per capita toxic waste generation > than 100 times the U.S. average of 883 lbs per capita.

ZIP CODE MEASURES OF SIZE, LEVELS OF AFFLUENCE AND QUALITY OF LIFE

1=Population (th.); 2= % White; 3=Households (th.); 4=% Owner Occupied; 5=Mean Income Per Household (th.$); 6=Mean Monthly Rent ($)*; 7=Mean Home Value (th.$)*; 8=% under 5; 9=% 65 and over; 10=% White Males, 65 and over; 11=% White Males, 65+; 12=# Toxic Waste Sites; 13=Toxic Waste Relative to US(883 lbs.per capita)**.

SOUTH DAKOTA

ZIPCODE	1	2	3	4	5	6	7	8	9	10	11	12	13
MITCHEL													
57374	.7	0	.3	82	14.8	223	24.9	7	21	.0	0	0	.0
57375	1.0	0	.4	76	14.1	201	28.9	8	14	.0	0	0	.0
57376	1.5	99	.6	88	16.4	267	38.4	6	25	.7	23	0	.0
57379	.2	100	.1	78	14.1	154	23.0	11	24	.1	22	0	.0
57380	3.2	74	1.1	72	17.0	186	44.1	9	17	1.1	18	0	.0
57381	1.2	100	.5	81	18.8	211	32.5	7	16	.6	16	0	.3
57382	2.3	0	.8	75	17.8	189	37.5	9	19	.0	0	0	.2
57383	1.0	0	.4	83	17.9	139	26.0	6	24	.0	0	0	.0
57384	.8	0	.3	78	18.6	261	42.5	7	9	.0	0	0	.0
57385	1.7	98	.6	78	14.9	217	26.9	8	20	.8	19	1	.0
57386	.3	100	.1	87	16.6	126	50.3	9	7	.1	5	0	.0
ABERDEEN													
57401	29.8	97	11.0	64	23.2	273	78.3	8	12	13.5	10	1	.4
57421	.4	100	.1	54	16.5	132	27.1	5	10	.1	9	0	.6
57422	.4	100	.2	88	18.6	121	23.4	4	18	.2	13	0	.0
57423	.2	100	.1	91	12.9	148*	15.4	9	2	.1	4	0	.0
57424	.3	100	.1	83	19.1	152	29.1	6	18	.2	14	0	.0
57427	.5	99	.1	88	19.1	364	53.6	10	8	.3	9	0	.0
57428	.9	100	.4	77	14.1	199	36.0	6	25	.4	21	1	1.1
57430	2.8	0	1.0	74	19.3	220	54.2	7	20	.6	20	0	.4
57431	.2	100	.1	86	13.7	158*	13.1	7	16	.1	11	0	.3
57432	.5	100	.2	79	22.0	125	24.4	9	12	.2	12	0	.0
57433	.5	100	.2	79	19.6	225*	30.4	10	11	.3	12	0	.0
57434	.6	100	.2	71	18.0	156	25.4	7	18	.3	17	0	.0
57435	.4	100	.2	82	17.3	199	34.3	11	10	.2	9	0	.0
57437	.7	100	.3	76	20.3	229	24.3	7	14	.3	10	0	.0
57438	2.0	100	.8	83	17.3	205	47.5	6	24	1.0	21	0	.0
57439	1.4	0	.6	77	16.3	176	47.3	5	25	.0	0	1	.2
57440	.7	0	.2	87	17.5	224	20.5	7	14	.0	0	0	.0
57441	.8	100	.3	86	15.5	163	45.1	4	15	.4	15	0	.0
57442	2.5	89	.9	70	19.0	194	47.2	8	17	1.1	16	0	.1
57445	2.0	0	.7	74	19.8	191	55.9	6	21	.0	0	0	.0
57446	.8	100	.3	75	19.7	159	28.5	7	13	.4	13	0	.5
57448	.7	100	.2	86	16.9	169	23.4	6	15	.3	25	0	.0
57449	.3	100	.1	74	21.5	247*	25.3	10	15	.1	12	0	.0
57450	1.2	100	.4	86	16.5	208	47.6	11	11	.6	10	0	.0
57451	2.0	100	.6	72	17.9	210	45.9	9	16	1.0	13	0	.5
57452	.6	99	.3	94	13.0	122	19.2	7	22	.3	19	0	.0
57454	.8	0	.3	75	20.4	192	25.7	6	15	.0	0	0	.2
57455	.3	100	.1	83	14.2	160	19.5	8	16	.2	15	0	.0
57456	1.1	100	.4	88	14.1	130	35.4	5	22	.6	20	0	.0
57457	.3	100	.1	78	15.1	133	26.1	5	19	.2	15	0	.0
57460	.5	0	.2	87	24.1	276*	35.7	8	9	.1	9	0	.5
57461	.5	98	.2	85	21.4	288	29.8	7	17	.2	16	0	.0
57462	.5	0	.2	94	23.3	314	86.6	8	7	.0	0	0	.0
57465	.3	100	.1	86	17.0	195*	33.9	5	21	.2	16	0	.0
57466	.3	100	.1	93	12.3	141*	29.9	9	11	.2	15	0	.0
57467	.6	0	.2	86	12.7	354	27.6	12	10	.0	0	0	.6
57468	.4	0	.1	86	17.8	75	20.7	10	16	.0	0	0	.0
ABERDEEN (cont.)													
57469	4.4	99	1.6	68	19.9	244	52.1	7	18	2.1	14	1	.0
57470	.3	0	.4	85	20.9	275	13.1	6	17	.0	0	0	.0
57471	1.0	100	.4	90	16.3	184	24.9	6	16	.5	14	0	.0
57472	1.4	99	.5	81	22.0	189	44.5	6	21	.7	19	0	.0
57473	.3	96	.1	85	19.9	215	17.9	7	10	.2	10	0	.0
57474	.3	0	.1	84	16.2	186*	24.8	9	15	.0	0	0	.0
57475	.3	100	.1	87	9.7	62	35.1	4	25	.1	24	0	.0
57476	.6	100	.2	79	19.0	208	38.3	6	13	.3	13	0	.0
57477	.3	100	.1	63	18.7	169	23.0	8	13	.1	7	0	.0
57479	.5	98	.2	81	23.3	319	68.0	14	7	.3	7	0	.0
57480	.3	100	.1	51	11.0	126*	13.1	13	9	.2	8	0	.0
57481	.4	100	.1	96	19.7	226*	36.1	10	9	.2	10	0	.0
57482	.4	100	.1	62	9.2	105*	13.1	10	6	.2	7	0	.0
57483	.2	100	.1	75	18.3	210*	13.1	7	12	.1	13	0	.0
PIERRE													
57501	13.5	94	4.9	67	27.2	282	86.9	9	9	6.0	8	0	.1
57520	.3	100	.1	88	15.6	194	37.5	15	18	.1	22	0	.0
57521	.2	0	.2	88	18.0	206*	35.2	2	26	.0	0	0	.0
57522	.6	0	.2	77	18.7	215	36.1	7	18	.0	0	0	.1
57523	1.3	99	.5	74	15.9	144	46.5	10	20	.6	17	0	.0
57526	.3	0	.1	80	19.3	48	21.9	8	7	.0	0	0	.0
57528	1.0	0	.3	80	16.9	341	32.1	11	14	.0	0	0	.0
57529	.7	100	.2	89	17.4	276	23.2	8	13	.4	15	0	.0
57531	.7	100	.2	80	23.3	223	34.9	7	17	.2	21	0	.0
57532	1.9	95	.7	75	23.5	276	68.0	10	10	.9	11	0	.0
57533	2.2	98	.9	74	16.1	199	47.7	7	23	1.0	21	0	.0
57536	.3	0	.3	92	21.3	245*	105.4	12	8	.7	9	0	.2
57537	.2	82	.3	80	16.6	137	32.7	9	7	.3	7	0	.0
57538	.4	0	.2	74	21.6	249*	43.8	9	10	.2	20	0	.0
57540	.4	91	.4	88	14.7	212	26.9	10	17	.1	17	0	.1
57541	.3	100	.2	77	14.2	163*	29.9	13	11	.1	9	0	.0
57544	.5	92	.4	66	18.8	37	13.1	17	5	.5	14	0	.5
57547	.3	64	.2	76	21.0	204	52.7	9	14	.3	13	0	.0
57548	.3	0	.2	70	58.4	118	37.2	14	4	.1	2	0	.0
57551	2.0	73	.7	69	16.3	177	48.2	9	16	1.0	21	0	.0
57552	.6	100	.6	70	17.5	185	49.9	9	11	.1	9	0	.0
57553	.3	100	.3	89	18.3	176	34.8	13	11	.5	13	0	.0
57554	.2	0	.1	67	12.6	144*	44.8*	10	6	.1	4	0	.0
57555	2.8	0	.8	54	16.3	187*	57.9*	13	13	.7	13	0	.0
57559	.9	12	.4	79	18.5	234	40.2	9	13	.1	16	0	.6
57560	.5	37	.9	68	17.5	152	41.5	8	16	.1	8	0	.6
57563	.3	100	.3	80	15.6	94	25.6	14	8	.7	18	0	.0
57564	1.4	99	.5	74	10.5	173	16.4	11	2	.7	12	0	.0
57566	.9	12	.9	58	19.7	177	55.2	7	14	.1	12	0	.6
57567	1.9	98	.7	78	20.1	219	57.4	11	14	1.0	12	0	.6
57568	1.1	100	.4	79	17.8	216	48.0	9	16	.5	15	0	.0
57569	.6	93	.2	89	12.4	215	42.0	7	17	.3	17	0	.0

*=Estimated **1.0=883 lbs per person; 100++ indicates per capita toxic waste generation > than 100 times the U.S. average of 883 lbs per capita.

ZIP CODE MEASURES OF SIZE, LEVELS OF AFFLUENCE AND QUALITY OF LIFE

1=Population (th.); 2= % White; 3=Households (th.); 4=% Owner Occupied; 5=Mean Income Per Household (th.$)*; 6=Mean Monthly Rent ($)*; 7=Mean Home Value (th.$)*; 8=% under 5; 9=% 65 and over; 10=% White Males (th.); 11=% White Males, 65+; 12=# Toxic Waste Sites; 13=Toxic Waste Relative to US(883 lbs.per capita)**.

SOUTH DAKOTA

ZIPCODE	1	2	3	4	5	6	7	8	9	10	11	12	13
PIERRE													
57570	1.2	3	.3	33	13.9	159	19.0	18	5	.0	0	0	.0
57571	.2	53	.1	47	15.4	162	35.0	6	18	.1	32	0	.0
57572	1.5	6	.3	58	15.0	163	19.6	16	4	.0	4	0	.0
57574	.2	0	.1	87	14.9	172*	21.6	6	12	.0	0	0	.0
57576	.3	100	.1	87	25.4	63	28.2	2	12	.1	15	0	.0
57577	1.0	0	.2	35	16.9	181	13.9	13	6	.0	0	0	.0
57579	1.4	63	.4	69	16.2	209	35.7	10	14	.4	18	0	.0
57580	4.5	90	1.7	71	20.0	233	61.7	8	16	2.0	15	0	.0
57581	.3	100	.1	91	25.1	288*	33.1	5	17	.1	19	0	.0
57585	.3	80	.1	76	15.7	145	17.4	9	13	.1	10	0	.0
MOBRIDGE													
57601	4.8	85	1.8	71	19.7	240	56.4	9	16	1.9	15	1	.0
57620	.7	100	.3	79	19.9	192	43.9	6	18	.3	17	0	.2
57622	.4	0	.1	31	11.0	124	13.1	22	4	.0	0	0	.0
57623	1.0	50	.3	61	16.8	146	31.4	10	10	.3	12	0	.0
57625	2.7	0	.8	43	18.4	159	41.3	13	5	.0	0	0	.0
57626	1.4	81	.4	76	18.4	189	60.3	11	10	.5	9	0	.0
57631	.4	0	.1	85	17.9	277	30.2	3	19	.1	0	0	.1
57632	1.0	100	.3	87	13.3	232	29.2	5	20	.5	17	0	.0
57633	.8	81	.3	80	14.2	96	18.3	11	16	.3	17	0	.0
57634	2.4	100	.9	79	14.4	166*	51.4*	17	9	.1	7	0	.0
57638	2.4	98	.9	75	21.6	205	56.2	7	15	1.1	12	0	.1
57639	.4	0	.1	56	21.6	128	76.8*	15	4	.1	12	0	.1
57640	.2	100	.1	90	18.3	210*	13.1	13	21	.2	19	0	.0
57641	.7	78	.2	82	16.7	159	27.5	6	9	.3	9	0	.4
57642	2.1	52	.6	52	18.5	174	48.0	14	8	.6	7	0	.0
57644	.2	6	.1	86	20.4	308	24.5	12	12	.0	15	0	.0
57645	.3	87	.1	81	17.6	145	23.4	13	16	.1	0	0	.0
57646	.4	100	.1	90	17.0	204*	17.0	7	13	.2	9	0	.0
57648	.4	0	.2	82	16.8	256	40.3	7	25	.3	12	0	.4
57649	.3	100	.1	92	21.8	250*	21.9	11	15	.2	15	0	.0
57650	.2	100	.1	90	13.9	160*	13.1	5	24	.2	22	0	.0
57652	.3	37	.1	92	18.5	212*	39.4	19	6	.1	0	0	.0
57653	.4	100	.1	86	19.4	223*	13.1	10	10	.2	9	0	.0
57656	1.2	79	.4	70	16.4	135	41.8	8	11	.5	11	0	.1
57658	.5	0	.1	42	13.8	161	32.1	10	10	.0	0	0	.0
RAPID CITY													
57701	64.2	93	23.0	67	25.5	296	91.7	9	8	29.7	7	7	.1
57706	8.3	84	2.0	2	18.3	311	77.0	16	0	3.9	0	1	.0
57714	.6	12	.1	50	12.1	172	13.1	16	4	.0	10	0	.0
57715	.9	0	.1	34	13.1	137	34.3	14	5	.0	0	0	.0
57716	.7	19	.1	48	22.0	243	29.5	11	6	.1	7	0	.0
57717	5.8	96	2.2	67	21.4	226	71.7	8	16	2.7	14	0	.7
57718	.6	0	.2	76	16.1	267	65.8	18	8	.0	0	0	.0
57719	1.1	94	.4	62	18.4	265	69.5	11	4	.5	5	0	.0
57720	.8	0	.3	70	20.7	133	50.6	10	11	.1	5	0	.0
57722	.4	82	.2	86	18.8	238	29.5	7	17	.2	23	0	.0

SOUTH DAKOTA

ZIPCODE	1	2	3	4	5	6	7	8	9	10	11	12	13
RAPID CITY													
57724	.2	0	.1	78	17.7	165	33.0	4	9	.0	0	0	.0
57725	.2	100	.1	80	64.5	741*	166.3	6	12	.1	16	0	.0
57730	4.3	97	1.5	68	23.2	257	73.6	8	12	2.1	10	0	.0
57732	3.1	99	1.0	65	20.1	219	68.4	7	16	1.5	12	0	.1
57735	2.1	96	.8	70	22.3	270	53.9	9	11	1.0	10	4	.8
57736	.2	100	.1	85	21.9	252*	78.1*	6	0	.4	10	0	.0
57741	.5	94	.1	21	42.0	309	83.1	1	18	.4	25	1	.0
57742	.2	100	.1	72	29.1	185	40.7	14	3	.1	1	0	.0
57744	1.1	85	.4	77	19.4	244	64.2	13	12	.5	13	0	.0
57745	1.5	96	.6	71	18.1	230	66.9	8	14	.7	16	1	1.3
57747	5.8	94	2.0	66	22.1	220	64.5	7	20	2.8	19	0	.0
57750	.4	49	.1	71	15.5	207	14.5	8	11	.1	11	0	.0
57751	.4	0	.2	83	20.7	206	52.5	8	15	.0	0	0	.1
57752	1.0	7	.3	61	12.9	239	34.0	16	5	.0	0	0	.0
57754	4.8	97	1.8	73	24.1	222	51.5	8	13	2.3	10	2	.0
57755	.9	100	.1	77	18.5	293	66.1*	7	15	.1	18	0	.0
57756	2.7	0	.8	47	29.8	183	16.0	14	6	.0	0	0	.0
57760	1.4	99	.5	80	16.4	240	43.7	10	14	.7	12	0	.0
57761	.9	98	.3	79	14.7	189	47.6	8	19	.4	20	0	.0
57762	.7	97	.2	82	20.2	212	29.2	9	8	.3	7	0	.0
57763	.4	0	.1	91	22.4	119	27.1	11	8	.0	0	0	.0
57764	1.5	2	.3	47	16.1	170	13.1	10	7	.1	17	0	.0
57765	.3	100	.1	87	18.0	206*	63.9*	0	16	.1	0	0	.1
57766	.3	0	.1	77	21.3	368	37.9	9	22	.7	12	0	.0
57767	.2	100	.1	96	24.7	283*	13.1	6	20	.8	22	0	.0
57769	1.7	96	.5	78	26.5	333	94.7	7	7	.8	8	0	.0
57770	4.3	6	1.0	39	17.2	179	29.4	14	6	.1	16	0	.1
57772	1.3	6	.3	58	16.4	183	58.5*	10	3	.1	0	0	.0
57773	.3	0	.1	89	25.7	357	68.3	7	5	.1	0	0	.0
57775	.3	100	.1	81	34.6	398*	34.9	9	21	.2	22	0	.1
57779	.3	96	.1	79	20.7	257	48.1	12	8	.2	8	0	.0
57780	.2	91	.1	93	14.5	167*	15.3	6	21	.1	16	0	.0
57783	8.4	97	3.1	61	19.0	268	85.1	8	14	3.9	11	0	.0
57785	7.6	99	2.8	72	22.3	233	79.3	8	14	3.7	12	0	.0
57787	.2	100	.1	86	15.8	181*	21.9	21	11	.1	4	0	.0
57788	.5	100	.1	80	21.0	86	40.4	4	16	.2	13	0	.0
57790	1.1	0	.5	71	18.2	161	61.7	8	18	.1	0	0	.0
57791	.2	100	.1	77	13.9	291	25.4	2	21	.1	21	0	.0
57793	1.3	0	.4	81	21.6	265	57.8	10	11	.2	0	0	1.1
57794	.6	0	.1	28	17.2	190	74.4	16	1	.0	0	0	.0
JAMESTOWN													
58439	.2	100	.1	87	9.8	112*	34.8*	14	10	.1	11	0	.0
VALENTINE													
69201	.4	87	.1	82	17.6	202*	62.7*	11	9	.2	8	0	.0
69212	.2	0	.1	59	21.4	246*	76.4*	19	8	.0	0	0	.0

*=Estimated **1.0=883 lbs per person; 100++ indicates per capita toxic waste generation > than 100 times the U.S. average of 883 lbs per capita.

ZIP CODE MEASURES OF SIZE, LEVELS OF AFFLUENCE AND QUALITY OF LIFE

1=Population (th.); 2= % White; 3=Households (th.); 4=% Owner Occupied; 5=Mean Income Per Household (th.$); 6=Mean Monthly Rent ($)*; 7=Mean Home Value (th.$)*;
8=% under 5; 9=% 65 and over; 10=White Males (th.); 11=% White Males, 65+; 12=# Toxic Waste Sites; 13=Toxic Waste Relative to US(883 lbs.per capita)**.

TENNESSEE

ZIPCODE	1	2	3	4	5	6	7	8	9	10	11	12	13
BRISTOL													
24210	.2	100	.1	52	9.7	208	21.9	5	7	.1	0	0	.0
24248	.3	100	.1	68	9.4	108*	13.1	1	20	.1	15	0	.0
HUNTSVILLE													
35740	.2	100	.1	93	21.5	247*	30.5	12	4	.1	2	0	.0
NASHVILLE													
37010	1.8	87	.6	74	19.9	238	52.9	8	15	.8	14	0	.0
37012	1.7	97	.7	86	18.0	165	48.8	6	20	.8	19	0	.0
37013	16.0	93	5.8	68	28.1	353	85.0	10	4	7.5	3	1	.0
37014	1.0	87	.3	77	28.8	235	101.9	8	11	.4	9	1	.0
37015	12.0	97	3.9	83	25.8	293	67.9	8	9	5.8	9	1	.3
37016	.5	0	.2	79	22.6	190	45.2	7	22	.0	0	0	.0
37018	.8	95	.3	72	15.9	110	44.6	3	22	.4	24	0	.0
37019	.6	86	.3	80	18.7	235	38.3	3	18	.4	18	0	.0
37020	2.3	88	.8	72	19.0	221	60.6	7	12	1.0	11	0	.0
37022	4.0	97	1.3	81	20.1	261	44.4	6	12	2.0	12	0	.0
37023	1.0	100	.3	92	15.5	299	45.2	7	10	.5	13	0	.0
37025	3.0	97	1.0	89	22.6	220	54.6	5	10	1.5	10	1	.1
37026	.9	0	.3	86	17.1	179	63.5	5	12	.0	0	2	.0
37027	13.4	97	4.1	91	48.6	517	179.0	6	5	6.5	5	3	.0
37029	.4	97	.2	89	16.9	240	39.1	7	9	.2	24	0	.0
37030	3.0	92	1.0	84	37.6	224	66.9	8	10	1.4	11	0	.0
37031	7.2	96	2.6	74	22.5	223	64.1	7	16	3.3	13	2	.3
37032	1.9	92	.6	80	30.1	269	86.9	9	7	.9	4	0	.0
37033	2.6	86	.7	82	23.1	256	54.1	7	12	1.1	12	0	.1
37034	6.0	94	2.1	77	20.2	278	50.9	9	13	2.8	10	1	.1
37035	2.5	96	.9	85	32.5	265	55.9	8	13	1.2	12	2	.1
37036	1.4	97	.5	84	20.7	219	63.0	8	10	.7	9	0	.0
37037	3.9	87	1.3	79	23.7	245	54.1	6	12	1.7	7	0	.0
37040	65.2	84	22.7	64	22.8	295	70.3	9	8	26.2	6	5	5.2
37046	2.2	81	.8	82	24.6	236	55.9	8	11	1.0	19	1	.3
37047	1.8	86	.6	79	19.4	215	47.0	5	18	.8	18	0	.4
37048	3.2	97	1.1	88	23.7	271	71.3	7	11	1.6	9	4	1.2
37049	1.8	86	.6	82	22.1	195	63.1	5	9	.9	8	0	3.0
37050	1.1	92	.4	78	22.8	139	47.7	7	19	.5	17	1	5.2
37051	2.2	0	.7	83	18.3	235	54.9	6	11	1.0	0	0	.6
37052	1.7	91	.6	89	21.0	253	54.7	6	15	.7	16	0	.1
37055	16.1	94	5.6	77	22.3	260	66.1	7	13	7.2	11	4	1.2
37057	.8	97	.3	86	21.6	276	68.6	13	17	.3	16	0	.0
37058	4.5	98	1.6	83	18.0	203	57.7	9	16	2.1	15	0	.3
37059	1.2	0	.4	84	18.0	135	47.8	7	14	.6	11	0	.6
37060	1.5	85	.6	70	19.8	216	58.5	5	12	.6	12	0	.1
37061	4.5	93	1.5	73	20.0	214	48.8	7	14	2.1	12	4	1.1
37062	6.0	99	1.9	84	25.9	321	70.5	8	7	3.0	8	1	.1
37064	31.5	87	10.5	75	33.9	343	118.7	8	13	13.4	9	4	.3
37066	24.4	84	8.5	70	25.8	292	81.2	8	11	10.0	8	6	.6
37072	18.3	97	6.2	77	27.5	382	91.3	7	9	8.7	8	0	.1
37073	7.5	99	2.5	85	27.5	318	67.0	8	10	3.8	9	1	.0
37074	5.4	85	2.0	67	22.4	274	58.6	7	14	2.3	12	1	.1

TENNESSEE

ZIPCODE	1	2	3	4	5	6	7	8	9	10	11	12	13
NASHVILLE													
37075	31.5	97	9.9	82	34.1	436	109.8	7	5	15.2	4	4	.1
37076	15.9	96	5.6	60	30.2	405	95.5	7	6	7.5	4	0	.0
37078	.5	100	.2	77	25.6	203	69.4	7	10	.3	11	0	.0
37079	1.7	95	.6	81	17.6	238	48.6	5	13	.8	10	0	.0
37080	6.6	99	2.1	79	25.4	339	77.4	7	8	3.3	7	1	.0
37082	3.4	95	1.1	87	27.7	296	78.3	8	9	1.6	7	0	.1
37083	9.4	100	3.5	81	19.3	248	56.5	7	13	4.6	11	0	.4
37085	1.8	92	.6	81	22.7	228	68.3	7	13	.9	10	0	.0
37086	6.4	94	2.1	81	24.5	338	69.3	8	7	3.0	4	2	2.0
37087	30.2	89	10.5	72	24.6	290	78.0	7	12	13.2	10	1	1.2
37091	14.5	89	5.4	69	21.2	234	55.6	7	16	6.2	12	3	1.0
37095	1.7	98	.6	76	15.8	173	36.6	8	14	.8	8	0	.0
37096	4.1	97	1.6	81	16.2	210	44.5	8	16	2.0	14	0	.5
37097	1.6	0	.6	83	23.7	259	47.7	4	14	.0	0	0	.0
37098	3.0	96	1.0	85	19.9	270	46.7	7	9	1.4	8	1	.0
NASHVILLE													
37101	4.2	99	1.5	82	19.5	164	51.4	6	14	2.1	12	0	.0
37110	27.0	96	9.8	73	19.9	217	58.6	7	13	12.5	11	2	.9
37115	30.0	94	11.9	52	25.5	333	81.9	7	12	13.0	9	3	.0
37118	.7	100	.2	88	23.0	335	73.0	10	17	.4	19	0	.2
37122	16.1	94	5.1	90	31.8	403	103.4	8	6	7.6	5	0	.4
37130	53.7	88	19.1	63	25.0	310	86.2	7	9	23.3	8	6	.4
37134	3.1	99	1.0	82	28.0	220	69.5	9	7	1.5	6	4	27.8
37135	2.1	83	.7	84	29.8	227	98.5	8	10	.9	7	0	.0
37137	1.3	100	.5	87	16.5	199	56.7	7	15	.7	17	0	.0
37138	16.4	93	5.9	81	29.5	299	93.8	8	13	7.4	12	2	12.6
37140	.8	70	.1	82	16.9	128	30.5	3	6	.5	6	0	.0
37141	.7	87	.3	87	20.8	250	49.7	5	17	.3	17	0	.0
37142	1.2	0	.4	85	19.7	127	53.0	5	22	.0	0	0	.0
37143	2.6	96	.8	81	28.8	269	79.2	9	9	1.3	5	0	.6
37144	2.7	91	1.0	82	19.5	143	40.2	7	15	1.1	14	0	.0
37145	1.9	100	.7	83	28.6	368	58.0	9	18	1.0	16	0	.0
37146	1.8	0	.6	84	29.0	316	66.4	5	10	.0	0	0	.0
37147	.5	100	.2	87	15.0	190	24.8	12	11	.9	8	0	.0
37148	10.3	97	3.6	80	22.1	238	55.5	7	14	4.9	13	4	.6
37149	1.6	96	.5	89	21.9	212	70.7	8	12	.8	12	0	.0
37150	4.7	100	1.6	82	19.4	130	47.1	7	16	2.3	14	0	.0
37151	.6	86	.2	77	24.5	331	54.9	6	15	.2	15	0	.1
37152	.8	0	.2	85	28.5	317	87.7	6	9	.0	0	0	.0
37153	2.0	95	.7	78	20.7	423	69.1	6	17	1.0	12	1	.0
37155	1.2	79	.4	60	24.5	420	78.9	0	18	.7	0	0	1.0
37160	21.3	70	7.7	70	24.7	240	63.4	7	15	9.0	12	0	.8
37165	.1	100	.1	76	12.0	270	27.3	0	44	.1	40	0	.0
37166	9.5	98	3.4	77	21.3	222	59.2	8	13	4.5	11	1	1.3
37167	11.8	92	3.8	67	26.4	321	81.3	8	5	5.4	5	7	6.0
37171	.9	92	.7	91	18.7	215*	63.4	13	9	.4	4	0	.0
37172	18.2	78	6.3	64	22.4	253	65.8	7	14	6.8	12	3	.1
37174	2.7	81	.9	80	25.2	275	58.7	8	6	1.1	0	0	.0
37175	.9	0	.4	86	15.9	136	35.8	6	22	.0	0	0	.1

*=Estimated **1.0=883 lbs per person; 100+ indicates per capita toxic waste generation > than 100 times the U.S. average of 883 lbs per capita.

ZIP CODE MEASURES OF SIZE, LEVELS OF AFFLUENCE AND QUALITY OF LIFE

1=Population (th.); 2= % White; 3=Households (th.); 4=% Owner Occupied; 5=Mean Income Per Household (th.$); 6=Mean Monthly Rent ($); 7=Mean Home Value (th.$); 8=% under 5; 9=% 65 and over; 10=White Males, 65+; 11=% White Males (th.); 12=# Toxic Waste Sites; 13=Toxic Waste Relative to US(883 lbs.per capita)**.

TENNESSEE

ZIP CODE	1	2	3	4	5	6	7	8	9	10	11	12	13
NASHVILLE													
37178	1.7	0	.6	86	20.4	218	48.5	8	11	.0	0	0	.0
37179	2.1	94	.8	85	25.6	252	72.4	7	12	1.0	11	0	.0
37180	1.2	96	.4	86	20.0	264	50.7	8	11	.5	10	0	.0
37181	1.0	100	.4	92	17.7	81	40.1	5	21	.5	24	0	.0
37183	1.9	87	.6	78	21.3	250	46.4	9	11	.8	8	1	.0
37184	4.4	94	1.6	84	19.5	194	48.0	5	16	2.1	14	0	.0
37185	8.1	93	3.0	76	22.2	216	63.4	8	14	3.6	13	0	.0
37186	5.8	0	2.1	80	18.2	269	43.4	8	12	.4	0	0	.2
37187	4.2	99	1.5	78	21.9	238	57.5	8	13	2.1	12	1	.0
37188	3.4	97	1.1	84	26.3	345	76.6	11	8	1.6	8	0	.1
37189	2.1	0	.7	84	29.2	377	75.8	7	11	.0	0	0	.0
37190	7.5	98	2.7	79	19.5	214	56.3	7	15	3.5	12	0	.0
37191	1.9	93	.6	75	19.1	317	53.2	9	8	.8	9	0	.0
NASHVILLE													
37203	19.9	41	5.9	19	14.9	249	57.8	4	14	4.0	11	1	.5
37204	13.3	63	5.4	55	26.3	322	104.5	6	18	1.3	15	1	.6
37205	23.2	98	9.4	74	46.8	487	171.7	5	14	10.4	11	0	.0
37206	31.9	70	11.7	52	18.7	268	55.9	8	13	1.6	12	2	.1
37207	35.2	49	11.5	63	22.7	282	65.5	9	9	.8	4	1	.1
37208	19.5	7	7.5	40	15.0	245	39.7	6	18	.6	22	2	.1
37209	34.4	73	13.0	52	21.3	318	66.2	8	10	12.2	9	10	.5
37211	56.7	92	22.7	52	26.1	380	78.8	6	7	24.8	3	6	1.8
37212	15.2	69	7.2	33	19.9	339	82.9	4	16	4.8	6	6	.3
37213	.7	73	.2	24	11.1	245	43.8	7	11	.3	8	1	2.9
37214	19.9	98	7.1	75	33.1	414	86.6	6	9	9.5	8	3	.0
37215	18.2	98	7.8	74	49.8	445	185.2	5	18	8.1	15	0	.0
37216	20.5	83	7.7	74	26.0	357	66.5	6	15	7.8	14	0	.0
37217	22.5	90	8.8	50	29.7	406	97.6	7	6	9.9	7	0	.6
37218	16.0	35	4.6	79	27.6	321	75.0	6	10	2.7	15	1	.0
37219	.8	88	.5	0	20.1	335	71.5*	5	19	.4	19	0	.5
37220	6.5	99	2.5	92	43.9	498	147.4	3	15	3.0	14	0	.0
37221	13.3	97	5.0	69	35.5	485	123.1	7	7	6.3	4	1	.0
CHATTANOOGA													
37301	1.0	0	.3	84	15.0	238	34.1	10	9	.0	0	0	.0
37302	.8	100	.3	78	20.7	312	60.0	4	10	.0	8	0	.0
37303	20.6	94	7.3	72	23.4	225	65.7	8	12	9.3	10	5	.5
37304	.3	100	.1	71	23.8	354	31.6	10	12	.2	10	0	.0
37305	.8	0	.3	77	12.5	167	35.8	10	8	.0	0	0	.0
37306	2.1	89	.7	75	22.0	198	51.9	7	13	1.0	15	0	.0
37307	3.0	0	.7	77	19.4	195	51.4	9	10	.0	0	0	.3
37308	1.5	0	.5	82	16.4	201	44.9	8	10	.0	0	0	.0
37309	1.5	100	.5	78	21.8	268	55.4	10	13	.7	12	0	7.1
37310	2.5	89	.9	80	22.4	248	70.6	8	13	1.1	11	1	10.4
37311	61.2	95	20.9	69	23.5	276	70.7	7	9	28.1	7	5	.5
37313	1.1	0	.4	89	17.7	121	44.6	8	17	.0	0	0	.0
37315	3.7	93	.8	62	27.4	305	85.4	4	5	1.7	5	0	.0
37316	.3	0	.7	74	18.0	108	52.1	8	10	.0	0	0	.0
37317	2.0	0	.7	84	21.1	207	51.3	4	11	.0	1	0	83.5

TENNESSEE

ZIP CODE	1	2	3	4	5	6	7	8	9	10	11	12	13
CHATTANOOGA													
37318	2.1	88	.8	76	19.2	223	46.5	7	14	.9	14	1	.0
37319	6.9	99	2.4	78	21.9	314	49.5	9	10	3.5	8	1	.4
37321	13.6	96	4.5	72	20.0	226	58.3	7	11	6.4	9	4	.3
37324	5.3	91	1.8	76	19.4	217	53.1	7	12	2.2	10	0	.1
37325	5.0	100	1.3	85	19.7	158	41.5	5	12	.7	10	0	.0
37326	1.3	100	.5	68	19.2	257	47.9	7	13	.4	10	0	.2
37327	.9	100	.3	79	17.6	246	49.8	8	12	3.3	9	1	.0
37328	7.0	98	2.4	76	21.4	178	46.9	6	9	.6	7	0	.0
37329	1.2	98	1.6	82	20.8	215	59.4	8	10	2.4	9	0	.0
37330	4.9	100	1.5	88	22.4	245	72.3	7	10	2.0	9	0	.1
37331	4.1	93	2.8	77	21.3	225	54.4	7	14	3.5	11	1	2.8
37332	7.7	100	.5	85	19.6	273	59.7	7	14	.8	13	0	.1
37333	1.6	100	.2	91	11.6	266	25.0	10	10	.3	13	0	.1
37334	.6	88	6.6	71	20.5	226	58.5	7	14	7.7	12	6	.6
37335	18.1	100	2.0	81	19.0	196	50.0	9	7	1.0	7	0	.0
37336	2.0	95	.6	86	21.4	236	69.8	8	8	1.0	5	0	.0
37337	2.1	82	.4	81	19.4	302	55.2	7	9	1.0	9	0	.3
37338	1.2	98	.7	84	16.5	227	40.6	7	10	1.0	9	0	.3
37339	2.1	100	.3	86	16.4	189	43.7	9	14	.5	11	0	.1
37340	1.1	0	.2	79	18.6	214	35.4	8	6	.0	0	0	.0
37341	.7	98	2.4	86	27.1	377	85.4	7	8	3.6	7	2	.7
37342	7.2	98	2.0	80	20.8	201	67.1	6	10	.0	2	0	1.9
37343	2.0	98	11.5	77	32.6	409	89.9	8	5	16.8	4	0	.0
37345	34.2	96	.1	84	25.7	243	54.1	8	12	1.1	10	0	.1
37346	2.2	100	.1	82	12.3	140	19.3	6	4	.1	0	0	.0
37347	.2	95	2.4	80	21.4	236	59.6	8	10	3.3	8	0	.3
37348	7.1	100	.4	74	15.0	224	37.3	4	13	.3	15	0	.3
37349	.6	100	.4	87	22.8	229	39.7	7	8	.6	6	0	.6
37350	1.2	93	.8	82	54.5	412	196.2	5	19	.8	15	0	.0
37351	1.5	100	.1	92	23.6	285	91.0	10	11	2	2	0	.5
37352	2.3	92	.8	85	22.4	276	81.6	8	13	1.0	11	0	.2
37353	2.5	99	.9	73	22.2	191	63.1	6	11	1.2	9	0	.0
37354	11.2	98	3.7	82	21.4	214	56.2	7	10	5.3	10	1	.1
37355	16.6	98	5.8	73	22.9	261	65.7	8	11	8.0	9	0	.0
37356	3.6	98	1.2	77	17.7	278	54.1	8	10	.8	8	0	.0
37357	3.6	97	1.2	82	18.5	120	54.0	6	15	1.8	16	0	.0
37359	.6	81	.3	77	13.8	252	32.1	6	24	.3	20	0	.0
37360	1.2	98	.4	87	21.0	178	52.1	8	13	.5	13	0	.0
37361	.8	0	.3	70	17.9	262	37.5	6	13	.0	0	0	.0
37362	2.0	100	.7	94	21.0	123	44.8	9	9	1.0	12	0	.0
37363	12.0	95	3.8	84	27.9	296	81.6	9	8	5.5	7	0	.0
37365	1.7	100	.5	87	15.7	193	33.4	9	12	.9	11	0	.0
37366	.9	100	.3	86	17.5	174	47.5	7	11	.4	16	0	.0
37367	8.1	96	2.5	77	18.2	194	47.5	7	11	3.9	10	1	.1
37369	.8	98	.3	79	13.1	110	25.6	6	13	.5	15	0	.2
37370	2.9	97	1.0	86	20.8	197	71.0	8	11	1.4	8	0	.0
37373	2.2	0	.7	89	30.1	180	48.5	9	11	.0	0	0	.0
37374	1.1	91	.4	91	18.4	132	48.5	7	7	.0	0	0	.0

*=Estimated **1.0=883 lbs. lbs per person; 100++ indicates per capita toxic waste generation > than 100 times the U.S. average of 883 lbs per capita.

ZIP CODE MEASURES OF SIZE, LEVELS OF AFFLUENCE AND QUALITY OF LIFE

1=Population (th.); 2= % White; 3=Households (th.); 4=% Owner Occupied; 5=Mean Income Per Household (th.$); 6=Mean Monthly Rent ($); 7=Mean Home Value (th.$);
8=% under 5; 9=% 65 and over; 10=White Males (th.); 11=% White Males, 65+; 12=# Toxic Waste Sites; 13=Toxic Waste Relative to US(883 lbs.per capita)**.

TENNESSEE

ZIPCODE	1	2	3	4	5	6	7	8	9	10	11	12	13
CHATTANOOGA													
37375	3.2	95	.9	66	22.1	264	68.1	4	10	1.6	7	0	.0
37376	.7	100	.2	79	19.8	186	30.4	9	11	.3	9	0	.0
37377	11.1	100	3.7	85	38.9	357	124.5	7	10	5.3	9	0	.0
37379	8.9	95	3.1	86	27.8	295	69.2	7	9	4.2	7	0	.0
37380	5.6	87	2.1	70	21.2	190	53.0	6	17	2.3	13	2	2.6
37381	7.0	97	2.5	75	20.4	239	63.3	8	12	3.3	11	2	.2
37382	.4	100	.1	44	13.1	253	59.2	20	8	.1	17	0	.0
37385	5.6	100	1.8	81	15.7	185	37.8	7	11	2.8	10	0	.0
37387	4.6	0	1.5	83	24.7	228	38.6	10	10	.0	0	0	.0
37388	20.1	94	7.2	69	24.4	260	73.2	7	11	9.3	9	1	.2
37391	1.4	100	.5	79	15.6	215	52.7	9	13	.4	10	0	.0
37394	.2	94	.1	74	16.3	172	41.1	7	24	.1	18	0	.0
37396	.4	100	.1	76	16.8	138	35.4	8	5	.2	5	0	.0
37397	8.1	98	2.7	82	17.5	255	46.1	8	10	.4	8	1	.0
37398	10.5	90	3.7	74	21.7	248	65.3	8	15	4.6	12	0	.4
CHATTANOOGA													
37402	2.4	84	1.5	1	14.7	227	107.1	0	41	.9	20	3	15.0
37403	7.7	19	3.2	9	10.4	201	54.6	6	19	.5	20	1	.5
37404	20.2	60	6.7	48	19.5	278	55.1	7	14	5.8	9	1	.4
37405	14.8	90	6.1	52	23.7	337	62.9	6	16	6.1	13	7	1.3
37406	18.5	30	6.1	52	17.7	266	48.2	9	11	2.5	15	7	3.3
37407	10.1	87	4.0	53	17.4	247	33.7	8	17	4.0	15	7	1.2
37409	3.8	3	1.2	16	10.0	179	32.0	8	17	.2	10	7	2.0
37410	8.0	0	2.5	31	10.9	192	31.4	10	15	.0	0	12	7.5
37411	19.3	64	7.6	70	25.2	353	64.4	7	16	5.5	17	0	.4
37412	21.1	99	8.3	69	28.1	394	67.1	5	12	9.7	10	0	.0
37415	22.1	98	9.0	65	26.9	330	72.8	6	11	10.3	10	2	.0
37416	14.0	82	4.6	76	29.2	416	82.0	7	6	5.6	5	1	.0
37419	5.6	99	1.8	80	29.3	331	71.9	7	8	2.8	6	0	.1
37421	26.8	92	9.0	77	31.4	329	93.1	7	7	12.1	8	3	.1
JOHNSON CITY													
37601	60.2	95	21.8	63	23.7	269	77.3	6	12	27.0	9	4	.6
37616	3.2	100	1.2	83	18.4	281	57.3	6	9	1.6	9	0	.0
37617	10.2	99	3.4	87	24.8	271	81.7	6	8	5.1	8	0	.1
37618	10.2	99	3.4	80	21.9	252	69.0	7	9	5.0	8	0	.0
37620	38.5	97	14.1	73	23.1	276	70.3	6	11	18.0	9	7	3.1
37640	3.5	0	1.2	87	14.3	200	38.9	6	10	.0	0	0	.0
37641	5.7	100	1.9	81	17.5	223	54.4	7	9	2.8	10	0	.0
37642	15.6	98	5.3	82	22.3	238	67.2	7	8	7.6	8	1	.0
37643	30.6	99	11.1	78	19.1	237	55.2	6	13	14.5	11	3	.9
37650	12.5	99	4.6	80	20.2	234	58.1	6	14	6.0	11	3	.0
37656	3.5	98	1.2	83	22.2	171	69.9	6	12	1.7	12	0	5.5
37657	1.2	100	.4	79	12.3	106	39.0	8	11	.6	11	0	.0
37658	4.0	100	1.4	82	16.1	220	46.9	8	11	.9	11	0	.2
37659	25.5	99	8.9	79	25.1	287	72.9	7	9	12.5	8	4	.0
37660	38.8	96	14.4	69	23.1	263	69.2	6	14	17.5	9	4	.0
37662	.5	100	.2	69	23.3	329	80.1	5	8	.2	12	4	100++
37663	11.9	99	4.1	82	31.8	309	97.7	7	7	5.8	6	0	.0

TENNESSEE

ZIPCODE	1	2	3	4	5	6	7	8	9	10	11	12	13
JOHNSON CITY													
37664	25.5	99	9.4	77	26.0	293	80.1	6	12	11.8	10	1	.0
37665	5.8	100	2.1	75	20.6	273	55.5	5	12	2.8	10	0	.0
37680	.9	100	.3	90	14.7	81	43.8	6	12	.5	10	0	.0
37681	4.2	99	1.4	78	19.1	173	66.2	7	12	2.1	9	0	.0
37682	8.7	98	.1	33	15.1	250	53.8	6	3	.3	3	0	.3
37683	8.7	99	3.1	81	16.2	224	52.6	7	14	4.2	13	0	.3
37686	4.0	0	1.4	86	24.7	289	72.4	8	9	.0	0	0	.7
37687	4.7	100	1.6	80	14.2	149	37.8	8	14	2.4	12	0	.0
37688	1.1	100	.4	74	16.7	305	45.2	6	13	.6	10	0	.0
37690	2.1	0	.7	86	20.1	148	51.7	6	14	.0	0	0	.0
37691	.9	0	.3	94	13.4	52	41.3	9	10	.0	0	0	.0
37692	3.0	0	1.0	75	19.1	294	66.0	7	10	.0	0	0	.0
37694	1.3	100	.4	89	19.9	245	58.0	6	9	.6	8	0	.0
KNOXVILLE													
37701	6.9	80	2.6	70	21.8	288	64.8	6	15	2.6	12	3	7.2
37705	3.0	100	1.0	88	22.0	227	56.7	6	16	1.5	14	0	.0
37707	.4	0	.1	82	17.5	136	58.8	4	7	.0	0	0	.0
37708	5.0	99	1.7	80	17.9	239	59.6	7	9	2.4	8	0	.0
37709	2.4	97	.8	81	18.5	214	47.4	9	11	.9	10	0	.0
37710	1.1	95	.2	64	14.3	159	32.5	7	8	.5	10	0	.0
37711	3.1		1.1	79	18.1	162	51.2	8	13	.0	0	0	.4
37712	.2	0	.1	82	12.2	146	55.3	8	28	.0	0	0	.0
37713	1.4	100	.5	77	14.4	80	34.5	4	9	.7	8	0	.0
37714	3.5	100	1.2	80	17.6	231	54.9	9	12	1.8	11	0	.0
37715	1.2	0	.3	63	15.7	119	28.8	9	8	.0	0	0	.0
37716	19.8	98	7.1	78	23.8	260	70.7	7	12	9.4	10	2	.4
37719	.2	100	.1	91	18.4	211*	55.6	11	12	.1	13	0	.0
37721	8.2	99	2.8	83	22.9	317	66.8	7	12	3.9	11	0	.0
37722	3.4	100	3.4	79	17.5	179	49.1	7	11	1.7	11	1	.0
37723	1.0	100	.3	73	13.0	187	36.7	8	16	.5	14	0	.1
37724	2.7	99	.7	81	18.1	187	64.6	8	10	1.0	8	0	.0
37725	7.7	96	2.7	81	18.9	231	59.7	6	13	3.7	12	0	.0
37726	1.6	0	.6	85	15.9	265	46.3	9	15	.0	0	0	.0
37727	2.1	0	.7	65	13.6	171	35.7	7	9	.0	0	0	.0
37729	1.7	100	.5	86	17.7	129	24.2	9	11	.9	10	0	.4
37730	.2	100	.1	61	15.4	197	37.0	11	7	.7	7	0	.0
37731	.7	100	.3	79	12.3	146	45.8	8	11	.4	14	0	.0
37732	.1	100	.1	70	13.7	185	21.4	13	8	.2	10	0	.0
37735	.2	65	.1	59	15.4	209	41.3	9	9	.1	8	0	.0
37737	2.9	99	1.0	85	22.1	256	63.1	6	11	2.2	8	0	.1
37738	4.5	100	1.8	69	23.7	334	100.3	6	13	2.8	9	0	.0
37742	3.1	100	1.1	82	18.5	207	61.3	8	14	2.1	12	0	1.1
37743	36.9	97	12.9	74	20.5	228	63.0	6	12	17.1	9	4	1.6
37748	18.6	96	6.4	73	20.9	205	57.9	8	12	8.5	10	1	1.5
37752	4.6	98	1.5	81	20.8	275	65.5	6	9	2.2	8	0	.0
37753	1.0	100	.3	75	11.5	198	25.5	5	9	.9	9	0	.0
37754	3.2	100	1.1	86	20.2	207	56.1	7	11	1.6	10	0	1.1
37755	2.7	100	.9	72	15.8	172	48.5	10	8	1.3	8	0	1.6
37756	3.2	99	1.0	77	18.5	163	40.4	11	7	1.6	6	0	.0

*=Estimated **1.0=883 lbs per person; 100++ indicates per capita toxic waste generation > than 100 times the U.S. average of 883 lbs per capita.

ZIP CODE MEASURES OF SIZE, LEVELS OF AFFLUENCE AND QUALITY OF LIFE

1=Population (th.); 2=% White; 3=Households (th.); 4=% Owner Occupied; 5=Mean Income Per Household (th.$); 6=Mean Monthly Rent ($); 7=Mean Home Value (th.$); 8=% under 5; 9=% 65 and over; 10=White Males (th.); 11=% White Males, 65+; 12=# Toxic Waste Sites; 13=Toxic Waste Relative to US(883 lbs.per capita)**.

TENNESSEE

KNOXVILLE

ZIP CODE	1	2	3	4	5	6	7	8	9	10	11	12	13
37757	5.2	100	1.9	77	18.3	204	60.8	9	13	2.5	12	0	.0
37760	10.5	96	3.5	70	20.3	229	63.8	5	11	4.9	9	1	.3
37762	4.0	99	1.6	68	14.5	158	45.9	7	18	1.8	15	0	.1
37763	12.0	99	4.3	83	25.8	302	74.4	7	9	5.9	8	1	.3
37764	2.7	0	1.0	75	19.4	248	66.5	6	9	.9	0	0	.0
37765	.8	100	.3	83	10.8	74	55.9	9	16	.3	12	0	.0
37766	17.4	99	6.0	73	18.2	221	51.2	6	13	8.2	11	1	.3
37769	6.6	99	2.2	72	17.9	237	46.6	7	13	3.1	11	0	.0
37770	2.2	0	.8	80	19.9	183	41.5	6	11	.9	11	0	.0
37771	18.5	99	6.7	79	24.0	265	70.5	6	11	8.9	9	2	.3
37774	8.6	97	3.1	77	21.2	232	58.3	7	15	3.9	13	4	2.4
37777	7.4	95	2.7	69	27.9	336	94.0	7	7	3.5	7	0	5.2
37779	3.7	0	1.2	83	15.9	201	48.7	8	10	.0	0	0	.0

KNOXVILLE

ZIP CODE	1	2	3	4	5	6	7	8	9	10	11	12	13
37801	49.4	99	17.8	75	24.1	265	76.7	6	12	23.3	10	0	.0
37806	2.9	0	.9	78	22.1	242	46.1	7	8	.0	0	9	.9
37807	5.5	100	2.0	77	18.7	211	58.0	6	11	2.7	10	0	.0
37809	1.7	98	.6	79	18.3	137	50.9	5	12	.8	12	0	.0
37810	1.6	99	.5	78	16.3	165	38.4	5	14	.8	14	0	.0
37811	2.1	0	.7	80	16.4	228	45.4	6	9	.0	0	0	.0
37812	.2	100	.1	68	12.2	145	18.2	3	11	.1	14	0	.0
37814	41.3	94	14.5	70	16.9	265	65.7	6	9	18.8	7	5	.6
37818	3.7	0	1.3	83	16.9	229	52.1	8	11	.0	0	0	.0
37819	1.1	100	.4	75	15.5	210	28.8	7	13	.5	13	0	.0
37820	3.6	96	1.3	83	20.6	192	56.3	6	11	1.6	9	1	.1
37821	18.6	97	6.6	71	17.3	213	53.1	7	11	8.5	10	7	3.0
37825	5.3	98	1.9	74	16.6	162	54.4	5	13	2.5	14	0	.0
37826	3.0	93	1.1	81	18.5	293	47.0	5	14	1.3	14	0	1.5
37828	1.7	99	.7	80	20.1	192	71.4	7	14	.8	14	0	.1
37829	1.6	99	.5	72	14.9	203	53.0	10	10	.0	0	0	.0
37830	28.2	91	11.2	65	31.4	305	86.4	6	10	12.3	9	7	100++
37840	10.2	98	3.4	83	22.9	224	57.5	7	14	4.8	8	0	.0
37841	8.7	100	2.9	73	23.5	238	56.0	7	13	4.3	11	1	.0
37843	3.0	97	1.1	75	17.7	171	48.0	7	11	1.5	11	0	.0
37845	1.2	88	.2	74	17.8	182	32.6	8	7	1.6	5	0	.0
37847	2.8	97	.9	77	22.5	236	48.6	8	10	1.4	8	0	.0
37848	1.1	99	.4	82	14.2	162	27.5	5	6	.5	6	0	.0
37849	.3	100	.1	80	14.5	61	45.3	10	15	.1	13	0	.0
37852	16.4	98	5.4	83	28.0	299	81.3	8	6	8.0	5	0	.0
37853	2.1	100	.7	72	14.9	203	33.8	10	14	1.1	15	0	.1
37854	3.3	92	1.2	75	33.6	242	65.9	7	14	1.4	9	0	.0
37857	11.3	96	4.1	75	21.1	205	50.0	7	14	5.1	11	0	.3
37860	17.0	97	6.0	76	17.9	230	56.2	7	13	8.0	10	1	.9
37861	2.2	94	.8	79	17.4	203	54.5	7	11	1.0	9	0	.2
37862	5.9	98	2.1	81	17.6	176	50.0	6	14	2.9	13	0	.6
37863	22.8	99	8.0	77	19.9	250	66.4	7	12	11.0	11	3	.0
37865	2.0	100	.8	70	21.8	295	88.7	7	11	.9	10	0	.0
37866	10.5	100	3.6	87	25.1	29	77.9	8	9	5.2	8	0	.3

TENNESSEE

KNOXVILLE

ZIP CODE	1	2	3	4	5	6	7	8	9	10	11	12	13
37867	.2	100	.1	75	19.3	255	51.3	9	21	.1	25	0	.0
37869	5.0	100	1.7	78	12.0	173	46.9	8	11	2.5	12	0	.0
37870	3.4	99	1.2	77	15.7	146	54.7	7	15	1.7	11	0	.2
37871	7.1	98	2.4	80	19.9	268	61.7	8	8	3.4	7	0	.3
37872	1.7	98	.6	78	16.3	154	34.0	8	13	.4	0	0	.0
37873	4.2	99	1.4	79	21.5	268	56.8	7	10	2.1	9	0	.2
37874	9.8	93	3.4	79	21.2	227	56.6	8	13	4.3	10	2	.0
37877	5.8	100	1.9	88	25.0	227	70.8	6	9	2.9	7	0	.0
37878	.3	100	.1	84	20.0	229*	26.1	0	25	.1	19	0	.0
37879	8.0	97	2.7	76	15.0	193	57.9	8	12	3.7	11	0	.0
37880	2.6	100	.9	85	21.5	149	68.3	6	9	1.4	9	0	.0
37881	1.5	96	.5	91	16.4	172	28.2	10	11	.7	10	0	.2
37882	1.9	99	.7	78	21.2	222	67.7	6	15	.9	15	0	.0
37883	.6	0	.7	71	16.9	87	23.2	7	12	.0	0	0	.0
37885	2.4	100	.8	79	16.4	163	56.2	8	12	1.2	11	0	.0
37886	2.2	100	.8	77	20.0	243	53.8	8	9	1.2	10	0	.0
37887	3.8	99	1.3	84	21.6	248	58.4	8	9	1.8	8	0	.2
37888	2.1	0	.7	84	14.5	159	48.1	9	14	.0	0	0	.0
37890	4.6	98	1.6	78	18.4	192	61.5	9	11	2.2	10	0	.1
37891	2.6	98	.9	77	20.4	216	48.1	6	10	1.2	9	0	.0
37892	1.5	97	.5	79	14.3	219	46.9	8	8	.8	3	0	.0

KNOXVILLE

ZIP CODE	1	2	3	4	5	6	7	8	9	10	11	12	13
37902	1.3	88	.7	4	8.6	167	74.4	1	15	.7	8	1	33.1
37912	16.7	97	6.8	56	25.3	349	66.9	6	9	7.6	8	0	.0
37914	30.7	71	11.2	73	23.2	291	61.7	6	14	10.5	12	4	.4
37915	7.5	0	3.3	21	11.6	194	54.7	8	16	6.4	2	1	.2
37916	13.1	88	3.4	7	12.2	284	74.1	1	3	6.4	0	0	.1
37917	28.9	93	12.3	56	17.7	256	46.7	5	20	12.0	15	2	.8
37918	38.2	98	13.7	67	20.2	304	77.5	6	12	17.9	9	0	.1
37919	54.4	96	21.5	54	32.3	344	117.6	6	10	24.9	7	6	.0
37920	39.3	97	14.6	69	23.2	277	68.2	6	12	18.5	10	2	.1
37921	37.5	84	12.9	66	20.9	241	64.2	8	10	15.2	9	4	3.2
37922	23.1	97	7.6	86	38.7	409	128.2	8	5	11.1	4	0	.2

MEMPHIS

ZIP CODE	1	2	3	4	5	6	7	8	9	10	11	12	13
38001	4.8	86	1.7	74	20.6	206	55.7	6	16	1.9	14	0	.1
38004	2.8	60	1.8	76	24.2	223	83.7	6	12	1.7	9	1	1.5
38006	4.6	74	1.4	73	24.3	258	70.2	9	7	1.7	5	0	.4
38007	4.6	73	1.6	72	17.4	237	51.5	8	15	1.6	14	2	.8
38008	.4	100	.2	70	17.4	308	37.1	7	13	.2	13	0	.1
38011	10.2	59	3.3	69	19.9	215	56.6	9	12	2.7	11	2	1.4
38012	5.8	83	1.8	75	23.8	255	70.7	9	10	2.5	8	1	.0
38015	14.4	52	4.7	67	19.6	215	59.3	9	14	3.5	13	1	.0
38017	2.0	87	.6	76	20.2	259	74.2	6	13	.9	11	1	.0
38018	10.8	74	3.1	77	28.9	319	91.4	9	7	3.9	5	2	1.7
38019	5.4	84	1.8	82	41.1	490	144.3	8	5	2.3	2	0	1.6
38021	12.3	69	4.2	65	20.9	248	65.3	8	14	4.0	12	0	.9
38023	.2	100	.1	74	22.8	293	35.0	11	13	.1	12	0	.0
38024	24.3	86	8.8	66	21.3	256	59.7	11	13	10.0	10	5	.3

*=Estimated **1.0=883 lbs per person; 100++ indicates per capita toxic waste generation > than 100 times the U.S. average of 883 lbs per capita.

ZIP CODE MEASURES OF SIZE, LEVELS OF AFFLUENCE AND QUALITY OF LIFE

1=Population (th.); 2= % White; 3=Households (th.); 4=% Owner Occupied; 5=Mean Income Per Household (th.$); 6=Mean Monthly Rent ($)*; 7=Mean Home Value (th.$)*;
8=% under 5; 9=% 65 and over; 10=% White Males (th.); 11=% White Males, 65+; 12=# Toxic Waste Sites; 13=Toxic Waste Relative to US(883 lbs.per capita)**

TENNESSEE

MEMPHIS

ZIPCODE	1	2	3	4	5	6	7	8	9	10	11	12	13
38028	2.5	69	.8	71	26.6	202	93.3	9	12	.8	9	0	.0
38029	1.0	64	.3	82	20.6	221	76.9	2	12	.3	6	0	.0
38030	1.4	100	.6	61	17.3	211	45.2	7	14	.7	13	0	.0
38033	.3	0	.1	87	17.3	310	42.8	4	25	.0	0	0	.0
38034	3.0	97	1.2	77	18.6	224	43.2	7	19	1.4	16	0	.0
38036	.8	45	.2	28	13.3	259	45.7	11	23	.2	30	0	.3
38037	1.5	77	.5	73	16.8	225	34.1	5	12	.6	9	0	.0
38039	1.9	31	.6	74	15.5	218	53.7	10	14	.7	15	0	.1
38040	6.0	80	2.1	68	19.1	228	48.3	8	16	2.3	14	1	.2
38041	2.6	40	.8	58	16.1	184	43.8	9	13	.5	15	0	.0
38042	.8	46	.3	67	18.3	235	48.0	7	14	.2	8	0	.0
38044	1.0	0	.3	78	16.4	142	43.9	7	11	.0	0	0	.0
38046	.5	62	.2	75	21.8	199	95.5	4	17	.2	10	0	.3
38047	.3	100	.1	64	11.7	113	29.8	4	18	.2	19	0	.0
38049	3.9	35	1.2	70	17.2	203	45.4	9	14	.7	15	0	.0
38050	1.0	56	.3	79	15.5	195	39.3	9	17	.2	15	0	.1
38052	3.1	92	1.1	77	16.6	167	45.9	7	17	1.5	16	0	.0
38053	23.7	78	7.4	52	22.5	280	76.8	10	5	9.1	4	13	.8
38057	2.9	52	.9	74	19.2	196	62.7	7	10	.7	13	0	1.4
38058	2.5	95	2.1	63	22.3	261	71.2	7	9	1.2	11	0	.1
38059	5.7	91	2.1	76	20.4	249	55.2	8	16	2.6	16	0	.0
38060	2.6	56	.8	79	20.9	206	57.2	7	10	.8	12	0	.1
38061	.9	100	.3	83	22.2	51	41.6	4	13	.5	11	0	.0
38063	16.3	69	5.6	67	18.4	193	52.9	8	15	5.4	13	2	2.0
38066	2.5	37	.8	66	18.9	194	57.6	8	12	.4	12	1	.1
38067	.7	83	.2	79	17.4	195	36.0	5	13	.3	9	0	.0
38068	9.4	48	2.7	70	19.1	185	62.8	9	14	2.2	11	0	.0
38069	3.7	0	1.2	59	13.9	177	43.4	10	16	.0	0	0	.0
38070	.2	37	.1	76	16.7	148	36.9	9	22	.0	17	0	.0
38071	.2	41	1.1	84	39.1	450*	47.5	6	7	.4	12	0	2.0
38075	3.3	43	1.1	70	16.5	166	41.7	9	16	.7	18	0	.0
38076	.7	51	.2	78	25.2	164	50.8	12	14	.2	9	0	.0
38077	.7	100	.2	63	17.0	183	32.4	8	18	.1	18	0	.0
38080	4.5	77	1.6	54	18.6	182	54.2	8	15	1.7	13	1	1.7

MEMPHIS

ZIPCODE	1	2	3	4	5	6	7	8	9	10	11	12	13
38103	2.6	54	1.0	5	14.4	198	13.1	4	23	.5	17	2	10.8
38104	27.8	78	14.2	28	19.7	259	86.9	5	21	9.7	15	2	.2
38105	12.9	21	5.2	11	11.7	179	42.7	9	16	1.4	12	4	.2
38106	50.4	9	15.5	55	15.5	213	41.5	8	13	.6	24	6	.4
38107	32.9	16	10.9	45	17.5	206	46.8	8	11	2.4	22	14	1.7
38108	30.6	25	9.8	61	17.4	218	40.6	8	11	3.8	8	13	7.5
38109	70.5	8	18.9	77	20.5	238	50.8	9	6	2.9	12	21	.7
38111	42.2	75	18.2	63	25.4	308	73.5	7	17	14.4	16	2	.0
38112	22.2	50	8.8	49	19.8	262	60.4	8	16	4.9	16	10	6.7
38114	45.5	9	15.0	52	17.5	251	45.3	9	10	1.9	22	6	.0
38116	48.6	65	18.6	48	18.6	351	87.7	8	7	15.3	8	8	.6
38117	40.7	98	15.9	85	43.5	445	115.0	5	14	18.6	13	1	.0
38118	59.6	83	22.5	53	29.0	376	81.4	8	4	24.1	3	30	.5

TENNESSEE

MEMPHIS

ZIPCODE	1	2	3	4	5	6	7	8	9	10	11	12	13
38122	25.6	97	11.1	70	22.4	319	55.9	6	17	11.5	13	1	.0
38126	19.5	0	6.4	15	8.2	142	33.5	11	11	.0	0	2	.3
38127	51.9	74	17.4	67	24.0	298	56.6	9	6	18.6	6	18	5.0
38128	37.0	85	12.9	63	28.3	359	83.8	9	5	15.4	4	6	.0
38134	43.2	92	13.4	77	34.0	392	102.0	8	6	19.8	3	8	.0
38138	56.3	96	19.0	73	47.0	470	161.0	7	3	26.7	2	11	.0

MCKENZIE

ZIPCODE	1	2	3	4	5	6	7	8	9	10	11	12	13
38201	9.2	90	3.4	76	20.4	229	56.6	7	14	4.1	12	0	.0
38220	2.2	84	.8	87	17.3	233	45.7	9	14	.9	12	0	.0
38221	2.8	100	1.1	85	15.9	146	52.5	5	17	1.4	17	0	.0
38222	1.7	0	.6	91	18.1	116	62.6	8	16	.0	0	0	.0
38224	.9	0	.3	78	20.6	111	53.2	3	17	.0	0	0	.1
38225	5.9	97	2.2	78	19.0	223	52.8	6	20	2.7	18	0	.3
38226	.5	100	.5	84	14.2	405	33.6	6	21	2.2	20	0	.0
38229	2.8	99	1.0	79	19.9	260	43.5	8	15	1.4	13	0	.0
38230	3.8	94	1.5	79	18.4	204	48.0	6	20	1.7	16	0	.1
38231	1.4	90	.5	84	20.0	211	45.2	9	17	.6	16	1	.0
38232	2.3	0	.8	71	18.0	190	43.4	8	14	.0	0	0	.1
38233	3.4	93	1.2	72	20.1	217	51.0	7	15	1.5	11	0	.0
38235	.4	86	.2	83	15.7	182	44.3	6	22	.3	20	0	.0
38236	.9	90	.2	97	20.3	233*	31.9	5	15	.3	15	0	.1
38237	14.5	88	4.7	63	20.2	266	67.9	6	11	6.3	10	0	.0
38240	2.6	94	1.0	74	19.7	213	47.5	7	17	1.2	13	0	.0
38241	1.2	100	.4	87	16.5	83	43.0	5	18	.7	19	0	.0
38242	18.4	85	7.1	71	20.2	232	62.1	7	17	7.4	14	5	1.2
38251	2.5	94	1.0	81	18.4	266	48.6	6	22	1.2	18	0	.0
38253	.9	96	.4	81	16.7	99	37.9	6	16	.5	16	0	.0
38255	2.7	93	1.0	78	20.8	222	48.9	6	18	1.2	16	0	.0
38256	2.3	98	.9	86	17.5	205	59.1	8	16	1.2	16	0	.0
38258	1.6	83	.6	83	17.9	241	45.9	10	17	.7	12	0	.0
38259	.9	97	.4	81	16.5	146	49.4	6	17	.4	15	0	.0
38260	3.0	100	1.1	85	20.9	222	58.8	6	17	1.4	15	0	.3
38261	16.2	88	6.0	67	24.4	249	67.3	7	14	6.7	12	1	.0
38271	2.9	76	.5	91	19.9	228*	43.5	5	23	1.3	17	0	.0

JACKSON

ZIPCODE	1	2	3	4	5	6	7	8	9	10	11	12	13
38301	63.1	69	22.8	64	23.0	265	72.7	8	13	20.7	11	9	.6
38310	4.9	96	1.7	85	19.6	201	57.9	7	16	2.2	12	1	.2
38311	.7	0	.3	82	20.5	95	44.2	6	26	.0	0	0	.0
38313	2.0	95	.7	87	21.6	176	60.3	7	12	.8	8	0	1.1
38314	3.9	90	.8	67	15.6	264	38.3	6	19	1.6	18	6	.0
38315	3.3	96	1.2	86	15.8	172	42.2	6	17	1.3	11	0	.0
38316	2.8	94	1.1	82	19.0	166	45.3	6	14	1.3	11	0	.0
38317	2.9	94	1.1	81	19.7	251	46.3	5	18	1.2	14	0	.0
38318	.8	0	.3	84	17.0	118	45.9	6	17	.0	0	0	.0
38320	10.4	97	3.9	81	21.4	215	58.8	6	17	4.7	15	0	.0
38321	2.4	82	.8	90	18.6	120	43.0	7	12	1.0	13	0	.0
38324		2	100	83	15.9	188	47.0	5	23	.1	17	0	.6
38326	1.7	0	.6	71	20.1	234	60.6	6	13	.0	0	2	4.5
38327	.5	100	.2	88	21.5	257	49.4	3	13	.2	15	0	1.1

*=Estimated **1.0=883 lbs per person; 100++ indicates per capita toxic waste generation > than 100 times the U.S. average of 883 lbs per capita.

PAGE 2.291

ZIP CODE MEASURES OF SIZE, LEVELS OF AFFLUENCE AND QUALITY OF LIFE

1=Population (th.); 2= % White; 3=Households (th.); 4=% Owner Occupied; 5=Mean Income Per Household (th.$); 6=Mean Monthly Rent ($)*; 7=Mean Home Value (th.$)*;
8=% under 5; 9=% 65 and over; 10=White Males (th.); 11=% White Males, 65+; 12=# Toxic Waste Sites; 13=Toxic Waste Relative to US(883 lbs.per capita)**.

TENNESSEE

JACKSON

ZIPCODE	1	2	3	4	5	6	7	8	9	10	11	12	13
38328	.7	100	.3	92	18.4	86	39.9	9	19	.3	23	0	.0
38329	3.2	95	1.2	80	16.6	195	51.6	8	16	1.5	15	0	.1
38330	4.5	89	1.7		19.1	198	49.9	6	17	1.9	14	0	.0
38332	1.0		.4	83	17.2	235	36.3	5	21			0	.0
38333	.4	100	.1	74	21.1	304	67.9	4	12	.2	8	0	.0
38334	1.5	96	.5	92	14.7	140	47.4	7	12	.7	13	0	.0
38337	1.3	81	.5	81	18.9	149	49.1	6	15	.5	18	0	.0
38338	.4	0	.1	79	19.9	213	48.7	7	10	.0	0	0	.0
38339	.6	0	.2	82	17.4	179	45.8	8	9			0	.0
38340	9.0	86	2.9	73	18.6	233	56.8	7	13	3.7	10	0	.1
38341	1.6	98	.5	77	19.2	117	51.3	8	11	.8	11	0	.0
38342	1.1	87	.4	83	16.9	166	41.3	9	15	.5	14	0	.0
38343	16.1	70	5.7	71	19.9	217	57.2	8	14	5.3	13	1	.8
38344	8.9	86	3.2	79	20.1	198	56.4	6	17	3.6	14	0	.1
38345	1.4	97	.4	85	17.4	275	48.9	14	11	.6	13	0	.0
38347	.4	0	.1	81	38.9	188	63.4	3	6			0	.0
38348	.7	91	.3	80	17.7	239	40.6	2	22	.3	17	0	.0
38351	13.3	89	4.8	77	19.9	235	59.8	8	13	5.8	11	2	1
38352	.5	87	.2	71	15.9	158	57.6	8	19	.2	12	0	.0
38355	2.1	93	.8	83	21.6	208	52.8	6	16	.9	13	0	.0
38356	2.0	60	.7	77	16.1	157	48.3	8	9	.6	11	0	.0
38357	2.7	65	1.0	76	16.1	215	44.7	7	13	1.3	13	0	.0
38358	11.9	83	4.3	72	20.8	244	59.8	7	15	4.6	12	3	3.5
38359	.3	100	.1	82	16.2	212	49.7	5	19	.1	16	0	.0
38361	.7	91	.3	78	17.1	199	40.7	6	20	.3	23	0	.0
38362	.4	70	.2	88	22.1	295	55.5	11	11	.2	9	0	.0
38363	5.2	96	2.0	77	18.9	185	61.3	6	15	2.4	13	0	.6
38366	2.0	88	.7	83	19.6	245	54.1	5	14	.8	16	0	.0
38367	2.5	86	.9	83	17.1	152	51.4	9	14	1.1	20	0	.0
38368	1.6	0	.5	81	14.7	169*	42.0	8	9	.7		0	.0
38369	2.2	86	.9	78	17.2	278	47.1	8	12	.9	19	0	6.8
38370	.8	80	.3	83	18.9	230	46.9	5	22	.3	19	0	.0
38371	1.3		.4	82	12.6	159	36.3	5	23	.1	18	0	.2
38372	15.1	96	5.3	76	16.5	167	44.9	8	18	6.9	12	0	.0
38374	2.0	100	.7	84	19.0	219*	51.7	8	16	.5	25	0	.0
38375	8.1	91	3.0	78	17.1	182	46.1	7	16	3.6	15	2	1.3
38376	.5	100	.2	81	21.0	243	55.5	5	12	.3	11	0	.0
38377	1.1	100	.4	76	18.9	127	62.5	5	17	.0	16	0	.0
38379	1.1	100	.4	78	14.8	185	43.5	5	35	.3	39	0	.0
38380	.3	100	.1	78	14.7	169	42.0	6	14	.6	12	0	.0
38381	1.6	68	.5	81	18.9	181	52.0	12	20	.2	23	0	.0
38382	9.9	82	3.7	74	19.8	222	42.6	12	11	.5	10	0	.0
38387	.4	100	.1	67	14.4	166*	53.0	6	21	.3	18	0	.0
38388	1.2	87	.4	84	19.0	219*	37.9	4	21	.5	25	0	.0
38390	.6	92	.2	88	16.7	123	48.4	11	15	.2	18	0	.0
38391	1.5	0	.5	64	14.2	184	48.1	9	15	.0	0	0	.0
38392	.9	64	.3	75	16.1	104	39.1	7	18	.3	18	0	.0

COLUMBIA

ZIPCODE	1	2	3	4	5	6	7	8	9	10	11	12	13
38401	37.5	83	13.6	70	23.9	275	67.2	7	13	15.0	10	9	3.7

TENNESSEE

COLUMBIA

ZIPCODE	1	2	3	4	5	6	7	8	9	10	11	12	13
38425	1.8	94	.7	70	16.7	235	36.6	8	15	.8	13	0	.0
38449	2.2	90	.7	75	19.3	203	52.3	6	15	1.0	14	1	.0
38450	2.8	100	1.0	84	18.6	194	47.7	8	12	1.4	12	0	.0
38451	2.0	98	.6	81	22.7	316	57.9	8	10	1.0	9	0	.0
38452	1.2	100	.4	91	20.6	147	37.6	10	13	.7	15	0	.0
38453	.2	69	.1	69	9.0	103*	31.8	6	10	.1	18	0	.0
38454	.7	89	.3	97	18.4	211*	49.1	1	26	.3	26	0	.0
38455	.4	72	.1	73	17.6	233	46.6	7	12	.1	9	0	.0
38456	3.2	100	1.0	76	18.0	236	45.7	8	10	1.6	10	0	.2
38457	.9	96	.3	70	18.1	170	31.1	8	15	.4	18	0	.2
38458	.3	100	.5	95	15.2	175*	56.2	16	16	.1	16	0	.1
38459	.4	100	.1	88	12.8	147*	25.6	8	18	.1	18	1	2.0
38460	1.0	0	.3	88	21.9	273	45.8	8	14	.0	0	0	.0
38461	1.0	91	.3	79	15.9	167	61.6	3	9	.4	11	0	.2
38462	7.6	98	2.7	76	17.6	192	47.6	7	14	3.5	12	1	.2
38463	2.3	0	.8	80	18.2	205	43.9	6	11	.0	0	1	.1
38464	18.6	97	6.7	74	20.5	237	64.5	8	14	8.7	11	2	2.0
38468	4.0	0	1.3	80	22.0	216	67.3	7	11	.0	0	0	.0
38469	3.4	0	1.1	82	22.5	232	59.7	7	9	.3	19	0	.0
38471	.6	100	.2	91	14.9	172*	30.6	5	17	.3	19	0	.0
38472	2.5	89	.8	77	21.1	137	43.7	7	16	1.1	15	0	.0
38473	1.2	95	.4	81	18.0	241	43.9	6	16	.6	13	0	.0
38474	7.0	77	2.5	72	19.7	207	48.4	7	15	2.7	10	10	14.1
38475	.4	100	.1	89	16.8	194*	32.9	9		.2	8	0	.0
38476	.6	0	.2	71	24.2	224	69.0	6	16	.3	23	0	.0
38477	2.0	83	.7	84	21.3	78	44.4	9	13	.8	12	0	.0
38478	15.3	83	5.7	68	20.7	229	60.7	6	15	6.1	12	1	2.2
38481	1.0	0	.4	78	21.1	153	46.5	7	14	.7	14	0	4.0
38482	1.5	96	.5	76	22.3	172	43.5	7	13	.7	10	0	.0
38483	4.2	99	1.9	88	18.9	210	41.8	13	8	2.1	9	0	.0
38485	5.9	99	2.0	81	18.8	229	50.6	7	12	2.8	11	2	.1
38486	1.0	96	.3	82	20.5	145	39.1	3	17	.6	16	0	.0
38487	.6	82	.2	76	22.4	155	64.7	4	11	.2	11	0	.0
38488	1.5	0	.6	74	20.3	264	57.0	7	15	.0	0	0	.0

COOKEVILLE

ZIPCODE	1	2	3	4	5	6	7	8	9	10	11	12	13
38501	39.9	97	14.1	66	21.1	268	80.0	6	11	19.1	9	3	.5
38504	1.1	100	.4	90	13.8	169	47.5	6	12	.6	9	0	.0
38541	1.5	100	.5	81	13.8	125	47.9	7	15	.7	14	0	.0
38543	.8	100	.3	85	14.1	245	60.9	10	6	.4	13	0	.0
38544	5.2	100	1.9	81	20.0	196	59.6	6	13	2.6	13	0	.0
38545	1.1	100	.3	92	18.7	145	42.9	12	9	.6	7	0	.0
38546	.5	100	.3	90	21.9	323	48.2	3	20	.2	25	0	.0
38547	1.0	100	.3	82	21.1	127	47.8	6	10	.5	12	0	.0
38548	.9	100	.3	85	19.2	150	44.2	6	13	.4	13	0	.0
38549	3.0	98	1.1	85	15.1	158	50.2	7	15	1.4	16	0	.0
38551	3.8	96	1.4	81	17.0	168	55.2	7	14	1.8	12	0	.0
38552	.4	100	.7	73	18.9	244	33.0	12	21	.2	22	0	.0
38553	2.2	100	.7	82	13.6	189	35.9	7	12	1.1	11	0	.0
38554	.3	85	.3	85	12.8	119	35.9	7	6	.5	3	0	.0

*=Estimated **1.0=883 lbs per person; 100++ indicates per capita toxic waste generation > than 100 times the U.S. average of 883 lbs per capita.

ZIP CODE MEASURES OF SIZE, LEVELS OF AFFLUENCE AND QUALITY OF LIFE

1=Population (th.); 2= % White; 3=Households (th.); 4=% Owner Occupied; 5=Mean Income Per Household (th.$); 6=Mean Monthly Rent ($)*; 7=Mean Home Value (th.$)*;
8=% under 5; 9=% 65 and over; 10=White Males (th.); 11=% White Males; 12=# Toxic Waste Sites; 13=Toxic Waste Relative to US(883 lbs.per capita)**.

TENNESSEE

ZIP CODE	1	2	3	4	5	6	7	8	9	10	11	12	13
COOKEVILLE													
38555	25.2	100	8.7	78	20.0	223	67.3	7	12	12.3	11	0	.0
38556	10.2	100	3.5	76	14.4	175	43.5	7	12	4.9	11	0	.0
38559	1.2	99	.4	90	17.4	212	44.3	7	17	.6	13	0	.0
38560	1.1	88	.4	72	21.1	174	42.2	5	17	.4	17	0	.0
38562	5.7	0	2.0	77	17.7	179	57.3	6	16	.0	0	0	.2
38563	1.6	0	.5	81	22.4	290	59.2	7	14	.2	0	0	.2
38564	.4	100	.2	90	14.9	82	60.4	5	24	.2	23	0	.0
38565	.4	100	.1	77	10.5	105	42.0	14	13	.2	11	0	.0
38567	.3	86	.1	100	19.4	223*	52.5	6	11	.1	11	0	.0
38568	1.5	100	.5	80	15.0	136	45.3	7	13	.8	12	0	.0
38570	8.7	99	3.2	79	18.4	199	56.0	7	15	4.2	13	0	.0
38573	1.8	100	.6	90	19.0	60	36.3	8	15	1.0	14	0	.0
38574	5.6	100	2.0	75	15.8	221	42.5	6	16	2.8	14	0	.0
38575	1.6	100	.5	73	14.1	247	36.8	5	13	.7	12	0	.0
38577	1.4	100	.4	78	12.4	207	45.8	5	16	.7	15	0	.0
38578	.5	0	.2	53	15.0	191	50.3	6	39	.0	0	0	.0
38579	.8	100	.3	88	22.4	202	38.6	2	17	.4	16	0	.0
38580	1.2	0	.4	76	17.0	267	49.1	9	8	.0	0	0	.0
38581	2.8	97	1.0	89	19.8	268	55.1	12	14	1.4	5	0	.0
38582	1.3	0	.4	88	16.7	127	47.1	8	14	.0	0	0	.1
38583	16.6	97	5.9	80	18.9	221	58.4	7	14	7.7	12	0	.0
38585	3.7	100	1.2	85	19.5	151	43.8	10	8	1.9	6	0	.2
38587	1.1	100	.4	89	18.8	354	49.9	6	12	.5	11	0	.0
	.8	0	.3	90	19.1	170	25.4	5	18	.7	15	0	.0
PADUCAH													
42041	5.0	82	1.9	78	21.8	226	52.4	7	17	1.9	15	0	.3
42049	.2	0	.1	100	23.1	265*	48.4	5	39	.0	0	0	.0
42050	.7	100	.2	91	21.4	302	47.3	9	6	.4	6	0	.0
BOWLING GREEN (EAST)													
42120	.5	100	.2	95	13.8	158*	33.3	5	11	.2	21	0	.0
BOWLING GREEN (WEST)													
42223	8.9	64	1.4	9	23.8	393	73.0	8	0	3.6	0	0	.0
42234	.8	63	.3	83	20.5	284	44.2	8	14	.3	8	0	.0
42262	.9	75	.3	83	22.7	284	77.9	11	2	.4	3	0	.0

TEXAS

ZIP CODE	1	2	3	4	5	6	7	8	9	10	11	12	13
SHREVEPORT													
71007	.4	84	.1	87	23.9	278	34.7	7	11	.2	7	0	.0
71046	.4	79	.1	93	25.8	296*	47.0	20	3	.1	4	0	.0
71049	.6	93	.2	91	17.5	143	33.2	9	15	.3	14	0	.0
LIBERAL													
73949	.5	90	.2	87	23.7	83	47.5	6	17	.2	18	0	.0
DALLAS													
75002	9.2	94	3.0	80	35.1	549	109.6	12	4	4.3	3	0	.0
75003	2.2	97	.7	76	27.4	248	61.5	9	13	1.0	12	0	.0
75004	1.7	0	.6	84	24.4	187	39.9	5	17	.0	0	1	.0
75005	2.0	85	.7	78	20.3	195	50.1	8	14	.9	14	2	.0
75006	31.2	92	11.4	65	37.7	452	122.2	8	4	14.0	3	4	2.6
75007	10.1	93	3.2	93	41.5	360	133.2	11	4	4.7	1	0	.0
75009	2.3	86	.9	76	26.0	211	53.9	6	21	.9	18	0	.0
75018	.5	0	.2	78	19.0	247	38.6	6	19	.0	0	0	.0
75019	3.3	95	1.1	84	37.5	386	128.4	8	4	1.6	4	0	.4
75020	29.7	90	11.4	71	24.2	281	55.8	7	15	12.8	12	4	.0
75023	21.3	95	6.3	86	44.6	588	161.0	11	1	10.2	1	0	.0
75028	2.5	99	.8	91	43.9	487	155.0	9	3	1.3	3	0	.0
75030	.1	100	.1	93	26.4	303*	51.1	3	24	.1	15	0	.0
75031	4.0	89	1.5	79	24.3	225	54.0	7	20	1.7	17	1	.0
75032	.4	90	.1	70	20.2	194	52.1	13	16	.2	13	0	.0
75034	6.5	90	2.2	73	29.9	319	93.7	9	7	3.0	7	2	2.7
75040	35.2	78	10.9	76	29.7	415	81.3	11	5	13.6	4	6	2.3
75041	24.9	97	9.0	69	31.3	405	83.5	7	7	11.8	6	6	.4
75042	48.4	92	16.5	70	33.3	432	100.3	9	4	21.8	3	2	.0
75043	31.7	95	9.9	86	38.0	560	112.0	10	2	14.8	2	0	.0
75050	26.4	89	9.2	66	30.7	350	88.7	9	7	11.5	7	10	2.0
75051	39.4	82	12.7	69	27.7	352	72.3	9	5	15.7	4	0	.2
75052	4.7	91	1.5	92	31.4	583	105.0	14	2	2.0	2	0	.0
75056	12.4	95	4.0	85	34.2	628	100.2	14	2	6.1	2	0	.0
75058	1.4	98	.4	67	23.8	240	49.6	8	26	.6	17	0	.0
75059	2.5	96	.8	71	26.0	278	56.9	13	8	1.2	11	3	.6
75060	35.4	93	12.5	62	27.9	389	82.4	9	6	16.0	5	3	.6
75061	34.7	91	13.0	48	29.2	386	95.6	7	6	16.1	5	5	.2
75062	40.6	95	15.1	51	35.4	437	114.2	6	3	18.9	3	1	.2
75064	.4	0	.2	78	31.3	209	42.9	9	15	.0	0	0	.0
75065	4.4	97	1.5	81	32.0	363	101.5	9	6	2.2	5	2	.0
75066	.3	96	.1	87	29.5	106	78.7	3	15	.1	17	0	.0
75067	29.2	95	9.3	78	35.7	401	110.8	9	5	13.8	4	2	.1
75068	.5	97	.2	61	25.2	378	83.5	10	7	.3	8	0	.6
75069	25.5	85	8.6	69	27.3	255	82.2	8	12	10.6	10	3	.6
75071	1.2	97	.4	87	22.2	330	45.4	9	9	.6	8	0	.6
75073	.9	81	.3	87	33.3	190	59.5	6	11	.3	5	1	.2
75074	24.7	90	7.8	71	32.4	418	109.9	9	4	11.0	3	1	.4
75075	28.2	97	8.6	80	44.3	454	167.7	8	2	13.8	1	1	.2
75076	3.6	100	1.4	82	24.6	329	65.7	5	16	1.8	15	0	.2
75077	2.8	98	1.0	75	23.2	276	56.1	8	11	1.3	11	1	.0
75078	.7	95	.2	76	25.7	306	63.8	5	13	.3	10	0	.4
75080	39.8	97	13.3	75	44.4	531	143.7	5	4	19.0	4	0	.4

*=Estimated **1.0=883 lbs per person; 100++ indicates per capita toxic waste generation > than 100 times the U.S. average of 883 lbs per capita.

ZIP CODE MEASURES OF SIZE, LEVELS OF AFFLUENCE AND QUALITY OF LIFE

1=Population (th.); 2= % White; 3=Households (th.); 4=% Owner Occupied; 5=Mean Income Per Household (th.$); 6=Mean Monthly Rent ($)*; 7=Mean Home Value (th.$)*;
8=% under 5; 9=% 65 and over; 10=White Males (th.); 11=% White Males, 65+; 12=# Toxic Waste Sites; 13=Toxic Waste Relative to US(883 lbs.per capita)**.

103001

TEXAS

DALLAS

ZIP CODE	1	2	3	4	5	6	7	8	9	10	11	12	13
75081	33.0	93	10.9	75	41.9	536	149.4	9	3	15.3	3	2	.1
75087	11.0	95	3.6	81	42.8	332	140.6	7	7	5.2	5	2	.9
75088	6.9	89	2.1	91	36.1	371	106.8	11	4	3.1	4	1	.0
75089	3.2	88	1.1	78	25.6	223	60.3	8	14	1.4	12	0	.0
75090	35.0	89	13.3	66	25.9	278	67.8	8	14	14.9	11	1	.8

DALLAS

ZIP CODE	1	2	3	4	5	6	7	8	9	10	11	12	13
75095	3.1	95	1.2	78	21.8	254	60.1	6	18	1.4	15	0	.0
75096	.3	100	.1	80	21.7	245	36.9	8	11	.2	8	0	.0
75098	7.8	98	2.5	85	30.4	309	95.1	7	9	3.7	7	2	.1

DALLAS

ZIP CODE	1	2	3	4	5	6	7	8	9	10	11	12	13
75101	.4	63	.1	81	21.8	249	33.7	8	15	.1	21	0	.0
75102	.7	94	.3	85	22.0	253*	49.0	6	26	.3	22	0	.0
75103	7.7	96	2.8	82	23.4	279	60.7	7	18	3.5	15	4	.0
75104	6.0	97	1.9	79	33.6	417	97.8	7	6	3.0	5	0	.0
75105	.3	85	.1	79	25.7	603	91.5*	13	15	.1	25	0	.0
75110	25.4	75	9.6	69	22.8	261	56.6	7	19	8.9	17	2	.4
75114	1.3	79	.4	81	36.2	252	53.2	7	13	.5	10	0	.3
75115	16.7	94	5.2	85	38.7	486	114.9	7	6	7.7	5	0	.0
75116	17.4	97	5.6	73	35.3	450	99.2	7	6	8.4	5	0	.1
75117	2.6	93	1.0	77	21.8	233	55.8	8	18	1.1	14	1	.0

DALLAS

ZIP CODE	1	2	3	4	5	6	7	8	9	10	11	12	13
75118	.2	100	.1	91	22.4	257*	40.6	9	9	.1	11	0	.0
75119	16.5	77	5.6	74	25.1	276	57.9	8	15	6.1	12	2	.6
75124	1.8	0	.7	80	21.1	238	52.6	5	19	.0	12	1	.0
75125	3.4	63	1.1	67	19.7	221	49.9	10	14	1.0	12	1	3.3
75126	4.5	93	1.6	83	31.1	286	88.8	7	7	2.0	7	0	.0
75127	.9	96	.3	75	20.4	244	48.2	5	15	.4	13	0	.0
75134	6.8	85	2.1	85	27.1	339	61.0	9	6	2.8	8	0	.0
75137	10.5	95	3.2	86	43.2	441	128.7	9	3	4.8	2	0	.0
75140	5.5	99	2.1	78	21.1	202	48.9	7	20	2.6	17	0	3.2
75141	2.7	62	.9	81	25.6	297	50.3	8	8	.9	12	0	.5
75142	8.1	84	2.8	77	26.7	266	60.2	7	14	3.1	12	4	.3
75143	7.6	96	2.9	87	23.5	214	68.2	6	16	3.6	16	0	.0
75144	2.9	66	1.1	77	17.4	189	36.8	7	21	.9	21	1	.0
75146	9.1	97	3.1	80	31.0	363	79.2	7	13	4.1	9	0	.5
75147	7.4	97	2.9	87	24.5	226	75.2	5	19	3.5	18	0	.0
75148	4.0	81	1.5	78	22.7	244	66.4	7	21	1.6	18	1	.0
75149	36.4	96	11.4	73	29.3	356	65.8	9	5	17.0	4	3	.3
75150	31.3	95	10.1	74	32.7	422	82.5	8	4	14.6	3	0	.2
75151	1.2	0	.6	70	25.5	293*	65.6	6	25	.0	18	0	.0
75152	1.9	87	.8	82	26.5	283	52.9	5	12	.8	10	3	.0
75153	.2	0	.1	81	19.7	133	58.1	3	15	.0	9	0	.5
75154	9.8	96	3.0	88	31.5	362	93.0	9	5	4.8	4	1	.0
75155	.7	95	.2	79	23.2	314	49.1	7	12	.3	11	0	1.0
75157	.3	0	.1	89	20.9	240*	34.6	9	13	.0	9	0	.0
75158	1.8	94	.6	93	26.4	162	60.0	7	8	.9	9	0	.0
75159	9.1	86	3.0	80	26.8	339	60.9	8	9	4.0	8	1	.0
75160	17.3	67	5.8	71	24.1	261	57.9	7	15	5.6	14	2	1.0
75163	1.4	86	.6	65	18.0	254	55.7	8	20	.3	18	0	.0
75165	18.0	78	6.2	67	24.7	270	67.3	8	15	6.7	12	7	.2
75169	8.2	92	3.1	82	23.1	246	58.1	6	16	3.8	16	1	.0

TEXAS

DALLAS

ZIP CODE	1	2	3	4	5	6	7	8	9	10	11	12	13
75172	2.4	74	.7	71	24.1	311	33.2	13	7	.9	9	1	.0
75180	13.6	94	3.9	82	26.9	379	52.9	10	6	6.3	5	1	.0
75181	2.5	99	.9	87	29.2	329	77.5	8	4	1.3	5	0	.0
75182	.9	0	.3	89	43.4	390	152.9	5	6	.0	0	0	.0

DALLAS

ZIP CODE	1	2	3	4	5	6	7	8	9	10	11	12	13
75201	3.0	45	1.0	16	30.8	296	65.5	4	15	.8	17	0	13.7
75202	2.2	56	.2	0	62.2	367	221.6*	0	5	1.0	5	2	.7
75203	21.9	22	8.0	29	16.3	247	38.1	10	9	2.5	10	2	.1
75204	18.5	36	8.0	17	17.9	261	76.0	9	9	3.7	17	1	.0
75205	24.2	96	10.2	51	51.3	448	290.9	3	14	10.4	10	4	.4
75206	32.9	81	18.4	25	23.2	406	86.6	5	13	12.3	9	1	.0
75207	.4	38	.1	40	15.3	341	51.3	4	10	.1	4	2	69.0
75208	29.6	68	11.5	49	23.1	277	70.4	9	16	9.1	16	0	.2
75209	15.2	60	5.2	57	33.4	357	145.9	6	17	4.4	16	0	.1
75210	14.0	1	4.6	31	12.8	219	31.0	17	0	.0	17	1	.1
75211	50.0	71	17.8	56	22.0	305	48.4	9	12	17.0	12	1	.2
75212	30.1	13	8.0	39	13.8	145	27.5	11	8	1.9	7	9	.0
75214	31.7	87	14.8	59	32.9	369	135.3	5	20	12.5	18	0	.6
75215	30.1	2	10.9	31	13.1	203	34.0	10	13	.3	21	1	.0
75216	65.6	6	19.1	57	19.9	298	41.7	10	8	1.8	28	3	.4
75217	54.1	70	17.7	69	23.2	310	49.0	8	8	18.5	13	4	.0
75218	22.9	96	9.8	68	32.0	421	103.6	6	16	10.0	13	0	.0
75219	19.0	69	10.9	17	25.0	371	130.2	5	9	7.1	5	0	.9
75220	24.4	83	11.8	37	32.9	408	130.3	6	8	10.3	7	3	2.3
75223	14.0	40	4.9	47	18.5	269	50.0	9	14	2.5	19	0	.1
75224	27.4	49	10.2	59	24.3	345	60.9	9	11	6.2	18	0	.1
75226	.8	64	.4	8	15.2	193	106.5	8	11	.2	23	0	40.2
75227	27.6	89	10.5	70	26.5	286	69.4	7	13	11.6	11	0	1.2
75228	47.8	92	18.1	65	30.2	404	85.1	7	9	20.7	8	2	.1
75229	30.2	93	11.0	75	58.3	470	183.6	8	8	13.8	8	6	.4
75230	23.2	97	12.1	55	47.8	510	218.4	6	15	10.2	15	0	.9
75231	30.4	91	19.5	13	27.0	413	200.4	3	13	13.7	2	1	.2
75232	30.4	34	9.7	74	30.3	338	81.3	5	9	4.9	12	0	.2
75233	11.0	57	4.1	55	32.1	449	94.4	7	10	3.1	10	0	.4
75234	42.7	93	16.4	56	38.4	455	137.9	6	6	19.2	7	1	1.5
75235	14.0	58	5.8	36	22.7	372	60.9	8	11	4.2	8	4	4.2
75236	2.2	93	.9	52	26.4	394	77.9	9	6	1.0	4	2	1.2
75237	2.9	32	1.2	32	30.0	441	102.7	8	7	.4	6	0	1.3
75238	25.2	96	9.0	65	41.5	409	147.9	7	13	11.5	11	1	.2
75239	4.0	3	1.1	85	17.5	292	31.2	9	9	.6	48	2	.0
75240	19.6	91	8.6	36	44.1	434	249.7	7	5	8.7	4	6	.0
75241	29.5	3	7.8	74	24.4	279	55.3	8	4	.4	14	1	1.5
75243	27.0	79	11.6	42	35.7	381	180.6	7	4	10.6	2	2	.0
75246	6.0	50	2.1	8	13.5	232	74.9	10	4	1.4	2	2	.1
75248	36.6	95	16.1	42	48.5	401	254.0	4	9	17.2	2	0	.4
75249	5.3	80	1.7	90	33.5	742	101.7	13	5	4.2	2	0	.1
75252	1.3	99	.5	93	54.8	175	232.7	8	3	2.1	3	0	.0
75253	5.6	96	1.9	71	22.8	335	50.8	11	7	2.7	7	1	.0

*=Estimated **1.0=883 lbs per person; 100+ indicates per capita toxic waste generation > than 100 times the U.S. average of 883 lbs per capita.

ZIP CODE MEASURES OF SIZE, LEVELS OF AFFLUENCE AND QUALITY OF LIFE

1=Population (th.); 2= % White; 3=Households (th.); 4=% Owner Occupied; 5=Mean Income Per Household (th.$); 6=Mean Monthly Rent ($)*; 7=Mean Home Value (th.$)*;
8=% under 5; 9=% 65 and over; 10=White Males (th.); 11=% White Males, 65+; 12=# Toxic Waste Sites; 13=Toxic Waste Relative to US(883 lbs.per capita)**.

TEXAS

GREENVILLE

ZIPCODE	1	2	3	4	5	6	7	8	9	10	11	12	13
75401	27.2	80	10.0	66	22.7	262	59.8	8	15	10.3	13	6	1.3
75410	1.9	0	.8	83	18.2	207	51.3	5	22	.0	0	0	.0
75411	1.1	96	.4	70	18.0	241	35.0	4	15	.5	12	0	.0
75412	.7	91	.3	86	18.2	127	26.8	7	23	.3	21	0	.0
75413	.2	100	.1	72	16.9	220	28.3	7	31	.1	27	0	.0
75414	1.7	98	.6	78	20.7	201	47.7	7	18	.8	15	1	.0
75415	.2	0	.1	70	16.0	221	21.9	4	34	.0	0	0	.0
75416	2.3	96	.8	84	19.1	174	39.6	8	14	1.1	13	0	.0
75417	2.8	98	1.0	78	16.8	180	33.0	6	29	1.3	24	0	.0
75418	9.8	92	3.8	72	21.2	225	47.4	6	23	4.4	21	2	1.6
75420	.5	100	.2	86	25.7	106	31.3	7	23	.3	16	0	.0
75421	.9	65	.3	88	15.7	217	28.9	9	15	.3	16	0	.0
75422	1.9	93	.5	91	24.3	211	70.4	10	14	.7	15	1	.0
75423	1.7	97	.6	81	20.2	133	37.1	7	18	.8	19	0	.0
75426	8.0	70	3.1	73	18.7	202	40.7	8	19	2.7	16	3	.3
75428	9.7	84	3.6	48	19.8	240	57.9	5	14	3.9	11	4	.0
75431	1.4	90	.6	80	19.1	223	37.7	5	22	.6	21	0	.0
75432	3.1	87	1.2	72	17.4	168	36.4	7	27	1.2	25	1	.0
75433	1.7	100	.7	83	20.9	197	48.1	7	21	.7	19	0	.0
75435	1.3	89	.5	74	20.7	177	40.8	6	21	.5	21	0	.1
75436	1.9	76	.7	76	14.3	148	27.5	5	19	.7	15	0	.0
75437	.7	97	.3	85	17.3	290	40.9	11	15	.3	14	0	.0
75438	.7	99	.2	83	26.1	263	31.7	6	22	.3	24	0	.0
75439	.7	99	.3	73	18.2	203	36.1	6	25	.3	25	0	.0
75440	2.6	90	1.0	78	22.1	220	48.9	7	18	1.1	18	0	.0
75443	.4	100	.1	89	20.4	234*	36.0	2	12	.2	8	0	.0
75446	.2	100	.1	83	17.0	359	42.7	12	34	.1	37	0	.0
75447	3.1	86	1.3	70	17.7	155	37.5	6	27	1.3	24	1	.0
75448	.7	100	.2	74	23.1	241	45.1	7	17	.4	15	1	.0
75449	.5	96	.2	90	16.3	282	33.5	3	29	.2	8	0	.0
75450	1.1	68	.4	78	15.5	140	26.6	4	16	.2	16	0	.0
75451	.4	100	.1	79	24.9	207	50.4	7	20	.3	10	0	.0
75452	2.6	74	1.0	80	20.8	424	50.8	7	17	1.1	17	0	.0
75453	1.6	93	.7	75	20.4	178	41.9	3	32	.7	20	2	.2
75455	18.8	83	6.7	74	24.3	270	59.1	9	15	7.5	13	2	.2
75457	3.9	89	1.5	76	22.1	239	53.5	8	20	1.6	17	0	.2
75460	31.0	82	11.8	65	20.3	247	48.5	8	14	12.1	15	5	.4
75468	.7	0	.2	75	22.8	155	41.1	6	21	.3	0	0	.0
75469	.4	94	.2	69	17.6	165	38.4	3	32	.2	30	1	.0
75471	.9	87	.3	74	18.5	120	41.5	10	14	.3	17	0	.0
75472	1.4	94	.5	80	22.9	204	42.9	6	19	.5	16	3	.2
75473	2.0	91	.6	87	23.1	288	52.2	7	11	.9	10	0	.0
75474	7.7	98	2.7	90	24.0	280	53.7	6	12	3.8	12	3	.0
75475	.2	94	.1	71	18.1	291	38.9	7	23	.7	16	0	.2
75476	1.0	0	.4	72	18.7	298	53.8	5	13	.0	0	1	.0
75477	.8	66	.3	69	15.5	168	33.6	5	26	.3	28	0	.0
75478	.8	96	.2	73	21.1	254	33.7	10	14	.4	12	0	.0

TEXAS

GREENVILLE

ZIPCODE	1	2	3	4	5	6	7	8	9	10	11	12	13
75479	1.5	97	.5	77	20.5	231	43.3	3	25	.7	22	0	.0
75480	.8	100	.3	92	48.0	185	76.7	4	15	.5	16	0	.0
75481	.3	100	.1	82	20.4	235*	60.9	5	22	.2	19	0	.0
75482	18.7	87	7.0	68	22.6	279	55.3	7	18	7.7	16	1	.1
75486	1.4	100	.5	89	19.9	155	52.1	9	10	.7	10	1	.0
75487	1.5	87	.6	77	17.7	201	28.2	6	20	.6	20	0	.0
75488	1.0	0	.4	83	15.2	159	35.5	6	18	.0	0	0	.0
75489	.8	0	.3	72	21.0	198	56.3	9	14	.0	0	0	.0
75490	.8	79	.3	74	18.5	195	40.6	8	22	.3	24	0	.1
75491	3.0	92	1.0	77	23.4	222	43.5	8	19	1.2	14	0	.0
75492	.5	83	.2	86	19.2	128	29.5	3	21	.2	19	0	.0
75493	.4	100	.2	87	21.0	219	45.3	10	18	.2	16	0	.1
75494	7.6	97	2.9	79	20.5	236	56.1	7	21	3.4	19	0	.0
75496	2.6	87	1.0	78	22.7	225	38.4	5	21	1.2	17	0	.0
75497	1.0	0	.4	80	24.4	219	51.2	7	16	.0	0	0	.0

TEXARKANA

ZIPCODE	1	2	3	4	5	6	7	8	9	10	11	12	13
75501	35.8	68	13.3	66	20.2	252	55.5	9	14	11.4	12	4	.6
75503	14.4	91	5.2	75	33.1	371	96.4	7	10	6.4	9	0	.0
75550	1.2	65	.4	81	18.0	200	34.9	8	15	.4	19	0	.1
75551	10.4	82	3.8	80	23.8	256	59.2	8	17	4.0	16	0	.0
75554	1.1	96	.4	79	17.9	140	37.4	7	18	.8	14	0	.0
75555	1.1	83	.4	88	20.9	282	49.0	8	12	.5	7	0	.0
75556	.8	84	.3	81	19.4	263	47.5	8	17	.3	11	0	.0
75557	.2	0	.1	100	22.4	257*	64.6	8	13	.0	0	0	.0
75558	.9	100	.3	81	27.8	356	36.1	4	16	.4	18	0	.0
75559	6.0	76	2.3	78	19.1	202	45.8	9	21	2.3	19	0	.0
75560	.4	48	.1	77	17.3	104	38.7	9	13	.3	7	0	.1
75561	4.6	81	1.7	80	21.2	280	47.6	7	13	1.8	10	0	.0
75562	.4	56	.1	86	29.3	337*	37.6	10	5	.1	10	0	.0
75563	4.4	82	1.6	75	21.2	226	49.6	7	18	1.7	14	1	.2
75564	.3	43	.1	88	26.9	309*	53.9	15	9	.1	11	0	.0
75565	.4	88	.1	89	35.1	89	40.9	6	22	.2	18	0	.0
75566	1.0	31	.3	85	18.6	207	33.3	7	17	.2	29	0	.0
75567	2.7	89	1.0	83	22.9	203	55.1	6	14	1.2	10	0	.0
75568	3.5	72	1.3	79	20.4	186	46.6	8	21	1.2	18	1	.0
75569	1.8	86	.6	81	23.9	230	58.2	9	7	.7	6	0	.6
75570	7.3	82	2.6	77	22.4	200	55.9	7	13	2.8	12	0	.0
75571	2.9	59	1.1	75	19.4	230	48.3	7	19	.8	19	0	.3
75572	3.0	77	1.0	77	19.1	260	46.3	7	15	1.1	11	0	.0
75573	1.3	86	.2	98	22.4	257*	53.8	7	15	.3	15	0	.0
75574	1.3	0	.3	79	19.3	163	33.4	6	11	.0	0	0	.0

LONGVIEW

ZIPCODE	1	2	3	4	5	6	7	8	9	10	11	12	13
75601	25.8	85	9.9	63	29.0	344	93.9	7	13	10.6	10	6	16.0
75602	18.6	52	6.4	66	22.0	293	55.5	9	12	4.9	12	3	.4
75603	6.8	76	2.5	73	23.4	334	71.4	9	9	2.6	8	1	.8
75604	21.9	94	7.6	66	30.0	352	87.0	9	7	10.3	5	3	.8
75605	6.9	93	2.3	80	29.8	394	96.4	8	6	3.2	4	0	.0
75630	2.5	77	.9	79	20.4	256	54.7	8	16	.9	17	0	.3
75631	2.5	83	.9	74	22.2	301	51.7	9	13	1.0	8	0	.0

*=Estimated **1.0=883 lbs per person; 100++ indicates per capita toxic waste generation > than 100 times the U.S. average of 883 lbs per capita.

ZIP CODE MEASURES OF SIZE, LEVELS OF AFFLUENCE AND QUALITY OF LIFE

1=Population (th.); 2= % White; 3=Households (th.); 4=% Owner Occupied; 5=Mean Income Per Household (th.$)*; 6=Mean Monthly Rent ($)*; 7=Mean Home Value (th.$)*; 8=% under 5; 9=% 65 and over; 10=White Males (th.); 11=% White Males (th.); 12=# Toxic Waste Sites; 13=Toxic Waste Relative to US(883 lbs.per capita)**.

TEXAS — LONGVIEW / TYLER

ZIP CODE	1	2	3	4	5	6	7	8	9	10	11	12	13
LONGVIEW													
75633	11.4	80	4.2	81	25.4	250	64.4	8	17	4.3	15	0	.0
75636	.4	40	.1	95	21.2	244*	40.0	7	15	.1	9	0	.0
75638	6.5	85	2.2	77	27.2	271	62.7	9	11	2.7	10	0	.0
75639	1.7	59	.6	90	18.1	71	40.8	9	14	.4	6	0	.0
75640	2.8	87	.9	85	24.6	311	63.9	8	11	1.2	10	0	.0
75641	.3	0	.1	81	12.6	438	28.1	17	9	.0	0	0	.0
75642	.3	79	.1	100	32.0	368*	60.6	17	10	.1	0	0	.0
75643	1.4	88	.5	82	20.4	201	39.5	7	15	.6	12	0	.0
75644	15.3	81	5.5	78	22.6	220	55.4	8	17	5.9	15	2	.0
75647	10.3	84	3.7	74	22.3	211	60.1	8	14	4.2	12	2	.2
75651	4.4	85	1.4	81	26.9	336	67.9	8	8	1.9	8	0	.0
75652	1.5	73	.4	85	20.0	163	48.3	11	9	.6	8	0	.0
75656	21.3	78	7.6	77	23.5	284	61.8	8	18	8.0	15	2	.0
75657	5.2	81	1.7	77	22.6	228	54.1	8	13	2.1	11	0	.0
75658	7.9	63	3.0	78	17.0	218	45.6	8	19	2.5	16	1	.0
75660	.3	64	.1	85	20.2	199	28.4	11	16	.1	6	0	.0
75661	2.8	0	.0	39	20.1	387	93.3	10	16	.0	8	0	5.9
75662	20.7	82	7.7	82	21.3	213	46.0	8	14	8.2	13	7	.8
75666	.6	0	.2	70	21.8	388	35.4	14	11	.0	0	0	.0
75667	1.2	65	.4	84	20.0	191	41.2	5	23	.4	29	0	.0
75668	2.2	98	.7	70	28.4	315	58.6	10	6	1.1	5	1	53.0
75670	32.7	70	11.7	82	13.7	265	58.5	8	16	9.5	31	6	3.6
75681	2.1	64	.8	83	22.5	192	47.7	5	22	.7	20	0	.1
75682	.8	95	.3	87	22.0	236	49.6	6	30	.3	24	0	4.3
75683	3.5	82	1.3	81	21.5	268	44.2	6	16	1.4	10	0	.0
75684	5.1	78	1.9	79	22.2	237	47.0	8	20	1.8	17	0	.0
75685	.2	0	.2	86	23.3	268*	54.3	4	23	.0	0	0	.0
75686	9.4	74	3.5	75	23.1	238	51.7	8	16	3.4	14	3	.1
75687	.2	0	.2	100	23.5	270*	38.6	10	25	.0	5	0	.0
75689	.3	100	.1	89	30.1	346*	47.6	9	10	1.2	8	0	.0
75691	3.1	76	1.0	76	22.1	275	49.0	10	13	1.2	8	0	.0
75692	3.7	69	1.2	77	24.2	281	65.0	8	11	1.3	9	1	.5
75693	4.2	100	1.4	71	30.1	345	78.4	9	8	2.1	7	1	.1
TYLER													
75701	32.6	84	12.0	69	31.1	374	88.7	7	16	12.7	13	2	1.2
75702	27.1	44	9.7	50	18.1	260	45.4	9	13	5.6	15	3	.0
75703	13.4	92	5.1	57	35.2	369	138.1	8	6	6.1	5	0	.0
75704	2.8	74	1.0	89	28.1	298	71.5	7	10	1.1	10	0	.1
75705	2.3	36	.7	83	23.9	268	58.2	8	10	.4	13	0	.0
75706	8.7	77	3.0	83	22.3	326	62.7	8	10	3.3	10	0	.0
75707	7.6	93	2.7	77	28.9	357	88.0	9	8	3.5	7	0	.0
75708	3.5	83	1.2	80	20.7	269	65.0	8	11	1.5	11	0	.0
75709	1.7	91	.5	84	33.9	470	104.4	11	4	.8	4	0	.0
75750	2.5	88	.9	85	23.2	238	51.4	7	14	1.1	12	0	.1
75751	17.1	86	6.2	73	23.3	239	63.6	7	16	7.0	13	3	.0
75754	3.1	87	1.1	89	17.1	190	51.3	5	18	1.3	22	0	.0
75755	4.0	88	1.4	77	21.3	219	55.2	9	15	1.7	20	0	.0

TEXAS — TYLER / PALESTINE

ZIP CODE	1	2	3	4	5	6	7	8	9	10	11	12	13
TYLER													
75756	2.1	100	.8	85	26.7	188	60.6	7	15	1.0	14	0	.0
75757	3.6	89	1.3	86	29.5	328	89.8	5	17	1.6	16	0	.0
75758	3.5	84	1.4	83	22.1	310	66.9	6	15	1.4	14	0	.0
75759	.2	0	.1	72	30.3	173	41.9	6	25	.1	0	0	.0
75760	2.3	74	.9	80	15.6	207	35.9	7	26	.8	23	0	.2
75762	3.3	90	1.1	88	32.0	389	102.2	7	10	1.5	8	0	.0
75763	4.1	82	1.5	84	22.1	263	56.5	7	18	1.6	17	0	.0
75764	.2	100	.1	84	14.7	167	50.8	6	26	.1	19	1	.0
75765	3.5	68	1.1	76	24.6	219	54.9	5	15	1.2	15	0	.0
75766	20.2	77	7.4	71	22.0	255	56.1	8	17	7.4	15	3	.6
75770	1.5	64	.6	84	15.5	267	53.3	8	21	.5	23	0	.0
75771	7.4	90	2.6	82	25.3	292	78.0	6	18	3.3	16	0	.0
75773	8.2	89	3.1	77	22.9	254	56.7	8	19	3.5	18	1	.5
75778	1.2	0	.5	86	21.5	311	52.4	3	19	.0	0	0	.0
75779	.3	100	.1	75	19.0	215	71.3	9	19	.1	10	0	.0
75780	.2	75	.1	54	23.3	243	45.0	0	22	.1	20	0	.0
75782	.2	87	.1	75	28.4	326	63.0	13	14	.1	9	0	.6
75783	4.5	92	1.7	81	23.2	269	66.8	9	15	2.0	20	0	.6
75784	.7	61	.2	90	17.6	306	40.6	9	19	.0	19	0	.0
75785	8.7	83	2.8	75	24.2	256	47.9	6	19	3.5	17	1	.1
75788	.1	0	.1	88	7.6	87*	16.8	0	52	.0	0	0	.0
75789	5.5	82	2.0	82	23.7	277	54.5	7	18	2.2	14	0	.9
75790	2.8	99	1.1	81	20.9	243	55.7	6	23	1.3	18	0	.0
75791	4.8	94	1.6	81	27.4	321	88.2	7	7	2.2	7	0	.0
75792	2.1	49	.8	82	19.1	171	46.0	7	16	.6	8	0	.3
PALESTINE													
75801	25.8	77	9.4	74	24.3	273	59.1	9	17	9.4	15	3	1.5
75831	2.7	87	1.0	82	21.4	246	49.2	7	20	1.1	18	1	.0
75832	.2	100	.1	77	22.6	260*	31.1	14	8	.1	10	0	.0
75833	1.9	70	.8	83	20.0	189	46.0	4	29	.6	21	0	.0
75835	11.4	63	4.2	67	19.7	213	60.8	7	21	3.3	21	1	.0
75838	.5	84	.2	91	25.1	152	41.3	6	19	.3	24	0	.0
75839	3.4	87	1.3	84	18.8	212	45.2	6	21	1.4	17	0	.0
75840	5.5	82	2.0	77	25.2	261	65.2	10	14	2.2	12	2	.0
75844	4.5	80	1.6	81	20.3	204	54.0	8	21	1.7	21	2	.3
75845	2.8	79	1.1	75	17.1	169	43.9	7	22	1.1	23	0	.0
75846	1.4	84	.5	89	20.4	302	49.2	5	25	.6	21	3	.0
75847	1.7	78	.6	78	14.8	253	33.8	6	21	.7	17	0	.0
75848	.2	0	.1	71	14.9	59	37.5	9	11	.1	10	0	.0
75849	.3	84	.1	93	22.1	254*	33.4	11	14	.1	9	0	.0
75850	.3	65	.1	79	18.8	356	43.3	10	15	.1	5	1	.0
75851	4.8	53	.7	73	19.8	181	42.0	3	8	1.9	7	0	.0
75852	3.5	46	.4	72	12.9	180	37.6	2	7	1.2	3	0	.0
75853	.6	78	.2	79	19.0	227	77.7	5	13	.6	8	0	.0
75855	2.4	43	.8	79	14.1	138	32.6	8	22	.4	19	0	.0
75856	.2	81	.1	69	13.9	323	21.4	0	31	.1	37	0	.0
75858	.2	50	.1	94	13.6	156*	32.2	17	9	.0	11	0	.0
75859	.9	74	.4	77	15.6	222	60.5	5	36	.3	26	0	.0
75860	4.8	82	1.9	81	21.3	187	51.5	6	25	1.8	20	0	.0

*=Estimated **1.0=883 lbs per person; 1p0++ indicates per capita toxic waste generation > than 100 times the U.S. average of 883 lbs per capita.

ZIP CODE MEASURES OF SIZE, LEVELS OF AFFLUENCE AND QUALITY OF LIFE

1=Population (th.); 2= % White; 3=Households (th.); 4=% Owner Occupied; 5=Mean Income Per Household (th.$); 6=Mean Monthly Rent ($)*; 7=Mean Home Value (th.$)*; 8=% under 5; 9=% 65 and over; 10=White Males (th.); 11=% White Males, 65+; 12=# Toxic Waste Sites; 13=Toxic Waste Relative to US(883 lbs.per capita)**.

TEXAS

ZIP CODE	1	2	3	4	5	6	7	8	9	10	11	12	13
PALESTINE													
75861	5.5	59	.4	69	20.5	111	61.8	1	3	2.8	2	0	.0
75862	5.1	78	2.1	76	19.8	211	57.8	7	20	1.9	19	0	1.4
75865	.2	79	.1	100	13.2	151*	38.0	0	31	.1	18	0	.0
LUFKIN													
75901	47.5	80	16.3	70	25.4	307	68.4	9	12	18.6	11	4	1.1
75925	3.7	71	1.4	70	17.0	200	38.3	8	18	1.2	18	4	.0
75926	.9	75	.4	78	16.7	261	35.8	5	17	.4	20	0	.0
75928	1.6	53	.5	74	18.4	206	33.3	6	9	.4	14	0	.5
75929	1.2	96	.5	87	18.0	224	42.1	6	21	.6	21	0	.0
75930	1.8	97	.6	89	18.1	171	34.5	8	13	.9	11	0	.0
75931	1.1	85	.4	89	17.7	86	58.3	7	18	.5	15	0	.0
75932	1.1	89	.4	87	19.5	78	50.2	9	14	.5	19	0	.0
75933	1.8	67	.6	82	19.7	181	32.1	9	14	.6	10	0	.0
75934	.3	25	.1	72	17.1	507	27.0	10	21	.1	13	0	.0
75935	12.4	79	4.6	75	21.4	214	52.9	7	17	4.8	15	0	.1
75936	1.0	79	.3	92	19.6	80	45.5	7	13	.4	13	0	.0
75937	1.3	86	.5	84	23.5	223	55.7	9	19	.5	24	0	.0
75938	1.7	90	.7	89	19.0	210	49.6	9	21	.7	20	1	.1
75941	3.6	74	1.3	65	19.3	219	44.4	12	14	1.3	14	1	.1
75942	7.7	67	2.2	65	24.0	236	57.3	11	11	2.5	18	3	.1
75943	.6	27	.2	72	17.8	204	46.2	5	11	.1	8	0	.0
75944	.6	84	.2	75	17.1	211	39.2	13	19	.2	20	0	.0
75946	.1	100	.1	83	18.6	214*	27.6	8	11	.1	28	0	.0
75947	3.1	71	1.1	80	20.0	188	50.3	7	18	1.0	16	0	.2
75948	3.9	85	1.6	79	18.1	166	60.3	5	22	1.6	23	0	.0
75949	4.9	94	1.8	85	21.7	199	46.5	7	15	2.3	13	0	.0
75951	15.1	70	5.3	74	23.1	266	58.2	8	14	5.2	13	3	.1
75954	2.8	95	.8	81	19.2	199	38.7	7	19	1.1	16	3	.1
75956	6.5	86	2.4	81	21.6	207	49.6	7	17	2.7	15	0	.0
75957	.3	33	.1	86	17.7	204*	25.9	10	22	.1	48	0	.0
75958	2.7	68	1.0	83	21.0	241*	49.9	6	24	.9	24	0	.0
75959	.6	91	.2	75	20.7	100	49.6	7	16	.3	26	0	.0
75960	.3	50	.1	100	23.3	268*	47.0	8	15	.1	6	0	.0
75961	39.2	80	13.6	59	22.5	285	74.5	9	27	15.3	30	0	.2
75962	.7	0	.3	0	10.4	198	37.1*	9	3	.0	0	0	.0
75966	4.2	75	1.5	82	19.5	179	51.1	9	18	1.5	17	0	.3
75969	2.1	83	.8	76	18.2	286	32.9	6	21	.8	19	0	.0
75971	.1	100	.1	87	16.1	185*	25.8	8	33	.1	42	0	.0
75972	7.4	60	2.7	77	18.9	180	49.6	7	20	2.1	22	0	.0
75973	2.7	68	1.0	83	20.0	106	46.3	4	23	.9	24	0	.0
75974	2.8	74	1.0	75	19.4	180	38.5	7	15	1.0	15	0	.0
75975	3.4	78	1.3	79	17.8	196	46.3	7	22	1.3	22	1	.0
75976	1.2	83	.4	70	20.2	227	44.3	8	15	.5	14	0	.0
75977	.7	20	.1	81	16.5	212	26.7	7	14	.1	43	0	.0
75978	.2	100	.1	60	17.6	232	59.5	4	30	.3	39	0	.1
75979	7.4	86	2.7	77	20.9	241	57.4	6	20	3.1	20	0	.0
75980	2.1	97	.9	84	16.2	209	34.7	5	22	1.0	24	2	1.1

TEXAS

ZIP CODE	1	2	3	4	5	6	7	8	9	10	11	12	13
FORT WORTH													
76008	3.5	97	1.2	86	34.0	302	103.8	7	7	1.7	6	1	.0
76009	6.9	92	2.3	80	25.8	307	65.9	7	11	3.2	9	1	.0
76010	39.4	91	15.6	42	24.9	354	69.1	6	6	17.6	4	1	2.5
76011	18.7	93	8.9	29	27.4	374	140.0	6	6	8.8	4	6	2.1
76012	22.4	95	7.4	78	41.7	401	145.5	5	6	10.4	4	0	.0
76013	28.0	95	10.5	61	34.4	375	122.2	6	6	13.1	5	0	.0
76014	16.6	91	5.2	80	33.0	535	95.6	10	3	7.7	1	0	.0
76015	11.5	95	3.8	70	32.7	474	112.8	9	3	5.4	3	0	.0
76016	17.4	97	5.4	90	41.4	588	137.1	11	2	8.5	1	0	.2
76017	9.3	98	3.0	93	41.7	575	149.9	11	2	4.6	2	2	.1
76020	8.1	97	2.9	82	29.0	315	80.8	7	11	3.9	10	1	.0
76021	21.5	98	7.1	78	39.6	440	124.8	7	3	10.3	2	1	.1
76024	8.6	96	3.4	84	25.8	264	64.9	8	17	3.7	14	0	.4
76026	7.1	96	2.6	76	26.8	281	61.6	7	12	3.3	12	0	.1
76027	.8	0	.3	72	17.7	212	31.2	12	18	.0	18	0	.0
76028	22.1	98	7.0	86	32.2	388	89.9	8	7	10.7	6	0	.1
76029	.4	88	.1	69	27.2	131	61.0	13	10	.2	11	1	.0
76030	2.0	0	.7	80	24.3	308	55.8	8	16	1.0	13	0	.0
76031	26.2	94	9.7	74	24.7	319	63.6	8	16	11.6	13	4	.2
76034	6.4	99	1.9	91	46.0	330	154.6	6	5	3.2	5	0	20.2
76035	.2	0	.1	67	42.3	266	61.1	13	28	.1	19	0	.0
76036	7.7	97	2.5	81	28.8	352	82.6	7	6	3.6	5	0	.1
76037	.2	100	.1	81	15.8	182*	56.4*	8	19	.1	13	12	.3
76039	24.7	95	9.1	52	30.9	412	93.3	7	3	11.8	3	4	.0
76041	.4	54	.2	96	21.5	247*	57.5	5	16	.1	17	0	.0
76043	3.4	94	1.2	66	25.7	235	50.9	9	14	1.6	13	0	.2
76044	2.0	95	.7	77	28.3	275	62.9	8	8	1.0	8	0	.0
76045	1.8	99	.7	78	28.2	213	53.1	4	20	.9	20	0	.0
76046	13.0	98	4.9	74	30.2	310	65.8	7	14	6.2	14	2	.0
76048	15.3	98	5.8	79	29.4	419	91.3	6	11	7.5	13	1	4.0
76050	3.3	95	1.2	79	27.0	220	57.1	7	14	1.5	12	2	.0
76052	.5	100	.2	66	33.5	339	121.8	9	4	.3	5	0	.0
76053	31.8	98	11.3	68	31.9	326	79.5	7	7	15.3	24	4	.3
76055	2.1	80	.8	73	35.4	375	102.3	9	25	.8	19	0	.3
76056	5.4	97	2.1	78	19.5	193	36.3	8	20	2.5	19	0	.4
76057	.2	100	.1	83	23.8	235	52.0	8	31	.1	38	0	.0
76058	5.4	98	1.8	81	16.2	186*	23.7	8	8	2.6	7	0	.5
76059	3.1	89	1.1	58	16.5	347	92.3	5	14	1.4	12	2	.0
76060	.8	95	.3	89	25.5	304	81.7	6	11	.4	11	0	.0
76062	.4	92	.1	86	24.5	249	57.3	7	19	.3	25	0	.0
76063	11.5	93	3.7	83	22.2	331	22.4	9	9	5.4	7	1	.0
76064	1.1	84	.3	75	32.2	366	94.6	9	8	.5	8	0	.2
76065	7.1	94	2.3	81	21.5	336	43.3	8	8	3.4	7	4	.0
76066	1.8	91	.6	82	30.5	314	84.8	7	9	.9	7	0	.3
76067	18.6	90	6.8	72	23.4	312	55.3	8	14	8.1	13	2	.3
76070	.2	0	.1	68	25.7	296*	91.9	14	27	.0	0	0	.0
76071	1.3	98	.4	89	21.8	216	59.4	8	11	.6	12	0	.0

*=Estimated **1.0=883 lbs per capita **1.0=883 lbs per person; 100++ indicates per capita toxic waste generation > than 100 times the U.S. average of 883 lbs per capita.

ZIP CODE MEASURES OF SIZE, LEVELS OF AFFLUENCE AND QUALITY OF LIFE

1=Population (th.); 2= % White; 3=Households (th.); 4=% Owner Occupied; 5=Mean Income Per Household (th.$); 6=Mean Monthly Rent ($); 7=Mean Home Value (th.$);
8=% under 5; 9=% 65 and over; 10=White Males (th.); 11=% White Males, 65+; 12=# Toxic Waste Sites; 13=Toxic Waste Relative to US(883 lbs.per capita)**.

TEXAS

FORT WORTH

ZIP CODE	1	2	3	4	5	6	7	8	9	10	11	12	13
76072	.7	94	.3	91	27.9	202	49.0	2	23	.3	21	0	.0
76073	1.2	94	.3	92	30.0	345*	60.0	5	13	.6	10	0	.0
76075	.6	100	.2	86	21.7	249*	44.8	3	16	.3	18	0	.0
76076	1.4	100	.5	93	28.5	327*	69.3	8	8	.7	9	0	.0
76077	.2	0	.1	81	27.6	367	98.0	3	9	.0	0	0	.0
76078	1.9	99	.7	82	27.2	257	54.6	4	11	1.0	11	0	.2
76082	11.1	99	3.8	87	28.5	283	78.0	7	8	5.5	8	0	.0
76083	1.4	93	.6	79	19.1	149	42.4	7	25	.6	24	0	.0
76084	1.0	94	.3	76	26.7	226	45.7	7	18	.4	15	2	.0
76086	27.1	96	9.8	77	25.9	289	74.3	7	14	12.6	12	2	.0
76090	.2	100		81	18.3	203	25.6	3	28	.1	29	0	.0
76091	.5	0	.2	87	23.0	114	30.0	4	27	.0	0	0	.0
76093	1.2	99	.4	78	26.2	237	54.3	7	11	.6	11	0	.0

FORT WORTH

ZIP CODE	1	2	3	4	5	6	7	8	9	10	11	12	13
76102	6.7	37	2.2	22	12.9	144	28.3	8	13	1.5	11	2	.3
76103	11.9	94	5.3	62	26.1	344	75.2	6	20	5.1	16	1	.2
76104	27.3	23	9.9	40	14.7	239	30.4	8	16	2.9	18	1	.2
76105	26.0	26	8.1	63	16.4	264	32.3	9	11	2.7	18	0	.1
76106	40.9	64	13.2	63	19.3	261	34.5	10	12	3.7	12	9	1.1
76107	28.3	72	13.2	53	29.4	336	95.0	6	19	9.3	15	9	.3
76108	16.2	95	5.6	71	25.8	329	62.5	8	8	7.6	7	1	.1
76109	15.7	98	7.0	72	48.8	420	151.7	5	19	7.2	15	0	.1
76110	27.3	76	10.8	59	21.5	283	53.4	8	16	9.6	14	1	.3
76111	17.9	84	7.2	71	21.1	269	50.2	7	15	7.2	15	2	1.2
76112	30.3	82	12.6	68	32.0	376	94.1	7	11	12.1	10	2	.1
76114	24.4	93	9.3	64	24.3	340	55.5	9	11	11.1	10	2	.1
76115	15.6	85	5.9	57	20.5	305	43.2	9	8	6.4	8	1	.5
76116	36.5	93	15.7	50	32.6	397	105.9	6	16	16.8	7	0	.1
76117	17.9	84	7.1	71	26.3	290	61.5	7	11	11.9	7	1	.2
76118	29.4	98	10.4	73	33.8	391	93.3	7	7	14.1	6	0	.3
76119	44.5	46	13.9	73	32.8	287	49.1	9	7	10.0	10	3	.2
76126	9.7	94	3.2	88	36.7	471	106.0	4	6	4.5	6	0	.0
76127	1.8	73	.2	0	22.3	333	79.6*	8	0	1.0	0	1	.2
76131	2.4	89	.7	86	27.9	417	56.8	10	8	1.1	3	0	.6
76132	4.2	95	1.8	51	42.8	499	151.8	7	8	1.9	6	0	.0
76133	32.2	94	11.3	80	37.6	433	106.4	7	7	14.5	6	0	.0
76134	13.9	66	4.3	86	33.5	444	85.4	7	5	6.4	6	0	.1
76135	13.7	97	4.8	75	31.3	334	99.8	7	9	6.7	8	1	.0
76137	2.6	93	.8	92	33.6	644	109.3	13	2	1.3	2	0	.0
76140	14.7	75	4.6	84	29.8	395	75.2	9	4	5.5	5	2	1.1
76148	12.7	96	3.7	83	30.4	623	75.5	12	4	6.2	1	0	.0
76179	7.5	96	2.5	79	29.7	269	86.9	8	6	3.5	5	0	.0
76180	8.3	98	2.7	85	35.9	505	107.9	10	4	4.1	3	0	.0

DENTON

ZIP CODE	1	2	3	4	5	6	7	8	9	10	11	12	13
76201	52.8	88	19.8	49	25.9	328	100.5	6	9	22.5	7	4	.3
76203	.8	76	.1	25	21.1	231	45.9	0	1	.4	0	0	.0
76225	1.5	97	.6	67	19.6	190	38.6	7	16	.7	15	0	.0
76226	2.5	99	.9	84	38.6	276	139.9	5	8	1.3	8	1	.0
76227	3.1	96	1.1	80	27.1	259	76.1	6	10	1.5	10	0	.0

TEXAS

DENTON

ZIP CODE	1	2	3	4	5	6	7	8	9	10	11	12	13
76228	1.1	100	.4	78	21.6	232	35.2	9	21	.5	18	0	.0
76230	8.9	99	3.5	79	22.5	261	53.7	7	20	4.1	18	0	.2
76233	1.5	100	.6	77	18.0	261	45.6	8	25	.7	23	1	.0
76234	7.4	92	2.6	72	25.0	236	65.0	8	17	3.2	14	0	.1
76238	.4	91	.1	76	30.0	248	60.5	8	6	.2	5	0	.0
76239	.5	100	.3	76	14.9	143	40.1	2	33	.3	28	0	.2
76240	21.4	92	7.9	70	24.1	283	64.7	4	15	9.6	13	1	1.3
76245	1.1	0	.5	85	19.3	277	43.7	4	30	.9	14	0	.0
76247	1.7	99	.6	76	26.4	280	71.0	6	14	.9	14	4	.0
76248	6.3	99	2.0	87	35.5	419	116.2	8	6	3.1	5	0	.1
76249	2.0	99	.7	83	27.9	317	69.3	8	9	1.0	9	0	.0
76250	.6	100	.6	78	24.8	304	63.6	9	6	.3	6	0	.0
76251	1.2	99	.2	97	17.1	197*	55.9	8	16	.3	14	0	.1
76252	2.7	100	.8	81	25.5	301	73.1	8	10	.3	14	0	.1
76253	.2	100	.1	78	17.3	200	31.7	12	15	.1	22	2	2.7
76255	5.0	99	2.0	75	19.9	177	46.0	6	24	2.3	21	1	.0
76258	3.1	93	1.1	73	26.8	223	64.6	9	18	1.4	16	0	.2
76259	.2	99	.1	80	25.4	385	67.3	9	15	.3	11	0	.1
76261	.2	100	.1	85	17.5	182	38.0	7	28	.1	20	0	.0
76262	7.6	97	2.4	90	42.6	344	151.3	7	5	3.8	4	0	.3
76264	.7	100	.3	84	23.0	217	37.2	2	17	.3	17	0	.1
76265	1.6	99	.6	77	17.7	135	42.3	6	24	.8	21	0	.1
76266	4.7	95	1.6	78	28.3	308	69.2	8	12	2.1	10	1	.1
76267	.2	100	.1	84	30.1	346*	69.4	8	17	.1	17	0	.1
76268	1.0	94	.4	73	20.4	186	32.4	6	9	.0	9	0	.0
76270	1.0	94	.4	77	18.8	241	37.2	5	23	.5	21	0	.1
76271	.8	99	.3	82	23.9	229	38.2	5	17	.4	19	2	.5
76272	1.4	97	.5	81	26.4	272	62.5	9	14	.7	13	0	.1
76273	5.5	100	2.1	78	25.1	236	53.3	6	19	2.6	16	0	.2

WICHITA FALLS

ZIP CODE	1	2	3	4	5	6	7	8	9	10	11	12	13
76301	22.7	71	9.5	57	18.3	231	43.4	8	18	7.6	15	2	.8
76302	9.5	97	3.4	77	32.0	358	81.0	8	11	4.5	11	0	.2
76303	4.2	55	1.5	67	19.2	242	38.4	11	7	1.2	9	1	.2
76304	4.9	58	1.8	52	14.1	195	31.8	10	12	1.3	15	1	.6
76305	7.7	90	2.7	71	24.5	329	51.6	9	6	3.4	6	0	.4
76306	4.6	85	1.6	54	25.3	366	82.3	11	1	2.0	1	0	.0
76308	16.1	97	6.1	73	38.8	371	111.6	6	10	7.6	9	2	.1
76309	12.9	95	5.4	64	24.2	299	64.5	7	17	5.5	13	0	.0
76310	7.5	97	2.5	85	34.6	336	86.9	8	5	3.6	6	3	.3
76311	9.7	79	1.3	0	20.2	345	71.9*	8	0	5.0	0	1	.0
76351	2.0	0	.8	77	23.2	213	51.0	7	20	.9	21	0	.0
76354	11.0	95	3.8	76	25.9	279	66.2	8	10	5.1	8	0	.2
76357	.8	100	.3	80	21.8	251	47.4	6	22	.4	21	0	.2
76359	.8	100		86	27.4	314*	53.8	6	29		28	1	.0
76360	4.5	94	.2	73	21.2	200	38.6	7	21	2.0	18	0	.8
76363	.5	62	.2	70	19.6	209	27.1	6	19	.2	27	0	.0
76364	.3	0	.1	79	33.9	195	22.2	4	22	.0	0	0	.2
76365	4.8	97	.9	81	24.1	237	51.7	6	19	2.3	16	0	.2
76366	1.9	96	1.1	80	23.5	247	55.15?	6	15	.9	14	0	.0

*=Estimated **1.0=883 lbs per person; 100++ indicates per capita toxic waste generation > than 100 times the U.S. average of 883 lbs per capita.

ZIP CODE MEASURES OF SIZE, LEVELS OF AFFLUENCE AND QUALITY OF LIFE

1=Population (th.); 2= % White; 3=Households (th.); 4=% Owner Occupied; 5=Mean Income Per Household (th.$); 6=Mean Monthly Rent ($)*; 7=Mean Home Value (th.$)*; 8=% under 5; 9=% 65 and over; 10=White Males (th.); 11=% White Males, 65+; 12=# Toxic Waste Sites; 13=Toxic Waste Relative to US(883 lbs.per capital)**.

TEXAS

ZIPCODE	1	2	3	4	5	6	7	8	9	10	11	12	13
WICHITA FALLS													
76367	8.2	98	2.8	80	27.9	305	61.4	8	10	4.0	8	2	.1
76369	.2	0	.1	76	38.2	32	44.1	6	20	.0	0	0	.0
76370	.5	94	.2	80	27.8	164	35.4	10	17	.3	15	0	.0
76371	2.4	78	.9	77	25.2	172	39.7	7	21	.9	21	3	.0
76372	.9	0	.4	74	19.3	180	29.9	7	23	.0	0	0	.0
76373	.2	0	.1	61	22.2	192	33.8	0	33	.0	0	0	.0
76377	5.2	92	2.1	71	26.4	203	47.8	7	23	2.2	20	2	.1
76379	.9	100	.3	84	25.9	213	38.1	7	16	.5	14	0	.0
76380	4.8	91	2.0	73	20.1	305	47.0	11	13	2.0	21	1	.0
76383	.1	100	.1	78	27.9	173	51.0	6	23	.1	29	0	.0
76384	15.1	85	5.7	68	22.2	320*	34.4	4	26	6.0	18	5	1.0
76388	.3	0	.1	78	26.8	131	43.4	7	24	.6	6	1	.0
76389	1.1	100	.3	80	30.4	223	75.2	11	6	.6	6	0	.0
FORT WORTH													
76401	16.0	95	6.3	68	24.2	251	63.2	7	18	7.4	14	1	.5
76430	3.0	94	1.1	75	25.6	245	55.2	8	20	1.4	16	1	.3
76432	1.1	0	.4	83	24.1	233	40.6	6	14	.0	0	0	.0
76433	.6	94	.2	80	14.3	155	42.8	9	20	.3	18	1	.0
76435	.7	0	.3	77	14.3	245	22.9	9	15	.0	0	0	.0
76436	.1	100	.1	45	11.5	68	32.0	0	32	.1	36	0	.0
76437	6.0	95	2.3	79	19.3	197	36.5	6	22	2.7	21	2	.1
76442	6.8	94	2.6	78	20.2	199	46.1	6	23	3.0	22	1	.2
76443	3.9	92	1.5	79	18.7	235	33.4	5	28	1.7	23	1	.0
76444	.4	100	.2	95	17.2	163	43.9	7	25	.1	24	1	.0
76445	5.5	96	2.1	71	21.3	198*	26.1	8	24	2.5	23	0	.0
76448	5.1	96	2.1	71	20.4	243	50.4	6	21	2.2	17	0	.0
76453	.8	100	.3	77	21.0	220	52.4	4	18	.4	17	0	.0
76454	1.9	96	.8	79	18.8	145	35.5	6	29	.0	0	0	.3
76455	.7	96	.3	85	14.9	153	33.5	3	26	.3	20	0	.0
76457	2.9	97	1.1	76	17.0	191	41.6	6	27	1.4	25	2	.0
76462	1.3	100	.5	77	24.3	219	42.2	8	14	.7	12	1	.0
76463	.3	0	.2	82	17.8	82	32.0	4	35	.0	0	0	.0
76464	.6	0	.2	79	18.8	217	25.5	6	27	.2	11	0	.0
76466	.3	100	.1	65	23.5	192	51.8	8	12	.2	11	0	.0
76469	.1	100	.1	75	16.3	153	19.7	3	23	.1	25	0	.0
76470	4.0	94	1.5	78	19.2	199	38.1	6	21	1.9	19	3	.7
76471	2.3	98	.9	80	16.7	154	30.7	7	29	1.1	26	0	.0
76472	.8	100	.3	85	21.7	198	32.7	5	25	.3	20	0	.3
76474	.7	96	.3	85	31.1	191	39.5	6	30	.2	32	0	.0
76475	.9	99	.4	72	17.8	124	32.9	5	23	.4	19	0	.0
76476	1.3	0	.5	85	22.5	322	45.1	10	13	.0	0	0	.0
WACO													
76501	47.8	80	18.1	63	23.9	292	70.2	8	14	18.4	13	3	.4
76511	2.1	68	.8	67	16.8	201	36.8	8	24	.6	21	0	.2
76518	20.0	87	6.9	66	22.4	257	69.2	9	10	8.6	9	2	.1
76519	1.2	88	.5	68	16.9	244	37.8	9	27	.5	26	0	.0

TEXAS

ZIPCODE	1	2	3	4	5	6	7	8	9	10	11	12	13
WACO													
76520	8.2	72	3.0	72	18.8	200	50.5	7	19	2.8	18	1	.0
76522	21.4	85	6.9	56	21.4	284	69.1	11	2	9.3	2	0	.0
76523	.2	100	.1	65	16.4	188*	41.1	25	19	.1	15	0	.0
76524	.8	91	.3	80	19.8	210	48.1	7	16	.3	17	0	.0
76525	1.0	95	.4	74	21.8	232	47.5	8	25	.5	23	0	.0
76526	.2	84	.1	90	22.7	261*	35.7	4	21	.1	40	0	.0
76527	1.7	91	.6	71	23.9	227	48.9	7	14	.8	11	1	.0
76528	10.5	91	3.8	75	20.4	196	50.5	6	19	4.4	18	1	.1
76530	2.0	80	.7	68	20.6	175	41.2	4	22	.7	20	0	.0
76531	5.1	96	2.1	80	20.0	194	46.9	5	28	2.3	25	0	.0
76533	.1	0	.1	82	22.1	272	44.1	4	16	.9	18	0	.0
76534	2.1	88	.7	77	19.8	153	39.5	6	18	.9	18	0	2.1
76537	1.0	89	.3	78	20.1	264	49.0	6	15	.5	15	0	.0
76538	.5	0	.2	77	19.0	315	44.3	11	24	.5	15	0	.0
76539	2.5	94	.8	82	25.6	229	96.8	10	8	1.3	8	0	.0
76541	60.2	71	21.5	46	20.9	270	76.0	12	3	21.9	4	1	.0
76544	20.4	64	5.2	1	17.8	341	81.1	19	0	6.8	0	1	.0
76550	8.3	90	3.1	74	20.3	257	56.1	7	19	3.5	17	0	.0
76554	.5	96	.2	77	19.2	265	50.2	6	16	.2	13	0	.0
76556	1.3	85	.5	85	18.2	182	33.6	9	20	.5	13	0	.0
76557	2.7	84	.9	77	20.1	214	42.4	6	17	1.1	15	0	.0
76558	.2	100	.1	86	37.0	45	57.6	0	9	.1	4	0	.0
76559	1.0	92	.4	58	16.5	207	47.5	11	7	.5	4	0	.0
76561	2.0	95	.7	79	24.1	313	65.2	10	11	1.0	10	0	.0
76565	.1	100	.1	87	12.8	147*	17.6	0	40	.0	33	0	.0
76566	.2	92	.1	83	12.8	147*	32.8	0	40	.1	33	0	.0
76567	8.4	84	3.0	75	22.9	246	56.9	9	15	3.4	14	0	.0
76569	2.0	87	.7	73	19.1	185	38.8	8	14	.9	14	0	.0
76570	3.5	75	1.4	72	16.9	175	46.0	5	28	1.3	26	0	.0
76571	1.4	0	.8	81	30.0	257	121.3	6	13	.0	0	0	.3
76574	12.4	89	4.4	72	22.1	249	57.9	8	18	4.1	18	3	.1
76577	2.3	70	.8	72	21.4	224	50.7	6	15	1.0	12	1	.0
76579	1.2	90	.5	73	20.4	185	47.6	5	19	.4	16	0	.0
WACO													
76621	.9	89	.3	71	22.1	250	53.7	6	17	.4	16	0	.0
76622	.6	89	.2	90	26.0	210	35.3	5	17	.2	22	0	.1
76623	.3	0	.1	77	19.1	236	33.1	16	12	.6	8	0	.0
76624	1.3	93	.5	91	23.6	167	50.0	5	13	.5	13	0	.0
76626	1.2	89	.4	76	15.6	168	40.1	6	27	.5	23	0	.0
76627	1.0	91	.4	76	30.4	179	39.3	7	13	.5	13	0	.0
76629	.9	80	.8	77	19.8	166	40.4	7	26	.8	25	0	.0
76630	.8	0	.3	85	23.5	184	56.6	8	15	.0	0	0	.0
76631	.3	90	.1	76	15.7	232	33.5	7	17	.5	17	0	.0
76632	1.5	71	.5	69	16.7	177	42.3	6	21	.5	19	0	.0
76633	1.9	96	.6	84	32.3	316	90.0	9	5	.9	5	1	.0
76634	5.5	95	2.3	80	20.7	200	57.3	5	30	2.4	31	0	.2
76635	1.3	57	.5	75	15.2	164	28.1	11	23	.4	19	0	.3
76636	1.0	0	.3	86	22.0	141	52.4	8	17	.0	0	0	.0

*=Estimated **1.0=883 lbs per person; 100++ indicates per capita toxic waste generation > than 100 times the U.S. average of 883 lbs per capita.

ZIP CODE MEASURES OF SIZE, LEVELS OF AFFLUENCE AND QUALITY OF LIFE

1=Population (th.); 2= % White; 3=Households (th.); 4=% Owner Occupied; 5=Income Per Household (th.$); 6=Mean Monthly Rent ($); 7=Mean Home Value (th.$); 8=% under 5; 9=% 65 and over; 10=% White Males (th.); 11=% White Males, 65+; 12=# Toxic Waste Sites; 13=Toxic Waste Relative to US(883 lbs.per capita)**.

TEXAS

WACO

ZIP CODE	1	2	3	4	5	6	7	8	9	10	11	12	13
76637	.6	96	.2	73	21.3	238	40.1	6	20	.3	22	1	.0
76638	1.4	94	.5	77	20.9	261	51.7	7	17	.6	16	0	.0
76639	1.1	79	.5	73	14.2	150	28.2	5	29	.9	24	0	.0
76640	2.1	87	.7	83	23.2	183	49.7	7	8	.9	8	0	.0
76641	1.2	90	.4	78	21.5	183	38.4	5	12	.5	9	0	.0
76642	4.2	77	1.7	75	19.0	215	50.3	7	26	1.5	25	0	.1
76643	5.4	96	1.7	80	32.1	441	86.5	12	3	2.5	3	0	.1
76645	9.4	80	3.6	67	19.9	232	47.7	7	22	3.4	19	2	.6
76648	2.2	79	.9	79	18.1	182	43.3	7	22	.8	20	2	.1
76649	.7	99	.3	83	18.5	202	37.5	8	28	.3	23	0	.0
76650	1	0	.1	89	15.7	180*	15.9	0	53	.0	0	0	.0
76651	1.9	75	.3	70	19.5	209	40.4	7	25	.7	25	0	.2
76652	.9	91	.3	81	17.7	249	51.6	4	14	.4	11	0	.2
76653	.9	74	.4	73	17.2	209	35.0	8	25	.3	27	0	.2
76654	.2	77	.1	89	22.3	256*	40.9	7	27	.1	30	0	.0
76655	3.7	92	1.3	89	27.7	203	77.0	8	10	1.6	16	0	.0
76656	1.8	81	.7	78	18.3	172	31.8	7	19	.7	16	0	.0
76657	6.2	82	2.2	74	22.4	257	56.7	8	17	2.4	14	1	.0
76660	.7	84	.2	80	22.1	188	34.9	3	17	.2	16	0	.0
76661	8.9	58	3.5	68	17.0	195	42.2	7	23	2.4	23	1	.0
76664	3.2	68	1.2	76	18.2	193	39.8	8	25	1.0	21	2	.0
76665	2.1	91	.8	71	19.4	165	54.7	6	26	.9	22	0	.1
76666	.3	100	.1	63	18.3	184	31.0	17	27	.3	30	0	.0
76667	12.0	72	4.1	75	19.1	216	44.9	6	20	3.9	16	0	.0
76670	1.0	72	.4	76	22.2	119	33.5	7	24	.4	23	1	.0
76671	2.4	97	.9	83	16.5	226	43.5	5	25	.6	25	0	.0
76673	1.0	84	.4	79	17.5	249	33.1	14	16	.4	18	0	.0
76675	.2	0	.1	81	22.0	253*	21.9	0	14	.2	7	0	1.4
76676	.4	90	.2	89	24.2	117	30.8	4	14	.2	7	0	.0
76678	.2	100	.1	72	11.4	253	24.3	12	24	.1	14	0	.0
76679	.8	87	.3	93	20.3	69	43.4	11	20	.3	24	0	.0
76680	.6	74	.2	82	18.7	206	32.5	10	22	.2	29	0	.0
76681	.4	84	.2	76	21.3	155	31.3	6	16	.2	13	0	.0
76682	2.0	85	.7	81	22.0	233	45.5	7	14	.8	14	0	.2
76687	1.3	90	.5	81	18.9	193	31.6	8	27	.5	22	1	.0
76689	2.4	93	.9	80	21.8	264	51.5	6	23	1.0	18	0	.0
76690	1.0	96	.4	70	19.1	232	30.8	6	25	.4	26	0	.0
76691	5.0	97	1.8	78	21.4	235	55.6	7	18	2.3	15	1	.0
76692	.6	96	2.0	81	19.3	228	49.8	5	25	2.3	24	0	.0
76693	1.5	79	.6	74	18.0	161	44.3	7	29	.5	26	0	.0

WACO

ZIP CODE	1	2	3	4	5	6	7	8	9	10	11	12	13
76701	2.4	74	.8	21	12.7	219	66.2	6	26	.8	22	1	.3
76703	4.4	92	.1	73	28.3	159	118.1	0	6	2.0	10	1	6.2
76704	10.4	5	3.6	51	13.3	191	33.7	10	14	.2	18	3	.0
76705	21.3	83	7.4	64	20.3	278	47.3	8	10	9.2	9	1	.2
76706	24.3	73	9.1	47	16.3	279	51.2	7	11	9.0	8	4	.0
76707	16.8	62	6.4	56	17.1	255	40.3	10	17	4.7	17	1	.0
76708	17.1	87	6.8	64	22.3	301	57.7	7	17	7.0	14	0	.0
76710	31.6	97	12.7	66	35.0	408	104.4	6	13	14.5	11	3	.4

TEXAS

WACO

ZIP CODE	1	2	3	4	5	6	7	8	9	10	11	12	13
76711	7.9	82	2.7	77	20.3	327	38.3	10	9	3.1	10	1	.0

ABILENE

ZIP CODE	1	2	3	4	5	6	7	8	9	10	11	12	13
76801	27.8	88	10.3	71	21.7	243	56.1	8	17	11.6	15	6	.2
76802		0		66	22.3	256*	79.5*	5	34				.0
76821	5.2	87	2.0	76	20.5	192	43.2	6	23	2.1	20	3	.1
76823	2.5	94	.9	80	18.5	202	43.2	6	23	1.0	22	0	.1
76825	7.3	87	2.9	75	18.6	223	48.4	7	25	3.0	22	0	.1
76827	.3	100	.1	84	29.4	251	43.5	3	7	.2	7	0	.0
76828	.5	90	.1	73	17.7	106	26.2	4	30	.1	22	0	.0
76832	.5	88	.2	78	26.4	180	58.0	5	17	.2	19	0	.0
76834	6.9	88	2.8	71	17.9	199	39.3	7	25	2.8	23	1	.0
76837	1.7	79	.6	75	22.1	136	51.1	7	23	.6	24	0	.2
76844	3.3	93	1.3	75	18.6	197	53.4	5	28	1.4	27	0	.2
76845	.2	100	.1	92	22.6	260*	74.4	9	18	.1	12	0	.0
76849	3.6	96	1.3	75	19.4	175	56.0	7	19	1.6	16	0	1.5
76853	1.3	0	.3	62	17.2	217	57.1	3	14	.0	0	0	.0
76854	.2	91	.5	70	16.4	176	39.6	9	19	.6	21	0	.0
76856	3.3	100	.1	98	19.3	222*	23.1	3	39	.1	40	0	.0
76857	.7	89	1.3	77	19.8	189	54.9	7	23	1.4	21	1	.0
76858	.4	100	.3	91	18.2	33	40.0	1	26	.3	26	0	.0
76859	2.2	93	.9	85	22.5	25	21.3	9	26	.2	18	0	.0
76861	1.7	89	.6	79	17.1	198	39.6	6	23	.9	22	1	.0
76862		96	.6	79	24.5	126	58.4	9	14	.8	24	0	.0
76864	.9	0		100	14.8	170*	84.4	8	21	.0	0	0	.0
76865	.2	100	.3	96	15.9	290	41.0	3	24	.1	33	0	.0
76866	.5	85	.1	88	26.8	308*	27.9	0	22	.1	10	0	.0
76869	.2	92	.2	68	15.9	82	37.3	7	12	.2	11	0	.0
76871	.8	97	.4	100	15.4	177*	18.6	1	32	.3	52	0	.0
76872	.7	100	.3	80	18.3	172	34.2	5	32	.3	31	0	.0
76875	.8	88	.3	87	18.3	211*	43.4	4	20	.4	19	0	.0
76877	4.6	85	1.7	76	18.0	98	51.5	9	15	1.9	22	1	.0
76878	2.0	87	.8	74	17.7	202	46.6	7	23	.8	24	0	.0
76882	.4	96	.1	80	19.6	166	31.1	7	25	.5	16	0	.1
76884	1.3		.3	84	19.4	86	25.8	7	36	.4	42	0	.0
76887		100				223*	23.1		33		33	0	.0
76890	.5	90	.2	79	19.7	178	28.5	10	20	.2	25	0	.0

MIDLAND

ZIP CODE	1	2	3	4	5	6	7	8	9	10	11	12	13
76901	48.9	92	17.4	67	29.4	376	80.2	7	11	21.7	9	6	.2
76902	.6	85	.2	84	32.4	198	62.8	6	4	.3	6	3	1.7
76903	31.7	73	11.7	59	18.5	252	43.9	9	14	10.8	14	1	1.7
76930	2.9	0	.1	69	19.3	359	20.2	8	14	.0	0	0	.0
76932	3.9	78	1.3	69	26.1	269	51.0	12	6	1.6	5	1	.1
76933	1.4	90	.5	79	23.2	160	42.0	5	26	.6	26	0	.0
76934	1.2	89	.3	79	32.7	187	27.7	7	15	.5	16	0	.2
76935	.8	94	.3	82	24.2	212	78.8	5	18	.4	14	1	.0
76936	2.7	94	1.0	77	24.7	214	48.4	9	14	1.3	12	0	.0
76937	.4	81	.1	81	26.6	171	30.0	9	27	.2	28	1	.0
76939	.2	72	.1	48	25.1	230	89.5*	9	6	.0	0	0	.0
76940	.2	66	.1	84	15.2	174*	36.7	7	3	.1	0	0	.4

*=Estimated **1.0=883 lbs per person; 100++ indicates per capita toxic waste generation > than 100 times the U.S. average of 883 lbs per capita.

ZIP CODE MEASURES OF SIZE, LEVELS OF AFFLUENCE AND QUALITY OF LIFE

1=Population (th.); 2= % White; 3=Households (th.); 4=% Owner Occupied; 5=Mean Income Per Household (th.$); 6=Mean Monthly Rent ($); 7=Mean Home Value (th.$); 8=% under 5; 9=% 65 and over; 10=% White Males, 65+; 11=% White Males (th.); 12=# Toxic Waste Sites; 13=Toxic Waste Relative to US(883 lbs.per capita)**.

TEXAS

MIDLAND

ZIPCODE	1	2	3	4	5	6	7	8	9	10	11	12	13
76941	1.2	97	.4	75	25.8	248	66.0	7	15	.6	15	0	.0
76943	4.4	70	1.5	68	26.9	224	63.2	10	10	1.5	10	1	.0
76945	1.6	85	.7	77	22.3	181	46.7	7	23	.7	22	0	.0
76950	5.1	96	1.7	70	33.2	308	55.0	10	7	2.5	7	0	.0
76951	1.2	94	.4	67	28.2	223	59.1	9	14	.5	12	0	.0
76957	.2	100	.1	88	41.6	478*	96.6	3	7	.1	7	1	.0
76958	.2	0	.1	78	44.7	514*	50.3	11	22	.0	0	0	.0

HOUSTON

ZIPCODE	1	2	3	4	5	6	7	8	9	10	11	12	13
77002	2.6	71	.9	10	19.7	309	165.6	1	15	1.4	14	0	17.5
77003	11.0	33	3.4	24	17.1	236	47.3	10	10	1.9	10	4	1.0
77004	45.5	10	17.0	24	17.9	259	76.0	7	11	2.6	9	0	.0
77005	18.7	98	8.8	70	41.2	473	187.4	6	19	8.4	15	0	.0
77006	16.5	85	9.7	24	26.8	387	168.1	3	9	8.3	8	1	.0
77007	30.8	60	10.6	31	21.6	325	72.8	9	10	9.6	5	1	.1
77008	31.9	79	13.1	50	25.6	355	84.8	7	15	12.1	13	5	.8
77009	46.7	54	15.7	50	22.2	319	63.4	9	12	12.5	12	1	.9
77011	25.3	48	7.1	41	21.1	292	52.7	11	7	6.4	8	4	.1
77012	19.5	52	6.3	37	22.1	313	47.3	11	7	5.4	7	7	1.4
77013	14.9	63	5.5	54	28.5	331	79.7	10	6	4.6	6	0	15.4
77014	.3	60	.9	64	36.1	37	118.1	7	9	.0	0	0	.4
77015	33.0	90	11.3	64	33.0	347	81.7	9	4	15.0	4	12	5.2
77016	41.0	10	11.2	71	24.5	336	54.1	9	5	2.0	10	2	6.6
77017	27.3	83	10.3	51	29.5	352	70.7	9	8	11.1	7	4	.3
77018	29.5	79	11.4	69	33.3	393	94.9	8	11	11.3	10	1	3.1
77019	20.3	63	9.0	32	44.4	341	279.9	6	12	6.7	10	1	.9
77020	34.6	26	10.5	43	17.9	241	45.3	10	10	4.5	8	5	.1
77021	31.9	8	10.8	54	22.5	293	64.1	8	7	1.2	18	3	1.0
77022	30.9	43	10.6	48	20.2	306	52.6	9	11	6.3	12	3	.8
77023	29.1	60	10.6	45	22.5	316	65.5	10	11	8.5	13	2	.9
77024	30.6	97	12.0	73	84.0	528	332.9	9	8	14.6	7	0	1.4
77025	24.5	77	11.6	41	34.5	413	139.3	5	14	8.9	14	0	.9
77026	39.4	6	12.9	39	16.8	269	44.2	9	9	1.1	15	8	.4
77027	10.8	94	6.3	40	49.2	444	255.8	4	15	4.7	12	0	5.1
77028	23.1	12	6.7	73	21.6	283	46.4	8	8	4.6	2	0	.6
77029	19.5	46	6.3	70	25.4	332	49.8	8	10	4.5	8	7	1.3
77030	11.7	76	5.6	38	35.2	421	235.9	3	12	4.3	11	2	4.1
77031	11.2	84	4.2	59	39.9	393	140.6	11	3	4.8	2	0	.0
77032	8.8	92	2.9	70	29.9	288	72.9	10	4	4.2	3	2	.0
77033	36.1	4	9.8	74	23.3	356	49.6	8	4	.6	13	0	.3
77034	20.4	90	7.5	56	32.4	398	78.1	8	9	9.3	4	3	.6
77035	23.7	73	9.1	54	35.2	409	117.7	9	5	8.6	6	1	.6
77036	45.9	83	23.0	23	28.6	389	136.6	5	6	18.6	3	0	1.3
77037	10.6	92	3.4	79	30.7	363	70.2	10	5	5.4	4	0	.4
77038	11.1	81	3.7	69	32.6	324	84.0	11	4	2.6	2	0	5.1
77039	19.2	75	5.6	71	31.3	407	74.8	11	3	7.1	3	0	.6
77040	21.6	92	7.1	67	38.4	433	125.2	10	3	10.1	1	2	1.3
77041	7.1	65	2.3	80	30.5	383	89.4	10	4	2.3	3	3	4.1
77042	25.5	91	11.6	36	41.6	411	221.6	6	3	11.8	3	1	2.1
77043	20.9	91	7.1	63	40.2	426	136.6	6	3	9.5	2	0	5.1

TEXAS

HOUSTON

ZIPCODE	1	2	3	4	5	6	7	8	9	10	11	12	13
77044	8.3	93	2.8	82	30.9	421	79.5	11	4	3.9	4	1	.0
77045	24.5	30	7.3	74	32.3	425	72.9	10	3	3.7	3	6	.8
77047	11.8	24	3.6	86	30.7	360	64.9	8	4	1.5	8	0	.1
77048	19.1	7	5.8	47	24.6	327	69.7	12	2	1.7	7	0	.6
77049	11.3	84	3.4	81	35.8	468	86.1	12	3	5.1	3	0	.1
77050	4.0	37	1.1	85	30.4	350	73.7	8	3	.8	11	0	.0
77051	17.7	0	5.4	62	19.4	284	43.7	8	9	.0	74	8	.0
77053	20.4	48	6.0	86	34.3	577	76.8	12	2	5.1	3	0	.0
77054	1.9	54	1.2	22	23.4	405	71.6	3	4	.6	5	7	13.5
77055	42.8	84	15.8	39	31.5	396	118.4	10	5	18.1	5	7	.7
77056	15.2	93	8.4	43	55.1	491	305.5	3	13	6.8	11	0	.3
77057	27.1	91	16.1	30	39.9	454	280.4	3	6	12.1	5	0	.1
77058	8.9	92	4.2	41	37.5	441	191.3	6	3	4.3	2	3	18.1
77059	6.2	94	1.8	93	57.9	852	190.6	8	1	2.9	0	0	.0
77060	27.3	89	11.1	37	28.1	314	81.7	6	8	12.6	3	0	.4
77061	20.3	77	9.8	36	30.7	371	103.1	8	8	7.3	9	2	.2
77062	15.2	94	5.3	63	40.6	474	134.1	6	2	7.3	2	1	.2
77063	22.2	88	12.6	29	36.4	487	189.8	3	8	9.6	1	0	1.7
77064	12.4	87	3.7	90	37.9	579	100.5	14	1	5.4	0	0	.1
77065	7.5	97	3.6	89	41.8	437	121.0	11	1	3.8	1	0	.0
77066	11.5	92	3.6	80	51.2	338	171.3	8	2	5.2	1	0	.0
77067	5.5	78	1.9	75	35.0	324	101.7	11	2	2.1	1	0	.0
77068	6.3	96	2.1	70	48.9	180	186.9	8	2	3.0	2	0	.0
77069	6.1	97	2.1	87	74.0	341	240.5	5	4	3.0	3	0	.0
77070	15.1	96	4.3	93	52.0	390	164.1	9	3	2.7	3	0	.1
77071	11.3	85	4.1	73	45.7	448	155.3	9	3	4.8	2	0	.0
77072	29.5	88	10.5	68	36.2	444	106.9	6	3	12.8	1	0	.0
77073	3.0	97	1.0	75	48.4	116	138.1	5	3	2.9	5	0	1.0
77074	30.0	85	13.5	37	29.9	428	108.0	7	5	12.5	4	1	.2
77075	13.7	81	5.1	62	29.6	393	84.2	10	5	5.5	5	4	.5
77076	25.6	80	9.2	61	26.4	367	59.8	9	7	10.0	7	1	.1
77077	22.6	93	8.7	63	47.1	402	184.8	10	2	10.5	1	0	.0
77078	14.3	41	4.3	70	27.8	389	61.2	11	3	2.9	5	1	.0
77079	33.3	95	11.1	69	60.1	492	234.6	5	3	15.3	3	0	.3
77080	37.2	89	13.3	52	35.6	350	114.4	7	3	16.4	3	1	.0
77081	29.0	73	15.9	8	22.7	361	126.3	6	3	11.1	3	1	.0
77082	3.2	85	1.2	83	46.2	607	140.8	8	4	1.4	1	0	.0
77083	5.5	83	1.7	93	51.0	858	142.4	12	0	2.3	0	0	.0
77084	16.3	92	5.3	91	43.7	483	123.0	13	1	7.6	1	0	.2
77085	6.3	47	2.0	62	28.8	397	76.0	11	2	1.5	4	0	.2
77086	6.6	86	2.1	77	34.4	465	95.4	13	3	2.9	3	1	1.2
77087	33.3	63	11.8	56	25.1	329	63.8	10	3	10.2	12	4	.3
77088	40.4	51	12.3	83	35.7	356	94.2	10	4	10.5	2	0	.4
77089	31.4	83	9.4	84	41.3	492	109.3	10	2	13.0	1	0	.2
77090	13.8	96	4.8	56	47.7	297	170.1	6	3	6.6	2	0	.2
77091	21.6	32	8.0	56	26.6	328	77.6	8	4	3.6	5	0	1.0
77092	32.9	88	13.9	41	30.5	443	93.7	8	4	14.8	3	3	.0
77093	49.0	55	14.5	63	24.2	324	49.7	10	6	13.3	8	1	1.0
77095	2.1	97	.7	98	50.7	662	156.5	13	0	1.0	0	0	.0

*=Estimated **1.0=883 lbs per person; 100++ indicates per capita toxic waste generation > than 100 times the U.S. average of 883 lbs per capita.

ZIP CODE MEASURES OF SIZE, LEVELS OF AFFLUENCE AND QUALITY OF LIFE

1=Population (th.); 2= % White; 3=Households (th.); 4=% Owner Occupied; 5=Mean Income Per Household (th.$); 6=Mean Monthly Rent ($); 7=Mean Home Value (th.$); 8=% under 5; 9=% 65 and over; 10=% White Males (th.); 11=% White Males, 65+; 12=# Toxic Waste Sites; 13=Toxic Waste Relative to US(883 lbs.per capita)**

TEXAS

ZIP CODE	1	2	3	4	5	6	7	8	9	10	11	12	13
HOUSTON													
77096	41.1	90	16.6	57	44.3	437	170.6	6	9	17.7	8	0	.0
77098	15.9	91	9.3	25	33.2	405	211.8	4	14	7.5	9	0	.9
77099	23.7	87	7.7	70	38.6	569	115.5	10	1	10.4	1	2	.0
HOUSTON													
77301	30.9	88	10.9	67	31.5	335	107.6	8	10	13.2	8	6	2.5
77302	17.6	95	5.4	89	35.8	335	108.3	7	6	8.6	5	2	.1
77326	.3	100	.1	82	21.0	294	88.5	19	5	.2	8	0	.0
77327	20.6	89	7.2	80	23.3	255	61.0	7	12	9.1	11	1	.2
77331	2.4	74	.9	91	20.2	199	64.1	5	18	.9	17	0	.2
77333	.4	67	.1	83	19.6	454	59.8	11	6	.1	11	0	.0
77334	.4	80	.1	78	24.1	225	33.9	7	19	.1	21	0	.0
77335	1.5	77	.6	80	15.9	229	48.3	7	21	.6	24	0	.0
77336	5.9	99	1.9	87	33.7	425	85.7	7	5	3.0	4	0	.0
77338	30.4	90	9.5	74	36.2	426	111.8	10	3	14.0	3	1	.2
77339	19.8	97	5.9	87	56.7	518	179.7	8	2	9.7	1	2	.0
77350	38.2	70	10.6	55	24.4	320	85.8	5	8	14.8	6	2	.0
77351	16.5	84	6.1	79	21.4	281	37.6	7	7	.7	7	2	.0
77355	10.5	96	3.3	89	33.6	323	121.3	9	6	5.2	5	2	.0
77356	6.9	89	2.6	86	32.0	246	110.2	6	14	3.0	12	1	.0
77357	9.8	96	3.0	90	30.9	406	87.1	8	5	4.7	5	0	.0
77358	2.9	58	1.0	80	20.2	217	50.2	8	16	.8	16	0	.0
77359	.6	67	.2	65	17.7	399	54.6	7	21	.2	17	2	.0
77360	.6	94	.3	90	15.7	271	72.4	8	17	.3	14	0	.0
77362	2.9	98	.9	93	33.5	518	112.8	9	9	1.5	7	0	.0
77363	.6	91	.2	89	23.5	99	62.6	9	10	.3	9	0	.0
77364	.9	55	.4	80	20.6	165	76.2	6	20	.3	24	0	.0
77365	10.0	99	3.1	89	33.7	363	90.0	10	6	5.0	5	0	.0
77368	.3	60	.1	83	12.2	140*	39.5	3	25	.1	27	1	.0
77369	1.1	0	.4	84	15.8	267	32.7	8	17	.7	0	0	.0
77371	3.6	85	1.2	87	18.5	260	44.6	9	13	1.5	12	0	.0
77372	7.4	100	2.3	87	27.3	338	70.6	10	6	3.8	6	0	.0
77373	51.1	95	14.9	88	44.9	423	132.6	10	2	24.7	2	3	6.7
77374	.2	100	.1	84	24.0	276*	41.6	9	11	.1	14	0	.0
77375	11.0	94	3.6	80	35.3	394	117.3	6	5	5.1	5	2	.0
77376	.3	100	.1	80	18.3	143	48.3	13	15	.2	14	0	.0
77378	8.2	87	2.8	78	28.0	344	84.6	8	11	3.5	10	1	.2
77379	17.8	97	5.2	91	46.9	546	150.3	8	2	8.7	2	0	.0
77380	12.1	99	3.9	75	44.5	439	143.0	9	3	5.9	2	0	.1
HOUSTON													
77401	15.0	95	6.0	77	37.0	566	117.3	6	12	6.8	11	2	.2
77411	1.1	54	.4	75	29.6	543	75.5	4	15	.7	10	1	.0
77414	23.3	74	8.2	60	28.7	353	80.5	10	10	8.6	8	5	6.7
77415	.4	0	.1	74	20.0	323	67.7	12	13	.4	0	0	.0
77417	1.3	70	.3	62	27.7	248	63.2	10	8	.4	6	0	.0
77418	5.7	83	2.2	78	26.1	318	78.4	6	22	2.3	18	1	1.2
77419	1.2	72	.4	64	28.4	357	63.3	10	7	.4	7	0	.0
77420	1.9	79	.7	79	24.7	248	63.8	6	19	.7	20	0	.1

TEXAS

ZIP CODE	1	2	3	4	5	6	7	8	9	10	11	12	13
HOUSTON													
77422	13.0	75	3.7	79	30.3	381	77.8	9	6	5.3	5	1	.0
77423	3.8	55	1.2	76	28.0	329	88.2	6	12	1.0	11	1	.6
77426	1.1	61	.4	79	26.2	283	62.2	2	26	.3	21	0	.0
77428	.1	100		90	21.8	251*	42.9	0	43	.1	47	0	.0
77429	11.9	96	3.6	92	49.0	622	142.9	8	2	5.8	2	0	.0
77430	1.6	0	.6	71	26.0	216	66.1	7	14		15	0	.0
77432	.2	100	.1	57	16.4	188*	90.8	25	14	.1	14	2	.0
77434	3.8	51	1.7	68	25.3	215	54.3	9	13	1.3	14	1	.0
77435	2.4	84	1.2	71	22.9	275	79.3	9	12	1.6	12	1	.0
77437	16.3	82	5.6	66	24.5	299	67.2	9	12	6.6	11	7	.1
77440	.7	78	.1	44	20.2	392	81.6	3	14	.1	21	0	.0
77441	.7	48	.2	86	30.3	260	106.4	12	12	.2	5	0	.0
77442	1.2	72	.4	79	26.0	284	54.4	8	13	.4	8	2	.1
77443	.8	0	.3	82	13.5	648	30.9	9	26	.0	0	0	.0
77444	.4	0	.2	74	26.7	358	40.8	10	11	.0	0	1	.0
77445	10.3	39	2.7	72	23.8	290	66.0	6	12	1.9	15	5	.2
77447	3.3	91	1.0	90	32.7	350	110.9	11	7	1.5	6	0	4.3
77448	.6	72	.2	92	17.3	206	48.1	9	24	.2	18	0	3.7
77450	26.1	92	8.0	88	44.7	571	132.9	11	3	12.1	2	2	.0
77451	.7	0	.2	70	16.1	187	44.1	14	7	.0	0	1	.0
77452	.2	68	.1	62	17.2	80	55.0	6	27	.1	29	0	.0
77453	.5	68	.2	70	16.5	262	47.3	7	7	.2	4	0	.0
77454	.3	100	.1	67	34.2	400	114.1	2	13	.2	17	0	.4
77455	1.9	92	.6	71	28.4	241	59.7	8	16	.8	13	0	.0
77456	2.2	80	.7	66	24.3	247	48.6	13	8	.9	7	1	.0
77457	1.0	88	.4	70	21.6	326	51.1	13	17	.5	17	0	.0
77458	.2	0	.1	77	29.4	278	34.7	18	13	.2	4	0	.0
77459	30.7	68	9.6	92	48.4	619	141.9	10	2	10.4	2	0	.4
77460	.2	0	.1	82	30.9	180	86.6	6	18	.3	13	0	.0
77461	5.4	81	1.8	79	26.8	312	82.8	8	11	2.2	10	2	3.1
77463	1.0	77	.4	50	31.7	244	58.0	9	6	.4	6	0	.0
77464	.8	82	.2	86	29.3	351	69.7	7	12	.3	14	0	5.5
77465	6.5	79	2.2	68	25.3	302	61.6	11	10	2.6	9	1	.0
77466	.3	55	.1	76	27.4	77	87.5	6	12	.1	15	1	.0
77467	.2	100	.1	77	34.2	393*	29.9	8	29	.1	32	0	.0
77468	.2	49	.1	76	15.5	131	42.9	2	15	.1	20	0	.0
77469	17.5	63	5.0	61	33.9	324	113.3	9	7	5.8	6	0	.0
77470	.1	81		81	20.6	237*	42.1	0	39	.0	8	0	.0
77471	20.3	77	6.5	63	28.2	347	86.5	10	8	7.9	7	2	.1
77473	.3	18	.1	85	22.6	181	41.9	5	14	.0	11	0	.0
77474	7.1	83	2.4	75	28.7	348	87.8	9	14	2.8	12	1	.1
77475	.7	0	.3	88	28.9	238	43.1	6	13	.4	0	0	.0
77476	1.0	80		69	44.4	383	187.4	8	8	.5	7	0	.0
77477	12.1	80	3.6	73	36.6	391	109.1	10	3	4.9	3	0	.0
77478	20.1	83	6.1	90	52.9	507	157.3	10	5	8.6	3	2	1.2
77480	6.4	86	2.1	78	32.2	322	77.3	9	9	2.7	8	1	1.6
77481	.4	30	.1	64	23.1	318	99.6	14	9	.1	0	0	10.7
77482	2.2	73	.7	81	30.3	347	62.8	10	6	.9	4	0	.0
77483	1.9	79	.7	79	23.4	383	52.9	14	11	.1	10	0	.0

*=Estimated **1.0=883 lbs per person; 100++ indicates per capita toxic waste generation > than 100 times the U.S. average of 883 lbs per capita.

ZIP CODE MEASURES OF SIZE, LEVELS OF AFFLUENCE AND QUALITY OF LIFE

1=Population (th.); 2= % White; 3=Households (th.); 4=% Owner Occupied; 5=Mean Income Per Household (th.$); 6=Mean Monthly Rent ($)*; 7=Mean Home Value (th.$)*; 8=% under 5; 9=% 65 and over; 10=White Males (th.); 11=% White Males, 65+; 12=# Toxic Waste Sites; 13=Toxic Waste Relative to US(883 lbs.per capita)**.

TEXAS

HOUSTON

ZIPCODE	1	2	3	4	5	6	7	8	9	10	11	12	13
77484	3.8	83	1.2	77	27.8	285	76.2	8	10	1.6	10	0	.1
77485	2.3	77	.8	77	21.4	217	71.2	9	15	.9	12	0	.0
77486	6.5	83	2.3	74	31.3	369	85.1	9	9	2.8	8	1	.0
77488	13.8	68	5.0	66	25.7	280	73.6	8	13	4.6	10	3	.0

HOUSTON

ZIPCODE	1	2	3	4	5	6	7	8	9	10	11	12	13
77502	29.7	95	10.0	67	37.9	401	88.9	7	6	13.9	5	4	
77503	21.6	89	7.0	59	30.6	343	75.1	11	3	9.9	3	0	1.1
77504	15.6	93	5.7	53	33.7	340	123.0	9	5	7.2	3	0	
77505	8.4	95	3.0	51	33.6	398	104.5	11	1	4.0	1	0	.0
77506	37.8	84	13.3	47	27.1	333	57.7	11	5	16.0	5	2	.0
77510	8.5	97	2.7	90	30.8	330	89.4	8	7	4.1	6	1	.2
77511	29.6	92	9.7	70	33.1	399	95.4	9	7	13.9	5	11	6.5
77514	4.3	78	1.6	70	27.8	257	64.5	9	13	1.6	12	3	
77515	22.2	83	7.0	69	34.0	388	84.8	9	9	9.6	5	3	.1
77517	3.8	96	1.2	86	28.7	377	76.8	7	7	1.8	5	2	.0
77518	4.1	96	1.5	73	28.1	362	65.7	10	8	2.0	8	0	.0
77519	1.0	100	.3	94	22.3	139	35.0	8	10	.5	9	0	.0
77520	44.6	77	15.8	60	30.5	354	76.5	9	5	16.9	9	10	12.8
77521	25.3	82	8.6	66	34.6	374	99.6	10	5	10.4	4	0	
77530	21.7	93	7.2	68	32.7	385	81.7	11	4	10.3	4	1	.1
77531	13.2	85	4.6	54	29.6	425	75.5	10	5	5.9	4	1	13.4
77532	13.1	72	4.3	86	33.4	288	95.5	10	6	4.7	6	4	.1
77533	1.4	98	.5	76	25.1	281	48.6	10	13	.7	10	0	1.3
77534	1.9	91	.6	76	32.3	423	83.7	10	6	.9	9	1	.0
77535	12.8	90	4.1	81	29.5	279	82.9	9	7	5.8	5	2	.2
77536	21.9	97	6.7	82	39.8	442	103.2	9	3	10.8	2	10	67.2
77539	.9	72	.3	83	22.9	192	54.0	10	12	1.6	11	2	
77541	18.4	79	6.4	74	33.9	294	96.9	8	7	7.8	6	3	.2
77545	19.8	71	6.7	58	29.0	363	67.3	10	6	8.1	6	13	100++
77546	1.4	94	.5	88	36.1	290	71.8	11	6	.6	4	0	.9
77547	19.1	94	5.8	85	45.9	481	131.2	8	3	8.9	2	2	.3
77550	9.0	69	4.6	72	28.2	366	55.6	9	15	3.6	13	1	6.4
77551	50.3	56	19.7	43	28.0	416	118.8	8	6	13.6	14	1	.4
77560	11.9	90	4.6	74	34.9	113	54.6	8	7	5.5	6	0	.0
77561	1.0	49	.3	88	20.6	401	62.3	11	7	.2	11	0	.2
77562	1.0	94	.4	82	27.5	355	78.8	8	8	.5	7	1	.0
77563	8.4	95	2.8	84	34.1	330	63.4	9	8	4.0	7	1	1.2
77564	8.1	66	2.9	77	28.6	250	45.4	6	10	2.7	10	5	.0
77565	1.8	99	.7	84	26.1	446	98.0	9	13	1.0	14	1	.0
77566	4.1	95	1.4	70	33.3	337	66.8	9	4	2.0	5	2	2.0
77568	20.4	94	6.9	68	41.3	407	95.4	9	9	9.7	3	0	.0
77571	15.1	72	5.4	75	29.2	404	99.3	9	4	5.4	7	1	.2
77573	23.4	88	7.4	75	35.6	330	69.9	10	6	10.3	5	2	.0
77575	15.6	93	5.0	77	36.7	372	82.6	9	11	7.3	9	0	.0
77577	13.2	76	4.6	74	28.6	125	107.8	8	11	5.0	9	5	3.3
77578	1.3	98	.5	69	28.0	359	33.3	11	10	1.6	11	0	100++
77579	4.3	97	1.3	90	34.7	125	107.8	6	7	2.0	7	0	.0
77580	2.0	89	.7	80	32.9	359	87.6	9	9	.9	10	1	6.9

TEXAS

HOUSTON

ZIPCODE	1	2	3	4	5	6	7	8	9	10	11	12	13
77581	23.3	92	7.5	81	38.9	410	117.3	8	5	10.9	4	2	.4
77582	.7	66	.2	87	25.9	261	72.7	7	11	.2	9	0	.0
77583	8.6	50	1.3	68	31.2	195	73.9	4	4	3.0	2	4	.0
77585	1.2	100	.4	76	22.5	209	36.3	8	14	4.6	14	0	.0
77586	12.9	95	4.5	70	43.9	394	155.4	3	3	6.4	3	3	5.8
77587	13.4	81	4.2	57	26.0	349	63.0	10	6	5.5	5	0	.0
77590	40.7	71	13.7	69	30.1	340	71.5	9	8	14.1	7	12	20.8
77597	.2	60	.1	82	26.2	301*	37.1	3	10	.1	11	1	.0
77598	5.7	86	2.3	52	31.0	363	103.9	9	6	2.5	4	0	1.0

BEAUMONT

ZIPCODE	1	2	3	4	5	6	7	8	9	10	11	12	13
77611	9.6	98	3.2	79	33.0	389	75.8	8	6	4.7	5	3	1.5
77612	7.2	96	2.3	83	24.4	223	49.4	9	10	3.3	9	1	.0
77613	1.4	72	.5	84	27.1	267	57.6	8	11	.5	10	0	.0
77614	1.5	0	.5	79	23.6	233	43.6	6	10	.0	5	0	.0
77615	1.2	100	.4	84	22.1	253	65.8	9	9	.6	7	0	1.7
77616	.7	0	.3	86	22.1	308	29.3	10	10	.0	6	0	.0
77617	.2	0	.1	100	18.3	210*	33.7	0	14	.0	0	0	.0
77618	.2	0	.1	98	28.6	328*	38.3	6	22	.0	8	0	.0
77619	17.2	99	6.3	77	31.9	394	64.8	7	11	8.3	9	1	.8
77622	.8	100	.3	87	32.2	213	62.6	4	7	.4	5	0	.0
77623	.6	100	.2	78	27.1	333	42.1	7	11	.3	9	0	.0
77624	.8	73	.3	86	23.3	152	53.1	7	27	.3	32	0	.0
77625	6.8	86	2.3	81	25.3	239	57.1	8	10	2.9	10	0	1.7
77626	1.5	91	.5	90	27.5	160	62.9	8	5	.0	0	0	.0
77627	23.9	96	8.3	81	32.3	383	71.4	7	7	11.5	5	1	3.4
77629	.8	61	.3	66	23.9	290	69.7	10	11	.9	7	1	.0
77630	46.7	84	15.9	71	28.4	297	67.3	8	9	19.4	7	11	13.4
77639	1.1	100	.3	78	32.1	229	46.6	9	8	.5	8	1	.0
77640	62.2	56	22.6	69	24.4	283	48.1	8	14	16.7	16	13	18.1
77650	1.8	99	.7	72	21.6	280	47.2	7	15	.9	16	0	.0
77651	14.4	97	4.9	75	34.6	354	81.7	7	7	7.0	7	10	39.4
77655	.8	97	.3	78	26.3	363	36.9	7	7	.4	6	0	.0
77656	25.8	88	8.7	82	27.5	296	66.8	9	10	11.3	9	3	.7
77659	3.8	95	1.3	90	30.7	297	79.2	8	11	1.7	10	1	.0
77660	1.2	97	.4	93	17.4	311	48.8	10	13	.5	12	0	.0
77661	.8	49	.3	86	24.6	197	41.3	5	11	.2	14	0	.0
77662	26.8	99	8.6	82	28.4	299	61.7	9	7	13.3	6	0	.0
77663	.8	0	.3	91	28.7	243	92.1	6	26	.0	0	0	.0
77664	2.3	87	.8	82	26.9	240	56.2	7	13	1.0	14	0	.0
77665	5.1	92	1.6	74	28.8	328	63.3	8	6	2.4	5	2	1.5

BEAUMONT

ZIPCODE	1	2	3	4	5	6	7	8	9	10	11	12	13
77701	23.7	33	8.7	49	17.9	241	37.0	9	13	3.8	18	11	.0
77702	4.0	85	2.1	39	24.6	345	75.0	5	23	1.5	18	1	.7
77703	19.0	41	6.9	63	21.0	261	43.4	10	13	3.6	15	1	.0
77704	.8	81	.2	84	29.3	307	54.5	7	23	.4	17	3	100++
77705	28.3	53	10.1	67	23.0	360	50.9	8	11	7.4	12	3	3.3
77706	25.4	96	9.5	75	43.7	451	122.5	7	9	12.0	8	1	1.4
77707	15.3	94	5.3	77	35.8	470	82.6	8	9	6.9	7	1	.0
77708	10.6	67	3.5	75	30.9	325	70.5	11	5	3.5	5	0	.0

*=Estimated **1.0=883 lbs per capita. 100++ indicates per capita toxic waste generation > than 100 times the U.S. average of 883 lbs per capita.

ZIP CODE MEASURES OF SIZE, LEVELS OF AFFLUENCE AND QUALITY OF LIFE

1=Population (th.); 2= % White; 3=Households (th.); 4=% Owner Occupied; 5=Mean Income Per Household (th.$); 6=Mean Monthly Rent ($)*; 7=Mean Home Value (th.$)*;
8=% under 5, 9=% 65 and over; 10=%White Males (th.); 11=% White Males, 65+; 12=# Toxic Waste Sites; 13=Toxic Waste Relative to US(883 lbs.per capita)**.

TEXAS

ZIP CODE	1	2	3	4	5	6	7	8	9	10	11	12	13
BEAUMONT													
77709	.5	70	.1	80	24.0	260	48.9	6	24	.1	23	0	.0
77711	.8	0	.3	90	29.7	153	83.8	8	5	.0	0	0	.0
BRYAN													
77801	55.1	77	20.2	60	23.8	338	83.4	8	10	21.7	8	4	.5
77830	1.4	71	.5	86	22.1	88	47.5	6	20	.5	19	0	.0
77831	1.3	84	.5	74	31.4	320	41.9	7	21	.5	17	0	.0
77833	17.9	79	6.2	72	26.7	267	79.0	7	17	6.8	15	2	.1
77835	1.9	80	.7	82	21.5	187	57.2	7	29	.8	29	0	.1
77836	7.5	76	2.7	76	21.5	238	54.3	7	20	2.7	18	0	.1
77837	2.1	41	.9	71	13.5	180	30.8	7	28	.4	26	0	.0
77839	.4	0	.1	81	22.1	218	31.6	16	13	.0	0	0	.0
77840	29.6	91	12.0	27	19.1	396	107.6	5	3	15.0	2	5	.0
77852	1.0	100	.3	81	18.1	208*	43.7	6	22	.1	5	0	.0
77853	1.0	67	.3	79	20.2	283	51.1	8	16	.3	17	1	.0
77855	.2	100	.1	68	22.5	237	109.4	5	5	.1	10	1	.0
77856	2.5	85	1.1	80	20.9	216	53.1	6	24	1.1	20	0	.0
77857	.4	85	.2	81	16.9	130	25.9	13	26	.2	31	0	.0
77859	7.1	53	2.6	66	20.5	218	46.0	9	17	1.7	16	3	.5
77861	.9	94	.3	87	18.4	211*	54.5	9	15	.4	16	0	.0
77863	.2	76	.1	78	12.4	99	36.3	0	42	.1	41	0	.0
77864	5.6	76	2.0	73	24.8	254	65.2	8	19	2.0	18	1	.1
77866	.8	93	.3	74	21.2	188	44.5	5	15	.4	11	0	.0
77867	.2	78	.1	90	22.5	259*	43.4	3	8	.1	7	0	.0
77868	9.0	0	3.1	68	12.0	195	41.6	11	0	.0	0	0	.0
77870	.2	78	.1	81	21.6	256	56.9	9	17	.1	19	0	.5
77871	2.2	89	1.0	79	17.4	138*	42.8*	6	30	.9	25	0	.0
77872	1.0	89	.4	84	20.3	286	60.8	6	26	.9	26	0	.0
77873	.7	69	.3	78	16.5	138	56.8	4	28	.2	28	0	.0
77876	.3	52	.1	100	16.9	194*	25.9	3	28	.1	23	0	.0
77878	.3	75	.1	68	20.4	289	55.9	8	18	.2	15	1	.0
77879	3.4	68	1.2	80	20.6	249	43.3	7	17	1.2	18	3	.0
77880	1.3	45	.5	81	17.4	188	60.0	5	14	.3	10	0	.0
77881	.2	62	.1	81	15.9	182	69.1	10	6	.1	7	2	.0
77882	.5	0	.2	81	28.9	203	62.1	10	14	.0	0	0	.0
VICTORIA													
77901	63.4	80	21.1	65	29.2	351	78.8	9	9	25.1	7	5	2.5
77950	.4	88	.1	66	24.2	281	49.2	6	14	.2	13	0	.0
77951	2.1	76	.6	76	23.9	261	43.8	10	9	.8	7	0	.0
77954	9.6	76	3.5	71	20.4	219	48.4	8	20	3.4	18	1	.0
77957	7.9	77	2.8	74	24.0	253	62.1	8	14	3.1	11	1	.0
77960	.2	61	.1	89	27.3	314*	87.7	10	11	.0	9	0	.0
77961	.2	100	.1	77	20.1	225	29.1	8	10	.1	18	0	.0
77962	3.0	90	1.1	76	23.3	247	65.4	9	16	1.3	15	1	.0
77963	4.3	74	1.4	74	21.0	271	54.9	7	16	1.5	15	0	.0
77964	7.0	90	2.6	78	21.2	233	57.9	7	23	3.0	20	0	.0
77968	1.6	86	.5	85	26.9	200	80.8	6	11	.7	9	0	.0
77970	.4	94	.2	53	15.8	326	35.7	9	15	.2	11	2	.0
77971	.7	100	.2	76	26.5	356	60.2	7	8	.3	6	0	.0

TEXAS

ZIP CODE	1	2	3	4	5	6	7	8	9	10	11	12	13
VICTORIA													
77974	.3	0	.1	89	26.8	248	61.5	15	7	.0	0	0	.0
77975	1.9	97	.7	77	18.6	230	58.2	6	29	.9	25	0	.1
77976	.3	83	.1	73	25.5	251	60.1	10	3	.1	0	0	.0
77977	.8	66	.2	65	25.9	291	43.6	15	5	.2	6	0	.0
77978	1.2	96	.4	83	44.9	409	50.2	7	6	.6	6	1	100++
77979	15.3	86	4.9	71	28.5	306	65.4	9	8	6.4	7	0	1.8
77982	1.0	94	.4	78	21.5	257	61.9	7	10	.5	6	2	.0
77983	2.1	84	.7	68	21.1	286	43.4	9	9	.9	11	0	.0
77984	4.1	90	1.6	80	18.3	173	52.8	7	25	1.8	20	0	.1
77987	.2	79	.1	91	11.1	281	29.3	10	16	.1	18	0	.0
77988	.7	93	.3	81	23.8	267	73.9	11	6	.3	7	0	.0
77989	.2	100	.1	71	30.8	128	37.9	4	5	.1	9	0	.0
77990	.8	88	.3	62	21.6	208	48.5	9	12	.3	14	1	.0
77991	.7	82	.2	74	25.4	177	36.2	6	5	.3	6	0	.0
77993	.2	100	.1	75	33.3	382*	58.0	11	5	.1	5	0	.0
77994	.4	88	.2	85	13.0	240	23.8	3	35	.2	32	0	.0
77995	9.1	83	3.3	75	20.7	196	51.2	8	19	3.6	17	0	.0
SAN ANTONIO (WEST)													
78002	3.3	77	.9	82	19.8	166	41.1	7	9	1.3	10	0	.0
78003	3.1	97	1.3	78	20.5	241	67.5	6	24	1.3	23	0	.0
78005	9.5	95	3.4	82	32.2	287	120.6	5	14	4.4	12	1	.0
78006	.4	88	.4	74	22.5	164	42.4	7	20	.2	22	0	.0
78008	.4	0	.2	66	31.3	131	26.4	6	7	.3	6	0	.4
78009	2.7	93	.8	81	24.7	227	64.2	8	12	1.2	9	0	.0
78010	1.8	97	.6	78	20.2	248	61.5	7	13	.9	10	0	.0
78011	2.0	92	.7	78	21.4	198	29.5	11	10	1.0	10	0	.0
78012	.4	90	.2	78	13.8	229	21.6	11	11	.4	11	0	.0
78013	2.7	90	1.0	77	20.3	167	76.4	8	17	1.1	16	0	.0
78014	4.4	82	1.4	73	17.8	158	33.9	9	12	1.7	12	0	.0
78016	6.5	93	2.1	82	23.8	216	45.4	8	12	3.1	11	1	.3
78017	3.1	90	1.0	70	17.9	229	35.5	10	11	1.4	9	3	.0
78019	.9	92	.2	64	15.1	143	19.2	10	11	.4	13	0	.0
78021	.2	100	.2	79	29.2	369	13.1	5	8	.1	7	0	.0
78022	4.1	95	1.4	86	24.5	240	59.1	11	9	1.9	9	0	6.3
78023	2.0	96	.7	63	36.5	417	130.8	4	8	1.0	8	0	.0
78024	.8	99	.3	76	30.5	400	104.4	7	14	.4	18	1	.0
78025	2.5	97	.9	76	23.6	266	66.3	8	20	1.2	19	0	.0
78026	2.9	90	1.0	81	21.8	235	46.0	8	12	1.3	10	0	.4
78027	.3	0	.1	82	23.4	269*	83.4*	0	33	.0	33	0	.0
78028	23.2	91	9.0	72	25.5	330	85.9	5	25	9.7	25	1	.1
78039	1.3	93	.4	81	22.1	163	41.7	5	13	.6	12	0	.3
78040	70.7	92	18.6	59	18.1	244	57.3	10	10	30.5	12	3	.2
78041	27.1	91	6.9	91	25.9	355	86.0	10	12	12.1	4	0	.0
78050	.7	89	.2	80	19.1	190	47.0	9	9	.4	9	0	.0
78052	2.9	88	.9	80	21.2	218	53.9	9	12	1.3	13	0	.0
78053	.2	0	.1	76	16.8	193*	13.1	0	27	.0	0	2	.0
78054	.5	91	.3	81	16.8	253	22.1	11	10	.2	11	2	.0
78055	1.0	97	.3	97	22.3	263	37.4	6	16	.5	15	0	.0

*=Estimated **1.0=883 lbs per person; 100++ indicates per capita toxic waste generation > than 100 times the U.S. average of 883 lbs per capita.

ZIP CODE MEASURES OF SIZE, LEVELS OF AFFLUENCE AND QUALITY OF LIFE

1=Population (th.); 2= % White; 3=Households (th.); 4=% Owner Occupied; 5=Mean Income Per Household (th.$); 6=Mean Monthly Rent ($)*; 7=Mean Home Value (th.$)*;
8=% under 5; 9=% 65 and over; 10=White Males; 11=% White Males, 65+; 12=# Toxic Waste Sites; 13=Toxic Waste Relative to US(883 lbs.per capita)**.

TEXAS

ZIPCODE	1	2	3	4	5	6	7	8	9	10	11	12	13
SAN ANTONIO (WEST)													
78056	.2	100	.1	82	19.6	211	50.4	6	47	.1	55	0	.0
78057	.9	0	.3	86	17.8	309	45.6	4	11	.0	0	0	.0
78058	.3	85	.1	49	44.9	516*	100.6	6	7	.1	9	0	.0
78059	2.5	86	.8	73	15.5	236	31.0	9	10	1.1	12	0	.0
78061	9.6	78	2.7	68	20.0	182	46.6	12	10	3.7	10	1	.0
78063	2.4	98	.9	91	24.9	192	73.4	6	12	1.2	12	0	.0
78064	9.6	90	3.2	74	22.6	241	55.6	10	13	4.3	12	0	.0
78065	5.8	91	1.7	76	17.6	186	33.1	3	11	2.6	12	0	.0
78066	.2	100		65	23.4	408	136.3	3	11	1	14	0	.8
78067	.9	90	.3	86	14.1	95	24.4	15	10	.5	9	0	.0
78069	1.4	89	.5	73	21.3	220	46.4	8	9	.6	9	0	.0
78070	.6	100	.2	95	25.3	193	86.2	8	15	.3	17	0	.0
78071	3.3	90	1.2	75	25.3	230	50.6	10	16	1.5	16	0	5.9
78072	.6	0	.2	80	29.7	176	42.1	5	14	.0	0	0	9.9
78073	4.1	92	1.2	77	19.8	239	38.9	9	10	2.0	9	0	.0
78075	.2	100	.1	68	23.2	153	56.9	0	24	.1	17	0	.0
78076	5.5	94	1.7	83	19.6	207	53.5	9	16	2.6	18	1	1.0
SAN ANTONIO (EAST)													
78101	3.9	93	1.3	89	24.9	274	76.8	7	9	1.9	9	0	.0
78102	21.5	84	6.7	61	22.3	286	60.4	10	9	8.9	7	1	.0
78107	.2	48	.1	79	18.4	53	24.6	6	6	.0	22	0	.0
78108	2.3	90	.8	87	25.3	276	77.1	7	10	1.0	9	0	.0
78109	6.2	85	1.9	79	25.8	361	74.9	10	5	2.7	5	0	.1
78112	1.4	88	.5	84	18.1	129	42.5	8	13	.6	11	0	.0
78113	1.9	97	.6	78	23.3	211	48.6	7	13	.9	14	0	3.4
78114	8.0	88	2.6	75	21.3	235	55.3	9	12	3.5	10	2	.0
78115	.2	0	.1	100	24.5	282*	40.8	4	20	.0	0	0	.0
78116	.2	0	.1	78	17.4	113	80.4	8	5	.0	0	0	.0
78117	.5	100	.2	84	26.2	506	31.0	4	25	.3	21	0	69.6
78118	4.3	87	1.4	77	20.9	214	45.5	8	15	1.8	13	0	.3
78119	5.8	80	1.9	72	22.7	222	49.6	9	15	2.2	16	0	.0
78121	2.2	87	.8	81	24.2	272	58.9	6	15	1.0	16	0	.0
78122	.3	83	.1	96	17.9	206*	24.3	9	19	.6	12	0	.0
78123	.8	87	.3	84	23.0	211	85.6	10	8	.4	8	0	.1
78124	2.9	90	1.0	73	24.3	242	65.7	6	12	1.3	10	0	.0
78125	.2	0	.1	77	20.2	232*	22.1	7	32	.0	0	0	.0
78130	34.8	92	12.5	76	25.9	343	80.2	7	15	15.5	15	5	.1
78140	3.1	80	1.1	69	18.9	206	33.2	9	17	1.2	13	0	1.2
78141	.5	91	.2	88	16.0	215	39.7	3	31	.3	21	0	.0
78142	.2	0	.1	71	27.9	90	43.5	8	14	.0	0	0	.0
78145	.5	60	.1	74	21.5	161	25.0	6	18	.2	5	0	.0
78146	.5	90	.3	68	25.3	203	44.0	9	20	.4	16	0	.0
78147	1.5	86	.5	76	21.8	218	46.9	9	13	.6	12	0	.2
78148	15.6	88	4.9	48	27.9	388	99.6	9	2	7.0	2	0	.0
78151	1.7	76	.6	73	18.7	178	35.1	8	17	.7	14	0	.0
78153	.3	57	.1	47	15.2	168	26.4	5	14	1	24	0	.0
78154	7.7	90	2.5	71	26.0	324	75.4	7	5	3.4	5	2	.0
78155	28.1	82	9.4	72	23.1	268	67.6	8	12	11.2	10	3	.2
78159	1.0	88	.3	77	19.3	135	33.2	5	16	.4	15	0	.0

TEXAS

ZIPCODE	1	2	3	4	5	6	7	8	9	10	11	12	13
SAN ANTONIO (EAST)													
78160	2.5	86	.8	77	20.8	180	46.0	6	18	1.1	14	0	.0
78161	.9	0	.3	100	16.2	187*	31.8	17	4	.0	0	0	.0
78162	.5	89	.1	84	26.3	468	54.4	4	19	.2	17	0	.0
78163	2.8	0	.9	88	40.0	448	135.4	7	7	.0	0	0	.0
78164	4.5	88	1.7	75	20.5	192	52.3	7	21	2.0	18	0	.1
SAN ANTONIO													
78201	43.8	85	16.7	55	19.7	294	50.0	7	16	16.9	13	0	.0
78202	13.2	22	4.9	56	13.4	202	31.8	7	18	1.3	17	1	.0
78203	8.2	29	2.9	48	12.3	183	30.3	8	19	1.1	13	0	.0
78204	13.1	80	4.1	59	16.9	210	35.7	8	14	4.8	13	0	.8
78205	2.0	79	1.0	4	10.4	185	67.8	2	28	1.1	20	1	1.6
78207	61.8	77	17.8	48	13.4	176	30.1	11	12	22.4	10	1	.2
78208	6.0	59	1.9	34	11.6	196	28.0	12	10	1.7	12	1	.1
78209	36.8	90	16.9	54	34.1	357	132.0	6	20	14.7	18	2	.3
78210	39.5	71	13.3	61	16.6	194	40.2	10	15	12.9	14	1	.4
78211	34.3	79	8.8	69	16.4	217	30.2	11	7	13.0	6	2	.1
78212	32.2	82	13.1	45	22.9	259	83.8	6	18	12.3	14	0	.0
78213	30.3	91	11.3	72	30.2	360	84.4	6	10	12.9	9	0	.2
78214	24.0	83	7.6	64	16.7	219	34.2	10	12	9.6	10	2	3.1
78215	1.8	78	.8	17	12.7	211	45.6	5	17	.6	17	1	.0
78216	27.6	94	12.3	42	28.2	374	102.4	5	12	12.0	10	2	.0
78217	20.2	95	7.8	58	35.0	408	103.8	6	7	9.1	6	1	.6
78218	28.7	85	9.9	63	25.7	348	72.7	8	5	11.9	5	1	.3
78219	12.4	63	4.0	72	23.7	267	60.4	7	5	3.9	5	2	2.9
78220	21.1	34	6.7	73	21.2	250	48.1	10	10	3.5	12	1	.1
78221	37.7	82	10.5	74	20.5	248	39.8	9	7	15.1	7	3	.0
78222	10.0	81	3.2	75	26.8	352	70.3	8	10	4.0	8	0	.0
78223	37.1	85	13.0	63	21.2	280	46.4	8	8	15.2	8	1	.0
78224	12.6	79	3.1	81	21.7	254	45.4	11	3	4.9	3	0	.2
78225	14.9	83	4.5	72	19.2	239	35.7	8	12	5.9	11	0	.0
78226	9.4	72	2.8	40	19.1	317	37.3	13	3	3.3	4	0	.0
78227	40.8	81	12.0	66	22.5	342	53.6	10	3	16.5	3	2	.1
78228	62.3	82	18.2	73	24.8	299	61.7	9	7	24.9	7	4	.0
78229	14.8	90	7.0	29	31.7	353	136.5	5	12	3.9	6	0	.0
78230	24.7	95	9.2	68	42.5	357	141.9	5	11	6.2	10	0	.1
78231	2.8	97	.9	99	59.6	685*	193.7	6	5	1.4	5	0	.0
78232	18.0	98	5.6	97	49.7	664	158.9	7	4	8.6	4	1	.0
78233	27.1	91	8.2	84	30.9	473	85.5	10	2	12.3	2	0	.0
78234	6.8	64	.8	0	27.2	404	97.0*	6	0	2.5	0	4	.2
78235	.9	83	.6	2	28.0	408	99.8*11	1	.4	0	0	.0	
78236	15.9	79	.6	65	18.9	322	76.9	3	9	.4	0	0	.0
78237	42.7	73	10.4	65	16.4	186	31.3	11	7	15.1	6	1	.0
78238	19.4	88	6.4	79	30.8	356	95.8	10	3	8.4	3	1	.0
78239	18.2	87	6.0	83	38.2	510	122.2	7	6	7.6	6	0	.2
78240	16.3	94	6.2	57	29.7	378	113.1	7	4	7.5	4	0	.0
78242	22.0	76	6.5	64	21.1	363	54.0	13	2	8.3	2	1	.0
78244	1.7	87	.5	94	34.4	651	101.5	8	1	.8	1	0	.0
78245	7.3	78	2.1	90	31.6	608	93.0	7	1	2.8	0	0	.0
78247	8.2	94	2.7	94	38.1	643	113.6	11	2	3.8	2	0	.0

*=Estimated **1.0=883 lbs per person; 100++ indicates per capita toxic waste generation > than 100 times the U.S. average of 883 lbs per capita.

ZIP CODE MEASURES OF SIZE, LEVELS OF AFFLUENCE AND QUALITY OF LIFE

1=Population (th.); 2= % White; 3=Households (th.); 4=% Owner Occupied; 5=Mean Income Per Household (th.$); 6=Mean Monthly Rent ($)*; 7=Mean Home Value (th.$)*;
8=% under 5; 9=% 65 and over; 10=White Males (th.); 11=% White Males, 65+; 12=# Toxic Waste Sites; 13=Toxic Waste Relative to US(883 lbs.per capita)**.

TEXAS

SAN ANTONIO

ZIP CODE	1	2	3	4	5	6	7	8	9	10	11	12	13
78248	1.0	0	.3	97	57.4	381	202.4	6	3	.0	0	0	.0
78249	6.6	91	2.3	78	33.9	392	109.3	11	3	3.0	3	0	.0
78250	4.7	93	1.5	96	34.6	655	104.6	12	1	2.2	1	1	.0
78251	4.5	84	1.4	91	31.2	698	93.6	11	2	2.2	2	1	.0
78255	1.3	98	.4	95	46.7	653	137.6	5	4	.6	4	0	.0
78256	.6	93	.3	0	17.8	283	63.3*	4	1	.3	0	0	.0
78257	.6	100	.3	86	27.6	420	70.4	1	22	.3	19	1	.0
78260	.4	100	.1	95	48.9	562*	134.6	12	0	.2	0	0	.0
78263	.4	93	.2	86	21.9	171	77.5	5	8	.2	9	0	.0

CORPUS CHRISTI

ZIP CODE	1	2	3	4	5	6	7	8	9	10	11	12	13
78330	1.2	89	.4	78	26.2	273	59.4	10	9	.5	9	0	.0
78332	27.7	89	8.4	73	25.5	277	53.3	10	10	12.1	9	2	.1
78336	9.5	88	3.1	69	23.8	257	67.6	10	12	4.0	11	1	.5
78338	.2	70	.1	6	14.2	233	50.5*	7	8	.1	3	0	.0
78339	.4	72	.2	46	33.5	385*	74.4	9	4	.1	0	0	.0
78340	.5	0	.2	82	22.4	261	47.5	7	16	.1	0	0	.0
78341	2.2	90	.7	85	19.2	185	29.6	10	14	1.0	12	0	.0
78342	.4	0	.1	93	23.0	265*	37.2	4	11	.0	0	0	.0
78343	4.9	88	1.6	76	25.4	260	58.3	9	11	2.2	8	1	.0
78344	.5	80	.1	86	17.6	101	28.1	11	23	.2	8	1	45.1
78347	.3	0	.1	0	21.4	246*	76.2*	10	19	.0	0	0	75.0
78349	.7	89	.3	94	18.1	208*	32.3	6	22	.2	8	0	.0
78351	.7	90	.2	90	21.4	246	41.4	8	10	.3	9	0	.0
78352	.7	67	.2	57	17.6	183	28.8	11	13	.3	12	0	.0
78353	.9	92	.3	73	12.6	100	27.1	10	17	.4	17	0	.0
78355	8.0	87	2.5	75	20.6	181	40.9	9	12	3.4	10	0	.0
78357	3.9	97	1.1	80	23.3	205	38.5	10	8	1.9	8	0	1.3
78358	1.4	95	.7	78	18.5	213	69.1	4	28	.7	28	1	.0
78359	2.8	58	.7	71	20.9	230	36.9	12	5	.8	5	1	.0
78361	5.1	95	1.6	76	21.5	242	41.3	9	12	2.3	11	1	.7
78362	5.8	89	1.8	70	28.5	374	72.0	9	9	2.5	8	1	15.6
78363	32.0	83	9.8	57	23.6	277	66.4	10	7	13.5	5	2	.0
78368	9.0	88	2.6	76	19.5	236	42.5	9	10	3.8	10	1	.0
78369	.6	91	.2	65	38.9	230	30.9	6	6	.3	5	0	.0
78370	3.7	95	1.1	80	28.1	256	54.1	8	8	1.7	7	0	.1
78371	.3	100	.1	81	15.6	179*	17.2	0	20	.1	13	0	.0
78372	2.5	93	.8	79	24.9	273	48.8	8	8	1.2	7	0	.0
78373	2.1	98	.9	71	27.9	103	88.3	4	14	1.0	14	0	.0
78374	12.6	94	4.0	68	36.7	458	105.2	8	3	5.9	3	1	.0
78375	3.7	95	1.2	80	21.6	206	38.5	7	13	1.7	12	0	.1
78376	.7	82	.2	75	16.3	129	22.9	9	24	.3	26	0	.0
78377	4.9	81	1.7	72	25.4	192	57.4	7	13	1.9	12	0	.0
78379	1.4	100	.5	74	22.4	204	44.7	5	14	.7	12	0	.0
78380	21.9	79	5.8	71	23.3	233	53.9	10	8	8.3	7	3	.0
78382	11.5	89	4.0	79	27.5	302	86.7	8	14	5.2	15	0	.1
78383	.7	95	.1	83	26.4	341	75.5	5	16	.9	19	0	.0
78384	5.9	94	1.6	83	17.0	162	32.4	10	14	2.6	13	0	.0
78385	.3	0	.1	36	65.6	754*	34.5	8	15	.3	8	0	.0
78387	9.1	86	2.8	67	23.3	247	53.2	10	11	3.8	9	4	.1

TEXAS

CORPUS CHRISTI

ZIP CODE	1	2	3	4	5	6	7	8	9	10	11	12	13
78389	1.6	87	.5	74	21.0	208	51.5	9	9	.7	9	0	.0
78390	7.0	74	2.0	69	24.8	255	55.4	10	11	2.6	11	1	.0
78391	.4	73	.1	52	13.2	174	32.6	6	14	.1	12	1	.0
78393	2.9	84	.9	69	23.4	227	53.0	9	14	1.2	13	0	.0

CORPUS CHRISTI

ZIP CODE	1	2	3	4	5	6	7	8	9	10	11	12	13
78401	7.3	51	2.8	13	12.7	199	52.8	11	12	1.9	12	2	.9
78402	1.0	90	.5	22	28.9	194	23.7	8	11	.5	12	0	.0
78404	20.2	84	7.2	54	24.9	308	75.5	8	16	7.9	13	0	5.5
78405	19.0	73	5.5	57	15.2	220	33.0	10	10	6.8	10	2	.3
78407	6.2	49	2.0	60	20.4	253	46.4	11	9	1.6	9	0	.0
78408	12.9	74	4.2	58	20.4	281	49.5	10	11	4.9	11	5	13.5
78409	3.5	77	1.1	69	24.5	379	74.8	12	4	1.4	5	2	.0
78410	14.6	93	4.6	75	31.9	406	85.4	9	6	6.7	5	1	.1
78411	28.7	91	10.4	68	32.6	399	89.1	8	10	12.6	9	0	.0
78412	32.2	91	11.5	62	34.6	445	99.2	8	6	14.3	6	4	.0
78413	15.7	93	6.0	54	44.5	453	148.1	8	4	7.3	4	2	.0
78415	37.3	84	11.7	60	24.8	373	64.2	10	7	15.1	6	0	.0
78416	19.0	65	4.8	75	21.4	274	42.1	12	6	6.1	6	0	.0
78417	3.0	64	.7	56	21.0	292	40.1	12	4	.9	5	0	.2
78418	12.3	93	4.2	61	26.9	343	88.1	8	6	5.9	5	0	.0
78419	3.7	81	.8	2	19.5	346	69.4*	13	0	1.8	0	2	.2

MCALLEN

ZIP CODE	1	2	3	4	5	6	7	8	9	10	11	12	13
78501	69.8	89	20.5	63	26.1	294	82.2	10	9	29.6	9	2	.1
78516	10.1	90	2.8	77	16.2	200	38.5	11	11	4.4	12	3	.0
78520	49.1	81	13.7	58	20.2	262	58.4	10	10	18.8	9	3	.8
78521	50.4	78	12.9	59	20.7	313	63.0	12	6	19.1	7	0	.0
78535	1.2	88	.3	69	16.5	254	39.0	11	6	.5	6	0	.0
78536	.4	82	.1	94	20.7	238*	32.1	6	22	.1	26	0	.0
78537	16.2	84	4.0	74	17.3	178	36.5	11	8	6.5	10	2	.0
78538	6.1	76	1.5	71	15.1	157	29.4	11	9	2.1	9	0	.0
78539	39.0	84	10.5	67	20.3	254	55.8	10	8	15.7	7	0	.0
78543	5.7	86	1.4	75	14.6	167	32.3	11	7	2.5	6	0	.0
78547	.5	0	.2	90	10.4	179	20.4	6	10	.0	9	0	.0
78548	1.6	85	.4	84	11.6	115	20.7	8	8	.7	8	0	.0
78549	1.0	92	.1	74	15.6	120	21.5	9	8	.5	10	1	.0
78557	54.2	80	16.5	65	22.8	276	58.2	12	12	20.6	12	7	.2
78558	2.7	85	.6	55	13.5	184	50.2	12	5	1.1	5	3	.0
78559	5.9	87	.1	90	22.8	272	56.0	4	9	.2	11	0	.0
78560	2.2	80	.5	76	18.7	207	43.1	9	15	2.1	15	1	6.1
78561	.5	60	.1	72	15.2	184	28.3	11	4	.8	5	0	.0
78562	1.7	94	.3	78	13.0	157	27.3	11	7	.1	7	0	.0
78563	.4	100	.1	51	15.2	172	25.3	13	8	.6	6	0	.0
78564	.2	78	.1	100	22.2	192	18.0	8	17	.2	18	0	.0
78565	.8	0	.2	88	9.3	107*	26.2	11	29	.1	35	0	.0
78566	3.6	72	1.0	77	16.3	147	25.3	8	5	1.2	8	3	.0
78567	.8	87	.2	94	24.2	284	76.2	9	8	.2	3	0	.0
78568	.5	87	.1	75	16.1	185*	26.5	11	5	.3	2	0	.0

*=Estimated **1.0=883 lbs per person; 100++ indicates per capita toxic waste generation > than 100 times the U.S. average of 883 lbs per capita.

ZIP CODE MEASURES OF SIZE, LEVELS OF AFFLUENCE AND QUALITY OF LIFE

1=Population (th.); 2= % White; 3=Households (th.); 4=% Owner Occupied; 5=Mean Income Per Household (th.$); 6=Mean Monthly Rent ($)*; 7=Mean Home Value (th.$)*; 8=% under 5; 9=% 65 and over; 10=%White Males (th.); 11=% White Males, 65+; 12=# Toxic Waste Sites; 13=Toxic Waste Relative to US(883 lbs.per capita)**.

TEXAS

MCALLEN

ZIPCODE	1	2	3	4	5	6	7	8	9	10	11	12	13
78570	16.8	75	4.5	70	16.7	147	37.2	11	11	6.2	11	5	.0
78572	37.5	89	10.2	76	19.6	207	50.7	11	11	16.2	11	6	.0
78575	1.4	75	.4	86	21.3	162	68.9	9	8	.5	10	0	.0
78576	.6	91	.2	78	11.2	124	36.9	13	11	.3	16	0	.0
78577	26.7	82	6.7	70	17.2	215	41.8	12	7	10.6	8	0	.0
78578	6.0	80	1.7	66	20.2	287	63.1	10	9	2.4	8	1	.2
78579	1.9	81	.4	62	21.2	135	31.5	8	4	.8	3	1	.0
78580	12.1	74	3.3	72	21.9	200	40.5	10	11	4.4	11	3	.0
78582	17.3	88	4.3	80	14.7	172	33.0	12	9	7.6	8	1	.0
78583	3.2	68	.9	76	18.2	195	48.8	11	13	1.0	15	5	.0
78584	5.9	94	1.5	73	13.5	213	36.1	8	7	2.6	7	0	.0
78585	.4	85	.1	92	7.4	85*	15.9	15	13	.3	20	0	.0
78586	28.0	74	7.7	75	18.6	189	43.0	10	10	9.0	10	6	.0
78588	.3	79	.2	78	18.3	211*	51.2	6	7	.1	10	0	.0
78589	12.4	81	3.1	77	18.2	203	40.7	11	8	4.9	7	0	.0
78590	.4	68	.1	78	15.8	135	24.4	14	9	.1	18	0	.0
78591	.6	73	.2	78	21.3	275	35.9	8	6	.2	10	0	.0
78592	.8	72	.2	74	14.2	89	26.1	15	6	.3	8	0	.0
78593	3.6	75	.9	82	15.0	138	30.0	12	8	1.3	10	1	.0
78594	1.6	48	.4	84	16.5	136	25.2	12	11	.4	11	0	.0
78595	1.5	89	.4	90	15.2	120	24.3	9	4	.7	3	0	.0
78596	29.4	82	7.9	72	18.4	243	48.5	10	11	11.5	11	4	.0
78597	.8	100	.4	63	30.9	242	126.3	7	15	.4	14	0	.0

AUSTIN

ZIPCODE	1	2	3	4	5	6	7	8	9	10	11	12	13
78602	7.6	72	2.6	77	21.4	256	62.2	8	16	2.8	14	3	.0
78605	1.6	93	.6	83	19.5	277	43.6	7	18	.7	15	0	.0
78606	2.5	95	1.0	77	23.9	265	72.6	5	19	1.2	17	0	.0
78607	.7	100	.1	77	21.5	383	76.1	0	34	.1	33	0	.0
78608	.3	100	.1	66	16.7	225	41.1	11	15	.1	17	0	.0
78609	1.4	96	.6	85	21.9	282	81.4	8	40	.6	46	0	.0
78610	2.8	89	.9	79	31.2	318	80.4	11	8	1.3	8	0	.0
78611	6.5	95	2.6	81	21.6	241	68.9	9	23	3.0	23	0	.0
78612	2.1	89	.7	90	23.1	390	57.6	7	14	1.0	11	0	.0
78613	3.4	96	1.1	90	28.5	380	93.7	8	4	1.7	4	0	.9
78614	.4	96	.1	95	24.4	280*	53.8	3	19	.2	22	1	.0
78615	.6	84	.2	80	22.1	228	60.5	11	12	.3	12	0	.0
78616	1.6	91	.5	82	20.7	311	56.6	10	10	.7	8	0	.0
78617	5.2	70	1.6	72	23.3	292	56.6	12	5	1.8	7	0	.0
78619	.7	0	.3	82	22.9	209	114.2	7	13	.1	8	0	.1
78620	2.0	96	.7	90	29.1	357	95.1	8	12	1.0	13	0	.0
78621	7.4	68	2.5	75	22.9	276	53.9	9	14	2.5	14	0	.1
78622	.4	92	.1	79	24.1	379	35.3	2	13	.2	14	0	.0
78623	.3	100	.1	65	15.6	448	86.6	6	26	.1	18	0	.0
78624	11.6	96	4.5	81	21.2	296	79.6	6	23	5.4	22	1	.0
78626	17.4	88	5.7	74	30.2	329	94.7	8	13	7.4	11	1	.0
78629	10.4	82	3.6	68	21.2	223	58.2	8	17	4.1	14	0	.0
78631	1.1	100	.4	82	15.4	326	75.5	13	20	.6	21	0	.1
78632	.3	0	.1	78	21.2	197	28.5	2	34	.0	0	0	.0
78634	1.4	78	.5	75	24.1	241	62.5	8	9	.6	8	0	.0

TEXAS

AUSTIN

ZIPCODE	1	2	3	4	5	6	7	8	9	10	11	12	13
78636	1.7	97	.7	71	24.8	189	60.6	6	22	.8	18	0	.6
78638	1.2	83	.4	75	21.1	289	43.9	9	12	.5	11	0	.1
78639	2.8	98	1.3	88	21.1	301	79.8	2	40	1.3	42	0	.0
78640	4.2	77	1.3	73	23.4	272	57.5	9	8	1.6	7	0	.0
78641	7.0	97	2.5	84	29.3	405	98.6	7	7	3.5	7	0	.0
78642	2.1	89	.7	82	26.9	291	69.5	8	10	.8	11	3	.0
78643	4.7	95	1.9	76	20.6	220	68.4	6	24	2.1	20	2	.0
78644	10.0	78	3.3	72	21.4	246	54.4	8	16	3.7	14	2	.1
78648	6.4	80	2.4	69	19.5	227	44.3	8	21	2.5	17	0	.0
78650	.7	100	.3	79	22.3	336	42.2	8	19	.3	19	0	.0
78652	2.7	95	.8	90	37.8	385	120.5	6	2	1.3	1	0	.0
78653	3.5	73	1.0	79	25.1	242	62.9	9	10	1.3	11	0	.0
78654	8.6	95	3.4	81	24.3	269	83.2	6	22	4.0	23	0	.0
78655	1.1	64	.3	71	24.1	274	49.4	5	10	.3	8	0	.0
78656	1.0	73	.3	71	24.9	228	61.3	6	8	.4	12	0	.0
78659	.7	0	.3	82	18.5	219	62.9	3	27	.0	0	0	.0
78660	2.7	93	.9	81	30.4	314	102.9	9	6	1.3	4	0	.7
78661	.2	71	.1	89	23.1	386	45.1	8	20	.1	32	0	.0
78662	.8	0	.3	90	20.7	150	52.8	9	15	.0	0	0	.0
78663	23.1	100	.1	88	25.1	288*	56.9	8	16	.1	13	0	.0
78664	23.1	91	7.1	81	32.9	375	109.3	10	5	10.7	4	0	.7
78666	31.4	76	8.6	51	20.0	358	81.2	5	7	11.5	5	2	.1
78669	1.5	99	.6	91	25.7	336	87.1	4	15	.7	16	0	.0
78670	.3	48	.1	36	13.1	201	32.0	7	8	.1	9	0	.0
78671	.4	0	.1	79	19.6	103	77.4	4	10	.0	0	0	.0
78672	.7	100	.4	92	14.1	239	57.9	4	46	.3	50	0	.0
78674	.2	100	.1	63	19.5	386	48.7	7	25	.1	28	0	.0
78676	2.7	98	1.1	72	25.7	261	111.9	7	15	1.3	13	0	.5

AUSTIN

ZIPCODE	1	2	3	4	5	6	7	8	9	10	11	12	13
78701	3.1	86	1.6	14	23.1	336	176.7	2	18	1.5	11	0	.0
78702	25.9	22	8.1	42	14.0	225	39.7	10	14	2.7	15	3	.0
78703	18.3	94	9.0	47	30.4	362	165.4	5	15	8.2	12	0	.0
78704	36.4	79	15.7	36	22.1	356	81.9	7	8	14.0	8	1	.1
78705	22.4	91	7.5	12	12.0	358	121.8	1	4	10.6	2	0	.0
78721	10.2	15	2.9	61	20.0	280	45.7	10	7	.8	6	0	.5
78722	6.6	57	2.9	48	19.3	319	65.3	6	14	1.9	11	0	.0
78723	23.2	65	8.5	54	27.1	389	81.1	7	6	7.4	6	1	.0
78724	4.2	42	1.3	74	25.1	454	75.6	10	5	.9	7	0	.0
78725	1.1	24	.3	86	28.0	332	61.1	8	1	.5	1	0	.0
78731	19.8	97	8.8	58	41.6	434	176.5	4	9	9.2	8	0	.0
78732	1.1	0	.5	64	34.8	369	140.1	7	7	.0	0	0	.0
78734	2.7	98	1.2	84	39.7	305	176.8	5	14	1.3	16	0	.0
78735	2.9	97	1.0	87	33.2	411	119.8	9	6	1.4	8	1	.1
78736	3.4	95	1.2	83	37.5	465	113.4	7	4	1.6	4	0	.0
78737	1.3	0	.4	99	39.5	454*	136.3	4	5	.0	0	5	.0
78741	23.0	68	9.5	22	17.3	311	67.7	6	14	8.6	11	1	.1
78742	1.0	75	.1	61	15.2	371	50.5	13	9	.3	4	1	.0
78743	5.1	65	1.1	25	21.6	346	77.1	12	1	2.0	1	2	.0
78744	14.1	80	4.6	73	25.5	481	74.1	12	2	5.7	2	0	.0

*=Estimated **1.0=883 lbs per capita. *=883 lbs per person; 100++ indicates per capita toxic waste generation > than 100 times the U.S. average of 883 lbs per capita.

ZIP CODE MEASURES OF SIZE, LEVELS OF AFFLUENCE AND QUALITY OF LIFE

1=Population (th.); 2= % White; 3=Households (th.); 4=% Owner Occupied; 5=Mean Income Per Household (th.$); 6=Mean Monthly Rent ($); 7=Mean Home Value (th.$); 8=% under 5; 9=% 65 and over; 10=% White Males, 65+; 11=% White Males (th.); 12=# Toxic Waste Sites; 13=Toxic Waste Relative to US(883 lbs.per capita)**

TEXAS

ZIPCODE	1	2	3	4	5	6	7	8	9	10	11	12	13
AUSTIN													
78745	41.7	86	13.6	72	29.4	446	85.4	9	4	17.8	4	0	.0
78746	12.0	98	4.5	70	49.9	341	184.4	6	6	6.0	5	0	.0
78747	1.8	91	.6	85	48.5	461	189.7	8	7	.8	7	1	.0
78748	.3	100	.1	94	40.3	463*	124.4	5	2	.7	0	0	.0
78749	3.0	94	1.0	84	37.6	511	136.3	10	2	1.4	2	0	.0
78750	9.8	96	3.0	86	44.3	626	156.3	7	3	4.7	2	0	.0
78751	13.2	89	6.7	25	15.0	364	71.6	4	11	6.1	8	0	.0
78752	10.9	75	4.8	33	22.4	371	68.9	7	6	4.0	6	1	.0
78753	17.8	87	6.7	58	27.4	365	87.9	9	5	7.6	4	0	.0
78754	1.0	94	.3	87	35.0	328	115.7	3	5	.5	6	0	.0
78756	7.2	92	3.8	35	19.2	361	80.1	5	19	3.2	13	0	.0
78757	12.5	95	5.1	64	26.9	417	78.1	6	11	5.5	10	0	.5
78758	29.5	90	11.4	50	29.5	407	95.8	8	4	12.9	3	3	.0
78759	17.4	95	7.5	75	41.1	519	139.5	8	5	7.9	4	0	2.6
78764	.9	97	.3	95	33.0	422	146.3	9	9	.4	10	0	1.1
SAN ANTONIO													
78801	18.9	82	5.8	69	20.7	247	58.6	9	11	7.5	10	2	.0
78827	1.8	79	.5	81	12.5	149	19.5	11	12	.7	13	0	.0
78828	.3	100	.1	56	14.2	44	39.1	2	35	.1	30	0	4.6
78829	1.6	85	.4	82	13.5	123	26.2	10	13	.7	9	0	.0
78830	1.1	87	.3	78	10.9	162	27.0	10	10	.5	16	0	.0
78832	2.2	80	.7	70	17.0	159	43.8	7	14	.9	15	0	.0
78833	1.3	96	.4	74	15.8	183	39.1	8	11	.6	8	0	.1
78834	8.1	82	2.3	75	21.7	218	43.2	11	9	3.4	9	0	.0
78836	.2	81	.1	71	12.9	148*	15.6	1	15	.7	7	2	.0
78837	.2	0	.	56	17.3	98	32.3	8	24	.	0	0	.0
78838	.2	100	.1	82	21.4	246*	85.1	5	27	.5	19	0	.0
78839	8.7	77	2.3	72	15.9	160	33.3	10	10	3.3	3	0	.0
78840	35.6	84	10.4	62	20.5	251	62.5	10	7	14.8	7	2	.1
78850	.9	100	.3	79	16.5	170	51.6	8	13	.6	8	0	.0
78851	.2	0	.1	49	46.6	86	15.6	13	3	.5	0	0	.0
78852	30.2	80	7.4	64	16.6	249*	89.6	11	8	11.7	6	0	.0
78861	7.8	86	2.5	78	20.8	241	52.6	11	6	3.3	13	0	.1
78870	.6	93	.2	91	19.3	264	36.8	8	15	.3	13	0	.0
78872	1.5	93	.5	82	18.7	144	29.1	13	10	.7	16	0	.0
78873	1.2	95	.4	73	17.9	206	58.9	4	17	.5	18	0	.1
78877	1.0	89	.3	80	22.4	210	37.4	7	15	.4	16	0	.0
78879	.	100	.1	78	19.6	315	81.8	4	29	.1	27	0	.0
78880	1.5	80	.5	70	20.4	197	39.1	8	13	.6	14	0	.1
78881	2.2	81	.7	76	16.8	237	37.4	9	14	.9	13	0	.1
78883	.3	0	.1	86	21.7	249*	89.6	11	3	.0	9	0	.0
78884	.5	100	.2	90	19.7	226*	61.1	0	29	.3	22	0	.0
78885	.1	100	.1	85	23.6	272*	51.0	12	39	.1	54	0	.0
78886	.3	100	.1	66	15.2	175*	28.8	4	27	.1	23	0	.0
AUSTIN													
78931	.3	100	.1	100	22.5	259*	79.0	14	18	.2	22	0	.0
78932	.6	89	.3	84	18.5	142	54.3	6	30	.2	33	0	.0
78933	.7	100	.3	84	23.6	113	95.8	4	22	.4	20	0	.0
78934	6.1	82	2.2	72	23.8	310	67.1	8	18	2.5	14	0	.1

TEXAS

ZIPCODE	1	2	3	4	5	6	7	8	9	10	11	12	13
AUSTIN													
78935	.4	57	.2	83	17.0	119	38.6	2	17	.1	14	0	.4
78938	.3	87	.1	72	18.3	173	37.2	2	22	.1	14	0	.0
78940	1.9	98	.8	80	19.0	196	54.6	6	26	1.0	24	0	.0
78941	1.9	86	.8	75	19.0	177	53.7	4	26	.9	26	0	1.3
78942	3.0	81	2.1	78	23.7	329	65.9	8	18	2.5	15	0	.3
78944	.6	74	.2	81	14.9	266	36.8	6	27	.2	25	0	.0
78945	.5	87	3.1	75	22.8	285	76.0	7	20	.3	16	0	.1
78946	.5	70	.	75	12.3	191	43.7*12	20	3.4	20	0		.0
78947	2.5	70	1.0	85	22.6	268	61.9	6	17	1.2	15	0	.0
78948	.7	94	.3	82	14.3	398	88.1	8	21	1	15	0	.0
78949	.3	85	.1	76	23.1	200	35.0	9	20	1	20	1	.0
78950	1.4	88	.6	91	18.8	91	58.6	6	26	.7	28	0	.5
78952	.2	56	.1	100	24.0	276*	66.8	6	18	.0	0	0	.0
78953	.3	97	.1	85	21.8	366	28.7	3	19	.2	17	0	.0
78954	.5	88	.3	93	22.6	83	61.0	2	44	.9	45	0	2.6
78956	4.5	90	1.8	78	18.7	182	54.0	7	27	1.9	24	0	1.1
78957	5.2	78	2.0	76	23.1	209	56.3	7	20	1.9	17	0	.6
78959	1.4	60	.6	70	11.6	163	27.6	6	26	.4	21	0	.0
78960	.1	0	.1	86	13.3	153*	47.4*	0	68	.	0	0	.0
78962	4.0	85	1.6	80	22.8	244	63.9	6	23	1.6	22	0	.2
78963	.4	91	.2	66	16.0	249	50.4	7	26	.2	26	0	.2
AMARILLO													
79001	.3	0	.1	70	21.4	192	36.7	8	8	.0	0	0	1.0
79002	.2	0	.1	76	21.1	113	29.2	0	18	.0	0	0	.0
79003	.3	100	.1	81	25.0	195	54.5	8	13	.1	12	0	12.2
79005	1.5	94	.5	72	29.0	358	68.2	8	9	.7	7	0	.0
79007	17.6	91	6.8	75	28.0	285	52.1	9	13	7.9	12	11	8.5
79009	2.7	74	1.0	74	20.6	248	51.2	9	13	.9	13	3	.0
79011	.3	100	.	12	25.1	289*	89.5*18	1	.0				.0
79012	.4	0	.1	79	48.1	334	65.9	8	8	.2	7	0	.0
79013	.1	71	.3	38	24.8	200	19.2	16	2	.3	4	0	.4
79014	5.1	95	1.8	69	30.5	336	81.9	11	10	2.5	9	0	.0
79015	10.6	95	4.1	62	25.3	280	80.6	7	9	4.9	8	1	.0
79016	1.0	88	.3	49	25.5	198	124.0	12	13	.8	0	0	.0
79018	1.0	98	.3	63	22.2	119	53.7	3	12	.7	10	0	.3
79019	1.7	99	.7	84	25.9	210	56.1	7	20	.8	17	0	.0
79022	8.7	90	3.2	72	23.4	240	64.9	9	12	3.9	12	6	.0
79024	.6	0	.2	67	26.7	245	51.2	12	13	.	0	0	.1
79027	6.6	72	2.0	67	22.5	230	65.6	10	9	2.3	9	8	.8
79029	13.2	94	4.6	72	28.3	297	65.1	10	8	6.1	8	10	.2
79031	2.0	66	.7	67	21.4	268	45.2	11	10	.7	12	0	.0
79032	.3	80	.1	33	20.6	267	38.2	12	8	.1	11	0	.3
79033	.	100	.	53	20.0	317	34.4	3	15	.	0	0	.0
79034	.8	100	.3	80	23.7	189	60.9	9	14	.4	11	0	.0
AUSTIN													
79035	6.2	87	1.9	69	24.0	258	60.9	10	9	2.7	9	6	.2
79036	4.6	98	1.6	85	27.8	312	57.0	9	10	2.3	10	0	.0
79039	.3	99	.1	69	23.8	199	53.8	10	14	.6	12	1	.3
79040	2.1	93	.4	71	32.2	259	65.3	8	10	1.0	8	4	.0

*=Estimated **1.0=883 lbs per person; 100++ indicates per capita toxic waste generation > than 100 times the U.S. average of 883 lbs per capita.

ZIP CODE MEASURES OF SIZE, LEVELS OF AFFLUENCE AND QUALITY OF LIFE

1=Population (th.); 2= % White; 3=Households (th.); 4=% Owner Occupied; 5=Mean Income Per Household (th.$); 6=Mean Monthly Rent ($); 7=Mean Home Value (th.$); 8=% under 5, 9=% 65 and over; 10=% White Males (th.); 11=% White Males, 65+; 12=# Toxic Waste Sites; 13=Toxic Waste Relative to US(883 lbs.per capita)**.

TEXAS

AMARILLO

ZIPCODE	1	2	3	4	5	6	7	8	9	10	11	12	13
79041	4.6	77	1.4	63	21.2	202	50.6	10	13	1.8	13	2	.0
79042	1.3	97	.5	71	22.2	198	41.3	7	16	.6	14	1	.0
79043	2.2	68	.6	54	25.1	219	62.7	12	7	.7	9	2	.0
79044	.5	0	.1	55	32.1	182	57.0	7	11	.7	0	0	.0
79045	21.1	83	6.4	69	24.7	286	65.8	11	8	8.6	8	6	.2
79046	.8	99	.3	73	23.0	230	49.5	10	20	.4	19	0	.0
79052	2.0	78	.6	64	22.3	313	57.3	6	7	.8	8	1	.0
79053	.2	85	.2	16	16.9	194*	26.3	9	9	.2	1	5	.0
79054	1.0	99	.4	75	38.8	244	39.6	8	14	.5	13	0	.0
79056	.1	100	.1	87	22.9	264*	50.3	5	37	.1	46	0	.0
79057	1.7	97	.7	72	20.8	178	39.3	5	27	.8	25	0	.1
79059	1.0	99	.4	75	31.4	281	55.7	8	13	.5	12	1	.0
79061	.5	100	.2	79	25.0	203	31.1	6	18	.2	20	1	.0
79062	.3	82	.1	50	33.9	266	47.5	13	5	.1	8	1	.0
79063	.8	0	.2	79	21.1	185	59.4	9	11	.0	11	0	.0
79064	3.0	73	1.1	71	21.3	192	53.2	10	15	1.1	18	2	.0
79065	23.8	93	9.2	77	27.3	303	54.4	8	14	10.7	12	2	4.3
79068	2.9	98	1.0	80	29.0	286	61.2	7	14	1.4	12	4	.0
79070	9.2	96	3.3	71	31.6	329	71.6	10	9	4.5	7	3	.1
79071	.8	100	.3	95	28.4	202	25.3	11	19	.1	1	0	.2
79072	27.5	76	9.3	64	23.4	283	63.5	10	11	10.1	11	8	.0
79079	3.9	90	1.5	74	27.6	220	40.6	9	14	.0	0	1	.0
79080	1.1	99	.4	83	25.0	253	42.3	7	20	1.7	18	3	.1
79081	4.1	93	1.5	76	25.8	247	68.2	10	10	1.9	11	6	.0
79082	.6	75	.2	50	28.6	220	34.4	11	13	.2	22	2	.0
79083	2.7	96	1.0	79	21.2	170	75.8	6	16	1.3	10	1	.0
79084	2.5	92	.9	77	25.1	264	42.4	9	11	1.1	10	3	.0
79086	2.3	97	.8	72	28.7	267	59.8	8	11	1.1	9	6	.0
79087	.7	95	.2	69	43.3	285	48.1	10	9	.3	18	6	29.0
79088	7.3	81	2.5	70	25.8	205	39.5	12	17	1.9	13	6	.4
79090	.2	100	.1	77	20.9	219	58.1	9	13	2.8	14	0	.0
79091	1.1	100	.1	66	32.2	86	32.4	4	26	.1	30	0	.0
79092	1.3	100	.5	70	28.0	322*	74.8	0	42	.7	1	56	0	.0
79095	3.9	84	1.5	78	19.5	181	43.8	6	22	1.5	20	2	.2
79096	2.5	98	.9	75	31.2	292	62.2	11	17	1.2	15	0	.0
79097	1.5	97	.5	81	29.0	281	55.6	8	12	.7	10	0	2.3
79098	.5	0	.1	63	25.3	115	80.9	9	5	.0	0	0	.0

AMARILLO

ZIPCODE	1	2	3	4	5	6	7	8	9	10	11	12	13
79101	4.0	82	2.0	35	21.1	225	92.1	7	17	1.6	13	2	.3
79102	9.8	89	4.4	54	24.6	286	62.6	8	18	4.0	15	1	.0
79103	10.1	91	3.2	84	29.3	367	48.9	10	4	4.6	5	2	.0
79104	7.4	80	2.4	68	20.0	280	34.6	11	8	2.7	8	2	.8
79105	.2	100	.1	69	39.7	456*	150.3	8	0	.1	0	1	100++
79106	28.3	95	11.5	67	28.1	309	72.9	7	14	12.7	12	3	.1
79107	32.1	72	10.9	68	19.8	251	36.8	11	8	11.3	7	7	.0
79108	7.8	98	2.6	86	26.5	267	62.8	7	9	3.8	9	0	.0
79109	36.7	96	14.3	67	37.2	383	99.4	7	10	16.9	8	1	.0
79110	16.0	97	5.8	79	27.3	336	58.1	10	7	7.6	6	6	.0

TEXAS

AMARILLO

ZIPCODE	1	2	3	4	5	6	7	8	9	10	11	12	13
79111	2.4	89	.5	0	24.7	390	87.9*	11	0	1.0	0	0	.1
79118	2.4	98	.8	83	31.4	351	108.9	6	4	1.2	2	1	.0
79119	1.1	0	.4	90	38.2	405	103.0	6	9	.0	0	0	.0
79121	2.0	96	.7	88	41.8	359	112.8	15	1	1.0	1	0	.0
79124	.2	100	.1	83	44.3	509*	171.1	21	0	.1	0	0	.0

CHILDRESS

ZIPCODE	1	2	3	4	5	6	7	8	9	10	11	12	13
79201	6.7	91	2.7	75	19.5	224	45.0	7	22	2.9	19	2	.1
79220	1.4	84	.5	52	15.8	182*	50.5	10	16	.0	0	3	.0
79225	1.4	84	.5	71	20.9	228	34.7	8	28	.5	26	3	.0
79226	3.3	93	1.3	70	22.9	194	51.9	6	20	1.5	18	1	.0
79227	2.1	89	.8	75	21.0	155	36.9	6	26	.9	26	0	.0
79229	.5	96	.2	85	15.9	223	29.3	5	18	.3	19	0	.0
79230	.9	82	.2	71	13.5	285	23.5	6	25	.1	36	0	.0
79233	.4	92	.1	65	20.8	152	32.7	13	25	.2	20	0	.5
79234	.3	100	.1	84	33.8	234	54.4	7	16	1.9	16	1	.0
79235	5.8	70	2.0	73	20.6	233	50.2	8	15	1.9	16	1	.0
79236	.2	94	.1	36	17.4	176	30.6	9	8	.1	8	0	.0
79237	.7	0	.3	78	14.2	163	31.0	7	30	.0	0	1	.0
79239	.5	0	.2	75	19.4	125	33.1	6	15	.0	0	0	.1
79240	.8	82	.2	84	21.4	245*	42.9	12	14	.1	8	0	.2
79241	3.6	76	1.2	66	21.9	201	36.9	9	14	1.3	16	5	.3
79243	.5	90	.2	61	16.1	170	43.1	7	21	.2	21	1	.0
79244	1.3	88	.6	76	17.8	167	43.4	7	25	.5	23	0	.1
79245	3.7	84	1.5	78	18.7	149	50.5	9	23	.3	18	0	.0
79248	2.9	89	1.1	68	23.7	154	47.1	8	22	1.2	20	1	.0
79250	2.2	72	.7	59	18.4	53	42.1	9	13	.2	8	5	.3
79252	5.1	89	2.0	77	23.1	213	38.7	7	20	2.1	17	3	.2
79255	1.1	84	.4	73	15.7	142	39.0	9	17	.4	15	1	.0
79256	.5	95	.2	85	18.5	133	27.0	4	21	.3	18	0	.0
79257	1.4	92	.6	77	22.3	205	47.9	7	18	.6	16	3	.0
79258	.2	100	.1	38	22.5	53	37.2	9	5	.1	9	1	.0
79259	.2	100	.1	80	15.5	178*	57.6	13	24	.1	26	0	.0
79260	.2	0	.1	83	34.7	210	27.8	8	32	.0	0	0	.0
79261	.9	89	.3	77	19.1	162	32.3	4	24	.4	25	0	.3

LUBBOCK

ZIPCODE	1	2	3	4	5	6	7	8	9	10	11	12	13
79311	4.0	84	1.3	70	22.1	261	56.2	8	11	1.7	11	0	.0
79312	1.9	84	.7	70	23.1	237	38.8	10	12	.8	12	0	.0
79313	2.0	86	.7	70	22.8	269	44.6	9	12	.9	11	0	.0
79314	.1	44	18.2	316	16.8	27	10	.0	0				.0
79316	13.1	84	4.4	72	23.3	259	58.1	7	10	5.3	11	7	.3
79322	2.8	80	1.0	74	23.1	236	48.4	8	17	1.1	15	2	.0
79323	6.1	85	2.0	72	26.6	279	56.0	12	7	2.7	7	2	.8
79325	1.3	83	.4	53	21.4	378	65.5	9	8	.5	8	3	.0
79327	.2	79	.1	37	17.8	245	63.3*	12	3	.1	7	0	.0
79328	1.2	79	.4	0	18.7	337	66.5*	18	9	.5	0	3	.1
79329	3.5	86	1.1	71	24.8	268	68.1	9	11	1.4	11	3	.0
79331	15.2	84	5.2	73	24.2	229	55.3	10	14	6.1	13	6	.0
79336	17.2	83	5.5	71	25.0	291	63.9	11	9	7.2	9	1	.0
79339	9.1	74	3.2	73	22.5	297	50.6	9	16	3.2	17	6	.3

*=Estimated **1.0=883 lbs per person; 100++ indicates per capita toxic waste generation > than 100 times the U.S. average of 883 lbs per capita.

ZIP CODE MEASURES OF SIZE, LEVELS OF AFFLUENCE AND QUALITY OF LIFE

1=Population (th.); 2= % White; 3=Households (th.); 4=% Owner Occupied; 5=Mean Income Per Household (th.$); 6=Mean Monthly Rent ($); 7=Mean Home Value (th.$); 8=% under 5; 9=% 65 and over; 10=White Males (th.); 11=% White Males, 65+; 12=# Toxic Waste Sites; 13=Toxic Waste Relative to US(883 lbs.per capita)**.

TEXAS

LUBBOCK

ZIP CODE	1	2	3	4	5	6	7	8	9	10	11	12	13
79342	.3	100	.1	89	47.3	544*	59.5	7	21	.2	21	1	.0
79343	2.1	74	.7	64	21.0	211	46.8	8	12	.8	14	2	.0
79344	.2	0	.1	48	16.5	53	50.3	5	10	.0	0	0	.0
79345	1.2	79	.4	71	25.3	142	54.9	7	14	.5	16	0	.0
79346	3.9	67	1.3	72	25.5	190	39.8	8	12	1.3	14	7	.0
79347	8.0	78	2.6	71	22.5	229	56.8	10	11	3.1	12	5	.0
79350	.5	77	.7	58	17.6	235	49.9	15	6	.2	12	1	.0
79351	2.2	72	.7	62	19.4	244	41.6	10	13	.8	14	0	.0
79355	1.9	92	.7	72	24.8	222	57.5	9	10	.9	11	0	.0
79356	5.5	75	1.9	70	25.3	219	42.5	8	14	2.0	15	0	.0
79357	3.5	67	1.1	65	20.7	234	48.9	9	13	1.2	14	1	.0
79358	1.1	81	.4	64	21.4	242	41.3	7	16	.5	18	2	.0
79359	3.9	80	1.3	71	22.7	197	40.9	8	11	1.5	13	4	.6
79360	8.8	92	2.8	73	25.5	276	61.4	11	8	4.0	7	4	.6
79363	3.6	88	1.1	74	23.5	266	68.8	8	10	1.7	10	0	.0
79364	9.6	74	3.2	73	26.1	250	59.5	9	12	3.4	12	1	.1
79367	.6	92	.1	76	22.1	267	48.2	8	5	.3	6	0	.0
79368	.1	0	.1	72	34.3	318	39.8	0	26	.0	0	0	.0
79370	2.6	79	1.0	74	17.2	204	37.5	9	23	.9	25	1	.2
79371	1.7	85	.5	72	21.9	264	45.5	9	15	.7	16	1	.0
79372	1.6	92	.5	70	24.8	268	45.2	11	10	.7	9	0	7.8
79373	4.6	80	1.5	72	21.0	243	52.6	8	14	1.7	15	2	.0
79376	.4	85	.1	53	20.0	230*	43.0	15	8	.2	6	0	.3
79377	.4	69	.1	66	18.5	212*	48.5	8	9	.2	4	1	.0
79378	.2	0	.1	46	22.3	154	52.9	9	3	.0	0	0	.0
79379	.7	84	.2	63	22.6	201	33.1	7	8	.3	8	2	.0
79380	.3	57	.1	82	17.5	93	32.4	19	11	.1	9	0	.0
79381	1.4	75	.4	65	18.5	204	47.0	12	10	.6	10	3	.0
79382	1.8	82	.6	77	25.9	315	65.4	8	7	.7	7	0	.0
79383	.3	64	.1	55	23.3	149	75.1	14	7	.1	9	0	2.0

LUBBOCK

ZIP CODE	1	2	3	4	5	6	7	8	9	10	11	12	13
79401	14.5	74	6.1	28	15.2	248	48.8	8	8	6.1	6	3	.0
79403	15.5	34	3.2	73	18.8	260	38.1	10	7	2.6	10	0	.1
79404	11.0	56	3.4	61	19.8	189	42.1	10	8	3.1	8	2	.3
79405	3.4	62	1.3	35	16.2	269	30.9	13	11	1.0	13	0	.1
79407	15.5	94	5.2	68	30.0	344	95.3	9	6	7.2	5	2	.0
79410	10.3	95	4.5	60	28.3	351	70.5	6	15	4.6	12	0	.1
79411	4.8	90	2.3	47	18.8	333	56.6	7	18	2.1	14	1	.0
79412	15.7	90	6.1	58	25.8	362	63.8	9	9	6.7	8	0	.0
79413	24.0	97	9.0	74	36.3	420	91.5	5	11	11.2	9	1	.0
79414	15.9	94	6.1	51	25.2	405	46.2	7	8	7.2	5	1	.0
79415	16.2	66	5.3	49	17.3	259	38.0	11	6	5.4	7	1	.1
79416	13.9	93	5.2	63	32.5	368	99.7	8	7	6.4	5	0	.0
79423	12.3	94	4.2	82	38.1	481	104.7	11	3	5.8	3	0	.0
79424	9.0	95	3.1	75	42.0	456	122.5	10	3	4.4	2	0	.0
79490	.2	61	.1	89	19.4	223*	44.7	2	11	.1	6	1	.0

ABILENE

ZIP CODE	1	2	3	4	5	6	7	8	9	10	11	12	13
79501	4.0	83	1.5	76	21.2	167	40.7	8	20	1.6	19	1	.0
79502	1.9	94	.7	75	20.0	201	43.9	8	22	.8	18	2	.0

TEXAS

ABILENE

ZIP CODE	1	2	3	4	5	6	7	8	9	10	11	12	13
79503	.3	100	.1	81	19.7	226*	43.1	10	22	.2	21	0	.0
79504	2.5	93	1.0	78	22.1	189	46.1	6	22	1.1	20	0	.0
79505	.3	97	.1	75	20.6	138	35.2	5	19	.1	18	0	.0
79506	.5	98	.2	85	21.7	173	34.2	6	27	.2	23	0	.0
79508	.5	97	.2	79	20.0	253	49.6	10	14	.2	14	0	.0
79510	6.0	99	2.1	85	23.6	270	61.7	8	16	2.8	14	0	.0
79511	1.6	87	.5	77	27.8	226	47.8	9	8	.7	7	0	.0
79512	7.4	81	2.7	78	22.4	248	39.6	8	19	2.8	19	1	.0
79517	.3	97	.3	69	27.0	310*	58.3	10	24	.1	15	0	.0
79518	.2	92	.1	75	20.6	323	42.5	4	16	.1	17	0	.0
79520	3.9	80	1.4	78	23.8	198	41.7	8	20	1.5	19	1	.0
79521	4.5	88	1.7	77	21.9	161	45.1	8	25	2.0	22	1	.0
79525	1.9	98	.6	89	24.8	269	52.4	6	10	.9	12	1	.0
79526	1.4	89	.5	82	21.0	218	44.4	5	17	.6	18	0	.0
79527	.5	91	.3	78	23.6	292	48.9	11	19	.2	18	0	.0
79528	.8	93	.3	79	22.8	213	43.0	5	24	.4	19	1	.0
79529	1.8	83	.7	80	22.8	186	38.8	7	23	.7	21	1	.0
79530	.7	94	.2	85	18.8	145	31.9	7	21	.3	21	0	.0
79532	1.2	72	.5	74	19.2	169	41.3	9	25	.4	24	0	.0
79533	.6	0	.3	81	17.4	161	22.8	7	27	.0	0	1	.0
79534	.3	100	.1	89	26.5	129	39.4	6	18	.1	17	0	.1
79535	.2	100	.1	41	16.7	148	27.3	10	6	.1	6	1	.0
79536	4.4	93	1.7	75	21.7	211	51.0	8	17	1.9	15	0	.1
79537	.2	100	.1	100	17.2	198*	36.5	4	14	.1	7	0	.0
79538	.7	98	.1	79	18.4	163	26.3	4	28	.1	18	0	.0
79539	.4	70	.1	69	27.9	236	38.7	8	11	.1	15	0	.0
79540	.3	0	.1	75	23.4	232	32.4	8	18	.1	16	0	.0
79541	.6	100	.2	84	29.4	337*	38.2	4	16	.3	16	0	.0
79543	1.5	91	.6	77	22.5	175	47.1	6	22	.3	23	0	.0
79544	.8	77	.3	79	21.2	165	33.4	4	18	.3	19	0	.0
79545	2.5	80	.8	78	26.9	226	55.5	8	16	1.0	16	2	.9
79546	3.2	81	1.2	75	26.7	145	40.4	7	22	1.2	18	3	.1
79547	1.3	79	.5	82	21.8	128	44.2	8	18	.5	19	0	.0
79548	.4	62	.2	83	23.2	266*	40.1	7	29	.1	31	0	.1
79549	16.2	83	5.7	74	27.3	302	58.3	9	11	6.5	11	0	.0
79553	5.2	80	2.0	77	22.2	200	42.7	6	21	2.0	22	1	.0
79556	14.4	84	5.5	72	22.8	231	48.6	8	16	5.7	15	0	.1
79560	.3	92	.1	91	19.3	222*	28.5	7	27	.1	32	1	.1
79561	.7	0	.3	78	25.1	169	41.0	5	25	.0	0	0	.0
79562	1.2	0	.1	83	20.1	167	43.0	7	18	.0	0	0	.0
79563	1.3	93	.4	54	19.7	256	39.2	12	8	.6	8	1	.0
79565	.4	91	.2	78	22.3	180	26.0	8	16	.6	12	0	.0
79566	.5	70	.2	88	15.7	161	37.5	6	29	.2	41	0	.0
79567	4.3	90	1.7	75	19.5	179	38.5	8	19	1.8	18	1	.4

ABILENE

ZIP CODE	1	2	3	4	5	6	7	8	9	10	11	12	13
79601	20.4	83	7.0	56	22.0	274	68.1	6	11	8.0	9	3	.3
79602	10.8	82	4.3	62	20.2	249	55.0	9	15	4.2	13	0	.3
79603	25.7	81	8.7	71	24.4	325	56.9	9	10	9.9	10	0	.0

*=Estimated **1.0=883 lbs per person; 100++ indicates per capita toxic waste generation > than 100 times the U.S. average of 883 lbs per capita.

ZIP CODE MEASURES OF SIZE, LEVELS OF AFFLUENCE AND QUALITY OF LIFE

1=Population (th.); 2= % White; 3=Households (th.); 4= % Owner Occupied; 5=Mean Income Per Household (th.$); 6=Mean Monthly Rent ($)*; 7=Mean Home Value (th.$)*; 8=% under 5, 9=% 65 and over; 10=White Males (th.), 11=% White Males, 65+; 12=# Toxic Waste Sites, 13=Toxic Waste Relative to US(883 lbs.per capita)**.

TEXAS

ZIP CODE	1	2	3	4	5	6	7	8	9	10	11	12	13
ABILENE													
79604	1.7	79	.1	75	29.9	575	65.6	3	7	.7	6	2	9.7
79605	34.6	92	12.7	70	31.0	381	84.4	8	10	15.3	9	1	.1
79606	5.4	97	2.0	63	33.9	419	116.5	10	2	2.6	2	0	.0
79607	5.2	73	1.0	.0	18.3	337	65.2*	2	0	2.4	0	1	.0
MIDLAND													
79701	58.8	77	21.0	69	39.3	370	99.8	9	8	22.2	8	11	.2
79702	.4	91	.1	86	26.9	423	98.4	6	0	.1	0	0	.8
79703	22.9	97	8.2	75	34.9	500	89.1	10	5	11.0	4	0	.0
79713	.8	90	.3	64	39.4	121	57.6	4	14	.4	16	0	.0
79714	13.3	86	4.4	74	28.2	321	59.1	10	8	5.7	7	1	.3
79718	1.0	90	.3	68	14.1	129	26.9	10	17	.5	16	0	.0
79719	.2	71	.2	86	24.0	238	25.3	8	8	.3	6	0	.0
79720	31.5	80	11.4	70	25.0	254	51.3	8	13	12.2	12	5	4.4
79730	.4	89	.1	26	23.8	128	41.6	9	1	.2	1	0	.0
79731	4.6	84	1.5	73	24.7	241	47.8	10	8	1.9	8	2	2.1
79733	.3	93	.1	80	23.3	126	36.6	4	15	.1	12	0	.0
79734	1.2	96	.5	74	17.7	199	51.4	7	18	.5	19	0	.0
79735	11.7	77	3.6	71	25.1	252	60.4	10	7	4.5	6	1	.0
79739	1.1	86	.3	65	30.9	70	31.4	15	10	.5	7	1	.0
79741	.8	94	.3	64	23.7	140	25.9	13	10	.4	14	1	.0
79742	.8	72	.2	58	19.5	125	26.6	10	15	.3	16	0	.0
79743	.6	100	.2	74	18.9	190	24.0	13	10	.7	7	0	.0
79744	1.4	92	.6	63	26.6	220	44.0	10	10	.3	8	2	.0
79745	8.6	77	3.0	60	24.3	237	43.3	10	10	3.3	11	0	.0
79748	.3	48	.1	71	29.3	337	104.4*	19	12	.2	0	0	.0
79749	.3	100	.1	53	48.8	264	70.6	4	19	.2	20	0	.0
79752	2.9	72	.9	79	24.0	206	32.1	10	12	1.0	12	0	.0
79755	.5	87	.1	17	24.5	91	87.1*	1	1	.2	3	1	.0
79756	11.6	84	3.9	76	24.4	251	51.2	10	9	4.9	8	2	.0
79758	.8	100	.3	84	31.1	244	88.6	6	6	.4	8	0	.0
79760	.7	92	.2	79	30.3	432	71.1	10	9	.9	11	3	.0
79761	24.0	91	9.8	52	30.0	388	82.0	8	9	10.9	9	4	100++
79762	42.3	95	14.8	71	32.8	420	76.0	9	6	19.9	5	4	.2
79763	47.2	74	15.4	71	26.3	317	61.0	10	7	17.5	7	6	.0
79772	13.9	63	4.2	71	22.7	224	45.1	11	7	4.3	3	6	.0
79777	.2	100	.1	71	23.3	151	17.7	3	11	.1	4	0	.0
79778	1.3	89	.5	66	23.5	195	36.3	11	9	.6	8	0	.0
79780	.5	74	.1	70	15.8	143	18.7	9	7	.3	7	0	.0
79781	.6	100	.2	59	25.3	229	14.7	13	7	.3	7	0	.0
79782	3.5	79	1.2	73	25.3	229	52.9	10	13	1.4	11	0	.0
79783	.3	89	.1	27	36.6	83	28.4	11	2	.1	1	1	.0
79785	.2	0	.1	60	13.2	123	24.2	10	21	.0	0	0	.0
79788	.7	95	.2	83	25.0	255	28.8	7	13	.3	13	0	.7
79789	1.3	91	.4	74	21.1	221	35.9	9	10	.6	9	0	.0
EL PASO													
79830	6.6	85	2.3	61	18.9	222	59.1	6	11	2.8	11	0	.0
79834	.3	88	.1	12	25.6	224	41.6	15	3	.1	6	0	.0
79835	5.2	71	1.4	74	19.9	244	53.1	11	6	1.8	8	2	.0

TEXAS

ZIP CODE	1	2	3	4	5	6	7	8	9	10	11	12	13
EL PASO													
79836	3.7	61	.9	73	21.4	208	60.1	12	5	1.1	3	0	.8
79837	1.0	91	.3	44	18.9	256	49.8	11	4	.5	5	0	.0
79838	5.2	74	1.4	64	18.0	198	36.9	11	8	1.9	7	0	.0
79839	.7	90	.2	65	17.6	209	22.3	11	10	.3	10	1	.0
79842	.7	46	.2	67	12.3	177	26.8	10	17	.2	21	1	.0
79843	3.1	81	1.1	68	16.6	180	50.1	8	17	1.2	16	0	.0
79845	1.9	87	.5	60	14.1	152	27.7	8	11	.8	11	0	.0
79846	.2	21	.1	61	8.5	96	13.1	5	11	.0	13	0	.3
79847	.2	100	.1	20	30.3	37	108.0*	5	3	.1	3	0	.0
79848	1.4	91	.5	74	21.5	143	42.2	8	14	.6	13	0	.0
79849	1.4	56	.3	84	15.1	193	51.5	11	7	.4	5	0	.0
79851	.7	96	.2	73	21.2	249	34.8	10	12	.4	11	0	.3
79852	.1	100	.1	21	11.4	53	41.6	7	15	.0	0	0	.0
79853	.8	65	.2	46	19.2	123	24.5	9	4	.3	6	0	.0
79854	.4	76	.1	51	16.2	135	18.8	13	5	.1	5	0	.0
79855	3.3	88	1.0	66	18.2	263	40.6	10	8	1.5	5	0	.2
EL PASO													
79901	17.9	68	5.8	10	8.3	135	42.5	10	12	5.4	12	1	.3
79902	23.2	77	9.1	38	23.6	259	102.3	7	16	8.1	14	1	.2
79903	20.0	75	6.8	62	18.6	241	61.1	8	16	6.9	14	0	.0
79904	30.7	73	9.6	52	21.7	295	75.0	11	5	11.1	6	0	.0
79905	35.5	67	9.5	50	15.9	191	50.2	9	8	11.1	7	4	.4
79906	6.9	62	1.9	0	17.0	243	60.5*	22	0	2.2	4	0	.0
79907	49.7	60	12.1	72	19.6	234	59.0	12	4	14.2	4	1	.1
79912	28.1	85	10.5	55	37.1	363	131.2	8	7	11.6	6	0	.1
79915	44.3	60	10.9	68		232	54.9	9	5	12.9	5	1	.0
79916	13.4	58	1.2	0	18.3	346	65.3*	6	0	6.0	0	1	.0
79917	7.4	87	.1	94	18.5	213*	62.8	12	7	3	0	1	4.3
79922	7.4	78	.1	83	42.8	249	139.6	9	5	2.8	3	0	.1
79924	49.7	80	14.9	75	24.3	340	67.9	8	4	19.7	4	2	.1
79925	40.4	84	13.8	64	30.9	395	94.6	7	6	16.4	6	1	.0
79927	14.9	72	3.7	84	21.4	278	65.6	11	4	5.2	5	2	.0
79930	30.2	68	9.9	55	20.1	291	63.5	9	12	9.5	12	0	.1
79932	10.8	61	2.9	79	34.4	187	123.3	9	3	3.5	4	0	.0
79934	.4	78	.1	79	19.3	310	62.5	17	5	1.1	10	0	.1
79935	29.3	79	9.4	68	32.0	410	109.2	11	3	11.4	2	1	.0
79936	5.8	75	1.7	92	30.9	419	97.9	15	1	2.1	1	0	.2
LAS CRUCES													
88021	3.3	70	.8	69	19.8	219	54.8	8	7	1.3	7	0	.0

*=Estimated **1.0=883 lbs per person; 100++ indicates per capita toxic waste generation > than 100 times the U.S. average of 883 lbs per capita.

ZIP CODE MEASURES OF SIZE, LEVELS OF AFFLUENCE AND QUALITY OF LIFE

1=Population (th.); 2= % White; 3=Households (th.); 4=% Owner Occupied; 5=Mean Income Per Household (th.$); 6=Mean Monthly Rent ($); 7=Mean Home Value (th.$); 8=% under 5; 9=% 65 and over; 10=White Males (th.); 11=% White Males, 65+; 12=# Toxic Waste Sites; 13=Toxic Waste Relative to US(883 lbs.per capita)**.

UTAH

SALT LAKE CITY

ZIP CODE	1	2	3	4	5	6	7	8	9	10	11	12	13
84001	.7	0	.2	72	25.6	359	88.7	13	10	.0	0	0	.0
84002	.2	100	.1	100	26.7	307*	81.0	14	9	.0	8	0	.0
84003	20.6	99	5.0	83	29.8	348	124.9	16	6	10.0	5	0	.0
84006	.6	100	.3	76	21.6	225	72.7	6	25	.3	24	1	10.8
84007	.5	100	.1	97	27.5	316*	76.7	15	8	.3	8	0	.0
84010	40.6	98	11.2	77	34.8	381	142.9	11	6	19.7	6	1	.1
84012	.2	100	.1	62	14.6	398	52.2*	18	7	.1	7	0	.0
84013	.4	0	.1	90	33.5	167	82.3	21	7	.1	5	0	.3
84014	8.0	100	2.2	88	34.5	380	140.2	16	4	3.9	3	1	.0
84015	26.8	93	7.8	76	26.7	377	95.4	15	5	12.5	4	1	.2
84017	2.0	99	.7	79	26.8	327	91.7	14	12	1.0	10	0	.0
84020	5.4	95	1.2	82	30.7	368	143.4	10	6	2.9	5	1	.0
84021	2.3	98	.7	72	26.4	247	79.1	13	5	1.2	5	1	.0
84022	1.7	89	.5	7	30.5	251	42.9	11	1	.8	1	1	.1
84023	.3	0	.1	25	25.4	251	90.3*	10	3	.8	1	1	.1
84025	5.0	99	1.2	82	31.8	392	148.6	14	6	2.5	5	0	.0
84026	.4	0	.1	64	23.7	241	61.3	11	1	.2	0	0	.0
84028	.4	0	.1	77	19.6	359	90.2	14	12	.2	13	0	.2
84029	4.6	95	1.3	80	27.4	309	89.8	15	5	2.2	5	2	.7
84030	30.6	93	8.6	82	29.3	383	112.0	14	14	14.3	10	0	.0
84031	.2	100	.1	85	19.1	284	13.1	16	15	.1	18	0	.0
84032	6.6	99	2.0	77	24.5	282*	83.1	24	7	3.3	9	1	5.3
84033	.6	0	.2	84	22.8	317	101.5	14	10	.2	0	0	.2
84035	.7	94	.2	90	21.9	319	80.8	15	16	.3	0	0	.0
84036	2.3	97	.7	80	24.5	298	95.6	17	9	1.1	5	0	.3
84037	13.9	98	3.8	83	27.6	273	94.9	12	7	6.8	8	0	.1
84038	4.0	100	1.1	72	32.9	349	137.5	14	4	.2	4	0	.2
84039	.5	96	.1	72	23.5	296	89.3	18	10	.2	13	0	.0
84041	30.6	93	8.6	82	29.3	383	112.0	14	14	14.3	10	0	.0
84043	8.7	98	2.3	81	26.9	336	106.0	15	7	4.2	5	0	.5
84044	14.3	95	4.2	84	25.8	342	81.5	19	5	6.7	5	4	5.3
84046	4.5	100	.5	72	23.1	206	95.4	15	9	.2	11	0	.0
84047	19.9	93	6.6	61	25.7	378	98.6	12	7	9.0	7	1	.0
84049	1.3	97	.4	80	28.8	341	95.6	14	9	.6	9	0	.0
84050	4.9	99	1.3	83	30.9	321	94.3	12	7	2.4	7	1	.1
84051	.2	0	.1	82	35.6	410	76.7	11	10	.0	0	0	.0
84052	1.2	93	.3	88	19.1	341	64.2	18	6	.6	8	0	.0
84053	.5	93	.3	99	28.1	323*	95.7	11	9	.3	5	0	2.5
84054	5.2	97	1.6	81	28.9	345	112.3	16	9	2.5	5	2	.0
84055	.4	100	.1	85	25.2	407	102.4	14	5	.2	4	0	.0
84056	5.4	79	1.2	2	19.9	313	108.3	15	0	2.5	0	1	.0
84057	52.5	97	14.0	69	26.8	358	121.9	18	5	25.0	4	2	1.5
84060	4.5	99	1.6	67	42.8	340	229.1	9	3	2.2	3	5	.5
84061	.3	100	.1	89	25.6	294*	85.4	10	10	.2	13	0	.0
84062	14.5	98	3.7	82	28.4	352	125.3	17	6	7.1	5	0	.1
84063	.9	42	.3	75	16.4	203	44.0	13	7	.6	12	0	.0
84064	.9	98	.3	79	27.8	311	74.2	17	6	.5	6	0	.0
84065	16.9	99	4.2	87	30.5	380	137.7	16	3	8.5	3	0	.0
84066	7.1	95	2.0	82	26.9	322	88.6	14	7	3.4	7	3	.0

SALT LAKE CITY

ZIP CODE	1	2	3	4	5	6	7	8	9	10	11	12	13
84067	20.9	95	6.2	80	29.7	378	106.9	12	5	9.8	4	0	.0
84069	.4	0	.1	87	32.1	210	86.6	11	10	.0	2	0	.0
84070	74.2	97	19.0	87	34.3	436	139.3	16	6	36.6	2	0	.1
84071	.8	92	.2	73		356	63.5	16	9	.4	7	2	.0
84072	.3	0	.1	75	16.3	312	62.8	11	14	.0	6	0	.0
84074	17.2	93	5.5	79	28.6	355	94.9	12	7	7.9	6	4	.3
84076	.3	0	.1	74	25.8	296*	48.4	18	11	.0	0	0	.0
84078	15.5	98	4.7	78	28.2	392	97.9	15	6	7.7	5	1	.0
84080	.5	100	.1	74	25.4	292*	74.2	8	2	.3	3	0	.0
84082	1.1	70	.4	45	26.5	310	130.3	16	4	.3	3	0	8.2
84083	.5	95	.1	90	22.5	288	75.0	12	2	.3	2	0	.3
84084	30.3	95	7.6	90	28.9	435	112.6	20	2	14.5	2	0	.0
84085	.5	29	.1	88	16.8	90	61.8	24	4	.1	16	0	.0
84086	.1	100	.1	74	28.0	428	71.2	13	14	.2	11	0	.0
84087	7.2	99	1.8	86	30.8	382	115.4	18	2	3.5	2	5	4.3

SALT LAKE CITY

ZIP CODE	1	2	3	4	5	6	7	8	9	10	11	12	13
84101	2.2	69	1.0	28	12.8	230	60.0	10	17	.8	10	0	9.2
84102	16.9	89	8.6	24	17.0	301	96.1	6	16	7.2	11	0	.1
84103	22.5	93	10.5	37	25.7	298	172.8	8	13	9.9	10	5	3.1
84104	16.7	82	5.6	68	22.4	345	73.0	11	11	6.6	11	0	.0
84105	23.3	93	10.1	59	23.3	348	103.5	9	18	9.9	16	0	.0
84106	31.2	96	12.4	64	26.3	384	103.3	9	16	14.2	14	0	.3
84107	46.5	96	16.4	68	28.6	397	128.8	10	7	21.7	7	2	.3
84108	20.9	96	7.5	70	38.7	383	172.5	8	10	9.6	10	0	.0
84109	25.7	98	8.5	76	37.7	440	144.4	8	10	12.3	9	0	.6
84111	8.8	83	4.7	20	13.6	228	68.9	7	24	3.6	19	0	.7
84112	1.5	87	.2	0	13.4	0	47.9*	16	0	.7	1	0	.0
84113	.2	91	.1	0	24.3	363	86.7*	16	0	.1	0	0	6.4
84115	21.4	92	9.4	40	18.3	319	71.5	10	15	9.4	12	2	1.7
84116	21.9	85	7.6	64	23.4	322	82.2	12	8	9.1	8	7	2.2
84117	43.8	98	14.6	73	39.1	424	167.9	9	8	20.9	8	0	.0
84118	40.8	95	10.8	91	28.4	480	91.4	18	2	19.4	2	0	.4
84119	32.8	93	9.8	72	27.4	394	96.7	13	4	15.1	3	6	.0
84120	42.2	95	11.1	81	29.1	405	97.6	17	9	20.0	2	1	.0
84121	37.9	98	10.4	87	40.8	474	154.0	11	4	18.5	4	0	.0

OGDEN

ZIP CODE	1	2	3	4	5	6	7	8	9	10	11	12	13
84301	.6	0	.2	96	23.8	274*	98.5	13	11	.6	0	0	.0
84302	19.1	91	5.7	75	28.0	308	103.3	12	8	8.6	8	0	1.5
84305	.6	0	.2	96	22.2	255*	80.5	13	16	.2	8	0	.0
84306	.2	100	.1	55	27.1	53	70.2	0	7	.1	16	0	.0
84307	1.1	87	.3	80	26.6	304	86.7	16	8	.5	7	0	.0
84309	.3	0	.1	81	17.7	144	69.4	28	12	.0	8	0	.0
84310	1.4	100	.4	84	18.0	279	90.4	15	13	.3	0	0	.0
84311	.6	0	.1	90	34.4	341	139.3	13	6	.4	5	0	.0
84312	2.2	98	.6	86	22.1	390	109.7	15	6	1.1	6	0	.0
84314	.9	91	.6	85	24.0	295	85.7	17	11	1.1	11	0	.0
84315	3.7	97	.9	93	24.7	279	96.8	13	11	1.8	9	0	.0
84317	1.6	95	.4	87	31.6	400	140.5	12	8	.0	5	0	.0

*=Estimated **1.0=883 lbs per person; 100++ indicates per capita toxic waste generation > than 100 times the U.S. average of 883 lbs per capita.

ZIP CODE MEASURES OF SIZE, LEVELS OF AFFLUENCE AND QUALITY OF LIFE

1=Population (th.); 2= % White; 3=Households (th.); 4=% Owner Occupied; 5=Mean Income Per Household (th.$); 6=Mean Monthly Rent ($)*; 7=Mean Home Value (th.$)*;
8=% under 5; 9=% 65 and over; 10=White Males (th.); 11=% White Males, 65+; 12=# Toxic Waste Sites; 13=Toxic Waste Relative to US(883 lbs.per capita)**.

UTAH

ZIPCODE	1	2	3	4	5	6	7	8	9	10	11	12	13
OGDEN													
84318	1.5	100	.4	88	27.3	313	114.5	16	8	.8	7	0	.2
84319	4.1	99	1.1	87	23.3	335	97.6	17	7	2.0	6	0	.2
84320	1.4	99	.4	88	23.7	335	79.0	14	13	.7	12	0	.2
84321	32.4	96	10.6	53	22.4	290	113.8	11	10	15.	1	1	.2
84325	.8	100	.2	91	25.7	238	112.9	13	10	.4	8	0	.0
84326	.9	0	.2	89	24.9	383	101.6	20	7	.0	0	0	.0
84327	.7	100	.2	92	21.6	380	94.3	19	11	.4	9	0	.0
84328	1.0	0	.3	87	25.7	272	94.7	14	8	.0	0	0	.0
84329	.3	100	.1	100	20.2	232*	103.7	15	16	.2	13	0	.0
84330	.2	100	.1	89	20.4	235*	67.2	16	15	.1	18	0	25.6
84331	.3	0	.1	95	20.1	231*	67.7	10	7	.0	0	0	.0
84332	2.7	99	.7	88	29.4	380	121.2	14	6	1.4	5	0	.0
84333	2.1	99	.6	81	22.9	317	93.3	13	12	1.0	11	0	.1
84334	.2	0	.1	89	26.9	309*	79.9	19	3	.0	0	0	.0
84335	6.1	99	1.7	85	25.0	263	100.0	16	8	3.1	7	0	.2
84336	.4	0	.1	85	23.0	387	75.1	13	5	.0	0	0	.0
84337	5.8	94	1.7	81	24.9	286	90.8	14	9	2.7	9	0	.0
84338	.5	98	.1	87	21.5	237	70.6	16	8	.2	7	0	.0
84339	2.3	99	.6	85	25.5	334	94.9	16	9	1.2	7	0	.2
84340	1.1	98	.3	83	25.9	317	96.5	13	10	.5	9	0	.0
OGDEN													
84401	26.1	86	10.0	51	19.3	258	81.2	11	13	11.0	11	2	.6
84403	48.1	95	16.5	72	29.0	344	114.0	10	10	22.1	9	1	.1
84404	44.8	96	13.8	79	27.6	339	102.7	12	8	21.3	7	3	.0
PROVO													
84501	13.2	96	4.3	73	28.7	359	100.5	13	9	6.2	7	0	.1
84510	.7	0	.2	74	10.1	299	83.7	15	4	.0	0	0	.5
84511	4.2	75	1.1	75	22.0	277	85.8	16	18	1.6	4	2	.5
84512	.7	26	.2	81	9.0	231	25.5	8	18	.1	72	0	.0
84513	2.0	97	.6	78	30.3	394	92.4	17	8	1.0	4	0	.0
84518	.9	0	.2	93	27.5	396	77.0	15	8	.7	15	0	.0
84520	1.7	87	.6	85	25.1	315	50.0	13	14	.7	2	0	.0
84521	.4	94	.1	89	28.5	440	85.4	13	7	.2	0	0	.0
84522	.4	0	.1	83	22.7	287	60.2	18	18	.0	0	0	.0
84523	1.9	98	.5	77	28.4	424	101.4	17	8	.9	6	1	.0
84525	.6	96	.1	71	21.5	309	68.7	11	7	.6	9	1	.0
84526	4.7	97	1.6	80	28.8	325	83.5	10	12	2.3	12	1	.0
84527	.2	89	.1	0	31.9	145	113.7*	22	0	.0	0	0	.0
84528	3.0	98	.9	78	28.3	330	90.3	17	6	1.5	5	1	.0
84529	.3	100	.1	90	11.9	530	42.3	17	14	.1	15	0	.0
84530	.5	83	.1	79	23.9	275*	108.3	19	5	.0	0	0	.0
84531	.5	15	.1	85	15.3	211	26.2	21	6	.2	0	0	.0
84532	8.0	96	2.7	78	26.4	347	96.2	12	6	3.9	6	2	4.5
84534	1.6	8	.3	59	20.8	202	95.4	12	1	.0	6	0	.0
84535	2.5	92	.7	81	24.9	308	85.1	17	5	1.1	5	3	.5
84536	.6	0	.1	59	14.0	159	26.2	16	11	.0	0	0	.0
84537	1.4	0	.4	81	27.8	438	95.4	19	7	.4	11	1	.0
84539	.8	87	.3	85	28.4	321	48.1	9	8	.4	11	1	.0
84542	1.3	99	.4	83	27.1	402	77.1	14	7	.7	5	1	.0

UTAH

ZIPCODE	1	2	3	4	5	6	7	8	9	10	11	12	13
PROVO													
84601	71.7	96	20.4	45	22.7	304	132.7	12	6	32.9	6	2	.2
84620	.9	0	.3	87	26.4	491	83.7	17	8	.0	0	0	.0
84621	.2	100	.1	96	17.7	203*	55.9	5	12	.1	14	0	.0
84622	.8	99	.2	83	17.7	277	66.6	17	11	.4	9	0	.0
84624	3.3	99	1.0	82	23.0	291	82.8	15	12	1.7	11	0	.5
84627	2.9	95	.7	75	20.3	243	81.5	11	9	1.3	9	0	.2
84628	.9	100	.3	96	19.5	248	43.3	11	15	.5	13	0	1.8
84629	1.4	99	.4	86	21.2	283	80.9	13	14	.6	13	0	.0
84630	.3	100	.1	88	19.8	227*	71.8	13	18	.1	15	0	.0
84631	2.5	91	.8	80	20.9	352	78.1	14	13	1.1	11	0	.0
84632	.6	0	.2	90	17.7	186	67.5	16	18	.0	0	0	.0
84633	.6	98	.2	89	21.0	189	74.3	11	15	.3	11	0	.1
84634	1.3	97	.4	87	21.7	262	78.0	14	11	.6	11	0	.0
84635	.7	99	.2	82	22.8	385	67.4	12	8	.3	7	0	.0
84636	.5	0	.1	91	19.0	93	72.4	12	14	.2	15	0	.2
84637	.5	87	.1	87	18.9	183	65.4	14	15	.2	15	0	.0
84639	.5	100	.1	84	19.9	185	61.5	18	2	.3	2	0	.0
84642	2.2	97	.7	84	17.9	215	73.8	15	17	1.0	16	0	.0
84643	.4	89	.1	89	23.1	385	79.0	14	16	.2	21	0	.2
84644	.3	0	.1	84	18.6	357	63.0	14	16	.0	0	0	.0
84645	.6	100	.2	85	19.8	224	80.1	19	13	.3	16	0	.0
84646	1.2	93	.4	86	21.2	292	77.6	14	13	.6	13	0	.0
84647	2.2	98	.7	81	20.4	312	75.3	14	14	1.1	13	0	.1
84648	3.4	99	1.0	83	25.0	272	80.1	12	14	1.6	13	0	.1
84649	.4	0	.1	96	20.3	233*	80.4	12	13	.0	0	0	.0
84651	10.5	98	2.8	83	26.7	280	99.4	17	7	5.0	6	0	.0
84652	.6	0	.2	91	21.6	243	72.0	19	11	.0	0	0	.0
84653	2.6	99	.7	89	28.5	321	126.9	16	11	1.3	6	0	.0
84654	2.0	100	.7	89	28.1	302	85.8	15	12	1.1	11	0	1.4
84655	3.1	97	.8	83	21.5	275	85.5	17	7	1.5	6	1	.0
84656	.3	100	.1	98	19.4	223*	88.5	12	20	.1	22	0	.0
84657	.4	100	.1	89	20.9	203	81.9	12	8	.2	5	0	.5
84660	13.1	98	3.6	80	27.2	302	105.0	15	9	6.4	8	0	.0
84662	.8	100	.8	91	15.4	499	74.2	12	16	.4	13	1	.0
84663	15.9	98	4.6	74	25.9	305	119.8	14	8	7.7	8	0	.0
84665	.3	0	.1	87	17.8	305	68.6	13	12	.0	0	0	.0
84667	.2	0	.1	81	18.7	215*	48.4	17	17	.0	0	0	.0
PROVO													
84701	6.1	98	1.9	81	24.7	301	89.5	13	12	3.0	10	0	.0
84711	.5	0	.1	91	22.5	381	87.1	19	9	.1	12	0	.0
84713	2.2	99	.7	83	18.5	214	80.7	12	14	1.1	12	0	.4
84714	.3	69	.1	71	16.3	145	65.0	17	14	.1	16	0	.0
84715	.4	0	.1	76	19.9	230	78.1	8	13	.1	13	0	.0
84718	.2	100	.1	86	14.5	167*	86.2	17	15	.1	6	0	.0
84720	13.9	96	4.1	74	23.6	299	97.1	13	6	6.7	6	1	.0
84722	.3	100	.1	82	22.7	253	81.8	14	8	.2	3	0	.0
84723	.1	0	.1	83	18.7	287	65.6	10	16	.0	0	0	.0
84724	.8	0	.2	88	17.6	248	66.2	13	11	.0	0	0	.0
84725	.9	0	.4	83	20.0	203	86.5	17	7	.0	0	0	1.4

*=Estimated **1.0=883 lbs per person; 100++ indicates per capita toxic waste generation > than 100 times the U.S. average of 883 lbs per capita.

ZIP CODE MEASURES OF SIZE, LEVELS OF AFFLUENCE AND QUALITY OF LIFE

1=Population (th.); 2= % White; 3=Households (th.); 4=% Owner Occupied; 5=Mean Income Per Household (th.$); 6=Mean Monthly Rent ($)*; 7=Mean Home Value (th.$)*; 8=% under 5, 9=% 65 and over; 10=White Males (th.); 11=% White Males, 65+; 12=# Toxic Waste Sites; 13=Toxic Waste Relative to US(883 lbs.per capita)**.

UTAH

ZIP CODE	1	2	3	4	5	6	7	8	9	10	11	12	13
PROVO													
84726	.8	99	.3	79	17.0	229	70.0	11	15	.4	14	0	.0
84729	.3	100	.1	89	19.5	224*	71.6	16	12	.1	12	0	.0
84730	.5	0	.1	91	21.1	336	72.2	19	7	.0	0	0	.0
84734	.5	96	.2	58	24.6	145	58.8	12	3	.3	4	0	.0
84735	.2	100	.1	97	18.2	209*	51.7	5	17	.1	15	0	3.8
84737	2.8	98	.9	84	19.4	285	104.7	14	14	1.4	14	0	.0
84738	.6	0	.1	96	20.5	236*	78.7	15	9	.0	0	0	.0
84739	.3	0	.1	94	22.8	262*	66.9	9	16	.0	0	0	.0
84740	.1	100	.1	91	13.7	158*	45.5	15	26	.1	19	0	.0
84741	3.0	99	1.0	80	19.4	235	93.3	13	11	1.5	11	0	.0
84742	.2	100	.1	96	16.7	192*	78.0	10	18	.1	22	0	.0
84744	.2	0	.1	94	20.7	238*	56.4	15	15	.0	0	0	.0
84745	1.0	99	.3	91	19.7	350	87.1	15	17	.5	18	0	.0
84746	.4	0	.1	79	20.1	360	113.4	5	25	.0	0	0	.0
84747	.6	99	.2	88	16.9	157	71.9	14	16	.3	14	0	.0
84749	.2	0	.1	92	21.0	241*	64.7	15	14	.0	0	0	.0
84750	.5	0	.2	89	22.2	144	72.6	10	19	.0	0	0	.0
84751	1.5	98	.5	82	23.9	241	61.3	12	15	.7	14	0	.0
84752	.6	99	.2	91	19.2	218	76.2	18	11	.3	11	0	.0
84754	2.3	99	.8	89	20.5	292	87.8	11	16	1.1	16	0	.0
84756	.3	100	.1	79	23.6	170	70.3	14	6	.2	12	0	.0
84757	.2	100	.1	81	35.9	201	82.2	12	12	.1	11	0	.0
84758	.4	0	.1	92	21.3	240	61.0	9	12	.0	0	0	.0
84759	1.5	96	.5	83	21.3	256	70.7	13	11	.7	11	0	.0
84760	.2	99	.1	85	19.4	375	65.2	7	14	.1	10	0	.0
84761	2.1	98	.6	86	19.3	236	84.5	14	11	1.0	11	0	.0
84763	.2	100	.1	67	11.5	185	79.6	9	27	.1	25	0	.0
84765	1.1	98	.3	92	29.3	410	124.8	15	9	.5	11	0	.0
84767	.3	100	.1	66	21.9	308	101.6	6	20	.2	21	0	.0
84770	13.8	99	4.4	72	22.4	321	125.3	12	15	6.6	15	0	.0
84773	.3	0	.1	83	32.9	206	85.6	13	18	.0	0	0	.0
84774	.3	100	.1	81	19.6	308	101.7	8	27	.1	30	0	.0
84775	.3	98	.1	73	12.7	131	65.8	16	15	.0	16	0	.0
84776	.4	0	.1	87	19.1	129	74.3	10	15	.0	0	0	.0
84779	.2	100	.1	89	18.5	213*	75.9	14	8	.1	10	0	.0
84780	2.8	99	.8	87	19.8	323	98.3	17	10	1.4	11	0	.0
FLAGSTAFF													
86021	1.1	100	.1	2	17.3	199*	61.6*	21	1	.5	1	0	.0
86044	.3	0	.1	62	13.5	207	13.1	14	0	0	0		.0
GALLUP													
86514	.3	0	.1	100	14.0	161*	13.1	20		.0	0	0	.0

VERMONT

ZIP CODE	1	2	3	4	5	6	7	8	9	10	11	12	13
PITTSFIELD													
01247	.8	100	.2	91	30.4	356	75.4	6	11	.4	9	0	.0
LITTLETON													
03576	.2	0	.1	81	20.3	263	45.6	6	7	.0	0	0	.0
03590	.3	0	.1	78	17.1	214	45.4	9	12	.0	0	0	.0
WHITE RIVER JUNCTION													
05001	5.1	98	1.9	67	24.2	319	79.5	6	15	2.4	12	0	.1
05030	.5	100	.2	84	23.1	348	71.3	7	9	.3	8	0	.0
05031	.2	100	.1	69	24.3	376	130.6	3	9	.1	7	0	.0
05032	2.4	99	.9	77	20.1	220	73.5	8	11	1.2	11	0	.2
05033	.8	0	.8	73	20.8	268	70.5	9	16	.0	0	0	.0
05034	.3	0	.1	84	23.4	355	67.3	9	9	.0	0	0	.0
05035	.5	100	.2	79	20.1	418	64.9	9	11	.3	11	0	.0
05036	.5	0	.2	91	24.5	175	71.0	10	12	.0	0	0	.0
05037	.4	0	.4	76	28.2	360	95.5	4	9	.0	0	0	.0
05038	1.1	100	.4	80	18.3	280	55.8	8	14	.6	13	0	.2
05039	.5	0	.2	84	19.4	302	47.7	8	9	.0	0	0	.0
05040	.5	100	.2	84	18.3	244	66.3	9	15	.3	12	0	.0
05041	.3	100	.1	70	20.2	456	76.9	8	12	.2	16	0	.0
05042	.4	98	.3	92	19.9	368	52.4	14	11	.2	14	0	1.2
05043	.9	0	.3	66	24.9	359	87.8	11	9	.0	0	0	.0
05044	.4	99	.2	75	19.0	337	74.9	11	9	.2	9	0	.0
05045	.6	0	.4	56	17.6	372	87.2	7	12	.0	0	0	.0
05046	1.1	100	.4	82	19.0	211	61.4	8	12	.6	10	0	.3
05047	.8	100	.3	56	26.2	370	85.5	9	6	.4	10	0	.0
05048	1.3	0	.4	79	25.7	397	83.9	9	9	.0	0	0	.1
05049	.2	100	.2	67	25.6	334	65.4	7	5	.1	5	0	.0
05051	.4	100	.2	66	19.5	313	60.4	9	18	.2	14	0	.0
05052	.2	0	.1	79	23.8	450	78.6	5	12	.0	0	0	.0
05053	.3	0	.1	85	28.7	399	90.6	9	12	.0	0	0	.0
05054	.2	93	.8	74	24.8	373	65.7	6	11	.0	9	0	.0
05055	2.1	100	.8	75	35.2	466	142.0	6	11	1.0	9	0	.1
05056	.2	0	.1	61	18.5	156	86.8	4	15	.0	0	0	.0
05058	.2	100	.2	80	24.2	434	89.0	8	10	.2	8	0	.0
05059	.6	100	.2	78	41.1	505	171.1	6	8	.3	6	0	.0
05060	4.3	0	1.6	69	20.2	270	70.8	8	15	.0	0	0	.6
05061	1.6	0	.3	79	20.4	354	68.4	5	5	.0	0	0	.0
05062	.7	100	.3	79	24.5	311	70.7	8	16	.6	13	0	.0
05065	.7	100	.2	80	23.4	416	77.9	8	10	.3	12	0	.0
05067	.1	0	.1	71	29.6	493	103	4	12	.2	14	0	.0
05068	2.4	99	.9	65	18.7	345	69.6	8	10	1.2	8	0	.0
05069	.6	0	.1	78	19.5	243	55.3	8	13	.0	0	0	.0
05070	.3	97	.1	78	21.2	490	76.0	15	13	.1	12	0	.0
05071	.3	100	.1	79	39.5	454*	72.1	5	13	.2	5	0	.0
05072	.3	0	.1	87	23.0	376	93.7	8	13	.0	0	0	.0
05073	.1	100	.1	72	23.7	119	168.8	0	19	.1	9	0	.0
05074	.2	0	.1	71	23.3	354	123.5	6	11	.0	0	0	.0
05075	.7	100	.3	76	23.8	322	77.6	7	10	.3	12	0	.0
05077	.8	0	.3	84	20.5	238	62.7	9	13	.2	9	0	.0
05079	.4	100	.1	67	18.1	114	48.2	10	8	.2	9	0	.0

*=Estimated **1.0=883 lbs per person; 100++ indicates per capita toxic waste generation > than 100 times the U.S. average of 883 lbs per capita.

ZIP CODE MEASURES OF SIZE, LEVELS OF AFFLUENCE AND QUALITY OF LIFE

1=Population (th.); 2=% White; 3=Households (th.); 4=% Owner Occupied; 5=Mean Income Per Household (th.$); 6=Mean Monthly Rent ($)*; 7=Mean Home Value (th.$)*; 8=% under 5; 9=% 65 and over; 10=% White Males (th.); 11=% White Males, 65+ ; 12=# Toxic Waste Sites; 13=Toxic Waste Relative to US(883 lbs.per capita)**.

VERMONT

ZIPCODE	1	2	3	4	5	6	7	8	9	10	11	12	13
WHITE RIVER JUNCTION													
05081	.8	99	.3	71	17.9	209	63.3	7	18	.4	16	0	.2
05083	.3	100	.1	77	18.7	473	64.9	6	8	.1	6	0	.0
05084	.3	100	.1	85	17.9	234	60.4	7	12	.1	13	0	.0
05086	.7	0	.2	89	21.7	327	58.3	8	7	.0	0	0	.0
05088	1.2	100	.4	72	23.6	353	80.8	5	9	.5	4	0	.0
05089	4.9	99	1.8	65	21.8	282	68.6	7	16	2.4	12	1	2.2
05091	3.5	100	1.4	71	26.2	369	97.0	6	17	1.7	14	0	.1
BELLOWS FALLS													
05101	5.1	100	2.0	56	19.8	292	59.8	7	14	2.4	11	1	.7
05142	.6	100	.2	87	25.2	264	56.0	7	15	.3	15	0	.2
05143	2.6	100	.9	73	22.4	337	70.6	7	12	1.3	11	0	.0
05144	1.9	98	.7	86	22.2	347	64.0	7	9	.9	8	3	.0
05146	.6	100	.2	77	24.2	385	93.9	5	17	.3	16	0	.0
05148	1.0	100	.4	81	25.9	356	98.0	5	11	.5	9	0	.0
05149	2.6	100	1.0	67	20.4	285	74.8	6	18	1.3	15	0	.1
05150	1.4	100	.5	75	27.5	342	70.2	6	12	.7	10	0	.8
05151	1.0	100	.4	80	22.6	354	69.5	8	12	.5	11	0	.0
05152	.3	100	.1	79	30.3	257	106.5	4	10	.2	9	0	.0
05153	.8	100	.3	71	23.2	371	63.7	6	15	.4	13	0	.0
05154	.9	99	.3	78	22.1	272	71.0	6	13	.4	11	0	.1
05155	.8	0	.3	68	26.5	381	91.4	7	14	.4	0	0	.0
05156	8.5	99	3.3	67	24.6	280	69.8	6	16	4.2	14	0	3.5
05158	.5	100	.1	64	23.6	360	62.4	9	8	.2	6	0	.0
05161	.6	100	.2	80	24.9	440	107.0	3	19	.3	16	0	.0
BENNINGTON													
05201	15.3	100	5.3	63	22.7	311	76.1	7	14	7.2	12	4	.3
05250	2.6	99	1.0	78	22.7	353	76.8	7	14	1.3	13	0	.1
05251	.8	0	.3	83	36.0	440	141.3	5	26	.6	0	0	1.1
05252	.5	100	.2	80	21.9	362	66.4	6	20	.3	16	0	.7
05253	.6	100	.3	75	27.7	288	84.8	4	14	.3	11	0	.0
05254	.8	0	.3	83	36.0	331	115.6	4	23	.4	0	0	.0
05255	2.6	98	1.1	63	23.4	321	98.5	6	13	1.3	12	0	.2
05257	2.2	99	.8	73	24.9	366	77.1	6	14	1.0	12	0	.0
05260	.6	100	.2	75	19.7	322	46.5	12	6	.3	8	0	.6
05261	2.3	100	.9	77	21.7	289	78.1	7	9	1.2	8	0	.0
05262	2.0	98	.7	81	24.7	379	77.7	8	11	1.0	9	0	.7
05263	.2	100	.1	83	23.4	278	79.9	7	22	.1	20	0	.0
BRATTLEBORG													
05301	14.3	99	5.5	56	23.1	314	77.8	7	15	6.6	11	0	.3
05340	.3	100	.1	52	28.2	459	107.3	8	17	.1	15	0	.0
05341	.8	100	.3	83	18.8	384	62.6	9	9	.4	12	0	.1
05342	.6	0	.2	83	21.1	299	64.4	6	16	.0	0	0	.0
05343	.5	100	.2	75	18.7	228	75.2	7	18	.3	16	0	.0
05344	.4	98	.1	51	21.9	389	81.1	5	7	.2	6	0	.0
05345	1.1	100	.4	80	23.6	327	77.9	7	10	.5	9	0	.0
05346	3.6	99	1.3	72	23.8	273	72.7	8	9	1.8	7	0	.4
05350	.6	100	.2	74	23.0	250	58.7	5	16	.3	15	0	.0
05351	.6	0	.1	80	26.7	350	83.8	2	18	.0	0	0	.0
05353	.6	0	.2	77	21.1	377	74.4	7	18	.0	0	0	.3

VERMONT

ZIPCODE	1	2	3	4	5	6	7	8	9	10	11	12	13
BRATTLEBORG													
05354	1.2	100	.4	73	23.4	259	82.8	6	20	.6	14	0	.9
05355	.3	100	.1	90	16.8	300	74.7	4	19	.0	0	0	.0
05356	.4	0	.2	58	25.8	293	87.4	5	6	.0	0	0	.0
05357	.2	100	.1	67	21.2	269	67.6	9	10	.1	7	0	.0
05358	.3	100	.1	75	19.2	245	49.9	12	8	.2	8	0	.0
05359	.4	0	.2	70	18.0	258	60.1	9	17	.0	0	0	.0
05360	.1	100	.1	65	23.1	273	84.2	8	8	.0	9	0	.0
05361	.5		.2	83	23.2	416	53.7	5	12	.0	0	0	.1
05362	.2	100	.1	81	23.5	312	82.0	7	13	.1	10	0	.2
05363	1.9	99	.7	63	20.4	266	86.4	7	9	.9	7	0	.9
BURLINGTON													
05401	48.8	99	16.9	50	25.0	380	101.9	5	10	22.3	8	3	.4
05404	8.6	98	2.8	43	20.0	362	80.0	6	9	4.0	7	0	.9
05440	1.4	98	.5	79	18.9	277	66.0	8	12	.6	12	0	.0
05441	.4	100	.1	76	23.3	315	65.2	9	10	.2	10	0	.1
05442	.2	100	.1	82	24.6	325	61.4	9	15	.1	9	0	.8
05443	5.0	99	1.7	75	20.8	309	73.4	9	10	2.5	9	0	.0
05444	1.4	100	.4	81	24.7	301	82.4	10	8	.7	7	0	.0
05445	2.0	99	.7	79	37.3	410	117.7	7	7	1.0	6	0	.1
05446	10.0	99	3.3	79	29.0	445	100.2	8	5	5.1	4	0	.2
05447	.2	100	.1	77	17.0	173	41.9	9	8	.1	16	0	.0
05448	.6	99	.2	79	22.6	259	59.0	10	8	.3	10	0	.0
05450	3.6	100	1.2	74	21.2	248	57.5	8	14	1.7	12	0	.0
05451	.5	100	.1	82	23.4	413	90.9	6	5	.2	5	0	.0
05452	13.8	98	4.6	72	32.4	418	101.5	7	5	6.6	4	1	.9
05454	2.0	100	.6	83	28.0	338	79.4	8	5	1.0	4	0	.3
05455	.8	100	.6	71	23.4	309	68.9	9	9	.3	8	0	.1
05456	.8	100	.3	87	24.4	463	89.8	6	9	.4	8	0	.1
05457	1.1	0	.3	85	24.2	259	56.6	9	13	.7	6	0	.7
05458	1.2	97	.4	82	25.2	343	82.6	7	9	.7	8	0	.0
05459	1.4	0	.4	81	20.2	335	51.3	7	9	.7	8	0	.0
05461	1.9	0	.6	77	28.8	422	91.4	8	5	.7	4	0	.2
05462	1.5	100	.5	86	21.0	449	75.7	10	7	.7	4	0	.6
05463	.4	100	.5	96	21.5	247*	67.9	10	15	.2	15	0	.0
05464	1.3	99	.5	76	24.3	387	76.9	7	10	.7	8	0	.0
05465	2.8	0	.8	86	30.9	437	97.3	9	5	.6	7	0	.7
05466	.2	0	.1	81	23.6	322	60.9	9	2	.0	0	0	.0
05468	9.2	100	2.8	84	26.1	390	85.6	10	5	4.6	4	0	.0
05471	.5	100	.2	82	17.7	181	64.4	8	13	.1	11	0	.3
05472	.2	0	.1	80	21.9	330	76.0	8	10	.0	4	0	.0
05473	1.4	98	.5	81	24.9	321	89.3	8	7	.7	7	0	.1
05474	.5	0	.2	76	25.4	326	98.9	6	16	.3	12	0	.0
05476	2.6	100	.9	72	18.4	255	38.5	9	14	1.3	12	0	.1
05477	3.8	99	1.2	81	27.8	324	92.7	8	5	2.0	4	0	.3
05478	11.7	99	4.1	60	22.8	300	73.6	7	14	5.4	11	1	.3
05481	.2	100	.2	79	20.4	363	62.4	10	6	.1	8	0	.4
05482	5.3	100	1.8	83	35.7	467	129.4	6	7	2.6	7	0	.1
05483	1.4	99	.4	84	23.3	326	61.1	9	8	.7	6	0	.0
05485	.3	100	.1	75	23.6	319	47.0	7	6	.2	5	0	4.9

*=Estimated **1.0=883 lbs per person; 100++ indicates per capita toxic waste generation > than 100 times the U.S. average of 883 lbs per capita.

ZIP CODE MEASURES OF SIZE, LEVELS OF AFFLUENCE AND QUALITY OF LIFE

1=Population (th.); 2= % White; 3=Households (th.); 4=% Owner Occupied; 5=Mean Income Per Household (th.$); 6=Mean Monthly Rent ($); 7=Mean Home Value (th.$);
8=% under 5; 9=% 65 and over; 10=White Males (th.); 11=% White Males, 65+; 12=# Toxic Waste Sites; 13=Toxic Waste Relative to US(883 lbs.per capita)**.

VERMONT

BURLINGTON

ZIP CODE	1	2	3	4	5	6	7	8	9	10	11	12	13
05486	1.2	99	.4	77	24.3	359	96.0	9	11	.6	11	0	.0
05487	1.0	99	.3	82	23.3	312	72.8	10	8		8	0	.0
05488	5.8	96	1.9	78	22.6	351	68.9	9	9	2.8	8	0	.2
05489	2.6	99	.8	92	32.9	491	107.6	7	6	1.3	5	0	.0
05490	.4	0	.1	79	34.1	462	107.5	9	3	.0	0	0	.0
05491	5.1	100	1.7	76	22.5	323	79.3	9	11	2.5	9	0	.8
05492	.6	99	.2	89	21.3	277	66.2	8	11	.3	12	0	.0
05494	.7	0	.2	83	26.1	376	88.5	9	5	.0	0	0	.0
05495	4.4	98	1.4	84	34.0	453	103.4	8	5	2.2	5	0	.1

MONTPELIER

ZIP CODE	1	2	3	4	5	6	7	8	9	10	11	12	13
05602	12.1	100	4.6	65	23.7	296	77.5	6	15	5.5	11	0	.0
05640	.1	0	.1	94	24.5	282*	70.0	8	9	.0	0	0	.0
05641	15.2	99	5.7	62	22.0	279	74.6	6	15	7.0	11	0	.4
05647	.7	99	.2	82	18.8	218	56.5	5	12	.4	0	0	.1
05648	.3	0	.1	89	24.0	390	76.9	13	6	.0	0	0	.0
05649	1.0	0	.3	88	25.0	412	63.6	9	11	.0	0	0	.0
05650	.6	100	.2	80	20.0	281	57.6	9	12	.3	10	0	.0
05651	1.2	0	.4	86	26.4	331	76.5	7	10	.3	0	0	.0
05652	.1	100	.1	78	18.5	282	43.3	10	15	.1	15	0	.0
05653	1.2	100	.5	85	20.1	249	56.8	8	4	.1	5	0	.0
05654	1.2	0	.4	74	22.0	298	57.2	11	9	.0	0	0	.0
05655	1.8	0	.6	81	20.3	354	69.9	9	9	.1	7	0	.0
05656	2.8	100	.9	63	19.5	283	65.4	7	8	1.4	6	0	.1
05657	.1	0	.1	90	18.3	210*	66.4	10	10	.4	13	0	.0
05658	.9	99	.3	76	18.3	202	51.1	6	10	.5	0	0	.0
05660	1.1	99	.7	70	22.5	355	83.5	9	6	.8	8	0	.0
05661	4.5	99	1.6	65	20.3	274	72.3	7	15	2.2	12	0	1.1
05662	.2	100	.1	63	32.3	391	99.1	5	8	.2	12	0	.2
05663	5.3	98	1.5	71	22.1	281	69.8	5	11	1.4	9	0	.2
05664	.6	0	.2	71	19.0	242	62.1	7	8	.0	0	0	.0
05665	.2	100	.1	77	18.7	330	60.3	10	7	.1	7	0	.0
05667	2.2	98	.7	74	22.0	274	62.7	7	9	1.1	8	0	.0
05669	.5	100	.2	77	19.6	283	50.6	10	17	.3	14	0	.1
05670	.8	100	.3	84	23.9	323	68.8	11	18	.3	16	0	.0
05672	2.9	0	1.2	58	23.5	354	122.8	6	8	.8	8	0	.0
05673	1.6	98	.7	70	25.1	370	112.2	6	8	.5	8	0	.0
05674	.9	100	.4	71	23.9	391	117.0	7	8	.3	8	0	.0
05675	.6	100	.2	91	18.4	249	59.2	9	10	.5	8	0	.0
05676	4.5	99	1.6	68	22.0	306	69.3	7	12	2.9	9	0	.1
05677	1.4	100	.5	88	25.6	384	81.3	8	7	.7	5	0	.1
05678	.4	100	.1	74	19.7	356	47.6	6	6	.2	5	0	.0
05679	2.1	0	.7	79	20.3	245	63.3	8	10	.5	0	0	.0
05680	1.2	100	.4	86	17.5	216	53.7	10	9	.6	10	0	.0
05681	.2	0	.1	80	16.4	424	43.8	4	7	.0	6	0	.0
05682	.8	99	.3	78	20.9	297	59.3	10	6	.4	6	0	.0

RUTLAND

ZIP CODE	1	2	3	4	5	6	7	8	9	10	11	12	13
05701	22.3	99	8.3	59	23.7	323	83.9	6	15	10.2	12	1	1.4
05730	.2	100	.1	68	30.0	293	103.2	10	16	1.13	13	0	.0
05731	.5	98	.2	75	20.4	305	62.3	9	10	.2	8	0	.0
05732	.8	100	.3	60	18.5	313	73.1	8	15	.4	13	0	.0
05733	5.2	100	1.8	73	19.7	299	68.0	7	13	2.6	11	0	.0
05734	.8	98	.8	79	24.3	376	79.5	10	11	.4	11	0	.0
05735	2.5	100	.6	72	21.9	281	74.9	3	9	1.2	8	0	.0
05736	.5	100	.2	84	25.0	291	72.3	7	23	.3	25	0	.0
05737	.5	0	.2	81	26.6	420	77.4	4	10	.0	0	0	.0
05738	.9	0	.3	85	26.7	335	72.5	7	9	.0	0	0	.0
05739	1.1	0	.4	82	21.8	277	60.2	7	13	.0	12	0	.0
05740	.5	100	.5	78	17.8	261	78.2	7	16	.2	12	0	.1
05742	.5	99	.2	78	22.3	377	71.9	8	12	.2	10	0	.1
05743	3.3	99	.1	72	20.5	319	62.5	8	12	1.6	10	0	.3
05744	.4	100	.1	76	20.3	270	60.2	3	10	.2	10	0	31.9
05745	.3	100	.1	79	17.5	212	60.3	6	21	.2	17	0	.2
05746	.2	0	.1	69	18.9	309	69.1	6	8	.0	0	0	.1
05747	.2	100	.2	80	21.0	272	48.6	10	8	.1	5	0	.1
05748	.2	0	.1	75	19.9	260	57.5	6	11	.0	6	0	.6
05750	.4	100	.1	71	18.4	471	48.0	5	7	.2	4	0	.0
05751	.9	0	.4	62	31.3	357	142.4	4	3	.0	2	0	.0
05753	8.8	99	2.5	66	25.5	358	93.5	5	10	4.2	8	0	3.4
05757	.8	99	.3	78	24.4	302	67.8	5	17	.4	18	0	.0
05758	.5	99	.2	80	22.0	372	68.6	8	10	.2	10	0	.0
05759	2.1	99	.6	80	23.1	302	70.0	8	8	1.0	7	0	.1
05760	.8	100	.3	84	22.4	273	76.0	8	13	.4	13	0	.0
05761	.9	0	.3	72	20.8	263	91.0	8	13	.4	13	0	.0
05762	.4	0	.2	76	26.2	372	96.4	7	11	.6	10	0	.0
05763	.8	0	.8	73	24.2	336	87.1	7	11	.3	16	0	.0
05764	3.3	99	1.1	75	21.2	290	60.5	7	12	1.4	10	0	.3
05765	2.0	99	.7	74	25.6	343	74.8	5	17	.9	15	0	.2
05766	.3	0	.3	77	20.6	220	73.1	7	4	.6	0	0	.1
05767	1.2	100	.5	65	20.7	264	76.3	8	11	.6	10	0	.0
05769	1.0	0	.3	83	23.3	319	76.6	5	10	.1	7	0	.0
05770	.9	100	.3	79	23.8	304	76.2	7	9	.4	8	0	.0
05773	1.8	100	.6	82	21.7	326	69.9	7	9	.9	8	0	3.7
05774	.9	0	.3	79	23.2	310	82.7	8	15	.4	9	0	.0
05775	.6	100	.2	77	20.3	309	61.2	6	18	.3	16	0	.0
05776	.6	100	.1	80	22.1	261	54.3	1	22	.1	22	0	.0
05777	3.2	0	1.1	79	22.0	310	64.8	8	13	1.4	10	0	.3
05778	.6	100	.2	77	26.0	251	71.2	8	8	.9	15	0	.2

SAINT JOHNSBURY

ZIP CODE	1	2	3	4	5	6	7	8	9	10	11	12	13
05819	8.6	100	3.3	54	21.3	268	64.4	8	15	4.1	12	0	1.8
05820	.3	100	.1	84	21.0	386	42.1	11	9	.2	9	0	.0
05821	.8	100	.7	74	20.2	334	60.1	5	19	.4	19	0	.0
05824	2.0	0	.3	66	17.4	271	55.4	10	16	.0	0	0	.0
05825	.8	100	.3	78	19.3	249	47.8	9	12	.4	7	0	.0
05826	.2	99	.1	86	20.7	238*	51.7	3	12	.2	15	0	.0
05827	.4	100	.2	73	18.9	239	54.4	6	13	.2	13	0	.0
05828	.5	99	.2	80	20.5	300	64.5	9	7	.2	6	0	.0
05829	1.1	0	.4	82	22.0	219	63.8	8	10	.3	5	0	.0

*=Estimated **1.0=883 lbs per person; 100++ indicates per capita toxic waste generation > than 100 times the U.S. average of 883 lbs per capita.

ZIP CODE MEASURES OF SIZE, LEVELS OF AFFLUENCE AND QUALITY OF LIFE

1=Population (th.); 2= % White; 3=Households (th.); 4=% Owner Occupied; 5=Mean Income Per Household (th.$); 6=Mean Monthly Rent ($); 7=Mean Home Value (th.$); 8=% under 5; 9=% 65 and over; 10=% White Males; 11=% White Males, 65+; 12=# Toxic Waste Sites; 13=Toxic Waste Relative to US(883 lbs.per capita)**.

VERMONT

SAINT JOHNSBURY

ZIPCODE	1	2	3	4	5	6	7	8	9	10	11	12	13
05830	1.6	100	.5	69	26.0	259	65.4	7	10	.8	7	0	2.5
05832	.7	100	.2	83	21.6	261	60.7	7	7	.3	7	0	.0
05836	.7	100	.2	90	19.5	196	48.8	10	10	.3	11	0	.0
05837	.4	100	.1	82	19.7	349	45.7	8	5	.2	3	0	.0
05838	.3	100	.1	95	25.1	289*	53.1	7	11	.1	10	0	.0
05839	.6	0	.2	81	19.8	305	55.3	9	14	.0	0	0	.0
05841	.4	0	.1	71	21.7	271	99.0	8	23	.0	0	0	.0
05842	.4	100	.1	85	17.0	228	50.8	8	12	.2	12	0	.0
05843	2.4	99	.8	68	15.3	218	49.7	9	11	1.2	9	0	.0
05845	.8	0	.3	79	20.4	298	54.3	9	9	.0	0	0	.2
05846	1.6	0	.5	72	18.1	261	46.0	10	14	.0	0	0	.0
05847	.5	0	.2	78	17.6	222	52.5	6	10	.0	0	0	.0
05848	.2	0	.1	96	29.6	341*	80.1	1	20	.0	1	0	.0
05849	.4	100	.1	65	24.5	300	60.2	6	7	.2	5	1	.0
05850	.4	0	.1	47	18.3	280	64.7	9	2	.0	0	0	.0
05851	4.7	100	1.6	68	19.6	267	64.2	9	11	2.4	9	1	1.4
05853	.2	100	.1	80	27.4	251	68.1	4	14	.1	10	0	.0
05854	.2	100	.1	80	23.6	354	67.3	4	13	.1	15	0	.0
05855	6.8	0	2.5	63	20.1	258	59.8	8	14	.0	0	0	.1
05857	1.1	0	.3	86	22.8	238	59.7	9	9	.4	9	0	.0
05858	.4	0	.1	83	17.2	301	56.6	9	15	.0	0	0	.0
05859	1.6	0	.5	75	18.8	234	54.4	9	11	.0	0	0	.2
05860	2.2	100	.8	75	17.8	245	52.8	9	12	1.1	11	0	.5
05861	.5	0	.2	83	22.4	324	57.0	11	10	.0	0	1	.0
05862	.3	100	.1	89	29.1	223	75.3	7	18	.1	17	0	.8
05863	.2	100	.1	92	28.1	323*	53.3	3	0	.1	6	0	.0
05866	.4	100	.1	82	16.3	321	36.5	6	14	.2	13	0	.0
05867	.5	0	.2	79	20.1	278	49.7	9	9	.0	0	0	.0
05868	.3	100	.1	80	17.2	272	56.7	9	10	.1	7	0	.0
05871	1.1	0	.4	83	21.0	242	51.4	9	10	.2	7	1	2.6
05872	.7	99	.2	86	19.9	357	50.8	9	10	.3	8	0	.0
05873	.3	100	.2	80	19.8	211	64.8	7	12	.4	10	0	.0
05874	.4	100	.1	91	23.7	289	53.6	9	12	.2	12	0	1.6
05875	.3	98	.1	92	19.3	222*	54.8	7	3	.2	3	0	.0

LITTLETON

ZIPCODE	1	2	3	4	5	6	7	8	9	10	11	12	13
05902	.3	100	.1	67	23.1	223	54.1	7	5	.2	7	1	2.6
05903	.7	100	.2	68	17.3	285	61.8	10	8	.3	8	0	.0
05904	.4	100	.2	77	19.6	259	34.6	5	19	.4	10	0	3.5
05905	.1	100	.1	82	23.7	281	38.2	7	31	.2	14	1	.0
05906	.9	99	.3	84	22.4	283	44.7	7	13	.4	12	0	.0
05907	.2	100	.1	69	19.2	158	54.0	3	18	.1	17	0	.0

VIRGINIA

NORTHERN VIRGINIA

ZIPCODE	1	2	3	4	5	6	7	8	9	10	11	12	13
22001	1.3	84	.4	71	38.7	494	103.1	6	8	.6	7	0	.0
22002	1.8	85	.6	73	25.7	332	87.9	7	12	.8	15	0	.0
22003	53.7	93	19.2	65	46.1	575	186.2	5	6	24.1	4	0	.0
22010	.2	100	.1	59	27.3	680	80.5	0	18	.1	10	0	.0
22011	.9	89	.2	61	30.8	539	144.0	6	6	.4	5	0	.0
22012	.9	91	.3	73	26.6	365	118.9	8	13	.4	14	0	.0
22013	1.1	81	.3	88	37.3	558	126.5	4	7	.4	4	0	.0
22014	1.4	88	.4	82	43.6	330	175.3	6	9	.6	6	0	.0
22015	23.7	93	7.3	87	47.4	726	176.4	10	1	11.1	1	0	.0
22016	.3	0	.1	76	29.3	369	122.3	5	6	.0	0	0	.0
22017	.4	81	.1	78	37.5	282	116.1	3	3	.2	0	0	.0
22018	.7	96	.2	95	49.8	744	195.2	6	1	.4	0	0	.0
22019	3.2	87	1.0	72	28.6	384	103.4	6	8	1.4	6	0	.1
22020	9.0	93	2.9	75	37.6	562	132.6	9	3	4.2	3	0	.0
22021	6.8	94	2.2	86	37.8	579	137.7	8	4	3.2	3	0	.1
22024	2.4	98	.7	92	56.0	576	238.1	4	5	1.2	5	0	.0
22025	.6	72	.2	60	29.7	272	127.6	4	15	.2	15	0	.0
22026	8.0	87	2.5	74	37.1	408	149.2	10	2	3.5	3	0	.0
22027	.8	95	.2	82	49.9	689	209.9	3	16	.4	13	0	.1
22030	44.1	94	14.6	71	41.7	569	165.1	5	4	20.5	3	0	.0
22031	12.8	94	4.7	62	53.4	577	209.2	5	4	5.9	4	0	.0
22032	15.2	93	4.2	89	50.8	816	178.8	7	2	7.1	1	0	.0
22039	3.6	94	1.0	92	60.0	674	295.2	6	4	1.7	5	0	.0
22041	16.2	77	7.2	40	36.3	461	209.7	7	9	5.8	10	0	.1
22042	26.4	84	9.5	62	37.2	520	145.3	7	6	11.0	6	0	.0
22043	19.6	85	7.2	56	38.4	537	154.8	6	5	8.0	4	0	.0
22044	10.4	83	5.0	29	35.5	466	241.9	4	9	4.8	8	0	.0
22046	13.0	93	5.2	67	40.5	549	162.8	5	12	5.8	9	0	.1
22060	8.2	69	1.8	1	22.5	348	83.1	12	0	3.4	0	0	.8
22065	3.7	87	1.2	80	36.3	424	138.7	9	6	1.6	7	0	.0
22066	9.0	96	2.7	94	65.7	774	294.3	7	4	4.3	4	0	.0
22068	2.2	87	.7	80	36.3	368	122.9	8	10	1.9	9	0	.0
22069	3.9	96	1.1	89	45.6	429	163.7	7	4	1.9	3	0	.0
22070	23.4	89	7.7	72	39.9	502	151.7	11	3	10.4	2	0	.1
22075	14.0	88	4.9	57	34.3	386	135.4	7	9	5.9	7	2	.0
22078	.2	63	.1	56	17.4	364	127.5	5	8	.0	31	0	.0
22079	7.5	93	2.6	71	41.2	547	152.1	8	3	3.6	3	0	.1
22080	2.9	0	.9	85	34.7	384	118.7	9	10	.0	0	0	.1
22090	17.8	89	6.6	51	42.6	524	173.5	8	4	7.7	2	0	.3
22091	17.4	86	6.2	65	42.8	464	180.0	9	3	7.4	2	0	.0

NORTHERN VIRGINIA

ZIPCODE	1	2	3	4	5	6	7	8	9	10	11	12	13
22101	28.7	93	9.6	82	65.7	810	264.2	5	8	13.1	7	0	.0
22102	10.0	93	4.2	56	52.0	618	329.9	4	5	4.4	5	0	.1
22110	56.7	92	17.7	71	34.9	433	118.5	9	4	26.1	3	0	.1
22115	3.6	82	1.3	67	26.0	442	93.5	7	11	1.5	10	0	.0
22117	3.0	75	1.1	54	35.7	352	130.1	4	3	1.1	10	0	.0
22123	5.0	97	1.5	81	39.4	403	151.9	8	13	2.5	2	0	.0
22124	8.7	97	2.8	87	59.6	719	242.5	6	4	4.2	3	0	.3
22125	.3	93	.1	47	31.4	302	125.3	2	15	.1	6	0	.0

*=Estimated **1.0=883 lbs per person; 100++ indicates per capita toxic waste generation > than 100 times the U.S. average of 883 lbs per capita.

ZIP CODE MEASURES OF SIZE, LEVELS OF AFFLUENCE AND QUALITY OF LIFE

1=Population (th.); 2=% White; 3=Households (th.); 4=% Owner Occupied; 5=Mean Income Per Household (th.$); 6=Mean Monthly Rent ($); 7=Mean Home Value (th.$);
8=% under 5; 9=% 65 and over; 10=White Males; 11=% White Males, 65+; 12=# Toxic Waste Sites; 13=Toxic Waste Relative to US(883 lbs.per capita)**;

VIRGINIA

NORTHERN VIRGINIA

ZIPCODE	1	2	3	4	5	6	7	8	9	10	11	12	13
22128	.1	75	.1	35	21.9	252*	78.0*	5	14	.0	14	0	.0
22129	.3	0	.1	73	29.1	450	75.8	6	14	.0	0	0	.0
22130	.3	84	.1	45	23.0	239	91.1	12	15	.1	20	0	.8
22131	.3	0	.1	82	30.9	456	116.3	5	16	.0	0	0	.0
22132	4.3	89	1.5	74	35.1	415	136.6	5	12	2.0	11	0	.0
22134	9.1	78	1.9	4	21.4	340	76.9	13	1	4.4	0	1	.0
22140	.2	77	.1	48	28.8	397	161.1	6	2	.1	8	0	.0
22141	1.5	94	.5	77	34.3	346	117.4	4	10	.7	7	0	.0
22150	14.5	89	4.9	73	40.8	581	143.6	6	4	6.5	4	0	.0
22151	16.9	95	5.7	80	47.5	660	153.5	6	4	8.0	3	0	.1
22152	21.1	94	6.8	81	50.5	680	183.4	5	2	9.7	1	0	.0
22153	17.6	80	4.6	88	48.6	787	179.9	7	1	7.1	1	0	.0
22170	23.9	93	7.3	83	41.3	644	129.4	9	2	11.1	1	0	.2
22171	1.8	85	.6	47	27.2	387	121.7	9	10	.8	12	0	.0
22172	5.3	79	2.0	36	24.6	362	115.6	10	4	2.1	2	1	.0
22176	.9	79	.3	46	27.7	309	94.9	5	16	.3	12	0	.0
22180	46.0	92	14.7	77	50.1	580	195.7	5	5	21.1	3	0	.0
22186	13.4	82	4.4	65	32.3	415	132.9	7	10	5.3	7	1	.0
22190	.9	0	.3	81	49.4	783	214.0	4	7	.0	0	0	.0
22191	27.5	90	8.5	70	35.4	453	103.9	9	3	12.6	1	0	.2
22192	15.6	93	5.1	79	41.0	523	150.1	9	1	7.3	0	0	.0
22193	32.8	85	9.2	84	37.9	622	112.6	10	1	14.1	1	0	.1

ARLINGTON

ZIPCODE	1	2	3	4	5	6	7	8	9	10	11	12	13
22201	18.6	88	9.6	27	29.5	432	174.9	5	12	7.7	8	1	.0
22202	13.3	93	7.9	24	41.2	565	216.8	2	15	5.8	11	0	.1
22203	12.0	85	5.8	34	31.9	436	162.4	5	16	4.7	14	0	.0
22204	37.8	74	18.3	28	28.8	463	138.3	5	10	12.4	9	0	.0
22205	15.0	95	6.0	72	41.6	548	167.7	5	13	7.0	11	0	.0
22206	14.6	73	7.5	43	35.1	495	129.9	5	5	4.9	5	2	.3
22207	27.8	91	10.8	75	51.9	587	219.5	4	15	11.8	13	0	.2
22209	8.0	81	5.1	3	24.8	429	181.2	4	6	3.4	5	0	.1
22211	3.0	59	.2	0	29.8	437	106.2*	3	0	1.3	0	1	.0
22213	2.1	97	.8	75	48.0	728	171.1	3	12	1.0	14	0	.0

ALEXANDRIA

ZIPCODE	1	2	3	4	5	6	7	8	9	10	11	12	13
22301	11.6	74	4.8	60	31.6	442	152.6	6	13	4.1	12	1	.0
22302	14.2	85	6.9	48	37.5	536	202.9	5	12	5.4	9	0	.0
22303	10.7	85	4.8	41	28.6	479	114.3	7	4	4.6	4	0	.0
22304	27.5	81	13.4	38	37.3	510	189.1	5	6	10.7	5	2	.0
22305	13.0	55	5.6	32	29.8	447	155.3	6	6	3.6	7	1	.3
22306	24.9	77	9.7	49	32.0	469	158.8	8	8	9.4	5	0	.0
22307	10.6	86	4.3	61	44.0	511	209.8	5	11	4.5	10	0	.0
22308	13.6	90	4.3	86	59.0	660	207.3	4	6	5.9	6	0	.0
22309	24.1	86	8.5	68	40.8	551	179.1	7	4	10.3	4	0	.0
22310	23.4	92	7.6	81	44.9	601	151.3	5	4	10.8	3	1	.0
22311	11.4	88	5.9	12	32.0	480	172.7	4	13	4.3	7	0	.0
22312	18.8	82	7.9	43	35.6	529	165.4	4	7	7.3	4	0	.0
22314	21.8	55	10.3	33	33.2	420	228.7	5	11	5.5	9	2	.1

FREDERICKBURG

ZIPCODE	1	2	3	4	5	6	7	8	9	10	11	12	13
22401	57.6	88	19.5	70	28.8	361	97.0	8	9	23.9	8	2	.1

VIRGINIA

FREDERICKBURG

ZIPCODE	1	2	3	4	5	6	7	8	9	10	11	12	13
22427	3.2	61	1.0	76	24.4	307	75.6	7	9	1.0	5	1	.0
22432	.4	56	.2	75	15.2	252	64.1	2	31	.1	39	0	.8
22435	2.0	76	.7	94	22.7	271	76.5	8	18	.8	18	0	.0
22436	.6	45	.2	74	24.0	201	50.9	8	14	.1	20	0	.0
22437	.6	61	.2	90	24.0	168	71.6	6	9	.2	7	0	.0
22438	.5	36	.1	67	14.7	122	54.8	12	3	.1	0	0	.0
22443	5.6	76	2.1	84	21.3	342	76.8	6	18	2.0	20	0	.0
22446	.3	83		50	16.6	204	59.0*22	0		.1	0	0	.0
22448	2.1	81	.7	56	30.9	396	110.6	9	6	.8	5	1	.1
22454	.9	65	.7	90	24.9	225	77.6	7	23	.3	23	0	.0
22452	1.9	67	.7	88	20.7	273	54.6	6	17	.7	20	0	.0
22469	1.3	0	.5	78	20.5	268	55.0	4	16	.8	5	0	.0
22471	1.7	89	.5	87	31.6	938	106.1	5	6	.8	5	0	.2
22472	.3	76	.1	80	25.0	242	78.1	3	10	.1	9	0	.0
22473	2.8	51	1.1	84	17.3	212	67.5	4	21	.7	27	0	.1
22475	.5	84	.2	86	18.2	192	55.8	9	16	.2	13	0	.0
22476	.3	0	.1	69	12.9	123	30.5	5	9	.0	18	0	.0
22480	.6	91	.3	84	29.0	430	126.1	4	23	.3	18	0	.0
22482	2.6	75	1.0	86	31.5	309	106.0	6	24	.8	22	0	.0
22485	5.8	76	1.9	79	27.2	354	87.7	8	10	2.2	8	0	.0
22488	1.5	46	.5	90	24.8	188	74.6	8	16	.3	19	1	.0

FREDERICKBURG

ZIPCODE	1	2	3	4	5	6	7	8	9	10	11	12	13
22501	.4	33	.1	82	22.9	402	51.8	3	9	.0	17	0	.6
22503	2.9	55	1.1	88	20.1	186	80.7	7	20	.8	22	0	.0
22504	.2	53	.1	69	15.3	176*	62.2	0	26	.1	17	0	.0
22507	.3	90	.2	81	17.1	265	79.1	3	32	.1	17	0	.0
22508	2.3	90	.8	82	32.4	480	121.9	5	8	1.0	11	0	.0
22509	.3	87	.1	83	29.5	339*	110.7	4	9	.1	8	0	.0
22511	1.0	74	.1	80	20.4	234*	56.9	12	16	.4	18	0	.1
22514	2.0	61	.8	87	23.3	282	61.8	6	8	.6	11	2	.6
22517	.3	34	.1	94	21.2	244*	96.5	2	12	.1	25	0	.0
22520	4.0	59	1.4	84	22.5	275	69.3	7	14	1.2	14	1	.2
22523	.2	52	.1	77	15.7	359	46.8	0	16	.1	33	0	.0
22524	.3	28	.1	74	23.6	176	82.2	9	15	.0	68	0	.0
22529	.3	26	.3	77	25.5	269	48.3	8	11	.0	41	0	.4
22532	.3	44	.1	81	29.2	156	63.4	8	4	.0	0	0	.0
22534	.9	95	.3	95	27.5	608	62.8	8	9	.4	10	0	.0
22535	.4	56	.1	70	24.9	220	64.6	7	15	.1	11	0	.0
22538	.1	71	.1	80	20.4	234*	56.9	12	16	.4	18	0	.1
22539	1.9	75	.8	93	27.5	237	88.7	5	21	.7	19	0	.1
22542	.8	76	.3	83	21.4	325	69.6	10	16	.3	16	0	.0
22546	5.9	54	2.0	80	22.0	356	67.2	8	9	1.6	8	0	.0
22547	.3	20	.1	60	17.1	262	37.4	8	15	.1	0	0	.0
22548	.2	73	.1	74	27.1	410	88.7	10	24	.1	26	0	.0
22553	10.2	77	3.0	85	25.9	357	78.9	8	15	4.0	53	3	.0
22554	18.0	90	5.4	84	31.7	376	119.1	9	4	8.3	3	0	.0
22559	.3	20	.1	94	22.7	261*	41.1	5	7	.3	3	0	.0
22560	.3	65	1.7	77	24.3	300	91.3	6	18	1.3	16	1	.9
22565	.2	81	.5	85	27.1	514	70.1	3	0	.1	0	1	.0

*=Estimated **1.0=883 lbs per person; 100++ indicates per capita toxic waste generation > than 100 times the U.S. average of 883 lbs per capita.

ZIP CODE MEASURES OF SIZE, LEVELS OF AFFLUENCE AND QUALITY OF LIFE

1=Population (th.); 2= % White; 3=Households (th.); 4=% Owner Occupied; 5=Mean Income Per Household (th.$); 6=Mean Monthly Rent ($)*; 7=Mean Home Value (th.$)*; 8=% under 5; 9=% 65 and over; 10=White Males (th.), 11=% White Males, 65+; 12=# Toxic Waste Sites, 65+; 13=Toxic Waste Relative to US883 lbs.per capita**.

VIRGINIA

FREDERICKSBURG

ZIP CODE	1	2	3	4	5	6	7	8	9	10	11	12	13
22567	1.5	88	.6	80	18.2	250	70.7	5	15	.6	15	0	.0
22568	.3	100	.1	97	18.6	214*	79.1	2	17	.1	13	0	.0
22572	5.0	68	1.7	83	23.7	342	69.1	7	14	1.6	11	2	.1
22576	1.7	68	.6	86	23.9	240	104.4	5	23	.6	26	0	.4
22577	.3	0		79	13.6	86	39.9	5	21	.0	0	0	.0
22578	2.2	71	.8	83	27.7	317	107.0	6	21	.7	16	0	.0
22579	.4	53	.2	70	30.6	228	116.8	5	7	.1	13	0	.0
22580	4.1	66	1.3	81	23.9	196	57.5	7	11	1.3	15	0	.0

WINCHESTER

ZIP CODE	1	2	3	4	5	6	7	8	9	10	11	12	13
22601	39.6	94	14.6	65	25.7	328	87.9	7	12	18.0	10	2	2.1
22610	1.4	98	.5	76	21.1	220	66.7	8	13	.6	13	1	.0
22611	7.0	91	2.4	74	28.5	342	86.7	6	15	3.1	12	1	.0
22620	1.6	85	.6	73	31.7	278	78.0	4	11	.7	10	0	.0
22623	.4	100	.1	78	25.6	276	59.8	2	9	.1	9	0	.2
22624	1.8	98	.6	82	24.1	379	74.9	9	6	.9	5	0	.5
22625	.5	100	.2	86	30.1	304	99.6	4	9	.3	11	0	.0
22627	.8	91	.3	81	29.5	286	98.5	6	12	.4	10	0	.0
22630	18.0	93	6.6	69	22.9	294	79.4	6	12	8.1	11	2	3.5
22637	1.1	100		74	18.7	217	63.4	9	8	.5	6	0	.0
22639	.4	87	.2	96	36.8	423*	105.3	1	14	.2	4	0	.0
22640	.3	0	.1	63	38.2	134	56.9	3	9	.0	0	0	.0
22642	.9	85	.4	73	32.0	347	82.7	5	12	.4	11	0	.2
22643	.2	80		44	16.2	235	41.4	12	4	.1	0	0	.0
22644	1.4	100	.5	83	25.3	299	73.6	6	19	.7	20	0	.0
22645	2.3	99	.9	73	22.8	344	74.2	6	12	1.1	12	0	35.8
22646	.1	51		83	41.3	475*	59.1	4	19	.0	31	0	.0
22650	.9	100	.3	78	15.9	312	57.1	9	9	.0	7	0	.0
22651	.3	0		77	24.7	176	71.4	6	18	.0	0	0	.2
22652	.5	100	.2	78	21.4	246*	85.5	3	14	.2	8	0	.0
22654	.4	100	.2	85	21.1	242*	73.5	3	17	.2	11	1	.0
22655	5.8	96	1.8	88	16.9	197	94.2	6	12	2.6	15	0	.0
22656	1.9	99	.7	82	27.7	346	90.0	9	7	1.0	6	0	.1
22657	6.4	98	2.3	76	23.9	325	86.2	5	7	3.0	5	1	.0
22660	1.1	98	.4	80	20.6	266	69.5	5	12	.5	11	1	.0
22662	.6	0	.2	80	16.7	399	61.8	7	10	.5	9	0	.0
22663	1.2	89	.4	60	20.9	168	69.0	7	6	.0	0	0	.0
22664	5.5	97	2.0	72	21.3	302	87.0	8	10	.6	10	0	.2

CULPEPER

ZIP CODE	1	2	3	4	5	6	7	8	9	10	11	12	13
22701	16.0	83	5.5	69	25.3	317	90.5	7	14	6.4	11	1	.5
22709	.8	90	.2	86	19.7	374	86.3	8	19	.3	15	0	.0
22711	.2	100	.1	90	19.6	225*	59.3	5	4	.1	5	0	.0
22712	2.5	87	.8	71	25.7	382	104.5	9	7	1.1	7	0	.2
22713	.7	90	.3	76	23.2	275	101.8	4	19	.3	20	0	.0
22714	.8	67	.2	58	18.5	338	54.8	7	13	.3	10	0	.0
22715	.6	92	.3	84	19.7	320	73.9	3	11	.4	12	0	.0
22716	.5	93	.2	77	23.4	478	91.5	5	11	.2	10	0	.0
22718	.6	85	.2	78	25.2	432	71.8	11	12	.3	11	0	.0
22719	.4	100	.1	82	23.8	330	59.7	14	18	.2	17	0	.0

VIRGINIA

CULPEPER

ZIP CODE	1	2	3	4	5	6	7	8	9	10	11	12	13
22720	.5	87	.1	74	25.6	528	99.2	12	7	.2	5	0	.0
22722	.2	0	.1	78	17.2	197*	86.4	5	18	.0	0	0	.0
22724	.7	36	.2	65	23.3	446	87.5	13	8	.1	19	0	.0
22726	.5	79	.5	87	22.8	384	75.6	2	21	.2	25	0	.0
22727	3.2	77	1.1	75	21.4	279	79.5	6	12	1.2	11	1	.1
22728	2.0	77	.6	71	27.1	308	108.2	9	8	.8	6	0	.8
22729	.3	70	.2	70	20.8	383	66.2	8	9	.8	11	0	.0
22731	.2	62	.1	86	28.1	323*	79.6	7	15	.1	37	0	.0
22732	.3	28	.3	82	18.9	148	76.4	4	17	.0	21	0	.0
22733	1.0	47	.3	70	21.2	251	69.3	7	13	.3	13	0	.0
22734	1.5	81	.5	62	25.2	325	98.9	6	12	.6	12	0	.0
22735	1.0	85	.3	86	20.0	444	79.6	4	18	.4	23	0	.0
22737	1.6	86	.5	91	28.6	123	77.6	7	7	.7	6	0	.0
22738	.5	75	.2	77	24.0	237	66.5	8	14	.7	12	0	.0
22740	1.2	91	.4	69	19.2	204	67.7	6	14	.5	12	0	.0
22741	.2	38	.1	66	26.3	360	26.8	4	13	.0	30	0	.0
22742	.6	100	.2	87	33.6	270	114.3	10	5	.3	5	0	.0
22743	.3	100	.1	64	24.6	283*	76.9	4	19	.2	20	0	.0
22746	.2	0	.1	60	24.8	230	91.1	10	13	.1	0	0	.0
22747	1.3	77	.5	60	24.6	261	74.5	7	15	.5	13	0	.3
22748	.5	63	.2	77	16.1	247	59.6	4	16	.1	12	0	.0
22749	.2	76	.1	60	25.4	142	113.0	0	18	.1	20	0	.0

HARRISONBURG

ZIP CODE	1	2	3	4	5	6	7	8	9	10	11	12	13
22801	34.7	96	11.0	60	24.5	333	99.5	5	10	15.6	8	0	.3
22810	.4	0	.2	97	35.9	412*	106.8	5	17	.0	0	0	.0
22811	.4	100	.2	93	16.7	192*	47.6	8	18	.2	19	0	.0
22812	6.2	98	2.0	76	25.6	320	86.3	6	14	2.9	11	0	.1
22815	5.4	98	1.9	78	24.2	288	74.4	7	9	2.6	8	0	.0
22820	.2	100	.1	87	16.4	188*	37.2	3	20	.2	28	0	.0
22821	4.5	100	1.4	76	28.8	332	78.8	9	11	2.2	10	0	.0
22824	4.8	100	1.7	78	19.0	275	72.9	6	13	2.3	11	0	.0
22827	8.6	96	2.9	82	21.5	253	64.1	6	11	4.1	9	1	6.7
22830	1.4	100	.3	84	26.3	214	68.3	6	11	.7	10	0	.0
22831	.8	100	.3	67	31.0	262	71.7	6	6	.4	7	0	.0
22832	1.0	100	.4	74	22.6	322	69.6	5	14	.5	10	0	.0
22834	1.3	0	.4	80	23.2	208	55.2	10	14	.3	11	0	.0
22835	9.4	95	3.4	75	21.2	253	73.3	6	15	4.3	13	1	.0
22840	2.0	0	.6	77	28.8	316	80.9	8	9	.0	11	0	.0
22841	2.2	99	.6	78	24.3	373	69.4	6	12	1.0	11	0	.2
22842	3.5	99	1.4	77	19.5	283	66.5	6	15	1.7	13	0	1.8
22843	1.7	97	.2	84	22.9	65	67.8	9	10	.3	8	0	.0
22844	3.0	99	1.1	67	20.7	319	75.7	5	15	1.5	15	0	.4
22846	.8	95	.3	84	26.4	341	108.6	6	11	.4	10	0	.0
22847	1.0	0	.3	89	25.0	351	58.1	6	13	.3	0	0	.0
22849	4.2	99	1.4	81	20.1	267	58.2	8	10	1.9	9	0	.2
22850	.2	100	.2	88	18.1	370	46.6	6	16	.1	9	0	.0
22851	4.8	93	1.6	79	20.3	256	58.5	8	12	.0	5	1	.0
22853	3.9	99	1.4	82	21.0	304	64.9	8	11	1.9	9	0	.1

*=Estimated **1.0=883 lbs per person; 100++ indicates per capita toxic waste generation > than 100 times the U.S. average of 883 lbs per capita.

ZIP CODE MEASURES OF SIZE, LEVELS OF AFFLUENCE AND QUALITY OF LIFE

1=Population (th.); 2= % White; 3=Households (th.); 4=% Owner Occupied; 5=Mean Income Per Household (th.$); 6=Mean Monthly Rent ($); 7=Mean Home Value (th.$); 8=% under 5; 9=% 65 and over; 10=White Males (th.); 11=% White Males, 65+; 12=# Toxic Waste Sites; 13=Toxic Waste Relative to US(883 lbs.per capita)**.

VIRGINIA — CHARLOTTESVILLE

ZIPCODE	1	2	3	4	5	6	7	8	9	10	11	12	13
22901	57.9	84	21.9	52	28.4	414	117.6	6	10	23.4	7	1	.1
22902	.1	100	.1	57	37.2	450	98.2	0	15	.1	18	1	1.8
22903	15.8	84	5.4	33	23.2	419	116.5	4	7	6.6	5	0	.0
22920	3.0	93	1.0	78	24.8	222	64.8	6	11	1.4	9	0	.1
22922	1.5	68	.5	75	19.3	207	50.6	7	16	.5	9	0	.0
22923	2.3	84	.8	79	23.3	267	70.1	7	10	1.0	8	0	.0
22924	.2	0	.1	73	33.0	379*	46.4	4	16	.0	0	0	.0
22929	.2	43	.1	77	46.5	534*	66.1	6	13	.0	18	1	.0
22931	.3	81	.1	82	24.2	337	67.1	11	9	.1	5	1	.0
22932	4.6	89	1.5	71	29.4	332	84.0	7	12	1.9	9	1	1.2
22935	.8	0	.3	69	26.6	306*	63.7	5	13	.0	0	0	.0
22936	2.4	94	.8	88	34.6	382	130.7	6	7	1.1	7	1	1.4
22937	1.3	38	.4	59	16.9	235	43.3	8	12	.2	9	0	.0
22938	1.5	71	.5	78	29.2	220	89.8	8	11	.6	14	0	.0
22939	2.6	87	.7	80	24.1	238	71.1	5	10	1.3	10	0	1.5
22940	.9	0	.3	69	66.0	348	79.5	8	8	.2	11	0	.0
22942	5.0	78	1.7	78	21.9	268	67.1	6	12	2.0	11	0	.0
22943	1.0	75	.3	59	19.7	311	76.4	8	10	.3	7	1	.0
22945	.5	86	.2	80	32.7	335	105.0	5	14	.2	18	1	.0
22946	.2	65	.1	76	13.9	323	50.2	3	16	.1	20	0	.0
22947	2.3	81	.8	71	30.7	381	96.7	5	11	1.0	11	0	.0
22948	.4	100	.1	58	19.6	343	61.1	8	8	.2	7	0	.0
22949	1.3	85	.5	74	25.4	253	66.6	4	19	.5	23	0	.0
22951	.6	84	.2	85	23.3	112	43.5	3	15	.2	9	0	.0
22952	1.9	91	.6	84	24.3	338	73.2	9	6	.9	5	0	.0
22954	.2	44	.1	87	17.7	204*	44.6	6	8	.1	0	0	.0
22957	.2	0	.1	54	17.8	204*	49.8	7	16	.0	0	0	.0
22958	.2	100	.1	68	23.2	295	50.5	7	15	.1	13	0	.0
22959	1.6	78	.6	73	27.5	273	63.6	4	13	.2	12	0	.0
22960	8.2	80	2.9	72	20.8	256	74.1	8	15	3.2	12	1	.7
22963	3.2	68	1.1	82	23.3	338	84.1	8	12	1.1	12	0	.0
22964	.4	89	.1	56	19.0	244	60.1	8	8	.2	9	0	.0
22967	1.4	66	.4	78	17.0	157	50.8	7	21	.4	27	0	.0
22968	3.3	96	1.1	80	25.8	290	91.2	10	7	1.6	5	0	.0
22969	1.1	87	.3	77	16.5	257	44.8	11	13	.4	12	0	.0
22971	1.1	67	.4	85	17.5	188	42.3	4	14	.4	9	0	.0
22972	.6	73	.2	48	21.8	284	89.0	8	11	.2	9	0	.0
22973	3.3	91	1.1	82	20.8	301	74.6	6	12	1.5	12	0	.0
22974	2.2	82	.8	80	23.4	339	80.4	9	11	.9	11	0	.0
22976	.4	87	.1	69	14.3	213	27.2	2	19	.2	18	0	.1
22980	25.4	93	9.2	70	27.6	311	85.2	6	12	11.3	10	6	7.1
22987	.6	73	.2	54	17.6	312	77.2	11	10	.1	10	0	.0
22989	.2	82	.1	58	24.2	278*	75.4	0	0	.1	0	0	.0

RICHMOND

ZIPCODE	1	2	3	4	5	6	7	8	9	10	11	12	13
23001	.4	100	.1	88	22.5	368	69.6	3	14	.2	12	0	.0
23002	6.7	64	2.2	80	22.7	237	61.4	7	12	2.1	11	1	.0
23003	.3	62	.1	82	33.7	482	66.4	0	8	.1	6	0	.0
23004	1.2	37	.3	73	14.8	160	32.1	10	11	.2	11	0	.0
23005	11.3	81	3.7	70	29.8	328	88.6	5	11	4.5	11	0	.2

VIRGINIA — RICHMOND

ZIPCODE	1	2	3	4	5	6	7	8	9	10	11	12	13
23009	2.3	65	.7	85	25.6	177	85.0	9	6	.7	1	0	.0
23011	.8	56	.3	78	24.5	215	70.0	7	10	.2	13	0	.0
23013	.2	100	.1	100	31.6	363*	107.8	0	14	.1	13	0	.0
23015	2.7	79	.9	81	25.8	282	72.4	8	11	1.1	9	1	.0
23016	.2	46	.2	100	14.8	170*	56.7	6	17	.0	18	0	.0
23018	.6	93	.2	90	24.3	354	98.2	6	11	.3	2	0	.0
23020	.3	85	.1	77	17.9	416	53.9	7	31	.1	24	0	.0
23021	.3	0	.3	95	36.6	421*	83.3	3	26	.0	0	0	.0
23022	.9	22	.2	69	18.7	392	44.8	7	12	.1	17	0	.0
23023	.3	79	.1	80	26.1	194	73.5	12	19	.1	23	0	.0
23024	3.2	84	1.1	83	20.3	233	73.3	8	12	1.4	10	0	.0
23025	.1	0	.1	75	15.8	221	49.0	7	20	.3	19	0	.0
23027	1.1	62	.3	86	18.3	210	72.3	6	12	.3	19	0	.0
23029	.2	24	.1	69	16.0	173	41.8	0	6	.0	50	0	.0
23030	4.6	20	1.3	83	26.5	260	53.7	7	8	.5	9	0	.1
23032	.3	29	.1	91	14.9	172*	49.3	5	8	.3	0	0	.0
23035	.5	90	.1	84	27.2	206	83.7	7	27	.1	17	0	.0
23037	.2	38	.1	100	21.6	248*	64.7	8	5	.1	0	0	.0
23038	1.3	0	.4	75	19.5	277	46.9	8	18	.0	0	0	.1
23039	.7	57	.2	83	27.1	494	115.8	4	18	.2	13	0	.0
23040	3.3	53	1.1	82	17.9	192	63.3	6	15	.9	9	0	.0
23042	.3	52	.1	67	17.6	224	41.3	11	13	.1	24	0	.0
23043	1.3	93	.5	88	18.4	330	92.8	4	26	.6	22	0	.0
23045	.2	100	.1	63	19.0	597	42.1	5	14	.1	15	0	.0
23047	1.9	63	.6	84	30.3	337	75.7	8	11	.6	12	1	.0
23050	.4	81	.1	88	19.0	218*	57.8	5	21	.1	21	0	.0
23054	.2	53	.1	63	31.9	147	30.6	16	13	.0	10	0	.0
23055	1.0	83	.4	68	22.3	285	80.6	6	12	.4	10	0	.8
23056	.2	0	.1	71	17.0	378	66.7	19	14	.2	0	0	.0
23060	11.1	80	3.6	86	30.4	364	92.8	7	9	4.4	8	0	.0
23062	6.2	79	2.3	83	24.5	318	87.0	6	14	2.5	10	0	.0
23063	2.5	94	.9	74	30.2	348	118.6	8	11	1.2	9	0	.0
23063	3.3	52	1.0	80	23.7	305	63.6	6	11	.8	11	0	.0
23064	.2	100	.1	86	27.3	313*	122.1	7	10	.1	11	1	.0
23065	.9	63	.3	100	23.5	270*	70.0	14	9	.3	8	0	.0
23066	.4	0	.2	77	15.7	281	76.5	4	32	.0	0	0	.0
23068	.2	83	.1	94	24.9	286*	89.3	6	22	.0	25	0	.0
23069	3.0	55	.9	74	29.5	287	82.0	6	10	.9	4	0	.0
23071	.2	64	.2	91	16.6	345	76.0	7	28	.2	28	0	.0
23072	5.7	90	2.0	85	23.3	359	87.4	7	10	2.6	8	0	.0
23075	9.9	87	3.6	70	27.6	395	71.7	8	8	4.1	7	0	.0
23076	.4	76	.2	85	23.2	261	104.6	4	12	.1	11	0	.0
23077	.1	0	.1	80	22.3	182	45.6	0	9	.0	0	0	.0
23079	.2	79	.1	80	14.2	163*	73.4	13	10	.2	5	0	.0
23080	.3	38	.1	94	19.6	225*	50.1	4	30	.1	40	0	.0
23083	1.1	57	.4	83	19.1	137	62.9	4	19	.3	9	0	.0
23084	1.0	66	.4	88	22.1	193	65.8	2	12	.4	9	0	.0
23085	.5	64	.2	87	17.6	218	79.0	9	13	.1	7	0	.0
23086	1.4	43	.5	43	21.6	320	57.3	7	12	.3	9	0	.0

*=Estimated **1.0=883 lbs; 100++ indicates per capita toxic waste generation > than 100 times the U.S. average of 883 lbs per capita.

ZIP CODE MEASURES OF SIZE, LEVELS OF AFFLUENCE AND QUALITY OF LIFE

1=Population (th.); 2= % White; 3=Households (th.); 4=% Owner Occupied; 5=Mean Income Per Household (th.$); 6=Mean Monthly Rent ($)*; 7=Mean Home Value (th.$)*;
8=% under 5; 9=% 65 and over; 10=White Males (th.); 11=% White Males, 65+; 12=# Toxic Waste Sites; 13=Toxic Waste Relative to US(883 lbs.per capita)**.

VIRGINIA

ZIP CODE	1	2	3	4	5	6	7	8	9	10	11	12	13
RICHMOND													
23089	2.2	74	.7	85	24.6	304	67.0	6	10	.9	8	0	.0
23090	.4	0	.1	74	22.7	301	56.3	7	1	.0	0	0	.0
23091	.3	36	.1	95	30.0	344*	60.3	3	18	.1	10	0	.0
23092	.5	0	.0	81	27.7	317	55.9	3	28	.0	0	0	.0
23093	6.2	68	2.1	78	21.5	273	65.1	6	13	2.1	13	0	.0
RICHMOND													
23102	.7	60	.2	82	27.5	385	84.3	9	7	.3	10	0	.0
23103	2.4	76	.8	81	41.5	349	115.7	5	10	.9	8	1	.0
23106	.9	63	.3	67	32.2	176	81.2	9	11	.3	11	0	.0
23109	1.6	79	.7	79	27.2	302	97.9	3	17	.5	15	1	.0
23111	26.4	94	8.5	90	34.1	397	99.9	6	8	12.2	7	1	.0
23113	17.9	94	5.4	94	46.0	647	139.7	8	4	8.4	2	0	.0
23114	.2	20	.1	100	26.8	308*	76.9	0	22	.0	0	0	.0
23115	.3	59	.1	75	24.4	302	72.0	7	10	.1	21	0	.0
23117	5.0	63	1.6	80	23.4	198	60.7	7	12	1.5	11	0	1.4
23118	.2	80	.1	83	26.5	374	77.7	7	9	.1	0	0	.0
23119	.3	0	.1	93	26.5	305*	87.6	4	26	.0	0	0	.0
23120	1.6	85	.5	87	25.3	246	87.6	5	11	.6	7	0	.0
23123	1.5	63	.5	76	17.8	180	59.4	5	11	.5	8	1	.0
23124	1.1	76	.4	81	23.1	244	91.0	4	12	.4	13	2	.0
23125	.3	0	.1	90	19.3	163	86.7	5	59	.0	0	0	.0
23126	.3	0	.1	76	20.7	200	47.0	7	13	.0	0	0	3.1
23127	.3	74	.1	74	29.6	352	98.3	4	14	.1	0	0	.0
23128	.5	64	.2	91	23.6	241	106.1	1	13	.1	11	0	.0
23129	.3	52	.1	63	48.6	698	83.9	4	13	.1	12	0	.0
23130	.3	100	.1	80	21.4	492	61.7	3	20	.1	19	0	.0
23131	.5	70	.2	90	31.5	461	61.9	9	11	.3	3	0	.0
23137	.7	68	.1	83	23.8	274	52.7	7	14	.3	18	0	.0
23138	.6	87	.2	96	27.0	310*	76.7	7	29	.2	24	0	.0
23139	10.6	80	3.3	86	28.4	366	83.1	7	7	4.2	7	0	.0
23140	3.1	38	.9	87	27.4	351	69.2	6	7	.6	11	2	.1
23141	3.9	83	1.3	86	28.9	425	90.3	8	7	1.6	5	0	.0
23146	1.7	80	.6	91	30.4	466	97.8	7	10	.7	8	0	.0
23147	.2	0	.1	81	26.0	137	54.6	4	25	.0	0	0	.0
23148	1.2	0	.4	73	19.4	186	56.4	9	10	.0	0	0	.0
23149	1.8	63	.6	80	23.9	262	57.8	6	17	.5	12	1	.0
23150	9.2	94	3.1	83	29.9	383	77.7	7	7	4.3	6	0	.0
23153	.7	50	.2	92	26.4	303*	75.1	7	10	.1	11	0	.0
23156	.3	30	.1	76	19.9	397	61.3	13	8	.0	0	0	.0
23163	.2	69	.1	92	30.1	346*	47.3	3	16	.1	21	0	.0
23165	.2	0	.1	100	16.9	195*	60.4	0	27	.0	0	0	.0
23168	2.5	53	.8	77	23.1	341	73.1	7	8	.7	6	0	.0
23169	.6	79	.2	91	30.4	522	90.0	8	12	.3	14	0	.0
23170	1.5	40	.5	81	20.0	276	52.2	4	13	.3	13	0	.0
23175	1.9	68	.7	78	23.9	264	80.7	6	19	.6	18	0	.0
23176	.3	78	.1	86	17.4	263	88.4	5	14	.1	18	0	.0
23177	.6	63	.1	84	21.5	152	71.5	7	15	.2	17	0	.0
23178	.2	0	.1	92	31.5	396*	236.6	3	26	.9	15	0	.0

VIRGINIA

ZIP CODE	1	2	3	4	5	6	7	8	9	10	11	12	13
RICHMOND													
23179	.2	83	.1	94	15.2	175*	60.8	5	15	.1	20	0	.0
23180	.3	79	.1	81	24.9	74	71.8	11	13	.1	17	0	.0
23181	4.7	69	1.6	82	27.9	262	78.3	6	14	1.6	14	0	1.5
23183	.4	61	.2	92	18.1	395	85.2	4	27	.1	16	0	.0
23184	1.1	95	.4	63	21.9	315	92.5	8	8	.5	6	0	.9
23185	36.2	77	11.6	63	30.4	359	116.6	9	8	13.3	8	4	.9
23190	.7	63	.2	95	21.2	243*	97.1	6	0	.0	0	0	.0
23191	.2	0	.1	46	27.1	323	129.9	0	15	.0	0	1	.0
23192	.9	62	.3	83	25.5	241	78.2	6	9	1.1	10	1	.0
RICHMOND													
23219	4.2	33	1.0	13	11.4	189	36.2	2	13	.9	6	1	.5
23220	33.6	48	14.2	27	18.7	301	81.6	4	14	7.4	9	0	3.6
23221	15.0	83	7.6	45	28.9	360	112.4	3	23	5.2	18	0	.1
23222	33.1	15	11.2	62	22.1	315	58.1	7	12	2.2	19	0	.1
23223	44.8	17	15.3	44	19.1	280	55.3	8	19	3.5	9	3	.1
23224	34.8	46	12.6	49	21.0	325	55.4	8	9	7.5	11	3	1.2
23225	36.3	73	16.0	48	26.7	392	82.2	7	13	12.1	12	0	.0
23226	17.5	95	7.3	75	39.8	438	113.3	5	21	7.5	17	0	.1
23227	22.9	79	10.1	52	27.5	378	95.3	4	23	7.5	17	0	.1
23228	28.5	90	11.7	58	27.1	423	78.3	5	12	11.7	10	1	.1
23229	42.5	96	15.7	66	38.1	470	121.0	5	9	19.4	8	1	.1
23230	7.1	88	3.0	51	26.4	411	80.7	5	17	2.8	15	0	6.7
23231	21.1	75	7.5	72	25.1	344	70.4	7	12	7.5	11	6	.2
23233	16.9	94	5.9	69	39.3	415	143.9	8	6	7.6	4	0	.0
23234	48.0	81	17.3	63	27.9	380	79.5	8	5	19.1	5	9	.3
23235	42.3	96	13.5	89	41.7	501	115.1	7	4	19.9	4	1	.0
NORFOLK													
23301	1.8	0	.6	68	21.3	255	54.8	6	18	.0	0	0	.0
23302	.2	32	.2	55	13.1	175	88.3	2	33	.0	62	0	.0
23303	.7	44	.2	91	25.5	178	61.5	7	6	.2	9	0	.0
23304	.3	65	.2	82	25.6	227	63.9	7	12	.1	17	0	.2
23306	1.1	66	.4	67	25.2	210	67.7	6	14	.4	8	0	.1
23307	.8	27	.2	69	16.8	159	42.3	8	7	.4	20	2	.2
23308	1.3	73	.6	75	21.8	222	38.0	4	19	.4	13	0	.7
23310	3.4	53	1.3	51	15.6	267	46.3	9	16	.9	15	3	.0
23314	2.4	79	.8	84	28.8	297	103.5	8	10	1.0	7	0	.0
23315	1.3	65	.4	69	21.6	349	71.1	8	12	.4	9	0	.0
23316	1.6	0	.6	57	13.0	180	49.3	6	20	.4	7	0	.2
23320	26.7	76	8.6	76	26.4	392	99.7	8	6	10.2	5	3	1.1
23321	19.2	82	5.8	83	34.5	440	106.6	8	4	7.8	4	0	.2
23322	8.4	80	2.4	78	29.1	355	110.4	7	7	3.5	6	1	.2
23323	20.4	65	8.0	75	26.8	380	74.7	9	8	6.4	6	0	.7
23324	24.0	51	8.0	57	21.6	316	60.6	9	8	5.9	6	0	.3
23336	15.8	85	5.4	75	27.9	398	84.5	8	12	6.7	14	0	.7
23337	3.6	99	1.5	78	18.9	276	61.3	5	18	1.8	14	0	.7
23341	.3	100	.1	100	31.4	361**	109.2	3	0	.1	7	0	.0
23347	1.6	45	.6	67	24.2	302	52.5	4	3	.3	14	0	.2
23350	3.1	60	1.2	63	16.7	209	57.5	6	16	.9	15	0	.7

*=Estimated **1.0=883 lbs per person; 100+ indicates per capita toxic waste generation > than 100 times the U.S. average of 883 lbs per capita.

ZIP CODE MEASURES OF SIZE, LEVELS OF AFFLUENCE AND QUALITY OF LIFE

1=Population (th.); 2= % White; 3=Households (th.); 4=% Owner Occupied; 5=Mean Income Per Household (th.$); 6=Mean Monthly Rent ($); 7=Mean Home Value (th.$); 8=% under 5; 9=% 65 and over; 10=White Males (th.); 11=% White Males, 65+; 12=# Toxic Waste Sites; 13=Toxic Waste Relative to US(883 lbs.per capita)**.

VIRGINIA

NORFOLK

ZIPCODE	1	2	3	4	5	6	7	8	9	10	11	12	13
23354	.4	30	.1	61	21.4	179	62.4	17	14	.1	12	0	.0
23356	.3	100	.1	100	15.4	177*	37.4	12	22	.1	19	0	.0
23357	.6	50	.2	50	20.5	223	67.2	6	18	.1	16	0	.0
23359	.6	85	.3	68	17.3	220	40.9	6	18	.2	16	0	.3
23389	.2	0	.1	82	32.0	469	75.1	14	30	.2	16	0	.3
23395	.4	12	.1	65	25.0	170	44.2	8	4	.0	0	0	.0
23396	.2	17	.1	67	14.6	150	46.2	21	11	.0	0	0	.0
23398	.2	59	.1	67	19.5	129	92.2	0	14	.1	65	0	.0
23399	.3	39	.1	73	12.8	240	22.0	10	12	.1	23	0	.1

NORFOLK

ZIPCODE	1	2	3	4	5	6	7	8	9	10	11	12	13
23401	.7	0	.2	78	19.4	338	49.6	9	13	.0	0	0	.0
23403	.1	100	.1	82	23.1	266*	54.7	0	22	.1	17	0	.2
23405	.9	40	.3	79	16.8	165	60.2	6	22	.2	30	0	.0
23407	.5	0	.2	74	21.5	272	36.0	8	10	.0	0	0	.0
23410	1.6		.5	80	18.5	238	58.6	10	14	.0	0	0	.3
23412	.7	54	.4	74	18.4	117	43.0	8	43	.0	63	0	.0
23413	1.0	37	.1	68	19.7	205	65.7	9	14	.2	12	0	.0
23414	.1	60	.1	82	19.9	401	60.1	8	15	.0	25	0	.0
23415	.8	54	.3	61	18.7	308	56.5	7	13	.2	14	0	.2
23416	.5	64	.2	75	17.5	223	56.7	3	18	.2	19	0	.0
23417	3.6	69	1.4	74	20.7	269	65.0	5	22	1.1	21	0	.0
23418	.9	76	.3	74	23.6	272	67.0	9	18	.3	22	0	.2
23419	.3	100	.1	63	17.0	219	36.1	6	9	.0	7	0	.0
23420	1.8	0	.7	71	12.9	234	40.0	7	15	.0	6	0	.9
23421	3.9	62	1.4	69	19.3	257	53.8	8	15	1.2	14	0	.0
23422	.4	74	.2	70	18.0	182	88.7	4	23	.1	25	0	.0
23423	.3	0	.1	76	23.4	136	53.8	9	23	.0	0	0	.0
23424	.3	81	.1	72	19.4	325	60.7	7	22	.1	15	0	.0
23426	.2	0	.1	83	16.4	255	34.0	15	29	.0	0	0	.0
23427	.5	100	.2	96	16.1	185*	33.5	3	20	.2	17	0	.0
23430	9.8	0	3.1	79	26.0	290	80.8	8	8	.0	0	0	.2
23432	1.4	49	.4	73	24.8	333	106.1	7	11	.3	9	0	.0
23433	.9	0	.3	87	33.5	313	126.9	8	9	.0	0	0	.4
23434	32.3	47	10.9	45	30.8	371	172.4	6	9	13.1	8	0	.0
23435	6.7	69	2.2	64	32.1	496	108.0	8	4	22.4	11	0	.0
23436	.7	42	.2	86	34.2	412	139.4	10	5	.1	3	0	.1
23437	4.0	0	1.3	71	21.3	464	116.5	7	6	.0	5	0	.0
23438	1.3	70	.4	77	22.6	423	105.6	10	3	.1	9	0	.0
23440	.8	100	.3	90	17.6	393	91.0	7	9	.4	2	0	.0
23441	.8	53	.1	59	20.6	183	54.2	11	10	.1	6	0	.9
23442	.8	53	.1	73	24.8	254	55.4	12	8	.2	6	0	.0
23443	.6	0	.2	89	18.6	205	49.9	4	19	.0	0	0	.4
23451	30.7	86	12.9	45	30.8	371	172.4	6	9	13.1	8	0	.4
23452	51.8	88	16.1	74	32.1	496	108.0	8	4	22.4	11	8	.0
23454	30.1	91	10.4	55	29.4	412	139.4	10	5	13.4	3	9	1.0
23455	35.6	90	12.6	58	31.0	464	116.5	7	6	15.8	5	1	.0
23456	22.8	86	7.0	65	26.6	423	105.6	10	3	9.9	2	2	3.6
23457	3.6	83	1.1	74	32.0	393	91.0	7	9	1.5	8	3	.4
23459	1.0	60	.2	0	16.0	329	57.1*10	0	7	.4	0	2	.1

VIRGINIA

NORFOLK

ZIPCODE	1	2	3	4	5	6	7	8	9	10	11	12	13
23462	77.0	85	24.6	75	32.4	496	110.0	8	3	32.6	3	0	.0
23480	.5	88	.2	80	18.3	300	52.7	3	26	.2	19	0	.0
23483	.3	38	.1	70	19.2	107	56.1	4	16	.0	22	0	.0
23486	.6	83	.3	82	15.8	315	38.7	5	19	.1	13	0	.0
23487	.2	68	.1	73	22.6	242	73.6	7	11	1.5	9	0	.0
23488	.4	19	.5	70	17.0	180	74.6	6	14	.0	0	0	.0

NORFOLK

ZIPCODE	1	2	3	4	5	6	7	8	9	10	11	12	13
23502	20.0	67	6.9	64	26.8	411	79.7	9	8	6.6	8	0	.1
23503	32.3	85	12.8	41	20.7	326	72.9	11	13	13.9	7	0	.0
23504	30.8	5	10.6	27	14.0	237	50.6	8	14	.6	18	0	.0
23505	27.1	81	10.9	43	24.2	350	98.8	10	13	10.0	12	0	.5
23507	5.7	96	2.8	35	32.2	376	150.9	3	19	2.5	13	0	.5
23508	20.1	50	7.0	50	23.1	355	93.8	6	11	5.0	11	0	.3
23509	14.4	62	5.3	64	22.0	348	67.9	8	14	4.2	16	0	.1
23510	3.6	24	1.4	3	15.4	248	228.8	7	14	.6	17	0	3.4
23511	5.9	79	.3	0	38.4	535	136.9*	2	0	3.7	0	0	.0
23513	33.5	49	12.1	49	20.0	330	60.9	10	8	8.0	9	0	.0
23517	2.0	62	2.1	24	22.8	318	92.7	6	22	1.0	9	0	.2
23518	34.8	86	13.1	48	24.4	344	86.8	10	14	1.9	5	0	.1
23521	5.7	80	.3	36	19.8	379	70.6*	3	14	.9	0	0	.1
23523	9.8	0	3.1	36	14.8	247	49.9	8	11	.3	0	0	4.4

NEWPORT NEWS

ZIPCODE	1	2	3	4	5	6	7	8	9	10	11	12	13
23601	22.8	90	9.0	59	27.1	372	84.0	7	12	9.8	10	2	.0
23602	52.1	80	17.7	62	29.5	406	96.0	9	4	21.1	3	3	.0
23603	2.2	78	.8	30	20.0	394	70.5	13	5	.8	2	0	.0
23604	7.9	63	1.3	2	19.2	347	68.6*12	6	3	.2	0	1	.0
23605	17.0	68	6.8	45	22.1	306	59.9	9	6	5.9	6	0	.3
23606	17.8	93	7.0	64	32.4	374	117.1	6	10	8.1	8	0	.0
23607	32.0	13	11.5	37	16.3	234	48.3	7	13	2.2	18	0	.1
23651	.4	77	.4	2	25.4	366	90.6*14	6	0	.6	0	0	.0
23661	15.5	42	5.8	75	25.0	350	62.1	6	15	3.1	18	0	.0
23662	8.8	99	2.8	88	33.8	431	113.2	7	7	4.3	6	2	.0
23663	15.2	64	5.0	61	23.1	359	59.9	8	6	4.9	5	0	.1
23664	8.5	86	3.1	63	23.9	337	74.4	8	7	3.6	6	0	.0
23665	35.7	72	1.7	2	23.5	374	83.7*	9	0	3.6	0	1	.0
23666	35.7	68	12.5	61	28.9	399	79.7	7	5	12.0	4	0	.0
23669	39.0	66	14.0	59	26.5	332	81.6	8	7	12.7	2	0	.0
23690	5.5	79	1.6	74	31.8	270	119.4	6	5	2.6	4	1	4.4
23691	.5	83	.1	12	34.4	512	122.5*	3	0	.3	0	0	.0
23692	7.3	92	2.4	89	34.8	437	118.2	5	6	3.3	5	1	.0
23694	.5	19	.2	67	18.8	252	46.1	7	7	.1	0	0	.0
23696	2.8	97	.9	89	32.9	299	109.4	4	8	1.3	7	0	.0

PORTSMOUTH

ZIPCODE	1	2	3	4	5	6	7	8	9	10	11	12	13
23701	32.3	49	11.0	65	24.5	357	68.6	8	8	7.5	8	2	.0
23702	11.6	83	4.4	56	20.5	309	55.2	11	11	4.7	9	1	.0
23703	18.4	82	6.3	73	32.6	436	99.5	8	7	7.4	7	2	3.6
23704	24.8	20	8.5	41	16.6	269	50.1	8	14	2.2	16	3	.4
23707	16.4	63	6.5	54	20.9	281	66.2	8	17	4.8	16	2	.1

*=Estimated **1.0=883 lbs per person; 100++ indicates per capita toxic waste generation > than 100 times the U.S. average of 883 lbs per capita.

ZIP CODE MEASURES OF SIZE, LEVELS OF AFFLUENCE AND QUALITY OF LIFE

1=Population (th.); 2= % White; 3=Households (th.); 4=% Owner Occupied; 5=Mean Income Per Household (th.$); 6=Mean Monthly Rent ($); 7=Mean Home Value (th.$);
8=% under 5; 9=% 65 and over; 10=White Males (th.); 11=% White Males, 65+; 12=# Toxic Waste Sites; 13=Toxic Waste Relative to US(883 lbs.per capita)**.

VIRGINIA

PETERSBURG

ZIPCODE	1	2	3	4	5	6	7	8	9	10	11	12	13
23801	9.8	52	1.6	1	21.3	369	91.9	9	0		3.1	0	.0
23803	63.8	45	21.0	61	24.3	319	67.3	6	11	14.0	10	2	.1
23821	1.7	58	.6	73	21.9	213	51.3	8	15	.5	15	0	.0
23824	7.1	58	2.4	73	21.5	266	55.0	6	17	2.0	13	1	.2
23827	1.8	0	.7	57	27.4	177	61.7	6	15	.0	0	0	.0
23828	.7	25	.2	59	19.7	156	49.8	6	11	.1	14	0	.0
23829	2.4	36	.4	54	16.9	226	59.3	4	5	.7	2	0	.0
23830	1.1	56	.4	79	25.5	276	62.7	4	15	.3	10	0	.0
23831	19.5	94	6.4	81	33.8	406	96.7	7	5	9.2	4	4	.0
23832	13.5	89	4.0	88	33.3	423	93.0	9	5	5.9	4	5	13.9
23833	1.9	70	.5	81	25.9	209	73.4	7	7	.9	9	0	4.2
23834	19.0	93	6.8	74	29.5	376	84.9	6	8	8.3	6	0	.1
23837	3.4	57	1.2	74	22.8	239	76.7	6	11	1.0	10	1	.0
23839	.8	28	.3	83	17.6	122	37.7	10	13	.1	21	0	.0
23840	1.4	59	.4	88	28.5	179	53.9	8	9	.5	10	0	.0
23841	3.2	0	1.0	80	24.8	251	62.7	6	11	.0	0	0	.0
23842	4.0	62	1.2	77	24.3	280	75.1	7	7	1.2	7	0	.0
23843	.8	43	.3	57	14.4	177	61.2	6	14	.2	5	0	.0
23844	.9	34	.3	76	16.2	256	56.7	8	14	.2	9	0	.0
23845	.2	75	.1	77	17.4	158	59.1	2	32	.1	33	0	.0
23846	.6	51	.2	76	31.5	204	52.1	0	15	.2	9	0	.0
23847	14.2	47	4.7	66	20.1	243	61.5	7	13	3.3	13	1	.1
23850	1.2	45	.3	74	23.2	227	55.1	7	10	.3	10	0	.0
23851	13.1	52	4.3	62	23.4	273	73.8	7	12	3.3	10	3	2.3
23856	.9	15	.4	53	14.2	192	51.5	8	8	.1	15	0	.0
23857	.5	88	.2	78	23.5	172	38.6	9	20	.2	14	0	.0
23860	26.2	79	9.5	64	24.3	314	68.8	8	10	10.0	9	12	44.8
23866	1.8	58	.6	73	24.1	222	57.9	5	12	.6	9	0	.0
23867	2.7	0	.8	75	22.6	252	51.5	6	11	.0	0	0	.3
23868	5.8	42	1.8	75	20.0	207	64.3	6	11	1.2	10	0	.0
23872	2.3	48	.7	78	22.3	270	56.6	5	12	.5	10	3	.6
23874	1.4	0	.5	71	19.5	175	51.2	6	14	.4	11	0	.0
23875	5.6	85	1.9	83	29.8	359	94.3	7	4	2.4	2	1	.0
23876	.7	21	.2	73	17.1	143	57.1	5	7	.1	1	0	.0
23878	1.1	53	.4	64	19.6	247	58.3	9	13	.3	5	0	.1
23879	1.0	29	.3	82	17.7	167	48.6	6	13	.2	12	0	.0
23881	1.4	28	.4	68	20.3	165	52.8	9	15	.2	16	0	.0
23882	3.0	0	.9	72	22.8	221	58.4	4	11	.0	0	0	.0
23883	2.7	0	.9	74	26.6	285	65.9	5	11	.0	0	0	3.1
23885	1.6	60	.5	89	31.6	90	94.3	6	6	.3	6	0	.0
23887	.4	37	.2	84	16.5	117	97.3	2	17	.1	12	0	.0
23888	2.5	0	.8	68	21.3	220	57.5	6	11	.2	10	3	.0
23889	.6	38	.2	90	18.5	425	63.4	9	3	.1	2	0	.0
23890	4.2	45	1.5	72	20.6	240	58.7	6	15	.9	16	1	.0
23894	.6	47	.2	70	18.2	157	51.2	7	11	.2	24	0	.0
23897	.5	66	.2	85	21.2	228	78.0	8	20	.1	20	0	.0
23898	.7	48	.2	90	20.1	230*	44.8	5	9	.2	14	0	.0
23899	1.9	57	.6	74	28.2	170	71.2	7	10	.5	12	0	.0
	.4	77	.2	74	23.8	340	63.2	6	16	.2	20	0	.0

VIRGINIA

FARMVILLE

ZIPCODE	1	2	3	4	5	6	7	8	9	10	11	12	13
23901	12.4	68	3.9	69	21.3	261	69.8	6	13	3.4	12	1	.1
23915	.8	51	.3	76	18.8	140	40.6	8	15	.2	19	0	.0
23916	.3	37	.1	93	20.7	238*	49.7	5	6	.0	19	0	.0
23917	2.5	49	.7	74	20.1	183	53.2	5	17	.6	19	0	.2
23919	.6	66	.2	81	26.9	208	77.6	4	20	.2	17	0	.2
23920	.7	44	.9	81	16.7	146	41.3	6	15	.6	13	0	.0
23921	2.6	53	.6	85	16.7	247	51.0	6	20	.4	22	0	.2
23922	2.6	57	.8	75	21.0	200	45.7	6	18	.8	18	0	.0
23923	2.1	54	.7	81	18.5	294	49.4	9	17	.5	20	0	.1
23924	6.6	64	2.4	73	19.7	220	47.4	6	14	2.0	11	0	.0
23927	3.8	70	1.4	76	22.1	237	74.3	5	14	1.2	14	0	.3
23930	5.6	67	2.0	79	20.9	269	56.8	7	16	1.8	15	0	.2
23936	.6	64	.2	87	20.5	235*	45.1	5	17	1.2	22	1	.0
23937	1.8	57	1.6	71	21.2	230	63.9	6	12	1.3	14	0	.0
23938	.6	68	.6	80	20.6	141	57.0	6	10	.6	8	0	.3
23939	.2	60	.2	80	18.7	147	54.7	3	19	.2	15	0	.0
23940	.2	0	.1	70	25.9	258	58.0	10	2	.0	0	0	.0
23942	.6	62	.2	100	20.8	239*	53.4	7	10	.2	5	0	.0
23943	.2	0	.2	81	17.3	135	48.0	7	15	.2	9	0	.0
23944	4.9	0	1.7	22	34.0	376	91.9	1	7	.0	2	0	.0
23947	3.9	74	1.4	71	19.7	194	60.1	6	13	1.4	11	0	.7
23950	2.6	53	.9	66	17.2	190	42.1	7	14	.7	14	0	.1
23952	.1	80	.1	72	17.8	282	37.2	15	4	.7	14	0	.0
23954	1.6	0	.5	76	15.7	221	53.8	7	18	.6	8	0	.0
23957	.5	38	.1	65	14.6	65	63.0	4	9	.2	15	0	.3
23958	.2	0	.1	87	22.4	213	49.0	8	11	.0	0	0	.0
23959	2.7	73	.8	76	19.4	142	61.4	5	16	.8	16	0	.2
23960	1.2	73	.4	83	15.9	239	51.2	4	18	.4	17	0	.0
23962	1.3	53	.5	72	12.5	144*	42.1	7	14	.3	12	1	.1
23963	.5	67	.2	44	18.9	225	30.7	7	7	.2	16	0	.2
23964	.5	28	.1	73	15.2	152	52.4	7	7	.1	11	0	.0
23966	1.1	57	.4	83	18.4	235	53.2	9	16	.3	21	0	.0
23967	1.6	57	.5	76	16.8	115	39.7	5	11	.5	10	0	.0
23968	1.5	46	.4	69	21.1	147	45.1	7	7	.3	7	0	.1
23970	7.0	65	2.4	64	21.4	272	63.2	8	15	2.2	12	0	.2
23973	.9	41	.3	62	18.5	172	40.6	9	11	.2	9	0	.0
23974	3.8	71	1.4	76	19.6	246	50.0	6	13	1.3	12	0	.1
23976	.4	38	.2	65	21.5	154	46.1	16	9	.1	18	0	.0

ROANOKE

ZIPCODE	1	2	3	4	5	6	7	8	9	10	11	12	13
24012	27.0	90	10.7	64	23.3	284	65.6	6	17	11.2	14	1	1.1
24013	8.6	98	3.4	62	15.5	241	32.6	7	19	3.9	15	1	.2
24014	19.9	95	7.8	61	30.7	323	100.7	6	13	8.9	10	0	.0
24015	15.8	98	7.3	64	25.0	280	78.1	5	21	6.7	16	0	.7
24016	10.9	58	4.7	31	15.3	222	33.3	6	19	3.0	12	1	.5
24017	26.5	48	9.4	63	21.4	276	55.8	7	11	6.0	11	0	.0
24018	22.1	98	7.9	80	37.6	389	114.5	5	9	10.6	8	0	.0
24019	17.2	97	6.0	86	30.6	393	85.0	6	7	8.2	6	0	1.0
24051	.2	100	.1	82	15.3	176*	87.5	13	16	.1	18	0	.0

*=Estimated **1.0=883 lbs per person; 100++ indicates per capita toxic waste generation > than 100 times the U.S. average of 883 lbs per capita.

ZIP CODE MEASURES OF SIZE, LEVELS OF AFFLUENCE AND QUALITY OF LIFE

1=Population (th.); 2= % White; 3=Households (th.); 4=% Owner Occupied; 5=Mean Income Per Household (th.$); 6=Mean Monthly Rent ($)*; 7=Mean Home Value (th.$)*;
8=% under 5; 9=% 65 and over; 10=White Males (th.); 11=% White Males, 65+; 12=# Toxic Waste Sites; 13=Toxic Waste Relative to US(883 lbs.per capita)**.

VIRGINIA

ROANOKE

ZIP CODE	1	2	3	4	5	6	7	8	9	10	11	12	13
24053	2.7	95	.9	79	18.2	268	54.5	7	12	1.3	12	0	.0
24054	5.5	54	1.8	84	21.8	203	53.8	7	9	1.4	9	0	.0
24055	14.6	85	5.0	80	22.7	204	56.3	7	10	6.2	10	0	.8
24058	.3	100	.1	96	22.6	260*	50.6	4	16	.3	13	0	.8
24059	.5	100	.2	85	24.7	292	72.2	7	9	.3	5	0	.0
24060	35.9	95	11.0	41	21.3	349	104.1	4	9	18.8	3	1	.1
24064	3.1	98	1.1	82	24.7	258	85.5	5	7	1.5	9	0	.1
24065	4.5	92	1.5	85	25.2	235	63.5	6	15	2.1	14	0	.0
24066	4.6	95	1.7	79	21.8	208	55.6	6	13	2.2	10	0	.0
24067	1.4	94	.5	89	22.9	152	60.0	8	11	.6	9	0	.0
24069	1.9	47	.6	85	23.0	179	46.9	8	6	.4	7	1	.0
24070	1.3	96	.3	82	20.1	264	64.5	4	28	.6	25	0	.1
24072	.8	100	.1	92	17.9	107	55.2	12	12	.4	12	0	.0
24076	17.9	96	6.5	74	22.6	269	71.0	6	10	8.4	8	0	.0
24077	.8	0	.3	80	16.1	340	59.7	4	21	.0	0	0	.0
24078	.5	0	.2	61	21.0	50	50.0	5	10	.0	0	0	.2
24079	7.1	99	2.6	74	26.8	264	74.9	6	6	3.4	5	1	.3
24082	1.8	89	.6	89	18.7	177	63.5	6	14	.8	12	0	.0
24083	.3	56	.1	77	20.8	84	91.3	13	19	.1	35	0	.0
24085	1.2	100	.4	89	37.1	296	139.2	4	8	.6	8	0	.8
24086	10.3	97	3.4	77	23.9	293	70.4	7	8	4.9	7	2	.0
24087	2.4	93	.9	83	20.2	235	51.0	6	13	1.2	10	0	.8
24088	.2	0	.1	78	21.4	246*	42.3	9	21	.2	7	0	.0
24089	2.6	93	.9	81	24.8	331	58.9	10	9	1.2	9	0	.0
24090	4.9	91	1.2	73	19.1	214	58.4	5	13	2.4	8	1	.0
24091	3.8	73	1.4	82	23.4	232	53.8	5	13	1.2	12	0	.9
24092	2.7	95	1.0	82	26.2	250	76.5	4	13	1.3	12	0	.0
24093	4.9	96	1.9	81	19.8	244	66.8	5	19	2.3	17	0	.0
24094	1.9	91	.7	79	22.3	200	72.7	11	8	.7	11	0	.2
24095	.2	0	.3	62	19.0	264	54.2	6	17	.0	0	0	15.3

ROANOKE

ZIP CODE	1	2	3	4	5	6	7	8	9	10	11	12	13
24101	2.7	95	.9	88	23.8	251	86.1	7	10	1.3	10	0	.0
24102	1.1	94	.4	97	20.6	236*	60.9	5	11	.5	9	0	.0
24104	1.7	93	.7	89	21.7	191	89.3	7	20	.8	20	0	2.9
24105	.4	100	.1	88	16.1	185*	48.4	8	20	.2	4	0	.0
24108	.3	100	.1	94	18.8	216*	57.8	6	4	.2	2	0	.0
24111	.3	100	.1	86	29.9	325	63.0	2	16	.2	13	0	.0
24112	37.4	67	13.1	74	24.2	261	68.8	6	12	12.0	11	3	6.6
24120	1.7	100	.7	87	18.9	181	54.0	4	17	.8	14	0	.0
24121	3.8	90	1.3	87	23.9	213	97.2	5	11	1.8	11	0	.0
24122	1.7	92	.5	86	20.2	241	54.2	5	12	.8	11	0	.0
24124	5.3	99	1.8	84	20.6	264	55.4	7	13	2.5	12	0	.0
24126	.1	100	.1	77	16.2	417	70.7	0	9	.0	0	0	.0
24127	3.2	100	1.2	82	20.4	194	59.0	6	12	1.6	10	0	.0
24128	1.7	0	.6	82	21.3	174	68.7	6	10	.0	0	0	.0
24129	.3	32	.1	90	13.1	208	41.1	8	33	.0	54	0	.0
24131	.2	100	.1	65	17.6	202*	62.7*	6	17	.1	29	0	.0

VIRGINIA

ROANOKE

ZIP CODE	1	2	3	4	5	6	7	8	9	10	11	12	13
24132	.6	100	.2	74	20.6	261	34.5	10	6	.3	5	0	.0
24133	2.5	96	.9	86	19.6	229	51.4	5	11	1.2	11	0	.0
24134	5.6	98	2.0	81	22.0	251	65.7	5	12	2.7	11	0	4.4
24136	3.1	92	1.0	80	20.1	213	58.9	6	10	1.4	9	0	.0
24137	1.8	65	.6	78	20.8	153	73.8	8	16	.6	19	0	.0
24138	1.1		.4	88	21.7	383	59.4	6	9	.0	0	0	.0
24139	.6	57	.2	81	21.1	260	33.7	6	9	.2	10	0	.0
24141	18.7	95	5.9	69	24.5	298	71.9	5	9	7.7	9	2	8.4
24147	1.2	100	.4	72	21.2	230	64.7	6	11	.6	11	0	1.0
24148	7.5	84	2.5	83	24.6	261	67.8	6	7	3.0	8	0	.1
24149	2.5		.6	83	21.1	283	60.3	7	11	.0	0	0	.0
24150	.6	100	.2	86	25.4	215	51.4	6	9	.3	6	0	.0
24151	14.6	85	5.1	77	22.1	227	61.7	7	11	6.0	9	1	.4
24153	35.2	96	12.3	71	28.3	341	84.1	5	12	16.3	10	4	.9
24161	.4	84	.1	68	18.9	308	51.3	10	17	.2	22	0	.0
24162	2.6	98	.8	74	23.8	277	65.7	6	13	1.2	11	0	.0
24165	2.1	69	.7	88	25.7	249	57.0	8	7	.8	8	0	.0
24167	.4	0	.1	77	20.9	212	55.7	11	9	.4	8	0	.0
24168	.6	100	.6	84	22.1	294	52.8	5	12	.3	5	1	3.7
24171	8.2	91	2.8	82	23.6	195	61.8	6	12	3.6	10	0	.1
24174	1.5	97	.5	85	21.8	196	47.4	6	11	.7	10	0	.0
24175	6.3	96	2.1	86	30.4	314	91.1	6	9	3.1	6	0	.1
24176	6.7	66	.7	92	32.3	50	104.5	7	13	.2	16	0	.0
24179	16.2	98	5.9	90	16.6	191*	62.9	4	23	.1	15	0	.0
24184	2.2	92	.7	75	25.1	286	78.7	7	10	7.5	8	0	.0
24185	.8	95	.3	90	27.2	287	77.7	7	11	1.0	11	0	.2

BRISTOL

ZIP CODE	1	2	3	4	5	6	7	8	9	10	11	12	13
24201	30.5	96	11.1	72	22.0	241	67.4	6	12	13.7	10	2	.7
24210	19.7	98	6.9	77	23.0	282	82.5	6	12	9.3	10	1	.3
24215	.3		.3	88	21.1	206	37.0	11	17	.0	0	0	.0
24216	3.7	98	1.3	71	20.5	256	46.2	8	13	1.7	10	1	.0
24217	.8	100	.2	88	19.6	164	44.1	14	8	.4	6	0	.0
24218	1	100	.1	86	15.3	216	34.5	1	35	.1	29	0	2.6
24219	9.9	96	3.4	77	24.0	307	68.9	8	12	4.7	4	0	.0
24220	1.1		.5	73	22.4	261	49.8	8	10	.5	4	0	.0
24221	1.1		.5	73	11.6	148	61.5	8	21	.0	0	0	.0
24224	5.9	0	2.0	81	20.6	245	61.5	8	10	.0	0	0	.0
24225	2.7	100	.9	83	18.6	230	55.7	7	13	1.4	12	0	.0
24226	1.8	96	.5	84	16.2	165	38.6	7	13	.8	14	0	1.4
24227	3.6	99	1.2	78	14.7	177	44.1	5	14	1.7	12	0	.0
24228	8.6	100	2.9	81	23.5	230	65.5	8	10	4.3	9	0	.0
24230	10.3	96	3.3	83	21.3	234	59.3	9	11	4.9	9	0	.4
24236	3.2	99	.9	82	18.0	211	53.7	5	14	1.5	12	0	1.6
24237	2.2	93	.7	87	20.1	183	30.2	5	11	1.0	11	0	.0
24239	.6	100	.2	67	20.9	180	49.3	13	6	.3	3	0	.0
24243	2.2	0	.7	84	22.8	282	56.0	7	18	.0	0	0	.4
24244	.6		.6	84	17.2	123	48.7	13	7	.0	0	0	.0
24245	1.5	100	.5	76	15.5	229	42.8	8	11	.7	9	0	.0

*=Estimated **1.0=883 lbs per person; 100++ indicates per capita toxic waste generation > than 100 times the U.S. average of 883 lbs per capita.

ZIP CODE MEASURES OF SIZE, LEVELS OF AFFLUENCE AND QUALITY OF LIFE

1=Population (th.); 2= % White; 3=Households (th.); 4=% Owner Occupied; 5=Mean Income Per Household (th.$); 6=Mean Monthly Rent ($)*; 7=Mean Home Value (th.$)*; 8=% under 5; 9=% 65 and over; 10=% White Males (th.); 11=% White Males, 65+; 12=# Toxic Waste Sites; 13=Toxic Waste Relative to US(883 lbs.per capita)**.

VIRGINIA

BRISTOL

ZIPCODE	1	2	3	4	5	6	7	8	9	10	11	12	13
24246	.9	0	.3	81	17.9	198	58.7	14	7	.0	0	0	.0
24248	3.0	0	1.0	77	17.3	228	52.1	7	11	.0	0	0	.0
24249	.5	100	.2	100	21.4	246*	25.5	6	10	.2	2	0	.0
24250	1.5	100	.5	80	13.4	58	27.8	6	13	.8	11	0	.0
24251	11.2	99	4.0	76	20.4	231	60.7	6	14	5.4	11	1	.0
24256	4.4	100	1.4	82	19.9	215	67.8	9	9	2.2	7	0	.0
24258	1.4	100	.5	75	18.0	155	46.8	6	13	.7	11	0	.0
24260	7.8	0	2.5	84	18.7	204	57.9	8	9	.7	0	0	.0
24263	5.7	0	2.0	77	18.4	250	64.5	7	15		0	0	.0
24265	1.3	100	.4	82	18.0	327	37.8	8	7	.7	5	0	.0
24266	8.8	99	3.0	78	25.0	293	73.5	7	11	4.3	8	0	.0
24269	.6	100	.2	65	20.7	296	35.3	4	13	.3	6	0	.0
24270	.7	100	.2	70	13.5	160	41.2	13	4	.4	19	0	.0
24271	2.8	100	1.0	78	17.5	216	53.7	6	15	1.4	15	0	.0
24272	.7	100	.2	76	22.7	180	45.6	11	11	.4	8	0	.0
24273	7.6	96	2.5	73	22.9	288	64.2	8	11	3.5	8	0	.6
24274	.2	100	.1	82	12.9	333	36.0	11	23	.1	27	0	.0
24277	6.8	98	2.4	72	18.5	233	51.7	7	14	3.2	13	0	.1
24279	5.6	100	1.9	82	22.3	287	60.6	7	11	2.7	10	0	.0
24280	.6	100	.2	76	28.5	301	119.6	7	14	.3	12	0	.0
24281	2.4	0	.9	76	14.1	198	41.3	6	20	.3	10	0	.0
24282	1.6	100	.5	73	14.8	166	25.3	10	9	.8	6	0	.0
24283	3.7	99	1.3	73	21.2	251	60.1	7	9	1.8	8	0	.0
24285	.3	76	.1	85	22.1	274	40.5	8	11	.1	13	0	.0
24289	.4	100	.2	26	15.6	132	23.1	5	10	.2	6	0	.0
24292	.7	100	.2	88	18.0	207*	27.8	8	10	.4	10	0	.0
24293	10.0	98	3.3	77	24.8	333	79.7	9	8	4.8	6	0	.0

PULASKI

ZIPCODE	1	2	3	4	5	6	7	8	9	10	11	12	13
24301	16.3	92	6.0	69	20.9	275	55.9	6	13	7.3	10	3	1.0
24310	.4	83	.1	77	13.7	157*	31.6	13	24	.1	29	0	.0
24311	1.7	0	.6	74	19.1	228	52.0	6	11	.0	0	0	.2
24312	2.4	0	.9	75	17.9	168	48.8	7	12	.0	1	0	.7
24313	.7	0	.2	89	19.3	227	24.5	11	5	.0	0	0	.0
24314	1.5	100	.6	87	20.3	353	60.2	6	14	.8	11	0	.0
24315	3.1	96	.9	86	19.5	235	60.4	5	12	1.6	11	0	.4
24316	.2	100	.1	100	21.6	249*	53.8	9	19	.1	17	0	.0
24317	1.7	100	.6	80	15.7	256	51.4	6	11	.8	8	0	.0
24318	.9	100	.2	68	16.6	319	27.8	11	11	.4	12	0	.0
24319	6.4	98	2.2	76	23.4	257	59.2	7	11	3.1	9	0	.2
24322	.2	0	.1	90	14.2	163*	21.0	5	15	.5	0	0	.0
24323	.7	100	.2	74	21.3	255	43.6	6	15	.3	15	0	.0
24324	2.2	98	.7	82	24.5	168	65.3	6	13	1.1	13	0	.0
24325	.9	100	.4	78	17.1	143	52.6	5	21	.5	21	0	.0
24326	1.2	96	.5	87	19.8	131	60.9	6	16	.6	11	0	.0
24327	1.0	98	.4	79	24.6	247	102.5	1	5	.5	4	0	.0
24328	1.9	100	.6	85	19.7	253	57.2	7	11	.9	11	0	.0
24330	4.3	98	1.5	84	18.7	182	37.8	8	15	2.0	13	0	.3
24333	15.5	96	5.9	79	21.1	216	56.7	6	14	7.1	12	0	.2
24340	4.8	95	1.7	78	23.3	261	61.2	7	13	2.2	11	0	.5

VIRGINIA

PULASKI

ZIPCODE	1	2	3	4	5	6	7	8	9	10	11	12	13
24343	8.7	99	3.2	81	20.3	235	60.0	6	15	4.2	13	0	.3
24347	1.2	0	.4	86	20.6	205	49.1	4	15	.0	1	0	2.8
24348	3.7	96	1.4	79	18.4	224	60.1	6	15	1.7	15	1	.1
24350	1.4	95	.5	83	21.2	116	37.0	9	13	.6	14	0	.0
24351	.3	100	.1	82	13.5	232	34.2	4	27	.1	31	0	.0
24352	.9	100	.3	89	16.6	308	45.8	2	19	.4	14	0	.0
24354	15.9	97	5.4	74	22.4	254	64.9	6	13	7.3	12	0	.2
24360	4.6	98	1.5	87	20.4	198	51.8	8	11	2.2	10	0	.0
24361	4.0	96	1.4	82	19.3	209	56.3	7	13	1.9	11	0	.0
24363	1.3	97	.5	77	17.1	125	54.0	4	18	.6	16	0	.0
24366	1.0	90	.3	81	21.3	254	70.0	8	12	.4	10	0	.3
24368	3.7	98	1.3	81	19.5	237	60.2	7	13	1.8	12	0	.3
24370	8.1	99	2.8	80	18.6	228	39.5	6	14	3.9	12	3	.0
24373	.2	100	.1	90	19.5	224*	47.3	7	7	.1	7	0	.0
24374	1.2	96	.4	92	17.7	82	47.3	5	12	.6	7	0	.6
24375	1.5	99	.6	76	16.5	219	55.1	5	13	.8	12	0	.6
24377	.4	100	.1	94	26.7	307*	41.7	10	12	.2	13	0	.0
24378	.5	100	.5	80	17.3	117	39.7	6	16	.8	13	0	.1
24379	.9	89	.9	89	19.6	120	58.1	6	16	.8	14	0	.0
24381	3.4	97	1.1	86	20.3	186	48.5	5	12	1.2	8	0	.0
24382	12.9	95	4.6	71	22.7	256	69.3	6	14	5.7	10	0	.3

STAUNTON

ZIPCODE	1	2	3	4	5	6	7	8	9	10	11	12	13
24401	31.9	90	11.4	68	25.6	299	78.4	5	16	13.2	12	2	1.0
24411	.3	0	.1	71	15.6	171	53.6	8	18	.0	0	1	1.7
24413	.4	100	.1	82	21.6	212	59.9	8	13	.2	6	0	.0
24415	.4	61	.1	94	19.5	224*	73.0	6	31	.0	40	0	.0
24416	8.6	96	2.9	76	20.7	259	59.9	6	11	4.0	9	4	.6
24421	3.0	98	1.0	88	23.4	236	65.2	7	8	1.5	7	0	.0
24422	8.0	89	2.9	76	23.1	247	57.6	6	17	3.3	11	0	.1
24426	18.5	92	6.6	74	22.9	276	59.9	6	14	8.3	11	0	16.7
24430	1.3	98	.5	75	20.5	224	45.5	5	12	.7	11	0	.0
24431	1.8	97	.6	80	23.3	294	71.6	8	6	.9	5	0	.0
24432	.4	0	.2	61	14.9	180	51.6	5	26	.0	0	0	.0
24435	1.3	0	.4	75	19.8	277	71.1	7	13	.8	0	0	.0
24437	.6	0	.2	77	27.2	155	96.0	6	15	1.1	0	0	.0
24438	.2	0	.1	71	26.8	465	48.1	8	12	.1	0	0	.0
24439	1.1	94	.4	82	18.1	149	43.3	7	13	.5	13	1	.7
24440	1.8	95	.6	77	24.5	284	68.5	6	11	.3	10	0	.0
24441	3.6	95	1.3	85	23.3	278	69.6	6	11	1.7	9	1	.1
24444	.2	100	.1	76	23.8	312	58.7	11	13	1.1	9	0	.0
24445	3.1	87	1.0	75	22.6	302	56.8	6	13	1.3	12	0	.0
24448	.9	85	.3	69	18.3	244	40.8	9	14	.4	16	0	.2
24450	14.3	93	4.7	64	21.9	254	83.8	5	11	7.6	8	0	.0
24457	.4	91	.2	70	25.5	160	30.0	4	11	.2	5	0	.0
24458	.5	100	.3	78	21.1	252	66.6	9	14	.2	9	0	.0
24459	.8	95	.3	62	20.0	251	51.3	6	12	.4	14	0	.0
24460	1.6	96	.5	75	23.5	281	57.8	9	13	.8	11	0	.0
24465	1.5	99	.6	78	23.4	354	61.1	7	16	.7	15	0	.0
24467	1.6	100	.6	78	29.9	344	93.1	5	9	.8	10	0	.0

*=Estimated **1.0=883 lbs per person; 100++ indicates per capita toxic waste generation > than 100 times the U.S. average of 883 lbs per capita.

ZIP CODE MEASURES OF SIZE, LEVELS OF AFFLUENCE AND QUALITY OF LIFE

1=Population (th.); 2= % White; 3=Households (th.); 4=% Owner Occupied; 5=Mean Income Per Household (th.$); 6=Mean Monthly Rent ($); 7=Mean Home Value (th.$);
8=% under 5; 9=% 65 and over; 10=White Males (th.); 11=% White Males, 65+; 12=# Toxic Waste Sites; 13=Toxic Waste Relative to US(883 lbs.per capita)**.

VIRGINIA

STAUNTON

ZIP CODE	1	2	3	4	5	6	7	8	9	10	11	12	13
24469	.2	100	.1	72	29.5	257	63.4	5	9	.1	8	0	.0
24471	1.2	97	.4	88	23.2	310	83.7	11	10	.5	8	0	.0
24472	1.7	0	.6	86	21.6	136	53.6	9	14	.0	0	0	.0
24473	.5	100	.6	79	29.9	138	71.0	5	22	.3	19	0	.0
24474	.6	100	.2	86	19.2	375	35.4	7	11	.3	5	1	.0
24475	.3	0	.1	69	17.2	147	96.9	4	5	.0	0	0	.0
24477	5.5	96	1.8	79	25.2	320	75.2	7	8	2.5	6	0	.1
24479	1.3	97	.5	76	22.9	255	77.0	6	12	.7	11	0	.0
24482	3.9	96	1.3	77	23.3	316	71.5	10	6	1.8	6	0	.0
24483	.7	0	.2	74	18.9	299	52.5	7	13	.0	0	0	.0
24484	1.2	92	.4	60	22.9	371	56.7	4	16	.6	12	0	.0
24485	.3	100	.1	91	37.5	431*	46.7	3	22	.1	17	0	.0
24486	1.6	0	.5	80	27.9	268	87.5	6	9	.0	0	0	5.4
24487	.2	100	.1	93	20.6	237*	48.4	5	18	.1	20	0	.0

LYNCHBURG

ZIP CODE	1	2	3	4	5	6	7	8	9	10	11	12	13
24501	24.3	73	9.3	56	19.9	296	49.4	7	14	8.2	12	2	.2
24502	29.3	94	10.3	76	29.8	332	84.3	7	10	13.2	8	1	.3
24503	15.8	88	6.0	70	36.0	349	111.3	5	16	6.1	13	0	.0
24504	12.7	39	4.0	54	17.6	243	38.6	6	14	2.3	13	4	.1
24505	3.8	92	.1	33	18.6	108	35.2	0	4	1.8	3	2	62.3
24506	.8	0	.3	85	26.2	382	80.8	4	2	.0	0	1	5.7
24507	.8	100	.1	94	38.7	445*	112.4	3	0	.1	0	0	.0
24517	6.1	84	2.3	71	23.0	271	65.2	7	13	2.6	13	0	8.2
24520	1.8	52	.6	68	20.9	138	51.2	7	12	.5	14	0	.0
24521	7.9	68	2.6	82	17.7	72	45.9	11	29	.1	49	0	.0
24522	7.8	77	2.7	85	23.8	240	67.6	7	13	1.3	6	0	.0
24523	15.2	83	5.4	77	24.4	256	66.6	7	13	2.9	12	0	.1
24526	1.7	82	.6	77	21.7	212	66.3	6	17	6.1	17	3	.1
24527	2.2	58	.7	79	20.0	125	48.2	7	14	.7	16	0	1.1
24528	3.7	69	1.2	86	20.9	158	64.8	7	10	.0	11	0	.0
24529	1.7	65	.6	71	22.5	249	58.0	6	13	1.2	12	1	.1
24530	1.2	67	.3	71	19.7	160	54.5	7	13	.6	12	0	.0
24531	8.9	60	3.1	76	20.6	124	51.8	9	12	.4	18	0	.0
24534	1.8	52	.6	68	21.7	186	54.7	5	14	2.5	15	3	.6
24536	.2	79	.1	82	18.3	187	45.8	6	15	.4	16	0	.0
24538	3.3	79	1.0	85	17.7	72	45.9	11	29	.1	49	0	.0
24539	.3	48	.4	77	13.4	144	43.1	5	21	.1	19	0	.0
24541	68.9	72	25.5	67	22.8	240	59.5	6	13	23.2	12	9	.5
24549	2.7	74	.9	76	20.9	251	55.4	6	15	1.0	14	0	.0
24550	4.5	84	1.5	86	22.1	248	65.8	8	9	1.9	9	0	.0
24551	5.3	87	1.6	82	31.3	300	110.8	8	7	2.3	5	0	.0
24554	3.6	68	1.1	87	22.6	212	48.7	7	14	.6	17	0	.0
24555	2.1	88	.8	83	21.9	181	52.8	9	11	1.4	11	0	.9
24556	1.4	91	.4	87	27.3	362	98.7	6	5	.7	7	1	.0
24557	7.7	70	2.7	76	24.2	221	52.0	6	12	2.7	12	0	.0
24558	6.6	64	2.2	73	21.8	237	62.2	6	12	2.0	12	0	.1
24562	.2	71	.1	84	18.3	211*	57.9	13	28	.1	29	0	.3
24563	6.0	83	2.0	80	21.6	247	54.5	7	18	2.4	10	1	.3

LYNCHBURG (continued)

ZIP CODE	1	2	3	4	5	6	7	8	9	10	11	12	13
24565	1.5	29	.4	67	20.9	168	46.3	9	8	.2	10	0	.0
24566	1.2	74	.4	83	23.1	181	56.2	8	10	.4	6	0	.0
24569	1.2	42	.3	78	21.7	118	53.5	5	9	.3	10	0	.0
24571	1.7	67	.5	86	20.2	165	44.5	6	11	.6	11	0	.0
24572	14.4	81	4.8	81	26.6	327	66.2	7	9	5.7	8	0	.0
24574	2.9	81	1.0	76	20.9	304	63.9	7	12	1.3	9	0	.1
24576	.2	23	.1	90	18.1	208*	50.7	11	7	.0	0	0	.0
24577	5.5	55	1.8	71	17.6	159	45.1	7	16	1.5	18	0	.0
24578	.7	100	.3	77	24.1	158	62.6	3	14	.3	10	0	.0
24579	1.8	99	.6	82	20.3	222	48.3	6	10	.9	10	0	.0
24580	.6	71	.2	76	23.2	275	56.1	5	16	.2	21	1	.0
24588	5.3	66	1.8	74	21.3	213	55.2	7	11	1.7	10	0	.0
24589	7.7	81	2.4	84	26.4	269	68.6	7	7	3.0	6	0	.0
24590	2.1	69	.7	75	17.5	172	43.6	7	10	.7	8	0	.0
24592	4.7	85	1.6	83	19.4	265	64.6	8	12	2.0	11	0	.0
24593	14.4	61	5.0	72	21.0	235	60.5	7	13	4.1	10	3	.9
24594	1.6	78	.5	79	24.6	353	62.3	6	13	.6	12	0	.0
24595	.7	62	.1	83	24.1	176	37.0	4	14	.5	16	0	.3
24597	1.1	95	.4	46	22.4	284	65.2	6	4	.3	6	0	.6
24598	1.9	59	.7	73	17.5	138	56.5	5	13	.7	18	0	.3
24599	.6	80	.2	76	20.5	177	56.0	7	19	.7	18	0	.7

BLUEFIELD

ZIP CODE	1	2	3	4	5	6	7	8	9	10	11	12	13
24601	.2	0	.1	81	20.0	126	36.7	9	14	.0	13	0	.0
24603	1.3	100	.4	85	17.7	168	38.8	6	10	.4	6	0	.1
24604	.6	93	.1	84	22.1	279	53.5	9	5	.3	12	0	.3
24605	10.3	94	3.6	80	24.2	184	33.5	9	5	4.8	11	0	.6
24606	.6	100	.2	82	18.2	277	75.3	7	12	.3	18	0	.1
24607	.4	100	.1	80	23.4	199	31.0	8	8	.2	11	0	.0
24609	6.5	100	2.2	80	23.4	217	60.4	4	10	3.0	15	0	.1
24611	.3	100	.1	74	26.0	302	66.4	9	10	.1	12	0	.0
24612	1.1	100	.3	79	22.5	223	35.0	15	2	.4	4	0	.6
24613	.9	99	.3	83	22.6	265	71.5	6	6	.5	7	0	.6
24614	9.9	99	3.2	76	27.6	245	50.7	8	9	4.9	5	0	1.2
24616	1.1	0	.3	75	19.7	254	83.0	9	7	.0	6	0	.0
24618	.9	100	.3	88	26.0	276	91.9	6	8	.4	6	0	.0
24620	3.6	100	1.1	80	24.5	167	54.4	5	9	1.8	5	0	.0
24622	1.5	100	.5	78	24.5	131	52.5	6	6	.6	8	0	.9
24623	.3	100	.1	42	44.3	154	48.6	6	11	.2	6	0	.0
24624	.5	100	.2	78	31.6	153	55.0	8	9	.2	8	0	.0
24627	.4	100	.1	78	19.3	193	90.2	8	7	.2	8	0	.0
24628	.5	100	.1	78	25.1	129	56.1	6	18	.2	15	0	.0
24630	7.2	96	2.4	80	21.1	245	38.7	11	8	3.4	7	0	.9
24631	1.9	100	.7	85	25.8	315	68.8	6	11	1.0	11	0	1.2
24633	.3	100	.1	86	26.0	162	58.2	6	7	.2	9	0	.0
24634	1.0	100	.3	83	19.9	269	30.0	8	9	.5	8	0	.0
24635	1.1	92	.4	78	19.4	143	40.3	10	4	.5	3	0	.0
24637	.5	98	.5	86	23.4	178	35.7	6	14	.9	9	0	.0

*=Estimated **1.0=883 lbs per person; 100++ indicates per capita toxic waste generation > than 100 times the U.S. average of 883 lbs per capita.

ZIP CODE MEASURES OF SIZE, LEVELS OF AFFLUENCE AND QUALITY OF LIFE

1=Population (th.); 2= % White; 3=Households (th.); 4=% Owner Occupied; 5=Mean Income Per Household (th.$); 6=Mean Monthly Rent ($)*; 7=Mean Home Value (th.$)*; 8=% under 5; 9=% 65 and over; 10=White Males (th.); 11=% White Males, 65+; 12=# Toxic Waste Sites; 13=Toxic Waste Relative to US(883 lbs.per capita)**.

VIRGINIA

ZIP CODE	1	2	3	4	5	6	7	8	9	10	11	12	13
BLUEFIELD													
24638	1.4	100	.4	89	23.4	190	55.5	9	9	.8	10	0	.0
24639	5.7	99	1.7	79	23.6	287	65.2	9	5	2.9	3	0	.0
24640	.4	100	.1	86	15.0	202	25.3	8	4	.2	0	0	.0
24641	7.8	99	2.7	71	23.0	298	80.3	8	8	3.7	7	0	.9
24646	1.5	100	.5	87	20.2	303	47.1	6	7	.8	0	0	.0
24647	.2	100	.1	92	24.9	286*	72.7	5	4	.1	4	0	.0
24649	2.6	100	.8	88	22.1	181	53.1	7	7	1.3	6	1	.0
24651	6.2	96	2.1	73	25.3	312	78.7	8	12	2.8	10	0	.8
24656	6.0	99	1.9	80	23.3	271	66.9	9	8	2.9	8	0	.0
24657	.7	100	.3	69	17.3	232	54.0	8	7	.4	8	0	.0
24658	.6	100	.2	78	23.2	382	59.0	7	8	.3	7	0	.0
MARTINSBURG													
25425	.3	100	.1	71	22.2	526	104.5	6	14	.2	12	0	.0
GREENSBORO (WEST)													
27030	1.9	100	.6	91	18.3	167	45.9	9	9	.9	9	0	.0
GREENSBORO (EAST)													
27305	.5	51	.2	81	15.6	221	59.1	6	10	.1	11	0	.0
RALEIGH													
27563	.6	16	.2	80	14.6	125	52.9	12	19	.0	55	0	.0
HICKORY													
28631	.1	100	.1	86	11.7	134*	64.2	9	35	.1	34	0	.0
JOHNSON CITY													
37660	.9	100	.3	88	19.4	275	63.0	6	16	.5	15	0	.0
KNOXVILLE													
37765	.1	100	.1	80	11.1	127*	39.5*	9	24	.1	23	0	.0

WASHINGTON

ZIP CODE	1	2	3	4	5	6	7	8	9	10	11	12	13
SPOKANE													
83843	.3	100	.1	67	31.5	294	170.6	10	11	.1	9	0	.0
SEATTLE													
98002	53.6	95	18.7	67	31.7	395	122.0	8	7	25.5	5	4	.8
98003	46.0	94	16.2	70	35.5	474	139.5	8	5	21.4	4	4	.0
98004	22.9	96	8.8	71	53.9	518	224.4	4	11	10.7	10	0	.8
98005	13.5	94	5.0	63	44.6	486	216.3	4	5	6.4	4	3	.1
98006	23.4	92	7.4	87	51.3	654	192.2	6	5	10.9	3	3	.0
98007	18.8	93	8.2	42	51.8	502	151.8	5	5	8.4	4	2	.0
98008	23.2	94	7.6	78	43.9	610	165.5	6	4	10.8	4	0	.0
98010	1.4	97	.5	86	26.4	354	107.9	8	12	.7	11	3	.0
98011	52.2	96	17.6	85	36.1	509	147.2	9	6	25.1	6	2	.0
98013	2.5	99	1.0	77	42.9	459	172.3	6	11	1.3	9	1	.0
98014	3.3	96	1.1	72	27.2	343	121.8	8	6	1.6	5	1	.1
98019	2.4	98	.9	78	26.7	421	118.3	8	6	1.5	5	1	.1
98022	46.1	96	16.5	74	38.1	499	160.8	8	8	21.5	7	1	.2
98024	14.1	98	4.9	75	31.7	356	124.3	8	11	6.9	10	2	.2
98025	3.3	98	1.1	84	29.7	414	127.6	9	10	1.7	9	0	.0
98027	.2	100	.2	100	39.3	452*	91.1	0	16	.1	12	0	.1
98031	20.6	98	6.8	80	41.7	432	187.4	7	6	10.1	4	8	.1
98033	80.9	95	28.3	70	34.2	416	136.7	8	8	38.5	11	11	1.1
98036	55.5	96	20.0	71	36.2	526	148.0	8	6	26.2	5	4	.5
98038	47.3	94	17.3	67	30.6	469	128.7	8	6	22.1	5	1	.0
98040	8.0	97	2.6	86	36.6	437	146.5	7	5	4.0	5	1	.0
98043	21.5	93	7.6	79	56.4	542	257.9	5	8	9.9	7	0	.0
98045	17.1	92	6.0	68	30.9	494	107.9	8	5	7.9	4	1	.7
98047	7.2	99	2.6	78	28.6	392	104.3	11	9	3.5	8	1	.0
98050	2.5	93	.2	69	27.3	397	102.5	9	8	1.2	7	1	.0
98051	.3	100	.1	77	32.8	551	129.8	8	10	.2	10	0	.2
98052	1.7	0	.5	80	39.9	576	167.9	8	5	.9	4	2	.5
98055	34.6	96	11.9	72	33.6	422	127.3	8	6	16.5	5	5	3.7
98061	78.9	93	28.0	89	42.8	484	202.3	7	9	37.1	6	6	.0
98065	.3	0	.1	76	33.4	366	91.5	6	9	.2	9	0	.0
98070	3.1	97	1.0	74	30.1	375	149.2	7	12	1.5	11	1	.0
98072	14.4	97	6.3	91	42.6	609	179.5	9	4	7.0	2	2	.0
SEATTLE													
98101	7.0	84	4.2	7	18.1	305	240.6	1	33	3.2	23	0	1.2
98102	17.5	89	11.1	21	22.9	377	180.7	2	16	7.4	11	1	.1
98103	36.2	92	17.1	49	24.9	424	106.5	5	15	15.9	12	5	.3
98104	8.0	58	4.6	1	13.3	221	47.4*	2	28	2.9	20	2	6.0
98105	32.1	88	12.9	41	28.3	407	174.4	3	10	13.9	8	2	.0
98106	16.0	81	6.3	58	24.3	358	88.1	9	10	6.3	11	5	2.5
98107	16.8	94	8.5	42	23.8	401	104.2	5	19	7.4	16	4	1.2
98108	16.6	53	6.6	59	24.2	304	92.2	7	14	4.2	18	17	5.7
98109	12.8	94	7.4	30	26.2	396	157.8	3	16	5.7	12	3	.6
98110	12.0	95	4.4	77	39.4	462	211.3	6	12	5.5	11	1	.1
98112	20.5	77	8.9	55	35.4	419	203.4	5	14	7.5	11	1	.0
98115	42.2	92	17.3	72	32.1	476	132.6	4	16	19.2	13	0	.0
98116	19.8	96	9.2	59	29.9	434	124.3	5	17	8.8	14	2	.0

*=Estimated **1.0=883 lbs per person; 100++ indicates per capita toxic waste generation > than 100 times the U.S. average of 883 lbs per capita.

ZIP CODE MEASURES OF SIZE, LEVELS OF AFFLUENCE AND QUALITY OF LIFE

1=Population (th.); 2= % White; 3=Households (th.); 4=% Owner Occupied; 5=Mean Income Per Household (th.$); 6=Mean Monthly Rent ($); 7=Mean Home Value (th.$); 8=% under 5; 9=% 65 and over; 10=% White Males; 11=% White Males, 65+; 12=# Toxic Waste Sites; 13=Toxic Waste Relative to US(883 lbs.per capita)**

WASHINGTON

SEATTLE

ZIPCODE	1	2	3	4	5	6	7	8	9	10	11	12	13
98117	29.0	95	12.5	74	28.5	464	118.5	5	19	13.1	17	0	.0
98118	35.1	45	13.3	61	27.5	359	111.0	8	11	7.6	17	3	.0
98119	17.7	94	8.9	37	26.2	406	148.4	3	18	7.4	14	4	.3
98121	3.3	90	2.5		15.3	263	54.5*	0	37	1.6	27	4	.5
98122	25.3	43	11.7	30	18.3	296	113.5	6	12	5.7	12	2	.0
98125	29.4	90	12.8	57	30.2	432	131.6	5	14	12.5	12	0	.0
98126	18.0	83	7.2	63	26.9	347	101.9	7	15	7.1	13	2	.0
98133	34.3	92	14.2	62	29.4	426	118.3	5	14	14.7	11	3	.0
98134		64	.1	25	20.4	289	72.8*	5*	7	.7	7	16	100++
98136	13.5	94	6.0	68	31.3	415	133.7	5	19	6.1	17	1	.0
98144	22.5	36	8.8	52	26.2	344	118.1	7	15	3.9	16	1	.1
98146	22.5	92	8.4	68	33.4	396	124.6	7	10	10.1	9	1	.0
98148	12.7	96	4.8	66	33.2	451	119.7	6	5	5.9	5	0	.0
98155	36.4	94	12.9	74	36.2	488	142.3	6	9	16.8	7	1	1.8
98166	19.7	96	7.5	69	36.5	423	165.8	5	9	9.5	8	0	.0
98168	27.7	93	11.2	61	30.1	412	102.8	7	10	12.9	8	1	.1
98177	19.2	97	7.0	85	49.0	501	184.3	4	11	9.1	11	1	.0
98178	19.2	79	7.3	75	33.0	451	117.4	6	10	7.5	11	1	.7
98188	30.0	94	12.5	52	31.3	435	121.2	5	11	13.6	8	2	.2
98199	18.4	94	8.3	65	39.1	502	172.6	4	18	8.2	16	0	.3

EVERETT

ZIPCODE	1	2	3	4	5	6	7	8	9	10	11	12	13
98201	24.3	94	10.5	45	21.0	335	91.7	8	18	10.6	15	4	.5
98203	23.7	96	9.3	67	31.3	441	118.8	7	12	11.1	13	1	.1
98204	32.7	95	11.5	71	31.8	421	132.6	9	6	15.8	6	1	1.8
98205	9.0	97	3.0	79	31.1	431	120.3	9	7	4.4	8	0	.0
98206	.8	100	.1	83	39.8	333	289.0	10	7	.1	10	0	41.1
98220	.8	95	.2	83	29.1	239	70.8	7	7	.4	6	1	.0
98221	12.0	98	4.7	73	28.0	334	109.0	9	11	5.7	16	1	.0
98223	16.3	98	5.5	79	28.1	362	116.3	9	9	8.0	5	0	7.9
98225	65.6	96	25.4	61	25.2	354	114.6	6	12	30.5	10	11	.3
98230	5.5	98	2.1	67	25.1	329	103.9	7	12	2.7	12	0	.0
98232	2.4	92	.9	79	26.6	305	114.8	6	12	1.1	15	0	.0
98233	8.0	94	3.0	73	28.3	342	98.3	8	13	3.8	11	0	.0
98235	.7	92	.3	70	19.8	331	79.3	4	14	.3	16	3	.0
98236	3.1	99	.1	85	37.9	313	144.5	9	11	1.5	10	0	.0
98237	1.8	97	.6	79	22.0	267	71.3	9	10	.8	14	0	.0
98239	3.2	97	1.3	75	25.6	354	124.9	5	17	1.0	11	0	.0
98240	2.0	99	.6	81	27.0	405	110.5	9	8	1.0	5	0	.0
98241	1.8	98	.7	76	24.1	248	77.1	9	9	.9	8	0	.3
98243	.2	0	.1	80	26.3	303*	169.6	19	25	.0	8	11	.3
98244	1.8	93	.6	77	25.9	291	96.0	8	8	.9	8	0	.0
98245	1.5	0	.6	68	25.4	342	189.2	6	12	1.1	15	0	.0
98247	4.7	94	1.6	77	28.5	331	105.6	9	8	2.2	7	3	.0
98248	11.7	93	4.0	72	27.6	344	107.9	9	7	5.5	6	3	6.4
98249	2.3	99	1.0	84	25.5	350	150.4	5	25	1.1	26	0	.2
98250	3.9	99	1.6	67	27.3	331	184.0	6	16	2.0	14	0	.0
98251	1.1	97	.4	78	18.7	325	90.6	11	13	.5	13	0	.0
98252	2.7	99	1.0	75	22.6	332	94.5	8	13	1.4	13	0	.0
98253	.8	0	.4	74	26.2	404	144.1	6	33	.0	0	0	.0

WASHINGTON

EVERETT

ZIPCODE	1	2	3	4	5	6	7	8	9	10	11	12	13
98255	.3	0	.1	59	20.7	279	64.8	12	4	.0	0	0	.0
98256	.3	98	.1	62	14.7	236	54.5	4	16	.1	10	0	.0
98257	2.0	81	.8	77	31.4	306	125.0	5	13	.8	13	0	.1
98258	8.4	82	2.8	82	32.6	416	132.8	5	13	4.1	6	1	.0
98260	2.9	99	1.1	68	24.2	354	123.7	6	18	1.3	15	0	.0
98261	1.2	100	.5	73	28.4	446	158.9	7	23	.6	27	0	.0
98262	.5	94	.2	73	16.9	276	125.0	6	21	.2	23	0	.0
98263	.4	0	.2	84	18.7	207	55.8	11	17	.0	0	0	.0
98264	10.2	98	3.4	75	28.3	370	106.0	10	13	4.9	11	1	.3
98266	.3	0	.1	63	22.1	311	78.8	11	11	.0	0	0	.0
98267	.3	0	.1	79	19.8	316	79.4	5	7	.0	0	0	.8
98268	.3	11	.1	63	22.4	474	47.0	14	2	.0	37	0	.0
98270	30.2	94	10.5	76	29.9	413	114.1	9	9	14.1	8	2	.1
98272	11.2	95	3.5	77	27.2	347	111.4	6	11	5.7	10	1	.4
98273	22.4	94	8.7	67	27.0	361	107.9	8	13	10.2	13	1	.0
98275	1.4	99	.1	79	37.3	510	176.1	4	11	.7	9	1	.0
98276	.3	93	.1	80	22.1	369	88.6	6	12	.1	12	0	.0
98277	26.7	90	8.8	57	24.3	342	118.4	10	5	12.8	5	6	.0
98279	.4	0	.2	83	21.4	260	153.3	5	24	.0	0	0	.0
98280	.3	94	.1	95	40.0	460*	222.5	0	20	.1	25	1	.0
98281	.5	100	.5	82	20.0	223	128.0	6	27	.2	22	1	.0
98283	.4	91	.2	43	22.5	270	61.0	0	11	.2	13	1	.0
98284	13.5	97	4.9	74	22.7	355	86.8	8	12	6.4	11	1	.4
98286	.1	100	.1	88	31.7	365*	178.6	0	6	.1	8	1	.0
98288	.3	0	.1	62	18.9	266	64.0	7	6	.0	0	3	.0
98290	24.4	97	8.1	79	30.8	376	131.9	9	8	11.9	7	5	.0
98292	13.6	98	5.1	76	26.2	353	135.4	6	18	6.7	18	1	.0
98294	2.4	98	.8	72	24.5	312	94.8	9	9	1.2	8	0	.0
98295	1.9	97	.6	73	38.4	274	85.2	10	11	.9	10	1	.0

TACOMA

ZIPCODE	1	2	3	4	5	6	7	8	9	10	11	12	13
98303	.3	100	.2	69	25.5	366	88.3	5	19	.2	17	0	.0
98304	.5	100	.2	61	29.4	209	90.6	6	6	.3	7	0	.0
98305	1.1	96	.4	69	26.2	308	78.7	13	7	.5	7	1	.0
98310	67.1	91	25.7	59	26.1	335	104.3	9	10	30.6	9	4	.0
98320	.8	0	.4	77	19.4	213	86.0	7	17	.0	0	0	.0
98321	6.5	98	2.0	81	28.9	350	94.6	7	8	3.2	8	0	.0
98322	.5	93	.2	96	28.5	327*	132.3	3	20	.3	21	0	.0
98323	.5	100	.2	84	26.5	350	49.2	13	13	.2	17	0	.3
98324	2.2	79	.1	87	13.8	158*	71.8	4	15	.1	19	0	.0
98325	.9	97	.3	80	34.7	219	113.8	5	14	.2	17	0	.0
98326	.9	97	.3	75	30.4	235	91.9	11	7	.5	7	0	.0
98327	.5	88	.2	50	20.9	374	85.8	9	10	.3	8	1	.0
98328	4.5	99	1.5	82	29.4	291	101.4	7	10	2.2	10	1	.0
98330	.3	100	.1	80	19.9	140	61.8	0	16	.1	21	0	.0
98331	7.1	93	2.4	67	30.5	378	104.5	12	3	3.5	2	0	.2
98333	1.5	98	.6	88	36.3	339	177.8	5	13	.8	13	0	.0
98335	22.1	97	7.9	76	34.7	409	150.8	8	9	10.7	8	0	.0
98336	1.1	99	.3	82	23.2	202	85.2	10	5	.5	6	0	.0
98338	8.5	98	2.7	88	32.4	322	125.3	10	5	4.2	5	0	.0

*=Estimated **1.0=883 lbs per person; 100++ indicates per capita toxic waste generation > than 100 times the U.S. average of 883 lbs. per capita.

ZIP CODE MEASURES OF SIZE, LEVELS OF AFFLUENCE AND QUALITY OF LIFE

1=Population (th.); 2= % White; 3=Households (th.); 4=% Owner Occupied; 5=Mean Income Per Household (th.$); 6=Mean Monthly Rent ($)*; 7=Mean Home Value (th.$)*; 8=% under 5, 9=% 65 and over; 10=White Males (th.); 11=% White Males, 65+; 12=# Toxic Waste Sites; 13=Toxic Waste Relative to US(883 lbs.per capita)**.

WASHINGTON

TACOMA

ZIPCODE	1	2	3	4	5	6	7	8	9	10	11	12	13
98339	.8	91	.3	68	22.8	281	110.4	10	5	.4	9	0	.0
98340	.9	0	.4	77	31.2	453	157.9	4	24	.0	0	0	.0
98342	.7	96	.3	79	31.7	336	129.1	10	11	.3	9	0	.0
98345	.6	84	.2	60	34.2	359	114.2	8	0	.3	0	1	.0
98346	3.9	89	1.4	80	29.3	359	130.1	9	10	1.8	12	0	.0
98349	1.7	98	.7	87	25.9	228	135.3	4	15	.8	16	0	.0
98350	.4	20	.1	77	15.8	380	68.5	16	0	.0	0	0	.0
98351	.5	100	.2	91	20.6	352	83.3	5	25	.2	23	0	.0
98353	3.6	81	1.2	75	30.5	380	116.2	1	4	2.7	2	1	.0
98354	2.1	98	.7	78	31.3	385	100.2	8	9	1.0	8	2	.0
98355	.5	0	.2	79	16.6	219	52.5	10	24	.2	0	0	.0
98356	2.4	98	.9	71	23.3	229	76.7	8	15	1.2	14	0	.0
98357	1.3	36	.5	61	22.3	286	70.1	13	7	.3	2	0	.0
98359	2.3	99	.8	80	27.1	406	107.6	9	9	.9	9	0	.0
98360	3.3	98	1.2	72	24.1	333	78.5	10	14	1.0	15	1	.5
98361	1.1	100	.5	71	22.6	226	76.8	7	14	.6	12	0	.1
98362	28.4	96	11.0	69	27.2	227	107.7	7	13	13.5	12	0	.3
98364	.3	91	.1	54	33.2	230	111.4	13	14	.1	14	0	.0
98365	2.8	97	1.2	77	30.0	191	142.0	6	18	1.4	20	0	.0
98366	32.8	95	11.2	76	27.5	389	106.5	9	8	15.7	7	1	.0
98368	8.2	98	3.4	76	24.5	314	102.6	6	17	4.0	16	1	.7
98370	13.9	98	5.1	72	30.6	377	137.3	7	12	6.8	11	0	.0
98371	58.0	97	20.4	75	29.8	397	113.0	8	10	27.6	8	3	.7
98376	1.5	95	.6	78	26.2	280	91.7	6	15	.7	18	1	.0
98377	2.0	98	.7	76	24.1	258	75.9	8	14	1.1	5	0	.0
98380	.5	100	.2	79	30.5	447	169.7	7	23	.3	25	0	.0
98381	.5	0	.2	67	31.8	370	114.0	7	8	.0	0	0	.0
98382	12.6	97	5.3	76	23.7	322	123.2	6	26	5.9	26	0	.0
98383	5.0	95	1.8	72	33.3	420	144.0	6	6	2.4	6	1	.1
98385	.3	100		81	30.2	342	97.9	5	18	.1	21	0	.0
98386	.3	0	.1	88	32.9	435	60.3	6	10	.0	0	0	.0
98387	15.3	90	5.3	96	40.8	469*	93.2	5	12	7.0	5	0	.4
98388	5.2	82	1.8	56	30.5	391	128.4	6	6	2.2	6	0	.4
98390	26.7	98	9.3	79	29.6	384	118.5	9	8	13.2	7	1	.0
98392	1.7	90	.6	81	29.8	432	104.3	9	7	.8	6	0	.0
98393	.6	95	.2	91	31.3	134	116.4	9	7	.3	5	0	.0
98394	.7	93	.3	87	28.4	290	143.9	10	17	.3	19	0	.0
98395	.1	100	.1	83	21.7	438	137.7	17	18	.1	25	0	.0
98396	.3	0	.1	82	18.6	269	56.0	9	18	.0	0	0	.0

TACOMA

ZIPCODE	1	2	3	4	5	6	7	8	9	10	11	12	13
98402	3.1	88	2.2	4	10.8	208	64.3	3	43	1.2	29	3	1.5
98403	8.1	92	4.2	31	23.3	292	130.2	5	20	3.3	14	0	.0
98404	24.7	75	8.4	67	23.3	313	72.7	10	10	9.0	11	2	.0
98405	21.9	67	9.1	48	18.2	279	65.3	8	15	9.5	15	0	.0
98406	21.2	94	8.1	70	28.0	354	104.1	6	13	9.5	11	0	.0
98407	18.1	94	7.1	74	29.2	328	100.2	7	14	8.1	11	1	1.0
98408	27.5	87	10.8	69	23.1	348	72.7	8	15	11.4	13	0	.0
98409	20.5	85	8.3	54	20.4	335	69.1	9	18	8.4	11	7	.4

WASHINGTON

TACOMA

ZIPCODE	1	2	3	4	5	6	7	8	9	10	11	12	13
98421	.4	60	.2	65	17.3	279	62.1	8	5	.2	10	26	100++
98422	7.2	94	2.4	83	38.5	479	145.0	7	6	3.6	5	3	.6
98424	3.8	92	1.5	59	28.6	351	111.0	7	10	1.8	9	4	.0
98433	23.3	65	3.2	1	19.0	336	118.1	11	0	10.4	1	0	.0
98439	7.1	71	2.2	9	16.0	323	91.4	18	1	2.7	0	0	.0
98443	4.8	94	1.7	87	30.6	393	106.8	7	9	2.2	9	1	.0
98444	22.2	89	8.7	51	27.7	339	83.5	7	8	6.8	7	1	.0
98445	15.0	90	4.9	80	27.7	390	100.0	7	8	6.8	8	1	.0
98446	6.6	95	2.1	85	31.2	356	114.7	7	8	3.2	8	0	.0
98465	6.3	88	2.8	51	30.8	339	122.3	6	12	2.7	11	1	.0
98466	21.5	95	8.4	65	33.6	443	129.0	6	9	9.6	8	0	.0
98467	7.2	91	2.7	57	33.3	385	144.3	9	4	3.4	4	0	.0
98498	25.4	84	9.7	60	32.6	385	134.2	7	6	10.6	6	1	.0
98499	20.2	77	8.3	44	26.5	344	118.8	10	7	7.9	7	6	.1

OLYMPIA

ZIPCODE	1	2	3	4	5	6	7	8	9	10	11	12	13
98501	20.9	96	8.5	61	28.5	343	109.8	6	12	9.6	10	4	.1
98502	29.6	96	11.4	67	29.9	359	123.3	7	10	13.9	9	2	.0
98503	30.8	93	11.2	64	28.2	414	110.0	8	10	13.9	8	1	.0
98505	.0	94			14.3	370	51.0*	4		.3	0	0	.0
98506	21.6	94	8.2	66	26.7	361	106.7	9	8	9.8	8	3	.0
98507	.3	100	.1	79	29.5	203	118.3	5	17		1	14	.0
98520	23.7	96	9.4	63	27.5	307	86.2	8	13	11.3	11	0	11.6
98524	1.3	98	.5	82	28.7	294	112.0	9	13	.7	17	0	.0
98526	.7	95	.7	79	26.2	218	138.8	3	10	.7	14	1	.0
98527	.2	0	.1	84	17.1	246	40.2	4	22				.0
98528	4.2	96	1.8	82	24.9	378	113.0	7	13	2.1	13	0	.0
98530	.6	99	.2	76	21.2	359	69.9	10	13		14	1	.0
98531	17.9	97	7.0	67	23.6	304	84.3	7	17	8.3	14	2	.0
98532	16.1	98	5.8	73	26.7	316	96.8	8	13	7.7	11	4	.1
98533	.2	0			19.3	415	57.5	11	19				.0
98535	.5	0	.2	70	19.4	238	105.8	5	13		0	0	.0
98536	.2	82	.1	71	18.0	341	45.8	7	10		1	0	.0
98537	2.3	97	.8	85	28.3	354	93.5	8	5		8	0	.0
98538	.3	100	.1	78	34.0	391*	71.5	10	10	1.1	12	0	.4
98539	.2	100	.2	91	22.2	255*	44.2	4	25		20	0	.0
98540	.2	100	.1	79	31.4	312	99.3	8	5		5	0	.0
98541	6.9	99	2.5	72	25.3	344	84.7	8	14	3.3	11	2	1.1
98542	.3	100	.1	73	19.5	228	118.1	9	17	.2	20	0	.0
98547	1.6	0	.6	85	25.1	467	98.9	2	16		0	0	.0
98548	1.1	96	.5	80	23.2	194	53.9	5	14	.6	16	0	.0
98550	12.5	96	4.7	74	21.2	305	106.8	8	16	.6	6	0	.0
98552	.3	0	.1	69	25.5	316	74.0	8	12	6.0	11	1	2.1
98555	.5	0		83	25.7	232	55.4	10	8		0	0	.0
98557	2.6	98	.9	80	20.4	381	75.9	8	20		0	0	.0
98558	.4	0	.1	79	27.2	347	79.3	9	12	1.3	12	0	.0
98560	.2	100	.1	55	17.2	485	104.1	9	11		0	0	.0
98561	.2	100	.1	62	14.9	241	109.4	11	7		12	0	.0
98562	.4	77	.2	60	17.2	253	66.3	10	20	.1	18	0	.0

*=Estimated **1.0=883 lbs per person; 100++ indicates per capita toxic waste generation > than 100 times the U.S. average of 883 lbs per capita.

ZIP CODE MEASURES OF SIZE, LEVELS OF AFFLUENCE AND QUALITY OF LIFE

1=Population (th.); 2= % White; 3=Households (th.); 4=% Owner Occupied; 5=Mean Income Per Household (th.$); 6=Mean Monthly Rent ($); 7=Mean Home Value (th.$); 8=% under 5; 9=% 65 and over; 10=White Males (th.); 11=% White Males, 65+; 12=# Toxic Waste Sites; 13=Toxic Waste Relative to US(883 lbs.per capita)**.

WASHINGTON

OLYMPIA

ZIP CODE	1	2	3	4	5	6	7	8	9	10	11	12	13
98563	7.2	98	2.6	77	29.0	318	96.2	8	11	3.6	9	0	.0
98564	1.8	0	.6	77	19.3	262	77.2	10	14	.0	0	0	.0
98565	.6	0	.2	79	23.4	250	81.5	9	10	.0	0	0	.0
98566	.2	0	.1	56	32.8	237	13.1	17	3	.0	0	0	.0
98568	1.7	89	.6	83	24.3	236	77.1	12	13	.8	12	0	.0
98569	2.1	97	.9	70	24.9	327	93.3	6	17	1.0	18	0	.0
98570	2.5	98	.8	80	26.4	365	70.0	10	10	1.2	10	0	.0
98571	.8	92	.3	52	28.0	298	89.1	9	10	.4	14	0	.0
98572	.8	98	.3	74	22.6	238	54.8	11	12	.4	11	0	.0
98575	.3	100	.1	63	25.5	254	70.3	6	6	.2	8	0	.0
98576	2.2	99	.7	84	26.4	338	91.9	9	8	1.1	7	0	.0
98577	6.1	98	2.3	76	24.7	356	62.9	8	15	2.9	14	0	.0
98579	5.2	98	1.8	77	24.5	356	85.1	11	9	1.5	9	0	.0
98580	3.8	97	1.2	86	29.3	312	104.7	8	9	1.9	10	0	.0
98581	.3	100	.1	100	14.6	168*	50.6	6	55	.1	70	0	.0
98582	.4	0	.2	88	25.0	202	55.2	5	12	.0	0	0	.0
98583	.3	80	.1	80	24.5	264	62.3	8	0	.1	0	0	.0
98584	19.6	94	6.9	75	25.5	319	89.3	7	11	9.4	10	1	.5
98585	.4	91	.1	92	25.6	294*	98.8	9	15	.4	15	0	.0
98586	2.3	94	.9	78	24.5	279	68.3	8	15	1.1	13	0	.0
98587	.9	0	.3	88	20.9	220	96.2	9	4	.0	0	0	.0
98588	.6	0	.3	88	20.9	180	93.0	10	17	.0	0	0	.0
98589	4.7	86	1.6	79	26.8	303	90.0	10	8	2.3	7	0	.0
98590	.2	86	.1	56	17.4	290	69.3	5	22	.0	0	0	3.7
98591	2.6	98	.8	82	26.4	330	82.3	9	10	1.3	10	0	.0
98592	.9	95	.4	85	25.7	313	136.9	7	29	.4	31	0	.0
98593	.7	0	.3	77	17.7	286	53.5	12	20	.0	0	0	.0
98595	3.1	98	1.4	72	22.1	276	86.4	7	15	1.5	15	0	.0
98596	5.0	96	1.7	77	23.6	258	70.2	9	11	2.3	11	0	.0
98597	6.8	96	2.3	78	24.8	307	87.8	9	7	3.2	7	0	.0

PORTLAND

ZIP CODE	1	2	3	4	5	6	7	8	9	10	11	12	13
98601	1.5	98	.5	80	23.7	301	87.1	10	7	.8	6	0	.0
98603	.5	100	.2	64	22.8	361	113.2	9	4	.3	4	0	.0
98604	11.2	98	3.4	83	30.8	315	126.3	9	9	5.5	7	0	.0
98605	1.1	95	.4	63	23.3	263	66.6	5	16	.5	16	0	.1
98606	4.7	97	1.4	87	32.3	366	140.8	10	6	2.3	5	0	.0
98607	10.7	96	3.8	74	29.3	320	106.0	8	11	5.1	9	0	3.7
98610	2.5	97	.9	70	29.3	291	87.5	9	9	2.2	8	0	.0
98611	7.6	97	2.7	79	27.9	290	94.9	8	10	3.8	10	0	.0
98612	2.5	97	.9	79	29.2	262	81.0	6	16	1.2	13	0	1.7
98613	.5	0	.1	83	25.7	282	29.5	12	7	.0	0	0	.0
98614	.6	0	.3	61	23.0	253	66.2	5	17	.0	0	0	.0
98617	.7	82	.2	83	26.0	132	81.2	12	10	.3	14	0	.0
98619	.6	92	.2	64	27.0	287	82.0	11	14	.5	18	0	.0
98620	5.6	93	2.0	71	24.4	279	77.3	8	12	2.6	11	1	1.7
98621	.3	0	.1	69	59.1	351	78.1	9	8	.3	8	0	.0
98622	.2	100	.1	100	38.1	438*	135.3	0	4	.1	7	0	.0
98624	1.1	98	.4	72	32.6	282	91.3	6	19	.5	18	0	8.0
98625	3.3	98	1.2	79	32.6	281	99.0	8	10	1.7	8	2	8.0

WASHINGTON

PORTLAND

ZIP CODE	1	2	3	4	5	6	7	8	9	10	11	12	13
98626	19.5	97	7.3	68	25.3	288	86.9	8	11	9.5	10	2	.1
98628	.5	100	.6	76	25.8	256	45.7	12	13	.3	16	0	.0
98629	2.7	98	.9	84	27.7	320	99.1	10	7	1.4	6	0	.0
98631	2.1	97	.9	70	22.9	237	93.7	6	26	1.0	24	0	1.0
98632	42.3	96	16.1	63	28.1	321	99.2	8	11	19.8	10	10	1.0
98635	1.1	96	.4	73	24.4	213	64.2	7	12	.5	12	0	.0
98637	.2	100	.1	91	32.4	372*	90.3	10	16	.7	11	0	.0
98638	1.4	95	.5	75	28.7	208	83.7	10	12	.7	13	0	.0
98639	.8	0	.2	0	22.5	383	110.2	8	15	.0	0	0	.0
98640	1.5	98	.7	83	21.2	213	82.7	3	24	.7	27	0	.0
98642	7.4	98	2.4	82	31.7	357	128.4	8	9	3.8	10	1	.3
98643	.4	0	.2	72	28.3	264	79.2	8	12	.0	0	0	.0
98644	.5	0	.2	67	32.1	235	84.8	8	15	.0	0	0	.0
98645	1.0	99	.3	87	30.2	427	104.4	9	2	.5	2	0	.0
98647	.4	93	.2	77	26.0	258	69.2	8	11	.2	17	0	.0
98648	2.5	99	.9	68	30.7	301	103.7	9	10	1.3	9	0	.0
98649	.8	92	.3	68	29.1	359	94.6	12	4	.4	6	0	.0
98650	.8	97	.3	64	27.1	195	57.2	8	15	.4	15	0	.0
98651	.6	98	.2	89	29.0	158	131.7	8	14	.5	2	0	.0
98660	9.6	94	4.5	46	18.4	260	78.2	7	17	4.3	17	2	4.3
98661	26.4	95	11.1	47	25.0	336	106.5	7	12	12.0	10	3	.3
98662	31.9	96	10.2	73	28.9	470	103.6	11	5	15.6	5	1	.0
98663	11.6	97	4.7	64	24.7	338	95.3	8	14	5.3	10	0	.1
98664	31.9	95	11.0	70	31.1	423	117.3	9	7	15.0	6	0	.0
98665	30.4	97	10.8	73	31.1	369	126.4	7	14	14.5	7	2	.0
98671	9.1	98	3.4	74	28.6	300	101.3	8	11	4.4	10	2	.1
98672	4.2	96	1.5	67	26.6	280	87.7	8	13	2.0	12	0	.0
98673	.5	83	.2	39	22.8	185	51.8	9	5	.2	6	0	.0
98674	6.1	98	2.1	72	29.2	312	106.2	8	12	3.0	12	0	.0
98675	2.2	96	.7	85	24.5	288	99.3	10	8	1.1	8	0	.0

WENATCHEE

ZIP CODE	1	2	3	4	5	6	7	8	9	10	11	12	13
98801	41.2	97	15.8	68	26.4	318	96.6	7	14	19.5	12	10	.5
98812	3.0	90	1.1	67	23.0	188	80.0	9	16	1.4	14	1	.0
98813	1.7	91	.6	72	25.4	169	57.7	8	15	.8	16	0	.8
98814	.3	100	.1	79	20.1	249	69.4	13	9	.1	10	0	.0
98815	5.3	98	2.0	71	25.8	273	87.8	8	15	2.6	13	1	.0
98816	4.7	95	1.9	62	22.4	259	108.3	8	16	2.2	16	1	.2
98817	.1	100	.1	82	22.6	273	80.9	8	18	.1	15	0	.0
98819	.1	96	.1	79	16.6	107	70.5	4	29	.1	30	0	.0
98821	.4	0	.2	79	20.2	331	83.2	3	21	.0	0	0	.0
98822	1.2	0	.4	69	24.0	183	75.5	10	9	.4	10	0	.1
98823	6.9	97	2.7	73	24.5	221	65.2	8	14	3.2	14	2	.2
98824	.4	0	.1	64	24.6	282	66.1	13	8	.0	0	0	.0
98826	4.0	99	1.6	74	23.1	266	100.8	6	14	2.0	12	0	.0
98827	.4	0	.2	76	23.1	318	67.4	11	16	.0	0	0	.0
98828	.9	0	.3	80	30.3	256	86.3	5	4	.0	0	0	.0
98829	.6	59	.2	68	19.4	61	56.7	8	3	.2	6	0	.0
98830	.6	99	.2	75	15.5	198	56.1	5	18	.3	12	0	.0
98831	1.6	98	.7	70	23.1	281	125.0	6	16	.7	18	0	.0

*=Estimated **1.0=883 lbs per person; 100++ indicates per capita toxic waste generation > than 100 times the U.S. average of 883 lbs per capita.

ZIP CODE MEASURES OF SIZE, LEVELS OF AFFLUENCE AND QUALITY OF LIFE

1=Population (th.); 2= % White; 3=Households (th.); 4=% Owner Occupied; 5=Mean Income Per Household (th.$); 6=Mean Monthly Rent ($); 7=Mean Home Value (th.$);
8=% under 5; 9=% 65 and over; 10=% White Males; 11=% White Males, 65+; 12=# Toxic Waste Sites; 13=Toxic Waste Relative to US(883 lbs.per capita)**.

WASHINGTON

ZIPCODE	1	2	3	4	5	6	7	8	9	10	11	12	13
WENATCHEE													
98832	.3	0	.1	80	27.2	39	26.4	3	11	.0	0	0	.0
98834	.3	100	.1	69	22.2	198	107.6	7	8	.1	0	5	.0
98836	.5	97	.2	62	25.7	188	90.5	10	21	.2	19	0	.0
98837	22.0	87	7.5	66	23.3	238	80.9	9	8	9.7	8	0	.2
98840	4.1	94	1.5	70	22.7	240	76.3	9	15	1.9	13	2	.0
98841	7.0	83	2.6	46	24.6	259	79.7	9	12	2.9	12	0	.0
98843	.8	98	.3	46	23.0	204	131.5	13	5	.4	2	0	.0
98844	3.6	95	1.4	67	19.2	206	77.7	8	16	1.7	16	2	.0
98846	.9	94	.4	60	24.4	225	69.4	4	15	1.5	14	0	.0
98847	1.1	94	.4	59	28.8	223	90.4	9	8	.5	8	0	.0
98849	6.3	92	2.1	67	24.4	241	70.7	10	9	2.9	10	2	.0
98850	.5	0	.2	88	24.4	235	68.2	4	10	.0	0	0	.0
98851	.5	96	.2	74	18.0	475	64.4	15	0	.2	1	0	.0
98855	2.7	97	1.1	69	19.5	133	63.6	6	22	1.3	22	0	5.2
98856	3.7	99	1.3	75	22.4	248	75.2	7	13	1.8	12	0	.0
98857	1.9	99	.8	73	18.0	248	71.9	8	15	1.0	15	1	.0
98858	2.7	77	.8	66	21.1	210	66.7	13	5	1.0	7	0	.0
98859	1.3	99	.5	78	19.9	174	67.1	7	15	.6	12	0	.0
98860	.5	89	.1	69	16.3	86	58.1*10		3	.2	5	0	.0
98862	.3	0	.1	64	21.8	192	51.2	2	8	.0	0	0	.0
98863	1.2	99	.5	68	20.7	245	70.5	7	9	.6	9	0	.0
TAKIMA													
98901	19.7	80	7.8	52	20.6	267	75.1	9	12	7.6	13	5	.7
98902	36.7	94	14.9	62	22.7	318	76.9	7	16	16.3	14	4	.1
98903	10.8	94	4.1	76	22.7	326	72.6	8	14	4.9	15	0	.8
98904	.1	100	.1	80	20.9	360	46.8	0	20	.1	25	0	.0
98908	22.7	97	8.1	73	33.5	401	128.0	7	9	10.7	9	0	.0
98921	.4	60	.1	72	18.0	193	27.9	10	14	.1	16	0	.0
98922	2.7	98	1.1	71	19.2	243	61.8	6	19	1.4	18	1	.1
98923	.2	85	.3	74	27.2	192	68.1	9	14	.3	16	0	.0
98925	.2	100	.1	75	25.3	291*	52.4	10	19	.1	12	1	.0
98926	19.0	97	7.2	54	23.6	276	88.5	6	11	9.0	10	3	.0
98930	10.6	77	3.5	72	23.6	299	79.1	10	12	3.9	14	0	.0
98932	3.3	65	1.0	67	19.8	257	57.5	11	11	1.0	14	0	.0
98933	.8	72	.3	60	26.1	300	54.9	15	7	.3	9	0	.1
98934	.9	0	.3	69	21.3	225	60.4	12	10	.3	0	0	.0
98935	3.3	54	1.0	64	19.0	261	52.7	13	10	.9	15	1	.0
98936	2.6	90	.8	82	27.1	320	81.5	10	8	.6	8	0	.0
98937	3.2	97	1.2	72	25.4	256	73.0	5	13	1.6	12	0	.0
98938	1.5	77	.5	80	18.1	165	64.5	11	8	.6	7	0	.0
98939	.3	88	.1	78	21.8	353	33.0	0	13	.1	13	0	.0
98940	.8	0	.1	75	16.1	327	29.7	8	22	.1	8	0	.0
98941	.8	97	.4	81	26.2	287	61.0	4	23	.4	19	0	.0
98942	12.7	97	4.2	77	28.5	312	107.3	8	8	.6	1	0	.0
98943	.5	0	.2	89	25.7	277	61.9	7	9	.0	0	0	.0
98944	14.4	74	4.9	65	24.4	291	78.8	10	11	5.2	12	2	.0
98946	.5	93	.2	78	34.5	218	43.7	7	4	.2	10	1	.0
98947	2.0	95	.7	71	24.9	251	73.2	9	13	.9	13	0	.0
98948	10.6	62	3.4	63	21.1	270	60.0	11	11	3.2	14	0	.0

WASHINGTON

ZIPCODE	1	2	3	4	5	6	7	8	9	10	11	12	13
TAKIMA													
98951	10.6	50	3.2	62	26.4	213	61.2	10	11	2.6	14	0	.0
98952	2.1	33	.5	66	23.0	201	77.7	9	5	.5	5	0	.0
98953	4.3	90	1.5	72	28.3	229	76.6	7	12	1.9	12	0	.1
SPOKANE													
99001	1.7	90	.7	57	18.3	262	59.2	10	3	.8	2	0	.0
99003	3.1	98	1.0	93	29.8	348	121.0	10	5	1.5	5	0	.0
99004	11.2	94	3.7	56	22.5	288	98.5	6	5	5.3	5	0	.0
99005	2.9	97	.9	89	31.1	368	156.5	5	6	1.5	6	0	.0
99006	6.2	99	2.0	81	25.1	255	84.5	7	10	3.0	11	0	.0
99008	.4	0	.1	56	33.4	260	70.3	10	9	.0	0	0	.0
99009	2.0	100	.6	89	26.3	214	77.2	5	7	1.1	7	0	.0
99010	.3	0	.1	94	29.8	342*144.5		3	3	.0	0	1	.0
99011	5.4	84	1.3	1	17.1	324	91.9	16	0	2.6	0	0	.0
99012	1.1	99	.4	65	26.9	270	70.3	9	23	.5	18	1	.0
99013	.7	59	.2	80	21.6	242	51.1	13	8	.2	10	0	.8
99014	.3	59	.1	88	23.2	193	90.0	7	5	.0	0	0	.0
99016	5.2	99	1.8	79	25.2	353	96.8	8	14	2.4	11	1	.0
99017	.2	0	.2	68	28.6	165	30.3	4	12	.0	0	1	.0
99018	.2	97	.1	78	21.4	107	36.6	5	20	.1	19	1	.0
99020	1.0	99	.6	83	39.0	402	155.9	5	6	.8	7	0	.0
99021	4.4	97	1.4	89	26.8	293	98.6	11	7	2.2	7	2	.0
99022	5.9	93	1.7	71	25.9	313	89.3	6	9	2.9	5	0	.0
99023	.3	0	.1	82	34.5	260	60.7	6	6	.0	0	0	.0
99025	2.9	99	.9	92	26.4	364	89.1	14	3	1.5	3	0	.0
99026	4.0	98	1.3	89	31.6	452	129.3	10	6	1.9	6	0	.0
99027	4.7	97	1.5	89	25.3	377	107.1	11	7	2.4	7	0	.0
99029	1.0	98	.4	78	24.1	241	67.4	6	15	.4	15	1	.1
99030	.8	98	.3	84	24.1	275	61.9	9	13	.4	10	0	.0
99031	2.0	99	.8	70	34.1	337	73.7	8	7	.5	9	2	.0
99032	.8	96	.3	67	22.4	202	39.6	8	16	.4	11	1	.0
99033	1.0	97	.3	79	21.1	247	56.2	6	21	.5	21	1	.0
99036	.9	98	.3	94	30.0	267	108.3	5	10	.4	11	0	.0
99037	7.1	97	2.2	83	34.7	346	114.6	10	4	3.4	4	0	.0
99040	.8	18	.2	62	27.1	107	60.4	14	3	.0	0	0	1.6
SPOKANE													
99101	1.0	99	.3	70	21.7	240	69.8	12	8	.5	9	1	.0
99102	.3	0	.1	74	25.5	288	91.2	13	6	.0	0	0	7.0
99103	.6	0	.2	66	24.5	231	61.7	8	13	.0	0	0	.0
99105	.1	100	.1	69	24.0	276*	13.1	0	25	.1	25	0	.0
99107	.2	100	.1	50	19.9	260	70.9*	4	10	.0	0	0	.0
99109	3.6	97	1.4	76	21.3	267	66.7	9	16	1.7	16	1	.0
99110	.8	100	.3	90	21.3	426	36.1	5	12	.4	13	0	.0
99111	3.9	99	1.6	66	26.5	247	71.6	7	20	1.9	17	0	.0
99113	.7	0	.3	75	23.9	253	85.0	10	14	.0	0	0	.0
99114	10.0	98	3.5	76	24.0	289	91.3	9	11	4.7	10	1	.1
99115	.9	93	.2	72	22.8	184	55.9	5	14	.5	12	1	.0
99116	1.8	92	.6	75	28.4	306	55.5	9	11	.8	12	0	.0
99117	.6	0	.2	71	30.5	144	55.5	7	7	.0	0	0	.0

*-=Estimated **1.0=883 lbs per person; 100++ indicates per capita toxic waste generation > than 100 times the U.S. average of 883 lbs per capita.

ZIP CODE MEASURES OF SIZE, LEVELS OF AFFLUENCE AND QUALITY OF LIFE

1=Population (th.); 2= % White; 3=Households (th.); 4=% Owner Occupied; 5=Mean Income Per Household (th.$); 6=Mean Monthly Rent ($); 7=Mean Home Value (th.$); 8=% under 5; 9=% 65 and over; 10=% White Males (th.); 11=% White Males, 65+; 12=# Toxic Waste Sites; 13=Toxic Waste Relative to US(883 lbs.per capita)**.

WASHINGTON

SPOKANE

ZIPCODE	1	2	3	4	5	6	7	8	9	10	11	12	13
99118	.5	0	.2	78	19.3	92	57.2	12	6	.0	0	0	.0
99119	.5	100	.1	84	17.2	252	45.3	5	6	.0	5	0	.1
99122	2.6	98	1.0	73	27.8	272	70.3	7	22	1.3	19	0	.0
99123	.9	93	.4	80	27.3	247	75.9	9	8	.4	7	0	.0
99124	.4	88	.1	83	30.4	313	82.2	11	14	.2	13	0	.0
99125	.5	0	.2	71	28.2	136	43.3	10	21	.0	0	1	.0
99126	.5	93	.1	87	16.0	291	65.1	4	0	.2	0	0	.4
99128	.3	100	.1	69	28.3	317	37.0	4	18	.2	17	0	.0
99129	.5	77	.2	86	23.1	238	89.3	3	3	.2	5	0	.0
99130	.9	0	.4	67	24.1	152	63.0	10	18	.0	0	0	1.1
99133	1.9	95	.8	72	21.0	183	60.7	8	14	.9	14	0	.1
99134	.7	100	.3	66	30.9	265	56.9	5	16	.3	16	0	.0
99135	.2	100	.1	73	26.2	121	47.7	8	17	.1	18	0	.0
99137	.4	0	.1	78	14.9	56	51.1	7	23	.0	0	0	.3
99138	1.1	51	.4	72	21.6	187	78.6	14	12	.3	12	0	.0
99139	1.3	98	.4	79	24.9	231	63.5	10	6	.7	6	0	.0
99140	.4	31	.1	59	18.3	223	79.2	15	6	.0	0	0	.5
99141	3.6	95	1.3	74	21.0	265	65.3	12	8	1.8	8	0	.0
99143	.9	100	.3	59	28.9	209	41.3	8	14	.4	14	0	.0
99149	1.1	97	.4	83	24.8	338	94.9	10	10	.5	11	0	.0
99150	.2	100	.2	90	14.8	170*	44.5	9	27	.1	30	0	.0
99152	.2	0	.2	76	21.3	80	45.9	5	0	.0	0	0	.0
99153	.2	0	.1	89	22.6	260*	47.3	5	23	.0	0	0	.0
99155	6	15	.3	63	19.0	81	50.6	6	20	1.2	18	1	5.9
99156	1.3	15	.3	63	19.8	191	58.5	13	5	1.1	11	0	.4
99157	4.7	99	1.7	77	17.5	236	69.6	9	13	2.3	12	0	.2
99158	.4	0	.1	79	17.5	129	42.8	7	20	.0	0	0	1.7
99159	.7	0	.3	72	24.6	199	62.1	5	19	.0	0	0	.0
99161	1.6	99	.6	77	25.7	221	59.6	5	21	.8	18	1	.0
99163	25.4	97	7.6	73	24.9	254	67.5	10	9	12.3	8	3	.0
99166	2.5	92	.9	36	21.3	340	118.1	4	11	1.2	8	0	.2
99167	2.6	97	.6	73	23.4	235	72.9	8	8	.0	9	0	.0
99170	1.1	0	1.1	86	18.7	203	100.6	11	10	1.2	11	1	.0
99171	1.2	98	.7	70	26.1	210	61.2	6	20	1.2	10	0	.4
99173	.8	100	.5	72	26.4	233	62.3	3	19	.6	18	1	.0
99174	.3	89	.4	73	30.5	196	57.9	6	16	.6	14	0	.0
99176	.5	100	.3	84	22.4	191	67.4	9	11	.4	14	0	.0
99179	.9	100	.1	65	15.6	217	33.7	11	23	.1	9	0	.0
99180	.5	100	.1	82	46.1	530*	63.5	6	15	.2	18	0	.0
99181	.9	84	.3	77	24.6	174	57.8	3	11	.3	10	0	.0
99185	1.3	0	.3	80	20.4	236	63.2	8	11	.3	4	26	.0

SPOKANE

ZIPCODE	1	2	3	4	5	6	7	8	9	10	11	12	13
99201	9.9	91	4.9	31	13.4	222	62.9	8	20	4.3	17	1	.1
99202	16.7	87	7.4	51	18.0	289	62.5	8	17	6.8	15	5	.8
99203	35.9	98	13.5	80	35.6	378	116.2	7	13	16.7	11	1	.0
99204	21.7	94	10.6	34	19.6	246	102.1	6	19	9.5	15	1	.1
99205	26.1	95	10.9	71	22.0	334	70.6	7	17	11.6	16	0	.0

WASHINGTON

SPOKANE

ZIPCODE	1	2	3	4	5	6	7	8	9	10	11	12	13
99206	44.6	98	16.8	71	27.2	326	96.0	7	10	21.3	8	3	.1
99207	44.7	95	17.6	65	20.2	344	63.2	8	14	20.3	12	9	.8
99208	41.1	97	14.7	80	29.0	382	94.1	7	8	19.1	8	0	.0
99216	17.8	97	6.0	74	29.0	374	95.2	8	8	8.4	7	4	.3
99218	11.1	98	3.7	73	35.3	366	134.0	7	6	5.2	5	0	.0

PASCO

ZIPCODE	1	2	3	4	5	6	7	8	9	10	11	12	13
99301	31.7	87	10.9	64	29.1	345	105.2	11	8	13.9	7	4	.0
99320	4.6	96	1.5	82	31.9	328	96.8	9	4	2.4	4	1	.0
99321	.2	100	.1	73	31.8	115	52.3	8	8	.1	14	0	.0
99323	.5	94	.2	80	27.5	258	92.0	5	12	.3	12	0	.1
99324	6.0	90	2.0	53	21.6	292	88.3	6	13	2.5	12	0	.0
99326	2.8	85	.9	65	26.0	293	69.8	13	5	1.2	7	0	.2
99328	3.6	98	1.4	75	22.1	227	61.7	6	19	1.7	16	0	.0
99329	.3	100	.1	100	26.0	299*	53.6	0	2	.1	4	0	.0
99330	.6	97	.6	87	27.7	262	81.7	9	7	.1	9	0	.0
99335	.5	99	.2	54	21.9	303	62.9	10	17	.3	16	0	.5
99336	55.6	96	20.0	66	32.3	386	112.7	10	5	27.0	5	7	.4
99341	.2	99	.4	61	27.4	229	60.1	8	11	.5	8	0	.0
99342	.2	0	.5	67	27.1	407	180.4	9	3	.0	5	0	.0
99343	1.5	92	.5	72	18.2	199	81.2	11	5	.8	5	0	.1
99344	10.7	84	3.3	68	25.6	267	86.7	12	6	4.5	6	0	.0
99345	.3	72	.1	49	20.9	332	120.4	15	1	.3	0	0	.0
99347	2.6	99	1.0	70	24.7	215	59.9	8	17	1.3	15	1	.0
99348	1.0	91	.3	42	21.8	250	60.8	14	8	.5	11	0	.4
99350	8.6	84	2.9	71	27.5	300	86.7	9	10	3.6	11	1	.1
99352	39.2	95	14.5	67	35.3	447	119.9	7	8	18.7	7	3	3.0
99356	.3	100	.5	49	30.0	242	60.3	12	13	.1	6	0	.0
99357	1.7	91	.5	68	26.0	215	30.6	12	7	.8	4	1	.0
99359	.3	96	.1	62	21.8	266	81.6	4	11	.4	8	0	.2
99360	.8	95	.3	63	28.8	382	81.6	4	11	.4	8	0	.2
99361	1.5	99	.6	70	23.7	288	71.0	7	18	.7	17	0	.1
99362	34.6	92	12.7	64	25.4	319	89.7	7	15	15.9	13	0	.0
99371	.4	100	.2	62	22.7	208	37.8	9	15	.7	13	0	.0

LEWISTON

ZIPCODE	1	2	3	4	5	6	7	8	9	10	11	12	13
99402	1.3	99	.5	77	24.6	293	83.6	10	10	.7	10	0	.0
99403	15.4	99	5.9	67	23.9	303	81.2	8	15	7.2	13	1	.0

*=Estimated **1.0=883 lbs per person; 100++ indicates per capita toxic waste generation > than 100 times the U.S. average of 883 lbs per capita.

ZIP CODE MEASURES OF SIZE, LEVELS OF AFFLUENCE AND QUALITY OF LIFE

1=Population (th.); 2= % White; 3=Households (th.); 4=% Owner Occupied; 5=Mean Income Per Household (th.$); 6=Mean Monthly Rent ($)*; 7=Mean Home Value (th.$)*;
8=% under 5; 9=% 65 and over; 10=White Males (th.); 11=% White Males, 65+; 12=# Toxic Waste Sites; 13=Toxic Waste Relative to US(883 lbs.per capita)**

WEST VIRGINIA

ZIPCODE	1	2	3	4	5	6	7	8	9	10	11	12	13
WASHINGTON													
15349	.2	100	.1	86	27.1	311*	87.2	8	0	.1	0	0	.0
15376	1.2	100	.4	83	22.5	334	90.4	8	11	.7	12	0	.0
CUMBERLAND													
21550	.2	100	.1	76	18.4	146	57.9	9	17	.1	10	0	.0
ROANOKE													
24093	.1	0	.1	100	18.3	210*	42.7	3	5	.0	0	0	.0
BLUEFIELD													
24604	.2	64	.1	89	20.1	231*	33.7	7	14	.1	11	0	.0
24619	.2	100	.1	78	19.5	128	19.1	7	18	.1	8	0	.0
BLUEFIELD													
24701	27.6	87	10.1	74	24.7	264	75.2	7	15	11.3	11	2	.2
24712	2.8	95	.8	62	22.0	219	85.6	6	8	1.3	6	0	.0
24715	.9	100	.1	100	18.0	207*	91.9	12	13	.1	24	0	.0
24716	.9	88	.3	73	21.0	255	43.0	8	16	.4	11	0	.0
24719	.5	100	.1	67	19.9	226	41.7	7	6	.2	4	0	.0
24721	.3	72	.1	100	24.0	276*	37.1	4	8	.1	12	0	.0
24722	.2	100	.1	100	18.3	210*	43.9	0	0	.1	0	0	.0
24724	.2	100	.1	74	23.8	225	46.1	5	12	.1	10	0	.0
24726	.9	78	.3	83	15.8	225	34.1	7	15	.3	10	0	.0
24727	.3	100	.1	86	22.6	251	39.7	12	4	.5	2	0	.0
24729	.2	100	.1	62	19.4	140	64.5	5	2	.2	0	0	.0
24731	.7	85	.2	92	14.1	162*	17.3	16	5	.1	0	0	.0
24733	.3	0	.1	84	20.6	281	51.4	10	11	.3	1	0	.0
24735	1.2	100	.2	92	20.8	254	40.7	9	5	.5	11	0	.0
24736	2.5	99	.8	71	13.7	157	34.7	10	12	.8	11	0	.0
24737	1.4	96	.4	80	18.6	160	34.7	9	11	1.2	5	0	.0
24738	.2	100	.1	91	15.7	257	36.7	9	11	.1	7	0	.0
24739	.3	100	.1	59	14.3	181*	34.9	0	5	.1	11	0	.0
24740	28.8	96	10.7	75	23.9	265	81.8	8	13	13.1	11	0	.0
24747	3.1	99	1.0	87	19.5	260	56.6	8	10	1.6	8	0	.0
24751	.1	37	.1	100	8.0	91*	31.7	16	33	.0	39	0	.0
BLUEFIELD													
24801	5.9	88	2.3	66	26.0	223	64.4	6	12	2.5	10	0	.0
24807	.2	41	.1	89	19.1	219*	30.9	9	9	.0	19	0	.0
24808	1.3	81	.4	75	20.6	132	29.9	10	12	.5	13	0	.0
24811	1.1	100	.3	81	19.4	145	27.8	8	4	.5	5	0	.0
24813	.7	0	.2	86	17.8	307	27.1	8	7	.0	0	0	.0
24815	.9	93	.2	86	18.6	261	26.8	13	10	.4	10	0	.0
24816	.5	87	.1	87	20.6	165	32.2	10	7	.3	7	0	.0
24817	1.7	100	.6	66	16.6	232	35.1	9	8	.8	5	0	.0
24818	1.6	100	.5	75	18.8	148	59.4	9	10	.8	8	0	.0
24819	.5	61	.1	90	14.3	164*	17.3	4	11	.0	14	0	.0
24820	.5	83	.1	63	14.7	235	19.8	12	13	.2	9	0	.0
24821	.8	84	.2	97	23.3	268*	28.9	10	8	.3	7	0	.0
24822	1.0	100	.3	86	21.7	253	63.8	10	15	.5	18	0	.0
24823	.6	100	.1	91	21.1	148	43.5	10	13	.4	8	0	.0
24824	1.2	84	.4	90	21.6	171	32.1	10	13	.4	8	0	.0
24825	.6	89	.2	97	17.7	203*	26.5	13	6	.3	4	0	.0

WEST VIRGINIA

ZIPCODE	1	2	3	4	5	6	7	8	9	10	11	12	13
BLUEFIELD													
24826	.2	100	.1	63	18.1	132	30.4	3	16	.1	23	0	.0
24827	1.9	100	.6	77	23.4	169	60.9	14	4	1.0	5	0	.0
24828	1.6	95	.5	63	18.3	196	32.1	8	11	.7	10	0	.0
24829	.6	36	.6	81	18.0	296	18.0	11	9	.1	10	0	.0
24830	.4	83	.1	98	30.2	346*	40.9	3	8	.1	5	0	.0
24831	.6	46	.2	86	18.7	231	29.5	6	16	.2	11	0	.0
24832	.6	0	.2	69	12.5	236	29.4	10	5	.0	0	0	.0
24834	.6	100	.2	97	26.4	304*	64.9	7	7	.3	8	0	.0
24836	1.4	68	.5	83	25.7	239	48.2	10	12	.3	5	0	.0
24839	1.6	100	.5	83	19.9	279	68.6	7	7	.8	6	0	.0
24841	.4	75	.1	80	17.4	234	35.6	10	9	.1	7	0	.0
24842	.8	66	.2	80	14.3	191	21.5	14	9	.2	9	0	.0
24843	.3	100	.1	78	17.4	151	47.5	5	13	.1	11	0	.0
24844	5.1	99	1.6	79	21.4	218	46.1	9	7	2.5	7	0	.0
24845	.5	100	.1	82	15.2	83	39.3	11	9	.3	3	0	.0
24847	.6	100	.2	96	29.1	335*	49.1	9	3	.3	4	0	.0
24848	.7	74	.2	92	18.2	194	16.3	6	10	.3	5	0	.0
24849	.4	100	.1	76	21.0	264	86.5	12	14	.2	17	0	.0
24850	2.2	0	.6	78	18.2	197	30.4	12	5	.0	0	1	.0
24851	.9	0	.3	78	21.1	256	51.1	8	9	.5	5	0	.0
24852	1.2	63	.4	60	17.3	170	35.0	11	20	.4	18	0	.0
24853	2.1	62	.7	68	20.3	208	35.1	6	12	.6	6	0	.0
24854	1.0	0	.3	87	27.2	330	54.8	11	5	.4	0	0	.0
24856	.3	100	.1	87	19.3	65	23.5	0	10	.2	11	0	.0
24857	1.0	100	.3	77	19.8	239	59.0	13	5	.5	6	0	.0
24858	.5	40	.1	69	19.0	342	22.2	18	8	.1	5	0	.0
24859	.5	100	.1	82	22.7	187	64.9	5	5	.2	5	0	.0
24860	.9	100	.3	87	20.4	230	61.9	15	8	.4	7	0	.0
24861	.7	70	.2	98	18.4	211*	27.3	7	10	.4	0	0	.0
24862	.9	100	.3	77	16.4	171	34.7	8	9	.4	6	0	.0
24866	.6	0	.1	87	18.1	287	26.2	6	20	.0	0	0	.0
24867	.7	100	.2	72	22.7	281	42.3	14	7	.3	5	0	.0
24868	1.2	60	.5	81	19.5	145	35.4	7	18	.4	19	0	.0
24869	.5	100	.5	72	22.4	271	68.9	16	2	.2	0	0	.0
24870	4.1	0	1.4	80	23.9	274	72.7	9	7	2.5	10	0	.0
24871	.4	78	.4	86	18.8	276	47.0	5	14	.1	13	0	.0
24872	1.7	0	.7	75	15.4	180	25.4	12	4	.5	5	0	.0
24873	.7	100	.2	80	21.2	132	47.0	4	4	.4	0	0	.0
24874	4.0	99	1.4	79	27.8	228	71.9	6	9	1.9	8	0	.0
24877	.3	0	.3	86	19.8	220	34.9	7	11	.0	7	0	.0
24878	.3	100	.1	92	24.6	288	25.0	17	8	.3	5	0	.0
24879	1.3	100	.4	81	18.4	205	30.5	8	7	.6	8	0	.0
24880	.4	100	.4	79	37.2	293	76.0	8	2	.3	14	0	.0
24881	1.3	97	.4	72	18.8	238	38.0	11	7	.6	9	0	.0
24882	1.2	95	.3	56	21.6	200	47.1	15	6	.6	6	0	.0
24883	.3	0	.3	68	22.8	152	47.9	0	9	.0	4	0	.0
24884	.7	96	.2	83	19.0	141	33.0	6	18	.3	13	0	.0
24886	.2	79	.1	54	21.9	300	67.8	22	6	.1	8	0	.0
24887	.3	73	.3	94	11.5	132*	21.9	22	17	.1	15	0	.0

*=Estimated **1.0=883 lbs per person; 100 indicates per capita toxic waste generation > than 100 times the U.S. average of 883 lbs per capita.

PAGE 2.333

ZIP CODE MEASURES OF SIZE, LEVELS OF AFFLUENCE AND QUALITY OF LIFE

1=Population (th.); 2=% White; 3=Households (th.); 4=% Owner Occupied; 5=Mean Income Per Household (th.$); 6=Mean Monthly Rent ($); 7=Mean Home Value (th.$); 8=% under 5; 9=% 65 and over; 10=White Males (th.); 11=% White Males, 65+; 12=# Toxic Waste Sites; 13=Toxic Waste Relative to US(883 lbs.per capita)**.

WEST VIRGINIA

BLUEFIELD

ZIP CODE	1	2	3	4	5	6	7	8	9	10	11	12	13
24888	.5	63	.2	86	26.0	279	43.7	10	8	.2	7	0	.0
24889	.3	100	.1	78	18.1	145	19.8	19	4	.2	5	0	.0
24890	.2	80	.1	79	23.6	240	36.5	7	18	.1	10	0	.0
24891	.2	53	.1	85	15.5	263	19.6	10	15	.1	0	0	.0
24892	2.2	93	.7	70	16.0	199	32.1	10	12	1.0	9	0	.1
24894	.5	0	.1	76	19.2	203	26.9	10	12	.0	0	0	.0
24895	.3	75	.1	68	20.8	151	32.5	7	7	.1	4	0	.0
24897	.3	63	.1	85	15.6	259	20.7	15	11	.1	0	0	.0
24898	.3	0	.1	100	22.9	263*	43.2	7	4	.0	0	0	.0
24899	.6	77	.2	72	23.6	292	30.9	14	7	.2	3	0	.0

LEWISBURG

ZIP CODE	1	2	3	4	5	6	7	8	9	10	11	12	13
24901	7.3	94	2.7	72	25.5	292	102.5	7	16	3.1	13	1	.2
24902	.6	100	.3	69	22.3	273	86.1	3	14	.3	8	0	.0
24910	4.8	82	1.4	81	18.4	251	61.4	5	15	1.9	17	0	.0
24915	.5	100	.1	87	22.5	176	72.0	6	11	.2	9	0	.0
24916	.4	100	.1	60	18.3	210*	64.4	13	6	.2	3	0	.0
24917	.1	100	.1	67	13.7	158*	78.8	0	4	.1	6	0	.0
24918	1.5	98	.5	83	17.3	167	67.4	7	13	.8	11	0	.0
24920	.4	0	.1	68	22.6	269	59.3	11	15	.0	0	0	.0
24923	.3	100	.1	87	14.1	162*	46.3	11	13	.1	16	0	.2
24924	.6	100	.1	78	25.7	210	53.8	6	15	.3	23	0	.0
24925	.9	95	.3	87	18.9	271	56.2	17	17	.4	13	0	.0
24927	.3	0	.1	77	24.1	229	38.8	7	23	.1	0	0	.0
24928	1.1	100	.3	85	19.5	28	62.5	5	11	.5	13	0	.5
24930	.2	100	.1	100	8.4	97*	30.9	4	10	.1	6	0	.1
24931	.4	100	.1	89	17.4	139	60.2	10	8	.2	6	0	.0
24933	.2	100	.1	91	13.1	150*	60.5	0	17	.1	14	0	.0
24934	.5	0	.2	80	17.8	169	45.2	7	22	.0	0	0	.0
24935	.4	100	.2	94	17.4	200*	61.0	3	28	.2	26	0	.0
24936	.2	100	.1	81	25.1	116	68.1	11	35	.1	29	0	.5
24937	.2	100	.1	42	16.7	267	25.2	6	8	.1	9	0	1.8
24938	1.4	100	.4	84	23.5	327	73.3	9	9	.7	7	0	.0
24941	.7	95	.3	86	18.4	129	65.1	10	8	.3	6	0	.0
24942	.1	100	.1	100	15.0	173*	41.6	5	30	.1	24	0	.0
24944	.6	100	.2	78	21.6	317	76.4	6	17	.3	22	0	.0
24945	.8	100	.3	79	15.9	216	34.2	9	10	.4	9	0	.0
24946	1.2	0	.4	79	15.3	173	62.8	6	30	.1	0	0	.1
24951	1.2	93	.4	87	15.9	248	56.2	9	11	.5	8	0	.0
24954	4.0	99	1.4	73	21.7	248	56.0	7	14	2.0	11	2	.1
24957	.3	100	.1	76	19.7	89	50.1	6	18	.2	16	0	.0
24959	.2	100	.1	79	15.7	180*	17.9	14	11	.1	15	0	.0
24960	.2	0	.1	79	17.7	536	57.8	10	17	.0	0	0	.0
24961	.2	100	.1	88	24.4	280*	73.0	3	16	.1	10	0	.0
24962	.4	93	.1	96	20.9	241*	73.0	4	18	.2	2	0	.3
24963	2.8	100	1.0	84	20.1	181	72.5	11	11	1.4	10	0	.0
24964	.3	100	.1	78	20.0	342	65.1	11	20	.2	15	0	.0
24966	1.3	0	.4	69	14.0	205	53.0	9	15	.0	0	0	.0
24970	4.7	95	1.6	78	19.9	269	67.4	7	16	2.2	12	2	.2
24974	.2	100	.1	89	22.3	256*	56.7	15	4	.1	7	0	.0

WEST VIRGINIA

LEWISBURG

ZIP CODE	1	2	3	4	5	6	7	8	9	10	11	12	13
24976	.7	100	.2	85	19.8	201	68.3	6	10	.4	13	0	.0
24977	.3	100	.1	68	16.2	357	48.9	10	25	.1	30	0	.0
24979	.2	100	.1	88	16.6	191*	41.6	3	8	.1	12	0	.0
24981	.4	77	.2	73	18.5	183	50.4	11	10	.2	13	0	.0
24983	2.3	99	.9	82	20.0	228	63.5	7	18	1.1	15	0	.0
24985	.3	0	.1	100	16.1	186*	42.9	0	25	.0	0	0	.0
24986	6.3	90	2.3	68	22.1	259	70.3	7	10	2.8	9	1	.0
24991	.5	100	.2	86	20.0	192	54.8	5	25	.2	25	0	.0

CHARLESTON

ZIP CODE	1	2	3	4	5	6	7	8	9	10	11	12	13
25003	.2	100	.6	70	24.6	257	92.2	9	24	.1	23	1	17.3
25004	1.7	100	.6	90	23.5	233	79.8	6	11	.8	11	0	.0
25005	.4	100	.1	60	19.1	249	41.0	9	14	.1	11	0	.0
25007	.8	100	.2	72	23.8	186	47.6	11	13	.4	13	0	.0
25008	.3	100	.1	79	17.3	206	36.2	16	9	.2	11	0	.0
25009	1.8	0	.6	74	22.5	201	52.6	4	7	.0	0	1	.0
25010	.5	100	.1	83	23.1	251	64.0	4	4	.2	3	0	.5
25011	.9	0	.3	79	19.3	228	61.3	7	9	.1	0	0	.0
25012	.2	100	.1	91	23.5	270*	46.3	3	3	.1	5	0	.0
25013	.8	100	.1	39	30.2	153	45.2	13	2	.4	0	0	.0
25014	.2	65	.2	79	15.0	377	29.4	0	9	.1	9	0	.0
25015	5.0	100	1.8	70	27.6	315	78.3	7	12	2.3	12	4	100++ 29.3
25018	.5	100	.4	74	12.8	175	37.6	7	7	.3	10	0	.0
25019	.6	100	.1	74	16.3	165	50.5	13	9	.3	8	0	.1
25021	.4	100	.1	82	26.9	239	57.6	8	11	.2	12	0	.0
25022	.7	98	.4	86	21.6	152	48.8	13	12	.3	10	0	.0
25024	.5	100	.2	60	20.3	214	46.0	9	10	.3	6	0	.0
25025	.4	100	.1	79	28.8	260	63.1	10	7	.2	7	0	.0
25028	.6	100	.2	74	27.5	222	59.1	9	6	.3	4	0	.1
25030	.5	100	.1	67	13.5	145	17.5	8	11	.2	12	0	.0
25031	1.0	80	.4	79	20.4	258	72.1	5	18	.4	18	0	.0
25033	2.0	0	.7	76	20.8	245	65.0	9	11	.3	6	0	.0
25035	2.0	99	.8	72	23.5	195	57.0	9	13	1.0	13	2	.0
25036	.9	87	.3	76	22.2	252	50.5	4	9	.4	5	0	.0
25037	.3	100	.1	68	28.6	239	32.6	20	4	.2	8	0	.1
25039	1.8	97	.6	58	23.0	224	61.3	8	12	.3	10	0	.0
25040	.6	100	.2	90	28.0	125	105.2	6	13	.3	7	0	.0
25043	2.3	100	.8	58	18.7	239	61.6	10	17	1.1	14	1	.0
25044	.4	100	.2	90	20.2	72	53.5	11	8	.2	5	0	.0
25045	6.3	99	2.1	76	20.9	215	67.4	7	13	3.1	12	0	.0
25046	.3	100	.1	91	15.8	181*	34.7	14	9	.1	6	0	.0
25047	.7	92	.2	81	20.5	227	43.6	7	9	.3	4	0	.0
25048	.6	100	.2	81	21.4	330	47.9	8	12	.3	11	0	.0
25049	.9	100	.3	68	23.8	262	49.2	8	8	.5	7	0	.0
25050	.2	100	.1	77	24.7	242	90.6	4	3	.1	0	0	.0
25051	.2	100	.1	92	21.5	246*	55.9	15	14	.1	11	0	.0
25052	.4	100	.1	31	24.6	225	33.5	9	7	.2	9	0	.0
25053	3.7	100	1.2	71	24.7	278	72.8	10	7	.0	0	0	.0

*=Estimated **1.0=883 lbs per person; 100++ indicates per capita toxic waste generation > than 100 times the U.S. average of 883 lbs per capita.

ZIP CODE MEASURES OF SIZE, LEVELS OF AFFLUENCE AND QUALITY OF LIFE

1=Population (th.); 2= % White; 3=Households (th.); 4=% Owner Occupied; 5=Mean Income Per Household (th.$); 6=Mean Monthly Rent ($)*; 7=Mean Home Value (th.$)*; 8=% under 5; 9=% 65 and over; 10=White Males (th.); 11=% White Males, 65+; 12=# Toxic Waste Sites; 13=Toxic Waste Relative to US(883 lbs.per capita)**.

WEST VIRGINIA

CHARLESTON

ZIP CODE	1	2	3	4	5	6	7	8	9	10	11	12	13
25054	.9	94	.3	76	23.9	122	44.3	4	13	.4	12	0	.0
25057	.6	74	.2	86	23.3	86	41.6	12	18	.2	22	0	.0
25059	.6	100	.2	77	26.1	162	49.9	16	5	.3	2	0	.0
25060	.5	100	.2	89	28.6	339	51.4	17	10	.3	8	0	11.3
25061	1.2	100	.4	62	16.6	208	42.9	11	13	.6	10	0	.0
25062	.5	100	.1	80	25.3	192	32.9	6	6	.3	8	0	.0
25063	.8	100	.2	71	20.4	158	75.5	7	8	.4	6	0	.0
25064	11.9	90	4.8	67	25.7	328	85.2	7	13	5.1	10	0	.0
25067	1.3	100	.4	77	25.9	290	78.5	8	10	.6	9	0	.0
25070	1.5	100	.5	84	26.2	313	86.7	8	10	.7	10	0	.1
25071	10.0	100	3.4	82	26.0	301	87.5	8	9	4.9	8	1	.0
25075	.2	100	.1	50	25.3	221	22.0	7	3	.0	1	0	.0
25076	.4	0	.1	35	27.5	311	97.5	8	6	.0	0	0	.0
25079	.3	100	.1	74	14.4	268	47.1	4	21	.1	14	1	.0
25080	.3	100	.1	89	28.3	325*	32.8	11	0	.2	0	0	.0
25081	1.0	100	.3	79	32.0	370	95.1	9	9	.4	7	0	.0
25082	.7	0	.2	82	28.5	418	92.2	7	6	.0	0	0	.0
25085	.8	85	.2	78	21.2	236	46.2	11	12	.3	6	0	.0
25086	1.6	100	.6	62	21.2	240	80.6	8	16	.8	13	0	.0
25088	1.3	100	.5	71	23.9	188*	13.1	5	15	.1	33	0	.0
25090	.2	100	.1	83	27.1	218	65.2	15	21	.1	22	0	.0
25093	.4	0	.1	90	19.4	250	48.6	4	17	.0	0	0	.0

CHARLESTON

ZIP CODE	1	2	3	4	5	6	7	8	9	10	11	12	13
25102	.6	93	.2	71	20.8	202	36.1	9	13	.3	6	0	.0
25103	.6	0	.2	70	22.8	199	66.8	12	9	.1	9	0	.0
25105	.3	100	.1	74	12.5	153	46.2	10	12	.1	9	0	.0
25106	1.0	99	.3	71	18.1	261	41.2	14	7	.5	5	0	.0
25107	1.0	100	.4	61	20.5	226	45.8	10	11	.6	13	0	.0
25108	1.2	0	.4	77	21.7	188	51.6	10	10	.0	0	0	.0
25109	1.0	100	.3	91	23.5	164	66.3	9	9	.5	8	0	.0
25110	.8	100	.3	68	22.8	196	50.1	11	8	.4	8	0	.0
25111	.7	100	.2	71	13.9	157	42.2	9	9	.3	10	0	.0
25112	1.5	27	.4	50	23.3	339	99.9	5	10	.2	5	0	.5
25113	.9	100	.3	83	14.9	254	59.4	7	16	.5	14	0	.0
25114	.7	100	.2	68	16.8	203	46.7	6	9	.4	8	0	.0
25115	.2	100	.1	41	13.6	273	56.7	10	19	.1	13	0	.0
25116	.2	100	.1	44	34.8	206	51.4	7	0	.1	0	0	.0
25118	.8	84	.3	81	22.9	231	47.9	5	10	.2	5	0	.0
25119	.7	89	.3	73	14.8	254	38.6	7	14	.4	11	0	.0
25121	.9	100	.3	77	19.7	164	75.1	6	6	.5	9	0	.0
25122	.7	100	.2	81	23.9	205	44.3	6	9	.4	9	0	.0
25123	2.0	100	.7	90	20.5	137	60.5	9	13	1.0	12	0	.0
25124	1.3	100	.4	91	17.8	204*	67.7	7	14	.7	14	0	.0
25125	.9	0	.3	83	16.4	189*	38.9	10	15	.0	0	0	.0
25126	.6	79	.2	57	21.3	289	57.6	6	13	.3	6	0	.0
25127	.2	79	.1	78	27.1	125	70.1	2	12	.1	14	0	.0
25130	4.8	93	1.7	70	27.1	287	86.1	8	11	2.2	8	1	.1
25132	.6	0	.2	90	23.4	223	27.6	5	14	.0	0	0	.0

WEST VIRGINIA

CHARLESTON

ZIP CODE	1	2	3	4	5	6	7	8	9	10	11	12	13
25133	.9	100	.3	70	17.3	188	48.7	9	5	.5	5	0	.0
25134	.6	100	.2	63	21.9	229	48.9	14	9	.2	6	0	.0
25135	.3	100	.1	84	32.6	101	24.6	2	13	.1	18	0	.0
25136	4.0	80	1.1	51	22.9	263	75.4	6	9	1.8	6	1	.3
25139	.5	0	.1	76	27.2	443	95.8	11	3	.0	0	0	.0
25140	1.1	100	.4	81	19.6	170	36.7	10	9	.5	7	0	.0
25142	.8	100	.2	89	18.7	326	38.6	8	18	.2	15	0	.0
25143	13.0	98	4.7	74	27.0	389	88.1	8	9	6.1	8	14	14.6
25147	.3	0	.1	95	21.2	244*	29.8	7	20	.0	0	0	.0
25148	.5	94	.2	82	24.3	125	50.6	11	6	.2	0	0	.0
25149	.3	100	.1	67	19.8	243	45.5	7	15	.2	7	0	.0
25152	.2	100	.1	70	15.8	182*	62.8	9	11	.1	9	0	.0
25154	.8	100	.3	76	23.5	250	77.7	18	14	.3	18	0	.0
25156	.8	100	.3	89	37.4	263	95.5	3	11	.3	16	0	.0
25158	.7	100	.2	75	18.9	401	63.7	12	11	.3	9	0	.0
25159	4.4	100	1.4	85	25.5	245	88.2	8	8	2.2	8	5	.0
25160	.4	0	.1	80	18.5	279	27.7	6	20	.0	0	0	.0
25161	1.4	90	.4	80	21.1	230	45.3	11	12	.6	10	0	.0
25162	.8	100	.3	72	30.6	352	91.5	8	11	.4	7	0	.0
25163	.4	100	.1	49	23.0	213	49.3	11	5	.1	3	0	.0
25164	1.0	100	.3	76	16.3	157	33.7	9	7	.5	9	0	.0
25165	.5	100	.2	64	33.4	221	90.7	13	12	.3	13	0	.0
25166	.5	100	.2	85	23.9	383	84.6	9	6	.2	5	0	.0
25168	1.6	100	.5	92	24.2	239	78.6	7	13	.8	13	0	1.2
25169	.7	100	.3	67	18.7	201	40.3	12	11	.3	6	0	.0
25172	.9	100	.3	76	17.3	201	53.9	12	4	.5	5	0	.0
25173	.3	0	.1	100	21.7	249*	41.5	8	18	.6	6	0	.0
25174	.5	100	.2	72	27.1	206	53.1	8	6	.3	2	0	.0
25177	28.3	97	10.2	79	28.7	345	90.9	8	10	13.4	3	0	.0
25180	.2	100	.1	52	18.3	155	81.5	14	9	.1	0	0	.0
25181	2.1	0	.7	76	25.7	214	67.0	7	13	.0	0	0	.0
25182	.3	100	.1	96	19.6	225*	37.2	3	13	.1	12	0	.0
25183	.7	0	.2	93	21.5	126	43.1	7	10	.2	9	5	.0
25184	.8	100	.3	77	26.3	260	70.4	6	9	.4	11	0	.0
25186	1.5	91	.5	43	21.8	246	66.7	8	11	.6	8	0	.0
25187	.7	100	.2	80	20.7	484	58.6	7	11	.4	11	0	.0
25189	.2	100	.1	39	17.0	166	51.4	4	23	.1	19	1	.0
25193	.6	100	.2	75	23.6	293	81.3	10	16	.3	17	0	.0

CHARLESTON

ZIP CODE	1	2	3	4	5	6	7	8	9	10	11	12	13
25201	.4	100	.1	57	15.2	213	46.7	15	14	.2	12	0	.0
25202	.9	100	.3	89	28.5	395	82.9	13	5	.4	3	0	.0
25204	.4	100	.1	78	20.0	190	43.0	12	15	.2	17	0	.0
25205	.6	100	.2	88	29.4	252	84.1	5	8	.3	4	0	.0
25206	1.0	100	.3	80	27.9	245	51.7	10	9	.5	9	0	.0
25208	.2	100	.1	36	26.5	164	60.8	8	4	.1	0	0	.0
25209	2.0	100	.7	65	22.9	223	51.2	3	14	1.0	11	0	.0
25211	.2	100	.1	77	11.8	147	17.5	3	21	.1	18	0	.0
25213	3.6	0	1.3	88	28.4	239	114.0	8	7	.0	0	0	.0

*=Estimated **1.0=883 lbs per person; 100++ indicates per capita toxic waste generation > than 100 times the U.S. average of 883 lbs per capita.

ZIP CODE MEASURES OF SIZE, LEVELS OF AFFLUENCE AND QUALITY OF LIFE

1=Population (th.); 2= % White; 3=Households (th.); 4=% Owner Occupied; 5=Mean Income Per Household (th.$); 6=Mean Monthly Rent ($)*; 7=Mean Home Value (th.$)*; 8=% under 5; 9=% 65 and over; 10=% White Males (th.); 11=% White Males, 65+; 12=# Toxic Waste Sites; 13=Toxic Waste Relative to US(883 lbs.per capita)**.

WEST VIRGINIA

CHARLESTON

ZIPCODE	1	2	3	4	5	6	7	8	9	10	11	12	13
25214	1.0	100	.3	79	23.0	203	55.0	8	6	.5	5	0	.0
25234	.7	100	.3	81	15.5	159	56.5	5	20	.4	23	0	.0
25235	.9	100	.3	78	14.0	188	48.8	11	4	.4	3	0	.0
25237	.2	100	.1	88	19.1	231	48.9	3	17	.1	11	0	.3
25239	1.4	0	.5	74	26.0	275	71.1	9	9	.0	0	0	.0
25241	1.2	0	.4	92	23.4	271	91.1	8	8	.0	0	0	.0
25244	.4	100	.1	75	20.4	285	61.8	4	13	.2	16	0	.0
25245	.7	100	.2	85	21.6	383	26.3	2	16	.4	16	0	.0
25246	.6	100	.2	83	26.0	453	115.0	7	5	.3	6	0	.0
25247	.6	100	.2	81	16.9	113	55.6	16	15	.3	16	0	.0
25248	2.2	100	.2	81	18.8	243	39.2	4	14	.3	14	0	.0
25249	.3	100	.7	86	19.7	225	65.7	7	9	1.1	9	1	.0
25251	.4	100	.1	94	15.2	174*	19.1	9	21	.2	14	0	.0
25252	.4	100	.1	82	15.0	182	13.1	12	21	.2	23	0	.0
25253	2.0	100	.7	89	17.5	405	67.3	17	8	1.0	9	0	.0
25255	.2	100	.2	88	25.0	223	55.0	7	14	.1	13	1	.0
25257	.6	100	.2	58	12.0	137*	13.1	10	12	.1	12	0	.0
25259	.5	99	.5	80	23.4	383	49.0	12	6	.3	6	0	.0
25260	1.9	99	.7	80	25.7	128	21.1	7	10	1.0	8	1	.1
25261	.5	100	.5	81	18.5	292	60.1	7	10	.2	17	0	.0
25262	.7	100	.7	83	34.1	338	50.0	9	20	.4	4	0	.0
25263	.3	100	.3	92	12.6	221	92.4	5	4	.1	16	0	.0
25264	.4	100	.4	88	22.9	128	21.9	2	15	.3	9	0	.5
25265	1.8	0	.6	84	26.4	162	62.6	13	9	.2	13	3	.8
25266	.5	100	.2	80	18.8	244	70.6	10	10	.3	10	0	.0
25267	.4	100	.1	72	18.0	131	63.0	6	12	.1	21	0	.0
25268	.3	100	.1	67	12.0	77	47.4	8	12	.2	19	0	.0
25270	1.1	100	.4	90	23.2	286	57.2	8	12	.6	12	0	.7
25271	6.8	0	2.4	90	25.6	320	92.3	8	12	.0	28	1	.0
25274	.2	100	.7	76	12.8	143	45.5*	7	22	.1	11	7	.0
25275	2.1	100	.7	87	21.7	292	78.6	9	11	1.0	11	7	75.1
25276	8.8	99	3.1	84	19.3	226	65.9	9	15	4.1	14	3	.1
25279	.3	100	.1	73	15.8	335	51.0	5	4	.2	4	0	.5
25280	.3	100	.1	85	11.0	87	45.0	10	31	.2	32	0	.2
25283	.4	100	.1	61	16.2	331	56.6	6	11	.2	11	0	.0
25285	.4	100	.4	74	13.7	179	73.4	9	10	.2	8	0	.0
25286	1.8	0	.6	84	17.0	188	58.0	9	13	.2	4	0	.0
25287	.7	100	.3	85	19.8	188	44.5	11	8	.3	5	0	.0

CHARLESTON

ZIPCODE	1	2	3	4	5	6	7	8	9	10	11	12	13
25301	4.6	63	2.4	90	16.2	245	68.3	4	28	1.2	23	1	.7
25302	20.1	94	8.4	76	25.8	323	87.7	6	18	8.5	14	0	.0
25303	9.5	94	3.8	87	31.0	351	108.8	6	11	4.1	11	7	75.1
25304	9.9	91	3.9	84	32.0	370	118.1	5	20	4.0	18	3	.1
25306	8.8	90	3.2	76	23.1	325	60.6	7	11	3.8	10	1	.2
25309	13.6	96	5.1	70	26.5	335	91.3	8	12	6.2	10	4	.0
25311	11.8	85	5.1	48	22.8	305	88.3	7	15	4.5	11	0	.0
25312	27.5	91	9.6	70	25.0	300	87.1	8	9	12.4	8	4	.0
25314	17.6	95	6.4	76	42.7	428	153.1	11	8	8.2	8	2	.0

WEST VIRGINIA

CHARLESTON

ZIPCODE	1	2	3	4	5	6	7	8	9	10	11	12	13
25315	5.0	93	1.9	64	24.5	308	67.2	6	12	2.2	11	1	.0
25320	6.4	100	2.0	83	26.4	332	87.4	9	7	3.3	6	0	.0

MARTINSBURG

ZIPCODE	1	2	3	4	5	6	7	8	9	10	11	12	13
25401	31.2	95	11.2	68	24.0	272	79.3	7	13	14.3	11	4	3.4
25410	.3	0	.1	87	28.2	274	138.0	4	10	3.7	0	0	1.0
25411	7.6	100	2.8	82	22.9	265	73.6	6	14	1.4	12	0	.0
25413	2.9	97	.9	85	26.3	284	80.3	7	7	3.6	11	0	.2
25414	8.7	88	3.0	70	24.1	288	92.6	9	12	3.6	11	0	.0
25419	2.4	0	.2	89	26.0	280	83.0	9	6	.0	0	0	.0
25420	1.3	100	.4	67	19.3	322	63.4	9	9	.7	9	0	.0
25421	.4	100	.1	78	19.5	401	66.8	11	8	.3	8	0	.0
25422	1.1	100	.3	73	39.1	229	48.4	11	6	.5	5	0	.0
25423	.3	100	.1	62	29.3	255	84.5	4	2	.0	0	0	3.8
25425	5.8	94	2.0	80	24.8	303	89.0	5	8	2.8	8	0	.0
25427	5.0	99	1.7	86	24.7	201	82.2	9	8	2.5	8	0	.0
25428	3.7	98	1.2	85	25.1	325	88.6	7	7	1.8	8	0	.0
25430	5.0	90	1.5	86	24.3	335	76.6	9	7	2.2	7	0	.0
25431	.4	100	.1	52	23.4	216	31.4	9	10	.1	9	0	.0
25434	1.8	95	.4	78	15.1	260	41.2	7	16	.8	14	0	.0
25437	.5	0	.1	73	20.9	183	39.2	11	12	.5	11	0	.0
25438	3.5	91	1.3	74	22.5	240*	34.7	10	13	1.6	11	0	.0
25441	.3	79	.1	83	28.0	281	66.4	6	21	.1	26	0	.0
25442	1.0	94	.3	77	23.7	260	66.1	9	11	.5	12	0	.0
25443	4.7	92	1.4	70	28.4	327	55.6	5	8	2.1	8	0	.8
25444	.3	100	.1	85	15.0	324	107.6	6	13	.2	19	0	.0
25446	.8	81	.3	55	27.0	173*	51.7	10	9	.3	7	0	.0

HUNTINGTON

ZIPCODE	1	2	3	4	5	6	7	8	9	10	11	12	13
25501	1.3	100	.4	78	17.1	344	63.4	9	9	.6	10	0	53.1
25502	1.1	100	.4	86	22.5	240	57.0	9	11	.5	9	0	.0
25503	.3	100	.1	89	16.8	258*	56.3	12	5	1.1	7	0	.0
25504	11.4	100	3.9	77	25.3	193*	68.3	9	9	5.6	7	1	.1
25505	.8	100	.2	77	14.3	315	87.1	15	3	.4	3	0	.0
25506	4.8	100	1.4	74	18.1	239	58.1	9	10	2.3	10	0	.5
25507	2.1	99	.7	62	26.9	220	50.5	8	10	1.0	8	0	.0
25508	6.4	99	2.1	80	21.9	326	83.5	10	8	3.3	8	0	.0
25509	.3	0	.1	60	19.7	287	76.7	14	6	.3	6	0	.0
25510	4.1	100	1.3	87	24.8	403	37.0	15	8	.0	8	0	.0
25511	1.1	100	.4	72	21.8	167	91.5	8	11	.5	10	0	.0
25512	1.8	100	.5	69	17.7	200	45.5	13	11	.9	9	0	.0
25513	.7	100	.2	94	16.5	252	53.8	9	11	.4	11	0	.0
25514	3.8	100	1.3	73	15.9	219	39.7	8	14	1.8	14	0	.0
25515	2.2	0	.8	77	21.8	236	52.6	5	7	.0	10	1	28.4
25517	1.5	0	.5	85	11.8	147	56.5	9	7	.0	7	0	.0
25520	1.8	100	.6	77	17.8	176	41.0	9	9	.9	8	0	.0
25521	1.0	100	.4	71	16.4	193	53.5	6	12	.5	11	0	.0
25523	2.5	0	.9	75	23.4	246	64.9	7	14	.0	14	0	.0
25524	2.7	100	.8	80	17.0	215	37.0	10	8	1.4	8	0	.0
25526	12.1	100	4.1	85	27.9	336	97.6	8	10	6.0	9	1	.1

*=Estimated **1.0=883 lbs per person; 100++ indicates per capita toxic waste generation > than 100 times the U.S. average of 883 lbs per capita.

ZIP CODE MEASURES OF SIZE, LEVELS OF AFFLUENCE AND QUALITY OF LIFE

1=Population (th.); 2= % White; 3=Households (th.); 4=% Owner Occupied; 5=Mean Income Per Household (th.$); 6=Mean Monthly Rent ($); 7=Mean Home Value (th.$)*;
8=% under 5; 9=% 65 and over; 10=White Males (th.); 11=% White Males, 65+; 12=# Toxic Waste Sites; 13=Toxic Waste Relative to US(883 lbs.per capita)**.

WEST VIRGINIA

HUNTINGTON

ZIPCODE	1	2	3	4	5	6	7	8	9	10	11	12	13
25529	.9	100	.3	71	20.4	211	43.4	10	12	.4	13	0	.0
25530	7.4	99	2.7	74	23.3	279	75.2	6	11	3.6	10	3	11.8
25535	2.5	100	.9	89	23.9	309	86.3	7	7	1.3	7	0	.0
25536	.4	100	.1	77	16.0	299	13.1	9	16	.2	14	0	.0
25537	2.2	100	.8	83	21.0	165	75.4	6	11	1.1	9	0	.0
25540	.5	100	.1	79	22.4	285	42.5	12	4	.2	3	0	.0
25541	8.9	99	3.0	79	24.2	294	93.0	7	12	4.4	10	0	.0
25542	.4	100	.1	74	22.5	239	50.1	7	4	.2	4	0	.0
25545	3.5	0	.1	90	27.3	270	93.6	10	8	.0	0	0	.0
25546	.2	100	.1	37	18.6*	214*	66.3*	6	6	.1	7	0	.0
25547	1.4	0	.4	66	19.0	248	67.9	9	9	.0	0	0	.0
25550	9.5	99	3.5	74	25.2	236	83.9	7	13	4.4	10	5	1.7
25555	1.9	100	.6	83	21.8	210	68.6	10	13	1.0	12	0	.0
25556	.1	100	.1	84	12.7	110	22.8	12	12	.2	17	0	.0
25557	2.2	100	.7	77	17.0	228	40.8	9	11	.7	13	0	.0
25559	2.1	0	.7	82	22.0	244	76.7	7	10	.0	0	0	.0
25560	4.0	100	1.3	90	32.6	398	136.3	7	7	1.9	6	0	.0
25561	.6	100	.1	91	17.0	233	51.2	9	6	.3	5	0	.0
25562	.2	100	.1	81	21.0	408	96.0	8	24	.1	12	0	.0
25563	.4	100	.1	64	13.2	101	30.2	8	8	.2	13	0	.0
25564	1.4	100	.5	80	21.0	240	52.7	8	9	.8	11	0	.0
25565	.5	100	.2	80	12.8	168	24.1	15	6	.3	3	0	.0
25567	.6	100	.2	87	19.9	119	40.8	3	11	.3	7	0	.0
25568	.2	100	.1	44	18.0	217	64.5	12	10	.1	2	0	.0
25570	6.3	100	2.1	77	23.1	252	74.8	7	11	3.2	10	0	.0
25571	2.7	0	.9	71	18.3	243	61.0	8	12	.0	1	0	.0
25572	.2	100	.1	65	12.8	178	85.5	11	18	.1	16	0	.0
25573	.9	100	.3	87	22.7	89	56.8	6	11	.5	10	0	.0

HUNTINGTON

ZIPCODE	1	2	3	4	5	6	7	8	9	10	11	12	13
25601	7.6	93	2.8	60	26.8	255	82.6	8	13	3.4	10	0	.2
25606	.8	95	.3	75	21.3	203	45.9	18	8	.4	8	0	.0
25607	.8	90	.3	81	21.8	232	52.1	15	5	.3	2	0	.0
25608	.5	0	.1	88	18.7	180	44.9	11	3	.0	0	0	.0
25609	.5	95	.2	90	24.7	267	59.9	8	12	.2	6	0	.0
25611	.9	100	.3	73	24.3	139	47.3	9	9	.5	9	0	.0
25612	.4	0	.1	81	34.9	245	105.9	7	9	.0	0	0	.0
25614	.4	34	.1	63	19.5	267	49.8	8	10	.0	1	0	.0
25616	.4	85	.1	84	19.2	195	34.6	17	7	.2	2	0	.0
25617	1.9	98	.6	80	25.2	256	74.0	10	7	.9	4	0	.0
25618	.4	90	.1	5	27.2	254	96.9*	8	6	.2	4	0	.0
25619	.7	0	.2	42	24.7	203	42.0	8	8	.1	7	0	.0
25621	3.2	100	1.0	74	29.1	256	74.1	11	6	1.7	5	0	.0
25623	.4	100	.1	83	25.4	94	70.4	7	4	.2	7	0	.0
25624	.8	0	.2	84	25.7	263	45.3	12	5	.0	0	0	.0
25625	2.6	90	.9	82	24.7	257	52.9	7	12	1.1	11	0	.1
25628	.8	87	.3	83	38.5	245	47.3	6	11	.3	7	0	.0
25629	.2	0	.1	88	22.0	278*	37.1	7	11	.0	0	0	.0
25630	.8	0	.2	85	22.1	282	44.5	10	6	.0	0	0	.0
25631	.5	0	.1	75	20.7	261	26.9	14	7	.0	0	0	.0

WEST VIRGINIA

HUNTINGTON

ZIPCODE	1	2	3	4	5	6	7	8	9	10	11	12	13
25632	.3	100	.1	51	16.5	142	40.2	12	19	.2	14	0	.0
25633	.5	100	.2	83	28.5	325	67.0	7	12	.3	9	0	.0
25634	2.8	90	.3	75	23.8	239	62.3	10	13	.3	9	0	.0
25635	2.8	99	.9	65	26.5	275	72.8	9	9	1.4	8	1	.1
25636	.7	0	.2	72	29.0	224	59.1	10	6	.0	0	0	.0
25637	2.4	96	.7	61	15.2	227	54.2	10	9	1.1	8	0	.0
25638	1.4	88	.5	77	21.6	209	49.3	6	11	.6	9	0	.0
25639	.9	0	.3	77	20.6	270	67.4	7	14	.0	0	0	.0
25642	.3	100	.1	95	21.6	248*	84.8	6	2	.1	5	0	.0
25643	.3	100	.1	92	22.4	257*	46.4	8	5	.2	5	0	.0
25644	.3	100	.1	53	20.9	302	53.0	13	9	.2	9	0	.0
25645	.4	77	.1	79	21.9	339	35.5	4	22	.1	13	0	.0
25646	.9	100	.3	72	26.4	240	80.0	9	7	.5	6	0	.0
25647	.9	95	.3	63	19.7	259	53.6	9	12	.4	9	0	.0
25649	1.7	0	.5	76	20.1	230	50.7	7	10	.0	0	0	.0
25650	.4	100	.1	76	24.1	128	68.4	5	5	.6	4	0	.0
25651	1.2	100	.4	81	22.7	239	59.5	8	5	.6	6	0	.0
25652	1.3	86	.4	77	26.8	300	63.3	10	11	.6	10	0	.0
25653	.5	0	.2	63	17.4	267	62.2	12	10	.1	4	0	.0
25654	.7	100	.2	23	24.8	249	56.9	13	4	.4	5	0	.0
25661	7.1	87	2.7	57	22.7	268	77.6	8	13	2.9	11	0	.0
25664	.3	100	.1	72	25.6	506	49.2	19	3	.1	1	0	.0
25665	.5	100	.1	80	20.7	312	69.0	10	4	.1	2	0	.0
25666	.4	100	.1	62	20.5	235*	50.0	5	10	.2	16	0	.0
25667	1.3	100	.4	81	17.9	276	69.1	10	6	.5	4	0	.0
25669	1.7	100	.9	73	16.4	261	39.2	13	5	.9	9	0	.0
25670	5.8	99	1.9	78	19.8	267	48.4	12	10	2.8	9	1	.0
25671	1.8	100	.5	71	16.0	186	42.3	11	3	.9	3	0	.0
25672	.3	100	.1	85	25.1	468	33.6	4	0	.9	0	0	.0
25674	3.7	100	1.2	68	22.8	229	52.6	8	9	1.9	9	0	.0
25676	1.4	100	.4	67	19.4	192	57.7	11	5	.7	6	0	.0
25678	1.1	97	.4	66	20.6	286	64.0	10	8	.5	5	0	.0
25682	.9	100	.3	70	19.7	167	50.6	5	14	.4	11	0	.0
25684	.3	100	.3	68	16.2	262	47.5	7	5	.1	5	0	.0
25685	.9	100	.3	77	19.7	230	50.7	10	6	.5	4	0	.0
25686	.4	0	.1	74	17.7	192	34.4	13	13	.3	17	0	.0
25687	.5	100	.1	77	20.3	174	73.8	14	8	.3	9	0	.0
25688	.6	100	.2	62	24.3	242	35.4	13	9	.3	5	0	.0
25690	.6	100	.2	75	20.2	420	39.6	8	8	.3	14	0	.0
25691	.5	100	.3	79	18.9	281	44.5	10	7	.3	5	0	.0
25692	1.0	85	.3	70	18.2	303	60.7	16	8	.3	6	0	.0
25693	.2	100	.1	69	20.5	183	29.5	8	4	.1	11	0	.0
25694	.3	100	.1	85	17.4	248	29.5	10	13	.2	15	0	.0
25696	.8	100	.2	81	18.0	338	59.9	8	8	.4	10	0	.0

HUNTINGTON

ZIPCODE	1	2	3	4	5	6	7	8	9	10	11	12	13
25701	27.8	91	12.1	54	24.5	290	102.5	5	18	11.5	14	3	.0
25702	11.5	99	4.4	66	20.6	299	67.6	6	17	5.2	13	0	1.1
25703	8.2	81	2.6	40	16.2	291	54.3	5	13	3.1	10	0	.1
25704	18.2	99	6.8	71	23.0	293	75.9	7	13	8.6	10	0	.6

*=Estimated **1.0=883 lbs per person; 100++ indicates per capita toxic waste generation > than 100 times the U.S. average of 883 lbs per capita.

ZIP CODE MEASURES OF SIZE, LEVELS OF AFFLUENCE AND QUALITY OF LIFE

1=Population (th.); 2= % White; 3=Households (th.); 4=% Owner Occupied; 5=Mean Income Per Household (th.$); 6=Mean Monthly Rent ($); 7=Mean Home Value (th.$); 8=% under 5; 9=% 65 and over; 10=White Males (th.); 11=% White Males, 65+; 12=# Toxic Waste Sites; 13=Toxic Waste Relative to US(883 lbs.per capita)**.

WEST VIRGINIA

HUNTINGTON

ZIPCODE	1	2	3	4	5	6	7	8	9	10	11	12	13
25705	23.1	97	8.3	74	28.6	299	101.3	7	11	10.6	9	1	.1

BECKLEY

ZIPCODE	1	2	3	4	5	6	7	8	9	10	11	12	13
25810	35.5	85	13.2	74	25.7	316	88.3	8	15	14.2	11	0	.2
25811	.5	60	.1	61	19.9	311	25.5	7	3	.0	0	0	.0
25812	2.5	97	.9	73	16.6	164	36.9	14	12	1.2	12	0	.0
25813	2.9	96	1.0	79	19.4	303	57.2	8	16	1.4	6	0	.0
25814	.3	0	.1	87	28.2	308	82.5	9	8	.0	0	0	.0
25816	.3	100	.1	67	16.1	338	48.2	21	10	.0	7	0	.0
25817	.6	100	.2	79	25.4	299	72.5	8	12	.3	6	0	.0
25818	1.4	97	.4	69	21.3	245	69.7	8	4	.6	8	0	.0
25820	.2	100	.1	88	24.3	238	72.0	7	11	.1	13	0	.0
25823	2.4	0	.8	100	26.5	304*	41.9	13	11	.0	0	0	.0
25825	1.4	99	.5	80	19.9	266	60.4	10	8	.7	9	0	.0
25826	.6	0	.1	81	20.8	305	87.8	7	9	.8	0	0	.0
25827	3.8	99	1.3	89	21.9	256	52.8	13	13	1.8	10	0	.0
25828	.2	100	.1	86	24.4	296	72.7	10	11	.1	6	0	.0
25830	.2	70	.1	93	22.2	256*	58.6	5	18	.1	0	0	.0
25831	1.1	100	.3	100	25.5	294*	30.6	2	2	.1	7	0	.0
25832	3.3	100	1	79	29.5	317	105.9	8	7	1.6	7	0	.1
25836	1.2	90	.4	90	29.0	333*	40.1	16	0	.5	11	0	.0
25837	.5	0	.1	80	17.4	286	45.2	7	11	.5	11	0	.0
25839	1.5	98	.5	79	21.6	286	32.6	12	8	.0	0	0	.0
25840	7.9	95	2.7	81	22.8	323	64.9	13	11	3.7	12	0	.0
25841	.7	100	.2	83	21.2	260	71.9	7	15	.4	8	0	.0
25843	.5	100	.2	80	21.6	95	53.4	13	8	.4	8	0	.0
25844	1.1	0	.4	83	24.1	301	58.6	6	13	.3	14	0	.0
25845	1.3	100	.3	84	24.1	226	66.7	10	6	.1	0	0	.0
25846	.7	73	.2	79	23.5	324	62.8	13	4	.6	5	0	.0
25847	1.1	0	.4	90	21.5	233	43.6	12	8	.3	5	1	.1
25848	.6	100	.2	70	22.6	270	63.6	9	6	.0	0	0	.0
25849	.7	69	.2	93	18.9	226	40.9	9	13	.3	4	0	.0
25851	.2	100	.1	82	18.4	183	41.6	12	4	.2	7	0	.0
25852	.2	56	.1	77	15.3	313	44.8	7	11	.1	6	0	.0
25853	.5	89	.1	58	20.4	281	42.2	21	6	.2	14	0	.0
25854	.6	0	.2	82	20.1	141	53.5	20	0	.6	6	0	.0
25855	.6	81	.2	66	14.0	219	36.0	17	14	.2	13	0	.0
25856	.3	70	.1	80	21.7	271	56.6	8	9	.2	6	0	.0
25857	.2	100	.1	74	18.3	210	28.0	6	9	.1	8	0	.1
25859	.5	86	.2	85	18.3	226	40.9	9	13	.2	4	0	.0
25860	.5	68	.2	85	16.9	183	49.4	5	6	.2	7	0	.0
25862	.4	100	.1	77	20.1	288	42.2	7	21	.2	6	0	.0
25864	.5	100	.2	66	14.0	219	36.0	17	14	.2	18	0	.0
25865	1.5	80	.5	80	21.7	271	56.6	8	9	.6	6	0	.0
25866	.4	87	.1	91	22.7	188	59.2	5	18	.2	13	0	.0
25867	.3	90	.1	74	16.9	145	49.4	5	6	.3	21	0	.0
25868	.6	100	.2	80	18.6	165	40.1	8	23	.3	21	0	.0
25870	.4	100	.1	81	19.9	165	48.5	12	12	.2	7	0	.0

WEST VIRGINIA

BECKLEY

ZIPCODE	1	2	3	4	5	6	7	8	9	10	11	12	13
25871	1.4	93	.5	77	20.9	295	55.8	8	14	.6	10	0	.0
25873	1.2	0	.4	89	20.6	344	67.3	6	12	.0	0	0	.0
25874	.2	100	.2	78	14.6	168*	52.8	12	24	.1	33	0	.0
25875	.3	100	.1	66	21.5	184	31.1	11	6	.2	6	0	.0
25878	.9	100	.3	90	27.1	278	61.1	9	7	.5	5	0	.0
25879	.8	87	.3	78	12.7	158	29.4	9	19	.3	14	1	.0
25880	5.4	91	1.9	79	20.3	227	58.5	9	13	2.3	9	0	.0
25882	3.0	96	1.1	73	26.6	233	66.4	9	11	1.4	11	0	.0

BECKLEY

ZIPCODE	1	2	3	4	5	6	7	8	9	10	11	12	13
25901	12.4	93	4.5	79	23.0	287	72.6	8	13	5.5	11	0	.4
25902	.4	100	.2	86	18.0	167	38.0	10	14	.2	8	0	.0
25904	.4	0	.2	51	17.2	256	45.7	12	14	.2	8	0	.0
25905	.4	100	.1	76	15.7	183	44.9	8	15	.2	17	0	.0
25906	.7	0	.3	68	17.9	273	54.1	6	12	.0	0	0	.0
25907	.2	100	.1	73	14.8	170*	34.5	3	18	.1	19	0	.0
25908	.7	92	.2	89	16.3	168	36.5	6	20	.4	19	0	.0
25909	.8	0	.2	82	21.3	358	73.9	13	8	.2	9	0	.1
25911	.7	78	.2	84	16.3	269	39.3	8	15	.3	11	0	.0
25912	.6	100	.2	80	16.6	242	51.6	12	14	.3	17	0	.0
25913	.7	100	.2	82	19.2	349	50.4	15	6	.3	9	0	.0
25914	.2	64	.1	100	16.6	190*	23.7	6	26	.1	8	0	.0
25915	.7	87	.2	75	16.9	227	24.5	8	11	.3	8	0	.0
25916	.3	100	.1	89	20.7	203	23.4	11	7	.2	9	0	.0
25917	2.9	90	1.0	83	18.0	260	45.1	10	18	1.3	15	0	.0
25918	2.9	100	.9	84	22.1	284	90.8	10	10	1.4	10	0	.0
25919	.3	0	.1	73	18.7	254	39.9	12	8	.0	6	0	.0
25920	.2	100	.1	43	16.4	223	73.4	9	14	.1	15	0	.0
25921	2.7	98	1.0	76	19.3	294	57.7	8	12	1.3	11	0	.0
25922	.3	100	.1	96	26.7	307*	103.5	2	9	.2	4	0	.0
25926	.1	73	.1	85	18.6	213*	50.7	5	9	.0	9	0	.0
25927	.6	88	.2	87	21.9	347	84.3	4	10	.3	10	0	.0
25928	1.0	100	.3	86	21.7	175	51.6	10	8	.5	6	0	.0
25930	.2	100	.1	100	17.3	199*	32.0	11	13	.1	8	0	.0
25931	.5	70	.2	90	16.2	187*	49.6	10	14	.2	17	0	.0
25932	.3	100	.1	66	22.2	319	58.7	11	21	.1	7	0	.0
25936	.2	95	.1	65	19.3	304	42.1	6	20	.2	16	0	.0
25938	1.1	0	.4	80	18.9	256	46.0	7	11	.0	3	0	.0
25942	.2	0	.1	47	8.2	134	13.1	13	23	.1	11	0	.0
25951	8.2	96	3.0	67	19.1	217	61.8	9	16	3.7	12	1	.0
25957	.2	100	.1	74	11.9	263	52.1	13	11	.1	8	0	.0
25958	.8	100	.3	91	17.6	233	44.3	6	20	.4	20	0	.0
25961	1.0	100	.2	74	20.3	288	30.4	13	8	.5	6	0	.0
25962	4.7	100	1.8	79	18.3	222	56.4	10	17	2.2	13	0	.1
25966	.1	100	.1	90	9.7	111*	65.9	0	37	.1	28	0	.0
25967	.4	100	.2	74	14.8	178	42.1	6	20	.2	16	0	.0
25969	1.0	0	.3	92	24.0	183	75.3	10	8	.0	0	0	.0
25970	.3	0	.1	79	17.8	174	47.0	11	14	.0	0	0	.0
25971	.8	100	.3	77	19.3	116	82.8	9	5	.4	7	0	.0
25972	.5	70	.2	91	19.0	110	22.1	7	6	.2	7	0	.0

*=Estimated **1.0=883 lbs per person; 100++ indicates per capita toxic waste generation > than 100 times the U.S. average of 883 lbs per capita.

103001

ZIP CODE MEASURES OF SIZE, LEVELS OF AFFLUENCE AND QUALITY OF LIFE

1=Population (th.); 2= % White; 3=Households (th.); 4=% Owner Occupied; 5=Mean Income Per Household (th.); 6=Mean Monthly Rent ($)*; 7=Mean Home Value (th.$)*; 8=% under 5; 9=% 65 and over; 10=White Males (th.); 11=% White Males, 65+; 12=# Toxic Waste Sites; 13=Toxic Waste Relative to US(883 lbs.per capita)**.

WEST VIRGINIA

BECKLEY

ZIPCODE	1	2	3	4	5	6	7	8	9	10	11	12	13
25973	.2	100	.1	73	27.4	315*	13.1	19	21	.1	17	0	.0
25975	.4	0	.1	72	17.1	260	30.9	8	4	.0	0	0	.0
25976	1.9	0	.7	79	16.1	197	48.9	5	14	.0	0	1	.0
25977	.3	100	.1	83	25.3	153	46.1	5	21	.1	18	0	.0
25978	.7	0	.2	81	23.5	241	68.8	10	6	.0	0	0	.0
25979	.8	100	.3	69	21.7	293	63.6	7	13	.0	13	0	.0
25981	.8	99	.3	71	20.8	231	45.4	7	18	.4	16	0	.0
25984	1.6	97	.6	79	19.9	269	61.4	8	17	.8	17	0	.0
25985	.7	100	.2	66	15.1	123	42.3	8	8	.3	7	0	.0
25986	.4	0	.2	91	16.2	267	47.3	4	9	.0	0	0	.0
25987	.3	82	.1	68	15.1	77	69.8	5	12	.1	16	0	.0
25988	.2	100	.1	64	14.3	150	65.0	13	4	.1	0	0	.0
25989	.3	0	.1	73	21.5	419	63.2	16	14	.0	0	0	.0

WHEELING

ZIPCODE	1	2	3	4	5	6	7	8	9	10	11	12	13
26003	58.7	97	22.5	65	25.4	268	84.9	6	16	26.3	13	5	.4
26030	1.0	99	.3	81	25.8	301	59.2	10	13	.5	12	0	.4
26031	3.0	97	1.1	69	25.0	192	59.4	7	15	1.4	14	0	.0
26032	1.7	97	.7	61	30.0	272	88.8	3	4	.9	3	1	.0
26033	4.0	0	1.5	77	20.1	161	45.2	8	16	.9	10	0	.0
26034	6.3	99	2.2	76	25.7	258	62.1	8	13	3.0	11	0	.3
26035	3.3	99	1.1	86	29.1	304	74.3	7	8	1.6	8	2	.0
26036	.5	0	.1	97	22.5	258*	63.2	9	6	.0	0	0	.3
26037	8.8	100	3.0	81	27.8	298	77.3	7	10	4.2	8	5	9.8
26038	3.6	98	1.3	83	36.3	384	105.7	7	12	1.6	11	3	.3
26039	1.2	0	.4	86	25.3	192	62.8	10	6	.0	0	0	.0
26040	2.4	0	1.0	76	21.4	259	58.2	5	17	.2	4	1	.0
26041	20.9	99	7.0	76	24.7	267	72.5	7	11	10.2	9	3	6.9
26047	7.9	100	2.6	82	29.0	274	74.7	7	8	3.9	8	0	.0
26050	2.5	100	.9	72	22.7	249	47.1	9	11	1.2	11	3	17.9

PARKERSBURG

ZIPCODE	1	2	3	4	5	6	7	8	9	10	11	12	13
26055	2.5	100	.8	83	27.5	176	71.3	8	8	1.2	8	1	.0
26056	.4	100	.1	94	32.1	369*	83.6	14	2	.2	4	1	.0
26058	.2	100	.1	71	23.8	784	40.4	0	14	.1	12	0	.5
26059	3.5	97	1.2	81	26.1	312	82.1	8	9	1.7	9	0	.0
26060	.6	100	.2	76	22.8	284	64.5	5	12	.3	10	1	.0
26062	27.4	96	10.0	74	32.5	323	86.1	6	13	12.7	11	4	6.6
26070	11.3	99	3.9	78	25.9	275	70.0	7	12	5.5	10	0	.2
26074	1.9	95	.3	51	23.2	291	60.6	3	3	.8	3	0	.0
26075	.6	100	.2	90	22.1	531	42.6	8	15	.3	13	0	.0
26101	56.8	98	21.3	67	23.7	288	73.1	7	14	26.4	11	10	8.3
26105	12.1	99	4.4	78	30.4	317	85.4	7	12	5.7	10	0	.5
26133	1.1	100	.3	86	18.5	170	56.8	8	12	.5	12	0	.0
26134	.7	0	.3	76	24.7	248	70.1	6	11	.0	0	0	.0
26135	.4	100	.2	81	27.3	145	42.7	2	13	.2	12	1	1.3
26136	.7	100	.2	82	16.8	191*	33.7	8	13	.3	15	0	.0
26137	.5	100	.1	94	16.8	193*	30.0	13	7	.3	3	0	.0
26141	.2	100	.1	79	7.0	174	32.1	4	27	.1	25	0	.0
26142	2.3	100	.8	84	21.7	401	64.5	5	12	1.1	9	0	.0
26143	4.8	100	1.6	84	20.8	204	65.3	8	12	2.4	11	0	.0

WEST VIRGINIA

PARKERSBURG

ZIPCODE	1	2	3	4	5	6	7	8	9	10	11	12	13
26145	.2	100	.1	77	11.7	158	21.9	15	27	.1	29	0	.0
26146	.9	100	.3	87	23.1	178	68.8	8	10	.5	9	0	.0
26147	2.6		1.0	67	21.8	213	66.0	8	18	.0	0	1	.0
26148	.1	100	.1	83	14.1	162*	39.1	10	20	.1	16	0	.0
26149	2.6	100	1.0	82	21.6	204	63.9	7	17	1.3	15	0	.0
26150	4.6	0	1.5	89	29.5	237	86.4	9	7	.0	0	0	.0
26151	.6	100	.2	75	17.5	135	76.4	3	23	.4	20	0	.0
26152	.2	100	.1	90	14.0	161*	23.1	8	15	.1	14	0	.0
26153	.5	100	.2	90	22.6	290	124.0	3	18	.3	22	0	.0
26154	.8	100	.3	85	22.7	129	76.5	7	12	.4	11	0	.0
26155	10.7	99	3.7	77	27.7	315	100.3	7	11	5.2	10	1	15.7
26158	.2	100	.1	100	14.2	163*	37.7	3	8	.1	10	0	.0
26159	3.8		1.3	81	25.9	274	76.3	6	11	.0	0	0	.0
26160	.6	95	.2	81	19.4	223*	51.2	7	12	.3	16	0	.0
26161	.5	100	.3	81	14.8	158	63.8	8	8	.2	8	0	.0
26164	7.5	98	2.5	78	29.2	291	86.8	7	9	3.6	7	1	1.3
26167	1.2	100	.4	70	19.8	243	69.3	9	8	.6	9	0	.0
26169	.8	100	.2	84	20.3	161	65.9	12	12	.4	12	0	.0
26170	6.8	99	2.2	77	22.8	243	76.2	7	12	3.3	12	1	2.6
26173	.4	100	1.6	100	17.8	204*	58.3	13	14	2.1	12	0	.0
26175	4.5	100	.3	77	23.6	242	74.1	7	13	2.1	11	0	8.6
26178	.8	100	.3	78	21.1	178	36.9	5	12	.4	13	0	.0
26179	.8	100	.1	100	16.5	189*	39.7	15	18	.1	22	0	.0
26180	2.1	0	.2	89	25.0	227	59.6	6	10	.0	0	0	.0
26181	5.0	100	1.5	90	32.3	291	96.5	8	6	2.5	6	3	.0
26184	2.2	99	.6	83	26.7	250	67.8	8	7	1.0	9	0	.4
26186	.6	100	.2	70	17.0	177	40.8	5	20	.3	18	0	.2
26187	5.6	100	1.9	84	28.4	347	80.8	7	10	2.7			.0

BUCKHANNON

ZIPCODE	1	2	3	4	5	6	7	8	9	10	11	12	13
26201	18.0	99	6.2	74	21.8	282	82.8	7	13	8.5	11	1	.0
26202	.9	100	.3	83	24.1	207	57.1	12	9	.5	7	0	.4
26203	.3	100	.2	70	13.5	159	47.4	6	12	.2	14	0	.2
26205	3.0	100	1.0	85	17.8	177	40.2	4	18	1.5	10	0	.2
26206	3.1	100	1.0	81	17.9	280	77.6	10	11	1.5	12	0	.0
26207	.8	100	.3	89	23.8	284	69.1	8	8	.4	8	0	.0
26208	1.1	100	.4	81	17.1	198	39.3	7	15	.5	15	0	.0
26210	.5	100	.1	61	13.5	368	35.1	7	17	.3	17	0	.0
26214	.2	100	.2	83	18.3	293	28.8	10	9	.1	9	0	.0
26217	.6	100	.6	74	18.4	185	43.6	8	13	.4	12	0	.0
26218	2.3	100	.6	86	16.8	206	62.0	9	10	1.1	10	0	.0
26222	.6	100	.6	60	16.4	159	47.4	9	11	.3	9	0	.0
26224	.3	100	.3	73	17.8	177	40.2	4	18	.2	12	0	.0
26228	.3	100	.1	71	10.2	118*	36.5*	0	6	.2		0	.0
26230	.3	100	.1	75	20.2	68	41.0	6	19	.2	21	0	.0
26234	1.3	100	.5	83	16.4	177	67.1	6	11	.7	10	0	.0
26237	.7	0	.7	76	17.2	199	59.4	9	11	.0	11	0	.0
26238	1.0	100	.3	79	22.9	441	53.4	4	11	.5	11	0	.0
26241	15.3	98	5.4	70	22.2	275	83.7	8	15	7.0	12	2	.0
26250	4.9	99	1.7	80	18.0	256	57.7	8	17	2.4	15	0	.0

*=Estimated **1.0=883 lbs per person; 100+ indicates per capita toxic waste generation > than 100 times the U.S. average of 883 lbs per capita.

ZIP CODE MEASURES OF SIZE, LEVELS OF AFFLUENCE AND QUALITY OF LIFE

1=Population (th.); 2= % White; 3=Households (th.); 4=% Owner Occupied; 5=Mean Income Per Household (th.$); 6=Mean Monthly Rent ($); 7=Mean Home Value (th.$); 8=% under 5; 9=% 65 and over; 10=White Males (th.); 11=% White Males, 65+; 12=# Toxic Waste Sites; 13=Toxic Waste Relative to US(883 lbs.per capita)**.

WEST VIRGINIA

BUCKHANNON

ZIPCODE	1	2	3	4	5	6	7	8	9	10	11	12	13
26253	2.4	99	.8	81	22.5	253	83.3	7	8	1.2	8	0	.1
26254	.2	0	.1	80	21.8	143	56.2	0	13	.0	0	0	.0
26257	.6	0	.2	81	20.7	325	44.8	8	7	.0	0	0	.0
26259	.4	100	.1	93	27.5	316*	61.3	14	12	.2	9	0	.0
26260	1.2	100	.5	67	21.1	294	63.2	10	15	.6	12	0	.5
26261	4.5	100	1.7	77	21.0	243	54.7	14	14	2.1	12	1	.0
26263	.3	100	.2	75	17.0	228	48.2	4	20	.4	13	0	.0
26264	.7	100	.2	65	19.4	254	49.6	10	13	.4	10	0	.0
26265	.2	0	.1	88	25.2	290*	43.1	7	10	.0	0	0	.0
26266	.5	100	.2	92	16.6	181	46.0	10	16	.2	8	0	.0
26267	.5	100	.1	58	15.9	183	25.7	6	12	.2	14	0	.0
26268	.1	100	.1	58	12.6	145*	43.8	0	15	.1	11	0	.0
26269	.8	100	.3	81	17.7	208	50.9	3	18	.4	17	0	.0
26270	.7	100	.2	72	17.0	197	47.8	13	22	.3	20	0	.0
26271	.5	0	.2	80	14.8	169	43.6	13	13	.0	0	0	.0
26273	1.3	96	.3	75	22.1	228	77.3	6	10	.8	7	0	.0
26275	.7	100	.3	82	15.3	159	42.1	8	17	.3	19	0	.0
26276	.5	100	.2	80	17.9	253	55.8	11	15	.3	17	0	.0
26278	.6	100	.2	88	64.7	303	33.5	11	2	.4	3	0	.0
26280	2.1	100	.7	72	18.8	209	47.0	9	12	1.0	12	0	.0
26281	.2	100	.1	66	26.2	301*	43.8	9	27	.1	26	0	.0
26283	1.2	100	.4	86	18.2	159	65.6	8	16	.6	16	0	.0
26285	.5	100	.2	88	18.4	270	35.9	4	10	.3	15	0	.0
26287	3.0	0	1.1	74	20.3	244	61.7	6	16	.0	0	1	1.9
26288	4.8	100	1.7	73	15.8	194	46.2	8	15	2.3	15	0	.0
26289	.2	100	.1	89	22.1	254*	74.4	12	18	.1	13	0	.0
26290	1.3	0	.4	75	16.7	278	36.6	8	8	.0	0	0	.0
26291	.2	100	.1	55	14.1	514	71.9	4	8	.1	8	0	.0
26292	1.1	0	.4	68	19.8	229	49.3	4	23	.0	0	0	.0
26293	.6	100	.2	87	21.0	242*	60.4	7	16	.3	16	0	.0
26294	.9	100	.3	76	16.0	147	44.9	11	14	.5	14	0	.0
26296	.4	100	.1	89	13.2	151*	22.7	0	16	.2	13	0	.0
26298	.2	100	.1	70	13.7	284	57.2	9	12	.1	6	0	.0

CLARKSBURG

ZIPCODE	1	2	3	4	5	6	7	8	9	10	11	12	13
26301	37.4	97	14.7	67	22.2	265	68.7	6	17	16.7	14	2	.3
26320	.9	0	.3	87	17.9	222	54.1	9	11	.0	0	0	.0
26321	.9	100	.3	63	19.1	147	13.1	5	13	.1	8	0	.0
26323	.9	98	.3	77	21.2	251	44.7	4	17	.4	14	0	.0
26325	.3	100	.1	65	15.2	86	21.9	4	10	.1	24	0	.0
26327	.1	100	.1	38	9.3	107*	21.9	9	20	.1	27	0	.0
26330	11.2	99	4.1	80	30.5	336	110.7	8	14	5.4	19	2	.3
26332	1.6	0	.5	72	20.2	297	84.4	7	11	.0	0	0	.0
26334	.3	0	.1	77	16.9	124	17.3	7	7	.0	0	0	.0
26335	1.1	100	.4	77	18.9	213	52.7	9	17	.5	16	0	.0
26336	.2	100	.1	100	18.8	216*	13.1	13	3	.1	5	0	.0
26337	1.6	100	.6	81	19.1	143	13.8	6	15	.0	0	0	.0
26338	.9	100	.3	81	21.2	181	69.2	7	7	.5	8	0	.0
26339	.2	100	.1	69	16.2	186*	36.3	14	26	.1	13	0	.0
26342	.5	100	.2	90	14.0	106	57.6	7	32	.2	32	0	.0

WEST VIRGINIA

CLARKSBURG

ZIPCODE	1	2	3	4	5	6	7	8	9	10	11	12	13
26343	.5	100	.2	71	17.8	278	44.0	13	18	.2	19	0	.0
26346	.8	100	.3	75	22.6	271	40.2	10	12	.4	9	0	.0
26347	1.9	96	.6	80	19.8	225	46.5	9	15	.9	15	0	.0
26348	.4	100	.1	95	22.5	259*	38.9	9	15	.2	11	0	.0
26349	.3	95	.1	75	13.8	187	26.0	14	12	.1	14	0	.0
26351	3.7	99	1.2	64	18.9	246	80.3	7	11	1.8	10	0	.0
26354	11.7	99	4.2	76	20.0	215	54.7	7	15	5.7	12	0	.0
26360	.7	100	.2	83	15.1	259	49.4	10	11	.3	10	0	.0
26361	.2	100	.1	55	15.4	281	23.5	7	26	.1	22	0	.0
26362	3.1	0	1.2	78	19.2	208	66.8	9	19	.0	0	0	.0
26366	.4	100	.1	93	20.4	234*	45.2	4	13	.2	5	0	.0
26369	.8	94	.3	83	17.3	257	43.2	6	15	.3	15	0	.0
26372	1.3	100	.2	83	22.0	458	81.5	4	10	.3	13	0	.0
26374	1.3	98	.5	79	20.2	268	57.0	8	8	.7	7	0	.0
26376	.5	100	.2	70	14.6	186	53.6	10	25	.3	26	0	.0
26377	.6	100	.2	79	20.3	199	44.7	9	11	.3	15	0	.0
26378	3.2	100	1.1	82	20.0	184	80.8	6	14	1.5	10	0	.0
26380	.5	100	.2	77	16.7	115	74.4	7	10	.3	9	0	.0
26384	.6	100	.2	79	16.8	212	56.4	4	12	.2	12	0	.0
26385	3.4	100	1.1	82	20.8	266	65.9	10	11	1.7	10	0	.0
26386	2.4	0	.8	82	18.1	242	58.0	7	12	.0	0	0	.0

CLARKSBURG

ZIPCODE	1	2	3	4	5	6	7	8	9	10	11	12	13
26401	.3	100	.1	93	22.4	258*	36.6	0	10	.1	11	0	.0
26404	.4	80	.1	72	22.2	166	55.4	2	19	.2	23	0	.0
26405	1.7	0	.6	84	18.8	181	41.0	9	12	.0	0	0	.0
26408	2.7	0	.9	87	22.3	233	68.1	8	10	.0	0	0	.0
26409	.1	100	.1	57	10.2	117*	13.1	5	19	.1	15	0	.0
26410	1.5	0	.4	76	18.8	253	41.4	5	13	.0	0	0	.0
26411	.7	100	.2	70	15.8	278	35.6	6	13	.4	12	0	.0
26412	.7	0	.2	77	14.8	272	59.1	12	19	.0	0	0	.0
26415	6.7	100	2.4	79	21.6	259	64.8	8	13	3.2	11	1	.1
26416	.2	100	.1	70	12.4	242	40.1	5	8	.1	0	0	.0
26419	6.7	98	2.3	75	20.7	270	70.9	6	13	3.0	11	1	.0
26421	.3	0	.1	76	18.5	208	51.9	6	15	.0	0	0	.0
26422	.6	100	.1	82	21.6	244	45.4	4	18	.3	5	0	.0
26423	.7	100	.3	77	18.1	107	54.7	4	20	.4	23	0	.0
26424	.5	0	.1	75	22.0	198	23.9	11	6	.0	0	0	.0
26425	1.4	100	.5	76	17.7	183	38.9	8	18	.7	15	0	.0
26426	6.0	99	1.9	74	18.2	212	54.3	8	12	2.9	11	0	.0
26430	.3	100	.1	71	14.8	272	59.1	12	19	.4	12	0	.0
26431	6.7	100	2.4	79	21.6	259	64.8	8	13	3.2	11	1	.1
26435	.2	100	.2	70	12.4	242	40.1	5	8	.1	0	0	.0
26436	.3	100	.1	85	22.5	270	49.5	7	9	.1	7	0	.0
26437	.7	0	.3	78	19.3	163	28.5	11	13	.3	0	0	.0
26438	.5	100	.2	86	16.4	301	39.0	6	15	.2	16	0	.0
26439	.9	100	.3	72	14.3	113	82.9	8	9	.2	6	0	.0
26440	1.0	100	.4	81	15.3	176*	47.0	11	19	.6	19	1	.0
26443	.4	100	.1	93	29.1	334*	47.0	8	18	.2	24	0	.0
26444	4.0	99	1.4	81	18.5	219	40.4	8	14	2.0	14	0	.0

*=Estimated **1.0=883 lbs per person; 100++ indicates per capita toxic waste generation > than 100 times the U.S. average of 883 lbs per capita.

ZIP CODE MEASURES OF SIZE, LEVELS OF AFFLUENCE AND QUALITY OF LIFE

1=Population (th.); 2= % White; 3=Households (th.); 4=% Owner Occupied; 5=Mean Income Per Household (th.$); 6=Mean Monthly Rent ($)*; 7=Mean Home Value (th.$)*; 8=% under 5; 9=% 65 and over; 10=%White Males; 11=% White Males, 65+; 12=# Toxic Waste Sites; 13=Toxic Waste Relative to US(883 lbs.per capita)**.

WEST VIRGINIA

ZIPCODE	1	2	3	4	5	6	7	8	9	10	11	12	13
CLARKSBURG													
26445	.2	100	.1	81	9.9	240	65.6	3	27	.1	5	0	.0
26447	.4	0	.1	83	18.6	214*	99.3	5	26	.0	0	0	.0
26448	1.6	0	.5	89	14.9	141	38.2	6	14	.0	0	0	.0
26451	.5	100	.2	82	22.8	317	60.9	7	13	.3	12	0	.0
26452	12.4	99	4.5	66	20.6	225	64.5	8	17	5.8	13	1	.0
26456	3.4	0	1.3	73	18.6	187	51.4	6	19	.0	0	0	.0
26459	.2	0	-	84	23.2	266*	65.6	6	10	.0	0	0	.0
26461	.5	85	.2	70	15.7	190	28.9	9	11	.2	12	0	.0
26462	.8	100	.3	88	22.9	239	60.7	5	16	.4	18	0	.0
26463	.2	100	.1	68	14.5	161	18.8	9	18	.1	13	0	.0
CLARKSBURG													
26505	64.2	96	23.4	60	24.1	349	101.4	6	9	30.5*	7	4	.5
26520	1.6	100	.5	82	19.1	199	49.0	8	12	.8	9	0	.0
26521	.9	100	.3	91	28.4	352	86.8	10	10	.4	7	0	.0
26522	.6	100	.2	75	27.7	263	58.3	6	12	.3	11	0	.0
26524	.4	0	.1	82	19.6	208	42.5	5	6	.0	0	0	.0
26525	3.1	100	1.0	33	15.0	242	48.4	9	9	.2	2	0	.0
26527	.8	100	.3	85	21.1	209	69.1	9	12	1.5	13	0	.0
26531	1.0	100	.3	73	17.9	285	41.3	8	11	.4	6	0	.0
26533	.3	100	.1	73	17.4	224	26.7	15	8	.1	11	0	.0
26534	.1	0	-	80	10.9	125*	15.3	6	6	.0	4	0	.0
26537	5.6	98	1.9	58	19.4	338	62.7	8	11	.5	10	0	.1
26541	1.1	0	.4	79	26.4	254	80.5	8	12	2.7	10	1	.1
26542	2.7	100	1.0	76	21.5	249	63.3	5	7	1.4	9	0	.0
26543	.7	64	.2	72	21.9	289	54.6	8	10	.8	8	0	.0
26544	.3	100	.1	69	22.0	276	36.0	11	11	.2	12	0	.0
26546	.3	0	.1	66	17.8	253	53.2	12	11	.1	10	0	.0
26547	1.4	0	.5	77	22.8	382	52.5	16	16	.0	0	0	.0
26554	44.3	95	16.7	71	23.2	289	69.6	6	9	19.9	12	8	.5
26559	1.8	95	.7	78	23.9	276	75.8	7	14	.8	9	0	.0
26560	.4	0	.1	74	22.9	253	67.6	7	13	.8	8	0	.0
26562	.5	100	.2	84	18.5	356	55.7	6	16	.3	13	0	.0
26563	.6	79	.2	91	21.1	172	46.2	6	19	.2	9	0	.0
26566	.2	100	.1	81	23.4	254	43.2	2	11	.1	15	0	.0
26568	.9	100	.3	73	22.1	389	68.7	9	11	.4	13	0	.0
26570	4.0	100	1.3	84	25.2	289	45.9	8	15	2.0	10	0	.0
26571	2.4	97	.9	86	19.3	196	55.9	6	13	1.1	12	0	.0
26572	.5	100	.3	67	16.0	193	52.4	8	6	.4	5	0	.0
26574	1.0	87	.3	80	21.2	177	16.5	8	6	.4	11	0	.0
26575	1.2	0	.5	68	16.5	263	50.4	8	14	.0	0	0	.0
26576	.5	100	.2	93	21.4	203	56.8	8	22	.3	22	0	.0
26578	.4	100	.1	90	23.3	280	56.7	9	21	.2	13	0	.0
26579	.2	100	.2	100	21.9	408	58.8	7	6	.1	15	0	.0
26581	.8	0	.3	74	21.9	252*	44.4	2	16	.2	9	0	.0
26582	6.3	100	2.3	77	19.5	222	37.4	9	16	3.0	13	0	.1
26585	.7	100	.2	83	21.0	228	52.6	7	16	.3	14	0	.0
26586	.2	0	.1	61	15.7	226	43.0	0	21	.0	0	0	.0

WEST VIRGINIA

ZIPCODE	1	2	3	4	5	6	7	8	9	10	11	12	13
CLARKSBURG													
26587	.5	88	.2	84	28.7	248	45.6	6	9	.3	7	0	.0
26588	3.3	99	1.2	79	21.3	242	58.4	6	15	1.5	14	0	.0
26589	.6	100	.2	86	24.7	181	63.8	10	9	.6	5	0	.0
26591	1.9	98	.7	75	17.6	279	45.7	8	13	.9	11	0	.0
GASSAWAY													
26601	3.7	98	1.4	74	17.5	249	71.8	8	15	1.8	13	1	.0
26610	1.3	100	.4	79	14.1	144	33.3	3	15	.6	13	0	.0
26611	.3	100	.1	94	13.7	158*	45.5	4	23	.2	23	0	.0
26615	.3	100	.1	90	8.9	102*	19.7	4	33	.2	34	0	.0
26616	.3	100	.1	73	12.6	117	41.6	10	19	.1	27	0	.0
26617	.4	100	.1	91	18.4	256	37.7	13	11	.2	10	0	.0
26619	.5	100	.1	89	15.5	179*	31.2	4	13	.2	14	1	.0
26621	.5	100	.2	78	19.3	256	63.5	5	28	.3	32	0	.0
26623	.7	100	.2	73	17.3	215	55.8	5	20	.4	17	0	.0
26624	3.1	100	1.1	78	18.7	249	64.4	7	17	1.5	14	0	.0
26625	.6	100	.1	67	18.8	216	109.4	10	13	.1	14	0	.0
26627	.6	100	.2	67	14.0	174	62.2	6	15	.3	14	0	.0
26629	.5	100	.2	83	15.1	168	47.4	10	7	.3	7	0	.0
26632	.3	100	.1	79	17.9	160	40.6	9	5	.1	7	0	.0
26633	.3	100	.1	70	16.9	201	39.4	13	8	.2	9	0	.0
26636	.3	100	.1	78	13.1	98	42.3	15	4	.2	6	0	.0
26639	.7	0	.2	85	17.9	55	59.9	5	11	.1	0	0	.0
26640	.1	100	-	69	14.1	70	18.5	5	22	.1	26	0	.0
26651	8.0	100	2.7	81	23.1	304	80.6	8	8	3.8	8	1	.1
26656	.9	100	.3	71	28.2	175	57.9	10	9	.5	9	0	.0
26660	.3	0	.1	100	26.4	303*	96.9	6	8	.0	0	0	.0
26662	.5	100	.2	89	22.7	71	83.3	13	4	.3	6	0	.0
26667	.6	100	.2	68	18.4	217	44.1	10	4	.3	2	0	.0
26671	.4	100	.1	61	14.6	211	44.6	11	9	.2	11	0	.0
26674	.5	100	.1	97	21.2	243*	39.0	7	9	.2	8	0	.1
26676	.8	0	.2	79	22.0	248	54.7	9	10	.2	8	8	.5
26678	.7	100	.2	82	26.1	238	56.6	11	8	.3	5	0	.0
26679	1.3	100	.4	83	17.4	280	68.1	12	10	.7	8	0	.0
26680	.6	100	.2	68	16.0	179	70.3	9	21	.1	15	0	.0
26681	1.8	100	.6	90	21.4	272	67.0	4	13	.9	13	0	.0
26689	.3	100	.1	81	20.7	215	60.2	2	5	.1	4	0	.0
26690	.3	100	.1	64	12.9	163	36.2	11	15	.1	16	0	.0
26691	.9	100	.3	87	19.3	140	40.0	8	12	.4	12	0	.0
CUMBERLAND													
26701	.2	100	.1	87	16.9	194*	45.4	8	12	.1	7	0	.0
26704	2.4	87	.8	79	19.5	331	66.2	10	14	.4	11	0	.0
26705	.8	0	.3	88	23.5	428	49.3	8	16	.0	0	0	.0
26707	.6	100	.3	82	19.2	298	43.3	7	16	.3	13	0	.0
26710	1.6	98	.6	78	18.4	305	64.7	9	15	.8	15	0	.0
26711	1.2	98	.4	85	23.9	267	63.7	7	12	.6	12	0	.0
26713	.2	100	.2	85	13.7	158*	27.1	10	10	.1	8	0	.0
26716	.3	100	.1	74	15.9	152	68.1	11	15	.2	14	0	.0
26717	1.4	100	.5	86	18.1	117	39.8	6	13	.0	0	0	.0
26719	1.6	100	.6	82	22.1	261	77.8	6	11	.8	7	0	.0

*=Estimated **1.0=883 lbs per capita. 100++ indicates per capita toxic waste generation > than 100 times the U.S. average of 883 lbs per capita.

ZIP CODE MEASURES OF SIZE, LEVELS OF AFFLUENCE AND QUALITY OF LIFE

1=Population (th.); 2= % White; 3=Households (th.); 4=% Owner Occupied; 5=Mean Income Per Household (th.$); 6=Mean Monthly Rent ($)*; 7=Mean Home Value (th.$)*; 8=% under 5; 9=% 65 and over; 10=White Males (th.); 11=% White Males, 65+; 12=# Toxic Waste Sites; 13=Toxic Waste Relative to US(883 lbs.per capital)**.

WEST VIRGINIA

ZIP CODE	1	2	3	4	5	6	7	8	9	10	11	12	13
CUMBERLAND													
26722	.6	100	.2	93	21.8	53	48.5	8	2	.3	3	1	1.4
26726	13.8	97	4.8	73	23.1	248	64.8	7	12	6.4	10	2	.0
26729	.3	100		83	11.0	258	64.0	4	22		27	0	.0
26739	1.0	0	.3	91	16.9	300	52.8	12	0	.0	0	0	.0
26743	1.4	100	.4	92	19.2	251	55.5	8	6	.8	6	0	.0
26746	.1	100		76	15.1	230	31.5	8	26	.1	21	0	.0
26750	1.4	77	.5	48	17.4	170	39.9	9	14	.5	13	0	.0
26753	5.4	99	1.9	84	23.7	232	66.7	8	9	2.7	9	0	.0
26755	.2	100	.1	82	13.9	159*	42.9	7	24		14	0	.0
26757	4.9	97	1.8	77	20.7	281	65.6	7	14	2.3	11	1	.0
26761	.7	0	.2	74	14.9	345	93.2	9	10	.0	0	0	7.0
26763	1.1	100	.4	89	22.3	315	61.5	4	17	.6	16	0	.0
26764	3.8	100	1.3	77	20.3	197	57.2	9	13	1.8	11	0	.0
26765	.9	100	.3	87	23.9	126	44.3	4	3	.2	6	0	.0
26767	.9	100	.3	87	21.5	280	53.4	2	14	.4	10	0	.0
26769	.5	100	.1	94	18.5	212*	54.3	5	12	.2	14	0	.0
PETERSBURG													
26801	1.0	100	.4	74	19.1	233	48.2	9	17	.5	16	0	.0
26802	.6	0	.2	69	13.0	300	49.9	7	32	.0	0	0	.0
26803	.5	100	.2	84	18.2	209*	26.4	5	6	.3	7	0	.0
26804	.3	100	.1	93	16.0	184*	58.6	12	10	.2	9	0	.0
26806	.3	100	.1	89	15.8	181*	59.5	14	11	.2	11	0	.0
26807	2.9	96	1.0	75	20.3	214	74.6	9	15	1.3	13	0	.0
26808	.2	100		71	17.4	192	88.3	12	13	.1	9	0	.0
26811	.4	100	.1	85	14.9	171*	47.2	9	9	.0	3	0	.0
26812	1.1	100	.4	89	17.8	155	53.5	5	16	.5	12	0	.0
26813	.3	80	.1	89	20.0	229*	68.0	3	15	.1	6	0	.0
26814	.6	100	.3	67	11.8	153	45.2	2	29	.3	30	0	.0
26815	.6	0		40	15.6	325	56.9	11	8	.0	0	0	.0
26816	.5	100	.2	87	17.5	318	58.4	10	22	.3	18	0	.0
26817	.2	100	.1	54	25.1	288*	65.6	8	0	.1	0	0	.0
26818	.3	100	.1	77	15.2	174*	54.8	7	9	.2	7	0	.0
26823	.3	100	.1	86	13.1	151*	33.9	10	9	.1	5	0	.0
26832	.3	100		90	16.5	123	47.4	5	9		9	0	.0
26833	1.6	100	.5	78	18.9	179	63.9	7	10	.8	11	0	.0
26835	.5	100	.2	77	17.3	143	47.1	3	15	.2	15	0	.0
26836	4.7	96	1.7	73	20.2	226	59.6	7	13	2.3	12	0	.0
26843	.1	100	.1	77	15.4	263	70.7	7	32	.1	20	0	.0
26845	.4	0	.1	81	19.5	149	65.1	4	10	.0	0	0	1.6
26847	4.0	98	1.4	77	20.4	279	69.7	6	14	1.9	12	1	.0
26851	1.4	98	.5	80	15.8	224	54.5	8	13	.7	14	0	.0
26852	.9	100	.3	88	19.4	246	56.1	5	15	.4	13	0	.0
26854	.3	100	.1	84	13.5	223	45.4	10	21	.1	22	0	.0
26855	.7	100	.2	90	17.5	201*	49.7	7	4	.0	4	0	.0
26865	.2	0		74	16.8	173	50.3	7	15	.0	0	0	.0
26866	1.0	100	.3	87	15.8	282	54.1	7	11	.5	12	0	.0
26884	.4	100	.1	81	20.3	183	100.4	9	6	.2	11	0	.0
26886	.4	100	.1	93	14.7	169*	60.5	3	26	.2	31	0	.0

WISCONSIN

ZIP CODE	1	2	3	4	5	6	7	8	9	10	11	12	13
IRON MOUNTAIN (EAST)													
49801	1.3	98	.4	85	21.9	286	66.8	8	11	.7	11	0	.0
IRON MOUNTAIN (WEST)													
49935	.3	0	.1	91	12.4	102	40.7	8	22	.0	0	0	.0
MILWAUKEE (NORTH)													
53001	1.8	100	.6	83	27.8	332	89.5	10	12	.9	11	0	.0
53002	2.0	100	.6	82	30.5	366	98.3	10	5	1.0	5	0	1.2
53003	.3	0	.1	85	32.5	384	88.8	4	11	.0	0	0	25.2
53004	2.2	99	.7	78	33.8	345	105.0	9	11	1.1	10	0	.1
53005	34.7	97	10.5	92	50.8	578	172.6	5	7	16.7	7	1	.9
53006	1.6	98	.6	76	30.6	293	93.6	10	10	.8	9	0	.0
53007	2.1	0	.8	54	27.2	305	99.8	7	14	.0	9	0	7.0
53010	6.3	100	1.9	79	28.2	344	91.9	9	12	3.1	9	0	.0
53011	1.7	99	.5	80	27.3	324	88.0	9	10	.8	9	0	.0
53012	15.2	99	5.0	73	36.5	428	146.8	7	9	7.5	7	0	.6
53013	2.5	99	.9	76	29.2	303	96.3	9	13	1.2	12	0	.2
53014	7.3	100	2.3	79	28.8	296	80.7	8	13	3.7	12	0	.8
53015	2.5	100	.8	83	29.3	314	86.6	9	10	1.3	9	0	.2
53016	.4	100	.1	75	26.8	287	69.8	7	13	.2	11	0	1.2
53017	4.2	99	1.2	91	42.3	493	144.3	9	4	2.1	4	0	.0
53018	4.1	100	1.3	84	39.4	442	153.4	10	7	2.0	7	0	.1
53019	1.7	99	.5	79	29.6	328	88.6	13	9	.9	8	0	.0
53020	3.5	100	1.1	79	32.2	343	105.7	9	10	1.7	10	0	.7
53021	3.5	0	.1	82	31.9	390	110.8	10	7	.0	0	0	1.5
53022	9.4	99	3.0	78	35.3	468	137.4	8	4	4.6	4	0	1.0
53023	1.2	0	.4	88	29.4	286	72.1	10	8	.0	8	0	.7
53024	12.5	99	4.1	70	36.1	434	135.2	7	6	6.2	5	0	1.6
53027	13.5	99	4.4	72	30.6	336	106.5	8	11	6.7	8	0	1.7
53029	12.5	99	4.0	71	40.9	447	165.3	8	6	6.2	5	0	.1
53031	.3	100	.5	82	31.0	293	79.4	21	11	.1	10	0	.0
53032	4.6	99	1.6	81	30.4	289	85.0	8	11	2.3	10	0	4.2
53033	4.5	0	1.3	94	37.7	463	136.4	7	4	.0	1	0	.0
53034	.9	100	.4	70	25.1	308	81.4	8	17	.5	15	0	1.0
53035	2.3	100	.7	83	27.9	365	84.1	10	9	1.2	9	0	.7
53036	1.8	100	.6	76	35.2	364	115.0	7	7	.9	7	0	.2
53037	3.4	99	1.2	66	29.4	433	116.7	8	8	1.7	8	0	4.7
53038	2.3	100	.8	79	27.1	319	87.7	8	11	1.2	10	0	1.1
53039	4.2	99	1.3	76	27.1	294	77.3	7	19	2.1	17	0	.2
53040	5.9	100	1.8	81	31.3	368	103.4	9	9	2.9	7	0	.8
53042	5.7	100	1.9	80	28.9	263	78.6	8	12	.9	9	0	1.2
53043	.5	100	.1	90	26.0	324	74.8	9	14	.2	13	0	.0
53044	1.8	100	.6	86	35.3	376	109.4	6	15	.9	12	1	12.5
53046	1.0	97	.4	79	30.7	297	110.3	7	10	.5	9	0	2.0
53048	2.0	100	.6	76	29.1	340	82.4	8	12	1.0	11	0	.4
53049	2.5	0	.7	87	29.1	304	93.7	10	12	.9	5	0	.0
53050	6.3	99	2.2	74	28.9	278	81.3	8	13	3.2	11	0	.9
53051	27.9	99	8.8	81	38.9	422	125.8	5	7	13.8	6	1	1.6
53056	.3	100	.1	77	30.9	335	100.6	5	9	.2	9	0	3.3
53057	1.8	99	.5	79	29.4	290	82.6	9	12	.9	10	0	.0
53058	2.2	100	.8	68	41.9	447	162.6	6	11	1.1	11	0	.0

*=Estimated **1.0=883 lbs per person; 100++ indicates per capita toxic waste generation > than 100 times the U.S. average of 883 lbs per capita.

ZIP CODE MEASURES OF SIZE, LEVELS OF AFFLUENCE AND QUALITY OF LIFE

1=Population (th.); 2= % White; 3=Households (th.); 4=% Owner Occupied; 5=Mean Income Per Household (th.$); 6=Mean Monthly Rent ($); 7=Mean Home Value (th.$);
8=% under 5; 9=% 65 and over; 10=% White Males, 65+; 11=% White Males; 12=# Toxic Waste Sites; 13=% Toxic Waste Relative to US(883 lbs.per capita)**.

WISCONSIN

MILWAUKEE (NORTH)

ZIPCODE	1	2	3	4	5	6	7	8	9	10	11	12	13
53059	1.7	100	.5	76	28.4	390	97.3	11	8	.9	7	0	.0
53060	.3	0	1	63	32.1	269	95.4	7	11	.0	0	0	1.9
53061	5.4	99	1.7	80	30.4	277	85.2	7	12	2.6	11	1	5.2
53063	1.7	99	5	88	34.9	286	86.5	9	12	.9	9	0	
53064	2.3	100	.9	83	27.8	360	128.4	5	15	.9	7	0	5.1
53065	2.3	99	.7	82	30.9	336	79.9	7	9	1.1	8	0	.1
53066	23.8	99	7.8	77	34.5	427	140.9	7	11	11.7	9	0	.2
53069	1.1	0	.4	74	28.1	465	104.5	6	10	.0	0	0	
53070	3.6	99	1.1	85	30.4	306	99.3	8	11	1.8	10	0	.2
53072	12.0	99	4.1	71	34.9	460	138.3	7	9	6.0	7	0	.6
53073	11.7	98	3.5	72	29.7	298	88.5	8	13	5.7	12	0	.9
53074	3.0	98	.9	70	31.8	380	112.6	7	11	5.0	9	1	
53075	3.0	98	.9	77	30.8	373	100.9	8	9	1.5	9	0	4.4
53076	2.8	100	.8	83	41.1	399	142.9	10	6	1.4	6	0	.9
53078	1.6	100	.4	83	35.8	390	102.0	9	9	.8	7	0	.5
53079	1.6	0	.5	86	30.1	314	83.2	9	9	.0	0	0	.6
53080	5.1	0	1.5	67	33.1	405	117.1	11	5	.0	0	3	4.6
53081	58.3	99	21.4	67	27.1	308	86.1	7	14	27.8	12	4	1.9
53085	9.8	100	3.3	77	28.3	323	86.5	7	12	4.9	11	1	.5
53086	3.4	0	1.1	79	29.9	366	106.1	8	8	.0	0	0	.5
53088	.4	97	.4	78	28.9	190	78.5	9	7	.2	5	0	
53089	10.1	99	3.0	87	38.3	429	136.8	7	6	5.0	6	0	
53090	.2	0	.2	100	25.9	297*	53.2	9	14	.0	0	0	.8
53091	1.7	100	.5	80	30.2	259	83.2	9	10	.8	10	0	
53092	19.5	97	6.3	82	52.3	494	187.1	6	9	9.4	8	0	1.3
53094	24.7	99	8.2	70	27.2	318	85.5	8	14	11.9	11	0	.6
53095	35.4	99	11.3	72	30.9	372	114.3	9	10	17.2	8	1	.8

MILWAUKEE (SOUTH)

ZIPCODE	1	2	3	4	5	6	7	8	9	10	11	12	13
53101	.2	100	.1	72	38.4	310	128.8	16	1	.1	2	0	.0
53103	3.6	99	1.0	89	33.1	431	128.3	10	6	1.9	6	0	1.2
53104	3.1	100	1.0	80	37.8	390	121.4	8	6	1.6	6	0	1.3
53105	21.2	99	7.0	75	29.7	364	102.1	8	10	10.3	9	0	.6
53108	3.8	99	1.1	90	36.4	419	112.5	5	5	1.9	9	2	
53109	.3	100	.1	63	28.0	342	85.7	2	25	.2	22	0	
53110	19.7	99	7.1	62	29.0	360	97.3	6	10	9.6	8	0	1.2
53114	1.7	96	.5	74	26.8	359	80.7	8	9	.8	7	1	1.3
53115	11.8	96	4.3	68	37.8	343	91.4	7	14	5.5	12	2	
53118	4.9	99	1.4	91	37.6	489	151.8	9	8	2.4	7	0	.6
53119	3.1	99	.9	88	32.1	453	126.7	9	8	1.5	8	0	.0
53120	7.1	100	2.3	76	29.7	399	113.6	10	9	3.6	9	2	.6
53121	11.2	99	3.8	72	27.0	347	104.1	7	13	5.4	11	3	.6
53122	6.8	99	2.2	87	77.4	518	222.5	3	14	3.2	10	0	
53125	1.9	99	.7	77	33.9	464	134.0	5	15	2.9	12	0	.4
53126	5.7	99	1.7	82	39.8	392	126.2	7	7	2.9	6	1	
53127	.3	100	.9	77	39.4	248	111.9	5	6	.2	6	0	5.5
53128	2.7	0	.9	77	26.3	377	108.3	7	15	.0	0	0	.0
53129	16.8	99	5.3	72	40.3	444	149.8	6	7	8.1	5	0	.0
53130	13.9	99	4.5	74	38.3	419	141.3	6	9	6.9	7	0	.0

WISCONSIN

MILWAUKEE (SOUTH)

ZIPCODE	1	2	3	4	5	6	7	8	9	10	11	12	13
53132	12.6	96	3.8	79	37.5	424	130.9	7	5	6.4	5	2	.2
53137	1.4	0	.4	79	26.9	232	92.8	9	8	.0	0	0	.0
53139	2.0	98	.6	81	30.5	419	95.6	8	9	1.0	8	0	.0
53140	53.8	93	19.6	63	27.0	305	82.5	7	12	24.3	10	1	3.7
53142	44.4	97	15.3	75	32.6	347	99.1	7	9	21.3	8	0	.1
53147	11.2	99	4.4	65	27.8	369	111.3	6	15	5.3	13	1	.2
53148	.5	98	.2	75	27.4	346	92.7	5	14	.3	11	0	.5
53149	12.0	99	3.7	83	35.3	427	125.8	10	6	6.0	5	0	.1
53150	12.7	100	3.8	87	37.4	502	136.3	7	5	15.0	4	0	.1
53151	30.3	99	9.3	87	41.6	490	136.3	7	5	15.0	4	2	.8
53153	1.0	99	.3	88	37.4	418	118.1	8	9	.0	0	0	.0
53154	16.7	98	5.5	69	33.7	366	118.1	8	6	8.2	5	0	2.8
53156	2.6	99	.9	73	28.1	280	99.4	7	13	1.3	12	1	.0
53157	1.5	0	.6	80	19.5	355	71.9	6	19	.0	0	0	.0
53159	.5	99	.3	71	32.4	405	114.9	7	18	.4	5	0	.0
53167	.8	99	.8	57	29.4	386	113.5	10	6	.0	0	0	.0
53168	5.6	99	1.9	83	29.3	405	87.2	9	10	2.8	8	0	.8
53170	1.6	99	.6	79	27.4	350	84.9	8	11	.8	11	0	.0
53171	.4	100	.1	78	36.5	418	99.6	6	2	.2	0	0	.6
53172	21.1	99	7.3	68	30.3	372	102.0	7	10	10.3	9	2	1.7
53176	1.1	0	.1	73	27.5	426	68.5	5	13	.0	0	0	.0
53177	6.5	99	2.0	69	31.7	397	95.9	8	7	3.3	7	3	.1
53178	2.3	99	.7	80	29.9	388	97.2	7	11	1.2	11	1	.0
53179	2.0	99	.6	85	27.7	406	82.5	6	13	.9	12	0	.5
53181	4.0	99	4.0	74	29.1	361	112.4	6	14	1.9	12	1	1.2
53182	8.2	99	2.4	75	31.8	347	105.4	7	8	4.2	7	1	.3
53183	2.6	94	.6	82	39.1	482	156.4	11	2	1.3	2	0	.8
53184	2.9	98	1.0	67	26.7	368	92.0	7	14	1.4	11	0	.0
53185	9.5	99	3.1	81	31.2	383	108.8	8	9	4.9	7	1	
53186	71.1	97	23.5	65	33.6	408	132.2	9	8	34.1	6	6	1.4
53190	15.5	97	4.4	56	24.5	346	93.3	5	8	7.4	6	0	.3
53191	1.9	99	.8	68	26.3	314	117.6	6	18	.9	15	0	.1
53192	.5	0	.2	83	29.1	358	103.4	9	10	.0	0	0	.0
53195	.2	93	.1	74	27.5	397	79.6	6	12	.0	0	0	2.5

MILWAUKEE

ZIPCODE	1	2	3	4	5	6	7	8	9	10	11	12	13
53202	20.9	91	12.4	10	20.1	317	69.0	2	25	8.7	17	0	1.8
53203	.5	80	.3	0	14.0	120	49.9*	0	19	.3	22	1	38.7
53204	35.9	84	13.1	35	19.9	303	48.3	10	12	14.5	11	4	1.7
53205	14.5	10	4.6	20	15.5	244	37.6	12	8	.7	20	0	.4
53206	45.4	3	13.6	42	19.8	336	40.6	10	6	.7	30	1	.0
53207	52.1	98	20.1	63	27.0	357	82.4	7	14	24.3	11	4	.5
53208	41.7	70	16.5	31	20.7	303	70.2	8	12	13.9	13	3	.3
53209	52.1	63	19.4	60	23.7	354	89.8	8	12	15.6	14	4	1.2
53211	36.3	96	15.7	38	31.3	439	148.1	4	15	15.5	10	1	.0
53212	39.4	35	14.4	31	18.4	312	44.6	9	13	6.5	13	1	1.5
53213	28.1	100	11.1	66	32.4	395	115.3	9	19	12.6	14	1	1.3
53214	36.9	98	14.8	60	26.1	366	85.7	7	13	17.4	11	3	5.0
53215	50.4	98	19.8	74	24.0	326	73.8	8	16	22.3	13	1	1.0

*=Estimated **1.0=883 lbs per person; 100++ indicates per capita toxic waste generation > than 100 times the U.S. average of 883 lbs. per capita.

ZIP CODE MEASURES OF SIZE, LEVELS OF AFFLUENCE AND QUALITY OF LIFE

1=Population (th.); 2= % White; 3=Households (th.); 4=% Owner Occupied; 5=Mean Income Per Household (th.); 6=Mean Monthly Rent ($); 7=Mean Home Value (th.$);
8=% under 5; 9=% 65 and over; 10=White Males (th.); 11=% White Males, 65+; 12=# Toxic Waste Sites; 13=Toxic Waste Relative to US(883 lbs.per capita)**.

WISCONSIN

MILWAUKEE

ZIP CODE	1	2	3	4	5	6	7	8	9	10	11	12	13
53216	33.7	65	13.8	60	25.0	353	77.5	7	17	10.0	21	2	.4
53217	30.7	98	10.9	83	58.2	532	184.9	5	14	14.1	12	0	.1
53218	42.4	83	15.3	64	27.4	376	78.5	8	11	16.7	11	0	.2
53219	37.0	99	15.2	66	28.6	369	93.2	5	17	17.2	14	0	1.2
53220	26.6	99	10.0	58	31.6	426	108.4	6	11	12.4	9	0	.0
53221	38.8	98	14.5	63	30.4	395	104.4	6	11	18.4	9	3	.2
53222	27.2	98	11.1	75	32.5	418	101.9	4	21	12.1	19	1	3.5
53223	29.8	90	10.6	63	33.2	423	112.9	6	10	12.9	7	0	.8
53224	14.6	90	4.9	63	34.0	463	113.6	9	4	6.5	4	0	.1
53225	26.8	94	10.0	45	30.1	450	101.3	8	11	11.9	9	1	.9
53226	20.9	99	7.7	69	38.2	508	129.4	5	17	9.3	15	1	.5
53227	24.2	99	9.5	57	30.2	392	108.9	6	14	11.3	11	1	.7
53228	12.1	98	4.2	65	34.2	483	118.2	7	7	5.9	6	0	.2
53233	15.2	68	6.2	4	12.3	252	46.4	4	10	5.8	10	1	1.1

RACINE

ZIP CODE	1	2	3	4	5	6	7	8	9	10	11	12	13
53402	31.6	96	11.2	73	35.0	380	107.3	8	10	14.5	8	0	.5
53403	26.6	72	10.0	60	26.6	303	78.1	8	10	9.3	10	3	10.1
53404	17.4	68	6.0	52	23.8	337	72.0	10	10	5.8	11	0	3.0
53405	28.1	96	10.2	77	32.7	383	91.6	7	13	12.9	11	1	.2
53406	18.3	94	6.1	66	33.4	360	121.2	7	11	8.3	8	1	.2

MADISON

ZIP CODE	1	2	3	4	5	6	7	8	9	10	11	12	13
53501	.3	100	.1	85	35.6	329	75.6	7	17	.1	17	0	.0
53502	1.9	99	.7	71	25.1	259	69.2	8	13	.9	11	0	.0
53503	1.5	99	.5	78	22.4	286	73.1	8	11	.7	10	0	.2
53504	2.2	99	.7	78	23.9	257	64.5	7	14	1.1	13	0	.5
53505	.5	100	.2	65	32.4	506	75.1	8	10	.3	9	0	.0
53506	1.1	0	.4	79	24.5	251	50.6	8	12	.0	0	0	.0
53507	1.3	99	.5	70	25.8	274	77.1	10	10	.7	9	0	.0
53508	3.0	0	1.0	79	29.9	349	86.4	7	11	.0	0	0	.3
53510	1.3	100	.5	71	24.0	263	68.5	9	12	.7	11	0	.0
53511	48.6	90	17.1	70	26.2	316	66.9	8	12	21.1	10	1	1.4
53515	2.0	99	.7	76	28.5	334	86.3	6	11	1.0	10	0	.0
53516	1.7	0	.6	79	21.8	236	60.1	8	18	.0	0	0	.0
53517	1.0	100	.3	64	23.3	315	91.2	9	10	.5	9	0	.2
53518	1.6	100	.5	83	20.4	246	48.4	8	15	.8	14	0	.7
53520	5.8	100	2.0	77	26.6	317	75.2	8	12	2.9	12	0	.3
53521	2.2	99	.7	81	27.2	348	93.1	8	9	1.1	9	0	.0
53522	1.0	0	.3	76	25.9	264	79.8	10	9	.0	0	0	.4
53523	3.9	99	1.4	76	28.6	323	99.8	7	12	1.9	11	0	.0
53525	3.6	99	1.2	71	28.8	327	86.6	8	13	1.7	11	0	.0
53526	1.5	100	.5	86	26.7	334	72.0	8	14	.3	8	0	14.6
53527	3.7	98	1.1	82	32.2	376	116.5	10	6	1.9	5	1	.0
53528	3.8	100	1.2	78	34.8	349	109.7	9	6	2.0	5	0	.0
53529	1.6	0	.5	76	30.0	404	95.8	9	9	.0	0	0	1.1
53530	4.6	100	1.6	74	23.7	263	70.3	8	16	2.2	13	0	.0
53531	2.6	98	.8	73	28.9	363	91.4	8	8	1.3	7	0	.3
53532	6.5	97	2.1	78	31.8	437	113.1	9	5	3.2	5	0	.5
53533	5.4	99	1.9	75	23.8	291	70.4	8	14	2.7	12	0	.0
53534	10.3	99	3.7	73	27.3	292	78.4	8	13	5.1	11	1	.2

MADISON (continued)

ZIP CODE	1	2	3	4	5	6	7	8	9	10	11	12	13
53536	5.5	100	2.0	73	30.0	273	79.3	8	13	2.8	11	0	.3
53537	.7	0	.2	77	26.4	301	73.6	8	10	.0	0	0	.3
53538	15.1	99	5.5	74	27.1	318	85.3	7	13	7.4	11	1	.8
53540	.2	100	.2	85	18.4	280	42.4	11	26	.1	30	0	.0
53541	1.0	100	.3	82	22.9	229	57.2	8	8	.5	7	0	.0
53542	.2	0	.1	89	27.6	264*	67.4	7	5	.2	0	0	2.3
53543	1.7	99	.5	78	23.2	255	59.5	9	11	.9	10	0	.0
53544	.8	100	.2	77	24.5	304	52.6	10	11	.4	10	0	.0
53545	60.1	99	21.2	69	29.4	338	89.2	8	10	29.1	8	3	1.0
53549	9.2	99	3.0	71	26.8	303	89.7	6	14	4.4	12	0	.1
53550	1.3	100	.4	72	27.5	371	69.7	9	8	.7	8	0	.0
53551	5.8	99	2.2	73	27.3	284	98.0	8	14	2.8	11	0	1.8
53553	.4	100	.1	80	22.0	211	38.6	9	12	.2	12	0	.0
53554	1.0	100	.4	80	25.0	269	58.9	8	13	.5	9	0	.0
53555	5.6	100	1.9	80	27.6	305	95.1	8	14	2.8	12	1	.0
53556	1.7	99	.6	81	20.4	255	57.7	8	15	.8	16	0	.2
53557	.5	97	.2	66	20.3	206	45.2	6	14	.2	12	1	.0
53558	6.1	99	2.0	81	34.5	356	113.7	9	4	3.0	4	1	.2
53559	4.2	99	1.4	79	28.4	338	101.2	9	8	.0	0	0	.1
53560	2.8	99	1.0	75	26.0	311	81.4	8	10	1.4	8	1	.0
53561	1.1	100	.4	79	22.1	294	94.0	6	18	.6	14	0	.2
53562	14.0	98	5.6	50	31.4	402	131.8	7	6	6.7	6	2	.7
53563	7.1	99	2.5	73	28.6	306	89.9	8	13	3.6	7	1	.0
53565	4.3	100	1.5	73	21.7	256	62.6	8	11	2.2	12	1	.2
53566	13.9	100	5.3	67	28.1	298	85.2	7	16	6.7	13	0	.6
53569	1.2	98	.4	77	22.8	274	55.0	7	14	.6	13	0	.0
53570	2.1	0	.7	72	25.0	278	72.8	9	13	.0	0	0	.7
53571	.3	100	.1	68	25.3	388	99.9	12	4	.2	0	0	.2
53572	5.5	99	1.9	74	28.2	338	99.1	7	13	2.7	11	0	.9
53573	3.3	0	1.1	80	21.0	251	60.3	7	17	.0	0	0	.0
53574	2.4	99	.9	73	27.2	269	83.5	8	19	.7	6	0	.2
53575	7.8	98	2.6	76	30.1	355	112.3	8	6	3.9	5	0	.0
53576	2.1	100	.7	77	27.1	341	76.5	8	9	1.1	9	0	.2
53577	1.5	99	.5	81	31.8	345	80.0	8	11	.8	9	0	.0
53578	3.4	100	1.2	75	26.8	336	92.8	8	12	1.7	12	0	.7
53579	1.6	99	.5	84	26.5	257	70.5	9	13	.8	9	0	.2
53580	.5	100	.2	76	23.6	294	44.4	8	12	.3	11	0	.0
53581	9.5	99	3.5	68	21.8	265	66.2	8	17	4.5	14	0	.4
53582	.9	100	.3	78	22.1	259	57.6	9	11	.9	11	0	.0
53583	4.8	100	1.6	73	26.7	320	86.6	7	15	2.3	14	0	.0
53584	.3	100	.1	82	23.3	273	60.6	9	7	.1	7	0	.9
53585	2.0	100	.7	74	26.1	345	75.7	9	10	1.0	9	0	.7
53586	2.7	100	.9	68	23.2	302	59.7	9	12	1.3	10	0	.0
53587	1.2	0	.4	72	24.3	341	62.2	9	12	.0	0	0	.0
53588	3.3	100	1.1	73	23.5	272	79.4	8	13	1.7	12	0	.0
53589	14.1	99	4.9	74	28.1	319	100.7	8	13	6.8	10	3	.9
53590	16.8	99	5.5	65	31.0	372	110.0	9	6	8.2	5	0	.3
53593	7.6	99	2.3	74	34.6	357	131.1	7	10	3.8	8	0	.3
53594	4.2	98	1.4	77	28.1	270	78.6	8	11	2.0	9	0	.3

*=Estimated **1.0=883 lbs per person; 100++ indicates per capita toxic waste generation > than 100 times the U.S. average of 883 lbs per capita.

ZIP CODE MEASURES OF SIZE, LEVELS OF AFFLUENCE AND QUALITY OF LIFE

1=Population (th.); 2= % White; 3=Households (th.); 4=% Owner Occupied; 5=Mean Income Per Household (th.$)*; 6=Mean Monthly Rent ($)*; 7=Mean Home Value (th.$)*;
8=% under 5; 9=% 65 and over; 10=White Males (th.); 11=% White Males, 65+; 12=# Toxic Waste Sites; 13=Toxic Waste Relative to US(883 lbs.per capita)**.

WISCONSIN

ZIPCODE	1	2	3	4	5	6	7	8	9	10	11	12	13
MADISON													
53597	7.7	100	2.4	71	34.3	392	120.7	8	7	3.8	6	0	.7
53598	1.7	0	.6	66	32.5	448	124.9	7	5	.0	0	0	.3
MADISON													
53703	25.8	94	11.2	11	14.4	362	95.4	1	7	12.9	4	0	.2
53704	38.3	96	15.4	59	27.7	356	99.3	6	10	17.5	8	1	.3
53705	29.2	94	12.3	50	33.3	383	138.7	5	13	12.7	11	0	.0
53711	38.1	97	13.8	68	35.0	420	121.0	7	8	17.8	7	0	.3
53713	18.6	89	8.8	22	22.9	372	124.4	7	4	7.9	4	0	.4
53714	16.4	97	5.8	69	28.8	384	89.8	7	7	8.7	7	1	.0
53715	9.2	89	4.2	27	16.9	334	83.9	2	17	3.8	12	0	4.1
53716	20.1	98	7.2	74	34.5	377	105.7	6	7	9.6	6	1	.0
53717	3.2	91	1.2	48	40.2	340	188.4	10	2	1.4	3	0	.0
53719	2.1	93	1.0	28	27.0	385	121.0	8	3	1.0	3	0	8.2
MADISON													
53801	.9	99	.3	82	24.9	121	43.7	6	14	.5	13	0	.0
53802	.1	100	.1	69	21.5	148	71.5	4	24	.1	24	0	.0
53803	1.2	0	.4	80	21.3	273	53.5	10	12	.0	0	0	.0
53804	1.6	100	.5	80	20.2	223	52.9	9	15	.8	12	0	.0
53805	4.8	99	1.7	74	20.6	244	59.5	9	15	2.3	15	1	.1
53806	2.4	100	.8	75	22.3	221	70.5	9	15	1.2	13	0	.0
53807	4.8	99	1.4	80	27.5	288	73.6	10	10	2.4	8	0	.0
53808	1.4	100	.4	72	32.6	278	87.5	11	8	.7	4	0	.0
53809	3.1	100	1.3	76	24.0	284	63.0	8	16	1.9	13	0	.0
53810	.7	100	.2	75	24.5	247	38.8	10	13	.5	12	0	.0
53811	3.3	0	1.0	79	28.8	312	82.4	8	8	.5	13	0	.0
53812	.5	100	.1	85	34.1	359	90.8	13	4	.1	24	0	.0
53813	6.7	100	2.3	72	24.4	286	71.3	10	16	3.2	13	0	.0
53816	.8	100	.3	72	21.2	271	50.6	9	13	.4	13	0	.0
53817	2.2	100	.1	66	19.0	185	50.6	9	15	.1	12	0	.0
53818	13.3	99	4.0	64	24.2	323	86.4	6	10	6.9	7	0	.0
53820	3.0	0	.9	81	24.9	310	71.2	8	9	.0	0	0	.0
53821	7.9	99	2.8	76	23.2	261	67.8	8	16	3.9	11	0	11.0
53825	.5	100	.2	88	21.6	131	51.8	7	11	.3	11	0	.0
53826	1.3	0	.4	75	22.6	211	55.1	12	12	.0	0	0	.0
53827	.5	0	.2	81	23.5	353	40.9	9	8	.0	0	0	.0
PORTAGE													
53901	11.0	99	4.3	71	22.9	282	73.8	7	16	5.3	13	0	2.1
53910	2.7	100	1.0	76	19.6	304	54.7	8	18	1.3	15	0	.0
53911	1.1	0	.4	72	28.4	394	83.3	10	10	.0	0	0	.0
53913	13.2	98	5.0	72	24.6	305	75.9	7	16	6.2	13	1	1.3
53916	19.6	99	7.2	71	26.3	335	82.2	7	15	9.4	13	3	.3
53919	2.7	0	.8	81	26.3	285	71.4	8	11	.0	0	0	.3
53920	.4	99	.2	84	22.4	345	71.5	5	15	.4	13	0	.1
53922	1.0	100	.3	80	27.6	189	83.9	6	8	.5	9	0	.0
53923	2.0	0	.7	73	24.2	254	58.8	9	13	.0	0	0	.0
53924	1.5	0	.5	81	21.3	264	60.8	7	11	.0	0	0	.0
53925	6.9	99	2.4	71	26.5	307	83.7	7	15	3.3	12	1	1.3
53926	1.0	100	.1	85	23.9	257	69.4	8	15	.5	15	0	.0
53927	.2	100	.1	88	19.9	346	69.4	5	8	.1	5	0	.0

WISCONSIN

ZIPCODE	1	2	3	4	5	6	7	8	9	10	11	12	13
PORTAGE													
53929	3.7	0	1.3	76	21.5	249	57.0	8	17	.0	0	0	.1
53930	1.2	0	.4	76	21.0	298	57.6	7	15	.0	0	0	.0
53931				88	22.8	365	57.0	9	14	.0	0	0	.3
53932	1.7	100	.6	73	25.0	310	76.0	7	12	.8	10	0	.5
53933	3.1	90	.9	77	22.7	282	72.1	6	13	1.5	13	0	.0
53934	3.2	98	1.2	78	20.3	294	67.6	6	23	1.5	23	0	.1
53935	.3	0	.1	94	27.3	313*	50.7	10	16	.0	0	0	.0
53936	.9	100	.4	90	19.0	268	54.8	8	19	.5	19	0	.0
53937	.3	99	.3	79	23.6	254	58.0	8	11	.4	9	0	.1
53939	.3	100	.1	84	23.6	281	62.9	6	25	.1	25	0	.0
53940	.8	95	.3	69	25.5	283	93.3	7	10	.4	9	0	.0
53941	2.1	0	.7	80	22.3	279	70.1	7	14	.0	0	0	.0
53942	.2	100	.1	80	25.5	308	49.0	8	12	.1	13	0	.0
53943	1.0	0	.3	67	24.2	255	57.8	6	12	.0	0	0	.0
53944	1.5	98	.5	76	19.0	255	54.8	8	15	.2	16	0	.0
53945	.1	100	.1	81	12.8	147*	39.1	4	47	.0	38	0	.0
53946	4.2	99	1.5	78	26.2	272	78.3	7	17	2.1	15	1	.0
53947	.2	0	.1	81	17.6	236	54.4	1	24	.0	0	0	.1
53948	6.7	99	2.5	75	20.8	265	62.2	7	17	3.2	15	0	.9
53949	4.5	99	1.7	80	19.9	272	66.7	7	19	2.2	18	0	.4
53950	3.5	99	1.3	80	20.5	248	59.0	8	18	1.7	17	0	.0
53951	1.9	100	.8	77	20.0	219	62.7	7	18	.9	17	0	.0
53952	2.8	89	.8	79	21.1	291	69.6	6	15	1.4	15	0	.0
53953	.3	100	.1	92	14.6	185	49.1	4	28	.0	0	0	.0
53954	4.4	99	1.6	81	24.6	301	81.9	7	13	2.2	12	0	.0
53955	4.4	99	1.5	79	25.9	328	88.3	8	11	2.2	9	0	.0
53956	3.4	100	1.1	80	24.5	278	71.0	8	16	1.7	14	2	2.1
53959	8.5	100	3.1	75	23.4	242	71.3	7	18	4.1	15	0	.4
53960	2.8	0	1.0	81	23.8	271	69.5	7	16	.0	0	0	.0
53961	.2	100	.3	86	25.3	303	53.8	8	16	.4	14	0	.0
53962	.2	0	.1	97	20.6	236*	58.4	7	13	.0	0	0	2.4
53963	11.2	93	3.5	77	27.3	300	75.1	7	12	5.4	10	0	.3
53964	2.6	98	1.0	80	20.1	272	63.4	8	18	1.3	17	0	.0
53965	6.5	97	2.4	77	21.2	288	82.2	6	16	3.1	15	0	.3
53969	1.6	0	.3	78	21.2	287	82.0	9	11	.2	0	0	.7
	.4	100	.1	70	22.3	320	69.9	3	40	.2	36	0	.0
SAINT PAUL													
54001	5.7	100	2.0	80	23.3	277	79.7	7	18	2.8	17	0	.1
54002	3.7	0	1.3	80	26.7	305	89.7	8	13	.0	0	2	.2
54003	1.0	0	.3	89	27.6	418	72.3	8	9	.0	0	0	.0
54004	2.0	0	.7	81	21.8	271	61.6	9	9	.0	0	0	.1
54005	2.6	100	.9	80	22.3	257	67.7	8	14	1.3	13	0	.1
54006	.8	99	.3	84	19.3	301	49.2	9	15	.4	13	0	.0
54007	1.2	99	.4	85	24.0	271	68.3	9	10	.6	12	1	.0
54008	.7	100	.2	88	24.8	380	96.4	11	11	.3	11	0	.2
54009	1.4	100	.5	79	26.3	268	76.7	9	11	.7	11	0	.0
54010	1.1	0	.4	59	22.2	321	77.0	6	32	.2	29	0	.2
54011	5.1	100	1.7	80	27.2	325	82.5	8	12	2.5	10	0	.0
54012	.8		.2	86	24.2	246	53.6	11	8	.0	0	0	.0

*=Estimated **1.0=883 lbs per person; 100++ indicates per capita toxic waste generation > than 100 times the U.S. average of 883 lbs per capita.

ZIP CODE MEASURES OF SIZE, LEVELS OF AFFLUENCE AND QUALITY OF LIFE

1=Population (th.); 2= % White; 3=Households (th.); 4=% Owner Occupied; 5=Mean Income Per Household (th.$); 6=Mean Monthly Rent ($)*; 7=Mean Home Value (th.$)*; 8=% under 5; 9=% 65 and over; 10=White Males (th.); 11=% White Males, 65+; 12=# Toxic Waste Sites; 13=Toxic Waste Relative to US(883 lbs.per capita)**.

WISCONSIN

SAINT PAUL

ZIPCODE	1	2	3	4	5	6	7	8	9	10	11	12	13
54013	2.3	100	.8	78	23.1	296	63.2	8	14	1.2	13	0	.1
54014	1.9	100	.6	89	27.4	319	81.6	8	11	1.0	10	0	.4
54015	1.7	100	.6	75	26.0	316	82.3	7	12	.9	11	0	.0
54016	11.9	98	3.9	74	33.7	355	123.9	8	7	5.8	6	1	.9
54017	9.5	100	3.1	74	27.3	318	92.3	9	11	4.7	9	0	.7
54020	3.9	99	1.3	78	25.1	247	87.5	9	11	2.0	10	0	.0
54021	3.8	0	1.2	78	29.5	346	108.1	7	8	.0	0	0	.0
54022	14.0	98	4.2	63	27.6	345	104.5	7	8	6.8	6	1	.0
54023	1.9	99	.6	82	29.2	377	96.3	10	7	1.0	7	0	.1
54024	3.4	100	1.2	77	23.7	281	85.9	7	16	1.7	14	0	.3
54025	2.8	0	.9	76	29.7	297	94.1	9	6	.0	0	0	.1
54026	1.3	100	.5	83	25.4	276	93.1	11	12	.7	11	0	.0
54027	.8	98	.3	89	25.8	321	44.7	5	10	.4	10	0	.0
54028	1.8	100	.6	85	26.0	259	72.8	10	16	.9	14	0	.1

GREEN BAY (WEST)

ZIPCODE	1	2	3	4	5	6	7	8	9	10	11	12	13
54101	1.6	0	.5	91	24.1	194	77.8	8	8	.0	0	0	.2
54102	.8	0	.3	87	19.5	192	52.7	8	12	.0	0	0	.0
54103	.5	99	.2	83	19.7	293	48.1	4	17	.3	19	0	.0
54104	.6	100	.2	92	16.4	203	57.8	5	16	.3	18	0	.0
54106	4.0	99	1.2	85	28.2	279	79.7	9	9	2.0	9	0	.3
54107	3.1	98	1.1	79	26.3	272	74.6	9	13	1.6	13	0	.3
54110	4.8	99	1.6	81	29.3	250	84.2	8	11	2.4	10	2	1.9
54111	2.0	99	.7	85	23.4	350	75.7	8	16	1.0	18	0	.0
54112	2.2	0	.7	77	20.8	262	71.0	8	13	.3	21	0	.3
54113	2.6	100	.9	90	30.2	316	81.5	8	2	1.3	2	0	.3
54114	4.2	100	1.5	82	18.7	246	65.8	6	19	2.1	19	0	1.6
54115	21.9	96	6.5	75	31.9	331	99.5	8	8	10.4	7	1	.5
54119	.5	0	.1	78	18.0	158	58.7	5	13	.0	0	0	.0
54120	.5	0	.1	81	14.2	234	62.6	4	18	.0	0	0	.5
54121	2.4	0	.3	80	20.2	206	70.0	7	21	.0	0	0	.0
54123	.1	100	.1	98	28.4	326*	63.4	10	14	.1	11	0	.0
54124	3.4	98	1.2	83	19.6	219	57.8	7	18	1.7	18	0	.0
54125	.7	99	.3	78	19.2	220	41.3	5	20	.3	21	0	.3
54126	3.3	0	.9	86	28.2	305	85.1	10	8	.7	17	0	.0
54128	1.6	80	.5	79	19.3	246	56.3	8	15	.7	17	0	.0
54129	3.4	100	1.0	82	30.7	262	77.2	9	9	1.7	8	0	1.9
54130	19.0	99	6.0	79	28.8	288	80.1	9	9	9.5	8	0	.0
54135	1.6	17	.4	76	18.3	220	63.3	10	8	.1	24	0	1.3
54136	5.9	99	2.0	79	27.8	262	76.1	8	8	2.9	7	0	1.7
54137	1.0	0	.3	85	25.1	289	72.0	9	11	.0	0	0	.0
54138	.5	0	.2	88	15.8	201	59.3	5	22	.0	0	0	.0
54139	3.2	100	1.0	81	22.8	256	65.6	8	11	1.6	11	0	.0
54140	6.6	99	2.1	77	28.1	332	78.3	10	9	3.2	8	0	.0
54141	2.5	0	.7	88	28.7	317	86.0	10	7	.0	0	0	.0
54143	15.7	100	6.0	74	22.1	268	62.4	8	16	7.5	13	4	1.6
54149	.9	0	.3	93	18.3	165	60.2	8	19	.0	0	0	.0
54150	1.4	0	.1	66	23.6	244	32.4	14	7	.0	0	0	.0
54151	2.8	100	1.0	85	24.1	318	63.5	7	15	1.4	13	0	1.9
54152	.3	100	.1	80	18.2	418	54.0	13	13	.1	16	0	.0

WISCONSIN

GREEN BAY (WEST)

ZIPCODE	1	2	3	4	5	6	7	8	9	10	11	12	13
54153	6.6	99	2.3	78	20.8	250	58.0	7	17	3.2	15	0	.6
54154	4.5	100	1.6	78	21.3	269	65.2	7	15	2.2	13	1	.7
54155	3.1	71	.8	83	30.8	240	113.6	9	6	1.1	5	0	.0
54156	1.3	0	.5	74	19.6	334	59.8	10	16	.0	0	0	.1
54157	5.1	100	1.7	80	24.7	300	73.3	10	18	2.5	16	1	.6
54159	1.3	100	.4	90	20.8	286	62.5	12	11	.6	11	0	.0
54160	.3	95	.1	76	27.4	308	72.3	6	13	.1	12	0	.0
54161	2.6	99	.9	81	22.1	276	65.3	10	14	1.3	15	0	.0
54162	5.8	100	1.8	83	28.2	262	79.3	8	10	3.0	9	0	4.1
54165	6.4	97	2.0	80	28.2	286	81.7	8	11	3.1	11	0	.5
54166	13.5	97	5.1	76	22.1	287	74.9	7	20	6.2	18	1	.2
54169	.4	100	.1	84	31.7	315	78.3	7	12	.2	12	0	.0
54170	3.0	100	.9	85	27.7	239	73.9	8	9	1.6	9	0	.0
54171	1.0	0	.3	93	26.3	118	95.6	10	8	.0	0	0	.0
54173	.5	0	.2	92	25.9	297	68.3	2	15	.2	0	0	.2
54174	3.0	91	1.0	81	19.1	225	60.6	8	15	1.4	16	0	.0
54175	.8	0	.3	90	16.1	244	58.9	8	25	.0	0	0	.0
54177	2.6	100	1.0	83	19.2	248	56.5	8	17	1.3	16	0	.0
54180	1.0	0	.3	82	26.3	306	79.9	11	11	.0	0	0	.0

GREEN BAY (EAST)

ZIPCODE	1	2	3	4	5	6	7	8	9	10	11	12	13
54201	5.7	0	2.2	75	23.9	244	69.3	7	18	.0	0	1	.2
54202	1.0	0	.4	86	23.1	317	110.9	6	20	.0	0	0	.0
54204	1.5	100	.5	84	24.9	219	58.9	10	15	.8	14	0	.0
54205	1.9	0	.6	84	27.2	250	70.8	9	12	.0	0	0	.0
54206	1.7	0	.6	89	30.0	284	69.3	9	8	.0	0	0	.2
54207	.2	100	.1	79	23.5	310	71.2	14	13	.1	13	0	.0
54208	5.2	0	1.6	84	27.4	275	77.1	8	11	.0	0	0	.0
54209	.9	100	.3	83	25.3	315	89.0	8	15	.5	14	0	.0
54210	.7	0	.3	83	22.2	151	81.7	6	21	.0	0	0	.0
54211	.3	100	.1	91	30.5	351*	137.8	5	26	1.4*	20	1	.0
54212	.7	0	.3	82	22.4	250	108.7	7	20	.0	0	0	.0
54213	1.3	98	.4	81	27.0	307	78.9	8	12	.7	12	0	.0
54214	.4	100	.2	78	28.0	255	80.3	10	13	.2	11	0	.0
54215	.3	100	.1	75	22.3	283	70.5	15	9	.1	7	0	.0
54216	6.2	100	1.7	82	26.0	195	68.7	8	15	.0	0	0	1.9
54217	5.6	100	1.7	85	29.0	292	83.6	9	9	2.9	9	0	.0
54220	40.4	99	14.8	70	25.9	269	78.1	7	16	19.0	14	1	1.2
54227	1.5	100	.4	87	26.2	279	81.6	10	10	.8	11	0	.0
54228	2.9	100	.9	81	28.3	266	74.5	8	9	1.5	8	0	.0
54229	2.1	99	.6	88	31.5	269	99.7	9	11	1.1	8	0	.0
54230	2.8	100	.8	77	29.8	240	76.2	9	11	1.4	10	0	.0
54232	.7	99	.2	82	24.1	185	67.2	6	14	.4	11	0	.0
54234	1.2	99	.5	80	23.5	245	115.3	7	24	.6	23	0	.0
54235	16.4	98	6.0	77	25.4	308	88.1	8	15	8.1	13	1	1.8
54241	17.3	99	6.0	76	25.5	270	71.9	8	12	8.4	11	1	1.5
54245	2.2	0	.7	82	32.7	278	82.2	10	10	.4	10	0	.0
54246	.5	99	.7	83	19.4	128	89.0	8	30	.3	29	0	.0
54247	2.1	100	.6	87	26.6	304	77.3	10	10	1.1	9	2	.0

*=Estimated **1.0=883 lbs per person; 100++ indicates per capita toxic waste generation > than 100 times the U.S. average of 883 lbs per capita.

ZIP CODE MEASURES OF SIZE, LEVELS OF AFFLUENCE AND QUALITY OF LIFE

1=Population (th.); 2= % White; 3=Households (th.); 4=% Owner Occupied; 5=Mean Income Per Household (th.$); 6=Mean Monthly Rent ($); 7=Mean Home Value (th.$); 8=% under 5; 9=% 65 and over; 10=White Males (th.); 11=% White Males, 65+; 12=# Toxic Waste Sites; 13=Toxic Waste Relative to US(883 lbs.per capita)**.

WISCONSIN

GREEN BAY

ZIPCODE	1	2	3	4	5	6	7	8	9	10	11	12	13
54301	38.2	97	13.3	67	30.1	317	102.1	8	11	17.8	9	2	.1
54302	24.5	97	9.7	62	23.6	325	80.9	8	11	11.4	10	1	.1
54303	44.6	98	15.8	67	27.0	332	90.1	8	9	21.2	7	2	.2
54304	28.9	99	9.9	69	27.8	357	86.2	8	8	13.7	7	0	.5

WAUSAU

ZIPCODE	1	2	3	4	5	6	7	8	9	10	11	12	13
54401	48.5	99	18.0	71	26.3	314	83.8	7	13	23.1	11	3	.5
54405	2.8	100	1.0	75	22.9	219	62.9	7	17	1.4	15	0	.1
54406	2.8	100	.9	82	23.9	266	78.7	10	11	1.4	11	0	.0
54407	1.4	0	.5	79	22.8	275	75.7	10	10			0	.0
54408	1.2	100	.4	87	22.6	212	52.6	8	11	.6	11	1	.0
54409	13.3	99	4.7	75	20.9	265	60.8	8	17	6.4	13	0	.4
54410	1.9	99	.6	83	23.8	279	58.5	11	13	1.0	12	0	.0
54411	3.8	0	1.1	85	23.7	228	62.9	9	12			0	.0
54412	2.1	100	.6	81	24.2	317	65.6	10	9	1.0	9	0	.0
54413	.3	0	.1	86	22.6	327	33.9	10	16			0	.0
54414	2.8	99	.9	85	22.5	251	58.6	10	12	1.4	11	0	.0
54416	1.5	70	.5	72	17.9	227	49.3	10	14	.5	17	0	.0
54417	1.1	100	.1	71	24.4	349	67.8	9	15	.1	13	0	14.0
54418	1.1	0	.3	84	22.7	214	59.8	9	11			0	.0
54420	1.0	0	.3	87	19.8	278	58.7	9	12			0	.3
54421	3.6	0	1.1	80	22.6	269	59.8	10	13			0	.0
54422	1.2	100	.3	84	21.8	305	51.2	14	10	.6	11	0	.0
54423	1.7	99	.5	87	26.3	379	80.5	11	11			0	.0
54424	1.6	0	.5	92	20.3	356	63.6	7	14			0	.0
54425	1.6	100	.5	81	24.5	302	56.9	9	13	.6	11	1	.0
54426	3.8	100	1.1	84	25.8	239	63.5	9	10	2.0	10	0	.1
54427	1.0	0	.3	89	25.7	251	55.8	8	13			0	.0
54428	.9	0	.4	88	18.9	292	63.2	9	21			0	.0
54429	.2	100	.1	63	17.2	282	56.2	9	15	.2	14	0	.0
54430	.2	100	.1	95	18.0	206*	64.8	9	11	.1	14	0	.0
54435	2.0	0	.7	88	21.3	255	51.7	7	15			0	.0
54436	1.9	0	.6	86	19.3	190	59.9	7	15			0	.0
54437	2.1	99	.7	84	20.9	290	61.5	8	13	1.1	14	0	.0
54438	3.1	100	1.0	87	19.8	254	56.9	7	15			0	.2
54440	1.0	99	.3	91	29.4	360	74.8	9	9	1.6	9	0	.0
54441	.3	100	.3	90	30.9	355*	80.0	14	8	.8	8	0	.0
54442	1.2	94	.3	90	22.1	144	63.1	7	14	.6	7	0	.0
54443	2.3	99	.7	87	23.6	245	64.2	10	10	1.2	9	0	.0
54445	.3	100	.1	90	14.4	94	54.3	9	24	.1	25	0	.0
54446	3.2	0	1.0	81	21.3	243	61.4	9	12	.0		0	.0
54447	.8	100	.3	77	17.4	202	44.1	9	13	.4	13	0	.0
54448	4.2	100	1.2	82	29.8	277	84.9	9	11	2.2	10	0	.0
54449	24.1	99	8.5	68	26.1	290	78.2	8	13	11.4	11	0	.2
54450	.4	100	.1	84	14.9	353	34.7	10	21	.0		0	.1
54451	9.9	100	3.3	78	25.9	294	72.4	8	13	5.0	12	0	.0
54452	17.4	100	6.1	77	23.6	255	66.4	8	14	8.6	12	0	.2
54454	1.2	0	.80	80	24.4	184	58.8	9	9	.0		0	.1
54455	12.3	100	4.0	83	27.2	338	86.7	10	10	6.2	8	2	.3

WISCONSIN

WAUSAU

ZIPCODE	1	2	3	4	5	6	7	8	9	10	11	12	13
54456	6.2	99	2.2	79	21.1	256	63.0	7	19	3.0	16	1	.3
54457	6.8	98	2.3	84	26.0	308	69.1	7	11	3.4	10	0	.7
54458	.2	100	.1	73	25.0	277	65.6	9	15	.1	16	0	.7
54459	1.4	0	.5	87	16.3	216	48.8	9	21			0	.0
54460	2.9	100	.9	79	18.8	219	50.4	7	22	1.5	20	0	.4
54462	.7	0	.3	76	18.0	343	50.6	9	15			0	.0
54463	.6	100	.3	83	17.8	164	73.5	5	28	.4	29	0	.0
54464	.2	0	.1	86	22.7	261*	46.7	7	12			0	.0
54465	.4	100	.2	88	17.2	62	66.9	4	29	.2	30	0	.0
54466	2.9	99	.9	83	22.5	305	59.7	9	13	1.4	12	1	.0
54467	4.9	100	1.6	77	27.5	300	94.9	10	5	2.5	3	0	.1
54469	2.0	0	.6	86	34.1	406	84.3	7	18			1	.0
54470	2.1	100	.7	82	19.2	261	52.3	8	17	.0	18	0	12.6
54471	.5	100	.1	93	32.6	375*	79.8	9	10	1.0	2	0	.0
54473	2.2	100	.7	84	22.5	219	65.3	9	14	1.1	13	0	.0
54474	3.9	99	1.3	80	31.0	357	89.1	9	7	1.9	6	0	2.1
54475	1.7	0	.5	87	30.2	302	80.3	7	8	.0		0	.0
54476	12.4	98	4.2	82	27.8	354	90.2	10	7	6.1	6	1	.0
54479	3.6	100	1.2	82	21.4	214	65.7	10	10	1.8	10	0	1.5
54480	1.2	99	.4	81	22.5	259	60.7	11	12	.0	11	0	.3
54481	37.2	98	11.9	68	26.1	320	84.9	7	10	18.0	8	2	.2
54484	4.2	0	1.3	84	24.7	254	66.9	9	11			0	.1
54485	.3	100	.1	84	18.2	315	61.3	5	26	.1	30	0	.0
54486	2.6	99	.9	80	19.1	215	49.9	8	14	1.3	14	0	.0
54487	8.4	99	3.0	79	25.3	252	73.3	9	16	4.1	15	0	.5
54488	1.4	0	.5	88	26.0	250	52.7	9	11			0	.0
54489	1.6	99	.5	86	25.5	242	69.5	10	12	.8	12	0	.0
54490	.9	100	.3	86	16.7	261	43.9	10	18	.5	19	0	.0
54491	1.1	0	.4	82	18.5	250	51.5	7	16			0	.0
54493	.8	100	.3	92	21.9	118	49.1	7	15	.4	14	0	.0
54494	33.2	99	11.6	76	27.7	326	72.3	8	11	16.0	10	3	.6
54498	1.1	100	.7	87	20.0	302	52.0	8	14	1.0	14	0	.0
54499	2.9	98	.9	79	22.0	258	59.3	8	16	1.4	14	0	.0

RHINELANDER

ZIPCODE	1	2	3	4	5	6	7	8	9	10	11	12	13
54501	19.3	99	6.9	76	23.5	292	76.2	7	13	9.3	12	1	.9
54510	.2	0	.1	78	16.8	438	92.1	5	17	.0		0	.0
54511	1.0	100	.3	89	18.7	244	56.1	8	12	.5	13	0	.0
54512	.7	100	.3	84	21.2	265	99.2	6	25	.3	25	0	.0
54513	.7	100	.2	89	16.2	186*	48.5	7	16	.3	15	0	.0
54514	2.1	100	.7	87	20.1	256	55.2	9	14	1.1	14	0	.0
54515	.7	0	.2	84	21.4	275	47.5	9	13	.0		0	.0
54517	.1	0	.1	81	15.3	244	50.1	3	20	.0		0	.0
54518	.2	100	.1	82	20.5	235	67.9	7	11	.1	13	0	.0
54519	.8	97	.3	89	22.6	264	83.4	4	19	.4	20	0	.0
54520	3.4	90	1.1	76	16.9	194	66.9	9	16	1.5	16	0	.9
54521	6.0	99	2.3	81	19.7	285	85.8	6	20	2.9	19	0	.0
54524	.6	0	.2	81	22.1	263	46.7	8	11	.0		0	.0
54525	.3	0	.1	80	15.4	237	33.6	6	21	.0		0	.0
54526	.9	100	.2	92	18.5	428	47.6	10	11	.0		0	.0

*=Estimated **1.0-883 lbs per person; 100++ indicates per capita toxic waste generation > than 100 times the U.S. average of 883 lbs per capita.

ZIP CODE MEASURES OF SIZE, LEVELS OF AFFLUENCE AND QUALITY OF LIFE

1=Population (th.); 2= % White; 3=Households (th.); 4=% Owner Occupied; 5=Mean Income Per Household (th.$); 6=Mean Monthly Rent ($); 7=Mean Home Value (th.$);
8=% under 5, 9=% 65 and over; 10=White Males (th.); 11=% White Males, 65+; 12=# Toxic Waste Sites, 13=Toxic Waste Relative to US(883 lbs.per capita)**.

WISCONSIN

RHINELANDER

ZIP CODE	1	2	3	4	5	6	7	8	9	10	11	12	13
54527	1.4	0	.5	82	17.3	169	48.8	7	17	.0	0	0	.0
54529	.6	0	.2	87	20.0	264	69.9	7	15	.0	0	0	.0
54530	1.0	100	.3	86	20.6	252	46.5	7	12	.5	11	0	.0
54531	.8	0	.3	92	22.5	234	89.5	7	16	.5	11	0	.7
54534	2.9	99	1.2	72	15.5	210	45.2	7	22	1.4	19	0	.0
54536	.3	100	.1	96	14.9	172*	36.6	3	39	.1	43	0	.0
54537	.5	100	.2	79	15.3	267	52.2	9	12	.3	11	0	.0
54538	2.0	45	.6	64	19.4	272	80.7	8	16	.5	27	0	.6
54539	.9	99	.3	84	20.2	208	87.8	5	15	.5	16	0	.0
54540	.9	0	.3	80	18.9	239	93.9	6	18	.0	0	0	1.6
54541	1.9	94	.6	76	18.5	250	54.4	7	16	.9	15	0	.0
54542	.2	100	.1	77	13.6	206	47.9	9	10	.1	14	0	.0
54543	.2	0	.1	90	20.3	316	89.1	8	21	.0	0	0	.0
54545	.9	0	.4	84	24.0	248	105.2	5	31	.0	0	0	.0
54546	1.6	0	.6	74	18.3	164	38.9	9	14	.0	0	0	.0
54547	1.4	0	.6	79	15.8	209	68.7	5	20	.0	0	0	.2
54548	3.3	99	1.3	78	24.5	345	110.8	5	17	1.6	16	0	.0
54549	.3	100	.1	81	15.3	306	60.5	7	11	.1	10	0	.0
54550	.6	0	.2	85	17.7	203	40.7	9	16	.0	0	0	.0
54551	.2	100	.6	87	15.8	273	46.4	6	20	.1	21	0	1.0
54552	5.2	99	1.9	78	21.1	220	62.3	7	18	2.6	16	1	.0
54554	.2	100	.4	94	15.4	177*	40.0	2	23	.1	19	0	1.0
54555	1.0	98	.4	76	20.7	176	71.6	2	23	.5	21	0	.0
54556	4.8	0	1.8	81	19.2	235	65.6	7	19	.0	0	0	1.3
54557	1.3	99	.5	82	17.4	237	57.1	7	17	.6	19	0	3.0
54558	.4	100	.2	89	19.9	209	84.2	5	15	.2	15	0	.0
54559	1.2	0	.5	89	20.9	315	97.3	4	19	.0	0	0	.0
54560	.5	0	.2	85	19.5	235	67.1	6	16	.0	0	0	.0
54562	1.6	0	.6	85	19.0	245	92.1	6	21	.2	15	0	.0
54563	.7	0	.2	85	19.1	288	71.6	7	12	.0	0	0	.0
54564	.5	100	.2	84	15.9	115	49.7	4	14	.2	18	0	.0
54566	1.5	95	.5	78	17.6	250	56.4	7	17	.7	18	0	.0
54567	.2	100	.1	95	13.3	153*	65.0	3	19	.1	18	0	.0
54568	3.8	99	1.4	84	21.7	293	93.4	7	14	1.9	18	0	.0

LA CROSSE

ZIP CODE	1	2	3	4	5	6	7	8	9	10	11	12	13
54601	60.7	99	22.1	60	24.9	326	89.8	6	14	27.8	11	1	.7
54610	2.1	0	.8	78	24.4	227	63.2	7	14	.0	0	0	.0
54611	1.1	0	.4	72	20.6	264	45.5	7	16	.0	0	0	.0
54612	4.5	0	1.5	74	22.2	272	67.4	7	15	.0	0	0	.1
54613	2.5	99	.4	82	19.8	262	52.2	6	18	.0	0	0	.0
54614	2.5	99	.8	80	30.1	280	70.5	8	11	1.2	10	0	.0
54615	8.0	95	2.9	72	21.3	266	62.1	8	17	3.7	16	1	.3
54616	2.7	0	.9	77	21.2	242	61.9	9	19	.0	0	0	.0
54618	2.1	99	.7	80	21.2	287	57.1	9	12	1.1	11	1	.0
54619	3.2	100	1.0	83	23.9	229	51.5	8	13	1.7	12	0	.0
54621	1.0	0	.3	80	25.6	264	67.3	8	10	.0	0	0	.0
54622	2.4	0	.7	81	22.8	262	68.8	7	19	.0	0	0	.0
54623	1.9	100	.7	88	26.0	277	75.4	7	14	1.0	11	0	.0

WISCONSIN

LA CROSSE

ZIP CODE	1	2	3	4	5	6	7	8	9	10	11	12	13
54624	1.1	99	.4	80	21.6	228	60.0	5	19	.6	20	0	.0
54625	.2	100	.1	80	19.6	77	59.4	6	19	.1	19	0	.0
54626	1.2	100	.7	80	18.8	253	51.4	10	13	.6	16	0	.0
54627	2.2	100	.7	83	21.5	264	65.7	7	13	1.2	14	0	.0
54628	1.2	100	.4	78	21.2	249	56.1	6	14	.6	14	0	.0
54629	2.4	100	.8	79	24.7	258	71.5	7	15	1.3	14	1	.0
54630	3.1	99	1.1	74	21.9	257	71.4	8	15	1.6	13	0	.1
54631	1.1	0	.7	76	19.3	212	50.8	8	12	.0	0	0	.1
54632	.9	0	.3	85	24.1	204	63.6	8	12	.0	0	0	1.6
54633	.4	100	1.1	83	26.3	246	47.6	7	10	.2	12	0	.0
54634	2.8	100	1.1	77	20.7	277	64.2	5	21	1.3	17	0	.0
54635	1.7	99	.6	82	20.1	228	55.0	8	15	.8	17	0	.0
54636	5.2	100	1.6	83	26.5	321	86.9	10	7	2.6	7	0	.0
54637	1.1	100	.1	79	13.3	326	31.4	9	27	.0	0	0	.0
54638	1.5	100	.5	80	24.4	217	56.6	9	14	.7	16	0	.0
54639	2.1	100	.8	76	17.4	249	44.5	8	16	1.1	16	0	.0
54640	1.9	100	.7	93	17.6	202*	51.4	0	19	.1	14	0	.0
54642	1.0	100	.7	81	22.7	242	59.1	7	12	.1	11	0	.0
54643	.2	0	.1	77	18.3	347	51.8	8	14	.0	0	0	.0
54644	1.2	0	.4	79	21.1	305	55.2	8	15	.0	0	0	.0
54645	.1	100	.1	85	18.2	209*	48.3	2	31	.1	25	0	.0
54646	2.6	99	.9	84	20.7	279	58.7	8	15	1.3	16	0	.2
54648	1.6	100	.5	76	22.8	168	59.9	8	12	.8	10	0	.2
54650	14.6	99	4.9	80	27.8	388	99.6	10	7	7.2	6	0	.0
54651	.9	100	.4	78	20.1	204	47.2	10	19	.5	17	0	.0
54652	.8	100	.3	81	17.1	327	35.5	5	21	.4	18	0	.0
54653	.8	100	.3	86	24.2	304	69.2	9	8	.5	9	0	.2
54654	.2	100	.1	90	27.7	319*	52.5	12	14	.1	16	0	.5
54655	1.9	99	.8	77	18.8	213	52.0	7	18	1.0	17	0	.0
54656	12.5	99	4.4	74	23.2	276	69.5	8	14	6.0	12	1	1.9
54657	.4	100	.4	78	19.2	186	37.2	13	8	.2	6	0	.0
54658	2.3	100	.7	89	27.9	396	93.9	9	8	1.1	8	0	.0
54659	1.1	0	.4	80	17.2	238	48.4	8	17	.0	0	0	.0
54660	12.4	98	4.2	74	25.1	297	74.2	7	15	6.2	14	5	.5
54661	2.3	100	.8	80	22.4	304	73.9	9	9	1.1	9	0	.0
54664	1.4	0	.5	79	18.8	204	44.6	8	20	.0	0	0	.2
54665	7.6	100	2.9	75	21.6	231	70.2	7	19	3.6	16	0	.0
54666	1.8	98	.6	78	22.3	311	64.7	8	12	.9	11	0	.0
54667	3.9	100	1.4	81	21.2	219	71.4	7	19	2.0	18	0	.0
54669	5.1	100	1.6	80	26.4	308	91.9	9	13	2.5	12	0	.2
54670	1.6	0	.5	77	21.5	202	44.0	10	9	.0	0	0	.0
54672	.8	0	.3	86	33.7	349	42.3	9	11	.0	0	0	.0

EAU CLAIRE

ZIP CODE	1	2	3	4	5	6	7	8	9	10	11	12	13
54701	64	99	22.6	65	24.8	333	81.0	6	11	30.1	9	2	.2
54720	4.6	98	1.7	70	24.5	325	78.9	8	9	2.2	8	0	.0
54721	1.5	98	.5	80	21.5	284	56.4	9	13	.7	11	0	.0
54722	3.5	99	1.2	80	21.0	266	53.5	8	17	1.7	16	0	.1
54723	1.2	98	.4	80	26.0	329	65.3	8	9	.6	8	0	.0
54724	1.9	100	2.1	80	23.8	246	66.8	8	14	3.2	12	0	.0

*=Estimated **1.0=883 lbs per person; 100++ indicates per capita toxic waste generation > than 100 times the U.S. average of 883 lbs per capita.

ZIP CODE MEASURES OF SIZE, LEVELS OF AFFLUENCE AND QUALITY OF LIFE

1=Population (th.); 2= % White; 3=Households (th.); 4=% Owner Occupied; 5=Mean Income Per Household (th.$); 6=Mean Monthly Rent ($); 7=Mean Home Value (th.$);
8=% under 5; 9=% 65 and over; 10=% White Males (th.); 11=% White Males, 65+; 12=# Toxic Waste Sites; 13=Toxic Waste Relative to US(883 lbs.per capita)**.

WISCONSIN — EAU CLAIRE

ZIPCODE	1	2	3	4	5	6	7	8	9	10	11	12	13
54725	2.5	100	.9	78	19.6	281	54.1	8	15	1.3	15	0	.2
54726	2.0	100	.6	85	22.8	254	49.5	10	15	1.0	15	0	.0
54727	4.0	100	1.2	80	25.5	245	62.1	11	10	2.0	10	0	.0
54728	4.9	100	1.8	80	18.7	263	65.5	8	21	2.5	20	1	.0
54729	25.0	99	8.5	74	24.5	292	72.1	7	13	12.1	11	0	.4
54730	3.8	100	1.3	81	22.6	294	68.0	9	15	1.9	13	0	.0
54731	.8	100	.2	87	20.4	319	50.8	7	10	.4	11	0	.0
54732	3.0	100	1.0	81	20.4	267	58.1	9	14	1.4	14	0	.3
54733	.8	0	.2	79	18.8	263	43.1	10	19	.0	0	0	.0
54734	.8	100	.2	90	24.1	188	57.0	11	12	.4	11	0	.0
54736	4.0	100	1.4	73	22.9	267	67.7	9	16	2.0	15	0	.0
54737	.5	100	.1	82	22.4	239	56.7	10	16	.2	15	0	.0
54738	2.8	0	.9	83	22.9	267	65.3	8	11	.0	0	0	.0
54739	3.1	99	.9	82	24.3	270	73.8	11	7	1.5	6	0	.0
54740	2.4	100	.8	80	21.8	250	54.6	7	17	1.2	15	0	.0
54741	1.4	0	.5	86	19.4	229	37.2	7	16	.0	0	0	.0
54742	3.9	100	1.3	84	23.8	267	73.4	9	11	2.0	9	0	.0
54744	.5	98	.2	87	21.4	333	47.0	12	9	.3	10	0	.0
54745	2.0	0	.7	89	16.7	248	63.1	8	14	.0	0	0	.0
54746	.7	95	.2	76	20.3	285	41.0	10	14	.3	15	0	.0
54747	2.6	0	.9	76	24.1	235	54.6	7	15	.0	0	0	.2
54748	1.4	100	.4	81	27.0	349	67.8	9	10	.7	11	0	.0
54749	1.0	99	.4	84	21.8	252	50.7	8	14	.5	13	0	.3
54750	1.5	99	.4	79	23.8	246	51.0	8	12	.5	13	0	.3
54751	19.8	98	6.1	62	22.7	343	79.4	6	11	9.5	9	0	.6
54754	1.3	98	.5	80	18.8	252	57.4	9	16	.6	16	0	.0
54755	6.4	100	2.2	76	21.3	248	60.9	7	17	3.2	15	0	.0
54756	1.1	100	.4	82	20.4	297	58.5	8	17	.6	17	0	.0
54757	2.5	0	.9	82	19.6	185	61.0	8	15	.0	0	0	.0
54758	4.0	100	1.4	79	21.0	271	59.8	10	14	2.0	15	0	.2
54759	1.6	100	.6	77	20.5	276	65.0	7	22	.8	19	0	.0
54760	.3	100	.1	64	22.3	237	47.5	8	33	.1	30	0	.3
54761	1.2	100	.4	78	22.4	218	63.3	8	16	.6	13	0	.0
54762	1.3	0	.4	82	21.0	221	64.0	8	16	.0	0	0	.1
54763	1.2	0	.4	78	24.0	202	53.3	10	14	.0	0	0	.6
54765	.2	100	.1	77	15.9	174	49.8	5	25	.1	13	0	.0
54766	1.7	99	.5	85	19.4	210	47.5	7	12	.9	11	0	.0
54767	2.7	100	.9	78	22.4	265	65.7	8	16	1.3	14	0	.0
54768	4.4	100	1.5	81	21.0	205	54.2	8	17	2.2	15	0	.0
54769	.5	100	.2	92	19.8	105	65.4	7	16	.3	18	0	.0
54770	2.1	100	.7	77	19.9	296	64.7	6	18	1.1	18	0	.0
54771	3.9	100	1.4	80	21.3	254	63.4	9	16	1.9	14	0	.1
54772	.8	100	.3	75	18.1	278	49.7	7	13	.4	16	0	.0
54773	3.2	100	1.1	84	21.7	245	63.5	6	19	1.6	16	0	.0

WISCONSIN — SPOONER

ZIPCODE	1	2	3	4	5	6	7	8	9	10	11	12	13
54801	5.4	99	2.1	78	20.0	271	71.7	7	19	2.6	17	0	.0
54805	1.3	100	.5	81	20.6	261	59.0	9	18	.6	17	0	.1
54806	12.0	93	4.4	72	19.8	239	57.0	7	18	5.4	16	0	.3
54810	1.9	97	.7	84	21.6	245	84.2	8	16	.9	18	0	.0
54812	4.7	100	1.7	76	21.9	250	69.0	7	17	2.3	15	0	.2
54813	.5	100	.2	88	19.6	293	39.7	6	9	.3	10	0	.0
54814	2.2	63	.7	70	19.3	229	64.6	7	14	.7	19	0	.0
54815	.3	0	.1	95	24.1	277*	49.6	6	9	.0	0	0	.0
54817	1.5	100	.6	80	18.3	192	68.3	6	20	.8	20	0	.0
54819	2.7	100	1.0	80	18.8	253	58.6	9	16	1.4	15	0	.1
54820	.7	100	.3	87	18.8	349	67.1	7	20	.4	18	0	.0
54821	1.3	0	.5	77	17.6	318	84.9	6	17	.0	0	0	.0
54822	2.9	99	1.0	78	19.3	283	65.9	10	12	1.4	12	0	.0
54824	1.6	100	.5	80	20.6	256	67.5	8	14	.8	12	0	.0
54826	.7	100	.2	83	19.2	313	60.4	8	18	.4	15	0	.0
54827	.2	100	.1	81	17.9	251	54.2	11	23	.1	29	0	.0
54828	.6	53	.2	79	15.9	251	62.4	6	12	.1	17	0	.0
54829	4.7	98	1.7	78	22.3	273	73.7	7	14	2.3	13	0	.5
54830	1.5	94	.6	90	17.9	179	67.5	5	20	.7	20	0	.0
54832	.3	0	.1	74	13.5	216	52.9	12	26	.0	0	0	.0
54835	1.1	100	.4	85	15.8	158	41.6	8	18	.6	21	0	.0
54836	1.0	0	.3	95	28.1	207	77.7	9	10	.0	0	0	.0
54837	3.4	99	1.2	80	19.5	244	65.8	7	18	1.7	16	0	.0
54838	.9	99	.3	90	15.2	180	63.3	4	18	.5	18	0	.0
54839	.3	0	.1	96	17.5	201*	50.6	8	16	.0	0	0	.0
54840	3.5	99	1.3	81	20.8	249	63.1	7	16	1.8	15	1	.4
54841	.3	0	.1	81	18.0	171	65.1	7	20	.0	0	0	.0
54842	.4	0	.1	80	23.6	336	61.3	6	34	.0	0	0	.6
54843	7.7	90	2.8	76	20.4	278	75.9	7	17	3.5	18	0	.3
54844	.3	100	.1	86	12.8	109	44.3	6	24	.3	26	0	.0
54845	.2	87	.1	97	16.9	194*	48.1	3	13	.1	13	0	.0
54846	.5	0	.2	87	16.4	189*	52.7	9	15	.0	0	0	.0
54847	1.9	99	.5	83	17.6	236	62.8	7	19	1.0	20	0	.6
54848	6.8	99	2.4	74	20.3	239	60.4	8	16	3.2	14	0	.3
54849	1.4	99	.5	84	22.5	338	74.8	7	13	.7	14	0	.0
54850	.2	0	.1	61	15.3	202	54.9	4	8	.1	13	0	.0
54851	1.5	0	.2	88	17.3	199*	49.0	11	18	.1	18	0	.0
54852	.2	100	.1	76	16.3	134	50.9	5	16	.1	16	0	.0
54853	3.1	96	1.1	77	19.9	265	67.3	8	19	1.5	19	0	.1
54854	.9	100	.3	87	20.8	262	54.4	8	12	.5	13	0	.0
54855	.5	100	.2	91	17.1	104	52.8	12	17	.3	18	0	.0
54856	1.5	0	.5	88	19.5	278	62.7	8	14	1.1	18	0	.0
54857	.2	100	.1	76	15.7	110	57.1	5	19	.1	16	0	.0
54858	1.3	100	.5	79	17.2	214	66.4	8	23	.6	21	0	.0
54859	1.7	98	.6	82	18.8	284	64.8	8	15	.9	15	0	.1
54861	.4	0	.2	47	16.7	231	28.2	11	8	.0	0	0	.0
54862	.3	100	.1	90	17.0	117	57.6	4	18	.1	21	0	.1
54864	1.2	100	.4	88	25.2	267	55.7	10	10	.6	9	0	.0
54865	.5	0	.2	89	17.2	192	55.6	8	24	.0	0	0	.0
54867	.5	0	.2	73	14.5	243	52.1	9	23	.0	0	0	.0
54868	13.4	99	4.8	71	22.8	286	76.2	8	14	6.5	12	1	.3
54870	1.1	99	.4	83	21.9	216	80.1	10	12	.6	15	0	.0
54871	2.6	99	1.0	77	18.7	229	66.9	9	17	1.3	16	0	.0

*=Estimated **1.0=883 lbs per person; 100++ indicates per capita toxic waste generation > than 100 times the U.S. average of 883 lbs per capita.

ZIP CODE MEASURES OF SIZE, LEVELS OF AFFLUENCE AND QUALITY OF LIFE

1=Population (th.); 2= % White; 3=Households (th.); 4=% Owner Occupied; 5=Mean Income Per Household (th.$); 6=Mean Monthly Rent ($)*; 7=Mean Home Value (th.$)*; 8=% under 5; 9=% 65 and over; 10=White Males (th.); 11=% White Males, 65+; 12=# Toxic Waste Sites; 13=Toxic Waste Relative to US(883 lbs.per capita)**.

WISCONSIN

SPOONER

ZIP CODE	1	2	3	4	5	6	7	8	9	10	11	12	13
54872	2.4	98	.9	76	16.4	273	63.0	7	22	1.1	22	0	.6
54873	1.8	0	.7	83	19.9	293	66.7	8	17	.0	0	0	.0
54874	1.6	99	.5	95	26.4	258	54.8	8	6	.8	7	0	.0
54875	.9	0	.3	83	18.2	238	40.1	4	13	.0	0	0	.0
54876	1.4	75	.5	78	17.9	272	73.8	7	16	.5	20	0	.0
54880	32.7	98	12.4	65	23.0	288	58.1	7	15	15.4	12	3	.8
54888	1.1	99	.4	86	16.6	298	68.8	7	19	.6	20	0	.0
54889	2.2	0	.8	80	19.8	261	62.8	7	16	.0	0	0	.3
54891	3.1	96	1.2	76	20.2	264	64.5	8	18	1.5	18	0	.0
54892	2.3	100	.9	81	15.2	310	73.3	7	30	.1	35	0	.0
54893	2.8	93	1.0	81	17.5	246	66.6	8	18	1.3	18	0	.0
54894	1.7	99	.5	93	23.5	281	60.1	9	10	.9	10	0	.0
54895	1.1	100	.4	84	18.6	230	49.8	5	16	.6	15	0	.0
54896	1.2	99	.5	75	15.9	195	57.5	6	17	.6	17	0	.0

OSHKOSH

ZIP CODE	1	2	3	4	5	6	7	8	9	10	11	12	13
54901	62.0	99	22.5	65	25.8	311	81.9	6	13	29.1	10	3	.8
54909	1.7	99	.6	84	25.2	251	57.5	9	13	.9	11	0	.0
54911	79.3	99	27.9	69	30.1	333	89.4	8	10	38.2	8	2	.6
54921	1.3	97	.4	82	20.8	350	57.5	10	9	.7	8	0	.0
54922	1.6	0	.5	87	24.4	296	54.3	9	12	.0	0	0	.0
54923	8.6	100	3.0	78	23.6	288	69.8	8	16	4.2	13	0	.3
54927	.5	100	.2	83	31.2	316	101.1	5	8	.2	6	0	.1
54928	.4	0	.2	84	19.0	350	56.0	7	16	.0	0	0	.0
54929	8.0	99	3.0	79	22.7	265	65.7	7	18	3.9	16	1	2.1
54930	1.3	0	.5	82	26.7	252	58.8	7	18	.0	0	0	.0
54931	.5	0	.2	88	30.3	298	74.5	7	13	.0	0	0	.0
54932	1.1	0	.3	89	27.3	365	78.4	11	9	.0	0	0	.0
54933	.4	0	.1	85	24.2	281	61.3	4	31	.0	0	0	.0
54934	.2	100	.1	87	21.6	255	60.4	5	20	.1	16	0	.0
54935	50.5	99	17.6	72	27.1	315	77.7	8	13	23.7	10	1	1.0
54940	3.0	99	1.1	86	25.0	308	77.6	7	15	1.5	15	0	.0
54941	2.5	0	1.0	78	25.4	314	103.7	5	19	.0	0	0	.2
54942	.5	0	.1	88	29.9	363	98.5	6	6	.0	0	0	.0
54943	1.6	97	.6	88	19.8	332	55.4	7	17	.8	17	0	.0
54944	5.4	100	1.6	81	28.5	301	82.9	10	9	2.7	8	1	.2
54945	2.6	100	1.0	81	20.4	203	66.8	6	21	1.3	21	0	.0
54947	1.8	99	.6	85	27.7	273	87.4	7	11	.9	11	0	.0
54948	.3	0	.1	83	19.7	129	58.5	9	13	.0	0	0	.0
54949	3.0	99	1.0	79	24.1	276	68.7	7	16	1.5	13	0	1.5
54950	3.0	100	1.1	81	22.6	239	66.2	8	12	1.5	10	0	.3
54952	21.7	99	7.7	71	27.8	319	82.3	8	11	10.6	9	5	1.0
54956	32.5	99	11.2	76	31.7	328	90.8	7	9	15.7	7	3	1.0
54960	1.7	99	.7	85	20.2	275	65.3	5	22	.9	21	0	.0
54961	11.3	99	3.8	77	25.3	292	77.8	9	13	5.5	10	1	.2
54962	1.0	100	.3	86	22.5	220	55.0	8	16	.5	11	0	.0
54963	5.3	100	1.8	81	26.1	305	69.4	7	13	2.7	12	1	.0
54964	.9	100	.3	82	28.7	279	91.7	8	10	.5	10	0	.0
54965	1.2	0	.4	91	24.7	399	63.2	7	9	.0	0	0	.2
54966	1.9	98	.7	79	23.4	273	60.0	9	16	.9	14	0	.0

WISCONSIN

OSHKOSH

ZIP CODE	1	2	3	4	5	6	7	8	9	10	11	12	13
54967	.4	100	.2	87	17.3	288	53.3	7	26	.2	24	1	.0
54968	2.8	100	1.1	80	20.4	277	65.3	7	21	1.4	19	0	.0
54969	.2	100	.1	87	26.0	298*	70.5	4	17	.1	11	0	.0
54970	2.1	99	.8	86	18.8	244	58.8	8	17	1.0	17	0	.0
54971	10.2	99	3.5	73	24.0	282	81.0	6	14	4.9	11	2	1.0
54974	1.4	100	.4	83	26.7	365	80.2	8	11	.7	9	0	.0
54977	1.0	100	.3	79	23.4	293	65.9	10	13	.5	11	0	.0
54979	1.7	0	.5	86	27.2	376	78.8	9	9	.0	0	0	.0
54980	.2	100	.1	78	21.9	355	60.9	6	7	.1	6	0	.0
54981	10.0	99	3.7	75	23.7	276	77.0	8	17	4.8	15	0	.5
54982	5.4	99	2.1	78	20.9	277	74.4	6	21	2.6	20	1	1.5
54983	4.1	100	1.4	82	24.2	273	71.7	7	18	2.0	15	0	.0
54984	2.4	99	.9	79	19.2	284	69.2	6	21	1.2	20	0	.0
54986	3.6	100	1.3	81	24.9	272	88.1	7	12	1.8	11	0	1.1

SAINT PAUL

ZIP CODE	1	2	3	4	5	6	7	8	9	10	11	12	13
55066	.1	0	.1	63	20.2	309	53.3	10	12	.0	0	0	.0
55082	.9	99	.3	92	38.0	426	124.0	10	6	.5	5	0	.0

NORTH SUBURBAN

ZIP CODE	1	2	3	4	5	6	7	8	9	10	11	12	13
60002	1.2	100	.5	71	24.0	338	78.8	9	21	.6	18	0	.0

ROCKFORD

ZIP CODE	1	2	3	4	5	6	7	8	9	10	11	12	13
61087	.2	0	.1	65	26.6	281	62.3	8	11	.0	0	0	.0

*=Estimated **1.0=883 lbs per person; 100++ indicates per capita toxic waste generation > than 100 times the U.S. average of 883 lbs. per capita.

103001

ZIP CODE MEASURES OF SIZE, LEVELS OF AFFLUENCE AND QUALITY OF LIFE

1=Population (th.); 2= % White; 3=Households (th.); 4=% Owner Occupied; 5=Mean Income Per Household (th.$); 6=Mean Monthly Rent ($)*; 7=Mean Home Value (th.$)*;
8=% under 5; 9=% 65 and over; 10=White Males (th.); 11=% White Males, 65+; 12=# Toxic Waste Sites; 13=Toxic Waste Relative to US(883 lbs.per capita)**.

WYOMING

ZIPCODE	1	2	3	4	5	6	7	8	9	10	11	12	13
BILLINGS													
59008	.3	100	.1	61	30.5	351*	126.9	3	14	.1	17	0	.0
ALLIANCE													
69352	.3	100	.1	51	21.7	249*	135.6	0	14	.1	18	0	.0
CHEYENNE													
82001	65.5	92	24.1	67	28.2	309	104.1	9	8	30.3	7	3	1.0
82050	.3	0	.1	75	25.2	225	33.5	4	16	.0	0	0	.0
82053	.6	0	.2	74	24.7	320	73.6	9	16	.0	0	0	.0
82054	.3	0	.1	76	24.1	276*	41.6	5	8	.0	0	0	.0
82055	.2	0	.1	54	25.7	343	131.0	6	14	.0	0	0	.0
82060	.1	100	.1	100	19.7	227*	60.2	5	19	.1	19	1	.0
82070	28.0	94	10.3	54	23.6	321	103.7	7	7	13.7	6	4	.0
82080	.1	100	.1	70	23.7	393	21.9	10	7	.1	0	1	.0
82082	1.5	97	.6	74	23.4	231	79.1	7	14	.7	13	0	.0
82083	.5	96	.1	76	24.2	182	66.1	16	12	.3	10	0	.0
YELLOWSTONE NATIONAL PARK													
82190	.4	100	.1	0	33.8	214	120.4*	0	0	.2	0	0	.0
WHEATLAND													
82201	8.9	98	3.3	72	28.4	365	91.8	10	9	4.6	7	0	.0
82210	.5	97	.2	63	18.9	203	42.6	9	20	.3	19	0	.0
82212	.7	98	.3	81	18.1	232	65.0	5	14	.4	13	0	.0
82213	.8	100	.3	63	24.0	366	56.1	5	9	.4	10	0	.0
82214	1.6	98	.6	74	25.5	251	77.7	8	11	.8	10	0	.0
82215	.3	0	.1	76	27.8	128	47.7	4	11	.0	0	0	.0
82217	.2	100	.1	55	40.8	239	45.9	16	8	.1	3	0	.0
82221	.5	0	.2	65	22.1	373	30.1	18	0	.2	0	0	.0
82222	.3	100	.1	60	27.6	213	21.9	10	10	.2	12	0	.0
82223	.9	99	.3	67	28.3	230	73.5	10	15	.5	15	0	.0
82225	2.3	100	.9	68	20.9	235	68.8	8	19	1.1	16	1	.0
82227	.1	100	.1	85	27.1	312*	45.1	4	8	.1	5	0	.0
82240	8.5	94	3.2	71	22.2	242	79.5	9	16	3.8	14	0	.0
82243	.2	100	.1	48	21.7	128	77.2*	6	13	.1	10	0	.0
82244	.4	100	.1	83	23.2	282	44.5	9	5	.2	5	0	.0
RAWLINS													
82301	12.3	87	4.1	67	31.9	399	110.9	11	7	5.7	6	2	.1
82310	2.4	98	.8	51	33.9	200	125.4	14	1	1.3	1	3	2.7
82321	.6	96	.2	63	26.7	397	94.1	8	8	.3	8	0	.0
82322	.2	100	.1	71	28.8	377	43.0	15	0	.1	0	1	.0
82323	.1	0	.1	64	33.3	320	56.9	7	27	.0	0	0	.0
82324	.3	93	.1	70	28.4	194	108.8	12	12	.2	14	0	.0
82325	.9	96	.3	73	25.4	247	92.6	12	8	.4	11	0	.0
82327	2.3	95	.7	76	33.9	343	94.5	13	3	1.1	2	0	.0
82329	1.0	97	.4	68	36.1	392	97.0	10	6	.5	4	0	.0
82331	2.8	99	1.0	71	31.7	360	106.6	11	8	1.4	7	0	.0
82332	.2	100	.1	40	34.4	395*	122.5*	14	7	.1	7	1	.0
82334	.6	95	.2	88	33.6	429	87.4	11	9	.3	11	1	28.6
82335	.1	100	.1	78	32.6	374*	148.8	0	0	.1	0	0	.0
82336	.8	0	.3	61	35.7	242	91.9	14	1	.0	0	0	.3
WORLAND													
82401	8.7	93	3.0	72	28.2	298	96.9	10	10	4.1	10	0	.3

WYOMING (continued)

ZIPCODE	1	2	3	4	5	6	7	8	9	10	11	12	13
WORLAND													
82410	1.9	98	.7	78	24.4	248	79.6	9	17	.9	15	0	.0
82411	.5	87	.2	72	19.4	239	40.7	7	16	.2	16	0	.0
82412	.6	100	.2	86	20.6	277	67.7	12	11	.3	10	0	.0
82414	10.8	98	4.0	71	28.7	309	110.4	9	10	5.2	9	2	1.1
82420	.3	0	.2	75	22.0	252	80.5	9	15	.0	0	0	.0
82421	.6	0	.1	81	19.0	218	58.7	13	9	.0	0	0	.0
82423	.2	0	.1	68	19.5	283	46.2	9	14	.0	0	0	.0
82426	3.1	100	1.2	69	24.4	251	75.8	9	14	1.5	12	1	.3
82428	.1	0	.1	59	20.5	165	74.4	13	11	.0	0	0	.0
82430	.2	0	.1	82	36.1	128	58.5	9	16	.1	0	0	.1
82431	3.7	98	1.2	74	22.5	245	75.0	11	13	1.8	11	2	.0
82433	.2	100	.1	68	36.6	287	44.0	8	8	.1	9	0	.4
82434	.9	98	.3	52	20.5	251	77.7	8	11	.5	10	0	.0
82435	8.9	97	3.0	73	25.8	297	88.2	9	11	4.2	10	0	.1
82440	.2	100	.1	71	11.1	207	90.8	8	13	.1	7	0	.0
82441	.1	100	.1	89	12.4	143*	110.8	6	23	.0	16	0	.0
82442	.6	96	.3	69	21.3	230	73.2	5	11	.4	10	0	.0
82443	5.5	98	2.1	65	24.6	255	93.4	8	16	2.7	15	1	.4
82450	.2	100	.1	56	11.3	360	196.9	22	8	.1	5	0	.0
RIVERTON													
82501	17.6	91	5.9	71	30.7	397	109.0	11	7	8.3	6	6	.9
82510	.8	30	.2	74	22.9	319	20.3	10	0	.1	0	0	.0
82512	.3	43	.1	87	25.6	294*	91.0*	16	13	.1	15	0	.0
82513	1.6	98	.6	72	25.2	275	112.5	10	8	.8	9	0	.1
82514	1.4	0	.4	46	19.4	252	77.8	11	5	.4	8	0	.0
82515	.6	98	.2	77	31.7	396	71.3	12	8	.3	8	0	.0
82516	.5	93	.1	76	26.3	143	101.1	8	6	.2	8	0	.0
82520	11.0	89	3.7	75	29.9	340	107.2	9	8	4.8	7	3	.0
82523	.9	94	.3	76	25.1	568	55.2	8	8	.5	10	0	.0
82524	.3	22	.1	79	30.1	347	107.1*	11	6	.3	0	0	.0
CASPER													
82601	63.1	96	23.0	72	35.4	437	135.2	9	7	30.9	5	12	1.3
82615	.6	0	.2	94	35.8	411*	56.9	10	1	.0	0	0	7.7
82620	.4	100	.1	59	27.4	342	74.4	8	8	.2	11	0	.0
82633	9.3	98	3.2	73	32.3	397	123.0	11	7	4.7	6	0	.0
82635	.6	97	.2	80	26.4	418	60.4	10	7	.3	9	0	.0
82636	3.1	96	.9	84	32.3	584	126.3	12	3	1.5	2	3	9.4
82637	4.4	97	1.4	76	32.7	414	113.8	12	4	2.2	3	6	.7
82639	.8	0	.3	74	27.5	268	99.0	9	12	.0	0	0	.0
82640	.2	100	.1	91	40.2	462*	33.4	8	0	.1	0	0	.0
82642	2.0	100	.7	71	29.7	341*	114.1	9	3	.1	9	0	.0
82643	.6	0	.2	65	26.5	384	50.4	5	9	.1	0	0	.5
82644	3.9	97	1.4	79	32.1	410	113.3	10	5	2.0	5	3	.0
82648	.1	100	.1	81	15.5	520	136.5	9	29	.1	27	0	.0
NEW CASTLE													
82701	5.1	99	1.4	95	23.9	342	76.9	11	9	.7	8	0	2.6
82710	.3	100	.1	86	28.3	325*	64.1	12	12	.1	9	0	.0

*=Estimated **1.0=883 lbs per person; 100++ indicates per capita toxic waste generation > than 100 times the U.S. average of 883 lbs per capita.

ZIP CODE MEASURES OF SIZE, LEVELS OF AFFLUENCE AND QUALITY OF LIFE

1=Population (th.); 2= % White; 3=Households (th.); 4=% Owner Occupied; 5=Mean Income Per Household (th.$); 6=Mean Monthly Rent ($)*; 7=Mean Home Value (th.$)*;
8=% under 5; 9=% 65 and over; 10=White Males (th.); 11=% White Males, 65+; 12=# Toxic Waste Sites; 13=Toxic Waste Relative to US(883 lbs.per capita)**.

WYOMING

ZIPCODE	1	2	3	4	5	6	7	8	9	10	11	12	13
NEW CASTLE													
82712	.2	0	.1	79	24.5	337	67.4	6	18	.0	0	0	.0
82716	22.2	98	7.3	74	38.1	441	134.2	12	3	11.5	2	4	.0
82720	.8	98	.3	78	22.2	243	61.0	13	11	.4	9	0	.0
82721	1.8	0	.6	78	32.7	258	102.0	11	5	.0	0	0	.0
82723	.4	100	.1	96	27.2	313*	69.0	5	8	.2	10	1	.5
82724	.2	0	.1	70	30.6	352*	109.1*	6	26	.2	10	0	.0
82725	.2	100	.1	100	32.3	371*	114.9*	3	13	.1	15	0	.0
82727	.5	92	.2	70	40.7	443	148.8	17	2	.2	6	0	.0
82729	1.8	100	.7	79	24.6	300	92.3	8	11	.9	10	0	.0
82730	1.6	97	.6	78	27.2	336	80.6	14	6	.8	6	0	.3
82732	1.2	98	.4	55	33.0	325	136.2	14	1	.6	0	0	.0
SHERIDAN													
82801	20.8	99	7.8	68	27.5	339	113.3	8	12	10.2	10	0	.1
82831	.2	100	.1	52	25.0	155	89.1*	7	15	.1	10	0	.0
82832	.3	100	.1	75	32.9	437	117.0*	16	2	.1	0	0	.0
82833	.6	0	.2	64	26.7	389	140.6	9	15	.0	0	0	.0
82834	5.5	99	2.1	68	28.7	316	111.7	8	14	2.7	13	0	.0
82835	.4	98	.1	68	21.4	266	67.1	8	14	.2	17	0	.0
82836	1.0	100	.3	65	24.7	336	93.2	10	9	.5	10	0	.0
82839	1.0	94	.4	74	34.3	378	105.2	10	6	.5	7	0	.0
82842	.8	0	.3	74	30.2	328	116.5	9	11	.0	0	0	.0
ROCK SPRINGS													
82901	24.4	95	8.7	66	35.0	391	110.9	11	6	12.3	5	3	.1
82923	.2	100	.1	69	21.8	428	64.5	7	15	.1	14	0	.0
82926	.2	0	.1	81	34.5	218	91.9	6	22	.0	0	0	.0
82929	.2	100	.1	13	24.5	255	87.2*	12	0	.0	0	0	.0
82930	7.6	98	2.5	72	32.3	367	106.6	11	7	3.8	6	0	.0
82932	.4	100	.1	83	16.9	420	65.6	20	3	.2	6	0	.0
82933	.8	100	.2	63	27.6	418	95.3	14	3	.4	4	0	.0
82934	.2	0	.1	49	24.3	164	61.9	13	7	.0	0	0	.0
82935	13.4	95	4.3	71	36.2	409	117.6	13	3	6.6	3	3	12.5
82937	3.3	98	1.0	86	31.6	361	106.5	16	4	1.7	3	0	.0
82939	1.2	99	.4	75	30.3	270	83.2	14	5	1.7	4	0	.0
82941	2.0	99	.7	73	25.7	358	111.2	8	11	1.0	10	0	.0
82942	.3	95	.2	69	24.3	279*	86.5*	8	3	.2	0	0	5.4
82943	.6	0	.1	88	33.0	410	58.4	8	5	.0	0	0	.0
82945	.6	0	.2	74	29.0	321	36.5	17	10	.0	0	0	.0
ROCK SPRINGS													
83001	7.0	99	2.8	59	30.6	379	187.9	7	5	3.5	4	0	.0
83011	.1	0	.1	8	20.2	310	72.0*	3	27	.0	0	0	.0
83012	.3	0	.1	24	24.5	356	213.5	2	8	.0	0	0	.0
83013	.3	0	.1	38	32.3	111	148.8	3	7	.0	0	0	.0
83014	.7	100	.4	58	30.8	364	179.6	4	11	.4	11	0	.0
83025	6.0	100	.3	49	34.6	542	333.3	2	0	.4	0	0	.0
ROCK SPRINGS													
83101	3.6	95	1.3	71	33.0	433	110.0	13	8	1.8	6	2	2.5
83110	3.3	100	1.0	86	23.2	283	103.5	15	8	1.7	8	0	.1
83111	.3	100	.1	84	17.5	425	85.4	24	0	.2	0	0	.0
83112	.5	100	.1	96	19.6	225*	57.8	5	11	.3	12	0	.0
ROCK SPRINGS													
83113	1.8	99	.6	70	29.7	313	99.8	10	5	1.0	5	0	.0
83114	.9	96	.3	71	24.5	302	85.3	13	9	.4	11	0	.0
83115	.3	100	.1	62	28.6	440	77.2	9	13	.1	15	0	.0
83116	.7	100	.3	85	28.9	541	74.3	12	8	.4	8	0	.0
83118	.2	100	.1	92	19.2	221*	104.5	6	14	.1	12	0	.9
83120	.2	100	.1	63	19.1	374	74.4	4	9	.2	7	0	.0
83121	.3	0	.2	58	31.1	338	35.4	10	11	.0	0	0	.0
83122	.2	100	.1	100	14.3	165*	74.4	10	33	.1	33	0	.0
83123	.4	0	.2	74	29.5	248	80.6	8	8	.0	0	0	.3
83126	.2	100	.1	71	16.4	188*	77.2	16	11	.1	7	0	.0
83127	.7	99	.2	87	22.5	224	84.6	22	4	.4	3	0	.0
83128	.2	0	.1	79	27.7	275	142.1	18	5	.0	0	0	.3
POCATELLO													
83422	.2	100	.1	58	19.1	741	276.2	28	0	.1	0	0	0

*=Estimated   **1.0=883 lbs per person; 100++ indicates per capita toxic waste generation > than 100 times the U.S. average of 883 lbs per capita.

ABOUT THE COUNCIL ON ECONOMIC PRIORITIES

The Council on Economic Priorities is a public service research organization dedicated to accurate and impartial analysis of some of the most vital issues facing our country today. The CEP is nonaligned, independent, and nonprofit.

Founded in 1969, the CEP believes that a well-informed community can express its convictions and play a far more effective and influential role in molding public policy when it is acting upon carefully conducted, documented, and factual research.

A clear and primary goal of the Council is to enhance corporate performance as it affects society in the critically important areas of: energy, the costs and consequences of military spending, political influence, fair employment practices, and environmental impact. The CEP acts as a clearinghouse for corporate responsibility issues, documents corporate activities, and monitors the role of government as it relates to these social issues.

Credibility is absolutely essential to the work of the Council. Our achievements can be measured by the frequency with which Congressional committees and administrative agencies invite CEP staff to testify. The national press reports regularly and extensively on the Council's work. A broad spectrum of corporations, libraries, and government agencies are institutional subscribers. We receive support from individuals and foundations who share our concerns and beliefs.

The remarkable impact of CEP studies on policymakers, the media, and government is a result of careful unbiased research. But the Council is far more than a research and reporting organization. Once a completed study points to a course of action that we believe to be correct, we are willing to adopt that point of view and press vigorously for its wide acceptance.

Our country is faced with issues of unimaginable magnitude and complexity. The role of the Council on Economic Priorities is to assist in uncovering the facts behind these issues and to bring them to the attention of both the public and the government in such a way that they can be effectively resolved in a logical, humane, and public-spirited manner.

Alice Tepper Marlin
President

THE COUNCIL
ON ECONOMIC PRIORITIES

CEP
COUNCIL ON
ECONOMIC
PRIORITIES

30 Irving Place
New York, NY 10003
212-420-1133

Join CEP Today

You Can Make a Difference!

☐ **Please enroll me as a Donor Member of CEP** and send me copies of all CEP publications — **Studies, Reports** and **Newsletters**. Membership $100. (Tax deductible.)

☐ **Please enroll me as a Sustaining Member of CEP** and send me a copy of all CEP **Reports** and **Newsletters**. Membership $50. (Tax deductible.)

☐ **Please enroll me as a Regular Member of CEP** and send me a copy of all CEP **Newsletters**. Membership $25. Students, unemployed and retired persons $15. (Tax deductible.)

☐ Please send me information on Institutional and Public Library subscriptions.

☐ Please send me a complete list of CEP publications.

Name _____

Street _____ **Apt.** _____

City _____

State _____ **Zip** _____

Phone No. (_____ **)** _____

(All contributions are tax deductible.)

Council on Economic Priorities, 30 Irving Pl., New York, NY 10003